Given to the

BRITISH MUSEUM

by

Dr Michael Rogers

ENCYCLOPÆDIA IRANICA

ACKNOWLEDGEMENTS

The preparation of this fascicle was made possible by a grant from:
the Program for Research Tools and Reference Works of the National Endowment for the Humanities, an independent federal agency;
Dr. Mansur Sharif-Zandieh;
and Bibliotheca Persica.

ENCYCLOPÆDIA IRANICA

EDITED BY

EHSAN YARSHATER

Volume III

ĀTAŠ—BAYHAQĪ

Routledge & Kegan Paul
London and New York
1989

First published in one volume 1989
by Routledge & Kegan Paul Ltd
11 New Fetter Lane
London EC4P4EE
Printed in Great Britain by
Unwin Brothers Ltd

ISBN 0 7100 9121 4

AUTHORS OF ARTICLES IN VOLUME III

ABBAS, IHSAN, University of Jordan, Amman. 164, 806.

ABED, SHUKRI B., Alexandria, Virginia. 70.

ACHENA, M., Bois Colombes, France. 99.

AFSAR, KERĀMAT-ALLĀH, Department of Archeology, Iran (emeritus). 399, 682.

AFŠĀR, ĪRAJ, University of Tehran (emeritus). 131, 133, 874.

AHMAD, QEYAMUDDIN, Patna University. 259, 787.

A'LAM, HŪŠANG, Tehran. 647, 656, 665, 724.

ALBRIGHT, CHARLOTTE F., University of Washington, Seattle. 569.

ALGAR, HAMID, University of California, Berkeley. 119, 278, 294, 295, 361, 380, 392, 410, 431, 433, 504, 754, 755, 776.

ALVI, SAJIDA S., McGill University, Montreal. 541.

AMANAT, ABBAS, Yale University, New Haven, Connecticut. 263, 726.

AMANAT, MEHRDAD, University of California, Los Angeles. 152, 525.

AMIN, S. H., Glasgow College of Technology. 586.

ĀMŪZGĀR, ŽĀLA, University of Tehran. 524.

ANSARI, the late N. H., University of Delhi. 494.

ASMUSSEN, JES PETER, University of Copenhagen. 168, 737, 801, 821, 845.

AUBAILE-SALLENAVE, Françoise, Centre National de la Recherche Scientifique, Paris. 14, 366.

AZADI, SIAWOSCH, Hamburg. 645.

BAEVSKIĬ, S. I., Institute for Oriental Studies, Leningrad. 381.

BAGLEY, F. R. C., University of Durham (emeritus). 379.

BAILEY, SIR HAROLD W., Cambridge University (emeritus). 403, 649.

BALLAND, DANIEL, University of Paris—Sorbonne. 323, 336, 360, 372, 417, 563, 567, 594, 596, 660, 692, 742, 745, 786, 788, 803, 818.

BANANI, AMIN, University of California, Los Angeles. 446.

BAQIR, MUHAMMAD, University of the Panjab, Lahore (emeritus). 6, 257, 259.

BARNETT, R. B., University of Virginia, Charlottesville. 30.

BARTH, FREDRIK, University of Bergen, Norway. 843.

BASSEER, POTKIN A., Fairleigh Dickinson University, Rutherford, N. J. 698.

BĀSTĀNĪ PĀRĪZĪ, MOḤAMMAD-EBRĀHĪM, University of Tehran. 651.

BAZIN, MARCEL, University of Reims, France. 170, 393, 802.

BAZMEE ANSARI, A. S., Central Institute of Islamic Research, Karachi. 364.

BEHN, WOLFGANG, Staatsbibliothek, Preussischer Kulturbesitz, Berlin. 307, 840.

BERNARD, PAUL, Centre National de la Recherche Scientifique, Paris. 124.

BĪNEŠ, TAQĪ, Tehran. 740.

BIVAR, A. DAVID H., School of Oriental and African Studies, University of London. 416.

BLAIR, SHEILA S., Harvard University, Cambridge, Massachusetts. 318.

BOEHMER, R. M., Deutsches Archäologisches Institut, Berlin and Baghdad. 859.

BOSWORTH, C. EDMUND, University of Manchester. 16, 18, 29, 177, 179, 224, 306, 370, 391, 526, 533, 570, 573, 582, 583, 588, 668, 721, 766, 774, 779, 797, 800, 825, 888, 895.

BOYCE, MARY, University of London (emeritus). 1, 6, 7, 9, 11, 16, 62, 126, 128, 273, 717, 756.

BÖWERING, GERHARD, Yale University, New Haven, Connecticut. 140, 722.

BREGEL, YURI, Indiana University, Bloomington. 830, 869.

BROMBERGER, CHRISTIAN, Université de Provence, Aix-en-Provence. 709.

DE BRUIJN, J. T. P., Rijksuniversiteit te Leiden. 372, 571, 877.

BUDDRUSS, GEORG, Johannes Gutenberg-Universität, Mainz. 827.

BULLIET, RICHARD, Columbia University, New York. 486, 586.

BURRILL, KATHLEEN, Columbia University, New York. 251.

BÜRGEL, J. CHRISTOPH, University of Bern. 265.

CAHEN, CLAUDE, Université de la Sorbonne Nouvelle, Paris (emeritus). 159.

CALMARD, JEAN, École Pratique des Hautes Études—Sorbonne, Paris. 137, 174, 261, 856.

CARDASCIA, GUILLAUME, Université de Droit, d'Économie et de Sciences Sociales de Paris. 325, 822.

DE CARDI, BEATRICE, Society of Antiquaries, London. 662.

CATON, MARGARET, Los Angeles. 669, 884, 885.

CHAUMONT, MARIE LOUISE, Centre National de la Recherche Scientifique, Paris. 17, 28, 169, 574, 579, 580.

CHITTICK, W. C., State University of New York, Stonybrook, New York. 114, 285.

CLAWSON, P., The World Bank, Washington, D.C. 504, 708.

CLINTON, JEROME W., Princeton University. 353.

COLE, JUAN, The University of Michigan, Ann Arbor. 422, 438.

CORBIN, the late HENRY, École Pratique des Hautes Études—Sorbonne, Paris. 183.

CRANE, HOWARD, The Ohio State University, Columbus. 382.

Dabīrsīāqī, Moḥammad, Mo'assasa-ye Loḡat-nāma-ye Dehḵodā, Tehran. 380, 382, 503, 542, 851, 882.

Daftary, Farhad, Institute of Ismaili Studies, London. 809.

Daiber, H., Vrije Universiteit, Amsterdam. 501.

Dandamayev, Muhammad A., Institute for Oriental Studies, Leningrad. 29, 205, 326, 418, 762, 785, 799.

Dānešpažūh, Moḥammad-Taqī, Fontenay-aux-Roses, France. 886.

DeBlase, Anthony F., San Francisco. 870.

Digard, Jean-Pierre, Centre National de la Recherche Scientifique, Ivry-sur-Seine, France. 548, 549, 551, 553.

Doerfer, Gerhard, Georg-August-Universität, Göttingen. 245, 882.

Donner, Fred M., The University of Chicago. 851.

Duchesne-Guillemin, Jacques, University of Liège, Belgium (emeritus). 12, 126.

Dupree, Louis, Duke University, Durham, North Carolina. 134.

Dupree, Nancy, Duke University, Durham, North Carolina. 396.

During, Jean, Centre National de la Recherche Scientifique, Paris. 255, 758, 858, 884.

Eaton, Richard M., The University of Arizona, Tucson. 530, 798.

Edwards, Robert W., Dumbarton Oaks, Washington, D.C. 886.

Ehlers, Eckart, University of Bonn. 538, 551.

Eilers, Wilhelm, University of Würzburg (emeritus). 123, 124, 361, 392, 536, 574, 649, 682, 685, 714, 729, 839.

EIr. 759.

Ekbal, Kamran, University of Bochum. 850.

Elāhī, 'Etrat, Berkeley, California. 368.

Elfenbein, Josef, Johannes Gutenberg-Universität, Mainz. 633.

Elwell-Sutton, the late Lawrence P., University of Edinburgh. 132, 294, 296, 476, 522, 814.

Emmerick, Ronald E., University of Hamburg. 30, 32.

Ende, Werner, Albert-Ludwigs-Universität, Freiburg im Breisgau. 130.

van Ess, Josef, University of Tübingen. 26, 179, 269, 409.

Farhūdī, Ḥosayn, Toronto. 735.

Fatemi, Nasrollah, S., Fairleigh Dickinson University, New Jersey. 540.

Fleischer, Cornell, Washington University, St. Louis, Missouri. 436.

Floor, Willem M., The World Bank, Washington, D.C. 115, 504, 531, 708, 768, 814, 838, 863.

Fourniau, Vincent, Levallois, France. 591.

Friedmann, Johannan, Hebrew University, Jerusalem. 381.

Frye, Richard N., Harvard University, Cambridge, Massachusetts. 298.

Gaffary, Farrokh, Paris. 539, 729.

Gheissari, Ali, University of California, San Diego. 437.

Gignoux, Philippe, École Pratique des Hautes Études—Sorbonne, Paris. 190, 488.

Gnoli, Gherardo, Istituto Italiano per il Medio e Estremo Oriente, Rome. 44, 334, 510, 689.

Grabar, Oleg, Harvard University, Cambridge, Massachusetts. 153.

Grenet, Frantz, Centre National de la Recherche Scientifique, Paris. 343, 415, 594.

Gropp, Gerd, University of Hamburg. 585.

Gutas, Dimitri, University of Crete, Rethymno. 67, 79.

ter Haar, J. G. J., University of Leiden. 728.

Ḥabībī, the late 'Abd-al-Ḥayy. 181.

Halm, Heinz J., University of Tübingen. 861, 894, 895.

Hanaway, William L., Jr., University of Pennsylvania, Philadelphia. 161, 395, 499, 519, 564.

Hardy, P., School of Oriental and African Studies, University of London. 753.

Hassanpour, Amir, Don Mills, Ontario. 485, 739.

Hawting, G. R., School of Oriental and African Studies, University of London. 205.

Henrickson, Robert C., Royal Ontario Museum, Toronto. 292.

Herrenschmidt, Clarisse, Université de la Sorbonne Nouvelle. 683.

Hewsen, Robert H., Glassboro State College, Glassboro, New Jersey. 32, 150, 406, 407, 408.

Hitchins, Keith, University of Illinois, Urbana-Champaign. 144.

Hoffmann, Karl, University of Erlangen (emeritus). 47, 51, 56.

Hourcade, Bernard, Centre National de la Recherche Scientifique, Paris. 788, 814.

Humphreys, R. S., University of Wisconsin, Madison. 164.

Ittig, Anette, Canadian Heritage Information Network, Ottawa, Canada. 561.

Jackson, Peter, University of Keele, Great Britain. 535, 669.

Jamzadeh, Parivash, Orinda, California. 513.

Janata, Alfred, Museum für Völkerkunde, Vienna. 136.

Javadi, Hasan, University of California, Berkeley. 251.

Johanson, Lars, Johannes Gutenberg-Universität, Mainz. 248.

Joslin, Paul, Brookfield Zoo, Brookfield, Illinois. 323.

Kanga, the late M. F., Vedic Research Institute, Poona. 123, 825.

Kārang, the late 'Abd-al-'Alī, University of Tabrīz. 190.

Karimi-Hakkak, Ahmad, University of Washington, Seattle. 13.

Kasheff, Manouchehr, Columbia University, New York. 293.

KEALL, EDWARD J., Royal Ontario Museum, Toronto. 155.

KECHICHIAN, JOSEPH A., University of Virginia, Charlottesville. 415, 508.

KELLENS, JEAN, University of Liège, Belgium. 35.

KENNEDY, HUGH, University of St. Andrews, St. Andrews, Fife, Great Britain. 412.

KHALEGHI-MOTLAGH, DJALAL, University of Hamburg. 119, 167, 174, 178, 199, 272, 324, 365, 489, 522, 523, 525, 730, 809, 841.

KIEFFER, CHARLES, Centre National de la Recherche Scientifique, Paris. 741, 788.

KLEISS, WOLFGANG, Deutsches Archäologisches Institut, Berlin and Tehran. 215, 824, 836, 867.

KLÍMA, OTAKAR, Academy of Sciences, Prague. 517, 518.

KOCH, HEIDEMARIE, Philipps-Universität, Marburg. 870.

KOHLBERG, ETAN, The Hebrew University of Jerusalem. 429, 527, 529, 572, 738.

KOTWAL, FIROZE M., Bombay. 6, 11.

KUNIHOLM, BRUCE R., Duke University, Durham, North Carolina. 231.

KUWAYAMA, SHOSHIN, Kyoto University. 843.

LEHMANN, FRITZ, The University of British Columbia, Vancouver, B.C., Canada. 320.

LERICHE, PIERRE, Ecole Normale Supérieure, Paris. 339.

LERNER, JUDITH, New York. 680.

LORAINE, MICHAEL B., University of Washington, Seattle. 476.

MAC DOWALL, DAVID W., University of Durham, Great Britain. 257, 258.

MACEOIN, DENIS M., University of Newcastle-upon-Tyne, Great Britain. 129, 179, 277, 278, 309, 315, 376, 447, 461, 471, 583, 740, 794, 878.

MACKENZIE, DAVID NEIL, Georg-August-Universität, Göttingen. 110, 111.

MACUCH, MARIA, Freie Universität Berlin. 763.

MADELUNG, WILFERD, Oxford University. 120, 354, 385, 528, 529, 718, 725, 873.

MAḤBŪBĪ ARDAKĀNĪ, the late ḤOSAYN, University of Tehran. 271, 272.

MAHDI, MUHSIN, Harvard University, Cambridge, Massachusetts. 66, 84.

MAḤMŪDĪ, Ḥ. 845.

MALANDRA, W. W., University of Minnesota, Minneapolis. 17.

MALTI-DOUGLAS, FEDWA, University of Texas, Austin. 377.

MARDŪḴ, ʿABD-ALLĀH, Paris. 665.

MARMURA, MICHAEL E., University of Toronto. 73.

MASSOUDIEH, M. T., University of Tehran. 644.

MATĪNĪ, JALĀL, Foundation for Iranian Studies, Washington, D.C. 117, 133, 183, 478, 501.

MAYRHOFER, MANFRED, University of Vienna. 26, 836.

MCCHESNEY, R. D., New York University, N.Y. 379, 800.

MCDERMOTT, MARTIN J., Université Saint-Joseph, Beirut. 112.

MELIKIAN-CHIRVANI, ASADULLAH SOUREN, Paris. 291, 712, 795.

MOHĀJER, PARVĪZ, New York, 132.

MOMEN, MOOJAN, Biggleswade, Bedfordshire, England. 364, 376, 470, 475, 649.

MORONY, MICHAEL, University of California, Los Angeles. 352, 479, 490, 494.

MOTTAHEDEH, ROY, Harvard University, Cambridge, Massachusetts. 265.

MUSALLAM, BASIM, University of Cambridge. 94.

NARTEN, JOHANNA, University of Erlangen. 487.

NAVĀʾĪ, ʿA.-Ḥ. Tehran. 490, 491, 524, 548, 549, 550.

NETZER, AMNON, The Hebrew University of Jerusalem. 297, 298, 339.

OBERLING, PIERRE, Hunter College, New York, 143, 151, 482, 484, 486, 532, 693, 875, 887.

OMIDSALAR, MAHMOUD, University of California, Los Angeles. 203.

PANDITA, K. N., University of Kashmir, Srinagar. 171.

PARSA, AHMAD, University of Tehran (emeritus). 110, 794.

PARVIN, NASSEREDDIN, Fondation Culturelle Mahvi, Geneva, Switzerland. 5, 177, 182, 187, 260, 540, 569, 654, 656, 664, 823.

PELLAT, CHARLES, University of Paris—Sorbonne. 760.

PERRY, JOHN R., University of Chicago. 173, 694, 695, 696, 876.

PIEMONTESE, ANGIOLELLO M., Université des Sciences Humaines, Strasbourg. 758.

PINGREE, DAVID, Brown University, Providence, Rhode Island. 431, 715, 716.

DE PLANHOL, XAVIER, University of Paris—Sorbonne. 205, 317, 319, 349, 355, 362, 385, 417, 500, 506, 507, 587, 592, 650, 657, 660, 679, 681, 682, 685, 688, 689.

POONAWALA, ISMAIL K., University of California, Los Angeles. 163.

RADTKE, BERND, Karlsruhe. 859.

RAFATI, VAHID, Haifa, Israel. 454, 460, 465, 467.

RAHIMOV (RAGIMOV), A. H., Institute of Oriental Studies, Azerbaijan SSR Academy of Sciences, Baku. 383.

RAHMAN, the late FAZLUR, University of Chicago. 83.

RAJĀʾĪ, the late A.-ʿA., Āstān-e Qods-e Rażawī, Mašhad. 189.

RAMAZANI, NESTA, Charlottesville, Virginia. 363, 657, 729.

REINERT, BENEDIKT, University of Zurich. 20.

RICHARD, FRANCIS, Bibliothèque Nationale, Paris. 830.

RICHTER-BERNBURG, LUTZ, Georg-August-Universität, Göttingen. 350.

ROAF, SUSAN, Oxford Polytechnic, England. 368.

RUSSELL, JAMES R., Columbia University, New York. 18, 204, 277.

SAFA, ZABIHOLLAH, University of Tehran (emeritus). 12, 118, 291, 362, 377, 383, 430, 499, 526, 534, 667, 855, 856.
SAHBA, FARIBORZ, Vancouver, B.C., Canada. 465.
SAID, HAKIM MOHAMMED, Hamdard Foundation, Azimabad and Karachi. 796.
SAʿĪDĪ SĪRJĀNĪ, ʿALĪ-AKBAR, Tehran. 399, 402, 480, 543, 654, 662, 690, 844.
SALIBA, GEORGE, Columbia University, New York. 88.
ṢĀNEʿĪ, MANŪČEHR, Nice. 844.
SCHIPPMANN, KLAUS, Georg-August-Universität, Göttingen. 221, 574, 761.
SCHLERATH, BERNFRIED, Freie Universität Berlin. 122.
SCHMITT, RÜDIGER, University of Saarland, Saarbrücken. 13, 29, 408, 832.
SCHÜTZINGER, HEINRICH, University of Bonn. 407, 598, 821.
SHAFFER, JIM G., Case Western Reserve University, Cleveland, Ohio. 632.
SHAHBAZI, A. SHAPUR, Eastern Oregon State College, La Grande. 284, 515, 516, 519.
SHAKED, SHAUL, The Hebrew University of Jerusalem. 127, 537, 837.
SHAKI, MANSUR, University of Prague. 149, 261.
SIDDIQI, I. H., Aligarh Muslim University. 481.
SIDDIQI, MOAZZAM, Voice of America, Washington, D.C. 171.
SIDDIQUI, M. ZAMIRUDDIN, Aligarh Muslim University. 121.
SIMS, ELEANOR G., Islamic Art Foundation, New York. 20.
SIMS-WILLIAMS, NICHOLAS, School of Oriental and African Studies, University of London. 277, 309, 344, 404, 823.
SKJÆRVØ, PRODS OKTOR, Columbia University, New York. 191, 400, 406, 780, 799, 827, 846.
SMIRNOVA, LIDIA P., Institute of Oriental Studies, Leningrad. 258.
SMITH, J. M., Jr., University of California, Berkeley. 126.
SMITH, PETER, University of Lancaster, Great Britain. 449.
SOUCEK, PRISCILLA P., Institute of Fine Arts, New York University. 292, 295, 523.
SOUCEK, SVAT, New York Public Library. 565.
SPOONER, BRIAN J., University of Pennsylvania, Philadelphia. 598, 841.
SPULER, BERTOLD, University of Hamburg (emeritus). 887.
STOLPER, MATTHEW W., University of Chicago, Illinois. 113.
SUBTELNY, MARIA, University of Toronto. 319, 377.
SUNDERMANN, WERNER, Akademie der Wissenschaften der DDR, Berlin. 492, 678, 873.
SUNY, RONALD G., University of Michigan, Ann Arbor. 566.
TAFAŻŻOLĪ, AḤMAD, University of Tehran. 123, 124, 173, 260, 539, 663, 757, 858.
TAPPER, RICHARD L., School of Oriental and African Studies, University of London. 234.
TARZI, ZEMARYALAI, Paris. 658.
THORDARSON, FRIDRIK, University of Oslo. 876, 886.
TOUMANOFF, CYRIL, Rome. 170, 419.
TSUGE, GEN'ICHI, Kunitachi College of Music, Tokyo. 32.

VAN RIET, SIMONE, Université Catholique de Louvain, Belgium. 104.
VANDEN BERGHE, LOUIS, Rijksuniversiteit-Gent, Belgium. 664, 761, 805.
VÖÖBUS, the late ARTHUR, The Institute of Syriac Manuscript Studies, Lutheran School of Theology at Chicago. 307, 308, 317, 824.

WALBRIDGE, JOHN, ESCABANA, Michigan. 464.
WALEY, MUHAMMAD ISA, British Library, London. 435.
WEISSER, URSULA, Johannes Gutenberg-Universität, Mainz. 107.
WICKENS, G. MICHAEL, University of Toronto (emeritus). 122, 479.
WIDENGREN, GEO, University of Uppsala (emeritus). 27.
WILLIAMS, ALAN V., University of Manchester. 531.
WINDFUHR, GERNOT L., University of Michigan, Ann Arbor. 559.
WRIGHT O., School of Oriental and African Studies, University of London. 92.

YARSHATER, EHSAN, Columbia University, New York. 238, 383.
YAGANEH, MOHAMMAD, Potomac, Maryland. 696.
YŪSOFĪ, ḠOLĀM-ḤOSAYN, University of Mašhad (emeritus). 299, 366, 401, 475, 889.

ZABIH, SEPEHR, St. Mary's College, Moraga, California. 542.
ZAIDI, N. H., Al-Husain Hospital, Lahore. 135.
ZAND, MICHAEL, The Hebrew University of Jerusalem. 534.
ZIEME, PETER, Akademie der Wissenschaften der DDR, Berlin. 691.
ZIMMER, STEFAN, Freie Universität Berlin. 405.

ADDENDA AND CORRIGENDA

Volume I

P. 431b ACTS OF THE PERSIAN MARTYRS, l. 24 *for* Wiesner *read* Wiessner.
P. 457a ADIABENE, l. 17 *for* Lekider *read* Le Rider;
P. 459a l. 13 *for* Artsunis *read* Artsrunis; l. 34 *for* persischen *read* persischer.
P. 461b ADĪB ṬĀLAQĀNI, l. 9 *for* 2 September 1919 *read* 4 August 1919.
P. 609b AGATHIAS, l. 30 *for* 1969 *read* 1964.
P. 742b ĀL, *add to the bibliography* M. Bahmanbeygī, "Āl," *Āyanda* 13/1-2, 1366 Š./1987, pp. 83-87.
P. 806b ALBANIA, l. 45 *for* Wesendonck *read* Wesendonk.
P. 807a l. 45 *for* Karkazskoĭ *read* Kavkazskoĭ.
P. 807b l. 48 *for* Dasxuvancʿi *read* Dasxurancʿi.
P. 831a ALEXANDRIA, l. 5 *for* Ammianus Marcellinus 13.6 *read* Ammianus Marcellinus 23.6; ll. 15-16 *for* Ammianus Marcellinus 33.6 *read* Ammianus Marcellinus 23.6; l. 48 *for Städtegrunden read Städtegründungen*.
P. 895a ALLIANCE, *add to the bibliography* E. Joseph, "Andar talāš-e sawādāmūzī wa yād-ī az maktab-ḵānahā-ye qadīm (Remembrance of the Past. The Task of Study in the Old Days)," *Rahāvard* 16-17, 1366 Š./1988, pp. 176-84.
P. 906a ALQĀB VA ʿANĀWĪN, l. 6 *remove parenthesis after* Qajars.
P. 937b L. 13 *for* AMĪD-AL-DĪN *read* ʿAMĪD-AL-DĪN.
P. 938b AMIDA, l. 35 *for* Thompson *read* Thomson; l. 36 *for* Amminus Marcelinus *read* Ammianus Marcellinus; l. 40 *for* Bercham *read* Berchem; *for* Strzygowsky *read* Strzygowski; 1.54 *for* Tigrisgebid *read* Tigrisgebiet.
P. 939b L. 19 *for* MOḤAMMAD-ḤOSAYAN *read* MOḤAMMAD-ḤOSAYN.
P. 943b AMĪN-AL-DAWLA, ll. 13-14 *for rasāʾ el-ekāṣṣa read rasāʾel-e ḵāṣṣa*; l. 31 *for* p. 83 *read* p. 91.
P. 967a AMĪR(-E) NEẒĀM GARRŪSĪ, l. 3 *for* Effandi *read* Effendi; l. 4 *for* Wilmett *read* Wilmette.
P. 977b AMMIANUS MARCELLINUS, l. 50 *for* 93 to 353 *read* 96 to 353;
P. 978a l. 15 *for* 539 *read* 359; l. 49 *for Syria* 28, 1962 *read Syria* **38**, 1961;
P. 978b l. 13 *add in the parenthesis* revised in *Byzantine Studies and Other Essays*, 1955; l. 43 *for Jahrbuch read Jahrbücher*; l. 49 *for Hermes* 40, 1914 *read Hermes* 41, 1906;
P. 979a l. 6 *for Syria* 28 *read Syria* 38; l. 10 *for* 1964 *read* 1967; l. 19 for M. Z. Chaumont read M. L. Chaumont.
P. 993b AMR BE MAʿRŪF, l. 24 *for* whith *read* with.
P. 1010b ANĀHĪD, in the caption of Plate XXXIX *for* ḵosrow *read* Ḵosrow; *for* Ohrmazed *read* Ohrmazd.

Volume II

P. 5a ANBĀR, l. 32 *for* Gordian IV in 243 *read* Gordian III in 244.
P. 416a ARMAVIR, l. 12 *for* 1966 *read* 1969.
P. 419b ARMENIA AND IRAN II, l. 11 *for Istambuler read Istanbuler*;
P. 424b l. 36 *for* Manadian *read* Manandian; l. 54 *for* Esbroek *read* Esbroeck;
P. 427a l. 31-32 *for* Armenian court *read* Roman court;
P. 427b ll. 20-21 *for Constantantini read Constantini*;
P. 428a l. 30 *for* 5.53 *read* 4.53;
P. 428b ll. 28-29 *for* Pomperini *read* Temporini;
P. 429b l. 14 *for* Kałakatuarecʿi *read* Kałankatuacʿi; l. 55 *for* Mercerian *read* Mécérian;
P. 431a l. 11 *for* Inglesian *read* Inglisian;
P. 440b l. 28 *for* Breckhins *read* Boeckhius.
P. 698b ASADĀBĀD, l. 4 *for* Dadūna *read* Dandūna.
P. 742a ʿĀŠEQ, *add to the bibliography* C. Albright, "The Azerbaijani *ʿĀshiq*. A Musician's Adaptations to a Changing Society," *Edebiyat* 2/1-2, 1988, pp. 205-17.
P. 763b ASIA MINOR, *add to the bibliography* P. Briant, "Les iraniens d'Asie Mineure après la chute de l'empire achéménide," *Dialogues d'histoire ancienne* 11, 1985, pp. 167-95 (on administrative continuities).
P. 773a AṢNĀF, l. 26 *for* Yat-il *read* Y a-t-il;
P. 773b l. 44 *for* Baṭūṭṭa *read* Baṭṭūṭa; l. 50 *for* Baṭṭūṭṭa *read* Baṭṭūṭa;
P. 775b l. 53 *for* except *read* exempt.
P. 840a ASTARĀBĀD, l. 19 *add* According to the census of 1355 Š./1976 Gorgān/Astarābād had a population of 88,033, and the statistical yearbook for Māzandarān gives an estimate of 132,000 for 1363 Š./1984. (M. Bazin)
P. 847b ĀŠTĪĀN, l. 48 *add* According to the census of 1355 Š./1976 Āštīān had a population of 5,738. Since 1359 Š./1980 Āštīān is the chef-lieu of the *šahrestān* of Āštīān (519 km²), comprising a *bakš* and two *dehestāns*. In 1355 Š./1976 it had a population of 20,742. (M. Bazin)
P. 851a AŠTIŠAT, l. 24 *for* armenichen *read* armenischen.

Volume III

P. 9ᵇ   ĀTAŠKADA, l. 19, *for* Fars *read* Fārs.

P. 19ᵇ   ATSÏZ ĠARČA'Ī, l. 22 *for* Qoṭb-al-din *read* Qoṭb-al-dīn.

P. 29ᵇ   AUTOPHRADATES, l. 16 *for* surrended *read* surrendered.

P. 44ᵇ   AVESTAN GEOGRAPHY, l. 15 *for* bərə-zaiti *read* bərəzaiti.

P. 70ᵇ   AVICENNA II, l. 27 *for* 'aqlī- *read* 'aqlī; *add to the bibliography* A. Reżwānī, *Abū 'Alī Sīnā*, Tehran, 1344 Š./1965.

P. 83ᵃ   AVICENNA V, *add to the bibliography* The existence of mystical views in Avicenna has also been recently disputed by M. Türker-Küyel, "İbn Sînâ ve 'mistik' denen görüşler," in A. Sayılı, ed., *İbn Sînâ. Doğumunun bininci yılı armağanı*, Ankara, 1984, pp. 749-92.

P. 101ᵇ   AVICENNA XI, l. 50 *for* be-'aynehī *read* be-'ayneh.

P. 110ᵃ   AVICENNA XIII, *add to the bibliography* N. G. Siraisi, *Avicenna in Renaissance Italy. The* Canon *and Medical Teaching in Italian Universities after 1500*, Princeton, 1987.

P. 122ᵇ   AWṢĀF AL-AŠRĀF, *add to the bibliography* W. Madelung, "Naṣīr ad-Dīn Ṭūsī's Ethics between Philosophy, Shi'ism, and Sufism," in R. G. Hovanissian, ed., *Ethics in Islam*, Malibu, Calif., 1985, pp. 85-101.

P. 123ᵇ   AXTARMĀR, l. 55 *for* Nīmruž *read* Nīmrūz.

P. 127ᵇ   AYĀDGĀR Ī JĀMĀSPĪG, *add to the bibliography* T. Olsson, "The Apocalyptic Activity. The Case of the Jāmāsp Nāmag," in D. Hellholm, ed., *Apocalypticism in the Mediterranean World and the Near East*, Proceedings of the International Colloquium on Apocalypticism, Uppsala, August 12-17, 1979, Tübingen, 1983, pp. 21-49.

P. 129ᵇ   AYĀDGĀR Ī ZARĒRĀN, *add to the bibliography* M. Shaki, "Observations on the Ayādgār ī Zarērān," *Archív Orientální* 54, 1986, pp. 257-71.

P. 150ᵃ   AYRARAT, ll. 4-5 *for* Genesis 12:20, Jeremiah 15:13 *read* Genesis 8:4, Jeremiah 51:27;

P. 151ᵇ   l. 16 *for* 1829 *read* 1828.

P. 155ᵇ   AYVĀN-E KESRĀ, in the caption *read* Figure 1.

P. 188ᵃ   ĀẔARBĀYJĀN, ll. 10, 12 *for* Ebtehāj *read* Eḥtīāj.

P. 204ᵇ   AŽDAHĀ IV, l. 14 *for* Kostaneance' *read* Kostaneanc'.

P. 207ᵃ   AZERBAIJAN I, l. 14 *for* Danişman *read* Danışman.

P. 215ᵇ   l. 20 *for* SSSR *read* SSR.

P. 226ᵃ   AZERBAIJAN IV, l. 58 *for* Balāḏarī *read* Balāḏorī.

P. 233ᵃ   AZERBAIJAN V, l. 6 *for* portested *read* protested;

P. 234ᵃ   l. 41 *for* fifteen *read* fifteenth;

P. 234ᵇ   l. 6 *for* Romazani *read* Ramazani.

P. 257ᵇ   AZES, l. 23 *for* MACDOWELL *read* MAC DOWALL.

P. 257ᵇ   AẒFARĪ GŪRGĀNĪ, MOḤAMMAD, l. 49 *for* Azfarī *read* Aẓfarī.

P. 261ᵃ   AZIŠMĀND, l. 57 *for* dādesṭān *read* dādestān.

P. 263ᵃ   'AZĪZ KHAN MOKRĪ, ll. 41-44 *replace the sentence* According to Eastwick... his career. *with* Since he was a Sunnite and of humble origin Amīr Kabīr's support was decisive for his future ascendancy (Eqbāl, art. cit., pp. 59f., quoting Eastwick).

P. 264ᵇ   'AZĪZ-AL-SOLṬĀN, l. 9 *for* Kāṭerāt *read* Kāṭerāt.

P. 292ᵃ   BĀBĀ JĀN ḴORĀSĀNĪ, l. 50 *for* Dost *read* Dōst.

P. 294ᵇ   BĀBĀ ŠAMAL, *add to the bibliography* R. Ganjaʾī, "Nāma-ye Bābā Šamal wa gardūna-ye pīškešī," *Āyanda* 13, 1366 Š./1987, pp. 655-57.

P. 306ᵃ   BĀBAK ḴORRAMĪ, l. 13. The attestation of Ḵorramīs under Ażod-al-Dawla is based upon what seems to be a misreading of Jorūmīya as Ḵorramīya, see Madelung in *EI²*, p. 65a supra.

P. 325ᵃ   BABR-E BAYĀN, *add to the bibliography* Sh. Shahbazi, "Babr-e Bayān-e Rostam," *Āyanda* 13, 1366 Š./1987, pp. 54-58. J. Ḵāleqī-Moṭlaq, "Babr-e Bayān (rūyīntanī wa gūnahā-ye ān)," *Īrān-nāma* 6/2, 1366 Š./1988, pp. 200-27.

P. 357ᵃ   BADAḴŠĀN I, l. 19 *for* Junipersus *read* Juniperus.

P. 367ᵇ   BĀDENJĀN I, l. 40 *for* le-l'mofradāt *read* le'l-mofradāt.

P. 380ᵃ   BADĪHA-SARĀʾĪ, l. 22 *for* Mīrza *read* Mīrzā.

P. 409ᵃ   BAGAZUŠTA, l. 5 *for* PBṢ *read* PBS.

P. 430ᵇ   BAHĀʾ-AL-DĪN 'ĀMELĪ, *add to the bibliography*: S. Amir Arjomand, *The Shadow of God and the Hidden Imam. Religion, Political Order, and Societal Changes in Shi'ite Iran from the Beginning to 1890*, Chicago, 1984 (index, s.v.). A. Newman, "Towards a Reconsideration of the 'Isfahān School of Philosophy'. Shaykh Bahāʾī and the Role of the Safawid 'ulamāʾ," *Studia Iranica* 15, 1986, pp. 165-99.

P. 435ᵇ   BAHĀʾ-AL-DĪN NAQŠBAND, l. 10 *for* armağani *read* armağanı.

P. 473ᵇ   BAHAI FAITH XII, l. 8 *for* REŻWAN *read* REŻWĀN;

P. 475ᵇ   BAHĀR, l. 30 for Šawwāl, 1338 June, 1920 *read* Šawwāl, 1338/June, 1920.

P. 476b BAHĀR, MALEK-AL-ŠOʿARĀʾ I, l. 8 *add* Bahār used his pen-name in his private letters (see, e.g., *Īrān-nāma* 5, 1366 Š./1987, pp. 703-13) before the use of the family name became mandatory by law for all Persians.

P. 479a BAHĀR, MALEK-AL-ŠOʿARĀʾ II, l. 27 *add* In literary criticism Bahār was one of the first Persian literateurs to adopt Western methodology and scholarship in the appreciation of Persian literary works (J. Matīnī, "Ṣadomīn sāl-e walādat-e Bahār," *Īrān-nāma* 5, 1366 Š./1987, pp. 556ff.). He also wrote some poetry in his native dialect of Mašhad.

P. 490b BAHMAN MĪRZĀ, l. 24 *for* Allāhyāṛ *read* Allāhyār.

P. 495b BAHMANID DYNASTY, l. 15 *for* Jālāl-al-Dīn *read* Jalāl-al-Dīn.

P. 515 BAHRĀM, Figure 11 *for* Bahrām II (274-97) *read* Bahrām II (274-93); *for* Bahrām III (292) *read* Bahrām III (293); *for* Narseh I (292-301) *read* Narseh I (293-301).

P. 527b BAHRĀMŠĀH, l. 11 *for* it final phase *read* its final phase.

P. 575a BALĀŠ, l. 47 *for* Cesennius Paeta *read* Caesennius Paetus;

P. 577b l. 40 *for* Weiskopf *read* Welskopf;

P. 578a l. 23 *for* Arabus *read* Arabicus;

P. 578b l. 11 *for* Commodus *read* Caracalla;

P. 580a l. 57 *for* 1886 *read* 1866.

P. 629b BALUCHISTAN I, *add to the bibliography* I. Afšār, "Bīst šahr o hazār farsang," *Yaġmā* 19, 1345 Š./1966, pp. 87-94, 255-62, 314-19.

P. 664a BĀMŠĀD, ll. 13-15 *replace the sentence* The weekly... magazine. *by* The weekly *Bāmšād* was brought out in Ḵordād, 1335 Š./June-July, 1956, as a publication of the newspaper *Īrān-e mā*, but after three issues a special permission from A. ʿAlam, minister of the interior, allowed it to be published as an independent weekly magazine without official licence. The licence was issued toward the end of that summer; l. 28 *after* arrest *add* and imprisonment for 40 days; *replace* II. 30-35 (until... 42 cm; its) *by* even after Pūrwālī's release from prison. Only the newspaper was allowed to continue publication and at the outset of 1343 Š./1964 was changed to a weekly news magazine of twenty, seven-column pages, measuring 29 × 42 cm. This magazine was at its most popular during the tenure of Prime Minister ʿAlī Amīnī. Its... ; l. 39 *for* 1347 *read* 1348.

P. 688a BANDAR-E GAZ, l. 30 *for* Rail road *read* Railroad.

P. 689b BANG I, l. 36 *for Pouru, baŋha read Pouru.baŋha.*

P. 692 *In running head for* BANGAŠ *read* BANGAṢ.

P. 712b BANNERS, l. 52 *for* crosshatched *read* cross-hatched;

P. 714b l. 22 *add* A systematic survey of banners illustrated in dated manuscripts should yield further information on their evolution. At this stage it appears that figural images were in use from as early as the 5th/11th century. As there is only one known illustrated manuscript surviving from before the Mongol invasion, it is not yet possible to state with certainty when such explicitly Islamic elements as Koranic inscriptions and possibly representations of angels were first adopted; both can be found in miniatures of the 8th/14th century.

P. 741b BARAKĪ BARAK, ll. 51-52 *for* Fallestudien *read* Fallstudien.

P. 755b BARĀQ BĀBĀ, l. 5 *for* Bektas-i *read* Bektaş-i.

P. 768b BARDA AND BARDADĀRĪ IV, l. 36 *for* others," Black *read* others." Black.

P. 776b BARDA AND BARDADĀRĪ V, l. 3 *for* Ghulām *read* G͟hulām.

P. 785 BARDESANES, *add to the bibliography* E. Beck, *Ephräms Polemik gegen Mani und die Manichäer im Rahmen der Zeitgenössischen griechischen Polemik und der des Augustinus*, CSCO 391, subs. 55, Louvain, 1978. Idem, "Bardaiṣan und seine Schule bei Ephräm," *Le muséon* 91, 1978, pp. 271-333. B. Aland, "Mani und Bardesanes—Zur Entstehung des manichäischen Systems," in A. Dietrich, ed., *Synkretismus im syrischpersischen Kulturgebiet. Bericht über ein Symposion in Reinhausen bei Göttingen in der Zeit vom 4. bis 8. Oktober 1971*, Göttingen, 1975, pp. 122-43. H. J. W. Drijvers, "Bardaiṣān von Edessa als Repräsentant des syrischen Synkretismus im 2, Jahrhundert n. Chr.," ibid., pp. 109-22 K. Rudolph, *Gnosis. The Nature and History of Gnosticism*, tr. and ed. by R. M. Wilson, San Francisco, 1987.

P. 855b BAṢRA, l. 11 *for al-ejtemāʿīya read al-ejtemāʿīya.*

P. 856b BAST, l. 22 *for zāwia read zāwīa*;

P. 857b l. 24 *after* by force *insert* (*Šekastan-e bast*); l. 25 *after* trespassers *add* This was the case of the Afsharid Nāder Mīrzā, who showed disrespect to the shrine of Imam Reżā and to the *ʿolamāʾ* (Algar, pp. 33, 47f.). After he had killed the *mojtahed* Mīrzā Moḥammad Mahdī he was tortured and put to death (Nāʾīnī, *Jāmeʿ-e jaʿfarī*, ed. Ī. Afšār, Tehran, 1343 Š./1964, pp. 111ff.; M.-Ḥ. Qoddūsī, *Nāder-nāma*, Mašhad, 1339 Š./1960, p. 441). He had also killed a *bastī* hidden in his stables (Malcolm, II, p. 559 n.). His mischief was recalled by Ayatollah Ṭabāṭabāʾī at the time of the Constitutional movement, when *bast* was broken by Qajar troops at Mašhad and Shiraz (Algar, p. 249).

P. 863a BĀṬENĪYA, l. 36 *for* Ğulāt *read* Ġulāt.

P. 867b BATHHOUSES I, l. 9 *for Gūša-i read Gūša-ī.*

P. 894a BAYHAQĪ, ABU'L-FAŻL, l. 16 *for* noqta *read* noqṭa; l. 31 *for soobshcheni-ya read soobschcheniya*; l. 48 after *Yaġmā* 23, *add* 1349 Š./1970.

EDITORIAL NOTE

In view of the expanding literature on Iranian studies and in the light of our experience of the past twelve years, it was felt that a revised short titles list would prove helpful. This has been placed at the beginning of this volume. It accommodates a number of frequently mentioned sources not included in the earlier list.

Beginning with letter B two slight modifications in transliteration have been made in order to bring it closer to the more common practice in the Iranian field and to ease a proofreading problem. These consist of the removal of the haček from *j* and beginning the second member of an Arabic compound name following *al-* consistently with a capital letter (thus Nāser-al-Dīn). In all Persian words of Arabic origin, *w* is being used rather than *v*. Also Ḥājī, the common Persian form of Ḥājj, will be used rather than Ḥājjī.

In the choice of titles for entries, increasing consideration has been given to choosing the title which comes first in alphabetical order, whether English or Iranian. Thus, the article on Bread is placed under this title rather than under Nān, whereas the article on Rice is placed under Berenj. Adequate cross-references however are provided to ensure that no article will be missed on account of its chosen title.

SHORT REFERENCES AND ABBREVIATIONS OF BOOKS AND PERIODICLAS

ʿAbd-al-Karīm Bok̲ārī
Charles Schefer, ed. and tr., *Histoire de l'Asie Centrale par Mir Abdoul Kerim Boukhary: Afghanistan, Boukhara, Khiva, Khoqand depuis les dernières années de règne de Nadir Chah (1153), jusqu'en 1233 de l'Hégire (1740-1818 A.D.)*, Publications de l'École des langues orientales vivantes, le série; I, text, Būlāq, 1290/1873; II, introd., tr., notes, Paris, 1876; repr. in one vol., Amsterdam, 1970.

Abh.
Abhandlungen.

Abu'l-Fedā, *Taqwīm*
Abu'l-Fedā Esmāʿīl b. ʿAlī b. Maḥmūd ʿEmād-al-Dīn Ayyūbī, *Taqwīm al-boldān*, ed. J.-T. Reinaud and M. de Slane, Paris, 1840.

Abu'l-Fedā, *Taqwīm*, tr. Reinaud
Abu'l-Fedā Esmāʿīl b. ʿAlī b. Maḥmūd ʿEmād-al-Dīn Ayyūbī, *Taqwīm al-boldān*, tr. J.-T. Reinaud, *Géographie d'Aboulfeda, traduite de l'arabe en français*, I and II/1, Paris, 1848; II/2, tr. S. Guyard, Paris, 1883.

Abu'l-Ḡāzī, *Šajara-ye tork*
Abu'l-Ḡāzī, *Šajara-ye tork*, ed. and tr. J. J. P. Desmaisons, *Histoire des Mongols et des Tatares par Aboul-Ghâzi Bèhâdour Khân, souverain de Kharezm et historien Djaghataï, 1603-1664*, 2 vols., St. Petersburg, 1871-74.

ADTD
Ankara Üniversitesi, Dil ve tarih-coğrafya fakültesi dergisi.

***Aḡānī*[1,2,3] (Cairo)**
Abu'l-Faraj ʿAlī b. al-Ḥosayn Qorašī Eṣfahānī, *Ketāb al-aḡānī*, 1st ed., Būlāq, 1285/1868-69; 2nd ed., Cairo, 1323/1905-06; 3rd ed., Cairo, 1345-/1926-.

Agathangelos, *History*, tr. Thomson
Agatʿangełay, *Patmutʿiwn Hayocʿ*, tr. R. W. Thomson, *History of the Armenians*, Albany, New York, 1976 (except pars. 259-715).

Agathangelos, *Patmutʿiwn Hayocʿ*
Agatʿangełay, *Patmutʿiwn Hayocʿ*, ed. G. Tēr-Mkrtʿean and St. Kanayeancʿ, Tiflis, 1909; repr. in Classical Armenian Text Reprint Series, Delmar, New York, 1979.

Agathangelos, *The Teaching of St. Gregory*
Agatʿangełay, *Patmutʿiwn Hayocʿ*, tr. R. W. Thomson, *The Teaching of St. Gregory, an Early Armenian Catechism*, Cambridge, Massachusetts, 1970 (pars. 259-715).

***Āʾīn-e akbarī*, ed. Blochmann**
Abu'l-Fażl ʿAllāmī, *Āʾīn-e akbarī*, ed. H. Blochmann, Bib. Ind., 2 vols., Calcutta, 1867-77.

***Āʾīn-e akbarī*, ed. Phillott**
Abu'l-Fażl ʿAllāmī, *Āʾīn-e akbarī*, rev. ed. and tr., D. C. Phillott, 3 vols., Calcutta, 1939-49.

***Āʾīn-e akbarī*, tr. Blochmann**
Abu'l-Fażl ʿAllāmī, *Āʾīn-e akbarī* I, tr. H. Blochmann; II-III, tr. H. S. Jarrett, Bib. Ind., Calcutta, 1868-94.

AirWb.
Christian Bartholomae, *Altiranisches Wörterbuch*, Strassburg, 1904; repr. Berlin, 1961.

AIUON
Annali dell'Istituto universitario orientale di Napoli.

AJA
American Journal of Archaeology.

AJSLL
American Journal of Semitic Languages and Literature.

Akbar-nāma
Abu'l-Fażl ʿAllāmī, *Akbar-nāma*, ed. Ā. Aḥmad-ʿAlī and M. ʿAbd-al-Raḥīm, 3 vols., Bib. Ind., Calcutta, 1873-86.

***Akbar-nāma*, tr. Beveridge**
Abu'l-Fażl ʿAllāmī, *Akbar-nāma*, tr. H. Beveridge, 3 vols., Bib. Ind., Calcutta, 1897-1939.

AKM
Abhandlungen für die Kunde des Morgenlandes.

Aʿlām al-šīʿa
Āḡā Bozorg Ṭehrānī, *Ṭabaqāt aʿlām al-šīʿa*, Najaf, 1373/1954.

AMI
Archäologische Mitteilungen aus Iran.

***ANRW* II**
Aufstieg und Niedergang der römischen Welt. Geschichte und Kultur Roms im Spiegel der neueren Forschung II: *Principat*, ed. H. Temporini and W. Haase, Berlin and New York, 1974-.

Anz.
Anzeiger.

AOASH
Acta Orientalia Academiae Scientiarum Hungaricae.

APAW
Abhandlungen der Preussischen Akademie der Wissenschaften.

ARW
Archiv für Religionswissenschaft.

Āryanpūr, *Az Ṣabā tā Nīmā*
Y. Āryanpūr, *Az Ṣabā tā Nīmā*, 2 vols., Tehran, 1351 Š./1973.

Aš'arī, *Maqālāt*
Abu'l-Ḥasan 'Alī b. Esmā'īl Aš'arī, *Maqālāt al-eslāmīyīn*, ed. H. Ritter, Istanbul, 1929-33.

Ātaškada
Loṭf-'Alī Bīg Āḏar (Āẕar), *Ātaškada*, ed. Ḥ. Sādāt-e Nāṣerī, 3 vols., Tehran, 1337-41 Š./1958-62.

Ateş, *Eserler*
A. Ateş, *İstanbul kütüphanelerinde farsça manzum eserler* I, Istanbul, 1968.

***Avesta*, ed. Geldner**
K. F. Geldner, ed., *Avesta, the Sacred Books of the Parsis*, Stuttgart, 3 vols., 1891-96.

***Avesta*, tr. Darmesteter**
J. Darmesteter, *Zend-Avesta: Traduction nouvelle avec commentaire historique et philologique*, 3 vols., Paris, 1899-93; repr. 1960.

***Avesta*, tr. Wolff**
F. Wolff, *Avesta, die heiligen Bücher der Parsen, übersetzt auf der Grundlage von Chr. Bartholomaes Altiranischem Wörterbuch*, Berlin and Leipzig, 1924.

'Awfī, *Lobāb*
Moḥammad 'Awfī, *Lobāb al-albāb*, ed. E. G. Browne and M. Qazvīnī, Leiden and London, 1906.

'Awfī, *Lobāb*, ed. Nafīsī
Moḥammad 'Awfī, *Lobāb al-albāb*, ed. S. Nafīsī, Tehran, 1335 Š./1956.

A'yān al-šī'a
Moḥsen Amīn 'Āmelī, *A'yān al-šī'a*, Damascus, 1935-.

Badā'ūnī, *Montaḵab*
'Abd-al-Qāder Badā'ūnī, *Montaḵab al-tawārīḵ*, ed. A.-'A. Kabīr-al-Dīn Aḥmad and W. Nassau Lees, 2 vols., Calcutta, 1864-69.

Badā'ūnī, *Montaḵab*, tr. Ranking et al.
'Abd-al-Qāder Badā'ūnī, *Montaḵab al-tawārīḵ*, tr. G. S. A. Ranking, W. H. Lowe, and W. Haig, 3 vols., Calcutta, 1884-1925; repr. Patna, 1973.

Baḡdādī, *Farq*, ed. Badr
Abū Manṣūr 'Abd-al-Qāher b. Ṭāher b. Moḥammad Baḡdādī, *al-Farq bayn al-feraq*, ed. M. Badr, Cairo, 1328/1910.

Baḡdādī, *Farq*, ed. 'Abd-al-Ḥamīd
Abū Manṣūr 'Abd-al-Qāher b. Ṭāher b. Moḥammad Baḡdādī, *al-Farq bayn al-feraq*, ed. M. M. 'Abd-al-Ḥamīd, Cairo, 1964.

Bahār, *Sabk-šenāsī*
M.-T. Bahār, *Sabk-šenāsī*, 3 vols., Tehran, 1321 Š./1942.

Bailey, *Dictionary*
H. W. Bailey, *Dictionary of Khotan Saka*, Cambridge, etc., 1979.

Bailey, *Zoroastrian Problems*
H. W. Bailey, *Zoroastrian Problems in the Ninth-Century Books*, Oxford, 1943; repr. with a new introd., 1971.

Balāḏorī, *Ansāb*
Abu'l-'Abbās Aḥmad b. Yaḥyā b. Jāber Balāḏorī, *Ansāb al-ašrāf* IVb, V, ed. M. Schlössinger and S. D. F. Goitein, Jerusalem, 1936-38.

Balāḏorī, *Fotūḥ*
Abu'l-'Abbās Aḥmad b. Yaḥyā b. Jāber Balāḏorī, *Fotūḥ al-boldān*, ed. M. J. de Goeje, Leiden, 1886; 2nd ed. 1968.

Balāḏorī, *Fotūḥ*, ed. Monajjed
Abu'l-'Abbās Aḥmad b. Yaḥyā b. Jāber Balāḏorī, *Fotūḥ al-boldān*, ed. Ṣ. Monajjed, Cairo, 1956-61.

Bal'amī, ed. Bahār
Abū 'Alī Moḥammad Bal'amī, *Tārīḵ-e Bal'amī*, ed. M. T. Bahār, Tehran, I, 1341 Š./1962.

Bal'amī, tr. Zotenberg
Abū 'Alī Moḥammad Bal'amī, *Chronique de... Tabari traduite sur la version persane d'Abou-'Ali Mo'hammad Bel'ami*, tr. H. Zotenberg, 4 vols., Paris, 1867-74.

Bāmdād, *Rejāl*
M. Bāmdād, *Šarḥ-e ḥāl-e rejāl-e Īrān dar qorūn-e davāzdahom wa sīzdahom wa čahārdahom-e hejrī*, Tehran, 6 vols., 1347-57 Š./1966-78.

Barthold, *Turkestan*[2,3]
W. W. Barthold, *Turkestan down to the Mongol Invasion*, 2nd ed., London, 1958; 3rd ed., London, 1969.

Bayānī, *Ḵošnevīsān*
M. Bayānī, *Aḥwāl o āṯār-e ḵošnevīsān: nasta'līqnevīsān*, 3 vols., Tehran, 1345-48 Š./1966-69.

Bayhaqī, ed. Fayyāż
Abu'l-Fażl Bayhaqī, *Tārīḵ-e mas'ūdī*, ed. 'A. Fayyāż, Mašhad, 1350 Š./1971.

Bayhaqī, ed. Nafīsī
Abu'l-Fażl Bayhaqī, *Tārīḵ-e mas'ūdī*, ed. S. Nafīsī, 3 vols., Tehran, 1319-32 Š./1940-53.

Bd.
See *Bundahišn*.

Belgrāmī, *Ḵezāna*
Āzād Belgrāmī, *Ḵezāna-ye 'āmera*, Cawnpore, 1871.

BGA
Bibliotheca Geographorum Arabicorum, ed. M. J. de Goeje, 8 vols. in 4, Leiden, 1870-94.

Bib. Ind.
Bibliotheca Indica, published by the Asiatic Society of Bengal, Calcutta.

Bib. Pers.
Bibliotheca Persica.

Bīrūnī, *Āṯār*
Abū Rayḥān Bīrūnī, *Ketāb al-āṯār al-bāqīa ʿan al-qorūn al-ḵālīa*, ed. E. Sachau, *Chronologie orientalischer Völker von Albêrûnî*, Leipzig, 1878; repr. 1923 and Baghdad, 1963.

Bīrūnī, *Āṯār*, tr. Sachau
Abū Rayḥān Bīrūnī, *Ketāb al-āṯār al-bāqīa ʿan al-qorūn al-ḵālīa*, tr. E. Sachau, *The Chronology of the Ancient Nations*, London, 1879.

BNF
Beiträge zur Namenforschung.

***Borhān-e qāṭeʿ*, ed. Moʿīn**
Moḥammad Ḥosayn b. Ḵalaf Tabrīzī, *Borhān-e qāṭeʿ*, ed. M. Moʿīn, 6 vols., Tehran, 1342-52 Š./1963-73.

Bosworth, *Ghaznavids*
C. E. Bosworth, *The Ghaznavids: Their Empire in Afghanistan and Eastern Iran 944-1040*, Edinburgh, 1963.

Bosworth, *Later Ghaznavids*
C. E. Bosworth, *The Later Ghaznavids, Splendour and Decay: the Dynasty in Afghanistan and Northern India 1040-1186*, Edinburgh and New York, 1977.

Boyce, "Middle Persian Literature"
M. Boyce, "Middle Persian Literature," in *HO* I, iv, 2/1, Leiden and Cologne, 1968, pp. 31-66.

Boyce, *Reader*
M. Boyce, *A Reader in Manichaean Middle Persian and Parthian*, Acta Iranica 9, Tehran and Liège, 1975.

Boyce, *Stronghold*
M. Boyce, *A Persian Stronghold of Zoroastrianism*, Oxford, 1977.

Boyce, *Zoroastrianism*
M. Boyce, *A History of Zoroastrianism*, HO I, viii, 1/2, 2A, Leiden and Cologne, 1975-.

Brockelmann, *GAL*
C. Brockelmann, *Geschichte der Arabischen Literatur*, Leiden, I-II, 2nd ed., 1943-49; S. (Supplement) I-III, 1937-42.

Browne, *Lit. Hist. Persia*
E. G. Browne, *A Literary History of Persia*, 4 vols., London, 1902-24.

Browne, *Persian Revolution*
E. G. Browne, *The Persian Revolution of 1905-1909*, London, 1910.

Browne, *Press and Poetry*
E. G. Browne, *The Press and Poetry of Modern Persia Partly Based on the Manuscript Work of Mírzá Muḥammad ʿAlí Khán "Tarbiyat" of Tabríz*, Cambridge, 1914.

BSL
Bulletin de la Société de linguistique de Paris.

BSO(A)S
Bulletin of the School of Oriental (and African) Studies.

BTNK
Bongāh-e tarjama wa našr-e ketāb, Tehran.

***Bundahišn* (DH)**
P. Anklesaria, ed., *The Codex DH, Being a Facsimile Edition of Bondahesh, Zand-e Vohuman Yasht, and Parts of the Denkard*, Tehran, [1350 Š./1971].

***Bundahišn* (TD_1)**
P. Anklesaria, ed., *The Bondahesh, Being a Facsimile Edition of the Manuscript* TD_1, Tehran, [1350 Š./1971].

***Bundahišn* (TD_2)**
T. D. Anklesaria, ed., *The Bûndahishn, Being a Facsimile of the TD Manuscript No. 2...*, Bombay, 1908.

***Bundahišn*, tr. Anklesaria**
B. T. Anklesaria, ed. and tr., *Zand-Ākāsīh: Iranian or Greater Bundahišn*, Bombay, 1956.

Caetani, *Annali*
L. Caetani, *Annali dell'Islam*, 10 vols. in 12, Milan, 1905-26; repr. 1986.

***CAH*[2,3]**
Cambridge Ancient History, 2nd ed., 12 vols., Cambridge, 1928-39; 3rd ed., vols. 1 and 2 in 4, 1970-75.

***Čahār maqāla*, ed. Qazvīnī**
Aḥmad b. ʿOmar b. ʿAlī Neẓāmī ʿArūżī Samarqandī, *Čahār maqāla*, ed. M. Qazvīnī, rev. ed. M. Moʿīn, Tehran, 1331 Š./1952.

Camb. Hist. Iran
The Cambridge History of Iran, Cambridge, etc., 1968-.

Cat. Bankipore
Catalogue of the Arabic and Persian Manuscripts in the Oriental Public Library at Bankipore, 29 vols., Calcutta, 1908-20; Patna, 1918-71.

Cat. Bibliothèque Nationale
E. Blochet, *Catalogue des manuscrits persan de la Bibliothèque Nationale*, 4 vols., Paris, 1905-34.

Cat. Bodleian Library
E. Sachau, H. Ethé, and A. F. L. Beeston, eds., *Catalogue of the Persian, Turkish, Hindustani, and Pushtu Manuscripts in the Bodleian Library*, 3 vols., Oxford, 1889, 1930, 1954.

Cat. Chester Beatty Library
The Chester Beatty Library: a Catalogue of the Persian Manuscripts and Miniatures, Dublin, I, ed. A. J. Arberry, M. Minovi, and E. Blochet, 1959; II-III, ed. M. Minovi, B. W. Robinson, J. W. S. Wilkinson, and E. Blochet, 1960, 1962.

CDAFI
Cahiers de la Délégation archéologique française en Iran.

Christensen, *Contributions*
A. Christensen, *Contributions à la dialectologie iranienne*, Det Kgl. Danske Videnskabernes Selskab, Hist.-fil. Medd., Copenhagen; I: *Dialecte guilākī de Recht, dialectes de Färizänd, de Yaran et de Natanz. . .*, 1930; II: *Dialectes de la région de Sèmnān. . .*, 1935.

Christensen, *Iran Sass.*
A. Christensen, *L'Iran sous les Sassanides*, 2nd ed., Copenhagen, 1944.

Col. Lect. Series.
Columbia Lectures Series on Iranian Studies.

Corpus Inscr. Iran.
Corpus Inscriptionum Iranicarum, London, 1955-.

CSCO
Corpus Scriptorum Christianorum Orientalium.

Curzon, *Persian Question*
G. N. Curzon, *Persia and the Persian Question*, 2 vols., London, 1892.

***Dādistān ī dēnīg*, pt. 1**
T. D. Anklesaria, ed., *The Dadistan-i Dinik, Part I, Pursishn I-XL*, Bombay, 1913.

Dāneš-nāma
Dāneš-nāma-ye Īrān o Eslām, Tehran, 1976-.

al-Ḏarīʿa
Āqā Bozorg Ṭehrānī, *al-Ḏarīʿa elā taṣānīf al-šīʿa*, Najaf (Tehran), 1355-/1936-.

Dawlatābādī, *Ḥayāt-e Yaḥyā*
Y. Dawlatābādī, *Tārīḵ-e moʿāṣer yā ḥayāt-e Yaḥyā*, 4 vols., Tehran, n.d.

Dawlatšāh, ed. Browne
Dawlatšāh, *Taḏkerat al-šoʿarāʾ*, ed. E. G. Browne, *The Tadhkiratu 'shshuʿará ("Memoirs of the Poets") of Dawlatsháh. . .*, Leiden and London, 1901.

Dehḵodā
ʿAlī-Akbar Dehḵodā, *Loğat-nāma*, Tehran, 1325-[58] Š./1946-[79].

***Dēnkard*, ed. Dresden**
M. J. Dresden, ed., *Dēnkart, a Pahlavi Text. Facsimile Edition of the Manuscript B of the K. R. Cama Royal Institute Bombay*, Wiesbaden, 1966.

***Dēnkard*, ed. Madan**
D. M. Madan, ed., *The Complete Text of the Pahlavi Dinkard*, 2 vols., Bombay, 1874-1928.

***Dēnkard*, ed. Sanjana**
D. D. P. Sanjana and P. D. B. Sanjana, *The Dinkard*, 19 vols., Bombay, 1874-28.

Dīnavarī, ed. Guirgass
Abū Ḥanīfa Dīnavarī, *al-Aḵbār al-ṭewāl*, ed. V. Guirgass, Leiden, 1888.

Doerfer
G. Doerfer, *Türkische und mongolische Elemente im Neupersischen*, 4 vols., Wiesbaden, 1963-76.

Ebn al-Aṯīr
ʿEzz-al-Dīn b. al-Aṯīr, *al-Kāmel fi'l-taʾrīḵ*, ed. C. J. Tornberg, 12 vols., Leiden, 1851-76; repr. Beirut, 1965.

Ebn al-Balḵī
Ebn al-Balḵī, *Fārs-nāma*, ed. G. Le Strange and R. A. Nicholson, *The Fársnáma of Ibnu'l-Balkhí*, GMS, Cambridge, 1912.

Ebn Baṭṭūṭa
Abū ʿAbd-Allāh Moḥammad b. Moḥammad Lawātī Ṭanjī b. Baṭṭūṭa, *Toḥfat al-noẓẓār fī ğarāʾeb al-amṣār wa ʿajāʾeb al-asfār*, ed. and tr. C. Defremery and B. R. Sanguinetti, *Voyages d'Ibn Batouta*, 4 vols., Paris, 1853-58.

Ebn Baṭṭūṭa, tr. Gibb
Abū ʿAbd-Allāh Moḥammad b. Moḥammad Lawātī Ṭanjī b. Baṭṭūṭa, *Toḥfat al-noẓẓār fī ğarāʾeb al-amṣār wa ʿajāʾeb al-asfār*, tr. H. A. R. Gibb, 3 vols., Cambridge, 1958-71.

Ebn Esfandīār
Moḥammad b. Ḥasan b. Esfandīār, *Tārīḵ-e Ṭabarestān*, ed. ʿA. Eqbāl, 2 vols., Tehran, 1320 Š./1941.

Ebn Esfandīār, tr. Browne
Moḥammad b. Ḥasan b. Esfandīār, *Tārīḵ-e Ṭabarestān*, abridged tr., E. G. Browne, Leyden and London, 1905.

Ebn al-Faqīh,
Abū Bakr Aḥmad b. Moḥammad Hamaḏānī "Ebn al-Faqīh," *Moḵtaṣar Ketāb al-boldān*, ed. M. J. de Goeje, BGA, Leiden, 1886.

Ebn Ḥawqal
Ebn Ḥawqal, *Ketāb ṣūrat al-arż*, ed. J. H. Kramers, BGA, 2nd ed., Leiden, 1938-39.

Ebn Ḥawqal, tr. Kramers
Ebn Ḥawqal, *Ketāb ṣūrat al-arż*, tr. J. H. Kramers and G. Wiet, *Configuration de la terre*, 2 vols., Paris and Beirut, 1964.

Ebn al-Jawzī, *Montaẓam*
ʿAbd-al-Raḥmān b. ʿAlī b. al-Jawzī, *al-Montaẓam fī taʾrīḵ al-molūk wa'l-omam*, Hyderabad, 1357-59/1938-40.

Ebn Ḵallekān, ed. ʿAbbās
Ebn Ḵallekān, *Wafayāt al-aʿyān wa anbāʾ abnāʾ al-zamān*, ed. E. ʿAbbās (I. Abbas), 8 vols., Beirut, 1968-72.

Ebn Ḵallekān, ed. Wüstenfeld
Ebn Ḵallekān, *Wafayāt al-aʿyān wa anbāʾ abnāʾ al-zamān*, ed. F. Wüstenfeld, Göttingen, 1835-50.

Ebn Ḵallekān, tr. de Slane
Ebn Ḵallekān, *Wafayāt al-aʿyān wa anbāʾ abnāʾ al-zamān*, tr. Baron M. de Slane, *Ibn*

Khallikan's Biographical Dictionary, 4 vols., Paris, 1842-71.

Ebn Ḵordāḏbeh
Ebn Ḵordāḏbeh, *al-Masālek wa'l-mamālek*, ed. M. J. de Goeje, BGA, Leiden, 1889; 2nd ed., 1967.

Ebn Meskawayh, *Tajāreb*
Ebn Meskawayh, *Tajāreb al-omam*. See Margoliouth and Amedroz, *Eclipse*.

Ebn al-Mortażā, *Ṭabaqāt*
Ebn al-Mortażā, *Ṭabaqāt al-moʿtazela*, ed. S. Diwald-Wilzer, Beirut and Wiesbaden, 1961.

Ebn al-Nadīm, ed. Flügel
Ebn al-Nadīm, *Ketāb al-fehrest*, ed. G. Flügel, Leipzig, 1871-72.

Ebn al-Nadīm, ed. Tajaddod
Ebn al-Nadīm, *Ketāb al-fehrest*, ed. M. R. Tajaddod, Tehran, 1st ed., 1971, 2nd ed., 1973.

Ebn al-Nadīm, tr. Dodge
Ebn-al-Nadīm, *Ketāb al-fehrest*, tr. B. Dodge, *The Fihrist of al-Nadīm*, 2 vols., New York and London, 1970.

Ebn Rosta
Ebn Rosta, *al-Aʿlāq al-nafīsa*, ed. M. J. de Goeje, BGA, Leiden, 1892; 2nd ed., 1967.

Ebn Rosta, tr. Wiet
Ebn Rosta, *al-Aʿlāq al-nafīsa*, tr. G. Wiet, *Les atours précieux*, Cairo, 1955.

Ebn Saʿd
Ebn Saʿd, *al-Ṭabaqāt al-kobrā*, ed. H. Sachau et al., 9 vols., Leiden, 1905-40.

Ebn Serapion. See **Sohrāb.**

Ebn Taḡrīberdī
Ebn Taḡrīberdī, *al-Nojūm al-zāhera fī molūk Meṣr wa'l-Qāhera*, Cairo, 1348-1929.

Edrīsī
Edrīsī, ed. E. Cerulli et al., *Opus Geographicum*, 6 vols., Naples, 1970-76.

Edrīsī, tr. Jaubert
P. A. Jaubert, tr., *Géographie d'Edrisi*, 2 vols., Paris, 1836-40.

***EI*[1,2]**
The Encyclopaedia of Islam, London and Leiden; 1st ed., 4 vols. and a supplement, 1908-36; 2nd ed., 1960-.

EIr.
Encyclopaedia Iranica, ed. E. Yarshater, London, etc., 1982-.

Ełišē, ed. Tēr-Minasean
Ełišē, *Ełišēi vasn Vardanay ew Hayocʿ paterazmin*, ed. E. Tēr-Minasean, Erevan, 1957.

Ełišē, tr. Thomson
Ełišē, *Ełišēi vasn Vardanay ew Hayocʿ paterazmin*, tr. R. W. Thomson, *History of Vardan and the Armenian War*, Cambridge, Massachusetts, 1982.

Elliot, *History of India*
H. M. Elliot and J. Dowson, eds., *The History of India as Told by its Own Historians*, 8 vols., London, 1867-77.

Eqbāl, *Tārīḵ-e Moḡol*
ʿAbbās Eqbāl, *Tārīḵ-e mofaṣṣal-e Īrān az estīlā-ye Moḡol tā eʿlān-e mašrūṭīyat* I, Tehran, 1320 Š./1941; 2nd ed., 1341 Š./1962.

Eskandar Beg
Eskandar Beg Torkamān, *Tārīḵ-e ʿālamārā-ye ʿabbāsī*, 2 vols., Tehran, 1334-35 Š./1955-56.

Eskandar Beg, tr. Savory
Eskandar Beg Monšī, *Tārīḵ-e ʿālamārā-ye ʿabbāsī*, tr. R. M. Savory, *History of Shah ʿAbbas the Great I-II*, PHS, Boulder, Colorado, 1979; III (index), Bib. Pers., New York, 1986.

Eṣṭaḵrī
Abū Esḥāq Eṣṭaḵrī, *Ketāb masālek al-mamālek*, ed. M. J. de Goeje, BGA, Leiden, 1870; 2nd ed., 1927; 3rd ed., 1967.

Eʿtemād-al-Salṭana, *Rūz-nāma-ye ḵāṭerāt*
Moḥammad-Ḥasan Khan Ṣanīʿ-al-Dawla Eʿtemād-al-Salṭana, *Rūz-nāma-ye ḵāṭerāt-e Eʿtemād-al-Salṭana*, ed. Ī. Afšār, 3rd ed., Tehran, 2536 = 1356 Š./1977.

Eʿtemād-al-Salṭana, *Montaẓam-e nāṣerī*
Moḥammad-Ḥasan Khan Ṣanīʿ-al-Dawla Eʿtemād-al-Salṭana, *Tārīḵ-e montaẓam-e nāṣerī*, 3 vols., Tehran, 1298/1881.

Eʿtemād-al-Salṭana, *Montaẓam-e nāṣerī*, ed. Reżwānī
Moḥammad-Ḥasan Khan Ṣanīʿ-al-Dawla Eʿtemād-al-Salṭana, *Tārīḵ-e montaẓam-e nāṣerī*, ed. M. E. Reżwānī, 1363 Š.-/1984-.

Ethé, Catalogue
H. Ethé, *Catalogue of the Persian Manuscripts in the Library of the India Office*, Oxford, 1903.

Eznik, ed. Mariès and Mercier
Eznik Kołbacʿi, *Ełc ałandocʿ* (Refutation of sects), ed. and tr. L. Mariès and C. Mercier, *Eznik de Kołb, De Deo*, PO 28/3-4, Paris, 1959.

Fasāʾī
Ḥasan b. Ḥasan Fasāʾī, *Fārs-nāma-ye nāṣerī*, Tehran, 2 vols. in 1, 1312-13/1895-96.

Fasāʾī, tr. Busse
Ḥasan b. Ḥasan Fasāʾī, *Fārs-nāma-ye nāṣerī*, tr. H. Busse, *History of Persia under Qajar Rule*, PHS, New York, 1972.

Faustus, ed. Patkanean
Pʿawstos Buzand, *Patmutʿiwn Hayocʿ*, ed. Kʿ. Patkanean, St. Petersburg, 1883; repr. in Classical Armenian Text Reprint Series, Delmar, New York, 1984.

Faustus, tr. Garsoïan
Pʿawstos Buzand, *Patmutʿiwn Hayocʿ*, tr. N. Garsoïan, Cambridge, Massachusetts, forthcoming.

Fehrest. See **Ebn al-Nadīm**

Fehrest... Āṣafīya
Fehrest-e kotob-e ʿarabī fārsī wa ordū, makzūn-e kotob-kāna-ye Āṣafīya, Hyderabad, 1332-33/1914-15.

Feraq al-šīʿa
Ḥasan b. Mūsā Nawbaktī, *Ketāb feraq al-šīʿa*, ed. H. R. Ritter, Leipzig and Istanbul, 1931.

Ferešta
Moḥammad Qāsem Hendūšāh Astarābādī Ferešta, *Golšan-e ebrāhīmī*, ed. J. Briggs, 2 vols., Bombay and Poona, 1831.

Ferešta, tr. Briggs
Moḥammad Qāsem Hendūšāh Astarābādī Ferešta, *Golšan-e ebrāhīmī*, tr. J. Briggs, *History of the Rise of the Mohamedan Power in India*, 4 vols., London, 1829; repr. Calcutta, 1908-10, 1966.

FIZ
Farhang-e Īrān-zamīn.

Gardīzī, ed. Ḥabībī
Abū Saʿīd ʿAbd-al-Ḥayy Gardīzī, *Zayn al-akbār*, ed. ʿA. Ḥabībī, Tehran, 1347 Š./1968.

Gardīzī, ed. Nazim
Abū Saʿīd ʿAbd-al-Ḥayy Gardīzī, *Zayn al-akbār*, ed. M. Nazim, Berlin, 1928.

Gazetteer of Afghanistan
L. W. Adamec, ed., *Historical and Political Gazetteer of Afghanistan*, Graz, 1972-.

Gazetteer of Iran
L. W. Adamec, *Historical Gazetteer of Iran*, Graz, 1976-.

GMS
E. J. W. Gibb Memorial Series.

Golčīn-e Maʿānī, *Tadkerahā*
A. Golčīn-e Maʿānī, *Tārīk-e tadkerahā-ye fārsī*, 2 vols., Tehran, 1348-50 Š./1969-71.

Gray, *Foundations*
L. Gray, *Foundations of the Iranian Religions*, K. R. Cama Oriental Institute Publication 5 (repr. from *Journal of the Cama Oriental Institute* 15, 1929), Bombay, 1930.

Grundriss
W. Geiger and E. Kuhn, eds., *Grundriss der Iranischen Philologie*, 2 vols., Strassburg, 1895-1901.

***Ḥabīb al-sīar* (Bombay)**
Ḡīāt-al-Dīn Moḥammad Kᵛāndamīr, *Tārīk-e ḥabīb al-sīar*, Bombay, 3 vols., 1272/1955-56.

***Ḥabīb al-sīar* (Tehran)**
Ḡīāt-al-Dīn Moḥammad Kᵛāndamīr, *Tārīk-e ḥabīb al-sīar*, Tehran, 4 vols., 1333 Š./1954.

Haft eqlīm
Amīn Aḥmad Rāzī, *Haft eqlīm*, ed. J. Fāżel, 3 vols., Tehran, 1340 Š./1961.

Ḥamza
Abu'l-Ḥasan Ḥamza Eṣfahānī, *Ketāb ta'rīk senī molūk al-arż wa'l-anbīā'*, ed. and Latin tr. J. M. E. Gottwaldt, 2 vols., St. Petersburg and Leipzig, 1844-48.

Ḥasan Rūmlū, ed. Navā'ī
Ḥasan Rūmlū, *Aḥsan al-tawārīk*, ed. ʿA. Navā'ī, Tehran, 1349 Š./1970; II, Tehran, 1357 Š./1979.

Ḥasan Rūmlū, ed. Seddon
Ḥasan Rūmlū, *Aḥsan al-tawārīk*, ed. C. N. Seddon, 2 vols., Calcutta, 1931.

Hedāyat, *Rawżat al-ṣafā*
Reżāqolī Khan Hedāyat, *Tārīk-e rawżat al-ṣafā-ye nāṣerī*, 2 vols., Tehran, 1270-74/1853-56 (=vols. 9-10 of Mīrkᵛānd, *Tārīk-e rawżat al-ṣafā*); vol. 11: index by M.-J. Maškūr, 1351 Š./1972.

Henning, "Mitteliranisch"
W. B. Henning, "Mitteliranisch," in *HO* I, iv, 1, Leiden and Cologne, 1958, pp. 20-130.

Highlights of Persian Art
R. Ettinghausen and E. Yarshater, eds., *Highlights of Persian Art*, Boulder, Colorado, 1979 (publ. by Bib. Pers., New York, 1982).

HJAS
Harvard Journal of Asiatic Studies.

HO
B. Spuler et al., eds., *Handbuch der Orientalistik*, Abt. I: *Der nahe und der mittlere Osten*, Leiden and Cologne.

***Ḥodūd al-ʿālam*, ed. Sotūda**
M. Sotūda, ed., *Ḥodūd al-ʿālam*, Tehran, 1340 Š./1961.

***Ḥodūd al-ʿālam*, tr. Minorsky**
V. Minorsky, tr., *Ḥudūd al-ʿĀlam "The Regions of the World,"* 2nd ed., GMS, London, 1970.

Honarfar, *Eṣfahān*
L. Honarfar, *Ganjīna-ye āṯār-e tārīkī-e Eṣfahān*, Tehran, 1344 Š./1965.

Horn, *Etymologie*
P. Horn, *Grundriss der neupersischen Etymologie*, Strassburg, 1893.

Houtsma, *Recueil*
N. Th. Houtsma, *Recueil de textes relatifs à l'histoire des Seljoucides*, Leiden, 1886-1902.

Hübschmann, *Armenische Grammatik*
H. Hübschmann, *Armenische Grammatik. Erster Teil: Armenische Etymologie*, Leipzig, 1897.

Hübschmann, *Persische Studien*
H. Hübschmann, *Persische Studien*, Strassburg, 1895.

İA
İslam ansiklopedisi, Istanbul, 1965.

Ibn. See Ebn.

IF
Indogermanische Forschungen.

IHQ
Indian Historical Quarterly.

IIJ
Indo-Iranian Journal.

IJMES
International Journal of Middle East Studies.

Iran
Iran. Journal of the British Institute of Persian Studies.

Iranian Studies
Iranian Studies. Journal of the Society for Iranian Studies.

Iranisches Personennamenbuch
M. Mayrhofer and R. Schmitt, eds., *Iranisches Personennamenbuch*, Vienna, 1977-.

Īrān-nāma
Īrān-nāma. Majalla-ye taḥqīqāt-e īrān-šenāsī. English title: *Iran Nameh. A Persian Journal of Iranian Studies.*

Ivanov, *Catalogue*
W. Ivanov, *Concise Descriptive Catalogue of the Persian Manuscripts in the Collection of the Asiatic Society of Bengal*, Calcutta, 1924.

JA
Journal asiatique.

Jacoby, *Fragmente*
F. Jacoby, *Die Fragmente der griechischen Historiker*, Berlin, 1923-58.

***Jāmeʿ al-tawārīḵ*.** See **Rašīd-al-Dīn**.

Jāmī, *Nafaḥāt*
ʿAbd-al-Raḥmān Jāmī, *Nafaḥāt al-ons*, ed. M. Tawḥīdīpūr, Tehran, 1336 Š./1957.

JAOS
Journal of the American Oriental Society.

JESHO
Journal of the Economic and Social History of the Orient.

JNES
Journal of Near Eastern Studies.

Jovaynī, ed. Qazvīnī
ʿAlāʾ-al-Dīn ʿAṭā Malek Jovaynī, *Tārīḵ-e jahāngošā*, ed. M. Qazvīnī, GMS, 3 vols., Leiden and London, 1906-37.

Jovaynī, tr. Boyle
ʿAlāʾ-al-Dīn ʿAṭā Malek Jovaynī, *Tārīḵ-e jahāngošā*, tr. J. A. Boyle, *The History of the World-Conqueror*, Manchester, 2 vols., 1958.

JPHS
Journal of the Pakistan Historical Society.

JRAS
Journal of the Royal Asiatic Society.

J(R)ASB
Journal of the (Royal) Asiatic Society of Bengal.

JRGS
Journal of the Royal Geographical Society.

Justi, *Namenbuch*
F. Justi, *Iranisches Namenbuch*, Marburg, 1895.

Jūzjānī, *Ṭabaqāt*
Menhāj-e Serāj Jūzjānī, *Ṭabaqāt-e nāṣerī*, ed. ʿA. Ḥabībī, 2nd ed., 2 vols., Kabul, 1342-43 Š./1963-64.

Jūzjānī, *Ṭabaqāt*, tr. Raverty
Menhāj-e Serāj Jūzjānī, *Ṭabaqāt-e nāṣerī*, tr. H. G. Raverty, Bib. Ind., 2 vols., London, 1881-99.

Kaḥḥāla
ʿOmar Reżā Kaḥḥāla, *Moʿjam al-moʾallefīn*, 15 vols., Damascus, 1957-61.

Karatay, *Katalog*
F. E. Karatay, *Topkapı Sarayı Müzesi Kütüphanesi farsça yazmalar kataloğu*, Istanbul, 1961.

***Kār-nāmag*, ed. Antia**
E. K. Antia, ed., *Kârnâmak-i Artakhshîr Pâpakân, the Original Pahlavi Text, with Translation in Avesta Characters, Translations into English and Gujarati, and Selections from the Shâhnâmeh*, Bombay, 1900.

***Kār-nāmag*, ed. Sanjana**
D. D. P. Sanjana, ed., *The Kârnâmê î Artakhshîr Pâpakân... The Original Pahlavi Text Edited for the First Time... Translations into English and Gujarati Lanuages...*, Bombay, 1896.

***Kašf al-ẓonūn*, ed. Flügel**
Ḥājī Ḵalīfa, *Kašf al-ẓonūn*, ed. G. Flügel, 7 vols., Leipzig, 1835-58.

***Kašf al-ẓonūn*, ed. Yaltkaya and Bilge**
Ḥājī Ḵalīfa, *Kašf al-ẓonūn*, ed. S. Yaltkaya and K. R. Bilge, 2 vols., Istanbul, 1941-43.

Kašf al-ẓonūn: Ḏayl
Esmāʿīl Pasha Baḡdādī, *Ketāb Īżāḥ al-maknūn fi'l-ḏayl ʿalā Kašf al-ẓonūn ʿan asāmi'l-kotob wa'l-fonūn*, 2 vols., Istanbul, 1945-47.

Kasrawī, *Āḏarbāyjān*
Aḥmad Kasrawī, *Tārīḵ-e hejda-sāla-ye Āḏarbāyjān*, Tehran, 2nd ed., 1333 Š./1954 (several reprints).

Kasrawī, *Mašrūta*[3]
Aḥmad Kasrawī, *Tārīḵ-e mašrūṭa-ye Īrān*, 3rd ed., 3 vols. in one, Tehran, 1330 Š./1951 (several reprints).

Kayhān, *Joḡrāfīā*
Masʿūd Kayhān, *Joḡrāfīā-ye mofaṣṣal-e Īrān*, 3 vols., 1310-11 Š./1931-32.

Ḵayyāmpūr, *Soḵanvarān*
ʿAbd-al-Rasūl Ḵayyāmpūr, *Farhang-e soḵanvarān*, Tabrīz, 1340 Š./1961.

Kent, *Old Persian*
R. G. Kent, *Old Persian. Grammar, Texts, Lexicon*, 2nd ed., New Haven, 1953.

Lambton, *Continuity*
A. K. S. Lambton, *Continuity and Change: Aspects of Social and Administrative History in Persia*, Col. Lect., Albany, New York, 1987.

Lambton, *Landlord and Peasant*
A. K. S. Lambton, *Landlord and Peasant in Persia*, London, etc., 1953.

Langlois, *Historiens*
Victor Langlois, tr., *Collections des historiens anciens et modernes de l'Arménie*, 2 vols., Paris, 1868-69.

Laufer, *Sino-Iranica*
B. Laufer, *Sino-Iranica. Chinese Contributions to the History of Civilization in Ancient Iran*, Chicago, 1919.

Lazard, *Premiers poètes*
G. Lazard, *Les premiers poètes persans (IXe-Xe siècle): Fragments rassemblés, édités et traduits*, 2 vols., Tehran and Liège, 1964.

Le Strange, *Lands*
G. Le Strange, *The Lands of the Eastern Caliphate*, 2nd ed., Cambridge, 1930.

***Loḡat-e fors*, ed. Dabīrsīāqī**
Asadī Ṭūsī, *Loḡat-e fors*, ed. M. Dabīrsīāqī from the edition of Paul Horn, Tehran, 1336 Š./1957.

***Loḡat-e fors*, ed. Eqbāl**
Asadī Ṭūsī, *Loḡat-e fors*, ed. ʿA. Eqbāl, Tehran, 1319 Š./1940.

Lorimer, *Gazetteer*
J. G. Lorimer, *Gazetteer of the Persian Gulf, 'Omān, and Central Arabia*, compl. and ed. L. Birdwood, 2 vols., Calcutta, 1908-15; repr., 2 vols. in 6, 1970.

***Maʾāṯer al-omarāʾ* (Calcutta)**
ʿAbd-al-Razzāq Šāhnavāz Khan Awrangābādī, *Maʾāṯer al-omarāʾ*, Bib. Ind., 3 vols., Calcutta, 1888-91.

***Maʾāṯer al-omarāʾ*, tr. Beveridge**
ʿAbd-al-Razzāq Šāhnavāz Khan Awrangābādī, *Maʾāṯer al-omarāʾ*, tr. H. Beveridge, rev. B. Prashad, Bib. Ind., 3 vols., Calcutta 1911-64; repr. Patna, 1979.

***Mādayān*, pt. 1**
Mâdigân-i-hazâr Dâtistân, ed. J. J. Modi (facs. ed. of pt. 1, fols. 1-55), Bombay, 1901.

***Mādayān*, pt. 2**
The Social Code of the Parsees in Sasanian Times of the Mâdigân-i-hazâr Dâtistân, Part II, ed. T. D. Anklesaria, Bombay, 1912.

Maḥbūbī, *Moʾassasāt*
Ḥosayn Maḥbūbī Ardakānī, *Tārīḵ-e moʾassasāt-e tamaddonī-e jadīd dar Īrān*, Tehran, I 1356 Š./1975, II, 2537 = 1357 Š./1978.

Majāles al-nafāʾes
ʿAlī Šīr Navāʾī, *Majāles al-nafāʾes*, Pers. tr. Faḵrī Herātī and Ḥakīm Shah Moḥammad Qazvīnī, ed. ʿA.-A. Ḥekmat, Tehran, 1323 Š./1944.

Majmaʿ al-foṣaḥāʾ
Reżāqolī Khan Hedāyat, *Majmaʿ al-foṣaḥāʾ*, ed. M. Moṣaffā, 2 vols. in 6, Tehran, 1336-40 Š./1957-61.

Malekzāda
M. Malekzāda, *Tārīḵ-e enqelāb-e mašrūṭīyat-e Īrān*, 7 vols., Tehran, 1327-35 Š./1948-56.

Mann, *Kurdisch-persische Forschungen*
O. Mann, *Kurdisch-persische Forschungen*. Pt. 1: *Die Tâjîk-Mundarten der Provinz Fârs*, Berlin, 1909. Pt. 2: *Die Mundarten der Lur-Stämme im südwestlichen Persien*, Berlin, 1910. Pt. 3: *Nordwestiranisch*, vol. 1: *Die Mundarten von Khunsâr...*, ed. K. Hadank, Berlin and Leipzig, 1926; vol. 2: *Mundarten der Gûrân...*, ed. K. Hadank, 1930; vol. 3: *Die Mundart der Mukri-Kurden*, 2 vols., 1906-09; vol. 4: *Die Mundarten der Zâzâ...*, ed. K. Hadank, Berlin, 1932.

Maqdesī, *Badʾ*
Moṭahhar b. Ṭāher Maqdesī, *Ketāb al-badʾ wa'l-taʾrīḵ*, ed. and tr. Claude Huart, *Le livre de la création et de l'histoire*, 6 vols., Paris, 1899-1919.

Margoliouth and Amedroz, *Eclipse*
D. S. Margoliouth and H. F. Amedroz, ed. and tr., *The Eclipse of the Abbasid Caliphate: Original Chronicles of the Fourth Islamic Century*, 7 vols., Oxford, 1921-22.

Markwart, *Ērānšahr*
J. Markwart (Marquart), *Ērānšahr nach der Geographie des Ps. Moses Xorenacʿi*, Abh. Ak. Wiss. zu Göttingen, N.S. 3/2, 1901.

Markwart, *Provincial Capitals*
J. Markwart, *A Catalogue of the Provincial Capitals of Ērānshahr (Pahlavi Text, Version and Commentary)*, ed. G. Messina, Analecta Orientalia 3, Rome, 1931.

Marshall, *Mughals in India*
D. N. Marshall, *Mughals in India: A Bibliographic Survey* I: *Manuscripts*, Bombay, 1967.

MASI
Memoirs of the Archaeological Survey of India.

Massé, *Croyances*
H. Massé, *Croyances et coutumes persanes suivies de contes et chansons populaires*, Les littératures populaires de toutes les nations 4, 2 vols., Paris, 1938.

Massignon, *Essai*
L. Massignon, *Essai sur les origines du lexique technique de la mystique musulmane*, new ed., Paris, 1954.

Masʿūdī, *Morūj*
Masʿūdī, *Morūj al-ḏahab*, ed. and tr. C. Barbier de Meynard and Pavet de Courteille, *Les prairies d'or*, 9 vols., Paris, 1861-1917.

Mas'ūdī, *Morūj*, ed. Pellat
Mas'ūdī, *Morūj*, rev. ed. Ch. Pellat, 7 vols., Beirut, 1962-79.

Mas'ūdī, *Tanbīh*
Mas'ūdī, *Ketāb al-tanbīh wa'l-ešrāf*, ed. M. J. de Goeje, BGA, Leiden, 1894.

***Maṭla'-e sa'dayn*, ed. Šafī'**
Kamāl-al-Dīn 'Abd-al-Razzāq b. Jalāl-al-Dīn Esḥaq Samarqandī, *Maṭla' al-sa'dayn wa majma' al-baḥrayn*, ed. M. Šafī', 2 vols., Lahore, 1360-68/1941-49.

Maṭla' al-šams
E'temād-al-Salṭana Moḥammad-Ḥasan Khan Marāḡa'ī, *Maṭla' al-šams*, 3 vols., Tehran, 1300-03/1883-85; repr. Tehran, 2535 = 1355 Š./1976.

Mayrhofer, *Dictionary*
M. Mayrhofer, *A Concise Etymological Sanskrit Dictionary* (*Kurzgefasstes etymologisches Wörterbuch des Altindischen*), 3 vols., Heidelberg, 1956-76.

MDAF
Majalla-ye Dāneškada-ye adabīyāt o 'olūm-e ensānī-e Dānešgāh-e Ferdowsī.

MDAFA
Mémoires de la Délégation archéologique française en Afghanistan.

MDAFI
Mémoires de la Délégation archéologique française en Iran.

MDAM
Majalla-ye Dāneškada-ye adabīyāt (o 'olūm-e ensānī-)e Dānešgāh-e Mašhad.

MDAT
Majalla-ye Dāneškada-ye adabīyāt (o 'olūm-e ensānī-)e Dānešgāh-e Tehrān.

MDA Tabrīz
Majalla-ye Dāneškada-ye adabīyāt (o 'olūm-e ensānī-)e Dānešgāh-e Tabrīz

MDOG
Mitteilungen der Deutschen Orient-Gesellschaft.

***Mēnōg ī xrad*, ed. Anklesaria**
Dânâk-u mainyô-i khard, ed. T. D. Anklesaria, Bombay, 1913.

***Meykāna*, ed. Golčīn-e Ma'ānī**
'Abd-al-Nabī Qazvīnī, *Taḏkera-ye meyḵāna*, ed. A. Golčīn-e Ma'ānī, Tehran, 1340 Š./1961.

***Meyḵāna*, ed. Šafī'**
'Abd-al-Nabī Qazvīnī, *Taḏkera-ye meyḵāna*, ed. M. Šafī', Lahore, 1926.

MIDEO
Mélanges de l'Institut dominicain d'études orientales du Caire.

Mir. Man.
F. C. Andreas and W. B. Henning, *Mitteliranische Manichaica aus Chinesisch-Turkestan*, SPAW, I, 1932, 10; II, 1933, 7; III, 1934, 27.

Mīrḵ̌ānd (Bombay)
Mīr Moḥammad b. Sayyed Borhān-al-Dīn Ḵ̌āvandšāh Mīrḵ̌ānd, *Tārīḵ-e rawżat al-ṣafā*, Bombay, 1266/1849.

Mīrḵ̌ānd (Tehran)
Mīr Moḥammad b. Sayyed Borhān-al-Dīn Ḵ̌āvandšāh Mīrḵ̌ānd, *Tārīḵ-e rawżat al-ṣafā*, 8 vols., Tehran, 1339 Š./1960; vol. 11: index by M.-J. Maškūr, 1351 Š./1972 (published with Hedāyat, *Rawżat al-ṣafā*, q.v.)

MO
Le monde oriental.

***Mojmal*, ed. Bahār**
M.-T. Bahār, ed., *Mojmal al-tawārīḵ wa'l-qeṣaṣ*, Tehran, 1318 Š./1939.

Monzawī, *Nosḵahā*
A. Monzawī, *Fehrest-e nosḵahā-ye ḵaṭṭī-e fārsī*, 6 vols., Tehran, 1348-53 Š./1969-74.

Moqaddasī
Moqaddasī, *Aḥsan al-taqāsīm fī ma'refat al-aqālīm*, ed. M. J. de Goeje, BGA, Leiden, 1877.

Moreley, *Catalogue*
W. H. Moreley, *A Descriptive Catalogue of the... Manuscripts in the Arabic and Persian Languages Preserved in the Library of the Royal Asiatic Society*, London, 1854.

Mošār, *Fehrest*
Fehrest-e ketābhā-ye čāpī-e fārsī, based on the catalogue by Ḵ. Mošār and the catalogues of the Anjoman-e Ketāb, 3 vols., Tehran, 1352 Š./1973.

Mošār, *Mo'allefīn*
Ḵ. Mošār, *Mo'allefīn-e kotob-e čāpī-e fārsī wa 'arabī*, 6 vols., Tehran, 1340-44 Š./1961-65.

Moses of Khorene
Movsēs Xorenac'i, *Patmut'iwn Hayoc'*, ed. M. Abełean and S. Yarut'iwnean, Tiflis, 1913; repr. in Classical Armenian Text Reprint Series, Delmar, New York, 1981.

Moses of Khorene, tr. Thomson
Movsēs Xorenac'i, *Patmut'iwn Hayoc'*, tr. R. W. Thomson, Moses Khorenats'i, *History of the Armenians*, Cambridge, Massachusetts, 1978.

Mostawfī, *Šarḥ-e zendagānī*
'Abd-Allāh Mostawfī, *Šarḥ-e zendagānī-e man yā tārīḵ-e ejtemā'ī o edārī-e dawra-ye qājārīya*, 3 vols., 2nd ed., Tehran, 1343 Š./1964.

Movsēs Xorenac'i. See **Moses of Khorene.**

MSL
Mémoires de la Société de linguistique de Paris.

MSS
Münchener Studien zur Sprachwissenschaft.

Müller, *Fragmenta*
C. Müller, ed., *Fragmenta Historicorum Graecorum*, 3 vols., Paris, 1860-81.

Nachr.
Nachrichten.

Nafīsī, *Naẓm o naṯr*
S. Nafīsī, *Tārīḵ-e naẓm o naṯr dar Īrān*, 2 vols., Tehran, 1344 Š./1965.

Nafīsī, *Rūdakī*
S. Nafīsī, *Aḥwāl o ašʿār-e Rūdakī*, Tehran, 1309-19 Š./1930-40; rev. ed. 1341 Š./1962.

Naršaḵī
Abū Bakr Jaʿfar Naršaḵī, *Tārīḵ-e Boḵārā*, ed. M. Rażawī, Tehran, 1319 Š./1940; 2nd ed. 1351 Š./1972.

Naršaḵī, tr. Frye
Abū Bakr Jaʿfar Naršaḵī, *Tārīḵ-e Boḵārā*, tr. R. N. Frye, *The History of Bukhara*, Cambridge, Mass., 1954.

NC
Numismatic Chronicle.

NDA Tabrīz
Našrīya-ye Dāneškada-ye adabīyāt (o ʿolūm-e ensānī)-e Dānešgāh-e Tabrīz.

Nöldeke, *Geschichte der Perser*
T. Nöldeke, *Geschichte der Perser und Araber zur Zeit der Sasaniden, aus der arabischen Chronik des Tabari übersetzt*, Leiden, 1879.

***Nozhat al-qolūb*, ed. Le Strange**
Ḥamd-Allāh Mostawfī, *Nozhat al-qolūb*, ed. and tr. G. Le Strange, GMS, 2 vols., Leiden and London, 1916-19.

NTS
Norsk tidsskrift for sprogvidenskap.

Nyberg, *Manual*
H. S. Nyberg, *A Manual of Pahlavi*, Wiesbaden, I, 1964; II, 1974.

OGI
W. Dittenberger, ed., *Orientalis Graeci Inscriptiones Selectae*, Leipzig, 1903-05.

OLZ
Orientalistische Literaturzeitung.

Osnovy
Osnovy iranskogo yazykoznaniya, gen. ed. V. A. Abaev, Moscow, 1979-.

***Pahlavi Rivayat*, ed. Dhabhar**
B. N. Dhabhar, ed., *The Pahlavi Rivâyat Accompanying the Dâdestân-î Dînîk*, Bombay, 1913.

***Pahlavi Texts*, ed. Jamasp-Asana**
J. M. Jamasp-Asana, ed., *The Pahlavi Texts Contained in the Codex MK*, 2 vols., Bombay, 1897-1913.

Pauly-Wissowa
G. Wissowa, W. Kroll, and K. Mittelhaus, eds., *Paulys Real-Encyclopädie der classischen Altertumswissenschaft*, Stuttgart, 1894-1970; Munich, 1973-74.

Pʿawstos Buzand. See **Faustus.**

Persian Literature
E. Yarshater, ed., *Persian Literature*, Albany, New York, forthcoming.

***Persian Rivayats*, ed. Unvala**
M. R. Unvala, ed., *Dârâb Hormazyâr's Rivâyat*, 2 vols., Bombay, 1922.

***Persian Rivayats*, tr. Dhabhar**
B. N. Dhabhar, tr., *The Persian Rivayats of Hormazyar Framarz and Others*, Bombay, 1932.

PHS
Persian Heritage Series.

Pokorny
J. Pokorny, *Indogermanisches etymologisches Wörterbuch*, 2 vols., Berne and Munich, 1959, 1969.

PRGS
Proceedings of the Royal Geographical Society.

Qāżī Aḥmad
Qāżī Aḥmad, *Golestān-e honar*, ed. A. S. Ḵᵛānsārī, Tehran, 1352 Š./1973.

Qāżī Aḥmad, tr. Minorsky
Qāżī Aḥmad, *Golestān-e honar*, tr. V. Minorsky, *Calligraphers and Painters*, Washington, D.C., 1959.

Qodāma, *Ketāb al-ḵarāj*
Qodāma b. Jaʿfar, *Ketāb al-ḵarāj*, ed. M. J. de Goeje, BGA, Leiden, 1889; repr. 1967.

RA
Revue d'assyriologie et d'archéologie orientale.

RAA
Revue des arts asiatiques.

Rādūyānī
Moḥammad b. ʿOmar Rādūyānī, *Tarjomān al-balāḡa*, ed. A. Ateş, İstanbul üniversitesi yayınlarından no. 395, Istanbul, 1949.

Rāmī, *Ḥaqāʾeq*, ed. Emām
Šaraf-al-Dīn Ḥasan b. Moḥammad Rāmī, *Ḥaqāʾeq al-ḥadāʾeq*, ed. M.-K. Emām, Tehran, 1341 Š./1962.

Rašīd-al-Dīn, *Jāmeʿ al-tawārīḵ* (Baku)
Ḵᵛāja Rašīd-al-Dīn Fażl-Allāh b. ʿEmād-al-Dawla Abu'l-Ḵayr, *Jāmeʿ al-tawārīḵ*, text ed. A. A. Ali-Zade, tr. A. K. Arends, vol. 3, Baku, 1957.

Rašīd-al-Dīn, *Jāmeʿ al-tawārīḵ* (Moscow)
Ḵᵛāja Rašīd-al-Dīn Fażl-Allāh b. ʿEmād-al-Dawla Abu'l-Ḵayr, *Jāmeʿ al-tawārīḵ*, text ed. A. A. Romaskevicha, A. A. Khetagurova, and A.A. Ali-Zade, vol. 1, Moscow, 1968.

Rašīd-al-Dīn, *Tārīḵ-e ḡāzānī*
Ḵᵛāja Rašīd-al-Dīn Fażl-Allāh b. ʿEmād-al-Dawla Abu'l-Ḵayr, *Tārīḵ-e mobārak-e ḡāzānī*, ed. K. Jahn, *Geschichte Ġāzān-Ḫān's*, GMS, London, 1940.

Razmārā, *Farhang*
Ḥ. ʿA. Razmārā, ed., *Farhang-e joḡrāfīāʾī-e Īrān: Ābādīhā*, 10 vols., Tehran, 1328-32 Š./1949-54.

REA
Revue des études arméniennes.

REI
Revue des études islamiques.

RHR
Revue de l'histoire des religions.

Rieu, *Persian Manuscripts*
C. Rieu, *Catalogue of the Persian Manuscripts in the British Museum*, 3 vols. and a supplement, London, 1876-95.

RIA
E. Ebeling, B. Meissner, et al., eds., *Reallexicon der Assyriologie und vorderasiatischen Archäologie* I-V, Berlin and Leipzig, 1928-77.

RMM
Revue du monde musulman.

Rypka, *Hist. Iran. Lit.*
J. Rypka et al., *History of Iranian Literature*, ed. K. Jahn, Dordrecht, 1968.

Ṣadr Hāšemī, *Jarāʾed o majallāt*
S. M. Ṣadr Hāšemī, *Tārīḵ-e jarāʾed o majallāt-e Īrān*, Isfahan, 1327-32 Š./1948-53.

Ṣafā, *Adabīyāt*
Ḏ. Ṣafā (Z. Safa), *Tārīḵ-e adabīyāt dar Īrān*, 1332 Š./1953-, with reprints of individual vols.; rev. ed. of vol. 1, Tehran, 1335 Š./1956.

***Šāh-nāma*, Borūḵīm ed.**
Abu'l-Qāsem Ferdowsī, *Šāh-nāma*, ed. ʿA. Eqbāl, S. Nafīsī, et al., 10 vols. in 5, Tehran, 1313-15 Š./1934-35.

***Šāh-nāma*, ed. Khaleghi**
Abu'l-Qāsem Ferdowsī, *Šāh-nāma*, ed. Dj. Khaleghi-Motlagh, Persian Text Series, n.s. 1, Bib. Pers., New York, 1987-.

***Šāh-nāma*, ed. Mohl**
Abu'l-Qāsem Ferdowsī, *Šāh-nāma*, ed. and tr. J. Mohl, 7 vols., Paris, 1838-78.

***Šāh-nāma* (Moscow)**
Abu'l-Qāsem Ferdowsī, *Šāh-nāma*, gen. ed. E. E. Bertel's, ʿA.-Ḥ. Nūšīn, et al., 9 vols., Moscow, 1960-71. New ed. R. M. Aliev and M.-N. O. Osmanov, Tehran, 1350- Š./1971-.

Šahrestānī
Šahrestānī, *Ketāb al-melal wa'l-neḥal*, ed. W. Cureton, London, 1846.

Samʿānī, ed. Margoliouth
Abū Saʿd ʿAbd-al-Karīm b. Moḥammad b. Manṣūr Tamīmī Samʿānī, *Ketāb al-ansāb* facs. ed. D. S. Margoliouth, GMS, Leiden, 1912.

Samʿānī, ed. Yamānī
Abū Saʿd ʿAbd-al-Karīm b. Moḥammad b. Manṣūr Tamīmī Samʿānī, *Ketāb-al-ansāb*, ed. ʿA. Yamānī, 7 vols., Hyderabad, 1382-86/1962-76.

Šams-al-Dīn Rāzī, *Moʿjam*
Šams-al-Dīn Moḥammad b. Qays Rāzī, *al-Moʿjam fī maʿāʾīr ašʿār al-ʿajam*, ed. M. Qazvīnī and M. Rażawī, Tehran, 1338 Š./1959.

Šāyest nē šāyest
J. C. Tavadia, ed. and tr., *Šāyast nē Šāyast, a Pahlavi Text on Religious Customs*, Hamburg, 1930.

***Šāyest nē šāyest*, suppl.**
F. M. Kotwal, ed. and tr., *The Supplementary Texts to the Šāyest nē-šāyest*, Copenhagen, 1969.

Sb.
Sitzungsberichte.

SBE
Sacred Books of the East.

Schlimmer
J. H. Schlimmer, *Terminologie médico-pharmaceutique et anthropologique française-persane*, Tehran, 1874; repr. 1970.

Schwarz, *Iran*
P. Schwarz, *Iran im Mittelalter nach den arabischen Geographen*, Leipzig, 1896-1935.

Sezgin, *GAS*
F. Sezgin, *Geschichte des arabischen Schrifttums*, Leiden, 1957-.

Siroux, *Anciennes voies et monuments*
M. Siroux, *Anciennes voies et monuments routiers de la région d'Ispahan*, Cairo, 1971.

Sobkī, *Ṭabaqāt* (Cairo[1])
Abū Naṣr ʿAbd-al-Wahhāb b. ʿAlī b. ʿAbd-al-Kāfī Tāj-al-Dīn Sobkī, *Ṭabaqāt al-šāfeʿīya al-kobrā*, 6 vols., Cairo, 1906.

Sobkī, *Ṭabaqāt* (Cairo[2])
Abū Naṣr ʿAbd-al-Wahhāb b. ʿAlī b. ʿAbd-al-Kāfī Tāj-al-Dīn Sobkī, *Ṭabaqāt al-šāfeʿīya al-kobrā*, ed. ʿA. M. Ḥolw and M. M. Tanāḥī, 9 vols. published, Cairo, 1964-.

Sofra-ye aṭʿema
Mīrzā ʿAlī-Akbar Āšpazbāšī, *Sofra-ye aṭʿema*, Tehran, 1353 Š./1974.

Sohrāb, tr. Le Strange
G. Le Strange, "Description of Mesopotamia and Baghdad, Written about 900 A.D. by Ibn Serapion," *JRAS*, 1895, nos. 1-3.

Solamī, *Ṭabaqāt*
Moḥammad b. Ḥosayn Solamī, *Ketāb ṭabaqāt al-ṣūfīya*, ed. J. Pedersen, Leiden, 1960.

SPAW
Sitzungsberichte der Preussischen Akademie der Wissenschaften.

Spuler, *Iran*
B. Spuler, *Iran in früh-islamischer Zeit*, Wiesbaden, 1952.

Spuler, *Mongolen*[2,3,4]
B. Spuler, *Die Mongolen in Iran*, Berlin, 2nd ed., 1955; 3rd ed., 1968; 4th ed., 1985.

Stchoukine, *Îl-khâns*
I. V. Stchoukine, *La peinture iranienne sous les derniers ʿAbbâsides et les Îl-khâns*, Bruges, 1936.

Stchoukine, *Safavis*
I. V. Stchoukine, *Les peintures des manuscrits safavis de 1502 à 1587*, Paris, 1959.

Stchoukine, *Tîmûrides*
I. V. Stchoukine, *Les peintures des manuscrits de Shâh 'Abbâs 1er à la fin des ṣafavîs*, Paris, 1964.

Storey
C. A. Storey, *Persian Literature: A Bio-bibliographical Survey*, Leiden, 1927-.

Storey-Bregel
C. A. Storey, *Persidskaya literatura: Bio-bibliograficheskiĭ obzor*, ed. and tr. Yu. E. Bregel, 3 vols., Moscow, 1972.

Stud. Ir.
Studia Iranica.

Stud. Isl.
Studia Islamica.

Stud. Or.
Studia Orientalia.

Survey of Persian Art
A. U. Pope and P. Ackerman, eds., *A Survey of Persian Art from Prehistoric Times to the Present*, 4 vols., London, 1938-39; 2nd ed., 16 vols., Tehran, 1964 with addenda 1967; 3rd ed. with bibliography and addenda, Tehran, 2535 = 1355 Š./1977.

Suter, *Mathematiker*
H. Suter, *Die Mathematiker und Astronomen der Araber und ihre Werke*, Leipzig, 1900.

Sykes, *History of Persia*
Sir Percy Sykes, *A History of Persia*, 2 vols., 3rd ed. with suppl. essays, London, 1930; repr. 1951, 1958.

T̲a'ālebī, *Ḡorar*
Abū Manṣūr T̲a'ālebī, *Ḡorar ak̲bār molūk al-fors*, ed. and tr. H. Zotenberg, *Histoire des rois des Perses*, Paris, 1900.

T̲a'ālebī, *Yatīma* (Damascus)
Abū Manṣūr T̲a'ālebī, *Yatīmat al-dahr fī maḥāsen ahl al-'aṣr*, Damascus, 1304/1886-87.

T̲a'ālebī, *Yatīma*, ed. 'Abd-al-Ḥamīd
Abū Manṣūr Ṯa'ālebī, *Yatīmat al-dahr fī maḥāsen ahl al-'aṣr*, ed. M. M. 'Abd-al-Ḥamīd, Cairo, 1377/1957-68.

Ṭabarī
Moḥammad b. Jarīr Ṭabarī, *Ketāb ta'rīk̲ al-rosol wa'l-molūk*, ed. M. J. de Goeje et al., 15 vols., Leiden, 1879-1901; 2nd ed., 1964.

Ṭabarī (Cairo[1])
Moḥammad b. Jarīr Ṭabarī, *Ketāb ta'rīk̲ al-rosol wa'l-molūk*, 13 vols., Cairo, 1326/1908; repr. Beirut, 6 vols., 1970.

Ṭabarī (Cairo[2])
Moḥammad b. Jarīr Ṭabarī, *Ketāb ta'rīk̲ al-rosol wa'l-molūk*, ed. M. A. Ebrāhīm, 9 vols., Cairo, 1960-68; repr. Beirut, 6 vols., 1970.

Ṭabarī, tr.
Moḥammad b. Jarīr Ṭabarī, *Ketāb ta'rīk̲ al-rosol wa'l-molūk*, tr. by various scholars, *The History of al-Ṭabarī*, gen. ed. E. Yar-Shater, New York, 1985-.

***Tad̲kerat al-molūk*, ed. Minorsky**
V. Minorsky, facs. ed. and tr., *Tadhkirat al-mulūk: A Manual of Ṣafavid Administration* (circa *1137/1725*), GMS, London, 1943.

Tarbīat, *Dānešmandān-e Ād̲arbāyjān*
M. 'A. Tarbīat, *Dānešmandān-e Ād̲arbāyjān*, Tehran, 1314 Š./1935.

Ta'rīk̲ Baḡdād
K̲aṭīb Baḡdādī, *Ta'rīk̲ Baḡdād*, 14 vols., Cairo, 1349/1931.

***Tārīk̲-e bīdārī*, ed. Sa'īdī Sīrjānī**
Nāẓem-al-Eslām Kermānī, *Tārīk̲-e bīdārī-e īrānīān*, ed. 'A.-A. Sa'īdī Sīrjānī, 2vols., Tehran, 1st ed., 1346 Š./1967; 2nd ed., 1362 Š./1983.

***Tārīk̲-e ḡāzānī*. See Rašīd-al-Dīn.**

***Tārīk̲-e gozīda*, ed. Browne**
Ḥamd-Allāh Mostawfī, *Tārīk̲-e gozīda*, facs. ed. E. G. Browne, GMS, Leiden and London, 1910.

Tārīk̲-e Sīstān
M. T. Bahār, ed., *Tārīk̲-e Sīstān*, Tehran, 1314 Š./1935.

***Tārīk̲-e Sīstān*, tr. Gold**
M. Gold, tr., *The Tārikh-e Sistān*, PHS, Rome, 1976.

Tārīk̲-e Waṣṣāf
Šehāb-al-Dīn 'Abd-Allāh Waṣṣāf al-Ḥażra, *Tajzīat al-amṣār wa tazjīat al-a'ṣār* Bombay, 1269/1853.

Tavadia
J. C. Tavadia, *Die mittelpersische Sprache und Literatur der Zarathustrier*, Wiesbaden, 1956.

TDED
İstanbul Üniversitesi, Edebiyat fakültesi türk dili ve edebiyat dergisi.

Tedesco, "Dialektologie"
P. Tedesco "Dialektologie der westiranischen Turfantexte," *MO* 15, 1921, pp. 184-257.

Toḥfa-ye sāmī
Sām Mīrzā Ṣafawī, *Toḥfa-ye sāmī*, ed. Ḥ. Waḥīd Dastgerdī, Tehran, 1314 Š./1935.

Toumanoff, *Généalogie*
C. Toumanoff, *Manuel de généalogie et de chronologie pour l'histoire de la Caucasie chrétienne*, Rome, 1977, supplement, 1978.

TPS
Transactions of the Philological Society.

Ṭūsī, *Fehrest*
Abū Ja'far Ṭūsī, *Fehrest kotob šī'a wa asmā' al-mo'allefīn*, ed. Sprenger, Calcutta, 1853-55.

Ṭūsī, *Rejāl*
Abū Ja'far Ṭūsī, *Ketāb al-rejāl*, ed. M. Ṣ. Āl

Baḥr-al-ʿOlūm, Najaf, 1381/1961.

Vd.

Vīdēvdād, Vendidad, a text of the Avesta.

VDI

Vestnik drevniĭ istorii.

Wolff, *Glossar*

F. Wolff, *Glossar zu Ferdosis Schahname*, Berlin, 1935; repr. Hildesheim, 1965.

Wulff, *Crafts*

H. E. Wulff, *The Traditional Crafts of Persia*, Cambridge, Mass., and London, 1966.

WZKM

Wiener Zeitschrift für die Kunde des Morgenlandes.

Y.

Yasna, a group of texts of the Avesta.

Yaʿqūbī, *Ta'rīḵ*

Aḥmad b. Abī Yaʿqūb b. Jaʿfar b. Wahb b. Wāżeḥ Yaʿqūbī, *Ta'rīḵ*, ed. M. T. Houtsma, *Historiae*, Leiden, 1883.

Yaʿqūbī, *Boldān*

Aḥmad b. Abī Yaʿqūb b. Jaʿfar b. Wahb b. Wāżeḥ Yaʿqūbī, *Ketāb al-boldān*, ed. M. J. de Goeje, BGA, Leiden, 1892; 2nd ed., 1967.

Yaʿqūbī, tr. Āyatī

Aḥmad b. Abī Yaʿqūb b. Jaʿfar b. Wahb b. Wāżeḥ Yaʿqūbī, *Ketāb al-boldān*, tr. M.-E. Āyatī, Tehran, 1347 Š./1968.

Yaʿqūbī, tr. Wiet

Aḥmad b. Abī Yaʿqūb b. Jaʿfar b. Wahb b. Wāżeḥ Yaʿqūbī, *Ketāb al-boldān*, tr. G. Wiet, *Les pays*, Cairo, 1937.

Yāqūt, *Boldān*

Šehāb-al-Dīn Abū ʿAbd-Allāh Yāqūt b. ʿAbd-Allāh Ḥamawī, *Moʿjam al-boldān*, ed. F. Wüstenfeld, 6 vols., Leipzig, 1866-73.

Yāqūt, *Boldān* (Beirut)

Šehāb-al-Dīn Abū ʿAbd-Allāh Yāqūt b. ʿAbd-Allāh Ḥamawī, *Moʿjam al-boldān*, 5 vols., Beirut, 1955-57.

Yāqūt, *Eršād al-arīb*. See **Yāqūt, *Odabā'*.**

Yāqūt, *Odabā'*

Šehāb-al-Dīn Abū ʿAbd-Allāh Yāqūt b. ʿAbd-Allāh Ḥamawī, *Moʿjam al-odabā'*, ed. D. S. Margoliouth, GMS, 7 vols., Leiden, 1907-31.

Yt.

Yašt, a text of the Avesta.

ZA

Zeitschrift für Assyriologie.

Zambaur

E. de Zambaur, *Manuel de généologie et de chronologie pour l'histoire de l'Islam*, Hanover, 1927.

Zādspram

B. T. Anklesaria, ed., *Vichitakiha-i Zatasparam, Part I*, Bombay, 1964.

ZDMG

Zeitschrift der Deutschen Morgenländischen Gesellschaft.

Zereklī, *Aʿlām*[1,2]

Zereklī, *al-Aʿlām*, Cairo, 1st ed., 1927-; 2nd ed., 1954-59.

Zhukovskiĭ, *Materialy*

V. A. Zhukovskiĭ, *Materialy dlya izucheniya persidskikh" narechiĭ*, 3 vols., St. Petersburg, 1888-22; repr. in 1 vol., Tehran, 1976.

ZII

Zeitschrift für Indologie und Iranistik.

ZVS

Zeitschrift für vergleichende Sprachforschung.

ĀTAŠ (Book Pahlavi and New Persian) "fire," Book Pahlavi also *ātaxš*, both from the Avestan nominative singular *ātarš*; the regular Middle Persian and Parthian form is *ādur* (also Book Pahlavi), whence New Persian *ādar*. The etymology of Avestan *ātar-* is unknown. For examples of usage see S. Wikander, *Feuerpriester in Kleinasien und Iran*, Lund, 1946, pp. 104-12.

PLATE I

A Parsi priest before a ritual fire placed in a vessel called an *āfrīnagān* (cf. under *ātašdān*). For "inner" religious ceremonies such a fire is regularly made with embers from a temple fire (before which no rituals may be performed except in its own veneration). For "outer" ceremonies the embers may be taken from any pure fire. The priest wears the muslin robe (*jāma*) proper for "outer" ceremonies, and the mouth-veil (*padān*), which prevents his breath reaching the fire, now consecrated by prayer, while he offers incense (*bōy*) on a flat metal ladle (*čamač*).

Zoroastrian veneration of fire plainly has its origin in an Indo-Iranian cult of the hearth fire, going back in all probability to Indo-European times. The hearth fire, providing warmth, light and comfort, was regarded by the ancient Iranians as the visible embodiment of the divinity Ātar, who lived among men as their servant and master; and in return for his constant help they made him regular offerings (see *ātaš-zōhr*). Fire was also present at their religious ceremonies, and the ancient *Yasna Haptaŋhāiti* seems to have its origins in a pre-Zoroastrian liturgy accompanying priestly offerings to fire and water.

Fire was also used judicially in ancient Iran. Those accused of lying or breach of contract (*miθra-*) might be required as an ultimate test to establish their innocence by submitting to a solemnly administered ordeal by fire. In one such ordeal the accused had to pass through fire, in another molten metal was poured on his bare breast; and there are said to have been some 30 kinds of fiery tests in all. (For the literature see M. Boyce, "On Mithra, Lord of Fire," *Monumentum H. S. Nyberg* I, Acta Iranica 4, 1975, pp. 70-72; *Vd.* 4.46; *Zātspram* 22.11.12; *Pahl. Rivāyat*, 18.d.4; Fakr-al-dīn Gorgānī, *Vīs o Rāmīn*, tr. G. Morrison, *Vis and Ramin*, New York and London, 1972, pp. 132-39.) In each case if the accused died, he was held to have been guilty; if he survived, he was innocent, having been protected by Mithra and the other divine beings. The mildest form of such ordeals required the accused to take a solemn oath, and as he did so to drink a potion containing sulphur (Av. *saokant*, Mid. Pers. *sōgand*, NPers. *sowgand*), a fiery substance which, it was thought, would burn him inwardly if he committed perjury. Fire thus acquired an association with truth, and hence with *aša* (q.v.). The ancient Iranian cosmogonists regarded fire moreover as the seventh "creation," forming the life-force, as it were, within the other six, and so animating the world (see *Bundahišn*, tr., chaps, 3.7-8; 6g. 1; *Zātspram*, chap. 3.77-83). Fire was thus of great theoretical, ethical, ritual, and practical importance in ancient Iranian life and thought.

Zoroaster developed this cultural inheritance yet further when he apprehended fire as the creation of Aša Vahišta (q.v.), and when he saw fire as the instrument of God's judgment at the Last Day. Then a fiery flood of molten metal will cover the earth, and men will undergo thereby a last judicial ordeal (see Frašegird). The cult of fire thus became for the prophet one of profound moral and spiritual significance. As he says in *Yasna* 43.9: "At the offering made in reverence (to fire) I shall think of truth (*aša*) to the utmost of my power;" and it was enjoined on his followers that they should always pray in the presence of fire—either a terrestrial fire, or sun or moon on high (*Mēnōg ī xrad*, chap. 53.3-5.)

The terrestrial fire could be hearth or ritual fire. Traditionally each man established his own hearth fire when he set up house independently, and this was not allowed to go out as long as he lived. To this extent the cult of domestic fire was one of ever-burning fire. The Greeks too had a cult of the hearth fire, and although Herodotus (3.16) mentions the great veneration in which the Persians held fire, he does not single them out as being in any remarkable way "fire-worshippers," nor does he know of temples of any kind among them (1.131). A Zoroastrian temple cult of fire seems to have been first instituted in the later Achaemenid period, being probably established by the orthodox as a counter-move to the innovation of a temple-cult, with statues of "Anāhīt." (See Anaitis and Arədvī Sūrā Anāhitā; for details about fire temples see *ātaškada*.) The temple cult of fire was essentially an extension of that of the hearth fire: the sacred fire, "enthroned" (*nišāst*; cf. the expression *takt-nešīnī* "enthronement" used of the fire) on an altar-like stand (see *ātašdān*), was still a wood fire, and still received the traditional offerings, five times a day. These offerings were made to it by a priest, its purity being most strictly guarded. There is no information from the Achaemenid period itself about categories of sacred fires, or how such fires were constituted; but it seems probably that the temple cult was instituted with as much pomp and dignity as possible, to rival the magnificent image-cult Anāhīt, and, accordingly, that the most exalted type of sacred fire is probably also the oldest. By a tradition which is first recorded in post-Sasanian times such a fire is created from embers taken from many fires, including lightning fire, which are purified over and over again before being combined and consecrated. (See Modi, *Ceremonies*, pp. 200 ff.) The sacred fire is then carried in procession to be installed in its sanctuary *pad wahrāmīh* "victoriously" (see Boyce, "On the Sacred Fires of the Zoroastrians," *BSOAS* 31, 1968, pp. 52-68 and pp. 287-88.) The priests escorting it carry swords and maces; and after the ceremony some of these weapons are hung on the sanctuary walls, to symbolize the warrior nature of the fire, and its ceaseless fight against all that is opposed to aša "truth." This martial symbolism is admirably expressive of a spirit of Zoroastrianism, which is a courageous and active faith, but it has no antecedent in the domestic cult of fire. It seems likely therefore that it was deliberately developed in connection with the temple fires in rivalry to the Anāhīt cult, since Anāhīt was worshipped as a goddess of war, and had probably been regularly invoked by the Achaemenids for victory in battle. The original name for a great temple fire was presumably *ātar- vərəθraγan* "victorious fire;" and already in the late Achaemenid period the custom (continued by the Sasanians) had developed of carrying embers from a sacred fire as a palladium before the Persian army (see Curtius Rufus, *History of Alexander*, 3.8ff.). In Middle Persian, however, the adjective *vərəθraγan-* fell together with the substantive *vərəθraγan-* "victory," and the name of these fires was then understood to mean "fire of Wahrām/Bahrām," i.e., was interpreted as fire belonging to the immensely popular *yazata* of victory (see Boyce, *Zoroastrianism* II, pp. 222ff.)

Remains of so-called "fire altars," i.e., raised fire-holders of characteristic Zoroastrian type, are known from Pasargadae at the time of Cyrus the Great; and it is possible that one of these held the Great King's hearth fire, which, thus exalted, was regarded as his dynastic fire, burning as long as he himself reigned. (For these and other fire-holders see further under *ātašdān*.) No certain traces have yet been found of any fire temple from Achaemenid times (see *ātaškada*). Literary and linguistic evidence, however, shows that by the end of that epoch fire temples had been established all across Iranian territories from Asia Minor to the Indian satrapies. Many of these appear to have survived Alexander's conquest, and the subsequent alien domination. Diodorus Siculus (17.114) records that when Alexander performed the funerary ceremonies for his friend Hephaistion, he ordered that "all the inhabitants of Asia should carefully extinguish the fire that the Persians call sacred," this being their custom at the death of one of their own kings. This statement is usually taken to refer to temple fires, but it seems more probably that individual hearth fires were meant, all unpolluted fire being sacred to Zoroastrians.

A literary reference from the third century A.D. (*Letter of Tansar*, ed. M. Mīnovī, Tehran, 1936, p. 22, tr. M. Boyce, Rome, 1968, p. 47) establishes that the Parthians allowed their vassal kings to found dynastic fires; and it seems possible that the Arsacids' own dynastic fire was the one mentioned by Isidore of Charax (*Parthian Stations* 11) as burning at Asaak in northeastern Iran, "where Arsaces was first proclaimed king." A general term attested for a fire temple in the Parthian language was **ātarōšan* (preserved in Armenian as *atrušan*), interpreted as meaning "place of burning fire" (see Wikander, *Feuerpriester*, pp. 98, 219; E. Benveniste, *JA*, 1964, p. 57); and in the Parthian version of an inscription of the Sasanian king Šāpūr (Šābuhr) I the term for a great sacred fire is given as *ādur warahrān* (see his inscription on the Kaʿba-ye Zardošt, Parthian l. 22; M. Back, *Die sassanidischen Staatsinschriften*, Acta Iranica 18, Tehran and Liège, 1978, p. 330). Descriptions exist of temple fires maintained by Persian congregations under alien rule in Asia Minor during the Parthian period. Starbo (*Geography* 15.3.15) writes of two kinds of "temples of the magi" in Cappadocia in his day (around the beginning of the Christian era). Some were "temples of the Persian gods" (containing presumably cult images), others were "pyratheia," i.e., fire temples, "noteworthy enclosures; and in the midst of these there is an altar, on which there is a large quantity of ashes and where the magi keep the fire ever burning. And there, entering daily, they make incantations for about an hour, holding before the fire their bundle of rods [= the *barsom*]." Pausanias, writing in the second century A.D., states (*Description of Greece* 5.27.3) that Persian communities maintained temples in two cities in Lydia. "In each of these temples there is an inner chamber, and in this an altar upon which are some ashes of a color unlike that of ordinary ashes. A magus enters the chamber, bringing dry wood which he places on the altar. After this he... intones an invocation... in a barbarian tongue... This...inevitably causes the wood to catch fire and break out into a bright flame." Both these accounts seem to be of lesser fires, which unlike the "victorious fires" (kept always burning bright) are often allowed "to sleep" (*xuft*) under a cover of hot ash between the times appointed for prayer and offerings. Dry wood placed on these hot ashes will in the course of nature catch fire after a little time. Although their temple fires are always wood fires, Zoroastrians also offered reverence to the naptha fires which burnt in various parts of Iran. In the Jewish II Maccabees 1:18-36 there is an account of a naptha well being enclosed as sacred by a Parthian king; and at the end of a chapter on fires in the *Bundahišn* (p. 128, tr. pp. 162 f., chap. 18.23-24) mention is made of two venerated fires which burned without fuel. In the same chapter there is also reference to the three oldest sacred fires known by name in Zoroastrian history. These are Ādur Burzēn-Mihr, Ādur Farnbāg and Ādur Gušnasp (qq.v). All three are held to be invoked indirectly in a late section (5-6) of the Ātaš Niyayišn (see under Ādur Gušnasp); and they must have been established not later than the Parthian period, since in Sasanian times they had become invested with an aura of immense antiquity. The temples of all three were set on hills, whereby the tradition of worship in high places (Herodotus, 1.131) was maintained; and in Sasanian times they were established respectively in Parthia, Persia, and Media. A fourth fire which was much venerated was that of karkūy in Sīstān (see K. Schippmann, *Die iranischen Feuerheiligtümer*, Berlin, 1971, pp. 37ff.), each quarter of Iran having thus its own great fire. This fire too appears to have been set on a hill; and archeologists have uncovered the remains of an impressive Parthian fire temple on the Kūh-e K̲ʷāja, a hill rising out of the shallows of the Hāmūn lake (see ibid., pp. 57ff.). These are at present the oldest known remains of an undisputed Zoroastrian fire temple.

It was perhaps in the Parthian period that Zoroastrian priestly scholars evolved a fivefold theoretical classification of fires. The five categories are invoked, in ascending order of dignity, in *Y.* 17.11 (a late section of the *Yasna* liturgy). First is the fire called *bərəzi.savah* "of high benefit," identified in the Pahlavi commentary as present in Ātaš Bahrāms; second, *vohu fryāna* probably "loving the good," the fire or life-force in men; third, *urvāzišta* "the most joyful," that which is in plants; fourth, *vazišta* "the swiftest (?)," which is lightning fire; and lastly *spə̄ništa* "the holiest," which burns in the presence of Ohrmazd himself. This classification is evidently purely scholastic. The names of the last three types of fire are common Avestan adjectives, two of which occur as cult-epithets of fire in *Yasna Haptaŋhāiti*. Of these *urvāzišta* has presumably been associated with plants, *urvara*, because of the identity of the first syllables of the words. The epithets *bərəzi.savah* and *vohu.fryāna* are known only from Y. 17. The identifications of the five fires are the same in *Zātspram*, pp. 40-41, chap. 3.77-82, but in the *Bundahišn*, pp. 123-24; tr. pp. 156-59, chap. 18.2-7, *bərəzi.savah* is held to be the fire which burns before Ohrmazd, and *spə̄ništa* that which is present in Ātaš Bahrāms, and other earthly fires.

In Zoroastrian worship the use of cult-images, instituted under the later Achaemenids, was evidently encouraged by Greek influences in Hellenistic times; but an iconoclastic movement, linked with the founding of more and more sacred fires, appears to have been in existence at least by the late Parthian period. (See M. Boyce, "Iconoclasm Among the Zoroastrians," *Christianity, Judaism and other Greco-Roman Cults, Studies for Morton Smith at Sixty*, ed. J. Neusner, IV, Leiden, 1975, pp. 93-111.) A Parthian king, Valaxš/Vologeses I (ca. A.D. 51-80) set a fire-holder on the reverse of bronze coin-issues, rather than the statue of a *yazata* (G. F. Hill, *Catalogue of Greek Coins* 28, London, 1922, pp. 29.11-12); and the evidence of the proper name Ādur-Ahāhīd "Anāhīd of the fire," borne by a granddaughter of Ardašīr I (Šāpur I on the Kaʿba-ye Zardošt, Mid. Pers. 1. 25, Parth, 1. 20, Greek 1. 47; see A. Maricq, *Syria* 35, 1958, pp. 318-19, 333 = *Classica et Orientalia*, Paris, 1965, pp. 60-61, 75), suggests that at least by the outset of the Sasanian era a sacred fire had replaced the cult-image in the temple of Anāhīt at Staxr (Eṣṭak̲r), of which the Sasanian family had been the hereditary guardians. The Sasanian kings in their turn regularly set a fire-holder on the reverse of their coins. The beginning of each king's reign was associated with the lighting of his regnal fire (cf. R. Ghirshman, "Inscription du monument de Chapour ler," *RAA* 10, 1937, pp. 123-29); and in the representations on coins a royal diadem is sometimes shown tied round the shaft of the fire-holder, to indicate that the fire thus displayed was the king's personal one.

In early Sasanian inscriptions there are references to the founding of many fires, the nomenclature still, it seems, reflecting the period of Parthian domination. Thus mention is made of "victorious fires" as *ādur ī wahrām* (e.g., Kirdēr, Kaʿba-ye Zardošt, line 2; Back, *Die sassanidischen Staatsinschriften*, p. 388); and of lesser temple fires simply as *ādurān* (ibid., line 2, Back, op. cit., p. 389). Šāpūr I records founding *ādurān* for the benefit of his own soul, and for the souls of his queen of queens and three of his sons. (Šāpūr's inscription on the *Kaʿba-ye Zardošt*, Mid. Pers. ll. 22-23; Back, op. cit., pp. 331-35); and this custom is attested again later in the Sasanian period, and indeed down into the twentieth century. The founder of a fire endowed it, usually with lands (see the account of Šāpūr's foundations, and those of the great Sasanian prime minister, Mihr-Narseh, Nöldeke, *Geschichte der Perser*, pp. 111-12; and for other similar foundations Boyce, "On the Sacred Fires," pp. 56ff.). The founders of such fire temples usually retained the patronage of them in their own families, with the right to manage their incomes, whether from endowments or offerings, and to appoint their priests, and litigation sometimes arose over these matters, which is recorded as case-history in the Sasanian law-book, the *Mādayān ī Hazār Dādestān* (see J. P. de Menasce, *Les feux et fondations pieuses sous les Sassanides*, Paris, 1966; Boyce, art.cit.) From these case-histories it becomes clear that the Sasanians recognized a third category of temple fire, namely the Ādurōg ī pad dādgāh or "minor fire in an appointed place," called in modern usage Ātaš-e dādgāh, or just Dādgāh. Such a fire can be formed simply from embers taken from an unsullied Zoroastrian hearth fire, and may be tended at need by a lay person, provided that he or she is in a state of purity. The Ādurōg sometimes figures in the law-books as an element in the iconoclastic campaign, waged, it seems, throughout the Sasanian epoch; for when a cult-statue was removed from a shrine, then a sacred fire was, it seems, regularly installed in its place--an Ataš ī wahrām in the case of a great temple such as that of Anāhīd at Staxr, an Ādurōg at some small local one, when no great new costs could be imposed on the patron or community (see Boyce, "Iconoclasm," pp. 63-64), It is recorded of one of the sons of Šāpūr I, Hormizd-Ardašīr, that in Armenia he set a sacred fire (presumably in place of a statue) in the temple of Ohrmazd at Pakaran (Movsēs Xorenacʻi, II, p. 77; V. Langlois, *Collection des historiens... de l'Arménie* II, Paris, 1869, p. 119); and Kirdēr records that by him "images were overthrown and the dens of demons [i.e. image shrines] were destroyed, and the places and abodes of *yazad*s [i.e. fire temples] were established" (*Kaʻba-ye Zardošt*, l. 10; Back, op. cit., pp. 415-16). But as late as the reign of Ḵosrow II (591-628) a case is recorded where "in accordance with the order and injunction of the mōbads" an image was removed from a privately endowed shrine and an Ādurōg was installed there at the expense of the Dīwān ī Kardagān (ministry of sacred works); ultimately the patrons of the shrine voluntarily themselves took over the maintenance of the Ādurōg, with due endowments (T. D. Anklesaria, ed., *The Social Code of the Parsees in Sasanian Times*, pt. 2, Bombay, 1912, p. 37.2-8). It has been suggested that Zoroastrian sacred fires were sometimes also set in image shrines taken over from other religions, cf. the Buddhist shrine at Kara Tepe at Termez in ancient Bactria, where a hastily constructed mud-brick fire-holder has been found in a niche in which a Buddhist statue once stood (see B. Y. Staviskiĭ, *Kushanskaya Baktriya*, Moscow, 1977, p. 176).

During the Sasanian epoch temple fires were still maintained beyond Iran's borders by groups of Zoroastrians descended from colonists of Achaemenid times. Kirdēr records the existence of sacred fires tended by Zoroastrian priests in regions overrun by Šāpūr I in his Roman campaigns, namely Syria, Cilicia, Cappadocia, Armenia, Georgia and Albania (*Kaʻba-ye Zardošt*, ll. 11-13; Back, op. cit., pp. 422-29). In the following century, when most of these scattered congregations were living under Christian rule, St. Basil (*Collected Letters*, no. 258) wrote of their tenacity in holding to their own beliefs and ways; but they were to suffer thereafter from Christian persecution, and in the fifth century king Pērēz complained that the Byzantines harassed their Zoroastrian subjects and would not permit them to maintain sacred fires (see J. Labourt, *Le Christianisme dans l'empire perse*, Paris, 1904, p. 129 n. 5).

The founding of sacred fires within Iran itself continued throughout the Sasanian period; and in later sources it is said that in the last great reign, that of Ḵosrow II, the king himself both built fire temples and appointed 12,000 priests to pray at such temples throughout his realm (Nöldeke, *Geschichte der Perser*, p. 353). It seems probable, from later evidence, that the main concentration of fire temples was in western Iran, and perhaps in the province of Pārs itself. It is there that Muslim geographers chiefly noted the existence of "fire houses;" and Abū Zayd Balḵī, writing in the ninth century stated that then there was still one in nearly every town and village in the province (*Bibliotheca geographorum arabicorum* I, pp. 100, 118-19; cited by H. S. Nyberg, *Journal of the K. R. Cama Oriental Institute* 39, 1958, p. 9). It is also there that archeologists in the present century have found the most remains of fire temples (see under *ātaškada*). Details of the observances which had evolved to link the ancient cult of the hearth fire to that of temple fires are first recorded in Islamic times, but must go back at least to the Sasanian period. The three categories of temple fires were in Islamic times called Ātaš Bahrām, Ādor-e Ādorān (or simply Ādorān) and Dādgāh. The doctrine behind the observances has been admirably formulated by J. Darmesteter (SBE IV, p. 115 n. 2): "As the earthly representative of the heavenly fire (the Bahrām fire) is the sacred center to which every earthly fire longs to return, in order to be united again, as much as possible, with its native abode. The more it has been defiled by worldly uses, the greater is the merit acquired by freeing it from defilement." Despite all care, the priests held, a hearth fire could not wholly escape impurity; so at intervals, varying according to different authorities from every third day to after every baking of bread, embers from it should be carried to the local fire temple, there to grow cold in the presence of the sacred fire. Embers from all fires used in ritual observances, and also from the great Sada fire, were likewise taken into the presence of the temple fire. (For the literature, and details of actual observances, see Boyce, *Stronghold*, pp. 72 ff., 182-83). Once a year embers from a Dādgāh fire should be taken into the presence of an Ādorān, and those from an Ādorān into the presence of an Ātaš Bahrām, thus completing the links of the chain (see Boyce, *Acta Orientalia* 30, 1966, pp. 63-64.) There was further the general ritual of rescuing embers from fires which had been actually polluted (in smiths' shops and the like), purifying them by lighting nine successive fires from these embers, each intermediate one being allowed to go out, and then taking the ninth fire, consecrated by prayer, to a temple fire. This ritual is still regularly carried out as an act of merit by Zoroastrians in Fārs, especially in Āḏar Māh, the month dedicated to fire (see Boyce, *Stronghold*, pp. 175, 186-90). Its technical name is the rite of "exalting the fire," *ātaš bozorg kardan*; and it was probably performed even before temple fires were founded (cf. *Vd.* 8.73 ff.). Another way in which the temple fires were made of central importance was that priests insisted that ash from an Ātaš Bahrām was needed for the major rites of purification, whereas formerly ash from a hearth fire (*ātaxš ī kadagīg*) could have been used (cf. the Pahl. commentary to *Vd.* 5.51).

This last usage is common to the Zoroastrians of Iran and India; and the Parsis duly established an Ātaš Bahrām (the Sanjana Ātaš Bahrām or "Īrānšāh," which now burns at Uḍwada) as soon as possible after their settlement at Sanjan in A.D. 936. This remained their only temple fire for some 500 years (see F. M. Kotwal, "Some observations on the history of the Parsi *Dar-i Mihr*," *BSOAS* 37, 1974, pp. 664-69); and so for most Parsis the hearth fire was necessarily the focus of their observances. The founding fathers of their community had come from Khorasan, i.e., ancient Parthian territory; and it seems possible that fewer sacred fires had been founded there than in Pārs, and that the need for more than one was not felt. Prosperity, and closer connections again with the Iranian Zoroastrians, led the Parsis to found many more sacred fires, of all three categories, from the seventeenth century onwards; but in spite of instructions from Persia they did not adopt any of the chain observances just described. Even the rite of "exalting the fire" is not recorded among them; but this may have been one of the ancient observances which seem to have been lost by the migrant community.

In Iran the spread of Islam after the Arab conquest led to the extinction of most sacred fires during the next 600 years, their temples being razed or turned into mosques. Eventually (perhaps in the late thirteenth century A.D.) the Dastūr Dastūrān, head of the dwindling community of Zoroastrians, sought haven in the village of Torkābād, at the northern end of the Yazdī plain; and probably at the same time two Ātaš Bahrāms were established in the neighboring village of Šarīfābād, where they still burn, though now conjoined. It is highly probably that these represent the two greatest fires of Persia proper, namely Ādur-Anāhīd from Stak̠r and Ādur Farnbāg taken from their former sanctuaries and preserved in hiding by their priests. Like all the sacred fires which survive, these were kept during the centuries of oppression in small mud-brick buildings, looking outwardly like any poor man's house. Moreover, for safety's sake the Iranian Zoroastrians abandoned the custom (maintained by the Parsis) of enthroning a sacred fire conspicuously in a central sanctuary, with open grills, and instead hid it away in a small side-room, entered by a tiny cupboard-like door. Priests crept through this door to serve the fire, but the laity gave up entirely the joy of seeing it, for the better chance of its survival. If Muslims broke into the temple, all that they saw in its main hall was an empty fire-holder, so that it seemed as if the sacred fire were already extinguished. In this holder (resembling a pillar-altar) fire would be set on occasion for public or private worship, embers being brought from the sacred fire for the purpose, and carried back afterwards to grow cold in its presence. Down the centuries both Šarīfābād and Kermān managed to preserve Ātaš Bahrāms, and there were Ādorāns or Dādgāh fires in Yazd and most Zoroastrian villages. Later, after the Dastūr Dastūrān had moved to Yazd, a new Ātaš Bahrām was established there also, with Parsi help; and in the twentieth century, with the shift of the majority of Zoroastrians to Tehran, an Ātaš Bahrām was installed there also, with embers carried by priests on foot across the Central Desert (Dašt-e Kavīr) from the Ātaš Bahrām of Yazd (although this method of creating a new sacred fire would have been frowned on by the orthopraxy of an earlier age, see B. N. Dhabhar, *The Persian Rivayats of Hormazyar Framarz and others*, Bombay, 1932, p. 72). By the end of the nineteenth century the Parsis had eight Ātaš Bahrāms (each individually consecrated), which are still maintained, and nearly 150 lesser fires, although with the fading away of their village communities in the present century some of these have been brought to burn in one temple (though always in separate rooms). Only in India and in Tehran is it still possible to have four priests serving each Ātaš Bahrām, as is ritually desirable. Almost all village fires, in both communities, are Dādgāh fires, often tended by the laity. It is still the general custom to maintain a Dādgāh fire in a small building near every funerary tower, for the benefit of the departed souls, but a lamp may be substituted.

Probably ever since the establishment of the temple cult of fire Zoroastrians have been known to those of other faiths as "fire worshippers," a title which they themselves have as regularly repudiated, on the grounds that fire is for them simply an icon, helping them to fix their thoughts on God and truth, as enjoined by their prophet. Nevertheless fire, so seemingly alive, perhaps attracts veneration even more readily than the static icons of other faiths; and undoubtedly over the millennia the cherishing of fire has contributed a special element to Zoroastrian worship.

Bibliography: Given in the text.

(M. Boyce)

ĀTAŠ, AḤMAD (Turkish AHMET ATEŞ), Turkish Iranist. See Supplement.

ĀTAŠ (Fire), a Persian journal of news and political comment, published at Tehran 1325-39 Š./1946-60. Publication began on 29 Farvardīn 1325 Š./19 April 1946. One issue per week was printed until the autumn of the first year, thereafter one issue per day until the beginning of the second year; then it was published first as a weekly, later bi-weekly and then again a weekly journal. Its publication was terminated in 1339 Š./1960. The holder of the publication license was Sayyed Mahdī Mīrašrāfī (1287-1358 Š./1907-79), a former army officer, Majlis deputy during the 15th, 16th, and 17th sessions, and a businessman and factory owner, with interest mostly in Isfahan. After the 1979 revolution, he was charged with political and financial corruption and brought before the revolutionary tribunal of Isfahan. Invocation of his links with Ayatollah Abu'l-Qāsem Kāšanī (q.v.) and their collaboration leading to the downfall of Mosaddeq (q.v.) in 1332 Š./1953 coup d'état did not win him a reprieve from death; he was executed by a firing squad in Āḏar, 1358 Š./December, 1979, in Isfahan.

The editor for the better part of the paper's life was Šams Qanātābādī, a former Majlis deputy, who heavily influenced the political orientation of the journal, and Anūšīravān Maʿālī in the journal's last year.

Ātaš was a very controversial right-leaning journal whose licencee was known to have been involved in a host of dubious political dealings and intrigues. Having vehemently opposed Prime Minister Aḥmad Qawām (q.v.) the headquarters of the journal were set on fire in Tīr, 1326 Š./June, 1947. Again, in Āḏar, 1330 Š./

December, 1951, when the offices of some right-wing and communist-affiliated papers were attacked by Mosaddeq followers, the offices of the journal were ransacked. *Ātaš* was banned four times in 1325 Š./1946 and 1327 Š./1948 but came out under other names, then only occasionally failed to appear before it ceased publication in Farvardīn, 1339 Š./March, 1960. A reappearance under the direct supervision of Qanātābadī after the revolution in 1979, proved unsuccessful and short-lived.

Ātaš consisted initially of eight six-column pages, later of four or eight pages measuring 36 × 50 cm. It carried illustrations and advertisements. The price was from one to two rials.

Ātaš appeared as a weekly magazine from 14 Ordībehešt 1337 Š./4 May 1958 to 22 Esfand 1337 Š./13 March 1959 in 45 issues, initially supervised by Sīāmak Pūrzand, later edited by Aḥmad Sorūš. The issues at first consisted of 40 to 48 pages each of 21 × 27 cm, later 24 × 32 cm, with colored cover. The price was 5 rials.

An incomplete set of *Ātāš* is preserved in the Library of Congress in Washington D. C.

According to Ṣadr-Hāšemī two other Persian journals had appeared under the name *Ātaš*, one at Tehran in 1303 Š./1923-24 and another outside Iran in 1309 Š./1929-30 (?), which was probably edited by the famous poet and journalist Farroḵī Yazdī (q.v.)

Bibliography: Jāmī, *Goḏašta čerāḡ-e rāh-e āyanda ast*, Tehran, 1362 Š./1983, p. 597. M. Ṣadr-Hāšemī, *Tārīḵ-e jarāyed o majallāt-e Īrān*, Isfahan, 1327-32 Š./1948-53, nos. 29, 357. L. P. Elwell-Sutton, "The Iranian Press 1941-47," *Iran* 6/7, 1968, p. 71.

(N. PARVĪN)

"ĀTAŠ," ḴᵛĀJA ʿALĪ ḤAYDAR B. ḴᵛĀJA ʿALĪ BAḴŠ, late eighteenth-early nineteenth-century Indo-Muslim poet in Persian and Urdu. He belonged to a respectable family of Delhi which claimed descent from Ḵᵛāja ʿObaydallāh Aḥrār (fl. 806-96-1404-90, q.v.), the noted Naqšbandī saint of Khorasan. His father moved from Delhi to Fayzabad in the time of Nawab Šojāʿ-al-dawla (1754-75) and settled in Maḥalla Moḡolpora. Ātaš was born in Fayzabad in 1192/1778. His father died when Ātaš was only a boy. His education neglected, he became a *bānka* (leisure companion) of Nawab Moḥammad-Taqī, who brought him to Lucknow sometime after 1815. Following the death of the nawab, Ātaš resigned his post.

From early youth Ātaš was poetically inclined and submitted his neophyte efforts to Ḡolām Hamadānī Moṣḥafī (d. 1240/1824) for correction. According to the vogue of the day, he started writing verses in Persian even though not a learned man. Later he also composed verses in Urdu.

Ātaš led an unaffected life, free from all conventions and formalities. A lover of beauty he was himself a handsome, fair-complexioned man. He dressed like a soldier and carried a sword with him even in poetical gatherings. Disdaining patronage and wealth, he led a life of resignation and contentment. On his death in 1263/1847 he left behind a host of pupils, some of whom later attained to the rank of poetical master. The most famous among them were Nawab Mīrzā Šawq, Dayā, Šankar Nasīm, Wājed-ʿAlī Šāh Aḵtar, Mīr Dōst-ʿAlī Ḵalīl, Āḡā, Ḥajjū Šaraf, Nawab Moḥammad Khan Rend, and Wazīr-ʿAlī Ṣabā. His own son, Moḥammad-ʿAlī Jōš, was a poet of moderate distinction.

Ātaš also left behind three *dīvān*s, two in Urdu and one in Persian. He wrote only *ḡazal*s, eschewing *qaṣīda*s and all other forms of composition. The great merit of his work is its vivid portrayal of emotions in elegant and attractive phrases.

Bibliography: Ḵᵛāja ʿAlī Ḥaydar Ātaš, *Kollīyāt-e Ātaš*, Kanpur, 1871. Ḡolām Hamadānī Moṣḥafī, *Rīāż al-foṣaḥāʾ*, Delhi, 1934, pp. 4-9. Ṣāfer Belgrāmī, *Jelwa-ye Ḵeżr*, Agra, 1884, II, p. 106. Ḵᵛāja ʿAbd-al-Raʾūf ʿEšrat, *Āb-e baqā*, Lucknow, 1918, pp. 9-11. Emdād Emām Aṯar, *Kāšef al-ḥaqāʾeq*, Lahore, 1956, II, p. 162. ʿAbd-al-Raʾūf ʿOrūj, *Taḏkera-ye fārsī o šoʿarā-ye ordū*, Lahore, 1971, pp. 124-26. E. G. Browne, *A Suppl. Handlist of Muhammadan MSS.*, Cambridge, 1922, p. 85. R. B. Saksena, *A History of Urdu Literature*, repr. Lahore, 1975, pp. 111-13.

(M. BAQIR)

ĀTAŠ NIYĀYIŠN, the fifth in a group of five Zoroastrian prayers (*niyāyišn*, q.v.), which is addressed to fire and its divinity (see *ādur*). It has seventeen "verses" or sections, and like almost all Avestan texts is a composite work. *ĀNy.* 7-16 corresponds to *Y.* 62.1-10, a part of the *yasna* service which is devoted to the veneration of fire. The complete *ĀNy.* is found in the Ḵorda Avesta (q.v.), since it is regularly recited during private prayers by both laity and priests. It is also said while tending a fire, whether a hearth or a temple one.

The opening and closing sections of *ĀNy.* consist of verses from Zoroaster's *Gāthās*, i.e., *ĀNy.* 1-3 = *Y.* 33.12-14, *ĀNy.* 17 = *Y.* 34.4. These sections are not found in *Y.* 62, presumably because the entire *Gāthās* have been recited earlier in the *yasna* liturgy. There are sections of *ĀNy.*, i.e., vv. 7, 13, and 16, which are addressed specifically to the hearth fire, and which may be older in content than the *Gāthās*, although the language is Younger Avestan. It seems reasonable to conjecture that in its earliest from the *ĀNy.* consisted of these apparently very ancient verses enclosed by those from the *Gāthās*, the whole forming a brief liturgy to accompany the regular offerings made to fire (see *ātaš-zōhr*). On this conjecture, the incorporation of most of the *ĀNy.* into *Y.* 62 would be a secondary development, as would the general devotional use of the text.

In its existing from *ĀNy.* includes such generally recurring elements as the short profession of faith (see *fravarāne*) and the prayer appropriate to the time of day (*gāh*, q.v.), both in v.4. It also embodies the *xšnūman* or ritual dedication to Ātar, vv. 5-6, which corresponds to *Sīrōza* 1.9. Several other verses contain petitions to Fire. Some, being strikingly defective in grammar, are clearly late.

A Pahlavi translation of the Avestan text, with

glosses, is assigned to the late Sasanian period. In glosses on vv. 5-6 the references to Fire, son of Ahura Mazdā, and to Xᵛarənah; to Mount Asnavant; and to Mount Raēvant, are interpreted as referring respectively to Ādur Farnbāg, Ādur Gušnasp and Ādur Burzēn-mihr (qq.v), the three greatest sacred fires of that epoch. The Avestan verses are accordingly held by priests to express veneration for these three fires. A Sanskrit rendering of the *ĀNy.*, based mainly on the Pahlavi but with occasional direct use of the Avestan text, was made about A.D. 1200 by the Parsi priestly scholar, Neryosang Dhaval (q.v.). A Persian translation was made from the Pahlavi sometime between 1600 and 1800, and a Gujarati one in 1818.

In making the offerings to a temple fire of the lowest grade, a Dādgāh fire (q.v.), a single *ĀNy.* suffices, as it does for offerings to a hearth fire. For those to an Ātaš-e Ādorān Parsi priests recite three *ĀNy.*, while for those to an Ātaš Bahrām they vary the number according to the watch (*gāh*), i.e. eleven in Hāvan Gāh; nine in Rapiθwin/Second Hāvan; seven in Uzērin and Aiwisrūθrim; and nine in Ušahin. In general, it is declared that anyone unable to recite the *ĀNy.* can acquire the same merit by saying the *Ahunwar* (q.v.) sixty-five times.

Bibliography: M. N. Dhalla, ed. and tr., *The Nyaishes or Zoroastrian Litanies, Avestan Text with the Pahlavi, Sanskrit, Persian and Gujarati Versions*, New York, 1908, repr. 1965, pp. 135-87, B. N. Dhabhar, ed., *Zand-i Khūrtak Avistāk*, Bombay, 1927, pp. 36-46, 299-312; tr., *Translation of Zand-i Khūrtak Avistāk*, Bombay, 1963, pp. 64-82. Z. Taraf, ed. and tr., *Der Awesta-Text Niyāyiš mit Pahlavi- und Sanskritübersetzung*, Munich, 1981, pp. 96-109, 152-54.

(M. Boyce and F. M. Kotwal)

ĀTAŠDĀN (Zoroastrian Pahlavi) "place of fire, fire-holder," designates the altar-like repository for a sacred wood-fire in a Zoroastrian place of worship. *Ādurgāh*, *ātašgāh*, and *ādišt* (today *ādošt*) are synonyms of *ātašdān*; *ādišt* (literally "fire-place") is also attested in the Zoroastrian Pahlavi books for a domestic hearth. Nowadays the Zoroastrians of Yazd commonly use the term *kalak*, which is a dialect word for a brazier or container of fire, and those of Kermān employ *magreb*, a word whose origin has still to be satisfactorily explained. The other Zoroastrian terms all appear to be factual ones, without the specifically religious connotations attached to the standard Western rendering of "fire-alter." No Avestan term is known, but the temple cult of fire was evidently a relatively late introduction in Zoroastrianism (see under *ātaš*).

An object which looks as if it might be a prototype of one of the standard forms of *ātašdān* has been excavated in a Median building attributed to the eighth century B.C. at Nūš-e Jān Tepe, Hamadān. This alter is made of mud-brick, and coated with fine white plaster, which gives it the appearance of stone. The square shaft is surmounted at about waist-height by a broad stepped top, each of the four steps projecting outward above the one below. In the top is a shallow bowl, with traces of charring round the rim. Its cavity is too small to have held an ever-burning wood-fire, which needs a deep bed of hot ashes to sustain it; what rites this Median altar served remain unknown. Fragments of two, or possibly three, *ātašdāns* which somewhat resemble it in profile have been discovered as surface finds at the Achaemenid site of Pasargadae. These, as reconstructed, consisted of a three-stepped top and a three-stepped base, joined by a slender rectangular shaft. The distinctive feature which shows them to have been Zoroastrian fire-holders, and not altars, is that the top was hollow, i.e., designed evidently to hold a quantity of ash. These fire-holders were finely wrought in white stone, and have been assigned on technical grounds to the time of Cyrus the Great (sixth century B.C.). The impressive pair of plinths which still stand on the Pasargadae plain are attributed to the same period, but are evidently not *ātašdāns*, for not only do they lack a deep fire-bowl, but excavation has established that they have always stood unsheltered in the open, and so could not have served the cult of ever-burning fire.

Fire-holders with exactly the same profile as the Pasargadae ones appear on the funerary monuments of Darius the Great and his successors. There the king is shown standing before an *ātašdān* which bears a pyramid of leaping flames. The *ātašdān* has again a three-stepped top and base, and the shaft is now decorated with threefold recessed vertical panels. A humbler mud-brick fire-holder of the later Achaemenid period has been found in a house in a farming village near Dahān-e Ḡolāmān in Sīstān. This has a big broad top with six steps, set on a slender round shaft which rises from a small, plain base. In the top is "a central hemispherical receptacle for the fire" (Scerrato, p. 727). In another house in this village there was found a low, square "stepped pyramid" (ibid.), with the third, and topmost, step being hollow. This too the excavators have identified as a fire-holder. If this is so, it is of an otherwise unattested type.

Representations of fire-holders appearing on seals of the Achaemenid period show two types. One is similar to that of the royal monuments. The other consists of a broad rectangular column, usually with a crenelated top, whose merlons have presumably the function of containing the embers. In some representations a thin column of flame appears between them; and sometimes a person or persons appear beside the column, reverencing the fire. These fire-holders are without known antecedent.

Another fire-holder was recovered from the ruins of the fire temple on the Kūh-e Ḵᵛāja Sīstān (q.v.). This may have been coeval with the Sasanian building, or have survived from the older Parthian structure there. It again was of the Pasargadae type, with three-stepped top and base; but it seems subsequently to have disappeared, and no measurements are recorded for the depth of its bowl. Otherwise fire-holders of the Parthian period are known only from representations. A carving at Bīsotūn (Behistun) shows a worshipper in Parthian dress beside a small Pasargadae-type one; and another fire-holder of this type is shown on a seal with a Parthian inscription from Seleucia-on-the-Tigris (*Survey of Persian Art* I, p. 473 fig. 126, t). An engraved gem from Nisa shows a worshipper venerating fire rising from a holder with slim shaft, plain top and two-stepped base, above which two projections spring out like upward-pointing brances on either side. A variety of fire-holders of different shapes and sizes are shown on the *Frātadāra coins of Pārs during the Parthian period. The first series portrays so-called "tower altars," solid rectangular blocks rising above the heads of the worshippers who stand beside them. These "altars" are set on two steps, and are decorated with recessed vertical panels. The earliest have flat tops which, perplexingly, are crowned in several instances by three miniature "altars" of exactly the same type as themselves, but bearing what look like twin horns—presumably either merlons or stylized flames. Other fire-holders have crenelated tops, like those on Achaemenid seals. In the last coin-series are shown fire-holders like those on the Achaemenid tombs, with threefold recessed panels on their shafts. Other coins of this series present a worshipper standing before what looks like a slender metal fire-holder, with flame rising from it.

The Arsacid Valaxš I was the first Iranian king to set a fire-holder on the reverse of bronze coin issues (G. F. Hill, *Catalogue of Greek Coins* 28, London, 1922, pl. 29.11-12); this became the standard practice of the Sasanians. Their *ātašdān* bore, as the coin-legends show, the personal fires of the kings; and they are shown as very big, like the "tower altars" of the early *Frātadāra coins, rising well above the heads of the figures beside them. The basic type has a two-stepped base and two- or three-stepped top, but other details vary. Thus the shaft is sometimes thick, sometimes slender; and when it is slender there are occasionally elaborate little side-columns, curiously wrought, to support the outer step of the top. Usually flames are shown leaping up, and often there is a diadem tied round the shaft, presumably to declare the fire a royal one.

Seals and rock-carvings of the Sasanian period show other *ātašdān*s of this basic type, but smaller than the royal ones, usually about waist-high. Small knee-high *ātašdān*s are also shown, which were presumably used for ritual purposes, being probably ancient specimens of what the Zoroastrians now call *āfrīnagān*, i.e., portable holders of fire for religious observances. A number of remains of Sasanian fire-holders are known, notably from the ruins of the temple Ādur Gušnasp (q.v.). Here the square three-stepped pedestal of the *ātašdān* of the great fire itself has been found, with the stone base of a round shaft rising from it; and other smaller *ātašdān*s and little stone *āfrīnagān*s have been dug out of the temple ruins. Big open-air "altars" also survive in Fars, the best known specimens being a pair at Naqš-e Rostam. These could only have been used for especial occasions and relatively brief observances, when fire set on them would have been constantly tended, and not exposed to harsh weather.

Most fire temples were eventually destroyed after the coming of Islam, or incorporated into mosques; but in the dark, lowly places of worship which were all that were ultimately left to the Zoroastrians, the *ātašdān* was still an essential feature. The relatively old specimens which still survive in Yazd, Kermān and their villages are big solid pillar-type ones, waist-high or a little taller, and round, hexagonal or octagonal in shape. Nearly all are made of mud-brick coated with a fine hard plaster, which gives a finish like stone; but at Šarīfābād-e Ardakān there is a little stone one, brought from the now-destroyed fire temple at Aḥmadābād nearby (see Boyce, *Stronghold*, pp. 8 n. 19, 76-77), which consists of a slender solid shaft with a deep cavity in the top. Around the rim of this cavity there are hollows to hold oil for lamps, and smaller ones to receive candles. When the Parsi agent, Manekji Limji Hataria, helped the Zoroastrians of Yazd to rebuild their Ātaš Bahrām in 1754, he set in it an old *ātašdān* (excavated near the city's *da<u>k</u>ma*s) made for it out of a solid block of stone, fashioned to form a deep round bowl (see Boyce, "The Fire-temples," p. 57). In india, however, the Parsis themselves had already by then broken with the old tradition of a stone *ātašdān* or its equivalent, and had taken to placing their sacred fires in big metal vases, made of brass or German silver. These were placed on a low square stone, to which the old name of *ādošt* was still applied (ibid., pp. 57-58). This development probably took place in the late fifteenth century, when for more than a decade the Parsis had to carry their one sacred fire, an Ātaš Bahrām, from place to place for safety during Muslim campaigns of conquest. When eventually it was brought to a more permanent abiding place at Navsari, a new *ātašdān* was probably made for it on the model of the portable *āfrīnagān* in which it had been kept for so long; since this was then the only sacred fire which the Parsis possessed (see further under *ātaš*), a pattern was thus set which was followed later for all sacred fires in their community. From the latter part of the nineteenth century Parsi influence has been strong on their Iranian co-religionists, and gradually the old traditional *ātašdān* of the Iranian fire temples have been replaced by handsome metal vases imported from India, which are now to be seen in the main fire temples of Yazd, Kermān and Tehran, as well as in a number of villages. The traditional type of *ātašdān* is now found in less prominent sanctuaries and in disused fire temples. In village sanctuaries there is regularly an *ātašdān* of this old type in the outer hall, in which fire is kindled at festivals and for special observances. In areas around Yazd where Zoroastrianism long survived, even bigger fire-holders (*kalak*s) are to be seen here and there in village squares, in which fires are lit by Muslims on festive occasions, in a manner which seems to carry on an ancient Zoroastrian tradition.

Bibliography: D. Stronach, *Iran* 7, 1969, pp. 1-20, and with M. Roaf, ibid., 11, 1973, pp. 129-39, fig. 6, for the Nūš-e Jān Tepe alter. D. Stronach, *JNES* 26, 1967, p. 287, and *Pasargadae*, Oxford, 1978, p. 141 with pl. 107, for the Pasargadae fire-holders. U.

Scerrato, *South Asian Archaeology 1977*, ed. M. Taddei, Naples, 1979, II, pp. 727-29, for the Dahān-e Ḡolāmān fire-holders. E. Schmidt, *Persepolis* II, Chicago, 1957, for Achaemenid seals. Idem, *Persepolis* III, Chicago, 1971, for plates of the Achaemenid funerary sculptures. *Survey of Persian Art*, IV, plates, for seals, coins, and monumental representations of fire-holders. K. Schippmann, *Die iranischen Feuerheiligtümer*, Berlin and New York, 1971, pp. 194-96 (with further references), for the *Frātadāra "tower altars." D. Stronach, "The Kuh-i Shahrak fire alter," *JNES* 25, 1966, pp. 217-27, for open-air fire-holders. R. Naumann, "Die sasanidischen Feueraltare," *Iranica Antiqua* 7, 1967, pp. 72-76. M. Boyce, "The fire-temples of Kerman," *Acta Orientalia* 30, 1966, pp. 56-58. W. Eilers, "Herd and Feuerstätte in Iran," *Innsbrucker Beiträge zur Sprachwissenschaft* 12, 1974, pp. 307-38. Y. Yamamoto, "The Zoroastrian temple cult of fire in archaeology and literature," pt. 1, *Orient* 15, 1979, pp. 19-53; pt. 2, ibid., 17, 1981, pp. 67-104.

(M. Boyce)

ĀTAŠKADA (New Persian) "house of fire," Mid. Pers. *ātaxš-kadag*, *kadag ī ātaxš*, a Zoroastrian term for a consecrated building in which there is an ever-burning sacred fire (see *ātaš*); the name is less commonly attested in the Zoroastrian Pahlavi books than the synonymous *mān ī ātaxš*, *xānag ī ātaxš*. Western scholars usually render all three terms by "fire-temple." The temple-cult of fire appears to have been instituted only in the latter part of the Achaemenian period (4th century B.C.), and there is no allusion to it in the Avesta, nor is any Old Pers. word known for a fire-temple. The Parthians appear to have called such a building an **ātarōšan* "place of burning fire" (the term survives as a loanword in Armenian *atrušan*), and there are a number of foreign literary references to fire-temples in their epoch. The prosaic nature of the Mid. Pers. names (*kadag*, *mān*, and *xānag* are all words used for an ordinary house) perhaps reflects a desire on the part of those who fostered the temple-cult in Pārs to keep it as close as possible in character to the age-old cult of the hearth-fire, and to discourage elaboration (see *ātašdān*).

After the Arab conquest a different name for a fire-temple came into general use among the Zoroastrians, namely Dar-e Mehr (q.v.), and eventually this entirely replaced the older terms for the Irani Zoroastrians. The Parsis, on settling in India, adopted also the Gujarati term *agiary* (*agīārī*), a literal translation of *ātaškada*, which they use side by side with Dar-e Mehr. In the 20th century the Faslis, a reformist group among the Parsis, revived the term *ātaškada* as a name for their new fire-temple in Bombay. This term is also now used by the Zoroastrians of Tehran for their chief fire-temple. As a descriptive one it is readily understood by Muslim Persians, who down the centuries have applied it locally to various ruins which are held to be those of fire-temples.

The oldest identified remains of a fire-temple in Iran are those on the Kūh-e K̲ʷāja in Sīstān where a stone fire alter is present. Only traces survive of the ground-plan of the oldest building, which has been assigned tentatively to Seleucid or early Parthian times. This temple was rebuilt later in the Parthian period, and further enlarged and remodeled in the Sasanian epoch. A relatively large number of ruins of fire-temples are known from the latter period, mostly in southwestern Iran (Fārs, Kermān, and ʿIrāq-e ʿAjamī), but the biggest and most impressive are those of Ādur Gušnasp (q.v.) in Azerbaijan. The characteristic feature of the Sasanian *ātaškada* was a domed sanctuary or *gombad* in which the fire itself was established. This had a square ground-plan and four corner-pillars which supported the dome (the *gombad* proper) on squinches. On a number of sites the *gombad*, made usually of rubble masonry with courses of stone, is all that survives, and so such ruins are popularly called in Fars *čahār-ṭāq* or "four arches." Archeological traces, and literary evidence, suggest that the *gombad* was regularly surrounded by a passage-way or ambulatory, for the use presumably both of the priests who tended the fire, and the worshippers. A typical small *ātaškada* appears to have consisted of the fire-sanctuary itself, with this passage-way; a smaller room or rooms for storing fire-wood, incense and utensils; and a *yazišn-gāh* or "place of worship" where the priest or priests would celebrate the rituals of the faith. These were never performed within the *gombad*, where no veneration might be offered except directly to the fire itself. There are also at some sites the traces of a large hall, no doubt a place where a congregation would gather to celebrate the *gāhāmbārs* (q.v.) and other feasts.

Modern usage shows that embers from a sacred fire might be taken into such a hall to make a fire there for congregational worship; but there is no evidence, literary, archeological or traditional, to suggest that a sacred fire itself, once established on its pillar-alter in the *gombad*, was ever moved except in its own interests (i.e., when the sanctuary needed to be cleaned or repaired, or for the fire's safety, when danger threatened). The theory, first put forward by A. Godard, "Les monuments du feu," *Āt̲h̲ār-é Iran* 3, 1938, p. 12, and widely adopted among archeologists, that a sacred fire was ordinarily kept hidden in a secret place, to be brought into the *gombad* only on festive days, or for other special occasions, not only lacks any solid evidence to support it, but runs counter to Zoroastrian concepts of the dignity of a sacred fire. This, once "enthroned" (*nišāst*; see *ātaš*, as the idiom is, with solemn rituals in its own sanctuary, should burn there "victoriously" (*pad wahrāmīh*) in perpetuity, as fixed and firm in its sanctified abode as the household fire upon the hearth (see M. Boyce, "The Sacred Fires of the Zoroastrians," *BSOAS* 31, 1968, pp. 52-53 with n. 9).

At the great fire-temple of Ādur Gušnasp at Tak̲t-e Solaymān in Azerbaijan, archeologists uncovered at the end of a series of pillared halls, traces of a *gombad*, which seems to have replaced an earlier flat-roofed sanctuary, and the base of a great stone fire-alter; also the remains of an elaborate complex of structures including courtyards, domed rooms, passage-ways and porticoes, as well as lesser fire-chambers. The building materials here were dressed stone and baked brick, and there are traces of rich adornment—panelling of thin leaves of marble, and, in the *gombad* itself, frescoes of white stucco, with more than life-size figures. The Sasanians did not permit the use of cult-images in worship, but tolerated representations of divine beings in high relief; and it is probably such representations which Masʿūdī refers to in his account of the ruins of the great fire temple at Istakhr (Eṣṭaḵr). These he describes as being of a very imposing building, with pillars made from huge blocks of stone, with carved capitals, the whole surrounded by a wide open space enclosed by a stone wall, covered with fine representational carvings. "The neighboring inhabitants" (he says) "saw in these the figures of the prophets" (Masʿūdī, *Morūj*, ed. Pellat, II, p. 400, par. 1403). All traces of this fire temple, already in ruins in the ninth century A.D., have since vanished; and the same is true of the magnificent temple at Karkūy, whose fire appears to have been extinguished in the Mongol invasions of the thirteenth century. Just before that time Qazvīnī describes the lofty twin domes of the temple, each crowned with a single horn, curving inwards, so that together they resembled the horns of a huge bull (*Kosmographie*, ed. Wüstenfeld, Göttingen, 1848, II, p. 165).

In Islamic times the fire-temples of Iran were all either demolished (the ruins, if any remained, having since generally disappeared), or replaced by mosques, some of which incorporated and effectively swallowed the older buildings. Only here and there the *gombad* of an old *ātaškada* can still be discerned within a Muslim place of worship. A notable example was to be seen till recently in the village mosque of Yazd-e Ḵāst in Fārs (described by M. Siroux, *Bulletin de l'Institut français d'archéologie orientale* 44, 1947, pp. 105-66); others also exist in area of Yazd (see M. Shokoohy, "Two Fire Temples Converted to Mosques in Central Iran," in *Papers in Honour of Professor Mary Boyce* II, Acta Iranica 25, Leiden, 1985, pp. 545-72). The Zoroastrians themselves had to keep those sacred fires which they managed to preserve in low mud-brick buildings, indistinguishable from humble dwelling-houses. Here, as a further precaution, the fire chamber was often hidden away among the recesses of the thick walls, and took various shapes accordingly, being sometimes rectangular and barrel-vaulted. In every case the small chamber had a double roof, to protect the purity of the fire, and the little holes for the smoke were set at angles to prevent rain or any small object falling into the sanctuary. The fire chamber was always paved (often with a pebble flooring), whereas the rest of the building frequently had only dirt floors.

To judge from travelers' descriptions, the Parsi *agiarys* in Gujarat, which was mostly under Muslim rule from the fourteenth century, were equally humble until British domination brought greater security to the community. The old Dar-e Mehr at Navsari (essentially a place of worship rather than a fire-temple) remains a building of this character, though much enlarged; but no Parsi sacred fire proper is housed in a building older than the late eighteenth century. Most of the Parsi temples belong to the nineteenth and early twentieth centuries, and are constructed in a pleasant blend of local styles, with an element occasionally of British Victorian. The fire itself is regularly installed in a central sanctuary, square, and pierced on three sides by window-openings, through which the worshippers can see it. (The principle thus appears to be the same as that of the Sasanian *čahār-tāq*, which similarly allowed the fire to be viewed through apertures.) Only the priests who tend it being allowed, with their extra purity, to enter the sanctuary itself. For the ground-plan of a typical small *agiary* see Avesta, tr. Darmesteter, I, pl. I.

The Zoroastrians of Iran began rebuilding their Dar-e Mehrs on a larger scale in the late nineteenth century, when the Muslim oppression started slowly to lessen. Some of their new buildings, in baked brick and stone, were of impressive size, and pleasing appearance. Muslim architects had necessarily to be employed for their construction, and they were often built in the general idiom of Iranian architecture. (Hence the larger fire-temple at the village of Šarīfābād, built in fact at the beginning of the present century, has been tentatively assigned by M. Siroux, on stylistic grounds, to the Safavid period [*Āṯār-é Īrān* III, 1938, pp. 83-87; cf. Boyce, *Stronghold*, pp. 77-78 n. 25].) A number of the Iranian fire-temples were reconstructed, however, on the Parsi plan. Both in Iran and India there are modern fire-temples which are embellished with adornments consciously inspired by the Achaemenid ruins at Persepolis, notably the winged figure in a disc, bull-capitals, and (in one instance in Bombay) impressive guardian animals.

Bibliography: See also for the *ātaškada* of pre-Islamic times the standard work of reference K. Schippmann, *Die iranischen Feuerheiligtümer*, Berlin and New York, 1971. This contains detailed studies, with bibliographies of all ruins, and putative ruins, of old Iranian fire-temples known in 1970. For some subsequent discussion, and further excavation reports, see R. Naumann and D. Huff, "Takht-i Suleiman," *Bastan Chenassi va Honar-e Iran* 9-10, 1972, pp. 7ff.; D. Huff, "Sasanian čahār tāqs in Fars," *Proceedings of the IIIrd Annual Symposium on Archaeological Research in Iran, 1974*, Tehran, 1975, pp. 243-54; M. Boyce, "On the Zoroastrian temple-cult of fire," *JAOS* 90, 1975, pp. 454-63. On the fire-temples of the Islamic period see M. Boyce, "The fire temples of Kerman," *Acta Orientalia* 30, 1966, pp. 51-72; idem, *A Persian Stronghold of Zoroastrianism*, Oxford, 1977, chap. 4; G. Gropp, "Die Funktion des Feuertempels der Zoroastrier," *AMI*, N.F. 2, 1969, pp. 147-75; idem, "Die rezenten Feuertempel der Zarathustrier," ibid., 4, 1971, pp. 263-88; F. M. Kotwal, "Some Observations on the History of the Parsi Dar-i Mihrs," *BSOAS* 37, 1974, pp. 664-69.

(M. Boyce)

ĀTAŠ-ZŌHR, or *ātaš-zōr* (Persian *zōr-e ātaš*), a Middle Persian term for the Zoroastrian ritual offering to fire of fat from a sacrificial animal, in which the fat caused the flames to leap up, and itself dissolved completely. The rite, now abandoned, appears to go back to at least the Indo-Iranian period, i.e., to at least the third millennium B.C., since the same offering (characteristically of the omentum, one of the fattiest parts of the entrails) was made also by the Brahmins of India (see J. Schwab, *Das altindische Thieropfer*, Erlangen, 1886, pp. 112f.; H. Oldenberg, *Die Religion des Veda*, 2nd ed., Berlin, 1917, repr. 1970, pp. 358-60). The ritual thus long pre-dates the founding of Zoroastrian temple fires, and presumably has its origin in the rewarding of the spirit of the hearth fire for cooking the household meal. Cf. *Ātaš Niyāyišn* (q.v.), v. 8, where the *zōhr* is referred to as the "meal" (*-piθwa-*) of the fire. (Down to the early twentieth century the Zoroastrians of Iran followed the ancient custom of eating meat only from an animal that had been ritually sacrificed. This custom can be traced among the Parsis also down to early modern times, see the *Sanskrit Ślokas* of Aka Adhyasu, v. 10, apud M. Boyce, *Textual Sources for the Study of Zoroastrianism*, Manchester UP, 1985, p. 123).

The earliest historical reference to the *ātaš-zōhr* is by Strabo, who, writing around the beginning of the Christian era, reports of the Persians (15.3.14) that "to fire they offer sacrifice by adding dry wood without the bark and by placing fat on top of it." Some writers, he says (15.3.13), describe the fat as being a portion of the omentum. Another independent attestation of the practice is provided by a Middle Persian Manichean text of the Sasanian period (M 95 V 1-6. see *Mir. Man.* II, pp. 28-29 [319-20] and W. B. Henning, *BSOAS* 11, 1943, p. 217 n. 7). There are numerous references to the rite in the Pahlavi books, some dateless, others (as in the writings of Manuščihr) belonging to the post-Sasanian period. From these references it appears that the rite was obligatory on the following occasions: at the enthronement of an Ātaš Bahrām (q.v.), and regularly thereafter in the maintenance of this most sacred of temple fires; at each of the six *gāhāmbārs* (q.v.); at the ceremony at dawn of the fourth day after death (see *čahārom*); at the still ill-defined *hamāg-dēn* ceremony; at various rites of expiation for grievous sins; and in thank-offering for the birth of a son (and presumably after other highly auspicious events). The offering might on occasion be made to any "fire of Ohrmazd," i.e., any pure fire, a hearth or ritual one as well as temple fire. *Zōhr* might not be given which had been "robbed and carried off" (*duzīdag ud appurdag*), i.e., taken from a stolen animal. Cost ensured that the offering was usually from a sheep or goat; but *zōhr* from any creature of Bahman, i.e. any "clean" animal, was acceptable. Sheep, goat, pig, donkey, and cow are explicitly mentioned in connection with the *ātaš-zōhr* in Pahlavi and Persian Zoroastrian texts (see Boyce, "Ātaš-zōhr," pp. 103-05); and horse, cow, and sheep sacrifices are repeatedly referred to in the Avesta.

Religious services performed with animal sacrifice were termed *pad zōhr*, and to provide for their celebration was held to be highly meritorious. Indeed, in the list of the "four best things" revealed by Ohrmazd to Zoroaster the second is "to give to fire fuel, incense and *zōhr*" (*ātaxš ēzm bōy ud zōhr dādan*, B. N. Dhabhar, ed., *The Pahlavi Rivāyat accompanying the Dādistān ī Dīnīk*, Bombay, 1913, chap. VIII, p. 11; E. W. West, tr., SBE XVIII, p. 417). In another text it is said that fire in its bodily form requires these three things of its servitors, as they in turn look to it in its spirit form for protection from powers of evil (see A. Barthélemy, ed. and tr., *Gujastak Abalish*, Paris, 1887, chap. VI.15-16).

Offerings of the *ātaš-zōhr* on most of the occasions listed above are attested in modern times. In the seventeenth century the Italian traveler J. F. Gemelli recorded the offering of "the fat of a sheep's tail" to a temple fire in Isfahan (see Awnsham Churchill, *A Collection of Voyages and Travels*, London, 1704, IV, p. 143a); and in a long Gujarati song composed to celebrate the founding of the Bhagaria Ātaš Bahrām at Navsari in A.D. 1765 there are adjurations to "bring a pair of goats . . . slaughter a goat for the Ātaš Bahrām" (see S. H. Chikan, *Pārsī strī garbā*, Bombay, 1879, pp. 346, 352). Animal sacrifice with *zōhr* was still performed by traditional Zoroastrians in Iran at religious services for the six *gāhāmbārs* well into the present century; and in the nineteenth century M. Haug had found this practice still a living memory among Parsi priests (see his *Essays*, 3rd ed., London, 1884, p. 281). The offering of the *ātaš-zōhr* for the dawn-ceremony of the *čahārom* persisted in both branches of the Zoroastrian community well into the present century. Anquetil du Perron refers to the practice in Surat in the eighteenth century, with fat from a sheep (*Zend-Avesta, ouvrage de Zoroastre*, Paris, 1771, II, pp. 586-87); and in 1823 the Bhagaria Anjoman of Navsari, answering an inquiry from Parsis in Bombay, laid it down that this observance was so important that maintaining it overrode the keeping of one of the Zoroastrian non-slaughtering days, should the death-ceremony and such a day coincide. The *zōhr*, it was then declared, was to be offered to an Ātaš Bahrām or an Ātaš-e Ādorān, together with frankincense and aloewood. In Surat the *čahārom* offering, from a white sheep or goat, was still made by Parsi priestly families in the 1930s; and the practice was continued a little longer in Zoroastrian villages around Yazd. As for the usage on auspicious occasions, in a Gujarati song which Parsi women of Navsari used to sing on the third day of wedding ceremonies, there is again the exhortation to "Bring a pair of goats, offer sacrifice to the Ātaš Bahrām" (see Chikan, op. cit., p. 407). Nowadays the conscious substitution is made on all these occasions of incense or fragrant woods.

Bibliography: See also Avesta, tr. Darmesteter, I, p. lxvi; II, pp. 154, 254 n. 69. T. D. Anklesaria and S. D. Bharucha, *Dādēstānē-dīnīnō tarjumō* (Translation of the *Dādestān ī dēnīg*), Bombay, 1926, appendix, pp. 17-30. M. Boyce, "Ātaš-zōhr and Āb-zōhr," *JRAS*, 1966, pp. 100-10. Idem, "Haoma, priest of the sacrifice," *W. B. Henning Memorial Volume*, ed. I. Gershevitch and M. Boyce, London, 1970, pp. 62-80. Idem, *Zoroastrianism* I, pp. 153-55.

(M. Boyce and F. M. Kotwal)

ATHENAIOS of **NAUCRATIS,** wrote the *Deipnosophistai* (Sophists at dinner; q.v.), his only extant work, in which in about a hundred passages he deals with things Persian. Athenaios was born in Naucratis, Egypt, and lived in Rome, possibly at the beginning of the third century A.D. "If the Ulpian of his dialogue is really modelled on the celebrated Ulpian of Tyre, the able jurist who, as praetorian prefect, undertook to carry on the reforms of Alexander Severus and was murdered in the emperor's presence by the mutinous guards in 228, the completion of the work the Deipnosophistai may be dated not long after 228." (Gulick, Introduction, p. viii.)

Bibliography: Wentzel, "Athenaios aus Naukratis," Pauly-Wissowa, II/2, cols. 2026-33. C. B. Gulick, ed. and tr., Athenaeus, *The Deipnosophists*, Harvard, 1961, 7 vols.

(J. Duchesne-Guillemin)

AṮĪR AKSĪKATĪ, a poet of the 6th/12th century with a distinctive style. According to late sources such as *Majmaʿ al-foṣahāʾ* (I, p. 269), Aṯīr-al-dīn was his personal name. His *nesba* indicates that he came from Aksīkat, then the chief town of Fargāna in Central Asia. He began his poetic career in the east, but on account of the troubles in Khorasan following the collapse of Sanjar's régime and the sultan's death in 552/1157, he moved to the west and entered the service of Moʿezz-al-dīn Arslān b. Ṭoḡrel; he has left an ode congratulating Arslān on his accession to the Saljuq sultanate of ʿErāq in 556/1161. Thereafter Aṯīr resided in ʿErāq-e ʿAjamī, Jebāl, and Azerbaijan, and won some fame in that region. In addition to the Saljuq sultan of ʿErāq, Arslān (556/1161-571/1176), the *atābak*s of Azerbaijan, Šams-al-dīn Ildegiz (531/1137-571/1175), Moḥammad Jahān-pahlavān (571/1175-581/1186), and Qezel Arslān ʿOṯmān (581/1186-587/1191) were recipients of his eulogies. He found particular favor with Ildegiz and Qezel Arslān, and is said to have replaced Mojīr-al-dīn Baylaqānī as Qezel Arslān's court poet (ʿAwfī, *Lobāb* II, p. 223). Aṯīr was in touch with a number of leading local poets such as Kāqānī, Mojīr-al-dīn Baylaqānī, and Asharī Nīšāpūrī. His claim to parity of talent with Kāqānī led to exchanges of abuse and sarcasm between the two. It has even been stated (Dawlatšāh, ed. Browne, p. 80) that Atīr traveled from Khorasan to Šervān for the purpose of challenging Kāqānī. Nor did Aṯīr hesitate to decry Mojīr-al-dīn for "plundering loot from the caravan of his poetry." This remark by Aṯīr is reprehended by the historian Rāvandī (*Rāḥat al-ṣodūr*, p. 327).

The date of Aṯīr's death is given as 577/1181 by Moḥammad Ṣādeq b. Ṣāleḥ, the compiler of the *Šāhed-e ṣādeq*, as 579/1183 (*Yādgār* 2/6, 1324 Š./1946, p. 29) by Āḏar Bīgdelī (*Āteškada*, p. 318), and as 563/1167 by Hedāyat (*Majmaʿ al-foṣaḥā*, loc. cit.); either 577/1181 or 579/1183 is likely to be correct, because Aṯīr wrote odes in praise of the *atābak* Moḥammad Jahān-pahlavān whose reign began in 571/1175.

The old literary critics placed Aṯīr in the top rank of *qaṣīda*-writers. His skills in producing rhymes with a *radīf* (appended refrain word or words) or other clever but unnecessary artifices, in handling difficult ideas, and in overcoming various snags which face poets, immediately strike the eye. He certainly did not attain parity with Kāqānī, whom he abused unjustifiably; but he was sometimes able to conceive lofty thoughts, make novel combinations of ideas, and use his wide learning in the creation of new themes, and in these respects he sometimes fell not far short of the great poet of Šervān. Although his work, like that of many contemporary poets, is predominantly erudite, there are some pleasing verses in his *dīvān*, particularly in his graceful *ḡazal*s. ʿAwfī (*Lobāb* II, p. 224) wrote that Aṯīr's poetry "is embellished and pleasant, and has a wealth of ideas." His *dīvān*, with a biographical introduction, has been published (ed. R. Homāyūn Farrok, Tehran, 1337 Š./1958).

Bibliography: See also Šams al-dīn Rāzī, *Moʿjam*, pp. 228, 236. *Majmaʿ al-foṣaḥāʾ* I, pp. 269ff. Dawlatšāh, ed. Browne, pp. 121-25. Loṭf-ʿAlī Beg Āḏar, *Āteškada*, Bombay, 1299/1882, pp. 318-19. B. Forūzānfar, *Sokan wa sokanvarān*, 2nd ed., Tehran, 1350 Š./1971, pp. 532-47. M. ʿA. Rāvandī, *Rāḥat al-ṣodūr*, ed. M. Eqbāl, Leiden, 1921, pp. 327-30. Ṣafā, *Adabīyāt* II, pp. 707-15. Kayyāmpūr, *Sokanvarān*, p. 26. Rypka, *Hist. Iran. Lit.*, p. 209. Nafīsī, *Naẓm o naṯr* I, p. 107.

(Z. Safa)

AṮĪR OWMĀNĪ, Aṯīr-al-dīn ʿAbdallāh, a poet of the ʿErāqī (western Iranian) school of the 7th/13th century (d. 665/1266).

He came from the village of Owmān near Hamadān, and is said to have been a pupil of the Kʷāja Naṣīr-al-dīn Ṭūsī though firm evidence of this is lacking. He spent most of his career at Baghdad but lived at times in Kordestān and Lorestān and also at Isfahan, where he was friendly with the poet Kamāl-al-dīn Esmāʿīl (d. 635/1237) and the latter's contemporary, Rafīʿ-al-dīn Lonbānī. His principal patron was the last Ildegizid ruler of Azerbaijan, the *atābak* Ozbek (r. 607-22/1210-25) son of the *atābak* Moḥammad Jahān-pahlavān. The poet also wrote eulogies of the prince of the Little Lors (Lor-e Kūček), Ḥosām-al-dīn Kalīl b. Badr b. Šojāʿ, while simultaneously courting and praising the latter's opponent Šehāb-al-dīn Solaymānšāh Īvāʾī, chief of the Kurdish Īvāʾī tribe and a chief minister of the caliph al-Mostaʿṣem Be'llāh; it was in hope of gaining this man's favor that Aṯīr Owmānī spent so much time at Baghdad. Solaymānšāh and his son were put to death after Hūlāgū's (Hülegü) conquest of Baghdad in 656/1258. Aṯīr Owmānī has described the fall of Baghdad and the accompanying slaughter and destruction in a very sorrowful *qaṣīda*. He died in 665/1266. His *dīvān* survives and is estimated at about 5,000 verses. He composed poems in Arabic as well as Persian. In poetic technique he tended to follow Anwarī. He attempted to enliven his odes by using a simple, fluent style and a forceful, well-chosen vocabulary, and at the same time, like Anwarī, to create poetic themes by using his knowledge of science, mathematics, medicine, and philosophy, but without going too far in this direction.

Bibliography: *Ḥabīb al-sīar* (Tehran) III, pp. 106-07. Dawlatšāh, ed. Browne, pp. 155, 157, 172-73. Loṭf-ʿAlī Beg Āḏar (Āẕar Bīgdelī), *Ātaškada*, Bombay, 1299/1882, pp. 253-54. ʿA. Eqbāl Āštīānī, *Tārīḵ-e mofaṣṣal-e Īrān* I: *Az ḥamla-ye Čangīz tā taškīl-e dawlat-e teymūrī*, 2nd ed., Tehran, 1341 Š./1962, pp. 533-34. *Majmaʿ al-foṣaḥāʾ* I, pp. 280-82. Ṣafā, *Adabīyāt* III/1, pp. 394-408. Nafīsī, *Naẓm o naṯr* I, p. 158. Ḵayyāmpūr, *Soḵanvarān*, p. 26. Dehḵodā, s.v. Aṯīr Owmānī.

(Z. SAFA)

AṮĪR-AL-DĪN AL-MOFAŻŻAL B. ʿOMAR B. AL-MOFAŻŻAL **ABHARĪ** SAMARQANDĪ. See ABHARĪ SAMARQANDĪ, AṮĪR-AL-DĪN

ATKINSON, DR. JAMES A. (1780-1852), a notable British Orientalist, a scholar of the Persian language and literature, and the translator of Ferdowsī's *Rostam o Sohrāb*, Neẓāmī's *Laylī o Majnūn*, the popular Persian romance of *Ḥātem Ṭāʾī*, and others. Atkinson was born in Durham on 9 March 1780, and demonstrated early on an exceptional talent for versification. He studied medicine in Edinburgh and London, and was appointed assistant surgeon in the Bengal establishment in 1805. He studied Persian in his free time and in 1810 began his verse translation of the story of Sohrāb. The work was published as *Soohrab, a Poem* in 1814 in Calcutta where a year earlier Lord Minto, the Governor General, had appointed Atkinson to the post of assistant assay master at the mint, a position he retained until 1828, except for two brief intervals, in 1818 when he took up the deputy chair of Persian in Fort William College, and the period 1826-27 which he spent in England. In 1817 Atkinson was also entrusted with the superintendency of the *Government Gazette*, the official British journal in India. The next year he published his edition of *Ḥātem Ṭāʾī: Hatim Taee, a Popular Romance*, Calcutta, 1818. After 1823, when the government severed its formal ties with the journal, the *Gazette*—and the newly founded *Press*—were placed under his charge.

Atkinson spent the years 1828-33 in England where he completed his abridged verse and prose translation of the *Šāh-nāma*. The work, to which a revised version of *Soohrab* had been appended, was published by the Oriental Translation Fund in 1832, and won the Fund's gold medal. Four years later the Fund published Atkinson's verse translation in epitome of Neẓāmī's celebrated romance under the title of *Laili and Mejnun* (1836). Meanwhile, Atkinson had returned to his duties in India, and in 1838 accompanied the British army of occupation into Afghanistan, where he remained stationed until the defeat and surrender of Dōst Moḥammad in 1841. Atkinson retired in 1847 after forty-two years of active service, returned to England shortly afterwards and died of apoplexy on 7 August 1852.

Atkinson's translations from the *Šāh-nāma* suffer from his over-zealous attempt to prove Ferdowsī closer in substance and utterance to Western epic conventions than was generally realized. In *The Shah Nameh* which is an abridgment in verse and in prose, he employs a variety of meters and measures, creating an uneven pace and, consequently, a false impression of the *Šāh-nāma*. The work thus conveys little of the majesty and poetic air of the original.

Atkinson's other translations from Persian include *The Aubid: An Eastern Tale* (Calcutta, 1819), a verse translation of a contemporary Indian romance, and *The Customs and Manners of the Women of Persia and Their Domestic Superstitions* (Oriental Translation Fund, 1832), a loose prose translation of Āqā Jamāl Ḵᵛānsārī's *Ketāb-e Kolṯūm Nana*.

Although these translations reveal the many pitfalls of pioneer work in the field, still they are a marked improvement over the cumbersome phraseology and elaborate diction of such late eighteenth-century translators of the *Šāh-nāma* as Joseph Champion. This tendency in turn reflects the departure in English Romanticism from the neo-Classical attitude towards Oriental literatures in general and towards epic poetry and poetic translation in particular.

In addition to his Persian translations, Atkinson is the author of two fascinating travelogues (*Expedition into Afghanistan* and *Sketches in Afghanistan*, London, 1842), many valuable essays of statistical and topographical importance in the *Gazette* and the *Press*, and other works that are outside Iranian studies.

Bibliography: *Proceedings of the Thirtieth Anniversary of the Royal Asiatic Society of Great Britain and Ireland*, London, 1853. *The Dictionary of National Biography*, ed. Sir Leslie Stephen and Sir Sidney Lee, Oxford, 1917. J. Atkinson, *Soohrab: A Poem Freely Translated from the Original Persian of Firdousee*, Calcutta, 1814; repr. as *Suhrab and Rustam*, Delmar, N.Y., 1972. Idem, *The Shah Nameh of the Persian Poet Firdausi*, London, 1832; repr; London, 1886, 1892. Idem, *Laili and Majnun: A Poem from the Original Persian of Nizami*, London, 1836; 2nd ed., 1894; reissued in L. Crammer-Byng, ed., *Love Stories of the East*, London, 1905. A. J. Arberry, ed., *British Contributions to Persian Studies*, London, 1942. J. D. Yohannan, *Persian Poetry in England and America: A 200-Year History*, Delmar, N.Y., 1977, pp. 80-82. A. Karimi-Hakkak, *The Shāhnāmeh of Firdawsī in France and England 1770-1860: A Study of the European Response to the Persian Epic of Kings*, doctoral dissertation, Rutgers University, New Brunswick, N. J., 1979

(A. KARIMI-HAKKAK)

ATOSSA, Achaemenid queen. The Greek form of the name may reflect Old Pers. *Utauθā (= Av. Hutaosā, possibly "well trickling" or "well granting" (see M. Mayrhofer, *Iranisches Personennamenbuch* I, Vienna, 1979, p. I/52, no. 179). The most famous bearer of this name was the daughter of Cyrus the Great—probably his eldest; her mother may have been Cassandane. Atossa lived ca. 550-475 B.C.; Aeschylus' *Persae* would indicate that she was still alive when Xerxes invaded Greece. (The fact that her name is not found in the Persepolis fortification tablets certainly does not prove that she was dead at that time as suggested by W. Hinz, *Orientalia*, N.S. 39, 1970, p. 423.) Atossa was consort to her brother Cambyses II; and, after his death, she somehow passed into the harem of Gaumāta (the Pseudo-Smerdis). Eventually Darius took possession of the harem, married Atossa, and made her his main consort and queen (Herodotus 3.88.2). A prominent motive may have been Darius' wish to legitimize the accession of his own collateral Achaemenid line by joining with a member of Cyrus' family. Atossa, according to an anecdote of Herodotus (3.134.1-6), induced Darius to make war on the Greeks; because she wanted to have Attic, Argive, and Corinthian maidservants (see also Aelian, *Natura Animalium* 11.27). At her instigation a Persian expedition reconnoitered the Greek coasts and surveyed Greek naval power. It was guided by Democedes of Croton, her own and Darius' private physician. (He had treated Darius successfully for a dislocated ankle and Atossa for a breast tumor; Herodotus 3.129.1-130.4, 3.133.1). Although the expedition was successful, Democedes took the opportunity to escape (Herodotus 3.134-138, Timaeus apud Athenaeus 3.152. 10ff.).

Atossa had four sons by Darius (Herodotus 7.7.2). Xerxes was the eldest; the others were Hystaspes, leader of the Bactrian and Saka troops in Xerxes' army, Masistes, one of Xerxes' commanding generals, and Achaemenes, admiral of the Egyptian fleet (Herodotus 7.3.2, 7.64.2, 7.82, 7.97). Because of her lineage and by her intelligence, Atossa exercised great influence on her husband and at court generally. Ca. 487, in a harem struggle, she won Darius' support for the succession of Xerxes. Xerxes was the first son born to Darius after his seizure of the kingship, but not the eldest of all. Darius had three sons by his first wife, the daughter of Gobryas (Herodotus 7.2.2). Xerxes' appointment as commander-in-chief of the Persian army was made to strengthen his position as prospective successor (Herodotus 7.2.1-3.4; Plutarch, *De fraterno amore* 18). The smooth transition to Xerxes' rule after Darius' death must have been due in part to Atossa's great authority. During her son's reign she held the high status of queen-mother. Her reputation is clearly reflected in Aeschylus' *Persae*, where her dignified figure is at the heart of the play's action (lines 159ff., 290ff., 598ff., 703.). Her personality is impressively represented and drawn with esteem; Darius, called up from Hades by the chorus, explicitly approves of her influence over her son (lines 832ff.).

The name Atossa was apparently a traditional one in the Achaemenid clan. According to the genealogy of the kings of Cappadocia, it was borne by a sister of Cambyses I (Diodorus Siculus 31.19.1). A sister and wife of Artaxerxes II was also so named (Plutarch, *Life of Artaxerxes* 23.26f.).

Bibliography: See also Justi, *Namenbuch*, p. 50.

F. Cauer, "Atossa," Pauly-Wissowa, II/2, col. 2133.

E. Kornemann, *Grosse Frauen des Altertums*, Wiesbaden, 1952 (4th ed.).

(R. Schmitt)

'AṬR "perfume" (Arabic *'eṭr*, plur. *'oṭūr*; in Persian also *'aṭrīyāt*, perfumes), a Semitic term also attested in Syriac and Amharic. The word originally designated a perfume exhaled from a person or a plant or aromatic substances in general (synonym *ṭīb*). Ebn Ḵordāḏbeh (3rd/9th cent.) speaks about the land where *'oṭūr* grew and Ebrāhīm b. Wāṣef Šāh (5th/11th cent.) about the islands of *ṭīb* near Java (Ferrand, *Textes arabes*, pp. 28, 152). But *'aṭr* also designated various kinds of perfumes made by an *'aṭṭār*: maceration oils, enfleurage fats and oils, unguents, and distilled waters. After the discovery of essential oils in the beginning of the seventeenth century *'aṭr* was used for perfume made from essential oil only, or, more precisely, for the essential oil of roses, *'eṭr al-ward*, *gol-'aṭr*, English *otto*.

*'Aṭr*s were compounded and obtained from scented substances, *Jawāher al-ṭīb al-mofrada*, taken from vegetal products (fruit-pulp, juice, rind—flowers, leaves, roots, woods, bark, seeds, resin, moss) as well as from animal products (ambergris, musk, civet, operculum of some gasteropods, castoreum, etc.) The most expensive substances were of course extensively counterfeited. They came in three principal forms, all three attested from old times: more or less thick unguents for rubbing, liquid oils of flowers for anointing, and distilled waters for sprinkling. There were four principal ways of extracting them: absorption or enfleurage (no heating), *naq'*; maceration (at medium or high temperature), *ṭabḵ*; fumigation, *tabḵīr*, *tadḵīn*; distillation *taqṭīr*, *taṣ'īdāt*.

Absorption and enfleurage. Most perfumes based upon oils (*dohn*, plur. *adhān*) were extracted by this process from fresh flowers. Absorption consisted in soaking, without preheating, fresh petals of flowers (jasmine, rose, violet, sour orange, henna, stock, etc.) in the base oils—from sesame (*ḥall, semsem*), olive, sweet almonds, cotton seeds, apricot, and peach kernels, *ban*, *Moringa aptera* Gaertn. (which was excellent for its neutral odor and did not go rancid), etc. These petals were changed every three or four days, five or six times in all; the oil was then filtered in a linen or silk material and placed in a well-closed glass bottle.

Enfleurage. In this process violets, roses, nenufar, narcissus, or Egyptian willow blossom (*bīdmešk*) were exposed to layers of sesame seeds, sweet almonds pulp, or *ban* seeds and changed several times. The seeds were then crushed and the extract was clarified by settling, *reqqa* (Ebn al-Bayṭār, I, p. 107).

Maceration. By this process perfume oils were obtained from hard vegetal substances: spices (cloves, nutmeg, cardamom, saffron, etc.), wood shavings, sawdust (*nošārat*) from white, yellow, or red sandal wood, aloewood, etc., pulp of fruit, rind (lemon, citron, Syrian apple), seeds of rose or lemon, dry petals of rose, dry leaves of myrtle, mint, etc. Each of these substances was moistened (*ball, naddā*) and the pulverized (*saḥq, deqqa*) in mortar (*hāvan*) or with a grinding stone (*ṣalāyat*). They were then thrown one by one into the oil and heated; alternatively they were all kneaded together and left for two or three days, then put in a cooking pot (*tenǰar, ṭūr*). Sometimes rose-water was added, in which case the water had to evaporate by boiling at low heat; it was then taken off the fire and allowed to settle for one or two days, and finally filtered into well-closed flasks.

Fumigation. In the preparation of unguents, the base substance may be fumigated with aloewood, costus or *aḏfār* (operculum of some gasteropods).

Unguents. The principal unguents were *ʿabīr, ḡālīyat, ḵalūq,* Persian *malāb, moṯallaṯa,* and *sokk.* They contained more or less the same ingredients as the perfume oils, but were thick. The base substance, *rokn,* was a paste made from oak-gall, resin, wax, pudding starch, *našāstaǰ al-fālūḏaǰ* (al-Kendī, no. 25), pith of palm-tree root, bitter almonds, purified vegetal tar, *qeṭrān,* or litharge (*mordāsanǰ*), etc. The base substance was gently heated and the ingredients (powdered vegetal substances as above, perfumed oils, ambergris, musk, civet, etc.) were added one by one and gently cooked; if all the vegetal ingredients and oils were first kneaded together the resulting paste could be dried and pulverized before adding the base substance. Ambergris, musk, or civet were in general added at the end of the process when they were introduced in powder form. The preparation was then taken off the heat and allowed to cool down somewhat before the mixing. The unguents were kept in glass bottles or flattened (*dalk*) into small disks and dried.

Distillation. The preparation methods described above appear to have been in use since antiquity. The process of distillation, which is far more complex, was known at least from the beginning of Islam, and may date back to the Greek Alexandrian alchemists, who knew the art from the Egyptians. Until the discovery of the essential oil, distilled "waters" were exclusively fabricated by this process. It involves two techniques: the dry technique, corresponding to the medieval *destillatio per descensum* (the cucurbit is in a cooking pot full of ash or is exposed to the fire directly), and the bain-marie (the boiler hangs in a cooking pot full of water) corresponding to the *destillatio per ascensum.* J̌āber b. Ḥayyān from Kūfa (2nd/8th cent.), al-Kendī from Baṣra (ca. 260/873), and especially al-Zahrāwī from Cordoba (ca. 404/1013) have left good descriptions of the various kinds of apparatus used. They, however, employed the bain-marie distillation (*taqṭīr be'l-roṭūbat*) for flower water and preferred charcoal fire to wood fire.

Yaʿqūb b. Eṣḥāq al-Kendī, a philosopher, mathematician, astronomer, and physician who lived at the court of Ma'mūn, in his book *Ketāb kīmīā' al-ʿeṭr wa'l-taṣʿīdāt,* shows the great variety of rich perfumes, and describes the distillation of many flowers: red rose, myrtle, jasmine, spikenard, willow blossm (giving the well-known *ʿaraq-e bīdmešk*), stock, and also lemon, Syrian apple peel, saffron, camphor, etc. Rose-water was added to intensify, enrich, and fix the fragrance, and was itself intensified with sandal, musk, etc. The distilled substances could also be impregnated before distillation, e.g., saffron with musk, in a kind of enfleurage.

Abu'l-Qāsem Ḵalaf b. ʿAbbās al-Zahrāwī, a physician and surgeon, in the twenty-eight section of his *Ketāb-al-taṣrīf le man ʿaǰeza ʿan al-ta'līf,* chiefly describes various kinds of rose-water (*golāb*) distillation. The bain-marie method he describes was in use in Iraq (Ebn al-ʿAwwām, II, p. 380), but unlike al-Kendī he always treats rose petals without water in the cucurbit, which must have been a risky procedure.

There is little information about the distillation output. Ebn al-ʿAwwām quoting at-Zahrāwī says it was from one half to three quarter the weight of the roses in the waterless process (II, p. 390). For a better concentration the water would be distilled two or three times.

The imperfection of the utensils certainly required careful adjustment in assembling the still, in order to get a low continuous fire and to guard the perfume from the smoke, but the effect of the smell of smoke could be helped some with amber, marjoram prepared with salt, or alum (Ebn al-ʿAwwām, II, p. 390). For a long time one had nothing but experience to guide one and so the correct adjustment of the equipment and the correct proportions in the mixtures remained a problem.

Though *golāb* "rose-water," by far the most popular perfume, was for a long time produced almost exclusively in Persia, the essential oil and its preparation were apparently discovered, more or less by chance, in Hindustan. The discovery took place in 1020-21/1611-12 at the court of the Mughal king J̌ahāngīr with its strong Persian influence, where the *ʿeṭr al-ward,* called *ʿaṭr-e ǰahāngīrī,* is first mentioned. The king himself in his memoirs relates how the discovery was made by the mother of Nūr J̌ahān Begum, his favorite Persian wife: "When she was making rose-water a scum formed on the surface of the dishes into which the hot rose-water was poured from the jugs. She collected this scum little by little... It is of such strength in perfume that if one drop be rubbed on the palm of the hand it scents a whole assembly and it appears as if many rose buds had bloomed at once" (*Tozok-e J̌ahāngīrī* I, pp. 270-71). In Europe, Arnold of Villeneuve (1235-1312) had isolated rosemary oil and used it in an alcoholic solution as a medicine (*Opera omnia,* pp. 589-90), but, curiously enough, though large quantities of rose-water were regularly distilled in Persian and Iraq at least from the ninth century, it was not known that *gol-ʿaṭr,* when cooled, like all essential oils floats upon the water in small quantities. Only during the seventeenth and eighteenth centuries was this knowledge extended to the entire Islamic world. European travelers in the seventeenth century noticed it and described it as a product unknown to them. Chardin speaks of a rose oil called *atre* which was very expensive, since from forty pounds of rose-water barely half a drachm of that oil was extracted. They left the rose-water for twenty-four hours in the open air in a large vat, and a brownish oil gathered on the surface of it and was removed with a straw (Chardin, II, p. 66).

See also anbar; gol; and ʿūd.

Bibliography: The main book of reference for the study of the preparation of perfumes is al-Kendī, *Ketāb kīmīā' al-ʿeṭr wa'l-tasʿīdāt*, ed. and tr. K. Garbers, *Buch über die Chemie des Perfüms und die Destillation*, Leipzig, 1948. Other: Arnold of Villanova, *Opera omnia*, Venice, 1505. Ebn al-Bayṭār, *al-Ketāb al-Jāmeʿ fi'l-adwīa al-mofrada*, 4 vols. in two, ed. Bulaq, Cairo, 1874-75; tr. L. Leclerc, *Traité des simples*, 3 vols., Paris, 1877-83. Jāber b. Ḥayyān, whose book about perfumes is not extant, discussed distillation in the *Ketāb al-ḵawāṣṣ al-kabīr* (see P. Krauss, "Jâbir ibn Hayyân. Contribution à l'histoire des idées scientifiques dans l'Islam," *Mémoires de l'Institut d'Égypte* 45, 1941, p. 9) and in *Ketāb al-sabʿīn* 41, fol. 151⁰ (P. Kraus, ibid., p. 22). Al-Zahrāwī, *Ketāb al-taṣrīf le man ʿajeza ʿan al-ta'līf*, 28th sec., in: (1) Ebn al-ʿAwwām, *Ketāb al-felāḥat*, tr. J. J. Clement-Mullet, *Le livre de l'agriculture*, 3 vols., Paris, 1964-67; (2) a Latin tr. from the late 13th cent.: *Liber servitoris sive Liber XXVIII translatus a Simone Januense interprete Abraam Iudeo Tortuosiensi* in Mesuë, *Liber de medicina*, tr. Gerard of Cremona, Venice, 1471, ff. 338-50. *Tūzok-e Jahāngīrī*, tr. A. Rodgers and H. Beveridge, *Memoirs of Jahângîr*, Delhi, 1909-14, 2 vols.; 2nd ed., Delhi, 1968, 2 vols. in one. J. Chardin, *Voyages en Perse, et autres lieux de l'Orient*, 3 vols., Amsterdam, 1711; ed. L. Langlès, *Les voyages du Chevalier Chardin, en Perse, et autres lieux de l'Orient*, 10 vols., Paris. 1811. G. Ferrand, *Textes arabes relatifs à l'Extrême Orient*, Paris, I, 1913, II, 1914. Note also the works of E. Wiedemann, especially "Beiträge zur Geschichte der Naturwissenschaften: zur Chemie bei den Arabern," *Sb. d. Physikalisch-Medizinischen Sozietät* 43, Erlangen, 1911, pp. 72-113.

(F. AUBAILE-SALLENAVE)

ATRAK, river of northern Khorasan, flowing first northwest, and then southwest into the Caspian Sea. Its course is some 320 miles (according to Ḥamdallāh Mostawfī, 120 *farsaḵs*); the upper two-thirds drain the wide trough between the mountain chains of the Kopet-Dag and the Kūh-e Hazār Masjed to the north and the Kūh-e ʿAlī, Kūh-e Šāh Jahān and Kūh-e Bīnālūd to the south. The Atrak actually rises in the Kūh-e Hazār Masjed, and all this part of its course lies today within Persian territory; it does receive some minor right-bank affluents which rise near the Soviet-Persian border running along the ridge of the Kopet-Dag. The trough between the two series of mountain chains continues to the southeast, over a low watershed, into the basin of the Kašaf River and the region of Herat in northwestern Afghanistan. The whole corridor has always been a historic route connecting the Caspian shores with northern Khorasan, and the part of it drained by the Atrak contains today the important market towns of Qūčān (q.v.) or Ḵabūšān and Bojnūrd and the medieval district of Ostovā (q.v.), as well as smaller places like Qatleš, Šervān and Sīsāb. The lower third of the Atrak's course has formed the Russian-Persian boundary since the delimitation of 1882. The river here flows through a shallow gorge (presumably caused by the fall in the level of the Caspian) across the arid steppelands before debouching through a marshy stretch into the Caspian. The only significant affluent here is the Sīmbār River flowing in from the north where the Atrak begins to from the political boundary. Until the present century there were virtually no settlements in this lower part of the river valley, owing to the insecurity of life caused by Göklen and Yomut Turkmen raiders, but in 1869 the Imperial Russian government established a fort at Chikishlyar near the Atrak mouth and within a few years subjugated the Turkmens; remnants of irrigation works here nevertheless show that the region cannot always have been so infertile and deserted as in recent times. The Atrak was anciently called the "Sarnois" (Strabo 11.8.1; Pliny, *Natural History* 6.36 gives "Zonius"), i.e., "the Golden (River)" (J. Markwart, *Wehrot und Arang*, Leiden, 1938, p. 128; cf. Avestan *zaranya* "gold"). Strabo refers to it as the boundary between Hyrcania (Gorgān), to the south, and the desert. In the medieval Islamic period, the lower Atrak separated the province of Gorgān to the south from Dehestān (the classical land of the Dahae) to the north. The early Muslim geographers seem to have been remarkably hazy about the Atrak's course and do not mention it under this name. Thus the author of the *Ḥodūd al-ʿālam* (372/982) calls its upper course the Herand River, but then confuses its lower course with the Gorgān River somewhat to the south (tr. Minorsky, p. 77, par. 6.50, and p. 133, par. 32.1). Mostawfī, *Nozhat al-qolūb*, p. 212, tr. p. 205, seems to be the first to mention the Atrak under this name; later, popular etymology explained it as "the river of the Turks" (*Atrāk*).

Bibliography: See also Le Strange, *Lands*, p. 377. *Admiralty handbook, Persia*, 1945, index. *Camb. Hist. Iran* I, index, *EI*² I, pp. 349-59. J. Markwart, *Ērānšahr*, p. 221. W. W. Tarn, *The Greeks in Bactria and India*, 2nd ed., Cambridge, 1951, pp. 113, 489.

(C. E. BOSWORTH)

ĀΘRAVAN- (Avestan) "priest" (strong stem *āθravan-*, weak stem *aθaurun-*), Mid. Pers. *āsrōn*. Its Vedic counterpart is *átharvan-* (for the phonetical development of **aθarvan-* to *āθravan-*, cf. Vedic *aramati-*, but Av. *ārmaiti*). Attempts have been made to connect the term with Avestan *ātar-* "fire" (not attested in Vedic); but these have been prompted by what is probably a mistaken assumption of the importance of fire in the ancient Indo-Iranian religion. The evidence points rather to fire having acquired such importance later, in India through the part played by fire (*agni-*) in the cult, in Iran through Zoroaster's reform. Even in Zoroastrianism, however, the temple cult of fire does not appear to have been established until the fourth century B. C. (see further under *ātaš*); and it was only with the development of this cult that priests were appointed whose sole office was tending the sacred fire. The probability is therefore that the word *āθravan* has a different derivation. (H. W. Bailey, *TPS*, 1956, pp. 88-90, has suggested connection with Av. *āθi-* "terror." The *āθravan* could then be assumed to be in origin an apotropaeist, one able to ward off supernatural evil.)

In the Avesta, *āθravan* is regularly used to designate the priests as a social "class" one of the three into which ancient Iranian society was theoretically divided; and in the pious schematizations by which the "classes" were related to the prophet himself, homage is offered to Zoroaster as "the first priest (*paoiryāi aθaurune*), the first warrior, the first herdsman" (*Yašt* 13.88). The priests as a group were further set under the symbolic leadership of his eldest son, Isaṯ.vāstra, Pahlavi Isadvāstr (*Bundahišn*, p. 235.7-13; tr. chap. 35-56, *Indian Bundahišn*, ed. F. Justi, Leipzig, 1868, repr. Hildesheim and New York, 1976, tr. p. 45, text p. 79). Apart from these artificial associations, the tradition recognizes Zoroaster as having in fact been an *āθravan* (see *Yašt* 13.94), while in the *Gāthās* he refers to himself as a *zaotar*, that is, as a fully qualified priest, one able to solemnize all ritual acts.

The oldest attestation of the word *āθravan* is in the *Yasna Haptaŋhāiti*, where the worshippers honor "the return of the priests who go afar (to those who) seek righteousness in other lands," that is, it seems to *āθravans* acting as Zoroastrian missionaries (*Y.* 42.6). In due course, by their endeavors, Zoroastrianism, first established in eastern Iran, reached western Iran also, to be adopted there by the hereditary priests of the Medes and the Persians, known to the Greco-Roman world as the "magi." Accordingly under the Achaemenids the standard word in western Iran for a Zoroastrian priest came to be *magu*. Under the Parthians, who represented an eastern tradition, an old Avestan term, *aēθrapati*, meaning apparently a learned priest or teacher, seems to have been widely used, in the form *ērbed* (*ēhrbed*), as an honorific for a leading priest, side by side with Middle Persian *magbed* (*mogbed*) "chief priest;" and these two words, in their later forms of *hērbad*/*ērvad* and *mōbad*, survive as the titles of Zoroastrian priests today. The Pahlavi term *āsrōn* or *āsrō* (a learned descendant of *āθravă*, cf. *ašō* "righteous" from *ašavă*) is never recorded as a title; but it occurs frequently in the Pahlavi books, always, it seems, in connection with priests as a social "class," with the abstract *āsrōrōnīh* denoting the priestly office. As *athornan* the Avestan word is regularly used by Parsi priests to denote a member of their own fraternity, and it is sometimes rendered by them into English as "fire priest."

The term is not attested in Old Persian (like many other Zoroastrian terms); however, it has been proposed to interpret several words in Elamite script from the Persepolis treasury and fortification tablets as transcriptions of an Old Pers. **aθarva*, thus I. Gershevitch in the case of Elam. *ad-da-ir-ma* and *at-tar-ru-ma, ha-tur-ma* and *at-tur-ma* (*an-tar-ma*), and *at-sa-ir-ma* (*at-sa-ma*) (in *Studia Classica et Orientalia Antonino Pagliaro Oblata*, Rome, 1969, pp. 189 f.; *TPS*, 1969, pp. 186 f.; see also M. Mayrhofer, *Onomastica Persepolitana*, Vienna, 1973, nos. 8.14, 148, 499; and W. Hinz, *Altiranisches Sprachgut der Nebenüberlieferungen*, Wiesbaden, 1975, p. 50); and *ha-tur-ma-bat-ti-iš* (and other spellings), which he interprets as **aθarva-patiš* (*TPS*, 1969, p. 170; cf. Hinz, op. cit., p. 50). However, in view of the ambiguity inherent in the Elamite rendering of Iranian words a possible etymology does not alone prove the correctness of an interpretation otherwise unsupported, e.g., by the context—note Gershevitch's first interpretation of Elam. *ad-da-ir-ma* as **a-darma-* "the undiminishing" (*Studia Classica*, p. 189)—so that the only certain attestations of the term in Iranian are in the Zoroastrian scriptures, the Avesta and the Pahlavi books.

See also Class system.

Bibliography: See also *AirWb.*, cols. 65-66. M. Mayrhofer, *A Concise Etymological Sanskrit Dictionary III*, 1974, p. 626. Modi, *Ceremonies*, index s.v. *athornan*.

(M. Boyce)

ĀTRƎVAXŠ (Mid. Pers *ādurwaxš*), one of the eight Zoroastrian priests (*ratu*) necessary for performance of the *yasna* ritual. As the name indicates, his primary function was to tend to (lit., "augment," *vaxš-*) the sacred fire (*ātar*). According to *Nirangistan* 73 he also had to cleanse three sides of the fire altar; and he made response to the *zaotar* during the ritual in the same way that, in more recent times, the *rāspīg* has answered to the *zōd*. The station of the *ātrəvaxš* within the sacrificial area was the southwest corner and facing the fire. The *ātrəvaxš* is today reckoned as one of the "invisible" priests, his functions having been taken over by the *rāspīg*.

Bibliography: *AirWb.*, cols. 318 f. Avesta, tr. Darmesteter, I, pp. lxxi, 453; III, pp. 129, 131, 133. D. D. P. Sanjana, *Nirangistan*, fol. 155 b.4-12. J. J. Modi, *Ceremonies*, pp. 316-19.

(W. W. Malandra)

ATROPATENE. See Azerbaijan.

ATROPATES (Āturpāt, lit., "protected by the fire," cf. Av. Ātərəpāta), The satrap of Media, Commander of the troops from Media, Albania, and Sacasene at the battle of Gaugamela in 331 B.C. (Arrian, *Anabasis* 3.8.4). He remained faithful to Darius III until the latter's death in 330, after which he went over to the Macedonian camp. Alexander, when passing through Ecbatana (Hamadān) earlier in the same year, had already transferred the governorship of Media to Oxydates (ibid., 3.20.3; Quintus Curtius, *Historiae*

6.2.11); but in 328-27 B. C. Alexander dismissed Oxy-dates, whose loyalty he no longer trusted, and reinstated Atropates (Arrian, 4.18.3; Quintus Curtius, 8.3.17, where Atropates is erroneously named Arsaces). As satrap of Media, Atropates delivered Baryaxes, a defeated rebel from that province, to Alexander at Pasargadae in 325-324 (Arrian, 6.29.3). He rose so high in the conqueror's esteem that his daughter was soon afterward married to Alexander's confidant Perdiccas (Arrian, 7.4.5; Justin, *Historiae* 13.4.13). He had a last interview with Alexander in Media in 324-323 (Arrian, 7.13.2, 6).

Under the territorial dispensation arranged at Babylon after Alexander's death in 323, the satrapy of Media was divided into two parts, of which only Little Media (the northwestern part) was left to Atropates while Great Media (the eastern part) was assigned to Pytho (Diodorus Siculus, 18.3.3; Justin, 13.4.13). Eventually Atropates refused allegiance to any of the Macedonian generals and made his satrapy an inde-pendent kingdom (Strabo, *Geography* 11.13.1). There-after this part of Media was known to the Greeks as Media Atropatene or simply Atropatene, like Parthian and Middle Persian Āturpātakān (whence Armenian Atrpatakan), later Ādurbādagān, NPers. Ād̲arbāyǰān.

Atropates founded a dynasty which was to rule in Atropatene for several centuries (cf. Strabo, 11.13.1). See also Azerbaijan.

Bibliography: Sources: Arrian, *Anabasis*. Diodorus Siculus, *Bibliotheca Historica*, bk. 18. Strabo, *Geography*, bk. 11. Modern authors: H. Berve, *Alexanderreich* II, 1926, no. 180. A. von Gutschmid, *Geschichte Irans und seiner Nachbarlän-der*, Tübingen, 1888. Justi, *Namenbuch*, p. 49. J. Kaerst, "Atropates," in Pauly-Wissowa, II/2, col. 2150. Th. Nöldeke, "Atropatene," *ZDMG* 34, 1880, pp. 692 f. On the name see M. Mayrhofer, *Iranisches Personennamenbuch* I/1, Vienna, 1977, p. I/29 no. 70.

(M. L. CHAUMONT)

ATRUŠAN, the Armenian word for "fire temple," a loan-word from Parthian (see H. Hübschmann, *Armen. Etymologie*, p. 110 and more recently H. W. Bailey, *Dictionary of Khotan Saka*, Cambridge, 1979, p. 309, s.v. *byuyāre*). Armenian Zoroastrians worshipped at both fire temples and image-shrines, the latter called *bagin-kʿ*. In the first century B.C., Strabo described the Magian temple cult of fire in Cappadocia, to the west of Armenia (*Geography* 15.3.15), and in the fourth century A.D. the Armenian historian Agathangelos referred to the *moxrapaštutʿiwn naxneacʿ merocʿ* "ash-worship of our ancestors" (*History of the Armenians*, tr. R. W. Thomson, Albany, 1976, par. 89). This is apparently a reference to the mounds of ash heaped upon fire-altars to keep the living coals hot between temple services, when the fire was made to blaze up, or it refers to the Zoroastrian practice of bringing ashes from hearth fires to the fire temple. Pits filled with wood ash have been excavated next to the sites of pre-Christian shrines at Duin (Dvin)), the capital of Persian Armenia in the

sixth century A.D. The shrines were probably fire temples, for we are told by the historian Yovhannēs of Drasxanakert that two prominent Armenian noblemen, Šawasp Arcruni and Vndoy of Duin, apostasized Christianity and built *zmeheann Ormzdakan ew ztun hrapaštutʿean* "the Temple of Ormizd and the house of fire-worship" (Drasxanakertcʿi, *Patmutʿiwn Hayocʿ*, Tiflis, 1912, p. 59; on the excavations, see A. A. Kʿalantʿaryan, *Dvini nyutʿakan mšakuytʿə 4-8 dd.* (Material culture of Dvin in the 4th-8th centuries), Hayastani hnagitakan hušarjannerə (Armenian arche-ological monuments) 5, Erevan, 1970 and K. G. Łafa-daryan, "Dvin kʿalakʿi himnadrman žamanaki ev mijnaberdi hetʿanosakan mehyani masin," *Patma-banasirakan Handes*, Erevan, 1966, p. 2). The form Ormizd above, corresponding to Sasanian Middle Persian rather than the Parthian form Aramazd of the Armenian pre-Christian cult, indicates that the fire temple at Duin was built under Persian auspices. The remains of a fire-altar, constructed most likely during the proselytizing compaign of Yazdegerd II in the mid-fifth century against the Christian Armenians, were found directly beneath the main altar Ēǰmiacin Cathe-dral, the Mother See of the Armenian Church (see A. Sahinyan, "Recherches scientifiques sous les voûtes de la Cathédrale d'Étchmiadzine," *Revue des études arméniennes*, N. S. 3, 1966). According to the Armenian historian Movsēs Xorenacʿi (*History of the Armenians*, tr. R. W. Thomson, Cambridge, Mass., 1978, II, p. 277), Ardašīr I (224-41) invaded Armenia, destroyed the *baginkʿ*, but commanded that the *hurn ormzdakan* "fire of Ormizd" be kept burning conti-nuously. No fire temple has been found in Armenia which can be assigned definitely to pre-Sasanian times, before the iconoclastic movement of the third century (see M. Boyce, "Iconoclasm among the Zoroastrians," in J. Neusner, ed., *Studies for Morton Smith at Sixty* IV, Leiden, 1975, pp. 93-111), but a tenth-century writer mentions a fire temple called Hurbak; Hübschmann (op. cit., p. 181) suggests that this is the Armenian rendering of the name of Ādur-Farnbag, but more likely it is an Armenian form of a Pahlavi term for a fire temple, *dar-ī ātaxšān*, found in Dēnkard VI (ed. S. Shaked, *The Wisdom of the Sasanian Sages*, Boulder, 1979, pp. 128-29 and xxvii), "court of the fire (s)."

(J. R. RUSSELL)

ATSĬZ B. ʿALĀʾ-AL-DĪN ḤOSAYN, **ʿALĀʾ-AL-DĪN.** See ʿALĀʾ-AL-DĪN ATSĬZ B. ʿALĀʾ-AL-DĪN ḤOSAYN.

ATSĬZ ĠARČAʾĬ, ʿALĀʾ-AL-DĪN WAʾL-DAWLA ABUʾL-MOẒAFFAR B. MOḤAMMAD B. ANŪŠTIGIN, ruler of Ḵᵛārazm with the traditional title Ḵᵛārazmšāh, 521 or 522/1127 or 1128 to 551/1156. His family was of Turkish *ḡolām* origin; his grandfather was appointed governor of Ḵᵛārazm by the Saljuq Sultan Malekšāh; and his father Qoṭb-al-dīn Moḥammad succeeded in the office. In effect, the governorship thus became heredi-tary in Anūštigin's line; but Atsĭz was able, in the course of his reign, to pursue a policy of greater independence from his Saljuq suzerain Sultan Sanjar. He may accordingly be regarded as the founder of a henceforth independent dynasty of K̲ᵛārazmšāhs, who at the opening of the 7th/13th century were briefly able to constitute themselves the greatest power in the eastern Islamic world before the Mongol cataclysm.

A task of all rulers in K̲ᵛārazm was to preserve the lengthy and exposed frontiers of the province against pressure from the nomads of the surrounding steppes—in Atsïz's time largely Ǭḡūz and Qïpčaq (Qepčāq) who were still pagan in considerable proportion. Already during his father's lifetime, he began a policy of securing the steppes between the Aral and Caspian Seas, occupying the Manqešlāq peninsula, an important concentration-point for the nomads. He also seized the strategically important town of Jand near the mouth of the Syr Darya, from where he made incursions against the infidel Turks over the ensuing years, earning for himself the designation of *ḡāzī* (fighter for the faith). During the next decades, Atsïz pursued a skillful military and diplomatic policy vis-à-vis Sanjar, and after 536/1141, against the invading Qara K̲iṭay (Qarā-K̲etāy) in Central Asia. He originally showed himself perfectly loyal to the Saljuq sultan, accompanying Sanjar on campaigns in Transoxania in 524/1130 and to Ḡazna against the rebellious Ghaznavid sultan Bahrām Shah in 529/1135. Relations then began to deteriorate, as Atsïz felt his way towards a more independent policy. In 533/1138 he rebelled openly but was driven out of K̲ᵛārazm to Gorgān by a Saljuq punitive expedition; he returned in the next year to K̲ᵛārazm, but eventually deemed it expedient to submit to Sanjar.

In 536/1141 the Qara K̲iṭay inflicted a sharp defeat on Sanjar in Transoxania at the battle of the Qaṭvān steppe, with a resultant blow to Sanjar's prestige and authority in Central Asia. The reverse came so conveniently for Atsïz that several sources accuse him of deliberately inciting the Qara K̲iṭay against Sanjar; this seems dubious, especially as K̲ᵛārazm itself also suffered from the ravages of a Qara K̲iṭay invasion at this point. Atsïz ambitions now led him to covet the Saljuq possessions in northern Khorasan, including Sarak̲s, Marv, Nīšāpūr, and Bayhaq, which his troops briefly occupied in 536/1141-42. Yet Sanjar re-established his authority over the next few years, twice invading K̲ᵛārazam again and bringing Atsïz to a reluctant submission. Atsïz accordingly returned to his original direction of expansion, into the northern steppes, and in 547/1152 recaptured Jand, which had fallen into the hands of the Qarakhanid prince Kamāl-al-dīn b. Arslān Khan Maḥmūd. Sanjar's capture and imprisonment by the rebellious Oḡūz of Khorasan in 548/1153 was obviously opportune for the furtherance of Atsïz's ambitions, but he in fact acted with restraint. A Khwarazmian army invaded as far as Bayhaq in 548-49/1154; and Atsïz himself came to Khorasan in 551/1156 to quell the Oḡūz at the invitation of Sanjar's nephew, the Qarakhanid Maḥmūd Khan. However Sanjar escaped from captivity and resumed power; and shortly afterwards, in the same year, Atsïz died at the age of 59 (26 Rabīʿ I 552/9 May 1157). The power of the K̲ᵛārazmšāhs was at that point still largely confined to K̲ᵛārazm, and Atsïz was paying tribute to the Qara K̲iṭay; yet he had laid the firm foundations for the subsequent imperialist expansion by his successors.

Jovaynī and ʿAwfī praise Atsïz for his literacy and his personal skill as a poet in Persian, and the literary circle at his court seems to have been quite distinguished. Saljuq poets like Adīb Ṣāber (q.v.) addressed odes to him, but especially connected with Atsïz is the poet and prose stylist Rašīd-al-dīn Vaṭvāṭ (q.v.), who functioned as court poet and propagandist. He engaged for instance, in poetic contests with Sanjar's panegyrist Anwarī. The Khwarazmian grammarian and lexicographer Jārallāh Maḥmūd Zamak̲šarī dedicated his dictionary the *Moqaddemat al-adab* to Atsïz, and the physician Zayn-al-dīn Jorjānī composed for one of Atsïz viziers his *Aḡrāż al-ṭebb*, a revision of his celebrated *D̲ak̲īra-ye K̲ᵛārazmšāhī* written earlier for Atsïz's father Qoṭb-al-din Moḥammad.

Bibliography: Primary sources: The principal ones are Jovaynī's *Tārīk̲-e jahāngošāy*, section on the origins of the K̲ᵛārazmšāhs, II, pp. 3-14; tr. Boyle, I, pp. 277-87 (who states that he drew upon the *Mašāreb al-tajāreb* of the local historian of Khorasan, Ebn Fondoq), followed by, e.g., Mīrk̲ᵛānd, *Rawżat al-ṣafā*. Sources for Saljuq history, which describe the course of Saljuq-Khwarazmian relations, include Ṣadr-al-dīn Ḥosaynī, Bondārī, Rāvandī, Ẓahīr-al-dīn Nīšāpūrī, Ebn al-At̲īr, and a local history like Ebn Fondoq's *Tārīk̲-e Bayhaq*. For Atsïz as patron of learning, see ʿAwfī, *Lobāb*, pp. 36-38.

Secondary sources: E. Sachau, "Zur Geschichte und Chronologie von Khwârazm," *Sb. Akad. Wiss.* 74, Vienna, 1873, pp. 316 ff. Barthold, *Turkestan*[3], pp. 324-31, and the documents (including important ones from *enšāʾ* collections) in the text volume of the original Russian ed. (*Turkestan v ėpokhu mongol'skago nashestviya*, St. Petersberg 1900). Idem, *Histoire des Turcs d'Asie Centrale*, Paris, 1945, pp. 109 ff. S. P. Tolstov, *Auf den Spuren der altchoresmischen Kultur*, Berlin, 1953, pp. 295-96. M. A. Köymen, *Büyük Selçuklu imparatorluğu tarihi. II: İkinci imparatorluğu tarihi*, Ankara, 1954, pp. 311-53, 445 ff. I. Kafesoğlu, *Harezmşahlar devleti tarihi (485-617/1092-1229)*, Ankara, 1956, pp. 44-72. H. Horst, *Die Staatsverwaltung der Grosselḡūqen und Ḫōrazmšāhs (1038-1231): Eine Untersuchung nach Urkundenformularen der Zeit*, Wiesbaden, 1964, index (s.v. Atsïz.Ḫōrazmašāh). C. E. Bosworth, in *Camb. Hist. Iran* V, pp. 143 ff. For the literary aspect, see Browne, *Lit. Hist. Persia* II, pp. 307-10, 330-33; and Rypka, *Hist. Iran. Lit.*, pp. 200, 432. For chronology see Zambaur, pp. 208-09, and Bosworth, *The Islamic dynasties*, Edinburgh, 1967, pp. 107-10.

(C. E. Bosworth)

'ATTĀBĪ, one of many names for cloth used by medieval Islamic writers. The specific qualities of *'attābī* are not entirely clear from these references, although a general picture of the textile can be deduced from the few concrete phrases occurring in the texts. The word has passed into a number of European languages as a name for cloth, sometimes general and sometimes quite precise: *attabi* in Spanish; *tabis* in French; *tabì* in Italian; *tabyn* in Dutch; and *tabby* in English. In 17th and 18th-century England, *tabby*, or *taby*, was understood as being a substantial silk fabric with a watered, *moiré*-like finish. Dr. Johnson's *Dictionary* of 1755 not only defines *tabby* as "a kind of waved silk" but notes that cats with brindled markings on the fur are, by extension, tabby-cats.

In contemporary textile terminology, *tabby* is a description of a cloth structure formed by the simplest of weaving techniques, one warp thread passed alternatingly over and under one weft thread in succession. The usual synonym for *tabby* is now *plain-weave*, although when and where this usage first occurred has not been firmly established. Irene Emery has pointed to a glossary definition of *tabby*, in Luther Hooper's *Hand-loom Weaving* of 1910, as "plain weaving," that appears to be among the earliest recorded uses of the term. She further notes that in modern textile terminology, *tabby* is usually accompanied by at least a parenthetical reference to *plain weave* while the opposite is not generally the case.

To medieval Islamic writers, however, *'attābī* was anything but plain. For Ebn Jobayr, in the late twelfth-century account of his pilgrimage to Mecca, the *reḥla*, *'attābī* was woven of silk or cotton and in various colors. For Ḡarnāṭī, writing in the *Toḥfat al-albāb*, slightly earlier in the same century, *'attābī* was "... striped cloth (*moḵaṭṭaṭ*) with black and white in regular stripes (*ḵoṭūṭ*) ... of ibrism-silk ..." Abu'l-Qāsem, at the beginning of the fourteenth century, speaks of a kind of *'attabī*, *'attābī dabīkī*, as having borders embroidered with gold. That stripes were typical of some kinds of *'attābī* is shown by a reference to the quality of *'attābī* lying in the fineness of the threads in the stripe. Dozy has described *'attābī* as being a sort of heavy silk taffeta with a watered effect. Le Strange provides the fullest explanation for the name: A district of Baghdad just west of the Round City was named after 'Attāb, a companion of the prophet and governor of Mecca, because his descendants, 'Attābīyīn, later settled there. Fabrics woven in 'Attābīya naturally came to be called *'attābī*, especially striped and watered ones. Serjeant's collected references suggest that *'attābī* was also produced all over Iran, in Isfahan, Kermān, Nīšāpūr, Hamadān, and Tabrīz; as well as in Antioch and possibly Damascus; and also in great quantities in Almeria. Finally, *'attābī* figured in the extensive cloth-trade of medieval Islam, for Ebn Esfandīār, on the basis of a tenth-century reference, says that priceless *'attābī* was exported to Ṭabarestān, whence it was then traded "... to the most distant countries in the earth."

See also Textiles.

Bibliography: R. P. A. Dozy, *Dictionnaire détaillé des noms des vêtements chez les Arabes*, Amsterdam, 1845, p. 110. Idem, *Supplément aux dictionnaires Arabes*, Leiden, 1881, II, p. 93. G. Le Strange, *Baghdad During the Abbasid Caliphate*, Oxford, 1900, pp. 137-38 and passim. *EI*[1] I, p. 513, C. J. Lamm, *Cotton in Medieval Textiles of the Near East*, Paris, 1937, pp. 123, 210, 219. R. B. Serjeant, "Material for a History of Islamic Textiles up to the Mongol Conquest," *Ars Islamica* 9, pp. 81-82; 10, pp. 99-100; 11-12, pp. 102, 107-08, 116, 138; 13-14, p. 111; 15-16, pp. 33-34, 66. CIETA, *Fabrics: A Vocabulary of Technical Terms: English, French, Italian*, Lyon, 1959, p. 30. I. Emery, *The Primary Structure of Fabrics: An Illustrated Classification*, Washington, D.C., 1966 and 1980, pp. 76, 85-86. M. Lombard, *Les textiles dans le monde Musulman du VIIe au XIIe siècle*, Paris, 1978, pp. 246-47. M. Hardingham, *Illustrated Dictionary of Fabrics*, London, 1978, pp. 148-49, with the clearest technical diagram of *tabby*. D. K. Burnham, *Warp and Weft: A Textile Terminology*, Toronto, 1980, p. 139 and frontispiece-illustration of *tabby*.

(E. SIMS)

'AṬṬĀR, SHAIKH **FARĪD**-AL-**DĪN,** Persian poet, Sufi, theoretician of mysticism, and hagiographer, born ca. 540/1145-46 at Nīšāpūr, and died there in 618/1221. His name was Abū Ḥāmed Moḥammad b. Abī Bakr Ebrāhīm or, according to Ebn al-Fowaṭī, b. Sa'd b. Yūsof. 'Aṭṭār and Farīd-al-dīn were his pen-names. (B. Forūzānfar, *Šarḥ-e aḥwāl wa naqd o taḥlīl-e āṯār-e Šayḵ Farīd-al-dīn Moḥammad 'Aṭṭār Nīšābūrī*, Tehran, 1339-40 Š./1960-61, repr., Tehran, 1353 Š./1975, pp. 1-3).

Reliable information on 'Aṭṭār's life is scarce. He is mentioned by only two contemporaries, 'Awfī (d. after 620/1223) and Ḵ᷾āja Naṣīr-al-dīn Ṭūsī (597/1200-672/1273); the latter's statement is quoted in a work by his pupil 'Abd-al-Razzāq b. Fowaṭī. The next notice of 'Aṭṭār is in Ḥamdallāh Mostawfī's *Tārīḵ-e gozīda*, which was completed in 730/1330 (see M. Qazvīnī's introd. to the *Taḏkerat al-awlīā'*, p. *wāw*). In all these sources 'Aṭṭār is described as a man of Nīšāpūr. Ṭūsī visited him there at some time, according to Forūzānfar's reckoning (*Šarḥ-e aḥwāl*, pp. 13 f.), between 612/1215 and 618/1221. 'Aṭṭār was then an old man. This fits in with 'Awfī's placing of 'Aṭṭār in his chapter on poets of the Saljuq period (*Lobāb*, Tehran, pp. 480-82). He must therefore have been in his prime during the second half of the 6th/12th century. Forūzānfar calculates that he was born about 540/1145-46 (ibid., pp. 7-16). The only biographical date which 'Aṭṭār himself mentions in his writings, namely 573/1177 as the year of his completion of the *Manṭeq al-ṭayr*, is consistent with the foregoing but cannot be taken as conclusive evidence because the verse in question does not appear in all the manuscripts.

While 'Aṭṭār's works say little else about his life, they tell us that he practiced the profession of pharmacy and personally attended to a very large number of customers (see especially *Asrār-nāma*, p. 170; cf. Forūzānfar, ibid., p. 39). He evidently started writing certain books—the *Moṣībat-nāma* and the *Elāhī-nāma*—while at work in the pharmacy (2nd introd. to the *K̲osrow-nāma*; see H. Ritter, "philologika X," *Der Islam* 25, 1939, p. 148, verse 40). Anyway he was fortunate in not depending on his muse for his livelihood. He could afford to spurn the art of the court eulogist (see idem, *Das Meer der Seele: Mensch, Welt und Gott in den Geschichten des Farīduddīn 'Aṭṭār*, Leiden, 1955, p. 156). His placid existence as a pharmacist and a Sufi does not appear to have ever been interrupted by journeys. In his later years he lived a very retired life (*Elāhī-nāma*, ed. Ritter, p. 366.11ff.). He reached an age well over seventy (see Forūzānfar, p. 107). The prolificacy sometimes laid to his charge (Qazvīnī, op. cit., p. *yā'-jīm*. 8 from the bottom) was noticed by Ṭūsī, who met him in his old age (see Ritter, "Philologika XIV," *Oriens* 11, 1958, p. 5. 5 from the bottom). He died a violent death in the massacre which the Mongols inflicted on Nīšāpūr in Ṣafar, 618/April, 1221 (see Forūzānfar, p. 91).

It seems that 'Aṭṭār was not well known as a poet in his own lifetime, except at Nīšāpūr. 'Awfī, who traveled widely, may have heard about him while staying there (*Lobāb*, introd. p. twenty-two), or perhaps from Majd-al-dīn Baḡdādī if this Majd-al-dīn was their common Sufi mentor, though 'Awfī appears to have only known about 'Aṭṭār's lyric poetry (*Lobāb*, p. 481.3f.). Ṭūsī likewise speaks mainly about 'Aṭṭār's impressive *dīvān* and mentions only one of his narrative poems, the *Manṭeq al-ṭayr* (passage quoted in Ritter, "Philologika XIV," p. 5). From the second half of the 7th/13th century onward, 'Aṭṭār's prose work, the *Taḏkerat al-awlīā'*, came to be widely read (list of mss. in Ritter, ibid., pp. 64ff.), but his greatness as a mystic, a poet, and a master of narrative was not discovered until the 9th/15th century. It was then that 'Aṭṭār's career became a matter of interest and was embroidered with fantastic myths, for instance in the biographical notices written by Jāmī and Dawlatšāh and in the inscription in the mausoleum of 'Aṭṭār built at Nīšāpūr, by 'Alī Šīr Navā'ī.

A favorite theme of this myth-making was 'Aṭṭār's initiation into Sufi faith. Examples have been collected by Sa'īd Nafīsī (*Jostojū dar aḥwāl o āṯār-e Farīd-al-dīn-e 'Aṭṭār Nīšābūrī*, Tehran, 1320 Š./1941, pp. *lām-dāl*ff.). Forūzānfar has convincingly shown that Najm-al-dīn Kobrā cannot have been 'Aṭṭār's spiritual guide, and that the tales of 'Aṭṭār's being a pupil of Qoṭb-al-dīn Ḥaydar, Sa'd-al-dīn b. Ḥammūya, and Rokn-al-dīn 'Akkāf are inventions which were prompted by various misunderstandings (*Šarḥ-e aḥwāl*, pp. 20-28; 31.5ff., 34.6ff., 30.7ff.). Of all the famous Sufi shaikhs supposed to have been teachers of 'Aṭṭār, only Majd-al-dīn Baḡdādī comes within the bounds of possibility, and the only certainty is 'Aṭṭār's own statement that he once met Majd-al-dīn (*Taḏkerat al-awlīā'*, pp. 1, 6, 21). Forūzānfar has also noted that 'Aṭṭār, in the introduction to his *K̲osrow-nāma*, extols a certain Sa'd-al-dīn b. Rabīb, the son of a vizier, in terms which normally denoted the relationship of a disciple to his shaikh (ibid., pp. 33.20ff., 37.7ff.) but in the absence of any information about this man's identity and Sufi status, the fact does not bring the problem nearer to solution. There remains the possibility that 'Aṭṭār did not have a shaikh in the literal sense at all, but became a Sufi through an *owaysī* affiliation, i.e., an inward relationship to a (deceased) Sufi, shaikh or the Prophet Moḥammad. Jāmī states in his *Nafaḥāt al-ons* that there were persons who said this of 'Aṭṭār. Forūzānfar substantiates the point by referring to 'Aṭṭār's own acknowledgement of a special spiritual relationship linking him to Abū Sa'īd b. Abi'l-K̲ayr (q.v.), which could indeed be taken to mean an *owaysī* affiliation (ibid., p. 32.8ff.; cf. F. Meier, *Abū Sa'īd Abū'l-Ḫayr*, Acta Iranica 11, Leiden, 1976, p. 464). It must, however, be noted that in certain passages 'Aṭṭār stresses the indispensability of an immediate shaikh (*Manṭeq al-ṭayr*, p. 109.1ff.; *Moṣībat-nāma* p. 63.2ff.). In any case it can be taken for granted that from childhood onward 'Aṭṭār, encouraged by his father, was interested in the Sufis and their sayings and way of life, and regarded their saints as his spiritual guides (*Taḏkerat al-awlīā'*, pp. 1, 55, 23 ff.).

The thought-world depicted in 'Aṭṭār's works reflects the whole evolution of the Sufi movement in its experiential, speculative, practical, and educational-initiatory ramifications. The starting point is the idea that the body-bound soul's awaited release and return to its source in the other world can be experienced during the present life in mystic union attainable through inward purification (F. Meier, "Der Geistmensch bei dem persischen Dichter 'Aṭṭār," *Eranos-Jahrbuch* 13, 1945, pp. 286ff.). Aspects and problems of this *via purgativa* form the central theme of 'Aṭṭār's mystic writings. He propounds them in theoretical discussions and exhortatory homilies and through the medium of exemplary facts or events, drawing his material not only from specifically Sufi but also from older ascetic legacies. Although his heroes are for the most part Sufis and ascetics, he also introduces stories from historical chronicles, collections of anecdotes, and all types of *adab* literature. He has no objection to putting his words of wisdom into the mouths of fools and madmen (cf. Ritter, *Das Meer der Seele*, pp. 165ff.). His talent for perception of deeper meanings behind outward appearances enables him to turn details of everyday life into illustrations of his thoughts. The idiosyncrasy of 'Aṭṭār's presentations invalidates his works as sources for study of the historical persons whom he introduces. As sources on the hagiology and phenomenology of Sufism, however, his works have immense value.

In regard to 'Aṭṭār's general education and culture, no adequate picture can be obtained from his writings. In his riper years he esteemed only the Islamic sciences of *feqh* (jurisprudence), *tafsīr* (Koranic exegesis), and Hadith (*Moṣībat-nāma*, p. 54), while viewing the ancient aristotelian heritage with scepticism and dislike (*Moṣībat-nāma*, p. 54.6ff.; *Asrār-nāma*, pp. 50, 794ff.).

Significantly, he did not want to uncover the secrets of nature. Although there are some indications that in his younger years he had paid attention to this and other fields of non-religious knowledge (see Forūzānfar, *Šarḥ-e aḥwāl*, p. 42), any traces of such knowledge in his writings are minimal. This is particularly remarkable in the case of medicine, which fell within the scope of his profession. On the other hand, he obviously had no motive for showing off his secular knowledge in the manner customary among court panegyrists (cf. Neẓāmī 'Arūżī, *Čahār maqāla*, ed. M. Mo'īn, p. 56.4f.), whose type of poetizing he despised and never practiced. Such knowledge is only brought into his works in contexts where the theme of a story touches on a branch of natural science, for instance when he describes the constellations at the end of a story about a poor man's impressions of the sky's phases (*Asrār-nāma*, pp. 108f.), or when he cites as an example of a polymath's erudition his skill in removing a brain tumor (*Elāhī-nāma*, ed. Ritter, p. 75.8ff.; tr. Boyle, pp. 72-73).

'Aṭṭār speaks of his own poetry in various contexts including the epilogues of his long narrative poems. He confirms the guess likely to be made by every reader that he possessed an inexhaustible fund of thematic and verbal inspiration; when he composed his poems, more ideas came into his mind than he could possibly use (*Asrār-nāma*, p. 185, verse 3146, and p. 186, verse 3151). He also states that the effort of poetical composition threw him into a state of trance in which he could not sleep (*Asrār-nāma*, p. 185, verse 3148). He does not seem to have been so aware of his proficiency in the art of narrative or of his peculiar gift of economy in the use of rhetoric combined with mastery of all its potentialities. When he boasts of his ability to conceive and express ideas, he generally does so in ways comparable with those of contemporary panegyrists such as Ḵāqānī. Like the latter, he is not only convinced that his poetry has far surpassed all previous poetry (*Elāhī-nāma*, p. 365.6; *Moṣībat-nāma*, p. 365.1), but even believes it to be intrinsically unsurpassable at any time in the future (*Elāhī-nāma*, p. 365.8), seeing himself as the "seal of the poets" (*Moṣībat-nāma*, p. 364, line 2 from bottom) and his poetry as the "seal of speech" (*Dīvān*, ed. Nafīsī, p. 361, line 2 from bottom; *Manṭeq al-ṭayr*, p. 288.7). He thinks that he exhausted the entire stock of poetical themes and artifices (*Moṣībat-nāma*, p. 365.5). Ḵāqānī's claims of finding eternally fresh themes and of subtlety in presenting them reappear in verses by 'Aṭṭār (*Asrār-nāma*, verses 3157 and 3164). The model for these shared notions of the two poets may have been provided by Sanā'ī.

A problem which has greatly occupied researchers on 'Aṭṭār is the question whether all the works that have been ascribed to him are really from his pen. It was brought to the fore by the observation of two facts; firstly, there are considerable differences of style among these works, secondly, some of them indicate a Sunnite, and others a Shi'ite, allegiance of the author. Classification of the various works by these two criteria yields virtually identical results. Ritter at first thought that the problem could be explained by a spiritual evolution of the poet; he distinguished three phases of 'Aṭṭār's creativity and surmised that the last phase, that of old age, was coincidental with a conversion to Shi'ism ("Philologika X," pp. 143f.), but in 1320 Š./1941, Nafīsī was able to prove that the works of the third phase in Ritter's classification were written by another 'Aṭṭār who lived about two hundred and fifty years later at Mašhad and was a native of Tūn (*Jostojū*, pp. 145ff.). Ritter accepted this finding in the main, but doubted whether Nafīsī was right in attributing the works of the second group also to this 'Aṭṭār of Tūn. One of Ritter's arguments is that the principal figure in the second group is not 'Alī, as in the third group, but Ḥallāj, and that there is nothing in the explicit content of the second group to indicate a Shi'ite allegiance of the author; another is the important chronological point that a manuscript of the *Jawhar al-ḏāt*, the chief work in the second group, bears the date 735 (= 1334-35). While 'Aṭṭār of Tūn's authorship of the second group is untenable, Nafīsī was certainly right in concluding that the style difference (already observed by Ritter) between the works in the first group and those in the second group is too great to be explained by a spiritual evolution of the author. The authorship of the second group remains an unsolved problem. Ritter in his first article ("Philologika X," p. 157) thought it possible that a poet with the name 'Aṭṭār lived in the later years of the 7th/13th century; but there is no concrete evidence to identify the poet in question as the author of the second group. As regards Nafīsī's suggestion of a certain Zayn-al-'ābedīn Moḥammad 'Aṭṭār Hamadānī who died in 727/1326-27, Ritter demonstrated that this putative individual came into being through a typographical error ("Philologika XIV," pp. 2f.).

After these subtractions from the huge total (reputedly equaling the number of the Koranic suras) which legend gave to 'Aṭṭār's works, the next question is the authenticity of the remainder. 'Aṭṭār himself, in the introductions of the *Ḵosrow-nāma* and the *Moḵtār-nāma*, lists the titles of further products of his pen as follows: *Dīvān*, *Asrār-nāma*, *Maqāmāt-e ṭoyūr* (= *Manṭeq al-ṭayr*), *Moṣībat-nāma*, *Elāhī-nāma*, *Jawāher-nāma*, and *Šarḥ al-qalb* (quoted in "Philologika X," pp. 147-53). He also states, in the introduction of the *Moḵtār-nāma*, that he destroyed the *Jawāher-nāma* and the *Šarḥ al-qalb* with his own hand. Although the contemporary sources confirm only 'Aṭṭār's authorship of the *Dīvān* and the *Manṭeq al-ṭayr*, there are no grounds for doubting the authenticity of the *Ḵosrow-nāma* and *Moḵtār-nāma* and their prefaces. One work is missing from these lists, namely the *Taḏkerat al-awlīā'*, which was probably omitted because it is a prose work; its attribution to 'Aṭṭār is scarcely open to question. In its introduction 'Aṭṭār mentions three other works of his, including one entitled *Šarḥ al-qalb*, presumably the same that he destroyed; the nature of the other two, entitled *Kašf al-asrār* and *Ma'refat al-nafs*, remains unknown (see Ritter, "Philologika XIV," p. 63). In the rest of this article the authentic works are discussed separately.

Dīvān. This consists almost entirely of poems in the *ḡazal* form, as he collected his *robāʿīs* in a separate work, the *Mok̲tār-nāma*. There are also some *qaṣīdas*, but they amount to less than one-seventh of the *Dīvān*; their infrequency can be partly explained by 'Aṭṭār's abstention from panegyric poetizing. His *qaṣīdas* expound mystic and ethical themes and practical moral precepts, and are to some extent modeled on those of Sanā'ī; the *qaṣīda Čašm bogšā ke jelwa-ye deldār* is a reply to Sanā'ī's *Konūz al-ḥekma* in exactly the same number of verses. The *ḡazals* often seem from their outward vocabulary just to be love and wine songs with a predilection for libertine imagery (*qalandarīyāt*; cf. Ritter, "Philologika XV," pp. 14 ff.), but generally imply spiritual experiences in the familiar symbolic language of classical Islamic mysticism (see Forūzānfar, *Šarḥ-e aḥwāl*, p. 82). Incidentally 'Aṭṭār's lyrics express the same ideas that are elaborated in his epics. Normally the verses in each poem are coherent. In many cases the poem goes into different aspects of a core-theme. The language of 'Aṭṭār's lyric poetry does not significantly differ from that of his narrative poetry, and the same may be said of the rhetoric and imagery.

Editions are S. Nafīsī, Tehran, 1319 Š./1940, 1335 Š./1956, 1339 Š./1960; T. Tafażżolī, Tehran 1341 Š./1962, 1345 Š./1966.

Mok̲tār-nāma. This is a collection of quatrains arranged by subject. After 'Aṭṭār's friends had complained of difficulty in finding their way through the great store of verses in the *Dīvān*, he picked roughly a third of its 6000 verses and arranged them in fifty chapters. This was done after the completion of four of his narrative poems, the *K̲osrow-nāma*, *Asrār-nāma*, *Manṭeq al-ṭayr*, and *Moṣībat-nāma*, but before the composition of the *Elāhī-nāma*. Two-fifths of the chapters (nos. 30-49) are about different aspects of the theme of love, and of these half portray the lover's state and the beloved's bearing, and half describe things used as elements of erotic sybolism such as the beloved's eyes, brows, down, mole, and lips, or rose, dawn, moth, and candle. In chapter 44 some space is given to *qalandarīyāt* on the ground of their connection with erotic themes. Chapters 12-29 are on matters of practical morals and general or Sufi ethics. The specifically Sufi themes of pantheism, self-effacement, and bewilderment (cf. the *Moṣībat-nāma*) are discussed in earlier chapters (4-9). The first three chapters are on *tawḥīd* (God's oneness), *naʿt* (the Prophet Moḥammad's glories), and *manāqeb* (merits of the Prophet's companions). In the last chapter, the poet's own hope is expressed.

Text in the lithographed *Kollīyāt*, Lucknow, 1872. M. R. Šafīʿī Kadkanī, ed., Tehran, 1358 Š./1979 (with detailed introduction and notes). Partial tr. H. Ritter, "Philologika XVI," *Oriens* 13, 1961, pp. 195-228.

Tad̲kerat al-awlīā'. This is 'Aṭṭār's only prose work; it is a collection of biographies dedicated to exponents and pioneers of classical Sufism, beginning with Imam Jaʿfar al-Ṣādeq, Oways Qaranī, and Ḥasan Baṣrī, and ending with Ḥallāj, whom 'Aṭṭār evidently felt to be the perfector of Sufism. The biographies of later Sufis, including 'Aṭṭār's favorite mentor Abū Saʿīd b. Abi'l-K̲ayr, are not from his own pen. The word gives a sort of hagiographic summary of his career in the ethical and experiential world of the Sufis (see above). It is to be regretted that he hardly ever names his sources. He appears to have relied almost entirely, if not exclusively, on written sources. In his choice and narration of edifying and memorable stories, he shows a distinctive taste of his own. Comparisons with versions of the same material in works by other authors suggest that he presented and interpreted the stories somewhat idiosyncratically (Ritter, "Philologika XIV," p. 63). On the other hand, he translated sayings of his Sufis, which had come down in Arabic, very faithfully into Persian. The work has also interested Iranian scholars as a specimen of early Persian prose (G. Lazard, *La Langue des plus anciens monuments de la prose persane*, Paris, 1963, p. 121.

Editions are R. A. Nicholson, with introd. by M. Qazvīnī, 2 vols., London and Leiden, 1905-07, repr. without notes, etc. Tehran, 1336 Š./1957; M. Esteʿlāmī, Tehran, 1346 Š./1965; particulars of older eds. in Mošār, *Fehrest*, p. 378. Translations: E. Hermelin, Stockholm, 1931-32; A. J. Arberry, *Muslim Saints and Mystics*, London, 1966, 1973; lives of several saints in *Türkische Bibliothek* 20 and 24; particulars of Turkish tr. in Ritter, "Philologika XIV," *Oriens* 11, 1958, pp. 70-76; Uigur tr., Paris, 1889.

K̲osrow-nāma. This stands apart from 'Aṭṭār's other works, as it is not a mystic poem but a courtly romance. Being about two lovers named Gol and Hormoz (later renamed K̲osrow), it also bears the titles *Gol o Hormoz*, *Gol o K̲osrow*, *K̲osrow o Gol* (Ritter, "Philologika X," p. 144). Gol is the daughter of the king of Ahvāz, Hormoz is an illegitimate son of the Caesar of Rūm (Byzantium). For protection against the jealousy of the Caesar's wife Hormoz is brought up at Ahvāz in the house of the court gardener. The two see each other and fall in love, but neither knows of the other's love. This situation provides the background for an eventful and exciting story of self-denial and self-discovery culminating in the marriage of the lovers (abstract in Ritter, "Philologika X," pp. 161-71). 'Aṭṭār's model was a prose work by an otherwise unknown author, named by 'Aṭṭār as Badr Ahvāzī, which one of 'Aṭṭār's friends had asked him to versify. Ritter has noted the significance of this author's surname (Ritter, ibid, p. 161). The location of the romance's opening at Ahvāz and the prevalence of folkloric types of adventure in the episodes suggest that the work was built on a foundation of local legends. Two versions of the *K̲osrow-nāma* exist: an older one composed by the poet before the completion of his *Manṭeq al-ṭayr* (in 573/1178 or 583/1187), and a later, abridged one, which he brought out after his four mystical narrative poems. No philological investigation of this matter has yet been undertaken. The latest printed edition does not distinguished between the two versions. It is therefore not yet possible to answer the question whether or how far the second version was influenced by Neẓāmī's *Ḵosrow o Šīrīn*, which was composed in the years 573-76. Although certain thematic parallels strike the eye, such as the hero's discomposure at the end of his very stormy courtship (*Ḵosrow-nāma*, pp. 121ff.; *Ḵosrow o Šīrīn*, pp. 142ff.), the wonderful time which the lovers have together after their reunion (*Ḵosrow-nāma*, pp. 231ff.; *Ḵosrow o Šīrīn*, pp. 115ff.), or the heroine's love-distraught death on the tomb of her beloved, the correspondence does not extend to details and cannot therefore be taken as a sufficient argument for any dependence of 'Aṭṭār on Neẓāmī.

Edition: A. Sohaylī Ḵ'ānsārī, Tehran, 1340 Š./1961.

Asrār-nāma. This is the earliest of 'Aṭṭār's mystical narrative poems (see Boyle, "The Religious *Mathnavīs* of Farīd al-Dīn 'Aṭṭār," *Iran* 17, 1979, pp. 9f.); it has attracted less scholarly attention than the other three. This may be partly due to its lack of a frame-story. The contents are arranged in 22 discourses (*maqāla*s) in random order, without regard to sequence of ideas. Each *maqāla* begins with an outline of an idea, which is then developed by means of short anecdotes. Frequently the anecdotes are accompanied by reflections which lead into thematically related fields or, in some cases, stray quite far from the basic idea. The work thus lacks a definite conceptual structure. Its concluding message is the hope of release of man's spiritual substance from the world's grasp. In no other work does 'Aṭṭār propound the gnostic concept of the soul's fall and the duty to free it from worldly and material bonds so comprehensively and forcefully as in the *Asrār-nāma*. The resultant belief that this work influenced the preamble of the *Maṯnawī-e ma'nawī*, probably gave rise to the legend that the aged 'Aṭṭār donated it to the young Jalāl-al-dīn Rūmī as his testament (Ritter, *Das Meer der Seele*, p. 30). The concluding message naturally leads the author into moralizing reflections of the world's transience, vanity, and depravity, which fill whole chapters in the last third of the work (chap. 14 onward). After the three introductory chapters on *tawḥīd*, *na't*, and *manāqeb*, the fundamentals of the gnostic concept are expounded; certain aspects are elaborated in chapters 8 and 11, and in chapter 5 the favorite theme of reason and love (*'aql o 'ešq*) is introduced. Chapter 12 also seems worthy of special mention, because it is about the impenetrability of celestial and extramundane secrets (*asrār*) and is thus more pertinent to the book's title than the rest.

Editions: Ṣ. Gowharīn, Tehran, 1338 Š./1959 (reviewed in *Rāhnamā-ye ketāb* 25, 1338 Š./1959, pp. 716-24); particulars of older eds. in Mošār, *Fehrest*, col. 95.

Manṭeq al-ṭayr, also entitled *Maqāmāt-e ṭoyūr*. This work has a frame-story, inspired by the *Resālat al-ṭayr* of Aḥmad or his brother Moḥammad Ğazālī (Ritter, *Das Meer der Seele*, pp. 8f.), which combines two well-known themes, the assembly of birds to choose the worthiest of them as their leader, and the journey of the birds to the distant seat of the bird-king. Forūzānfar (*Šarḥ-e aḥwāl*, pp. 336-45) has traced the second theme back to the *Resālat al-ṭayr* of Ebn Sīnā. 'Aṭṭār embellished and expanded the allegory of Ğazālī and gave it a deeper meaning, but kept the frame. The birds achnowledge the Sīmorḡ as their king. Smitten with desire to see him, they decide to set out for his faraway palace. The journey costs the lives of many of them. The few birds, according to 'Aṭṭār only thirty, who survive to reach their goal are made aware of the Sīmorḡ's inaccessability and self-sufficient majesty. Only after they have apprehended the vastness of the gulf between their own dependence and the Sīmorḡ's independence are they granted admission for an audience. 'Aṭṭār then consummates the epic with an affirmation of his cherished belief that man will find the sought supreme being within himself, and he expresses his meaning through an ingenious pun: The thirty birds (*sī morḡ*) find to their amazement that the Sīmorḡ is none other than their own selves (*maqāla* 45). In contrast with the birds of Ğazālī, 'Aṭṭār's birds are not an anonymous flock, but often come onto the scene as individuals concerned with problems of the venture (*maqāla*s 3-12 and elsewhere). Their leader, the *hodhod* hoopoe, (mentioned in Koran 27: 20 as Solomon's messenger) is the moving spirit of the whole enterprise. 'Aṭṭār also interweaves numerous tales and anecdotes into the frame-story just as he does in his other mystical narrative poems, for the purpose of developing the various themes. Sometimes the role of reciter is given to an actor in the main drama as a means of keeping the plot on course; for example, it is after hearing the hoopoe tell the tale of Shaikh Ṣan'ān's fateful love (*maqāla* 14; analysis in Forūzānfar, *Šarḥ-e aḥwāl*, pp. 320-26) that the birds decide to set out on their quest for the Sīmorḡ (*maqāla* 15).

Editions, manuscripts, and translation are described in Ritter, "Philologika XIV," pp. 49-56; to these must be added the eds. by M. J. Maškūr, Tehran, 1341 Š./1962, and Ṣ. Gowharīn, Tehran 1342 Š./1963, and the tr. by R. P. Masani, *The Conference of the Birds: A Sufi Allegory, Being an Abridged Version of Farid-ud-din Attar's Mantiqut-Tayr*, London, 1924, and C. S. Nott, *The Conference of the Birds*, London, 1954 and 1961.

Moṣībat-nāma. This expounds a basic theme of 'Aṭṭār's world of thought, namely the inner restlessness and bewilderment from which deliverance is attainable on the Sufi path (see Ritter, *Das Meer der Seele*, pp. 245ff.). In the *Moṣībat-nāma*, the person who has these experiences is a *sālek* (wayfarer) guided by a master. 'Aṭṭār insists explicitly here on the necessity of guidance by a master (ed. Weṣāl, pp. 63.2ff., and passim). He identifies the *sālek* with the ideal mystic, and relates this ideal to remembrance of God (ibid., p. 57.2). Mystical experiences in the privacy of vigils probably form the background of the whole work (Ritter, ibid., p. 18), as the forty stages traversed by the *sālek* apparently correspond to the forty days of a religious vigil (*čella*). The idealized *sālek* appeals to forty celestial and terrestrial beings for advice on deliverance from his tormented state of mind: They are Gabriel and the other angels (pp. 1-5), God's throne and its pedestal (pp. 6-7), the tablet and the reed-pen (pp. 8-9), paradise and hell (pp. 10-11), the sky, sun, and moon (pp. 12-14), the four elements (pp. 15-18), the mountains and seas (pp. 19-20), minerals, plants, and different orders of animals (pp. 21-25), demons, sprites, and human (p. 26-28), Adam and the other prophets to Moḥammad (pp. 29-35), the faculties of perception, imagination, reason, and heart, i.e., emotion (pp. 36-39), and finally the universal soul (*rūḥ*). All but one give him the same answer in the unspoken language of mood (*zabān-e ḥāl*; ibid., p. 56.4ff.): they are in no better state than he is. Only from the universal soul does he get the salutary advice that he can find the deliverance he seeks nowhere except in himself. He must cast himself into the ocean of the soul and utterly efface himself (*maqāla* 40). From time to time the *sālek*'s appeals to the different beings and their replies lead the poet into rhetorical disquisitions in the panegyric verse style about ideas and themes associated with the particular luminaries. Sometimes the *sālek*, after one of his conversations with a being, gets comments on it from his master; this also probably reflects a practice in Sufi vigils. The various beings are transformed into symbols or occasions for explanation of specific aspects of mystical progress or Sufi ethics. Also instrumental to this end, as in ʿAṭṭār's other mystical narrative poems, are more or less lengthy interposed stories which he explains and discusses as the occasion requires.

Manuscripts and translations are described in Ritter, "Philologika XIV," 36-60. Printed ed. by N. Weṣāl, Tehran, 1338 Š./1959. Particulars of older printed eds. in Mošār, *Fehrest*, col. 1448.

Elāhī-nāma. This work owes its name to the poet's intention that it should open the "door to the divine treasure" (*dar-e ganj-e elāhī*; ed. Ritter, p. 366.5). The frame-story tells of a caliph who has six sons and asks each about his heart's desire. The first son longs for the daughter of the king of the fairies, the second for mastery of the art of magic, the third for the *Jām-e Jam*, the world-reflecting cup of Jamšīd, the fourth for the water of life, the fifth for the demon-controlling ring of Solomon, and sixth for knowledge of alchemy. The ruler discusses each son's desire with him, trying to explain to him not only that it is absurd if viewed *sub specie aeternitatis*, but that it may also, if interpreted esoterically, have a deeper meaning and be capable of fulfillment within himself. The fairy princess may be one's own purified soul (p. 76.7ff.), magic may consist of turning the devil which one carries in one's self (p. 128.3ff.) into a Muslim (p. 139.1 ff.). Jamšīd's cup may be the mystic who in the state of union becomes the mirror of reality (p. 185.5 ff.), the water of life may be esoteric knowledge (p. 218.15 ff.), Solomon's ring may be contentment with one's lot (p. 286.10 ff.), and the true elixir may, in ʿAṭṭār's words, be the "light of God" which transforms everything (p. 361.16 ff.). In another passage, typical of ʿAṭṭār's reinterpretations, he makes alchemy mean transformation of body into heart and of heart into pain (p. 355.12)—words which echo the theme of the *Moṣībat-nāma*. In substance the *Elāhī-nāma* conveys the same message as the *Manṭeq al-ṭayr*, namely that the goal which man seeks is latent within himself. The outline of this basic idea is enriched with numerous apposite stories of varying length (from 3 to over 400 verses). In other words, a wealth of edifying anecdotal material is fitted into a frame-story, as in the *Manṭeq al-ṭayr*.

Editions: H. Ritter, *Ilahi-Name: Die Gespräche des Königs mit seinen sechs Söhnen. Eine mystische Dichtung von Faridaddin ʿAṭṭār*, Leipzig and Istanbul, 1940 (Bibliotheca Islamica 12); F. Rūḥānī, Tehran, 1339 Š./1960. Translations: F. Rouhani (Rūḥānī), *Le livre divin*, Paris, 1961; J. A. Boyle, The *Ilāhī-nāma or Book of God*, Manchester, 1976 (Persian Heritage Series, 29). For interpretation of the frame-story, see also F. Meier, "Geistmensch," *Eranos-Jahrbuch* 13, p. 346.

Four more *maṯnawī* poems are placed by Ritter in the first group of ʿAṭṭār's authentic works. Two of them, the *Meʿrāj-nāma* and the *Jomjoma-nāma*, are very short and look as if they may be pieces from a larger narrative poem, the former being part of *naʿt*, and the latter being an illustrative story about Jesus's reanimation of the skull of a heathen king who then tells him of the horrors of the tomb and hell's punishments (see Ritter's ed. of the *Elāhī-nāma*, p. 10 b). The third poem, the *Bolbol-nāma*, tells how the nightingale, after being hauled before Solomon for singing love-songs to the rose, defends and finally vindicates himself (Ritter, "ʿAṭṭār," in *EI*² I, p. 754, no. 10; Nafīsī, *Jostojū*, pp. 106f.); this work is judged by Nafīsī, on stylistic grounds, to be spurious. On the other hand, Nafīsī surprisingly upholds the authenticity of the fourth of these *maṯnawīs*, the *Pand-nāma* (*Jostojū*, pp. 108f.), even though there are no indications of ʿAṭṭār's authorship in the text of this short work (Ritter, "Philologika XVI," pp. 228 f.) and no traces of its existence before the 9th/15th century. In content it does not display any of the characteristically stock of ideas of ʿAṭṭār, being a dry moral rule-book in abrupt and grammatically very simple language with trite wording. Only the nine verses of the conclusion (*Ḵātema*) are worthy of ʿAṭṭār. Nevertheless this work won great popularity, particularly among the Turks; it has been printed, often with commentaries, and translated into Turkish many times (Ritter, "Philologika XVI," pp. 228-38).

As for the works in Ritter's second group, Nafīsī has convincingly shown that they cannot, for reasons of style, be from ʿAṭṭār's pen. (*Jostojū*, pp. 105 ff., 114, 128, 132 f.). The works in question are entitled *Oštor-nāma*, *Jawhar* (or *Jawāher*) *al-ḏāt Haylāj-nāma*, *Manṣūr-nāma*, and *Bīsar-nāma*. To these must be added the *Maẓhar al-ʿajāʾeb* and *Lesān al-ḡayb* from the third group, in addition to the following which are judged also by Ritter to be indisputably apocryphal: *Ḵayyāṭ-nāma*, *Waṣlat-nāma*, *Kanz al-asrār*, *Meftāḥ al-fotūḥ*, *Waṣīyat-nāma*, *Kanz al-ḥaqāʾeq* (see *EI*², s.v. *ʿAṭṭār*).

Bibliography: Given in the text. See also *Colloquio italiano-iranico sul poeta mistico Farīd uddīn ʿAṭṭār*, Rome, 1978.

(B. REINERT)

ʿAṬṬĀŠ (or EBN ʿAṬṬĀŠ), AḤMAD B. ʿABD-AL-MALEK, Ismaʿili leader during the time of Sultan Barkīāroq (Berk-yaruq, d. 498/1104) and contemporary of Ḥasan Ṣabbāḥ. His father, a famous calligrapher and obviously a man of some scholarly reputation, had held the function of *dāʿī al-ʿErāqayn* and had lived in Isfahan until forced to leave because of his Ismaʿili activity. He went to Ray, where in 464/1072 he introduced Ḥasan Ṣabbāḥ into the cadres of the *daʿwa* and sent him as his deputy to Egypt. He is also reported to have engaged Raʾīs Moẓaffar of Gerdkūh, another famous leader of the Nezārī movement, for the Ismaʿili cause. His son managed to stay in Isfahan, obviously by feigning serious differences with his father's ideas. He penetrated the garrison of a fortress about 30 km southwest of Isfahan called Šāhdez (or Qalʿa-ye Jalālī), allegedly as a schoolteacher for the children of the soldiers. These were Daylamis and as such probably prepared for Shiʿite ideas (the Fatimids used to recruit part of their troops in Daylam cf. C. E. Bosworth in *Oriens* 18-19, 1967, pp. 158f.; Y. Lev in *Asian and African Studies* 14, 1980, p. 174 n. 32). They seem to have come to Isfahan only during the time of Sultan Malekšāh (465-85/1072-92), when the fortress was built. Ḥasan Ṣabbāḥ's takeover of Alamūt (in Daylam) in 483/1090 may have facilitated ʿAṭṭāš's success; after having won over the entire garrison and parts of the surrounding population, he was able to retain independent control of the area for several years (twelve years according to Rašīd-al-dīn, i.e., from ca. 488/1095 onward). He managed to get hold of K̲ālanjān, another fortress in the neighborhood. ʿObaydallāh b. ʿAlī K̲aṭībī, the Hanafite *qāżī* and "mayor" of Isfahan (the *raʾīs*, i.e., *raʾīs al-mad̲hab* or *raʾīs al-balad*), had to make arrangements with him (cf. Bondārī, *Zobdat al-noṣra* ed. Houtsma, pp. 90ff. Cairo, 1318/1900-01, pp. 83ff.). Only when he started to levy taxes, as the Saljuq government had done before, did agitation start against him in the town. Barkīāroq, who had enough to do with the internal dissensions of the Saljuqs during this period, was rather lenient towards the Ismaʿilis, at least until the last years of his reign. The situation changed definitely under Moḥammad b. Malekšāh who, immediately after Barkīāroq'a death in 498/1104, started attacking the Ismaʿili strongholds. Šāhdez was besieged for almost one year. ʿAṭṭāš tried to avoid the hopeless fight by pointing to the fact that his followers accepted the fundamental tenets of Islam and could therefore not be an object of war; they differed from Sunnite opinion only concerning the tenet of *emāma*, and here they were ready to recognize Saljuq suzerainty. This may already have been the legal basis of arrangement applied by K̲aṭībī; it was obviously brought forth in a discussion which took place in Isfahan in the presence of the sultan (cf. Qazvīnī, *Ketāb al-naqż*, p. 48.16ff.). Moḥammad b. Malekšāh, however, did not agree with this interpretation. Šāhdez was conquered in 500/1107 and ʿAṭṭāš was captured together with his son; his wife had precipitated herself from the walls of the fortress. He was paraded through the streets of Isfahan, ridiculed by a song which, antithetically, attested his former prestige. Finally he was skinned alive; his head and his son's were sent to Baghdad. The victory was important enough to be reported to Damascus in an official letter (Ebn al-Qalānesī, *D̲ayl taʾrīk̲ Demašq*, ed. Amedroz, Beirut, 1908, p. 151.13ff.; French tr. R. Le Tourneau, *Damas de 1075 à 1154*, Damascus, 1952, pp. 66ff.). The poet Nāṣeḥ-al-dīn Arrajānī (d. 544/1149; *GAL*[2] I, p. 254, S. I, p. 448) praised it in a panegyric on the conqueror, Moḥammad b. Malekšāh's vizier Saʿd-al-molk Ābī (ʿA. Eqbāl, *Wezārat*, p. 161). K̲aṭībī was assasinated by an Ismaʿili shortly afterwards, in 502/1109 (Ebn Abu'l-Wafāʾ, *al-Jawāher al-možīʾa*, Hyderabad, 1332/1913, I, pp. 338f.). ʿAṭṭāš, in contrast to his father, who had composed an Ismaʿili propaganda treatise called *al-ʿAqīqa*, is not known for any literary activity.

Bibliography: Moḥammad b. ʿAlī Rāvandī, *Rāḥat al-ṣodūr*, ed. M. Eqbāl, London, 1921, pp. 155ff.; Turkish tr. A. Ateş, Ankara, 1957, I, pp. 151ff. Abu'l-Fatḥ Bondārī, *Zobdat al-noṣra wa nok̲bat al-ʿoṣra*, ed. M. Th. Houtsma, in *Recueil de textes relatifs à l'histoire des Seldjoucides* II, Leiden, 1889. Ebn al-Jawzī, *Montaẓam*, Hyderabad, 1938-40, IX, pp. 190f. ʿAbd-al-Jalīl Qazvīnī, *Ketāb al-naqż*, ed. J. Moḥaddet̲ Ormavī, Tehran, 1371/1951-52, pp. 91, 176.11ff. Ẓahīr-al-dīn Nīšābūrī, *Saljūq-nāma*, Tehran, 1332 Š./1953-54, pp. 40ff. (depends on Rāvandī). Ebn al-At̲īr, X, pp. 215ff., 299ff. K̲ᵛāja Rašīd-al-dīn Fażlallāh, *Jāmeʿ al-tawārīk̲, qesmat-e Esmāʿīlīān*, ed. M. T. Dānešpažūh, Tehran, 1338 Š./1959, p. 122. Mostawfī, *Tārīk̲-e gozīda*, pp. 454f. (depends on Rāvandī). ʿA. Eqbāl, *Wezārat dar ʿahd-e salāṭīn-e bozorg-e saljūqī*, Tehran, 1338 Š./1959-60, pp. 157ff. M. G. S. Hodgson, *The Order of the Assassins*, The Hague, 1955, pp. 85f. M. Ḡāleb, *Aʿlām al-Esmāʿīlīya*, Beirut, 1964, pp. 114f. B. Lewis, *The Assassins*, London, 1967, pp. 39, 50ff. Idem, "Ibn ʿAṭṭās̲h̲," *EI*[2] III, p. 725. On the fortress of Sahdez see L. Honarfarr, *Ganjīna-ye āt̲ār-e tārīk̲ī-e Eṣfahān*, Isfahan, 1350 Š./1971, pp. 63ff. Mehryār, *Našrīya-ye Dāneškada-ye Adabīyāt-e Eṣfahān* 1, 1965, pp. 115f., 156f. C. O. Minasian, *Shah Diz of Ismaʿili Fame: Its Siege and Destruction*, London, 1971. For a picture see *Isfahan, City of Light: Catalogue of the Exhibition in the British Museum 6 May—11 July 1976*, pp. 21f.

(J. VAN ESS)

ATTAŠAMA, personal name in the Nuzi texts (at-ta-aš-ša-ma), see I. J. Gelb, P. M. Purves, and A. A. MacRae, *Nuzi Personal Names*, Chicago, 1943, p. 38b. An (Indo-) Aryan origin was proposed for this name by P. -E. Dumont (apud R. T. O'Callaghan, *Aram Naharaim*, Rome, 1948, pp. 58a, 150a), but the etymologies suggested (*āpta-sāman "having gained wealth" or *āpta-kṣāman "having obtained the earth") presuppose a middle Indian source for the name and can not be taken seriously.

(M. MAYRHOFER)

ĀTUR, fire. See ĀDUR and ĀTAŠ.

AΘURĀ, Achaemenid province. See ASSYRIA.

ĀΘVIYA, in the Avestan *Hōm Yašt* (*Y.* 9.7) the second mortal to press the *haoma* and the father of Θraētaona (Ferīdūn). See ĀBTĪN. Additional bibliography: M. Boyce, *Zoroastrianism* I, pp. 97ff. M. Mayrhofer, *Iranisches Personennamenbuch* I/1, Vienna, 1977, p. I/30, no. 75.

AUDH. See AVADH.

AUGUSTINE, prominent Christian theologian and philosopher, born 354 in Thagaste, Numidia. In 373 he became a Manichean and for nine years belonged to their church as a layman, *auditor*. His profession as a rhetor and his intellectual curiosity made him ponder over Manichean doctrines from a philosophical point of view. The reading of Cicero's work *Hortensius* incited him to find real Wisdom. It was the pretension of the Manicheans to possess Wisdom that induced Augustine to be one of them. Pursuing his philosophical studies, in an eclectic way based upon the Academy, Aristotelian logic, the Stoa, and Neo-platonism, Augustine soon discovered that Manicheism was in no way built upon philosophical premises, but on the preaching of its founder, Mani. Augustine urged the leading Manichean theologians of his community to answer his questions concerning crucial points of the doctrine but was constantly referred to the foremost Manichean thinker, Faustus of Mileve, then living in Italy. When Faustus ultimately appeared, he frankly admitted that he was unable to solve Augustine's problems. Augustine's astronomical studies had revealed the non-rational nature of the Manichean explanation of the universe and celestial phenomena (*Confessiones* 5.5.8). Their so-called "Wisdom" turned out to be a mixture of myths and rather childish speculations. This does not mean, however, that during his nine years as an *auditor* he was only halfway a Manichean, as he later tried to make believe. He was sceptical, but still a believer.

The conversation with Faustus had a decisive influence on his attitude towards Manicheism. His *Confessiones* show that up to this time he had scrupulously obeyed the Manichean commandments (*Confessiones* 3.10; 4.1). He refused with horror to kill even a fly (4.2.3). He used to defend the Manichean doctrines and was active in making proselytes (6.7.12). In that way he influenced his friend Alypius. He even wrote a treatise *De pulchro et apto*, based upon Manichean doctrines (4.13).

Augustine's intellectual difficulties were in part due to strong pressure from his mother Monica, a Christian, and some close friends. Monica had never ceased to hope that Augustine would ultimately embrace Christianity, under the influence of which he had been brought up, and his friend Nebridius pointed out the great logical difficulties inherent in the system of Mani. Under the influence of another friend he abandoned belief in astrology, which made him disbelieve Mani's astrological doctrines. In the West the Manicheans claimed to preach the true Christianity and on the basis of Marcion's criticism of both the Old and the New Testament, they argued in their exegesis that many important scriptural passages had been falsified. But they were not able to prove their assertions. Undoubtedly, Augustine was also impressed by the attitude of the majority of the population and the malevolent rumors spread among Christians about alleged sexual excesses among the *electi*. However, such rumors constitute a common topic of criticism and can not be relied upon. After the discussion with Faustus Augustine, already withdrawing from Manicheism, left North Africa for Italy, accompanied by his son, mother, and friends. After a stay at Rome, where he still had contacts with the Manichean community, he took up a position at Milan as professor of rhetoric. It was here that he abandoned Manicheism in favor of the ancient philosophers. The influence of Ambrosius, bishop of Milan, the tears of his mother, the study of Neoplatonism as expounded by the Christian philosopher Marius Victorinus carried him now definitely back to Christianity where he once had been a catechumen. At Easter 387 he was baptized by Ambrosius together with his son Adeodatus and his friend Alypius. He then returned via Ostia—where his mother died—to Africa with the intention to devote himself to the service of the Church. Appointed presbyter in 391, he was elected bishop of Hippo in 395. He died there in 430 during the invasion of the Teutonic Vandals.

After his conversion Augustine attacked Manicheism in a series of writings. In public disputations he exposed the Manichean dogmas to trenchant criticisms with the skill and ruthlessness of a trained rhetor and the dialectical ability of a philosopher. His most important anti-Manichean works are: *De diversis quaestionibus ad Simplicianum, De genesi contra Manichaeos, De moribus Manichaeorum, De utilitate credendi, De duabus animabus, Contra Fortunatum, Contra Adimantum, Contra Epistulam Fundamenti, Contra Faustum, Contra Felicem, Contra Secundinum, De natura boni, De haeresibus 46*. Augustine also composed an abjuration formula to be used by former Manicheans. (See also *De libero arbitrio, De moribus Ecclesiae Catholicae, De vera religione, Enchiridion.*)

In his polemic Augustine discusses such problems as had caused him difficulties during his period as an *auditor*. He accordingly attacks those aspects of Manichean dogmatics he finds weak from a philosophical point of view, above all the lack of perfection he discovers in the idea of God and his kingdom in comparison with his enemy, the kingdom of Darkness with its redoubtable prince. Since God according to Mani is limited in so far as his kingdom borders on Darkness, Augustine argues that he is not perfect. Further, how can God be a pure spirit and incorporeal if he has a common border with a corporeal being? The Manichean theologians were unable to answer these objections for they lacked their opponent's philosophical training and had to defend a religious system based upon inherited Iranian mythology. In vain they tried to attack weak points in Christian dogmatics. Their position in the West was unfavorable, as they tried to teach Manicheism as the esoteric, true Christian doctrine; but in doing so they had recourse to Marcion's thesis of falsification of Scriptures without being able to demonstrate the correctness of this allegation. They were on safer ground when trying to show—after Marcion—the great difference between the Old and the New Testament. Their argumentation here followed arguments Mani had taken over from Marcion. In their argumentation with Augustine the Manicheans relied on exegesis whereas Augustine was especially strong in his philosophical arguments. With sharp irony Augustine criticizes the Manichean pantheon as well as the rich mythology of the system. The Manichean myths appear to him as a collection of naive, absurd, and partly obscene fables. Here again his opponents were placed in an impossible situation because they were not able to give a satisfactory interpretation of the inherited myths. As to the founder Mani's own position, Augustine underlines the fact that no Christian text mentions Mani as Apostle and still less as the promised Paraclete, a claim essential to his attitude vis-à-vis Christianity. Here again the Manicheans could only fall back on Mani's own assertions. Even though the Manichean Fortunatus displayed great skill in his disputation with Augustine, the general impression is that the Manicheans were helpless against an opponent who possessed the same dogmatic knowledge of their religion as they themselves and who used all the methods dialectics could give him. Augustine's attacks are, on the whole, not unfair but he shows no understanding of the great religious problem at the bottom of the system, namely the necessity to explain the existence and cause of evil. Augustine's own solution that evil is only a privation of good, *privatio boni*, is dictated by his Neoplatonic position and is at least as difficult to justify as the Manichean position. On the whole, the nine years Augustine belonged to Manicheism, although leaving some traces in his Christian thinking, as is emphasized by some scholars (Baur, Harnack), influenced him much less strongly and deeply than Neoplatonism (see the summary given by Capelle).

For the study of Latin-speaking Manicheism Augustine remains an invaluable source, but it should always be remembered that the Manicheism he describes is not the original system as developed by Mani, but a later adaptation to Christianity. This fundamental fact is sometimes forgotten (e.g., by Decret). To Augustine himself it was always clear that Manicheism was a *fabula persica* (*Contra Secundinum*, chap. 2).

Bibliography: Editions of Augustine's works: J. P. Migne, ed., *Patrologiae cursus completus, series Latina* XXXII-XLVI, *Sancti Aurelii Augustini . . . opera omnia*, Paris, 1841-42. *Corpus Scriptorum Ecclesiasticorum Latinorum*, distributed between vols. XII and LXXXV, Vienna, 1887-1974. Ed. and tr. R. Jolivet and L. M. Jourjon, *Oeuvres de Saint Augustin* XVII (Bibliothèque Augustinienne): *Six traités anti-Manichéens*, Paris, 1961. M. Dods, tr., *The Works of Aurelius Augustine. Bishop of Hippo* V: *Writings in Connection with the Manichaean Heresy*, Edinburgh, 1872.

Studies of Augustine and his relation to Manicheism: A. Adam, "Das Fortwirken des Manichäismus bei Augustin," *Zeitschrift für Kirchengeschichte* 69, 1958, pp. 1-25. P. Alfaric, *L'évolution intellectuelle de saint Augustin*, Paris, 1918. F. C. Baur, *Das manichäische Religionssystem*, Tübingen, 1831. P. Brown, *Augustine of Hippo*, Berkeley, 1969. Idem, *Religion and Society in the Age of Saint Augustine*, New York, 1972. E. Buonaiuti, "Manichaeism and Augustine's Idea of 'Massa Perditionis'," *Harvard Theological Review* 20, 1927, pp. 117-27. B. Capelle, "Augustinus," *Reallexikon für Antike und Christentum* I, Stuttgart, 1950, pp. 981-93. P. Courcelle, *Recherches sur les Confessions de saint Augustin*, Paris, 1950. F. Decret, *Aspects du manichéisme dans l'Afrique romaine*, Paris, 1970. A. von Harnack, *Lehrbuch der Dogmengeschichte* I, 5th ed., Tübingen, 1931. J. P. de Menasce, "Augustin manichéen," *Freundesgabe für Ernst Robert Curtius*, Berne, 1956, pp. 79-93.

(G. Widengren)

AURELIUS VICTOR, SEXTUS, born in Africa ca. 325/330, held high positions under Julian and Theodosius. He was a contemporary of Ammianus Marcellinus. Of the several works attributed to him, only one survives: the *Liber de Caesaribus* or "Book of Emperors," an abridgment of imperial biographies from Augustus to Constantius II. Aurelius is classed with the epitomists (abbreviators), a group of writers well represented in the fourth century. His accounts, of course, are second hand. Among the sources he may have used are Suetonius, Tacitus, the imperial biographer Marius Maximus, and perhaps—directly or indirectly—Dio Cassius and Flavius Josephus. He makes only brief mention of Roman relations with the Persians. In most cases, he condenses and simplifies enormously the accounts of his sources. Trajan's Parthian war, for instance, is reduced to a simple delivery of hostages (13.7), and Lucius Verus's campaign against the Parthians is despatched in a single sentence (16.4). The "Book of Emperors" contains a number of distortions of historical facts: Xerxes (= Ardašīr) is defeated by Alexander Severus (24.2), Narseh is captured by Maximinianus Galerius (39.35; in fact, Narseh ran away). It is also difficult to believe the author when he reports a war between Vespasian and Vologeses I (9.10). In dealing with Valerian's capture by the Persians, he echoes an unverifiable tradition according to which the emperor suffered flaying on Šāpūr I's order. In general, Aurelius Victor records few of the many episodes in the Romans' struggle with Iran, though it spanned centuries; his interests lie elsewhere. It is therefore highly characteristic that he should say not a word about the incessant battling which his contemporary, Emperor Constantius II, carried on against the Sasanian Šāpūr

II. On the subject of Romano-Parthian and Romano-Persian (i.e., Sasanian) relations, the "Book of Emperors" is highly uninformative compared with the contemporary "breviaries" of Eutropus and Festus Rufus.

Bibliography: Principal editions: *Historia romana*, ed. J. Arntzen, Amsterdam, 1733. *Liber de Caesaribus*, ed. F. Pichlmayr and R. Gründel (Teubner), Leipzig, 1961, 1966. Ed. P. Dufraigne (Budé), Paris, 1975. Translations: M. N. Dubois, Paris, 1846. A. Closs, 3 vols. in 1, Stuttgart, 1837-38. Secondary sources: W. Den Boer, *Some Minor Roman Historians*, Leiden, 1972, pp. 18-113. C. G. Starr, "Aurelius Victor, Historian of Empire," *American Historical Review* 61, 1955, pp. 574-86. F. Wolflin, "Aurelius Victor," *Rheinisches Museum*, N.S. 29, 1874, pp. 282-308. A. H. M. Jones et al., *The Prosopography of the Later Roman Empire* I, Cambridge, 1971, p. 960.

(M. L. CHAUMONT)

AUTIYĀRA, name of a district (Old Persian *dahyāuš*) of the satrapy Armina of the Achaemenid empire; this Old Persian form (attested only in DB 2.58f.; see Kent, *Old Persian*, pp. 122, 124) is rendered as Elamite h.Ha-u-ti-ya-ru-iš and Babylonian ^{KUR}ú-ti-ia-a-ri (completely preserved only in the fragment BE 3627, line 2; see E. N. von Voigtlander, *The Bisitun Inscription of Darius the Great. Babylonian Version*, in *Corp. Inscr. Iran.* I/II, *Texts* I, London, 1978, p. 63). In this region, Vaumisa, one of the generals loyal to Darius I, overthrew the Armenian rebel army, which he had already defeated some months before in Assyria. The localization of the district and the etymological interpretation of its name remain uncertain; the connection with that of the Tīārī Kurds (proposed by H. C. Rawlinson, *JRAS* 11, 1849, pp. 71f.) is wholly speculative.

Bibliography: R. Schmitt, "'Armenische' Namen in altpersischen Quellen," *Annual of Armenian Linguistics* 1, 1980, p. 12

(R. SCHMITT)

AUTOPHRADATES (Greek rendering of Old Persian *Vāta-fradāta, Lycian Wataprddata). The bearers of this name include: 1. A satrap of Lydia under Artaxerxes II, from 391 B.C. until the late 350s. Some coins with his portrait come from the cities Lampsacus and Cyme, which belonged to his satrapy. In an inscription from Lycia, which was in the sphere of his influence, he is called "Vātafradāta, the Persian satrap." He is also pictured at Xanthos on the sarcophagus of Paiawa, a Lycian commander. Autophradates and Hecatomnos, satrap of Caria, were ordered to put down the rebellion of Evagoras, king of Cyprian Salamis, who since 390 B.C. was in open revolt against Artaxerxes II. Only after ten years did Evagoras surrender on the terms which were offered by himself. When ca. 368 B.C. Datames, satrap of Cilicia and Cappadocia, revolted against Artaxerxes II, and the next year Ariobarzanes, satrap of Hellespont Phrygia, joined him, Autophradates was ordered to put down both rebellions. But with the help of Athens and Sparta the rebellion spread further, and about 364 all the satraps of Asia Minor and Orontes, satrap of Armenia, joined the rebels, and in 362 even Autophradates was compelled to desert to them. In 360 Ariobarzanes was betrayed by one of his sons, Datames was attacked by his own soldiers, and Orontes surrended to Artaxerxes, and only then did Autophradates manage to put down the Satraps' Revolt.

2. A Persian general who together with Pharnabazus, nephew of Memnon, in 333-32 B.C. restored the Persian rule over the islands of the Aegean Sea and the coast of Asia Minor which had been conquered by Alexander the Great (Arrian, *Anabasis* 2.1-2).

3. A Satrap of Tapurians. In 330 B.C. he surrended to Alexander the Great in Hyrcania and was granted his satrapy, but about 328 refused to obey him and was deprived of his office. Curtius calls him Phradates (Arrian, *Anabasis* 3.24.3; 4.18.2; Curtius 4.12.9; 6.4.24-25; 6.5.21; 8.3.17).

Bibliography: K. J. Beloch, *Griechische Geschichte*^{2}, Strassburg, 1912-27, III/2, pp. 135-36. W. A. P. Childs, "Lycian Relations with Persians and Greeks in the Fifth and Fourth Centuries Re-examined," *Anatolian Studies* 31, London, 1981, pp. 72-76. Diodorus 15.90-93. J. Friedrich, *Kleinasiatische Sprachdenkmäler*, Berlin, 1932, no. 40. E. Meyer, *Geschichte des Altertums* V, Stuttgart and Berlin, 1933, pp. 311-17, 454-57, 485-87. A. T. Olmstead, *History of the Persian Empire*, Chicago, 1948, pp. 391-92, 412-13, 421-22. A. Sh. Shahbazi, *The Irano-Lycian Monuments*, Persepolis, 1975, pp. 146f. For the name see Justi, *Namenbuch*, pp. 52-53. E. Benveniste, *Titres et noms propres en iranien ancien*, Paris, 1966, p. 102. W. Hinz, *Altiranisches Sprachgut der Nebenüberlieferungen*, Wiesbaden, 1975, p. 258. M. Mayrhofer and R. Schmitt, eds., *Iranisches Personennamenbuch* V/4, pp. IV/26-27.

(M. A. DANDAMAYEV)

ĀVA, the basic modern form (and the older spoken form) of the name of two small towns of northern Persia, normally written Āba in medieval Islamic sources. The geographers of that time had difficulty in distinguishing the two places, but usually designate them by the names "Āba of Hamadān" (Maqdesī, pp. 25, 51, "Āba of Qazvīn") and "Āba of Sāva."

1. Āba (now Āvaj) of Hamadān. This, the more northerly of the two, lies on the Qazvīn-Hamadān road approximately halfway between the two, 49° 15′ east longitude and 35° 35′ north latitude, on a high plateau, and was considered as belonging to the *sardsīr* or cold regions. Ḥamdallāh Mostawfī reckons it as belonging to the district of "the two Ḵarraqāns," dependent administratively on Hamadān and comprising forty villages, of which Āba was one of the chief (*Nozhat al-qolūb*, p. 73, tr. p. 76). The present town, now known as Āvaj, had 1,800 inhabitants, Persian- and Turkish-speaking, in 1950.

2. Āba of Sāva (with which town Āba of Hamadān was usually linked). This seems to have been the more important of the two in medieval times. The town lies in 50° 20′ east longitude and 34° 45′ north latitude, on the Zarrīn-rūd (or Qara-sū, former Garmāsa-rūd or Garmās-āb), which rises in the Alvand district of Hamadān and flows down to the plain of Āba and Sāva; there it was, in Saljuq times, dammed and the waters stored used for irrigation in the summer (*Nozhat al-qolūb*, p. 221, tr. pp. 212-13). The *Ḥodūd al-ʿālam* (tr. Minorsky, p. 133, sec. 31.22) describes Sāva and Āva as two flourishing towns on the pilgrimage route from Khorasan; Yāqūt (pp. 57-58) mentions that the people of Āba were ardent Shiʿites and frequently at odds with their Sunnite neighbors in Sāva. It was from Āba that two celebrated statesmen of the 5th/11th century sprang, both with the *nesba* al-Ābī: Abū Saʿd Manṣūr b. Ḥosayn, protégé of the Ṣāḥeb Esmāʿīl b. ʿAbbād (vizier to the last Buyid amir of Ray and Jebāl, Majd-al-dawla Rostam) and author of an *adab* work, the *Ketāb naṯr al-dorar* (extant) and a lost *Taʾrīḵ al-Rayy*. He died in 421/1030 (Brockelmann, *GAL*[2] I, pp. 429-30; Sezgin, *GAS* II, p. 646). 2. His brother, Abū Manṣūr Moḥammad was vizier to "the king of Ṭabarestān" (one of the Ziyarids?). In the early 6th/12th century, the governor of Āba and Sāva on behalf of the Great Saljuqs was the *atābak* Anūštigin Šīrgīr, builder of the dam on the Garmāsa-rūd (see above), and active against the Ismaʿilis of the Alborz mountains; in the later part of this century, the Shiʿite *madrasas* of ʿEzz-al-molk, ʿArabšāh, and others are mentioned at Āba (C. E. Bosworth and A. Bausani in *Camb. Hist. Iran* V, pp. 118-19, 294-95). Although attacked by the Mongols, like Sāva, Āba apparently regained its importance, for we possess a fair number of coins minted at Āba (presumably Āba of Sāva) in the post-Mongol period under the Il-khanids, Jalayerids, Mozaffarids, and Timurids (E. von Zambaur, *Die Münzprägungen des Islams, zeitlich und örtlich geordnet* I, Wiesbaden, 1968, p. 138; earlier, coins were minted at Āba by the Samanids briefly and more extensively by the Buyids, see von Zambaur, loc. cit.). The present small town or village of Āba had 885 inhabitants in 1950.

Bibliography: See also Le Strange, *Lands*, pp. 196, 211. Schwarz, *Iran* pp. 549-50 (Āba of Hamadān), 542-43 (Āba of Sāva). Razmārā, *Farhang* I, pp. 26-27. L. W. Adamec, ed., *Historical Gazetteer of Iran* I: *Tehran and Northwestern Iran*, Graz, 1976, p. 57 (Āba of Sāva). Kayhān, *Joḡrāfīā* II, pp. 374, 398.

(C. E. BOSWORTH)

AVADĀNA, Sanskrit term for a category of Buddhist narrative literature. Three such popular Buddhist stories are known through fragments of Khotanese paraphrases: the *Aśokāvadāna* (see Aśoka iii), the *Nandāvadāna* (q.v.), and the *Sudhanāvadāna* (q.v.). The Khotanese texts of all three have been published in transcription by H. W. Bailey (*Khotanese Buddhist Texts*, 1st ed., London, 1951, 2nd ed., Cambridge, 1981). The Aśoka legend was translated by Bailey in *Bulletin of Tibetology* 3/3, 1966, pp. 5-11; the Nanda story by R. E. Emmerick in *BSOAS* 33/1, 1970, pp. 72-81; and the Sudhana story by Bailey in *BSOAS* 29/3, 1966, pp. 506-32.

Bibliography: Given in the text. See also R. E. Emmerick, *A Guide to the Literature of Khotan*, Tokyo, 1979, pp. 17f., 24f., 30.

(R. E. EMMERICK)

AVADH (English also Audh or Oudh), an ancient cultural and administrative region lying between the Himalayas and the Ganges in North India, named after Ayodhyā, the setting of the Sanskrit epic *Rāmāyana*. By the 700s/1300s, Avadh proper had become a province of all the major Islamic dynasties in India (except the Šarqī sultanate of Jaunpur, which controlled only the eastern half of it). What may be called Greater Avadh emerged as an autonomous political system in the process of Mugal decline in the 12th/18th century, expanding to more than twice its original size under the rule of Nīšāpūri *sayyeds*. In 1189/1775 it was almost as large as the modern state of Uttar Pradesh.

Throughout seven centuries of Muslim domination in North India, Avadh remained a fertile area in which military and administrative elites from Iran and Transoxiana could settle and develop the legal, intellectual, and religious activities of their *qaṣabas*. The best known of these settlements is Belgrām, in Hardōī district near the Ganges in southwest Avadh, which has produced a number of remarkable men such as the poet in Persian and Arabic ʿAbd-al-Jalīl Belgrāmī (fl. 1071-1138/1660-1725), the author in Persian and Arabic Āzād Belgrāmī (fl. 1116-1200/1704-86; q.v.), and the historian Belgrāmī, author of Sawāneḥ-e Akbarī.

On the opposite side of Hardōī district lies the isolated *qaṣaba* of Gopāmaw, which contains the ruins of numerous *ḵānaqāh*s, *madrasas*, tombs, and inns, bearing testimony to earlier cultural activities.

Nine miles west of Lucknow lies Kākorī which for many generations has been the home of eminent scholars of theology, law, and literature; some families have a 600 year-long tradition of scholarly activities. In Lucknow itself, a relatively small settlement until the late 12th/18th century and the home of Turkic immigrants who came during the Delhi Sultanate, scholarly training has been uninterrupted since high Mughal times.

It was with the decline of Delhi in the early 1700s that Avadh came into its own as the main source of literary, artistic, and religious patronage in North India. Its rulers, called nawabs, were Iranian Shiʿites from Nīšāpur, who not only encouraged the existing Persian-language belle-lettrist activity to shift from Delhi, but also invited, and received, a steady stream of scholars, poets, jurists, architects, and painters from Iran. Although Urdu was at this time becoming more widely used both for artistic expression and for everyday speech, Persian remained the medium of government, academic instruction, high culture, and the court language until the mid-13th/19th century. The best Urdu poets produced *dīvān*s in Persian, often under a different pen-name from that used in their Urdu composition, competing with the Iranian immigrants who criticized the relatively ornate *sabk-e hendī*, or "Indian style."

A primary source of patronage and encouragement was, naturally, the nawabi family itself. Šojāʿ-al-dawla (r. 1754-75), though primarily interested in military affairs, nevertheless supported the cultural and scholarly activity at his capital in Fayżābād. There jurists at his court, Sayyed Sarīʿ-al-dīn, Mollā ʿAṭāʾallāh, and Mawlawī Majīd, were famous well beyond Avadh's borders, and two Hindu historians, Harčaran Dās and the Marāthā Kāšī Rāj, wrote polished Persian narratives of his important reign. One court physician, Ḥakīm Ṣādeq Moḥammad Moʿālej Khan, was also a scholar of Hadith and *feqh*.

Several poets in Persian at Šojāʿ's court, or supported by his Mughal in-laws, deserve mention: Serāj-al-dīn ʿAlī Khan Ārzū who received a monthly allowance of Rs. 300 (£30) from the nawab's treasury; Rāe Sarap Singh Khatrī Dīvāna and Mīrzā Moḥammad Fāḵer Makīn, both refugees from Delhi; Shaikh ʿAbd-al-Reżā b. ʿAbdallāh Matīn Eṣfahānī, himself the author of a 5,000-verse *dīvān* and sometime tutor to Dīvāna, spent decades wandering around India in search of a Sufi master, until he found Sayyed Moḥammad ʿĀref Neʿmatallāhī of the Qāderīya *selsela* (who received a stipend granted by Šojāʿ's uncle, the nawab Ṣafdar Jang) in Lucknow. An interesting bilingual poet was the Belgrāmi aristocrat, Moḥammad-ʿĀref Jān, who wrote in Persian as ʿĀref, and in Hindi as Jān; he was a close friend to Āzād, and studied Sanskrit as well as Arabic.

Early in Āṣaf-al-dawla's reign (1775-97), the realm changed from a military patronage state to a partially demilitarized protectorate under the subsidiary alliance with the English East India Company. By controlling Avadh's foreign policy, border security, and army, the British guaranteed the survival of the régime against external and internal enemies, while in effect depriving it of all but cultural and internal administrative activity. Lucknow, Āṣaf's new capital, became as a consequence the major source of patronage in all of North India, a haven for writers and artists fleeing unsettled conditions elsewhere. Although Urdu was strengthening its hold on the public imagination, partly due to a reaction against the growing attacks on *sabk-e hendī* by Iranians, Persian retained a large following and remained the supreme test of literary accomplishment.

Shiʿite influence grew immensely from this period, Moḥarram becoming a lavishly sponsored ceremony for all communities, including non-Muslims, as well as a rite of cultural legitimation for the régime. With it arose the genre, increasingly however in Urdu, of the *marṯīa* (q.v.) or tragic elegy on the martyrdom at Karbalā of Imam Ḥosayn and his family. Āṣaf supported theologians such as Deldār ʿAlī b. Moḥammad Moʿīn-al-dīn Lakhnavī, whose sermons are preserved in *Mawāʿeẓ-e Ḥasanīya*, and whose son, Mawlawī Sayyed Moḥammad, founded a madrasa for Shiʿite theology called the Solṭān-al-madāres. To this Mīrzā Bahādōr Mīrzā added the Madrasa-ye mašāʾeḵ al-šarāʾī, also in Lucknow.

The poets of Persian retained their social position throughout the reigns of Āṣaf, his brother Saʿādat ʿAlī Khan (r. 1798-1814), and the latter's five descendants—who ruled Avadh until its annexation by the British in 1856—yet no author or poet wrote exclusively in Persian.

Until Ḡāleb in the 13th/19th century, Persian was primarily employed in the compilation of *taḏkera*s or biographical anthologies, dictionaries, compendia of usages and idioms, commentaries, and histories. A plateau in literary creativity in Persian had been reached in the late 12th/18th century, in which writers sought to preserve, compare and evaluate the works of their predecessors, reform their own use of language, and influence the direction of Urdu itself; as a matter of fact, our present knowledge of much Arabic and Turkish as well as Persian poetry owes much to the conserving and evaluative work of this period. At the same time the genre of literary memoirs gained momentum with the Persian *Ḏekr-e Mīr* of the poet Mīr Moḥammad-Taqī Mīr, known primarily for his Urdu compositions.

The enthusiasm for defining and appreciating Indian Muslims' classical literary and religious traditions led Ḡāzī-al-dīn Ḥaydar (r. 1814-27) to found the Maṭbaʿ-e Šāhī or Royal Press in the Dawlat-ḵāna on the Gomtī river. One of its first publications was the *Haft qolzom*, a seven-volume Persian dictionary compiled under the king's own supervision. The *Tāj al-loḡāt*, an Arabic-Persian dictionary in seven large folio volumes, was the result of the work of scholars under the reigns of three successive rulers. In the 1830s publishing expanded greatly as lithography was introduced, and works of classical literary, artistic, and religious importance gained wide acceptance along with more popular tracts and minor works. By the late 1840s there were no fewer than twelve private lithographic publishing houses in Lucknow and Kanpur, which produced over 700 separate works, some of them in more than ten editions. This was especially important for Koran and Hadith studies, which contributed to the social and religious reform movements launched by Indian Muslims, in Avadh and elsewhere. Thus, by mid-century, the political and military importance of the region had been eclipsed by its more lasting achievements in the realms of social awareness, literary conservation, and religious reform.

Bibliography: Mīr Ḡolām ʿAlī Khan Belgrāmī Āzād, *Ḵezāna-ye ʿĀmera*, wr. 1762-63, Kanpur, 1871. Bhagvān Dās Hindī, *Safīna-ye Hendī*, wr. 1804, Patna, 1958. Bahādōr Singh, *Yādgār-e Bahādorī*, wr. 1833, Uttar Pradesh State Archives, Allahabad, fols. 269-71, 273-83, 557a-606b. Deldār ʿAlī b. Moḥammad Moʿīn-al-dīn Lakhnavī, *Mawāʿeẓ-e Ḥasanīya*, Asiatic Society of Bengal MS, IV, II, no. 1049. Harčaran Dās, *Čahār golzār-e Šojāʿī*, wr. 1787, British Museum Or. Ms. 1732. Harnām Singh Nāmī,

Tārīḵ-e Saʿādat-e Jāvīd, wr. 1806, British Museum Or. Ms. 1820, fols. 197-221. Enʿām ʿAlī, *Awṣāf al-Āṣaf*, wr. 1785, British Museum Or. Ms. 1707; Aligarh Muslim University Library, *żamīma fārsī tārīḵ*, no. 25, fols. 53a-109b. Mīr Taqī Mīr, *Ḏekr-e Mīr*, ed. ʿAbd-al-Ḥaqq, Aurangabad, 1928. Moḥammad Fayż Bakš, *Resāla dar aḥwāl-e zamīndārān-e Kākōrī*, wr. ca. 1815, Asiatic Society of Bengal MS, Ivanow catalog of the Curzon Collection, number 87. Ḡolām Hamadānī Moṣḥafī, *ʿEqd-e Ṯorayyā*, wr. 1784, Aurangabad, 1934. Solṭān ʿAlī Ḥosaynī Ṣafawī, *Maʿdan al-saʿādat*, wr. 1804, British Museum Or. Ms. 2057, fols. 123-46; Asiatic Society of Bengal MS, Ivanow catalog number 181, vol. four. Rājā Ratan Singh Zaḵmī, *Solṭān al-tawārīḵ*, wr. 1842, British Museum Or. Ms. 1876, fols. 1-8b, 112b-273b. Mawlawī ʿEnāyatallāh, *Taḏkera-ye ʿOlamāʾ-e Ferangī Maḥal* (in Urdu), Lucknow, 1930. A. Sprenger, *A Catalogue of the Arabic, Persian and Hindustani Manuscripts of the Libraries of the King of Oudh*, Calcutta, 1854. See also C. Collin Davies in *EI*² I, pp. 756-58.

(R. B. Barnett)

AVALOKITEŚVARA-DHĀRAṆĪ, name given by H. W. Bailey to a Buddhist text written in archaizing Late Khotanese (q.v.). The text was so called because it ends with a *dhāraṇī* (Skt. "spell, sacred formula") that is preceded by homage to the bodhisattvas headed by the bodhisattva Avalokiteśvara. It has been published so far in transcription only (H. W. Bailey, *Khotanese Texts* III, Cambridge, 1956, pp. 1-13). It may be a translation from a Sanskrit original, but no source text has so far been identified. In the nineteen surviving folios the bodhisattva Avalokiteśvara is frequently addressed in the vocative. Great emphasis is laid in the text on his compassion, and it is on account of this quality in particular that he became popular not only in Tibet, China, and Japan, but also in Ceylon and elsewhere in southeast Asia.

Bibliography: See also R. E. Emmerick, *A Guide to the Literature of Khotan*, Tokyo, 1979, p. 38.

(R. E. Emmerick)

AVARAYR, a village in Armenia in the principality of Artaz southeast of the Iranian town of Mākū. The plain of Avarayr, located in the extreme northwest of Iran near the Soviet frontier, was the scene of an important battle which took place during an Armenian uprising against the Persians in the mid-fifth century A.D. The cause of the rebellion was a decree issued in 449 by the Sasanian king, Yazdegerd II (439-57), in which he ordered the Armenians, the bulk of whose country had become a vassal state of Iran at the Romano-Persian partition of 387, to convert from Christianity to Zoroastrianism. The Armenians refused and were forced to take up arms to defend their stand. In the course of this conflict, the Persians attempted an invasion of Armenia which was met by a combined force of Persarmenian nobles on the field of Avarayr lying along the banks of the Tłmut River (Rūd-e Zangemār), apparently the Armeno-Persian frontier at that time.

The battle took place on the Feast of Pentecost, 2 June 451. Its essential details were set down soon after by Łazar Pʿarpecʿi; a more elaborate and probably somewhat fictionalized account was recorded by Ełišē (Elisaeus) late in the same century or possibly early in the next. According to the story, an Armenian army of 60,000 men, led by Vardan Mamikonean, met a force of 200,000 Persians, including the elite corps known as the Immortals led by Muškan Niwsalawurt. The Armenians had appealed to the Byzantines for aid without success and were further weakened by the defection of several noble houses led by Vasak, Lord of Siwnikʿ, the most important principality in Armenia. In spite of these disadvantages, the Armenians were holding their own until the Persians drew up their elephant corps. Through this tactic the Armenians were crushed, and Vardan and eight other generals were slain, together with the flower of the Armenian nobility and a large number of common soldiers. So spirited was the Armenian defense, however, that the Persians suffered enormous losses as well. Their victory was pyrrhic and the king, faced with troubles elsewhere, was forced, at least for the time being, to allow the Armenians to worship as they chose.

The battle of Avarayr has become the Armenian national holiday; its anniversary is a festival of the Armenian Church, and Vardan Mamikonean has become one of its saints. The defense of the Christian faith by the Armenians has been hailed as a landmark in the history of the struggle for religious freedom, and the fallen of Avarayr have been held up as examples of heroism, patriotism, and Christian virtue to generations of young Armenians. Contrary to popular belief, however, the battle was not decisive. The Persians persecuted Christianity in Armenia again within two generations, and the Armenians were forced to rise a second time under Vardan's nephew Vahan Mamikonean (481-84). Of greater significance is the social aspect of the original uprising, for, although several princely houses defected from the Armenian cause, the movement cut across class lines and appears to have had the support, not only of the bulk of the nobility and the church but of the common people as well.

Bibliography: Łazar Pʿarpecʿi (Lazarus of Pʿarpi), *Patmutʿiwn Hayocʿ* (History of the Armenians), Tiflis, 1907; tr. Langlois, *Historiens* II, pp. 255-368. Ełišē (Elisaeus), *Patmutʿiwn Vardanancʿ* (History of the Vardanians), Tiflis, 1913; tr. Langlois, *Historiens* II, pp. 179-254; Engl. tr. R. W. Thomson, Cambridge, Mass., 1982. *Camb. Hist. Iran* III/1, pp. 146-47.

(R. Hewsen)

ĀVĀZ, in modern Persian "song" (of any kind) or, more broadly, "music." In use it thus resembles Arabic *ḡenāʾ* (singing), which has "stood for both 'song' in particular and 'music' in general" (Farmer, *History of*

Arabian Music, p. 152). The word is derived from OIr. *vač-* "to voice, utter, speak," and is related to Av. *vāč-* "voice," NPers. *vāža* "word, vocabulary item" (see J. Pokorny, *Indogermanisches etymologisches Wörterbuch*, Berne and Munich, 1959, I, pp. 1135-36).

Āvāz as a musical term has three basic meanings: (1) The classical vocal style of Iran, which is based on the elaborate modal system called *dastgāh* and sung mainly to classical Persian verses. (2) "Tune." This term is used to denote an auxiliary mode in the *dastgāh* system. *Āvāz-e Abū ʿAṭā, āvāz-e Afšārī, āvāz-e Daštī, āvāz-e Bayāt-e Tork* and *āvāz-e Bayāt-e Eṣfahān* are used in contemporary music theory (R. Ḵāleqī, *Naẓar-ī be mūsīqī*, p. 111). However, some music theoreticians such as ʿAlī-Naqī Wazīrī use the Arabic term *naḡma* (melody) in this sense, as in *naḡma-ye Daštī*, instead of *āvāz* (ʿA. Wazīrī, *Āvāz-šenāsī*, p. 35). Use of the Persian term *āvāz* (in Arabic *āwāz*, plur. *āwāzāt*) for secondary mode is old, going back to the 7th/13th-century theoretician Ṣafī-al-dīn ʿAbd-al-Moʾmen Ormavī. In his *Ketāb al-adwār* (633/1235?), he mentions six *āwāzāt: Kavāšt, Kardānīya, Salmak, Nowrūz, Māya*, and *Šahnāz*. In this sense, the term *āvāz* is almost equivalent to the Arabic terms for "branch mode," such as *šoʿba* (plur. *šoʿab*) or *farʿ* (plur. *forūʿ*) (Farmer, op. cit., pp. 203-05). (3) Most importantly, *āvāz* is used to specify the unique rhythmic texture of the non-metric vocal style of Iran. In this sense, instrumental music, which has been developed primarily as accompaniment to the *āvāz* per se in the *dastgāh* system, might well be called *āvāz*, provided that it is executed in non-metric *rubato* style. In particular the term refers to improvised passages following the original vocal style and adapting it into the instrumental version. In this context, the term *āvāz* is contrasted to *żarbī*, which is characterized as a section played in a fixed meter (usually with the *tonbak/żarb* or drum accompaniment). Since the *bī-żarb* (non-metric) rhythmic texture predominates and constitutes the main body of the so-called *dastgāh* music, the term *āvāz* is sometimes used in the sense of "classical Iranian music," both vocal and instrumental. On the other hand, *āvāz* may be contrasted to the term *taṣnīf*, which generally implies a kind of strophic song composed in a fixed meter. The *taṣnīf* also presents a striking contrast to the *āvāz* in respect to the verses employed. The verses sung in the *āvāz* are usually composed in the *ʿarūż* (q.v.) system of Arabo-Persian versification, whereas those employed in the *taṣnīf* are often non-*ʿarūż* poems which are sometimes called "syllabic" verses (*ašʿār-e hejāʾī*).

Rapport with the poetic meter. In the *āvāz*, the *ḡazal*s of Ḥāfeẓ and Saʿdī and the *maṯnawī* of Rūmī are among the most frequently sung verses. As far as the non-metric portion is concerned, theoretically a verse composed in any kind of poetic meter may be sung. However, in practice, some special meters are preferred: *Mojtaṯṯ-e moṯamman-e maḵbūn-e maqṣūr* (∪ – ∪ – / ∪ ∪ – – / ∪ – ∪ – / ∪ ∪ – //*bis*) and its variations; *Hazaǰ-e moṯamman-e sālem* (∪ – – – / ∪ – – – / ∪ – – – / ∪ – – – //*bis*); *Hazaǰ-e mosaddas-e maḥḏūf* (∪ – – – / ∪ – – – / ∪ – – //*bis*); *Hazaǰ-e moṯamman-e aḵrab-e makfūf* (– – ∪ / ∪ – – ∪ / ∪ – – ∪ / – //*bis*) and its variations; *Ramal-e moṯamman-e maḥḏūf* (– ∪ – – / ∪ ∪ – – / ∪ ∪ – – / ∪ ∪ – //*bis*) and its variations; *Ramal-e mosaddas-e maḥḏūf-e maqṣūr* (– ∪ – – / – ∪ – – / – ∪ – //*bis*); and *Możāreʿ-e moṯamman-e aḵrab-e makfūf-e maḥḏūf* (– – ∪ / – ∪ – ∪ / ∪ – – ∪ / – ∪ – //*bis*). The meter of *Motaqāreb-e moṯamman-e maḥḏūf-e maqṣūr* (∪ – – / ∪ – – / ∪ – – / ∪ – //*bis*) is also sometimes found in the *āvāz*. The particular reference for the *Mojtaṯṯ*-type meters is rather easily explained. The combination of short and long syllables in this poetic meter coincides exactly with that of the musical meter called *Kerešma*.

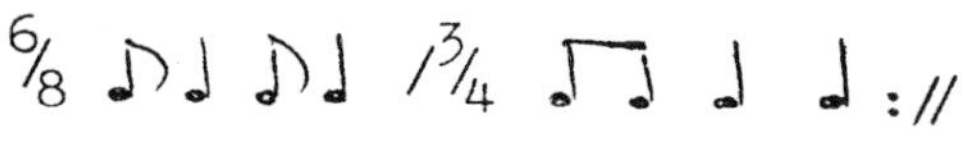

This is one of the most typical rhythmic patterns of Iranian music. This distinctive rhythmic pattern is held so important in the *āvāz* that it appears at various points. The so-called *Šāh-gūša* (king *gūša*) has usually a section named *Kerešma* which is performed with a more or less clearly fixed metric rhythm. This rhythmical meter serves as relaxation and diversion to set off the non-metric *āvāz* texture which is rather serious and tight.

The preference for *Hazaǰ*-type meters may be explained in terms of their relationship to folk verses and songs. The meter of *Hazaǰ* and its variations are among the ones most frequently found in folk poetry such as *do-baytī* and lullabies (*lālāʾī*). The meter of *Hazaǰ-e mosaddas-e maḥḏūf-e maqṣūr*, which is the meter of *do-baytī* (or *čār-baytī* in regional dialects), is particularly often sung in the *āvāz-e Daštī*, which is closely associated with Iranian folk tunes.

Ramal-e mosaddas-e maḥḏūf-e maqṣūr is the meter of Jalāl-al-dīn Rūmī's *Maṯnawī-e maʿnawī*, couplets from which are often sung in the *āvāz* of *Afšārī, Bayāt-e Tork, Abū ʿAṭā* (*Gabrī*), *Daštī, Šūr, Bayāt-e Eṣfahān, Māhūr*, and of *Segāh* (*Moḵālef*). A few other *Ramal*-type meters such as *Ramal-e moṯamman-e maḵbūn-e maḥḏūf-e aslam* are frequently found in the *ḡazal*s of Ḥāfeẓ and Saʿdī, which are most favorably sung in the *āvāz*.

There are some other types of poetic meter which are associated with the specific *āvāz: Motaqāreb-e moṯamman-e maḥḏūf-e maqṣūr* is the meter of Ferdowsī's *Šāh-nāma*, and of the *Sāqī-nāma*s of Ḥāfeẓ and Rażī-al-dīn Artīmānī. Verses chosen from either book are sung in the *āvāz*. When these verses are sung in more or less fixed meter, this meter of *Motaqāreb* is usually treated in the unique rhythmic mode of duple (or square) meter.

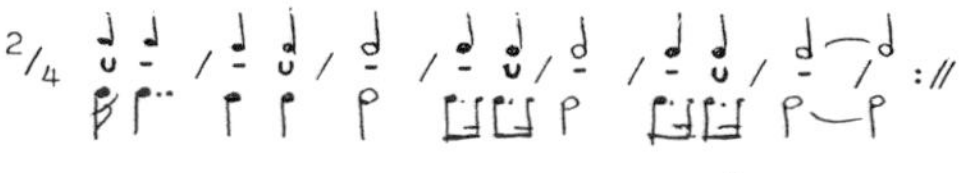

The verses sung in the *gūša* entitled *Čahār-bāḡ* are composed in the poetic meter called *Kāmel-e moṯamman-e sālem*, a not very popular meter in Persian literature. The verses *Če šavad be čehra-ye zard-e man, naẓar-ī ze rāh-e ḵodā konī,....*/ by Aḥmad Hātef Eṣfahānī (d. 1198/1783-84) are among the few examples.

Rhythmic characteristics. The most distinct rhythmic factor in the *āvāz* of course comes from the verse. Thus, the rhythmic organization of the *āvāz* is primarily based upon the poetic meter of the *ʿarūż* system, which is a recurrent cycle of short and long syllables. The pattern and length of a poetic meter, once chosen, remains constant as a kind of rhythmic mode; however, the stress accents of words chosen in a line do not necessarily follow those of the model. "The contrapuntal interplay between the stress patterns of a meter and the stress pattern of normal speech makes for a much needed variety in a strait-jacket of strict quantitative meter" (Yar-Shater, "Affinities," p. 72). In a way, the *āvāz* melody reinforces features of the poetic meter, elaborates it, and gives rise to the mood of the verse. However, its resultant rhythmic texture is rather complex.

A close examination of several descriptive transcriptions of sung *āvāz* reveals the following rhythmic principles: (1) The primal unit of recurring elements of the unmeasured rhythmic texture is a phrase. The accent of the phrase is an inseparable pair of a short syllable and a long syllable (an iamb). (2) Generally speaking, a phrase unit coincides with a foot of the poetic meter, which has usually one iambic pattern (= the accent). (3) In most cases this iambic pattern is found at the very beginning of a phrase. (4) When certain numbers of syllables precede the accent, they are treated rather as neutral syllables in terms of length. (5) From (3) and (4) it is obvious that words are usually articulated at the beginning of a phrase. Then, the following long syllable(s) may be prolonged as far as the sustaining energy permits. (6) At the end of a phrase, the *taḥrīr* technique (elaborate melismatic singing) is preferred; this must constitute one of the recurring elements of a phrase in *āvāz* (Tsuge, "Rhythmic Aspects," pp. 223-24).

Form. The close affinity between Persian poetry and *āvāz* is difficult to overstate. The skeleton of *āvāz* form comes from the basic structure of Persian verses: (1) Each line or *bayt* (couplet) consists of two hemistichs of equal length and identical syllabic pattern. (2) In regard to rhythm, a couplet is based on six or eight poetic feet (*ajzāʾ*) with a cesura in the middle, hence six or eight recurrent accents. This is the core of the *āvāz* which is called *šeʿr* (verse). The *āvāz* is usually preceded by an introduction called *darāmad*, which is usually sung without verse text as such but with vocables such as *āy, ey, del ey del, amān, jān, yār, jānam*, and *ʿazīz-e man*.

The singing of the verse is usually followed by an extensive *taḥrīr* to demonstrate the singer's (*āvāzḵʷān*) vocal technique with vocables, a feature which is very characteristic of Persian *āvāz*. This ornamental vocal technique is such an important aspect of the *āvāz* that no *āvāzḵʷān* is considered proficient without mastery in it. Each *āvāzḵʷān* has freedom to create his own elaborate and tasteful *taḥrīr*. Certain styles of *taḥrīr* are called by such appellations as *Taḥrīr-e bolbolī* (song of nightingale), *Taḥrir-e čakošī* (brazier's hammer), etc. (Caron and Safvate, *Les traditions*, p. 160)

Thus, the most basic form of the *āvāz* in one *gūša* may be outlined as follows: (1) *darāmad*, (2) *šeʿr*, (3) *taḥrīr*. However, in contemporary performance practice of the *āvāz*, several (usually two to five or six) *gūšas* are chosen from one *dastgāh*; instrumental sections are inserted; and its overall musical form has become much more complex. A typical scheme of the *āvāz* in a given *dastgāh* is as follows: (1) *Pīšdarāmad*, a "prelude" or orchestral ensemble piece composed in the *dastgāh* with fixed meter. (2) *Čahār-mežrāb*, an instrumental piece performed in improvisatory manner, demonstrating the soloist's technical virtuosity. It is usually accompanied by a *tonbak* player. (3) *Āvāz*, singing of the verses by a solo singer in the manner of improvisation, going through various *gūšas*. It is the main body of the entire *āvāz* performance. This portion is usually accompanied by a solo instrument such as *tār, santūr, kamānča* or *violon, nay*, or less often, *piano*. (4) *Taṣnīf*, a composed song in the *dastgāh*, often featuring characteristics of a particular *gūša*. It has a fixed meter and is accompanied by an orchestral ensemble including a *tonbak*. (5) *Reng*, a dance piece composed in the *dastgāh*, most frequently in the compound duple meter of 6/8 which often appears in the form of 6/8 + 3/4, giving a hemiola effect. It is performed by the orchestra as a finale.

In fact, this format is not too far from the classical Turkish suite called *fasil*, which consists of *peşrev, taksim, kâr, beste, ağir-semaî, şarki, yürük- semaî*, and *saz-semaî* in a given *makam*. The practice of the Azerbaijan *moğām* and ʿErāqi *maqām* appears to resemble more closely that of the Persian *āvāz*. These musical styles are most probably descended from the *nawba* (or *nawbat*) of medieval Islamic courts, though their evolution and exact relationship can not be determined in detail.

See also entries for each *dastgāh*; Music.

Bibliography: M. Barkechli and M. Maʿaroufi, *La musique traditionnelle de l'Iran* (*Radīf-e mūsīqī-e īrānī*), Tehran, 1341 Š./1963; repr, *Les systèmes de la musique traditionelle de l'Iran* (*Radīf-e haft dastgāh-e mūsīqī-e īrānī*, Tehran, 1352 Š./1973). N. Caron and D. Safvate, *Les traditions musicales: Iran*, Paris, 1966, p. 160. H. Farhat, *The Dastgāh Concept in Persian Music*, doctoral thesis, University of California, Los Angeles, 1965 (on the modal aspects of the *āvāz*). H. G. Farmer, *A History of Arabian Music to the XIIIth Century*, London, 1929, pp. 152, 203-05. M. N. Forṣat Šīrāzī *Boḥūr al-alḥān*, Bombay, 1332/1914, pp. 4-44 and passim. R. Ḵāleqī, *Naẓar-ī be mūsīqī* II, Tehran, 1317 Š./1938, pp. 111-12. Idem, *Sargoḏašt-e mūsīqī-e Īrān* I, Tehran, 1333 Š./1955, pp. 366-84 and passim. Kh. Khatschi, *Der Dastgāh. Studien zur neuen persischen Musik*, Regensburg, 1962, pp. 117-28. M. T. Massoudieh, *Āwāz-e-Šūr: zur Melodiebildung in der persischen Kunstmusik*, Regensburg, 1968, p. 10. Idem, "Tradition und Wandel in der persischen Musik des 19. Jahrhunderts," in R. Günther, ed., *Musikkulturen Asiens, Afrikas und Ozeaniens im 19. Jahrhundert*, Regensburg, 1973, pp. 73-93. Idem, *Radīf-e āvāzī-e mūsīqī-e sonnatī-e*

Īrān, Tehran, 1978. B. Nettl, "Aspects of Form in the Instrumental Performance of the Persian Āvāz," *Ethnomusicology* 18/3, 1974, pp. 405-14. G. Tsuge, "Rhythmic Aspects of the Āvāz in Persian Music," *Ethnomusicology* 142, 1970, pp. 205-07. Idem, *Āvāz: A Study of the Rhythmic Aspects in Classical Iranian Music*, doctoral thesis, Wesleyan University, Middletown, Conn., 1974, pp. 23-28 and passim. ʿA. Wazīrī, *Āvāz-šenāsī* (part 2 of *Mūsīqī-e naẓarī*), Tehran, 1313 Š./1934, p. 35. E. Yar-Shater, "Affinities between Persian Poetry and Music," in P. J. Chelkowski, ed., *Studies in Art and Literature of the Near East*, Salt Lake City, 1974, pp. 59-78. E. Zonis, *Classical Persian Music: An Introduction*, Cambridge, Mass., 1973, pp. 126-31, 136-37.

(G. Tsuge)

AVESTA, the holy book of the Zoroastrians. Avesta is the name the Mazdean (Mazdayasnian) religious tradition gives to the collection of its sacred texts. The etymology and the exact meaning of the name (Pahlavi *ʾp(y)stʾk/abestāg*) can not be considered established, although, despite a recent study by W. Belardi ("Il nome dell' 'Avesta'"), Bartholomae's hypothesis (*Die Gatha's*, p. 108) still seems to be very convincing: we should read *abestāg* and derive this from Old Iranian **upa-stāvaka-* "praise." Properly speaking *Avesta* is the collection of texts in Avestan, and *Zand* their translation and commentary in Book Pahlavi. The interest of the book of Avesta is twofold; on the one hand, it transmits to us the first Mazdean speculations and, on the other hand, it contains the only evidence for Avestan, an Old Iranian language which together with Old Persian constitutes the Iranian sub-division of the Indo-Iranian branch of Indo-European. The Avesta is a compilation of ancient texts, which we owe to the collaboration of the Mazdean priesthood and the Sasanian political power, but of which, unfortunately, only a fraction has been transmitted to us by the Parsi communities of India and Iran, which still remain true to the old religion. The corpus which Western scholarship has reconstituted is found in manuscripts that all date from this millennium; the most ancient (K 7a) dates from A.D. 1288.

The indigenous history of the sacred books is told in several Pahlavi texts. In essence it is as follows: The twenty-one *nasks* "books" of the Avesta, which were created by Ahura Mazdā, were brought by Zaraθuštra to king Vištāspa. The latter or, according to another tradition, Dārā Dārāyān, had two copies of them written down, one of which was deposited in the **Šasabīgān* (thus Bailey, *Zoroastrian Problems*, pp. 230-31; Markwart, *Provincial Capitals*, p. 108, gives *Šapīkān* or *Šīčīkān*; Nyberg, *Manual* II, Wiesbaden, 1974, p. 186, prefers *Šēčīkān*) treasury, the other in the "house of the archives" (*Diz ī nibišt*). At the time of Alexander's conquest, the Avesta was destroyed or dispersed by the Greeks, who translated into their own language the scientific passages of which they could make use. The first attempt at restoring the Avesta was made under the Arsacids, when a king Valaxš had the fragments collected, both those which had been written down as well as those which had been transmitted only orally. This undertaking was carried on in four phases under the Sasanians: Ardašēr (226-41) ordered the high priest Tansar (or Tōsar) to complete the work of collecting the fragments that had begun under the Arsacids and gave official protection for this undertaking; Šāpūr I (241-72) initiated a search for the scientific documents that had been dispersed by the Greeks and the Indians and had them reintroduced into the Avesta; under Šāpūr II (309-79) Ādurbād ī Mahraspandān made the general revision of the canon and ensured its orthodox character against sectarian divergences by submitting himself successfully to the ordeal by fire at the time of a general controversy; finally, a revision of the Pahlavi translation took place under K̲osrow I (531-79).

The testimony of the Mazdean religious tradition is often incoherent and can not be taken literally; it must necessarily be confronted with the results of modern scholarship, which leads to the following picture of the different stages of the formation and transmission of the Avestan texts.

The origin of the Avestan texts. It is on this point that the testimony of the *Dēnkard* and the *Ardā Wirāz-nāmag* is obviously the most based on legends and so the least trustworthy; there never was an Avesta set down under the Achaemenids and destroyed or dispersed by the Greek invaders. The Avestan texts can not be dated accurately, nor can their language be located geographically. Its phonetic characteristics prove with absolute certainty only that this is not the dialect of Pārs/Fārs. One can locate it almost anywhere else without having to face serious counterarguments. Thus scholars have located it in the northwest (Tedesco, "Dialektologie"), the northeast (Morgenstierne, *Report*), Chorasmia (Henning, *Zoroaster*), Margiana-Bactria (Humbach, "Al-Biruni"), or Sīstān (Gnoli, *Ricerche*).

The texts which form the canon were not all written at the same period. We must at least make a chronological distinction between the Old Avestan texts (the *Gāθās*—*Y.* 28-34, 43-51, 53; the *Yasna Haptaŋhāiti*—*Y.* 35-41; and the four great prayers of *Y.* 27) and the remaining, Young Avestan, texts. The Old Avestan texts are probably several centuries older than the others, although a precise date can not yet be justified. In the last ten years a general consensus has gradually emerged in favor of placing the *Gāθās* around A.D. 1000 and assuming that the composition of the best texts of the recent Avesta is more or less contemporary with the Old Persian monuments. The *Vidēvdād* seems to be more recent than the *Yašts* or the *Yasna* and it has also been suggested that it belongs to a particular liturgical school; however, no linguistic or textual argument allows us to attain any degree of certainty in these matters. The earliest transmission of the Avesta must have been oral only, since no Iranian people seems to have used writing in early times. Only with the invention of the cuneiform Old Persian script (probably under Darius) would it have been possible to codify the religious texts. However, there is no evidence that the Achaemenids actually did this. Until the advent of the Sasanians, and even under their regime, Iran was a country in which written documents were conspicuously rare, so as far as the religious tradition is concerned, it faithfully carries on the old Indo-Iranian tradition which established the pre-eminence of a precise and careful oral textual transmission and made learning by heart of the sacred texts an essential element of an adequate cult. Thus, until the beginning of our era, at least, the liturgical texts of Mazdaism could only have formed the subject of an oral tradition preserved by theological schools such as that of Eṣṭaḵr, of which the tradition was not entirely forgotten. It is clear that the writers of the Pahlavi books shared our ignorance of the prehistory of the Avesta. However, we can concede that it does preserve the memory (though in legendary form) of a real break in the religious tradition, or of its splitting into sects, as a result of the absence of a unifying political power after the Greek conquest.

The "Arsacid Avesta." The existence of a written Arsacid canon was at the center of one of the most important disputes in the history of Iranian studies. In 1902 Friedrich-Carl Andreas enunciated the hypothesis that the Avestan Vulgate was full of mistakes resulting from a clumsy transcription in a differentiated phonetic alphabet of a text originally written in a script of the Pahlavi type, i.e., the vowels were not usually marked and the same letter was used for different consonants. Thus the analysis of a modern scholar agreed with the teachings of the *Dēnkard* in postulating the existence of an Arsacid archetype. As a matter of fact, early testimonies are at variance in the question of Mazdean books in the first centuries of our era. Saint Basil states that the magi had no books and the *Ardā Wirāz-nāmag* relates that Ardašēr collected the Avestan texts as they had been memorized by priests who had been summoned for this purpose; however, according to a passage from the Coptic *Kephalaia*, Mani reported that Zaraθuštra's disciples wrote his words down "in the books they are reading today." By a curious coincidence, three outstanding Iranian scholars, more or less simultaneously, published strong criticism of the theory, denying either the existence or at least the relevance of the "Arsacid Avesta": H. W. Bailey (*JRAS*, 1939, p. 112) stated that "the hypothetical Arsacid text will probably prove to be unreal, and the alleged transcribers not to have existed." G. Morgenstierne ("Orthography and Sound-system," pp. 30-31) and W. B. Henning ("Disintegration," pp. 47-48) did not deny the existence of an Arsacid text, but its practical importance. Whatever may be the truth about the Arsacid Avesta, the linguistic evidence shows that even if it did exist, it can not have had any practical influence, since no linguistic form in the Vulgate can be explained with certainty as resulting from wrong transcription and the number of doubtful cases is minimal; in fact it is being steadily reduced. Though the existence of an Arsacid archetype is not impossible, it has proved to contribute nothing to Avestan philology.

The Sasanian Avesta. It has now been established beyond any doubt that the known Avestan Vulgate originates from a canon which was arranged and written down under the Sasanians in an alphabet typologically similar to the Greek alphabet, invented ad hoc in order to render with extreme precision the slightest nuances of the liturgical recitation. The comparison of the Avestan letters with those of Pahlavi allowed K. Hoffmann (*Henning Memorial Volume*, p. 275) to date the fixing of the canon and its writing down to the fourth century, i.e., approximately under Šāpūr II. This enterprise, which is indicative of a Mazdean revival and of the establishment of a strict orthodoxy closely connected with the political power, was probably caused by the desire to compete more effectively with Buddhists, Christians, and Manicheans, whose faith was based on a revealed book. The earliest reference to the Avesta in Sasanian times is perhaps to be found in the inscriptions of Kirdēr (Kartēr), see P. O. Skjærvø, *AMI* 16, 1983 [1985], pp. 269-306.

Of the history of the Avestan texts from the collapse of the Sasanian empire and the oldest manuscripts in our possession little is known. We know that the Muslim conquest and the dispersal of the Mazdean communities caused a weakening of the religious tradition and a decline of the liturgical elocution, which caused damage to the written transmission of the Avesta. Also, examination of the manuscripts reveals mistakes which prove that all of them derive from a single common ancestor, which K. Hoffmann (*Aufsätze* II, p. 515) calls the "base manuscript" and places in the ninth to tenth century A.D. This was proved definitively by K. Hoffmann for the transmission of the *Yasna*, and by H. Humbach ("Beobachtungen") for that of the *Yašt*s and the *Vidēvdād*, but already Nyberg (*Die Religionen des alten Iran*, p. 13) had assumed that all extant Avesta manuscripts derive from a single Sasanian archetype, and Morgenstierne ("Orthography and Sound-system," p. 32 n. 6) had adduced material from the *Yasna, Yašt*s, and *Vidēvdād* in support of Nyberg's hypothesis.

Contents of the Avesta. The Sasanian collection of the Avesta and its commentary (*zand*) is described in chap. 8 of the *Dēnkard*; it was probably composed of three books of seven chapters as shown in Table 27: the left column gives the names as recorded in the *Dēnkard*; the middle column shows which texts are still extant; the third column indicates the contents of the texts. The *Dēnkard* probably does not give us a reliable and credible image of the Sasanian archetype, since it is deficient on several points. Most importantly, the analysis in the *Dēnkard* is based on the Pahlavi translation of the Avestan texts and so may have left out texts without Pahlavi versions on the one hand and included post-Avestan texts on the other. Thus it takes into account Avestan texts that we know to be late compilations; e.g., the *Vištāsp Yašt*, which is considered by this tradition to be Zaraθuštra's teaching to Vištāspa, is just a poorly fabricated medley of quotations from the *Vidēvdād*. It is certain that only a

Table 1

CONTENTS OF THE AVESTA ACCORDING TO THE *DĒNKARD*

I. The *Gāsānīg*, the seven Gāθic nasks, contained the text of the *Gāθās* and their commentaries:

1. *Stōt Yašt*	*Y.* 14-16, 22-27, 28-54, 56 (complete)	
2. *Sūtkar*	a few fragments?	commentaries on the *Gāθās*
3. *Varštmānsar*		commentaries on the *Gāθās*
4. *Bag*	*Y.* 19-21, originally 22 chapters	commentaries on the *Gāθās*
5. *Vaštag*	lost	not analysed
6. *Hādōxt*	Only *Y.* 58, *Yt.* 11, *Az.*, and *H.* 1, 2 left	various texts
7. *Spand*	a few fragments	legend of Zaraθuštra

II. The *Hadag-mānsarīg* (Av. *haδa-mąθra*) contained the sacred formulas connected with the ritual:

1. *Dāmdād*	a few fragments?	cosmogony
2. *Nāxtar*	lost	not analysed
3. *Pājag*	only *Gāh* and *Sīrōza* left	connections of the liturgy with the divisions of the day and of the year
4. *Raθβištāiti*	a few fragments	arrangement of the sacrifice
5. *Bariš*	a few fragments	points of religious ethics
6. *Kaškaysraw*	a few fragments	how to annul a badly made sacrifice
7. *Vištāsp-Yašt*	only *Az.* and *Vyt.* left	legend of Vištāsp's conversion

III. The *Dātīg* contained the books of laws.

1. *Nikātum*	a few fragments	law books
2. *Duzd-sar-nizad*	a few fragments	law books
3. *Huspārām*	only *Nīrangistān* left	law books
4. *Sakātum*	a few fragments	law books
5. *Vidēvdād*	complete	law books
6. *Čihrdād*	a few fragments	mythical history of Iran
7. *Bagān Yašt*	only *Y.* 9-11, 57; *Yt.* 5-19 left	hymn to the deities

part of the Avestan texts collected in the Sasanian archetype is now extant. Duchesne-Guillemin (*La religion de l'Iran ancien*, p. 31) suggested that we only know one quarter of it, since only about one-fourth of the Avestan quotations in the Pahlavi commentary are found in the extant Avesta. However, fragments such as the *Pursišnīhā* and the *Vaēθā Nask* indicate that an indeterminable quantity of juridical literature similar to that of the *Vidēvdād* has been lost. On the other hand, it is not improbable that the oldest texts, i.e., the Old Avestan texts and the old *Yašt*s, that were known to the Sasanian priesthood, have come down to us in their entirety. Not only are no quotations from lost *Yašt*s to be found, it is also clear that the Parsis would have paid particular attention to the transmission of the most venerable parts of the sacred canon.

The extant Avesta comprises the following texts:

I. The *Yasna* (*Y.*) "sacrifice," which is composed of 72 *hād*s "chapters" (from Av. *hāiti* "cut"), is a heterogeneous collection of liturgical texts recited during the ceremony of the preparation and offering of *haoma*.

Y. 1-8 are written in the form of an enumeration: the deities are invited to the sacrifice (1), the libation and the *barəsman* are presented to them (2), then the other offerings (3-8: *Srōš ḍarūn*).

Y. 9-11 form the *Hōm Yašt* "hymn to Haoma." *Y.* 9 begins with a dialogue between Zaraθuštra and the *haoma* personified. In it Indo-Iranian myths are reflected: the first four to pour the *haoma* were in chronological order Vīuuaŋhan, Yima's father, Āθβiia, Θraētaona's father, Θrita, father of Uruuaxšaiia and Kərəsāspa, and lastly, Pourušāspa, Zaraθuštra's father. The core of the *Hōm Yašt* is a series of prayers and eulogies. *Y.* 11 reports the curses of the cow, the horse, and the *haoma* on those who do not treat them as prescribed and mentions the parts which are attributed to Haoma during the bloody sacrifice (the cheeks, the tongue, and the left eye).

Y. 12-13 constitute the Mazdean profession of faith, which opens with the *frauuarāne* declaration "I wish solemnly to declare myself (a Mazdean, etc.)." The passage is in pseudo-Gathic, i.e., it imperfectly imitates the characteristics of the language of the *Gāθās*.

Y. 14-18, a series of invocations comparable to *Y.* 1-8 which serve as introduction to a section called *Staota Yesniia*, which extends to *Y.* 59.

Y. 19-21 or *Bagān Yašt* provide a commentary on the three prayers *Yaθā ahū vairiiō* (called *Ahuna vairiia*),

Aṣ̌əm vohū, and *Yeŋ́he hātąm*. These three very special chapters, the only ones in the Avesta which represent the kind of commentary typified by the commentaries of Sāyaṇa in India, have not yet been fully interpreted.

Y. 22-26 contain another series of invocations.

Y. 27 gives the text of the three prayers which are commented upon in *Y.* 19-21.

Y. 28-53 constitute a collection of texts written in a more ancient dialect than that of the rest of the book. This dialect is called Gathic or Old Avestan. The different chapters are arranged in unities characterized by a similar meter. The *Gāθās* are the only Avestan texts which are clearly composed in verse, using meters based on the number of syllables. In detail:

Y. 28-34 *Gāθā Ahunauuaitī* (named after the *Ahuna Vairiia* in *Y.* 27): stanzas of 3 verses of 7 + 9 syllables.

Y. 35-41 *Yasna Haptaŋhāiti* in prose.

Y. 43-46 *Gāθā Uštauuaitī* (from the beginning of *Y.* 43, *uštā ahmāi*): stanzas of 5 verses of 4 + 7 syllables.

Y. 47-50 *Gāθā Spəṇtamainiiū* (from the beginning of *Y.* 47, *spəṇtā mainiiū*): stanzas of 4 verses of 4 + 7 syllables.

Y. 51 *Gāθā Vohuxšaθrā* (from the beginning of *Y.* 51, *vohū xšaθrəm*): stanzas of 3 verses of 7 + 7 syllables.

Y. 53 *Gāθā Vahištōištī* (from the beginning of *Y.* 53, *vahištā ištiš*): stanzas of 4 verses, 2 of 7 + 5 syllables followed by 2 of 7 + 7 + 5 syllables.

We see that the *Yasna Haptaŋhāiti* or "Yasna of the seven chapters" is inserted in the *Gāθās* properly speaking. It is written in Gathic, but in prose. On the other hand, *Y.* 42, an invocation of the elements, and *Y.* 52, a praise of Aṣ̌i, are texts in the later language that have been secondarily inserted among the *Gāθās*.

Y. 54 gives the text of the prayer *ā airiiə̄mā išiiō* already mentioned in *Y.* 27.

Y. 55 praises the *Gāθās* and the *Staota Yesniia*.

Y. 56 appeals to the deities for attention.

Y. 57 constitutes the *Srōš Yašt*, a hymn to Sraoša, the genius of religious discipline. Its formulas are closely related to and partly borrowed from *Yašt* 10 to Miθra. (See K. Dehghan, *Der Awesta-Text Srōš Yašt.*)

Y. 58 praises the "prayer" (*nəmah*).

Y. 59 repeats some of the invocations of *Y.* 17 and 26.

Y. 60 contains a series of blessings of the abode of the just.

Y. 61 extols the anti-demoniacal power of the *Ahuna Vairiia*, *Aṣ̌əm vohū*, *Yeŋ́he hātąm*, and *Āfrīnagān dahmān*.

Y. 62 is a praise of the fire (*Ātaxš Niyāyišn*).

Y. 63-69 constitute the prayers which accompany the ritual of the waters (*Āb Zōhr*): praise in 65, offering in 66-67, invocation in 68-69 (they are invoked under the name, among others, of *ahurānīs* "Ahura's wives").

Y. 70-72 again contain a series of invocations.

II. The *Visprad* (*Vr.*) "(prayer to) all the patrons" (from Av. *vīspe ratauuō*), composed of twenty-four sections (*kardag*), supplements the *Yasna* with invocations and appeals to the patrons (*ratu-*).

III. The *K̲orda Avesta* "little Avesta" contains the prayers which are recited by the faithful on everyday occasions as opposed to those which are recited by the priest. The name of this book is not mentioned in the Pahlavi literature and therefore it is difficult to estimate its age. It comprises:

1. Five introductory chapters (Intr.), quotations from different passages of the *Yasna*.

2. Five *Niyāyišns* (*Ny.*) "praises," addressed to the sun, Miθra, the moon, the waters, and the fire, composed of excerpts from the corresponding *Yašts*, the last from *Y.* 62. (See Z. Taraf, *Der Awesta-Text Niyāyiš.*)

3. Five *Gāhs* (*G.*) "moments of the day," addressed to the genii presiding over the great divisions of the day: *hāuuana-* "the morning," *rapiθβina-* "midday," *uzaiieirina-* "the afternoon," *aiβisrūθrima-* "the night, from midnight up to the dawn."

4. Four *Āfrinagāns* (*A.*) "blessings" which are recited respectively in honor of the dead, at the five epagomenal days which end the year, at the six feasts of seasons, at the beginning or the end of summer.

IV. The *Sīrōza* "thirty days" enumerates the deities who patronize the thirty days of the month. It exists in two forms, the "little" *Sīrōza* and the "great" *Sīrōza*. The former consists in incomplete formulas containing only the name of the deity and his epithets in the genitive (e.g., *ahurahe mazdå raēuuatō xᵛarənaŋhuṇtō*), whereas the latter contains independent sentences in which *yazamaide* "we sacrifice to" governs the same formulas in the accusative (*ahurəm mazdąm raēuuaṇtəm xᵛarənaŋhuṇtəm yazamaide*).

V. The *Yašts* (*Yt.*) are hymns addressed to the principal deities. There are twenty-one *Yašts*, unequal in size and interest; among them we find those texts which in addition to the *Gāθās* provide the most information about the origins of Mazdaism and its doctrine at the time of its early development. All of them are written in what appears to be prose, but which, for a large part, may originally have been a (basically) eight-syllable verse, oscillating between four and thirteen syllables, and most often between seven and nine (Gropp, *Wiederholungsformen*, p. 137; G. Lazard, "La métrique de l'Avesta récent," in *Orientalia J. Duchesne-Guillemin Emerito Oblata*, Acta Iranica 23, Leiden, 1984, pp. 284-300).

Yt. 1-4 are mediocre, meaningless texts, composed in incoherent language; they probably result from a very late expansion of the *Yašt* collection. *Yt.* 1 (33 verses) to Ahura Mazdā; *Yt.* 2 (15 verses) to the *Aməṣ̌a Spəṇtas*; *Yt.* 3 (19 verses) to Aṣ̌a; *Yt.* 4 (11 verses) to Hauruuatāt.

Yt. 5 (132 verses) is an important hymn addressed to Arəduuī Sūrā Anāhitā, goddess of the waters. It falls into five principal sections: verses 1-5, praise of the goddess; 16-83, enumeration of the mythical sacrificers with allusions to their feats; 84-96, Anāhitā informs Zaraθuštra of her sacrificial requirements; 97-118, enumeration of the sacrificers of the circle of the prophet: Zaraθuštra, Vištāspa, Zairiuuairi; 119-32, description of the goddess as a beautiful noble maiden.

Yt. 6 (7 verses) to the sun.

Yt. 7 (7 verses) to the moon.

Yt. 8 (62 verses) to Tištriia, the star which controls the mechanism of rain, relates the myth of his fight against Apaoša, demon of drought.

Yt. 9 (33 verses) where Druuāspā, the goddess who ensures the health of horses, is extolled with formulas borrowed from *Yt.* 5, enumerating the prestigious sacrificers of the past.

Yt. 10 (145 verses) to Miθra, who is described as the strict guardian of the contract, patron of warriors, master of the entirety of the Iranian countries, inciter of the dawn, and god of the diurnal heaven, which he travels through in a chariot surrounded by an escort of attendants. (See I. Gershevitch, *The Avestan Hymn to Mithra.*)

Yt. 11 (23 verses) and *Yt.* 12 (47 verses) are dedicated to Sraoša and Rašnu, attendants of Miθra.

Yt. 13 (158 verses) to the *frauuašis* falls into two parts. Verses 1-84 praise the *frauuašis* by presenting them as agents of the creation who witnessed its early moments and saw then to its permanence (these passages constitute the only known elements of ancient Mazdean cosmogony), as protectors in battle and distributers of water to their fatherland. The second part enumerates in seven groups the *frauuašis* of the heroes of Mazdaism from Gaiiō Marətan to Saošiiaṇt: verses 85-95, *frauuašis* of the deities, the first man Gaiiō Marətan, the prophet Zaraθuštra, and his first disciple Maiδiiōi.mā̊ŋha; 96-100, *frauuašis* of the early Zoroastrians (circle of Vištāspa); 111-117, *frauuašis* of the heroes of Pouruδāxšti's circle; 118-128, *frauuašis* of the heroes of the non-Iranian countries; 129, *frauuaši* of Saošiiaṇt Astuuaṱ.ərəta; 130-138, *frauuašis* of the mythical heroes; 139-142, *frauuašis* of the holy women of Mazdaism. (See J. Kellens, *Fravardīn Yašt.*)

Yt. 14 (64 verses) to Vərəθraγna relates the ten incarnations in which the deity appeared to Zaraθuštra (1-28); enumerates the powers that he bestows on Zaraθuštra in return for his cult (31-33); describes the magic of a particular feather which makes invulnerable in fighting (34-46); and ends with a praise (47-64).

Yt. 15 (58 verses), in spite of its title *Rām Yašt* (hymn to Rāma X̌āstra, attendant of Miθra), is dedicated to Vāiiu, god of the stormy wind, who belongs partly to good, partly to evil. The hymn falls into two clearly distinct parts: 1-41 draw upon the formulas of *Yt.* 5 which enumerate the famous sacrificers; 42-58 list the names of the deity, most of which are very obscure.

Yt. 16 (20 verses), *Dēn Yašt*, praises Čistā, the wisdom which impregnates the Mazdean religion.

Yt. 17 (62 verses) to Aši Vaŋ̌hī "good fortune:" 1-22 describe the benefits the goddess lavishes on pious houses; 23-52 enumerate her sacrificers in the manner of *Yt.* 5; 53-62 describe those who are to be excluded from her cult.

Yt. 18 (9 verses), *Aštād Yašt*, praises the *Airiiana x̌arənah* "Aryan Glory."

Yt. 19 (97 verses) justifies its title *Zamyād Yašt* "hymn to the earth" with the first eight verses, which relate the creation of the mountains. The rest is a hymn to the *x̌arənah*: it enumerates its holders, tells how Yima lost it, describes the fight of the two spirits for its possession, and announces the use the final savior will make of it.

Yt. 20 (3 verses) to Haoma is a short excerpt from *Y.* 9-11.

Yt. 21 (2 verses) is a brief praise of the star Vanaṇt.

Some scholars have tried to discern distinct strata in the material of the *Yašts*. S. Wikander endeavored to define material proper to the clan of the Friiāna characterized by dialectal peculiarities and the pre-eminence of the cults of Vāiiu and Anāhitā. His conclusions were adopted by S. Hartmann, who reinforced them by adding his views concerning a tradition impregnated with Zurvanism, and by J. Kellens (*Études mithriaques*), who thinks a distinction can be established between the *Yašts* of the type of *Yt.* 10, which are essentially moral and written in the first person present tense (invocation containing *yazamaide*), and those of the type of *Yt.* 5, which are epico-historical and written in the third person preterite (invocation containing *yazata*). This distinction, if correct, reveals a duality of tradition in primitive Mazdaism based on deep divergences of formulary.

VI. The *Vidēvdād* (*V.*) "law of breaking off with the demons" (see Benveniste, "Que signifie *Vidēvdāt*?" pp. 71f.) comprises twenty-two chapters, the first two explaining the origin of the book, the rest containing diverse rules and regulations, with the exception of chap. 19 which contains the temptation of Zaraθuštra.

Chap. 1 is a prelude explaining the successive creation by Ahura Mazdā of the different provinces of Iran, each of which Aŋra Mainiiu, in response, afflicts with a specific countercreation or adversary.

Chap. 2 relates how Yima refused to accept the Mazdean law and to transmit it to men, confining himself to ensuring their immortality and their prosperity. He completes his mission by building an artificial cave (*vara*) as a refuge from the great winter that was to ravage the world.

Chap. 3 contains rules concerning the earth, its working, and injunctions not to defile it.

Chap. 4 contains rules concerning contracts and attacks on people

Chap. 5-12 deal with the impurity due to contact with a corpse and the purifications which are prescribed in this case.

Chap. 13 praises the dog.

Chap. 14 concerns the crime of killing an otter.

Chap. 15 deals with the five sins which deserve death (to make apostate, to give a dog noxious food, to cause the death of a pregnant bitch, to have sexual intercourse with a menstruating or a pregnant woman); a man's obligations to a natural child and its mother; the cares owed to a pregnant bitch; and the breeding of dogs.

Chap. 16 concerns the impurity of women during menstruation.

Chap. 17 describes what one should do with cut hair and nails.

Chap. 18 deals with the unworthy priest, the saintliness of the cock, the four sins which make the Druj "deceit" pregnant with a progeny of demons (to refuse to give alms to one of the faithful, to urinate standing, to have a nocturnal emission, not to wear the sacred belt and shirt after the age of fifteen); the evil caused by the prostitute; and the atonement for the sin of having sexual intercourse with a menstruating woman.

Chap. 19 relates the temptation of Zaraθuštra, who, urged by Aŋra Mainiiu to forswear the good religion, turns towards Ahura Mazdā and solicits him for his teaching.

Chaps. 20-22 expound a trifunctional conception of medicine: treatment by means of incantation, with a knife, or with plants.

The Avestan texts described above have reached us in a version that is, if not complete, at least continuous. They were edited by Geldner in his monumental edition of the Avesta. The entire Avesta, including all the fragments known to him, was translated into French by James Darmesteter. Fritz Wolff, basing himself on the dictionary by Bartholomae, translated into German Geldner's corpus, with the exception of the *Gāθās*, which had been translated by Bartholomae himself. As a rule, Wolff is more reliable than Darmesteter, whose translation follows the Pahlavi version. Darmesteter is sometimes superior in his understanding of the *Vidēvdād*.

VII. The fragments. In addition to the complete texts, more than twenty groups of fragments are known (cf. *AirWb.*, pp. viii-x).

1. *Nīrangistān* (*N.*) "precepts concerning the organization of the cult." The first eighteen fragments comprise the *Ēhrbadistān* "precepts concerning the priest's activity." (Ed. see bibliography.)

2. *Pursišnīhā* (*P.*) "questions" (Darmesteter's "Fragments Tahmuras") is a small Mazdean catechism. (Ed. Humbach and JamaspAsa.)

3. *Aogəmadaēčā* (*Aog.*) lit. "we accept," is a treatise on death. (Ed. Geiger; JamaspAsa.)

4. *Hādōxt Nask* (*H.*) "book of the scriptures" is made up of two lengthy fragments, the first celebrating the prayer *Ašəm vohū*, the second relating the soul's destiny after death. (Ed. Haug and West.)

5. *Frahang ī ōīm* (*FiO.*), Avestan-Pahlavi lexicon. (Ed. Reichelt; Klingenschmitt.)

6. *Āfrīn ī Zardušt* (*Az.*), a blessing which was pronounced, according to the legend, by Zaraθuštra upon King Vištāspa. (Ed. Westergaard, *Zendavesta*, pp. 300-01, *Yt.* 23.)

7. *Vištāsp Yašt* (*Vyt.*), a medley of quotations from the *Vidēvdād*. (Ed. Westergaard, pp. 302-17, *Yt.* 24).

8. *Nīrang ī Ātaxš* (*Any.*) "precepts concerning the fire cult." (Ed. Westergaard, p. 317.)

9. *Vaēθā Nask* (*Vn.*) concerns some points of law and religious ethics. (Ed. K. M. JamaspAsa and H. Humbach, Wiesbaden, 1969.)

10. Westergaard's fragments (*FrW.*). (*Zendavesta*, pp. 331-34.)

11. Darmesteter's fragments (*FrD.*). (*Zend-Avesta* III, pp. 149-53; frag. no. 3 restored by Hoffmann, *Aufsätze* I, pp. 221-27.)

12. Geldner's fragments (*FrG.*). ("Yasna 36," pp. 587-88 n. 6; *AirWb.*, cols. 329 s.v. *āparō*, 1071 s.v. *nəmrōnāi*, 1697 s.v. *zimata.*)

13. Barthélémy's fragments (*FrB.*). (*Gujastak Abalish*, Paris, 1887, pp. 55-56; *AirWb.*, col. 1168 s.v. *mānō.*)

14. West's fragments (*SlZ.*). (J. C. Tavadia, *Šāyast-nē-šāyast*, Hamburg, 1930, chap. 8.22; F. M. P. Kotwal, *The Supplementary Texts to the Šāyest nē-šāyest*, Copenhagen, 1969, pp. 116-18; SBE V, pp. 307, 338, 366; cf. *AirWb.*, col. 579 s.v. *čaθruš.*)

15. Sanjana's fragments (*DkB.*). (*Dēnkard* III, p. 131; ed. Madan, pp. 113-14; ed. Dresden, p. 749; see *AirWb.*, col. 1125 s.v. ²*man-*, end of article.)

16. Fragment from the *Aogəmadaēčā* (*Aog.* 81 D; cf. *AirWb.*, cols. 221-22 s.v. *a-srāuayat̰.gāθā-*.)

17. Fragments Gš. (P. B. Sanjana, *Ganjesháyagán*, Bombay, 1885, pp. 19f.)

18. Fragments from the *Bundahišn* (pp. 224-25; tr. 34.15, pp. 288-89; *AirWb.*, col. 549 s.v. *xšapan*, end of article.

19. Fragments from the *Vidēvdād Sāda* (*Vs.*). (H. Brockhaus, *Vendidad Sade*, Leipzig, 1850.)

20. Fragments which are contained in the Pahlavi or Sanskrit translations of Avestan texts. (Cf. Darmesteter, *Zend-Avesta* III, pp. 29-52.)

21. Fragments in the *Vizīrkard ī Dēnīg* (*Vd.*) (Ed. Bartholomae, *Indogermanische Forschungen* 12, 1901, pp. 93-101.)

22. Anklesaria's fragments (*FrA.*). (Ed. G. Klingenschmitt, *Münchener Studien zur Sprachwissenschaft* 29, 1971, pp. 111-74.)

A few more fragments are listed by Schlerath, *Avesta-Wörterbuch*, pp. viii-ix, 242-56; see also A. V. W. Jackson, *Index Verborum of the Fragments of the Avesta*, New York, 1901, repr. 1965.

Careful analysis and sifting of the Pahlavi books would no doubt reveal much more material quoted from the Sasanian *Avesta and Zand*. These books contain a large number of explicit quotations from various *nasks*, but the summary in the *Dēnkard* allows us to approximately identify much other material as well. Thus, much of the *Spand* was probably incorporated into book seven of the *Dēnkard* (the legend of Zaraθuštra, see, e.g., M. Molé's edition pp. 5-6, and J. de Menasce, *Le Dēnkart*, p. 64) and in the description of hell in the *Ardā Wirāz-nāmag* (see Darmesteter, *Zend-Avesta* III, pp. xiif.). The *Bundahišn* probably contains material from the *Čihrdād* and *Dāmdād* (see Darmesteter, ibid., pp. xivf.).

The manuscripts of the Avesta. The entirety of the known handwritten tradition was the subject of a definitive analysis by Geldner in the *Prolegomena* to his critical edition, where the names of the manuscript families indicate the text (*Yasna, Visprad*, etc.), their origin (Indian or Iranian), and whether they contain a Pahlavi or Sanskrit translation. The manuscripts that contain only the Avestan text are called *sāda* "pure." The *Vidēvdād sāda* family contains the entirety of the texts recited during the liturgy of the *visprad*, i.e., the *Yasna* enlarged by the formulas of the *Visprad* and followed by the *Vidēvdād*.

(a) The *Yasna* is the book for which we have at our disposal the largest number of independent testimonies. We distinguish six manuscript families:

1. The Sanskrit *Yasna*: S1 and J3, old undated manuscripts; P11 and K6 derive from J3.

2. The Indian Pahlavi *Yasna*: J2 and K5, both dated 1323; B3, M1, and L17 derive from K5.

3. The Iranian Pahlavi *Yasna*: Mf1 (1741), Pt4 (1780), and Mf4, which Geldner does not quote (facsimile published K. M. JamaspAsa, 1976). F11 and Br2 derive from Mf1.

4. The Iranian *Vidēvdād sāda*: Mf2 (1618), Jpl (1638), and K4 (1723).

5-6. The Indian *Vidēvdād sāda* (K10, L1, etc.) and the *Yasna sāda* (C1, H1, etc.) contain few important readings.

(b) The *Visprad* rests on two manuscript families:

1. All the manuscripts of the Pahlavi *Visprad* (M6, J15, M4, Pt4) derive from K7a (1278).

2. Those of the *Visprad sāda* (H1, J8, Jm4, K11, L27, Pt3, P12) derive from a common ancestor.

(c) The *K̲orda Avesta* is transmitted in two manuscript families:

1. The ancestor of the Indian *K̲orda Avesta* is Jm4 (1352). J9 and H2 contain a Sanskrit translation.

2. The Iranian *K̲orda Avesta*, which is more recent, is divided into three families: (i) F2, Mf3, K36, K38; (ii) K18a, K37, W1, W3, Pd, Kh2, L25, Lb5, Lb6; (iii) K13, H5, and M12 (modern codex written in Arabic alphabet).

(d) Most of the *Yašts* are transmitted in a small number of manuscripts.

1. The most important manuscript if F1 (Nausari 1591). Pt1 and E1 are copies of F1; P13, K19, L18 derive from Pt1, and K15, K16, H3 from E1.

2. The Pt1 family gives a version that is independent of F1 in *Yt*. 4, 9, and 14, but agrees with E1 in *Yt*. 1, 2, 3, and 16.

3. J10, a bad modern manuscript, contains the only independent testimony for the entire *Yašt* collection. In this manuscript a source anterior to F1 shows through. D represents this tradition for *Yt*. 19.

4. The *K̲orda Avesta* transmits independently the text of some *Yašts*; both branches contain *Yt*. 1, 2, 3, 9, 14 (J9 gives the Sanskrit translation of *Yt*. 1, 11); the Indian branch also contains *Yt*. 4, 6, 7, 12, 16, 18; the Iranian branch also *Yt*. 13.

5. The modern manuscript H4 (1820), which probably influenced K40, gives an independent version of *Yt*. 10 and appears to agree with the now unknown manuscript Jm2 that Darmesteter used.

(e) The *Vidēvdād* is transmitted in three manuscript families:

1. The (Indian) Pahlavi *Vidēvdād* is represented by two incomplete ancient manuscripts: L4 (1323), of which Pt2 is a copy, and K1 (1324), from which M13 (1594), B1, K3a, K3b, P2, and M3 derive.

2. The Iranian *Vidēvdād sāda* (see the *Yasna*).

3. The Indian *Vidēvdād sāda* is divided into two branches, that of Br1, L2, and K10, a collection of manuscripts from the eighteenth century, and that of L1, M2, O2, B2, and P1, which are all of poorer quality.

History of Avestan studies. A specimen of the *Vidēvdād sāda*, which was given to a merchant by the Parsis of Surat, reached the Bodleian Library in Oxford in 1723: the West thus learned that Zoroaster's book was not lost. It had only to be collected and interpreted, which could be done only with the cooperation of the Parsi priesthood. This was the work of Anquetil-Duperron. He went to India in 1755, succeeded in overcoming the reticence of the Parsis, and on 15 May 1762, deposited the 180 Avestan, Pahlavi, Persian, and Sanskrit manuscripts in the King's library. He then began to analyze the documents he had gathered and prepared a translation of the Avesta, which was published in 1771. The following years saw no progress in Avestan studies, mainly on account of the long polemics concerning the authenticity of the text brought back by Anquetil, though already in 1776-1777 there appeared a German translation of Anquetil's works. Also, the notion was entertained for a long time by William Jones, Paulin de Saint-Barthélemy, and others, that the Avesta was written in a Sanskrit or Prakrit dialect. The works of Emmanuel Rask and Eugène Burnouf not only established an adequate method for a philological approach to the text, but also proved conclusively that though Avestan was a language with an Iranian phonetic system, it was not the direct ancestor of Modern Persian. The deciphering of the Old Persian inscriptions finally proved, by revealing an Iranian language closely akin to Avestan and dating from the Achaemenid period, that the language of the Avesta was an antique representative of an independent Indo-European language, which was however more closely related to Indian than to any other branch of the family. The publication of a complete edition of the Avesta, by Nicolas Westergaard, a follower of Rask, concluded this first stage of the research.

Avestan studies were particularly active during the second half of the nineteenth century and became involved in a fierce polemic between the "traditional" school represented by scholars such as Spiegel and Darmesteter, who considered that the Avesta could only become clear with the help of the native Pahlavi commentary, and the "Vedic" school, of which Karl-Friedrich Geldner was the most famous representative. The latter school, sceptical about the commentary, which in its view was no more reliable a guide to the Avesta than was Sāyaṇa's commentary to the Rigveda was convinced that the best approach to the true meaning of the Avesta was the etymological one, for which Vedic provided abundant material. During the last years of the century the discord was, if not dissipated, at least mollified: The representatives of both schools became aware that their respective methods were legitimate and dangerous at the same time, and, above all, they had learned to rate the Pahlavi commentary at its true value. This estimate of the Pahlavi commentary has not changed since that time

(Klingenschmitt, "Die Pahlavi-Version"); it is essential for the understanding of the *Vidēvdād* and some fragments such as the *Nīrangistān*, but absolutely devoid of any value as to the *Yasna* and texts such as the *Vištāsp Yašt*. The scholars of that generation gave Avestan philology its great monuments, which still have not been superseded. We must mention Darmesteter's translation (1892-1893), Geldner's monumental critical edition (1889-1896), which was based upon the analysis of more than 120 manuscripts, the grammatical description of Avestan in the *Grundriss der Iranischen Philologie* (1896), and the *Altiranisches Wörterbuch* (1904) by Christian Bartholomae.

The year 1902 opened a new period in the history of Avestan philology. That year, at the congress in Hamburg, Friedrich-Carl Andreas stated the hypothesis that the Avesta, as it is transmitted to us, was a clumsy transcription in a differentiated phonetic alphabet of a text—the Arsacid archetype—that had been recorded in a script that omitted vowels and confused some consonants (see Andreas iii). From this he logically concluded that the only adequate philological approach to rediscover the authentic aspect of a form consisted in imagining the manner in which it was written in the Arsacid archetype. For more than forty years this principle of graphic restoration was universally applied. It was not until counterarguments were brought to light during World War II by Henning ("Disintegration"), Bailey (*Zoroastrian Problems*), and Morgenstierne ("Orthography and Sound-system") that confidence in Andreas' principle was lost. But harm had been done. Avestan philology had gone off on a wrong track precisely during the important fifty years in which the Vedic, Greek, or Latin philologies accomplished progress of prime importance and produced reference books of paramount value. Only two important works were published during that period: *Les infinitifs avestiques* by Émile Benveniste (Paris, 1935) and *Les composés de l'Avesta* by Jacques Duchesne-Guillemin (Paris and Liège, 1936), works which achieved results of value because their authors, while claiming to apply Andreas' methods, only rarely did so.

Progress in Avestan studies from 1902 until about 1965 was confined largely to the elucidation of particular facts, almost always from the etymological point of view. Two approaches were available: etymology "from above," from Vedic and Indo-European, and etymology "from below," from Middle Iranian dialects that became known in the course of this century. The two approaches did not give scope for a confrontation, as had happened in the nineteenth century, because their fields of research were not the same. Comparison with Vedic and Indo-European allows us to explain morphological facts and is more fruitful in the analysis of the most ancient parts of the Avesta, while the Middle Iranian languages help clarify the phonetic and semantic aspects. Two outstanding works, both published in 1959, illustrate this point in a striking way. In his new translation of the *Gāθās*, H. Humbach exploited to the full the "Vedic" approach (it was used later by S. Insler in his translation of the *Gāθās*). On the other hand, I. Gershevitch, in his edition of *Yt.* 10, shed much light on the text by comparing the Middle Iranian languages.

Over the last twenty years K. Hoffmann has been in the center of the renewal of an adequate philological approach to the *Avesta*. His critical investigations have resulted in his delineating convincingly the history of the formation of the canon and in his establishing an important point of methodology, namely that the extant Avesta is not that of the authors but that of the Sasanian diascevasts. Thus the primary task of the philologist is to determine exactly what was written in the canon that the Sasanian priesthood collected in the course of the fourth century. The only sound way to answer this question is to combine the traditional methods of philological analysis with the handling of a linguistic postulate. The different readings must be evaluated on the basis of criticism of the manuscripts, and the reading which must be considered as genuine in the sense that it belonged to the Sasanian archetype must be confronted with the linguistic postulate, i.e., with the form which comparison with Vedic leads one to expect. If both agree, we can consider it as a proof.

Bibliography: For the history of the Avesta see Darmesteter, *Zend-Avesta* III, pp. xx-xxxvi, and especially the comprehensive discussion by H. W. Bailey, *Zoroastrian Problems in the Ninth-Century Books*, Oxford, 1943, pp. 149-76 (chapter on *patvand*), which contains the relevant Mazdean texts with translations. A short outline, with references, can be found in J. Duchesne-Guillemin, *La religion de l'Iran ancien*, Paris, 1962, pp. 40-46. Some of the Pahlavi texts containing the history of the sacred books are conveniently gathered in H. S. Nyberg, *A Manual of Pahlavi* I, Wiesbaden, 1964, pp. 107-12 (*Ardā Wirāz-nāmag; Dēnkard*, books 3, 4, 5). On the Avesta in Persis, see the suggestions by K. Hoffmann in J. Harmatta, ed., *Prolegomena to the Sources on the History of Pre-Islamic Central Asia*, Budapest, 1979, pp. 89-93. On the *Zand*, see, e.g., M. Boyce in *HO* I/IV: *Iranistik* 2, *Literatur*, Leiden and Cologne, 1968, pp. 33-38. J. C. Tavadia, *Die mittelpersische Sprache und Literatur der Zarathustrier*, Leipzig, 1956, pp. 13-35. Also Bailey, *Zoroastrian Problems*, pp. 151-60. J. de Menasce, *Une encyclopédie mazdéenne. Le Dēnkart*, Paris, 1958, pp. 64-67.

The analysis of the Sasanian *Avesta and Zand* in the *Dēnkard* is summarized in Darmesteter, *Zend-Avesta* III, pp. vii-xix. Complete editions and translations: N. L. Westergaard, *Zendavesta or the Religious Book of the Zoroastrians* I, Copenhagen, 1852-1854. K. F. Geldner, *Avesta, the Sacred Books of the Parsis*, Stuttgart, 1889-1896. J. Darmesteter, *Le Zend-Avesta* I-III, Paris, 1892-1893. F. Wolff, *Avesta, die heiligen Bücher der Parsen*, Leipzig, 1910 (except the *Gāθās*, see below). Part editions and translations (select titles): H. Reichelt, *Avesta Reader*, Strassburg, 1911, repr. Berlin, 1968 (90 pages of texts with commentary and glossary). K. Barr, tr., *Avesta*,

Copenhagen, 1954 (select translations in Danish). The *Gāθās*: Chr. Bartholomae, *Die Gatha's des Awesta. Zarathushtra's Verspredigten*, Strassburg, 1905. H. Humbach, *Die Gathas des Zarathustra* I-II, Heidelberg, 1959 (a revised, English translation, including all the Old-Avestan texts, is forthcoming). S. Insler, *The Gāthās of Zarathustra*, Tehran and Liège, 1975. *Yasna Haptaŋhāiti*: ed. J. Narten, Wiesbaden, 1986. (Also included in H. Humbach's revised translation of the *Gāθās*). On the sacred prayers, see most recently H. Humbach, "A Western Approach to Zarathustra," *Journal of the K. R. Cama Oriental Institute* 51, 1984, pp. 48-54 (*Ašəm Vohū*), and idem, in *Orientalia J. Duchesne-Guillemin Emerito Oblata*, Acta Iranica 23, Leiden, 1984, pp. 225-41 (*Ahuna vairiia*); see also Ahunvar; Airyaman Išya; Ašəm Vohū. The *Yasna*: J. M. Unvala, *Neryosangh's Sanskrit Version of the Hōm Yašt (Yasn IX-XI)*, Vienna, 1924 (Avestan, Pahlavi, Sanskrit, with Sanskrit glossary, Pahlavi index). K. Dehghan, *Der Awesta-Text Srōš Yašt (Yasna 57) mit Pahlavi- und Sanskritübersetzung*, Munich, 1982. The *K̠orda Avesta*, the *Niyāyišns*: M. N. Dhalla, *The Nyaishes or Zoroastrian Litanies*, New York, 1965 (Avestan, Pahlavi, Sanskrit, Persian, Gujarati). Z. Taraf, *Der Awesta-Text Niyāyiš mit Pahlavi-und Sanskritübersetzung*, Munich, 1981. The *Yašts*: H. Lommel, *Die Yäst's des Awesta*, Göttingen and Leipzig, 1927. I. Gershevitch, *The Avestan Hymn to Mithra*, Cambridge, 1959. J. Kellens, *Fravardīn Yašt (1-70)*, Wiesbaden, 1975. The *Vidēvdād*: A. Christensen, *Le premier chapitre du Vendidad et l'histoire primitive des tribus iraniennes*, Copenhagen, 1943. *Nīrangistān*: Darmesteter, *Zend-Avesta* III, pp. 78-148. D. P. Sanjana, *Nirangistan. A Photozincographed Facsimile*, Bombay, 1895. A. Waag, *Nirangistan. Der Awestatraktat über die rituellen Vorschriften*, Leipzig, 1941. S. J. Bulsara, *Aêrpatastân and Nîrangastân*, Bombay, 1915. (A new, critical edition and translation of *Nīrangistān* are badly needed.) The *Pursišnīhā*: Darmesteter, *Zend-Avesta* III, pp. 53-77. K. M. JamaspAsa and H. Humbach, *Pursišnīhā. A Zoroastrian Catechism* I-II, Wiesbaden, 1971. The *Aogəmadaēčā*: ed., tr. W. Geiger, Leipzig and Erlangen, 1878, repr. Hildesheim, 1971. K. M. JamaspAsa, *Aogəmadaēčā. A Zoroastrian Liturgy*, Vienna, 1982. The *Hādōxt Nask*: Westergaard, *Zendavesta*, pp. 294ff., *Yt*. 21-22. M. Haug and E. W. West, *The Book of Arda Viraf*, Bombay and London, 1872, repr. Amsterdam, 1971, Appendix II: *The Three Fargards of the Hâdôkht Nask*.., ed. M. Haug, pp. 301-16 (Avestan and Pahlavi). The *Frahang ī Ōīm*: Darmesteter, *Zend-Avesta* III, pp. 13-28. H. Reichelt, "Der Frahang i oīm (Zand-Pahlavi Glossary)," *WZKM* 14, 1900, pp. 177-213; 15, 1901, pp. 117-86. G. Klingenschmitt, *Farhang-i ōīm, Edition und Kommentar*, Erlangen, 1968 (unpublished). For the remaining fragments see bibliography in the text. Pahlavi versions: B. N. Dhabhar, *Pahlavi Yasna and Visperad*, Bombay, 1949 (text, glossary, and index). Idem, *Zand-i Khūrtak Avistāk*, Bombay, 1927 (text); tr., Bombay, 1963. H. J. Jamasp, *Vendidâd* I: *The Texts*, II: *Glossarial Index*, Bombay, 1907 (Avestan and Pahlavi). D. D. Kapadia, tr., *Pahlavi Vendidâd*, 1949. Idem, *Glossary of Pahlavi Vendidad*, Bombay, 1953. Sanskrit versions: F. Spiegel, *Neriosengh's Sanskrituebersetzung des Yaçna*. Leipzig, 1861. Sh. D. Barucha, *Collected Sanskrit Writings of the Parsis* II: *Ijisni (Yasna)*, Bombay, 1910. See also Boyce, *HO*, pp. 33-38. Dictionary: Chr. Bartholomae, *Altiranisches Wörterbuch*, Strassburg, 1904, with additions and corrections in *Zum Altiranischen Wörterbuch*, Strassburg, 1906. A complete bibliography of editions and studies up to about 1965 is in B. Schlerath, *Awesta-Wörterbuch. Vorarbeiten* I, Wiesbaden, 1968. A very useful survey of Avestan studies in the twentieth century is J. Duchesne-Guillemin, *Kratylos* 7, 1962, pp. 1-44, continued by J. Kellens, ibid., 16, 1971, pp. 1-30, and 18, 1973, pp. 1-5.

On the manuscript tradition, see the fundamental remarks by K. Hoffmann in I. Gershevitch and M. Boyce, eds., *W. B. Henning Memorial Volume*, London, 1970, pp. 187-200, esp. pp. 188f. n. 2 (*Aufsätze zur Indoiranistik* I, Wiesbaden, 1975, pp. 274-87). Further K. Hoffmann, "Zur Yasna-Überlieferung," *MSS* 26, 1969, pp. 35-38 (*Aufsätze zur Indoiranistik* II, Wiesbaden, 1976, pp. 513-15). H. Humbach, "Beobachtungen zur Überlieferungsgeschichte des Awesta," *MSS* 31, 1973, pp. 109-22.

On the history of Avestan studies, see the comprehensive survey up to about 1960 in J. Duchesne-Guillemin, *La religion de l'Iran ancien*, pp. 384-99; and his and Kellens' articles in *Kratylos* (see above).

Select studies: W. Belardi, "Il nome dell' Avesta: alla ricerca di un significato perduto," *Accademia nazionale dei Lincei*, Serie VIII, 24, Roma, 1979, pp. 251-74 E. Benveniste, "Que signifie *Vidēvāt*?" in I. Gershevitch and M. Boyce, eds., *W. B. Henning Memorial Volume*, London, 1970, pp. 37-42. G. Gnoli, *Ricerche storiche sul Sīstān antico*, Roma, 1967. G. Gropp, *Wiederholungsformen im Jung-Awesta*, Hamburg, 1967. S. S. Hartmann. *Gayōmart. Étude sur le syncrétisme dans l'Iran ancien*, Uppsala, 1953. W. B. Henning, "The Disintegration of the Avestic Studies," *TPS*, 1942, pp. 40-56 (*Selected Papers* II, Acta Iranica 16, Tehran and Liège, 1977, pp. 151-67). K. Hoffmann, *Aufsätze zur Indoiranistik* I, Wiesbaden, 1975; II, Wiesbaden, 1976. H. Humbach, "Al-Biruni und die Sieben Strome (*sic*) des Awesta," *Bulletin of the Iranian Culture Foundation* 1/2, 1973, pp. 47-52. J. Kellens, "Caractères differentiels du Mihr Yast," in J. R. Hinnells, ed., *Études Mithriaques*, Tehran and Liège, 1978, pp. 261-70. G. Klingenschmitt, "Die Pahlavi-Version des Avesta," *ZDMG*, Suppl. I, Wiesbaden, 1969, pp. 993-97. M. Molé, *La légende de Zoroastre d'après les livres pehlevis*, Paris, 1967. G. Morgenstierne, *Report on a Linguistic Mission to Afghanistan*, Oslo, 1926. Idem, "Orthography and

Sound-system of the Avesta," *NTS* 12, 1942 [1944], pp. 30-82. H. S. Nyberg, *Die Religionen des alten Iran*, tr. H. H. Schaeder, Osnabruck, 1938, repr. 1966. P. Tedesco, "Dialektologie der westiranischen Turfantexte," *Le Monde Oriental* 15, Uppsala, 1921, pp. 184-258. S. Wikander, *Vayu* I, Lund, 1941. Idem, *Feuerpriester in Kleinasien und Iran*, Lund, 1946.

(J. Kellens)

AVESTAN GEOGRAPHY. It is impossible to attribute a precise geographical location to the language of the Avesta. The Avestan texts, however, provide some useful pointers, while their comparison with Old Persian inscriptions offer further evidence: Geographical references in the Avesta are limited to the regions on the eastern Iranian plateau and on the Indo-Iranian border. Moreover, the Old Persian inscriptions are written in a language different from that of the Avesta. With the exception of an important study by P. Tedesco ("Dialektologie der westiranischen Turfantexte," *Le Monde Oriental* 15, 1921, pp. 184ff.), who advances the theory of an "Avestan homeland" in northwestern Iran, Iranian scholars of the twentieth century have looked increasingly to eastern Iran for the origins of the Avestan language (e.g., G. Morgenstierne, *Report on a Linguistic Mission to Afghanistan*, Oslo, 1926, pp. 29f.; W. B. Henning, *Zoroaster, Politician or Witch-doctor?*, London, 1951, pp. 44f.; K. Hoffmann, "Altiranisch," in *HO* I, 4: *Iranistik* 1, *Linguistik*, Leiden and Cologne, 1958, p. 6); and today there is general agreement that the area in question was in eastern Iran—a fact that emerges clearly from every passage in the Avesta that sheds any light on its historical and geographical background. Many scholars have maintained (see, for example, D. Monchi-Zadeh, *Topographisch-historische Studien zum iranischen Nationalepos*, Wiesbaden, 1975, p. 126) that the Avesta mentions a place in the so-called Raghian Media, Raγa (*Vd.* 1.15; *Y.* 19.18), but there is no foundation (G. Gnoli, *Zoroaster's Time and Homeland*, Naples, 1980, pp. 59ff.) to the theory that the first chapter of *Vīdēvdāt* (*Vendidād*) conserves the names of some western lands in boustrophedonic order (H. S. Nyberg, *Die Religionen des alten Iran*, German tr. H. H. Schaeder, Leipzig, 1938, pp. 324ff.). Moreover, the question of the identification of Avestan Raγa with the Raga in the inscription of Darius I at Bīstūn (DB 2.71-72; 3.2-3), with the Rhágai of the Greeks, the al-Rayy of the Arabs, and finally with Ray (J. Markwart, *A Catalogue of the Provincial Capitals of Ērānshahr*, ed. G. Messina, Rome, 1931, pp. 112-14) has by no means been settled; in fact, there is considerable evidence that this is not the case (see below).

The first stumbling-block in the study of Avestan geography is the mixture of mythical and historical elements characterizing all the data we have at our disposal. Actually the tendency has often been to interpret as mythical a good deal of data that probably have historical significance. When tackling Avestan geography, the practice has been to assume that historical elements were superimposed on a body of myths. It was common among the Indo-Iranians to identify concepts or features of traditional cosmography—mountains, lakes, rivers, etc.—with their concrete historical and geographical situation as they migrated and settled in various places.

There are many shared elements of undoubted significance in Indo-Iranian cosmography. Comparison of the various ancient Indian cosmographic systems (cf. W. Kirfel, *Die Kosmographie der Inder nach den Quellen dargestellt*, Bonn and Leipzig, 1920, pp. 1ff., 178ff., 208ff.) and the Avesta or, indeed, the whole body of Zoroastrian writings, including the Pahlavi literature of the ninth century, reveals a number of common features: the concept of Mount Harā, or Haraitī, barəz-/bərəz or bərə-zaitī "high" (cf. W. Eilers, *Geographische Namengebung in und um Iran*, Munich, 1982, p. 42), and that of Mount Meru, or Sumeru, in Brahmanical, Buddhist, and Jainist cosmography; the idea of the seven regions of the earth, the Iranian *karšvar-* (Pahlavi *kešwar*) and the Indian *dvīpa*; the idea of a central region, X^{v}aniraθa (Pahlavi Xwanirah) and Jambūdvīpa; the idea of the "Tree of All Seeds" in the Vourukaša sea, south of the Peak of Harā and the *Jambū* tree, south of Mount Meru (for the connection of Iranian cosmography with the Indo-Iranian background, cf. M. Boyce, *Zoroastrianism* I, pp. 130ff.). These elements, common to the Iranian and Indo-Aryan vision of the earth, are certainly to be considered essentially mythical when related to the historical periods during which these groups were living on one side or the other of the Indus. Yet they do not seem to be totally devoid of any geographical reference if the so-called nordic cycle of Indo-Iranian mythology is anything to go by. According to some Soviet scholars, the ancestors of the Avestan Iranians and the Vedic Indians, before migrating to the lands they eventually settled in, had lived side by side with Finno-Ugric populations. This would account for their "nordic representations," the sacred mountains in the north, the Nordic Ocean and the "polar" lands (G. M. Bongard-Levin and E. A. Grantovskij, *De la Scythie à l'Inde. Énigmes de l'histoire des anciens Aryens*, French tr. Ph. Gignoux, Paris, 1981, p. 112).

As far as these points are concerned, we must at any rate bear in mind that the great mountain ranges running from the Hindu Kush to the Pamir and the Himalayas could, with their arctic temperatures, have inspired the various successive identifications of nordic, polar elements with the ancient cosmology and traditional geography of the Aryans (G. Gnoli, *De Zoroastre à Mani. Quatre lecons au Collège de France*, Paris, 1985, p. 17). This could be the explanation of the story of the severe climate of Airyana Vaējah (see below) rather than that deriving from theories about nordic origins and reminiscences favored by Bongard-Levin and Grantovskij (op. cit., p. 56).

There are not many passages in the Avesta that refer to historical geography, but they raise a great many problems. In the first place, they are of various kinds because, together with specifically "geographical" texts like the first chapter of the *Vīdēvdāt*, there are short passages mentioning real geographical features included in all sorts of contexts. The places where the hero offers sacrifices to the gods, a river-bank, for example, or the peak of a mountain visited by the god Mithra, provide occasions for fleeting references, at times containing interesting geographical information. In other cases names of places or areas are associated with names of peoples or characters famous in other periods. This information is found not only in Avestan texts, especially in the *Yašt*s, but also in Pahlavi literature, whether of direct Avestan derivation, like the commentaries on the Avesta, or, at least from the textual point of view, independent of it. Examples of the latter category are to be found in some chapters of the *Bundahišn* (IX-XII) and some brief works like the *Abdīh ud sahīgīh ī Sagistān* (The wonders and magnificence of Sīstān) (recently published by B. Utas, "The Pahlavi Treatise *Avdēh u sahīkēh ī Sakistān*," *Acta Antiqua Academiae Scientiarum Hungaricae* 28, 1983, pp. 259-67). These are of great use in the reconstruction of Avestan geography.

As already pointed out, the main Avestan text of geographical interest is the first chapter of the *Vīdēvdāt*. This consists of a list of sixteen districts (*asah-* and *šōiθra-*) created by Ahura Mazdā and threatened by a corresponding number of countercreations that Aŋra Mainyu set up against them (*paityāra–*). The structure of this chapter is very simple: Twenty paragraphs, consisting of an introduction, fourteen paragraphs dedicated to one district each, four dedicated to two districts (two paragraphs for each of the two districts), and a final paragraph stating that there existed still more districts worthy of praise. It is likely that paragraphs 2 and 14, dealing with Airyana Vaējah and Haētumant are interpolations or later additions, as they interrupt the flow of the whole text which gives one single paragraph to each district. In fact, paragraphs 2 and 13 deal with Airyana Vaējah and Haētumant respectively. The period the text belongs to is uncertain: While the contents and lack of any reference to western Iran suggest that it should date back to the pre-Achaemenian period, the form in which it survives would seem to place it in the Parthian period.

Set right at the beginning of a whole *nask* of the Avesta, dedicated to prescriptions for purification and the rules for the atonement of sins, the first chapter of the *Vīdēvdāt* probably has the same purpose as the lists of the sixteen Great Districts, *Ṣoḍaśa mahājanapada*, in the Buddhist and Jainist sources and the epic poetry of India in the sixth century B.C., which were subject to the Aryan element. It seems likely that this geographical part of the Avesta was intended to show the extent of the territory that had been acquired in a period that can not be well defined but that must at any rate have been between Zoroaster's reforms and the beginning of the Achaemenian empire. The likely dating is therefore between the ninth and seventh centuries B.C., starting from the period of the domination of the Aryan followers of Ahura Mazdā (Gnoli, *De Zoroastre à Mani*, pp. 24ff.). In any case, there is considerable disagreement among the interpretations that have been attempted: H. S. Nyberg (op. cit., p. 326) read into it the stages of Zoroaster's mission; S. Wikander (*Vayu* I, Lund, 1942, pp. 202ff.) those of the cult of Vayu or of Vayu/Anāhitā; A. Christensen (*Le premier chapitre du Vendidad et l'histoire primitive des tribus iraniennes*, Copenhagen, 1943, pp. 78ff.) the progressive expansion of the Aryan tribes; E. Herzfeld (*Zoroaster and His World*, Princeton, 1947, pp. 744ff.) a list of the provinces of the Parthian kingdom; M. Molé ("La structure du premier chapitre du Videvdat," *JA* 229, 1951, pp. 283-98) a geographical "structure" that conformed to Dumézil's theory of a tripartite ideology; F. Altheim (*Geschichte der Hunnen* IV, Berlin, 1975, 2nd ed., pp. 166-82) a sign of the Zoroastrian renaissance that was to take shape around the middle of the seventh century A.D.

The first of the sixteen districts, Airyana Vaējah, presents a particular problem which is dealt with below. The other fifteen districts are, in order: 2. Gava = Sogdiana; 3. Mōuru = Margiana; 4. Bāxδī = Bactria; 5. Nisāya = a district between Margiana and Bactria, perhaps Maimana (W. Geiger, *Ostiranische Kultur im Altertum*, Erlangen, 1982, p. 31 n. 1); 6. Harōiva = Areia, Herat; 7. *Vaēkərəta* = Gandhāra (S. Levi, "Le catalogue géographique des Yakṣa dans la Mahāmāyūrī," *JA* 5, 1915, pp. 67ff.; Christensen, op. cit., p. 28; W. B. Henning, "Two Manichaean Magical Texts," *BSOAS* 12, 1947, pp. 52f.); 8. Urvā = probably the Ḡaznī region (Christensen, op. cit., pp. 33f.; Gnoli, *Zoroaster's Time and Homeland*, pp. 26-39; 9. Xnənta = a region defined as *vəhrkānō.šayana-* "the dwelling place of the Vəhrkāna," where Marquart placed the Barkánioi of Ctesias (Photius, *Bibliotheca*, Cod. 72, 36b-37a), an ethnicon analogous with that of Old Persian Varkāna, the inhabitants of Hyrcania, the present Gorgān (J. Marquart, *Die Assyriaka des Ktesias*, Göttingen, 1892, p. 616; idem, *Untersuchungen zur Geschichte von Eran* I, Göttingen, 1896, p. 514, II, Göttingen, 1905, p. 143 n. 1; idem, *Ērānšahr nach der Geographie des Ps. Moses Xorenacʻi*, Berlin, 1901, p. 72 n. 3; Gnoli, *Zoroaster's Time and Homeland*, pp. 39, 235, 236, 239; see Eilers, op. cit., p. 19 on the name *Gorgān*) or, less probably, Hyrcania; 10. Haraxᵛaitī = Arachosia; 11. Haētumant = the region of Helmand roughly corresponding to the Achaemenian Drangiana (Zranka) (G. Gnoli, *Ricerche storiche sul Sīstān antico*, Rome, 1967, p. 78 and n. 3); 12. Raγa = a district north of Haraxᵛaitī and Haētumant in the direction of the district of Čaxra (Gnoli, ibid., pp. 65-68, 77-78; idem, *Zoroaster's Time and Homeland*, pp. 23-26, 64-66), to be distinguished, given its position in the list (I. Gershevitch, "Zoroaster's Own Contribution," *JNES* 23, 1964, pp. 36f.) from Median *Ragā* (see above) and probably also from Raγa *zaraθuštri-* of *Y.* 19.18 (Boyce, *Zoroastrianism* II, pp. 8-9 and cf. pp. 40, 42, 66, 254, 279; G. Gnoli, "Ragha la zoroastriana," *Papers in Honour of Professor Mary Boyce*, Leiden, 1985, I. pp. 226ff.); 13. Čaxra = Čarx between Ḡaznī and Kabul, in the valley of Lōgar (Gnoli, *Ricerche storiche sul Sīstān antico*, pp. 72-74;

idem, *Zoroaster's Time and Homeland*, pp. 42-44; D. Monchi-Zadeh, op. cit., pp. 126-27), not Māzandarān, as Christensen thought (op. cit., pp. 47-48); 14. Varəna = Bunēr (S. Levi, art. cit., p. 38; Henning, art. cit., pp. 52f.; but cf. also Monchi-Zadeh, op. cit., pp. 127-30), the Varṇu of the *Mahāmāyūrī*, the 'Aornos of Alexander the Great, the homeland of Θraētaona/Frēdōn/Afrīdūn (Gnoli, *Zoroaster's Time and Homeland*, pp. 47-50); 15. Hapta Həndu = Sapta Sindhavaḥ in Vedic geography, the northeastern region of Panjab (Monchi-Zadeh, op. cit., p. 130; but cf. also H. Humbach, "Al-Bīrūnī und die sieben Strome [*sic*] des Awesta," *Bulletin of the Iranian Culture Foundation* I, 2, 1973, pp. 47-52); 16. Raŋhā = Rasā in Vedic geography, at times mentioned together with Kubhā (Kabul) and Krumu (Kurram), as in *RV.* 5.53.9 (Gnoli, *Ricerche storiche sul Sīstān antico*, pp. 76f.; idem, *Zoroaster's Time and Homeland*, pp. 50-53; and cf. also H. Lommel, "Rasā," *ZII* 4, 1926, pp. 194-206), a river situated in a mountainous area (Monchi-Zadeh, op. cit., p. 130, who associates it with the Pamir), probably connected with the Indus, not with the Jaxartes (Geiger, op. cit., pp. 34ff.; Nyberg, op. cit., p. 323) or with the Volga (J. Markwart, *Wehrot und Arang*, ed. H. H. Schaeder, Leiden, 1938, pp. 133ff.).

There is further geographical interest to be found in another passage from the Avesta *Yt.* 10.13-14, where the whole region inhabited by the Aryans (*airyō.šayana-*) is described. The description begins with Mount Harā, the peak of which is reached by Mithra as he precedes the immortal sun: The entire Aryan homeland, according to this passage, consisted of the districts of Iškata and Peruta, Margiana and Areia, Gava, Sogdiana, and Chorasmia. The names of Sogdiana, Suxδəm, and Chorasmia, X̌āirizəm, appear here, as E. Benveniste has demonstrated "L'Ērān-vēž et l'origine légendaire des iraniens," *BSOAS* 7, 1933-35, pp. 269f.), in Medo-Iranian forms; this suggests that they were later additions (G. Gnoli, "Airyō.šayana," *RSO* 41, 1966, p. 68; idem, *De Zoroastre à Mani*, p. 21). The geographical extension of *Mihr Yašt* (the subject of an analytical study by Gershevitch, *The Avestan Hymn to Mithra*, Cambridge, 1959, pp. 174ff.), covered the eastern part of the Iranian territory, the central part being occupied by the regions of the Hindu Kush, represented by Mount Harā, Iškata (Kūh-e Bābā?), Paruta (Ḡūr?), the district of Herodutus's Aparútai (3.91) or Ptolemy's Paroûtai or Párautoi (6.17.3).

Like the *Mihr Yašt*, the *Farvardīn Yašt* also contains some passages of use in the reconstruction of Avestan geography, in particular *Yt.* 13.125 and *Yt.* 13.127, where some characters are mentioned because of their venerable *fravaši*. For each of these the birthplace is given: Mužā, Raoždyā, Tanyā, Aŋhvī, Apaxšīrā. Only the first of these place-names can perhaps be identified because Mužā recalls the Sanskrit Mūjavant, which should be in a region between the Hindu Kush and the Pamir (W. Eilers, "Der Name Demawend," *Archiv Orientální* 22, 1954, pp. 277, 324 n. 74; T. Burrow, "The Proto-Indoaryans," *JRAS*, 1973, p. 138 n. 31; Gnoli, *Zoroaster's Time and Homeland*, pp. 59f.; M. Witzel, "Early Eastern Iran and the Atharvaveda," *Persica* 9, 1980, p. 87 and n. 16). But it should be borne in mind that the character related to the land of Apaxšīrā, Paršat̰.gav, may be connected with a Sīstāni tradition (Gnoli, *Ricerche storiche sul Sīstān antico*, p. 80 and n. 4) and that the passage in *Yt.* 13.125 is dedicated to the *fravaši* of members of the family of Saēna, the son of Ahūm.stūt̰, who also had connections with Sīstān (Gnoli, *Zoroaster's Time and Homeland*, pp. 138f.).

There is no justification for the supposition expressed by M. Boyce (op. cit., I, p. 250) that the districts in *Yt.* 13.125 and 127 belonged to regions "in the remote northeast, at some distant time in the prehistory of that area": It seems more than likely that they belonged to the same geographical area as the great *Yašts* and the first chapter of *Vīdēvdāt*.

The *Zamyād Yašt*, dedicated to X̌arənah, is of very great importance for Avestan geography as it provides a surprisingly well-detailed description of the hydrography of the Helmand region, in particular of Hāmūn-e Helmand. In *Yt.* 19.66-77 nine rivers are mentioned: X̌āstrā, Hvaspā, Fradaθā, X̌arənahvaitī, Uštavaitī, Urvaδā, Ərəzī, Zarənumaitī, and Haētumant; six of these are known from the *Tārīk̲-e Sīstān* (ed. M. Bahār, Tehran, 1935, pp. 15-16). Other features of Sīstāni geography recur in the same *yašt*, like the Kąsaoya lake (Pahlavi Kayānsih) or Mount Uši.δām (Kūh-e K̲ˇāja), both closely bound up with Zoroastrian eschatology, so that with the help of comparisons with Pahlavi and classical sources, mainly Pliny and Ptolemy (cf. A. Stein, "Afghanistan in Avestic Geography," *Indian Antiquary* 15, 1886, pp. 21-23; Markwart, *Wehrot und Arang*, pp. 19ff.; E. Herzfeld, "Zarathustra. Teil V. Awestische Topographie," *AMI* 2, 1930, pp. 92f.), we can conclude that the *Zamyād Yašt* describes Sīstān with great care and attention. In Avestan geography no other region has received such treatment. There is an echo of Sīstān's importance in Avestan geography in the brief Pahlavi treatise *Abdīh ud sahīgīh ī Sagistān*.

Yet another reference to Sīstān is to be found in another passage of the great *yašts*, *Yt.* 5.108, in which Kavi Vīštāspa, prince and patron of Zoroaster, is represented in the act of making sacrifice to Arədvī Sūrā Anāhitā near Frazdānu, the Frazdān of Pahlavi literature, that is, one of the wonders of Sīstān; it can probably be identified with Gowd-e Zera (A. V. W. Jackson, *Zoroastrian Studies*, New York, 1928, p. 283; Herzfeld, "Zarathustra, Teil V," p. 91; idem, *Zoroaster and His World*, p. 762; Gnoli, *Ricerche storiche sul Sīstān antico*, pp. 14ff.).

If we compare the first chapter of the *Vīdēvdāt* with the passages of geographical interest that we come across mainly in the great *yašts*, we can conclude that the geographical area of Avesta was dominated by the Hindu Kush range at the center, the western boundary being marked by the districts of Margiana, Areia, and Drangiana, the eastern one by the Indo-Iranian frontier regions such as Gandhāra, Bunēr, the land of the "Seven Rivers." Sogdiana and, possibly, Chorasmia (which, however, is at the extreme limits) mark the boundary to the north, Sīstān and Baluchistan to the south.

One of the old, thorny problems in studies on Avestan geography is represented by Airyana Vaējah (Pahlavi: Ērānwēz), "the area of the Aryans" and first of the sixteen districts in *Vd.* 1, the original name of which was *airyanəm vaējō vaŋhuyå dāityayå*, "the Aryan extension of Vaŋuhī Dāityā (Benveniste, art. cit., pp. 267f.; against Christensen, op. cit., p. 74; Herzfeld, *Zoroaster and His World*, p. 698), where Vaŋuhī Dāityā "the good Dāityā" is the name of a river connected with the religious "law" (*dāta-*). The concept of Airyana Vaējah is not equivalent to that of *airyō.šayana-* in *Yt.* 10.13, or to the group of *airyå daiŋ́hāvō* "the Aryan lands" which is recurrent in the *yašts*; this, in fact, refers to just one of the Aryan lands, as the first chapter of the *Vīdēvdāt* clearly shows. It does not designate "the traditional homeland" (Boyce, op. cit., I, p. 275) or "the ancient homeland" (R. N. Frye, *The History of Ancient Iran*, Munich, 1984, p. 61) of the Iranians. These definitions perpetuate old interpretations of the Airyana Vaējah as "Urheimat des Awestavolkes" (Geiger, op. cit., p. 32), "Urland" of the Indo-Iranians (F. Spiegel, *Die arische Periode und ihre Zustände*, Leipzig, 1887, p. 123), "Wiege aller iranischen Arier" (J. von Prášek, *Geschichte der Meder und Perser bis zur makedonischen Eroberung* I, Gotha, 1906, p. 29), drawing from the texts more than the contents really warrant. Airyana Vaējah is only the homeland of Zaraθuštra and of Zoroastrianism (Nyberg, op. cit., pp. 326f.; Henning, *Zoroaster*, p. 43). According to Zoroastrian tradition Ērānwēz is situated at the center of the world; on the shores of its river, Weh Dāitī (Av. Vaŋuhī Dāityā), there were created the *gāw ī ēw-dād* (Av. *gav aēvō.dāta*) "uniquely created bull" and Gayōmard (Av. Gayō.marətan) "mortal life," the first man; there rises the Čagād ī Dāidīg, the "lawful Summit," the Peak of Harā, in Avestan also called *hukairya* "of good activity"; the Činvat Bridge is there, and there too, Yima and Zoroaster became famous. Taken all together, these data show that Zoroastrianism superimposed the concept of Airyana Vaējah onto the traditional one of a center of the world where the Peak of Harā rises (see above). The fact that Airyana Vaējah is situated in a mountainous region explains its severe climate (*Vd.* 1.2.3) better than does its supposed location in Chorasmia (Markwart, *Ērānšahr*, p. 155). This is not surprising if we consider the analogy between the Iranian concept of the Peak of Harā with the Indian one of Mount Meru or Sumeru. The Manicheans identified Aryān-waižan with the region at the foot of Mount Sumeru that Wištāsp reigned over (W. B. Henning, "The Book of the Giants," *BSOAS* 11, 1943, pp. 68f.), and the Khotanese texts record the identification of Mount Sumeru in Buddhist mythology with the Peak of Harā (*ttaira haraysä*) in the Avestan tradition (H. W. Bailey, *Indo-Scythian Studies. Khotanese Texts* IV, Cambridge, 1961, p. 12; idem, *Dictionary of Khotan Saka*, Cambridge, 1979, p. 467). All this leads us to suppose that the concept of Airyana Vaējah was an invention of Zoroastrianism which gave a new guise to a traditional idea of Indo-Iranian cosmography (Gnoli, *Ricerche storiche sul Sīstān antico*, pp. 86ff.). At any rate, identifications of Airyana Vaējah with Chorasmia are quite unfounded (Markwart, loc. cit.; H. W. Bailey, "Iranian Studies I," *BSOAS* 6, 1930-32, pp. 948-53; idem, "Iranian Studies IV," *BSOAS* 7, 1933-35, pp. 764-68; Benveniste, art. cit.; Nyberg, op. cit., p. 326; Christensen, op. cit., pp. 66-76; Monchi-Zadeh, op. cit., pp. 115f.), whether this is understood to refer to K̲ᵛārazm itself or to a "greater Chorasmia" (Henning, *Zoroaster*, pp. 42ff.; Gershevitch, *The Avestan Hymn to Mithra*, pp. 14ff.). As for the river of Religious Law, it is not at all easy to identify (see H. Humbach, "About Gōpatšāh, His Country, and the Khwārezmian Hypothesis," *Papers in Honour of Mary Boyce* I, p. 330): The most likely hypotheses seem to be those that identify it with the Oxus, or rather the Helmand, which at times appears to be in a curious "competition" with the Oxus (Markwart, *Wehrot und Arang*, pp. 122 n. 3, 159 note; Gnoli, *Ricerche storiche sul Sīstān antico*, pp. 13, 38, 87) in the Zoroastrian tradition.

Bibliography: Given in the text. See also F. Justi, *Beiträge zur alten Geographie Persiens*, Marburg, 1869. W. Tomaschek, "Zur historischen Topographie von Persien," *Sb. d. Wiener Akad. d. Wiss., Phil.-hist. Kl.*, 102, 1883, pp. 146-231; 108, 1885, pp. 583-652 (repr. Osnabrück, 1972). W. Geiger, "Geographie von Iran," in Geiger and Kuhn, *Grundr. Ir. Phil.* II, 3, pp. 371-94. H. Lommel, "Anahita-Sarasvati," in *Asiatica. Festschrift Friedrich Weller*, Leipzig, 1954, pp. 15-32. H. Humbach, "Die awestische Länderliste," *Wiener Zeitschrift für die Kunde Süd- und Ostasiens* 4, 1960, pp. 34-46. Idem, "Ptolemaios-Studien," ibid., 5, 1961, pp. 68-74. G. Gnoli, "᾿Αριανή. Postilla ad *Airyō.šayana*," *RSO* 41, 1966, pp. 329-34. Idem, "More on the Sistanic Hypothesis," *East and West* 27, 1977, pp. 309-20. H. Humbach, "A Western Approach to Zarathushtra," *Journal of the K. R. Cama Oriental Institute* 51, Bombay, 1984, pp. 15-32. W. Barthold, *Istoriko-geograficheskiĭ obzor Irana*, Moscow, 1971; Eng. tr. S. Soucek, *An Historical Geography of Iran*, Princeton, New Jersey, 1984.

(G. Gnoli)

AVESTAN LANGUAGE, the language of the Avesta (q.v.), an Old Iranian language.

i. *The Avestan script.*
ii. *The phonology of Avestan.*
iii. *The grammar of Avestan.*

i. The Avestan Script

The Avestan script is known from manuscripts written in Iran (at Yazd and Kerman) and in India (in Gujarat, e.g., Cambay, Broach, Ankleshwar, Surat, and Navsari). The earliest manuscript dates from A.D. 1288. The script consists in 14 (or 16) letters for vowels

Table 2

THE AVESTAN SCRIPT

1	𐬀	*a*	17	𐬐	*k*	35	𐬢	*ŋ*
2	𐬁	*ā*	18	𐬑	*x*	36	𐬣	*ŋ́*
3	𐬂	*å*	19	𐬒	*x́*	37	𐬤	*ŋᵛ*
4	𐬃	*ā̊*	20	𐬓	*xᵛ*	38	𐬥	*n*
5	𐬄	*ą*	21	𐬔	*g*	39	𐬦/𐬦	*ń*
6	𐬅/𐬅	*ą̇*	22	𐬕	*ġ*	40	𐬧	*ṇ*
7	𐬆	*ə*	23	𐬖	*γ*	41	𐬨	*m*
8	𐬇	*ə̄*	24	𐬗	*c*	42	𐬩	*m̨*
9	𐬈	*e*	25	𐬘	*j*	43	𐬪	*y*
10	𐬉	*ē*	26	𐬙	*t*	44	𐬬	*v*
11	𐬊	*o*	27	𐬚	*ϑ*	45	𐬭	*r*
12	𐬋	*ō*	28	𐬛	*d*	46	𐬴	*ṣ̌*
13	𐬌	*i*	29	𐬜/𐬜	*δ*	47	𐬯	*s*
14	𐬍	*ī*	30	𐬝/𐬝	*t̰*	48	𐬰	*z*
15	𐬎	*u*	31	𐬞	*p*	49	𐬱	*š*
16	𐬏	*ū*	32	𐬟	*f*	50	𐬲	*ž*
			33	𐬠	*b*	51	𐬳	*š́*
			34	𐬡	*β*	52	𐬫	*y*
						53	𐬵(𐬵)	*h*

and 37 letters for consonants, see Table 28. In printed texts the letters *å*, *ġ*, *ŋ́*, *ń*, *m̨*, and *ẏ* are not used. The transliteration given in Table 28 differs in some points from that almost universally used until recently. Thus, it has been usual to use *h'* for *x́*; *č* and *ǰ* for *c* and *j*; *w* for *β*; *n* for both *n* and *ṇ*; *š* for *š*, *ś*, and *ṣ̌*; *y* for both *y* (*ẏ*) and *ii*; *v* for both *v* and *uu*. The signs for *ą*, *ġ*, *ŋ́*, *ń*, *ṇ*, *m*, *ś*, and *ṣ̌* were not used at all until recently.

The letters are written from right to left and are not connected. Ligatures (e.g., *šk*, *šc*, *št*, *ša*) are rare and clearly of secondary origin. A point (dot) is used to indicate the end of a word or the end of the first member of a compound, no distinction being made between the two. The letters have almost the same shapes in all manuscripts. Only some Indian manuscripts show peculiarities: H2 (A.D. 1415), S1 and J9 (14/15th century A.D.).

The large number of letters used suggests that their invention resulted from an attempt to record an orally recited text with all its phonetic nuances. For that reason the Avestan script must have been the deliberate invention or creation of a scholar or of a group of scholars (see, e.g., Morgenstierne, "Orthography and Sound-system," pp. 31-33; Henning, "Disintegration," p. 44).

The Avestan script is based on the Pahlavi (q.v.) script in its cursive form as used by theologians of the Zoroastrian church when writing their books. The earliest Pahlavi manuscripts date from the fourteenth century A.D., but the Pahlavi cursive script must have developed from the Aramaic script already in the first centuries A.D. This is proved for example by the fact that an early inscription on the lid of a sarcophagus found in Istanbul that for archeological reasons can not be dated later than A.D. 430 already shows the characteristic written forms of the Pahlavi cursive script with two insignificant exceptions (*k* and *s*). (See the bibliography in Ph. Gignoux, *Glossaire des inscriptions pehlevies et parthes*, Corp. Inscr. Iran., Suppl. Ser. I, London, 1972, p. 14.) In the Pahlavi cursive script almost all the letters represent several different sounds. This ambiguity is due in part to inadequacies of the Aramaic alphabet from which it developed, in part to the phonological development of the Middle Persian language ("historical spelling"), and in part to the graphic coalescence of signs. In addition, many individual letters of a word are joined to one another, with the result that extremely ambiguous ligatures occur.

Apart from the Pahlavi cursive script as used in the Zoroastrian church there was a still older kind of script that was to some extent less ambiguous. This script, called here the "Psalter script," is known to us from a manuscript from the seventh or eighth century A.D. containing a "Christian" Pahlavi translation of the Psalms. (See D. N. MacKenzie, *A Concise Pahlavi Dictionary*, London, 1971, pp. xi, xiii, for tables of the Pahlavi and Psalter scripts; and Aramaic, i.)

The creator of the Avestan script took over from the Pahlavi cursive script the letters *a*, *i*, *k*, *t*, *p*, *b*, *m*, *n*, *r*, *s*, *z*, *š*, and *x*ᵛ to represent the same sounds as in Pahlavi. The sign (28) for *d* derives likewise from the unambiguous Psalter script. In Pahlavi the sign for *k* (17) represented both the sounds *k* and *γ* because *k* had developed to *γ* in word-interior position. In the Psalter script the sign for *k* differed from that of the Pahlavi cursive in that the Psalter sign ended in a flourish towards the right. The creator of the Avestan script made use of this variation in the shape of the letters by assigning to the Pahlavi form (17) the fixed value *k* and to the Psalter form (23) the fixed value *γ*. In this way the flourish could be reinterpreted as a diacritical mark, which the creator of the script put to further use. The Pahlavi Psalter sign (25) for *c*/*j*/*z*/*ž* had a similar flourish and was accordingly adopted to represent the voiced sound *j*. By removing the flourish the creator of the script obtained the sign (24) for *c*, which has a different shape in the Pahlavi cursive script. Pahlavi *p* represented the sounds *p*/(*f*)/*β*. It was retained unchanged in Avestan for *p* (31) while an initial flourish converted it into the sign for *β* (34). The addition of a flourish to Pahlavi *t* (26) either initially or finally was not used, as might be expected, to represent *δ* but to represent a word-final *t̰* (30) that was probably implosive. The Pahlavi *alef* was adopted as *a* (1) in the Avestan alphabet. In Pahlavi, *alef* had coalesced graphically with *h*, from which it was still distinguished in the Psalter script. Thus, Pahlavi had only one sign to represent *alef*, *h*, and *x*. In order to represent the sound *x*ᵛ in Avestan, use was made of an ambiguous Pahlavi ligature (20) of '/*h* + *w*/*n*/*r*, which among many others had the value *xw*. The shape of the ligature *hw* adopted for Avestan *x*ᵛ is characteristic not only of the Pahlavi books but is found already in the inscription on the sarcophagus lid from Istanbul whereas the ligature has a different shape in the Psalter script. In the Avestan script a flourish was added to distinguish *x́* (19) from *x*ᵛ (20). An unusual diacritic in the form of a loop at the end of a curved flourish was used to distinguish *h* (53) from *a* (1). The loop may have been a secondary addition providing graphical resemblance to *p* (31) since a variant form of *h* (53 in brackets) without the loop is found in such manuscripts as H2 and J9. By extending the curve further upwards than in the unlooped variety of *h* it was possible to distinguish *x* (18) from both *a* (1) and *h* (53). The curved upwards flourish was further used to create Avestan *f* (32) out of Pahlavi *p* (31) and is seen in the voiceless fricative *θ* (27). The basic shape to which the curved upwards flourish was added in the case of *θ* is to be seen in the form taken by final *s* in Pahlavi words such as *g's* for Avestan *gāθā*, in which *s* represents Avestan *θ* (MacKenzie, *Pahlavi Dictionary*, p. xiii, the second *s*, to the right).

The Avestan letter *ā* (2) is also derived from the Pahlavi script, where this sign was used for '*y* at the end of a word (already in the Istanbul sarcophagus inscription). However, as early as in Middle Persian inscriptions from the third century A.D., '*y* was used to represent the final -*ā* of foreign names as in *swly'y* for (Greek) *Sūriā*, and the Pahlavi Psalter confirms that this convention continued to be adopted as the Psalter itself has the spelling *'plt'y* for Syriac *'prt'*, that is (Greek) Ephrathá (Bethlehem).

The Avestan letter *o* (11) corresponds in graphic spape to a special form of Pahlavi *l* that is found only in Aramaic heterograms. The commonest of those heterograms is the preposition *'L* "to, at," which was read in Middle Persian as *ō* (MacKenzie, *Pahlavi Dictionary*, p. 187, left column, 3rd line from the top). It looks as though the creator of the Avestan script used this special form of *l* without the initial *'ayn* to represent the sound *o*. The letter *e* (9) seems to have a similar origin. Pahlavi *ēw* "one" was probably pronounced simply as *ē* already at an early date. This pronunciation is actually attested in the later Pahlavi literature. Avestan *e* differs from the Pahlavi ligature *ēw* only by the absence of a small initial hook which was indispensable for Pahlavi but unnecessary for Avestan. (Words with initial *ēw-/ ēn-* in MacKenzie, *Pahlavi Dictionary*, pp. 232f.)

The original (Aramaic) letters *n*, *w*, *r*, and *'* (*'ayn*) coalesced in a single short vertical stroke in Pahlavi. This sign was taken over unchanged for *n* in the Avestan alphabet (38). A slight bend in the stroke was made to distinguish Avestan *u* (15) from *n* since Pahlavi *w* was used in internal position also to designate the sound *u*.

The Pahlavi script had very inadequate means to designate the vowel sounds. By contrast the creator of the Avestan script quite clearly invented a special sign for every vowel distinguished in the oral tradition. No doubt the Greek script had provided a model; the Greek script was well known in Iran as is shown by the fact that already under Šāpūr I (241-72 A.D.) Greek translations accompanied the royal inscriptions. Thus Avestan *ə* (7) could have been adopted from Greek minuscules, which had a comparable form already in the fourth century. The sign for *ā* (2) probably came directly from Pahlavi but the letters for the remaining long vowels were evidently formed by adding diacritics to letters for the corresponding short vowels. *ə̄* (8) was accordingly formed by adding to *ə* (7) a flourish to the left, while *ē* (10) was formed by adding to *e* (9) a flourish to the right. The letters for *ō* (12), *ī* (14), and *ū* (16) were distinguished from the letters for the corresponding short vowels by the addition of a short vertical stroke at the bottom. It is likely that the creator of the script based the sign for *ō* (12) on the Pahlavi heterogram *'L*, which was pronounced *ō*, by placing the *'ayn*, the vertical stroke on the right, under the *L*. The sign for the short vowel was then formed by treating the vertical stroke as a diacritic denoting length. The same stroke may subsequently have been used by analogy in order to differentiate between *ī* and *i* and between *ū* and *u*.

As yet few plausible statements can be made concerning the origin of the remaining letters of the Avestan alphabet, but it must be accepted that the creator of a script is free to invent letters or diacritics arbitrarily.

ā̊ (4), which looks like a ligature of *ā* + *ə*, was differentiated from *ā*. Short *å* (3) has been found in one manuscript only (Pd, where it is used instead of *ą* before *ŋh*; see Salemann, "Parsenhandschrift," p. 510). *ą* (5) seems to be a free invention. In some manuscripts (e.g., Mf4, ed. in facsimile by K. M. JamaspAsa) *ą̇* (6) is found instead of *ą* (5). There is some slight evidence that *ą* and *ą̇* were not just graphic variants but two different letters. *ą* may have been a nasalized long *ą̄* and *ą̇* a nasalized short *ə*. The original form of *ą̇* may have been the left variant of no. 6 in the table.

The Avestan script originally possessed also the letter *ġ* (22). All the known Avestan alphabets, most of which are very corrupt, begin with the letters *g*, *ġ*, *γ* (21-23). *ġ* is seldom found in the manuscripts but relatively often in final *-ə̄ŋ̇ġ*, especially in the manuscripts S1 and J3. This suggests that *ġ* was implosive, like *t̰*, the only other final stop in Avestan.

Avestan *g* (21) may be a modification of the corresponding Pahlavi letter. Neither of the forms of *δ* (29) appears to be based on Pahlavi letters.

Among the nasal signs *ŋ* (35), the labialized nasal *ŋ́* (37), and the uvular nasal *ṇ* (40) appear to be free inventions. Both forms of palatalized *ń* (39)—that on the right in the table is found only in MS K7—are modifications of *n* (38). The voiceless *m̨* (42) is simply *m* (41) plus a diacritic.

The sign for initial *ẏ* (43) and *v* (44) are free inventions.

The left part of *ž* (50) resembles the Pahlavi ligature *'c* (written like 53). The reason for that could be that *c* in Pahlavi *'cydh'k* was pronounced by theologians in agreement with Avestan *aži- dahāka-* as *až(i)dahāγ* (for genuine Middle Persian *azdahāγ*).

š́ (51) is simply *š* (49) plus a diacritic. In Indian manuscripts initial *ẏ* (43) is replaced by initial *y* (52), which looks like *š* (49) with a slightly different diacritic. If the sign originally had the phonetic value palatal *ž*, that may in fact have been its origin. Even *ṣ̌* (46) could be a modification of *š* (49) if the sound it represents was already some kind of *š* sound at the time the script was invented (see on phonology below).

It is generally considered that the Avestan script dates to the Sasanian period (224-651 A.D.). The evidence of the Istanbul sarcophagus inscription (before A.D. 430) suggests that it may have been invented already by the fourth century A.D., perhaps even under Šāpūr II (310-379 A.D.). Note, however, that none of the letters of the alphabet used in the monumental Mid. Pers. inscriptions seem to have been borrowed for the Avestan alphabet (table in MacKenzie, *Pahlavi Dictionary*, p. xi).

It may be assumed that the Avestan texts were written down shortly after the invention of the script, which was designed to provide a special sign for each sound used in the traditional pronunciation of Avestan. In this first notation of the Avestan texts, the so-called "Sasanian archetype," the aim of the inventor of the script must have been put into practice.

In the post-Sasanian period there took place a serious deterioration in what had become a manuscript tradition. There must have been numerous errors even in the manuscripts written in the ninth or tenth century, from which ultimately the extant manuscripts descend. Thus, for example, the letters *š*, *š́*, and *ṣ̌* were only in part correctly employed and *ŋuh* or *ŋh* was written instead of *ŋ'h*. The manuscripts themselves constantly betray a marked deterioration in the pronunciation of the vulgate.

Bibliography: C. F. Andreas, "Die Entstehung des Awesta-Alphabetes und sein ursprünglicher Lautwert," *Verhandlungen des XIII. internationalen Orientalisten-Kongresses, Hamburg, September 1902*, Leiden, 1904, pp. 99-106. W. B. Henning "The Disintegration of the Avestic Studies," *TPS*, 1942, pp. 40-56 (*Selected Papers* II, Acta Iranica 15, pp. 151-67). Idem, "Mitteliranisch," p. 52. K. Hoffmann, "Zum Zeicheninventar der Avesta-Schrift," in *Festgabe deutscher Iranisten zur 2500 Jahrfeier Irans*, Stuttgart, 1971, pp. 64-73 (*Aufsätze zur Indoiranistik* I, Wiesbaden, 1975, pp. 316-25). A. V. W. Jackson, *The Avestan Alphabet and its Transcription*, Stuttgart, 1890. K. M. JamaspAsa, *Manuscript D90: Yasnā with its Pahlavi Translation* I-II, Shiraz, 1976 (facsimile of Geldner's ms. Mf4). G. Morgenstierne, "Orthography and Sound-system of the Avesta," *NTS* 12, 1942, pp. 30-82 (*Irano-Dardica*, Wiesbaden, 1973, pp. 31-79). C. Salemann, "Ueber eine Parsenhandschrift der Kaiserlichen Oeffentlichen Bibliothek zu St. Petersburg," *Travaux de la troisième session du Congrès international des Orientalistes 1876* II, St. Petersburg and Leiden, 1879, pp. 508-19. G. Windfuhr, "Diacritic and Distinctive Features in Avestan," *JAOS* 91, 1971, pp. 104-24 (somewhat speculative). See also J. Duchesne-Guillemin, *Kratylos* 7, 1962, pp. 4-9.

(K. HOFFMANN)

ii. THE PHONOLOGY OF AVESTAN

Attested forms and stages of development. Avestan is attested in two forms, known respectively as Old Avestan (OAv.) or Gathic Avestan and Young Avestan (YAv.). They differ from each other not only chronologically but also dialectally. Avestan, which is associated with northeastern Iran, and Old Persian, which belongs to the southwest, together constitute what is called Old Iranian. It is possible to some extent to reconstruct Proto-Iranian by comparing Avestan with Old Persian. This Proto-Iranian is closely related to the Vedic language of ancient India. Both Proto-Iranian and Vedic go back to Proto-Indo-Iranian or Proto-Aryan, which in turn descends from Proto-Indo-European.

By comparison with Vedic, whose phonemes are consistently recorded, Avestan in the form in which it has been handed down in manuscripts from 1288 A.D. onwards is attested in a very irregular notation. Apart from errors introduced in the post-Sasanian period, the essential features of the manuscript tradition of the Avesta must have been present already in the Sasanian archetype. When the Avestan texts were first recorded, perhaps as early as the fourth century A.D., each sound of the current Avestan pronunciation was designated by a special letter. The fact that a phonetic notation was used rather than a phonemic one means that it is possible to assess the linguistic significance of the individual spellings with regard to both the synchronic description of the language and its historical development.

Every Avestan text, whether composed originally in Old Avestan or in Young Avestan, went through several stages of transmission before it was recorded in the extant manuscripts. During the course of transmission many changes took place.

For Old Avestan the following stages may be assumed: 1. The original language of the Zarathustrian *Gāθās*, the *Yasna Haptaŋhāiti*, and the four sacred prayers; 2. Changes involved by the practice of slow chanting; 3. Changes due to transmission by YAv. priests, who introduced many YAv. sound forms into the OAv. texts; 4. Deliberate alteration of the text in the course of an orthoepic revision ("School text"); 5. Continued transmission of the OAv. texts along with the YAv. texts.

Young Avestan went through the following stages: 1. The original language of the composers of grammatically correct YAv. texts; perhaps in Marv or Herat; 2. Dialect influences as a result of the transfer of the Av. texts to Southeast Iran (Arachosia ?); 3. Transfer of the Avesta to Persis in Southwest Iran, possibly earlier than 500 B.C.; 4. Transmission of the Avesta in a Southwest Iranian theological school, probably in Eṣṭaḵr: Old Pers. and Mid. Pers. influences, the insistence on fantastic pronunciations by semi-learned schoolmasters (Av. *aēθrapaiti-*), the composition of ungrammatical late Av. texts, the adaptation of portions of texts taken from other regions where they were recited; 5. The end of the oral transmission: phonetic notation of the Avestan texts in the Sasanian archetype, probably in the fourth century A.D.; 6. Post-Sasanian deterioration of the written transmission due to incorrect pronunciation (Vulgate); 7. In the ninth and tenth centuries A.D. the manuscript copies of individual texts were made on which the extant manuscripts are based; 8. Earlier manuscripts were copied in manuscripts dating from A.D. 1288 till the nineteenth century by scribes who introduced errors and corruptions. These are the manuscripts extant today.

Many phonetic features can not be ascribed with certainty to a particular stage since there may be more than one possibility. Every phonetic form that can be ascribed to the Sasanian archetype on the basis of critical assessment of the manuscript evidence must have gone through the stages mentioned above so that "Old Avestan" and "Young Avestan" really mean no more than "Old Avestan and Young Avestan of the Sasanian period."

The vowels. The Proto-Indo-Ir. vowels *a*, *ā*, *i*, *ī*, *u*, *ū* and the diphthongs *ai̯*, *āi̯*, *au̯*, *āu̯* (= Vedic *e*, *ai*, *o*, *au*) remained unchanged in Proto-Iranian. Proto-Indo-Ir. *i* that arose from Proto-IE. *ə* (the vocalization of a consonantal laryngal *H*) is attested by such forms as Av. *pitár-* "father;" OAv. *sīšā* "teach," cf. Vedic *śiṣat*, from Proto-IE. **ḱəse-*; OAv. *-maidī*, cf. Vedic *-mahi*, 1 plur. verb ending, from Proto-IE. *$*$-medʰə*. But Proto-IE. *H* was maintained under certain accentual conditions in Proto-Ir. and was lost in Av. Hence we find such contrasting forms as Av. *draonah-* "possession" beside Vedic *drávinas-*; OAv. *dugədar-* "daughter" beside Vedic *duhitár-*; OAv. *vərəṇtē* "he wishes" beside Vedic *vr̥ṇīte*; OAv. *fəδrōi* "to the father" beside OAv. *piθrē*. Proto-Indo-Ir. sonant *r̥* (= Vedic *r̥*) became in Proto-Ir. and Av. *ər* but before *š* the tradition introduced the YAv. spelling *ar(š)* also into OAv. texts. The corresponding long vowel *r̥̄* from Proto-IE. *r̥H* developed in Proto-Ir. and Av. to *ar* whereas Vedic had either *ir/ur* or *īr/ūr*.

There is a wide variety in the representation of the vowels in the manuscripts. Most of these features were already present in the Sasanian archetype.

Numerous anaptyctic vowels, represented mostly by *ə* but also by *a*, *ō*, and other vowel signs, were used to simplify consonant clusters especially after *r*: *arəθa-*, *karapan-*, *vīžibiiō*, *θβarōždūm* etc. These anaptyctic vowels were introduced during the course of transmission in order to account for the pronunciation used in the slow chanting of the texts.

A late feature, perhaps arising in Southwest Iran, is the use of epenthetic *i* before consonants that are followed by *i*, *ii* or *ē̆*: *aiti*, *mrūitē*, *irista-*, *iθiiejah-*. This epenthesis is not found before *ń*, *ŋ́*, *st*, *št*, *m*, *hm*, but it does occur before *rm*: *zairimiia-* "house," cf. Vedic *harmⁱyá-*; *airime* "quiet" beside *armaēᵒ*. Anaptyxis and epenthesis may occur together: YAv. *kərəiti-*; OAv. *daibitā*.

Epenthetic *u* occurs only before *ru*, *ru̯*: *uruθβarə*, *pouru*. It is a genuine YAv. development in the case of *-uri-* arising from older **-urui̯-*: YAv. *paoiriia-* "first" from **pauriia-* from older **paruiia-*, cf. OAv. *paouruuiia-*; YAv. *tūiriia-* "father's brother" from **təuriia-* from older **təruiia-* and ultimately from Proto-Indo-Ir. **pHtr̥uiia-*, cf. Vedic *pitr̥vⁱya-*. (On the phonological status of epenthetic *i* and *u*, see Morgenstierne, "Orthography and Sound-system," pp. 55-58 par, ix.)

There is a consistent pattern in the representation of the quantities of the vowels *a*, *ā*, *ə*, *ə̄*, *i*, *ī*, *u*, *ū*, *e*, *ē*, *o*, *ō* in final position: in OAv. they are always long, that is, both original *a* and *ā* are written *ā*, etc., while in YAv. they are always short, expect for *-ō*, *-ə̄* (the YAv. final *-ą* is always long) and in monosyllabic words. The short vowels were probably closed, the long open, as in Attic Greek. Hence in the Sasanian archetype short and long vowels were often used to indicate degrees of openness of the vowels rather than their quantities. Thus we find *vīspa-* "all" with *ī* indicating a (short) open vowel: cf. Vedic *víśva-*. Similarly explainable are the spellings of *ahura-* "lord," with (long ?) closed *u*, beside the derivative *ahūiri-* with (short ?) open *u* (through dissimilation with the closed *i* ?); note also *ao* from **au̯* beside *aē* from **ai̯*.

Qualitative changes are seldom found in the case of *ī̆* and *ū̆* but note OAv. *ə̄nəiti-* from **əniiti-* and *drəguuaṇt-* from **druguant-*. As in East Iranian dialects, Av. **-īu̯-* became *-uu̯-* in *juua-* "living," cf. Vedic *jīvá-*, and *cuuaṇt-* "how much, how big" from **čīu̯ant-*.

Proto-Ir. *a* suffered very many changes: to *ā*, *ə*, *ə̄*, *e*, *o*, *ō*. These came about partly due to phonological development caused by the surrounding sounds, partly due to the liturgical chanting, and partly due to dialect influence. Before final *-n* and *-m*, *a* always became *ə̆̄*. This was originally the case also in word-interior position but *ə* was often replaced by *a* in this position in YAv., from where it was introduced also into OAv. Thus both OAv. and YAv. have *nəmah-* beside *manah-*. Before *-ŋh-* (*-ŋgh-*) where the nasal is etymological (*-ŋh-* from **-ns-*), OAv. has only *ə̆̄* in *sə̄ŋgha-* "pronouncement," cf. Vedic *śáṁsa-*. But before *-ŋh-* where the nasal is secondary (*-ŋh-* from **-s-*), OAv. has only *a* e.g. in *manaŋhā*, cf. Vedic *mánasā*. In both cases YAv. has *a*: *saŋha-*, *manaŋha*. In final position **-ans* became *-ə̄ṇg* in OAV. and *-ə̄* in YAv.

In YAv. *ə* developed further to *i* after *i̯*, *č*, *ǰ*: YAv. *yim* beside OAv. *yə̄m*; YAv. *drujim*, beside OAv. *drujə̄m*. Postconsonantal **-i̯ə-* became first **-ii-*, then YAv. *-ī̆-*, which was introduced from YAv. into OAv.: YAv. *ainim*, OAv. *aniiə̄m*, *ainīm*, cf. Vedic *anyám* "other." Similarly **-u̯ə-* became *-u̯u* and then *ū̆*: YAv. *tūm*, OAv. *tuuə̄m*, cf. Vedic *tvám* "you." Note that *-aiiu̯ə-* became *-ōiiu-* by umlaut: YAv. *ōiium* from *aēuua-* "one;" YAv. *vīdōiium* from *vīdaēuua-* "abjuring the devils;" YAv. *Harōiium* beside OPers. *Haraiva-*. An exception is *daēum* (not **dōiium*!) from *daēuua-* "devil." Proto-Av. **ai̯ə*, **āi̯ə*, **au̯ə*, and **āu̯ə* before *n*, *m* were reduced in YAv. to the disyllabic diphthongs *aē*, *āi*, *ao*, *āu* respectively: YAv. *aem* beside OAv. *aiiə̄m* "this;" YAv. *daēnā-* "religion" (from **dai̯ənā-*) was introduced into OAv.

Before **-u̯i-*, *a* became *ə*: *səuuišta-* "strongest," cf. Vedic *śáviṣṭha-*. In certain environments *a* became *e*: between *i̯* and *j*, cf. *iθiiejah-* "abandonment;" between *i̯* and a syllable containing *ī̆*, *ii*, or *ē̆*, cf. *yesne*, loc. sing. from *yasna-* "veneration." In some environments *a* became *o*: between *p*, *m*, *u̯* and a syllable containing *u* (but not *u̯*): *pouru* "much;" *mošū* "soon;" *vohu* "good," but there are exceptions: *vaŋhuš* "good;" *pasu-* "cattle;" *maδu-* "wine."

Proto-Ir. **ā̆n* became *ą* before spirants *x*, *θ*, *f*, *s*, *z*, *š*, *hi*: *mąθra-* "sacred utterance," cf. Vedic *mántra-*; *ąsa-* "party," cf. Vedic *áṁśa-*; *mąsta* "he thought," cf. Vedic *maṁsta*; *ązō* "narrowness," cf. Vedic *áṁhas-*; *dąhišta-* "most versed," cf. Vedic *dáṁsiṣṭha-*; *vąs* "he prevailed" (from **u̯ānst*); *sąstā* (2 plur. imv.) "appear," cf. Vedic *á-chāntta*; *frąš* "forward" (from **prāŋᵏš*).

In OAv. final *-ah* (cf. Vedic *-aḥ* from *-as*) became *-ə̄* but it has in most cases been replaced by YAv. *-ō*. That even YAv. originally had *-ə̄* (cf. Khot. *-ä* [ə] from **-ah*) is indicated by such forms as YAv. *vacə̄bīš* (instr. plur.) based on nom. sing. OAv. *vacə̄* (= Vedic *vácaḥ*).

We often find long, that is, open (*back*) *ā* instead of closed (*front*) *a* in initial position: *ārmaiti-* "right-mindedness," cf. Vedic *arámati-*; *kāuuaiiō* "princes," cf. Vedic *kaváyaḥ* "seers;" *srāuuahiieitī* "he desires fame," cf. Vedic śravasyáti; *hātąm* (gen. plur.) "of the existing (ones)," cf. Vedic *satā́m*. Note also *ā* for *a* after *i* and *u*: *vii-ādarəsəm* "I have seen," cf. Vedic *adarśam*;

vərəziiātąm, nīdiiātąm, višiiātā, hāmiiāsaite, paitiiāmraot̰, aiβii-āma-, drəguuātā, drəguuāitē (but *drəguuatō*), etc.

Proto-Ir. **ai̯* usually becomes *aē* in open syllables (*vaēdā̆* "he knows") but *ōi* in closed syllables (*vōistā̆* "you know"). In final position it appears as *-ōi* in OAv. but as *-e* in YAv. The spelling *-ē* in OAv. is due to YAv. YAv. has *-ōi* only in *yōi* and *maiδiiōi*. The dat. sing. forms OAv. *axtōiiōi* and YAv. *anumatōe* point to an original **-ə̄i̯ə̄i̯* from Proto-Indo-Ir. **-ai̯ai̯*, cf. Vedic. *-aye*.

Proto-Ir. *au̯* became *ao*, but before final *-š* it usually became *ə̄u* in OAv. and YAv.: *gə̄uš, mańiiə̄uš, mərəθiiaoš*. In final position *-au̯* became sometimes *-u̯ō*, sometimes *-ō* (cf. Vedic *-o*): OAv. *huuō* "yonder" (from **hau̯*, cf. OPers. *hauv*); *ərəzuuō* (voc. sing.) "O straight one;" *huxratuuō* (voc. sing.) "O skilful one," cf. Vedic *sukrato*; but *mainiiō* (voc. sing.) "O spirit," cf. Vedic *manyo*; *aŋhuuō* (loc. sing.) "in the life;" *gātuuō* "in the place;" *daŋ́huuō* "in the land" beside *daŋ́hō*; *haētō* "on the bridge;" *šātō* "in peace;" *vaštō* "in the wish;" *həṇtō* "in gain," cf. Vedic *sánitau*.

Many changes are found in the case of Proto-Ir. *ā*, e.g. *ą*: *uruuąnō* "souls" beside *uruuānō*; in final position always *ąm, ąn*); *å*: *mazåṇtəm* (acc. sing.) "great;" *måŋhəm* (acc. sing) "moon;" *e*: *aiienī* "I shall go," cf. Vedic *ayāni*; *zbaiiemi* "I call," cf. Vedic *hvayāmi*. Final *-āh* became *-å* (cf. Vedic. *-āḥ* from *-ās*); *sāsnå* "commandments" (by analogy also *sāsnås-ca* "and commandments").

Original *ā* is often shortened, as in *dātaras-ca* beside *dātārō* "creators;" *-anąm*, gen. plur. ending with disyllabic *-ąm*, cf. Vedic and OPers. *-ānām*; *aētaŋhąm*, cf. Vedic *etā́sām*: *-at̰.haca* (instead of **-āt̰.haca*), but *-āat̰cā̆* in *ašāat̰cā̆*.

Before a vowel, *āi̯* and *āu̯* are often shortened to *ai̯* and *au̯*, a feature shared by Avestan with East Iranian dialects such as Sogdian: *vaiiu-* "wind," cf. Vedic *vāyú-*; *zaiiata* "he was born," cf. Vedic *jāyata*; *-aiiå*, gen. sing. fem. ending, cf. Vedic *-āyāḥ*; *-aiiāi*, dat. sing. fem. ending, cf. Vedic *-āyai*; *nauuāza-* "boatman," cf. Vedic *nāvājá-*; *yauuaṇt-* "as great, as much," cf. Vedic *yāvant-*; *ašauuā* "righteous," cf. Vedic *r̥tāvā*.

The consonants: (a) *Semivowels*. In the Sasanian archetype the semivowels *i̯* and *u̯* were always written *ẏ* and *v* in word-initial position. These sounds probably represent an intermediate stage in the development of initial *i̯* and *u̯* to *j* and *b* as seen in NPers. In the Indian manuscripts *ẏ* is replaced by *y*, whose original value was probably palatal *ź*. In medial position the manuscripts have *ii, uu* and not *y, v* as earlier transcriptions seemed to indicate, (e.g., *vayu-* for *vaiiu-*). The graphs *ii* and *uu* are to be interpreted phonetically as *ii̯* and *uu̯*: *friia-* "dear," cf. Vedic *priyá-*; *druua-* "firm," cf. Vedic *dhruvá-*. The fact that *jiia* "bowstring" and *kuua* "where" were disyllabic in YAv., cf. Vedic *jⁱyā́* and *kᵘvà* respectively, is proved by their being written with a short final vowel, since the final vowel of monosyllables was regularly written long in YAv. *ii̯* and *uu̯* may have developed in West Iran under the influence of Old Persian, where every postconsonantal *i̯* and *u̯* became *iy* and *uv* respectively: Av. *ańiia-* (from **ani̯a-*, cf. Vedic *anyá-*) like OPers. *aniya-*; Av. *hauruua-* (from **haru̯a-*, cf. Vedic *sárva-*) like OPers. *haruva-*. Even intervocalic *i̯* and *u̯* are sometimes written *iy* and *uv* in OPers. Thus Av. *dāraiia-* and *bauuaiti* correspond to OPers. *adāraiya* and *bauvatiy*. Note too that intervocalic *ii* and *uu* may even be etymologically justified: OAv. *āiiāt* from **āii̯āt*, cf. Vedic *iyāt*, Av. *sraiiah-* "more excellent," cf. Vedic *śréyas-* (from Proto-Indo-Ir. **śrai̯Hi̯as-*); *gauuāstriia-* "belonging to the cattle pasture" from **gau̯-u̯āstrii̯a-*. In the manuscripts the sequences *-iiuu-* (from **-i̯u̯-*) and *-uuii-* (from **-u̯i̯*) are usually simplified to *-iuu-* and *-uii-* or else expanded to *-iiauu-* and *-uuaii-*, but the original spellings are sometimes still attested: *mańiiuuå*, that is, **mańii̯uu̯å*, from **mańiᵘu̯āh* "of the two (evil) spirits;" *paouruuiia-*, that is, **paouruu̯ii̯a-*, from **pauru̯ii̯a-* "first," cf. OPers. *paruviya-*.

Internal *i̯* was lost in YAv. before *e*: YAv. *vaheh̄ī-* (fem.) "the better," from **u̯ahi̯ehī-*, cf. Vedic *vásyasī-*; *-ahe*, gen. sing. masc. ending, cf. Vedic *-asya*; *kaine* "girl," cf. Vedic *kanⁱyā̆*; *bāzuβe* "with both arms," from **bāzuβi̯a*, cf. Vedic *bāhúbhyām*; YAv. *-ə̄e*, dat. sing. ending, cf. Vedic *-aye*.

A late but consistent change is that of *-u̯e* (from earlier **-u̯ai̯* and **-u̯ai̯*) to *-uiie*: OAv. *mruiiē*, YAv. *mruiie* "I say," cf. Vedic *bruve*; OAv. *vīduiiē* "to know" from **u̯idu̯ai̯*.

In some cases Proto-Ir. *i̯* and *u̯* combine with a preceding consonant. Proto-Indo-Ir. **či̯* became **śi̯* in original OAv. and then *śii* in the Sasanian archetype. In original YAv. it became *ś* but is mostly written *š* or *ṣ̌* in the manuscripts. Thus we have: OAv. *śiiāta-* beside YAv. *śāto* (mostly written *šāto* or *ṣ̌ātō*).

Proto-Ir. *hi̯-* from Proto-Indo-Ir. *-si̯-* remained unchanged in original OAv. but became *-hii-* in the Sasanian archetype. After the change of *h* to *ŋh*, Proto-Ir. *-hi̯* developed in original YAv. to *-ŋ́h-* from **-ŋhi̯-*. Thus we have: OAv. *vahiiō* beside YAv. *vaŋ́hō* (wrongly written *vaŋhō*), cf. Vedic *vásyaḥ* "better." In the same way Proto-Ir. *-hu̯-* (from Proto-Indo-Ir. *-su̯-*) developed into OAv. *-huu-* (from *-hu̯-*) and original YAv. *-ŋᵛh-* (often written *-ŋuh-*or-*ŋh*-in the MSS): OAv. *gūšahuuā*; YAv. *pərəsaŋha* (often written *pərəsaŋuha, pərəsaŋha*). Initially **hu̯-* became in Av. *xᵛ-*: *xᵛafna-* "sleep," cf. Vedic *svápna-*. On *xᵛ* see also under (f) below.

After certain consonants Proto-Ir. *u̯* underwent further changes. Proto-Ir. *śu̯* became *sp* in Avestan and Median: *aspa-* "horse," cf. Vedic *áśva-*. Proto-Ir. *źu̯* became *zb* in Av. and Median: *zbaiia-* "to call," cf. Vedic *hvaya-*, from Proto-Indo-Ir. **ǰʰu̯ai̯a-*. Proto-Ir. *θu̯* became *θβ* in Av.: *caθβārō* "four," cf. Vedic *catvā́raḥ*, Sogd. and Parth. *ctf'r*. Proto-Ir. *δu̯* became in YAv. *δβ* (*ərəδβa-* "upright" beside *ərəduua-* from **ərdu̯a-*) but initial **du̯i-* became OAv. *dbi-* (*daibišiiant-* but *duuaēšah-*, cf. Vedic *dvéṣas-* "hatred") and YAv. *t̰bi-* (*t̰bišiiant-* and by analogy *t̰baēšah-*). From initial **du̯i-* YAv. has also *bi-* perhaps by dissimilation; *bitiia-* "second" beside OAv. *daibitiia-*, cf. Vedic *dvitī́ya-*.

Initial **u̯r-* was metathesized to **ru̯-* and written

uruu- in Av.: *uruuata-* "commandment," cf. Vedic *vratá-*.

(b) *Liquids* (only *r*).

Consonantal *r* and original syllabic **r̥* fell together in Avestan, syllabic **r̥* becoming *ər*. After *t* the *ə* was usually dropped: *ātrəm* (acc. sing.) "fire" from **ātərəm*; *strə̄š* (acc. plur.) "stars" from **stərə̄š*; *striia-* "to sin" from **stəri̯a-*, where the *ə* must have been lost before *i*-epenthesis could take place. Immediately following the Proto-Indo-Ir. accent *rk* became *hrk* and *rp* became *hrp*: *mahrka-* "destruction," cf. Vedic *márka-*; *vəhrka-* "wolf," cf. Vedic *vŕ̥ka-*; *kəhrpəm* "body" from **kŕ̥pam*. Instead of the expected **hrt* from **rt* we find *ṣ̌*: *maṣ̌iia-* "man," cf. Vedic *mártⁱya-*; *aməṣ̌a-* "immortal," cf. Vedic *amŕ̥ta-*. From the third century A.D. Mid. Pers. loanwords from Av. are attested which have *hr*/*hl* for Av. *ṣ̌*: Mid. Pers. *'hlw* [*ahlaw*] from Av. *aṣ̌auua*. *ṣ̌* will accordingly have been pronounced originally as a voiceless *l*-like lateral fricative, which, at any rate in the post-Sasanian period, merged with *ṣ̌*.

(c) *Nasals*.

On the whole the nasals *n* and *m* remained unchanged in Av., but they are regularly written *n̨* before *t, d, k, g, c, j, b*. The letter *n̨* probably represents a uvular nasal that was articulated just by lowering the soft palate. It is indicated in this article by *N* in reconstructions. The same sound no doubt occurred in OPers. but it was not written: Av. *an̨tarə* "inside" but OPers. *a-ta-ra* [*aⁿtar*]. The dorsal nasal was, however, retained in YAv. *paŋtaŋhum* "a fifth" from **paŋᵏtahu̯əm*. An unusual metathesis is attested by YAv. *mərəγən̨te* "he destroys" for **mərəŋte from* **mr̥ŋᵏtai̯*. Proto-Indo-Ir. *ns* before *ā̆* resulted in Av. *ŋ(g)h*: YAv. *saŋha-*, OAv. *sə̄ŋgha-*, cf. Vedic *śáṃsa-*.

For discussion of Av. *-aŋha-*, *-aŋ́ha-*, *aŋʷha*, and *-aŋ́hi-* see above under (a) and below under (f).

Before *i̯*, *n* was palatalized to *ń* but in the manuscripts *ń* is usually replaced by *n*: *ańiia-*, cf. Vedic *anyá-*. The manuscripts often have *m̨* instead of *hm*, which makes it probable that *m̨* was a voiceless *m*. Final *-m* is found for *-n* when the syllable in question had a labial initial: OAv. *dāmą̇m*, *nāmą̇m*: YAv. *uruθβą̇m*, *θrizafəm*, *aṣ̌āum* (from **aṣ̌āu̯ən*).

Phonetically Av. *ą* was probably nasalized *ə̄*. Not only did it develop from Proto-Indo-Ir. *ā̆n* (*ā̆N*) before *s* and *š* as seen above on the vowels but it occurs also in OAv. *ərą̇š* from *-*ərəNš* from older *-*rNš*: *nərą̇š*, *mātərą̇š*, *mərą̇ždiiāi*. Note also *mərą̇ṣ̌iiāt̰* from **mərəNṣ̌i̯āt* from older **mr̥nči̯āt*. As in the case of the OAv. and YAv. acc. plur. endings *-ī̆š* and *-ū̆š* from *-*iNš* and *-*uNš*, the nasalization is not attested in the acc. plur. of consonant stems in YAv.: *nərə̄š*, *strə̄š*, and *pairiiaētrə̄š-ca*. In the manuscripts these forms are often miswritten, e.g., *nərə̄uš* for *nərə̄š*.

(d) *Occlusives*.

The Proto-Indo-Ir. occlusives *p, t, k*, became *f, θ, x* in Proto-Ir. before a consonant. Proto-Indo-Ir. *pʰ, tʰ, kʰ* also became *f, θ, x* before a vowel. However, Av. shows certain peculiarities. After *s* and *š* it has only *p, t, k*. Moreover, Av. has *pt* instead of the expected **ft*; *fδ* and *xδ* for expected **fθ* and **xθ*; *ši* and *še* for expected **xi* and **xi̯ai̯* in *haši* and *haše* corresponding to Vedic *sákhi* and *sákhye*.

It is characteristic of OAv. that it has preserved *b, d, g* from Proto-Indo-Ir. *b, d, g* and *bʰ, dʰ, gʰ*. In YAv., *b, d, g* are retained only in initial position while in medial position they were replaced by the voiced fricatives *β, δ, γ* except after a nasal or a sibilant. Thus, OAv. *dugədar-* "daughter" contrasts with YAv. *duγδar-*. There are, however, a number of exceptions. Note OAv. *-βž-* and *γž-*, YAv. *γž-*, *γəm-*, and *γən-*. Proto-Ir. *-dn-* became *-n-*: OAv. and YAv. *bū̆na-* "bottom," cf. Vedic *budhná-*. Proto-Ir. *dm-* was retained in OAv. but became *n̂m-* in YAv.: OAv. *dəmāna-* "house" beside YAv. *nmāna-*. In YAv., *γ* was lost before *u* and *u̯*: *Mourum*, cf. OPers. *Margum*; *raom*, cf. Vedic *raghúm*; *druuan̨t-* from **druγu̯ant-*, cf. OAv. *drəguuan̨t-*. In YAv. *driγūm* "pauper," the *γ* was restored by analogy with other forms of the paradigm such as gen. sing. *driγaoš*.

The YAv. change of *β* to *u̯* is dialectal, perhaps Arachosian; it may also have belonged to the colloquial language. Examples are: *gəuruuaiia-* "to seize" from **gərβāi̯a-*, cf. Vedic *gr̥bhāyá-*; the prep. *auui* "to," which is also written *aoui*, *aoi*, from **aβi* contrasting with *aiβi-* in nominal compounds, cf. OAv. *aibī* and Vedic *abhí*; the adj. *uuaiia*, *uuaēm* "on both sides," cf. Vedic *ubháya-*; *uua* "both," cf. Vedic *ubhā́* (masc. dual); *uiie* from **uu̯e*, cf. Vedic *ubhé* (neuter dual); *nəruiiō* "to the men" beside *nərəbiiō*, cf. Vedic *nŕ̥bhyaḥ*; *aṣ̌auuaoiiō* "to the righteous" from **aṣ̌au̯aβi̯ō*. In some cases the spellings seem to be arbitrary: YAv. *māuuōiia* "to me" from **mau̯i̯a* from older **maβi̯a*, cf. OAv. *maibiiā*; *huuāuuōiia* "to (your)self" from **huu̯au̯i̯a* from older **huu̯aβi̯a*, cf. original *-*u̯i̯-* in *hāuuōiia* (inst. sing.) "with the left (hand)" from **hau̯i̯ā*, cf. Vedic *savyā́*.

The occasional replacement of *δ* by *θ* appears also to be dialectal, perhaps West Iranian. In the athematic *daδāiti* "he puts; he gives," cf. Vedic *dad(h)āti*, *δ* is retained but in the thematic new formation *daθaiti* earlier *δ* has been replaced by *θ*. The gen. sing. of *daδuuå* "creator" is *daθušō*, which is confirmed by *dathousa* (in Greek script) in the Cappadocian calendar. Note also *h* from *θ* in Parth. *dh-*, NPers. *dah-* "to give." *θ* is attested also in East Iranian in Khot. *parāth-* "to sell" from **parā-daθa-*, cf. Av. *para.daθa-*.

Proto-Indo-Ir. *t* was lost before *s*: Av. *masiia-* "fish," cf. Vedic *mátsya-*. Similarly, Av. has *st* from *-*tˢt-* from *t*/*d* + *t* as in *vista-* "found" from **u̯idˢtá-*, cf. Vedic *vittá-* and *zd* from *-*dᶻdʰ-* from *dʰ* + *t* as in *vərəzda-* "grown" from **u̯rdᶻdʰá-*, cf. Vedic *vr̥ddhá-*.

Final *-t* was lost after *n*, probably already in Proto-Indo-Ir., and also after *s*. Examples are: YAv. *ās* "he was" from **āst*; OAv. *cinas* "she assigns" with *-s* from *-*st*; *vą̇s* "it prevailed" from **vān-s-t*; OAv. *są̇s* "it seemed" from **sśānd-s-t*. However, both *-st* and *-št* are also found: OAv. *urūraost* "he wailed (?)" from **ruraudˢt*; YAv. *nāist* "he cursed" from **nāid-s-t*; OAv. *vaxšt* "he made grow," *cōišt* "he assigned," *tāšt* "he shaped." In all other cases *-t* became *-t̰* (probably an implosive): YAv. *barat̰* OAv. *cōrət̰* from **čart*; OAv.

yaogət "he harnessed" from **i̯augd* (?) from older **i̯aukt*. The graph *-gət* may represent an implosive *-k/-g* in YAv. *paragət̰* "apart from," cf. Vedic *párāk*; YAv. *aṣ̌iš.hāgət̰* "following Aṣ̌i;" OAv. *paitiiaogət̰* "responding."

(e) *Affricates*.

The palatal affricates of Proto-Indo-Ir. *č, ǰ, ǰʰ*, which in Vedic became *c, j, h*, survived in Av. as *c, j, j*. On the development of Proto-Indo-Ir **či̯* to OAv. *śii* and YAv. *ś* see above on the vowels. The YAv. change of *j* to the palatal **ž́*, always written *ž*, is dialectal, perhaps Arachosian: *druža-* "to deceive" from **druji̯a-*, cf. OAv. *a-drujiiant-*; *snaēža-* "to snow;" *draža-* "to hold;" *daža-* "to burn;" *baža-* "to distribute;" *naēnižaiti* "he washes." It occurs very rarely in nouns: *aži-* "snake;" *tiži-⁰* "sharp;" *snaēžana-* "slavering;" *a-družąm* (gen. plur.) "of the deceitless" (otherwise only *druj-*).

The primary palatal affricates of Proto-Indo-Ir., namely *ć, ȷ́* and *ȷ́ʰ* from Proto-IE. *ḱ, ǵ, ǵʰ*, developed via Proto-Ir. *ś, ź, ź* to Av. *s, z, z* corresponding to Vedic *ś, j*, and *h* respectively: Av. *satəm* "hundred," cf. Vedic *śatám*; *zaoša-* "pleasure," cf. Vedic *jóṣa-*; *zaotar-* "priest," cf. Vedic *hotár-*. Before *t, dʰ*, and *bʰ*, ć and ȷ́ developed already in Proto-Indo-Ir. to *š* and *ž* respectively: OAv. *vaštī* "he wishes" beside *vasəmī* "I wish," cf. Vedic *váṣṭi* beside *váśmi*; OAv. *važdra-* "pulling" from *vaz-* "to pull," cf. Vedic *voḍhár-* "draught (i.e., pulling) animal" from *vah-*; OAv. and YAv. *vīžibiiō*, abl. plur. from *vīs-* "tribe," cf. Vedic *viḍbhyáḥ* from *víś-*. In initial position *źn-* became *žn-* in YAv. (= OPers. *xšn-*): *žnātar-* "knower," cf. Vedic *jñātár-* "knower," OPers. *xšnā-* "to know;" *žnu-* "knee," cf. Vedic *jñu-⁰*. Internally both *śn* and *źn* became *šn*: YAv. *frašna-* "question," cf. Vedic *praśná-*; YAv. *baršna* "in height, depth" (= OPers. *baršnā*) from **barźnā* from older **bʰarȷ́ʰnā*. But *sn* is found instead of *šn* in some cases due to the influence of other forms: OAv. *vasnā* "according to wish" (= OPers. *vašnā*) from *vas-*; OAv. and YAv. *yasna-* "veneration" (cf. Vedic *yajñá-*), from *yaz-*.

The Proto-Indo-Ir. clusters *sć* and *šć* from Proto-IE. *sḱ* developed via Proto-Ir. *sś* and *šś* to Av. *s* (= Vedic *ch*): Av. *pərəsa-* "to ask," cf. Vedic *pṛchá-*. Similarly, *ćš* and *ȷ́žʰ*, from Proto-IE. *ḱs, ḱþ* and *ǵʰs, ǵʰþ* respectively, developed via Proto-Ir. *śš* and *źž* to Av. *š* and *ž*: Av. *šōiθra-* "dwelling-place," cf. Vedic *kṣétra-*; *uz-uuažat̰* "he drew out," cf. Vedic *vákṣat* (subj.) from Proto-IE. *u̯eǵʰ-se-* (see next paragraph).

(*f*) *Sibilants*.

Proto-Indo-Ir. *s* and *z* were maintained in Av. before *n* and occlusives, and after *t* and *d*, which were lost in that position as noted above. Thus we find: YAv. *snāuuarə* "sinew," cf. Vedic *snā́van-*; *asti* "he is," cf. Vedic *asti*; *masiia-* "fish," cf. Vedic *mátsya-*; YAv. *mazga-* "marrow" from Proto-IE. *mozgʰo-*; YAv. *aspasca* "and the horse," cf. Vedic *áśvaś-ca*; OAv. *zdī* (2 sing. imv.) "be," cf. Vedic *edhi*, from Indo-Ir. *azdʰī*; *vərəzda-* "grown" from **u̯rdᶻdʰā-*, cf. Vedic *vṛddhá-*.

After Proto-Indo-Ir. *ĭ* (*i̯*), *ŭ* (*u̯*), *r* (*r̥*), *k/g/gʰ*, and *ć/ȷ́/ȷ́ʰ* (from Proto-IE. *ḱ/ǵ/ǵʰ*), Proto-Indo-Ir. *s* and *z* became *š* and *ž*: Av. *vīša-* "poison," cf. Vedic *viṣá-*; *mīžda-* "reward," cf. Vedic *mīḍhá-*; *zušta-* "loved," cf. Vedic *júṣṭa-*; *aršti-* "spear," cf. Vedic *ṛṣṭí-*; *uxšan-* "bull," cf. Vedic *ukṣáṇ-*; OAv. *aoγžā* "you say" from **au̯gʰ-sa*; *vašī* "you wish," cf. Vedic *vakṣi*, from Proto-IE. *u̯eḱ-si*; *tašan-* "fashioner," cf. Vedic *tákṣan-*, from Proto-IE. *téḱþon-*. In Proto-Ir. this development took place also in clusters with labials. Thus Av. has *fš* from **ps* and **pś*: Av. *drafša-* "banner," cf. Vedic *drapsá-*; *fšu-* from **pśu-* to *pasu-* "cattle." Similarly Av. has *βž* from **bzʰ*: *diβža-* "to deceive," cf. Vedic *dípsa-*, from Proto-Indo-Ir. *dʰibzʰa-*; *vaβžaka-* "wasp" from **u̯abzʰa-* from Proto-IE. *u̯obʰso-*.

In all other positions Proto-Indo-Ir. *s* became Proto-Ir. *h*. This *h* was kept initially before a vowel: *hafta* "seven," cf. Vedic *saptá*. But **hi̯* became *x́ii-* in OAv.: *x́iiāt̰* "he should be," cf. YAv.; *hiiāt̰*, Vedic *syāt*; and **hu̯* became *xᵛ* in both OAv. and YAv.: *xᵛafna-* "sleep," cf. Vedic *svápna-*. Medial *h* was unchanged only before *i* and *u*: *ahī* "you are;" *ahura-* "lord." In OAv. medial *h* remained unchanged also before *i̯* and *u̯*: OAv. *ahiiā*, cf. Vedic *ásya*; *gūšahuuā* with the ending *-ahuuā* corresponding to Vedic *-asva*. In the sequence *ăha*, *h* probably became voiced and resulted in *ŋh*: *aŋhat̰*, cf. Vedic *ásat*; *ăŋharə*, cf. Vedic *āsur*. That this *ŋ* was phonemically significant is shown by the fact that it was extended from the gen. sing. *vaŋhāuš* from **u̯ahauš* (= Vedic *vásoḥ*) to the nom. sing. masc. *vaŋhuš* although it is not found in the neuter *vohū̆* or when *m* or *n* follow as in *vohūm* and *vohunąm*. In medial position *hi̯* and *hu̯* developed in YAv. to *ŋ́h* and *ŋᵛh*: see (a) above. (See also Hoffmann, *Aufsätze* II, pp. 595-96).

In OAv. the gen. sing. ending *-ahiiā* is always written with *x́* before enclitic *-cā* "and:" *-ax́iiā-cā*. This pronunciation may reflect the secondary accentuation **ahi̯á-ca*. *-x́ii-* is also found elsewhere for *-hi̯-*: OAv. *dax́iiāuš* "of the land" but YAv. *daŋ́hāuš*; both OAv. and YAv. *dax́iiūm* (acc. sing.) and *dax́iiunąm* (gen. plur.).

The use of *-xᵛ-* for internal *-hu̯-* in YAv. *Haraxᵛaitī-* "Arachosia" and OAv. *nəmaxᵛaitī-* "respectful" may be dialectal, perhaps Arachosian. The same applies to the use of *xᵛ* for unaccented syllabic *huu̯-* in the following: *Xᵛāstrā-*, name of an Archosian river, from **hu-u̯āstrā-*; OAv. *xᵛāθra-* "welfare" from **hu-āθra-*, cf. *duž-āθra-* "discomfort;" *xᵛə̄ng* (gen. sing.) from **huu̯ə̄ŋh* to *huuarə* "sun," cf. Vedic *suvár*; *xᵛaēta-* "easy to walk along" from **hu-ā-ita-*; *xᵛīti-* "easy walking." (See also Hoffmann, "Das Avesta in der Persis," pp. 92-93.)

Proto-Ir. *hm* is retained internally as in *ahmi* "I am" but the *h* is lost in initial position: *mahi* "we are," cf. Vedic *smasi*. Proto-Indo-Ir. *sr* appears to have become *θr* in YAv. in initial position: *θraotō.stāc-* "flowing in rivers," from **srautas-tāč-*, cf. Vedic *srótas-* but OPers. *rautah-*. Medially *hr* became *ŋr* in YAv.: *aŋra-* "evil," cf. Vedic *asrá-* "painful;" *daŋra-* "knowing," cf. Vedic *dasrá-*. These forms were introduced from YAv. into OAv., where one also finds the spellings *aŋ̇gra-* and *daŋ̇gra-*.

For the loss of final *-h* see above on the vowels.

Bibliography: Chr. Bartholomae, in Geiger and Kuhn, *Grundr. Ir. Phil* I/I, pp. 1-48,

152-88. W. B. Henning, "The Disintegration of the Avestic Studies," *TPS*, 1942, pp. 40-56. London, 1944 (*Selected Papers* II, Acta Iranica 15, Leiden, 1977, pp. 151-67). K. Hoffmann, "Altiranisch," in *HO* IV, 1, Leiden and Cologne, 1958, pp. 1-19 (*Aufsätze* I, pp. 58-76). Idem, "Das Avesta in der Persis," in J. Harmatta, ed., *Prolegomena to the Sources on the History of Pre-Islamic Central Asia*, Budapest, 1979, pp. 89-93. Idem, *Aufsätze zur Indoiranistik* I-II, Wiesbaden, 1975-76. G. Morgenstierne, "Orthography and Sound-system of the Avesta," *NTS* 12, 1942, pp. 30-78 (*Irano-Dardica*, Wiesbaden, 1973, pp. 31-79). (This was the only comprehensive phonetic and phonemic analysis of Avestan until 1979.) H. Reichelt, *Awestisches Elementarbuch*, Heidelberg, 1909, pp. 28-89. S. N. Sokolov, "Yazyk Avesty," in V. J. Abaev, ed., *Osnovy iranskogo yazykoznaniya* I: *Drevneiranskie yazyki*, Moscow, 1979, pp. 136-60. G. Windfuhr, "Diacritic and Distinctive Features in Avestan," *JAOS* 91, 1971, pp. 104-24. Idem, "Some Avestan Rules and Their Signs," ibid., 92, 1972, pp. 52-59. See also J. Duchesne-Guillemin, *Kratylos* 7, 1962, pp. 4-11. J. Kellens, ibid., 16, 1971, pp. 4-6; 18, 1973, p. 1.

(K. HOFFMANN)

iii. THE GRAMMAR OF AVESTAN

The morphology of Avestan nouns, adjectives, pronouns, and verbs is, like that of the closely related Old Persian, inherited from Proto-Indo-European via Proto-Indo-Iranian (Proto-Aryan), and agrees largely with that of Vedic, the oldest known form of Indo-Aryan. The interpretation of the transmitted Avestan texts presents in many cases considerable difficulty for various reasons both with respect to their contexts and their grammar. Accordingly, systematic comparison with Vedic is of much assistance in determining and explaining Avestan grammatical forms.

Old Avestan (OAv.) or Gathic Avestan, the language of Zarathustra, the founder of the Zoroastrian religion, is particularly archaic. Young Avestan (YAv.) is the language of the later texts, the earliest of which may date from the sixth century B.C. It already shows numerous innovations when compared with OAv.

A particular difficulty of Avestan is caused by the fact that many sound changes took place which obscure the original structure of the forms. Note that words ending in *-ā*, *-ī*, *-ū*, *-ē* are OAv. while those ending in *-a*, *-i*, *-u -e* are YAv. Forms that are otherwise identical in OAv. and YAv. are indicated by *-ā̆*, *-ī̆*, *-ū̆*, *-ē̆*. Apart from forms with these endings, forms that are common to both OAv. and YAv. are not specified.

1. Nominal inflection.

Like Vedic and Proto-IE., Avestan distinguishes three genders: masculine, feminine, and neuter. Words designating male and female beings are masculine and feminine respectively, but also many words that designate inanimate objects and concepts are masculine or feminine and not neuter as might be expected. Avestan has three numbers: singular, dual, and plural. The dual is used to refer to two persons or objects. Avestan has eight cases: nominative for the subject, accusative for the direct object, dative for the indirect object, genitive to indicate possession or relation, instrumental to indicate means or association, ablative to indicate separation, locative to indicate location, and vocative used in addressing a person, less commonly a thing.

The basis of the nominal inflection is the noun stem, which not only conveys the lexical meaning but in most cases also the gender. In general, inflectional categories are marked by endings, most of which indicate at the same time number, case, and, in part, gender. Thus a particular ending may be characteristic of the genitive sing. masc. Neuter nouns are inflected like masc. nouns except that they have different endings in the nom. and acc. for all three numbers. The nom. and acc. of neuter nouns are always identical. Some noun stems remain unchanged throughout the paradigm whereas others have different ablaut grades according to the case.

The paradigm followed by a noun or adjective is usually determined by the final sound of its stem. Thus, there are masculines and neuters in *-a-*, feminines in *-ā-*, *-ī-*, *-ū-*, masculines and feminines in *-i-*, *-u-*, masculines in *-n-* and *-r-*, neuters in *-man-* and *-ah-*, and words of all three genders ending in consonants (e.g., *-p-*, *-t-*, *-k-*, *-g-*, *-s-*).

The addition of the case ending to the final sound of the stem often involves special sound changes. Thus, the original Proto-IE. ending of the nom. sing. masc. and fem. of most noun stems is *-s*, and this *-s* is retained in the case of *-a-* stems before *-cā̆* "and" (in sandhi), but otherwise *-as* developed via *-ah* to *-ō*. After *-ī̆-*, *-ū̆-* and some consonants, *-s* became *-š*, e.g., *gairiš* "mountain," *aŋhuš* "life," *vāxš* "voice" (< **u̯āk + s*).

a-stems. The thematic stems in *-a-* are particularly numerous. Examples are masc. nouns: *ahura-* "lord," *maṣ̌iia* "mortal," *yasna-* "worship," *vīra-* "man," *zasta-* "hand;" neuter nouns: *aṣ̌a-* "truth," *uxδa-* "word," *xšaθra-* "rule," *š́iiaoθna* "action;" and adjectives: *aka-* "bad," *aniia-* "other," *hauruua-* "entire."

The masc. *a*-stem inflection is as follows. Sing.: nom. *ahurō, yasnas-ca*;—acc. *ahurəm* (*maṣ̌īm* < **maṣ̌iiəm*; *haurum* < **hauruəm*),—inst. *ahurā̆*;—dat. *ahurāi*, OAv. *ahurāi.ā*; abl. *yasnāt̰*, *yasnāat̰-ca*, *-at̰ haca*;—gen. OAv. *ahurahiiā*, *-ax́iiā-cā*, YAv. *ahurahe*;—loc. *yesnē̆* (*zastaiia* < **-ai̯ + ā*); OAv. *ōi*;—voc. *ahurā̆*.—Dual: nom. *ahurā̆*;—inst./dat./abl. *ahuraēibiia*;—gen. *vīraiiā̊*;—loc. OAv. *zastaiiō*.—Plur.: nom. *maṣ̌iiā*, *maṣ̌iiā̊ŋhō*, *ahura-ca*;—acc. OAv. *maṣ̌iiə̄ṇg*, *maṣ̌iią̄s-ca*, YAv. *-ą*/*-ə̄* (*zastə̄*);—inst. *zastāiš*;—dat./abl. OAv. *-ōibiiō*, YAv. *-aēibiiō*;—gen. *yasnanąm*;—loc. *maṣ̌iiaēšū*, YAv. *-aēšuua* (< **-aišu + ā*);—voc. OAv. *ahurā̊ŋhō*.

Neuter *a*-stem inflection differs from masc. *a*-stem inflection only in having special forms in the nom./acc., e.g. sing. *xšaθrəm* "rule;" dual OAv. *š́iiaoθnōi* "the two actions;" plur. *uxδā* "words."

ā- and ī-stems. The inflection of fem. *ā*-stem words, e.g., *gaēθā-* "living being," *daēnā-* "religion," and the inflection of fem. *ī*-stem words, e.g., *nāirī-* "woman," *aṣ̌aonī-* "righteous" (fem. adjective from *aṣ̌auuan-*) are largely parallel.

The fem. *ā*-and *ī*-stem inflection is as follows. Sing.: nom. *daēnā̆, nāirī*;—acc. *daēnąm, aṣ̌aonīm*;—inst. *daēnā̆, daēnaiiā̆, -iiā̆*; dat. *daēnaiiāi, aṣ̌aoniiāi*;—abl. YAv. *-aiiāt̰*, YAv. *-iiāt̰*;—gen. *daēnaiiå, nāiriiå*;—loc. *grīuuaiia* "on the neck;"—voc. *daēne, sūra, aṣ̌aoni*.—Plur.: nom./acc./voc. *gaēθå, aṣ̌aonīš*;—inst. *gaēθābīš*;—dat./abl. *gaēθābiiō, aṣ̌aonibiiō*;—gen. *gaēθanąm, aṣ̌aoninąm*;—loc. *gaēθāhu, gaēθāhuua, -išu, -išuua*.

i- and u-stems. Similarly formed are the paradigms of masc. and fem. stems ending in *-i-* (e.g., *aṣ̌i-* "reward," *axti-* "pain," *gairi-* "mountain," *paiti-* "master") and in *-u-* (e.g., *aŋhu-* "life," *xratu-* "mental vigor," *daxiiu-/daŋ́hu-* "land, country," *mainiiu-* "spirit," *vaŋhu-/vohu-* "good"). The stem final shows the ablaut grades *-i-*, *-ai̯-*, *-āi̯-* and *-u-*, *-au̯-*, *-āu̯-* respectively.

The *i*- and *u*-stems inflect as follows. Sing.: nom. *aṣ̌iš, xratuš*;—acc. *aṣ̌īm, xratum*;—inst. *aṣ̌ī, xratū*;—dat. (< **-ai̯-ai̯*) OAv. *axtōiiōi*, YAv. *°patōe*; (< **-au̯-ai̯*) *vaŋhauuē*;—abl. YAv. *garōit̰, xrataot̰*;—gen. (< **-ai̯-š*) *patōiš*; (< **-au̯-š*) *xratəuš*;—loc. (**-ā* < **-ā(i̯)*) *gara*; *vaŋhāu*;—voc. (< **-ai̯*) *paite*; (< **-au̯*) *mainiiō*.—Dual: nom./acc. *paiti, mainiiū*;—inst. *aṣ̌ibiiā, ahubiiā*;—gen. *mainiuuå* (< **maniu̯u̯-āh*);—loc. *aŋhuuō* (< **ahuu̯-au̯*).—Plur.: nom. (< **-ai̯-ah*) *garaiiō*; (< **-au̯-ah*) *xratauuō*;—acc. (< **-i-Nš*) *gairīš*; (< *-u-Nš*) *xratūš*;—dat. *gairibiiō, daŋ́hubiiō*;—gen. *gairinąm, vohunąm*;—loc. *vaŋhušu*.

The nom./acc. of neuter stems in *-i-* and *-u-* has in all three genders the endings *-ī̆* and *-ū̆* respectively.

The only *i*-stem word that is declined irregularly is *paiti-* in the sense of "husband," which in the dat. sing. has the ending *-i̯-ai̯* instead of *-ai̯-ai̯*: YAv. *paiθiiaē-ca, paiθe* (Vedic *pátye*). Several *u*-stem words have exceptional forms: nom. sing. OAv. *darəgō.bāzāuš* "long-armed;" inst. sing. *xraθβā* (Vedic *krátvā*); dat. sing. *xraθβe* (Vedic *krátve*), OAv. *aŋhuiiē*, YAv. *aŋ̇he* (< **ahu̯-ai̯*); loc. sing. *daŋ́huuō, daŋ́hauua* (< **dahi̯au̯ + ā*, cf. Vedic *dásyav-i*) reflecting the ending **-au̯* (+ *ā*).

Root nouns, etc. A large group of masc. and fem. nouns are monosyllabic "root nouns" (that is, nouns whose stem consists of the root alone), and other nouns, not all monosyllabic, that end in *-ā-*, *-ī-*, *-ū-* (e.g., *xā-* "source," *ərəžə-jī-* "right-living," *tanū-* "body") or in a consonant (except *-n-* and *-r-*). The case endings are the same in almost all paradigms. As mentioned above, the original ending *-s* of the nom. sing. appears in various forms: *-ā + s > -āh >* Av. *-å* (*raθaē-štå* "charioteer"); *-ī + s, -ū + s >* Av. *-īš, -ūš* (*ərəžə-jīš, tanūš*) *-p + s >* Av. *-fš* (*afš < ā̆p-* "water"); *-k (g) + s >* Av. *-xš* (*vāxš < vā̆c-* "voice," *druxš < druj-* "lie"); *-ś + s >* Av. *-š* (*vīš < vis-*, Vedic *víś-*, "settlement"); *-t (d) + s >* Av. *-s* (*hauruuatās < hauruuatāt-* "completeness").

The other endings of this group are: Sing.: acc. *-əm* (*āpəm, vācəm*), *-im* (*drujim*);—inst. *-ā̆* (*visa* = Vedic *viśā*);—dat. OAv. *-ōi, -ē*, YAv. *-ē* = **-ai̯* (*vīse* = Vedic *viśé*);—abl. (OAv. = gen.), YAv. *-at̰* (*vīsat̰*);—gen. *-ō* < **-ah* < **-as* (*vīsō* = Vedic *viśáḥ*);—loc. *-ī, -iia* < **-i + ā* (*vīsi, vīsiia*; Vedic *viśí*).—Dual: nom./acc. *-ā̆* (*ratu-friia* "delighting the Ratus");—inst./dat./abl. *-biiā̆* (*vaγžibiia*);—gen./loc. *-å* (*amərətātå*).—Plur.: nom. *-ō* < **-ah* < **-as* < Proto-IE. **-es* (*āpō*);—acc. *-ō* < Proto-IE. **n̥s* (*vīsō*);—inst. *-bī̆š* (*vaγžibiš*);—dat./abl. *-biiō* (*vīžibiiō*);—gen. *-ąm* (*vīsąm*);—loc. *-hu/-šu* < Proto-IE. **-su* (*nafšu* "among the grandsons" < **napt-su*).

In a number of paradigms the noun stem shows ablaut. The "strong" cases are the sing. nom., acc., and loc.; the dual nom.-acc.; and the plur. nom. The remaining cases are "weak," that is, they show zero grade or a short vowel in the stem. Thus, among the root nouns, we find nom. sing. *āfš, vāxš*; acc. sing. *āpəm, vācim*, but inst. sing. *apa, vaca*.

Ablaut is particulary well preserved in the case of the possessive suffixes **-u̯ant-/*-mant-* "having," which in the "week" cases appear as **-u̯at-/*-mat-* (< Proto-IE. **-u̯n̥t-/*-mn̥t-*). Thus, OAv. has acc. sing. *drəguuaṇtəm* but gen. sing. *drəguuatō* from *drəguuaṇt-* "deceitful." The same ablaut is found in the case of the participles of athematic temporal stems (**-ant-*: **-at-*) and in the case of the adjective *bərəzaṇt-/bərəzat-* "high." The nom. sing. masc. takes various forms. The participles have *-ą̇s* in OAv. (< **-ant-s*: *pərəsą̇s* "asking," *hą̇s* "being") but usually *-ō* in YAv. (*pərəsō, bərəzō*), only rarely *-ą* (*hą* "being"). The expected form **-u̯ąs/*-mąs* (< **-u̯ant-s *-mant-s*) is attested only in OAv. *θβāuuą̇s* "like you" and in YAv. *cuuą̇s* "how big" (< **cī-u̯ant-s*). Elsewhere it is replaced by **-uuå/*-må* (< **-u̯āh/*-māh*): OAv. *drəguuå*, YAv. *druuå* "deceitful" (< **drugu̯āh*); YAv. *xratumå* "having mental vigor."

Stems in -an- and -ar-. Masc. and fem. stems in *-an-* (*-man-*, *-u̯an-*) and in *-ar-* (*-tar-*) form the nom. sing in *-ā* (YAv. *-a*) < Proto-IE. **-ē/*-ō* with loss of the final consonant, e.g., *tašā* "carpenter" (Vedic *tákṣā*, Greek *téktōn*); OAv. *ptā*, YAv. *pita* "father" (Vedic *pitā́*, Greek *patḗr*). In the other "strong" cases we find both *-an-*, *-ar-* (< Proto-IE. **-en-*, **-er-*) and *-ān-*, *-ār-* (< Proto-IE. **-on-*, **-or-*), e.g., OAv. *tašānəm* (Vedic *tákṣāṇam*, Greek *téktona*); OAv. *patarəm*, YAv. *pitarəm* (Vedic *pitáram*, Greek *patéra*). In the "weak" cases the stem ends in simple *-n-*, *-r-* before an ending beginning with a vowel but in *-a-* (< Proto-IE. **-n̥-*), *-ər-* (< Proto-IE. **-r̥-*) before an ending beginning with a consonant, e.g., dat. sing. *tašne* (Vedic *tákṣṇe*); OAv. *aṣ̌āunē* (Vedic *r̥tā́vne*) "to the righteous one;" OAv. *fəδrōi*, OAv., YAv. *piθrē̆* (Vedic *pitré*);—dat. plur. *aṣ̌auuabiiō* (with *-u̯abiiō* < **-u̯n̥-bʰios*); YAv. *ptərəbiiō* (Vedic *pitŕ̥bhyaḥ*). The rare gen. sing. YAv. *-arš* (< *-r̥-š*) corresponds to Vedic *-ur*: *zaotarš* "of the sacrificer" = Vedic *hótur*.

Neuter *n*-stems have in the nom.-acc. sing. *-ā̆* (< Proto-IE. **-n̥*), e.g., YAv. *nąma* "name" (Vedic *nā́ma*, Latin *nōmen*), in the nom.-acc. plur. both *-ə̄nī̆*, e.g., *nāmə̄nī̆* and *-ąn* (*-mąn/-mąm*), e.g., *nāmąm*. A peculiarity of the nt. *n*-stems is the formation of the gen. sing. in OAv. *-ə̄ŋg*, YAv. *-ą[n]* (< **-ənh* < **-an-s*), e.g., *cašmə̄ŋg* < *cašman-* "eye;" *barəsmąn* < *barəsman-* "bundle of twigs." Note also YAv. *zrū* gen. sing. of *zruuan-* masc. "time," from **zruu̯ū* < **zruu̯ō* < **zruu̯əŋh*, and abl. sing. *barəsmən* < **-man + t*.

Neuter *r*-stems are well attested in Avestan in the nom.-acc. sing. with the ending *-arə*, e.g., *aiiarə* "day" Vedic *áhar*), *karšuuarə* "continent," *yākarə* "liver" (Vedic *yákr̥t*, Greek *hēpar*), *vadarə* "weapon" (Vedic *vádhar*). The remaining cases were formed from an *n*-stem in Proto-IE. and Proto-Aryan. Only a few such forms are attested in Avestan, e.g., OAv. *rāzarə* "directive" has *n*-stem forms in the inst. sing. (*rāšnā*), gen. sing. (*rāzə̄ng*), and gen. plur. (*rāšnąm*); *huuarə* "sun" (Vedic *súvar*) contrasts with gen. sing. OAv. *x᷈ə̄ng* (disyllabic, < **huu̯ə̄ŋh*), YAv. *hū* (< **huu̯ū* < **huu̯ə̄* < **huu̯əŋh*); YAv. *aiiarə* "day" contrasts with gen. sing. *aiiąn* (< **ai̯əŋh*); **azar* "day" (Vedic *áhar*) contrasts with dat. sing. *asne* (Vedic *áhne*) and gen. plur. *asnąm* (Vedic *áhnām*). In the nom.-acc. plur. we find both *-ārə* and *-ąn*, *-ə̄ni*, e.g., OAv. *aiiārə* "days," YAv. *aiiąn* (cf. Vedic *áhāni*).

h-stems. Neuter *h*-stem words with *-ah-* < **-as-* have in the nom.-acc. sing. the ending *-ō* < **-ah*, e.g., *manō* "thought" (Vedic *mánaḥ*, Greek *ménos*). Before endings beginning with a vowel, *-ah-* usually becomes *-aŋh-*, e.g., inst. sing. *manaŋhā*, dat. sing. *manaŋhe*, gen. sing. *manaŋhō*. Noteworthy are: nom.-acc. plur. OAv. *manā̊* with *-ā̊* < **-ās*, inst. YAv. *manə̄biš*, and loc. plur. YAv. *ązahu* "in distresses" (Vedic *áṁhasu*). When *ah*-stems are used as masculines, e.g., in the case of the comparative suffix *-i̯ah-*, the nom. sing. ends in *-ā̊* < **āh*, e.g., OAv. *vax́iiā̊*, YAv. *naŋhā̊* < **u̯ahi̯āh* "the better one." Contrast the neuter sing. OAv. *vahiiō*, YAv. *vaŋhō*, Vedic *vásyaḥ*.

The suffix *-u̯āh-* of the perfect participle active takes the form *-uš-* in the "weak" cases. Sing.: nom. masc. OAv. *vīduuā̊* "knowing" (cf. Vedic *vidvā́n*)—acc. YAv. *vīδuuā̊ŋhəm* (Vedic *vidvā́ṁsam*);—dat. OAv. *vīdušē* (Vedic *vidúṣe*);—gen. OAv. *vīdušō* (Vedic *vidúṣaḥ*).—Plur.: nom. YAv. *vīδuuā̊ŋhō* (Vedic *vidvā́ṁsaḥ*).

Irregular nouns. For historical reasons a number of words are inflected irregularly. The most important are:

Mazdā- (*Ahura-*) "the Wise (Lord)." Voc. *Mazdā*, nom. *Mazdā̊*, acc. *Mazdąm*, dat. *Mazdāi*, gen. *Mazdā̊*. The last three cases have disyllabic endings *-ąm*, *-āi*, *-ā̊*.

pantā-/*paθ-* "way, path." Sing.: nom. *pantā̊* (cf. Vedic *pánthāḥ*), acc. *pantąm* (cf. Vedic *pánthām*), inst. *paθa* (Vedic *pathā́*), gen. *paθō* (Vedic *patháḥ*), loc. *paiθī* (Vedic *pathí*).—Plur.: acc. *paθō* (Vedic *patháḥ*), inst. *padəbīš* (cf. Vedic *pathíbhiḥ*), gen. *paθąm* (Vedic *pathā́m*).

kauuaii- "seer" and *haxāii-* "companion." Sing.: nom. *kauuā*, *huš.haxā*, YAv. *haxa* (Vedic *sákhā*); acc. *kauuaēm*, *huš.haxāim* (Vedic *sákhāyam*); inst. YAv. *haša* (Vedic *sákhyā*); dat. YAv. *haše* (Vedic *sákhye*).—Plur.: nom. OAv. *kāuuaiias-cīṯ* (Vedic *kávayaḥ*), YAv. *haxaiiō* (Vedic *sákhāyah*); gen. YAv. *kaoiiąm* (< **kau̯i̯ām*), *hašąm* (< **sákhi̯-ām*).

**raii-* "wealth" has "weak" stem **rāi̯-*. Sing.: acc. YAv. *raēm* (Vedic *rayím*), inst. YAv. *raiia* (Vedic *rāyā́*), gen. OAv. *rāiiō* (Vedic *rāyáḥ*).—Plur.: gen. YAv. *raiiąm* (Vedic *rāyā́m*).

āiiū "life" (nom.-acc. sing. nt.) has oblique forms in OAv.: inst. *yauuā*, dat. *yauuōi*, *yauuē*, gen. *yaoš*. *dāuru* "wood" (Vedic *dā́ru*) has gen. sing. YAv. *draoš* (Vedic *dróḥ*). *zānu* "knee" (Vedic *jā́nu*) has abl. plur. YAv. *žnubiias-ciṯ*.

gauu- masc. fem. "ox, cow." Sing.: nom. *gāuš* (Vedic *gáuḥ*), acc. *gąm* (Vedic *gā́m*), inst. *gauua* (Vedic *gávā*), dat. OAv. *gauuōi*, YAv. *gauue* (Vedic *gáve*); abl. OAv. *gə̄uš* (Vedic *góḥ*), YAv. *gaoṯ*, gen. *gə̄uš* (Vedic *góḥ*), voc. YAv. *gao-spəṇta*.—Dual: nom. *gāuuā* (Vedic *gā́vā*).—Plur.: nom. YAv. *gauuō* (Vedic *gā́vaḥ*), acc. *gā̊* (Vedic *gā́ḥ*), inst. *gaobīš* (Vedic *góbhiḥ*), gen. *gauuąm* (Vedic *gávām*).

zam- "earth," *ziiam-* "winter," *dam-* "house," *ham-* "summer." Sing.: nom. *zā̊* (Vedic *kṣā́ḥ*), *ziiā̊*; acc. *ząm* (Vedic *kṣā́m*), *ziiąm*; inst. YAv. *zəmā* (Vedic *jmā́*), *hama*; abl. YAv. *zəmaṯ*; gen. *zəmō* (Vedic *jmáḥ*), *zimō*, OAv. *də̄ng* (Vedic *dán* < **dám-s*); loc. *zəmē* (Vedic *kṣmay-ā́*), *zəmi* (Vedic *kṣámi*), OAv. *dąm*, YAv. *dąmi*.

-jan-/*-γn-* "striking," in *vərəθra-jan-* "breaking the resistance." Sing.: nom. masc. *vərəθra-jā* (Vedic *vr̥tra-hā́*); acc. *vərəθrā-janəm* (Vedic *vr̥tra-hánam*); dat. *vərəθra-γne* (Vedic *vr̥tra-ghné*).

YAv. *span-*/*sun-* "dog." Sing.: nom. *spā* (Vedic *śvā́*); acc. *spānəm* (Vedic *śvā́nam*); dat. *sūne* (Vedic *śúne*); gen. *sūnō* (Vedic *śúnaḥ*).—Dual: nom. *spāna* (Vedic *śvā́nā*).—Plur.: nom. *spānō* (Vedic *śvā́naḥ*); gen. *sunąm* (Vedic *śúnām*).

nar- "man" and *star-* "star." Sing.: nom. OAv. *nā*, acc. *narəm* (Vedic *náram*), YAv. *stārəm*; dat. OAv. *narōi*, YAv. *naire* (Vedic *náre*); gen. OAv. *nərəš*, YAv. *narš*; voc. YAv. *narə*.—Plur.: nom. OAv. *narō* (Vedic *náraḥ*), YAv. *stārō*; acc. OAv. *nərąš*, YAv. *nərə̄š*, incorrect *nərə̄uš* (cf. Vedic *nr̥̄́n*), YAv. *strə̄š*, incorrect *strə̄uš*; dat. OAv. *nərəbiias-cā*, YAv. *nərəbiiō*, *nəruiiō* (Vedic *nr̥bhyaḥ*); abl. *stərəbiiō*; gen. YAv. *narąm* (Vedic *nárām*); OAv. *strə̄m-cā*, YAv. *strąm*.

ātar- masc. "fire" has been remodeled from an old neuter. Sing.: nom. OAv., YAv. *ātarš* (< **ātr̥-š*); acc. OAv. *ātrə̄m*, YAv. *ātrəm* (< **ātr̥-m*); inst. OAv. *āθrā* (< **āθr-ā*); dat. YAv. *āθre*; abl. OAv. *āθras-cā*, YAv. *āθraṯ*; gen. OAv., YAv. *āθrō*; voc. OAv., YAv. *ātarə* (< **ātr̥*).—Plur.: acc. (< nom.) YAv. *ātaro*; inst. YAv. *ātərəbiiō*; gen. YAv. *āθrąm*.

Pronouns. The irregularity of the Avestan pronominal inflection is almost entirely inherited from Proto-Indo-Ir. and Proto-IE. Thus the personal pronouns for the first and second persons have in all three numbers stem forms in the nominative differing from the stems of the remaining cases (cf. English I : me, we : us). In the case of the personal pronouns no distinction of gender is made, but masculine, feminine, and neuter are distinguished in the demonstrative, relative, and interrogative pronouns.

Personal pronoun for the first person ("I, we both, we"). Sing.: nom. *azə̄m*; acc. *mąm*; dat. OAv. *maibiiā* *maibiiō*, YAv. *māuuōiia*, *māuuaiia-ca* (< **mau̯i̯a* < **maβi̯a*); abl. *maṯ* (OPers. *-ma*); gen. OAv. *mə̄.nā*, YAv. *mana* (OPers. *manā*). Enclitic forms: acc. *mā*; gen., dat. OAv. *mōi*, YAv. *mē* (OPers. *-maiy*).—Dual: nom. OAv. *vā*; acc. *āuuā*. Enclitic gen. *nā*.—Plur.: nom. *vaēm* (< **u̯ai̯əm*, cf. OPers. *vayam*); acc. OAv. *ə̄hmā*, YAv.

ahma; inst. OAv. *ə̄hmā*; dat. OAv. *ahmaibiiā*; abl. OAv. *ahmat̰*; gen. YAv. *ahmākəm*. Enclitic forms: acc. OAv. *nā̊*, YAv. *nō*; gen., dat. OAv. *nə̄*, YAv. *nō*.

Personal pronoun for the second person ("you"). Sing.: nom. OAv., YAv. *tū*, OAv. *tuuə̄m*, YAv. *tūm* (OPers. *tuvam*); acc. *θβąm* (OPers. *θuvām*); inst. *θβā*; dat. OAv. *taibiiā-cā*, *taibiiō*; abl. OAv. *θβat̰*; gen. *tauuā̆*. Enclitic forms: acc. *θβā*; gen., dat. OAv. *tōi*, YAv. *tē* (OPers. *-taiy*).—Dual: gen. YAv. *yauuākəm*.—Plur.: nom. *yūžəm*, OAv. *yūš*; inst. OAv. *xšmā*; dat. OAv. *xšmaibiiā*, YAv. *xšmāuuōiia*; OAv. *yūšmaibiiā*, YAv. *yūšmaoiiō*; abl. OAv. *xšmat̰*, OAv., YAv. *yūšmat̰*; gen. OAv., YAv. *xšmākəm*, YAv. *yūšmākəm*. Enclitic forms: acc. OAv. *vā̊*, YAv. *vō*; gen., dat. OAv. *və̄*, YAv. *vō*.

Personal pronouns for the third person ("he, she, it; they") are represented by various forms of the stems *i-*, *h(i)-/š(i)-*, *di-*. All forms are enclitic except for OAv. *hī* (sing. nom. fem. and dual nom. nt.). Sing.: acc. masc. fem. *īm*, *hīm*, YAv. *dim* (OPers. *dim*); gen., dat. OAv. *hōi*, YAv. *hē/šē* (OPers. *-šaiy*).—Dual: acc. OAv. *ī*.—Plur.: acc. OAv. *īš*, OAv., YAv. *hīš* (OPers. *-šīš*), YAv. *dīš* (OPers. *-dīš*).—Neuter forms: acc. sing. OAv. *īt̰*, YAv. *it̰*, *dit̰*; plur. YAv. *ī*, *dī*.—Reflexive sing. dat. YAv. *huuāuuōiia* (< **hu̯au̯aβi̯a*).

Demonstrative pronouns: *ta-* "this," *aēta-* "this," *auua-* "that one over there (yonder);" relative pronoun *ya-* "who, which;" interrogative pronoun *ka-/ca-* "who, which" (when followed by the enclitics *-cā̆*, *cit̰*, this becomes an indefinite pronoun "whoever, whichever"). The case endings of all these pronouns are largely the same in the masc. and nt. as those of the *a*-declension nouns and in the fem. as those of the *ā*-declension nouns. Examples: masc. sing. nom. OAv. *yə̄*, *kə̄*, YAv. *yō*, *kō*; acc. *təm*, *kəm*, OAv. *yə̄m*, YAv. *yim*, *aom* (< **au̯əm*, OPers. *avam*); gen. YAv. *aētahe*, *auuaŋhe*, OAv. *yehiiā*, YAv. *yeŋ́he*, OAv. *kahiiā*, *cahiiā*, YAv. *kahe*, *kahiiā-cit̰*;—plur. acc. OAv. *tə̄ṇg*, *tą*, YAv. *tə̄*, *tą*, YAv. *auuū*, *aū* (< **au̯ə̄*).

Characteristic pronominal forms are, e.g., masc. sing. (from the pronoun *ta-*, *aēta-*) YAv. *hā*, *hō* (Vedic *sá*), YAv. *aēšō* (Vedic *eṣá*); (from the pronoun *auua-*) OAv. *huuō* (< **hau̯*), YAv. *hāu* (= fem.) (OPers. *hauv*);—inst. *kana*;—dat. *aētahmāi*, *yahmāi*, *kahmāi*, *cahmāi* (Vedic *yásmai*, *kásmai*);—abl. *aētahmāt̰*, *yahmāt̰*, *kahmāt̰* (Vedic *yásmāt*);—loc. *aētahmi*, *yahmī̆*, *kahmi*, *cahmi* (cf. Vedic *yásmin*, *kásmin*).—Plur. nom. OAv. *tōi*, YAv. *tē*, *aēte* (Vedic *té*, *eté*), *auue* (OPers. *avaiy*), OAv., YAv. *yōi*, *kōi* (Vedic *yé*, *ké*);—gen. *aētaēšąm* (OPers. *avaišām*), *yaēšąm* (Vedic *yéṣām*).—Neuter sing. nom./acc. OAv., YAv. *tat̰* (Vedic *tát*), YAv. *auuat̰*, OAv. *hiiat̰*, YAv. *yat̰* (Vedic *yát*), *kat̰* (Vedic *kát*).—Fem. sing. nom. *hā*, *aēša* (Vedic *sā́*, *eṣā́*), YAv. *hāu* (OPers. *hauv*);—inst. *aētaiia* (Vedic *etáyā*);—dat. YAv. *auuaŋhāi* (< **au̯ahi̯āi*);—abl. *auuaŋhat̰*;—gen. *aētaŋhā̊* (< *aitahi̯āh*, Vedic *etásyāḥ*);—loc. *yeŋ́he* (< **i̯ahi̯ā*, cf. Vedic *etásyām*).—Plur. gen. YAv. *aētaŋhąm* (Vedic *etā́sām*).

A special pronoun with the meaning "this one here" is based on the stems *a-* and *i-/ai̯-*: masc. sing. nom. OAv. *aiiə̄m*, YAv. *aēm* (Vedic *ayám*);—acc. YAv. *iməm*;—inst. *anā* (OPers. *anā*);—dat. *ahmāi* (Vedic *asmai*);—abl. *ahmāt̰*;—gen. OAv. *ahiiā*, YAv. *ahe*, *aŋ́he* (Vedic *ásya*);—loc. *ahmī̆* *ahmiia*.—Dual nom./acc. *ima*;—dat. *ābiia*;—gen. *aiiā̊*.—Plur. nom. *ime*;—acc. *ima*;—inst. OAv. *āiš*, *anāiš*, YAv. *aēibiš*;—dat. *aēbiiō*;—gen. *aēšąm*;—loc. *aēšu*, *aēšuua*.—Neuter sing. nom./acc. *imat̰*.—Plur. nom./acc. OAv. *ī*, *imā̆*.—Fem. sing. nom YAv. *īm* (* < *i̯iəm*, Vedic *iyám*);—acc. *imąm*;—inst. OAv. *ōiiā*, YAv. *ā̆iia* (Vedic *ayā́*);—dat. OAv. *ax́iiāi*, YAv. *aŋ́hāi* (Vedic *asyái*);—abl. *aŋ́hāt̰*;—gen. *aŋ́hā̊*;—loc. *aŋ́he* (< *ahi̯ā*).—Dual dat. OAv. *ābiiā*.—Plur. nom./acc. *imā̊*;—inst. OAv. *ābīš*;—dat. *ābiiō*;—gen. *ā̊ŋhąm* (Vedic *āsā́m*);—loc. *āhū*, *āhuua*.

In addition to the interrogative pronoun *ka-/ca-* there is a stem *ci-* (*ci-* + *cā̆* "someone," *naē-ci-* "no one"): sing. nom. masc. *ciš*, *ciš-cā̆*, *naē-ciš* (Latin *quis*, *quis-que*, *nīquis*);—acc. *cīm*, *naē-cim*.—Nom./acc. nt. *cit̰* (Latin *quid*), *naē-cit̰*.—Plur. nom. masc. *caiiō*, *caiias-cā*;—nom./acc. nt. *cī̆-cā̆*.

The possessive pronouns OAv. *ma-* "my," OAv. *θβa-* "your" (sing.), and OAv., YAv. *x́ᵛa-*, YAv. *hauua-*, *huua-* "one's own" also have some pronominal endings, e.g., masc. sing *θβahmāi*, *θβahmāt̰*, *θβahmī*, *x́ᵛahmi*.—Plur. nom. *θβōi*.—Fem. sing. nom. *θβōi* (< **tu̯ā* + *i*), *x́ᵛaē-cā* (< **su̯ā* + *i*);—inst. *maiiā*;—dat. OAv. *x́ᵛax́iiāi*;—gen. *θβax́iiā̊*. Note also the pronominal endings used with *aēuua-* "one," *aniia-* "other," and *vīspa-* "all:" sing. *aniiahmāi*, *vīspəmāi* (< *-*əhmāi*, Vedic *viśvasmai*), *aēuuahmāt̰*, *aēuuahmi*.—Plur. *aniie*, *vīspe* (Vedic *anye*, *viśve*), *aniiaēšąm*, *vīspaēšąm*, (Vedic *anyéṣām*, *viśveṣām*).—Fem. sing. gen. *aēuuaŋhā̊*.

2. Verbal inflection.

Many Avestan verbal forms have counterparts in the Vedic language. Since Vedic is attested by an extensive literature that enables its grammatical forms to be determined with exactitude, it is possible to establish the complicated Avestan verbal system with considerable certainty by comparing it systematically with Vedic. With the exception of certain nominal forms such as participles, every verbal form terminates with a personal ending. The personal endings determine the first, second, and third persons in singular, dual, and plural. In addition, they indicate at the same time the diatheses active (e.g., English "I praise") and middle (e.g., English "I praise in my own interest, we praise each other, I am praised"). The middle may be reflexive, reciprocal, or passive, etc.There are four kinds of personal endings: the primary and secondary endings, the imperative endings, and the perfect endings. The secondary endings indicate only the person and the diathesis whereas the primary endings indicate also present time (e.g., English "I am praising"). The special perfect endings indicate, together with the perfect stem, the state arrived at as a result of an action ("I have praised"). The basis of a verb form is the so-called "verb root," which conveys the lexical meaning of the verb. By means of changes of the verb root or by the addition of suffixes the so-called "tense stems" are formed. These are known as the present, aorist, and perfect stems. The future stem is typologically a present stem.

When an imperative ending is added to a present stem the verb form expresses a command (imperative present). The addition of a primary ending to the present stem results in an indicative present whereas the addition of a secondary ending to the present stem results in an injunctive present. The injunctive present is used to mention an action without reference to time, one which is general or adhortative, past or future. The preterite is expressed by the imperfect, which is formed by prefixing to the verbal stem the augment *a-*. Whereas the augment *a-* is common in Vedic and OPers., it is seldom found in Avestan.

Originally the aorist stem was used to indicate the perfective aspect of an action, that is the view of a completed action in its entirety, but this function of the aorist is usually no longer evident in the Avestan texts. The aorist stem can take only imperative or secondary endings. With secondary endings the aorist is known as the injunctive aorist, which has functions corresponding to those of the injunctive present. The aorist stem with prefixed augment *a-* and secondary endings forms the indicative aorist, which has preterite meaning.

The moods of the verb are: indicative, injunctive, imperative, subjunctive, and optative. The subjunctive expresses volition and futurity. It is characterized by the addition of the suffix *-a-* to the high-grade present, aorist, and perfect stems. The subjunctive may take either primary or secondary endings, no difference in meaning being discernible. The optative expresses volition and potentiality. It is formed by adding to the low-grade tense stems the suffix *-i̯ā-/-ī-* and the secondary endings.

The present system. Since the Proto-IE. period, present stems have been formed in many different ways, but it has in most cases not been possible to determine the reason for any particular formation. From the point of view of morphology two broad groups can be distinguished: the thematic and the athematic present stems. The thematic present stems end in the thematic vowel *-a-*, which with certain variations is retained before the personal endings. In the case of the athematic present stems the personal endings and the suffixes for subjunctive and optative are added directly to the various present stems instead of being preceded by the thematic vowel.

Thematic present stems. To the full or zero grade of the verb root is added the thematic vowel *-a-* alone or a suffix ending in *-a-*: *-i̯a-*, *-ai̯a-*, *-sa-* (= Vedic *-cha-*). Examples: *bar-a-* "carry," *spas-iia-* "espy," *kir-iia-* (passive) "be done," *xš-aiia-* "rule," *vaxš-aiia-* (causative) "make grow," *ja-sa-* "come" (= Vedic *gáccha-* < Proto-IE. *gʷm̥-sk̂é-*). The root can receive an infixed *-n-*, e.g., *kərənta-* "cut" (Vedic *kr̥-n-ta-*). The desideratives are characterized by reduplication and the addition of the suffix **-sa-* (*-ha-*, *-ša-*), e.g., *su-srū-ša-* "wish to hear." In some cases the present stems look quite different from the root, e.g., *sixša-* (Vedic *śikṣa-*) "wish to be able (*sak*), learn," *diβža-* (Vedic *dipsa-*) "wish to cheat (*dab*). The future stem in **-si̯a-* (*-hi̯a-*, *-ši̯a-*) can also be classified as a thematic present, e.g., *vax-šiiā* "I shall say."

Inflection of the thematic present stems. Active: indic. pres. sing. 1. *barāmi* (OAv. *pərəsā* "I ask"), 2. *barahi*, 3. *baraitī.*—Dual 3. *baratō.*—Plur. 1. *barāmahi*, 2. *-aθā*, 3. *barəṇti.*—Inj. pres. sing. 1. *barəm*, 2. *barō*, 3. *barat̰.*—Dual 3. *-atəm.*—Plur. 2. *-ata*, 3. *barən.*—Subj. pres. sing. 1. *barāni*, 2. *barāhi*, 3. *-āiti*, *barāt̰.*—Dual 1. *-āuua*, 3. *barātō.*—Plur. 1. *barāma*, 2. *āθā*, 3. *barą̊ṇti*, *barąn.*—Opt. pres. sing. 2. *barōiš*, 3. *barōit̰.*—Plur. 1. *-aēma*, 2. *-aēta*, 3. *baraiiən.*—Imv. pres. sing. 2. *bara*, 3. *baratu.*—Plur. 2. *barata*, 3. *barəṇtu.*—Part. pres. *barəṇt-*.

Middle: indic. pres. sing. 1. *baire*, 2. *-ahe*, 3. *baraite.*—Dual 3. *baraēte.*—Plur. 1. *barāmaide*, 2. OAv. *dīdraγžō.duiiē* "you wish to fasten" (< **-a-du̯ai̯*, Vedic *-a-dhve*), 3. *barəṇte.*—Inj. pres. sing. 1. *baire*, 2. *-aŋha* (< **-a-sa*), 3. *barata.*—Dual 3. *-aētəm.*—Plur. 3. *-əṇta.*—Subj. Pres. sing. 1. *-āi*, *āne*, 2. *-ą̊ŋhe* (< **-āhai̯*), 3. *-āite.*—Plur. 3. *-ą̊ṇte.*—Opt. pres. sing. 2. *-aēša*, 3. *baraēta.*—Plur. 1. *-ōimaidī*, 2. *-ōiδβəm*, 3. *-aiiaṇta.*—Imv. pres. sing. 2. *baraŋᵛha*, 3. OAv. *vərəziiātąm* (< **-a-tąm*).—Plur. 2. OAv. *gūšōdum* "listen" (< **-a-du̯əm*), 3. *-əṇtąm.*—Part. pres. *barəmna-*.

Athematic present stems. In the case of the athematic present stems the personal endings are added to the root or to the present suffix directly, that is, without the intervention of the thematic vowel *-a-*. The most important classes of these present stems are: 1. the root presents; 2. the reduplicated presents; 3. the present stems containing infixed *-n-*; 4. the present stems ending in *-nā-*; 5. the present stems ending in *-nu-*. These present stems are affected by ablaut: they have the full grade of the root or the infix or suffixes in the case of the active singular forms of the indic., the inj., and, in part, of the imv. as well as throughout the active and middle paradigms of the subj. The remaining forms have the zero grade as far as that is phonologically possible.

1. The root presents. In this case the pres. stem is identical with the verb root, e.g., *ah-/h-* "to be" (Vedic *as-/s-*), *mrauu-/mrū-* "to speak" (Vedic *bravⁱ-/brū-*); *vas-/us-* "to wish" (Vedic *vaś-/uś-*). A subgroup has the long grade in the act. sing. indic. and inj. and otherwise the full grade, e.g., *stāuu-/stauu-* "to praise," *tāš-/taš-* "to fashion;" *aog-* "to speak;" *sāh-* "to instruct."

Active inflection: indic. pres. sing. 1. *ahmī*, *mraomī*, *vasəmī*; *stāumi*, 2, *ahī̆*, *vašī̆*, 3. *astī̆*, *mraoiti*, *vaštī*; *tāšti*, *sāstī.*—Dual 1. *usuuahī*, 3. *stō* (Vedic *s-taḥ*), *mrūtō.*—Plur. 1. *mahī̆* < **hmahi* (Vedic *s-masi*), *usə̄mahī* (Vedic *uśmási*), 2. *stā* (Vedic *s-tha*), *uštā*, 3. *həṇtī̆* (Vedic *s-ánti*).—Inj. pres. sing. 1. *mraom*, 2. *mraoš*, 3 *mraot̰*; *tāšt.*—Plur. 2 *mraotā*, *uštā*—Subj. pres. sing. 1 *aŋhā*, *mrauua*, *mrauuāni*, 2. *aŋhō*, 3. *aŋhat̰*, *aŋhaitī*, *vasat̰.*—Plur. 1. *ą̊ŋhāmā* (< **aŋhāma*), 3. *aŋhən*, *vasən.*—Opt. pres. sing. 1. OAv. *x́iiə̄m* (Vedic *s-yā́-m*), 2. *x́iią̊*, *mruiią̊*, 3. *x́iiāt̰*/YAv. *hiiāt̰*, *usiiāt̰*, *sāhīt̰*,—Plur. 1. *x́iiāmā*, 2. *x́iiātā*, 3. YAv. *hiiārə.*—Imv. pres. sing. 2. OAv. *zdī* (< **s + dʰi*) "be!," *mrūiδi*, 3. *astū*, *mraotū̆.*—Plur. 2. *staota*, 3. *hə̄ṇtu.*—Part. pres. *haṇt-* (sing. nom. masc. *hąs*, acc. *həṇtəm*, gen. *hatō.*—Plur. gen. *hātąm.*—Fem.

stem *hāiti-*), *usaṇt-*; *stauuat-* (< **stéu̯-n̥t-*).

Middle inflection: indic. pres. sing. 1. *mruiie* (< *mruu̯ai̯*); *aojōi*, 3. *mrūite*.—Plur. 1. *mrūmaidē*; *aogəmadaē-cā*, *staomaide*, 3. *aojaite* (Vedic *óhate* < *-*n̥toi̯*).—Inj. pres. sing. 1. *aojī*, 2. *aoγžā* (< **aug^h* + *sa*), 3. OAv. *aogədā* (< **aug^h* + *ta*), YAv. *aoxta*, *staota*.—Subj. pres. sing. 1. *aojāi*, *mrauuāne*, *stauuāne*.—Opt. pres. sing. 2. *mruuiša*, 3. *mruuīta*; *aojīta*.—Part. pres. *mruuāna-*, *aojana-*.

2. Reduplicated present stems. The commonest such verb is **da-dā-*, which continues both Indo-Ir. *dā* "to give" and *d^{h}ā* "to put."

Active inflection: indic. pres. sing. 1. *daδąmi*, 2. *daδāhi*, 3. *dadāitī*, *daδāiti*.—Plur. 1. *dadəmahī*, YAv. *dąnmahi*, 3. *dadaitī* (Vedic *dád(h)ati* with -*ati* from *-*n̥ti*).—Inj. pres. sing. 1. *daδam*, 2. OAv. *dadå*, 3. OAv. *dadāt̰*, YAv. *daδāt̰*.—Plur. 3. *dadat̰* (< **d*(^{h})*a*-*d*(^{h})-*n̥t*).—Subj. pres. sing. 1. *daθāni*, 3. OAv. *dadat̰*, YAv. *daθat̰*.—Plur. 1. *daθāma*, 3. *daθən*.—Opt. pres. sing. 1. *daiδiiąm*, 2. *daidīš*, *daiθiiå*, 3. OAv. *daidīt̰*, YAv. *daiδīt̰*, YAv. *daiδiiāt̰*, *daiθiiāt̰*.—Dual 3. *daiδītəm*.—Plur. 3. *daiθiiąn*, *daiθiiārəš*.—Imv. pres. sing. 2. *dazdi* (< **d*(^{h})*a*-*d*(^{h})^z-*d^{h}i*), 3 *dadātū*.—Plur. 2. *dasta*.—Part. pres. *daδat-* (sing. nom. masc. *daδō*, *daθō*).

Middle inflection: indic. pres. sing. 1. *dadē*, *daiθe*, 3. *dastē* (Vedic *datté*), *dazdē* (< **d^h a-d^{hz}* + *tai*).—Plur. *dadəmaidē*.—Inj. pres. sing. 3. *dazdā* (< **d^{h}a-d^{hz}* + *ta*), *dasta*.—Subj. pres. sing. 3. *daθaite*.—Plur. 3. *dadəṇtē*.—Opt. pres. sing. 2. *daiθīša*, 3. *daidītā*, *daiθīta*.—Imv. pres. sing. 2. *dasuuā* (Vedic *d(h)atsva*).—Plur. 2. *mąz-dazdūm* (< **d^{h}a-d^{hz}-d^{h}u̯am*) "bear in mind!"—Part. pres. *daθāna-*.

3. Present stems containing infixed -*n*-. In the act. sing. forms of the indic. and inj. and throughout the subj., -*na*- is infixed but elsewhere only -*n*-, e.g., *vi-na-d-*/*vi-n̥-d-* "to find," *ci-na-h-*, *ci-na-s-*/*cīš-* (< *ci-N-š-*) "to assign," *mərə-n̥-c-* "to destroy."

Active inflection: indic. pres. sing. 1. *cinahmi*, 3. *cinasti*, *vinasti*.—Plur. 1. *cīšmahī*, 3. *viṇdəṇti*.—Inj. pres. sing. 3. *cinas*.—Plur. 3. *viṇdən*.—Opt. pres. sing. 3. *cīšiiāt̰*, *mərąsiiāt̰* (< **mr̥nčiāt*).—Plur. 3. *cīšiiąn*.—Imv. sing. 2. *cīždī*.

Middle inflection: indic. pres. sing. 3. *mərəγəṇte* (< **mərəŋ(g)te*).—Plur. 1. *cīšmaide*, 2. *mərəngəduiiē* (< **mr̥ng-d^{h}u̯ai*), 3. *mərəṇcaitē* (with -*aitē* < *-*n̥toi*),—Opt. pres. sing. 3. *mərəṇcīta*, *viṇdīta*.—Part. pres. *viṇdāna-*.

4. Present stems in -*nā*-. In the act. sing. forms of the indic. and inj. and throughout the subj. the affix -*nā*- is used but elsewhere only -*n*-, e.g., *frī-nā-*/*frī-n-*. "to delight," *gərəβ-nā-*/*gərəβ-n-* "to seize," *pərə-nā-*/*pərə-n-* "to drive away," *vərə-n-* "to choose."

Active inflection: indic. pres. sing. 1. *frīnāmi*, 3. *gərəβnāiti*.—Plur. 1. *friiąnmahī* (< **frinmahi*), 3. *frīnəṇti*.—Subj. pres. sing. 1. *frīnāni*, 3. *frīnāt̰*.—Plur. 3. *gərəβnąn*.—Imv. plur. 3. *frīnəṇtu*.

Middle inflection: indic. pres. sing. 1. *vərənē*, 3. *vərəṇtē*.—Inj. pres. sing. 3. *vərəṇta*.—Plur. 3. OAv. *vərənātā* (with -*ātā* < *-*ata*).—Subj. pres. sing. 1. *frīnai*, *pərənāne*, 3. *pərənāite*.

5. Present stems in -*nu*-. The suffix appears in the full grade as -*nau̯*- in the sing. forms of the indic. and inj. active. In the subj. it takes the form -*nau̯-a*- and elsewhere it appears as *nu*- or -*nu̯*-. The commonest such verb is *kar* "to make, do."

Active inflection: indic. pres. sing. 1. *kərənaomi*, 3. *kərənaoiti*.—Plur. 3. *kərənuuaiṇti*.—Inj. pres. sing. 3. (*a*-)*kərənaot̰*.—Subj. pres. sing. 1. *kərənauuāni*.—Plur. 3. *kərənaon* (with -*naon* < *-*nau̯ən*).—Opt. pres. sing. 3. *kərənuiiāt̰*.—Imv. pres. 2. *kərənūiδi*.—Part. pres. *kərənaṇt-*.

The aorist system. As shown by Vedic, the aorist stem indicates the perfective aspect. Apart from the consideration of aspect, the inj., subj., opt., and imv. forms of the aorist have the same functions as the corresponding forms in the present system. The indic. aor. is formed by prefixing the augment *a*- to the injunctive. The indic. aor. is restricted to the past. Three types of aorist are found in Avestan: 1. thematic aorists, 2. athematic root aorists, 3. sigmatic aorists.

1. The thematic aorist. There are three kinds of thematic aorist. The thematic vowel may be added to the full grade of the root (e.g., *taša*- "to fashion," Vedic *tákṣa-*; *hana*- "to acquire," Vedic *sána-*) or to the zero grade of the root (e.g., *sīša*- "to instruct," Vedic *śiṣa-*, from the root *sāh*, Vedic *śās*; *xša*- "to rule" from the root *xšā*, Vedic *kṣā*; *xsa*- "to look" from the root *xsā*, Vedic *kśa*) or to the reduplicated root (e.g., *vaoca*- "to speak," Vedic *vóca*- < **u̯a-u̯č-a*- from *vac*).

The thematic aorist inflection corresponds to that of the thematic present stems. Noteworthy forms are: active inj. *ā-xsō* "look at," *tašat̰* "he fashioned," *ā-uuaocāma* (Vedic *á-vocāma*) "we spoke."—Subj. *hanānī* "I shall acquire," *fra-uuaocāmā* "we will proclaim."—Opt. *sīšōit̰* "may he instruct," *hanaēmā* "may we earn." Middle inj. *mā* . . . *xšəṇtā* "they shall not rule."—Subj. *xsāi* "I shall look."—Opt. *xšaētā* "may he rule."—Imv. *xšəṇtąm* "let them rule."

2. The athematic root aorist. Thirty-seven verbs use the verb root as aorist stem without the addition of any further morphological feature. Their inflection is largely the same as that of the athematic root present stems. The following examples are attested forms of *dā* 1. "to give," 2. "to put" and *gam* "to go."

Active inflection: inj. aor. sing. 3. *dāt̰*.—Plur. 2. *dāta*, 3. *dąn*, *gmən*.—Subj. aor. sing. 1. *jimā*, 2. *dāhī*, 3. *dāitī*, *dāt̰*, *jimaitī*, *jimat̰*.—Plur. 1. *dāmā*, 3. *daiṇtī*, *dąn*, *jimən*.—Opt. aor sing. 1. OAv. *diiąm*, 2. *jamiiå*, 3. *diiāt̰*, *jəmiiāt̰*.—Plur. 1. *jamiiāmā*, 2. *dāiiata*, 3. YAv. *jamiiąn*, *jamiiārəš*.—Imv. aor. sing. 2. *dāidī*, *gaidī*, 3. *dātū*.—Plur. 2. *dātā*.—Part. pres. *daṇt-*.

Middle inflection: inj. aor. sing. 2. *dåŋhā*, 3. *dātā*.—Dual. 1. *duuaidī* (< **d^h-u̯ad^{h}i*) "we two destined."—Subj. aor. sing. 1. *dānē*, 2. *dåŋhē*, 3. *dāitē*.—Dual 3. *jamaētē*.—Plur. 2. *daduiiē* (< *d^h-a-d^{h}u̯ai*), 3. *dåṇtē*.—Opt. aor. sing. 1. *diiā* (< **d^h-īi̯a*) 2. *dīšā*.—Imv. aor. sing. 2. *dāhuuā*.

Some special forms for the 3. sing. passive also belong to the root aorist: *a-uuācī* "it has been called," *srāuuī* "it has been heard;" *ərəž-ucam* (imv. sing. 3.) "it shall be correctly told" (from the root *vac*).

3. The sigmatic aorist. Whereas the thematic aorist and the athematic root aorist can be distinguished from similarly formed present stems only on the basis of comparison with Vedic, the sigmatic aorist is clearly marked. Proto-IE. *-s-*, which may appear in Avestan as *-h-* or *-š-*, is affixed to the verb root. The root has the long grade in the indic. and inj. but the full grade elsewhere. The inflection is athematic. About twenty-seven verbs have attested sigmatic aorists. The following verbs have been selected to illustrate the inflection: *xšnu* "to satisfy" (*xšnāuš-*/*xšnaoš-*), *dis* "to show" (*dāiš-*/*dōiš-*), *fras* "to ask" (*fraš-*), *man* "to consider (*məngh-*, *mąs-*), *van* "to overcome" (*vəngh-*, *vąs-*), *varz* "to work" (*varš-*), *rā* "to present" (*rāh-*, *rā̊ŋh-*), *uruuaj* "to walk" (*uruuāxš-*), *sand* "to appear" (*sąs-*, Vedic *chā̃nts-*).

Active inflection: inj. aor. sing. 2. *dāiš*, 3. *xšnāuš*, *sąs*.—Plur. 3. *uruuāxšat̰* (with *-at̰* from **-n̥t*).—Subj. aor. sing. 1. *dōišā*, 3. *vǝ̄nghaitī*, *vǝ̄nghat̰*, *varǝšaiti*.—Plur. 3. *xšnaošǝn*.—Imv. aor. 2. *dōišī* (< *daiš* + *ši*).—Plur. 2. *sąstā* (< *sśānd-s-ta*).

Middle inflection: inj. aor. sing. 1. *frašī*, *mǝ̄ŋghī*, 3. *fraštā*, *mąstā*.—Plur. 1. (*a-*)*mǝ̄hmaidī*.—Subj. aor. sing. 1. *mǝ̄ŋghāi*, *varǝšānē*, 2. *rā̊ŋhaŋhōi*, 3. *varǝšaitē*. —Plur. 2. *maz-dā̊ŋhō.dūm*.—Imv. aor. sing. 2. *fǝrašuuā*.—Part. aor. *maŋhāna-*.

The perfect system. The perfect originally designated the state arrived at as the result of an action but it came to be used as a preterite tense. It is found with fifty-six verbs in Avestan. In the perfect stem the verb root has the full grade in the sing. forms of the active and throughout the subj. but elsewhere it has the zero grade. With the one exception of *vaēd-*/*vid-* "to know" all the perf. forms are reduplicated, that is, the first consonant of the root followed by the vowel *-ă-* (occasionally *-i-*, *-u-*) is prefixed to the root. The perf. differs from the present-aorist system also in having special endings in the indic. active and middle. The following are examples of perf. stems: *āh-* (< *ah* "to be"), *dadā-*/*dāδ-* (< *dā* "to give; put"), *mamn-* (< *man* "to think"), *yaiiat-*/*yaēt-*, *yōit-* (< *yat* "to take a firm stand"), *vāuuarǝz-*/*vāuuǝrǝz-* (< *varz* "to work"), *vaēd-*/*vid-* (< *vid* "to know").

Active inflection: indic. perf. sing. 1. *vaēdā*, 2. *vōistā*, *dadāθā*, 3. *vaēdā*.—Dual 3. *yaētarǝ*.—Plur. 1. *yōiθmā*, 3. *ā̊ŋharǝ̄*, *vīδarǝ*.—Opt. perf. sing. 1. *daiδiiąm*, 3. *vīdiiāt̰*.—Dual. 3. *aŋ́hāt̰.tǝm* (< **āh-i̯ā-tām*).—Part. perf. (suffix *-u̯āh-*, *-uš-*, fem. *-ušī-*) sing. nom. masc. *vīduuā̊*, *daδuuā̊*, gen. *vīdušō*, *dadušō*, fem. *vīθušī-*.

Middle inflection (rare): indic. perf. sing. 3. *vāuuǝrǝzōi* "it has been worked."—Dual 3. *mamnāitē*.—Opt. perf. plur. 3. *vaozirǝm* "they would have driven" (from root *vaz*).—Part. perf. *mamnāna-* "having thought," *vāuuǝrǝzāna-* "having been done."

Infinitives. Infinitives are formed by the addition of various suffixes either directly to the root or to a tense stem: **-ai*: OAv. *pōi* (< **pH-aí*) "to protect," YAv *buiie* (< **buu̯-ai*) "to become;" **-u̯ai*: OAv. *dāuuōi* "to give," *vīduiiē* (< **u̯id-u̯ai*) "to know;" **-u̯anai*: OAv. *vīduuanōi* "to know;" **-tai*: OAv. *itē* "to go," *mrūitē* "to say," *stōi* 'to be;" **-ah*: OAv. *auuō* "to aid," *vǝrǝziiō* "to work;" **-ahai*: OAv. *vaocaŋ́hē* "to say" (from aorist stem *vaoca-*), *srāuuaiieŋ́he* "to recite" (from caus. stem *srāuuaiia-*), **-dʰi̯āi* (Vedic *-dhyai*): OAv. *jaidiiāi* "to be killed" (from root *jan*), *diβžaidiiāi* "to be deceived," *vǝrǝziieidiiāi* "to do, be done."

Verbal adjectives. Verbal adjectives ending in *-ta* have almost always passive meaning, but there are exceptions such as *gata-* (= Vedic *gatá-*) "gone." If phonologically possible the root appears in the zero grade, e.g., *-uxta-* "said" (Vedic *uktá-* < *vac*); *vista-* "found" (< **u̯idᶻ-tá-*, cf. Vedic *vittá-* < *vid*); *vǝrǝzda-* "increased" (Vedic *vr̥ddhá-* < **u̯r̥dᶻdʰá-* < **u̯r̥dʰᶻ-tó-*); *jata-*"slain" (Vedic *hatá-* < *han*) from root *jan*; *zāta-* "born" (Vedic *jātá-* with *-ā-* < *n̥H-*) from root *zanH*. Roots ending in *-ā-* do not show ablaut, e.g., *dāta-* "given; put" (But Vedic *hitá* < **dʰǝ-tó-*).

Bibliography: Chr. Bartholomae, *Awestasprache und Altpersisch*, in Geiger and Kuhn, *Grundr. Ir. Phil.* I, pp. 188-241. A. V. W. Jackson, *An Avesta Grammar in Comparison with Sanskrit*, Stuttgart, 1892, repr. Darmstadt, 1968, pp. 62-200. H. Reichelt, *Awestisches Elementarbuch*, Heidelberg, 1909, repr. Darmstadt, 1967. H. G. Herzenberg, *Morfologicheskaya struktura slova v drevnikh indoiranskikh yazykakh*, Leningrad, 1972. S. Sokolov. "Yazyk Avesty," in V. I. Abaev, ed., *Osnovy iranskogo yazykoznaniya* I: *Drevneiranskie yazyki*, Moscow, 1979, pp. 161-94. E. Benveniste, *Les infinitifs avestiques*, Paris, 1935. J. Kellens, *Les noms-racines de l'Avesta*, Wiesbaden, 1974. Idem, *Le verbe avestique*, Wiesbaden, 1985. On other aspects of Avestan grammar, not treated here, consult the works listed above. On composition see J. Duchesne-Guillemin, *Les composés de l'Avesta*, Liège and Paris, 1936. See also J. Duchesne-Guillemin, *Kratylos* 7, 1962, pp. 11-38; J. Kellens, ibid., 16, 1971, pp. 9-17; 18, 1973, pp. 1-2. K. Hoffmann, *Aufsätze zur Indoiranistik* I-II, Wiesbaden, 1975-76 (consult the index pp. 688-704).

(K. HOFFMANN)

AVESTAN PEOPLE. The term Avestan people is used here to include both Zoroaster's own tribe, with that of his patron, Kavi Vištāspa, and those peoples settled in Eastern Iran who, though not all "Avestan"-speaking, were "of the Avesta" in that they shared in transmitting, and in part composing, the holy texts. Of these texts, the linguistically later ones were handed down in fluid oral transmission—it seems well into the Achaemenian era—and reflect accordingly social conditions from over a long period, often anachronistically blended. Only Zoroaster's *Gāθās*, strictly memorized from the time of their composition, provide evidence for a particular period and place; but since they form only a small body of texts, their data have generally been interpreted in the light of more abundant Younger Avestan materials.

With regard to Old Avestan society, i.e., that reflected

in the *Gāθās*, W. Geiger, studying it in the nineteenth century, saw it as a simple, archaic one, divided essentially between priests and other men, with "every peasant . . . at the same time a fighting man, who was ready to defend his property against enemies in times of danger" (*Civilization of the Eastern Iranians in Ancient Times*, tr. D. P. Sanjana, London, 1886, II, p. 64). Subsequent linguistic studies established that the "other men" were not in fact peasant-farmers but cattle-tending pastoralists, Zoroaster's terms for them being "herdsman, pasturer" (*vāstrya, vāstar, vāstrya fšuyant*). Archaeologists have shown that some farming was practised on the Inner Asian steppes (presumed to be the homeland of the proto-Indo-Iranians) already in the third millennium B.C., as well as a mixed pastoralism (with cows, sheep, goats, camels, and horses); but a parallel has repeatedly been drawn in this respect between the Indo-Iranians and certain East African tribes, who also have a mixed pastoral economy, but for whom too the cow is of unique social and even religious importance (see B. Lincoln, *Priests, Warriors and Cattle*, University of California Press, 1981, pp. 13ff. with nn. 38-40 for earlier studies). These African tribes are likewise divided into two social groups, priests and warrior-herdsmen. The Younger Avestan people recognized, however, three social divisions, priests, warriors, and herdsmen-farmers (*āθravan, raθaēštar, vāstryō.fšuyant*); and attempts were subsequently made to transfer this clearly and frequently articulated pattern to Old Avestan society also, notably by supposing that *nar* "man," used on occasion, it seems, by Zoroaster (*Y.* 28.8) to mean "brave man, hero," could also (*Y.* 48.10, cf. 40.3), mean in the plural specifically "warriors," and so be a class-designation (see C. Bartholomae, *AirWb.*, col. 1048; E. Benveniste, "Les classes sociales dans la tradition avestique," *JA*, 1932, p. 122; contra, M. Boyce, "The Bipartite Society of the Ancient Iranians," in *Societies and Languages of the Ancient Near East: Studies in Honour of I. M. Diakonoff*, ed. M. A. Dandamayev et al., Warminster, 1982, pp. 33-34; J. Narten, *Der Yasna Haptaŋhāiti*, Wiesbaden, 1986, pp. 276-79). In 1930 G. Dumézil put forward the theory that the tripartite divisions of Younger Avestan and Vedic society shared a proto-Indo-Iranian origin, despite the wholly different terminology (Vedic *brahmán, kṣatríya, vaíśya*) ("La préhistoire indo-iranienne des castes," *JA*, 1930, pp. 109-30). Ergo, Gathic society must have known the same divisions, even if again differently named. Against Dumézil, E. C. Polomé maintained that a classless society would have been characteristic generally of Indo-European peoples in their pastoral period: "The trifunctional hierarchization of society . . . [has] to be viewed diachronically as part of a dynamic process of development . . . . In the older pastoral society, we rather expect *unranked* descent groups. As the community grows and *diversifies*, the extended family 'swarms' for economic reasons; moving to establish new settlements leads to profound social changes with *ranked* descent groups and full-time craft specialization" ("Indo-European Culture, with Special Attention to Religion," in E. C. Polomé, ed., *The Indo-Europeans in the Fourth and Third Millennia*, Michigan, 1982, p. 170). The *Gāθās* appear indeed to mirror ancient Iranian society still at this pastoral stage, the community of "cattle and men" (*pasu vira*, *Y.* 31.15, 45.9), experiencing violent changes but not yet driven to the "swarming" represented by the great migrations from the steppes southwards into Iran, which led, it seems, to the evolution of social classes (with a parallel but independent development in Vedic India).

For the priesthood the *Gāθās* yield, frequently, the word *karapan*, generally held to designate ordinary working priests who performed rituals and were castigated by Zoroaster (presumably because they were hostile to his teachings and supported those whom he regarded as wicked); once, *zaotar*, for an officiating priest (*Y.* 33.6); and, repeatedly, *mąθran*, for one uttering inspired words. *Usig* also occurs once, on which see below. There is nothing to indicate whether or not the priesthood was hereditary; but the *Gāθās* attest the existence of a learned, subtle, technically complex religious poetry, whose cultivation clearly required years of study. (The widespread composition also of secular oral poetry may be assumed from allusions in the Younger Avesta to ancient epic themes.)

The *Gāθās* have two series of terms for social groupings. One is *xvaētu* "family," *vərəzə̄na* "community," *airyaman* "clan" (*Y.* 32.1; 33.3; 46.1; 49.7). (Attempts to equate this series with YAv. *āθravan, raθaēštar, vāstryō.fšuyant* were justly criticized by Benveniste, art. cit., pp. 121-22). The other is *dəmāna* "dwelling," *vīs* "settlement," *šōiθra* "district," *dahyu* "land" (*Y.* 31.18, cf. 31.16, 46.4). The last term presumably defined that region lived in or wandered over by related clans. There are no allusions to towns or commerce. Payments for services were by gifts of livestock (cf. *Y.* 44.18; 46.19). The importance of family and communal ties is emphasized particularly in *Y.* 53.4, where the prophet pledges his daughter, on marrying, to serve not only father and husband but also "herdsmen and family" (*vāstryaēibyō at̰čā x^vaētaovē*); and in *Y.* 46.1, where he grieves at his own exclusion from "family and clan" (*x^vaētə̄uš airyamanasčā*). The existence of a code of laws (*dāta-*), regulating presumably both individual and communal actions, is expressly indicated in *Y.* 51.14; and Zoroaster makes recurrent use of the concepts of judgment and judging, wrongdoing and punishment, and draws frequently on that of the judicial ordeal by fire and by molten metal (*Y.* 30.7; 31.3, 19; 43.4; 47.6; 51.9).

The form of wrongdoing uppermost in his thought was evidently that of violent attack by "slayers of men, harmers of men," on "(peacefully)-dwelling settlements" (*Y.* 53.8; cf. 48.10). These cruel assailants of law-abiding (*ašavan-*) herdsmen are led by "fury" (*aēšəma-*, *Y.* 29.1; 30.6; 48.7; 49.4); and as well as killing, they steal and rob (*Y.* 32.14), and above all harm and carry off cattle (e.g., *Y.* 29.1, 51.14). They are under the authority of "evil rulers" (*dušəxšaθra-*, *Y.* 48.10), wicked lords who themselves plunder the just man (*Y.* 30.11); and they are aided by priests—the *karapan* and *usig* (*Y.* 44.20). The latter was perhaps employed to perform special rites to bring martial success, cf. Vedic *uśij* (see Lincoln, op. cit., pp. 61-62), and presumably shared in the spoils of a raid. Zoroaster uses no specific term for the raiders themselves (who are evidently fellow-Iranians), but defines them negatively as "non-herdsmen" (*avāstrya-*, *Y.* 31.10), "non-pastors" (*afšuyant-*, *Y.* 49.4), seeing them, it seems, as those who had broken away from the accepted social order to live ruthlessly from plunder alone (*Y.* 31.15). This suggests that for the "Gathic" people such lawless raiding was a recent phenomenon, a breach with established ways.

A terminus post quem for this social upheaval is provided by Zoroaster's use in metaphor of "yoked" (i.e., harnessed) horses, racing ahead(*Y.* 50.7, cf. 30.10) and of "charioteer" (*raiθī-*, *Y.* 50.6). The horse-drawn chariot was evolved in the Near East early in the second millennium B.C. (see M.A. Littauer and J.H. Crouwel, "Wheeled Vehicles and Ridden Animals in the Ancient Near East," in *HO* VII. 1. 2. B. 1, Leiden, 1979, pp. 51ff.), and chariotry was then developed, it seems, by diverse peoples there, including the Indo-Aryan aristocrats of Mitanni, with chariot-riding noblemen coming to be widely known as *maryanni*/*maryannu*. F.C. Andreas suggested a possible connection here with Vedic *márya*, meaning primarily "young man" (see apud H. Winckler, *OLZ*, 1910, p. 291 with n. 1); and debate continues as to whether the Mitannian word is indeed Indo-Aryan acc. plur. *máryān* with a Hurrian suffix, or a purely Hurrian word, accidentally similar to *márya* in form and meaning (see Littauer and Crouwel, op. cit., pp. 68-71 with n. 93 for the literature). One of the specific meanings of Vedic *márya*, and its Av. cognate *mairya*, was "fighting man, warrior;" and this meaning probably attached already to proto-Indo-Iranian **marya*. As a fighter, the Vedic *márya* rode in a chariot (see W.F. Albright, "Mitannian Maryannu, 'chariot-warrior'. . . .," *Archiv für Orientforschung*, 1931, p. 220; S. Wikander, *Der arische Männerbund*, Lund, 1938, pp. 22ff.); and this was probably true also of Av. Fraŋrasyan (who lived before Zoroaster, see AFRĀSĪĀB) and of Arəjat̰.aspa (the prophet's contemporary), both fighting chieftains for whom *mairya* is a fixed epithet. Before the Bronze Age reached the Asian steppes (from ca. 1700 B.C.), the *márya*/*mairya*, i.e., the young warrior-herdsmen, had fought necessarily on foot, with the hunter-herdsman's ancient weapons: club, sling-stones, bow, and arrows. With more effective, and costly, bronze weapons, and the also costly chariot (giving mobility), social revolution came to the steppes. The earliest known chariots there, from "not later than 1500 B.C.," were found in the Sintashta graves, in the Cheliabinsk region on the eastern flank of the Central Urals (see V.F. Gening, "Le champ funéraire de Sintachta et le problême des anciennes tribus indo-iranniennes," *Sovetskaya Arkheologiya*, 1977, 4, pp. 53-75, with French summary). The excavators found several reasons to identify the Sintashta community (which supported itself by pastoralism, with a little farming) as Iranian; and there is diversity there in ways of disposing of the corpse (i.e., burial both of the integral body, and of disarticulated bones after excarnation) which suggests differing beliefs about the after-life, such as might have provided the seedbed for Zoroaster's new teachings. There is also a lack of any sign of class-divisions. In the associated settlement there were only large communal houses; and in the cemetery, pit-graves of the one kind were made for all alike. The presence of chariots in four tombs show that there were individuals with the means and enterprise to acquire and maintain such vehicles; but they were apparently no more than leading members of a still essentially homogeneous society. The *Gāθās* suggest, however, that gradually more and more *mairya*s (some perhaps returned mercenaries from Near Eastern wars, cf. H.M. Chadwick, *The Heroic Age*, Cambridge, 1911, pp. 444ff.) acquired chariots and the new bronze weaponry, and, attaching themselves to war-lords, the *dušəxšaθra* of *Y.* 48.10, began to live by plundering their fellows. Thus, it seems, were created the conditions for the Iranian Heroic Age, which, like any other, had its dark and brutal side. Eventually many Iranian tribes, some doubtless impoverished (this was also, apparently, a period of drought on the steppes, see H. H. Lamb, *Climate, History and the Modern World*, London. 1982, pp. 132-40), "swarmed," probably from around 1200-1000 B.C., moving south into Iran.

During the course of these events the more warlike "Younger Avestan" society evolved. Priest-poets equipped the gods themselves with war-chariots, and entreated them repeatedly for help in battle; and the chariot-riding *mairya*s established their social dominance. A new term was coined for these now professional fighting men, *raθaēštar*, "one standing in a chariot;" and *mairya* in the sense of "warrior" was superseded by it, as Vedic *márya* was by *kṣatríya*. (Both words survive with this meaning only in certain fixed usages.) These facts were obscured for Wikander (op. cit.) because he subordinated his study of the *mairya*/*márya* to trying to establish the existence of a hypothetical Indo-Iranian institution, the "Männerbund." He ignored both the *Gāθās* (because the word *mairya* does not occur in them) and archaeological evidence; and treated Iranian society as static, simply projecting Bronze Age conditions back into the early second millennium, and assuming (with others) that a professional warrior-class had existed already then. In this he was followed by Lincoln, op. cit. (For a more detailed discussion of both their works see Boyce, "Priests, Cattle and Men," *BSOAS* 50/3, 1987). Their findings were largely accepted by G. Gnoli (see his *Zoroaster's Time and Homeland*, Naples, 1980, Index s.v. "Männerbund"), who sought to place Zoroaster in Eastern Iran about 1000 B.C., i.e., after the main migrations, thus again making no distinction between Old and Younger Avestan society (op. cit., pp. 59ff.; *De Zoroastre à Mani*, Paris, 1985, pp. 15ff.); but, all other considerations apart, it would be strange if at that epoch immigrant Iranians had been savagely raiding one another, instead of seeking to subdue the alien peoples among whom they then found themselves.

In the *Gāθās* women figure as dependent socially on men (father, husband) whom they look after (*Y.* 53.4), but as spiritually their equals (*Y.* 46.10). The Avestan people had a short initiation rite which in pre-Zoroastrian days had probably been undergone only by youths, being then as much social as religious, marking entry into adult life (see Geiger, op. cit., I, pp. 58-59). In Zoroastrianism this rite is essentially religious, and so is administered to both sexes. It is first attested in the Younger Avesta, but may reasonably be presumed to be old. It was performed at fifteen (*Vd.* 18.54, 58-59), which was regarded as the ideal age (cf. e.g., *Yt.* 8.13; *Y.* 9.5); and it consisted essentially of investing the candidate with a sacred girdle (*aiwyå̄ŋhana-*) to be worn thereafter day and night, but untied and retied with prayers at prescribed moments. The rite remained common to priests and to the laity of both Young Avestan classes (Wikander, op. cit., pp. 67ff., was unable to produce any evidence for his postulated separate "warrior" initiation); and this is a further indication of the homogeneity of Old Avestan society. In that society marriage evidently followed on initiation, with, ideally, the speedy begetting of children, so that a man could hope to see his first grandson soon after he himself reached the ripe age of thirty. The Avestan people attached immense importance to lineage, and venerated the souls of their ancestors (see FRAVAŠI), which they believed protected them if duly worshipped (*Yt.* 13.49-52; see further Boyce, *Zoroastrianism* I, pp. 119ff., with references). Such worship was carried out in the home; and the daily prayers were said either there, before the hearth fire, or in the open. The Avesta has no words for a consecrated building or temple fire. Communal worship, with merrymaking, took place at festivals scattered irregularly through the year, which, to judge from their Young Avestan names (see GĀHĀMBĀR), were associated originally with events in the pastoral and farming year. The tradition that "spring butter" (*zaramaya- raoγna-*) was the best of all foods (*Hāδōxt Nask* 2.38) clearly goes back to Old Avestan times, and the joy of a pastoral people in fresh products from their cows after winter's deprivations. The staple food then was evidently meat (*pitu-*), cf. the expression *arəm-piθwā* (*Y.* 44.5) "time for preparing meat," i.e., midday, which again suggests dependence on flocks and herds.

The Younger Avesta, though preserving many archaic elements, reflects various stages of a later, more complex society, with a different social structure and economic basis. Known regions in Eastern Iran are named (see AVESTAN GEOGRAPHY), and the three classes are firmly established, their foundation being piously attributed to Zoroaster himself (*Yt.* 13.88). Although the term *vāstryō.fšuyant* is used for the third class, its dominant representative is now the farmer. The merit is stressed of irrigating, draining, tilling the soil, sowing corn, and cultivating fruits (*Vd.* 3.4, 23-31), since all these activities reduced barrenness, in which Aŋra Mainyu (see AHRIMAN) was held to rejoice. "Corn (*yava-*) shall man eat" Ahura Mazdā is made to declare (*Vd.* 5.20), which indicates the change from meat to bread as the basic diet. In *Vd.* 14.7-11 the equipment is listed proper to members of each class. That of the *vāstryō.fšuyant* includes a spade, plough, and wine-press, while the *raθaēštar* has spear and sword and, instead of the chariot which gave him his name, a saddle and full armor. Riding began to replace the chariot in warfare from the ninth century B.C.; and the *yašt*s duly contain references to mounted *raθaēštar*s (see I. Gershevitch, *The Avestan Hymn to Mithra*, Cambridge, 1959, repr. 1967, pp. 69-70). There is still no mention of town-life, but in a late passage a fourth class is recognized, that of the *hūiti*, the craftsman or artisan (*Y.* 19.17). This presumably included not only smiths, but also potters, weavers, and the like, all now become specialized workers. The use of metals was evidently steadily increasing, e.g., beside the traditional stone pestle and mortar (*hāvana-*) others of metal (*āyah-*) are mentioned (*Y.* 22.2); but payments were still reckoned in traditional manner in units of livestock (e.g., *Vd.* 9.37-38). In *Vd.* 7.41-42 a scale of rewards is listed for physician and surgeon; and here a donkey (*kaθwā-*) appears, a southern animal unknown of old on the steppes.

Indications of a more complex political organization, with perhaps at its apex a council of chiefs of diverse "lands" (*dahyu-*) occur in *Yt.* 10.18, 87, 145 (see Gershevitch, op. cit., pp. 296-99) with possibly, locally at least, a parallel priestly hierarchy (*Yt.* 10.115, with Gershevitch's commentary, op. cit., p. 265). Daily life included a number of observances, developed on the basis of Zoroastrian dualism as means of repelling or reducing evil. One was the regular utterance of *bāj* (q.v.); another the killing of *xrafstra*s, noxious or repulsive creatures such as snakes, frogs, ants, worms (*Vd.* 14.5-6), regarded as belonging to Aŋra Mainyu. The dog on the contrary was highly esteemed (*Vd.* 13.39-40, 44-49), probably since the Old Avestan pastoralists had relied on herd-dogs. There was also a wide-ranging code of purity laws (*Vd.* 3ff.). Some (e.g., those relating to contamination from a corpse, or a flow of blood) are of a kind found commonly in ancient or primitive societies, and may be presumed to have existed among the Old Avestan people. Others appear to have evolved under Zoroastrianism as yet another means of countering evil. There were also rituals for recovering lost purity, with an elaborate one, *barašnom* (q.v.), for serious pollutions.

According to Zoroastrianism the active struggle against "evil" (physical, moral, and spiritual) was incumbent on every believer, and was best waged by the prosperous, provided they acted justly. A rich man was considered "better," i.e., more effective, than a poor one, a man who had eaten than one who had fasted (*Vd.* 4.47.49), since they had more means and energy to combat what seemed wrong in the world, and to extend the good. It was meritorious also to marry and have children (see ibid.), who would carry on the good fight.

The Younger Avestan people appear accordingly philoprogenitive, energetic and purposeful, confident that they, as followers of Zoroaster, had a divinely appointed part to play in improving the world, and that they were supported in it by *x'arənah* (see FARR), the heaven-sent power that made them superior to all other peoples (cf. *Yt.* 19.56; *Vd.* 19.39).

Bibliography: Given in the text.

(M. BOYCE)

AVICENNA, the Latin form of the name of the celebrated philosopher and physician of the Islamic world, Abū ʿAlī Ḥosayn Ebn Sīnā (b. Bukhara 370/980[?], d. Hamadān 428/1037).

i. *Introductory note.*
ii. *Biography.*
iii. *Logic.*
iv. *Metaphysics.*
v. *Mysticism.*
vi. *Psychology.*
vii. *Practical sciences.*
viii. *Mathematics and physical sciences.*
ix. *Music.*
x. *Medicine and biology.*
xi. *Persian works.*
xii. *The impact of Avicenna's philosophical works on the West.*
xiii. *The influence of Avicenna on medical studies in the West.*

i. INTRODUCTION

The generally accepted view that the Islamic philosophic tradition established by Fārābī (d. 339/950) came to an end with Ebn Rošd (Averroes, fl. 520-95/1126-98) has been challenged by scholars who have pointed to the continuity of that tradition in the East, principally in Iran, to the present day. In order to understand the point at issue, one must begin with Avicenna, as a disciple of Fārābī, which in many ways he was, but also as a thinker who attempted to redefine the course of Islamic philosophy and channel it into new directions. For to the extent that the post-Averroistic tradition remained philosophic, it moved in the directions charted for it by Avicenna in the investigation of both theoretical and practical sciences.

If one looks at the broad movement of Islamic philosophy since Fārābī one can see that it began with the formulation of its principles and moved progressively toward greater elaboration and application of these principles to the study of the relation between philosophy and religion, but also toward a closer and more detailed examination of the various aspects of the phenomenon of religion, such as prophecy, revelation, the divine or religious law, and of what one might call the varieties of religious experience. Fārābī avoided explicit examination of Islam or any other particular religion and always spoke of religion in general. (As far as the reader is concerned, he could have been speaking about someone else's religion or some hypothetical religion.) This enabled him to speak boldly, if cautiously, about the relation between philosophy and religion, state the principles of a philosophic or scientific approach to the study of religion, include the science of religion within political philosophy, and identify religion with the city.

With Avicenna one finds the beginnings of a movement away from explicitness about the central question of the relation between philosophy and religion, and toward treating this question either in the form of myths, poems, and stories, or else obliquely by means of suggestive hints. Instead, there emerges what might be called a philosophic interpretation of religion: The various aspects of the phenomenon of religion in general, and of Islam in particular, are explained in a way that, broadly speaking, bears out Fārābī's view of religion, but without stating the original formulation of that view or its political framework. The Koran, the Tradition of Moḥammad (*Sonna*), the political history of the Muslim Community (*Omma*), the Islamic Law (*Šarīʿa*), Islamic theology (*kalām*), and such questions as prophecy and revelation are now examined directly, not as a hypothetical case, or as the "universals" or "general rules," as was the case in Fārābī's political science, but as this specifically determined revelation and as these doctrines and texts and men and situations. This required him to make certain concessions, especially in areas such as the resurrection of the body, where reason can not validate religious doctrine. But it enabled him to domesticate philosophy in the Islamic world and present it in a way that could now be appreciated, not only by the select few, but by a wide range of educated Muslims.

Two generations after Avicenna, Abū Ḥāmed Ḡazālī (fl. 450-505/1058-1111) testifies to the fact that no serious Muslim thinker could ignore the claim of philosophy as a way to the highest and most comprehensive knowledge available to man and as a way to the Truth. He also testifies to the fact that, at least as far as he was concerned, philosophy for all practical purposes meant Avicenna's philosophy. When he set about to learn what philosophy was, he read Avicenna's works. When he tried to present the intentions of the philosophers, he wrote a summary of Avicenna's philosophy. And when he tried to show the incoherence of the philosophers, he wrote a refutation of Avicenna's doctrines. Similarly, when Moḥammad Šahrestānī (d. 548/1153) came to give an account of the doctrines of "the philosophers of Islam" (*falāsefat al-Eslām*), as distinguished from the doctrines of Greek or Indian philosophers, he simply summarized the doctrines of "the most distinguished ... Avicenna" (ed. A. Fahmī Moḥammad, 3 vols., Cairo, 1368/1949, 3.3, 3.43). Most of the later Muslim theologians and mystics who tried to harmonize philosophy and theology, or philosophy and mysticism, and, later on, philosophy and theology and mysticism, also made use of Avicenna. All this testifies to his success in popularizing philosophy in the

Islamic community. Later philosophers, especially in the Islamic West, perceived that Avicenna's success was achieved at the expense of the integrity and purity of philosophy, by concessions to theology and mysticism, and by the creation of a hybrid mixture which led to confusion and exposed philosophy to attacks and criticisms by men like Ḡazālī. Within philosophic circles, there arose an anti-Avicennan, pro-Farabian tradition which accused Avicenna of engaging in too much rhetoric and dialectic and of making too many adjustments to popular views. His popularity with non-philosophers was matched, among his fellow philosophers, by a certain opposition to his temper, manner of writing, and lack of prudence. But the public did not, of course, listen to these philosophers. Avicenna's writings spread like fire and continued until today to form the basis of philosophic education in the Islamic world.

However all this may be, the central question is how Avicenna took the crucial step or steps from Fārābī's general science of religion to a science of this particular religion which is Islam. Avicenna wrote a vast body of specialized tracts on religious matters, including commentaries on Koranic passages, and discussions of subjects like prayer, prophecy, and the hereafter. Most of these, however, represent a movement from particular religious doctrines and ideas to their theoretical principles, without explaining the place of these specialized discussions within the whole body of human knowledge. And he wrote encyclopedic works on logic, natural sciences, mathematics, and metaphysics, in which practical science occupies a subordinate position.

(M. MAHDI)

ii. BIOGRAPHY

Sources. Avicenna's biography presents the paradox that although more material is available for its study than is average for a Muslim scholar of his caliber, it has received little critical attention. The very existence of the autobiography and Jūzjānī's biography, both retold, paraphrased, and elaborated upon, seems to have inhibited from the very beginning further research into additional sources and critical analysis of those available. The assessment first made by Ebn Abī Oṣaybeʿa in the middle of the 7th/13th century has been valid ever since for both Muslim and Western scholars: Avicenna "mentioned his personal circumstances and described his own life in a way that relieves others of describing it again" (*Ketāb ʿoyūn al-anbāʾ fī ṭabaqāt al-aṭebbāʾ*, ed. A. Müller, Cairo, 1882-84, II, p. 2).

A comprehensive and critical study of Avicenna's life will have to draw on the following four categories of sources:

1. The autobiography/biography complex and its recensions and derivatives. Avicenna's autobiography covers the period from his birth until after his encounter with Abū ʿObayd ʿAbd-al-Wāḥed Jūzjānī, his disciple and constant companion. Jūzjānī wrote down the autobiography (either from dictation, according to Ebn al-Qefṭī, *Tārīḵ al-ḥokamāʾ*, ed. J. Lippert, Leipzig, 1903, p. 413, or from a draft originally penned by Avicenna), and appended to it the biography, covering the rest of Avicenna's life. This combined original document, in Arabic, exists in at least two recensions. One is embedded in the accounts of Avicenna by Ebn al-Qefṭī (pp. 413-26) and Ebn Abī Oṣaybeʿa (II, pp. 2-9), and the other exists independently in various manuscripts, in some of which it is also given the Persian title, *Sargoḏašt*. The relationship of the two recensions to Jūzjānī's text and to each other is not entirely clear. W. E. Gohlman, the editor of the *Sargoḏašt*, tends to think that it is closer to the original (Gohlman, *The Life of Ibn Sina*, p. 6).

Jūzjānī's edition of the autobiography/biography forms the only source for all subsequently narrative accounts of Avicenna's life. There is no indication that there ever was an original rival biography, and all later retellings merely repeat Jūzjānī's account in different degrees of fidelity to his (and Avicenna's) wording. These retellings differ only in the various details they introduce, which, however, have to be proven authentic in each case before they can be accepted. Even during his lifetime Avicenna had achieved great fame or notoriety (depending on the viewer's standpoint), and stories about him with essentially hagiographic or demonographic content doubtless began to circulate soon after his death. The trend continued until later popular tradition made of him either a saint and a mystic or a magician.

The most important retelling of the autobiography/biography, which sometimes is erroneously treated as an independent source, is that by Ẓahīr-al-dīn Abu'l-Ḥasan Bayhaqī in the *Tatemmat ṣewān al-ḥekma*. Bayhaqī recasts the autobiography in the third person, slightly paraphrases the biography, omits certain details, mostly of a bibliographic nature, and adds some others. These additions, which in Šafīʿ's, edition (Lahore, 1935) are conveniently enclosed in double brackets, occur mostly in the autobiography part, and are informative (provide names of personalities mentioned, refer to historical events), bibliographic (report on the fate of some of Avicenna's lost books), calumniatory (blame Avicenna for being the first philosopher to indulge in wine and sex, and to frequent royal courts), and anecdotal (e.g., the story of ʿAlāʾ-al-dawla's sister and the Ghaznavid Sultan Masʿūd, pp. 55-56 and Avicenna and the youth from Ray, pp. 59-61). Except for the bibliographic reports about the survival of some of Avicenna's books, not much of this additional information can be taken at face value. Bayhaqī's gratuitous comments on Avicenna's alleged debauchery, his arbitrary extrapolations from the material at hand, such as the mention that Avicenna used to study the *Rasāʾel Eḵwān al-Ṣafāʾ*, and the anecdotal material merit little credence; but even the information about the names of certain personalities should be questioned. There is no reason why the names of Avicenna's mother, and of the greengrocer from whom Avicenna learned arithmetic as a young boy, should have survived unaltered, or at all, for more than

150 years until Bayhaqī's time. Such information, even if it had survived orally in the popular tradition, lends itself easily to falsification.

Similar criticism must be applied to all details added in the derivatives of Jūzjānī's edition of the autobiography/biography. These derivatives are the accounts of Avicenna's life by subsequent biographers, from Ebn Ḵallekān (*Wafayāt al-aʿyān*) and Šahrazūrī (*Nozhat al-arwāḥ*) to Ebn al-ʿEmād (*Šaḏarāt al-ḏahab*) and Ḵᵛāndamīr (*Ḥabīb al-sīar* and *Dostūr al-wozarāʾ*).

The manuscript tradition of Jūzjānī's edition also shows accretions and contaminations from various sources. In one instance, the recension in Ebn al-Qefṭī/Ebn Abī Oṣaybeʿa is contaminated with the version of Bayhaqī, in the Vienna MS Ar. Mixt. 866, 8 (H. Loebenstein, *Katalog der arabischen Handschriften der österreichischen Nationalbibliothek*, Vienna, 1970, p. 212, no. 2430).

2. Private writings by Avicenna and his disciples. These constitute a reliable source about numerous details of Avicenna's life. They consist of his many autobiographical references in the prologues, epilogues, and occasionally even in the body of his own works, of his correspondence, and of similar writings by his disciples, including Jūzjanī's introduction to the *Šefāʾ* (*Madḵal*, Cairo, 1952, pp. 1-4). This material, which has been virtually untapped for Avicenna's life, is preserved partly in the collection of his *Nachlass* known under the title *al-Mobāḥaṯāt*, one recension of which was edited by ʿA. Badawī, (*Aresṭū ʿend al-ʿArab*, Cairo, 1947, pp. 119-249), and partly independently in the MSS, and remains mostly unpublished.

3. Historical works. As a rule they have little information to add to Avicenna's life, but they are useful for providing the background for many of the social and political events referred to or hinted at in the autobiography/biography.

4. Legendary and hagiographic stories. These belong not to his biography proper but to a study of the transformation of his image in popular tradition after his death. This played a role in the reception of his authentic works in the Persian- and Turkish-speaking areas of the Islamic world and has to be studied as a separate subject. The pride of place among the legendary material belongs to Neẓāmī ʿArūżī's *Čahār maqāla* (tr. E. G. Browne, London, index, s.v.). For later material see A. Süheyl Ünver, "Şark folklorun'da İbni Sina hakkında yaşayan ve kaybolan efsaneler," in his *İbni Sina, Hayatı ve Eserleri Hakkında Çalışmalar*, Istanbul, 1955, pp. 62-70.

Analysis of the autobiography. For the fitst part of Avicenna's life, our sole source of information is the autobiography. The real purpose of this document is philosophical: While purporting to give details about his early life—details which, in the absence of contrary, or any other, evidence, may have to be taken at face value—Avicenna is providing a concrete illustration of his epistemological theory. This centers on the ability of some individuals with powerful souls to acquire intelligible knowledge all by themselves and without the help of a teacher through their propensity to hit spontaneously upon the middle terms of syllogisms, *ḥads* (see below Mysticism: Avicenna and Sufism). The autobiography is written from the perspective of a philosopher who does not belong by training to any school of thought and is therefore not beholden to defending it blindly, who established truth through his independent verification (*ḥads*) and found that for the most part this truth is contained in the philosophical sciences as classified and transmitted in the Aristotelian tradition, and who is therefore in a position both to teach this more accurate version of truth—or revised Aristotelian philosophy—and to judge the attainment in philosophy of others.

For this reason, when the autobiography is reduced to its bare essentials, it appears as a transcript of Aristotelian studies and a model curriculum vitae in a Peripatetic program. Avicenna reports in it basically that he studied the philosophical sciences according to their classification in the Aristotelian tradition, and that he studied them in three successive stages at increasingly advanced levels. Everything else that Avicenna says he studied was studied not for its own sake but for that of the philosophical sciences, in whose terms it is to be seen. The elementary courses in the Koran, literature, and arithmetic are preparatory subjects for the philosophical sciences. Avicenna's rejection of the Ismaʿili teachings is intended to indicate that already at an early age he could refuse, through his own reflection, authoritative knowledge, *taqlīd.* (Bayhaqī's unwarranted addition at this point, that Avicenna would read and reflect on the *Rasāʾel*, as already mentioned, caused many a misunderstanding and generated the myth of the Ismaʿili Avicenna. Avicenna nowhere indicates that he had any interest in the doctrine or in the kind of thinking it involved.) His study of *feqh* with the Hanafite jurist Esmāʿīl Zāhed (d. 402/1012) is mentioned only to refer to the method of the discipline and to justify his knowledge of and practice in Aristotelian dialectics (as expounded in the *Topics* 8). On this basis is Avicenna then able to analyze the question "What is it?" and amaze his teacher Nātelī. Medicine, finally, though it belongs to the canon of sciences in the Greek Aristotelian tradition, is not a theoretical, but a practical science. Therefore it is easy, i.e., its acquisition does not require the solution of syllogisms by hitting upon middle terms, but merely reading the texts and medical practice. Avicenna then says that he studied the philosophical sciences—logic, mathematics, physics, metaphysics, in that order—in three stages: first, initially with Nātelī and finally on his own, second, entirely on his own, and third, at a research level, in the physicians' library in the palace of the Samanid ruler.

The systematic nature of Avicenna's presentation of the actual course of his studies, and its close correspondence to the theoretical classification of the philosophical sciences, raise the question whether Avicenna presented a stylized autobiography in which the chronology of events is bent to fit the theoretical classification of the sciences. The issue can not be resolved, insofar as the classification of the sciences in the Aristotelian tradition influenced actual educational practice which in turn is presented in an autobiographical account reproducing that very classification in order to promote it. However, the exact historical sequence of events in Avicenna's studies is not as important as the point which the autobiography intends to make, as discussed in the first paragraph of this section.

Avicenna's life. Bukhara (370/980[?]-389/999[?]). Avicenna was born around the year 370/980 and most likely quite a few years earlier than that. It has not yet been possible to establish the date of his birth with greater precision; there are enough inconsistencies and contradictions in the transmitted chronology, however, to make the traditional date of 370/980 rather untenable (Sellheim, *Oriens*, p. 238). He was born in Afšana, a village near Bukhara. His father, who had moved in from Balḵ a few years previously, was the Samanid governor of nearby Ḵarmayṯan. A few years after his birth, the family moved to Bukhara. The intellectually active capital attracted scholars, and Avicenna had an excellent education. Although for the reasons mentioned in the preceding section Avicenna is reticent about his teachers, it is almost certain the he studied with more scholars than the Nātelī that he mentions in the autobiography; the names of the physicians Abū Manṣūr Qomrī and Abū Sahl Masīḥī are also mentioned among his teachers. Given the availability of teachers and libraries, his father's high position in the Samanid administration, and his own application and precocity, Avicenna was perfectly schooled in the Greek sciences by the time he was eighteen.

Avicenna began his professional career around the age of seventeen, when he was enrolled as a physician in the service of the Samanid Nūḥ b. Manṣūr (r. 365/976-387/997) whom he was summoned to treat. After the death of his father a few years later—according to the chronological sequence of the events as described in the autobiography, after he was twenty-one—he was also given an administrative post, perhaps a district governorship. The fact that in the autobiography the death of his father and his assumption of administrative duties are mentioned closely together justifies the speculation that he may have succeeded his father as governor of Ḵarmayṯan. By a relatively early age Avicenna was established, in his twin capacity as physician and political administrator, in a profession that he was to practice in the courts of various Iranian rulers, heads of the numerous successor states that emerged during the period of the disintegration of ʿAbbasid authority.

Gorgānǰ (ca. 389/999[?]-402/1012). Avicenna remained in Bukhara until, as he puts it, "necessity called" him to leave for Gorgānǰ in Ḵᵛārazm, where he joined the service of the Maʾmunid Abu'l-Ḥasan ʿAlī b. Maʾmūn (see Āl-e Maʾmūn). Since the latter reigned from 387/997 to 399/1009, Avicenna could have moved to Gorgānǰ any time between these two dates; but the fact that the "necessity" to which he refers can be interpreted in any satisfactory way only in political terms suggests the following. The Samanid state was overthrown by the Turkish Qarakhanids who entered Bukhara in 389/999 and took ʿAbd-al-Malek II, the last amir, prisoner. Avicenna, a high functionary of the fallen state and strongly identified with the Samanid dynasty, may have found his position, to say nothing of his job, difficult to maintain. Furthermore, it may not be entirely fortuitous that soon after the fall of Bukhara to the Qarakhanids, Esmāʿīl Montaṣer, the Samanid prince, also went to Ḵᵛārazm to seek support for a political comeback. Avicenna may or may not have been involved in the undertaking, but it appears that it was the events of 389/999 and those immediately following them that generated the circumstances which made Avicenna's departure from his home town necessary (cf. Lüling, "Ein anderer Avicenna," p. 499).

From Gorgānǰ to J̌orǰān (402/1012-403/1013). Avicenna left Gorgānǰ for the same unspecified reason—"necessity called" him—and traveled south into Khorasan and then west. During the journey he passed through Nasā, Abīvard, Ṭūs, Samangān, J̌āǰarm, and arrived at J̌orǰān (Gorgān) only to find that the Ziyarid amir Qābūs b. Vošmgīr, his prospective patron, had died in the meantime (winter months of 403/January-March, 1013). Avicenna's report in the autobiography is too brief to provide any hints about the reasons behind this odyssey, although political considerations would again seem to be the only plausible answer. As for the duration of his travels, Avicenna does not mention that he stayed or worked in any of these locations, so in all likelihood he left Gorgānǰ in 402/1012. In J̌orǰān (403/1013-ca. 404/1014) Avicenna met J̌ūzǰānī. He spent little time there, apparently in the employ of Manūčehr b. Qābūs, and lived in the house of a private patron.

Ray (ca. 404/1014-405/1015). From J̌orǰān Avicenna moved to Ray, where he joined the service of the Buyid Maǰd-al-dawla Rostam and his mother Sayyeda, the power behind the throne. Although he had with him letters of recommendation for his new employers, it appears that he gained access to the political elite of the J̌ebāl again through his skill as a physician. He treated Maǰd-al-dawla who was suffering from a black bile disease.

Hamadān (405/1015-ca. 415/1024). Avicenna remained in Ray until the Buyid Šams-al-dawla, Maǰd-al-dawla's brother, attacked the city after Ḏu'l-qaʿda, 405/April, 1015. Then he left for Qazvīn, again for reasons unspecified, and finally arrived in Hamadān where he was summoned to treat Šams-al-dawla. Inevitably Avicenna became also Šams-al-dawla's vizier and acted in this capacity (with an occasional conflict with the amir's troops) until the latter's death in 412/1021. The new amir, Samāʾ-al-dawla, asked Avicenna to stay on as vizier, but "Avicenna saw fit not to remain in the same state nor to resume the same duties, and trusted that the prudent thing to do ... would be to hide in anticipation of an opportunity to leave that region" (J̌ūzǰānī, *Šefāʾ*, *Madḵal*, p. 2). He secretly corresponded with the Kakuyid ʿAlāʾ-al-dawla in Isfahan about this matter. The Buyid court in Hamadān, and especially Tāj-al-molk, the Kurdish vizier, suspected Avicenna of treachery because of these moves, and they arrested and imprisoned him in a castle outside of Hamadān called Fardajān. Avicenna remained in prison for four months until ʿAlāʾ-al-dawla marched toward Hamadān and ended Samāʾ-al-dawla's rule there (414/1023). Released from prison in the wake of these developments, Avicenna was again offered an administrative position in Hamadān, but he declined. Some time later he decided to move to Isfahan and he left Hamadān with his brother, Jūzjānī, and two slaves, dressed like Sufis.

Isfahan (ca. 415/1024-428/1037). ʿAlāʾ-al-dawla received Avicenna with honors, and gave him, in Jūzjānī's words, "the respect and esteem which someone like him deserved." Avicenna finally settled in Isfahan and remained in ʿAlāʾ-al-dawla's employ until his death. He accompanied his master in most of his campaigns and trips, and indeed it was during one such trip to Hamadān that he died, in 428/1037, of colic, after a protracted series of recoveries and relapses. He was buried in Hamadān.

Apart from his scholarly persona, which is one of unprecedented energy and sharpness, we get almost no glimpse of Avicenna's character. He was a self-conscious boy prodigy, professionally successful at an early age; also at an early age he became a permanent exile from a home that ceased to exist; he was forced to serve petty rulers most of whom not only did not appreciate his special genius but did not even esteem him as an intellectual; and yet he somehow stayed with these rulers and seems to have been determined to avoid, for whatever reasons, the Ghaznavid court. The combination of these factors, among many others, could produce either a hero or a villain: it does not help to speculate before all the available evidence, especially his private writings, is assessed. One thing, though, is certain, and this has again to do with his scholarly self: When it came to intellectual matters, Avicenna could accept no rival and decline no challenge. When he was slighted for his ignorance of Arabic lexicography, he answered the affront by memorizing Azharī's *Tahḏīb al-loḡa*, forging three epistles in the styles of famed authors, and submitting them for identification to the person who had insulted him. That person failed to recognize the forgery. This also, however, depending on the surrounding circumstances, which we do not know, could be interpreted either as extreme arrogance, or proper estimation of self worth, or even as an exaggerated sense of humor. Avicenna the person is hardly distinguishable behind the brilliance of Avicenna the mind. But for Avicenna, who saw the supreme happiness in the contact of the human intellect with the active intellect during the split-second of hitting upon the middle term, perhaps this is just the way it should be.

Bibliography: The only critical edition of the Arabic autobiography/biography in the independent recension (*Sargoḏašt*) is that by W. E. Gohlman, *The Life of Ibn Sina*, Albany, N.Y., 1974. This edition, which contains a facing English translation, has to be used in conjunction with the review by M. Ullmann in *Der Islam* 52, 1975, pp. 148-51. Among scholarly translations, the earliest, and one of the most accurate, is that by P. Kraus, "Eine arabische Biographie Avicennas," *Klinische Wochenschrift* 11, 1932, pp. 1880b-1882b. The very readable, but not always as accurate, English translation by A. J. Arberry was first published in his *Avicenna on Theology*, London, 1951, pp. 9-24, and later reprinted in a number of publications (listed by Gohlman on p. 117, note 28). There are also a French translation by M. Achena and H. Massé, *Le livre de science*, Paris, 1955, I, pp. 6-11, and a Persian Translation by Ḡ. Ḥ. Sadīqī, *Sargoḏašt-e Ebn Sīnā*, Tehran, 1331 Š./1952.

The bibliography on the autobiography/biography is extensive. There is a useful collection of the traditional material in Saʿīd Nafīsī, *Zendagī o kār o andīša o rūzgār-e pūr-e Sīnā*, Tehran, 1333 Š./1954. A list of western European publications is given in Gohlman and supplemented by Ullmann in his review. References to eastern European publications can be found in B. and S. Brentjes, *Ibn Sina (Avicenna), der fürstliche Meister aus Buḫārā*, Leipzig, 1979, and A. V. Sagadeev, *Ibn-Sina*, Moscow, 1980. See also S. M. Afnan, *Avicenna: His Life and Works*, London, 1958. Ḏ. Ṣafā, *Jašn-nāma-ye Ebn Sīnā* I, Tehran, 1331 Š./1952. Idem. *Tārīḵ -e ʿolūm-e ʿaqlī-dar tamaddon-e eslāmī* I, Tehran, 1331 Š./1952, pp. 206-81.

Jūzjānī's biography has not yet been subjected to a critical study. Particularly perceptive analyses of the autobiography, on the other hand, are offered by R. Sellheim in his review of Ergin's Avicenna bibliography, *Oriens* 11, 1958, pp. 231-39, and by G. Lüling, "Ein anderer Avicenna. Kritik Seiner Autobiographie and ihrer bisherigen Behandlung," *ZDMG* Suppl. 3/1, 1977, pp. 496-513. D. Gutas, *Avicenna and the Aristotelian Tradition. Introduction to Reading Avicenna's Philosophical Works*, (forthcoming) contains a translation and an analysis of the autobiography.

(D. GUTAS)

iii. LOGIC

Avicenna's works on logic. Many of Avicenna's works on logic are extant and most of them have been published. With the exception of two Persian works, *Dāneš-nāma-ye ʿalāʾī* and *Andar dāneš-e rag* (see below, xi), all of his works are written in Arabic.

The nine parts that make up the first treatise of *Ketāb al-šefāʾ* (Book of the healing [of the soul]), Avicenna's philosophical summa, are devoted to logical matters. The first of these parts, the *Madḵal*, is an introduction to the other eight, each of which corresponds to one of the Aristotelian logical works, collectively known as the *Organon* or "instrument of science." The *Madḵal*, on the other hand, corresponds to Prophyry's *Isagoge*, a work that strongly influenced the writings of Islamic logicians as well as those of medieval Latin logicians. In addition to these works, the first part of Avicenna's *Ešārāt* as well as the first part of the *Najāt* are summaries of Avicenna's version of Aristotelian logic.

The last work that Avicenna wrote on the subject of logic, which like the *Najāt* and the *Ešārāt* is a summary of his logic, is called *Manṭeq al-Mašreqīyīn*. It is the only extant portion of a philosophical encyclopedia he reportedly wrote or meant to write.

Avicenna on the subject matter of logic. Avicenna's works on logic usually begin with a discourse on the utility and the subject matter of logic. Logic for him is an instrument (*āla*) that has numerous functions. Thus in the *Najāt* (p. 3) which is an abridgement of the *Šefā'*, he writes: "I start with a detailed description of the art of logic because it is the instrument which prevents the mind from committing errors both in conception (*taṣawwor*) and in judgment (*taṣdīq*). It is the instrument that leads to true beliefs as well as to the reasons for and the right way to achieve them." By the "right way" Avicenna is referring to the methods by which one can reach a proper definition, as well as to the mastering of the theory of the syllogism and other methods which guard the mind against committing errors in judgment, i.e., in composing propositions. Knowing how to define leads to conceptual soundness, whereas knowing the methods that lead from the known to the unknown guarantees that one makes sound judgments. That which leads to a clear and definite conception (*taṣawwor mostaḥṣal*) is the expository statement (*qawl šāreḥ*) which can be either an essential definition (*ḥadd*) or a descriptive definition (*rasm*). That which leads to a definite judgment (*taṣdīq yostaḥṣal*) is an argument (*ḥojja*) which can be either a syllogism (*qīās*), an induction (*esteqrā'*), or an analogy (*tamṯīl*) (*Ešārāt*, pp. 181-85; *Manṭeq*, p. 10). According to Avicenna the latter can help identify not only what is true and valid, but also what is false and invalid (*Manṭeq*, pp. 5-6). Moreover, these methods are a necessary condition not only for scientific or theoretical inquiry, but also for the "salvation of man," which, according to Avicenna, lies in the purity of man's soul (*Treatise*, p. 14): "This purity of the soul is attainable by contemplating the pure form and avoiding this-worldy inclinations. And the way to these two is science. And no science which can not be examined by the balance of logic is certain and exact." This statement indicates that mastering the science of logic is, in Avicenna's view, a necessary condition for the knowledge of any discipline, be it theoretical or practical. In either case the purpose is knowledge: knowledge of the truth (*ḥaqq*) in the former case and of the good (*ḵayr*) in the latter (*Madḵal*, p. 149).

This raises a question concerning Avicenna's views on the age-old debate about whether logic is a part or an instrument of philosophy. Avicenna argues (*Qīās*, p. 10) that there is no contradiction (*tanāqoż*) between those who maintain that logic is part of philosophy (i.e., the Stoics) and those who hold that logic is an introduction to and a tool for philosophy (i.e., the Peripatetics). The answer to this question depends, according to him, on one's definition and understanding of the subject matter of philosophy, and any quarrel about this issue is both meaningless (*bāṭel*) and futile (*fożūl*) (*Madḵal*, p. 16).

As for the subject matter of logic, Avicenna maintains that the secondary intelligibles (or concepts) (*al-ma'ānī al-ma'qūla al-ṯānīa*) are the proper subject matter of logic (*Elāhīyāt* I, p. 10).

These secondary concepts depend on the primary concepts, Avicenna argues. By this he means that the former come about by abstraction (*tajrīd*) from the latter, i.e., they become ideas remote from the particular content which they have as primary concepts. The secondary concepts, in other words, are remote from the sensible forms (*hay'āt maḥsūsa*) or from the particular material objects (*'Ebāra*, p. 2, line 1). The primary concepts, on the other hand, are associated with the sensible material objects of which they are pictures (*ṣowar*) (ibid., p. 1, line 1).

Logic and language. The distinction between primary and secondary intelligibles occurs in several Arabic logical texts much before Avicenna's time. As many scholars have already pointed out, it occurs in (the Arabic translation) of Porphyry's *Isagoge* as well as in the writings of Fārābī and other Arab thinkers of the tenth and eleventh centuries. Yet, probably due to historical circumstances, it is Avicenna who is credited as the originator of this distinction, which remained a central issue in logical debate for several centuries.

This distinction, to which the modern distinction between object language and metalanguage is related, is of great importance for logicians. First it defines as the subject matter of logic those concepts which, in Avicenna's language, "have a mental existence that is not attached to matter at all or is attached to non-corporeal matter" (*Elāhīyāt*, p. 11). These are the secondary concepts and not the primary concepts. The latter, because they are descriptions of the *accidental* aspects of things, can not be the subject matter of logic.

Secondly, this distinction is an extension and a development of the Aristotelian theme concerning the three modes of discourse—written, spoken, and mental. Avicenna discusses these in the first chapter of his *'Ebāra* under the section heading: "On the Relationship Between Things (*omūr*), Conceptions (*taṣawworāt*), Spoken Utterances (*alfāẓ*), and the Written [Form]," thus making the threefold Aristotelian division a fourfold division by adding the dimension of external things. Avicenna describes the relationships between the four modes as follows (paraphrased):

Due to a special faculty with which mankind is equipped (*qowwa ḥessīya*) external things are imprinted (*tartasem*) in the mind (*nafs*, soul). These imprints are present in the mind without the presence of the material object which they depict; this is the stage of abstraction (*tajrīd*). Thus, things have two modes of existence: an external existence (*wojūd fi'l -a'yān*), i.e., the individual material objects, and a mental existence (*wojūd fi'l-nafs*). The argument then describes the need for a tool to communicate, thus adding the third dimension (spoken). The fourth dimension (the written word) is explained through the need for continuity of ideas (*'Ebāra*, pp. 1-2). The third dimension (speech) and its relation to thought (the second mode) is a major theme in many of the logical writings of medieval philosophers, both Arab and Latin, many of whom claim that logicians are supposed to deal with utterances insofar as they signify thought.

According to Avicenna, however, language should on no account be considered an issue for logicians in their logical inquiries. Logicians, he says (*'Ebāra*, p. 5) are concerned with utterances (*lafẓ*) only accidentally (*be'l-'araż*) and only insofar as these utterances signify the concepts themselves (*al-ma'ānī anfosohā*), which are the proper subject matter of logic. Elsewhere, (*Madkal*, p. 22) Avicenna says that logicians need (natural) languages only in order to be able to address logical issues and to communicate with others about these issues. Logic, according to him, does not deal with utterances per se because these are only a tool and can theoretically be replaced by some other device (*ḥīla*) through which one can express logical relations without the mediation of a natural language. Avicenna criticizes those who think of language as an integral part of logic. By this he refers to the logicians of the tenth century (led by Fārābī) who adopted this view.

Yet, in the same passage of his *Madkal*, Avicenna states that "utterances have various modes (*aḥwāl*) on account of which the modes of the notions corresponding to them in the soul vary so as to acquire qualifications (*aḥkām*) which would not have existed without the utterances." From this statement, it is easy to infer—as has A. I. Sabra, for example (p. 763)—that "the secondary concepts, the proper object of logic, not only are reflected in language, but are generated by it." How can we reconcile these two positions of Avicenna concerning the thought-language relationship?

In the *Ešārāt* (p. 181) Avicenna modifies his initial position concerning the accidental nature of the relationship between logic and language by stating that languages have a universal side (*jāneb moṭlaq*) which is not confined to any particular language. It is this universal side of language with which logicians should be concerned. Unfortunately, Avicenna does not explain what counts as a universal feature of a language.

Whether in the final analysis utterances are a subject for logical inquiry or not, however, Avicenna devotes much of his logical theory to the *relationship* between language and thought or logic.

Utterances can signify either a universal notion ('man' or 'animal', each of which is predicated of many individuals) or a particular one ('Zayd', i.e., a particular man). Like all the logicians, he adopts the Porphyrian division of general terms into the following categories: genus (*jens*), differentia (*faṣl*), species (*naw'*), property (*kāṣṣa*), and accident (*'araż 'āmm*).

The list of five predicables, as these are called, is the subject matter of logic for it includes all the secondary concepts (or, to be more exact, the terms that signify these concepts).

Utterances, Avicenna says (*Ešārāt*, p. 187; *Manṭeq*, p. 14) can signify concepts in three different ways:

(1) By correspondence (*moṭābaqa*), i.e., when a certain term directly signifies the concept for which it was coined or designed (*mawżū'*), as in the term 'triangle' which signifies the notion of a three-sided figure or 'man' which signifies the notion of a rational animal.

(2) By inclusion (*tażammon*), i.e., when a concept is included in the meaning of a term. 'Man', for example, means and corresponds to the notion 'rational animal'. Thus both 'rational' and 'animal' are included in the meaning of 'man'.

(3) By implication (*eltezām*), i.e., when the meaning is only implied by the term (it neither corresponds to it nor is it part of its meaning), as in the relationship between the term 'ceiling' and the concept of wall (*Madkal*, p. 43; *'Ebāra*, p. 3).

Having dealt with individual terms, Avicenna next discusses how these terms combine to produce sentences. Like all logicians, however, his concern is not with the syntactical features of sentences as such, but rather with the statements (*qażīya*, *qawl jāzem*) that these sentences represent.

A statement is either predicative (*ḥamlīya*) ('S is P') or conditional (*šarṭīya*). The latter is a combination of two or more predicative statements and can be either a conjunctive conditional (*šarṭī mottaṣel*) (if . . . , then . . .) or a disjunctive conditional (*šarṭī monfaṣel*) (either . . . or).

Avicenna's explanations of the different types of predicative statements, the division according to their quality, quantity and modality, and finally their different combinations in a syllogism are Aristotelian. His treatment of these same issues in relation to the conditionals relies heavily and perhaps exclusively on the Stoics who developed this branch of logic. Yet, Avicenna exhibits a superb understanding of these problems and presents them in a very coherent, systematic and clear style to the student of logic. His writings are, no doubt, the encyclopedia of Arabic logic.

Bibliography: Works by Avicenna: *al-Šefā', al-Manṭeq*, Cairo, I: *al-Madkal*, ed. G. C. Anawati et al., 1952; II: *al-Maqūlāt*, ed. G. C. Anawati et al., 1959; III: *al-'Ebāra*, ed. M. Kodayrī, 1970; IV: *al-Qīās*, ed. S. Zāyed, 1964; V: *al-Borhān*, ed. A. 'Afīfī, 1956; VI: *al-Jadal*, ed. A. Ahwānī, 1965; VII: *al-Safsaṭa*, ed. idem, 1958; VIII: al-*kaṭāba*, ed. M. S. Sālem, 1954; IX: *al-Še'r*, ed. idem, 1969. *Al-Šefā', al-Elāhīyāt*, ed. G. C. Anawati and S. Zāyed, Cairo, 1960. *Al-Najāt*, ed. Kordī, 2nd ed., Cairo, 1938. *Al-Ešārāt wa'l-tanbīhāt*, ed. S. Donyā, Cairo, 1960. *Manṭeq al-mašreqīyīn*, Cairo, 1910. *Ketāb al-ḥodūd*, ed. and French tr. A. M. Goichon, Cairo, 1963. *Treatise on Logic*, ed. with Engl. tr. of pt. 1 of the original Persian *Dāneš-nāma-ye 'alā'ī* by F. Zabeeh, The Hague, 1971. *Fī aqsām al-'olūm al-'aqlīya* in *Tes' rasā'el*, Cairo, 1908; Engl. tr. in *Medieval Political Philosophy*, ed. R. Lerner and M. Mahdi, New York, 1972, pp. 95-97.

Secondary sources: S. M. Afnān, *Avicenna. His*

Life and Works, London, 1958. G. C. Anawati, *Mo'allafāt Ebn Sīnā*, Cairo, 1950. W. Gohlman, ed., *The Life of Ibn-Sina*, Albany, N.Y., 1974. K. Gyekye, "The Terms 'Prima Intentio' and 'Secunda Intentio' in Arabic Logic," *Speculum* 46, 1971, pp. 32-38. A. I. Sabra, "Avicenna on the Subject Matter of Logic," *The Journal of Philosophy* 77, 1980, pp. 746-64. N. Shehaby, *The Propositional Logic of Avicenna*, Boston, 1973.

For comparison with Islamic logicians who dealt with similar problems see Ebn al-Ṭayyeb (980-1043), *Commentary on Porphyry's Eisagoge*, ed. K. Gyekye, Beirut, 1975. Ebn-Sowār (943-1020), "Commentary on the Arabic Translation of Aristotle's Commentary," in *Manṭeq Aresṭū*, ed. ʿA. Badawī, Kuwait and Beirut, 1981, 1, pp. 77ff. Fārābī (d. 950), *Eḥṣāʾ al-ʿolūm*, ed. ʿO. Amīn, 3rd ed., Cairo, 1968, Idem, *Šarḥ le-ketāb Arestūṭālīs fi'l-ʿEbāra*, ed. W. Kutsch and S. Marrow, Beirut, 1960. Idem, *Ketāb al-ḥorūf*, ed. M. Mahdi, Beirut, 1970. Yaḥyā b. ʿAdī (893-974), "On the Difference between Philosophical Logic and Arabic Grammar," ed. G. Endress, in *The Journal of the History of Arabic Science* 2, 1978, pp. 38-50.

(Sh. B. Abed)

iv. Metaphysics

General characteristics. Avicenna's metaphysical system is one of the most comprehensive and detailed in the history of philosophy. Its ingredients, its conceptual building blocks, so to speak, are largely Aristotelian and Neoplatonic, but the final structure is other than the sum of its parts. Avicenna himself hints at this when in introducing his magnum opus, the voluminous *Šefāʾ* (Healing), he writes: "There is nothing in the books of the ancients but we have included in this our book. If something is not found in a place where it is normally found, it would be found in another place where I judge it more fit to be in. I have added to this what I have apprehended with my thought and attained through my reflection, particularly in physics, metaphysics and logic" (*Šefāʾ*, *Isagoge*, pp. 9-10).

While the ingredients of his metaphysics derive "from the books of the ancients," Avicenna criticizes, selects and refines this material, but above all, informs it with his own insights to construct a world-view that has a character all its own. He also injects into it a pattern of deductive reasoning that anticipates the kind of thinking encountered in seventeenth-century European rationalist philosophies. At the same time, it should be remembered that his metaphysics is part of medieval Islam's intellectual history. It represents a climactic development of medieval Islamic Aristotelian and Neoplatonic thought. It also has to be understood (in part, at least) as a response to doctrines encountered in Islamic theology (*kalām*).

The Islamic philosopher who influenced Avicenna most was Fārābī (d. 339/950). Avicenna was indebted to Fārābī's various exegeses of Aristotle's works, logical and philosophical. He was also greatly influenced by the Neoplatonic emanative scheme Fārābī outlines in some of his more popular works. Avicenna, however, introduces important modifications to this scheme, gives a more comprehensive and detailed account of the descent of beings from God, and makes the connection between his version of emanation and the essence-existence distinction explicit and intimate. Thus the two schemes while closely related remain distinct. It should also be added that Avicenna's theory of the state, which is connected with his metaphysics, is grounded in Fārābī's political philosophy. There is, moreover, in Avicenna's metaphysics an underlying Farabian motif, namely, that the quest after philosophical knowledge is for the sake of perfecting one's soul and hence for the attainment of happiness in this world and the next.

As to the Islamic theologians, the *motakallemūn*, his criticism of their doctrines tends to be muted. Nonetheless, it represents an important undercurrent of his metaphysical writings. He refers to the theologians by name when criticizing their interpretation of the meaning of the term "origination," *ḥodūṯ*, and the doctrine of the world's creation ex nihilo it implies. In other instances, however, he makes no explicit mention of the *motakallemūn*, but the doctrines he criticizes are definitely identifiable as held by one of their schools. Thus, for example, he criticizes the doctrine of latency (*komūn*), a theory that has Stoic antecedents, but which in Islam was developed by the Muʿtazilite theologian Ebrāhīm Naẓẓām (d. ca. 840) and identified with him and his followers. Avicenna is also highly critical of the notorious Muʿtazilite argument for bodily resurrection and the doctrine on which it is based, namely that non-existence (*ʿadam*) is "a thing" (*šayʾ*). Again, in his discussions of efficient causality, he answers typical arguments used by the Ashʿarite occasionalist theologians to deny secondary causes. It should be added that as an Aristotelian, Avicenna criticizes and rejects atomism, his criticism, no doubt, being directed at the Greek atomists. But was it not aimed at *kalām* atomism as well? Here, again, there is no reference to the *motakallemūn*, the vast majority of whom were atomists. It is true that their doctrine of the transient atom, temporally created ex nihilo, contrasts sharply with the Greek concept of eternal atoms. But Avicenna's criticism is logically applicable to both versions of atomism. Taking into account that he opposed a number of the doctrines of the *motakallemūn*, including that of the world's creation ex nihilo, intimately related to their atomism, it seems unlikely that he did not intend his criticism of atomism to include its *kalām* version.

Criticism in Avicenna's metaphysical writings, by no means confined to the *kalām* or to atomism, is a manifestation of a very characteristic aspect of these writings, the analytic. It is here that one encounters his distinctions, clarifications and hard-headed attempts to solve problems. This is complemented by a synthetic aspect, where he strives to construct a deductive system. Both aspects, however, interweave, the system he constructs being constantly buttressed by the analyses and distinctions he makes. This system is admittedly an ambitious one, particularly as it includes a cosmological scheme in which he endeavors to infer from the First Principle, God, the Ptolomaic astronomical scheme to which he subscribes. Such an attempt, wide open as it is to serious criticism, serves to reveal a facet of his rationalist approach, namely, his belief that in principle, at least, some human minds, whether intuitively or "naturally," as with prophets, or through arduous processes of discursive reasoning, are capable of grasping the basic structure of reality as it emanates from its Source.

This brings us to the "rationalist" character of Avicenna's philosophy, manifest in what he holds to be (a) the object of our knowledge and (b) the manner of attaining it. The principle of all existence, God, for Avicenna, is pure intellect (*ʿaql maḥż*) and hence the highest object of human knowledge is intellect. All other existents, whether minds, souls or bodies, emanate from the pure intellect, God. They form an orderly hierarchical chain of causes and effects that are necessarily connected and hence (when all necessary conditions obtain) are rationally inferrable from each other. Knowledge by its very definition is conceptual, intellectual, consisting (on the human level) of the mind's reception of the intelligibles (*maʿqūlāt*). One class of these intelligibles which includes the self-evident truths of logic are received directly by all men from the Active Intellect, the last of the celestial intelligences emanating from God. They are received "directly" in the sense that this reception requires neither observation of the external world nor the thinking processes associated with such observation. Another class of intelligibles, less simple and less general, the secondary, consisting of universal concepts and inferences, are normally "acquired" in a different manner. Normally, they require the presence of the self-evident logical truths and observation of the external world with concomitant thinking activities on the sensory, imaginative, particular levels. Observation and its accompanying thinking activities, however, do not themselves in the real sense acquire the secondary intelligibles. Rather, they are activities that prepare the soul for the reception of the secondary intelligibles from the Active Intellect. Only prophets can receive the secondary intelligibles directly, without the need of the preparatory activities of the soul and the learning processes that accompany them. Thus the object of knowledge is the intelligible, received from a rational principle, the Active Intellect.

But this is not all. To fully appreciate the extent of Avicenna's rationalism it should be noted that he also includes with the class of intelligibles that normally do not require for their reception perception of the external world primary concepts that are the most general—the concepts of "the existent," "the thing," and "the necessary." These, like the self-evident propositional truths of logic, are "impressed on the soul in a primary manner." This class of intelligibles, consisting of the primary concepts and the self-evident truths of logic, are sufficient in Avicenna's system for formulating a proof leading to the existence of God, demonstrating His uniqueness, and for inferring the existing of the world (with its order) from God. Thus the highest form of metaphysical knowledge is attainable rationally, independently of our perception of the external world.

The affinity of this rationalism to seventeenth-century continental European modes of philosophizing has often been noted, particularly the similarity between the Cartesian *Cogito* and Avicenna's hypothetical example of a human floating in space (cf. Psychology). According to this example, if we imagine ourselves to be born all at once, fully mature, but suspended in space in such a manner that we are totally unaware of our physical and bodily circumstances, we would still be aware of ourselves as individual selves. Without denying parallels between this example and aspects of Descartes's process of systematic doubting of the senses, it is important to recognize a difference quite fundamental for understanding Avicenna's metaphysical approach.

Avicenna's metaphysical starting point is not doubt. (The primary intention of the example of a person suspended in space is to show that the human rational soul is immaterial and individual.) As has been noted, the concept of "the existent" for him is a primary concept, intuited immediately. It is indubitable. He begins one version of his proof from contingency for God's existence with the statement: "There is no doubt that there is existence" (*lā šakka anna hāhonā wojūdan*). But existence, as he points out, divides into that which is in itself necessary and that which in itself is only possible. The existents immediately encountered (including ourselves) are in themselves only possible. They can exist or not exist. Yet in fact they do exist. Why is this the case? In his metaphysics, Avicenna, in effect, seeks an answer to this very question, namely, why is it that that which in itself is only possible (and this includes the whole world as distinct from God) exists at all?

Definition and scope of metaphysics. Although the question of why is it that that which in itself is only possible exists at all is at the heart of Avicenna's metaphysics, it does not constitute its starting point. In the *Metaphysics* of the *Šefāʾ*, for example, it suggests itself quite unobtrusively when Avicenna is establishing one of his basic premises for his proof of God's existence. Nor is the existence of God and the simplicitly of His essence "the subject matter" of metaphysics. Rather, as will be shortly seen, these are among the things "sought after" in metaphysics. Avicenna's starting point and conception of metaphysics are Aristotelian. This Aristotelianism is clearly seen in the distinction he draws between metaphysics and the two other theoretical sciences, physics and mathematics. He makes this distinction in terms of two related criteria: (a) the relation of the objects of knowledge belonging to each of these sciences to matter and motion; (b) the subject matter, in its broadest sense, of each of these disciplines.

The objects of knowledge of both physics and mathematics are always "mixed" with matter (and motion), but in different ways. With physics, the object is always "mixed" with a specific kind of matter. A human being, for example, as the object of natural science, can not be separated from a specific kind of matter, from the material body of the genus, animal. Again, the object may be of a different sort that can be separated from matter—causality, for example. But when it is the object of natural science, it must be associated, not only with matter, but with matter of a specific kind. The physicist is concerned with the cause of motion of this or that specific kind of matter, not with causality as such. In the case of mathematics, on the other hand, although its object is always "mixed" with matter, it is not "mixed" with a specific kind of matter. Triangles and squares in external non-mental existence must be of some kind of material, but not confined to a specific kind. As such, as objects of knowledge, they undergo a degree of abstraction, whereby the mathematician can consider them dissociated from a specific kind of matter. Other objects of mathematical knowledge, such as plurality or unity, can be separated from matter. But as objects of mathematical inquiry, they are treated as associated with matter, but not of a specific kind. Again, there is a degree of abstraction. But they are not regarded in pure abstraction. The mathematician considers them in terms of quantity, related to some kind of matter or another, but not confined to a specific kind.

Metaphysics, however, always has as its object that which is not "mixed" with matter. The object may be necessarily immaterial, as with God and mind. It can, however, consist of objects that can mix with matter. The metaphysician, however, is concerned with these objects in themselves, *men ḥayṯo hīa hīa*, abstractly and immaterially. Thus to take causality again as an example, unlike the natural scientist who is concerned with the cause of a specific kind of matter, the metaphysician is concerned with causality as such and with causality as one of the concomitants of the existent considered as such. This brings us to the second criterion for the distinction between the three theoretical sciences: their respective subject matter.

All three theoretical sciences have for their subject matter the existent, but with a difference. Physics is concerned with the existent inasmuch as it is in motion or in its relation to motion. Mathematics is concerned with the existent inasmuch as it is quantified or relates to measure and quantity. Metaphysics, on the other hand, has for its object the existent without qualification. Its subject matter is the existent inasmuch as it exists (*al-mawǰūd be mā howa mawǰūd*), or, as Avicenna puts it in his *Naǰāt*, "absolute existence" (*al-woǰūd al-moṭlaq*). Metaphysics undertakes investigating the relation of the existent to the ten categories, the states that affect it, and the concomitants (*lawāḥeq*) that adhere to it. Following the methodology of the *Posterior Analytics*, Avicenna distinguishes between "the subject matter" (*mawżūʿ*) of metaphysics and that which "is sought in it" (*maṭlūb*). Among the things that are sought after and established in metaphysics are the principles presupposed in natural science and mathematics. In this sense, physics and mathematics receive "their credentials," as it were, from metaphysics.

Among the things "sought after" in metaphysics are the four causes (material, formal, efficient, and final) of existing things and the ultimate cause of all existence, God. Hence, investigating the four causes and the existence and nature of God do not constitute "the subject matter" of metaphysics. This, as has been pointed out, is the existent inasmuch as it exists. But the concept of the existent qua existent as the subject matter of metaphysics raises a methodological difficulty regarding the quest in it for the principles of existing things. "If the existent is made the subject of this science," it could be argued, writes Avicenna, "then the principles of the existent can not be established in it, since in every science, investigation is of things concomitant to its subject, not of its principles" (*Šefāʾ*, *Metaphysics*, p. 14).

In the endeavor to resolve this problem, Avicenna maintains that "theoretical inquiry of the principles is also an investigation of the cocurrent concomitants (*ʿawāreż*) of this subject." For, being a principle is not a defining characteristic of "the existent." He then adds a qualification: The principle sought after is not the principle "of the whole of existence." Otherwise the principle would be a principle of itself. The principle that is sought after is hence the principle of the existent that is caused. God, to paraphrase Avicenna, can not be the principle of His own existence, but is the principle and cause of all other existents.

This brings us to the ultimate quest, ultimate principle sought after in metaphysics, the existence of God. This existence, Avicenna asserts, is not self-evident, but has to be demonstrated. Furthermore, its demonstration belongs solely to metaphysics, not to any other theoretical science. Assertions relating to God's existence in the *Physics* of the *Šefāʾ*, he states, were out of their place, put there only to whet the reader's appetite. As indicated earlier, Avicenna offers not only a rational proof for God's existence, but also a rational deduction from this existence of the world's existence and order. Proof and deduction, however, employ the distinction between essence and existence, for which Avicenna is noted. This distinction underlies his very significant theory of universals, as well as his theory of efficient causality. For this reason, before turning to the proof of God's existence, it is perhaps best to begin with this distinction as it relates to his theory of universals and also say something supplementary about his theory of efficient causality.

The essence-existence distinction. For Avicenna, the distinction between essence and existence applies to all existents, actual and potential, other than God. At the heart of this distinction is the theory of the essence, quiddity, or nature of such existents considered strictly in itself. An essence, Avicenna states, may exist in external reality, associated with circumstances peculiar to that reality. These circumstances associate with it to form a particular existent. The essence may also exist as a concept in the mind where in this mental existence it also is associated with circumstances peculiar to this existence—for example, circumstances that render it a subject or a predicate. But, he maintains, there is also "a consideration of the essence inasmuch as it is that essence, without being related to the two [kinds of] existence" (*Šefāʾ*, *Isagoge*, p. 15). In itself, or as such, the essence does not include the idea of existence, whether this is external or mental existence. Existence is not a defining characteristic of essences. From what a thing is, it can not be inferred that it exists.

According to Avicenna, the quiddity (or essence) considered simply as a quiddity, excludes not only the idea of existence, but also the concomitants of existence, unity and plurality. Thus in his typical example of "horseness" as a quiddity considered in itself, he states that "it is neither one nor many, exists neither externally nor in the soul." Moreover, he maintains, the quiddity considered in itself excludes the ideas of universality and particularity. In short, the quiddity as such excludes the ideas of existence, unity, plurality, particularity, and universality.

Avicenna uses this concept of the quiddity considered in itself and the distinction between essence and existence that it carries with it to resolve two problems pertaining to universals. The first is a logical problem that has to do with the predication of a quiddity of a subject. If the quiddity as such included universality and particularity, the results would be odd indeed. For then universality or particularity (but not both, since they are mutually exclusive) would form part of the very definition of the quiddity. To use his example, if animality includes universality in its very definition, then we can not predicate it of a particular animal. If, on the other hand, particularity is included in the definition of animality, then this would not merely exclude its predication of a universal subject, but of any individual other than the one specified in the quiddity's definition.

The answer Avicenna finds is in the concept of aquiddity which, when considered in itself, is devoid of the notions of universality and particularity. Universality and particularity are then added to it when it is conceived in the mind. This brings us to Avicenna's important theory of the universal, which for him is always a concept in the mind. The quiddity as such is not a universal. It is, however, a component of the universal. For the universal is compounded of two things, the quiddity as such and universality, that quality that renders the quiddity predicable of many instances. The general framework of this theory is Aristotelian. But Avicenna introduces refinements and the distinction between the quiddity as such and universality. He also adds to it a Neoplatonic dimension by maintaining that quiddities have existence in the celestial intelligences, as well as in the particulars of sense and in the human minds.

The second problem relating to universals which Avicenna strove to resolve is metaphysical. This is the problem of the one and the many, in an Avicennian context. How can the selfsame quiddity be "found in many," to use his own words, and not be many? To answer this, Avicenna again invokes the concept of the quiddity considered as such. For although a quiddity can exist in external reality associated with particular circumstances, rendering it in this association an individual, it can be considered in itself, for what it is, in dissociation from these circumstances. When thus considered, it excludes the ideas of unity and plurality: These become totally inapplicable to it. Thus if one asks whether a quiddity like humanity is one or many, Avicenna's reaction to such a question is that "there is no need for a reply because inasmuch as it is the defining identity (*howīya*) of humanity it is other than the two alternatives. In the definition of that thing, there is nothing except humanity alone" (*Šefāʾ*, *Metaphysics*, pp. 197-98).

If, then, existence (and its concomitants) are extraneous to the quiddity as such, the quiddity is existentially neutral, so to speak. There is nothing in it to tip the balance in favor of its existence rather than its non-existence. Its existence and non-existence are equally possible. That a quiddity which in itself is only possible in fact exists calls for explanation. The explanation that Avicenna offers includes his establishing a premise necessary for his proof of God's existence. This is the premise that the existent that in itself is only possible is causally necessitated by another existent. The argument to establish this premise, as will be shortly seen, is a metaphysical argument. It is, however, complemented by an epistemological argument (which was later adopted by Latin scholastics) that should be noted. This is the argument from the observation of regularities in nature. Avicenna is only too well aware that such observation alone is insufficient to establish the principle of necessary causal connection. Such observation, he asserts, leads only to concomitance. Something else is needed. This is hidden premise (*qīās ḵafīy*) to the effect that if the regularities were accidental or coincidental they would not have happened always or for the most part (cf. Aristotle, *Physics* 2.5.156b.10-16). From this he concludes that these regularities are the necessary outcome of inherent essential casual properties in things. It should be added that Avicenna subscribes to the four Aristotelian causes. Unlike Aristotle, however, he does not confine efficient causality to the production of motion, but maintains that, as with God in producing the world, it is productive of existence itself.

God's existence and the world's emanation. Demonstrating God's existence, His utter oneness and the manner of the world's emanation from Him are the high points of Avicenna's metaphysical endeavor. The proof he offers is his proof from contingency, noted for its a priori character, that is, for its total dependence on reason. Thus, he does not argue for the contingency of things on the basis of our observation of change in the world. For the concept of the possible is either a primary concept, immediately intuited by the mind, or rationally derived from a primary concept, immediately intuited by the mind, the concept of the necessary. It is also a metaphysical proof, as distinct from a proof in *Physics*. Thus it is not based on the observation of motion in the world, leading ultimately to the Prime Mover. It is not in any sense a proof that infers God's existence from the observation of His handiwork. On this Avicenna is explicit. After giving one version of his proof from contingency, for example, he writes: "Reflect on how our proof for the existence and oneness of the First and His being free from attributes did not require reflection on anything except his existence itself and how it did not require any consideration of His creation and acting, even though the latter [provide] evidential proof (*dalīl*) for Him. This mode, however, is more reliable and noble, that is, where when we consider the state of existence, we find that existence inasmuch as it is existence bears witness to Him, while He thereafter bears witness to all that comes after Him in existence" (*Ešārāt*, p. 482).

Although Avicenna gives closely related but somewhat different versions of the proof, they all share its a priori character. Underlying these versions is Avicenna's theory that there are primary concepts, those of "the existent," "the thing," and "the necessary," that are rationally intuited without the need for perceptual experience of the external world. These parallel the self-evident propositional logical truths that, again, are purely rational. The versions of the proof also share basically the same structure. An existent in itself is either necessary or only possible. If necessary, then this is the existent we are seeking, God. If only possible, then it can be demonstrated that such a contingent being ultimately requires the existent that is necessary in Himself. In either case, there must be an existent necessary in Himself, the one God.

The version of the proof in the *Metaphysics* of the *Šefā'*, although it is dispersed in different places in this work and has to be reassembled, remains the most detailed and comprehensive. It is also the one that argues explicitly for the causal premise presupposed in the other versions. The proof in this version can be summed up as follows. Existents are either such that their existence is in itself necessary or only possible. If we suppose an existent that in itself is necessary, then, it can be shown that it would not be caused, would necessarily be one, unique and without multiplicity in its being. If we suppose an existent that in itself is only possible, then it can be shown that it would require for its existence the existent that is necessary in Himself. For an existent that in itself is only possible can equally exist or not exist. Why, then, if we suppose it to exist, should it exist at all? An external cause would be needed to explain why it had been "specified" with existence rather than non-existence. Now if in relation to the supposed cause, the existence of the contingent is not "necessitated," then it would remain purely possible and no explanation for its existence would have been given. Another cause would have to be posited and if this is not a necessitating cause, yet another, and so on *ad infinitum*. Even if, for the sake of argument, the infinity of such causes is allowed, they would still not explain why the contingent exists. Hence, since we have supposed it to exist, then the extraneous cause would have to necessitate it. In other words, Avicenna is arguing not merely that if the contingent exists, it must have an extraneous cause, but that this extraneous cause necessitates its existence. Thus the existence of such a contingent, while in itself only possible, would be necessary through another.

The cause that necessitates its effect, for Avicenna, is the essential cause. It is the accidental cause that precedes its effect in time and as such a chain of accidental causes and effects can be infinite. A chain of such accidental causes would not constitute an actual infinite. Not so with the chain of essential causes and their effects. The essential cause coexists with its effect, its priority to the effect being ontological not temporal. A series of coexisting causes and effects can not be infinite. For the infinite they would constitute would be an actual infinite, which, for Avicenna, is demonstrably impossible. The chain must have a first cause, the existent necessary for Himself, God.

That Avicenna also wishes to "infer" the existence of the world and its order (though not in all its detail) from God's existence, in the way in demonstration the effect is inferred from the cause, is clear from the following statement of intention early in the *Metaphysics* of the *Šefā'*: "It will become clear to you anon through an intimation that we have a way of proving the First Principle, not by the method of evidential inference (*estedlāl*) from the things perceived by the senses, but by way of universal rational premises that render it necessary that there is for existence a principle that is necessary in its existence, that makes it impossible for this principle to be in any way multiple, and makes it necessary that the whole is necessitated by Him according to the order possessed by the whole. Because of our incapacity, however, we are unable to adopt this demonstrative method which is the method of arriving at the secondary existents from the primary principles and the effect from the cause, except with some groupings of the ranks of existing things, not in detail" (*Šefā'*, *Metaphysics*, p. 21).

There can be little doubt that the "groupings of the ranks of existing things" in the last sentence above refers to the celestial triads which, according to Avicenna, emanate from the first intelligence that proceeds directly from God. In explaining this emanative scheme, he employs the concepts of the necessary in itself, the necessary through another, and the possible in itself, the latter two being the consequence of his essence-existence distinction.

God, according to Avicenna, undergoes an eternal act of self-knowledge, resulting in a necessitated effect, a first intelligence. Involved here is the principle that from the one only one proceeds. The first intelligence then encounters the three facts of existence: (1) God's being necessary in Himself; (2) its own existence as necessitated; (3) its own existence as in itself only possible. It conceives each of these facts of existence. Since from the one only one proceeds, each of these three acts of cognition produce one existent—hence the triads. Its act of knowing (1) produces another intelligence; of knowing

(2) a celestial soul; of (3) a celestial body, the outermost sphere of the universe. The second intelligence undertakes a similar cognitive process resulting in the emanation from it of the sphere of the fixed stars. This cognitive activity is repeated by successive intelligences, giving rise to successive triads. The bodily components of these triads include the planetary spheres and the spheres of the sun and the moon. The last of the celestial intelligences is the Active Intellect, from which our world of generation and corruption emanates. In each of the celestial triads, the intellect acts as the teleological cause of that triad: The soul within the triad desires the intellect, causing the eternal circular motion of the third component of the triad, the celestial sphere. It should be added that the emanative process is eternal. God, the eternal necessitating cause, ever in act, necessitates the existence of an eternal effect, the world.

Divine knowledge, providence, and prophethood. The world thus emanates from God as a consequence of His self-knowledge. This self-knowledge entails His knowing Himself as the cause of all existents, and hence knowing the consequent effects of His causality. Avicenna states that in this way God knows all particular existents, but "in a universal way." This type of knowing the particular also belongs to the celestial intelligences, as distinct from the celestial souls that know particulars in their particularity. To understand what knowing the particular "in a universal way" means, one must consider a peculiarity of the Avicennian celestial triads.

This peculiarity, a consequence of the principle that from the one only one proceeds, consists in the fact that in this system each existent in each of the celestial triads is the only member of its species. This is in total contrast with the existents in the terrestrial world, where a triad of existents may be said to continue. But this would be a triad of kinds only, not of individuals each of which is the sole member of its species. Thus there are numerous human intellects of a species, numerous souls and numerous bodies of various species. Now Avicenna holds that divine knowledge is conceptual, eternal, and changeless. Its object is the universal. In the case of the celestial triads, God knows the species of each individual of the triad and, moreover, that each individual is the only member of that species. In this sense, knowing the universal species means knowing the one member of this species. This applies also to celestial events like eclipses whose occurrences are mapped out eternally for God, so to speak, without this involving any change in Him. This is also possible because the event is related to individuals that are the only members of their species. When it comes to the terrestrial world, where the individual is not the only member of its species, God (and the celestial intelligences) knows only the kinds of existents, not their individual members. Of the celestial beings, only the souls in the triads know the particulars of the terrestrial world as particulars. These souls are instrumental in causing particular temporal events in the terrestrial world. Not only do they know the particulars in this world as particulars, but have foreknowledge of future terrestrial temporal events.

Closely associated with Avicenna's doctrine of divine knowledge is his doctrine of divine providence. He writes: "Providence consists in the First's knowing in Himself [the mode] of the good order, in His being in Himself a cause of goodness and perfection in terms of what is possible, and in His being satisfied with [its having the order] in the manner that has been mentioned. He would then conceive the good order in the best possible manner. Consequently, what He conceives in the best possible manner would emanate from Him in the manner—in terms of what is possible—that is most completely conducive to order" (*Šefāʾ*, *Metaphysics*, p. 415).

This is not to deny the existence of evil which enters the world of generation and corruption, associated with terrestrial matter and potency. In a detailed analysis of the different types of mundane evils, moral and physical, Avicenna maintains that they affect individuals, not the species and that, although numerous, they are not predominant. Most evils are accidental consequences of what produces the greater good. Fire, for example, is basically beneficial, but on occasion harms individuals. Could not God then have created the world free from such harm, such evil? Not this type of world, Avicenna answers, since then, to take the example of fire, he would have to create a fire that neither warms nor burns, a contradiction. A world free from evil is possible in a different mode of existence. But the creation of such a world would exclude the creation of ours which, though not without evils, would have greater good than the former. For Avicenna, this is the best of all possible worlds.

Political philosophy. The concept of divine providence relates Avicenna's metaphysics to his political philosophy. This political philosophy, essentially Farabian, rests on the theory of prophethood and revelation. The law, revealed through prophets, is not only necessary for the existence of human society, but for the very survival of man. It consists of the truths of theoretical and practical philosophy, conveyed, however, in language which the vast, non-philosopher, majority of humanity can understand. This is the language of the particular example, instead of the abstract universal concept, of the image and the symbol. Without prophets and the law they reveal the good order will not be realized in the terrestrial world of men. The existence of the law-revealing prophet is the necessary consequence of God's knowledge of the good order, an expression of His providence.

The appearance of prophets on the historical scene, however, is very infrequent. This has practical implications regarding the setting down of institutions and traditions to ensure the continuance of the good order once the prophet is gone. But the infrequency of the appearance of prophets has a metaphysical side, a metaphysical explanation involving Avicenna's doctrine of the human soul. This soul, individual and immaterial, emanates from the celestial intelligences. It is created with the body, but not imprinted in it. Its association with the body is conditioned by the material compositions that receive it. These compositions vary and their variance determines the quality of the souls that are created with them. The bodily composition that induces the reception of a prophetic soul, which is the highest quality of human souls, occurs very infrequently, Avicenna tells us. This soul is endowed with exceptional cognitive powers. Some prophetic souls receive symbolic knowledge directly from the celestial souls. Others (of a still higher rank) receive from the Active Intellect all or most of the intelligibles instantaneously. These intelligibles are then conveyed in the language of imagery, example, and symbol understood by all.

In the hierarchy of existents, the prophet stands highest in the world of generation and corruption. In Avicenna's cosmology he is, in effect, a link between the celestial and terrestrial worlds. It is perhaps no accident that Avicenna concludes the *Metaphysics*, which is the last part of the encyclopedic *Šefāʾ*, with the following words: "If one combines with justice speculative wisdom, he is the happy man. Whoever, in addition to this, wins the prophetic qualities becomes almost a human god. Worship of him, after worship of God, becomes almost allowed. He is indeed the world's earthly master and God's deputy in it."

Bibliography: Works by Avicenna. The most comprehensive expression of Avicenna's metaphysics is given in the *Metaphysics* of his *Šefāʾ*, complemented by other parts of this work. Critical editions of the Arabic text of the *Šefāʾ* by a team of scholars under the supervision of E. Madkūr have been appearing at Cairo since 1952. Of these the most pertinent for Avicenna's metaphysical thought include the following books: *al-Madkal* (*Isagoge*), 1952; *al-Maqūlāt* (Categories), 1959; *al-Borhān* (Demonstration), 1955; *al-Nafs* (Psychology), 1975; *Elāhīyāt* (Metaphysics), 2 vols., 1960. Vol. I of G. C. Anawati's French translation of the *Elāhīyāt* was published in Paris, 1979.

Among Avicenna's numerous shorter Arabic works pertaining to metaphysics, special attention must be given to the following two books: (1) *Ketāb al-ešārāt wa'l-tanbīhāt*. This was edited by J. Forget, Leiden, 1882, and recently by S. Donyā, Cairo, 1958. Donyā's edition includes the very important commentary on this work by Naṣīr-al-dīn Ṭūsī (d. 1274). For a French translation, of the *Ešārāt*, see *Ibn Sīnā* (*Avicenne*), *Le livre des directions et remarques*, tr. A. M. Goichon, Paris, 1955. (2) *Ketāb al-najāt*, Cairo, 1938. For a translation of the part on the soul of this work, see F. Rahman, *Avicenna's Psychology*, London, 1952, repr. Westport, Conn. 1981. For an English translation of the *Metaphysics* of Avicenna's most important work in Persian, his *Dāneš-nāma-ye ʿalāʾī*, see P. Morewedge, *The Metaphysics of Avicenna* (*Ibn Sīnā*), New York, 1973.

Studies. M.-T. d'Alverny, "Anniya-Anitas," *Mélanges offerts à Étienne Gilson*, Paris and Toronto, 1959. M. Cruz Hernandes, *La metafisica de Avicena*, Granada, 1949. L. Gardet, *La pensée religieuse d'Avicenne* (*Ibn Sīnā*), Paris, 1951. A. M. Goichon, *La distinction de l'essence et de l'existence d'après Ibn Sīnā* (*Avicenne*), Paris, 1937. G. F. Hourani, "Ibn Sīnā's 'Essay on the Secret of Destiny'," *BSOAS* 29, 1966, pp. 25-48. "Ibn Sīnā on Necessary and Possible Existence," *The Philosophical Forum* 4/1, 1972, pp. 74-86. M. E. Marmura, "Some Aspects of Avicenna's Theory of God's Knowledge of Particulars," *JAOS* 82/3, 1962, pp. 299-312; "Avicenna's Chapter on Universals in the *Isagoge* of his *Shifāʾ*," in *Islam Past Influence and Present Challenge*, ed. A. T. Welch and P. Cachia, Edinburgh, 1979, pp. 34-56; "Avicenna's Proof from Contingency for God's Existence in the *Metaphysics* of the *Shifāʾ*," *Mediaeval Studies* 42, 1980, pp. 337-52; "Avicenna on the Division of the Sciences in the *Isagoge* of his *Shifāʾ*," *Journal of the History of Arabic Science* 4, 1980, pp. 241-51. P. Morewedge, "Philosophical Analysis and Ibn Sīnā's 'Essence-Existence' Distinction," *JAOS* 92/3, 1972, pp. 425-35. S. H. Nasr, *Islamic Cosmological Doctrines*, Cambridge, Mass., 1964. J. Owens, "Common Nature: A Point of Comparison between Thomistic and Scotistic Metaphysics," *Mediaeval Studies* 19, 1957, pp. 1-14. F. Rahman, "Essence and Existence in Avicenna," *Mediaeval and Renaissance Studies* 4, 1958. Dj. Saliba, *Étude sur la métaphysique d'Avicenne*, Paris, 1926.

(M. E. MARMURA)

v. MYSTICISM

Avicenna and Sufism. Avicenna's philosophical system, rooted in the Aristotelian tradition, is thoroughly rationalistic and intrinsically alien to the principles of Sufism as it had developed until his time. It is also self-consistent and unified, and therefore free of any other mystical or esoteric aspect—however these terms are understood—that would represent a different form or body of knowledge and create a dichotomy within the system. Avicenna, however, did maintain the validity of Sufism, just as he maintained the validity of other manifestations of Islamic religious life, but he interpreted it, just as he interpreted them, in terms of his own system.

Avicenna's epistemological theory revolves around the pivotal concept of *ḥads*. All knowledge consists of the totality of the intelligibles contained in the intellects of the celestial spheres, and is structured in a syllogistic fashion; that is, it contains the extreme terms of syllogisms along with the middle terms which cause, or explain the conclusions. The acquisition of this knowledge, which is the goal of all human activity because the misery or bliss of the immortal rational soul in the hereafter depends directly upon it, proceeds accordingly by the consecutive discovery of middle terms. The capacity to hit spontaneously upon the middle term in any syllogism is called *ḥads*. It is a mental act whereby the human intellect comes into contact (*etteṣāl*) with the active intellect (*ʿaql faʿʿāl*) and receives what Avicenna frequently describes as "divine effluence" (*fayż elāhī*), i.e., knowledge of the intelligibles through the acquisition of the middle terms. *Ḥads* constitutes the *only* point of epistemological contact, in Avicenna's thought, between the sublunar and the supralunar realms, or between the mundane and the transcendental, and it refers to a strict and precise syllogistic process. Avicenna admits no other way to a knowledge of the intelligible world and ultimately of the Necessary Existent (*wājeb al-wojūd*).

Avicenna derived the concept of *ḥads* directly from a passage in Aristotle's *Posterior Analytics* (89b.10-11, *eustochia* = *ḥosno ḥadsen* in the Arabic translation, ʿA. Badawī, *Manṭeq Aresṭū*, Cairo, 1948, p. 406), to which he added Galen's idea that the different degrees of acumen in people are consequent upon the temperament of the body (I. Müller, *Galeni Scripta Minora*, Leipzig, 1891, II, p. 79 = H. H. Biesterfeldt, *Ketāb fī anna qowa'l-nafs*..., *AKM* 40/4, p. 43). The resulting theory in its final form, Avicenna's original creation, enabled him not only to rank people on the basis of their capacity for *ḥads*, but also to suggest the means whereby one could improve one's standing on that scale. If, as Galen taught, the faculties or powers of the soul follow the humoral temperament of the body, then clearly the more balanced temperaments would have a greater predisposition for hitting upon the middle terms. One should therefore strive to acquire a balanced temperament, or, in religious terminology, a pure soul. At the lower end of the scale there is thus the impure dullard, and at the upper end the pure person who can consistently hit upon the middle terms. This is the prophet. In his case, "the forms of all things contained in the active intellect (i.e., the intelligibles) are imprinted on his soul either at once or nearly so. This imprinting is not an uncritical reception of the forms merely on authority (*taqlīd*), but rather occurs in an order which includes the middle terms" (A. F. Ahwānī, ed., *Aḥwāl al-nafs*, Cairo, 1371/1952, p. 123 = *al-Šefāʾ*, *al-Nafs*, ed. F. Rahman, London, 1959, pp. 249-50 = *al-Najāt*, Cairo, 1331, pp. 273-74).

In order for those at the lower end of the scale of *ḥads* to gain any of this knowledge, it is obvious that their only recourse is to acquire a balanced temperament (a pure soul) in anticipation of a later or posthumous understanding, and to learn something about this knowledge in terms familiar to them. This is the function of religious life in all its manifestations. The prophet communicates the knowledge of the intelligible world in symbols and in language accessible to the masses because syllogistic discourse, the medium in which he himself received this knowledge, is unintelligible to them; and he lays down legislation whose purpose is to purify their souls. This is the reason for the efficacity of religious prescriptions like fasting and ritual prayer, of popular religious practices such as the visitation of saints' tombs, and of the ascetic practices of the Sufis. Needless to say, these practices are beneficial not only to the dull masses but also to philosophers when they are faced with a difficulty and can not find a middle term. This is the reason for Avicenna's recourse to prayer in similar circumstances, as recounted in his autobiography (W. E. Gohlman, *The Life of Ibn Sina*, Albany, New York, 1974, p. 29).

Avicenna composed his works in a variety of styles for the same reason, i.e., in order to reach different layers of audience with the same knowledge, not the same audience with a different, "esoteric," knowledge. He used symbol and allegory, and some terminology from Sufism, in order to convey this knowledge that grants salvation to those best disposed to receive it in such a medium. Otherwise the symbols and Sufi terms correspond exactly to the philosophical concepts of his system. The *ʿāref* mentioned in the final chapters of the *Ešārāt*, for example, refers to the person whose rational soul has reached the stage of the acquired intellect. In the case of the allegory, *Ḥayy b. Yaqẓān*, it corresponds precisely to Avicenna's theory of the soul, as demonstrated by A.-M. Goichon (*Le récit de Ḥayy ibn Yaqẓān commenté par des textes d'Avicenne*, Paris, 1959). In all these instances there is no reference to another knowledge (there is none, other than that contained in the active intellect), nor to another way of acquiring it (there is none, other than through hitting upon middle terms, *ḥads*).

This is the context in which the treatises listed by G. C. Anawati under *taṣawwof* ought to be seen (*Moʾallafāt Ebn Sīnā*, Cairo, 1950, nos. 213-44). *Taṣawwof* is not a proper label for these treatises, for they do not treat Sufism in terms of Sufism; they deal, rather, with the workings of the rational soul in Avicenna's philosophical system, its relationship to the active intellect, and the influence which the latter exerts on the former, and its results (prophecy, miracles, wonders, etc.). Metaphysics of the rational soul would be a more accurate category, for in his philosophical summae Avicenna treated these very subjects in the section on metaphysics right after theology. Apart from these subjects which he incorporated in his philosophical system and explained in the fashion described, Avicenna had no relation with Sufism, or indeed, with Sufis. The celebrated meeting with the Sufi Abū Saʿīd Abi'l-Ḵayr in all likelihood never took place; only the correspondence appears to be genuine (F. Meier, *Abū Saʿīd-i Abū l-Ḫayr (357-440/967-1049): Wirklichkeit und Legende*, Acta Iranica 11, Tehran and Liège, 1976, pp. 26-28). Popular tradition in the East after Avicenna's death, however, partly misled by the Sufi terminology in some of his works, and partly through a misunderstanding of his theory of *ḥads* as mystical illumination, considered him a mystic and occasionally even somebody who claimed to be a prophet; but this has nothing to do with the historical Avicenna (see Biography).

The question of the Easterners (*Mašreqīyūn*). Avicenna's development of an epistemological theory, whereby the intelligibles are acquired either by personally hitting upon the middle terms or by receiving them from a teacher who himself successfully traversed part of the syllogistic process mirroring the structure of the intelligible world, enabled him to have a progressive view of the history of philosophy. Although the knowledge to be acquired, the intelligibles, in itself and on a transcendental plane is a closed system and static, on a human level and in history it is evolutionary: Each philosopher, through his own syllogistic prowess, modifies and completes the work of his predecessors, thus presenting a body of knowledge that is an ever closer approximation of the intelligible world, and hence of truth itself. For Avicenna, the philosophical tradition that had achieved this best was the Aristotelian, and he saw himself as essentially belonging to it while at the same time revising and modifying it on the basis of his own syllogistic analyses. In the introduction to his *Mašreqīyūn* he specifically says that the Peripatetics are the philosophical school most worthy of adherence, but he criticizes his predecessors for having failed to revise Aristotle's system despite the fact that the truth, i.e., the intelligibles contained in the active intellect, "can be discovered by anybody who examines a lot, reflects long, and has almost fully developed the ability to hit upon the middle terms" (*ḥads*). He himself claims to have done so because, he says, he acquired knowledge, i.e., the philosophical sciences reflecting the intelligible world, "from a direction (*jeha*) other than that of the Greeks," i.e., not from teachers and their books (the Greeks), but from the direction of *ḥads*, or of the active intellect, by coming into contact with it while hitting upon middle terms (*Manṭeq al-Mašreqīyīn*, Cairo, 1910, pp. 3-4). In the *Dāneš-nāma* (*Ṭabīʿīyāt-e Dāneš-nāma-ye ʿalāʾī*, ed. S. M. Meškāt, Tehran, 1331 Š./1952, pp. 144-45) he makes an obvious autobiographical reference to this effect, while the autobiography itself is an illustration of the very concept of *ḥads* (see Biography: Analysis of the Autobiography). Avicenna did not, however, claim to have acquired all the knowledge contained in the active intellect; in other writings he bemoans the limitations of human knowledge and urges his readers to continue with the task of improving philosophy and adding to the store of knowledge.

This was Avicenna's theoretical position regarding the piecemeal acquisition of knowledge by successive philosophers. In actual practice, this manifested itself in a tendency, observable in all his major philosophical works, to follow a course increasingly more independent from the transmitted formats of exposition and discussion in the Greco-Arabic Aristotelian tradition. With each successive stage in his literary career, the treatment of the traditional material, as well as of his own revisions, became more systematic, and this was accompanied either by an attenuated emphasis on the historical aspects of a question, or by a sharper contrast between the traditional positions and his own. The texts on Eastern philosophy and the Easterners represent one of the later, but temporary stages of this development. These texts are the following:

1. *Ketāb al-Mašreqīyīn* (The book of the Easterners). It was written after the *Šefāʾ*, in 418-19/1027-28, and the greater part of the first and only draft was lost in 425/1034. The title of the work, as given above, is the only one attested in the oldest and most reliable MS containing the extant part on logic (Cairo, Dār al-Kotob, Ḥekma 6M, f. 116v); the expressions *al-ḥekma al-mašreqīya* and *al-falsafa al-mašreqīya* which are occasionally used by Avicenna and others seem to be designations of the contents of the work rather than verbatim references to the title. *Manṭeq al-Mašreqīyīn* is the title invented by the Cairene publisher of the extant part on logic. The work was another summa of philosophy in the Aristotelian tradition, as revised by Avicenna on the basis of his syllogistic emendations (*ḥads*). It was parallel to the *Šefāʾ* in content, except that it was systematic in method, whereas the *Šefāʾ* also treated views which traditionally formed part of the discussion on a given subject, but which were either disproved by Avicenna or no longer possessed, in his estimation, any intrinsic value. Avicenna referred to this stylistic difference between the two books in his prologue to the *Šefāʾ*, a prologue that was written after both books had been completed (*Madḵal*, Cairo, 1952, p. 10). Because of the parallel content of the two books, Avicenna did not repeat in the *Mašreqīyūn* those parts of the philosophical sciences for which he had nothing new to offer. The book thus contained logic (i.e., the "instrumental science," *al-ʿelm al-ālī*, the other name for *manṭeq* referred to in the introduction, p. 3), metaphysics (in its two major subdivisions, universal science and theology), some parts of physics, and some of ethics (p. 8). The part that has survived contains the introduction and logic, from the beginning to the section corresponding to the *Prior Analytics*. A section containing the part on physics and identified in some MSS as belonging to this work needs to be investigated further (G. C. Anawati in *MIDEO* 1, 1954, pp. 164-65).

2. *Ketāb al-enṣāf* (The book of fair judgment). It was drafted between 15 Day 397/19 December 1018 and 30 Ḵordād 398/7 June 1019, and this first draft was lost in Moḥarram, 421/January, 1030. The work was a detailed commentary on the Aristotelian corpus, including the Plotinian *Theologia Aristotelis*, in which Avicenna came to grips with the very texts and did not merely present their teachings in his own words. In a way it was the historical counterpart of the systematic *Ketāb al-Mašreqīyīn*. There he had presented his own systematic revision of Aristotelian philosophy without direct reference to or argumentation against his predecessors; here he juxtaposed the transmitted texts in the entire Greco-Arabic Aristotelian tradition, which he called that of the Westerners (*Maḡrebīyūn*), with his own systematic elaborations, which he attributed to the Easterners (*Mašreqīyūn*). The extant portions of the work consist of the commentary on *Metaphysics*, *Lambda* (ed. ʿA. Badawī, *Aresṭū ʿend al-ʿArab*, Cairo, 1947, pp. 22-33), and two partially overlapping recensions of the commentary on the *Theologia Aristotelis* (ed. Badawī, *Aresṭū*, pp. 37-74).

3. *Al-Taʿlīqāt ʿalā ḥawāšī Ketāb al-nafs*, (Marginal notes on *De anima*) (ed. Badawī, *Aresṭū*, pp. 75-116). The title is by the scribe of the MS in which the work has been preserved (Cairo, Ḥekma 6M), and describes the

provenance of the notes. They are comments written by Avicenna in the margins of his own copy of Aristotle's *De anima*, and were later transcribed cleanly and consecutively by the scribe of the MS, or his immediate source, who omitted the Aristotelian text. Although these notes follow the same principles of composition as the *Enṣāf*, they are not part of it; they were written either immediately before it and directly occasioned it by whetting the appetite of Avicenna's disciples for a similar but more extensive composition, or immediately afterwards, in partial compensation for its loss.

In these texts Avicenna wished to designate by a different name his revised systematization of theoretical knowledge as transmitted in the Aristotelian tradition in order to emphasize the more advanced level which the history of philosophy had reached through his efforts. The name he chose reflected appropriately his background in the East (*mašreq*) of the Islamic world, i.e., Khorasan, and the philosophical tradition he generated was accordingly Eastern, i.e., the Khorasani school of Aristotelian philosophy. This designation, however, appears to have met with little approval and generated even less interest among his disciples and colleagues (perhaps because not all of them were from Khorasan?), and Avicenna decided to abandon the idea. He stopped referring to the easterners as a live concept by about 422/1031, six years before his death; with the sole exception of a couple of bibliographical references in his private correspondence, there is not a single mention of them in any of his subsequent writings. Their absence is particularly noteworthy in the *Ešārāt*, a work in which he achieved the highest degree of independence from traditional models of presentation and discussion, but in which he claims, in the epilogue, to have presented neither Western nor Eastern philosophy, but just the truth (*ḥaqq*) and philosophical points (*ḥekam*).

In the context of Avicenna's own work, the significance of the concept of Eastern philosophy lies in displaying his attitude toward his philosophical achievement and toward his position in the history of philosophy, during a specific and limited period of his career (418/1027-422/1031). Variants of this attitude are also observable in other stages of his philosophical activity. As for the texts on Eastern philosophy, the loss of most of them has resulted only in the loss of variant reformulations of the same positions taken in other works. In substantial terms nothing seems to have been lost.

This impression is also reflected by Avicenna's immediate posterity. There is no reference to the whole issue of Eastern philosophy in what is known of the works of Avicenna's disciples, or, a few scattered bibliographical notes excepted, in subsequent philosophical tradition in the Islamic East, where the surviving fragments of the Eastern texts were available. Sohravardī, as a matter of fact, who read these fragments, rebuked Avicenna for taking in vain the name of the east for his revised Aristotelianism (*al-Mašāreʿ wa'l-moṭāraḥāt*, in H. Corbin, *Šihābaddīn Yaḥyā as-Suhrawardī: Opera Metaphisica et Mystica* I, Leipzig and Istanbul, 1945, p. 195).

It was only in the West, both in medieval Andalus and contemporary Europe, where the fragments were not available until recently, that the creative imagination of some scholars, prompted by the suggestive name, the East, and unchecked by any documentation, fashioned visionary recitals about Avicenna's mysticism. Ebn Ṭofayl's *Ḥayy b. Yaqẓān* proved to be particularly misleading. Ebn Ṭofayl, for his own purposes, misinterpreted as a difference of substance the stylistic contrast which Avicenna drew in the prologue of the *Šefāʾ* between that book and the *Ketāb al-Mašreqīyīn*, and created the impression, through the whole tenor of his own introduction, that the Eastern philosophy has somehow to do with mysticism. The subtitle of his work *Fī asrār al-ḥekma al-mašreqīya*, (On the secrets of eastern philosophy) also contributed to this effect. The suggestion was not lost on contemporary European scholars. Ebn Ṭofayl's subtitle was appropriated at the end of last century by M. A. F. Mehren who used it arbitrarily as the Arabic title of his own edition of the last chapters of the *Ešārāt* and a number of smaller treatises (*Rasāʾel . . . Ebn Sīnā fī asrār al-ḥekma al-mašreqīya*, Leiden, 1889-99). This created the unfounded notion that these works deal with Eastern philosophy. To compound the error, Mehren translated in the same volume his Arabic title into French as, *Traités mystiques . . . d'Avicenne*, associating this time, again without any basis, Eastern philosophy with mysticism. Once it gained printed legitimacy in this fashion, the myth of Avicenna's mystical Eastern philosophy has since reappeared in a number of variations that bear no relationship to the extant Eastern texts and are irrelevant to Avicenna's thought.

Bibliography: Different theories have been put forward about Avicenna's alleged mysticism. The standard Catholic version of Avicenna's "natural" mysticism is that by L. Gardet, "La connaissance mystique chez Ibn Sīnā et ses présupposés philosophiques," *Mémorial Avicenne* II, Cairo, 1952, incorporated in a revised form in the same author's *La pensée religieuse d'Avicenne* (*Ibn Sīnā*), Paris, 1951, pp. 143-96. There is a brief review of the theories on this subject by S. H. Nasr, *Islamic Cosmological Doctrines*, 2nd ed., London, 1978, pp. 191-95, and, in greater detail, by S. Gómez Nogales, "El misticismo persa de Avicena y su influencia en al misticismo español," *Cuadernos del Seminario de Estudios de Filosofía y Pensamiento Islámicos* II, Madrid, 1981, pp. 65-88. H. Corbin's own version of Avicenna's light mysticism is set forth in his classic, *Avicenna and the Visionary Recital*, New York, 1960. Corbin also gives a brief discussion of the history of scholarship on the subject on pp. 271 ff. A review of the various theories that have been put forward about the "Oriental" philosophy of Avicenna is given by S. H. Nasr in his *Cosmological Doctrines*, pp. 185-90; see also R. Macuch, "Greek and Oriental Sources of Avicenna's and Sohrawardi's Theosophies," *Graeco-Arabica* (Athens) 2, 1983, pp. 9-13.

The critical study of the question of Avicenna's Eastern philosophy was inaugurated by C. A. Nallino's "Filosofia 'Orientale' od 'illuminativa' d'Avicenna?," *RSO* 10, 1923-25, pp. 433-67, and continued by S. Pines, "La 'philosophie orientale' d'Avicenne et sa polémique contre les Bagdadiens," *Archives d'histoire doctrinale et littéraire du Moyen Âge* 27, 1952, pp. 5-37. For a full discussion of the question and the bibliographical details about the Eastern texts, as well as Avicenna's epistemological theory and the concept of *ḥads*, see D. Gutas, *Avicenna and the Aristotelian Tradition: Introduction to Reading Avicenna's Philosophical Works* (forthcoming).

(D. Gutas)

vi. Psychology

Like his metaphysics, Avicenna's psychology or doctrine of the soul has an Aristotelian base with a strong Neoplatonic superstructure. This we can see already in his definition of the soul. While Aristotle defines the soul as an entelechy or form of an organized natural body, Avicenna interprets the term entelechy in the sense in which a pilot is the entelechy of the ship (*De anima*, Ar. text, p. 6.13ff.). This example we find already in Aristotle but Aristotle does not offer it as his doctrine.

Avicenna gives a proof for the substantiality of the soul that renders it capable of existing by itself apart from the body. This proof was famous in medieval times, in Europe also, and is called the "proof of the suspended man." Avicenna asks us to suppose a person to be born adult and suspended in a vacuum where there is no air to resist him and, finally, to suppose that the parts of his body are so situated vis-à-vis each other that no part can touch others, then in that case such a person will not affirm the existence of anything external to him nor yet of his own body but he will still say, "I am." This assertion of self-consciousness apart from the body is the basis upon which the existence of the soul as a purely spiritual being is established (ibid., p. 15.12ff.). The striking affinity of this proof with the Cartesian proof is unmistakable.

Avicenna's theory of knowledge exhibits the same character, namely an Aristotelian starting point and a highly neoplatonized superstructure. His theory of sense-perception, imagination, and intellect have all an Aristotelian point of departure. First of all, Avicenna elaborates on the basis of Aristotelian suggestions that knowledge comes about by abstraction (Rahman, *Avicenna's Psychology*, pp. 38ff.). In sense-preception, for example, the matter of the perceived object is left out, but the form of the object is perceived. The next step in abstraction is reached in imagination because imagination can preserve an image which is free from matter. Although perception is not free from material attachments, imagination is free even from material relationships and attachments. The final stage of abstraction is reached in conception because a concept applies indifferently to all the members of a species: It is completely abstracted from the particulars of that species and is therefore universal. Just as there are five external senses—vision, audition, touch, taste, and smell—so there are five internal senses. Avicenna seems to be the originator of this theory. The first of the internal senses is the *sensus communis* which fuses information coming from different external senses into an object or a percept. The second internal sense is what he calls imagination or, rather, the memory-image (*ḵayāl*). This is the faculty which contains the image of the object perceived after that object is removed from direct perception. Next comes the faculty which Avicenna calls *taḵayyol*, which literally means "imagining" as a verb. The function of this faculty is to combine images retained in the memory and to separate them from one another. Thanks to this faculty, fantastic images can be formed, for example, that of a golden mountain by combining that of gold with that of mountain. While much of the activity of this faculty, as we shall presently see, is non-rational and, in fact, recalcitrant to the control of reason, it plays a fundamental role in rational activity because thinking never comes about without the interplay of images.

The fourth faculty among the internal senses appears to be an innovation of Avicenna's because it is not found in any other earlier philosopher, either Greek, Christian, or Muslim. This faculty he terms *wahm* (ibid., p. 31.13ff.; *De anima*, pp. 166ff.) which is translated into Latin by the term *estimatio*. While the external perception perceives the physical form of the thing, its inner meaning is perceived by an internal sense; for example, when a sheep sees a wolf for the first time, it runs away in fear. Now the external perception of the sheep only perceives the form and the shape of the wolf. That the wolf is dangerous is conveyed to the sheep not by external perceptions but by an inner faculty.

Lastly, the fifth internal sense consists of a faculty which retains not the forms of perceived things, but their meanings and ideas as perceived by the faculty of *wahm*. This faculty, which is a storehouse of ideas and meanings rather than that of externally perceived forms must be clearly noted because it retains individual meanings, just as the faculty of memory preserves individual forms.

In his doctrine of intellection, Avicenna again starts from the Aristotelian distinction between the active and the passive intellect. The human intellect is at first only potential and is gradually actualized by the operations of the faculties of perception and particularly imagination. The faculty of imagination helps intellection in that the intellect compares and contrasts the images stored in the mind. Through this exercise of comparing and contrasting, the universal emerges from those particular images. This emergence of the universal from particular images is thanks to the action upon the human mind of the Active Intellect, which is the lowest in the series of ten incorporeal and cosmic intelligences below God. Avicenna emphasizes that the universal does not emerge *from* the images, but that due to the activity of comparing and contrasting the images and combining them also with the meanings that are retained in the mind, the universal emerges into the human mind from the Active Intellect. Thus the mind's activity of comparing and contrasting the images is an exercise which prepares the soul for the reception of the universal intelligence from the cosmic intelligence. It is in this connection that Avicenna asserts that the mind has no storehouse or memory for the universal or abstract ideas as it has for particular forms and meanings. Therefore when the human mind wants to remember or recall universals, it reestablishes a contact with this universal Active Intelligence and receives the intelligible afresh, but whereas in the first instance it had to go through the whole exercise of camparing and contrasting images, this time it does not have to rehearse all the activity; its mere attention to the Active Intelligence is sufficient (ibid., pp. 116ff.)

Avicenna is also the author of a famous doctrine about the intellect, according to which the human mind, when it contacts the Active Intelligence, receives from the latter a power which he calls "simple knowledge" (known in the medieval Latin West as *scientia simplex*; *De anima*, p. 243.9ff. This doctrine asserts that a person may be asked a question about a matter he had never thought of before a detail, yet he is sure that he possesses the ability to answer the question. This assurance that the person has that he can definitely answer the question in detail means that he knows the answer already—this is simple knowledge. But as he begins to answer the question of the questioner in detail, he comes to know it in a different way than in a simple unanalyzed form. The first kind of knowledge is the creative simple knowledge on the pattern of God's knowledge, while the second form of knowledge is termed by Avicenna "psychic knowledge" or discursive knowledge. This doctrine of the simple intellect exercised a good deal of influence on the development of Islamic mysticism as well.

Avicenna also strenuously denied the transmigration of souls (*Psychology*, chap. 14 with notes) because the soul, through its association and experiences with a certain given body, becomes permanently individuated. Hence, it can not pass into another body. Indeed, according to Avicenna, a particular soul comes into existence at a time when a certain body with a particular temperament comes into existence and is prepared to receive this soul. Therefore, there is an initial reciprocity that is further strengthened by individual experiences and, hence, any talk of one soul entering another new body, whether human or non-human, is absurd. But for Avicenna there is no survival of the body after its death at the end of this life (Rahman, *Prophecy*, pp. 42-44). He believed that the soul survives by itself. Those souls which have become intellectually developed do not need the body at all and therefore do not need to seek physical survival or indeed revival on the day of resurrection. Such intellectually developed souls form a kind of paradise wherein they enjoy each other. As for those human souls which have not become intellectually fully developed and still need some sort of physical support, they will survive through their imagination because they are unable to go beyond the level of imagination. Such souls experience in the future life physical pleasures and pains just as described graphically in the Koran—the tortures of the fire of hell and the enjoyment of a physical paradise. Whether such souls have the opportunity of further development in the afterlife, Avicenna does not discuss.

Avicenna also formulated a comprehensive and elaborate theory of prophethood and prophetic revelation, several elements of which were taken from Greek thought and which had earlier been welded in some form by the philosopher Fārābī. (On the forms of prophethood see ibid., chaps. 1 and 2; Gardet, *La pensée*, chap. 4) Avicenna's prophetic faculty or power has three aspects: intellectual, imaginative, and practical. Whereas by the first, the prophet receives intellective revelation or wisdom, this results in the verbal revelation (for example, the Koran) thanks to the strong prophetic power of imagination which transforms intellective knowledge into moving images. Whereas the prophet shares the first with the philosopher, he is distinguished from the philosopher by the power of imagination. The third aspect of prophethood concerns the production of miracles, on the one hand, and the founding of the state and giving the law on the other.

Bibliography: Avicenna, *De anima* (Ar. text), ed. F. Rahman, Oxford, 1959, F. Rahman, *Avicenna's Psychology*, Oxford, 1952, repr. Westport, Conn., 1981. Idem, *Prophecy in Islam—Philosophy and Orthodoxy*, repr. Chicago, 1979. L. Gardet, *Le pensée religieuse d'Avicenne*, Paris, 1951. Works in Arabic: F. Ḵolayf, *Ebn Sīnā wa maḏhaboho fi'l-nafs* (Avicenna on psychology), Beirut, 1974. A. Nadir, *al-Nafs al-bašarīya 'enda Ebn Sīnā*, Beirut, 1968 (an anthology of Arabic texts on the human soul by Avicenna.

(F. RAHMAN)

vii. PRACTICAL SCIENCE

Avicenna's account of practical science is laconic and dispersed in minor tracts and in the opening and closing passages of his comprehensive encyclopedic works. The hope that he might some day write a comprehensive account of practical science, which he expresses at the beginning of the *Šefāʾ* (Healing), was never fulfilled. This was not because he was incapable of fulfilling it, but because it served his purpose, or so it seems, to remain laconic and to offer his views on the subject in bits and pieces, in a form lacking clarity, order, or completeness, and with intentions that remaind inaccessible to many of his contemporaries and readers of his encyclopedic works such as the *Šefāʾ*. Such, for instance, was the case of the person who requested that Avicenna give a comprehensive, clear, and orderly account of the rational sciences, for whom he wrote the short treatise entitled (*Fī aqsām al-ʿolūm al-ʿaqlīya*) (On the division of the rational sciences).

Departing from his usual practice of confining himself to praising God as the bestower of the intellect, Avicenna begins and concludes this treatise with extended professions of faith and prayers for the prophet Moḥammad. The organization of this treatise is curious also in that it does not conform to the organization of the sciences presented in Avicenna's encyclopedic works. (These normally begin with logic, proceed to natural science and mathematics, and conclude with metaphysics, with a brief account of practical science as an appendage of metaphysics.) After defining wisdom and presenting its primary divisions (secs. 1-2), he presents the tripartite division of theoretical and the tripartite division of practical wisdom (secs. 3-4), concluding what appears to be the first part of the treatise. Then, and without having prepared the reader for what follows, he gives an account of the principal and subsidiary divisions of natural science, mathematics, and metaphysics, devoting two sections to each of these three theoretical sciences (secs. 5-10: the subsidiary divisions of metaphysics are knowledge of revelation and resurrection). One would expect this second part of the treatise to be followed by an account of the principal and subsidiary divisions of the three practical sciences. But Avicenna says nothing about these. Instead, he concludes with the statement that this part dealt with the principal and subsidiary divisions of wisdom, not just of theoretical wisdom, and proceeds to give an account of the instrument, logic, that leads to the acquisition of both theoretical and practical wisdom (sec. 11: this third part concludes with an account of rhetoric and poetry). Thus despite the weight given to the theoretical sciences (it is only in sec. 4 that practical science is treated in any detail) all three parts of the treatise conclude with things that are of primary practical political importance.

Avicenna restates the Aristotelian division of philosophic knowledge or wisdom into theoretical and practical sciences in a seemingly emphatic and positive fashion. This deserves particular attention, in view of the fact that his predecessor Fārābī—praised by Avicenna as "perhaps the most excellent" of his predecessors among the philosophers (*Mobāḥaṯāt*, p. 122.4)—had kept this Aristotelian division largely in the background and hinted at its problematical character. What, then, did Avicenna mean to achieve by reintroducing this perhaps concise and orderly division with the claim that it is clear, complete, and precise as well? And what are we to make of the additional claim, with which he concludes the treatise, that this division of wisdom into theoretical and practical rational sciences has made it apparent that none of them "contains what contradicts the [Islamic divine] Law" and that those who pursue these sciences and "deviate" from the path of the Law "err of their own accord, because of their incompetence and failing, not because the art [of philosophy or wisdom] itself requires it—the art is not responsible for them" (p. 118.9-12)? To see how Avicenna succeeds in removing all contradiction between any of the philosophic rational sciences and the Islamic Law, we need to take a closer look at his reformulation of the Aristotelian division of the sciences in general and at his new view of practical science and its relation to the religious Law.

At first sight Avicenna seems to contradict himself by presenting two incompatible views of practical science. In the first he holds to the notion that wisdom is one, not many; it may have many parts, but they all participate in and are directed toward the one wisdom, which is a theoretical art of inquiry by which man pursues two things: Knowledge of what all being is in itself and that kind of activity which is necessary, and only as far as it is necessary, to render his soul noble and perfect so as to become an "intelligible world" corresponding to the world of being and ready for the highest or ultimate happiness (pp. 104.13-105.3). The aims is one: Knowledge of the things that are. To pursue this man needs to know and do certain practical things that are indispensable if he is to achieve his aim. These necessary conditions of the pursuit of theoretical knowledge make him noble and perfect, not as such, but as an instrument, one may say, of theoretical inquiry. This practical science and the activity it points to have no independent end or a horizon within which goodness and nobility are ends in themselves; goodness and nobility are defined in terms of what is useful and necessary for the pursuit of theoretical knowledge. Practical life, whether man's life by himself or in association with others, is subordinated to theoretical life. The emphasis is clearly on private rather than public life; and ethics (knowledge of goodness and nobility) is somehow divorced from politics, which is not even mentioned in this context. This is one direction in which Avicenna moves. It emphasizes ethics and subordinates practical life to theoretical life. The code names are "ultimate" and "other-wordly" happiness, which mean the same thing as perfect theoretical knowledge of all the beings as far as this is possible for man.

The second direction emerges in sec. 4 (pp. 107.4-108.10) where Avicenna gives the divisions of practical wisdom. The point of departure is "human governance," which is divided into (1) single individual and (2) in partnership with others, which is subdivided into (a) the household and (b) the city. (1) Ethics now covers man's happiness here (his first perfection) as well as in the hereafter. This is said to be contained in Aristotle's *Ethics*. (2a) The aim of household management is a well-ordered life, which merely "enables man" (that is, places him in a position) to gain happiness (presumably both kinds); it is clearly subordinated to ethics and conceived as a preparatory stage that makes possible the moral habits and activities that make men happy in this and the other life. (2b) Politics deals with the classes of political régimes, rulerships, and associations, good and bad; how each is preserved, the cause of its disintegration, and how it is transformed. And although as part of practical wisdom political science aims at the "good" (vs. the truth), Avicenna does not say that it aims at "happiness," either directly as in the case of ethics, or indirectly, as in the case of household management.

Then he singles out "rulership" and divides it into "kingship" and "prophecy and the Law," stating that each is contained in two books written by Plato and Aristotle respectively. He insists that what the philosophers (Plato and Aristotle) mean by *nomos* (plur. *nomoi*) in their two books on the subject is precisely the *Šarīʿa* (the religious divine Law) and the coming down of revelation; and he defends this philosophic view of the *nomoi* against a vulgar view, which is that the *nomos* is "nothing but a device and deceit." (In fact, this was not a "vulgar" view, but the view of those philosophers with whom Avicenna disagrees and whom he likes to call "vulgar people," e.g., the physician al-Rāzī.) According to the philosophers (Plato and Aristotle), *nomos* is the way of life (*Sonna*) and the norm (*meṯāl*) established by the coming down of revelation, which seems to be confirmed by the use of the Arabized form of *nomos*, *nāmūs*, as a name for the angel of revelation. The vulgar view assumed that the philosophers considered the *nomoi* (including prophecy and revelation) as "nothing but a device and deceit." Avicenna could have criticized this view by saying that the philosophers (Plato and Aristotle) did not speak about this kind of prophecy, revelation, and divine Laws. Instead, he counters it by assuming that this is exactly what Plato and Aristotle wrote about.

Now while it may be true that Plato and Aristotle did not write about this particular prophet or revelation or divine Law, there seem to be certain things about all prophecy, revelation, and the divine Laws which can be learned, that is, known scientifically, only in political science and nowhere else. The list which follows is important because it presents a program which Avicenna did not elaborate elsewhere in the same context: Political science, and no theoretical or practical philosophic or religious science other than political science, enables one to know the following:

(1) The necessity (*wojūb*) of prophecy and the human species' need of the divine Law (*Šarīʿa*) for its existence, preservation, and final destiny. This ambiguous statement indicates that prophecy and the divine Law are necessary and indispensable for the very existence and preservation of human life (of the species), which seems absurd, yet it is confirmed by the Persian compendium written for the king ʿAlāʾ-al-dawla, where Avicenna says that within political science, the science of the Law is the root and the science of the régime the branch (*Dāneš-nāma-ye ʿalāʾī* [*Elāhīyāt*], chaps. 1-2). It can also mean that political science shows whether, to what extent, and for what reason prophecy and the divine Law are necessary, which may make better sense. Political science was said to deal with the classes of régims and rulerships. Two types of rulerships were cited: royal and prophetic. So the question whether and under what conditions prophecy (and the Law) rather than kingship is necessary or needed for man's existence and preservation, properly belongs to political science.

(2) The "wisdom" of the (particular) prescriptions or determinations (*ḥodūd*, cf. *ʿOyūn al-ḥekma*, p. 16.10), both the ones common to all Laws and the ones that pertain to particular Laws, having to do with particular peoples and particular times. That is, why prescriptions in general, and why prescriptions should be different in different Laws, for different peoples, and in different times.

(3) It is through political science that one knows the difference between "divine prophecy and false claims to it." Avicenna does not explain how political science, whose subject matter is good and bad régimes and rulerships, can tell the difference between divine prophecy and false claims to it. After all, "divine" things are not the subject of political science, which is part of practical wisdom. He could have reserved this subject for divine science, but does not even mention it there. Nor does he explain on what basis political science can tell the difference between genuine and false prophecy, or whether all prophecy is "divine" prophecy, all revelation "divine" revelation, or all laws "divine" Laws.

Now political science as political science presumably makes known whether a political régime or rulership is virtuous or bad, how it is preserved, the cause of its disintegration, and how it is transformed. So presumably the only way it can tell the difference between "divine prophecy and false claims to it" is by whether or not the régime and rulership and laws are excellent, well made, and lasting. But surely one can not say that excellent régimes and divine Laws are necessary, required for the very existence and preservation of the human species; for ordinary régimes and laws can preserve it just as well. Is the conclusion, then, that what is necessary is prophecy and laws of any kind, good or bad, divine or false, provided they contain appropriate workable prescriptions? The only thing that is clear is that the answers to such questions are to be found in political science, in the writings of Plato and Aristotle, who wrote two books each on the kingship and the *nomoi* respectively.

On the surface it appears that Avicenna has concluded the account of practical science; he will now move to give an account of the principal and subsidiary divisions of the three theoretical sciences and an account of logic; unlike the theoretical sciences, practical science has no subsidiary divisions. Yet in fact the account of things practical, as against practical "wisdom" or "philosophy," is far from having been completed. To begin with, there are numerous references to what might be called the theoretical foundations of prophecy, revelation, and the divine Law in the principal divisions of natural science and divine science (secs. 5, 9). These include the "divine art" that underlies the overall order of nature and the immortality of the human soul (sec. 5); and the account of God's unity and attributes, the ranks and functions of the angels, and the overall order of the universe and its essential goodness. These matters, like everything contained in the principal divisions of the theoretical sciences, are all known by demonstration and with certainty.

The subsidiary divisions of the theoretical sciences, in

contrast, are not said to be known demonstratively and with certainty; in many cases their method is characterized as proceeding through guesswork (*takmīn*), recognition through signs (*estedlāl*), or simply as production or making (*'amal*) (pp. 110.10, 15 and 112.6-7). All the subsidiary divisions of the theoretical sciences can in fact be seen as applied or practical arts, and thus can be considered as subsidiary divisions of practical science as well. This is obviously the case in the practical arts that form the subsidiary divisions of natural science (such as medicine or astrology) and of mathematics (such as mechanical devices or musical instruments), but the case is perhaps not so obvious in the subsidiary divisions of divine science, to which we shall now turn.

All five principal divisions of divine science were said to be contained in Aristotle's *Metaphysics* and to be known with certainty by means of demonstration (114.8); neither of the two subsidiary divisions of divine science selected by Avicenna (he does not give an exhaustive account of these but only a selection introduced by *men ḏāleka*, p. 114.10, 16-17) are said to be know by demonstration or with certainty.

The first subsidiary division of divine science deals with revelation, prophecy, miracles, inspiration, and the angles of revelation, all of which are related or made to correspond to what was known demonstratively in the theoretical divisions of divine science, yet they are not to be found in Aristotle's *Metaphysics*. One can, however, find there certain things with which these matters can be identified or on the basis of which they can be explained. Nothing is said in this connection about the divine Law. This looks like "applied" or "special" metaphysics, where the general view of the universe found in Aristotle's *Metaphysics* (including, of course, Book *Lambda*) is used to show that revelation, miracles, and inspiration are possible. The main theme of this subsidiary division of divine science is not "what" these matters are, but "how" they take place, e.g., how the angel of revelation comes to be seen or heard.

The second subsidiary division of divine science deals with the "science of return" or the afterlife, a subject treated with unusual length in sec. 10 (pp. 114.16-116.2.) The reason seems to be this. As a rational science, the "science of return" can make known the immortality of the soul and the rewards and punishments awaiting it after death. But the rewards or punishments that await the soul after death are meted out, not only for holding true or false beliefs in this life, but for whether or not one has performed the good deeds "prescribed by both the divine Law and reason." But the divine Law makes known also the resurrection of the body and promises rewards and punishments in respect of both the soul and the body. Reason and the divine Law thus agree with respect to the immortality of the soul, but the divine Law provides in addition for the resurrection of the body and for bodily rewards and punishment in the hereafter, something that is in God's power to do if and when He wills, but that reason can not prove or show its necessity. Avicenna goes further. He suggests the following formula for whatever reason can not prove: "Whatever reason can not assert that it exists or prove its necessity (as far as reason is concerned, it is only possible), then it is prophecy that settles the question whether it does or does not exist" (pp. 115.16-116.1).

But this assumes a true prophecy rather than false claims to it, and we recall that the difference between true prophecy and false claims to prophecy is one of the tasks of political science, which is a practical science. Political science must first judge whether the divine Law legislated by the prophet is a true divine Law revealed to a genuine or truthful prophet, after which, it seems, it must admit the validity of whatever is legislated by the prophet, including things that reason can not know, and this seems to apply in particular to the resurrection of the body and to bodily rewards and punishments in the hereafter. It is perhaps not necessary to add that, as a rational science, practical science must judge the truthfulness of prophecy through the character of the prophet's legislation insofar as it promotes the welfare of the city, of the souls and bodies of the citizens in this world, and their ultimate or higher happiness—the happiness of their souls—in the hereafter, rather than insofar as it promotes the happiness of their bodies in the hereafter. And since what promotes the happiness of the soul in the hereafter (what Avicenna calls the higher or nobler happiness of man) is correct beliefs and good deeds in this world, practical science can only judge the truthfulness of prophecy by whether and to what extent the prophet's Law promotes correct beliefs and good actions in this world.

The non-demonstrative account of the subsidiary or applied divisions of divine science points to the complex relationship between the theoretical and practical rational sciences on the one hand and the beliefs and practices legislated in the divine Law on the other. The beliefs legislated by the divine Law find their counterparts in the theoretical sciences, which can demonstrate some of them, but not all, e.g., it can not know anything about the resurrection of the body and bodily rewards and punishments in the hereafter. The practical prescriptions of the divine Law find their counterpart in practical science (and in the subsidiary divisions of the theoretical sciences). But practical science can not make known the entire wisdom of the prescriptions common to all divine Laws or of those that pertain to a particular divine Law legislated for a particular people at a particular time. The divine Law contains beliefs and practices that are not accessible to reason, largely because they deal with bodily affairs or with particular prescriptions that are not rational or can not be known by reason or with certainty. Nevertheless, they seem to be essential to the welfare of the city and to man's life on earth, where the soul does not exist independently of body and of bodily concerns.

The treatise *On the Divisions of the Rational Sciences* culminates in a third part that gives an account of logic, which tries to explain the method that must be employed in all investigations, both the ones that admit of demonstration and the ones that do not, such as arguments in favor of what is praiseworthy and arguments against what is blameworthy, the useful ways of addressing the multitude, and imaginative representations—that is, dialectic, rhetoric, and poetry. In this way what is not accessible to reason becomes accessible to methods of investigation which, while not fully rational and to some degree even based on exploiting the human passions, are not wholly devoid of rational elements.

All this points to the fact that Avicenna was fully aware of the range of investigations in which practical science can engage following the models presented in the political works of Plato, Aristotle, and Fārābī. Yet he chose not to follow these models but to chart a new path that assumes the validity of these models and applies their conclusions to particular aspects of the Islamic divine Law. To do so, he had to move backwards, as it were, from the beliefs and practices prescribed by the divine Law to the spiritual, moral, and rational purpose and meaning that lay behind them. To perform this task safely and effectively, he found it prudent to abandon the Platonic and Farabian views of political science as the architectonic practical science if not the architectonic science simply, and revive the practical Aristotelian division of wisdom or philosophy into theoretical and practical sciences.

Taking his cue from the concerns of the divine Law with the body and bodily matters, Avicenna revived another ancient (Platonic, Aristotelian, as well as Farabian) view of political science. This view emphasized the usefulness of political science in respect of promoting the welfare of the bodies (*maṣāleḥ al-abdān*) and the preservation of the human species (*'Oyūn al-ḥekma*, p. 16.14). At first sight, this view seems to distinguish political science from ethics, which is said to be useful in purifying the soul. But purifying the soul means freeing it from bodily concerns, and the virtues and vices with which Avicenna deals in his ethical writings involve the control of the soul's desires, passions, etc., which are occasioned by the soul's connection to the body. Further, purification does not necessarily mean complete detachment from the body, an event that does not occur until the final separation with the death of the body.

Nevertheless, Avicenna's sharp division in practical science between the human governance that pertains to a *single* individual (ethics) and that which does not pertain to a single individual but takes place through partnership (household management and politics) points to the importance he placed on private perfection and thus to the subordination of practical science as a whole to the pursuit of theoretical knowledge. This, however, was enough to initiate the decline of political philosophy among those who maintained the Islamic philosophic tradition in the East until modern times, with the result that the Muslim community finds itself meeting the practical political challenge of the modern world with only a faint memory of an indigenous political-phylosophic tradition.

Bibliography: Works by Avicenna, *Fī aqsām al-'olūm al-'aqlīya*, in *Tes' rasā'el*, Cairo, 1326/1908, pp. 104-18. *'Oyūn al-ḥekma* (*Fontes sapientiae*), ed. 'A. Badawī, Institut francais d'archeologie orientale du Cairo [*Mémorial Avicenne* V], Cairo, 1954. *Dāneš-nāma-ye 'alā'ī* (*Elāhīyāt*), ed. M. Mo'īn, Tehran, 1331 Š./1952. *Al-Mobāḥaṯāt*, in *Aresṭū 'enda'l-'Arab*, ed. 'A. Badawī, Cairo, 1947, pp. 117ff.

(M. MAHDI)

viii. MATHEMATICS AND PHYSICAL SCIENCES

Introduction. What is understood by mathematics and physical sciences in this context is what Avicenna himself referred to in his encyclopedic work the *Šefā'*, as the mathematical sciences, which included both mathematics and astronomy, and the physical sciences (*ṭabī'īyāt*), which included the usual Aristotelian disciplines designated as the Physics, the Heavens, Generation and Corruption, Meteorologica (the fourth part of which is treated separately under the title *al-fe'l wa'l-enfe'āl*), the Soul, the Plants, and the Animals.

A few other works have been attributed to Avicenna in the literature such as: *ḥall-e moškelāt-e mo'īnīya* (Anawati, p. 227), *taḥrīr al-majesṭī* (Mahdawī, p. 263), which can now be definitely determined as being by later authors, the first being the work of Naṣīr-al-dīn Ṭūsī (d. 1274) and the second being the work of Mo'ayyad-al-dīn 'Orżī (d. 1266).

Mathematical works. The third treatise (*jomla*) of the *Šefā'* is devoted to the mathematical sciences. The Avicennian division is that of Aristotle, and thus the mathematical sciences included four parts (*fann*), namely, Geometry, Arithmetic, Music and Astronomy.

The two major works in this treatise are the one devoted to geometry and that devoted to astronomy. The Arithmetic and the treatise on music are simply renditions of the elementary principles of these two disciplines and need not concern us here, except to say that in the Arithmetic, Avicenna manages, in his eclectic style, to include results reached by earlier mathematicians such as Ṯābet b. Qorra and others. In the same book he also combines material from Euclid's *Elements*, Diophantus' *Arithmetic*, and the contemporary algebraists. The influence of the latter is especially significant, for it reveals the impact of the Arabic discipline of algebra on Greek arithmetical theory.

Geometry. In the part of Geometry, Avicenna wrote what could be properly called a *taḥrīr* of Euclid's *Elements*, in spite of the fact that he called his work an abridgment (*eḵteṣār*), thus feeling free to reorganize the material, to supply alternate proofs for theorems, to restate the conditions and the theorems themselves, and to add any "corrections" that he saw fit. The editor of this part of the *Šefā'* has established beyond doubt that Avicenna although staying close to the order of the *Elements*, had taken the liberty to rearrange the theorems, to combine proofs, to add new ones, and change the statement of the contents to agree with his own style and taste.

All this deliberate "tampering" with the text of the *Elements* should, however, be understood in terms of the Arabic translations of the *Elements*, which, from very early times, included the addition of material that was thought to belong to it, such as the two treatises fourteen and fifteen, attributed to Esqlābes (Hypsicles), but actually authored by Hypsicles and an anonymous author respectively, and not by Euclid. In addition to these translations the Arabic tradition also included commentaries that were sometimes composed of lengthy explanations of the text together with an attempt to put the material in a historical perspective. These commentaries also "took liberties" with the text in the sense that they grouped together theorems and proofs that were seen as closely related, and at times omitted other proofs or parts thereof, because they were thought to be redundant. Avicenna's work falls within this tradition and is actually closer to a *taḥrīr* than to an *ek̲teṣār*.

As an example of the free use of the text and the additional remarks appended to it, we note the additional definition of the irrationals given by Avicenna at the beginning of book ten of his version of the *Elements*. After defining the commensurable and the incommensurable in almost the same terminology as the one used by Euclid, Avicenna goes on to say that "there are no magnitudes that are irrational or rational (*aṣamm* or *monṭaq*) by themselves (*be-d̲ātehe*), but are so only in relation to the assumed (unit) magnitude. If it (i.e. the magnitude) is commensurable with that (unit) magnitude then it is rational, otherwise it is irrational. This same irrational could become rational in relation to another (unit) magnitude; and the original (unit) magnitude would then become irrational." There is no such comment in the Euclidean text or in the Arabic translations of that text, it is obviously an interpolation by Avicenna. It shows the degree to which the Euclidian text was being reorganized and could very well show the indebtedness of Avicenna to the earlier commentators who may have elaborated the text at this point.

Astronomy. Avicenna's works on astronomy are of the same nature as his work on geometry. In this part of the *Šefāʾ*, he gives his own version of what he thought were the contents of Ptolemy's *Almagest*. The Avicennian text is again called *talk̲īṣ* and, like the *ek̲teṣār* of the *Elements*, it contains a rearrangement of the material, an abridgment, and several explanatory notes. Treatises nine, ten, and eleven of the *Almagest* are treated by Avicenna in one chapter, for they all deal with the particulars of the dimensions of the models that Ptolemy proposed for the planets. Many of the lengthy proofs of the *Almagest* are summarized, and they are all recast in a simplified language, without loosing any of the mathematical rigor of the *Almagest*. The observations that were used by Ptolemy, for example, to determine the eccentricities of the upper planets Saturn, Jupiter, and Mars are grouped together by Avicenna at the beginning of the fourth chapter of his unified treatise, instead of being spread in X, 7 (Mars), XI, 1 (Jupiter), and XI, 5 (Saturn) as in the *Almagest*.

On the other hand, the method used by Ptolemy to determine the eccentricities of the models of each of these upper planets is essentially the same for each one of them. It involves a rather sophisticated iteration method. Once this method is mastered for the case of Mars, one needs no longer repeat it for the other two. Ptolemy, however, repeats this iteration method for each one of these planets in essentially the same terms although in somewhat shortened form. Avicenna, on the other hand, must have seen that the theoretical contents of these procedures used for each planet are the same; the only variation being really in the details of the observations leading to the variation in the computed results for each model. As a result, he must have felt that the Ptolemaic exposition contains some redundancy and hence can be better restated. This would then explain why he treated these three treatises, namely, nine, ten, and eleven, in one chapter.

The same method is followed by Avicenna throughout the book, and one could easily follow the Ptolemaic results from the Avicennian exposition of the *Almagest*. The only parts of the *Almagest* that are not included here are the numerical tables and the star catalogue.

From another perspective, the theoretical and mainly philosophical foundation of the *Almagest* is not touched upon by Avicenna throughout the whole book. These theoretical issues had motivated other Islamic astronomers, e.g., the contemporary of Avicenna, Ebn al-Hayt̲am, to write a full treatise devoted to their analysis and refutation. Ebn al-Hayt̲am's treatise *al-Šokūk ʿalā Baṭlamyūs* managed to isolate what was perceived to be a contradiction in Ptolemaic astronomy in the sense that that astronomy did not harmonize the mathematical and the physical aspects of the world. This does not mean that Avicenna was not interested in these issues or that he did not notice them.

In a treatise written by his student Abū ʿObayd J̌ūzǰānī about the contradiction in Ptolemaic astronomy that came to be known as the problem (*eškāl*) of the equant, the student says that his teacher Avicenna had even succeeded in solving at least this Ptolemaic contradiction, namely, the problem of the equant. The student further claims that he had asked Avicenna about the veracity of that claim, only to be told by his teacher that it was indeed true, but that he wanted the student to find the solution for himself. The student proceeds to observe that he, i.e., the student, was the first to succeed in obtaining a mathematical solution for the problem of the equant. Here are the student's own words: "When I asked him (i.e., Avicenna) about this problem (i.e., that of the equant), he said: 'I came to understand this problem after great effort and much toil, and I will not teach it to anybody. Apply yourself to it and it may be revealed to you as it was revealed to me'. I suspect that I was the first to achieve these results." However, a closer analysis of the student's work, which was published recently, shows that he too was not quite successful in establishing a valid solution of the problem.

Should this anecdote be true, then one must admit that by our modern standards the moral attitude of Avicenna left a lot to be desired. But what it also shows is the fact that within the circle of Avicenna, he and his students were at least discussing these same issues, which, as we have seen, had motivated Ebn al-Hayṯam to devote a special treatise to them, and thus to formulate the main program of research for later Islamic astronomers for centuries to come, extending well into the fifteenth century as far as we can now tell.

As for the parameters that were reported in the *Almagest* and were later found to be contradicted by observational facts, we find Avicenna discussing them in an appendix that is usually attached to his *talḵīṣ*, and which also included what Avicenna thought were defects in Ptolemaic astronomy. In its introduction, he says that one ought to contrast the statements of the *Almagest* with those of the rational part of natural science. One must further show the method by which the motions of the planets could take place. Thirdly, Avicenna reports some of the observational results reached after the writing of the *Almagest* and still in agreement with the theoretical statements of the *Almagest*.

In the body of this appendix, he begins by showing how it is possible for a sphere embedded within another sphere to move by its own motion in spite of the fact that it has to follow the surrounding sphere in the latter's motion. But if both spheres have the same axis, then it is impossible for the inner sphere to move by its own motion, and to move accidentally with the motion of the surrounding one in such a way that the two motions are opposite in direction. He then analyzes the two cases when the two axes are not identical, namely, (1) when the two axes intersect at the center or (2) when they do not.

Avicenna then takes up the issue of the observational results reached after the writing of the *Almagest*, which affected the validity of the *Almagest* statements themselves. In this category, he takes the parameter for the inclination of the obliquity, determined by Ptolemy to have been 23;51 degrees, and reports the results reached by the astronomers working during the reign of the caliph al-Ma'mūn (813-833) as being 23;35. He then claims that it had "decreased" after that by some one minute, and that he himself had observed the inclination and found it in his own days to be less than that by another amount equal to half a minute approximately. These results for the obliquity of the ecliptic were much closer to the true value, as derivable from modern computations, than the value found by Ptolemy.

The next two interrelated parameters of precession and solar apogee were also noted as having been found to be at variance with the results found by Ptolemy. In the first case, Ptolemy found precession to be one degree in one hundred years while the more precise value, which was determined afterwards and was reported by Avicenna, was found to be one degree in every sixty-six years approximately. This also determined the motion of the solar apogee, which was found by Ptolemy to have been stationary at five degrees of Gemini, but was found by later astronomers to have been moving primarily with precession. By Avicenna's time, the solar apogee must have been around the eighteenth degree of Gemini, instead of the fifth.

The size of the solar disk was also found to be less than the size computed for it, "with some approximation," by Ptolemy.

Avicenna concludes this appendix by stating that other parameters were also at variance with the results reached by Ptolemy, but that he had no observational results to determine them with any certainty. This means that, although there are claims in Avicenna's works of direct observations, he did not seem to have had access to a functional observatory, nor did he seem to have had a systematic program of observations that he wished to complete.

Finally, Avicenna's *talḵīṣ* of the *Almagest* includes a very curious note about his alleged observation of the disk of Venus being like "a mole on the face of the sun." There are several citations in medieval Arabic sources of the transit of Venus, and this would have been just another one of them, had it not been for its crucial importance in the argument for the relative order of the planetary spheres. The problem had already started with Ptolemy when he could not cite a positive proof for the order of the planetary spheres, and finally opted for a proper order that placed the sun in the middle with both Venus and Mercury as inferior planets, while Mars, Jupiter, and Saturn were taken as the superior ones. The planetary distances, which were computed by Ptolemy for each of these spheres included an approximation that allowed someone like J̌āber b. Aflaḥ (fl. first half of the 12th century) and later Mo'ayyad-al-dīn 'Orżī (d. 1266) to conclude that according to the Ptolemaic computations Venus should fall above the sun, and hence could not be seen "as a mole on the face of the sun."

Whether Avicenna had actually seen Venus in transit or not is immaterial, for he was then quoted by later astronomers as confirming Ptolemy's arrangement of the planets. Among those astronomers who quoted this observation specifically for that purpose were the thirteenth-century astronomer Naṣīr-al-dīn Ṭūsī (d. 1274) and the much later astronomer Cyriacus (ca. 1482), to name only two.

Physical Science. We shall confine ourselves to an account of the disciplines treated by Avicenna in the vast field covered by natural science: alchemy, astrology, and theory of vision.

In his explanation of the theory of metal formation in the *Ṭabīʿīyāt* section of the *Šefāʾ* (Cairo ed., part 5, chap. 5, pp. 22f.), Avicenna proposes two different theories: (1) the familiar Aristotelian theory of condensed vapors as being responsible for the formation of the various metals, and which is followed immediately by (2) the mercury-sulphur theory, commonly attributed to J̌āber b. Ḥayyān (8th-9th century) (E. J. Holmyard, *Alchemy*, London, 1957, repr. 1968, pp. 75, 94). In the mercury-sulphur theory, Avicenna argues successfully for the production of all metals through balancing the relationship of the Aristotelian qualities—hot, dry, wet, and cold—in the substances mercury and sulphur. "If," he says, "the mercury be pure, and if it be commingled with and solidified by the virtue of a white sulphur which neither induces combustion nor is impure, but on the contrary, is more excellent than that prepared by the adepts (i.e., Alchemists), then the product is silver." (Holmyard and Mandeville, *Congelatione*, p. 39). "If," he continues, "the sulphur besides being pure is even better than that just described, and whiter, and if in addition it possesses a tinctorial, fiery, subtle, and non-combustive virtue—in short, if it is superior to that which the adepts can prepare—it will solidify the mercury into gold" (ibid.).

One would have expected that once Avicenna had recognized the difference between silver and gold as a difference in the qualities of the two substances—one requiring only a purer sulphur than the other—and not the substances themselves, he would have followed the path of the alchemists who simply held the same opinion. But in a strange twist, Avicenna went on to say: "As to the claims of the alchemists, it must be clearly understood that it is not in their power to bring about any true change of species" (ibid., p. 41), thereby redefining the metals as separate concrete species as distinct as the species horse and dog, as one of his critics best put it (ibid., p. 7).

This generally confused argument of Avicenna against alchemy was duly noted and attacked by Ṭoḡrā'ī (d. 1121). And as much as Ebn Ḵaldūn would have wanted Avicenna's attack against alchemy to have been successful, he nevertheless found himself obliged to agree with Ṭoḡrā'ī's criticism of Avicenna's argument (*Moqaddema* III, pp. 273-74).

On the subject of astrology, he was not much clearer, in spite of the fact that he had written a treatise especially devoted to the attack of astrology (*Resāla fī ebṭāl aḥkām al-nojūm*). After classifying astrology as a refutable science, he went on to say that although it was true that each planet had some influence on the earth, it was doubtful whether one could tell of the nature of this effect. The next argument that he put forth was that the astrologers were incapable of determining the exact influence of the stars, although he agreed with them that according to what he called "the scientists" each star did have an influence on the earth.

In essence, Avicenna did not refute astrology, but denied man's ability to know of the effects of the stars on the sublunar matter. With that, he did not refute the essential dogma of astrology, as someone like the Ash'arite Bāqellānī, close to a generation earlier, did, but only refuted our ability to know the principles of that science. If one developed better methods and techniques of gauging the influence of the stars on man's life and earthly events, then Avicenna would, in principle, have accepted that that would have been possible.

Avicenna's theory of vision is an explicit restatement of the Aristotelian theory. In terms of intramission versus extramission, this theory occupied the middle grounds. For neither Aristotle nor Avicenna after him could subscribe to the extramission theory by accepting the ability of the eye to issue forth a ray that will have to reach as far as the stars to explain their visibility. For similar reasons, they could not accept the ability of the eye to receive anything from the outside to explain its visibility. The middle ground would therefore be that vision occurs in the medium that separates the eye from the visible object. For vision to take place, the object must have the ability to affect the medium separating it from the eye; and this medium must be transparent; and the perceptive faculty in the eye must sense this change or affectation.

In his treatise *On The Soul*, Avicenna states the problem in the following terms: "Among them (i.e. the doctrines of vision) is the doctrine of the one who thinks that, like other sensed objects, which are not perceived (*edrāk*) due to anything coming out toward them from the senses and touching them or by sending a messenger to them, so is vision. It takes place, not by the issuing of any ray whatsoever that meets the seen (object), but rather by the transmission of the form (*ṣūra*) of the seen (object) to the eye (*baṣar*) through the transparency (*al-šaffāf*) that delivers it" (*Šefā'*, *Ṭabī'īyat*, *Nafs* III, 5, p. 102).

Later on in the same treatise, he elaborates further the nature of the visibility of the lit objects and the media that separate them from the eye, by saying: "It is characteristic of the body that is bright by itself, or the one that is lit and colored, that it imprints (*yaf'al*) upon the body facing it—if it were capable of receiving the form (*šabaḥ*) in the same way the eye is, and having a colorless body between them—an effect, that is, a form (*ṣūra*) similar to its own form, without having any effect on the intermediary, for it (the intermediary) is transparent and is incapable of reception" (ibid., p. 128).

This terminology is indeed very reminiscent of the Aristotelian version of the theory of vision as it was expressed in so many words in *De anima*, and in *Parva naturalia*. In *De anima*, "Seeing is due to an affection or change of what has the perceptive faculty, and it can not be affected by the seen color itself; it remains that it must be affected by what comes between" (419a.19). In the *Parva naturalia*, "vision is caused by a process through this medium (that separates the object from the eye)" (438b.4).

In Themistius' commentary on *De anima*, which was available in Arabic, vision is explained as "the ability to accept the essence (*ma'ānī*) of the colors that are in the transparent medium that is separate from it (i.e., vision)" (Themistius, *De anima* 98.12).

With this understanding of Avicenna's explanation of the theory of vision, it is not surprising to find Roger Bacon classifying Avicenna together with Ebn al-Hayṯam (Alhazen) and Ebn Rošd (Averroes) as the Arab philosophers who were opposed to the theory of the extramission of light (*Opus maius* V, 1, Distinction 7, chap. 3-4).

Bibliography: The major bibliographical works dealing with the Avicennian corpus are that of G. Anawati, *Essai de bibliographie avicennienne*, Ligue Arabe, Direction Culturelle, Cairo, 1950, and that of Y. Mahdawī, *Fehrest-e nosk̲ahā-ye moṣannafāt-e Ebn Sīnā*, Tehran, 1333 Š. /1955.

A critical edition of the various parts of Avicenna's *al-Šefā'* was published in Cairo from 1952 to 1983 under the general editorship of Ebrāhīm Madkūr. The critical editions of the mathematical and the physical works used in the present survey are those produced by this project.

For elementary treatises on music and arithmetic, the reader is refferred to the French translation of the *Dāneš-nāma, Le livre de science* II, by M. Achena and H. Massé, Paris, 1958. See also the study of this treatise presented by R. Rashed, "Mathématiques et philosophie chez Avicenne," presented at the Millenniary Colloquium of Avicenna in New Delhi, 1981.

For the work of Avicenna's student Abū 'Obayd Jūzjānī on the problem of the Ptolemaic equant, see the edition, translation and commentary by G. Saliba, "Ibn Sīnā and Abū 'Ubayd al-Jūzjānī: The Problem of the Ptolemaic Equant," *Journal for the History of Arabic Science* 4, 1980, pp. 376-403.

Avicenna's note on alchemy is in the fifth chapter of the first treatise of his *Meteorologica*, which itself is the fifth part of the *Ṭabī'īyāt*. It was translated by E. J. Holmyard and D. C. Mandeville, in *Avicennae De Congelatione et Conglutinatione Lapidum*, Paris, 1927.

The treatise on astrology was published by H. Z. Ülken, *Ibn Sīnā Risāleleri* 2, Istanbul Üniversitesi Edebiyat Fakültesi Yayınlarından, no. 552, 1953, pp. 49-67, but was already studied by M. A. F. Mehren, "Vue d'Avicenne sur l'astrologie...," *Le Muséon* 3, 1884, pp. 383-403.

(G. Saliba)

ix. Music

Islamic writings on music are often theoretical treatises concerned with the analysis of pitch and duration, the constituent elements of melody. They are conceived less as descriptive accounts of contemporary practice than as systematizations of possible structures, utilizing, in the case of pitch, mathematical formulations derived from the Greek legacy. Among the most impressive examples of such writings are the relevant chapters in Avicenna's *Ketāb al-najāt*, *Dāneš-nāma-ye 'alā'ī*, and *Ketāb al-šefā'*, where music is considered as one of the mathematical sciences (the medieval *quadrivium*).

Not unexpectedly, matters of incidental relevance occur in other works also. Thus the *Resāla fi'l-nafs* contains a passage on the perception of sound (*ZDMG*, 1875, pp. 355-56); the first chapter of the *Resāla fī mak̲ārej al-ḥorūf* concerns itself with the physics of sound production; and the *Qānūn fi'l-ṭebb* discusses the pulse by analogy with musical proportion conceived, interestingly, not only in terms of rhythm but also of intervallic relationships (ed. Cairo, 1294/1877, I, pp. 125-26; see also the parallel passage in *Ragšenāsī*, ed. M. Meškāt, Tehran, 1370/1951, pp. 31-36). There is, further, a brief definition of the scope of the science (*'elm*) of music in *Fī bayān aqsām al-'olūm al-ḥekmīya wa'l-'aqlīya* (BM. MS. Add. 7528, fol. 44v).

Nevertheless, any assessment of Avicenna as a theorist of music must concern itself essentially with the chapters on music in the *Najāt*, *Dāneš-nāma*, and *Šefā'*, and for our purposes they may be considered together, as representing more or less extensive versions of the same analysis. The expositions in the *Dāneš-nāma* and in the *Najāt* (which also occurs separately, with a few minor omissions, as the *Resāla fi'l-mūsīqī*) may be regarded as Persian and Arabic versions of the same text, and they contain virtually nothing that is not examined in greater depth in the *Šefā'*. The nature and quality of Avicenna's treatment of the subject may thus best be demonstrated by specific reference to this work, presenting as it does the most detailed theoretical analysis to appear between the *Ketāb al-mūsīqī al-kabīr* of Fārābī (d. 339/950) and the treatises of Ṣafī-al-dīn Ormavī (d. 693/1294).

Avicenna's general approach in the *Šefā'* is, not unexpectedly, similar to that of Fārābī. (The scope is undeniably narrower, but his formulations are sometimes more succinct and his organization of material more rigorously logical.) Noteworthy among the introductory remarks are peremptory dismissal of the doctrine of ethos (prominent in Kendī [d. ca. 260/874] and central to the Ek̲wān al-Ṣafā' [second half of the fourth/tenth century]), and an interesting discussion of the nature of sound viewed first functionally (as a signaling device aiding, ultimately, the survival of the species) and then as a means of expression with, in its more strictly musical form, a particular esthetic potential. The main body of the chapter then falls into two parts in accordance with the initial definition of the subject as a science concerned with notes (*nağam*) and the times separating them (*al-azmena al-motak̲allela baynahā*), its ultimate goal being knowledge of compositional procedures (*kayf yo'allaf al-laḥn*).

The first part, dealing with notes, begins with a discussion of the physical causes of differences in pitch, and provides definitions of the basic concepts of note, interval (*bo'd*), genus (*jens*), and group (*jamā'a*), the last three of which are then amplified in subsequent sections. Intervals are handled in terms of the mathematical ratios by which they may be represented, and are ranked according to their relative degrees of consonance. Two categories are recognized. The first is divided into large (octave), medium (fifth and fourth), and small (the series of superpartial intervals from the major third down to an approximate quartertone), with the small being subject to a further threefold division. The second consists of combinations of the above (e.g., octave plus fourth). The mathematical emphasis is equally apparent in two further sections dealing respectively with the addition and subtraction of intervals and their doubling and halving, and culminates in the extensive survey of the genera or tetrachord types. An initial discussion of the esthetics of different interval sizes considered in relation to melodic function gives pride of place to the class of small intervals, and these are then variously combined into 16 tetrachords (yielding a possible 48 permutations in all) grouped according to the usual categories of strong (*qawī*), chromatic, and enharmonic. Here, oddly, Avicenna reverses the normal terminology, calling the chromatic *rāsem* and the enharmonic *molawwan*. The first part ends with an outline of the notion of group, essentially the various combinations of tetrachords and whole-tones within the Greek two-octave Greater Perfect System, and with a brief schematic survey of elementary types of melodic movement.

The material elaborated in the course of this analysis should not be thought of as constituting a description of the modal structure of the contemporary Arabo-Persian musical system. It is explicitly stated, for example, that the chromatic and enharmonic tetrachord species portrayed in such detail were not in normal use. We are thus presented here not with the results of empirical observation, but with a sophisticated adaptation and development of material derived from the Greek theorists. In the less technical areas there are, predictably, Aristotelian echoes, and Avicenna himself refers to Euclid and to the more important figure, in musical theory, of Ptolemy. While problems remain with regard to the way in which the material was transmitted, there are fewer difficulties in identifying the ultimate sources, and a comprehensive survey of these may be consulted in the appendix to D'Erlanger's translation of the music chapter in the *Šefāʾ* (*La musique arabe* II, pp. 258-306).

Seemingly less remote from contemporary practice, even if just as schematic, is the second major part, on rhythm (*īqāʿ*). Nevertheless, it is only at the end that some indication is given of which particular cycles were in current use: The main body of this section, for which Fārābī is again the model, presents a set of possible structures in terms of which rhythms could be formulated. Greek influence recedes, and the main analytical tools are derived rather from the Arab science of prosody, so that there is nothing unexpected in finding certain sequences discussed in terms of their varying suitability for verbal as against instrumental articulation, or the inclusion (specifically in the *Šefāʾ*) of a section devoted to prosody. The theoretical introduction begins with the notion of a basic recurring pulse to which can be related the concept of a minimum (indivisible) time unit, defined in articulatory (prosodic) terms as CV (*ḥarf motaḥarrek*) and symbolized as *ta*, and alternatively in relation to the circular physical movement of a player's hand between one percussion and the next. Discussion of the maximum possible number of time units between two precussions involves psychological considerations, the definition being that it must not be so great as to undermine the subjectively perceived relation between them. With regard to the structure of the rhythmic cycles, an immediate distinction is drawn between conjunct (*mowaṣṣal*) and disjunct (*mofaṣṣal*). The former, generically termed *hazaǰ*, are speedily dismissed, being equated with the basic recurring pulse (in different tempi), and attention is focused on the more flexible and complex patterns of the latter.

Each cycle is analysed as a set (*dawr*) of primary percussions separated from the next set by a disjunction (*fāṣela*). The number of primary percussions ranges from two to six, distributed over two to ten time units (sets with more time units are mentioned, only to be rejected as too long). Alterations to which the set may be subject involve the elimination of percussions (with or without deletion of the related time unit) and adding secondary percussions to otherwise unmarked time units, this latter feature being associated particularly with the slower rhythms. It should be noted, too, that the disjunction is also a variable. A given rhythmic type could thus comprise a number of cycles differing not only in the internal patterning of percussions but also in the total number of time units.

It is in the briefer final section that attention is turned more specifically to aspects of contemporary practice. The opening passage on the process of composition is an essentially abstract formulation, but includes nevertheless references to such techniques as trills and glissandi, and was to have ended with a specimen melody in *hazaǰ* rhythm, the notation for which, if it ever existed, has unfortunately failed to survive. There follows a short survey of instruments in which chrodophones figure prominently, being divided organologically according to both the way of mounting the strings (thus contrasting, e.g., harps and zithers) and the way of playing them: stopped or free, plucked or bowed. Aerophones are differentiated by whether the air stream passes through a hole, across a free beating reed, or is produced by means of an air reservoir. Only one (hammered) percussion instrument is mentioned, those of unturned pitch being ignored. Avicenna gives finally a fretting for the lute, called both *ʿūd* and *barbaṭ* (details in Farmer, *Lute scale*, and Manik, *Tonsystem*, pp. 47-52), and then (in the *Šefāʾ* only) defines, largely in terms of that fretting, the intervallic structure of the more common melodic modes of his time. These show an interesting transitional phase between the early diatonic system and that described by Ṣafī-al-dīn; thus alongside purely diatonic modes are found others utilizing, in addition or exclusively, genera containing three quarter-tone intervals (associated with the *wosṭā zalzal* fret) and including, Arabized as *mostaqīm*, the earliest recorded version of the mode *rāst*.

Bibliography: Texts: Z. Yūsof, ed., *al-Šefāʾ, al-rīāžīyāt, 3, ǰawāmeʿ ʿelm al-mūsīqī*, Cairo, 1376/1956; tr. R. D'Erlanger, *La musique arabe* II, Paris, 1935, pp. 103-245. *Dāneš-nāma-ye ʿalāʾī*: tr. M. Achena and H. Massé, *Le livre de science* II, Paris, 1958, pp. 217-39. *Ketāb al-naǰāt*, chap. on music, ed. M. El-Hefny (see below). *Resāla fi'l-mūsīqī*, in *Maǰmūʿ resāʾel ... Ebn Sīnā*, Hyderabad, 1353/1934. For further details see A. Shiloah, *The Theory of Music in Arabic Writings (c. 900-1900)*, Munich, 1979, pp. 137-143.

Studies: H. G. Farmer, "The Lute Scale of Avicenna," *JRAS*, 1937, pp. 245-57. M. El-Hefny, *Ibn Sīnās Musiklehre*, Berlin, 1931. M. Cruz Hernández, "La teoría musical de Ibn Sīnā en el Kitāb al-šifāʾ,"

Milenario de Avicenna II, Madrid, 1981, pp. 27-36. H. Husmann, *Grundlagen der antiken und orientalischen Musikkultur*, Berlin, 1961, pp. 88-134. L. Manik, *Das arabische Tonsystem im Mitterlalter*, Leiden, 1969, pp. 47-52. A. Shiloah, "'Ên-Kol'—commentaire hébraïque de Šem Tov Ibn Šaprût sur le Canon d'Avicenne," *Yuval* 3, 1974, pp. 267-87.

(O. Wright)

x. Biology and Medicine

Introduction: Avicenna between Aristotle and Galen. At the time of Avicenna natural philosophy and medicine overlapped, sharing a large area of the field that today we call biology. But they were two distinct traditions, in the important sense that each had its own literature and leading authorities, primarily Aristotle (Arestātālīs) for philosophy and Hippocrates (Boqrāṭ) and Galen (Jālīnūs) for medicine.

Galen, whose dominance of medicine was nearly complete, had differed sharply with Aristotle on some questions, the most central of which was whether the powers that control animal life have one single source (the heart, as Aristotle believed) or three distinct sources (the brain, heart, and liver, as Galen argued). He also forcefully challenged Aristotle's views on the male and female roles in sexual generation. These differences fueled a fierce dispute between the followers of Aristotle (the natural philosophers) and the followers of Galen (the physicians) for centuries.

Nowhere in medieval thought was the contest between Galen and Aristotle as dramatic as in the works of Avicenna, where the two great traditions intersected. Avicenna wrote the medieval textbook of Galenic medicine the *Qānūn* (the *Canon*), as well as the central medieval statement of Aristotelian biology (the *Ḥayawān*, the biological section of the *Šefā'*). In both works he confronted the problem of the Aristotelian-Galenic division, and settling the contest between the two titanic authorities became the cardinal interest of his life-work in medicine and biology.

Already in book 1 of the *Canon* (composed before 405/1015, when he was thirty-five years old). Avicenna had taken Aristotle's side in the theoretical controversies, with the ironical result that this most influential Galenic document of the Middle Ages was written by someone openly committed to the Aristotelian point of view. This apparent irony only deepens when we realize that the *Ḥayawān*, arguably Avicenna's most explicitly Aristotelian work, harbored a massive amount of purely Galenic material. In fact, Avicenna's synthesis depended on accepting the new (post-Aristotle) Galenic evidence in anatomy and physiology, and equally on interpreting it so as to fit Aristotelian theory.

The Canon. Galen (and Hippocrates as presented by Galen) had generally dominated Islamic medicine from its beginnings. Galen's positive ideas about anatomy, physiology, disease, and treatment of disease have the pride of place in the *Canon*, as they do in all of Islamic medicine.

The *Canon* has been accurately described as a "monumental unity," and "the clear and ordered 'summa' of all the medical knowledge of Ibn Sīnā's time" (A.-M. Goichon, "Ibn Sīnā," *EI*² III, p. 942). In this, Avicenna did not break new ground. As a magisterial exposition of Galenic medicine the *Canon* is not unique, nor was it the first in Arabic. Islamic medicine had developed for two centuries before Avicenna: Ḥonayn b. Esḥāq (fl. 192-260/808-73) and his associates had firmly established its sources and Arabic terminology, and 'Alī b. Sahl Rabbān Ṭabarī, Moḥammad b. Zakarīyā' Rāzī, and 'Alī b. 'Abbās Majūsī (q.v.) had all published systematic and sophisticated medical works. Majūsī's *Kāmel al-ṣenā'a al-ṭebbīya*, in particular, rivals and *Canon* in size as well as in the clarity and authority of its exposition of Galenic medicine.

The *Canon* is organized into five books. Book 1 (the *Kollīyāt*) covers the basic principles of medicine, and is in four parts. Part 1 discusses the constitution of the body (What is it made of? The four elements: earth, water, air, and fire, and the four humors: blood, phlegm, yellow bile, and black bile, whose mixture determines the temperament of every individual); the anatomy of uniform parts (the bones, muscles, nerves, veins, and arteries); and general physiology (How does the body function?). Part 2 deals with the causes and symptoms of disease. Part 3 is devoted to preventive medicine (*ḥefẓ al-ṣeḥḥa* "the maintenance of health"), principally through disciplined living and diet. Part 4 deals with the treatment of disease, again with emphasis on regimen and diet, and on medicines only when these fail.

Avicenna devoted two of the *Canon*'s five books to medicines: Book 2 comprises the Materia Medica, which lists about 800 individual drugs, mostly of vegetable origin (but with many animal and mineral substances); and book 5 (the Formulary), which contains some 650 compounded prescriptions—theriacs, electuaries, potions, syrups, etc.

The diseases of particular organs, starting from the head and moving down to the toes, are systematically discussed in book 3. Book 4 deals with medical conditions that affect the body as a whole (fevers, poisons) or that could happen to any part of it (wounds, fractures). It concludes with a treatise on personal hygiene, emphasizing care of the hair, skin, nails, body odor, and the treatment of overweight or underweight persons.

Medicine and natural philosophy. No doubt the *Canon*'s dominance of later medicine owed much to Avicenna's general influence. Yet it is possible that the *Canon*'s special perspective on Galenic medicine contributed to its popularity among the learned. This perspective can best be appreciated when contrasted with that of Majūsī's *Kāmel al-ṣenā'a*, its closest rival. Majūsī began his book with a history of medicine from the ancient Greeks to his own day, and justified his work without reference to anything else. In contrast, Avicenna avoided the history of medicine, and instead took extraordinary pains in the *Canon* itself to circumscribe medicine to what he considered to be its proper domain. By defining the place of medicine in the hierarchy of the sciences, something which Majūsī had failed to do, Avicenna increased the appeal of his work as a textbook for teachers of the medieval curriculum.

Since in practice the content of medicine and natural philosophy overlapped, Avicenna wished to delineate clearly their respective areas of competence. He devoted the first chapter of the *Canon* to this task, and repeatedly returned to it afterwards. Medicine for him was indeed an independent science with its own special subject, as the first sentence of the *Canon* makes clear: "Medicine is a science by which we learn about the conditions of the human body in health and in the absence of health, in order to maintain health or to restore it." However, medicine begins with a set of basic concepts (including the "elements," "humors," temperaments," and "faculties," i.e., the common vocabulary of Galenic medicine) which it borrows from natural philosophy. The actual investigation of these theoretical concepts falls outside the purview of medicine, belonging instead to natural philosophy. According to Avicenna, the physician could not independently answer such questions as: Do the elements exist? What are the humors? How many faculties are there? He persistently admonishes the physician to leave this task to the natural philosopher. When Galen dealt with such questions, Avicenna writes, he did so "not as a physician, but as someone who wanted to be a philosopher" (*Canon* I, pp. 4, 5, 6, 17, 19, 21, 67, 71, 72).

A certain urgent purpose emerges through Avicenna's repeated admonitions, namely his desire to safeguard natural philosophy, and the authority of its master Aristotle, from the inroads of Galenism. But his emphasis on the difference between the two sciences amounted to little more than a holding action. For the real source of the trouble was that medicine and natural philosophy, though distinct, were nevertheless joined together like Siamese twins by anatomy—the common material on which all medical and biological discussion depended. And since anatomical knowledge was supposed to be based strictly on "experience and dissection" (ibid., I, p. 5), there were no grounds for asking the physician to defer to the philosopher in arguments about anatomical facts. It is this which had given Galen's challenge its cutting edge, for he was the beneficiary of centuries of anatomical discoveries after Aristotle.

The essence of the problem for Avicenna was that Aristotle's anatomy was comparatively primitive, and had enfeebled his whole biological system. Ultimately Avicenna was able to deflect Galen's challenge only by rebuilding the Aristotelian system on the firmer basis of the new anatomy. But what he did in the *Canon* was principally to recognize the problem, his normal practice being (1) to say that a controversy exists (on generation or the heart) between Galen (or the physicians) and Aristotle (or the philosophers), and to state briefly the two positions, and (2) to say either that he will resolve the dispute in his philosophical works (ibid., I, p. 22), or that "serious analysis" will show that Aristotle's view is the correct one (p. 67). It was only in the *Ḥayawān*, much later, that he confronted the problem head on.

The Ḥayawān. The *Ketāb al-ḥayawān* (Book of animals) is the last and largest part of the "Physics" (*Ṭabīʿīyāt*) of the *Šefāʾ*. The *Šefāʾ* itself is highly original in conception, being the first all-inclusive work in philosophical literature, giving a detailed exposition of all the Greek, primarily Aristotelian sciences. Avicenna's purpose in the *Šefāʾ* was not to write a commentary on Aristotle, but to restate the Aristotelian arguments convincingly. His method is more clearly evident in the *Ḥayawān* than in any other part of the *Šefāʾ*.

The *Ḥayawān* is organized into nineteen books following the scheme of Aristotle's own "Book of animals." This was a translation of the three treatises, *Historia animalium*, *De partibus animalium*, and *De generatione animalium*. The Arabic translation, traditionally ascribed to Ebn al-Beṭrīq, regarded the three treatises as one corpus, in 19 *maqālas* (books). Books 1-10 represented the *Historia*, books 11-14 the *De partibus*, and books 15-19 the *De generatione*. The *Historia* contained Aristotle's descriptions of some 500 animals and their behavior, mostly raw material that could be augmented without raising any theoretical problems. He took up the difficult problems of the classification of animals and their anatomy in the *De partibus*, and it was here that Galen had seriously encroached on his system. The same situation held for the *De generatione*, the most significant of his biological works. The *Ḥayawān* text treats the Aristotelian biology in three ways: summary, new synthesis, and outright substitution.

a. Summary. Ebn al-Beṭrīq's translation of Aristotle was especially poor. Avicenna's *Ḥayawān* provided a more accessible account of the Aristotelian biology, in the form of clear summaries of (1) the *Historia* (*Ḥayawān*, books 1-8, pp. 1-140, except chapter 2, book 1, pp. 10-19, and chapter 1, book 3, pp. 40-46) and (2) of the *De generatione* (*Ḥayawān*, books 15-19, pp. 384-433). There is little doubt that Avicenna based his summaries on Ebn al-Beṭrīq's translation, to judge from his direct quotations from it (e.g., *Ḥayawān*, p. 398). Three centuries later Ebn Qayyem J̌awzīya also quoted directly the same translation (*Meftāḥ* II, pp. 155-56) which suggests that it was the only available one (published in the various volumes of Brugman and Drossaart Lulofs, Kruk, and Badawī).

b. New synthesis. In the *Ḥayawān* Avicenna was firmly committed to Aristotle's theoretical conclusions, and equally determined to modernize Aristotelian biology. The new material consisted almost entirely of the later anatomy of the Hellenistic physicians which Galen had inherited and elaborated, and Avicenna had already taught in the *Canon*. Joining the fray openly as the loyal champion of Aristotle, he was able to win for Aristotelian theory a new lease on life, but only by accepting a large portion of Galen's positive contribution, his intemperate attacks on him notwithstanding ("Let us then look at Galen's contradictions, and show that he did and said nothing well, that even when he thought he presented proof, he did not convince; and that he is extremely weak in the principles [of philosophy], even though he is very productive in the branches of medicine." *Ḥayawān*, pp. 146, 155).

In the first part of the *Ḥayawān* (pp. 1-140) Avicenna had essentially followed Aristotle's outline by selecting material from the *Historia* on the behavior of animals and adding similar observations of his own. However, there is early in book 1 a significant departure from this method where chapter 2 (pp. 10-19) consists of non-Aristotelian anatomical material lifted verbatim out of the *Canon* (I, book 1, pp. 19-24). This is a harbinger of the major textual transplant that will occur in later sections of the *Hayawān* to be discussed below. Of more immediate interest is chapter 1, book 3 where at last Avicenna deals with the problem of the heart, fulfilling the promise he had made in the *Canon* (e.g., I, p. 22) as well as in *Ketāb al-nafs* (p. 234), the *De anima* of the *Šefāʾ*.

Aristotle believed the heart to be the central location of the soul—the organizing principle of all the functions of the body, including digestion ("concocting" food into blood), sensation, and movement. He made little distinction between the veins and arteries, calling them both by the same term, *phlebes* (blood vessels). Being convinced of the need for a central focus for all sensation, and writing before the discovery of the nervous system, he also assigned that role to the heart. In brief, Aristotelian biology asserted that the heart was the origin, anatomically, of the arteries, veins, and nerves.

The Hellenistic physicians after Aristotle made major advances in anatomy. Praxagoras of Cos (fl. ca. 300 B.C.) distinguished clearly between the arteries and the veins; Herophilus of Chalcedon (fl. ca. 300 B.C.) discovered the nervous system; and Erasistratus (fl. 258 B.C.) gave the blood-making faculty to the liver, not the heart. By Galen's time, scientific opinion saw the brain as the origin of the nerves (and the faculty of sensation), the liver as the origin of the veins (and the faculty of digestion), and the heart as the origin of the arteries only. Galen summed up the arguments forcefully in his *De placitis Hippocratis et Platonis*.

Avicenna, in a typical example of his general method in the *Ḥayawān*, managed to accept the new anatomy and, at the same time, hold firmly to the Aristotelian theory that the heart is the origin of all the body's faculties. He argued that Galen's anatomical facts, where indeed the nerves appear to "grow" from the brain and spinal cord, and the veins from the liver, derived from dissection of the completely formed animal. Avicenna interpreted Aristotle to mean that the heart is the origin of all the organs and their faculties in embryological development, where it is the first organ to be formed by the soul, and all else is formed later through its agency (*Ḥayawān*, pp. 40-46).

The shift of the argument to embryological development was not entirely tactical on Avicenna's part, for in fact it pointed to his and Aristotle's primary concern in biology, namely the problem of sexual generation and development of the fetus. Aristotle had set about to answer such questions as: What is it that tells the fetus to develop into dog, or human, or horse? How does the fetus know how to develop the organs? How does it know the order of their development and differentiation? In brief, what is the organizing principle? Aristotle found the answer in the soul, whose connection to the heart and to the male semen is the backbone of the Aristotelian-Avicennan biology.

In book 9, while still in the part ostensibly devoted to the *Historia*, Avicenna abruptly departed from Aristotle's model to discuss, with some urgency, "the controversies about semen and the fetus—not according to Aristotle's scheme, but following what we consider more appropriate in our own time (pp. 144-45)." The discussion of sexual generation which followed became the pivotal discussion of the *Ḥayawān* and determined Avicenna's method in the biology as a whole.

The normal location of this discussion would have been in books 15-19 of the *Ḥayawān* (where Avicenna made a masterly abridgment of the *De generatione*, repeating briefly some of the arguments of book 9). Clearly Galen's challenge had forced him to confront the issue early on. The titles of the first three chapters of book 9 give a palpable sense of a drama to this central section of the *Ḥayawān*: (1) "On puberty, semen, menses, and the controversy about them." (2) "On Galen's criticism of Aristotle, and the refutation of that criticism, and the establishment of its fatuousness." (3) "The return to the Aristotelian source, and the proof that women do not really have semen, and that the female matter called semen has no formative faculty, but only a passive faculty..."

The Greek thinkers had disagreed radically on the question of parental contribution to sexual reproduction. Hippocrates maintained that both male and female contribute "semen," reasoning that the child's resemblance to both of its parents means that both contribute similar reproductive material to it (*Hippocratic Writings*, p. 322). Aristotle categorically rejected this theory, and formulated a radical distinction between the male and female contributions, asserting that the female provides only the passive material (menstrual blood) which the male semen, as sole carrier of the soul, forms into the fetus. He maintained that semen was a residue of the blood, which only the male, by virtue of his adequate vital heat, could transform into semen. The female, lacking this ability because she is not "hot" enough, discharges her contribution as menstrual blood (*De generatione*, 728a, 726b, 730b, 738b).

Galen re-affirmed the original Hippocratic idea of equal contribution, and supported it with new evidence. Although he agreed with Aristotle that semen was a residue of the blood, he insisted that women as well as men could produce it. According to him, both male and female semina contributed equally to the "form" as well as to the "matter" of the fetus. His new evidence was the discovery (probably first made by Herophilus of Chalcedon) of the ovaries which he called "female testicles." Aristotle had had no notion of these organs and had also denied that the male testicles contributed to the actual production of semen. Galen re-affirmed the direct relevance of the testicles to reproduction and was able to point to their existence in both sexes (*De semine* 1.5 (ed. Kuhn, vol. IV), pp. 527ff.).

By Avicenna's time the discovery of the ovaries had long been incroporated into the body of scientific knowledge. His first statement of the problem made clear the degree to which Aristotelians were on the defensive, and the extent to which Galenism had come to define the basic issues of generation (*Ḥayawān*, pp. 145-46). In what was a critical departure in Aristotelian biology, Avicenna's response was to accept the existence of the ovaries and the argument that it is the female semen, and not menstrual blood, which represents the basic female contribution to reproduction (ibid., pp. 145, 161, 388-90). But in what sense, then, can we still speak of Avicenna's biology as Aristotelian? What remained of the original Aristotle? Nearly everything that mattered. Avicenna applied to the female semen Aristotle's central hypothesis, giving it exactly the same role that Aristotle had assigned to the menstrual blood: "Clearly the seed of women is fit to be matter, but not fit to be the principle of movement. The seed of men is the principle of movement" (ibid., p. 399).

There were purists among the Aristotelians after Avicenna, for example Ebn Rošd, who held fast to the letter of Aristotle ("As to the 'testicles' which Galen claims women have, it is possible that they play no role in generation—if the 'semen' they produce has no role in generation. This is not strange when you consider that breasts in the female are organs of generation, but do not have such a function in the male.... If the female semen could do what the male can, a female should be able to generate by herself, and there would be no need for the male." Ebn Rošd, *Kollīyāt*, p. 30). However, most medieval Aristotelians, East and West, attest to the success of Avicenna's solution, for they elected to view their biology through him (Sarton, *Introduction* II, 1, p. 63), even though the original Aristotle was available to them in both Arabic and Latin. Avicenna's version was much less vulnerable to Galenic attack than the original.

c. Substitution. Fitting the ovaries into Aristotle's anatomy was the cardinal example of Avicenna's treatment, but—as we have already noted—the first anatomical discussion in the *Ḥayawān* came directly from the *Canon*. Similarly, the chapter on the development of the embryo (book 9, chap. 5, pp. 172-78), and the anatomy of the penis and the uterus (book 15, chap. 1, pp. 387, 388-89, 390) were also taken verbatim from the *Canon*.

The attempt to update Aristotle's data is especially blatant in books 11-14 of the *Ḥayawān*, the sections which parallel Aristotle's *De partibus animalium* (pp. 188-383). Here there took place a wholesale substitution: Most of the original Aristotelian text was simply discarded and replaced by Galenic material lifted out in bulk from the *Canon*. The substituted text included all the anatomy of uniform parts from book 1 of the *Canon* (I, pp. 6-66) and nine sections on the anatomy of the organs from book 3 (II, pp. 2-5, 108-110, 208-10, 261-62, 283-86, 349-50, 418-21, 555-56, and 557-62).

Over seventy-five percent of the text of books 11-14 (150/195 pages) and fully forty percent of the text of the whole *Ḥayawān* (170/433 pages) came from the *Canon*. The transplanted material—aside from its critical implications for the establishment of Avicenna's texts—radically changed the original balance of Aristotle's biology. In Bekker's edition of the greek text of the three treatises, the *De partibus* occupies only twnety-one percent of the pages; in the Cairo edition of the *Ḥayawān*, books 11-14 (representing the *De partibus*) fill forty-five percent of the pages. In the process of updating Aristotle, the space devoted to anatomy was more than doubled.

The *Ḥayawān* changed the emphasis of Aristotle's biology in another important way. Aristotle, although emphasizing man, considered the whole animal kingdom as his subject. The anatomy transplanted from the *Canon* was exclusively human anatomy, tending to narrow the focus of biology from the living creation as a whole to man. This was the clearest effect on natural philosophy of Avicenna the physician.

d. Composition of the *Ḥayawān*. The substitution of the new anatomy for the old carried out—with vengeance—Avicenna's evident design to modernize Aristotle. Yet the size and extraordinary crudeness of this textual transplant are startling, and raise a question about the extent of Avicenna's direct responsibility for it.

The text of the *Ḥayawān* is uneven. Books 1-10 and 15-19 (representing the *Historia* and the *De generatione*) are clearly more finished than books 11-14. Their borrowings from the *Canon* are limited (a total of twenty pages) and well integrated either into genuine summaries of Aristotle (books 1-8 and 15-19), or into a new synthesis (books 9-10). In contrast, the transplanted text of books 12-14 (book 11 poses a special problem to be discussed below) was merely adjusted to the *Ḥayawān*'s different arrangement of subjects, as Table 31 shows.

There is a revealing record of the checkered fortunes of the *Šefā'* in general and the *Ḥayawān* in particular. According to Abū 'Obayd Jūzjānī, Avicenna's companion and biographer, the *Šefā'* took seventeen years to write, with many interruptions, and with the *Ḥayawān* always left to the end. Avicenna worked on the *Šefā'* during three separate periods. The first was in 406/1015: "I asked him to comment on the works of Aristotle... and so he began with the "Physics" of a work he called the *Šefā'*." However, he made little progress and dropped the project for six years. The second period was in 412/1021, when he "finished all of the 'Physics' and 'Metaphysics', with the exception of the book on Animals." Lastly, during his years in Isfahan after

Table 3

CONCORDANCE BETWEEN THE TEXTS OF THE *ḤAYAWĀN* AND THE *QĀNŪN*

Ḥayawān	*Qānūn*
Book 1:	
1. General anatomy, pp. 10-19.	I, pp. 19-24.
Book 9:	
2. Development of the embryo, pp. 172-78.	II, pp. 557-62.
Book 12:	
3. The temperaments, pp. 192-204.	I, pp. 6-13.
4. The humors, pp. 205-18.	I, pp. 17-19, 13-17.
5. The brain, pp. 226-33.	II, pp. 2-5.
6. The nerves and spinal cord, pp. 235-46.	I, pp. 53-59.
7. The bones, pp. 248-49, 251-54.	I, pp. 24-26.
8. The eyes and their muscles, pp. 255-60.	II, pp. 108-10.
9. Movements and muscles of the head, pp. 266-69.	I, pp. 42-43, 40, 41.
Book 13:	
10. The teeth, pp. 270-71.	I, p. 28.
11. The organs of breathing, pp. 277-82.	II, pp. 208-09; I, p. 44; II, pp. 209-10.
12. The heart and its arteries, pp. 283-91.	II, p. 261; I, pp. 59-61; II, pp. 261-62.
13. The organs of digestion, pp. 292-96.	II, pp. 283-86.
14. The intestines, pp. 300-07.	II, pp. 418-21; I, p. 50; II, p. 421.
15. The liver and veins, pp. 308-19.	II, pp. 349-50; I, pp. 62-66.
Book 14:	
16. The collarbone, shoulder, arms, pp. 330-37.	I, pp. 33-37.
17. The spine and neck, pp. 338-41.	I, pp. 28-30.
18. The backbone and the chest-cargo, pp. 342-47.	I, pp. 30-32.
19. The ribs, pp. 348-50.	I, pp. 33, 37.
20. Their muscles, pp. 351-59.	I, pp. 49, 45-49.
21. The leg, pp. 360-69.	I, pp. 37-39, 51-53.
22. The jaw, pp. 376-77.	I, pp. 26-27.
23. The check and lips, pp. 378-81.	I, pp. 41-42.
Book 15:	
24. The penis and the uterus, pp. 387, 388-89, 360.	I, p. 50; II, pp. 555-56.

415/1024, "he finished the *Šefāʾ*, except for the two books on the Plants and the Animals, which he wrote on the way in the year that ʿAlāʾ-al-dawla attacked Sābūr K̲ᵛāst (most probably 423/1032). He also wrote the *Najāt* en route." (Gohlman, Life, pp. 54-67).

Was it true that Avicenna wrote the *Najāt* and the *Ḥayawān* together on the same trip? Curiously the *Najāt*, which he composed by simply selecting material from all parts of the *Šefāʾ*, has preserved no memory of the *Ḥayawān*. It would be easier to understand why the *Najāt* omitted the biology if we were to assume that when he composed it, Avicenna was not working on the *Ḥayawān* and considered it unfinished.

Did Avicenna ever finish the *Ḥayawān*? Here the case of book 11 is the most telling. It exists, if this is the right word, as one paragraph of less than six lines. The nature of this paragraph is not entirely a mystery. In 1021, the second time he began working on the *Šefāʾ*, Avicenna first produced an outline of "the main topics" of the whole work. (When Jūzjānī later said, in his introduction to the *Šefāʾ*, that Avicenna finished the book when he was forty years old—Avicenna was born in 370/980—he could have only been referring to this completed outline.) As it now stands, book 11 represents literally the "main topic" from Avicenna's original outline of 412/1021, and nothing more. The subject of book 11 is of critical importance. In the original *De partibus* it contained Aristotle's theoretical justification for his system of classification and anatomy, and it attracted lengthy commentaries by Ebn Bajja (Avempace) and Ebn Rošd. It is tempting to suggest that when Avicenna and Jūzjānī took the road to Sābūr K̲ᵛāst in 1032, books 11 to 14 of the *Ḥayawān* were still unwritten. Ultimately, books 12, 13, and 14 were "finished" by raiding the *Canon*. But there was no such convenient source for book 11 of the *Ḥayawān*, since Avicenna had not dealt with the subject anywhere else in his writings. Neither Avicenna on the road, nor Jūzjānī after him, ever finished it.

Bibliography: References to Avicenna's works are to the Cairo editions: (1) *Ketāb al-qānūn fi'l-ṭebb*, 3 vols., Būlāq and Cairo, 1877. The *Qānūn* has not been critically edited, and there are differences between the Cairo-Būlāq edition and the Rome edition of 1593. Book 1 is available in English, based on the twelfth-century Latin translation of Gerard of Cremona (with its own departures from the Arabic text) in O. C. Gruner, *A Treatise on the Canon of Medicine, Incorporating a Translation of the First Book*, London, 1930. Gruner omits the anatomy, which is included in M. A. Shah's more recent translation of book 1, *The General Principles of Avicenna's Canon of Medicine*, Karachi, 1966. (2) *Al-Ḥayawān*, section 8 of the *Ṭabīʿīyāt* of the *Šefāʾ*, ed. Montaṣer, Zāyed, and Esmāʿīl, Cairo, 1970. This is easier to read than the Tehran lithograph of 1886 (the *Šefāʾ*, including the *Ḥayawān*, pp. 507ff.), but does not otherwise improve on it, principally because the editors are unaware of the relationship of their text to that of the *Qānūn*. (3) *Ketāb al-nafs*, section 6 of the *Ṭabīʿīyāt* of the *Šefāʾ*, ed. G. C. Anawati and S. Zāyed (Cairo, 1974).

References to the works of Aristotle are to the Loeb Classical Library editions, edited and translated by A. L. Peck, *Historia animalium* (Cambridge and London, 1965-), *Parts of Animals* (Cambridge and London, 1968), and *Generation of Animals* (Cambridge and London, 1942). The Greek text was established by August Immanuel Bekker in the Berlin edition of Aristotle (Berlin, 1831), vol. 1: *Historia*, pp. 486-638, *De partibus*, pp. 639-97, *De generatione*, pp. 715-89. The Arabic translation ascribed to Ebn al-Beṭrīq: *Ṭebāʿ al-ḥayawān* (*Historia*), ed. ʿA. Badawī, Kuwait, 1977; idem., *Ajzāʾ al-ḥayawān* (*De partibus*), Kuwait, 1977, and separately by R. Kruk, Amsterdam, 1978; *Fī kawn al-ḥayawān* (*De generatione*) ed. J. Brugman and H. J. Drossaart Lulofs, Leiden, 1971. Ebn Qayyem Jawzīya quotes from this translation in his *Meftāḥ dār al-saʿāda*, 2 vols., Beirut, repr. of the Cairo edition, n.d. Ebn Rošd defends the original Aristotelian position on sexual generation in his *al-Kollīyāt*, ed. A. Bustani, Spanish Morocco, 1939.

The most important Hippocratic writings for Islamic medicine and biology are *The Seed and The Nature of the Child*, translated by I. M. Lonie in G. E. R. Lloyd, ed., *Hippocratic Writings*, London, 1978. The medieval Arabic translation has been edited by M. C. Lyons and J. N. Mattock, *Ketāb al-ajenna le-Boqrāṭ*, Arabic Technical and Scientific Texts 7, Cambridge, 1978. Galen's *De semine* is in C.G. Kuhn, ed., *Claudii Galeni opera omnia*, 20 vols., Leipzig, 1822, vol. IV, pp. 512-651; his *De placitis Hippocratis et Platonis* has been edited and translated by P. H. De Lacy, *Galen: On the Doctrines of Hippocrates and Plato*, 3 parts, Corpus Medicorum Graecorum, vols. 4, 1, 2, Berlin 1980-84.

ʿAlī b. ʿAbbās Majūsī's *Kāmel al-ṣenāʿa al-ṭebbīya*, 2 vols. Būlāq and Cairo, 1294/1877, was studied by M. Ullmann, e.g., *Islamic Medicine*, Edinburgh, 1978. Avicenna's autobiography, covering his career until the age of 30, and Jūzjānī's biography which covers the rest of his career have been edited and translated by W. E. Gohlman, *The Life of Ibn Sina*, Albany, 1974. The significance of Avicenna's biology for medieval Europe is succinctly stated by G. Sarton, *Introduction to the History of Science*, 5 vols., Baltimore, 1927-48, II, I, p. 63. Islamic medicine after Avicenna is surveyed, with bibliography, in S. H. Nasr, *Islamic Science*, London, 1976, chap. 8. The relation of Avicenna's *Ḥayawān* to Islamic religious thought and to later Islamic natural philosophy is discussed in B. F. Musallam, *Sex and Society in Islam*, Cambridge, 1983, chap. 3, with notes and bibliography.

(B. MUSALLAM)

xi. PERSIAN WORKS.

Only two works in the Persian language by Avicenna have come down to us: a short book entitled *Andar dāneš-e rag* (On the science of the pulse, also known as *Resāla-ye nabż*), and a treatise on philosophy in the broadest sense entitled *Dāneš-nāma* (Book of science).

Authenticity. No problem of authenticity exists in the case of either work. Avicenna's authorship was confirmed by his disciple and friend Abū ʿObayd ʿAbd-al-Wāḥed b. Moḥammad Jūzjānī (Gowzgānī) and has never been called in question (Ebn al-Qefṭī, *Taʾrīḵ al-ḥokamāʾ*, p. 418; Ebn Abī Oṣaybeʿa, *ʿOyūn* II, p. 2; Ẓahīr-al-dīn Bayhaqī, *Taʾrīḵ*, pp. 59-60). The prefaces of the two works show that both were written at the request of ʿAlāʾ-al-dawla Kākūya, the Buyid ruler of Isfahan, i.e., during the last fourteen years of Avicenna's life, which he spent in that city. Comparison of these prefaces, both addressed in eulogistic language to the ruler of Isfahan, indicates that *Dāneš-e rag* was probably composed before the *Dāneš-nāma* because Avicenna states in the preface to the latter that "in that prince's shadow he had achieved all his ambitions—for security, dignity, respect for science. . ." This implies that he had spent many happy years at Isfahan before he completed the *Dāneš-nāma*.

General description. Avicenna's writings in Arabic, the language of religion and scientific expression in the entire Muslim world at that time, were intended for his disciples and other specialists and may be described as "advanced textbooks." In marked contrast, his two books in Persian, the spoken and literary language of the Iranian peoples, are introductory manuals written for the use of an uninitiated person and possessing the appropriate qualities: Clear language, near-colloquial phraseology (Arabic technical terms being replaced with Persian equivalents in the *Dāneš-nāma* and given together with Persian equivalents in *Dāneš-e rag*), choice of themes and questions which give access to relatively elementary knowledge in each field, exclusion of subjects which could only be of interest to specialists, reduction of chapter lengths, and frequent use of explanatory description rather than logical definition. These are among the common characteristics of the two works. The contents of each are outlined below.

Andar dāneš-e rag (ed. S. M. Meškāt, *Rag-šenāsī yā resāla andar nabż*, Tehran, 1330 Š. /1952, with a list of technical terms). The book's first three chapters are a prologue to its main subject, study of the pulse. They describe (1) the substances which, when in harmonious synthesis, constitute the human body, the vital spirits which animate it, and the soul (*ravān, nafs*) which dwells in it; (2) the necessity of inhalation, nutrition, and elimination; (3) the functions of the lungs, heart, and arteries as regulators of the pulse, illustrated by the example of the blacksmith's bellows, and the way in which, at every beat, these regulators cause movements of expansion and contraction, each followed by a pause.

The study of the pulse as such is commenced in chapter four and pursued in chapters five and six. Here the author gives simplified summaries of the thorny problems which he had examined in detail in the first chapter of the third lesson of the eleventh section (*fann*) of the first volume of the *Qānūn fi'l-ṭebb*, namely, (1) why every beat comprises the aforesaid four moments; (2) a list of ten types of pulse condition with descriptions of symptoms which permit diagnosis of each; (3) explanation of the causes of these ten types and of varieties and sub-varieties to be found in each, together with the appropriate Persian and Arabic technical terms, such as long (*derāz*) pulse and short (*kūtāh*) pulse in conditions identifiable by the length (*andāza*) of the beat, rapid (*tīz*) and slow (*derangī*) in conditions identifiable by its frequency, even (*hamvār*) and uneven in conditions identifiable by the symmetry or dissymmetry (*mostawī-mānanda būdan wa nabūdan*) of the beats. Chapter seven is a summary of the discussion of regular and irregular (*mostawī wa mok̲talef*) pulse behavior in the second chapter of the above-mentioned third lesson in the *Qānūn*, and chapter eight, which enumerates varieties and name of composite pulse conditions, is a summary of the third chapter of the same lesson. Some of the descriptive terms for pulse conditions used in this book correspond to those used in modern medical textbooks, e.g., *mūrčagī* (Ar. *al-namlī*, formicant), *setabr 'aẓīm* (large), *dom-e mūšī* (myurous), *mawjī* (bounding, undulating) *do-zak̲mī* (dicrotic).

Chapter nine, which concludes the work, is a summary of all the questions studied in the remaining sixteen chapters of the lesson in the *Qānūn*, namely, the best pulse condition, the constituents of the pulse, the factors which influence these constituents, the pulse in males, females, and pregnant females, the pulse in different ages, life-stages, seasons, temperatures, and temperaments, and the effects of climates, sleep, being awake, bathing, physical exercise, pain, inflammations, and emotions on the pulse.

This short book's plan of three introductory chapters, three chapters on the more difficult problems, and one final chapter dealing concisely with easier matters shows that Avicenna intended it to be a condensed synopsis. He accomplished his task with great skill.

Dāneš-nāma. This work, like the *Šefā'* and the *Najāt* (but unlike the *Ketāb al-ešārāt* which deals only with logic and metaphysics) is a comprehensive treatise on seven sciences grouped in four sections: logic (ed. S. M. Meškāt and M. Mo'īn, *Manṭeq-e Dāneš-nāma-ye 'alā'ī*, Tehran, 1331 Š./1952), metaphysics (ed. M. Mo'īn, *Elāhīyāt-e Dāneš-nāma-ye 'alā'ī*, Tehran, 1331 Š./1952), natural science (ed. S. M. Meškāt, *Ṭabī'īyāt-e Dāneš-nāma-ye 'alā'ī*, Tehran, 1331 Š./1952) and mathematics (the last-named consisting of geometry, astronomy, arithmetic, and music). The original section on mathematics was lost in Avicenna's lifetime, and the extant text (ed. M. Mīnovī, *Rīāżīyāt-e Dāneš-nāma-ye 'alā'ī*, Tehran, 1331 Š./1952) is a reconstituted version which his disciple 'Abd-al-Wāḥed Jūzjānī put together by translating into Persian the master's short monographs on the same subjects. (The original Arabic monographs constitute the mathematical section of the *Ketāb al-najāt*, which was not edited by Avicenna himself).

The *Dāneš-nāma* should not be compared with the *Šefā'*, an encyclopedic work in which the number and diversity of the problems and theories under discussion is very great and the number of the chapters is very large. Although comparable to the *Najāt* in general content, the *Dāneš-nāma* differs from it in the relative lengths and specific topics of the chapters and the order of the sections. Its exposition of logic, in two parts on definition and proof respectively, follows the plan of the *Ešārāt* rather than that of the *Najāt*. Although most of its chapters are summaries or abridgments of chapters in the *Najāt*, there are some which give longer and fuller explanations. The abridgment is generally done through combination of two or more chapters into a single chapter with a composite title, e.g., the chapter on "Explanation of genus, species, difference, common property, and accident" (*Bāz namūdan-e jens, naw', faṣl, k̲āṣṣa wa a'rāż-e 'āmm*). In some cases, however, the abridgment is done through suppression of chapters interesting only to academicians and specialists, e.g., that on the theory of the contents of propositions and the three modalities of judgment (possible [*šāyad būdan, momken*], necessary [*żarūrī*], and impossible [*na-šāyad būdan, momtane'*]). This theory, which is one of the bases of Avicenna's logic of judgment, receives only ten lines of explanation in the *Dāneš-nāma* compared with ten pages in the *Najāt* and twelve pages in the *Ešārāt*. Also drastically pruned is the treatment of contradiction and conversion, which are here reduced to their absolute forms; Avicenna preferred to omit from the *Dāneš-nāma* any discussion of contradiction and conversion in modal propositions. The discussion of the four figures of the syllogism is equally brief. On the other hand, Avicenna writes at considerable length in this book on a subject passed over in silence in the *Ešārāt*, namely reasoning by analogy (*meṯāl*); he here denounces this method of reasoning dear to the scholastic theologians whom he describes as "dialecticians" (*jadalīān*). He also writes at some length on the "subject-matter of the syllogism," one of his main innovations which forms the epistemological aspect of his logic and is its most strikingly original contribution, being concerned with search for the sources of human knowledge and evaluation of its degrees of certainty.

As regards metaphysics, a noteworthy feature of the *Dāneš-nāma* is the placing of this subject immediately after logic, whereas in both the *Najāt* and the *Šefā'* the metaphysical discussions form the concluding and crowning section of the work. The different arrangement in the *Dāneš-nāma* is not fortuitous. This book was written in order to acquaint an uninitiated mind with the notion of science and its subject and object, and with the division of the sciences into speculative and practical disciplines and the subjects and objects of each. For this purpose there was need of an introductory prologue which could only be placed straight after the section on logic and at the head of the section on metaphysics. The generalized outline of the subjects and objects of the sciences leads on to define explanations of the subject of higher science (*'elm-e barīn*), i.e., metaphysics, namely, being qua being, and of its object, namely, the states of being qua being. These states are presented as pairs of opposites. They provide the chapter headings and the content of the metaphysical section of the work as follows: substance (*jawhar*) and accident (*'araż*), universal (*kollī*) and particular (*joz'ī*), single (*wāḥed*) and multiple (*kaṯīr*), cause (*'ellat*) and effect (*ma'lūl*), action (*fe'l*) and potentiality (*qowwa*), possible (*momken*) and necessary (*wājeb*); these are predicates of being qua being.

By starting with the study of substance and accident as the first pair of states of being qua being, Avicenna breaks more frankly here than in the *Šefā'* with the Aristotelian conceptions and traditions regarding the theory of substance and its categories of accidents and the position of these ten highest genera of "things." In the *Dāneš-nāma* he integrates this study with metaphysics, while in the *Najāt* he examines the categories together with the thoery of definition in the section on logic. Now this idea of substance and its nine categories conceived as the ten highest genera of "things" is directly linked to another idea which is fundamental to Avicenna's metaphysics, i.e., the idea of the accidentality of existence; for saying that such and such a substance or accident exists is tantamount to saying that existence is not the element which constitutes the essence (quiddity) of any of these ten highest genera of "things," in other words that existence is not logically conceivable as other than an accidental predicate of the essence. The presentation of this original theory is all the more noteworthy because Avicenna begins his discourse with a criticism of "persons who lack sharp insight," i.e., scholastic theologians, in the *Najāt* called *motakallemān*. At the same time this idea of existence as an accidental predicate of the essence is closely connected with the last pair of states of being qua being, namely the contingent and the necessary.

The study of these two states forms the introduction to the second area of metaphysics, which Avicenna calls "the science of divine sovereignty." Forty chapters are devoted to the search for the Necessarily Existent Being (*Wājeb al-wojūd*) and His attributes (*ṣefāt*. These chapters occupy more than two thirds of the metaphysical section of the *Dāneš-nāma* and form the longest dissertation in the whole book. The relative extent of the section is a measure of the importance which Avicenna attached to it and the more remarkable because the book does not contain any lengthy chapters (such as are found in the *Šefā'* and the *Najāt*) on purely theological matters like human bodily resurrection, divine inspiration, proofs of prophethood, etc. This makes the treatment of metaphysics more akin to that in the *Ešārāt* than that in the *Najāt*. Moreover, the *Dāneš-nāma* sometimes echoes the former's directives (*ešārāt*), notably those of chapter six on the purposes of principles and order and chapter seven on detachment (*tajrīd*).

The most distinctive feature of the *Dāneš-nāma*, however, is its style, which is much simpler, easier, less formal, and more lively than that of the Arabic works. In this book Avicenna again takes issue with his adversaries, the scholastic theologians. In the *Najāt* he describes some of them as "weak" (*żo'afā' al-motakallemīn*) (*Najāt*, p. 213), but here he goes further and speaks disparagingly of them as "dialecticians" (*jadalīān*). He ironically ridicules their method of proving the existence of the invisible (*ḡāyeb*), from the existence of the witness (*šāhed*), and in a pretended exposition of their reasoning, ascribes to them actions which expose the logical absurdity of their words, for example in the section on logic (*manṭeq*): "Then they went and gazed at the sky and found that it resembled a house..." (pp. 96 ff.). Many more words and phrases carry, in the context, an ironic sting, e.g., "they thought of a subterfuge," "some who were a little wilier" (ibid., p. 98). In the section on metaphysics, the criticism is directed at Plato and the Platonic "ideas." In the *Najāt* Avicenna alludes discreetly and very briefly to the Platonic "ideas." In the *Šefā'* he devotes a rather long and very closely and forcefully reasoned chapter to their refutation. In the *Dāneš-nāma* he does not refute them but ridicules them. He invites us to imagine the idea of an "idea," that of a unique and real "humanness" (*mardomī*) which would exist per se (*be-'aynehī*) in every human individual and would be Plato after acquiring knowledge and someone else if remaining ignorant. Even more astonishing would be the idea of "animal," at once mobile and immobile, flying and flightless, quadruped and biped.

In conclusion, it must be emphasized that the *Dāneš-nāma* is an original work and that its originality does not lie solely in its being written in Persian. After the *Ešārāt*, which Avicenna composed in the same period of his career, it is the most personal of his writings. His intention to give this book a different stamp from his other works is revealed by his preference for certain themes and the number and length of the chapters which he devoted to them, notably to contingent and necessary, cause and effect, and the Necessary Being and His attributes. Another feature is that he does not include under metaphysics any discussion of extra-philosophical theses such as life after death, missions and miracles of prophets, and marvels of saints, but only touches very briefly on these matters in the section on natural science. His great veneration for Aristotle, "the chief of the sages" (*emām-e ḥakīmān*), "the guide and master of the philosophers" (*dastūr o āmūzgār-e fīlsūfān*) (*Elāhīyāt*, p. 110; *Ṭabīʿīyāt*, pp. 59 and 90), his spontaneous humor, and his genial irony with regard to the scholastic theologians (*motakallemān* or *jadalīān*) give us clues to understanding of the man. This book was, of course, written for a patron who must be spared the bother of reading pedantic disquisitions. Even so, and despite all the abridgments and suppressions, nothing of real importance is omitted. It is a comprehensive treatise on philosophy, unique in its kind among Persian writings in this field.

Editions of the Dāneš-nāma-ye ʿalāʾī. 1. Lithographed, under the title *Māya-ye Dāneš-e ʿalāʾī mašhūr be'l-Ḥekmat al-ʿalāʾīya*, Hyderabad (Deccan), 1309/1891, comprising three parts—logic, metaphysics, and natural science. Marred by too many errors, but noteworthy as the first published edition. 2. Edited by A. K̲orāsānī under the title *Dāneš-nāma-ye ʿalāʾī yā ḥekmat-e Bū ʿAlī*, Tehran, 1315 Š./1926. Critical text based on four mss., comprising two parts—logic (*manṭeq*) and metaphysics (*ʿelm-e barīn*)—preceded by a preface made up of (1) K̲orāsānī's translations of the autobiography of Avicenna and the supplementary biography of him by Abū ʿObayd b. ʿAbd-al-Wāḥed Jūzjānī (Gawzgānī), (2) some poems attributed to Avicenna, namely, two short pieces in Arabic and four quatrains and a short piece about wine in Persian, (3) a list of Avicenna's works, and (4) a brief study of features of the language of the *Dāneš-nāma* and a glossary of the Persian technical terms in the *Dāneš-nāma* with their Arabic equivalents. 3. Edited by M. Moʿīn and S. M. Meškāt, published for the Avicenna Millenary celebration at Tehran in 1331 Š./1952; consists of the first three parts in separate volumes, namely, (1) logic (*Resāla-ye manṭeq*), ed. Moʿīn and Meškāt, (2) metaphysics (*Elāhīyāt-e Dāneš-nāma-ye ʿalāʾī*), ed. Meškāt, (3) natural science (*Ṭabīʿīyāt-e Dāneš-nāma-ye ʿalāʾī*), ed. Meškāt. The critical text based on ten mss. on the whole concurs with that of K̲orāsānī despite numerous variants. Appended to each volume is a combined list of Persian and Arabic technical terms in alphabetic order.

The language aspects of the *Dāneš-nāma* and of *Andar dāneš-e rag*, above all the originality of their Persian vocabulary, were noted by K̲orāsānī and are of great interest to Iranian philologists. This subject was discussed in two communications to the Avicenna Millenary conference at Tehran, one by Ḥ. K̲aṭībī on Avicenna's Persian prose style in the context of the Persian prose of the late 4th/10th and early 5th/11th centuries, the other by M. Moʿīn on Avicenna's Persian vocabulary and its influence on Persian literature (see D̲. Ṣafā ed., *Jašn-nāma-ye Ebn Sīnā* II, Tehran, 1334 Š./1955, pp. 316-28, 342-90). Holding that the Persian language at the time when Avicenna wrote was more influenced by Pahlavi than by Arabic, Ḥ. K̲aṭībī credited Avicenna with the invention of Persian scientific-philosophic terminology and diction; he cites as examples of the distinctiveness of Avicenna's prose style the frequent use of the particles *mar* and *andar*, of the verbal prefix *hamī* instead of *mī*, and the word order of the often terse, but always precise, sentences. M. Moʿīn studied Avicenna's creation of a Persian scientific-philosophic vocabulary, his sources and methods, and the varieties of this vocabulary used by his disciples in their translation of his works and later by other thinkers such as Nāṣer (-e) K̲osrow, Afżal-dīn (Bābā Afżal) Kāšānī, and Abū Ḥāmed Moḥammad Ḡazālī.

Translations of the Dāneš-nāma-ye ʿalāʾī. 1. Arabic. The *Maqāṣed al-falāsefa* of Moḥammad Ḡazālī (d. 505/1111) may be regarded as the Arabic translation of the *Dāneš-nāma* because its structure and content are in general on the same lines. 2. French. Translation of all four parts by M. Achena and H. Massé, under the title *Le livre de science*, 2 vols., Paris, 1955-58; vol. I logic and metaphysics, vol. II natural science and mathematics. Appended to vol. I is an analysis of the metaphysics by Achena. A revised and corrected new edition came out in 1985; to this has been added a prolog comprising translations of Avicenna's autobiography and Jūzjānī's biography, an introduction to the logic, and a revised and amplified version of the same analysis of the metaphysics as in the first edition. 3. English. Translation with commentary by P. Morewedge, entitled *The Metaphysica of Avicenna (Ibn Sīnā): A Critical Translation-Commentary and Analysis of the Fundamental Arguments in Avicenna's Metaphysica in the Dānis̲h̲ Nāma-i ʿAlāʾī*, PHS, London, 1973. [The present writer has not seen this book.] 4. Russian. Translation by Bugutdinov, Stalinabad (Dushanbe), 1973.

Avicenna's Persian poems. Avicenna is the reputed author of Persian quatrains and *qeṭʿas* (short poems) quoted in anthologies and miscellanies. Their number and quality vary with the source. There is every reason to believe that Avicenna possessed poetic talent and wrote poems in his spare time, particularly when in captivity. This is attested by the undoubtedly authentic opening verses which are all that remain of two Arabic odes (*qaṣīdas*) which he composed (see *Le livre de science*, Prolog, p. 11). That he should have written poems in Persian, his native and everyday language, is probable, but can not be proved. H. Ethé collected twelve quatrains and two *qeṭʿas* which are ascribed to Avicenna in anthologies and other sources, and published the texts with German translations (*Nachrichten von der Kgl. Gesellschaft der Wissenschaften und der Georg-August-Universität zu Göttingen*, no. 21, 1 September 1875, pp. 555-67). E. G. Browne gives translations of two quatrains from Ethé's collection (*Lit. Hist. Persia* II, pp. 108-109, 267). S. Nafīsī included in his book on Avicenna's life and works (*Pūr-e Sīnā*, Tehran, 1333 Š./1954) all poems known to have been ascribed to Avicenna, with particulars of the source of each. It may be added that the Bibliothèque Nationale in Paris possesses the following two manuscripts: (1) ms. Suppl. Pers. 793, a small anthology which, on folio 103, contains the quatrain "*Mā-īm be-loṭf-e to tamannā karda*" found in many anthologies and attributed in some to Avicenna, in others to K̲ayyām, and following it a quatrain attributed to Abū Saʿīd b. Abi'l-K̲ayr (cf. Nafīsī, op. cit., p. 47); (2) ms. Suppl. Pers. 1777, a selection of poems by three poets, Qāsem al-Anwār, ʿAṭṭār, and Nāṣer K̲osrow, in which have been inserted, on the margin of folio 326, six quatrains said to be by Avicenna, though none is cited by Nafīsī. This manuscript is dated 25 Ṣafar 825/1422. D̲. Ṣafā has published a collection of Persian poetry ascribed to Avicenna (*Jašn-nāma-ye Ebn Sīnā* I, Tehran, 1331 Š./1952, pp. 111-15).

Apocryphal treatises. At the time of the millenary celebrations in 1331 Š./1952, the Anjoman-e Āṯār-e Mellī (q.v.) in Tehran published a series of Persian *resāla*s (treatises), all short, which are stated in the manuscripts to be from the pen of Avicenna. All, however, contain evidence which throws doubt on the attribution, and none are mentioned in the list of Avicenna's works. G. Lazard had demonstrated the spuriousness of these *resāla*s in a detailed study ("Publications iraniennes à l'occasion du millénaire d'Avicenne," *REI* 22, 1954, pp. 153-55). Brief indications of the content of each are given below.

(1) *Resāla-ye nafs*, ed. M. ʿAmīd, Tehran, 1331 Š./1952. This is in fact one of two existing Persian translations of Avicenna's Arabic treatise on the soul, which bears six different titles in different manuscripts (see Y. Mahdawī, *Ketāb-šenāsī-e Ebn Sīnā*, Tehran, 1333 Š./1954, p. 244). ʿAmīd states that all the manuscripts which he used in preparing his edition attribute the translation to Avicenna himself. The language of this translation, however, differs greatly from that of the *Dāneš-nāma*, being full of Arabic words and technical terms not found in corresponding passages in the latter, such as *edrāk* (perception) on p. 19 instead of *andaryāft* as in the *Dāneš-nāma*, *Ṭabīʿīyāt*, p. 101; *qowwat-e ʿāmela* (agential faculty) on p. 24 instead of *qowwat-e konā'ī*; *qowwat-e ʿālema* (cognitive faculty) on p. 24 instead of *qowwat-e andaryāft-e naẓarī*. Furthermore we know from a statment of the translator of the other Persian version that Avicenna did not personally translate his treatise from Arabic into Persian; in the words of this translator in his preface, "A learned man had translated this *resāla* (here entitled *al-Maʿād*) into Persian, but on comparing the translation with the original text he found it defective, erroneous, and incomplete, and therefore, at a friend's request, made a new and more complete and accurate translation" (see Mahdawī, op. cit., p. 247).

(2) *Resāla andar ḥaqīqīyat wa kayfīyat-e selsela-ye mawjūdāt wa tasalsol-e asbāb wa mosabbabāt* (Treatise on reality and the mode of connection of beings and the interconnection of causes and effects), ed. M. ʿAmīd, Tehran, 1331 Š./1952. This *resāla* is written in the form of questions and answers—a form not normally used by Avicenna. It is certainly apocryphal, not only because the vocabulary and phrasing, the constant reference to the Koran and citation of its verses in support of arguments, and the imprecision and logical unsoundness of the premises and inferences are untypical of Avicenna's authentic works, but above all because the assertions contradict Avicenna's teachings. The words *mostaʿār* (borrowed or metaphorical), *mostafād* (understood), *jā'ez* (allowed), *jā'ez al-wojūd* (allowed to exist), which recur from the answer to the first question onward, are not only un-Avicennian but also have meanings which conflict with Avicenna's concepts of *momken* (potential) and *momken al-wojūd* (potentially existent). The question whether the existence of the creator can be inferred from that of created beings is answered with the assertion of creation ex nihilo (*ebdāʿ*), which the Ashʿarite theologians postulated and Avicenna always rejected, counterposing his own theory of process (*ṣonʿ*) (*Dāneš-nāma*, [*Manṭeq*, *rāh-e jadalīān* ...] p. 95; *Ešārāt*, the whole chapter "Fi'l-ṣonʿ wa'l-ebdāʿ;" and especially "Tanbīh," p. 153).

(3) *Meʿyār al-ʿoqūl* (Assay of minds), ed. J. Homā'ī, Tehran, 1331 Š./1952. The subject-matter, which is far removed from Avicenna's interests, and the use of Arabic terms such as *ṣolb* (spine), *ṯeql* (weight), *rasan* (rope), which are not found in Avicenna's Persian prose, are sufficient proof of the inauthenticity of this *resāla*.

(4) *Qorāża-ye ṭabīʿīyāt* (Scrap of the natural science), ed. Ḡ. -Ḥ. Ṣadīqī, Tehran, 1331 Š./1952. In the first lines of his preface the editor acknowledges that this *resāla* has nothing in common, aside from the form, with Avicenna's Persian works. The presentation of problems, the advocacy of certain theories such as the teleological theory, the abundance of Arabic terms, and the peculiarities of the language, all prove that this short treatise is spurious.

(5) *Konūz al-moʿaẓẓamīn* (Treasures for great men), ed. J. Homā'ī, Tehran, 1331 Š./1952, a small manual on practical use of charms. There is also an Arabic version entitled *al-Nīranjāt* (Mahdawī, op. cit., p. 251). On the ground that all the manuscripts bear Avicenna's name, Homā'ī thought that this *resāla* must be authentic. It is difficult, however, to believe that Avicenna, who placed treatises on logic at the head of all his philosophical works and based his logic on axioms of pure reason, could have been led to teach magic arts with such conviction. Further proofs of inauthenticity are the differences of style and language from those of Avicenna's Persian writings, and the advice given in the preface to "keep this book away from the indiscretion of unqualified and unworthy persons."

(6). *Resāla-ye jūdīya*, ed. M. Najmābādī, Tehran, 1330 Š./1951, a short advice-book on prevention and, above all, cure of afflictions ranging from sneezes to fly-swarms and including snake-bites. The editor, himself a doctor of medicine, is to be commended for the painstaking erudition with which he explains and comments on the recommended remedies. He accepts the attribution to Avicenna as authentic, and thinks that the title ought correctly to be *Resāla-ye maḥmūdīya* because the work is dedicated to the sultan Maḥmūd Ḡaznavī. Its prose, however, is in no way comparable with that of Avicenna's Persian works, and its counsels and remedies are too simple and credulous to be from the pen of any medical practitioner, even a country doctor, let alone the author of the canon of medicine. The dedication linking Avicenna to the sultan Maḥmūd is a further illustration of the forger's naïveté.

(7) *Ẓafar-nāma*, ed. Ḡ. -Ḥ. Ṣadīqī, Tehran, 1331 Š./1952, a small collection of maxims said to have been enunciated by Bozorgmehr in reply to questions put to him by K̲osrow I Anōšīrvān. If so, it must have been translated from a Pahlavi text. The only external source in which the translation is attributed to Avicenna is Ḥājjī K̲alīfa's *Kašf al-ẓonūn*, according to which the Samanid prince Nūḥ b. Manṣūr commissioned his minister Ebn Sīnā to render this collection of maxims from Pahlavi into Persian. All the evidence points to a confusion or a fictitious attribution. Avicenna did not know Pahlavi and was not Nūḥ b. Manṣūr's minister. Moreover, the language is not comparable with that of Avicenna's Persian works. Ṣadīqī writes interestingly on possible explanations in his excellent preface.

To the above list must be added a *resāla* called *Meʿrāj-nāma* [not seen by the present writer]. According to Mahdawī (op. cit., p. 297), the text has twice been published: first in facsimile, secondly in print ed. by Ḡ.-Ḥ. Ṣadīqī in the Anjoman-e Āṯār-e Mellī series (Tehran, 1331 Š./1952. For a further list of works in Persian attributed to Avicenna see D̲. Ṣafā, *Tārīk̲-e ʿolūm-e ʿaqlī dar tamaddon-e eslāmī* I, 4th ed., Tehran, 1356 Š./1977, pp. 231-35 and idem, ed., *Jašn-nāma* I, pp. 57-63.

Bibliography: Works by Ebn Sīnā; *Dāneš-nāma-ye ʿalāʾī*, ed. S. M. Meškāt and M. Moʿīn, repr. Tehran, 1353 Š./1974. *Ketāb al-najāt*, Cairo, 1960 *Ketāb al-šefāʾ*, Cairo, 1952-83. *Ketāb al-ešārāt wa'l-tanbīhāt*, ed. Forget, Leiden, 1892. *Al-Qānūn fi'l-ṭebb*, Būlāq, 1294/1877; Eng. tr. by Q. C. Gruner. Ẓahīr-al-dīn Bayhaqī, *Taʾrīk̲ ḥokamāʾ al-eslām*, Damascus, 1946. Ebn Abī Oṣaybeʿa, *Oyūn al-anbāʾ fī ṭabaqāt al-aṭebbāʾ*, ed. von Müller, Cairo, 1299/1882. Ebn al-Qefṭī, *Taʾrīk̲ al-ḥokamāʾ*, Leipzig, 1903. Ṣafā, *Adabīyāt* II, pp. 625-28.

(M. ACHENA)

xii. THE IMPACT OF AVICENNA'S PHILOSOPHICAL WORKS IN THE WEST

Western European acquaintance with Avicenna began when Latin versions of some of his Arabic works came out in the period between the mid-twelfth and the late thirteenth century. These versions were products of a great translation movement which brought into being a large corpus of philosophical and scientific literature of Greek, Arabic, and Jewish origin and greatly influenced medieval thought in the thirteenth century.

The best known of Avicenna's philosophical works in the Middle Ages was his encyclopedic *Ketāb al-šefāʾ* (Book of healing). This consists of a biography of Avicenna in a preface by his pupil Jūzjānī and of four *Summae*, i.e., collections (*jomal*, sing. *jomla*), dealing with particular disciplines, namely logic, physics, mathematics, and metaphysics. Each *jomla* is divided into *fonūn* (sing. *fann*), i.e., specialities or sections. Almost all of the Physics (*Ṭabīʿīyāt*, i.e., branches of natural science) and the whole of the Metaphysics (*Elāhīyāt*, i.e., branches of knowledge of God) were translated into Latin. The Mathematics (*Rīāżīyāt*) were not translated. The only parts of the Logic (*Manṭeq*) which were translated were the introduction (*Madk̲al*), a chapter from section 5 on proof (*borhān*, i.e., by syllogism), and two passages from section 8 on rhetoric (*k̲eṭāba*); in all, about one tenth of the Arabic text.

Some of the translations were made during the second half of the twelfth century at Toledo, namely, (1) the introduction (*Madk̲al*) to the Logic, preceded by the preface to the *Šefāʾ* and the chapter from the section on proof; (2) from the Natural Science, three quarters of section 1 (*al-fann al-awwal*) on physics in the strict sense (*al-Samāʿ al-ṭabīʿī*) and section 6 (*al-fann al-sādes*) which forms the Treatise on the Soul (*Ketāb al-nafs*); (3) the entire Metaphysics, i.e., the whole of the fourth *jomla*.

Section 8 (*al-fann al-ṯāmen*) of the Natural Science, which forms the Treatise on Animals (*Ḥayawān*) was translated about 1230 for the emperor Frederick II, King of Sicily.

The two passages on rhetoric were translated about 1240 for John, Bishop of Burgos.

Also at Burgos, translation of the Natural Science was resumed under the auspices of Bishop Gonzalvo Garcia de Gudiel, beginning with the part of section 1 which had been left unfinished at Toledo: Despite the work done at Burgos, the Latin text does not amount to a full translation of the Arabic text. The other translated parts of the Natural Science are sections 2, 3, 4, and 5, on the Heaven and the World (*al-Samāʾ wa'l-ʿālam*), Generation and Corruption (*al-Kawn wa'l-fasād*), Actions and Reactions arising from elemental qualities (*al-Afʿāl wa'l-enfeʿālāt*), and Meteorology, i.e., atmospheric phenomena (*al-Āṯār al-ʿolwīya*), respectively. Three chapters of the last-mentioned section had been separately translated toward the end of the twelfth century; we thus have a version of this part earlier than the Burgos version.

Section 7 of the Natural Science, which constitutes the short Treatise on Plants (*al-Nabāt*), was translated under the title *Liber de vegetabilibus*; this title is mentioned in the inventory of the great fourteenth-century library of the Sorbonne compiled in 1338, but it has not yet come to light (M. Th. d'Alverny, *Notes*, p. 348).

The names of almost all the chief translators of the *Šefāʾ* (though not of their assistants) are definitely known. They were Avendauth, an "Israelita philosophus," and the archdeacon Dominic Gundisalvi or

Gundissalinus, both mentioned in the letter dedicating the Treatise on the Soul to the archbishop John of Toledo; Michael Scotus, who dedicated the Treatise on Animals to Frederick II; Master John Gunsalvi and Salomon, mentioned in the part of the Natural Science translated at Burgos; Herrmann the German, mentioned in the preface to his translation of Aristotle's Rhetoric into which he inserted passages from Avicenna's *Šefā'*; and Alfred of Sareshel or Alfred the Englishman, the translator of the three extracts from the Meteorology (section 5 of the Natural Science).

On the other hand, the Latin manuscripts give contradictory indications of the role of Gerard of Cremona, who resided at Toledo contemporaneously with Dominic Gundisalvi and translated Avicenna's *Canon* on medicine. Some of the Latin terms used in the translation of the Metaphysics suggest that perhaps Gerard had a hand in it, but only one of the twenty-four known manuscripts names him as the translator. In three other manuscripts the translation is attributed to Dominic Gundisalvi, but these are not independent sources (Van Riet, *Liber de philosophia prima* I-IV, p. 123).

In addition to the *Šefā'*, another philosophical work by Avicenna was known to the medieval Europeans, namely *al-Adwīa al-qalbīya* (Medicaments of the Heart), an essay on certain subjects also discussed in the *Ketāb al-nafs*. This short work was translated into Latin early in the fourteenth century by Arnaud de Villeneuve at Barcelona in 1306. Avicenna's disciple Jūzjānī had inserted a part of the essay into the Arabic text of the *Ketāb al-nafs* in view of the relatedness of the subject matter, and these chapters had already been translated into Latin at the same time as the whole of the *De anima* in the twelfth century (Van Riet, *De medicinis cordialibus, fragmentum*, in *De anima* IV-V, pp. 98*-99*, 115*-118*, 187-210).

Finally there are mentions of two more works of Avicenna in the book *Pugio fidei* written by the Dominican friar Raymond Martin in 1278. One is the *Alixarat*, i.e., the *Ketāb al-ešārāt wa'l-tanbīhāt*; the title is interpreted by Raymond Martin as *Liber invitationum vel nutuum* or as *Liber invitationum et exercitationum*, and ten lines in Latin translation are quoted. The other is *Annage*, i.e., *al-Najāt*, one page of which is translated into Latin (Cortabarria, *L'étude des langues*, pp. 233-34).

Avicenna's philosophical works formed the core of a large body of literature comprising other translations from Arabic and compilations in which Avicenna's translated writings were lumped together with texts of Christian and Neoplatonist authors. Dominic Gundisalvi himself also translated the *Summa philosophiae* of Algazel (Ḡazālī) and the *Fons vitae* of Ebn Gabirol, and reputedly compiled several treatises containing quotations of paraphrases from works by Avicenna such as *De anima* and *De divisione philosophiae*.

There is general agreement that a work falsely attributed to Avicenna, bearing the title *Liber Avicennae in primis et secundis substantiis et de fluxu entis* should be placed in the category of compilations modeled on those of Dominic Gundisalvi. This work is included in the *Opera philosophica* of Avicenna printed at Venice in 1508 (pp. 64v-67v). Other copies with the title *De causa causarum et fluxu earum* were made and are to be found following *De anima* in several manuscripts (d'Alverny, *Les traductions d'Avicenne*, p. 81; cf. *Avicenna latinus*). As Gilson (*Les sources gréco-arabes*, pp. 92-93) observed, "it is almost certainly a Christian work written by an author who borrowed at random from writings of Dionysius, St. Augustine, Erigena, and Avicenna. Such unthinking and unrestrained imitation of Avicenna only appeared in the last two-thirds of the 13th century." The author propounds the concept of the soul's illumination through a separate substance, as taught by Fārābī and Avicenna, and attempts to synthesize this with St. Augustine's teaching; Avicenna's active intellect (*dator formarum*) is identified with St. Augustine's illuminator-God, who thus becomes the active intellect of the human species. The complex of ideas prevalent in this historic phase, as attested by the syntheses of Arab and Christian Neoplatonism, is called "Avicennizing Augustinism" by Gilson (op. cit., p. 103) and "Latin Avicennism" by de Vaux (*Notes et Textes*, pp. 63f.). These terms are questioned by certain historians of thirteenth-century philosophy (Van Steenberghen, *La philosophie*, pp. 17-18 and 185-87). In any case the doctrine identifying the active intellect, as a separate substance, with the Father of Light or Word of God continued for decades to be attractive to many minds, e.g., Roger Marston and Marsilio Ficino (Goichon, *La philosophie d'Avicenne*, pp. 113-14).

In the first third of the thirteenth century, Avicenna's works were no longer studied only in connection with writers of Neoplatonic inspiration such as pseudo-Dionysius, St. Augustine, John Duns Scotus, or Erigena; they were also used in the study of Aristotle. Avicenna's own paraphrases of Aristotle "met the needs of the first Aristotle-interpreters until superseded by Averroes's literal commentaries. Before the Western Christians became acquainted with Averroes, Avicenna's influence on Latin Aristotelianism was very marked" (Van Steenberghen, *La philosophie*, pp. 186-87).

As early as 1210, a synod at Paris banned the reading of Aristotle's "libri de naturali philosophia" and "commenta" thereon. In 1215 the ban was reaffirmed and clarified by Robert de Courcel, the legate of Pope Innocent III, in one of the regulations specifying what might be taught in the faculty of arts: "Non legantur libri Aristotelis de metaphisica et de naturali philosophia nec summae de eisdem" (Aristotles' books on metaphysics and natural philosophy must not be read, nor the "summaries" of same). Historians suggest somewhat divergent explanations of these bans, having regard to the circumstances and to the identities of the suspect teachers (Amaury of Bène, David of Dinant, and others), but all agree that the words "commenta" and "summae" refer definitely, if not exclusively, to the paraphrases of Avicenna. It is noteworthy that the prohibition applied only to the teaching of these texts, not to personal reading and use of them, and that its scope was strictly local. Thus in 1229 the books of Aristotle and commentaries thereon which were under interdict at Paris could be read and taught at the nascent university of Toulouse (Van Steenberghen, *La philosophie*, p. 92).

Several writers active about 1240, such as Guillaume of Auvergne, Alexandre of Hales, Jean of La Rochelle, show in their comments or censures that they had precise knowledge of Avicenna's *De anima*, of his analysis of the faculties of the soul, his theory of abstraction, and his classification of intellects.

Various works of Avicenna enter prominently into the great philosophical-scientific encyclopedia of Albertus Magnus, who started work on it toward the middle of the thirteenth century, just at the time when Aristotelianism was triumphing at Paris. His wish was to "rehash Aristotle for use by the Latins" and to "place within reach of the studious all the scientific findings made by the human mind up to his own time" (Mandonnet, *Siger* I, pp. 37-39). Rather than the literal commentaries on Aristotle's works, he cites the paraphrases of Avicenna. He also makes frequent use of Avicenna's own works, most often not explicitly, in quotations which have not yet all been identified (Van Riet, *Liber de philosophia prima* I-IV, pp. 159*-163*). The philosophy of Albertus Magnus, as presented in his encyclopedia, may therefore be described as a Neoplatonized , and above all Avicennized, Aristotelianism (Van Steenberghen, *La philosophie*, p. 303).

Thomas Aquinas's writings contain more than 400 explicit quotations of Avicenna, drawn mainly from *De anima* (section 6 of *De naturalibus*) and the *Metaphysica* and in some cases from the Physics in the strict sense (*Sufficientia*). On the basis of a solid exegesis of Aristotle made in the light of Averroes' criticisms, Thomas Aquinas endorses or rejects the quoted theses of Avicenna, thereby putting them into sharper perspective. He does this in his discussions of God the Creator, God's providence, the real distinction between essence and existence in finite beings, the analogy of being, and the notion of the necessary (which he drops in his list of the transcendental attributes) (Verbeke, *Le statut*, p. 36).

Following the examples set by Albertus Magnus and Thomas Aquinas after him, it became customary to incorporate the gist of the Toledan translations of Avicenna and also materials from the *Liber de animalibus* in large-scale syntheses and thus to engulf them in a mass of texts of other authors such as Aristotle, Boethius, Proclus, and Averroes. This at least facilitated comparisons of different doctrines, with fruitful effects on the works of later writers such as Henry of Ghent, Godefroid of Fontaines, John Duns Scotus, Marsilio Ficino, Caietano, and others. Avicenna's future standing in the West was to be tied to that of the works in which so many ideas taken from him had been integrated (Goichon, *La philosophie*, p. 127).

Less is known about the process of diffusion of the *Libri naturales*, sections 2 to 5, which were translated at Burgos after the death of Thomas Aquinas in 1274 and probably not long before that of Albertus Magnus in 1280. The texts of these books are not included in the *Opera philosophica* of Avicenna printed at Venice in 1508 and have not yet been systematically studied.

In the sixteenth century, several short philosophical works of Avicenna were translated from Arabic into Latin by the physician-philosopher Andrea Alpago of Belluno, but these new translations did not have any leavening effect on contemporary Western thought.

The tally of the work done in the past thirty years gives promise of a revival of Avicennian studies in the West in the coming decades, with particular attention to the *Šefāʾ*. The new Arabic edition of the *Šefāʾ*, which the Ebn Sīnā Committee at Cairo began to publish in 1952, was completed with the printing of the *Physics* (*al-fann al-awwal men al-Ṭabīʿīyāt*) in 1983. This edition provides the essential basis for studies of the Latin versions. The inventory of the Latin manuscripts begun by M. d'Alverny in 1952 has also been completed. The first critical editions of *De anima* and the *Metaphysica*, prepared by S. Van Riet, came out in 1968-72 and 1977-80-83 respectively. A critical edition of the *Libri naturales* is in progress.

Bibliography: Andrea Alpago, *Avicenna philosophi... Compendium de anima. De Mahad... Aphorismi de anima. De diffinitionibus et quaesitis. De divisione scientiarum...*, Venetiis, apud Juntas, 1546. M.-Th. d'Alverny, "Notes sur les traductions médiévales d'Avicenne," *Archives* 19, 1952, pp. 337-58. Idem, "Avendauth," in *Homenaje a Millas Vallicrosa* I, 1954, pp. 19-43. Idem, "Les traductions d'Avicenna (Moyen Age et Renaissance)," in *Avicenna nella storia della cultura medievale*, Accademia Nazionale dei Lincei 304, 1957, pp. 71-87. Idem, "Avicenna Latinus I à XI," *Archives* 28-39, 1961-72. Idem, "Les traductions d'Avicenne. Quelques résultats d'une enquête," *Correspondance d'Orient*, no. 11 (Actes du Ve congrès international d'arabisants et islamisants), Brussels, 1970, pp. 151-58. L. Baur, Dominicus Gundissalinus, "De divisione philosophiae," *Beiträge zur Geschichte der Philosophie des Mittelalters* IV, 2-3, Münster, 1903. A. Cortabarria Beitia, "L'étude des langues au Moyen Age chez les Dominicains," *MIDEO* 10, 1970, pp. 189-248. Ét. Gilson, "Avicenne et le point de départ de Duns Scot," *Archives* 2, 1927, pp. 89-149. Idem, "Les sources gréco-arabes de l'augustinisme avicennisant," *Archives* 4, 1929, pp. 5-149. A. M. Goichon, *La philosophie d'Avicenne et son influence en Europe médiévale*, 2nd ed., Paris, 1951. P. Mandonnet, *Siger de Brabant et l'averroïsme latin au XIIIe siècle*, Louvain, 1908-11. J. T. Muckle, "The treatise 'De Anima' of Dominicus Gundissalinus," *Mediaeval Studies* 2, 1940, pp. 23-103. S. Van Riet, *Avicenna latinus. Édition critique de la traduction latine médiévale: Liber de anima seu Sextus de naturalibus* I-V, Louvain and Leiden, 2 vols., 1968-72; *Liber de philosophia prima sive scientia divina* I-X, 2 vols., Louvain and Leiden, 1977-80; *Lexiques*, 1 vol., Louvain-la-Neuve and Leiden, 1983. F. Van Steenberghen, *La philosophie au XIII siècle*, Philosophes médiévaux 9, Louvain and Paris, 1966. C. Vansteenkiste, "Avicenna-citaten bij S. Thomas," *Tijdschrift voor Philosophie* 15, 1953, pp. 457-507. R. de Vaux, *Notes et textes sur l'avicennisme latin aux confins des XIIe-XIIIe siècles*, Bibliothèque Thomiste 20, Paris, 1934. G. Verbeke, "Introductions doctrinales" in *Avicenna latinus*, ed. S. Van Riet: "Une conception spiritualiste de l'homme" in *De anima*, 1968, pp. 1*-73*; "Science de l'âme et perception sensible" in *De anima*, 1972, pp. 1*-90*; "Le statut de la métaphysique" in *Liber de philosophia prima*, 1977, pp. 1*-122*; "Une nouvelle théologie philosophique" in *Liber de philosophia prima*, 1980, pp. 1*-80*.

(S. Van Riet)

xiii. The Influence of Avicenna on Medical Studies in the West

From the early fourteenth to the mid-sixteenth century Avicenna held a high place in western European medical studies, ranking together with Hippocrates and Galen as an acknowledged authority. His works had a formative influence on the scholastic medicine of the later Middle Ages, and at some places continued to be used for teaching up to the eighteenth century.

Although Avicenna was more of a philosopher and natural scientist than a physician, the Europeans saw him primarily as the *princeps medicorum* (prince of physicians), in contrast with the Muslims who revered him as the *šayk̲-al-ra'īs* (chief master, i.e., of all the sciences). It is not yet possible, however, to assess his impact on the rise of scientific medicine in the West because systematic studies of the various fields are still, on the whole, lacking. A catalogue of the manuscripts of Latin versions of Avicenna's writings on medicine is still a desideratum, and there is no critical bibliography of the printed editions which came out in the fifteenth, sixteenth, and seventeenth centuries.

Three medical works by Avicenna were available in Latin versions in the later Middle Ages: *al-Qānūn fi'l-ṭebb*, a five-book medical encyclopedia translated as *Canon medicinae* and provided with a glossary by Gerard of Cremona (d. 1187) at Toledo in the second half of the twelfth century; *al-Adwīa al-qalbīya*, a treatise on psychiatry translated as *De viribus cordis* (On the powers of the heart) by Arnald of Villanova (d. 1311) at Barcelona in 1306; *al-Orjuza fi'l-ṭebb*, a medical manual in verse rendered into Latin prose under the title *Cantica* by Arnald's nephew Armengaud Blasius (d. 1312) at Montpellier in 1294, together with Ebn Rošd's commentary thereon. The last two translations were wrongly attributed to Gerard in certain early printed editions.

The *Canon* translation was one of the fruits of the endeavors of the twelfth-century Toledan school of translators to open up the whole range of Arabic learning. They took particular interest in philosophical and theoretical writings. This phase in the Western reception of Greco-Arabic medicine had been preceded in southern Italy about a century earlier by one of greater concern with practical matters. Starting from Salerno, early scholastic medicine with a scientific approach based on Arabic material had spread into the medical schools and the new universities of France and Italy (Baader, "Reformdenken," pp. 268f.), preparing the ground for acceptance of the *Canon*. This work met the needs of the new scholastic medicine in three respects: (1) with its immense wealth of information, it provided Western physicians with a synopsis of virtually all the knowledge amassed in the preceding 1500 years and stimulated them to work further on their own; (2) with its systematic incorporation of every subject, down to the smallest detail, in a well-ordered theoretical framework, it greatly facilitated the adoption of its contents for teaching and at the same time satisfied the scholastic liking for a logical classification of subject matter; (3) last but not least, Avicenna linked the medicine of Galen to the natural philosophy and theory of science of Aristotle, who from the thirteenth century onward dominated intellectual life in Europe. Avicenna's Aristotelian views on basic questions of biology (e.g., the central organ of the body, the roles of the sexes in reproduction) provided starting points for discussions, typical of the scholastic medicine of the time, about the discrepancies between philosophers and physicians, i.e., between Aristotle and Galen, and thereby prompted new efforts to solve old problems.

The *Canon* came into use among medical scholars during the thirteenth century (mainly the second half) and in university courses during the fourteenth century, when commentaries providing the groundwork for interpretation by professors (*magistri*) first became available. Key roles in this field appear to have been played by pupils of Taddeo Alderotti (d. 1295) at Bologna, particularly by Dino del Garbo (d. 1327) who for the first time systematically elucidated large parts of the *Canon* (Siraisi, pp. 96f., 105-09). As to the first introduction of the *Canon* into academic curricula, direct evidence is lacking for the Italian universities. The earliest testimony is a syllabus for mastership candidates at the university of Montpellier included in a papal bull of 1309. The *Canon* is recommended in this document as one of a number of optional textbooks. By 1340, however, it had been firmly established in the various course programs. Arabic science was long to maintain a strong position at Montpellier, where lectures on Avicenna's works often went far beyond what was required by the syllabus; as late as 1545 he still clearly ranked above the ancient Greek authorities (Germain, *La médecine*, pp. 9-12). At Paris the *Canon* is first mentioned as lecture material in 1330, and it also appears in the library catalogue of the medical faculty made in 1395 (Seidler, *Die Heilkunde*, pp. 49f.). Following the example of Paris, German universities founded in the fourteenth and fifteenth centuries also admitted the *Canon* to their programs of study.

Academically trained physicians in the later Middle Ages undoubtedly were familiar with the entire *Canon*. Lectures, however, were concentrated on certain parts of the work, with slight local variations in choice and range. The compulsory teaching matter always included the part on physiology in the first *fen* (transcription of the Arabic *fann*) of book 1, which expounds the general principles of medicine, and the theory of fevers (*Canon* 4.1), sometimes together with the theory of crises (4.2). Often the three remaining *fens* of book 1—on etiology and symptomatology, dietetics and general therapy—were also prescribed. Book 3, on the specifics of pathology and therapy, was by reason of its vast range less often used as lecture material, and then only in excerpts, but it was a favorite source for examination questions. In some universities book 2 on materia medica was read together with other pharmaceutical treatises of Arabic origin. For surgical training, in so far as this took place on the academic level, Avicenna's surgery (*Canon* 4.3-5) was among the standard textbooks.

This selection was of course influenced by the wealth of commentaries on the *Canon*, which in the absence of a systematic inventory (a first attempt by Eckleben has left many gaps) can not yet be adequately surveyed. The most numerous are exegeses of *Canon* 1.1 and 4.1. No Latin commentary on the entire work is known to exist. The most comprehensive commentary, produced by Jacques Despars (d. 1458) after more than twenty years' work and printed *in toto* at Lyons in 1497-98, deals only with *Canon* 1.3 and 4 (Jacquart, *Un médecin*, pp. 109-12). Outstanding among the numerous exponents who wrote in the heyday of *Canon*-exegesis in the fourteenth and fifteenth centuries were certain professors of the then pre-eminent north Italian universities, whose commentaries were widely used as textbooks and quite frequently printed after the introduction of printing in the mid-fifteenth century. In addition to Dino del Garbo (see above), Gentile of Foligno (d. 1348), Ugo Benzi of Siena (d. 1439), and Jacopo of Forlì (d. 1414) dealt with several parts of the *Canon*; others, like Giovanni Matteo Ferrari of Grado (d. 1472) and Giovanni Arcolani (d. 1458), commented only upon individual sections. Leonardo of Bertapaglia wrote a commentary on the surgical chapters in 1424 (Thorndike, *Science and Thought*, pp. 60-65). As Jacquart (*Le regard*, pp. 43-76) has shown in the case of Despars, the exegetic writings were often amplified with personal observations and experiences of their authors. These hitherto neglected sources are therefore likely to provide interesting evidence of the ways in which the *Canon* stimulated new developments in Western medicine. It was a main source for many medical manuals and monographs and it was sometimes also taken as a model of form; for example, the collection of medical counsels by Ferrari of Grado (Venice, 1514 and several times reedited) is arranged according to the method of Avicenna.

The *Canon* was one of the medical books most frequently printed in the fifteenth and sixteenth centuries. Incunabula from before 1500 were for the most part printed in Italy; they comprise eleven complete editions (among which the five-volume Venice edition of 1490-95 is supplemented with commentaries by various authors) and two partial editions. The earliest printed edition (1472) consists only of *Canon* 3, the Bologna edition (1482) only of *Canon* 4.1, 3-5. A Hebrew version was printed at Naples in 1491-92. Up to 1608, fourteen more complete editions of the Latin version were printed, including three with commentaries, as well as an epitome by Michael Capella (*Flores Avicennae*, Lyons, 1508, 1514) and an alphabetically arranged adaptation by Gabriel of Tarrega (Bordeaux, 1520, 1524). To these must be added excerpts published in compilations, particularly collected doctrines of the three principal authorities, Avicenna, Galen, and Hippocrates, and the lemmata in the numerous commentaries. The original Arabic text was printed at Rome at 1593, but like all products of the Medici press was intended primarily for export to the East.

Most of the printed editions of the *Canon* included two other works of Avicenna which played a minor role in university teaching. These were *De viribus cordis* (initially in the Paduan edition of 1476, but also printed separately at Lyons in 1527 with a commentary by Jaime López of Calatayud) and the *Cantica* (initially in the Venetian edition of 1482-83). The *Cantica* and Ebn Rošd's (Averroes') commentary on them were printed together at Venice, 1483, and in Ebn Rošd's *Opera* at Venice, 1484, and were included with the other principal texts from the *Canon* in some printings of the textbook *Articella* (e.g., Venice, 1509; Lyons, 1519, 1534).

From the end of the fifteenth century onward, efforts were made to remedy the linguistic deficiencies of the medieval version of the *Canon*, e.g., its clumsy word-for-word renderings and many transliterated borrowings of Arabic terms. Andrea Alpago (d. 1522), who had acquired a deep understanding of both the language and the subject during his thirty years of service as physician to the Venetian embassy at Damascus, supplied emendations derived from Arabic manuscripts to the Latin versions of the *Canon*, the *Cantica*, and *De viribus cordis* (which he more accurately entitled *De medicamentis cordialibus*), and compiled a new glossary, mainly of Arabic names of drugs. His corrections were published posthumously in 1527 by his nephew Paolo in the first edition of the *Canon* from the Giunta press at Venice (d'Alverny, "Avicenne," pp. 184-89). The later Giuntine editions of the 1544, 1555 (reprinted at Basel in 1556), 1562, 1582, 1595, and 1608 were based on Alpago's revised text, from 1555 onward augmented by marginal notes—taken from Alpago's manuscript—by Benedetto Rinio, which show parallel readings in ancient Greek and Arabic works (d'Alverny, pp. 196f.). To facilitate reference, an index by Giulio Palamede was also printed (Venice, 1557, 1584).

Alpago's was to be the only textual revision of the entire *Canon*. Andrea Grazioli brought out a new version of only book 1 (Venice, 1580) based on an unfinished translation by Girolamo Ramnusio (d. 1486), Alpago's predecessor at Damascus (d'Alverny, pp. 182-84). Another translation by Miguel Jerónimo Ledesma (Valencia, 1546) went no further than *Canon* 1.1. Jacob Mantino's translations of *Canan* 1.4 (five editions between 1530 and 1555) and Canon 3.1.1.29 (on headache; Bruges, 1538) and the translation of excerpts from Canon 3.1-2 by Jean Cinqarbres (Paris, 1570, 1572) are not from the original Arabic but from the Hebrew version, while Jean Bruyerin's new rendering of the book on heart drugs (Lyons, 1559) was from the Arabic.

Western Europe also has to thank Andrea Alpago for his translation of two other medical treatises by Avicenna, *De removendis nocumentis quae accidunt in regimine sanitatis* (On harmful things in the regulation of health which have to be prevented—*Daf' al-mażārr al-kollīya 'an al-abdān al-ensānīya*) and *De syrupo acetoso* (On oxymel—*sekanjabīn*), as well as the only Latin versions of two Arabic commentaries on the *Canon*, those of Qoṭb-al-dīn Šīrāzī on books 2, 3, and part of book 4, and of Ebn al-Nafīs on book 5 (pharmacopeia), in which, incidentally, there is no mention of Ebn al-Nafīs's discovery of pulmonary circulation. These four texts were published by Paolo Alpago at Venice in 1547; the first two were also appended to several later editions of the *Canon*.

But even the availability of these new texts and the improved versions of previously known works could not arrest the growing rejection of Avicenna's authority in the universities. In the context of humanist efforts to reform medicine, criticism of the *Canon* spread and gained strength in the course of the sixteenth century. The most spectacular onslaught was the public burning of the *Canon* by Paracelsus in the Midsummer-Day bonfire at Basel in 1527—though a gesture admittedly motivated by his rejection of all written authorities, and by no means typical of the age. In general the humanist critics of Arabic medicine, who made Avicenna their prime target, strove for a revival of ancient Greek and Roman medicine. Scholars such as Niccolò Leoniceno, Giovanni Manardi, Symphorien Champier, Janus Cornarius, and Leonhart Fuchs, who were intent on demolishing the medieval system, dismissed its textbooks of Arabic origin as verbal and factual misrepresentations of ancient teachings and replaced them by newly recovered Greek and Latin medical writings. Their criticism of detail focused mainly on Avicenna's prescriptions, where the indications and dosages differed from the ancient traditions. On the other hand, Avicenna's innovations were praised as practical advances by his defenders, such as Sébastien Monteux, Bernhard Unger, and Lorenz Fries.

Although the scholastic features of academic medicine were not finally discarded until the eighteenth century, in the choice of subjects for study it was the humanistic tendency that prevailed. In the second half of the sixteenth century, the *Canon* gradually fell out of the syllabus at most European universities, though it was still taught by individual professors, e.g., by Werner Rolfinck at Jena in 1670. It remained obligatory well into the eighteenth century at the Spanish universities of Valladolid and Salamanca (Gonzalez, p. 20) and likewise at Padua, where Giovanni Battista Morgagni, the founder of morbid anatomy, still lectured on its first book in 1712-15—just as Santorio Santorio, one of the pioneers of experimental medicine, had done a century before him (Pazzini, "Manoscritti," pp. 179-82). It would appear, however, that these teachers used the set text mainly as background for the presentation of more recent knowledge; for example, Santorio in his commentary (Venice, 1625, 1626) describes instruments which he himself had invented (clinical thermometer, pulse meter).

Work on the preparation of more accurate Latin versions continued in the seventeenth century. Preoccupation with Arabic on the part of physicians seeking better comprehension of the *Canon* even contributed to the advance of Arabic philology at that time (Fück, pp. 57-59). In 1624 Zacharias Rosenbach attempted to introduce an Arabic language course for medical students at the Herborn academy (Grün, pp. 64f.). In 1609 Peter Kirsten, a physician of Breslau, brought out an Arabic-Latin edition of the materia medica (*Canon* 2). Vopiscus Fortunatus Plemp, who lectured on Avicenna at the university of Louvain, could not fulfill his plan to retranslate the whole of the *Canon* but published new translations of books 1 and 2 and part of book 4 in 1658. At Paris in 1659 a translation by Pierre Vattier of 16 chapters from *Canon* 3.3-4 on mental diseases (one of the highlights of the work on account of its penetrating differentiations) appeared under the title *De morbis mentis*. Georg Hieronymus Welsch in his *Exercitatio de vene medinensi* (Augsburg, 1674), an overexpanded commentary on Avicenna's short discussion of the Medina worm (*Canon* 4.3.8.4), quotes passages in the original Arabic accompanied by his own translations. Finally Avicenna's didactic poem *al-Orjūza* was retranslated into Latin by the Netherlander Anton Deusing under the title *Canticum* (Groningen, 1645). These philological as well as medical contributions already mark the transition to a purely historical interest in the *Canon*.

Bibliography: M.-Th. d'Alverny, "Avicenne et les médecins de Venise," in *Medioevo e rinascimento. Studi in onore di Bruno Nardi*, Florence, 1955, pp. 177-98 (Pubblicazioni dell'Istituto di Filosofia dell'Università di Roma 1). G. Baader, "Medizinisches Reformdenken und Arabismus im Deutschland des 16. jahrhunderts," *Sudhoffs Archiv* 63, 1979, pp. 261-96. S. Brentjes, "Spuren des Einflusses wissenschaftlicher Schriften aus der islamischen Welt auf den Lehrbetrieb an der Universität Leipzig im 15. und 16. Jahrhundert," *Schriftenreihe für Geschichte der Naturwissenschaften, Technik und Medizin* 17/2, 1980, pp. 59-64. L. Dulieu, *La médecine à Montpellier*, Paris, I, 1975, pp. 88-94; II, 1978, pp. 140-50. W. Eckleben, *Die abendländischen Avicenna-Kommentare*, Leipzig, 1921 (doctoral thesis). L. Elaut, "Der Avicenna-Kommentar des Chirurgen Leonardo da Bertapaglia," *Sudhoffs Archiv* 41, 1957, pp. 18-26. J. Fück, *Die arabischen Studien in Europa bis in den Anfang des 20. Jahrhunderts*, Leipzig, 1955, pp. 45-55, 57-60. A. Germain, *La médecine arabe et la médecine grecque à Montpellier*, Montpellier, 1897. R. Gonzalez Castrillo, *Rhazes y Avicena en la Biblioteca de la Facultad de Medicina de la Universidad Complutense*, Madrid, 1984, pp. 27-35, 135-334. H. Grün, "Die Medizinische Fakultät der Hohen Schule Herborn," *Nassauische Annalen* 70, 1959, pp. 55-144. D. Jacquart, "Un médecin parisien du XVe siècle: Jacques Depars (1380-1458)," *École nationale des chartes, positions des thèses... de 1971*, Paris, pp. 107-13. Idem, "Le regard d'un médecin sur son temps: Jacques Despars (1380?-1458)," *Bibliothèque de l'école des chartes* 138, 1980, pp. 35-86. F. Klein-Franke, *Die klassische Antike in der Tradition des Islam*, Erträge der Forschung 136, Darmstadt, 1980, pp. 17-53. F. Lucchetta, *Il medico e filosofo bellunese Andrea Alpago* (†1522), *traduttore di Avicenna*, Padua, 1964 (index, s.v. Avicenna). A. Pazzini, "I manoscritti 'laurenziani' di G. B. Morgagni, noti, ma ignorati," *Rivista di storia delle scienze mediche e naturali* 44, 1953, pp. 165-86. H. Schipperges, "Zur Rezeption und Assimilation arabischer Medizin im frühen Toledo," *Sudhoffs Archiv* 39, 1955, pp. 261-83. Idem, *Die Assimilation der arabischen Medizin durch das lateinische Mittelalter*, Sudhoffs Archiv, Beiheft 3, Wiesbaden, 1964 (index, s.v. Avicenna). E. Seidler, *Die Heilkunde des ausgehenden Mittelalters in Paris*, Sudhoffs Archiv, Beiheft 8, Wiesbaden, 1967, pp. 49-50, 58-61. N. G. Siraisi, *Taddeo Alderotti and his Pupils*, Princeton, 1981 (index, s.v. Avicenna). L. Thorndike, *Science and Thought in the Fifteenth Century*, New York and London, 1963, pp. 59-80, 268-77. S. Van Riet, "Trois traductions latines d'un texte d'Avicenne 'Al-Adwiya al-qalbiyya'," *Actas do IV Congresso de Estudos Árabes e Islâmicos, Coimbra-Lisboa 1968*, Leiden, 1971, pp. 339-44. E. Wickersheimer, "Une liste, dressée au XVe siècle, des commentateurs du Ier Livre du Canon d'Avicenna et du livre des Aphorismes d'Hippocrate," *Janus* 34, 1930, pp. 33-37. Idem, Die 'Apologetica epistola pro defensione Arabum medicorum von Bernhard Unger aus Tübingen (1533)," *Sudhoffs Archiv* 38, 1954, pp. 322-28.

(U. WEISSER)

ĀVĪŠAN, wild thyme. The genus *Thymus* of the family *Labiatae* (Mint) comprises a number of fragrant aromatic undershrubs, with very small leaves and whorls of small purplish, nectar-bearing flowers in the axils of the leaves or at the ends of the branches. The Kotschy thyme (*āvīšan-e bārīk, Thymus kotschyanus* Boiss. et Hohen., locally called *avīšam, avšam, ābšan, āyšūm* [Alborz, Lār], *odšan, ūšan, ošna-ye kūhī, ṣaʿtar, kaklik-oti* [Šarafḵāna in Azerbaijan], *kālvāš* [some northern districts], *āzorba* [Ganjnāma of Hamadān, used for both *Thymus kotschyanus* and *Thymus serpillum*], *jowšan-e šīrāzī* [in the bazaars of Tehran], Ar. *ṣaʿtar/saʿtar*) is a low perennial, strongly aromatic, wild undershrub with many varieties distributed in the higher regions of northwest Iran, in the Alborz mountains, and in Khorasan. Dried leaves and floral tops, which contain oil of thyme, are used for flavoring soups, sausages, sauces, and various vegetable and meat dishes. Aqua or *ʿaraq-e āvīšan*, used for flavoring sherbets, is obtained by soaking dried leaves and floral tops in water. Around Tehran dried *āvīšan* is used with a refreshing drink made of a mixture of yogurt, water, and salt (*dūḡ*).

Mother-of-thyme (*Thymus serpillum*, locally *ošm, ošma, āzorba*) in another widespread thyme of Iran. Both thymes are carminative, stomachic, diuretic, digestive, and flatulent. They may be used for liver and respiratory disorders. *Maḵzan al-adwīa* (p. 256) and *Toḥfa-ye Ḥakīm Moʾmen* (pp. 563-64) attribute the aperitive, diuretic, vermifuge, emmenagogue, and anti-acid properties of thyme.

Āvīšan-e Šīrāzī is one of the species of the genus Zataria.

Bibliography: M. ʿAlī-Akbar Khan Āšpaz-bāšī, *Sofra-ye aṭʿema*, Tehran, 1353 Š./1974, p. 83. J. Jalas, "Thymus," in K. H. Rechinger, *Flora Iranica*, Cont. 150, Graz, 1982. Ḥakīm Moḥammad Moʾmen Tonokābonī, *Toḥfa-ye Ḥakīm Moʾmen*, Tehran, (1402/1981. Sayyed Moḥammad-Ḥosayn ʿAlawī Ḵorāsānī Šīrāzī, *Maḵzan al-adwīa* together with *Qarābādīn-e kabīr*, Tehran, 1349 Š./1970, p. 273. Ḥ. Ṯābetī, *Deraḵthā wa deraḵtčahā-ye jangalī-e Īrān* (Forest trees and shrubs of Iran), 2nd ed., Tehran, 1355 Š./1976, pp. 747ff.

(R. A. PARSA)

AVROMAN (Hawrāmān, Persian Owrāmān), a mountainous region on the western frontier of Persian Kurdistan. It extends for approximately 50 km, from a point west of Marīvān (46° 0′ east longitude, 35° 30′ north latitude) south-eastwards to the confluence of the two branches of the river Sīrvān (46° 20′ east longitude, 35° 10′ north latitude). The Kūh-e Owrāmān range has several peaks of over 2,000 m, the highest being Kūh-e Taḵt, 2985 m. It is continued south of the Sīrvān by the Kūh-e Šāhō, which rises to 3,223 m. Parallel to these, east of the Sīrvān, is the Kūh-e Sālān, 2,597 m. The chief products of the area are various orchard fruits, walnuts, gall-apples (for tanning), and terebinth mastic.

The territory has four divisions: Owrāmān-e Lohon, southwest of the main range; main village, Nowsūd: Owrāmān-e Taḵt, north of Kūh-e Taḵt; main village, Šahr (Šār)-e Owrāmān: Dezlī, further north: Razāb (Razāw), around the Kūh-e Sālān. The population of the valley numbers perhaps 10,000 persons. They are distinguished from the Kurds, who surround them on all sides, to some extent by their traditional dress, but especially by their language (see Avromani), which is an archaic dialect of the Gōrāni group. They pay allegiance to branches of the Bagzāda family, which traces its descent back through at least three centuries in the first instance, and ultimately to legendary kings of Iran. The chieftains often use the title Sān, i.e., sultan, dating from Safavid times. The main divisions are the Ḥama-Saʿīd-Sānī family in Lohon, the Ḥasan-Sānī in Taḵt, the Bahrām-Bagī in Dezlī, and the Moṣṭafā-Sānī in Razāb. At the beginning of this century all branches of the Bagzāda family succeeded in extending their sway over a number of non-Avromani villages adjoining their homelands. The Lohoni branch, in particular, acquired Bīāra and Tawēla, both the seats of Naqšbandī shaikhs, among other villages in Iraq, and Pāva, to the south of the Sīrvān. (The men of Pāva, like their neighbors of Ḥajīj in Lohōn proper, are known as wandering pedlars, who formerly traveled the length and breadth of the Caliphate.) With the increase of the power of central government in Iran and Iraq after the First World War, however, their depredations ceased and several chieftains were dispossessed and exiled.

Bibliography: C. J. Edmonds, *Kurds, Turks, and Arabs*, London, 1957 (index s.v. Hewrámán). M. Mardūḵ Kordestānī, *Ketāb-e tārīḵ-e Mardūḵ* II, Tehran, n.d.

(D. N. MacKenzie)

AVROMAN DOCUMENTS, three parchments found in a cave in the Kūh-e Sālān, near Šār-e Owrāmān (see Avroman), and brought in 1913 by Dr. Saʿīd Khan Kordestānī to London, where they were acquired by the British Museum. Two of the documents, dated 225 and 291 of the Seleucid era (= 88-87 and 22-21 B.C.), are written in Greek, one with a barely legible Parthian endorsement. The third, dated in (H)arwatāt of the year 300, presumably of the Arsacid era (= January-February, A.D. 33), is in Parthian. The Greek documents are deeds of sale of half a vineyard (*bāḡ*, *raz*) called Dādbakān (GK. Dadbakabag, Dadbakanras) belonging to the village Kop(h)anis, which may have been the modern Kōpī in Qara Dāḡ, the range west of the Šahrezūr plain. In the Parthian document, however, another name occurs: it appears to refer to "a half part of the vineyard Asmak, which (is) by the ploughland" (*KRMʾ ʾsmk MH ʾbykškn PLG yʾt*) being sold by Pātaspak, son of Tīrēn, from Bōd (*ptspk BRY tyryn ZY MN bwdy*) to Awīl, son of Bašnīn, and his brother (*ʾwyl BRY bšnyn nzd ʾḤY*) for 65 drachmae. Several witnesses are named.

The discovery of these documents may also have given rise to the modern legend that a Kurdish parchment dating from the time of the Muslim invasion has been discovered in the area. The published "early Kurdish" text of this fictional document is completely spurious.

Bibliography: E. H. Minns, "Parchments of the Parthian Period from Avroman in Kurdistan," *Journal of Hellenic Studies* 35, 1915, pp. 22-65. C. J. Edmonds, "The Place-names of the Avroman Parchments," *BSOAS* 14, 1952, pp. 478-82. W. B. Henning, "Mitteliranisch," pp. 28-30. D. N. Mackenzie, "Pseudoprotokurdica," *BSOAS* 26, 1963, pp. 170-73. See also Ph. Gignoux, *Glossaire des inscriptions pehlevies et parthes*, Corp. Inscr. Iran., suppl. ser. I, London, 1972, pp. 43-44.

(D. N. MacKenzie)

AVROMANI, the dialect of Avroman (q.v.) properly Hawrāmi, is the most archaic of the Gōrāni (q.v.) group. All Gōrāni dialects exhibit a number of phonological features which link them with the dialects of central Iran and distinguish them from Kurdish. While the main Gōrāni language area, to the west of Kermānšāh, is an island in a sea of chiefly Kurdish dialects, the Hawrāmān now forms a separate islet to the north. It is clear, however, that the neighboring Kurdish dialects have encroached on a much wider Gōrāni area and have been considerably affected in the process. There has also been much interchange of vocabulary.

Phonologically Hawrāmi is distinguished from Kurdish and Persian alike by (i) the preservation of initial *y-* and *w-*, (ii) the development of *hw-* to *w-*, (iii) *wy-* to *y-*, (iv) *x-* to *h-*, and (v) *dw-* to *b-*, e.g. (i) *yawa* 'barley', *yahar* 'liver', *wā* 'wind', *wahār* 'spring', *wīs* 'twenty', (ii) *wārday* 'to eat', *wāstay*, *wāz-* 'to want', *witay*, *ūs-* 'to sleep', *wē-* 'self', (iii) *yāgē* 'place', *yāw-* 'arrive' (< **wy-āp-*), (iv) *har* 'ass', *hāna* 'spring, source', (v) *bara* 'door'. In common with Kurdish, etc., it has (vi) the preservation of *s*, *z* < IE, *ḱ*, *ǵ* and (vii) the development of *j-* to *ž-*, e.g., (vi) *āsin* 'iron', *āska* 'gazelle', *zānāy* 'to know', *zamā* 'bridegroom', (vii) *žanī* 'woman', *žīw-* 'to live'. The preservation of intervocalic *-č-*, especially in some verb stems, is noteworthy, e.g., *sōč-* 'burn', *wāč-* 'speak', *wēč-* 'sift'; otherwise to *-ž*, or lost, e.g., *tēž* 'sharp', *miž-* 'to suck', *rō* 'day' (perhaps loanwords).

The vowel system comprises seven long and three short vowels, with a distinction, morphologically important, between open and close *e* and *o*, thus *ī ē ɛ̄ ā ɔ̄ ū*, *i a u*. The consonant phonemes, 26 in number, are similar to those of the neighboring Kurdish dialects, particularly the continuant allophones of *d* and *t*, the distinction between flapped *r* and rolled *r̄*, and *l* and *ł*. Stress plays a vital part in the morphology, often distinguishing otherwise identical forms, e.g., *č'anī* 'needle': *čan'ī* 'with', *lū'ɛ̄* 'they went': *l'ūɛ̄* 'if he had gone' (cf. *lū'ē* 'he was going').

The dialect preserves a distinction of number (singular and plural), gender (masculine and feminine), and case (direct and oblique) for nouns, pronouns, and adjectives (including the "indefinite article" suffix, masc. *-ēw*, fem. *-ēwa*): thus, *kitēb* (*-ēw*) *-ī sī'āw* '(a) black book', plur. *kitēbē sī'āwē*, *tawanī* (*tawanēwa-y*) *sī'āwa* '(a) black stone', plur. *tawanī sī'āwē*, obl. *ja tawanē sī'āwē* 'from black stone'; *dagā-y gawr'ē* 'a big village', plur. *dagɛ̄ gawr'ē*. Besides the epithetic particle *ī* there is a genitival (*eżāfa*) *ū*: *yāna-y* (*yānēw-ī*) *gawr'a* '(a) big house', *yāna-w šūān'ay* 'the shepherd's house'.

In conjunction with various defining and pronominal suffixes these endings form some very intricate inflexional patterns.

The verbal system presents further complications, having two distinct sets of personal endings used with each of the present and past stems. They are (i-a) Present sing. 1 -*ū*, 2 -*ī*, 3 -*ō*, plur. 1 -(*y*)*mē*, 2 -(*y*)*dē*, 3 -*ā*, (i-b) Imperfect, -'*ēnē*, -*ēnī*, -*ē*, -*ēnmē*, -*ēndē*, -*ēnē*, (ii-a) Past, -*ā*(*nē*), -*ī*, -*ϕ* masc. ~ -*a* fem., -*īmē*, -*īdē*, -*ē*, and (ii-b) Past Conditional *ɛ̄nē*, etc. (like i-b).

The copula is characterized by the presence of *n*, thus -*anā*, -*anī*, -*ā*/-*n*(a) masc. ~ -*ana* fem., -*anmē*, -*andē*, -*anē*.

The modal prefixes, *m*(*i*)- pres. indicative, *b*(*i*)- subjunctive, are regularly omitted with some verbs, thus *m-ūs'ū* 'I sleep', *b'i-daw* 'should I give', but *kar'ū* 'I do', *k'arū* 'if I do': the corresponding negative forms are generally *ma-*, *na-* respectively, thus *m'a-wsū*, *n'a-daw*, *m'a-karū*, *n'a-karū*. Verbs may also take adverbial suffixes and a pronominal suffix, as agent in the regular construction of the past tenses of transitive verbs, otherwise as object, e.g., *wizū-š-arāwa wār* 'I shall throw it (-*š*) down (-*ara*) again (-*awa*)', *wist-im-ara wār* 'I threw it down', *warō-š-ɔ̄* 'if he drinks it', *agar na-wārda-bīɛ-m-ɔ̄* 'if I had not drunk it'.

Bibliography: D. N. MacKenzie, *The Dialect of Awroman* (*Hawrāmān-ī Luhōn*), Hist.-Filos. Skr. Dan. Vid. Selsk. 4, no. 3, Copenhagen, 1966 (with earlier literature).

(D. N. MacKenzie)

AWĀ'EL AL-MAQĀLĀT FI'L-MAḎĀHEB AL-MOḴTĀRĀT (Principal theses of selected doctrines), a Shi'ite doctrinal work written in Baghdad by Shaikh Abū 'Abdallāh Moḥammad b. Moḥammad b. No'mān al-Mofīd (d. 413/1022; q.v.) probably between the years 396 and 406/1005-16. In it (p. 1) Shaikh al-Mofīd defines his position, which he calls that of the "justice party" among the Shi'ites (*al-'adlīya men al-šī'a*), on the entire spectrum of theological (*kalām*) questions by comparison and contrast with other schools.

Important in the history of the Imamite creed, especially for its relation to Mu'tazilism, the *Awā'el* is neither a systematically argued theological treatise nor a detailed heresiography. Rather it is a practical catalogue of Imamite positions on disputed questions composed for a *naqīb* of the 'Alids, probably Šarīf Rażī. The important problems fall naturally at the beginning, and questions on the finer points are strung out towards the end. In designating opponents and supporters of his theses, Shaikh al-Mofīd does not name any of his own contemporaries.

The essence of Shi'ism is defined as loyal adherence to 'Alī and repudiation of the three caliphs preceding him; the essence of Mu'tazilism is the "middle position," between the faithful (*mo'men*) and the infidel (*kāfer*), assigned to the grave sinner. No one who rejects this latter thesis is a Mu'tazilite, no matter how much he may agree with them on other points.

The *Awā'el* insists that revelation is needed to assist reason both for establishing the premises and for assuring the reasoning process in the fundamentals of religion. Its other main points of opposition to all Mu'tazilites concern: the indefectibility and infallibility of the imams; the Return (*raj'a*) to life of many of the best of the Shi'ites and the worst of their enemies, expected at the time of the Mahdi's reappearance in order to fight a final battle where the Mahdi's forces will be victorious; the thesis that the grave sinner within the Shi'ite community is nonetheless a believer (against the Mu'tazilite "middle position" which calls him neither a believer nor an unbeliever); and the thesis that the grave sinner of the community, being a believer, will not be punished forever in the Fire (against the Mu'tazilite doctrine of "the promise and the threat").

On questions of God's Oneness and Justice the position taken coincides with Mu'tazilism and in detail agrees with the Baghdad school against the Basran. Thus with the Baghdad Mu'tazilites the *Awā'el* refuses to apply to God attributes derived from reason but not found in the Koran or traditions; Abū Hāšem Jobbā'ī's theory of "states" is rejected; God does not will in the same sense as man wills; God is bound by His nobility and generosity, not by justice, to look after man's best interests. The Baghdad Mu'tazilite most frequently cited is Abu'l-Qāsem Balḵī Ka'bī (q.v.).

The *Awā'el* attributes, as did Abū Esḥāq Naẓẓām (q.v.), the miraculous aspect of the Koran to God's preventing others from imitating it, not to its intrinsic inimitability. It says rather hesitantly that the current text of the Koran is probably integral. This implies a re-interpretation of Imamite tradition and goes counter to the accusations of some—but not all—contemporary Imamites that the Sunnites had left ommissions or even forged additions to the sacred text. Shaikh al-Mofīd himself had in fact argued in a previous work ("al-Masā'el al-Sarawīya," in *al-Ṯaqalān*: *Al-Ketāb wa'l-'etra*, Najaf, n.d., p. 59) that there were omissions in the current text.

Following the main questions comes a series of related minor points such as repentance, the interpretation and binding force of traditions, eschatology, etc. After this, the second edition of the *Awā'el* contains two further series of questions on the fine points of theology, many of them dealing with atomism and other points of natural philosophy, which may originally have been separate treatises but which fit in very well as part of this work.

The theory that things are composed of atoms and accidents was necessary to the theologians as a basis for their proof of God's existence from the temporality of the world. The atomism of the *Awā'el*, except for one inconsistency (that atoms are extended), follows the Baghdad Mu'tazilites against the Basrans. The most notable differences are the Baghdad Mu'tazilites'—and the *Awā'el's*—denial of the existence of a void (*ḵalā'*), and their assertion that there are natural qualities (*ṭab'*, plur. *ṭebā'*) in things which dispose them to act the way they do.

Finally, the *Awā'el* goes counter to the materialism of most Baghdad and Basran Mu'tazilites in defining man as "a thing produced in time, self-subsistent, outside the categories of atom and accident." This means, as Shaikh al-Mofīd explains in another work, that the essential part of man is spirit ("al-Masā'el," p. 52).

Bibliography: Edition: *Awāʾel al-maqālāt fi'l-madāheb al-moktārāt*, ed. ʿA. Wajdī, Tabrīz, 1363/1944; revised and augmented 1371/1951-52. Translation of the first section: D. Sourdel, "L'Imamisme vu par le Cheikh al-Mufīd," *REI* 40, 1972, pp. 217-96. *Al-Darīʿa* II, pp. 472-73. W. Madelung, "Imamism and Muʿtazilite Theology," in *Le shīʿisme imâmite*, ed. T. Fahd., Paris, 1972, pp. 22-25. M. J. McDermott, *The Theology of al-Shaikh al-Mufīd*, Persian Studies Series 9, Beirut, 1978.

(M. J. McDermott)

AWAN, name of a place in ancient western Iran, the nominal dynastic seat of Elamite rulers in the late third millennium B. C.; its location is unknown.

Three rulers of Awan form the fourth post-diluvian "dynasty" in at least four manuscripts of the Sumerian King List. Only the beginning of the third ruler's name is preserved (Ku-u [l-...]). The King List attributes a reign of 36 years to him, and a total of 356 years of rule to the kingdom of Awan. One fragmentary copy may record an abbreviated tradition of only two kings of Awan. (Jacobsen, *The Sumerian King List*, pp. 94 f., iv. 6-616; Kraus, "Zur Liste der älteren Könige," p. 34 and n. 2; Nissen, "Eine neue Version," pp. 1-5). The King List is a schematic and tendentious document (possibly compiled as early as 2100 B.C., though extant manuscripts are two to four centuries younger); and these numbers have no chronographic worth, but the context of the Awan section suggests that it was meant to refer to a period beginning ca. 2500-2400 B. C. Its historicity is questionable. No known ancient text provides an independent reference to this "dynasty" (V. Scheil's suggestion ["Dynasties élamites," pp. 8 f.] that an exercise tablet from Susa does so is unverifiable.)

A second, shorter king list from Susa supplies twelve personal names, summarized in Akkadian as "twelve kings of Awan," without indicating lengths of reign or filiation (Scheil, "Dynasties élamites" = Scheil, MDP 23, p. iv. 1-13). The date of composition of this list is unknown; the unique manuscript of it dates from ca. 1800-1600 B.C. There is no point of concord between the Awan "dynasties" of the Sumerian King List and the Susa list; the latter probably refers to a second series of rulers, rather than an extension of the tradition recorded in the former. Independent textual evidence dates the eighth ruler in the Susa sequence, Luḫḫiššan, to ca. 2300 B.C. and the twelfth ruler, Puzur-Inšušinak, to ca. 2100 B.C., but there is no assurance that the Susa list records a complete and uninterrupted series of rulers of equal stature.

An Old Akkadian votive inscription of Sargon of Akkad (2334-2279 B.C.), preserved in an Old Babylonian copy, commemorates military triumphs over Elam and Baraḫši, naming among Sargon's defeated opponents Luḫ-iššan, son of Ḫišiprašini, king of Elam, and referring to booty (?) taken from Awan (Hirsch, "Die Inschriften," p. 47, xii.10-13, 36-37). Awan is given no special emphasis to distinguish it from other toponyms similarly mentioned (Susa among them), nor does it appear in the Elamite ruler's title. The Luḫ-iššan of this text, however, is identical with the eighth king of Awan named on the Susa list, and his patronym, Ḫišiprašini, is an orthographic or grammatical variant of the ninth name on the Susa list, Ḫišep-ratep. (The discrepancy in the order of the names may reflect error in one of the sources, or the existence of two distinct but nearly homonymous individuals, or eccentricity in the royal succession at Awan.)

Old Babylonian copies also preserve two Old Akkadian inscriptions of Sargon's successor Rimuš (2278-70 B.C.), again commemorating victories over Baraḫši and the subjugation of Elam, without referring to a king of Elam or Awan, but mentioning the capture of enemy leaders "between Awan and Susa, on the middle (?) (or: upper) river" (ibid., pp. 62f., xxiii.11-16, p. 67, xxv.50-56).

Two Akkadian stelae from Susa claim for Puzur-Inšušinak the titles "mighty one" and "king of Awan" (Scheil, MDP 11, pl. 3, 1a. 3-5; 2.5-6; cf. Gelb, *Old Akkadian Writing*, p. 46; Boehmer, "Datierung," p. 345; Edzard, *Répertoire* 1, p. 21). These are the only contemporary occurrences of the toponym in royal titulature from southwestern Iran. An unpublished Mesopotamian text (in Summerian and Akkadian) indicates that Puzur-Inšušinak was a contemporary of Ur-Nammu of Ur (2112-95 B.C.; C. Wilcke, personal communication, citing 1B 1537; despite Boehmer, "Datierung," p. 345).

Awan is conspicuous by its absence from routine contexts in Sumerian administrative texts from the Third Dynasty of Ur (2112-04 B.C.), but a date formula of the last Ur III ruler, Ibbi-Sin (2028-04 B.C.) names a "year in which Ibbi-Sin, king of Ur, roared like a storm in Susa, Adamdun, and the land of Awan, subdued them in a single day, and took their lords captive (cf. Sollberger, "Ibbī-Suen," p. 7), and the same phrase recurs in two votive inscriptions of the same ruler (Gadd, Legrain, and Smith, *Royal Inscriptions*, pp. 210.4, 289 xiii.42; cf. Edzard and Farber, *Répertoire* II, p. 20).

The toponym Awal is not a variant of Awan (despite Goetze, "Šakkanakkus," p. 5 n. 46; Edzard and Farber, op. cit., p. 20) but the name of another place, now securely located in the Hamrin basin (Whiting, "Tiš-atal," p. 180; Steinkeller, "Early History," p. 164). The Šaykān inscription near Qaṣr-e Šīrīn may record a conquest of the "land of Awan (?) (or Aban)," but the reading of the toponym and the historical context of the inscription are wholly uncertain, and its date is later than that of any other text mentioning Awan (Herzfeld, *Persian Empire*, pp. 154f., n. 2; Gelb, *Glossary*, p. 293; Farber, "Zur Datierung," pp. 47-50; Calmeyer, "Ḫūrīn Šaiḫān," p. 504).

Only two of these references have geographical, rather than political import. The Rimuš texts that locate an event "between Awan and Susa" suggest that Awan indicates a place close enough to Susa to render such a phrase meaningful, and the Ibbi-Sin date formula, even understood as royal hyperbole, implies that Awan was a region that abutted Susa and its territory. Poebel and Goetze held that Awan was in Elam (by which they meant Khuzistan), not far from Susa (Poebel, *Miscellaneous Studies*, p. 40 n. 9; Goetze, op. cit., p. 5; similarly Miroschedji, "Le dieu élamite," p. 132; and others). Hinz proposed the vicinity of Dezfūl (*Das Reich Elam*, p. 62; "Persia," p. 647). Hansman, supposing a meaningful complementary distribution between references to Awan and Anshan (q.v.), suggested with reservations that Awan indicates a region of which the capital was Anshan, in the *dehestān* Bayżā in Fārs (Hansman, "Elamites," p. 101, 115), and Vallat conjectures that the region of Awan applied to an uncertain extent of Zagros valley systems in Luristan, perhaps as far north as Kurdistan ("Suse et l'Élam," map 4).

The texts are sparing of information on Awan's actual political role at any moment. The king lists take retrospective views of Awan as the enduring dynastic seat of the outstanding western Iranian state in Early Dynastic and Old Akkadian times. The Old Akkadian inscriptions consider the kings of this state to be the rulers of Elam, but they name Awan only as one of several defeated places, with no indication of political primacy.

Puzur-Inšušinak's stelae, like the king lists, use the place name to mark royal status, but the inscriptions themselves come from Susa. In the mid-third millennium B.C., at any rate, a state centered on Awan engaged in political and military competition with Mesopotamian city states, with enough success to earn a place in the Sumerian King List. Awan may have continued to be the political center of leading Elamite rulers in the later third millennium, justifying the retrospective use of "King of Awan" in the Old Babylonian king list from Susa. Later rulers named in the Susa list were adversaries of Sargon of Akkad and his descendants; despite the Akkadian claims of early success, it was probably still a King of Awan with whom Naram-Sin of Akkad (2254-18 B.C.) concluded an entente and drew up a treaty, the Elamite text of which was found at Susa (Scheil, MDP 11, pp. 1ff.; cf. Hinz, "Elams Vertrag," pp. 66ff.; Kammenhuber, "Historisch-geographische Nachrichten," p. 180; Vallat, "Suse et l'Élam," p. 5). During the period of interstate struggle that preceded the hegemony of Ur in Mesopotamia and parts of western Iran Puzur-Inšušinak of Awan brought Susa under his control, but subsequently Awan disappeared from the political scene, eclipsed and presumably absorbed by the state and "dynasty" of Šimaški. Ibbi-Sin's use of the toponym is merely geographical, and probably already archaic.

Bibliography: R. M. Boehmer, "Die Datierung des Puzur/Kutik-Inšušinak und einige sich daraus ergebende Konsequenzen," *Orientalia*, N.S. 35, 1966, pp. 345-76. P. Calmeyer, "Ḫūrīn Šaiḫān," *Reallexikon der Assyriologie* IV/6-7, 1975, pp. 504-05. D. O. Edzard, *Répertoire géographique des textes cunéiformes* I: *Die Orts- und Gewässernamen der präsargonischen und sargonischen Zeit*, Beihefte zum Tübinger Atlas des Vorderen Orients, Series B, no. 7/1, Wiesbaden, 1977, p. 21. Idem and G. Farber, *Répertoire géographique des textes cunéiformes* II: *Die Orts- und Gewässernamen der Zeit der 3. Dynastie von Ur*, Beihefte zum Tübinger Atlas des Vordern Orients, Series B, no. 7/2, Wiesbaden, 1974, p. 20. W. Farber, "Zur Datierung der Felsinschrift von Šaiḫ-ḫān," *AMI*, N.S. 8, 1975, pp. 47-51. C. J. Gadd, L. Legrain, and S. Smith, *Royal Inscriptions*, Ur Excavations, Texts, I, London, Trustees of the British Museum, 1928, nos. 210, 289. I. J. Gleb, *Glossary of Old Akkadian*, Materials for the Assyrian Dictionary, no. 3, Chicago, 1957. Idem, *Old Akkadian Writing and Grammar*, Materials for the Assyrian Dictionary, no. 2, 2nd ed., Chicago, 1961. A. Goetze, "Šakkanakkus of the Ur III Empire," *Journal of Cuneiform Studies* 17, 1963, pp. 1-31. J. Hansman, "Elamites, Achaemenians and Anshan," *Iran* 10, 1972, pp. 101-25. E. Herzfeld, *The Persian Empire, Studies in the Geography and Ethnography of the Ancient Near East*, ed. G. Walser, Wiesbaden, 1968, pp. 154-56. W. Hinz, *Des Reich Elam*, Urban-Bücher 82, Stuttgart, 1964, pp. 58-66. Idem, "Persia, c. 2400-1800 B.C.," in *CAH*³ 1/2, pp. 644-53. Idem, "Elams Vertrag mit Narâm-Sîn von Akkade," *ZA* 58, 1967, pp. 66-96. H. Hirsch, "Die Inschriften der Könige von Agade," *Archiv für Orientforschung* 20, 1963, pp. 1-82. T. Jacobsen, *The Sumerian King List*, Assyriological Studies 11, Chicago, 1939. A. Kammenhuber, "Historisch-geographische Nachrichten aus der althurritischen Überlieferung, dem Altelamischen und den Inschriften der Könige von Akkad . . . ," *Acta Antiqua Academiae Scientiarum Hungaricae* 22, 1974, pp. 157-247. F. R. Kraus, "Zur Liste der älteren Könige von Babylonien," *ZA* 50, 1952, pp. 29-60. P. de Miroschedji, "Le dieu élamite Napirisha," *Revue d'assyriologie* 74, 1980, pp. 129-43. H. J. Nissen, "Eine neue Version der Sumerischen Königsliste," *ZA* 57, 1965, pp. 1-5. A. Poebel, *Miscellaneous Studies*, Assyriological Studies 14, Chicago, 1947. V. Scheil, *Textes élamites-sémitques*, MDP 11, Paris, 1908. Idem, "Dynasties élamites d'Awan et de Simaš," *Revue d'assyriologie* 28, 1931, pp. 1-8. Idem, *Actes juridiques susiens*, MDP 23, Paris, 1932. E. Sollberger, "Ibbī-Suen," *Reallexikon der Assyriologie* V/1-2, 1976, pp. 1-8. P. Steinkeller, "Early History of the Hamrin Basin in the Light of Textual Evidence," in *Üch Tepe* I: *Tell Razuk, Tell Ahmed al-Mughir, Tell Ajamat*, ed. McG. Gibson, Chicago and Copenhagen, 1981, pp. 163-68. E. Unger and E. Ebeling, "Awan," *Reallexikon der Assyriologie* 1/3, 1929, p. 324. F. Vallat, "Suse et l'Élam," *Recherche sur les grandes civilisations*, Mémoire no. 1, Paris, 1980. R. M. Whiting, "Tiš-atal of Nineveh and Babati, Uncle of Šu-Sin," *Journal of Cuneiform Studies* 28, 1976, pp. 173-82.

(M. W. STOLPER)

'AWĀREF AL-MA'ĀREF (Kind gifts of [mystic] knowledge), a classic work on Sufism by Šehāb-al-dīn

Abū Ḥafṣ 'Omar b. Moḥammad Sohravardī (b. 539/1145 in Sohravard near Zanjān, d. 632/1234 in Baghdad, a Shafi'ite *faqīh*, celebrated Sufi master, and *šayḵ-al-šoyūḵ* (dean of Sufi masters) of Baghdad (appointed by the caliph al-Nāṣer in 599/1202-03). Šehāb-al-dīn has sometimes been confused with his paternal uncle and spiritual guide, Abu'l-Najīb 'Abd-al-Qāher b. 'Abdallāh Sohravardī (d. 563/1168), the founder of the Sohravardi Order, and with the Illuminationist (*ešrāqī*) theosopher Šehāb-al-dīn Yaḥyā b. Ḥabaš Sohravardī Maqtūl (d. 587/1191).

Sohravardī's work demonstrates the increasing tendency of Sufis to organize and systematize their teachings; it soon gained wide acceptance as the standard manual for matters pertaining to the duties of masters and disciples. It was translated into Persian by Qāsem Dāwūd Ḵaṭīb Darāča in ca. 639/1241-42, and by Esmā'īl b. 'Abd-al-Mo'men b. 'Abd-al-Jalīl b. Abī Manṣūr Mãšāda in 665/1266 (ed. Q. Anṣārī, Tehran, 1364 Š./1985; cf. N. Māyel Heravī, "Tarjama-ye 'Awāref al-ma'āref-e Sohravardī," *Našr-e dāneš* 6, 1364 Š./1985-86, pp. 114-120). Other Persian translations were made by Ẓahīr-al-dīn 'Abd-al-Raḥmān b. Shaikh Najīb-al-dīn 'Alī b. Bozgoš (d. 716/1316; cf. Brockelmann, *GAL*, S. II, p. 789), Ṣadr-al-dīn Jonayd b. Fażlallāh b. 'Abd-al-Raḥmān Šīrāzī (d. 791/1389, including a commentary called *Ḏayl al-ma'āref*), Kamāl-zāda Čalabī, and Behbūd 'Alī Ḵorāsānī (13th/19th century). All these works are extant (Mā'el Heravī, art. cit., p. 117). Ḥājjī Ḵalīfa cites an addendum (*ta'līqa*) by the famous theologian and philosopher Sayyed Šarīf Jorjānī (d. 816/1413-14), an abridgment by Moḥebb-al-dīn Aḥmad b. 'Abdallāh Ṭabarī Makkī Šāfe'ī (d. 694/1294-95), and a Turkish translation by 'Ārefī (*Kašf al-ẓonūn* [Istanbul], cols. 1177-78; Brockelmann mentions a Turkish translation by Moḥammad b. Aḥmad b. 'Alī Ḵabbāz completed in 938/1531). The *'Awāref* is said to have been introduced into Indian Sufism through a summary written by Farīd-al-dīn Mas'ūd Ganj-e Šekar (d. 664/1265; *EI*² II, p. 796). In India as elsewhere it remained one of the most popular Sufi manuals (A. Schimmel, *Mystical Dimensions of Islam*, Chapel Hill, 1975, p. 348).

Most sources, including Ḥājjī Ḵalīfa, refer to *Meṣbāḥ al-hedāya* by 'Ezz-al-dīn Maḥmūd b. 'Alī Kāšānī (d. 735/1335) as a Persian translation of *'Awāref* (hence the title of *Meṣbāḥ*'s awkward and partial English translation by H. Wilberforce Clarke: *The 'Awarif-l-Ma'arif*, Calcutta, 1891; repr. New York, 1970). Kāšānī himself writes that he had received an "influx" (*wāred*) from the Unseen World telling him to compose an independent work based on the words of the great masters and including his own intuitions (*'endīyat*) and inspirations (*fotūḥāt*) "such that most of the roots and branches of *'Awāref al-ma'āref* would be included" (*Meṣbāḥ al-hedāya*, ed. J. Homā'ī, Tehran, 1324 Š /1945, pp. 7-8; cf. Homā'ī's introd., p. 37). Comparison of the tables of contents of *'Awāref* and *Meṣbāḥ* is enough to show that the two works bear little resemblance in structure, while those passages which are indeed based upon *'Awāref* (often indicated by reference to "Šayḵ-al-eslām") have usually been expanded and/or rewritten.

Sohravardī displays a deep concern to defend Sufism from its detractors and to demonstrate its roots in the Koran and Hadith. He provides detailed quotations from earlier authorities (many of them not known as Sufis) with full chains of authority (*esnād*). He criticizes those who have falsely attached themselves to Sufism (chap. 9) and identifies true Sufis with "the people brought nigh to God" (*al-moqarrabūn*) mentioned in the Koran (chap. 1. Beirut, 1966, p. 18). Much of the text is taken up by quotations and *esnāds*, but Sohravardī's own contributions are far from insignificant. He demonstrates skill in formulating sophisticated and fresh explanations of well-known terms, weaving together elements from the authorities he has quoted and from his own understanding and intuition (see, for example, his explanation of the terms *nafs*, *rūḥ*, *qalb*, and *serr*, chapter 56, [pp. 449-55]; compare this with Kāšānī's much expanded version, *Meṣbāḥ*, pp. 82-103).

The sixty-three chapters (*bāb*) of the *'Awāref* can be divided into five major sections: Chapters 1-9: the term "Sufism" (*taṣawwof*); what sets Sufis apart from other Muslims. Chapters 10-28: specific institutions and practices connected with Sufism, including the Shaikh, the spiritual companion (*ḵādem*), the cloak of initiation (*ḵerqa*), and the Sufi center (*rebāṭ*); traveling (*safar*) as opposed to staying in the *rebāṭ*; marrying (*ta'ahhol*) as opposed to staying single (*tajarrod*); listening to music (*samā'*); spiritual retreats (*arba'īnīya*). Chapters 29-30: the character traits (*aḵlāq*) of the Sufis, such as humility (*tawāżo'*), kindliness (*modārāt*), charity (*īṯār*), forgiveness (*tajāwoz*), cheerfulness (*ṭalāqat al-wajh*), indulgence (*sohūla*), abandoning affectations (*tark al-takallof*), and contentment (*qanā'a*). Chapters 31-55: propriety and proper conduct (*adab*), including the Sufi's attitude toward God; the performance of the specific ritual practices such as ablutions (*ṭahāra*), prayer (*ṣalāt*), and fasting (*ṣawm*) common to all Muslims; everyday activities such as eating (*akl*) and sleeping (*nawm*); vigils (*qīām al-layl*); relationship between shaikh and disciple (*morīd*). Chapters 56-63: the different kinds of knowledge (*ma'refa*) and inspiration (*ḵawāṭer*); the states (*aḥwāl*) and the stations (*maqāmāt*) of the spiritual travelers.

Bibliography: The text has often been printed in commercial editions, e.g., Beirut, 1966; and on the margin of Ḡazālī's *Eḥyā' 'olūm al-dīn*, Cairo, 1327/1909. German translation by R. Gramlich, *Die Gaben der Erkenntnisse des Umar as-Suhrawardi* (*'Awaref al-ma'aref*), Wiesbaden, 1978. See also H. Ritter, "Philologika IX. Die vier Suhrawardī. Ihre Werke in Stambuler Handschriften," *Islam* 24, 1937, pp. 270-86; 25, 1939, pp. 35-86, esp. pp. 36-43. J. S. Trimingham, *The Sufi Orders in Islam*, Oxford, 1971, pp. 29-30.

(W. C. CHITTICK)

'AWĀREŻ, term used since 4th/10th century to

denote extraordinary imposts of various kinds, the nature of which differed per area and historic period. *ʿAwāreż* (sing. *ʿāreża)* was used as a singular, so that in later times we encounter the pluralized form *ʿawāreżāt*. K͟ᵛārazmī (*Mafātīḥ*, p. 61) referred to extraordinary contributions as *ʿawāreż*. In the beginning the imposition of *ʿawāreż* probably was limited to contributions exacted by the king's army as a punitive measure when it had to appear to put down some unrest or in case of some delay in paying the taxes (Bosworth, *Ghaznavids*, p. 80). It appears, however, that *ʿawāreż* was imposed with more regularity than it was supposed to be. The impost was collected either from a town, village, region, or a distinct group such as a guild. Such tax categories could also be exempted from paying *ʿawāreż*. Aḥmad b. Ḥasan Maymandī, the Ghaznavid grand vizier, for example, is reported to have exempted for two years the town of Lomḡān from payment of *ʿawāreż* (Neẓāmī ʿArūżī, *Čahār maqāla*, text, pp. 29-31). Under the Saljuqs and K͟ᵛārazmšāhs *ʿawāreż* seems to have been collected almost like a regular impost. Sanjar in a decree to a local *raʾīs* (governor) instructed the latter to avoid collecting *ʿawāreż*, if possible. If it was unavoidable the burden had to be distributed equitably among the subjects (H. Horst, *Die Staatsverwaltung der Grosselǧuqes und Ḫorezmšahs (1032-1231)*, Wiesbaden, 1964, pp. 77, 78). Under the Mongols *ʿawāreż* continued to be collected regularly. Jovaynī, when describing the organization of the Mongol horde, mentions certain contributions they were liable to make, including *ʿawāreżāt*. He also mentions that the Mongols exempted the most learned of every religion (*aḥbār-e ak͟yār*) from every kind of *ʿawāreżāt* (I, pp. 11, 22; tr. Boyle, I, pp. 16, 30). The burden of the imposition of *ʿawāreżāt* was so heavy that Rašīd-al-dīn goes so far as to say that it was one of the causes of the ruinous state of Iran. *ʿAwāreżāt*, moreover, were collected in cash, which increased the burden, since peasants who were forced to sell their produce found themselves in a disadvantageous bargaining position. (Rašīd-al-dīn Fażlallāh, *Mokātabāt-e rašīdī*, p. 28; see also Waṣṣāf, *Tārīk͟-e Waṣṣāf*, p. 197). In the 8th/14th and 9th/15th centuries under the Jalayerids and Timurids *ʿawāreż* continues to be levied. Nak͟javānī gives various instances of its imposition. He also indicates that in many cases *ʿawāreż* was levied illegally, in which case the wronged subjects were invited to complain to the central government (*dīvān-e bozorg*) in order to get a compensation (Moḥammad b. Hendūšāh Nak͟javānī, *Dostūr al-kāteb fī taʿyīn al-marāteb*, ed. ʿA. ʿA. ʿAlīzāda, Moscow, 1964, I, pp. 64. 110, 535, 685; I/2, p. 467; II, 1976, pp. 89, 280, 282, 301; for the Timurids see H. R. Roemer, *Staatsschreiben der Timuridenzeit*, Wiesbaden, 1970, pp. 78, 165, 166).

Under the Aq Qoyunlū and Qara Qoyunlū the imposition or the exemption from payment of *ʿawāreżāt* is mentioned in several documents. By that time the term *ʿawāreżāt-e dīvānī* is also found in decrees issued by the Qara Qoyunlū Jahānšāh and Ḥasan-ʿAlī, and the Āq Qoyunlū Uzun Ḥasan (G. A. Bourhoutian, *Eastern Armenia in the Last Decade of Persian Rule*, Malibu, 1982, p. 124; A. D. Papazian, *Persidskie dokumenti Matenaderana*, I, Ukazi, pp. 223, 230; H. Busse, *Untersuchungen zum islamischen Kanzleiwesen*, Cairo, 1959, p. 104). In Herat in 1298/698 Fak͟r-al-dīn the Karti ruler of Herat granted exemption to the people of Herat of inter alia *ʿawāreż-e dīvānī* (Sayfī Heravī, *Tārīk͟-nāma-ye Herāt*, ed. Moḥammed Zobayr Seddīqī, Calcutta, 1943, p. 439).

Safavid practice does not greatly differ from that of the previous dynasties. According to Minorsky *ʿawāreż-e dīvānī* was imposed for the upkeep of ambassadors, for public festivities, and fireworks (V. Minorsky, *Tad͟kerat al-molūk*, p. 181). Based on the practice in the Caucasus, he states, quoting Kaempfer, that in case of imposition on rural communities the peasants had to provide additional imposts (ibid., p. 22; idem, "A Soyūrghāl of Qāsim b. Jahāngīr Aq-qoyunlu (903/1498)," *BSOAS* 9/4, 1939, pp. 930, 946f.) which were four times higher than for urban subjects (Anonymous, *A Chronicle of the Carmelites*, London, 1939, p. 116). Throughout the Safavid period *ʿawāreż(āt)* were levied as attested by many documents.

Busse concludes from a study of chancellery documents that the term *ʿawāreż(āt)* is used as a generic term in either the introductory or concluding fiscal formulas in government decrees. Almost invariably *ʿawāreż* is mentioned together with other generic fiscal terms. The texts state, for example, that so-and-so is exempt from the imposition of cesses, imposts, duties or other state duties and imposts of the kingdom (*zawāyed o ʿawāreż o ek͟rājāt* or *sāyer-e ek͟rājāt o ʿawāreżāt-e mamlakatī*). This chancellery practice can already be discerned among the Saljuqs and continues till the 12th/18th century (see Horst, op. cit., pp. 77, 78; Busse, op. cit., pp. 104-05; Nak͟javānī, ibid.). This string of generic fiscal terms is usually concluded with another generic term "*wa sāyer-e takālīf-e dīvānī*" (and other *dīvān* taxes, see Busse, op. cit., pp. 104).

Safavid texts also indicate that *ʿawareż(āt)* could either be imposed by decree or by other means (*ʿawāreżāt-e ḥokmī o ḡayr-e ḥokmī*) (A. K. S. Lambton, *Landlord and Peasant*, London, 1953, p. 116) as is clear from a decree issued by Shah Esmāʿīl I in 918-1512-13. A similar terminology is used by Shah ʿAbbās I exempting the hairdresser guild from inter alia *ʿawāreżāt* in 1628/1038 where the text states duties imposted by decree or other means (*k͟ārejāt-e ḥokmī o ḡayr-e ḥokmī*; Honarfar, *Esfahān*, 2nd ed., Tehran, 1350 Š./1971, p. 436). The use of this terminology probably also refers to illegal or excessive imposition of *ʿawāreżāt*. Most decrees exhort the officials not to levy this or other imposts from the tax categories that had been exempted from it "under any guise whatsoever" (Lambton, op. cit., p. 116; S. ʿA. Bāybūrdī, *Tārīk͟-e Arasbārān*, Tehran, 1341 Š./1962, p. 160). Shah Sultan Ḥosayn (r. 1105-35/1694-1722) is even more explicit when he speaks about *ʿawāreżāt-e k͟elāf-e ḥokm o ḥesāb* (Moḥammad-Ḥasan Khan Eʿtemād-al-salṭana. *Merʾāt al-boldān*, Tehran, 1294/1877, I, p. 337). Although a generic term, sometimes the texts indicate what they mean by *'awāreż*. The decree by Shah Sultan Ḥosayn specifically refers to "*'alafa, 'olūfa, šekār, bīgār*, etc." when he mentions the *'awāreżāt-e mazbūra* (aforementioned imposts) (ibid.). Shah 'Abbās I in his decree exempting the hairdresser guild of Isfahan from *'awāreżāt* uses the term *'awāreżāt-e masdūdat al-abwāb* (the following imposts) to refer to the same imposts as mentioned in Shah Sultan Ḥosayn's decree (Honarfar, op. cit., pp. 435-36). Other decrees also imply or explicitly indicate a similar identification of the particular indirect tax they are referring to (see Busse, op. cit., p. 104). M. E. Bāstānī Pārīzī (*Sīāsat o eqteṣād-e 'aṣr-e Ṣafawī*, Tehran, 1357 Š./1978, 2nd ed., p. 183) mentions the term *'awāreż-e rosūm-e dār al-marz*, which, however, is a misreading of Mīrzā Rafī'ā's *Dostūr al-molūk* that clearly states *'aważ* (ed. M. T. Dānešpažūh, Tehran, 1346 Š./1967, p. 58).

The term *'awāreż(āt)* is less frequently used after the Safavid era. In the latter half of the 12th/18th century *'awāreż* was an expected supplementary tax burden, which, in many cases, however, was not only neglected but positively repudiated by Karīm Khan Zand once he came to power (J. R. Perry, *Karim Khan Zand*, Chicago, 1979, p. 236).

In Qajar times the term *'awāreż* is seldom used and then only in the general sense for tax (see, e.g., 'Abd-al-Raḥmān Żarrābī, *Tārīḵ-e Kāšān*, p. 315). Oddly enough its use increases after the Persian revolution of 1906 when the term is regularly used in fiscal laws to denote any kind of indirect tax or more specifically as a customs or road/transportation tax. A decree by Moẓaffar-al-dīn Shah (9 Ḏu'l-ḥejja 1318/31 March 1901) concerning customs and road tax tariffs (*mālīāt o 'awāreż-e gomrokī*) mentions in article 1 *woṣūl-e ḥoqūq-e rāhdārī o ḵānāt o qapāndārī o sāyer-e 'awāreż-ī har-ča būda ast* (for levying road duties, octroi, weighbridge tax, and other similar imposts of whatever nature may have been) (Majīd Yaktā'ī, *Tārīḵ-e gomrok*, Tehran, 1355 Š./1976, pp. 60-61). The tax laws enacted after the constitutional revolution of 1906 in Iran continue this practice. The law of 22 Tīr 1320 Š./1941 states *ḥoqūq-e gomrokī o 'awāreż-e dīgar* (customs duties and other imposts), and similar terminology (*mālīāt-e rāh o ḥoqūq-e gomrok o 'awāreż-e dawlatī*, i.e., road taxes, customs duties, and state imposts) is used in the tax laws of 20 Āḏar 1307 Š./1928 and 22 Tīr 1320 Š./1941. The law of 3 Day 1312 Š./1933 mentions *'awāreż-e bandarī* (port duties), while the law of 4 Šahrīvar 1309 Š./1930 states all kinds of other imposts such as road duties (*har gūna 'awāreż-e dīgar-ī az qabīl-e 'awāreż-e rāh*), etc. Especially the law of 19 Bahman 1304 Š./1926 lists a large number of indirect taxes, referring generically to them as *'awāreż-e ḏayl* "the following imposts." Nowadays the term *'awāreż* is commonly used and refers to any kind of extraordinary indirect tax. Often it is used in combination with *mālīāt*.

Bibliography: Abū 'Abdallāh Moḥammad b. Aḥmad Ḵ'ārazmī, *Mafātīḥ al-'olūm*, ed. G. van Vloten, n.p., n.d. Neẓāmī 'Arūżī Samarqandī, *Čahār maqāla*, ed. M. Qazvīnī and M. Mo'īn, 3rd ed., Tehran, 1333 Š./1954. Ḵ'āja Rašīd-al-dīn Fażlallāh, *Mokātabāt-e rašīdī*, ed. M. Š. Lāhūrī, Lahore, 1367/1947. Šehāb-al-dīn 'Abdallāh Waṣṣāf Šīrāzī, *Tārīḵ-e Waṣṣāf*, lith. ed., Bombay, 1269/1853.

(W. Floor)

'AWFĪ, SADĪD-AL-DĪN (NŪR-AL-DĪN, or JAMĀL-AL-DĪN) MOḤAMMAD B. MOḤAMMAD B. YAḤYĀ B. ṬĀHER B. 'OṮMĀN BOḴĀRĪ ḤANAFĪ, an important Persian writer of the late 6th/12th and early 7th/13th centuries. The little that we know about 'Awfī's life comes mainly from his own writings. He appears to have been born around the middle of the second half of the 6th/12th century. His birthplace was Bukhara according to all the sources expect Ferešta (I, p. 117), who gives Nīšāpūr. 'Awfī claimed direct descent from 'Abd-al-Raḥmān b. 'Awf, a companion of the Prophet Moḥammad, whom he mentions in his *Jawāme' al-ḥekāyāt* (*Lobāb* I, p. *yḥ*). 'Awfī's grandfather, Qāżī Šaraf-al-dīn Abū Ṭāher Yaḥyā b. Ṭāher was a leading scholar in Transoxiana, and his maternal uncle, Majd-al-dīn Moḥammad b. Żīā'-al-dīn 'Adnān Sorḵkatī, was the personal physician (hence his title Malek-al-aṭebbā') of the Qarakhanid (Ilek-khanid) ruler of Transoxiana, Sultan Qïlïč Ṭamḡāč Khan Ebrāhīm b. Ḥosayn; he also wrote poetry and was the author of two books, one of which was on the history of the Qarakhanids (ibid., I, pp. 44, 178-181, 300-01, 337-38).

After finishing his preliminary studies at Bukhara, 'Awfī traveled extensively in Transoxiana, Khorasan, and India, visiting Samarkand, Āmū, Ḵ'ārazm, Marv, Nīšāpūr, Herāt, Asfezār, Esfarāyīn, Šahr-e Now (between Astarābād and Ḵ'ārazm), Sajestan, Farāh, Ḡaznīn, Lahore, Cambay (Kanbāyat), Nahrvāla, and Delhi, and received permission to transmit Hadith from a number of scholars that he met. He also preached sermons and conducted *ḏekr* sessions. The long list of his teachers and mentors include Imam Borhān-al-eslām Tāj-al-dīn 'Omar b. Mas'ūd b. Aḥmad (of the politically influential Borhān family, see Āl-e Borhān), Imam Rokn-al-dīn Mas'ūd b. Moḥammad Emāmzāda, and Shaikh Majd-al-dīn Šaraf b. Mo'ayyad Baḡdādī (a prominent mystic and a disciple of Shaikh Najm-al-dīn Kobrā), some of whose poems 'Awfī has preserved, having heard them directly from him.

Apparently 'Awfī first went to Samarkand and, through the help of his maternal uncle who was in the service of the sultan Qïlïč Ṭamḡāč Khan, got an introduction to the latter's son Solṭān-al-salāṭīn, Qïlïč Arslān Ḵāqān Noṣrat-al-dīn 'Oṯmān b. Ebrāhīm, then heir apparent. Finding 'Awfī to be learned, resourceful, and shrewd, this prince put him in charge of his correspondence office (*dīvān-e enšā'*). 'Awfī must have left Samarkand before 600/1204, because he was at Nesā in that year. In 603/1206 he was at Nīšāpūr, in 607/1210 at Asfezār, and during one of his journeys he lost all his belongings to highwaymen.

Some time after 607/1210, 'Awfī decided, apparently after hearing the first rumors of an imminent Mongol invasion, to migrate to India. In 617/1220 he was at the court of Nāṣer-al-dīn Qabāǰa (a *mamlūk* of the Ghurid sultan Šehāb-al-dīn or Mo'ezz-al-dīn Moḥammad), who was governor of Sind and Mūltān from 602/1205 to 625/1228. He stayed at Ucch, Qabāǰa's capital, until 625/1228. During this period he compiled the *Lobāb al-albāb* and dedicated it to Nāṣer-al-dīn Qabāǰa's vizier, 'Ayn-al-molk Faḵr-al-dīn Ḥosayn b. Šaraf-al-molk Rażī-al-dīn Abū Bakr Aš'arī.

In 625/1258 Šams-al-dīn Iltutmiš (a *mamlūk* of the Ghurids and the architect of the slave sultanate of Delhi) put an end to Qabāǰa's rule in Sind, annexing his territory to the Delhi Sultanate. 'Awfī, who had already begun the compilation of the *J̌awāme' al-ḥekāyāt* at the request of Nāṣer-al-dīn Qabāǰa, stayed with his master until the last day, but was quick to enter the service of the victorious Sams-al-dīn Iltutmiš. When he completed the work he dedicated it to the sultan Šams-al-dīn's vizier, Neẓām-al-molk Qewām-al-dīn Moḥammad b. Abī Sa'd J̌onaydī (*Lobāb* I, pp. yḥ-kā). Nothing is known about 'Awfī's life after 625/1258 except that he must have been living in 628/1230-31, because in the *J̌awāme' al-ḥekāyāt* he mentions an event of that year, namely the defeat of Malek Eḵtīār-al-dīn Dawlatšāh Bolkā b. Ḥosām-al-dīn (or Ḡīāt-al-dīn) 'Eważ Ḵalǰī, who had rebelled, and his execution by order of Iltutmiš. Moḥammad Qazvīnī maintained that 'Awfī lived at least until 630/1232-33 (ibid., p. *kb*).

'Awfī's surviving works are:

1. *Lobāb al-albāb*, the oldest *taḏkerat al-šo'arā'* (anthology with biographies of the poets) in the Persian language, consisting of 12 sections, apparently completed in 618/1221 (ed. E. G. Browne, 2 vols., London, 1903-06; ed. S. Nafīsī, Tehran, 1335 Š./1956). The work is important mainly for two reasons: (1) 'Awfī gives biographies and quotes verses of contemporary poets who had received him in various towns and are not mentioned in any other works; (2) he gives information, not found anywhere else, about certain poets of the Ghaznavid, Samanid, Saffarid, and Taherid periods. He is uncritical in his appraisals of the poets, being often loquacious and rhetorical. His selections are not well balanced and often show poor taste.

2. *J̌awāme' al-ḥekāyāt wa lawāme' al-rewāyāt*, a collection of prose anecdotes in 4 sections, each made up of 25 chapters. In compiling this very large collection, 'Awfī took material from books on history, belles lettres, stories and reports, available data on poets and prose-writers, etc. Some of the sources which he used are lost. This compilation is not only valuable as a literary work but also has historical and other aspects of considerable importance (selections published by M. T. Bahār, Tehran, 1324 Š./1945; partial edition [sec. 1, chap. 1] by M. Nizamuddin, Hyderabad (Deccan), 1960; partial edition [sec. 3, chap. 1 and sec. 2, chap. 3] by B. Moṣaffā Karīmī, Tehran, 1352 Š./1973 and 1353 Š./1974).

'Awfī states in the *J̌awāme' al-ḥekāyāt* that he completed two other works: a Persian translation of the Arabic book *al-Faraǰ ba'd al-šedda* by Qāżī Abū 'Alī Moḥsen b. 'Alī b. Moḥammad b. Dā'ūd Tanūḵī

(d. 384/994) (ref. to this tr. in sec. 4, chap. 7), and a panegyric entitled *Madā'eḥ al-solṭān* in the meter and style of Sanā'ī's *Ḥadīqat al-ḥaqīqa* (ref. and quotation of two verses in sec. 1, chap. 12). Both works are lost.

'Awfī's prose style is not uniform. In the prefaces of his two surviving works and in the opening lines of the biography of each poet in the *Lobāb*, he uses the artificial, ornate style fashionable in his times, whereas in the text of the *J̌awāme' al-ḥekāyāt* and some parts of the *Lobāb* he writes in a language much simpler than any normally found in works from the 6th/12th and 7th/13th countries. 'Awfī composed other poems as well. He has inserted examples in the *Lobāb al-albāb* and the *J̌awāme' al-ḥekāyāt*, and at the end of each chapter of the *J̌awāme' al-ḥekāyāt* he has added a short or long verse piece by himself in praise of the vizier Neẓām-al-molk J̌onaydī; these suffice to show that he lacked poetic talent.

Bibliography: 'Awfī, *Lobāb* I, pp. yb-kh (introd. by M. Qazvīnī with ample references to manuscript sources); II, pp. j-w; Tehran ed., 1335 Š./1956 (with introd. by S. Nafīsī). N. Bland, "On the Earliest Persian Biography of Poets, by Muhammad Aúfi, and on Some Other Works of the Class Called Tazkirat ul Shuârá," *JRAS*, 1848, pp. 111-76. R. N. Nicholson, "An Early Persian Anthology," in his *Studies in Islamic Poetry*, Cambridge, 1921, pp. 1-42. J̌āmī, *Nafaḥāt al-ons*, Calcutta, 1859, pp. 487-92. Browne, *Lit. Hist. Persia* II, pp. 477-79. Ṣafā, *Adab-īyāt* II, pp. 1023-30. Nafīsī, *Naẓm o natr* I, pp. 97-98. Rypka, *Hist. Iran. Lit.*, pp. 132, 222. Storey, 1/2, pp. 781-84. *EI*¹, p. 764.

(J̌. MATĪNĪ)

AWḤAD-AL-DĪN KERMĀNĪ, ḤĀMED b. Abi'l-Faḵr, a famous mystic of the 6th/12th century. Dates of his death given in different sources range from 562/1166 to 635/1238. Since he was a contemporary of Shaikh Šehāb-al-dīn Sohravardī (d. 632/1235) and Moḥyī-al-dīn b. 'Arabī (d. 638/1241), the most probable of these given dates must be 634/1237 or 635/1238. J̌āmī (*Nafaḥāt*, p. 588) states that Awḥad-al-dīn was a disciple of Shaik Rokn-al-dīn Saǰǰāsī and that he met and conversed with Moḥyī-al-dīn b. 'Arabī, and Ebn 'Arabī himself speaks (in chapter 8 of his *Fotūḥāt al-makkīya*) of an event which Awḥad-al-dīn Kermānī had related to him. Dawlatšāh states that Awḥad-al-dīn was a disciple of Šehāb-al-dīn Sohravardī, but we know that the two differed in their religious views and that Sohravardī regarded Awḥad-al-dīn as an innovator (*mobtade'*). It is alleged (Ma'ṣūm-'Alīšāh, *Ṭarā'eq al-ḥaqā'eq* II, p. 281) that he had recourse to contemplation of outward appearances of forms in his quest for insight into the truth and perceived absolute beauty in concrete things.

Awḥad-al-dīn spent parts of his life in Kermān, Azerbaijan, and Baghdad where the 'Abbasid caliph al-Mostanṣer Be'llāh (624/1227-640/1242) conferred a robe of honor on him and put him in charge of the Marzbānīya *rebāṭ* so that he might spend all his time there in prayer and remembrance of God.

Some poems of Awḥad-al-dīn Kermānī are quoted in various works. A narrative *maṯnawī* poem entitled *Meṣbāḥ al-arwāḥ* (in the *hazaj mosaddas aḵrab maqbūż* meter, that of Neẓāmī's *Laylī o Majnūn*) is attributed to him in most of the sources, but has been shown by B. Forūzānfar (in the preface to his edition of the *Meṣbāḥ al-arwāḥ*, Tehran, 1347 Š./1968) to be the work of Šams-al-dīn Moḥammad b. Ṭoḡān Bardsīrī Kermānī, a poet of the 6th/12th century mentioned by ʿAwfī (*Lobāb* I, p. 279-81). An edition with English translation of 120 *robāʿī*s by Awḥad-al-dīn Kermānī has been published (B. M. Weischer and P. L. Wilson, *Heart's Witness: The Sufi Quatrains of Awḥaddudīn Kermānī*, Tehran, 1978).

Bibliography: Chief among the many sources in which Awḥad-al-dīn Kermānī is mentioned are Jāmī, *Nafaḥāt*, pp. 588-92. Dawlatšāh, ed. Browne, pp. 210, 223; ed. M. Ramażānī, Tehran, 1338 Š./1959, pp. 612-14 and notes. *Ḥabīb al-sīar* III, p. 116. *Kašf al-ẓonūn* (Istanbul) V, par. 1705. *Haft eqlīm* I, p. 265. Āḏar, *Ātaškada*, Bombay, 1277/1860-61, pp. 118-19. Maʿṣūm-ʿAlīšāh, *Ṭarāʾeq al-ḥaqāʾeq*, Tehran, 1318-19/1900-01, 11, pp. 281-83. *Majmaʿ al-foṣaḥāʾ* I, pp. 89-94. See also *Manāqeb-e Awḥad-al-dīn*, ed. B. Forūzānfar, Tehran, 1347 Š./1968. B. Forūzanfar, ed., *Manẓūma-ye Meṣbāḥ al-arwāḥ*, Tehran, 1349 Š./1970. Q. Ḡanī, *Baḥṯ dar āṯār o afkār o aḥwāl-e Ḥāfeẓ* II, Tehran, 1340 Š./1961, pp. 402-04, 502. Ḵayyāmpūr, *Soḵanvarān*, p. 70.

(Z. SAFA)

AWḤADĪ MARĀḠAʾĪ, SHAIKH AWḤAD-AL-DĪN (or ROKN-AL-DĪN) B. ḤOSAYN (born ca. 673/1274-75 in Marāḡa and died there in 738/1338), a poet who flourished in the reign of Abū Saʿīd Bahādor Khan (r. 716/1316-736/1335; q.v.), the ninth Mongol Il-khan of Iran. He is usually surnamed Marāḡaʾī, but also mentioned as Awḥadī Eṣfahānī because his father hailed from Isfahan and he himself spent part of his life there. He first chose the pen-name Ṣāfī, but changed it to Awḥadī after becoming a devotee of the school of the famous mystic Shaikh Abū Ḥāmed Awḥad-al-dīn Kermānī (q.v.).

Awḥadī has left a *dīvān* (ed. A. S. Usha, Madras, 1951) of more than 8,000 verses comprising *qaṣīda*s, *ḡazal*s, *tarjīʿ-band*s, and *robāʿī*s. Most of the *qaṣīda*s are in praise of Abū Saʿīd and his vizier Ḡīāṯ-al-dīn Moḥammad (son of Rašīd-al-dīn Fażlallāh). Most of the other poems are on mystic, ethical, and religious subjects. Awḥadī is at his best in his *marṯīa*s (elegies) and his *ḡazal*s, where his style prefigures that of Ḥāfeẓ. In addition to the *dīvān*, he has left two narrative poems, the *Dah-nāma* or *Manṭeq al-ʿoššāq* (about 600 verses, ed. with biographical notes by M. Farroḵ, Mašhad, 1335 Š./1956), which he wrote in 706/1307 for Wajīh-al-dīn Yūsof, a grandson of Ḵᵛāja Naṣīr-al-dīn Ṭūsī, and the *Jām-e Jam* or *Jām-e jahānbīn* (ed. Waḥīd Dastgerdī, Tehran, 1307 Š./1928), which he wrote in the manner of Sanāʾī's *Ḥadīqat al-ḥaqīqa* in 733/1333 and dedicated to Sultan Abū Saʿīd Bahādor Khan. The *Jām-e Jam* (Cup of Jamšīd), which runs to approximately 5,000 verses, is a treatise on mysticism but also includes discussions of social, ethical, and educational matters; all considered, it is Awḥadī's best work. According to Dawlatšāh (ed. Browne, p. 213) the *Jām-e Jam* won such fame that in the first month 400 manuscripts of it were sold at high prices, but adds that in his own time (later part of the 9th/15th century) it appeared to have lost popularity. Awḥadī died in 738/1338 and is buried at Marāḡa, where his tomb is still in place (Ṣafā *Adabīyāt* III/2, p. 834). The dates 554/1159 (*Majmaʿ al-foṣaḥāʾ* I, p. 249) and 697/1297-98 (Dawlatšāh, loc. cit.) are evidently wrong.

Bibliography: For manuscripts of Awḥadī's work see Rieu, *Pers. Man.*, supp., p. 258, and Monzawī, *Noskahā* III, pp. 1847, 2242-43; IV, pp. 2735-37, 2818-19. See also Browne *Lit. Hist. Persia* III, pp. 141-46. Ḵayyāmpūr, *Soḵanvarān*, pp. 69-70. Nafīsī, *Naẓm o naṯr* I, pp. 173, 199; II, p. 760. Rypka, *Hist. Iran. Lit.*, pp. 254-55. Ṣafā, *Adabīyāt* III/2, Tehran, 1352 Š./1973, pp. 831-44.

(DJ. KHALEGHI-MOTLAGH)

AWLĪĀʾ (more fully, *awlīāʾallāh*, the "friends of God"), a term commonly translated in European languages as "saints" or the equivalent. The term, of which the singular is *walī*, derives from Koran 10:62: "Varely the friends of God—there is no fear upon them, neither shall they grieve." It occurs also in a number of *aḥādīṯ qodsīya*, such as "whoever harms a friend (*walī*) of Mine, I declare war against him" (Zayn-al-dīn Ḥaddādī, *al-Etḥāfāt al-sanīya*, Cairo, 1388/1968, p. 166) and "My friends are beneath my domes; none knows them but I" (B. Forūzānfar, *Aḥādīṯ-e maṯnawī*, Tehran, 1348 Š./1969, p. 52). These scriptural texts (*noṣūṣ*) have provided the basis for Sufi writing and speculation on the nature of the *walī* and the quality (*welāya*) that he possesses.

An early definition of the *walī* was that supplied by Abu'l-Qāsem Qošayrī (d. 467/1074-75): "The word *walī* has two meanings. The first is passive, and designates the one whose affairs are totally directed by God Almighty... He does not entrust himself with his affairs for a single moment; rather God Almighty assumes their administration. The second meaning is active and emphatic, and designates the one who takes it one himself to worship God and obey Him: his worship is continual and uninterrupted by sin. Both meanings must be present in the *walī* for him truly to be a *walī*" (*al-Resāla al-qošayrīya*, ed. ʿAbd-al-Ḥalīm Maḥmūd and Maḥmūd b. Šarīf, Cairo, 1385/1965-66, pp. 519-20). This definition was incorporated by Šarīf Jorjānī (d. 817/1414) in his celebrated *Ketāb al-taʿrīfāt* (Beirut, 1969, p. 275) and repeated, with some elaboration, by ʿAbd-al-Raḥmān Jāmī (d. 897/1492) in the prologue to *Nafaḥāt al-ons* (pp. 5-6).

An alternative definition, stressing the concept of friendship inherent in the word *walī*, was given by Najm-al-dīn Dāya in his commentary on Koran 10-62: "The *awlīāʾ* are the lovers of God and the enemies of their souls. For *welāya* is the knowledge of God and the knowledge of one's own soul; knowledge of God means looking upon Him with the gaze of love, and knowledge of the soul means looking upon it with the gaze of enmity, once the veils constituted by the states and attributes of the soul are removed" (*al-Ta'wīlāt al-najmīya*, quoted in Esmā'īl Ḥaqqī Borūsawī, *Rūḥ al-bayān*, Istanbul, 1389/1970, IV, p. 58). The notion of "closeness" has also been discerned as part of the meaning of the word *walī*: "The *walī* means 'he who is close'; the meaning of *awlīā'allāh* is, then, the elect among the believers, so designated because of their spiritual proximity to God Almighty" (Abu'l-So'ūd Efendī, quoted in *Rūḥ al-bayān* IV, p. 58).

A particular problem in the definition of the *walī* and his attributes has been the relationship between him and the prophet (*nabī*). It appears that in the 3rd/9th century, the notion arose that the *walī* is superior to the prophet. Abū Bakr Ḵarrāz (d. 286/899) wrote a brief treatise in refutation of this belief (*Kašf al-bayān*, contained in *Rasā'el*, ed. Q. Sāmarrā'ī, Baghdad, 1967), and was followed soon after by Ḥakīm Termeḏī (d. between 295/907 and 310/922), who wrote the most important single treatise on *welāya*, *Ketāb ḵatm al-awlīā'* (ed. 'O. Yaḥyā, Beirut, 1965). In addition to affirming the superiority of prophethood to *welāya*, Termeḏī set forth the various categories of *awlīā'*, propounded the idea of a "seal of the saints," corresponding to the seal of the prophets, and made a division of *welāya* into *welāya 'āmma* (embracing the totality of the believers) and *welāya ḵāṣṣa* (pertaining exclusively to the spiritual elect).

This division of *welāya* into "general" and "particular" is reminiscent of certain Shi'ite formulations deriving from the particular status accorded to the imams, and the claim has been made that it is an unacknowledged borrowing from Shi'ism. Corbin speaks, indeed, of "the paradox of a *welāya* deprived of imamology" (see his discussion of Termeḏī in *Histoire de la philosophie islamique*, Paris, 1964, pp. 273-75). It has been pointed out, however, that Termeḏī's sole points of reference are the Koran and mystical experience; there is no Shi'ite flavor to his writing (Paul Nwyia, *Exégèse coranique et langage mystique*, Beirut, 1970, p. 241). Termeḏī was, in any event, the author of a brief but harsh polemic against the Shi'ites, which would seem to exclude the likelihood of influence (Ahmed Subhi Furat, "al-Ḥakīm al-Tirmizī ve al-Radd 'alā'l-Rāfiẓa adlı risalesi," *Şarkiyat Mecmuası* VI, 1966, pp. 23-35).

The relationship of the *walī* and the *nabī* also form an important theme in the writings of Ebn al-'Arabī. According to him, while the prophet is indeed superior to the *walī*, he is himself a *walī* in addition to being prophet, and the *walī*-dimension of his being is superior to the *nabī*-dimension (A. E. Affifi, *The Mystical Philosophy of Muhyid Din Ibnul 'Arabi*, Lahore, 1964, pp. 95 ff.). This view was confirmed and elaborated by one who in other respects rejected Ebn al-Arabī's doctrines, Shaikh Aḥmad Serhendī (d. 1033/1624) (see Y. Friedmann, *Shaykh Aḥmad Sirhindī*, Montreal, 1971, chap. 4: "Prophecy and Sainthood").

Another problem connected with *welāya* is the "knowability" or "unknowability" of the *walī*. Abū 'Abdallāh Sālemī said that the *awlīā'* are recognizable by "their gentleness of speech, their good character, their pleasant demeanor, their generosity, their refraining from all objection, their acceptance of whatever excuse be proffered them, and their compassion to all men, the good and the bad alike" (Jāmī *Nafaḥāt*, p. 121). More generally, the *awlīā'* are deemed knowable by the inspiration (*elhām*) they receive, the charismatic deeds (*karāmāt*) they perform, and the quality of protected (*maḥfūẓ*) they possess, these three corresponding to the revelation (*waḥy*), miracles (*mo'jezāt*) and sinlessness (*'eṣma*) of the prophets. Others hold that the *awlīā'*, as the friends of God, are hidden by the veil of their intimacy with Him. A complete discussion of the question is to be found in the introduction to Y. Nabhānī's *Jāme' karāmāt al-awlīā'*, Cairo, 1381/1962, I, pp. 27-48.

Finally, it may be noted that Sufi writers of Shi'ite allegiance draw a distinction between "solar *welāya*" and "lunar *welāya*;" the former belongs to the imams, and the latter, its reflection, to the pole (*qoṭb*) that stands at the head of each Shi'ite Sufi order (R. Gramlich, "Pol und Scheich im heutigen Derwischtum der Schia," in *Le shi'isme imamite*, Paris, 1970, p. 175).

See also ABDĀL.

Bibliography: See also Abū Naṣr Sarrāj, *Ketāb al-loma'*, ed. R. A. Nicholson, Leiden, 1914, pp. 422-24. 'Alī b. 'Oṯmān Hojvīrī, *Kašf al-maḥjūb*, Samarkand, 1330/1910, pp. 259-69, Moḥammad b. Ṣalāḥ Boḵārī, *Anīs al-ṭālebīn wa 'oddat al-sālekīn*, ms. Bodleian, Persian e 37, fols. 46a-47b. 'Azīz Nasafī, *Ketāb al-ensān al-kāmel*, ed. M. Molé, Paris and Tehran, 1962, pp. 317-22. Ḥāfeẓ Ḥosayn Karbalā'ī Tabrīzī, *Rawżat al-jenān wa jannāt al-janān*, ed. J. Solṭān-al-qorrā'ī, Tehran, 1349 Š./1970, II, pp. 511-15. Qoṭb-al-dīn Amīr Abū Manṣūr 'Abbādī, *al-Tasfīa fī aḥwāl al-motaṣawwefa*, ed. Ḡ.-Ḥ. Yūsofī, Tehran, 1347 Š./1968.

(H. ALGAR)

AWLĪĀ'ALLĀH ĀMOLĪ, the author of the history of Rūyān, *Tārīḵ-e Rūyān*, written about 760/1359. Nothing is known about his life except for a few data mentioned in his book. He was born and lived in Āmol in Māzandarān until 750/1349 when he fled because of the upheaval in the town following the murder of the last Bavandid king of Māzandarān, Faḵr-al-dawla Ḥasan, by the sons of Kīā Afrāsīāb Čalābī. Awlīā'allāh had evidently been a partisan of the Bavandid and now sought refuge in Rūyān with the Ostandār Jalāl-al-dawla Eskandar (734/1334-761/1360) who was an active champion of a Bavandid restoration. He became closely attached to Eskandar's brother and later successor, Faḵal-dawla Šāh-Ḡāzī (ruled 761/1360-781/1379), who at this time governed Nātelrostāq. The latter suggested to him writing his history of Rūyān. Awlīā'allāh was evidently an Imami Shi'ite and mentions that he visited the tombs of the imams in Najaf, Karbalā', and Baghdad. Nothing is known about his life after the completion of his book.

The *Tārīk-e Rūyān* is preserved in a single manuscript and has been edited twice, by 'Abbās Kalīlī (Tehran, 1313 Š./1934) and by Manūčehr Sotūda (Tehran, 1338 Š./1969). The text of the manuscript appears to be in some places in disorder and perhaps incomplete. The book was evidently composed under the reign of the Ostandār Eskandar whose name is regularly followed by formulas indicating that he was alive. There is no account of his death and of the succession of Šāh-Gāzī, Awlīā'allāh's patron. The last date mentioned in the main text is 759/1358. It is commonly assumed that the date of writing, 1 Moḥarram 764/21 October 1362, given at the end of the manuscript together with some appended notes on much later events, marks the author's completion of his book, but this assumption must be questioned. For the early history of Rūyān, the author relied on various literary sources, most extensively on Ebn Esfandīār's *Tārīk-e Ṭabarestān*. For the history after the end of the latter work (ca. 613/1216), he provides a virtually unique account. It is, however, summary and inadequate, especially for the time before the author's life. The reliability even of the dates of reigns during that period must be considered doubtful.

The unpublished continuation of Ebn Esfandīār's *Tārīk-e Ṭabarestān* contained in most manuscripts of that book is known to be largely taken from Awlīā'allāh's *Tārīk-e Rūyān*. It has been suggested that Awlīā'allāh himself composed and added it to the work of his predecessor. A close comparison, however, has not yet been made.

Bibliography: Storey, I, p. 361. Storey-Bregel, pp. 1070, 1072-73. M. Sotūda, introd. to his edition of *Tārīk-e Rūyān*. Ṣafā, *Adabīyāt* III/2, pp. 1303-04.

(W. MADELUNG)

AWQĀF. See WAQF.

AWRANGĀBĀDĪ, 'ABD-AL-ḤAYY. See 'ABD-AL-ḤAYY B. 'ABD-AL-RAZZĀQ, "ṢĀREM" AWRANGĀBĀDĪ.

AWRANGĀBĀDĪ, 'ABD-AL-RAZZĀQ. See 'ABD-AL-RAZZĀQ AWRANGĀBĀDĪ.

AWRANGĀBĀDĪ, SHAH NEẒĀM-AL-DĪN, the celebrated Češtī saint said to be a descendant of Abū Bakr, the first caliph, in the line of Šehāb-al-dīn Sohravardī (Raḥīmbakš, *Šajarat al-anwār*, fol. 383a). According to Mawlawī Elāhbakš (*Kātam-e solaymānī*, Lahore, 1325/1907) he was born in 1076/1665-66 while Najm-al-dīn Češtī (*Manāqeb al-maḥbūbīn*, p. 47) implicitly puts it at 1060/1650. Controversy shrouds his original home as well. Contemporary and near-contemporary works mention both Kakorī and Nograon (Najm-al-dīn Češtī, op. cit., p. 47; Moḥammad-Ḥosayn Morādābādī, *Anwār al-'ārefīn*, p. 430) while K'āja Gol Moḥammad Aḥmadpūrī (*Takmela-ye sīar al-awlīā'*, p. 180) avers that he or his ancestors hailed from Gūr.

After finishing elementary education in his home town, Awrangābādī went to Delhi in pursuit of higher learning and attended the lectures of Shah Kalīmallāh on theology. Subsequently the latter initiated him in the mystic discipline as his disciple in fulfillment of the prophecy once spoken by Shah Kalīmallāh's mentor, Shaikh Yaḥyā Madanī (Raḥīmbakš, *Šajarat al-anwār*, fol. 384b).

Upon the completion of his study with Shah Kalīmallāh, Shah Neẓām-al-dīn was deputed by him to propagate the doctrine of the Češtī *selsela* (order) in the Deccan with particular stress to concentrate his efforts in the Imperial forces in operation there (Moḥammad-Qāsem Kalīmī, *Maktūbāt-e Kalīmī*, p. 26; Raḥīmbakš, *Šajarat al-anwār*, fol. 415a). He traveled a great deal in search of a permanent abode, and finally established his headquarters at Aurangabad, where he drew a large number of disciples from all classes of people (Raḥīmbakš, op. cit., fol. 422b; 'Emād-al-molk, *Manāqeb al-fakrīya*, fol. 3a). With the establishment of his *kānaqāh* at Aurangabad, Deccan became the focal point of the efflorescence of the Češtī *selsela* in south India, and on Shah Kalīmallāh's death on 17 October 1729, Awrangābādī became the head of the central organization of the *selsela* which now moved from Delhi to the Deccan. His efforts to revitalize the Češtī *selsela* turned his *kānaqāh* into the rallying center of the devotees from far and near in the peninsula. He paid much attention to building up the moral and spiritual personality of his disciples. They were trained as a disciplined band of dedicated votaries of the order, undergoing penances and self-abstemious exercises to attain piety, resorting to the arduous practice of *dekr-e johr* (vocal and loud recollections) by night in the company of two to three hundred disciples either in a mosque or in wilderness with a view to arousing ecstatic love of God and fervor among the devotees (Kalīmī, op. cit., pp. 25, 34, 37; Raḥīmbakš, op. cit., fol. 388a). Other practices such as divine recollection with control of breath, keeping night vigils in devotions, etc., were also recommended (Raḥīmbakš, op. cit., fols. 388-93). Another point of emphasis was the need to control the emotional life rather than attaching too much importance to the external forms of behavior. As an individual, Awrangābādī was amiable in manners, lavish in hospitality, and humane in disposition and demeanor (K. A. Nizami, *Tārīk-e mašā'ek*, pp. 439, 440, 443, 445; Gol Moḥammad Aḥmadpūrī, op. cit., p. 101; Kāmgār Khan, *Aḥsan al-šamāyel*, fols. 75, 77).

Awrangābādī's mentor, Shah Kalīmallāh, ceaselessly urged on him to expand the order and attempt to gain more adherents, even from among the rich and the powerful whom he first preferred to avoid. Eventually a number of them became his disciples. His *kānaqāh* is said to have had ten gates, over each of which a scribe was posted to write down the supplications of the needy which were affixed with Awrangābādī's seal. The bearers of such notes would take them to the nobles who would respond to their need in order to earn religious merit (Fak̲rī, *Fak̲r al-ṭālebīn*, fol. 88; Gol Moḥammad Aḥmadpūrī, op. cit., fol. 88; Mawlānā Emām-al-dīn, *Nāfeʿ al-sālekīn*, Lahore, 1286/1869, p. 107; Kāmgār Khan, op. cit., fol. 77).

Awrangābādī is also author of a book *Neẓāam al-qolūb* (Delhi, 1309/1891) in which he made a systematic exposition of the doctrines and the ritualistic practices of the *selsela*. Its contents embody the metaphysical postulates and the basic tenets of the mystic ideology of the order. Another important work on the ideology of the *selsela* and the life and work of Awrangābādī, entitled *Aḥsan al-šamāyel*, was composed by one of his chief deputies, K̲ᵛāja Kāmgār Khan. A similar work, *Rašk-e golestān-e eram*, by his disciple Neẓām-al-molk Āṣafjāh I (Raḥīmbak̲š, fol. 305b) seems to be lost.

Shaikh Neẓām-al-dīn married twice and had five sons and one daughter. One of his sons, Shah Fak̲r-al-dīn Dehlavī, became his successor and attained celebrity as one of the eminent saints of India (*Tārīk̲-e mašāʾek̲-e Češt*, p. 428).

Bibliography: See also K̲ᵛāja Kāmgār Khan, *Aḥsan al-šamāyel*, Ms. Aligarh Muslim University, fols. 1-82, Raḥīmbak̲š, *Šajarat al-anwār*, Ms. Aligarh Muslim University, fols. 383a-423a. K̲ᵛāja Gol Moḥammad Aḥmadpūrī, *Takmela-ye sīar al-awlīāʾ*, Delhi, 1312/1894, pp. 94-104. Najm-al-dīn Češtī, *Manāqeb al-maḥbūbīn*, Lahore, 1312/1894, pp. 47-49. Moḥammad-Ḥosayn Morādābādī, *Anwār al-ʿārefīn*, Bareilly, 1290/1873, pp. 430-31. Moḥammad-Qāsem Kalīmī, *Maktūbāt-e Kalīmī*, Delhi, 1301/1884, pp. 10, 22, 25, 28, 29, 34, 37, 44, 45, 48, 52, 67, 72, 101. ʿEmād-al-molk Ḡāzī-al-dīn, *Manāqeb al-fak̲rīya*, Ms. Aligarh Muslim University, fols. 3a-5b. Sayyed Nūr-al-dīn Ḥosayn Fak̲rī, *Fak̲r al-ṭālebīn*, Ms. personal collection, K. A. Nizami. K. A. Nizami, *Tārīk̲-e mašāʾek̲-e Češt*, Delhi, 1953, pp. 427-59.

(M. Z. Siddiqui)

AWRANGZĒB. See Supplement.

AWRŌMĀN, AWRŌMĀNI. See AVROMAN; AVROMANI.

AWṢĀF AL-AŠRĀF, a short mystical-ethical work in Persian by Naṣīr-al-dīn Ṭūsī, written late in life, ca. 670/1271-72. According to its introduction, it was composed after the *Ak̲lāq-e nāṣerī* (q.v.) for Ṣāḥeb-e Dīvān Šams-al-dīn Moḥammad Jovaynī, statesman and brother of the historian ʿAlāʾ-al-dīn ʿAṭā Malek. Its genuineness is questioned by those who feel it contrasts too strongly with Ṭūsī's life and with his other writings. While a few would doubt its actual authenticity, many others only too easily assert (cf. A. J. Arberry, *Classical Persian Literature*, London, 1958, p. 262) that the author himself could not have been "sincere" when writing it. In the nature of the case, nothing conclusive is likely to emerge. One might observe that a measure of inconsistency or (perhaps better) development is a natural part of human existence; as the experience of many rational thinkers would suggest (Plato, Plotinus, Ḡazālī, Avicenna, and St. Thomas Aquinas are but a few), there is no essential dichotomy as between pragmatic living and philosophy on the one hand and mystical intuition on the other. On internal evidence, the linguistic features of the work (especially the use of the Arabic component) have much in common with those of the *Ak̲lāq-e nāṣerī*. The same holds for a good part of the content and the treatment; cf. especially the latter work's Discourse Three, Section Two, on love.

The treatise is not really original or concerned with the technicalities of mystical discipline and experience; rather does it seek to apply, in fairly standard fashion, the fruits of the mystical lifestyle to moral situations. It is divided into six *bāb*s (chapters), each of which except the last (a very short piece), is subdivided into six *faṣl*s (sections), of varying length. Chapter one (on motion) comprises faith, constancy, intention, truthfulness, conversion, and sincerity. Chapters two (on removing hindrances from the spiritual path) includes repentance, abstinence, poverty, discipline, self-examination, and piety. Chapter three (on the mystical path and the search for perfection) has solitude, reflection, fear and sadness, hope, fortitude, and gratitude. Chapter four is on the states associated with the way-stages until perfection is attained and comprises will, yearning, love (*maḥabbat*), knowledge (*maʿrefat*), certainty, and repose. Chapter five (on the states befalling those who attain) includes reliance on God, acceptance, surrender to God, monotheistic affirmation (*tawḥīd*), union with God (*etteḥād*), and unity (*waḥdat*). Chapter six is on self-annihilation (*fanā*).

The work has been copied, lithographed, and printed many times, never critically. A Berlin (Kāvīāni) edition of 1306 Š./1927 was republished in Tehran 1345 Š./1966. Prepared by Ḥ. Sayyed Naṣrallāh Taqawī, it is a facsimile of the calligraphy of Mīrzā Ḥosayn Khan Sayfī ʿEmād-al-kottāb. It has a page-by-page Arabic equivalent by Rokn-al-dīn Moḥammad b. ʿAlī Jorjānī and a somewhat far-ranging introduction on philosophy and mysticism, in east and west, by Moḥammad Modarresī. There is no complete western-language translation, nor would one add much to the body of Islamic mystical lore already available.

Bibliography: Monzawī, *Nosk̲ahā* I, pp. 1057-59. Mošār, *Fehrest* I, cols. 403-04.

(G. M. Wickens)

AWTĀD. See ABDĀL; AWLĪĀʾ.

ĀXŠTI (Avestan) "Peace, contract of peace." The existence of a late Avestan divinity Āxšti (fem.) is doubtful. The common noun, "peace," occurs several times (*Yt.* 10.29, 11.14; *Y.* 60.5; *Pursišnīhā* 26) but personified only in the Young Avestan litanies, in which a large number of abstract notions are personified: as direct object of *yaz-* "to revere" (*yazamaidē*, "we revere," *Yt.* 11.15; *V*[*ispe*]*r*[*ed*] 7.1: *S*[*īrōza*] 2.2; and *yazāi* "I shall revere," *Yt.* 15.1), or of *āvaēδayamahī* ("we invite," *Vr.* 11.16), and associated with Vohu Manah (*S.* 1.18, 2.2). In Middle Persian literature there seems to be no trace of a divinity Āštīh "Peace." In the Avestan litanies *āxšti* is accompanied by *hąm.vaintī* which Bartholomae (*AirWb.*, col. 311) took as an adjective "victorious" (conceivably by haplology from the present participle **hąm.vanaintī*) but which is more likely to be the substantive "victory" (with an unusual full grade of the root before the suffix *-ti*).

Bibliography: *AirWb.*, col., 311. Gray, *Foundations*, pp. 138ff. E. Benveniste and L. Renou, *Vṛtra et Vṛθragna*, Paris, 1934, pp. 54ff. H.-P. Schmidt, *Vedish* vratá *und awestisch* urvata, Hamburg, 1958, p. 137 n. 67 (with criticism of Benveniste and Renou). On *hąm-vaintī* see also K. F. Geldner, *Studien zum Avesta*, Strassburg, 1882, p. 119. S. Wikander, *Vayu*, Lund, 1942, pp. 16ff. J. Kellens, *Les noms-racines de l'Avesta*, Wiesbaden, 1974, pp. 44ff.

(B. SCHLERATH)

AXT (Av. Axtya), a sorcerer and, according to Zoroastrian tradition, a vehement, early opponent of the Religion. He was defeated in a verbal contest by Yōšt ī Friyān (Yōišta of the Fryānas), who had sacrificed to Ardvī Sūrā Anāhitā, asking "that I may be victorious over the false Axt of dark existence (*duždå təmaŋ'hå*; Pahlavi in *Dēnkard: dušdēn ī tam-axw*) and may reply to his 99 difficult questions asked in enmity" (*Yt.* 5.81-83). The Pahlavi text *Mādayān ī Yōšt ī Friyān* (q.v.) elaborates the legend but attributes only 33 riddles to Axt. It relates how the sorcerer had previously slain many people who failed to correctly answer his questions. In the course of the contest Axt was impelled to slay his own brother, as well as Hufraš—his own wife and Yōšt ī Friyān's sister. After answering the questions (with divine assistance), Axt in his turn is unable to solve Yōšt ī Friyān's three riddles. Ahriman, fearing a magical loss of efficacy, refuses Axt the answers; and the defeated sorcerer is ritually slain by Yōšt ī Friyān. The *Selections of Zātspram* (25.10, ed. Anklesaria, p. 92) places this event in year 80 of the Religion. Axt is there given the epithet *wššp'y*. The Sasanian Avesta may have contained additional legends about Axt. *Fragard* 21 of the *Warštmānsr Nask* dealt with his hostility to Zaraθuštra (*Dēnkard*, ed. Sanjana, XVIII, p. 43.14; ed. Madan, II, p. 869.8-9; ed. Dresden, p. 154.6-7). *Dēnkard* 3.196 attributes to Axt "of evil knowledge" 10 admonitions against the Religion (ed. Madan, I, pp. 210-12; J. de Menasce, *Le troisième livre du Dēnkart*, Paris, 1972, pp. 203-05). Axt is there depicted as espousing the reverse of Zaraθuštra's commands: hostility to the gods, friendship with the demons, and the practice of evil works, sorcery, and harm to people.

(M. F. KANGA)

AXTAR (Middle and New Persian) "star" or "constellation." This word, which first appears in Pahlavi, is an early back-formation from Middle Persian *apāxtar* (*abāxtar*) (planet) produced by artificial dropping of the first component (false deglutination). This was made possible by a notion that *apāxtar* meant "off-star" or "unstar" (*nē-axtar*), whereas in reality *apāxtar* can be traced through the Old Iranian **apāxtara* (backward-turning, retrograde) to Aryan **apāk-* or **apānk-* "backward." The planets were regarded as abnormal stars because their courses appear to be in the opposite direction to the general eastward motion of the firmament.

Also derived from *apāxtar* is the New Persian word *bāḵtar*, which means "west" in the context of an eastward orientation and "north" in that of a southward orientation. If the speaker means "west," he turns his back on the rising sun; if north, on the noon sun.

These matters were first elucidated by W. Eilers in "Stern—Planet—Regenbogen—Ein Beitrag zur vorderasiatischen Himmelskunde," in *Der Orient in der Forschung. Festschrift für Otto Spies*, Wiesbaden, 1967, pp. 112ff.; also in *Abhandlungen der Göttinger Akademie der Wissenschaften*, Phil-hist. Kl. 3, 98, 1976, pp. 115ff., and more fully in *Sinn und Herkunft der Planetennamen*, Sitzungsberichte der Bayerischen Akademie der Wissenschaften, Phil.-hist. Kl. 5, 1975, pp. 8ff.

Compounds of *axtar* with verbal stems indicating "count" or "know" mean "astrologer;" e.g. *axtar-(ā)mār* (q.v.), NPers. *aḵtaršenās*. The occasional (NPers.) reading *aḵtar-e āmār* or *aḵtar-e mār* with a senseless *eżāfa* is of course incorrect.

(W. EILERS)

AXTARMĀR (or AXTARĀMĀR, Pahlavi; AXTARMAR, Man. Mid. Persian) "astronomer." The astronomers were included in the category of the third of the four Sasanian social classes, i.e., the class of the scribes, together with the physicians and poets (*Nāma-ye Tansar*, p. 12; *ʿAhd-e Ardašīr*, p. 54; *Ketāb al-tāj*, p. 25). In the *Kār-nāmag* (ed. Antia, p. 11, par. 4, p. 13, par. 10) the astronomers are mentioned in conjuction with the wise men. Their head had the title *Axtarmārān sālār* (*Kār-nāmag*, p. 12, par. 5, p. 16, par. 6). The astronomers studied the positions of the stars, established and defined horoscopes, and predicted events (*Bundahišn*, pp. 50.15, 57.11, 60.3, 66.9). This last duty gave them special respect and influence at the royal court, where they would foretell the future of a new-born prince and read his horoscope (Ṭabarī, II, pp. 854, 1052ff.; Ṯaʿālebī, *Ḡorar*, pp. 539, 712; Dīnavarī, p. 113). According to Ṭabarī (pp. 1009-10), Ḵosrow Parvēz kept 360 priests, magicians, and astrologers around him, and when he was concerned about a matter, he would ask for their opinions. Unfavorable opinions concerning someone close to the king usually brought unpleasant consequences for that person; when Ḵosrow's astrologers predicted that his death would be by the hand of someone from Nīmrūz, Mardānšāh, the governor of Nīmruž, was executed (Ṭabarī, II, pp. 1058ff.). In Sogdian sources the *'nyrks'yt* "astronomers" were charged with similar responsibilities (*Vessantara Jātaka*, ed. E. Benveniste, Paris, 1946, p. 104).

Similar terms are Pahl. (Parthian) **simaspār* "soothsayer" (*Ayādgār ī Zarērān*, in *Pahlavi Texts*, p. 7, par. 2), Sogd. *sambatsar* (D. N. Mackenzie, in *Acta Iranica* 23, pp. 284-85); Pahl. *kēd* "soothsayer, astrologer" (*Kār-nāmag*, ed. Antia, p. 52, par. 2, etc.), Man. Parth. *qydyg* (W. B. Henning, *BSO(A)S* 9/1, 1937, pp. 84, 91-92); Pahl. and Man. Mid. Pers. *kandāg* "magician" (Henning, ibid., p. 84).

See also ASTRONOMY AND ASTROLOGY.

Bibliography: *Nāma-ye Tansar*, ed. M. Mīnovī, Tehran, 1311 Š./1932. M. Grignaschi, "Quelques spécimens de la littérature sasanide," (*'Ahd-e Ardašīr*) *JA* 254, 1966, pp. 1-142. Jāḥeẓ, *Ketāb al-tāj*, ed. A. Z. Pāšā, Cairo, 1914.

(A. TAFAŻŻOLĪ)

ĀXWARR (NPers. ĀḴOR), Middle Persian term meaning "manger" or "stall" and borrowed into Armenian as *axoṙ*. It is derived from *ā-xwarna*, a combination of *xwar-* (drink, eat) with the preverb *ā*. Since ancient times a Near Eastern manger has normally been a recess hollowed out of a thick mud-brick wall so as to form a trough before which the feeding animal (ass, horse, or camel) stands. The surrounding stable is called *ṭawīla* or *sotūrgāh*.

In dialectical variants such as *owḵor*, and also in the Avestan *avō.xᵛarəna-* (place for watering animals, Bartholomae, *AirWb.*, col. 180), *ā* is obviously rivaled by *āb* (water) as the first component. In place-names it is often impossible to distinguish between original *āḵᵛar* (manger, stall) and another *āḵᵛar* contracted from *āb-ḵᵛar* (water-drinking). The latter usually does not refer to a place's inhabitants but denotes the limited area of its fields and orchards which "drinks," i.e., is irrigated by, some source such as a spring, *qanāt*, stream, or river. The New Persian *ābḵᵛar* (*ābḵor*) is thus virtually synonymous with the much commoner *ābād* (Pahl. *āpāta*), if this means "watered," (see Eilers, *MSS* 45, 1985, pp. 23f.) and with *čam*, (from *čamīdan*, to drink, sip) which in some districts is quite frequent.

The contraction of *ābḵᵛar* to *āḵor* with consequent distortion of the meaning to "manger" probably lies at the root of certain legends about site origins, which in Iran as elsewhere have a charm of their own. In the not infrequent place-name Āḵor-e Rostam, the meaning is clearly "manger" because Rostam's steed, Raḵš, is said to have been lodged in a cave in the locality (e.g., in a cave near Persepolis). Many other names are problematic; e.g., two places mentioned in medieval sources, Āḵūr in Gorgān and Āḵūrīn between Semnān and Dāmḡān; Āḵūr-sar (Razmārā, *Farhang* III, p. 6); and the area called Āḵora in the *šahrestān* of Farīdan in the *ostān* of Isfahan, with its villages of Āḵora-pā'īn and Bādajān Āḵora (ibid., x, pp. 4-5, 31).

Interpretation of the following names with *āḵor* as the second component is particularly difficult: Čegāḵor, west of Isfahan (cf. Curzon, *Persia* II, p. 298; *čegā* means mound or hill), Čīlāḵor and Mīrāḵor (lit. stablemaster) near Zanjān, the two villages Golāḵor in the *šahrestāns* of Ahar and Tabrīz, Pīšāḵor near Kadkan in Khorasan (*pīš* may perhaps here mean dwarf palm), and Sīlāḵor in the *šahrestān* of Borūjerd (probably *seyl-āḵor*, flood-irrigated (Razmārā, op. cit., II, pp. 87, 299; IV, p. 452; VI, p. 46; IX, p. 80; Kayhān, *Jogrāfīā* II, pp. 443-44). There is no question, however, that the names Ābḵᵛāra (ibid., IV, p. 1) and Ābḵᵛara (ibid., I, p. 1) refer to irrigation.

See also ĀXWARRBED.

Bibliography: See also Horn, *Etymologie* no. 8. H. Hübschmann, *Armen. Etymologie* I, p. 93, no. 6. On *āb-ḵᵛar*: W. Eilers, *Die Sprache* 6, 1960, p. 128 n. 94. Idem, "Kyros," *Beiträge zur Namenforschung* 15, 1964, p. 220. Idem, *Semiramis*, Vienna, 1971, p. 61 n. 111. Idem, "Toponymische Übertragung," *Onoma* 21, 1977, p. 299. Idem, *Westiranische Mundarten aus der Sammlung Wilhelm Eilers* [I]: *Die Mundart von Chunsar*, Wiesbaden, 1976 (with U. Schapka), pp. 280 n. 45 and 374. Idem, *Geographische Namengebung in und um Iran*, Munich, 1982, pp. 26, 41 n. 147.

(W. EILERS)

ĀXWARRBED, Middle Iranian term for the "Stablemaster, Royal Equerry," lit. "lord of the manger" (see ĀXWARR), an official in charge of the royal stables and transport. It is attested in the inscription of Šāpūr I on the Ka'ba-ye Zardošt (ŠKZ Parth. 1. 24, the Mid. Pers. is lost): *Wrdn 'hwrpty* "Wardan the Stablemaster," Greek version (1.58) OUARDAN TOU EPI TĒS PATHNĒS (see A. Maricq, *Syria* 35, 1958, pp. 324-25, repr. in *Classica et Orientalia*, Paris, 1965, pp. 66-67); in Sogdian in the Mug documents as *''γwyrpt* (*Sogdiĭskie dokumenty s gory Mug* III, ed. M. N. Bogulyubov and O. I. Smirnova, Moscow, 1963, p. 89); and borrowed in Armenian as *axoṙapet* (Hübschmann, *Armen. Etymologie*, p. 93). In later Sasanian and early Islamic times there is a corresponding title Mid. Pers. *āxwarr-sālār* "Chief of the Stable," NPers. *āḵor-sālār* (*Ayādgār ī Zarērān*, in *Pahlavi Texts*, p. 11.18; *Šāh-nāma* [*sālār-e āḵᵛar*], see M. Dabīrsīāqī et al., eds., *Loḡat-nāma-ye fārsī* I/3, Tehran, 1362 Š./1983, p. 288). Similar titles are **āxwarr-dār* "stable-holder," in Aramaic *'ḥwryyr'* (S. Telegdi, *JA*, 1935 p. 226); **āxwarr-bān* "stable-keeper," in Arm. *axoṙapan*; finally, Ḵᵛārazmī (*Mafātīḥ al-'olūm*, ed. G. van Vloten, Leiden, 1895, p. 118) and Ḥamza Eṣfahānī (*al-Tanbīh 'alā ḥodūṯ al-taṣḥīf*, ed. Āl-e Yāsīn, Baghdad, 1967, p. 66) list the office (*dafīra*) of *āhorhamār* "Accountant of the Stables." A similar office was that of the Sasanian *stōrbān* "horse-keeper" (*Kār-nāmag*, ed. Antia, p. 15 par. 2). It is not known whether the different titles implied differences in duties and rank. In later Islamic times the term *mīrāḵor* was used for the "Royal Marshall" or "Equerry" (W. Eilers in *Acta Iranica* 1, 1974, p. 286, proposes a derivation of *mīr-* from OIr. **marya*, not from Ar.-Pers. *amīr*) and recently *mehtar* or *mehtar-e asb* has been used to designate the groom or horse-keeper (Dehḵodā, s.v. *mehtar*).

(A. TAFAŻŻOLĪ)

ĀY ḴĀNOM or AÏ KHANUM (Tepe), a local Uzbek name (lit. Lady Moon hill) designating the site of an important Greek colonial city in northern Afghanistan excavated since 1965 by a French mission and which belonged to a powerful hellenistic state born of Alexander's conquest in Central Asia (329-27 B.C.). Centered around Bactriana, the middle valley of the Oxus (Amu Darya), this colonized area was first part of the Seleucid empire, then, around 250 B.C., it became an independent kingdom which remained under Greek rule until approximately 150 B.C. when it was destroyed by nomad invasions from the northern steppes. The city of Aï Khanum which controlled a fertile agricultural plain irrigated by an extensive system of canals (J. -Cl. Gardin and P. Gentelle, *Bulletin de l'Ecole française d'Extrême Orient*, 1976, pp. 59-99) and a mountainous back-country (Badaḵšān) rich in minerals and semi-precious stones (rubies, lapis), was built at the junction of the Oxus river and of one of its left-bank affluents, the Kokča. Roughly triangular in shape (1800 by 1600 m), it encompassed within a girt of powerful mud-brick ramparts (P. Leriche, *Fouilles d'Aï Khanoum IV: les remparts d'Aï Khanoum*, Paris, 1986) a lower town where most of the buildings were located and an acropolis on a hill (P. Bernard and D. Schlumberger, *Bulletin de correspondance hellénique*, 1965, pp. 595-657; P. Bernard, *Proc. British Academy*, 1967, p. 71-95). Outside the ramparts lay a suburb and the necropolis. Although the Greek colonists kept their national language and way of life, the architecture of the tówn, combining mud-brick walls and stone columns and pillars, reveals a mixture of Greek and oriental traditions (P. Bernard, *Comptes rendus de l'Académie des inscriptions et belles letters*, 1966, pp. 127-33; 1967, pp. 306-24; 1968, pp. 263-79; 1969, pp. 313-55; 1970, pp. 301-49; 1971, pp. 387-452; 1972, pp. 605-32; 1974, pp. 280-308; 1975, pp. 167-97; 1976, pp. 287-322; idem, *JA*, 1976, pp. 245-75; P. Bernard et al., *Fouilles d'Aï Khanoum* I, pp. 1-120; *Bulletin de l'École française d'Extrême Orient*, 1976, pp. 6-51). Columnated porticoes of the Corinthian, Doric, and more rarely Ionic orders (P. Bernard, *Syria*, 1968, pp. 111-51) bespeak the hellenistic tradition as do the antefixes and tiles of the roofs and such typical buildings as a gymnasium, a theater, a fountain, and funerary monuments. The gymnasium, of colossal proportions, consisted of several courtyards surrounded by rooms, of which the two principal ones were devoted to physical training and intellectual activities, and included extensive bath-facilities (S. Veuwe, *Fouilles d'Aï Khanoum VI: Le gymnase*, Paris, 1987). In the theater, made entirely of mud bricks and as large as the one in Babylon, the usual tiered rows of seats were interrupted by loggias for prominent people. In a fountain a water-spout carved to represent one of the characters of Greek comedy proves that the theatrical repertory itself was Greek. Funerary monuments for eminent citizens were built inside the ramparts and imitated Hellenic temples. In the most ancient of them—and the most modest—a certain Kineas was buried, who may have been the city's founder. In the precinct of this heroon a stele, on which was engraved a copy of the famous Delphic maxims which embody Greek wisdom, had been erected (L. Robert in *Fouilles d'Aï Khanoum* I, pp. 207-37). Alongside these buildings of Hellenic types there were others of Oriental tradition in which local elements were fused with Iranian and even Mesopotamian ones. Three temples have been discovered, none of which has a Greek plan. One of them, a simple stepped podium in open air on the acropolis, is clearly related to Iranian and Central Asian sanctuaries of the Achaemenid period. Another, standing on a three-stepped platform, with a square plan and a broad vestibule leading to a smaller cella flanked by two sacristies, and whose walls are decorated with indented recesses, is also purely Oriental and can be compared with certain Parthian temples at Dura Europos. A third temple with a triple cella has the same wall-decoration and stepped platform. Although the official pantheon, as it appears on the coinage of the Greco-Bactrian kingdom, was, with a few exceptions, purely Greek (Cl. Petitot, *RN*, 1975, pp. 23-57; P. Bernard, ibid., pp. 58-69; 1973, pp. 238-89; 1974, pp. 6-41; *Fouilles d'Aï Khanoum IV*: *Les monnaies hors trésors*, Paris, 1985, this typė of religious architecture implies a strong influx of local beliefs in the city-cults and suggests divinities of a syncretic nature. The vast patrician mansions, with their front courtyard and the disposition of the secondary rooms grouped around the principal one which is usually surrounded by a peripheral corridor, except for the spacious bath-rooms, have nothing to do with the traditional Greek houses (P. Bernard, *JA*, 1976, pp. 257-66). A huge arsenal housed the military equipment (F. Grenet, *Bulletin de l'École française d'Extrême Orient*, 1980, pp. 51-63). The city's main building was a monumental palace—probably the governor's—approximately 300 m^2, which was situated in the middle of the lower town. It comprised several courtyards, two of them possessed columned porticoes, residential quarters, administrative sections with offices and reception rooms, and also a treasury in which was found a large number of storage jars, several of them bearing economic inscriptions in Greek (Cl. Rapin, *Bulletin de correspondence hellénique*, 1983, pp. 315-72), a large amount of fragments of cut and uncut semi-precious stones, among them a great quantity of lapis lazuli, and fragments of Greek literary papyri. Although the columns and antefixes give a certain Greek aura, the compact aggregation of several ensembles in the same compound linked by a complex criss-crossing of corridors, the plan of certain units, the monumentality of proportions, and the repetitious symmetry, all point to Oriental conceptions. Similarly the pottery offers examples of Greek types as well as purely local forms (J. -Cl. Gardin in *Fouilles d'Aï Khanoum* I, pp. 121-88). In the field of fine arts, the Greek colonists were much more conservative and seemed to have been satisfied with traditional Greek productions, as can be seen from fragments of stone statuettes, from the water-spouts of a fountain representing respectively a dolphin-head, a dog-head and a comic mask, and from the pebble-mosaics which paved the bath-rooms of the palace and were decorated with floral and animal designs (P. Bernard, *Bulletin, de l'École française d'Extrême Orient*, 1976, pp. 6-24). A beautiful medallion in gilt silver, figuring the goddess Cybele on her lion-driven chariot, followed by one of her priests holding an umbrella over her and facing another one who sacrifices at an altar, represents, through its flat Hieratic style, a rare exception to this general trend (P. Bernard, *Computes rendus de l'Académie des inscriptions et belles lettres*, 1970, pp. 339-47). Fragments of life-size statues modeled in clay or stucco attest the introduction of a technique which was subsequently spread all over Central Asia. As one might expect in such a wealthy and urbanized society, workshops were active in producing all kinds of artifacts both for utilitarian purposes, for example grindstones of a specifically Greek type, and for the luxury market such as carved ivories (P. Bernard, *Syria*, 1970, pp. 327-43) and vessels of dark schist inlaid with colored stones (H. -P. Francfort, *Arts Asiatiques*, 1976, pp. 91-95).

See also AFGHANISTAN VIII: ARCHEOLOGY; IX: PRE-ISLAMIC ART.

Bibliography: See also *EIr*. I, p. 530. *Camb. Hist. Iran* III, pp. 188, 822, 866, 1032-35, 1037, 1040. O. Guillaume, *Fouilles d'Aï Khanoum* II: *Les propytees de la rue principale*, Paris, 1983. H. -P. Francfort, ibid., III: *Le sanctuaire du Temple à niches indentées. 2. Les trouvailles*, Paris, 1984.

(O. BERNARD)

AY TĪMŪR (or TEYMŪR), MOḤAMMAD, Sarbadār commander and ruler, "the son of a slave" (probably one of the Turkish *ḡolāms* that Mas'ūd, the previous Sarbadār leader, recruited to supplement his bandit and Shi'ite dervish soldiery). Mas'ūd left Ay Tīmūr governing Sabzavār when campaigning against Herat (743/1342) and Māzandarān (summer, 745/1344). When Mas'ūd and his army fell in Māzandarān, Ay Tīmūr found himself the ruler. To defend Sabzavār and Nīšāpūr against Ṭaḡāy Tīmūr (for the reading of this name, see Smith, *History*, pp. 181-82) and Arḡūnšāh Jāūnī Qorbānī (Mong. Je'ün Gurban), Ay Tīmūr had to acknowledge Ṭaḡāy Tīmūr's sovereignty (Sabzavār coin of 746), station his good troops on the frontiers, and eke out their numbers with the Shi'ite dervishes demobilized after Mas'ūd murdered their leader, Ḥasan Jūrī. These measures led to military success and political failure. Ay Tīmūr remained unguarded against the dervishes, who hated him as Mas'ūd's man, and the gentry of Bāštīn (whence came the first Sarbadār leaders, 'Abd-al-Razzāq and Mas'ūd) and aristocrats of Sabzavār (especially Šams-al-dīn 'Alī), who despised him. Alleging his disrespect for the dervishes, preference for "the commons and the mob," and the impropriety of rule by "the son of a slave," these deposed and, instigated by Šams-al-dīn 'Alī, murdered Ay Tīmūr in Jomādā I, 747/August-September, 1346.

Bibliography: A lost *Tārīḵ-e Sarbadārān* is partly reproduced in *Mojmal-e faṣīḥī*, Mašhad, 1339 Š./1960, pp. 70-74. Mīrḵānd (Tehran), pp. 614-17. Dawlatšāh, ed. Browne, p. 281. See also F. Tauer, ed., *Cinq opuscules de Ḥāfiẓ-i Abrū*, Prague, 1959, notes, p. 16. J. M. Smith, Jr., *The History of the Sarbadār Dynasty, 1336-1381 A.D., and Its Sources*, The Hague and Paris, 1970, pp. 126-30, and index.

(J. M. SMITH, JR.)

ĀYADANA "place of cult." The term occurs once in the Old Persian Bīstūn inscription of Darius I (DB 1.63f.): *āyadanā tayā Gaumāta haya maguš viyaka adam niyaçārayam* "the places of cult which Gaumāta the mage had destroyed, I restored." The *āyadana*s can hardly have been temples, since we know from Herodotus that the Iranians, even in his time, had no temples, and since statues of gods (and therefore presumably temples to house them) were not introduced until the time of Artaxerxes II. There is absolutely no proof that the so-called Ka'ba-ye Zardošt at Naqš-e Rostam, and the similar structures at Pasargadae and Nūrābād, ever were fire temples as suggested by W. Hinz ("Altpersische Feuerheiligtümer," *Geistige Arbeit* 9/2, 1942, pp. 1f.) and called *āyadana* (see also E. Schmidt, *Persepolis* III, Chicago, 1970, p. 45, and D. Stronach, *Iran* 3, 1965, pp. 16f.). The term must therefore have designated podiums, terraces such as those excavated by R. Ghirshman (*Terrasses sacrées de Bard-è Neshande et Masjid-i Soleiman*, Paris, 1976). To what gods the *āyadana*s that Gaumāta destroyed were consecrated is a moot question. Gaumāta's gesture has often been interpreted as reflecting a religious conflict, either a Zoroastrian revolt of the magi (thus. e.g., L. H. Gray, in *Encyclopaedia of Religion and Ethics*, ed. J. Hastings, I, Edinburgh, 1908, p. 71) or, on the contrary, an attempt on the part of the magi to suppress Zoroastrianism (see, e.g., R. N. Frye, *The Heritage of Persia*, Cleveland and New York, 1963, p. 88, and J. Duchesne-Guillemin, in *Acta Iranica* 3, 1974, p. 19). It has even been suggested that the conflict between Gaumāta and Darius reflected a class struggle, Darius being helped by the noblemen (M. Dandamayev, *Iran pri pervykh akhemenidakh*, Moscow, 1963, pp. 256f.). But this hypothesis too runs up against major difficulties since one would expect Darius to name the gods whose places of cult he restored (gods of the aristocrats, such as Vərəθraγna, the god of war). In fact, he only names Ahura Mazdā.

Bibliography: See also M. Boyce, "On the Zoroastrian Temple Cult of Fire," *JAOS*, 1975, pp. 454f. Idem, *Zoroastrianism* II, pp. 88-89. G. Widengren, *Die Religionen Irans*, Stuttgart, 1965, p. 141.

(J. DUCHESNE-GUILLEMIN)

AYĀDGĀR Ī JĀMĀSPĪG "Memorial of Jāmāsp," a short but important Zoroastrian work in Middle Persian, also known as the *Jāmāspī-* and *Jāmāsp-nāma*. Fragments from a damaged manuscript survive in Pahlavi script, but the complete text exists only in Pāzand (i.e., Middle Persian written in Avestan script), with many inaccuracies. There is also a later Pārsī version (i.e., a transcription in Arabic script), with

Persian and Gujarati paraphrases. The Pahlavi fragments were published by E. W. West in *Avesta, Pahlavi and Ancient Persian Studies in Honour of ... P. B. Sanjana* I, Strasbourg and Leipzig, 1904, pp. 97-116; and the various versions by J. J. Modi, *Jāmāspī, Pahlavi, Pazend and Persian Texts with ... English and Gujarati Translation*, Bombay, 1903. G. Messina, in *Libro apocalittico persiano Ayātkār ī Žāmāspīk*, Rome, 1939. published the Pāzand together with a complete Pahlavi text (of which the missing sections were reconstructed from the Pāzand and Pārsī versions), together with translation and notes. (See the review by A. Pagliaro, *RSO*, 1922, pp. 147-54.)

The work is cast in the form of question and answer between Wištāsp (Zoroaster's princely patron) and Jāmāsp (the prophet's kinsman through his marriage to Hvōvī). The latter figures in Zoroastrian tradition as the greatest of seers, divinely endued with all knowledge. A description of what his superhuman wisdom can reveal (*Ayādgār ī Jāmāspīg* 1.10-13) has a parallel in *Ayādgār ī Zarērān* (q.v.), pars. 35-38. The *Ayādgār ī Jāmāspīg*, written in simple, direct style, may have been intended as a compendium of essential doctrine, together with basic myth, legend, history, and some miscellaneous matter, for the enlightenment of the laity, and it has been deservedly popular. As is usual with Pahlavi texts, its sources are diverse. A brief account of creation and of duality (chaps. 2-3, cf. the *Bundahišn*) derives ultimately from lost Avestan works. Here (chap. 3.6-7) there occurs a striking theological statement, that Ohrmazd's creation of the six Amašaspands was like lamps being lit one from another, none being diminished thereby. A standard list (as found in the *Bundahišn* and Ferdowsī's *Šāh-nāma*) is given of the ancient rulers of Iran, from Gayōmard to Wištāsp himself (chap. 4); and there is another of the kings who are to follow him (chap. 15). In chap. 15.5-6 it is said that after Alexander rule will pass to the "renowned Parthians" (*husraw Partawān*), under whom Iran will prosper again. This is at odds with the usual late Sasanian propaganda about the evils of Arsacid rule, and suggests a Parthian transmission of some of the material. This possibility is strengthened by the fact that Jāmāsp is given throughout the Parthian title of *bidaxš*, which still in early Sasanian times meant the highest in the land after the king, but then lost this significance (see O. Szemerényi, in *Acta Iranica* 5, 1975, pp. 360-66, 375, 391). Other matter is clearly of Persian origin, notably the Sasanian king-list down to Yazdegerd III (chap. 15.7-27). During remarks about Arabs, Chinese, etc., there are interesting implications that there were Zoroastrians among the Hindus (chap. 8.4, 5) and Turks (chap. 12.9).

Chapter 16, which is preserved in Pahlavi, consists of prophecy about the end of Zoroaster's millennium, with the coming of Pišyōtan and Ušēdar (see APOCALYPTIC: ZOROASTRIAN). As in the *Zand ī Wahman Yašt* (see BAHMAN YAŠT), there is perhaps a blending of old prophecies, made after Alexander's conquest, with later ones foretelling the downfall of Arab, Turk, and "Roman;" but there are details, some puzzling, which are peculiar to *Ayādgār ī Jāmāspīg*. The chapter was edited by H. W. Bailey, "To the Zamasp-Namak I, II," *BSOS* 6, 1930-32, pp. 55-85, 581-600, with addenda, pp. 822-24, 948 (reprinted without the addenda in H. W. Bailey, *Opera Minora. Articles on Iranian Studies*, ed. M. Nawabi, I, Shiraz, 1981, pp. 22-55, 57-76). In an important study ("Une apocalypse pehlevie: Le Žāmāsp-Nāmak," *RHR* 106, 1932, pp. 337-80) E. Benveniste established that this chapter is in verse, and linked it with other apocalyptic texts, Iranian and non-Iranian. Chapter 17, surviving only in Pāzand, is of the same character, and also contains some unique materials. In it Jāmāsp foretells events of the millennia of Ušēdar and Ušēdarmāh, and those of the last days.

Bibliography: See also J. C. Tavadia, *Die mittelpersische Sprache und Literatur der Zarathustrier*, Leipzig, 1956, pp. 124-26. B. Utas, "On the Composition of the Ayyātkār ī Zarērān," in *Acta Iranica* 5, 1975, pp. 409-11. J. P. de Menasce, "Zoroastrian Pahlavi Writings," *Camb. Hist. Iran* II/2, pp. 1194-95.

(M. BOYCE)

AYĀDGĀR Ī WUZURGMIHR, a popular-religious *andarz* composition in Pahlavi, attributed to one of the best-known sages of the Sasanian period, Wuzurgmihr (Bozorgmehr) ī Buxtagān, who was active at the court of Ḵosrow I Anōšīravān (531-79 A.D.). Nothing in the work itself is at variance with such a dating, and the unity of the composition points to a single author.

The work is preserved in what seems to be its original Pahlavi form (ed. J. M. Jamasp-Asana, *Pahlavi Texts*, Bombay, 1897-1913, pp. 85-101), as well as in an Arabic version of a fairly early period, which reflects quite closely the Pahlavi original (in Meskawayh's [Meskūya] *Jāvīdān ḵerad*, cf. Abū ʿAlī Aḥmad b. Moḥammad Meskawayh, *al-Ḥekma al-ḵāleda*. ed. ʿA. Badawī, Cairo, 1952, pp. 29-41). The substance of the composition occurs also in verse form in Ferdowsī's *Šāh-nāma* (ed. Borūḵīm, VIII, pp. 2448ff.). Several other later elaborations and versifications are found both in Arabic and in Persian; most of them are unpublished. Many short quotations from the work are found scattered throughout the Arabic and Persian *adab* (q.v.) works, mostly deriving, as it seems, from the version known through Meskawayh but some are culled from other redactions. One of the more interesting independent versions of the work in Arabic was published from a manuscript by Louis Cheikho under the title *Ḥekam Bozorjmehr* (see *Machriq* 6, 1903, pp. 203-07, 250-54). Meskawayh's book itself contains other collections of sayings attributed to Wuzurgmihr, and several further such collections are known from other Arabic sources (e.g., Pseudo-Aṣmaʿī, *Nehāyat al-ʿarab*, Ms. British Museum Add. 23.298, fol. 193bff.), but their literary relationship to this composition is not easy to establish. Short anecdotes and sayings, as well as short collections of sayings attributed to Wuzurgmihr are scattered in the Arabic and Persian *adab* works (Masʿūdī's *Morūj*, Ṯaʿālebī's *Ḡorar*, etc.) as well as in medieval works in

Ethiopian (*Maṣḥafa falāsefa ṭabībān*, cf. F. Altheim, *Geschichte der Hunnen*, Berlin, 1963, V, pp. 215f.), Syriac (e.g. Bar Hebraeus. *The Laughable Stories*, ed. E.A.W. Budge, London, 1897, p. 17), and other languages.

The clearly structured composition begins with a short introduction, in which the author is described by a series of titles and epithets, some of which are not entirely clear: *wēnān* (or *nēwān*?) **pad *tan šabistān*, a chief courtier, of the town of Ōstīgān-Xusraw (cf. *Monumentum H. S. Nyberg* II, Acta Iranica 5, Leiden, Tehran, and Liège, 1975, pp. 223f.; also *Irano-Judaica*, ed. S. Shaked, Jerusalem, 1982, pp. 299f. Differently, H. W. Bailey, *Zoroastrian Problems in the Ninth-Century Books*, 2nd ed., London, 1971, introd. p. xliii). An unconvincing attempt was made by A. Christensen (*Acta Orientalia* 8, 1930, pp. 81-128) to identify Wuzurgmihr with the physician Borzūya, the reputed Sasanian author of the introduction to Ebn al-Moqaffaʿ's version of *Kalīla wa Demna.*

The opening section of the work states that it was written at the command of K̲osrow the King of Kings for the instruction of those "who, by accepting the [decree of] those above, have been created in a well-fashioned and worthy manner." The treatise was deposited, according to the opening section, in the royal treasury.

The next section, which constitutes the beginning of the treatise itself, is devoted to the theme of the futility and transience of the things of this world. The bulk of the treatise consists of an exposition of the main tenets of the Zoroastrian religion in the form of questions and answers. This part of the treatise contains, among other things, a list of the worst demons created by Ahriman to mislead man, and the faculties of wisdom and virtue which were created by Ohrmazd in order to counter the demons.

There follows a long section which consists of questions concerning abstract notions, such as what is the best nature, which custom is best, and so on. The answers, like the rest of the treatise, display a sort of pragmatic piety: Although the main tenor of the work is pious, there is little emphasis on observance and ritual; the main concern is with the moral and personal qualities connected with the religious life.

See also ANDARZ.

Bibliography: F. Muller, *WZKM* 12, 1898, pp. 55-58 (translation of the first part). J. C. Tarapore, *Pahlavi Andarz Nāmak*, Bombay, 1933, pp. 38-57 (a transcription and translation into English). A. Christensen, *Acta Orientalia* 8, 1930, pp. 81-128, (contains a discussion of the person of Bozorgmehr, and a partial translation of the text). M. Nawabi, *Revue de la Faculté des Lettres de l'Université de Tabriz* (*MDA Tabrīz*) 11/3, 1338 Š./1959, pp. 302-33 (the Pahlavi text with a translation into Persian; Arabic tr. of Nawabi's Persian tr. A. Tarǰānīzāda, ibid., 11/4, 1338 Š./1960, pp. 377-89). On the relationship of the Pahlavi and the Arabic text of Meskawayh cf. W. B. Henning, *ZDMG* 106, 1956, pp. 76f.

(S. SHAKED)

AYĀDGĀR Ī ZARĒRĀN "Memorial of Zarēr," a short Pahlavi text which is the only surviving specimen in that language of ancient Iranian epic poetry. It is preserved in a unique manuscript, written in A.D. 1322. The chief editions are those of J. M. Jamasp-Asana, *The Pahlavi Texts Contained in the Codex MK* II, Bombay, 1913, repr. Tehran, [1971-72], pp. 1-16; Pagliaro, *Il testo pahlavico Ayātkār-i Zarērān*, Rome, 1925; and D. Monchi-Zadeh, *Die Geschichte Zarēr's*, Uppsala, 1981 (reviewed by D. N. MacKenzie, *IIJ* 27, 1984, pp. 155-63). For other editions, translations, and commentaries see Monchi-Zadeh's edition and MacKenzie's review, pp. 9-10 and p. 163 n. 1.

The *Ayādgār ī Zarērān* celebrates an event in the early history of Zoroastrianism. Wištāsp, having accepted the "pure religion of the Mazda-worshippers" (*dēn ī abēzag ī māzdēsnān*), is challenged on this account by Arǰāsp, lord of the Hyōns. The wise J̌āmāsp foretells that Wištāsp's brother Zarēr and many others of his kin will die in the coming encounter. Nevertheless battle is joined. Zarēr, after fighting heroically, is foully slain by a Hyōn, Wīdrafš the sorcerer. His son Bastwar, forbidden by Wištāsp to go to the battle-field because of his youth, flouts this command, finds his father's body, and utters a moving lament over it. He slays many Hyōns in revenge, and shoots an arrow through Wīdrafš' heart. His cousin Spandyād, Wištāsp's son, ends the battle by capturing Arǰāsp, mutilating him, and sending him abject away.

There are numerous traces in the Pahlavi text of an older Parthian version, with Parthian words, phrases and grammatical usages scattered through it (for these see most fully MacKenzie, loc. cit.). Parthian, and other apparently archaic, certainly obscure, elements are most concentrated in passages of reported speech, notably par. 92, Bastwar's incantation over the arrow with which he is to shoot Wīdrafš; par. 41, an oath-taking formula; and pars. 84-87, Bastwar's elegy for his father. C. Bartholomae (*Zur Kenntnis der mitteliranischen Mundarten* IV, Sb. Heidelberger Ak. d. Wissenschaften, 1922, 6. Abh., p. 22) suggested that this elegy might come from an epic poem. Subsequently E. Benveniste ("Le mémorial de Zarēr," *JA*, 1932, pp. 245-93) argued convincingly that virtually the whole *Ayādgār ī Zarērān* is a heroic poem, a Sasanian adaptation of an Arsacid original, although his attempt to reconstruct a series of regular six-syllable lines has had to be abandoned in the light of subsequent work (initiated by W. B. Henning) on Pahlavi verse. (For a survey of this see S. Shaked in *W. B. Henning Memorial Volume*, London, 1970, pp. 395-405. For some further remarks on the metrics of *Ayādgār ī Zarērān* see B. Utas, "On the Composition of the Ayyātkār ī Zarēran," in *Acta Iranica* 5, 1975, pp. 399-418; and G. Lazard, "La métrique de la poésie parthe," in *Acta Iranica* 25, 1985, pp. 371-99).

Avestan allusions to the struggle of Vištāspa and Zairivairi (whose name, irregularly, developed into "Zarēr") against the "wicked Arəǰat.aspa" (*Yašt* 5.108, 112, 117, cf. *Yašt* 19.87) establish the antiquity of this story of "Wištāsp's battle" (*razm ī wištāspān*, *Ayādgār ī Zarērān*, par. 39). Bastwar also appears in the Avesta, as Bastavairi (*Yašt* 13.103); and various well-known Avestan characters have a part in the *Ayādgār ī Zarērān*, namely Spəntōδāta, J̌āmāspa, Hutaosa, and Humāya. It is reasonable to assume that Vištāspa's victory was first celebrated at his own court by minstrel lays in the Old Avestan tongue; and that because that victory was linked with the survival of the faith, it continued to be celebrated at Zoroastrian courts and castles down the ages, passing presumably through a Younger Avestan transmission into various other Iranian languages, until Parthian minstrels finally taught it to Sasanian singers (see M. Boyce, "The Parthian *Gōsān* and Iranian Minstrel Tradition," *JRAS*, 1957, pp. 10-45; "Zariadres and Zarēr," *BSOAS* 17, 1955, pp. 463-77). The tale became part of the materials amassed by Persian priests for the Sasanian royal chronicle, the *Xwadāy-nāmag*; and partly on the basis of that work, partly perhaps from a still living oral tradition in north-eastern Iran, Daqīqī turned it into rhymed verse in the tenth century A.D. His poem was incorporated by Ferdowsī in his *Šāh-nāma* ed. Borūk̲īm, VI, pp. 1497ff. Monchi-Zadeh (op. cit., pp. 75-121) has re-edited Daqīqī's lines, with a textual commentary. For a systematic comparison of Daqīqī's version with the *Ayādgār ī Zarērān* see A. G. and E. Warner, *The Shāhnāma of Firdausi* V, London, 1910, pp. 24-7; and for some further details B. Utas, art. cit. Other versions of the story are to be found in T̲aʿālebī, *Histoire des rois des Perses*, ed. and tr. H. Zotenberg, Paris, 1910, repr. Tehran, 1963, pp. 262ff., and Ṭabarī, *Taʾrīk̲ al-rosol waʾl-molūk*, ed. M. J. de Goeje, 1, Leiden, 1879, pp. 676ff., on which see Monchi-Zadeh, op. cit., pp. 10-11. The last-named version, which is the shortest, is the closest of these later renderings to the *Ayādgār ī Zarērān*. The *Ayādgār ī Zarērān* records the battle as the event of a day; and it is predominantly a celebration of the deeds of Zarēr and his son. The *Šāh-nāma* describes a prolonged campaign, and gives accounts of letters, speeches, and single combats at greater length. Moreover, it attributes the killing of Wīdrafš not to Bastwar ("Nastūr" in Daqīqī's rendering) but to the more famous Esfandīār (Av. Spəntōδāta, Pahl. Spandyād).

Despite the religious connection which evidently secured the story its immensely long survival, the interest in religion in the *Ayādgār ī Zarērān* is perfunctory, and the material and its handling belong essentially to heroic epic. As is usual in oral tradition, the incidentals of the tale have been changed to suit changing conditions, and the taste of successive audiences. The original lay presumably celebrated a battle between tribal chieftains, well before the Iranians adopted writing; but in the *Ayādgār ī Zarērān* Arǰāsp sends a letter to Wištāsp, and Zarēr dictates an answer to the chief scribe, *dibīrān mahist* (par. 9), whose name appears as *ʾpľhym*. (Former editors have interpreted this as Ebrāhīm, taking the name to refer to the early employment of Semitic scribes by Iranians; Monchi-Zadeh, op. cit., p. 53, emends to *ʾplsʾm*, i.e., Aparsām/Abarsām.) Descriptions of embassage and formal audience, and the titles of courtiers and court officials are details likely to have interested aristocratic listeners, while the battle itself has been developed from a local encounter between chariot-fighters of old to the clash of imperial armies, with huge numbers engaged, and Wištāsp holding a great military review in which war-elephants and mail-clad cavalry take part. Despite such anachronisms, suited to the Arsacid and Sasanian periods, the *Ayādgār ī Zarērān* retains the conventions of heroic epic, with rich hyperbole, fixed epithets, and an abundance of similes and formal repetitions. It thus attests, in both subject-matter and treatment, the long cultivation of Iranian minstrel poetry.

Bibliography: See also J. C. Tavadia, *Die mittelpersische Sprache und Literatur der Zarathustrier*, Leipzig, 1956, pp. 135-37. M. Boyce, *Camb. Hist. Iran* III/2, pp. 1157-58. Idem, *Textual Sources for the Study of Zoroastrianism*, Manchester, 1984, pp. 77-80.

(M. BOYCE)

AYĀDĪ-E AMR ALLĀH, "Hands of the Cause of God" (sing. also *ayādī*, normally preceded by the reverential term *ḥażrat*), term used in Baha'ism to designate the highest rank of the appointed religious hierarchy. In early Babism, an attempt was made to establish a hierarchical system based on eighteen groups of nineteen believers under the overall authority of a nineteenth group consisting of the Bāb (q.v.) and his first eighteen disciples, the Letters of the Living (*ḥorūf al-ḥayy*) or Foregoers (*ṣābeqūn*); but there is no evidence that, apart from the latter group, this system was ever made effective. Later Bābi writings such as the Persian *Bayān* (q.v.) and *Panj šaʾn* speak of "mirrors" (*marāyā*), "glasses" (*bolūrīyāt*), "guides" (*adellāʾ*), "letters" (*ḥorūf*, *ḥorūfāt*), and "witnesses" (*šohadāʾ*) (see *Panj šaʾn*, pp. 34, 63, 102, 120, 128, 131, 134-35, 136, 149, 163, 176, 184-85, 193, 200, 209, 235, 247, 257, 280; *Bayān-e fārsī*, pp. 82, 89, 90, 91, 165, 180); but no systematic attempt seems to have been made to create an organized structure based on any of these groupings. In the 1850s, Mīrzā Yaḥyā Ṣobḥ-e Azal, as the generally-recognized successor of the Bāb, did attempt to organize a system of agents, to whom he gave the title *šohadāʾ*, but this never developed into a permanent leadership cadre. With the emergence of Baha'ism in a context of conflicting claims to leadership within the Bābi community, any attempt to formalize a hierarchy was abandoned. In reinforcement of his own claim to be the messianic fulfillment of Babism, Bahā'allāh (q.v.) argued that the Bāb had abrogated the rank of successor (*waṣī*) and that in the *Bayān* only "letters" and "mirrors" had been named, the latter being "unlimited" (*mārāyā rā ham maḥdūd na-farmūda-and*; *Lawḥ-e serāj*, p. 40). As the new movement developed, however, it became necessary to delegate certain essential religious functions to various individuals and, towards the end of Bahā'allāh's life, two small groups emerged as possible nuclei for a more developed hierarchical structure. These were known as Names of God (*asmā' Allāh*; e.g., *esm-Allāh al-mīm*, *esm Allāh al-jamāl*) and Hands of the Cause of God. The latter group consisted of four individuals: Ḥājjī Mollā 'Alī-Akbar Šahmīrzādī (q.v.), Ḥājjī Mīrzā Moḥammad-Taqī Abharī (Ebn Abhar), Mīrzā Moḥammad-Ḥasan Adīb-al-'olamā', and Mīrzā 'Alī-Moḥammad (Ebn Aṣdaq). Their functions seem to have been to promulgate Baha'ism, to organize the community of believers in Iran, to advance arguments against opponents (particularly against the Azali Bābis), and to preserve doctrinal unity.

On the death of Bahā'allāh in 1892, the rank of *esm Allāh* seems to have fallen into desuetude (partly through defection), but the four Hands continued to function under the direction of Bahā'allāh's son and successor 'Abd-al-Bahā'. The latter referred in writing to a number of individuals as *ayādī*, but made no formal appointments to this position. He did, however, define their functions more clearly in his Will and Testament (*Alwāḥ-e waṣāyā*), where he also indicated that his successor, the future Guardian of the Cause (*walīy-e amr Allāh*), was to appoint such individuals and direct their activities. In effect, these Hands were to form a religious aristocracy under the leadership of the head of the faith. Shoghi Effendi, who succeeded to the position of *walī* in 1921, made only eight posthumous appointments, for the most part westerners, between then and 1951. In that year, he appointed twelve living Hands, three each in Israel, Iran, America, and Europe. In 1952 the number was raised to nineteen, a figure maintained by new appointments following the deaths of several individuals until 1957, when the total was again raised to twenty-seven. On the death of Shoghi Effendi in November, 1957, it was the Hands as a whole rather than the International Bahā'i Council in Haifa which assumed interim control of the affairs of the religion. Following a Conclave in Haifa in late November, it was announced that Shoghi Effendi had left no will and no heir and that there could be no succession. A body of nine Hands, designated Custodians of the Faith, remained in Israel to direct Bahā'i affairs internationally; these include Mason Remey, president of the International Bahā'i Council, who in 1960 claimed to be the "Second Guardian" of the faith, as a result of which he was excommunicated by his fellow Hands. Further Conclaves of the entire body of Hands were held annually (except for 1962) until 1963, when the election of the first Universal House of Justice (*bayt al-'adl al-a'ẓam*) took place. This latter body now took overall charge of the Bahā'i community, including the direction of the work of the Hands which was now concerned principally with the areas of propagation and protection of the faith. Significantly, the authority to excommunicate or reinstate dissidents continued to rest with the body of the Hands, subject to the approval of the House of Justice.

In 1968 an important development occurred when the House of Justice, seeking to overcome the problems raised by the fact that they could not, technically, appoint further Hands (something only another Guardian could do), established eleven Continental Boards of Counsellors (*hay'āt-e mošāwerīn-e qārra'ī*) in order to extend the functions of the Hands into the future. This new institution has since grown in numbers and influence, with responsibility for regionally-appointed Auxiliary Boards (*hay'āt-e mo'āwenat*, originally created in 1954 to assist the Hands), themselves now seconded by Assistants (*mosā'edān*) in individual localities. An International Teaching Center (*dār al-tablīḡ-e bayn-al-melalī*), composed of Hands and Counsellors and based in Haifa, was created in 1973. As the surviving Hands die out, the influence and authority of the Counsellors appear to grow.

It is of interest to note how this increased administrative complexity has been interpreted in official Bahā'i pronouncements. The Universal House of Justice, National Assemblies, and Local Assemblies together constitute the rulers (*omarā'*) of the community (and, of course, of the predicted Bahā'i World State), while the Hands, Counsellors and Auxiliary Board Members (with their Assistants) are the learned (*'olamā'*). Thus, although according to the prescriptive theory Bahā'ism is without a formal clergy, there does, in fact, exist a hierarchical organization which differs from the clergy of other religions only to the extent that one clergy does from another. Trained scholars for the purpose, however, are conspicuous by their absence from the ranks of the Bahā'i *'olamā'*, a fact of sociological significance. Although the members of this hierarchy have little official power, they do, in fact, wield considerable influence within the Bahā'i community and are treated with considerable deference.

Bibliography: Sayyed 'Alī-Moḥammad Šīrāzī, the Bāb, *Ketāb-e panj ša'n*, n.p. [Tehran], n.d. Idem, *Bayān-e fārsī*, n.p. [Tehran], n.d. See also *The Bahā'ī World* 13, 14, 15 (Haifa, 1970, 1974, 1976). 'Abd-al-'Alī 'Alā'ī, *Mo'assasa-ye ayādī-e amr-Allāh*, Tehran, 1974. Mīrzā Moḥammad Nabīl Zarandī, *The Dawn-Breakers: Nabīl's Narrative of the Early Days of the Bahā'ī Revelation*, ed. and tr. Shoghi Effendi, Wilmette, Ill., 1932, p. 123. Mīrzā Ḥosayn-'Alī Bahā'allāh "Lawḥ-e serāj," in 'Abd-al-Ḥamīd Ešrāq Ḵāvarī, ed., *Mā'eda-ye āsmānī* VII, Tehran, 1973, p. 40. Mīrzā Asadallāh Fāżel Māzandarānī, *Asrār al-āṯār* I, Tehran, 1968, p. 126. For details of the Bābi hierarchical system, see D. MacEoin, "Authority, Hierarchy, and Eschatology in Early Bābī Thought," in P. Smith and M. Momen, eds., *Studies in Babi and Baha'i History* III, Los Angeles, 1986.

(D. M. MacEoin)

A'YĀN AL-ŠĪ'A, a monumental dictionary (56 vols. altogether) of Shi'ite celebrities and learned men compiled by the Shi'ite scholar Sayyed Moḥsen Amīn 'Āmelī (d. 1952), the spiritual leader of the Imami community in Damascus since 1901 and a member of the Arab Academy of Damascus from 1942. The first volume, in two parts (1st ed. Damascus, 1935), is a collection of articles written by Moḥsen Amīn in defence of both the Imami Shi'ite doctrine and a view of history against what he considered to be unfair or polemic statements by non-Shi'ite classical and modern authors. About half of part one has been translated into Persian by Kamāl Mūsawī and published with additional material provided by Ḥasan Amīn (*Dāyerat al-ma'āref-e šī'a*, Tehran, 1345 Š./1967). The second volume is devoted to the life of the Prophet and his daughter Fāṭema, while the next two volumes deal with the lives of the imams up to Ḥasan al-'Askarī. From the fifth volume onwards, the biographies (many of them only a few lines in length) are arranged in alphabetical order according to the name of each individual presented. The fortieth volume (Saida, 1957), however, is devoted to Sayyed Moḥsen himself. It contains his autobiography with a list of his writings (pp. 98-102) and a great number of articles by contemporaries in praise of his achievements as a modernist religious scholar and author. Starting with this volume, the work is edited by the author's son, Sayyed Ḥasan Amīn, and printed in Beirut and/or Saida. Volumes 53 (1962) to 56 (1963) are supplements. In 1969 the first instalment (32 pp.) of another supplement (ed. Ḥasan Amīn) appeared in Beirut. Some of the earlier volumes have been reprinted several times. A new edition in folio format and six volumes was published in Tehran in1980.

Apart from the *A'yān*, 'Āmelī produced a considerable number of other important writings, ranging in topic from the historical geography of Jabal 'Āmel to a diary of his travels to Iraq, Iran, Egypt, and the Hejaz.

Bibliography: In addition to vol. 40 of the *A'yān*, see Mošār, *Mo'allefīn* V, cols. 206-10. Kaḥḥāla, VIII, pp. 183-85; XIII, p. 416. Yūsof As'ad Dāğer, *Maṣāder al-derāsa al-adabīya* II/1, Beirut, 1956, pp. 141-46. Adham Jondī, *A'lām al-adab wa'l-fann* I, Damascus, 1954, pp. 230-32. 'Alī Ḵāqānī, *Šo'arā' al-ğarīy* VII, Najaf, 1955, pp. 255-73. Ja'far Ḵalīlī, *Hākaḏā 'araftohom* I, Baghdad, 1963, pp. 204-24. W. Ende, "The Flagellations of Muḥarram and the Shi'ite 'Ulamā'," *Der Islam* 55, 1978, pp. 19-36.

(W. Ende)

ĀYANDA, Persian journal which began publication in Tīr, 1304 Š./June-July, 1925, under the editorship of its founder, Maḥmūd Afšār (1893-1983). Its proclaimed purpose (1/1, pp. 3-15) was to strengthen national unity and cohesion, particularly through the promotion of the Persian language and public education throughout the country. Among its contributors figured some politicians and scholars of note, such as Sayyed Ḥasan Taqīzāda, Aḥmad Kasravī, Moḥammad-'Alī Forūğī, Dr. Moḥammad Moṣaddeq, 'Alī-Akbar Dāvar, 'Alī Daštī, Moḥammad-Taqī Bahār, Sa'īd Nafīsī, Rašīd Yāsamī, Moḥammad Qazvīnī, Mojtabā Mīnovī, and Naṣrallāh Falsafī.

This phase of the magazine's existence came to an end after two years, during which period twenty-four issues were published, and the journal achieved considerable success. A second series of sixteen issues appeared in the same style from 1323 Š./1944 to 1324 Š./1945. During this phase, its contributors included political figures like Mostašār-al-dawla Ṣādeq, Allāhyār Ṣāleḥ, Maḥmūd Narīmān, and 'Alī-Aṣğar Ḥekmat. *Āyanda* was revived with the publication of the fourth volume in 1334 Š./1955, but only six issues appeared. After the revolution of 1979 and the closing down of the *Rāhnemā-ye ketāb* (q.v.), *Āyanda* was revived and resumed publication with the fifth volume under the editorship of Īraj Afšār, the founder's son, and as a continuation of the *Rahnemā-ye ketāb*. After four quarterly issues, the journal became bi-monthly, and since 1983, it has been published monthly. Adopting the format, purpose, and style of *Rahnemā-ye ketāb*, the journal's main aim in the new phase has been to publish research articles in the fields of Iranian history, literature, and bibliography.

[The reputation of the old *Āyanda* rests on its first phase, which coincided with the rise of Reżā Shah to power and the dissolution of the Qajar dynasty. It reflected the views of the reform-minded nationalists who, tired of the ineffectual governments that followed one another under Aḥmad Shah and encouraged by the effective de facto rule of Reżā Khan between 1921 and 1924, were now looking forward to a strong nationalist government which would secure national unity and embark on modernizing the country. Among the interesting events reported in the pages of *Āyanda* (1/4, pp. 217-39) were the speeches of the supporters and opponents of the bill which led to the dissolution of the Qajar dynasty and relegated the rulership of the country to Reżā Khan.

The second and the third phases of *Āyanda* proved to be unsuccessful attempts at regaining the prominence the periodical had enjoyed during the first phase. Its editor, an essayist, poet, and a business and real estate man who had studied in India and Switzerland, and who had espoused nationalistic causes, had somewhat lost touch with the realities of the post-war period, and his journal remained outside the mainstream of cultural, literary, and political currents.

The fourth phase, with its entirely different format and as a continuation of the *Rahnemā-ye ketāb*, of which Īraj Afšār had been the defacto editor since 1961, is a survivor of the Pahlavi period. With the closing of *Soḵan, Yağmā, Waḥīd*, and the like after the 1979 revolution, *Āyanda* has been practically the only periodical of its kind that has maintained a secular and independent stance from the Islamic Republic. Of interest among the contents of the new *Āyanda* are the obituaries of men of learning in Iranian studies, Iranian or otherwise; correspondences and documents bearing on the modern history of Iran; and listings of chief Persian and foreign publications, the latter on an ad hoc basis. With regard to literature, *Āyanda*'s approach is a traditional one. *E.Ir.*]

Bibliography: J. Rypka, *Hist. Iran. Lit.*, pp. 382, 402. Franciszek Machalski, "La presse en Iran sous le régime des Alliés 1942-1946," *Acta Orientalia* 30, 1966, p. 145. R. Cottam, *Nationalism in Iran*, Pittsburgh, 1964, pp. 32, 87, 114, 137. M. Ṣ. Hāšemī,

Tārīḵ-e jarāyed o majallāt-e Īrān I, p 350. L. P. Elwell-Sutton, "The Iranian Press, 1941-1947," *Iran* 6, 1968, p. 76. Ḡ.-Ḥ. Ṣāleḥyār, *Čehra-ye maṭbūʿāt-e moʿāṣer*, Tehran, 1973, pp. 4-5. J. Šayḵ-al-eslāmī, "Be yād-e bonyāngoḏār-e "Āyanda," *Āyanda* 9/10-11, 1362 Š./1984, pp. 716ff.

(Ī. Afšār)

ĀYANDAGĀN, a daily morning newspaper that first appeared in Tehran on 16 December, 1967. Ḥosayn Aharī, Masʿūd Behnūd, and Dāryūš Homāyūn were listed as the founder, the editor, and the general manager of the paper, respectively, but *Āyandagān* was in fact the brainchild of Homāyūn and a number of aspiring journalists who had for some time been entertaining the idea of publishing a morning paper. From the very outset, *Āyandagān* pursued a more serious journalistic approach in presenting news and commentary than that employed by other papers, offering a challenge to the dominating position held by the two long-established evening papers *Eṭṭelāʿāt* and *Keyhān*. Enjoying a relative freedom of action—within a tightly controlled and mostly lethargic press—it introduced a new mode of reporting which subsequently found considerable following. News and articles in *Āyandagān* were less circumscribed, while commentary was more bold and thought-provoking.

Stylistic innovations, especially in editorial writing—mostly by Homāyūn—set it apart from other daily papers; these involved the introduction and extensive use of newly coined Persian equivalents of journalistic words and phrases prevalent in the Western press. *Āyandagān* tried serious visual art, opera, and music criticism, featured interesting cultural, economic, and sports sections, and presented a more spirited analytical news reporting.

Within the confines of the political control of the press exercised by the regime, *Āyandagān* professed a nationalistic and liberal leaning, aiming at liberalization of the Iranian political system and promoting political dialogue. Its staunch anti-communist and pro-establishment stance plus its real and presumed links with high authorities, however, cast a suspicion over its motives and won *Āyandagān* the grudge and emnity of both leftist and anti-regime intellectuals. In terms of circulation, the paper was no match for the two big evening newspapers, but it carried considerable weight with the political elite of the right and the center in Iran, and the views expressed—especially in its editorials—were held to influence the policy decisions within the government.

Āyandagān produced also two weekly editions: a special rural edition, *Ayandagān-e rūstā*, intended for farmers, and a literary edition, *Āyandagān-e adabī*, featuring book reviews, literary works of Iranian writers, and translations of the works of non-Iranian writers.

With the departure of Homāyūn in 1977 to assume a ministerial post in the cabinet of Jamšīd Āmūzgār, *Āyandagān*'s management was entrusted to a five-member board of editors and writers headed by Hūšang Wazīrī. This change of hand coincided with the rise of agitations against the government and the spread of revolutionary fervor which led in the fall of 1978 to the paper's take-over by a group of left-leaning and pro-revolutionary journalists headed by Fīrūz Gūrān. The victory of the revolution in Iran in February, 1979 brought *Āyandagān* unprecedented prominence.

Assuming an uncompromising anti-dictatorial stance right from the beginning of the revolution, however, *Āyandagān* set a course leading to an unavoidable head-on collision with the politically active clergy and their followers who were striving for nothing less than a total control of the press, and as it turned out, complete submission or destruction of the dissent within it. For the first six months after the revolution, a relentless and often violent tug of war ensued between *Āyandagān* and its supporters on the one side and the forces of the revolutionary government which loathed its anti-clerical, leftist, and liberal positions on the other. Although run mostly by a group of leftist journalists, *Āyandagān* represented a much wider, spectrum of approaches and ideas. Its attainment of national prominance during this phase may be explained by the fact that it gradually became the focal point and spokesman for all those who felt threatened with and feared a monopolistic take-over by Islamic radicals. With the notable exception of the Pro-Moscow Tūda (Communist) party, various groups from the extreme left, such as Fadāʾīān-e Ḵalq, religious revolutionaries such as Mojāhedīn-e Ḵalq, progressive liberals such as the National Democratic Front, liberal centerists like the National Front, to a host of artists, writers, other groups and factions representing minorities, women, etc., found a vehicle in *Āyandagān* to express their views and air their grievances. Proliferation and the relative freedom of opposition newspapers in the first few months after the revolution did not diminish the significance of *Āyandagān* which enjoyed a substantial national readership. It only reinforced the determination of anti-*Āyandagān* forces to bring the paper under control as soon as possible. The process took several months and passed through several stages. It started from verbal threats, harassment of the writers, the occasional vandalising of its premises, and led to physical violence against its writers and supporters, destruction of its publications, and finally, burning and lootings of its offices. The leader of the revolution, Āyatallāh Ḵomeynī, personally set the stage for the final assault against *Āyandagān* by declaring that "he would not read *Āyandagān*," which amounted to an official banning of the paper. Finally following several pro- and anti- demonstrations in the spring and early summer of 1979, the offices of *Āyandagān* were taken over, some of its writers arrested and jailed, and its printing offices expropriated (16 Mordād 1358 Š./7 August 1979). The *Āyandagān* establishment was soon utilized to publish a pro-Islamic Republic newspaper called *Ṣobḥ-e āzādagān* (The dawn of the free) and *Āyandagān* ceased to exist.

Bibliography: For *Āyandagān* before the 1979 revolution see M. Barzīn, *Maṭbūʿāt-e Īrān*. 1354 Š./1976, Tehran, pp. 33, 250. Ḡ.-Ḥ. Ṣāleḥyār, *Čehra-ye maṭbūʿāt-e moʿāṣer*, Tehran, 1973, pp. 6, 68, 140, 145, 231. Idem. *Čašmandāz-e jahānī wa vīžagīhā-ye īrānī-e maṭbūʿāt*, Tehran, 1977, pp. 175-77, 193.

(L. P. Elwell-Sutton and P. Mohajer)

ĀYATALLĀH (Sign of God), an honorific title awarded by popular usage to *mojtaheds*, particularly the foremost among them, presumably with ultimate reference to Koran 41:53, "We shall show them Our signs on the horizons and in their own selves." The sense of the title is that the one to whom it is awarded manifests qualities of piety and learning that indicate God's purposes in creation (compare the analogous title of *ḥojjat al-eslām*). It is a title of recent origin, borne in the distant past by Ḥasan b. Moṭahhar Ḥellī (d. 776/1374), but not entering general usage until recent decades. Certain modern biographical compendia of Shiʿite *ʿolamāʾ* (e.g., Ḥājj Shaikh Moḥammad Šarīf Rāzī, *Ganjīna-ye dānešmandān*, Tehran, 1352 Š./1973, 7 vols.), apply it retrospectively to *ʿolamāʾ* of the past, but there is no indication that the persons in question were known to their contemporaries as *āyatallāh*. The title appears to have been used sporadically in the 1930s, possibly as an indirect result of the reform and strengthening of the religious institution in Qom inaugurated by Shaikh ʿAbd-al-Karīm Ḥāʾerī (d. 1355/1936). Ḥāʾerī may, indeed, have been the first *mojtahed* to bear the title of *āyatallāh* (see Mīrzā Moḥammad-ʿAlī Modarres, *Rayḥānat al-adab*, Tabrīz, n.d., I, p. 66). With the emergence in the postwar period of influential figures such as Āyatallāh Borūjerdī and Āyatallāh Kāšānī, use of the title became increasingly common. Virtually all *mojtaheds* came to be designated as *āyatallāh*, so that recourse has been had to the elative *al-ʿoẓmā* (the supreme) in order to distinguish the most prominent *mojtaheds*. Even this, however, has not been able to prevent a certain devaluation of the title in recent years. Partly because of the cheapening of the title, and partly because of his assumption functions that transcend by far the traditional activity of the *mojtahed*, the most celebrated person ever to have been designated as *āyatallāh*, Āyatallāh Rūḥallāh Ḵomeynī, has come to be known as Imam Ḵomeynī in the wake of the Islamic Revolution of 1357 Š./1978-79. The title *āyatallāh* appears to be unknown among the Shiʿites of Lebanon. Pakistan, and India, and even in Iraq it is applied only to *ʿolamāʾ* of Iranian origin. It should finally be noted that such is the ubiquity of the term in Iran that it is applied even to Sunni religious dignitaries, to whose vocabulary it is totally alien.

Bibliography: ʿAbd-al-ʿAzīz Ṣāḥeb-jawāhar, *Dāʾerat al-maʿāref-e eslāmīya-ye Īrān*, Tehran, n.d., I, pp. 86-87. J. Calmard, "Ayatullāh," in *EI*[2], Suppl. 1-2, pp. 103-04. J. Matīnī, "Baḥt-ī dar bāra-ye sābeqa-ye tārīḵī-e alqāb o ʿanāwīn-e ʿolamāʾ dar maḏhab-e Šīʿa," *Iran Nameh* I/4, 1362 Š./1983, pp. 560-608.

(H. Algar)

ĀYATĪ, ʿABD-AL-ḤOSAYN (b. 1288/1871; d. 1332 Š./1953), son of Mollā Moḥammad-Taqī Āḵūnd Taftī, Bahāʾi missionary, journalist, author, and teacher. After receiving traditional education in Yazd and in Iraq, he became the leader of the Friday prayer (*emām-e Jomʿa*) in Yazd until he converted to Bahaʾism. Then for eighteen years he acted as a missionary (*moballeḡ*) for his new faith in Turkestan, the Caucasus, the Ottoman Empire, and Egypt, during which time he met and associated with ʿAbd-al-Bahāʾ (q.v.), and also wrote his *al-Kawākeb al-dorrīya fī maʾāṯer al-bahāʾīya* in two volumes (Cairo, 1914; Arabic tr. by Aḥmad Fāʾeq, Cairo, 1343/1924) on the history of Bahaʾism. This is still one of the major works on the subject. He received the title Raʾīs-al-moballeḡīn (chief of missionaries) but later turned against Bahaʾism, thereby being counted by the Bahāʾis among the *nāqeżīn* or apostates. (Ṣadr Hāšemī, *Tārīḵ* IV, pp. 310-11). He returned to Tehran in 1343/1924 and served as a teacher in secondary schools for the rest of his life. During this period he wrote *Kašf al-ḥīal* in three volumes (Tehran, 1307-10 Š./1928-31 with several reprints) in refutation of Bahaʾism. He also published the periodical *Namakdān* for six years and was a founding member of the Literary Society (Anjoman-e Adabī) of Yazd.

In his poetry he used the *taḵalloṣes* Āvāra, Żīāʾī, and Āyatī. In prose he tried to use only purely Persian words. He has seventeen book titles to his credit (see Mošār, *Moʾallefīn* III, cols. 718-20) of which a useful history of Yazd (*Ātaškada-ye yazdān*, Yazd, 1317 Š./1928) and *Ketāb-e nabīy yā Qorʾān-e fārsī* (3 vols., Yazd, 1324-26 Š./1945-47) may be noted here.

Bibliography: M. Rastgār, "Aḥwāl o āṯār-e ʿAbd-al-Ḥosayn Āyatī," *Waḥīd*, 1353 Š./1974, no. 242, pp. 29-34; no. 243, pp. 52-55; no. 245, pp. 17-18, 65. M. Esḥāq, *Soḵanvarān-e Īrān dar ʿaṣr-e ḥāżer*, Delhi, 1352/1933. ʿE. Nāʾīnī, *Madīnat al-adab*, ms., Majlis Library, Tehran. S. M.-B. Borqaʿī, *Soḵanvarān-e nāmī-e moʿāṣer* II, 1330 Š./1951. ʿA. Ḵalḵālī, *Taḏkera-ye šoʿarā-ye moʿāṣer-e Īrān* II, Tehran, 1337 Š./1958. A. Ḵāżeʿ, *Taḏkera-ye soḵanvarān-e Yazd*, Bombay, 1341. M. Hedāyat, *Golzār-e jāvīdān* I, Tehran, 1353 Š./1974. S. M. Ṣadr Hāšemī, *Tārīḵ-e jarāyed o majallāt-e Īrān* IV, Isfahan, 1332, pp. 309-11. A. Golčīn-e Maʿānī, *Golzār-e maʿānī*, 2nd ed., Tehran 1363 Š./1984, pp. 52-64 (specimens of Āyatī's prose and poetry).

(Ī. Afšār)

AYĀZ, ABU'L-NAJM B. ŪYMĀQ, favorite Turkish slave of the Ghaznavid Sultan Maḥmūd, whose passion for Ayāz is a recurrent theme in Persian poetry, where he is also called Ayās or Āyāz. Information about Ayāz's life is very scarce, his real personality being hidden behind a veil of tales. As the chief royal cupbearer (*sāqī*), he enjoyed Maḥmūd's trust and probably was given some important assignments (Bayhaqī, 2nd ed., pp. 329, 527). After Maḥmūd's death, Ayāz refused to join Moḥammad, the designated heir to the throne, and together with two other prominent men and "most of the palace slaves" left Ḡaznī to join Masʿūd, the rival claimant, at Nīšāpūr. This move must have had importance, because Masʿūd mentioned it in a letter which he wrote to the Qarakhanid amir Qader Khan (Bayhaqī, p. 94). Ayāz continued to enjoy favor in Masʿūd's reign. Aḥmad b. Ḥasan Maymandī recommended Ayāz for the governorship of Ray, a prestigious and hazardous post, but the sultan decided otherwise on the ground of his inexperience (ibid., p. 346). Later in Masʿūd's reign, however, Ayāz was appointed governor of Qoṣdār and Kermān. Ebn al-Aṯīr gives the year of Ayāz's death as 449/1057 (IX, p. 638). The tomb of the Ghaznavid governor Arslān J̌āḏeb near Mašhad is locally referred to as Gūr-e Ayāz (the tomb of Ayāz; see ĀSTĀN-E QODS-E RAŻAWĪ).

In Persian literature, much has been written about Ayāz's good looks and his qualities of valor, shrewdness, sincerity, and loyalty, though a few authors deny that he was good-looking. Farroḵī, one of Maḥmūd's court poets, panegyrized Ayāz in a *qaṣīda*, describing him as valiant, brave, and handsome. A passage in the *Tārīḵ-e Bayhaqī* (p. 527) suggests that Maḥmūd probably wearied of Ayāz's frivolous behavior but does not make clear why. Sultan Maḥmūd's relationship with this Turkish *ḡolām* had many parallels in the category of royal love for a slave, but this one was presented in Persian literature as something different and exceptional. Neẓāmī ʿArūżī in his *Čahār maqāla* (text, pp. 55-57), written just over a century after Ayāz's death, tells a story which is meant to absolve Maḥmūd of sinful love for Ayāz, but confirms the sultan's great fondness for this slave. In other literary works, however, and particularly in Sufi writings, where the love of Maḥmūd and Ayāz often comes up, Ayāz is presented as a paragon of purity and sincerity: e.g., in the story of Ayāz's shoes and fur coat as told in ʿAṭṭār's *Moṣībat-nāma*, Rūmī's *Maṯnawī*, and several other works. Sufi writers also drew mystic inferences from the love of Maḥmūd and Ayāz. The subject was pursued and poetically interpreted in various ways in the works of many Persian poets and several prose-writers. The consequence of this extraordinary fame was that in Persian literature Maḥmūd and Ayāz came to be placed in the same category as Laylī and Majnūn, Ḵosrow and Šīrīn, Vīs and Rāmīn, and Yūsof and Zolayḵā. Long *maṯnawī* poems about the love of Maḥmūd and Ayāz were written by littérateurs such as Faḵr-al-dīn ʿAlī b. Ḥosayn Wāʿeẓ Kāšefī, Anīsī Šāmlū, Zolālī Ḵᵛānsārī; another was once wrongly ascribed to ʿAṭṭār.

Bibliography: Neẓāmī ʿArūżī, *Čahār maqāla*, ed. M. Qazvīnī and M. Moʿīn, 3rd ed., Tehran, 1333 Š./1954, notes, pp. 175, 176. *Ātaškada* I, pp. 44-45. Farroḵī Sīstānī, *Dīvān*, ed. ʿA. ʿAbd-al-Rasūlī, Tehran, 1311 Š./1932, pp. 163-65. Nafīsī, *Naẓm o naṯr*, pp. 115, 248, 285, 424. J̌alāl-al-dīn Rūmī, *Maṯnawī*, ed. R. A. Nicholson, 8 vols., Leiden, 1925-40, V, p. 118. Browne, *Lit. Hist. Persia* III, p. 504. Rypka, *Hist. Iran. Lit.*, p. 301. Ḡ.-Ḥ. Yūsofī, *Farroḵī Sīstānī*, Mašhad, 1341 Š./1962. A. Sohaylī Ḵᵛānsārī, "Maḥmūd o Ayāz," *Yaḡmā* 4, 1330 Š./1951, pp. 262-69, 328-31, 355-60. Idem, "Maḥmūd o Ayāz," *Dāneš* 3, 1331 Š./1952, pp. 33-40, 97-104, 189-96. Dehḵodā, s.v. Ayāz.

(J̌. MATĪNĪ)

AYBAK (Uzbek "cave dweller"), now called Samangān, capital of Samangān province, associated with several important archeological sites (N. H. Dupree, *The Road to Balk*; see also AFGHANISTAN VIII: ARCHEOLOGY). Modern ethnic groups in the area include Hazāra, Uzbek, Tājīk, and a smattering of Pashtun.

Several doubtful Lower Paleolithic implements of an amorphous "Clactonian" nature were reported by Puglisi ("Preliminary Report") from the Hazār Som (Thousand caves) area, about 16 km north of Aybak. The earliest verifiable evidence for human occupation comes from the rock shelter of Qara Kamar, near Hażrat Solṭān, about twenty-three km north of Aybak (Coon, *The Seven Caves*). Qara Kamar was the first Paleolithic site excavated in Afghanistan. (Its name, Black Belt, refers to the blackened roof and walls of the rock shelter, caused by smoke from the fires of generations of nomads who have camped inside.) Coon identified four cultural assemblages; but the sequence is based on a small number of finds, so little sophisticated interpretation is possible (Davis. *The Late Paleolithic of Northern Afghanistan* and "The Paleolithic of Afghanistan"). Qara Kamar IV, the lowest and oldest assemblage, is represented by ten flint flakes and blades, not enough to be diagnostic, but separated from the overlying Upper Paleolithic by a 50 cm—thick sterile deposit Qara Kamar III which Coon and others call "Aurignacian," dates to about 32,000 years ago (Coon and Ralph, "Radiocarbon Dates"); it yielded eighty-two worked flint implements (carinated or nosed scrapers/bladelet cores, blades and bladelets, a drill), three bone awls, plus animal bones (wild sheep, horses), and mollusks.

Qara Kamar II presents another amorphous industry with a limited number (17) of worked flints, three flake cores, and nine core fragments. This area appears to include at least elements of an intrusive industry. Qara Karmar II, however, is stratigraphically distinct from Qara Kamar I, which represents a very late Upper Paleolithic (Epipaleolithic or, as Coon refers to it, Mesolithic), dating to about 10,000 years ago (Coon and Ralph, "Radiocarbon Dates"). Although a micro-component exists in Qara Kamar I, normal-sized flakes and blades dominate, including six endscrapers, four notched pieces, and two burins. Two other, apparently later, Epipaleolithic sites occur. Darra Kalon, a rock shelter about twenty km south-southeast of Qara Kamar, has a single carbon-14 date of about 9,500 years ago (Alessio et al., in *Radiocarbon* 9). The microblade (including pressure retouch on edges), regular flake, and blade implements resemble those of the Kuprukian farther west. Only forty-three implements have been tabulated to date by Puglisi, including burins, endscrapers, denticulates, and *perçoirs* (Davis, *The Late Paleolithic*, pp. 64-67).

Kokǰar, eight km due south of Qara Kamar, is an open-air site situated on a mesa, from which several hundred flint specimens were surface-collected, including a wide range of worked and unworked flakes and blades, plus an extensive microblade element. The virtual absence of flake and blade cores or nodules indicates, possibly, a temporary hunting site; but excavations must be undertaken before this can be determined.

A gap occurs from between 9,500 years ago and the B. C.-A. D. line, although the third millennium B. C. Bronze Age finds farther east at Tape Follōl (K̲oš Tepe) indicate a need for further surveys into this period (Dupree et al., "The Khosh Tapa Hoard," p. 34).

Puglisi (personal communication) has identified an "urban complex" of more than 200 multi-roomed, multi-storyed cave dwellings in Hazār Som Valley. Many exhibit painted designs, bas reliefs, and petroglyphs. Possibly the oldest dwellings date about the first century. A. D., with the climax period between the second to third centuries A. D. The erosion of Kūšān power from the third century A. D. may account for the apparent decline of this presumably important caravan way station. Early Islam may have precipitated another peak period between the seventh and thirteenth centuries A. D., when the area seems to have been abandoned and only sporadically occupied by passing nomads (Mizuno, ed., *Hazarsum*, p. 1).

The Chinese Buddhist pilgrim, Hsuan-Tsang (ca. A. D. 630) mentions Sih-min-Kien (Samangān), as do early Islamic geographers (S. Beal, *Buddhist Records of the Western World*, London, 1884, I, p. 43; Markwart, *Ērānšahr*, p. 81).

A Buddhist site, Tak̲t-e Rostam, is located two km southeast of Aybak. Dating about the fourth to fifth centuries A. D., the site consists of a rock-cut cave monastery complex and an adjacent stupa cut out of limestone, a unique edifice in Afghanistan (N. H. Dupree, *The Road to Balkh*, pp. 23-25; Mizuno, ed., *Haibak*, pp. 85-94), but comparable to similar finds in India (Fischer, *Schöpfungen*, pp. 123-24; idem et al., *Architektur*, ills.).

Bibliography: M. Alessio et al., "University of Rome Carbon-14 Dates V," *Radiocarbon* 9, 1967, p. 360. C, S. Coon, *The Seven Caves*, New York, 1957. Idem and E. Ralph, "Radiocarbon Dates from Kara Kamar, Afghanistan," *Science* 122, 1955, pp. 921-22. R. S. Davis, *The Late Paleolithic of Northern Afghanistan*, Ph.D. thesis in Anthropology, Columbia University, 1974. Idem, "The Paleolithic of Afghanistan," in N. Hammond and R. Allchin, eds., *The Archaeology of Afghanistan*. Academic Press, 1978, pp. 37-70. L. Dupree et al., "The Khosh Tapa Hoard from Afghanistan," *Archaeology* 24, 1971, pp. 28-34. N. H. Dupree, *The Road to Balkh*, Kabul, 1967, pp. 21-27. K. Fischer, *Schöpfungen indischer Kunst*, Cologne, 1959. K. Fischer, M. Jansen, and J. Pieper, *Architektur des indischen Subkontinents im Überblick*, Darmstadt, 1986. S. Mizuno, ed., *Haibak and Kashmir-Smast, Buddhist Cave Temples in Afghanistan and Pakistan Surveyed in 1960* (Japanese and English text), Kyoto University, 1962. Idem, *Hazar-sum and Fil Khana, Cave Sites in Afghanistan Surveyed in 1962*, Kyoto, 1967. S. Puglisi, "Preliminary Report on the Researches at Hazar Sum (Samangan)," *East and West*, N.S. 14/1-2, 1963, pp. 1-8.

(L. DUPREE)

AYBAK, QOṬB-AL-DĪN, founder of the Moʿezzī or Slave Dynasty and the first Muslim king of India, also called Ībak (moon chieftain) and Aybak Šel (lit., of the damaged little finger; this interpretation of the name is preferred by Thomas, *Pathān Kings of Delhi*, p. 32). In the second half of the 6th/12th century, while still a boy, he was brought from Turkestan to Nīšāpūr and sold to Qāżī Fak̲r-al-dīn ʿAbd-al-ʿAzīz Kūfī, the governor, who brought him up and provided for him the training and soldierly arts and some religious education (J̌ūzǰānī, *Ṭabaqāt*, p. 487). He was again sold, as a youth, to the Ghurid sultan Moʿezz-al-dīn Šehāb-al-dīn Moḥammad (r.569-602/1173-1206); he was in charge of the forage supply for the Ghurid army in their battle of 586/1190 against the K̲ᵛārazmšāh Solṭānšāh and in 588/1192, when Moʿezz-al-dīn Moḥammad conquered northern India, the latter posted him as governor at Kohrām (ʿEṣāmī, *Fotūḥ*, p. 71). In the same year Aybak occupied the forts of Meerut (Mīrat) and Delhi; the latter became the seat of Muslim rule.

In 590/1194 he reinforced Moʿezz-al-dīn with 50,000 troops in an attack against Jai Chand of Qannauj and the next year took the forts of Thankar (identified with Bayana by Ferešta, tr. Briggs, I, pp. 100-02), Kaliwar (Kālenjar or Gwalior), Budaun (Badāʾūn), and Kol (Aligarh), and conquered Nahrwala (Gujarat). In 593/1197 Anhalwara was subdued and in 599/1203 Ranthambor fell. In 601/1205 Moʿezz-al-dīn personally moved against the Khokar tribes who infested western Punjab and threatened the Ghurid line of communication and was joined by Aybak. The rebels were subdued and Aybak was confirmed as Moʿezz-al-dīn's viceroy in India (J̌ūzǰānī, *Ṭabaqāt* 1, pp. 445-50). On Moʿezz-al-dīn's assassination on 3 Šaʿbān 602/15 March 1206, the local governors acknowledged Aybak as the supreme ruler of India, and this was confirmed a few months later by the Ghurid court at Ḡazna (J̌ūzǰānī, tr. Raverty, p. 525). The province of Punjab was still claimed by Tāǰ-al-dīn Yildiz of Ḡazna and Nāṣer-al-dīn Qobāča of Multan-Sindh, who were Aybak's father-in-law and son-in-law respectively, as well as his rivals for the control of the Ghurid conquest of India. In order to check them, Aybak left Delhi for Lahore, where he reportedly proclaimed himself king on 18 D̲u'l-qaʿda 602/27 June 1206.

Aybak was a just and liberal ruler, celebrated for his disciplined administration, orthodoxy, and munificence, qualities that have been attributed to his early training at Nīšāpūr under the supervision of Qāżī

Fak̲r-al-dīn. His compassion and lack of prejudice earned him the respect of the Hindus, the majority of his subjects. The peace and comfort enjoyed during his reign attracted scores of scholars, poets, theologians, and spiritual leaders to Lahore, and trade, industry, agriculture, and education flourished (ʿAbd-al-Ḥaqq. *Ak̲bār al-ak̲yār*, pp. 29-37). He died in mid-Jomādā, 607/October, 1210, in Lahore from an accident at a polo game (ʿEṣāmī, *Fotūḥ*, p. 101).

His tomb with its impressive dome was built by his successor Šams-al-dīn Iltutmiš (*Tārīk̲-e mobārakšāhī*, p. 16) at the back of Anarkali Market. After the establishment of English rule in Punjab (1848), it served to house a library and a church (Jūzjānī, tr. Raverty, p. 529). It seems that the tomb was then neglected until the new government had it restored in 1947; in 1970 an imposing tomb was raised on the model of K̲aljī and Slave Dynasty architecture.

Aybak is credited with the construction of the first two mosques in India, the Qowwat-al-eslām mosque in Delhi in 587/1191-92 (on a temple plinth), and another one at Ajmer at about the same time (actually a converted Hindu college). Both were built using materials taken from Hindu temples. After the additions made by Iltutmiš (Iletmiš), the Qowwat-al-eslām mosque had a total area, including courtyard, of about 50,000 sq ft, with gilded domes and pointed arches 52 ft high. In 602/1206 Aybak built the white palace which is mentioned in histories up to the reign of Ḡīāt̲-al-dīn Balban (r. 664-86/1266-87).

The most famous of his architectural undertakings is the Qoṭb Menār in Delhi, originally meant to be a tower for the call to prayer. The tower was extended by Iltutmiš to the total height of 69.7 m. In 1794 it stood 242 ft high but later on the sixth and seventh storeys, damaged by an earthquake, were removed to avoid their possible collapse (sir Sayyed Aḥmad Khan, *Āt̲ār al-ṣanādīd*, ed. S. Moʿīn-al-ḥaqq, Karachi, 1966, p. 69).

Aybak was succeeded in Lahore by his adopted son Ārāmbak̲š Shah, whom the nobility raised to the throne (Jūzjānī, tr. Raverty, pp. 529-30), but he was soon killed during a march on Delhi where Iltumiš, Aybak's son-in-law, had been proclaimed king.

Aybak, like the other Turkish generals of Moʿezz-al-dīn continued to uphold Ghurid policies and traditions in India (C. E. Bosworth, *The Islamic Dynastics*, Edinburgh, 1967, p. 185) and contributed to the spreading of Persian language and culture on the subcontinent.

Bibliography: ʿAbd-al-Ḥaqq Moḥaddet̲ Dehlavī, *Ak̲bār al-ak̲yār*, Delhi, 1332/1914. Żīāʾ-al-dīn Barnī, *Tārīk̲-e fīrūzšāhī*, Calcutta, 1862. Fak̲r-e Modabber Ḡaznavī, *Tārīk̲-e mobārakšāhī*, ed. D. Ross, London, 1927. J. Ferguson, *History of Indian and Eastern Architecture* II, London, 1910. Hāšemī Farīdābādī, *Tārīk̲-e mosalmānān* I, Lahore, 1949. ʿAbd-al-Malek ʿEṣāmī, *Fotūḥ al-salāṭīn*, ed. M. Ḥosayn, Agra, 1938. Nūr Aḥmad, *Taḥqīqāt-e češtī*, Lahore, 1865. M. Ḥ. Neẓāmī. *Tāj al-maʾāt̲er*, MS, see Rieu, *Pers. Man.* I, p. 239. E. Thomas, *The Chronicles of the Pathān Kings of Delhi*, London, 1871. Yaḥyā b. Aḥmad Serhendī, *Tārīk̲-e mobārakšāhī*, Calcutta, 1931.

(N. H. Zaidi)

AYMĀQ (Turk. OYMAQ), a term designating tribal peoples in Khorasan and Afghanistan, mostly semi-nomadic or semi-sedentary, in contrast to the fully sedentary, non-tribal population of the area. The local dialects of the Aymāq are very close either to the Fārsī of east Khorasan province or to the Herātī idiom of Fārsī Darī. The Čār Aymāq in western Afghanistan live in contiguous areas from Bādḡīs, north of Herat, to the south of Ḡūr. Their habitat is drained by the headwaters of the K̲oškāb, Harī-rūd, Morḡāb, and Farāh-rūd. From northwest to southwest they comprise 40,000 Jamšīdī, 60,000 Aymāq-Hazāra, 100,000 Fīrūzkūhī, and 180,000 Taymanī.

These tribes are ethnic formations of the 10th/16th and 11th/17th centuries; their grouping as four is in consequence a more recent administrative measure. There is consensus as to the composition of this grouping, among its members as well as among the other Aymāq. Ethnic groups of Iranian, Čaḡatāy, Uzbek, Qepčāq, Eastern Turkic, Arab, and other origins have been unified by chiefs who originated outside their area. Among the Jamšīdī it was a branch of the Kayānī from Sīstān (tracing descent to the legendary hero Jamšīd, whence the tribal name has been derived), who had been invested as "Wardens of the Marches" in Bādḡīs by Shah ʿAbbās II (*Tad̲kerat al-molūk*, tr. V. Minorsky, p. 16). A Kākaṛ Pashtun from Baluchistan, Tayman, formed a coalition in Ḡūr around 1650 (*Historical and Political Gazetteer of Afghanistan* III, Graz, 1975, p. 260; *Baluchistan District Gazetteer* I, Bombay, 1907, p. 69). The traditional chiefs of the northern Fīrūzkūhī, Zay Ḥākem, claim descent from Ačakzay Pashtun ancestors, whereas the tribe takes its name from Fīrūzkūh, the capital of the Ghurid dynasty. After the downfall of the Safavid power and during the struggle for Herat in the 12th/18th and 13th/19th centuries, Bādḡīs was haunted by marauding Turkmen; and all Aymāq at one time or another were involved in these international affairs. Changing intratribal coalitions and opportunistic siding with either of the contending powers resulted in intertribal feuds which facilitated the centralizing efforts of Amīr ʿAbd-al-Raḥmān at the end of the 13th/19th century and led to the breakdown of the power of tribal aristocracies. A new type of charismatic leader arose whose descendants still are of paramount importance in local politics. Members of the former aristocracy are still high ranking in prestige, holding government positions at various levels.

The events of the past 200 years forced the northern Aymāq to lead a nomadic life. The Jamšīdī, forcibly moved from one exile to the other, became indistinguishable from Turkmen in their way of life (Yate, *Northern Afghanistan*, p. 122). During this period, small groups of Aymāq-Hazāra and Jamšīdī settled in Persian Khorasan and Turkmenistan. (They now number about

2,000.) At the base of social organization, the extended family is still intact, functioning as a patriarchal household and also as a minimal economic unit. The tribes are segmented patrilineally into *ṭāʾefa*s, the larger ones subdivided into *awlād*, most frequently bearing the name of the fictitious founder or of the place of origin. There are 68 Jamšīdī *ṭāʾefa*s, 39 Aymāq-Hazāra, 44 Fīrūzkūhī, and 101 Taymanī. As far as their history can be traced, tribal unity never existed. Political power at the local level was maintained by coalitions based on marriage allegiances of the *ṭāʾefa* chiefs. This pattern still prevails. Jamšīdī and Aymāq-Hazāra may be classed as semi-sedentary whereas Fīrūzkūhī and Taymanī are semi-nomadic. All the tribes use temporary housing during the summer season at varying degrees. In Bādḡīs water and appropriate soil for irrigated agriculture are plentiful, and dry farming is also practised. Conditions for herding are optimal, since the cattle can be kept grazing all year round (de Planhol, "La frontière," pp. 1-16). Together with carpet weaving, these activities permit the production of a considerable surplus that can be sold at the markets of Herat and Qalʿa-ye Now. The narrow defiles of Ḡūr provide only limited space for irrigated agriculture, and, due to scarce and irregular rain-falls, yields from dry-farming are poor. Severe winters with heavy snows limit the number of cattle.

Other semi-sedentary, semi-nomadic or nomadic Aymāq in western Afghanistan, chiefly in Herat province, are the Ḡalmanī (600), Malekī (12,000), Mīšmast (5,000), Sīāmūsā (300), Ṭāherī (17,000), Tīmūrī (33,000), and Zūrī (15,000). Another 25,000 Tīmūrī, descendants of nineteenth-century immigrants, live in Iranian Khorasan. They have incorporated small groups of Jamšīdī and Zūrī. Some now fully sedentary ethnic groups consider themselves, and are classified by the Herātī, as Aymāq: Bādḡīsī (1,000), Čengīzī (6,000), Čaḡatāy (2,000), Dāmanregī (200) Ḡōrī (1,000), Kākerī (1,000), Maraydār (200), Mobarī (1,500), Qepčāq (17,000), and Ḵamedī (200). All of them have preserved their ethnic identity; but linguistically, economically, and in social structure and religion, they are fully assimilated to the Sunnite population of western Afghanistan. The Tīmūrī, once the most powerful of the "lesser" Aymāq, had their original homeland in western Bādḡīs. Besides those still living there or in Khorasan, there are settled Tīmūrī south of Herat and near Šendand, as well as to the north of Ḡaznī in Shiʿite Hazāra country. A group of Pashtunized nomadic Tīmūrī has its winter quarters near Baḡlān in northeastern Afghanistan. Some of the best qualities of "Herat Baluch" carpets are woven by Tīmūrī in Bādḡīs, classified by the name of the respective *ṭāʾefa* such as Kawdanī, Šērḵānī, Yaʿqūbḵānī, or Zakanī.

See also AFGHANISTAN IV: ETHNOGRAPHY; V: LANGUAGES

Bibliography: C. E. Yate, *Northern Afghanistan, or Letters from the Afghan Boundary Commission*, Edinburgh and London, 1888. A. A. Semenov, *Dzhemshidi i ikh strana*, Izvestiya turkestanskogo otdela russkogo geograficheskogo obshchestva 16, 1923. W. Ivanov "Notes on the Ethnology of Khurasan," *The Geographical Journal* 67, 1926, pp. 143-58. E. G. Gafferberg, "Formy braka i svadebnye obrady u Dzhemshidov i Khasare," *Sovetskaya Etnografiya* 1, 1936. Idem, "Zhilishche Dzhemshidov Kushkinskogo rayona," ibid., 4, 1948, pp. 124-43. N. A. Kislyakov and A. I. Pershits, *Narody Peredneĭ Azii*, Moscow, 1957, pp. 124-33. A Janata, "Die Bevölkerung von Ghor. Beiträge zur Ethnographie der Aimaq," *Archiv für Völkerkunde* 17-18, 1962-63, pp. 73-156. H. F. Schurman, *The Mongols of Afghanistan. An Ethnography of the Moghôls of Afghanistan*, The Hague, 1962. K. Ferdinand, "Ethnographical Notes on Chahār Aimāq, Hazāra and Moghōl," *Acta Orientalia* 28, 1964, pp. 175-203. M. Kuhn, *A Report on Village Society in the Chakhcharan District of Afghanistan*, M. A. thesis, London University, SOAS, 1970. A. Janata, "Völkerkundliche Forschungen in Westafghanistan." *Bustan* 2-3, 1970, pp. 50-61. Idem, "On the Origin of the Firuzkuhis in Western Afghanistan," *Archiv für. Völkerkunde* 25, 1971, pp. 57-65. G. Mandersloot and J. Powell, *Firozkohi, een afghaans reisjournaal*, Rotterdam, 1971. M. Barry, *Western Afghanistan's Outback*, USAID, Afghanistan, 1972. A. Singer, "The Jamshīdī of Khurasan: An Historical Note," *Iran* 10, 1972, pp. 151-55. X. de Planhol, "Sur la frontière Turkmène de l'Afghanistan," *Revue géographique de l'est*, 1973, 1-2, pp. 1-16.

(A. JANATA)

ʿAYN-AL-DAWLA, SOLṬĀN **ʿABD-AL-MAJĪD MĪRZĀ** ATĀBAK-E AʿẒAM (1261-1345/1845-1926) son of Solṭān Aḥmad Mīrzā ʿAżod-al-dawla, Fatḥ-ʿAlī Shah's forty-eighth son and a prominent political figure of Moẓaffar-al-dīn Shah's reign (1313-24/1896-1907). He is mainly remembered in modern Iranian history for his "reactionary stubborn character" which, as pointed out by Sykes (*History* II, p. 399), was often considered a major cause of the conflicts leading to the Constitutional Revolution. Although opinions on him generally remained negative, recent reappraisals (see below) tend to partly rehabilitate him and his political actions which continued, on a lesser scale, after the granting of a constitution.

He was educated by a private tutor but his lack of academic motivation led to his removal from Dār al-Fonūn (the Tehran Polytechnic). He was then sent to Tabrīz to the crown prince's service where he learnt administrative skills and calligraphy (Sykes, ibid.; Mostawfī, *Zendagānī* II, pp. 54f.; Ṣafāʾī, *Rahbarān* II, p. 357). He was proud of his royal descent and renowned for his haughtiness, ostentatiousness, extorsions, and meanness (Mostawfī, op. cit., p. 56). Reportedly, he was a hot-tempered, rude, and greedy courtier (Bāmdād, *Rejāl* II, p. 93). In 1289/1872-73, he married one of the crown prince's daughters, Anīs-al-dawla, who died without giving him any child. His only son was from a temporary (*ṣīḡa*) wife (see below).

He began his career at Moẓaffar-al-dīn Mīrzā's court at Tabrīz as *nāyeb-e eṣṭabl*, a deputy to the *amīr(-e) āḵōr* (stablemaster) whom he eventually replaced in 1303/1885-86. He then obtained several governorates in Azerbaijan (Mostawfī, ibid.; Bāmdād, ibid.), In 1306/1890, while he held the governorate of Qarājadāḡ (Arasbārān), Nāṣer-al-dīn Shah on his return from his third European tour fell ill in Azerbaijan and was saved *in extremis* by Doctor Feuvrier (September, 1890). Allegedly ʿAyn-al-dawla announced the shah's imminent death to the crown prince and was severely castigated for his rashness after the shah's recovery (Eʿtemād-al-salṭana, *Rūz-nāma*, p. 665; Molkārā, *Šarḥ-e ḥāl*, p. 107; Bāmdād, op. cit., pp. 93 ff.; Feuvrier, *Trois ans*, pp. 66f.). In 1309/1891-92, along with the post of stablemaster, he received the governorship of Ardabīl, Mešgīn and Qarājadāḡ with the rank of *amīr(-e) tūmān* (q.v.) as well as being in charge of the crown properties (*ḵāleṣajāt*) in Azerbaijan. In 1310/1892-93, he was given the title ʿAyn-al-dawla by Nāṣer-al-dīn Shah (Bāmdād, op. cit., p. 95).

By the time of Moẓaffar-al-dīn Shah's accession (Ḏu'l-ḥejja, 1313/May-June, 1896), he had been for some time the head of the crown prince's court in Azerbaijan (Dawlatābādī, *Ḥayāt-e Yaḥyā* I, p. 150). Already in September, 1895, he was reluctantly given by Nāṣer-al-dīn Shah the *pīškārī* of Azerbaijan (Ṣafāʾī, *Rahbarān* II, pp. 258ff.; according to Amīn-al-dawla, *Ḵāṭerāt*, p. 263, his *pīškārī* was only semi-official). Although he enjoyed Moẓaffar-al-dīn's confidence and was influential among the Azerbaijani retinue of the new king (the Turk of Tabrīz party according to Mostawfī, op. cit., p. 56), his ascendancy was temporarily barred by powerful rivals. ʿAlī-Aṣḡar Khan Amīn-al-solṭān (*ṣadr-e aʿẓam* until Jomādā II, 1314/November, see ATĀBAK-E AʿẒAM) managed to send him as governor to Māzandarān. But under Farmānfarmā's cabinet (November, 1896-April, 1897), he resigned and left his governorate unexpectedly to go on pilgrimage to the *ʿatabāt* (Dawlatābādī, op. cit., I, p. 168; Amīn-al-dawla, op. cit., pp. 232f.; Ṣafāʾī, op. cit., p. 361). In 1317/1899, he was governor (*wālī*) of Lorestān and Ḵūzestān where he was able to bring about a degree of stability (Ṣafāʾī, op. cit., pp. 362f.). His decisive step to power came with his appointment as the governor of Tehran (1319/1901). Together with his brother Wajīhallāh Mīrzā Amīr Khan Sardār (then *sephsālār*), they were considered the most powerful enemies of Amīn-al-solṭān Atābak-e Aʿẓam. During Moẓaffar-al-dīn Shah's second European tour (1902), the two brothers were entrusted with the task of vice regency. ʿAyn-al-dawla was in contact with anti-Atābak *ʿolamāʾ* and journalists and was considered as the "prime instigator" of the anti-Atābak drive. While the shah promised him the premiership, he tried to bar Moḥammad-ʿAlī Mīrzā from the succession (Dawlatābādī, op. cit., pp. 299, 317; Keddie, "Iranian Politics," I, p. 26, II, p. 153; Ṣafāʾī, op. cit., pp. 363f.; Bāmdād, *Rejāl* II, p. 96). Whereas popular discontent continued, he made profit by putting arbitrary taxes on bakeries and slaughterhouses. Through his contacts with the *atābak*'s opponents, he was involved in the circumstances leading to the latter's second dismissal (Jomādā II, 1321/September 1903), notably the *takfīr-nāma* (text in Kasravī, *Mašrūṭa*[2] I, p. 45). He also incited the *atābak* to dismiss his rival Ḥakīm-al-molk (Dawlatābādī, op. cit., I, p. 317; Malekzāda, *Tārīḵ-e enqelāb* I, p. 272; Amīn-al-dawla, op. cit., p. 317; Keddie, op. cit., II, p. 156; see also ATĀBAK-E AʿẒAM). Having abandoned the *atābak*, their former faithful supporter, the British now favored his enemies, notably ʿAyn-al-dawla and his brother Wajīhallāh Mīrzā who both convinced the shah that they could maintain security and order. Appointed minister of the interior (September, 1903), ʿAyn-al-dawla was made *wazīr-e aʿẓam* (chief minister; January, 1904) and *ṣadr-e aʿẓam* (prime minister; September, 1904). Shortly afterwards, he was granted his predecessor's title of Atābak-e Aʿẓam (Bāmdād, ibid.).

His firm hand on court and provincial affairs at first enabled him to prevent a general spread of disorders. Although he could then enjoy the support of some of the opponents of Mīrzā ʿAlī-Aṣḡar Khan Atābak, his rough attitude towards the clergy, notably the *ṭollāb*, undermined his position. Leading *ʿolamāʾ* were soon divided into ʿAyn-al-dawla's partisans and opponents, some of the latter working for the ex-*atābak*'s restoration. His authoritative measures to resolve the inherited financial crisis (such as reduction of court expenses, imposition of new taxes), the increasing influence of Belgian officials on customs and other departments, and his own greediness and private hoarding were factors which made him meet, like his predecessors, the opposition of many vested interests (Keddie, op. cit., II, pp. 234ff.). Opponents to the Russians, the Belgians, and ʿAyn-al-dawla's policy were encouraged by the news of Tsarist Russia's difficulties (defeat against Japan in 1904-05, revolution of 1905). A vast campaign united merchants, modernists, and *ʿolamāʾ* (some of whom being regrouped in secret societies) against ʿAyn-al-dawla and the Belgian Joseph Naus who held several top-level official positions (Naus's photograph in a *mollā*'s dress taken at a costume ball caused great uproar among the clergy). News of a third royal European tour added to the discontent. This time (summer 1905), ʿAyn-al-dawla accompanied the shah while government at Tehran was secured by the harsh measures introduced by the crown prince Moḥammad-ʿAlī Mīrzā. From the beginning of 1905, secret societies helped to provoke further discontent among merchants and *ʿolamāʾ*, notably at Mašhad, Tabrīz, and Tehran (*bast* at Shah ʿAbd-al-ʿAẓīm, April, 1905). Disturbances sometimes took a racial or religious character against the Jews, the Babis, the Armenians, and others. A factional strife raged at Kermān between *šayḵīs* and *bālāsarīs* (see G. Scarcia, "Kermān 1905: la 'guerra tra šeiḫī e bālāsarī'," *AION*, N.S. 13, 1963, pp. 195-238).

There were serious demonstrations against the construction of a new building for the Russian Bank on *waqf* land at Tehran (November, 1905) and revolutionary activities began to flare up throughout Iran. After his return, the bastinado inflicted on some Tehran merchants (mostly sugar dealers) by the governor Mīrzā Aḥmad Khan 'Alā'-al-dawla, applying 'Ayn-al-dawla's policy (December, 1905), initiated the chain of events leading to the granting of a constitution. Repression of demonstrations provoked a massive *bast* of the *'olamā'* in Tehran and at Shah 'Abd-al-'Aẓīm (January, 1906) which resulted in 'Alā'-al-dawla's dismissal and the promise of an *'adālat-ḵāna* (house of justice). Further protests and repressions in Tehran and the provinces led to the great emigration (*hejrat-e kobrā*) of the *'olamā'* to Qom and the massive *bast* of merchants, *ṭollāb*, preachers, and others at the summer quarters of the British Legation at Golhak (July-August, 1906). Along with the demands for an *'adālat-ḵāna* and eventually a *majles-e šūrā-ye mellī*, national consultative assembly, and a constitution (*mašrūṭa*), 'Ayn-al-dawla and Naus's dismissal were consistently insisted upon. Even before the issuing of the *mašrūṭa* decree, 'Ayn-al-dawla was dismissed (9 Jomādā II 1324/31 July 1906) and replaced by Mīrzā Naṣrallāh Khan Nā'īnī Mošīr-al-dawla (Algar, *Religion and State*, pp. 240ff.; Browne, *Revolution*, pp. 105ff.; Kasravī, op. cit., I, pp. 31ff.; Keddie, op. cit., II, pp. 234-50; Nāẓem-al-eslām Kermānī, *Bīdārī-e Īrānīān* I, pp. 243ff.; Ṣafā'ī, op. cit., pp. 368f.).

'Ayn-al-dawla then went to Mobārakābād and Varāmīn and finally settled at Farīmān, his personal estate in Khorasan, and remained politically inactive for nearly two years. After the bombardment of the Majlis (June, 1908) and the intensification of the resistance at Tabrīz, he was sent to Azerbaijan as governor together with Moḥammad-Walī Khan Tonokābonī Sepahdār-e A'ẓam to quell the revolt. His efforts to induce the nationalists to surrender or negotiate failed and on a few occasions governmental forces were defeated by nationalists on the outskirts of Tabrīz (October, 1908). Moḥammad-Walī Khan Sepahdār-e A'ẓam joined the nationalists and 'Ayn-al-dawla was not even recognized as governor by the provincial *anjoman* and was forced to settle at Bāsmenj. When after months of siege Tsarist troops entered Tabrīz, 'Ayn-al-dawla went to Tehran and reported to Moḥammad-'Alī Shah about the provincial *anjoman*'s attitude and Tabrīz diplomats' lack of support (June, 1909). He then retired to his house in expectation (Ṣafā'ī, op. cit., pp. 369ff.; Browne, op. cit., pp. 256ff.; Kasravī, op. cit., I, pp. 198ff.).

When Tehran was captured by constitutionalist forces (July, 1909), 'Ayn-al-dawla refused any foreign protection and dearly bought his liberty by giving his estates in Qarabāḡ to the revolutionary government. He was, however, promised the government of Fārs for which he gave a heavy *pīškeš*. But his appointment was canceled because of Taqīzāda's strong protest (Ṣafā'ī, op. cit., p. 371; Browne, op. cit., pp. 315ff.). Although he was invited to the opening of the second Majlis (November, 1909) he had to remain out of office for four years while being prosecuted on the ground of forgery for the purchase of his Farīmān estate. In Ṣafar, 1331/January, 1913, in Mīrzā Moḥammad-'Alī Khan 'Alā'-al-salṭana's cabinet, he was appointed minister of the interior and paid particular attention to news given about Iran in European newspapers. He kept his office under the subsequent government of Mostawfī-al-mamālek but was again idle after the latter's resignation (March, 1913). He was appointed prime minister and minister of war (Jomādā II, 1333/April, 1915), but after he granted his support to his minister of the interior Farmānfarmā (who committed a political error by being hostile to the Ottomans), he was interpellated and compelled to resign (July, 1915). During the famine of 1915, he had bread made from the wheat of his own estates baked in Tehran and distributed freely among the needy. In Ṣafar, 1336/November, 1917, he was again chief minister, but because of the British disapproval, the hostility of the Tehran democrats, and criticism of his ministers by Azerbaijani deputies, he again resigned (Rabī' I, 1336/January, 1918). Under Woṯūq-al-dawla's second cabinet (1297-99/1918-20), he was again Azerbaijan's governor and had to cope with Shaikh Moḥammad Ḵīābānī's rebellion. He had no further official appointment (Ṣafā'ī, op. cit., pp. 371ff.; Kasravī, *Āḏarbāyjān*, pp. 51ff.).

In the coup d'état of 1299 Š./1921, he was among the officials who were arrested and was heavily fined. Although he had gathered a certain amount of wealth through inheritance and official appointments, he was deep in debt from having borrowed money to cover state expenses during his first tenure. Contrary to the customs of the Qajar government, Moẓaffar-al-dīn Shah held him personally responsible for these debts, which were said to amount of three *korūr* (1,500,000) tomans. This paralysed his life, for his creditors kept harassing him, especially after his loss of influence. He died on 7 Jomādā I, 1345/10 Ābān, 1306 Š./23 November, 1926.

'Ayn-al-dawla was dismissed by most of his contemporaries, and still is by modern authors, as a mere reactionary, being generally described as an unscrupulous "Russian creature" whose fortune came from speculation, extortions, and malversations. Although he was less friendly to Naus than Atābak Amīn-al-solṭān, he still embodied Qajar autocracy and symbolized the past which had to be destroyed by revolutionary forces (Destrée, *Les functionnaires*, pp. 5f., 113ff.). But he had to pay more dearly than Naus—who retained his position for some time—for his stubborn resistance to both foreign influence and internal rebellion. Although he was later somewhat more liberal and showed a certain courage, his contemporaries only saw in his change of attitude (notably towards the poor, which included the foundation of an asylum in Tehran) a means to maintain his political influence (Ṣafā'ī, op. cit., pp. 373f. quoting Mostawfī). There have been recent attempts at his partial rehabilitation, including praise for his courage and chivalry (*Javānmardī*, see Ṣafā'ī, ibid.), his opposition to foreign influence, his partial success on the economic plan notably by cutting down court expenses. His repression was mainly directed against discontented *bāzārī*s rather than radical intellectuals (Ādamīyat, *Īde'oložī*, pp. 126ff., cf. Bagley,

"New Light," pp. 49ff.).

ʿAyn-al-dawla's only son Mīrzā Moḥammad Šams-al-molk ʿAżod-al-dawla was a pleasure-seeking courtier who dissipated what remained from his father's fortune and ended as a pauper (Bāmdād, *Rejāl* II, p. 99, V, p. 198; Ṣafāʾī, op. cit., p. 376). Photographs of ʿAyn-al-dawla have been published many times (see, e.g., Dawlatābādī, *Ḥayāt-e Yaḥyā* I, p. 150; Nāẓem-al-eslām Kermānī, *Bīdārī-e Īrānīān* I, opposite p. 169; Malekzāda, *Tārīḵ-e enqelāb* I, p. 269; Bāmdād, *Rejāl* II, pp. 93ff., IV, p. 122, V, p. 144; Ṣafāʾī, op. cit., p. 356). A street in Tehran was named after him (Mostawfī, *Zendagānī* I, p. 258).

Bibliography: Sources in Persian: F. Ādamīyat, *Fekr-e āzādī o moqaddama-ye nahżat-e mašrūṭīyat-e Īrān*, Tehran, 1340 Š./1961. Idem, *Īdeʾoložī-e nahżat-e mašrūṭīyat-e Īrān*, Tehran, 2535 = 1355 Š./1976. Idem and H. Nāṭeq, *Afkār-e ejtemāʿī o sīāsī dar āṯār-e montašer na-šoda-ye dawra-ye qājārīya*, Tehran, 2535 = 1355 Š./1976. Ī. Afšār, ed., *Awrāq-e tāzayāb-e mašrūṭīyat marbūṭ ba sālhā-ye 1325-1330 qamarī*, Tehran, 1359 Š./1980. Idem, ed., *Awrāq-e tāzayāb-e mašrūṭīyat o naqš-e Taqīzāda*, Tehran, 1359 Š./1980, pp. 143-57. Idem, ed., *Mobāraza bā Moḥammad-ʿAlī Šāh: Asnād az faʿʿālīyathā-ye āzādīḵʷāhān-e Īrān dar Orūpā o Estānbol*, Tehran, 1359 Š./1980. Ḡ. Ḥ. Afżal-al-molk, *Afżal al-tawārīḵ*, ed. M. Etteḥādīya and S. Saʿdvandīān, Tehran, 1361 Š./1982. Mīrzā ʿAlī Khan Amīn-al-dawla, *Ḵāṭerāt-e sīāsī*, ed. Ḥ. Farmānfarmāʾīān, Tehran, 1341 Š./1962. M. Amīrī, *Zendagī-e sīāsī-e Atābak-e Aʿẓam*, Tehran, 1346 Š./1967. Bāmdād, *Rejāl* II, pp. 93-99. M. Dāwūdī, *ʿAyn-al-dawla wa režīm-e mašrūṭa*, Tehran, 1341 Š./1962. Y. Dawlatābādī, *Tārīḵ-e moʿāṣer yā ḥayāt-e Yaḥyā*, 4 vols., Tehran, 1361 Š./1982. M. Ḥ. Eʿtemād-al-salṭana, *Rūz-nāma-ye ḵāṭerāt*, ed. Ī. Afšār, Tehran, 2536 = 1356 Š./1977. M. ʿA. Farīd-al-molk, *Ḵāṭerāt-e Farīd*, Tehran, 1354 Š./1975. Q. Ḡanī, *Yāddāšthā-ye Doktor Qāsem Ḡanī*, 12 vols., London, 1980-84. M. Moḵber-al-salṭana Hedāyat, *Gozāreš-e Īrān*, 3 vols., n.p., n.d., Idem, *Ḵāṭerāt o ḵaṭarāt*, 2nd ed., Tehran, 1344 Š./1965. M. Kašmīrī, "Čand telegrāf-e tārīḵī az ʿAyn-al-dawla ba wālī-e Fārs," *Barrasīhā-ye tārīḵī* 5/6, 1349 Š./1970, pp. 145-92. Ḵān Malek Sāsānī, *Sīāsatgarān-e dawra-ye Qājār* II, Tehran, 1346 Š./1967. M. Maḥmūd, *Tārīḵ-e rawābeṭ-e Īrān o Engelīs dar qarn-e nūzdahom-e mīlādī*, 8 vols., Tehran, 1328-29 Š./1949-50. M. Malekzāda, *Tārīḵ-e enqelāb-e mašrūṭīyat*, 7 vols., Tehran, 1327-35 Š./1948-56. (Moḥammad-ʿAlī Shah), "Telegrāf ba ʿAyn-al-dawla," *Waḥīd* 6, 1348 Š./1969, p. 959. Ḥ. Moḥīṭ Māfī, *Tārīḵ-e enqelāb-e Īrān* I. *Moqaddamāt-e mašrūṭīyat*, ed. M. Tafrešī and J. Jānfedā, Tehran, 1363 Š./1984. ʿA. Molkārā, *Šarḥ-e ḥāl*, ed. ʿA. Navāʾī, Tehran, 1325 Š./1946. ʿA. Mostawfī, *Šarḥ-e zendagānī-e man yā tārīḵ-e ejtemāʿī o edārī-e dawra-ye qājārīya*, 3 vols., Tehran, 1343 Š./1964. Moẓaffar-al-dīn Shah, "Dastḵaṭṭ ba ʿAyn-al-dawla," *Waḥīd* 4, 1346 Š./1967, pp. 477f. M. Nāẓem-al-eslām Kermānī, *Tārīḵ-e bīdārī-e Īrānīān*, ed. ʿA. A. Saʿīdī Sīrjānī, 2 vols., Tehran, 1357 Š./1978. E. Ṣafāʾī, *Asnād-e bargozīda*, Tehran, 1325 Š./1946. Idem, *Asnād-e mašrūṭa*, Tehran, 2535 = 1355 Š./1976. Idem, *Asnād-e now-yāfta*, Tehran, 1349 Š./1970. Idem, *Asnād-e sīāsī-e dawrān-e qājārīya*, Tehran, 1346 Š./1967. Idem, *Nāmahā-ye tārīḵī*, Tehran, 2535 = 1355 Š./1976. Idem, *Panjāh nāma-ye tārīḵī*, Tehran, 2535 = 1355 Š./1976. Idem, *Rahbarān-e mašrūṭa*, 2 vols., Tehran, 1344-46 Š./1965-67, II, pp. 355-77. M. M. Šarīf Kāšānī, *Wāqeʿāt-e ettefāqīya dar rūzgār*, 3 vols., Tehran, 1362 Š./1983. N. Šāh-Ḥosaynī, ed., "Do nāma az marḥūm Sayyed Ṭabāṭabāʾī ba ʿAyn-al-dawla," *Eṭṭelāʿāt-e māhāna* 3/6, 1329 Š./1950, pp. 23ff.. ʿA. ʿAlī Khan Tafrešī Ḥosaynī, *Rūz-nāma-ye aḵbār-e mašrūṭīyat*, ed. Ī. Afšār, Tehran, 1351 Š./1972. ʿAlī Khan Ẓahīr-al-dawla, *Ḵāṭerāt o asnād*, ed. Ī. Afšār, Tehran, 1351 Š./1972.

Sources in other languages: H. Algar, *Religion and State in Iran 1786-1906*, Berkeley and Los Angeles, 1969. E. Aubin, *La Perse d'aujourd'hui*, Paris, 1908. F. R. C. Bagley, "New Light on the Iranian Constitutional Movement," in *Qajar Iran 1800-1925: Studies Presented to Professor L. P. Elwell-Sutton*, ed. E. Bosworth and C. Hillenbrand, Edinburgh, 1983, pp. 48-64. S. Bakhash, "The Failure of Reform: the Prime Ministership of Amîn al-Dawla, 1897-8," ibid., pp. 14-33. E. G. Browne, *The Persian Revolution of 1905-1906*, London, 1966. Idem, *The Press and Poetry of Modern Persia*, Cambridge, 1914. A. Destrée, *Les fonctionnaires belges au service de la Perse*, Acta Iranica 13, Tehran and Liège, 1976. J. B. Feuvrier, *Trois ans à la cour de Perse*, Paris, n.d.. A. Hardinge, *A Diplomatist in the East*, London, 1928. F. Kazemzadeh, *Russia and Britain in Persia 1864-1914*, New Haven and London, 1968. N. R. Keddie, "Iranian Politics 1900-1905: Background to Revolution," *Middle Eastern Studies* 5, 1969, 1, pp. 3-31; 2, pp. 151-67; 3, pp. 234-50. A. K. S. Lambton, "Secret Societies and the Persian Revolution of 1905-1906," *St. Anthony's Papers* 4, 1958, pp. 43-60. Idem, "Persian Political Societies 1906-1911," ibid., 3, 1963, pp. 41-89. Idem, "The Persian ʿUlama and Constitutional Reform," in T. Fahd, ed., *Le Shîʿisme imâmite*, Paris, 1970, pp. 245-69. P. Sykes, *A History of Persia*, London, 1951[3], vol. II.

(J. CALMARD)

ʿAYN-AL-QOŻĀT HAMADĀNĪ, ABU'L-MAʿĀLĪ ʿABDALLĀH B. ABĪ BAKR MOḤAMMAD MAYĀNEJĪ (492/1098-526/1131), brilliant mystic philosopher and Sufi martyr. Born at Hamadān, he was a descendant in a line of scholars from Mīāna, a small town between Tabrīz and Marāḡa in Azerbaijan. His immediate ancestors were a family of judges of Hamadān with a legacy of loyalties shifting from Shiʿism to Shafiʿism and a history of violent death—his grandfather was executed as *qāżī* of Hamadān and his father also came to a violent end. As a young man ʿAyn-al-qożāt qualified for appointment as *qāżī* and, in his writings, preferred to call himself "the Judge of

Hamadān" though he came to be known in the Sufi milieu as *ʿayn-al-qożāt* "the pearl of the judges."

ʿAyn-al-qożāt studied Arabic grammar, law, philosophy, and theology, became bilingual in Arabic and Persian, and composed his first original work at a precocious age. While as yet an adolescent he turned to Sufism and received Sufi instruction, apparently also from a certain Baraka of Hamadān who is repeatedly cited in ʿAyn-al-qożāt's letters (see also Jāmī, *Nafaḥāt*, p. 416). His best known Sufi teachers, however, were Moḥammad b. Hammūya and Aḥmad Ḡazālī (d. 520/1126), the brother of the great theologian Moḥammad Ḡazālī (d. 505/1111). Moḥammad b. Hammūya's line of Sufi affiliation can be traced through Abu'l-Ḥosayn Bostī to Abū ʿAlī Fāramaḏī (d. 477/1084), a representative of the Khorasanian Sufi tradition influenced by Abū Saʿīd b. Abi'l-Ḵayr (d. 440/1049). Aḥmad Ḡazālī was a disciple of Abū Bakr Nassāj (d. 487/1094), himself a pupil of Abu'l-Qāsem Korrakānī (alias Jorjānī, d. 469/1076), who was affiliated with the Iraqi tradition of Sufism traced back to Jonayd (d. 297/910).

ʿAyn-al-qożāt turned to Aḥmad Ḡazālī's spiritual guidance in 516/1122 after an intensive study of Moḥammad Ḡazālī's *Eḥyāʾ ʿolūm al-dīn*. In person and through his works on mystical love, Aḥmad Ḡazālī had a powerful influence on ʿAyn-al-qożāt's life. He initiated him into religious dance and Sufi meditation, inspired many facets of his mystic philosophy and, until his death, remained in constant contact with him, occasionally by meeting and frequently by letter as attested by extant specimens of the correspondence between master and disciple (*Mokātabāt*). ʿAyn-al-qożāt was married and had at least one son, by the name of Aḥmad.

ʿAyn-al-qożāt's reputation as a Sufi teacher attracted many disciples whom he instructed in oral teaching sessions or by correspondence. Sometimes he taught as many as seven or eight sessions a day and found himself compelled to recuperate from the exhaustion for two or three months. His teaching aroused the opposition and hostility of the *ʿolamāʾ* who laid a formal complaint against him at Baghdad. There, he was incarcerated by Qewām-al-dīn Nāṣer b. ʿAlī Dargazīnī, the Saljuq vizier of Iraq and rival of ʿAzīz b. Rajā, a protector of ʿAyn-al-qożāt's. While in prison he wrote his Arabic defense, *Šakwa'l-ḡarīb* against the charges of heresy brought by his accusers. The major offenses listed in ʿAyn-al-qożāt's apologia included his theory on the nature of sainthood as a stage beyond reason, preparatory to prophethood; his interpretation of eschatological events as psychological realities experienced within the human soul; his teaching on the unconditional submission of the disciple to the spiritual instructor, in which his detractors perceived an insistence on the heretical doctrine of Ismaʿili initiatory teaching; and his view that God, the source and origin of all being, is the All, that He is the Real Being, and that all other than He is perishing and non-existent. ʿAyn-al-qożāt's defense against the charges was based on his Arabic *Zobdat al-ḥaqāʾeq*. His accusers apparently were unaware of many extremely offensive passages in his Persian writings. Some of these, enumerated by A. J. Arberry (*A Sufi Martyr*, London, 1969, pp. 99-101), climax in ʿAyn-al-qożāt's defense of the Sufi statement attributed to Bāyazīd Besṭāmī (d. 261/875), *al-ṣūfī howa'llāh* "the Sufi is God" (*Tamhīdāt*, pp. 300, 313-14).

After some months' detention in Baghdad, ʿAyn-al-qożāt was sent back to Hamadān. There, on the night of the arrival of the Saljuq sultan Maḥmūd, he was tortured and put to death at the age of 33—flayed, crucified, rolled up in a mat, and burnt alive—by order of the sultan on 6-7 Jomādā II 525/6-7 May 1131, along with several high officials with whom he had close ties, notably the atabeg Šīrgīr of Abhar (see also L. Massignon, *The passion of al-Ḥallāj* II, Princeton, 1982, pp. 63, 167).

ʿAyn-al-qożāt's authentic list of his Arabic writings (*Šakwa'l-ḡarīb*, p. 40) enumerates eight works beside the apologia itself and includes writings on philosophy and mathematics. Of these eight, only the *Zobdat al-ḥaqāʾeq*, written in clear and beautiful Arabic when the author was 24 years old, appears to be extant. This philosophical treatise is a testimony to ʿAyn-al-qożāt's struggle for the truth as he tries to detach himself from the theological reasoning of Moḥammad Ḡazālī and adopt the mystical intuition of Aḥmad Ḡazālī. In it he also finds fault with emanationist philosophy and Avicennian thought and upholds the priority of the Necessary Being on the grounds that, situated beyond time, God is simultaneously present to everything. It is not by His action in time that God possesses knowledge of everything but by His very Being (*howīya*) to which everything else has a purely existential relation symbolized by the sunbeams radiating from the sun. The mystic alone understands the relation between the One and the many by spiritual perception (*baṣīra*) resembling the taste (*ḏawq*) of poetic experience.

ʿAyn-al-qożāt's principal Persian writings are the *Tamhīdāt*, the *Lawāyeḥ*, and the *Maktūbāt* or *Nāmahā*. The Persian *Ḡāyat al-emkān*, attributed to him, appears to be work of Šams-al-dīn Deylamī (fl. end of 6th/12th century) revised by Tāj-al-dīn Maḥmūd Ošnohī (fl. 7th/13th century at Herat). The *Resāla-ye Yazdānšenāḵt*, which more commonly is attributed to Yaḥyā Sohravardī (d. 587/1191; see *Opera metaphysica et mystica* III, treatise 13), may be the work of an intermediary between the two authors.

The most important Persian work of ʿAyn-al-qożāt, commonly known as *Tamhīdāt* (Preludes), is entitled *Zobdat al-ḥaqāʾeq fī kašf al-ḵalāʾeq* by the author himself and divided into ten *tamhīd*s illustrating Sufi life and thought. The work discusses the inner attitudes, religious experiences and philosophical assumptions of the mystic and supports them by the interpretation of Koranic verses and classical Sufi sayings. ʿAyn-al-qożāt expresses his profound ideas in precious poetic language and exhibits a high erudition in the literary and religious traditions of his time. The work reveals the author's unconventional spirit and paradoxical reconciliation of belief and unbelief. The symbol of the conjunction of *īmān* and *kofr* is the devil Eblīs, who refused to obey God's command and bow before the creature Adam. Though prototype of unbelief, Satan also personifies the guardian of divine oneness and mad lover of God since his disobedience professes the ultimate goal of monotheism, worship of God alone, and the final aim of mysticism, pure love of God. This theme of 'Ayn-al-qożāt is clearly influenced by Ḥallāǰ (d. 309/922) whose *Ṭawāsīn* he is the first to cite by name and author (see, L. Massignon, *The Passion of al-Ḥallāj* I, Princeton, 1982, p. 42).

'Ayn-al-qożāt's conception of the divine Being is seen against the background of the Iranian dualism of light and darkness which he neither rejects nor avows. "The Divinity is two: one is Yazdān, Light, the other Ahriman, Darkness. Light is that which commands the Good, Darkness that which commands Evil. Light is the primordial Time of Day, Darkness the Final Time of Night. Unbelief results from one, faith from the other." (*Tamhīdāt*, p. 305). Transcending the dualism of light and darkness, 'Ayn-al-qożāt transposes the dichotomy into God and combines it with the figures of Moḥammad and Eblīs. "When the point of divine Magnitude expanded from the one divine Essence to the horizons of pre-eternity and post-eternity, it did not stop anywhere. So it was in the world of the Essence that the range of the attributes unfolded, namely divine beauty, homolog of Moḥammad, and divine majesty, homolog of Eblīs." (*Tamhīdāt*, p. 73). Adopting the opaque notion of the black light (*nūr-e sīāh*) that lies beyond the divine throne (*Tamhīdāt*, p. 118), 'Ayn-al-qożāt fuses the dualist trends of his thought into a paradoxical unity. The black light is both "the shadow of Moḥammad" (*Tamhīdāt*, p. 248) whose nature is pure luminosity and "the light of Eblīs" (*Tamhīdāt*, p. 118) conventionally called "darkness" only because of its sharp contrast to God's light. The notion of the black light is taken from a quatrain of Abu'l-Ḥosayn Bostī, quoted twice in the *Tamhīdāt* (pp. 119, 248) and qualified as "well-known and difficult" by J̌āmī (*Nafaḥāt*, p. 413). It describes the black light as being "higher than the point of 'no' (*lā*)" beyond which "there is neither this nor that" (for one possible interpretation of the verse, see H. Ritter, *Das Meer der Seele*, Leiden, 1978, p. 541). The *Tamhīdāt* were translated twice into Turkish at the end of the 10th/16th century by anonymous scholars (see F. Meier, *Der Islam* 24, 1937, p. 5). It had a considerable influence on the Češtī Sufi order in India through a commentary written on it by Moḥammad b. Yūsof Gīsūderāz (d. 825/1422). Another commentary was compiled by Allāh-Nūr in the 11th/17th century, while Mīrān Ḥosayn Šāh (d. 1080/1669) translated it into Dakhnī Urdu (see A. Schimmel, *Mystical Dimensions of Islam*, Chapel Hill, 1975, p. 296). It also may be noted that 'Ayn-al-qożāt's Češtī admirer, Mas'ūd Bakk, was executed in Delhi in 800/1397. 'Ayn-al-qożāt's treatise, entitled *Lawāyeḥ* (Flashes), is modelled on the *Sawāneḥ* (Thoughts), Aḥmad Ḡazālī's subtle treatise on mystical love (ed. H. Ritter, Leipzig, 1942). The authenticity of the *Lawāyeḥ* was called into question by H. Ritter (*Der Islam* 21, 1933, p. 94). F. Meier spotted its attribution to 'Ayn-al-qożāt in the *Maǰāles al-'oššāq* (*Der Islam* 24, 1937, p. 2), while R. Farmaneš advocated its authenticity in the introduction to his edition of the text (Tehran, 1337 Š./1958). Many stray reflections in the *Lawāyeḥ* agree with 'Ayn-al-qożāt's Sufi themes in style and content; e.g., the admiration of Satan's disobedience and the claim that it is better not to obey God in case He gave the command that one should be occupied with other than Him (*Lawāyeḥ*, pp. 22-23); the idea that hell is better for the mystic than paradise because the mystic lover is lonelier among those who are separated from God than in the community of those drawn near to God (*Lawāyeḥ*, p. 27); the phrase, "the Beloved is I, although I am without I (*bī-k̲īštan*), probably coined by 'Ayn-al-qożāt (*Lawāyeḥ*, p. 40), and the view that the apex of mystical love is reached in death brought about by the cruelty of the Beloved who readies the executioner's mat for the lover's beheading while the lover, rapt in the Beloved's beauty, exclaims: "He is about to slay me, and I only admire His beauty as He draws the sword" (*Lawāyeḥ*, pp. 62, 101). 'Ayn-al-qożāt's collected letters, *Nāmahā* (also known in Sufi literature as *Maktūbāt*), numbering 127, were published in two volumes (Beirut, 1969-72). They are addressed to disciples and fellow Sufis who remain anonymous. In one letter (vol. I, p. 400 no. 50), 'Ayn-al-qożāt mentions that he read through a bundle of his letters himself, in another, that he did not write letters directly to individual disciples but sent them to his son Aḥmad and had them copied so as to assure their wide distribution and safe preservation (vol. I, p. 363 no. 48). With his letters, it appears, 'Ayn-al-qożāt became one of the first Sufi masters to institute the systematic writing of letters as a means of Sufi instruction in Persian. The letters deal with a great variety of Sufi life and doctrine and convey 'Ayn-al-qożāt's fine Persian style of writing. In content, the letters are both inspired and illustrated by interpretations of Koranic verses, Hadith statements, Sufi sayings, and Persian (sometimes also Arabic) poetry. Although some blocks of letters linked by subject matter can be perceived in the collection, it appears to be impossible to put these epistles into any clear logical or chronological order. Three letters (nos. 59-61) are focused on the interpretation of Koran 35:3 and may give an inkling of the esoteric type of Koran commentary 'Ayn-al-qożāt planned to compile (see *Šakwa'l-ḡarīb*, p. 41) but was prevented from doing by his early death.

'Ayn-al-qożāt was a highly original thinker known for his excellent diction. His factual information and historical judgement, however, are highly suspect. He arbitrarily ascribes a work called *Maṣābīḥ* and many poems to Abū Sa'īd b. Abi'l-K̲ayr, which are uncritically listed by R. Farmaneš (*Aḥwāl o āṯār-e 'Ayn-al-qożāt*, Tehran, 1338 Š./1959, pp. 292-312). It is impossible to maintain 'Ayn-al-qożāt's distinction made in the apologia between Sufis who lectured on mysticism in public and those who discoursed on it exclusively before their disciples. Contrary to the common assumption of Sufi sources that Abū Hāšem Ṣūfī, a contemporary of Sofyān Ṯawrī (d. 161/778) was the first to adopt the name "Sufi," 'Ayn-al-qożāt puts the spread of the name in the 3rd/9th century and claims that 'Abdak Ṣūfī (d. ca. 210/825) was the first to be called by that name in Baghdad (*Šakwa'l-ḡarīb*, pp. 17-18). Sufi literature, however, is hardly concerned with the reliability of 'Ayn-al-qożāt's historical information. It focuses its criticism on his daring thought and accords it reproachful admiration that may be summed up in the succinct and pointed axiom coined in this century by Ma'ṣūm 'Alīšāh (d. 1344/1926): 'Ayn-al-qożāt was '*īsawī al-mašrab wa manṣūrī al-maslak*, "Christian by inspiration and Hallajian by orientation" (see *Ṭarā'eq al-ḥaqā'eq* II, Tehran, 1318-1319/1901, p. 568).

Bibliography: Works: The bulk of 'Ayn-al-qożāt's works has been edited by the tireless efforts of 'Afīf 'Osayrān under the collective title, *Moṣannafāt-e 'Ayn-al-qożāt*, Tehran, 1341 Š./1962, including three separate works: *Zobdat al-ḥaqā'eq* with a lengthy introduction (pp. 1-73), Tehran, 1361/1961; *Šakwa'l-ḡarīb* with an introduction (pp. 1-38), Tehran, 1382/1962; and *Tamhīdāt* with an important introduction on 'Ayn-al-qożāt's life and thought (pp. 1-192), a detailed index (pp. 418-523), and selections from Gīsūderāz's commentary (pp. 355-417), Tehran, 1382/1962. Gīsūderāz's entire commentary, *Šarḥ-e Tamhīdāt*, was edited by Ḥāfeẓ Sayyed 'Aṭā' Ḥosayn, Hyderabad, 1324/1906. The first critical edition of *Šakwa'l-ḡarīb*, with French translation and introduction, was prepared by Mohammed Ben Abd El-Jalil, *JA* 216, 1930, pp. 1-76 and 193-297. A. J. Arberry translated it into English with a brief introduction, *A Sufi Martyr*, London, 1969. The *Resāla-ye lawāyeḥ* (Tehran, 1337 Š./1958) was edited by R. Farmaneš who added a separate study on 'Ayn-al-qożāt's life and work, *Aḥwāl o āṯār-e 'Ayn-al-qożāt*, Tehran, 1338 Š./1959. R. Farmaneš also edited *Ḡāyat al-emkān fī derāyat al-makān*, Tehran, 1339 Š./1960, but wrongly attributed it to 'Ayn-al-qożāt. 'Ayn-al-qożāt's *Maktūbāt* were edited jointly by 'Alī-Naqī Monzawī and 'Afīf 'Osayrān under the title *Nāmahā-ye 'Ayn-al-qożāt Hamadānī*, 2 vols., Beirut, 1969-72, while the correspondence between 'Ayn-al-qożāt and Aḥmad Ḡazālī, *Mokātabāt*, was edited by N. Pūrjavādī, Tehran, 1398/1978. The spurious *Resāla-ye Yazdānšenāḵt* was edited by B. Karīmī, Tehran, 1327 Š./1948 and S. H. Nasr in: Yaḥyā Sohravardī, *Opera metaphysica et mystica*, Tehran, 1327 Š./1948, III, treatise 13.

Studies: L. Massignon, *Recueil de textes inédites*, Paris, 1929, pp. 98-102. H. Ritter, "Philologika VII," *Der Islam* 21, 1933, pp. 84-109. F. Meier, "Stambuler Handschriften dreier persischer Mystiker," *Der Islam* 24, 1937, pp. 1-42 (a ground-breaking study). 'Abd-al-Ḥosayn Navā'ī, "'Ayn-al-qożāt Hamadānī," *Yādgār* 3, 1946-47, no. 2, pp. 63-70. T. Izutsu, "Mysticism and the Linguistic Problem of Equivocation," *Studia Islamica* 31, 1970, pp. 153-70. Idem, "Creation and the Timeless Order of Things," *The Philosophical Forum* 4, 1972, pp. 124-40. H. Landolt, "Mystique iranienne," in *Iranian Civilization and Culture*, ed. C. J. Adams, Montreal, 1972, pp. 23-37. Idem, "Two Types of Mystical Thought in Muslim Iran," *Muslim World* 68, 1978, pp. 187-204 (with stimulating observations on 'Ayn-al-qożāt's thought). The major references to 'Ayn-al-qożāt in the *Ṭabaqāt* literature are cited by Brockelmann, *GAL* I, p. 490 and S. I, pp. 674-75 and Dehḵodā, s.v.; see also *Farhang-e fārsī* V, pp. 1227-28.

(G. Böwering)

AYNALLŪ (or Īnallū, Īnālū, Īmānlū), a tribe of Ḡozz Turkic origin inhabiting Azerbaijan, central Iran and Fārs. The name of this tribe, Minorsky believed, was derived from the Turkic title *īnāl*, or *yenāl*. He suggested that the original Aynallūs might have constituted the family and retinue of Ebrāhīm Yenāl, the half-brother of the Saljuq ruler Ṭoḡrel. When the tribe was later incorporated into the Shi'ite Šāhsevan tribal confederacy, its name was changed to Īmānlū, "Those of the faith," and Īnānlū, from the Turkish verb *īnān* "to believe." As for the subsequent evolution of the name into Aynallū, Minorsky maintained it was probably influenced by the sobriquet of the Austrian Wrendl rifle, *ā'īnalū* (having mirrors, see Minorsky, "Äịnallu/Inallu," pp. 1-11). In any case, the tribe was already known as Aynallū in the early 1800s (J. M. Jouannin's list of tribes in Dupré, *Voyage* II, p. 460).

The Aynallū tribe probably settled down in southeastern Anatolia or Azerbaijan in Saljuq times. Later, it was absorbed by the powerful Afšār tribe (q.v.) and became one of its major components. On the list of notables during the reign of Shah 'Abbās I (r. 996-1038/1588-1629), the Aynallū amirs are to be found among the Afšārs (cf. *Tadhkirat al-molūk*, p. 16). The Aynallūs backed the Safavids, first as *qezelbāš* and then as Šāhsevan (R. Tapper, "Shahsevan," pp. 339-40).

The Aynallūs form one of the chief clans of the Afšār tribe of Urmia (Nikitine, "Les Afšārs d'Urumiyeh," pp. 105-08) and of the Šāhsevan tribe of northeastern Azerbaijan (Oberling, *The Turkic Peoples*, pp. 6, 13, 26). Kalb-e 'Alī Khan Īmānlū was given the Urmia region as a fief by Shah 'Abbās I and he was followed by a series of other Aynallū governors (Nikitine, op. cit., pp. 73, 105, 106). A third group of Aynallūs belongs to the Šāhsevans of central Iran. According to H. Field, these Aynallūs were forced to move into the area from northeastern Azerbaijan by Āqā Moḥammad Khan Qājār (q.v., r. 1193-1212/1779-97) (*Contributions*, p. 171). Field estimated their number at from 5,000 to 6,000 families (ibid.) and Kayhān at 10,000 families (*Joḡrāfīā* II, p. 112). Their winter quarters are near Sāva; their summer quarters are near Qazvīn. Many have settled down in villages in the *baḵšes* of Zarand and Ābyak (Razmārā, *Farhang* I, pp. 72, 194, 234).

A fourth group of Aynallūs inhabits southeastern

Fārs. These Aynallūs almost certainly came to Fārs by way of central Iran. Ḥasan Fasā'ī's list of the clans of the Aynallūs of Fārs (II, p. 310) includes several names which suggest a past connection with that region, e.g., Gūkpar (which is also one of the clans of the Aynallūs of Sāva and Qazvīn), Qūrt Beglū (which is also one of the clans of the Šāhsevans of central Iran), and Zarandqolī. In addition, the list contains the name of Afšār Ūšāgī, which recalls the tribe's past association with the Afšār tribe. When it was still nomadic, the Aynallū tribe of Fārs had its winter quarters in the *bolūk*s of Kafr, Dārāb, and Fasā, and its summer quarters in the *bolūk*s of Rāmjerd and Marvdašt (cf. Fasā'ī, p. 309). In 1278/1861-62, when the Ḵamsa (q.v.) tribal confederacy was formed to counterbalance the growing influence of the Qašqā'ī (q.v.) tribal confederacy, the Aynallū tribe was one of the five tribes selected for that purpose. It thereby fell under the domination of the wealthy Qawām family of Shiraz, which had been placed in charge of the new confederacy. The Aynallūs of Fārs were accomplished raiders and banditti. But in 1293/1876 they were severely punished by Mo'tamed-al-dawla Farhād Mīrzā, the governor general of Fārs, and were forced to become sedentary (Fasā'ī, pp. 309-10; G. Demorgny, "Les réformes," p. 102). Before World War I, Demorgny estimated their number at 5,000 families (op. cit., p. 102), and A. T. Wilson at 4,000 families (*Report*, p. 48). Today, these Aynallūs inhabit several villages on the open country east of Fasā (Razmārā, *Farhang* VII, pp. 59, 113, 159, 171).

Bibliography: L. W. Adamec, ed., *Historical Gazetteer of Iran* I: *Tehran and Northwestern Iran*, Graz, 1976, pp. 589-91. G. Demorgny, "Les réformes administratives en Perse: Les tribus du Fars," *Revue du monde musulman* 22, 1913, pp. 85-150. H. Field, *Contributions to the Anthropology of Iran*, Chicago, 1939. L. S. Fortescue, *Military Report on Tehran and Adjacent Provinces of North-Western Persia*, Calcutta, 1922. M. S. Ivanov, *Plemena Farsa*, Moscow, 1961. J. M. Jouannin's list of the tribes of Iran, in A. Dupré, *Voyage en Perse*, Paris, 1819, II, pp. 456-68. T. Kowalski, "Sir Aurel Stein's Sprachaufzeichnungen im Äinallu-Dialekt aus Südpersien," *Polska Akademia Umietjetności* 29, 1937. B. V. Miller, "Kocheviya plemena Farsistana," *Vostochniĭ Sbornik* 2, 1916, pp. 200-23. V. Minorsky, "Äinallu/Inallu," *Rocznik Orientalistyczny* 17, 1953, pp. 1-11. B. Nikitine, "Les Afšārs d'Urumiyeh," *JA*, January-March, 1929, pp. 67-123. P. Oberling, *The Turkic Peoples of Azerbayjan*, American Council of Learned Societies, 1964. R. Tapper, "Shahsevan in Ṣafavid Persia," *BSOAS* 37/2, 1974, pp. 321-54. A. G. Tumansky, "Ot Kapiĭskago morya k Hormuzdskomu prolivu i obratno," *Sbornik Materialov po Azii* 65, 1986, pp. 76-81. A. T. Wilson, *Report on Fars*, Simla, 1916.

(P. OBERLING)

'AYNĪ, ṢADR-AL-DĪN (1878-1954), poet, novelist, and the leading figure of Soviet Tajik literature, born 18 Rabī' II 1295/15 April 1878 in the village of Sāktarī in the emirate of Bukhara, a Russian protectorate. His father, Saidmurad-hoja, (Sayyed Morād ḵ^vāja), a village craftsman, influenced his son's early intellectual development. Although his formal education had amounted to no more than a brief stay in a *madrasa*, he read classical Persian poetry as an avocation and instilled in his son a love of heroic legends and popular songs ('Aynī, *Yoddoštho* (*Yāddāšthā*) I, pp. 22-43, 131-40).

The death of 'Aynī's parents in 1889 brought his village childhood to an end. He moved to Bukhara in 1890 as a ward of a high emirate functionary, Šarifjon Maḵdum (Šarīfjān Maḵdūm) who wrote poetry under the pseudonym, Sadri Ziyo (Ṣadr-e Zīā'), and had been impressed by 'Aynī's skill at impromptu versification. Except for short absences, 'Aynī remained in Bukhara until the First World War, integrating himself fully into its varied intellectual life. He studied at several *madrasa*s, but their narrow curricula, dominated by conservative religious ideals, and their emphasis upon rote learning repelled him. To satisfy his intellectual curiosity he joined small groups of students who secretly indulged in "secular" studies—history, literature, and geography—and who read newspapers, an activity forbidden by the amir. From time to time 'Aynī attended the literary salon held at Šarifjon Maḵdum's home. The discussions ranged widely over classical and contemporary literature, and it was here that 'Aynī, by his own account, acquired the foundations of his literary education ('Aynī, op. cit., III, pp. 3-37).

By the mid-1890s, 'Aynī had become engrossed in poetry. He was attracted to the classical Persian poets, especially Jāmī and Ḥāfeẓ, and the Perso-Jaḡatay master, 'Alī-Šīr Navā'ī. He was also influenced by contemporary Tajik poets such as Šamsiddin Maḵdum Šohin (Šams-al-dīn Maḵdūm Šāhīn) (1859-94), a skilled satirist and critic of the emir's regime, and he became good friends with Muhammad Siddiq Hairat (Moḥammad Ṣeddīq Ḥayrat, fl. 1878-1902), a writer of simple, direct verse, who deepened 'Aynī's knowledge of prosody. 'Aynī composed his first poems in 1895. Being of a reticent nature, he used various pseudonyms and at first shared his work only with Hairat. But as his poems circulated more widely under the by now sole pseudonym, 'Aynī, which he liked most (ibid., p. 250), he attracted the attention of Bukhara's intellectual elite and began to be invited to their literary salons. This early poetry consisted mainly of love poems, *ḡazal*s written in the classical manner with complex rhyme schemes. Later he also wrote *qaṣīda*s, *qeṭ'a*s, and *robā'ī*s and delighted in composing *moḵammas*es on the *ḡazal*s of Ḥāfeẓ and Bīdel. The mood of some poems was melancholy, expressing deep loneliness and a pervasive sense of the injustice of life. Occasionally, he turned to satire and parody, which were in vogue among Central Asian writers of the time as instruments of social commentary. Whatever their subject, all these poems displayed a freshness of conception and a mastery of the *'arūż* (q.v.).

At this time 'Aynī's intellectual horizons were broadening and after the turn of the century he became increasingly interested in social issues. His sense of responsibility towards others grew, and he was persuaded that he could change the conditions of life for the better through his own knowledge and work. Of critical importance for the development of his social consciousness were the writings of Ahmad Doniš (Aḥmad Dāneš, fl. 1827-97), the most influential Tajik social critic of his day. Doniš's *Navodir ul-vaqoe'* (*Nawāder al-waqā'e'*), a wide-ranging examination of Central Asian society, was a revelation to him ('Aynī, *Bu̱koro inqilobi tari̱ki učun materiallar* [Materials for a history of the Bukhara revolution], in *Asarlar* I, Tashkent, 1963, p. 198). Doniš's faith in progress and his advocacy of knowledge and reason as the means of promoting it drastically affected 'Aynī's relations with the mullahs and channeled his own frustration with the obscurantism practiced in the *madrasas* into a sustained effort at educational reform. But his disenchantment with Muslim religious leaders did not lead to indifference or atheism. Islam remained a guiding priciple of his literary and educational activities at least until the Bolshevik Revolution in 1917, but the Islam to which he owed allegiance was the enlightened, socially conscious form advocated by Doniš and his circle.

'Aynī's commitment to educational and religious reform was strengthened by contact with the new currents of social thought that were emerging throughout the Muslim Middle East. He avidly read the burgeoning newspaper press, from the satirical Azeri *Mollā Naṣr-al-dīn* published by J̌alīl Mamedkulized (Moḥammad-qolī-zāda) in Tbilisi beginning in 1906, to occasional newspapers (*Čehranamā*, *Ḥabl al-matīn*) from Egypt and India. Most influential of all was *Tarǰomān*, the organ of Muslim reformers published in the Crimea since 1883. Through its pages and other publications from Kazan, Tashkent, and Samarkand in Tatar and Uzbek he became acquainted with the tenets of Jadidism (modernism), a movement among Turkic intellectuals in the Russian empire for school reform and general public "enlightenment." 'Aynī was one of numerous Tajik intellectuals who were attracted to its causes. The fact that the Jadids (modernists) were often Pan-Turks did not deter Tajiks from joining in their activities, for at this time a distinct Tajik national consciousness did not exist. Moreover, any nascent ethnic rivalry was assuaged by the supra-national character of Jadidism, which expressed itself in strong Pan-Islamic sentiments. The Jadid movement had important immediate consequences for Tajik intellectual and cultural life, notably the creation of the Tajik-language press. Although the Jadid newspapers in Central Asia appeared mainly in Uzbek, several of them such as *Samarkand* (1913) and *Oina* (mirror, 1913-15) carried articles and poetry in Tajik. *Bu̱koroi šarif* (*Bo̱kārā-ye šarīf*, 1912-13) was the principal Tajik newspaper.

'Aynī wholeheartedly embraced the Jadid educational program. His own sharing of the hard life of artisans in Bukhara and his travels in the surrounding villages, where poverty and ignorance abounded, had convinced him that change must come primarily from education. But he was equally certain that benefits could not be expected from the traditional *madrasa* but only from the "new-method" schools being promoted by the Jadids. He joined the Tarbiyati Atfol (Tarbīat-e Aṭfāl), a secret Jadid society committed to the establishment of schools and the promotion of various literary activities ('Aynī, *Mu̱ktasari tarǰumai holi ḵudam* [*Mo̱ktaṣar-e tarǰama-ye ḥāl-e ḵ^v odam* "My short biography"], in *Kulliyot* [*Kollīyāt*] I, pp. 85-86). He taught in a new-method school which had been established for Tatar children in Bukhara in 1907, and a year later he founded a separate school for Tajiks. The elementary textbook, *Tahzib us-sibyon* ([*Tahḏīb al-ṣebyān* "Education of the youth"] 1909), which he composed for it, offered a variety of readings based upon new-method principles. Within the religious and moral framework of Islam, it taught pupils to revere school as a holy place and to pursue learning as a salvation from evil in this world. Another of 'Aynī's textbooks, *Zaruriyoti din* (*Żarūrīyāt-e dīn* "Requirements of religion" 1914), reveals his continued preoccupation with religion as an indispensable moral accompaniment to secular learning. Like his fellow Jadids, 'Aynī also used the press to disseminate his pedagogical ideas and contributed regularly to *Bu̱koroi šarif* and *Oina*.

'Aynī continued to write poetry in both Tajik and Uzbek. Although the form remained classical, the themes reflected his growing involvement in current social questions, and the language showed a further move towards a more colloquial diction. Sometimes sadness showed through as he meditated on human irrationality and ignorance. In "Fojiai shea va sunni" ([Fāǰe'a-ye šī'a wa sonnī "The Šī'a-Sunni tragedy"), written in 1910 shortly after a bloody clash between Sunnis and Shi'ites in Bukhara, he expressed horror at the killing of Muslims by Muslims in the name of religion. In "Hasrat" (Ḥasrat "Grief"), a long poem in Uzbek, he lamented the lack of modern educational opportunities for the peoples of Central Asia and warned that if reforms were not soon forthcoming Turkestan would be transformed into a "graveyard."

During the First World War 'Aynī remained active in Jadid educational activities. His most important didactic publication was the second edition of his 1909 school reader. It contained a new story illustrative of the development of his own ideas and art, one told by means of letters passed between a young man and his family. Entitled "Ḵonadoni ḵušbaḵt" (Ḵānadān-e ḵošbaḵt "Fortunate family"), it was intended to impress upon young readers the need for serious study ('Aynī, *Tahzib us-sibyon*, Samarkand, 1917, pp. 44-46). It was 'Aynī's first piece of realistic prose, a modest work, but one in which straightforward dialogue, in contrast to the flowery narrative style of the time, allowed the characters to reveal their distinct personalities.

The Russian revolutions of February and October, 1917 changed the direction, if not always the substance, of 'Aynī's art. After a brief imprisonment and severe beating by the amir's men in Bukhara in April, he went to Samarkand, which was under Russian control and where he came into contact with Muslim organizations linked to the local soviet. These experiences and his belief that revolution had opened the way to intellectual freedom and the enlightenment of the masses made him a fervent supporter of the new regime. He served it as poet, journalist, and teacher.

The poetry he wrote between 1917 and 1920 faithfully chronicled the growth of his militancy. His first poems after his arrival in Samarkand were filled with a sense of hopelessness at being uprooted from familiar places. But by the end of 1917 he had rediscovered his vocation as a teacher and reformer. He attacked the amir's regime in harsh, uncompromising verses and composed a series of marches extolling the accomplishments of the October revolution. Notable among them was "Surudi ozodi" (Sorūd-e āzādī "Song of freedom"), composed in October, 1918, which was revolutionary for Tajik poetry not only in theme but also in its rhythms. He sensed an awakening of the entire East and in marches written in 1919 in Uzbek and Tajik he summoned its peoples to rise up together against the old order.

'Aynī also used the columns of the new Soviet Tajik press to rally support for the revolution and social and economic reform. Almost daily between 1919 and 1921 he published articles in *Šu'lai inqilob* (*Šo'la-ye enqelāb*), the organ of the Samarkand Communist Party regional committee, explaining the party's objectives and urging support for the Red Army. On the delicate national question he followed the Bolshevik line, which called for autonomy for Turkestan on Soviet rather than "bourgeois nationalist" foundations. Yet, the idea underlying these articles was the promise of new freedom and well-being under the Soviet system, which 'Aynī argued, could prosper only by eliminating "darkness" (*torikī*). He thus pursued his old theme of enlightenment as the way to progress, praising the opening of new schools and the printing of more books and newspapers ("Hukumati shuroi ba mo chi dod [Ḥokūmat-e šūrā'ī ba mā če dād]?" *Šu'lai inqilob*, December 15, 1919, in 'Aynī, *Aknun navbati qalam ast* [*Aknūn nawbat-e qalam ast*] I, pp. 105-09).

The reform of education remained 'Aynī's constant preoccupation. He founded the first Soviet school in Samarkand and taught in it himself and wrote new textbooks, which were widely used in Tajik and Uzbek schools. Characteristic of these readers was *Qizbola yo ki K̲olida* ("The little girl or K̲olida" Berlin, 1924), written in Uzbek in 1922 for girls' primary schools. In thirty lessons it traced the maturinng of K̲olida from a spoiled little girl into a devoted, self-reliant teacher, who was the prototype of later heroines of 'Aynī's novels—the liberated woman.

The early 1920s were a period of literary transition for 'Aynī. Although he continued to write poetry, he had by now decided that prose would be his principal means of artistic expression. He evidently thought prose better suited than poetry to depict the fundamental social changes taking place under the new regime, for he confessed that he found the meters and rhythms of classical prosody inhibiting. In 1922 he completed his first realistic story, *Jallodoni Buk̲oro* ([*J̌allādān-e Bok̲ārā* "The executioners of Bukhara"] in *Kulliyot* I, pp. 101-82; *Sobranie* III, pp. 7-66), an indictment of the amir and his circle told through the conversations of prison guards, and in 1924 he began the publication of his first critical success in prose, the short novel, *Sarguzašti yak tojiki kambağal* (*Sargod̲ašt-e yak tāǰīk-e kam-bağal* "The story of a poor Tajik"), better known by its hero's name, Odina. His marches in 1918 and 1919 may have been an initial attempt to bridge the perceived gap between poetical form and social reality.

The political and social changes that had taken place in Central Asia after the revolution and civil war had a profound effect on the development of Tajik literature in general and 'Aynī's creativity in particular. The recognition of a distinct Tajik ethnic and political nation through the establishment of the Tajik Autonomous Soviet Socialist Republic in 1924 and of the Union Republic in 1929 provided a framework within which a "national" literature could be nurtured. The new regime, which had embarked upon rapid industrialization and collectivization, mobilized writers to promote its ambitious economic and social goals. The creation of the Tajik Union of Writers in 1933 gave it an instrument capable of directing all aspects of literary production. 'Aynī was its first president. He also served on various local governmental bodies, but, preferring the quiet of his study, he does not seem to have been an "activist."

After 1925 'Aynī devoted himself primarily to literary and scholarly pursuits. In the latter 1920s and the 1930s, the most creative period of his life, he produced three major novels: *Dok̲unda* (1930), *Ğulomon* ([*Ğolāmān* "Slaves"] 1934 in Uzbek; 1935 in Tajik), and *Margi sudk̲ur* ([*Marg-e sūd-k̲or* "the usurer's death"] 1939). He wrote another novel, *Yatim* ("Orphan;" Stalinabad, 1940, in *Kulliyot* IV, pp. 183-345; *Sobranie* III, pp. 321-432), about a Tajik boy's separation from his mother and subsequent adventures with Soviet border guards in their struggle against counterrevolutionaries. The plot is melodramatic and the characters are predictable, but the scenes of early family life are charming. 'Aynī's main poetical work during the period was *J̌angi odamu ob* ([*J̌ang-e ādam o āb* "Man's struggle with water"] 1937), a *doston* in the old Iranian *motaqāreb* meter, which described in heroic terms the taming of the Vak̲š river to serve the needs of the new collective farms.

During the Second World War 'Aynī voiced his patriotism in numerous short poems and prose works, but unlike the majority of Soviet writers, who focused their attention on contemporary events, 'Aynī turned to the past. In his condemnation of Hitler and the German invaders he drew upon heroic episodes of Perso-Tajik history. Characteristic were the stories, *Qahramoni halqi tojik Temurmalik* ([*Qahramān-e k̲alq-e tāǰīk Tīmūr Malek* "The hero of the Tajik people, Tīmūr Malek"] Stalinabad (Dushanbe), 1944; *Kulliyot* V, pp. 141-218; *Sobranie* VI, pp. 104-41), which told of the defense of

K̲ojand against the armies of Genghis Khan, and *'Isyoni Muqanna* ([*'Eṣyān-e Moqanna'* "Moqanna''s uprising"] Stalinabad, 1944, in *Kulliyot* X, pp. 194-284; *Sobranie* VI, pp. 7-78), a tale of resistance by the ancestors of the Tajiks to the Arab invasion of the eighth century.

After the war 'Aynī's literary activities remained focused on that past. Although numerous civic honors were bestowed upon him—he became president of the newly established Tajik Academy of Sciences in 1951—he refused to join in the adulation of Stalin or to turn out production novels as prescribed by party ideologues. Rather, he intensified his study of Tajik and Central Asian literatures and wrote four volumes of his memoirs, which by the time of his death he had brought down to 1900.

'Aynī's reputation as a creative writer rests primarily upon four novels published between 1924 and 1939. Forming a panorama of Tajik society between the first half of the nineteenth century and the early 1930s, they are concerned mainly with the lives of ordinary people. 'Aynī was clearly influenced by the general evolution of Soviet fiction during the period, but his principal debt was to the Tajik ethnic experience and the Tajik literary tradition.

Odina (*Kulliyot* I, pp. 183-327; *Sobranie* III, pp. 67-132) is concerned with the mountain peasants of eastern Bukhara and the changes brought about in their traditional way of life by the revolution. 'Aynī displayed an intimate knowledge of the *dehqon* (*dehqān*) and described sympathetically the struggles and ultimate failure of the hero to make a new life for himself. Odina was thus far removed from the positive hero of socialist realist art. He remained a traditional figure, undergoing no inner evolution as a result of his experiences and allowing fate to take its course. Many other features of traditional prose were also present—the loose construction and the accumulation of casual incidents, the abundance of poetic interventions, and the idealized pair of lovers (Odina and Gulbibi). Yet, a transition to modern techniques is discernible. *Odina* was indeed unlike anything that had appeared before in Tajik prose: The main characters were poor peasants, the past was recent and unheroic, the images and style were down-to-earth, and the language was the rich vernacular.

The positive hero made his appearance in Tajik fiction in *Dok̲unda* (*Kulliyot* II; *Sobranie* I, pp. 121-494). Yodgor was a poor peasant, but unlike Odina, he struggled to reshape the village in accordance with Communist values. Artistically, Yodgor is a more successful creation than Odina. While the latter was a static figure, the former evolved from a submissive mountaineer eager to obtain the good things of life only for himself into a class-conscious revolutionary dedicated to improving his community. But this is no five-year-plan novel written to ideological specifications. Tradition retained its hold on 'Aynī. He digresed frequently, and his portrayal of life in the village before the revolution is a masterpiece of affectionate detail.

Gulomon (*Kulliyot* III; *Sobranie* II) chronicles the life of Tajik peasants from the early nineteenth century to the triumph of the kolkhoz in the 1930s. Perhaps 'Aynī's finest novel and certainly the major work of Tajik fiction before the Second World War, it combines his deep knowledge of Tajik history and sympathetic understanding of Tajik rural life with continued faith in the new economic order as the key to prosperity and social justice. It also brings 'Aynī's art closer to the ideals of socialist realism. Society is divided into opposing classes, and the heroes and villains stand in stark contrast to one another. Here, no middle ground exists between good and evil. 'Aynī also contrasts the individualistic labor of the old society, which brought neither material rewards nor spiritual happiness, with the collective labor of the new, which ennobled man. Here the "new man" of Soviet society reaches maturity in the persons of the kolkhoz member Hasan (Ḥasan), the son of slaves, and Fotima (Fāṭema), a Komsomol member and a tractor driver. Their superior moral and social qualities and optimistic view of life stamp them as citizens of the future. But they are not merely embodiments of an idea. In 'Aynī's hands, they are also creatures of flesh and blood.

The short novel, *Margi sudk̲ur* (*Kulliyot* IV, pp. 6-182; *Sobranie* III, pp. 183-320), added a new dimension to 'Aynī's art—psychological analysis. He probes the character of a moneylender against the background of Bukharan society before the revolution. Through numerous episodes in Qurī Iškamba's business and religious life 'Aynī fashions a portrait of utter baseness and hypocrisy. The moneylender, who exhibits no redeeming qualities, symbolizes a society for which there is no hope, and at the end of the novel Qorī himself falls dead at reports that the Bolsheviks have seized power.

All of 'Aynī's works of fiction were, in a sense, studies of Tajik history and society, but he also investigated his people's cultural development and ethnic character in numerous works of original scholarship. He was, for example, intent upon proving the antiquity of Tajik literature and argued that it had had its beginnings in the ninth century and that the great poets from Rūdakī to J̌āmī were the common heritage of both Tajiks and Persians. To persuade doubters and to give the lie to the claims of Pan-Turks that the Tajiks were merely Turks who had lost their language because of Iranian domination ('Aynī, *Muk̲tasari tarǰumai holi k̲udam*, *Kulliyot* I, p. 97), he assembled a critical anthology, *Namunai adabiyoti tojik* ([*Namūna-ye adabīyāt-e tāǰīk* "A picture of Tajik literature"] Moscow, 1926), covering a thousand years of writing. 'Aynī's comments on classical and modern authors make it the first work of Tajik literary criticism. To his earlier, shorter studies of classical verse in *Ustod Rudaki* ([*Ostād Rūdakī*] Stalinabad, 1940; *Sobranie* VI, pp. 79-103), *Dar borai Firdavsī va "Šohnoma"-i u* ([*Dar bāra-ye Ferdowsī wa Šāh-nāma-ye ū* "About Ferdowsī and his *Šāh-nāma*"] Leningrad, 1940; *Kulliyot* XI/1, pp. 7-50), and *Šaik̲ Muslihiddin Sa'dīi Šerozii* ([*Šayk̲ Moṣleḥ-al-dīn Sa'dī Šīrāzī*] Stalinabad, 1942; *Sobranie* VI, pp. 142-68) he now added large-scale monographs—*Alisher Navoi* ([*'Alī-Šīr Navā'ī*] Stalinabad, 1948; *Kulliyot* XI/1, pp. 265-470) and *Mirzo Abdulqodiri Bedil* ([*Mīrzā 'Abd-al-Qāder Bīdel*] Stalinabad, 1954; *Kulliyot* XI/2, pp. 9-327; *Sobranie* VI, pp. 194-265). The former was the culmination of his longstanding interest in the relations between Tajik and Jağatāy-Uzbek literatures and of his appreciation of Navā'ī's influence throughout the Middle East; the latter was the first scholarly biography of Bīdel and detailed analysis of his work, and, in a sense, it reintroduced him into Tajik literature.

'Aynī's historical writings are mainly to be found interspersed in his memoirs and fiction, where materials for a social history of the Tajiks abound. His view of history as a teaching tool and a political weapon is evident in his two principal historical works: *Ta'riki amironi manğitiyai Bukhoro* ([*Tārīk-e amīrān-e manğītī-e Bokārā* "The history of the Mangit amirs of Bukhara"] Tashkent, 1923; *Kulliyot* X, pp. 5-191; *Sobranie* VI, pp. 266-312) dwelled upon the corruption of the Bukharan ruling dynasty between the middle of the eighteenth century and 1920 and was undoubtedly intended to justify its recent overthrow: *Bukoro inqilobi tariki učun materiallar* (Moscow, 1926; 'Aynī, *Asarlar* I, pp. 181-349) reveals 'Aynī as a skillful chronicler of contemporary events and polemicist and should be read in conjunction with his newspaper columns of the same period. Drawing upon diverse sources relating to the period 1900-18, he shows why and how revolution came to Central Asia.

'Aynī, more than any other individual, was responsible for establishing the norms of the modern Tajik literary language. His works of fiction winnowed out elaborate phraseology and obsolete vocabulary and spoke directly to the growing mass audience (N. Ma'sumi, *Očerkho oid ba inkišofi zaboni adabii tojīk* [*Očerkhā 'āyed ba enkešāf-e zabān-e adabī-e tājīk* "Sketches concerning the development of a Tajik literary language"], Stalinabad, 1959, pp. 145-59, 231-60). Of particular importance was dialogue, a major component of his fiction, which elevated everyday speech to the level of art. 'Aynī also intervened directly in the debates among Tajik intellectuals in the 1920s and 1930s over the nature and future development of the Tajik literary language. He favored its modernization through the gradual elimination of unnecessary Arabic and Uzbek words and expressions and the replacement of the "complicated" Arabic by the "more appropriate" Latin alphabet. Yet, he urged that changes be made with due consideration for the Tajik cultural heritage and warned against the artificial replacement of Arabic terms that had become an integral part of the Tajik language ('Aynī, *Mas'alahoi zaboni tojikī* [*Mas'alahā-ye zabān-e tājīkī* "Problems of the Tajik language"], *Kulliyot* XI/2, pp. 335-86). His goals were practical—to provide contemporary writers with a suitable tool and the public with ready access to enlightenment. His pioneering works of lexicography, notably his massive *Luğati nimtafsili tojikī baroi zaboni adabii tojik* ([*Loğat-e nīm-tafṣīl-e tājīkī barā-ye zabān-e adabī-e tājīk* "A half-comprehensive Tajik dictionary for the literary Tajik language"] Dushanbe, 1976; *Kulliyot* XII), were intended to set the new literary language on a solid foundation.

'Aynī's final major work, *Yoddoštho* (*Kulliyot* VI, VII; *Sobranie* IV, V), may be read on several levels—as a remembrance of childhood and young manhood, as an inquiry into the meaning of his own life, and as an attempt to comprehend the underlying forces at work in social change. At the same time, the four parts, which span a period between the 1880s and 1900, provide a synthesis of all his previous literary work. In subject matter, the varied individual types and groups of Tajik society from his novels—the artisans of Bukhara, the mountain peasants, and those who exploited them—are all there. In form, the memoirs resemble a succession of stories, each complete within itself and confirming once again 'Aynī's mastery of short fiction. His technique varies from the sober, almost scholarly exposition of events (the description of his life in the *madrasa*) to the lyrical "*ğazal* in prose" (the death of his mother and father). Perhaps most striking is the directness with which great and small events alike are related, an apparent simplicity that suggests profound truth.

'Aynī died on July 15, 1984 in Dushanbe. His contributions to Tajik fiction, literary history and criticism, and language were pioneering. They are the starting-point for any study of twentieth-century Tajik literature.

Bibliography: (A) Works. Publication of a complete edition of 'Aynī's works in Tajik in 15 volumes has been underway for some time: *Kulliyot* I-VII, IX-XIII, Stalinabad (Dushanbe), 1958-77. The first edition of *Yoddoštho* I-IV was published in Stalinabad, 1949-54; a fine Persian edition was published in one volume in Tehran (ed. 'A. A. Sa'īdī Sīrjānī, 1362 Š./1983) with an introduction, a glossary of Tajik words (pp. 834-945), and indexes. Ample selections of his works are available in Russian: *Sobranie sochinenii* I-VI, Moscow, 1971-75, and in Uzbek: *Asarlar* I-VIII, Tashkent, 1963-67. In Uzbek there is also *Tanlangan ilmiy asarlar*, Tashkent, 1978. Noteworthy among other anthologies are S. 'Aynī, *Akgari inqilob*, Dushanbe, 1974, a collection of lesser known poems and newspaper articles, and S. 'Aynī, *Aknun navbati qalam ast* I-II, Dushanbe, 1977-78, which contains newspaper articles, especially those from *Šu'lai inqilob*, and literary works. Little of 'Aynī's work has been translated into Western languages. His memoirs have appeared in German: *Erinnerungen* (Leipzig, 1955) and in French: (*Boukhara* by S. Borodine and P. Korotkine, Paris, 1956, the first two parts only). *Pages from My Own Story* (Moscow, 1958) is a translation by G. H. Hanna of 'Aynī's *Muktasari tarjumai holi kudam*. There is also S. 'Aynī, *La mort de l'usurier*, Paris, 1957.

(B) Studies of his life and work. Among recent general surveys are I. Braginskiĭ, *Sadriddin Aini. Zhizn' i tvorchestvo*, 2nd ed., Moscow, 1978, and Jiří

Bečka, *Sadriddin Aini, Father of Tajik Culture*, Naples, 1980. On 'Aynī's poetry, Kh. N. Niyazov, *Put' Sadriddina Aini—poet*, Moscow, 1965, is indispensable. The realist elements in 'Aynī's novels have received continuous attention. Useful are A. Saifulloev, *Romani ustod Sadriddin Ayni "Do͟kunda"* (*Român-e Ostād Ṣadr-al-dīn 'Aynī "Do͟kunda"*), Dushanbe, 1966; H. Husainov, *Zabon va uslobi "Odina"-i ustod Ayni* (*Zabān wa oslūb-e "Odina"-ye Ostād 'Aynī*), Dushanbe, 1973; and A. Saifulloev, *Maktabi Ayni* (*Maktab-e 'Aynī*), Dushanbe, 1978. For a discussion of 'Aynī's fiction and memoirs within the broad framework of modern Tajik prose, see *Ta'riki adabiyoti sovetii tojik* (*Tārīk͟-e adabīyāt-e sāvetī-e tājīk*) II: L. N. Demidchik, *Nasri solhoi 30* (*Nat͟r-e sālhā-ye 30*), Dushanbe, 1978, pp. 46-161, passim, and IV: M. Shukurov, *Nasri solhoi 1945-1974* (*Nat͟r-e sālhā-ye 1945-74*), Dushanbe, 1980, pp. 198-219, passim. 'Aynī's views on the modern Tajik literary language are amply discussed in N. Ma'sumi, *Očerkho oid ba inkišofi zaboni adabii tojik*, Stalinabad, 1959, which analyzes *Margi sudk͟ur*, and S. Halimov, *Sadriddin Aynī va ba'ze mas'alahoi inkišofi zabone adabii tojik* (*Ṣadr-al-dīn 'Aynī wa ba'ż-ī mas'alahā-ye enkešāf-e zabān-e adabī-e tājīk*), Dushanbe, 1974. On the problems of translating 'Aynī's prose into Russian see Z. Mullodzhanova, *Still' originala i perevod*, Dushanbe, 1976. Articles in Tajik and Russian on all aspects of 'Aynī's life and work are contained in the series *Jašnnomai Aynī* (*Jašn-nāma-ye 'Aynī*) I-V, Stalinabad (Dushanbe), 1960-78. Essential research tools are the bibliographies of over 4,500 items by J. Azizqulov and Z. Mullojonova, *Fehrasti asarhoi S. Aynī va adabiyoti oid ba u to okhiri soli 1961* (*Fehrest-e at͟arhā-ye Ṣ. 'Aynī wa adabīyāt-e 'āyed ba ū tā ak͟er-e sāl-e 1961*), Dushanbe, 1963 and by Z. Mullojonova and N. Faizulloev, *Fehrasti asarhoi S. Aynī va adabiyoti oid ba ū, solhoi 1962-1976*, Dushanbe, 1978. See also Rypka, *Hist. Iran. Lit.*, pp. 535, 559-64, 602-03, and index.

(K. Hitchins)

AYŌKĒN, a Middle Persian legal term denoting the category of persons to whom descends the obligation of *stūrīh* (marriage by proxy or substitution; q.v.). The term is from the beginning words of the Avestan technical phrase *yō hē pasčaēta* "he to whom afterwards" (i.e., after the decease of a man without male issue) descends the obligation of *stūrīh*. The entire Avestan phrase is found transcribed in the Pahlavi alphabet in the *Mādayān ī hazār dādestān* (pt. 1, p. 22.8), but more commonly the formula was reduced to the two words *yō hē*, transcribed as *ayōk-hē* and then corrupted to *ayōkēn* in the *Riwāyat ī Ēmēd ī Ašawahištān* (chap. 4). Other spellings found in the *Mādayān* are *yōk hē* and *ayōk-kēn'*; the Pahlavi model marriage contract (*Paymān ī zanīh*, in *Pahlavi Texts*, p. 141-43) has *ayōkānīh*; in the *Persian Rivayats* (ed. M. R. Unvala, *Dârâb Hormazyâr's Rivâyat*, Bombay, 1922, I, pp. 180f.) it is written *ayūk*, *ayūkan*, and *ayūkī*.

The persons referred to as *ayōkēn* are one's own (*pādixšāyīhā*) "virile" (*zahāg*) son, who is an immediate and direct progeny and successor, and then in the order of priority a *pādixšāyīhā* widow whose *ayōkēn stūrīh* for her deceased issueless husband is also called *čakarīh* (q.v.); an adopted son (*pus ī padīriftag*); a designate *stūr* (*stūr ī kardag*) who is instituted by the deceased in his lifetime to undertake his successorship; and an associate brother (*brād ī hambāy*). In default of these, the obligation of *stūrīh* descends to the eldest *pādixšāyīhā* daughter, or to the one who has not yet married, and finally to a sister.

An obligated successor (*ayōkēn*) assuming an *ayōkēn stūrīh* enjoys special proprietary rights. That is the reason why *ayōkēnīh* is referred to as a special form of marriage in the Pahlavi marriage contract (*Pahlavi Texts*, p. 141) and why the *Mādayān ī hazār dādestān* has devoted a separate chapter to it: *Dar ī ayōkēn yō hē pasčaēta* (pt. 1, p. 21.4-5).

The case of an only *pādixšāyīhā* daughter, succeeding to her father's obligated successorship, is erroneously given by the *Riwāyat ī Ēmēd ī Ašawahištān* (chap. 44) as the only case of *ayōkēnīh* (ed. B. T. Anklesaria, *Rivâyat-î Hêmît-î Asavahistân*, Bombay, 1962). This idea was repeated by the *Persian Rivayats* (I, pp. 180f.) and provided the basis for the various faulty readings and interpretations of the term as *yūkān* "the only child" (West, in *SBE* 18, p. 185 n. 3); *aêvakkîn* "marriage in condition of the only child" (Bulsara, *The Laws of the Ancient Persians*, p. 153); *ēvakēn* "le mariage de la fille unique" (J. de Menasce, *Feux et fondations pieuses dans le droit sassanide*, Paris, 1964, pp. 35-57); *ēwgānīh* "submission" (see D. N. MacKenzie, "The Model Marriage Contract in Pahlavi," in *K. R. Cama Oriental Institute Golden Jubilee Volume*, Bombay, 1969, pp. 103-09, and with A. G. Perikhanian, ibid., p. 110); as derived from Av. **aēnō.kaēna* "expiator," interpreted as *epiklēros* "(the only) heiress" (Perikhanian, in *W. B. Henning Memorial Volume*, ed. M. Boyce and I. Gershevitch, London, 1970, p. 352, and with MacKenzie, in *K. R. Cama Oriental Institute Golden Jubilee Volume*, pp. 110-12); and *ēnōkēn* "under the obligation to continue her father's line" (D. N. MacKenzie, *A Concise Pahlavi Dictionary*, London, 1971, p. 30).

Bibliography: Editions of the *Mādayān ī hazār dādestān*: J. J. Modi, facs. ed. of the first part (fols. 1-55), Bombay, 1901. S. J. Bulsara, tr., *The Laws of the Ancient Persians as Found in the 'Mâtikân ê hazâr Dâtastân' or the Digest of a Thousand Points of Law*, 2 vols., Bombay, 1937. Further references in M. Boyce, "Middle Persian Literature," in *Handbuch der Orientalistik* I, IV, 2, 1, Leiden and Cologne, 1968, pp. 61f. See also M. Shaki, "The Sasanian Matrimonial Relations," *Archiv Orientální* 39, 1971, pp. 332-33. Idem, "The Concept of Obligated Successorship in the Mādiyān ī Hazār Dādistān," in *Monumentum H. S. Nyberg* II, Acta Iranica 5, Tehran and Liège, 1975, pp. 227-42.

(M. Shaki)

AYRARAT, region of central Armenia in the broad plain of the upper Araxes (q.v.); the name is undoubtedly connected with the Assyrian Urautri, later Urartu, the biblical Ararat (Genesis 12:20, Jeremiah 15:13), and with the people called Alarodioi by Herodotus (3.94) in the fifth century B.C. The name Ayrarat is unknown to classical authors who were well acquainted with Armenia, and it appears to have been in purely local usage to describe the central lands of Armenia which formed the royal domains of the Arsacid kings and probably those of their Orontid and Artaxiad predecessors. In this case it may well represent the Araxenōn Pediōn (Araxena plain) of Strabo (11.14.3), which in its Armenian form Erasxajor was otherwise restricted to one district within Aurarat.

Geography. Although the anonymous seventh-century *Armenian Geography* depicts Ayrarat as a vast province containing twenty-two districts, this account appears to reflect the situation only after the Byzantine reorganization at the time of the Byzantine-Persian partition of Armenia in A.D. 591. The original domains of the Armenian kings appear to have consisted of only the following fourteen districts (for details see also Eremyan, *Hayastanə*):

1. Erasxajor (Araxes valley), i.e., Greater Aršarunik', the plain along both banks of the upper course of the Araxes which subsequently broke into the four separate principalities Abełeank', Gabełeank', Hawnunik', and (lesser) Aršarunik'. 2. Bagrewand or Bagrəvand (Greek Bagravandēnē, on which see Markwart, *Südarmenien*, p. 11) in the valley of the upper Aracani river (Greek Arsanias, Turkish Murad-su) in the modern plain of Alaškert (Turkish Eleşkirt). 3. Całkotn (lit., foot of Całke, Urartian Luša, Georgian Kalkoitni) located at the northern foot of the Całkē mountains (Turkish Ala Dağ). 4. Kogovit (Kog valley), the district west of Mount Ararat centered at the castle of Daroynk' (also Dariwnk' or Darewnc'berd, Turkish Bayazid, now Doğu Bayazit), where in Arsacid times a part of the royal treasure was kept. 5. Čakatk' in the valleys of the streams Vardamarg and Agarak, right-bank tributaries of the Araxes, and centered at the town of Kołb. 6. Aragacotn (lit., foot of Aragac), the plain along the left bank of the Araxes between Maseac'otn and the slopes of Mount Aragac. 7. Nig or Nigatun (land of Nig, Greek Nigē) corresponds to the modern raion of Abaran in the valley of the K'asał river north of Aragacotn. 8. Mazaz, the upper course of the Hrazdan river (Turkish Zanga) which flows from Lake Sevan to the Araxes. Originally this district probably included Varažnunik', which later became a separate entity under the princely house of that name (see below). 9. Kotayk' (Greek Kotaia), the left bank of the valley of the lower course of the Hrazdan river. Here was located the fortress of Erevan (Urartian Erebuni), now capital of Soviet Armenia. 10. Ostan Hayoc' (capital/court of Armenia), the municipal territory of the city of Artašat (Greek Artaxata), which for most of the Hellenistic and Roman periods was the capital of the Armenian kingdom. Located in the valley of the Azat river (Garni-chay), it included the city of Dvin (Byzantine Doubios or Tibiōn, Arabic Dabīl), capital of Armenia from the fifth to the ninth centuries, and the fortress of Garni, summer capital of the Arsacid kings. 11. Urc or Urcajor, the valley of the Urcajor river (modern Vedi), left tributary of the Araxes, southeast of Ostan Hayoc' and centered around the castle of Sagerberd and the locality of Urcajor. 12. Arac or Aracoy *kołmn* (district of Arac') in the foothills of the Siwnik' mountains southeast of Urc along the right bank of the Arp'aneal river. 13. Šarur or Šarur Dašt (Šarūr plain), along the lower course of the Arp'aneal river, centered in the locality of Marawan (lit., Mede town) near modern Norašen. 14. Maseac'otn (lit., foot of Masis, i.e., Mount Ararat), a broad area along the right bank of the Araxes river northeast of Mount Ararat. This was the region called Erikuahi or Irkua by the Urartians, and here were found the town of C'olakert or Jołakert (Greek Zogokara, Latin Coloceia or Zotozeta) and the village of Anhatakan Ałbiwr (Anahit's spring).

History. The chief characteristic of the history of Ayrarat is its gradual partitioning among various princely houses related to the Armenian kings. The Bagratids (q.v.), for example, were almost certainly a branch of the Orontid dynasty of Armenia; it appears likely that the emergence of their principality took place under the Artaxiads (ca. 189 B.C.-A.D. 14) or, if the Artaxiads were an Orontid offshoot, as now seems likely, then under their successors, the Arsacids. The new dynasty, unable to oust the Bagratids, probably gave them as an appanage the land of Bagrewand which may previously have been a part of Erasxajor. In some way unknown to us the Bagratids lost Bagrewand to the pagan religious establishment, possibly being recompensed with the large district of Sper where later we find them ruling. After the conversion of Armenia to Christianity ca. 314, however, Bagrewand passed to the house of St. Gregory the Illuminator and, upon the death of the his last male descendant, St. Isaac, in 438, to his son-in-law of the house of Mamikonean (q.v.), from whom the Bagratids regained the district in 855/862.

Similarly, under the Arsacid Tiridates II (216-17 to 252) the district of Nig was granted to the house of Gnt'uni, while Całkotn at some time was held by the house of Gnuni. Again, at a date unknown to us but prior to 555, a portion of the royal domains formerly probably a part of Mazaz was granted to the house of Varažnunik', from whom it took its name (not to be confused with their earlier land, also called Varažnunik', in south central Armenia). By the fourth century A.D. all of Erasxajor appears in the possession of the house of Kamsarakan, itself an Arsacid branch which had probably received the territory as an appanage from the senior line of the family. Besides these three houses, there were others which owned lands within the royal domains, but whose holdings were not territorial units and probably consisted of large estates. It seems likely that such houses were generally offshoots of the royal dynasty.

After the fall of the Arsacid monarchy in A.D. 428,

Ayrarat rapidly broke up into separate principalities, Erasxajor alone dividing into four units (see above), each under a homonymous branch of the Kamsarakan house, while in the southwest the princes of Urc emerge with a separate state which probably included the adjacent but princeless lands of Arac and Šarur. By the seventh century we find Kogovit in the possession of the Bagratids, who probably also held Całkotn, which by then appears to have been part of Bagrewand (Adontz, *Armenia*, p. 241). The eastern lands of the old royal domains (with the possible exceptions of Varažnunikʿ, and Nig, each of which had its own princely house) apparently remained under the direct jurisdiction of the *marzpan*s (Persian governors-general) of Armenia after the fall of the monarchy.

After the Byzantine-Persian partition of Armenia in A.D. 591, the emperor Maurice organized his newly acquired territories in east central Armenia into a Byzantine province, which, probably from its elevation relative to the rest of Armenia, was designated Lower Armenia (Armenia Inferior). This province appears to have included the four Kamsarakan principalities, the Bagratid principality (Bagrewand-Całkotn-Kogovit), the principality of Varažnunikʿ (without Mazaz), the principality of Nig, and most of the lands formerly lying under the jurisdiction of the *marzpan* (Maseacʿotn, Aragacotn, Čakatkʿ; and Kotaykʿ); however, Mazaz, Ostan Hayocʿ, and the principality of Urc (with Arac and Šarur) remained across the new frontier in Persarmenia. To these eleven lands were added at this time the following principalities: (1) Basean (with Daroynkʿ and Salkʿora); (2) Vanand with the fortress city of Kars, and the town of Zarišat; (3) Širak (with Širakavan or Erazgawors, Širakašat—Byzantine Maurikopolis; Tk. Mevrek—and the fortified cities of Kumayri and later Ani; (4) Ašocʿk (with Ašocʿkʿ castle); and (5) the land of Upper Tašir (Eremyan, *Hayastanə*, p. 85), which, like Ašocʿkʿ, was formerly a part of the viceroyalty of Gugarkʿ (Gk. Gogarenē), which had passed to Iberian, i.e., East Georgian, suzerainty at the earlier Roman-Persian partition of Armenia in A.D. 387. It is this much larger entity of sixteen units (Byzantine Lower Armenia) which the *Armenian Geography* calls Ayrarat in the seventh century; its author fails to mention Upper Tašir but does include Mazaz, Ostan Hayocʿ, Urc, Arac, and Šarur, probably because the latter five lands, while still in Persian lands, had always been held to be part of the royal demesne and ipso facto a part of Ayrarat whatever the current political division.

During the almost 250 years of Arab rule in Armenia (7th-9th cents.), the Bagratids gradually assumed the paramount position among the surviving Armenian princes and ca. 884 were able to establish a new monarchy in central Armenia which included all of Lower Armenia and considerably more territory in eastern Armenia as well. Originally centered at Bagaran, the capital was moved to Kars and then to Ani in 961. In 962 an independent Bagratid kingdom emerged in Vanand with its capital at Kars, and in 982 yet another in Tašir centered at Loṙi. The remaining territory of the original Bagratid kingdom was annexed by the Byzantines in 1045 and then conquered by the Saljuk Turks in 1064-71; thereafter the term Ayrarat gradually fell out of use. In the Geography of Vardan (13th cent.; ed. Berberean, p. 13) it is used solely for the region of Kałzuan (i.e., Erasxajor and Aršarunikʿ), Basean, Gabełeankʿ, Abełeankʿ, and Apahunikʿ and does not include any of the other lands of the old royal domains. The territory of Ayrarat was under Georgian domination in the later 12th-early 13th centuries, but was then conquered by the Mongols (ca. 1240), after which it passed under Turkman rule in the 14th-15th centuries. The former Ayrarat was then partitioned between Ottoman Turkey and Safavid Iran in 1512 and again in 1639. In 1827 Persian Armenia was conquered by Russia, and in 1829 and again in 1878 certain portions of Ayrarat lying in Turkey also were taken by Russia. In 1921 the acquisitions of 1878 were returned to Turkey and the Turkish-Soviet frontier dividing Ayrarat in half follows largely the line of 1639.

See also ARARAT.

Bibliography: Anonymous, *Armenian Geography* (*Ašxarhacʿoycʿ*), French tr. of the short recension in J. Saint-Martin, *Mémoires historiques et géographiques sur l'Arménie* II, Paris, 1819, pp. 301-94; ed. and tr. of the long recension in A. Soukry, *Géographie de Moïse de Chorène d'après Ptolémée*, Venice, 1881, cf. Adontz and Garsoïan below for relevant passages. Vardan Vartabed, *Ašxarhacʿoycʿ* (Geography), ed. H. Berberean, Paris, 1960. L. Ališan, *Širak*, Venice, 1881. Idem, *Ayrarat bnašxarh Hayastangeaycʿ* (Ayrarat, homeland of the Armenians), Venice, 1890. H. Hübschmann, *Die altarmenischen Ortsnamen*, Strassburg, 1904, repr. Amsterdam, 1969, pp. 278-83, 361-66. N. Adontz, *Armeniya v èpokhu Yustiniana*, St. Petersburg, 1908; tr. N. G. Garsoïan, *Armenia in the Period of Justinian*, Lisbon, 1970, pp. 179-80, 236-41 passim. J. Markwart, *Südarmenien und die Tigrisquellen*, Vienna, 1930. E. Honigmann, *Die Ostgrenze des byzantinischen Reiches von 363 bis 1071*, Brussels, 1935. H. Manandyan, *O torgovle i gorodakh Armenii v svyazi s mirovoĭ torgovleĭ drevnikh vremyon*, Erevan, 1945; tr. N. G. Garsoïan, *Trade and Cities of Armenia in Relation to World Trade in Ancient Times*, Lisbon, 1965, S. T. Eremyan, *Hayastanə əst "Ašxarhacʿoycʿ"-i* (Armenia according to the "Geography"), Erevan, 1963, pp. 35, 118. C. Toumanoff, *Studies in Christian Caucasian History*, Washington, D. C., 1963, passim. S. T. Eremyan, "Ayrarat," in *Haykakan sovetakan hanragitaran* (Soviet Armenian Encyclopedia) I, Erevan, 1974, pp. 110-11. T. X. Hakobyan, *Hayastani patmakan ašxarhagrutʿyun* (Historical geography of Armenia), 2nd ed., Erevan, 1968, pp. 121-58. Toumanoff, *Généologie*, pp. 266-70.

(R. H. HEWSEN)

ĀYRĪMLŪ (in Persian often Āyromlū), Turkic tribe of western Azerbaijan. Following the treaty of Torkamānčāy (q.v.) in 1243/1828 through which Iran lost the provinces of Īravān (Erevan) and Naḵǰavān,

ʿAbbās Mīrzā (q.v.), the crown prince, who valued the fighting ability of Turkic tribesmen, encouraged several Turkic tribes which dwelled in the ceded provinces to settle down south of the Aras (Araxes) river, offering them fertile lands and lush pastures as a reward. One of these was the Āyrīmlū tribe, which moved from its ancestral holdings in the vicinity of Gümrü (later Alexandropol, and later still Leninakan) to Āvājīq, a district to the west of Mākū (cf. Stewart, *Through Persia*, p. 183). The Āyrīmlūs were described by at least two nineteenth-century travelers, Fraser (*A Winter's Journey* I, pp. 327-28) and de Gobineau (*Trois ans* II, pp. 266-69). Their principal village is Kalīsā Kandī. Other villages occupied by them are Qara Bolāḡ, Pīr Aḥmad Kandī, Sīāh Čašma, Sangī Tapa, ʿArab Dīzačī, Jamāl Kandī, and Beyg Kandī. They are now completely sedentary (cf. Oberling, *The Turkic Peoples*, p. 63). Ḥājjī Mīrzā Āqāsī (q.v.), the prime minister of Moḥammad Shah Qājār, and General Moḥammad Ḥosayn Āyrom (q.v.), the commander-in-chief of the Iranian police under Reżā Shah Pahlavī, were members of the Āyrīmlū tribe.

Bibliography: C. E. Stewart, *Through Persia in Disguise*, London, 1911. J. B. Fraser, *A Winter's Journey from Constantinople to Tehran*, London, 1838. J.-A. de Gobineau, *Trois ans en Asie de 1855 à 1858*, Paris, 1922. P. Oberling, *The Turkic Peoples of Iranian Azerbayjan*, American Council of Learned Societies, 1964.

(P. OBERLING)

ĀYROM, MOḤAMMAD-ḤOSAYN KHAN, army commander and the head of the police under Reżā Shah (r. 1304-20 Š./1925-41). A native of the Caucasus (see Āyrīmlū) he joined the Cossak division where he became an associate of Reżā Khan. As an officer and a Russian translator he rose to the rank of *sartīp* (brigadier general) (Wilber, *Riza Shah*, p. 102; Ḵᵛājanūrī, *Bāzīgarān*, p. 71). He is reported to have spent some years in Russia prior to the Bolshevik Revolution, where he served as an officer in the Tsarist army (*Paykār* 1/6). Upon his return to Iran in 1921, he was appointed commander of the northern army where his attempts at putting down the Turkman rebellion had little success (Farroḵ, *Ḵāṭerāt*, p. 359). In July, 1925, he replaced General ʿAbdallāh Amīr Ṭahmāsbī as commander of the northwest army (Wilber, *Riza Shah*, p. 118). Soon after, he joined other pro-Reżā Khan provincial army commanders in organizing a campaign aimed at the final overthrow of Qajar rule including sending intimidating telegrams to opposition Majlis deputies (Makkī, *Tārīḵ* II, p. 549). In spite of these services, in August, 1926, Reżā Shah dismissed Āyrom from his posts, apparently for his failure to effectively suppress the Kurdish rebellion (Wilber, *Riza Shah*, p. 118; Eʿẓām Qodsī, *Ḵāṭerāt* II, p. 87). He was then demoted to the position of the head of the military police and later, the army's special inspector (Ḵᵛājanūrī, *Bāzīgarān*, p. 89).

On 22 March 1931, Āyrom was appointed head of the national police force, a division within the armed forces (Ṣadīq, *Yādgār* II, p. 327). This was the third appointment made by the shah after the arrest of Moḥammad Khan Dargāhī, a former chief of police, in December, 1929. At a time when the state's suppression of the oppositional elements was increasing, Āyrom was considered resolute enough not to be bound by legal restraints (Rezun, *Soviet Union*, pp. 175-77). The duties of chief of police under Reżā Shah went beyond the mere establishment of law and order and included counter-espionage, intelligence gathering, intimidation of ordinary citizens, and the elimination of opponents of the shah. Moreover, the shah used the office of the chief of police to check the power of other high officials and to spy on their activities. Using this powerful position, Āyrom managed to become one of the shah's closest confidants. He established kinship ties with the shah through the marriage of his son to the shah's sister-in law (Ṣadīq, *Yādgār* II, p. 327). More importantly, he shrewdly catered to the shah's growing avidity for intelligence by reporting on high-ranking officials (Makkī, *Tārīḵ* VI, p. 109). This way, he also caused the fall from favor of some of his own opponents and rivals such as General Būḏarjomehrī, an old collaborator of Reżā Shah and Tehran's mayor (M. Ṣadr, in *Sāl-nāma-ye donyā*, Tehran, 1346 Š./1968; Makkī, *Tārīḵ* VI, pp. 112-13). Sources indicate that he had an active role in the downfall and murder of such key political figures as ʿAbd-al-Ḥosayn Teymūrtāš and Jaʿfar-qolī Khan Sardār Asʿad Baḵtīārī (Ḡanī, *Ḵāṭerāt* I, p. 221; Eskandarī, *Ārezū* I, pp. 24-26).

Āyrom's brutal conduct allowed him to comply with the shah's unrealistic and unreasonable demands such as the immediate identification and arrest of suspected criminals or political opponents (Makkī, *Tārīḵ* VI, p. 238; Ṣadīq, *Yādgār* II, p. 327). Equally important in gaining the shah's good favor was Āyrom's active role in accumulating wealth and property for the shah, including expropriation of land in Māzandarān which reached its peak under Āyrom (Makkī, *Tārīḵ* VI, pp. 252-59; F.O. 371, 1932, *Annual Report*, p. 55). After General Karīm Būḏarjomehrī was dismissed from his duties as the manager of royal properties, Āyrom took over his post (Makkī, *Tārīḵ* VI, pp. 112-13). He also replaced Teymūrtāš as the shah's unofficial press liaison. Lacking his predecessor's ability to maintain a reformist image of the shah, on occasion he was blamed by the monarch for the inability of the press to present the state's modernizing policies with adequate effect (Daštī, *Ayyām*, p. 252; Bahār, *Tārīḵ*, introd., p. *yd*). Āyrom's efforts for gaining the shah's good favor by organizing a costly carnival to celebrate the shah's birthday, only angered the shah (*Eṭṭelāʿāt dar yak robʿ-e qarn*, pp. 227-29; Makkī, *Tārīḵ* V, pp. 151-52).

Unlike numerous other close aids to Reżā Shah who faced their deaths in prison, Āyrom managed to escape the shah's wrath, as soon as the signs of dissatisfaction became apparent, by obtaining permission to leave the country in 1314 Š./1935 ostensibly to receive medical treatment in Europe. The shah's attempt to persuade him to return through financial incentives were unsuccessful

(Farrok̲, *K̲āṭerāt*, p. 367).

During World War II, Āyrom actively tried to form a German-backed government in exile in Berlin under the name of *Īrān-e āzād* (free Iran) to conduct anti-allied activity, and to take over Iran after a German victory (Makkī, *Tārīk̲* VI, pp. 230-38). When it led to the arrest of German sympathizers in Iran, Āyrom was arrested and confined to a village in Germany. He died in 1948 in Liechtenstein—where he had become a citizen—far away from his numerous enemies (Ḡanī, *K̲āṭerāt* VIII, p. 314; Makkī, *Tārīk̲* VI, p. 238). Among Āyrom's contemporaries, even the most ardent supporters of Reżā Shah have had nothing good to say about him, since to them he represented the darkest side of Reżā Shah's rule. Nevertheless, he was an important part of the coalition of army officers which played the determinant role in Reżā Khan's bid for ultimate power. Later, as a police chief, he developed the security apparatus which enabled the state to exercise a stronger control over nearly all aspects of the life of the people.

Bibliography: ʿA. Amīr Ṭahmāsbī, *Tārīk̲-e šāhanšāhī Aʿlāḥażrat Reżā Šāh Pahlavī*, Tehran, [1305 Š./1926?]. M. T. Bahār, *Tārīk̲-e mok̲taṣar-e aḥzāb-e sīāsī*, Tehran, 1323 Š./1944. Bāmdād, *Rejāl* III, pp. 373-74; VI, p. 108. ʿA. Daštī, *Ayyām-e maḥbas*, 3rd ed., Tehran, 1339 Š./1960. ʿA. Eskandarī, *Ketāb-e ārezū* I, Tehran, n.d. *Eṭṭelāʿāt dar yak robʿ-e qarn*, Tehran, 1329 Š./1950. Ḥ. Eʿẓām Qodsī, *Ketāb-e k̲āṭerāt-e man yā rowšan šodan-e tārīk̲-e ṣad sāla* II, Tehran, 1342 Š./1963. M. Farrok̲, *K̲āṭerāt-e sīāsī-e Farrok̲*, Tehran, 1347 Š./1969, pp. 351-68. Ḥ. Fāṭemī, in *Mard-e emrūz* 5/115, 1326 Š./1947. Q. Ḡanī, *K̲āṭerāt-e Doktor Qāsem Ḡanī*, 12 vols., London, 1980-84. E. Kʷājanūrī, *Bāzīgarān-e ʿaṣr-e ṭalāʾī*, Tehran, 1357 Š./1978. Ḥ. Makkī, *Tārīk̲-e bīst sāla-ye Īrān* II-VI, Tehran, 1357-62 Š./1978-83. P. L. Mok̲tārī, *Tārīk̲-e haftād sāla-ye polīs-e Īrān*, Tehran, 1329 Š./1950. *Paykār* 1/6, apud K. Šākerī (D. Bozorgue), *Historical Documents: The Workers, Social Democratic, and Communist Movement in Iran* VI, Tehran, 1358 Š./1979, pp. 158-59. M. Rezun, *The Soviet Union and Iran: Soviet Policy in Iran from the Beginning of the Pahlavi Dynasty until the Soviet Invasion in 1941*, Geneva, 1981. ʿĪ. Ṣadīq, *Yādgār-e ʿomr* I, Tehran, n.d. D. Wilber, *Riza Shah: The Resurrection and Reconstruction of Iran*, Hicksville, N.Y., 1975.

(M. AMANAT)

AYVĀN (palace, veranda, balcony, portico), a Persian word used also in Arabic (*īwān, līwān*) and Turkish. In classical Persian or Arabic texts, *ayvān* refers most of the time to a palatial function, either a whole palace or the most important and formal part of a palace. By extension, it can mean the most official or impressive part of any building. It has been suggested that the word derives from Old Persian *apadāna* (q.v.; W. B. Henning, "Bráhman," *TPS*, 1944, p. 109 n.1 = *Acta Iranica* 6, p. 195; W. Eilers, in *Camb. Hist. Iran* III, p. 495), but this derivation is no longer securely established. The most celebrated literary use of the term for a standing secular monument occurs with respect to the remains of the Sasanian palace, Ayvān-e Kesrā (q.v.), in Ctesiphon, where it is synonymous with *ṭāq*, the latter term referring to a form rather than to a function. The other examples of the use of the term in texts can rarely be associated with a specific form. In descriptions of ʿAbbasid palaces the *ayvān* was the main reception and audience hall of a larger establishment with only hypothetical formal equivalents. However, a four-storeyed *ayvān*, presumably a discrete building, was erected by the Muzaffarid Shah Yaḥyā (r. 789-95/1387-93) in Yazd (Aḥmad b. Ḥosayn Kāteb, *Tārīk̲-e jadīd-e Yazd*, ed. Ī. Afšār, Tehran, 1345 Š./1966, p. 86). In the *Šāh-nāma*, the word is consistently and almost exclusively used for palaces or for audience halls. At some still undetermined time, it is possible that the word *ayvān* acquired the more technically narrow meaning of the architectural form to be discussed below. Thus in an inscription dated in 768/1366-67, the eastern hall of the Great Mosque in Isfahan is described as "this high *ayvān*" (Honarfar, *Eṣfahān*, p. 137). Whether the reference is to a form or to a place of particular distinction is not clear, as ʿAlī-Šīr Navāʾī, for instance mentions an *ayvān* with many columns, which certainly does not correspond to the vault of Isfahan. The matter will only be resolved after a careful survey of literary sources in proper chronological order.

The second common meaning of the word was developed by western art historians and archeologists, possibly under the impact of the monument at Ctesiphon. In this sense, the *ayvān* is a single large vaulted hall walled on three sides and opening directly to the outside on the fourth. Seen strictly as a unit of architectural composition, the *ayvān* is obviously one of the most consistent features of Iranian architecture since Parthian times. From Iran it was allegedly exported both eastward and westward, as in many buildings of thirteenth- and fourteenth-century Anatolia and Syria, in the *madrasa* of Sultan Ḥasan in Cairo, or in monuments of Islamic India. Within the Iranian world it is found in palaces, houses, mosques, *madrasa*s, sanctuaries, and caravanserais. In mosques it is usually called *ṣoffa*. In pre-Islamic and early Islamic monuments, a single *ayvān* appears frequently associated with a domed hall, but its most conspicuous and celebrated use is in the combination of four *ayvān*s around a court. More than any other architectural element, this combination became the modular axis around which decorative and architectonic compositions were organized. Initially, as with the Great Mosque of Isfahan, these compositions were centered exclusively on the inner courtyard, defining the most characteristic Iranian architectural esthetic of the interior facade. Later, as in Timurid or Safavid masterpieces like the K̲argerd *madrasa*, the Bībī K̲ānom mosque in Samarqand, or the Masjed-e Šāh in Isfahan, the *ayvān* also appears on the exterior of the monument, as a forecast of its interior forms. The exact history of these formal developments is still to be investigated as are the cultural or other reasons for whatever changes occurred in the use of *ayvān*s. But, regardless of the results of future scholarship on these issues, the ubiquitous importance of the *ayvān* is obvious enough.

Within this general definition and shortened survey of the *ayvān* in Iran several problems have attracted the attention of scholarship and require elaboration. Three of them are particularly important: 1. origins of the form; 2. the problem of the four *ayvān*s; 3. practical, symbolic, and esthetic properties of the *ayvān*.

1. Origins. The origins of the *ayvān* are virtually unknown.

The earliest known examples are found in the Parthian and Parthian-inspired monuments of Iraq. The most celebrated ones are the well-preserved single ones from Hatra (first century B.C.-second century A.D.), but recent investigations by E. S. Keall among others have shown that by the first century A.D. it was a common form in temples, palaces, and residences and that already at that time it was used singly, as two similar units facing each other, or even (Ashuz) as four units around a courtyard. Earlier research had tended to see in the *ayvān* an indigenous Mesopotamian development, possibly when technical innovations in vaulting made it possible and desirable in lands without wood to imitate the more formal buildings of the Iranian plateau. Some even saw its origins in the vernacular reed constructions of Mesopotamia, but this kind of explanation is no longer accepted. More recently it has been thought that this *ayvān* grew out of the impact on the Near East of Mediterranean architectural forms and that it is merely an adaptation to Mesopotamian or Iranian constructional techniques of the *tablinum* at court. Historically and culturally this is a reasonable hypothesis, since Parthian times are precisely the period when Hellenistic motifs were incorporated into the traditions of Iran or Mesopotamia. Its assumption, however, is that it was in Iran and/or Iraq that monumental vaulting first developed and this assumption has been questioned recently by historians of Mediterranean vaulting. It is curious, also, that the otherwise spectacular monuments from Parthian Nisa in Central Asia show extraordinary domes but no *ayvān*s.

To decide between these hypotheses is well-nigh impossible at this time, and one reason is the absence of adequate information from Iran itself and especially from its northeastern and Central Asian provinces. These are the provinces where the *ayvān* was to become particularly important in later times, but their Parthian and even later pre-Islamic monuments show, until now, only one identifiable *ayvān*, in the presumably Parthian palace at Kūh-e K̲ᵛāja in Iranian Sīstān. But the exploration of these vast regions has barely begun.

The form of the *ayvān* appears at the beginning of the Christian era and is almost immediately used for different functions and in varying arrangements, especially in Iraq. Whether or not it was a form imported from farther east can not be demonstrated.

2. The problem of the four *ayvān*s. A special problem in Islamic architecture is posed by the plan of a court with four *ayvān*s. The reason is that the spread of this particular plan has been related by many scholars to the growth of a major new Islamic function, the *madrasa*. The classical reasoning (Godard) is that the *madrasa* appeared first in northeastern Iran, that its functions were initially accomplished in private houses, that the original Khorasan house was one with four *ayvān*s, and that this house type became monumentalized in the Neẓāmīyas (one of which is alleged to have been traceable in K̲argerd fifty years ago) and subsequently transferred into the standard plan for all possible functions of monumental architecture.

In this simplified form the scheme is not acceptable. The examples of four-*ayvān* private houses in eastern Iran are neither very numerous nor consistent enough to be used as models for later architecture; in addition, houses with exactly the same plan are known in ninth-century Iraq as well. What remains of the K̲argerd *madrasa* is hardly sufficient for an acceptable reconstruction; and the assumption that four *ayvān*s were a convenient arrangement for the purposes of religious teaching is a fallacious extrapolation based on the ecumenical meaning of a few later *madrasas*. Most early *madrasas* were devoted to a single, or at most, to two religions.

Yet, even if the scheme as such is wrong, two of its features have some historical validity. The increasing popularity of the four-*ayvān* plan in religious architecture, as it appears for instance in a group of twelfth-century mosques in western Iran (Zavāra, Ardestān, Bersīān, Isfahan), indeed corresponds to the time of the spread of the institution of the *madrasa*, and inscriptions at Ardestān (q.v.) and literary sources at Isfahan (Honarfar, passim) indicate some sort of new relationship between the traditional Muslim place of prayer and specialized teaching functions, especially in Iran. The second feature is the northeastern Iranian background of the plan. The discovery at Ajina Tepe (q.v.) of a Buddhist monastery with four *ayvān*s as well as the number of formal variations in the *ayvān*s (including four around a court) found in presumably early Islamic houses in Sīstān suggest that Khorasan in its broadest sense may well have been the area where the monumental use of four *ayvān*s really originated or that it was revived there in Islamic times. Already it was used there for palaces (Laškarī Bāzār and Termed̲) as well as for religious monuments.

3. Practical, symbolic, and esthetic properties of the *ayvān*. The *ayvān* was rarely used alone (partial exceptions in the sanctuary of Pīr-e Bakrān at Lenjān near Isfahan or the mosque of Nīrīz in Fārs) and was not therefore a discrete, individually meaningful, form. In Sasanian times it appears most commonly in combination with a dome and this *ayvān*-dome combination remained a most consistent feature of Iranian architecture. Alternately, it is the dominant feature of a court, in later times flanked by minarets. It is with two minarets that the *ayvān* is frequently used as a gateway.

Since we are not able to equate the Persian and Arabic word *ayvān* with the form called *ayvān* by art historians, the official meanings and associations of the former can not automatically be transferred to the latter. Yet it is likely that *ayvāns* in their art-historical sense did have specific practical and occasionally symbolic functions. In Sasanian times they were almost certainly the place of formal royal appearances, as the imperial crown was hung from the apex of the vault and a curtain stretched in front of the *ayvān* was opened to reveal the royal presence to the people assembled in the court. It is impossible to reconstruct the proper architectural setting for Islamic royal practices, except in fairly early times, when, in Baghdad or Marv, Sasanian practices and forms were probably maintained. But the exact use of all four *ayvāns* at a palace like Laškarī Bāzār is difficult to imagine. Honorific meanings can also be assumed for the *ayvān* in such examples as the sanctuaries of Lenjān and of Gāzorgāh, although for pious and commemorative architecture the *ayvān* never acquired the importance of the dome.

It is difficult to define the practical attributes of *ayvāns*. The single *ayvān* has the advantage of creating a single large space and its communal usefulness is obvious. But in a large building with several *ayvāns*, the unit is on the contrary a means to break up large spaces into small parts, each one with its individual focus. Whether or not the development of multi-*ayvān* mosques or caravanserais is a reflection of internal social or other divisions is still a moot question. Yet it is clear that the form itself would be used in very flexible fashion and its adoption in Islamic times corresponds to the whole culture's concern for forms which could be used in many different ways and which would not become straitjackets. Finally it should be noted that, just as the *ayvān* would not have been possible without the development of vaulting, so also it became during the centuries one of the best vehicles for Iranian construction techniques.

Two themes predominate in a definition of the *ayvān*'s esthetic value. One is that it becomes a screen between interior and exterior worlds, controlling, as it does, the compositional rhythms of all walls and often their decoration as well. It is the place where inscriptions proclaim whatever secular or pious function a building had and the glory of its founders. Yet the *ayvān* is also a passageway, as the shadow of its interior intimates other parts of buildings. Hence it is not an accident that the *ayvān* became a gateway and that its decoration occasionally resembles that of a magnified *mehrāb*. Its value as a frame made it a characteristic form of architecture in miniatures.

Bibliography: There is no real study of the *ayvān*; the following works may be consulted: O. Grabar, "Īwān," *EI*². Honarfar, *Esfahān*, pp. 86ff., 137. N. V. D'yakonova and O. I. Smirnova, "K voprosu ob istolkovaniĭ pendzhikentskiĭ rospisi," *Sbornik v chesti I. A. Orbeli*, Leningrad, 1960. F. Oelmann, "Hilani und Liwanhaus," *Bonner Jahrbücher* 127, 1922. G. Gullini, *Architettura iranica*, Turin, 1964, pp. 326ff. . L. Golombek, *The Timurid Shrine at Gazur Gah*, Toronto, 1969. A. Godard, "La mosquée," *Ars Islamica* 6, 1951. B. A. Litvinskiĭ and T. I. Zeĭmal, *Adzhina-tepe*, Moscow, 1971. E. J. Keall, *The Significance of Late Parthian Nippur*, doctoral thesis, University of Michigan, Ann Arbor, 1970. H. Behrens and M. Klinkott, "Das Ivan-Hofhaus in Afghanisch-Sistan," *AMI*, N.S. 6, 1973. N. Ardalan and L. Bakhtiar, *The Sense of Unity*, Chicago, 1973. *Camb. Hist. Iran* III, pp. 489, 495, 1058-80 (passim), 1147, 1149.

(O. Grabar)

AYVĀN (or **ṬĀQ**)-E **KESRĀ** (the Palace of Ḵosrow), the most famous of all Sasanian monuments and a landmark in the history of architecture, now only an imposing brick ruin. While actually belonging to the city of Asbānbar on the east bank of the Tigris below Baghdad, the Ayvān-e Kesrā (also called Ayvān-e Madā'en) is usually associated with the name of Ctesiphon, which lies immediately to the north of Asbānbar and is another of the cities which made up the multiple complex of Madā'en (Figure 1). Situated near the modern settlement of Salmān-e Pāk, the Ayvān-e Kesrā is the legendary throne hall of the Sasanian kings of kings.

Pertinent studies of the monuments include the invaluable photographic record that was published in Dieulafoy (V, sec. 6) before the floods of 1888 destroyed one third of the standing ruin (Plate xxxiii); the investigations of Herzfeld in 1907-08 from which he produced a plan based on the traces of walls above ground and the shapes of the surrounding ruins (Sarre and Herzfeld, *Archäologische Reise*, p. 61, fig. 167); the excavations of the German expedition of 1928-29 which confirmed some of Herzfeld's projections, as well as unearthing other features in the area (Reuther, *Ausgrabungen*, pp. 17ff.); and the probes, conducted in 1964 by the Italian Mission in Iraq, which were designed to prepare the ground for restoration (Bruno, "The Preservation," pp. 89ff.). In 1972 the Directorate-

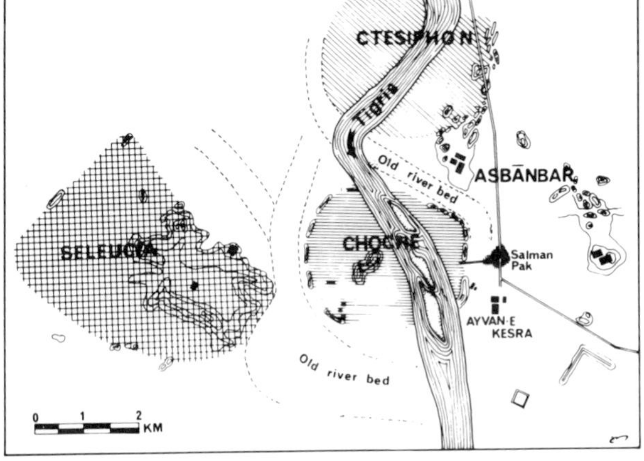

Figure 2. Topography of Al-Madā'en showing location of Ayvān-e Kesrā. After Fiey (*Sumer* 23, 1967) and Mesopotamia 1, 1966

Elevation of the great arch and the north and south wings of Ayvān-e Kesrā, prior to 1888. From Dieulafoy, 1884

General of Antiquities of Iraq completed the restoration of the south wing, and in 1975 work began on the reconstruction of the collapsed north wing (Madhloom, "Restorations," pp. 119ff.).

The standing monument consists of a large *ayvān* 43.50 m deep by 25.50 m wide, penetrating a blind facade that stretches 46 m in either direction from the center line of the *ayvān* and stood originally 35 m above ground level to the height of its cornice (Plates II-III). The articulation of the blindfacade is formed by a series of six stories of brickwork, consisting of columns, entablatures, and arched niches. The *ayvān* is roofed by a parabolic vault, with the side walls tapering from 7 m to 4 m and brought forward by slight corbeling below the impost in order to reduce the enormous width to be spanned. The true part of the vault, for which slanting lays of brick on edge were employed (permitting the construction of a vault without centering), is confined to the upper third of the structure; this arch tapers from 1.80 m at the point of the spring line to 1.30 m at the crown. The great arch dominates the layout, but the area behind the facade can be shown to be taken up by a pair of large rectangular and square chambers on either side (if one can assume symmetry of plan) which are separated from the axial *ayvān* by a vaulted corridor system (Figure 2). Access to the corridor is gained through a doorway which penetrates the facade. Behind the *ayvān*, and connected to it by a narrow door, is an arrangement of rooms which are remarkable for their comparatively small dimensions. Through a cross passage and the central chamber one can enter the large hall at the rear of the complex. It is a later addition and measures 26 m wide by 38 m deep.

The great arch and its facade have aroused comments that generally have acknowledged its impressive qualities. Ebn al-Faqīh (p. 255) considered it to be one of the marvels of the world. Ṭabarī (III, p. 320) reports that the caliph al-Manṣūr was advised by his minister Ḵāled b. Barmak not to attempt its demolition. This advice reflects both the building's prodigious dimensions and its reputation as a monument. In spite, however, of the past and present notoriety surrounding the Ayvān-e Kesrā, including the observations of Arab geographers, the accounts of travelers, and the attention of archeologists, it is still only largely circumstantial evidence which permits investigators to propose a specific date for the building's construction. That such a problem is a crucial issue stems from the fact that any

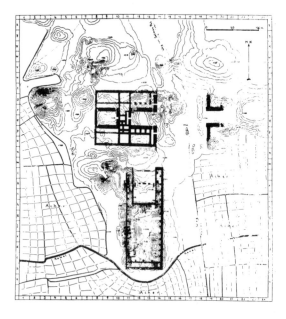

Figure 2. Plan of Ayvān-e Kesrā and adjacent features. From "The German Excavations," *Antiquity* 3, 1929

Elevation of the great arch and south facade of Ayvān-e Kesrā prior to 1928. From *Antiquity* 3, 1929

interpretation of the building's significance in the history of architecture depends entirely upon knowing when it was built.

The problem of identifying the building's sponsor began at least as early as the time of Ḥamza Eṣfahānī (mid-4th/10th century A. D.) who, as cited by Yāqūt (I, pp. 425-26), quotes a passage translated by Ebn al-Moqaffaʿ from a Pahlavi chronicle, the *K͟ʷadāy-nāmag*, which states that the Ayvān at Madāʾen was built by Šāpūr I (r. 241-72 A. D.). This date was preferred by Herzfeld (*Archäologische Reise*, p. 76). Ḥamza himself favored a different view, based on information received from a Zoroastrian priest, Omayd b. Ašūhast, who claimed that the Ayvān was the work of K͟osrow II Parvēz (r. 590-628). In other sources it is K͟osrow I Anōšīravān (r. 531-79) who is claimed as the founder. This attribution has received the most support in recent times for stylistic reasons as well. Yāqūt said that it was the work of several kings (loc. cit.). The problem is compounded by the fact that late medieval writers confuse the Ayvān-e Kesrā with the "White Palace." The confusion may stem from the fact that, according to Ṭabarī (I, p. 2441), when the victorious Moslem general Saʿd b. Abī Waqqāṣ occupied Madāʾen in 16/637 "he resided in the White Palace and took his prayers in the Ayvān." By the time of Yāqūt the White Palace had long since been demolished for the re-use of its building materials, and there may have been a tendency to think of the two structures as belonging to same complex, though it is clear from the early writers (e.g., Yaʿqūbī, *Boldān*, p. 321, and the *Taʾrīk͟ Bağdād* I, p. 128) that the White Palace was in the ʿAtīqa section of Madāʾen, while the Ayvān was in Asbānbar. The picture is further clouded by the way that the personal name Kesrā was used in post-Sasanian times as the generic title for all Sasanian kings of kings. The problem is only slightly alleviated by the theory advanced by O. Grabar (see AYVĀN) that the latter term was used in the medieval period to refer to a throne palace and had no specific connotations of architectural form. Thus, any reference to an *ayvān* in Madāʾen should presumably automatically relate to the Ayvān-e Kesrā.

Reuther arrived at a sixth century date, i.e., that of K͟osrow I, on the grounds of the facade's style (*Survey of Persian Art*, pp. 515-16). He argued that three of the decorative principles employed in the facade's decorations are unknown in the eastern Mediterranean area before the sixth century. These include the combination of large and small elements of the same type in an arcade where stories of markedly different scale are linked by a "colossal order" of engaged columns; the rejection of vertical alignment for the elements of superimposed stories; and the use of a decorative arcade motif on the archivolt of the arch. Naturally, this argument presupposes that all these developments had to have taken place first in Syria. It relied heavily upon the accounts of Byzantine historians such as Theophylaktos Simokatta (*Histories* 5.6, ed. C. de Boor, Leipzig, 1887, cf. *Šāh-nāma*, ed. Borūk͟īm, IX, pp. 2886 ff.), who went to great lengths to emphasize the contribution made by Greek, i.e., Byzantine, architects. "Ctesiphon is the biggest of the royal residences in Persia. It is said that the emperor Justinian sent Greek stone, as well as architects who were experts in building and experienced in vaulting, to K̲osrow the son of Kavād (K̲osrow I). And they built the royal palace not far from Ctesiphon in the Byzantine manner."

While one can not dispute that marble, as well as artisans and even architects, were in all probability brought to the royal court of K̲osrow I for his foundation of New-Antioch after his capture of the mother city in 540 A.D., it is entirely to be disputed whether these individuals were involved in the conceptual planning of the Ayvān-e Kesrā monument. It would be natural for any Byzantine writer like Theophylaktos, with his obvious bias, to have made the smallest contribution by a western architect (even redecoration with marble slabs) seem like control over the entire project. It would be wrong, too, to deny that the origins of the individual elements of the decorative facade are to be found in the vocabulary of the Hellenistic and Roman architecture of the West. But these principles of decoration had long been adopted and even developed by the Parthian architects of Mesopotamia, as demonstrated by the facade of the Parthian palace at Ashur. In fact, one could argue that the types of liberties which eastern architects were already accustomed to taking with the strict Classical concepts, in the second century A.D., naturally permitted the decorative arrangement of the Ayvān-e Kesrā to have been conceived long before the era of K̲osrow I.

Herzfeld and others relied heavily upon this argument, being inclined to accept the *K̲ᵛadāy-nāmag̲* source which attributed the building to Šāpūr I. Gullini has acknowledged the obvious similarity between the Ayvān-e Kesrā and the Ashur palace in terms of the use of a blind facade to decorate a building, but he argues that the Sasanian example lacks "the uniform rhythmic vertical cadence" which distinguishes the Parthian version. Following basically the same stylistic argument as Reuther he is inclined to favour a sixth century date (Bruno et al., *Mesopotamia* 1, p. 92).

Reuther's interpretation also depended upon evidence unearthed by the 1928 excavations. But it should be emphasized that this evidence is circumstantial in the extreme. Thwarted by the lack of material by which they could study the monument in detail, and with considerations of safety in mind, the German excavators turned their attention to the Tell al-D̲abāʿī mounds that lay immediately to the south of the south wing of the Ayvān-e Kesrā. Extensive fragments of architectural decorations were found on the surface, mostly of colored marble, mosaic glass cubes, and ornamental stucco. The stucco was dated to the sixth century on stylistic grounds. By an unacceptable line of argument the hypothesized friezes of human and animal figures were interpreted as being appropriate remnants of the White Palace, with the Ayvān-e Kesrā (in which, according to Ṭabarī, I, p. 2441, Saʿd took his prayers) located conveniently close by. The similarities of pavement level between the two areas were seen by the excavators as additional supportive evidence for dating the Ayvān-e Kesrā to the sixth century.

A possible solution to the dilemma might be found if it could be determined that the great arch actually dated from the third century, while the decorations (in particular the marble slabs from Antioch) merely represented later refurbishings. The later addition of the enclosed chamber at the rear of the complex suggested by the different level of foundations, might even fit nearly into this arrangement—the greater mystique associated with the imperial throne and the closed draperies of the reign of K̲osrow I would have been well served by the addition of this more secluded chamber behind the public audience hall.

Recent probes, however, by the Italian Mission around the footings of Ayvān-e Kesrā—designed specifically as studies to plan the restoration of the monument—have demonstrated fairly strongly that there is no archeological evidence for such suggested refurbishings. The Mission reports that the only major changes visible from the probes appear to have occurred after the tearing-out of the precious wall facings (presumably after the Moslem conquest). It would be surprising if all traces of earlier phases had been completely removed, even if the hypothetical sixth-century refacing had involved the complete removal of the earlier pavements. Virtually no finds were recovered from the fill associated with the footings which could in any way provide a satisfactory date, although the universally problematic greenish-blue glazed pottery was found in the upper layers and assigned "a definite early Islamic" date (*Mesopotamia* 1, p. 103). The recent restoration projects on the Ayvān-e Kesrā itself seem to imply that no further refinement of this date will be possible using conventional stratigraphic excavation techniques, unless some of the small side and rear chambers can be safely excavated, with the chance that more diagnostic dating material can be found in them. Excavations in the general area will advance considerably our knowledge of the history of Madā'en, but barring a laboratory breakthrough such as in the realm of thermoluminescence for the dating of its bricks, the date and therefore significance of the great arch is likely to remain somewhat elusive.

Ayvān-e Kesrā has been mentioned and often described in Arabic and Persian sources and it is the subject of a moving *qaṣīda* by the poet K̲āqānī who visited its ruins in mid-6th/12th century.

Bibliography: A Bruno, with contributions by G. Gullini and M. Cavallero, "The Preservation and Restoration of Taq-i Kisra," *Mesopotamia* 1, 1966, pp. 89-108, pls. xvii-xxv, figs. 35-59. *Camb. Hist. Iran* III, pp. 1062-64. Christensen, *Iran Sass.*, pp. 386, 389ff., 504ff. M. Dieulafoy, *L'art antique de la Perse*, Paris, 1884, V, pp. 71-74. J. M. Fiey, "Topography of al-Mada'in," *Sumer* 23, 1967, pp. 3-38. E. Kühnel, *Die Ausgrabungen der zweiten Ktesiphon-Expedition*, with English summary by S. Dimand, Berlin, 1933, pp. 1-35. O. Kurz, "The Date of the Taq-i Kisra," *JRAS*,

1941, pp. 37-41. H. Lacoste, "L'arc de Ctésiphon ou Taq Kesra (Mesopotamie)," *Sumer* 10, 1954, pp. 3-22. T. Madhloom, "Mada'in (Ctesiphon), 1970-71," *Sumer* 27, 1971, Arabic section, pp. 129-46. Idem, "Al-Mada'in," *Sumer* 31, 1975, Arabic section, pp. 165-70. Idem, "Restorations in al-Mada'in 1975-77," *Sumer* 34, 1978, Arabic section, pp. 119-29. O. Reuther, *Die Ausgrabungen der deutschen Ktesiphon-Expedition im Winter 1928-29*, Berlin, 1930. Idem, "The German Excavations at Ctesiphon," *Antiquity* 3, 1929, pp. 424-51. Idem, "Sasanian Architecture," in *Survey of Persian Art*, pp. 493-578. A. Saleh, "Al-Mada'in and its Surrounding Area in Arabic Literary Sources," *Mesopotamia* 3-4, 1968-69, pp. 417-39. F. Sarre and E. Herzfeld, *Archäologische Reise im Euphrat- und Tigris-Gebiet* II, Berlin, 1920. J. H. Schmidt, "L'expéditon de Ctesiphon en 1931-1932," *Syria* 15, 1934, pp. 1-23.

(E. J. KEALL)

'AYYĀR, a noun meaning literally "vagabond," applied to members of medieval *fotowwa* (*fotūwa*) brotherhoods and comparable popular organizations.

i. *General.*

ii. 'Ayyār *in Persian sources.*

i. GENERAL

The history of *'ayyārs* and *'ayyārī* presents a paradox. On the one hand, there can be little doubt as to their pre-Islamic origin, not only because in later times they were said to have certain distinctively Iranian customs, but above all because in the Islamic period up to the Mongol invasion they were only to be found in territories which had once belonged to the Sasanian empire. On the other hand, our scanty documentation on that empire does not appear to contain anything about them. The early Islamic sources present difficulties because they combine different traditions—Arab, Iranian, urban, rural-aristocratic—under the same name.

In the pre-Islamic Arab tradition, the noun *fatā* (plur. *fetyān*), literally "young man," was applied to any individual claiming the specific qualities of youth (*fotowwa*). The latter noun also acquired the collective meaning of a group of such individuals, though this usage is not attested before the 2nd/8th century. The qualities were essentially courage, generosity, and chivalry. In the Iranian aristocratic tradition, the noun *javānmard*, also literally "young man," or its Arabic equivalent *fatā* meant a sort of knight-errant, in whom similar qualities were expected. The urban brotherhoods were evidently influenced by these ideas and words, but to what extent we do not know; in any case they were different in their recruitment, corporate organization, and confinement to towns.

Comprehension of the urban *fotowwa* movement is hampered by the fact that the sources are of two different kinds. As will be seen, the *fotowwa* brotherhoods at a certain stage of their development began to absorb ideas of mystic origin, and this trend found expression in writings which prompted a long-held belief among modern scholars that the movement was essentially ideological. Although F. Taeschner, who collected almost all our documentation, and L. Massignon, who set Islamic socio-religious problems in the context of his personal understanding, did not ignore certain aspects of recruitment conducive to this ideology, neither could really explain the position of the *fotowwa* brotherhoods in the social contexts of their times. Research faces the difficulty that for the early Islamic period we possess no texts emanating from *fotowwa* circles, and that for later times we possess little except ideologically slanted writings. Our only information about social aspects of the *fotowwa* movement in early Islamic times comes in works by authors connected with aristocratic circles, who take no interest in it except in cases of its involvement in disorders, when they describe it as a bandit organization; they never credit it with ideological motives. Nevertheless it seems possible, if clear questions are asked, to extract sufficient evidence from the sources to permit the piecing together of an interesting social record.

The picture is one of groups of young men (*fetyān*) aspiring towards a better life. Although the members were not required to quit after growing older and acquiring wives and children, they were for the most part bachelors, which led their adversaries to accuse them of homosexuality. They lived more or less together, ate together, and held joint entertainments. In short they were "comrades," bound by a strong sense of group loyalty (*'aṣabīya*), who saw themselves as "smarter" than other men and apparently had demanding notions of personal and group honor. Although it appears (contrary to some opinions) that they did not admit non-Moslems, who may have had similar groups of their own, religious belief was clearly not the main bond. The evidence shows only that particular groups were associated with different persuasions. The *fetyān* have often been portrayed as artisans or proletarians, but it should be borne in mind that *fotowwa* groups were not organized on a craft basis before late medieval times, and then only in the Turco-Iranian lands; also that the *fetyān*, while clearly for the most part of humble origin, included and would increasingly include influential notables, who found membership useful in building up clientèles for furtherance of their ambitions.

In historical chronicles and other writings, the *fetyān* generally appear as trouble-makers, ready in times of breakdown of authority to harass rich merchants and other worthies by pillaging or threatening to pillage the shops or premises of any who would not pay them fixed sums of protection-money. Being subject to police surveillance even in undisturbed times, the *fetyān* pressed for appointments of police chiefs sympathetic to them and even applied for enrollment in the police, which would assure them of regular pay as well as impunity. At Baghdad they achieved these goals for a short time in the 5th/11th century, but never did so in the subsequent period of Turkish rule when urban policing was in the hands of the army. In provincial towns where the central government's grip was less tight, the *fetyān* in the early period often made themselves the real masters, no doubt after admitting a "bourgeois" element into their ranks. In the subsequent period when political fragmentation permitted the rise of local lordships, *fetyān* groups were more than once able to bring their own candidate to power.

It is a well-known fact that medieval Moslem cities were often torn by strife between factions whose sectarian labels must have masked social cleavages not easily detectable today. The *fetyān*, with their group loyalties (*'aṣabīyāt*), frequently appear as militant wings of broader movements. Like the sans-culottes of the French revolution, they often proudly appropriated insulting or contemptuous names given to them by their adversaries—names which varied from century to century. It would therefore be hazardous to dissociate them from those to whom the texts give names such as *'ayyār* (vagabond), *šāṭer* (adroit), *rend* (rogue), and in the nineteenth century *lūṭī* (pederast, rowdy).

Sometimes there were separate and rival *fotowwa* groups in a town. On the other hand, groups in different towns maintained a degree of solidarity, notably through hospitality to traveling comrades. The Isma'ilis may have tried to infiltrate *fotowwa* groups in this way, but (despite certain suppositions) there is no evidence that they had any success.

The *fetyān* or *'ayyārān* have often been confused with the *ḡāzīs*. This is incorrect but explicable. The *ḡāzīs*, being volunteers for holy war, were only important in frontier regions, at first mainly in Central Asia where they faced the pagan Turks. Although they were recruited from town-dwellers and concentrated in towns, they had no links with the urban social organizations. Conversely the *'ayyārān* had nothing to do with holy war. In the frontier regions, however, the two elements were obviously bound to become more or less intermixed, whereas in the towns on the Iranian plateau no such process occurred. Where intermixing did take place, it was fostered by the popular institution of the *zūrḵāna* (gymnasium), in which young men practiced archery and other sports.

It has already been mentioned that from the 5th/11th century onward, some of the *fotowwa* groups began to adopt an ideology which brought them into contact with mystic circles then seeking corporate forms, and that this trend gave rise to a considerable literary output. The groups thus acquired an increasing cultural role in contemporary society. As a result they began, during the 6th/12th century, to attract favorable attention from official and clerical quarters hitherto hostile to them. Finally the caliph al-Nāṣer (575/1180-622/1225) decided to support them while planning to use their organizations as instruments for integrating them in a social framework which would transcend sectarian difference and be held together by the aristocracy and the caliphate. Literature written under official auspices to promote this policy is the source of such knowledge as we possess concerning initiation ceremonies and patron saints ('Alī, Salmān) in the ritual of various groups. It is significant that Šehāb-al-dīn Sohravardī, one of the chief exponents of *fotowwa* teachings, was also the founder of a mystic order. In later times we find occasional mentions of notables who combined mystic literary activity with leadership of more or less violent protest-groups.

The originality of the caliph al-Nāṣer's *fotowwa* policy lay in its being on the one hand an effort to promote unity and discipline, and on the other hand an attempt to win over the notables by giving them exclusive control of sports and thereby enabling them to acquire popular clienteles. Al-Nāṣer not only pursued this policy in his own domains but also persuaded most of the leading Moslem princes in the east to adopt it. The fact that the orientalist J. von Hammer-Purgstall happened to find the manuscript of a "Court *fotowwa*" text at a time (in the mid-19th century) when no other *fotowwa* texts were known, gave rise to the long-held notion that the *fotowwa* was initially a sort of order of chivalry. In Iraq, the city and therewith the *fotowwa* of Baghdad were soon afterward destroyed by the Mongol invasion. Somewhat suprisingly this was just the time when the *fotowwa* achieved a remarkable and long-lasting spread into Asia Minor and Azerbaijan in the new and perhaps original form of the brotherhoods mentioned under the name *aḵī* (plur. *aḵīān*). We do not have such clear information about what happened in the rest of Iran and in Central Asia under the various Mongol and Turkish régimes of the next two and a half centuries. The outstanding development in the Turco-Iranian sphere as a whole in this period is the increasingly (though unevenly) close linkage between *fotowwa* groups and guilds. The *fetyān* began to identify and organize themselves on the basis of their craft or trade, and thus to gain control of the respective guilds. This system subsequently spread to the Arab countries as a result of the Ottoman conquest.

In later times the *fotowwa* tended to become semi-official. *Fotowwa* catechisms and guild rule-books had virtually identical titles and contents. Popular dislike of this tendency may perhaps have been an underlying cause of the Sarbadār revolt in Khorasan in the 8th/14th century; in Qajar Iran it was voiced by the *lūṭīs* (rowdies) and by men of the type made known to Europeans and Americans through J. Morier's portrayal of Hajji Baba of Isfahan.

Bibliography: The largest number of original texts as well as the most important and the greatest number of studies bearing on the *'ayyārs* and *fotowwa* were published by Franz Taeschner; nearly all of these are now assembled in a posthumous volume edited by Heinz Halm under the title of *Zünfte und Bruderschaften im Islam*, Artemis Verlag, Zürich and Munich, 1979. See also "Futuwwa" by Claude Cahen and Franz Taeschner in *EI*[2]. Most of the references to studies on the subject are found in Claude Cahen, "Mouvements populaires et autonomisme urbain dans l'Asie musulmane du Moyen Age, *Arabica*, 1958-59, also printed separately, Leiden, 1960. Despite the

Iranian nature of the *fotowwa* and the *'ayyār*s the majority of the relevant works are in Arabic and concern the Arab world. In addition to major Arabic histories, mention should be made of *Ketāb al-dakā'er wa'l-tohaf* by the Egyptian Rašīd b. Zobayr, ed. Ḥamīdallāh, Kuwait, 1959. (For Persian sources and studies see the Bibliography of the following article.)

(CL. CAHEN)

ii. 'AYYĀR IN PERSIAN SOURCES

In Persian sources the term *'ayyār* varies widely in meaning with time and context. It appears in prose texts and poetry of all periods, and is used literally and metaphorically with both positive and negative connotations. No succinct definition can cover all occurrences of the term, but three broad areas of meaning can be distinguished: (1) In a neutral or negative sense, mostly in historical works, *'ayyār* can mean irregular fighter, rogue, highwayman, robber, troublemaker. (2) In a sense ranging from somewhat negative to somewhat positive, mostly in poetry, it can mean strong, fast, or rough; a night prowler, a deceiver, or a coquette. (3) In a wholly positive sense it can mean a noble-minded highwayman, or a generous, clever, brave, modest, pious, chaste, hospitable, generally upright person. This last image is found mostly in poetry, in *adab* and Sufi texts, and popular romances. The meaning of *'ayyār* often reflects the social point of view of the author of the text in which it appears, so it can be found with quite different meanings in the same period. Further complicating the problem of definition is the fact that at times *'ayyār* is synonymous with *javānmard* (q.v.), and the abstract noun *'ayyārī* is synonymous with *javānmardī* and *fotowwa* (*fotūwa*). Rather than attempt a chronological or generic survey of the term, this article will examine the three large areas of meaning mentioned above, and the sources for each.

1. *'Ayyār*s portrayed in a neutral or negative sense appear in early historical texts as irregular fighting men. *Tārīk-e Sīstān* mentions Ṣāleḥ b. Naṣr, a local *'ayyār*, who rose to power in Bost in 238/852-53 and that "all of his army's strength came from Ya'qūb b. Layt and the *'ayyār*s of Sīstān" (p. 193; tr., p. 153). *Qābūs-nāma* describes what sort of songs to sing on particular occasions, and says "If you see [in your audience] soldiers and *'ayyār*s, sing quatrains in the Transoxanian style about war and bloodshed, and in praise of *'ayyār*s" (pp. 195-96; tr., p. 189). Qaṭrān of Tabrīz, in a *qaṣīda* praising a ruler's military prowess, says of an enemy fortress that it was as wide and high as the sky and filled with fighting men, each one chosen for his bloodthirstiness and *'ayyārī* (*Dīvān*, p. 397). In the story of Ardašīr and Haftvād, Ferdowsī says: "There was an ambitious man named Šāhōy / who was of bad character and ill-spoken" (*Šāh-nāma* [Moscow] VII, p. 145), and: "There was also Šāhōy, [Haftvād's] *'ayyār* / who was his eldest son and his commander" (loc. cit., p. 153).

*'Ayyār*s acting in groups appear to have been led by *sarhang*s. Gardīzī, discussing Ya'qūb b. Layt, says, "After being a coppersmith he turned to *'ayyārī*, and from there to stealing and highway robbery. Then he became a *sarhang*, acquired a following, and gradually became a commander (*amīr*). He was the first to be given the leadership (*sarhangī*) of Bost" (*Zayn al-akbār*, ed. Ḥabībī, p. 139). *Tārīk-e Sīstān* describes how in 248/862-63 Ya'qūb b. Layt promised rewards to defecting Kharejites: "Ya'qūb gave their leaders robes of honor and praised them saying that 'whoever of you is a *sarhang* I shall make an *amīr*, and whoever is a cavalryman I shall make a *sarhang*, and whoever is a footsoldier I shall make a cavalryman'" (p. 205, tr., pp. 162-63).

Groups of *'ayyār*s often acted independently, siding with or against the established authority. When the Saffarid Ṭāher b. Kalaf revolted in 393/1002-03 against his father Kalaf b. Aḥmad, and Kalaf captured Ṭāher after swearing a false oath, "The people of Sistān (i.e., Zaranj) and Ṭāher's army and the *'ayyār*s closed up the city, turned against Kalaf, and proclaimed their allegiance to the Ghaznavid Sultan Maḥmūd" (*Tārīk-e Sīstān*, p. 350, tr. p. 285). In contrast, in 635/1237-38 the ruler of Herat with a group of *'ayyār*s from the city went five farsangs out of Herat to greet the amir 'Ezz-al-dīn Moqaddam and welcomed him warmly (Asfezārī, *Rawżāt al-jannāt* II, p. 110).

In times of weak central authority, groups of *'ayyār*s would often harass local populations. After the death of Maḥmūd of Ğazna in 421/1030 "Turmoil appeared on the earth and the world was disturbed.... The *'ayyār*s took the city and engaged in fighting and factionalism. . .and burned and plundered the houses of Imam Fāker b. Ma'ād and his sons" (*Tārīk-e Sīstān*, p. 362, tr. p. 295). In 423/1031-32 affairs were still in turmoil, but "[Bū Sa'd Jīmartī] had arrived and the uproar of the *'ayyār*s had lessened because he had cut in half a number of them, and 'Azīz [Fūšanjī, who had arrived earlier] had arrested the *sarhang*s and whipped them, and had decapitated and cut in two their leaders" (ibid., p. 363, tr. p. 296). Similarly, in the troubled times following the death of the Saljuq Sultan Malekšāh in 485/1092 the *'ayyār*s harassed Bayhaq, and Fakr-al-dīn Abu'l-Qāsem Faryūmadī patrolled the city with cavalry and foot soldiers for five months to protect the families and property there (Ebn Fondoq, *Tārīk-e Bayhaq*, pp. 101, 478).

A number of individual *'ayyār*s appear in the historical texts as local strongmen and troublemakers. A dark view of *'ayyār*s is taken by Ebn Esfandīār: "Much trouble broke out in Khorasan at the hands of *rend*s and *'ayyār*s.... The most prominent of all was Ya'qūb b. al-Layt the Coppersmith, who was originally of lowly origin and an *'ayyār*" (*Tārīk-e Ṭabarestān* I, p. 245, tr. pp. 180-81). A particularly troublesome individual was 'Alī Qohandezī who operated in the area of Jūzjānān. Gardīzī calls him "an *'ayyār* and a malefactor" (*mardī 'ayyār o mofsed*; *Zayn al-akbār*, p. 202), and Bayhaqī says that "he had spent some time in that district and had robbed and plundered and made trouble; several clever fellows had allied themselves with him and they used to raid caravans and plunder villages" (2nd ed., pp. 741-43). The reputation of *ʿayyār*s for this sort of behavior is echoed in a line from Saʿdī where he says "If that city-disturbing *ʿayyār* should ask about me one day / Say 'He can't sleep at night because of [the disturbance caused by] the *ʿayyār*s'" (*Ḡazalhā* II, no. 456, p. 151). Here the *ʿayyār* is, of course, the beloved, and what is disturbed is peace of mind, patience, sobriety, and sleep. In addition to the above, the sources contain many references to *ʿayyār*s as deceivers, thieves, or worse. Ebn Fondoq says that Ṭūs was famous for its *ʿayyār*s (op. cit., p. 46), and Gardīzī related that when Alptigin passed through the environs of Ṭūs in 350/1961-62 some of his baggage was left behind and the *ʿayyār*s and *sarhang*s plundered it and carried it off (op. cit., p. 162). The fourteenth-century historian Karīm Āqsarāʾī explains the origins of a popular expression with an anecdote about a trusting monk and a thievish *ʿayyār* (*Mosāmarat al-aḵbār*, p. 69). This view of *ʿayyār*s is also found in Ḥāfeẓ' line "Depend not on the night-prowling star; for this *ʿayyār* / Has stolen Kāvūs's crown and Kayḵosrow's belt" (*Dīvan*, no. 407, p. 281). Similarly, Masʿūd-e Saʿd-e Salmān says "My heart-stealer, like an *ʿayyār*, has stolen my heart/Yes, stealing has always been the business of *ʿayyār*s" (*Dīvān*, p. 277), and again, "I do not know why I have been imprisoned / I know that I am neither a thief nor an *ʿayyār*" (ibid., p. 357). Moʿezzī likewise says "Nowrūz spread a new display in the flower gardens / And stole yesterday's display from the garden like an *ʿayyār*" (*Dīvān*, p. 674). This attitude is seen at its most extreme in the scandalous tales recounted by Moḥammad-Hāšem Āṣaf of court life during the reign of Shah Sultan Ḥosayn (r. 1105-35/1694-1722), emphasizing the decadent morality of the time. He links *ʿayyār*s with popular champions, wrestlers, night prowlers, imposters, rogues, dare-devils, and swindlers (*Rostam al-tawārīḵ*, pp. 103, 108-09, 153).

2. *ʿAyyār*s are not always portrayed as thoroughly bad: Often they are viewed ambivalently. Sometimes they are described as strong, quick, or rough as in a quatrain written by a famous *rend* after witnessing the *samāʿ* of the Mawlawī (Turk. Mevlevi) dervishes: "Those who associate with (*barḵordār-and*) that Noble One / Are quick and bold and ʿayyarish / Beware, do not grapple with them, for / They have defeated and taken as slaves a hundred like you" (Aflākī, *Manāqeb al-ʿārefīn*, p. 840). In the same vein, Nāṣer(-e) Ḵosrow says "The sober man is helpless in the hands of drunks/Even if he is like an *ʿayyār*" (*Dīvān*, no. 167, p. 352), the image representing the sober but "unawakened" man in the clutches of this world. The *ʿayyār* as spy or night prowler is seen in an anecdote in *Manāqeb al-ʿārefīn* when Jalāl-al-dīn Ḵʷārazmšāh says of ʿAlāʾ-al-dīn Kayqobād that "in *ʿayyārī* and night prowling he is a wonder" (pp. 49-50). Nāṣer Ḵosrow says of solitude, his "companion" in Yomgān "You will never see him nor hear what he says / Nobody has ever seen such an *ʿayyār*" (*Dīvān*, no. 127, p. 272); and Ḥāfeẓ, about his beloved: "What hard-hearted one taught her these ʿayyarish ways / For from the first when she came out she has robbed the night-people (*šab zendadārān: Dīvān*, no. 153, p. 104). The *ʿayyār* as coquette or deceiver is seen in Ṣāʾeb's verse: "Although that eye appears to be ill/Do not be deceived by its tricks: It might be an *ʿayyār*" (*Kollīyat*, no. 879, p. 322), and in this verse from Solṭān Ebrāhīm Mīrzā: "Don't think that her eye knows not the ways of *ʿayyārī* / It just presents itself so that you would think not" (*Maktab-e woqūʿ*, p. 5).

3. *ʿAyyār*s are presented in a strongly positive sense in many sources. *Qābūs-nāma* has a story about an *ʿayyār* from Khorasan who is described as "very respectable, of good character, and well known" (p. 145, tr., p. 133). *Sīar al-molūk* has Yaʿqūb b. Layṯ describe his rise to power and fortune as due to bravery and *ʿayyārī*, not to inheritance (p. 24, tr., p. 18). In *Čahār maqāla* the Amir Abu'l-Moẓaffar Čaḡānī says to the poet Farroḵī (regarding a herd of horses), "You are a Sīstāni and an *ʿayyār*; you can have as many as you can catch" (p. 64). *ʿAyyārī* means skill in Ḥāfeẓ's lines "It is natural that I be oppressed by that curly lock / But what fear of her bonds and chains is there for one with the ways of an *ʿayyār*?" (*Dīvān*, no. 191, p. 129), and "Thinking of your locks is not for the inexperienced / For escaping from chains is the way of *ʿayyārī*" (ibid., no. 66, p. 46).

From the time of the earliest appearances of *ʿayyārī* in Persian texts, the word has also been linked with *javānmardī*. Early definitions of *javānmardī* often involve *ʿayyārī*. Abu'l-Ḥasan ʿAlī Hojvīrī relates an anecdote about the Sufi Ḥamdūn-e Qaṣṣār who met in Nīšāpūr an *ʿayyār* named Nūḥ and asked him the definition of *javānmardī*. Nūḥ defined it in mystical terms (*Kašf al-maḥjūb*, p. 228; ʿAṭṭār repeats this story in his *Taḏkerat al-awlīāʾ*, pp. 401-02). *Qābūs-nāma* discusses *ʿayyār*s and puts forth a theory of *javānmardī*, which it divides into three levels. The first level is the *javānmardī-e ʿayyārī*, possessed by *ʿayyār*s, soldiers, and merchants (p. 243 ff., tr., p. 239 ff.). In the chapter "On Being a Merchant" in the same work, the author advises his son to associate with three types of persons while traveling: *ʿAyyār*s and persons who practice *javānmardī*; wealthy and generous persons; and those who know the roads and the local area (p. 170, tr., p. 161). The importance of the ethical code of *javānmardī* is stressed in an anecdote related by Hojvīrī about Fożayl b. ʿEyāż, a noble-minded *ʿayyār* who guarded faithfully money entrusted to him by a merchant from the very caravan that he was robbing (op. cit., p. 120; also in ʿAṭṭār, op. cit., pp. 89-90, tr., pp. 53-54). A story making the same point is found in *Qābūs-nāma*, pp. 108-09, tr., pp. 96-97).

The richest and most extensive representation of *ʿayyār*s in the positive sense is in the pre-Safavid storytellers' romances, where the *ʿayyār*s are popular heros, deeply motivated by the ideals of *javānmardī*. One of the functions of these romances must have been to portray and transmit the ideals of *ʿayyārī* and *javānmardī* to an illiterate population. In doing so, they present a view of 'ayyārs quite at odds with that found in the works of court historians. The earliest of these romances, and the one in which the ethical code, and the rituals of the 'ayyārs are most clearly set out, is Samak -e 'ayyār (q.v.). Explicit descriptions can be found in vol. I/1, pp. 44-45, 48-49, and 65. From these, and from descriptions of the garb and equipment of 'ayyārs (e.g., ibid., I/1, pp. 44, 104; Dārāb-nāma I, p. 685) and references to initiations (ibid., II, p. 310), it is clear that in addition to engaging in the traditional activities of 'ayyārs, these 'ayyārs are being shown as members of a corporate, initiatory organization apparently similar to organizations of craftsmen, and Sufi orders in the Iranian world.

In the storytellers' romances of the Safavid period, the 'ayyārs become almost fantastic figures. The most famous of these, Mehtar Nesīm in Eskandar-nāma and 'Amr-e Omayya in Romūz-e Ḥamza, no longer, represent the ethical ideals of javānmardī, but become essentially comic figures and vehicles for the creative imagination of the oral narrators who told these tales. They still embody a non- or even anti-courtly view of society, however, and are a balance to the early court historians who looked on 'ayyārs as threats to public order and established power. By the Qajar period, 'ayyārs are no longer mentioned in popular romances.

Bibliography: Šams-al-dīn Aḥmad Aflākī, Manāqeb al-'ārefīn, ed. T. Yazıcı, Ankara, 1976. Karīm Āqsarā'ī, Mosāmarat al-akbār, ed. O. Turan, Ankara, 1944. Moḥammad-Hāšem Āṣaf, Rostam al-tawārīk, ed. M. Mošīrī, Tehran, 1348 Š./1969. Shaikh Farīd-al-dīn 'Aṭṭār, Taḏkerat al-awlīā', ed. M. Este'lāmī, Tehran, 1346 Š./1967; abridged Eng. tr. A. J. Arberry, Chicago, 1966. Shaikh Moḥammad b. Aḥmad Bīgamī, Dārāb-nāma, 2 vols., ed. Ḏ. Ṣafā, Tehran, 1339-41 Š./1960-63; abridged Eng. tr. W. L. Hanaway, Jr., Delmar, N.Y., 1974. Ebn Esfandīār, Tārīk-e Ṭabarestān I, abridged Eng. tr. E. G. Browne, Leiden and London, 1905. Mo'īn-al-dīn Moḥammad Asfezārī, Rawżāt al-jannāt, 2 vols., ed. K. Emām, Tehran, 1338-39 Š./1959-60. Eskandar-nāma, Tehran, 1327 Š./1948. Farāmarz b. Kodādād Arrajānī, Samak-e 'ayyār, 5 vols., ed. P. N. Kānlarī, Tehran, 1338-53 Š./1959-74. Ebn Fondoq, Tārīk-e Bayhaq, ed. K. Ḥosaynī, Hyderabad (Deccan), 1968. Ḥāfeẓ, Dīvān, ed. M. Qazvīnī and Q. Ḡanī, Tehran, 1320 Š./1941. Abu'l-Ḥasan 'Alī b. 'Oṯmān Hojvīrī, Kašf al-mahjūb, ed. V. Zhukovsky, Tehran, 1336 Š./1957, Eng. tr. R. A. Nicholson, London, 1911. A. Golčīn-e Ma'ānī, Maktab-e woqū', Tehran, 1348 Š./1969. Mas'ūd-e Sa'd-e Salmān, Dīvān, ed. R. Yāsamī, Tehran, 1339 Š./1960. Mo'ezzī, Dīvān, ed. 'A. Eqbāl, Tehran, 1318 Š./1939. Nāṣer(-e) Kosrow, Dīvān, ed. M. Mīnovī and M. Moḥaqqeq, Tehran, 1353 Š./1974. Neẓām-al-molk, Sīar al-molūk, ed. H. Darke, Tehran, 1340 Š./1962, Eng. tr. H. Darke, London, 1960. Neẓāmī 'Arūżī Samarqandī, Čahār maqāla, ed. M. Mo'īn, Tehran, 1333 Š./1954. 'Onṣor-al-ma'ālī Kaykāvūs, Qābūs-nāma, ed. Ḡ.-Ḥ. Yūsofī, Tehran, 1345 Š./1967, Eng. tr. R. Levy, New York,

1951. Qaṭrān Tabrīzī, Dīvān, ed. M. Nakjavānī, Tehran, 1333 Š./1954. Romūz-e Ḥamza, Tabrīz, 1321/1903-04. Sa'dī, Ḡazalhā, 2 vols., ed. N. Īrānparast, Tehran, 2535 = 1355 Š./1976-1357 Š./1978. Ṣā'eb Tabrīzī, Kollīyāt, ed. B. Taraqqī, Tehran, 1333 Š./1954.

Studies: C. E. Bosworth, "The Armies of the Ṣaffārids," BSOAS 31, 1968, pp. 534-54. Idem, "The Political and Dynastic History of the Iranian World (A.D. 1000-1217)," in Camb. Hist. Iran V, pp. 1-202. Idem, Sīstān under the Arabs, Rome, 1968. Idem, "The Ṭāhirids and Ṣaffārids," in Camb. Hist. Iran IV, pp. 90-135. (General historical works with many references to 'ayyārs, mostly in eastern Iran.) Cl. Cahen, "Mouvements populaires et autonomisme urbain dans l'Asie musulmane du moyen âge," Arabica 5, 1958, pp. 225-50; 6, 1959, pp. 25-56, 233-65, and EI² s.vv. "Aḥdāth," "Akhī," "'Ayyār," "Futuwwa," "Ghāzī," are useful for indicating connections between 'ayyārs and other organizations. W. Hanaway, "Formal Elements in the Persian Popular Romances," Review of National Literatures 2/1, 1971, pp. 139-60, discusses 'ayyārs in storytellers' romances. Ḥosayn Wā'eẓ Kāšefī, Fotowwat-nāma-ye solṭānī, ed. M. J. Maḥjūb, Tehran, 1350 Š./1971 (Maḥjūb's lengthy introduction includes many mentions of 'ayyārs). K. Kāẓemaynī, 'Ayyārān, Tehran, 1349 Š./1970 (stories of 'ayyārs from Romūz-e Ḥamza; not scholarly). P. N. Kānlarī, "Ā'īn-e 'ayyārī," Sokan 18, 1347-48 Š./1968-69, pp. 1071-77; 19, 1348-49 Š./1969-70, pp. 19-26, 113-22, 263-67, 477-80 (discussion of 'ayyārs in historical and literary sources). M. J̌. Maḥjūb, "Ā'īn-e 'ayyārī," Sokan 19, 1348-49 Š./1969-70, pp. 869-83, 1059-73, 1182-95; 20, 1349-50 Š./1970-71, pp. 38-51, 173-99, 301-11 (continues Kānlarī's discussion, focusing more on popular literature). Idem, "Ravešhā-ye 'ayyārī wa nofūḏ-e kār wa kerdār-e 'ayyārān dar Šāh-nāma," Honar o mardom 15, 2536 = 1356 Š./1977, nos. 177-78, pp. 2-13 (incidents when the heroes of the Šāh-nāma behave in the manner of 'ayyārs. F. Taeschner, "Futuwwa, eine gemeinschaftbildende Idee im mittelalterlichen Orient und ihre verschiedene Erscheinungsformen," Schweizerisches Archiv für Volkskunde 52, 1956, pp. 122-58 (fundamental study of the subject, with references to 'ayyārs as they relate to fotowwa in the Islamic world; comprehensive bibliography). See also E. Narāqī, Āyīn-e javānmardī, Tehran, 1363 Š./1984, basically a Persian translation of H. Corbin's introduction of M. Ṣarrāf's Rasā'el-e javānmardān, but with the addition of 19 articles on 'ayyārs and fotowwa by mostly Persian scholars.

(W. L. HANAWAY, JR.)

'AYYĀŠĪ, ABU'L-NAŻR MOḤAMMAD B. MAS'ŪD B. MOḤAMMAD B. AL-'AYYĀŠ AL-SOLAMĪ SAMARQANDĪ, Imami jurist and scholar of the 3rd-4th/9th-10th centuries. It is said that he descended from the tribe of Tamīm and was born and raised as a Sunni, but while still young he was converted to the Shi'ite

Imami faith. He studied with the disciples of 'Alī b. Ḥasan b. Fażżāl and 'Abdallāh b. Moḥammad Ṭayālesī, the leading Imami scholars of the third/ninth century as well as with other prominent scholars of Kūfa, Baghdad, and Qom. It is reported that he spent his whole inheritance of 300,000 dinars in pursuit of scholarship and tradition and that his house, which had become a center of learning, was always filled with people. Although he is said to have related traditions on weak authorities, he is regarded as an eminent, trustworthy figure, like that of Kolaynī (q.v.), among the early Imamis. He was one of the main sources for his student Kaššī's *Rejāl* (Bombay, 1317, passim; Najāšī, *Ketāb al-rejāl*, Bombay, 1317, pp. 247-50).

Ebn al-Nadīm states that 'Ayyāšī was one of the most learned of his time and that his books carried great weight in Khorasan. He was a prolific author and Ebn al-Nadīm has given a comprehensive list of his works based on the authority of Jonayd b. No'aym comprising over 200 titles (*Fehrest*, pp. 244-46; see also Ṭūsī, *Fehrest*, ed. Moḥammad-Ṣādeq Āl Baḥr-al-'olūm, Najaf, 1381/1961, pp. 163-65; Ebn Šahrāšūb, *Ma'ālem al-'olamā'*, ed. 'A. Eqbāl, Tehran, 1353/1934, pp. 88-89; Astarābādī, *Menhāj al-maqāl*, Tehran, 1306, pp. 319-20). Though most of his works dealt with jurisprudence, they covered a wide range of subjects from typical Shi'ite themes, such as *dalā'el al-a'emma*, *taqīya*, *ḡaybe* and *raj'a*, to medicine, poetry, dreams, stars, and divination. He also wrote biographies of the first three caliphs and Mo'āwīa drawing on Sunni sources. His commentary of the Koran (*tafsīr*), wherein the moral excellence (*fażā'el*) of Ahl al-Bayt (q.v.) is emphasized, enjoyed wide popularity with the Imamis and was used both by Ṭabrasī (6th/12th century) and Majlesī (11th/17th) as a source for their *Majma' al-bayān fī tafsīr al-Qor'ān* (Tehran, 1379/1959, I, p. 17) and *Beḥār al-anwār* (Tehran, 1376/1956, I, pp. 97-100) respectively. Unfortunately, all his works except the first half of the *tafsīr* are lost (Mīrzā Moḥammad-Bāqer Ḵᵛānsārī, *Rawżāt al-jannāt fī aḥwāl al-'olamā' wa'l-sādāt*, ed. A. Esmā'īlīān, Tehran, 1390/1970, VI, pp. 129-31; *al-Ḏarī'a* IV, p. 295).

Bibliography: See also Kaḥḥāla, XII, p. 20. Zereklī, *al-A'lām²* VII, p. 316. Brockelmann, *GAL*, I, p. 704. S. F. Sezgin, *GAS* I, p. 42. *EI²*, pp. 794-95.

(I. K. POONAWALA)

AYYOHA'L-WALAD, a short treatise by Abū Ḥāmed Moḥammad Ḡazālī Ṭūsī (fl. 450-505/1058-1111), originally composed in Persian, but, except for one line of Persian poetry, only its Arabic translation is extant. It was written sometime after his *Eḥyā' 'olūm al-dīn* to which it makes many references. The introduction, written by a later commentator, states that Ḡazālī wrote this tract to answer a pupil who had enquired about which science would benefit him most in the hereafter and other matters. However, more probably Ḡazālī chose to address his views in this manner in order to give the work a more personal touch and to give more liveliness to some of the views expounded in detail in his *Eḥyā'*. The pupil also asked about submissiveness, trust in God, and sincerity. Some questions Ḡazālī did not answer, either because they were answered in the *Eḥyā'* and other writings or because he could not.

Ḡazālī's answer to the question about the real knowledge which would be most beneficial in the hereafter is the knowledge that leads one to follow the right path, i.e., the Sufi way. Ḡazālī thinks that theoretical knowledge does not lead to salvation. Knowledge must be combined with action and both must be kept in conformity with the *Šarī'a*—Law. To be on the right path, one needs to observe the four obligations of pure belief, sincere repentance, satisfaction of adversaries, and acquiring the necessary amount of knowledge of the *Šarī'a* and some other useful science.

Arriving at this stage, the disciple can start his initiation in Sufism which is defined as righteousness with God and longanimity with men. Here the disciple needs a Shaikh (i.e., a master) to direct him. The disciple's respect for his master must be absolute and total. After combining submissiveness, trust in God, and sincerity with his total respect for the Shaikh, the disciple is instructed what to avoid (arguments, becoming a preacher, accepting gifts, and mingling with princes) and what to perform (in connection with God, other people, himself, and possession of goods).

Although the tract allows for some digression in its structure, the quarternary units that prevail in it grant it some coherence. It is full of quotations from the Koran, the Hadith, the Gospels, the sayings of outstanding Sufis, and poems. Some scholars have tended to treat *Ayyoha'l-walad* as a treatise on education. It emphasizes the spiritual aspect in education in contrast to scientific wordly knowledge. In some respects it can be anti-educational in conveying a rather negative attitude towards the sciences in particular, and temporal life in general.

Bibliography: For information about manuscripts, editions, translations, and commentaries, see Brockelmann, *GAL*, S. I, pp. 750 (no. 32), and A. Badawi, *Les oeuvres d'al-Ghazali* (in Arabic), Cairo, 1961, pp. 179-83. See also F. H. Foster, "Ghazali on the Inner Secret and Outward Expression of Religion in his 'Child'," *Muslim World* 23, 1983, pp. 378-96. M. Ben Cheneb, "Lettre sur l'education des enfants," *Revue africaine*, 1901, pp. 101-10. The text used in this study is the one published with a French translation by Toufic Sabbagh, Beirut, 1959.

(I. ABBAS)

AYYŪB KHAN, MOḤAMMAD B. AMĪR ŠĒR 'ALĪ KHAN. See MOḤAMMAD AYYŪB KHAN.

AYYUBIDS (Ar. Banū Ayyūb), a Kurdish family who first became prominent as members of the Zangid military establishment in Syria in the mid-sixth/twelfth century. Seizing power in Egypt in 564/1168, they were soon able to extend their dominion to the Yemen, Syria, and much of the Jazīra. However, they lost the bulk of their lands during the crises of the mid-seventh/thirteenth century, though they did continue to hold two minor principalities for some time thereafter (Ḥamā until 740/1341, Ḥeṣn Kayfā until 866/1462). In addition, many members of the family continued to be maintained in Egypt as pensioners of the Mamluk sultanate until the early eighth/fourteenth century.

The Ayyubids traced their ancestry back to Šāḏī, a notable of the Kurdo-Armenian town of Dvin (Ar. Dabīl) in the first quarter of the sixth/twelfth century. Ebn Ḵallekān [Beirut, I, pp. 255-56, tr. de Slane, p. 243] identifies him as belonging "to one of the most eminent and respectable families of Duwîn" (*men ahl Dowīn wa men abnāʾ aʿyānehā waʾl-moʿtabarīn behā*). Šāḏī's father is commonly called Marwān, but nothing whatever is known about him. It does seem clear, however, that Šāḏī was a member of the Rawādīya section of the powerful Haḏbānīya tribe, and that the Rawādīya were the dominant Kurdish group in the Dvin district. It is quite evident that the progenitor of the Ayyubids was no simple pastoralist, but a member of the sedentary political-military elite of a marginal but very complex region.

Once the Ayyubids were ensconced in power, some of them sponsored genealogies showing that they were not Kurds, but rather of noble Arab descent, stemming from the Morra b. ʿAwf—or even from the Banū Omayya: On one level, such genealogies are obviously fictions. However, Minorsky (*Studies in Caucasian History*, pp. 114-16, 123, 128-30) argues that the Rawādīya Kurds should perhaps be connected to the descendants of the Arab general Rawwād Azdī, who was governor of Tabrīz ca. 200/815. These men, having become Kurdicized, emerge in the late fourth/tenth century as the paramount clan among the powerful Haḏbānīya tribe in Azerbaijan, whence one branch moved to take up residence in the district of Dvin at some point in the eleventh century. If Minorsky's speculations are sound, then the fictitious Arab genealogies of the Ayyubids not only contain a kernel of truth but preserve an authentic folk memory.

The rise of the Ayyubids really begins with the exile of Šāḏī from Dvin, perhaps in 524/1130, when a Turkish general seized the town from its Kurdish prince. Šāḏī migrated to Iraq with his two adult sons, Najm-al-dīn Ayyūb and Asad-al-dīn Šīrkūh, and was appointed commandant of Takrīt by an old friend from Dvin, Mojāhed-al-dīn Behrūz, who had become the *šeḥna* of Iraq under the Saljuqs. But Šāḏī soon died, and his place was taken by his elder son Ayyūb. Political vicissitudes soon compelled another exile, however, and in 532/1138 Ayyūb and Šīrkūh took service with the powerful *atābak* of Mosul (Mawṣel), ʿEmād-al-dīn Zangī, and were quickly numbered among his most powerful and influential officers—a status which they retained also under his son Nūr-al-dīn Maḥmūd (r. 541/1146-569/1174).

In 564/1168 Šīrkūh was given command of Nūr-al-dīn's third expeditionary force to Egypt, and succeeded in compelling the helpless Fatimid caliph al-ʿĀżed to name him vizier. Dying a few months thereafter (Jomādā II, 564/March, 1169), he was succeeded by his newphew Ṣalāḥ-al-dīn Yūsof b. Ayyūb. It is this man, known in the West as Saladin, who was the real founder of his family's power. With great skill, Ṣalāḥ-al-dīn first suppressed all effective opposition in Egypt, and then, after his master Nūr-al-dīn's death in 569/1174, began to take control of Syria piece by piece. In 579/1183 he occupied Alepo (Ḥalab), the last center of Zangid power in Syria, and in 581/1186 he was able to reduce even Mosul to client status. Ṣalāḥ-al-dīn is of course best known for his wars against the Crusaders, and these dominated the rest of this reign until his death (589/1193). Though his heirs would extend their hegemony in the Jazīra and Armenia, it is nevertheless true to say that Ṣalāḥ-al-dīn's wars marked out the Ayyubid sphere of influence in the Middle East.

In the present context, however, Ṣalāḥ-al-dīn is most significant to us as the creator of a political system which would provide the framework of attitudes, expectations, and goals which governed the conduct of his successors for the next half-century. This political system, which may be called the family confederation, was closely modeled on Saljuq and Zangid practice, and had affinities as well to the political structures which his grandfather, father, and uncle had known in Armenia. The fundamental (and generally unspoken) principle in this system was that political authority within a state should not be the sole possession of one man, but rather should be shared among the leading male members of the ruling family. This sharing of authority was accomplished by assigning to each suitable prince an appanage of his own, which he would govern as a hereditary and autonomous principality. One member of the ruling family might indeed be recognized as its head, and as such would be accorded a certain degree of deference by the other princes. But in spite of the grandiloquent titles which commonly accompanied such a dignity, there were seldom any regular administrative mechanisms by which the senior ruler could translate his primacy of honor into effective power. Control and coordination within the confederation could be achieved only if the senior ruler commanded a preponderance of military force, or if he enjoyed a high degree of natural familial authority over the other princes. That is, a man who was the father of his "colleagues" could expect to have far more authority than an uncle or older brother. In this kind of system, kinship links among the princes were certainly the primary (though of course not the only) determinant of their political behavior. (The first to identify this system of politics seems to have been Barthold [*Turkestan*[3], pp. 268, 306-07]. Further discussion of this tradition in Humphreys, *From Saladin to the Mongols*, pp. 66-75.)

If one accepts that Ṣalāḥ-al-dīn's political outlook was largely shaped by such considerations, his decision (after his conquest of Aleppo in 579/1183) to parcel out his vast conquests as appanage states will come as no surprise. Likewise, the rationale behind his choice of his major heirs will be clear: three of his sons, a nephew, and his younger brother al-Malek al-ʿĀdel Sayf-al-dīn.

The history of Ṣalāḥ-al-dīn's successors is extremely complex: however, it can be summed up in the observation that his two principal successors as chiefs of the Ayyubid confederation made no significant changes in the structure of politics which he had established, but were rahther content to manipulate it for their own ends. Thus his brother al-Malek al-ʿĀdel Sayf-al-dīn (r. 596/1200-615/1218) was able to ensure his authority by assigning the major appanages to his own sons. On the other hand, al-Malek al-Kāmel Nāṣer-al-dīn (r. 615/1218-635/1238), who was older brother or cousin to the other princes, was able to achieve a modicum of control over the confederation only through his superb diplomacy and an occasional resort to military force. Like his predecessors, al-Kāmel divided the lands he controlled between two sons, al-Malek al-ʿĀdel II and al-Malek al-Ṣāleḥ Najm-al-dīn Ayyūb. And as before there was a protracted struggle to determine the hierarchy of power and prestige within the confederation. But the issue this time was drastically different, for the series of wars between 635/1238 and 643/1245 led to a fundamental alteration of the Ayyubid constitution.

This change of political structure is linked to the name of al-Ṣāleḥ Ayyūb, the nominal head of the Ayyubid kingdom from 637/1240 to 647/1249. In crude terms, what al-Ṣāleḥ did was to wrench the confederation—or at least those parts of it which he controlled—into a unitary state governed by men who were his functionaries rather than his colleagues, and who were not members of the Ayyubid family. The motive force for al-Ṣāleḥ's changes may be attributable to his domineering temperament and his deep-seated sense of alienation from his kinsmen and their traditions. On the other hand, this alienation was not merely a question of personality, but must also be seen in the context of family structure. First, al-Ṣāleḥ's reign represented the fourth generation of Ayyubid dominion, and the ruling princes were no longer close kin, but in effect autonomous dynasts who shared a common eponymous ancestor. Second, al-Ṣāleḥ himself—the nominal head of the Ayyubid house—was only a cousin or nephew to the other princes, and there was no one else of sufficient seniority and prestige to assume his role. The general applicability of these facts can be seen in the similar (though more tentative) policy of administrative centralization being carried out simultaneously in north and central Syria by al-Nāṣer Yūsof of Aleppo (634/1236-658/1260).

The full significance of al-Ṣāleḥ's centralizing policy emerged only after his death. Just six months later, his elite Baḥrīya regiment (composed of his personal *mamlūks*) seized power in Egypt and promoted one of its own members, ʿEzz-al-dīn Aybak, to the throne. When the Mongol cataclysm of 658/1260 destroyed the Syrian Ayyubid kingdom of al-Nāṣer, the Mamluk regime was able to occupy his former dominions. These were then incorporated in a highly centralized state controlled from Cairo, in which formal authority was vested in a single autocrat. This policy should occasion no surprise. The new rulers' training as royal *mamlūks* had taught them to think of authority as embodied in one man. Likewise, their whole political education and experience had been as instruments of al-Ṣāleḥ's policy, and they knew no political system other than his.

In the light of the above outline, is it proper to think of the Ayyubid confederation as a specifically "Kurdish" state? On the level of political structure, the governing attitudes of the Ayyubid confederation can certainly be related to the political institutions of their original homeland. On the other hand, these institutions do not differ significantly from the underlying structures of contemporary Turkish states, and in many ways the Ayyubids can be understood simply as a successor kingdom to the Saljuqs.

On the level of his culture, the matter is equally ambiguous. The Ayyubids ruled a predominantly Arabic-speaking region, and many of their princes became very proficient in Arabic letters and in the religious sciences, However, we see many signs of a continuing connection with their homeland and with Iranian culture generally. Thus, it is clear that al-Malek al-ʿĀdel and his son al-Malek al-Moʿaẓẓam ʿĪsā (d. 624/1227) still spoke Kurdish or even New Persian. And al-Moʿaẓẓam's particular interest in Iran is seen in his patronage of two works (in Arabic) by Fatḥ b.ʿAlī Bondārī (q.v.): one, a translation of the *Šāh-nāma* (ed. ʿA. Aʿẓam, Cairo, 1350/1931); the second, the standard abridgment of ʿEmād-al-dīn Kāteb Eṣfahānī's history of the Saljuqs (ed. M. Th. Houtsma, *Recueil de textes relatifs à l'histoire des Seldjoucides*, Leiden, 1886-1902, II). Still, there is no evidence of any widespread translation movement among the Ayyubids, or of any general devotion to the Persian classics.

It is true, however, that the personal influence of Iranian scholars was very much felt in the religious sciences. Dominique Sourdel has shown that almost one-third of the *madrasa* professors in Aleppo between about A.D. 1150 and 1250 were of Kurdish of Iranian origin. The same figures would not hold for Damascus, let alone Egypt, but their presence in these places was far from negligeable. However, most of these men had come to Syria not under the Kurdish Ayyubids, but under the Turkish Zangids, particularly Nūr-al-dīn Maḥmūd, in the third quarter of the sixth/twelfth century (D. Sourdel, "Les professeurs de madrasa à Alep aux XIIe-XIIIe siècles d'après Ibn Šaddād," *Bulletin d'études orientales* 13, 1949-51, pp. 85-115).

The most visible and distinctive Kurdish presence was in the army. This process too had begun long before the Ayyubid seizure of power, when the *atābak* ʿEmād-al-dīn Zangī had begun trying to control the Kurdish-dominated mountains north of Mosul in order to ensure reglular access to Kurdish recruits. Though the Kurds were viewed with some disdain by Turkish troopers, they were adept at the same mode of warfare (mounted archery) and on a tactical if not social level were easily integrated into the regular Zangid forces. The policy of Kurdish recruitment was doubtless inspired by two problems: 1) That Syria and the Jazīra were unable to obtain many Turkish *ḡolāms* from Central Asia at this time, and thus could not rely on chiefly *mamlūk* forces; 2) while Turkman tribesmen were plentiful in this region, their primary loyalties were to their tribes, and they could not be subjected to regular discipline. In this light, Kurdish mercenaries might well seem relatively cheap and reliable.

In spite of the importance of Kurdish recruitment for the Zangid armies, one should not suppose that the Kurds were ever more than a minority of these forces. And though Kurdish troops become more visible than ever before in the reign of Ṣalāḥ-al-dīn, they certainly remained a minority, constituting at the highest possible estimate one-third of his forces. The Kurds in Ṣalāḥ-al-dīn's armies were sometimes recruited and placed as individuals, but they are more commonly found as members of tribally organized units, of which the sources name four: the Hakkārīya (certainly the largest and most powerful), the Mehrānīya, the Ḥomaydīya, and the Zarzārīya (see, e.g., Abū Šāma, *Ketāb al-Rawżatayn* II, pp. 144, 179). After Ṣalāḥ-al-dīn's death, however, such tribal units are rarely recorded, and Kurdish soldiers appear either as individuals or under the collective appellation "*al-Akrād*." After Ṣalāḥ-al-dīn, in fact, the Kurds seem to have become a far less prominent part of the Ayyubid military establishment; their amirs are less often members of the political elite, which becomes increasingly Turkish.

In the last two decades of Ayyubid history, however, the Kurds re-emerged as a major political and military force. This was due chiefly to two new Kurdish migrations into Syria (in which both groups appear to carry names of regional origin rather than tribal names). The first of these were the Qaymarīya, who arrived in the train of the Khwarazmian marauders who swept through Syria in 642-43/1244-46; from them were drawn several of the most prominent amirs under al-Nāṣer Yūsof, and they remained a significant force under the Mamluk sultan Rokn-al-dīn Baybars (r. 658/1260-676/1277). The second group was the Šahrazūrīya, fleeing before the Mongols in 657/1259. Though numerous (3,000 mounted warriors), the Šahrazūrīya could not be integrated into the regular forces of al-Nāṣer; they were simply an element in the vast human debris thrown up by the Mongol invasion. In the final analysis, then, the Ayyubids did make a considerable use of Kurdish troops, as had their Turkish predecessors and rivals (the Zangids and Artuqids), but we cannot say that theirs was a Kurdish army.

Bibliography: The narrative sources for the history of the Ayyubids are very numerous, but the essential texts—more or less in order of composition—are as follows. 'Emād-al-dīn Moḥammad Kāteb Eṣfahānī, *al-Barq al-šāmī* (Bodleian, Bruce 11 and Marsh 425; see H. A. R. Gibb, "Al-Barq al-Shāmī; The History of Saladin by the Kātib 'Imād-al-Dīn al-Iṣfahānī," *WZKM* 52, 1953, pp. 93-115 for a resumé of the contents). Idem, *al-Fatḥ al-qossī fi'l-fatḥ al-qodsī*, ed. Landberg, Leiden, 1888; tr. H. Massé, Paris, 1972. Bahā'-al-dīn b. Šaddād, *al-Nawāder al-solṭānīya wa'l-maḥāsen al-yūsofīya* or *Sīrat Salāḥ-al-dīn*, ed. J. Šayyāl, Cairo, 1964; tr. Wilson and C. R. Conder, *The Life of Saladin*, London, 1897. Ebn al-Aṯīr, vols. XI-XII. Ebn Ḵallekān (Beriut), I, pp. 255-57; VII, pp. 139-45 (the most important statements concerning the family's origin). Abū Šāma, *Ketāb al-Rawżatayn fī akbār al-dawlatayn*, 2 vols., Būlāq, 1287-92/1871-75. Idem, *al-Ḏayl 'ala'l-Rawżatayn*, ed. Kawṯarī, Cairo, 1336/1947. Sebṭ b. Jawzī, *Mer'āt al-zamān fī ta'rīḵ al-a'yān*, ed. Jewett, Chicago, 1907. Ebn Wāṣel, *Mofarrej al-korūb fī akbār Banī Ayyūb*, ed. J. Šayyāl, 5 vols. (in progress), Cairo 1953-.

R. S. Humphreys, *From Saladin to the Mongols: the Ayyubids of Damascus, 1193-1260*, Albany, 1977, so far the only full-length attempt to deal with the whole period of Ayyubid rule. C. Cahen, "Ayyubids," in *EI*² I, pp. 796-807 (a superb short account with a geneological table, to be supplemented by H. A. R. Gibb, "The Aiyubids," in K. M. Setton, ed., *History of the Crusades* II, Madison, 1969, pp. 693-714. On the origins of the Ayyubids, see V. Minorsky, *Studies in Caucasian History*, London, 1953, pp. 107-57. On the careers of Ayyūb and Šīrkūh, see N. Elisséeff, *Nūr al-dīn*, II, Damascus, 1967, passim. On Ṣalāḥ-al-dīn, the most useful studies are recent ones: H. A. R. Gibb, *The Life of Saladin*, Oxford, 1973, A. S. Ehrenkreutz, *Saladin*, Albany, 1972 (an interpretation diametrically opposed to Gibb's), and M. C. Lyons and D. E. P. Jackson, *Saladin: the Politics of the Holy War*, Cambridge, 1982. On the later rulers, see F.-J. Dahlmanns, *al-Malik al-'Ādil*, Giessen, 1975, H. L. Gottschalk, *al-Malik al-Kāmil und seine Zeit*, Wiesbaden, 1958 (very important). G. Schregle, *Die Sultanin von Ägypten*, Wiesbaden, 1961. Finally, on the Kurds and the Ayyubid army, see D. Ayalon, Aspects of the Mamluk Phenomenon. II," *Islam* 54, 1977, pp. 1-32. R. S. Humphreys, "The Emergence of the Mamluk Army," *Stud. Isl.* 45, 1977, pp. 89-93, 46, 1977, pp. 150-52, 155-57.

(R. S. HUMPHREYS)

'AYYŪQĪ, a poet of the fifth/eleventh century who versified the romance of *Varqa o Golšāh*. In it he gives his name as 'Ayyūqī (ed. Ṣafā, pp. 3, 122) and complains in the concluding section (p. 116) about ill-treatment by the people of his town. Apart from this, no reliable information about him has come down. In the preface (p. 3) he eulogizes the *ḡāzī* sultan Abu'l-Qāsem Maḥmūd, i.e., the Ghaznavid ruler Maḥmūd b. Sübüktegin (r. 389/999-421/1030). In view of the manifest influence of Ferdowsī's style on many passages, *Varqa o Golšāh* is likely to have been composed after the *Šāh-nāma*; and the use of archaic words, pronunciation, and certain grammatical peculiarities point to the early fifth/eleventh century as the date of its composition. Lexical and grammatical inconsistencies found in the text may be due to clerical tampering with the text or the influence of the spoken language of the time. ('Ayyūqī seems to have been a man of little education, without full mastery of the literary idiom of his time.)

Two verses by 'Ayyūqī, not from *Varqa o Golšāh*, quoted on the margin of a single manuscript of *Loḡat-e fors*, indicate that he also wrote *qaṣīdas* (odes) and perhaps another narrative poem in the *ramal* meter (Ṣafā, *Adabīyāt* I, p. 603).

Varqa o Golšāh is a romance of love and adventure, running to approximately 2,250 verses in the *motaqāreb* meter. Many words are vocalized, which makes the work important for Persian philology. The work survives in a unique manuscript at Istanbul (Topkapı Sarayı Müzesi, Hazine 841), which is adorned with seventy-one illustrations in color; it bears no date but the handwriting must be from not later than the seventh/thirteenth century. (A facsimile edition is to be produced at Graz, Austria.) A feature of the work is that ten *ḡazals*, all in the *motaqāreb* meter, are interspersed in the narrative. This method had not hitherto been used in Persian poetry, but was subsequently imitated, e.g., in 'Obayd Zākānī's *'Oššāq-nāma*, a narrative poem written in 751/1350. 'Ayyūqī's romance of Varqa and Golšāh is a mediocre work, lacking the thematic development and intensity of emotion that is found, for example, in the almost similar romance of *Laylī o Majnūn* by Neẓāmī.

'Ayyūqī's theme is the love between a youth named Varqa and a maiden named Golšāh. Their fathers are two Arab brothers named Homām and Helāl, who are the chiefs of a tribe, the Banū Šabīh. On the day fixed for Golšāh's marriage to Varqa, she is abducted by enemies under the leadership of Rabī' b. 'Adnān. Numerous fights, in which Varqa's father and Rabī' and his two sons are killed, take place before Golšāh is rescued. Golšāh's father, however, now withholds consent for her marriage to Varqa because Varqa is too poor. Varqa therefore goes to the court of his maternal uncle, Monḏer king of the Yemen, in the hope of making money. During his absence, the king of Syria induces Golšāh's mother to give him her daughter in marriage. When Varqa comes home with much wealth, he is told that Golšāh is dead. He discovers this to be a lie, and goes to Syria in search of Golšāh, but receives so much hospitality and kindness from the Syrian king that he cannot honorably break the bond of gratitude and is therefore obliged to part from Golšāh. Soon afterward he dies of grief. When Golšāh learns of his death, she goes to his grave and, while lamenting there, also passes away. Their tomb becomes a place of pilgrimage to which both Jews and Muslims resort. One year after the tragedy, the Prophet Moḥammad passes by the place. After requiring the Jews to become Muslims, he resurrects Varqa and Golšāh, who then at last are united.

The story, as 'Ayyūqī states (pp. 4-5, 122), was taken from Arabic sources. It is based on the adventures of 'Orwa b. Ḥeẓām 'Oḏrī, an Arab poet, and 'Afrā, the daughter of his paternal uncle 'Eqāl, whose romance was already famous before the 4th/10th century; a book of *'Orwa wa 'Afrā* is mentioned in Ebn al-Nadīm's *Fehrest* (p. 306). 'Ayyūqī claims to have produced the first Persian version of this romance. In later times, further renderings were brought out: at least one more in Persian (in the *hazaj* meter), one in Kurdish, and several in Turkish. A Turkish version, entitled *Varqā wa Golšāh* with the same meter as Neẓāmī's *Laylī o Majnūn*, was written by a poet named Mosīḥī for the Safavid ruler Shah 'Abbās I in the late 10th/16th or early 11th/17th century. In Anatolia a version in western Turkish had been composed by a poet named Yūsof Maddāḥ in 770/1369. A translation by 'Abdallāh b. Ḥājji b. Mīr Karīm from Persian into eastern Turkish, under the title *Ḥekāya-ī 'ajība az aḥwāl-e Golšāh wa Varqa*, was printed at Tashkent in 1324/1906.

The story also entered into Spanish and French literature. Its elements, other than the resurrection of the lovers, form the substance of *Floire et Blancheflor*, a romance which was popular in the twelfth century.

Bibliography: A. Ateş, "Yak maṯnawī-e gomšoda az dawra-ye ḡaznavīān, Varqa o Golšāh-e 'Ayyūqī," *MDAT* 1/4, 1333 Š./1954, pp. 1-13. Ṣ. Kīā, "Āyā maṯnawī-e Varqa o Golšāh-e 'Ayyūqī hamzamān bā Šāh-nāma-ye Ferdowsī ast?" ibid., 2/1, 1334 Š./1955, pp. 49-50. 'Ayyūqī, *Varqa o Golšāh*, ed. Ḏ. Ṣafā, Tehran 1343 Š./1964. A. S. Melikian-Chirvani, "Le roman de Varqe et Golšāh," *Arts asiatiques* 22, 1970, pp. 1-262 (primarily a discussion of the miniatures in the manuscript with full bibliographical review and a discussion of its connection with the romance *Floire et Blancheflor*). Ṣafā, *Adabīyāt* I, pp. 601-03.

(DJ. KHALEGHI-MOTLAGH)

ĀZ, Iranian demon known from Zoroastrian, Zurvanite, and, especially, Manichean sources. Avestan Āzi- (not in the *Gāθās*) derives from the root *āz-* "Strive for, endeavor to" (used *in bonam partem*). New Persian continues Mid. Ir. *āz* but without mythological significance, apart from the conception of Āz as demon of death implied by the expression "the door of Āz" (*dar-e āz*; see R. C. Zaehner, *Zurvan, A Zoroastrian Dilemma*, Oxford, 1955, p. 172). Ferdowsī, for example, uses the phrases *āz o nīāz*, "avarice and want," and *āz o ranj*, "avarice and distress" (Wolff, *Glossar zu Firdosis Schahname*, Berlin, 1935, p. 10). Āz is Greed, Lust, Avarice, Avidity, Concupiscence—the demon both in its mythological (metaphysical) aspect and in its psychological (religious) aspect realized in man. In the Avesta the demon Āzi is the opponent of Ātar (Fire) (*Vd.* 18.19, 21, 22) but is overcome by the milk and fat of the sacrifice (*Y.* 16.8 = 68.8) or by X^{v}arənah (*Yt.* 18.1). Āz is there unimportant, religiously as well as mythologically. In the Zoroastrian Mid. Pers. texts, including those possibly based on lost Avestan material, Āz especially represents gluttony as opposed to contentment (*hunsandīh*). As an abuse of a natural and legitimate function, it is the most serious menace to pious striving (*tuxšagīh*) in the service of Ahura Mazdā. It brings about death as it destroys man's physical strength and so keeps him from fulfilling the whole range of religious duties (his *xwēškārīh*). In Zoroastrian mythology Āz is let loose already on Gayōmard, the Primordial Man (*Bundahišn* 43.10); according to the eschatology, it and Ahriman are the last demons to be defeated, their special adversaries being Srōš and Ohrmazd. In Zurvanite theology (represented by Zātspram, 9th/10th-century high priest of Sīrkān and author of the *Wizīdagīhā ī Zātspram*), Āz has a primary importance as leader of the demonic host. This Zurvanite conception explains the great role played by the Manichean Āz; According to a Parthian text, she is "mother of the demons (*mād čē dēwān*), from whom every sin has come" (M 183 in Sundermann, 1973, p. 63).

The Manichean Āz formed the human body and imprisoned in it the soul (i.e., the particle of light, God's substance), Āz is Hylē, Matter, Evil itself; as an active, invisible power (*mēnōgīh*) of the body, this demon tries to make man forget his divine origin, thus excluding him (and God) from salvation. It is no wonder that in Uighur Buddhism *az* could render *tṛṣṇā* "thirst, desire" that causes rebirth (see, e.g., the *nidāna*-chain in F. W. K. Müller, *Uighurica II*, 1910, no. 3, pp. 11f., 14.). The principal text on Āz is the Mid. Pers. text T III 260, "possibly from the *Šābuhragān*, or from a translation of another work by Mani" (Boyce, *Cat. Man. Script*, p. 132; ed. in *Mir. Man.* I, pp. 177ff.): The Third Messenger and/or the Maiden of Light (or the twelve Maidens of Light) arouse the lust of the demons by appearing in male shape before the females and in female shape before the males; the demons, by shedding semen, will release the Light previously swallowed by them. Āz becomes enraged and enters "the male Āsrēštār [q.v.] and the female Āsrēštār, lion-shaped, lustful and savage, sinful and ravaging" (*Mir. Man.* I, p. 194). Āz teaches them and all demons to feel desire and mate, effecting through them the creation of Adam and Eve in the image of the Third Messenger/Maiden of Light (J. P. Asmussen, *Xᵘāstvānīft. Studies in Manichaeism*, Copenhagen, 1965, pp. 247ff.). She thus attempts to preserve some of the captive particles of Light and to keep man from receiving the knowledge (*gnōsis*) of salvation. (For the fundamental role of Āz as Matter, see W. B. Henning, "Ein manichäischer kosmogonischer Hymnus," *Nachr. Gött. Gesell. Wiss.*, 1932, pp. 214ff., with the Mid. Pers. text S 9.)

The Manichean Āz is unambiguously feminine, whereas the Avestan Āzi is determined as masculine by the form of its epithet *daēvō.dāta-* "demon-created." Perhaps Āzi/Āz was originally hermaphroditic.

Bibliography: See also J. P. Asmussen, "Some Remarks on Sasanian Demonology," in *Acta Iranica* 1, Tehran and Liège, 1974, pp. 236ff., W. Sundermann, *Mittelpersische und parthische kosmogonische und Parabeltexte der Manichäer*, Schriften zur Geschichte und Kultur des Alten Orients. Berliner Turfantexte IV, Berlin, 1973.

(J. P. ASMUSSEN)

ĀZĀD (older ĀZĀT), a class of the Iranian nobility. The word (Mid. Pers. *'z't*, *'c't*, plur. obl. *'z't'n*, *'c't'n*, Parth. *'z't*, plur. obl. *'z'tn*) literally means "free," and by extension also "noble."

i. *In ancient Iran.*

ii. *Armenian* azat.

i. IN ANCIENT IRAN

The division of the Iranian society into four privileged classes antedates the advent of the Sasanians, who inherited it from the Parthians; however, A. Christensen's suggestion that the term *āzād* goes back to the Aryan conquerors, who adopted it to distinguish themselves from the indigenous population, is disputable (*Iran Sass.*, p. 111). This fourfold division of the nobility is attested in inscriptions from the Sasanian period, which show that in Sasanian times the *āzād*s constituted the fourth and last rank of nobles. They were preceded by the *šahryār*s (Mid. Pers. *šhrd'r*, Parth. *hštrdr*) "kings" or "dynasts," the *wispuhrs* (*BRBYTA*[*n*]) "princes of the royal blood, members of the great families," and the *wuzurgs* (*LBA*[*n*], *RBA*[*n*], Mid. Pers. plur. obl. also *wclk'n*) "grandees" (qq.v). (See H. Hübschmann, *Armen. Etymologie*, p. 91, but also A. Perikhanian, *Revue des études arméniennes*, N.S. 8, 1968, pp. 11f.).

The attestations of *āzād* in the inscriptions are: the bilingual (Middle Persian and Parthian) inscription of Šāpūr I at Ḥājjīābād (see D. N. MacKenzie, "Shapur's Shooting," *BSOAS* 41, 1978, pp. 499-511, with references to previous literature) and the inscription of Narseh I at Paikuli, Kurdistan (see H. Humbach and P. O. Skjærvø, *The Sassanian Inscription of Paikuli* I-III, Wiesbaden, 1978-83, III, 2, pp. 45-46). In the Paikuli inscription, which was composed and engraved to commemorate the accession of Narseh I in A.D. 293, the *āzād*s are mentioned several times together with other categories of the nobility (Mid. Pers./Parth. lines 3/2, 7/6, 8/7, 16-17/15, 30/27, 37/34[twice], 38/35, 40/38 [41-42/39], see ibid., p. 46 and III, 1, pp. 29-68, 77). In the Middle Persian inscription of Šāpūr II at Meškīnšahr, Azerbaijan, only the *šahryār*s, the *wuzurg*s, and the *āzād*s are mentioned (G. Gropp, "Die sasanidische Inschrift von Mishkinshahr in Āzarbaidjān," *AMI*, N.F. 1, 1968, p. 152).

In a parchment from Dura Europos, dated A.D. 121, the *strategos* Manesus, son of Phraates, with the rank of *batesa*, is said to belong to the *eleutheroi* "the free" (C. Bradford Welles in *The Excavations at Dura-Europos. Final Report* V, New Haven, 1959, pp. 115-16, no. 20.4-5; see also idem and M. I. Rostovtzeff, "A Parchment from Dura," *Yale Classical Studies* 2, 1931, pp. 5-6, 52), probably the Greek equivalent of Iranian *āzād.* This shows that the *āzād*s at that time comprised members of the high nobility.

According to Classical and Armenian authors a cavalry regiment was picked from the *āzād*s both under the Parthians and the Sasanians. Flavius Josephus (*Bellum Judaicum* 1.13.3) says that a regiment consisting of *eleutheroi* was under the command of Prince Pacorus, son of Orodes II during the invasion of Judea in 40 B. C.

Justinian (*History of Trogus Pompeius* 41.2) is less clear, stating that among the 50,000 horsemen confronting Antony's army (36 B.C.) only 400 were *liberi* "free." In Sasanian times, we are told that the royal bodyguard at the court of Šāpūr II was composed mainly of an "army of free men" (P'awstos Biwzand, *History* 4.53, Venice, 1933, p. 171 = V. Langlois, *Collection des historiens arméniens* I, p. 269: *azatagund puštipan zawracn*). To designate these regiments of free men, the Armenian authors used the terms *azatagund*, *azatakoyt*, and *azatazawr*.

In Sasanian Iran the *āzād*s seem to have included, at least in later centuries, the *šahrīg*s "heads of districts" and the *dehgān*s "heads of villages" (Nöldeke, *Geschichte der Perser*, pp. 446-47; Christensen, *Iran Sass.*, pp. 112, 138, 140 n. 3). The Arab authors sometimes use the term *banu'l-aḥrār* or *aḥrār* (q.v.) to designate this class.

In Arsacid Armenia the term *azatk'* (plur.) came to designate the middle and lower nobility in general, in contrast to the *naxararak'* who were the satraps and the great lords. The *azatk'* had their share in the major events of the country, such as at the election of the patriarch (P'awstos Biwzand, *History* 4.3, Venice ed., p. 77 = V. Langlois, *Collection* I, p. 236). Elsewhere they are contrasted with the *šinakank'* (< Parth. **šēnakān*), the rural lower class of peasants and villagers (P'awstos Biwzand, *History* 5.30, 44, Venice ed., p. 91 = V. Langlois, *Collection* I, pp. 296, 306; Eḷišē Vardapet, pars. 3, 8, Venice, 1950, p. 91; cf. Hübschmann, *Armen. Etymologie*, p. 91; Adontz, "L'aspect iranien du servage," p. 155; Widengren, *Der Feudalismus*, pp. 112-14). (See also ii below.)

Outside of Iran proper, we find the *āzād*s as a privileged class in Sogdia, see G. A. Koshelenko, "Les cavaliers parthes," *Dialogues d'histoire ancienne* 6, Paris, 1980, pp. 177-99; O. I. Smirnova, "Azatan as a Social Category of Sogdian Population," in *The Near and Middle Orient* (for the 70th Anniversary of Professor M. Petrushewski), Moscow, 1970, pp. 148-49.

Bibliography: See also N. Adontz, "L'aspect iranien du servage," in *Recueils de la société Jean Bodin* 2, 1937, pp. 100, 111f., 140. E. Herzfeld, *Paikuli* I, Berlin, 1924, p. 129 no. 34. P. O. Skjærvø, "Case in Inscriptional Middle Persian, Inscriptional Parthian and the Pahlavi Psalter," *Studia Iranica* 12/1, 1983, pp. 60-61. G. Widengren, *Der Feudalismus im alten Iran*, Cologne and Opladen, 1969, pp. 31, 113f., 126f., 140. Idem in H. Temporini and W. Haase, eds., *Aufstieg und Niedergang der römischen Welt* II, 9/1, 1976, pp. 239-40, 248. *Camb. Hist. Iran* III, pp. 394, 632-34, 644-46, 700, 703, 1276.

(M. L. CHAUMONT)

ii. ARMENIAN AZAT

The Armenian term *azat*, derived from the Iranian *zan-* "to be born," originally signifying "born (into the clan)" and, by extension, "noble" and "free," a congener of the Iranian term *āzāt* (*āzād*), was its exact etymological and sociological equivalent. In the dichotomous structure of the Armenian—and Caucasian—nobility, it designated members of the lesser nobility, standing below the group of the dynastic princes, descendants of the tribal chiefs of prehistoric times. The *azatk'* (plur.) were presumably descended (a) from heads of smaller clans and family-heads of tribal times, (b) from a section of the tribal army-people that had remained free, (c) from the war-bands of the dynasts, and (d) possibly illegitimately from the princes themselves. This was a class of noble landowners directly subordinate to the princes and to the king, as prince of his own demesne, and at the same time a class of noble warriors, an *ordo equester*, whose vassalage to the dynasts was expressed, first of all, in the duty, which was also a privilege, of serving the feudal cavalry of their suzerains, as well as in other obligations. It seems plausible that they enjoyed certain minor governmental rights on their own lands. Their equivalence with the medieval Western knights was immediately recognized when, as during the Crusades, the two societies, Armenian and Frankish, existed side by side. Thus the Armeno-Cilician Code of the Constable Smbat (after 1275) explains the meaning of *azat* by *jiawar*, an Armenian adaptation of *chevalier*. Together with the princes, these lesser nobles formed a social group that was wholly distinct from the rest of the people, and their oneness as a class was shown by the fact that derivatives of the term *azat* were used to designate the entire body of the nobility.

Bibliography: N. Adontz, "L'aspect iranien du servage," *Recueil de la Société Jean Bodin* 2, 1937, pp. 143-45. Idem, *Armenia in the Period of Justinian*, tr. and rev. by N. Garsoïan, Lisbon, 1970, pp. 305, 332-33, 342-43. R. Grousset, *Histoire de l'Arménie, des origines à 1071*, Paris, 1947, p. 294. R. Kherumian, "Esquisse d'une féodalité oubliée," *Vostan* 1, 1948-49, pp. 7-56. Y. Manandian, *P'eodalizmə hin Hayastanum. Aršakunineri ew marzpantut'yan šrǰan* (Feudalism in ancient Armenia. The period of the Arsacids and of the *marzpans*), Erevan, 1934, passim. Idem, *The Trade and Cities of Armenia in Relation to Ancient World Trade*, tr. N. Garsoïan Lisbon, 1965, pp. 70-71, 175. C. Toumanoff, *Studies in Christian Caucasian History*, Georgetown, 1963, pp. 93-94, 123-27.

(C. TOUMANOFF)

ĀZĀD, *Zelkova crenata* or Siberian elm, a tree of the *Ulmaceae* family, for which also other scientific names, such as *Zelkova carpinifolia*, *Zelkova hyrcana*, *Planera crenata*, and *Planera Richardi*, have been proposed. It is one of the most typical trees of the hyrcanian forest and is found, always mixed with many other species, in the humid Caspian forests of low altitude, from the Lankarān lowlands to the Golī Dāḡ, where it reaches 900 meters above the sea level (Ḥ. Ṯābetī, *Deraḵtān-e jangalī-e Īrān*, Tehran, 1326 Š./1947-48, pp. 28-29), as well as in the Colchidian forests. It is one of the endemic species of the Euxino-Hyrcanian botanical province inside the Euro-Siberian territory, which are relics of the Arcto-Tertiary flora that was elsewhere destroyed during the Quaternary cold periods (K. H. Rechinger, "Grundzüge der Pflanzenverbreitung im Iran," *Verhandlungen der zoologischen-botanischen Gesellschaft in Wien*, 1951, p. 187; M. Zohary, "On the Geobotanical Structure of Iran," *Bulletin of the Research Council of Israel*, section D, Botany, 11 D, supp., March, 1963, pp. 22-28; a. Noirfalise and M. H. Djazirei, "Contribution à la phytogéographie de la forêt caspienne," *Bulletin de la Société Royale Botanique de Belgique* 98, 1965, pp. 205-07).

The tree is called *āzād* (noble, free) in Persian and Gīlakī, *nīl* in northern Ṭāleš, *sək* or *sīyā dōr* in central and southern Ṭāleš, *azedār* or *azzār* in Māzandarān and Gorgān and *āqča āḡāj* in Golī Dāḡ (Ṯābetī, op. cit., pp. 154-55).

Its leaves, serrate-edged and downy like those of the elm, but smaller, are often given to livestock as fodder. Siberian elms are sometimes kept up in that purpose, together with other forest trees, amidst fields and pastures, in a park-like landscape (M. Bazin, *Le Tâlech, une région ethnique au nord de l'Iran*, Paris, 1980, I, pp. 146-47).

Other majestic *Zelkova*, some of them exceeding 30 m in height or 1.80 m in diameter, have been preserved around many sanctuaries in Gīlān, and often seem to have been an object of worship before the erection of the *emāmzāda* (M. Sotūda, *Az Āstārā tā Astarābād* I, Tehran, 1349 Š./1971, passim; M. Bazin, "Le culte des arbres et des montagnes dans le Tâleš (Iran du nord-ouest)," in *Quand le crible était dans la paille*..., *Hommage à P. N. Boratav*, Paris, 1978, pp. 96-98).

The Siberian elm gives a hard wood of high quality. Gīlak peasants make from it their shoulder-stick called *čānčū* (Ḥ. Ṯābetī, *Jangalhā-ye Īrān*, Tehran, 1346 Š./1967-68, p. 116), and carpenters regard it as the best building timber.

Bibliography: See also H. Bobek, *Die natürlichen Wälder und Gehölzfluren Irans*, Bonn, 1951, pp. 16-17.

(M. Bazin)

ĀZĀD, MOḤAMMAD-ḤOSAYN, scholar and writer in Urdu and Persian, born about 1834 in Delhi. Āzād cultivated literary and Islamic studies under his father, Mawlānā Moḥammad-Bāqer, a leading journalist in north India, and under the poet Moḥammad-Ebrāhīm Ḏawq. After the Mutiny of 1857, which resulted in his father's execution by the British, he left Delhi and finally settled in Lahore, where he was employed by the Punjab Education Department. In 1867 he became secretary to the Anjoman-e Panjāb, a literary society founded in 1865 by Dr. G. W. Leitner, the director of the government college, aiming at inducting realistic themes in Urdu poetry. His journeys to Central Asia (on a secret mission for the government of India) and Iran in 1865 and 1883 gave him insight into the life of those regions. In 1887 the British government of India honored him for his services to literature and education. He died at Lahore in 1910.

Āzād's literary interests touch upon history, biography, literary criticism, journalism, and story-telling, making him an outstanding figure in the nineteenth-century history of Urdu and Persian literature in India. His prose writings are noted for their picturesque style.

Works. The better known of his nearly seventeen published works in Urdu are: *Qeṣaṣ-e Hend* (Lahore, 1872, repr. Lahore, 1961, Karachi, 1962), a collection of stories from Indian history; *Neyrang-e ḵayāl* (Karachi, 1961), a collection of allegorical stories in moral science adapted from the essays of Samuel Johnson and Joseph Addison (*Tārīḵ-e adabīyāt-e mosalmānān-e Pākestān wa Hend* IX, pp. 308ff.); *Āb-e ḥayāt* (Lahore, 1881, 1950, Fayżābād, 1966), a history of Urdu poetry written in a colorful style; *Soḵandān-e Pārs* (Lahore, 1907), dealing with Indo-Iranian philology, traditions, and the development of Persian prose style (M. Ṣādeq, *Āb-e ḥayāt kī ḥemāyat mayn* [Ṣādeq, in the defence of the *Āb-e ḥayāt*], Lahore, 1967, pp. 382-84); *Darbār-e akbarī* (ed. Mīr Momtāz ʿAlī, Lahore, 1898, ed. Moḥammad-Ebrāhīm, Lahore, 1910, Lucknow, ca. 1965), a biographical work on some courtiers of the emperor Akbar of India (ibid.); *Negārestān-e Pārs* (Lahore, 1922) on nearly thirty-six Persian poets of Iran and India from Rūdakī to Ārzū. The *Dīvān* of Ḏawq Dehlavī, edited by Āzād, carries useful notes. A selection of Āzād's articles has been published by Āḡā Moḥammad-Bāqer, *Maqālāt-e Mawlānā Moḥammad Ḥosayn Āzād*, Lahore, 1966. His *Dīvān* was published under the title *Naẓm-e Āzād*, Lahore, 1910.

Bibliography: *Tārīḵ-e adabīyāt-e mosalmānān-e Pākestān wa Hend*, ed. S. F. Maḥmūd and ʿE. Barelvi, Lahore, IX, 1972, pp. 308ff. B. A. Saksena, *A History of Urdu Literature*, Allahabad, 1927, pt. 2, pp. 46ff. Moḥammad-Yaḥyā Tanhā, *Sīar al-moṣannefīn*, Delhi, 1924, pt. 2, p. 158. Shaikh ʿAbd-al-Qāder, *New School of Urdu Literature*, Lahore, 1921, pp. 31-49. Ḡolām Ḥosayn, *Oriental College Magazine*, Lahore, May, 1962, p. 139. M. Šafīʿ, "Šams-al-ʿolamāʾ Mawlānā Moḥammad Ḥosayn Āzād," ibid., February, 1961, pp. 19-29. *Dāʾerat al-maʿāref-e eslāmī* I, Lahore, 1972, pp. 110-14. M. Bāqer, *Supplement to the Oriental College Magazine*, Lahore, February, 1939. M. Ṣādeq, *Muhammad Husain Azad: His Life and Work*, Lahore, 1965. Idem, *History of Urdu Literature*, London, 1964, pp. 288-302. Jahān Bānū Begom, *Moḥammad-Ḥosayn Āzād*, Hyderabad (Deccan), 1940 (in Urdu). Rażawī Masʿūd Ḥasan, *Āb-e ḥayāt kā tanqīd moṭālaʿa* (A critical Study of the *Āb-e ḥayāt*). Lucknow, 1953. *EI*², Supp., p. 107.

(K. N. Pandita)

ĀZĀD BELGRĀMĪ, MĪR ḠOLĀM-ʿALĪ B. MOḤAMMAD NŪḤ ḤOSAYNĪ WĀSEṬĪ, major eighteenth century Indo-Muslim poet, biographer, and composer of chronograms, also known as Ḥassān-al-Hend (fl. 1116-1200/1704-86). Born into a family of scholars in Belgrām, he studied with his maternal grandfather, Mīr ʿAbd-al-Jalīl Belgrāmī, a noted scholar and poet of

Persian, Arabic, Turkish, and Hindi, and his maternal uncle, Mīr Moḥammad Belgrāmī.

In 1142/1730 Āzād left for Sehwan in Sind where his uncle Mīr Moḥammad was *mīr bak̲sī* and *waqā'e'-negār*. He worked in Sehwan for four years as a deputy (*nā'eb*) to his uncle. In 1150/1737 he set out on a pilgrimage to the Ḥejāz and remained there for the next two years, studying the *Ṣaḥīḥ* of Bok̲ārī under Moḥammad Ḥayāt Sindi (d. 1750). On his return from the Ḥejaz in 1152/1739 he went to Aurangabad and spent the next seven years of his life in total seclusion at the tomb of Shah Mosāfer Ḡojdovānī. Soon after emerging from seclusion, he met Nawab Neẓām-al-dawla Nāṣer Jang, the second son of Neẓām-al-molk Āṣafjāh and the future nizam. They became fast friends. It is likely that Āzād received stipendiary support from the nizam, but he never accepted any service at court. Neither did he ever compose panegyrics for the king of Deccani nobility; he reserved this kind of poetry for the praises of the prophet and saints, which in fact earned him the title Ḥassān-al-Hend (after Ḥassān b. T̲ābet, the panegyrist of the prophet).

Āzād also had a very close friendship with the prime minister of Hyderabad, Ṣamṣām-al-dawla Shah Navāz Khan. When in 1170/1757 Ṣamṣām-al-dawla fell from grace, it was Āzād who took an active role in restoring him to favor, and it was Āzād again who recovered most of the unfinished manuscript of Ṣamṣām-al-dawla's *Ma'āt̲er al-omarā'*, after he had been assassinated and his house plundered. Āzād later published this work, though in a fragmentary form. He died in 1200/1786, and was buried at Rawża (or K̲oldabad) near Daulatabad (See T. W. Haig, *Historic Landmarks of the Deccan*, Allahabad, 1907, pp. 56-58).

Āzād wrote in Arabic, Persian, and reportedly Urdu. His Arabic writings comprise a commentary on the *Ṣaḥīḥ* of Bok̲ārī, an Arabic *dīvān* consisting of more than 3,000 couplets, a Sufi *mat̲nawī* titled *Mak̲zan al-barakāt*, a commentary on Motanabbī's poetry, and the *Sobḥat al-marjān fī āt̲ār Hendostān*, a compilation of three books originally written as independent works and later put together as the four chapters of *Sobḥat al-marjān*. Later, Āzād made a Persian translation of the fourth chapter under the title *Ḡezlān al-Hend*. The first and second chapters were also later translated into Persian by Shah Wāret̲ 'Alī Ḥasanī Ḥosaynī Banārasī at the request of the Raja of Benares, Mahārāj Īšarī Paršād (Storey, I/2, p. 860).

Āzād's Persian writings include, besides the above-mentioned *Ḡezlān al-Hend*, a *dīvān*, a few *tad̲keras* (see below), two rather long *mat̲nawīs* (*Mat̲nawī be-jawāb-e mat̲nawī-e Mīr 'Abd-al-Jalīl Belgrāmī* and *Mat̲nawī-e sarāpā-ye ma'šūq*), and some letters written in a simple elegant style. His Persian *dīvān* is a good specimen of the eighteenth-century post-Bidelian (see Bīdel) style of Indo-Persian poetry; Āzād makes skillful use of rhetorical devices and employs traditional images in a highly broken and intellectualized fashion—a trend common to all Indo-Persian poets of the eighteenth century and later; it was transferred to Urdu poetry as part of the enduring legacy of Bīdel. In the Persian *dīvān* of Āzād one comes across many images and expressions borrowed from Bīdel whom Āzād knew personally.

His biographical works include: *Ma'āt̲er al-kerām tārīk̲-e Belgrām*, a book divided into two chapters dealing with the lives of about 150 saints, mystics, and savants connected in some remote sense with Belgrām. *Sarv-e āzād*, considered as the second volume of the *Ma'āt̲er*, likewise consists of two chapters and is principally devoted to the lives of 143 poets who were born in India or visited India after 1000/1591-1592, including some from Belgrām. Chapter two of *Sarv-e āzād* provides an account of eight *rēk̲ta* (Urdu) poets. *Yad-e bayżā'*, the most protracted of Āzād's Persian *tad̲keras*, contains the lives of 532 ancient and modern poets, arranged in alphabetical sequence. Originally begun at Sehwan in 1145/1732 when Āzād was working for his uncle, it was later enlarged twice, first in Allahabad in 1148/1735 and then again after his return from Mecca in 1152/1739.

By far the best known and most valuable *tad̲kera* of Āzād, from a literary, historical, cultural, or sociological perspective, is *K̲ezāna-ye 'āmera*. Written in 1176/1762-63, it contains alphabetically arranged notices on about 135 ancient and modern poets. But the major importance of *K̲ezāna-ye 'āmera* rests on the prelimary section of the book where Āzād details the biographies of Āṣafjāh together with his sons, Nāṣer Jang and Moẓaffar Jang, and then gives an historical overview of Āṣafjāh, Aḥmad Shah Dorrānī, and the Marathas. The result is a uniquely valuable historical document for the study of eighteenth-century south India, especially since Āzād personally knew the people about whom we talks in the book, and was an eyewitness to many of the pivotal events he narrates. Also included among Āzād's Persian works are two relatively short *tad̲keras*: *Šajara-ye ṭayyeba*, a brief account of the pedigrees and lives of the shaikhs of Belgrām, and *Rawżat al-awlīā'*, a recapitulation of the lives of ten saints buried at Rawża (K̲oldābād).

Āzād lived at a time when Urdu was rapidly displacing Persian as the major literary vehicle for Indo-Muslim culture, and he is said to have authored a book in Urdu, which has not survived.

Bibliography: Āzād Belgrāmī, *K̲ezāna-ye 'āmera*, Cawnpore, 1871, 1900 (with several translated extracts; Storey, I/2, p. 865). *Ma'āt̲er al-kerām*, Hyderabad, 1910. *Sarv-e āzād*, Lahore, 1913. *Sobḥat al-marjān*, Bombay, 1886. *Rawżat al-awlīā'*, Aurangabad, 1892-93. Storey, I/2, pp. 855-66. Z. Ahmad, *Contribution of Indo-Pakistan to Arabic Literature*, repr. Lahore, 1968, see index. A. Schimmel. *Islamic Literatures of India*, Wiesbaden, 1973, pp. 45-46. W. Chambers, *Asiatick Miscellany* I, Calcutta, 1785, pp. 496-97, Sayyed Wajahat Ḥosayn, "Āzād Bilgrāmī," *JRASB*, 3rd ser., Letters, 2, 1936, pp. 119-30. Maqbūl Aḥmad Ṣamdānnī, *Ḥayāt-e Jalīl Belgrāmī* (Urdu) II, Allahabad, 1929, pp. 163-77. Šams-allāh Qāderī, *Qāmūs al-a'lām* (Urdu), pt. 1, Hyderabad, 1935, cols. 32-35. Moḥyī-al-dīn Qāderī Zor,

Ġolām-ʿAlī Āzād Belgrāmī (Urdu), Hyderabad, n.d. *EI*² I, p. 808.

(M. Siddiqi)

ĀZĀD FĪRŪZ, governor of Bahrain and the surrounding area in the time of K̲osrow (probably K̲osrow II Parvēz). His name occurs as Āzād Ferūz (variants Azād Afrūz, Azād Fīrūz, both unpointed; Ṭabarī, I, p. 985), Azād Fīrūz (Ebn al-At̲īr [repr.], I, p. 468), Dād Ferūz (Ḥamza, pp. 138, 143), and Fīrūz (Balād̲orī, *Fotūḥ*, p. 85), The original form was probably Āzād Pērōz, Arabicized as Āzād Ferūz and Dād Ferūz, apparently a misreading for Zād Ferūz (Zād being a shortened form of Āzād). The Arabs called him Mokaʿber (mutilator) because he would cut off peoples' hands and feet (Ṭabarī, ibid.). According to the tradition, a caravan of tributes sent by Vahrēz, the Sasanian governor of Yemen, to K̲osrow II (see below) was raided in the territories of Banū Yarbūʿ (one of the tribes of the Tamīm), whereupon K̲osrow ordered Āzād Fīrūz, the son of Gošnasp (Ar. J̌ošnas, J̌ošnasf [Ḥamza], J̌ošayš [Balād̲orī]) to chastise this tribe. Once the Banū Tamīm went to Hajar, Āzād Fīrūz invited them into the castle of Mošaqqar, where he killed all their men and sent all their boys in captivity to Eṣṭak̲r (Ṭabarī, ibid.; Ebn al-At̲īr, ibid.; Nöldeke, *Geschichte der Perser*, pp. 259ff.). Ṭabarī places this event in the time of K̲osrow I (r. 531-79); and Balʿamī, (*Tārīk̲*, p. 1075) and Ebn al-At̲īr have followed him. However, others (e.g., Ḥamza, p. 143, and Yāqūt, III, p. 401) have placed the event in the time of K̲osrow II (r. 590-628). This seems more plausible, because Āzād Fīrūz lived until the time of the caliphate of ʿOmar and converted to Islam (Balād̲orī, ibid.), and because also some other individuals mentioned in connection with these events lived past the time of the death of Moḥammad (Nöldeke, op. cit., p. 257 n. 3).

Bibliography: See also Justi, *Namenbuch*, p. 53.

(A. Tafażżolī)

ĀZĀD KHAN AFĠĀN (d. 1195/1781), a major contender for supremacy in western Iran after the death of Nāder Shah Afšār (r. 1148-60/1736-47).

Āzād was the son of Solaymān of the Ġalzay (also written Ġalīčaʾī, Ġalǰī) Pashtuns of Kabul. He joined Nāder Shah's army, probably after the fall of Kabul in 1738, and participated in subsequent campaigns in India and Iran. At the time of Nāder's assassination in 1160/1747 he was second-in-command to Amīr Aṣlān Khan Qerqlū Afšār, the *sardār* (governor) of Azerbaijan. He defected in the field to Nāder's nephew and would-be successor, Ebrāhīm Mīrzā, thus helping to defeat Aṣlān Khan's bid for power and earning for himself the sobriquet of khan (Donbolī, *Taǰreba* I, p. 491). When in 1749 Ebrāhīm was in turn defeated by the forces of Šāhrok̲ Shah, Āzād Khan attached himself and his 10-15,000 Afghan cavalry to Mīr Sayyed Moḥammad, the superintendant of the shrine at Mašhad, who ordered him to withdraw toward Qazvīn (Golestāna, *Moǰmal*, pp. 35-36). He withdrew to the western frontier and took service with K̲āled Pasha, the Kurd governor of Ottoman-ruled Šahrezūr. Āzād next aided Naqī Khan Qāsemlū Afšār to oust his brother Mahdī Khan from Tabrīz. By dint of alliances with other local Kurd and Turk leaders, and a politic of submission to Erekle (Īraklī Khan) the regent of Kartli-Kakheti (Gorǰestān)—whose daughter he married—Āzād rose by 1165/1752 to control all the territory between Ardabīl and Urmia (Olivier, *Voyage*, pp. 18-19, 35).

However, Erekle's power kept Āzād from expanding north of the Aras, and in spring, 1166/1753 he seized an opportunity to annex the central Zagros provinces and perhaps win a controlling interest in a restored Iranian monarchy. He was invited by the Bak̲tīārī leader ʿAlī-Mardān Khan and his allies, who were advancing from Baghdad with a Safavid pretender in tow, to assist them in capturing the strategic fortress of Kermānšāh, then held by the de facto regent of western Iran, Karīm Khan of the Zand tribe. However, the Zand army defeated this force before Āzād could effect a junction, and the Afghans opted for a quiet retreat. Karīm Khan pursued and attacked them, but was completely routed (Golestāna, op. cit., pp. 260, 270-73; Nāmī, *Gītīgošā*, pp. 35-36). Āzād swiftly marched on the Zands' home fortress of Parī, near Malāyer, captured it by trickery, and sent seventeen Zand khans and fifty women and children—including Karīm Khan's mother—as captives toward Urmia. However, these overpowered their guards en route, escaped, and rejoined Karīm Khan at Borūǰerd (Golestāna, op. cit., pp. 279-83).

In spring, 1167/1754 Āzād and Fatḥ-ʿAlī Khan Afšār dislodged Karīm Khan from his winter base of Qomeša and, having occupied Shiraz, harried him progressively to the very edge of the Iranian plateau near Kāzerūn. But with the help of a local leader, Rostam Khan K̲eštī, the Zands ambushed and routed Fatḥ-ʿAlī's forces in the steep defile of Kamāreǰ; Shiraz was delivered to the Zands by fifth columnists on 13 Ṣafar 1168/29 November 1754 (Nāmī, op. cit., pp. 44-46; Golestāna, op. cit., pp. 287-90, 315; Malcolm, *History*, pp. 123-25), and Āzād's fortunes were henceforth to decline. Threatened by the Qajars of Māzandarān under Moḥammad-Ḥasan Khan, Āzād fell back from Isfahan and, by early 1756, to Urmia. In August he took advantage of an unsuccessful Qajar siege of Shiraz to reoccupy Isfahan, then pursued the retreating Qajars to the Caspian coast. But in a surprise winter attack at Rašt, Moḥammad-Ḥasan drove Āzād back into Azerbaijan. First Tabrīz fell then, after a last pitched battle in June, 1757, Urmia surrendered to the Qajars, and Āzād fled with a few followers to refuge in Baghdad (Nāmī, op. cit., p. 60).

During 1759-60 Āzād made at least one further attempt, with the encouragement of Solaymān Pasha of Baghdad and Erekle of Georgia, to regain his hegemony in Azerbaijan; but his erstwhile allies, including Fatḥ-ʿAlī Khan Afšār, combined to defeat him decisively near Marāġa. Āzād took refuge at the court of Erekle in

Tbilisi for the next two years (Ḡaffārī, *Golšan*, pp. 70-73; Donbolī, op. cit., II, pp. 31-35). In 1762 Karīm Khan, having subjugated all of northern Iran, invited Āzād to surrender. The Afghan ended his days comfortably in Shiraz as an honored pensioner of the generous Zand ruler, and on his death in 1195/1781 was taken to Kabul to be buried in accordance with his will (Nāmī, op. cit., pp. 113-14; Donbolī, op. cit., II, p. 39).

Āzād is characterized as brave and chivalrous (Ḡaffārī, op. cit., pp. 111-12). He appears to have harbored ambitions to carve out a neo-Safavid, or even neo-Ḡalzay, Iranian empire; but unlike his rivals for power, he remained an alien without any lasting source of support in western Iran—a Sunni Afghan with no urban or tribal-territorial base, and who was never able to acquire a Safavid scion to legitimize his authority. The Ḡalzay in Afghanistan had been destroyed as a power by Nāder, and were replaced in the 1750s by the Abdālī (later known as Dorrānī). Most of Āzād's Ḡalzay followers in Iran, both troops and non-combattant settlers, were massacred in 1171-72/1758-59 during his Baghdad exile—first by the Qajar governor of Māzandarān (Nāmī, op. cit., pp. 67-68) and then by the Zands (Golestāna op. cit., p. 322).

Bibliography: ʿAbd-al-Razzāq Beg Donbolī, *Tajrebat al-aḥrār wa taslīat al-abrār*, 2 vols., ed. Ḥ. Qāżī Ṭabāṭabāʾī, Tabrīz, 1349-50 Š./1970-71. Mīrzā Abu'l-Ḥasan Ḡaffārī, *Golšan-e morād*, B. M. ms. Or. 3592. Abu'l-Ḥasan Golestāna, *Mojmal al-tawārīḵ*, ed. M. T. Modarres Rażawī, Tehran, 1344 Š./1965. Sir John Malcolm, *The History of Persia*, London, 1815, vol. II. J. R. Perry, *Karim Khan Zand*, Chicago, 1979. Guillaume-Antoine Olivier, *Voyage dans l'Empire Ottomane, l'Egypte et la Perse*, Paris, 1807, vol. VI. Mīrzā Moḥammad-Ṣādeq Nāmī, *Tārīḵ-e gītī-gošā*, ed. S. Nafīsī, Tehran, 1317 Š./1938.

(J. R. Perry)

ĀZĀDA, name of a Roman slave-girl of Bahrām Gōr. According to Ferdowsī (*Šāh-nāma* [Moscow] VII, p. 273, vv. 153ff.) and Ṯaʿālebī (*Ḡorar*, pp. 541f.) Bahrām Gōr, during his stay as a young man at the court of his Arab mentor the Lakhmid Monḏer b. Noʿmān, became the owner of Āzāda (Āzādvār in *Ḡorar*), who was a fine harpist. Whenever a hunt was arranged, Bahrām would place her behind himself on his camel and take her with him to the hunting ground. On one such day Āzāda expressed sympathy for the gazelles instead of praise for Bahrām's prowess. Bahrām took offense, flung her to the ground, and let his camel trample her. According to Ṯaʿālebī, Monḏer had the event painted in the palace of Ḵʷarnaq at Ḥīra. Neẓāmī incorporated the story into his *Haft paykar* (ed. H. Ritter and J. Rypka. Istanbul, 1934, p. 87, vv. 1f.), but altered the girl's name to Fetna and gave the story a happy ending. The hunting scene has been a popular theme for miniaturists.

(Dj. Khaleghi-Motlagh)

ʿAZĀDĀRĪ, to hold a commemoration of the dead, by extension, mourning, a word deriving from Arabic *ʿazāʾ*, which means commemorating the dead. This is also the basic meaning of the cognate *taʿzīa*, (q.v.), which came to designate in addition the passion plays mounted in Moḥarram. Details of the commemoration of the dead as regulated by *feqh* are to be found in the chapters headed *al-janāʾez* (funerals) in the handbooks of all the legal schools.

Because of diverse historical, geographical, and cultural factors, a great variety of funerary rites and death customs has developed in Iran. Despite a series of political and religious changes, beliefs and customs regarding death have been deeply influenced by the distant past. A general survey of pre-Islamic funerary practices on the Iranian plateau has not yet been made, but an extensive archeological survey of sedentary Central Asia—a vast area of Iranian culture—has demonstrated the existence of a great diversity in the disposal of the dead (see F. Grenet, *Les pratiques funeraires dans l'Asie centrale sédentaire de la conquête grecque à l'islamisation*, Paris, 1984, which discusses cremation, funerary towers, burial pits, embalmment, inhumation, ossuaries, and cinerary urns). Mourning customs in Central Asia generally followed non-Zoroastrian patterns (ibid., pp. 253 ff.). References to pre-Islamic funerary practices are to be found in various versions of the Iranian national epic, as reflected in both textual and visual materials. Some of these practices may have continued to exercise an influence in the Islamic period. A case in point is the cult of kings and heroes such as Sīāvoš, tentatively identified by Russian scholars as the figure being mourned in a Panjikent wall painting (see E. Yarshater "Taʿziyeh and Pre-Islamic Mourning Rites in Iran," in P. J. Chelkowski, ed., *Taʿziyeh. Ritual and Drama in Iran*, New York, 1979, pp. 88-94, and in *Camb. Hist. Iran* III/1, pp. 449, 450, n. 2, and F. Grenet, op. cit., pls. XLVII and XLVIII). The cult of Sīāvoš may have influenced the Shiʿite mourning rituals of Moḥarram (Yarshater, ibid., p. 151); some connection has also been found between this wall painting and mourning scenes found in the iconography of Ferdowsī's *Šāh-nāma* (O. Grabar, "Notes on the Iconography of the 'Demotte' Shah-Nama," in R. Pinder-Wilson, ed., *Paintings from Islamic Lands*, Oxford, 1969, pp. 32-47, 45 ff.; N. M. Titley, *Miniatures from Persian Manuscripts*, London, 1977, subject index under coffins, funerals, mourners, processions, etc.; J. Norgren and D. Davis, *Preliminary Index of Shah-nameh illustration*, Ann Arbor, 1969). The *Šāh-nāma* abounds in references to ancient funerary beliefs and customs such as so-called Scythian Practices (see ASB ii. AMONG THE SCYTHIANS); in addition to mummification and embalmment, they include a cult of the horses of the dead prince or hero (see J̌. Ḵāleqī Moṭlaq, "Yak-ī daḵma kard-aš ze somm-e sotūr," *Našrīya-ye Dāneškada-ye adabīyāt wa ʿolūm-e ensānī*, Dānešgāh-e Āḏarābādagān, 1357 Š./1978, no. 124, pp. 462-70; idem, "Yakī dāstān ast por āb-e čašm," *Iran Nameh* 1/2, 1983, pp. 164-205; F. Wolff, *Glossar zu Firdosis Schahname*, Berlin, 1935, under *asp*, *summ*, *Raxš*, etc.) as well as the destruction of possessions and the suicide of wives, concubines, and slaves (see, e.g., *Šāh-nāma* [Moscow] IV, p. 65 vv. 888 ff.). Customs such as dishevelling, cutting or pulling out the hair, and biting or ripping the flesh off the arms, are also attested in the *Šāh-nāma* (see VI, p. 315 vv. 1558ff., and F. Wolff, op. cit., under *sōg*).

Certain features of ancient practices persisted into the Islamic period, such as the use of banners (*a'lām*, see 'ALAM VA ALĀMAT) and horses in funeral processions (see H. Massé. *Croyances et coutumes persanes*, Paris, 1938, I, pp. 86 ff.). Mourning colors tended to remain dark: blue and purple were especially favored, with black, grey, and brown also being used (for the currency of these colors in pre-Islamic Iran, see H. Massé, *Firdousi et l'épopée nationale*, Paris, 1935, p. 204; Wolff, op. cit., under *banafš, kabūd, sīāh*). Self-laceration and the tearing of clothes—practices condemned by Islam—persisted well into the Islamic period, being practised especially by rural women. The practice of repairing tombs eight days before Now-rūz is an obvious link of funerary customs of the Islamic period with ancient times (see Massé, *Croyances et coutumes* I, p. 115). Finally, mention may be made of funerary dances—pre-Islamic in origin—which persisted until recently in Tajikistan (see Grenet, op. cit., p. 259).

In general, however, Islamic tenets and practices relating to death have predominated: Belief in Azrael, the angel of death; Monkar and Nakīr, the interrogating angels; the torment of the tomb; and the entry of the soul after death into the *barzak̠* (an intermediary realm) have determined popular conceptions of death and the passage into the hereafter (see Massé, op. cit., I, pp. 113 ff.; B. A. Donaldson, *The Wild Rue*, London, 1938, pp. 70 ff.).

When death approaches, the expiring person pronounces the *šahāda*, encouraged and accompanied by those around him. His body is laid out in the direction of the Ka'ba, and to ease his passage into the hereafter the *sūra yā-sīn* (Koran 36) is recited. The body is ritually washed (*ḡosl-e mayyet*) by the *morda-šūr* (corpse-washer) according to precise regulations and then wrapped in a series of funerary garments of which the outer-most is the *kafan* (shroud) before being placed in a *tābūt* or *nak̠l* (bier). Martyrs are not washed and are buried in the clothes in which they met their death (Massé. *Croyances et coutumes* I, p. 95). Following the tradition established by the Prophet, most schools of law—including the Ja'farī—recommend prompt burial, generally on the day following death. This is held to have led on occasion to fatal errors, with apparently dead persons being buried alive (see Y. Ragib, "Faux morts et enterrés vifs dans l'espace musulman," *Stud. Isl.* 57, 1983, pp. 5-30; Massé, op. cit., I, p. 95). Sometimes the bier is placed on a hearse (*na'š-keš*), but more often it is carried by young men on their shoulders, walking quickly. Passers-by participate in this meritorious act by helping to carry it for a few steps, meanwhile reciting the *šahāda* (ibid., pp. 98 ff). Once in the cemetery (*gūrestān/qabrestān*), the corpse is laid in the tomb, without bier, lying on its right side and facing the Ka'ba. Canonical prayers for the dead (*namāz-e mayyet* or *ṣalāt al-janāza*) are followed by supplicatory prayers on his behalf (*do'ā-ye amwāt*).

Post-burial rites vary from a simple funeral gathering, known as *majles-e tarḥīm* (assembly for invoking mercy on the deceased) or *fāteḥa-k̠ʷānī* (recitation of *sūrat al-fāteḥa*), to a full *k̠atm* (reading of the entire Koran), with separate ceremonies for men and women, known respectively as *k̠atm-e mardāna* and *k̠atm-e zanāna*. Those attending such gatherings are served food and drinks (generally tea or coffee). The *k̠atm* takes place at the latest three days after the funeral (Massé, op. cit., I, p. 104). Sometimes a Koran reading takes place at the graveside, three days after burial; this is designed to assist the deceased in his interrogation by Monkar and Nakīr (see Donaldson, op. cit., p. 74; cf. the Zoroastrian parallel with the three days' judgement by Srōš and Rašn; see I. Goldziher, *Muhammedanische Studien*, p. 247, tr. C. R. Barber and S. M. Stern, *Muslim Studies*, New York, 1977, I, p. 224 n. 3). Further ceremonies are held one week (*hafta* or *pā-gereftan*), forty days (*čella or arba'īn*), and one year (*sāl*) after death, and optional ceremonies in commemoration of the dead are held in the cemeteries on the occasion of various religious festivals. It is also customary for women to visit tombs every Thursday evening (Massé, op. cit., I, pp. 106 ff.). Prayers and passages from the Koran are recited, and food—mostly *ḥalwā*—and alms are distributed (Donaldson, op. cit., pp. 74 ff. nn. 11 to 18; Massé, op. cit., I, pp. 111ff.). Sometimes complete meals (*sofra*) are offered in memory of the dead.

Although not viewed as forbidden (*ḥarām*) by most legal schools—including the Ja'farī—the construction of buildings over tombs, as well as decorating and inscribing them, is regarded as reprehensible (*makrūh*). Nonetheless, Iran—like other Muslim countries—has seen a proliferation of richly laid-out tombs, mausolea, and sanctuaries (see "Ḳabr," "Ḳubba," "Maḳbara" in *EI*[2]; Massé, op. cit., I, pp. 102, 114 ff.). A distinctively Iranian trait, found at tombs in tribal and other areas, is the presence of funerary effigies of lions or rams as symbols of bravery, connected, perhaps, both with the proverbial valor of 'Alī b. Abī Ṭāleb (Asadallāh "the lion of God") and with pre-Islamic cults and beliefs (ibid., pp. 116 ff.).

In literature, mourning has inspired the genres of eulogy (*fażā'el* or *manāqeb*), dirge (*nūḥa/nawḥa*), and elegy (*mart̠īa*).

Iran's adherence to Shi'ism from the Safavid period onward introduced new elements into Iranian funerary practice. Dust gathered from the tomb of Imam Ḥosayn (*torbat*) at Karbalā would be mixed with water to form a beverage given to the dying. Burial at the Shi'ite shrines in the *'atabāt* (q.v.) in Iraq and at Mašhad and Qom within Iran has been regarded as highly desirable. From Qajar times onward, the transport of corpses over long distances for interment in sacred territory became a common practice, one involving both legal and sanitary problems (Massé, op. cit., I, p. 102 n. 2). Bodies buried in Mašhad would often be carried around the tomb of

Imam Rezā in a kind of *ṭawāf* before interment (E. Šakūrzāda, *'Aqāyed o rosūm-e 'āmma-ye mardom-e Korāsān*, Tehran, 1346 Š./1967, pp. 180ff.). Finally, various aspects of the Moḥarram rituals have been imitated in general Iranian funerary practice (see I. Lassy, *The Muharram Mysteries among the Azerbeijan Turks of Caucasia*, Helsingfors, 1916, pp. 132-209).

The mourning ceremonies of Moḥarram, commemorating the martyrdom of Imam Ḥosayn at Karbalā in 61/680 and reaching their climax on the tenth day of the month ('Āšūrā', q.v.), originated in Arab Iraq (see M. Ayoub, *Redemptive Suffering in Islam: A Study of the Devotional Aspects of 'Āshūrā' in Twelver Shi'ism*, The Hague, 1978). However, they were held in Iran as early as the twelfth century, when both Sunnites and Shi'ites participated in them (see J. Calmard, *Le culte de l'Imam Husayn*, thesis, Paris, 1975, pp. 434-49). In the Safavid period, the annual mourning ceremonies for Imam Ḥosayn, combined with the ritual cursing of his enemies, acquired the status of a national institution. Expressions of grief such as *sīna-zanī* (beating the chest), *zanjīr-zanī* (beating oneself with chains), and *tīg-zanī* or *qama-zanī* (mortifying onself with swords or knives) emerged as common features of the proliferating mourning-processions (*dasta-gardānī*). In some towns these processions often led to clashes between rival factions known as *ḥaydarī*s and *ne'matī*s (q.v.). Mourning for the martyred imam also took place in assemblies held in buildings erected especially for the purpose, known either as *ḥosaynīya*s or *takīa*s (tekkes), as well as in moques and private houses. At these assemblies, called either *rawża-k̲ʷānī* (the recitation of *Rawżat al-šohadā'* by Ḥosayn Wā'eẓ Kāšefī (d. 910/1504-05) or similar works on martyrs of the Imamite line) or *mart̲īa-k̲ʷānī* (the recitation of elegies), professional reciters and preachers would recount the deeds of the martyrs and curse their enemies, arousing the emotions of the mourners who responded by singing dirges at appropriate intervals in the narrative (see M. J. Mahjūb "Az fażā'el o manāqeb-k̲ʷānī tā rawża-k̲ʷānī," *Iran Nameh*. 2/3, 1984, pp. 402-31). Theatrical representations of the tragedy at Karbalā (*šabīh-k̲ʷānī* or *ta'zīa*)—possibly the most remarkable feature of the entire corpus of Moḥarram ritual—also made their appearance in the Safavid period (on this significant development, see the works listed in P. Chelkowski, ed., *Ta'ziyeh: Ritual and Drama in Iran*, New York, 1979, pp. 255-68 ("Bibliographical Spectrum"), and J. Calmard, "Moḥarram Ceremonies and Diplomacy," in E. Bosworth and C. Hillenbrand, eds., *Qajar Iran: Political, Social and Cultural Change, 1800-1925*, Edinburgh, 1983, p. 224).

Commemoration of the drama at Karbalā reached its apogee in the mid-nineteenth century. By then it had spread across a vast area, extending from the Middle East and the Caucasus eastwards to India, Indonesia, and Thailand, and it had even been established in Trinidad by Indian Muslim migrants. In Iran, the memory of Karbalā came to permeate social and cultural life, with mourning assemblies and dramatic performances being organized throughout the year, not only in Moḥarram. The occasion might be furnished by the death of a revered person or the need to fulfill a vow. Gatherings known as *sofra* (lit. tablecloth), in which the preparation and serving of food played a focal role, were exclusively feminine: the preachers as well as the mourners were all women, and the lives and tribulations of women such as Fāṭema and Zaynab were the principal topic of commemoration. Gatherings of this type appear to have originated in the late nineteenth century.

From the period of the Constitutional Revolution (1905-11) onward, mourning gatherings increasingly assumed a political aspect. Following an old established tradition, preachers compared the oppressors of the time with Imam Ḥosayn's enemies, the Omayyads (see J. Calmard, "L'Iran sous Naseroddin Chah et les derniers Qadjars," in J. Aubin, ed., *Le monde iranien et l'Islam* IV, Paris, 1976-77, pp. 189-94; A. Fathi, "Preachers as Substitutes for Mass Media: The Case of Iran 1905-1909," in E. Kedourie and S. G. Haim, eds., *Towards a Modern Iran: Studies in Thought, Politics and Society*, London, 1980, pp. 169-84).

The political function of Moḥarram observances was very marked in the years leading up to the Islamic Revolution of 1357 Š./1978-79, as well as during the revolution itself. In addition, the implicit self-identification of the Muslim revolutionaries with Imam Ḥosayn led to a blossoming of the cult of the martyr, expressed most vividly, perhaps, in the vast cemetery of Behešt-e Zahrā, to the south of Tehran, where the martyrs of the revolution and the war against Iraq are buried (on the connection between recent events and the Moḥarram cult in Iran, see E. Neubauer, "Muharram-Bräuche im heutigen Persien," *Der Islam* 49/2, 1972, pp. 250-72; G. E. Thaiss, *Religious Symbolism and Social Change: The Drama of Husayn*, Ph.D. thesis, Washington University, 1973; P. J. Chelkowski, "Iran: Mourning Becomes Revolution," *Asia* 3, May-June, 1980, pp. 30-37; M. J. Fisher, *Iran: From Religious Dispute to Revolution*, Cambridge, Mass., and London, 1980, pp. 136ff.; H. G. Kippenberg, "Jeder Tag 'Ashura, jedes Grab Kerbala. Zur Ritualisierung der Strassenkämpfe im Iran," in K. Greussing, ed., *Religion und Politik im Iran*, Frankfurt am Main, 1981, pp. 217-56; M. E. Hooglund, "Hoseyn als Vermittler, Hoseyn als Vorbild. Anpassung und Revolution im iranischen Dorf," ibid., pp. 257-76; M. Momen, *An Introduction to Shi'i Islam*, New Haven and London, 1985, pp. 233ff.).

Finally among modern developments, it may be noted that the legitimacy of some forms of self-mortification and of dramatic performances has been a subject of controversy among Shi'ite communities in Syria, Lebanon, and Iraq (see W. Ende, "The Flagellations of Muḥarram and the Shi'ite 'Ulamā'," *Der Islam*, 55/1, 1978, pp. 19-36. See also 'ĀŠŪRĀ'; MOḤARRAM; and MOURNING.

Bibliography: For details of Shi'ite burial regulations see Moḥaqqeq Ḥellī, *Šarā'e' al-eslām*, tr. A. Querry, *Recueil des lois concernant les musulmans chyites*, 2 vols., Paris, 1872, I, pp. 27-36, 96-100. On regional and tribal beliefs and customs, which are often quite distinct from those generally prevailing in Iran, see ʿA. Bolūkbāšī, "Āyīn-e be ḵāk sepordan-e morda wa sūgvārī-e ān," *Payām-e novīn* 7/9, 1344 Š./1965, pp. 73-84. Ṣ. Homāyūnī, *Farhang-e mardom-e Sarvestān*, Tehran, 1349 Š./1960, pp. 520-22. Y. Majīdzāda et al., "Āyīn-e sūgvārī dar Delfān-e Lorestān," *Honar o. mardom*, N. S., 25, pp. 8-13. G. H. Nawwābī, "Rasm-e taʿzīat dar Šaḡānān," *Āryānā* 12/4, p. 241. M. Šafīānī and B. Dāvarī, "Marāsem-e ʿazādārī dar Baḵtīārī," *Ketāb-e hafta* 78, pp. 115-16. E. Šakūrzāda, *ʿAqāyed o rosūm-e ʿāmma-ye mardom-e Ḵorāsān*, Tehran, 1346 Š./1967, pp. 177-93.

(J. CALMARD)

ĀZĀḎBEH B. BĀNEGĀN (MĀHĀN?) B. MEHR-BONDĀD a *dehqān* (landowner) of Hamadān, *marzbān* (governor) in the former Lakhmid capital of Ḥīra in central Iraq during the years preceding the Arab conquest of that province. Ṭabarī's account of his governorship cites as source Hešām b. Moḥammad Kalbī and this same historian says that he governed Ḥīra for seventeen years after the rule there of the Arab Īās b. Qabīṣa Ṭāʾī and the Persian co-ruler, Naḵīragān. Since he was killed in 12/633, the beginning of his governorship should probably be placed in A.D. 617 or 618. Āzāḏbeh represents the Sasanian policy of imposing, in effect, direct rule on Ḥīra after the deposition of the last Lakhmid king Noʿmān V b. Monḏer. His tenure of power there spanned the troubled reigns of Ḵosrow II, Šērōya, Ardašīr III, Pūrān, Hormozd V, and Yazdegerd III. The Arabs appeared in Iraq during Abū Bakr's caliphate (soon after the suppression of the Redda wars) under Ḵāled b. Walīd and Moṯannā b. Ḥāreṯa Šaybānī. In 12/633 Azāḏbeh was defeated by the Arabs, and his son killed in the fighting; the Arabs then proceeded to besiege Ḥīra, while Āzāḏbeh fled. Nothing is recorded in the Arabic sources of his ultimate fate.

Bibliography: Ṭabarī, I, pp. 1038, 2019. Balāḏorī, *Fotūḥ*, pp. 242-43. Ḥamza, p. 112. Ebn al-Aṯīr (repr.), II, p. 390 (A.H. 12). Nöldeke, *Geschichte der Perser*, pp. 347-48. Justi, *Namenbuch*, p. 53. ʿA. Zarrīnkūb in *Camb. Hist. Iran* IV, pp. 7-8.

(C. E. BOSWORTH)

ĀZĀDĪ (Freedom) was the name of the following Persian journals: (1) A journal published at Tehran during the *estebdād-e saḡīr* (lesser autocracy, June 1908-July 1909). No copies have been found and no details are available. (2) A journal published at Istanbul in 1909. No copies are known to have been preserved, but some facts are on record. The first issue, consisting of four printed (not lithographed) pages of three columns each, was dated 8 Moḥarram 1327/30 January 1909 and edited by Ḥasan Nājī Qāsemzāda, an Iranian from Ḵoy. Its declared purpose was to be "a defender of constitutionalism and the country's policies and rights, and a propagator of the ideas of those who seek freedom for Iran." Two issues per month were promised, but his journal did not survive beyond its first issue. (3) A Political-satirical weekly of reformist outlook published at Tehran in the months of Jawzā and Saraṭān, 1302 Š./June and July, 1923. The license-holder and editor was Maḥmūd Āzādī. After the seventh issue dated 30 Saraṭān/23 July, further publication was banned. Nevertheless Maḥmūd Āzādī brought out another issue under the title *Bohlūl*, using the license of a political-satirical journal of that name which had been published at Tehran in 1329/1911 by a licensee named Ḥasan Khan Meʿmār. The same Ḥasan Khan was the licensee, and Maḥmūd Āzādī was the editor, of the *Bohlūl*, which presented itself as *Āzādī's* successor. *Āzādī* consisted of four printed pages measuring 36 × 49 cm with four columns per page. Its price was four *šāhīs*. Copies are preserved in various national libraries in Iran. (4) A Journal of news and social comment published initially at Mašhad in Šahrīvar, 1304 Š./September, 1925, and subsequently at Tehran from 1313 Š./1934 to 1314 Š./1935. It was intended to be a daily, but no more than four issues per week were ever achieved in practice. The publication license was held by ʿAlī Akbar Golšan-e Āzādī (1319/1901-1353 Š./1974), a poet and writer, formerly home news editor of the newspaper *Fekr-e āzād*. In Bahman, 1321 Š./February, 1943. *Āzādī* was banned, but after a long pause publication was resumed in the autumn of 1344 Š./1965. Now a weekly, *Āzādī* came out irregularly until the winter of 1352 Š./1974. Its size and format varied in its successive phases, but most often it had four pages measuring 45 × 49 cm with six columns per page. Its price was 35 *dīnārs* in the first phase and two *rīāls* in the last year of its existence. Copies which it has been possible to examine contain small numbers of illustrations and large numbers of official notices. *Āzādī's* political comments were always more or less favorable to the government of the day.

Outside Iran, an incomplete set of this journal is held in the Library of Congress at Washington, D.C.

Bibliography: E. G. Browne, *The Press and Poetry of Modern Persia*, Cambridge, 1914, p. 30. M. Ṣadr-Hāšemī, *Tārīḵ-e jarāyed wa majallāt-e Īrān*, Isfahan, 1327 Š./1948-1332 Š./1953, nos. 104-107. L. P. Elwell-Sutton, "The Iranian Press, 1941-1947," *Iran* 6, 1968, p. 75. Ali Norouze, "Registre analytique annoté de la presse persane," *Revue du monde musulman* 60, 1925, p. 57. R. Lescot, "Notes sur la presse iranienne," *Revue des études islamiques* 2-3, 1938, p. 273. M. Barzīn, *Sayr-ī dar maṭbūʿāt-e Īrān*, Tehran, 1344 Š./1965, p. 155.

(N. PARVĪN)

ĀZĀDĪSTĀN (ĀZĀDĪESTĀN), the title of a Persian educational magazine which came out at Tabrīz in Jawzā, 1299/June-August, 1920.

The magazine was in fact the mouthpiece of Shaikh Moḥammad Ḵīābānī's rebel government in the educational-cultural field. Ḵīābānī seized power at Tabrīz in April 1920 and controlled the provincial government of Azerbaijan until his defeat and death in September of that year. The first issue of the magazine was brought out on 15 Jawzā 1299/5 June 1920, one month after the historic province had been renamed "Āzādīstān" (Land of freedom) by Ḵīābānī and his followers as a gesture of protest against the giving of the name "Azerbaijan" to the part of Caucasia centered on Bākū.

The magazine was printed under the supervision of the poet and writer Moḥammad Taqī Raf'at (b. at Tabrīz 1890-91, d. at Qezel Dīzaj September 1920). After completing his studies at Istanbul, Raf'at had served as a teacher at Trabzon and then at Tabrīz. From the start of the revolt he worked closely with Ḵīābānī. Through articles and poems in *Tajaddod* (Regeneration), the newspaper which Ḵīābānī published at Tabrīz from April 1917 to August 1920, Raf'at and other like-minded writers had attempted to initiate a reform of Persian literature and had engaged in controversy with the Tehran periodical *Dāneškada*. For *Āzādīstān*, Raf'at wrote under both his own name and a pseudonym, "Femina." Shortly after the sanguinary crushing of the revolt and killing of its leader Ḵīābānī, he committed suicide at a village near Tabrīz when little more than thirty years old.

Āzādīstān has a special importance in the history of modern Persian literature. It not only sought to give its readers new educational and social insights, but also contributed to the modernization of Persian prose and, above all, to the transformation of the language, content, and form of Persian poetry. The poems of Taqī Raf'at and the poetess Šams Kasmā'ī which appeared in *Āzādīstān* are the earliest examples of modernist Persian verse.

Beneath the title on the cover were printed the words "a magazine devoted to the regeneration of literature." In the first issue of *Āzādīstān*, Taqī Raf'at emphasized this point with calls for "sincerity and boldness of innovation" and for a "literary revolution." The nature of the desirable innovations became a matter of dispute between *Āzādīstān* and the periodical *Kāva* (published at Berlin). For various reasons, particularly semantic imprecision and overuse of words borrowed from modern Ottoman Turkish, as well as resistance by conservative elements, the literary reform efforts of *Tajaddod* and *Āzādīstān* made no impact at the time. Nevertheless credit is due to these two publications for their pioneering attempt to find new forms and styles of expression.

Āzādīstān was meant to come out once a fortnight, but in the circumstances this was impossible. The first issue bears the date 15 Jawzā 1299/15 June 1920. Some authorities, following Ṣadr-Hāšemī, place its start on 15 Saraṭān, which is a month too late. Altogether three issues of *Āzādīstān* came out in the course of three months. The fourth issue, dated 21 Sonbola 1299/12 September 1920, was in the press at the time of the suppression of Ḵīābānī's revolt, but some passages from it are quoted in Y. Āryanpūr's *Az Ṣabā tā Nīmā*.

Āzādīstān consisted of fourteen two-column pages measuring 30.5 × 23 cm. Contrary to M.M. Tarbīat's statement (*Dānešmandān*, p. 405), it was not lithographed but printed. No illustrations and no advertisements were carried. The price per copy was 30 *šāhīs*. Annual subscription rates of 18 *qerān*s in Tabrīz, 20 in other Iranian cities, and 25 abroad were announced.

Incomplete sets of *Āzādīstān* are preserved in the National Library of Tabrīz and the Central Library of Tehran University.

Bibliography: Y. Āryanpūr, *Az Ṣabā tā Nīmā* II, Tehran, 1350 Š./1971, pp. 446-64. M. Ṣadr-Hāšemī, *Tārīḵ-e jarā'ed wa majallāt-e Īrān*, Isfahan, 1327 Š./1948-1332 Š./1953, no. 111. M. M. Tarbīat, *Dānešmandān-e Āḏarbāījān*, Tehran, 1314 Š./1935, p. 405.

(N. Parvīn)

ĀZĀDSARV. Two bearers of this name are known.

1. A *mōbad* in the reign of Ḵosrow I Anōšīravān and one of the emissaries whom Ḵosrow sent to all corners of the kingdom in search of a dream interpreter (*Šāh-nāma* [Moscow] VIII, p. 111 vv. 990f.). Āzādsarv went to Marv, found in a school in the town, the youthful Bozorgmehr who claimed this ability, and brought him to the royal presence.

2. A scholar in the entourage of Aḥmad b. Sahl (d. 307/920; q.v.), governor of Marv in the second half of the 3rd/9th century. In the surviving national legends, Āzādsarv is named as the source of three stories: the story of Rostam and Šaḡād (*Šāh-nāma* VI, p. 322 vv. 1f.), The *Farāmarz-nāma* (mss. B.M. and Bib. Nat.), and the *Dāstān-e Šabrang* (ms. B.M.). The fact that all these stories belong to the Sīstān legend cycle lends credence to Ferdowsī's remark that Āzādsarv "knew many of Rostam's (battles by heart" (loc. cit., v. 4). The writings of Āzādsarv probably comprised more than the three stories just mentioned; it seems highly probable that all or most of the Sīstān legends, i.e., stories of Rostam and his family, recounted in the *Šāh-nāma* and elsewhere stem directly or indirectly from Āzādsarv.

Āzādsarv resided and did his literary work at Marv, although Ferdowsī's assertion that Āzādsarv "traced his ancestry to Sām son of Narīmān" (loc. cit., v. 4) could be interpreted as implying that he was of Sīstāni origin. He is described in the *Farāmarz-nāma* as the "cypress (*sarv*) of Māhān of Marv" and in the *Dāstān-e Šabrang* as the "foremost lamp of Māhān of Marv." Māhān, which is also mentioned in the *Šāh-nāma* (loc. cit., v. 30), is probably identical with Mīr Māhān, a suburban village of Marv (Eṣṭaḵrī, p. 260; Moqaddasī, p. 231; Yāqūt, IV, p. 714).

Bibliography: See also Ebn al-Aṯīr, repr. Gardīzī, ed. 'A. Ḥ. Ḥabībī. S. Ḥ. Taqīzāda, "Mašāhīr-e šo'arā-ye Īrān," *Kāva*, repr. in Ḥ. Yaḡmā'ī, ed., *Ferdowsī wa Šāh-nāma-ye ū*, Tehran, 1349 Š./1970. Ḏ. Ṣafā, *Ḥamāsa-sarā'ī dar Īrān*, Tehran, 1333 Š./1954.

(Dj. Khaleghi-Motlagh)

ĀZĀDVĀR (or ĀZADVĀR), a small town of Khorasan in the district (*kūra, rostāq*) of Jovayn, which flourished in medieval Islamic times, apparently down to the Il-khanid period. It lay eight farsakhs from Jājarm and at the western end of the very fertile Jovayn corridor between the Kūh-e Čaḡatāy to the south and the Kūh-e ʿAlī to the north, hence on the road connecting Besṭām and Gorgān with Nīšāpūr. The medieval geographers describe it as the chief town (*qaṣaba, madīna*) of Jovayn, populous and prosperous; 189 villages depended on it; it had fine mosques, markets, and a caravanserai; and it was surrounded by rich agricultural land producing cereals and fruits. Irrigation was mainly by *qanāt*s led down from the hills to the south. Maqdesī (Moqaddasī) describes the inhabitants of the district as cultured (*ahl adab*) and *aṣḥāb ḥadīṯ*, i.e., Shafiʿites; and from this district stemmed one of the greatest families of Shafiʿite *ʿolamāʾ* in Nīšāpūr—that of Abū Moḥammad ʿAbdallāh Jovaynī (d. 438/1047) and his son Abu'l-Maʿālī ʿAbd-al-Malek, the Emām al-Ḥaramayn (d. 478/1085). Samʿānī (*Ansāb* [Hyderabad] I, p. 76) names a considerable number of scholars and theologians with the *nesba* Āzādvār. The family of the historian ʿAlāʾ-al-dīn ʿAṭā Malek Jovaynī and his brother, the statesman Šams-al-dīn Moḥammad Ṣāḥeb(-e) Dīvān also hailed from Āzādvār. The poet Ašraf Ḡaznavī is buried there. During the eighth/fourteenth century, however, Āzādvār apparently declined; and Faryūmad, some distance to its south, replaced it as the center of the Jovayn district. Āzādvār is now the name of a subdistrict (*dehestān*) and its administrative center in the *bakš* of Jağatāy of the Sabzavār *šahrestān*. Near the present-day Āzādvār, in the center of the valley, are the remains of the medieval city, which were still marked by the remains of a lofty brick building in 1897 when Yate visited the area. A stage on the Tehran-Mašhad railroad is also called Āzādvār.

Bibliography: Eṣṭakrī, pp. 257, 284. Ebn Ḥawqal, pp. 428, 433, 456; tr. Kramers, pp. 414, 419, 440. Maqdesī, pp. 50, 318. *Ḥodūd al-ʿālam*, tr. Minorsky, p. 102, sec. 23. Yāqūt, I, p. 61; II, pp. 164-66. *Nozhat al-qolūb*, p. 174; tr. Le Strange, p. 169. ʿA. Mawlawī, *Āṯār-e bāstānī-e Korāsān* I, Mašhad, 2535 = 1355 Š./1976, p. 361. Le Strange, *Lands*, pp. 391-92. H. Halm, *Die Ausbreitung der šāfiʿitischen Rechtsschule von den Anfängen bis zum 8/14 Jahrhundert*, Wiesbaden, 1974, p. 77. J. Aubin, "Réseau pastoral et réseau caravanier: Les grand'routes du Khurassan à l'époque mongole," *Le monde iranien et l'Islam* I, Geneva and Paris, 1971, pp. 128-29. C. E. Yate, *Khurasan and Sistan*, London, 1900, pp. 390-91. Razmārā, *Farhang* IX, p. 14.

(C. E. BOSWORTH)

AZAL, Arabic theological term derived from Pahlavi *a-sar* "without head" and meaning, already in early Muʿtazilite *kalām*, "eternity *a parte ante*," as opposite to *abad* (q.v.), "eternity *a parte post*." It corresponds to the Greek term *ánarchon*. The etymology frequently brought up by Arab lexicographers which connects *azal* with *lam yazal* "he did not cease (being or doing something)" is certainly wrong (cf., e.g., Aḥmad b. Fāres, *Maqāyīs al-loḡa*, ed. ʿAbd-al-Salām Moḥammad Hārūn, Cairo, 1366-/1946- I, p. 97). But the assonance may account for the fact that the early Muslim theologians always circumscribed the eternal existence of God's attributes, etc., with the verbal expression *lam yazal.... wa-lā yazālo* (*ʿāleman, qāderan*, etc.; cf., among innumerable examples, Ašʿarī, *Maqālāt*, p. 156, l. 4). Nöldeke proposes to derive the word from Syr. *ezal*.

Bibliography: See also "Abad" and "Ḳedam" in *EI²* (with further references). For the etymology see G. Monnot, *Penseurs musulmans et religions iraniennes*, Paris, 1974, p. 152 n. 6; Th. Nöldeke, *Belegwörterbuch der klassischen arabischen Sprache*, Berlin, 1952, p. 21b; and cf. H. S. Nyberg, *A Manual of Pahlavi* II, Wiesbaden, 1974, p. 31.

(J. VAN ESS)

AZALI BABISM, designation of a religious faction which takes its name from Mīrzā Yaḥyā Nūrī Ṣobḥ-e Azal (about 1246-1330/1830-1912), considered by his followers to have been the legitimate successor to the Bāb (q.v.). A son of Mīrzā Bozorg Nūrī, a court official in the reign of Fatḥ-ʿAlī Shah, Yaḥyā was converted to Babism around 1260/1844, probably by his older half-brother, Mīrzā Ḥosayn-ʿAlī, the future Bahāʾallāh (q.v.), founder of the Bahai religion. From about 1848, Mīrzā Yaḥyā Ṣobḥ-e Azal was in regular contact with the Bāb, who was then in prison in Azerbaijan. His letters were well received by the Bāb, who claimed to find in them evidence of divine inspiration. Numerous references in writings by the Bāb from this period seem to provide strong evidence that Azal (also referred to as al-Waḥīd, Ṭalʿat al-Nūr, and al-Ṯamara) was regarded by him as his chief deputy following the deaths of most of the original Babi hierarchy, and as the future head of the movement. Earlier criteria for leadership within the sect had been priority of belief and membership of the *ʿolamāʾ* class, but Azal appears to have been selected on account of his innate capacity (*feṭra*) to receive divine knowledge and his ability to reveal verses—as had been the case with the Bāb himself.

After the Bāb's death in 1266/1850, Ṣobḥ-e Azal came to be regarded as the central authority within the movement, to whom its followers looked for some form of continuing revelation. Recognition of his authority was, however, only one of a number of doctrinal positions adopted by Babis in the 1850s and early 1860s. Numerous other claimants to theophanic status emerged in this period, some of whom were seen by Azal as rivals, while others appear to have been regarded as reflections enhancing the prestige of the original theophany (in accordance with the Bāb's theories concerning limitless descending emanations or manifestations of the Primal Will). It is particularly significant that, with few exceptions, these claimants were from non-clerical backgrounds like the Bāb and Azal—an indication of the new social role now emerging for Babism in its second phase.

Following the attempt by several Babis on the life of Nāṣer-al-dīn Shah in 1852 and an abortive uprising organized by Azal in the same year, he and other Babis chose to go into exile in Baghdad. Here he lived as generally-acknowledged head of the community until their removal to Istanbul in 1863. By adopting a policy of seclusion (*ḡayba*), Ṣobḥ-e Azal gradually alienated himself from a large proportion of the exiles, who began to give their allegiance to other claimants, notably Azal's half-brother, Bahā'allāh. During this period, Azal set up a network of agents (termed *šohadā'* "witnesses," i.e., of the Bayān) in Iraq and Iran. But this attempt to routinize further the charismatic authority of the faith seems to have clashed with the continuing appeal of original charisma within the movement and further weakened Azal's position.

In Edirne in 1866, Bahā'allāh made public his claim to be *man yoẓheroho'llāh* (he whom God shall manifest), the messianic figure of the *Bayān* (q.v.). Ṣobḥ-e Azal responded by asserting his own claims and resisting the wholesale changes in doctrine and practice introduced by his brother. His attempt to preserve traditional Babism proved largely unpopular, however, and his followers were soon in the minority. In 1868, bitter feuding between the two factions, leading to violence on both sides, induced Ottoman authorities to exile the Babis yet further. Bahā'allāh and his followers (now known as Bahais) were sent to Acre in Palestine, and Azal with his family and some adherents to Famagusta in Cyprus, where he remained until his death on 29 April 1912.

Ṣobḥ-e Azal, like his brother, was a prolific writer, his works consisting primarily of interpretations and elaborations of existing Babi doctrine, together with very large quantities of devotional pieces and poems. His best-known writings include the early *Ketāb-e nūr*, *Mostayqeẓ* (a refutation of claims advanced by Mīrzā Asadallāh K̲ū'ī Dayyān), the *Motammem-e Bayān* (a continuation of the Bāb's unfinished Persian *Bayān*), and the *Naḡamāt al-rūḥ*. One list of his writings gives 102 titles, some in several volumes, others very short.

Azali Babism represents the conservative core of the original Babi movement, opposed to innovation and preaching a religion for a non-clerical gnostic elite rather than the masses. It also retains the original Babi antagonism to the Qajar state and a commitment to political activism, in distinction to the quietist stance of Baha'ism. Paradoxically, Azali conservatism in religious matters seems to have provided a matrix within which radical social and political ideas could be propounded. If Babism represented the politicization of dissent within Shi'ism (Bayat, chap. 4) and Baha'ism stood for a return to earlier Shi'ite ideals of political quietism (MacEoin, "Babism to Baha'ism"), the Azali movement became a sort of bridge between earlier Babi militancy and the secularizing reform movements of the late Qajar period.

The first generation of Azalis were largely established Babis like Sayyed Moḥammad Eṣfahānī, Mollā Rajab-'Alī Qāher Eṣfahānī, Mollā Moḥammad Ja'far Narāqī, and Ḥājī Mīrzā Aḥmad Kāšānī. In the writings of men like Qāher and Narāqī, as in those of Azal, we find an abiding concern with sometimes obscure religious themes that remain well within the tradition established in the Bāb's later writings. But for the second generation of Azal's followers, "Azalī Babism provided... a creed which seemingly justified their political activism and growing nationalist consciousness" (Bayat, p. 130). Often loosely applied, Babi affiliation (which came increasingly to mean Azali affiliation) was applied to or used as a badge by several important individuals active in demanding social change in Iran, in a manner paralleling the connection with Freemasonry used by Malkom Khan and others. It is, in fact, important to remember that the *farāmūš-k̲ānas* were regarded by many as centers for Babi recruitment and prozelytization (Gobineau, *Religions et philosophies*, p. 274).

The best known of the early Azali nationalist reformers were Shaikh Aḥmad Rūḥī Kermānī (1272/1856-1314/1896) and Mīrzā 'Abd-al-Ḥosayn Kermānī (Āqā Khan Kermānī, q.v.), both of whom were executed along with Mīrza Ḥasan Khan K̲abīr al-Molk following the assassination of Nāṣer-al-dīn Shah in 1896. Rūḥī's father, Mollā Moḥammad Ja'far Tahbāḡallāhī Šayk̲-al-'olamā' (1241/1826-1311/1893) was an eminent *'ālem* from Kermān who had been an early convert to Babism; he is described by Browne as "one of the early promoters of the Liberal Movement in Persia" (*Persian Revolution*, p. 414). Rūḥī and Āqā Khan formed the core of a group of Azalis resident in Istanbul in the 1880s and 90s who had close links with political activists such as Mīrzā Malkom Khan (q.v.) and Sayyed Jamāl-al-dīn Afḡānī (q.v.). A number of Azalis, particularly Āqā Khan, were closely associated with the influential Persian-language newspaper *Ak̲tar* (q.v.), published in Istanbul under the editorship of Mīrzā Moḥammad Ṭāher Tabrīzī. Both Rūḥī and Āqā Khan wrote on Babism (they collaborated on the well-known work *Hašt behešt*) and were married to daughters of Ṣobḥ-e Azal, but it would be a mistake to overstress the importance of their Babi affiliation in their wider activities. Like other Azalis of this period, they seem to have used Babism as a motif for dissent, much as Malkom Khan or Afḡānī (and, indeed, Āqā Khan at times) used Islam. It is chiefly (one might say, properly) as free-thinkers and secularist reformers rather than as thoroughgoing Babis that they made their impact on contemporary affairs.

Edward Browne noted that it was "a remarkable fact that several very prominent supporters of the Persian Constitutional Movement were, or had the reputation of being, Azalīs" (*Materials for the Study of the Bābī Religion*, p. 221). Notable among these were: Mīrzā Jahāngīr Khan Šīrāzī (1292/1875-1326/1908), a teacher at the Dār al-Fonūn in Tehran and a member of various *anjomans*, who edited the important Constitutionalist newspaper *Ṣūr-e Esrāfīl* and was executed following the coup d'état of 1908; Mīrzā Naṣrallāh Eṣfahānī Malek-al-motakallemīn (1277/1861-1326/1908), a pro-Constitution cleric also killed in 1908, who was active with other free-thinking 'olamā' in promoting reform ideas; Shaikh Mahdī Šarīf Kāšānī (d. 1301 Š./1922), author of the Tārīk-e Ja'farī and Tārīk-e waqāye'-e mašrūṭīyat and a son of the important Azali cleric Mollā Moḥammad Ja'far Narāqī, who was a member of the Anǰoman-e Ma'āref in Tehran and head of the Šaraf school; Shaikh Moḥammad Afżal-al-molk Kermānī (1267/1851-1322/1904), a brother of Shaikh Aḥmad Rūḥī and a close associate of Afḡānī in Istanbul; his brother Shaikh Mahdī Baḥr-al-'olūm Kermānī, a member of the first and second Majlis; and Ḥāǰǰ Mīrzā Yaḥyā Dawlatābādī (1279/1862-1359/1939, q.v.), the well-known educationalist who served as a member of the second and fifth Majlis.

It is important to remember that these men, like their predecessors, acted as individuals rather than Azalis and that their ideas were frequently more secularist than religious in orientation. It must also be stressed that many individuals who have been suspected of harboring Babi sympathies or even of being Babis, such as Sayyed Jamāl-al-dīn Eṣfahānī, were hardly true converts: the mere suggestion of heretical leanings or association with known Azalis were often enough to earn a man the name. Neither Jamāl-al-dīn Afḡānī nor Mīrzā Moḥammad Reżā Kermānī, the assassin of Nāṣer-al-dīn Shah, were Babis, although both were often described as such. Abu'l-Ḥasan Mīrzā Šayk al-Ra'īs, a member of the Qajar family who was an outstanding reformer of the Constitutional period, has sometimes been called an Azali, whereas there is ample evidence that he was, in fact, a Baha'i.

Yaḥyā Dawlatābādī was appointed Ṣobḥ-e Azal's successor after the death of his own father, Ḥāǰǰ Mīrzā Hādī, but there is little evidence that he was actively involved in organizing the affairs of the sect. He did not write on Babi subjects, nor did any other Azalis of note emerge after the death of Azal to produce significant writing on the topic or to develop the original ideas of the religion. With the deaths of those Azalis who were active in the Constitutional period, Azali Babism entered a phase of stagnation from which it has never recovered. There is now no acknowledged leader nor, to the knowledge of the present writer, any central organization. Members tend to be secretive about their affiliation, converts are rare, and association appears to run along family lines. It is difficult to estimate current numbers, but these are unlikely to exceed one or two thousand, almost all of whom reside in Iran.

Bibliography: Apart from general works on Babism, the following may be consulted: Shaikh Aḥmad Rūḥī Kermānī and Āqā Khan Kermānī, *Hašt behešt*, n.p. (Tehran), n.d.; 'Ezzīya Kānom, *Tanbīh al-nā'emīn*, n.p. (Tehran), n.d., with a section by Aḥmad Rūḥī; Mollā Moḥammad Ja'far Narāqī, *Taḏkerat al-ḡāfelīn*, ms. Cambridge U.L., Browne F. 63; Mollā Rajab-'Alī Qāher, *Ketāb-e Mollā Rajab-'Alī Qahīr*, mss. Cambridge U. L., Browne F. 24. Lists of the works of Ṣobḥ-e Azal may be found in E. G. Browne, ed., *Materials for the Study of the Bābī Religion*, Cambridge, 1918, pp. 211-20; idem and R. A. Nicholson, *A Descriptive Catalogue of the Oriental MSS Belonging to the late E. G. Browne*, Cambridge, 1932, pp. 69-75. Manuscripts of numerous works by Azal are located in the Browne Collection at Cambridge, the British Library, and the Bibliothèque Nationale. The following have been published, all in Tehran without date: *Mostayqeẓ*, *Motammem-e Bayān*, and *Majmū'aī az āṯār-e Noqṭa-ye Ūlā wa Ṣobḥ-e Azal*. Further references may be found in: Mangol Bayat, *Mysticism and Dissent*, Syracuse, 1982, pp. 87, 129-31, 140-42, 149, 157-62, 167, 179, 180-83; H. Algar, *Mirza Malkum Khan*, Berkeley, Los Angeles, and London, 1973, pp. 46, 58-59, 215-16, 221-25; H. M. Balyuzi, *Bahā'u'llāh the King of Glory*, Oxford, 1980, chap. 40; idem, *Edward Granville Browne and the Bahā'ī Faith*, London, 1970, pp. 18-41, 45-46, 50-52; Bāmdād, *Rejāl* (on individuals mentioned); Yaḥyā Dawlatābādī, *Tārīk-e mo'āṣer yā ḥayāt-e Yaḥyā*, 3 vols., Tehran, 1336 Š./1957; Nāẓem-al-eslām Kermānī, *Tārīk-e bīdārī-e Īrānīān*, Tehran, 1332 Š./1953; N. Keddie, "Religion and Irreligion in Early Iranian Nationalism," *Comparative Studies in Society and History* 4, 1962, pp. 265-95, esp. pp. 273-74, 284-89, 292-95; D. MacEoin, "From Babism to Baha'ism," *Religion* 13, 1983, pp. 219-55.

(D. M. MacEoin)

A'ẒAM KHAN, AMIR MOḤAMMAD, the fifth son of Amir Dōst Moḥammad Khan and the third amir of the Moḥammadzay line, ruler of Afghanistan in 1284/1867-1285/1868. Born at Kabul in 1236/1820 from a daughter of Mollā Ṣādeq 'Alī, the *sardār* of the Bangaš tribe, he received a thorough education under his father's supervision (Fayż Moḥammad, *Serāj al-tawārīk*, p. 251; Kāfī, *Pādešāhān-e mota'akker* I, p. 197). A'ẓam Khan was with his father at the time of the latter's defeat in the first Anglo-Afghan war (q.v.) on 1 Jomādā II 1255/12 August 1839 and his subsequent flight to Bukhara. In 1256/1840 Dōst Moḥammad returned to Afghanistan and was eventually sent in exile to Calcutta, while A'ẓam Khan worked with other Afghan chiefs to stir the Andar and Solaymān-kēl tribes around Ḡazna against the British domination, later joining his father in India (*Serāj*, p. 160; Farrok, *Tārīk-e sīāsī*, p. 133). When general uprising forced the British to evacuate Afghanistan, Dōst Moḥammad Khan was allowed to return to Kabul, where he reascended the throne in 1259/1843 and appointed his sons to governorships of provinces, making A'ẓam Khan governor of Lōgar, south of Kabul. In 1268/1851, during the amir's absence on a campaign to subdue a revolt of the Tūkī and Hōtakī tribes, A'ẓam Khan was acting governor of Kabul (*Serāj*, p. 200; *Tārīk-e sīāsī*, p. 169). In 1272/1855 he subdued members of the royal family who were resisting his father at Qandahār. Later he was governor of Kūram (Kurram) and Kōst, south of Kabul. In

1274/1857 he was commissioned to pacify the lands north of the Hindu Kush range and to help his brother Amir Moḥammad Afżal Khan (q.v.; *Serāj*, pp. 220-31; *Tārīḵ-e sīāsī*, p. 173; *Pādešāhān-e mota'akker* I, p. 200). In Šawwāl, 1278/1862 he accompanied his father on the successful expedition to Herat, where Amir Dōst Moḥammad died on 21 Ḏu'l-ḥejja 1279/9 June 1863. From among his twenty-seven sons, Šēr-'Alī was chosen on 24 Ḏu'l-ḥejja to be the next amir. Although Moḥammad A'ẓam Khan is said to have obtained oaths of allegiance to Šēr-'Alī from the people in the Great Mosque of Herat, he secretly wrote to his elder brother Afżal Khan at Balḵ urging the latter to seize Kabul, he himself assuming governorship of Kūram and Ḵōst (*Pādešāhān-e mota'akker* I, p. 40; *Serāj* I, p. 252; *Tārīḵ-e sīāsī*, p. 202). Amir Šēr-'Alī Khan faced opposition from brothers and relatives on all sides, not least from A'ẓam Khan in Kūram who marched against Kabul in 1281/1864, but was defeated by a strong force sent out under the command of Moḥammad-Rafīq Khan Lūdīn, forcing him to escape to Rawalpindi in India (*Serāj* I, p. 264; *Tārīḵ-e sīāsī*, p. 203). When his nephew Sardar 'Abd-al-Raḥmān Khan, who had gone to Bukhara after suffering defeat in a battle at Bājgāh in Moḥarram, 1281/1864, sent a letter urging him to proceed to Balḵ, he immediately left Rawalpindi and made his way thither through Swat, Chitral, and Badakšān, arriving just at the time when Balḵ fell to 'Abd-al-Raḥmān (*Serāj* II, pp. 268, 278, 281, 289; Āṣaf Khan, *Tārīḵ-e Swāt*, p. 116). The two then marched on Kabul, captured the city, and released Afżal Khan from imprisonment at Ḡazna and placed him on the throne (*Serāj*, p. 289; Ḡobār, *Afḡānestān*, p. 591; *Tārīḵ-e sīāsī*, p. 210). A'ẓam Khan also captured Qandahār in Ramażān, 1283/1866; but facing resistance from Šēr-'Alī at Herat and hearing the news of A'ẓam Khan's illness he had to return to Kabul. Afżal Khan died at Kabul in Jomādā II 1284/1867 and Moḥammad A'ẓam Khan succeeded him as the amir (*Serāj*, p. 295; *Tārīḵ-e sīāsī*, p. 215; *Pādešahān-e mota'akker* I, p. 197; Afḡānī, *Tatemmat al-bayān*, p. 135; *Afḡānestān*, p. 591); and his accession was officially recognised by the Governor General of India on 26 Ša'bān 1284/1867 (Lahore Archives). At this time Sayyed Jamāl-al-dīn Afḡānī (Asadābādī) was attached to his court at Kabul (Afḡānī, *Asnād o madārek*, p. 156).

A'ẓam Khan's rule was marked by civil war and atrocities committed by his sons (Nūrī, *Golšan-e emārat*, p. 127). Šēr-'Alī marched from Herat against Qandahār and Kabul, defeating A'ẓam in battles at Šeš-gāv and Zana-ḵān. A'ẓam left Kabul in Jomādā I 1285/1868, escaping to Sīstān and eventually reaching Mašhad (1286/1869) via Bīrjand (*Serāj* II, pp. 296, 307, 314). Late in the same year he set out for Tehran, but fell ill when he reached Šāhrūd and died there at the age of fifty. His remains were buried in the nearby cemetery of Bāyazīd Besṭāmī (*Serāj* II, p. 325; *Tārīḵ-e sīāsī*, p. 228). The length of his reign was eleven months.

Bibliography: N. M. Nūrī, *Golšan-e emārat*, Kabul, 1335 S./1956. Y. 'A. Ḵāfī, *Padešāhān-e mota'akker-e Afḡānestān*, Kabul, 1334 Š./1955. M. M. Ḡobār, *Afḡānestān dar masīr-e tārīḵ*, Kabul, 1346 Š./1967. Fayż Moḥammad, *Serāj al-tawārīḵ* II, Kabul, 1331/1913. M. Farroḵ, *Tārīḵ-e sīāsī-e Afḡānestān* I, Tehran, 1315 Š./1935. Moḥammad Zardār Khan Nāgār *Ṣawlat-e afḡānī* (in Urdu), Lucknow, 1876. Amir 'Abd-al-Raḥmān Khan, *Pand-nāma-ye donyā wa dīn*, Kabul, n.d. Sayyed Jamāl-al-dīn Afḡānī (Asadābādī), *Tatemmat al-bayān fī ta'rīḵ al-Afḡān*, Cairo, 1901. Ī. Afšār and A. Mahdawī, eds., *Majmū'a-ye asnād o madārek-e čāp našoda dar bāra-ye Sayyed Jamāl-al-dīn mašhūr ba Afḡānī*, Tehran, 1342 Š./1963. M. Āṣaf Khan, *Tārīḵ-e Swāt* (in Paštō), Peshawar, 1959. D. R. Munawwar Khan, *Anglo-Afghan Relations*, Peshawar, 1964.

('A. Ḥabībī)

ĀŽANG (Wrinkle), a Persian newspaper which commenced publication in Esfand, 1332 Š./February, 1954, and lasted until 1353 Š./1974. The license-holder and director was Sayyed Kāẓem Mas'ūdī. Featuring news and political comments, *Āžang* was one of the twelve licenced dailies in Tehran at that time, but in most years only three or four issues per week were actually produced. It consisted initially of four and later of eight pages measuring 35 × 50 cm with seven columns per page. Illustrations and numerous official notices filled much of the space. The first editor, was Īraj Nabawī, who was followed by Reżā'Azmī. Though not an organ of the Mellīyūn Party (the governmental party during the premiership of Manūčehr Eqbāl 1336 Š./1957-1339 Š./1960), *Āžang* strongly supported its policies. Sayyed Kāẓem Mas'ūdī was elected to the 22nd Majlis in 1346 Š./1967 and to the 23rd Majlis in 1350 Š./1971 on the then ruling Īrān-e Novīn party's ticket.

Under the same publication license, a weekly newspaper for Iranians living abroad, named *Āžang-e havā'ī*, was launched in 1344 Š./1965 and kept afloat for over ten years. Edited by Farīda Malekī and Reżā 'Azmī, it had twelve pages measuring 21 × 22 cm.

Also on the strength of *Āžang*'s license, another weekly, *Āžang-e jom'a*, was published in the years 1342 Š./1963-1347 Š./1968 under the direction of Farhang Farrahī. Mainly cultural in content, it had eight to twelve pages of the same size as those of the daily *Āžang*. This weekly paid special attention to modern literature both Persian and Western, and attracted considerable interest. Several modernist poets and authors contributed to it.

In addition to copies preserved in libraries in Iran, there is an incomplete set of the daily *Āžang* in the Library of Congress at Washington.

Bibliography: M. Barzīn, *Sayr-ī dar maṭbū'āt-e Īrān 1343-53*, Tehran, 1344 Š./1965, pp. 33, 38-39.

(N. Parvīn)

AẒAR "fire." See articles under ĀDUR.

ĀZAR, father of Abraham. See EBRĀHĪM.

ĀẔAR (ĀḎAR) **BĪGDELĪ**, ḤĀJJ LOṬF-ʿALĪ BĪG B. ĀQĀ KHAN BĪGDELĪ ŠĀMLŪ (fl. 1134/1721-1195/1781), poet and author of a *taḏkera* (biographical anthology) of about 850 Persian poets, complied in 1174/1760 and dedicated to Karīm Khan Zand (r. 1163/1750-1193/1779).

Āẕar belonged to the Syrian (Šāmlū) branch of the Bīgdelī (Begdīllū) tribe, which had moved to Iran in Tīmūr's time. Some of his relatives were men of distinction: Three were sent on embassies to the Ottoman empire during his lifetime, and several held important offices. He was born in Isfahan, where his family had lived since the early Safavid period. His birth almost coincided with the Afghan invasion of Iran and the fall of Isfahan, which prompted his whole family to flee to Qom, where he stayed fourteen years. Later in about 1148/1736, his father was appointed governor of Lār and the coasts of Fārs by Nāder Shah. After his father's death, Āẕar made a pilgrimage to Mecca, visited the holy places in Iraq, and later on went to Mašhad, where his arrival coincided with Nāder's return from India. He accompanied Nāder's troops to Māzandarān, Azerbaijan, and ʿErāq-e ʿAjam, and finally settled at Isfahan. After the assassination of Nāder, he joined the services of the Afsharid ʿĀdel Shah (q.v.) and Ebrāhīm Shah and the Safavid Esmāʿīl III and Solaymān III, and eventually retired to his small estate near Qom and turned his attention to poetry. He reportedly lost 7,000 verses of his poetry during the sack of Isfahan by ʿAlī-Mardān Khan Baḵtīārī, but a *dīvān* comprising *qaṣīdas*, *ḡazals*, and *qeṭʿas*, and a *maṯnawī*, *Yūsof o Zolayḵā*, have reached us. He was much influenced by his paternal uncle Walī (Walīy) Moḥammad Khan Bīgdelī (killed 1177/1763) and Mīr Sayyed ʿAlī Moštāq Eṣfahānī (d. 1192/1778) who was his master in the art of poetry.

Āẕar is known mainly because of his *taḏkera*, the *Ātaškada-ye Āḏar* (Āẕar's fire temple). Using terms relevant to fire he has divided it into two main chapters which he has called *majmeras* (cansers). The first *majmera* is further divided into a *šoʿla* (flame) on the poetry of kings, princes, and amirs; three *aḵgars* (embers) on the poets of Iran, Tūrān (Central Asia), and India; and a *forūḡ* (light) on poetesses. The three *aḵgars* are further divided, in terms of geographical divisions, into five, three, and three *šarāras* (sparks) respectively, opening each one with a brief description of the region involved. The second *majmera* comprises two *partows* (beams); the first *partow* treats poets contemporary with the author and the second one contains the author's biography and a selection of his poetry. Poets are represented under their pen-names, not their personal names, and the book is generally arranged in alphabetical order. The cited verses of each poet are ordered according to the rhyme.

Āẕar's prose in the *Ātaškada*, despite containing certain weaknesses common to Persian writings of the 12th/18th century, is generally simple and fluent. In the preface, he uses rhymed prose, into which he fits words having some connection with "fire;" his theme is the defense of poetry. The long introduction to the account of contemporary poets contains some fine passages of poetic prose. For contemporary poetry, his principle was to give first choice to verses which he had heard directly from the poets themselves, but his claims that, in his selection from earlier poets, he had carefully studied their *dīvāns* is discredited by careful examination of earlier *taḏkeras* available to him (see Golčīn-e Maʿānī, *Taḏkerahā* I, p. 4).

Āẕar was one of the pioneers of the revulsion against the so-called *sabk-e hendī*, Indian style (see BĀZGAŠT-E ADABĪ), and as such is frankly censorious of the poetry of Ṣāʾeb and his followers; but for those such as Moštāq, who rejected the Indian style and sought to revive the idiom of the early poets, he has nothing but praise. For some poets, he gives detailed biographies, but for most he finds two or three lines sufficient; he is equally sparing in his selections from their work.

Bibliography: Āẕar Bīgdelī, *Ātaškada*, lithog. ed., Bombay, 1277/1860; ed. Ḥ. Sādāt Nāṣerī, 3 vols., Tehran, 1337 Š./1958-1341 Š./1962. M. T. Bahār (Malek-al-šoʿarā), *Sabkšenāsī* III, Tehran 1337 Š./1958, p. 318. M. Dabīrsīāqī, in *Dāneš-nāma* I/1, Tehran, 1355 Š./1976, p. 15. Browne, *Lit. Hist. Persia* IV, pp. 282-84. Ḵayyāmpūr, *Soḵanvarān*, p. 2. Golčīn-e Maʿānī, *Taḏkerahā* I, pp. 14-17.

(J. MATĪNĪ)

ĀẔAR (ĀḎAR) KAYVĀN (b. between 1529 and 1533; d. between 1609 and 1618), a Zoroastrian high priest and native of Fārs who emigrated to India and became the founder of the Zoroastrian *Ešrāqī* or illuminative School. The literature produced by this school constitutes a Zoroastrian *Ešrāqī* literature. It is dominated by *Ešrāqī* doctrine and terminology and is the Zoroastrian response to the great project of Šayḵ al-Ešrāq Šehāb-al-dīn Yaḥyā Sohravardī (q.v.; d. 587/1191), which was the revival in Islamic Iran of the philosophy of Light taught by reputed sages of ancient Persia. Āẕar Kayvān and his immediate successor Kay Ḵosrow b. Esfandīār, were designated as the heads of the *Ešrāqī* School.

The Islamic response to Sohravardī was given by his first commentators, and above all with the development under the Safavid dynasty of the School of Isfahan, with which Āẕar Kayvān and his disciples were contemporaries, by Ṣadr-al-dīn Šīrāzī (Mollā Ṣadrā) (d. 1050/1640) and his students. Thus there is a synchronism in the development of the philosophy or theosophy of the "Light of the East" (*Ḥekmat al-ešrāq*) among the Shiʿite thinkers of Iran and these Zoroastrian spiritual leaders. This synchronism is partially explained by the strong cultural and spiritual contacts between India and Iran occasioned by the "ecumenical" religious reform undertaken by the Mughal emperor of India, Akbar Shah (q.v.; r. 963-1014/1556-1605). This helped produce a sort of philosophical and mystical revival in the Zoroastrian milieu, which up to that time seems to have remained largely outside the main currents of thought that had enlivened Iranian Islam. It was only then that the entire system of cosmology, anthropology, psychology, and mystical theosophy of Iranian Islam became included in this Zoroastrian *Ešrāqī* literature. Admittedly, it would be anachronistic to try to trace these elements back to the pre-Islamic era, yet these books had so many Zoroastrian resonances that the Parsis of India took an interest in them, considered them as at least "semi-Parsi" works, and published them.

Methodology. It is very important to be clear about the methodological postulate underlying Zoroastrian *Ešrāqī* literature. This is an area in which historical criticism has no useful role. If we want to deal with anything other than apocryphal or "fictitious" writings we must use the kind of method designated by the German term *Formgeschichte*, which concerns itself with literary forms and types of composition. One of the results of Sohravardī's work was to bind together the prophetic tradition of Zoroaster and the ecstatic holy sovereigns (Ferēdūn, Kay Ḵosrow), with the Semitic prophetic tradition of the Bible and the Koran. This combination was achieved by means of the coincidence between the concepts of the Zoroastrian "Light of Glory" (*X'arnah*, Persian *Ḵorra*), the "Muhammadan Light" (*Nūr-e Moḥammadī*), and the *Sakīna* (the Hebrew *Shekhina*, "Presence of the Divine Glory") as sources of the prophetic charisma. Thus it is understandable how a circle such as that of Āẕar Kayvān might have felt the need for something like a "Bible" of the prophets (*vaḵšūrān, vaḵšvārān*) of ancient Iran. The disciples of Āẕar Kayvān believed that they received in visionary encounters the teachings of the ancient sages of Persia, Greece, and India, and as a result their literary productions belong to a type of hierology quite familiar in other systems of gnosis. The facts and events of their works do not belong to the actual, empirical history of this world; instead, they have that reality *sui generis* of facts which take place and unfold in that intermediate world which the *Ešrāqīān* called the *mundus imaginalis* (*'ālam al-meṯāl*). It is from this perspective that we must also understand the lengthy chains of ancestry, all of them going back to the great figures of the pre-Islamic era, which these disciples gave themselves. For each member of a religious community is free to choose his own spiritual ancestry, to choose his "patron saint" and the "heavenly witness" under whose protection he places himself and who serves for him as model and guide. In other words, we are dealing here with biographies based on the style of hagiographies, and the method of purely historical criticism is of no use in dealing with such compositions if one wishes to understand their intentions and the experiences which they wish to express by means of the genealogies they adopt, the stories they tell, etc.

Sources. Concerning the sources at our disposal, we are caught in a bit of a circle. On the one hand, we owe the better part of our information concerning Āẕar Kayvān and his disciples to the *Dabestān-e maḏāheb* (The school of religious doctrines; q.v.), a source rich in facts and information not found elsewhere. On the other hand, the principle sources for the *Dabestān* in this area are either the books of those very disciples, or even the author's personal encounters with some of them. It was written in India, not by a certain "Moḥsen Fānī" (as was long believed), but by Mōbed Šāh (1615-70), during the reign of Awrangzēb (1658-1707; q.v.). The author made many journeys through today's Pakistan, and undoubtedly went as far as Mašhad in Iran. He was acquainted with a great number of religious and scientific personalities from Parsism, Hinduism, Judaism, Christianity, Islam. A bad English translation of the *Dabestān* was done by Shea and Troyer (Paris, 1843; partial repr.: New York, 1937). The two translators, who did not work together, seem to have been quite ignorant of any of the technical vocabulary involved, and their work is full of gaps and mistaken readings. Hence the *Dabestān* still needs a critical edition and rigorous translation, as is also true of the Zoroastrian *Ešrāqī* literature in its entirety.

The *Dabestān* is divided into twelve books. Each of these books is called a *ta'līm* (instruction), and is subdivided into chapters called *naẓar* (insight). In the first book, comprising fifteen *naẓar*s the author informs us as to the condition and the doctrine of the Parsis (*Pārsīān*), as they were known to him at his time and in the areas with which he was acquainted. He groups the Parsis into fourteen different communities (*gorūh*), each with various names. The *Dabestān* is our only source for this information. The first of these communities were the Sepāsīān, also known as the Yazdānīān, (present-day) Ābādīān, Āẕar Hūšangīān, etc. This is the group to which Āẕar Kayvān is supposed to have belonged.

The hagiography of Āẕar Kayvān, son of Āẕar Gašasb, traces his ancestry back to Sāsān the Fifth (cf. the *Dasātīr-nāma*, see below) then through Sāsān the First to the Kayanids, Gayōmart, and finally to Mahābād, the figure who appeared at the very beginning of the great cycle of prophecy, according to the "Bible of the Prophets of Ancient Iran," and who seems to be none other than the primordial Adam. His mother was named Šīrīn; her ancestry goes back to Ḵosrow I Anōšīravān. Already as a young boy, Āẕar Kayvān showed signs of his calling to the contemplative life. Through dream visions, he received the teaching of the ancient sages, which allowed him to give extraordinary replies to the questions which were asked of him at the *madrasa* where he was a student, and which won him the nickname *Ḏu'l-'olūm* (master of the sciences). Certain references allow us to determine that his residence was at Eṣṭaḵr (about a hundred kilometers north of Shiraz), where he spent the first thirty or forty years of his life in contemplation and where he assembled his first disciples. Around 1570, drawn by the religious revival which was taking place in India around Akbar Shah, he left with them to settle down in Patna, where he lived until he died at around eighty-five years of age.

Already at Eṣṭaḵr, the most diverse personalities, including certain Muslim figures, had come to ask his spiritual advice: One day, for instance, someone expressed to him his surprise at hearing the Shi'ites attack and vilify two such eminent personages as Abū Bakr and ʿOmar, the first two caliphs, who were highly honored by all the Sunnites. Āẕar Kayvān replied that even though the Iranians had formed their Shiʿite faith by incorporating into it a great many elements of their ancient Zoroastrian faith, they could still not forget that the Arabs had attacked and ravaged the religion of their forefathers and destroyed its monuments.

Āẕar Kayvān and his disciples avoided, so we are told, all contact with the profane and observed a strict esotericism. They advised people to keep and to deepen their own religion, because following the same spiritual path as themselves in no way depended on some external act of "conversion."

This last characteristic helps us to understand the special attraction for Āẕar Kayvān of the project of religious reform which was pursued by Akbar Shah. Akbar, a man of profoundly mystical temperament, had conceived the notion of a "divine religion" (*dīn-e elāhī*), a sort of "ecumenicism," which would be able to assemble all religious spirits in a single spiritual community capable of overcoming all confessional barriers and limits. Around him he set up a sort of academy made up of scholars, artists, and representatives of all the different religions. This circle included Parsi *dastūr*s and *mōbed*s, Christian friars, and representatives of Hinduism and Islam, especially, in the latter case, of Sufism. Until then no one has sufficiently emphasized the influence of the *Ešrāqī* doctrine of Sohravardī in the spirit of this ecumenicism. One witness to that influence, among others, is the literature created by the School of Āẕar Kayvān. However, Āẕar Kayvān himself does not seem to have had any direct contact with the court of Akbar. He was content to set up residence at Patna (a site which also evokes the most ancient memories of Buddhism in India), in the company of his disciples, both old and new.

The author of the *Dabestān* gives us a considerable amount of firsthand, detailed information concerning these disciples, several of whom he knew personally. Some of them were Zoroastrians, others were not. Of this latter group, our author mentions seven Muslims, two Jewish Rabbis, a Christian, and a Brahmin. The majority of the Zoroastrians were *mōbed*s, from the priestly class. The *Dabestān* gives a lengthy account of around twelve Zoroastrians whom the author had known personally and mentions another twelve. Below is a list of authors of Persian books that have survived to our own day. These are the authors of the "Zoroastrian *Ešrāqī* literature," and the author of the *Dabestān* states (book 11) that everything professed by the *Ešrāqīān* is in complete concordance with what he has explained (in book 1) concerning the ancient religion of the Iranians. First are listed their names and biographical data, and then the titles and contents of their works.

Authors. Kay Ḵosrow b. Esfandīār, though not Āẕar Kayvān's son, was his spiritual successor at the head of his school, and inspired the composition or "translation" several books.

Farzāna Bahrām b. Farhād b. Esfandīār traced his ancestry back as far as Gōdarz Kešvād, the minister of King Kay Ḵosrow. He knew Pahlavi, Persian, and Arabic, was well versed in philosophy, theology, mystical theosophy, and alchemy, and is the author of an important work entitled *Šārestān*. . . . He was the close confidant of Āẕar Kayvān, whom he met at Patna, rather than in Persia. He states that it was Āẕar Kayvān who first opened for him the way to the angelic worlds. Earlier, in Persia, he had been in close contact with Ḵʷāja Jamāl-al-dīn Maḥmūd a disciple of Jalāl-al-dīn Davānī, the famous commentator of Sohravardī's *Book of the Temples of Light*. He died at Lahore in 1624 A.D.

Mōbed Sorūš b. Kayvān b. Kamgār, who traced his paternal ancestry to the prophet Zoroaster and his maternal ancestry to Jāmāsp, was a student of Āẕar Kayvān and of Farzāna Bahrām, who taught him the Islamic sciences. He led an ascetic life, marked by thaumaturgical deeds. He is the author of the *Zar-e dast-afšār* and of two other books which are known to us today only by their titles. He died shortly after 1627.

Mōbed Ḵodājūy (He who searches for God) b. Nāmdār. A native of Herat, he joined Āẕar Kayvān at Eṣṭaḵr, after seeing him in a dream. He is the author of the *Jām-e Kay Ḵosrow*. He died in Kashmir in 1631, the same year in which the author of the *Dabestān* had encountered him there.

Mōbed Ḵūšī for many years searched for a guide among the masters of the different religions; each of them sought to convert him to his own way. Finally the angel Sorūš advised him in a dream that until that time he had only investigated the tiny brooks and tributary streams; now he must await the great river, or rather, the ocean itself. This ocean was the spiritual teaching of Āẕar Kayvān, whom he went to meet in the company of Mōbed Ḵodājūy. He is the author of the *Zāyanda-rūd*.

Farzāna Bahrām b. Faršād, called Bahrām "Junior" (*kūčak*), so as not to confuse him with the Farzāna Bahrām already mentioned above. The author of the *Dabestān* met him in Kashmir in 1622. Learned in Arabic, Persian, Hindi, and even Farangī, he translated into Persian all the Arabic works of Sohravardī. He also wrote a book entitled *Aržang-e Mānī* (Mani's picture book). However, no manuscript of any of these works has been discovered. Bahrām "Junior" died at Lahore in 1638.

Mōbed Hūš, whom the author of the *Dabestān* also met in Kashmir in 1622, was himself the author of the *Ḵʷēš-tāb*. It is possible that he was not an immediate disciple of Āẕar Kayvān, but belonged to his school.

Two individuals originally from Shiraz who are mentioned in the *Dabestān* (book 9) are Ḥakīm Elāhī Hērbad, a Zoroastrian, and Ḥakīm Mīrzā, a *sayyed* from Shiraz. Both of them are designated as *Ešrāqīān*. The works of Sohravardī were as familiar to them as they were to Farzāna Bahrām "Junior," and they had made Sohravardī's "Book of Hours" the scripture for their own personal spiritual practice.

Works. At the head of these books comes the *Dasātīr-nāma* (The book of sages; in fact, the original term is *vaḵšūr*, or prophet, which recurs repeatedly in the text).

This "Bible of the prophets of ancient Iran" (cf. the methodological remarks above) is one of the basic sources on which the *Dabestān* bases its account of the theological situation of the Parsis in its own time, to such a degree that the two works are really inseparable from each other. This book, after having been praised to the skies at the time of its discovery—by the Orientalist William Jones, among others, as a document of ancient Persia and a complement of the Avesta, was then just as quickly relegated to oblivion as a cheap apocryphal trick. The truth of the matter is that this book deserved neither that original excess of honor nor its subsequent indignity and neglect. Although it has nothing to do with the theology of the Avesta, on the other hand, even though it does not bear the name of any author, it does have all the interest of the sort of book that could blossom forth in the entourage of Āẕar Kayvān. The work presents itself in two languages. The first has not been deciphered. It may be in a secret code or cipher (in which one letter is substituted for another), a special jargon, or in one of the dialects which was current in certain Zoroastrian communities. This "original" text is matched by a commentary and second version in very pure Persian, avoiding the use of any Arabic words. Both this Persian version and its commentary are stated to be the work of one "Sāsān the Fifth," whose own book concludes this "Bible" and who is supposed to have lived under the Sasanian ruler K̲osrow Parvēz (r. A.D. 590-628).

All the other books of the School of Āẕar Kayvān also claim to be the work of very ancient personages; the mōbeds mentioned above only claim to be their "translators." In general, these other books only repeat or amplify themes that are already given in the *Dasātīr-nāma*. However, even though this "Bible" of the prophets of ancient Iran has a speculative rather than a historical origin, it does contain allusions to a great many events which were familiar parts of the traditional histories. What actually predominates in this work is the influence of Sohravardī's "Zoroastrian Neoplatonism." The philosopher can have no doubt about this, once he has read the "Book of Mahābād" and the "Book of Sāsān the First." From the very beginning, it is the entire Avicennan cosmology and angelology, as revised by Sohravardī, that finds its expression in this text and commentary. Only the Arabic vocabulary has been completely changed over to Persian words. Thus the *Ešrāqīān* are here the *Gašasbīān* or the *Partovīān*. The hierarchical Intelligences are designated by the names of the *Amahraspandān*, or Zoroastrian archangels. The Angel or "Lord" of each species (*rabb al-naw'*, which Sohravardī identified with the Platonic idea-archetype of each species) is translated by *Parvadgar-ferešta* or "guardian angel" (cf. the Avestan concepts of *fravarti* or *fravaši*, and *ratu*). The "Light of Lights" (*Nūr al-anwār*) here becomes *Šēdān-šēd*; the subtle, imperishable body of the beings of Paradise is here called the *tan-e bartar*, etc.

Jām-e Kay K̲osrow (the "Cup, or Grail, of Kay-K̲osrow"), written by Mōbed K̲odājūy. Several other disciples had asked him to give a commentary on the contemplative visions of Āẕar Kayvān, the "guide of the *Ešrāqīān*." Since one of those who made this request was Kay K̲osrow b. Esfandīār, Āẕar Kayvān's successor, the author dedicated the book to him. The title, while containing the name of the man to whom it was dedicated, also evokes a famous theme in the heroic and mystical epic literature of Iran. The book is also known as *Mokāšafāt-e Kayvān* (The visionary experiences of Āẕar Kayvān). The Persian text was published in 1848, along with a Gujarati translation, by Sayyed 'Abd-al-Fattāḥ, known as Mīr Ašraf 'Alī.

Šārestān (*Šahrestān*)*-e dāneš wa golestān-e bīneš*, (The city of knowledge and the rose garden of vision), the work of Farzāna Bahrām b. Farhād, more commonly known as ***Šārestān-e čahār čaman*** (The city of four gardens). It is a voluminous work of some 800 pages divided into four books: 1. Cosmogony (Sohravardī is cited as early as p. 4) and traditional history of the prophet-kings of ancient Iran, from Hūšang up to Kay Qobād; 2. The Kayanid kings, from Kay K̲osrow b. Kay Qobād up to Lohrāsp; the prophet Zoroaster and the *Ešrāqīān* theosophers; Esfandīār, up to Dārāb (Darius) and Alexander; 3. The Arsacids (*Aškānīān*) and the Sasanians; 4. Cosmography and geography. This is the type of work in which the insertion of the philosophy of *Ešrāq* into the sacred history of the prophets of ancient Iran is already an accomplished fact, and the Avesta and other traditions are interpreted in light of the teachings of the Šayk̲ al-Ešrāq. This corresponds to what had already become the traditional conception of the history of philosophy in Šahrazūrī (13th cent.), including the Iranian origin of the *Ešrāqīān*, the destruction of all the documents of the ancient Zoroastrian religion as a result of Alexander's conquests, etc.

The following four books were published together in a collection entitled *Āyīn-e Hūšang* (The religion of Hūšang).

K̲ᵛēš-tāb (Burning by itself), a term equivalent to *K̲ᵛod-sūz*, the name of a fire-temple in Azerbaijan. The book was supposedly written by one Ḥakīm K̲ᵛēštāb, a disciple of Sāsān the Fifth, during the reign of K̲osrow II Parvēz (590-628); it was originally entitled *Garzan-e dāneš* (Crown of knowledge). The actual author, who claims to be only the Persian "translator" of his own day, is the Mōbed Hūš (see above), a disciple of Āẕar Kayvān, who also began this work at the request of Kay K̲osrow b. Esfandīār.

Zar-e dastafšār by Mōbed Sorūš is a commentary on the sayings of the prophets and sages of ancient Persia, various aspects of *Ešrāqī* cosmology and angelology, etc. The title literally means "gold which has been brought to such a malleable state that it can be worked by hand," and may refer to a certain gold which was part of the treasure of K̲osrow Parvēz. The alchemical allusion in this title may actually refer to Āẕar Kayvān himself. (J. J. Modi, for some reason, read the title as *Daštafšār*, while Shea and Troyer made it out to be *Zardošt afšar* "Companion of Zoroaster"!)

Zāyanda-rūd (The river that gives life) was supposedly written by a sage by the name of Zenda Āzarm in the time of K̲osrow II Parvēz. The "translator"-author is in fact Mōbed K̲ūšī (see above), who wrote this work at the request of Kay K̲osrow b. Esfandīār, Āẕar Kayvān's successor. J. J. Modi mentions it under the title *Zenda-rūd* ("The living river" or "The river of life"); this is also the name of the river which goes through Isfahan. In either case, the allusion is the same, and agrees with the original title of the book, which is supposed to have been *Čašma-ye zendagī* (The fountain of life, Arabic *'Ayn al-ḥayāt*), a traditional term which appears in all the treatises of mystical theosophy and Sufism.

Zawra or *Zawra-ye bāstān*, a short treatise which closes this collection. A marginal note explains that *zawra* is the equivalent of *sūra* "sura" or chapter of the Koran. This "Ancient chapter" was supposedly the work of one *Āẕarpažūh* (Fire-seeker).

The biographical and bibliographical notices above all concern Āẕar Kayvān's Zoroastrian disciples. We have also briefly mentioned above some of his non-Zoroastrian disciples, whose presence is an illustration of the non-confessional character of his school. Among these non-Zoroastrian disciples, it is important to point out at least the names of two eminent personalities of Shi'ite Iran. One was Mīr Abu'l-Qāsem Fendereskī, a contemporary of Mīr Dāmād and Mollā Ṣadrā Šīrāzī, and a major figure in the School of Isfahan, notorious for his boldness in metaphysics as well as in his social behavior. He was also involved in the project of translating Sanskrit texts into Persian. The other was the eminent *mojtahed* and great figure in Imamite Shi'ism during the Safavid period; Shaikh Bahā'-al-dīn 'Āmelī, "Šayk̲-e Bahā'ī," the close friend of Mīr Dāmād, and like him, one of the intellectual masters of a great number of the students of the School of Isfahan. According to the account which Farzāna Bahrām "Junior" gave directly to the author of the *Dabestān*, Shaikh Bahā'-al-dīn's encounter with Āẕar Kayvān was so successful that the Shaikh considered himself as belonging to Āẕar Kayvān's circle. This is a little known feature in the biography of this famous *mojtahed*.

Thus we can perceive the outlines of a remarkable cultural cycle, as Iranism, preserved first in Iran itself, moves to India in a pilgrimage toward those who will keep alive its flame there, and then returns to the very heart of Iran, in the person of these masters of the School of Isfahan.

Bibliography: *Dabestān-e maḏāheb*, litho., Bombay, 1267/1850-51. *The Desātīr, or the Sacred Writings of the Ancient Persian Prophets, together with the Commentary of the Fifth Sāsān*, tr. Mulla Firuz bin Kaus, 2nd ed., Dhunjeebhoy Jamsetjee Medhora, Bombay, 1888. (The first edition of the "original" text of this work, with the Persian version and an English translation of the *Dasātīr-Nāma* by the Dastūr Mollā Fīrūz, was published at Bombay in 1818, in two volumes. A new lithographed edition of the text and Persion version was made in Iran, under the title *Dasātīr-e āsmānī*, without any date other than the words "under the reign of Nāṣer-al-dīn Shah Qājār."). *Jām-e Kay K̲osrow*, ed. Mīr Ašraf 'Alī, [Bombay], 1848. Farzāna Bahrām b. Farhād, *Ketāb-e šarestān-e kollīyāt-e čahār čaman*, ed. Mōbed Bahrām Bēžan, Mōbed K̲odādād, Mōbed Ardašīr K̲odābanda, and Rostam Pūr Bahrām Sorūš, Bombay, 1279/1862, 2nd ed., 1328/1919. *Ā'īn-e Hūšang*, a collection of four Parsi-Persian treatises published by Mīrzā Bahrām Rostam Naṣrābādī, Bombay, 1295/1878. Jivanji Mamshedhi Modi, "A Parsi High Priest (Dastūr Azar Kaiwan, 1529-1614 A.D.) with his Zoroashtrian Disciples in Patna, in the 16th and 17th Century A.C.," *Journal of the K. R. Cama Oriental Institute* 20, 1932, pp. 1-85. Shihāboddīn Yaḥyā Sohravardī, Shaykh-e Ishrāq, *Œuvres philosophiques et mystiques* I, ed. with French prolegomena by H. Corbin; 2nd ed., Tehran, 1976, pp. lvff. of the French section. H. Corbin, *En Islam iranien: aspects spirituels et philosophiques*, Paris, 1971-72, II: *Sohravardī et les Platoniciens de Perse*, pp. 354ff.

(H. CORBIN)

[The *Dasātīr*, mentioned in this article, has been proved a fabrication of the time of the Mughal emperor, Akbar, and was almost certainly written in India, apparently when Akbar's search for an ecumenical religion encouraged religious invention. Its contents have no relation to Zoroastrianism as embodied in the authentic literature of that religion. It contains gross absurdities, and claims, names and events born of fantastic imagination. Its text consists of unintelligible gibberish and the so-called commentary is in affected "pure" Persian, devoid of any Arabic words. (See Sheriarji D. Bharucha, *The Dasâtîr*, Bombay, 1907; and E. Pūredāvūd, "Dasātīr," *Farhang-e Īrān-e bāstān*, 1326 Š./1947, pp. 17-51.) However, the falseness of the *Dasātīr* did not hinder its impact on some Zoroastrian factions. Mollā Kāvūs and his son, Mollā Fīrūz, were both deceived by it and through them its influence increased. Many of its faked "pure Persian words" found their way into Persian dictionaries, including the *Borhān-e qāṭe'*, *Farhang-e anjomanārā-ye nāṣerī*, and *Farhang-e nafīsī* (of Nāẓem al-Aṭṭebā') and were also employed by some late Qajar poets. Its use as a basis of Zoroastrian esoteric beliefs and its contamination of Persian during the period when that language was being affected by chauvinistic considerations remain a fact. *EIr*.]

ĀẔAR K̲ORDĀD. See ĀDUR FARNBAG.

ĀẔARBĀDAGĀN. See AZERBAIJAN.

ĀẔARBĀY(E)JĀN. See AZERBAIJAN.

ĀẔARBĀYJĀN (ĀḎARBĀY[E]JĀN), the title of a satirical-political journal published at Tabrīz in 1907.

Among the many newspapers and periodicals published in Azerbaijan and Caucasia which have borne the name *"Āẕarbāyjān,"* this bilingual Persian and Azeri

Turkish journal is the most memorable. Launched at Tabrīz a month after the coronation of Moḥammad-ʿAlī Shah, it combined politics with humor in a sufficiently varied mix to make it worthy of the description "magazine." Its tone was strongly liberal and nationalistic.

The manager and editor of *Āẕarbāyjān* was ʿAlī-qolī Khan Safarov, who had already made himself known at Tabrīz as the issuer of illegal leaflets in 1892-93 and publisher of progressive news-sheets named *Ebtehāj* and *Eqbāl* in 1898. In the imprint of *Āẕarbāyjān* he is named as ʿAlī-qolī Khan, former editor of *Ebtehāj*. He had spent part of his early career in Caucasia and later had been employed at the headquarters of the Crown Prince Moḥammad-ʿAlī Mīrzā as a "*rāportčī-bāšī*" (chief intelligence agent). Despite this, he had always sympathized with the freedom-seekers.

Up to issue no. 15, communications to and from *Āẕarbāyjān* were handled by Ḥājj Mīrzā Āqā Tabrīzī (Bolūrī), a liberal-minded merchant and prominent backer of the constitutionalists, particularly the patriotic journalists, in Tabrīz at the time. Kasravī considers him to have been the founder of *Āẕarbāyjān*. Bolūrī owned a printing press, which he had earlier bought from the Crown Prince Moḥammad-ʿAlī Mīrzā, and he placed this press, which used movable type and was called the Nāmūs Press, at *Āẕarbāyjān*'s disposal. The first and last pages, however, being made up of caricatures, were lithographed and run off at another establishment, the Eskandānī Press. From the fifteenth issue onward, the recipient and sender of the communications bore the pseudonym Ḥājjī Bābā Tabrīzī. Like its contemporary, the satirical journal *Mollā Naṣr-al-dīn* published at Tiflis, *Āẕarbāyjān* frequently attributed items to an imaginary figure, in its case named Ḥājjī Bābā. The example was to be followed by later humorous and semi-humorous publications in Iran. Ḥājjī Bābā appears in the majority of *Āẕarbāyjān*'s caricatures. He is an elderly man, clad in the then usual garb of an Azerbaijani city-dweller; often he is flanked by another imaginary figure, his friend Ūlmāz (Azeri Turkish for "Can't be done").

Āẕarbāyjān is the third satirical journal in the history of the Persian press, having been preceded by *Šāhsevan* (Istanbul, 1888 or 1889) and *Ṭolūʿ* (Būšehr, 1900); but if the time of *Āẕarbāyjān*'s appearance, the extent of its circulation, and various special features are taken into account, it deserves to be rated as the first important Persian satirical journal.

Not all the contents of *Āẕarbāyjān* are satirical. Most of the leading articles, and some of the poems, reviews, and announcements which were printed in it, are unmistakably serious. Like many later humorous or semi-humorous publications launched in Iran, it was greatly influenced by the already mentioned journal *Mollā Naṣr-al-dīn* of Tiflis. It never equaled *Mollā Naṣr-al-dīn* in the quality and presentation of its subject-matter, but was more courageous than the latter in its critical comments on internal politics—in its case, Iranian politics. Amongst other things, *Āẕarbāyjān* engaged in a debate with its Tiflis counterpart, and in an article headed *Mollā Naṣr-al-dīn javābı* condemned the latter's support for the contemporary Iranian prime minister, ʿAlī Aṣḡar Khan Atābak.

Āẕarbāyjān was opposed to autocracy, sympathetic to Iranian nationalism, and eager for moral and social reforms. On the first point, it directly attacked Moḥammad-ʿAlī Shah in biting lampoons, poems, and caricatures, going to greater extremes than any other contemporary publication. It also showed more awareness of popular feelings. Among the subjects in which *Āẕarbāyjān* took interest were social problems such as usurpation of peasants' rights by landlords, drug addiction, and hoarding and overpricing of essential goods.

Āẕarbāyjān vigorously advocated freedom of oral and written expression. It spoke up in defense of the free press of Iran and Caucasia and in praise of liberal journalism. Some of its angriest protests and lampoons were over the sale of Iranian girls from Qūčān to Turkmen who were Russian subjects—a scandal in which high-ranking Iranian officials were involved (nos. 6, 13, 14, 16, 17).

Unlike other liberal-nationalist journals of the time, *Āẕarbāyjān* refrained from using religious expressions and arguments to explain and popularize its liberal ideals. Indeed it called on the Iranians to change their habits as a sign of release from the bonds of tyranny, in particular to celebrate the Nowrūz festival of that year (1335 Q.) even though it fell in the month of Ṣafar during the customary forty days of mourning for the Imam Ḥosayn (no. 3, p. 5).

Āẕarbāyjān's opinions about foreigners were far from favorable. Russian and Ottoman Turkish policies were sharply criticized, and the Ottoman sultan was personally lampooned (no. 17, p. 6). The Anglo-Russian agreement of 1907 for partition of Iran into spheres of influence naturally incurred severe condemnation. *Āẕarbāyjān* also took a poor view of Joseph Naus and the other Belgian officials in the Iranian government's service (no. 15, p. 7).

Āẕarbāyjān was the first Iranian publication to appear in both the national language and a local language. The example was followed a fortnight later by another liberal journal, *Faryād* (published at Orūmīya [Urmia] during 1907). It must be added that the Persian content of *Āẕarbāyjān* greatly exceeded the Azeri Turkish content, and that one of its articles expressed preference for the use of Persian in writing.

The intention was that *Āẕarbāyjān* should appear weekly, but this proved impracticable. The first issue was published on 6 Moḥarram 1325/19 February 1907. The date 1324 printed conspicuously in the vignette of this issue refers to the grant of the constitution in that year. At least 23 issues came out before publication of *Āẕarbāyjān* ceased, probably as a result of the death of ʿAlī-qolī Safarov. Issue no. 21 was printed on 22 Šawwāl 1325/29 November 1907, but nos. 22 and 23 are undated. Since the interval between each issue from no. 15 onward ran to over a fortnight, it can be inferred that the last issue was probably printed at the end of Ḏu'l-ḥejja or beginning of Ṣafar 1325 (early January 1908); if so, Kasravī's surmise that *Āzarbāyjān* lasted one year is not far off the mark. Only three months after the demise of *Āzarbāyjan*, publication of a successor journal began; this was *Ḥašarāt al-arż*, which came out at Tabrīz between March, 1908, and January, 1911.

Āzarbāyjān's vignette was a lion with the sun on its right side and the name *Āzarbāyjān* showing through the sun's rays. In the second and subsequent issues, the national emblem of the lion and sun was added in the form of an internal vignette at the top of page 2. The first and last pages were occupied by caricatures, which were in color and lithographed; the name of the caricaturist remains unknown.

Āzarbāyjān carried advertisements. It consisted of eight two-column pages measuring 35 × 24 cm. The price per copy was 14 *šāhīs*. The annual rate for subscribers in Tabrīz was four *tūmāns*; no rate for subscribers elsewhere was notified.

Sets of *Āzarbāyjān* are preserved in a number of important libraries of Iran, the Cambridge University Library, and Bibliotheque Nationale (Versailles).

Bibliography: E. G. Browne, *Press and Poetry of Modern Iran*, Cambridge, 1914, pp. 27, 36, 44, 108, 257-59 (nos. 2, 31, 44). M. Ṣadr-Hāšemī, *Tārīḵ-e jarā'ed wa majallāt-e Īrān*, Isfahan, 1327-32 Š./1948-53, no. 72. A. Kasrawī, *Tārīḵ-e mašrūṭa-ye Īrān*, 2nd ed., Tehran, 1333 Š./1954, pp. 151, 269, 272-73. Y. Āryanpūr, *Az Ṣabā tā Nīmā*, Tehran, 1350 Š./1971, II, pp. 23, 26, 27. M. M. Tarbīat, *Dānešmandān-e Āḏarbāyjān*, Tehran, 1314 Š./1935, p. 405. H. L. Rabino, *Ṣūrat-e jarā'ed-e Īran*, Rašt, 1911, no. 13. Ghilan (H. L. Rabino), "Le club national de Tauris," *RMM* 3, 1907, pp. 109-14. Idem, "La décomposition du corps social en Perse," *RMM* 4, 1908, p. 90. L. Bouvat, "La caricature à Téhéran," *RMM* 3, 1907, p. 554. Idem, Azèrbâïdjân," *RMM* 2, 1907, pp. 65-69.

(N. PARVĪN)

ĀẔARĪ, the ancient language of Azerbaijan. See AZERBAIJAN vii.

ĀẔARĪ (ĀḎARĪ) **ṬŪSĪ,** NŪR-AL-DĪN (or FAḴR-AL-DĪN) ḤAMZA B. ʿALĪ MALEK ESFARĀYENĪ BAYHAQĪ, Shiʿite Sufi poet (fl. 784-866/1382-1462). He was born in Esfarāyen (Khorasan), where his father was of some importance under the Sarbadārs (Dawlatšāh, p. 398). He showed an early inclination toward poetry and soon gained the favor of Šāhroḵ (r. 807-50/1405-47) after a competition with Ḵ˘āja ʿAbd-al-Qāder ʿŪdī, in which he was required to compose *qaṣīda*s in the manner of Salmān Sāvajī (d. 778/1376-77). He was promised the position of poet-laureate at the Timurid court but, about the same time, came under the influence of the Sufi, Shaikh Moḥyī-al-dīn Ṭūsī Ḡazālī. He made the pilgrimage to Mecca with his teacher; and, while there, he wrote *Saʿy al-ṣafā*, a history of the Kaʿba with description of the *ḥājj* ceremonies (Dawlatšāh, pp. 398-409). On the return journey Shaikh Moḥyī-al-dīn died at Aleppo (830/1426-27), and Āẕarī then became the disciple of Shah Neʿmatallāh Walīy. He made the pilgrimage again with the latter, from whom he received the Sufi's cloak (*ḵerqa*; see Nafīsī, *Naẓm o naṯr* I, p. 294; Qāżī Nūrallāh Šūštarī, *Majāles al-mo'menīn*, Tehran, 1335 Š./1956, II, p. 125).

Āẕarī then traveled to India. In 832/1428-29 he became attached to the court of Aḥmad Shah Bahmanī (820-38/1417-35) in the Deccan, and the king bestowed on him the title of poet laureate. Āẕarī began work on a history of the dynasty, the *Bahman-nāma*. He eventually sought permission to return home but promised to continue work on the history. By the time of his death he had carried it down to the reign of Sultan ʿAlā'-al-dīn Homāyūn Shah (862-65/1457-61); other poets, such as Naẓīrī and Sāmeʿī, continued the project (Nafīsī, op. cit., II, p. 786). On his departure from India, Āẕarī received a gift of 60,000 silver tankas, five slaves, and a robe of honor.

Āẕarī returned to Esfarāyen and spent the remaining thirty years of his life in seclusion. He largely turned from the writing of panegyric to verse in praise of the Prophet and his descendants. He also had built, and provided endowments for, houses and hospices to serve dervishes, the poor, pilgrims, and students. When the Timurid Sultan Moḥammad b. Bāysonqor passed through in 850/1446-47 (after Šāhroḵ's death, on his way to assume the rule of Fārs, ʿErāq-e ʿAjam, and Māzandarān), he called on the revered Sufi elder. Āẕarī offered advice but declined a bag of gold. In 852/1448-49 Āẕarī had another royal interview in Esfarāyen, with Ulug̣ Beg (Dawlatšāh, p. 363). Āẕarī died there in 866/1461-62 and was buried in one of his foundations. His death date was found in the chronograms *ḵosrow* (by Aḥmad Mostawfī, see M. ʿA. Modarres, *Rayḥānat al-adab* I, 3rd ed., Tabrīz, n.d., p. 46) and *ḵorūs* (ʿAlī-Šīr Navā'ī, *Majāles al-nafā'es*, ed. ʿA. A. Ḥekmat, Tehran, 1332 Š./1954, p. 186).

Āẕarī's other literary works were: *Mafātīḥ* (or *Meftāḥ*) *al-asrār*, written in 830/1426-27, apparently lost; *Jawāher al-asrār*, an abridgement of the preceding, done ten years later (H. Ethé in Geiger and Kuhn, *Grundr. Ir. Phil.* II, p. 304), published Tehran, 1353/1934; *Ṭog̣rā-ye homāyūn*; and *Maṯnawī-e mer'āt*, comprising *Tāmmat al-kobrā*, *ʿAjā'eb al-donyā*, *ʿAjā'eb al-aʿlā*, and *Saʿy al-ṣafā*. The third of these has been tentatively identified with an *ʿAjā'eb al-ġarā'eb* in the Majlis Library, Tehran (Ebn Yūsof, *Fehrest-e ketāb-ḵāna-ye Majles* III, Tehran, 1312-18 Š./1933-39, p. 513) by Āqā Bozorg Ṭehrānī (*al-Ḏarīʿa* IX/1, pp. 3-4, XV, p. 218). Āẕarī may have written other works; S. Nafīsī attributed to him a *Maṯnawī-e emāmīya* and *Maṯnawī-e ṯamarāt* (op. cit., I, p. 294).

Bibliography: See also Dawlatšāh, ed. Browne, pp. 398-412. *Majāles al-ʿoššāq*, lith., Lucknow, n.d., pp. 245-47. *Ḥabīb al-sīar* IV, p. 61. *Majmaʿ al-foṣaḥā'* I, p. 8. Moḥammad Qodratallāh Gōpāmavī, *Natā'ej al-afkār*, Bombay, 1336/1917-18, pp. 30-32. Browne, *Lit. Hist. Persia* III, pp. 398, 502-03. Ḵayyāmpūr, *Soḵanvarān*, p. 3. Rypka, *Hist. Iran. Lit.*, p. 720. Ṣafā,

Adabīyāt IV, Tehran, 2536 = 1356 Š./1977, pp. 323-33.

(A. ʿA. RAJĀʾĪ)

ĀZARMĪGDUXT (Pers. *Āzarmīdokt, Arzmīdokt, Arzmīndokt, Āzarūmīddokt*), Sasanian queen who according to Ṭabarī ruled for a few months in 630. She was the sister of Queen Pūrān (r. 630 or 631), daughter of King Ḵosrow II Parvēz. Her name, meaning "daughter of the respected one," refers to her father (see Nöldeke, *Geschichte*, p. 393 n. 2). We know little about this figure, who belongs to the troubled period at the end of the Sasanian monarchy, but her existence is confirmed by the evidence of coins.

M. I. Moshiri discovered and published a coin of this queen (*Études* I, pp. 11-16); it was struck in the year 1 at a mint called WYHC, which has been thought to be Veh-az-Amīd-Kavād (= Arrajān). The piece bears the effigy of a man. Moshiri explains this anomaly by suggesting that it is the figure of Farroḵ-Hormozd, who supposedly wished to seize power, and who actually obtained it under the name Hormozd VI (cf. *Étude* II, pp. 209-12). He was able to reign simultaneously with the queen for a little more than a year. There are no coins of Hormozd VI struck in the year 1, only examples dated in the years 2 and 3. Two other coins of the queen are in the Bibliothèque Nationale (Paris), and the late M. Foroughi also possessed one. Only the mint WYHC is attested.

The Islamic sources give the length of her reign variously as six months (Ṭabarī, I, p. 1065; Yaʿqūbī, I, p. 198; Bīrūnī, *Chronology*, p. 123; Ḥamza, p. 28; Ebn Meskawayh, *Tajāreb* I, p. 270), four months (Maqdesī, *Badʾ* III, p. 173; Kasrawī, apud Ḥamza, p. 22 [cf. p. 28]). and sixteen months (Masʿūdī, *Morūj* [ed. Pellat] I, p. 322; Ḥamza, p. 16; *Mojmal*, p. 83).

Ṭabarī (I, pp. 1064-65) relates that Farroḵ-Hormozd, the military commander of Khorasan, asked for her in marriage. Not daring to refuse, the queen invited him to her private quarters, where she had him killed. To avenge him, his son Rostam apparently captured the capital Ctesiphon, then dethroned the queen and had her blinded and killed.

The Islamic sources describe the queen as a clever and very attractive woman. The *Ketāb ṣowar molūk Banī Sāsān* (The Sasanian picture book) depicted her as seated, wearing a red embroidered gown and sky-blue studded (*mowaššaḥ*) trousers, grasping a battle-axe in her right hand and leaning on a sword held in her left hand (Ḥamza, p. 62). She is also credited with the foundation of a fire temple in Abḵāz and a castle at Asadābād (*Mojmal*, p. 83). Her title was "the Just." The *Šāh-nāma*, which calls her Āzarmdoḵt and reports her reign briefly, relates her throne speech saying that her power was broken in the fifth month of her reign; it is not specific about the manner of her death (ed. Mohl, VII, p. 422). The Christian sources mentioned below also record her reign, distorting her name in various ways.

Bibliography: For the numismatic sources, see: Ph. Gignoux, "Noms propres sassanides en moyen-perse épigraphique," in M. Mayrhofer and R. Schmitt, eds., *Iranisches Personennamenbuch* II/2, Vienna, 1986, no. 167. M. I. Moshiri, *Étude[s] de numismatique iranienne sous les sassanides*, Tehran, I, 1972; II, 1977. Literary sources, Pre-Islamic: Eutychius, *Annales* II, ed. L. Cheikho et al., repr. Louvain, 1954, p. 9. *The Chronography of Bar Hebraeus*, tr. E. A. Wallis Budge, Oxford, 1932, I, p. 93. *Chronique de Michel le Syrien*, tr. J.-B. Chabot, Paris, 1901, II, p. 410. Islamic: Balʿamī, *Tārīḵ*, pp. 1201-06. Dīnavarī, p. 125. Ebn al-Aṯīr (repr.), I, pp. 497, 500; II, pp. 416, 434. Ebn Meskawayh, *Tajāreb* I, ed. L. Caetani, London, 1901, pp. 269-70. Abū ʿAbdallāh Moḥammad Ḵʷārazmī, *Mafātīḥ al-ʿolūm*, ed. G. van Vloten, Leiden, 1895, p. 104. Masʿūdī, *Morūj* (ed. Pellat) I, p. 326. Ṯaʿālebī, *Ḡorar*, pp. 736-37. Ṭabarī, I, pp. 1061, 1064-66, 2119, 2121, 2163, 2165. Yaʿqūbī, I, pp. 198-99. See also *Camb. Hist. Iran* III, p. 171. Christensen, *Iran Sass.*, pp. 499-500. R. Gyselen. *Studia Iranica* 8, 1979, pp. 189-212. Justi, *Namenbuch*, p. 54. Nöldeke, *Geschichte der Perser*, pp. 286, 385, 390, 393-95, 398, 434.

(PH. GIGNOUX)

ĀẔARŠAHR (or DEHḴʷĀRAQĀN; in the local Azeri Turkish: Toḵarḡan), a town and a district (*baḵš*) of the *šahrestān* of Tabrīz, bounded on the north and east by the district of Oskū, on the south by the sub-district (*dehestān*) of Sarājū, and on the west by Lake Urmia (Razmārā, *Farhang* IV, p. 226). The old name Deh-ḵʷāraqān was changed to Āẕaršahr in the early Pahlavī period, only to be officially reinstated later (M. J. Maškūr, *Naẓar-ī be tārīḵ-e Āḏarbāyjān*, Tehran, 1349 Š./1971, p. 27). It comprises four sub-districts with forty-eight villages: Āẕaršahr (19 villages, 1,787 households, 10,229 inhabitants), Šīrāmīn (9 villages, 1,1336 households, 7,139 inhabitants), Gāvgān (19 villages, 2,188 households, 12,042 inhabitants), and Mamaqān (1 village, 1,427 households, 7,290 inhabitants) (ibid., pp. 434, 509, 519). The eastern part of the Āẕaršahr district is mountainous, reaching up to the slopes of Sahand-kūh (3,722 m/12,211 ft), and enjoys a salubrious climate. The western part is flat land extending along the eastern shore of Lake Urmia, where the summers tend to be hot. Irrigation for the district's numerous farms and gardens is provided by the Deh-ḵʷāraqān and Īška (Bārīk) rivers, as well as underground channels (*qanāt*s), natural springs, and deep wells.

The administrative center of the district is the town of Āẕaršahr, situated at 45° 85′ 39″ east longitude and 37° 46′ 15″ north latitude at an elevation of 1,468 m/4,816 ft above sea level. It stands on the main highway from Tabrīz to Marāḡa, lying some 54 km southwest of Tabrīz. According to the 1345 Š./1966 census (*Koṣūṣīyat-e asāsī-e šahrhā-ye Īrān*, Tehran, 1350 Š./1971), the population of the town numbers 15,318 persons, the majority of whom are engaged in agriculture and small businesses.

Āẕaršahr is an old town, referred to by early sources

as Dāḵarraqān (Ṭabarī, III, p. 1380; Eṣṭaḵrī, pp. 181, 190, 194; Ebn Ḥawqal, pp. 333, 336, 345; tr. Kramers, pp. 326, 329, 339; Ebn Ḵordāḏbeh, p. 120; Moqaddasī, pp. 51, 374), Ḵarraqān (Moqaddasī, p. 383), and Deh al-Ḵarraqān (Qodāma b. Ja'far, BGA, p. 213). Both *Ḥodūd al-ʿālam* (tr. Minorsky, p. 143) and Moqaddasī (p. 374) mention it as a part of Armenia although it lay only two stages from Marāḡa and only nine leagues to the southwest of Tabrīz, both of them historically and geographically parts of Azerbaijan. Yāqūt (II, p. 636) calls it Deh-Naḵīrjān and derives the name from that of Naḵīrjān, the treasurer of Ḵosrow (II?). Ḥamdallāh Mostawfī (mid-8th/14th century), who calls it Deh-ḵᵛāraqān (Dehḵᵛārakān in Rašīd-al-dīn Fażlallāh's *Tārīḵ-e mobārak-e Ḡāzānī*, ed. K. Yahn, London, 1940, p. 94), refers to it as a small town with eight dependent villages and speaks of the abundance of its gardens and grape-arbors, and extols the excellent grains, cotton, and fruits produced there. The people of Āẕaršahr were fair-complexioned and belonged to the Shafi'ite sect of Sunni Islam; its total revenue assessment was 23,600 dinars (*Nozhat al-qolūb*, p. 86).

The district of Āẕaršahr contains a number of monuments and sites of historical interest, the most important being Tappa-ye Pīr-e Qaṭrān, Tappa-ye Moṣallā, the cemetery of Pīr-e Ḥayrān, the Čārsū and Rūmīān mosques, the Meḥrāb mosque of Āẕaršahr, the ancient cave and burial sites at Bādāmyār and Tūrāmīn, the mosque of Tūrāmīn, the Awlīā' mausoleum in the village of Qāżī Jahān, the mausoleum of Pīr-e Jāber, etc. ('A. 'A. Kārang, *Āṯār-e tārīḵī-e šahrestān-e Tabrīz* I, Tabrīz, 1351 Š./1972, pp. 470-514).

Bibliography: See also Le Strange, *Lands*, p. 164. Kayhān, *Joḡrāfīā* I, p. 80; II, p. 155; III, pp. 119, 156, 157. Markwart, *Ērānšahr*, p. 24.

('A. 'A. Kārang)

AŽDAHĀ "dragon," various kinds of snake-like, mostly gigantic, monsters living in the air, on earth, or in the sea (also designated by other terms) sometimes connected with natural phenomena, especially rain and eclipses.

i. *In Old and Middle Iranian.*
ii. *In Persian literature.*
iii. *In Iranian folktales.*
iv. *Armenian* aždahak.

i. In Old and Middle Iranian

At the time of the Indo-Iranian unity, the Indo-Iranians must have imagined dragons restraining the heavenly waters and causing drought, and not releasing them until slain by a god or hero, as in the Rigvedic myth of Indra and Vr̥tra. In the Iranian Zoroastrian literature, however, other than Gandarəβa who lives in the Vourukaṣ̌a Sea, dragons are rarely mentioned in connection with water, though they are sometimes said to dwell by rivers. The demon which causes drought seems not to be a dragon (Av. Apaoša, Mid. Pers. Apōš, q.v.); instead, the Zoroastrian dragons, materially huge monsters with ravenous appetites for men and horses, have been given their place in the Mazdayasnian view of the world, in which all monsters are the creations of evil and thus antagonists of the true, Mazdayasnian religion. Still but sketched, or briefly alluded to, in the extant Avesta, this aspect of the Iranian dragons is elaborated throughout the later religious writings. In Manichean myths, however, we notice a change in the concept of the monsters, which are now located in the oceans, presumably as the result of Mesopotamian influence.

The most common Indo-Iranian word for dragon, Indian *ahi*, Avestan *aži*, originally meant only "snake," a meaning which Avestan *aži* still has beside "dragon." These two words are etymologically related to words in other Indo-European languages such as Latin *anguis* (hence *anguilla*, related to Germanic "eel;" see further Mayrhofer, *Etymological Dictionary* I, p. 68, and III, p. 638). In later Iranian the word *aži* has mostly been replaced, partly for reasons of linguistic taboo, partly probably for phonetic reasons. Thus only Yidgha and Munji still have (*y*)*īž* < *aži*; Middle and New Persian have *mār*, which may derive from **marθra* "killer" (though there are phonetic difficulties in such a derivation) and *kirm*/*kerm* "worm", Av. *kərəma*, Sogd. *kyrm-* (translating Mid. Pers. *azdahāg*, Parth. *aždahāg*, see Henning, *Sogdica*, pp. 21f.); Shughni has *sāǰ*, which may be from **sušnā* "the hisser;" etc. (see Morgenstierne, "An Ancient Indo-Iranian Word for 'Dragon'" on this and other words for "snake" and "dragon" in Iranian; on "snake" in Indo-Aryan, see G. Buddruss, "Zur Benennung der Schlange").

Other dragons or dragon-like monsters in Old and Middle Iranian are the Avestan Gandarəβa (Pahlavi Gandarb/Gandarw), the Pahlavi Kirm (battled and vanquished by Ardašīr I, see below, AŽDAHĀ II), the Zoroastrian Middle Persian Gōčihr and Mūšparīg, and some of the Manichean Middle Persian *mazans*.

Indo-European and Indo-Iranian connections. Myths of dragons and the slaying of dragons were common among both other Indo-European peoples and the Near-Eastern peoples with whom the Iranians came into contact from the first half of the first millennium B.C. We need only recall the Teutonic myths of the Nibelungen and Beowulf on the one hand, and the Babylonian dragon-slaying myths on the other. The myth which relates how Dahāg was chained to Mount Demāvand by Ferēdūn but is unchained at the end of time (see below) may reflect Indo-European myths of monsters which are vanquished by a god or hero and imprisoned or chained, but sometimes are liberated at the end of time and come forth to wreak havoc among gods and men. In Greek mythology Zeus battles the Titans and imprisons them in Tartarus; according to some authors, he later set them free (see, e.g., Harvey, *The Oxford Companion*, p. 126a). In the Scandinavian mythology, the monstrous Fenris wolf is chained by the god Týr, but at Ragnarokk (Götterdämmerung) it is unchained and is fought by Óðinn, whom it swallows, but is itself slain by Óðinn's son (see. e.g., Davidson,

Gods and Myths, pp. 38, 59). It is of course difficult to establish detailed connections between these various Indo-European myths, and some scholars prefer to see individual developments rather than elements inherited from a distant past (see, e.g., Boyce, *Zoroastrianism* I, p. 283).

In Indian mythology the only dragon of importance is the snake/dragon (*ahi*) vanquished by Indra and usually referred to as Vṛtra. The origin of the name has been much discussed and is important for Indian as well as Iranian mythology since in Iranian the standing epithet of Indra, *vṛtra-han*/*Vṛtra-han* "smiter of obstacles or defences/slayer of Vṛtra," corresponding to Av. *vərəθraγan*, was thematicized and came to designate one of the most important gods in the Iranian pantheon: Av. Vərəθraγna, Mid. Pers. Wahrām, NPers. Bahrām (q.v.). The *ahi* Vṛtra is described in the Rigveda as keeping the (heavenly) waters imprisoned in caves in the mountains. With the *vajra* (in the Avesta *vazra* is the chief weapon of Miθra), Indra smites him on the neck, splits his head thus freeing the waters, which immediately rush out like cows and run to the sea. In India the epithet is given also to Agni (the fire-god) and Soma; in the Avesta also to Haoma. In the Avesta and the Zoroastrian Pahlavi texts, however, the epithet is never given to any of the dragon-slaying heroes and no gods (including Vərəθraγna) slay dragons. Nevertheless, this concept may have had a place in the mythology of at least some of the Iranian peoples since in Manichean cosmology the dragon-slaying god Adamas is called Wšγnyy in Sogdian (< OIr. Wrθragna; see further below) and also elsewhere in the later tradition some local counterparts of Vərəθraγna preserve traces of his dragon-killing function: Thus, e.g., Armenian Vahagn kills a dragon (see also Duchesne-Guillemin, *La religion*, pp. 175-78; and BAHRĀM).

Whereas in the Indian myths the dragon-slayer is the warrior god, in the Zoroastrian myths the dragon-slayers are superhuman heroes: Θraētaona, who slays Aži Dahāka, and Kərəsāspa, who slays Aži Sruuara, the horned dragon. Kərəsāspa seems to have no parallel in Indian myths; however, Θraētaona, son of Āθβiia, appears to be related to another Avestan hero, Θrita, whose name corresponds formally to the Indian Trita Āptya; the patronym Āptya, however, corresponds to that of the Avestan Θraētaona. In the *Hōm yašt* (*Y.* 9) the first mortals to press the *haoma* are enumerated: the first was Vīuuaŋʰhan, father of Yima, the second Āθβiia, father of Θraētaona, and the third was Θrita (literally "the third"), father of Uruuāxšaiia and Kərəsāspa. In the Rigveda, Trita Āptya is portrayed as the first sacrificer to prepare the *soma*. Clearly these various mythical persons are related (see Boyce, *Zoroastrianism* I, pp. 99f.). The Rigvedic Trita Āptya is no dragon-slayer but he does appear in a myth which bears great similarity to that of Indra's slaying of Vṛtra: In addition to this feat, Indra also liberates some cows which are held imprisoned in a cave by a certain Vala (whose name may or may not be etymologically related to Vṛtra: IE. root *u̯el-, cf. Eng. "wall") but sometimes this feat is ascribed to Trita Āptya.

It therefore seems clear that although dragon-slaying gods and heroes were part of Indo-Iranian mythology, India and Iran developed distinct myths early, changing, deleting, and adding details. In India dragon-slaying was made a characteristic feature of the god Indra. The notion of a god of victory **Vrtraǵhan-* "smiter of obstacles/defences" was probably also common heritage, but whereas the epithet in Iran became the name of the god himself, in India it was given to the warrior god Indra, prompted by his connection with the dragon-slaying (cf., e.g., *Rigveda* 1.32.2 *ahann ahim* "he struck/slew the dragon," with the same verb *han-*/*ghn-*, Av. *jan-*/*γn-* "to strike, kill," as in *vṛtra-han-*/*ghn-*, *vərəθra-jan*/*γn(a)-*). For succinct overviews of the arguments and various theories, see Duchesne-Guillemin, *La religion*, pp. 175-78; Boyce, *Zoroastrianism* I, pp. 63f., especially p. 64 nn. 279-80; see also BAHRĀM).

The only other dragon/snake mentioned in the Rigveda is the "dragon of the deep" (*ahi budhnya*), who is mentioned in lists of lesser divinities and said to dwell at the bottom of heavenly rivers (*budhne nadīnāṃ rajaḥsu sīdan*; Grassmann, *Wörterbuch*, cols. 909f.).

In India the dragon-fight was symbolically connected with New-year and the end of drought but in ancient Iran there is no trace of a connection between the killing of the dragon and Now Rūz. Scholars attempting to see such a connection (e.g. Dumézil, *Le problème des centaures*, pp. 72f., and Widengren, *Religionen*, pp. 41-49) have failed to prove it (Boyce, *Zoroastrianism* I, p. 102 n. 110).

In Mithraism a reference to a simulated dragon-slaying is found in a passage from Lampridius (*Commodus* 9), quoted from Loisy by Widengren, *Religionen*, pp. 44f. n. 16, but otherwise this myth seems to be quite absent from Mithraism, where the snake apparently was "a symbol of a beneficial, life-giving force" (Hinnells, "Reflections," p. 295).

Dragons and dragonlike monsters in the Zoroastrian scriptures. 1. *Ažis*. 2. Gandarəβa. (On Gōčihr and Mūšparīg see *Dragons in astrology*, below.)

1. *Ažis*. Physical descriptions are found of several *ažis* in the Avesta:

Aži Dahāka had three mouths (*θrizafanəm*), three heads (*θrikamarəδəm*), and six eyes (*xšuuaš.ašīm*). (See further on *Aži Dahāka* below.)

Aži Sruuara, the horned dragon, also called Aži Zairita. was the yellow dragon that Kərəsāspa slew (*Y.* 9.1; *Yt.* 19.40; see on the *Legend of Kərəsāspa* below) "who swallowed horses (*aspō.gar-*), who swallowed men (*nərə.gar-*), the poisonous yellow one, over whom poison flowed the height of a spear;" also described as (*Y.* 9.30) "the terrifying (*sima-*), poison-spitting (*vīšō.vaēpa-*) dragon." The *Dādestān ī dēnīg* (71) appears to have preserved two more old epithets of Aži Sruuara no longer found in the Avesta; here we read that Az ī Srūwar was one of the seven worst sinners (two of the others being Dahāg and his mother Wadag, see below), being close to Ahriman himself, and that in addition to swallowing men and horses in a terrifying way (*sahmgenīhā... asp ud mard-ōbārīh kard*), it was also a highway robber (*rāhdārī ud rāh-bīmēnīdārīh... kard*; cf. the dragon in *Aogəmadaēcā* below and note *Pahlavi Rivayat*, p. 69 par. 16, where Kirsāsp tells Ohrmazd that he has killed seven gigantic *rāhdārs*). In the *Dēnkard* it is said to be skilled in witchcraft (Dresden, p. 91 [109.6]; Madan, p. 747.20; tr. West, 8.5.23, p. 111; it is spelled *slwbl yz* and *slwblyz*). There seem to be no similar creatures in the old Indian mythology; however, in Sumero-Semitic culture, art and literature, horned and multi-headed dragons and other monsters are common-place. The number of heads is often seven (see, e.g., the illustrations in Heidel, *The Babylonian Genesis*; see also Christensen, *Démonologie*, pp. 20-23).

A dragon guarding a road is described in *Aogəmadaēcā* 78, where it is compared with Vayu: "the road which a dragon guards, horse-*crushing (*aspaŋhāδō*), man-*crushing (*vīraŋhāδō*), man-slaying (*vīraja*), without compassion." (The element *-hāδa-* may belong to the root *had-*, Olnd. *sad-* "to treat roughly" according to H. W. Bailey, "Arya", p. 526, who quotes *Yt.* 14.56 where we find the parallels *jana... nōiṭ janən haδa... nōiṭ haδən*). The descriptions of *ažis* in the *Vidēvdād* are of snakes rather than of dragons: "of the snakes that crawl on their bellies (*ažinąm udarō.θrąsanąm*)" (*Vd.* 145; on *θrąsa-* see Hoffmann, *Aufsätze* I, p. 197 n. 2); "swift snakes (*ažaiiō xšuuaēβåŋhō*)" (*Vd.* 18.65).

The Aži Raoiδita, the red dragon (in contradistinction to the Aži Zairita "yellow dragon" = Aži Sruuara), ought to have been one of the most important Avestan dragons (excepting Aži Dahāka, see below) since it was, together with the "daēuua-created winter" (*ziiąmca daēuuō.dātəm*), Aŋra Mainiiu's counter-creation (*paitiiārəm frākərəṇtaṭ*) to Ahura Mazdā's creation of Airiiana Vaējah (*Vd.* 1.2; see Christensen, *Le premier chapitre du Vendidad*, pp. 23, 26-27), and thus should by rights have been the most loathed creature in the original home of the Iranians. However, it is mentioned only here. The Aži Raoiδita was probably not identical with Aži Dahāka. As dragons, the only point they had in common was that they were created by Aŋra Mainiiu as the worst thing in the world, but Aži Dahāka is nowhere said to be red, and is nowhere connected with winter. The Pahlavi translation and commentary has *az-iz i rōdīg; was bawēd* "and the river snake; there is a large number" without further comments. The corresponding text in the *Bundahišn* (chap. 31) describes the dragon of the counter-creation as *mār ī pad parrag ud ān-iz ī nē pad parrag* "the snake with wings and the one with no wings" (TD_1, p. 176.1-2; TD_2, p. 205.7-8; tr. Anklesaria, pp. 264f.; cf. Christensen, op. cit., p. 27).

An Aži Višāpa is mentioned in *Nirangistan* 48, where it is said that the act of offering libations to the waters between sunset and sunrise is no better than throwing them into the *mouth of the Aži Višāpa. The two manuscripts of the *Nirangistan* (neither of them old and trustworthy) have *vṣ̌āpahe* (TD) and *viṣ̌āpahe* (HJ), the Pahlavi rendering has *MYA Y ŠPYL* "good water," which may or may not be a scribal corruption of *'p Y wš*, i.e., *az ī wiš* "poison snake," as suggested by Waag (p. 109; see Sanjana's text p. 197, variants listed on p. 43). The epithet *višāpa* is commonly interpreted as containing the word *vīša-* "poison" (Bartholomae, *AirWb.*, col. 1473 "whose juices are poison," Boyce, *Zoroastrianism* I, p. 91 n. 42 "dragon with poisonous slaver," etc.) and although such an interpretation lies close at hand in view of the other dragons' association with poison, the Armenian form of the word, *višap* (Georgian *vešapi*, also a fabulous serpent; Syriac *wšp'*) must be derived from **vēšāp* (Hübschmann, *Armen. Etymologie*, p. 247; Benveniste, "L'origine"), i.e., Old Iranian **u̯aiš-* (Benveniste, p. 7, reconstructs **vāišapa-* but still assumes some derivative of "poison"). The etymology of the term is still unclear; besides the older proposals (cf. *AirWb.*) note that Rigvedic has two verbs *viṣ* "to pour out" (intr.) and "seize," both used in the context of "water" and the second in a context involving Indra, the *vajra*, and the dragon *ahi*, but neither verb gives a totally satisfactory meaning for the term. Perhaps we should compare Avestan *vaēšah* "foulness," so that this dragon was originally the dragon "of foul waters" or the dragon "which fouls the waters." The importance of the epithet lies in the fact that Armenian *višap* has become the designation of a whole class of dragons (see Benveniste, "L'origine") and the hero Vahagn is there called *višapakʻal* "dragon-slaying."

In the Middle Iranian period, an *aždahā* was often depicted on banners to frighten the enemy by its ferocious aspect. Such banners are referred to several times in the *Šāh-nāma* as *aždahā-peykar* (e.g., ed. Borūkīm, II, p. 480 v. 775, IV, p. 924 v. 949). An early reference to them is found in Lucian (*De historia conscribenda* 29, pp. 42f.), where we are told that the Parthians used banners with different emblems to differentiate divisions of their army, a dragon-banner (*drákōn*) preceding—Lucian believes—a thousand-man division. (See also AZDAHĀ II.)

2. Gandarəβa/Gandarw (or Gandarb, spelled *gndlp*). Among the other various noxious creatures depicted in the Zoroastrian Pahlavi literature we find the sea monster Gandarəβa, which may have been a dragon of the sea, though descriptions as to its exact nature are lacking. It was a monster with yellow heals (*Zairipāšna-*) and living in the sea (*upāpa-*), which, on emerging to destroy the entire creation of Aša, was fought and vanquished by Kərəsāspa (*Yt.* 5, 38, 15.28 19.41; cf. Christensen, *Démonologie*, pp. 18f., and see below). Like the other dragons it had a ravenous appetite, even more so since it was able to swallow twelve provinces at once (*pad ēw-bār 12 deh bē jūd*; *Pahlavi Rivayat*, p. 67 par. 9). Etymologically the name equals Olnd. *gandharva* a beneficent mythical being, said to be surrounded by the heavenly waters—which flow down at his look—sometimes (in later literature, usually) portrayed as a heavenly musician. It is through the "Iranian polarization" of the inherited Aryan mythological concepts, it seems, that *gandarəβa* has been turned into a sea monster. Of

all the Old Iranian monsters Gandarəβa is the most reminiscent of Near-Eastern, Semitic, sea monsters. (On the Olnd. *gandharva* see, e.g., Oldenberg, *Die Religion des Veda*, pp. 248ff.; Grassmann, *Wörterbuch*, col. 378; Dumézil, *Le problème*, devotes several chapters to this monster.) It also recalls the Manichean water dragons, the *mazans* (see below). The *gandarəβa* survives in Sogdian as *γntrw* (for genuine Iranian **γntrβ* through Indian influence) and the entire Avestan phrase (*upāpō gandarəβō*) as *wp'pγntrw* (P 3.131, see Henning, "Sogdian Tales," pp. 481f.); it has survived in modern Shughni dialects as the designation of a monster or dragon, but also a werewolf (see Morgenstierne, *Etymological Vocabulary*, p. 110).

Aži Dahāka. Aži Dahāka (Pahl. Az[i]dahāg, spelled *'cydh'k*, or Dahāg) belongs to the realm of mythologized history or historicized mythology. He is depicted in the Avesta as a dragon-like (*aži*) monster with three mouths (*θrizafanəm*), three heads (*θrikamarəδəm*), six eyes (*xšuuaš.ašīm*), with a thousand viles (*hazaŋrā.yaoxštīm*), very strong (*aš.aojaŋhəm*), a demoniac devil (*daēuuīm drujim*). For the rest he behaves like the other heroes and non-heroes of the Avestan mythological prehistory, and it is not clear whether he was originally considered as a human in dragon-shape or a dragon in man-shape. The former alternative is suggested by his epithet *dahāka-* if it means "man (-like)" (Schwartz, *Orientalia* 49, pp. 123f., who for the word formation compares *maṣ̌iia-* and *maṣ̌iiāka-*, and for the meaning compares Khotanese *daha-* "male," Wakhi *δāi* "man," and translates Aži Dahāka as "the hominoid serpent, the Snake-man"). However, the traditional connection of Av. *dahāka* with the Olnd. *dāsa*s and *dasyu*s, who are also among the opponents of Indra and who are usually assumed to be the indigenous pre-Aryan inhabitants of northwestern India can not be wholly discarded. (Note that Pashto *lōy* "big" is likely to be from *dahāka*, which may point to an original meaning "big, huge.") (See also Christensen, *Démonologie*, pp. 20ff.)

A number of elements of the myth of Aži Dahāka have been preserved in the Zoroastrian texts: In their struggle to regain the *x'arənah* after it left Yima, Ahura Mazdā and Aŋrō Mainiiu each employed their best helpers. Ātar and Aži Dahāka with his brother Spitiiura here faced one another and threatened one another, but the threats of Ātar were the most efficient ones, and Evil's attempt was foiled. According to the Avestan myth Spitiiura sawed Yima in half (*Yt.* 19.46 *yimo.kərəṇtəm* "the Yima-cutter"), but the *Bundahišn* states that he did it together with Aži Dahāka (TD_1, p. 196. 13-14; TD_2, p. 228.12; tr. Anklesaria, pp. 292f.; tr. West, p. 131; see also Darmesteter, *Zend-Avesta* III, p. 629 n. 76). According to the *Pahlavi Rivayat* (46.35, p. 136), it was as a recompense (*pāddāšn*) for his success against Dahāg that Ādur Farnbag was established victoriously in K̲ˇārazm, and the *Bundahišn* says that when Jam was cut in half, the *xwarrah* of Jam saved Ādur Farnbag from the hand of Dahāg (TD_1, p. 102.15-17; TD_2, pp. 124.14-125.1; tr. Anklesaria, pp. 158f.; tr. West, p. 63).

In the Avesta (*Yt.* 5.29-35 and 15.19-21) we are told that Aži Dahāka worshipped Arduuī Sūrā in the land of Baβri and Vaiiu in the inaccessible (*dužita*) Kuuiriṇta. The tradition has interpreted Baβri as Babylon, Old Persian Bab(a)iruš (Mid. Pers. Bābēl) and Kuuiriṇta as Aži Dahāka's castle in Babylon. The *Bundahišn*, in a list of dwellings (*mānīhā*) made by the *kays*, reports that Dahāg made a dwelling in Bābēl called Kuling *dušdīd* (TD_1, p. 179.11-12; TD_2, p. 209.8; tr. Anklesaria, pp. 268f.; see further Darmesteter, *Zend-Avesta* II, pp. 584f. n. 16). In the *Dēnkard* (7.4.72) it is told that Dahāg by sorcery had made many wonderful things (*widimās*) in Bābēl, which induced people to idolatry, in order to destroy the world but that Zardošt recited the words of the Religion and thus rendered nought Dahāg's efforts (Dresden p. 119 [54]; Madan, p. 639.5-10; Molé, *La légende*, pp. 56f.). These interpretations are of doubtful historical and geographical value, not least because of the Avestan form of the name, Baβri, which differs from the others; nevertheless it is understandable that the Iranians, after they came into contact with Near-Eastern, especially Semitic culture, located Aži Dahāka, the big dragon, in Babylon, which must have been notorious for its dragons, in literature and artistic representations. Another mansion was constructed by Dahāg in *Šambarān (wr. *y'mbl'n*; cf. *Šāhnāma* Šambarān) and one in India (TD_1, p. 179.15; TD_2, p. 209.11-12; tr. Anklesaria, pp. 270f.). Only once, it seems, is Dahāg associated with a river, namely in the chapter on rivers in the *Bundahišn* where he is said to have asked a favor from Ahriman and the demons by the river Spēd in Azerbaijan (TD_1, p. 82.15-17; TD_2, p. 88.3; tr. Anklesaria, pp. 108f.; tr. West, p. 80).

Aži Dahāka's prayer to Arduuī Sūrā and Vaiiu was for them to give him the power to render unpopulated (*amaṣ̌iia-*) the seven climes, i.e., the entire world; Arduuī Sūrā and Vaiiu of course did not grant this prayer; on the contrary, when Θraētaona subsequently worshipped them, asking them to grant him the power to overcome Aži Dahāka, it was him they granted his wish. The same two passages contain another fragment of the myth: At the same time, Θraētaona asked and was granted the power to lead away Sauuaŋhauuāci and Arənauuāci, the two most beautiful women in the world, whom the later tradition represented as Yima's sisters or daughters and as having been captured and detained by Aži Dahāka (further on the capture of beautiful women by dragons, see AŽDAHĀ II). More information originally contained in the Avesta is to be found in the later Pahlavi texts, especially in the resumes of the *nasks* given in the *Dēnkard* (books 8 and 9, tr. West, SBE 37, and elsewhere); in particular, the twentieth *fragard* of the *Sūdgar nask*, called *Vohuxšaθrəm*, was devoted in its entirety to the rule of Dahāg.

In the Pahlavi texts Dahāg is portrayed as the embodiment and originator of the bad religion, i.e., the opposite of the Good Mazdayasnian Religion. In *Dēnkard* 3.229 we are told that the bad religion and the non-law was codified by Dahāg in the writings of Judaism (the *'wlyt'*, Syriac *Urāyθā*, i.e., the *Pentateuch*), and that from Dahāg it went to Abraham, the *dastūr* of the Jews (tr. Menasce, p. 243; cf. Zaehner, *Zurvan*, p. 30). In the *Sūdgar nask* Dahāg was said to have possessed five defects (greediness, want of energy, indolence, defilement, and illicit intercourse), the opposites of the best qualities wisdom, instructed eloquence, diligence, and energetic effort (according to the resumé in *Dēnkard* 9.5.1-2, DH, p. 172.8-9; Madan, p. 789.1518; tr. West, p. 177). In *Dēnkard* 3.308 Dahāg, destroyer of the world is said to have been of Arabic (*tāj*) race. *Dēnkard* 3.287-88 lists ten good counsels to mankind given by Jam followed by ten bad, counter-counsels by Dahāg, which are referred to also elsewhere in the *Dēnkard* (tr. Menasce, pp. 243, 283-85; the *'Olamā'-e eslām* contains a note that the name Dahāk actually means "ten sins," see *Persian Rivayat*, p. 454, and Zaehner, *Zurvan*, p. 413). In the *Dādestān ī dēnīg* (71) Dahāg is said to have been one of the seven worst sinners ever, i.e., those who are close to Ahriman himself (two more being the Az ī Srūwar and Dahāg's mother Wadag); here Dahāg is said to be the first who lauded (*stāyīd*) sorcery (*jādūgīh*) (cf. also *Dēnkard* 8.35.13 and 9.10.2-3; tr. West, pp. 111, 185). He is often referred to as Bēwarasp in the Pahlavi texts (e.g., *Dēnkard* 9.21.7; tr. West, p. 214; *Mēnōg ī xrad* 7.29, 26.34, 35, 38; tr. West, pp. 35, 60f.; *Bundahišn* TD_1, p. 66.7-8; TD_2, p. 80.6-7; tr. Anklesaria, pp. 98f.; tr. West, p. 40).

A curious note is found in *Mēnōg ī xrad*, chap. 27, in which the sage asks about the benefit of all the ancient rulers. About Azdahāg the *Mēnog ī xrad* says that the advantage (*sūd*) of Azdahāg Bēwarasp and Frāsyāg the Turanian was that if they had not received the rule it would have gone to Xešm (wrath) and then it could not have been taken from him till the end of the world because Xešm has no bodily existence.

The Pahlavi texts moreover provide Dahāg with a mother, who is the embodiment of evil and sinfulness and is one of the seven worst sinners ever (see *Dādestān ī dēnīg* 71, 77). Her name is variously given as Ōdag, Wadag, etc. She was the first to have practised whoredom (*rōspīgīh*) and incestuous adultery, having intercourse with her son while her husband Arwadasp/Urwadasp (or Xrūdasp as West, tr., *Bundahišn*, p. 131?) was still alive, and without his sanction (*adastūrīhā*) and unlawfully (*adādestānīha*) (TD_1, p. 196.17-197.3; TD_2, pp. 228.15-229.4; tr. Anklesaria, pp. 292f.; tr. West, pp. 131f.). (In the same vein one might expect Dahāg to have instituted the heinous sin of sodomy, but that had of course already been done by Ahriman, when he performed it on himself to create "demons and lies and other abortions," see *Mēnōg ī xrad* 7.10, tr, West, pp. 32f.; Zaehner, *Zurvan*, pp. 368f.) She is described in some detail in *Dēnkard* 9.21.4-5, which seems to allude to some relationship between her and Jamšēd (DH, p. 188.18-21; Dresden, p. 58 [175]; Madan, p. 810.19ff.; tr. West, pp. 212-13 n. 5). Being the most sinful of females, by one commentator of *Vd.* 18.30 Ōda is identified with the *druj*. that tells Srōš who are the four males who make her pregnant. However, this is probably a late interpretation since the summary of *Vd.* 18 in the *Dēnkard* has only *druz* (see Darmesteter, *Zend-Avesta* II, pp. 248f. and n. 43) in *Vd.* 19.6, Aŋra Mainiiu promises Zaraθuštra a boon such as the one the ruler (*daiŋ́hupaiti*) Vaδaγana got, if he foreswears the Mazdayasnian religion. The passage is found also in *Mēnōg ī xrad* where Wadagān *dahibed* is glossed by Dahāg (56.24-25, pp. 154f.; tr. West, p. 103 with n. 3). This means that the tradition took Av. *vaδaγana* to be a matronymic referring to Aži Dahāka, and it is possible, of course, that the whole character of Wadag/Ōda is built upon this interpretation.

The rule of Aži Dahāka. From the Pahlavi texts onwards, Dahāg is inserted into the list of mythical Pīšdādīān (Pēšdādīān) rulers of Iran, i.e., the rulers descended from Hōšang ī Pēš-dād (Haošiiaŋha Paraδāta), succeeding Jam ī Xšēd (Yima Xšaēta) and preceding Frēdōn (Θraētaona). The Avesta does not say explicitly whether Dahāg was a king or not, but from the way he was mentioned among the early rulers of the Iranians, it was quite natural that he should be considered as such. An attempt was made by S. Wikander to trace the triple succession of Yima-Aži Dahāka-Θraētaona back to Indo-European patterns, comparing the Greek myth of the Ouranides, according to which Zeus conquered Kronos and the Titans and established a reign of order; however, Duchesne-Guillemin (*La religion*, pp. 336f. with references) has convincingly argued against such a connection, pointing out the differences between the Greek and Iranian myths and, most importantly, pointing out the fact that there is no trace of this kind of triple succession in India, which precludes an Indo-Iranian date for it. It seems better to assume that it is a post-Avestan creation, due to a certain interpretation of the Avestan texts.

In the Pahlavi texts the reign of terror of Dahāg is described in some detail (see, e.g., *Dēnkard* 9.21.12-16). His genealogy is given in the *Bundahišn* chap. 31.6, which traces it back to the Evil Spirit himself (TD_1, pp. 196.17-197.3; TD_2, pp. 228.15-229.4; tr. Anklesaria, pp. 292f.; tr. West, p. 131f.). About his rule we read in the *Bundahišn* that a hundred years after the *xwarrah* left Jam the millennium reign (*hazārag xwadāyīh*) came to Scorpio (Gazdumb) and then Dahāg ruled for a thousand years., until the millennium rule came to Sagittarius (Nēmasp) and the five hundred-year rule of Frēdōn (TD_1, p. 206.1-2; TD_2, p. 239.4-5; tr. Anklesaria, pp. 306f.; tr. West, p. 150; briefly mentioned in *Dēnkard* 3.329, Menasce, p. 308; *Mēnōg ī xrad* 57.25). In the *'Olamā'-e eslām* we are told that after Jamšēd became deranged, he was seized and slewn by the Arab Dahāk who made himself king and reigned a thousand years, mixing men and demons, and working much sorcery, until Ferēdūn, son of Ātfī, came and bound him (*Persian Rivayat*, p. 454; Zaehner, *Zurvan*, p. 413).

Aži Dahāka and Θraētaona. The Avesta contains several references to Θraētaona's victory over Aži Dahāka (*Y.* 9.8, *Yt.* 5.29-35, 14.40, 15.23-25, 19.37, 92,

Vd. 1.17), but there is little detail, except in the case of his liberating Arənauuāci and Sauuaŋhauuāci. The Pahlavi texts contain some further details: In the *Dēnkard* (7.1.25-26) we are told that by the power of the *xwarrah*, which came to him while he was still in the womb of his mother, Frēdōn was able at the age of nine to go forth and vanquish Dahāg and to deliver Xwanirah from the ravages of the lands (*dehān*) of Māzandarān (Dresden, p. 359; Madan, p. 596.2-12; tr. Molé, p. 9; see also *Dēnkard* 9.21.17-24, DH, pp. 190.8-191.21; Dresden, pp. 55-57 [178-82]; Madan, pp. 812.19-815.1; tr. West, pp. 217ff.). The *Dēnkard* (9.21.8-10) relates how Frēdōn first struck Dahāg with his club upon the shoulder (*frēg*), the heart, and the skull, without killing him, and that he then hewed him with a sword three times, which caused the body of Dahāg to turn into (*gaštan*) various noxious creatures. Seeing this Ohrmazd told Frēdōn not to cut Dahāg so that the world should not become flooded with reptiles and other noxious creatures (DH, p. 189.8-14; Dresden, p. 58 [176-77]; Madan, p. 811.13-21; tr. West, p. 214). This curious episode is hard to explain, but one is reminded of cosmogonical myths in which a giant is partitioned to give rise to the various elements of the world, as the Indian primeval Man, Puruṣa. Maybe the episode reflects some early element of the story of the creation by the Evil Spirit.

But most importantly the Pahlavi texts attribute to Aži Dahāka and Frēdōn/Kərəsāspa an eschatological role: Aži Dahāka is not killed by Frēdōn, but captured and chained "with awful fetters, in the most grievous punishment of confinement" at Mount Demāvand (*Dēnkard* 9.21.10, tr. West, p. 214; see also, e.g., *Bundahišn* TD_1, p. 66.7-9; TD_2, p. 80.6-7; tr. Anklesaria, pp. 98f.; tr. West, p. 40; *Mēnōg ī xrad* 26.38; tr. West, p. 61). At the beginning of the millennium of Ušēdarmāh, the *druz* of the seed of dragons (*az-tōhmag*) will be destroyed. Aži Dahāka breaks loose from the fetters and rushes out to terrorize the world, devouring one third of men, oxen, sheep, and other creatures of Ohrmazd, and smiting the water, the fire, and the plants. The last three then request from Ohrmazd that Frēdōn should be resuscitated to combat him. In the event, however, it is not Frēdōn but Kirsāsp (in the texts variously called Sām or son of Sām) who is reawakened and kills the dragon. The reason for this is not clear though it may be connected with the statement (see above) found in the Pahlavi texts that Ohrmazd refused Frēdōn permission to slay Dahāg because as a result the earth would have been flooded with noxious creatures (*xrafstar*). (See *Bundahišn* TD_1, pp. 188.12-189.1; TD_2, pp. 219.14-220.5; tr. Anklesaria, pp. 180-83; tr. West, p. 119; and see also, e.g., *Bahman yašt*, p. 128; *Dēnkard* 6.B4 [ed. Shaked, pp. 134f.], 9.15.2; *Šāyest nē šāyest* 20.18, ed. Kotwal, pp. 87f.; A. Christensen, *Démonologie*, pp. 20-25, 52). That this role was early assigned to Kirsāsp/Sām is clear from *Yt.* 13.61 and *Mēnōg ī xrad* 61.20-24 (tr. West, p. 110), where it is told that the body of Sām is protected by 99,999 *fravaši*s of the righteous so that demons and fiends may not harm it.

The legend of Kərəsāspa/Kirsāsp. Kərəsāspa's slayings of the Aži Sruuara and the Gandarəβa are only alluded to in the Avesta itself, but elaborated in the later Pahlavi writings. His slaying of Dahāg is recounted only in the Pahlavi and later texts. The Pahlavi texts contain two versions of the legend of Kirsāsp (spelled *krssp*; also Krišāsp, Grišāsp spelled *klyššp*, *glyš(')sp*), one in the 14th *fragard* of the *Sūdgar nask* as retold in the *Dēnkard* (DH, pp. 182.7-83.2 [*kls'sp*, *gls'sp*]; Dresden, pp. 65-66 [*klyš'sp*]; Madan, pp. 802.14-803.12; tr. West, 9.15, pp. 196-99), another in the *Pahlavi Rivayat* (ed. Dhabhar, pp. 65-74). Both accounts were edited and translated by Nyberg, "La légende."

From the Avesta we only learn that Kərəsāspa for some reason or other had settled upon the back of the dragon—presumably thinking it to be a hill—to cook his midday meal (*Y.* 9.1, *Yt.* 19.40) and that the heat from his fire made the dragon hot and sweaty and finally woke him up, whereupon he jumped up from underneath the cooking pot, scattering the boiling water, and frightening Kərəsāspa, who fled, but eventually slew the dragon. The account in the *Sūdgar* only states that Kirsāsp killed the horned dragon, but the one in the *Pahlavi Rivayat* adds a few details (this version is also found in *Dârâb Hormazyâr's Rivâyat*, p. 62, not translated in Unvala, *Persian Rivayat*): Kirsasp tells Ohrmazd that there was a horned dragon (Pers. *aždahā-ī*), swallowing men and horses, which has teeth as large as his arm, ears as large as fourteen *nmt*'s, eyes as large as a chariot, and a horn as large as a *š'k* (Pers. *haštād araš* "eighty ells"). He ran after it (*pad pušt hamē tazīd*; Pers. *bar pošt-e vey* "on its back") for half a day until he caught up with its head, struck his mace at its neck and killed it. The *Persian Rivayat* adds that when he looked into its mouth he saw men hanging from its teeth, a feature which the *Pahlavi Rivayat* reserves for Gandarəβa/Gandarw. Kirsāsp tells Ohrmazd that Gandarw, large enough to devour twelve provinces at once (and so tall that the sea reached him to the knee and his head reached the sun according to the *Persian Rivayat*), seized him by the beard and pulled him into the sea where they fought for nine days and nights, when Kirsāsp managed to seize him by the foot and promptly pulled off his skin from his feet to his head and used it to bind the monster, which he left to his friend Axrūrag to guard. Then, after eating fifteen horses, Kirsāsp fell asleep under a tree and Gandarw pulled Axrūrag and Kirsāsp's wife and parents into the sea. All the people came and roused him and he ran down to the sea taking a thousand strides in one. Arriving at the sea he delivered those abducted, seized Gandarw, and killed him. The eschatological role played by Kirsāsp is not mentioned in the *Pahlavi Rivayat* but the *Sūdgar* tells how, when Dahāg runs free of the fetters to destroy the world, he (i.e., Kirsāsp) is awakened (*hangēzīhēd*) to vanquish the powerful demon (*Dēnkard*, DH p. 182.16-18; Dresden, p. 65 [161]; Madan, p. 803.3-6; tr. West. pp. 198f., See also Christensen, *Démonologie*, pp. 17f., 51).

Dragons in astrology. Zoroastrian and Manichean

astrology know of several dragons or snake-like monsters.

Gōčihr and Mūšparīg. In the *Bundahišn* the snake-like (*mār homānāg*) Gōčihr and Mūšparīg with the tail (*dumbōmand*) and wings (*parrwar*) are said to be the evil opponents of the sun, moon and stars. These two harmful beings were bound to the sun so as not to run free and cause harm (*Bundahišn* TD_1, p. 43.11-17; TD_2, pp. 52.12-53, 13; cf. *Bundahišn* TD_1, p. 159.12ff.; TD_2, p. 188.4ff.; tr. Anklesaria, pp. 242f.; tr. West, pp. 113f.; MacKenzie, "Zoroastrian Astrology," pp. 513, 516; Zaehner, *Zurvan*, pp. 159, 164). Both are probably derived from Avestan concepts: In the Avesta *gaociθra* is an epithet of the moon and Mūš Pairikā "the witch Mūš" is found in *Y.* 16.8, where she is mentioned in connection with Āzi, the demon of greed (see ĀZ) and the heretic (*aṣ̌əmaoγa*).

In the Pahlavi cosmogony Gōčihr is described as "similar to a snake with the head in Gemini (*dō-pahikar*) and the tail in Centaurus (*Nēmasp*), so that at all times there are six constellations between its head and tail." It runs retrograde, so that every ten years the head and tail have changed place. It is said to be standing in the middle of the sky, an expression which may refer to the polar region of the sky and so perhaps contain a reminiscence of the constellation Draco, which circles the pole (see MacKenzie, "Zoroastrian Astrology," pp. 515f. with notes). In the *ʿOlamāʾ-e eslām* it is stated that the heaven of Gōčihr is below the heaven of the moon (Zaehner, *Zurvan*, p. 417; cf. *Persian Rivayat*, p. 429 bottom; see also *Škand-gumānīg wizār*, ed. Menasce, pp. 47, 55, 60).

At the end of time Gōčihr will fall down on the earth, which it will terrify like a wolf does a sheep; its fire and halo will then melt the metal of Šahrewar in the hills and mountains, thus providing the river of molten metal necessary for the purification of men. (Gōčihr appears to be the only fiery dragon in ancient Iran.) At the end, after Ohrmazd himself has come down to earth to send Āz and Ahriman back to the Darkness whence they had come, Gōčihr the serpent burns in the molten metal and the pollution of Hell burns and Hell becomes pure (*Bundahišn* TD_1, pp. 193.11-16, 195.17-196.2; TD_2, pp. 225.3-8, 227.12-15; tr. Anklesaria, pp. 288-91; tr. West, pp. 125f., 129).

Mūšparīg may originally have been considered the demon who causes the eclipses of the moon, as is indicated by its name Mūš meaning "mouse" but originally also probably "thief," cf. Olnd. *muṣ* "to steal" (see Darmesteter I, *Zend-Avesta*, pp. 144 n. 15).

In the Manichean cosmogony these two dragons are simply called "two dragons" (*dō azdahāg*); they were hung up (*āgust*) and fettered (*gišt*) in the lowest heaven and two angels (*frēstag*), male and female, were put in charge to make them revolve ceaselessly, i.e., presumably to make the firmament turn so as to keep the Manichean salvation machine going (Jackson, *Researches*, 30f., 31f.; Boyce, *Reader*, p. 60 text *y* 1 with note).

In later literature, the seven planets are sometimes called *aždahā* (see Eilers, *Sinn und Herkunft*, p. 11).

Dragons and dragon-like monsters in Manichean writings. The Manichean texts mention dragons in general terms (Mid. Pers. *azdahāg*, Parth. *aždahāg*) but they play no prominent role. Thus in *Mir. Man.* I (p. 22[194] = Boyce, *Reader*, p. 72 y 39) we read that the female and male *mazans* (q.v.) and *āsrēštārs* (q.v.) copulate to produce dragon brats (*ʾwzdhʾg zhg*) and in *Mir. Man.* III (p. 30 [875]) the Living Soul complains that it was seized and mangled by innumerable demons, including "dark, ugly, stinking, black dragons" (*tʾryg ʾjdhʾg dwrcyhr gndʾgʾwd syʾw*).

More important in Manichean cosmology is the class of demoniacal beings called *mazans*. In the Zoroastrian writings these are clearly only "giants," whom the ocean reaches to the knees. In the Manichean myths, however, they are definitely connected with the ocean and though most of them are indeterminate "giants" (e.g., the *mazans* which usually accompany the *āsrēštārs*, some are sea dragons or dragon-like sea monsters (see below).

For the history of Iranian mythology, however, the most important fact is that the dragon-killing episode has been fitted into the Manichean cosmological scheme: Here we find the third son of the Living Spirit (Mihryazd), Adamas of Light (Syr. Adamos Nuhrā), being sent by his father (*Mir. Man.* I, p. 10 [182], Boyce, *Reader*, p. 65 text y 14), to throw down the *mazan*, stretching it out from east to west, and putting his foot upon it so that it could do not harm, and, in another text (M 472v, Boyce, *Reader*, p. 80 text z 16), we are told that he suppressed (*nyrʾft*) the giant dragon (*azdahāg ī mazan*), which corresponds to "giant of the sea" (*mzn ʿy zrhyg*) in a Manichean Middle Persian text; this is the *gigas tēs thalássēs* in the *Kephalaia* (I, pp. 113ff.), which is responsible for ebb and flow (see Henning, "Book of the Giants," p. 54 and n. 3, and cf. Boyce, *Reader*, pp. 6, 62 text y5 with note; and Sundermann, *Parabelbuch*, pp. 21f. with n. 30). Adamas's Iranian heritage is evident in his Sogdian name, Wšγnyy Bγyy (M 583 I r8 in Waldschmidt and Lentz, *Manichäische Dogmatik*, p. 68 [545], with comm. 88 [565], from *wr̥θragna-); whether this name implies that the Sogdians had preserved traditions of a demon-slaying Vərəθraγna or whether it is due to Indian influence, has not yet been investigated. The Greco-Syriac name Adamas/Adamos probably means "indomitable, adamant" (Cumont, "Adamas"). Augustine calls him "the belligerous indomitable hero (or "the hero Adamas") who holds a spear in his right and a shield in his left" (*adamantem heroam belligerum*; *Contra Faustum* quoted by Cumont, p. 79). In the Chinese text edited by Waldschmidt (Waldschmidt and Lentz, pp. 9, 33 [486, 510]) he is called "the brave, strong, equipped with the ten powers, demon-subduing emissary." This god is also called, for reasons as yet not understood, Wisbed Yazd (three other sons of the Living Spirit being the Dahibed, Zandbed, and Mānbed Yazds), and the god with four forms (*yazd ī taskirb*; see Sundermann, "The Five sons," passim, and "Namen von Göttern," pp. 101f., 127 n. 166, 131 n. 226). The *mazan* which he suppresses is that formed by that part of the ejected seed of the

Archons which fell on the moist, and became a horrible monster (*Mir. Man.* I, p. 10 [182]; Syriac *hywt' snyt'* "a terrible beast" in the likeness of the King of Darkness (see Theodore Bar Konay in Jackson, *Researches*, p. 247); note that Ebn al-Nadīm reports that the King of Darkness had "the head of a lion" and a "body like the body of a dragon (*tannīn*)" (*Fehrest*, tr. Dodge, II, p. 778; Taqīzāda, *Mānī wa dīn-e ū*, p. 151 infra). In the Manichean Psalm-book (p. 138.41-42) it is stated explicitly that Adamas subdues the Hyle (i.e., Matter, in Iranian texts called Āz), and in the *Kephalaia* Adamas conquers a "sea giant" which had been formed out of those elements of the Darkness which were thrown into the sea by the Living Spirit and caused its saltiness and bitterness (*Kephalaia*, pp. 114-15). In another Middle Persian text concerning Adamas and his fight with this sea-monster, the monster is not named (Sundermann, *Kosmogonische Texte*, pp. 47ff.).

The battle between a god and a sea monster is of course well known from the Babylonian creation myths (see e.g., the translation by Heidel, *The Babylonian Genesis*, pp. 40ff.) In these the young god Marduk conquers Ti'âmat, the primeval salt-water ocean personified (cf. the Manichean myth just quoted), by shooting an arrow into her mouth which she was unable to close because Marduk had let the evil wind loose into here face (cf. the Persian versions of the dragon-slaying described below in AŽDAHĀ II). It is also found in the Bible, where the Lord is described as having slain Leviathan, the serpent and the *tannīnīm* (crocodiles) in the sea (see, e.g., Heidel, op. cit., pp. 102ff.). With Hebrew *tannīnīm* compare Ebn al-Nadīm's use of Ar. *tannīn* in his description of the Evil Spirit quoted above and note Middle Persian *TNYNA: possibly attested in *Dēnkard*, Madan, p. 816.13, and *Pahlavi Rivayat*, p. 22.10 (see Henning, "Two Manichean Magical Texts," p. 42 and Bailey, *Zoroastrian Problems*, pp. 29f., 2nd ed., p. xxxiii.)

Clearly a large number of elements from different sources, literary and oral, combined to form the various concepts of dragons. These elements and their various connections and interactions, especially those stemming from the Iranian and the Semitic traditions still have to be investigated in detail.

Bibliography: Texts (Old and Middle Iranian, Classical): A. Adam, *Texte zum Manichäismus*, Berlin, 1969. C.R.C. Allberry, *A Manichean Psalm-Book* II, Manichean Manuscripts in the Chester Beatty Collection 2, Stuttgart, 1938. P. K. Anklesaria, *A Critical Edition of the Unedited Portion of the Dādestān-i Dīnīk*, doctoral thesis, University of London, 1958. T. D. Anklesaria, ed., *Dânâk-u Mainyô-i Khard*, Bombay, 1913. M. Boyce, *A Reader in Manichaean Middle Persian and Parthian*, Acta Iranica 9, Tehran and Liège, 1975. *Bundahišn* 1. *The Bondahesh, Being a Facsimile Edition of the Manuscript* TD_1, Tehran, [1350-51 Š./1971-72]. 2. *The Codex DH, Being a Facsimile Edition of Bondahesh, Zand-e Vohuman Yasht, and Parts of Denkard*, Tehran, [1350-51 Š./1971-72]. B. N. Dhabhar, ed., *The Pahlavi Rivâyat accompanying the Dâdestân-î Dînîk*, Bombay, 1913. Idem, ed., *The Persian Rivayats of Hormazyar Framarz and Others*, Bombay, 1932. M. Dresden, ed., *Dēnkart, a Pahlavi Text, Facsimile Edition of the Manuscript B of the K. R. Cama Oriental Institute Bombay*, Wiesbaden, 1966. W. B. Henning, "The Book of the Giants," *BSOAS* 11, 1943, pp. 52-74 (repr. in *W. B. Henning—Selected Papers* II, Tehran and Liège, 1977, pp. 115-37). Idem, *Sogdica*, London, 1940 (repr. ibid., pp. 1-68). K. M. JamaspAsa, *Aogəmadaēcā. A Zoroastrian Liturgy*, Österr. Ak. Wiss., Phil.-hist. Kl., 397, Vienna, 1982. F. M. P. Kotwal, *The Supplementary Texts to the Šāyest nē-šāyest*, Copenhagen, 1969. Lucian, *Quomodo historia conscribenda sit* 29, ed. K. Kilburn, London, 1968. D. N. MacKenzie, "Mani's *Šābuhragān*," pt. 1 (text and translation), *BSOAS* 42/3, 1979, pp. 500-34; pt. 2 (glossary and plates), *BSOAS* 43/2, 1980, pp. 288-310. J. de Menasce, Sh*kand gumânîk* v*ichâr: Texte pazand-pehlevi transcrit, traduit et commenté*, Fribourg, 1945. Idem, *Le troisième livre du Dēnkart*, Paris, 1973. M. Molé, *La légende de Zoroastre selon les textes pehlevis*, Paris, 1967. H. S. Nyberg, *A Manual of Pahlavi*, Wiesbaden, I, 1964 (texts of the legend of Kirsāsp according to the *Pahlavi Rivayat* pp. 31-35), II, 1974. Idem, "La légende de Keresāspa: Transcription des textes pehlevis, avec une traduction nouvelle et des notes philologiques," in *Oriental Studies in Honour of Cursetji Erachji Pavry*, London, 1933, pp. 336-52 (repr. in *Monumentum H. S. Nyberg* IV, Acta Iranica 7, pp. 379-95). C. Schmidt ed., *Kephalaia* I, Manichäische Handschriften der staatlichen Museen Berlin I, Stuttgart, 1940. S. Shaked, *The Wisdom of the Sasanian Sages* (*Dēnkard VI*), Boulder, Colorado, 1979. W. Sundermann, *Mittelpersische und parthische kosmogonische und parabeltexte der Manichäer*, Berliner Turfantexte 4, Berlin, 1973. Idem, *Ein manichäisch-sogdisches Parabelbuch*, Berliner Turfantexte 15, Berlin, 1985. M. R. Unvala, *Dârâb Hormazyâr's Rivâyat* I, Bombay, 1922. A. Waag, *Nirangistan. Der Awestatraktat über die rituellen Vorschriften*, Leipzig, 1941. W. E. West, tr., *Pahlavi Texts* I-V, in SBE 5, 18, 24, 37, 47, Oxford, 1880-87, repr. Delhi, etc., 1965.

Secondary literature: H. W. Bailey, "Arya," *BSOAS* 21, 1958, pp. 522-45. Idem, *Zoroastrian Problems in the Ninth-Century Books*, Oxford, 1943, 2nd ed., 1971. E. Benveniste, "L'origine du *višap* arménien," *Revue des études arméniennes* 7, 1927, pp. 7-91. M. Boyce, *Zoroastrianism* I, see index pp. 336-37 s.vv. Aži Dahāka and dragons. G. Buddruss, "Zur Benennung der Schlange in einigen nordwestindischen Sprachen," *MSS* 33, 1975, pp. 7-14. A. Christensen, *Essai sur la démonologie iranienne*, Copenhagen, 1941. Idem, *Le premier chapitre du Vendidad et l'histoire primitive des tribus iraniennes*, Copenhagen, 1943. F. Cumont, "Adamas, génie manichéen," in *Philologie et linguistique, mélanges offerts à Louis Havet*, Paris, 1909, pp. 79-82.

H. R. E. Davidson, *Gods and Myths of Northern Europe*, Penguin Books, 1964. J. Duchesne-Guillemin, *La religion de l'Iran ancien*, Paris, 1962. G. Dumézil, *Le problème des centaures*, Paris, 1929. W. Eilers, *Sinn und Herkunft der Planetennamen*, Sb. Bayer. Ak. Wiss., Phil.-hist. Kl., 1975, 5, Munich, 1976. H. Grassmann, *Wörterbuch zum Rig-Veda*, 5th ed., Wiesbaden, 1976. L. H. Gray, *Foundations*, pp. 187-91. P. Harvey, *The Oxford Companion to Classical Literature*, Oxford [many editions]. A. Heidel, *The Babylonian Genesis*, 2nd ed., Chicago and London, 1951. W. B. Henning, "Two Manichaean Magical texts...," *BSOAS* 12, 1947, pp. 39-66 (repr. in *W. B. Henning—Selected Papers* II, Tehran and Liège, 1977, Acta Iranica 15, pp. 273-300). J. R. Hinnells, "Reflections on the Bull-slaying Scene," in J. R. Hinnells, ed., *Mithraic Studies* I, Manchester, 1975, pp. 290-312. K. Hoffmann, *Aufsätze zur Indoiranistik* I, ed. J. Narten, Wiesbaden, 1975. A. V. W. Jackson, *Researches in Manichaeism*, New York, 1932, repr. 1966. D. N. MacKenzie, "Zoroastrian Astrology in the *Bundahišn*," *BSOAS* 27, 1964, pp. 511-29. M. Mayrhofer, *A Concise Etymological Sanskrit Dictionary*, 3 vols., Heidelberg, 1956-76. G. Morgenstierne, "An Ancient Indo-Iranian Word for 'Dragon'," in *Dr. J. M. Unvala Memorial Volume*, Bombay, 1964, pp. 95-98 (repr. with additions in *Irano-Dardica*, Wiesbaden, 1973, pp. 24-30). Idem, *Etymological Vocabulary of the Shughni Group*, Wiesbaden, 1974. R. V. Oldenberg, *Die Religion des Veda*, Stuttgart and Berlin, pp. 248ff. H.-C. Puech, *Le manichéisme, son fondateur, sa doctrine*, Paris, 1949. M. Schwartz, review of M. Mayrhofer, *Iranisches Personennamenbuch* I: *Die altiranischen Namen* I: *Die awestischen Namen*, Vienna, 1977, in *Orientalia* 49, 1, 1980, pp. 123-26. W. Sundermann, "The Five Sons of the Manichaean God Mithra," in *Mysteria Mithrae*, ed. U. Bianchi, Rome, 1979, pp. 777-87. Idem, "Namen von Göttern, Dämonen und Menschen in iranischen Versionen des manichäischen Mythos," *Altorientalische Forschungen* 6, 1979, pp. 95-133. S. Ḥ. Taqīzāda, *Mānī wa dīn-e ū*, Tehran, 1335 Š./1956-57. E. Waldschmidt and W. Lentz, *Manichäische Dogmatik aus chinesischen und iranischen Texten*, *SPAW*, Phil.-hist. Kl., 1933, 13, Berlin, 1933, pp. 478-607. G. Widengren, *Die Religionen Irans*, Stuttgart, 1965. R. C. Zaehner, *Zurvan, a Zoroastrian Dilemma*, Oxford, 1955, repr. New York, 1972.

(P. O. Skjærvø)

ii. In Persian Literature

In Persian literature the *aždahā* (also *aždar*, *aždarhā*, *aždahāk*, in modern East-Iranian dialects also *aždār*, etc.) is pictured as a giant snake or lizard with wings.

Descriptions of dragons. The principal texts containing descriptions of *aždahā*s are *Sad dar-e naṯr and sad dar-e Bondaheš* (ed. B. N. Dhabhar, Bombay, 1909, p. 86: the legend of Garšāsp); *Šāh-nāma* ([Moscow], I, pp. 202-04, vv. 1016-22, 1029-31, 1034, 1051; II, p. 96 vv. 274-81; VI, pp. 40 v. 530, 174-75 vv. 133-34, 155, 158; VII, pp. 72-73 vv. 1195, 1214, IX, p. 145 v. 2287-88; XI, p. 149 v. 2360), Asadī Ṭūsī, *Garšāsp-nāma* (ed. Ḥ. Yaḡmā'ī, Tehran, 1354 Š./1975, p. 53 vv. 50, 60-62, 64-65, 67; p. 54 vv. 66, 68-72; p. 57 vv. 4-15, 20-22; p. 58 vv. 28-31, 33-35, 38; p. 59 v. 43; p. 165 vv. 4, 6). In these texts the dragons are variously described: In the Persian epics it is sometimes described as a wolf, a tiger, *šīr-e kappī*, i.e., a sort of sphinx (combined lion and ape), or simply as a *patyāra* (maleficent creature), or a black cloud. In the epics it has one head and mouth, exhaling fire and smoke from its hellish mouth, and inhaling with enough force to suck in a horse and rider, or a crocodile from the water, or an eagle from the sky. In other texts, as in the Old and Middle Iranian texts, it has several heads. (In a verse by Labībī quoted in M. Dabīrsīāqī, *Ganj-e bāz yāfta*, Tehran, 2535 = 1355 Š./1976, its seven heads represent the heavenly spheres and the universe.) The enormous size of the beast is described in the *Šāh-nāma* and the *Garšāsp-nāma*, with elements also found in the Avesta and the Pahlavi literature: It is big as a mountain. Its head resembles a thicket of hair and its bristles stretch down to the ground like nooses. It has two horns the size of the branch of a tree, ten *gaz* or eightly cubits long. Its eyes are the size of wagon wheels or like two tanks of blood. They shine from afar as brightly as stars at night, as two glittering diamonds, as two blazing torches, or as two mirrors held beneath the sun. It has two tusks, each the length of the hero's arm or of a stag's horns. Humans and animals hang from its teeth. When it sticks its long, black tongue out of its mouth it hangs down onto the road like a black tree. Its skin has scales like a fish, each as big as a shield. It has eight feet, though most often it drags itself over the ground, and when it moves it makes the valleys and plains tremble, and a river of yellow poison as deep as a spear flows from its tail and nose. Its color is variously described, e.g., as dark yellow or grey, black, blue. It can not be touched with water, fire, or any weapon. According to one legend it can even speak human language (*Šāh-nāma* 11, p. 96 vv. 274-81). Its lair, guarded day and night, is on a mountain (usually said to be near the sea, whence the *aždahā* itself originated) or rock the same color as its body and is shunned by all living things, animals and plants. The sources variously locate it on the Kašaf-rūd near Ṭūs, on Mount Šekāvand in Kabul, India, "Māzandarān," on Mount Saqīlā in the land of the Romans, Mount Zahāb in the Yaman, or in Ṭabarestān.

Aždahā in Persian legends. Several Iranian heroes battle and slay the dragons. This old literary theme, common to many civilizations and known from both Old Indian and Old Iranian, was elaborated in later times in the national legends on the basis of popular, in some instances perhaps pre-Avestan, legends of Ferēdūn and Garšāsp, and underwent changes due to new social and ideological conditions.

The legends know of a number of other dragon-slaying heroes other than Ferēdūn and Garšāsp, e.g.,

Sām (= Garšāsp), Rostam, Farāmarz, Borzū, Āḏar Barzīn, Šahrīār, Goštāsp, Esfandīār, Bahman, Alexander, Ardašīr, Bahrām Gōr, and Bahrām Čōbīn.

Ferēdun. This is the great dragon-slayer in the Avesta, where he is said to have slain Aži Dahāka. In the national legends, however, Ferēdun has lost the role of a dragon-slayer, no doubt because his opponent Żaḥḥāk was transformed more strongly into a pseudo-historical person, though he is still described as having two snakes growing from his shoulders, a reminiscence of his once reptilian body. In another legend Ferēdūn transforms himself into a dragon to test his sons (*Šāh-nāma* I, p. 256 l. 1; see further below).

Garšāsp and Sām. Unlike Ferēdūn, Garšāsp has retained his dragon-slaying role in the national legends, and the Avestan story of Kərəsāspa has left a trace in later traditions about Garšāsp in Bayhaqī (p. 666). In addition to the older legends, the *Garšāsp-nāma* relates that Garšāsp, at the age of fourteen, was requested by Żaḥḥāk to slay a dragon which had come out of the sea after a storm and made its abode on Mount Šekāvand. Garšāsp ate some *teryāk* (antidote) and set out to fight the dragon. In the fight he shot an arrow from a specially made bow at the dragon's throat, then thrust a spear into its mouth, and finally clubbed it to death. (The club is said to be carved in the shape of a dragon's head, ibid., p. 269 v. 10.) Thereafter Garšāsp lost his skin and consciousness for a while (cf. the similar episode of Sām in *Šāh-nāma* I, pp. 202-04, and see below, Borzū). When he regained his consciousness, he gave thanks to an angel. The dragon's carcass was carried to the city on twenty hitched wagons, and celebrations were held to mark the event. Garšāsp, now honored as *jahān-pahlavān* (chief hero), commemorated his feat by making a flag adorned with a figure of the dragon in black and a pole tipped with a golden lion and a moon above it (*Garšāsp-nāma*, pp. 49-63). This flag afterwords passed to Garšāsp's descendants and was his family's coat of arms (cf. the flag of Rostam, also adorned with a dragon figure, in the *Šāh-nāma* II, p. 214 v. 566). The story is retold once (*Garšāsp-nāma*, p. 165). (A flag with a dragon emblem appears in a picture from the seventh or eighth century A.D. found in eastern Iran, see G. Widengren, *Der Feudalismus im alten Iran*, pl. 13).

In the *Šāh-nāma* (I, p. 202 vv. 1015-51) Sām slays a dragon which has come out of the Kašaf-rūd. (The same feat is attributed to Rostam in the *Jahāngīr-nāma*, ms. Bibl. Nat., Supp. Pers. 498, fols. 62f.) Ebn Esfandīār (I, p. 89) has recorded a legend from Māzandarān in which Sām had slain a dragon there at a place called Kāva Kalāda near the sea. The dragon was fifty ells (*gaz*) long and was killed with a single blow of a specially made mace. The episode was put into Ṭabarī verse, a line of which has been preserved by Ebn Esfandīār (ibid.). (A picture of a dragon trying to coil its tail around the hero has been preserved, see Widengren, op. cit., pls. 11 and 12.)

Rostam. There are several legends about dragon-slaying by Rostam, the most famous ones being Rostam and the *babr-e bayān* (q.v.) and the third of Rostam's *haft-ḵᵛān*. The legend of Rostam and the *babr-e bayān* is found in two versions in a manuscript of the *Šāh-nāma* in the British Museum (Or. 2926, fols. 112b-115a and 118b-122b) and is also current in Iranian oral folklore (A. Enjavī, *Mardom o Šāh-nāma*, Tehran, 1355 Š./1976, pp. 217f.) as well as among the Mandeans of Iraq (H. Petermann, *Reisen im Orient*, 2nd ed., Leipzig, 1965, II, pp. 107-08). The scene of the slaying of the *babr-e bayān* (*patyāra* in the variant story in the B.M. ms.) is in the far east—India in the *Šāh-nāma*, China in the Mandean legend—and Rostam is but a youngster (fourteen and twelve respectively). In both variants Rostam kills the dragon by making it swallow something (a ruse suggested to him by his mentor Gōdarz according to the *Šāh-nāma*, but by a demon captured by him in the Mandean legend): In the first *Šāh-nāma* story Rostam fills ox hides with quicklime and stones and carries them to the place where the dragon comes out of the sea once a week. The dragon swallows them and its stomach bursts. Rostam then has the dragon flayed and makes a coat from its hide called the *babr-e bayān*. In the variant story Rostam does not get into the box but has fastened poisoned blades on it which kill the dragon. Rostam then remains unconscious for two days and nights, but is guarded by his steed Raḵš. On reviving he washes himself in a spring (cf. below, Borzū and Āḏar Barzīn). In the Mandean legend Rostam himself hides in a box, is swallowed by the dragon, and kills it from inside its belly. As a reward the king of China gives Rostam his daughter in marriage. (Cf. below, Farāmarz.)

The story in Rostam's *haft-ḵᵛān* (*Šāh-nāma* II, p. 94 vv. 345ff.) differs. This dragon lives underground on the road to Māzandarān (= India) and Rostam unwittingly enters the dragon's territory. The (talking) dragon attacks him while asleep but Raḵš wakes him and helps him overcome the beast.

Farāmarz. One of the most widely disseminated dragon-slaying stories in Persian tells how Rostam's son Farāmarz with the help of Bīžan slew a dragon called the *mār-e jowšā* (the hissing serpent), which dwelt on a granite mountain in India, by hiding in two boxes and letting themselves be swallowed by the dragon. Beforehand they took doses of *teryāk* against its poison and stuck ambergris and musk up their noses against the stench (*Farāmarz-nāma*, ms. B.M., Or. 2946, fols. 24f.; see also Dj. Khaleghi-Motlagh, "Farāmarz-nāma," *Iran Nameh* 1/1, Washington, D.C., 1361 Š./1982, pp. 22-45).

Borzū, son of Sohrāb. Seeking the hand of the daughter of the king of Yaman, Borzū was required to slay the dragon on Mount Zahāb. He drank *teryāk* and milk against the poison (cf. above, Garšāsp and Farāmarz), went to the dragon's lair, hurled into its mouth an iron ball which choked it, shot arrows into its eyes and blinded it, and clubbed it on the head and killed it. Borzū's armor then cracked and fell off and he lost consciousness (cf. above, Garšāsp). Reviving he washed himself at a spring (cf. above, Rostam, and below, Āḏar Barzīn). The people celebrated this day in the same way as the new year (*Borzū-nāma*, ms. Bib. Nat., Supp. Pers. 1023, fols. 242f.).

Āḏar Barzīn, son of Farāmarz. Looking for a black cloud which came out of a mountain every year in spring and forced the daughter of the local ruler, Bēvarasp, to have intercourse, Āḏar Barzīn found that the cloud was a dragon and slew it with arrows. He then washed at a spring (*Bahman-nāma*, B.M. Or. 2780, fols. 180f.; cf. above, Rostam, Borzū).

Šahrīār, grandson of Rostam. This is another dragon-slayer (*Šahrīār-nāma*, ed. Ḡ.-Ḥ. Bīgdelī, Tehran, 1358 Š./1979, pp. 96f.).

Goštāsp. According to the *Šāh-nāma* (VI, pp. 26 v. 292, 36 vv. 461ff.), while living incognito in the land of the Romans, Goštāsp slew a wolf with the features of a dragon and later a dragon at the requests of the heroes Mīrān and Ahran who both wished to marry the Caesar's daughter.

Esfandīār. In the third of his seven exploits on his journey to rescue his sisters from Arjāsp's prison Esfandīār slew a dragon by means of the box ruse, then became unconscious and on reviving washed himself (*Šāh-nāma* VI, p. 173 vv. 126f.; cf. above, Rostam, Borzū, and Āḏar Barzīn).

Bahman son of Esfandīār. According to the *Bahman-nāma* (B.M. ms. Or. 2780, fols. 186f.), a dragon named Abr-e Sīāh (Black cloud) swallowed Bahman while he was out hunting. The defeat of the hero may symbolize the loss of the crown of an Iranian king to a foreign invader, perhaps Alexander.

Alexander. In the *Šāh-nāma* (VII, p. 71 vv. 1190f.) it is told that Alexander killed a dragon on a mountain by feeding the dragon five ox-hides stuffed with poison and naphtha, but with quicklime, bitumen, lead, and sulphur according to the Syriac Alexander romance. Th. Nöldeke, in his study of the Alexander romance noted the similarity of the Syriac version to the story of Daniel's slaying a dragon with balls of bitumen, dough, and hair, and to the killing of the snake-king Sapor (Šāpūr II, r. 309-79?) through use of camel hides stuffed with straw and charcoal (Jerusalem Talmud, Ned. 3.2; "Beiträge zur Geschichte des Alexanderromans," in *Denkschriften d. Königlichen Akad. d. Wiss.*, Phil.-hist. Kl., 38, Vienna, 1890, pp. 22, 25).

Of the Sasanian kings Ardašīr and Bahrām Gōr slew dragons: Ardašīr (r. 226-41) slew a worm (*kerm*) who protected the owner Haftvād of the castle Kojāran on the Persian Gulf coast, by pouring molten zinc and lead into its mouth (*Kār-nāmag* 7, *Šāh-nāma* VII, pp. 139ff.). Bahrām V Gōr (r. 420-38) on his journey to India as the royal envoy slew a dragon on the seashore (*Šāh-nāma* VII, p. 464 vv. 2111f.) and was given permission to marry one of the Indian king's three daughters. In addition, Bahrām Čōbīn, the Sasanian general and claimant to the throne slew a dragon in Turkistan, which had swallowed the daughter of the ḵāqān and which would become invulnerable if it went to a certain spring and wetted its hair (*Šāh-nāma* IX, p. 145 vv. 2285ff.).

Symbolism of the dragon-slaying. The dragon in Iranian mythology is a destructive demoniacal force and a symbol of drought. Various theories about the dragon-slaying theme in both Indo-European and Indo-Iranian mythology have been advanced. One theory links the Indo-Iranian legends with solar and lunar eclipses and with lunar waxing and waning, which lay at the root of moon worship. The popular explanation for these phenomena was that a dragon comes up from hell every month on the eastern side of the sky and swallows a piece of the moon's disc every night until the night comes when no part of the moon can be seen. Then the moon-god kills the dragon from inside its belly and triumphantly reemerges. In later times, however, the sun took over the moon's role in the celestial combats, and it was the sun which slew the dragon and rescued the moon from the dragon's belly twelve times every year. Later still the celestial combats were brought down to earth. The sun-god or god of light was replaced by a hero, and the belief in the dragon's swallowing of the moon was transformed into the myth of the dragon's swallowing of a maiden (for detailed discussion see Stiecke, *Drachenkämpfe*; Hüsing, *Iranische Überlieferung* and *Krsaaspa*).

In the Persian epics there is no hint of a belief in entry of the moon or sun into a dragon's belly, but in legends and certain poems, particularly those of Neẓāmī, a few vestiges can be traced (see A. Moṣaffā, *Farhang-e esṭelāḥāt-e nojūmī*, Tabrīz, 1357 Š./1978, pp. 36, 693; also Faḵr-al-dīn Gorgānī, *Vīs o Rāmīn*, pp. 180 v. 8, 265 v. 115). In Iran people imagined eclipses to be swallowings of the sun or the moon by a dragon, and they therefore went up onto the flat roofs of their houses at those times and thumped their washtubs in prayer for the sun's or moon's release (Moṣaffā, op. cit , p. 693).

Another interpretation of the dragon-slaying by Indo-Iranian gods is that the god in question was a god of thunder and lightning, that the dragon was a black cloud, and that by slaying the dragon, the god released water impounded in its stomach to fall as rain.

In the Iranian texts there is no direct reference to drought, but all the Persian tales describe the country for many parasangs around the dragon's lair as an arid, burning desert devoid of humans, animals, and plants. At the same time, these legends are silent on the subject of rainfall after the slaying of the dragon and release of water [which the dragon had impounded], but in all the stories the dragon's lair is close to either a spring or the sea, and in most of them, a woman plays a part. It would appear that the woman in the Iranian legends has replaced water and rain as the symbol of fertility and life. The theme of the feast held after the victory over the dragon—note especially the feast of Mehragān held after Ferēdūn's victory over Żaḥḥāk (*Šāh-nāma* I, p. 79, 1.1)—can be traced to the legend of the slaying of a dragon by the god Mehr (Mithras), though no clear and direct link between the ritual and worship and the theme of dragon-slaying has been found.

Structural changes. The main novelty of the Iranian legends is the introduction of the theme of "the maiden and the dragon," in which the dragon becomes a historical person, sometimes a foreign usurper such as Żaḥḥāk, sometimes simply a foreign enemy such as Arǰāsp in the story in the seven labors of Esfandīār. (The story of Ṭā'er and Māleka in the *Šāh-nāma* (VII, p. 220, vv. 26ff.) may be another example, see 'A. Zaryāb Ḵūyī, "Afsāna-ye fatḥ al-ḥażar," in *Šāh-nāma-šenāsī* I, Tehran, 1356 Š./1977, pp. 187-201). The kidnapped maiden always disappears and the hero, after slaying the dragon, is rewarded with marriage to another maiden, with no connection with the dragon. It appears that, as the mythology of dragon-slaying evolved, the maiden was removed from the dragon's belly in order to make the story more realistic and so it became necessary to invent a reason other than rescue of the maiden for the hero's entry into the dragon's belly, namely the invulnerability of the dragon's hide. Because of this, the hero's attacks are always aimed either at the inside of its stomach or at its mouth, eyes, or skull. He has to kill the dragon from within himself, or, in a later development, kill the dragon by feeding it skins stuffed with deadly substances. The pouring of molten lead into the dragon's mouth concurs with Iranian notions about execution of demoniacal beings in the next world by means of molten metal (this may well have been a method of torturing and killing enemies in use among the Iranians themselves, see Wikander, *Männerbund*, pp. 106 f.). Against this, Christensen (*Iran Sass.*, p. 96) derives the story of Ardašīr's dragon-slaying from the legend of the Babylonians' god, Marduk, who called up a terrible wind which entered the mouth of Ti'âmat and killed her. In the Avestan account of Garšāsp's dragon-slaying, a long time has to elapse before the fire's heat begins to affect the dragon's hide. This suggests that belief in the invulnerability of dragon hide was a very old component of the myth.

After slaying the dragon, the hero makes a coat for himself out of its invulnerable hide. As already noted, in several stories the name of some other animal is applied to the dragon in order to give variety to the hero's exploits. In the story of the *babr-e bayān* (q.v.), the tiger (*babr*) is either a dragon whose name has been changed or a beast which was originally a tiger but has been endowed with dragon-like features. The fact that Rostam's coat is also called a leopard skin (*palangīna*) in the *Šāh-nāma* (IV, p. 286 v. 1188) and in a Sogdian legend (E. Benveniste, *Textes Sogdiens*, Paris, 1940, pp. 134-36) supports the interpretation of *babr* in *babr-e bayān* as "tiger." It may be significant that in Greek mythology, the lion which Hercules strangled (because its skin was invulnerable), and whose skin he thereafter wore (like Rostam's *babr-e bayān*) on his shoulders, is called the Nemean lion after the place (Nemea) which the lion had infested. In another surviving legend, the *babr-e bayān* is said to have been a coat sent from heaven (see AKVĀN-E DĪV).

When the dragon is presented as a historical person, the invulnerability of the dragon's hide is transformed into the impregnability of the enemy's castle, which the hero can only seize by stealth. Similarly in the Greek legend of Troy, Epeios, the designer of the wooden horse, plays the same part as the demon in the Mandean legend and as Gōdarz in the Iranian legend of the *babr-e bayān*. In some of the Iranian legends, however, the hero himself devises the ruse (story of the *patyāra* and elsewhere). Several different stratagems for the capture of the castle are mentioned, e.g., entry in the disguise of a merchant (cf. also the story of Esfandīār's capture of the castle of Rū'īn Dež, *Šāh-nāma* VI, p. 192 vv. 452f.), seizure of the enemy's signet-ring (the story of Qāren's capture of the castle of the Ālān people, *Šāh-nāma*, p. 126 vv. 799f.), making the castle's guards drunk (cf. also Šāpūr and Ṭā'er, *Šāh-nāma* V, 224 vv 81f.), etc. In legends where the dragon is presented as a historical person, the maiden is imprisoned by the enemy and set free by the hero, cf. Helen of Troy, Jamšīd's sisters in Ferēdūn's struggle against Żaḥḥāk, Esfandīār's sisters in the story of Esfandīār and Arǰāsp, Māleka in the story of Ṭā'er and Māleka.

The dragon-slaying legends in the Avesta by comparison with the Rigveda, have lost their mythico-religious importance. In the national legends this development is carried much further, to the point where the theme of dragon-slaying has nothing whatever to do with service to religion and becomes an instrument of royal or heroic ideology. Thus in the Iranian legends dragon-slaying comes first among the marvels and bold feats required as proofs of the king's or hero's legitimacy (Khaleghi-Motlagh, *Farāmarz-nāma*, p. 43 n. 23). In general it can be said that the dragon-slaying exploit of Ferēdūn is the model for kings and that of Garšāsp the model for heroes. The requirement that every king or hero should demonstrate the legitimacy of his status by slaying a dragon or doing some other fabulous deed or receiving miraculous aid prompted not only the tendency to historicize mythology but also a contrary tendency to mythologize history.

In the matter of royal ideology, special emphasis was laid on the king's legitimacy at times when his position was contested and insecure. This was the case in the reign of Ardašīr I (r. 241-66). After the overthrow of the long-established Parthian dynasty, the new regime's legitimacy had to be asserted, and this was done in various ways: notably by invention of the genealogy which makes Ardašīr a descendant of the Achaemenids (as in the *Šāh-nāma*, *Kār-nāmag*, and other sources), and by propagation of the stories about the worm (*kerm*); similarly in the case of Bahrām Čōbīn, the general of Hormozd IV (r. 578-90) and rival of Ḵosrow II. According to the version in the *Šāh-nāma* (IX, p. 150 v. 2376), all the people with one voice acclaimed Bahrām as "Shah of Iran" after he had proved his legitimacy by slaying the *šīr-e kappī* in Turkistan. The same purpose is apparent in the stories about Bahrām V (r. 434-60), the renowned Bahrām Gōr. From the accounts in the available sources, it is clear that the Iranians had greatly resented the conduct of his father, Yazdegerd I (399-420) and were unwilling, after the latter's death, to acknowledge the succession of his son, Bahrām; they therefore made a certain Ḵosrow king for a while, until Bahrām recovered his crown and throne with the help of the ruler of Ḥīra. It was because of this situation that Bahrām's legitimacy is so strongly and frequently stressed in stories of his exploits, including his slaying of dragons. In the case of Alexander, unlike the Zoroastrian priests who never acknowledged the Macedonian conqueror, the court historians attempted to justify Alexander's rule in Iran with all sorts of arguments for his legitimacy. In the Alexander romance written by Pseudo-Callisthenes, many wondrous feats and bold deeds are ascribed to Alexander, such as going disguised as his own ambassador on a mission to Darius, making the ice break after crossing a river, seeing marvels, etc.; all stemmed from stories which the Iranians themselves had invented for the purpose of legitimizing Alexander. Later, when this romance was translated into Pahlavi, the translator saw fit to add two further themes, not present in the original but of great importance for Alexander's legitimization in Iran: Alexander's Iranian lineage and his slaying of a dragon.

One particularly interesting example of the importance of dragon mythology in assertion of royal legitimacy is the story in the *Šāh-nāma* (I, p. 256 vv. 1ff.) that Ferēdūn turned himself into a dragon and then barred the path of his sons in order to see how each would react. In this trial, the youngest son, Ēraj, comes out best because he chooses the middle road, halfway between hesitancy and impetuosity, the inhibitive element of earth and the stimulative element of fire being equally balanced in Ēraj's constitution. Ferēdūn therefore judges him worthier than the other two, and in dividing the empire he allots its middle and best part, Iran, to Ēraj.

A recent psychoanalytic interpretation of the dragon-slaying theme, propounded by Otto Rank, a pupil of Sigmund Freud, deserves mention. Rank thinks that the entry of heroes into the belly of the dragon is a symbolic expression of the desire of sons to reenter the womb of the mother. Among other evidence for his theory he cites Iranian dragon-slaying legends.

Bibliography: See also E. Stiecke, *Drachenkämpfe: Untersuchungen zur indogermanischen Sagenkunde*, Leipzig, 1907. G. Hüsing, *Die iranische Überlieferung und das arische System*, Leipzig, 1909. Idem, *Krsaaspa im Schlangenleib*, Leipzig, 1911. O. Rank, *Das Inzest-Motiv in Dichtung und Sage*, 3rd ed., Darmstadt, 1974. G. Dumézil, *Le problème des centaures*, Paris, 1929. Idem, *Horace et les Curiaces*, Paris, 1942. H. Lommel, *Der arische Kriegsgott*, Frankfurt, 1939. S. Wikander, *Der arische Männerbund*, Lund, 1938. Idem, *Vayu*, Lund, 1941. G. Widengren, *Die Religionen Irans*, Stuttgart, 1965. (with further references). Idem, *Der Feudalismus im alten Iran*, Cologne and Opladen, 1969, pp. 15ff. (with reproductions of pictures of dragon-slayings). W. Knauth, *Das altiranische Fürstenideal von Xenophon bis Ferdousi*, Wiesbaden, 1975, pp. 95f. N. M. Titley, *Dragons in Persian, Mughal and Turkish Art*, London, 1981.

(Dj. Khaleghi-Motlagh)

iii. In Iranian Folktales

The dragon is a well-attested motif in the lore of the Indo-European peoples (see Hartland; Róheim, 1912; Smith; Fontenrose; and Lutz). In Persian folklore, the dragon (*aždahā*) appears mostly in tales of magic and in legends. It is curiously missing in myths which are narratives concerned with creation (see Bascom). (In the following all motif numbers refer to Thompson, 1955).

The *aždahā* of the Persian folktales is a fantastic animal of serpentine variety, usually of enormous size (Thompson, B11.2.12; and see, e.g., Anjavī, 1975, p. 80; 1979, pp. 147, 205, 221, etc.), and fire-breathing (B11.2.11; Anjavī, 1979, p. 216; 1975, p. 170; 1984, p. 85, etc.), which resides in or near water (e.g., at the bottom of the sea; motif B11.3.1; in a lake: B11.3.1.1, etc.) Sometimes the *aždahā* resides in an underground cavern (B11.3.5; Anjavī, 1984, p. 85) or in a mountain (Anjavī, 1984, pp. 7, 199-200). It is endowed with powers of magical invisibility (B11.5.2; Anjavī, 1975, p. 80), and speech (N11.4.5; Anjavī, 1974, p. 17; 1979, pp. 20-23; Šakūrzāda, 1967, pp. 304-07; Behrangī, 1965, pp. 35-36). It usually guards a treasure (B11.6.2; Anjavī, 1974, pp. 252-54), or a magical tree or object (D950.0.1; H133.6; Anjavī, 1979, p. 205). In many folktales, it controls the water-supply of a town or a country (B11.7.1; Anjavī, 1974, p. 87; 1975, p. 139; 1979, pp. 147, 177; Eškevarī, 1973, pp. 101-05; Ṣobḥī, 1946, pp. 104-05; Behrangī, 1978, pp. 281-92) forcing the inhabitants to sacrifice a maiden or a princess, by offering her as food to the *aždahā* in order to find access to water.

The tale types 300-303 (Aarne and Thompson; Marzolph), i.e., "The dragon slayer," which demonstrate the dragon-fight motif (B11.11ff.; see Róheim, 1940) are quite common in Persian folk narratives. In these tales the protagonist slays the *aždahā* in order to rescue the princess or maiden about to be sacrificed to the beast (R111.1.3). Such episodes may betray the sexual nature of the dragon-fight because from the standpoint of nutritive value, plump matrons would make more sense than fair maidens (Lutz, p. 208). In the course of the fight with the *aždahā*, the hero is sometimes overcome by the poisonous fumes of the slain beast's venomous blood (B11.2.13.1; Anjavī, 1979, p. 147). *Aždahā* is often used as a metaphor for evil in folk legends (B11.9; Anjavī, 1975, p. 160). In these legends, the saint/hero metaphorically overcomes evil by slaying a dragon (cf. Saint George in Christian tradition; see Aufhauser and Panzer).

In some folktales, the *aždahā* appears as a grateful animal (B350). In a version of the tale type 1165, "The evil woman thrown into the pit" (Anjavī, 1979, pp. 20-23) for instance, an *aždahā* helps its rescuer to marry a princess. In another story, it devours threatening wild animals on behalf of the protagonist (Anjavī, 1974, p. 268). In a version of the tale type 563, "The table, the ass, and the stick," the stick is magically turned into an *aždahā*, by the help of which the hero recovers his stolen magical objects (Anjavī, 1974, p. 299). Sometimes the grateful *aždahā* is itself the bestower of magical gifts (Anjavī, 1975, p. 362).

The most common allomotifs (see Dundes) for the *aždahā* in Persian folklore are snakes (Anjavī, 1975, pp. 360-66; 1979, pp. 7-23, 363), lions (Anjavī, 1974, p. 99), and fish (Anjavī 1974, p. 180). Some folk legends in Iran speak of an aquatic beast which bears a feline name but also has all of the typical draconic features (cf. Omidsalar).

For collections of Persian folktales in western languages see Christensen, 1958; Elwell-Sutton, 1950; and Boulvin, 1975.

Bibliography: A. Aarne and S. Thompson, *The Types of The Folktale*, Folklore Fellows Communications 184, Helsinki, 1973. S. A. Anjavī, *Qeṣṣahā-ye īrānī*, Tehran, 1974. Idem, *Mardom wa Šāh-nāma*, Tehran, 1975. Idem, *Mardom wa Ferdowsī*, Tehran, 1976. Idem, *Gol ba Ṣenowbar če kard? Qeṣṣahā-ye īrānī*, Tehran, 1979, I/1. Idem, *Ferdowsī-nāma: mardom wa qahremānān-e Šāh-nāma* III, Tehran, 1984. J. B. Aufhauser, *Das Drachenwunder der heiligen Georg in der griechischen und lateinischen Überlieferung*, Leipzig, 1911. W. Bascom, "The Forms of Folklore: Prose Narratives," *Journal of American Folklore* 78, 1965, pp. 3-20. Ṣ. Behrangī, *Afsānahā-ye Āḏarbāyjān* I, Tehran, 1965. S. Behrangī and B. Dehqānī, *Afsānahā-ye Āḏarbāyjān* II, Tehran, 1978. A. Boulvin, *Contes populaires persans du Khorassan*, 2 vols., Paris, 1970 and 1975. A. Christensen, *Persische Märchen*, Düsseldorf and Cologne, 1958. A. Dundes, "The Symbolic Equivalence of Allomotifs in the Rabbit-Herd (AT 570)," *Arv* 36, 1982, pp. 91-98. L. P. Elwell-Sutton, *The Wonderful Sea-Horse and Other Persian Tales*, London, 1950. K. S. Eškevarī, *Afsānahā-ye Eškevar-e Bālā*, Tehran, 1973. J. Fontenrose, *Python: A Study of Delphic Myth and Its Origins*, Berkeley, 1980. E. S. Hartland, *The Legend of Perseus: A Study of Tradition in Story, Custom, and Belief* III: *Andromeda, Medusa*, London, 1896. R. Lutz, "Problems of Dragon Lore," in *Folklore on Two Continents. Essays in Honor of Linda Dégh*, ed. Nikolai Burlakoff and Carl Lindahl, Bloomington, 1980, pp. 205-10. U. Marzolph, *Typologie des persischen Volksmärchens*, Beirut, 1984. M. Omidsalar, "Invulnerable Armour as a Compromise Formation in Persian Folklore," *International Review of Psycho-Analysis* 11, 1984, pp. 441-52. F. Panzer, *Studien zur germanischen Sagengeschichte* I: *Bewulf*, Munich, 1910. G. Róheim, *Drachen und Drachenkämpfer*, Berlin, 1912. Idem, "The Dragon and the Hero," *American Imago* 1, 1940, 2, pp. 40-69; 3, pp. 61-94. E. Šakūrzāda, *ʿAqāyed wa rosūm-e ʿāmma-ye mardom-e Ḵorāsān*, Tehran, 1967. G. E. Smith, *The Evolution of the Dragon*, London, 1919. F. Ṣobḥī, *Afsānahā* II, Tehran, 1946. S. Thompson, *Motif-Index of Folk-Literature*, 6 vols., 2nd ed., Bloomington, 1955-58.

(M. Omidsalar)

iv. Armenian Aždahak

Aždahak is the Armenian form, borrowed from Parthian (cf. Man. Parth. *ʾjdhʾg*), of the name of the Avestan demon Aži Dahāka, who in Iranian mythology is said to be chained in Mount Damāvand, from which he will burst forth at the end of days only to be slaughtered by the hero Θraētaona. In the *Šāh-nāma*, Żoḥḥāk (an arabicized form of the name) is depicted as a tyrannical foreign ruler of Iran of demonic aspect: serpents sprout from his shoulders. In Armenian mythology, King Artawazd is said to be imprisoned in Mt. Ararat, like Aži Dahāka in Damāvand (the comparison is drawn by the eleventh-century Armenian scholar Grigor Magistros, *Tʿłtʿerə*, ed. Kostaneanceʿ, Alexandropol, 1910, letter 36). The Armenian historian Movsēs Xorenacʿi relates the same legend as the *Šāh-nāma*, apparently in a Northwest Iranian form (the name of Θraētaona, Mid. Pers. Frēdōn, is found as Hṙudēn), in an appendix to book 1 of his *History of Armenia*, but also identifies Aždahak (without the epithet *Biwrasp*, Pahl. *Bēwarasp* "with ten thousand horses" found in the *Bundahišn*) with Astyages, the king of the Medes against whom the Armenian Tigran rebelled.

In varying Armenian and Iranian applications, Aždahak is seen thus as the embodiment of foreign tyranny. He is also seen as a symbol of wickedness and heresy: Xorenacʿi condemns certain communistic practices of Biwrasp Aždahak; this is interpreted as a reference to the Mazdakite heresy (see N. Akinean, "Biwraspi Aždahak ew hamaynavarn Mazdak hay awandavēpi mēǰ ǝst Movsēs Xorenacʿway" [Biwrasp Aždahak and the communist Mazdak in the Armenian epic according to Movsēs Xorenacʿi], *Handēs Amsoreay*, Vienna, 50, 1936). In an anonymous southern Armenian chronicle dated to the 11th-12th centuries, Moḥammad is described as one possessed by demons and breaking free from confinement; the Arab prophet is shown as a heresiarch in terms reminiscent of Aždahak (see M. H. Darbinyan-Melikʿyan, ed., *Patmutʿiwn Ananun Zrucʿagri karcecʿeal Šapuh Bagratuni*, Erevan, 1971, pp. 40-43).

The depiction of Żoḥḥāk in manuscript illuminations of the *Šāh-nāma* conforms to the Avestan descriptions of the demon as *θrizafanəm θrikamərəδəm xšvašašīm* "three-mouthed, three-headed, six-eyed" (*Yt.* 9.8), but appears to derive from Mesopotamian iconography, as in the late representation of Nergal at Hatra. In Armenia, the fourth-century A.D. king Pap, who persecuted the Church and practised sodomy, is described by the historian Pʿawstos Biwzand as having serpents springing from his breasts (*Patmutʿiwn Hayocʿ*, Erevan, 1968, 4.44, 5.22). A terra-cotta figurine in the Hermitage, probably made in Sogdia in the 7th-8th centuries A.D., shows a man, enthroned and wearing a jewelled tiara, with two snakes springing from his shoulders at the base of the neck (see N. V. D'yakonova, "Terrakotovaya figurka Zakhaka,"

Trudy otdela Vostoka gosudarstvennogo Ermitazha 3, 1940, pp. 195-205 fig. 1). In modern Armenia, the steles with snakes and other figures carved on them are called *višap* "dragon" by the Armenians, but *aždahā* by the Kurds.

In Zoroastrian thinking, temporal values of righteous kingship are closely bound to spiritual righteousness and the sovereignty of Ahura Mazdā; the development of the image of the demonic creature Aži Dahāka as the human Aždahak, a tyrant and heresiarch with visibly demonic attributes, is logical in a Zoroastrian framework.

(J. R. RUSSELL)

AZDĀKARA (from Old Persian *azdā-* "announcement" and *kara-* "maker"), officials of the Achaemenid chancery, the heralds, who made known the government edicts, court sentences, etc. The word is first attested in the form *'zdkr(y)'* in an Aramaic letter, sent in 428 B.C. to Aršāma (q.v.), satrap of Egypt (Cowley, no. 17.5, 7). The corresponding verbal expression is attested in Cowley no. 27.8-9 as *'zd' ytʿbd* "it is made known, it is announced." In Old Persian we have (DNb 50) *azdā kušuvā* corresponding to *hwdʿ* in the Aramaic version (N. Sims-Williams, *BSOAS* 44/1, 1981, p. 4); and (DB 1.32, DNa 43, 45) *azdā bav-* "to become known." In later Iranian we find Christian Sogdian *'zd'qry'* "announcing" (F. W. K. Müller and W. Lentz, *Soghdische Texte* II, SPAW, 1934, p. 526, text 3.42) and Khotanese *āysda* (i.e., /*āzda*/) *yan-* "to protect, look after" with the noun *āysdagaraa-* "protector" (H. W. Bailey, *Dictionary of Khotanese Saka*, Cambridge etc., 1979, pp. 21f.).

Bibliography: A. Cowley, *Aramaic Papyri of the Fifth Century B.C.*, Oxford, 1923. W. Eilers, "Iranisches Lehngut im arabischen Lexikon," *IIJ* 5, 1962, p. 225. P. Grelot, *Documents araméens d'Égypte*, Paris, 1972, p. 282. W. Hinz, *Altiranisches Sprachgut der Nebenüberlieferungen*, Wiesbaden, 1975, p. 52. B. Porten, *Archives from Elephantine*, Berkeley, 1968, p. 52. H. H. Schaeder, *Iranische Beiträge* I, Halle, 1930, p. 264. O. Szemerényi, "Iranica II," *Die Sprache* 12, 1966, p. 204.

(M. DANDAMAYEV)

AZDĪ, MOḤAMMAD B. RAWWĀD, a notable of Azerbaijan at the beginning of the 3rd/9th century, known mainly in connexion with the revolt of Bābak (q.v.), the leader of the K̲orrami movement.

According to the *Fehrest*, Bābak was in Ebn al-Rawwād's service in Tabrīz for two years between the ages of sixteen and eighteen. Probably a variant of this, cited by Ṭabarī, says that Bābak's mother was a servant of Ebn al-Rawwād. Ṭabarī also refers to Wajnā' b. Rawwād, probably Moḥammad's brother, and to the *rostāq* of Dāk̲arraqān, i.e., Dehk̲ᵛāraqān (see ĀẕARŠAHR) to the east of Lake Urmia, as "the *belād* of Moḥammad b. al-Rawwād." Yaʿqūbī mentions Ebn al-Rawwād as one of the Azerbaijani notables who helped the caliph's forces against Bābak in 206/821-22.

Bibliography: *Fehrest*, p. 343. Ṭabarī, III, pp. 1172, 1232, 1380. Yaʿqūbī, II, p. 564. G. H. Sadighi, *Les movements religieux iraniens au IIe et IIIe siècle de l'hégire*, Paris, 1983, pp. 239, 241-42, 247. E. M. Wright, "Bābak of Badhdh and al-Afshīn during the Years A.D. 816-841; Symbols of Iranian Persistence against Islamic Penetration in North Iran," *Muslim World* 38, 1948, p. 46. S. Nafīsī, *Bābak-e K̲orram-dīn*, Tehran, 1348 Š./1969, pp. 9, 57, 88, 145.

(G. R. HAWTING)

AZERBAIJAN (Āḏarbāy[e]jān), region of northwestern Iran, divided between the present-day territories of Iran and the Soviet Union since the treaties of Golestān (1813) and Torkamānčāy (1828).

i. *Geography.*
ii. *Archeology.*
iii. *Pre-Islamic history.*
iv. *Islamic history to 1941.*
v. *History from 1941-1947.*
vi. *Population and its occupations and culture.*
vii. *The Iranian language of Azerbaijan.*
viii. *Azeri (Āḏarī) Turkish.*
ix. *Iranian Elements in Azeri Turkish.*
x. *Azeri literature.*
xi. *Music of Azerbaijan.*

i. GEOGRAPHY

I. The geographic concept of Azerbaijan.

A. The name of the country is derived from that of the Achaemenian satrap of Media Atropates (Strabo 11.523) who was retained by Alexander in the government of western Media and preserved it under his successors, thus founding a principality which maintained itself in a state of independence or at least semi-independence until the second century B.C., and was only definitively reunited with the Persian empire under the Sasanian king of kings Šāpūr I along with Armenia (cf. Markwart, *Ērānšahr*, pp. 111-12). From the name of this man comes the Greek forms (Atropatene, Atropatios Mēdia [Strabo loc. cit.], Tropatene [Ptolemy 6.2], the Armenian form Atrpatakan (Movsēs Xorenacʿi, cf. Markwart. *Ērānšahr*, pp. 108-14), the Middle Persian form Āturpātakān (cf. Schwarz, *Iran*, p. 960), the New Persian forms Āḏarbāyjān and Āḏarbāygān. The medieval Arab geographers were already giving it different meanings, deriving it from the personal name Āḏarbāḏor forging popular etymologies, like "fire temple" or "guardian of the fire" (from *āḏar*, "fire" and *bāykān*, "guardian," Yāqūt, I, p. 172).

B. From antiquity until the time of the Arab conquest the name of this country, an independent principality or province first under the Sasanians, then of the caliphate, was thus perceived as that of a political circumscription whose frontiers were always changing as a result of political occurrences. However, the heart of the area was always the mountainous country to the east of lake Urmia (Reżā'īya). The ancient summer capital was located there at Ganzaca (Ganzak) (Strabo, loc. cit.), the present-day Taḵt-e Solaymān. At the time of the Arab conquest, the (summer) capital was located at Ardabīl. In the third century B.C., Atropatene had probably extended toward the north to the Pontic regions Phasia and Colchis (Markwart, op. cit., p. 108) but normally its boundaries were limited by the basin of the Araxes. In the Middle Ages, Masʿūdī (Morūǰ I, p. 100.18) indicates that Azerbaijan extended to the north of the river. To the northeast, the soil basins of Moḡān (the plain to the south of the Araxes) were included in Azerbaijan by Masʿūdī and by Ebn Ḵordāḏbeh, but were excluded by other geographers. Varṯān on the Araxes was the farthest locality attached to Azerbaijan to the northeast, according to Ebn al-Faqīh (p. 286). In the third century of our era, the western frontier bordering Armenia was moved by the union of the cantons of "Persian Armenia" with Azerbaijan to the west of the lake (Markwart, op. cit., pp. 109-10) and was subsequently localized in the mountainous countries between the two lakes Urmia and Van. To the south Azerbaijan extended at one period to Sīsar, present day Sanandaǰ. Subsequently, its main eastern boundary was situated at the bed of the Safīd-rūd, which separated it from the province of J̌ebāl and then at the mountain chain of the western Alborz which separated it from the humid, forested regions of Gīlān.

Thus, at the time of the early Arab geographers, Azerbaijan consisted essentially of a northwestern fragment of the high interior Iranian plateau within limits that did not differ much from the frontiers of present-day Iran and that, in any case, from the side of the low lands of the Transcaucasus, scarcely exceeded the bed of the Araxes. The imprecise and sometimes contradictory information given by Yāqūt in the beginning of the 7th/13th century, occasionally extends Azerbaijan to the west to Erzinjan (Arzanǰān). On the other hand in certain passages, he annexes to it, in addition to the steppes of Moḡān, all of the province of Arrān, bringing the frontier of the country up to Kor, indicating, however, that from this period the conception of Azerbaijan tended to be extended to the north and that its meaning was being rapidly transformed.

C. The Turkification of Azerbaijan: an ethnic region. This country of crude mountain peoples, still poorly acculturated to the rest of the Iranian world (even if it is an exaggeration for Moqaddasī to affirm [p. 375.2] that in Sabalān seventy different dialects were spoken), underwent, as a result of the Turkish invasions, a profound ethno-linguistic transformation. The essential cause for this was the geographical situation of Azerbaijan, where the Turkish tribes newly arrived from Central Asia assembled for the holy war on the western frontiers of the Islamic domain. They had traveled the route of the steppes, overrun by the nomads and opposed by the Christians of the humid, wooded lowlands of Christian Georgia in western Transcausia and of the empire of Trebizond in the Pontic forest. Azerbaijan at the end of the major migration route of the nomad tribesmen—along the dry southern watershed of the Alborz to the

south of the Caspian forest—was an area where the newcomers could collect and become dominant.

But the process was long and complex. Although isolated Turkish groups had doubtlessly appeared in Transcaucasia repeatedly from the beginning of the seventh century A.D., it was only in the 5th/11th and 6th/12th centuries that the first massive settlements occurred. This happened in particular in the semi-arid steppes of eastern Transcaucasia, north of present-day Azerbaijan, in the provinces of Arrān and of Moḡān, but outside the state of the Kesranids of Šervān, which remained relatively untouched. The Turkification of these northern centers was rapid. Even before the Mongol invasion, the Turkmen "swarmed like ants" in Arrān and Moḡān (Nasavī, Sīrat al-Solṭān J̌alāl-al-dīn, ed. Houdas, Paris, 1891, p. 225). Moḡān (Mūqān), still known as the name of a city by the first Arab geographers (Ebn al-Faqīh, p. 285; Esṭaḵrī, p. 182; Ebn Ḥawqal, p. 239; cf. Schwartz, Iran, pp. 1089-94), was in the beginning of the 7th/13th century according to Yāqūt (IV, p. 686) only a region where the villages alternated with pasturage and populated exclusively by Turkmen. In the second half of the thirteenth century, according to Qazvīnī (Kosmographie, ed. Wüstenfeld, Göttingen, 1848, II, p. 379.8) it was no more than a winter passage for Turkman nomads. In this period Turkmen were found to the west of Lake Urmia and some groups were found in the area of Kurdistan in the region of Šahrazūr, but, generally, there were few throughout the south of Azerbaijan, where the effect of the accumulation along the frontier did not have any effect.

At the time of the Mongol invasion, most of the first arrivals had passed on to Anatolia, but new groups of Turks or Turkified Mongols are to be noted in numbers in southern Azerbaijan, in the regions of Marāḡa, Ḵoy, around Lake Urmia, as well as in the J̌ebāl in the regions of Qazvīn and Zanǰān. In addition, after the death of Abū Saʿīd, the Turks who had moved to Anatolia began to return to Iran (J̌alāyerī and Čūpānlū). This movement continued under the Qara Qoyunlū and the Āq Qoyunlū, and the linguistic Turkification had by then certainly progressed to an advanced degree. But the decisive period no doubt occurred in the Safavid period with the adoption of Shiʿism as the state religion of Iran, while the Ottoman state remained faithful to Sunnism. Soon Shiʿite propaganda among the tribes located outside of the urban centers of orthodoxy, prompted the Anatolian nomad tribes to return to Iran. This migration began in 1500 when Shah Esmāʿīl assembled the Qezelbāš tribes in the region of Erzincan. The attraction made itself felt as far as the region of Antalya, whence came the Tekelū, who were to play an important role in Iran, in mass along with 15,000 camels. Nomads undoubtedly constituted the majority of the movement, though it also affected semi-nomads and even peasants. At the end of the 11th/16th century, Shah ʿAbbās I's organization of the great confederation of the Šāhseven precipitated the massive entry of Turks into Azerbaijan, and the area became definitively Turkish in this period, with the exception of some isolated Tati-speaking communities. From the time of Shah ʿAbbās to that of Nāder Shah, many Azeris were moved eastward into Khorasan to guard the frontier against the Uzbeks. But this did not influence significantly the definitive settlement of the Turkish nomads. During this period the Azeri language came to be spoken as far east as Abhar, near Qazvīn (Chardin, *Voyages... en Perse*, ed. Langlès, Paris, 1830, IV, pp. 179-80; the observations date from 1665-77). At the time of Evlīā Čelebī, who traveled in Azerbaijan in 1645, Turkish, largely predominant in Tabrīz among the lower classes (*Seyâhatnāmesī*, ed. Z. Danişman, 15 vols., Istanbul, 1969-71, esp. III, p. 247), was spoken in Qazvīn along with Persian. The delimitation of the languages on the Iranian plateau has on the whole remained the same until the present time. Elsewhere, however, the progress of Azeri Turkish has continued until the present. In the course of the last two generations the entire southern part of Iranian Ṭāleš, the coastal fringe of the Caspian, has adopted Turkish as the common language of commerce and in some places it has become the mother tongue of the majority of the population. This was a consequence both of a return of Azeris to northern Azerbaijan after the Soviet revolution and of a large present-day migration of Turks of the high leeward slope of the Alborz who have settled on the shore plain (M. Bazin, "Le Tâlech et les Tâlech: Ethnie et région dans le Nord-Ouest de l'Iran," *Bulletin de l'Association de géographes français*, no. 417-418, May-June, 1974, pp. 161-70). The area of the Azeri language in Iran, even omitting the numerous Azeri minorities scattered in various provinces (especially Khorasan) and other Turkish-speaking minorities of Iran (Turkmen, Ḵalač, Qašqāʾī), thus goes well beyond the political boundaries of the provinces of Western Azerbaijan (center: Urmia [Reżāʾīya]) and Eastern Azerbaijan (center: Tabrīz). (Their respective populations, according to a 1976 census, were 1,408,875 and 3,194,543 inhabitants.) The linguistic area comprises, along with most of the province of Zanjān (579,000) important portions of the central province (to the west of, and around, Qazvīn) and even of the province of Gīlān. The Azeri-speaking population in northwest Iran today probably exceeds 6 million persons. This human geographical area defines most exactly the geographical concept of Azerbaijan today.

In the region of the Soviet Socialist Republic of Azerbaijan, the same process of linguistic and cultural assimilation has taken place. The total population of Soviet Azerbaijan (86,600 km^2), which includes the autonomous Republic of Nakhichevan (which separates Soviet Azerbaijan from Soviet Armenia) and the autonomous oblast of Upper Karabakh, counted, in 1979, 6,028,000 inhabitants (of which 3,195,000 [53 percent] were urban) as compared to 3,700,000 (1,770,000 urban population) in 1959 and 2,340,000 (570,000 urban) in 1913. In this total, the proportion of Azeris, which was 67.5 percent in 1959, rose to 73.82 percent in 1970 and 78.1 per cent in 1979; this increase reflects the now almost complete assimilation of the Iranian-speaking populations of northern Ṭāleš. In the Armenian minority (9.42 percent in 1970 from 12 percent in 1959) and various Caucasian minorities the same assimilation is in progress. At the same time, in Soviet Azerbaijan the proportion of the population of Russian nationality decreased from 13.6 percent in 1959 to 10 percent in 1970 and 7.9 percent in 1979. In addition, more than 750,000 Azeris are settled outside Soviet Azerbaijan itself. The total number of Azeris in the Soviet Union rose to 4,380,000 in 1970 and 5,477,000 in 1979 (numerically, the seventh largest nationality). Their relative weight (but not their importance) is considerably less than that of the Azeris in Iran. (For the statistics see Y. V. Bromleĭ et al., *Processus ethniques en U.R.S.S.*, Moscow, 1982, passim, more up to date than the Russian edition 1975.)

Thus the Azeri people, being the result of a blending process in which the Turanian elements are few (Schoch, *Beiträge*), is the product of a multi-secular cultural Turkification that is actively pursued still. Although split in two by a recent and artificial boundary, the Azeri ethnic group remains vigorous, and exceeds on all sides the territorial limits accorded to it. Nevertheless, both in Iran and the U.S.S.R., the political-administrative entities that today bear the name Azerbaijan constitute the nuclei of this ethnic region.

II. Physical geography.

Stretching from the extreme east of the Caucasus to the north to the northern confines of the Zagros to the south, Azerbaijan includes natural environments of great contrasts. Between the high mountain blocks, where sufficient rain permits rain-fed agriculture, lie low basins, where arid climatic conditions prevail and where the agriculture depends on irrigation.

A. Morphological unities, sharply defined in Soviet Azerbaijan, are much less clear in Iranian Azerbaijan.

1. To the north, Soviet Azerbaijan extends to the southeastern extremity of the chain of the Caucasus, the marginal border of the Russian platform, resulting from an Eocene folding supplemented by vertical movements at the end of the Tertiary period. A vast and complex anticlinorium running northwest to southeast, with a Jurassic-Cretaceous sedimentary osseous frame, cut by longitudinal faults, constitute its axis, with high summits chiseled by the Quaternary glaciation (Bābā-Jūzī, 4,480 m, on the frontier of Dagestan; Bābā-dāğ, 3,632 m). Overthrusts and imbricate structures appear on the southern slopes. The southeastern termination of the Caucasus, in the hills of Gobystan (400 m) and the peninsula of Apsheron are marked by structures of short domes with which are associated mud volcanoes and diapirs (piercement folds) with petroleum beds.

2. The plain of the Kura (Kor) and the Araxes (Aras), the eastern extremity of the Transcaucasian trench, is an alluvial basin that was filled primarily in the Quaternary, in a regular slope from

west to east, divided by large water courses: the steppe of Šervān to the north of the Kura; the steppe of Karabakh and the steppe of Milskaja between the Kura and Araxes; the steppe of Moğān to the south of the Araxes, the last partially extending into Iranian territory.

3. The lesser Caucasus running in the general direction of northwest to southeast like the Caucasus, has a more complicated structure than the latter. The Cretacean and Jurassic sediments are mixed with numerous secondary and tertiary granite batholiths and ultrabasic intrusions (gabbroes, perioditites) that are aligned along the chains of the Shachdag (Ginaldag, 3,367 m; Gyamyshdag, 3,724 m) and of Karabakh (Dalidag, 3,616 m). The whole system culminates in the Sang-e Sūr mountains (Mt. Kopydzhikh, 3,916 m), with material that is essentially Eocene (volcanic-sedimentary facies); their southwest slopes define the autonomous region of Nakhichevan (Nak̲ǰavān), beyond the Soviet Socialist Republic of Armenia. Vast Neocene volcanic overflows crown the edifice.

4. The chains of the Ṭāleš, reaching heights of 2,400 m, constitute the Iranian-Soviet border. They extend from northwest to southeast, south of the Araxes, in the direction of the Caspian sea, delimiting the triangular plain of Lankarān (Soviet Talysh) situated between the sea and the mountains. The predominence of Eocene volcanic-sedimentary material relates them to the lesser Caucasus and the Alborz, of which they are the northwestern termination.

5. To the south of the frontier, the mountain blocks of Iranian Azerbaijan are characterized by volcanic constructions, the result of considerable eruptions which took place in the Neocene and Quaternary epochs, in conjunction with the fracturing of the northwest sector of the high Iranian plateau. This activity occurred along the "volcanic cicatrix" that follows the internal ridge of the Zagros and marks its contact with the central Iranian plateau. The large andesitic cones of Sabalān (4, 740 m) to the west of Ardabīl, and of Sahand (3,710 m) between Tabrīz and Marāğa, bear the marks of the Quaternary glacier; Sabalān now also bears minor glaciers (its permanent snows lie above ca. 4.400 to 4,500 m). They dominate the lower plateaus, untouched by the glaciers, of the Kūh-e Bozqūš (3,305 m) between Sarāb and Mīāna, and Kīāmakī-dāğ, to the north east of Marand.

6. Beneath these recent volcanic eruptions, the substratum presents a complex structure. There are folded volcanic-sedimentary Eocene layers to the northeast and to the east, in the prolongation of the chains of the Alborz and Ṭāleš: Qarāğa-dāğ or Qara-dāğ to the northwest of Ahar (2,880 m), and the hills of Kūh-e Ṣalawāt to the north of Sabalān, continued by Neocene hills limited by the eastwest anticline of the K̲orūžlū-dāğ (700 m), which dominates the Moğān steppe to the south.

In the northwest, west, and south are exposed older elements of consolidation wherein are mixed fragments of an infra-Cambrian base and sedimentary Paleozoic and Mesozoic series associated with ultrabasic intrusions folded at the end of the Cretaceous and before the Eocene. These form the osseous frame of the massifs that, to the west of Lake Urmia, constitute the Turko-Iranian border (Kūh-e Zakī, 3,100 m.) and to the north, separate the basin of the Araxes (Kūh-e Mesow, 3,155 m). This is the northwestern extremity of the large tectonic unity of central Iran which here is limited between the orogens of the Alborz and the Zagros, raised and divided by numerous fractures.

7. The tectonic division of the northwest of the Iranian plateau, is further marked by the existence, between the raised masses, of sunken depressions with Neocene and Quarternary filling (gypsum and saline formations, conglomerates, still sharply corrugated), which contain the principal centers of urban life. These are the basin of Ardabīl (1,350 m), between Sabalān and the chains of Ṭāleš; the depression of Qara-sū and Ahar (1,300-1,000 m) which runs in an eastwest direction, to the north of Sabalān; the basin of Sarāb (1,700-1,900 m) parallel to that of Qara-sū, to the north of Sabalān; and especially the heart of Azerbaijan: the vast basin of Lake Urmia (1,275 m—with more than thirty-five islands), which is broken up by small volcanic reliefs: Kūh-e Čoboqlū (2,175 m) in the peninsula of Šāhī on the eastern shore; Mount Bezow (1,947 m) and Mount Zanbīl (1,610 m), both isolated on the plain to the northwest of Lake Urmia.

B. Climate. Azerbaijan presents a varied range of climatic conditions, being situated at the limits of the subtropical zone and of the temperate zone, and both connected to the Euroasian continental mass and subject to the influence of the Near Eastern bodies of water. However, its fundamental characteristic is aridity. The cyclonic depressions arriving from the west, having dropped their moisture for the most part on the slopes of the Colchian watershed of the Transcaucasus, reach this area almost entirely without water.

Precipitation depends primarily on the relief of the mountains and the altitude. The high chains of the eastern Caucasus probably receive nearly a meter of precipitation a year, and the lesser Caucasus, the chains of the Turco-Iranian frontier to the west of lake Urmia, and the summits of Qarāǰa-dāğ, Sabalān, and Sahand, more than 600 mm. But the low plains of the Kura and the Araxes, which are deeply wedged into the mountainous mass, receive in total a mere 2-300 mm, and the annual total is even less than 200 mm over the rivers of the Caspian to the south of the peninsula of Apsheron (Aliat-Pristan, on the coast south of Baku, 189 mm) as well as in a section in the heart of the Iranian steppe of Moğān on the windward side of the Qarāǰa-dāğ (Mošīrān, 156 mm at an altitude of 667 m). The figures are scarcely higher for the more elevated, Iranian part of the Araxes basin (K̲oy, 277 mm at 1139 m of altitude). The southern basins of Iranian Azerbaijan, even more elevated, receive slightly more rainfall (Ardabīl, 356 mm at an altitude of 1,350 m; Mīāna, 359 mm at an altitude of 1,057 m), but precipitation also sinks to less than 300 mm in the greater area of the basin of Lake Urmia

(Mīāndoāb, 262 mm), although the city of Urmia itself receives 405 mm (Tabrīz, 312 mm) as does the basin of Sarāb (286 mm at Sarāb itself). The first slopes of the volcanic reliefs are barely more favored (Līqvān at an altitude of 2,000 m on the northern watershed of Sahand, 362 mm). Only the Soviet coast of Ṭāleš enjoys an exceptionally high rainfall because there the orographic effect (the discharge of the rainy winds from the east, filled with moisture gathered in the course of their passage over the Caspian, as well as when the Cyclonic depressions pass along the coast on the slopes of the Ṭāleš chain) are added to the intense activity of the cyclones over the southern bank of the Caspian and yield considerable precipitation (Lankarān, 1,250 mm.)

The periods of rainfall are characterized generally by two high points, one in the spring (May, or less often, April) connected with the convectional rains that develop in the barometrically low point preceding the establishment of the hot and dry flow of summer. The second is in autumn or the beginning of winter (most often in October) which is connected with the cyclonic rains from the west. Their highest frequency occurs with the onset of the winter thermic anti-cyclone. The spring maximum is the higher of the two in most areas, including Iranian Azerbaijan, which is more closely connected to the continental land mass, while the autumnal rains dominate slightly in the eastern part of the Transcaucasian basin, on the northeast watershed of the Caucasus and in Soviet Ṭāleš, where the influence of the Caspian on the genesis of autumnal cyclones is apparent.

As regards temperatures, the moderating influence of the Caspian is significantly felt in the summer. Thus, Ardabīl at an altitude of 1,350 m has an average temperature of 20.9° in August in comparison with 24.8° in Tabrīz, which is situated at almost the same altitude (1,362 m), but which is more closely connected with the interior land, and 24° in July in Urmia (1,329 m). On the Caspian shore, at an altitude of 21 m, Baku registers only 25.5° in July, and Lankarān 26° in August, as opposed to 28.9° in July in Kyurdamir (442 m altitude, located in the Kura plain). The mean temperature of the hottest months remains below 27° almost everywhere in the Kura and Araxes plains. In winter the difference is less apparent, both in the high basin of Iranian Azerbaijan (Ardabīl has minus 20° in January, as compared with minus 2° in Urmia and minus 2.7° in Tabrīz) and in the Kura and Araxes plains where Baku registers 3.6° in January (and Lankarān 3.3°) as compared with 1.3° at Kyurdamir, a contrast that represents only the difference in altitude. On the Caspian coastal regions, the absolute extremes do not drop below minus 15° while they remain around minus 25° in the interior of the plain.

C. Hydrology. The two great rivers of Azerbaijan are the Kura, which flows along the axis of the Transcaucasian ditch (length 1515 km; watershed basin 188,000 km²) and its tributary on the right bank, the Araxes (length 1072 km; watershed basin 102,000 km²) which in its long course constitutes first the Turco-Soviet border, then the Irano-Soviet border. Both rivers originate in the highlands of eastern Anatolia and, partially supplied by Caucasian tributaries, for the most part escape the effects of the aridity of the regions downstream. The Kura's mean discharge is 397 m³ per second at Mingechaur and 586 m³ per second at Ṣabīrābād after the Araxes has joined it (the mean discharge of the latter is 222 m³ per second at Karadonlu shortly after its entry into Soviet territory). Both water courses reach their maximum level in May, as a result of the melting of snow in the highlands and secondarily as a result of the spring rains, and they reach their minimum level in August-September; however, in summer the high waters of the Kura (month of second-highest level June) surpass those of the Araxes (month of second- highest level April). This is due to the fact that most of the Kura's water comes from the western and central Caucasus and its glaciers. Moreover, the Kura reaches a secondary peak in November as a result of the autumnal rains and then declines to a secondary low in January-February due to glacial water retention, while the Araxes has a simple "two-time" regime.

The water courses of Iranian Azerbaijan are much more modest. The Safīd-rūd (Qezel Üzen), the principal water course of the northwestern part of the Iranian plateau, only skirts the edges of its southeastern borders. Most of the region belongs to the endoreic basin of Lake Urmia (51,000 km²), a shallow body of water (16 m at the maximum level, generally 6 to 8 m) and very saline; various analyses have estimated the salinity to range from 18.8 to 29.1 percent. Its surface, which is extremely variable, can range from 4,750 to 6,100 km² between periods of high and low water and this closely reflects the annual variations of rainfall. Thus the lake underwent a maximum regression in 1962 and had extremely high levels in 1909-14 and 1969. The principal water courses that supply it are the Zarrīna-rūd to the south (watershed basin 7,890 km²; mean discharge 50 m³ per second) and the Ājī-čāy (Talḵa-rūd) to the east (watershed basin 8,100 km²; mean discharge 13 m³ per second). Both reach their peak in May-April while the low is in August (Ājī-čāy) or in September (Zarrīna-rūd, which is farther south and influenced by the summer aridity of the Zagros Mediterranean-type climate).

D. Plant cover and ecological regions. In theory the mountainous massifs in their natural state produce a woody vegetation. In the southern chains of Iranian Azerbaijan, forests of oaks with deciduous leaves (*Quercus Brantii, Quercus Libani, Quercus infectoria, Quercus iberica*) are mixed with junipers (*Juniperus excelsa, Juniperus oxycedrus*) at an altitude from 1,600-700 to 2,200 m. These trees are well-adapted to aridity and cold winters. In Karabakh and the lesser Caucasus, this forest indicates greater humidity and becomes more complex, containing oaks (*Quercus macranthera, Quercus castaneifolia, Quercus iberica, Quercus araxina*), yoke-elms (*Carpinus orientalis, Carpinus betulus*), and maples at altitudes from 1,500 to 2,300 m, while beech trees (*Fagus orientalis*) are found at a higher level.

The lower level, with oaks, elms, and maples, in their natural state probably covered both the Qarāja-dāḡ and the eastern and northern slopes of Sabalān. In the Caucasus, the beech tree forests are found along the whole axis of the mountain chain, above the level of oaks (*Quercus robur, Quercus longipes*). Lastly, the chains of Soviet Ṭāleš present a particularly rich forest in which the chestut leafed oak (*Quercus castaneifolia*) predominates. This species is associated with the yoke elms and also with various endemic species (*Gleditschia caspica*) which already hint at the botanic complexity of the Hyrcanian forest (the southern region of the Caspian).

The present reality differs from the theory, however. Only the best watered chains (Caucasus, Lesser Caucasus, Ṭāleš) still possess appreciable stretches of forests. Soviet Karabakh has already been deforested, and throughout Iranian Azerbaijan the forests have been reduced to miniscule relics or isolated trees which barely allow us to reconstruct the original plant covering. The steppe, which is native to the low plains of the Transcaucasia and in the high basin of Iranian Azerbaijan below the forest line, has been greatly extended as a consequence of man's activity.

This strong deforestation of the Iranian mountains represents the thousand year-old settlement of dense agricultural civilizations in the mountain valleys above the forbidding plains. Like the semi-desert steppes of the Kura and Araxes, the high, closed, semi-arid basins of Iranian Azerbaijan are not in fact suited for cultivation of grains dependent on rain. In fact, the combination of summer aridity and winter frost that curtails the growing season and makes useless a certain percentage of the rainfalls makes such cultivation impossible. The boundary of nonirrigated culture is located, therefore, in the proximity of isohyets of 300 to 500 mm of rain per year. Sedentary life is hardly possible below these figures except in scattered places in conjunction with irrigation. This situation influences the whole human geography of the area.

III. Human and economic geography.

A. The nomads and their sedentarization. Azerbaijan combines plains devoted to a large extent to the winter migration of tribes and mountains suited to shelter a dense agricultural population, but also offers attractive summer pasturages at an altitude above the forest line. For the Turco-Mongol nomads this was ideal and Azerbaijan has remained until the present time, in its Iranian section at least, a nomadic area.

The Šāhsevan have always constituted the primary ethnic group in eastern Azerbaijan, and studies in connection with the development of irrigation in the Moḡān steppe, give a rather precise idea of their contemporary evolution and present situation. From 1886 when the Russian government closed its frontiers to their migrations, thus depriving perhaps as many as three-fifths of them of their winter pasturage in the low plain of the Araxes, sedentarization, already spontaneously begun in the nineteenth century, began to progress rapidly. At the same time the migration routes were definitively fixed in a general north-south direction, between the section of the Moḡān steppe that remained Iranian (winter quarters) and the main summer pasturages of Sabalān and Kūh-e Bozqūš and a smaller summer pasturage in the Bāḡrow-dāḡ to the southeast of Ardabil. A second essential phase was initiated by the policy of control and enforced settlement carried out by Reżā Shah in the 1930s, which resulted in the creation of numerous villages, particularly in the winter quarters, but also along the migration routes in the high country. However, a large group of the Šāhsevan resumed their group migrations from the last years of the reign of Reżā Shah. In 1965, the most realistic evaluations still counted about one hundred thousand pure nomads dwelling both summer and winter in felt tents in the shape of a semi-cupola (*ālāčūq*), grouped in *oba* of two to twelve tents both in the summer pasturages (*yeylāq*) and in the winter pasturages (*qešlāq*). Data collected in areas now being converted to agriculture by irrigation (see below) suggest that approximately 800,000 sheep and goats must spend the winter in the 4,000 km^2 of the steppe winter quarters of Moḡān. To this figure must be added the animals of transport, like camels and horses. At the present, the Šāhsevan are an inextricable mixture of pure nomads, living year-round in felt tents, of semi-nomads inhabiting village houses and spending only summers under tents in the mountains, and of sedentary peoples who entrust their herds to the care of a small number of migrating shepherds. The length of time spent in the *yeylāq*s of the mountains is inversely proportional to the importance of cultivation in the winter quarters and of the existence of permanent villages. For the pure nomad, the sojourn lasts from between five to seven months (including the time of the migration, three to four weeks in each direction) generally in the time period extending from May to the end of October. It can be considerably shorter for the shepherds and for the semi-nomads. But the cultural and economic unity of the group, in spite of these innumerable variables, remain very clear. It is marked especially by the adoption of a calender of pairing and parturition of the sheep, beginning with the lambing toward the end of autumn; this custom is the opposite of that practiced almost universally among the natives of the Middle East but by placing the period of lactation in winter, when the Šāhsevan are in the plain, it permits massive sale of milk products (especially white cheese) to Tabrīz and Tehran. The problems of collection and transport in the mountains would make this practice impossible in summer. Thus the Šāhsevan constitute a type of nomad closely integrated with the economy of the sedentary populations.

A new and final phase of sedentarizaton has been initiated since 1951 in connection with the development of the areas irrigated by the Araxes dams (see below). In 1968, 1,452 families, either from the true nomads or from semi-nomads already partially sedentarized, were installed on 11,787 ha in 15 new villages, with cultivable lots ranging from 3 to 12 ha. The movement has been continued following the construction of the large dam Aṣlāndūz (see below), although it is not possible to give a precisely balanced figures. But the evolution toward sedentarization seems irreversible and the proportion of sedentary peoples who are content to have their flocks moved with the shepherds is increasing constantly.

Other large nomad groups still exist in Iranian Azerbaijan, especially in the Qarāja-dāḡ and on the heights of the Sahand, where their summer pasturages are mixed with those of the sedentary villages and of the semi-nomads who are much more numerous. They have not yet been the object of an in-depth study.

Today in Soviet Azerbaijan, nomadism, properly speaking, has almost entirely disappeared. However, important pastural migrations still take place that indicate the attraction of the pasturage of the low steppe basins of the Kura and the Araxes. Thus, in winter many mountain villages send their flocks with shepherds to the plains, which also accommodate an equal number of transhumant flocks coming from the neighboring countries of Georgia and Armenia, where the cold-season pasturages are very inadequate.

B. The types of mountain life. If exception is made of a small number of irrigated centers that have resisted the generalized nomadization of the plains, the most stable seats of sedentary life are situated in the better watered mountainous areas. In these areas, the toponomy has remained largely Iranian in the villages located at higher altitudes, underlining the continuity of occupation with the soil. In fact, most of the characteristics of human geography are connected to the ancient autochthonous agricultural tradition: Valley floors converted into terraces irrigated by small derivation dams and kept in continuous cultivation by a rotating system in which especially grazing crops (alfalfa, clover) along with cereals are continued for several years, providing fodder for a large number of cattle, which, in winter, are kept in stables that are partly or wholly underground (e.g., in the areas of soft volcanic tufts). Traditionally, only short summer migrations were undertaken to the lower neighboring slopes so that the higher summits remained open to the nomads. Excepting the ethno-linguistic transformation, cultural traits of nomadic background, such as the use of black tents as summer dwellings are rare.

The expansion of most of the mountain areas, resulting from the development of the areas of rain-fed cultivation surrounding the irrigated areas of the valleys, appears to have reached its limits forty to fifty years ago. As a result the present demographic pressure has led especially to the development of pastoral life and the exploitation of the complementary seasonal resources offered by the superposed zones of elevation. The people of the large village of Sahand, which, fifty years ago, was mainly agricultural and limited pastoral migrations to the immediate neighborhoods, have considerably increased the number of rented livestock and now practice summer migrations of much longer duration, which involved them in more elevated areas of the mountain. The last nomads have gradually been driven from these areas and at the same time currents of inverse spring transhumance leading the flocks to the plain of Tabrīz have appeared. Formerly self-contained high-country villages rather than real mountain villages, they are now turning to advantage the totality of their natural environment in complex rhythms. About thirty-five years ago labor began to migrate towards the centers of Tehran or the Caspian. At first this occurred at the end of spring when provisions would grow scarce, but gradually they became year-round.

C. Agriculture on the plain and the large-scale irrigation works. The agricultural activity of the high basins of Azerbaijan, like the plains of the Kura and the Araxes, has traditionally been considerably less than that of the mountain valleys, and has been limited to precise sites of the irrigated oases of the piedmont, or the cones of volcanic overflow that are fed by small local water courses rathern than by large rivers, once not utilized at all, or by *qanāts*, which are rare throughout Azerbaijan. These irrigated grounds are almost never dense enough to give the impression of continuous cultivation, with outer areas of rain-fed agriculture adjoining each other. The most remarkable example is that of the western border of the basin of Lake Urmia (and to a smaller extent the borders to the north and to the south, the plain of Tabrīz to the east being almost barren with the exception of the large oasis of the city itself located at the mouth of Ājī-čāy). Here the numerous small water courses have furnished the basis for the existence of a unique area that has continually remained thoroughly humanized, and marked by a strong cultural individuality. Certain distinctive agricultural techniques (especially use of rural wagons that are rare throughout the rest of Iran) bring it closer to the high Armenian or Anatolian lands. On the other hand, it has also sheltered, for a long period of time, a Christian minority, the Assyro-Chaldeans, who speak a Syriac language. At the beginning of World War I, it numbered some 40,000 to 50,000 adherents. It was almost completely wiped out or dispersed by the war, but has been partially reconstituted by people who have returned and, around 1950, the number stabilized at approximately 15,000 people. At that time it remained an essentially rural population settled to the west of Lake Urmia. Later it was deeply affected by emigration to the cities (Urmia itself, but especially Tehran) and abroad (especially the United States and Australia) and today probably numbers only 5,000 people in Azerbaijan, half of them in the city of Urmia.

The contemporary demographic pressure in the semi-steppe plains has led to extensive development of pluvial agricultural, at least in areas where the relatively mild winters permit it to profit maximally from the rainfalls by prolonging the growing season. Thus, from the 1920s we have witnessed the multiplication or sizeable increase of villages that subsist almost exclusively on rain-fed agriculture, both in the northeast of Iranian Azerbaijan (the basin of the Qara-sū to the north of Sabalān) and in the high basins that are relatively well watered (south of the plain of Ardabīl). But essentially the contemporary development has been connected with the large-scale irrigation works. The earliest and most spectacular of these projects were carried out in Soviet Azerbaijan. In 1860-63, the Tsarist government devoted itself to establishing a unified plan for irrigating the eastern Transcaucasian steppe after the model of the large irrigation systems of antiquity (Giaur-Arch), doubtlessly going back to Sasanian times, whose remains can still be seen in the Karabakh steppe. The Marian canal in the Karajasy steppe dates from this period. In the course of the following decades, derivative canals, supplied by the high waters of the Kura, were restored or newly excavated, to partially irrigate the steppes of Šervān, Moḡān, and Karabakh. In 1914, the Romanov canal permitted the exploitation of 176,000 ha in the Moḡān steppe, which was also irrigated (to the amount of 77,000 ha in 1913) by three canals leading off from the Araxes. After an abatement of work between the two wars, the high point of the development of eastern Transcaucasia was the construction of the major dam of Mingechaur, completed in 1953 in the mid-sector of the plain (reservoir of 16 km^3; lake of 625 km^3; hydro-electric power plant with a generating capacity of 360,000 kw). Two main canals lead off from it; the canal of Verkhne-Karabakh on the right bank (possible discharge 110 m^3 per second) and the canal Verkhne-Šervān on the left bank (discharge 175 m^3 per second), each of which encompass a perimeter of approximately 100,000 ha. Similarly, the other parts of the Transcaucasia benefit from a variety of irrigation schemes: Small local barrages and canals along all the minor water courses descending from the greater and lesser Caucasus, permit the development of the cones filled with volcanic overflow on the piedmont; the canal of Samur-Divichi which distributes the waters of the Samur over all the northeastern watershed of the Caucasus along the Caspian; the water-lifting machines that mark the course of the Kura and assure the irrigation of a long stretch of river bank; wells that furnish water in the peninsula of Apsheron; artesian wells in the middle sector of the plain. This complex organization, uniting all the partial possibilities, now ensures the almost complete use of the waters of eastern Transcaucasia.

In Iranian Azerbaijan irrigation schemes did not start until much later. From 1951 two small canals were constructed on the Araxes, 25 km downstream from the Qara-sū. They have made possible the irrigation respectively of 4,000 and 18,000 ha of the Moḡān steppe (discharge 4 and 17 m^3 per second) and the settlement of the Šāhsevan (see above). In 1963, the conclusion of a Perso-Soviet agreement on the integrated use of the waters of the Araxes opened up much broader prespectives: A dam serving as a regulating reservoir (capacity 1.35 km^3; lake of 145 km^2) was completed in 1971 close to the Iranian city of Qezel Qešlāq, not far from the Soviet city of Naḵjavān. The Aṣlāndūz dam was completed in 1972, at the confluence of the Qara-sū shortly after the Araxes enters the lowlands of Moḡān; from this dam, two canals of identical capacity lead off to the Iranian side and the Soviet side (80 m^3 per second). The perimeter irrigated on the Iranian bank would thus approach a total of 56,000 ha, to which we can add 6,000 ha irrigated by pumps. The newly claimed lands are developed essentially in the form of 42 large cooperative unities of exploitation (1000 ha each); each unity harbors 50 families of colonists. Here is also the most important hydro-electric installation of northwest Iran with 42,000 kw of generating capacity (150 million kwh). Other projects are in the process of realization around lake Urmia, and ensure an integral regulation of the entire basin. There is a reservoir of 0.6 km^3 on the Zarrīna-rūd, with two canals of 28 m^3 per second for the irrigation of Mīāndoāb plain to the southeast of the lake (perimeter of 85,000 ha); a reservoir on the Mahābād river (Mahābād-čāy) for the irrigation of 21,000 ha in the plain of Mahābād to the south of the lake; a reservoir on the Zolū river (Zolā-čāy) for the irrigation of the plain of Šāhpūr to the northwest (32,00 ha); and finally a series of three reservoir dams providing for the irrigation of 80,000 ha in the plain of Urmia to the west of the lake.

D. Agricultural production. Up to now, the high basins of Iranian Azerbaijan have remained largely devoted to growing cereals (wheat and barley), up to approximately 2,500 m. Lentils are the food-crop raised at the highest altitude: 2,500 m on the southeastern watershed of Sabalān. Industrial crops always have to be irrigated; they are represented in particular by sugar beets, which are processed locally; tobacco in the plain of Urmia; grape vine for wine and raisins up to 1,500 m (the stems are buried during the winter to protect them from the cold); fruit trees, especially apricot and almond, which require scarcely any irrigation. Potatoes, which would suit the climate of these high cold lands, are hardly grown at all. The newly irrigated areas around lake Urmia will be devoted in particular to fruits and legumes, along with cereals and fodder. In the northeast of the country, the agricultural crops vary as the altitude diminishes. Rice appears below 1,200 m in the Qara-sū basin. Vineyards and melons in open fields become more important. Cotton production is not profitable above 250 m of altitude and is chiefly limited to the Moḡān steppe, although it is to be found occasionally in higher areas (the Mīāndoāb plain.)

The climate and abundant water resources explain why agriculture is much more industrialized and commercialized in the Transcaucasus, where cotton occupies 20 percent of the cultivated area. Other crops include grapes, fruits (apricots, peaches, walnuts, citrus fruits), tea (20,000 ha), olives (especially in the Apsheron peninsula), and silk in the hills bordering the Greater and Lesser Caucasus.

E. Cities and industrialization. The high lands of Iranian Azerbaijan have produced a flourishing urban life. Each basin has at least one important urban center: Around the Urmia lake, they become more numerous, controlling access to the plain and command various alluvial plains with irrigated agriculture. Most of the cities, in spite of an often glorious past, are today rural markets with an essentially regional function. Ardabīl (147,000 inhabitants in 1976; q.v.), ensconced in its oasis where fruit trees characteristic of the moderate cold climate predominate (pears and apples). Here was the cradle of the Safavids and it still preserves in its layout a circular boulevard which traces the wall that the French general Gardanne had built in the beginning of the nineteenth century. At this time the city was an important caravan stop between eastern and central Transcaucasia and Tehran and Isfahan. The closing of the Russian borders, following the annexation of the Transcaucasus by the Tsarist Russia, left it with a purely local role. Urmia, more important today because of its population (163,000), never had any long distance relations. K̲oy (population 70,000), to the north of the lake, remains somewhat outside the important international route from Turkey to Iran. Tabrīz is currently in rapid decline as the center of a network of communications and roads, the fact which explains its previous prosperity. It developed in the long corridor of Ājī-čāy, between Sahand to the south and the Qarāja-dāḡ to the north, not far from the northern point of Lake Urmia where the principal southeast-northwest route is intersected by a north-south route paralleling the eastern bank of the lake and leading to the valley of the Araxes and to Transcaucasia. It was finally fixed at the farthest point where the river valley is still contained between two firm shores before spreading out into the bottom of the marshy basin near the confluence of the Maydān-rūd, flowing down from Sahand, whose waters irrigate the gardens of the city. Tabrīz was the capital of Iran in the Mongol period, then again at the beginning of the Safavid period, before the wars with the Ottomans forced them to look for a less exposed site for the capital, and was still very prosperous in the seventeenth century when it must have counted 150,000 inhabitants. However, the city had only 15,000 in the beginning of the nineteenth century after a series of epidemics and earthquakes. At this time, with the progressive opening of Iran to the West, it was at the peak of its prosperity. It was the gateway of the country to the outside and an important stage for caravans going toward Trebizond and the Black Sea, which was henceforth open to European commerce, until the railroad that linked it to the Russian network at J̌olfā and Tiflis was completed. The Russian revolution interrupted travel to the West across Soviet territory and almost totally destroyed this prosperity, and in the 1930s the construction of the Trans-Iranian Railway eventually made Iran turn back toward the Persian Gulf. It was connected with the Turkish railroad system in 1970, but the connection remains inpractical and slow, and has not really changed the situation. With 598,000 inhabitants in 1976, Tabrīz ranks today as the fourth largest city in Iran, although it was still the second some fifteen years ago. Essentially it exists from its role as regional capital and from its numerous crafts (few industries of importance: especially carpet wearing, leather, wood, and food supplies) although many sections of its important bazaar have today fallen into disrepair, especially the southern parts, close to the bed of the Ājī-čāy.

Russian influence has deeply modified the urban network of the eastern Transcaucasus, assuring the predominence of Baku. This was only the second capital of the Šervāšāhs whose principal residence was Shemakha (Šemāk̲ī) on the first slopes of the Caucasus, in a better irrigated area with a gentler climate. Baku, a strategically located capital controlling the passage east to the Caucasus along the shores of the Caspian, competed on this route with other centers lying farther to the south (Darbent) and remained a very modest city until the Russian conquest. The development of relations between Russia and Transcaucasia destined it to become the seat of Russian administration. A second element of its prosperity was furnished at the beginning of the nineteenth century by the extraction of oil, a process that sub-marine exploitations in the Caspian have prolonged until the present time despite the depletion of the first layers (the production is still 18 million tons in comparison with 22 in 1940). The agglomeration of Baku, with 1,300,000 inhabitants and 80 percent of the industry of Azerbaijan (the only other large industrial center is Kirovabad), represents the centralization of an already very urbanized region (the percentage of the total urban population reaches 50 percent) and its level of development and type of territorial organization today differ profoundly from that of Iranian Azerbaijan.

Bibliography: I. Historical geography. The concept of Azerbaijan. Antiquity: F. Spiegel, *Eranische Altertumskunde* I, Leipzig, 1871, passim and especially pp. 125-37. Markwart, *Ērānšahr*, pp. 108-14. Middle Ages: for the exhaustive description given by the geographers see Schwarz, *Iran*, pp. 959-1340; for a shorter treatment see Le Strange, *Lands*, pp. 159-71 and the map on p. 86. Geohistorical aspects of Turkicization: Z.V. Togan, "Azerbaican," in *İA* II, pp. 91-118. M. F. Köprülü, "Azeri," ibid., pp. 118-51. F. Sümer, "Azerbaycan' ın türkleşmesi tarihine umumi bir bakış," *Belleten* 21, 1957, pp. 429-47. R. Housseinov, "Superpositions ethniques en Transcaucasie aux XIe et XIIe siècles," *Turcica* 2, 1970, pp. 71-81. Anthropological aspects of the Azeri ethnogeny: E. O. Schoch, *Beiträge zur Anthropologie der Aderbeidshan-Türken, Usbeken und Kazaken*, Oosterhout N. B., 1969, Studien und Materialen aus dem Institut für Menschheit und Menschheitskunde, Series Maior, I, pp. 11-39. See also ʿA. Kārang *Āt̲ār-e bāstānī-e Ād̲arbāyjān* I, Tehran, 1351 Š./1972. M. J̌. Maškūr, *Naẓar-ī ejmālī ba tārīk̲-e Ād̲arbāyjān*, Tehran, 1349 Š./1971.

II. Iranian Azerbaijan. A. General description of the country and routes of exploration. The geographic knowledge of Azerbaijan has not yet gone beyond the stage of local exploratory analyses and we can rely only on rare specialized monographs. Existing syntheses are out-dated: C. Ritter, *Die Erdkunde von Asien* VI, 2: *Iranische Welt*, Berlin, 1840, pp. 763-1048 (also very useful for historical geography). G. N. Curzon, *Persia and the Persian Question*, 2 vols., London, 1892, I, chap. XVI, pp. 514-49 and the bibliography of previous travel accounts, p. 570. J. de Morgan, *Mission scientifique en Perse* I: *Etudes géographiques*, Paris, 1894, pp. 279-88, 289-355 (the valley of the Araxes and the Qara-dāḡ). Among the more recent travel accounts and descriptions see H. Binder, *Au Kurdistan, en Mésopotamie et en Perse*, Paris, 1887, pp. 43-107. P. Müller-Simonis and H. Hyvernat, *Du Caucase au Golfe Persique à travers l'Arménie, le Kurdistan et la Mésopotamie*, Paris, 1892, chaps. 5-10. W. B. Harris, *From Batum to Baghdad*, Edinburgh, 1896, pp. 85-173. E. Zugmayer, *Eine Reise durch Vorderasien im Jahre 1904*, Berlin, 1905, pp. 65-220. R. de Macquenem, "Le lac d'Ourmiah," *Annales de géographie*, 1908, pp. 128-44 (in fact it treats the whole region around the lake). A. V. W. Jackson, *Persia, Past and Present*, New York, 1909, esp. pp. 33-143. H. Grothe, *Wanderungen in Persien*, Berlin, 1910, pp. 293-321. C. F. Lehmann-Haupt, *Armenien einst und jetzt: Reisen und Forschungen von Lehmann-Haupt* I, Berlin, 1910, pp. 181-323. A. Stein, *Old Routes of Western Iran*, London, 1940, pp. 361-404. We can reconstitute the history of the discovery and the succession of the first European travelers thanks to A. Gabriel, *Die Erforschung Persiens*, Vienna, 1952, see the index under Adherbaidjan. The present writer is not aware of any recent monograph on the geography of Azerbaijan. M. Bazin, *Le Tâlesh. Une région ethnique au nord de l'Iran*, 2 vols., Paris, 1980, contains much information on relations with Azerbaijan. W. B. Fisher et al., in *Camb. Hist. Iran* I (index s.v. Āzarbāijān) is a very general study and excludes any regional analysis. See also E. Ehlers, *Iran: Grundzüge einer geographischen Landeskunde*, Darmstadt, 1980, index, s.v. Kayhān, *Joḡrāfīā* II-III. Razmārā, *Farhang* IV.

B. Physical geography. There are a few geological, geomorphic, and morpho-climatic monographs: H. Rieben, "Contribution à la géologie de l'Azerbaidjan persan," *Bulletin de la Société neuchâteloise des sciences naturelles* 59, 1935, pp. 1-144. H. Bobek, "Die Rolle der Eiszeit in Nordwestiran," *Zeitschrift für Gletscherkunde* 25, 1937, pp. 130-83. Idem, "Forschungen im zentralkurdischen Hochgebirge zwischen Van- und Urmia-See (Südostanatolien und West-Azerbaičan)," *Petermanns geographische Mitteilungen* 84, 1938, pp. 152-62, 215-28. B. Damm, *Geologie des Zendan-i Suleiman un seiner Umgebung, südöstliches Balqash-Gebirge, Nordwest-Iran*, Beiträge zur Archeologie und Geologie des Zendan-i Suleiman I, Wiesbaden, 1968. F. Plattner, "Über den Salzgehalt des Urmia-Sees," *Petermanns geographische Mitteilungen*, 1955, pp.276-78. Idem, "Mehrjahrige Beobachtungen über die Spiegel- und Salzgehaltschwankungen des Urmia-Sees," *Erdkunde*, 1970, pp. 134-39. G. Schweizer, "Der Kuh-e Sabalan (Nordwestiran): Beiträge zur Gletscherkunde und Glazialgeomorphologie vorderasiatischer Hochgebirge," *Beiträge zur Geographie der Tropen und Subtropen. Festschrift für H. Wilhelmy*, Tübinger geographische Studien 34, Tübingen, 1970, pp. 163-78. Idem, *Untersuchungen zur Phisio-geographie von Ostanatolien und Nordwestiran: geomorphologische, klima- und hydrogeographische Studien im Vansee und Rezaiyehsee-Gebiet*, Tübinger geographische Studien 60, Tübingen, 1975 (contains an exhaustive bibliography of older studies on the Urmia lake and its region). M. Berberian and J. S. Tchalenkov, "Field Study and Documentation of the 1930 Salmas (Shahpur-Azarbaidjan) Earthquake," in M. Berberian, ed., *Contribution to the Seismotectonics of Iran*, pt. II, Geological Survey of Iran, report no. 39, Tehran, 1976, pp. 271-342. There does not exist any systematic physical description of the region.

Studies covering the entirety of Iran: Structure and relief: J. W. Schroeder, "Essai sur la structure de l'Iran," *Eclogae Geologicae Helveticae*, 1944, pp. 37-81. J. Stöcklin, "Structural History and Tectonics of Iran: A Review," *Bulletin of the American Association of Petroleum Geologists* 52, 1968, pp. 1229-59. Climate: M. H. Ganji, "The Climates of Iran," *Bulletin de la Société de géographie d'Egypte* 28, September, 1955, pp. 195-299. Ch. Djavadi, *Climats de l'Iran*, Monographies de la météorologie nationale 59, Paris, 1966. Vegetation and ecological regions: H. Bobek, *Die natürlichen Wälder und Gehölzfluren Irans*, Bonner geographische Abhandlungen 8, Bonn, 1951. Idem, "Die Verbreitung des Regenfeldbaues in Iran," in *Geographische Studien. Festschrift Johann Sölch*, Vienna, 1951, pp. 9-30. Idem, "Beiträge zur klima-ökologischen Gliederung Irans," *Erdkunde*, 1952, pp. 65-84. Kayhān, *Joḡrāfīā*, vol. I. M. Zohary, "On the Geobotanical Structure of Iran," *Bulletin of the Research Council of Israel*, Section D, Botany, Volume 11D, Supplement, March, 1963. Hydrology: P. Beaumont, *River Regimes in Iran*, Department of Geography, University of Durham, Occasional Publications, N.S. 1, Durham, 1963. See also ĀB; ĀB-E GARM; ĀBYĀRĪ.

C. Human geography. 1. Nomadism and sedentarization of the Šāhsevan. Development of the Moḡān steppe: P. Bessaignet, "Shah Sevan: Un exemple de sédentarisation de tribu nomade avec transplantation culturelle," *Colloque sur la conservation et la restauration des sols tenu à Téhéran du 21 mai au 11 juin 1960*, Paris, pp. 140-58. C. Op't Land, *The Shah-savan of Azarbaijan. A Preliminary Report*, University of Tehran, Institute of Social Studies and Research, Tehran, 1961. Idem, *The Permanent Settlement of the Dachte Moghan-Area. A Preliminary Report*, pub. ibid., Tehran, 1961. Idem, "The Admirable Tents of the Shah Savan," *International Archives of Ethnography* 50, 1964-66, pp. 237-43. G. Schweizer, "Nordost-Azerbaidschan und Shah-Sevan Nomaden," in E. Ehlers et al., *Strukturwandlungen im nomadisch-bäuerlichen Lebensraum des Orients*, Erdkundliches Wissen 26, Wiesbaden. 1970, pp. 81-148. Idem, "Lebens- und Wirtschaftsformen iranischer Bergnomaden im Strukturwandel. Das Beispiel der Shah Sevan," in C. Rathjens, et al., eds., *Vergleichende Kulturgeographie der Hochgebirge des südlichen Asien*, Erdwissenschaftliche Forschung 5, Wiesbaden, 1973, pp. 168-73. Idem, "Das Aras-Moghan-Entwicklungsprojekt in Nordwestiran und die Probleme der Nomadenansiedlung," *Zeitschrift für ausländische Landwirtschaft*, 1973, pp. 60-75. R. Tapper, *Pasture and Politics: Economics, Conflict and Ritual among Shahsevan Nomads of Northwestern Iran*, London, 1979. See also 'AŠĀYER.

2. Types of mountain life. Only the Sahand has been the object of detailed analyses: X. de Planhol, "La vie de montagne dans le Sahend (Azerbaidjan iranien)," *Bulletin de l'Association de géographes français* 271-72, January-February, 1958, pp. 7-16. Idem, "Un village de montagne de l'Azerbaidjan iranien, Lighwan (versant nord du Sahend)," *Revue de géographie de Lyon*, 1960, pp. 395-418. Idem, "Aspects of Mountain Life in Anatolia and Iran," in S. R. Eyre and G. R. J. Jones, eds., *Geography as Human Ecology*, London, 1966, pp. 291-308 (concerning the Sahand and containing a toponymic map of this mountain). P. Oberling, "The Tribes of Qarāca Dāğ: A Brief History," *Oriens* 17, 1964, pp. 60-95 (primarily ethno-historical). M. Bazin, "Le Qara Dāğ d'après Asghar Nazarian," *Revue géographique de l'est*, 1982, pp. 19-60.

3. Agriculture of the plains. J. Koch et al., "Neue Bewässerungs- und Entwicklungsprojekte in Iran. Das Beispiel der Provinz West-Azerbaidschan," *Orient* 15, 1974, pp. 8-16.

4. Assyro-Chaldeans. E. Berthaud, "La vie rurale dans quelques villages chrétiens de l'Azerbaidjan occidental," *Revue de géographie de Lyon*, 1968, pp. 291-331. Idem, "Chrétiens d'Iran," *Orient* 45-46, Paris, 1969, pp. 23-26 (contains a map of the Christian villages to the west of Lake Urmia). H. de Mauroy, "Mouvements de population dans la communauté Assyro-Chaldéenne en Iran," *Revue de géographie de Lyon*, 1968, pp. 333-56. Idem, "Les minorités non-musulmanes dans la population iranienne," ibid., 1973, pp. 165-206, cf. pp. 189-96. Idem, "Lieux de culte (anciens et actuels) des églises 'syriennes orientales' dans le diocèse d'Ourmiah-Salmas en Iran (Azerbaidjan occidental)," *Parole de l'Orient* 3, 1972, pp. 313-51. Idem, *Les assyro-chaldéens dans l'Iran d'aujourd'hui*, Publications du Département de géographie de l'Université de Paris-Sorbonne 6, Paris, 1978 (contains a very complete bibliography of previous works). J. M. Fiey, "Aḏarbāyğān chrétien," *Le Museon*, 1973, pp. 397-435.

5. Towns. M. J̌. Maškūr, *Tārīḵ-e Tabrīz tā pāyān-e qarn-e nohom-e hejrī*, Tehran, 1352 Š./1973. S. Schafaghi, *Die Stadt Tabriz und ihr Hinterland*, Doctoral thesis, Cologne, 1965. G. Schweizer, "Tabriz (Nordwest-Iran) und der Tabrizer Basar," *Erdkunde*, 1972, pp. 32.46.

III. Soviet Azerbaijan. The problems of documentation are of a very different nature from those of the Iranian sector. We shall mention here first general syntheses and comprehensive studies in Russian that provide a guide to more detailed works. The basic source for the geography of the country is the *Atlas Azerbaĭdzhanskoĭ Sovetskoĭ Sotsialisticheskoĭ Respubliki*, Akademia Nauk Azerbaĭdzhanskoĭ, SSR, Institut Geografii, Baku and Moscow, 1963. The accompanying maps, commentaries, and very detailed descriptions constitute a complete analysis of the country. A more comprehensive and synthetic description of the natural environment can be found in general treatises or manuals of physical geography of the USSR; for the regions in the Caucasus see for example, A. M. Alpatev et al., *Fizicheskaya geografiya SSSR*, Moscow, 1976, I, pp. 187-239 and F. I. Milkov and N. A. Gvozdechkiĭ, ibid., pp. 343-420. Some geomorphological monographic studies are collected in *Voprosy istorii razvitiya rel'efa i landshafty Azerbaĭdzhanskoĭ SSSR*, Akademia Nauk Azerbaĭdzhanskoĭ SSR. Trudy Instituta Geografii 16, Baku, 1976. Among the works in Western languages, A. Büdel, *Transkaukasien, eine technische Geographie*, Petermanns Mitteilungen, Ergänzungsheft 189, Gotha, 1926, is still useful.

The works cited above are of a didactic character and rather abstract. For a concrete approach to the traditional styles of life and descriptions of the land, one should refer to the numerous itineraries and travelogues in Western languages, written at the end of the last century, among which we can mention in particular: J. Abercromby, *A Trip through Eastern Caucasus*, London, 1889. G. Radde, *Reisen an der persisch-russichen Grenze. Talysch und seine Bewohner*, Leipzig, 1886 (it also treats *pro parte* the Iranian section Ardabīl and the Sabalān). Idem, *Karabagh. Bericht über die im Sommer 1890 im russischen Karabagh von Dr... und Dr. Jean Valentin ausgeführte Reise*, Petermanns Mitteilungen, Ergänzungsheft no. 100, Gotha, 1890. Mme B. Chantre, *A travers l'Arménie russe*, Paris, 1893 (to a great extent concerned with Azerbaijan). M. Rikli, ed., *Natur- und Kulturbilder aus den Kaukasusländern und Hocharmenien*, Zurich, 1914. More recent and systematical is M. Bazin and C. Bromberger, *Gilân et Âzarbâyjân oriental, cartes et documents ethnographiques*, Paris, 1982 (Institut français d'iranologie de Téhéran, Bibliothèque iranienne 24).

(X. de Planhol)

ii. Archeology

The region to be discussed comprises the two Iranian provinces of West Azerbaijan and East Azerbaijan, with administrative centers at Urmia (before 1979 Reżā'īya) and Tabrīz respectively; it does not include "Northern Azerbaijan," centered on Baku, which since 1829 has belonged to the Russian empire.

The modern provincial and international boundaries do not correspond to limits of ethnic or tribal areas. The border between the provinces of Kurdistan and West Azerbaijan and the frontier on the Aras (Araxes) river between East Azerbaijan and Russian Azerbaijan cut across such areas. Before the partition in the nineteenth century, Iranian and Russian Azerbaijan constituted a single cultural entity. In ancient times, however, the two provinces now belonging to Iran had formed a distinct cultural region, known as Media Atropatene because, after the collapse of the Achaemenid empire, the satrap Atropates secured the political independence of this part of the former satrapy of Media (Pauly-Wissowa, II, col. 2150).

Azerbaijan is a mountainous region where routes of ancient origin interesect. It has thus been, throughout the centuries, both a pole of attraction for migrating peoples and warring armies and a center of commercial and cultural exchange. It was the bridge from Mesopotamia to the metal-rich lands of the Caucasus and from the Anatolian plateau to central Iran, with further links to Transcaucasia and India.

Ancient sites. From the pre-historic period onward, Azerbaijan was at least sparsely populated. The oldest known traces of human settlement are paleolithic cave-dwellings, such as the cave at Tamtama, north of Urmia in West Azerbaijan, found by C. Coon (*Cave Explorations in Iran 1949*, Philadelphia, 1951, pp. 15-20), and the caves which, together with some open-air sites, have been found in the Sahand massif south of Tabrīz in East Azerbaijan (survey report in *Iran* 14, 1976, p. 154). It was apparently not until the late neolithic period, from 6,000 B.C. onward, that Azerbaijan came under closer human occupation. Evidence of this has been brought to light by the British excavations at Yanīk Tepe on the east shore of Lake Urmia (C. A. Burney, "Excavations at Yanik Tepe, North-West-Iran," *Iraq* 23, 1961, pp. 138ff.) and by the findings of the American Ḥasanlū project in the Soldūz plain and at Ḥasanlū itself (see R. H. Dyson, "Hasanlu 1974. The Ninth Century B. C. Gateway," in *Proceedings of the 3rd Annual Symposium on Archaeological Research in Iran 1974*, Tehran, 1975, pp. 179ff.; I. E. Reade, "Hasanlu, Gilzanu and Related Considerations," *AMI* 12, 1979, pp. 175ff.; Vanden Berghe, *Bibliographie analytique*, pp. 157ff., and *Supplément* 1, pp. 46ff.). Pottery from then on shows vigorous development of both shape and decoration. Azerbaijan in the phase of incipient continuous settlement offers one of the Near East's most interesting fields for archeological exploration, as can be seen from the results of the fruitful efforts made mainly between the end of the Second World War and the Islamic revolution (ca. 1950-78). Surveys and test diggings have produced evidence of close settlement in different periods around Lake Urmia and of inhabited sites and forts in vallyes leading up into the mountains.

The population of the west bank of Lake Urmia became denser from the fourth millennium B.C. onward. Surveys conducted by Italian archeologists in an area west of Urmia (P. E. Pecorella and M. Salvini, *Fra lo Zagros e l'Urmia: Ricerche storiche ed archeologiche nell'Azerbaigian Iraniano*, Rome, 1984), by the German Archeological Institute in the northwest of Azerbaijan (Vanden Berghe, op. cit., nos. 1964-70, 1973, 2240-54), and by several smaller expeditions have revealed numerous sites of settlements of the third and second millennia in Azerbaijan. As yet it has been possible only to take measurements, but not to start excavations, at Ravaz, a relatively large settlement north of Sīah Čašma, and at Yaḵvalī, a fort settlement east of Mākū (W. Kleiss and S. Kroll, *AMI* 12, 1979, pp. 27ff.). Each is from the third millennium, having round houses of a type already known from the excavations of the third millennium sites at Haftavān Tepe and Yanīk Tepe. Both belong to the Early Caucasian culture (early Bronze Age).

Ravaz presents a vivid picture of a big and important settlement in the third millennium. It was defended by a thick stone wall, later supplemented with stout semicircular towers in front. Access to the houses was through a single tongue-shaped gateway. The houses were packed tightly together, but traces of streets are discernible. This site was never built over in later times. Outside the main settlement lay an extensive periphery of seemingly terraced fields or gardens with single round houses. Lines of roads can be recognized in this area also.

Yaḵvalī, on the other hand, is a small fort settlement. It too had a solid defensive wall, but without any towers. The access gateway was of simple design. Outside the fort lay some separate groups of round houses.

Bolūrābād, northeast of Besṭām, is another fort settlement from the third millennium B.C. (idem, *AMI*, N.S. 8, 1975, pp. 15ff.). Its surrounding wall was 3 m thick and of quarried stone. Remains of round houses can be seen inside. In a second phase of building, probably still in the third millennium, the wall was strengthened at its most vulnerable point by the addition of an external box-like structure which was filled with earth. At this site also, only measurement has so far been possible.

In the northwestern part of the province of West Azerbaijan, measurements of extensive tumulus clusters at Maḵand, Qara Żīā'-al-dīn/Besṭām, and Maryam northeast and east of Mākū, and of a single tumulus at Vār west of Ḵoy, have been carried out (Kleiss, ibid., 11, 1978, pp. 13ff.). Although none of these tumuli have yet been opened, there can be no doubt that they date from a period extending from the second into the first millennium B.C., as do the graveyard sites in northeastern Azerbaijan between Meškīnšahr and Ardabīl and in the Ṭāleš mountains on the Caspian west coast. The abundance of tumuli in the pastureland of the Aras plain between Mākū and Besṭām indicates that they were graves of the equestrian nomadic peoples who roamed in this area before the arrival of the Urartians ca. 800 B.C. For this reason no remains of settlements connected with the tumuli are likely to be found. Different methods of tumulus erection have been noted, those at Maḵand being made of earth with stone trimmings (the commonest type), those at Maryam made of earth and stones, and those at Qara Żīā'-al-dīn/Besṭām made entirely of stones.

Finds of importance for knowledge of the general development of architecture, ceramics, and burial practices have emerged from the excavation of Kordlar Tepe by Austrian archeologists (A. Lippert, "Die Österreichischen Ausgrabungen am Kordlar-Tepe in Persisch—Westaserbeidschan (1971-78)," *AMI* 12, 1979, pp. 103ff.). Most of the finds are from the early Iron Age (11th century B.C.). This settlement had a central building of fort-like design.

Haftavān Tepe, which was explored by British archeologists, is potentially one of the more important sites in the northwest of Iran, having been inhabited from the fourth millennium through the Urartian period right down to Sasanian times (C. A. Burney, "The Fifth Season of Excavations at Haftvan Tappeh: Brief Summary of Principal Results," in *Proceedings of the 4th Annual Symposium on Archaeological Research in Iran 1975*, Tehran, 1976, pp. 257ff.). The British excavations at Goy (Gök) Tepe south of Urmia have yielded interesting evidence of cultural links between the plain on the west bank of Lake Urmia, Mesopotamia, Anatolia, and Central Iran in the second and first millennia B.C. (T. Burton-Brown, "Geoy Tepe," in *Excavations in Iran, the British Contribution*, Oxford, 1972, pp. 9-10). Also noteworthy are the investigations done by J. and H. de Morgan in cemeteries of the third to second millennia in the Ṭāleš district in the northeast of Azerbaijan (H. de Morgan, "Recherches au Talyche persan," in *MDAP* VIII, 1905, pp. 251ff.).

The biggest and richest prehistoric burial site in Azerbaijan, however, is the one at Ḥasanlū (q.v.). The adjoining settlement, already occupied from the third to the sixth millennium, was strengthened in a later period (Ḥasanlū IV) with a citadel and annexes. These so-called "burned buildings" mark a significant step in the evolution of large-room construction from the Hittite architecture of the fortress at Boğazköy to the later Urartian architecture and thence to the Median halls at Godīn Tepe west of Hamadān (T. Cuyler Young, "The Chronology of the Late Third and Second Millennium in Central Western Iran as Seen from Godin Tepe," *American Journal of Archaeology* 73, 1969, pp. 287ff.) and the Achaemenid *apadānas* (q.v.) at Persepolis and Susa (E. F. Schmidt, *Persepolis* I, Chicago, 1953). The layout of the Ḥasanlū IV citadel foreshadows the fortress architecture of the first millennium B.C., and the rich finds of metallic and ceramic objects are typical of its early centuries (R. H. Dyson, "Architecture of the Iron I Period at Hasanlu in Western Iran and Its Implications for Theories of Migration on the Iranian Plateau," in *Le Plateau iranien et l'Asie Centrale*, Paris, 1977, pp. 155ff.). Ḥasanlū was probably conquered, plundered, and destroyed by the Urartians ca. 800 B.C., but some time later it was rebuilt as a strong Urartian fortress.

Urartian period. From ca. 800 to the mid-7th century B.C., the Urartians held the districts southwest, west, northwest, and northeast of Lake Urmia. Thus the whole of the modern province of west Azerbaijan except the southern district around Mīāndoāb, and the western part of East Azerbaijan up to somewhere near Ahar, belonged to Urartu. By 1978 a total of 101 Urartian forts, settlements and other sites, and inscriptions had been indentified, including six inscriptions on rocks and buildings already known before 1967 (Kleiss and Kroll "Vermessene urartäische Plätze in Iran (West-Azerbaidjan) und neufunde (Stand der Forschung 1978)," *AMI* 12, 1979, pp. 183ff.). The principal excavations were done at Besṭām/Rusa-i URU.TUR (Vanden Berghe, op. cit., nos. 2217-40 and 4278-300; on Sangar see also *Istanbuler Mitteilungen* 18, 1968, pp. 1f.), Haftavān Tepe (Ch. Burney, "Excavations at Haftavan Tepe 1969," *Iran* 10, 1972, pp. 127ff.), Qalʿa-ye Esmāʿīl Āqā (Pecorella and Salvini, *Fra lo Zagros e l'Urmia*, pp. 215ff.), Ḥasanlū and Agrab Tepe (O. W. Muscarella, "Excavations at Agrab Tepe, Iran," *The Metropolitan Museum Journal* 8, 1973, pp. 47ff.), and Moḥammadābād southwest of Urmia (the Iranian excavations are not yet published; W. Kleiss, *AMI*, N.S. 9, 1976, pp. 36ff.; the inscription has been published by M. Salvini, *AMI*, N.S. 10, 1977, pp. 125ff. and in Pecorella and Salvini, op. cit., pp. 77f.).

Besṭām was founded by the Urartian king Rusa II (685-645 B.C.), who has left an inscription on stone from a building. According to the inscription, which has been moved from Besṭām to the Mūza-ye Īrān-e Bāstān at Tehran, the name of the newly founded settlement was Rusa-i URU.TUR "Rusa's town." Here a brief description of the Urartian site at Besṭām will suffice (see BESṬĀM).

Besṭām consists of a citadel, a craftsmen's and tradesmen's quarter, and a square walled enclosure at the foot of the citadel hill probably used for keeping horses. The citadel comprised a lower part, reserved mainly for the garrison but also containing stables, business premises, and a guest house; a middle part, stretching up the slope of the hill, with large storage areas for supplies needed in the fortress, and on the upper levels ceremonial halls and the temple of the urartian god Haldi (which is mentioned in the inscription); and a highest part or acropolis which was used as a royal lodging and as a last refuge in emergencies. Besṭām/Rusa-i URU.TUR appears to have been the regional base from which the itinerant king or his governors controlled Urartu's eastern territories. The citadel at Besṭām is the biggest-known building complex of the Urartians, covering a larger area than the citadels of their capitals at Van and Toprak Kale in Turkey. The most recent excavation in 1978 produced evidence that Besṭām was probably plundered and burned during civil wars in the second half of the seventh century B.C.

No Urartian cemeteries have been found at or near Besṭām, but some Urartian rock-chamber tombs in Azerbaijan are known. The most impressive is a series of three chambers in the vicinity of a rather small Urartian fort at Sangar, west of Mākū (Kleiss, *Istanbuler Mitteilungen* 18, 1968, pp. 1ff.). Access is by a 1.10 m wide staircase of thirty steps cut in the rock face. The tomb-chambers consist of a main chamber, 3.15 m in height and 5.45 × 3.90 m² in area, with niches in the walls and a big niche-like recess, 2.00 m in height and 2.30 × 1.30 m² in area, and of two side chambers reachable from the main chamber through doorways. The dimensions of the recess at the back of the main chamber are sufficient to take a sarcophagus. In the middle of the rear wall of the recess a slab-shaped alcove has been chiseled out, perhaps for the placing of a stela.

The Urartian sites are sufficiently numerous to permit the drawing of a rough map of the Urartian road network. The roads connected the various places to each other and led westward to the heartland of Urartu around the capital Tuspa (Van in Turkey). It has also been possible to locate a number of staging posts, some close to passes. One of these, at Tepe Dosoğ near the pass between Urmia and Ošanavīya, prefigures the courtyard type of hostelry which, in its eventual development, was to become important as the normal form of the oriental caravansary (Kleiss and Kroll, *AMI* 12, 1979, pp. 195f.). Still to be seen near the fort and settlement at Verak̲ram are vestiges of an Urartian bridge over the Aras (now the river frontier with U.S.S.R.); this is the oldest bridge known to have existed in Azerbaijan (ibid., p. 221).

Somewhat antedating or perhaps contemporary with the Urartian period in Azerbaijan is the probably Mannean sanctuary at Zendān-e Solaymān, which lay beyond Urartu's southern limits. The German excavations at this site have shown that it had an unusual layout, with a surrounding wall in the form of a series of box-like structures not yet seen elsewhere in the region. The wall surrounded a natural crater-lake formed by sinter deposits. Consturction took place mainly in two phases. The sanctuary, a terraced structure, was built first, in the eighth century B.C. Later the sanctuary was abandoned and the site was walled and fortified to serve as a safe haven for the Manneans (Kleiss, *Zendan-i Suleiman: Die Bauwerke*, Wiesbaden, 1971). The artifacts found at Zendān-e Solaymān resemble those found at Zīvīya (Ziwiyeh) in the nearby province of Kurdistan (A. Godard, *Le Trésor de Ziwiye (Kurdistan)*, Haarlem, 1950, p. 136).

Armenian monuments. In connection with the Armenians, certain forts in the area north to northeast of Mākū deserve mention. Because of the architectural features of the remains and the pottery found in them, they must be dated from the sixth century B.C. It has been possible to take measurements of two of them Īlān Qara II and Qalʿa-ye Ḥājjestān (despite the superimposition of a medieval Armenian castle on the latter site). They have the salient-reentrant wall lines typical of Azerbaijan in the sixth century B.C. Both must therefore be classified as purely Urartain forts. But since the territory and culture of the Urartians were taken over by the Armenians, sites such as Īlān Qara II and Qalʿa-ye Ḥājjestān are likely to have become early (pre-Christian) Armenian forts. Elsewhere in West Azerbaijan there are remains of other forts of prehistoric origin which remained in use until the later Middle Ages. Some names of Aremenian castles in the Armenian province of Vaspurakan are known from old writings but difficult to pin on ruins visible today. For example, it has not yet been possible to find the name of the Armenian castle which stood on top of the Urartian ruins at Besṭām from the ninth to the fifteenth century A.D. (see also further below).

Median period. It is not yet possible, in the present state of knowledge, to describe the political changes which led to the ending of Urartian rule in Azerbaijan in the middle or the second half of the 7th century B.C. Some clues, however, have been provided by archeological investigations in the northwestern part of West Azerbaijan. A change in the method of fortress defence is indicated by the construction of massive walls, with the rectilinear, sailent, and reentrant lines of ramparts, on the irregular contours of citadel hills. The pottery also shows change, with the development of the painted, so-called "triangle ware." In many cases the dating of architectural and ceramic remains in the transition from the Urartian to the Median and subsequent Achaemenid periods has not yet been satisfactorily worked out. There is reason to believe that certain remains of settlements at Besṭām and in its vicinity are Median. Investigations have shown, however, that the rock-tomb at Fak̲raka south of Lake Urmia, which was once thought to be Median, is of considerably more recent, probably late Achaemenid, origin (H. von Gall, "Zu den 'Medischen' Felsgräbern in Nordwestiran and iraqi Kurdestan," *Archäologischer Anzeiger*, 1966, pp. 20ff.).

Achaemenid period. Azerbaijan was annexed to the empire of the Achaemenids some time in the second half of the sixth century B.C. They have left very few relics in this province compared with others. Some graves and houses of the period have been discovered at Tak̲t-e Solaymān and other cemetery sites (R. and E. Naumann, 'Takht-i Suleiman," in *Katalog der Ausstellung München 1976*, p. 26). Finds of Achaemenid pottery have been made at Qalʿa-ye Żaḥḥāk (Kleiss, *AMI*, N. S. 6, 1973, pp. 163ff.)

Seleucid and Parthian periods. The Seleucids (312-129 B.C.) have left no significant vestiges in Azerbaijan. From the Parthian period (191 B.C.-A. D. 225), however, remains of settlements and cemeteries are widely scattered throughout the region. Numerous graveyards of the first century A. D. have been found in the Ṭāleš district around Germī north of Ardabīl (Iranian excavations directed by S. Kāmbak̲š-e Fard, unpublished report). At Tak̲t-e Solaymān, however, the excavations have yielded so little in the way of Parthian pottery that the identification of this site with the Parthian fortress Phraaspa, which the Roman general Mark Antony besieged without success in 36 B.C., is no longer tenable (R. and E. Naumann, op. cit., p. 11). Phraaspa is more likely to be traceable in the Marāḡa district. At Qalʿa-ye Żaḥḥāk south of Sīāh Čaman (Qara Čaman) in East Azerbaijan, extensive ruins of buildings from the Parthian period, including an almost wholly intact brick-walled pavilion of the first century A. D., await detailed examination (Kleiss, *AMI*, N. S. 6, 1973, pp. 163ff.). The design of the pavilion's facade exhibits a blend of old Iranian traditions of building inherited from Achaemenid times with influences from Roman architecture. There are strong grounds for the hypothesis, first propounded by V. Minorsky (*BSOAS* 9, 1943-46, p. 262) that Qal'a-ye Żaḥḥāk is to be identified with the Parthian town Phanaspa mentioned by Ptolemy (*Geography*, ed. F. W. Wilberg, VI, 2, Essendiae, 1838-45, p. 393).

Sasanian period. The Sasanian period (A. D. 240-642) is represented in Azerbaijan by clearly identifiable remains of settlements, including one at Besṭām, by parts of mosques, such as the Masǰed-e J̌omʿa at Urmia, and by ruins of fortresses. Many old castles are believed to be of Sasanian origin, and in some of them Sasanian brick or stone work can be recognized, but more often the belief rests on speculation rather than factual evidence of Sasanian characteristics of the walls. No solution has yet been found to the problem of distinguishing Sasanian from Islamic fortification techniques. The same is true of pottery designs.

The most important legacy of Sasanian art in Azerbaijan is the rock-carving at Salmās (formerly Šāhpūr). This dates from the third century A. D. and probably represents an act of homage or acceptance of vassalage by the Armenians in the presence of Ardašīr I and the crown prince Šāpūr. The lowness of the relief sets it apart from the more sculptural Sasanian rock-carvings in other regions (W. Hinz, "Das Sasanidische Felsrelief von Salmās," *Iranica Antiqua* 5, 1965, pp. 148ff.). A Sasanian rock-inscription survives in the Meškīnšahr district in East Azerbaijan (ibid., nos. 2266-67).

The German excavations at Taḵt-e Solaymān, the site of the Sasanian sanctuary of Ādur Gušnasp (q.v.), have thrown light on one of the most important and interesting cult centers of the Zoroastrian religion (R. Naumann, "Die Ruinen von Tacht-e Soleiman und Zendan-e Suleiman und Umgebung," in *Führer zu archäologischen Plätzen in Iran* II, Berlin, 1977. D. Huff, "Recherches archéologiques à Takht-i Suleiman, centre religieux royal sassanide," *Comptes rendus de l'Académie des inscriptions et belles-lettres*, 1978, pp. 774ff.). The fire sanctuary, known as the sanctuary of Šīz, had originally stood at Ganzak (probably identifiable with the Laylān) and was apparently moved to the plateau now called Taḵt-e Solaymān (Solomon's throne) by Ḵosrow I in the middle of the sixth century A.D. The fire temple, which was the focal point of the complex, evidently suffered at least partial destruction at the hands of the Byzantine army of the emperor Heraclius in 624, although according to Abū Dolaf Mesʿar b. Mohalhel (q.v.), who wrote in the mid 4th/10th century, the fire had been burning for seven hundred years and was still alight in his time. The excavations have produced evidence that the fire sanctuary buildings which finally took shape on the Taḵt-e Solaymān plateau remained intact for only about one hundred years, from Ḵosrow I's to Ḵosrow II's reign. Before then, perhaps in the fifth century during the reign of Pērōz I, the plateau had been fortified for the first time with the construction of a mud-brick wall, and mud-brick buildings had been erected inside the sacred enclosure. The plan devised at that time was on a large scale, and the builders in the later Sasanian period adhered to its general lines. The plateau is a terrace of sinter built up by lime deposition from a powerful spring, the impounded waters of which form a small lake or pond in the middle of the terrace. The original mud-brick buildings and surrounding wall of the sanctuary were replaced from ca. 500 onward by structures of hewn stone with baked brick vaults. Sasanian building activity at Taḵt-e Solaymān certainly reached its peak in the reign of Ḵosrow I (531-79), when the Ādur Gušnasp fire was relocated and suitably housed at this site, then called Šīz. After the destruction by the Byzantines and the subsequent conquest of Iran by the Arabs, practice of the fire cult at Taḵt-e Solaymān continued for a long time, despite the establishment and gradual expansion of a Muslim settlement on the plateau in the ʿAbbasid period. Even so, Taḵt-e Solaymān lost the religious eminence which it had enjoyed under the Sasanians. It did not regain any sort of importance until ca. 1271, when the il-khan Abaqa (Abāqā; q.v.) built a summer palace on top of the ruins, partly incorporating walls and surviving chambers of the former fire sanctuary.

Islamic period. Azerbaijan, with the rest of Iran, fell to the Muslims in the mid-seventh century A.D. Its history in the first four centuries of the Islamic period is to a large extent obscure. The oldest surviving Islamic edifices were built in the Saljuq period, e.g., the Se Gonbad tomb-tower at Urmia which dates from 1180 and is notable for the fine stalactitic stucco ornamentation over its portal. The domed hall of the great mosque (Masǰed-e J̌omʿa) at Urmia is conceptually derived from the Sasanian *čahār-ṭāq* (dome on four arches over a fire altar) and evidently stands on pre-Islamic foundations. This mosque's *meḥrāb* dating from 1277 and another at Marand dating from the fourteenth century are fine examples of the use of stucco for niche-decoration in the Il-khanid period, comparable in the delicacy of their carving with the *meḥrāb* in the Masǰed-e J̌omʿa of Isfahan. Also important are the remains of the Masǰed-e J̌omʿa and its minaret at Ardabīl from the Saljuq or the Īl-khanid period (12th or 13th century). The tomb-tower at Meškīnšahr from the Il-khanid period or the time of Tīmūr (13th or 14th century) is the last big tomb-tower left in Azerbaijan since the destruction of the one at Salmās in an earthquake in 1930. Several smaller tomb-towers, mostly of later date, also exist and have been surveyed. (On the Islamic architecture in general, see *Survey of Persian Art* I-IX, London 1938; XIV, New York and Tehran 1967; XV, Tehran, 1977. For the survey reports, see Kleiss in *AMI*, N.S. 2-6, 1969-73.) At Tabrīz, nothing from the early Islamic period remains, and the Masǰed-e J̌omʿa in the bazaar, though originally built in the Saljuq period, underwent drastic alteration in the fifteenth century. Of the five architecturally important tomb-towers at Marāḡa, the Qoy-borǰ (Tower of the ram) from the Timurid period has collapsed; three of those still standing are from the Saljuq period, namely the Gonbad-e Sorḵ (Red dome) completed in 1148, which is the oldest, the Gonbad-e Kabūd (Blue dome), and a round tower, while the fourth, known as the Gonbad-e Ḡaffārīya, is from the time of the Il-khans (early 14th-century).

As already mentioned, the il-khan Abaqa (1265-81), whose capital was at Marāḡa, had a hunting lodge, named Saturiq, built on the Taḵt-e Solaymān plateau. The walls of its main rooms were richly adorned with carved stucco and glazed tiles (R. and E. Naumann, "Takht-i Suleiman," pp. 43ff., 61ff.). Being built on top of the Sasanian ruins, the Mongol palace on the whole conformed to the plan of the Zoroastrian sanctuary with the pond at the center of the layout, but the main entrance was shifted from the north to the south side of the defensive wall around the plateau. Pillared galleries were built around the pond on all four sides, probably also as in Sasanian times. Behind the arcades lay rooms with differing but commodious dimensions. On the site of the former fire-temple, a large and conspicuous chamber with a north-south orientation was erected, possibly for use as an audience hall, and made accessible by means of a flight of steps. Among the decorative objects found in the Il-khanid palace at Taḵt-e Solaymān, a marble capital with the acanthus design is particularly interesting; it is typical of the late Roman period and likely to have been imported from northern Syria. Remains of kilns and potters' workshops at Taḵt-e Solaymān indicate that the wall tiles were manufactured on the spot. Taḵt-e Solaymān was abandoned early in the fourteenth century and Abaqa Khan's palace then fell into ruin (ibid., p. 12).

As regards the dating of the foundation of Azerbaijan's main towns, no clear evidence is available. Despite the lack of definite proof, it can be taken for certain that Urmia is of pre-Islamic origin. There are no archeological remains to show that Tabrīz existed in pre-Islamic times, and the earliest date of its establishment given in a literary source is 175/791 during the caliphate of Hārūn al-Rašīd (*Nozhat al-qolūb*, p. 75). In general the larger towns of Azerbaijan appear to have come into being soon after the spread of islam in Iran, because most of them contain buildings or remains of the early Islamic period. Tabrīz was the capital of the il-khans in the 7th/13th century and of the Qara Qoyunlū and Āq Qoyunlū Turkman dynasties in the 9th/15th century. Surviving from the Turkman period are the remains of the Masǰed-e Kabūd (Blue Mosque) and from the Il-khanid period those of the Masǰed-e ʿAlīšāh, whose massive *qebla* wall dominates the city's skyline. For a long time the remains of the latter mosque were used as the citadel (*arg*) of Tabrīz (see ARG-E ʿALĪŠĀH); after the Revolution of 1979 they were restored to their original purpose and made into an enclosure for public prayers in the open air.

Parts of the north of Iranian Azerbaijan were inhabited by Armenians before the mass expulsions and emigrations of the First World War. Numerous churches and ruins of churches attest the density of this population, particularly in the area northwest of Lake Urmia. Some are of considerable artistic and historical interest, such as the church at Moǰombār near Tabrīz which probably dates from the 4th/10th century. The church of St. Thaddeus, locally called the Qara Kelīsā, on the site of the saint's tomb is partly 4th/10th century (the east end); it was largely rebuilt after an earthquake in 1318 and greatly extended in the 13th/19th century. There were hopes on the Iranian side at that time that the monastery of St. Thaddeus, if suitably enlarged, might become the seat of the Catholicos, but when political factors rendered these hopes vain, the nineteenth century building work was left unfinished; even so, this is one of the most interesting Armenian churches. Equally noteworthy is the monastery of St. Stephanos on the frontier-river Aras; parts of it go back to the 3rd-4th/9th-10th centuries, but most of what remains today dates from the 10th-11th/16th-17th centuries and gives interesting evidence of mutual interactions between Christian and Islamic art in that period. (For reports of surveys of Armenian churches in Azerbaijan, see *AMI*, N.S. 2, 1969, pp. 8ff., 12, 1979, pp. 361ff.; on St. Thaddeus, *Documenti di architettura Armena* 4, Milan, 1973; on St. Stefanos, ibid., 10, 1980.) Armenian influence on Iranian architecture is apparent in the gateway of the bazaar entrance to the town of Ḵoy, probably built by Armenian masons in the early 13th/19th century when the town's walls were broadened to form "French-type" fortifications; the use of alternate layers of different-colored stone is typical of Armenian stonework.

The most impressive relics of Safavid architecture and fine art in Azerbaijan are the tile-clad mausoleum of the dynasty's founder Shaikh Ṣafī at Ardabīl (q.v.) and the adjoining chamber which was built to house the royal collection of Chinese porcelain. Lesser buildings of the Safavid and likewise the Qajar period in Azerbaijan give the impression that the province made no significant cultural advance in the 11th/17th and subsequent centuries. When the central government left Tabrīz, Azerbaijan was relegated to a subordinate role and all the artistic talent of Iran was drawn to the succeeding capital cities, first Qazvīn, then Isfahan, and finally Tehran.

Trade routes across Azerbaijan have long been important. Stretches of some of them were described in ancient times by Ptolemy. Economic growth in the Middle Ages gave rise to increasing intercontinental traffic, particularly on the branch of the "silk road" crossing Azerbaijan from east to west. Although in general nothing much was done in Azerbaijan to improve the state of the roads, construction of bridges and caravanserais was essential.

The Aras was bridged at a number of places. Remains of a Qajar (19th century) bridge on the Tabrīz-Baku road and of a probably Safavid (17th century) bridge at Ḵodā-āfarīn survive in fairly good condition (see *AMI* 18, 1985). Also well preserved is the remarkable walled approach ramp of another probably Safavid bridge over the Aras west of Julfa (J̌olfā) on the road from Tabrīz to Yerevan (Īravān). A bridge east of Mākū bearing an Armenian inscription is still intact. The old bridge near Tabrīz and another near Āḏaršahr deserve mention, and the bridge called the Pol-e Qāflān-kūh over the Safīd-rūd near Mīāna is particularly interesting as an inscription records the date of its completion in 888/1484 (Kleiss, *AMI* 16, 1983, pp. 363ff.). Dating of bridges which lack an inscription is difficult, but in general it appears that the surviving old bridges or ruins of bridges date from the Qajar period (19th century) or less frequently the Safavid period (17th century).

Azerbaijan is not so rich in caravanserais as are the areas around the central Iranian desert, the Dašt-e Kavīr, and along the cross-desert routes. The main road from Yerevan through J̌olfā, Marand, Tabrīz, and Mīāna to Qazvīn and Tehran was endowed with Safavid and Qajar caravanserais as well as the J̌olfā and Pol-e Qāflān-kūh bridges. Remains of the tile-adorned portal of a Timurid (14th-15th century) caravanserai can be seen between J̌olfā and Marand (Kleiss, *AMI*, N.S. 5, 1972, pl. 53.3). Most of the caravanserais are of the courtyard type with four *ayvān*s (arched portals), the commonest form of caravanserai in Iran. On roads which cross the frontier to Turkey through high passes, particularly the Tabrīz-Ḵoy-Van road, some caravanserais of the completely covered type remain, and there is also one close to the pass on the Tabrīz-Ahar road; they were built to give shelter from avalanches and snowstorms and therefore have no courtyard, all the rooms and stables being interconnected and vaulted.

Azerbaijan has a large number of medieval castles, mainly in mountainous areas. Many stand on pre-Islamic fort sites. They were built to guard and control lines of communication, to overlook and protect cultivated areas, and to dominate cities and towns. Certain castles, such as the Qalʿa-ye Doḵtar above the Pol-e Qāflān-kūh, have architectural peculiarities which suggest that they were built by the Assassians to secure the communications between their headquarters at Alamūt northeast of Qazvīn and their outposts in Syria.

Much work remains to be done on the archeology of Azerbaijan from pre-historic to recent times. Insecurity on the roads, and thereafter wars and their sequels, kept archeologists away for many decades. Between 1950 and 1978 promising excavations and wide-ranging surveys in Azerbaijan were planned and implemented in an international cooperative effort. Political developments in Iran since 1357/1979 have brought all these undertakings to a temporary halt.

Bibliography: Given in the text. On the pre-Islamic period, consult L. Vanden Berghe, *Bibliographie analytique de l'archéologie de l'Iran ancien*, Leiden, 1979, and *Supplément 1. 1978-1980*, Leiden, 1981. On the Islamic period, see the survey reports in *Archäologische Mitteilungen aus Iran*, N.S. 1, Berlin, 1968, and subsequent volumes. See also ʿA. Kārang, *Āṯār-e bāstānī-e Āḏarbāyjān* I: *Āṯār o abnīa-ye tārīḵī-e šahrestān-e Tabrīz*, Tabrīz, 1351 Š./1972, and S. J̌. Torābī Ṭabāṭabāʾī, *Āṯār-e bāstānī-e Āḏarbāyjān* II: *Āṯār o abnīa-ye tārīkī-e šahrestānhā-ye Ardabīl, Arasbārān, Ḵalḵāl, Sarāb, Meškīnšahr, Moḡān*. Tabrīz, 2535 = 1355 Š./1976.

(W. Kleiss)

iii. Pre-Islamic History

Like other parts of Iran, the northwestern province of Azerbaijan can look back on a long history. For the earliest periods, however, archeological research has barely begun.

Before the Achaemenids. In 1949 C. Coon discovered a cave of the paleolithic period at Tamtama, north of Urmia (Reżāʾīya) (Coon, *Cave Exploration in Iran 1949*, Philadelphia, 1951, pp. 15-20, 36-37, 44, 65). No indications of paleolithic settlement, however, were found in the first larger-scale surveys in the west of the province made by R. R. B. Kearton (see *Iran* 7, 1969, pp. 186-87) and R. S. Solecki (ibid., pp. 189-90) in 1968. Opinions differed on the question why no paleolithic sites had been discovered in this seemingly favorable region. D. Perkins, Jr. (ibid., p. 189) surmised that scarcity of "raw chipping material, such as flint," in the region might be the explanation, but Solecki considered this improbable because flint was certainly available in the local mountains and spark-flints had been found at later neolithic sites; in Solecki's opinion, the lack of paleolithic settlements was more likely to be due to ecological factors. Investigations by B. G. Campbell in the Tabrīz-Marāḡa-Mīāna triangle in 1974 and 1975 yielded evidence to the contrary for this area, as three caves and seven "open air localities" of the lower paleolithic period were discovered (H. Sadek-Kooros, "Earliest Hominid Traces in Azerbaijan," *Iran* 14, 1976, p. 154; idem, *Proceedings of the 4th Annual Symposium on Archaeological Research in Iran 1975*, Tehran, 1976, pp. 1ff.). The University of Pennsylvania's large-scale expedition, called the "Ḥasanlū Project," to the Soldūz valley under the leadership of R. B. Dyson, Jr., in 1965 produced evidence that the effective human occupation of this area began ca. 6000 B.C. (*Bibliotheca Mesopotamica* VIII, 1977; also L. Vanden Berghe, *Bibliographie analytique de l'archéologie de l'Iran ancien*, Leiden, 1979, and idem and E. Haerinck, *Supplément 1: 1978-80*, Leiden, 1981). Other excavations in Azerbaijan, e.g., by C. Burney at Yanik Tepe and later at Haftavān and by A. Lippert at Kordlar Tepe, point to widespread settlement in Azerbaijan in the neolithic and chalcolithic periods.

For historical times, which in Azerbaijan begin roughly in the seventh century B.C., new archeological data have come to hand from the investigations of W. Kleiss, who excavated the big Urartian fortress of Besṭām (Basṭām) and from 1967 onward conducted systematic surveys in several parts of the province. Thanks mainly to Kleiss's surveys, we now know that Azerbaijan, in particular the western region, was densely populated by Urartians—something that would not have been believed twenty years ago. In addition,

Kleiss's surveys brought to light many other large and small settlements of early historical times (see his successive articles in *AMI*, N.S., 1967 and later; and Vanden Berghe and Haerinck's bibliographies). Also worthy of mention here is the fact that the long known rock chamber of Karaftū, twenty km west of Takāb, with its inscription "Hercules dwells here, let nothing evil enter," has now been dated, in the light of its paleographic characteristics, from the late fourth or early third century B.C. (H. van Gall, *AMI*, N.S. 11, 1978, pp. 91ff.; P. Bernard, *Studia Iranica* 9, 1980, pp. 301ff.).

Achaemenid period. In the Achaemenid period Azerbaijan was part of the satrapy of Media. When the Achaemenid empire collapsed, Atropates, the Persian satrap of Media, made himself independent in the northwest of this region in 321 B.C. (thus H. H. Schmitt, *Untersuchungen zur Geschichte Antiochos' des Grossen und seiner Zeit*, Wiesbaden, 1964, p. 61; in 328 according to V. Minorsky in *EI*^{2} I, p. 188, or 328-27 according to Kaerst, in Pauly-Wissowa, II, col. 2150). Thereafter Greek and Latin writers named the territory Media Atropatene or, less frequently, Media Minor (e.g. Strabo 11.13.1; Justin 23.4.13). The Middle Persian form of the name was (early) Āturpātakān, (later) Ādurbādagān) whence the New Persian Āḏarbāyǰān (on the name Atropatene and its derivation, see Minorsky, loc. cit.; Andreas, "Adarbigana," in Pauly-Wissowa, I, cols. 345ff.; Weissbach, "Atropatene," in Pauly-Wissowa, II, cols. 2149-50, and Streck, in Pauly-Wissowa, Suppl. I, cols. 223-24; Schwarz, *Iran*, repr. 1969, pp. 959ff.).

Atropates managed to keep on good terms with Alexander. At the famous mass wedding at Susa in 324, his daughter was married to Perdiccas (Arrian 6.4.5). After Alexander's death he was left in command of his territory (Diodorus Siculus 18.3.3). He founded a dynasty which was to last long. The exact extent of the state of Media Minor or Media Atropatene is not known; in the opinion of Schwarz (op. cit., p. 61) it probably reached the Caspian, but how much of the coast it embraced is debatable.

Seleucid period. A successor of Atropates known to us from Greek sources is Artabazanes, who was contemporary with the Seleucid ruler Antiochus III (223 or 242-187). On the basis of a statement of Polybius (5.44.8 and 5.55.27) that Atropatene stretched to the Caucasus mountains, E. Herzfeld (*AMI* 4, 1931-32, p. 56) described Artabazanes as ruler of "Armenia and Atropatene." Antiochus III, after his successful campaign against Molon, satrap of Media, who had rebelled, decided to march against Artabazanes with the intention to warn all concerned against supporting rebels with troops or arms (Polybius 5.55.1-2). Whether Artabazanes had in fact sent troops to help Molon is doubtful (Schmitt, op. cit., p. 124). Artabazanes, who was growing old, did not put up much resistance and appears to have acquiesced in submission to Seleucid suzerainty, in return for which he was probably confirmed in his rulership of Atropatene (Schmitt, op. cit., p. 149).

Parthian period. The exact date of Atropatene's incorporation in the Parthian empire is not known. Most probably it occurred in the reign of Mithridates I (ca. 171-139/38 B.C.) when this Parthian great king, taking advantage of the Seleucid empire's weakness after the defeat of Antiochus III by the Romans at Magnesia in 190 B.C., moved to extend his sway eastward and northward. Presumably Media Atropatene became a vassal state under Parthian suzerainty at the same time as the rest of Media. This must have been after 148 B.C. because the Seleucid rock-inscription at Bīsotūn (Behistun) shows that there was then still a Seleucid governor of the "Upper Satrapies," which certainly included Media (K. Schippmann, *Grundzüge der parthischen Geschichte*, Darmstadt, 1980, p. 24). It seems, however, that the small state of Atropatene kept a good measure of autonomy. Descendants of Atropates are said to have "married into the (Arsacid) royal house" (Minorsky, in *EI*^{2} I, p. 188).

The next mention of Media Atropatene comes in reports that after the death of Mithridates II in 88-87 B.C., the Armenians succeeded in recovering lands which they had earlier lost to the Parthians. According to Strabo (11.14.15) and Plutarch (*Lucullus* 26), the Armenians occupied Atropatene at this time.

Atropatene's history in the following years is confused. Dio Cassius (36.14) states that a certain Mithridates, king of Media and son-in-low of the Armenian king Tiridates, supported the latter when he went to war with the Romans and invaded Cappadocia in 67 B.C. Quite possibly this Mithridates was the future Parthian monarch Mithridates III, who together with his brother Orodes murdered their father Phraates III in 58-57 (Dio Cassius 39.56.2). He has been described, on the strength of Dio Cassius's statement, as "king of Media Atropatene" in several works by modern scholars (e.g., A. Gutschmid, *Geschichte Irans und seiner Nachbarländer*, Tübingen, 1888, p. 98; H. Volkmann, in *Der Kleine Pauly-Wissowa* III, col. 1358; Geyer, with reservations in Pauly-Wissowa, XV, 2, col. 2207), though in fact he is called by Dio Cassius (36.14 and 39.56.2) simply "king of Media" (see also C. Le Rider, *Suse sous les séleucides et les parthes, MADFI* 38, 1965, p. 400; E. Herzfeld, *AMI* 4, 1932, p. 72).

In some sources (Appian, *Mithridatica* 106, 117; Diodorus Siculus 12.40.4), the Romans under Pompey are reported to have attacked a certain Darius, king of Media, in 65 B.C. Here again this person has been described as "ruler of Media Atropatene" by some modern writers (N. C. Debevoise, *A Political History of Parthia*, New York, 1938, p. 74; Gutschmid, op. cit., p. 98; less explicitly Herzfeld, art. cit., p. 56), whereas in the sources only Media is given. Acceptance of the supposition that he ruled Media Atropatene is also made difficult by the evidence of other sources (*Monumentum Ancyranum* VI, 11f.; see also Wilcken in Pauly-Wissowa, II, col. 1309) which speak of Artavasdes king of Atropatene, born in 59 B.C. or a little earlier, son of Ariobarzanes, king of Atropatene. This suggests that the father had come to the throne some time before 59

B.C. If so, the time-scale would appear to preclude a reign of this Darius in Media Atropatene.

The Greco-Roman writers have left much more detailed and precise accounts of the expedition led by Mark Antony against the Parthians in 36 B.C. Having obtained the support of the Armenian king Artavasdes, Antony made Armenia his base for an invasion of Media Atropatene, whose identically named (and just mentioned) king Artavasdes was an ally of the Parthians. As is well known, the Roman campaign was bungled and ended ignominiously. After a Parthian attack which destroyed his rearguard and siege-train, Antony had to abandon his siege of Atropatene's capital city Phraata (in some sources Praaspa or Phraaspa) and flee back to Armenia. It has not yet been possible to determine where Phraata lay; the often mooted identification with Takt-e Solaymān southeast of Lake Urmia where the German Archeological Institute conducted excavations in 1959 and subsequently, remains unproven (K. Schippmann, *Die iranischen Feuerheiligtümer*, New York and Berlin, 1971, pp. 309ff.; H. Bengtson, *Zum Parther-Feldzug des Antonius*, Munich, 1974, pp. 24ff.).

Soon after the defeat of the Romans, so Plutarch (*Antonius* 52-53) and Dio Cassius (49.33) state, enmity arose between Artavasdes of Media Atropatene and Phraates, the Parthian great king, over the division of the spoils and the fears of Artavasdes concerning his autonomy, with the result that the Median king offered Antony an alliance. The offer was accepted in 33 B.C. (K.-H. Ziegler, *Die Beziehungen zwischen Rom und dem Partherreich*, Wiesbaden, 1964, p. 36). It was very welcome to Antony who, in the belief that Artavasdes of Armenia had left him down in his campaign, now planned a pincer movement against Armenia while also cherishing hopes of Atropatenian support in his continuing war with the Parthians and impending contest with Octavian (for an assessment of the different motives, see Bengtson, op. cit., pp. 43-44). Troop detachments were exchanged and at the same time some Armenian territory, consisting mainly of the Sambyke district which had earlier belonged to Atropatene, was ceded to the Median ruler. To strengthen the bonds, a son of Antony was betrothed to Iotape, a daughter of Artavasdes. The alliance at first proved advantageous to Artavasdes of Atropatene, who with the help of the Roman reinforcements repulsed an offensive launched jointly by Artaxes, a son of Artavasdes of Armenia, and the Parthians.

These dealings indicate that not only Artavasdes, but also previous rulers of Media Atropatene, were more or less independent of the Parthian great kings. No doubt the geography of this relatively inaccessible mountain region facilitated the maintenance of its autonomy.

Artavasdes, however, could no longer hold out against the Parthians when Antony withdrew the Roman detachment from Media because he needed the men for his war with Octavian. In 30 B.C. Artavasdes was taken prisoner, but later he contrived to escape, probably as a result of the outbreak of civil war between Phraates IV and Tiridates, a rival claimant to the Parthian throne. He took refuge with Octavian, now Augustus, who gave him a friendly reception. He is reported to have died at Rome shortly before 20 B.C. (see Wilcken in Pauly-Wissowa, II, col. 1311).

Soon afterward, probably in 20 B.C., Augustus is said to have nominated Ariobarzanes II, the son of Artavasdes, to be king of Media Atropatene. At some later date, Ariobarzanes was appointed king of Armenia also. (Thus E. Meyer in Pauly-Wissowa, Suppl. I, col. 130; M. L. Chaumont in H. Temporini and W. Haase, eds., *Aufstieg und Niedergang der römischen Welt*, Berlin, 1976-81, II, *Principat* 9.1; J. G. L. Anderson in *CAH* X, pp. 264, 276. Between 20 B.C. and A.D. 2 in the opinion of Gutschmid, op. cit., p. 116. For a different interpretation, see U. Kahrstedt, *Artabanos III und seine Erben*, Bern, 1950, pp. 15-16). The actual induction of Ariobarzanes took place much later, namely in A.D. 9 following the accession of Vonones to the Parthian throne with Roman support (Ziegler, op. cit., p. 57 n. 81).

Ariobarzanes II was succeeded, on the thrones of both Media Atropatene and Armenia, by his son Artavasdes (Artavasdes II in the reckoning of Herzfeld, art. cit., p. 57; III in that of Chaumont, op. cit., p. 82, with many bibliographic references). Not long afterward, according to M. L. Chaumont in A.D. 19 or 20, this king was murdered. The event marks the virtual end of the rule of the dynasty founded by Atropates over Media Atropatene. It may have been consequent on the negotiation of the peace treaty of A.D. 18-19 between Germanicus, the Roman commander, and Artabanus II, the Parthian monarch since A.D. 10-11 (on whose background see below). Peace with Rome evidently gave Artabanus a free hand to deal with internal issues. Media Atropatene was one of a number of vassal kingdoms where the indigenous dynasts were eliminated and replaced with Arsacid younger sons (Kahrstedt, op. cit., p. 18; Ziegler, op. cit., p. 60 n. 104, basically agrees but points out that the sources for the treaty contain no word of any Roman promise of nonintervantion in Media Atropatene). The later princes of the Atropatenian dynasty probably lived in exile in Italy. Two inscriptions bearing the name Artavasdes which were found in Rome are probably epitaphs of the son and grandson of an Atropatenian king Ariobarzanes, whether Ariobarzanes I or II being uncertain (Meyer in Pauly-Wissowa, Suppl. I, col. 130; Kahrstedt, op. cit., pp. 15, 17; Herzfeld, art. cit., p. 57).

It is necessary to comment here on the assertion, which has been frequently made (e.g., by Gutschmid, op. cit., p. 119; Herzfeld, art. cit., p. 74; Anderson in *CAH* X, p. 278) and is based on a passage in Josephus's *Antiquitates Judaicae* (18.48), that Artabanos had been king of Media Atropatene before he became the great king of the Parthians. Kahrstedt (op. cit., pp. 11ff.) has found ample and convincing evidence that this is not so and that Artabanus probably stemmed from eastern Iran.

For the following period few events involving Atropatene are reported in the sources. Josephus (20.74) mentions that the first official act of the Parthian monarch Vologases I (A.D. ca. 51–ca. 76 or 80) was to appoint his brother Pacorus king of Media Atropatene (for a different interpretation, see R. Hanslik, in Pauly-Wissowa, IX, cols. 1839-40; Vonones II may have previously assigned the throne of Media Atropatene to Vologases, see Chaumont, op. cit., p. 97). When the Alans invaded Atropatene A.D. ca. 72, Pacorus had to flee into the trackless mountains (Debevoise, op. cit., p. 200; Chaumont, op. cit., p. 126). Another Alan invasion took place between A.D. 134 and 136.

Information about Atropatene (Azerbaijan) is then lacking until the last years of Parthian rule, when the conflict with Ardašīr, the founder of the Sasanian dynasty, had already begun. Artabanus IV, the last Parthian great king, was simultaneously engaged in a contest for the throne with his brother Vologases VI. His supporters were strongest in Media (where his coins appear to have been minted, probably at Ecbatana, the present-day Hamadān) and in Azerbaijan, Ḵūzestān, and Adiabene (G. Widengren, in *La Persia nel Medioevo*, Accademia Nazionale dei Lincei, Quaderno 160, Rome, 1971, pp. 711ff., esp. p. 741). Widengren has found evidence, however, that the common people of Media Atropatene were allies of Ardašīr (p. 749). In any case Azerbaijan submitted with little resistance to Ardašīr once he had defeated and killed Artabanus in 226 (the date preferred by Widengren, pp. 748-49). The well-known Sasanian rock relief at Salmās, not far from lake Urmia in which Aradšīr and others are depicted, is in Widengren's opinion quite possibly a monument to this success (but see Chaumont, *Recherches sur l'histoire d'Arménie de l'avènement des sassanides à la conversion du royaume*, Paris, 1969, pp. 173ff.); the opinion of W. Hinz (*Iranica Antiqua* 5, 1965, p. 159) that it commemorates Ardašīr's conquest of Armenia seems less well grounded.

Sasanian period. The next information given in the sources is that Šāpūr I, in the first year of his reign, i.e., 241-42, conducted two campaigns, first against the Khwarazmians then against the "Medes in the mountains," which evidently means in Azerbaijan (Christensen, *Iran Sass.*, p. 219). Thereafter Azerbaijan appears to have been pacified, because no more campaigns against its inhabitants are reported in the sources.

Atropatene/Āturpātakān, as the province appears to have been officially named throughout the Sasanian period (M. Streck, in *EI*[1] I, p. 142) was governed on behalf of the Sasanian monarchs by a *marzbān* (margrave) who had all the authority of a satrap. It was a religious center, the principal temple being at Šīz, now Taḵt-e Solaymān. This was the hearth of Ādur Gušnasp (q.v.), one of the empire's three most sacred fires. The name Šīz often appears in linkage with other names, particularly Ganzaca (Ganzak) and Thebarmais, but the supposition that all refer to the same place is questionable (Schippmann, *Feuerheiligtümer*, pp. 341ff.; D. Huff, *Comptes rendus de l'Académie des inscriptions et belles-lettres*, 1978, pp. 774ff.). As a result of the existence of this great fire-temple, so revered that every newly crowned Sasanian king had to walk all the way to it on foot, and of the establishment of a royal palace in the province, Azerbaijan became a tightly integrated part of the empire instead of a loosely attached vassal state as in Parthian times. Herzfeld (art. cit., p. 57 n. 2) thought that "personal names incorporating *gušnasp*, the name of the sacred fire of Ganzak, were distinctively Atropatenian;" if so, this province produced many men of worth who held high office in the four centuries of Sasanian rule (Herzfeld, loc. cit.; Christensen, *Iran Sass.*, pp. 518ff.).

Azerbaijan reenters the historical scene at the end of the Sasanian period. In A.D. 590 the decisive battle in the contest for the throne between the usurper Bahrām Čōbīn and Ḵosrow II was fought at Ganzak in Azerbaijan, ending in victory for Ḵosrow. In 628, on Easter day, the Byzantine emperor Heraclius captured Ganzak. Sasanian authority then began to collapse. Azerbaijan fell to the Arabs between A.D 639 and 643 (Minorsky, in *EI*[2] I, p. 190), and a new phase of its history began.

Bibliography: Given in the text.

(K. Schippmann)

iv. Islamic History to 1941

Background. Azerbaijan formed a separate province of the early Islamic caliphate, but its precise borders varied in different periods. In the north, the Aras or Araxes river (q.v.) formed a clear natural boundary between Azerbaijan and Arrān (q.v.) or Caucasian Albania, whilst the low-lying region of Mūḡān/Mūqān (Moḡān; q.v.), lying between the lower reaches of the Aras-Kor river system and the western shore of the Caspian Sea was usually considered administratively as part of Azerbaijan. In the south, the Safīd-rūd formed in general the boundary with the province of Jebāl, with the northwestern continuation of the Alburz (Alborz; q.v.) chain separating Azerbaijan from Gīlān (q.v.) and the Caspian coastlands. The western boundary was less determinate, but the northern extension of the Zagros mountains running up through Kurdistan and the modern Turkish *welāyat*s of Hakārī and Van, separating the basins of lakes Urmia and Van, was generally held to be the boundary. But Azerbaijan and the tributary but often in practice largely independent province of Armenia (q.v.) were often taken as one vast province—their configuration, as the term given to them of *reḥāb* "the upland plains, plateaux" shows, being essentially similar—and placed under a single governor; the geographer Moqaddasī, pp. 373-74, includes under the *eqlīm al-Reḥāb* Azerbaijan, Arrān, and Armenia, cf. A. Miquel, *Aḥsan al-taqāsīm fī maʿrefat al-aqālīm* (*La meilleure répartition pour la connaissance des provinces*), Damascus, 1963, p. 318. However, at times, Azerbaijan might be linked also with Jebāl or with the provinces of Mosul and Jazīra, demonstrating the fluidity of administrative arrangements in the first two or three centuries of Islam. It should further be noted that the classical Arabic and

Persian geographers of the 3rd/9th and 4th/10th centuries often distinguish an eastern and a western administrative division of Azerbaijan: the eastern one with Marāḡa as its center, and the western one administered from Ardabīl, which was considered to be the capital of Azerbaijan in general.

The Arabic geographers and historians noted too that the broken nature of the terrain, whose plateaux and mountains gave the province a notoriously harsh climate (the geographers placed it partly in the fourth and partly in the fifth clime), was reflected in a heterogeneity in linguistic, ethnic, social, and religious matters. We need not take seriously Moqaddasī's assertion (p. 375) that Azerbaijan had seventy languages, a state of affairs more correctly applicable to the Caucasus region to the north; but the basically Iranian population spoke an aberrant, dialectical form of Persian (called by Mas'ūdī al-āḏarīya) as well as standard Persian, and the geographers state that the former was difficult to understand. North of the Aras, the distinct, presumably Iranian, speech of Arrān long survived, called by Ebn Ḥawqal (p. 349, tr. Kramers, p. 342) al-Rānīya, and in the northeastern districts of Azerbaijan Armenian was of course found. In the west of the province, around Lake Urmia, Kurdish must have been known, for the Kurds are frequently mentioned as an ethnic component of Azerbaijan and were to play a significant political role there from the time of the Rawwadids onwards (see below). As Arabic settlement increased, Arabic became well-known, at least as an urban speech. Ebn Ḥawqal (loc. cit.) states that most Persian speakers could also understand Arabic (an assertion doubtlessly only valid for town dwellers) and that the merchants and landowning classes spoke it excellently; such social classes would, of course, require a knowledge of Arabic for their commercial contacts and for their political links with the Arab military and official classes. It was only the ethnic Turkicization of Azerbaijan, from the 5th/11th century onwards, which made Turkish the major language of Azerbaijan, as it is today (see below).

Concerning the religious pattern of Azerbaijan, Zoroastrianism had held a pre-eminent position in pre-Islamic times, and the Arabic sources frequently report that the province was Zoroaster's birthplace; Balāḏorī and Ebn Ḵordāḏbeh both, for instance, specify Urmia for this, and Yāqūt and Qazvīnī mention Šīz. The formerly numerous fire temples of Azerbaijan led many Arabic authorities to explain the name itself of the province as meaning something like "fire temple" (e.g., Yāqūt [Beirut], I, p. 128: "fire-keeper" > "fire temple"). The great shrine at Šīz (q.v.) (perhaps to be located at Taḵt-e Solaymān, to the southeast of Lake Urmia), was the local spiritual center of Zoroastrianism at the time of the Arab conquest, and the rights of the Zoroastrian community, as *ahl al-ḏemma*, to the free exercise of their religion were secured at that juncture (see below). The 4th/10th-century traveler Abū Dolaf speaks of the fire temple as being still in existence then, with the detail that "on the summit of its cupola there is a silver crescent which forms its talisman. Both amirs and usurpers wished to remove it, but did not succeed;" but Minorsky was probably right to doubt the truth of this account and to suggest that only the ruins were visible by then (*Second Resāla = Abū-Dulaf Mis'ar Ibn Muhalhil's Travels in Iran (circa A.D. 950)*, Cairo, 1955, text par. 5, tr. pp. 31-32, comm. pp. 67-68; see also A. Godard, "Les monuments du feu," *Āṯār-é Īrān* 3, 1938, pp. 45ff., and B. M. Tirmidhi, "Zoroastrians and their Fire-temples in Iran and Adjoining Countries," *Islamic Culture* 24, 1950, pp. 271-84). If Zoroastrianism disappeared as a distinct faith in Azerbaijan, its former adherents, and those of Mazdakism (the latter known to be a numerous element in later Sasanian Azerbaijan), very probably contributed to the strongly heterodox flavor of Azerbaijan and Arrān in the early Islamic centuries, seen in the strength there of socio-religious protest movements and revolutionary upheavals, above all, in that of Bābak and the Ḵorramīya (see below).

Whilst Zoroastrianism clearly declined, Christianity was for long vital and flourishing, as is attested by the frequent mention of bishops of Azerbaijan in Syriac sources and by the apparent presence of monastic institutions and of hermits; the *'ahd* "agreement" between the incoming Arabs and the people of Azerbaijan (see below) mentions the exclusion from payment of the *jezya* or poll-tax of, amongst others, "the pious devotee and anchorite, who has no possessions" (Ṭabarī, I, p. 2662). When the Jacobite Maphrian or head of the church in the Persian lands, the celebrated Barhebraeus, died at Marāḡa in 1286, local Nestorians, Melkites, and Armenians joined with the Jacobites in mourning him. In the Mongol period, indeed, the Christian communities enjoyed at the outset a comparative florescence and toleration; in the time of the Great Khan Güyük (r. 1246-49), the influence within the Mongol horde of the Syrian monk Simeon Rabban Ata secured the building of churches in strongly Muslim towns like Tabrīz and Nakhchevan (Naḵjavān), until the conversion to Islam of Ḡāzān (r. 694-703/1295-1304) brought about a reversal of this favor (see Spuler, *Mongolen*, pp. 203ff.). Thereafter, Christianity in Azerbaijan declined to the point of extinction, with the exception of the vestigial Nestorian or Assyrian Christian Neo-Syriac-speaking communities of the Lake Urmia region which have survived till today. As for the Jews, these are virtually unmentioned in the early centuries, though they may well have formed part of the urban communities.

From the Arab conquest to the Saljuqs. The Arab conquest of Azerbaijan took place in 'Omar's caliphate at a date variously given as between 18/639 and 22/643, after battles such as Nehāvand and Jalūlā had opened up the possibility of invading Jebāl from Iraq, and it was undertaken essentially by troops from the newly-founded *meṣr* of Kūfa in central Iraq. The Armenian historian Sebeos states that the Espahbaḏ of Atrpatakan of Azerbaijan in the last years of the Sasanian monarchy was Farroḵ-Hormezd (d. 630), whose sons Rostam and Farroḵzād or Ḵorrazād then led resistance to the Arabs (see Markwart, *Ērānšahr*, pp. 112-14). Of the Arabic sources, we have the fullest accounts from Balāḏorī, citing the shaikhs of the capital Ardabīl and Madā'enī (*Fotūḥ* [Cairo], pp. 321-26) and from Ṭabarī citing Sayf b. ʿOmar (I, pp. 2647-50, 2660-62).

The Arabs seem to have attached considerable importance to the over-running of Azerbaijan. A saying attributed to the *dehqān* Hormozān, consulted by the caliph ʿOmar, describes Azerbaijan as being, with Fārs, one of the two wings on each side of the key point, the head, of Isfahan, all three of them being interconnected (Masʿūdī, *Morūj* IV, p. 230, ed. Pellat, par. 1563). Once the base of Hamadān had been secured during the governorship in Kūfa of Moḡīra b. Šoʿba, the whole of northern Persia was laid open to attack. Balāḏorī's account makes Ḥoḏayfa b. Yamān the first commander of the expedition into Azerbaijan. Ḥoḏayfa was opposed by the *marzbān* of Azerbaijan at Ardabīl, supported by the men of Bājarvān, Mīmaḏ, Sarāt or Sarāb, Šīz, Mayānaj, etc., but triumphed militarily, and made a peace agreement on the basis of an annual tribute of 800,000 derhams in return for the preservation of the people's lives; no enslavement; respect for the sanctity of the fire temples (in particular, the people of Šīz were to continue freely to hold their festivals); and protection for the population against the predatory Kurds of Balāsajān, Sabalān, and Šātrūḏān (Balāḏorī, *Fotūḥ*, p. 321). Ḥoḏayfa was subsequently replaced by ʿOtba b. Farqad Solamī, who had to subdue the countryside of Azerbaijan, whilst the new governor appointed by the caliph ʿOṯmān, his kinsman Walīd b. ʿOtba b. Abī Moʿayṭ, had further to quell a rebellion in 25/645-46 and re-impose the *ʿahd* of Ḥoḏayfa. Ṭabarī's account attributes the preliminary stages of the conquest, made in the face of strenuous opposition from the Espahbaḏ Rostam's brother Esfandīār and then from Bahrām b. Farroḵzād, to the efforts of Arab generals like Bokayr b. ʿAbdallāh before ʿOtba b. Farqad arrived, after when Bokayr was despatched northwards against Arrān and Bāb al-Abwāb or Darband (q.v.). The text of the *ʿahd* document, made when a general peace was established in Azerbaijan, is given verbatim by Ṭabarī; it provided for payment of the *jezya* in return for *amān*, i.e., liberty of property, laws and faith (Ṭabarī, I, pp. 2661-62).

From ʿOṯmān's reign onwards, Arab warriors began to settle in the towns of Azerbaijan, with Ardabīl as their administrative center. Settlers from Kūfa and Baṣra and from Syria purchased land from the indigenous population, and received the voluntary submission of many villages in return for protection (*ḥemāya*, *talje'a*). The Islamization of the province must now have got under way too. Some details are given by Balāḏorī of the pattern of Arab settlement in the towns over the first two centuries or so of Arab domination. Arab colonists were settled in Ardabīl, where a mosque was built by the chief of Kenda, Ašʿaṯ b. Qays, the governor of Azerbaijan for the caliph ʿAlī b. Abī Ṭāleb (Balāḏarī, *Fotūḥ*, p. 329). Warṯān on the Aras river was developed by the Omayyad prince Marwān b. Moḥammad b. ʿAbd-al-Malek (eventually the last Omayyad caliph, Marwān al-Ḥemār, 127-32/744-50), who also held property at Marāḡa; his Warṯān estates passed after the ʿAbbasid revolution ultimately to the caliph al-Mahdī's daughter Omm Jaʿfar Zobayda, wife of Hārūn al-Rašīd (Yāqūt, IV, pp. 919-20). Marand was settled, probably in early ʿAbbasid times, by an Arab colony under the grandfather of Moḥammad b. Baʿīṯ Rabīʿī; under this last, a rebellion of this town against the caliph al-Motawakkel's authority is mentioned (Balāḏorī, *Fotūḥ*, pp. 325-26). Urmia was subdued by Ṣadaqa b. ʿAlī, a *mawlā* of the tribe of Azd. Tribesmen of Hamdān were settled at Mayānaj and Ḵalbāṯā early in al-Manṣūr's reign by the governor of Azerbaijan Yazīd b. Ḥātem Mohallabī. Men of Kenda from the following of Ašʿaṯ b. Qays took over Sarāt or Sarāb. Tabrīz was a place of little importance at this time, having been largely destroyed in the Armeno-Persian wars of the fourth century (see V. Minorsky, "Tabrīz," in *EI*[1] IV). Its revival was the work of another Azdī, Rawwād b. Moṯannā and his son Wajnā', who were granted by Yazīd b. Ḥātem the lands stretching from Tabrīz to Baḏḏ and who rebuilt the citadel, town walls, etc. of Tabrīz (Balāḏorī, *Fotūḥ*, p. 326; Yaʿqūbī, II, p. 13).

During the Omayyad period, Azerbaijan was only thinly settled by the Arabs and was very much a frontier zone. In particular, it formed a base for the Arab governors to mount their operations against the Caucasian peoples and into the Cis-Caucasian steppe lands, the lure here being above all the hope of tapping the plentiful reservoirs of slaves in the Caucasus region and the Khazar steppes. Although Darband had early been reached (see above), for more than two centuries the Arabs' way was blocked by the indigenous mountaineers of the Caucasus, such as the Alans, and beyond, them, by the Turkish Khazars of south Russia. The swaying fortunes of war in these regions meant that Armenia, Arrān, and Azerbaijan at times suffered invasion and devastation by these more northerly peoples. There were Khazar raids in the caliphates of Yazīd I (60-64/680-83) and ʿAbd-al-malek (65-86/685-705), and particularly violent incursion took place in 112/730 when the Khazars poured down through the Alan Gate, overran Armenia and Azerbaijan, killed Hešām's governor Jarrāḥ b. ʿAbdallāh Ḥakamī Maḏḥejī at Ardabīl, and penetrated as far as Dīārbakr and Jazīra (D. M. Dunlop, *History of the Jewish Khazars*, New York, 1967, pp. 69-73, 76).

Under the early ʿAbbasids, northern Azerbaijan was the epicentre of the prolonged and dangerous rebellion against the caliphate led by Bābak Ḵorramī (q.v.), which affected much of northwestern Persia and which lasted over twenty years, from ca. 201/816-17 till the sack of his capital Baḏḏ, just to the south of the Aras and in the modern Qarāja-dāḡ, in 222/837. The rebellion certainly had a religious basis (see below), but there may also have been social and economic factors at work, such as local discontent at the prospecting and mining activities in these highland districts by Arabs from Jazīra under Ṣadaqa b. ʿAlī Azdī and his son

Zorayq, in the suggestion of H. Kennedy, *The Early Abbasid Caliphate, a Political History*, London, 1981, pp. 170-74, citing Azdī's *Ta'rīḵ Mawṣel*. Bābak's uprising was favored at the outset by the rebelliousness of the local Arab governor, Ḥātem b. Hartama b. A'yan (d. 203/818-19), and in 217/832 Bābak had the active support of the governor 'Alī. b. Hešām, but he was clearly also able to utilize a great deal of Iranian, anti-Arab feeling in Azerbaijan. Strongly anti-Islamic elements in the Ḵorramīya, perhaps going back to Mazdakism, demonstrate that Islam had by no means completely overlaid the older faiths of northwestern Iran, and for a long time after the suppression of Bābak's movement by Mo'taṣem's generals, and certainly until the 5th/11th century, remnants of the Ḵorramīya who venerated the memory of Bābak and who expected his return as a promised Mahdī, survived there (see Gh. H. Sadighi, *Les mouvements religieux iraniens au IIe et au IIIe siècle de l'hégire*, Paris, 1938, pp. 229-80; B. S. Amoretti, in *Camb. Hist. Iran* IV, pp. 503-09).

An episode like Bābak's uprising showed the continuing strength in Azerbaijan of ancestral Iranian local feelings. There was also internal dissent in the Muslim community there, seen for instance in a rising at Ardabīl in 251/865 in Favor of a Talebid claimant from the Caspian region, 'Alī b. 'Abdallāh Mar'ašī (cf. Ṭabarī, III, p. 1584), and in Kharejite activity spilling over from Jazīra at times. There were the ambitions of Arab governors and of Arab tribal groups settled in the towns of Azerbaijan, and an upsurge in the attempts of neighboring Kurdish and Daylami chiefs to extend their authority over the fringes of the province. All these factors combined to abstract Azerbaijan from direct caliphal control once the personal power of the Baghdad rulers started to decline, as it did in the later 3rd/9th century. The province was still a frontier zone, liable to attack from the Caucasus direction and to harassment by the independent-minded, though nominal vassals of the Muslims, Bagratid princes of Armenia. In ca. 279/892 the claiph Mo'tażed appointed one of his generals, Moḥammad b. Abi'l-Sāj, an Iranian from Central Asia, as governor of Azerbaijan and Armenia, and the family of the Sajids (q.v.) took their place as one of the virtually autonomous lines of provincial governors, headed by the earlier Taherid governors in Khorasan, who rose to prominence during the period of the decline of the central power in Baghdad. For nearly forty years, until the killing of Fatḥ b. Moḥammad b. Abi'l-Sāj in 317/929, members of the family ruled Azerbaijan and Armenia first from Marāḡa and Barḏa'a and then from Ardabīl. They reduced refractory Armenian princes to submission, but themselves sporadically withheld allegiance to Baghdad and suspended the payment of tribute; after the end of the Sajids, direct caliphal control was never restored in northwestern Iran (see W. Madelung, in *Camb. Hist. Iran* IV, pp. 228-32).

For the next century or so, until the coming of the Saljuq Turks, the history of Azerbaijan is a component of the so-called "Daylami interlude" of Iranian history, when hitherto submerged peoples like the Daylamis, the Kurds, the Baluch, etc., rose momentarily to the surface and often assumed political control in different parts of Iran.

In the years immediately after the end of the Sajids, a Kurdish chief, Daysam b. Ebrāhīm b. Šāḏlūya, mentioned as having Kharejite sympathies, tried to establish his authority in Azerbaijan, but had to yield in 330/941-42 to the Mosaferid or Sallarid ruler of Ṭārom in the mountains of Daylam, Marzobān b. Moḥammad b. Mosāfer. Marzobān extended his military power as far as Dvin in Armenia, finally capturing and jailing Daysam just before his own death in 346/957, and he fought off attempts by the Arab Hamdanids of Mosul to invade Azerbaijan. It was during Marzobān's reign that the Rūs (mixed Scandinavian and Slav adventures?), who had already harried the coasts of Ṭabarestān and Gīlān from the Caspian Sea, appeared in Arrān and Azerbaijan (332/943-44). They sailed up the Kor, defeated Marzobān's forces, and sacked and occupied Barḏa'a; it is unclear whether Ardabīl also suffered, although this seems probable (Meskawayh, *Tajāreb* II, pp. 62-67, tr. V, pp. 67-74, the most detailed source; Mas'ūdī, *Morūj* II, pp. 20-21, ed. Pellat, par. 459; Ebn al-Aṯīr (repr.), VIII, pp. 412-15; D. S. Margoliouth, "The Russian seizure of Bardha'ah in 943 A.D.," *BSOAS* 3, 1918, pp. 82-95). Marzobān's brother and successor Vahsūdān had to struggle against the ambitions for power of his nephews Jostān and Ebrāhīm b. Marzobān; in the course of these disputes, much of Azerbaijan was devastated, and by Vahsūdān's death in 373/983, Mosaferid control over Azerbaijan was clearly weakening (see Madelung, op. cit., pp. 232-36; and on the Mosaferids in general, Cl. Huart, "Les Mosâfirides de l'Adherbaïdjân," in *'Ajab-náma, a Volume of Oriental Studies Presented to E. G. Browne*..., Cambridge, 1922, pp. 228-56; S. A. Kasrawī, *Šahrīārān-e gomnām*[2], Tehran, 1335 Š./1956, I, pp. 52-120; Bosworth, *The Islamic Dynasties*, pp. 86-87).

After then, authority in the province passed largely to the rival power of the Rawwadids of Tabrīz, descendants of the Azdī Arabs who had been allotted Tabrīz in early 'Abbasid times (see above), but by now apparently largely Kurdicized, doubtless through the process of intermarriage. Abu'l-Hayjā' Ḥosayn b. Moḥammad (d. 378/988-89) and his son Mamlān or Moḥammad (d. 393/1001) and their descendants pushed the Mosaferids back into their original homeland of Daylam, and ruled the whole of Azerbaijan from Tabrīz, thus bringing that town into prominence for the first time in Islam. Much of their time was spent combatting the resurgent forces of the Christian rulers of Armenia and Georgia, until in the reign of Abū Manṣūr Vahsūdān b. Mamlān (416-51/1025-59) a new element appeared in the politics of Azerbaijan which was to mark a decisive change in the ethnic complexion of the province, namely the Oğuz or Ǧuzz Turks (see Madelung, op. cit., pp. 236-37; Kasrawī, op. cit., pp. 130-45; V. Minorsky, *Studies in Caucasian History*, London, 1953, pp. 114-16; Bosworth, op. cit., pp. 88-89).

The Arabic geographers give useful accounts of Azerbaijan and its towns during the 4th/10th century. The position of the province on the trade routes running north from Hamdān and Zanjān to Arrān and the Caucasus, and running westwards to Mosul and Āmed, gave it a commercial importance. The transit traffic in slaves (Greek, Armenian, Pecheneg, Khazar, and Ṣaqlābī, i.e., Slav and Ugrian ones, according to the *Ḥodūd al-ʿālam*, par. 35, tr. Minorsky, p. 142) was naturally significant, as was the trade in carpets and textiles (especially silks dyed with the crimson tincture of the *qermez* insect) and the production of salted fish (*šūr-māhī*) from the rivers and lakes. Ardabīl is described as the largest town of the province, in Moqaddasī's phrase, "the *qaṣaba* of Azerbaijan and the *meṣr* of the region," although this same author is scathing about the avarice, fecklessness and treachery of its people, the paucity of scholars there, and the filthiness of the whole place ("one of the latrines of the world," pp. 377-78). Moreover, Ebn Ḥawqal, writing a generation before Moqaddasī, states that Ardabīl's prosperity had been shattered by the warfare of Daysam and Marzobān, when the town's walls had been destroyed, so that "it is at this time like a sick person in comparison with its former prosperity" (p. 334, tr. Kramers, pp. 326-27; cf. also Le Strange, *Lands*, pp. 59-71, 184; Schwarz, *Iran*, pp. 959-1388).

Under the Saljuqs. It was during the Rawwadid Vahsūdān's reign that there arrived in Azerbaijan the first waves of the Oğuz Turkmen, the so-called "ʿErāqī ones (from ʿErāq ʿAjamī, i.e., western Persia), formerly the followers of Arslān Esrāʾīl b. Saljūq, expelled from Khorasan in 419/1028 by the Ghaznavid Sultan Maḥmūd. The first group appeared in 420/1029, and the Turkman mounted archers were taken into Vahsūdān's service as auxiliaries for use against the Christians of Armenia and Georgia and against the rival Muslim family of the Kurdish Shaddadids (q.v.) of Ganja in Arrān and of Dvin. But their indiscipline made them uncontrollable, and the depredations of their flocks disturbed the agrarian system of Azerbaijan, so that shortly after the Oğuz had sacked Marāğa in 429/1038, Vahsūdān allied with Abu'l-Hayjāʾ b. Rabīb-al-dawla of the Hadbānī Kurds and slew many of them. Some of these "ʿErāqī" Turkmen eventually moved on to Mosul and Jazīra, but increasing waves of new arrivals meant that independent bands of marauders were gradually becoming established in Azerbaijan. In 446/1054 Vahsūdān and then in 454/1062 his son and successor Mamlān II were forced to acknowledge the suzerainty of Ṭoğrel Beg when the Saljuq leader arrived to assert his authority in Azerbaijan and Arrān. On his return from the Anatolian campaign and the Mantzikert victory, Alp Arslān deposed Mamlān (463/1071), but a later member of the family, Aḥmadīl b. Ebrāhīm b. Vahsūdān, held Marāğa as a fief of the Saljuqs, and his name was perpetuated after his death in 510/1116 by the Aḥmadīlī atabegs there (Madelung, op. cit., pp. 237-39; Bosworth, in *Camb. Hist. Iran* V, pp. 32-34). Alp Arslān's assertion of authority at this time in northwestern Iran also proved fatal to the senior line of the Shaddadids in Arrān (although a junior branch was to survive as Saljuq vassal in Ānī), for in 460/1068 and then in 468/1075 under Malekšāh, the slave commander Savtigin penetrated to Arrān and on the second occasion incorporated the territories there of the Shaddadid Fażlūn III into the Saljuq empire (Minorsky, *Studies in Caucasian History* I: *New Light on the Shaddādids of Ganja (A.D. 951-1075)*, pp. 1-77).

The personal concern of the Great Saljuq sultans was in the main to secure the rich Iranian heartlands of Khorasan, Jebāl, and Fārs, and then to extend their power into Iraq. Azerbaijan and the lands towards the Caucasus tended to be left to their slave commanders or to bands of Turkman adventurers who could carry on raids against the Christians of Anatolia and Transcaucasia. Much of Azerbaijan was parceled out as *eqṭāʿ*s among the Saljuq military commanders, and in the later 6th/12th century, was generally controlled by Turkish atabegs, the guardians of youthful Saljuq princes. The period of Great Saljuq decline, with internecine warfare between various contenders for the throne, meant that Azerbaijan and its resources were frequently controlled by Saljuq claimants at odds with the supreme sultans in Baghdad or Hamadān. Thus under Maḥmūd b. Moḥammad (511-25/1118-31), Maḥmūd's brother Ṭoğrel held Qazvīn, Daylam, Gīlān, and Arrān, whilst another brother, Masʿūd (subsequently sultan 529-47/1134-52), was *malek* of Azerbaijan, Mosul, and Jazīra. Also, after Maḥmūd's death in 525/1131, his young son Dāwūd was proclaimed sultan at Hamadān, but was able to establish his power in Azerbaijan only against the superior might of his uncle Masʿūd, sultan in Iraq and Jabāl; from this base, however, Dāwūd secured the support there of the deposed ʿAbbasid caliph Rāšed in 530/1136, and maintained himself in Azerbaijan for the rest of his life, i.e., until 538/1143-44. Thenceforth, the substance of power in Azerbaijan until the advent of the Ḵʷārazmšāhs was shared by the two atabeg lines of the Aḥmadīlīs of Marāğa, the family of Aq Sonqor, atabeg to the Rawwadid Aḥmadīl b. Ebrāhīm of Tabrīz, and, more importantly, that of the Ildegozids (Eldigüzids or Ildenizids; q.v.), who controlled most of Azerbaijan, Arrān, and Jebāl. Šams-al-dīn Eldigüz was originally atabeg for the Saljuq prince Arslān b. Ṭoğrel (r. 556-71/1161-76). In the Saljuq family disputes, the Aḥmadīlīs generally supported the claims of Malek Moḥammad b. Maḥmūd b. Moḥammad, but in 605/1208-09 almost all their lands fell to the Ildegozid Noṣrat-al-dīn Abū Bakr b. Pahlavān; the Aḥmadīlī atabeg ʿAlāʾ-al-dīn Qara Sonqor is nevertheless significant as a patron of the poet Neẓāmī. The Ildegozids reached a position of great influence in northwestern Iran as defenders of the Muslim cause against the expanding Georgian monarchy, and at one point, Moẓaffar-al-dīn Qezel Arslān (581-87/1186-91) laid claim to the whole sultanate of Persia and Iraq for himself against the last Saljuq sultan Ṭoğrel III b.

Arslān b. Ṭoḡrel II. Various members of the line were patrons of great poets like Ḵāqānī and Neẓāmī, and the petty courts of Azerbaijan were thus at this time considerable centers of culture and focuses of intellectual activity (see Bosworth, op. cit., pp. 176ff.).

Under the Mongols. All the local rulers of Azerbaijan and adjacent lands were engulfed when first the Ḵʷārazmšāhs and then the Mongols swept into northwestern Iran. It was the Ildegozid Qotloḡ Inanč who, involved in an internal dynastic dispute, summoned in the Ḵʷārazmšāh Tekeš, and it was eventually Sultan Jalāl-al-dīn who gave the coup de grace to the dynasty by capturing Tabrīz in 622/1225 and deposing Moẓaffar-al-dīn Özbeg. After 617/1220-21 the Mongols turned northwards from Hamadān and in 618/1222 sacked Marāḡa, slaughtering the males and enslaving the women, and there was a further siege in 628/1231. The Ildegozid Özbeg bought off the Mongols from Tabrīz in 617/1220-21. Jalāl-al-dīn then defended it, but after his departure for Anatolia in 628/1231, the whole of Azerbaijan passed under the control of the Great Khan Ögedey (1227-41), and from the time of Güyük onwards (1246-49), Azerbaijan and Arrān were governed by Malek Ṣadr-al-dīn, according to Jovaynī (tr. Boyle, II, p. 518).

After the conquest of Baghdad in 656/1258, Hülegü made Marāḡa the capital of the Il-Khanid dominions in Persia and Iraq. He built a fortress for his accumulated treasures and spoils on the nearby island of Šāhī in Lake Urmia, where he was in fact to be buried (the Gūr Qalʿa), and ordered the contruction of the famous observatory of Marāḡa to the plans of the philosopher and scientist Ḵʷāja Naṣīr-al-dīn Ṭūsī (q.v.). The fertility of the Marāḡa district and its eminence now as a place of learning doubtless explain why, in the 8th/14th century, the traveler Ebn Baṭṭūṭa (I, p. 171, tr. Gibb, I, p. 108) was to describe it as the "Little Damascus" of ʿErāq ʿAjamī. Then under Hülegü's successor Abaqā (663-80/1265-82), the capital was moved to Tabrīz. Tabrīz suffered a severe earthquake in 671/1273 (see C. Melville, "Historical Monuments and Earthquakes in Tabriz," *Iran* 19, 1981, pp. 162-63), but thereafter the khans set about beautifying the town and erecting splendid buildings, such as the mosques and *madrasas* and the mausoleum built by Ḡāzān for himself. In this period of the religiously tolerant early Mongols, Christianity enjoyed a period of revival and florescence in Azerbaijan, and the khan Argūn had his son baptized in the church at Marāḡa. But under the Muslim convert Ḡāzān, disfavor fell upon all non-Muslim groups; in 705/1306 Öljeytü permanently re-imposed the *jezya* on the *ḏemmīs*, and from this time, there begins the decline and eventual near-disappearance of Christianity from Azerbaijan. It was likewise Öljeytü (703-17/1304-17) who began construction of a new summer capital called Solṭānīya at a spot lying between Zanjān and Abhar, in a region of rich pasture, and this was completed in 713/1313 with many fine buildings, including the khan's own tomb. Solṭānīya was still the capital under his successor Abū Saʿīd, but thereafter, Tabrīz re-asserted itself as the natural capital of the region. Thus it was at Tabrīz that the Turkman chief Ḥasan Bozorg Jalāyer in 736/1336 established his candidate for the Il-khanid throne, Moḥammad, and there that Ḥasan Kūček Čūpānī in 740/1340 placed in power his own candidate Solaymān. We now have numerous descriptions of Tabrīz by both European and Islamic travelers and writers; the Spaniard Clavijo states that in 1403 it had 200,000 households or families, i.e., approaching one million inhabitants, but this must be a great exaggeration.

During this later medieval period, the gradual Turkicization of Azerbaijan was favored by the Il-Khanids' policy of allotting to their leading commanders land grants (*eqṭāʿ*s, *soyurḡāls*) (cf. I. P. Petrushevsky, in *Camb. Hist. Iran* V, pp. 518ff.); by the presence of the khans themselves and their entourages in these favored regions of upland pasture, and then of their Turkman epigoni, beginning with the Jalayerids; and finally, by the incoming of fresh waves of Central Asian nomads accompanying Tīmūr on his campaigns to the west. The Jalayerids seem to have achieved among the population of Azerbaijan a measure of support; there was, for instance, public rejoicing when in 809/1406-07 Aḥmad Jalāyer regained power in Tabrīz, for Azerbaijan had suffered considerably from such events as the invasion through the Caucasus of Tīmūr's rival, the Golden Horde khan Toqtamiš, in 787/1385 and the unbridled excesses of Tīmūr's debauched son Mīrānšāh when he was governor in Tabrīz (among other things, he exhumed the corpse of the great vizier of the Il-khanids Rašīd-al-dīn). But after four years, Aḥmad was defeated in battle and executed by the Qara Qoyunlū leader Qara Yūsof, and Tabrīz now became the capital of the Black Sheep Turkmen; under Jahānšāh b. Qara Yūsof (841-72/1438-67), Tabrīz became the capital of a kingdom stretching from Anatolia to Herat, and was enriched by such splendid buildings as the Blue Mosque. Then after 873/1468 Azerbaijan passed to the rival Āq Qoyunlū leader Uzun Ḥasan and his successors, for whose reigns we possess important accounts of the beauties of Tabrīz from Venetian envoys anxious to forge an alliance with the White Sheep Turkmen against the Ottomans.

Under the Safavids. Azerbaijan was necessarily of importance in the early Safavid period which now followed, for Shaikh Ṣafī-al-dīn Esḥāq, founder of the Ṣafawīya Sufi order, was a native of Ardabīl, and his shrine there was subsequently to be developed under the Safavid shahs into a superb complex of richly-endowed religious and charitable buildings, as the accounts of Western travelers attest (see ARDABĪL). The Safavid Esmāʿīl I (q.v.) successfully overthrew the Šervānšāhs (q.v.) and then marched on Tabrīz in 906/1501, after routing in battle the Āq Qoyunlū Alvand Mīrzā; there he was proclaimed shah in 907/1501-02 (see R. M. Savory, "The Struggle for Supremacy in Persia after the Death of Tīmūr," *Der Islam* 40, 1964, pp. 63-64). Jaʿfarī Shiʿism was forcibly imposed on the inhabitants of Tabrīz, and Tabrīz became the

Safavid capital until its exposure to attack from the Safavids' enemies the Ottomans (it was temporarily occupied by Sultan Selīm's forces after the Ottoman victory at Čālderān in northwestern Azerbaijan in 920/1514) led Shah Ṭahmāsp I (q.v.) to transfer the capital to Qazvīn in 962/1555, after a further Ottoman occupation of Tabrīz.

In the 10th/16th century, Azerbaijan was ruled by a governor (*beglarbegī*) who normally combined control of this strategically-vital province with the highest military rank of *sepahsālār*. Both Azerbaijan and the province of Qarābāḡ (q.v.), i.e., the region between the Aras and the Kor, medieval Arrān, to the north (this last province later found as a separate governorate, with its capital at Ganja, see *Tadhkirat al-Mulūk, a Manual of Ṣafavid Administration*, tr. Minorsky, London, 1943, p. 44, comm. pp. 166-67) were still further settled by Turkman elements belonging to such tribes as the Afšār, the Īnāllū, and Šāmlū, etc., making up the Safavids' early backing of the Qezelbāš (q.v.). Financial administration in Azerbaijan was regulated by a vizier, who was in the 10th/16th century responsible for all the northwestern provinces; thus in 966/1559 Mīrzā ʿAṭāʾallāh Ḵūzānī Eṣfahānī had the oversight of Azerbaijan, Georgia, Šervān, and Šakkī (see K. M. Röhrborn, *Provinzen und Zentralgewalt Persiens im 16. und 17. Jahrhundert*, Berlin, 1966, p. 104).

During the two centuries or more of Safavid rule, Azerbaijan was on several occasions plundered by invading Ottoman forces, and during the years 993-1012/1585-1603 Tabrīz and the western half of Azerbaijan was permanently occupied by them, becoming a province (*īālat*) of the Ottoman empire during those years (cf. A. Birken, *Die Provinzen des osmanischen Reiches*, Wiesbaden, 1976, p. 172); only the eastern part remained in Persian hands, being ruled from Ardabīl. According to the Ottoman-Persian agreement of the Year of the Hare 1000/1591-92, Shah ʿAbbās I had to cede to the Ottomans their conquests in Transcaucasia, Qarabāḡ and western Azerbaijan, the frontier being fixed at the village of Areštanāb twelve farsakhs to the southeast of Tabrīz (Röhrborn, op. cit., pp. 6-9; on this place see Razmārā, *Farhang* IV, p. 15). Tabrīz and western Azerbaijan were returned to Shah ʿAbbās by the treaty of 1022/1613, but further Ottoman incursions took place all through the century. In the reign of Shah Ṣafī I, Sultan Morād IV occupied and devastated Tabrīz (1045/1635-36), although it was extensively rebuilt later in the century, as the accounts of Western diplomatic envoys and travelers confirm. There were nevertheless periods of peace, and the province developed commercially as a result of its position on the Trebizond-Tabrīz-central Persia communications and trade route.

The confusion within Persia caused in the early 12th/18th century by the loss of control by the Safavids and the consequent invasions of the Afghans gave the Ottomans fresh opportunities (cf. L. Lockhart, *The Fall of the Ṣafavī Dynasty and the Afghan Occupation of Persia*, Cambridge, 1958, pp. 212ff.). In 1135-36/1723-24 the desperate Ṭahmāsp II was compelled, in return for promised Turkish and Russian support in enforcing his claims to the throne, to cede Šervān and the eastern Caucasian provinces to Peter the Great; the Ottomans occupied Qarabāḡ and western Azerbaijan yet again, with ʿAbdallāh Köprülü Pasha taking Tabrīz, By an agreement of 1140/1727-28 with the Afghan cheif Ašraf, the Ottomans were awarded northwestern Persia as far as Solṭānīya and Abhar, and by 1142/1730 they had occupied Georgia, Armenia, Azerbaijan, Persian Kurdistan, and ʿErāq-e ʿAjamī, and had divided Šervān and Dāgestān with Russia. Azerbaijan was regained by Persia when Nāder Shah Afšār vanquished the Afghans and in 1146/1734 regained the province from the Ottomans (Lockhart, *Nadir Shah, a Critical Study*, London, 1938, pp. 80ff.); Nāder then entrusted Azerbaijan to his brother Moḥammad Ebrāhīm Khan (ibid., pp. 169ff.).

Under the Qajars. The history of Azerbaijan in the ensuing Zand period is obscure, with Zand control there disputed by Afghan and Qajar Turkman chiefs and by local potentates such as the Domboli Kurdish chiefs of Ḵoy. In 1205/1790-91 Āḡā Moḥammad Khan, founder of the Qajar dynasty, asserted his power there, but during his reign and the early part of that of his nephew Fatḥ-ʿAlī Shah, this power was disputed by the Dombolis, who on several occasions held Tabrīz itself. There now began the practice, adopted in view of the province's strategic importance vis-à-vis the Ottomans and Russians, of entrusting the governorship of Azerbaijan to the heir-apparent to the throne, e.g., in 1213/1799 to Fatḥ-ʿAlī's son ʿAbbās Mīrzā, and in the second quarter of the nineteenth century, to Moḥammad Shah's son Nāṣer-al-dīn.

In the early nineteenth century, intense pressure—military, diplomatic, and economic—began to be exerted on Azerbaijan by Russia. The frontier there with Russia was finally fixed by the Treaty of Torkamānčāy (q.v.) of 1828, confirming the arrangements of the Golestān Treaty of 1813, so that Persia was forced reluctantly to abandon her eastern Caucasian provinces for ever. Russia also exacted under the terms of the treaty fiscal and commercial privileges on a "most favored nation" basis, so that Russian economic penetration of northern Persia via Azerbaijan now had free rein. The reports of the Russian commercial adviser in Tabrīz for the years 1833-47 show how disastrous for Persia was her balance of trade with Russia: Russian imports were estimated at 250 million paper roubles during these fifteen years, with Persian exports only at 90 million (see Minorsky, *BSO(A)S* 11, 1946, pp. 878-80). Also, ʿAbbās Mīrzā, the local governor, was willy-nilly susceptible to Russian pressure whilst ever the war indemnity stipulated in the treaty as payable to Russia remained not fully paid, as was generally the case. Until the accession of Moḥammad Shah in 1250/1834, Tabrīz was the normal seat of the Russian and British diplomatic missions to Persia, and their transfer to Tehran thereafter marked the latter city's definite assumption of the status of political capital. Nevertheless, Tabrīz remained the commercial center and entrepôt for Persia, especially as southern Persia had not yet fully recovered from the devastations of the Zand and early Qajar periods and was comparatively neglected by the northern-based Qajar government.

It further remained the second city of Persia as the seat of the *walī'ahd* or heir to the throne, with his own court circle, and was always more open than other centers to European and outside influences and ideas. Hence it is not surprising that Tabrīz played a leading role in the period of storm and stress inaugurated by the constitutional movement of 1906 when Moẓaffar-al-dīn Shah was compelled to grant a constitution. It was a focus too for Persian national feeling and resentment against outside pressures, fanned by the settlement in Azerbaijan of many *mohājerīn*, Muslims who had emigrated in the course of the nineteenth century from the Russian-occupied Caucasus and Caspian provinces (cf. P. Avery, *Modern Iran*, London, 1967, pp. 135-37). Hence when Moḥammad-ʿAlī Shah and his Cossack Brigade, encouraged by Russian support, closed the Majles in 1908, rebellion broke out in Tabrīz, leading to the Russian military occupation of 1909. From then onwards, and despite the "second constitutional period" of 1909-11, during which the Russians continued to support the intrigues of the deposed despot Moḥammad-ʿAlī Shah, Russian influence was paramount in Azerbaijan, with nationalist and democratic leaders arrested and executed in Tabrīz (for the constitutional period and the ensuing years in Azerbaijan, see Kasravī, *Ādarbāyjān*, Tehran, 1318-19 Š./1939-40).

Only the entry of Ottoman Turkey into World War I on the side of the Central Powers in November, 1914, compelled the withdrawal of Russian forces from Azerbaijan at the end of 1914 under the threat of invasion by Ottoman-backed Kurdish irregular troops, although they returned early in 1915. The outbreak of the Russian Revolution in 1917 led to a withdrawal of Russian troops at the opening of 1918, and the Bolsheviks proclaimed that the new Russia no longer had any political or territorial ambitions in Persia. The Russian military departure enabled the Ottoman army to advance into Azerbaijan and to occupy Tabrīz in summer 1918. Meanwhile, a democratic party under Shaikh Moḥammad Ḵīābānī (q.v.) had arisen in Tabrīz, and after the end of the war, disputed control of Azerbaijan with the central government of Woṯūq-al-dawla in Tehran. Early in 1920 Ḵīābānī proclaimed Azerbaijan to be Āzādīstān "Land of the free" (q.v.), but his movement was suppressed militarily in September, 1920, and the control of Tehran re-asserted there, only momentarily to be challenged in February, 1922, by the brief revolt of the gendarmerie officer Abu'l-Qāsem Lāhūtī (q.v.) against the commander in chief Reżā Khan (later Reżā Shah), suppressed by the latter.

Shortly before the abdication under Allied pressure of Reżā Shah Pahlavī in September, 1941, during World War II, British and Russian forces, later joined by American ones, occupied Persia, with Russia controlling the northern provinces, including Azerbaijan. Already, earlier in the century, there had been signs of a stirring of Azerbaijani self-consciousness and feelings of distinctness. The Ottomans in 1918 had encouraged pan-Turkish cultural and linguistic feelings there, and there was a feeling in Azerbaijan to kinship with the Turkish and Muslim peoples of the eastern Caucasus, which in some cases entailed political sympathies with the communist régime now dominant there. Under the sixteen years' rule of Reżā Shah, Azerbaijan felt comparatively neglected, and use of the local language, Azeri Turkish, was forbidden for official purposes in favor of Persian. Now, with the Russians controlling northern Persia, the old feelings which has broken out after World War I in the shape of the Gīlān and Azerbaijan movements re-emerged. Under the veteran Persian communist leader J̌aʿfar Pīšavarī (q.v.), who had been an old ʿAdālat Party member in Baku in 1918 and commissar for internal affairs in the Bolshevik republic of Gīlān 1920-21, a coup by the pro-Soviet Democrat Party of Azerbaijan (Ferqa-ye Demokrāt-e Ādarbāyjān), to which the local Tūda Party speedily affiliated itself, took place in Ābān, 1324 Š./November, 1945, against the central government in Tehran (see AZERBAIJAN, v). The Russians prevented the Persian government troops from advancing beyond Qazvīn, and in the next month, a Russian-protected autonomous republic of Azerbaijan was proclaimed. Simultaneously, an autonomous Kurdish republic was proclaimed at Mahābād in southwestern Azerbaijan under Qāżī Moḥammad (q.v.), and in April, 1946, it concluded a treaty of alliance and support with the Tabrīz régime.

Under a 1942 agreement of the Allies, all foreign troops were to be withdrawn from Iranian soil by six months after the end of the War. In fact, by March, 1946, the troops of the Western Allies were withdrawn, but the Russian ones did not leave till May. By November-December, 1946, the central government army was able to move into Azerbaijan; the Provincial Assembly abandoned resistance, and Pīšavarī fled to the USSR, where he later allegedly died in an accident. The Mahābād Kurdish régime collapsed early in 1947 (G. Lenczowski, *Russia and the West in Iran 1918-1948*, pp. 286ff.; R. Rossow, "The Battle of Azerbaijan, 1946," *Middle East Journal* 10, 1956, pp. 17-32). The authority of the central government in Tehran was reestablished, and in the ensuing years, signs of recrudescent Azerbaijani seccessionist feeling were closely watched and the use of Azeri was once more discouraged.

Bibliography: Given in the text.

(C. E. Bosworth)

v. History from 1941 to 1947

The United Kingdom and the Soviet Union invaded Iran on 3 Šahrīvar 1320 Š./25 August 1941, invoking an unsatisfactory response to parallel demands for expulsion of four-fifths of the 1,500 Germans in Iran. Approximately 40,000 Soviet troops entered Iran from the north, occupying Azerbaijan and Mašhad, while 19,000 British troops entered from the south along a six hundred-mile front to protect the oil fields in Ḵūzestān. Reasons for the occupation included creation of a supply route from the Persian Gulf to Russia and protection of allied interests from the threat posed by the Germans. The significance of the supply route is suggested by the fact that 7,900,000 long tons of imports crossed Iran into the Soviet Union in the years 1941-45, including 180,000 trucks and 4,874 airplanes.

The dispersal of the Iranian army undermined Reżā Shah's earlier efforts to consolidate or repress the centrifugal forces (political, administrative, religious, tribal, and economic) in his country, leaving the central government vulnerable to them and aggravating mutual suspicions between central and provincial administrations. The collapse of government control in Azerbaijan, meanwhile, created the opportunity for local forces to come to the fore. Soviet occupation, meanwhile, resulted in Soviet control over many aspects of the province's internal affairs and revived traditional rivalries among the great powers.

Upon entering Iran, the Soviets dismantled frontier and customs posts between Iran and the USSR, and set up military posts on the southern border of the Soviet occupied zone. The de facto result was extension of the Soviet frontier into Iran. The terms of occupation, meanwhile, were set in the Tripartite Treaty of Alliance (29 January, 1942), under which Britain and Russia agreed to respect the territorial integrity, sovereignty, and political independence of Iran (Art. 1) and to withdraw from Iran within six months of an armistice between the allied and axis powers (Art. 5). In spite of this treaty, however, and the Declaration Regarding Iran (1 December, 1943), which provided for British, Russian, and American commitments to Iran's sovereignty and territorial integrity, Soviet policies ignored Iran's political independence. In Azerbaijan, wartime conditions combined with scarce resources to cause widespread hunger and insecurity among the region's communal groups. The Soviets exacerbated these problems and imposed a number of unfavorable agreements on the Azerbaijanis. They influenced the trade unions, which they infiltrated, and reinforced the power of both the Central Council of Federated Trade Unions and Azerbaijan's Communist Tūda (Tudeh) Party, which, because it saw Azerbaijan as a nation and not one among many diverse nationalities, had serious differences with the Tūda leadership in Tehran (Kuniholm, *Origins*, pp. 130-213; Abrahamian, *Iran*, pp. 388-415; Meister, *Soviet Policy in Iran*, pp. 147, 654-73). The Soviets also prevented the central government from maintaining order and exercised control over local populations through town commandants, who were responsible to the Soviet consul in Tabrīz.

In October, 1944, the Russian vice commissar of foreign affairs S. Kavtaradze, reacting perhaps to apprehension over potential American penetration of Iran (encouraged by the central government as a counterweight to Soviet and British influence), asked for exclusive exploration rights for five years along Iran's northern, Caspian coast from the Russian border in Azerbaijan to Khorasan. Fearing the proposal was only a cover for infiltrating the area, the Iranian cabinet on October 8 postponed oil concessions until after the war. Despite Soviet intimidation, Moḥammad Moṣaddeq led the Majlis on 2 December, 1944, to pass a law forbidding oil negotiations between cabinets and foreigners; thereafter, concessions were to be dependent on the Majlis (Ramazani, *Iran's Foreign Policy*, pp. 103ff.; *Foreign Relations of the United State, 1944* V, Washington, D.C., 1966, pp. 452-54).

In 1945, the United States and Britain repeatedly sought the early withdrawal of all foreign troops from Iran, but the Russians refused to discuss the matter; instead, they encouraged dissolution of the Tūda Party in Azerbaijan and, in order to build a wider base of support, the establishment in its place of the Democratic Party of Azerbaijan (Ferqa-ye Demokrāt-e Āḏarbāyǰān). The social bases, interests, and policies of the two parties were very different. J̌aʿfar Pīšavarī, the Democratic Party's founder, was contemptuous of the Tūda Party and its Persian intellectuals whose Western European Marxism contrasted with the Leninism of his Azeri followers. His own party, however, was even more susceptible to Soviet manipulation (Ramazani, "Autonomous Republic," pp. 448-74; Abrahamian, op. cit., pp. 388-415; Kuniholm, op. cit., pp. 270-82).

In western Azerbaijan, the Soviet commander at Mīāndoāb summoned the Kurdish chieftains and transported them to Baku in southern Russia. There, in late September, 1945, the Prime Minister of the Azerbaijan SSR told them that neither their own nationalist party, the Komala-ye Žīān-e Kordestān, nor the Tūda Party was looked on favorably, that they should seek their goals within Azerbaijani autonomy, and that they should call themselves the Democratic Party of Kurdistan (Ḥezb-e Demokrāt-e Kordestān; see Eagleton, *The Kurdish Republic*, pp. 43-46; Roosevelt, "Kurdish Republic," pp. 256-57).

The Azerbaijan movement, one must keep in mind, was not created solely by Soviet pressures. While benefitting from Soviet support, the Azeris were partly reacting to the process of centralization instituted under Reżā Shah and to the central government's incompetence, corruption, and discrimination against the province; the Kurds opposed, among other things, the government's attempts at detribalization. Thus, a concern for identity within their own communal groups seemed logical to both Kurds and Azeris in the aftermath of the Soviet occupation in 1941. Characterizing in terms of class what were primarily communal and regional differences (Azerbaijan had only twelve towns with a population of 10,000 or more and there was a substantial number of factory workers only in Tabrīz), the Tūda Party gained support in Azerbaijan under the aegis of the Soviet occupation and, when Soviet tactics dictated a shift, provided what became the Democratic Party with a ready group of supporters (although only one of nine cabinet ministers were former Tūda members).

After the armistice with Japan on 2 September 1945, open Soviet sympathy for the Azerbaijan movement, and repeated incidents of interference in the province, were protested by the Iranians and ignored by the Soviets who only replied with a renewed demand for oil concessions. In the fall, the Soviets distributed arms in key areas, and in October and November sponsored large-scale uprisings throughout the province. When Britain and Russia occupied Iran in 1941, the British captured the Iranian Army arsenal in Teheran. When the Soviets expressed a desire for the weapons in it, the British handed them over, but only after recording their serial numbers. Rifles collected from the *fedāʾīyīn* in Tabrīz after the fall of the Democratic Republic in almost every case matched those handed over to the Red Army (Kuniholm, op. cit., pp. 278-79. See also, Meister, op. cit., p. 186; Eagleton, op. cit., p. 55; Abrahamian, op. cit., pp. 389-400). When the Iranian gendarmerie tried to control the newly armed rebels, the Soviets challenged them and forced them to retire. By November 19, all major routes entering the province had been seized by the Democratic Party; communications had been cut, and an Iranian force of 1,500 troops was stopped at Qazvīn by the Soviets. By December 10, Tabrīz was in the hands of the Democratic Party; shortly thereafter, a newly inaugurated "National Assembly" proclaimed the Autonomous Government of Azerbaijan with Pīšavarī as Premier. On December 15, Qāżī Moḥammad, an hereditary judge and religious leader of Mahābād, inaugurated the Kurdish Republic (Roosevelt, op. cit., pp. 256-57; Eagleton, op. cit., p. 60).

Figure 3. Northwest Iran, December, 1945–December, 1946 (From Kuniholm, *The Origins,* p.283)

Stalin's stated reason for maintaining approximately 30,000 troops in Azerbaijan after the war was that they served as a precaution against sabotage and "hostile" actions. More likely, he was protecting security interests on his southern flank, preventing Anglo-American influence in what he felt to be his sphere of influence, exploiting several of the opportunities that occupation afforded him with a view to controlling the government in Tehran and, perhaps, creating conditions that, in the long run, would give the Soviet Union access to warm water ports. A friendly government in Azerbaijan and oil concessions were both means to the same end.

Within Azerbaijan, Pīšavarī played down class differences, focused on communal conflict, and with Soviet backing instituted two reforms: redistribution of non-Azerbaijani-owned land (which was confiscated in 687 out of a total of over 7,000 villages) and nationalization of the larger banks. He also began badly needed work on roads, established workers' welfare pensions, and declared Azeri Turkish the official language of Azerbaijan. These reforms—or at least the intentions which motivated them—were popular, but economic difficulties (the result, primarily, of bad weather and a bad harvest) forced him to demand even more money from farmers and landlords than previously exacted under the old system. With a police force modeled after the Soviet NKVD, Azerbaijan became a police state. Even those friendly to Pīšavarī's rule denounced his abuse of power (Hooglund, *Land and Revolution*, pp. 41-42; Abrahamian, op. cit., pp. 409-412; Kuniholm, op. cit., p. 309; Meister, op. cit., p. 256; Rossow, "The Battle of Azerbaijan," p. 19; Lenczowski, *Russia and the West*, p. 290; *Foreign Relations of the United States*, 1946 VII, Washington, D.C., 1969, pp. 332-34).

On 19 January 1946, meanwhile, Iran called for investigation of Russian interference in Iran's internal affairs. In February and March, 1946, the Soviets attempted to pressure prime Minister Aḥmad Qawām (Qawām-al-salṭana) to recognize the autonomy of the Democratic Party and to acquiesce in the creation of an Irano-Soviet petroleum company; in contravention of the Tripartite Treaty, they also indicated that they would not evacuate Azerbaijan until order had been restored and Iran's "hostile" attitude had ceased. By March 2, the date set under the Tripartite Treaty for the withdrawl of all foreign troops from Iran, British and U.S. troops had withdrawn, but Soviet troops had not. Rather, in the course of the next three weeks, Soviet reinforcements of at least 200 tanks and 3,500 trucks arrived in Tabrīz and were deployed south toward Qazvīn, west toward the Turkish border, and southwest toward the Iraqi border (see Kuniholm, op. cit., pp. 318-19 and nn. 40-41). Subsequent developments are subject to differing interpretations. Whatever Soviet motives, and their movements suggest the possibility of a coup d'etat, they were thwarted by masterful Iranian diplomacy and by firm U.S. support for the Iranian case at the United Nations. The Soviets finally agreed to withdraw, but not before extended debate of the issue in the United Nations and a commitment by Qawām to ratify within seven months an Irano-Soviet agreement to exploit oil in northern Iran (ibid., pp. 303-42).

The Democratic Party, meanwhile, was still ensconced in Azerbaijan. Without a Soviet presence, however, its authority began to erode. In spite of a tentative agreement with the central government that granted Azerbaijan considerable autonomy and allowed the Democratic Party to remain in full control, negotiations broke down. The influence of both Qawām and the Shah in resolving the situation in Azerbaijan was crucial and can be quickly summarized: Departure of the Soviets made it possible for the military to arm opponents of the Tabrīz regime; a revolt by the Qašqā'ī and Baḵtīārī tribes in the South made it possible for Qawām to assert the central government's authority throughout Iran and to order the military into Azerbaijan to maintain order during elections (which could be held only with security forces present). In the face of Soviet threats and with the unqualified support of the United States in the Security Council if complications arose, Iranian troops began moving into Azerbaijan on 9 Decmber 1946. By 21 Āḏar 1325 Š./13 December 1946, Pīšavarī had fled to Baku and Iranian forces entered Tabrīz. Two days later, on December 15, Qāżī Moḥammad announced the surrender of Mahābād. Almost a year to the day after the republics had been founded, they collapsed. In the process, several hundred rebels were killed, while approximately one thousand Azerbaijanis and as many as 10,000 Kurds under Mollā Moṣṭafā Bārzānī fled to the Soviet Union. Grim reminders of the regimes were embodied for months afterward in rows of bodies swinging from crude gibbets in many public squares of Azerbaijan and northern Kurdistan. In Iran, a complicated election process that had begun in January ended in June, 1947. The fifteen Majles did not open until July, and did not vote on the controversial oil agreement with the Soviet Union until October. Then, by a vote of 102 to 2, the agreement was rejected and the issues generated by the Soviet occupation of Azerbaijan were finally resolved (ibid., pp. 342-50, 383-98, 414).

See also FERQA-YE DEMOKRĀT-E ĀḎARBĀYJĀN; PĪŠAVARĪ; and QAWĀM AL-SALṬANA.

Bibliography: U.S. Department of State Decimal File, S.D. 891.6363/10-1144/11-1244/12-1144. E. Abrahamian, *Iran between two Revolutions*, Princeton, 1982, pp. 169-246, 281-312, 326-415. W. Eagleton, *The Kurdish Republic of 1946*, London, 1963. E. Hooglund, *Land and Revolution in Iran, 1960-1980*, Austin, 1982. A. Ḵāma'ī, *Ḵāṭerāt-e Anwar Ḵāma'ī* II: *Forṣat-e bozorg-e az dast rafta*, Tehran, 1362 Š./1984, passim. B. Kuniholm, *The Origins of the Cold War in the Near East: Great Power Conflict and Diplomacy in Iran, Turkey, and Greece*, Princeton, 1980, pp. 140-216, 270-350, 376-99, 425-31. G. Lenczowski, *Russia and the West in Iran 1918-1948*, Ithaca, 1949. I. Meister, *Soviet Policy in Iran, 1917-1950: A Case Study in Techniques*, Ph. D. dissertation, Fletcher School of Law and Deplomacy, Tufts University, 1954. R. Romazani, *Iran's Foreign Policy, 1941-1973: A Study of Foreign Policy in Modernizing Nations*, Charlottesville, 1975, pp. 91-178. Idem, "The Autonomous Republic of Azerbaijan and the Kurdish People's Republic: Their Rise and Fall," in *The Anatomy of Communist Takeovers*, T. Hammond, ed., New Haven, 1975, pp. 448-74. A Rosevelt, Jr., "The Kurdish Republic of Mahabad," *The Middle East Journal* 1/3, July, 1947, pp. 256-57. R. Rossow, "The Battle of Azerbaijan, 1946," *The Middle East Journal* 10, Winter, 1956, pp. 17-32.

(B. KUNIHOLM)

vi. POPULATION AND ITS OCCUPATIONS AND CULTURE

Population. Azerbaijan, the main Turkic-speaking area and one of the richest and most densely populated regions of Iran, presents a picture of ethnic distinctiveness and homogeneity that is perhaps misleading. Not only are there various linguistic, religious, and tribal minority groups, but Azerbaijanis themselves have settled widely outside the region.

The great majority of the people of Azerbaijan are native speakers of the language known as Azerbaijani Turkish or Azeri (q.v.). Kurdish speakers are mainly found in the border districts of western Azerbaijan. Iranian Tāti (Tati) dialects are still spoken in small communities south of J̌olfā, east of Mīāna, and in Qaradāḡ (see AZERBAIJAN VII and Bazin, 1980, II, p.85 for references to studies by Henning, Yarshater, and Kārang).

Tribalism is no longer of great social relevance for most Azerbaijanis, but most have a recent history of tribal allegiances, whether Turkish or Kurdish. The main Turkish tribal groups that can still be identified are the Šāhsevans of Meškīn and Ardabīl, the Afšārs of Urmia and Ṣā'īn Qal'a, and the Bayāt and others of Mākū. Kurdish tribal groups (from north to south along the frontier) include the Ḥaydarānlū, Mīlān, Ṣakāk, Herkī, Begzāda, Zarza, Māmāš, Pīrān, Mangūr, and Dehbokrī.

Tribal groups in this region were essentially political groups, bearing the names of dominant chiefly sections. The chiefs were not necessarily linked culturally or genealogically with the "commoners," who frequently changed allegiances, although a long association with one tribe often led to the adoption of the chiefs' language and culture and possibly the invention of a common pedigree. Whole tribes have sometimes changed identity, particularly when re-located as a linguistic or religious minority in a new area. Thus, several Turkish-speaking groups are known to have more or less recent Kurdish origins, for example the Donbolī of Ḵoy, the Lek of Salmās, the Šaqāqī and related tribes of Mīāna and Kalkāl, most of the tribes of Qaradāğ, and some of the Šāhsevan. The Korasūnnī of Dowl and Salmās appear to be mixed, while some of the Kalkāl groups are reported to speak Kurdish at home. The Qarapapak and Šamsaldīnlū of Soldūz, on the other hand, are of Turkish origins but nearly assimilated to Kurdish language and culture. The Čārdowlī of Ṣā'īn Qal'a finally, are Turkicized Lors, immigrant from Fārs (see Oberling, 1964a and 1964b; Tapper, 1974 and 1983).

Almost all Turkish-speaking Azerbaijanis are Shi'ite Muslims, like the large majority of Iranians. Kurdish speakers are mainly Sunni, as are the few Ṭāleši villages northeast of Ardabīl, and some at least of the Turkicized Kurds of Kalkāl and the Kurdicized Turks of Soldūz. There are some Ahl-e Ḥaqq (q.v.) or 'Alī-Elāhī villages, notably Īlkčī south of Mount Sahand (Sā'edī, 1964), the Qara Qoyunlū of Mākū (Oberling, 1964a, p. 62) and some Qaradāği (Melikoff, 1975). Christian minorities, Armenian, and Assyrian/Chaldean, live west of Lake Urmia and near Delmān.

Azerbaijanis have emigrated and resettled in large numbers, some in Baku and Istanbul, but mainly in Tehran, Khorasan, Qom, and other Iranian cities and provinces; wherever they have settled they have become prominent not only among urban and industrial working classes but also in commercial, administrative, political, religious, and intellectual circles. Azerbaijani Turkish, moreover, is spoken widely in provinces to the south and east stretching to the vicinities of Hamadān and Tehran, while both the official language of Soviet Azerbaijan and the Turkish spoken in eastern Anatolia are very close to the Azerbaijani of Iran.

Some writers are of the opinion that the Turkicization of Azerbaijan has been relatively superficial, citing as evidence both the persistence of Tāti dialects and the "bastardization" of the Turkish language, notably the loss of vowel harmony characteristic of Tabrīzi speech (Minorsky in *EI*[2] I, p. 191).

Nonetheless Azerbaijanis, despite their insistence on their Iranian identity, generally call themselves, and are called, "Türk," by contrast with "Kürt" (speakers of Kurdish), and "Fārs/Pārs" (Persian-speakers), the major ethnic groups with whom they have most contact. Otherwise, opposed to various Christian groups or the Soviets they are "Musulman;" as distinct from the Sunni Turks of Anatolia, they are firmly Shi'ite, an identity which more than anything else has kept them loyal to Iran. Within the region, people claim a variety of local and tribal identities, according to context. One of these is "Tat (Tāt)," a term with two main meanings: the first, synonymous with "Tājīk," "non-Turkish speaker," is used by Turkish groups inside and outside Azerbaijan and conforms with both the linguistic term for the dialects mentioned above, and the ethnonym "Tājīk" prevalent in Afghanistan and Tajikistan. The second meaning of Tat, peculiar to Azerbaijan, designates the Turkish-speaking, settled, non-tribal population by contrast with nomadic tribal groups, especially the Šāhsevan, from whom they otherwise differ little in language, religion or, culture (see Tapper, 1979; Sā'edī, 1965). In fact, although no systematic comparison of regional Azerbaijani Turkish dialects has been published, there is evidence that in some respects, for example vowel-harmony, the nomad Šāhsevan speak a "purer" Turkish than their settled Tat neighbors.

Iranian society has been characterized for centuries by a cleavage between the Turks (dominant but "uncouth" tribes, mainly from Azerbaijan) and the Persians (subordinate but "civilized" townspeople and peasants of the central provinces). This ethnic division is marked by a number of stereotypes on both sides. Turks, for example, are often seen by Persians as slow and dull, while their martial, commercial, and organizational capacities are recognized. Iran was politically dominated by Turkish rulers since medieval times, with Azerbaijan, on the frontiers of the Ottoman and later the Russian empires, economically and politically the most important province outside the capital. The Persians, however, gained the upper hand by the end of the nineteenth century. Azerbaijanis were prominent in the Tobacco Protest of 1908, the Constitutional Revolution of 1906-11, and ensuing political struggles and movements, but under the Pahlavi Shahs Azerbaijan as a whole lost its primacy, while central regions were favored, Persian language and culture were strongly promoted, and publication in Turkish (except for poetry and folk literature) was banned. Nonetheless, despite various separatist movements in this century, some fostered by Turkey or the Soviet Union, Azerbaijanis have remained strongly committed to Iran. Having played a significant role during the 1978-79 Revolution the Azerbaijanis were granted some cultural freedom afterward, but greater autonomy sought by some among them for the region and minorities have been denied.

Tabrīz, by far the largest city of Azerbaijan, was for long the second city of Iran. As the major commercial entrepôt on the main routes from Europe through Turkey and Russia, and also the seat of the Heir Apparent in Qajar times, Tabrīz developed a substantial middle class of merchants, clerics and intellectuals. Tabrīzis acquired a reputation for liberal nationalism, through active involvement in the Tobacco Protest, the Constitutional Revolution, and Kīābānī's Āzādestān movement. Later, however, suffering from the curtailment of transit trade through and from Russia and from changes under the Pahlavis, Tabrīz declined. Restored to favor somewhat during the 1970s, Tabrīz was by 1980 the fourth largest city with a population of some 600,000. Capital of western Azerbaijan is Urmia: (Reżā'īya), with about 170,000 people, the center of the Afšār tribe, located near the Kurdish borderlands and noted too for the nearby Christian minority. In the northeast Ardabīl (population 150,000) owes its importance originally to the presence of the Safavid shrines but also to its location as trading entrepôt between western Iran, the Caspian, and Russia. Somewhat smaller is the old Mongol capital, Marāğa, in the west. Other towns of any size are local market centers or staging points along the main routes.

Azerbaijan has long been noted as Iran's "bread-basket," as well as a major source of tax revenue and military recruits. Nearly two thirds of the population of about five million (both provinces) are still rural. It is a region of high mountains, fertile valleys, and broad rolling upland plains; of extensive pastures and farmlands, favored with adequate rainfall if cold winters. Villages (*känd*, denoting the houses and the lands) are sometimes very large, with thousands rather than hundreds of inhabitants. They grow a variety of crops; an abundance of wheat, but also barley, cotton, fruit, vegetables, and nuts; the honey produced in the neighborhood of Mount Sabalān is nationally renowned. Although some areas in the west and north are wooded, considerable amounts of timber are imported from the Caspian forests through Ardabīl.

Before the Land Reform of Moḥemmad Reżā Shah in 1963, much of the land in Azerbaijan was owned by absentee landlords, including tribal chiefs and city-dwelling clerics, merchants, officials, and professionals. These owned shares in one or several villages; often large landed proprietors owned scores of villages. Small landowners and peasant proprietors were relatively rare except in Urmia and Qaradāḡ. *Awqāf* (pious endowments) were uncommon except near Ardabīl, and there was little *kāleṣa* (state land) except in certain frontier districts (Lambton, 1953).

Peasant families in a village formed two classes, the contracted, crop-sharing cultivators (*jütčī*) and the landless laborers and others collectively known as *ḵošnešīn*, in about equal proportions. Landlords collected around a quarter of the crop, and extracted in addition a variety of customary dues, rarely giving in return loans, protection, and patronage. The peasants' shares in the crops were barely sufficient for subsistence, and had to be supplemented through livestock-rearing and the production of woven goods for sale. The general picture was one of great incomes accruing to the wealthier landowners, while peasants possessed a capacity for survival though in extreme poverty and debt. The village headman was either elected by the cultivators, or chosen from among them by the landowner; sometimes two different men were appointed to balance the factions into which villages were very commonly split. The headman was often assisted by the body of village elders (the *aq-saqal*s). Other officials were elected or appointed on a short-term basis, such as the *mīrāb* who supervised the distribution of irrigation water and negotiated with other villages sharing the same source.

Lambton refers to the Soviet-inspired separatist Ferqa-ye Demokrāt (Democratic Party) which held sway in Azerbaijan in 1946, and under whom the lands were expropriated, and writes that, after the fall of the Democrat government, "there was, broadly speaking, a reversion to the *status quo ante* in matters of land tenure and rural organization. The position of the landlords in Azerbaijan was, nevertheless, considerably shaken by this episode" (1969, p. 37).

Until recently, communications were poor, mountain ranges presented formidable barriers to intercourse, and villages were isolated and inward-looking. Houses clustered together, often within a village wall which, though now crumbling, once gave some protection against nomad raiders. This danger ceased in the 1920s, but the narrow alleys, another defence against mounted raiders, are still present-day village features. Most marriages are still contracted within the village. However, the years since the 1920s have on several occasions brought close contact with the neighboring Soviet regime and socialist ideas with some salutary effects. Lambton's remarks on Ardabīl are more widely valid: "The peasants were more aware of the outside world than in many other districts and less amenable to pressure by landlords and others" (1969, p. 127).

Occupations and culture. With the establishment of comparative security and government control, communications improved, mobility increased, and villages became less isolated. Economic exchanges have proliferated along new all-weather roads; new market-centers have grown up; and every village has acquired at least one store, besides schools and other government sponsored services and administrative arrangements. Most important have been measures like the Land Reform, which brought considerable change to the structure of society in Azerbaijan. The reform was indeed first implemented in Azerbaijan, in Marāḡa and surrounding districts, and Ardabīl and Ahar were also among the first districts in the country to be affected. Other large-scale developments under the Pahlavi regime involved irrigation schemes at half a dozen sites in the region.

Such schemes, as well as increasingly mechanized dry-farming, have now decisively reduced the grazing available to livestock, both in the plains and on the lower reaches of the mountain pastures. Pastoralism continues, however, as the climate and geography of much of Azerbaijan are even better suited to this form of production than to cultivation. The mountain meadows of Sabalān and Sahand, Qaradāḡ and the Kurdish frontier districts, and the rich winter pastures of Moḡān in particular, long ago attracted the first Turkish and Mongol nomad invaders. Most livestock raising is now done by settled or semi-settled villagers. The only remaining major nomadic group are the Šāhsevan of Moḡān, while in other districts smaller nomadic and semi-nomadic groups continue to migrate between winter and summer quarters. Nowadays, in much of the region Šāhsevan is synonymous with tented nomad, much as Kurd once was.

Livestock-rearing, by nomads or others, has always been geared to regional and national marketing systems, but now, with vastly improved communications and increased demand, this integration is vital to both the pastoralists and the national economy. Though the producers sometimes take their own livestock for sale to Tabrīz or even Tehran, city-based cheese-makers, wool merchants, and livestock dealers visit the camps at various points in the year, buying up large quantities of pastoral produce to meet an insatiable urban demand. During the 1960s, the tribal chiefs, who had usually been among the large landowners, lost both this economic base and their official government appointments, and turned more to livestock-raising, which they developed on a commercial scale.

The categories Šāhsevan and Tāt, mentioned above, are locally held to imply a whole complex of cultural differences beyond the basic nomad/settled and pastoral/agricultural distinctions. For example, the Šāhsevan claim they lead by comparison with Tāt a cleaner, healthier, and more profitable way of life, maintain stricter moral standards, achieve a more direct approach to God, and are generally braver and more generous in nature. Tāt of course claim most of these qualities as their own, but lay special emphasis on supposed village characteristics such as more varied diet, more orthodox religious practices, and more law-abiding habits. These attitudes are greatly fostered by mutual ignorance. Šāhsevan and Tāt have little social interaction, even when linked by marriage (nomads give twenty percent of their daughters to villagers, and receive ten percent of their wives from them).

To the observer there are in fact only small differences between nomad and villager in dialect, religious beliefs and practices, oral literature, and customs such as life-cycle ceremonies. In many cases differences are less than those between districts. (The foregoing descriptions of village agriculture and pastoralism are drawn from northeast Azerbaijan but apply very broadly to the rest of the region.)

Azerbaijan is a region of cultural variation and contrast, differences between districts and between city, town, and countryside being greater than those between the region as a whole and other parts of Iran. Some distinctive features arise from Azerbaijan's combining elements from Central Asia and the Middle East, as shown in the meeting not only of Turkish with Iranian languages but of the Bactrian camel with the one-humped dromedary, which are here crossed to produce the larger and much prized hybrid (Tapper, 1985); or of the round, felt-covered *alačīḡ* of the Šāhsevan and Qaradāḡ nomads (see Andrews, 1978) with the rectangular black tent of the Kurds and others. Otherwise, in conformity with the climate, the traditional village house is a single-storey, mud-brick building set in a courtyard and with a south-facing, pillared verandah. Bread, whether oven or griddle-baked, is basic in the diet of rural people at least, while the distinctive cuisine includes a wide variety of *āš* and *šorbā* dishes. Several districts of Azerbaijan have produced some of the varieties of Persian carpet best known in the West, especially Ardabīl, Herīs, Qaradāḡ, Tabrīz, and the Kurdish areas. Recently the subtle flat-weaves of the Šāhsevan nomads have acquired a considerable reputation.

In rural areas large patriarchal households are preferred, though not often achieved in practice. It is uncommon for married sons to leave their father's house, and even brothers often continue in a cooperative household for some time after their parents' deaths. In tribal contexts and in families of religious or other notable descent, lineal pedigrees are important, but usually both sides of the family are balanced in day-to-day life, though the maternal uncle (*dāʾī*) is a very different relation from a paternal one (*ʿamū*). If there is a particular theme in Azerbaijani kinship relations it is one of respect to age and seniority, to the head of household and to an older brother.

In all classes, especially close-knit village and tribal communities, marriage with cousins is common, but boys marry maternal cousins as frequently as paternal. Azerbaijani women have a reputation in the rest of the country for beauty and for being good cooks and household managers; locally they are expected to be strong, capable of running a home in the absence of their husband, and of organizing public activities (see M.-J. DelVecchio Good on urban women of Marāḡa, and N. Tapper on Šāhsevan nomad women, in Beck and Keddie, 1978).

Beyond kinship and marriage, individuals are linked in a variety of ties of personal friendship and pseudo-kinship, for example *siqäqardašlïx* (akin to blood-brotherhood) or the more purpose-based *qonaḡlïq* (contact). A third kind of relation, *kirvälik*, may approach the disinterested amity ideal of both friendship and kinship, though it often has distinctly political overtones. The *kirvä*'s role is to hold a small boy when he is being circumcised, but socially he approximates the godfather in many Christian societies. The boy's father will seek an influential friend for the purpose, thereby inaugurating a lifelong tie of patronage and support. The range of social relationships is summed up explicitly in the concept of *xeyr-ü-šärr* (lit. good and evil), denoting relations of reciprocal attendance at life-cycle feasts and also the personal networks so formed. "My *xeyr-ü-šärr*" means all those whose ceremonies I attend and who attend mine.

Though the major themes in Azerbaijani life-cycle ceremonies are similar to those elsewhere in Iran, there are variations in detail that distinguish districts and classes of society. The main occasions for joyful celebration and gatherings of large numbers of people are parties (*toy*) at circumcisions and weddings, when the host arranges feasting, music, dancing, and games for days on end, but with contributions made by all *xeyr-ü-šärr* guests. *Xeyr-ü-šärr* also contribute to the expenses of funeral feasts and the journeys of pilgrims to Mecca. In effect, *xeyr-ü-šärr* networks constitute a form of rotating credit association (see Tapper, 1979, pp. 150-52).

Religious practices among Azerbaijanis are not significantly different from those of other Iranian Shiʿites, though they are reputed to be more than usually pious. The religious classes of the major cities of the region exercise considerable control over belief and practice throughout the countryside. In some towns and villages the Moḥarram passion plays have been regularly performed (see Good, 1984 on Marāḡa); otherwise, dramatic and highly emotional *rawżaḵᵛānī* are put on for special occasions or in fulfillment of vows, but especially during the ten days of Moḥarram together with processions and dirges (*dästä/dasta, nowhä/nawḥa, märsiä/marṯīa*) (see Tapper, 1979, pp. 159-63; Lassy, 1916). Other religious occasions are Ramażān and the concluding feast of *fitr-bayramï*, the feast of sacrifice (*qorban-bayramï*), and in some places the festival of *ʿOmar-bayramï*, when an effigy of the Caliph ʿOmar is burned (Sāʿedī, 1965, p. 152). As in the rest of Iran, Nowrūz is a major festival, preceded on the Wednesdays of the last month by special ceremonies, including fire-jumping. Shrines of varying importance are common in town and countryside, from Shaikh Ṣafī's tomb at Ardabīl to wayside "rooms" (*ojaḡ*) and praying trees (*pir*). Women especially make pilgrimages to these, seeking cures, remedies and intercessions. Mullahs, wandering sayyeds, and dervishes may act as prayer-writers (*doʿayazan*), providing more or less "unorthodox" cures, protections, and exorcisms. Modern cosmopolitan medicine, with government personnel, hospitals and health centers, has during the present century all but driven underground the traditional *ḥakīm*s and other specialists in *torkidava* (herbal and humoral medicine, see B. Good, 1981). In the realm of popular culture, Azerbaijan is known for distinctive dresses, music, dances, and oral literature. One particular tradition associated with Azerbaijan, as well as neighboring areas of the Caucasus and Anatolia, is that of the *āšeq* (q.v.), wandering minstrels with a wide and well-loved repertoire of songs, ballads, and folk epics.

In the twentieth century, Azerbaijan, like other parts of Iran, has undergone enormous social changes. In particular there has been a sharpening of distinctions of wealth and status, as well as a growing divergence between those who favor more traditional attitudes and ways of life, with roots in the countryside, religion, and the bazaar, and those who seek a more cosmopolitan "modernity," through secular education, the professions, the civil service, and government-sponsored industry and commerce. (See B and M.-J. DelVecchio Good, 1984).

Bibliography: P. A. Andrews. "Âlâčïx and küme, the Felt Tents of Âzarbâijan," *Mardomšenāsī wa farhang-e ʿāmma-ye Īrān* 3, 1977-78, pp. 19-45. M. Bazin, *Le Ṭâlich. Une région ethnique au nord de l'Iran*, Paris, 1980, 2 vols. Sarhang ʿA. Bāybūrdī, *Tārīḵ-e Arasbārān*, Tehran, 1341 Š./1962-63. L. Beck and N. Keddie, eds., *Women in the Muslim World*, Cambridge Mass., 1978. M. van Bruinessen, *Agha, Shaikh and State: On the Social and Political Organization of Kurdistan*, Utrecht, 1978. B. Good, "The Transformation of Health Care in Modern Iranian History," in M. E. Bonine and N. Keddie, eds., *Modern Iran: the Dialectics of Continuity and Change*, Albany, 1981, pp. 59-82. B. Good and M.-J. DelVecchio Good, "Azeri (Iran)," in R. Weekes, ed., *Muslim Peoples: A World Ethnographic Survey*, 2nd ed., Westport, Greenwood, 1984, II, pp. 67-73 (and see bibliography of their writings on Marāḡa). Z. Z. Abdullaev et al., "Azerbaijan," in N. A. Kislyakov and A. I. Pershits, eds., *Narody Peredneĭ Azii*, Moscow, 1957, pp. 284-300. A. K. S. Lambton, *Landlord and Peasant in Persia*, Oxford, 1953. Idem, *The Persian Land Reform 1962-1966*, Oxford, 1969. I. Lassy, *The Muharram Mysteries among the Azerbaijan Turks of Caucasia*, Helsingfors, 1916. I. Mélikoff, "Le problème kızılbaş," *Turcica* 6, 1975, pp. 49-67. V. Minorsky, "Āḏharbaydjān," in *EI²* I, and other articles by the same author on, e.g., "Mākū," "Marāgha," "Tabrīz," "Urmīya." B. Nikitine, "Les Afšārs d'Urumiyeh," *JA* 214, 1929, pp. 109-23. Idem, *Les Kurdes*, Paris, 1956. P. Oberling, *The Turkic Peoples of Iranian Azerbaijan*, American Council of Learned Societies, Research and Studies in Uralic and Altaic Languages Project no. 51, 1964a. Idem, "The Tribes of Qarāca Dāġ," *Oriens* 17, 1964b, pp. 60-95. X. de Planhol, "Un village de montagne de l'Azerbaïdjan iranien," *Revue géographique de Lyon*, 1960, pp. 395-418. Research Group, "A Study of the Rural Economic Problems of East and West Azarbaijan," *Taḥqīqāt-e eqteṣādī* 5, 1968, pp. 149-238. W. Rudolph, "Grundzüge sozialer Organisation bei den westiranischen Kurden," *Sociologus*, N.S. 17/1, 1967, pp. 19-39. B. Ṣafarī, *Ardabīl dar goḏargāh-e tārīḵ*, 2 vols., Tehran, 1350 Š./1971-72 and 1353 Š./1974-75. Ḡ.-Ḥ. Sāʿedī, *Īlḵčī*, Tehran, 1342 Š./1963. Idem, *Ḵīāv yā Meškīnšahr: Kaʿba-ye yeylāqāt-e Šāhsevan*, Tehran, 1344 Š./1965. G. Schweizer, "Nordost-Azerbaidschan und Shah Sevan-Nomaden," in E. Ehlers et al., eds., *Strukturwandlungen im nomadisch-bäuerlichen Lebensraum des Orients*, Wiesbaden, pp. 81-148. Idem, "Tabriz und seine Bazaare," *Erdkunde* 27, 1972, pp. 32-46. R. Tapper, "Shahsevan in Ṣafavid Persia," *BSOAS* 37, 1974, pp. 321-54. Idem, *Pasture and Politics: Economics, Conflict and Ritual among Shahsevan Nomads of Northwestern Iran*, London, 1979. Idem, ed., *The Conflict of Tribe and State in Iran and Afghanistan*, London, 1983, introd., pp. 1-82. Idem, "One Hump or Two? Hybrid Camels and Pastoral Cultures," *Production pastorale et société* 16, 1985, pp. 55-69. Z. V. Togan, "Azerbaycan," in *İA* I.

(R. TAPPER)

vii. THE IRANIAN LANGUAGE OF AZERBAIJAN

Āḏarī (Ar. *al-āḏarīya*) was the Iranian language of Azerbaijan before the spread of the Turkish language, commonly called Azeri, in the region. The currency of Āḏarī in Azerbaijan during the first centuries of the Islamic period is attested by contemporary sources. The earliest reference to Āḏarī is the statement by Ebn al-Moqaffaʿ (d. 142/759), quoted by Ebn al-Nadīm (*Fehrest*, p. 13), to the effect that the language of Azerbaijan was Fahlawī (*al-fahlawīya*) "pertaining to Fahla," and that Fahla was the region comprised of Isfahan, Ray, Hamadān, Māh Nahāvand, and Azerbaijan. A similar statement, on the authority of Ḥamza Eṣfahānī, and obviously deriving from the same source, occurs in Yāqūt's *Moʿjam al-boldān* (III, p. 925, s.v. "Fahlaw"), and also in Ḵʷārazmī's *Mafātīḥ al-ʿolūm* (ed. van Vloten, pp. 116-17).

Next to Ebn al-Moqaffa''s the oldest reference to Ādarī, though no name is given the language, occurs in Balāḏorī's *Fotūḥ al-boldān* (p. 328; cf. Qazvīnī, *Bīst maqāla* I, p. 145), composed in 255/869. He quotes the word *ḫān*, meaning "house" or "caravanserai" (Ar. *ḫā'er*), as belonging to the "language of the people of Azerbaijan." (This word shows the development in Ādarī of Middle Iranian *x* to *h*, see below.) The oldest mention of the specific term Ādarī occurs in Yaʿqūbī's *Ketāb al-boldān*, composed in 276/891, p. 272; the population of Azerbaijan is described here as a mixture of Iranian Ādarī (*al-ʿajam al-ādarīya*) and old Jāvedānis (*al-jāwedānīya al-qedam*). By these terms he apparently means the Muslim Azerbaijanis and the Ḵorramdīnis or Jāvedānis, the followers of Jāvedān and Bābak, the neo-Mazdakite leaders who had held sway in Azerbaijan under al-Maʾmūn. It thus appears that the term Ādarī was applied to both the population of Azerbaijan and their language.

The next testimony is the statement by Masʿūdī (d. 345/956) which points to the original unity of the language of the Iranians and its later differentiation into separate languages, such as Fahlawī, Darī, and Ādarī—obviously the most prominent Iranian dialects in his estimation (*Tanbīh*, p. 78). Next we have the statement of Ebn Ḥawqal (d. ca. 981/371) that "the language of the people of Azerbaijan and most of the people of Armenia (*sic*; he probably means the Iranian Armenia) is Iranian (*al-fāresīya*), which binds them together, while Arabic is also used among them; among those who speak *al-fāresīya* (here he seemingly means Persian, spoken by the elite of the urban population), there are few who do not understand Arabic; and some merchants and landowners are even adept in it" (p. 348). Despite the exaggeration concerning the spread of Iranian languages into Armenia and the currency of Arabic in Azerbaijan, the statement clearly attests to the fact that the language of Azerbaijan in the 4th/10th century was Iranian. Moqaddasī (d. late 4th/10th cent.) also affirms that the language of Azerbaijan was Iranian (*al-ʿajamīya*), saying that it was partly Darī and partly "convoluted (*monqaleq*)"; he means no doubt to distinguish between the administrative lingua franca, i.e., Darī Persian, and the local dialects (*Aḥsan al-taqāsīm*, p. 259). Further he says that the language of the Azerbaijanis "is not pretty... but their Persian is intelligible, and in articulation (*fī'l-ḥorūf*) it is similar to the Persian of Khorasan" (p. 378). Again he must mean Darī Persian, which then, as now, must have been current in the urban centers of Azerbaijan.

An anecdote preserved by Samʿānī (*Ansāb*, s.v. Tanūḵī) concerning Abū Zakarīyā Kāteb Tabrīzī (d. 502/1109) and his teacher Abu'l-ʿAlāʾ Maʿarrī refers again to the vernacular of Azerbaijan in the 5th/12th century. While Kāteb Tabrīzī was in Maʿarrat al-Noʿmān in Syria, he met a fellow-countryman and conversed with him in a language which Abu'l-ʿAlāʾ could not understand. When Abu'l-ʿAlāʾ asked him to identify the language, Kāteb told him it was the language of the people of Azerbaijan (read *al-*

ādarīya in the Hyderabad ed., III, p. 93; and *al-adarbījīya* [unpointed] in the Leiden ed.; c.f. A. Kasravī, *Ādarī*, p. 13 n. 1). The statement of Yāqūt (d. 626/1229) to the effect that "The people of Azerbaijan have a language which they call *al-ādarīya*, and it is intelligible only to themselves" (*Moʿjam al-boldān* I, p. 172) makes it clear that Ādarī was still current in Azerbaijan on the eve of the Mongol invasion.

From Zakarīyā b. Moḥammad Qazvīnī's report in *Ātār al-belād*, composed in 674/1275, that "no town has escaped being taken over by the Turks except Tabrīz" (Beirut ed., 1960, p. 339) one may infer that at least Tabrīz had remained aloof from the influence of Turkish until the time of Abaqa. Ḥamdallāh Mostawfī writing in the 740/1340s calls the language of Marāḡa "modified Pahlavi" (*pahlavī-e moḡayyar*, as in Dabīrsīāqī's reading, *Nozhat al-qolūb*, Tehran, 1336 Š./1957, p. 100; the reading *pahlavī-e moʿarrab* "arabicized Pahlavi" in Le Strange's edition, p. 87, is not likely). Mostawfī also calls (ibid., p. 62) the language of Zanjān "straight Pahlavi" (*pahlavī-e rāst*) and the language of the Goštasfī province on the western side of the Caspian (i.e., north of the Persian Ṭāleš and south of Šīrvān) a Pahlavi close to the language of Gīlān (ibid., p. 92). By Pahlavi he, like Ebn al-Moqaffaʿ, obviously means in a general way the vernacular of northwestern and central Iran (an area coinciding with ancient Media). This language, however, was not, contrary to Marquart's view (Markwart, *Ērānšahr*, p. 132 n. 5) the same as Parthian, as is evident from the written remains and surviving dialects of Ādarī (see below).

These various testimonies, in spite of their being occasionally imprecise and uncritical, indicate that the population of Azerbaijan spoke a major Iranian language, termed Ādarī after the name of the region. It formed a group with the dialects of Ray, Hamadān, and Isfahan and remained the prevalent language of Azerbaijan until the 8th/14th century and probably for some time thereafter.

The spread of Turkish in Azerbaijan.

The gradual weakening of Ādarī began with the penetration of the Persian Azerbaijan by speakers of Turkish. The first of these entered the region in the time of Maḥmūd of Ḡazna (Ebn al-Atīr [repr.], IX, pp. 383ff.). But it was in the Saljuq period that Turkish tribes began to migrate to Azerbaijan in considerable numbers and settle there (A, Kasravī, *Šahrīārān-e gomnām*, Tehran, 1335 Š./1956, III, pp. 43ff., and idem, *Ādarī*, pp. 18-25). The Turkic population continued to grow under the Ildegozid atabegs of Azerbaijan (531-622/1136-1225), but more particularly under the Mongol il-khans (654-750/1256-1349), the majority of whose soldiery was of Turkic stock and who made Azerbaijan their political center. The almost continuous warfare and turbulence which reigned in Azerbaijan for about 150 years, between the collapse of the Il-khanids and the rise of the Safavids, attracted yet more Turkic military elements to the area. In this period, under the

Qara Qoyunlū and Āq Qoyunlū Turkmen (780-874/1378-1469 and 874-908/1469-1502 respectively), Āḏarī lost ground at a faster pace than before, so that even the Safavids, originally an Iranian-speaking clan (as evidenced by the quatrains of Shaikh Ṣafī-al-dīn, their eponymous ancestor, and by his biography), became Turkified and adopted Turkish as their vernacular.

The Safavid rule (905-1135/1499-1722), which was initially based on the support of Turkish tribes and the continued backing and influence of the Qezelbāš even after the regime had achieved a broader base, helped further the spread of Turkish at the detriment of Āḏarī, which receded and ceased to be used, at least in the major urban centers, and Turkish was gradually recognized as the language of Azerbaijan. Consequently the term Āḏarī, or more commonly Azeri, came to be applied by some Turkish authors and, following them, some Western orientalists, to the Turkish of Azerbaijan (see EI^{1-2}, s.v. "Ād̲h̲arī").

Āḏarī survivals.

These are of three kinds: (1) words, phrases, poems, and scattered verses, recorded in various written sources; (2) the present-day dialects which continue Āḏarī, spoken mainly on the periphery of Azerbaijan to the south and southeast, but also in isolated pockets in the north and the center; and (3) vocabulary borrowed from Āḏarī into the Turkish of Azerbaijan. The credit for first bringing together a collection of Āḏarī survivals belongs to Aḥmad Kasravī (d. 1324 Š./1946; see *Āḏarī yā zabān-e bāstān-e Āḏarbāygān*, Tehran, 1304 Š./1925). He also sketched the Āḏarī background and a history of the gradual spread of Turkish in Azerbaijan. Although his linguistic observations and methods can not always be supported, his general conclusions were essentially valid and dispelled a widespread notion that no information was available on the original language of Azerbaijan beyond Turkish. (See the reflection of his research in *İslâm Ansiklopedisi*, s.v. "Âzerî," where *Âzerî-Fârisî lehcesi* "Iranian Azeri dialect" is distinguished from *Âzerî-Türk lehcesi* "Turkish Azeri dialect".) Later, other Āḏarī survivals were detected.

1. *Āḏarī in written sources.* These include the following: (1) A sentence in "the language of Tabrīz" in Ḥamdallāh Mostawfī's *Nozhat al-qolūb* (ed. Dabīrsīāqī, p. 98). (2) A sentence in the "Tabrīzi" language and two sentences attributed to Shaikh Ṣafī-al-dīn of Ardabīl, two double distichs (*dobaytī*s) probably by him, another *dobaytī* apparently in the language of Ardabīl, and one in the language of Ḵalḵāl, all of these in the *Ṣafwat al-ṣafā* of Ebn Bazzāz, a contemporary of Shaikh Ṣadr-al-dīn, the son of Shaikh Ṣafī-al-dīn, and therefore of the 8th/14th century (Bombay ed., 1329/1911, pp. 25, 107, 191, 220). (3) Eleven double *dobaytī*s by Shaikh Ṣafī-al-dīn, and therefore apparently in the language of Ardabīl, in the *Selselat al-nasab-e Ṣafawīya* of Shaikh Ḥosayn, a descendant of Shaikh Zāhed Gīlānī, the mentor (*morād*) of Shaikh Ṣafī-al-dīn (Berlin, 1343/1924-25, pp. 29-33). (4) A macaronic *ḡazal* by Homām Tabrīzī (d. 714/1314) in Persian and a local language which must be that of Tabrīz (see M. Moḥīṭ Ṭabāṭabā'ī, "Dar pīrāmūn-e zabān-e fārsī," *Majalla-ye āmūzeš o parvareš* 8/10, 1317 Š./1938, p. 10; M. Ḥ. Adīb Ṭūsī, *NDA Tabrīz* 7/3, 1334 Š./1955, pp. 260-62). This specimen differs, however, from the sentence in Tabrīzi given by Ebn Bazzāz with respect to one important phonological feature: In Homām's poem, the enclitic pronoun of the second person singular is *-t*, while in Ebn Bazzāz's sentence it is *-r* (see below). (5) Two anonymous *qaṣīda*s in a manuscript written in 730/1329-30 and preserved in the Aya Sofia library in Istanbul (see Adīb Ṭūsī, ibid., 10/4, 1337 Š./1958, pp. 367-417); the dialect of these, judging from their phonology and some of the vocabulary which can be read with certainty appears to belong to the north-central Persian Azerbaijan, probably the Tabrīz-Marand region (see below). (6) One *ḡazal* and thirteen *dobaytī*s by Maḡrebī Tabrīzī (d. ca. 809/1406-07; see Adīb Ṭūsī, ibid., 8/12, 1335 Š./1956, pp. 121-27). (7) A text probably by Māmā 'Eṣmat, a mystical woman-poet of Tabrīz (d. 9th/15th cent.), which occurs in a manuscript, preserved in Turkey, concerning the shrines of saints in Tabrīz (see M. Nawwābī, ibid., 7/1, 1334 Š./1955, pp. 41-44; cf. Adīb Ṭūsī, "Fahlawīyāt-e Māmā 'Eṣmat wa Kašf-ī be-zabān-e āḏarī—eṣṭelāḥ-e rāžī yā šahrī," *NDA Tabrīz* 8/3, 1335 Š./1957, pp. 242-57). (8) Three poems in the dialects of Ḵamsa and Qazvīn, quoted by Ḥamdallāh Mostawfī in *Nozhat al-qolūb* which, although not belonging to Azerbaijan in the narrow sense of the term, should be grouped with the other remnants of Āḏarī in accord with the classification of the modern Iranian dialects of the Qazvīn and Zanjān areas. These poems consist of a *dobaytī* by Abu'l-Majīd Bāygānī in the dialect of an environ of Qazvīn; two *dobaytī*s by Jūlāha of Abhar, apparently a contemporary of Mostawfī, in the dialect of Abhar, a town in Ḵamsa, and a fragment of nine *dobaytī*s, by a certain Uyanj or Utanj, in the dialect of Zanjān. The text of all three is extremely corrupt (E. G. Browne, *JRAS*, 1900, pp. 738-41). (9) Two *dobaytī*s by Kašfī, a *ḡazal* and seven *dobaytī*s by Ma'ālī, five *dobaytī*s by Ādam, and seven by Ḵalīfa Ṣādeq from a *jong* (a manuscript of personal selections) found in Ṭāleš, and another *jong* from the Ḵalḵāl area (Kasravī, *Āḏarī*, 5th ed., pp. 57-61). Information is lacking concerning their authors and their dates of composition, but linguistically they are all close to the verses of Shaikh Ṣafī. (10) Ten words from the language of "Āḏarbāḏakān" in contrast to Persian, quoted in an old manuscript of Asadī Ṭūsī's *Loḡat-e fors* in the Malek Library (no. 5839) (Ṣ. Kīā, "Kohnatarīn dastnevīs-e 'Loḡat-e fors'-e Asadī Ṭūsī", *MDAT* 3/3, 1335 Š./1956, pp. 4-5; idem, *Āḏarīgān: āgāhīhā-ī dar bāra-ye gūyeš-e āḏarī*, Tehran, 1354 Š./1975). (11) Two short *ḡazal*s, five lines each, by Badr Šīrvānī (*Dīvān*, ed. A. H. Rahimov, Moscow, 1985, pp. 665f.) in the language of "Kanār Āb," in a local dialect of Šīrvān and possibly the mother tongue of the poet who was born in Šamāḵī. The language of these poems is almost identical to that of Shaikh Ṣafī-al-

dīn's *dobaytīs* (see below); notice *čəman* "my," *-r*, the 2nd singular enclitic pronoun (read *mehr-ər* "your love," cf. *ğam-ər* "your sorrow"), *až* "from," *vī* "without," *kar-*, the present stem of "to do," *vāč-*, the present stem of "to say."

It should be noted that the final section of Rūḥī Anārjānī's 11th/17th-century *Resāla*, a literary miscellany, entitled "On the Terms and Phrases of Ladies, Grandees, and Dandies of Tabrīz" which has been assumed by a number of scholars to be in Āḏarī dialect ('Abbās Eqbāl, "Yak sanad-e mohemm dar bāb-e zabān-e āḏarī," *Yādgār* 2/3, 1324 Š./1945, pp. 43-50; M. Moğdam [Moqaddam], *Iran Kūda* 10, 1327 Š./1948, pp. 1-18; Saʿīd Nafīsī, ed., "Resāla-ye Rūḥī Anārjānī," *FIZ* 2, 1333 Š./1954, pp. 329-72; Y. M. Nawwābī, *NDA Tabrīz* 9, 1336 Š./1957, pp. 221-32, 396-426; M. J. Maškūr, *Naẓar-ī ba tārīḵ-e Āḏarbāyjān wa āṯār-e bāstānī wa jamʿīyatšenāsī-e ān*, Anjoman-e Āṯār-e Mellī, Tehran, 1349 Š./1971, pp. 221ff.; M. Mortażawī, *Zabān-e dīrīn-e Āḏarbāyjān*, Tehran, 1360 Š./1981, p. 35), bears no relationship to Āḏarī, but as W. B. Henning ingeniously realized ("The Ancient Language of Azerbaijan," *TPS*, 1954-55, p. 176 n. 5) refers to a vulgar form of New Persian, and actually attests to the continued currency of this language in Tabrīz even in the sixteenth century.

Of the written remains of Āḏarī, the *dobaytīs* of Shaikh Ṣafī-al-dīn are the most important: They are relatively old, their linguistic area and their author are known, and they are accompanied by a paraphrase in Persian which helps their understanding. Despite Ardabīl's location at the eastern edge of Azarbaijan, in view of its significance both before and after the advent of Islam, its language must have been one of the more important dialects of Āḏarī. Before it fell into the hands of the Arabs, Ardabīl was the *madīna*, i.e., the metropolis, of Azerbaijan; it was the center of its fiscal administration and the seat of the Sasanian *marzbān* (Balāḏorī, *Fotūḥ al-boldān*, p. 325; Yāqūt, *Moʿjam-al-boldān* I, p. 197) and was confirmed as the capital of the region by Ašʿaṯ b. Qays during 'Alī's caliphate (Balāḏorī, *Fotūḥ*, p. 329). Some three centuries later Ebn Ḥawqal (*Ṣūrat-al-arż*, p. 334) still mentions it as the center and the largest city of Azerbaijan (cf. Moqaddasī, *Aḥsan al-taqāsīm*, p. 375); Eṣṭaḵrī (*Masālek*, p. 181) refers to it as the largest city, the seat of the government (*dār al-emāra*), and the military encampment (*moʿaskar*) of the region (see further Qodāma b. Jaʿfar, *Ketāb al-ḵarāj*, p. 244 and Ebn Rosta, *Aʿlāq*, p. 106).

2. *Words borrowed from Āḏarī into Azeri Turkish.* These include *dardažar* "ailing" and **kušn* "field", which occur in Shaikh Ṣafī's *dobaytīs* (see Kasravī, *Āḏarī*, p. 41). Kārang (*Jahān-e aḵlāq* 4, 1956, pp. 84ff.) notes a number of Tati words used also in Azeri Turkish, e.g., *dīm* "face," *zamī* "land, field," *olis*, Azeri *ulas* "charcoal." But to determine the full extent of such borrowings requires further research. Several authors, notably Adīb Ṭūsī ("Nomūna-ī čand az loğat-e āḏarī," *NDA Tabrīz* 8/4, 1335 Š./1957, pp. 310-49; 9/2, 3, 4, 1336 Š./1957, pp. 135-68, 242-60, 361-89; cf. M. Aržangī, ibid., 9/1, 2, pp. 73-108, 182-201; 10/1, 1337 Š./1958, pp. 81-93) have collected the large number of non-Turkish words used in the Azeri Turkish of the various parts of Azerbaijan (See Maškūr, op. cit., p. 263 for a count); but, ignoring proper linguistic criteria, they have taken them to be Āḏarī, whereas in fact, they are, by and large, Persian (or Arabic, borrowed through Persian), a fact which shows that Āḏarī, unlike Persian, has not affected the lexicon of Azeri Turkish significantly. The assumption of these researchers that the material in the last chapter of Rūḥī Anārjānī's *Resāla* is Āḏarī (see above) has also tended to vitiate their conclusions. (for a listing of Azeri vocabulary see Y. M. Nawwābī, *Zabān-e konūnī-e Āḏarbāyjān* [Bibl.]; and Koichi Haneda and Ali Ganjelu, *Tabrizi Vocabulary, An Azeri-Turkish Dialect in Iran*, Studia Culturae Islamicae, no. 13, Tokyo, 1979).

3. *Present-day dialects of Āḏarī.* Despite its continued decline over the centuries, Āḏarī has not died out and its descendants are found as modern dialects, mostly called Tati, sharing a wide range of phonological and grammatical features. Proceeding from north to south, these are: (1) The dialect of Kalāsūr and Ḵoynarūd, two villages of the Ḥasanow (Ḥasanābād) district of Ahar; (2) the dialect of Karīngān, a village of eastern Dīzmār in the Vazraqān district (*baḵš*) of Ahar sub-province (*šahrestān*); (3) the dialect of Galīnqaya, a village of the Harzand rural area (*dehestān*) in the district of Zonūz, Marand sub-province; (4) the Ḵalḵāli dialects spoken in the chief villages of the Šāhrūd *baḵš* (i.e., Askestān, Asbū, Derow, Kolūr, Šāl, Dīz, Karīn, Lerd, Kehel, Ṭahārom, Gelūzān, Gīlavān, and Gandomābād), in Karnaq, in the Ḵoreš-e Rostam *baḵš*, and in Kajal in the Kāğaḏkonān *baḵš* of Ḵalḵāl; (5) the Tati dialects of the Upper Ṭārom (principally in the villages of Nowkīān, Sīāvarūd, Kalāsar, Hazārrūd, Jamābād, Bāklūr, Čarza, and Jeyšābād); (6) the Tati dialects of Rāmand and Zahrā, southwest and south of Qazvīn (i.e., the dialects of Tākestān, Čāl, Esfarvarīn, Ḵīāraj, Ḵᵛoznīn, Dānesfān, Ebrāhīmābād, and Sagzābād) which are close to the Tati of Ḵalḵāl and Ṭārom; (7) the dialects of Ṭāleš, from Allāhbaḵš Maḥalla and Šāndermīn on the border of Gīlān in the south to the Soviet Ṭāleš in the north, including the dialect of 'Anbarān in the Namīn district of Ardabīl; all connected with the Tati dialects of Šāhrūd. This list does not necessarily exhaust the Āḏarī-speaking villages of Azerbaijan, and there may exist villages which the writer has not been able to visit, and where Tati is still understood (see A. A. Kārang, *Tātī wa harzanī*, pp. 27; he mentions a number of villages in Dīzmār and Ḥasanābad districts, including Arzīn, where the dialect was still understood in the 1940s; on the continued waning of Āḏarī, see below).

To the same group of dialects belong in a broad sense: (1) the dialect of Māsūla in the Fūmenāt district of Gīlān; (2) the language spoken in the Rūdbār of Gīlān (Raḥmatābād, Rostamābād, etc.), in the Rūdbār of Alamūt (Dekīn, Mūšqīn, Garmārūd, and Bolūkān), and in Alamūt (Moʿallem Kelāya, Estalbar, Gāzarḵān,

Avānak, etc.); (3) the dialect of K̲o'īn and Safīdkamar in the Ījrūd of Zanjān, and a few villages in the Kūhpāya of Qazvīn (Zerejerd, Nowdeh, Asbemard, Ḥeṣār, etc.); (4) the dialect of Vafs, between Hamadān and Arāk. There are also a number of border dialects, such as the dialect of Ṭāleqān villages between Qazvīn and Karaj, and the dialects of Āmora and Āštīān, all much affected by Persian, that have close affinities with the group. In fact, the demarcation line between these dialects and their more northerly cognates cannot be sharply drawn. Kurdish, however, spoken in Mahābād in southwestern Azerbaijan and scattered in several other areas in the region, which some have supposed to be a descendant of Median, does not belong to this group and exhibits some clear differences with it. (See D. N. Mackenzie, "The Origins of Kurdish," *TPS*, 1961, pp. 67-83).

The fact that these dialects are so relatively abundant and are spoken in contiguous areas over a vast territory confirms their being indigenous to these areas and speaks strongly against the possibility that they spread into Azerbaijan and its border regions from other areas. Their shared linguistic features place them in a well-defined group of North-West Iranian, with affinities with the Central dialects, spoken to the south and southeast of the Ad̲arī language area. Ād̲arī and the language termed Fahlawī in the medieval Islamic sources refer in fact to the northern and southern branches of the language spoken in the territory of ancient Media, broadly corresponding to their modern continuations, namely the Tati or Ād̲arī dialects in central and western Iran (excluding Kurdish and Luri). On the analogy of New Persian one may call them New Median (see further below).

That only meager traces of the language spoken in the central regions of Azerbaijan have survived is only natural, since a language that comes under pressure from other languages disappears faster in the center than in the periphery. The fact that while there are some meager remains of Ād̲arī from the north, the center, the east, and south of Azerbaijan, yet the western part of the province yields no comparable material, is no doubt due to the dominance in these regions, before the spread of Turkish, of other languages, such as Neo-Aramaic and Kurdish.

The process of the linguistic Turkification of Azerbaijan continues to this day, and even in the border areas the original dialects keep giving way to Turkish. In the course of his study of these dialects in the 1960s, the writer met a number of elderly people who could remember or had been told by their fathers or grandfathers that villages now speaking Turkish formerly spoke the Iranian dialect. In Ḥalab, a village in Ījrūd on the way from Zanjān to Bījār, he met in 1964 the last three men who still retained some shaky memory of their Tati, and in Galīnqaya there was in 1972 only one old man who could speak the native dialect fluently. (See also Kārang, *Tātī wa harzanī*, pp. 27-29; idem, "K̲alk̲ālī," *Jahān-e ak̲lāq* 4, 1335 Š./1956, p. 83; D̲okā', *Gūyeš-e Galīnqaya*, p. 6.)

Linguistic features.

The absence of vocalization, the deficiencies of the Arabic alphabet in indicating the details of pronunciation, scribal errors, and the influence of classical Persian make the reading of the literary Ād̲arī remains difficult. Nevertheless they reveal some genuine features of the phonology, grammar, and vocabulary of the language in which they are written. Here the features of two written remains are explored.

A. *Shaikh Ṣafī-al-dīn's* dobaytīs. 1. Old Iranian intervocalic *t* > *r*. Examples: *žir* "life" (< **jit*-, cf. Parthian *jydg*); the enclitic 2nd singular pronoun -(*a*)*r* (Pers. -[*a*]*t*); past tense forms: *āmarim* "I came" (< **āmat*-), *bori* or *beri* "he was" (< **būt*-), *šoram* or *šeram* "I went" (< **šut*-), and *žar* "struck" (< *jat*-, Pers. *zad*) in *dara žar* "was pained" (Parthian *drdjd*; Henning, "Ancient Language," p. 176 n. 4). The same sound change is found in two Tati dialects: Harzandi and the dialect of Kalāsūr and K̲oynarūd; cf. Harzandi *amārā* "he came" (other examples: *vör* "wind" < **wāt*-, *kar* "house" < **kat*-, *jörö-tan* "stranger" < *(*wi*)*yut*-, Pers. *jodā* "separate"); Kalāsūri *umarim* "I came," and *šerim* "I went" (other examples: *vur* "wind," *jeru* "separate," *purez* "autumn" < **pātēz* [Pers. *pā'īz*], *zura* "boy, son" < **zātak*-). In other dialects, this change occurs only sporadically; cf., e.g., Kajali *kerom* "which" (< **katām*-, Pers. *kodām*), and in the dialect of Derow in K̲alk̲āl *šera* "he went." The enclitic pronoun of the 2nd singular is -*r* in Kajali and Šāhrūdi of K̲alk̲āl, also in Asālemi and Māsāli in the central and southern Iranian Ṭāleš area (but not in northern Ṭāleši or 'Anbarāni). In the sentence in the dialect of Tabrīz recorded by Ebn Bazzāz as uttered by a contemporary of Shaikh Ṣafī-al-dīn, we find *ḥarīf-ar žāta* "your contender has come." One can not measure the extent of this rule in the defunct dialect of Tabrīz by this instance alone, but note also the Iranian word *därdäjär* "sick, ailing" in Azeri Turkish, and the Azerbaijani placename Esparak̲ūn, colloquial for Safīdak̲ān, a village in Bostānābād, east of Tabrīz, probably "White spring," with *espara* < **spētak*- (Pers. *safīd* "white"). The change of intervocalic *t* to *r* is seen also in the so-called Tati, but actually (archaic) New Persian dialect of the Iranian-speaking Jews in the Apsheron peninsula and the northeast of the Azerbaijan S.S.R. The change, on the other hand, is not effected in the dialects of Ṭārom, K̲o'īn, Rāmand, and Alamūt areas to the south.

2. Old Iranian intervocalic *č* > *j*. Examples: *riji* "he pours," (Av. *raēca*-), and *navāji* "you [sing.] do not say" (Parth. *w'c*-). The same change is seen in the modern dialects of Šāhrūd, Kajal and Asālem: Šāhrūdi *verijam* "we flee," *vāje* "he says;" Kajali *mivrije* "he flees;" and Asālemi *bivrij* "flee!" By contrast, in the dialects of Kalāsūr and K̲oynarūd, Ṭāleš, Karīngān, and Harzand, *č* has become *ž*: cf. Kalāsūri *ruž* "day," *namuž* "prayer;" 'Anbarāni *ruža* "fast," *nəmož* "prayer;" Ṭāleši as spoken in the Soviet Union: *tož* "to rush, gallop," *bad-vož* "defamer, slanderer;" Karīngāni *vuž* "say!;" Harzandi *ruž* "sun."

3. A vowel phoneme /ö/ə/ is indicated by the variant

spellings *-w* and *-h*: *čw* and *čh*, i.e., */čə/* "from" (< **hača*, Pers. *az*); and *'štw* and *'čth*, i.e., */aštə/* or */ačtə/* "yours" (2nd sing., rendered by Pers. *māl-e to*, lit., "your property"). A similar phoneme is found in the modern dialects of Harzand, Ṭāleš, Kajal, and Šāhrūd (not in word-final position in Šāhrūdi).

4. Old Iranian initial *j* > *ž*. Examples: *žir* "life," and *žar* "struck." The same sound change is seen in the modern dialects of Kalāsūr and Ḵoynarūd: *žan* "woman," *žare* "to hit," *žāte* "to arrive"; Ṭāleši *žen* "woman," *žae* "to hit"; Arazini *žen* and Kajali *žan* "woman," *bežana* "strike!" The form *žāta* in Ebn Bazzāz's sentence shows that this feature extended to the dialect of Tabrīz. In the dialects of Karīngān and Harzand, however, initial *ž* has become *y*: Karīngāni *yan* "woman" and "strike!," *yaz/yat-* "to arrive," and Harzandi *yan* "woman," *yare* "to strike."

5. Old Iranian *x, xw* > *h* in *harda* "he ate;" cf. *sohrāb* "rouge" in the manuscript of the *Loḡat-e fors* mentioned above (Kīā, p. 4). This development is regular in Kajali: (*hardan* "to eat," *hára* "ass," *heriār* "buyer," *howlig* "sister") but sporadic in the Šāhrūdi group: Šāli *(h)ardan*, cf. Gīlavāni *ha* "sister," *hezə* "he wants" (Parth. *wxāz-, wxāšt*, but Pers. *k̲ᵛāh-, k̲ᵛāst*); but Šāli *k̲ri-* "to buy," *k̲es/k̲el* "to sleep," etc. Cf. also Karīngāni *hārdan* "to eat," *haraši* "sun" (Pers. *k̲ᵛaršīd*): Harzandi *horde* "to eat," *hösn/höst* "to want," *hištan* "self" (Pers. *k̲ᵛīštan*); Kalāsūri *horma* "I ate," *hāmma* "I read" (Pers. *k̲ᵛāndam*); and in most Ṭāleši dialects: Asālemi *hard-*, ʿAnbarāni *hāna bim* "I was eating, used to eat," and Northern Ṭāleši *hova* "sister". But in Asālemi we find *ženā-xāzī* (Pers. *k̲ᵛāstgārī*), and in the dialect of Māsāl in southern Ṭāleš we find *xa* "sister," *xəšk* "dry," etc.

6. Old Iranian *fr* > *hr* in *ahrā* "tomorrow" (Pers. *fardā* < **fra-*, cf. G. Lazard, *La langue des plus anciens monuments de la prose persane*, Paris, 1963, p. 145). In the modern dialects we find Kajali *a(h)rā*, Harzandi *ohra* (cf. also *heraš/heröt* "to sell" < **frawaxš-/frawaxt*, Pers. *forūš/forūk̲t*), Ḵīāraji of Rāmand *ahrā*, Šāli *paš-arā* "the day after tomorrow," Šāndermīni and Māsāli *pašerā*, Tākestāni *sarā* "day after tomorrow," Northern Ṭāleši *havate* "to sell," *hamue* "to order" (< **framāt-*, Pers. *framūdan*).

7. Oblique case/genitive in **-i* (or so-called inverted *eżāfa* construction). This ending is written only in *öyān-i banda* "the servant of the Lord" (*dobaytī* 11; on *öyān* < Tk. *oyan*, see Henning, "The Ancient Language," p. 176 n. 4; it is not a plural of *oy* "he," as Kasravī thought) but may also be assumed in other cases, e.g., *oyān(i) k̲āṣṣān* "special friends of god," *čowgān(i) gur-im* "I am the ball of the polo stick" (i.e., resigned to the divine will), and *qodrat(i) zanjir-im* "I am the chain of power" (*dobaytī* 3). Among modern dialects, Kalāsūri and Asālemi have accusative and genitive in *-i*, Ḵalk̲āli in *-e*.

8. The personal pronouns have four forms:

	Direct	Oblique	Possessive	Enclitic
1st	*az*	*man*	—	*-m*
2nd	—	*te* or *tö*	*eštö*	*-r*

This feature is shared by the dialects of Ḵalk̲āl and Ṭāleš, For instance, the corresponding forms in the Šāli dialect of Šāhrūd are:

1st	*az*	*man*	*čeman*	*-m*
2nd	*te*	*te*	*ešte*	*-r*

In Kajali the forms are:

1st	*az*	*aman*	*čəman*	*-m*
2nd	*tə*	*tə*	*əštə*	*-r*

and in Asālem:

1st	*az*	*man*	*čəmən*	*-m*
2nd	*tə*	*tə*	*əštə*	*-r*

A similar scheme is found in the dialect of Čāl in Rāmand. In the rest of the Rāmand area, however, the oblique form is no longer used. The dialects of upper Ṭārom, e.g., Nowkīāni and Hazārrūdi, have a system of actually five pronominal forms (the pronouns for the direct object and the "logical direct object" in passive constructions are differentiated; see Yarshater, "The Tati Dialects of Ṭārom"). In Karīngāni and Harzandi the direct pronoun has been replaced by the originally oblique form, as in Persian.

9. The 2nd person singular ending is *-i* in the present indicative (*riji* "you pour," *navāji* "you do not say"), but *-š* in the present subjunctive (*mavāješ* "you may not say"). A 2nd person singular ending *-š* is found in several Tati dialects. In Karīngāni, in particular, it is the common form; in Kalāsūr, it is found in the present indicative (*bežareš* "you strike"); in Šāhrūdi (Šāli and Kolūri), everywhere except the present indicative and the imperative (*bešiš* "you went," *age bevrijāš* "if you should flee"); in Asālem, everywhere except in the imperative and the present subjunctive (*biš* "you were," *bebaš* "be!"); in ʿAnbarāni, in the continuous past tense; and in Northern Ṭāleši throughout the verbal system. In Harzandi the ending *-š* does not occur.

10. A continuous present is made from the past stem if indeed, as it appears, the verbs in the fourth *dobaytī* are present tense, wrongly rendered by the past tense in the paraphrase of the *Selselat al-nasab*: *be-koštim* "I kill," *be-heštim* "I let/leave," and *na-daštim* "I am not harming" (on the last verb, see Henning, "The Ancient Language," p. 176 n. 4). The same kind of formation is found in the dialects of Karīngān, Harzand, and Kalāsūr, Northern Ṭāleši, and in Asālemi, but not in the dialects of Southern Ṭāleši: Karīngāni *heteine* "I am sleeping" (cf. *fesene* "I sleep" < **xwafs-*), Harzandi *bāvāštān* "he is carrying," *bo-hordān* "he is eating," Kalāsūri *ba-durem* "I am giving" (< **dāt-*), *be-žareš* "you (sing.) are striking," *ba-šem* "I am going," Asālemi *ba-vindiše* "you (sing.) are seeing," *ba-bramastim* "we are weeping."

11. Vocabulary. Note *asra* "tear" (cf. Šāhrūdi *asərk*, Asālemi, Māsāli, and ʿAnbarāni *asərg*, Harzandi *ösör*, Karīngāni *aster*; cf. also *ásra* [fem.] in the dialects of Rāmand and *ars* in the Persian dictionaries) and *ahra* "tomorrow" (see above, no. 6). The question whether *-a* in *asra* is a feminine marker (as it is in Rāmandi) and

whether Ādarī of Ardabīl distinguished grammatical gender, can not be determined on the basis of the material at hand. Its affinities lie mostly with modern dialects which do not have the category of gender (see below).

It can be seen from the foregoing that the language of the *dobaytīs* is not identical with any one modern descendant of Ādarī. Its greatest affinity seems to be on the one hand with the Tati dialects of Kalāsūr and Koynarūd to the northwest (*t* > *r*, *j* > *ž*, 2nd singular -*š*, continuous present from the past stem), and on the other with the dialects of the central Ṭāleš area to the east (*j* > *ž*, four-fold personal pronoun, 2nd singular -*š*, continuous present from the past stem), and Kalkāli (*t* > *r* in some instances, *j* > *ž* in Kajali, four-fold personal pronoun). This agrees well with Ardabīl's geographical position. By contrast, the dialects of Harzand and Karīngān, the Āstārā region, and of Soviet Ṭāleš to the north that B. V. Miller (*Talyshskiĭ yazyk*, Moscow, 1953, pp. 253ff.) for lack of information about Tati and southern Ṭālešī dialects thought were closest to Ādarī, are relatively remoter. (Northern Ṭālešī is characterized by the dropping or greatly reducing of unstressed syllables, *t* does not become *r*, the enclitic pronouns are -*ə* and -*əon* for 2nd singular and plural, respectively).

Another conclusion that can be drawn from these comparisons is that Ṭālešī should not be grouped with the Caspian dialects, as is commonly done on the basis of their geographical location, but rather with the Tati dialects of Azerbaijan, particularly Šāhrūdī.

B. *The Istanbul* qaṣīdas. The phonology and vocabulary of the language attested in this poem link it with the area of Tabrīz and Marand. Note the following features.

1. Old Iranian *ā* > *ū* in *āžūr* "free" (Pers. *āzād*), *dūr* "hold!" (Pers. *dār*), *gūn* "soul" (Parth. and Mid Pers. *gyān*, NPers. *jān*), **huzdan* "to ask, want" (Pers. *k̲ᵛāstan*), *pūydūr* "permanent" (Pers. *pāydār*), and *vad-nehūd* "bad-natured" (Pers. *bad-nehād*).

2. Old Iranian intervocalic *t* > *r* in *āžūr*, -*r* "you" (Pers. -*t*), *zūnar* "he knows" (< **zān-*, Pers. *dānad*), and *žaran* "to strike" (< **jat-*, Pers. *zadan*).

3. Old Iranian intervocalic *č* > *j* in *jeman* "my own" (< Old Iranian *hača-*).

4. Old Iranian *x*, *xw* > *h* in *harda* "eaten" (Pers. *k̲ᵛorda*), **hūzdan* "toask, want"; cf. *hošk* "dry" (< Old Iranian **huška*).

5. Vocabulary. Note *gūn* "soul," **karend* "they do, make" (Parth. *kar-*), *sag* "stone" (Pers. *sang*), and *vūn* "blood" (Av. *vohunī*, Pers. *k̲ūn*).

The position of Ādarī among the Iranian languages.

It is obvious that the language of as broad an area as Azerbaijan could not have been uniform throughout and must have exhibited a variety of local dialects. The statement by Moqaddasī (*Aḥsan al-taqāsīm*, p. 375) to the effect that seventy dialects were spoken in the region of Ardabīl, despite its gross exaggeration, has to be taken to refer to the variety of its local subdialects. On the other hand, the fact that the language of the entire Azerbaijan has been called Ādarī in the early sources and placed alongside Darī and Pahlavi implies that the dialects of the region were similar enough to be called by a single name.

Azerbaijan and the "Jebāl" of the medieval geographers, that is, the mountainous west-central part of the Iranian plateau, coincide geographically with ancient Media and was inhabited by Median tribes in ancient times. Although no independent written document in ancient Median has yet come to light, its fundamental phonological features are known from the Median words and names which occur in Old Persian inscriptions and, less frequently, in Greek (e.g., IE. *ĝ*, and *ĝh* < Med(ian) *z*, OPers. *d*; IE. *k̂u̯* > Med. *sp*, OPers. *s*; IE. *tr* and *tl* > Med. *θr*, OPers. *ç*; see Kent, *Old Persian*, secs. 8-9; M. Mayrhofer, *Die Rekonstruktion des Medischen*, Anz. d. Österreichischen Akad. d. Wiss., Phil.-hist. Kl., 1968, 1, Vienna; G. L. Windfuhr, "Isoglosses: A Sketch on Persians and Parthians, Kurds and Medes," in *Monumentum H. S. Nyberg* II, Acta Iranica 5, Tehran and Liège, 1975, pp. 457-72). All these features are characteristic also of Ādarī and its modern relatives. Thus there are no linguistic arguments against the derivation of Ādarī from Median, which is based upon compelling geographical and historical evidence (see below), and such a conclusion can in no way be invalidated by the fact that the phonological peculiarities of Median are found, by and large, in all northwestern branches of Iranian, including Parthian, or by the fact that it has not been possible to find exclusive Median isoglosses (see P. O. Skjærvø, *BSL* 78, pp. 244-51). It will be noted that Ādarī differs from Parthian in some important respects, e.g. "came" is from **ā(g)mata-* (as in Persian) against Parthian *āγad* < **āgata-*; Parthian has a suffix -*īft* and the *eżāfa čē*, both unknown in Ādarī.

Likewise, the fact that the Ādarī group of dialects shares a few isoglosses with some geographically and linguistically distant dialects in southeastern Iran, namely Lāri and Baškardi, which, like Persian belong to the South-Western Iranian dialects does not affect our conclusion with regard to the derivation and provenience of Ādarī. The isoglosses shared with Lāri are the 2nd singular ending -*š* and the continuous present from the past stem; cf. Lāri *ačedāeš* "you are going," *čedeš* "you went" (A. Eqtedārī, *Farhang-e lārestānī*, Tehran, 1334 Š./1955, p. 269); the isoglosses shared with Baškardi are: *t* > *r* in North Baškardi (e.g., *zar-* "to strike") and the continuous present based on the past stem (e.g., North Baškardi *akerdénom*, South Baškardi *bekert(en)om* "I am doing," see G. Morgenstierne in *HO* I, iv, 1: *Linguistik*, Leiden, 1958, p. 178). There is no need for assuming any special historico-geographical connection between the Ādarī group and Lāri and Baškardi to explain these isoglosses. Indeed, since Ādarī is phonetically a typical North-Western dialect but Lāri and Baškardi typical South-Western dialects, such an assumption would create more problems for historical Iranian linguistics than it would solve. In the case of other Iranian languages and dialects, too, we occasionally find isoglosses crossing other, fundamental, isoglosses and spanning large distances. One typical case is that of Sogdian and Old Persian (see Henning, *Mitteliranisch*, p. 108).

Historically, Media was divided into Greater Media, which was the area where today the Central dialects are spoken, and Lesser Media or Azerbaijan. Doubtless it is this geographical division which is reflected in the linguistic distinction between *al-āḏarīya* and *al-fahlawīya* of our medieval sources. (The fact that while there are some meager remains of Āḏarī from the north, the center, the east, and the south of Azerbaijan, yet the western part of the province yields no comparable material, is no doubt due to the dominance in these regions, before the spread of Turkish, of other languages, such as Neo-Aramaic and Kurdish.) Since there is no historical evidence that the population of the Median territories was ever dislocated on a significant scale, or that its language was superceded by any other language than Persian (in the urban centers) and Turkish (in Azerbaijan), the conclusion is inevitable that the affiliated Iranian dialects spoken in Azerbaijan, Kamsa, Qazvīn, Ṭāleš, Hamadān, Nahāvand, Kᵛānsār, Kāšān, Isfahan, and Semnān, to mention only the chief regions, can be none other than the descendants of the Old Median language, today divided roughly into a northern, Āḏarī, group and a southern, "Fahlawī" or "Central" group of dialects.

Bibliography: Given in the text. The dialect materials referred to in the article, except for the Ṭāleši of the Soviet Union, Arazīni, Baškardi, and Lārī, were collected by the author between 1955-72. See also M. Qazvīnī's review of Kasravī, *Āḏarī*, repr. in *Bīst maqāla*, Tehran, 1332 Š./1953, I, pp. 178-86. On the modern dialects see 'A. Kārang's pioneering treatise on the dialects of Karīngān and Galīnqaya, *Tātī wa harzanī, do lahja az zabān-e bāstān-e Āḏarbāyjān*, Tabrīz, 1333 Š./1954. Y. Ḏokā', *Karīngānī*, Tehran, 1332 Š./1954. Idem, *Gūyeš-e Galīnqaya, 'harzandī*,' Tehran, 1336 Š./1957. J. Matīnī, "Daqīqī, zabān-e darī wa lahja-ye āḏarī," *MDAM* 11/4, 1354 Š./1975, pp. 559-75. M. Mortażawī, "Nokta-ī čand az zabān-e harzanī," *NDA Tabrīz* 6/3, 1333 Š./1954, pp. 304-14. Idem, *Feʿl dar zabān-e harzanī*, Tabrīz, 1342 Š./1963. Y. M. Nawwābī, *Zabān-e konūnī-e Āḏarbāyjān*, Tabrīz, 1334 Š./1955 (published earlier as a series of articles in *NDA Tabrīz* 5 and 6, 1332-33 Š./1953-54). E. Yarshater, "The Tati Dialect of Shāhrud (Khalkhāl)," *BSOAS* 22, 1959, pp. 52-68. Idem "The Tati Dialect of Kajal," *BSOAS* 23, 1960, pp. 275-68. Idem, "The Tati Dialects of Rāmand," in *A Locust's Leg. Studies in Honour of S. H. Taqizadeh*, ed. W. B. Henning and E. Yarshater, London, 1962, pp. 240-45. Idem, "Marāḡīān-e Alamūt wa Rūdbār wa zabān-e ānhā," *Majalla-ye Īrānšenāsī* 1, 1346 Š./1967. Idem, *A Grammar of Southern Tati Dialects* (*Median Dialect Studies* I), The Hague and Paris, 1969. Idem, "The Tati Dialects of Ṭārom," in *W. B. Henning Memorial Volume*, ed. M. Boyce and I. Gershevitch, London, 1970, pp. 451-

67. M. Mortażawī provides a listing of the Persian articles on topics related to Āḏarī in *Zabān-e dīrīn-e Āḏarbāyjān*, pp. 56ff.; of interest is a paper he entitled "Bīst vāža-ye āḏarī dar ḥawāšī-e noska-ye kattī-e *Ketāb al-bolḡa*" (Twenty Āḏarī words on the margin of the MS. of the *K. al-bolḡa*) read by M. Mīnovī at the sixth conference of Iranian studies (1974?), but apparently not yet published. On Median and the "Median" dialects see also A. Meillet, *Grammaire du vieux perse*, 2nd ed. by E. Benveniste, Paris, 1931, p. 7, par. 8; I. Gershevitch, "Dialect Variation in Early Persian," *TPS*, 1964 [1965], pp. 1-29; P. O. Skjærvø, "*Farnah*: mot mède en vieux-perse?" *BSL* 79, 1984, pp. 241-59. On the dialectology of Middle Iranian see also W. Lentz, "Die nordiranischen Elemente in der neupersischen Literatursprache bei Firdosi," *ZII* 4, 1926, pp. 252-316, and P. Tedesco, "Dialektologie der westiranischen Turfantexte," *Monde oriental* 15, 1921, pp. 184-258.

(E. YARSHATER)

viii. AZERI (ĀḎARĪ) TURKISH

Azeri belongs to the Oghuz branch of the Turkic language family. In the eleventh century the "Tūrān" defeated Ērān and a broad wave of Oghuz Turks flooded first Khorasan, then all the rest of Iran, and finally Anatolia, which they made a base for vast conquests. The Oghuz have always been the most important and numerous group of the Turks; in Iran they have assimilated many Turks of other origins and even Iranians.

Oghuz languages were earlier grouped into Turkish (of Turkey), Azeri, and Turkmen, but recent research has modified this simple picture. Today we may provisionally distinguish the following languages: Turkish of Turkey (including Crimean Osmanli and Balkan dialects, such as Gagauz), Azeri, "Afsharoid" dialects (spoken east and south of the provinces of Azerbaijan; there is a broad area of either transitional Azeri-"Afsharoid" dialects or of mixed territories between Qazvīn and Kalajestān, and south of a line Hamadān-Qom, including Qašqāʾī and Aynallū, "Afsharoid" dialects dominate; Afshar is also spoken in Kabul), Khorasan Turkic (northeastern Iran, Turkmenistan and northwestern Afghanistan), and Turkmen (in Turkmenistan, northern Afghanistan and close to the southeastern shore of the Caspian Sea). Some features of Oghuz were described by Maḥmūd Kāšḡarī (11th century), e.g., the sound change *t- > d-* (*dävä* 'camel' = *tävä*, or similar, of other Turkic branches). But it is very difficult to draw a clear line between the East Anatolian dialects of Turkish and Azeri, on the one hand, and between Azeri and "Afsharoid" dialects or even Khorasan Turkic, on the other hand. There is a plethora of transitional phenomena among all Oghuz idioms. Thus one possibility would be to range East Anatolian as Azeri; however, the personal forms of the predicate show clear, and apparently archaic, distinctions among these five groups (Doerfer, 1982, pp. 109-

15). The most distant of the Oghuz dialects is Turkmen; therefore the Iranian designations *torkī* (i.e., all Oghuz dialects except Turkmen) and/versus *torkamānī* (i.e., Turkmen are rather appropriate.

Azeri is spoken in the Soviet Union (above all, in the AzSSR = Azerbaijan Soviet Socialist Republic), Iran (above all, in the northwestern provinces East and West Azerbaijan, but also on the southeastern shore of the Caspian Sea: Galūgāh, 36° 43′ north latitude, 53° 49′ east longitude), and in northern Iraq (e.g., in Kerkuk).

The early Azeri texts are a part of the Old Osmanli literature (the difference between Azeri and Turkish was then extremely small). The oldest poet of the Azeri literature known so far (and indubitably of Azeri, not of East Anatolian of Khorasani, origin) is 'Emād-al-dīn Nasīmī (about 1369-1404, q.v.). Other important Azeri authors were Shah Esmāʿīl Ṣafawī "Ḵaṭāʾī" (1487-1524), and Fożūlī (about 1494-1556, q.v.), an outstanding Azeri poet. During the 17th-20th centuries a rich Azeri literature continued to flourish but classical Persian exercized a great influence on the language and its literary expression. On the other hand, many Azeri words (about 1,200) entered Persian (still more in Kurdish), since Iran was governed mostly by Azeri-speaking rulers and soldiers since the 16th century (Doerfer, 1963-75); these loanwords refer mainly to administration, titles, and conduct of war. This long-lasting Iranian-Azeri symbiosis must be borne in mind if one is to understand the modern history of Iran and its language correctly.

Azeri dialects. We may distinguish the following Azeri dialects (see Širaliev, 1941 and 1947): (1) eastern group: Derbent (Darband), Kuba, Shemakha (Šamāḵī), Baku, Salyani (Salyānī), and Lenkoran (Lankarān), (2) western group: Kazakh (not to be confounded with the Kipchak-Turkic language of the same name), the dialect of the Ayrïm (Āyrom) tribe (which, however, resembles Turkish), and the dialect spoken in the region of the Borchala river; (3) northern group: Zakataly, Nukha, and Kutkashen; (4) southern group: Yerevan (Īravān), Nakhichevan (Naḵjavān), and Ordubad (Ordūbād); (5) central group: Ganja (Kirovabad) and Shusha; (6) North Iraqi dialects; (7) Northwest Iranian dialects: Tabrīz, Reżāʾīya (Urmia), etc., extended east to about Qazvīn; (8) Southeast Caspian dialect (Galūgāh). Optionally, we may adjoin as Azeri (or "Azeroid") dialects; (9) East Anatolian, (10) Qašqāʾī, (11) Aynallū, (12) Sonqorī, (13) dialects south of Qom, (14) Kabul Afšārī.

Modern literary Azeri has been constructed on the basis of the eastern group in the Soviet part of the Azeri area; this does not mean that it is identical with the dialect of Baku. It became the official language of the AzSSR after its establishment in 1936 and many thousand works have been published in this language.

This situation is different in the Azeri-speaking territory of Iran (Doerfer, 1970, p. 226): Very few native, European, or American scholars have worked on the Iranian type of Azeri. Most literary works there are produced in a language which resembles the dialect of the main city, Tabrīz. But the official language is Persian, and a large part of the population is bilingual. The only linguistic studies are some small vocabularies, grammars, and handbooks (for the use of Iranians) composed mostly in the 1960s by native authors (see the bibliography). New efforts at shaping a standard Azeri literary language have been made since the Islamic Revolution. Curiously enough, the most recent Azeri-Persian dictionary (Peyfūn) is based on the language of the AzSSR; the Persian word *īstgāh*, 'railway station', e.g., has been replaced by *vağzal* (< Russian *vokzal* < English Vauxhall).

The script. The older Azeri literature was written in the Arabic alphabet. In North (Soviet) Azerbaijan the Latin alphabet was introduced in 1925, three variants of it were in use, or at least tried out. In 1939 the Latin alphabet was replaced by an alphabet based on the Cyrillic alphabet. Subsequently, five different variants of this system came into use, the fifth in 1958; this means that between 1925-58 nine different writing systems existed (see Ismailova). In South (Iranian) Azerbaijan the Arabic alphabet is still used (Peyfūn, however, distinguishes ö from the other labial vowels by adding a *hamza* to *wāw*).

The language. The linguistic structure of Azeri is very similar to that of Turkish. Therefore, it will be sufficient to characterize the main differences between these languages.

The modern literary language has nine vowels in initial syllables of Turkic words. Like the Anatolian and Khorasani dialects it has preserved the ancient Turkic opposition *ä* ~ *e*, lost in Turkish of Turkey; in most cases *e* is from Old Turkic *e:* Non-initial syllables have vowel harmony, as in Turkish; many dialects, however, show signs of a dissolution of the vowel harmony (e.g., *gäl-max* 'to come' instead of *gäl-mäk*). In consonantism, Azeri shows usual Oghuz features, such as *t-* > *d-*, *k-* > *g-*; but the frequent elision of *y-* before high vowels *i, ï, ü* is peculiar to Azeri (*it-* 'to be lost' < *yit-*, *il* 'year' < *yïl*, *üz* 'face' < *yüz*). A few of the twenty-four Russian letters for Azeri consonants mark allophones, e.g., *g* (front) and *q* (back; only initially; pronounced like Persian *q*), both belonging to the /G/ phoneme; other allophones, such as the back and front *l*, *lenes* and *madiae lenes*, are not distinguished in writing.

Grammatical structure. All the Turkic languages, including Azeri, are highly synthetic, i.e., words are inflected by means of affixes and suffixes (not, e.g., by umlaut and other internal inflection), cf. the typical example *türk-lä-š-dir-äbil-sä-x* 'if we can make (somebody) become like Turks', literally "Turk + verbal derivative (*-lä-*) + cooperative (*-š-*) + causative (*-dir-*) + possibilitive (*-äbil-*) + conditional (*-sä-*) + 1 person plural (*-x*)."

Azeri has many productive and non-productive suffixes both for nominal and verbal derivation. The Azeri literary language has six main cases (dialects show up to ten). Just as the other Turkic languages, Azeri has no special category of pre- or postpositions; instead it uses inflected "space nouns," e.g., *kändin ičindä* 'within the village', literally "village's-inside-its-LOCATIVE;" some of these space nouns are of Persian or Arabic (via Persian) origin; these loans were facilitated by the fact that Persian itself uses such "space nouns" as *tū-ye*, *mīān-e* contrasting with genuine prepositions such as *be*, *dar*. Many dialects have a comparative case form in *-rAx*.

Whereas Azeri nominal morphology, generally speaking, is quite similar to that of Turkish, verbal morphology shows some distinctive features. We may distinguish five diatheses: active, passive, reflexive (nonproductive), reciprocal-cooperative, and causative. Each of them may be positive, negative, or possibilitive; the impossibilitive base form is, in contrast to Turkish, a simple combination of possibilitive + negative. We may distinguish the following "tense" forms: aorist (always in *-Ar*, in contrast to Turkish), present (*-Ir*), future (*-ǰAK*), perfect (*-mIš* ~ *-Ib*, varying in the dialects), preterite (*-dI*), durative present (*-mAkdA*, also *-AdU* and similar forms in the dialects). Furthermore, we may distinguish five moods: indicative, voluntative-imperative (vocative verbal form), optative (*-A*), necessitative (*-mAlI*, *-AsI*), and conditional. From a Turkic point of view, however, there is no structural difference between moods and tenses, cf., *al-a* 'may he take' and *al-mïš* 'he took, he has taken'. It is therefore better to operate with only one category "tense-mood," rather than the two categories "tense" and "mood." Real past tense forms can be formed analytically by adding *(i)di* or *(i)miš* 'was' to the tense-mood forms, e.g., *al-mïš-dï* 'he had taken'.

On the vocabulary see IRANIAN ELEMENTS IN AZERI TURKISH below.

The state of research. Soviet Azeri has been fairly well researched, although as yet no large Azeri dictionary has been produced and the available collections of dialect words are by no means comparable to the Turkish *Derleme sözlüğü* (Ankara, 1963-82, 12 vols.). However, the investigation of other parts of the language: phonology, grammar, etc., is satisfactory.

In contrast, Iranian Azeri is still but poorly known. In 1970, Doerfer stated that there existed at least 1,442 works on Soviet Azeri but only 18 on Iranian Azeri. Nevertheless, the publication of material from several Azeri dialects of Azerbaijan, Ḵalaǰestān, and Galūgāh (as well as quite comprehensive material from Afsharoid and Khorasani Turkic), based upon the Göttingen expeditions of 1968, 1969, and 1973, is planned for the near future.

Bibliography: 1. General works: A. Caferoğlu, "Şarkta ve garpta azeri lehçesi tetkikleri," *Azerbaycan yurt bilgisi* (Istanbul) 3, 1934, pp. 96-102, 136-41, 197-200, 233-38. Idem and G. Doerfer, "Das Aserbaidschanische," *Philologiae Turcicae Fundamenta* 1, Aquis Mattiacis, 1959, pp. 280-307. G. Doerfer, "Irano-Altaistica," in *Current Trends in Linguistics* VI, ed. Th. A. Sebeok, The Hague and Paris, 1970, pp. 217-34. Idem, "Ein türkischer Dialekt aus der Gegend von Hamadān," *Acta Orientalia Hungarica* 36, 1982, pp. 99-124. G. G. Ismailova, "K istorii azerbaĭdzhanskogo alfavita," in *Voprosy sovershenstvovaniya alfavitov tyurkskikh yazykov SSSR*, Moscow, 1972, pp. 28-40. S. Sä'diyev, *Azärbayǰan dilčiliyinä dair ädäbiyyatïn bibliografiyasï* (*Sovet dövrü*), Baku, 1960.

2. Dictionaries: Kh. A. Azizbekov, *Azerbaĭdzhansko-russkiĭ slovar'*, Baku, 1965 (the best available dictionary). G. Doerfer, *Türkische und mongolische Elemente im Neupersischen*, 4 vols., Wiesbaden, 1963-75. G. Guseĭnov, *Russko-azerbaĭdzhanskiĭ slovar'*, 4 vols., Baku, 1960-66. N. Z. Hatämi and M. Š. Širäliyev, *Farsǰa-azärbayǰanǰa danïšïq kitabčasï*, Baku, 1983. H. H. Hüseynov, *Azärbayǰanǰa-rusǰa lüğät*, Baku, 1941. M. J̌avadova, *Šah Ismayïl Xätainin leksikasï*, Baku, 1977. J̌. M. J̌äfärov, *Almanǰa-azärbayǰanǰa lüğät*, (*Deutsch-aserbaidschanisches Wörterbuch*), Baku, 1971 (the best available non-Russian-Azeri dictionary). Yu. Mirbabaev et. al., *Kratkiĭ persidsko-russko-azerbaĭdzhanskiĭ slovar'*, Baku, 1945. Ä. Ä. Oruǰov, *Azärbayǰan dilinin orfografiya lüğäti*, Baku, 1975. Idem, *Azärbayǰan dilinin izahlï lüğäti*, 3 vols., Baku, 1964-83. Idem, *Russko-azerbaĭdzhanskiĭ slovar'*, 3 vols., Baku, 1971-78. Ä. N. Orudzhov, S. D. Melikov, and A. A. Efendiev, *Russko-azerbaĭdzhanskiĭ slovar'*, 2 vols., Baku, 1956-59. J̌. Qährämanov, *Näsimi divanïnïn leksikasï*, Baku, 1970. R. Ä. Rüstämov and M. Š. Širäliyev, *Azärbayǰan dilinin dialektoloži lüğäti*, Baku, 1964. H. Zärinäzadä, *Fars dilindä azärbayǰan sözläri*, Baku, 1962.

3. Grammars: Z. Budagova, *Azerbaĭdzhanskiĭ yazyk* (*kratkiĭ ocherk*), Baku, 1982. Idem, *Müasir azärbayǰan dili* II: *Morfologiya*, Baku, 1980. G. Fraenkel, *A Generative Grammar of Azerbaijani*, doctoral thesis, Indiana University, Bloomington, 1962 (Dissertation abstracts XXIII, 1963). N. Z. Gadzhieva, "Azerbaĭdzhanskiĭ yazyk," in *Yazyki narodov SSSR* II: *Tyurkskie yazyki*, Moscow, 1966, pp. 66-90. R. Ä. Rüstämov, *Grammatika azerbaĭdzhanskogo yazyka*, 2 vols., Baku, 1959-60. M. Š. Širäliev and Ė. V. Sevortyan, *Grammatika azerbaĭdzhanskogo yazyka*, Baku, 1971.

4. Linguistic studies: Ä. Z. Abdullaev, *Müasir azärbayǰan dilindä tabeli müräkkäb ǰümlälär*, 2 vols., Baku, 1964-74. N. G. Agazade, *Sistema glagol'nykh naklonenii v sovremennom azerbaĭdzhanskom literaturnom yazyke*, Baku, 1967. Ehliman Ahundov, ed. with a foreword by Semih Tezcan, *Azerbaycan halk yazını örnekleri*, Ankara, 1978 (this contains interesting texts with a concise linguistic introduction and dictionary). A. Axundov, *Azärbayǰan dilinin fonemlär sistemi*, Baku, 1973. Idem, *Azärbayǰan dilinin tarixi fonetikasï*, Baku, 1973. A. K. Alekperov, *Fonematicheskaya sistema sovremennogo azerbaĭdzhanskogo yazyka*, Baku, 1971. Z. Älizadä, *Müasir azärbayǰan dilindä modal sözlär*, Baku, 1965. Z. I. Budagova, *Müasir azärbayǰan ädäbi dilindä sadä ǰümlä*, Baku, 1963. Ä. M. Dämirčizadä, *Müasir azärbayǰan dilinin fonetikasï*, Baku, 1960. Idem, *Azärbayǰan ädäbi dilinin tarixi*, Baku, 1979. A. Djaferoglu, "75 azärbaj-

ğanische Lieder 'Bajatv' in der Mundart von Gänǰä, nebst einer sprachlichen Erklärung," *Mitteilungen des Seminars für Orientalische Sprachen zu Berlin, Westasiatische Studien* 32, 1929, pp. 55-79; 33, 1930, pp. 105-29. N. Z. Gadzhieva, *Sintaksis slozhnopodchinennogo predlozheniya v azerbaĭdzhanskom yazyke*, Moscow, 1963. M. Hüseynzadä, *Müasir azärbayǰan dili*, Baku, 1963. R. J̌. Mähärrämova and M. P. J̌ahangirov, *Azärbayǰan dilinin tarixi sintaksisinä dair materiallar*, Baku, 1962, H. Mirzäzadä, *Azärbayǰan dilinin tarixi morfologiyasï*, Baku, 1962. Idem, *Azärbayǰan dilinin tarixi grammatikasïna aid materiallar*, Baku, 1953. M. Rähimov, *Azärbayǰan dilindä fe'l šäkillärinin formalašmasï tarixi*, Baku, 1965. R. Ä. Rüstämov, *Azärbayǰan dili dialekt vä šivälärindä fe'l*, Baku, 1965 (important work). È. V. Sevortyan, *Affiksy glagoloobrazovaniya v azerbaĭdzhanskom yazyke*, Moscow, 1962 (important work). Idem, *Affiksy imennogo slovoobrazovaniya v azerbaĭdzhanskom yazyke*, Moscow, 1966 (important work). Z. N. Verdieva et al., *Azärbayǰan dilinin semasiologiyasï*, Baku, 1979.

5. Dialects: M. Amirpur-Ahrandjani, *Der aserbaidschanische Dialekt von Schapur, Phonologie und Morphologie*, Freiburg, 1971. N. I. Ashmarin, *Obshchiĭ obzor narodnykh tyurkskikh govorov gor Nukhi*, Baku, 1926. S. Buluç, "Tellâfer Türkçesi üzerine," *Türk dili araştırmaları yıl'lığı, Belleten*, 1973-74, pp. 49-57. Idem, "Kerkük ḫoyratlarına dair," *Reşit Rahmeti Arat için*, Ankara, 1966, pp. 142-54. G. Doerfer, "Zum Vokabular eines aserbaidschanischen Dialektes in Zentralpersien," in *Voprosy tyurkologii*, Baku, 1971, pp. 33-62. V. T. Dzhangidze, *Dmanisskiĭ govor kazakhskogo dialekta azerbaĭdzhanskogo yazyka*, Baku, 1965. Dj. B. Hadjibeyli, "Le dialecte et le folk-lore du Karabagh," *JA* 222, 1933, pp. 31-144. Hussin Shahbaz Hassan, *Kerkük ağzı*, dissertation, Istanbul, 1979. Choban Khıdır Haydar, *İrak türkmen ağızları*, dissertation, Istanbul, 1979. A. Hüseynov, *Azärbayǰan dialektologiyasï*, Baku, 1958. M. Islamov, *Azärbayǰan dilinin Nuxa dialekti*, Baku, 1968. V. Monteil, "Sur le dialecte turc de l'Azerbâydjân iranien," *JA* 244, 1956, pp. 1-77. K. T. Ramazanov, *Azärbayǰan dilinin Muğan grupu šivä-läri*, Baku, 1955. Idem, *Azärbayǰan dilinin Naxčïvan grupu dialekt vä šiväläri*, Baku, 1962. H. Ritter, "Azerbaidschanische Texte zur nordpersischen Volkskunde," *Der Islam* 11, 1921, pp. 181-212; 25, 1939, pp. 234-68. R. Ä. Rüstämov, *Guba dialekti*, Baku, 1961. Idem and M. Š. Širäliev, *Azärbayǰan dilinin qärb grupu dialekt vä šiväläri* 1, Baku, 1967. M. Š. Širäliev, "K voprosu ob izuchenii i klassifikatsii azerbaĭdzhanskikh dialektov," *Izvestiya azerbaĭdzhanskogo filiala Akademii Nauk SSSR*, 1941, 4. Idem, "Izuchenie dialektov azerbaĭdzhanskogo yazyka," *Izvestiya Akademii Nauk SSSR* 4, 1947, pp. 431-36. Idem, *Azärbayǰan dialektologiyasï*, 2 pts., Baku, 1942-43. Idem, *Bakï dialekti*, Baku, 2nd ed., 1957. Idem, *Azärbayǰan dilinin Naxčïvan grupu dialekt vä šiväläri*, Baku, 1962. Idem, *Azärbayǰan dialektologiyasïnïn äsaslarï*, Baku, 1962 (indispensable description of Azeri dialects). H. S. Szapszal, *Próby literatury ludowej Turków Azerbajdżanu perskiego*, Kraków, 1935. S. Taliphanbeyli, "Karabağ-Istanbul şivelerinin savtiyet cihetinden mukayesesi," *Azerbaycan yurt bilgisi* 2, 1933, pp. 23-41, 65-71, 212-19, 380-85.

6. Manuals: Fr. W. Householder, with M. Lotfi, *Basic Course in Azerbaijani*, Bloomington and The Hague, 1965 (excellent practical introduction). C. G. Simpson, *The Turkish Language of Soviet Azerbaijan*, Oxford, 1957.

7. Important older works: K. Foy, "Azerbajğanische Studien mit einer Charakteristik des Südtürkischen," *Mitteilungen des Seminars für Orientalische Sprachen zu Berlin, Westasiatische Studien* 6, 1903, pp. 126-93; 7, 1904, pp. 197-265. A. Kazembek, *Obshchaya grammatika turetsko-tatarskago yazyka*, 2nd ed., Kazan', 1846. L. Lazarev, *Turetsko-tatarsko-russkiĭ slovar', s prilozheniem kratkoĭ grammatiki*, Moscow, 1846. D. F. M. Maggio, *Syntagma linguarum orientalium, quae in Georgiae regionibus audiuntur, liber secundus, complectens Arabum et Turcarum orthographiam et turcicae linguae institutiones*, Rome, 1643 (2nd ed., 1670).

8. Selected studies in Persian: anonymous, *K̲ʿodāmūz-e torkī yā mokālamāt-e rūz-marra-ye zabān-e torkī*, Tabrīz, 1339 Š./1960. M. A. Farzāna, *Mabānī-e dastūr-e zabān-e Ād̲arbāyǰān*, Tabrīz, 1344 Š./1965. S. J̌āvīd, *K̲ʿodāmūz-e zabān-e ād̲arbāyǰānī wa fārsī*, Tehran, 1343 Š./1964. ʿA. Kārang, *Dastūr-e zabān-e konūnī-e Ād̲arabāyǰān*, Tabrīz, 1340 Š./1961. M. Moğdam, *Gūyešhā-ye Vafs o Āštīān*, Tehran, 1318 Y./1949. M. Peyfūn, *Farhang-e ād̲arbāyǰānī-fārsī*, Tehran, 1361 Š./1982 (based on Soviet Azeri material). M. R. Šeʿār, *Bah̲t̲-ī dar bāra-ye zabān-e Ād̲arbāyǰān*, Tabrīz, 1346 Š./1967. M. T. Z. (*sic*), *Iran türkčäsinin ṣärfi*, n.p., 1355 Š./1976.

See also D. Sinor, *Introduction à l'étude de l'Eurasie Centrale*, Wiesbaden, 1963, pp. 62-64. J. Benzing, *Einführung in das Studium der altaischen Philologie und der Turkologie*, Wiesbaden, 1953, pp. 90-93.

(G. DOERFER)

ix. IRANIAN ELEMENTS IN AZERI TURKISH

Azeri is, perhaps after Uzbek, the Turkic language upon which Iranian has exerted the strongest impact—mainly in phonology, syntax and vocabulary, less in morphology. Much of the Iranian interference is also present, albeit less strongly in other Turkic languages, e.g., Ottoman Turkish, but many features are specific to Azeri. The strong Iranian influence upon Oghuz Turkic began already in Central Asia. Since Persian Azerbaijan had been Iranian-speaking long before the Turkic immigration, there has been a thorough sub- and adstrative Iranian impact upon dialects of the area: some of them, such as Aynallū and Qašqā'ī (though these are sometimes classified as non-Azeri idioms), are particularly strongly Iranized. Furthermore, Persian as the culturally dominant language played a superstrative—or "roofing"—role which is obvious still today in southern Azerbaijan with its lack of linguistic standardization and long-standing general bilingualism.

Though generally recognized the Iranian influence on Azeri has not yet been investigated. For proper research in this field more information is required not only about different variants of Azeri but also about the local Iranian dialects of the contact regions, such as Tati and Ṭālеši.

Phonology. There is considerable interference at the phonological level. For example, all Azeri dialects spoken in Iran display phonotactic perturbations, partly due to Iranian influence. Especially affected is the Turkic sound harmony, although less than in Uzbek. We find, e.g., non-harmonic, i.e., invariable suffixes like *-max* (infinitive suffix): *bil-max* 'to know', etc. This and other similar phenomena are usually explained as results of Iranization, i.e., a break-down of vowel harmony and a tendency to neutralize vowels and pronounce them centrally. However, not all deviations from the vowel harmony rules of Standard Turkish can be attributed to external factors.

Another exception to a common Turkic phonotactic tendency, heard mainly in educated speech, is the simplification of consonant clusters. Thus, [*fikr*] 'thought' is heard instead of the integrated form [*fikir*], etc.

In phonetics there are several examples of presumably Iranian influence:

Vocalism. A tendency (also known in 'Iranized' Turkic dialects of Central Asia) towards a fronted pronunciation of vowels, e.g., the shift of *a* > *ä* (K. Foy, 1903, p. 185). Accordingly, the short *a* in Arabic and Persian loanwords is rendered as a front vowel more often than in Turkish even in the neighborhood of emphatic and dorso-velar consonants, e.g., *bäxt* 'happiness' (Turkish *baht*). The tendency may be valid also for the unrounded high vowels. Even if, as in Uzbek, New Uigur, etc., the phonetic distance between the front *i* and the back *ï* has been diminished, the phonological opposition is still maintained. (Gagauz and Karaim similarly have a fronted pronunciation of Common Turkic *ï* under Slavic influence.) In several Azeri dialects, *ï* is pronounced with the tongue slightly more advanced than in Turkish. However, this phenomenon is difficult to diagnose in terms of interference, since it is observed also in Kipchak languages (Kazakh, Karakalpak, and Tatar). There are also reasons to suppose the existence of a neutral *schwa* in some Azeri dialects; M. V. Monteil mentions a sound "à peu près l'*e* fermé persan," e.g., *mäne* 'me', *ade* 'his name' (instead of *mäni, adï*; cf. L. Johanson, 1978-79).

The tendency towards front pronunciation is also manifest in the shift of *yï-* > *i-* in words like *ilan* 'snake' (Turkish *yïlan*). The southern dialects show strongly palatalized forms of *k*, *g* and *l*, e.g., [*ćöć*] for Common Turkic *kök* 'root'. Thus, in spite of 'disturbances' of the vowel system, the basic syllabic palatal correlation is maintained also in Azeri dialects.

The relatively open pronunciation of *ä* approaches that of Persian *a*. According to L. Ligeti's observations, "cette voyelle azéri cherche toujours à se conformer, du moins en Perse et en Afghanistan, à la prononciation de l'*a* persan (ou tadjik) local" (1957, p. 114). In some Azeri dialects, as in Uzbek, the long *a:* is more or less rounded, e.g., [*yå:d*] 'memory'. Typically Turkic vowels alien to Persian are sometimes replaced by more familiar sounds, i.e., *ö* > *o*, *ü* > *u* (M. Širäliyev, 1968, pp. 43f.), in non-initial syllables *ï* > *u*, etc. It is still an open question whether in some dialects remnants of Turkic vowel quantity oppositions have been preserved under the influence of the Persian long vowels. Whereas Turkish shows an aversion against Persian *ow* (< *aw*), this diphthong occurs frequently in Azeri (as well as Turkmen) dialects. Parallel to the Persian development *ow* < *aw*, even in native Turkic words low vowels are labialized in front of a labial element: *aw* > *ow* (often > *o:*), e.g., *dowšan* or *do:šan* 'rabbit' (< **taβïšγa:n*, cf. Turkish *tavšan*).

Consonantism. An Iranian feature in the consonantism is the palatalization of certain consonants (notably *k*, *g*, *l*) mentioned above. As in Turkman and many Anatolian dialects, there is a regular substitution of the un-Persian fortis *q*: initially by voicing, e.g., *gal-* 'to remain', *guš* 'bird', non-initially usually by spirantization, e.g., *yaxïn* 'near', *yatax* 'bed'. (In Standard Azeri the latter change is restricted to the first syllable boundary.) Azeri, as Persian, but contrary to modern Turkish, has boh [*x*] and [*h*]. There is no resistance to *z* (with substitution by *g*, as in some other Turkic languages). Initial fricative *γ-*, which does not occur in Turkish, is accepted to some extent, essentially in educated speech: *γeyrät* 'zeal' (cf. Turkish *gayrät*), etc. The un-Turkic sound *f* is not only accepted in loanwords (*häftä* 'week' against Kazakh *apta*), but also replaces native *p* in some dialects: e.g., *if* 'thread'. (This phonetical development is also met with in Turkmen and Uzbek dialects.)

Suprasegmental features. In some dialects a special intonation pattern at the end of yes/no-questions, possibly due to Iranian influence, replaces the interrogative particle *mI*.

Morphology. Iranian derivational suffixes found in Azeri are *-baz*, *-dan*, *-dar*, *-i*, *-kar*, *-keš*, *-päräst*, *-stan*, and *-xana*, etc. Iranian prefixes such as *bi-* ~ *be-* and *na-* still play a rôle in word-formation. (All these elements were frequent in Ottoman Turkish but have now been largely abandoned.) The copula of the first person singular *-(y)Am* is usually explained as influenced by the corresponding Persian personal ending *-am*. Optatives like *al-a-m* 'I (may) take' resemble in their structure the Persian subjunctive (present stem + personal endings, e.g. *bar-am* 'I take'). The Persian perfect of the type *āmada* (*ast*) 'he has come' (past participle [+ copula]) may have corroborated the use of *-(U)b(dUr)* as the usual perfect form among the Turks of Iran. (For the various perfect forms, see M. Širäliyev, 1967, pp. 213-20.) Sonqori, Aynallū and Qašqā'ī (possibly not classifiable as Azeri dialects) use Persian *-tar* as a comparative suffix, e.g., Aynallū *yektär* 'better'. Iranian may also have influenced the aspect and temporal values, notably of the perfect forms, which function very much like the Persian perfect tense, e.g., *yazmïšam* "I have written', *gälibsän* "you have arrived'. (For Azeri and Turkish *-mIš*, see L. Johanson, *Aspect im Türkischen*, Mainz, 1971, pp. 289f.).

Syntax. The impact of Iranian on Azeri syntax is particularly clear in the structure of complex sentences, especially in the sociolects of the educated. (Note that most of the features concerned occurred more frequently in Ottoman but have been given up in modern Standard Turkish; some subsist as substandard varieties.) There is a sort of replica syntax: Imitations of Indo-european language-type subordinative constructions are used instead of Turkic, left-branching, constructions, in which the subordinated elements are more or less expanded sentence constituents, morphologically based on verbal nouns, participles, and gerunds, cf. *Bilirsänmi män kimäm*? 'Do you know who I am?' (instead of *Mänim kim olduγumu bilirsänmi?*); *Heč kim dinmirdi, ondan ötrü ki, hamïnïn bu išdän xäbäri var idi* (Mirzä Ibrahimov) 'No one said anything, because everyone knew about this affair' (instead of *Hamïnïn bu išdän xäbär olduγu üčün heč kim dinmirdi*). As in Ottoman and Chaghatay, Persian subordinative conjunctions, alien to Turkic sentence structure, are widely used, particularly *ki*, which appears as a connective device between sentences of different kinds, e.g., *Görmüšäm ki, onlar xošbäxt olublar* 'I have seen that they have become happy' (instead of *Onlarïn xošbäxt oldugларïnï görmüšäm*); *Bir ata ki, bu išlär ilä mäšγul olan, onun oγlu da išgüzar olar* 'Also the son of a father who occupies himself with these things becomes skilful' (instead of *Bu išlär ilä mäšγul olan atanïn oγlu da išgüzar olar*); *Sizin väzifäniz budur ki, tä'lim veräsiz* 'It is your duty to teach' (instead of *Sizin väzifeniz, tä'lim vermäkdir*); *Män istärdim ki, sän gälsän* 'I would like you to come' (instead of *Sänin gälmäyini istärdim*); *Atasï ona pul verir ki, o gedä bilsin* 'His father gives him money in order that he may be able to go' (instead of *O, gedä bilsin deyä, atasï ona pul verir*); *Kitabï ačïrdïm ki, gapï döyüldü* 'I was just opening the book as there was a knock at the door' (instead of *Kitabï ačdïgda gapï döyüldü*). Like the Iranian subjunctive the optative is often used as a sort of subordinative mood.

Several conjunctions (and/or connective adverbs) of Persian origin are used even in Standard Azeri, e.g., *ägär* 'if', *čünki* 'for', *gah . . . gah* 'now . . . now', *häm* 'also', *hämčinin* 'also', *härčänd* 'although', *härgah* 'if', *nä . . . nä* 'neither . . . nor', *näinki* 'not only', *yainki* 'or', *yaxud* 'or', *zira* 'for'. However, both these and conjunctions of Arabic origin occur frequently only in educated speech. Other frequent adverbs, modal words, and particles are *bäli* 'yes', *bälkä* 'perhaps', *bäs* 'well', *hä* 'yes', *hämišä* 'always', *mägär* 'really', etc.

Lexicon. The Iranian elements in Azeri are especially numerous at the lexical level. Azeri posesses a large number of Iranian loanwords missing or rarely used in Turkish (*asan* 'easy', *bar* 'fruit', *ǰavan* 'young', *čäp* 'crooked', *girdä* 'round', *huš* 'consciousness', *kar* 'deaf', *köhnä* 'old', *küčä* 'street', *mis* 'copper', *payïz* 'autumn, fall', *šänbä* 'Saturday', *turš* 'sour', etc.); idioms, e.g., *xahiš ediräm* 'please', *güzäšt elä* 'excuse me', *xudahafiz* 'good-bye'; numerous calques in phraseology (*xoš gäl-* 'to please', coined on Persian *xoš āmadan*, etc.); morphological contaminations as *tanïš ol-* 'to know' = *tanï-*, cf. Persian *dāneš* 'knowledge'. Some indefinite pronouns are of Persian origin, e.g., *hämin* 'the same', *här* 'every', *här käs* 'everyone', *heč* 'any'. It must be left to further research to sort out the different layers of elements borrowed in the course of the long Irano-Turkic symbiosis. There may be some phonetic criteria, e.g., the *majhūl* vowel in forms like *dost* 'friend' (Modern Persian *dūst* < *dōst*) points to an early date of borrowing, whereas *ruzi* 'daily bread' (cf. Persian *rūzī* < *rōzī*) is a relatively late loanword.

The quantity of Iranian lexical elements differs significantly in the various forms of Azeri. Persian is more dominant in written than in spoken Azeri; the dominance is also more evident in the language of the educated. As for the innovatory vocabulary, northern Azeri often prefers Russian loanwords (e.g., *vaγzal* 'railway station'), where southern Azeri chooses Persian ones or accepts European words through the intermediary of Persian or Turkish (e.g., *istgah, gar, istasyon*). Since, for several decades, there has been little, if any, cultural exchange between the two parts of Azerbaijan, the mutual intelligibility is decreasing. Whereas in Soviet Azerbaijan, the puristic efforts have yielded considerable results, the Azerbaijani language of Iran, through school education and the growing influence of Persian mass media, remains very dependent upon Persian.

Bibliography: As G. Doerfer remarks in "Irano-Altaistica: Turkish and Mongolian Languages of Persia and Afghanistan" (in Th. A. Sebeok, ed., *Current Trends in Linguistics* VI, The Hague, 1970, pp. 217-34), there are "only sporadic remarks about the influence of Iranian on the Irano-Altaic languages." (For details, see the bibliography added to Doerfer's article.) A basic work on Azeri of Persian Azerbaijan is K. Foy: "Azerbajğanische Studien mit einer Charakteristik des Südtürkischen," *Mitteilungen des Seminars für Orientalische Sprachen zu Berlin, Westasiatische Studien* 6, 1903, pp. 126-94; 7, 1904, pp. 197-265. Important remarks are found in T. Kowalski, *Sir Aurel Stein's Sprachaufzeichnungen im Äinallu-Dialekt aus Südpersien*, Kraków, 1939; L. Ligeti: "Sur la langue des Afchars d'Afghanistan," *Acta Orientalia Hungarica* 7, 1957, pp. 110-56; V. Monteil: "Sur le dialecte turc de l'Azerbâydjân iranien," *JA* 244, 1956, pp. 1-77. General problems of Iranian influence are treated in K. H. Menges, "Indo-European Influences on Ural-Altaic Languages," *Word* 1, 1933, pp. 188-93. See also L. Johanson: "Die westoghusische Labialharmonie," *Orientalia Suecana* 27-28, 1978-79, pp. 63-107 and "Reproduktion, Widerstand und Anpassung: Zur lautlichen

Iranisierung im Türkischen," in R. Schmitt and P. O. Skjærvø, eds., *Studia Grammatica Iranica. Festschrift für Helmut Humbach*, Munich, 1986, pp. 185-201. Y. Z. Širvani, *Äräb vä fars sözläri lüγäti*, Baku, 1967. A standard work on Azerbaijani dialectology is M. Širäliyev, *Azärbayǰan dialektologiyasïnïn äsaslarï*, Baku, 1967. See also G. Windfuhr, *Persian Grammar*, The Hague, Paris, and New York, 1979, pp. 188-89.

(L. Johanson)

x. Azeri Literature in Iran

The language spoken today in Azerbaijan is one of the branches of Oghuz Turkic. It was introduced into Iran by Turks entering the area in the 5th/11th and 6th/12th centuries and underwent a gradual development before assuming its present form. For two centuries after their appearance in Iran, the Oghuz Turks seem to have had only an oral literature. The origins of the stories attributed to Dädä Qorqut, which are about the heroic age of the Oghuz Turks, probably lie back in this period. The accepted text, however, was compiled only in the 9th/15th century. A written, classical Azeri literature began after the Mongol invasion, and developed strongly in the 10th/16th century after the Safavid dynasty established its dominance in Iran. From the beginning it was under the strong impact of Persian letters. Many poets produced works in both Persian and Azeri and, due to bilingualism among the educated Turkic-speaking people of the area, the use of Azeri prose was widespread until the reign of Reżā Shah Pahlavī (1304-20 Š./1925-41), when publishing in Azeri was banned.

The history of Azeri literature in Iranian Azerbaijan can be divided into four main periods:

1) From the 7th/13th century to 1243/1828 when, as a result of the defeat suffered by Iran in the Perso-Russian wars (q.v.), a number of regions north of Azerbaijan, where Azeri was spoken, were ceded to Russia (now Azerbaijan Soviet Socialist Republic).

2) From 1243/1828 to the mid- 1300s Š./1920s, when the Soviets and the Pahlavi dynasty came to power in Russia and Iran. This includes the Constitutional era (1324-44/1906-25).

3) The Pahlavi era (1304-57 Š./1925-79) when, except for a brief period from 1941 to 1946 when the country was occupied by the Allied forces, the ban on Azeri publications was in effect and the official use of the language discouraged in Iran. Furthermore, because of the change of alphabet in Soviet Azerbaijan and due to that region's being in the Soviet bloc, communication between the two Azerbaijans became more difficult. Only a few audacious poets managed to get some of their works secretly printed.

4) From the advent of the revolution of 1357 Š./1979 to the present. Though the desire of some fervent Azerbaijanis to make Azeri their official language has not been fulfilled, there is no longer a ban on Azeri publications in Iran, and more than 200 works in Azeri have appeared.

It was in the 7th/13th and 8th/14th centuries that a stylized poetry began to develop, partly due to Eastern Turkic traditions brought from Khorasan during the Mongol occupation. An example is the poetry of Khorasani Shaikh ʿEzz-al-dīn Esfarāʾīnī, known as Ḥasanoğlū or Pūr(-e) Ḥasan (late 7th/13th and early 8th/14th century), two of whose Turkic and Persian *ğazal*s have survived (cf. J. Heyat, *Azerbaijan ädäbiyat tarixinä bir baxiš*, Tehran, 1979, p. 26). Two poets of the 8th/14th century, Qāżī Aḥmad Borhān-al-dīn (an East Anatolian) and the Hurufi ʿEmād-al-dīn Nasīmī played significant roles in the development of Azeri poetry. It is said that Nasīmī was originally from Šīrvān and, coming to Tabrīz, met Fażlallāh Naʿīmī who converted him to Hurufism. He was put to death in Aleppo around 810/1407 because of his fervent propagation of the Hurufi beliefs. The influence of Rūmī, Neẓāmī Ganǰavī, and Shaikh ʿAṭṭār is noticeable in his poetry, and he mentions Ḥāfeẓ in his Persian *Dīvān*. Another bilingual Azeri poet, one whose Persian poetry takes precedence over his Azeri, is Moʿīn-al-dīn ʿAlī Shah Qāsem-e Anwār (b. 757/1356 in Sarāb, educated in Tabrīz). He was a pupil of Shaikh Ṣadr-al-dīn Mūsā b. Shaikh Ṣafī-al-dīn Ardabīlī, and established his Sufi order in Herat under the Timurid Šāhrok̲. Shah Qāsem-e Anwār wrote *ğazals*, *molammaʿ*s, and *tuyuğs* in a simple Azeri (see M. Fuad Köprülü, "Azerî edebiyatının tekâmülü," in *İA* II, p. 131a). There are also a few poems in Azeri by ʿAbd-al-Qāder Marāğī, a man known essentially as a musical composer (Köprülü, loc. cit.). The 9th/15th century saw the beginning of a more important period in Azeri cultural history. The position of the literary language was reinforced under the Qara Qoyunlūs (1400-68), who had their capital in Tabrīz. J̌ahān Shah (r. 841-72/1438-68) himself wrote lyrical poems in Azeri using the pen name of Ḥaqīqī. He sent his *Dīvān* of Persian and Azeri poems to ʿAbd-al-Raḥmān J̌āmī, who praised their form as well as their content (see J. Heyat, op. cit., p. 31).

Another poet-ruler of great significance is Shah Esmāʿīl I (892-930/1487-1524), founder of the Safavid dynasty, who established Shiʿism as the state religion of Iran. The strong adherence of the Turks of Azerbaijan to Shiʿism was among the factors that were to weaken their ties with the rest of the Turkic world, giving Azeri literature a local identity and restricting it to Azerbaijan and the area just north of it (now Soviet Azerbaijan). Writing with the pen name of K̲aṭāʾī, Shah Esmāʿīl declared his own devotion to ʿAlī and his family in passionately ecstatic *ğazals*. His *dīvān* also includes *robāʿī*s and *maṯnawī*s and a didactic "*Naṣīḥat-nāma*." His *Dah-nāma* (Ten letters; comp. 911/1506), a *maṯnawī* of more than 1,400 distichs, contains ten love letters exchanged between the lover (i.e., the poet) and his beloved. The poetry of Shah Esmāʿīl shows the influence of the folk poetry and the *ʿāšeq* (q.v.) style.

Among the Azeri poets of the 9th/15th century mention should be made of K̲aṭāʾī Tabrīzī. He wrote a *maṯnawī* entitled *Yūsof wa Zoleyk̲ā*, and dedicated it to the Āq Qoyunlū Sultan Yaʿqūb (r. 883-96/1478-90), who himself wrote poetry in Azeri. The most important poet of this period is Ḥabībī. He was the poet laureate of Shah Esmāʿīl but in 1514, when the Ottoman army occupied Tabrīz, he went to Turkey and died in Istanbul in 925/1519. Another Sufi poet is Shaikh Alvan of Shiraz who translated the *Golšan-e rāz* of Shaikh Maḥmūd Šabestarī into Azeri verse.

The reigns of Shah Esmāʿīl and his son Ṭahmāsb (r. 930-84/1524-86) are considered the most brilliant period in the history of Azeri language and literature at this stage of its development. The great poet Moḥammad b. Solaymān Fożūlī of Baghdad (ca. 885-963/1480-1556; q.v.), who wrote in Turkish, Persian, and Arabic, played an important role in the development of Azeri poetry in Iran. As F. Köprülü has pointed out ("Fuzûlî," in *İA* IV, p. 697), very few Turkish poets had the far-reaching influence that Fożūlī had on later generations. One of his followers was Moḥammad Amānī (d. ca. 951/1544-45), whose work is also a useful historical source, as he took an active part in Safavid campaigns. He wrote poems in both the classical and popular *ʿāšeq* style and provided the first examples of Azeri narrative verse with a religious content (*Ḥātem wa Ǧarīb*, *ʿAlī wa šīr*; see A. Caferoğlu, "Die aserbeidschanische Literatur," in *Philologiae Turcicae Fundamenta*, Aquis Mattiacis (Wiesbaden), 1964, II, p. 645). Another disciple of the Fożūlī school is Ṣādeqī Afšār (b. 939/1532), the author of a *taḏkera* entitled *Majmaʿ al-ḵawāṣṣ*, which was modeled on Amir ʿAlī Šīr Navāʾī's *Majāles al-nafāʾes* and written in Chaghatai Turkish (see ʿA. R. Ḵayyāmpūr, tr., *Taḏkera-ye majmaʿ al-ḵawāṣṣ*, Tabrīz, 1327 Š./1948). In this work, Ṣādeqī deals not only with Azeri poets, but also with Chaghatai and Ottoman poets and writers. Among the Safavid poets mentioned in the *taḏkera*s reference should be made to Qāżī ʿAbdallāh Ḵoʾī, Kalb(-e) ʿAlī Tabrīzī and Yaʿqūb Ardabīlī.

There was also considerable development in the popular literature, especially *bayātī*s (four-lined poems) and long narrative poems. The best-known folk poem of the period, *Koroğlï dästanï*, reflects the resentment of the people against the tyrannical rulers of the time. Other ballad-like compositions such as *Šāh Esmāʿīl*, *ʿĀšeq ǧarīb*, and *Aṣlī wa Karam* are accounts of romantic love and heroic deeds. Qorbānī is considered the foremost *ʿāšeq* of this century (see A. Caferoğlu, op. cit., pp. 646f.). Finally, an interesting document related to folk literature in this period is a short work by Rūḥī Anārjānī (from a village near Tabrīz). The writer gives a humorous account of conversations between various common people in Tabrīz. These are not in Azeri, Turkish, but in the old Persian dialect of Azerbaijan, showing that during the reign of Shah ʿAbbās I (996-1038/1587-1629) bilingualism was prevalent in Azerbaijan (see above, Azerbaijan vii).

In the 11th/17th century, although the transfer of the capital to Isfahan favored Persian at the court, Azeri poetry in the style of Fożūlī and the Chaghatai poet Navāʾī still flourished. ʿAlījān Esmāʿīloğlū Qawsī Tabrīzī (born in Tabrīz and educated in Isfahan), was an important poet who combined classical refinement with the candor of popular poetry. Rokn-al-dīn Masʿūd Masīḥī (d. 1656), was a musician and poet who wrote three romantic *maṯnawī*s—*Dām wa dāna*, *Zanbūr-e ʿasal*, and *Varqa wa Golšāh*. The last was modeled on a Persian work of the same name by ʿAyyūqī (q.v.). In addition to his Persian works, the great poet of the period Mīrzā Moḥammad-ʿAlī Ṣāʾeb Tabrīzī (d. Isfahan, 1081/1670) wrote 17 *ǧazal*s and *molammaʿ*s in his native Azeri (see T. Yazıcı, "Sâib," in *İA* X, pp. 75-77).

Shah ʿAbbās II (r. 1052-77/1642-66; q.v.) was himself a poet, writing Turkic verse with the pen name of Ṯānī. In the same century Ṭarzī Afšār, who was from Ray, wrote a small *dīvān* of humorous poems in a mixture of Persian and Azeri. This type of poetry, known as *tarzilik*, became quite popular at the Isfahan court for a while. The poets Darūnī and Mīrza Moḥsen Taʾṯīr were natives of Tabrīz, their families having migrated to Isfahan in the reign of Shah ʿAbbās I. Moḥsen Taʾṯīr became a notable courtier and poet at the courts of Shah Solaymān (r. 1077-1105/1667-94) and Shah Sultan Ḥosayn (r. 1105-35/1694-1722), devoting most of his Turkish and Persian poetry to eulogy of the imams. This was a practice greatly encouraged by the Safavid kings. Other Azeri poets of the period include Reżā-qolī Khan, the governor of Bandar ʿAbbās, Mīrzā Jalāl Šahrestānī, Mīrzā Ṣāleḥ, the Šayḵ-al-eslām of Tabrīz, Waḥīdī Tabrīzī, the historian of ʿAbbās II, and lastly Mālek Beg "Awjī," who was influenced by Fożūlī and Ṣāʾeb.

Due to political events, the 12th/18th century was a period of decline in the Azeri literature of Azerbaijan. In the north, however, the forerunners of modern Azeri literature, Mollā Panāh Wāqef (1717-97) and Wadādī (1709-1809), were active. In fact, a contrast is seen in this period in that whereas bilingualism continues to be practiced in Azerbaijan, writing is almost exclusively in Azeri in the north. In general the time from the fall of the Safavids (1135/1722) to the end of the century is a period of stagnation in Azerbaijan. However, there is an abundant Shiʿite literature, especially elegies and *taʿzīa* poems. Well-known authors of such dirges are Neẓām-al-dīn Moḥammad Dehḵāraqānī (d. 1756), Sayyed Fattāḥ Ešrāq Marāǧī (d. 1175/1761-62), and Ḥājjī Ḵodāverdī Tāʾeb Ḵoʾī (d. 1201/1786). Other poets of this period include Mīrzā ʿAbd-al-Razzāq Našʾa Tabrīzī (d. 1158/1745), who was greatly influenced by Ṣāʾeb, Mortażā-qolī Khan Nāmī, who went as an envoy to Istanbul in 1721, and the famous Loṭf-ʿAlī Bīg Āḏar, author of the *Ātaškada* (q.v.), the well-known Persian *taḏkera* (see M. F. Köprülü, in *İA* II, p. 139; J. Heyat, op. cit., pp. 67-68).

In the nineteenth century under the Qajars, when Turkish was used at court once again, literary activity was intensified. A revival of interest in Ottoman and Chaghatai poetry and philology is evidenced by such works as *Bahjat al-loǧat* by Fatḥ-ʿAlī Qājār Qazvīnī and *Āl tamǧā-ye nāṣerī* by Moḥammad Ṣāleḥ Eṣfahānī, a work dedicated to Nāṣer-al-dīn Shah. Among Azeri poets of the period, mention should be made of Mīrzā

Moḥammad Rażī Tabrīzī, with the pen name of Banda, who was a calligrapher and poet at the court of Fatḥ-ʿAlī Shah, Ḥosayn-qolī Khan Čāker Ḵamsa'ī, and Ḵalīfa Moḥammad ʿĀjez Sarābī whose *dīvān* was published in Tabrīz in 1856. Others are Mollā Mehr-ʿAlī from Ḵoy, Ātašī Marāḡa'ī, Mollā Ṣādeq Čartāb Tabrīzī, and the poetess Ḥayrān Ḵānom Donbolī (d. 1167/1753).

There was also a significant crop of elegy (*marṯīa*) literature, the most outstanding poets in this respect being Āḵūnd Mollā Ḥosayn Daḵīl Marāḡa'ī, Mīrzā Abu'l-Ḥasan Rājī Tabrīzī (1247-93/1831-76), and Moḥammad Amīn Delsūz Tabrīzī whose Azeri *dīvān* was printed in Tabrīz.

The second half of the 13th/19th century brought a period of transition in Azerbaijan, both in social and political thinking and in literature. The literary movements of the north (as well as those occurring in the Ottoman empire) are reflected to some extent in the south. Publications from the north, namely, the more realistic works of Qāsem Beg Ḏāker (1784-1857), ʿAbbās-qolī Āḡā Qodsī Baqīḵānov (Bakïxanlï; 1794-1847), Mīrzā Šafīʿ Wāżeḥ (b. 1794-1852), Esmāʿīl Beg Gotgašīnlī (Gutgašïnlï; 1806-61), Mīrzā Fatḥ-ʿAlī Āḵūndzāda (1812-78; q.v.), and others, have some influence on the works written in the south. Several authors celebrate—in a noticeably simpler language and style—the values of enlightenment, liberty, and patriotism. At the same time, one of the most outstanding poets of Azerbaijan in this period is Sayyed Abu'l-Qāsem Nabātī (1812-73), a Sufi who wrote in both Persian and Azeri. he was influenced by Nasīmī, Jalāl-al-dīn Rūmī and Ḥāfeẓ, producing a famous *sāqī-nāma* on the model of that of Ḥāfeẓ. He also has numerous poems in the *ʿāšeq* style.

Another important poet is Mīrzā ʿAlī Khan Laʿlī, who was born in Erevan in 1261/1845, and came to Tabrīz as a young man. After completing his medical studies in Istanbul, he worked as a doctor in Tabrīz where he died in 1325/1907. Known as Ḥakīm Laʿlī, he wrote satirical poetry in the traditional style (see the introduction to *Dīvān-e Ḥakīm Laʿlī* by Moḥammad-ʿAlī Ṣafwat, Tabrīz, n.d.). Ḥājjī Reżā Ṣarrāf (1271-1325/1854-1907) and Ḥājjī Mahdī Šokūhī (d. 1314/1896) are mostly known for their elegy poetry. Moḥammad-Kāẓem ʿAlīšāh Asrār Tabrīzī (b. 1265/1848-49) was a Neʿmatallāhī Sufi and poet, who compiled two anthologies of Azeri poets: *Bahjat al-šoʿarā'* and *Ḥadīqat al-šoʿarā'* (1298/1881). The latter is a selection made from the former and is mostly devoted to satirical and humorous poetry. The former includes the works of eighty-six poets (for an account of these two unpublished works, see J. Heyat, op. cit., p. 137). Another poet of some significance is Mīrzā Moḥammad-Bāqer Ḵalḵālī, who was a *mojtahed* and wrote a well-known *maṯnawī* called *Ṯaʿlabī'a* (1893). The style and the structure of this work somewhat resemble the *Maṯnawī* of Rūmī, and within the framework of a main story Ḵalḵālī brings in many folkloric stories, always trying to present a moralistic view (see H. Ṣādeq, *Haft maqāla dar pīrāmūn-e folklor wa mardom-e Āḏarbāyjān*, Tehran, 1978, pp. 142-98).

In the twentieth century the Azeri literature of Iran has continued to reflect the political and social development of the country as a whole, but has been influenced especially by official attitudes and policies toward the use of Turkic as a literary language. In contrast to the flourishing of Turkic literature in Soviet Azerbaijan, therefore, Azeri literature in Iran has had a limited development. Many Azeri writers are better known for their contributions to Persian literature than to Azeri.

The Constitutional period, with its background of liberal and democratic ideas, proved a productive one for Azeri Turkic, both as a vehicle for poetry and in journalism. Of eight newspapers published in Tabrīz and Urmia at that time, five were in Turkic, three bilingual (see S. Berengian, *Poets and Writers from Iranian Azerbaijan in the Twentieth Century*, Ph.D. dissertation, Columbia University, 1965, p. 38). A number of journals also were published, the most outstanding and influential being *Mollā Naṣr-al-dīn* (first appearing in 1906). Although published in Tiflis, it counted many southern poets among its contributors, including the great satirist Mīrzā ʿAlī-Akbar Ṣāber (1862-1911). Ṣāber had a strong influence not only on other Azeri poets but also on Persian poets such as Abu'l-Qāsem Lāhūtī (1887-1957), Sayyed Ašraf Gīlānī (1287/1870-1313 Š./1934; q.v.), and ʿAlī-Akbar Dehḵodā (1297/1879-1334 Š./1956). In spite of the ban imposed by the government of Moḥammad-ʿAlī Shah aimed at stopping the journal from entering Iran, *Mollā Naṣr-al-dīn* and the poetry of Ṣāber in particular were extremely popular in Azerbaijan. The Constitutionalists fighting the Royalist forces in Tabrīz would recite the poems of Ṣāber to keep up their morale, and his poems touching on Iranian affairs would occasionally be answered by the journal *Āḏarbāyjān* (see *Āzarbāyjān*), published in Tabrīz in Azeri and Persian during 1906 and 1907. Jalīl Moḥammad-qolīzāda (Mämmädguluzade; 1869-1932) who, like Ṣāber, had deep-rooted associations with Iran, went to Tabrīz in 1921 and published eight issues of *Mollā Naṣr-al-dīn* there. Due to police interference, however, he returned to Baku, where he continued to publish the journal until 1929. In a letter dated April 26, 1906, Moḥammad-qolīzāda states that half of *Mollā Naṣr-al-dīn*'s fifteen thousand readers were in Iran (see S. Sardarınıa, "Mollā Nasreddīn in Iran," *Vārleq*, January-April, 1986, p. 110).

The most outstanding poet of Azerbaijan to be influenced by Ṣāber was Mīrza ʿAlī Moʿjez (1873-1934). One of the few Azeri poets to come close to the greatness of Ṣāber as a satirist, Moʿjez went to Istanbul at the age of sixteen and spent fourteen years there working as a bookseller and becoming acquainted with the literary and social currents in the Ottoman empire at that time. When he was thirty he returned to his native Šabestar and began to write biting satires in criticism of the absolutist rule in Iran and the backwardness of his countrymen. Prominent themes of his satires, which are written in a simple poetic language, include the abject condition of women, and religious hypocrisy and fanaticism (see ŠABESTARĪ).

The case of Moʿjez, who ended his days in self exile in Šāhrūd, serves as a good example of the restrictions imposed upon Azeri poets and writers under Pahlavi rule. Pursuing a policy of national unification, Reżā Shah aimed at suppressing the use of Azeri as a literary medium. Thus, although the poems of Moʿjez were very popular, permission for the publication of his *dīvān* was withheld until after the abdication of Reżā Shah in 1320 Š./1941. Between then and 1325 Š./1946 it went through several editions. These years correspond to a period of weak central government and a strong Soviet military presence in Iranian Azerbaijan. With the active support of Soviet military forces, a local government was established in 1324 Š./1945 under Sayyed Jaʿfar Pīšavarī, only to be overthrown by a government force in December 1325 Š./1946. Short though it was, the period was a significant one for the cultural and literary life of the area. Azeri was recognized as the official language of the province and a number of newspapers and journals appeared in that language. New collections of poetry were published and many old *dīvān*s reissued. The nature of the literature produced was a combination of basic Persian literary conventions, Azeri folk and popular traditions, and Soviet-inspired socialist realism (see Berengian, op. cit., pp. vi-vii). One interesting development was the revival of syllabic meters. Many Azeri poets, including Ṣāber and Moʿjez, had used prosodic meters. Now, under the influence of folk poetry and *ʿāšeq* compositions in particular, some modern poets experimented with the syllabic tradition. Of the poets of this period, Ḥaddād and Karīm Marāḡaʾī are very much followers of Ṣāber and Moʿjez. Authors under Soviet Azerbaijani influence include Balaš Āḏaroḡlī (Azäroğlu; b. 1921 in Ardabīl), Madīna Golgūn (Gülgün; b. 1926), Ḥokūma Bolūrī (Bülluri; b. 1926 in Zanjān), ʿAlī Javāndāda "Tūda" (b. 1924; spent the years 1938-46 in Azerbaijan), and the political publicist Fereydūn Ebrāhīmī (b. 1919 in Āstārā, d. 1947 in Tabrīz). Many older writers also became active, including the satirical poet Ebrāhīm Ḏāker (b. 1891 near Ardabīl), ʿAlī Feṭrat (b. 1890 in Tabrīz, d. 1948), the poet and educator Mīr Mahdī Eʿtemād (b. 1900 in Tabrīz, d. 1981), and ʿĀšeq Ḥosayn Javān (b. 1916 in Azerbaijan).

With the fall of Pīšavarī's government, the ban against the public use of Azeri was renewed, a ban that was in force for more than half a century overall. Even when, on rare occasions, a publication was allowed, the authorities had to be appeased. For instance, when ʿAlī-Aṣḡar Mojtahedī (1905-72) published his collection of Azeri proverbs and their Persian translations, he was not allowed to use the word "Azeri" on the title page. The book thus appeared as *Amṯāl wa ḥekam dar lahja-ye maḥallī-e Āḏarbāyjān* (2nd ed. by Ḥ. Javādī, Piedmont, California, 1984). Between 1326 Š./1947 and the Revolution of 1357 Š./1978-79, publications in Azeri were extremely rare in Iran. The most important poet of this period is Sayyed Moḥammad-Ḥosayn Šahrīār (b. 1285/1907-08 in Ḵošganāb, near Tabrīz). Known earlier for his Persian *ḡazal*s, mainly written in the tradition of Ḥāfeẓ, in the 1320s Š./1940s he began to develop his colloquial Azeri idiom into a masterful literary language. His long lyric poem *Heydär Babaya sälam* (*Ḥaydar Bābāya salām* "Greetings to Ḥaydar Bābā," published in two parts: I, 2nd ed., Tabrīz, 1954; II, Tabrīz, 1966) quickly became famous not only in Azerbaijan but across the rest of the Turkic world (see Muharrem Ergin, "Şehriyâr'a selâm," *Türk kültürü* 29/3, 1965, p. 293; Ahmet Ateş, *Sehriyâr ve Haydar-Baba'ya selâm*, Ankara, 1964). Written in a lively, stanzaic form, the poem recalls memories from the poet's childhood in a mountain village of the Tabrīz region. Bolūd Garāčorlī Sahand (Bulud Garačorlu Sähänd; b. 1926 in Marāḡa, d. 1979) is known for his excellent verse adaptation of the "Book of Dädä Qorqut" (4 vols.). Ḥabīb Sāher (b. 1903, Tabrīz, d. 1983, Tehran) began to publish his poems in the 1320s Š./1940s and continued his literary activities until the end of his life. Classified as one of the Haydar Baba School, he was educated in Istanbul, and the influence of both classical and modern Turkish poetry is noticeable in his poetry. As a result of the 1324-25 Š./1945-46 political events in Azerbaijan, his subsequent works became considerably more political. Other poets and writers of this period include Moḥammad-ʿAlī Maḥzūn (Mämmädali Mähzun; who joined the ranks of those writing in praise of events in the Pīšavarī period), Moḥammad Bīrīā (b. Tabrīz, 1918) who was a minister in the Democratic Party government, Ṣamad Behrangī (q.v.), who occasionally wrote poems, ʿAbbās Bārez, Jabbār Bāḡčabān, and Noṣratallāh Fatḥī (see M. ʿA. Farzāna, "Češmandāz-e šeʿr-e mobārez-e Āḏarbāyjān dar dawrān-e eḵtenāq," *Vārleq* 3-4, June-July, 1985).

Since 1357 Š./1978 there has been much literary activity again, especially in Tabrīz. A few Azeri periodicals began to appear just after the revolution, such as *Mollā Naṣr-al-dīn* (a satirical weekly published in Tabrīz in 1979) and *Saṭṭār Ḵān Bayrāqī* (a political monthly, Tabrīz, 1979; originally published in West Germany). None of them, however, lasted very long. An important journal now is *Vārleq* (*Varlïg*), currently in its seventh year of publication in Tehran. This serves as a forum for leading Azeri intellectuals and writers such as Ḥāmed Noṭqī, M. ʿA. Farzāna, Jawād Ḥayāt (its editor), Moḥammad Payfūn (author of a recent Azeri-Persian dictionary), and many others. Contemporary literature mainly consists of poetry, written in both *ʿarūż* and the syllabic meter. It is influenced by the poetry of both Soviet Azerbaijan and modern Turkey, and concentrates thematically upon social and cultural questions.

Many Soviet Azerbaijan authors (some of whom originate from southern Azerbaijan) have dealt with Iranian Azerbaijan in their works. Jalīl Moḥammad-qolīzāda (Mämmädguluzade) was proud of the fact that his forefathers were from Iran, and he considered himself an Iranian (see Sardarınıa, op. cit., p. 109). Moḥammad (*Mämmäd*) Saʿīd Ordūbādī (1872-1950) described Tabrīz in *Bädbäxt milyonču* (The unlucky millionaire; 1907) and the revolutionary movement of 1906-09, which he himself witnessed, in *Dumanlı Täbriz* (Misty Tabriz; 1933-1948). Bayrām-ʿAlī ʿAbbāszāda (1859-1926), who participated in the Constitutional Revolution, later wrote satirical poems in northern Azerbaijan that treated Iranian themes. Many works by the northern Azerbaijani author ʿAlī Naẓmī (1878-1946) also deal with the revolutionary movements in the south. The novel *Gün gäläjäk* (The day will come) by Mīrzā Ebrāhīmov (b. 1911, in Sarāb), is also about events during the Constitutional period. It was published in 1948 and has been translated into several languages. The poetry of Osman Sarïvelli (b. 1905) contains personal impressions of the south during the war, for example *İki sahil* (Two shores; 1950), which contrasts Iranian and Soviet Azerbaijan. Moḥammad (Mämmäd) Raḥīm (b. 1907) describes the south in a poetic cycle *Täbrizdä* (in Tabrīz). Anwār Moḥammad-ḵānlī (Mämmädxanlï; b. 1913), who also served with the Soviet army in Iran, deals with similar matters in short stories from Tabrīz and in the drama *Od ičindä* (In the fire; 1951).

Bibliography: See also M. ʿĀref, *Adabīyāt-e Āḏarbāyjān*, 1958. Idem [M. Arif], *Istoriya azerbaĭdzhanskoĭ literatury*, Baku, 1971. Ä. Axundov, *Azerbaĭdzhanskie skazki*, Baku, 1955. Idem, ed., *Azärbayjan folkloru antologiyasï*, 2 vols., Baku, 1968. Ankara, 1978. Idem, *Azärbayjan ašïglarï vä el šairläri*, 2 vols., Baku, 1983-84. Idem et al., eds., *Azärbayjan dastanlarï*, 5 vols., Baku, 1965-72. M. F. Axundov (Āḵūndzāda), *Äsärlär*, 3 vols., Baku, 1938. N. Axundov, *Azärbaijan satira jurnallarï 1906-1920*, Baku, 1968. R. Azadä, *Azärbayjan épik še'rinin inkišaf yollarï (XII-XVII äsrlär)*, Baku, 1975. *Azärbayjan šifahi xalg ädäbiyyatïna dair tädgiglär*, 6 vols., Baku, 1961-81. A. H. Billuri, *Razvitie realisticheskoĭ demokraticheskoĭ poezii iranskogo Azerbaĭdzhana (1945-1960 gg.)*, Baku, 1972. A. Caferoğlu, "Āḏharī," in *EI²* I, pp. 192-94. Idem, "Die aserbaidschanische Literatur," in *Philologiae Turcicae Fundamenta* II, Aquis Mattiacis (Wiesbaden), 1964, pp. 635-99. M. Ergin, *Azerî türkçesi*, Istanbul, 1971 (this work contains the text of "Heydar Babaya sälam" in Latin characters). Fuzuli, *Divan*, ed. K. Akyüz et al., Ankara, 1958. Idem, *Leyli vä Mäjnun*, 2 vols., Baku, 1958. T. Gandjeï, ed., *Il canzoniere di Šāh Ismāʿīl Ḫaṭāʾī*, Naples, 1959. F. and Y. Gedikli, *Çağdaş azerî şiir antolojisi*, Istanbul, 1983. J. Heyat, "20'inci asırda Güney Azerbaycan edebiyatı," *Beşinci milletler arası türkoloji kongresi. Tebliğler* II: *Türk edebiyatı* I, Istanbul, 1985, pp. 119-29. A. Ibrahimov, *Azärbayjan klassik ädäbiyyatï*, Baku, I: *Xalg ädäbiyyatï*, 1982; II: *Imadäddin Näsimi*, 1985. Idem, ed., *Azerbaĭdzhanskaya poeziya*, Moscow, n.d. (after 1969). Salāmallāh Jāvīd, *Dostlar görüšü*, n.p., 1980 (interesting collection of poems by contemporary Azeri poets in Iran with a short account of their lives). F. B. Köčärli, *Azärbayjan ädäbiyyatï* I, Baku, 1978. F. Köprülü, "Azeri edebiyatına notlar," *Darülfünun Edebiyat Fakültesi Mecmuası* 4, 1925, pp. 68-77. P. Makulu, *Adabi maʿlumat jadvalï*, Baku, 1962. I. Näsimi, *Üč jilddä äsärlär*, Baku, 1973. Ḥāmed Noṭqī, "Honar-e Šahrīār," *Vārleq* 3, April-May, 1984, pp. 1-15; 9-12, January-April, 1986 (devoted to Sāher). Mīrzā ʿAlī Moʿjez Šabestarī, *Taza tapïlan šiʿirlär*, Tabrīz, n.d. B. R. Sahand, *Sazmyn sözü*, n.p. [Tehran?], n.d. (anthology of Azeri poetry from Iran). M. H. Tähmasib, *Azärbayjan xalq dastanlarï*, Baku, 1972. Idem et al., *Azärbayjan nağïllarï*, 5 vols., Baku, 1961-64. Idem et al., *Azärbayjan mahabbat dastanlarï*, Baku, 1979. M. ʿA. Tarbīat, *Dānešmandān-e Āḏarbāyjān*, Tehran, 1314 Š./1935. A. P. Vekilov, *Narodnaya poéziya Azerbaĭdzhana*, Leningrad, 1978. S. Vurğun et al., *Azärbayjan ädäbiyyatï tarixi*, 2 vols., Baku, 1960.

(H. JAVADI AND K. BURRILL)

xi. Music of Azerbaijan

History. The art music of Azerbaijan is connected with the Irano-Arabo-Turkish art of the *maqām*, of which the great theoreticians were notably Ṣafī-al-dīn Ormavī (d. 693/1294) and ʿAbd-al-Qāder b. Ḡaybī Marāḡī (d. 838/1435), who were originally from Urmia and Marāḡa in Azerbaijan. According to Hajibekov, this tradition collapsed at the end of the fourteenth century (with the Mongol rule), and subsequently each national group reconstructed its own system from the debris (1945, p. 18). The names were preserved, but the realities to which they applied varied from one tradition to another. In the same way the old rhythmic patterns (*oṣūl*) disappeared in favor of several simple formulas, mainly in 6/8 and 4/4. It seems, however, more correct to locate the break in the traditional chain of transmission in the 12th/18th century. This period was followed, at the beginning of the 13th/19th century, by a revival, in the course of which the remains of the old system were enriched by popular contributions. In the course of this evolution the art music of Azerbaijan remained intimately linked with that of Iran, to which it is still very close. In the absence of documents, this process of revival still remains quite obscure, but it may be located in the southwest and northwest of Iran. In the northwest, it was particularly the town of Šūša in the Qarabāḡ mountains that was the focus of musical life, but it was at Tiflis that Caucasian musicians found the widest audience. Since the beginning of the century the most active musical center has been Baku.

The Iranian elements in the development of the Azeri tradition were numerous, as is shown by modern terminology (*čahār meżrāb*, *bardāšt*), as well as by certain pieces in the repertoire, recent *gūša* and *maqām* that have Iranian names (Bayāt-e Šīrāz, Šūštar, Delkaš, Šekasta-ye Fārs, Bayāt-e Qājār). Conversely, Azerbayjani elements are found in Iranian music, particularly in dance pieces (*reng*). (see also M. Rezvani, *Le théâtre et la danse en Iran*, Paris, 1962, p. 149). Azeri art music is also played in other regions of the Caucasus, especially among the Armenians, who have adopted the system of *maqām* and the instruments *kamānča* and *tār*. Aside from these recent and older Iranian elements (the majority of the names of the *maqām* are already found in such Safavid sources as *Behjat al-rūḥ*, attributed to ʿAbd-al-Mo'men b. Ṣafī-al-dīn), a certain number of *maqām* and melodic patterns are typically Azeri or have gradually become so (e.g. Segāh, Čārgāh, Welāyetī, Qaṭār, Mobarqaʿ, and Kord-Šahnāz).

The traditions musical of Azerbaijan were already distinct from those of the area now known as Soviet Azerbaijan, but they became definitively separated toward the end of the 13th/19th century. Iranian Azerbaijan opting for the purely Iranian style. Subsequently the music of the Soviet Azerbaijan underwent a period of Western acculturation marked by the reduction of the seventeen intervals in the octave to twelve tempered half-tones, the integration of Western instruments, polyphony, and orchestration. On the other hand, a music that is Western in form but national in style developed, integrating such traditional elements as instruments (*tār*, *kamānča*, *daf*, and *bālamān*), rhythms, modes, and melodies. The founder of this new school was Hajibekov (1895-1948).

Ultimately acculturation has not deeply affected the old music. which is still performed by great interpreters faithful to their tradition. In the popular domain, the *ʿāšeq* (q.v.) bards have never stopped singing in cafés and at family celebrations, accompanying themselves on the *sāz* (*čoğūr* in Azarbaijani Persian) and also accompanied by the reed flute (*bālamān*) and the tambourine (*qaw[w]āl*).

Bases of Azeri music. The scales in Azeri music are constructed from the following intervals, reproducing the octave division on the neck of the *tār* lute:

Scale	Intervals (in cents)
Do	90
si	112
si b	90
La	22
la –	90
la b	90
Sol	90
Sol b	22
fa #	90
Fa	70
mi +	40
mi t	70
mi b +	40
mi b	70
Re	22
re –	70
re b	112
Do	

Other, more abstract divisions are given in *Grove's Dictionary of Music*. This scale, which incorporates popular elements (the *ʿāšeq* tradition), is distinct from the Persian, Turkish, and Arab traditions, It may have been inspired by that of Ṣafī-al-dīn, whom the Azeris knew. (In the 13th/19th century Ḥājjī Sayyed Aḥmad Qarabāğī of Šūša compiled a small work on musical terms, entitled *wożūḥ al-ağrām*, from older sources.)

The art music tradition transmitted through several generations in the Mansurov family includes twelve principal modes (Rašt, Māhūr-e hendī, Segāh-Zābol, Čārgāh, Homāyūn, Šūštar, Bayāt-e Šīrāz, Šūr, Bayāt-e Kord, Bayāt-e Qājār, Rahāb, Navā-Nīšāpūr) and ten secondary modes (Delkaš, Kord-Šahnāz, Dogāh, Qaṭār. Eṣfahān, Čobān Bayātī, Orta-Māhūr, Orta-Segāh, K̲ārej-Segāh, Mīrzā Ḥosayn-Segāh, the last four being variants of Māhūr and Segāh). Beside these a certain number of small *maqāms*, generally played within the framework of a more important *maqām*, can be mentioned: Ḥosaynī, Welāyatī, K̲ojasta, Šekasta-ye Fārs, ʿErāq, Panjgāh, Rāk, Sāranj, Zābol, Basta-Negār, Ḥasār, Mok̲ālef, Manṣūrī, ʿOššāq, Samā-ye Šams, Mobarqaʿ, Rahāb. Ḥejāz, Daštī.

The majority of these *maqāms* can be taken as types of such modal compositions as the rhythmic introduction to a mode (*darāmad*), songs (*taṣnīf*), and dance tunes (*reng*, *derenga*). Finally, there are about 100 melodic types (*šoʿba* and *gūša*) that never serve as modal patterns for compositions but are interpreted in the course of development of the principal *maqām*. Some of them are rhythmically unmarked melodies; others are rhythmic transitions. Each of the twelve great *maqāms* includes between ten and twenty of these sequences, each of which has a name. Altogether they constitute an ideal repertoire, serving as a basis for improvisation and composition, which is quite comparable to the Persian *radīf* and embodies the originality of this system in relation to neighboring traditions.

A certain number of established classical compositions for voice and instruments, the *żarbī maqāmlar*, stand outside the range of the *maqām*. They are Arazbāra, Ot̲mānlī (or Mānī), Owšār, Heyrātī, Heyrātī-Kābolī (instrumental), ʿErāq-Kābolī, Samā-ye Šams, Manṣūrīya, Ḥaydarī, and Ozzāl-Żarbī.

Bibliography: Ch. Albright, *The Music of Professional Musicians of Northwest Iran (Azerbayjan)*, Ph.D. thesis, University of Washington, 1976. R. At'ayan, "Azerbaijan," in *The New Grove's Dictionary of Music and Musicians*, ed. S. Sadie, vol. 19, London, 1980, pp. 349-52. A. Badalbeyli, *Musigi lugati*, Baku, 1969. B. M. Belaev, "Muzikal'naya kul'tura Azerbaĭdzhana," in *Ocherki po istorii musiki narodov SSSR*, ed. G. A. Balter, II, Moscow, 1963, pp. 5-81. E. M. Eldarova, "Iskusstvo azerbaĭdzhanskikh ashugov," in *Azerbaĭdzhanskaya narodnaya musika*, Baku, 1981. U. Hajibekov, *Principles of Azerbaijan Folk Music*, Baku, 1985. M. Ismailov, *Zhanry azerbaĭdzhanskoĭ narodnoĭ musiki*, Baku, 1960. R. K̲āleqī, *Sargod̲ašt-e mūsīqī-e Īrān*, Tehran, 1353 Š./1974. M. H. ʿOd̲d̲ārī, *Tārīk̲-e panjāh sāl-e honarmandān-e mūsīqī-e Īrān dar Ād̲arbāyjān*, Tabrīz, 1972. S. Rustamov, F. Amirov, and T. Kuliev, *Azerbaĭjan khalg mahrïlarï*, 2 vols., Baku, 1956, 1958. Z. Safarova, *Ouzéir Hadjibekov*, Baku, 1985. F. Shushinski, *Seyid Shushinski*, Baku, 1966. J. Spector,

"Musical Tradition and Innovation," in *Central Asia. A Century of Russian Rule*, ed. E. Allworth, New York, 1967, pp. 434-84. R. Zohraov, *Azerbaĭdzhanskie tesnify*, Moscow, 1983.

(J. DURING)

AZES, the name of two Indo-Scythian kings of the major dynasty ruling an empire based on the Punjab and Indus valley from about 50 B.C. to A.D. 30. Regarded as Parthian by some scholars and Scythian by others, the dynasty is probably Scytho-Parthian, a composite people using both Śaka and Pahlava names, derived from the Scythian settlement in the Parthian province of Sīstān. Numismatists have distinguished the existence of two kings. Azes I has the obverse coin type of the king on horseback holding a couched spear, while Azes II has the horseman holding an upright whip. Bronze coins of Azes I are overstruck by Azilises (q.v.), showing that Azes I preceded Azilises; the coinage of Azes II is debased into billon, is copied by Gondophares, and is found in the later strata at Taxila.

Belonging to the Azes dynasty is the group of early Kharoṣṭhī inscriptions dated in the old Śaka era. Van Lohuizen de Leeuw (*The 'Scythian' Period*, Leiden, 1949, pp. 1-50) relates the era to the Yue-chi conquest of Bactria in 129 B.C.; but most scholars refer them to the Vikrama era of 58 B.C. The Taxila silver vase referring to a great Kushan king, like the Shahdaur inscription, has a high number date (136) with "Ayasa." J. H. Marshall ("The Date of Kanishka," *JRAS*, 1914, pp. 973-86) interpreted this as "in the era of Azes." If correct, Azes' accession would be in 58 B.C.

Azes I succeeded as king of kings to the empire previously ruled by Maues. His coinage was struck in three principal mints—at Pushkalavati in Gandhara, at Taxila, and in the middle Indus province (not Arachosia, where finds rarely contain his coinage). He retained the silver denominations and square coppers with legends in Greek and Kharoṣṭhī that the Indo-Greeks had used, but instead of a royal portrait his obverse type was a mounted horseman with a couched lance.

Azes II succeeded the intervening ruler Azilises as king of kings in the north, but lost the middle Indus province, where Spalahores and Spalagadames struck coins with Vonones as king of kings (probably the same as the Parthian emperor from A.D. 8 to 12). Azes II probably added Jalālābād and Gard to the empire. An inscription of Tīravharṇa the satrap in year 83 (i.e., A.D. 25) was found at Jalālābād, and hoards of copper coins of Azes II are reported (*NC*, 1861, pp. 72-78). Azes II used the Zeus Nikephoros reverse for silver issues from Taxila and the Pallas types for his mint in Gandhara and experimented with the metrology of his new round copper denominations. At the end of his reign there was a major debasement of his silver coinage datable before A.D. 42 (MacDowall, "The Azes Hoard from Shaikhan Dheri," *South Asian Archaeology*, London, 1973, p. 228). Drachms of Azes II of the Zeus Nikephoros type, first in silver then in billon, were struck in large quantities and are very common in finds from north Pakistan.

The empire was governed by satraps; and when the empire of Azes II began to break up, we find independent coinages of satraps such as Jihonika and Rajuvula, as well as of the *stratēgos* Aspavarma and the Kushan king Kujula, which copy the denominations and types of Azes II. Their Indo-Parthian and Kushan successors continued to use the old Śaka era of Azes for some time, presumably claiming some continuity with Azes.

Bibliography: R. B. Whitehead, *Catalogue of Coins in the Punjab Museum* I, Oxford, 1914, pp. 104-32. G. K. Jenkins, "Indo-Scythic mints", *JNSI*, 1955, pp. 1-26. S. Konow, *Corpus Inscriptionum Indicarum* II/1, Calcutta, 1929, pp. xxxiv-xliv. J. Marshall, *Taxila*, Cambridge, 1951, especially pp. 769-85. W. W. Tarn, *The Greeks in Bactria and India*, 2nd ed., Cambridge, 1951, pp. 91, 335 n. 4, 344 n. 2, 346-49, 353, 398-99, 401-02, 498, 502. *Camb. Hist. Iran* III, pp. 41 n. 2, 194, 196, 1030. N. C. Debevoise, *A Political History of Parthia*, repr. New York, 1968, pp. 63-65.

(D. W. MACDOWELL)

AẒFARĪ GŪRGĀNĪ, MOḤAMMAD ẒAHĪR-AL-DĪN MĪRZĀ ʿALĪ BAḴT, B. SOLṬĀN MOḤAMMAD-WALĪ (Walīy) also called MĪRZĀ-YE KALĀN, Indo-Persian poet and lexicographer. He was of royal descent, born 1172/1758 in the Red Fort at Delhi, where he was brought up and educated. He escaped from the Fort on 3 Rabīʿ I 1203/2 December 1788 and reached Lucknow, where he was warmly received by Āṣaf-al-dawla, the ruler of Avadh. Aẓfarī stayed in Lucknow for about seven years, and his family joined him there. He received allowances from Āṣaf-al-dawla as well as from the East Indian Company. At the end of 1211/1797 Aẓfarī moved from Lucknow to Maqṣūdābād (now Murshidabad) and later on (23 Ḏu'l-qaʿda 1212/9 May 1798) to Madras, 'Omdat-al-omarā'. He died there in 1234/1818 at the age of sixty.

Aẓfarī was fluent in Arabic, Persian, Turkish, and Urdu, and during his stay in Madras he also learned a little English. He had mastered nearly all the sciences of the day, namely medicine, astrology, prosody, geomancy, and metrics, but he was primarily a poet and lexicographer. In addition to an Urdu *dīvān*, he left behind large collections (mostly lost) of Persian and Turkish poetry.

In 1211/1797, he began to write his memoirs, *Wāqeʿāt-e Azfarī* which are an account in Persian of the overthrow of the Mughals in 1788 by Ḡolām Qāder Rohella, the author's escape from captivity, and his wanderings until 1221/1806. In the *Ḵātema*, Aẓfarī mentions his other works: (1) *Loḡat-e torkī-e čaḡatāʾī* (or *Farhang-e Aẓfarī*), a Turkish-Persian and Persian-Turkish dictionary; (2) *Marḡūb al-foʾād*, an enlarged Persian translation of Mīr ʿAlī-Šīr Navāʾī's *Maḥbūb al-qolūb*, completed in 1208/1793; (3) *Neṣāb al-torkī*, a Turkish textbook; (4) *Tengrī Tārī*, a Turkish-Hindi imitation of the *Ḵāleq Bārī*, ascribed to Amīr Ḵosrow;

(5) *Resāla-ye qabrīya* (or *ʿAlāmāt al-qażāyā*), a Persian metrical translation of a treatise on the signs of approaching death ascribed to Hippocrates; (6) *Noskẖa-ye sāneḥāt*, a parenetic work comprising 119 anecdotes; (7) a second Čağatāy *Neṣāb* in 452 verses; (8) *Fawāʾed al-aṭfāl*, on medicine; (9) *Fawāʾed al-mobtadī*, on verbs; (10) *Mīzān-e torkī*, a Turkish grammar; (11) *ʿArūż-zāda*, a versified Turkish treatise on prosody, composed in 1198/1783 and based on Bādor's *ʿArūż resāla sī*; (12) *Dīvān-e ḡazalīyāt-e Ordū* (lost); (13) *Dīvān-e Ordū*; and (14) *Dīvān-e fārsī o torkī o rēḵta*.

Bibliography: *EI²* I, p. 813. Storey, I/1, pp. 642-43, 1322. Moḥammad Ḡawṯ Khan, *Ṣobḥ-e waṭan*, Madras, 1258/1842. Idem, *Golzār-e aʿẓam*, Madras, 1272/1855. Garcin de Tassy, *Histoire de la littérature Hindouie et Hindoustani*, Paris, 1870, I, p. 265. H. M. Elliott and H. Dowson, *History of India as Told by its Own Historians*, Delhi, 1964, VIII, p. 234. A. Sprenger, *Oudh Catalogue*, Calcutta, 1854, p. 2. S. ʿAbd-al-Raḥmān, *Bazm-e tīmūrīya*, Azamgarh, 1948, pp. 426-27. Srī Rām Dehlavī, *Ḵomḵāna-ye jāvīd*, Lahore, 1908, I, p. 331. Moḥammad-Karīm, *Sawāneḥāt-e momtāz*, Central Library Hyderabad (Dn.), MS., fols. 332-37. *The Urdū*, Delhi, April, 1940, pp. 171-221. ʿA. Orūj, *Taḏkera-ye fārsīgū šoʿarā-ye ordū*, Lahore, 1971, pp. 121-22. Marshall, *Mughals in India*, p. 95.

(M. BAQIR)

AZHAR B. YAḤĀ B. ZOHAYR B. FARQAD, nicknamed **AZHAR-E ḴAR** "Azhar the ass," third cousin, and military commander of the Saffarid amirs Yaʿqūb and ʿAmr b. Layṯ; like them, he was provided by the author of the *Tārīḵ-e Sīstān* (p. 204) with a patently spurious genealogy going back to the Sasanian king of kings Ḵosrow II Aparvēz. Neither the date of his birth nor of his death are known, but he flourished in the second half of the 3rd/9th century.

He was the confidant and aide of both Yaʿqūb (r. 253-65/867-79) and ʿAmr (r. 265-88/879-901) during their amirates, being not only described as a mighty warrior but also as highly literate, an *adīb*, and a *dabīr* or secretary (ibid., p. 269). In an anecdote in the *Qābūs-nāma* of Kay Kāvūs b. Eskandar (ed. Ḡ. -Ḥ. Yūsofī, 3rd ed., Tehran, 1364 Š./1985, p. 96), he is described as giving good counsel to ʿAmr about the dangers of exposing himself to injury and thus harming the state. One suspects from the anecdotes given about him in the local *Tārīḵ-e Sīstān* and from his nickname Azhar-e ḵar that he deliberately cultivated a mask of obtuseness in order to disarm and confuse potential opponents.

When the amir was outside Sīstān, he seems regularly to have been entrusted with the government of the homeland. Thus in 261/875, when Yaʿqūb b. Layṯ was absent in Fārs, Azhar acted as his deputy in Sīstān; and in the crisis of Ramażān, 276/January, 890, when ʿAmr was away in Fārs also and his brother ʿAlī b. Layṯ escaped from confinement in Bam, collected an army, and threatened to march on Sīstān, Azhar and Aḥmad b. Šahfūr rallied the defence and deflected ʿAlī into Khorasan (ibid., p. 247). Before this, he had acted as Yaʿqūb's agent in 248/862 in winning over the leaders of the Kharijites in Sīstān, thereby securing for him an accession of troops for his ambitions of external expansion (ibid., pp. 204-05); he had fought at the side of Yaʿqūb in Kermān in 254-55/868-69 when the Saffarid amir had attacked the caliphal governor there, ʿAlī b. Ḥosayn, personally capturing in battle ʿAlī's commander Ṭawq b. Moḡalles (ibid., p. 213); and he had taken part in an expedition against the local ruler of Zamīn(-e) Dāvar in southeastern Afghanistan, the Zonbīl, distinguishing himself in battle.

Bibliography: See also *Tārīḵ-e Sīstān*, pp. 213, 225, 269-71; tr. M. Gold, pp. 162-63, 169, 178-79, 196, 214-17. Rašīd-al-dīn Vaṭvāṭ, *Ḥadāʾeq al-seḥr fī daqāʾeq al-šeʿr*, ed. ʿA. Eqbāl Āštīānī, Tehran, 1308 Š./1929, pp. 105-07.

(L. P. SMIRNOVA)

AŽI and **AŽI DAHĀKA.** See AŽDAHĀ; ŻAḤḤĀK.

AZILISES, Indo-Scythian king of the dynasty of Azes (q.v.) in the Indus valley about the beginning of the Christian era. Rare joint coins have the name of Azes as "great king of kings" in Greek or Kharoṣṭhī script and Azilises as "great king of kings" in the second legend (Whitehead, *Punjab*, p. 132). Herzfeld, *AMI* 4, 1931-32, pp. 97-98) makes these all references to one king, while Tarn (*The Greeks in Bactria and India*, Cambridge, 1951, p. 348) argued from this that Azes I associated Azilises with himself as co-ruler; but the supposed joint coinage is rare and may simply to be the continued use of old dies at Azilises' accession. The independent evidence of overstrikes and stratified finds establishes that Azes I was succeeded by Azilises and then by Azes II. Azilises struck coins with obverse legends in Greek and Kharoṣṭhī in the three mints that Azes I had used at Taxila, at Pushkalavati in Gandhara, and in the middle Indus; his copper coins have the same square denomination that Azes I had used. Silver tetradrachms of Azilises have been found in hoards with those of the Indo-Greek king Hippostratus in north Pakistan and Kashmir (Whitehead, *NC*, 1923, p. 338), and with silver coins of Azes I, Azes II, Hermaeus, and the Parthian king Orodes II (57-37 B. C.) in the hoard from Mohmand, north of Shabkadar in Gandhara. (G. K. Jenkins, *JNSI*, 1955, pp. 23-25). In stupa 4 at the Dharmarajika at Taxila, a silver drachm of Azilises was found in a votive deposit with a silver denarius of the Roman emperor Augustus, struck in Gaul between 2 B. C. and A. D. 14 (J. H. Marshall, *Taxila*, Cambridge, 1951, pp. 277, 292). Azilises succeeded Azes I as king of kings in the Indus provinces towards the end of the first century B. C. and continued to use his obverse coin type of the king as a horseman with a spear couched. He subsequently introduced a new obverse type of the king as a horseman holding a whip which was continued by his successor Azes II.

Bibliography: See also R. B. Whitehead,

Catalogue of Coins in the Punjab Museum I, Oxford. 1914, pp. 132-41. G. K. Jenkins, "Indo Scythic Mints," *JNSI*, 1955, pp. 1-26. *Camb. Hist. Iran* III, pp. 196-97, 1030.

(D. W. MacDowall)

ʿAẒĪM NAVĀZ KHAN BAHĀDOR, MOʿTAMED JANG ʿOMDAT-AL-ʿOLAMĀʾ MAWLAWĪ MOḤAMMAD SEBḠATALLĀH B. MOḤAMMAD ḠAWṮ (fl. 1859), the author of a Sunni account in Persian of the martyrdom of Imam Ḥosayn called *Dāstān-e ḡam* (completed in 1250/1834-35; Madras, 1843) and the superintendent of the compilation of the *ʿAẓīm al-tawārīḵ*, a political and natural history of the Carnatic and of India in general. He was an official in the service of the nawabs of the Carnatic ʿAẓīm-al-dawla (1801-19) and Aʿẓam Jāh (1820-25). The latter entrusted him with the project of the *ʿAẓīm al-tawārīḵ*. ʿAẓīm Navāz Khan selected proper collaborators for various parts of the project and applied himself particularly to the history of the rulers of the Carnatic, from Moḥammad Saʿādatallāh Khan I (1700-32) to Nawab Moḥammad-ʿAlī Khan Bahādor Vālājāh (1749-95). The nawab's death, however, on 12 November 1825, left the work unfinished.

There is only one—incomplete—manuscript of *ʿAẓīm al-tawārīḵ* extant, now in the India Office Library, London (MS 3216). It was originally planned to consist of seven *maqāla*s and five *moqaddema*s, but the seventh *maqāla* (the Carnatic and Maysore history) is missing from the manuscript. It comprises (1) general introduction on the value of historiography, the sources of the Hindu period, and an outline of pre-Muhammadan Indian history; (2) history of the creation, the patriarchs, the Hindu rajas, and the rise of Islam in India; (3) the Ghaznavids; (4) the Delhi sultans to ʿAlāʾ-al-dīn Ḵaljī; (5) the Delhi sultans from Bahlūl Lōdī; and (6) the Mughal emperors to Moḥammad Shah. These *maqāla*s are followed by a portion called *Jāmeʿ al-ašyāʿ* or *Hašt čaman* on natural history.

Bibliography: C. H. Philips, *Handbook of Oriental History*, London, 1951, p. 93. Storey, I, pp. 222-23, 482, 897, 1039, 1188, 1263. Ethé, *Cat. Ind. Off.* I, p. 162. C. E. Buckland, *Dictionary of Indian Biography*, London, 1906, pp. 73-74.

(M. Baqir)

ʿAẒĪMĀBĀD (Patna), ancient Pataliputra, present capital of Bihar state in northeast India. After its great days as the capital of the Mauryas (321-185 B.C.) and the Guptas (A.D. 319-550) Pataliputra got relegated to the position of a small town. Its fortune revived when Šēr Shah (r. 947-52/1540-45), impressed by the strategic location of the site, had a fort built there in about 948/1541. The town, Patna, subsequently developed and became the capital of Bihar (ʿAbdallāh, *Tārīḵ-e dāʾūdī*, ed. Shaikh ʿAbd-al-Rašīd, Aligarh, 1389/1969, p. 150). During the next two centuries Patna emerged as an important political, commercial, and cultural center.

It was the headquarters of a long line of governors (*ṣūbadār*s), including Mughal princes, many of whom built new buildings there, including public facilities, administrative centers, mausoleums, mosques, etc. The most notable builders were Sayf Khan (1038-42/1628-32), whose *madrasa* and *ʿīdgāh* have partly survived, and Šāʾesta Khan (1049-53/1639-43), some of whose mosques are extant and the site of whose shopping center (*katra*) can still be identified (see Q. Aḥmad, *Corpus of Arabic and Persian Inscriptions of Bihar*, Patna, 1973, passim).

Patna obtained a new name, ʿAẓīmābād, and greater splendor during the governorship of Prince ʿAẓīm (1115-19/1703-07), a grandson of Awrangzēb (r. 1658-1707; q.v.) and better known as ʿAẓīm-al-šaʾn. Coins bearing the new name are available from the year 1117-18/1705-06 onwards. The district (*pargana*) was also renamed ʿAẓīmābād.

The town spread lengthwise along the southern bank of the Ganges river at the point where it joins the river Punpun, which flows parallel to it a little further south. It was walled and had several gates, of which the eastern and the western ones are still marked.

The town's population (474,000 according to the 1971 census, 12 percent of whom were Muslims) was estimated by S. Manrique in 1051/1641 at 200,000 (two *lakh*s; *Travels of Manrique 1629-43*, tr. F. Luard and H. Hosten, London, 1927, II, p. 140); it had started spilling beyond the wall since the eighteenth century, if not earlier. During the British period the westward expansion began. The East India Company's civil station and cantonment were built on that side. A conspicuous monument of the period is the Golghar (Rose-house), a granary built in 1200/1786 by Warren Hastings; it is 96 feet high with two staircases on the outside winding to the top. In modern times the town has also expanded southwards, cutting across the railway which used to mark the southern boundary. The eastern part represents the old, walled town; elderly people still call it ʿAẓīmābād or simply Šahr (the city).

ʿAẓīmābād was located at the confluence of three rivers, well connected to overland trade routes, and serving as a vital commercial link to the fertile province of Bengal, and so turned into an industrial and commercial center which attracted European entrepreneurs. Its industries comprised textiles, paper, sugar, carpets, gilded glass, earthenware, vermillion, indigo, later also opium (see H. K. Naqvi, *Urban Centers and Industries in Upper India, 1556-1803*, New York, 1968). It also served as a cultural and educational center. Moḥammad-Ṣādeq, the author of *Ṣobḥ-e ṣādeq*, mentions many eminent litterateurs, teachers, magistrates, physicians, calligraphists, and musicians from whom he received his education. It appears that many Persian migrants who passed through Bihar en route to service in Bengal returned to settle in ʿAẓīmābād upon their retirement. The *madrasa* of Sayf Khan was well-endowed, providing residential arrangements for many of its teachers and students. The presence and patronage of ʿAẓīm-al-šaʾn attracted many notable persons in various fields. Later, during the political upheavals of

1119-34/1707-22 and after Nāder Shah's invasion of 1152/1739 many of Delhi's élite and non-élite began to emigrate to other parts of Hindustan, particularly 'Aẓīmābād. Many Sufis, poets, historians, and scholars lived and flourished there, among others, Mīrzā 'Abd-al-Qāder Bīdel (1054-1133/1644-1721; q.v.), Ḡolām-Ḥosayn Khan, author of *Sīar al-mota'akkerīn*, 'Alī Ebrāhīm Khan, compiler of an anthology of Persian poets entitled *Ṣoḥof-e Ebrāhīm*, and Abu'l-Ḥasan Fard, the poet-saint of the Phulwari *kānaqāh*. Non-Muslims, too, achieved axcellence in Persian. The *Dīvān* of the Persian verses of Raja Ram Narain, pen-name Mawzūn, *nā'eb nāẓem* of Bihar (1169-74/1756-60), a disciple of Shaikh Ḥazīm, who visited 'Aẓīmābād in 1163/1750, as also the history *Kolāṣat al-tawārīk*, of Maharaja Kaliyan Singh, are well known. There were many others whose works have either been lost or lie neglected in manuscript collections (for a partial listing see 'Ebratī's *Rīāż al-afkār*, Khuda Bakhsh Oriental Public Library, Patna, ms. copy). 'Aẓīmābād is also the home of a library donated by Mawlawī Kodābakš (d. 1326/1908), known for its excellent collection of rare Persian and Arabic manuscripts.

A new phase in the town's history began in the mid-12th/18th century. From his base at 'Aẓīmābād, 'Alīverdī Khan founded the virtually independent kingdom of Bengal, to which Bihar was appended. Outside of the control of Delhi, Bihar was drawn into the whirlpool of mid-12th/18th-century Bengal politics. When the British won the crucial battles of Plassey and Buxar, the fugitive Prince 'Alī Gawhar, later Shah 'Ālam II (r. 1172-1220/1759-1806; q.v.) came to 'Aẓīmābād in a bid to seize the town and assert his sovereignty. He failed and the British assumed economical control throughout the region. 'Aẓīmābād was a center for the Uprising of 1857 and also for the socio-political reform movement popularly known as the Wahhabi Movement.

During the early 14th/late 19th century Bihar, and with it 'Aẓīmābād, suffered as it became incorporated into a large, populous administrative unit. The laying of railways (1279/1862) adversely affected the river-borne commercial traffic on which the town's prosperity had depended. Meanwhile, with the expansion of the British educational system and the emergence of a vocal middle class, there was increasing demand for a more equitable distribution of resources and services in the Bihar sub-province. In response to this condition and for a variety of other reasons, the British opted to parcel up Bengal. In 1921 Bihar was constituted as a separate province of British India, and 'Aẓīmābād, once again labeled Patna, reverted to its status as a provincial capital.

Bibliography: See also Q. Ahmad, ed., *Patna through the Ages*, Patna, 1986. M. Archer, *Patna Painting*, London, 1948. J. D. Beglar, "Report of a Tour through the Bengal Provinces in 1872-3," in A. Cunningham, *Archaeological Survey of India Reports* VIII, Calcutta, 1879. H. Beveridge, "The City of Patna," *The Calcutta Review*, 1884, pp. 211-22. F. Buchanan, *An Account of the Districts of Bihar and Patna in 1811-12*, Patna, 1896. N. Kumar, *Image of Patna*, Patna, 1971. Ramji Misra, ed., *Patna Municipal Centenary Celebration Souvenir*, Patna, 1965. L. S. S. O'Malley, *Bihar and Orissa Gazetteers: Patna*, Patna, 1917. J. N. Sarkar and J. C. Jha, *A History of the Patna College, (1863-1963)*, Patna, 1963. *The New Encyclopædia Britannica*, 15th ed., 1980, vol. 13, p. 1076.

(Q. AHMAD)

ĀZĪN (ĀḎĪN) **JOŠNAS,** a military commander of the Sasanian Hormazd IV (r. A.D. 579-90), killed in Hamadān on his way to fight the rebellious general Bahrām Čōbēn (Ṭabarī, I, p. 995; Ya'qūbī, I, p. 190; Bal'amī, *Tārīk*, p. 1079; *Šāh-nāma* [Moscow] VIII, pp. 394, 428). He has also been referred to as minister (*wazīr*) (Mas'udī, *Morūj* I, sec. 634; Gardīzī, ed. Ḥabībī, p. 34), chief minister (Dīnavarī, p. 85), or scribe (*dabīr*) (*Šāh-nāma* VIII, p. 394) of the king. Ṯa'ālebī (*Ḡorar*, p. 659) says the king consulted with him but does not specify his official title. The title *dabīr* does not seem appropriate since he seems to have belonged, as most sources confirm, to the warrior class. He has been referred to as Kūzī, i.e., native of Kūzestān, by Mas'ūdī (ibid.) and Ḥūrī (Jūrī?) by Gardīzī (ibid.).

Most sources report that when the news of Bahrām's victory over Šāva, the king (*kāqān*) of the Turks, arrived at the court with war booties, Āzīn Jošnas, envious of Bahrām's achievement, accused him of having kept the best and most of the spoils for himself, sending only a token share to the king. Other sources, however, make others such as Bahmūda, the *kāqān*'s son, who lived as a captive at the court (Y'aqūbī, p. 189) or some courtiers (Ṯa'ālebī, p. 657) responsible for the king's suspicion. According to Dīnavarī and Bal'amī Āzīn Jošnas was dispatched in order to apologize to Bahrām and console him, but death did not allow him to fulfill his mission.

The Arabicized form Āzīn Jošnas recorded by Ṭabarī (ibid.) and Ya'qūbī (p. 190) indicates that the original form of the name was Āzēn Gošnasp, which occurs as Āzīn Košasb in Ṯa'ālebī (p. 659) and Āyēn Gošasb in *Šāh-nāma* (ibid.). Other corrupted forms are Arīksīs (Mas'ūdī), Arḥasīs (Gardīzī), Yazdān Jošnas (Dīnavarī), and Yazdān Bakš (Bal'amī), etc.

Bibliography: See also Nöldeke, *Geschichte der Perser*, p. 276.

(A. TAFAŻŻOLĪ)

ĀŽĪR "Alarm bell," a radical leftist Persian newspaper which was printed at Tehran from Kordād, 1322 Š./May, 1943, to Kordād, 1324 Š./June, 1945. The holder of the publication license was Sayyed Ja'far Pīšavarī (q.v), a veteran revolutionary and communist (b. 1893 at Kalkāl in Iranian Azerbaijan, d. 1948? at Baku). He was also *Āžīr*'s editor and the author of articles in it under both his own name and the pseudonym Raštī.

In an earlier period, Pīšavarī had used the name Sayyed Ja'far Javādzāda and been active in the Baku-based 'Adālat party (Ferqa-ye 'Adālat), editor of its bilingual Azeri-Persian newspaper *Ḥorrīyat* "Freedom," and one of the founders of the Communist Party of Iran in 1920. He was commissar for internal affairs in the Soviet Republic of Gīlān and editor of the newspaper *Kāmūnīst*, printed at Rašt in 1920 and later the prime mover of the newspaper *Ḥaqīqat*, printed at Tehran in 1921-22.

Āžīr was closed down shortly after Pīšavarī's departure to Tabrīz, where a group calling itself the Democrat Party of Azerbaijan (Ferqa-ye demokrāt-e Āḏarbāyǰān) set up a pro-Soviet autonomous regime under his leadership in the summer of 1324 Š./1945.

Āžīr's contents included political and social topics, particularly debates of the fourteenth Majlis (parliament) which invalidated Pīšavarī's electoral mandate; criticisms of Reżā Shah's reign; attacks on non-leftist individuals and groups; criticism of new leftist organizations, groups, and individuals (accusing them of lack of revolutionary experience and drive); propaganda for Marxism-Leninism; and support for the Soviet Union, whose troops were then occupying parts of Iran. This newspaper in its first year, beginning on 1 Ḵordād 1322 Š./23 May 1943, consisted of two six-column pages measuring 29.5 × 40.5 cm and was published three times weekly on odd-numbered days and sold at the price of 1 1/2 rials. Illustrations were few. Advertisements filled about a quarter of the paper's space.

Sets of *Āžīr* are preserved in the National Library and the Majlis Library at Tehran and in the Library of Congress at Washington.

(N. PARVĪN)

AZIŠMĀND, one of the few Middle Persian exclusively legal terms designating "obstructed or hampered justice" (see Shaki, "The Obstruction of Justice," *Archív Orientální* 45, 1977, pp. 48-53). The *Mādayān ī hazār dādestān*, our only source of information, offers various instances of this juridical case and its judicial consequences in twenty-odd paragraphs, all of which seem to have originally been included in its chapter 22, entitled *Dar ī azišmānd*. Apart from the *Mādayān* the word occurs in connection with legal terminology once in the *Nīrangestān* (ed. D. D. P. Sanjana, Bombay, 1894, fol. 110r.4) and once in the *Dēnkard* (ed. Madan, p. 706.14-15: *zamān ī rāyēnišn . . . ud pād ud azišmānd ud ēraxtagīh padiš* "the time of process . . . and its observance and obstruction and the sentence thereby").

The evidence for the fundamental meaning of the term is provided by a few unambiguous passages of the *Mādayān*. In pt. 1, p. 12.9-13 the *azišmānd* is occasioned by the defendant's unwillingness to identify his own property; in pt. 1, p. 75.11-12 it is caused by the advocates (*jādag-gōw*) of one party contradicting each other. However, the conclusive support for the interpretation of the term as "obstructed or hampered justice" comes from the *Nīrangestān*, in which Av. *aδāiti frāraiθyanąm* "denial of right" (see *AirWb.*, col. 1020) rendered by Pahlavi *adahišnīh ī frāz dādeṣtān* "not according access to justice, i.e., the hampering of justice," is in turn glossed by its parallel expression *aziš mānd*. The relational pattern of the syntagm thus resolves into *az-iš mānd*, where the verb *māndan* is used in the sense of "to be hindered, hampered," and *-iš* refers to the legal process. Other, untenable, interpretations of the term include "interdictum" (A. Pagliaro, "Aspetti del diritto sāsānidico: *hačašmānd* 'interdetto'," *RSO* 24, 1949, p. 120) and "contumace" (A. Perikhanian, "Le contumace dans la procédure iranienne et les termes pehlevis *hačašmānd* et *srāδ*," in *Mémorial Jean de Menasce*, ed. Ph. Gignoux and A. Tafazzoli, Louvain, 1974, pp. 305-26).

In its extended sense *azišmānd* is employed in relation to the juridical implications of withholding a promised grant (*mādayān*, pt. 2, p. 9.3-5). It may also result from the default of one party (*pasēmāl ō gōw nē šawēd* "the defendant fails to appear in the court," *Mādayān*, pt. 1, pp. 73.13-74.1; *az pasēmāl nē *šudan azišmānd bawēd* "the process becomes obstructed because of the defendant's default," pt. 1, p. 73.10-12). It is also used to denote the prejudicing of one's right, a person's claim to the possession of a property (*azišmānd pad dārišn*, pt. 1, p. 10.12-13), or of one's claim to the ownership of his private property (*azišmānd pad xwēšīh dāštan wizūdan*, pt. 1, pp. 10.16-11.2).

The court may concede one to three instances of *azišmānd*, in accordance with the gravity of the case, beyond which it rules in favor of the offended party (*Mādayān*, pt. 1, pp. 10.12-13, 10.16-11.2, 11.16-12.9).

Bibliography: Editions of the *Mādayān ī hazār dādestān*: J. J. Modi, *Mâdigân-i-hazâr Dâtistân* (facs. ed. of pt. 1, fols. 1-55), Bombay, 1901. T. D. Anklesaria, *The Social Code of the Parsees in Sasanian Times or the Mâdigân-i-hazâr Dâtistân, Part II*, Bombay, 1912. S. J. Bulsara, tr., *The Laws of the Ancient Persians as Found in the 'Mâtikân ê hazâr Dâtastân' or the Digest of a Thousand Points of Law*, 2 vols., Bombay, 1937. A. G. Perikhanian, tr., *Sasanidskiĭ sudebnik*, Yerevan, 1973.

(M. SHAKI)

ʿAZĪZ KHAN MOKRĪ, SARDĀR-E KOLL (1207-87/1792-1871), an army chief and dignitary of Qajar Iran who occupied high-ranking positions from early in Nāṣer-al-dīn Shah's reign (1204-1313/1848-96).

ʿAzīz Khan was the son of Moḥammad Khan (also called Moḥammad Solṭān). He was *sardār* of the Bābā Mīrī family of the Mokrīs (Nikitine, *Les Kurdes*, p. 166; further genealogical information in Ḵormūjī, *Ḥaqāyeq*, pp. 293f.). He was born at Sardašt, southwest of Mahābād, in 1207/1792-93. Little is known about his youth. He married one of Amīr(-e) Kabīr's daughters, born from Amīr Kabīr's first wife (Eqbāl, "ʿAzīz Ḵān," p. 61), with whom he had three sons. His son Sayf-al-dīn Khan (d. 1308/1891-92) governed Sāvojbolāḡ several times and was succeeded as head of the Mokrīs by his son Ḥosayn Khan, who was killed when the Ottomans invaded Sāvojbolāḡ in 1332/1914 (ibid., pp. 61f.). ʿAzīz Khan went to Tabrīz in the attendance of his elder brother. As he was literate and had a good handwriting, he went into service in the sixth regiment (*fawj-e šešom*) of Azerbaijan at Tabrīz. He was in command of this regiment as *sarhang* at the protracted siege of Herat in 1253-54/1837-39. On behalf of Moḥammad Shah, he spent two days in vain negotiations with the besieged Yār Moḥammad Khan and Kāmrān Mīrzā. Left without any important political function after his Herat mission, he took an interest in Sufism (*faqr o darvīšī*), but at the same time began cultivating several influential personalities at the court (see Eqbāl, art. cit., p. 40; Bāmdād, loc. cit.). In 1256/1840-41, the people of Fārs rebelled against Ferīdūn Mīrzā Farmānfarmā, and Moḥammad Shah sent Mīrzā Nabī (Nabīy) Khan Qazvīnī to Shiraz. Upon Mīrza Naẓar-'Alī Ḥakīm-bāšī's recommendation, Nabī Khan brought 'Azīz Khan with him as a consultant (*rīš-safīd*) and took over the administration of Fārs. Again in 1259/1843 Nabī Khan took with him 'Azīz Khan to Fārs. Nabī Khan was succeeded the next year by Ḥosayn Khan Moqaddam Marāḡa'ī Ājūdān-bāšī who was appointed governor of Fārs and granted the title of *ṣāḥeb ektīār*. Through Ḥakīm-bāšī's support, 'Azīz Khan remained in office and Ḥosayn Khan, whom he knew from Tabrīz, made him first his consultant, then *taḥwīldār*, and finally *sarhang* of the fourth regiment of Tabrīz, located in Fārs. Ḥosayn Khan Ṣāḥeb Ektīār (later Neẓām-al-dawla) remained governor of Fārs until Moḥammad Shah's death in September, 1264/1848 and 'Azīz Khan remained at his service there (see Fasā'ī, I, p. 299; Bāmdād, op. cit., p. 328).

After Nāṣer-al-dīn Shah ascended the throne and made Mīrzā Taqī Khan Amīr Neẓām (Amīr Kabīr, q.v.) his grand vizier (*atābak-e a'ẓam*) in October, 1848, the people of Shiraz rebelled against Ḥosayn Khan Neẓām-al-dawla. 'Azīz Khan played an important role as negotiator between the opposing parties Fasā'ī, I, pp. 30ff.). This lead Amīr Kabīr to recognize his value and name him *ājūdān-bāšī-e koll-e 'asāker* (see ĀJŪDĀN-BĀŠĪ), in spite of his hostility towards 'Azīz Khan's protectors, Neẓām-al-dawla and Ḥakīm-bāšī. On the occasion of the Babi uprising of Zanjān led by Mollā Moḥammad-'Alī Zanjānī (begun in Rajab, 1266/April, 1850), Amīr Kabīr dispatched 'Azīz Khan to Zanjān to quell the revolt and, at the same time, to act as ambassador to Yerevan, where Prince Alexander Pavlovitch was putting down a local rebellion. After trying first to negotiate with the Babis and then to attack them, both in vain, 'Azīz Khan left it to Moḥammad Khan Amīr Tūmān; head of the troops in Zanjān, to suppress them and went himself to Yerevan (Kormūjī, op. cit., pp. 74f.; Eqbāl, art. cit., pp. 46ff.; Bāmdād, op. cit., p. 329), where he was warmly welcomed. Returning to Tehran on 9 Jomādā I 1267/12 March 1851, he was granted a cordial audience by the shah (Eqbāl, art. cit., pp. 47f.).

During the shah's journey to 'Erāq-e 'Ajam accompanied by Amīr Kabīr (Rajab to Ḏu'l-ḥejja, 1267/May to October, 1851), 'Azīz Khan was in command of the army and the citadel (Arg) at Tehran. The newly created police force of Tehran was entrusted to his son 'Alī Khan, who had Kurdish and other tribal forces under his command (Nikitine, op. cit., p. 166). After Amīr Kabīr's dismissal in Moḥarram, 1268/November, 1851, 'Azīz Khan remained in service. Having by now mastered the art of political survival, despite the enmity of the new *ṣadr-e a'ẓam*, Mīrzā Āqā Khan Nūrī, he was promoted to *sardār-e koll-e 'asāker* (commander in chief of the army) in an official ceremony on 3 Ḏu'l-qa'da 1269/8 August 1853. In the same month, he organized for the shah an impressive military parade at Solṭānīya (Eqbāl, art. cit., pp. 49f.). In 1268/1852 'Azīz Khan personally organized the execution of the Babi Fāṭema Barajānī Qorrat-al-'ayn in Tehran. Among other important functions, he was then entrusted with the administration of the Dār al-Fonūn (q.v.) at Tehran.

In 1270/1853-54, the Russian ambassador Prince Dolgorouky convinced Nāṣer-al-dīn Shah in a private interview to side with the Russians against the Ottomans and their allies in the coming Crimean war. Neither the shah nor Mīrzā Āqā Khan (who discovered this secret arrangement only later) was able, or willing, to adopt a clear pro-Russian policy. Two armies were sent to the Ottoman border—one to Kermānšāh and one, under 'Azīz Khan's command, to Azerbaijan—but had no millitary success. In the same year, 'Azīz Khan was put in charge of the administration of Azerbaijan until the new governor arrived (see Eqbāl, art. cit., pp. 50f.). In his absence, Mīrzā Āqā Khan kept intriguing with courtiers and the shah's favorite Jeyrān Kānom against 'Azīz Khan, which led to 'Azīz Khan's dismissal by the shah on 20 Šawwāl 1273/13 June 1857. His complete disgrace was announced in a court ceremony by 'Alī Khan Ḥājeb-al-dawla, the murderer of Amīr Kabīr (ibid., pp. 52f.). No precise charges, however, were leveled against him. 'Azīz Khan was cashiered, jailed, and asked to justify his accounts for four year's administration in Tabrīz (Gobineau, *Les dépêches*, pp. 107ff., no. 35). In Moḥarram, 1274/August-September, 1857, he was ordered to retire to Sardašt, but even there Mīrzā Āqā Khan did not leave him in peace. He dispatched Mīrzā Fażlallāh Nūrī to Azerbaijan to summon the ailing 'Azīz Khan to Tabrīz to prosecute and harass him (see Nāder Mīrzā, *Tārīk o jogrāfī*, pp. 208f.).

After Mīrzā Āqā Khan was removed from office on 20 Moḥarram 1275/30 August 1858, Nāṣer-al-dīn Shah entrusted the newly-created ministry of war (*wezārat-e jang; sepahsālārī-e qošūn*) to Mīrzā Moḥammad Khan Kešīkčī-bāšī. As soon as he was informed of 'Azīz Khan's recovery from illness, the shah reinstated him in his former dignities and conferred upon him increasing responsibilities in Azerbaijan, where he became general manager (*pīškār*) for the *wālī* (governor general) Bahrām Mīrzā, and in Tehran, where he was member of the cabinet in 1276/1859-60. When the governorship of Azerbaijan was transferred to the crown prince Moẓaffer-al-dīn Mīrzā in 1277/1860-61, 'Azīz Khan replaced him as minister of war and head of the armed forces, but lost his *pīškārī* of Azerbaijan. He then aspired towards high responsibilities in the retinue of the crown prince at Tabrīz, where he had accumulated considerable wealth and influence: *pīškārs* who did not follow his advice did not remain in office for long. In 1285/1868-69, the shah sent Ṭahmāsb Mīrzā Mo'ayyed-al-dawla to Tabrīz with full powers to jail Mīrzā Qahramān Amīn-e Laškar (q.v.), who was 'Azīz Khan's collaborator. He sent a detailed report on the two men to Tehran and demanded that Amīn-e Laškar should pay back 70,000 *tūmāns*. 'Azīz Khan interceded, accepting responsibility for the money. After further checking, the accountants found the money owed to be 150,000 *tūmāns*, which 'Azīz Khan was unable to pay. His properties were then confiscated and he was exiled for about one year to Solṭānābād (present-day Arāk), receiving only a small gratuity (Eqbāl, art. cit., pp. 55ff., quoting Nāder Mīrzā).

In 1286/1869-70, Nāṣer-al-dīn Shah restored his properties to him and entrusted 'Azīz Khan with the governorship of Māzandarān, the command of the fourth army of Tabrīz, and the governorship of Sāvoj-bolāḡ (Eqbāl, art. cit., pp. 54ff.).

'Azīz Khan was for the last time given the *pīškārī* of Azerbaijan in 1287/1870-71. But he was old and had no strength to cope with the courtiers surrounding the young crown prince, Moẓaffer-al-dīn. He died at Tabrīz on 18 Šawwāl 1287/11 January 1871. Nāṣer-al-dīn Shah, who was on a pilgrimage to Karbalā', is said to have been upset by the news of 'Azīz Khan's death (ibid., pp. 58f.). 'Azīz Khan's tomb lies near the Emāmzāda-ye Ḥamza in Tabrīz (see Qorrā'ī, "Maḥall-e qabr-e 'Azīz Ḵān," pp. 69f.).

Ḵormūjī praises 'Azīz Khan's sense of justice and chivalrous qualities (op. cit., pp. 294ff.; see also Eqbāl, art. cit., p. 59, and Bāmdād, op. cit., pp. 333f.). According to Gobineau (op. cit., pp. 108ff., 112), on the other hand, 'Azīz Khan reached his position as head of the army only through his incompetence. Eastwick saw him at Tabrīz in September, 1860, and described him as "a large brawny man, with bloodshot eyes, and inflamed features . . . he had lately walled up fourteen robbers, two of them with their heads downward, and so left them to perish." According to Eastwick (quoted by Eqbāl, art. cit., pp. 59f.) it was because of 'Azīz Khan's being a Sunnite and of humble origin that Amīr Kabīr had furthered his career.

For portraits and photographs of 'Azīz Khan see, e.g., Eqbāl, art. cit. and Bāmdād, op. cit. A square at Tehran which used to be part of 'Azīz Khan's living quarters bears his name: the Čahār-rāh-e 'Azīz Khan in the neighborhood of the Arg (Nikitine, op. cit., p. 166).

Bibliography: F. Ādamīyat, *Amīr-e Kabīr wa Īrān*, Tehran, 4th ed., 1354 Š./1975-76, pp. 23, 45, 207, 363, 453. Bāmdād, *Rejāl* II, pp. 326-36. E. B. Eastwick, *Journal of a Diplomate's Three Years' Residence in Persia*, London, 1864, I, pp. 185-87. 'A. Eqbāl, "'Azīz Ḵān Mokrī sardār-e koll," *Yādgār* 4, 1-2, 1326 Š./1947-48, pp. 37-62. Gobineau, *Les dépêches diplomatiques du Comte de Gobineau en Perse*, ed. A. D. Hytier, Paris and Geneva, 1959. R. Ḵ. Hedāyat, *Rawżat al-ṣafā-ye nāṣerī*, Tehran, 1339 Š./1960-61, pp. 562ff., 773ff. Ḵormūjī, *Ḥaqāyeq al-akbār-e nāṣerī*, ed. H. Ḵadīvjam, Tehran, 1344 Š./1965-66, index. Nāder Mīrzā, *Tārīḵ o joḡrāfī-e Dār al-Salṭana-ye Tabrīz*, ed. Sepehr, Tehran, 1323/1905. B. Nikitine, *Les kurdes*, Paris, 1956. J. Solṭān al-Qorrā'ī, "Maḥall-e qabr-e 'Azīz Ḵān sardār-e koll," *Yādgār* 4, 4, 1326 Š./1947-48, pp. 68-70.

(J. CALMARD)

'AZĪZ NASAFĪ. See NASAFĪ, 'AZĪZ.

'AZĪZ-AL-DĪN, MOSTAWFĪ. See ABŪ NAṢR MOSTAWFĪ.

'AZĪZ-AL-MOLK. See 'ALĪ EBRĀHĪM KHAN.

'AZĪZ-AL-SOLṬĀN, ḠOLĀM-'ALĪ KHAN (1297-1359/1879-1940) better known as **Malījak**(-e) Ṯānī [II], the boy favorite of Nāṣer-al-dīn Shah Qājār. He was the son of Mīrzā Moḥammad Khan Malījak Awwal [I] (later Amīn Ḵāqān)—himself a favored page of the private quarters (*ḵalwat*)—and grand-son of a Kurdish shepherd from the small village of Ḥalwā'ī in the Garrūs region. It is said that Nāṣer-al-dīn gave Moḥammad the nickname *malījak* (corruption of *melīčak* "little sparrow" in Kurdish [*melīč*: "bird, sparrow" with the diminutive ending *-ak*], later further corrupted to Manījak) when the unpolished Kurdish shepherd boy, upon seeing a sparrow exclaimed "*malījak*!" Moḥammad's one year-old son, Ḡolām 'Alī, first caught the attention of the Shah during the latter's visits to Zobayda Ḵānūm Amīna Aqdas (q.v.), the trusted and influential wife of Nāṣer-al-dīn Shah and the elder sister of Malījak I (Dūst-'Alī Khan Mo'ayyer-al-mamālek, *Rejāl-e 'aṣr-e nāṣerī*, Tehran, 1361 Š./1982, p. 240). The unattractive boy suffering from chronic trachoma and acute stammer (Tāj-al-salṭana, *Ḵāṭerāt*, ed. M. Etteḥādīya and S. Sa'dvandīān, Tehran, 1362 Š./1983, pp. 18, 23-24), apparently became the substitute for the shah's favorite cat, Babrī Khan, who had been put to death as a result of jealousy in the harem towards Amīna Aqdas, the honorary keeper of Babrī (Tāj-al-salṭana, *Ḵāṭerāt*, pp. 15, 17-18). There is little reason to doubt Mīrzā 'Alī Khan Amīn-al-dawla's remark (*Ḵāṭerāt-e sīāsī*, ed. Ḥ. Farmānfarmā'īān, Tehran, 1341 Š./1962, p. 87) concerning the intentions of Amīna Aqdas to bring Ḡolām 'Alī—whom he calls "the essence of dirt and the extract of filth and putridity"—to the inner quarters (*andarūn*) of the court as an instrument to retain her control over the ageing, and increasingly capricious monarch. Later, also his father and the eunuch 'Abdallāh Khan Ḵᵛāja, among others, would use him to further their wishes with the shah. The shah's almost obsessive love for Ḡolām 'Alī greatly annoyed everyone at the court and in the government, most of all his own children. Gradually in the early 1880s the inner court and to some extent the government, but above all Nāṣer-al-dīn himself became subservient to the whims of Malījak II, his petty wishes and his precarious health, always in grip of some mysterious illness and in convenient custody of his caring aunt Amīna Aqdas.

From early age Malīǰak was treated as the most precious belonging in the royal household, living in ultimate luxury. In addition to a large retinue of pages, servants, and guards as well as a house keeper, an esquire, a tutor, and a eunuch, he also enjoyed the company of several members of his own clan, the so-called Malāǰeka, as Eʿtemād-al-salṭana calls them, including his younger brother, Malīǰak III, his father, his maternal grandfather Abu'l-Qāsem Bazzāz (the clothier), his maternal uncle Āqā Mardak (Eʿtemād(-e) Ḥażrat), and a host of playmates. A children's music band was formed for his pleasure and a special music section was created in the Dār al-Fonūn. There was no limitation to his movements in and out of the *andarūn*, and he often intruded, together with his entourage, into formal audience. Every slight illness that affected Malīǰak soured the royal temper—even to the point of disrupting the shah's gastronomic habits—and every gesture of his delighted the shah. In the presence of the high officials, the shah showed little restraint to kiss, hug, and play with the young boy, and call him with words of endearment. He even had Malīǰak's milk tooth overlaid with gold and preserved in the palace museum (Moḥammad Ḥasan Khan Eʿtemād-al-salṭana, *Rūz-nāma-ye ḵāṭerāt*, ed. Ī. Afšār, Tehran, 1345 Š./1966, p. 611). Reportedly, he even promised Malīǰak that he would be the *sardār* (military chief) of Iran and hoped he would become his successor (ibid., p. 588).

In 1304/1886 Ḡolām ʿAlī received the title ʿAzīz-al-solṭān (the beloved of the sovereign). Eʿtemād-al-salṭana comments that by conferring a title similar to that of the chief minister, the shah made utter ridicule of Amīn-al-solṭān (*Rūz-nāma*, p. 531). A year later Malīǰak was given the high military rank of *amīr(-e) tūmān* (head of ten thousand, q.v.) with all its ceremonial privileges. When he was eleven years of age, the shah arranged for his engagement to his own eight year-old daughter Aḵtar-al-dawla (Tāj-al-salṭana *Ḵāṭerāt*, pp. 23-24) and they were married in 1312/1894 in a pompous wedding. Shortly before the marriage, the shah eventually consented to Malīǰak's circumcision. On that occasion Eʿtemād-al-salṭana was commissioned by the shah to write a short history of circumcision (*Rūz-nāma*, pp. 1096-97). In the same year Malīǰak replaced the young son of the *īl-ḵānī* of the Qajar tribe in the prestigious office of the *mohrdār* (keeper of the royal signet) and at the same time was promoted to the rank of *amīr(-e) nowyān* (the equivalent of Field Marshal, *Rūz-nāma*, p. 1213, cf. G. Curzon, *Persia and the Persian Question*, London, 1892, I, p. 400), the second highest military rank in a largely non-existent army. He was also granted the ownership of some confiscated properties in and around Tehran. These included the village of Behjatābād (1303/1886) which initially belonged to Mīrzā Yūsof Mostawfī-al-mamālek (*Rūz-nāma*, p. 493) and the private quarters of Mīrzā Ḥosayn Khan Sepahsālār which was renamed ʿAzīzīya and later became part of the compound of the Majles-e Šawrā-ye Mellī (Moʿayyer-al-mamālek, *Rejāl*, p. 243). The shah also transferred to him the ownership of one of his most valuable landed properties in the Varāmīn region (Amīn-al-dawla, *Ḵāṭerāt*, p. 174). After the death of Amīna Aqdas (1311/1894), contrary to the usual practice of confiscation, Nāṣer-al-dīn granted the total ownership of her vast estate, including a substantial sum in cash, to Malīǰak (Amīn-al-dawla, *Ḵāṭerāt*, p. 178, cf. Tāj-al-salṭana, *Ḵāṭerāt*, p. 30). His father, Malīǰak I, among other privileges received the ceremonial chieftainship of the royal bodyguards, the Čaganī cavalry detachment.

The behavior of Malīǰak was a constant source of aggravation within and outside the palace. Most sources portray him as an enfant terrible and as a pleasure-seeking adolescent with a passion for shooting, sexual excesses, and scandalous feasts. He learned foul language in the *andarūn* and on one occasion was reported to have called Nāṣer-al-dīn "son of a pimp" (Bāmdād, *Rejāl* III, p. 31). With no more respect he treated the long bearded Fatḥ-ʿAlī Shah when he saw his portray on the royal sword (*Rūz-nāma*, pp. 395, 404, cf. Bāmdād, *Rejāl* III, pp. 30-31). On another occasion he demanded reverence equal to that of the shah's sons. To appease him the shah authorized Malīǰak to "run sword" through those who failed to pay him proper respect (*Rūz-nāma*, p. 603; see ibid., pp. 290-91, and cf. ʿA. Mostawfī, *Šarḥ-e zendagānī-e man*, 2nd ed., 3 vols., Tehran, 1343 Š./1964, pp. 263-64, for Farhād Mīrzā's objection to the shah's special treatment of Malīǰak). It is small wonder that according to Eʿtemād-al-salṭana, on different occasions he actually murdered five innocent people, including his own bodyguards (*Rūz-nāma*, p. 1003). A more romantic side of ʿAzīz-al-solṭan and his love affair with the shah's other daughter, Tāj-al-salṭana, appears in the latter's memoirs (see, e.g., *Ḵāṭerāt*, pp. 40-42). His relationship with some of the concubines of the harem, including a famous Circassian slave, forced the shah to plead with Malīǰak to sleep outside the *andarūn* (on his bi- and homosexual experiences see *Rūz-nāma*, pp. 1003, 1055, 1142, 1179, 1186). According to Eʿtemād-al-salṭana, however, the shah himself had no sexual interest either in Malīǰak or his father (*Rūz-nāma*, p. 1053), but the rumors of the shah's sexual love for Malīǰak were so widespread, both at home and abroad, that the court Mollā, Mīrzā Moḥammad Ḏu'l-rīāsatayn, composed a treatise entitled *ʿAqā'ed al-moslemīn* to justify the permissiveness of the shah's infatuation (*ḡarāma*) for Malīǰak (Āqā Bozorg Ṭehrānī, *al-Ḏarīʿa* XV, p. 285).

In spite of objections from the women of the *andarūn*, most notably Anīs-al-dawla (the shah's most respected wife and an outspoken critic of Malīǰak; q.v.), Malīǰak was included in the royal retinue during the shah's third European tour (1306/1889), during which he was a subject of curiosity and criticism in the European press. He was granted an audience with Queen Victoria and other heads of state. It was later alleged that he had stolen some items during a visit to the house of the British banker Baron Rothschild.

Criticism of the relationship between Malījak and the shah was common in the later part of Nāṣer-al-dīn's rule. E'temad-al-salṭana who calls Malījak "*al-kannās*" [he who withdraws when the name of God is mentioned], and "blood thirsty wicked," clearly found him and his relatives repulsive, a sentiment he shared with other officials, e.g. the premier Mīrzā 'Alī Aṣğar Khan Amīn-al-solṭān, who used to call the shah's favorite in his absence "sheep-dung" (*pešgel*), yet used the shah's affection for 'Azīz-al-solṭān to tighten his own grip on the monarch, either by means of emotional blackmail or sheer cajolery. He apparently convinced the resident European envoys that the shah's excessive love for Malījak was a symptom of insanity (*Rūz-nāma*, p. 976). Outside government circles, the criticism of Malījak and the shah contributed to the growing general discontent. However, he was far less cursed by the public than Amīn-al-solṭān or Kārmān Mīrzā Nā'eb-al-salṭana. In 1307/1890 a *mojtahed* in Tehran, Mollā Fayżallāh Tork, alleged that this "Malījak business" (*malījak-bāzī*) was a "disgrace to the dignity of Islam" (*Rūz-nāma*, p. 796). Later, Mīrzā Reżā Kermānī, Nāṣer-al-dīn's assassin, gave the shah's devotion to 'Azīz-al-solṭān and his lavish spending for him and his entourage as one justification for the assassination (M. Nāẓem-al-eslām Kermānī, *Tārīḵ-e bīdārī-e Īrānīān*, 2nd ed., ed. 'A. A. Sa'īdī Sīrjānī, 3 vols., Tehran, 1346 Š./1967, I, pp. 102, 106). Nāẓem-al-eslām himself in a long poem entitled "lamentation on the present state of affairs" blamed Nāṣer-al-dīn: "He did not pay attention to the affairs of his subjects; he adored instead sometimes his cat and sometimes his Malījak." *Īrānīān* I, p. 182).

The rising tide of public discontent, the petty court rivalries, and the misconduct of government affairs all in one way or another stemmed from the shah's self-interest, profligacy, and hedonistic attitude. At forty-eight, Nāṣer-al-dīn was evidently suffering a mid-life crisis, being bored, insecure, and psychologically troubled, and the passion for Malījak no doubt gave him a welcome refuge from the troublesome world of the inner court, the state, and beyond. On one occasion he expressed his wishes that except for himself, Malījak, some maids of the *andarūn* and a fair supply of lamb and poultry, everything else—the whole universe—should turn into stone until the Day of Resurrection (*Rūz-nāma*, p. 967). On another occasion he confessed to his own helplessness in his infatuation for Malījak. Notwithstanding the obvious emotional undertones, the affection for 'Azīz-al-solṭān had a subtle rationale. It may have been that the shah wished to humiliate the notables, courtiers, and high officials, towards whom he had always felt helpless and despiteful, by excessively favoring the son of a court page with humble origin.

For some time after Nāṣer-al-dīn's death, 'Azīz-al-solṭān led a comfortable life. He maintained connections with the court and during the reign of Aḥmad Shah received the title of *sardār-e moḥtaram* but lost most of his fortune ('A. Mostawfī, *Šarḥ-e zendagānī-e man*, pp. 498-501). He died relatively poor in 1319 Š./1940 in Tehran.

Bibliography: Given in the text.

(A. AMANAT)

'AZĪZALLĀH BEN NA'ĪM. See JEWS, PERSIAN.

'AŻOD-AL-DAWLA, ABŪ ŠOJĀ' FANNĀ (PANĀH) ḴOSROW (or Ḵosrah, as on his coins) the greatest Buyid monarch and the most powerful ruler in the Islamic East in the last years of his life. He was born in Isfahan on 5 Ḏu'l-qa'da 324/24 September 936 to Rokn-al-dawla Ḥasan b. Būya, second eldest of the three Buyid brothers who established the original kingdoms of the Buyid dynasty.

The eldest of these brothers, 'Emād-al-dawla 'Alī b. Būya, the ruler of the Buyid kingdom of Fārs, who had no sons, chose as his heir to that province his nephew, Fannā Khosrow, the future 'Ażod-al-dawla, whom he summoned from the court of his brother Rokn-al-dawla at Rayy. 'Emād-al-dawla knew that some of his own officers who were of noble Daylami descent believed that they themselves had a better claim to the throne of Fārs than did the Buyids (who were also Daylamis but of humble origin); therefore he arrested a group of these officers before his nephew's arrival. When his nephew did arrive in Shiraz, the capital of Fārs, in 338/949 'Emād-al-dawla met him, seated him on the throne in his palace, and stood in his nephew's presence to oblige the other members of the court to do likewise. His effort for his nephew were either hopeless or too late; rebellion against Fannā Ḵosrow followed shortly after 'Emād-al-dawla's death on Jomādā I, 338/November, 949 (Ebn Meskawayh [Meskūya], *Tajāreb* II, p. 121-22; Ebn al-Aṯīr, VIII, pp. 245-363).

Rokn-al-dawla hurried south in 338 to save his son and to secure Buyid rule in southern Iran. He was met there by the vizier of Mo'ezz-al-dawla, sent from Iraq for the same purpose; and together they returned Fannā Ḵosrow to the throne. After transferring the district of Arrajān from the kingdom of Shiraz to his own dominions, Rokn-al-dawla left (Meskawayh, *Tajāreb* I, pp. 130, 137). From this time on, Fannā Ḵosrow, who received the title 'Ażod-al-dawla from the 'Abbasid caliph al-Moṭī' in 351/962, ruled Fārs without any apparent difficulty. Fārs had been the stablest of the Buyid kingdoms and was to remain so until Buyid rule disappeared; among its other advantages, its non-Buyid neighbors were not of the military calibre of the rulers of northern Iraq or Khorasan. In 356/967 'Ażod-al-dawla took advantage of the struggle between Abū 'Alī Moḥammad b. Elyās/Alyās (see ĀL-E ELYĀS) and the latter's sons in Kermān to conquer part of that province. He conquered the rest of Kermān in 357/968 and negotiated a peace with Abū Aḥmad Ḵalaf b. Aḥmad, the Saffarid ruler of Sīstān, who was then playing a vital role in weakening the perpetual enemies of the Buyids, the Samanids (Ebn Meskawayh, *Tajāreb* II, pp. 232, 249-53; Ebn al-Aṯīr, VIII, pp. 416-17; Hamadānī, *Takmela*, p. 176.)

The Samanids sent soldiers to support the attempt by Solaymān, the son of Moḥammad b. Elyās, to reconquer Kermān. But 'Ażod-al-dawla defeated him, and then on 10 Ṣafar 360/13 December 970 inflicted an even more important defeat on Solaymān's allies, the Kūč-Balūč, who had helped the Elyasids and earlier local rulers keep any Islamic central government from gaining full control of Kermān. The army of 'Ażod-al-dawla now marched through Kermān into the province of Tīz and Makrān and ended their victorious progress at the Persian Gulf port of Hormoz. Many tribes offered both obedience and conversion to Islam for the first time. In Ḏu'l-qaʿda, 360/August-September, 971, 'Ażod-al-dawla led a successful punitive expedition to subdue the Baluch (Balūč) who had gone back on their word; and after their decisive defeat on 11 Rabīʿ I 361/8 January 972 he settled farmers in the area to change the complexion of the province. One of the legacies of Buyid rule would be the conversion and assimilation of parts of Kermān, Makrān, and even areas of southern Pārs near the Gulf that had remained nearly untouched by Islamic central governments until the 4th/10th century. The successes of 'Ażod-al-dawla and his father, Rokn-al-dawla, led to a formal peace in 361 by the Buyids with the Samanids in which the Buyids agreed to pay 150,000 dinars a year to the Samanids. An expedition sent by 'Ażod-al-dawla in 364/975 to Kermān recaptured Bam from a renegade Samanid officer, then defeated a son of Moḥammad b. Elyās at Jīroft, after which the border between the Samanids and Buyid Kermān seems to have remained undisturbed until 'Ażod-al-dawla's death (Ebn al-Atīr, VIII, p. 461; Hamadānī, *Takmela*, p. 210; Meskawayh, *Tajāreb* II, pp. 298-300, 311, 360-62; Rūdrāvarī, *Ḏayl*, p. 189).

Moʿezz-al-dawla, the uncle of 'Ażod-al-dawla and the Buyid ruler of Iraq, gained control of Basra in Rabīʿ II, 336/November, 947, after which it became a natural objective of Buyid policy to control Oman, the rulers of which province could tax or hinder trade between the Gulf and the Indian Ocean. In 355/966 'Ażod-al-dawla and Moʿezz-al-dawla sent a joint expedition which imposed direct Buyid rule on Oman, but the representatives of the Buyids were expelled shortly afterwards. 'Ażod-al-dawla, after clearing the land route to Hormoz, the Gulf port in Iran opposite Oman, in the campaign of 360-61/970-72 against the Baluch, sent an army from Kermān and captured Sohar, the capital of Oman, in 362. In the succeeding year 'Ażod-al-dawla's commander conquered the mountains of Oman, which gave him fuller control of the provinces than any ruler had enjoyed in many years (Ebn al-Jawzī, *Montaẓam* II, p. 368; Hamadānī, *Takmela*, p. 187; Meskawayh, *Tajāreb* II, pp. 213, 217-18; Ebn al-Atīr, VII, p. 474).

On the death of Moʿezz-al-dawla in 356/967 the province of Iraq passed to that ruler's eldest son, 'Ezz-al-dawla Baktīār (q.v.), whose conflict with 'Ażod-al-dawla, his first cousin was to destroy the system of family cooperation that had been such a remarkable feature of the first generation of Buyid rule. In 363/974 'Ezz-al-dawla was trapped in Wāseṭ by a rebellion of his troops in both Baghdad, his capital, and Ḵūzestān. 'Ażod-al-dawla came from Fārs, defeated the rebels on

14 Jomādā I 364/30 January 975. But after reaching Baghdad he manipulated circumstances so that 'Ezz-al-dawla was forced to abdicate on 4 Jomādā II 364/12 March 975 in favor of his rescuer (Ebn Meskawayh, *Tajāreb* II, pp. 236, 246, 324, 326, 341, 343, 346; Ebn al-Atīr, VIII p. 450; Hamadānī, *Takmela*, p. 218).

Then Rokn-al-dawla, the last survivor of the three Buyid brothers who had founded the dynasty, by sheer exercise of parental authority made his son disgorge his conquests, restore 'Ezz-al-dawla, and retreat without compensation to Fārs. Rokn-al-dawla rewarded 'Ażod-al-dawla at least in part for his obedience. When the two met in 365/976 in Isfahan in Rokn-al-dawla's territory 'Ażod-al-dawla repeatedly kissed the ground before his father until permitted to kiss his hand. Then, at a banquet for all his sons and leading army officers Rokn-al-dawla declared his eldest son, 'Ażod-al-dawla, his heir apparent as head of Buyid family, and a document that acknowledged the priority of 'Ażod-al-dawla over his brothers was signed by the leading men of the Buyid kingdoms of western Iran (Ebn Meskawayh, *Tajāreb* II, pp. 350-52, 362-64; Ebn al-Atīr, VIII p. 492).

On 18 Moḥarram 366/16 September 976, with the death of Rokn-al-dawla, the last Buyid ruler to understand the family system as a matter of genuine affection as well as of policy, this system of mutual support among states ruled by relations disappeared, although for another eighty years its ghost continued to haunt Buyid politics, especially in the continual quarrels as to who had priority among Buyid rulers. 'Ezz-al-dawla prepared for a second round of fighting by forming an alliance with Faḵr-al-dawla, a son of Rokn-al-dawla and his father's successor to territories around Hamadān, with the Hamdanid dynasty of northern Iraq, the Kurdish ruler Ḥasanwayh (Ḥasanūya) Barzekānī, and 'Emrān b. Šāhīn the ruler of the marshes of southern Iraq. (Moʾayyed-al-dawla, another son of Rokn-al-dawla, and his father's successor to territories around Isfahan, remained loyal to his elder brother 'Ażod-al-dawla.) 'Ezz-al-dawla then abandoned all pretext of recognizing his cousin's precedence by stopping the mention of 'Ażod-al-dawla in the public prayer in Iraq. 'Ażod-al-dawla advanced into Ḵūzestān and easily defeated 'Ezz-al-dawla on 11 Ḏu'l-qaʿda 366/1 July 977 at Ahvāz. 'Ezz-al-dawla, an incompetent and irresolute ruler, after some vacillation asked and got 'Ażod-al-dawla's permission to withdraw and established himself in Syria, a politically very fragmented province in the later 4th/10th century. But on the way to Syria the Hamdanid Abū Taḡleb persuaded 'Ezz-al-dawla to fight his cousin again, and on 18 Šawwāl 367/29 May 978 in the battle which followed at Qaṣr al-Jaṣṣ near Samarra 'Ezz-al-dawla was defeated, captured, and sentenced to death by 'Ażod-al-dawla (Ebn Meskawayh, *Tajāreb* II, pp. 364-81; Hamadānī, *Takmela*, p. 232.)

'Ażod-al-dawla occupied the former Hamdanid stronghold of Mosul in 367/978 and, unlike former Buyid rulers who had occupied this city only temporarily, held onto it for the rest of his reign; the remainder of Hamdanid territory came directly under his control or was left in the hands of a Hamdanid ruler who offered his allegience. ʿAżod-al-dawla's armies then subjugated the Kurds of northern Iraq and western Iran, who had become semi-independent after the dissolution of ʿAbbasid power. It should be remembered that "Kurd" in the sources of the 4th-5th/10th-11th centuries refers to all the transhumants of the Zagros region including the Lors (Ebn Meskawayh, *Tajāreb* II, pp. 383, 392; Ebn al-Aṯīr, VIII, p. 521).

In Ḏu'l-qaʿda, 369/May-June, 979, ʿAżod-al-dawla advanced on the territory of his brother, Fak̲r-al-dawla who fled to Qazvīn and then to Nīšāpūr after many of his officers deserted. ʿAżod-al-dawla moved on to Kermānšāh where he installed Badr, a son of Ḥasanwayh, to rule the surrounding Kurdish territory as his representative. In Ṣafar, 370/August-September, 980, ʿAżod-al-dawla occupied Hamadān and soon subjugated the regions east and south of that city, which were now more fully under central control than they had been for at least half a century (Ebn Meskawayh, *Tajāreb* II, pp. 398, 414-15; Rūḏrāvarī, *Ḏayl*, pp. 9-10, 12; Ebn al-Jawzī, *Montaẓam* VII, p. 101).

Very shortly after ʿAżod-al-dawla's conquest of Hamadān the great minister of Mo'ayyed-al-dawla, Esmāʿīl b. ʿAbbād (q.v.), arrived from Rayy and stayed until Rabīʿ II, 370/October-November 980, to arrange the transfer of control of that city to his king. ʿAżod-al-dawla had other rewards for his younger brother's loyalty: He gave him Fak̲r-al-dawla's troops and later gave him even more troops to help him campaign against the Samanids, whose ally, the Ziyarid king Qābūs b. Vošmgīr, had just seized Ṭabarestān in time to welcome the fleeing Fak̲r-al-dawla. ʿAżod-al-dawla at first tried to get Qābūs to surrender Fak̲r-al-dawla; apparently, ʿAżod-al-dawla had supported Qābūs in the struggle among the sons of the Ziyarid king Vošmgīr, and expected some cooperation in return. When Qābūs refused, in Moḥarram, 371/July-August, 981, ʿAżod-al-dawla arranged for Mo'ayyed-al-dawla to receive an official appointment by the ʿAbbasid caliph as governor of Ṭabarestān and Gorgān, which provinces Mo'ayyed-al-dawla proceeded to conquer (Rūḏrāvarī, *Ḏayl*, pp. 10, 15-18.)

When ʿAżod-al-dawla died on 8 Šawwāl 372/26 March 983, he was not only the direct ruler of Fārs (the site of his capital, Shiraz), Iraq and parts of the Jazīra to the north of Iraq, but also controlled, through his brother, his sons, and vassals, territories from the border of Khorasan to the Byzantine border in Syria, and from Oman to the shores of the Caspian. He was, moreover, recognized by lesser kings as their overlord as far away as the Yemen and the shores of the Mediterranean. The Byzantines, who had for a period raided into Syria without fear of reprisals, had sought and gained a treaty in exchange for ʿAżod-al-dawla's promise not to support Bardos Scleros, the Byzantine pretender who had escaped to Baghdad. Similarly the Fatimids, who had been hostile to earlier Buyids, had tried to gain his good favor in order to avoid any contest of strength with him. The Samanids had more direct reason to fear him, since his support for Mo'ayyed-al-dawla had laid Khorasan open to his brother. No other Buyid ruler had been, or would be, nearly as successful in military matters (Ebn Meskawayh, *Tajāreb* II, pp. 409-10; Rūḏrāvarī, *Ḏayl*, p. 29; Ebn al-Aṯīr, VIII, pp. 513, 515; IX, p. 13; Ebn al-Jawzī, *Montaẓam* VIII, p. 105).

ʿAżod-al-dawla maintained as complete personal control over his administration as circumstances allowed. When his kingdom expanded he appointed a second vizier, Moṭahhar b. ʿAbdallāh, in addition to Naṣr b. Hārūn, a Christian whom he maintained in this office; and he also personally appointed a deputy vizier, who acted as the deputy of the king rather than of the viziers. He was punctilious about having government employees paid promptly at the beginning of each pay period, and staggered pay schedules so that such prompt payment would not be a burden on the treasury. Nevertheless, the fundamental changes in administration that had taken place at the end of the ʿAbbasid period, changes such as the introduction of the *eqṭāʿ* (q.v.), were not reversed by ʿAżod-al-dawla (Ebn Meskawayh, *Tajāreb* II, pp. 410, 412; Rūḏrāvarī, *Ḏayl*, pp. 43, 45).

While following the policy of earlier Buyid rulers in maintaining the ʿAbbasid caliphate in Baghdad (which gave legitimacy to Buyid rule in the eyes of some of their Sunni subjects) ʿAżod-al-dawla showed more interest than previous Buyid rulers in evoking the pre-Islamic Iranian precedents for Buyid kingship. He visited Persepolis and left an inscription there that showed his consciousness of the association of Buyid kingship with pre-Islamic Iran; and he assumed the title Šāhanšāh on his coins and in public ceremonial, probably the first Moslem king to do so since the fall of the Sassanians with whom he claimed a genealogical link. ʿAżod-al-dawla celebrated the ancient Iranian festivals of Sada and Mehragān (and, doubtless, Nowrūz as well, which last festival had been celebrated by numerous earlier Islamic rulers including the caliphs themselves). He also founded two festivals commemorating the foundation of Kard-e Fannā K̲osrow (see below).

However, like most of the Buyids he patronized Arabic authors, and there is very little evidence of his interest in the new Persian poetry of his time. He was an assiduous student of Arabic, wrote Arabic verse, and was proud that one of his teachers was the celebrated grammarian of Arabic, Abū ʿAlī Fāresī (q.v.). he studied many of the sciences of the time in Arabic, including geometry and astronomy; and, thanks to his patronage, many Arabic books were dedicated to him, including books in the fields of *feqh*, *tafsīr*, *kalām*, *ḥadīṯ*, genealogy, poetry, grammer, prosody, medicine, astronomy, and geometry. The very large and complete library he established in Shiraz had a separate list for each subject it included (Moqaddasī, pp. 10, 258-59, 448, 449). In his interest in higher learning in Arabic (to the apparent exclusion of Persian) ʿAżod-al-dawla followed the general pattern of intellectual life in his time in his home province, Fārs, where written culture was dominated by Arabic and Pahlavi (since the *mōbads* had no interest as yet in the "Islamic" idiom of new Persian).

Furthermore, like many of his Iranian contemporaries, he does not seem to have felt that his admiration for the pre-Islamic Iranian past contradicted his Islamic belief. He was probably a Shi'ite of some undefined variety, as were the great majority of Buyid rulers, and according to some accounts he repaired the shrine of Ḥosayn b. 'Alī at Karbalā' and built the shrine over the grave of 'Alī b. Abī Ṭāleb at Najaf where he asked to be buried. He is said to have shown great generosity to the eminent Shi'ite theologian, Shaikh Abū 'Abdallāh Moḥammad Mofīd. However, his religious policy was far from uniformly Shi'ite in character. He forced the 'Abbasid caliph to marry his daughter, supposedly with the hope of uniting the claim of the Sunni 'Abbasids and the Buyids in one line (a policy the caliph resisted by not consummating the marriage). In 369/979-80 he appointed a jurist in Fārs, Bešr b. Ḥosayn, chief judge in Baghdad, even though Bešr continued to reside in 'Ażod-al-dawla's capital province of Fārs, presumably in an attempt to further integrate one important remaining institution of Sunni 'Abbasid government into the Buyid state.

Ażod-al-dawla was a great builder. In Iraq his most important building was a large hospital which remained in operation at least as late as the Mongol invasion. The beautiful bazaars he had built near the congregational mosque of Rāmhormoz were unmatched (Moqaddasī, p. 413). But most of his constructions were in Fārs where he built caravansarais, cisterns, and dams in addition to buildings, and his principal beneficiary was Shiraz. Near this city on the river Kor he built a famous dam, Band-e 'Ażodī (now called Band-e Amīr), which brought a large area into cultivation and is still in use (Moqaddasī, p. 444; Ebn Balḵī, pp. 151-52). Within Shiraz he built a palace of three hundred and sixty rooms, with elaborate wind towers and water canals, and a hospital (Moqaddasī, p. 449). Shiraz became so crowded during his reign that he built a satellite city nearby for his army, the name of which, Kard-e Fannā Ḵosrow ("Fannā Ḵosrow made it"), consciously echoed the style of the names that Sasanian kings had given to the towns they founded (Moqaddasī, pp. 430-31; Ebn Balḵī, pp. 132-33; *Nozhat al-qolūb*, tr., p. 113). According to Bīrūnī (*Chronology*, p. 217) two annual festivals were held in the town (Jašn-e Kard-e Fannā Ḵosrow) on the day Serōš of the month of Farvardīn and the day Hormoz of the month Ābān. The former commemorated the day the water of the acqueduct reached the town from a distance of four leagues and the latter the day the construction of the town started. These two festivals were founded by 'Ażod-al-dawla on the model of the festival of Nowrūz in Isfahan which he had seen in his childhood there (Mofażżal b. Sa'd Māfarrūḵī, *Ketāb maḥāsen Esfahān*, ed. S. J. Ḥosaynī Ṭehrānī, Tehran, n.d., p. 93.). By his building activity in Fārs he strengthened a revival of that province which was so dramatic that, according to Ebn al-Jawzī, the tax income of Fārs in the time of 'Ażod-al-dawla was triple what it had been at the beginning of the 4th/10th century (*Montaẓam* VIII, p. 116). Shiraz, a comparatively unimportant town until the Saffarid invasion of Fārs in the 3rd/9th century, achieved under 'Ażod-al-dawla the economic and cultural importance it was to maintain throughout succeeding centuries.

Ażod-al-dawla's achievement in building a strong, unified Buyid state was not sustained by his successors. His execution of his cousin destroyed the Buyid family system. Nevertheless, his success in exerting Buyid power against almost all the rivals of the Buyids in the second generation of that dynasty gave this family of humble origin a legitimacy that helped them to survive until the middle of the 5th/11th century. More importantly, he contributed to the growing prosperity of Fārs which was to be a comparatively safe and prosperous haven for Iranian culture during the troubled Saljuq and Mongol periods.

Bibliography: The only book on 'Ażod-al-dawla is 'A. A. Faqīhī's *Šāhanšāhī-e 'Ażod-al-dawla*, Tehran, 1347 Š./1968, which uses a wide range of primary sources in Persian and Arabic and has a valuable bibliography of primary sources. The best survey of Buyid history, including a full treatment of the career of 'Ażod-al-dawla is H. Busse's "Iran under the Buyids," *Camb. Hist. Iran* IV, pp. 250-304 (with a good bibliography of secondary as well as primary sources). W. Madelung's magisterial article, "The Assumption of the Title Shahanshah by the Buyids," *JNES* 28, 1969, pp. 84-108 and 168-83 is important for all aspects of Buyid rule, in particular for the political circumstances surrounding this ruler's "Iranizing" policy. It is complemented by the important article by L. Richter-Bernburg, "*Amīr-Malik-Shāhānshāh*: 'Aḍud ad-Daula's Titulature Re-examined," *Iran* 18, 1980, pp. 83-102. J. C. Bürgel's *Die Hofkorrespondenz 'Aḍud ad-Daulas und ihr Verhältnis zu anderen historischen Quellen der frühen Buyiden*, Wiesbaden, 1965, analyzes 'Ażod-al-dawla's personal and often very tendentious interpretations of his actions and intentions as propagated in his official letters and in contradiction to the more or less critical accounts in the extant chronicles, even though some of these were influenced by the official propaganda or even written under pressure, as was the case with the *Tājī*, composed by Ebrāhīm b. Helāl al-Ṣābe'. Of the chronicles of the period, Ebn Meskawayh's *Tajāreb al-omam*, vol. II, Cairo, 1915 and Abū Šojā' Rūḏrāvarī's *Ḏayl Tajāreb al-omam*, Cairo, 1916, are by far the most important. Ebn al-Aṯīr's *Kāmel*, vols. VIII and IX; Ebn al-Jawzī's *al-Montaẓam*, Hyderabad, 1358/1939; and Moḥammad b. 'Abd-al-Malek Hamaḏānī's *Takmelat Ta'rīḵ al-Ṭabarī*, ed. A.Y. Kan'ān, Beirut, 1960, are also important. The numismatic evidence, which often provides the only accurate evidence as to who ruled when and where and under whose suzerainty, has never been properly drawn together except for

Richter-Bernburg's careful examination of its bearing on titulature. See also 'A. A. Faqīhī, *Āl-e Būya wa awżāʿ-e zamān-e īšān yā namūdār-ī az zendagī-e mardom-e ān ʿaṣr*, Tehran, 1357 Š./1978. For further bibliography see BUYIDS.

(CH. BÜRGEL AND R. MOTTAHEDEH)

ʿAŻOD-AL-DAWLA ŠĪRZĀD. See ŠĪRZĀD.

ʿAŻOD-AL-DĪN ĪJĪ, QĀŻĪ ABU'L-FAŻL ʿABD-AL-RAḤMĀN B. ROKN-AL-DĪN AḤMAD B. ʿABD-AL-ĠAFFĀR B. AḤMAD BAKRĪ MOṬARREZĪ ŠABĀNKĀRĪ ŠĪRĀZĪ, famous Shafiʿite jurist and Ashʿarite theologian. He was born at Īj (Īg or Īk), then the chief town of the district Šabānkāra in Fārs, in 680/1281 or shortly afterwards. (The later dates 708 or "after 700" given by such Arab biographers as Ebn al-ʿEmād, Ebn Ḥajar, Soyūṭī, and others, are plainly erroneous.) He was a descendant of a family which traced its genealogy back to the caliph Abū Bakr. Although he may have been sure of inheriting the office of his father, who had already been *qāżī* of the same place, he tried to make his fortune with Ḵᵛāja Rašīd-al-dīn Fażlallah, the influential vizier of the Il-khanids Ḡāzān Khan (694-703/1295-1304) and Öljeitü (Oljāytū) (703-16/1304-16). In 706/1306 he arrived in Solṭānīya, which had just been chosen as the new capital of the Il-khanid empire by Öljeitü. His older contemporary, Ebn al-Fowaṭī (642-723/1244-1323) reports in his *Majmaʿ al-ādāb fī moʿjam al-alqāb* (ed. Moṣṭafā Jawād, Damascus, 1962, IV, 1, pp. 444f. no. 634) some gossip about his licentious behavior and about his eventual removal from the court to Kermān. But he is mentioned together with his brother ʿEmād-al-dīn, his teacher Faḵr-al-dīn Aḥmad b. Ḥasan Čahārbartī (Jārabardī in Arabic sources, d. 746/1345), and the doyen of the Iranian *ʿolamāʾ* at the time, ʿAbdallāh b. ʿOmar Bayżāwī (d. 716/1316), in a list of fifty-one scholars whom Rašīd-al-dīn asked his son (Amīr ʿAlī, the governor of Baghdad) to present with copious donations; he himself was far away in Syria, obviously in 712/1312-13, during Öljeitü's only campaign against the Mamluks (cf. *Mokātabāt-e rašīdī* [Letters of Rašīd-al-dīn Fażlallāh], ed. M. Šafīʿ, Lahore, 1947, p. 59; Russ. tr. A. I. Falina, *Rashid ad-din. Perepiska*, Moscow, 1971, p. 126). The sequence of names in the latter seems to indicate that Ījī lived at that time in Tabrīz where his teacher Čahārbartī was acknowledged as the best authority in grammar and the religious sciences (Brockelmann, *GAL* II, p. 246, S. II, p. 257). We know however, through a passage in Ḥāfeẓ-e Abrū's *Majmaʿ al-tawārīḵ*, that during Öljeitü's reign he also belonged to the teaching staff of a mobile *madrasa* (*madrasa-ye sayyāra*) which had been established by the il-khan at the suggestion of Rašīd-al-dīn and which accompanied the army (*Ḏayl-e Jāmeʿ-al-tawārīḵ-e rašīdī*, ed. K. Bayānī, 1st ed., Tehran, 1317 Š./1938, p. 48 n. 1 [on p. 53]; 2nd ed., Tehran, 1350 Š./1971, p. 101 n.1 [on p. 104]: read *Ījī* instead of *Avajī*). The vizier mentions him again a few years later in his will (in 719/1319 or shortly before), in connection with two *madrasas* in Šabānkāra whose considerable endowment (*waqf*) income went to Ījī and his sons (Mokātabāt, p. 232, Russ. tr., p. 271).

At that time, however, the founder of the Muzaffarid dynasty, Mobārez-al-dīn Moḥammad, had already started to make himself master of Šabānkāra. This may have added to Ījī's readiness to return to the capital when Öljeitü's son Abū Saʿīd Bahādor Khan (r. 716-36/1316-35; q.v.) nominated him supreme judge of the Il-khanid empire (*qāżī al-mamālek*). He owed this promotion to the fact that Abū Saʿīd, in contrast to his father, no longer adhered to the Shiʿite creed; Shiʿite sources like Šūštarī's *Majāles al-moʾmenīn* or Ḵᵛānsārī's *Rawżāt al-jannāt* leave no doubt that Ījī always defended the Sunnite cause. He attached himself to Ḡīāṯ-al-dīn Moḥammad, the son of Rašīd-al-dīn, who became vizier in 727/1327; in the following years, until Ḡīāṯ-al-dīn's execution in 736/1336, he dedicated several works to him. His scholarly reputation spread far beyond the borders of Iran: he is called *pādešāh-e ʿolamāʾ wa ḵosrow-e dānešmandān* in the *Tārīḵ-e gozīda* (p. 654); he is also mentioned in the biographical dictionaries of the Mamluk empire (e.g., Ebn Ḥajar ʿAsqalānī and Ebn Taḡrīberdī), and Moḥammad b. Toḡloq, sultan of Delhi (r. 725-52/1325-51), sent him a donation without having ever met him (Ebn Baṭṭūṭa [Paris] III, p. 254; tr. Gibb, p. 677). Ījī's relations with his former teacher Čahārbartī deteriorated; he had asked him for an explanation of Zamaḵšarī's commentary on Sūra 2:23 in *Kaššāf* (for the transmission of which Čahārbartī was the best authority at that time); receiving a rather condescending answer, he had attacked him in a lengthy reply (cf. Sobkī, *Ṭabaqāt al-šāfeʿīya* IV, p. 108).

With Abū Saʿīd's death in 736/1335 and Ḡīāṯ-al-dīn's ensuing execution, Ījī lost his position as *qāżī al-mamālek*. After some years, which he seems to have spent in Šabānkāra, he joined the court of the Īnjū Abū Esḥāq at Shiraz, where he became a *qāżī al-qożāt*. It was here that he met Ḥāfeẓ and ʿObayd Zākānī; Ḥāfeẓ praised him, in retrospect, as one of the five most important people of his time in Fārs (*Dīvān*, ed. M. Qazvīnī and Q. Ḡanī, Tehran, 1320 Š./1941, pp. 363-67), whereas ʿObayd Zākānī tells some facetious anecdotes about him in his *Ḥekāyāt-e fārsī* (*Kollīyāt-e ʿObayd-e Zākānī*, ed. P. Atābakī, Tehran, 1321 Š./1942, pp. 311ff.). When after 750/1350, Abū Esḥāq found himself increasingly confined by Mobārez-al-dīn's expansion, he sent Ījī to negotiate with him. Ījī was received with great respect but the political mission was a complete failure; Mobārez-al-dīn was apparently too sure of his success to give in. Ījī seems to have adjusted himself to the new situation; before returning to Abū Esḥāq he received Mobārez-al-dīn as his guest in Šabānkāra; and when Shiraz was besieged by the Muzaffarid army in 754/1353, he managed to leave the town secretly. He retired to Šabānkāra where Mobārez-al-dīn's son Shah Šojāʿ visited him one year later, after having subdued a rebellion initiated by a certain ʿEmād-al-dīn Maḥmūd Kermānī in favor of Abū Esḥāq. Either this rebel or Malek Ardašīr, the last *atābak* of Šabānkāra (who, according to *EI*[1] IV, p. 242 rose against the Muzaffarids in 755/1355 or 756/1356, but who is reported to have lived much earlier according to other sources, cf. B. Spuler, *Mongolen*[3], p. 147), imprisoned Ījī in the fortress of Deraymīān at Īj, where he died in 756/1356.

Ījī's works, intended as systematic handbooks for teaching in *madrasas*, have no claim to originality, but they were well-organized and had profited from the long scholarly tradition which had survived the Mongol invasion. Their popularity is evident from the great number of commentaries. Most have not yet been intensively studied; the best bibliographical surveys are those by C. Brockelmann (*GAL* II, pp. 267ff., S. II, pp. 287ff.) and by A. Ateş ("Îcî," *İA* V, pp. 921ff.). They deal with the following disciplines:

A: Theology: (1) *al-Mawāqef fī 'elm al-kalām*, Ījī's most famous work, probably composed before 730/1330 (it is mentioned in the *Tārīḵ-e gozīda* [p. 808.15], which was written in that year) for Ġīāṯ-al-dīn Moḥammad b. Fażlallāh (*Kašf al-ẓonūn* [Istanbul], p. 1891), but subsequently dedicated to Abū Esḥāq. The book sets out in the style of a *summa theologica*, in concise language, the traditional ideas of late Ash'arite theology; it is based mainly on the *Moḥaṣṣal* of Faḵr-al-dīn Rāzī (d. 606/1209) and the *Abkār al-afkār* of Sayf-al-dīn Āmedī (d. 631/1233), in places also on the former's *Nehāyat al-'oqūl fī derāyat al-oṣūl*. The oldest commentary was written by Ījī's disciple, Šams-al-dīn Kermānī (d. 786/1384), but the commentary which always enjoyed the highest popularity was the one written by Šarīf Jorjānī and finished in 807/1404-05 at Samarkand (*GAL* II, p. 269; Ateş, op. cit., pp. 923ff.; L. Gardet and M.-M. Anawati, *Introduction à la théologie musulmane*, Paris, 1948, pp. 165ff., 370ff.). (2) *Jawāher al-('olūm fi'l-)kalām*, dedicated to Ġīāṯ-al-dīn Moḥammad and commented upon for the first time as early as 770/1368, for the Muzaffarid ruler Qoṭb-al-dīn Shah Maḥmūd, the brother of Shah Šojā' (*GAL* II, p. 270; ed. Abu'l-'Alā' 'Afīfī, *Majallat kollīāt al-ādāb* [Jāme'a Meṣrīya] II, 1934, pp. 133ff.). The exact relationship between the *Mawāqef* and the *Jawāher* has still to be investigated. Both works are structured after the same pattern and contain almost the same material, but the *Jawāher* is shorter. The commentary by 'Abd-al-Raḥmān b. 'Abd-al-Qāder Fāsī (d. 1096/1685) mentioned by Esmā'īl Pasha (*Īżāḥ al-maknūn*, Istanbul, 1945-47, p. 378) as having been finished on 18 Ša'bān 1078/2 February 1668, is preserved in a manuscript at Medina. (3) *Al-'Aqā'ed al-'ażodīya*, a short catechism which Ījī finished immediately before his death (cf. *GAL* II, p. 270; the last edition of the text together with the commentaries of Dav(v)ānî (d. 907/1501) and Moḥammad 'Abdoh [d. 1323/1905] is by Solaymān Donyā, *al-Šayḵ Moḥammad 'Abdoh bayn al-falāsefa wa'l-kalāmīyīn*, Cairo, 1377/1958).

B. Jurisprudence: (1) A commentary to Ebn al-Ḥājeb's (d. 646/1249) abridgement (*Moḵtaṣar*) of his own *Montaha 'l-so'ūl (sūl) wa'l-amal fī 'elmay al-oṣūl wa'l-jadal*, on *oṣūl al-feqh* and dialectics, finished 26 Ša'bān 734/2 May 1334 (*Kašf al-ẓonūn* [Istanbul], p. 1853; *GAL* I, p. 372, S. I, p. 537; Ateş, op. cit., p. 922). Ebn al-Ḥājeb had based himself on Āmedī's *Eḥkām fī oṣūl al-aḥkām* (cf. *GAL* I, p. 494, S. I, p. 678); both of them were Malikites. Ījī, on the contrary, was a Shafi'ite; in *oṣūl al-feqh* the difference of *maḏhab* did not matter very much. (2) *Resāla fī ādāb al-baḥṯ*, which may be subsumed here insofar as it treats the art of dialectics like the former work (cf. *GAL* II, p. 267). It seems note worthy that Ījī, in spite of his being supreme judge, did not write anything on *forū'*. The intellectual climate of the later Īl-khanid empire with its mixture of Mongol and Muslim law may have suggested a certain reserve.

C. *Tafsīr*: A commentary on Bayżāwī's *Anwār al-tanzīl wa asrār al-ta'wīl* entitled *Taḥqīq al-tafsīr fī takṯīr al-tanwīr* (cf. *GAL* II, p. 267; Ateş, op. cit., p. 922).

D. Ethics: *al-Resāla al-šāhīya fī 'elm al-aḵlāq* (dedicated to Abū Esḥāq Īnjū, who had the title Shah?). Cf. *GAL* II, p. 270. The work takes up a specific Iranian tradition represented, e.g., by Naṣīr-al-dīn Ṭūsī's *Aḵlāq-e nāṣerī* (completed 633/1235) and later by Davānī's (d. 907/1501) *Aḵlāq-e jalālī* (qq.v.). It treats, in concordance with the Greek pattern, the basic elements of the three branches of practical philosophy: individual ethics, economics, politics. The earliest commentary was written by Šams-al-dīn Kermānī (d. 786/1384; *Kašf al-ẓonūn* [Istanbul], p. 37). There is a Turkish translation by Moḥammad Amīn b. Moḥammad As'ad (Istanbul, 1281/1864; cf. Ateş, op. cit., p. 923).

E. Rhetoric and linguistics: (1) *al-Fawā'ed al-ġīāṯīya*, an abridgement of the section on rhetoric (i.e., part III) from Sakkākī's encyclopedic *Meftāḥ al-'olūm*, and dedicated to Ġīāṯ-al-dīn Moḥammad (cf. *GAL* II, p. 271). The oldest commentary was written for Shah Šojā' by Moḥammad b. Ḥājjī b. Moḥammad Boḵārī Sa'īdī and finished in 760/1359 (*Kašf al-zonūn* [Istanbul], p. 1299); another one was composed shortly afterwards by Šams-al-dīn Kermānī (d. 786/1384). (2) *Al-Modḵel fī 'elm al-ma'ānī wa'l-bayān wa'l-badā'e'* (cf. *GAL* II, p. 270). (3) *Al-Resāla al-waż'īya al-'ażodīya*, a short treatise with numerous commentaries, on *'elm al-waż'*, the reflection about the relation between expression and meaning, especially with regard to technical terms (cf. ibid., p. 268).

F. Historiography: *Ešrāq al-tawārīḵ*, a short survey of the historical facts relevant for a theologian, consisting of an introduction (on the lives of the prophets from Adam to Jesus) and three main chapters (on Moḥammad, on the *'ašara al-mobaššara*, and on the most important religious personalities from the Companions until Ġazālī). The work was translated in a slightly different form, under the title *Zobdat al-tawārīḵ*, into Turkish by the poet 'Ālī Čelebī (d. 1008/1600; cf. *EI*[2] I, p. 380; cf. *GAL* II, p. 271; Ateş, op. cit., pp. 922f.

Bibliography: See also Mo'īn-al-dīn Yazdī, *Mawāheb-e elāhī dar tārīḵ-e Āl-e Moẓaffar*, ed. S. Nafīsī, Tehran, 1326 Š./1947, I, pp. 92f., 241ff., 257. Maḥmūd Kotobī, continuation of *Tārīḵ-e gozīda*, ed.

E. G. Browne, London, 1910, pp. 654ff., 663. Mīrḵ̌ānd (Tehran), IV, pp. 484, 487, 494. *Ḥabīb al-sīar* (Tehran) III, pp. 197, 221, 224, 286, 288. Nūrallāh Šūštarī, *Majāles al-mo'menīn*, Tehran, 1375/1955, II, p. 214. Moḥammad-Bāqer Ḵ̌ānsārī, *Rawżāt al-jannāt*, lith. Tehran, 1263/1846-47, pp. 414f. Sobkī, *Ṭabaqāt*[1] VI, pp. 108ff., *Ṭabaqāt*[2] X, pp. 46ff. Asnavī, *Ṭabaqāt al-šāfe'īya*, ed. 'A. Jobūrī, Baghdad, 1391/1971, II, p. 238 no. 857. Ebn Ḥajar 'Asqalānī, *al-Dorar al-kāmena*, ed. M. S. Jād-al-ḥaqq, Cairo, 1385/1966, II, pp. 429f. no. 2278. Abu'l-Fażl 'Abd-al-Raḥmān Soyūṭī, *Boḡyat al-wo'āt*, ed. M. Abu'l-Fażl Ebrāhīm, Cairo, 1384/1964, II, pp. 75f. no. 1476. Abu'l 'Abbās Aḥmad Maqrīzī, al-*Solūk le-ma'refat dowal al-molūk*, ed. M. Moṣṭafā Zīāda, Cairo, 1956-, II, p. 885.10f. (s.a. 753); III, p. 16.7ff. (s.a. 755). Ebn Taḡrīberdī, *al-Nojūm al-ẓāhera* X, p. 288.4ff. Idem, *al-Manhal al-ṣāfī* (ms.). Ebn al-'Emād, *Šaḏarāt al-ḏahab*, Cairo, 1350-51/1931-32, VI, pp. 174f. Šawkānī, *al-Badr al-ṭāle'*, Cairo, 1348/1929-30, I, pp. 326f. no. 225. Qannawjī, *al-Tāj al-mokallal*, ed. 'A. Šaraf-al-dīn, Bombay, 1383/1963, pp. 379f. no. 408. Šehāb-al-dīn Aḥmad b. Qāżī, *Dorrat al-ḥejāl: Répertoire bibliographique d'Ahmad Ibn al-Qadi* ed. I. S. Allouche, Rabat, 1934-, p. 365 no. 1019. Taşköprüzade, *Meftāḥ al-sa'āda*, Cairo, 1968, I, pp. 169f. Zereklī, *A'lām*, Cairo, 1954-59, IV, p. 66. Kaḥḥāla, *Mo'jam al-mo'allefīn*, V, pp. 119f. Q. Ḡanī, *Baḥt dar āṯār o afkār o aḥwāl-e Ḥāfeẓ*, Tehran, 1321 Š./1942, I, pp. 29, 31, 75, 99ff. M. 'A. Modarres, *Rayḥānat al-adab*, Tehran, 1967-, IV, pp. 142ff. H. Halm, *Die Ausbreitung der šāfi'itischen Rechtsschule*, Wiesbaden, 1974, p. 152. J. van Ess, *Die Erkenntnislehre des 'Aḍudaddīn al-Īcī*, Wiesbaden, 1966. Idem, "Neue Materialien zur Biographie des 'Aḍudaddīn al-Īǧī," *Welt des Orients* 9, 1978, pp. 270ff.

(J. VAN ESS)

'AŻOD-AL-MOLK, 'ALĪ REŻĀ KHAN QĀJĀR, regent of Iran in 1327/1909-1328/1910. His father Mūsā Khan was a son of Solaymān Khan Qājār E'teżād-al-dawla and a first cousin of Mahd-e 'Olyā, the mother of Nāṣer-al-dīn Shah. He was born circa 1263/1847, because he is said to have been 35 years old on 1 Ḏu'l-qa'da 1298/1881 (E'temād-al-salṭana, *Rūz-nāma-ye ḵāṭerāt*, p. 134).

Following the usual practice, he became a court page (*ḡolām-bača*) early in Nāṣer-al-dīn Shah's reign. Allegedly he (with or without deliberate intent) transmitted information on harem affairs to the chief minister (*ṣadr-e a'ẓam*), Mīrzā Āqā Khan Nūrī, and warned the latter of the impending decision to dismiss him. When this came to light, 'Alī Reżā Khan was bastinadoed and expelled from the private quarters (*andarūn*), but on the intervention of Mahd-e 'Olyā, he was reinstated and later promoted to the rank of head page (*ḡolām-bāšī*) (ibid., p. 301). Being simple-hearted, uneducated, and very religious, he was considered trustworthy by the shah and gradually rose in favor. In his boyhood he massaged Nāṣer-al-dīn Shah's feet, and as he was a skillful and tireless masseur, the shah spent much time with him and they became close friends. In 1283/1866, when the shah decided to send gilded bricks for the Ḥaram al-'Askarīyayn (tomb of Imam Ḥasan al-'Askarī and place of occultation of the Twelfth Imam Moḥammad al-Mahdī) at Samarra, Mahd-e 'Olyā persuaded the shah to assign the task to 'Alī Reżā Khan, who then proceeded to the holy places in Iraq while the shah departed on a visit to Khorasan. On the shah's homeward journey, 'Alī Reżā Khan rejoined the royal entourage at Fīrūz Kūh, and after the return to Tehran, he was honored with the title *'ażod-al-molk* (the support of the state) in 1285/1868 (E'temād-al-salṭana, *Tārīḵ-e montaẓam-e nāṣerī* III, p. 308).

It was probably in 1288/1871 that 'Ażod-al-molk was appointed controller (*nāẓem*) of the royal household after the transfer of Amīr Aṣlān Khan Majd-al-dawla, a maternal uncle of the shah and first cousin of 'Ażod-al-molk, to the governorship of Ḵūzestān (*Montaẓam-e nāṣerī* III, p. 319). He is mentioned as the superintendent (*ḵān-e nāẓer*) in 1299/1882 (E'temād-al-salṭana, *Ḵāṭerāt*, p. 146). In Šawwāl, 1302/June-July, 1885, he was replaced in this position by Mahdī-qolī Khan Majd-al-dawla (*Ḵāṭerāt*, p. 424) but left in possession of two other offices which he also held at that time, namely those of keeper of the signet (*mohrdār*) (*Montaẓam* III, p. 309) and governor of Māzandarān, conferred on him in 1289/1872 and 1288/1871 respectively. He accompanied the shah on the latter's visit to the holy places in Iraq and two journeys to Europe. In 1290/1873, he was appointed chief (*īlḵānī*) of the Qajar tribe (*Montaẓam* III, p. 332). He in effect became minister of justice on 9 Ša'bān 1304/4 May 1887 (*Ḵāṭerāt*, p. 563). In 1305/1888 he held three offices in plurality: justice, the signet, and the Qajar chieftancy (*Ḵāṭerāt*, p. 629). Consequently he was able to amass wealth, and being disinclined to extravagance, or according to some accounts inclined to stinginess, he grew steadily richer. He bought some large landed properties, one of which was Solaymānīya, formerly named Eṣfahānak, on the Dūlāb in the outskirts of Tehran, which he equipped with a new *qanāt* costing 14,000 *tūmān*s and renamed after his son Solaymān Mīrzā (*Ḵāṭerāt*, p. 292, cf. Bāmdād, *Rejāl* I, p. 352).

In his manners, 'Ażod-al-molk was affable and very dignified. People spoke of him as the "emperor of China" (*ḵāqān-e Čīn*) ('Abdallāh Mostawfī, *Zendagānī-e man*, 2nd ed., Tehran, 1341 Š./1962-1343 Š./1964, I, p. 134). One peculiar trait was his quickness to weep and ability to bring tears to his eyes at will (E'temād-al-salṭana, *Ḵāṭerāt*, 1st ed., p. 134). These qualities, however, did not restrain him from beating men with intent to kill (ibid., pp. 184, 384). He was a habitual gambler (ibid., p. 317) and held gambling sessions at his house (ibid., p. 1209).

During the Tobacco protest of 1298-99/1891-92, 'Ażod-al-molk was one of the chief mediators between the shah and the *'olamā'* of Tehran. Because of his religiosity, he enjoyed the respect of the *'olmā'* and thus was a valuable asset to the desperate monarch. In Możaffar-al-dīn Shah's reign, he enjoyed the monarch's special respect (Ḵalīl Khan Ṯaqafī (A'lam-al-dawla), *Maqālāt-e gūnāgūn*, Tehran, 1322/1904-05, p. 155). His relations with Moḥammad 'Alī Mīrzā were not cordial (ibid., p. 157). After coming to the throne, however, the new shah was in no position to do him any harm. During the constitutional revolutions, his house was occasionally the gathering place for moderate constitutionalists (Dawlatābādī, *Ḥayāt-e Yaḥyā* II, p. 244). Here, too, he was accepted as a mediator between the shah and the constitutionalists (ibid., p. 250) though he was sometimes heeded by the shah (Malekzāda, *Tārīḵ-e enqelāb-e mašrūṭīyat* III, p. 238). On one occasion when the shah angrily rejected his advice, he walked out of the royal presence and as an expression of his displeasure went straight to Solaymānīya (Dawlatābādī, op. cit., II, p. 261).

After the deposition of Moḥammad 'Alī Shah on 28 Jomādā II 1327/16 July 1909, a regent had to be appointed because Aḥmad Shah was a minor. The choice fell on 'Ażod-al-molk. As a senior dignitary and the chief of the Qajar tribe, he enjoyed the respect of the constitutionalists and was in good relationship with the *'olamā'*. He served as regent for one year and three months until his death at the age of 65 (lunar years) on 17 Ramażān 1328/23 September 1910.

Bibliography: M. Ḥ. E'temād-al-salṭana, *Rūznāma-ye ḵāṭerāt-e E'temād-al-salṭana*, ed. Ī. Afšār, Tehran, 1345 Š./1966, passim, in particular the character sketch on p. 134. Idem, *Tārīḵ-e montaẓam-e nāṣerī*, 3 vols., Tehran, 1300/1883, vol. 3. Bāmdād, *Rejāl* II, pp. 435-42. A. Kasrawī, *Tārīḵ-e mašrūṭa-ye Īrān*, repr. Tehran, 1340 Š./1961. M. Malekzāda, *Tārīḵ-e enqelāb-e mašrūṭīyat-e Īrān*, 7 vols., Tehran, 1327 Š./1948. Yaḥyā Dawlatābādī, *Tārīḵ-e mo'āṣer yā ḥayāt-e Yaḥyā*, 4 vols., Tehran, 1331 Š./1952 (vol. 2 on the struggle for constitutional government).

(Ḥ. Maḥbūbī Ardakānī)

'AŻOD-AL-MOLK, MĪRZĀ MOḤAMMAD ḤOSAYN (d. 1284/1867), a senior official in the first part of Nāṣer-al-dīn Shah Qājār's reign. Both he and his father Mīrzā Fażlallāh Mollā-bāšī Qazvīnī were initially employed as clerical secretaries at the provincial government of the crown prince 'Abbās Mīrzā in Azerbaijan (Farhād Mīrzā, *Zanbīl*, Tehran, 1329/1911, p. 162). They claimed holy descendency through Mīr Sayyed Ḥosayn b. 'Alī Karakī Jabal-'Āmelī (M. Golrīz, *Mīnū-dar yā Bāb al-jannat-e Qazvīn*, Tehran, 1337 Š./1958, p. 327).

In 1267/1851, Mīrzā Moḥammad Ḥosayn, who then held the office of *ṣadr-e dīvān-ḵāna* (the chief official in charge of the state judicial administration), was appointed ambassador to Russia (Ḵormūjī, *Ḥaqā'eq al-aḵbār* II, p. 100; E'temād-al-salṭana, *Montaẓam-e nāṣerī* III, p. 210). Two years later he returned to Tehran (*Ḥaqā'eq al-aḵbār* II, p. 126), and in 1270/1854 he was honored with the title *'ażod-al-molk* and appointed minister of pensions and endowments (*waẓā'ef wa awqāf*) in one of the earliest attempts to reform the machinery of the state (*Montaẓam-e nāṣerī* III, pp. 230, 232). Having been deputed to express condolence and felicitation to the Russian embassy after the death of Nicholas I and accession of Alexander II in 1271/1855, he escorted the chargé d'affaires and other staff of the embassy to an audience with the shah (*Ḥaqā'eq al-aḵbār* II, p. 153). In 1272/1856, he was sent to Mašhad on appointment as the trustee (*motawallī-bāšī*) of the shrine and endowments of the Emām Reżā (ibid., p. 169; *Montaẓam-e nāṣerī* III, p. 244). It was he who, on orders from Tehran, arranged the construction and erection of a gold door for the tomb chamber in 1276/1860 (*Montaẓam-e nāṣerī* III, p. 266). He remained at Mašhad until 1278/1862, when Mīrzā Ja'far Khan Mošīr-al-dawla took over his office (ibid., p. 277). 'Ażod-al-molk became the trustee of the shrine for a second time in 1282/1866 after the death of the incumbent, Ḥājjī Qawām-al-molk Šīrāzī (ibid., p. 293). He himself died in 1284/1867 at Tehran. His remains were interred at Mašhad.

Bibliography: M. J. Ḵormūjī, *Ḥaqā'eq al-aḵbār-e nāṣerī*, ed. Ḥ. Ḵadīv Jam, 2 vols., Tehran, 1344 Š./1965. M. Ḥ. E'temād-al-salṭana, *Tārīḵ-e montaẓam-e nāṣerī*, 3 vols., Tehran, 1300/1883, vol. 3. Idem, *Mer'āt al-boldān*, 4 vols., Tehran, 1294/1877-1297/1880, vol. 3. Bāmdād, *Rejāl* III.

(Ḥ. Maḥbūbī Ardakānī)

AZRAQĪ HERAVĪ, the pen-name of Abū Bakr b. Esmā'īl Warrāq of Herat, a Persian poet of the 5th/11th century. His personal name is given as Abū Bakr by Neẓāmī 'Arūżī (*Čahār maqāla*, ed. M. Qazvīnī and M. Mo'īn, Tehran, 1333 Š./1954, p. 69), as Šaraf-al-zamān Abu'l-Maḥāsen by 'Awfī (*Lobāb al-albāb* [Tehran], p. 310). In some other *taḏkera*s the title Zayn-al-dīn is attributed to him. Neẓāmī 'Arūżī (op. cit., p. 80) states that Azraqī's father was a bookseller (*warrāq*) and that Ferdowsī, after fleeing from Maḥmūd Ḡaznavī's court, hid in this bookseller's house for six months.

As a young man, Azraqī won the favor of the Saljuq prince Šams-al-dawla Ṭoḡānšāh, who was governor of Khorasan, with headquarters at Herat, in the reign of his father, the sultan Alp Arslān (r. 455-65/1063-72); Azraqī became not only a poetic eulogist, but also a courtier and boon-companion of this prince. He was also in the good graces of Amīrānšāh, a son of the contemporary Saljuq ruler of Kermān, Qāvord b. Čaḡrī Beg (d. 466/1073); he has left a number of *qaṣīda*s in praise of Amīrānšāh.

The date of Azraqī's death is given as 526/1132 in Reżā-qolī Khan Hedāyat's *Majma' al-foṣaḥā'* and as 527/1133 in another *taḏkera*, Taqī-al-dīn Kāšī's *Ḵolāṣat al-aš'ār wa zobdat al-afkār*; Sa'īd Nafīsī (preface to Azraqī's *dīvān*, pp. vf.) considered these dates likely to be correct in view of certain passages in Azraqī's poems, but Moḥammad Qazvīnī (*Čahār maqāla*, notes, p. 218) found them unacceptable and reckoned that Azraqī must have died before 465/1073. The truth probably lies somewhere in between; Azraqī certainly lived until late in the 5th/11th century, but does not appear to have seen any events of the 6th/12th century.

The surviving poems of Azraqī are *qaṣīdas* and *robāʿīs*. In Nafīsī's edition (Tehran, 1336 Š./1957) they amount to 2,675 verses, but the attribution of some of them to Azraqī seems doubtful. In addition to the eulogies of Ṭoḡānšāh, Amīrānšāh, and other grandees, he has left some *qaṣīdas* which express admiration for the renowned mystic of Herat, ʿAbdallāh Anṣārī (d. 481/1088). His poetic style is close to that of ʿOnṣorī but distinctly independent, being marked by a fondness for abstract words and cerebral similes which some later poets liked and imitated but others (e.g., Rašīd Vaṭvāṭ apud Qazvīnī, notes to *Čahār maqāla*, pp. 218-19) found objectionable.

Azraqī not only composed a *dīvān*; he also, according to ʿAwfī and later *taḏkera*-writers such as Dawlatšāh (ed. Browne, p. 72) Ḥājjī Ḵalīfa (*Kašf al-ẓonūn* [Leipzig] III, pp. 620-21), and Amīn Aḥmad Rāzī (*Haft eqlīm* II, pp. 139ff.), and on the evidence of some of his own poems (*Dīvān*, verses 191, 1872-78, 2275), composed Persian verse renderings of the *Sendabād-nāma* (story of the seven viziers) and the *Alfīya wa šalfīya* for Ṭoḡānšāh and apparently intended (*Dīvān*, verses 1774-76) to versify another romance for Amīrānšāh. The text on which Azraqī based his rendering of the *Sendabād-nāma* is likely to have been the Persian prose translation from the Pahlavi made in 339/950 by Abu'l-Fawāres Qanārazī (on the correct spelling of this name, see *Čahār maqāla*, notes, p. 220 n. 3). Both Azraqī's and Qanārazī's versions are lost. The *Alfīya wa šalfīya* was an illustrated book on sexual matters based on Indian pornographic writings which had been translated into Pahlavi and therefrom into Arabic; Ebn al-Nadīm (*Fehrest*, p. 314) refers to part of this title in his mention of two Arabic books, the *Ketāb al-alfīya al-ṣaḡīr* and the *Ketāb al-alfīya al-kabīr*, as well as other such books of Pahlavi origin as *Ketāb Bonyāndoḵt*, *Ketāb Bahrāmdoḵt fi'l-bāh*, etc. It can be inferred from a remark in Bayhaqī's history (ed. Q. Ḡanī and ʿA. A. Fayyāż, pp. 121-22) and a verse in Manūčehrī's *dīvān* (ed. M. Dabīrsīāqī, Tehran, 1338 Š./1959, v. 1265) that these books had a smutty notoriety in the 5th/11th century.

Bayhaqī (ibid.) reports that the Ghaznavid Sultan Masʿūd had a pavilion in Herat (which was used for his afternoon nap) painted from top to bottom with erotic scenes from the *Alfīya wa šalfīya*.

Such books were quite popular in court circles (particularly during the Qajar period) and many more, versified and in prose, illustrated or not, were produced in subsequent centuries. Some are extant, including a manuscript in prose of anonymous authorship preserved in the Bibliothèque Nationale in Paris (see R. Surien and M. Horstmann, *Die Liebe in der Kunst. Deutsche Bearbeitung*, Genf, 1978, fig. 114; Q. Ḡanī, *Yāddāšthā-ye Doctor Qāsem Ḡanī*, ed. S. Ḡanī, London, 1982, p. 793).

Azraqī's verse rendering of the *Alfīya wa šalfīya* appears to be lost, though an illustrated manuscript with this title is said to have existed in the Royal Library at Tehran (*Čahār maqāla*, notes, p. 222 n. 3). The words *alfīya* and *šalfīya* may be onomatopoeic.

Bibliography: See also Browne, *Lit. Hist. Persia* II, p. 323. B. Forūzānfar, *Soḵan o soḵanvarān*, 2nd ed., 1350 Š./1971, pp. 202-07. Idem, *Majmūʿa-ye maqālāt o ašʿār*, ed. ʿE. Majīdī, pp. 17-19. Ḵayyāmpūr, *Soḵanvarān*, p. 37. Rypka, *Iran. Lit.*, p. 195. Ṣafā, *Adabīyāt* II, pp. 432-38.

(DJ. KHALEGHI MOTLAGH)

ĀZŪITI-, an Avestan word (cf. Skt. *āhuti-*) meaning "oblation of fat." It occurs twice in the *Gāθās*, once together with *īžā-* (q.v.; *Y.* 49.5), once, it seems, with particular reference to the ritual offering to fire (*Y.* 29.7; see *ātaš-zōhr*). In the younger Avesta milk and *āzūiti-* are reverenced together as the two offerings which make the waters flow and plants grow (*Y.* 16.8; cf. *Y.* 68.2). *Āzūiti-* (rendered in Pahlavi simply by *čarbīh* "fat") is also used for fat in an ordinary sense, as forming, with milk and flesh, suitable food for dogs (*Vd.* 13.28).

The word is grammatically feminine and from it there evolved the concept of a divine being representing Fatness or Plenty. In *Yasna Haptaŋhāiti* she is invoked among a group of female divinities who, with the Waters, represent the sustaining, fecund aspect of creation (*Y.* 38.2); and in *Vd.* 9.53 she is venerated with Īžā and other "abstract" divinities. She does not appear, however, to have had an active role in later Zoroastrianism as attested from the Sasanian period onwards.

Bibliography: *AirWb.*, cols. 343-44. I. Gershevitch, *JRAS*, 1952, p. 178. H. Humbach, *IF* 63, 1957, pp. 50-51. Idem, *Die Gathas des Zarathustra*, Heidelberg, 1959, I, p. 82 and II, p. 17. R. Zaehner, *The Dawn and Twilight of Zoroastrianism*, London, 1961, repr. 1975, p. 34 with n. 8 p. 325. M. Boyce, *BSOAS* 33, 1970, p. 32.

(M. BOYCE)

B

EDITORIAL NOTE

In view of the expanding literature on Iranian studies and in the light of our experience of the past twelve years, it was felt that a revised short titles list would prove helpful. This has been placed at the beginning of this volume. It accommodates a number of frequently mentioned sources not included in the earlier list.

Beginning with letter B two slight modifications in transliteration have been made in order to bring it closer to the more common practice in the Iranian field and to ease a proofreading problem. These consist of the removal of the haček from *j* and beginning the second member of an Arabic compound name following *al-* consistently with a capital letter (thus Nāṣer-al-Dīn). In all Persian words of Arabic origin, *w* is being used rather than *v*. Also Ḥājī, the common Persian form of Ḥājj, will be used rather than Ḥājjī.

In the choice of titles for entries, increasing consideration has been given to choosing the title which comes first in alphabetical order, whether English or Iranian. Thus, the article on Bread is placed under this title rather than under Nān, whereas the article on Rice is placed under Berenj. Adequate cross-references however are provided to ensure that no article will be missed on account of its chosen title.

BAAT, Middle Iranian personal name, borrowed in Armenian as Bat.

i. *Baat in Iranian sources.*

ii. *Armenian Bat.*

i. Baat in Iranian Sources

Baat is the name of a disciple of Mani mentioned several times in the Coptic "crucifixion narrative," where it is spelt Baat and (perhaps) Badia (H. J. Polotsky, *Manichäische Homilien*, Stuttgart, 1934, pp. 44.22, 45.5, 46.13), and in Parthian fragments of the Manichean missionary history, where he is called B't (W. B. Henning, "Mani's Last Journey," *BSOAS* 10, 1942, pp. 941-53; W. Sundermann, *Mitteliranische manichäische Texte kirchengeschichtlichen Inhalts*, Berliner Turfantexte XI, Berlin, 1981, pp. 79-81). According to these sources, Baat was a man of high rank, who was converted from Zoroastrianism and became a close associate of Mani during the last three years of the latter's life. Mani's conversion of Baat aroused the anger of Bahrām I, who summoned them both to Bēlāpāt; Baat accompanied the prophet for part of the way, but failed to appear before the king.

Although the name Bāt or Ba'āt (from *Baga-dāta- "God-given," cf. Arm. Bat beside Bagrat, see Henning, *BSOAS* 14, 1952, p. 511, and BAGA ii) is found elsewhere, there are no other certain references to the same historical personage. According to O. Klíma, "Baat the Manichee," *Archív orientální* 26, 1958, pp. 342-46, he may be identified with the ruler of this name (Mid. Pers. Bgdt, Parth. B'ty) mentioned in the Paikuli inscription (Henning, loc. cit.), and even with a certain Bāṭī bar Ṭōbī mentioned in the Babylonian Talmud as a contemporary of Šāpūr I. If the "Lord *Ptw*" mentioned in the Sogd. Manichean fragment L83a is the Baat of the Coptic homily, the fragment must be taken to recount the events leading up to his conversion (see N. Sims-Williams, *BSOAS* 44, 1981, pp. 238-39).

(N. Sims-Williams)

ii. Armenian Bat

In Armenian Bat is the name of the *nahapet* "family head" of the Šaharuni dynastic house in the fourth century A. D., according to the fifth-century historian P'awstos Buzand, 5.35. The name may be attested in Gk. Batis (Arrian) and Latin Betis (Quintus Curtius), but this is unlikely; according to W. B. Henning, Parthian *b'ty*, Bāt, is merely an allegro form of Bagdāt, via an intermediate Ba'āt—the Gk. form Baat is attested where in Middle Iranian parallel texts the name Bāt is found. From the title of B't, *šhrd'r* (Bāt the *šahrdār*), who accompanied Mani on his final journey it is apparent that he was a petty king or nobleman. Mani's mother belonged to the Kāmsarakān family, a branch of the noble Parthian house of Kārēn which had become established in Armenia. It is possible that Bāt may have been a family friend as a fellow nobleman, as well as a disciple, and an Armenian. In a Sogdian text, we are informed that Mani had written an epistle to the Armenians. The name Bat in Arm., would appear to be a loan of the Sasanian period, for an earlier, Parthian, form of Bag(a)dāt, Bagarat, is found as the name of the progenitor of the Bagratuni *naxarar*dom; Armenian intervocalic *-r-* is from Iranian *-d-*, which remained in Parthian but was lost or became *-y-* in Middle Persian, as in Ba'at > Bāt.

Bibliography: M. Boyce, *A Reader in Manichean Middle Persian and Parthian*, Acta Iranica 9, Leiden, 1975, p. 43. W. B. Henning, "A Farewell to the Khagan of the Aq-Aqatärān," *BSOAS* 14/3, 1952, p. 511 and n. 3. Idem, "Mani's Last Journey," *BSOAS* 10/4, 1942, p. 944. Idem, "The Book of the Giants," *BSOAS* 11/1, 1943, p. 52 n. 4. H. Hübschmann, *Armen. Etymologie*, p. 32. F. Justi, *Namenbuch*, pp. 65-66. P'awstos Buzand(ac'i), *Patmut'iwn Hayoc'* (History of the Armenians), Venice, 1933, pp. 239ff.

(J. Russell)

BĀB "door, gate, entrance": a term of varied application in Shi'ism and related movements. It is applied differently in several sects to a rank in the spiritual hierarchy, either as conceived in transcendent terms or as actually manifested in the religious system on earth. Thus, the Isma'ili hierarchy of *ḥodūd al-dīn* includes the *bāb* as fourth in rank after prophet, *asās*, and *emām* (Hollister, p. 260), while under the Fatimids *bāb* came to be used as a title for the chief *ḥojja*, immediately under the imam and responsible for the organization of the *da'wa* (Lewis, "Bāb"). In the Noṣayrī system, the *bāb* is the third element in the hierarchy after *ma'nā* and *esm*, in which the *ma'nā* is the equivalent of the Isma'ili "silent" (*ṣāmet*) imam, the *esm* the equivalent of the "speaking (*nāṭeq*) imam, and the *bāb* the gateway to the imam. The names of the *abwāb* are given for the first seven cycles and for the cycle of Islamic imams, beginning with Salmān al-Fāresī (with 'Alī and Moḥammad). (For lists of these names, see Massignon, "Nuṣairī"). In 245/859-60, Ebn Noṣayr proclaimed himself *bāb* of the tenth Shi'ite imam, 'Alī al-Naqī. The Druzes apply the term to the embodiment of the *'aql al-koll* who stands as the first of the hierarchy of five agents below the divinity; thus, Ḥamza b. 'Alī, their founder, claimed to be the *bāb* as the last incarnation of universal reason (Carra de Vaux, "Druzes").

Among the Twelver Shi'ites, the term is applied in a variety of ways to the imam, who is spoken of in traditions as *bāb Allāh*, *bāb al-hodā*, *bāb al-īmān*, and so forth, in which capacity he is the means of access to the knowledge of God and an intermediary for the passage of prayers and grace between the divine and human worlds (for numerous traditions on these themes together with Koranic verses interpreted accordingly, see Kermānī, *Mobīn* I, pp. 227-31; for commentary on the application of the term *abwāb al-īmān* to the imams in the *zīāra al-jāme'a al-kabīra*, see Aḥsā'ī, *Šarḥ* I, pp. 78-

85; for discussion of this theme in general, see Kermānī, *Eršād* I, pp. 338-69; idem, *Feṭra* II, pp. 198-213). ʿAlī is described in one tradition as the gate of the prophet, the latter being "the gate of God" (Kermānī, *Mobīn* I, p. 228), while a well-known *ḥadīṯ* (extant in several versions) ascribes to Moḥammad the words "I am the city of knowledge (*madīnat al-ʿelm*) and ʿAlī is the gate; will you enter the city other than by its gate?" (ibid., pp. 229-30). Shiʿite interpretation of Koran 2:58 and 7:161 identifies the imams with the *bāb* through which the Children of Israel are to pass after saying '*ḥeṭṭa*' (for traditions, see Kermānī, *Mobīn* I, p. 229; for commentary, see Aḥsāʾī, *Šarḥ* II, pp. 227-31; Šabestarī, *Šarḥ*, pp. 148-49).

The term also came to be used among the Imami Shiʿites to designate the representatives of the imam and is best known in its application to the four *abwāb* believed to have acted as intermediaries for the twelfth imam during his lesser occultation: Abū ʿAmr ʿOṯmān b. Saʿīd ʿOmarī, his son Abū Jaʿfar Moḥammad (d. 305/917), Abu'l-Qāsem Ḥosayn b. Rūḥ Nowbaḵtī (d. 326/937), and Abu'l-Ḥasan ʿAlī b. Moḥammad Sāmarrī (d. 329/940). (On these, see Maškūr, *Tārīḵ-e Šīʿa*, pp. 137-42; Hussain, *Occultation*, chaps. 4-7). Other claimants to this rank appeared during the same period (ibid., pp. 142-46), but in the end the system of *bābīya* was abandoned in favor of the theory of the greater occultation. During the nineteenth century, a section of the Shaikhi school (q.v.) came to regard Shaikh Aḥmad Aḥsāʾī (q.v.) and Sayyed Kāẓem Raštī (q.v.) as gates of the imam, a belief which led to the emergence of Babism (q.v.) following the application of the term *bāb* to Sayyed ʿAlī Moḥammad Šīrāzī (see BĀB, ʿALĪ MOḤAMMAD ŠĪRĀZĪ, below).

Bibliography: J. N. Hollister, *The Shīʿa of India*, London, 1953. B. Lewis, "Bāb," in *EI*[2] I. L. Massignon. "Nuṣairī," in *EI*[1] III. B. Carra de Vaux, "Druzes," in *EI*[1]. Ḥājj Moḥammad Khan Kermānī, *al-Ketāb al-mobīn*, 2nd ed., 2 vols., Kermān, 1354 Š./1975-76. Ḥājj Moḥammad Karīm Khan Kermānī, *Eršād al-ʿawāmm*, 4th ed., 4 vols. in 2, Kermān, 1380/1960-61. Idem, *al-Feṭra al-salīma*, 3rd ed., 3 vols. in 1, Kermān, 1378/1958-9. Shaikh Aḥmad Aḥsāʾī, *Šarḥ al-zīāra al-jāmeʿa al-kabīra*, 4th ed., 4 vols., Kermān, 1355 Š./1976. Ḥojjat-al-Eslām Ḥājī Sayyed Moḥammad Ḥosaynī Šabestarī, *Šarḥ-e zīārat-e jāmeʿa-ye kabīra*, Tehran, 1333 Š./1954. M. J. Maškūr, *Tārīḵ-e Šīʿa wa ferqahā-ye Eslām tā qarn-e čahārom*, Tehran, 2535 = 1355 Š./1976. J. M. Hussain, *The Occultation of the Twelfth Imam*, London, 1982. D. M. MacEoin, "Hierarchy, Authority and Eschatology in Early Bābī Thought," in P. Smith, ed., *In Iran: Studies in Bābī and Bahāʾī History* III. Los Angeles, 1986, esp. pp. 113-14.

(D. M. MacEoin)

BĀB, a title given to certain Sufi shaikhs of Central Asia. It appears to be a localized variant of *bābā* (father), a much more widely used appellation of Sufi elders, for *bāb* also is said to have the sense of father (see *Borhān-e qāṭeʿ*, ed. Moʿīn, I, p. 201). Hojvīrī (d. ca. 464/1071) writes of a certain Bāb ʿOmar, from the village of Salāmatak in the region of Farḡāna, and remarks that "all the dervishes and great shaikhs of that area are called *bāb*" (*Kašf al-maḥjūb*, Samarkand, 1330/1912, p. 287). Four centuries later we encounter mention of one Bāb-e Māčīn, not identified by personal name, who is said to "have come from Māčīn [south China or Indochina—perhaps Cham?] and settled in Tashkent" (Faḵr-al-Dīn ʿAlī Ṣafī, *Rašaḥāt ʿayn al-ḥayāt*, Tashkent, 1329/1911, p. 225). Supposedly four times a centenarian, Bāb-e Māčīn was credited with the ability of flying 24 farsangs a day. Made arrogant by his powers, Bāb-e Māčīn foolishly and baselessly charged the celebrated Aḥmad Yasavī (d. 562/1167) with bringing men and women together in his gatherings. By way of punishment, Yasavī had his disciples tie Bāb-e Māčīn to a pillar and give him 500 lashes, from the effect of which he was protected by the spirit-beings clustered on his back. Thereafter he became a faithful and even favored disciple of Yasavī. He was buried in the village of Farkat (Ahmed-i Yesevi, *Divan-i hikmet'ten seçmeler*, ed. K. Eraslan, Ankara, 1983, pp. 191, 365; Alî Şîr Nevâyî, *Nesâyimü'l-mahabbe min şemâyimi'l-fütüvve*, ed. K. Eraslan, Istanbul, 1979, p. 389—here the name Bāb-e Māčīn has been misread as Bāb-e Ḥosayn).

The Borhān-al-Dīn Ābrīz described in *Rašaḥāt* (loc. cit.) as a *morīd* of Bāb-e Māčīn may be identical with the Borhān-al-Dīn Sāḡarčī mentioned elsewhere; he too had links with China, and was buried there (see V. V. Bartol'd, *Sochineniya*, Moscow, 1964, II, 2, pp. 434-35). Mention may be made finally of Arslān Bāb (or Bāb Arslān), preceptor of Yasavī (d. 562/1167). Although numerous legends surround the name of Bāb Arslān, notably that he was a companion of the Prophet and lived for 400 or 700 years, it seems certain that he was a historical personality; he may, indeed, have been Yasavī's paternal uncle. Bāb Arslān was buried next to Yasavī in the city of Torkestān, and his son, Manṣūr Atā, was Yasavī's principal successor (see Fuad Köprülü, *Türk edebiyatında ilk mutasavvıflar*, new ed., Ankara, 1966, pp. 14, 22-24, 67, 73). Although Bāb ʿOmar, Bāb-e Māčīn, and Bāb Arslān were all either Turks or the inhabitants of Turkish-influenced regions, their common appellation appears to be Iranian in origin.

Bibliography: Concerning Bāb ʿOmar, see also Ḵʷāja ʿAbd-Allāh Anṣārī, *Ṭabaqāt al-ṣūfīya*, ed. ʿAbd-al-Ḥayy Ḥabībī, Kabul, 1341 Š./1962, pp. 176, 424, and Jāmī, *Nafaḥāt*, p. 282.

(H. Algar)

BĀB, SAYYED ʿALĪ MOḤAMMAD ŠĪRĀZĪ (1235/1819-1266/1850), the founder of Babism (q.v.). Born in Shiraz on 1 Moḥarram 1235/20 October 1819, he belonged to a family of Ḥosaynī *sayyeds*, most of whom were engaged in mercantile activities in Shiraz and Būšehr. Conflicting accounts indicate that the Bāb's father, Sayyed Reżā Bazzāz, died either when he was in infancy or when he was aged nine and that Bāb's guardianship was undertaken by a maternal uncle, Ḥājī Mīrzā Sayyed ʿAlī, who later became a disciple and was martyred in Tehran in 1850 (Balyuzi, *The Báb*, p. 32). The family had few direct links with the *ʿolamāʾ*, apart from Mīrzā Moḥammad Ḥasan Šīrāzī (the Mīrzā-ye Šīrāzī of the Tobacco Rebellion, q.v.) and Ḥājī Sayyed Jawād Šīrāzī (an *emām-e jomʿa* of Kermān), but several of them were active adherents of the Shaikhi school (q.v.; Zarandī, *Dawn-Breakers*, p. 30). After six or seven years schooling at a local *maktab*, the Bāb began work in the family business, entering into partnership at the age of fifteen, at which point he went to Būšehr with his guardian. References in some of his early writings, however, suggest that he had little love for business pursuits and instead applied himself to the study of religious literature, including works on *feqh*. At some point during the five or so years he remained in Būšehr, he began to compose prayers and sermons, an activity which seems to have excited unfavorable comment (Balyuzi, *The Báb*, p. 40). The Bāb's short period of study in Iraq, his composition of *tafāsīr* and works on *feqh* and *kalām*, his references to theological literature in his early writings, and his idiosyncratic, ungrammatical Arabic all serve to paint a picture of him in his early youth as a would be *ʿālem* with original aspirations and ideas, whose lack of *madrasa* education, however, excluded from the rank of the *ʿolamāʾ*.

In 1255/1839-40, he headed for the *ʿatabāt* (q.v.) in Iraq, where he spent a year, mostly in Karbalāʾ, where he regularly attended the classes of the then head of the Shaikhi school, Ḥājj Sayyed Kāẓem Raštī (q.v.) and where he became acquainted with several of the latter's younger disciples, including a number who later became his own followers. This obviously crucial period in his development remains virtually undocumented, however, and it is difficult to define the exact dimensions of the Bāb's relations with Shaikhism at this time. In 1256/1840-41, the Bāb returned reluctantly to Shiraz at the insistence of his family and in Rajab, 1258/August, 1842, married Ḵadīja Begom, a daughter of his mother's paternal uncle. A child, Aḥmad, was born in 1259/1843 but died in infancy or was, possibly, stillborn.

Some months later, Sayyed ʿAlī Moḥammad had what seems to have been the first of a number of dreams or visions through which he was convinced of a high spiritual station for himself; on the following day, he began the composition of his first major work, a *tafsīr* on the *sūra al-Baqara* (see BAYĀN). A second such experience occurred on 15 Rabīʿ II 1260/4 May 1844, which he describes as "the first day on which the spirit descended into his heart" (*Ketāb al-fehrest*, p. 286); this experience seems to have been accompanied or followed by a dream in which he imbibed blood from the severed head of the Imam Ḥosayn, to which he later attributed "the appearance of these verses, prayers and divine sciences" (*Ṣaḥīfa-ye ʿadlīya*, p. 14). It must have been immediately after this that he began the composition of his first work of an unconventional nature, the unusual *tafsīr* on the *sūra Yūsof* entitled *Qayyūm al-asmāʾ*. He continued to experience dreams or visions until at least Ramażān, 1260/September-October, 1844 (see MacEoin, *From Shaykhism*, p. 153 n. 134) and possibly much later, but their significance dwindled as he came to believe himself in a state of perpetual grace and a recipient of direct verbal inspiration from the twelfth imam or God Himself.

About the time of his second vision in Rabīʿ II, 1260/early May, 1844, Sayyed ʿAlī Moḥammad seems already to have been in contact with Mollā Moḥammad Ḥosayn Bošrūʾī (q.v.), a young Shaikhi who had come to Shiraz from Karbalāʾ following the death there of Sayyed Kāẓem Raštī on 11 Ḏu'l-ḥejja 1259/1 January 1844. In common with other Shaikhis, Bošrūʾī was searching for a possible successor to Raštī (see BABISM) and, on 5 Jomādā I/22 May, Sayyed ʿAlī Moḥammad told him privately that he was indeed Raštī's successor as the bearer of divine knowledge and, more specifically, the channel of communication with (or "gate to") the Hidden Imam (*bāb al-emām*), a theme which is pursued in the pages of the *Qayyūm al-asmāʾ*. This date is mentioned by the Bāb in several places, notably his Persian *Bayān* (2:7, p. 30). Bošrūʾī accepted these claims after some consideration, as did several other Shaikhis who arrived in Shiraz from Karbalāʾ shortly after this (see BABISM). A small group of disciples, to whom he gave the title *ḥorūf al-ḥayy* (Letters of the Living) was thus formed about the Bāb, instructed by him, and sent out as missionaries on his behalf to various parts of Iran and Iraq.

The Bāb claimed to be the "gate" (*bāb*) and "representative" (*nāʾeb*) of the Hidden Imam, succeeding Shaikh Aḥmad Aḥsāʾī (q.v.) and Sayyed Kāẓem Raštī (*Qayyūm al-asmāʾ*, fols. 41a, 64b, 139a; *resāla* in Iran National Bahai Archives 6003c, p. 321; see also MacEoin, "From Shaykhism," pp. 172-73). In his early works, he describes himself as the "remembrance" (*ḏekr*) of the imam, the "servant of the *baqīyat Allāh*" (i.e., of the Hidden Imam), and the "seal of the gates" (*ḵātem al-abwāb*) and makes it clear that he has been sent by the Hidden Imam to prepare men for his imminent advent. An anonymous Babi *resāla* dated 1848 speaks of how, during the lesser occultation of the imam, there appeared the "four appointed gates" (see BĀB) while, in the greater occultation, there were in every age "gates not appointed by name or connection" until the appearance of two further specific gates—Aḥsāʾī and Raštī (*resāla* in Iran National Bahai Archives, MS 6006. C, p. 8). The Bāb himself is the third of these gates (Qorrat-al-ʿAyn, *resāla* in Golpāyegānī, *Kašf*, p. 2), after whom the Qāʾem will appear (ibid., pp. 14-15). In several passages, however, the Bāb already identifies himself effectively with the imam, while retaining a distinction of function (MacEoin *From Shaykhism*, p. 174; for a full discussion of the earliest claims of the Bāb see MacEoin, ibid., chap. 5).

While his earliest disciples spread news of his appearance, the Bāb left Shiraz on 26 Šaʿbān 1260/10 September 1844, accompanied by Mollā Moḥammad ʿAlī Bārforūšī (q.v.) and an Ethiopian slave, heading for

Mecca by way of Būšehr. After performing the *ḥajj* and visiting Medina, he returned to Būšehr on 8 Jomādā I 1261/15 May 1845 and stayed there until around mid-Rajab/July. Before leaving for the *ḥajj*, he had sent instructions to his followers to gather in Karbalāʾ to await his arrival there, which would be a signal for the appearance of the imam and the waging of the final *jehād*. For reasons that are still unclear, but which may be linked to the arrest and despatch to Istanbul of his emissary to Karbalāʾ, Mollā ʿAlī Besṭāmī (q.v.), the Bāb decided to return instead to Shiraz. An incident there involving some Babis (including Bārforūšī, who had gone ahead from Būšehr) about mid-June led the governor, Mīrzā Ḥosayn Khan Moqaddam Marāḡaʾī Ājūdānbāšī, to seek the Bāb's arrest; the latter was, accordingly, taken into custody while en route from Būšehr at the end of June. Placed under house-arrest in his uncle's home, the Bāb occupied himself with writing and with meeting a stream of visitors now making their way to Shiraz, many of them Shaikhis from Karbalāʾ. Kept thus in communication with his followers in Iran and Iraq, he was able to direct the course of the growing movement which had by now taken its name from his principal title. Although the leaders of the Babi movement in the provinces played a significant part in the development of doctrine and the working out of policies, the role of the Bāb ought not to be underestimated. Successive imprisonments between 1261/1845 and 1267/1850 prevented him from active participation in the affairs of the sect, but his writings were copied and widely disseminated and large numbers of pilgrims succeeded in obtaining personal interviews with him, in spite of official disapproval. His authority over his followers remained supreme: Thus, during the controversies centered on the figure of Qorrat-al-ʿAyn (q.v.) which rocked the Babi community of Karbalāʾ in the early period, final appeal was made to the Bāb in person (Balyuzi, *The Báb*, p. 68; MacEoin, *From Shaykhism*, pp. 203, 207).

There is evidence that, in Būšehr and again in Shiraz, the Bāb adopted a policy of *taqīya*, which involved the public renunciation of his original claims (see Fayżī, *Ḵānedān*, pp. 25-28; Balyuzi, *The Báb*, pp. 94-98; Mīrzā Asad-Allāh Fāżel Māzandarānī, *Asrār-al-āṯār* I, Tehran, 124 B. (*Badīʿ*)/1968-69, pp. 179-82). In writings dating from this period and the one following, he denies that there can be an "appointed gate" (*bāb manṣūṣ*) for the Hidden Imam after the first four gates and argues that any "revelation" (*waḥy*) claimed by him is not comparable to that given to Moḥammad (see ibid.). On one occasion, he was pressed to make a public appearance in the Wakīl mosque of Shiraz, in the course of which he denied all claim to *bābīya* (see Balyuzi, *The Báb*, pp. 94-98).

During an outbreak of cholera in Shiraz in September, 1846, the Bāb succeeded in escaping to Isfahan, where he had already sent a number of disciples to await his arrival, and where he was favorably received in the home of the *emām-e jomʿa*. For a brief period, he was involved in public discussions of his claims, but growing opposition from the *ʿolamāʾ* ended in the issue of a *fatwā* for his execution. At that point he was secretly transferred to the residence of the governor, Manūčehr Khan Moʿtamed-al-Dawla, whose interest in the Bāb's message may have also been tinged by political considerations. Moʿtamed-al-Dawla's plans, which included the introduction of the Bāb to Moḥammad Shah (possibly with a view to his ultimately replacing Ḥājī Mīrzā Āqāsī [q.v.] as the king's advisor), collapsed on his death in February, 1847. The loss of his supporter, who had already protected him from the *ʿolamāʾ* of Isfahan by concealing him in his own residence, was a serious blow to the Bāb. Gorgīn Khan, Moʿtamed-al-Dawla's nephew and successor, discovered the prophet and sent him under escort to Tehran, notifying the court of his action. At Kolayn near the capital, however, instructions came that the Bāb was to be taken to the town of Mākū in Azerbaijan, where he arrived, after a stay of forty days in Tabrīz, about July, 1847. It has been suggested that the prime minister, Ḥājī Mīrzā Āqāsī, prevented the Bāb's arrival in Tehran out of fear that he might supplant him as an influence on Moḥammad Shah (Zarandī, *Dawn-Breakers*, pp. 231-32). In Mākū the Bāb was placed under what was originally close confinement in the castle overlooking the town, but before long conditions were sufficiently relaxed to permit the arrival of visitors and the resumption of communications between him and his followers.

The Bāb's growing popularity and the ease with which he was still able to orchestrate the movement for which he was the figurehead gave considerable cause for concern to Ḥājī Mīrzā Āqāsī. At this point, the Russian Minister in Tehran, Dolgorukov, began to exert pressure on the Prime Minister to have the Bāb removed from Mākū, which was located dangerously close to the Russian border; a recent messianic movement in the Caucasus had caused serious problems for the Russians and their fears of renewed chiliastic agitation in the region seem to have been behind their request for the Bāb's removal (see Momen, *Bābī and Bahāʾī Religions*, p. 72). From Mākū, the Bāb, was, accordingly, transferred to Čahrīq near Urmia, at a fair distance from the sensitive border region but still sufficiently far from the heart of Iran. He arrived there in early May, 1848, and was placed under strict confinement.

During the later period of the Bāb's confinement in Mākū, he began to advance claims even more startling than those of *bāb* and *nāʾeb*. In a letter written shortly before his transfer to Čahrīq, copies of which were soon distributed on his instructions among his followers, he proclaimed himself the Imam Mahdī in person and announced the abrogation of the laws of Islam (Māzandarānī, *Ẓohūr*, pp. 164-66). Not long after his arrival in Čahrīq, he was brought temporarily to Tabrīz, where he was examined by a tribunal of religious and civil dignitaries, including Nāṣer-al-Dīn Mīrzā, the crown prince, then governor of Azerbaijan. At this hearing, the Bāb made public his claim to be the return of the Hidden Imam and was unofficially sentenced to death by several of the *ʿolamāʾ* present. The charge of insanity was introduced in order to prevent his execution at this juncture.

In an account of the Bāb's interrogation possibly written by Amīr Aṣlān Khan Majd-al-Dawla, it is stated that, following his bastinado, the Bāb recanted his claims and gave a "sealed undertaking" that he would not repeat his errors. What appears to be the original of this latter document was discovered in the Iranian state archives after the deposition of Moḥammad-ʿAlī Shah in 1909; it is now understood to be preserved in the Majles Library. The authenticity of the recantation document seems to rest, not only on the handwriting, which bears comparison with that of the Bāb, but also on the explicit denial in it of specific vicegerency (*nīāba ḵāṣṣa*) on behalf of the imam, something the Bāb had already denied several times before. (Facsimiles of both these documents are reproduced by Browne in *Materials*, pp. 248-56.) The implications of his claim to *qāʾemīya* had already been made clear to the authorities when he was brought through Urmia en route to Tabrīz. Several accounts, including some by American missionaries, indicate that large numbers of people turned out to greet him with an enthusiasm bordering on acceptance of him as the imam in person (Momen, op. cit., pp. 73-74). Repeated scenes of this kind, were they to be allowed, could only lead in one direction. That direction was further indicated (almost simultaneously with the Bāb's examination in Tabrīz, see above) at a gathering of some eighty Babi activists in the village of Badašt in Māzandarān, where the Bāb's claim to be the Hidden Imam was announced together with a proclamation abrogating the Islamic *Šarīʿa*. The Badašt gathering seems to have acted as a signal, in concert with the Bāb's own announcement of his more developed claims, for the successive Babi-led risings in Māzandarān, Neyrīz (Nīrīz) and Zanjān, between 1848 and 1850 (see BABISM).

Following his return to Čahrīq in August, 1848, however, the Bāb devoted himself to the elaboration of a yet more radical development of his position. In the works written between then and his execution in July, 1850, notably in the later parts of the Persian *Bayān*, he claimed to be, not merely the Imam Mahdī, but a theophanic representation of the godhead, a divine manifestation (*maẓhar-e elāhī*) empowered to reveal a new *Šarīʿa*, the basic outline of which may be found in the Persian and Arabic *Bayān*s. It is unlikely that these claims of the Bāb were widely known to his followers in the period before his death (the *Bayān*, for example, was not much distributed before then), but they proved an important influence on later Babism with its numerous theophanic claimants, and, in particular, on Bahaism as it developed this strand of the Bāb's teaching from the 1860s. Several of the Bāb's writings during this period, such as the *Ketāb al-asmāʾ* and *Ketāb-e panj šaʾn* indicate growing doctrinal idiosyncrasy and a preoccupation with the amplification of ritual practices largely unrelated to the actual circumstances of the Babi community.

The struggle between a group of Babis and state forces in Māzandarān (September, 1848-May, 1849) caused considerable anxiety in the early months of Nāṣer-al-Dīn Shah's reign, but its eventual suppression and the fact that it had been restricted to a rural area lessened the fear of the government. When, however, violence broke out in the urban centers of Neyrīz and Zanjān in May, 1850, Mīrzā Taqī Khan Amīr Neẓām decided to take the extreme step of having the Bāb put to death. He was, accordingly, brought to Tabrīz at the end of June, 1850, and executed by firing squad in the barracks square there at noon on either July 8 or 9. (The Bahais celebrate this event on 9 July, stating that it occurred on 28 Šaʿbān 1266, but several contemporary sources give the date as 8 July—see Momen, op. cit., p. 78 and n.). Accounts of the execution exist, but none is a direct eye-witness description, although there are a few second-hand versions based on the testimony of eye-witnesses. The Bāb survived the first volley, when the bullets cut ropes suspending him and Mīrzā Moḥammad-ʿAlī Zonūzī, a disciple, condemned to death with him; a second regiment had to be brought in to complete the task. The corpses of the Bāb and his fellow-victim were thrown together into a ditch, where they were said to have been eaten by dogs, an action which prompted Justin Sheil, then British Minister in Tehran, to address a note to the prime minister expressing outrage at its barbarity (Momen, *Babi and Bahaʾi Religion*, p. 79). Babi sources maintain, however, that the bodies were removed from the ditch through the efforts of a certain Ḥājī Solaymān Khan Mīlānī and eventually brought to Tehran, where they were buried in secret at the Emāmzāda Ḥasan, in which location some modern Babis believe them to remain (Nicolas, *Sayyed Ali Mohammed*, pp. 379-85). Bahai accounts, however, state that the remains were at one point removed from the Emāmzāda on the instructions of Mīrzā Ḥosayn-ʿAlī Bahāʾ-Allāh (q.v.) and transferred from hiding-place to hiding-place for almost fifty years before being brought to Palestine in 1899. A shrine to house the remains was begun on Mt. Carmel by ʿAbbās Effendī ʿAbd-al-Bahāʾ (q.v.), who interred them there in 1908 (Balyuzi, *The Báb*, pp. 189-92). Some time later, a marble superstructure topped by a gold-tiled dome was erected over the original shrine and is today a well-known landmark in Haifa, forming the central feature of the complex of Bahai buildings there.

The Bāb's personality remains elusive in the absence of detailed contemporary descriptions and the presence of so much later hagiographical material. According to Dr. William Cormick, an Irish physician who treated the Bāb following his bastinado in Tabrīz in 1848, he was "a very mild and delicate-looking man, rather small in stature and very fair for a Persian, with a melodious soft voice, which struck me much. Being a Sayyid, he was dressed in the habits of that sect. . . . In fact his whole look and deportment went far to dispose me in his favour" (quoted in Browne, *Materials*, p. 262). This picture of the Bāb is borne out by more concrete evidence, such as a portrait preserved in the Bahai archives in Haifa, clothing and other personal effects, and examples of penmanship all testify to a highly-developed aesthetic temperament. The influence of this love of delicacy and fine things is apparent in many of the Bāb's injunctions in the Persian *Bayān* and elsewhere, including regular bathing and depilation, the use of perfumes, rose-water, and henna, the wearing of precious stones, the use of the best paper and calligraphy for writing the scriptures, the detailed rules for the washing, adornment, and burial of the dead, and even in the prohibition on beating children. Such an image must be balanced, however, by reference to the Bāb's obvious harshness in such matters as *jehād*, the treatment of unbelievers and their property (including religious shrines), and the destruction of non-Babi books.

During the nineteenth century, something of a myth of the Bāb was perpetuated in some intellectual and literary circles in Europe, largely owing to the widespread influence of the Comte de Gobineau's *Religions et philosophies dans l'Asie centrale* (Paris, 1865), which presented an extended and somewhat inaccurate picture of the Bāb not unlike that of Moḥammad popular during the French Enlightenment. This phenomenon is best described by the French journalist Jules Bois, who wrote of the Bāb's death: "All Europe was stirred to pity and indignation.... Among the littérateurs of my generation, in the Paris of 1890, the martyrdom of the Bāb was still as fresh a topic as had been the first news of his death. We wrote poems about him. Sarah Bernhardt entreated Catulle Mendes for a play on the theme of this historic tragedy" ("Babism and Baha'ism," *Forum* 74, 1925, quoted in Momen, op. cit., p. 50). Among others attracted to the Bāb in this period figured Matthew Arnold, Ernest Renan, and, in Russia, Turgenev and Tolstoy; little of this enthusiasm survived into the twentieth century (for further details, see Momen, op. cit., pp. 3-56).

The Bāb's fame has endured chiefly within the context of Bahaism (see BAHAI FAITH) in which he plays an important role as an independent divine manifestation in some respects equal, in others subordinate to, Mīrzā Ḥosayn-ʿAlī Bahā'-Allāh, for whom he is held to act as a herald (*mobašser*). Although Bahai accounts of the Bāb are more reliable than those of Gobineau and other early European writers, they are frequently edited in order to fit into the wider perspective of Bahai history and are often hagiographic. The standard account, on which all later versions are based to a greater or lesser extent, is Mollā Moḥammad Nabīl Zarandī's history available only in English translation as *The Dawn-Breakers* and subtitled *Nabil's Narrative of the Early Days of the Bahā'ī Revelation*. Among Western Bahais the image of the Bāb is frequently compared to the Christ of popular devotion and made to figure as the saint par excellence of the religion. Few references are made in the published materials to his early claims, his laws, his ritual innovations, or other matters felt to be inconsistent with this image.

For details of the Bāb's works, see BAYĀN.

Doctrines. It is difficult to summarize the doctrines taught by the Bāb, largely because these changed substantially between the earliest and latest periods of his career. In works written during the first years following his claim to be *bāb al-emām*, considerable stress is laid on the theme that his teachings represent the "true Islam" (*al-dīn al-ḵāleṣ*). Thus, "this religion is, before God, the essence of the religion of Moḥammad" (*Qayyūm al-asmā'*, fol. 78a), while God has "made this book the essence of the Koran, word for word" (ibid., fol. 72b; cf. fol. 53b) and "The pure faith is the Remembrance in security; whoever desires Islam, let him submit himself to his cause" (ibid., fol. 2a). The laws of Moḥammad and the imams were to remain binding "until the day of resurrection" (ibid., fol. 185b): Islamic injunctions as to what was *ḥarām* and *ḥalāl* were to remain in force (*Ṣaḥīfa-ye ʿadlīya*, pp. 5-6; cf.Balyuzi, *The Báb*, pp. 97-98). At the same time, the Bāb claimed authority to clarify obscure issues relating to the details of the *Šarīʿa*, such as *ṣalāt, zakāt*, and *jehād*, and also introduced some ordinances extending or intensifying the standard Koranic regulations. According to one of his followers, in his early letters, the Bāb "put desirable matters (*mostaḥabbāt*) in the place of obligatory (*wājebāt*), and undesirable matters (*makrūhāt*) in the place of forbidden (*moḥarramāt*). Thus, for example, he regarded it as obligatory to have four tablets (*mohr*) from the soil (from the shrine) of the prince of martyrs, [i.e., Imam Ḥosayn], on which to place the hands, forehead and nose during the prostration of *namāz*; he considered the pilgrimage of *ʿĀšūrā* (q.v.) a duty; he laid down prayers (*adʿīa*) and supererogatory observances (*taʿqībāt*); he proclaimed the obligation of Friday prayer... ; and he fashioned amulets (*hayākel*), charms (*aḥrāz*), and talismans (*ṭelasmāt*) such as are prepared among the people.... All his companions acted with the utmost circumspection according to the *oṣūl* and *forūʿ* of Islam" (Moḥammad-ʿAlī Zonūzī, quoted by Māzandarānī, op. cit., pp. 31-32). Several important supererogatory injunctions are to be found in the *Ḵaṣā'el-e sabʿa*, written by the Bāb during his *ḥajj* journey, and in another work of this period, the *Ṣaḥīfa bayn al-ḥaramayn*.

A wider picture of early doctrines may be found in the *Ṣaḥīfa-ye ʿadlīya*, which, among other things, condemns the concept of *waḥdat al-wojūd* as *šerk* (p. 16), lists the seven bases (*oṣūl*) of *maʿrefa* as *tawḥīd, maʿānī, abwāb, emāma, arkān, noqabā'*, and *nojabā'* (pp. 20-31); states that prayer through the imam or others is *kofr* (p. 20); denies that either Aḥsā'ī or Raštī prayed through ʿAlī or thought him the Creator (p. 22); regards the station of the imams as higher than that of the prophets (p. 24); states that most Twelver Shiʿites, because of their ignorance of the station of the *noqabā'*, will go to hell (p. 31); declares the enemies of Aḥsā'ī and Raštī to be unbelievers like the Sunnis (pp. 32-33); refers to the necessity of belief in a physical resurrection and *meʿrāj* (p. 34); condemns the idea of spiritual resurrection and maintains that Aḥsā'ī did not speak of it (p. 34); and, finally, speaks of obedience to himself, as the "servant" of the twelfth imam, as obligatory (p. 41).

Finally, it is worth noting that messianic expectation, although far from dominant in these early works, finds a place in them, notably in the *Qayyūm al-asmāʾ*, where it is frequently joined with exhortation to wage *jehād*, a fact to which reference must be made in any attempt to understand the Babi-state conflicts of 1848-50 (for full details, see MacEoin, "Bābī Concept of Holy War").

The Bāb's doctrines, which exhibit many of the gnostic and Neoplatonist features common to earlier Shiʿite sects such as the Ismaʿilis and Ḥorūfīs, tend to become more abstruse in the later periods. The crucial change occurs with the Bāb's abrogation of Islamic law in 1264/1848, followed by the elaboration of his own *Šarīʿa* and doctrinal system. This highly elaborated body of ideas, frequently expressed in oblique and allusive language and lacking any real organization, is not easy to summarize. There have been no later Babi theologians to analyse or systematize the elements of the Bāb's scattered thoughts. At the heart of the system is the belief that the divine or eternal essence (*ḏāt-e elāhī*, *ḏāt-e azal*) is unknowable, indescribable, and inaccessible (*Bayān-e fārsī* 3:7, p. 81; 4:1, p. 105; 4:2, p. 110). The revelation of God (*ẓohūr Allāh*) in this world is that of the Tree of Reality (*šajara-ye ḥaqīqat*) (ibid., 2:8, p. 37), a term frequently used for the Primal Will (*mašīyat-e awwalīya*) (ibid., 4:6, pp. 120-21) which has appeared in all the prophets (*Dalāʾel-e sabʿa*, pp. 2-3). The Bāb compares the Primal Will to the sun which remains single and unchanged, although appearing under different names and forms in the persons of the prophets in whom it is manifested, as if in a mirror (ibid.; *Čahār šaʾn*, quoted in *Āʾīn-e Bāb*, pp. 48-49; untitled *ṣaḥīfa*, quoted ibid., p. 49). This manifestation of the Primal Will is frequently referred to as the Point of Truth (*noqṭa-ye ḥaqīqat*) (*Bayān-e fārsī* 3:7, p. 81) or Primal Point (*noqṭa-ye ūlā*)—the latter term being the most common title used of the Bāb by his followers—from whom all things are originated (ibid., 1:1, p. 4; 3:8, p. 37) and by whom the prophets and books have been sent down (ibid., 2:8, p. 37). This Point possesses two stations; a divine station in which it is the manifestation of the divinity (*maẓhar-e olūhīyat*), and a human station in which it manifests its servitude (ibid., 4:1, pp. 105, 107). In his human form, the prophet is the apex of creation and the perfect man, since all things progress until they find their perfection in man and man develops until he culminates in the prophet (ibid., 2:1, pp. 14-15). It is only by meeting this theophany that man can be said to meet God (ibid., 2:7, p. 31; 2:6, p. 63; 3:7, p. 81); thus, references in the Koran to the meeting with God (*leqāʾ Allāh*) are, in reality, references to meeting Moḥammad (ibid., 3:7, p. 81). All things have been created to attain to this meeting (ibid., 6:232, p. 222; *Dalāʾel-e sabʿa*, p. 31). Since the time of the revelation of Adam to that of the Bāb, 12,210 years have elapsed, although God undoubtedly had unnumbered worlds and Adams before this cycle (*Bayān-e fārsī* 3:13, p. 95); but in every world, the manifestation of the Primal Will has always been the Point of the *Bayān*, the Bāb, for he is identical with Adam (ibid.); thus, "in the day of Noah, I was Noah, in the day of Abraham, I was Abraham" (untitled *ṣaḥīfa* quoted in *Āʾīn-e Bāb*, p. 49). Indeed, this same Point will appear again and again in future manifestations of the Primal Will (ibid.). Nevertheless, there is progress from one manifestation to the next: In each succeeding theophany, the appearance is nobler than in the one before; hence, all the revelations of the past were created for the appearance of Moḥammad, they and the revelation of Moḥammad were created for the appearance of the Bāb (Qāʾem), and so on into the future (*Bayān-e fārsī* 4:12, p. 136). Adam is compared to the human being in the state of a seed in the womb, the Bāb to a twelve-year old child (ibid., 3:13, p. 95).

One of the most important elements in the Bāb's thought is his elaborate symbolic interpretation of eschatological terms. Thus, resurrection (*qīāma*) is the appearance of the Primal Will in its latest manifestation (ibid., 2:7, p. 30); just as all things were originally created in one person, so all will be resurrected in one person, whereupon they will be individually resurrected in their various places (ibid., 2:11, p. 47). Physical resurrection of bodies from their graves, however, will not take place (ibid.). The Day of Resurrection extends from the moment of the appearance of the Tree of Truth in each age until his disappearance; thus, the resurrection of Moses took place from the appearance of Jesus until his Ascension (ibid., 2:7, p. 30). The resurrection of Islam began with the Bāb's announcement of his mission two hours and eleven minutes after sunset on the evening of 5 Jomādā I 1260 and will end at his death (ibid.). In this resurrection, the return (*rajʿa*) of Moḥammad, the imams, Fāṭema, and the four *abwāb*, has taken place in the persons of the eighteen *ḥorūf al-ḥayy*, the Bāb's first disciples (ibid., 1:2-19, pp. 6-10). After the death of the prophet, a *fatrat* intervenes, during which there are witnesses (*šohadāʾ*) until his return (ibid., 2:3, p. 22); during this *fatrat*, the Primal Will is within creation, but is not recognized outwardly (ibid., 2:9, pp. 44-45). When, however, the Point is again manifested, belief in him is paradise and unbelief hell (ibid., 2:9, p. 44); indeed, the first to believe is himself the essence of paradise and the first to disbelieve the essence of hell (ibid., 2:17, p. 68). All things are in a condition of either belief or denial (ibid., 2:3, p. 23), belonging to the "Letters of Exaltation" (*ḥorūf-e ʿelīyīn*) or their opposite (*ḥorūf-e dūn-e ʿelīyīn*) (ibid., 2:2, pp. 20-21). In another sense, all things find their paradise in their perfection (ibid., 5:4, p. 155). Other eschatological terms such as *qabr*, *ṣerāṭ*, *mīzān*, *ḥesāb*, *ketāb*, *sāʿa* are given similar interpretations (ibid., 2:10, 12, 13, 14, 15, 18).

A constant theme of the Persian *Bayān*—and one which was to have important implications for later developments—is that of *man yoẓheroho'llāh* (him whom God shall make manifest) the next embodiment of the Primal Will, whose appearance is anticipated sometime between 1511 and 2001 years in the future, or sooner if God wills. Many of the prescriptions of the *Bayān* are connected in some way to respect for *man yoẓheroho'llāh* or preparation for his appearance. The

Bāb also developed a complex legal system, much of which was clearly intended for implementation in the theocratic Babi state he anticipated; there is a marked contrast between regulations directed towards unbelievers and those applicable to Babis, the former being harsh, the latter milder than in Islam. There are regulations for marriage, burial, pilgrimage, prayer, and other devotional and ritual practices, often in detail. (Full descriptions of these may be found in MacEoin, "Ritual and Semi-Ritual Observances."

Bibliography: No really adequate biographical study on the Bāb exists. A. L. M. Nicolas, *Séyyèd Ali Mohammed dit le Bâb*, Paris, 1905, is a study of the movement more than the man. Similar in scope, but with rather more about the Bāb himself, are H. M. Balyuzi, *The Báb*, Oxford, 1973, and M. ʿA. Fayżī, *Ḥażrat-e Noqṭa-ye Ūlā*, Tehran, 1352 Š./1973-74, both of which depend largely upon Mollā Moḥammad Nabīl Zarandī, *The Dawn-Breakers: Nabíl's Narrative of the Early Days of the Baháʾí Revelation*, ed. and tr. Shoghi Effendi, Wilmette, Ill., 1932. On the Bāb's family in general, see M. ʿA. Fayżī, *K̲ānadān-e Afnān*, Tehran, 127 *Badīʿ*/1349 Š./1970-71. On the Bāb's first wife, see H. M. Balyuzi, *K̲hadíjih Bagum: The Wife of the Báb*, Oxford, 1981. See also A. Amanat *Resurrection and the Renewal of the Age: The Emergence of the Babi Movement in Qajar Iran (1844-1852)* (forthcoming). Anonymous, *Āʾīn-e Bāb*, n.p., n.d. E. G. Browne, ed., *Materials for the Study of the Bābī Religion*, Cambridge, 1918. J. A. de Gobineau, *Religions et philosophies dans l'Asie Centrale*, 10th ed., Paris, 1957. Mīrzā Abu'l-Fażl Moḥammad Golpāyegānī and Mīrzā Mahdī Golpāyegānī, *Kašf al-ḡeṭāʾ ʿan ḥīal al-aʿdāʾ*, Ashkhabad, n.d. F. Kazemzadeh, "Two Incidents in the Life of the Báb," *World Order* 5/3, 1971, pp. 21-24. S. Lambden, "An Incident in the Childhood of the Bab," in P. Smith, ed., *In Iran: Studies in Bábí and Bahá'í History* III, Los Angeles, 1986. D. M. MacEoin, *From Shaykhism to Babism: A Study in Charismatic Renewal in Shīʿī Islam*, Ph.D. thesis, Cambridge University, 1979 (University Microfilms 81-70,043). Idem, "The Bābī Concept of Holy War," *Religion* 12, 1982, pp. 93-129. Idem, "Ritual and Semi-Ritual Observances in Babism and Baha'ism," paper read to the Bahāʾī Studies Seminar 1980, University of Lancaster. Idem, *Early Babi Doctrine and History: A Survey of Source Materials* (forthcoming). Idem, "Early Shaykhí Reactions to the Báb and his Claims," in M. Momen, ed., *Studies in Bábí and Bahá'í History* I, Los Angeles, 1983. Mīrzā Asad-Allāh Fāżel Māzandarānī, *Ketāb-e ẓohūr al-ḥaqq* III, Cairo, n.d. Sayyed ʿAlī-Moḥammad Šīrāzī, *Bayān-e fārsī*, [Tehran], n.d. Idem, *Ṣaḥīfa-ye ʿadlīya*, [Tehran], n.d. Idem, *Qayyūm al-asmāʾ*, Cambridge University Library, ms., Browne Or. F. 11. Idem, *Resāla-ye forūʿ al-ʿadlīya*, Iran National Bahai Archives 5010.C. Idem, *Ketāb al-fehrest*, Iran National Bahai Archives 6003.C.

(D. M. MacEoin)

BĀB AL-ABWĀB. See DARBAND.

BĀB AL-BĀB. See BOŠRŪʾĪ.

BĀB-E FARḠĀNĪ. See BĀB (Sufi).

BĀB-E HOMĀYŪN (august [royal] gate), name of a gate and its connecting street in the Qajar citadel (Arg, q.v.) of Tehran. The southern half of the Arg housing the royal quarter was separated from the ministerial area in the north by a lane called Kūča Darb(-e) Andarūn, while a south-northerly street, K̲īābān Almāsīya (Diamond avenue, later [K̲īābān] Bāb-e Homāyūn), divided the ministerial area itself into two quarters. A gate, Sardar(-e) Almāsīya, at the southern end of K̲īābān Almāsīya, opened up in the center of Kūča Darb Andarūn; another, Darvāza Arg, a simple gate built during the Afghan occupation, connected it to the northern wall of the Arg. (V. Minorsky in *EI*[1] V, pp. 718 refers to an historically "important plan" of quarters in the Arg and Tehran prepared by Brezin in 1842.) In 1869-1874, Tehran saw radical development based on a plan prepared by the Austrian August Křiž (J. E. Polak, "Topographische Bemerkungen zur Karte der Umgebung und zu dem Plane von Teheran," in *Mitteilungen der K. K. geographischen Gesellschaft in Wien* 20, 1877, p. 218 and pl. III); it resulted in the extension of the town on all sides (P. G. Ahrens, *Die Entwicklung der Stadt Tehran*, Opladen, 1966, pp. 46f.). Meydān(-e) Tūpk̲āna (Artillery square) was created to the north of the Arg; the Arg's eastern ditch was filled to make room for a street (Nāṣerīya, later Nāṣer K̲osrow) intended to divert public access from Almāsīya Avenue (Moḥammad-Ḥasan Khan Ṣanīʿ-al-Dawla, *Merʾāt al-boldān* III, Tehran, 1296/1879, p. 44), and Almāsīya Avenue and its gates were renovated. This latter task was supervised by Moḥammad-Raḥīm Khan Qājār ʿAlāʾ-al-Dawla Amīr Neẓām, and in it older Iranian architectural traditions were combined with some European features (cf. G. N. Curzon, *Persia and the Persian Question*, London, 1892, pp. 306f.). Sardar Almāsīya was renamed Bāb-e Homāyūn (in obvious imitation of the Ottoman usage which applied the term, in the sense of "imperial gate," to the principal entrance in the outer wall of the sultan's new serail, Top-kapı Sarayı at Istanbul, see U. Heyd in *EI*[2] I, p. 836; the term saray is of Persian origin) and rebuilt as a two-storied structure. The lower level was partly dressed with ashlar masonry and partly faced with glazed tiles of brilliant colors. Access was gained through a large gateway crowned by a round arch and flanked by arcades, porticoes and guardrooms. The half-circular upper façade of the gateway was faced with glazed tiles representing floral designs surrounding the state and royal emblem, the Lion-and-Sun. The upper story contained a hall with two columns ornamented in plaster with spiral bands, and crowned with a semi-circular arch bearing various floral designs. Flanking this hall were two corner rooms or balconies with stained-glass openings and mirror-works. The Lion-and-

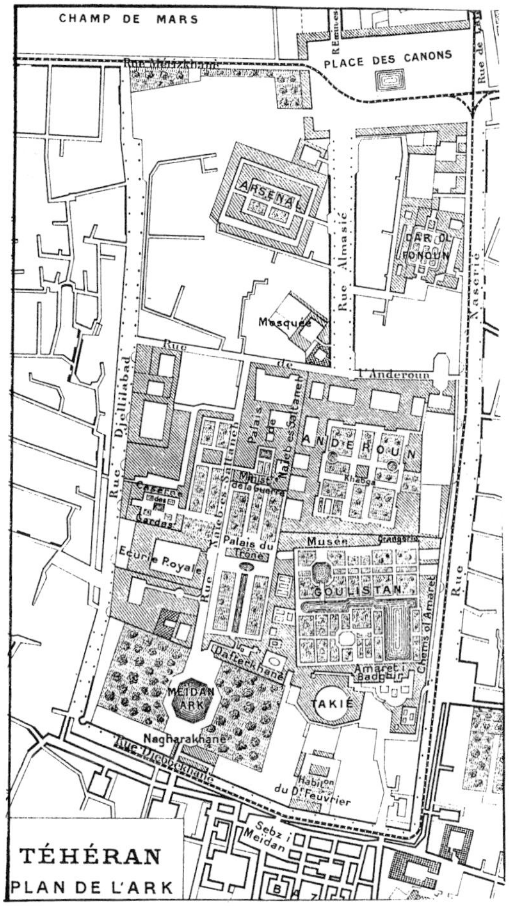

Figure 4. Plan of the Arg of Tehran (late nineteenth century). After Feuvrier, *Trois ans à la cour de Perse*, Paris, 1906

Sun flag floated upon this gate whenever the shah was in Tehran (Curzon, op. cit., pp. 307-08; Y. Ḏokā', *Tārīḵča-ye sāḵtemānhā-ye arg-e salṭanatī-e Tehrān wa rāhnamā-ye kāḵ-e Golestān*, Tehran, 1349 Š./1970, pp. 336ff., with the reproduction of a contemporary picture in fig. 149). The Almāsīya Avenue itself was renamed Ḵīābān Bāb-e Homāyūn (later also called Dālān(-e) Behešt [Paradise alley], or Ḵīābān Dawlat) and developed into a cobbled street, broad and straight, with footpaths, rows of trees, lamp-posts (containing oil-lamps) and metal fences. Two rows of uniformed shop units flanked the street, all with façades ornamented with circular arches and latticed arcades. The street gave access to major official buildings such as Madrasa-ye Neẓām (military college), The Qūrḵāna (arsenal), Anbār-e Ḡalla-ye Ḵāleṣa (royal grainery), and the Majma'-e Ṣanāye' (artisans' quarter) where various skilled workers and professional artists worked in their own workshops (E'temād-al-Salṭana, *Rūz-nāma-ye Īrān* 478, 1299/1882), as well as to Mahd 'Olyā' Mosque and, indirectly, to Dār al-Fonūn (Ḏokā', op. cit., pp. 338ff., with references and fig. 147 reproducing a water color by Maḥmūd Khan Malek-al-Šo'arā'). Darvāza Arg was now renamed Darvāza Dawlat, and rebuilt as a two-storied gatehouse, with a large gateway flanked by two smaller ones in the lower level and a columned portico crowned by a semicircular pinnacle and flanked by corner rooms. The main doors were of cast iron, and the whole structure was faced with glazed tiles in glittering patterns (Ḏokā', op. cit., pp. 339f.; Curzon, op. cit., pp. 306-07 and the figure opposite p. 306). A new development plan, carried out under Reżā Shah in 1934, wiped out the Arg's walls and gates (M. T. Moṣṭafawī, "Arg-e Tehran," *Eṭṭelā'āt-e māhāna* 6, no. 69, 1332 Š./1953, p. 26; H. Bobek, "Tehran," in *Geographische Forschungen = Schlern-Schriften 190: Festschrift zum 60. Geburtstag von Hans Kinzl*, Innsbruck, 1958, p. 18), leaving the Bāb-e Homāyūn Avenue fairly intact.

Bibliography: Given in the text.

(A. Sh. Shahbazi)

BĀB-e MĀČĪN. See Bāb (Sufi).

BĀBĀ AFŠĀR, Mīrzā. See Ḥakīmbāšī.

BĀBĀ AFŻAL-al-DĪN Moḥammad b. Ḥasan Maraqī Kāšānī, known as Bābā Afżal, poet and author of philosophical works in Persian. Several dates have been suggested for his death, the most likely being 610/1213-14 (M.-T. Modarres Rażawī, *Aḥwāl wa āṯār-e... Naṣīr-al-Dīn [Ṭūsī]*, Tehran, 1354 Š./1975, p. 207; cf. J. Rypka, "Bābā Afḍal," in *EI*² I, pp. 838-39). About his life practically nothing is known. His works (especially nos. 7 and 12, see below) suggest a disdain for officials, so it is not surprising that he is said to have once been imprisoned by the local governor on trumped-up charges of practicing sorcery (*seḥr*); a *qaṣīda* he wrote on the occasion has been published (M. Mīnovī and Y. Mahdawī, *Moṣannafāt-e Afżal-al-Dīn Moḥammad Maraqī Kāšānī*, 2 vols. [a promised third volume on his life and works has not been published], Tehran, 1331-37 Š./1952-58, pp. 731-32; cf. P. Bayżā'ī, "Ḥabsīya-ye Ḥakīm Afżal-al-Dīn Kāšānī," *Yaḡmā* 4, 1330 Š./1951, pp. 414-17; M. Moḥīṭ Ṭabāṭabā'ī, "Bābā Afżal Zendānī," *Moḥīṭ* 1, 1321 Š./1942, pp. 19-25). His tomb in Maraq, a village forty-two km northwest of Kāšān, is still a place of pilgrimage; a second grave is attributed locally to the *pādešāh* of Zang, who is said to have been a devoted disciple. The *taḏkera*s mention a family relationship and an exchange of quatrains (*robā'īs*) with Naṣīr-al-Dīn Ṭūsī, but these are next to impossible. The most that can be said is that in his *Šarḥ al-ešārāt* Ṭūsī refers to Bābā Afżal's opinion on a point of logic (ed. Maṭba'at al-Ḥaydarī, I, Tehran, 1377/1957-58, p. 283; cf. *Moṣannafāt*, pp. 573-74) and that in his *Sayr o solūk* Ṭūsī mentions that he studied various sciences with Kamāl-al-Dīn Moḥammad Ḥāseb, a student of Bābā Afżal (quoted in M. Fayżī, Ḥ. 'Āṭefī, 'A. Behnīā, and 'A. Šarīf, *Dīvān-e Ḥakīm Afżal-al-Dīn*

Moḥammad Maraqī Kāšānī (Bābā Afżal), Kāšān, 1351 Š./1972, p. 30).

Mīnovī suggests that Bābā Afżal may have been an Isma'ili (*Moṣannafāt*, introd., p. vii), but his prose works provide no evidence for this, and he alludes to Sunnism as the best of paths (ibid., p. 297). Several *robā'īs* mentioning 'Alī may or may not be genuine; one that refers to the exclusive truth of Twelve-Imam Shi'ism (*Dīvān*, no. 300) is certainly spurious. Though Bābā Afżal avoids terminology connected specifically with Sufism in his major prose works, much of his poetry and some of his letters are explicitly Sufi in tone, while various passages in his prose works point to the spiritual benefits the traveler (*sālek*)—a favorite Sufi term—will gain by studying; e.g., "He will find his own self, which is the treasury of the realities of all things and the leaven (*māya*) of infinite existence" (*Moṣannafāt*, p. 149; cf. pp. 321, 724). Bābā Afżal alludes in several places to the knowledge he has acquired through purifying his own soul; e.g., God gave him familiarity with the radiance of His own Being, making him into a mirror that reflected the whole of the universe (ibid., p. 83; cf. p. 259). In a letter he mentions spending sixty years in the world's darkness and discovering the water of life, which is intellect (*'aql, ḵerad*). "Since my tongue has tasted intellect's sweetness and savor, I have taken up residence at its wellspring" (ibid., pp. 698-99).

Bābā Afżal's most universally recognized contribution to Iranian culture lies in the field of literature. In poetry he has been considered one of the two or three greatest masters of the *robā'ī*, while in philosophical prose only Sohravardī stands on the same level. Though Bābā Afżal wrote none of the visionary treatises of the type for which Sohravardī is famous, his systematic expositions of the teachings of the Peripatetic philosophers surpass Sohravardī's similar works in clarity, smoothness, and liquidity. Like Ebn Sīnā (Avicenna; d. 428/1037) in the *Dāneš-nāma-ye 'alā'ī*, Bābā Afżal employs a great deal of Persian vocabulary where others would have used Arabic, but unlike Ebn Sīnā he chooses only attractive and mellifluous terms, making his works a delight to read; nor does he neglect to employ the corresponding Arabic terms where clarity demands them. That he was a careful stylist in his philosophical works is shown by his letters, which are written less formally and show a preponderance of Arabic words.

Bābā Afżal's influence on later thinkers has not been investigated, and only a careful comparison of his works with later writings will be able to uncover its extent. Given the fact that his works are clearly and beautifully written, they were probably a rich source of inspiration for philosophical writings not only in Persian but also in Arabic. Thus Mollā Ṣadrā (d. 1050/1640) modeled his Arabic *Eksīr al-'ārefīn* (Mollā Ṣadrā, *Rasā'el*, Tehran, 1302/1884-85, pp. 278-340; ed. and Japanese tr., S. Kamada, Tokyo, 1984) on Bābā Afżal's *Jāvedān-nāma*, though he did not mention this fact in the text, nor was it noticed by the work's editor; the tables of contents of the two treatises are practically identical, many—though by no means all—of Mollā Ṣadrā's arguments and examples are taken from Bābā Afżal's work, and a significant amount of the text is literally translated.

Philosophy. Bābā Afżal wrote during a period when several figures were bridging the gaps between philosophy and Sufism. Ebn Sīnā had shown some of the directions this movement could take in his visionary recitals and in the last sections of *al-Ešārāt wa'l-tanbīhāt*, while certain passages in the works of Ḡazālī (d. 506/1111) had combined Sufi and philosophical concerns (cf. work no. 55 below); 'Ayn-al-Qożāt Hamadānī (d. 525/1131) had employed philosophical terminology to express concepts derived from mystical unveiling (*kašf*). Among Bābā Afżal's contemporaries, Sohravardī (d. 587/1191) followed many of Ebn Sīnā's leads, while Ebn al-'Arabī (d. 638/1240) made full use of philosophical terminology to depict a universe transfigured by the presence of God. For his part, Bābā Afżal follows the philosophical and logical (not the visionary or gnostic [*'erfānī*]) terminology of Ebn Sīnā and shows no obvious inclination to move in the new directions mapped out by other philosophers, nor to follow any of the various schools of Sufism. But most of his works evoke a visionary aura in spite of their philosophical and logical exactitude. Perhaps his major predecessors were those philosophers interested in Hermes and the esoteric side of the Greek legacy; given the nature of those works attributed to Greek authors that he chose to translate, he certainly deserves the title "Hermetizing" given him by Henry Corbin (*Avicenna and the Visionary Recital*, London, 1960, p. 13; cf. below, works 50-53).

Bābā Afżal's major concern is to explain the salvific power of true knowledge, i.e., self-knowledge, or knowledge of the Self (*ḏāt* or *howwīyat*, God Himself viewed as the center of man's being). As S. H. Nasr has pointed out, Bābā Afżal's philosophy is basically an autology (*ḵ'od-šenāsī*; "Afdal al-Din Kashani and the Philosophical World of Khwaja Nasir al-Din Tusi," in M. E. Marmura, ed., *Islamic Theology and Philosophy: Studies in Honor of George F. Hourani*, Albany, 1983, p. 260). To know oneself is to know the everlasting reality that is consciousness, and to know it is to be it. In contrast to most philosophers and philosophically-minded Sufis, Bābā Afżal writes practically nothing about God and His attributes, while rarely referring to the nature of existence except in relation to self-knowledge. His ontology is simultaneously an epistemology, since the full actualization of the potentialities of the universe can only take place through the self-awareness of human beings (*mardom, ensān*), which in turn depends upon the training of the human soul, or education in the widest sense of the term.

Bābā Afżal's view of the structure of reality is set down most succinctly at the beginning of *Rahanjām-nāma* (*Moṣannafāt*, pp. 58ff.). Cleverly exploiting the meaning of the root *w-j-d*, he divides existence (*wojūd*) into two kinds, "being" (*būdan*) and "finding" (*yāftan*), each of which may be potential (*be-qowwa*) or actual (*be-fe'l*). Potential being is represented by the tree present in a seed, while actual being is the tree itself. Potential finding is life or the soul at whatever level it may be envisaged, from the mineral up to the human; actual finding is the self-consciousness of the intellect (*kerad*, *'aql*), where knowledge, knower, and known are identical. Existence that is only "being" lacks the perfection of "finding," while finding that is only potential has not yet become everlasting. Each higher level of existence contains the lower levels within itself; everything outside the intelligible world of the soul is an imperfect likeness (*metāl*) of what is found within (ibid., pp. 69ff., 83, 191, 241).

Like most Muslim cosmologists, Bābā Afżal discerns two movements in the universe, that from the origin (*āḡāz*, *mabda'*) to the world, or from "finding" to "being," and that from the world to the point of return (*anjām*, *ma'ād*), from being to finding. The descending movement is ruled by the First Intellect, which is one of God's two vicegerents (*kalīfa*) in the world and whose domain extends down through the spheres to the four elements. The ascending movement extends from nature (*ṭabī'a*) through the mineral, vegetal, and animal kingdoms up to man, God's second vicegerent (ibid., pp. 90-91). As the microcosm, man contains within himself all levels of the macrocosm; these he must actualize one by one to bring about the Return to God.

The goal of existence is for each thing to reach the full flowering of its own nature (ibid., pp. 6ff.). Perfected human nature encompasses every degree of existence found in the ascending movement of the universe. Both in the outside world and in man himself, the four elements, held in balance by nature, prepare the ground for the actualization of the pneumatic (*nafsānī*) and spiritual (*rūḥānī*) faculties of the soul, i.e., all the powers connected specifically with vegetal, animal, and human existence. In attaining to perfection (*kamāl*, *tamāmī*), man brings to fruition the specifically human faculty that is the intellect, which balances all the lower faculties on the basis of ethical norms (*farhang*, *adab*), thus giving rise to the virtues (*fażīlathā-ye kolqī*, ibid., pp. 94ff.). Hence ethics has a firm ontological basis; the moral virtues are a necessary stage in the universe's return to God. The intellect, having brought the soul into equilibrium, i.e., having established the positive character traits which define a true human being, allows the realization of absolute being, the Self (ibid., p. 75). The world is a tree whose fruit is man, man a tree whose fruit is soul, soul a tree whose fruit is intellect, and intellect a tree whose fruit is the meeting (*leqā'*) with God (ibid., p. 315).

Philosophy is valuable because people who meditate upon its truths will look within themselves and come to understand that they already possess everything they seek. "Man has no need of anything but himself" (ibid., p. 241). By classifying the kinds of knowledge and existents, philosophy awakens human souls from forgetfulness and incites them to reach the perfection of existence (ibid., p. 153). It prepares man for death by allowing him to undergo a cognitive separation from the body before it dies. "Until the soul knows its separation (*mofāraqat* [from the body]), no separation takes place, neither during life when the body's parts are joined together, nor after death when they decompose" (ibid., p. 701). Ignorance of its own nature is the cause of the soul's wretchedness (*šaqāwat*) in the next world.

Works. Works attributed to Bābā Afżal can be divided into four basic categories: poetry, prose, works of uncertain ascription, and works of incorrect ascription. All works are in Persian unless otherwise noted.

I. Poetry. 1. S. Nafīsī collected 483 quatrains ascribed to Bābā Afżal (*Robā'īyāt-e Afżal-al-Dīn*, Tehran, 1331 Š./1952), while Mīnovī and Mahdawī list 195 (*Moṣannafāt*, pp. 737-72, 674-76). M. Fayżī et al. (*Dīvān*) add to the sources employed by these earlier works a manuscript dated 1215/1801 from the Madrasa-ye Solṭānī in Kāšān (no. 141/2) and list more than 686 quatrains, while rejecting another 37 as definitely spurious. All these scholars refer to instances where quatrains have been ascribed to other authors, but none attempts a serious critical study. In addition to the quatrains, twelve *ḡazal*s and three *qaṣīda*s are mentioned (*Dīvān*, pp. 242-59; cf. ibid., pp. 731-36, 673). Though many of the quatrains would be unremarkable in any anthology of the genre, a large number reflect the specific philosophical concerns and language of Bābā Afżal's prose works. Recurring themes include warnings about the futility of involvement with the things of the corporeal world, the correspondence between microcosm and macrocosm, and self-knowledge as the goal of human existence.

II. Prose. A. Major original works. 2. *'Arż-nāma* (*Moṣannafāt*, pp. 147-253). This is Bābā Afżal's longest and most complete exposition of his philosophy, a masterly summa that brings together all topics related to the perfection of the soul. It is divided into four "displays" (*'arż*) arranged in an ascending order according to the four kinds of things in the universe: corporeal bodies (*ajsām*), which are acted upon (*kardahā*); agents or souls, which do the acting (*konandahā*); concepts or known things (*dānestahā*); and knowers (*dānandagān*). First *'arż*: On corporeal things and their different kinds, the four elements, the unity of corporeal substance, place, motion, time, causes of motion, discrepancies of natures, the mixture of the elements, the engendering of things, plants, animals, human bodies. Second *'arż*: On activity (*koneš*), agents, and acts; and on creation (*kalq*) and origination (*ebdā'*). Acts and motions in bodies derive from something other than the bodies themselves, i.e., nature or soul. Soul can only be perceived through intellect. Third *'arż*: On the world of knowledge and the concepts that are the objects of knowledge. Created things (*maklūqāt*) pertain to the corporeal world, which is an adulterated likeness or image, while originated things (*mobda'āt* belong to the intelligible world, which is pure reality (*ḥaqīqat*). On the nature of knowledge, the knower, and the known, and the degrees of awareness. The existence of the highest kind of known things can not be separated from the act of being known (*dānestagī*). By knowing a thing a person becomes it. The highest object of knowledge is the First Known Thing (*dānesta-ye awwal*), i.e., God. All universal objects of knowledge (*maʿlūmāt-e kollī*) go back to a single source; all sciences are embraced by the divine science (*ʿelm-e elāhī*). Fourth *ʿarż*: On the kinds of knowers. That which in essence (*be-ḏāt*) is knower, knowledge, and known is one thing, the utmost limit and perfection of existence. Intellect knows through its very essence, and "that which is aware of the Absolute Existent *is* the Absolute Existent" (p. 233).

3. *Jāvedān-nāma* (*Moṣannafāt*, pp. 259-326; also ed. N. Taqawī, Tehran, 1311 Š./1932). This relatively comprehensive work is Bābā Afżal's most specifically Islamic treatment of his favorite themes; it is the only work of certain ascription to him outside the letters that quotes and comments on Koran and Hadith. Bābā Afżal points out that here, in contrast to his other works, his aim is to admonish and remind (*taḏkīr*), not to prove and demonstrate (p. 322). In four chapters the work explains the different kinds of sciences, brings out the importance of self-knowledge, and elucidates the nature of the origin and the return. First chapter: On the kinds of knowledge and the superiority of otherworldly knowledge (*dāneš-e ān jahānī*), which is knowledge of the microcosm and the macrocosm ("the horizons and the souls" *āfāq wa anfos*) in relation to God. Second chapter: On self-knowledge. On the reasons for differences in schools of thought and in religions. The knowledge that is incumbent upon all human beings concerns (1) the meeting (*leqāʾ*) with God, i.e., *tawḥīd* or the profession of God's Unity, and (2) the creation of the world and man. The meeting with God takes place constantly in this life, though most people are unaware of it. The faculties of the soul in the microcosm correspond with the archangels in the macrocosm. Third chapter: On the origin. On space, time, and motion; on kinds of origins and returns. Further analysis of the relationship between the soul's faculties and the angels of the macrocosm. The meaning of the prostration of the angels before Adam and of Iblis's rebellion. On inspiration (*elhām*) and satanic whispering (*waswasa*), both of which bring profit to God's friends. Analysis of the two "I's," corporeal and pneumatic (*man-e jesmānī* and *nafsānī*) and explanation of their levels of growth and their ultimate unity. Fourth chapter: On knowledge of the return. The body holds back the soul's development in various ways that can only be overcome by meeting God in the microcosm and the macrocosm. By listening to God's word (the verses or "signs" *āyāt* given to the microcosm), a person can come to see God's signs (*āyāt*) in the macrocosm; vision of the truth follows upon hearing it. Felicity in the next world is for the soul to be resurrected in the best cognitive (*ʿelmī*) form, just as happiness in this world is for it to possess the best form of works (*ʿamalī*). The substance of felicity is knowledge and certainty, which are increased by the worship of God. Each transformation undergone by the soul is a death through which God forgives man; the "angel of death" at each level is the next higher stage of existence; e.g., the angel which takes away the animal soul is the human soul, and that which takes away the human soul is the intellect.

4. *Madārej al-kamāl* (*Moṣannafāt*, pp. 3-52). This is Bābā Afżal's most complete discussion of the development and transformation of the soul. In a postcript found in some manuscripts (pp. 671-72; cf. pp. 700-01), he explains that he had originally written the work in Arabic, but then two of his companions persuaded him to translate it into Persian; the Arabic text is extant but has not been published. The work is divided into eight chapters and several sections: (1) On the human substance, showing the several levels of existence within man, from nature to intellect. (2) On that which distinguishes human beings from other creatures, in particular the fact that human beings can strive to actualize all levels of existence, including the highest, which is self-knowledge. (3) On the degrees of human imperfection and perfection. Imperfection is not blameworthy so long as intellect is actively seeking to purify man from animal traits. The full actualization of perfection belongs to those who have actualized self through knowing God's Self. (4) All perception aids human beings in reaching perfection, since it belongs to the higher levels of existence that must be actualized. (5) Attachment to the desires of the body turns the soul away from its spiritual food, which is knowledge. (6) A perfect human being (*mardom-e tamām*) has actualized equilibrium among all the faculties of the soul on the basis of the intellect's rule. (7) Perfection can be reached through purification and spiritual discipline, meditation on the principles of certain knowledge, and actualization of the moral virtues. (8) Knowledge allows human beings to actualize their every potentiality and reach the unity of the intelligent agent, the intellect, and the object of intelligence (*etteḥād-e ʿāqel o ʿaql o maʿqūl*).

5. *Rahanjām-nāma* (*Moṣannafāt*, pp. 55-80; also ed. S. M. Meškāt, *Selsela-ye entešārāt-e Dāneškada-ye maʿqūl wa manqūl* 5, 1315 Š./1936, pp. 26-57). In three discourses this work explains self-knowledge as the road to human perfection. First discourse: On the self (*ḵ^vod*) and how it can be known. Characteristically the self perceives universal (*kollī*) things (as opposed to the particular [*jozwī*] things perceived by the animal faculties); the more universal the objects it perceives, the closer it comes to knowledge of its own nature. An understanding of the factors that bring about pneumatic existence leads to self-knowledge. The highest degree of understanding and self-awareness is intellect. Second discourse: On the nature of knowledge and awareness (*āgāhī*). All things exist in the soul; by knowing what is outside of itself, the soul comes to know itself. Third discourse: On the profit of knowledge. By coming to know itself, the soul reaches Self, which is the end of all ends, being, everlastingness, and perfection.

6. *Resāla dar ʿelm o noṭq* or *Menhāj-e mobīn* (*Moṣannafāt*, pp. 477-579). Written first in Arabic and then translated into Persian, this work, Bābā Afżal's second longest, shows the extreme importance he attached to logical thinking in the strict Aristotelian sense. Certain

authors have suggested that the original was by Aristotle or Avicenna, but in the Arabic text Bābā Afżal expresses his disagreement with Avicenna's definition of *qīās al-kolf* in a manner that suggests his own authorship (cf. ibid., p. 574). The editors quote sufficient sections from the original (pp. 580-82) to show that the Persian is much expanded and makes a thoroughly fresh contribution. Bābā Afżal explains that he wrote the work to clarify the two arts (*honar*) that are specific to human beings: knowing (*dānestan*) and speaking (*goftan*). In the relatively short section on knowing (16 pages), he provides important definitions of the basic terminology necessary for logical discussions, including, for example, the distinction between existence (*būd, hastī*) and quiddity or "thing" (*čīz, šay'*). The second part of the work provides a detailed exposition of the science of logic.

7. *Sāz o pīrāya-ye šāhān-e pormāya* (*Moṣannafāt*, pp. 83-110; also ed. [with no. 52] by Ḥ. Mobaṣṣer-al-Salṭana, Tehran, 1311 Š./1932). Hardly a typical "Mirror for princes," this treatise explains not only the perfect king but also the perfect soul. It is divided into an introduction, three discourses, and a conclusion. Introduction: Human beings are the most excellent of creatures, containing within themselves the characteristics of all other things. Among human faculties, speech is the highest, while the most useful speech is that which reaches the noblest of human beings, i.e., kings and rulers. First discourse: There are many kinds of kings. The soul is king over the four humors, the intellect over the soul, and God over the intellect. Second discourse: The function of humans is to take creation back to God, but only perfect human beings are able to achieve this. Intellect acts to bring all the soul's faculties into balance on the basis of ethical norms. In the many degrees of human existence, the perfect man is king over ordinary human beings, and the more perfect man king over the perfect man. The role of a king is to govern his subjects in such a way as to allow them to reach their highest perfection, i.e., the full actualization of intellect, upon which depends felicity in the next world. The king's moral qualities must include opposition to no one, gentleness and indulgence toward everyone, humility, and courage. Only a king illuminated by intellect can stay a king. Third discourse: The king's duty is to nurture (*parvardan*), i.e., to perfect those who have the aptitude for perfection. He achieves this on the basis of self-knowledge and his own perfection; only then can he discern the desired perfection of each thing and help in its actualization. Conclusion: Contemporary kings and rulers live in dreadful opposition to everything described in the present work, but if they should make it their guide, they can be freed from cares in this world and the next.

B. Minor works 8. *Mabādī-e mawjūdāt-e nafsānī* (*Moṣannafāt*, pp. 585-97; also published in *Jelwa* 1, 1324 Š./1945, pp. 121-28). Explains in five sections (1) the two basic kinds of existent things, natural (*ṭabīʿī*) and pneumatic (*nafsānī*), (2-4) some of the terminology related to the latter kind, including Aristotle's ten categories, and (5) the meaning of the most general of terms, *ḥaqīqat*, *čīz*, and *mawjūd*.

9. *Īmanī az boṭlān-e nafs dar panāh-e ḵerad* (*Moṣannafāt*, pp. 601-09). The food of the soul is knowledge, though the soul, in contrast to the body, can never eat enough. All knowledge is useless unless put into the service of knowledge of self, which in turn depends upon discernment among the three constituent elements of the human being (body, soul, and intellect). All things are found in the intellect, so nothing can oppose it or destroy it.

10. Answers to questions posed by Montaḵab-al-Dīn Harāskānī (*Moṣannafāt*, pp. 717-28). This important treatise touches on points not dealt with elsewhere; topics include the influence of the stars and planets on human beings, the role of the intellect in bringing the faculties of the soul into balance, the life of the soul through knowledge and its death through ignorance, and the futility of discussing religion and theology with worldly people. In one passage Bābā Afżal establishes a connection between his philosophical views and ideas current in Sufism by explaining that there are several successive levels of spirit (*rūḥ*) which man may actualize; the highest, the holy spirit (*rūḥ-e qodsī*), is the radiance of the Divine Essence and is mentioned in the Koranic verse, "I breathed into him [Adam] of My spirit" (15:29); in Bābā Afżal's own writings, it is referred to as intellect (*Moṣannafāt*, pp. 723-25).

11. Answer to a letter from Šams-al-Dīn Moḥammad Dozvākūš (*Moṣannafāt*, pp. 681-91; one of Bābā Afżal's "companions," *yār*, cf. pp. 671-72). Provides important clarifications of the recurrent theme that the intellect is the sheer actuality of knowing, or the unity of knower, knowledge, and known. The letter refers to the various kinds of seekers (*sālek*) on the path to God, dividing them into two broad categories according to their natural gifts. It insists on the necessity of following a spiritual guide and on the special nature of the training needed by the human soul as opposed to the vegetal and animal souls.

12. Answer to a letter from Majd-al-Dīn Moḥammad b. ʿObayd-Allāh (*Moṣannafāt*, pp. 692-99). Majd-al-Dīn was apparently an important official who had requested that Bābā Afżal write something appropriate with which to begin epistles and addresses; this letter should be read in conjunction with *Sāz o pīrāya* (no. 7, above) to appreciate Bābā Afżal's view of the imperfections of government. Bābā Afżal opens by discussing the nature of human language as the fruit of the tree of human nature. But the meaning of language can only be grasped fully by knowing the meaning of one's own self. To actualize the leaves and branches of the tree—the arts and social skills—a person must drive the tree's root (the soul) deep into the hidden water of the intellect. The natural world, where delusion and unconsciousness rule, stands in stark contrast to the pneumatic world of wakefulness; in his official capacities, Majd-al-Dīn should always choose the latter over the former.

13. Answer to a letter from Šams-al-Dīn Dozvākūš

(*Moṣannafāt*, pp. 700-06). Bābā Afżal points out the spiritual benefit to be found in *Madārej al-kamāl* (no. 4, above) and then turns to the specific question of the felicity (*sa'ādat*) or wretchedness (*šaqāwat*) of the soul in the next world. He provides important clarifications of the nature of the intellect as the actualization of the potentialities of the soul, and in the process strongly criticizes current views of the soul's nature (perhaps the only place in his works where he takes an explicitly critical approach).

14. Letter of condolence to Tāj-al-Dīn Moḥammad Nūšābādī (*Moṣannafāt*, pp. 706-09). Grief arises not from the loss of a loved one, but from our ignorance in being attached to false hopes. Bābā Afżal discusses the life of the soul, quoting from Edrīs as reported in *Zajr al-nafs* (no. 51, below).

15. Letter apparently to one Šams-al-Dīn (Dozvākūš?; *Moṣannafāt*, pp. 710-12). Speaks of the scarcity of true knowledge and refers to having sent a copy of *Zajr al-nafs*.

16. Letter apparently to the same Šams-al-Dīn (*Moṣannafāt*, pp. 713-17). In reply to a request to send anything new he had written, Bābā Afżal remarks that he has been kept too busy by his disciples (*aṣḥāb*) and family to write anything, but what he has already written is in any case sufficient. His works are not lengthy, but if they find a receptive heart, "they will turn it into a world" which will look upon this outside world as trivial. Bābā Afżal admonishes the recipient to keep up his spiritual discipline, since the worst disaster for a gifted person is laziness.

17-48. Miscellaneous pieces (*Moṣannafāt*, pp. 611-65). These thirty-two works range in length from two lines to six pages. Most of the subjects are covered in Bābā Afżal's longer works, some approaching verbatim repetitions (e.g., pp. 662 and 315; 646 and 320). About the only subject covered here and not found elsewhere is music (pp. 653-54).

49. *Āyāt al-ṣan'a fi'l-kašf 'an maṭāleb elāhīya sab'a* (ed. Moḥyī-al-Dīn Kordī, *Jāme' al-badāye'*, Cairo, 1919, pp. 201-04). Brief discussion in Arabic of intellect, soul, and body.

C. Translations. 50. *Resāla-ye nafs-e Aresṭūṭāles* (*Moṣannafāt*, pp. 389-458; also ed. S. M. Meškāt, with an introduction by Malek-al-Šo'arā' Bahār, 2nd ed., Isfahan, 1333 Š./1954). This is a Persian translation of one of the several Arabic epitomes of Aristotle's *De anima* (cf. F. E. Peters, *Aristoteles Arabus*, Leiden, 1968, p. 43). The Arabic text, attributed to Esḥāq b. Ḥonayn, was published by A. Ahwānī (*Ebn Rošd: Talḵīṣ ketāb al-nafs*, Cairo, 1950, pp. 128-75). M. Saghir Hasan has shown that Bābā Afżal's translation was based on a better Arabic text than the printed version ("Notes on the Edition of the *Kitāb al-nafs* Ascribed to Isḥāq ibn Ḥunayn," *JRAS*, 1956-57, p. 72).

51. *Yanbū' al-ḥayāt* (*Moṣannafāt*, pp. 331-85). The Arabic text, attributed to Hermes and sometimes also to Plato or Aristotle, is known by several other names as well, including *Mo'āḏalat al-nafs* and *Zajr al-nafs* (Sezgin, *GAS* IV, pp. 43-44); it was printed by 'A. Badawī (*al-Aflāṭūnīyat al-moḥdaṯa 'end al-'Arab*, Cairo, 1955, pp. 51-116). Latin and German translations were made in the nineteenth century, and an English translation was made from the Latin (W. Scott, *Hermetica* 4, Oxford, 1936, pp. 277-352; cf. Sezgin, ibid.). The work takes the form of thirteen chapters, each containing a series of admonitions addressed to the soul; many of the themes of Bābā Afżal's own works are clearly present, though without the systematic presentation and logical demonstrations: the things of this world are symbols and images of the intelligible world; this world is not to be blamed, only the soul's love for it; the goal of life is for the soul to bring the intellect into full actuality; the soul must love death, which is rebirth into the intelligible world; the intellect is the soul's father, teaching it ethical norms and correct modes of activity (*farhang o adab*); everything that must be known is already present in the soul.

52. *Resāla-ye toffāḥa* (*Moṣannafāt*, pp. 113-44; also ed. [with no. 7, above] by Ḥ. Mobaṣṣer-al-Salṭana, Tehran, 1311 Š./1932). This is the pseudo-Aristotelian *Liber de pomo*, well-known in Latin and Hebrew. In contrast to these two versions, Bābā Afżal's translation follows the original Arabic text closely (cf. Peters, *Aristoteles Arabus*, pp. 65-66; for the Arabic text with a study of its sources, cf. J. Kraemer, "Das arabische Original des *Liber de pomo*," in *Studi Orientali in onore de Giorgio Levi della Vida* I, Rome, 1956, pp. 484-506). Bābā Afżal's text was edited and translated into English by D. S. Margoliouth ("The Book of the Apple, Ascribed to Aristotle," *JRAS*, 1982, pp. 187-252). The work contains Aristotle's teachings and admonitions to his students on his death bed, dealing especially with the nature of the soul, its purification, the necessity of possessing the moral virtues, and the indispensability of knowledge for works to have any value.

53. *Moḵtaṣar-ī dar ḥāl-e nafs* (*Moṣannafāt*, pp. 461-66). The original is attributed to Ebn Sīnā; in seven chapters the treatise describes the attributes of the soul, such as its purity, simplicity, everlastingness, and cognitive power.

III. Works of uncertain ascription. 54. *Al-Mofīd le'l-mostafīd* (ed. N. Taqawī, Tehran, 1310 Š./1931, 93 pp. [not seen]). Apparently a synopsis of Bābā Afżal's teachings, it was printed from the manuscript in the Ketāb-ḵāna-ye Salṭanatī in Tehran; the copyist of a manuscript in Tehran University (1035) attributes it to Ḡazālī (Monzawī, *Noskahā* II, pp. 1689-90).

55. *Čahār 'onwān* (printed as an addendum to Jāmī, *Aše''at al-lama'āt*, 2nd ed. by Ḥ. Rabbānī, Tehran, 1352 Š./1973, pp. 338-58). This is a skillful abridgment and condensation of the first part of Ḡazālī's *Kīmīā-ye sa'ādat*, concerning the sign of being a Moslem (*'onwān-e mosalmānī*), which Ḡazālī himself divides into four *'onwāns*: knowledge of self, of God, of this world, and of the next world (ed. A. Ārām, Tehran, 1319 Š./1940, pp. 7-103). The abridgment takes material from *'onwān* I, introduction, sections 1-2, 4-8, 16; II, 1-3; III, 1-2; IV, 1-2, 12, 13, 15. Only the last paragraph of the work seems to be the independent contribution of the author.

Both the material selected and the last paragraph—which emphasizes the utmost importance of knowledge as an everlasting attribute of self—are consistent with Bābā Afżal's prose style and major concerns.

56. *Šarḥ Ḥayy b. Yaqẓān* (of Ebn Sīnā). Probably identical with the work by a contemporary of Ebn Sīnā edited and translated by Corbin (*Ebn Sīnā wa tamṯīlāt-e ʿerfānī* I, Tehran, 1331 Š./1952; *Avicenna and the Visionary Recital*; cf. Nasr, "Afdal al-Din," p. 255).

IV. Works of incorrect ascription. 1. *ʿElm-e wājeb*. A short unpublished treatise rejecting the Peripatetic idea that God does not know particular things. There is no reason to attribute this work to Bābā Afżal except that the sole manuscript is found with a number of his short works; the style is totally Arabized, and the content is too theological (cf. Monzawī, II, pp. 822-23; Nasr, "Afdal al-Din," p. 254).

2. *Šarḥ foṣūṣ al-ḥekam* (of Ebn al-ʿArabī; mentioned by Nafīsī in *Robāʿīyāt*, pp. 78-9). Bābā Afżal's dates, concerns, and terminological style preclude this work's authenticity.

Bibliography: Given in the text. See also M. T. Dānešpažūh, "Neveštahā-ye Bābā Afżal," *Mehr* 8, 1331 Š./1952, pp. 433-36, 499-502.

(W. CHITTICK)

BĀBĀ BEG. See JŪYĀ.

BĀBĀ FAĠĀNĪ, a Persian poet in the 9th/15th and early 10th/16th centuries. Born and brought up at Shiraz, he began work as a cutler in his father's and brother's shop. For this reason he chose the pen-name Sakkākī, but later on he used Faġānī instead. After the sultan Yaʿqūb Bāyondorī (Āq Qoyunlū) had given him the title *bābā* (an appellation of leading dervishes and *qalandar*s), he was most widely known as Bābā Faġānī. He left Shiraz when he was thirty years old and went first to Herat, where his poetry was not well received, then to Tabrīz, where he worked for the sultan Yaʿqūb and his successors until the Āq Qoyunlū régime began to disintegrate. He then returned to Shiraz, but at the time of Shah Esmāʿīl Ṣafawī's rise to power he moved to Khorasan, where he lived for a time at Abīvard and then at Mašhad. He died at Mašhad at an age of over sixty in 925/1519 or, according to some accounts, 922/1516.

Bābā Faġānī's *dīvān*, which has been printed, comprises *qaṣīdas*, *tarkīb-bands*, *tarjīʿ-bands*, *ġazal*s, and *robāʿī*s. All are pleasing and well-written. His *qaṣīda*s are in praise of Twelver Shiʿite imams and Bāyondorī sultans, particularly Yaʿqūb (d. 896/1490), Bāysonqor (d. 897/1491), and Rostam Beg (d. 902/1496); the last one which he wrote is a eulogy of the Safavid Shah Esmāʿīl. In all these *qaṣīda*s the simplicity of the poet's diction and the fluency and vividness of his rhetoric are impressive. He deserves praise for his attention to these qualities at a time when other poets were imitating abstruse odes of old masters or concocting purely cerebral lyric and narrative pieces. In his *ġazal*s the same fluency and objectivity are found together with new phrases and compounds, moving expressions of feeling, and original themes. This caused his style to be seen as different from that of his contemporaries and to be taken as a new and acceptable model. Literary critics even described him as a "Lesser Ḥāfeẓ." His method of *ġazal* writing, in particular, was widely studied in the 10th/16th, 11th/17th, and 12th/18th centuries and is reflected in the works of poets who regarded him as a master. In all fields Bābā Faġānī exercised a lasting influence on Persian poetic style in the Safavid period.

Bibliography: Bābā Faġānī, *Dīvān*, ed. with introd. A. Sohaylī Ḵʷānsārī, Tehran, 1317 Š./1938, repr. 1340 Š./1961. Sām Mīrzā, *Toḥfa-ye Sāmī*, Tehran, 1314 Š./1935, pp. 102-03. Qāżī Nūr-al-Dīn Šūštarī, *Majāles al-moʾmenīn*, lithographed, Tehran, n.d., p. 512. Rāzī, *Haft eqlīm*, ed. Jawād Fāżel, Tehran, 1340 Š./1961, vol. 1, pp. 219-20. Āḏar Bīgdelī, *Ātaškada*, Bombay ed., p. 291. Mīr ʿAbd-al-Razzāq Ḵʷāfī, Ṣamṣām-al-Dawla Šāhnavāz Khan, *Bahārestān-e soḵan*, Madras, 1958, pp. 528-31. Moḥammad Qodrat-Allāh Gōpāmavī Hendī, *Natāʾej al-afkār*, Bombay, 1334/1916, pp. 528-31. C. Rieu, *Catalogue* II, p. 651. Nafīsī, *Naẓm o naṯr*, pp. 437-38. Ṣafā, *Adabīyāt* IV², pp. 411-12.

(Z. SAFA)

BĀBĀ FARĪD. See FARĪD-AL-DĪN GANJ-E ŠEKAR.

BĀBĀ ḤĀTEM, 5/11th-century mausoleum in northern Afghanistan, popularly known as Bābā Ḥātom, at some 40 miles west of Balḵ (A. S. Melikian-Chirvani "Remarques préliminaires sur un mausolée ghaznévide," *Arts Asiatiques* 17, 1968, pp. 59-92). It follows the simple plan of the earliest Islamic mausoleums standing in the Iranian world, consisting of a single square room with a cupola resting on squinches. Precise measurements could not be taken, but the proportions seem to be all based on a modular unit. The only decoration on the stern and bold brick facade is calligraphic, leaving aside the trellice on the spandrels over the door. A band of raised calligraphy in knotted Kufic framing the door reads *Besmellāh al-Raḥmān al-Raḥīm, hāḏā mašhad Sālār Ḵalīl.* The door is of extraordinary size in proportion to the monument, the *hastae* being approximately ninety-five centimeters in length. The inscription identifies the structure as the mausoleum of a certain noble Sālār Ḵalīl who must have received a violent death but whose name has yet to be found in the sources. David Bivar has read the next few words as "*ṣanaʿhu umm ummihi*" ("The Inscription of Sālār Khalīl in Afghanistan," *JRAS*, 1977, 2, pp. 145-49), which does not quite fit what remains of the lettering. Inside, the carved three trompe l'oeil gesso niches including the *meḥrāb* emphasize the dependency of such mausoleums on earlier *čahār-ṭāq*s. The tomb in the center, badly plastered over in recent times. Still retains its pointed arch profile. The carved gesso decoration on the trilobate squinch arches and the arches above, offer the best preserved example of its kind in any 5/11th-century Iranian mausoleum with remarkable diversity in the variations on the formal motif which is, in effect, a stylized ibex head seen sideways. A long invocation in plain Kufic on the drum of the dome calls God's blessings on "the angels that surround God, the messenger prophets, the pure worshippers among those in heaven and earth, and on Moḥammad the Seal of prophets and the imam of the Lord of the worlds (*Emām Rabb al-ʿĀlamīn*)." The highly unusual formula raises the possibility of an Ismaʿili connection which sould be investigated. It is followed by the signature of an otherwise unrecorded artist Moḥammad b. Aḥmad b. Maḥmū[d] (A. S. Melikian-Chirvani, "Baba Hatem: Un chef d'œuvre inconnu d'époque ghaznévide en Afghanistan," in *The Memorial Volume of the Vth International Congress of Iranian Art and Archaeology*, ed. M. Y. Kiani and A. Tajvidi, Tehran, 1972, II, pp. 108-22). I originally wrote that the phrase *memman ʿamala[hu]* introducing the artist's name indicates that he must be the architect. I am now inclined to believe that this could equally well refer to the designer (*naqqāš*) or the calligrapher (*kāteb*), despite the lack of a term specifying such a qualification such as *naqaša* or *kataba*.

Bibliography: Given in the text. See also J. Sourdel-Thomine, "Le mausolée dit de Baba Hatim en Afghanistan," *REI* 39, 1971, pp. 293-320.

(A. S. MELIKIAN-CHIRVANI)

BĀBĀ JĀN ḴORĀSĀNĪ, also known as Ḥāfeẓ Bābā Jān Torbatī, calligrapher, poet, and craftsman the first half of the 10th/16th century. He was the son of Ḥāfeẓ ʿAbd-al-ʿAlī Torbatī, a religious figure connected with the court of Sultan Ḥosayn Bāyqarā. Bābā Jān's brother Ḥāfeẓ Qāsem was a noted singer and Bābā Jān himself was a gifted player of the *ʿūd*. Sām Mīrzā praises him not only as a musician and calligrapher but also as an expert in the inlaying of gold into ivory. Despite these references to his many skills the circumstances of Bābā Jān's life and the scope of his activities remain obscure. Qāżī Aḥmad states that the family moved from Herat to Iraq, but gives no further details. M. Bayānī suggests that he may have been associated with the Safavid prince Bahrām Mīrzā and that he can be identified with a certain "Bābā Jān Bahrāmī" whose calligraphy appears in the album prepared for Bahrām Mīrzā now in the Topkapı Sarayı Library, Istanbul. If Bābā Jān Ḵorāsānī was a well-known calligrapher at the court of Bahrām Mīrzā it is puzzling that his name does not appear in the preface to this album written by Dost Moḥammad.

Bibliography: Bayānī, *Ḵošnevīsān* I, pp. 83-84. Sām Mīrzā, *Toḥfa-ye Sāmī*, p. 82. Qāżī Aḥmad, *Golestān-e honar*, p. 82; tr. Minorsky, *Calligraphers and Painters*, p. 148.

(P. P. SOUCEK)

BĀBĀ JĀN TEPE (Tappa), an archeological site in northeastern Luristan (34° north latitude, 47° 56′ east longitude), on the southern edge of the Delfān plain at approximately 10 km from Nūrābād, important primarily for excavations of first-millennium B.C. levels conducted by C. Goff from 1966-69. Work concentrated on two mounds joined by a saddle. The East Mound (85 m in diameter, 9 m high) yielded a series of first-millennium B.C.buildings (Baba Jan III-I) above Bronze Age (Baba Jan IV) graves. On the Central Mound (120 m in diameter, 15 m high), excavation concentrated on the Baba Jan III Manor on the summit; an 8 × 6 m Deep Sounding provides a partial late fourth- to mid-second-millennium B.C. sequence (Baba Jan V-IV).

Baba Jan V. Levels 7-6 in the bottom 2 m of the Deep Sounding yielded late fourth-millennium B.C. chalcolithic pottery similar to Godin (Gowdīn) VI (Goff, 1971, fig. 7; Goff, 1976, pl. VIIIc-d).

Baba Jan IV. In the Deep Sounding on the Central Mound, two levels of domestic architecture (level 5, 2300-2100 B.C. and level 4, 1800-1500 B.C.) were separated by a period of abandonment during which four burials were dug into the area. Four other Baba Jan IV graves were cut into virgin soil on the East Mound; these date to the late third (Goff, 1976, fig. 11.10-13, 16-18) and mid-second millennium B.C. (ibid., fig. 11.19-23). The assemblage is comparable to that of period III at Godin Tepe.

Baba Jan III. On the Central Mound only the superimposed foundations from two phases of a Manor (30 × 35 m) survive. The earlier, level 2, consisted of a rectangular court with a north-south axis flanked by long narrow rooms, the whole with towers both at the corners and midpoints of all sides. When rebuilt in level 1, the Manor consisted of a central columned hall (one row of three columns) surrounded by long narrow rooms. On the East Mound the almost 2000 m^2 excavation yielded the Fort and Painted Chamber. The excavated portion of the Fort, whose walls survived to a height of 3-4 m, consisted of a large (12 m^2) room with four irregularly placed columns and surrounded by long rectangular chambers. A spiral ramp led either to a second storey or the roof. Further rooms extended to the south. The Painted Chamber (10 × 12 m) unit was added at the east end of the Fort. This ceremonial hall, which opened southward onto an enclosed courtyard, had two columns, a niche and doorway with reveals, white walls decorated with red paint, and a painted-tile ceiling. The Fort and Painted Chamber were probably the seat of a local ruler. The extent and nature of the settlement are uncertain. Fire destroyed this complex at the end of the eighth century B.C. The pottery evidence suggests that the East Mound buildings were built and used after the Central Mound Manors. The columned halls at Baba Jan are analogous to contemporary buildings of Hasanlu (Ḥasanlū) IV, Godin Tepe II, and Nush-i Jan (Nūš-e Jān).

Baba Jan III pottery, long known as Genre Luristan, was a handmade, turntable-finished buff ware with distinctive decoration in a thick red-brown matte paint. Typical motifs included ladders and pendant triangles with hatching or crosshatching. Common

Table 4

BABA JAN TEPE: CHRONOLOGICAL TABLE

Approximate date B.C	Level	East Mound	Central Mound
6-4th century	I	Village	
7th century	II	Squatter reoccupation	
9-8th century	III	Fort and Painted Chamber	Manors (levels 1-2); small stone houses (level 3)
2300-1400	IV	Graves	Deep Sounding levels 5-4
3500-3000	V		Deep Sounding, levels 6-7

vessel shapes were simple: wide-bodied jars with narrow necks, small bowls with incurved rims and horizontal loop handles, conical bowls, and cups. A range of iron weapons and tools were found, but classic Luristan bronze artifacts were uncommon.

Baba Jan II. The walls of the ruined Fort remained standing until late in Baba Jan II; squatters briefly reoccupied the eastern rooms. While the eastern wall of the Fort remained standing, three phases of small structures were built in the area of the Painted Chamber and its courtyard.

The Genre Luristan pottery of Baba Jan III continued with simpler decoration, but small quantities of a new type of wheelmade buff pottery with small golden mica inclusions appeared. The most common shapes were deep bowls with a thickened rim and horizontal handle, double-handled jars, and jars with a vertical handle and tubular spout with trefoil-mouth. This ware and characteristic shapes are very similar to Tepe Nush-i Jan level I (Malāyer plain). Baba Jan II probably dates to the seventh century B.C.

Baba Jan I. On the East Mound poorly preserved village house walls covered the summit and extended down the east slope in a series of terraces. Superposition of architectural remains suggests two to three phases. The buff ware Baba Jan I assemblage, whose closest affinities are with Period II at Godin Tepe (Kangāvar valley), is characterized by numerous bowl forms and is a development from the wheelmade pottery of Baba Jan II. Baba Jan III wares disappear. Baba Jan I probably falls within the Achaemenid period.

Bibliography: The final report on the excavations consists of a series of articles by C. Goff: "Excavations at Baba Jan: The Bronze Age Occupation," *Iran* 14, 1976, pp. 19-40; "Excavations at Baba Jan: The Architecture of the East Mound, Levels II and III," *Iran* 15, 1977, pp. 103-40; "Excavations at Baba Jan: The Pottery and Metal from Levels III and II," *Iran* 16, 1978, pp. 29-65; "Excavations at Baba Jan: The Architecture and Pottery of Level I," *Iran* 23, 1985, pp. 1-20. Goff also published substantial preliminary reports on the first three seasons of excavation (*Iran* 7, 1969, pp. 115-30; *Iran* 8, 1970, pp. 141-56; C. Goff Meade, *Iran* 6, 1968, pp. 105-26). On the Painted Chamber, cf. R. C. Henrickson, "A Reconstruction of the Painted Chamber Ceiling at Baba Jan," *Iranica Antiqua* 18, 1983, pp. 81-96, for an alternative reconstruction. For revised dates for Baba Jan IV material, see R. C. Henrickson, "A Regional Perspective on Godin III Cultural Developments in Central Western Iran," *Iran* 24, 1986, table 2 and fig. 2; for Baba Jan III-I, see L. D. Levine, "The Iron Age," in *Archaeological Perspectives on Western Iran*, ed. F. Hole (Smithsonian), in press.

(R. C. HENRICKSON)

BĀBĀ KŪHĪ, popular name of Shaikh Abū ʿAbd-Allāh Moḥammad b. ʿAbd-Allāh b. ʿObayd-Allāh Bākūya Šīrāzī, Sufi of the second half of the 4th/10th and the first quarter of the 5th/11th century, also (more correctly) known as Ebn Bākūya. Despite frequent references to him in Sufi literature, next to nothing is known about his life. He was probably born in Shiraz, where, as a young man, he met the famous mystic Abū ʿAbd-Allāh Moḥammad b. Ḵafīf (d. 371/982) and the Arab poet Motanabbī (in 354/965). He traveled extensively in search of stories concerning Sufi shaikhs and their sayings. During his travels he met with the leading Sufis of his time including Shaikh Abū Saʿīd Abi'l-Ḵayr and Abu'l-Qāsem ʿAbd-al-Karīm Qošayrī. He was still in Nīšāpūr in 426/1035, but he finally returned to Shiraz and retreated in a cave in a mountain (now called Bābā Kūhī) just north of the city, where he soon died and was buried in 428/1037 at a very advanced age. Until very recently, the cave was occupied by an old dervish who was known to the Shirazis as Bābā Kūhī.

The name Bābā Kūhī, apparently a popular corruption of Ebn Bākūya (Bābā Kūhī means old gaffer of the mountains) is first mentioned by the poet Saʿdī (*Būstān*, chap. 5). Faḵr al-Zamānī (*May-ḵāna*, pp. 86-88) records a legend according to which the young poet Ḥāfeẓ, an object of ridicule among his fellow citizens for his poor poetry, engaged in a vigil at the tomb of Bābā Kūhī for three nights. On the third night he was visited by Imam ʿAlī, who gave him a heavenly morsel, thereby opening the door of all knowledge to Ḥāfeẓ and endowing him with the gift of poetry. This obviously unfounded story is apparently an awkward attempt, as often is the case with Ḥāfeẓ's poetry, to explain a difficult poem.

Of his works a *resāla* on Ḥallāj called *Bedāyat ḥāl al-Ḥallāj wa nehāyatohu* (see Sezgin, *GAS* I, p. 652) has survived. Samʿānī mentions also the *Ketāb maqāmāt al-mašāyek̲* (apud Meier, *Abū Saʿīd*, p. 288). The Persian *Dīvān* attributed to him (Shiraz, 1347/1928, 2nd ed., Shiraz, 1332 Š./1953), as convincingly argued by M. Qazvīnī, must belong to a mediocre poet of a later date (probably 10th/17th century), whose *tak̲alloṣ* Kūhī has evidently been the cause of the false attribution.

Bibliography: M. Qazvīnī has listed most references to Ebn Bākūya in his edition of Moʿīn-al-Dīn Abu'l-Qāsem Jonayd Šīrāzī's *Šadd al-ezār fī ḥaṭṭ al-awzār ʿan zowwār al-mazār*, Tehran, 1328 Š./1949, pp. 380-84, 550-56. Idem, *Yāddāšthā* II, pp. 3-9. See also Brockelmann, *GAL*, S. I, p. 770. Mollā ʿAbd-al-Nabī Fak̲r-al-Zamānī, *Tad̲kera-ye may-k̲āna*, ed. A. Golčīn-e Maʿānī, Tehran, 1339 S./1960. L. Massignon, *Quatre textes inédits relatifs à la biographie d'al-Ḥosayn ibn Manṣour al-Ḥallāj*, Paris, 1919. F. Meier, *Abū Saʿīd-i Abū l-Ḫayr*, Tehran and Liège, 1976, pp. 52, 55, 112 and nn. 94 and 95, 256, 288-89, 290. Nafīsī, *Naẓm o naṯr* I, p. 57; II, p. 717. Moḥammad Ṣarīfīnī, *Montak̲ab men ketāb al-sīāq ·le taʾrīk̲ Naysābūr* (*The Histories of Nishapur*), ed. R. Frye, The Hague, 1965 (not consulted). For the poetry ascribed to him, see A. J. Arberry, *Shiraz: Persian City of Saints and Poets*, Norman, Oklahoma, 1960, pp. 81-82. *al-D̲arīʿa* IX, pp. 117-18. Ḵayyāmpūr, *Sok̲anvarān*, p. 493. Rypka, *Hist. Iran. Lit.*, pp. 234, 243 (bibliography).

(M. KASHEFF)

BĀBĀ ŠAMAL, weekly satirical periodical founded by Reżā Ganjaʾī (b. 1918 in Tabrīz) in Farvardīn, 1322 Š./April, 1943. It was published regularly until Mehr, 1324 Š./October, 1945, when Ganjaʾī left for Europe. A further fifty issues were published until Esfand, 1326 Š./March, 1947, after his return. The magazine, which was printed on eight 21 × 31 cm pages, had a wide circulation (a print order of 17,000 was claimed for it), and dealt with the political issues of the day in a racy colloquial style spiced with cartoons and caricatures, sometimes in color. An issue cost 2.5 rials; a yearly subscription was 150 rials. On the whole, its stance was independent, nationalistic, and middle of the road. It was impartially opposed to all foreign intervention and influence in Iran, and was particularly hostile to Sayyed Żīāʾ-al-Dīn Ṭabāṭabāʾī (q.v.) because of his reputation for being linked with Britain. At the same time it strongly opposed the Russian request in 1323 Š./1944 for an oil concession, and so incurred the hostility of the pro-Soviet Tūda (Tudeh) Party. The leader of the pro-Soviet separatist movement of Azerbaijan, Jaʿfar Pīšavarī (q.v.), was also highly distrustful of *Bābā Šamal*, whose founder he considered partly responsible for the campaign leading to the invalidation of his electoral mandate in the fourteenth Majles. *Bābā Šamal*'s strongly satirical methods earned it many enemies, especially in government circles, and the increasing pressure of censorship forced its closure in 1327 Š./1948. Reżā Ganjaʾī, an engineer by training, held important posts in the Ministries of Posts and Telegraphs and of Industry and Mines, in the railways, insurance, etc., but resigned from all his posts in 1341 Š./1962.

In publishing *Bābā Šamal*, Ganjaʾī was assisted by a talented staff of satirists, poets, and writers. Highly popular cartoons were rendered by Dāvarī and among Ganjaʾī's other collaborators were Rahī Moʿayyerī (pen-name Zāḡča), Eqteṣād (pen name Shaikh Pašm-al-Dīn), Fozūnī (pen-name Mohandes-al-Šoʿarāʾ), and Ṣahbā (pen-name Shaikh Sornā).

Bibliography: J. Āl-e Aḥmad, "Varšekastagī-e maṭbūʿat," in *Se maqāla-ye dīgar*, Tehran, 1342 Š./1963, pp. 35-36. L. P. Elwell-Sutton, "Iranian Press 1941-47," *Iran* 6, 1968, p. 80. A. Ḥālat, "Nāma-ye Bāba Šamal," *Talāš* 34, 1351 Š./1972, pp. 26-31. M. Nafīsī, "Bābā Šamal," *Taḥqīqāt-e rūz-nāma-negārī* 15, 1348 Š./1969, pp. 47-49. Ḡ.-Ḥ. Ṣāleḥyār, *Čehra-ye maṭbūʿāt-e moʿāṣer*, Tehran, 1351 Š./1972, p. 257.

(L. P. ELWELL-SUTTON)

BĀBĀ SAMMĀSĪ, K̲ᵛĀJA MOḤAMMAD, Central Asian Sufi of the line known as *selsela-ye k̲ᵛājagān* (line of the masters) which was inaugurated by K̲ᵛāja Abū Yaʿqūb Hamadānī (q.v.). Born in Sammās (or Sammāsī), a village in the region of Rāmītan, three *farsak̲s* distant from Bukhara, Sammāsī became a follower of K̲ᵛāja ʿAlī Rāmītanī ("Hażrat-e ʿAzīzān") early in his life. Most of Rāmītanī's life was spent in the environs of Bukhara, but he migrated to K̲ᵛārazm at a date that can not be precisely determined. Sammāsī appears to have stayed in the area of Bukhara, although he must have visited his master in K̲ᵛārazm at least once, for he was present when Rāmītanī, on his death bed, appointed him his sole successor in 721/1321.

The most important figure initiated into the "line of the masters" by Sammāsī was his own principal successor, Amīr Kolāl. Before entering the Sufi path, Amīr Kolāl was much given to wrestling, but he abandoned this pursuit and turned to Sufism when one day in Rāmītan he felt the powerful gaze of Bābā Sammāsī fixed on him during a bout. Thereafter Amīr Kolāl remained almost constantly in Sammāsī's company.

Bābā Sammāsī's main title to fame lies in his having adopted as his spiritual son K̲ᵛāja Bahāʾ-al-Dīn Naqšband, the eponym of the Naqšbandī order. It is said that when passing by Qaṣr-e Hendovān, a suburb of Bukhara, Bābā Sammāsī was in the habit of remarking that he could perceive a strong fragrance emerging from its soil, interpreting this to presage the birth of a great spiritual master. One day in 718/1318, he observed that the fragrance was stronger than ever before, and it turned out that Bahāʾ-al-Dīn had been born three days earlier. Bahāʾ-al-Dīn's grandfather, who was a *morīd* of Bābā Sammāsī, brought the infant to him to receive his blessing, whereupon he adopted him as his spiritual progeny. At the same time, however, he entrusted Amīr Kolāl with training Bahāʾ-al-Dīn when he attained maturity, and it is not clear whether Bahāʾ-al-Dīn saw Sammāsī again before the age of eighteen. It was then that Bahā'-al-Dīn's grandfather—evidently the foremost influence in his life—decided it was time for him to marry, and he dispatched him to Bābā Sammāsī to obtain his approval. Bahā'-al-Dīn witnessed a number of miraculous feats during this visit to Sammāsī, but it was not until Sammāsī himself paid a return visit to Qaṣr-e Hendovān that a bride was chosen and the marriage performed, under his direct supervision.

None of the early Naqšbandī sources give a date for Bābā Sammāsī's death, but the celebrated thirteenth/nineteenth-century hagiographical compendium, Ḡolām Sarvar Lāhūrī's *Ḵazīnat al-aṣfīā*, places it in 755/1354, and adds that he was buried in his native village.

After the death of his spiritual father, Bahā'-al-Dīn was taken by his grandfather to Samarkand to benefit from the Sufi masters of that city before being entrusted to Amīr Kolāl for his formal initiation and training, in accordance with Bābā Sammāsī's instructions.

In addition to Amīr Kolāl, Bāba Sammāsī left behind three successors: Ḵᵛāja Maḥmūd Sammāsī, his eldest son; Ḵᵛāja Ṣūfī Sūḵārī; and Mawlānā Dānešmand 'Alī. All that is known about Bābā Sammāsī, in addition to what has been related above, is that he was frequently subject to states of ecstasy that came upon him while he was working in his vineyard. No writings are attributed to him, and it appears that his importance in the history of the *selsela* is purely that of a transmitter, with the luster of his name enhanced by its proximity to that of Bahā'-al-Dīn Naqšband.

Bibliography: Ṣalāḥ-al-Dīn b. Mobārak Boḵārī, *Anīs al-ṭālebīn*, ms. Bodleian Persian e 37, ff. 47b-50b. Abu'l-Ḥasan Moḥammad-Bāqer b. Moḥammad-'Alī, *Maqāmāt-e Šāh-e Naqšband*, Bukhara, 1327/1909, pp. 5-7. Jāmī, *Nafaḥāt*, pp. 380-82. Ḡolām Sarvar Lāhūrī, *Ḵazīnat al-aṣfīā*, Lucknow, 1320/1902, I, pp. 545-46. Ḵᵛāja Moḥammad Pārsā, *Qodsīya*, ed. Aḥmad Ṭāherī 'Erāqī, Tehran, 1354 Š./1975, p. 9. Moḥammad b. Ḥosayn Qazvīnī, *Selsela-nāma-ye Ḵᵛājagān-e Naqšband*, ms. Laleli (Süleymaniye) 1381, f. 7b. Faḵr-al-Dīn 'Alī Ṣafī, *Rašaḥāt 'ayn al-ḥayāt*, Tashkent, 1329/1911, pp. 42-43. Mawlānā Šehāb-al-Dīn, *Manāqeb-e Amīr Kolāl*, ms. Zeytinoğlu (Tavşanlı) 169, ff. 12a-12b, 19a.

(H. ALGAR)

BĀBĀ SANKŪ (or SANGŪ), ecstatic Central Asian dervish of disorderly habits, contemporary with Tīmūr and one of several Sufis with whom Tīmūr chose to associate for reasons of state. The name Sankū does not yield any obvious meaning, and should perhaps be read as Süngü (Turk. "pike"); the dervish in question may have carried a pike as part of his accoutrement. He appears to have spent his entire life in Andḵūd (Transoxiana), where he was famous for his miraculous feats. When Tīmūr passed through Andḵūd in 728/1381, en route to his first campaign in Iran, he visited Bābā Sankū and sat down with him to eat. For no apparent reason, Bābā Sankū picked up a roast breast of lamb and threw it straight at Tīmūr. Delighted by this gesture, Tīmūr predicted that just as he had had the choicest part of the meat thrown at him, he would soon go on to conquer the choicest part of the globe, i.e., Khorasan. Bābā Sankū's tomb in Andḵūd became a place of visitation, and he was succeeded in his spiritual dignity first by Bābā Jān Bābā (*sic*) and then by Bābā Ebrāhīm. A *ḵānaqāh* was constructed near the tombs of the three men and remained in use for an unknown period.

Bibliography: *Ḥabīb al-sīar* (Tehran) III, p. 543. Alî Şîr Nevâyî, *Nesâyimü' l-mahabbe min şemâyimi' l-fütüvve*, ed. K. Eraslan, Istanbul, 1979, p. 392. Browne, *Lit. Hist. Persia* III, pp. 184-85. V. V. Bartol'd, *Sochineniya* II, 2, Moscow, 1964, p. 44.

(H. ALGAR)

BĀBĀ SHAH EṢFAHĀNĪ, calligrapher and poet who lived in Isfahan and Baghdad where he died in 996/1587-88. He was famous as a writer of the *nasta'līq* script. Said to have had an ascetic temperament, he also wrote poetry under the *taḵalloṣ* "Ḥālī." Virtually nothing is known about his personal life or professional training. Statements by Taqī-al-Dīn Moḥammad Kāšānī and Moṣṭafā-'Alī (apud Bayānī, *Ḵošnevīsān*, pp. 85-86) that he studied in Mašhad with Sayyed Aḥmad Mašhadī are disproven by Qāżī Aḥmad's silence on this matter. He associates Bābā Shah exclusively with Isfahan and Baghdad. Since Qāżī Aḥmad himself lived in Mašhad and studied with Sayyed Aḥmad Mašhadī he would certainly have mentioned it if Bābā Shah had done likewise.

Bābā Shah does not appear to have been connected with any royal or princely patrons. According to both Qāżī Aḥmad and Eskandar Beg he first went to Iraq to visit its shrines. Eskandar Beg Monšī mentions that Bābā Shah supported himself by his calligraphy during his residence in Iraq. The commercial value of his calligraphy is confirmed by Eskandar Beg's remark that his writing sold at a high price and had become difficult to obtain. An indirect confirmation of the wide dispersal of Bābā Shah's calligraphy is given by M. Bayānī who was only able to identify three specimens by Bābā Shah's hand.

Another facet of Bābā Shah's activity is his composition of a treatise on calligraphy entitled *Ādāb al-mašq*. Some copies of this text ascribe its composition to the later calligrapher Mīr 'Emād but an early copy now preserved in the library of Punjab University in Lahore confirms that Bābā Shah is indeed its author. In his preface Bābā Shah praises the writing of Solṭān-'Alī Mašhadī. The few published examples of Bābā Shah's calligraphy suggest that he may have modeled his own style on that of Solṭān-'Alī. Both calligraphers stress balance and harmony in both the formation of letter shapes and overall composition of a page.

Bibliography: Bayānī, *Ḵošnevīsān*, pp. 84-91. Eskandar Beg Monšī, *Tārīḵ-e 'ālamārā-ye 'abbāsī*, p. 121. Qāżī Aḥmad, *Golestān-e honar*, p. 119; tr. Minorsky, *Calligraphers and Painters*, pp. 165-66.

(P. P. SOUCEK)

BĀBĀ ṬĀHER, known as ʿORYĀN, a dervish poet from the area of Hamadān. This is almost all that is known of him; even his dates are a matter of dispute, estimates ranging from the 4th/10th to the 7th/13th centuries. His tomb in Hamadān, where his companion Fāṭema is also buried, is first mentioned in the *Nozhat al-qolūb* (p. 71); it was renovated in 1329-30 Š./1950-51 (for a picture, see *Farhang-e fārsī* V, p. 18). One story makes Bābā Ṭāher a contemporary of ʿAyn-al-Qożāt (d. 526/1131; q.v.), another of K̲ᵛāja Naṣīr-al-Dīn Ṭūsī (d. 672/1273-74). On the other hand Reżāqolī Khan Hedāyat in the *Majmaʿ al-foṣaḥāʾ* claims, without citing any evidence, that he predeceased Ferdowsī and ʿOnṣorī in 410/1019-20 (II, p. 845). A *do-baytī* attributed to him appears to contain a reference to a date: "I am that sea and have come into a bowl; I am that dot and have come into a letter; in every thousand one straight-as-an-*alef* (*alef-qadd*) appears; I am that straight one, for I came in a thousand." Mīrzā Mahdī Khan Kawkab calculated by *abjad* that this would give the date 326/937-38 for Bābā Ṭāher's birth, which would fit with Hedāyat's version. Rašīd Yāsamī, on the other hand, takes the third line to refer to the Zoroastrian belief that a spiritual leader will appear every thousand years; Bābā Ṭāher, he maintains, is claiming to be such a leader, having been born in A.D. 1000 (i.e., 391 A.H.). Mojtabā Mīnovī, however, dismisses this theory as too far-fetched: Bābā Ṭāher would scarcely have known his date of birth according to the Islamic calendar, let alone the Christian. The one story that has the ring of truth is to be found in the *Rāḥat al-ṣodūr* of Rāvandī (completed 603/1206), which, based on hearsay, describes a meeting between Bābā Ṭāher, in company with two other saints (*awlīāʾ*), and the Saljuq conqueror Ṭoḡrel (pp. 98-99). This meeting, if authentic, must have taken place between 447 and 450 (1055-58); the use of the term saint would suggest that Bābā Ṭāher must have been of an advanced age, which would bring his birth-date very close to that calculated by Yāsamī. The year 410/1019-20 given for his date of death (Reżāqolī Khan Hedāyat, *Rīāż al-ʿārefīn*, Tehran, 1316 Š./1937, p. 167) and accepted by Nafīsī (p. 24) is unlikely.

Bābā Ṭāher is best known for his *do-baytī*s, quatrains composed not in the standard *robāʿī* meter but in a simpler meter still widely used for popular verse (*hazaj mosaddas maḥdūf*: ⏑ – – – ⏑ – – – ⏑ – –), which Nyberg regards as having affinities with Middle Persian verse. The other characteristic of these verses is their use of what was probably the local dialect of the period, though in course of time so many corruptions have crept in through the ignorance or carelessness of copyists that it is impossible to be certain what the original form was. Most traditional sources call it loosely Lorī, while the name commonly applied from an early date to verses of this kind, *fahlavīyāt*, presumably implies that they were thought to be in a language related to the Middle Iranian dialect Pahlavi. Roubène Abrahamian however found a close affinity with the dialect spoken at the present time by the Jews of Hamadān.

When we come to the problem of assessing Bābā Ṭāher's view of the human predicament, we encounter an obstacle not dissimilar to that faced by students of ʿOmar K̲ayyām. Short dialect verses of the kind attributed to him have been composed by a number of well-known poets and many lesser ones. When Heron-Allen produced his edition in 1902 no more than some eighty quatrains were known. In 1927, however, Waḥīd Dastgerdī produced an edition of 296 *do-baytī*s, together with four *ḡazal*s and seventy additional quatrains of more doubtful authenticity. Many are found in the *dīvān*s of other poets. Nevertheless there is a certain consistency of feeling, even in the larger number, that encourages one to think that they could all have emanated from the same mind. The qualities that strike one most forcibly are simplicity, sincerity, humility; indeed the straightforward nature of his verse, unencumbered by intellectual conceits and artifices, could scarcely have found a better medium than the dialect quatrain, redolent of the wind-blown deserts, the towering mountains, the isolated valleys, the austere life of the nomad. All of Bābā Ṭāher's images are drawn from this environment. He is the humble, self-effacing wandering dervish, pouring out with earnestness and passion his love of God, whom he sees everywhere around him. Like many of his fellows, he is conscious of man's insignificance, of his rejection, loneliness, and isolation; but unlike K̲ayyām he sees the solution to this not in a hedonistic savoring of the pleasures of the world, but in *fanāʾ*, ultimate absorption and annihilation in God. Yet there is an earthy side to his poetry, too; his love is human as well as divine, and indeed his expression of it is more genuine than the somewhat artificial court verse of his contemporaries like ʿOnṣorī or Manūčehrī, who were writing to please a royal patron. He could be described as the first great poet of Sufi love in Persian literature. In the last two decades his *do-baytī*s have often been put to music.

Bābā Ṭāher was first and foremost a Sufi, and this comes out most vividly in the only other work, apart from a few *ḡazal*s, attributed to him—the *Kalemāt-e qeṣār*, a collection of nearly 400 aphorisms in Arabic, which has been the subject of commentaries, one allegedly by ʿAyn-al-Qożāt Hamadānī. If these are authentic (and no other authorship is claimed), Bābā Ṭāher must have had a considerable degree of education, and so can hardly have been the unlettered tribesman that his verse suggests. The aphorisms are divided into twenty-three chapters, covering all the themes of Sufi teaching from ʿ*elm* and *maʿrefa* to *ḥaraqa* and *taqdīr*: "Knowledge is the guide to gnosis, and when gnosis has come the vision of knowledge lapses and there remain only the movements of knowledge to gnosis"; "knowledge is the crown of the gnostic, and gnosis is the crown of knowledge"; whoever witnesses what is decreed by God remains motionless and powerless."

It has been argued that Bābā Ṭāher was a Shiʿite; this is deduced from a line "O God, by virtue of your eight and four...," which is taken to refer to the twelve imams revered by the Shiʿites. It should be said, however, that figures like this are open to various interpretations; they could mean, for instance, the eight heavens, the four elements, and so on. According to the Ahl-e Ḥaqq (q.v.), who use Bābā Ṭāher's verses in their rituals, he was an incarnation of one of the angels who accompanied the third manifestation of the Divinity. Many stories are told of his miracles and magical powers. One of the best-known relates how, stung by the mockery of students at a college in Hamadān, he spent the night in a frozen tank, and emerged in the morning filled with divine knowledge.

Bibliography: R. Abrahamian, *Dialecte des Israélites de Hamadan et d'Ispahan et dialecte de Baba Tahir*, Paris, 1936, pp. 155-70. Browne, *Lit. Hist. Persia* I, pp. 83-85; II, pp. 259-61. Waḥīd Dastgerdī, ed., *Dīvān-e kāmel-e Bābā Ṭāher ʿOryān*, Tehran, 1306 Š./1927 (repr. 1932, 1953), introd. by Ḡ.-R. Rašīd Yāsamī. Āzād Hamadānī, "Mašāhīr-e Hamadān," *Armaḡān* 17, 1315 Š./1936, pp. 433-40, 552-56. E. Heron-Allen, *Lament of Bábá Ṭáhir*, London, 1902. Cl. Huart, "Les quatrains de Bābā-Ṭāhir ʿUryān en pehlevi musulman," *JA*, ser. 8, no. 6, 1885, pp. 502-45. Idem, "Nouveaux quatrains de Bābā Ṭāhir," *Spiegel Memorial Volume*, ed. J. J. Modi, Bombay, 1908, pp. 290-302. P. N. Ḵānlarī, "Dobaytīhā-ye Bābā Ṭāher," *Payām-e now* 1/8-9, 1324 Š./1945, pp. 26-30, 37-39. Mīrzā Mahdī Khan Kawkab, "The Quatrains of Bābā-Ṭāhir," *J(R)ASB*, 1904, no. 1, pp. 1-29. G. L. Leszczynski, *Die Rubāʿīyāt des Bābā-Tāhir ʿUryān oder Die Gottestränen des Herzens...*, Munich, 1920. V. Minorsky, in *EI*² I, pp. 839-42 (full bibliography). Nafīsī, *Naẓm o naṯr*, pp. 715, 722. H. S. Nyberg, "Ein Hymnus auf Zervān im Bundahišn," *ZDMG* 82, 1928, pp. 217-35. A. Pagliaro and A. Bausani, *Storia della letteratura persiana*, Milan, 1960, pp. 554-56. Moḥammad b. ʿAlī Rāvandī, *Rāḥat al-ṣodūr wa āyat al-sorūr*, ed. M. Eqbāl, London, 1921. Rypka, *Hist. Iran. Lit.*, p. 234. Ṣafā, *Adabīyāt* II, pp. 383-86. Ṣ. Reżāzāda Šafaq, *Tārīḵ-e adabīyāt-e Īrān*, many editions. Ḡ.-R. Rašīd Yāsamī, "Bābā Ṭāher ʿOryān," *Armaḡān* 10, 1308 Š./1929, pp. 66-70.

(L. P. Elwell-Sutton)

BĀBĀʾĪ BEN FARHĀD, eighteenth-century author of a versified history of the Jews of Kāšān with brief references to the Jews of Isfahan and one or two other towns. Next to nothing is known about him except that he was probably a leader of the Jewish community in Kāšān and that he, together with other Jews of Kāšān, was converted to Islam by force for a period of seven months (at the beginning of the fall of 1142/1729), while he retained secretly his Jewish faith. According to Bābāʾī himself he was inspired in his work by his grandfather Bābāʾī Ben Loṭf (q.v.), the author of *Ketāb-e anūsī*. His history *Ketāb-e sargoḏašt-e Kāšān*, comprising approximately 1,300 verses in the *hazaj-e mosaddas-e maḥḏūf* meter, is in Persian using Hebrew script. It is the second (after *Ketāb-e anūsī*) and, so far as we know, the only other historical manuscript found among the Iranian Jews. It also takes note of some interesting details of the Afghans' attacks on Isfahan and Kāšān, as well as of Nāderqolī Khan's wars against them. It is interesting to note that Bābāʾī Ben Farhād mentions Maḥmūd and Ašraf, the leaders of the Afghans (especially the latter), favorably while he criticizes Nāderqolī (the future Nāder Shah) for his harsh measures, particularly against the Jews. We know from other historical sources that the Zoroastrians also mention favorably the Afghan conquests and had even helped in them (as in the occupation of Kermān). The Jews and Zoroastrians were accorded superior status to Shiʿites in the political structure of the Afghans. According to *Sargoḏašt-e Kāšān*, the Jewish community of Kāšān was wealthy, mostly involved in the silk trade. Bābāʾī mentions thirteen synagogues in Kāšān, a figure larger than the number of synagogues in most of the towns of Iran. He also observes with dissatisfaction the lack of religious observance among most of the Jews of his town.

Another Jew from Kāšān named Māšīaḥ Ben Rafāʾel appended approximately eighty verses to Bābāʾī's narrative in which he mentions favorably Mollā Ebrāhīm, the leader of the Jews of Kāšān, who together with a number of supporters, was instrumental in allowing the Jews who had been forced to accept Islam to return to Judaism.

Ketāb-e sargoḏašt-e Kāšān is the only known work of Bābāʾī Ben Farhād; three manuscripts are known to exist as appendices to the *Ketāb-e anūsī*.

Bibliography: W. Bacher, "Les Juifs de Perse aux xviie et xviiie siècles d'après les chroniques poétiques de Babai b. Loutf et de Babai b. Farhad," *Revue des études juives* 53, Paris, 1907, pp. 85-110. Ḥ. Levī, *Tārīḵ-e yahūd-e Īrān*, Tehran, 1334-39 Š./1955-60, III, pp. 448-54. A. Netzer, *Montaḵab-e ašʿār-e fārsī az āṯār-e yahūdīān-e Īrān*, Tehran, 1352 Š./1973, introd. p. 48. Idem, *Judeo-Persian Literature* I: *A Chronicle of Babai b. Farhad*, The Hebrew University of Jerusalem, 1978, pp. 1-38 (MS. no. 917 of Ben Zvi Institute photoprinted).

(A. Netzer)

BĀBĀʾĪ BEN LOṬF, the Jewish poet and historian of Kāšān during the first half of the 11th/17th century (d. after 1073/1662). According to his own words, he, along with the Jews of Kāšān, was forced to embrace Islam and was, for some years, openly a Muslim while retaining secretly his Jewish faith. He was unable to emigrate to Baghdad on account of his advanced age and out of concern for the safety of his large family. He left behind two works in verse: the history *Ketāb-e anūsī* (The book of a forced convert) and a short poem entitled *Monājāt-nāma* in praise of the prophet Elijah. Both these works are in Persian using Hebrew script. Nothing else is known about him.

The *Ketāb-e anūsī* (*anūsī* is a Hebrew word meaning a Jew forced to apostasize who remains secretly Jewish), a work of approximately 5,300 verses composed in the *hazaj-e mosaddas-e maḥḏūf* meter, is, so far as we know, the first historical work originating from an Iranian Jewish community. This work has not been published. There are approximately six manuscripts of it in some major libraries of the U.S., Europe, and Israel. Errors in versification and the use of obsolete words and colloquial language gives the *Ketāb-e anūsī* little literary merit. However, despite the disorderly chain of events recorded in it, it possesses incomparable value because of its content which can be divided as follows: 1. Description of the status of Iranian Jews from the years before 1022/1613 until the end of the reign of Shah ʿAbbās I in 1038/1629. During this period the Jews of Iran were subjected to persecution and molestation. A number of their religious leaders were killed for refusing to convert to Islam. Bābā'ī also mentions some of the wars of Shah ʿAbbās I with the Georgians, the foundation of the town of Faraḥābād by him in Māzandarān and the settling of the Georgian Jews and Christians there. He is corroborated in many details by his contemporaries, Eskandar Beg and, especially, Pietro della Valle. Bābā'ī speaks favorably of Shaikh Bahā'-al-Dīn ʿĀmelī and Shah Ṣafī I, and praises the former's intercession on behalf of rescuing the Jews of Isfahan. 2. The molesting and forced conversion of the Jews from the years 1067/1656 to 1073/1662 during the reign of Shah ʿAbbās II forms the most important part of the book. His narration is again confirmed by other sources such as the *ʿAbbās-nāma* of ʿEmād-al-Dīn Moḥammad Ṭāher b. Ḥosayn Khan Qazvīnī (*taḵalloṣ*: Waḥīd) and the history of the Iranian Armenians by the Armenian priest Arakel of Tabrīz. The good will and intercession of Mollā Moḥsen Fayż Kāšānī on behalf of the Jews is also mentioned with respect. 3. Also of importance is the information concerning the population, professions, economic situation, and communal organization of the Jews in Iran, especially in Isfahan and Kāšān, as well as some historical events such as the coronation of Shah Ṣafī and the war on Qandahār during the reign of Shah ʿAbbās II.

Bibliography: W. Bacher, "Les Juifs de Perse aux xviie et xviiie siècles d'après les chroniques poétiques de Babai b. Loutf et de Babai b. Farhad," *Revue des études juives* 51, 1906, pp. 121-36, 265-79; 52, 1906, pp. 77-97, 234-71. V. B. Moreen, *An Introductory Study of the Kitāb-i Anusī by Bābāī ibn Lutf*, Ph.D. Dissertation, Harvard University, 1978. A. Netzer, *Montaḵab-e ašʿār-e fārsī az āṯār-e yahūdīān-e Īrān*, Tehran, 1352 Š./1973, introd., pp. 46-48, text pp. 298-302. Idem, "Persecution of Iranian Jewry in the 17th Century," *Pe'amin* 6, 1980, pp. 32-56 (in Hebrew). Idem, *Tārīḵ-e yahūd dar ʿaṣr-e jadīd* (A history of the Jews in modern times), Tel Aviv, 1982, pp. 227-28.

(A. NETZER)

BĀBĀ'Ī BEN **NŪRĪ'EL,** a rabbi (*ḥāḵām*) from Isfahan who, at the behest of Nāder Shah Afšār (r. 1148-60/1736-47), translated the Pentateuch and the Psalms of David from Hebrew into Persian. Three other rabbis helped him in the translation, which was begun in Rabīʿ II, 1153/May, 1740, and completed in Jomādā I, 1154/June, 1741. At the same time, eight Muslim mollas and three European and five Armenian priests translated the Koran and the Gospels. The commission was supervised by Mīrzā Moḥammad Mahdī Khan Monšī, the court historiographer and author of the *Tārīḵ-e jahāngošā-ye nāderī*. Finished translations were presented to Nāder Shah in Qazvīn in June, 1741, who, however, was not impressed.

There had been previous translations of the Jewish holy books into Persian, but Bābā'ī's translation is notable for the accuracy of the Persian equivalents of Hebrew words, which has made it the subject of study by linguists. Bābā'ī's introduction to the translation of the Psalms of David is unique, and sheds a certain amount of light on the teaching methods of Iranian Jewish schools in eighteenth-century Iran. He is not known to have written anything else.

Bibliography: J. P. Asmussen, "Einige Bemerkungen zu Baba ben Nuriel's Psalmenübersetzung," *Acta Orientalia* 30, 1966, pp. 15-24. M. Mahdī Eṣfahānī, *Neṣf jahān fī taʿrīf al-Eṣfahān*, ed. M. Sotūda, Tehran, 1340 Š./1961, p. 256. W. J. Fischel, "The Bible in Persian Translation," *Harvard Theological Review*, Cambridge 1952, pp. 33-42. G. Margoliouth, *Catalogue of the Hebrew and Samaritan Manuscripts in the British Museum* I, London, 1899, pp. 120-21, nos. 159, 160, mss. Or. 4729 and Or. 2452. A. Netzer, *Montaḵab-e ašʿār-e fārsī az āṯār-e yahūdīān-e Īrān*, Tehran, 1352 Š./1973, introd. pp. 21-22.

(A. NETZER)

BABĀJĀ'Ī. See KURDISTAN TRIBES.

BĀBAK (Mid. Pers. Pāpak, Pābag), a ruler of Fārs at the beginning of the third century, father of Ardašīr (q.v.), the founder of the Sasanian dynasty. There are several traditions regarding the relationship of Bābak to Sāsān, who gave his name to the dynasty. One tradition, reported by Ṭabarī (I, p. 813) and other Islamic authors says that Bābak was the son of Sāsān, while another tradition found in the Middle Persian *Kār-nāmag ī Ardašīr Pābagān*, Ferdowsī's *Šāh-nāma*, and elsewhere claims that Bābak's daughter was given in marriage to Sāsān, a shepherd who had royal blood, and from this union Ardašīr was born. Variations of this theme occur in the *Bundahišn* (chap. 35, A232) where the genealogy of Ardašīr is given (*Artaxšahr ī Pābagān kē-š mād duxt ī Sāsān ī Weh-āfrīd*, etc.) "Ardašīr son of Bābak whose mother (was) the daughter of Sāsān son of Weh-āfrīd, etc.," and in Agathias (2.27.5), where Bābak is described as a shoemaker who allowed an itinerant soldier called Sāsān to sleep with his wife, from which Ardašīr was born. Later Bābak and Sāsān quarreled over the parentage of Ardašīr and then both agreed that the boy should be called the son of Bābak, but of the lineage of Sāsān.

Another version calls Ardašīr the son of the daughter of Bābak, for which reason he was called Ardašīr Bābakān. (For various quotations in New Persian sources see Dehḵodā s.v. Bābak.) According to the

Mojmal (p. 33) Bābak claimed Ardašīr as his son, from fear of revealing his true lineage to the Parthians. The *Ḡorar* of Ṯaʿālebī (p. 474), however, tells us that Sāsān was an officer of Bābak and his son-in-law, but Sāsān died early so Ardašīr was raised by his grandfather Bābak who sent the boy to the court of Ardavān where he remained until Bābak died.

It is hardly possible to determine which version about Ardašīr's parentage is correct, but the suspicion that Ṭabarī simply assumes that Sāsān is the father of Bābak is great. In the great trilingual inscription of Šāpūr I at Naqš-e Rostam near Persepolis (ed. A. Maricq, *Syria* 35, 1958, pp. 318-19 [= *Classica et Orientalia*, Paris, 1965]), Sāsān is merely a lord (Parth. *hwtwy*) while Bābak is a king (*MLKA*), Greek *kúrios* and *basiléōs* respectively (Greek 1.46, Mid. Pers. l. 25, Parth. l. 20). At the same time, the dynasty was called Sasanian, and not Babakian, as we see from the Paikuli inscription where the family or "seed of the Sasanians" is mentioned (ed. P. O. Skjærvø in H. Humbach and P. O. Skjærvø, *The Sassanian Inscription of Paikuli* III/1, Wiesbaden, 1983, p. 65 par. 80, Parth. l. 36, and pp. 122f.). Consequently, early in Sasanian rule Sāsān was considered the ancestor of the dynasty.

In any case Bābak was a local ruler in Fārs, with his capital at Istakhr (Eṣṭaḵr), who revolted against his Parthian overlord, probably in 205-06, as we may infer from a Mid. Pers. inscription on a pillar from Bīšāpūr (cf. R. Ghirshman, "Inscription du monument de Châpour Ier," *Revue des Arts Asiatiques* 10, 1937, pp. 123-29). As far as we know Bābak did not strike any coins, for those with his name on them, together with the name Ardašīr, were most probably issued by the latter (R. Göbl, *Sasanidische Numismatik*, Braunschweig, 1968, p. 42 and table I). Other than his name on coins and in later inscriptions, we have no contemporary sources on Bābak and are forced to rely on much later accounts, the most complete of which is the history of Ṭabarī (I, pp. 813ff.), presumably based for the most part on the lost *Xwadāy-nāmag*, or official history compiled under the Sasanians (see, e.g., M. Boyce in *HO* I, IV: *Iranistik* II: *Literatur*, Lief. 1, pp. 57ff.). According to Ṭabarī, Bābak was the ruler of Ḵīr (a district to the south of Istakhr on the edge of the salt lake, Baḵtagān). He continues that the wife of Sāsān, his father, called Rāmbehešt, was from the Bāzrangī (q.v.; Ar. al-Bāzranjī) family which ruled Fārs province, presumably as vassals of the Parthian rulers. Further, Sāsān became the director (*qayyem*) of the fire-temple in Istakhr which was called the fire-temple of Anāhīḏ. Bābak was born from Sāsān and Rāmbehešt. Bābak had long hair at his birth, a sign of future greatness. Later he followed his father Sāsān in rule and Ardašīr was his son. Ṭabarī continues that the king of Istakhr at the birth of Ardašīr was called Jūzehr (or Jozehr, Mid. Pers. *Gōčihr*) of the family of Bāzrangī. When Ardašīr was seven years old Bābak asked Jūzehr who resided at that time in the town of Bayżā, northwest of Istakhr, to give him to the care of his eunuch Tīrē who was in charge of the town of Dārābjerd. After subduing several local lords Ardašīr wrote to his father to revolt against Jūzehr, which he did and killed him. Then Bābak wrote to Ardavān (Artabanus), his Parthian overlord, requesting permission to grant the crown of Jūzehr to Bābak's son Šāpūr. The Parthian ruler refused but Bābak died and his son Šāpūr succeeded him (see also E. Herzfeld, *Paikuli* I, Berlin, 1924, pp. 35-36).

This account by Ṭabarī is the most detailed we have about Bābak but we can not check its veracity. No coins attributed to Gōčihr or to Bābak have been identified and the graffiti of a Sasanian prince on the wall of the Harem building, now the museum, at Persepolis, may or may not represent Bābak (see E. Schmidt, *Persepolis* I, Chicago, 1953, p. 258), but the style of clothes and crown, in any case, is very early Sasanian.

Bibliography: Given in the text. On the name see also E. Benveniste, *Titres et noms propres en iranien ancien*, Paris, 1966, p. 17, where it is suggested that Pāpakān should be interpreted as "(son) of Pāp," a name attested in Pahlavi and Armenian. More probably both Pāp and Pāpak formed the patronym Pāpakān.

(R. N. FRYE)

BĀBAK ḴORRAMĪ (d. Ṣafar, 223/January, 838), leader of the Ḵorramdīnī or Ḵorramī uprising in Azerbaijan in the early 3rd/9th century which engaged the forces of the caliph for twenty years before it was crushed in 222/837.

The fullest account of Bābak's career comes from a lost *Aḵbār Bābak* by Wāqed b. ʿAmr Tamīmī, which is quoted in the *Fehrest* of Ebn al-Nadīm (ed. Flügel, pp. 406-07) and was probably used by Maqdesī (*Badʾ* VI, pp. 114-18; see Sadighi, p. 234). Other accounts are less detailed and show variations.

The name Bābak is found in all the sources, but Masʿūdī also says that "Bābak's name was Ḥasan" (*Morūj* VII, p. 130, ed. Pellat, IV, sec. 2814). The statements about his parentage and background are unclear and inconsistent, sometimes fantastic and incredible. His father's name is variously given as Merdas/Merdās (Samʿānī, ed. Margoliouth, fol. 56a); ʿAbd-Allāh, a native of Madāʾen (*Fehrest*, p. 406); Maṭar, a vagabond (*men al-ṣaʿālīk*); Ṭabarī, III, p. 1232); and ʿĀmer b. Aḥad from the Sawād region who had gone to Ardabīl (Abu'l-Maʿālī, chap. 5). According to Wāqed, however, ʿAbd-Allāh, Bābak's father, was a cooking-oil vendor who had left his home town Madāʾen for the Azerbaijan frontier zone and settled in the village of Belālābād in the Maymaḏ district. His mother, according to Faṣīḥ (I, p. 283), was a one-eyed woman named Māhrū from a village in a district belonging to Azerbaijan. On the one hand the stories about ʿAbd-Allāh and Maṭar may imply that Bābak's father had an illicit relationship with this woman, but on the other hand Dīnavarī (p. 397) asserts: "What seems to us to be true and proven is that Bābak was a son of Moṭahhar, the son of Abū Moslem's daughter Fāṭema, and that the Fāṭemīya group of the Ḵorramīs took their name from this Fāṭema, not from

Fāṭema the daughter of God's Prophet." In Masʿūdī's *Morūj* (ed. Pellat, IV, p. 144, sec. 2398) Bābak is described simply as one of the Fāṭemīya group of the Ḵorramīs.

In most of these accounts, other than Dīnavarī's, a note of sarcasm and hostility can be perceived. Our information about Bābak and his revolt comes almost entirely from adversaries. Merdās is the name of Żaḥḥāk's father in Ferdowsī's *Šāh-nāma*, probably meaning "man-eater" (*mard-ās*; see R. Roth, "Die Sage von Dschemschid," *ZDMG* 4, 1850, pp. 417-33, esp. p. 423), however, this view was rejected by Nöldeke, who considered Merdās to be the same as Arabic Merdās (see Zereklī and Dehḵodā, s.v. Merdās); its attribution to Bābak may be a disguised reference to his and his henchmen's readiness to kill their enemies (Zarrīnkūb, 1355, p. 237). The coupling of his mother's name Māhrū "Belle" with the description "one-eyed" also looks like a sneer. There is no means of knowing whether the kinship with Abū Moslem, considered probable by Dīnavarī, was a fact or a pretense designed by Bābak (as by other rebel leaders) to gain support among people who cherished Abū Moslem's memory (Ḡ.-Ḥ. Yūsofī, *Abū Moslem, sardār-e Ḵorāsān*, Tehran, 1345 Š./1966, pp. 175-78, 165f.), or whether it was subsequently invented to argue a link between Abū Moslem's and Bābak's revolts or to explain the Ḵorramī veneration for Abū Moslem (cf. Neẓām-al-Molk, pp. 359, 367-68). Dīnavarī's mention of a Ḵorramī group named Fāṭemīya after Abū Moslem's daughter and of Bābak's membership of it is repeated in *Taʾrīḵ Baḡdād* (X, p. 207; see also Madelung, pp. 63-64, 65; Amoretti, pp. 503ff.).

According to Wāqed, Bābak's father, after the birth of Bābak, died from wounds suffered in a fight during a journey to the Sabalān district. His widow then earned her living as a wet-nurse for other people's infants, while Bābak worked as a cowherd until he was twelve years old. We are told that one afternoon his mother saw Bābak asleep under a tree, stark naked and with blood at the root of every hair on his head and chest; but when he woke and stood up, she saw no trace of blood and said, "I know that my son has a great task ahead" (*Fehrest*, p. 406; Maqdesī, *Badʾ* VI, pp. 114f.; ʿAwfī, pt. 1, chap. 5). Wāqed adds that Bābak in his youth worked as a groom and servant for Šebl b. Monaqqī (Moṯannā?) at the village of Sarāt (Sarāb?) and learned to play the *tanbūr* (drum or mandolin). This must be the source of the statement by Abu'l-Maʿālī (chap. 5, p. 299) that Bābak used to play the *tanbūr* and sing songs for the people while working as a fruit vendor in the village. When he had grown up he went to Tabrīz, where he spent two years in the service of Moḥammad b. Rawwād Azdī (q.v.) before returning at the age of eighteen to his home at Belālābād.

Wāqed's account of what happened next is, in summary, as follows. Two rich men named Jāvīdān b. Šahrak (or Sahrak) and Abū ʿEmrān were then living in the highland around the mountain of Badd and contending for the leadership of the highland's Ḵorramī

inhabitants. Jāvīdān, when stuck in the snow on his way back from Zanjān to Badd, had to seek shelter at Belālābād and happened to go into the house of Bābak's mother. Being poor, she could only light a fire for him, while Bābak looked after the guest's servants and horses and brought water for them. Jāvīdān then sent Bābak to buy food, wine, and fodder. When Bābak came back and spoke to Jāvīdān, he impressed Jāvīdān with his shrewdness despite his lack of fluency of speech. Jāvīdān therefore asked the woman for permission to take her son away to manage his farms and properties, and offered to send her fifty dirhams a month from Bābak's salary. The woman accepted and let Bābak go. It must have been then that he joined the Ḵorramīs.

In the *Fehrest* and elsewhere, Jāvīdān b. Šahrak is said to have been Bābak's teacher. From 192/807-08 until 201/816-17 he led a Ḵorramī group named Jāvīdānī after him (Yaʿqūbī, *Boldān*, p. 272; Masʿūdī, *Tanbīh*, pp. 321-22; Ebn al-Aṯīr, repr., VI, p. 328; Ebn al-ʿEbrī (Bar Hebraeus), p. 139; Ebn Ḵaldūn, events of 201/817; Fasīḥ, I, p. 270; see also G. Flügel, p. 539 nn. 2, 3, and Sadighi, pp. 107ff.).

Sometime after Bābak's entry into Jāvīdān's service, the rival chieftain Abū ʿEmrān sallied forth from his mountain stronghold against Jāvīdān and was defeated and killed, but Jāvīdān died three days after the battle from a wound. Some of the writers allege that Jāvīdān's wife was already enamored of Bābak, who is said to have been a handsome lad with a good voice (Abu'l-Maʿālī, chap. 5, p. 300). This allegation may have its root in the marriage of the two after Jāvīdān's death (see Sadighi, p. 244). The woman told Bābak of her husband's death and added that she was going to announce it to the community the next day, when she would also claim Bābak as Jāvīdān's successor, who would restore the religion of Mazdak and lead the community to triumph and prosperity. On the following day Bābak appeared before Jāvīdān's assembled warriors and followers. When they asked why Jāvīdān had not summoned them before uttering his last testament, she answered that since they lived in scattered places, sending out the message would have spread the news, which in turn might have compromised their security. After securing their obedience to Jāvīdān's instructions, she said that according to Jāvīdān's last testament the night before, his soul would upon his death enter Bābak's body and fuse with his soul (the Ḵorramīs believed in the transmigration of souls, see ḴORRAMDĪNĀN), and that anyone contesting this testament should be excommunicated. All those present acknowledged Jāvīdān's mandate to the young man, and at the woman's request they bound themselves by a ritual oath to give the same allegiance to Bābak's soul as they had given to Jāvīdān's soul. Then Jāvīdān's widow married Bābak in a simple ceremony in the presence of all (*Fehrest*, pp. 406-07; on the role of this woman and the position of women in Bābak's revolt in general, see Amoretti, pp. 517-18, 508). Abu'l-Maʿālī (chap. 5, p. 300) alleges that the woman poisoned Jāvīdān, while Ṭabarī (III, p. 1192) and Ebn al-Aṯīr (VI, p. 459) state that Jāvīdān had a son (Ebn Jāvīdān) whom the Muslims had captured and later released; Sadighi (pp. 244-45) wonders why this son was not chosen to succeed Jāvīdān. Wāqed and Ṭabarī depict Bābak as low-born, but Bābak's reply to his son's letter after his escape, and the words of his brother 'Abd-Allāh to Ebn Šarvīn Ṭabarī, the officer appointed to take him to Baghdad (Ṭabarī, III, pp. 1221, 1223), suggest that they were of noble family (Sadighi, pp. 239-41).

Bābak must have absorbed ideas and beliefs current among the Ḵorramīs after his entry into Jāvīdān's service and adhesion to the sect. The epithet Ḵorramī or Ḵorramdīn given to Bābak in the sources denotes membership of this sect. The name has been explained as referring to Ḵorrama, the wife of Mazdak (Sīāsat-nāma, p. 319; Mojmal al-tawārīk, p. 354) or to a village named Ḵorram near Ardabīl (surmise of Naṣr quoted by Yāqūt, Mo'jam II, p. 362), but these attributions are questionable. Other writers take ḵorram to be the adjective normally meaning "verdant" or "joyous" and interpret it as "permissive" or "libertine." Ḵorramdīn appears to be a compound analogous to dorostdīn (orthodox) and Behdīn ("Zoroastrian"; see Sadighi, p. 195; Nafīsī. p. 21; Madelung, p. 63), and since joy was one of the forces governing the world in the Mazdakite religion (see Yarshater, pp. 1005-06), the name Ḵorramdīn appears to confirm the assertion in several sources that the sect was an offshoot of Mazdak-ism (Mas'ūdī, Tanbīh, p. 322; Fehrest, pp. 405-06; Sīāsat-nāma, p. 319; Mojmal, pp. 353-54; Abu'l-Ma'ālī, chap. 5, p. 300; see also Sadighi, pp. 187f., 197; Yar-shater, pp. 1003-04; and Nafīsī, p. 21). Many modern scholars regard them as "neo-Mazdakites" (e.g., Madel-ung, p. 64; Amoretti, p. 503; Yarshater, p. 1011; Zar-rīnkūb, 1343 Š./1964, p. 544). Under Bābak's leader-ship the Ḵorramīs, who are described as having been before Bābak's time peaceful farmers, refraining from killing or harming other people (Maqdesī, Bad' IV, pp. 30-31; Fehrest, p. 406; 'Awfī, pt. 1, chap. 5), changed into militants eager to fight and kill, to seize or destroy villages, and to raid caravans (Dīnavarī, p. 397; Ṭabarī, s.a. 220/835; Abu'l-Ma'ālī, chap. 5). Bābak incited his followers to hate the Arabs and rise in rebellion against the caliphal regime. The reports state that Bābak called men to arms, seized castles and strong points, and ordered his warriors to kill people and destroy villages, thereby barring roads to his enemies and spreading fear. Gradually a large multitude joined him. There had long been groups of Ḵorramīs scattered in Isfahan, Azerbaijan, Ray, Hamadān, Armenia, Gor-gān, and elsewhere, and there had been some earlier Ḵorramī revolts, e.g., in Gorgān jointly with Red Banner (Sork-'alamān) Bāṭenīs in the caliph Mahdī's reign in 162/778-79, when 'Amr b. 'Alā', the governor of Ṭabarestān, was ordered to repulse them, and at Isfahan, Ray, Hamadān, and elsewhere in Hārūn al-Rašīd's realm, when 'Abd-Allāh b. Mālek and Abū Dolaf 'Ejlī put them down on the caliph's behalf (Sīāsat-nāma, pp. 359-60; Faṣīḥ, I, pp. 230-31; cf. Madelung, p. 64; Amoretti, pp. 504-05); but none had the scale and

duration of Bābak's revolt, which pinned down caliphal armies for twenty years. After his emergence, the Ḵorramī movement was centered in Azerbaijan and reinforced with volunteers from elsewhere, probably including descendants of Abū Moslem's supporters and other enemies of the 'Abbasid caliphate. The figures given for the strength of Bābak's army, such as 100,000 men (Abu'l-Ma'ālī), 200,000 (Mas'ūdī, Tanbīh, p. 323), or innumerable (Tabṣerat al-'awāmm, p. 184; Bağdādī, p. 267) are doubtless highly exaggerated but at least indicate that it was large.

In most of the sources the start of Bābak's revolt is placed in the year 201/816-17 in al-Ma'mūn's reign, when the Ḵorramīs began to infiltrate neighboring districts and create insecurity in Azerbaijan. On or before that date, according to some sources, Ḥātem b. Hartama, the governor of Armenia, learned that his father Hartama b. A'yan had, despite loyal service to al-Ma'mūn, been flogged and imprisoned on the ca-liph's order and been killed in prison at the behest of the minister Fażl b. Sahl (Ṭabarī, II, p. 1026). Ḥātem b. Hartama therefore planned to rebel and wrote letters to local commanders urging them to defy al-Ma'mūn, but at this juncture he died. One of those to whom he wrote was Bābak (or probably Jāvīdān), who was greatly encouraged thereby (Ebn Qotayba, p. 198; Ya'qūbī, II, p. 563; Sadighi, p. 238 n. 3).

Al-Ma'mūn at first paid scant attention to Bābak's revolt, evidently because he was living in distant Khorasan and preoccupied with matters such as the designation of his successor, the actions of Fażl b. Sahl, and the backlash at Baghdad. Thus contemporary circumstances as well as popular dislike of Arab rule favored Bābak and his followers.

In 204/819-20 al-Ma'mūn moved to Iraq, and after dealing with the dissidents at Baghdad, he sent Yaḥyā b. Mo'ād to subdue Bābak's revolt. This general fought Bābak in several battles but without success. Thereafter al-Ma'mūn showed more concern and regularly dis-patched well-armed forces to Azerbaijan. In 205/820-21 'Īsā b. Moḥammad b. Abī Ḵāled was appointed gover-nor of Armenia and Azerbaijan with responsibility for operations against Bābak, but his force was caught and smashed by Bābak's men in a narrow defile. 'Īsā either ran for his life or was killed by Bābak (Ṭabarī, III, p. 1072). In 209/824-25 al-Ma'mūn chose Zorayq b. 'Alī b. Ṣadaqa (Ṣadaqa b. 'Alī in Ṭabarī, 'Alī b. Ṣadaqa known as Zorayq according to Ebn al-Atīr) to govern Armenia and Azerbaijan and organize the war, and put Aḥmad b. Jonayd Eskāfī in command of an expedition against Bābak. Aḥmad b. Jonayd was taken prisoner by Bābak while Zorayq failed to pro-secute the war, and al-Ma'mūn then put Ebrāhīm b. Layt b. Fażl in charge. In 212/827-28 the caliph sent a force under Moḥammad b. Ḥomayd Ṭūsī to punish Zorayq, who had rebelled, and to subdue Bābak. This general succeeded after some delay in capturing Zorayq and dispersing his group of rebels and then, having obtained reinforcements and made thorough preparations, set out against Bābak. In the contest between them, which went on for six months, Moḥammad b. Ḥomayd won several victories, but in the last battle in 214/829 his troops, who in compliance with his strategy had advanced three parasangs into the mountains, were attacked in a steep pass by Bābak's men, who rushed down from an ambush higher up; the troops then fled, leaving behind only Moḥammad b. Ḥomayd and some officers, who were all killed. The death of this general prompted poetic laments such as a *qaṣīda* by Abū Tammām, two verses from which are quoted in Dīnavarī (p. 398). From the statements of Ṭabarī (s.a. 214/829), Yaʿqūbī, and others it appears that al-Ma'mūn then either appointed ʿAbd-Allāh b. Ṭāher to the governorship of Jebāl, Armenia, and Azerbaijan, or gave him the choice between this and the governorship of Khorasan. He in fact chose or was ordered to go to Khorasan (Sadighi, pp. 248-49) but according to one account (*Sīāsat-nāma*, p. 361) he first sent a force against Bābak, who took refuge in a castle. The caliph appointed ʿAlī b. Hešām, the governor of Jebāl, Qom, Isfahan, and Azerbaijan, with the responsibility to lead the operations against Bābak; allegedly he oppressed the inhabitants, killing men and confiscating properties, and even planned to kill al-Ma'mūn's emissary ʿOjayf b. ʿAnbasa and then to join Bābak; but he was arrested by ʿOjayf and delivered to al-Ma'mūn, who ordered his execution in 217/832 (Ṭabarī, III, pp. 1108f.). Al-Ma'mūn then entrusted the governorship of Jebāl and conduct of operations against the Ḵorramīs to Ṭaher b. Ebrāhīm. For the time being, however, the caliph's campaign against the Byzantines precluded large-scale action against the Ḵorramī rebels, who gained further ground. Al-Ma'mūn died on the campaign in 218/833. His moves against Bābak had failed, but his concern with the problem is revealed in his testamentary advice to his successor al-Moʿtaṣem in which al-Ma'mūn exhorts him not to spare any effort or resources to crush Bābak's revolt (Ṭabarī, III, p. 1138).

The persistence of Bābak's revolt and the failure of the caliphal generals and expeditionary forces to quell it had various reasons. His stronghold Baḏḏ was situated in impenetrable mountains with intricate defiles and passes, where, according to Balʿamī (see Kāmbaḵš Fard, *Barrasīhā-ye tārīḵī* 1/4, Dey, 1345 Š./November-December, 1966-67, pp. 9-10), a handful of men could stop thousands of advancing troops. Severe winter weather and heavy rain and snowfalls made operation against Baḏḏ impossible in winter. Often Bābak used his positional advantage to surprise the enemy and kill large numbers of them. While Balʿamī and others describe Bābak's following as made up of local farmers and poor people, several writers call them "thieves, heretics, and profligates" (ʿAwfī, pt. 1, chap. 5). It can be inferred that Bābak won wide support among peasants and poor villagers of the Azerbaijan highlands who hoped for a better future through the revolt's success (Amoretti, pp. 507-08), but it is not improbable that some joined for expediency or out of fear.

The Iranian Archeology Department has identified the site with ruins (called Qalʿa-ye Jomhūr, probably after the surrounding Jomhūr mountains) in the present district of Ahar, located 50 km from Ahar town on a height above the left bank of a tributary of the Qarasū 3 km southwest of the village of Kalībar (Report of the Department's mission in the summer of 1345 Š./1966). Aḥmad Kasrawī's researches had already pointed to the site near Kalībar (*Šahrīārān-e gomnām*, 2nd ed., Tehran, 1335 Š./1956, p. 149). The remains consisting of fortifications and a large building rest on a mountain-top 2,300-2,600 m above sea level, surrounded on all sides by ravines 400-600 m deep. The only access is by a very narrow track through gorges, up steep slopes, and across patches of dense forest. The final approach to the castle's gate is through a corridor-like defile wide enough for only one man to walk at a time. Old siege engines could not be brought up here. To reach the large building from the castle's walls one had to climb about 100 m higher up by a narrow path passable only by one man at a time along the ridge, which is surrounded by a forested ravine 400 feet deep (see Kāmbaḵš Fard, "Qalʿa-ye Jomhūr yā Dež-e Baḏḏ," *Honar o mardom* 50, Āḏar, 1345 Š./November-December, 1966, pp. 2-6; *Barrasīhā-ye tārīḵī* 1/4, pp. 3-18 and plates 2, 4, 5, 9, 11; Torbatī Ṭabāṭabā'ī, pp. 466-71; Flügel, p. 539 n. 1; Nafīsī, pp. 37-39; Abū Dolaf Mesʿar b. Mohalhel Ḵazrajī, *al-Resāla al-ṯānīa*, ed. V. Minorsky, Cairo, 1955, p. 6; for further details see BAḎḎ).

Bābak's hand was greatly strengthened by his possession of this inaccessible mountain stronghold, to which the Arabic poet Boḥtorī, amongst others, refers in verses quoted by Yāqūt (I, p. 361). Baḏḏ was not Bābak's only castle, however, as there are mentions of several others, some of which can be identified with surviving ruins (Nafīsī, pp. 69-71; Ṭabāṭabā'ī, pp. 472-75). At that time there were Ḵorramīs scattered in many regions besides Azerbaijan, reportedly in Ṭabarestān, Khorasan, Balḵ, Isfahan, Kāšān, Qom, Ray, Karaj, Hamadān, Lorestān, Ḵūzestān, Baṣra, and Armenia (Nafīsī, pp. 32-33). According to the *Fehrest* (pp. 405-06) and Masʿūdī (*Tanbīh*, p. 322), Bābak's sway at the height of his career extended "southward to near Ardabīl and Marand, eastward to the Caspian Sea and the Šamāḵī district and Šervān, northward to the Mūqān (Moğān) steppe and the Aras river bank, westward to the districts of Jolfā, Naḵjavān, and Marand" (see Nafīsī, p. 36 and map).

The Ḵorramī danger was thus a matter of a grave concern to al-Moʿtaṣem on his accession to the caliphate in Rajab, 218/August, 833, and all the more so when later in the same year a large number of men from Jebāl, Hamadān, and Isfahan went over to the Ḵorramī and encamped near Hamadān. To deal with them al-Moʿtaṣem sent a force under Esḥāq b. Ebrāhīm b. Moṣʿab, who was also made governor of Jebāl. In the subsequent battle near Hamadān several thousand (60,000 in Ṭabarī and Ebn al-Aṯīr) Ḵorramīs were killed, but a large number escaped to Byzantine territory, whence they came back later to resume their fight (Ṭabarī, III, p. 1165; Ebn al-Aṯīr, VI, p. 441; *Sīāsat-nāma*, pp. 362-63). In Jomādā I, 219/May, 834 many

Ḵorramī prisoners were brought by Esḥāq b. Ebrāhīm to Baghdad (Ṭabarī, III, p. 1166; Ebn al-Aṯīr, VI, p. 444). Bābak's revolt, however, was still in full swing, and the slaughter of so many Ḵorramīs seems to have strengthened his men's will to fight. In 220/835 al-Moʿtaṣem placed Ḥaydar b. Kāvūs Afšīn (q.v.), a senior general and a son of the vassal prince of Osrūšana, in command of an expedition to destroy Bābak. According to most of the sources, al-Moʿtaṣem not only made Afšīn governor of Azerbaijan and seconded high-ranking officers to serve under him, but also ordered exceptionally large salaries, expense allowances, and rations for him; Afšīn was to receive 10,000 dirhams per day spent on horseback and 5,000 dirhams per day not so spent. For rapid transmission of messages, the caliph ordered that a swift horse with a rider should be stationed at every parasang-pillar between Sāmarrā and the Ḥolwān (now Pā-ye Ṭāq) pass and beyond Ḥolwān as far as Azerbaijan watchmen should be posted on hills with the task of uttering a loud shout on the approach of a courier so that the rider at the nearby station might get ready to take the leather pouch (*ḵarīṭa*) and carry it to the next station; in this way the pouches were carried from Afšīn's camp to Sāmarrā in four days or less (Ṭabarī, III, p. 1229).

Before Afšīn's departure, al-Moʿtaṣem had sent Abū Saʿīd Moḥammad b. Yūsof Marvazī to Ardabīl with instructions to rebuild the forts between Zanjān and Ardabīl which Bābak had demolished and to make the roads safe by posting guards. Abū Saʿīd Moḥammad set about these tasks. A band of mounted Ḵorramī led by a certain Moʿāwīa broke into one sector, intending to surprise Abū Saʿīd Moḥammad with a night attack, but Abū Saʿīd Moḥammad and his soldiers got word and blocked Moʿāwīa's way; in the ensuing fight some Ḵorramīs were killed, others were captured, and the skulls and the prisoners were sent to Baghdad. Ṭabarī (III, p. 1171; cf. Ebn al-Aṯīr, VI, p. 447) records this as Bābak's first defeat. A later incident also boded ill for Bābak. Previously Moḥammad b. Boʿayṯ, the lord of a strong castle named Qalʿa-ye Šāhī, had been well-disposed to Bābak and willing to accommodate his men when they came to the neighborhood; but when Bābak sent a company under a captain named ʿEṣma, Moḥammad b. Boʿayṯ first made them drunk, then threw ʿEṣma into chains and enticed the men one by one into the castle and killed most of them, only a few being able to escape. ʿEṣma was sent to al-Moʿtaṣem, who before jailing him obtained useful information from him about Bābak's territory and tactics and about tracks in the area (Ṭabarī, III, p. 1172; Ebn al-Aṯīr, VI, pp. 447-48).

On arriving in Azerbaijan, Afšīn camped at a place on the Ardabīl road called Barzand at a distance of 15 parasangs from Ardabīl (Eṣṭaḵrī, p. 192; Moqaddasī, pp. 378, 381; Yāqūt, I, p. 382; *Nozhat al-qolūb*, pp. 90, 182). He repaired the forts between Barzand and Ardabīl and made traffic possible by providing road guards, caravan escorts, and halting places. He also spent a month at Ardabīl gathering knowledge of the topography and tracks from informants and spies. If he caught any of Bābak's spies, he pardoned them and paid them to spy for him at twice the rate that Bābak had paid. One such intelligence report was that Bābak knew that al-Moʿtaṣem had sent Boḡā the Elder (a senior general) with a large sum of money for the pay and expenses of the troops and was planning a raid to seize this money. Afšīn used this information to lure Bābak into a full engagement, in which many of Bābak's comrades were killed. Bābak himself got away to the Mūqān plain and thence to Badd (Ṭabarī, III, pp. 1174-78; Ebn al-Aṯīr, VI, pp. 449-51).

When Bābak came under attack from Afšīn's army, he is said to have written a letter to the Byzantine emperor Theophilus (r. 829-42), begging him to lead an expedition into Azerbaijan; but Theophilus's march into caliphal territory with a force including fugitive Ḵorramīs did not take place until after the capture and execution of Bābak in 223/838; the authenticity of Bābak's letter is open to question (Sadighi, p. 257 n. 3). Details of numerous engagements between Bābak's men and Afšīn's troops before the fall of Badd are given by Ṭabarī and Ebn al-Aṯīr (s.a. 220/835-222/837) and recapitulated by Nafīsī (pp. 97-117). Also mentioned are various precautions which Afšīn took at this time, such as trench-digging, patroling, hiring local highlanders as spies, and sending detachments to strategic points. Whenever he needed money or supplies, he informed al-Moʿtaṣem by means of swift couriers and soon got what he wanted. The caliph regularly sent him instructions on tactics and precautions, and gave him every encouragement. On one occasion al-Moʿtaṣem dispatched Jaʿfar Dīnār known as Ḵayyāṭ (the Tailor), who had been a senior general in al-Maʾmūn's reign, and Aytāḵ the Turk, a slave-soldier who superintended the caliphal kitchen, with reinforcements and money for Afšīn and also several ass-loads of iron spikes to be strewn around the camp as a precaution against night raids. When Bābak heard of the arrival of Jaʿfar and Aytāḵ, he is said to have informed Theophilus, "Moʿtaṣem has no one else left, so he has sent his tailor and his cook to fight me" (Sadighi, p. 257). Bābak and his men remained in control of the highland and with their ambushes and surprise attacks, often frustrated Afšīn's plans. They repeatedly captured supplies which Afšīn had ordered from Marāḡa and Šervān. Afšīn's tactics were to lure Bābak's men away from their mountain fastnesses and engage them in the open and to foil their ambushes by efficient reconnaissance. But his officers, eager to bring the matter to a head, complained of his inaction and even accused him of conniving with Bābak. More encounters took place with heavy losses to both sides and finally Afšīn reached the mountain facing the gate of Badd and camped there, only a mile away. Bābak, losing hope, came out to meet him and requested a safe-conduct from the caliph. According to Yaʿqūbī (*Taʾrīḵ* II, pp. 578f.), Afšīn refused, but when Afšīn demanded hostages, Bābak offered his son or others of his followers and asked Afšīn to restrain the troops from attacking. By then, however, fierce fighting with the castle's defenders had started, and in the end Afšīn's troops scaled the walls of Baḏḏ and hoisted their flags. Afšīn entered the castle and had it demolished after it had been plundered (Ṭabarī, III, pp. 1233-34; Masʿūdī, *Tanbīh*, pp. 93, 160). Many of Bābak's men scattered in the mountains and escaped. Bābak, together with some members of his family and a few of his warriors, slipped away by mountain tracks, heading for Armenia Baḏḏ fell on 9 Ramażān 222/15 August 837.

Afšīn, who had already dispatched a request to the caliph for a safe-conduct for Bābak, learned from spies that Bābak and his party were hiding in a forest-covered valley on the Azerbaijan-Armenian border, and he proceeded to blockade the area. When the caliph's safe-conduct arrived, Afšīn commissioned two Ḵorramīs to carry it to Bābak together with a letter from Bābak's son, who had been taken prisoner. Bābak rejected the document without opening it, and after sending the messengers away fled to Armenia with four or five male and female members of his family and one bodyguard. All except Bābak and his brother ʿAbd-Allāh and the guard were captured. Being close to starvation, Bābak sent the guard to a village to get food. The local ruler, Sahl b. Sonbāṭ (on whom see Nafīsī, pp. 135, 138, 175-76) was informed and received Bābak hospitably. Bābak, however, took the precaution of sending his brother ʿAbd-Allāh to ʿĪsā b. Yūsof b. Eṣṭefānūs (Ṭabarī, III, pp. 1223-24). Afšīn had already sent letters to the district promising a large reward for the capture of Bābak, and Sahl b. Sonbāṭ informed Afšīn of Bābak's presence. After verifying this, Afšīn sent a large force under Abū Saʿīd Moḥammad b. Yūsof to capture Bābak. He was arrested after going out at Sahl b. Sonbāṭ's suggestion to hunt (after being put in irons by Sahl b. Sonbāṭ according to Masʿūdī, *Morūj*, ed. Pellat, sec. 2807) and then taken to Afšīn's camp at Barzand on 10 Šawwāl 222/15 September 837. Many stories about Bābak's escape and adventures have come down (see Sadighi, p. 265 n. 3). According to Ṭabarī, he wore a white cloak at the hunting ground, and this has been taken as possibly symbolic of either purity and light or opposition to the ʿAbbasids whose flag was black (Sadighi, p. 264 n. 4). Afšīn also found out where Bābak's brother ʿAbd-Allāh had escaped and wrote to ʿĪsā b. Yūsof b. Eṣṭefānūs, who handed him over. Afšīn reported his success (by pigeon post according to Masʿūdī's *Morūj*, ed. Pellat, sec. 2809) to al-Moʿtaṣem, who in reply ordered him to bring the captives forthwith to Sāmarrā. Allegations that Afšīn deceived Bābak with conciliatory messages and feigned friendship (Nafīsī, pp. 66, 68; Zarrīnkūb, 1355, pp. 247-48; *Dāʾerat al-maʿāref-e fārsī*, s.v. *Bābak*) appear to derive from rumors that Afšīn was already in secret contact with anti-ʿAbbasid leaders such as Bābak and the ruler of Ṭabarestān, Māzyār b. Qāren, and perhaps also with the Byzantine emperor Theophilus. Another conjecture is that Afšīn sacrificed Bābak because he was afraid of being supplanted as commander of the anti-Ḵorramī expedition by his Taherid rivals (Nafīsī, p. 68).

Large numbers of men, women, and children from Bābak's side fell into Afšīn's hands, figures from 1,300 to 7,600 being mentioned (Ṭabarī, III, p. 1233). He released the men and returned the women and children to those shown to be their husbands, fathers, or guardians. Then he set out with Bābak and Bābak's brother and some Ḵorramī prisoners for al-Moʿtaṣem's capital Sāmarrā. (On the question why Afšīn remained in Azerbaijan for almost four months after the capture of Bābak, see Sadighi, p. 268.) They arrived on Thursday, or Wednesday night, 3 Ṣafar 223/4 January 838. Al-Wāṯeq, the heir to the throne, and other relatives of al-Moʿtaṣem as well as senior dignitaries went out at the caliph's command to meet Afšīn. Bayhaqī (2nd ed., pp. 168-69) tells how the minister Ḥasan b. Sahl, like several dignitaries, was reluctant to dismount and salute Afšīn but dared not disobey the caliph's command. Afšīn camped at Maṭīra (or at Qāṭūl five parasangs from Sāmarrā), and it is related that first the *qāżī* Aḥmad b. Abī Doʾād, then al-Moʿtaṣem himself went to the camp secretly in their impatience for a glimpse of Bābak (Ṭabarī, III, pp. 1229-30; Masʿūdī, *Morūj*, ed. Pellat, sec. 2809), a story which, if true, shows what a relief Bābak's fall had been for the caliphal government. To give the populace an exemplary lesson, a parade was held in the following week, most probably on Monday, 6 Ṣafar 223/7 January 838, in which Bābak, clad in an embroidered cloak and capped with a miter, was made to ride on an elephant which had been given to al-Maʾmūn by an Indian king, while his brother, ʿAbd-Allāh, also specially clad and capped, was mounted on a camel. Two verses of Moḥammad b. ʿAbd-al-Malek Zayyāt about this elephant are quoted by Ṭabarī (see Sadighi, p. 266 n. 2). The whole length of the street to the Bāb al-ʿĀmma was lined on both sides with cavalrymen and foot soldiers and huge numbers of people. Then al-Moʿtaṣem ordered the executioner to proceed. First Bābak's hands and feet were cut off, then at the caliph's command his mangled body was strung on a gibbet in the outskirts of Sāmarrā. According to some sources his head was later sent around for display in other cities and in Khorasan. Bābak was hanged in the same place that afterwards Māzyār b. Qāren, the rebel prince of Ṭabarestān, and Yāṭas Rūmī, the patricius of Amorium who had died in prison, were hanged; this is the subject of a poem by Abū Tammām quoted in Masʿūdī's *Morūj* (ed. Pellat, sec. 2821). Bābak's brother ʿAbd-Allāh was sent to Baghdad, where he was similarly executed and gibbeted by Esḥāq b. Ebrāhīm Moṣʿabī. According to some authors (e.g., Neẓām-al-Molk, *Sīāsat-nāma*, pp. 365-66), when one of Bābak's hands had been cut off, he made his face red by smearing blood on it with his other hand, and when al-Moʿtaṣem asked why, he answered that it was because loss of blood causes pallor and he did not want anyone to suppose that he was pale with fear (Sadighi, pp. 267-68). The poet ʿAṭṭār, however, attributes this gesture to the crucified mystic Ḥosayn b. Manṣūr Ḥallāj (*Manṭeq al-ṭayr*, ed. M. J. Maškūr, Tabrīz, 1336 Š./1957, pp. 156-57). A different story about Bābak's words to al-Moʿtaṣem appears in ʿAwfī's *Jawāmeʿ al-*

ḥekāyāt (pt. 1, chap. 5). Bābak's brother 'Abd-Allāh, according to Ṭabarī, met his death with similar calm assurance (Ṭabarī, III, p. 1231).

The cruelty of these killings as well as the enormous favor that al-Mo'taṣem lavished upon Afšīn (daily dispatch of horses and robes of honor on his way back from Barzand, gifts of a crown and jeweled insignia, 20,000 dirhams for himself and his troops, etc., ibid., pp. 1230, 1232, 1233) and others illustrate the importance which the caliph and his advisers placed on the suppression of Bābak's revolt. Among the court poets who lauded the victory of Afšīn and received rewards from al-Mo'taṣem were Esḥāq b. Ḵalaf (quoted in Dīnavarī, p. 399) and Abū Tammām Ṭā'ī, whose poem likened Afšīn to Ferēdūn and Bābak to Żaḥḥāk (Mas'ūdī, Tanbīh, p. 93). According to Mas'ūdī (Morūj, ed. Pellat, sec. 2815) al-Mo'taṣem gave Otroja, the daughter of a high-ranking Turkish officer named Ašnās, in marriage to Afšīn's son Ḥasan and laid on a splendid wedding party. Ḥasan b. Sonbāṭ was rewarded by the caliph with a gift of 100,000 dirhams, a jeweled belt, and the crown of a patricius, and his son Mo'āwīa also received 100,000 dirhams. Neẓām-al-Molk (Sīāsat-nāma, p. 366) reckons the defeats of Bābak, Māzyār, and the Byzantines to be three great victories for Islam won in al-Mo'taṣem's reign.

The number of Bābak's men taken prisoner is given as 3,309, and the number of his captured male and female relatives as 30 or more. Various figures, said to have been obtained from an executioner or executioners whom Bābak had employed, are given for those whose death he ordered in the course of his long revolt; the figure of 255,000 or more in most of the sources (Ṭabarī, III, p. 1233; Maqdesī, VI, p. 114; Sadighi, p. 271) is obviously an exaggeration, no doubt intended to impute cruelty and bloodthirstiness to Bābak. All the accounts of Bābak are biased, some begin with curses on him (e.g. Sayyed Mortaża, p. 184; Mostawfī, Tārīḵ-e gozīda, p. 316). Esṭaḵrī (p. 203) and Ebn Ḥawqal (p. 266) state that Ḵorramīs recited the Koran in mosques, but authors such as Baḡdādī (p. 269) describe this as a ruse to conceal disbelief under the pretense of being Muslim. Ḵorramī libertinism has probably also been exaggerated (Madelung, p. 65); for example, the public appearance of Bābak and Jāvīdān's widow at their wedding does not mean that they were unmindful of marriage obligations (see Sadighi, p. 214), and none of the allegations of libertinism made against Bābak and his followers can be taken as certain or trustworthy. All considered, it may be said that Bābak's motives and actions were anti-caliphal, anti-Arab, and to that extent anti-Muslim (Ṭabarī, III, p. 1226; Sadighi, pp. 265, 275; Amoretti, p. 509). The numerous revolts in the two or three centuries after the Arab conquest point to widespread discontent among the Iranian elements from whom the leaders, including Bābak, drew their support, and perhaps also to a desire to return to the past. Bābak's aims, however, were clearly not shared by the Iranian princes and nobles like Afšīn (except Māzyār), being incompatible with their ambition to regain power and wealth (Zarrīnkūb, 1355, p. 232). Most of them, including Afšīn who was one of their number, supported the caliph's action against Bābak. Modern scholars such as Sadighi (p. 229) and G. E. von Grunebaum (Medieval Islam, Chicago, 1961, p. 205) regard Bābak's revolt as a politico-religious movement, and Nafīsī, J. Homā'ī (in Mehr 3, p. 159), and D. Ṣafā have laid stress on its nationalistic aspect. Bābak's boldness, shrewdness, and efficiency in the military leadership of the long struggle, and the trust placed in him by his supporters are certainly remarkable (on his personality and ideas, see Sadighi, pp. 268-72). Ṭabarī states that none of the Ḵorramīs dared obey Afšīn's order to take the caliph's safe-conduct to Bābak and that when Afšīn's emissaries reached him, he said in an angry message to his son, "Perhaps I shall survive, perhaps not. I have been known as the commander. Wherever I am present or am mentioned, I am the king." The words show that he was a man of far-reaching ambition and enterprise. In his conversation with Sahl b. Sonbāṭ about the need to send away his brother 'Abd-Allāh, he said, according to Ṭabarī, "It is not right that my brother and I should stay in one place. One of us may be caught and the other may survive. I do not know what will happen. We have no successor to carry on our movement." The fact that Bābak sent his brother away when he himself took refuge with Sahl b. Sonbāṭ implies Bābak's hope for the continuation of the movement. Ṭabarī also states that Afšīn, when about to leave Azerbaijan, asked Bābak whether he would like anything before their departure, and Bābak replied that he would like to see his own town again. He was sent to Baḏḏ with some guards on a moonlight night and allowed to walk around the town. This gives proof of his great love for his homeland. In the same context Ṭabarī has a story that Afšīn granted a request from Bābak to spare him from surveillance by the appointed guard-officer, because this officer "was slippery-handed and slept beside him and stank unbearably." The statements of Ṭabarī (III, pp. 1177, 1205) and Ebn al-Aṯīr (s.a. 220/835 and 222/837) about Ḵorramī merry-making and wine drinking even in wartime confirm one of the sect's reputed characteristics (see Amoretti, p. 517), but their tales of Bābak's promiscuity and abduction of pretty Armenian girls seem inconsistent with another statement of Ṭabarī (III, p. 1227) that the women wept when they saw Bābak captive in Afšīn's camp.

The excitement over the fighting and the defeat of Bābak is echoed in contemporary Arabic literature, e.g., a verse description of Bābak on the gibbet quoted by Rāḡeb Eṣfahānī (Moḥāżarāt al-odabā', Beirut, 1961, III, p. 199), poems by Abū Moḥammad Esḥāq b. Ebrāhīm Mawṣelī (155/172-235/850) in praise of Esḥāq b. Ebrāhīm Moṣ'abī (see Ḥoṣrī Qayrawānī, Zahr al-ādāb, Cairo, III, pp. 13-14), the odes in Abū Tammām's dīvān, also his invectives against Afšīn after the latter's fall, and praises for Moḥammad b. Homayd Ṭūsī and his campaign against Bābak in the dīvān of Boḥtorī (see also Nafīsī, pp. 158-60).

Armenia was close to Bābak's territory and had contacts with him but occasionally suffered from his raids. The mentions of his doings in Armenian chronicles have been assembled by Nafīsī (pp. 135-41).

Bābak's defeat hit the Ḵorramīs hard but did not destroy them. Descendants of his followers evidently continued to live at Baḏḏ, as Abū Dolaf b. Mesʿar b. Mohalhel saw them there in the mid-4th/10th century. Further Ḵorramī stirrings are reported: in the reign of al-Moʿtaṣem's successor al-Wāṯeq and as late as 300/912-13 (Sīāsat-nāma, pp. 366-67); in 321/933 and again in 360/970 in the reigns of the Buyid amirs ʿEmād-al-Dawla and ʿAżod-al-Dawla and as late as the mid-6th/12th century (Margoliouth and Amedroz, Eclipse II, p. 299; Samʿānī, s.v. Bābakī; Bondārī in Houtsma, Recueil, p. 124); and even in the Mongol period. Many of the old writers, particularly those of Sunnite persuasion, assert that Ḵorramīs influenced and infiltrated the Qarmaṭī and Esmāʿīlī movements, and some modern scholars take the same view while others are more cautious (Madelung, p. 65; B. Lewis, The Origins of Ismailism, Cambridge, 1940, pp. 96-97). The suspicion probably gained credence because the three movements shared a common hostility to the ʿAbbasids and may have occasionally collaborated.

Bibliography: Abu'l-Maʿālī Moḥammad b. ʿObayd-Allāh, Bayān al-adyān, ed. M.-T. Dāneš-pažūh, FIZ 10, 1341 Š./1962, pp. 282-318. Abū Manṣūr Baḡdādī, al-Farq bayn al-feraq, ed. M. M. ʿAbd-al-Ḥamīd, Beirut, n.d., pp. 266-69. Abu'l-Moẓaffar Esferā'īnī, al-Tabṣīr fi'l-dīn, Cairo, 1359/1940. B. A. Amoretti in Camb. Hist. Iran IV, 1975, pp. 503-18. Moḥammad ʿAwfī, Jawāmeʿ al-ḥekāyāt, MS, Bib. Nat., supp. Pers., 906, fols. 95a-b, 202b, 70a. M. Azizi, La domination arabe et l'épanouissement du sentiment national en Iran, Paris, 1938. Dāʾerat al-maʿāref-e fārsī, ed. Ḡ.-H. Moṣāḥeb, Tehran, 1345 Š./1966, s.v. "Bābak-e Ḵorramdīn," "Ḵorramdīnān." Ebn al-ʿEbrī (Bar Hebraeus), Taʾrīḵ moḵtaṣar al-dowal Beirut, 1958, p. 139. Ebn Ḵaldūn, Ketāb al-ʿebar, Būlāq, 1284/1867, III, pp. 256-62. Ebn Meskawayh, Tajāreb I, pp. 233ff.; II, pp. 282ff. Faṣīḥ Ḵʿāfī, Mojmal-e faṣīḥī, ed. M. Farroḵ, Mašhad, 1341 Š./1962, I, pp. 283-96. G. Flügel, "Bābak, seine Abstammung und erstes Auftreten," ZDMG 23, 1869, pp. 531-42. Gardīzī, ed. Ḥabībī, pp. 76-79. ʿA.-R. Homāyūn-Farroḵ, "Dāstān-e tārīḵī-e Bābak wa Afšīn," Hūḵt, no. 13, 1341 Š./1962, n.s., pts. 4-12; no. 14, 1342 Š./1963, n.s., pts. 1-9, 11-12. C. Huart, "Bābak," in EI¹. W. Madelung, "Ḵhurramiyya," in EI² V. D. Margoliouth, "Ḵhorramiyya," in EI¹ II. S. Nafīsī, Bābak-e Ḵorramdīn, 2nd ed., Tehran, 1342 Š./1963 (comprehensive study with full list of sources; first published in Mehr 1-2, 1312-13 Š./1933-34). Idem, Māh-e Nakšab, Tehran, 1334 Š./1955, pp. 64-87. ʿA. Parvīz, "Ḵorramdīnān wa qīām-e Bābak barā-ye eḥyā-ye esteqlāl-e Īrān," Barrasīhā-ye tārīḵī 1, 1345 Š./1966, pp. 75-88. Ebn Qotayba, Ketāb al-maʿāref, ed. F. Wüstenfeld, Göttingen, 1850, p. 198. M. Rāvandī,

Tārīḵ-e taḥawwolāt-e ejtemāʿī III, Tehran, 1331 Š./1952. G. Sadighi, Les mouvements religieux iraniens au IIe et au IIIe siècle de l'hégire, Paris, 1938, pp. 187-280 (sources pp. 230-36). Ḏ. Ṣafā, "Bābak-e Ḵorramdīnī," Majalla-ye arteš 8, 1328 Š./1949, no. 8, pp. 19-23, no. 9, pp. 53-61, no. 10, pp. 46-49. Sayyed Mortażā b. Dāʿī, Tabṣerat al-ʿawāmm, ed. ʿA. Eqbāl, Tehran, 1313 Š./1934, p. 184. D. Sourdel, "Bābak," in EI² I. B. Spuler, Iran, Wiesbaden, 1952, pp. 61-64, 201-03. Ṭabarī, The Reign of al-Muʿtaṣim, tr. E. Marin, New Haven, 1951, index. S. J. Torābī Ṭabāṭabāʾī, Āṯār-e bāstānī-e Āḏarbāyjān II, Tehran, 2535 = 1355 Š./1957, pp. 466-71. Tanūḵī, Nešwār al-moḥāżara wa akbār al-modākara, ed. ʿA. Šāljī, 4 vols., Beirut, 1971-72, I, pp. 147-48. Neẓām-al-Molk Ṭūsī, Sīāsat-nāma, ed. J. Šeʿār, Tehran, 1348 Š./1969, pp. 319, 359-89. E.M. Wright, "Bābak of Badhdh and al-Afshīn during the Years A.D. 816-841...," Muslim World 38, 1948, pp. 43-59, 124-31. E. Yarshater in Camb. Hist. Iran III/2, pp. 991-1024, Pers. tr. in Īrān-nāma 2/1, 1362 Š./1983, pp. 6-42. ʿA.-Ḥ. Zarrīnkūb, Do qarn-e sokūt, 5th ed., Tehran, 1355 Š./1976, pp. 231-56. Idem, Tārīḵ-e Īrān baʿd az Eslām, Tehran, 1343 Š./1964, pp. 566-69.

(Ḡ.-Ḥ. Yūsofī)

BĀBAKĪYA. See ḴORRAMDĪNĪS.

BABAN (or Bavan), a small town in the medieval Islamic province of Bādḡīs (q.v.), to the north and west of Herat, more particularly, in the district of Ganj Rostāq (q.v.), which formed the eastern part of Bādḡīs. It must have been within the Herat welāyat of modern Afghanistan, just south of the border with the Turkmenistan S.S.R. and near the modern Afghan town of Košk.

The 4th/10th-century geographers link it with Kīf and Baḡšūr as the three main settlements in Ganj Rostāq. Baban was two stages from Herat, Kīf and Baḡšūr being respectively a stage and a day's journey further onwards. It was the most populous of the three and, as the qaṣaba or capital, the seat of the governor. The whole district is described as being agriculturally highly prosperous, obtaining its water from running streams from the hills and from wells, with grapes being a speciality; the Ḥodūd al-ʿālam mentions grape-syrup (došāb) from Baban. The place was still apparently prosperous in the later 6th/12th and early 7th/13th centuries, for both Samʿānī and Yāqūt visited it, the former hearing ḥadīṯ there from the local cadi (qāżī); both mention a prominent faqīh from the town, one Abū ʿAbd-Allāh Moḥammad b. Bešr Bavanī. After the Mongol invasions, however, it drops out of mention.

Bibliography: Eṣṭaḵrī, p. 269. Ebn Ḥawqal, pp. 441, 457; tr. Kramers, pp. 426, 441, Maqdesī, pp. 298, 308. Ḥodūd al-ʿālam, tr. Minorsky, p. 104, sec. 23.31. Samʿānī (Hyderabad), II, pp. 363-64. Yāqūt (Beirut) I, p. 512. Le Strange, Lands, p. 413. A description of the district as it was a century ago is given by C. E. Yate, *Northern Afghanistan or Letters from the Afghan Boundary Commission*, Edinburgh and London, 1888, pp. 67-68.

(C. E. Bosworth)

BĀBĀN (or Baban) name of a Kurdish princely family who from their center at Solaymānīya ruled over an area in Iraqi Kurdistan and western Iran (early 11th/17th—mid-13th/19th century) and was actively involved in the Perso-Ottoman struggles. The name occurs in Western travel accounts of the early nineteenth century variously as Bebah, Bebbeh, or Bebe. Modern Kurdish as well as Persian sources refer to them as Bābān or Āl-e Bābān, while the Turkish equivalents are Babanlar or Babanzadeler. The origins of the Bābān are clouded in obscurity. Some information on the relationship of the Bābān and Sorān up to 1005/1596 can be obtained from Šaraf Khan Bedlīsī, *Šaraf-nāma* (various mss., see Storey, I, pp. 367; recent editions: Arabic, Cairo, 1958; Persian, Tehran, 1343 Š./1964; Russian, Moscow, 1967-76; Turkish, Istanbul, 1975). The authorities are unanimous in their recognition of Aḥmad Faqīh (Kurdish Faqī Aḥmad) as the first known ancestor of the last of several successive dynasties of Bābān rulers originating from the region around Pīšdār. However, there is no agreement on the dynastic chronology or on their family relationship (for a detailed discussion of the sources for the history of the Bābān see Nebez, pp. 10-35). The real founder of the fortunes of the Bābān emirate was Solaymān Beg in the last quarter of the seventeenth century. Somewhat earlier, the Bābān had established their headquarters at Qalʿa-ye Čolān in the Šahrazūr region, where it remained until Maḥmūd Pasha Bābān founded Solaymānīya in 1195/1781. Though the exact date of the foundation is disputed, it is generally agreed that Solaymānīya owes its importance as the intellectual center to Bābān initiative. The history of the Bābān emirate from 1163/1750 to 1263/1847 is dominated by the rivalries among the Kurdish emirates of Bōtān, Sorān, and Bābān on the one side, and their reaction against the centripetal endeavors of the Ottomans and Qajars on the other. At the height of their power, the Bābān possessed all the signs of local autonomy and gave decisive military support to the Ottoman *wālī* of Baghdad in his campaigns against the Qajars. The ferocity accompanying the constant vicissitudes of the frontier warfare and the dynastic intrigues are reflected in the epic poem *Bayt-e ʿAbd-al-Raḥmān Pāšā Baba* (O. Mann, *Die Mundarten der Mukri-Kurden*, pt. 1, Berlin, 1906, pp. 53-58). Bābān autonomy came to an end with Aḥmad Pasha Bābān's defeat near Ḵoy in 1263/1847, after which the Šahrazūr region became permanently attached to Turkey. His brother ʿAbd-Allāh Pasha was put in charge of Solaymānīya, but expressedly as Ottoman *qāʾem-maqām*; he, too, was finally dismissed in favor of a Turkish administrator in 1267/1851. Descendants of the Bābān are still to be found in Solaymānīya.

Bibliography: ʿA. ʿAzzāwī, *ʿAšāʾer al-ʿErāq* II, Baghdad, 1366/1947. M. van Bruinessen, *Agha, Shaikh and State: On the Social and Political Organization of Kurdistan*, Ph.D. thesis, Utrecht, 1978. M. Dorra, *al-Qażīya al-kordīya*, 2nd ed., Beirut, 1966. C. J. Edmonds, *Kurds, Turks and Arabs*, London, 1957. S. H. Longrigg, "Bābān," *EI*² I, p. 845. Idem, *Four Centuries of Modern Iraq*, Oxford, 1925. H. Ḥoznī Mūkrīānī, *Āwarīkī pāšawa: tārīḵī ḥokmdārānī Bābān le Kūrdistānī Šārezūr Erdelanda le 636 tā 1274*, Revandoz, 1349/1931. J. Nebez, *Der kurdische Fürst Mīr Muhammad-ī Rawāndizī*, Ph.D. thesis, Hamburg, 1970. C. J. Rich, *Narrative of a Residence in Koordistan*, 2 vols., London, 1836. Moḥammad Amīn Zakī, *taʾrīḵ al-Solaymānīya wa anḥāʾehā*, Baghdad, 1951.

(W. Behn)

BĀBAY, catholicos (d. 502) elected at the synod at Seleucia in 497. Bābay was of Seleucia and had served as a secretary of the *marzbān* of Bēt Arāmāyē. He was quite advanced in years when he was elected catholicos in 497. As far as the outer conditions were concerned, his time was advantageous. His rule fell in an epoch during which the church could enjoy peace, and the relations of the catholicos with the court were friendly. The presence of the patriarch was even welcome in the royal court, since King Zāmāsp (496-498), it seems, sought help form the Christians against Mazdak, whose revolutionary message upset the Persian communities.

Bābay was a patriarch without much instruction and education but with the ability to handle the affairs of the church with prudence, skill, and firmness. The interregnum had threatened to split the church, but Bābay succeeded in enforcing reconciliation among the forces inimical to the unity of the church. The acts of the synod gathered in November, 497, in Seuleucia reflect the wisdom of the newly elected head of the church. The annulments of all the excommunications and suspensions which had taken place during the ecclesiastical turmoil of the preceding years, reveal his endeavors to mend entangled ties and to terminate mutual fighting through a formal act of reconciliation between the quarreling parties.

Practically, however, the decisions which were made at the synod of November, 497, moved in the direction of Barṣaumā's (q.v.) aspirations, being a renewal of the decisions adopted by the preceeding synods. When the patriarchal see became vacant after the death of Catholicos Bābōē (q.v.), the synod elected Aqāq catholicos in 484. Aqāq had been a companion-in-arms of Bābōē in the battle against Barṣaumā and rejected for himself the term "Nestorian" applied to him by ʾAksenāyā of Mabbūg. However, he realized the inevitability of the process and so the synod held in February, 486, in Seleucia-Ctesiphon sanctioned previous decisions and solemnly adopted the Nestorian creed. The process of Nestorianization was brought to its conclusion through Barṣaumā's friend Narsay (d. 507).

The adoption of previous decisions by the synod of

497 involved far-reaching decisions which reshaped the spiritual countenance and life of the church: The ancient ascetic ideals were to a great extent abandoned and the clergy, including the hierarchy, were obliged to marry. The canon adopted by the synod of 497 forbade monasteries in and near the towns. All this meant a transformation of the doctrine and the inner life of the Persian church and caused a complete isolation of the church in the East. Regarding the questions of faith and church life as well as ecclesiastical law, Bābay succeeded in establishing himself as the supreme head of the Persian church. He was able to put a restless and fermenting situation under control even after the Monophysites had resumed their activities in Iran, thanks to the propaganda activities of Šemʿōn of Bēt Aršām. This transformation, however, in which Barṣaumā of Nisibis stood at the forefront took place not without violence.

Bibliography: *Synodicon orientale*, ed. J. B. Chabot, Paris, 1902, pp. 62ff. A. Baumstark, *Geschichte der syrischen Literatur*, Bonn, 1922, p. 113. J. Labourt, *Le christianisme dans l'empire perse sous la dynastie sassanide*, Paris, 1904, pp. 154f. A. Vööbus, *Les messaliens et les réformes de Barṣauma de Nisibe dans l'église perse*, Pinneberg, 1947.

(A. Vööbus)

BĀBAY THE GREAT (d. 628), the head of the Nestorian church in Iran under Ḵosrow II.

Bābay, to whom the Nestorian church gave the epithet *Rabbā* "the Great," is the most eminent personality in Syrian monasticism and ecclesiastical life as well as in the area of literary culture in Iran during the last generations before the Islamic invasion. He was the first prolific author among the East Syrians.

Born in the village of Bēt ʿAynāṯā in Bēt Zabday, he received instruction in Persian and then started his medical studies at Nisibis, at the same time attending theological courses offered in the School of Nisibis (q.v.). Soon, he was drawn by the fame of Abraham of Kaškar (al-Wāseṭ), distinguished for his ascetic virtues and reforms in the Persian monasteries, and decided to devote his life to monasticism. He entered the monastery of Īzlā, then under the leadership of Abraham, which was later to become the scene of his activities. Later he founded a monastery in his home country on the estate of his well-to-do parents, adding to it a significant school. When Abbot Dādīšōʿ, successor of Abraham, died in 604, Bābay became the third abbot of the monastery of Īzlā, which had become the leading monastery in Persia.

Bābay is said to be the author of a number of works on monastic discipline, especially for novices, and on monastic asceticism for monks, but it is uncertain whether these works date to this period. The only document of this kind which can be ascribed to him with certainty is his rules for the community of his monastery, now extant only in Arabic translation (*Syriac and Arabic Documents*, pp. 179 ff.). Other extant works of his comprise commentaries on ascetic and mystical themes, the extensive Centuria of Evagrius Ponticus, and on the discourse of Marqos the monk on the spiritual law. However, according to ʿAbdīšōʿ's *Catalogus librorum*, pp. 88 ff., the first history of Syriac literature, his production was enormous, altogether 83 works in various fields. His exegetical work on the whole text of the Scripture has not survived, but the exposition of his important work on the Nestorian christology can be traced in the extant work. He paid especial attention to the monastico-historical genre. He himself testifies that he produced a large number of such biographies, including a work on a number of eminent monks of the monastic community of Īzlā. Only a few of his hagiographical works have survived; the rest are known only by titles. His literary legacy includes also liturgico-historical and liturgical works, metrical as well as in prose, the most outstanding being his works on commemorations and feasts throughout the ecclesiastical year. Thomas of Margā dedicated a chapter of his *Historia Monastica* (I, p. 27) to him, extolling his learning, prolific literary output, and sanctity of life. Bābay enjoyed an authority which exceeded that of all his contemporaries.

The rule of Ḵosrow brought heavy suppression and persecution to the church and after the death of Catholicos Grīgōr of Kaškar (607) until the death of Ḵosrow the church had no head. Under these circumstances it was impossible to elect a new catholicos and so the metropolitans of Nisibis, Ḥadiyab, and Karkā de-Bēt Ṣelōk (or Bēt Garmay) by a joint action authorized Bābay to act as inspector-general of the monasteries. Since it was common knowledge that he was a monk and not a bishop, he could carry out the ecclesiastical visitations without anybody suspecting that a new head of the church had been elected. They also needed Bābay to counter the infiltration of heterodox trends in the monastic communities. Bābay performed the entrusted task so well that after the death of Ḵosrow and during the rule of Šērōē (Šīrūya) when a new catholicos was to be elected, Bābay was regarded as the natural choice, and, not surprisingly, the Synod of 627-28 unanimously elected him to the dignity of catholicos. Bābay, however, declined. He died not much later at the age of 77 years. He had then ruled over his monastery for 24 years.

Bibliography: Thomas of Margā. *The Book of Governors: The Historia Monastica*, ed. E. A. W. Budge, London, 1893, II, pp. 27ff. Išōʿdenaḥ, *Le livre de la chasteté*, ed. I. B. Chabot, Paris and Rome, 1891, p. 25. ʿAbdīšōʿ, *Catalogus librorum*, ed. J. S. Assemani, in *Bibliotheca Orientalis*, Rome, 1725, III, 1, pp. 88f. A. Baumstark, *Geschichte der syrischen Literatur*, Bonn, 1922, pp. 137ff. J. Labourt, *Le christianisme dans l'empire perse sous la dynastie sassanide*, Paris, 1904, pp. 156ff. *Syriac and Arabic Documents*, ed. A. Vööbus, Stockholm, 1960, pp. 176ff. A. Vööbus, *History of the School of Nisibis*, Louvain, 1965.

(A. Vööbus)

BĀBAY OF **NISIBIS** (BĀBAY BAR NṢIBNĀYE), also known as Bābay the Less, Christian Syriac writer who flourished about the beginning of the seventh century A.D. He was the author of a number of hymns and poems, almost none of which have been published. A Sogdian version of one of his works, a metrical homily "On the Final Evil Hour," is partially preserved in the manuscript C2 (see SOGDIAN LITERATURE, CHRISTIAN). The Sogdian translation is of particular importance, since the Syriac original is not known to be extant.

Bibliography: N. Sims-Williams, *The Christian Sogdian Manuscript C2*, Berliner Turfantexte 12, Berlin, 1986, pp. 87-100.

(N. SIMS-WILLIAMS)

BĀBEL. See BABYLON.

BĀBIRUŠ. See BABYLON.

BABISM

i. *The Babi movement.*
ii. *Babi executions and uprisings.*

i. THE BABI MOVEMENT

Babism was a 13/19th-century messianic movement in Iran and Iraq under the overall charismatic leadership of Sayyed ʿAlī-Moḥammad Šīrāzī, the Bāb (1235/1819-1266/1850; q.v.). Babism was the only significant millenarian movement in Shiʿite Islam during the 13th/19th century and is of particular interest in that, unlike other Islamic messianic movements of approximately the same period, it involved, in its later stages, a wholesale break with Islam and an attempt to establish a new religious system. Although the Babi movement as such was rapidly crushed and rendered politically and religiously insignificant, the impetus towards the proclamation of a post-Islamic revelation was continued in Bahaism (q.v.) which began as a Babi sect in competition with that of the Azalī Babism (q.v.) during the 1860s. The relative success of Bahaism inside Iran (where it constitutes the largest religious minority) and in numerous other countries, where it claims the status of an independent religion, gives renewed significance to its Babi origins; indeed, Babi history and doctrine live on, albeit in a much revised form, in the literature and self-image of the modern Bahais.

The present article concerns itself with Babism up to about 1853, when the leadership of the sect moved from Iran to Iraq and internal developments began which led to the Bahai/Azalī split. For our purposes, Babism may be divided into two main periods: 1) from 1250/1844 to 1264/1848, when the Bāb claimed to be the gate preparing the way for the return of the Hidden Imam and the movement around him was characterized by intense Islamic piety and observance of the *Šarīʿa* or Islamic law; and 2) from 1264/1848 to 1269/1853, beginning with the Bāb's claim to be the Imam in person and the abrogation of the Islamic *Šarīʿa*, through his assumption of the role of an independent theophany and his promulgation of a new religious law, to his execution in Tabrīz, the collapse of the leadership of the movement, the proliferation of authority claims, and the dispersal of a hard core of the sect to Baghdad. This second period also witnessed the outbreak of clashes between Babis and state in several parts of Iran and the physical defeat of the movement as a challenge to the religio-political system.

1. 1260-64/1844-48. At its inception, Babism was an intense expression of certain radical tendencies in the Shaikhi school of Shiʿism which had come to the fore during the leadership of Sayyed Kāẓem Raštī (q.v.). During the seventeen years (1242-59/1826-44) that he acted as head of the school from its center in Karbalāʾ, Raštī stressed the essential orthodoxy of Shaikhi belief as originally expounded by the founder, Shaikh Aḥmad Aḥsāʾī (d. 1753/1826; q.v.), while teaching an elitist doctrine of the Shaikh as the *morawwej* or promoter of Islam in a new cycle of inward truth (*bāṭen*) following 1200 years of outward teaching (*ẓāher*). Raštī's death on 11 Ḏu'l-ḥejja 1259/1 January 1854 precipitated a serious internal crisis in the movement, bringing to the surface many concealed tensions, disagreements, rivalries, and ambitions within the Shaikhi community. His failure to appoint a clear successor and the absence of an agreed system for the selection of one led, inevitably, to much fragmentation, out of which two major schools emerged: that around Ḥājj Mollā Moḥammad-Karīm Khan Kermānī (1225/1810-1288/1871; q.v.) and another around Sayyed ʿAlī-Moḥammad Šīrāzī. These two factions expressed diametrically opposed tendencies within the Shaikhism of the period, the first wishing to preserve the name and identity of the school, emphasizing the continuing role of the Prophet and the imams and seeking accommodation with the Shiʿite majority by stressing its total adherence to Twelver Shiʿite orthodoxy and playing down the more unorthodox aspects of Shaikhi teaching; the second also regarding itself as wholly orthodox but adopting the name Bābīya and moving away from the outward practice of Islam towards a concentration on the expression of its inner realities and, ultimately, a new revelation of divine truth. It was some time, however, before this divergence of tendencies became quite clear and, in the earliest period, emphasis must be placed less on specific doctrinal views and more on claims to charismatic authority within the wider context of Shiʿism as a whole. (For a detailed study of the role of charisma in early Shaikhism and Babism see MacEoin, *From Shaykhism to Babism.*)

There is evidence that a section of the Shaikhi community at this period regarded Aḥsāʾī and Raštī as "gates" (*bābān*) of the imam, presumably fulfilling functions similar to those of the four *abwāb* (plur. of *bāb* "gate") traditionally regarded as channels of communication with the Hidden Imam during his "lesser occultation" (see BĀB) and possibly presaging the return of the imam himself. The development of a

Bābīya school within Shaikhism may be regarded as having begun even before the announcement by Sayyed ʿAlī-Moḥammad of his own claim to be the *bāb*. Various statements attributed to Raštī in the period just before his death suggest that chiliastic motifs were present in his teaching, and there is evidence that some of his followers expected the imminent appearance of an "affair" or "cause" (*amr*) somehow linked to the advent of the imam. It seems to have been a group of those Shaikhis most animated by messianic expectations who chose, in early Ṣafar, 1260/late February, 1844, to engage in prayerful withdrawal (*eʿtekāf*) in the main mosque of Kūfa, and it was from this group that the majority of the Bāb's earliest disciples emerged.

The first to enter *eʿtekāf* was Mollā Moḥammad-Ḥosayn Bošrūʾī (q.v.), a young Shaikhi *ʿālem* or mulla who had only recently returned to Iraq from a lengthy period in Iran and who was himself regarded by a section of the school as a potential successor to Raštī. Leaving Kūfa with a brother and cousin on or just after 12 Rabīʿ I 1260/1 April 1844, Bošrūʾī set out for Kermān, where he planned to consult with Moḥammad Karīm Khan (for references see MacEoin, "From Shaykhism," p. 144). En route he passed through Shiraz where he renewed an earlier acquaintance with Sayyed ʿAlī-Moḥammad Šīrāzī, a young merchant who had studied briefly with Raštī in Karbalāʾ a few years before and who had attracted some attention from a number of Shaikhis at the *ʿatabāt* (the Shiʾite holy shrines and cities in Iraq; q.v.) at that time. In recent months, Sayyed ʿAlī-Moḥammad had undergone a religious crisis culminating in at least two visions indicating a high spiritual station for himself. He had also begun the composition of works of a religious nature, including a commentary of sorts on the Koranic chapter (*sūra) al-Baqara*. After some weeks, during which Bošrūʾī seems to have read at least a part of these writings, on 5 Jomādā I/22 May, Sayyed ʿAlī-Moḥammad announced to him that he was the successor to Raštī and the *bāb* of the Hidden Imam. Some time after this, a second group of Shaikhis arrived in Shiraz from Karbalāʾ. Thirteen of these (according to one version, the entire group numbered thirteen) met the Bāb through Bošrūʾī and were converted, together with Bošrūʾī's brother and cousin (Zarandi, *Dawn-Breakers*, pp. 69-70, 80-81). Among this second group was a brother-in-law of Fāṭema K̲ānom Baragānī Qazvīnī (better known as Qorrat-al-ʿAyn and Janāb-e Ṭāhera; q.v.), a woman who had already won a reputation as an outstanding and radical Shaikhi cleric while herself resident in Karbalāʾ. Although then in Qazvīn, she was enrolled by the Bāb in the group of his first disciples, whose number was brought to eighteen by the late arrival of Mollā Moḥammad-ʿAlī Bārforūšī (q.v.), a young Shaikhi who was en route to Būšehr on a *ḥajj* or pilgrimage journey.

These eighteen disciples known as the "Letters of the Living" (*ḥorūf al-ḥayy*) constituted, together with the Bāb, the first "unity" (*waḥed* = 19) of a series of nineteen unities which would make up a body of three hundred and sixty-one individuals—a *kollo šayʾ* (= 361)—the first believers in the imam through the *bāb*. These *ḥorūf al-ḥayy* are regarded as identical with the "precursors" (*sābeqūn*) referred to in early works of the Bāb and his followers, both literally in preceding others in recognition of the Bāb and esoterically in being identified with the first group of mankind to respond to God's pre-eternal covenant, a group itself identified in Shiʿite belief with Moḥammad and the imams. It is, in fact, clear that the Bāb came to regard the *ḥorūf al-ḥayy* as incarnations of the Prophet, the twelve imams, the original four *abwāb* and Fāṭema, an identification which led to serious controversy in the early Babi community of Karbalāʾ (see MacEoin, "Hierarchy," pp. 104-09).

After a short period of instruction ending in early July, 1844, the Bāb instructed sixteen of the *ḥorūf al-ḥayy* to disperse in various directions, carrying transcriptions of parts of his early writings, notably his commentary on the Koranic chapter *Yūsof*, the *Qayyūm al-asmāʾ*. They were not to reveal his name or identity but merely to announce that the gate or agent (*nāʾeb*) of the Hidden Imam had appeared. Through these disciples and the men they met and converted—almost all, like themselves, *ʿolamāʾ* or Muslim divines—the claims of the Bāb were rapidly disseminated, principally to the Shaikhi communities in the areas they visited. In this way, a growing section of the Shaikhi school followed the Bāb in the period of his earliest claims. The unity of Shaikhism was irretrievably shattered and a core of convinced Babis brought into existence, eager to put into practice the radical changes implicit in the Bāb's claims.

The most immediate impact made by the dissemination of Babi propaganda on the Shiʿite world occurred at its heart in Karbalāʾ. The Bāb's message was brought to the region of the shrines in Iraq in the first instance by Mollā ʿAlī Besṭāmī (q.v.), whose preaching there precipitated a major uproar among both Shaikhis and non-Shaikhis, leading to his arrest, trial and eventual despatch to Istanbul. During his stay in Iraq, however, as is attested by contemporary diplomatic reports, Besṭāmī and other Babis awakened a widespread chiliastic fervor among the Shaikhis of the area (see Momen, *Babi and Baha'i Religions*, pp. 83-89). The *Qayyūm al-asmāʾ*, portions of which now began to circulate there, indicated that the Bāb had appeared on earth to prepare men for the imminent arrival of the imam and the waging of the final *jehād* or holy war against unbelief (which was widely interpreted to include not only Sunnism but non-Babi Shiʿism as well). News also arrived from Shiraz that the Bāb had left the town in September in order to perform the *ḥajj* and that, on his departure, he had said that he would reveal his cause in Mecca, after which he would enter Kūfa and Karbalāʾ and fulfill the prophecies. In various letters of this period, he called on his growing body of followers to assemble in Karbalāʾ in order to aid the imam on his appearance. A number of Babis appear to have traveled to Karbalāʾ with this hope and, following instructions in the *Qayyūm al-asmāʾ*, to have purchased arms in readiness for the *jehād* that would follow the Bāb's appearance and the advent of the imam. In the end, the Bāb failed to reach Karbalā' as promised, returning instead to Shiraz via Būšehr in the summer of 1261/1845. His arrest en route to his home town by agents of the governor of Shiraz considerably restricted his freedom of action and prevented even a late arrival in Iraq. As a result, a number of the newly-converted abandoned their allegiance, leaving only a small core of believers, who were forced to begin the work of proselytization once more (al-Qatīl b. al-Karbalā'ī, letter in Māzandarānī, *Ẓohūr al-ḥaqq* III, p. 503).

Although the Bāb remained at the heart of the movement, his personal activities were now restricted. He remained under house arrest in Shiraz until September, 1262/1846, when he escaped to Isfahan following an outbreak of cholera. There, with the support of the governor, Manūčehr Khan Mo'tamad-al-Dawla, he had greater freedom to write and meet disciples, but this interlude ended abruptly with the governor's death in February, 1847. The Bāb was summoned by Moḥammad Shah to Tehran but en route diverted to Mākū in Azerbaijan, where he remained in confinement until his transfer in May, 1848 to the fortress of Čahrīq, his place of imprisonment until shortly before his execution in 1266/1850. Although communications between him and his followers were never entirely severed, they were, at times, difficult, and it was, in any case, impossible to refer to him all questions for elucidation or arbitration.

The exposition of Babi doctrine (to the extent that we can speak of this in a period of considerable confusion) in a number of provincial centers fell increasingly to the leading followers of the Bāb, both *ḥorūf al-ḥayy* and other *'olamā'* in those areas: in Mašhad, Mollā Moḥammad-Ḥosayn Bošrū'ī, who was expressly appointed by the Bāb to answer questions on his behalf for the community as a whole; in Borūjerd, Kurdistan, Tehran, Qazvīn, Isfahan, Qom, and elsewhere, the peripatetic Sayyed Yaḥyā Dārābī (Waḥīd) (q.v.); in Tehran and, later, Zanjān, Mollā Moḥammad-'Alī Zanjānī (Ḥojjat) (q.v.); in Qazvīn, Mollā Jalīl Orūmī; and, perhaps the most important, in Karbalā' and, for a time, Baghdad, Qorrat-al-'Ayn. The role of these and a few other individuals must be stressed. Bošrū'ī, Dārābī, and Zanjānī were to lead the Babi insurrections in Māzandarān, Neyrīz, and Zanjān, while Qorrat-al-'Ayn was perhaps the guiding spirit behind the events at the enclave of Badašt (q.v.) in 1848, when a group of Babis proclaimed the abrogation of the Islamic *Šarī'a*. More importantly, the main figures of the Babi hierarchy formed what Berger calls a "charismatic field," playing roles of messianic significance ("From Sect to Church," pp. 161-62). Thus Bošrū'ī and Mollā Moḥammad-'Alī Bārforūšī Qoddūs were regarded by their followers at Ṭabarsī shrine as the "Qā'em-e Ḵorāsānī" and "Qā'em-e Jīlānī" respectively, while quasi-divine honors were paid to the latter (such as the circumambulation of his house and the direction of prayers towards him as the *qebla*). While in Karbalā', Qorrat-al-'Ayn claimed to be an incarnation of Fāṭema, whereas some regarded her as "the point of divine knowledge" after Raštī. Unfortunately, with the exception of some interesting treatises by Qorrat-al-'Ayn and a few fragments by Qoddūs, works penned by these individuals have been lost, and it is almost impossible to reconstruct the details of Babi doctrine as actually taught by them or to determine how far this may have coincided with or differed from the doctrine taught by the Bāb and carefully preserved in his writings.

The role played by Qorrat-al-'Ayn in Karbalā' was, as we have noted above, particularly significant. Residing in Raštī's home there, she assumed supreme control of the Shaikhi-Babi community of the region, stressing her authority as one of the *ḥorūf al-ḥayy* and the incarnation of Fāṭema. This led to the first serious crisis of authority in the movement, when her position was challenged by Mollā Aḥmad Ḵorāsānī and his followers who were particularly opposed to the leadership role of the *ḥorūf al-ḥayy*. The rift produced in the Babi community of Iraq by this conflict was further deepened by Qorrat-al-'Ayn's increasingly radical and unconventional behavior. In his early writings, the Bāb stressed the necessity for his followers to observe the laws of Islam and, indeed, to perform acts of supererogatory piety, and there is some evidence that the Babis of this period were as noted for the zeal of their adherence to tradition as they were later to be known for their rejection of it (for details see MacEoin, "From Shaykhism," pp. 208-10). There were, however, elements inherent in the claim of the Bāb to an authority direct from God which threatened to conflict with this more conservative position. Qorrat-al-'Ayn seems to have been particularly conscious of this and to have linked the concept of the Bāb's overriding authority in religious matters with ideas originating in Shaikhism, to which we have referred earlier—the advent of an age of inner truth succeeding that of outer observance. She seems to have made this link before the Bāb himself and by 1262/1846 had begun to stress the importance of inner realities at the expense of outward practice. In her classes attended by Babi men, she appeared unveiled, and on one occasion chose to celebrate the birth of the Bāb during the early days of Moḥarram. Mīrzā Moḥammad-'Alī Zonūzī states that, with the Bāb's permission, Qorrat-al-'Ayn "rendered all the previous laws and observances null and void" (letter in Māzandarānī, *Ẓohūr al-ḥaqq* III, p. 35). In a statement written after Rajab, 1262/June-July, 1846, she herself records that she began to call on her followers to "enter the gate of innovation" following the receipt of a letter from the Bāb in that month, which she interpreted to mean that Islam was to be abrogated (letter ibid., p. 349; for details, see MacEoin, "From Shaykhism," pp. 210-16).

Controversy ensued within the Babi community. Many were scandalized by Qorrat-al-'Ayn's behavior, particularly that of appearing before men without a veil, and wrote to the Bāb seeking support (which he would not give). Others, however, began to follow her example, and the controversy soon spread beyond the confines of the Babi community proper. In the end,

Qorrat-al-ʿAyn was arrested in Karbalā', forced to leave the city for Baghdad in 1263/1847, kept there for several months in the home of the Mufti, Shaikh Maḥmūd al-Ālūsī, and finally expelled from Iraq on orders sent from Istanbul. Traveling through Hamadān and Kermānšāh, where she carried on an extensive campaign of proselytization, she returned in Qazvīn in the late summer of 1263/1847.

The controversy surrounding Qorrat-al-ʿAyn and the growing challenge presented by Babi missionaries in all the major provinces of Iran, where the number of converts was growing rapidly, led to a hardening of attitudes towards the sect. In Kermān, Moḥammad Karīm Khan Kermānī, who had been acquainted with the Bāb's claims from an early date, was engaged in laying claim to the leadership of the Shaikhi school for himself. Among his activities in this respect was the composition of several works refuting the Bāb and his claims. Not only was the Bāb a threat to Kermānī's position within the school itself, but the obvious heterodoxy of his doctrines and the activities of his followers threatened, because of their close association with the school he purported to represent, to further damage Shaikhism in the eyes of the Shiʿite *ʿolamā'* at large. Kermānī's efforts, reinforced by the Bāb's own rejection of "orthodox" Shaikhism, led to a growing sense of an absolute split between the two movements and a greater sense of independent identity for Babism, together with a hardening of attitudes on both sides. An analysis of later Babi membership indicates that the original Shaikhi dominance within the sect began to decline and that Babism came to have a much wider appeal among the general Shiʿite public. The motives for conversion seem to have become less doctrinal and more social or economic as fewer *ʿolamā'* and greater numbers of the public at large entered the movement. This in itself, however, led to a growing attack on the sect from non-Shaikhi clergy confronted by the challenge of the Babi missionary enterprise.

Matters began to come to a head in Ḏu'l-qaʿda, 1263/October, 1847. Until then, violence directed against the Babis had been limited and no one had died. The Babis, for their part, despite exhortations to *jehād* in several works of the Bāb, still awaited the appearance of the Mahdī before commencing the holy war (a possible indication in itself of doctrinal rather than social motivation) and, in the meantime, contented themselves with issuing challenges to *mobāhala* or mutual cursing (for the development of the themes of *mobāhala* and *jehād* in the movement and the escalation of violence against and on behalf of the sect see MacEoin, "Bābī Concept of Holy War," pp. 109-11. Some months after Qorrat-al-ʿAyn's return to Qazvīn in the late summer of 1263/1847, a group of three Babis attacked her uncle, Ḥājj Mollā Moḥammad-Taqī Baragānī (q.v.), the leading cleric of the town; he died of his wounds three days later, on 16 Ḏu'l-qaʿda/27 October. There had already been a build-up of tension in Qazvīn, much aggravated by Baragānī's preaching against both Shaikhis and Babis. Now, large numbers of Babis were arrested, houses were broken into and looted, and several individuals were eventually put to death in retaliation for what was held to be a general Babi plot. At about the same time, relations between Babis and the civil authorities in Mašhad became strained, particularly after two incidents in which members of the movement tried to rescue two of their arrested correligionists by force.

2. 1264-69/1848-53. The situation changed radically when, in the early months of 1848, the Bab wrote a letter in which he proclaimed himself the promised imam in person and declared the abrogation of the laws of Islam. Announcement of the *qīāma* or resurrection, interpreted as a spiritual event, spread rapidly among the Babi communities of Iraq and Iran. In July, 1848, a gathering of some eighty Babi activists, including Qorrat-al-ʿAyn and Mollā Moḥammad-ʿAlī Bārforūšī, formally proclaimed the advent of the *qīāma*. Towards the end of the same month, the Bāb himself was brought from Čahrīq to Tabrīz, where he was interrogated by a council of *ʿolamā'* and state officials presided over by Nāṣer-al-Dīn Mīrzā (shortly to be made king). Conflicting accounts of this examination exist, but all are agreed that the Bāb insisted on his claim to be the Hidden Imam returned—a claim whose political implications would not have been missed.

Also in July, 1848, Bošrū'ī and a large body of followers left Mašhad, possibly headed for Azerbaijan to rescue the Bāb from prison. Swelled along the route by others, this band encountered opposition as they moved into Māzandarān in September. The residents of Bārforūš (Bābol), alarmed by the arrival of a body of armed men immediately after the death of Moḥammad Shah, offered fierce resistance to their entry to the town. Forced to travel on and attacked by a band of local horsemen, the Babis finally reached the shrine of Shaikh Abū ʿAlī Fażl Ṭabarsī, where they constructed a fort and were joined by other Babis from all parts of Iran, including Bārforūšī and seven other *ḥorūf al-ḥayy*, their numbers eventually reaching to near 500. A series of engagements soon ensued between the Babis and successive contingents of provincial and state troops until May, 1849, in the course of which all but a few of the defenders were killed. Two features of this incident stand out: the messianic overtones of the struggle, emphasized by the roles of Bošrū'ī and Bārforūšī as *qā'em*, the carrying of a black standard, the identification of the fort with Karbalā', its defenders with Ḥosayn and his followers, and their enemies with the Omayyad forces; and the related belief in the supreme authority of the Bāb and his lieutenants as against the illegitimacy of Qajar rule. Babism now clearly posed a direct threat to the established political and religious order.

Further outbreaks of mass violence followed after an interval in Neyrīz (Rajab-Šaʿbān, 1266/May-June, 1850) and Zanjān (Rajab, 1266-Rabīʿ I, 1267/May, 1850-January, 1851), although these differed from Shaikh Ṭabarsī in their distinctly urban character and in the relative absence (as far as our sources indicate) of messianic motifs. The character of these struggles in particular has suggested to some commentators that they were more of an expression of social and political discontent than of religious fervor, and there is undoubtedly a measure of truth in this, particularly in the case of Zanjān. Nevertheless, in a recent study ("The Social Basis of the Bābī Upheavals"), Momen has shown that it is difficult to reach clear conclusions as to the social composition of these outbreaks or of the Babi movement as a whole. Our emphasis must at present remain on the outwardly religious character of Babism, while recognizing the value of religious motifs as a means of socio-political expression in a society such as Qajar Iran. It should be stressed that the Babi leadership and much of the membership was drawn from the ranks of the *'olamā'* class, particularly its lower strata (for further details see ibid.).

In July, 1850, the Bāb was again brought to Tabrīz, where he was executed by firing squad on the 8th or 9th. Coupled with the debacles of Māzandarān, Neyrīz, and Zanjān, in the course of which some 2,000 to 3,000 Babis, including most of the provincial leadership, perished (on these figures see MacEoin, "From Babism to Baha'ism," p. 236), the Bāb's death spelt the end of the movement as a vital political force in Iran. That the "Mahdī" had been executed and his followers everywhere defeated seemed to most people clear evidence of the falsehood of the Bāb's claims, and the potential following which would certainly have accrued to the movement had even a measure of success attended its struggle with the state was drastically diminished. In a final act of desperation, on 15 August 1852, a small group of Babis attempted to assassinate Nāṣer-al-Dīn Shah. A plot led by Shaikh Mollā 'Alī Toršīzī was uncovered, large numbers of Babis in the capital and elsewhere arrested, and some fifty put to death. Among those arrested was Mīrzā Ḥosayn-'Alī Nūrī Bahā'-Allāh, a Babi from a wealthy family connected with the Qajar court. Ḥosayn Nūrī's father, Mīrzā 'Abbās Nūrī, had held various government posts (see Bāmdād, *Rejāl* VI, pp. 126-29), and he was distantly related to the prime minister, Mīrzā Āqā Khan Nūrī (Balyuzi, *Bahā'u'llāh*, p. 13). Released on the intervention of the Russian Minister in January, 1853 (Zarandi, *Dawn-Breakers*, p. 636), he was instructed to leave the country and chose to go to Baghdad, accompanied by members of his family and other Babis. Before long, he was followed by his younger half-brother, Mīrzā Yaḥyā Ṣobḥ-e Azal, appointed by the Bāb his successor and regarded by most of the surviving Babis as their leader. During the next decade, Baghdad became firmly established as the main center of Babism, giving refuge to a small community of Iranian émigrés who sought to perpetuate the movement. There was considerable doctrinal confusion, in part due to the idiosyncratic teachings and legal prescriptions expounded by the Bāb in his later works, notably the Persian *Bayān*, in which he attempted to codify a religious system destined to supplant Islam, with himself as the latest in a line of divine revelators. The system propounded by the Bāb depended for its implementation on the establishment of a Babi state, which was now only a very remote possibility. There was, moreover, a lack of certainty over the question of leadership. Although the consensus seemed to favor the acceptance of Ṣobḥ-e Azal as head of the faith, he appears to have lacked the qualities of a good leader and to have adopted a retiring mode of life. The concept of theophanies, already apparent in the roles ascribed to Bāb al-Bāb, Qoddūs, and Qorrat-al-'Ayn, led to a succession of at least twenty-four claimants to supreme authority in the movement, few of whom obtained a substantial following. A growing section of the Baghdad community, however, was willing to grant a measure of authority to Ṣobḥ-e Azal's elder half-brother, Bahā'-Allāh, a more experienced man of much less retiring temperament with a leaning towards Sufism and political quietism. Sometime in the 1860s, he claimed the status of *man yoẓheroho'llāh* (he whom God shall make manifest), a messianic figure referred to frequently in the Persian *Bayān*. The ensuing quarrel between him and Ṣobḥ-e Azal resulted in the splitting of the movement into the Bahai and Azalī factions, with the majority belonging to the former. Azalī Babism has remained essentially conservative, basing its tenets on the works of the Bāb and Ṣobḥ-e Azal, whereas Bahaism represents a radical solution to the problem of continuing the Babi movement (see MacEoin, "From Babism to Baha'ism"). The harsher and less practical teachings of the *Bayān* are either abolished or toned down, immediate pressure to create a Babi theocracy is transformed into a future Bahai world state to be created through peaceful conversion and indefinitely postponable, and the Babi legal system is extensively modified to suit "modern" conditions.

Babism is of considerable interest for the light it sheds on a number of problems in the sociology of religion, notably that of charismatic breakthrough. We can observe a process whereby an initial development of traditional charismatic roles is rapidly intensified by a more radical breakthrough still expressed in terms of traditional motifs but involving a sharp move away from established religious modes, leading finally to a wholesale charismatic renewal in which the norms of the religious environment are replaced by a fresh set of doctrines and practices deriving their authority wholly from the charismatic authority of the prophet-figure. Within the overall spectrum from Shi'ism through Shaikhism and Babism to Bahaism, Berger ("Motif messianique") has delineated a process of messianic expectation—fulfillment—renewed expectation, which indicates the importance of Babism as a case study in millenarianism. Within the context of modern Shi'ism, Babism provides valuable evidence of extreme tendencies in the religious establishment of mid-13th/19th-century Iran. To see Babism as an aberration or side issue in Qajar Shi'ism (as does Algar, *Religion and State*, p. 151) is to ignore its original orthodoxy and the role within it of religious motifs central to the Shi'ite tradition. Careful retrospection will show not only that Babism came close to upsetting the balance of Qajar political life but that it owed its ability to shake the foundations of society so forcefully and in such a short period less to a chance concatenation of events and more to its character as a vital response to deep-rooted expectations and needs of the Iranian people of the time. Far from having been a maverick or aberrant outgrowth of post-Safavid Shiʿism, Babism—especially when its early, semiorthodox phase is taken fully into consideration—may be regarded not only as a highly typical expression of certain strands of Shiʿite thought, but as particularly relevant to the social and religious circumstances of many Iranians at the time of its inception. It may, indeed, be argued that many later developments within the orthodox establishment (including the wide rejection of reformism) were reactions against Babism and the dangers it showed to be inherent in an extreme insistence on charismatic authority, in a situation where the religious hierarchy was engaged in a process of intensifying such authority (see further MacEoin, "Changes in Charismatic Authority"). Although extremist movements in other parts of the Muslim world in the nineteenth century (Tejānīya, Sudanese Mahdīya, even the Aḥmadīya) represented serious departures from orthodox norms and involved considerable *bedʿa*, or innovation, only Babism and its offshoot Bahaism present us with the phenomenon of outright severance from Islam and an attempt to introduce a new religious synthesis.

Bibliography: The bibliography of Babism, both published and unpublished, is vast and uneven. The reader should refer to D. M. MacEoin, "Babism," in L. P. Elwell-Sutton, ed., *Bibliographical Guide to Iran*. The most recent studies of early Babism are D. M. MacEoin, *From Shaykhism to Babism: A Study in Charismatic Renewal in Shīʿī Islam*, Ph.D. thesis, Cambridge University, 1979 (University Microfilms 81-70,043); A. Amanat, *The Early Years of the Babi Movement: Background and Development*, Ph.D. thesis, Oxford University, 1981; idem, *Resurrection and the Renewal of the Age: The Emergence of the Babi Movement in Qajar Iran (1844-1852)* (forthcoming); P. Smith, *A Sociological Study of the Babi and Bahaʾi Religions*, Ph.D. thesis, Lancaster University, 1982; and idem, *The Babi and Baha'i Religions*, Cambridge, 1986. Of early European studies the best are those of E. G. Browne, notably "The Bábís of Persia. I. Sketch of Their History, and Personal Experiences among Them. II. Their Literature And Doctrines," *JRAS* 21, 1889, pp. 485-526, 881-1009; article "Bāb, Bābīs" in J. Hastings, ed., *Encyclopaedia of Religion and Ethics*, and his notes to *A Traveller's Narrative Written to Illustrate the Episode of the Báb* (by ʿAbbās Effendi), 2 vols., Cambridge, 1891; *Táríkh-i-Jadíd or New History of Mírzá ʿAlí Muḥammed the Báb* (by Mīrzā Ḥosayn Hamadānī), Cambridge, 1893; and the *Kitáb-i-Nuqṭatu'l-Káf* (attributed to Ḥājjī Mīrzā Jānī Kāšānī), London, 1910. His *Materials for the Study of the Bábí Religion*, Cambridge, 1918, deals mostly with Bahaism in its separate phase of development. The earliest Babi history is the above-mentioned *Noqṭat al-kāf*, written in the early 1850s; the *Tārīḵ-e jadīd* is a Bahai version of this work with numerous omissions and additions. The most detailed history is a hagiographic work written by Mollā Moḥammad Nabīl Zarandī between 1888 and 1890 and published only in an edited English translation by the Bahai leader Shoghi Effendi as *The Dawn-Breakers: Nabíl's Narrative of the Early Days of the Bahá'í Revelation*, Wilmette, Ill., 1932. All subsequent Bahai accounts follow this closely (e.g., H. M. Balyuzi, *The Báb*, Oxford, 1973, and M.-ʿA. Fayżī, *Ḥażrat-e noqṭa-ye ūlā*, Tehran, 1354 Š./1975-76). Less systematic but more useful is Mīrzā Asad-Allāh Fāżel Māzandarānī, *Ketāb-e ẓohūr al-ḥaqq* III, Cairo,.n.d. Details of the various upheavals, other than those in the general histories, may be found in M.-ʿA. Malek Ḵosravī, *Tārīḵ-e šohadā-ye amr*, 3 vols., Tehran, 1352 Š./1973-74, Moḥammad Šafīʿ Rūḥānī Neyrīzī, *Lamaʿāt al-anwār*, 2 vols., Tehran, 1352-53 Š./1973-74, 1354-55 Š./1975-76, M.-ʿA. Fayżī *Neyrīz-e moškbīz*, Tehran, 1351-52 Š./1972-73), ʿAbd-al-Aḥad Zanjānī, "Personal Reminiscences of the Bābī Insurrection at Zanjān in 1850," tr. E. G. Browne, *JRAS* 29, 1897, pp. 761-827, Sayyed Moḥammad Ḥosayn Zavāraʾī, *Waqāyeʿ-e mīmīya* and *Majles-e šahādat-e ḥażrat-e awwal man āmana Qāʾem Ḵorāsānī*, and Loṭf-ʿAlī Mīrzā Šīrāzī, untitled history of the Māzandarān struggle, Cambridge University Library, ms., Browne Or. F. 28 (items 1, 2, 3). A study of the uprisings from a Marxist point of view exists by Mikhail Ivanov: *Babidskie vosstaniya v Irane*, Leningrad, 1939. Sources are dealt with in D. M. MacEoin, *Early Babi Doctrine and History: A Survey of the Sources* (forthcoming). Important contemporary documents are published in M. Momen, ed., *The Bábí and Bahá'í Religions (1844-1944): Some Contemporary Western Accounts*, Oxford, 1981. See also P. L. Berger, *From Sect to Church: A Sociological Interpretation of the Baha'i Movement*, Ph.D. thesis, New School for Social Research, 1954. Specific topics are dealt with in the following articles: MacEoin, "The Bābī Concept of Holy War," *Religion* 12, 1982, pp. 93-129; idem "Early Shaykhí Reactions to the Báb and his Claims," in M. Momen, ed., *Studies in Bábí and Bahá'í History* I, Los Angeles, 1983, pp. 1-47; idem, "From Babism to Baha'ism," *Religion* 13, 1983, pp. 219-55; idem, "Changes in Charismatic Authority in Qajar Shiʿism," in E. Bosworth and C. Hillenbrand, eds., *Qajar Iran: Political and Cultural Change*, Edinburgh, 1983, pp. 148-76; idem, "Hierarchy, Authority and Eschatology in Early Bábí Thought," in P. Smith, ed., *In Iran: Studies in Bábí and Bahá'í History* III, Los Angeles, 1986, pp. 95-155; idem, "Baha'i Fundamentalism and the Academic Study of the Babi Religion," *Religion* 16, 1986, pp. 57-84; idem, "Ritual and Semi-Ritual Practices in Babism and Baha'ism," paper read to the Bahāʾī Studies Seminar 1980, University of Lancaster; M. Momen, "The Social Basis of the Bābī Upheavals in

Iran (1848-1853)," *IJMES* 15, 1983, pp. 157-83; idem, "The Trial of Mullā ʿAlī Basṭāmī: A Combined Sunnī-Shīʿī Fatwā against the Bāb," *Iran* 20, 1982, pp. 113-43; idem and P. Smith, "The Social Location of the Babi movement," in P. Smith, ed., *In Iran*; S. Lambden, "An Incident in the Childhood of the Bab," ibid.; P. L. Berger, "Motif messianique et processus social dans le Bahaisme," *Archives de sociologie des religions* 4, 1957, pp. 93-107; Mirza Aleksandr Kazem-Beg, "Bab et les Babis," *JA* 7, 1866, pp. 329-84, 457-522, 8, 1866, pp. 196-252, 357-400, 473-507; F. Kazemi, "Some Preliminary Observations on the Early Development of Babism," *Muslim World*, 1973, pp. 119-31. For a bibliography of scriptural and related materials, see BAYĀN.

(D. M. MACEOIN)

ii. BABI EXECUTIONS AND UPRISINGS

In the 1840s and 1850s a series of violent incidents involving members of the Babi sect (see BABISM) and Shiʿites took place in Iran, the most serious of which were four military encounters at Shaikh Ṭabarsī in Māzandarān, Zanjān, and Neyrīz (twice). At the inception of the Babi movement in 1260/1844, an uprising (*k̲orūj*) against unbelievers was keenly anticipated; it was at first believed that this event would begin in 1261/1845 in Karbalāʾ, when the Hidden Imam would appear to lead the *jehād* in person. The Bāb's earliest major work, the *Qayyūm al-asmāʾ*, contains detailed regulations governing the conduct of *jehād* (*Qayyūm al-asmāʾ*, *sūra*s 96-101; see MacEoin, "Holy War," pp. 101-09). Up to 1264/1848, the sect's *jehād* doctrine was essentially that of orthodox Shiʿism, but after that date, with the Bāb's assumption of the role of Mahdī, a new legal system was promulgated in the Persian *Bayān* (q.v.) and other works. It appears that the entire Shiʿite population of Iran was now regarded as subject to *jehād*: non-Babis were to be forbidden to live in any of the five central provinces of Fārs, Iraq, Azerbaijan, Khorasan, and Māzandarān. More broadly, Babi law called for the destruction of the shrines and holy places of previous religions and, as one later Bahai source puts it, "the universal slaughter of all save those who believed and were faithful" (ʿAbbās Effendi, *Makātīb ʿAbd-al-Bahāʾ* II, Cairo, 1330/1912, p. 266).

From 1844 to 1848, tension between Babis and the rest of the population increased rapidly through several key incidents: the arrest and trial in Baghdad of the Bāb's emissary, Mollā ʿAlī Besṭāmī (q.v.) in 1260/1844-45; the arrest and punishment of three Babis in Shiraz in 1261/1845; the arrest of the Bāb on his return from the *ḥajj* in the same year; several challenges to *mobāhala* (mutual imprecation) issued by the Bāb and his followers to *ʿolamāʾ* in Iraq and Iran in 1262/1846 and 1263/1847; attacks on individual Babis in Hamadān, Qazvīn, Karbalāʾ, and Kermānšāh during the same period; and attacks on Babi merchants and *ʿolamāʾ* in Qazvīn in 1263/1847, leading to the assassination by three Babis of Mollā Moḥammad-Taqī Baraḡānī (q.v.) in October of that year. (For details of these incidents, see MacEoin, "Holy War," pp. 109-12).

Several sources indicate that Babis in different centers were collecting and manufacturing arms in readiness for the postponed *k̲orūj* on the imam's appearance (ibid., pp. 111-12; Māzandarānī, *Ẓohūr al-ḥaqq*, p. 374). The first serious incidents occurred in 1264/1848 in Mašhad, where armed members of the large Babi community clashed on two occasions with local soldiery. Expelled from Mašhad in Šaʿbān, 1264/July, 1848, a party of Babis under the leadership of Mollā Moḥammad-Ḥosayn Bošrūʾī (q.v.) headed into Māzandarān and in October of that year established themselves near Bārforūš at the shrine of Shaikh Abū ʿAlī al-Fażl Ṭabarsī, which they fortified. From an original total of about 300, the number of insurgents rose to between 540 and 600 (Momen, "Social Basis," pp. 161-65, esp. table 4). Leadership of the fort was in the hands of Bošrūʾī and another of the Bāb's original disciples, Mollā Moḥammad-ʿAlī Bārforūšī Qoddūs (q.v.). Between 14 D̲u'l-qaʿda 1264/13 October 1848 and 16 Jomādā II 1265/9 May 1849, the Babi defenders and state troops under the overall command of Mahdīqolī Mīrzā engaged in sporadic fighting, with heavy losses of life on both sides. The siege was finally ended by a ruse and the surviving Babis either executed or taken prisoner.

Following disturbances in Yazd, a prominent Babi *ʿālem* (scholar) named Sayyed Yaḥyā Dārābī Waḥīd (q.v.) moved to Neyrīz in Rajab, 1266/May, 1850; on his arrival he preached to large crowds and soon converted (or at least gained the support of) a sizeable part of the population of the Čenārsūk̲ta quarter. Existing tensions between the populace and the governor, Zayn-al-ʿĀbedīn Khan, seem to have been reformulated and exacerbated by Dārābī, who was regarded by his followers as an independent authority in the town. Fighting soon broke out, whereupon around 1,000 Babis occupied the fort of K̲ᵛāja outside Neyrīz, where they were besieged by troops sent by Fīrūz Mīrzā Noṣrat-al-Dawla (q.v.), the governor of Fārs. Hostilities continued until the capture of the fort by treachery in Šaʿbān/June; about 500 Babis were killed during the fighting and in the executions that followed.

The Zanjān episode of 1266-67/1850-51 was the most protracted and involved the largest numbers, with the town almost equally divided between the Babis and their opponents. The former, numbering over 2,000, were led by Mollā Moḥammad-ʿAlī Zanjānī Ḥojjat-al-Eslām (q.v.), a former Ak̲bārī *ʿālem* who had already been the center of religious controversy before his conversion and who seems to have advocated radical social changes. In the course of heavy fighting between the Babis and several contingents of state troops, from 1000 to 1800 Babis lost their lives and parts of the town were badly damaged.

Following the assassination by Babis of the governor of Neyrīz Ḥājī Zayn-al-ʿAbedīn Khan, early in 1269/1853, fighting continued for several months in the mountains outside the town, resulting in the deaths of some 350 Babis.

In addition to these outbreaks of large-scale violence, other incidents involving Babis occurred between 1850 and 1853: on 19 or 20 February 1850, seven Babis of relatively high social status were executed in Tehran; on 27 or 28 Šaʿbān 1266/8 or 9 July 1850, the Bāb himself was publicly shot with one companion in Tabrīz; in Ḏu'l-qaʿda, 1268/August-September, 1852, some 37 Babis, including leading figures such as Qorrat-al-ʿAyn Ṭāhera (q.v.), Mollā Shaikh ʿAlī Toršīzī, and Sayyed Ḥosayn Yazdī were executed in reprisal for the Babi attempt on the life of Nāṣer-al-Dīn Shah on 28, Šawwāl/15, August; at the same period, there were further attacks on Babis in Mīlān near Tabrīz, Tākor in Māzandarān, Yazd, Neyrīz, and possibly elsewhere.

In all, something like 3000 Babis died in these episodes, or, if we take the lower figure of 1000 deaths at Zanjān, just over 2000 in all. Later estimates of 20,000 and more found in some Bahai works do not, in fact, correspond to the more detailed figures given in Bahai historical sources. Similarly, the very high figures for both participants and casualties given in state chronicles like the *Nāsek̲ al-tawārīk̲* are manifestly exaggerated, probably in order to explain away the failure of the government forces to put down the disturbances rapidly.

It is impossible to identify a consistent pattern in these events. Ivanov's (1939) Marxist analysis shows serious limitations in its treatment of motives and its portrayal of the Babi participants in the struggles as "peasants, artisans, urban poor, and small tradespeople." More recent studies by Momen (1983), Smith (1982), and MacEoin (1982) reveal a more complex interplay of social, political, and religious factors at work. The Shaikh Ṭabarsī siege was the most markedly religious of the larger incidents, while the Zanjān and Neyrīz uprisings were more closely linked to local politics. It is arguable that, whereas those involved in the Shaikh Ṭabarsī struggle and in the smaller pogroms were convinced Babis, many of those who participated in the fighting at Zanjān, Yazd, or Neyrīz may have been vague about or indifferent to the specific religious issues propounded by the Babi leadership. At Shaikh Ṭabarsī, messianic ambitions were linked to a belief that, through martyrdom, the defenders were re-enacting the events of Karbalā'; the Qajar state and its forces were condemned as illegitimate and a defensive *jehād* proclaimed against them. At Zanjān, religious millenarianism was less marked, while puritan and egalitarian ideals were clearly in evidence.

Smallness of numbers, a limited social base, lack of a centralized or coordinated leadership, the absence of an agreed policy, and conflicts of motive all combined to rob the Babi uprisings of any potential they might otherwise have had of acting as catalysts for a broader movement for social, religious, or political change. Conversely, the military defeat of Babism all but stopped it in its tracks and forced the surviving leaders to reinterpret the religion and restate its goals, leading to the eventual emergence of Azalī Babism (q.v.) and Bahaism (q.v.). In the latter case, rejection of Babi militancy and the adoption of a pacifist orientation resulted initially in an emphasis on the absolute distinctiveness of the two movements; but as later doctrinal developments demanded increasing conflation of Babism and Bahaism, the Babi uprisings themselves were reinterpreted as defensive reactions to persecution by church and state (see, in particular, MacEoin, "From Babism to Baha'ism").

Bibliography: Accounts of specific incidents: Mollā Moḥammad Nabīl Zarandī, *The Dawn-Breakers*, ed. and tr. Shoghi Effendi, New York, 1932, chaps. 19-24, 26. Mīrzā Moḥammad-Taqī Lesān-al-Molk Sepehr, *Nāsek̲ al-tawārīk̲: Salāṭīn-e Qājārīya*, 4 vols. in 2, Tehran, 1385/1965-66, III, pp. 233-63, 285-97, 302-07, 337-42; IV, pp. 30-42, 72-73. Reżā Khan Lalabāšī, *Rawżat al-ṣafā-ye nāṣerī*, vols. 8-10, Tehran, 1274/1857; X, pp. 118, 121-33, 167-70. Joseph Arthur Comte de Gobineau, *Religions et philosophies dans l'Asie centrale*, 10th ed., Paris, 1957, chaps. 7-11. A. L. M. Nicolas, *Séyyèd Ali Mohemmed dit le Bâb*, Paris, 1905, chaps. 5-7, 9-12. Moḥammad-ʿAlī Malek K̲osravī, *Tārīk̲-e šohadā-ye amr*, 3 vols., Tehran, 130 B. (*Badīʿ*)/1973-74, I-II; III, pp. 39-334. ʿAlīqolī Mīrzā Eʿteżād-al-Salṭana, *Ketāb al-motanabbīyūn*, section published as *Fetna-ye Bāb*, ed. ʿAbd-al-Ḥosayn Navā'ī, 2nd ed., Tehran, 1351 Š./1972-73, pp. 33-106. M. Momen, *The Bábí and Bahá'í Religions, 1844-1944: Some Contemporary Western Accounts*, Oxford, 1981, chaps. 1-8. Shoghi Effendi, *God Passes By*, Wilmette, 1944, chaps. 3-5. Mīrzā Ḥosayn Hamadānī, *Tārīk̲-e jadīd*, tr. E. G. Browne, *The New History of Mírzá ʿAlí Muḥammed, the Báb*, Cambridge, 1893, pp. 44-110, 111-35, 135-68, 250-67, 293-312. Ḥājī Mīrzā Jānī Kāšānī, *Ketāb-e noqṭat al-kāf*, ed. E. G. Browne, London and Leiden, 1910, pp. 154-204, 215-23, 223-29, 230-38, 245-52. (ʿAbbās Effendi ʿAbd-al-Bahā'), *A Traveller's Narrative Written to Illustrate the Episode of the Bāb*, ed. and tr. E. G. Browne, 2 vols., Cambridge, 1891, I, pp. 211-18, 253-61, 306-09, 323-34. Mirza (Aleksandr) Kazem Beg, "Bab et les Babis," *Journal asiatique*, 6th ser., 7, 1866, pp. 457-522, 8, pp. 196-252 (cf. also idem, *Bab i Babidy i religiozno-politicheskaya smuty v Persii v 1844-1852 gg.*, St. Petersburg, 1865). ʿAbd-al-Ḥosayn Āvāra, *al-Kawākeb al-dorrīya*, 2 vols., Cairo, 1342/1924, I, chaps. 2-4. Moḥammad-Šafīʿ Rūḥānī Neyrīzī, *Lamaʿāt al-anwār* I, Tehran, 130 B./1973-74. Moḥammad-ʿAlī Fayżī, *Neyrīz-e moškbīz*, Tehran, 129 B./1972-73. ʿAbd-al-Aḥad Zanjānī, "Personal Reminiscences of the Bábí Insurrection at Zanján in 1850," tr. E. G. Browne, *JRAS* 29, 1897, pp. 761-827.

Broader analyses: M. S. Ivanov, *Babidskie vosstaniya v Irane (1848-1852)*, Moscow, 1939. M. Momen, "The Social Basis of the Bābī Upheavals in Iran (1848-53): A Preliminary Analysis," *IJMES* 15, 1983, pp. 157-83. Idem, "Some Problems Connected with the Yazd Episode of 1850," paper read to 3rd Bahai Studies Seminar, Lancaster University, 1977. D. M. MacEoin, "The Bābī Concept of Holy War,"

Religion 12, 1982, pp. 93-129. Idem, "From Babism to Baha'ism: Problems of Militancy, Quietism, and Conflation in the Construction of a Religion," *Religion* 13, 1983, pp. 219-55 (esp. pp. 236-37). Idem, "Bahāʾī Fundamentalism and the Academic Study of the Bābī Movement," *Religion* 16, 1986, pp. 57-84. Idem, "A Note on the Numbers of Babi and Baha'i Martyrs in Iran," *Baha'i Studies Bulletin* 2/2, 1983, pp. 84-88. M. Afnan and W. S. Hatcher, "Western Islamic Scholarship and Bahāʾī Origins," *Religion* 15, 1985, pp. 29-51. P. Smith, *A Sociological Study of the Babi and Baha'i Religions*, Ph.D. dissertation, University of Lancaster, 1982, chap. 5. Idem, "Millenialism in the Babi and Baha'i Religions," in R. Wallis, ed., *Millenialism and Charisma*, Belfast, 1982, pp. 231-83. Mangol Bayat, *Mysticism and Dissent: Socioreligious Thought in Qajar Iran*, Syracuse, 1982, chap. 4, esp. pp. 118-26.

For details of histories of Shaikh Ṭabarsī found in manuscripts, Neyrīz, Zanjān, and other incidents, see D. M. MacEoin, *Early Babi Doctrine and History: A Survey of Source Materials* (forthcoming).

(D. M. MacEoin)

BĀBŌĒ, catholicos (d. 481 or 484), orthodox leader of the Christian church in Iran under Pērōz, one of Barṣaumā's (q.v.) chief opponents. The rule of Catholicos Bābōē fell during an epoch seething with powerful forces which were working towards a complete reshaping of Christianity in Persia. He was the last head of the church who withstood the tremendous pressures which would mold the later history of Christianity in Persia.

Bābōē of Tellā at Ṣerṣer was a Mazda-believer who was converted to the Christian faith by a monk. He was elected catholicos for the see in Seleucia-Ctesiphon some time between 456 and 466. When the persecution of Christians broke out under Pērōz, he was imprisoned and was not released until peace was made between the king of the Persians and the Roman emperor (464). According to some sources his imprisonment lasted for two years; other sources indicate it lasted seven years.

More troubles awaited him after his release. Seleucia-Ctesiphon was no longer the spiritual center of the church, but Nisibis in the north where the Persian School, which had returned from Edessa, had taken its place. And since no other theological school could compete with the one in Nisibis, where the Nestorian theology and the Antiochian traditions were being cultivated, this hearth of spiritual culture was destined to shape the theological life and thought of the church. A number of teachers expelled from Edessa obtained episcopal sees in Persia. Among these was Barṣaumā, who became the most energetic agitator for the theological tenets of the School of Nisibis and worked relentlessly for the dissemination of Nestorianism, causing headaches for the catholicos and the bishops who rallied around him.

Moreover, the time had come when the church could not remain content with the ancient canons for its life. Thus, besides the propagation of the Nestorian tenets, Barṣaumā pursued other aims destined towards a reorientation of the basic ideals and inner tenets of Christian life, and a transformation of the inner countenance of the Persian church. The earliest form of Christianity in these areas had rested on the vigor of the spiritual elite of the ascetics, drawing its strength from these sources who had originated in Mesopotamia even before monasticism appeared in Egypt. These ascetic tenets stood in opposition to the Zoroastrian tenets of the Sasanian society, where marriage and richness of children were seen as religious obligations. In his pursuit of a reversal of the ancient tenets and anti-ascetic ideals, Barṣaumā could count on the power of the state and of Pērōz himself coming to his support.

Bābōē with his fondness for monasticism resisted also on this front. (A writing on monasticism, written to a priest Qyriaqos, is attributed to him. See also *Acta martyrum*, p. 633 for his relations to monasticism.) But in spite of his resistance, changes took place. Bābōē faced forces, too strong to fight against, aiming at the isolation of the Persian church from the west. At a schismatic synod under the direction of Barṣaumā, held in April, 484, at Bēt Lāpaṭ, the capital of Susiana—an important but always restless ecclesiastical province—the Nestorian creed was adopted. Bābōē's attempts to check its progress through a countersynod were in vain and further attempts ended in tragedy: Bābōē sent a letter to Emperor Zenon in order to arouse his interest in the plight of the church in Persia—this must be understood as a request for help in behalf of endangered orthodoxy. The letter was intercepted in Nisibis and handed over to Pērōz. The sources blame Barṣaumā, probably rightly so, for having had a hand in this affair. Pērōz threw Bābōē into prison, and after an imprisonment of two years, Bābōē was beaten to death in the twenty-fourth year of Pērōz, i.e., 484, but in 481 according to ʿAmr b. Mattā. A vivid account of the end of his life is found in *Acta martyrum* (pp. 631f.). His death removed the last obstacle to the realization of Barṣaumā's aspirations.

Bibliography: P. Bedjan, *Acta martyrum et sanctorum*, Paris, 1890, II, pp. 631ff. J. A. Baumstark, *Geschichte der syrischen Literatur*, Bonn, 1922, pp. 107f. J. Labourt, *Le christianisme dans l'empire perse sous la dynastie sassanide*, Paris, 1904, pp. 129, 141ff. A. Vööbus, *History of Asceticism in the Syrian Orient*, Louvain, 1958, I, pp. 120, 297, 323f.

(A. Vööbus)

BĀBOL, town in Māzanderān, formerly Bārforūš.

i. *The town.*

ii. *Islamic monuments.*

i. The Town

Bābol lies near the Bābol river, occupying a central position in the coastal plain. It was at first a small, local market-place, as indicated by the name Bārforūš (lit. [place where] loads are sold) which it bore until 1927. The settlement developed in early Safavid times on the site of the old town of Māmṭīr, and was favored by Shah ʿAbbās who built a garden there, Bāḡ-e Šāh or Bāḡ-e Eram. It nevertheless remained little more than a village till the beginning of the Qajar period. Pietro della Valle, writing in 1627, mentions it only as a village. Its growth began in the eighteenth century as a result of population increase in the Caspian plain and gained strength, particularly in the late eighteenth and early nineteenth centuries, from the rise of Russian trade with the Caspian coastlands (by the late nineteenth century Russia had a resident commercial consul there). In 1822 J. B. Fraser found Bārforūš very active and comparable in size to Isfahan, with a population which he estimated at 70,000. Thanks to its centrality on the plain and, above all, to its accessibility from the sea (the Bābol river being navigable by small craft), Bārforūš grew rapidly in the nineteenth century, thus becoming the chief commercial center of Māzandarān, exporting rice, cotton, silk, and timber, importing factory-made goods, and acting as the hub of modernization in the province. For several short spells it was also the seat of the provincial administration. After a sharp drop in the 1830s due to plague, the population recovered to 30-40,000 in the rest of the nineteenth century and the first quarter of the twentieth century, making it Māzandarān's biggest town in that period. Its links with the outside world may perhaps explain why the population at the start of the twentieth century included a relatively large number of Bahais and approximately 750 Jews.

During the Pahlavi period the town, renamed Bābol, grew much more slowly than the other towns in the region. It did not lie on the Trans-Iranian railroad, did not benefit much from Reżā Shah's promotion of modern industries, and had gradually lost its role in long-distance trade. Since then its commercial radius has been limited to the regional market. It was still the biggest town in the eastern part of the Caspian lowland at the time of the 1956 census, when it had 36,000 inhabitants, but in 1976 it was surpassed by Gorgān, Sārī, and Āmol, and ten years later probably also by Šāhī (new Qāʾemšahr). The censuses show that Bābol's population grew from 49,973 in 1966 to 69,790 in 1976, i.e., at an annual rate of 3.1 percent which barely exceeded the natural demographic increase; also that the proportion of its inhabitants born in other provinces was the smallest of any town of the Caspian region. This relative stagnation might have been remedied if the revolution of 1979 had not put an end to the project for a university of Māzandarān at Bābol. The town has kept a traditional appearance, particularly evident in the bazaar with its many intact warehouses (*ḵāns*) of the Qajar period and fine vaulted section not to be found elsewhere in the region.

Bibliography: G. N. Curzon, *Persia and the Persian Question* I, London, 1892, pp. 379-81. E. G. Browne, *Material for the Study of the Bábí Religion,* Cambridge, 1918, pp. 199, 208-11, 238-39, 241-43. H. L. Rabino, *Mázandarán and Astarábád*, London, 1945, pp. 151, 512-13. Razmārā, *Farhang* III, pp. 36-38. H. Kopp, *Städte im östlichen iranischen Kaspitiefland. Ein Beitrag zur Kenntnis der jüngeren Entwicklung orientalischer Mittel- und Kleinstädte*, Erlanger geographische Arbeiten 33, Mitt. d. Frankischen geographischen Ges. 20, 1973, Erlangen, 1973, pp. 33-197. L. Adamec, *Historical Gazetteer of Iran* I: *Tehran and Northwest Iran*, Graz, 1976, pp. 76-77, 91-92.

(X. DE PLANHOL)

ii. ISLAMIC MONUMENTS

Once the largest town in Māzandarān, Bābol was undoubtedly the site of numerous monuments. In the early seventh/thirteenth century, for example, the geographer Yāqūt (IV, p. 642) mentioned its congregational mosque and the historian Ebn Esfandīār reported visiting the tomb of Ḥasan b. Mahdī Māmṭīrī (p. 125; tr. E. G. Browne, *History of Ṭabaristān*, GMS 2, London, 1905, p. 76). At the beginning of this century, H. L. Rabino counted 63 quarters, 26 mosques, 8 *madrasas*, 31 *takīas* used during religious ceremonies in Moḥarram, 10 shrines, 3 graves of venerated darvishes, 31 caravanserais for merchants and 13 for caravans, 36 baths, many elementary schools, and 1,471 shops (*Mázandarán and Astarábád*, GMS, N.S., 7, London, 1928, p. 45 and n. 69). In addition, a royal garden lay outside the town to the southwest.

Yet today only two small ninth/fifteenth-century *emāmzādas* are classified as historical monuments and attest to this past: one to the east of the town, four kilometers from Šāhī (illustrated in D. Wilber, "Survey of Persian Architecture," *Bulletin of the American Institute for Iranian Art and Archeology* 5, 1937, figs. 6-7, and A. Hutt and L. Harrow, *Iran* II, London, 1978, pl. 101, p. 125) and the other in the town itself (Iranian National Monuments 67 and 342 respectively). Both are brick octagonal towers surmounted by pyramidal roofs and connected to rear rectangular prayer halls. The inscription on the cenotaph in the first states that it is the grave (*mašhad*) of Solṭān Moḥammed-Ṭāher b. Mūsā Kāẓem, that it was founded by the amir Mortażā Ḥosaynī who also provided the cenotaph (*ṣandūq*), and that the architect (*meʿmār*) was the master (*ostād*) Šams-al-Dīn b. Naṣr-Allāh Moṭahharī in 875/1470-71 (Pers. text in Rabino, pp. 18-19). The tomb tower's door is also dated 896/1490-91. The second mausoleum contains two cenotaphs, the main one dated 888/1483-84 and signed by the master Aḥmad, the carpenter from Sārī (*najjār al-Sāravī*).

Both of these buildings are typical of tomb towers in Māzandarān. The earliest Islamic examples dating from the Bavandid dynasty in the early fifth/eleventh century (Rādakān, Lājīm, and Resket) are round with *moqarnas* cornices underneath conical roofs (A. Godard, "Les tours de Ladjim et de Resget," *Aṯār-é Īrān* 1, 1936, pp. 109-24). Their Pahlavi inscriptions and decorative *moqarnas* suggest the maintenance of an earlier tradition. Later ninth/fifteenth-century examples are usually polygonal, with a composite cornice including a blind arcade, and some (like the two at Bābol) have rectangular prayer halls in the back (*Survey of Persian Art*, pp. 1163-64). The tradition continued until the eleventh/seventeenth century, but the ninth/fifteenth-century group, including the two at Bābol is noteworthy for its finely carved wooden doors and cenotaphs: Rabino mentioned sixteen in situ examples dating from 781/1379-80 to 906/1500-01 (passim, listed in L. Bronstein, "Decorative Woodwork of the Islamic Period," in *Survey of Persian Art*, pp. 2622-23; many more are published in M. Ḏabīḥī and M. Sotūda, *Az Āstārā tā Astārābād*, 7 vols., Tehran, 1349-54 Š./1970-75); similar fragments are found in museums in Iran, Europe, and America. These simple small towers are totally distinct from contemporary Timurid architecture in Khorasan and Transoxania with its sophisticated vaultings and spaces, bulbous domes, and glittering tile and stucco revetment. Rather, they bear witness to the relative isolation of Māzandarān and the importance of a local architectural tradition.

Bibliography: See also N. Meškātī, *Fehrest-e banāhā-ye tārīḵī o amāken-e bāstānī-e Īrān*, Tehran, 1349 Š./1970, pp. 181-82; Eng. tr. H. A. S. Pessyan, *A List of the Historical Sites and Ancient Monuments of Iran*, Tehran, 1353 Š./1974, pp. 169-70.

(S. BLAIR)

BĀBOLSAR, town on the Caspian coast in the province of Māzandarān. It acquired its present name in 1306 Š./1927, at the same time that Bārforūš, the important inland town 20 km to the south-southeast, was renamed Bābol. Its former name was Mašhad-(e) Sar. Initially a village arose at this site around the shrine of an *emāmzāda*, Ebrāhīm Abū Jawāb, which contains several inscriptions from the 9th/15th century. From the mid-18th century onward, Mašhad-e Sar became a busy commercial port, thanks to its position near the mouth of the small Bābol river and access by boat to Bārforūš (to which the river was brought nearer by a short westward diversion ca. 1850). We also know from Hanway's account that Mašhad-e Sar was the base for Nāder Shah's Caspian fleet. Its commercial importance culminated in the early years of the twentieth century. In 1909 its customs post, together with the subsidiary posts at smaller ports in Māzandarān, yielded 12 percent of the total customs revenue of Iran (H. Grothe, *Zur Natur und Wirtschaft von Vorderasien* I: *Persien*, Frankfurt, 1911, p. 115). This activity, however, was already exposed to competition from ports in Gīlān which had been connected to Tehran by a good road since 1895.

In Reżā Shah's reign, Bābolsar lost much of its remaining trade to the new port of Bandar-e Šāh at the terminus of the trans-Iranian railroad. The cargo handled at Bābolsar in 1314 Š./1935-36 was only 25,000 tons. On the other hand, a modern quarter and a big hotel were built at that time.

After World War II, Bābolsar gained a new vitality as a seaside resort (in the summer months) for people from Tehran. The tourism business gave rise to a new phase of rapid expansion. Bābolsar's population increased from about 3,500 in 1324 Š./1945 to 11,781 in 1345 Š./1966 and 18,810 in 1355 Š./1976.

Bibliography: J. Hanway, *An Historical Account of the British Trade over the Caspian Sea...*, 2 vols., Dublin, 1754 (journey in 1744), I, pp. 124, 178-79, 276-77. H. L. Rabino, "Report for the Year 1910-1911 on the Trade and General Condition of the City of Barfurush and the Province of Mazandaran," *Diplomatic and Consular Reports, Annual Series, Persia*, no. 4812, London, 1912, pp. 4-6. Idem, *Mázandarán and Astarábád*, London, 1928, pp. 46-48. Naval Intelligence Division, Geographical Handbook Series, *Persia*, London, 1945, pp. 512-13. P. Sommerville-Large, *Caviar Coast*, London, 1968, pp. 100-03. H. Kopp, *Städte im östlichen iranischen Kaspitiefland. Ein Beitrag zur Kenntnis der jüngeren Entwicklung orientalischer Mittel- und Kleinstädte*, Erlanger Geographische Arbeiten 33 = Mitteilungen der Fränkischen Geographischen Gesellschaft 20, 1973 (pp. 33-197), Erlangen, 1973, pp. 46-47.

(X. DE PLANHOL)

BĀBOR, ABU'L-QĀSEM MĪRZĀ B. BĀYSONQOR B. ŠĀHROḴ, Timurid prince (b. 825/1422), the youngest son of Bāysonqor, the eminent Timurid bibliophile and artistic patron, and a great-grandson of the conqueror Tīmūr. His mother was a concubine of Bāysonqor's by the name of Gowhar-nasab (*Moʿezz al-ansāb*, fol. 145b). According to Ḵᵛāndamīr, during the reign of his grandfather, Šāhroḵ, Bābor was not held in as high esteem as were his two older half-brothers, ʿAlāʾ-al-Dawla (q.v.) and Solṭān Moḥammad, and he had to content himself with living on the stipend assigned to him. In the struggle for power that ensued in Khorasan after Šāhroḵ's death in 850/1447, Bābor managed at first to have himself recognized as ruler of Māzandarān by Amīr Hendūka, who had been wintering in Jorjān on Šāhroḵ's orders. After an abortive battle with his elder half-brother, ʿAlāʾ-al-Dawla, who was holding Herat, the two agreed on Ḵabūšān (Qūčān) as the boundary between their respective kingdoms (*Ḥabīb al-sīar* IV, pp. 22-23).

After Šāhroḵ's son and legitimate heir, Uluḡ Beg, who had remained in Transoxiana but who was also vying for control of Khorasan, defeated ʿAlāʾ-al-Dawla at Tarnāb near Herat in 852/1448, the latter fled to Bābor, now established in Astarābād (ibid., p. 20). Bābor advanced into Khorasan against Uluḡ Beg and his son, ʿAbd-al-Laṭīf Mīrzā, by this time at odds with each other, and defeated Uluḡ who had left Herat for Transoxiana to try to counter the Uzbek threat to his Transoxanian possessions. Bābor captured Herat at the end of the month of Ḏu'l-ḥejja, 852/February, 1449, from the Qara Qoyunlū Turkmen chief, Yār-ʿAlī, who had been ruling there for only about twenty days. The conquest of Herat established Bābor on the throne of

Khorasan and he was now able to strike his own coinage and have his name mentioned in the Friday sermon (ibid., p. 30).

After the death of Ulug̱ Beg in 853/1449, Bābor's second brother, Solṭān Moḥammad, who was ruler of ʿErāq-e ʿAjam and Fārs, wrested Herat from Bābor after winning a battle against him at Jām (*Ketāb-e Dīārbakrīya* II, pp. 319-22). Bābor was forced to return to Astarābād, his former residence, where he soon welcomed many deserters from Solṭān Moḥammad's Herat which was experiencing not only a terrible famine that winter, but also the tyrannical exactions of one of Solṭān Moḥammad's amirs. Shortly thereafter, Solṭān Moḥammad was in turn defeated by Bābor and retreated to Iraq. In the meantime, ʿAlāʾ-al-Dawla had set himself up as ruler of Herat in 854/1450 (*Maṭlaʿ-e saʿdayn*, p. 1001). However, upon hearing that Bābor was returning to the city, he fled to Balḵ and Herat again passed to Bābor (*Ḥabīb al-sīar* IV, pp. 40-42). In 855/1451, at Čenārān, Bābor again defeated Solṭan Moḥammad who had made yet another attempt to take Khorasan from him, and after taking him prisoner, had him killed and his body sent to Herat to be buried next to that of their father, Bāysonqor (ibid., pp. 45-46; *Ketāb-e Dīārbakrīya* II, p. 325). Bābor then ordered that ʿAlāʾ-al-Dawla be blinded, but the operation was performed in such a way that his eyesight remained unimpaired (*Ḥabīb al-sīar* IV, p. 20).

As a consequence of his victory at Čenārān, Bābor came into possession of the provinces of ʿErāq-e ʿAjam and Fārs. But later that same year, ʿAlāʾ-al-Dawla rebelled in Khorasan and Bābor also had to contend with the Qara Qoyunlū Turkmen ruler, Jahānšāh, who had captured some of his Iraqi possessions. He succeeded in repulsing his brother who now fled from Khorasan and joined the Qara Qoyunlū court (ibid., p. 48). But he was unable to hold his own against Jahānšāh and his son, Pīr Bodāq, who in a short time captured all of ʿErāq-e ʿAjam and Fārs (*Maṭlaʿ-e saʿdayn*, pp. 1044-45). Bābor now tried to extend his power into Transoxiana where he had to face his formidable Mīrānšāhī cousin, Abū Saʿīd, from whom he tried unsuccessfully to capture Samarqand in Šawwāl, 858/October, 1454 (ibid., p. 1061). At the beginning of 859/1454, Bābor reconquered Sīstān from a rebellious vassal, Shah Ḥosayn, and also put down an insurrection in the fortress of ʿEmād (*Ḥabīb al-sīar* IV, pp. 53-55). After recovering from a serious illness at the beginning of 860/1455, he decided to make a pilgrimage to Mašhad where he arrived in the month of Ḏuʾl-qaʿda, 860/October, 1456. After spending the winter there, he died, probably of poisoning, in early spring on 25 Rabīʿ II 861/22 March 1457. He was buried in Mašhad near the tomb of Imam ʿAlī al-Reżā (ibid., p. 57).

Bābor was the first patron of the later Timurid sultan, Ḥosayn Bāyqarā (842-911/1438-1506), who entered his service in Herat at the age of fourteen and was joined there by his foster brother, ʿAlī-Šīr Navāʾī, whose father, according to Dawlatšāh, had occupied a high position in Bābor's government (ed. Browne, pp. 495-96).

Bābor is mentioned by Ḵᵛāndamīr as being a humble and unassuming person with a pleasant disposition (*Ḥabīb al-sīar* IV, p. 22). Like all of his Timurid relations, he was a cultivated prince and wrote poetry under the pen-name Bābor. Faḵrī Heravī, who calls him Bābor Qalandar, speaks of him as being inclined toward Sufism and as having studied the classical Sufi texts. He quotes a *robāʿī* of his on the subject of Sufism as well as a *g̱azal* he says was famous (*Rawżat al-salāṭīn*, pp. 34-35). In his memoirs, Ẓahīr-al-Dīn Moḥammad Bābor describes the pleasure house (*ṭarab-ḵāna*) he had built in Herat during his rule there (*Bābor-nāma*, fols. 188b-189).

Bibliography: Primary sources: Anonymous, *Moʿezz al-ansāb*, MS Bibliothèque Nationale, Paris, ancien fonds, persan, 467. Ẓahīr-al-Dīn Moḥammad Bābor, *Bābor-nāma*, ed. A. S. Beveridge, Leiden, 1905, fols. 188b-189. Solṭān Moḥammad Faḵrī Heravī, *Rawżat al-salāṭīn*, ed. ʿA. Ḵayyāmpūr, Tabrīz, 1345 Š./1966, pp. 34-35. Sām Mīrzā Ṣafawī, *Toḥfa-ye sāmī*, ed. W. Dastgerdī, Tehran, 1314 Š./1935, p. 179. ʿAbd-al-Razzāq Samarqandī, *Maṭlaʿ-e saʿdayn*, ed. M. Šafīʿ, 2 vols., continuous pagination (=*jeld* II, *jozʾ* 1-3), Lahore, 1360-65/1941-46. Abū Bakr Ṭehrānī, *Ketāb-e Dīārbakrīya*, ed. N. Lugal and F. Sümer, 2 vols., Ankara, 1962-64, II, pp. 316-27. Secondary sources: V. V. Bartol'd, *Sochineniya* II/2, Moscow, 1964, pp. 149-56, 214-18; Eng. tr. V. V. Barthold, *Four Studies on the History of Central Asia*, tr. V. and T. Minorsky, II, Leiden, 1958, pp. 146-55; III, Leiden, 1962, pp. 17-21, O. D. Chekhovich, "Oborona Samarkanda v 1454 godu," *Izvestiya Akademii nauk UzSSR*, 1960, no. 4, pp. 36-44. Ḵayyāmpūr, *Soḵanvarān*, pp. 73-74. R. M. Savory, "The Struggle for Supremacy in Persia after the Death of Tīmūr," *Der Islam* 40, 1964, pp. 44-47.

(M. E. Subtelny)

BĀBOR, ẒAHĪR-AL-DĪN MOḤAMMAD (6 Moḥarram 886–6 Jomādā I 937/14 February 1483–26 December 1530), Timurid prince, military genius, and literary craftsman who escaped the bloody political arena of his Central Asian birthplace to found the Mughal Empire in India. His origin, milieu, training, and education were steeped in Persian culture and so Bābor was largely responsible for the fostering of this culture by his descendants, the Mughals of India, and for the expansion of Persian cultural influence in the Indian subcontinent, with brilliant literary, artistic, and historiographical results.

Bābor's father, ʿOmar Šayḵ Mīrzā (d. 899/1494), ruled the kingdom of Fargāna along the headwaters of the Syr Darya, but as one of four brothers, direct fifth-generation descendants from the great Tīmūr, he entertained larger ambitions. The lack of a succession law and the presence of many Timurid males perpetuated an atmosphere of constant intrigue, often erupting into open warfare, between the descendants who vied for mastery in Khorasan and Central Asia, but they finally lost their patrimony when they proved incapable of cooperating to defend it against a common enemy. It was against that same enemy, namely, the Uzbeks under the brilliant Šaybānī Khan (d. 916/151), that Bābor himself learned his trade as a military leader in a long series of losing encounters. Bābor's mother, Qotlūk Negār Ḵanūm, was the daughter of Yūnos Khan of Tashkent and a direct descendant of Jengiz Khan. She and her mother, Aysān-Dawlat Bēgam, had great influence on Bābor during his early career. It was his grandmother, for instance, who taught Bābor many of his political and diplomatic skills (*Bābor-nāma*, tr., p. 43), thus initiating the long series of contributions by strong and intelligent women in the history of the Mughal Empire.

Bābor presumed that his descent from Tīmūr legitimized his claim to rule anywhere that Tīmūr had conquered, but like his father, the first prize he sought was Samarqand. He was plunged into the maelstorm of Timurid politics by his father's death in Ramażān, 899/June, 1494, when he was only eleven. Somehow he managed to survive the turbulent years that followed. Wars with his kinsmen, with the Mughals under Tanbal who ousted him from Andijan, the capital city of Fargāna, and especially with Šaybānī Khan Uzbek mostly went against him, but from the beginning he showed an ability to reach decisions quickly, to act firmly and to remain calm and collected in battle. He also tended to take people at their word and to view most situations optimistically rather than critically.

In Moḥarram, 910/June-July, 1504, at the age of twenty-one, Bābor, alone among the Timurids of his generation, opted to leave the Central Asian arena, in which he had lost everything, to seek a power base elsewhere, perhaps with the intention of returning to his homeland at a later date. Accompanied by his younger brothers, Jahāngīr and Nāṣer, he set out for Khorasan, but changed his plans and seized the kingdom of Kabul instead. In this campaign he began to think more seriously of his role as ruler of a state, shocking his troops by ordering plunderers beaten to death (*Bābor-nāma*, tr., p. 197). The mountain tribesmen in and around Fargāna with whom Bābor had frequently found shelter had come to accept him as their legitimate king. He had no such claims upon the loyalty of the Afghan tribes in Kabul, but he had learned much about human nature and the nomad mentality in his three prolonged periods of wandering among the shepherd tribes of Central Asia (during 903/1497-98, 907/1501-02, and 909/1503-04). He crushed all military opposition, even reviving the old Mongol shock tactic of putting up towers of the heads of slain foes, but he also made strenuous efforts to be fair and just, admitting, for instance, that his early estimates of food production and hence the levy of tributary taxes were excessive (*Bābor-nāma*, tr., p. 228).

At this point Bābor still saw Kabul as only a temporary base for re-entry to his ancestral domain, and he made several attempts to return in the period 912-18/1506-12. In 911/1505 his uncle Sultan Ḥosayn Mīrzā of Herat, the only remaining Timurid ruler besides Bābor, requested his aid against the Uzbeks—even though he himself had refused to aid Bābor on several previous occasions. His uncle died before Bābor arrived in Herat, but Bābor remained there till he became convinced that his cousins were incapable of offering effective resistance to Šaybānī Khan's Uzbeks.

While in Herat he sampled the sophistication of a brilliant court culture, acquiring a taste for wine, and also developing an appreciation for the refinements of urban culture, especially as exemplified in the literary works of Mīr ʿAlī-Šīr Navāʾī. During his stay in Herat Bābor occupied Navāʾī's former residence, prayed at Navāʾī's tomb, and recorded his admiration for the poet's vast corpus of Torkī verses, though he found most of the Persian verses to be "flat and poor" (*Bābor-nāma*, tr., p. 272). Navāʾī's pioneering literary work in Torkī, much of it based, of course, on Persian models, must have reinforced Bābor's own efforts to write in that medium.

In Rajab, 912/December, 1506, Bābor returned to Kabul in a terrible trek over snow-choked passes, during which several of his men lost hands or feet through frostbite. The event has been vividly described in his diary (*Bābor-nāma*, tr., pp. 307-11). As he had foreseen, the Uzbeks easily took Herat in the following summer's campaign, and Bābor indulged in one of his rare slips from objectivity when he recorded the campaign in his diary with some unfair vilification of Šaybānī Khan, his long standing nemesis (*Bābor-nāma*, tr., pp. 328-29).

Bābor next consolidated his base in Kabul, and added to it Qandahar. He dramatically put down a revolt by defeating, one by one in personal combat, five of the ringleaders—an event which his admiring young cousin Mīrzā Moḥammad Ḥaydar Doḡlat believed to be his greatest feat of arms (*Tārīḵ-e rašīdī*, tr., p. 204). Here again it seems that Bābor acted impetuously, but saved himself by his courage and strength; and such legend-making deeds solidified his charismatic hold on the men whom he had to lead in battle. Uncharacteristically, Bābor withdrew from Qandahar and Kabul at the rumor that Šaybānī Khan was coming. It was apparently the only time in his life when he lost confidence in himself. In fact, the Uzbek leader was defeated and killed by Shah Esmāʿīl Ṣafawī in 916/1510, and this opened the way for Bābor's last bid for a throne in Samarqand. From Rajab, 917 to Ṣafar, 918/October, 1511 to May, 1512, he held the city for the third time, but as a client of Shah Esmāʿīl, a condition that required him to make an outward profession of the Shiʿite faith and to adopt the Turkman costume of the Safavid troops.

Bābor's kinsmen and erstwhile subjects did not concur with his doctrinal realignment, however much it had been dictated by political circumstances. Moḥammad-Ḥaydar, a young man indebted to Bābor for both refuge and support, exulted at the Uzbek defeat of Bābor, thus demonstrating how unusual in that time and place were Bābor's breadth of vision and tolerance, qualities that became crucial to his later success in India. Breaking away from his Safavid allies, Bābor dallied in the Qunduz area, but he must have sensed that his chance to regain Samarqand was irretrievably lost.

It was only at this stage that he began to think of India as a serious goal, though after the conquest he wrote that his desire for Hindustan had been constant from 910/1504 (*Bābor-nāma*, tr., p. 478). With four raids beginning in 926/1519, he probed the Indian scene and discovered that dissension and mismanagement were rife in the Lōdī Sultanate. In the winter of 932/1525-26 he brought all his experience to bear on the great enterprise of the conquest of India. With the proverb "Ten friends are better than nine" in mind, he waited for all his allies before pressing his attack on Lahore (*Bābor-nāma*, tr., p. 433). His great skills at organization enabled him to move his 12,000 troops from 16 to 22 miles a day once he had crossed the Indus, and with brilliant leadership he defeated three much larger forces in the breathtaking campaigns that made him master of North India. First he maneuvered Sultan Ebrāhīm Lōdī into attacking his prepared position at the village of Panipat north of Delhi on 8 Rajab 932/20 April 1526. Although the Indian forces (he estimated them at 100,000; *Bābor-nāma*, tr., p. 480) heavily outnumbered Bābor's small army, they fought as a relatively inflexible and undisciplined mass and quickly disintegrated. Bābor considered Ebrāhīm to be an incompetent general, unworthy of comparison with the Uzbek khans, and a petty king, driven only by greed to pile up his treasure while leaving his army untrained and his great nobles disaffected (*Bābor-nāma*, tr., p. 470). Yet Bābor ordered a tomb to be built for him. He then swiftly occupied Delhi and Agra, first visiting the tombs of famous Sufi saints and previous Turkish kings, and characteristically laying out a garden. The garden provided him with such satisfaction that he later wrote: "to have grapes and melons grown in this way in Hindustan filled my measure of content" (*Bābor-nāma*, tr., p. 686).

His new kingdom was a different story. Bābor first had to solve the problem of disaffection among his troops. Like Alexander's army, they felt that they were a long way from home in a strange and unpleasant land. Bābor had planned the conquest intending to make India the base of his empire since Kabul's resources proved too limited to support his nobles and troops. He himself never returned to live in Kabul. But since he had permitted his troops to think that this was simply another raid for wealth and booty, he now had to persuade them otherwise, which was no easy chore (*Bābor-nāma*, tr., pp. 522-35). The infant Mughal state also had to fight for its life against a formidable confederation of the Rajput chiefs led by Mahārānā Sangā of Mewar. After a dramatic episode in which Bābor publicly foreswore alcohol (*Bābor-nāma*, tr., pp. 551-56), Bābor defeated the Rajputs at Khanwah on 13 Jomādā I 933/17 March 1527 with virtually the same tactics he had used at Panipat, but in this case the battle was far more closely contested. Bābor next campaigned down the Ganges River to Bengal against the Afghan lords, many of whom had refused to support Ebrāhīm Lōdī but also had no desire to surrender their autonomy to Bābor.

Even while rival powers threatened him on all sides—Rajputs and Afghans in India, Uzbeks at his rear in Kabul—Bābor's mind was turned to consolidation and government. He employed hundreds of stone masons to build up his new capital cities, while winning over much of the Indian nobility with his fair and conciliatory policies. He was anxiously grooming his sons to succeed him, not without some clashes of personality, when his eldest son Homāyūn (b. 913/1506) fell seriously ill in 937/1530. Another young son had already died in the unaccustomed Indian climate, and at this family crisis his daughter Golbadan wrote that Bābor offered his own life in place of his son's, walking seven times around the sickbed to confirm the vow (*Bābor-nāma*, translator's note, pp. 701-2). Bābor did not leave Agra again, and died there later that year on 6 Jomādā I 937/26 December 1530.

Bābor's diary, which has become one of the classic autobiographies of world literature, would be a major literary achievement even if the life it illuminates were not so remarkable. He wrote not only the *Bābor-nāma* but works on Sufism, law and prosody as well as a fine collection of poems in Čağatay Torkī. In all, he produced the most significant body of literature in that language after Navā'ī, and every piece reveals a clear, cultivated intelligence as well as an enormous breadth of interests. His *Dīvān* includes a score or more of poems in Persian, and with the long connection between the Mughals and the Safavid court begun by Bābor himself, the Persian language became not only the language of record but also the literary vehicle for his successors. It was his grandson Akbar who had the *Bābor-nāma* translated into Persian in order that his nobles and officers could have access to this dramatic account of the dynasty's founder.

Bābor did not introduce artillery into India—the Portugese had done that—and he himself noted that the Bengal armies had gunners (*Bābor-nāma*, tr., pp. 667-74). But his use of new technology was characteristic of his enquiring mind and enthusiasm for improvement. His Ottoman experts had only two cannon at Panipat, and Bābor personally witnessed the casting of another, probably the first to be cast in India, by Ostād ʿAlīqolī on 22 October 1526 (*Bābor-nāma*, tr., pp. 536-37). The piece did not become ready for test firing till 10 February 1527 when it shot stones about 1,600 yards, and during the subsequent campaigns against the Afghans down the Ganges, Bābor specifically mentions Ostād ʿAlīqolī getting off eight shots on the first day of the battle and sixteen on the next (*Bābor-nāma*, tr., p. 599). Quite obviously then it was not some technical superiority in weaponry, but Bābor's genius in using the discipline and mobility which he had created in his troops that won the crucial battles for him in India.

Bābor, however, was generally interested in improving technology, not only for warfare but also for agriculture. He tried to introduce new crops to the Indian terrain and to spread the use of improved water-lifting devices for irrigation (*Bābor-nāma*, tr., p. 531). His interest in improvement and change was facilitated by his generous nature. Though he had faults, they were outweighed by his attractive personality, cheerful in the direst adversity, and faithful to his friends. The loyalties he inspired enabled the Mughal Empire in India to survive his own early death and the fifteen-year exile of his son and successor, Homāyūn. The liberal traditions of the Mughal dynasty were Bābor's enduring legacy to his country by conquest.

Bibliography: Ẓahīr-al-Dīn Moḥammad Bābor, *Bābor-nāma*, ed. A. S. Beveridge, Leiden, 1905; tr. A. S. Beveridge, London, 1921, repr. New Delhi, 1971. J. B. Harrison, P. Hardy, and M. Fuad Köprülü, "Bābor," in *EI*² I, pp. 847-50. Golbadan Bēgam, *Homāyūn-nāma*, ed. and tr. A. S. Beveridge, London, 1902. S. K. Banerji, "Babur and the Hindus," *Journal of the United Provinces Historical Society* (Allahabad) 9/2, July, 1936, pp. 70-96. Mīrzā Moḥammad-Ḥaydar Doḡlat, *A History of the Moghuls of Central Asia, being the* Tarikh-I Rashidi, ed. N. Elias, tr. E. D. Ross, 2nd ed. London, 1898, repr. New York, 1972 and Patna, 1973. William Erskine, *A History of India under the Two First Sovereigns of the House of Taimur, Babur and Humayun* I: *Babur*, London, 1854, repr. Karachi, 1974. Fernand Grenard, *Baber: Fondateur de l'empire des Indes 1483-1530*, Paris, 1930, Eng. tr. H. White and R. Glaenzer, repr. Dehra Dun, 1971. R. D. Palsokar, *Babur: A Study in Generalship*, Poona, 1971. Kh. Khasanov, *Zahiriddin Muhammad Babir: Haeti va Geografik Merosi* (Uzbek), Tashkent, 1966.

(F. LEHMANN)

BĀBORĪ (or Bābor, Bābar; sing. Bāboray), a Paṣ̌tūn tribe originally from the Solaymān mountains, now widely dispersed. Its principal territory lies in Pakistan on the border between the Northwest Frontier Province and Baluchistan, extending over the Solaymān mountains into the Dērajāt foothills around Chaudhwan, where certain lineages are said to have been domiciled since the fourteenth century (H. A. Rose, *A Glossary of the Tribes and Castes of the Punjab and North-West Frontier Province*, Lahore, 1919, repr. Lahore, 1978, II, p. 31). Estimates of the tribe's strength at the end of the nineteenth century differ greatly; H. Raverty suggested a total of 6-7,000 families (*Notes on Afghanistan and Part of Baluchistan*, London, 1880-88, repr. Lahore, 1976, p. 328), which seems excessive, whereas the British Indian General Staff reckoned 700 fighting men, a figure implying a much lower total of only about 4-5,000 persons (*A Dictionary of the Pathan Tribes on the North-West Frontier of India*, Calcutta, 1899, p. 25).

Reports from the late eighteenth century onward give evidence of the tribe's participation in long-range trade between Central Asia and India (H. Raverty, op. cit., p. 329; M. Elphinstone, *An Account of the Kingdom of Caubul*, London, 1815, repr. Graz, 1969, p. 377). Commercial incentives stimulated an influx of Bāborī into the Peshawar district (D. Ibbetson, *Panjab Castes*, Lahore, 1916, repr. New Delhi, 1981, Lahore, 1982, p. 73) and above all into certain parts of Afghanistan, where they found openings in the annual gathering of asafetida gum (*heng*) and the trade in sheep and sheepskin jackets (*pūstīn*) (*Baluchistan through the Ages*, 1906, repr. Quetta, 1979, II, p. 49). In this connection, there is a reference in Moḥammad Ḥayāt Khan's work (*Afghanistan and its Inhabitants*, tr. from the "Hayat-i-Afghan" by H. Priestley, Lahore, 1874, repr. Lahore, 1981, p. 80) to the presence of some 500 Bāborī families scattered over the country, in the Arḡandāb, Lōgar, and Konar valleys, at Qandahār, and around Kābol. What happened to these settlements in later times is not known. There is a village named Bāborī in the province of Nangrahār (M. H. Nāheż, ed., *Qāmūs-e jograāfīā'ī-e Afḡānestān* I, Kabul, 1335 Š./1956, p. 189), but the name does not necessarily prove a connection. The nomadic survey of 1357 Š./1978 recorded fewer than one thousand Bāborī families (280 nomadic, 695 semi-nomadic), all in other parts of Afghanistan. Most of them live north of Qaysār (Fāryāb province) and around Šebergān (Jawzjān province) during the winter and in the upper Morḡāb region during the summer. Smaller groups live in the Dašt-e Arčī in the district of Qaṭaḡan, around Balḵ, along the middle course of the Harīrūd, and in the Helmand valley (D. Balland and A. de Benoist, *Nomades et semi-nomades d'Afghanistan* (forthcoming). On the Bāborī of Fāryāb, see also *Gazetteer of Afghanistan* IV, Graz, 1979, p. 291). There are mentions of the following Bāborī lineages in Afghanistan: Ḡōrḵēl (also Ḡōrīzī, which may be a variant form), Ebrāhīmḵēl, Malaḵēl, ʿOmrānḵēl. Only the first and second of these (the first in the forms Ḡōryāḵēl or Ḡōrāḵēl) have been recorded as also present in Pakistan (Ḥayāt Khan, op. cit., p. 77. Šēr Moḥammad Khan, *Tawārīḵ-e ḵ̌oršīd-e jahān*, Lahore, 1311/1894, p. 180. H. A. Rose, *Glossary* II, p. 31).

The Bāborī are treated by genealogists as a section of the Šērānī tribe. They are in fact the latter's neighbors in Pakistan, but so distinct that neither has any sense of common tribal solidarity; the Bāborī even collaborated with a British punitive expedition against the Šērānī in 1853 (*Frontier and Overseas Expeditions from India*, 1910, repr. Quetta, 1979, III, p. 179). The Bāborī of Afghanistan never speak of such a kinship. They simply describe themselves as Paṣ̌tūn and are almost wholly Pashtophone.

Bibliography: Given in the text.

(D. BALLAND)

BABR "tiger." The little evidence remaining suggests no more than tentative differences between the Caspian tiger (*Panthera tigris virgata*) and that of either the Indian tiger (*P.t. tigris*) or the Siberian tiger (*P.t. altaica*). Skins and photographs would suggest that it was of intermediate size. The stripes have been reported as not as wide, and more brownish on the sides. The Caspian tiger has been noted for its long winter coat. Little is known regarding the biology of the Caspian tiger. It was reported to reproduce once every 2 to 3 years, bearing 2 to 4 cubs per litter. No particular breeding season has been documented. In the Ili River Valley in Kazakhstan, tiger territories measured 20 by 50 km, while a male and two females were thought to have occupied an area measuring only 6 by 7 km. Their territories partially overlapped. In former times the Caspian tiger's range was extensive, ranging westward to the mountains of Ararat and the Caucasus and as far eastward as the Aral Sea and Lake Balkhash in Russian Kazakhstan. Material collected near Bagrash Kul in Chinese Turkestan may also belong to this race. At the beginning of the century the tiger was still found in Armenia, and one specimen was captured in Tiflis. In Iran it was formerly distributed throughout the moist Caspian region, inhabiting the reed-covered coastal plain and the forests on the northern slopes of the Alborz mountains in Gīlān, Māzandarān and western Khorasan provinces. Unlike the wild boar, its principal wild prey species, it was never recorded on the southern, drier slopes of the Alborz mountains. Clearing of the Caspian lowland forests and marshes for agricultural use along with direct persecution eliminated the tiger from these areas, the last of which were recorded in the remaining fragment of reed stands in the Southeast Caspian region, where they were poisoned because of reputed depredations on livestock. Increased hunting by military squads and the replacement of dense forests with cotton fields resulted in their decline in the Turkmenia region. Burning of the dense reed thickets in the river valleys in Kazakhstan is thought to have brought about its demise in Central Asia.

Between 1973 and 1976 extensive efforts were made by the biologists of the Iranian Department of Environment to determine if tigers remained in the forests of the Alborz Mountains. Casts of cat pug marks were collected throughout the region each winter. Almost all were easily identified as leopard. However in two of the more isolated areas the casts were sufficiently large as to be suggestive of tiger. A dozen bait stations with remote cameras were established in both regions over a two-winter period. Wolves, bears, innumerable leopards, and a host of other predators were recorded, but no tiger. Some unusually large cat tracks in partially melted snow conditions in conjunction with leopard photographs led to the conclusion that the original casts were those of leopard. Closer examination of the original casts also revealed that they were recorded while the animal or animals were descending down snow-covered slopes, at which time the toes were widely splayed, thus adding to their size. Why the tiger did not continue to survive in the more isolated forested mountain areas can only be conjectured. Perhaps it existed as a population in the mountains in former times only as a temporary surplus from the adjoining Caspian lowland. While prey in the form of wild boar were abundant in the mountains, so too were leopards, which may have served as more efficient predators under these conditions. This coupled with a combination of loss of the lowland population of tigers along with a modicum of direct persecution through hunting and poisoning may have reduced the mountain tiger population to a level that was incapable of surviving. Once the tiger's decline had become well recognized, laws were enacted both in Iran and the USSR giving it total protection. However, such actions did not come soon enough to save it in the wild. Apart from a Caspian tiger reportedly breeding and producing young twice in the Moscow Zoo over a two-year period, no effort was made to develop a captive breeding program, which might also have saved it from extinction. The last reliable report of a Caspian tiger was in 1958 within the forested mountain area of the former Moḥammad Reżā Shah National Park in northeastern Iran.

Bibliography: J. Fisher, N. Simon, V. Vincent, *The Red Book*, London, 1969. F. A. Harrington, ed., *A Guide to the Mammals of Iran*, Dept. of Environment, Tehran, 1977. P. Joslin, *Analysis of Track Measurement Data Collected during the Tiger Survey in the Alborz Mountains*, Dept. of Environment, Tehran, 1974. Idem, "Night Stalking," *Photo Life* 2/5, 1977, pp. 34-35. D. MacDonald, in *The Encyclopaedia of Mammals* I, London, 1984.

(P. JOSLIN)

BABR-E BAYĀN (or *babr*, also called *palangīna*), the name of the coat which Rostam wore in combat. It was fire-proof, water-proof, weapon-proof, dark-colored, and apparently hairy, because Rostam when wearing it is said to have looked as if he had "sprouted feathers" (*Šāh-nāma*, Moscow ed., II, p. 89 v. 244, III, p. 188 v. 2880, IV, pp. 200 vv. 1354-56, 281 vv. 1118-19, 286 vv. 1888-89, 319 v. 6).

Before going into battle, Rostam put on first a *zereh* (tunic of lightweight chainmail), then a *jowšan* or *gabr* (suit of thick armor made of iron plates), and lastly the *babr-e bayān* (*Šāh-nāma* IV, p. 202 v. 1404). According to the *Šāh-nāma*, the *babr-e bayān* had been made out of the skin of a leopard (*palang*) and was therefore also named *palangīna* (IV, p. 200 vv. 1354-55, p. 286 vv. 1888-89); this is confirmed by a description of the coat in a Sogdian text (E. Benveniste, *Textes Sogdiens*, Mission Pelliot III, Paris, 1940, pp. 134-36).

The first component of the name must therefore obviously be the noun *babr* (tiger). Ferdowsī also used *babr*, and in two passages (III, p. 224 v. 3417, IV, 52 v. 695) the full name *babr-e bayān*, with the meaning of "tiger." For the second component *bayān* various etymologies have been suggested (see Maḥmūd Omīdsālār, "Babr-e bayān," *Īrān-nāma* 3, 1362, Š./1983, pp. 447-58); but since the word does not mean anything in Persian and is not found in Pahlavi, none of the suggestions is convincing. Ferdowsī (III, p. 224 v. 3417, IV, p. 52 v. 695) himself evidently took *bayān* to have the same meaning as *žīān*, i.e., "fierce" or "raging."

In a different account which has come down to us (Asadī Ṭūsī, *Loḡat-e fors*, s.v. *babr-e bayān*), the coat is said to have been sent from heaven (see also AKVĀN-E DĪV). According to still another account by an unknown poet and inserted in a manuscript of the *Šāh-nāma* (British Library, ms. Or. 2926, fols. 112b-115a), Rostam, when fourteen years old, slew a dragon known as Babr-e Bayān in India. The dragon used to come out of the sea one day every week. Rostam made a coat for himself out of its skin and called the coat *babr-e bayān*. Similar accounts are found in oral folktales current among the Iranians and also the Mandeans and in some of the Persian epic literature (see AŽDAHĀ ii); in all of them the animal is described as coming from the sea, dwelling in India, and possessing an invulnerable hide.

The last of these three accounts appears to be the oldest; and the more plausible explanation of the word *bayān* is as a place-name. Most probably the place was the Indian city of Bayāna, which lay at a distance of some 70 km from the Yamuna river (the parallel tributary of the Ganges). It is also noteworthy that early geographers mention a town named Bayān on the Tigris in Ḵūzestān (e.g. Eṣṭaḵrī, pp. 88, 89; Moqaddasī, pp. 53, 114, 134, 419; *Ḥodūd al-ʿālam*, tr. Minorsky, pp. 139, 214); and that, in the Greek legends, Heracles strangled a lion, being unable to slay it in any other way because its skin was invulnerable, and subsequently wore the skin of this creature, called the Nemean lion from the place where it was slain, as a coat over his shoulders.

According to the *Farāmarz-nāma* (Bombay, 1324/1906, p. 294 v. 6), the *babr-e bayān* passed after Rostam's death to his son Farāmarz.

Bibliography: See also F. Wolff, *Glossar zu Ferdosis Schahname*, Hildesheim, 1965, pp. 115, 203. M. Bāqerī (Sarkārātī), "Babr-e bayān," *Āyanda* 12/1-3, 1365 Š./1986, pp. 6-19.

(DJ. KHALEGHI-MOTLAGH)

BABYLON under the Achaemenids. The economic and cultural history of Babylon under Persian rule matched the vicissitudes of its political life. Its citizens welcomed the first Achaemenids as liberators. Having been deeply offended by the sacrilegious innovations of Nabonidus, they opened its gates in 538 B.C. to Cyrus, who had already won Kubaru (Gobryas), the Babylonian governor of Gutium, over to his side (*Annals of Nabonidus* III, 15-20, in S. Smith, ed., *Babylonian Historical Texts*, London, 1924, pp. 98-123; Cylinder of Cyrus, in R. W. Rogers, *Cuneiform Parallels to the Old Testament*, Oxford, 1912, pp. 380-84; W. Eilers in *Festgabe deutscher Iranisten zur 2500 Jahrfeier Irans*, Stuttgart, 1971, pp. 156-66; Xenophon, *Cyropaedia* 7.5.26-30). With the god Marduk's blessing, the Persian king sent the foreign gods imported by the fallen ruler back to their home towns.

By touching Marduk's hand at the celebration of the New Year festival (Akîtu), Cyrus identified his cause with that of the god and took over the primary religious function of the former kings, which was to safeguard the country's prosperity by exorcizing the water-demons (S. Pallis, *The Babylonian Akîtu Festival*, Copenhagen, 1926, pp. 174ff.). To mark the importance which he attached to his conquest, he proceeded, perhaps in 537, to have his son, probably Cambyses, enthroned as "King of Babylon" (*Annals of Nabonidus* III, 24; F. E. Peiser, *Texte juristischen und geschäftlichen Inhalts*, Leipzig, 1896, p. 260, II), and later himself assumed the title "King of Babylon and the Countries." The former dominions of Nebuchadnezzar became a huge satrapy centered on Babylon, which was in fact the empire's western capital, on a par with Susa, the central capital, and Ecbatana, the eastern capital. The Persians had no lack of men fit to serve as generals and governors but, being short of middle-ranking and subordinate administrative personnel, they left the everyday affairs of Babylon to the officials whom they found there (E. Unger, *Babylon*, Berlin, 1931, p. 39 n. 6).

This favorable treatment was modified to some extent after the accession of Darius I, who in the space of one year (December, 522-November, 521) had to deal with two revolts led by purported sons of Nabonidus (Behistun [Bīsotūn] inscription, secs. 16-20, 49-50, in F. H. Weissbach, *Die Keilinschriften der Achämeniden*, Leipzig, 1911; Kent, *Old Persian*, pp. 118-23, 126-28). At the same time, and probably as a result of this political tension, local administrative functions, even at the lower levels, appear to have been transferred increasingly to Iranian hands. Nevertheless Darius continued to hold court at Babylon (Behistun inscription, section 31) and to reside in Nebuchadnezzar's palace (R. Koldewey, *Das wieder erstehende Babylon*, 4th ed., Leipzig, 1925, pp. 126ff. and figs. 78-80). He also began the construction of a new palace and had the Euphrates diverted for this purpose. It was at Babylon that his son Xerxes gained experience in handling state affairs (ibid.).

Three revolts of Babylonian pretenders caused Xerxes to drop the title "King of Babylon" in the early years of his reign. The third revolt, lasting from 480 to 476, was quelled after a siege of several months and punished with destruction of the Esagila, removal of the gold statue of Marduk, slaughter of priests, and deportation of many inhabitants (Herodotus, 1.183; Arrian, *Anabasis of Alexander* 7.17). It is impossible to judge whether the new centralizing trend of Achaemenid policy was a cause or a consequence of these revolts. In any case, the central government's tightening grip was detrimental to Babylon, which ceased to be a holy city and the seat of a "great satrapy." Nevertheless Babylon remained a major city by virtue of its large population, its economic activity, and its monuments, as attested by Herodotus who visited it in 450 and has left an interesting, if not wholly accurate, description (1.178-87; see O. E. Ravn, *Herodotus's Description of Babylon*, Copenhagen, 1942; F. Wetzel, "Babylon zur Zeit Herodotus," *ZA*, 1944, pp. 45-68). Moreover the Persian rulers did not consistently show such harshness. Parysatis, the wife of Darius II, was exiled to Babylon after a family quarrel (Plutarch, *Artaxerxes* 19); Artaxerxes II Mnemon received treatment there for wounds suffered at the battle of Cunaxa in 401, and built a temple of the goddess Anāhitā in the city (Berossus in Clement of Alexandria, *Protreptica* 5); Artaxerxes III Ochus built an *apadāna* on the site of a part of the palace of Darius (Diodorus Siculus, 2.8. See Koldewey, loc. cit.; Unger, op. cit., p. 40 n. 1). These facts do not, of course, prove that Babylon was restored to favor.

The commercial documents (on clay tablets) which have been found in Babylonia are too specialized to give a general picture of the city's economic life in the Achaemenid period. Most of them are from two sets of records. The oldest, consisting of records kept by the Egibi family, shows how these landowning businessmen resident at Babylon prospered through letting their lands and lending their money. The fact that they did business with the courts of the successive rulers from Neriglissar to Darius I confirms that the establishment of Persian rule took place without any economic or social disruption (S. Weingort, *Das Haus Egibi*, Berlin, 1939; J. A. Delaunay, ed., *MOLDENKE, Cuneiform Texts in the Metropolitan Museum of Art (New York)*, Paris, 1977, pp. 29-31). The other set consists of the records of the Murašû family, who were estate-managers resident not at Babylon but at Nippur (G. Cardascia, *Les archives des Murašû*, Paris, 1951). The vocabulary of their documents, compared with that of the Egibi documents which date from before the reign of Xerxes, gives evidence of increasing iranization, with the use of numerous Persian words in Akkadian adaptations in the administrative terminology (names of offices, taxes, types of land, etc.) (W. Eilers, *Iranische Beamtennamen in der keilschriftlichen Überlieferung*, Leipzig, 1940). Babylon must have shared in the economic destiny of Lower Mesopotamia as a whole. Like the rest of the country, the city profited from the prosperity of agriculture (Herodotus, 1.193) made possible by the canal-irrigation of the alluvial plain and intensive date-palm cultivation practiced by the Chaldeans; and like the rest of the country, it suffered from the tax-burden, which was heavy, because Babylonia paid an annual tribute of one thousand silver talents (Herodotus, 3.92) together with the upkeep of the court and the army for one third of the year (Herodotus, 1.192), and at the same time economically injurious, because it drained coins from local circulation into the Great King's treasury and thus gave rise to adverse price movements and excessively high interest rates (M. W. Stolper, *Management and Politics in Later Achaemenid Babylonia*, Ann Arbor, 1976).

The temples kept their important role in the economy, but they too suffered from the hardening of Achaemenid policy under and after Xerxes. They received fewer royal benefactions and lost their fiscal immunities (M. A. Dandamaev, "Politische und wirtschaftliche Geschichte," in G. Walser, ed., *Beiträge zur Achämeniden-geschichte*, Historia, Einzelschriften 18, Wiesbaden, 1972, pp. 52-53).

Nevertheless Babylon remained important, but only in the tertiary sector as a seat of governmental and private managerial functions, but also as a flourishing center of craft industries and of commerce. There can be no doubt that the scarcity of the written documentation now available to historians is due solely to the increasing displacement of durable clay tablets by perishable parchments in this period. Manifestly Babylon's commercial vitality was sustained by the advantages of its site at the junction of the north-south Mesopotamian axis and the Euphrates valley with the eastward route to Media by the Dīāla valley. While Ur, now cut off from the sea by silting, went into rapid decline, Babylon remained a busy focal point because the Persians preferred to do their trade by caravan. The reports of the astonishment of Alexander and his men at the sight of Babylon's riches give further proof of the city's contemporary preeminence in Mesopotamia (Diodorus Siculus, 17.66).

The influence of Babylonian culture on Achaemenid art is apparent in various remains: e.g., use of terraced platforms in palace construction, wall decoration with enameled bricks depicting flowers and animals, repoussé technique in metal work (A. Godard, *L'art de l'Iran*, Paris, 1962, pp. 109-36).

Bibliography: Given in the text. See also *Camb. Hist. Iran* II. G. Cameron, *History of Early Iran*, Chicago, 1936. C. Huart and L. Delaporte, *L'Iran antique*, Paris, 1943. M. Meuleau, "Mesopotamia in der Perserzeit," in *Fischer Weltgeschichte* V, ed. H. Bengtson, Frankfurt, 1965, pp. 330-55. A. T. Olmstead, *History of the Persian Empire*, Chicago, 1948. S. Pallis, "The History of Babylon (538-93 B.C.)," in *Studia Orientalia Iohanni Pedersen... Dicata*, Copenhagen, 1953, pp. 275-94. H. W. Saggs, *The Greatness that was Babylon*, London, 1962.

(G. CARDASCIA)

BABYLONIA, state in southern Mesopotamia, present-day Iraq.

i. *History of Babylonia in the Median and Achaemenid periods.*
ii. *Babylonian influences on Iran.*

i. HISTORY OF BABYLONIA IN THE MEDIAN AND ACHAEMENID PERIODS

I. Political history.

Babylonia came into being early in the second millennium B.C. and lasted until it was conquered by the Persians in 539 B.C. For the early history of Babylonia see ASSYRIA and ELAM.

In 729 B.C. Babylonia was taken by the Assyrians and, with a few brief interludes, remained dependent for a century. A revolt against Assyrian domination flared up in 626, headed by Nabopolassar, who had been appointed governor of the southern part of the country. Nabopolassar revitalized the traditional alliance of the Chaldean tribes of southern Babylonia with Elam. In November, 626, he was crowned in Babylon, thereby founding the Chaldean, or Neo-Babylonian, dynasty. There followed a protracted war between Babylonia and Assyria, with the advantage shifting from one side to the other and back again. No clear result emerged until 614, when Assyria was attacked by the Medes. The Medes, under their king Cyaxares, first seized the Assyrian province of Arrapha. Then, in the autumn of the same year, and after a fierce battle, they gained control of Assyria's ancient capital, Assur. Nabopolassar brought his Babylonian army and joined the Medes after Assur had fallen. The Medes and the Babylonians formed an alliance and cemented it through the marriage of Nabopolassar's son Nebuchadnezzar to Cyaxares' daughter Amytis. Greek tradition derived from the Babylonian historian Berossus records that behind his palace in Babylon, on terraces cut to look like natural hills, Nebuchadnezzar constructed the famous hanging gardens, in imitation of the mountain gardens of Media, so that Amytis would not pine for the scenery of her homeland. (See E. Unger, *Babylon. Die heilige Stadt nach der Beschreibung der Babylonier*, 2nd ed., Berlin, 1970, pp. 217-21; W. Nagel, "Wo lagen die 'Hängenden Gärten' in Babylon?" *MDOG* 110, 1978, pp. 19-28.)

In August 612 the combined forces of the Medes and the Babylonians took Nineveh, the greatest city in Assyria, though the remnants of the Assyrian army did manage to make their way through to the city of Harran in Upper Mesopotamia. Necho, the pharaoh of Egypt, sent troops to aid the Assyrians. Apparently Nabopolassar then turned to the Medes for further assistance. In November, according to the *Babylonian Chronicle*, an army of Umman-manda fought on the side of the Babylonians against the Assyrians. From the evidence of a letter of prince Nebuchadnezzar it would seem that these Umman-manda were Medes: the text states that "the king departed for Harran; substantial Median forces went with him" (F. Thureau-Dangin, "La fin de l'empire assyrien," *RA* 22, 1925, pp. 27-29). The Medes routed the Assyrians and took Harran. Babylonians also participated in the storming of the city, but in a minor capacity. (See I. M. D'yakonov [Diakonoff], *Istoriya Midii*, Moscow and Leningrad, 1956, p. 315.)

In 607 Nabopolassar handed over command of the army to his son Nebuchadnezzar, who in the spring of 605 crossed the Euphrates and attacked the city of Carchemish, annihilating its Egyptian garrison. In 604, the greater part of Syria and Palestine then capitulated to the Babylonians. Soon after Nebuchadnezzar II became king following the death of Nabopolassar in August 605, he seized the Phoenician cities as well. (See D. J. Wiseman, *Nebuchadnezzar and Babylon*, Oxford, 1985, pp. 25-29.)

In 598 Jehoiachin, king of Judah, was coaxed by Necho into seceding from Babylonia. Nebuchadnezzar took Jerusalem, in 597. Greek sources state that in the campaign against Jerusalem Nebuchadnezzar requested aid from Cyaxares, king of Media (G. G. Cameron, *History of Early Iran*, New York, 1936, p. 220). Judah again rebelled, and in 587 Nebuchadnezzar captured Jerusalem and removed thousands of its inhabitants to Babylonia in captivity.

During the reign of Nebuchadnezzar the culture and economy of Babylonia flourished. Mighty fortifications were erected in order to protect the country from future attacks. Nebuchadnezzar was wary of an over-powerful Media, and he well understood that sooner or later Media would change from ally into dangerous rival. For this reason he willingly accepted political refugees from Media, and Babylonian texts of the period 595-570 mention that Median refugees were allocated provisions from the royal stores. The same texts also mention the issue of provisions to seven hundred and thirteen Elamites and to three men from "the land of Parsumash," that is, to Persians (E. F. Weidner, "Jojachin, König von Juda, in babylonischen Keilschrifttexten," in *Mélanges syriens offerts à René Dussaud*, Paris, 1939, pp. 929-30). One letter addressed to Nebuchadnezzar indicates that in 591 relations between Media and Babylonia became strained. The letter states that a number of Babylonians fled to Media. A messenger from the king arrived with the order for them to return, but they refused to comply (R. P. Dougherty, *Archives from Erech, Neo-Babylonian and Persian Periods*, New York, 1933, no. 395). However, if Herodotus is to be believed, relations between Babylonia were still tolerably good in 585 when Media and Lydia concluded a peace-treaty through the agency of Syennesis, king of Cilicia, and a certain "Labynetos" of Babylonia (Herodotus, 1.74). The latter is usually but erroneously identified as the future king Nabonidus, see W. Röllig, "Erwägungen zu neuen Stelen König Nabonidus," *ZA* 56, 1964, p. 239.

After the death of Nebuchadnezzar II in 562 Babylon entered a period of political crisis caused partly by the conflict between Chaldean and Aramaic tribes, who had long been numerous in Mesopotamia, and partly by the tensions between priestly and military factions. Priestly interference in politics extended even to the deposition of kings thought to be unsuitable or unamenable. There was a succession of three kings in a few brief years until Nabonidus seized power in May, 556. Unlike the other Neo-Babylonian kings he was an Aramean, not a Chaldean. (See R. H. Sack, "The Nabonidus Legend," *RA* 77, 1983, pp. 59-67.)

Around 552, when Median troops were recalled from Harran during the war between Media and Persia. Nabonidus reinstated the temple of the moon god Sin in Harran. The revival of this shrine was an integral part of a program of major religious reforms which Nabonidus gradually put into effect. His aim was that precedence should go to the cult of Sin, which would eclipse the cult of the supreme Babylonian deity Marduk. These reforms brought Nabonidus into conflict with the priests of Marduk in Babylon. For ten years he himself stayed out of Babylon, handing over the administration of the territory to his son Belshazzar. Nabonidus spent these ten years at the oasis of Tema in the northern part of Central Arabia, where he appropriated extensive territories.

By 543 the long rivalry between Babylonia and Egypt had eased, as both countries had to prepare for imminent war with the Persians. Babylonia, however, was without allies. Only the pharaoh of Egypt, Amasis, might have provided aid, but he remained on the sidelines. Furthermore, the Babylonian army had been worn down by years of war on the Arabian peninsula, yet it had to do battle with the massive and well equipped Persian army which had already conquered many lands as far as the borders of India. And in Babylonia itself the position of Nabonidus was precarious. Influential sections of the priesthood were so dissatisfied with Nabonidus' policies that they were prepared to assist any external enemy of his. Besides this, Babylonia housed many thousands of assorted non-Babylonians who had been forcibly removed from their homelands and who viewed the Persians as their liberators. Nevertheless, the Persians still faced the task of breaching the mighty defensive fortifications within whose protective perimeter of one hundred and fifty kilometers lay such major towns as Sippar, Cutha, Babylon, and Borsippa. Babylon was especially well fortified. It was ringed by a double wall of dried and baked brick. The outer wall was 7.8 m high, 3.72 m thick, and $8\frac{1}{3}$ km in circumference. The inner wall, built 12 m from the outer wall, was 11-14 m high, 6.5 m thick, and 6 km in circumference. On top of the walls, at intervals of 20 m, there were fortified towers from which one could shoot down on attackers. In front of the outer wall was a deep moat. (See D. E. Ravn, *Herodotus' Description of Babylon*, Copenhagen, 1942, pp. 16-38.)

According to the *Babylonian Chronicle*, in the spring of 539 the Persian army set out on its campaign and started to move down the valley of the river Dīāla, where it was joined by Ugbaru, governor of the region of Gutium (probably Media). Nabonidus, concerned that the towns outside the fortifications might defect to the enemy, ordered that the idols of the gods be removed from them to Babylon. The point of this gesture was to make the outlying towns more dependent on Babylon both politically and in matters of religion. In August, 539, near the town of Opis on the Tigris, the army of Belshazzar was routed by the Persians. After the fall of Opis there were no major battles. The Persians crossed the Tigris to the south of Opis and surrounded Sippar, whose defence was supervised by Nabonidus himself, but which capitulated after token resistance, on October 10. Nabonidus fled to Babylon. Two days later the army of Ugbaru entered Babylon unopposed and Nabonidus was taken prisoner. Archeological evidence supports the assertion of the *Babylonian Chronicle* that the capital surrendered without a fight: no traces of fires and no signs of the violent destruction of houses have been uncovered in the layer for the period of the Persian invasion (O. Reuther, *Die Innenstadt von Babylon (Merkes)*, WVDOG 47, 1926, pp. 34-36). On 29 October 539 Cyrus himself entered Babylon and the people laid on a triumphal welcome for him (A. K. Grayson *Assyrian and Babylonian Chronicles*, Locust Valley, N.Y., 1975, pp. 109-10). The independence of Babylonia was lost forever.

The Babylonian historian Berossus presents Cyrus as having a rather more hostile attitude to the captured city: Cyrus apparently ordered that the outer walls of Babylon be destroyed so as to render the city less formidably impregnable (F. Jacoby, ed., *Fragmente der griechischen Historiker* III C, pp. 108-09). Yet other sources paint a wholly different picture of the fall of Babylon. Herodotus and Xenophon relate that the Babylonians did resist Cyrus and that the capital was taken only after fierce fighting. Herodotus (1.188-91) tells of how the Babylonians carefully prepared themselves for the siege, stocking up supplies to last several years; but the Persians demolished one of the dikes and diverted the waters of the Euphrates at the point where it entered Babylon; they then took the city by surprise, entering into it along the dried-out riverbed just as the inhabitants were relaxing in celebration of some festival. Herodotus also calls the Babylonian king Labynetos. According to Xenophon, the Persians dug a large trench around Babylon, along the outer wall; at night, while the citizens were celebrating one of the festivals, the attackers diverted the Euphrates into this trench and entered the capital along the old riverbed; they then disposed of the palace guards, penetrated to the inner rooms, and killed the (unnamed) Babylonian king (Xenophon, *Cyropaedia* 7.5.7-32, 58).

The *Book of Daniel* (chaps. 3-5) also gives an account of the last stage of the fall of Babylon: during a feast in his palace Belshazzar saw a fiery hand trace cryptic words on the wall, signifying that he was soon to perish.

Cyrus spared the life of Nabonidus but had Belshazzar killed. Soon the whole country was in Persian hands. The Persian administration put out meticulously coordinated propaganda: several contemporary Babylonian texts present Cyrus as the liberator of the land from its oppression under Nabonidus, while Nabonidus is said to have despised even the gods of his own country, to have committed crimes against the temples, and to have plundered the possessions of others (W. von Soden, "Kyros und Nabonid, Propaganda und Gegenpropaganda," *AMI*, Ergänzungsband 10, 1983, pp. 61-68). The *Cyrus Cylinder* relates that Marduk ordered Cyrus to enter Babylon and entrusted the country to him so as to guarantee its people peace and prosperity. The same claim is made in an inscription of Cyrus from Ur (C. J. Gadd, L. Legrain, and S. Smith, *Royal Inscriptions. Ur Excavations. Texts* I, London, 1928, p. 58, no. 198). The author of the *Book of Isiah*, a witness to the Persian conquest of Babylon, seems to have been well acquainted with Cyrus's broad political aims, and whole chapters are written in a mood similar to that of the Babylonian texts which stress the piety of Cyrus while condemning Nabonidus. Josephus Flavius states that extracts from the *Book of Isiah* dealing with Cyrus's conquest of Babylon were read aloud in Cyrus's presence (E. Bickerman, *Four Strange Books of the Bible*, New York, 1967, p. 62).

Yet all these texts are propagandistic in character. They were compiled by Babylonian priests on the orders either of the king or of his servants, and they were modeled on the earlier inscriptions of Assurbanipal. In his own inscriptions Nabonidus claims that Babylonia flourished under his rule. Several thousand administrative and private legal documents from the time of Nabonidus bear witness to the continuing economic prosperity of the country. (For these texts see M. A. Dandamaev, *Slavery in Babylonia*, DeKalb, Illinois, 1984, pp. 10-13.)

On Cyrus's orders the idols which had been brought to Babylon under Nabonidus were now dispatched back to the temples where they had previously resided. The images of foreign gods which earlier Babylonian kings had appropriated from Susa and the cities of northern Mesopotamia, were likewise returned to their old shrines. The run-down temples of Babylonia and of the former territory of Assyria were restored. Cyrus instructed Ugbaru to provide Babylon with defense against looters and to protect the sacred places. Foreigners who had been brought to Babylonia by force were now permitted to return home. Cyrus did not formally dismantle the Babylonian kingdom, nor did he tamper with the social structure. Instead he established his rule in the form of a personal union with the Babylonians, taking the official title "King of Babylon, King of the Countries." This title was retained by his successors down to the time of Xerxes. Babylon became one of the Achaemenid residences. In its economic life there are no perceptible changes before the beginning of the fifth century. The civil servants of the old regime kept their places in the bureaucracy, and the Persian administration accepted Babylonian law and the traditional methods of Babylonian government. (See M. A. Dandamaev, *Persien unter den ersten Achämeniden*, Wiesbaden, 1976, pp. 99-100.)

After Darius I seized the throne in 552 the Babylonians, with others, rose up in rebellion against him. According to the Bīsotūn inscription a certain Nidintu-Bel, son of Ainaira,took power, styling himself Nebuchadnezzar (III) and claiming to be the son of Nabonidus. On October 3 he was proclaimed king. Documents from Babylon, Borsippa, and Sippar name him as the current ruler. Darius took personal command of the campaign against the rebels. The first battle took place by the Tigris on 13 December 522. Five days later Darius won a second victory in the area of Zazana on the Euphrates. Nidintu-Bel fled to Babylon, where he was captured and executed.

When Darius was busy quelling revolts elsewhere, the Babylonians rebelled again. If the Bīsotūn inscription is to be believed, they were led by Araxa, son of Haldita, an Armenian who claimed to be Nebuchadnezzar (IV), son of Nabonidus. Araxa managed to gain control of the entire country, as witnessed by documents from Babylon, Sippar, and Borsippa in the north, and from Uruk in the south, all dated according to his reign. The earliest of these documents was written on 16 August 521. In order to pacify the Babylonians Darius sent an army under the command of Vindafarna, a Persian. On 27 November 521 Araxa was defeated, and subsequently executed. Herodotus (3.150-60) also gives an account of the Babylonian revolt against Darius. He writes that after taking Babylon Darius ordered that three thousand leading citizens be executed and that the walls of the city be demolished. Archeological excavations confirm that the outer wall of Babylon was indeed demolished, though references to the inner wall continue to be found in documents long after the rebellion was crushed. (See F. Wetzel, E. Schmidt, and A. Mallwitz, *Das Babylon der Spätzeit*, WVDOG 62, 1957, p. 70; F. M. Th. de Liagre Böhl, "Die babylonischen Prätendenten zur Anfangszeit des Darius I," *Bibliotheca Orientalis* 25, 1968, pp. 150-53.)

In June or July, 484, a fresh rebellion broke out in Babylon, headed by a certain Belshimanni. The rebels managed to capture Borsippa and Dilbat as well as Babylon itself. But they were easily defeated by Xerxes, king of Persia, possibly in the course of the mere two weeks during which documents were dated by the reign of Belshimanni. Nevertheless, in August, 482, the Babylonians rebelled yet again, this time led by Shamash-eriba. Major successes came quickly. The insurgents took Babylon, Borsippa, Dilbat, and other cities. Megabyzos, a relative of Xerxes, was given the task of suppressing the rebellion. His siege of Babylon lasted several months, probably until March, 481 (F. M. Th. de Liagre Böhl, "Die babylonischen Prätendenten zur Zeit des Xerxes," *Bibliotheca Orientalis* 19, 1962, pp. 110-14), and he exacted stern justice in his eventual victory. The city walls and other fortifications were razed to the ground. A number of priests were executed. Esagila, the main temple, was badly damaged. Many objects from the temple's treasury, objects donated by the Assyrian and Babylonian kings, were carried off to Persepolis (E. F. Schmidt, *Persepolis* I, Chicago, 1953, pp. 174, 179; II, 1957, pp. 56-67). The gold statue of the god Marduk was also removed, so that nobody could now claim to be the rightful king, since, by Babylonian tradition, a new ruler was obliged to receive his authority from the hands of Marduk in the Esagila temple during the festival of the new year. Thus Xerxes put an end even to the notional existence of the Babylonian kingdom. The old title of the Achaemenid rulers, "King of Babylon, King of the Countries," was now rendered meaningless. From Xerxes onwards the title became simply "King of the Countries." Babylonia was reduced to the level of an ordinary satrapy. Babylon itself forfeited forever its political significance. It also ceased to be a holy city. It did, however, manage to recover some of its status as the economic center of the country, and indeed Babylonia as a whole remained rich and prosperous through to the fourth century, as is clear from Xenophon's *Anabasis* (1.5.10, 2.4.21, etc.).

After the battle of Gaugamela on 1 October 331, Alexander the Great moved on Babylon, and the satrap Mazaios surrendered the city to him without a struggle. Alexander intended to make Babylon the capital of his empire, but the project was abandoned after his death in 323. In 321 Babylonia came under the rule of Seleucus I, one of Alexander's generals and the founder of the Seleucid state which included Mesopotamia, Media, Persia, Northern Syria, and part of Asia Minor. In 312 Seleucus founded the city of Seleucia-on-Tigris, which was formally declared the capital in 275, in the reign of Antiochus I Soter. Thenceforth Babylon was doomed to a gradual extinction. Mithradates I (ca. 170-139), founder of the Parthian empire, captured from the Seleucids Media and Babylonia up to the Euphrates. In the interminable wars between the Parthian kings and the Seleucids, Babylonia was devastated. There were nine changes of ruler in Babylon between the years 161 and 122. By the start of the second century A.D. the city was completely empty of inhabitants. Nothing was left of Babylon but its ruins. Mesopotamia became part of the Sasanian empire (224-651). (See S. A. Pallis, "The History of Babylon 538-93 B.C.," in *Studia Orientalia Ioanni Pedersen... Dicata*, Copenhagen, 1953, pp. 275-94.)

II. The Persian satrapy.

Supreme administrative power in Babylonia belonged to the Persian satrap. The first governor of the city of Babylon was Cyrus's general, Ugbaru, who in effect held power over the whole of Mesopotamia. Ugbaru died three weeks after the capture of Babylon. In 538 Cyrus appointed his own son, Cambyses, as king of Babylonia, keeping control of the rest of the empire for himself. The true extent of Cambyses' rule was in fact even more limited than it sounds: he was king only of the city of Babylon and of the northern part of the country, while central and southern Babylonia remained in the hands of Cyrus and his agents. Furthermore, Cambyses reigned for no more than about nine months. In 537, for unknown reasons, Cyrus removed him from his post. (See M. San Nicolò, *Beiträge zu einer Prosopographie neubabylonischer Beamten der Zivil- und Tempelverwaltung*, Munich, 1941, pp. 51-54; M. A. Dandamaev, *Politicheskaya istoriya Akhemenidskoĭ derzhavy*, Moscow, 1985, pp. 45-48.)

Cyrus retained as governor of Babylonia a native Babylonian, Nabu-ahhe-bullit, who had held the post before the Persian conquest, under Nabonidus. In 535, however, he created a single province comprised of Mesopotamia and the countries to the west of the Euphrates (Phoenicia, Syria, Palestine), and he appointed as satrap a Persian, Gubaru, who held this position until at least 525. The province itself, which included practically the entire territory of the former Neo-Babylonian empire, was designated Babylonia and Beyond the River. By March, 520, its governor was Ushtani, another Persian. But about 516 Darius I split the satrapy into two: Ushtani became governor of Babylonia, while Beyond the River was allocated to Tattenai, though Ushtani still ranked higher than Tattenai in the administration. In Herodotus's list of the satrapies of the Persian empire (3.91-92) the divided province appears as two distinct satrapies: Babylonia and the "rest of Assyria" constitute the ninth satrapy, and Beyond the River is the fifth. The Babylonian satrapy also included the heartland of old Assyria. Herodotus (3.155 etc.) does not differentiate between Assyria and Babylonia: he calls Babylon the capital of Assyria, and sometimes he styles the Babylonians themselves "Assyrians." (See O. Leuze, *Die Satrapieneinteilung in Syrien und im Zweistromlande von 530-320*, Halle, 1935, repr. Hildesheim, 1972, pp. 4-42; A. T. Olmstead, "Tattenai, Governor of 'Across the River'," *JNES* 3, 1944, p. 46; M. San Nicolò, *Beiträge*, pp. 54-64.)

Babylonia was the richest satrapy under Achaemenian rule, paying one thousand talents (about thirty tons) of silver to the Persian kings annually, as well as five hundred boys to serve at court as eunuchs. In addition, the Babylonians were required to maintain the army stationed in their country, and for four months of the year to provide provisions for the king and his entourage (Herodotus, 1.192, 3.92). On the Persepolis reliefs the Babylonians are depicted among the tributary peoples, bringing woven garments, vases and other vessels (G. Walser, *Die Völkerschaften auf den Reliefs von Persepolis*, Tehraner Forschungen 2, Berlin, 1966, pp. 77f.).

The Achaemenids spent part of the year in Babylon. They laid out gardens with pavilions, and in 345 Artaxerxes III ordered the construction of the *apadāna*. Fragments of trilingual inscriptions of Persian kings have also been found (F. Wetzel, E. Schmidt, and A. Mallwitz, *Das Babylon der Spätzeit*, pp. 48-49).

Although there was no sudden break in the local administrative, economic, and juridical traditions, nevertheless significant changes did gradually occur both in the structure of government itself and in the terminology of officialdom. Babylonian texts thus contain many administrative, juridical, economic, and military terms borrowed from Old Persian: *ahšadarapannu* (satrap), *arazapanatašu* (vineyard-keeper), *ardabu* (a measure of capacity), *aštabarru* (lance bearer), *bāra* (tax), *dāta* (law), *dātabara* (judge), *ganzabara* (treasurer), *hāmārakara* (bookkeeper), *iprasakku* (investigator), *pardēsu* (paradeisos), *umarzanapāta* (city governor), and many others (W. Eilers, *Iranische Beamtennamen in der keilschriftlichen Überlieferung*, Leipzig, 1940).

Under the Achaemenids Babylonian private law reached the peak of its development, providing the general model for the juridical norms among the countries of the Near East. In its dealings with the population of Babylonia the Achaemenid government observed local law, as did those Persians who began to participate in the administrative life of the country. Throughout the Achaemenid period private law and documentary conventions underwent no fundamental change, although Iranian influence did reach many state institutions, and private law was to some extent affected by the reforms in economic and state management introduced at the beginning of the reign of Darius I (G. Cardascia, *Les archives des Murašû*, Paris, 1951, pp. 5-8).

Soon after the Persian conquest of Babylonia, texts already refer to "judges of Cyrus" or "royal judges." Under Darius I and his successors there are also frequent references to Persian judges. For example, the late fifth-century documents from Nippur regularly mention Ishtubazanu, a judge from the district of the Sin canal. Ishtubazanu subsequently handed on his office to his son Humardatu. Under Darius I a contract between two Babylonians concerning a loan was drawn up in the presence of the Persian judge Ummadatu, son of Udunatu, while another text from the same period mentions a Persian judge Ammadatu (*Textes cunéiformes, Musée du Louvre* XIII, Paris, 1929, no. 193; J. N. Strassmaier, *Inschriften von Darius, König von Babylon*, Leipzig, 1892, no. 435).

Members of the royal family and certain Persian magnates with extensive land-holdings in Babylonia had recourse to their own legal and administrative apparatus, as may be seen from the case of Queen Parysatis, wife of Darius II: Parysatis retained in Babylonia a judge, who was styled in documents "judge of the estate of Parysatis" (*The Babylonian Expedition of the University of Pennsylvania*. Series A: *Cuneiform Texts* X, Philadelphia, 1904, nos. 97 etc.).

After the capture of Babylonia, and after the many rebellions had been put down, the Achaemenids confiscated part of the land from the local population, split it into large estates, and distributed these estates among members of the royal family and Persian nobility as their unencumbered and hereditary possessions. The fields around the city of Nippur, for example, were divided among Persian magnates. Many of the owners are mentioned in documents from the well-known business house of Murashu. In 429 Bagavira, a Persian, son of Mithradates, leased to Murashu for a period of sixty years his own field and land which had passed to him on the death of his father's brother Rushundatu. Both fields were close to Nippur, by the side of two canals, next to the field of another Persian, Rushunpati. At the same time Bagavira also leased out "residential buildings" near Nippur. The lessee paid in full when the contract was issued, a total of 1800 hectoliters of dates (*The Babylonian Expedition* IX, 1898, no. 48). Also close to Nippur, and also leased to the house of Murashu, were the fields of Queen Parysatis (*Publications of the Babylonian Section, University of Pennsylvania* 2/1, Philadelphia, 1912, nos. 50, 60, 75, etc.). According to Xenophon (*Anabasis* 2.4.27), Parysatis owned in addition "villages" situated six days away from the town of Opis. The Persian princes too had large land-holdings near Nippur and elsewhere.

Part of the land was in effect the property of the king. Indeed, the royal holdings became significantly more extensive than they had been in the previous period. Like the fields of the royal family, the king's lands were normally leased out. In 420, for example, a representative of the house of Murashu requested the overseer of the king's grain-fields along a number of canals near Nippur to lease him one field for three years. In return the lessee undertook to give an annual payment of thirty-three thousand liters of barley, three thousand liters of wheat, one and a half thousand liters of emmer, as well as one bull and ten sheep (*Texte und Materialen der Frau Professor Hilprecht Collection* II/3, Leipzig, 1933, no. 147). *Paradeisoi* (parks with fruit and other trees) of the Persian kings were located near the cities of Sippar, Nippur, and Uruk (M. Dandamayev, "Royal Paradeisoi in Babylonia," in *Orientalia J. Duchesne-Guillemin Emerito Oblata*, Acta Iranica 23, Leiden, 1984, pp. 113-17).

The king also owned many large canals, which were normally leased out by his managers. The royal canals around Nippur were leased to the house of Murashu, which in turn sub-leased them to smaller landowners. Thus in 439 seven landowners made a contract with three lessees of a royal canal. One of the lessees was the house of Murashu. This contract stipulated that the sub-lessees had the right to irrigate their fields with water from the canal for three days each month. In return they were obligated to pay the lessees one third of the harvest from the irrigated fields in "water tax," as well as a specified sum of money for each measure of land (*The Babylonian Expedition* IX, no. 7).

In Babylonia under the Achaemenids the king would allot portions of land to his soldiers. The soldiers settled on such allotments would work the land communally, in groups, part of whose military service was to pay a levy in money and kind. Such holdings were called allotments of the bow, allotments of the horse, and allotments of the chariot, and their holders were obliged to serve as archers, cavalrymen, and charioteers respectively. In time of war the allotment-owners (who included both Babylonians and non-Babylonians) had to present themselves together with the appropriate equipment. The system of military allotments first started to be introduced in the 530s, in the reign of Cambyses. Despite the fact that most of our information about it derives from documents produced in Nippur in the late fifth century, it did become a feature of Babylonia as a whole (G. Cardascia, "Lehenswesen in der Perserzeit," *RlA* 6, 1983, pp. 547-50). These lands were inalienable: they passed to the soldiers' descendants in the male line. Only if there were no such descendants did the land revert to the state.

During the Achaemenid period there were major changes in the policies towards the Babylonian temples. The temples were substantial owners of land and of slaves, as well as operating as traders and usurers. The Chaldean kings and their families had paid the temples an annual tithe in gold, silver, cattle, grain, dates, and the like. The Achaemenids, though they preserved the tithe as a compulsory tax on their subjects, ceased to pay it themselves. The Chaldean kings had rarely meddled directly in the affairs of the temples. Only a minimal portion of the state's income was derived from the temples, whereas the temples received royal gifts of land and slaves. Yet under the Achaemenids the temples were obliged to pay to the state large taxes in kind: in cattle, sheep, goats, grain, etc. For example, in the second year of the reign of Cambyses shepherds of the temple of Eanna in Uruk had to bring two hundred head of suckling lambs and kids "for the king's table in the palace in the city of Amanu." In the same year the temple of Eanna also provided the same palace with eighty "large sheep," with spices, and other goods. Two years later the temple of Eanna was obliged to deliver one hundred and fifty tons of firewood, again to the same palace. In addition, temples performed certain tasks for the state, sending slaves to work in the palaces of Babylon and other cities. To ensure that the temples did actually fulfill their commitments to the state, that taxes were paid on time and that duties were performed, royal and fiscal agents were installed in the temple administration. Royal agents were also delegated to keep a check on temple possessions, and inspections were frequent (M. Dandamayev, "State and Temple in Babylonia in the First Millennium B.C.," *State and Temple Economy in the Ancient Near East* 2, Leuven, 1979, pp. 589-96).

III. Links with Iran.

There were cultural and commercial links between Babylonia and Iran well before the Medes and Persians had established their states on the territory of Iran (P. Calmeyer, "Mesopotamien und Iran im II und I Jahrtausend," *Mesopotamien und seine Nachbarn*, ed. H.-J. Nissen and J. Renger, Berlin, 1982, pp. 339-48). From the twelfth to tenth centuries B.C. Babylonia had close ties with the countries to the east of the Tigris. During this period the Babylonians held sway in Namar, a region in the middle reaches of the river Dīāla, and their influence extended to western Iran (J. Brinkman, *A Political History of Post-Kassite Babylonia*, Rome, 1968, p. 200). As early as the twelfth century the Babylonians also set their sights on the colonization of areas bordering on Media, and one finds Babylonian influence in artifacts from western Iran (P. Calmeyer, *Reliefbronzen in babylonischem Stil*, Munich, 1973, pp. 227-32).

Among items of Luristan bronze there have been found thirty-eight pieces of weaponry (daggers, arrowheads, etc.) inscribed with the names of Babylonian kings who reigned from 1135 to 940. This may have been votive weaponry dedicated to Babylonian temples and subsequently captured by troops from Iran on their incursions into Mesopotamia. Yet it has also been suggested that the weapons were gifts presented for loyal service, from Babylonian rulers to troops from Iran (G. Dossin, "Bronzes inscrits du Luristan de la collection Foroughi," *Iranica Antiqua* 2, 1962, pp. 149-64; P. Calmeyer, *Datierbare Bronzen aus Luristan und Kirmanshah*, Berlin, 1969, pp. 161-74). The names of private individuals also appear on several of the Luristan bronzes, inscribed in cuneiform, in the Akkadian language, yet many of these inscriptions are in fact merely copied from older Babylonian oddments (mainly seals) by illiterate Luristan artisans (P. R. S. Moorey and W. G. Lambert, "An Inscribed Bronze Vessel from Luristan," *Iran* 10, 1972, pp. 161-63). Three Akkadian inscriptions have been found in Western Iran. One of them, cut on two sides of a bronze plate, was discovered not far from Hamadān and probably dates from the tenth or ninth century B.C. It refers to a king Shilisruh (we do not know of what country) who apparently released his subjects from certain taxes in kind (I. M. Diakonoff, "A Cuneiform Charter from Western Iran," in *Festschrift Lubor Matous* I, Budapest, 1978, pp. 51-68). The other two inscriptions were unearthed in excavations at Ḥasanlū. One of them may be dated paleographically to the ninth century, or perhaps earlier. It mentions the palace of Bauri, who seems to have been governor of the land of Ida. Ida, as Assyrian inscriptions show, was located in Zamua, one of the districts of western Iran (see ASSYRIA). The second inscription contains the name of Kadashman-Enlil, a Babylonian king of the Kassite dynasty, and it dates from the fourteenth or thirteenth century (both inscriptions in R. H. Dyson, "The Hasanlu Project 1961-67," in *The Memorial Volume of the Vth International Congress of Iranian Art and Archeology* I, Tehran, 1972, pp. 49-50). Since no texts in the Median language have been found, though literacy certainly did exist in the Median state, it is likely that the Medians used Akkadian cuneiform script and the Akkadian language. During the second millennium B.C. the Akkadian language and script were used sporadically, but widely, in southwestern Iran (see ELAM).

In its ethnic composition, Achaemenid Babylonia became increasingly mixed, and one can observe an emerging syncretism of the cultures and religious beliefs of its various peoples. This occurred partly because the Achaemenids founded ethnically heterogeneous military colonies in Mesopotamia. Often their administrative appointees were also of non-Babylonian origin. Babylonia thus came to contain a fair number of Egyptians, Lydians, Phrygians, Carians, and others. In the documents from the house of Murashu for the second half of the fifth century, about one third of all personal names are not Babylonian. There are dozens of Iranian names, mostly belonging to Persians, Medes, Sakai, and Areians, though some bearers of Iranian names were not actually of Iranian stock (R. Zadok, "Iranians and Individuals bearing Iranian Names in Achaemenian Babylonia," *Israel Oriental Studies* 7, 1977, pp. 89-138).

Persians took an ever more active part in local transactions, usually working through their agents who were for the most part Babylonians, Arameans, Egyptians, etc. Even Cambyses, while prince, became involved in usury, making loans through his steward (J. N. Strassmaier, *Inschriften von Cyrus, König von Babylon*, Leipzig, 1890, no. 177). Partammu, a Persian, bought a house in the center of Babylon (J. N. Strassmaier, *Inschriften von Darius*, no. 410). In Borsippa Arbatema the Persian leased out his secure storehouses (M. San Nicolò and A. Ungnad, *Neubabylonische Rechts- und Verwaltungsurkunden* I, Leipzig, 1929-37, no.138). In 423 the house of Murashu paid for the lease of a field belonging to the Persian Uhejagam, son of Parnak. The field was near Nippur, though its owner lived in Babylon, to where the payment had therefore to be sent (not, as was normal, in kind, but in money) (*Publications of the Babylonian Section* II/1, no. 5). One legal document was drawn up in Dilbat during the reign of

Darius I in the presence of several civil servants among whom was a Persian named Ahsheti, son of Kamakka (San Nicolò and Ungnad, *Neubabylonische*, no. 702).

Many Persians fell gradually under Babylonian influence. In fifth-century Nippur, for example, the Persians Artabarri, Bagadatu, Ishtubazanu, and others gave their sons typically Babylonian names such as Nidintu-Bel and Bel-ibni (*The Babylonian Expedition* IX, nos. 14, 76, 82, etc.). Conversely, Babylonians started to give their children foreign names. Thus the sons of Ninurta-eṭir, Bel-ibni, and others were given names like Tiridatu, Shatabarzana, Adabaga, or Aspabar (*The Babylonian Expedition* IX, nos. 39, 69, 74, etc.). Such onomastic borrowing frequently occurred in the context of mixed marriages, as in the case of the Persian Mithradates and his Babylonian wife Esagil-belit, who gave their son the Iranian name of Bagavira (*The Babylonian Expedition* IX, no. 48). Since all the cited Babylonian and Iranian names derive from the names of deities ("Ninurta the god-saved," "given by the god Mithra," etc.) it is likely that their bearers worshipped the foreign deities as well as their own. One might note in this context a building excavated in Uruk and thought to be a shrine of Mithra. A clay image of Mithra killing a bull has been found there (*Vorläufiger Bericht über die... in Uruk-Warka unternommenen Ausgrabungen* XIV, Berlin, 1958, pp. 18-20). Persian influence can also be detected in Babylonian seals of the Achaemenid period.

Medes, too, were deeply involved in Babylonian affairs. Early in the reign of Darius I a Median family living in Babylonia, Kakia and his wife Uhija, leased a house from one Babylonian dealer while from another they hired equipment and a slave-girl (Strassmaier, *Inschriften von Darius*, no. 51). Another Mede, Ninakku, a resident of Borsippa, pawned his slave-girl to a Babylonian (San Nicolò and Ungnad, *Neubabylonische*, no. 677).

Babylonian texts frequently mention *gimirrāya* (literally "Cimmerians"). The reference is probably to members of the Saka (Scythian) tribes of Central Asia, who spoke one of the Old Iranian dialects. In Achaemenid Babylonia they served in the king's army. Among the Sakai in the Persian army in Babylonia were those whose job it was to guard the boats carrying official cargoes by order of the Persian administration. A document of the year 524 mentions Scythians with the Iranian names Ušukaya and Tattakkaya (M. A. Dandamayev, "Saka Soldiers on Ships," *Iranica Antiqua* 22, 1982, pp. 101-02).

As early as the seventh century B.C. the Scythians had mounted raids on Western Asia, and a Scythian influence on Babylonian armor is noticeable even before the Persian conquest of Mesopotamia. The soldiers of Nebuchadnezzar II and Nabonidus were often equipped with Scythian bows, Scythian bronze- and iron-tipped arrows, and various other Scythian items including Scythian harnesses for their horses. In the pre-Persian levels at Babylon archeologists have found bronze arrowheads of the Scythian type. These technological borrowings occurred because the Scythian bows were vastly superior to the Babylonian in their ballistic qualities (M. A. Dandamayev, "Data of the Babylonian Documents from the 6th to the 5th Centuries B.C. on the Sakas," in *Prolegomena to the Sources on the History of Pre-Islamic Central Asia*, ed. J. Harmatta, Budapest, 1979, pp. 95-109). Among Babylonia's military colonists of Iranian extraction can also be found Areians (*arumāya*), who came originally from Haraiva in what is now Afghanistan.

A document from Babylon dated 508 B.C. mentions among the slaves of the business house of Egibi a girl from Gandara on Iran's border with India. In Sippar in 511 a Babylonian sold a slave-girl of Bactrian origin (T. G. Pinches "Babylonian Contract-Tablets with Historical References," *Records of the Past* IV, London, 1890, pp. 104-06).

The population of Babylonia also included many Elamites. They are frequently mentioned in business transactions either as contracting parties or as witnesses. Under Darius I, for example, a man with the Elamite name of Sammannapir gave his daughter to an Egyptian in marriage. In addition, Elamites often traveled for seasonal employment in Babylonian temples (M. A. Dandamayev, "Connections between Elam and Babylonia in the Achaemenid Period," in *The Memorial Volume* I, pp. 258-64; R. Zadok, "On the Connections between Iran and Babylonia in the Sixth Century B.C.," *Iran* 14, 1976, pp. 61-78). In a number of cases foreigners, and the military colonists in particular, occupied regions of Babylonia in groups substantial enough and homogeneous enough to have their own popular assemblies which acted as organs of local self-government alongside the assemblies of the Babylonian cities. The function of these assemblies of ethnic minorities was to resolve internal disputes. Thus a document from the time of Cambyses refers to the "assembly of the Elders of the Egyptians" in Babylon, which pronounced its verdict on some fields belonging to Egyptian colonists (M. A. Dandamayev, "The Neo-Babylonian Elders," in *Societies and Languages of the Ancient Near East: Studies in Honour of I. M. Diakonoff*, Warminster, 1982, p. 41). It would seem, therefore, that the *politeumata*, those popular assemblies of ethnic minorities, normally thought to be a purely Hellenistic institution, in fact made an embryonic appearance under the Achaemenids. For the most part, however, foreigners in Babylonia were dispersed throughout the country, living side by side with the local population, coming into contact through business and through intermarriage. The foreigners gradually became assimilated in their adopted land. They took Babylonian names, spoke Aramaic (which had become the standard spoken language of Mesopotamia), and in turn exerted a degree of their own cultural influence on the Babylonians. Akkadian, which was supplanted in oral communication by Aramaic, remained the language of literature, of religion, of some juridical documents, and, together with Old Persian and Elamite, of the royal inscriptions of the Achaemenids. During the Achaemenid period Old Persian borrowed a number of words from Akkadian, as, for example, *aguru* (kiln-fired brick), *maškā* (skin), and, via Elamite, *dipī* (inscription).

The administrative and economic expertise of the Babylonians, acquired over many centuries, was useful to and much used by the Persian kings in their government. Babylonians worked in the state bureaucracy in the late-sixth and early-fifth centuries, even in southwestern Iran. For example, the Babylonian Bel-eṭir was responsible for the delivery of the state post between Persepolis and Susa. Hitibel was a royal messenger. Marduka controlled a royal flour depot in the region of Liduma (R. T. Hallock, *Persepolis Fortification Tablets*, Chicago, 1969, nos. 81, 1381, etc.). Babylonian scribes on parchment, in groups of between three and thirty-one, also worked in Persepolis and in other cities of Iran, as did considerable numbers of Babylonian artisans (Hallock, *Persepolis*, nos. 868, 1807, 1810, 1811, 1821, 1828, etc.). At the construction of the palace of Darius I at Susa Babylonians were involved in earthworks, brick-moulding, and in cutting the reliefs (Kent, *Old Persian*, p. 142). Susa, capital of the Achaemenid empire, was home to many Babylonians. A document in Akkadian written at Susa in 447 mentions several people with Babylonian names, both as witnesses and as one of the contracting parties (M. Rutten, "Tablette No. 4," *Mémoires de la Mission Archéologique en Iran* 36, Paris, 1954, pp. 83-85). A slave sale contract written at Persepolis in Babylonian during the reign of Darius I has been preserved, in which the contracting parties as well as the witnesses, the scribe, and the slave himself, to judge from their names, were Babylonians (M. W. Stolper, "The Neo-Babylonian Text from the Persepolis Fortification," *JNES* 43, 1984, pp. 299-310).

In the Achaemenid period close trading links were established between Iran and Babylonia. In the late sixth century members of the house of Egibi and others traveled regularly to southwestern Iran to sell barley and clothing and to purchase slaves and various Elamite export wares (Dandamayev, "Connections," p. 259). Soon after the Persian conquest of Mesopotamia, Babylonian businessmen started traveling to Ecbatana, capital of Media, and to other cities in northwest Iran, for trade (Strassmaier, *Inschriften von Cyrus*, nos. 60, 227, etc.).

Bibliography: Given in the text. See also *Camb. Hist. Iran* II, esp. chaps. 3, 5, 10.

(M. A. DANDAMAYEV)

ii. BABYLONIAN INFLUENCES ON IRAN

Introduction. We can distinguish three periods in the influence of Mesopotamian civilization on pre-Islamic Iran: (1) the pre-Achaemenid period: before the conquest of Babylon by Cyrus the Great; (2) the Achaemenid period: before the conquest of the Persian empire by Alexander the Great; and (3) the Seleucid-Parthian-Sasanian period.

The first period was characterized by an influence on the Medes and the Persians that was often indirect and at times mediated by the Elamite world, with no more than a tendency towards eclecticism and syncretism (see Boyce, *Zoroastrianism* I, pp. 30ff., 141). The second period was one of direct contact probably favored by the presence of Iranian Magi in Babylon and of the elaboration of a religious syncretism which spread beyond Mesopotamia and Iran to reach Israel and Asia Minor. In this period, the influence of Babylonia was strong in the fields of the arts, science, religion, and religious policies, even affecting the concept of kingship (see G. Gnoli, "Politica religiosa e concezione della regalità sotto gli Achemenidi," in *Gururājamañjarikā. Studi in onore di Giuseppe Tucci*, Napoli, 1974, pp. 23-88). The third and longest period was distinguished by an influence that was both Mesopotamian and Semitic and Hellenistic. During this period the syncretistic features in all fields were still clearer and more obvious and the cultural influence in the broad sense was still more accentuated, especially under the Parthians (see G. Widengren, *Iranisch-semitische Kulturbegegnung in parthischer Zeit*, Cologne and Opladen, 1960), whereas influence on political concepts and, in particular, on the concept of kingship was weaker.

General. From the era of the supremacy of the Medes to the end of the Sasanian period, Mesopotamian civilization never ceased to influence the development in the Iranian world in religion, science, the arts, writing, political and administrative organization, and law, and with the conquest of Babylon in 539 B.C., Cyrus II became the head of an immense empire with traditions in these fields dating back over a thousand years.

Babylonian or Mesopotamian influence on Iranian art from the most ancient times is immediately obvious both in monumental art and sculpture, though these were also subject to Greek and Egyptian influences in the Achaemenid era (see A. Farkas, *Achaemenid Sculpture*, Istanbul, 1974; H. Frankfort, *The Art and Architecture of the Ancient Orient*, Harmondsworth, Middlesex, 1956, chap. 12; E. Porada, "Classic Achaemenian Architecture and Sculpture," in *Camb. Hist. Iran* II, 1985, pp. 793-831; M. C. Root, *The King and Kingship in Achaemenid Art*, Acta Iranica 19, Leiden, 1979).

Babylonian influence on the religious thought and the actual practices of worship in ancient Iran proved fertile in the meeting between the Iranian Magi and the Chaldeans, especially in Achaemenid Babylonia. References to this meeting are to be found in classical Greek and Latin sources (see G. Messina, *Der Ursprung der Magier und die zarathuštrische Religion*, Rome, 1930, pp. 48ff.; J. Bidez and F. Cumont, *Les Mages hellénisés*, Paris, 1938, I, pp. 34ff.) and an analysis of all the available sources enables us to reconstruct a fairly exhaustive picture of the influence of Mesopotamian religious thought on the doctrines of the Magi (see M. Boyce, op. cit., pp. 28ff., 66ff., 196ff., 201ff.).

The astral character of the Babylonian religion, in which the stars were considered divine entities to be worshipped, was increasingly accentuated in the course of the first millennium B.C. (see J. Bottéro, *La religion babylonienne*, Paris, 1952, pp. 142ff., and, more generally, B. Meissner, *Babylonien und Assyrien* II, Heidelberg, 1925, chap. 18) and even penetrated the other religions of the ancient Orient, the Iranian included. The characteristics and names of the stars were attributed to the gods and there was a growing conviction that their dominion over the world and over mankind was that of the astral forces themselves. Later, the mysterious, invincible, and all-pervading force called the *Heimarmene*, which had developed with particular vigor in the Hellenistic era, underwent a process of divinization and was placed at the center of the astral ideology's vision of the world and of life.

In Babylonian politics the Persians found a model which they used to further develop their own political structures.

It is a remarkable fact, however, that in spite of this strong cultural pressure Iran never lost its own originality or identity and developed autonomous structures with their own characteristics (see A. Bausani, *L'Iran e la sua tradizione millenaria*, Rome, 1971, pp. 9, 38).

In view of these facts it is obviously historically misleading to see the development of Iranian civilization solely in an Indo-European perspective, as has sometimes been done.

Zurvanism and dualism. The origin and development of the religious tendency which goes by the name of Zurvanism were in all probability inspired by the astral ideology of Babylonia (see Bidez and Cumont, op. cit., I, p. 64; G. Gnoli, *Zoroaster's Time and Homeland*, Naples, 1980, pp. 210ff., and *De Zoroastre à Mani*, Paris, 1985, pp. 71ff.). As it appears certain that Zurvanism was developed in the Achaemenid period and since it is quite likely that the religious tradition of Babylonia was at the heart of the syncretism which characterized the cultural history of the Near East in the first millennium B.C., even before the advent of Hellenism, we are led to recognize in the Iranian Zurwān (Avestan *Zrvan*; Pahlavi *Zurwān* and *Zamān* "Time") an influence from this ideology. The alternative hypothesis, that Zurvanism was an autonomous Iranian religion professed by the Median Magi and independent of Mazdaism, is less probable (see, e.g., G. Widengren, *Die Religionen Irans*, Stuttgart, 1965, pp. 149ff., 214ff.). Even less convincing are the attempts that have been made to trace its origins back to a Phoenician god of time supposed to be not only the source of the Chronos of Pherecides (mid-6th century B.C.) but also of the Indian Kāla (see Boyce, op. cit., pp. 150ff.).

It has been conjectured that Mesopotamian religion influenced Iranian dualism (G. Furlani, *Miti babilonesi e assiri*, Florence, 1958, p. 24 n. 2). This may certainly be true in the case of the particular role played in Mesopotamia and in Iran by demonology. The divine or extra-human world was seen as the scene of a struggle between contending powers that was reproduced and reflected on earth. However, Iranian dualism must be seen in a much broader historical perspective and it is necessary to distinguish clearly between different times and places.

In fact, Iranian dualism does not present a single body of doctrines remaining unchanged throughout the course of time. While the dualism of the *Gāθās* is expressed in the formula "Angra Mainyu versus Spənta Mainyu overshadowed by the figure of Ahura Mazdā, the god and creator of all things," the so-called Zurvanite dualism is characterized by the formula "Ahriman versus Ōhrmazd, overshadowed by Zurwān ī akanārag 'Boundless Time'." While in the Zoroastrian teachings the two opposing spirits are represented as twins, in the myth and doctrine of Zurvanism, Ahriman and Ōhrmazd himself are twin brothers.

It is quite probable that this profound transformation of Iranian dualism came about in the Achaemenid era through Mesopotamian influence. The formula "Oromasdes versus Areimanios," which is well documented in the most ancient Greek sources such as the *Peri philosophias* of Aristotle, Eudemus of Rhodes in Damascius, and *De Iside et Osiride* of Plutarch, most probably presupposes the presence of a dominating entity such as Zurwān (G. Gnoli, "L'évolution du dualisme iranien et le problème zurvanite," *RHR* 201, 1984, pp. 130ff.).

Astrology. It is generally acknowledged that Babylonian astrology was at the root of the spreading of astrology in ancient Iran, even though only one planet, Saturn, has preserved a Semitic name, Kaywān; the others are named after Iranian divinities: Ōhrmazd (Jupiter), Warahrān (Mars), Anāhīd (Venus), and Tīr (Mercury). The order of the planets, reproduced by Zādspram (30.12; cf. H. W. Bailey, *Zoroastrian Problems in the Ninth-Century Books*, Oxford, 1943, p. 211), reflects the order given them by the Greeks (see J. Duchesne-Guillemin, *La religion de l'Iran ancien*, Paris, 1962, p. 247). In Mazdean cosmology the planets were turned into devils, but probably only at a relatively late period, as is shown by the fact that they still bear the names of the greatest divine entities (cf. R. C. Zaehner, *Zurvan: A Zoroastrian Dilemma*, Oxford, 1955, pp. 152, 160ff.). This contradiction between the divine names and the diabolic nature of the planets may be one of the reflections in Iran of the astral religious thought of Babylonia.

The spreading of Chaldean astrology in Iran is generally dated to the Hellenistic or Parthian era because of the Greek influence evident in that period (see D. N. MacKenzie, "Zoroastrian Astrology in the *Bundahišn*," *BSOAS* 27, 1964, pp. 513-29) and, more particularly, in the astronomical notions that appear in the Pahlavi texts (see W. B. Henning, "An Astronomical Chapter of the Bundahišn," *JRAS*, 1942, pp. 229-48). We can not, however, exclude an earlier period for this event and, in fact, certain aspects of the astronomy of the second chapter of the *Bundahišn* date back to a pre-Achaemenid era (Henning, loc. cit., p. 230) while other aspects—the ecliptic, the zodiacal signs, and the planets—reveal an early Babylonian influence but also a relatively late (mid-Sasanian era) Greek influence, especially as regards the system of the lunar mansions.

At any rate, the renaming of the planets—e.g., Ōhrmazd for Marduk-Jupiter, Warahrān for Nergal-Mars, Anāhīd for Ištar-Venus, and Tīr for Nabû-Mercury—dates back to the Achaemenid era. In fact, the Achaemenid Iranian-Mesopotamian religious syncretism was only one, though perhaps the most important, aspect of a much vaster and more general phenomenon which affected the Western Semitic world, including Israel and Asia Minor. This syncretism finally made an indirect contribution to the religion of the Mysteries of Mithra (see F. Cumont, *Les mystères de Mithra*, 2nd ed., Brussels, 1902, p. 24, and G. Gnoli, "Sol Persice Mithra," in *Mysteria Mithrae*, ed. U. Bianchi, Leiden, 1979, pp. 725-40.)

Great gods. The three great Iranian divinities Ahura Mazdā, Miθra, and Anāhitā appear in Achaemenid inscriptions starting from the reign of Artaxerxes II (404-359 B.C.). As regards Anāhitā, we know from Berossus, quoted by Clement of Alexandria (C. Clemen, *Fontes historiae religionis persicae*, Bonn, 1920, p. 67), that it was Artaxerxes II himself who ordered images of Aphrodite Anaitis to be set up throughout his vast territories—in Babylon, Susa, Ecbatana, Persepolis, Bactra, Damascus, and Sardis—and who spread the worship of his new goddess. According to Herodotus (1.131) it was the "Assyrian" and "Arabian" influence which was supposed to have led to the spreading of the cult of Aphrodite Urania among the Persians. All this evidence points to Mesopotamian influence on the cult of Anāhitā, and it is probable that the Assyrian Ištar and the Elamite Nanā were forerunners of the Iranian goddess (cf. G. Gnoli, "Politica religiosa," pp. 31ff.) since her complex nature can not be explained from an Indo-Iranian viewpoint alone. It is for this reason that Boyce (op. cit., chaps. 2, 12, 13) proposes that we should recognize in this goddess as she appears in late-Achaemenid, Parthian, and Sasanian times the result of an identification of a Western Iranian divinity *Anāhiti strongly influenced by the Elamite and Mesopotamian goddess, and the Avestan *Harahvaitī Arədvī Sūrā Anāhitā. According to this hypothesis, the Babylonian influence would account for the strengthening of a cult which did not conform to orthodox Zoroastrianism, for the anthropomorphism, and for the founding of temples with divine images which were later to be countered by the spreading of the temple-cult of fire (M. Boyce, "Iconoclasm among the Zoroastrians," in *Studies for Morton Smith at Sixty*, ed. J. Neusner, Leiden, 1975, pp. 93-111).

Similarly Ahura Mazdā and Miθra were probably identified with Marduk, the principal god of Babylon, and Šamaš, the solar divinity, respectively (see Gnoli, "Politica religiosa," pp. 29f., 37f., 44 and Boyce, *Zoroastrianism* II, pp. 28f.); in the Babylonian calendar the seventh month was dedicated to Šamaš, in the Iranian calendar it was dedicated to Miθra (see Gnoli, "Sol Persice," pp. 734ff.).

Tīrī/Tīr (or perhaps *Tīriya, see M. Schwartz, "The Religion of Achaemenian Iran," in *Camb. Hist. Iran* II, p. 673), the god of the planet Mercury, was assimilated to the Mesopotamian Nabû (see G. Gnoli, "La stella Sirio e l'influenza dell'astrologia caldea nell'Iran antico," *Studi e Materiali di Storia delle Religioni* 34, 1963, pp. 237-45; Boyce, op. cit., pp. 31ff.).

Kingship. The special relationship that Ahura Mazdā, Miθra, and Anāhitā had with kingship is demonstrated by the appearance of their names in the royal inscriptions of the Achaemenids as well as by other evidence (see Gnoli, "Politica religiosa," pp. 31-43). It is probable that this relationship reflected Mesopotamian beliefs and customs, especially in the case of Marduk and Ištar (and her various namesakes). Moreover, the formula used in the Old Persian inscriptions to express the idea of the divine investiture of the king of kings, *vašnā Ahuramazdāha* "by the will of Ahura Mazdā" is quite probably of Mesopotamian inspiration (cf. Gnoli, *De Zoroastre à Mani*, p. 63 and n. 39). In it is contained the idea of the sovereign being elected by the supreme god, an idea which is similar to the Assyro-Babylonian concept of kingship but unlike the Avestan idea of the *kavi* who ruled by virtue of his *x*ᵛ*arənah*. The Achaemenid concept had to be adapted to the reality of a universal empire and an absolute monarchy, while the Avestan one perpetuated traditions proper to an essentially tribal, patriarchal, and pastoral society (see Gnoli, "Politica religiosa," pp. 72ff.). The Babylonian influence on the concept of kingship and on the royal ideology of ancient Iran also strongly affected institutional practice and court ceremonial, for instance, the adoption of co-regency and the introduction of elements of etiquette such as the *proskynesis* (see G. Widengren, "The Sacral Kingship of Iran," in *The Sacral Kingship*, Leiden, 1959, pp. 247ff.; Gnoli, *"Politica religiosa,"* pp. 25, 62ff.).

Mesopotamian influence continued until the end of the Sasanian period. It played an important part in the formation of Manicheism, whose founder, Mani, called himself the Apostle of Babylon and which professed a dualism of Iranian origin (see G. Widengren, *Mesopotamian Elements in Manichaeism*, Uppsala, 1946).

Bibliography: Given in the text. See also H. Frankfort, *Kingship and the Gods*, Chicago, 1955, 2nd ed., epilogue. C. Colpe, "Development of Religious Thought," in *Camb. Hist. Iran* III, 2, 1983, pp. 819-65. R. N. Frye, *The History of Ancient Iran*, Munich, 1984, pp. 133ff.

(G. GNOLI)

BAČČA-YE SAQQĀ (popularly Bače Saqqāw), "the water-carrier's child," the derogatory name given to the leader of a peasants' revolt which succeeded in placing him on the throne of Afghanistan in 1307 Š./1929. He reigned for nine months with the title Amīr Ḥabīb-Allāh Khan Ḵādem-e Dīn-e Rasūl Allāh.

Ḥabīb-Allāh was his real name. He was born about 1307/1870 into a poor family settled at Kalakān, a large Tajik village in the Kōhdāman district some 30 km north of Kabul His father had once been a water-carrier (*saqqā*) in the Afghan army. The son also enlisted, and in 1298 Š./1919 he fought in the third Anglo-Afghan war, serving in one of the best regiments and earning distinction for bravery and marksmanship. In 1303 Š./1924, however, he deserted, being unwilling to take part in the campaign against the Mangal tribe, whose antipathy to the régime of King Amān-Allāh he shared. After living for a few years as a fugitive in the tribal areas of northwestern of India, he reappeared in his native district in the role of a traditional Iranian *ʿayyār* (chivalrous bandit), attacking official convoys, holding rich travelers to ransom, and distributing part of his booty among the peasants. The insecurity which he caused throughout the strategic Samt-e Šamālī region at the head of his fellow outlaws was so troublesome that King Amān-Allāh several times sent troops on unsuccessful missions to capture him. Their reverses enhanced Bačča-ye Saqqā's popularity and brought more recruits to his cause, which, moreover, received active support from local Naqšbandī *mollās* and *ʿolamāʾ*, who were now calling in their sermons for disobedience to the central government, which in their eyes had become impious and therefore illegitimate.

The revolt of the Šīnwārī tribe in the Nangrahār district in ʿAqrab, 1307 Š./November, 1928, posed a grave threat to the régime. Out of concern for the few troops left behind in Kabul, King Amān-Allāh offered an amnesty to Bačča-ye Saqqā. The latter sent a pretended acceptance, but then took the chance to seize the fortress of Jabal al-Serāj on 19 Qaws/10 December. From this stronghold he immediately launched an offensive against Kabul, but failed to advance much further than the hill of Bāḡ-e Bālā, northwest of the capital, before being forced at the end of ten days of confused fighting to retreat toward Paḡmān and the Kōhdāman in order to regroup his forces. He resumed the offensive on 23 Jadī 1307 Š./13 January 1929 and this time his men, said to have been 15,000 strong, easily outflanked the few thousand royal troops left in Kabul. In desperation Amān-Allāh abdicated on the following day in favor of his elder half-brother ʿEnāyat-Allāh and fled from the capital by car, taking the main road to the south. His action shattered the morale of his remaining supporters. When the fallen king reached Qandahār, the water-carrier's son was in control of the capital except the Arg (citadel), which held out for a few more hours while the leading Naqšbandī *mollās* negotiated ʿEnāyat-Allāh's abdication. They then crowned Bačča-ye Saqqā amir of Afghanistan on 27 Jadī 1307 Š./17 January 1929.

The resumption of this old title, which Amān-Allāh had replaced with shah, epitomized the program of the new ruler of Kabul and the conservative forces which he represented. National traditions were to be reestablished through abolition of Amān-Allāh's modernizing reforms in the political, fiscal, judicial, and, above all, socio-cultural fields. Steps were to be taken for a return to the *Šarīʿa* and for immediate closure of state schools, removal of dress constraints, and reinstatement of the lunar calendar. (In point of fact, all coins minted for Amir Ḥabīb-Allāh bear the lunar year-date.)

At Kabul the change of régime proceeded rather smoothly. A considerable number of men of the political class, and even of the royal family, rallied to the new ruler through genuine sympathy or mere opportunism. Ḥabīb-Allāh himself, in an evident quest for legitimacy, contrived to get a place in the royal clan by taking a second wife from the collateral Eʿtemādī line. His staunchest supporters, however, were always the *mollās*, especially those in the Naqšbandī order to which he himself apparently belonged, and the Tajiks of the Samt-e Šamālī. After ten years of erratic effort to secularize Afghan society, the *mollās* got their revenge by recovering their influence and privileges. After two centuries of Paštūn ascendancy, the Tajiks turned the scales by looting the homes of Moḥammadzī princes in Kabul and obtaining all the ministerial posts. None of the foreign powers, however, gave the new régime de jure recognition, and most of them evacuated their nationals from Kabul as soon as they could arrange airlifts to Peshawar and Termez.

In Afghan historiography, the rise of Ḥabīb-Allāh, the water-carrier's son, is called the Saqqāwī movement or Saqqāwīya. Despite the narrowness of its power-base, his government was able to bring the greater part of Afghanistan under control within a few months. No serious opposition was encountered in the west, where Herat surrendered on 14 Ṯawr/4 May, or in the north, where the Aymāq, Uzbek, and Tajik ethnic groups supported him. In other regions events took different turns. The Hazāra people of the center of the country remained loyal to Amān-Allāh out of gratitude for his abolition of slavery and tolerant attitude to Shiʿism; the amir Ḥabīb-Allāh did not succeed in subduing them, but eventually got them to sign a cease-fire whereby they were to stop their harassment of his troops. As for the Paštūns of the south and east, although most of them undoubtedly disliked Amān-Allāh, they resented the enthronement of a non-Paštūn even more deeply. Several ill-prepared risings of Paštūn dissidents took place and successively collapsed, more because of internal dissensions and tribal rivalries than because of any military superiority of the Saqqāwī troops. The old enmity between the Dorrānī and Ḡelzī tribal confederations had been effectively rekindled by Naqšbandī preachers who had acquired great influence among the latter, and the resultant split was the direct cause of the failure of Amān-Allāh's attempt to reconquer the throne in the spring of 1929, after which he finally left the scene for exile abroad. With this event a spell of good fortune for Ḥabīb-Allāh set in. No longer having to face any serious adversary, he was able to establish his authority in almost all the Paštūn country, taking Qandahār on 10 Jawzā/31 May, and Gardēz on 5 Saraṭān/26 June.

The only irreducible stronghold of resistance was the Afghan part of the Solaymān mountains, where the tribes traditionally lived beyond the reach of the central government, whatever its complexion. It was in the area of one of them, the Jājī tribe, that Nāder Khan and his brothers of the Yaḥyā K̲ēl, a branch of the royal clan very distantly related to Amān-Allāh, established their base after returning hurriedly from exile in France. Spurning approaches from both Ḥabīb-Allāh and Amān-Allāh, they proceeded to organize anti-Saqqāwī operations for their own account. Their first thrusts toward Kabul in April and June failed.

Before long, however, the Saqqāwī government's position began to crumble as a result of lack of money, resentment of high tax demands by newly appointed provincial governors, and defections of influential *ʿolamāʾ* such as Fażl ʿOmar Mojaddedī, who swung the Ḡelzī tribes to Nāder's side. Further disorders in Paṣ̌tūn districts began at the end of the summer, and troops of the Kabul garrison had to be sent away to deal with them. Seeing the time ripe for another attempt on the capital, Nāder moved quickly. A three-week campaign ended with the capture of the Arg of Kabul by his younger brother and principal lieutenant, Šāh Walī Khan, on 21 Mīzān/13 October. Two days later Nāder entered the capital, and on 24 Mīzān/16 October he was proclaimed king by acclamation of his troops, whom he then let loose to pillage the city for three days. Ḥabīb-Allāh, now again only Bačča-ye Saqqā, had fled to the Kōhdāman, his main stronghold, but on 30 Mīzān/22 October he surrendered against the promise of an amnesty. The promise was not kept; he and some ten leading figures in his government were executed at Kabul on 10 ʿAqrab 1308 Š./1 November 1929.

The death of Bačča-ye Saqqā did not mark the end of the Saqqāwīya. The Kōhdāman again erupted in 1309 Š./1930 and was very harshly subdued by means of bombardments, the burning down of the bazaar of Sarā-ye Ḵᵛāja, summary executions, and seizures of cattle and women by bands of Aḥmadzī, Mangal, and Jājī tribesmen who were sent into the district. The repression was accompanied by systematic planting of Paṣ̌tūn settlers to counteract the local particularism. Such steps, however, could not eradicate memories of Bačča-ye Saqqā. Glorified as the "Lion of the mountains" (Šēr-e Kōhsār), he still remains alive in the folklore of the Kōhdāman. Men directly descended from Saqqāwī supporters are known to be active as local cadres of anti-communist movements in the 1980s.

Afghan official historiography has always portrayed the period of Saqqāwī rule as a deplorable and rather ridiculous interlude, an accident of history due to a temporary upsurge of obscurantist and reactionary forces. It is indeed true that Bačča-ye Saqqā and most of his ministers were illiterate. This portrait, however, is oversimplified. The Saqqāwīya was a genuinely popular movement of opposition to the central power and not so narrowly confined to the Tajik ethnic group as is often said, because several notables of the Kōhdāman, who were of Paṣ̌tūn descent but had become Persian-speaking, threw their weight behind it. On the other hand it was manipulated by *mollā*s to such an extent that it cannot be said to have been wholly spontaneous. Many commentators, in Afghanistan and elsewhere, hold that British secret agencies played a part in the destabilization and fall of Amān-Allāh's régime. Soviet historiography, in particular, asserts this thesis. While it can not be dismissed out of hand, the fact remains that no evidence to support it can be found in the copious British Indian archives pertaining to this period. There can be no doubt, however, that behind the stance of official neutrality which the British maintained throughout the crisis of 1929 lay an unwillingness to help Amān-Allāh to reconquer his throne and a benevolence toward the moves of Nāder Khan. While the Soviet authorities favored Amān-Allāh (though reluctantly) and aided a foray on his behalf by Ḡolām Nabī Čarḵī in the Balḵ region, the British authorities allowed Nāder Khan to reenter Afghanistan through India and to obtain a decisive addition of strength through his recruitment of thousands of armed Wazīr and Masʿūd frontier tribesmen. Also helpful was their decision to lift a restriction order, imposing residence at a fixed address in India, on Fażl ʿOmar Mojaddedī, who was to play an apparently decisive role in persuading the Naqšbandī *mollā*s of Afghanistan to change sides and later was to become Nāder Shah's first minister of justice. In short, while all the evidence indicates that Bačča-ye Saqqā's rise was due solely to the internal disintegration of King Amān-Allāh's régime, there can be no doubt that British policy, tacit rather than explicit, helped to bring about Bačča-ye Saqqā's fall. The sudden entry of such a character onto the stage was bound to cause internal instability in Afghanistan, and the British policymakers could not tolerate a long continuance of the threat which this would pose to the delicate geopolitical equilibrium of that part of Asia.

Bibliography: Sources for study of the Saqqāwīya are plentiful but not fully informative on all the episodes. Baččа-ye Saqqā's autobiography, available only in an English translation, *My Life: From Brigand to King. Autobiography of Amir Habibullah*, London, n.d. (1936), is in all probability apocryphal and certainly not objective. Reminiscences of several other participants have been published. The well-known poet Ḵ. Ḵalīlī (b. ca. 1906), who bore a personal grudge against Amān-Allāh and was treasurer (*mostawfī*) of Turkestan under Baččа-ye Saqqā. seeks to rehabilitate the Saqqāwīya in his recently published book *ʿAyyārī az Ḵorāsān: Amīr Ḥabīb-Allāh Ḵādem-e Dīn-e Rasūl Allāh*, Peshawar, n d. (1980). The views of the other side are expounded in the memoirs of Šāh Walī Khan. *Yāddašthā-ye man*, Kabul, 5th ed., 1344 Š./1965 (Russian tr., Moscow, 1960; Eng. tr., *My Memoirs*, Kabul, 1970), an apologia for the struggles against the "forces of ignorance and tyranny" with details of Nāder Khan's steps to form the tribal coalition which was to carry him to power. The same tone pervades two very detailed chronicles, one by Moḥyī-al-Dīn (Anīs), who recounts the events in strictly chronological order (*Borhān wa Nejāt*, Kabul, n.d., perhaps 1931), the other by B. Koškakī, who writes in a more convoluted way (*Nāder-e Afḡān*, Kabul, 1310 Š./1931).

Diplomatic dispatches, sent in large numbers from the foreign legations at Kabul before the evacuation of the foreigners, have been used by L. B. Poullada, *Reform and Rebellion in Afghanistan, 1919-1929*, Ithaca, 1973, and by L. W. Adamec, *Afghanistan's Foreign Affairs to the Mid-Twentieth Century*, Tucson, 1974 (both with a detailed list of documents). The sometimes thrilling account given by R. T. Stewart, *Fire in Afghanistan, 1914-1929*, Garden City, N.Y., 1973, is also based in the main on official sources but can not be used with confidence because she never cites them. K. Jäkel wrote his article "Reform und Reaktion in Afghanistan. Aufstieg und Fall Amānullāhs," *Mardom nameh* 3, Berlin, 1977, pp. 24-57, after obtaining access to unpublished Afghan sources which enabled him to draw attention, for the first time, to the importance of Bačča-ye Saqqā's links with the rural network of Sufi brotherhoods in the countryside of eastern Afghanistan. The only published account of Bačča-ye Saqqā's last days by a foreign eyewitness is in the book by A. Viollis (pseudonym of A. d'Ardenne de Tizac), *Tourmente sur l'Afghanistan*, Paris, 1930, a pompous record of events during her stay at Kabul as a journalist in October-November, 1929.

The latest findings of Soviet historiography on the subject are set forth in the work of V. G. Korgun, *Afghanistan v 20-30-gody XX v. Stranitsy politicheskoĭ istorii*, Moscow, 1979.

Selected texts of Saqqāwī-inspired folklore from the Kōhdāman have been published by L. Dupree in his book *Afghanistan*, Princeton, 1973, pp. 120ff. Also from this source is a quatrain (no. 81) collected by A. Farhādī, *Le persan parlé en Afghanistan*, Paris, 1955.

The Saqqāwī lineage of anti-communist groups active in the 1980s is documented by O. Roy, *L'Afghanistan. Islam et modernité politique*, Paris, 1985, p. 89.

(D. Balland)

BACHER, WILHELM (Bīnyāmīn Ze'ev) 1850-1913), was born in Liptószentmiklós, Hungary (today in Czechoslovakia). His father, Simon, was a Hebrew poet who translated a part of Sa'dī's *Golestān* into Hebrew (*Hebräische Dichtungen*, Vienna, 1894). In 1867 Bacher was admitted to the University of Budapest where he studied Oriental languages, history, and philosophy. The famous Ármin Vámbéry was one of Bacher's teachers. In 1870 he earned his doctorate writing a dissertation on the life and poetry of the Persian poet Neẓāmī (*Nizâmî's Leben und Werke und der zweite Theil des Nizâmîschen Alexanderbuches, mit persischen Texten als Anhang*, Leipzig, 1871; see also E. G. Browne, *Lit. Hist. Persia* II, p. 400). In 1876 Bacher was ordained a rabbi by Breslau Seminary and a year later was appointed by the Hungarian Government a professor at the newly founded Budapest Rabbinical Seminary, where he taught Bible, Jewish history, Midrash, Hebrew Poetry and Grammar. Bacher was one of the consulting editors of the *Jewish Encyclopaedia* (1901-05) where he published several articles on Judeo-Iranian subjects (see specially his "Judeo-Persian"). In 1907, Bacher was appointed head of the Seminary, which position he held until his death in 1913.

Bacher's scholarly output is exceptionally and outstandingly manysided (the bibliography of his published works, compiled by Ludwig Blau, lists 48 books and close to 700 articles). He was a master of Hebrew, Aramaic, Arabic, and Persian. He is known to Iranists especially through his many works on Judeo-Persian language and literature. Bacher's valuable works in Judeo-Persian are mainly based on the collection of Judeo-Persian manuscripts that Dr. Elkan Nathan Adler of England had bought during his travels to Central Asia, Afghanistan, and Iran at the end of the nineteenth century. The large part of this collection is now in the Jewish Theological Seminary of America in New York. About Bacher's list of important works on Judeo-Persian studies see Amnon Netzer, *Manuscripts of the Jews of Persia in the Ben Zvi Institute*, Jerusalem, 1985, p. 60.

(A. Netzer)

BACKGAMMON. See NARD.

BACTRA. See BACTRIA I; BALKH VI.

BACTRIA

i. *Pre-Islamic period.*
ii. *In the Avesta and in Zoroastrian tradition.*
(See also AFGHANISTAN VII and IX; and BALḴ.)

i. Pre-Islamic Period

Bactria, the territory of which Bactra was the capital, originally consisted of the plain between the Hindu Kush and the Āmū Daryā with its string of agricultural oases dependent on water taken from the rivers of Balḵ (Bactra), Tashkurgan, Kondūz, Sar-e Pol, and Šīrīn Tagāō. This region played a major role in Central Asian history. At certain times the political limits of Bactria stretched far beyond the geographic frame of the Bactrian plain.

Bactria in the Bronze and Iron Ages. The first mentions of Bactria occur in the list of Darius's conquests and in a fragment of the work of Ctesias of Cnidos—texts written after the region's incorporation in the Achaemenid empire. Ctesias, however, echoes earlier reports in his mention of campaigns by the Assyrian king Ninus and the latter's wife Semiramis (late 9th and early 8th century B.C.). Thereafter, he states, Bactria was a wealthy kingdom possessing many towns and governed from Bactra, a city with lofty ramparts. A similar picture is presented in the Zoroastrian tradition (*Avesta, Šāh-nāma*), which speaks of the protection given to Zoroaster by a powerful ruler of Bactra (see ii, below).

While the existence of such a kingdom remains hypothetical, archeological investigations have produced evidence of big oasis communities grouped around a fortress (Dašlī). These communities, like those of the oases in Margiana, were already practicing a well-developed system of irrigation and carrying on trade in products such as bronze and lapis lazuli with India and Mesopotamia.

Bactria under the Achaemenids. After annexation to the Persian empire by Cyrus in the sixth century, Bactria together with Margiana formed the Twelfth Satrapy. Apparently the annexation was not achieved through conquest but resulted from a personal union of the crowns. Indicative of this are the facts that the satrap was always a near kinsman of the great king and that the Achaemenid administrative system was not introduced. The local nobles played a big part and held all real power. Their wealth is attested by the opulence of the Oxus treasure. Bactra occupied a commanding position on the royal road to India. Profits from the east-west trade as well as from the outstandingly prosperous local agriculture enabled the province to pay a substantial tribute (360 talents of silver per annum).

The Bactrians also made an important contribution to the Persian army. At Salamis they were under the great king's direct command. At Gaugamela the Bactrian cavalry nearly turned the scales against the Macedonians. When Darius Codomannus, after his defeat in this battle, sought refuge in the Upper Satrapies, the Bactrian Bessos (q.v.) caused him to be murdered and then proclaimed himself king. Despite the resistance by scorched earth tactics conducted by Bessos, Bactria was conquered by the Macedonians and Bessos was delivered to them and put to death on Alexander's order. Bactra then served as Alexander's headquarters during his long compaign into Sogdia. After overcoming all the forces of resistance, Alexander took away 30,000 young Bactrians and Sogdians as hostages and incorporated a large number of Bactrians in his army. At the same time he settled many of his veterans in colonies planned to secure the Macedonian hold on Bactria.

Little information has been obtained from Achaemenid sites in Bactria. Bactra is deeply buried under the citadel (*bālā-ḥeṣār*) of present-day Balk̲. Drapsaca and Aornos, mentioned by the historians of Alexander, are usually identified with Kondūz and Tashkurgan, where excavations have yet to begin. More recently it has been suggested that Aornos may have been located at Altyn Delyār Tepe (Rtveladze, pp. 149-52), a site north of Balk̲ where excavation was started but could not be pursued. Other sites from the Achaemenid period are Kyzyl Tepe and Talaškan Tepe on the Sork̲ān Daryā, and Tak̲t-e Qobād (the probable source of the Oxus treasure) on the right bank of the Oxus, the citadel of Delbarjīn, and the circular town of Āy K̲ānom II on the left bank. All show traces of fortifications built of dried mud or large bricks on massive platforms. At none of them has thorough exploration yet been possible.

Hellenistic Bactria. The future of the Greek colonization of Bactria hung in the balance when the colonists rebelled in 326, after learning of Alexander's death, and again in 323; but they were reduced to obedience, and Bactria was then combined with Sogdia to form a satrapy under Philippos. After the establishment of the Seleucid regime, Bactra became for a time the headquarters of Seleucos I's son Antiochos, who was deputed to defend the eastern satrapies against the growing might of the Mauryan empire. The weakening of Seleucid power particularly in the reign of Antiochos II (261-247) enabled first Parthia, then Bactria to secede. The independent kingdom of Bactria was founded by Diodotos. On coins minted at Bactra the figure of Antiochos is replaced with that of Diodotos over the royal title (the figure on the reverse being Zeus brandishing a thunderbolt).

In 208 Antiochos III set out to reestablish Seleucid authority and marched into Bactria. After fending off a move by the Bactrian cavalry to halt his advance, he blockaded their king Euthydemos in the city of Bactra. The siege dragged on for two years, and in the end Antiochos had to recognize Bactria's independence and sign a treaty of alliance with Euthydemos.

The Greco-Bactrian kingdom was bounded in the south by the Paropamisadai (Hindu Kush) and in the east by the mountains of Badak̲šān. In the west it was in direct touch with the Parthians, who recovered Parthyene after the departure of Antiochos III and seized the Marv oasis. Scholars now generally accept the view that its northern frontier lay on the line of the Ḥeṣār mountains (between the Oxus and Zarafšān valleys; Bernard and Francfort, pp. 4-16) rather than the view, based on the rarity of finds of Greek coins north of the Oxus, that it lay on that river (Zeĭmal', pp. 279-90). These frontiers shifted in the course of the kingdom's career. In the north, Sogdia was annexed at an uncertain date. In the south, a campaign of conquest launched by Demetrios I about 190 led to the creation of a Greco-Indian kingdom with its center at Taxila, but relations did not remain close for long. The Greco-Indian kingdom survived for half a century after the collapse of the Greco-Bactrian kingdom.

The Hellenistic period appears to have been a prosperous time for Bactria. One indication of this is the high quality of its coin issues. Strabo echoes memories of the period when he speaks of "Bactria of the thousand towns." Until recently, however, archeological investigations, mainly at Balk̲ (Bactra) and Termed̲, were so fruitless that A. Foucher could speak of the "Bactrian mirage." The situation has been radically changed since 1964, when the remains of a large city were discovered at Āy K̲ānom (q.v.). Excavations, vigorously pursued until 1978, have shown that this city at the confluence of the Oxus and the Kūkča river was the capital of eastern Bactria. Strongly fortified and dominated by an acropolis and citadel, it was built on a regular plan well suited to the site and had a number of fine edifices typical of a Hellenistic city: a *heroon* (monument to the founder), gymnasium, theater, fountain with sculptures, and peristyle courts. On the other hand, the huge palace occupying the central position and the upper class dwellings are clearly influenced by Iranian concepts, while the temples and the fortifications show signs of Mesopotamian inspiration.

The abundant and datable material from Āy Ḵānom provided guidance for other site investigations, which were pursued with vigor on both sides of the Oxus. These have revealed the great scale of the irrigation projects undertaken to complete the already substantial works of the preceding periods. Furthermore several new sites of towns or fortified settlements were identified and provisionally excavated, though Termeḏ (probably a foundation of Demetrios) remained inaccessible. In general these are sites of towns founded in the later years of the kingdom's existence; they are smaller than those of the cities founded by the Seleucids and have a markedly military character, with a citadel overlooking a geometrically planned settlement surrounded by ramparts. Noteworthy are the quadrangular town of Delbarjīn in the north of the Balḵ oasis, and the fortresses of Kay Qobād Šāh, Ḵayrābād Tepe, Qalʿa-ye Kāfernegān, and Qarabāḡ Tepe on right bank tributaries of the Oxus. Somewhat later came the discovery of the site on the right bank of the Oxus called Taḵt-e Sangīn, which is surrounded by stone fortifications (most unusual in this region); excavations there have uncovered a sanctuary of the Oxus god and yielded abundant materials closely resembling those found at Āy Ḵānom (Litvinskij and Pitchikian, pp. 195-216).

The last period of the Greco-Bactrian kingdom is marked by the reign of Eucratides, who overthrew Demetrios and thereby started a long conflict with the descendants of Euthydemos who remained in power in India, which continued under his successors. The protracted hostilities probably explain, in part, why the kingdom lost strength and succumbed to a nomad invasion, which ended Greek rule in the region. It is known that Āy Ḵānom was abandoned by the Greeks and pillaged by neighboring populations in 147. According to the Chinese traveler Chang Chien, Ta Hsia (Bactria) in 130 consisted of a multitude of petty principalities, lacking a supreme chief but all under the domination of the Yüe Chih tribes whose camping grounds lay on the right bank of the Oxus.

Pre-Kushan Bactria. The subsequent period is extremely obscure. It is known from the Chinese historical work *Hou Han Shu* that the Yüe Chih occupied Lan Shih, which many scholars identify with Bactra. This is taken to mean that Bactria then came under the direct rule of the Yüe Chih. The exact date of the occupation is unknown. The work goes on to describe the political situation in Bactria: "The Yüe Chih... moved into Ta Hsia (Bactria) and divided this kingdom into five *hsi-hou* (*yabḡū*), namely those of Hsiu-mi, Shuang-mi, Kuei-shang, Hsi-tun, and Tu-mi." Strabo, who possessed only indirect information because the presence of the Parthian empire prevented contact, gives us to understand that Bactria was conquered by several nomad groups: the Asii/Asiani, the Tochari, and the Saraucae (*Geography* 11.511). Although Strabo's statement is difficult to reconcile with those in the Chinese sources, archeological evidence obtained from excavations of several large nomad cemeteries on the right bank of the Oxus shows that many of the newcomers were natives of the northwestern steppes and belonged to the Sauromatian/Sarmatian ethnic group.

According to Trogus Pompeius (quoted by Justin, *Prologi* 42), "the Asiani became the kings of the Tochari, and the Saraucae (Sacaraucae) were destroyed." This statement tallies with the account in the *Hou Han Shu* which tells how one of the chiefs who shared Ta Hsia overcame the others and founded the Kushan dynasty in Bactria: "More than a century after (the arrival of the nomads in Bactria), the *hsi-hou* of the Kuei-shang, named Ch'iu-tsiu-ch'ü, attacked the other four *hsi-hou*s. He proclaimed himself king. The name of his kingdom was Kuei-shang." Comparison of the two texts leaves no doubt as to the identity of the Asiani with the Kushans.

The Tochari, from whom eastern Bactria was to acquire the name Ṭoḵārestān, were for a long time thought to be identical with the Kushans. Their language may have belonged to the Indo-European "centum" group used in the oases of the Tarim basin. These matters, however, remain problematical and controversial.

As for the Sacaraucae, they are thought to have settled in western Bactria after they had pillaged Bactra. Probably attributable to a dynasty of chiefs of this tribe are the tombs discovered in 1978 at Ṭelā Tepe in the Šebergān district, a site in one of several oases along the Sar-e Pol river west of Bactra which were developed and settled at that time. The extraordinary profusion of the finds of jewelry and gold artifacts, often encrusted with precious stones, in these tombs has prompted comparison with the treasure of Peter the Great in the Hermitage Museum at Leningrad. All the items can be dated from the first century B.C. and first century A.D. The workmanship attests the continuing impact of Greek culture (e.g., buckles with figures of Ares or Dionysos in his chariot), the strength of Bactrian traditions akin to the art of the steppes (e.g., scabbards with encrusted dragon ornamentations, ear pendants in animal style), and the presence of East Asian influences (e.g., Chinese mirrors, Mongoloid features of human figures).

The archeological discoveries relating to pre-Kushan Bactria point to continuance of the agricultural and urban development observed in the later part of the Greco-Bactrian period. The case of Āy Ḵānom is exceptional; here the only occupants were now a small garrison lodged in the citadel, the role of chief city of eastern Bactria having reverted to Kondūz. In addition to finds made at nomad cemeteries, such as Tūlḵār, Bīškent, and Tūpḵāna (Litvinskiĭ and Sedov, 1984), materials have been unearthed from sites of towns founded in the previous period which continued to live and flourish without a break, such as Delbarjīn and Qalʿa-ye Kāfernegān. Other settlements of smaller size from this period were elaborately fortified with ramparts and covered galleries in a quadrangular layout, as at Kohna Qalʿa, Aĭrtam, and Saksanošūr. Real towns arose at Delvarzīn Tepe on the Sorḵān Daryā, at Zar

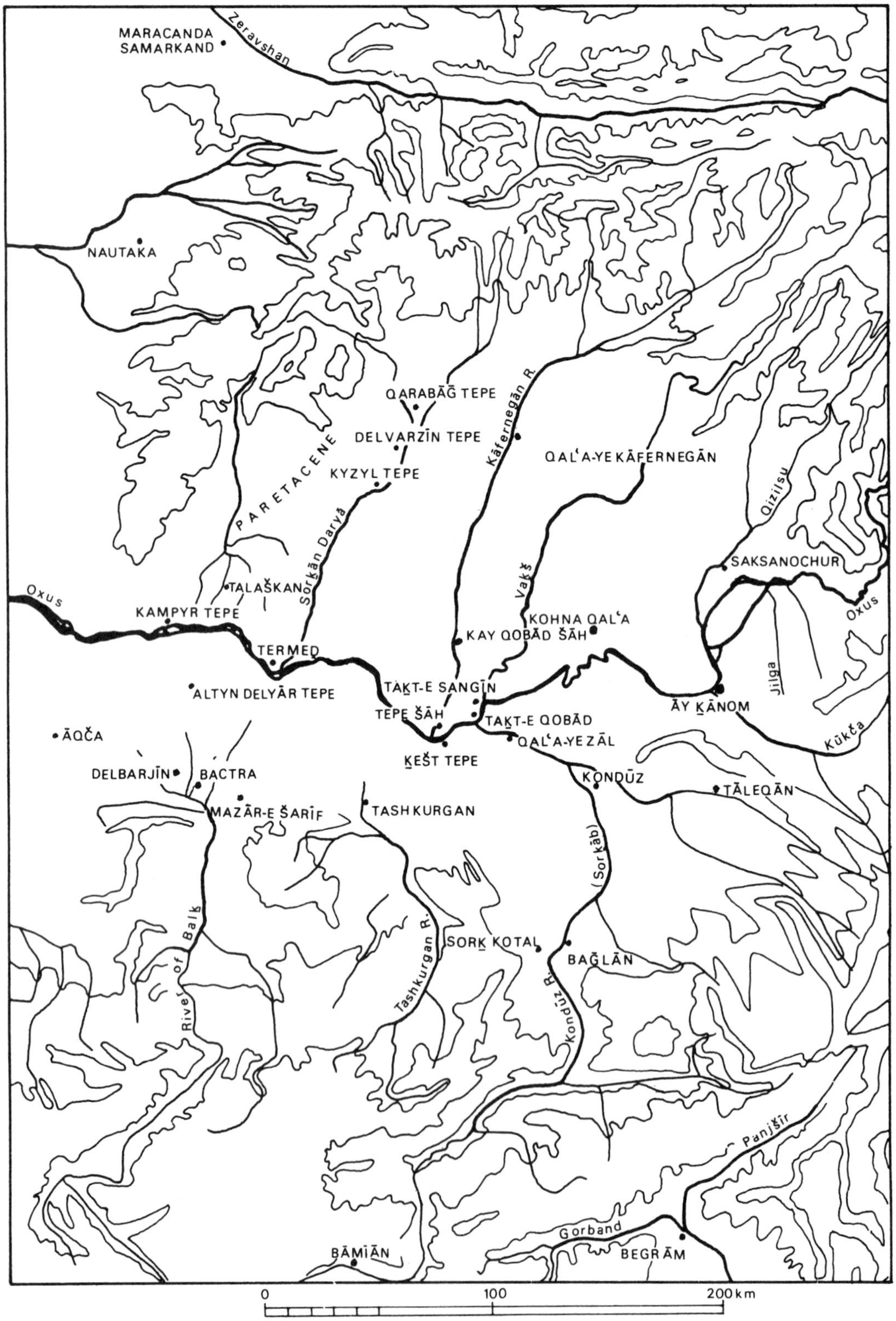

Figure 5. Pre-Islamic Bactria

Tepe on the right bank of the Oxus, and at Yemšī Tepe which was probably the seat of the local rulers interred at Ṭelā Tepe (Sarianidi).

Bactria under the Kushans. The history of the Kushan empire presents, as is well known, many difficulties due to the paucity and heterogeneity of the Greco-Roman, Syrian, Indian, and Chinese sources. The only documentation of Kushan origin consists of coin legends, seals, and votive inscriptions whose dating remains problematic because several different eras are used in them.

This empire spread far and wide from its nucleus in Bactria and finally comprised a vast area stretching from Central Asia to India. As a result, Bactria gradually lost its political importance and became merely one province among many others.

Even so, Bactria appears to have prospered during the Kushan period. Thanks to trade expansion made possible by the prevalence of peace, Bactra became a major commercial center. The city was one of the chief halts on the silk road and the crossroads of routes leading westward to Marv, northward to Termeḏ, Čaḡānīān, and Kāšgar, and south-eastward to Kondūz, Sorḵ Kotal, Begrām, and thence to India. People were able and willing to travel, and among them were Indian monks who brought the religion of the Buddha to Bactria with the encouragement, so it seems, of the powerful Kushan king Kanishka. Numerous monasteries were founded in the region at that time: at Termeḏ (Qara Tepe), Zar Tepe, Kondūz, Bāmīān, Begrām, and elsewhere. The art types of the Buddha flashing fire and the Buddha gushing water were probably conceived in the Bactrian monasteries under the influence of Mazdean and Zoroastrian concepts (Staviskii).

In the Kushan period a Bactrian alphabet based on the Greek was created for monumental use, and excavations at Delbarjīn and near Termeḏ have uncovered fragments of texts in a cursive Bactrian script. (See BACTRIAN LANGUAGE.)

A substantial increase of the area under cultivation in Bactria took place in the Kushan period. New lands were irrigated, e.g., at Bīškent and along the lower course of the Vaḵš, while the valleys of the Balḵ, Kondūz, and Sorḵān Daryā rivers were important producers. Urbanization showed similar progress. Some forty urban sites, including fifteen of more than 15 ha, have now been located; all have dimensions fit for medium-sized or large towns. Besides the main cities of Bactra (Zariaspa, Lan Shi), Kondūz, and Termeḏ (Qara Tepe), the following towns deserve mention: in southern Bactria, Delbarjīn, Begrām (famous for the find of a treasure-store containing objects from Alexandria in Egypt and from India), and the sanctuary Sorḵ Kotal (with a great temple at the top of a flight of steps, dedicated to an apparently eclectic collection of gods headed by a deity personifying the victory of the temple's founder Kanishka; Schlumberger, le Berre, and Fussman); north of the Oxus, Delvarzīn, Aĭrtam, Zar Tepe, Qalʿa-ye Kāfernegān, and Ḵalčajān. All these sites attest the remarkable development of urban life which characterized Kushan Bactria.

It was in the Kushan period, however, that the name Bactria fell out of use. We do not know what name the region then bore. The geographer Ptolemy, writing in the second half of the second century A.D., states that it was then inhabited mainly by Tochari. In Middle Persian and Armenian, the name Balḵ denotes only the capital city. By the end of the Kushan period, Bactria had come to be known as Ṭoḵārestān. After the conquest of the region by the Sasanians, Ṭoḵārestān formed the core of their province of Kūšānšahr. In the Chinese sources Tu Kho Lo, undoubtedly a transcription of the new name, replaces the older Ta Hsia.

Bibliography: Comprehensive surveys are now available in two fundamental works: A. D. H. Bivar, in *Camb. Hist. Iran* III, 2, Cambridge, 1983, pp. 181-209, and B.A. Staviskii, *La Bactriane kouchane*, Paris, 1986 (both with full and up-to-date bibliographies). Some further material is to be found in the recently published studies by P. Bernard, *Fouilles d'Aï Khanoum* IV: *Les monnaies hors trésor. Questions d'histoire gréco-bactrienne*, Paris, 1985; idem and H. P. Francfort, *Etudes de géographie historique sur la plaine d'Aï Khanoum*, Paris, 1978; G. A. Koshelenko, *Drevneĭshchie gosudarstva Kavkaza i Sredneĭ Azii*, Moscow, 1984; P. Leriche, *Fouilles d'Aï Khanoum* V: *Les remparts et les monuments associés*, Paris, 1986; B. A. Litvinskij and I. P. Pitchikian, "Découvertes dans un sanctuaire du dieu Oxus de la Bactriane septentrionale," *RA*, 1981, no. 2, pp. 195-216; B. A. Litvinskiĭ and A. Sedov, *Tepa i Sakh: Kul'tura i svyazy kushanskoĭ Baktrii*, Moscow, 1983; idem, *Kul'ty i ritualy kushanskoĭ Baktrii*, Moscow, 1984; T. V. Pyankov, *Baktriya v traditsii drevnosti*, Dushanbe, 1982; E. V. Rtveladze, "O mestopolozhenii baktriĭskogo goroda Aorna," *VDI*, 1982, no. 1, pp. 149-52; V. I. Sarianidi, *Zoloto Baktrii*, Moscow, 1985; D. Schlumberger, M. le Berre, and G. Fussman, *Surkh Kotal en Bactriane* I: *Les temples*, Paris, 1983; B. Staviskij, "Kara Tepe in Old Termez," *Acta Antiqua Academiae Scientiarum Hungaricae*, 1980, pp. 99-135; V. I. Zeĭmal', *Drevnie monety Tadzhikistan*, Dushanbe, 1985.

Still stimulating are the broad perspectives presented by A. Foucher, *La vieille route de l'Inde de Bactres à Taxila*, Paris, 1942; W. W. Tarn, *The Greeks in Bactria and India*, 2nd ed., Oxford, 1952; D. Schlumberger, *L'Orient hellénisé*, Paris, 1969.

(P. LERICHE)

ii. IN THE AVESTA AND IN ZOROASTRIAN TRADITION

In the Avesta Bactria is mentioned only in the list of countries in the first chapter of the *Vendīdād* (*Vd.* 1.6 and 7). It appears as Bāxδiš (from which Humbach [1966, p. 52] reconstitutes an original form *Bāxδriš in order to explain the western, probably Median, form Bāxtriš), and is qualified as *srīra-* "beautiful" and *uzgərəptō.drafša-* "with uplifted banners." The names of the two plagues sent to Bactria by Angra Mainyu, *barvara-* (or *bravara-*) and *usaδ-*, are puzzling and the corresponding names in the Pahlavi version are incomprehensible. *Barvara-*, if compared with Sanskrit *barbara-*, *varvara-*, Greek *barbaroi*, might designate non-Aryan peoples (indeed the name Barbar is still applied to some populations and places in Bactria, especially in the mountaneous area). *Usaδ*, used in the plural, is considered by Humbach (1960, pp. 38-39) as a graphic corruption of *usij-*, which in *Y.* 44.20 designates priests hostile to Zoroaster.

In the existing Pahlavi books, Bactria is mentioned in two contexts. In the *Bundahišn* (ed. and tr. B. T. Anklesaria, XI-A, p. 109) the Oxus, together with the Indus, is identified with the *Wehrōd*, the "Good River," which forms the boundary of Ērānšahr and is conceptually linked with the Avestan *Vaŋhvī Dāityā*, next to which the first upholders of the faith performed their sacrifices (meanwhile, the latter's proper Pahlavi transcription; *Dāitī*, is never identified with any real river in the Pahlavi texts). The *Šahrestānīhā ī Ērān* (8-9) associates Bactria with the Kayanid prince Spandyād (Esfandīār) and his victory in the holy war against Arjāsp, king of the Xyōn; he is purported to have built Bal<u>k</u> under the name Navāzag (Pers. Avāza, elsewhere identified with the Rū'īndež "brazen castle" and the town of Paykand), and to have established a "Wahrām fire" there. Both the Spandyād tradition and the Oxus-Wehrōd identification are found in the Armenian *History of Heraclius* attributed to Sebeos (ca. A.D. 660).

It is highly probable that by the end of the Sasanian period the lost national chronicle *Xwadāy-nāmag* had come to incorporate more substantial traditions on Bal<u>k</u>, linking it with the second Kayanid dynasty and with the preaching of Zoroaster under king Goštāsp (Kavi Vīštāspa). In fact, from Ṭabarī onwards, the last point is expressed by all the authors whose information is derived from the chronicle (see Jackson, pp. 199-201, 205-19). Some of them consider that Kay Kāvūs had already established the capital at Bal<u>k</u>, while the *Šāh-nāma* attributes this step to Goštāsp's father Lohrāsp (called "the Bactrian" by Bīrūnī). The idea that Bactria had been the setting of the prophet's activity was eventually reconciled with the claim by Azerbaijan to be his birth-place; it superseded other eastern traditions (especially those of Sīstān and Sogdiana), transmitted by some Pahlavi sources. This process can be explained by several factors: the long-lasting political pre-eminence of Bactria among eastern regions; its importance as a scene of the wars with "Turānian" peoples at the end of the sixth-beginning of the seventh century A.D. (reminiscences of these wars color Ferdowsī's account of Goštāsp's reign, and even more the section on Spandyād in the *Šahrestānīhā*); traditions proper to the local clergy, whose intervention is shown by the fact that a genuinely Bactrian name, Lohrāsp, was substituted for Aurvat̰aspa, the Avestan name of Vīštāspa's father.

Bibliography: A. Christensen, *Le premier chapitre du Vendidad et l'histoire primitive des tribus iraniennes*, Copenhagen, 1943, pp. 64-65. Gh. Gnoli, *Zoroaster's Time and Homeland*, Naples, 1980, pp. 62, 66-67. J. Harmatta, *Acta Orientalia Hungarica* 11, 1960, pp. 202-03. H. Humbach, "Die awestische Länderliste," *Wiener Zeitschrift für die Kunde Süd- und Ostasiens* 4, 1960, pp. 36-46. Idem, *Baktrische Sprachdenkmäler* I, Wiesbaden, 1966. A. V. W. Jackson, *Zoroaster, the Prophet of Ancient Iran*, New York, 1899, repr. 1965. G. Lazard, "Notes bactriennes," *Studia Iranica* 13, 1984, p. 223. J. Marquart, (Markwart), *Ērānšahr nach der Geographie des ps. Moses Xorenacʿi*, Berlin, 1901, repr. Göttingen, 1979, pp. 87-91. Idem, *A Catalogue of the Provincial Capitals of Ērānshahr*, Rome, 1931, pp. 10, 34-38. Idem, *Wehrot und Arang*, Leiden, 1938, pp. 31-52, 125-26, 143-44. S. Wikander, "Sur le fonds commun indo-iranien des épopées de la Perse et de l'Inde," *La Nouvelle Clio* 1-2, 1949-50, pp. 310-29.

(F. GRENET)

BACTRIAN LANGUAGE, the Iranian language of ancient Bactria (northern Afghanistan), attested by coins, seals, and inscriptions of the Kushan period (first to third centuries A.D.) and the following centuries and by a few manuscript fragments from a much later period, perhaps the eighth or ninth century. Instead of "Bactrian" some scholars have preferred terms such as "Greco-Bactrian" (emphasizing the use of a modified Greek script to write the language), "Kushan," or "Kushano-Bactrian." The name "Eteo-Tocharian," despite its eloquent defence by A. Maricq (*JA* 248, 1960, pp. 162ff.), can hardly be justified (see W. B. Henning, *BSOAS* 23, 1960, pp. 47f.); in any case it is to be avoided in view of the risk of confusion with the non-Iranian language already generally known as "Tocharian." A similar trap, into which some unwary bibliographers have fallen, results from the (long obsolete) use of the term "Old Bactrian" to refer to the Avestan Language.

Historical background. It is noteworthy that Bactrian is the only Middle Iranian language whose writing-system is based on the Greek alphabet, a fact ultimately attributable to Alexander's conquest of Bactria and to the maintenance of Greek rule for some 200 years after his death (323 B.C.). Soon after the middle of the second century B.C. Bactria was overrun by nomads from the north, notably by the Yüeh-chih or Tokharoi, who settled in northern Afghanistan and subsequently gave their name to the area (medieval Ṭo<u>k</u>ārestān). Early in the Christian era a tribe or family named Kushan obtained supremacy over the rest of the Tokharoi. The Kushan empire founded by Kujula Kadphises soon expanded into northern India.

Nothing is known for certain of the language of the Tokharoi/Yüeh-chih; in view of mounting evidence in favor of the much disputed connexion of the Tokharoi with the inhabitants of Agni and Kucha in Chinese Turkestan, it is not unlikely that it was in fact related to the language which modern scholars have named "Tocharian." (For some recent contributions to the long debate see Henning in G. L. Ulmen, ed., *Society and History: Essays in Honor of K. A. Wittfogel*, The Hague, 1978, pp. 215-30; H. W. Bailey, *JRAS*, 1970, pp. 121f.) It seems that the Kushans, upon becoming masters of Bactria, at first continued the traditional use of Greek as a medium of written communication. As a spoken language they had adopted Bactrian, the native idiom of the country, which they afterwards elevated to the status of a written language and employed for official purposes, perhaps as a result of increasing national or dynastic pride. The earliest known inscriptions in Bactrian (the "unfinished inscription" from Surkh Kotal, cf. A. D. H. Bivar, *BSOAS* 26, 1963, pp. 498-502, and the Dašt-e Nāvūr trilingual) belong to the reign of Vima Kadphises. A few decades later, early in the reign of Kanishka I, Bactrian replaced Greek on the Kushan coins. After this period Greek ceased to be used as an official language in Bactria (although later instances of its use by Greek settlers are known, cf. P. M. Fraser, *Afghan Studies* 3-4, 1982, pp. 77f.).

Sources. 1. Coins. The coins of Kujula and his immediate successors give the king's name and titulature in Greek, often with a Kharoṣṭhī version on the reverse. The earliest issues of Kanishka likewise bear on the obverse his name and title in Greek (*basileus basileōn kanēškou* "[coin] of Kanishka, king of kings"), while the reverses portray divinities named in Greek as Hēphaistos, Hēlios, Nanaia, and Selēnē. Later issues follow the same pattern, but the legends are henceforward in Bactrian rather than Greek. Kanishka's titulature appears (in its fullest form) as *šaonano šao kanēški košano* "of Kanishka, king of kings, the Kushan," that of his successor Huvishka as *šaonano šao ooēški košano*. The forms *kanēški* and *ooēški* (also *ouoēški, ooēške*) are in the oblique case, cf. the Greek gen. *kanēškou*; a few coins of Huvishka have the nom. form (*ooēško*), as do those of the succeeding rulers, Vasudeva (*bazodēo*), Kanishka II (*kanēško*), Vasishka (*bazēško*, cf. R. Göbl, *Dokumente zur Geschichte der iranischen Hunnen in Baktrien und Indien*, Wiesbaden, 1967, III, pl. 8), etc. Of the numerous divinities depicted on the coins of Kanishka I and Huvishka, most are given Iranian names, e.g., *ardoxšo* (Av. *ašiš vaŋuhī*), *aθšo* "fire," *farro* (Av. *x'arənah-*), *lrooaspo* (masc.; cf. Av. *drvāspā-*), *mao* "moon," *miiro* (in many spellings; Av. *miθra-*), *nana* (Sogd. *nny*), *oado* "wind," *oaxšo* "Oxus," *oēšo* (Av. *vayuš*, conflated with the Indian Śiva, see H. Humbach in *Monumentum H. S. Nyberg* I, Acta Iranica 4, Tehran and Liège, 1975, pp. 402-08), *ōoromozdo* (Av. *ahurō mazdå*), *orlagno* (Av. *vərəθraγna-*), and *teiro* (Mid. Pers. *tīr*). See further F. Grenet, "Notes sur le panthéon iranien des Kouchans," *Studia Iranica* 13, 1984, pp. 253-62. The coinage of Kanishka includes issues portraying *boddo* "Buddha," *sakamano boudo* "Śākyamuni," and *mētrago boudo* "Maitreya" (see J. Cribb, "A Re-examination of the Buddha Images on the Coins of King Kaniṣka. . . ," in *Studies in Buddhist Art of South Asia*, Delhi, 1985, pp. 59-87), while that of Huvishka attests foreign gods and demigods such as *ērakilo* "Heracles," *sarapo* "Sarapis," *maasēno* "Mahāsena," and *skando komaro* "Skanda Kumāra." After Huvishka the repertoire of reverse types contracts sharply, the only deities named on the coins of the last Kushans being *ardoxšo* and *oēšo*.

With the eclipse of the Kushan dynasty their lands west of the Indus fell into the hands of the Sasanians, under whom the administration of these provinces was entrusted to a governor styled Kušānšāh. In addition to coinage inscribed in Pahlavi and (occasionally) in Brāhmī, the Kušānšāhs issued coins with legends in cursive Greco-Bactrian script. The language of these latter is usually said to be Bactrian. However, most of the "Bactrian" legends are virtually identical in vocabulary and phraseology to their Pahlavi equivalents. A legend such as *bago pirōzo oazarko košano šauo* "Lord Pērōz, great Kušānšāh" may be compared with the Pahl. *mazdēsn bay Pērōz wazarg Kušān šāh*, while the usual reverse *borzaoando iazado* (variously spelt) corresponds precisely to Pahl. *burzāwand yazad*. Thus it is possible to regard these legends not as Bactrian but as Middle Persian, superficially adapted to local orthographic norms. It should therefore not be too readily assumed that the Bactrian language possessed words such as *oazarko* "great" or *iazado* "god," which are absent from the Bactrian of the Kushan period.

From the middle of the fourth century Bactria and northwestern India were overrun by Hunnish tribes, of whom the Hephthalites proved the most durable, maintaining their rule in parts of Afghanistan up to the Arab conquest in the seventh century. The "Bactrian" coin-legends and countermarks of the Hunnish period display a rich linguistic diversity, with titles deriving from Indian (*sri* "Śrī"), Turkish (*kagano* "Khaghan," *tarxano* "Tarkhan," *todono* "Tudun"), and even Latin (*fromo kēsaro* "Caesar of Rome"), as well as from Bactrian and Middle Persian (*bago, šauo, xoadēo*).

The plates accompanying R. Göbl, "Die Münzprägung der Kušān von Vima Kadphises bis Bahrām IV," in F. Altheim and R. Stiehl, *Finanzgeschichte der Spätantike*, Frankfurt am Main, 1957, pp. 173-256, offer a wide range of Kushan coin-legends; see also Göbl's comprehensive *System und Chronologie der Münzprägung des Kušānreiches*, Vienna, 1984. The Kushano-Sasanian coinage may be studied from Bivar, ed., *Corp. Inscr. Iran.*, part 3, vol. 6, portfolio I, London, 1968, pl. 4-10 (cf. Humbach, *ZDMG* 121, 1971, pp. 392f.). For the Hunnish coins see Göbl, *Dokumente*, esp. III, pl. 9-83; cf. also Humbach, *MSS* 22, 1967, pp. 39-56.

2. Seals. About forty seals inscribed with names and titles in Greco-Bactrian script have been published. The titulature attested on the seals is largely Western Iranian, e.g., *asbarobido* "chief of cavalry," *oazarko fromalaro* "great commander," *šaurabo* "satrap," and *uazaroxto* "chiliarch." (See Henning, *ZDMG* 115, 1965, pp. 80f.) Particularly important is the bulla of *mauo kanēško* "Moon-Kanishka" (ibid., pp. 85ff.; J. Brough in *W. B. Henning Memorial Volume*, ed. M. Boyce and I. Gershevitch, London, 1970, pp. 87f.). Almost all of

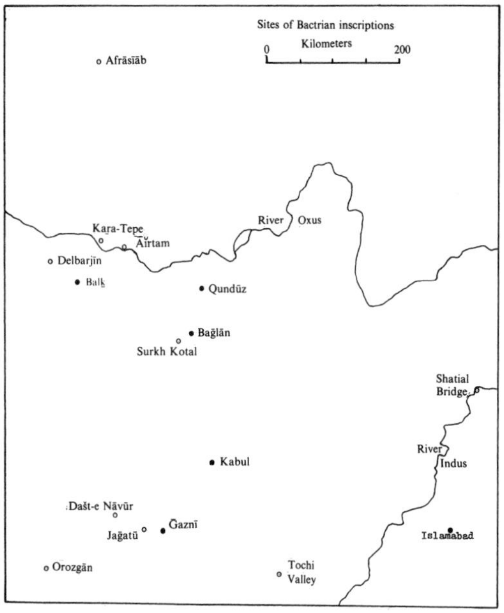

Figure 6. Sites at which Bactrian inscriptions have been found

the seals are illustrated by Bivar, op. cit., pl. 1-4, 27 (cf. Humbach, *MSS* 25, 1969, pp. 65-74).

3. Inscriptions. By far the most important surviving monument of the Bactrian language is the monolith found at Surkh Kotal. The undamaged 25-line inscription records construction work carried out early in the reign of Huvishka by the margrave (*karalraggo*, cf. Henning, op. cit., pp. 77ff.) Nokonzoko. It was first published by Maricq (*JA* 246, 1958, pp. 345-440) under the title "La grande inscription de Kaniṣka" (due to an unfortunate misunderstanding of the passage in which Kanishka's name is mentioned). Two slightly shorter copies of the same inscription, with interesting orthographic variants, were discovered later (see E. Benveniste, *JA* 249, 1961, pp. 113-52). The key to the interpretation of this text, and hence to the understanding of the Bactrian language, was provided by Henning's identification of many of the most common words (*BSOAS* 23, 1960, pp. 47-55). Further refinements are due to I. Gershevitch (*BSOAS* 26, 1963, pp. 193-96; *Asia Major*, N.S. 12, 1966, pp. 90-109; *Afghan Studies* 2, 1979, pp. 55-73), J. Harmatta (*Acta Antiqua Academiae Scientiarum Hungaricae* 12, 1964, pp. 373-471), N. Sims-Williams (*IF* 78, 1973, pp. 95-99; *BSOAS* 48, 1985, pp. 111-16), and G. Lazard, F. Grenet, and C. de Lamberterie (*Studia Iranica* 13, 1984, pp. 199-232). The aberrant interpretation put forward by Humbach in *Die Kaniška-Inschrift von Surkh-Kotal*, Wiesbaden, 1960, and later works has now been abandoned by its author.

Of the minor inscriptions of Surkh Kotal only the "Palamedes inscription" (cf. Henning, *BSOAS* 18, 1956, pp. 366f.) and the end of the "Inscription pariétale" (cf. Benveniste, op. cit., pp. 146-50) add anything to our knowledge of the Bactrian language.

The trilingual inscription of Dašt-e Nāvūr (in Bactrian, Kharoṣṭhī, and an undeciphered script) is of potential rather than actual linguistic significance. Little can be certainly read beyond the name of Vima (*ooēmo*) and the date (including the Macedonian month-name *gorpiaiou*). See G. Fussman, *Bulletin de l'École Française d'Extrême-Orient* 61, 1974, pp. 1-75, and cf. Bivar, *BSOAS* 39, 1976, pp. 333-40.

The inscription of Aĭrtam is dated early in the reign of Huvishka and resembles the almost contemporary Surkh Kotal monolith in vocabulary (e.g., *bagalaggo* "sanctuary," *ma liza* "the acropolis") and phraseology, ending with the clear statement: *oti eimo miirozada nibixto pido ia šod[.].a fromana* "And M. wrote this at the command of (the?) Š." See B. A. Turgunov, V. A. Livshits, and È. V. Rtveladze, *Obshchestvennye nauki v Uzbekistane*, 1981, no. 3, pp. 38-48; J. Harmatta in *Studia Grammatica. Festschrift für Helmut Humbach*, ed. R. Schmitt and P. O. Skjærvø, Munich, 1986, pp. 131-46.

The inscriptions of Delbarjīn (I. T. Kruglikova, ed., *Drevnyaya Baktriya*, 2 vols., Moscow, 1976, 1979) include substantial fragments of a monumental inscription of the early Kushan period (published by Livshits and Kruglikova, ibid., 2, pp. 98-112).

Several graffiti in cursive Bactrian script of the Kushano-Sasanian period have been found in the Buddhist cave-monastery of Kara-Tepe. Although they chiefly record names (*borzomiro, bōzano, ōromozdo*, etc.), words such as *odo* "and," *kaldo* "when," and *malo* "here" make it clear that their language is indeed Bactrian. They have been published by various scholars in B. Staviskiĭ, ed., *Materialy sovmestnoĭ arkheologicheskoĭ èkspeditsii na Kara-Tepe* 2-4, Moscow, 1969, 1972, 1975. For a similar inscription from Afrasiab see Livshits, ibid., 4, p. 50, n. 16.

Of the two inscriptions from Jaghatu, one, containing the *triratna* formula *namōo boda, namōo dauarma, namōo sagga*, may be regarded as Indian in Bactrian script. The other is largely incomprehensible, a remark which unfortunately applies to most late Bactrian inscriptions in cursive script, such as those from Uruzgan and the Tochi valley. Two very short rock-inscriptions from Shatial Bridge have been published by Humbach in *Allgemeine und vergleichende Archäologie, Beiträge [des Deutschen Archäologischen Instituts]* 2, 1980, pp. 210, 220.

4. Manuscripts. Of eight known manuscript fragments in Greco-Bactrian script, one (possibly of the fourth century) was found at Lou-lan and seven (of much later date) at Toyoq. Their content is largely obscure, though at least one, to judge from the words *rakšazano šao* "king of the *rākṣasas*" and *rakšazanzo* "*rākṣasī*," may contain a Buddhist text. All eight fragments are illustrated by Humbach, *Baktrische Sprachdenkmäler* II, Wiesbaden, 1967, pl. 28-32. Their reading and interpretation has been appreciably furthered by Gershevitch, *IF* 72, 1967, pp. 37-56.

More considerable is a unique fragment in Manichean script from Qočo (see idem, "The Bactrian Fragment in Manichean Script," *AAH* 28, 1980 [1984], pp. 273-80; cf. also N. Sims-Williams, *BSOAS* 49, 1986, p. 588). Although the less legible verso side presents severe problems, most of the recto can be interpreted. The fragment contains many new words and grammatical forms (e.g., *lh-* "to give," *xwyn-* "to call," *'z 'γdym* "I have come"), while the Manichean orthography of words already known in Greek script (*'s* = *aso* "from," *t̠''d* = *tado* "then," etc) provides valuable information on Bactrian phonology.

5. Indirect witnesses. The meagre remains of Bactrian so far described are usefully supplemented by some identifiable Bactrian loanwards in other, better-known languages. As well as words already attested in Bactrian (e.g., Pers, *xidēv* < Bactr. *xoadēo* "lord," Kroraina Prakrit personal name *Vaǵamareǵa* < *bago* "god" plus *marēgo* "servant") these include some new vocabulary. Amongst the most certain items are Kroraina Prakrit *lastana*, Khot. *lāstana-* "dispute" < **lastano*, Toch. A *lāstaṅk*, B *lastāṅk* "execution-block" < **lastaggo*, Toch. A. *ākāl*, B *akālk* "wish" < **agalgo* (see M. Schwartz in P. Gignoux and A. Tafazzoli, eds., *Mémorial J. de Menasce*, Louvain, 1974, pp. 399-411, and cf. L. Isebaert, *De Indo-Iraanse bestanddelen in de Tocharische woordenschat*, thesis, Leuven, 1980).

Script. The seventh-century Chinese traveler Hsüan-tsang reported that the language of Ṭok̲ārestān employed an alphabet of 25 letters, evidently the 24 of the standard Greek alphabet with the addition of Þ, sometimes referred to as *san*, to represent *š*. (Despite W. W. Tarn, *The Greeks in Bactria and India*, 2nd ed., Cambridge, 1951, pp. 508-10, the letter is probably not in fact *san* but a variant of *rho*, cf. Humbach, *Baktrische Sprachdenkmäler* I, 1966, p. 41). Of these letters, *ksi* and *psi* were not actually used for writing Bactrian, in which the sequences *ks* and *ps* do not occur. As in Greek, numerals are indicated by the letters of the alphabet, generally with the addition of some diacritic mark. For this purpose the extra letters *digamma* (= 6), *koppa* (= 90) (both possibly attested), and *sampi* (= 900) will no doubt have been required, as well as *ksi* (= 60) and *psi* (= 700).

For writing an Iranian language the Greek alphabet is not ideal. The Bactrians overcame some of its disadvantages by the introduction of the letter *š* and by the use of *u* (*upsilon*) for *h*. Ambiguities remain: Thus *i* (*iota*) represents both *i*, *ī*, and *y*; *o* (*omicron*) both *u*, *ū*, and *w*; *a* (*alpha*) both *a* and *ā*. Since there are no special signs for affricates, it is possible that *s* (*sigma*) and *z* (*zeta*) stand for *c* (*ts*) and *j* (*dz*) as well as for *s*, *z*/*ž*. As in Greek, *gg* represents *ŋg*. Of the vowel digraphs, *ei* seems to stand for *ī* and *ou* for *ū* (also *uh*, etc.); the value of final *-ēio* is not yet clear. Concerning the function of the vowel letters in final position see below.

The decipherment of the Bactrian cursive script (for which see G. D. Davary, *Baktrisch: ein Wörterbuch*, Heidelberg, 1982, pp. 45-52) is probably not yet complete. In this style, chiefly but not exclusively attested in the post-Kushan era, the forms of certain letters (e.g., *a*/*d*/*o*) are wholly or partially confounded. The reading of the "rectangular" script found on most of the coins and inscriptions of the Kushan period is comparatively straightforward, though confusions due to the influence of the cursive or simply to the engraver's ignorance are not infrequent.

The Manichean script (q.v.) of the manuscript from Qočo contains two letters with unusual diacritics, *š̈* and j̈. The function of the suprascript points is not clear.

Language. In the following paragraphs the symbols G and M will be employed to identify words cited from texts in Greco-Bactrian and in Manichean script respectively. Proposed phonetic interpretations will be indicated, where necessary, by square brackets.

1. Dialectal position. Bactrian belongs to the north-eastern group of the Iranian languages. This is clear from certain features of its phonological development, e.g., *ē* and *i* from palatalized *ā* and *a* respectively; *γd* from **xt*; *c* or *s* from **č*; *β* and *γ* from **b* and **g* (even in initial position). The development of **d* via **δ* to *l* is as in Pashto and Yidgha-Munji; it can also be shown to have occurred dialectally in Sogdian (cf. Sims-Williams, *JA* 269, 1981, p. 353). In word-formation and syntax Bactrian shows some particular affinities to Sogdian, for instance in possessing a fem. suffix G *-anzo* (in *rakšazanzo*) = Sogd. *-'nc*. But it also has more westerly connexions, as indicated by forms such as M *lh-* "to give," *l'hw'n* "gift" (Parth. *dh-*, *d'hw'n*) or by the employment of G *i* as *eżāfa* (cf. Persian and Choresmian). Bactrian thus "occupies an intermediary position between Pashto and Yidgha-Munji on the one hand, Sogdian, Choresmian, and Parthian on the other: it is thus in its natural and rightful place in Bactria" (Henning, *BSOAS* 23, 1960, p. 47).

2. Foreign elements. A non-Iranian element, presumably a remnant of the language which the Tokharoi had brought with them to Bactria, is clearly apparent in Kushan onomastics (Kujula Kadphises, Nokonzoko, etc.). The suffix *-šk* occurs frequently, especially in royal names: Kanēško, Ooēški, Bazēško, Kozgaški. Its similarity to the Kuchean (Tocharian B) suffix *-śke* (fem. *-śka*), the most characteristic name-formative in that language (cf. W. Krause, *Ural-Altaische Jahrbücher* 25, 1953, pp. 11ff.), can scarcely be coincidental (see V. V. Ivanov in *Narody Azii i Afriki*, 1967/3, pp. 106-18, English summary on pp. 234-35).

Perhaps surprisingly, Bactrian seems to have adopted little from Greek other than its alphabet. The month-name Gorpiaiou and the Greek divine names mentioned above come into the category of foreign vocabulary rather than that of loanwords. A more significant borrowing, if its derivation from Greek *khrónos* is correct (A. Thierfelder, apud Humbach, *Baktrische Sprachdenkmäler* I, p. 24, cf. also W. S. Allen, *Vox Graeca*, Cambridge, 1968, p. 41 n. 1), would be G *xšono* "year" (Khot. *kṣuṇa-*, Tumshuqese *xšana-*, Toch. B *kṣuṃ*, Kroraina Prakrit *kṣunami*). The title G *xoadēo* "lord" (Sogd. *xwt'w*, Mid. Pers. *xwadāy, xwadāwan*, etc., all from **xwa-* "self" plus forms of **taw-* "to be powerful") is a calque on Greek *auto-krátōr* (A. Meillet, *MSL* 17, 1911, pp. 109-12).

The presence of Indian divinities on the coins of Kanishka I and Huvishka has already been noted. The much later manuscript fragments, like other texts from Central Asia, contain many Indian (Buddhist) loanwords, e.g., M *mwwl* "root," *nrẖ* "hell," *pwwn* "merit," G **rakšazo* "*rākṣasa*" (in plur. *rakšazano*) and perhaps **marano* "death" (in adj. *maraniggo*, cf. Khot. *maraṇīnaa-*, Parth. *mrnyn*?).

3. Phonology. The development of **b, d, g* to *β, l, γ* may be illustrated by M *βrg* "fruit," G *lizo* "acropolis," and M *γ''w* "cow." Non-initial **t* and **k* become *d* and *g* (M *'wd* and *'wṯ* [ud] "and," *ywg* "one"), while **-p-* has further developed via **b* to *β* (M *y'β* "water"). The affricate **č* is depalatalized, giving G *s* (e.g., *sido* "which," *aso* "from"), which, to judge from M *'cyd* and *'s*, may sometimes represent [c] and sometimes [s]. Voiceless stops become voiced after nasals (G *oanindo* "victor," *bagolaggo* [-ŋg] "temple"), while **nč* presumably gives [ndz], written M *nǰ* (*y'wyd'nǰyg* "everlasting"), G *nz* or *ns* (cf. *uastiloganzeigo* beside *astiloganseigi*, meaning uncertain). Intervocalic **θ* survives in G *iθa* "so;" the *h* of M *lh-* "to give," etc., may be interpreted as a later development. However, the change of **θr* to *hr* is early, cf., G *miuro* [mihr] "Mithra," *uirso* [hirs] (< **hris*) "30." Bactrian *h*, of whatever origin, is unstable, so that one finds G *arougo, mao, miiro* beside *uarougo* [harūg] "whole," *mauo* [māh] "moon, month" and *miuro*.

Certain consonant groups deserve special mention. While **xt* becomes *γd* (e.g. G *pidorigdo* "abandoned"), **xšt* becomes *xt* (G *nobixto*, M *nβyxt-* "written," cf. Munji *nəwuxt-*). Simple **št* sometimes remains (M *rštyg* "just," etc.), but elsewhere it gives *t* (G *xoto* "dried up," etc.), as does **t + t* in secondary contact (G *oto, oti* "and," etc.); see Sims-Williams, "A Note on Bactrian Phonology," *BSOAS* 48, 1985, pp. 111-16. The place-name G *lrafo* (< **drafša-*) indicates that **fš* gives *f*. Initial **xš* becomes *š*, cf. G *šao* "king," etc. On (*h*)*r* < **θr* see above, but note also *rl* < **rθr* in G *orlagno* "Vərəθraγna" and *xl* < **xθr* in G *baxlo* "Bactra" (via **xδ(r)*, cf. Av. *bāxδī-*?). Metathesis, as in G *alošxalo* beside *alaxšalo* "merciful," *albargo* "water-tank" (*āl-βārg* < **āβ-lārg*), or *uirso* "30" (cf. above), is not uncommon.

Palatalization affects both vowels and consonants. On the possible interpretation of G *-ge, -gi, -ki* as [gʸ (γʸ), kʸ] see below. The development of *s* and *z* after palatal vowels to M *š* and *j/ǰ*, as in *wyšp* "all" and *prdyjg* "orchard," may be late or dialectal, contrast G *oispo* etc. Palatalization of *ā* to *ē* and of *a* to *i* may be exemplified by the present stem *-lēr-* "to hold" (in G *ablēr-*, meaning unknown, M *lynlyryg* = Mid. Pers. *dēndār*) and the preposition G *pido*, M *pyd*; cf. Khot. *pader-* and *väte* respectively. A remarkable form is G *nokonziki* (i.e. [-ikʸ] < **-əkī*?), obl. of the personal name *nokonzoko*. If the title G *loixobosaro* "helper of the country (?)" does indeed contain **dahyu-*, the first syllable shows both *i-* and *u*-umlaut.

Long **ā* generally remains unchanged in non-final syllables; **ai, aya,* (*i*)*ya* give G *ei* [ī] and *ē* (e.g., *ei*(*i*)*o*, *eido* "this," *frei-* "dear," but *zēnobido* "armorer," *marēgo* "servant"); **awa-* gives *ō-* (G *ōsogdo* "pure"), while **-wa-* sometimes remains uncontracted (G *froxoaš-* beside *froxōš-* "to withdraw," *xouzo, xozo* [xūž] "well," *uarougo, uarogo*(?) "whole"). G *iōgo*, M *ywg* "one" < **aiwaka-*, cf. Munji *yūγa*, is a special case.

Vocalic **ṛ* gives *ir* or *ur* according to phonetic context: G *kirdo* "made" vs. *borzomiuro* (personal name) < **bṛza-*. The remaining short vowels **a, i, u* are generally well preserved in stressed syllables (but note G *boo-* [βow-] "to become"). In unstressed syllables they tend to be weakened or lost (G *-maggo* [-māŋg] "-minded" < **-mānaka-*, proclitic article *mo* < **ima-*, *zooasti, azooasto, ozooasto* "led out" < **uzwăsta-*; before *nd* unstressed **a* often becomes *i* as in G *oanindo* "victor," M *wyšpz'nyndyg* "all-knowing"). In the Manichean fragment most polysyllabic words (other than those ending in *-y*(*y*)(*ẖ*) = G *-ēio* < **-ai*(*C*)) have lost their former final vowels. It is not clear whether this development had already taken place at the time of the inscriptions. In these, every word ends in a vowel-letter, but the original final vowels are largely confused, *-o* tending to usurp the place of all others (hence *iθo, sido*, (plur.) *bago* beside *iθa, sidi, bage*, etc.). It has been proposed to interpret this *-o*, and similarly the *-o-* which occurs internally in place of an earlier unstressed **a* or **i* (e.g., G *nošalmo* beside *nišalmo* "seat," *bagolaggo* beside *bagalaggo*, preverb *poro-* < **pari-*), as a reduced vowel [ə] (thus: *nəšalmə, βaγəlaŋgə, pərə-*[?]). But the fact that *-o* is added even to words already ending in a vowel (as in G *-ēio* < **-ai*(*C*), *namōo* for Skt. *namo*) suggests that, at least in some instances, G *o* has no phonetic value, functioning merely as a word- or morpheme-divider.

See also G. Morgenstierne, "Notes on Bactrian Phonology," *BSOAS* 33, 1970, pp. 125-31, and I. M. Steblin-Kamenskiĭ in *Osnovy iranskogo yazykoznaniya* II: *Sredneiranskie yazyki*, Moscow, 1981, pp. 335-41. For a different view on the interpretation of Bactrian vocalism, see G. Lazard, *Studia Iranica* 13, 1984, pp. 219-22.

4. Morphology. In its simplified morphology Bactrian resembles Western Middle Iranian. The only inflected form of nouns attested in the manuscript fragments is the plural in G *-ano*, M *-'(')n*. Coins and inscriptions up to the time of Huvishka show vestiges of a two-case system: sing. *-o*, obl. *-i* or *-e* (e.g. *karalraggi/°ge* "margrave," *ooēški/°ke*), plur. *-e* (*bage* "gods," *asagge* "stones"), obl. plur. *-ano* (e.g., *oadobargano* "living beings;" note also *šaonano*, obl. plur. of the *n*-stem *šao* "king"). Since the obl. and plur. endings *-i* and *-e* occur only after *k* and *g* (*γ*), it is possible that they indicate palatalization of the preceding consonant rather than distinct vowels. Fem. *ā*-stems are sometimes spelt with final *-a* but more often with *-o*: *fromano/°na* "command," *lizo/liza* "acropolis," etc. Similarly, the articles *i* and *mo* have fem. forms *ia* and

ma, but these are not used consistently. The neuter survives only in G *sido, sidi*, M *'cyd* "which" beside G *kido, kidi*, M *kyd* "who." Other notable pronominal forms are G *pideino* = NPers. *bad-īn* and the third person enclitics, sing. G *-ēio*, M *-y(y) (h)*, plur. G *-ano*, which display generalization of **-hai, *-hānām* (as in Choresmian and Khotanese) rather than of **-šai*, etc. (see Sims-Williams in R. E. Emmerick and P. O. Skjærvø, eds., *Studies in the Vocabulary of Khotanese* II, Vienna, 1987, pp. 74-75).

The verbal inflexion is very imperfectly known. Best attested is the 3 sing. pret., which consists of the simple past stem: *G kirdo, kirdi*, M *qyrd* "made," etc. The 1 sing. (M *'γdym* "came") and 3 plur. (G *froxortindo/°di* "withdrew," etc.) are formed with the enclitic auxiliary verb "to be." Note that the pret. of a trans. verb agrees with its logical object (the "ergative" construction). Of verbal forms based on the pres. stem, the following are securely attested: pres. indic. 3 sing. M *-y(y)d* (e.g., *'βyryyd* "produces"), 3 plur. M *-y(y)nd* (e.g., *'βyryynd*, cf. perhaps G *na-tirindo* "do not go(?)"); opt. 3 sing G *-ēio* (e.g., *booēio* "may be"), 3 plur. G *-ondēio, -indēio* (*froxoašondēio, froxōšindēio* "may withdraw").

5. Syntax. Three characteristic features, all of which appear also in Sogdian, may be mentioned here. (i) Two demonstrative elements may be used together, e.g., G *eiio mo* (whence also *eimo*?), *eido ma*. (ii) A preposition governing a series of appositional phrases may be repeated before each phrase, as in: G *amo borzomiuro amo kozgaški pouro* "with B. son of K." (see Sims-Williams, "A Note on Bactrian Syntax," *IF* 78, 1973, pp. 95-99). (iii) Throughout the great Surkh Kotal inscription the enclitic particle **uti* "so" (> *-do, -di*, etc.) is attached to the first word or phrase of every clause, giving rise to a series of compounds such as *kaldo, kaldi* "when" (= Sogd. *kδwty*), to which alone enclitic pronouns can be added (e.g., *kaldano*). See Sims-Williams, "A Note on Bactrian Phonology," *BSOAS* 48, 1985, pp. 111-16.

Bibliography: Most important publications are cited in the text. Fuller bibliography is given in G. D. Davary, *Baktrisch: ein Wörterbuch*, Heidelberg, 1982 (a work not without merits, but to be used with caution). I. M. Steblin-Kamenskiĭ, "Baktriĭskiĭ yazyk," in *Osnovy iranskogo yazykoznaniya* II: *Sredneiranskie yazyki*, Moscow, 1981, pp. 314-46, gives a balanced analytical survey of studies up to about 1977. Cf. also I. Gershevitch, "Bactrian Literature," in *Camb. Hist. Iran* III, pp. 1250-58, and N. Sims-Williams, "Bactrian," in *Compendium Linguarum Iranicarum*, ed. R. Schmitt, Wiesbaden (forthcoming).

(N. Sims-Williams)

BĀD (wind), phenomenon at ground level resulting from modifications of general airflows by local topographic factors. On the plateau of Iran and Afghanistan winds depend on a general régime of atmospheric pressures characterized, in the course of the year, by the succession of markedly distinct seasons with relatively stable barometric gradients. Local winds, channeled and strengthened by relief trends or regularly alternating under the influence of mountain blocks (up-valley and down-valley breezes) or sea coasts (on-shore and off-shore breezes), acquire particular importance under such a stable barometric régime and are often individually identified in popular speech. Thus the usual wind names referring to the four cardinal points are supplemented with an exceptionally rich stock of more vividly descriptive terms.

Winter winds. The entire Irano-Afghan plateau normally falls within the influence of the Asiatic high pressure center and consequently experiences fine, dry weather with a general airflow from the north and northeast. Resultant winds are in many places known simply as "north wind" (*šamāl*), in the Kermānšāh (Bāḵtarān) region as "black wind" (*bād-e sīāh*). This stable situation is more or less regularly interrupted by the passage of cyclonic depressions coming from the west, mainly along a northern track through Transcaucasia across the Caspian Sea to the north flank of the Khorasan and Hindu Kush mountains and a southern track down to the Persian Gulf. Their arrival gives rise to various types of unsettled weather. On the Caspian coast a wind called *sartūk* or *saltūk* blows straight from the northeast when such depressions pass in the autumn, but in mid-winter it bends around the depressions then occupying the southern basin of the sea and reaches the coast of Gīlān either directly from the sea as a north-northwest wind (known as *ḵazarī*) or along the shore as a northwest wind (known as *dašt-vā* or in districts further east as *vāreš-vā*, i.e., "rain wind"). On the Persian Gulf coast passage of depressions is followed by cool spells when a cold catabatic wind, similar to the Mediterranean mistral or bora, blows down from the Iranian plateau; in Fārs it is named the *gohra*. A similar phenomenon sometimes occurs on the plateau south of the Alborz when a depression moves along the southern flank of that range. On the other hand, föhn-type winds, reheated after crossing mountains, blow down the northern slopes of highland massifs when depressions pass. This phenomenon occurs at various plateau localities on the northeast side of the Zagros with winds which have already been reheated over Syria and Iraq, e.g., the *garmīš* at Mīāna and the *garmīj* at Ardabīl; it is particularly striking on the very steep north side of the Alborz, where the "hot wind" (*bād-e garm, garmeš, garmīš*) can cause forest-fires and sudden snow-melts with floods, whence its other name "snow-eater" (*barf-ḵ̌or*).

Summer winds. The weather in summer is generally hot, dry, and stable, in consequence of the extension of the subtropical high pressures. Barometric readings show a very regular gradient from the north and northwest down to the low-pressure center in the northwest of the Indian subcontinent. Thus in Ḵūzestān and on the Persian Gulf coast, the northwest wind called the *šamāl* blows throughout the hot season. In the east and southeast of the plateau (Sīstān, southern Khorasan, Lūt desert), the "wind of 120 days" (*bād-e sad-o-bīst-rūza*) blows from late in May to late in September with extraordinary regularity, at first only in the afternoon but in mid-season throughout the day and night; sometimes it is very violent, though it seldom exceeds 100-110 km per hour and often drops to 30-40 km per hour or less. The ruin-like buttes (*kalūts*) which this wind has sculpted from the soft sandstones of the southern Lūt have the same north-northwest-south-southeast alinement and give impressive testimony of its constancy and strength. Human use of it as an energy source began long ago, southern Khorasan and Sīstān having been important centers of windmill technology development. In the stable summer weather régime, local occurrences of regularly alternating up-valley and down-valley breezes or winds are important. Among these is the celebrated wind of Manjīl, on the Rašt-Qazvīn road in the Safīdrūd valley; it blows from north-east to southwest in the afternoon during the summer, often with enough force to make crossing the bridge over the river dangerous, as many travelers have found. In the Tehran district, the uphill breeze which blows in the afternoon from late March onward is supposed to make flowers bud and bloom more vigorously and known as the "rose wind" (*bād-e gol-e sork*). The only regions not subject to the stable summer régime are the Caspian side of the Alborz and the southeastern parts of Afghanistan which are touched by the tail end of the Indian monsoon. Summer storms emanating from the monsoon can occur in southeastern Iran and even in Fārs, but are exceptional. Normally the coastlands of southeastern Iran and the Persian Gulf are exposed in summer only to a sea breeze from the east (*šarqī*), which being moisture-laden makes the weather very oppressive but does not deliver any rainfall.

Spring winds. Unstable weather prevails only in the interval between the end of the winter régime and the start of the summer régime, i.e., in springtime. Local centers of low pressure then develop in basins on the Iranian plateau and in western Central Asia, giving rise to convectional rainstorms, duststorms, and sandstorms. This is the season of the greatest frequency of dustladen whirlwinds, which arise in the afternoon in basins subject to differential heating and in popular belief are stirred by the devil. They may also occur from time to time throughout the summer. On the other hand, Iran suffers relatively little from hot, dry south winds of the type of the khamsin which often afflicts Mediterranean countries in spring when a deep depression passes along that sea. The same phenomenon can occur in Kūzestān and even in Baluchistan, but the wind, having crossed the Persian Gulf or open sea, always carries some moisture.

Bibliography: (i) General. ʿA.-Ḥ. ʿAdl, *Āb o hawā-ye Īrān*, Tehran, 1339 Š./1960. Ch. Djavadi, *Climats de l'Iran*, Monographies de la météorologie nationale 54, Paris, 1966, pp. 12-16. E. Ehlers, *Iran. Grundzüge einer geographischen Landeskunde*, Darmstadt, 1980, pp. 64-68. M. H. Ganji, "The Climates of Iran," *Bulletin de la Société de géographie d'Égypte* 28, 1953, pp. 195-299. Idem, "Climate," *Camb. Hist. Iran* I, pp. 217-20. (ii) Regional studies: Southeast. G. Stratil-Sauer, "Die Sommerstürme Südostirans," *Archive für Meteorologie*, Ser. B, 4, 2, 1952, pp. 133-53. Idem, "Studien zum Klima der Wüste Lut und ihrer Randgebiete," *Sb. der Österreichischen Akademie der Wissenschaften, Math. -nat. Kl.*, Abt. 1, 161, 1, 1952, pp. 19-78. (iii) Caspian region. J. B. Tholozan, "Sur les vents du nord de la Perse et sur le foehn du Guilân," *Comptes rendus hebdomadaires des séances de l'Académie des sciences* 100, 1885, pp. 607-11. M.-Ḥ. Ganjī, "Tağyīrāt-e nāgāhī-e hawā-ye sāḥel-e jonūbī-e Baḥr-e Ḵazar," *Yādgār* 5, 4-5, 1327 Š./1949, pp. 148-50. M. Bazin, *Le Tâlech. Une région ethnique au nord de l'Iran*, Institut français d'iranologie de Téhéran, Bibliothèque iranienne 23, 2 vols., Paris, 1980, I, pp. 42-44. (iv) Winds in folklore. H. Massé, *Croyances et coutumes persanes*, 2 vols., Paris, 1938, I, pp. 177-79. (v) Use of winds. See ĀSĪĀB, BĀDGĪR.

(X. de PLANHOL)

BĀD (wind) in Perso-Islamic medicine: 1. wind as a medically relevant environmental factor; 2. "airiness" as internal physiological and pathological agent.

1. Following Hippocrates' "On airs, waters, places," Galen stressed the influence on human health of wind as of other ecological and climatic factors; the winds prevailing in a given locality were held to affect the temperament of its population, and more specifically, to transmit those miasmatic diseases thought to be caused by corrupted air or vapors. Each wind had certain characteristics ascribed to it, depending on changes of season or time of day, and some were considered more salubrious than others. In Arabic and Persian medical literature, wind as an external force acting on the organism was treated together with air in the discussion of the six non-naturals (*setta żarūrīya*).

2. In Galenic medicine, air entered the lungs through respiration and was there and in the left ventricle of the heart assimilated to the body as vital spirit (*pneuma zōtikon*, mistranslated into Arabic as *rūḥ ḥayawānī*), which arterial blood then carried throughout the body. For Galen this pneuma was not a substance, but a certain quality of the inhaled air, yet he also used the term *pneuma* to denote pathologically altered matter which, because of its mobility, sudden formation, and dissolution within the body, could not be understood as fluid or solid. According to this concept, *pneuma* in Galenic medicine did not only include flatulence in the gastrointestinal tract and its symptoms, such as eructation or colic-like aches, but was taken to act, in a variety of ways, on bone and muscle tissues as well as on organs like the brain, eyes, ears, spleen, and uterus. Manifestations of excess wind included disorders as diverse as epilepsy, pannus trachomatosus, earaches, splenomegaly, tympanitic dropsy, uterine swelling, and spontaneous abortion during the first three months of pregnancy, "phlegmatic tumors," bone fractures and

spinal tuberculosis (?); male impotence without an apparent deficiency of semen production was, conversely, thought to derive from a lack of "wind" and was to be treated by ingesting flatulence-inducing foods such as beans. In the Greek authors down to Paul of Aegina, there is no terminological differentiation between *pneuma* as a force of life and *pneuma* as a gaseous substance analogous to fluids and solids on the one hand and to the four humors on the other; often, *pneuma* is the product of disordered humors like phlegm and black bile. In the Arabic versions of the Greek texts, and consequently also in Persian medical literature, the ambivalence of *pneuma* no longer obtains; *pneuma* as a force of life is rendered as *rūḥ* (spirit), whereas airiness as a material component of the body becomes *rīḥ* or *bād* (wind); following Galen, it is often qualified as coarse (*ḡalīẓa*) when discussed as an agent of internal disorder. Wind, although frequently mentioned as a cause of disease different from the four humors and not just as the result of their pathological alteration, was never really incorporated into the system of humoral pathology. Ebn Sīnā (Avicenna) apparently was the first to list internal wind under a separate heading in his discussion of pain according to its causes, and Esmāʿīl Jorjānī then adopted this classification. The exact place of wind in Arabic and Persian medical writing remains to be examined, however, in particular as regards the possible influence of popular notions on the development of Islamic Galenic concepts of wind. As early as in Ebn Māsawayh's treatise on ophthalmology, *Dağal al-ʿayn*, pannus trachomatosus was called *rīḥ al-sabal*, and the Persian term *bād-e bakast* (fly-wind) appeared there as the current name of a symptom which the author related to nightblindness. In a later nonspecialist usage, *bād* reflects several vague notions about disease, not all of them necessarily derived from Galenic medicine either; a sudden onslaught of pain is implied in some (*Farhang-e fārsī* I, pp. 435-36 and ʿA. A. Nafīsī Nāẓem-al-Aṭebbāʾ, *Farhang-e Nafīsī* I, Tehran, 1355 Š./1976, pp. 498, 502, 503, s. vv. *bād*, *bād-e sork* [erysipelas], *bād-e gonjī* [colic], *bād-e fatq* [hernia], etc.).

Bibliography: The following list of references gives an easily expandable selection of sources and studies which can serve to illustrate the discussion of the topic in Islamic medicine.

(A) Sezgin, *GAS* III, pp. 36f., no. 8 (Hippocrates, *Ketāb al-ahwīa wa'l-azmena wa'l-mīāh wa'l-boldān*), 123f., no. 81 (Galen's commentary on Hippocrates' *De aeribus*). M. Ullmann, *Die Medizin im Islam*, HO 6, Leiden and Cologne, 1970, pp. 27f., no. 3 (Hippocrates), 61, no. 10 (Galen's commentary), ʿAlī b. Sahl Ṭabarī, *Ferdaws al-ḥekma*, ed. M. Z. Siddiqi, Berlin, 1928, pp. 23-27, 501. Pseudo-Ṯābet b. Qorra, *Ḏakīra fī ʿelm al-ṭebb*, ed. G. Sobhy, Cairo, 1928, pp. 167-69. ʿAlī b. ʿAbbās Majūsī, *Ketāb al-malakī* (*Kāmel al-ṣenāʿa al-ṭebbīya*), 2 vols., Būlāq, 1294/1887, I, pp. 154-70, esp. pp. 163f. Abū Bakr Rabīʿ b. Aḥmad Akawaynī, *Hedāyat al-motaʿallemīn*, ed. J. Matīnī, Mašhad, 1344 Š./1965, pp. 143-54. Ebn Sīnā, *Ketāb al-qānūn fi'l-ṭebb*, *ketāb* 1, *fann* 2, *taʿlīm* 2, *jomla* 1, *foṣūl* 2-10, esp. 9-10 (= 1.2.2.1.2-10; New Delhi, 1982, I, pp. 140-55, esp. pp. 152-55). Zayn-al-Dīn Abū Ebrāhīm Esmāʿīl Jorjānī, *Ḏakīra-ye ḵᵛārazmšāhī*, ed. J. Moṣṭafawī, III, Tehran, 1352 Š./1973, pp. 9-26. Ullmann, op. cit., pp. 244f.

(B) Claudius Galenus, *Opera omnia*, ed. C. G. Kühn, 20 vols., Leipzig, 1921-33 (repr. Hildesheim, 1966), VII, pp. 596f., 599 *tremore*), X, p. 879 (*De methodo medendi*), XI, p. 111 (*Ad Glauconem*), XVII, 2, p. 847 (*In Hippocratis Aphorismos*), XX (Index), s.vv. *flatulentia* and *spiritus*. Alexander Trallianus, ed. and German tr. Theodor Puschmann as *Alexander von Tralles, Original-Text und Übersetzung* ..., 2 vols., Vienna, 1878-79, esp. II, pp. 31 (eyeaches caused by *pneuma* obstructing pores), 439 (dropsy). Paulus Aegineta (Ar. Fūlos al-Ajānīṭī), ed. I. L. Heiberg, 2 vols., Leipzig and Berlin, 1921-24 (*Corpus medicorum Graecorum* IX, 1-2), esp. I, pp. 171 (bk. 3, chap. 22, on *pneuma*-caused eyeaches), 268 (bk. 3, chap. 57, on priapism), 287 (bk. 3, chap. 70, on uterine flatulence), 291ff. (bk. 3, chap. 74, on female sterility), 350 (bk. 4, chap. 28, on airy swellings: *emphusēmata*). Abū Zakarīyāʾ Yūḥannā b. Māsawayh, *Dağal al-ʿayn* (see C. Prüfer and M. Meyerhof, "Die Augenheilkunde des Jûḥannâ b. Mâsawaih," *Der Islam* 6, 1916, pp. 217-56, esp. pp. 236, 240f., 243f. [pannus, *bād-e bakast*]) ʿAlī b. Sahl, op. cit., p. 162.11ff. (pannus), 220f. (dropsy), 273ff. (uterine wind), 325 (swellings). Pseudo-Ṯābet b. Qorra, op. cit., pp. 28.11-15 (*rīāḥ al-afresa*: spinal tuberculosis?), 94.7-10, 96.8-11, 98.3f. (hepatic and splenic disorders); Majūsī, op. cit., p. 386.2-7 (uterine wind). Akawaynī, op. cit., pp. 227.12ff. (headache), 229.10ff. (splitting headache), 247-50 (melancholy, etc., epilepsy), 356.4, 359.11, 381ff., 385f. (stomachic disorders, e.g., eructation), 403.3, 424f., 430f. (intestinal colic etc.), 451, 458f. (dropsy), 472f., 475f. (splenic disorders), 509.14-18 (male impotence), 517 (uterine winds), 540 (hysteria), 547 (spontaneous abortion), 577f. (*rīāḥ al-afresa*), 598 (itching rash). Abū Manṣūr Mowaffaq Heravī, *Ketāb al-abnīa ʿan ḥaqāʾeq al-adwīa*, ed. A. Bahmanyār and Ḥ. Maḥbūbī Ardakānī, Tehran, 1346 Š./1967, pp. 60.8 (ear-wind), 66.9ff. (headache caused by coarse winds), 91.4f. (wind increasing sexual drive) 95.10f. (uterine flatulence), 101.5f. (hemorrhoidal winds), 147.6f. (head-wind), 149.14-17 (wind as general agent of internal disorder), 158.5f. (uterine winds), 164.12f. (flatulence increasing semen and milk), 171.5f. (winds in chest), 245 n. 2 (infantile epilepsy called *rīḥ al-ṣebyān*), 337.6f. (pannus trachomatosus), and index, s. vv. *bād*, *nafḵ*. Ebn Sīnā, op. cit., 1.2.2.2.16 (lesions of tissues), ibid., 26 (specificity of pains caused by winds), 1.2.3.9 (symptoms of winds; see New Delhi ed. I, pp. 177, 182, 197f.; quoted in Jorjānī, op. cit., II, Tehran, 1349 Š./1970, pp. 70f., 231, 238). Rudolph E. Siegel, *Galen's System of Physiology and Medicine*, Basel and New York, 1968, esp. p. 183 etc. and index, s.v. *Pneuma*.

(L. Richter-Bernburg)

AL-**BAD'** WA'L-**TA'RĪḴ** (The book of creation and history), an encyclopedic compilation of religious, historical, and philosophical knowledge written in Arabic by Abū Naṣr Moṭahhar b. al-Moṭahhar (or Ṭāher) Maqdesī in 355/966 at Bost in Sīstān for a Samanid prince. It survives in three Istanbul manuscripts. "Dâmâd Ebrahim 918" was copied by Ḵalīl b. Ḥosayn Kordī Walāšjerdī in 663/1265 and ascribes the work to Abū Zayd Aḥmad b. Sahl Balḵī (d. 322/934) on the title page. According to Sezgin (*GAS* I, p. 337), the rest of this text is in "Reis-ül-Küttâb 701", which was copied in 1006/1598. The "Yusof Ağa" summary (in "Süleymaniye 315"), copied in 670/1272 is also attributed to Balḵī, while "Ayasofya 3406" is an eighth/fourteenth-century copy ascribed to Maqdesī. The "Dâmâd Ebrahim" ms. was edited by Huart in six volumes and published by the École des langues orientales vivantes (Ser. IV, vol. 16/1-6, Paris, 1899-1919; repr. Baghdad, 1962) as *Le livre de la création et de l'histoire d'Abou Zaid A. b. Sahl al-Balkhī*, although by 1901 Huart was convinced that Maqdesī was the author. Huart's announced French translation appears never to have been published. A six-volume Persian translation of volumes IV-VI, *Āfarīneš wa tārīḵ*, was published by M. R. Šafīʿī Kadkanī (Tehran, 1349 Š./1970) with an index to each volume. Determining the date and authorship of this work is complicated by a reference (V, p. 78) to the discovery of the gold fields of Ḵašbājī in Sīstān in 390/1000, which is added to the book as a "wonder."

The published text is divided into twenty-two sections: (1) the nature of knowledge (I, pp. 18-55), (2) the unity of creation (I, pp. 56-94), (3) the attributes of the creator (I, pp. 95-108), (4) prophecy (I, pp. 109-144), (5) ideas about creation (I, pp. 115-50), (6) heaven and hell (I, pp. 161-208), (7) the creation of the material universe (II, pp. 1-73), (8) Adam (II, pp. 74-132), (9) the end of the world (II, pp. 143-241), (10) the prophets (II, pp. 1-37), (11) the Persian kings (*molūk al-ʿajam*; III, pp. 133-211), (12) the religions of the world (IV, pp. 1-48), (13) world geography (*aqsām al-arż*; IV, pp. 49-104), (14) Moḥammad at Mecca (IV, pp. 131-79), (16) Moḥammad at Medina (IV, pp. 180-242), (17) Moḥammad's character (V, pp. 1-69), (18) the Prophet's companions (*Saḥāba*; V, pp. 70-120), (19) sectarian divisions among Muslims (V, pp. 121-50), (20) the rightly guided caliphs (*ḵelāfat al-ṣaḥāba*; V, pp. 151-238), (21) the Omayyads (*welāyat Banī Ommaya*; VI, pp. 1-55), and (22) the ʿAbbasids (*ḵolafāʾ Banu'l-ʿAbbās* until 350/961; VI, pp. 65-127).

This work contains important supplementary information, some of it first-hand, relating to Iranian history and religion. The author describes his visit to an ancient fire temple in Ḵūz where he questioned the Zoroastrian priests who showed and recited a copy of the Avesta to him (I, pp. 62-3). He records the views of Zoroastrians (*majūs*) on creation (I, p. 143), on their own prophets (III, p. 7), and information about their laws (IV, pp. 26-30). Concerning the Mazdakīya there is an account of Qobād and Mazdak (III, pp. 167-8), the Ḵorramī view of creation (I, p. 143), the ascent of souls that he read in the Ḵorramī book (II, pp. 20-21), the subgroups of the Ḵorramīya and how he visited them in Māsabaḏān and Mehrajān Qaḏaq (IV, pp. 30-31), and the revolt of Bābak Ḵorramī (VI, pp. 114-20). The section on the *molūk al-ʿajam* contains an account of the legendary as well as the Parthian and Sasanian kings of Iran (III, pp. 138-73) in which three lines of Masʿūdī of Marv's *Šāh-nāma* are quoted (III, pp. 138, 173). The section on the *aqsām al-arż* includes a survey of Iranian geography (IV, pp. 76-81) and of cities founded by Iranian rulers (IV, pp. 98-100). The Muslim conquest of Iraq and Iran are recounted (V, pp. 169-88) as well as the death of Yazdegerd (V, pp. 196-99) and the conquest of Jorjān and Ṭabarestān under Solaymān b. ʿAbd-al-Malek (VI, pp. 42-43). There is also a short section on the Barāmeka viziers of the early ʿAbbasid caliphs (VI, pp. 104-07).

In addition, there is material relevant to Shiʿism on Salmān Fāresī (V, pp. 110-13), its sects (*feraq al-Šīʿa*; V, pp. 124-38), ʿAlī b. Abī Ṭāleb and his children (V, pp. 71-76, 208-38), the deaths of Ḥasan (VI, pp. 5-6) and Ḥosayn (VI, pp. 10-13), the revolts of Moḵtār (VI, pp. 20-25), Zayd b. ʿAlī b. al-Ḥosayn (VI, pp. 49-51), Yaḥyā b. Zayd (VI, pp. 52-53), and the ʿAbbasids (VI, pp. 56-69). There is also information about Abū Moslem (V, pp. 62ff., 80-82, 92-95), and the revolts of Sonfād (*sic*) Majūsī, the Rawandīya, Moḥammad and Ebrāhīm the Ḥosaynīs, and Ostādsīs (VI, pp. 82-87) that broke out after Abū Moslem's death.

The scope of Maqdesī's work, which ranges from creation to the author's time and embraces non-Islamic peoples, puts it among the new type of universal histories along with the work of Yaʿqūbī (d. ca. 284/897) and Masʿūdī (d. 345/956). Like them he gave a cultural treatment to pre-Islamic history and a dynastic presentation to Islamic history. His interest in ancient peoples and in India foreshadows that of Bīrūnī (d. 442/1051). As a Muʿtazilite he was concerned with the development of reason and revelation in history and urged that creation legends be taken symbolically rather than literally (II, p. 50); he interpreted the legends of the prophets allegorically (II, pp. 33-34).

Although much of Maqdesī's material parallels that in other works, Ṯaʿālebī (d. 429/1038) included the section on Indian religion in his *Ḡorar*, (p. 501), and Abu'l-Maʿālī Moḥammad b. ʿObayd-Allāh translated the section on the Avesta (I, p. 62) into Persian in his *Bayān al-adyān* (pp. 5, 6-7) in 485/1092. Moreover, Ebn al-Wardī included entire sections of Maqdesī's work in his ninth/fifteenth-century *Ḵarīdat al-ʿajāʾeb* (pp. 249-52) but ascribed them to Abū Zayd Balḵī.

Bibliography: Jūzjānī, *Ṭabaqāt* I, pp. 12, 21, 64, 106, 133-35, 138, 142, 157-158, 162-163, 170, 174-175, 181, 321. Cl. Huart, "Le véritable auteur du *Livre de la Création et de l'Histoire*," *JA*, Ser. 9, 18, 1901, pp. 16-21. Idem, *Littérature arabe*, Paris, 1902, tr. *A History of Arabic Literature*, Beirut, 1966, pp. 284, 291, 301. Cl. Cahen, "Les chroniques arabes concernant la Syrie, l'Egypte et la Mésopotamie de la conquête arabe à la conquête ottomane dans les bibliothèques d'Istambul," *Revue des études islamiques*, 1936, p. 336. Brockelmann, *GAL*, S. I, pp. 222, 408. Sezgin, *GAS* I, p. 337. T. Khalidi, *Islamic Historiography*, Albany, 1975, pp. xiii-xiv, xvi, 7-8, 57, 59, 68-69, 83, 114.

(M. Morony)

BĀDA (Pahl. *bātak*), one of several terms used in Persian poetry to mean wine, and, by extension, any intoxicating liquor. Others are, in approximate order of frequency, *mey, šarāb, ḵamr*, and *nabīḏ*. In meaning they are virtually interchangeable, but they are metrically different. Their use by poets was governed more by phonetic and linguistic considerations than by differences in sense.

Bāda and *mey* in particular appear in the terms for various kinds of wine, the implements necessary to make wine and prepare it for drinking, the place where it is drunk, and for wine-bibbers themselves. Double distilled wine is "wine of two fires" *bāda-ye do ātaša*, a tavern is a "wine-house" *mey-ḵāna, mey-kada*, and wine-drinkers are those who "drink," "worship," or "measure out" wine—*bādagosār, bādaparast, bādapeymā* (for these terms see, e.g., Dehḵodā, s.vv.).

Literary texts reflect very different views of wine and drunkenness than one might expect from the fierce temperance of Islamic injunctions against intoxicating beverages. In the *Šāh-nāma*, a work that is self-consciously pre-Islamic in its context and ideology, wine is an antidote to grief and misfortune and the necessary accompaniment of hospitality (*Šāh-nāma*, Moscow, II, pp. 173-74 ll. 52, 58, 197-98 ll. 353-54, 460-63). Drinking wine in company is the benign opposite of meeting in war or single combat. There are many scenes in which heroes either invite their foes to put aside their arms and hoist the cup of friendship instead, or in which warriors prepare for battle by a night of carousal (*Šāh-nāma*, Moscow, II, pp. 208-09 ll. 484-526 passim, 232 ll. 815, 830-34).

Nor is there any suggestion that drunken conviviality has unfortunate side effects. Kay Kāvūs is a rash and foolish monarch who makes many decisions he later repents, but never under the influence of drink. Finally, while Zoroastrian beliefs and practices are only vaguely and imperfectly adumbrated in the *Šāh-nāma*, there is no suggestion that wine-drinking is offensive to the new faith. Esfandīār does not hesitate to hoist a cup with Rostam although he is an exemplar of Zoroastrian piety (*Šāh-nāma*, Moscow, VI, p. 249 l. 528).

Poetry and other works written as part of courtly *adab*, acknowledge the immorality of drinking, but rather light-heartedly. While it is now immoral to drink with one's friends, drunkenness is still presented as a relief from pain and the focus of hospitality and celebration. Persian poets followed the example of Abū Nowās in playing upon the opposition of wine-drinking and piety for ironic or humorous effect. Manūčehrī, for example, parodies the ritual of morning prayer—the cock is the *mo'aḏḏen* of wine drinkers and wine not piety is the hope of the despairing—and begins another poem by describing the drunken feast that follows the conclusion of the fast of Ramażān (*Dīvān*, ed. M. Dabīrsīāqī, Tehran, 1338 Š./1959, pp. 88, 177). Nor were such convivial gatherings simply a poetic convention; Bayhaqī makes reference to gatherings at which the members of the court gathered to drink and enjoy music and singing as well (Bayhaqī, ed. Fayyāż, pp. 54, 527-29).

When wine-drinking is condemned, it is less for reasons of piety than for a practical recognition of its disastrous consequences on public conduct and policy. Stories about the evils of making important decisions while drunk abound, as does praise for those officials wise enough to reconsider on the sober morning after all decisions made while drunk (Ḵᵛāja Neẓām-al-Molk, *Sīār al-molūk*, ed. H. Darke, Tehran, 1347 Š./1968, chaps. 15, 17, 39). There is a certain truth in poets' fanciful derivation of *bāda* from *bād* "wind," meaning that it inflates the drinker with the "wind" of conceit and rashness (*bād-e ḡorūr*; see Dehḵodā, s.v.). Disapproval of drinking, however, is balanced by the acceptance of it as a common, if unfortunate, practice. Kaykāvus b. Eskandar includes a chapter on how to conduct oneself at a drinking party, along with gentle reproofs for those who so indulge themselves ('Onṣor-al-Ma'ālī Kaykāvūs b. Eskandar, *Qābūs-nāma*, ed. Ḡ.-Ḥ. Yūsofī, Tehran, 1345 Š./1967, chap. xi).

As the center of gravity in Persian poetry shifted from court to *ḵānaqāh*, *bāda* gained a new range of meanings which transformed the immorality of wine-drinking into an alternative mode of piety. In order to separate themselves from Islamic orthodoxy, Sufis created a world which, in their poetry in particular, was the diametric opposite of court and mosque. The well-established association of wine with intoxication, irrational behavior, the impious rejection of orthodoxy, and the joys of fellowship made wine-drinking a logical, even an inevitable symbol for the piety of mysticism. Wine-drinking and drunkenness came to stand both for the search for transcendent spiritual knowledge, and for the brotherhood of mystics. Wine was also widely believed by Muslim Iranians to be a part of Zoroastrian religious rituals, and this association with illicit or unconventional religious practices provided mystical poetry with an alternative clergy, the magian elder (*pīr-e moḡān*), and an alternative place of worship, the winehouse, that were in direct and shocking contrast with shaikh and mosque. And in the fusion of the "beloved" of the courtly *tašbīb* with the magian's acolyte, the cupbearer or *sāqī* who poured the wine, mystical poetry found its most powerful and attractive symbol—the metaphorical love (*'ešq-e majāzī*) for a beautiful youth which transformed the seductions and distractions of worldly joy into an allegory for the pursuit of transcendent union (Schimmel, pp. 284, 292). The association of worldly drunkenness with spiritual intoxication eventually became so firmly established in Persian poetry that wine drinking lost its original meaning of simple, worldly revelry.

Bibliography: Given in the text. See also A. G. Chejne, "The Boon-Companion in Early ʿAbbasid Times," *JAOS* 65, 1965, pp. 327-35 (discusses the tradition of the wine party in early ʿAbbasid times). A Schimmel, *Mystical Dimensions of Islam*, Chapel Hill, North Carolina, 1975. E. Yarshater, "The Theme of Wine-Drinking and the Concept of the Beloved in Early Persian Poetry," *Studia Islamica* 13, 1960, pp. 43-53 (contains numerous references to the treatment of wine-drinking in contemporary literary works).

(J. W. Clinton)

BADĀʾ (Ar. appearance, emergence), as a theological term denotes a change of a divine decision or ruling in response to the emergence of new circumstances. It is upheld in Imami Shiʿite doctrine and rejected by most other Shiʿite and Sunni schools. The notion of *badāʾ* is said to have been put forward first by Moḵtār b. Abī ʿObayd Ṯaqafī when he predicted the victory of his supporters in a battle against Moṣʿab b. Zobayr in 67/686-87, claiming to have received a promise of God to that effect and, after their defeat, explained that God had changed His decision (*badā lahū*). In support of this explanation he quoted Koran 13:39: "God deletes whatever He wishes and confirms" (Ṭabarī, II, p. 732). *Badāʾ* became a theological doctrine of the Kaysānīya, the followers of Moḵtār, and was then, like other Kaysānī doctrines, adopted by the nascent Emāmīya. The religious importance of the doctrine was emphasized in various traditions transmitted from the imams, especially Moḥammad al-Bāqer and Jaʿfar al-Ṣādeq. They affirmed that "God is not worshipped (*ʿabada*), or glorified (*ʿaẓẓama*), through anything as He is through (belief in) *badāʾ*," and that "if people knew what a reward there is for upholding *badāʾ* they would never tire of speaking about it." Imam ʿAlī al-Reżā is quoted as stating that "God has never sent a prophet without the prohibition of wine and without his affirming *badāʾ* of God." A practical application of *badāʾ* was given by Imam al-Ṣādeq when his son Esmāʿīl, who had been expected to succeed him, died before him. He is reported to have said: "God has never changed his decision (*mā badā le'llāh*) as in the case of my son Esmāʿīl." A variant of this tradition substituted "my father (*abī*)" for "my son (*ebnī*) Esmāʿīl," thus referring to Abraham's son Ishmael whom God decided to save after having commanded his father to sacrifice him. (See Majlesī, p. 107; Ebn Bābawayh, p. 275.)

Such traditions of the imams ensured that *badāʾ* remained a permanent Imami dogma though its precise significance has been subject to varying interpretations. *Badāʾ* was fully consistent with the early Imami *kalām* theology represented by Hešām b. Ḥakam (d. 179/795-96) and others who held that nothing could become subject to knowledge, either human or divine, before its existence. The emergence of new circumstances for God was thus reasonable, especially in respect to human acts. Constantly adjusting His decisions to the free choice of man, God, in their view, controlled the course of the world at any time without having predetermined it.

Badāʾ became theologically problematical when divine foreknowledge of all future events was accepted. Some traditions of the imams affirmed that *badāʾ*, too, was known to God before it occurred. Imam al-Ṣādeq was quoted as stating: "God has never changed a decision (*mā badā le'llāh*) about anything but that it was in His knowledge before He changed it" (Kolaynī). There was now the disturbing question whether God could inform man of a decision knowing that He would change it. Some traditions denied this suggesting that *badāʾ* could happen only in the hidden part of God's knowledge. To Imam al-Bāqer is attributed the statement: "(God's) knowledge is of two kinds: A knowledge that is stored (*maḵzūn*) with God of which He does not inform anyone of His creation, and a knowledge which He teaches His angels and Messengers (*rosol*). Whatever He teaches His angels and Messengers will happen; He will not turn Himself, His angels, and His Messengers into liars. But of the knowledge which is stored with Him, He may advance, postpone, and confirm whatever He wishes" (Kolaynī). This position was backed by a few Imami theologians. However, the prevalent position, upheld by Shaikh Abū Jaʿfar Ṭūsī (d. 460/1067), was that any information about future events given by God to His prophets and imams was conditional (*moštaraṭ*) unless it was stated to be definitely ordained (*maḥtūm*). This position was reflected in a tradition ascribed to Imam al-Ṣādeq: "God informed Moḥammad of everything that was since the existence of the world and that will be until the end of the world. He informed him of what is definitely ordained and declared everything else conditional (*estaṯnā ʿalayhe fīmā sewāho*)" (Kolaynī). On that basis Imami doctrine holds some of the signs announcing the advent of the Mahdi to be inevitable and others as subject to cancellation by God. A Koranic verse (6:2): "He fixed a (life's) term (*qażā ajalan*) and a term is stated (*mosamman*) in His keeping" was interpreted as distinguishing between a definitely ordained and a deferrable (*mawqūf*) life span. Traditions described God as keeping a book of future events in which He deletes and confirms in response to prayers. Whatever is recorded in the Omm al-Ketāb (Koran 13:39), however, can never be changed. In the Night of *al-Qadr* in Ramażān, the imam is annually informed of all of God's definite decisions for the coming year which had previously been conditional. (See Majlesī, pp. 102, 116-19.)

Imami theologians influenced by the Muʿtazilite concept of an immutable divine essence found it most difficult to accomodate the doctrine of *badāʾ*. They tended to associate it closely with *nasḵ*, abrogation of divine legislation, which was accepted by all Muslim theologians because of its foundation in the Koran. Ebn Bābawayh (d. 381/991) stresses that *badāʾ* did not imply a repentence (*nadāma*) of God. Anyone who admitted that God abrogated some of His laws in the best interest of His creatures and that He advanced or deferred the creation and annihilation of anything as He wished affirmed in fact *badāʾ*. Similarly Abū ʿAbd-Allāh Moḥammad Mofīd (d. 413/1022) identified *badā'* largely with *nask̲* and maintained that any difference between his doctrine and that of all Muslims in this regard was only verbal. Admitting the ambiguity of the term *badā'* he emphasized that he used it only because it occurred in accepted traditions of the imams, just as he used the anthropomorphic expressions occurring there. Like the latter *badā'* was to be understood metaphorically in consonance with reason. In so far as *badā'* implied the appearance of something unexpected, it meant an event unexpected by man rather than God. It applied to the conditional (*moštaraṭ*) in God's preordination. Šarīf Abu'l-Qāsem 'Alī Mortażā (d. 436/1044) considered the *badā'* recognized by the Emāmīya as identical with *nask̲* and repudiated any other concept of it. Later *kalām* works by Imami scholars inclining to Mu'tazilism generally ignored *badā'*.

The discussion of *badā'* was, however, resumed by the philosophical school of Isfahan in the Safavid age which tended to remove *badā'* from the essence of God locating its causes in the lower levels of the spiritual world. Mīr(-e) Dāmād (d. 1040/1630) held that *badā'* had the same function in temporal creation (*takwīn*) as had *nask̲* in legislation (*tašrī'*). *Badā'* does not occur in the realm of Ordainment (*qażā'*) nor does it affect God, the pure spiritual beings (*mofāreqāt*), and the backside of the aeon (*matn al-dahr*) which envelops the whole world of existence. Rather it arises in the realm of Premeasurement (*qadar*) and affects the physical world of time and space. Just as *nask̲* does not signify a cancellation (*raf'*), but rather a discontinuity, in the legislative process, *badā'* is a discontinuity in the creational process, not a cancellation or annulment. Mīr Dāmād's view was partly adopted and developed by his disciple Mollā Ṣadrā (d. 1050/1641), who also confined *badā'* to the realm of *qadar* where, in contrast to the realm of *qażā'*, substantive change, an indeterminacy of God's will, and possibility versus necessity prevail. More specifically *badā'* could result from the imperfect reflection of the divine omniscience in the lower heavenly soul from which the mind of prophets and imams receives its images. These images might change as a result of either changed conditions of the world or the rise of a new idea in the world soul. The resulting *badā'* or *nask̲* could be loosely ascribed to God since the heavenly souls are servants perfectly obedient to Him (F. Rahman, *The Philosophy of Mullā Ṣadrā*, Albany, 1975, pp. 180-84). Imami scholars have continued to deal with the subject of *badā'* in special treatises until recent times (see *al-D̲arī'a* III, pp. 51-57).

Imami apologists of *badā'* generally held that Sunni Hadith and theology supported belief in it in substance and merely rejected the term. The Jews, however, were criticized for repudiating the notion of *badā'* itself and for considering *nask̲*, the abrogation of divine laws, as a form of it. Traditions of the imams interpreted Koran 5:62: "The Jews say: The hand of God is fettered" as referring to their denial of *badā'* and their belief that God had finished with creation (*qad faraḡa men al-amr*) at the beginning of the world and does not bring forth anything new (see Majlesī).

Bibliography: Abu'l-Ḥosayn K̲ayyāṭ, *Ketāb al-enteṣār*, ed. H. S. Nyberg, Cairo, 1925, pp. 127-30. Ḥasan b. Mūsā Nawbak̲tī, *Feraq al-šī'a*, ed. H. Ritter, Istanbul, 1931, pp. 55, 62. Aš'arī, *Maqālāt*, pp. 36, 39, 221, 479, 491-92. Abū Ja'far Moḥammad Kolaynī, *al-Oṣūl men al-kāfī*, ed. 'Alī Akbar Ḡaffārī, Tehran, 1388/1968, I, pp. 146-49. Ebn Bābawayh, *Ketāb al-tawḥīd*, ed. Moḥammad-Mahdī K̲orsān, Najaf, 1386/1966, pp. 272-75. Baḡdādī, *Farq* (Cairo[1]), pp. 35-37. 'Abd-al-Jabbār (correctly: Mānekdīm), *Šarḥ al-oṣūl al-k̲amsa*, ed. 'Abd-al-Karīm Ot̲mān, Cairo, 1384/1965, pp. 583-85. Abu'l-Ḥosayn Baṣrī, *al-Mo'tamad*, ed. M. Hamidullah, Damascus, 1964, pp. 398-99. Shaikh Abū Ja'far Moḥammad Ṭūsī, *al-Ḡayba*, Najaf, 1385/1965, pp. 363-65. Šahrestānī, p. 110. Moḥammad-Bāqer Majlesī, *Beḥār al-anwār*, Tehran, 1376-1405/1957-85, IV, pp. 92-134. W. Madelung, "Imāmism and Mu'tazilite Theology," in *Le shî'isme imâmite*, ed. T. Fahd, Paris, 1970, pp. 13-27. Idem, "The Shiite and Khārijite Contribution to pre-Ash'arite *Kalām*," in *Islamic Philosophical Theology*, ed. P. Morewedge, Albany, 1979, pp. 123-24. J. van Ess, *Frühe mu'tazilitische Häresiographie*, Beirut, 1971, p. 64, Ar. text, p. 75. M. J. McDermott, *The Theology of al-Shaikh al-Mufīd*, Beirut, 1978, pp. 302, 329-39, 392-93. See also *EI*[2] I, pp. 850f. [Mahmoud Ayoub, "Divine Preordination and Human Hope. A Study of the Concept of *Badā'* in Imāmī Shī'ī Tradition," *JAOS* 106/4, 1986, pp. 623-32.]

(W. MADELUNG)

BADAK̲ŠĀN, the name of an area and modern province of northeastern Afghanistan (q.v.), situated between the upper Amu Darya to the north, the Hindu Kush to the south, and the Kondūz river to the west.

i. *Geography and ethnography.*
ii. *Modern province.*
iii. *The name.*

i. GEOGRAPHY AND ETHNOGRAPHY

Geographical meaning and administrative divisions. The name Badak̲šān first occurs, in the form Po-to-chang-na, in a seventh-century Chinese source (journey of Hüan Tsang in 629 A.D.; see S. Beal, *Si-Yu-Ki, Buddhist Records of the Western World*, 2 vols., London, 1884, I, p. 42, and II, p. 291). The area described is small (200 *li* = approximately 75 miles or 120 km in circumference) and appears to have consisted of the lower basin of the Kokča river; if so, it must have lain entirely on the left bank of the upper Oxus, of which the Kokča is the principal left bank tributary. A distinction is made between the lower part and the upper part of the Kokča valley (Yamgān, above Jorm, probably the Chinese traveler's Im-po-kin); Korān, above Sar-e Sang, probably his Kiu-lang-na). No further information is to be found in more recent Chinese sources from the fifteenth and sixteenth centuries (E. Bretschneider,

Mediaeval Researches from Eastern Asiatic Sources, 2 vols., Leiden, 1888, II, pp. 276-78). These describe the area as a land of passage but do not give any precise information about its limits.

For the Arabic geographers of the classical period, however, Badakšān has a considerably wider meaning. They often write vaguely about this area, of which they evidently had little knowledge, as the routes east of Balk which they mention generally end in Ṭokārestān (the area then called Ṭālaqān, Ṭāraqān, or Ṭāyagān and still known as Ṭaleqān [Tālaqān], corresponding to the modern province of Qaṭaḡān together with the districts of Kolm and Baḡlān) and in the Kottal area north of the Oxus. There are also some discrepancies and contradictions in the accounts of the successive authors. Nevertheless it is clear that in their estimation Badakšān meant the entire Kokča basin (for a rough summary of their statements, see Le Strange, *Lands*, pp. 432ff.; also V. Minorsky's notes on p. 349 of his tr. of the *Ḥodūd al-ʿālam*). They describe Badakšān as a mountainous, mineral-rich country where lapis lazuli (see below), balas rubies, asbestos, rock crystal, and bezoar stones are found. The term "balas," applied to a sort of ruby (spinel), is derived from al-Balakš, an Arabic dialect-form of the area's name which was noted by Ebn Baṭṭūṭa (see P. Pelliot, *Notes on Marco Polo* I, Paris, 1959, p. 63). There are no grounds for the supposition of J. Markwart (*Ērānšahr*, p. 279) that, on the contrary, the precious stone's name might have been the source of the country's name (see BADAKŠĀN iii, below). Marco Polo (I, p. 29; tr. H. Yule, ed. H. Cordier, 3rd ed., London, 1921, I, pp. 157-63) has a similar concept of Badakšān, except that he explicitly excludes from it the district of "Casem" (Kešm), i.e., the lower Kokča basin. Probably the name Badakšān was first applied to the less elevated areas, later extended gradually to the mountains upstream which supplied the mineral products for sale elsewhere after transportation through the Oxus valley and plain, and finally limited to the highland which was the source of the country's world-wide fame. In any case the political influence of Badakšān then reached into the Pamir and the Wākān (Wakhan, upper Oxus) valley, whose inhabitants, according to Marco Polo (tr. Yule, I, p. 217), paid tribute to the prince of Badakšān. It seems, however, that Badakšān was not then thought to include the lowland valleys downstream from the northward bend of the Oxus, still less those on the great river's right bank.

In later times the concept evolved in the opposite way, probably for historical and political reasons. Early in the sixteenth century Bābor (*Bābor-nāma*, tr. A. S. Beveridge, London, 1922, p. 1) regarded Badakšān as adjoining Farḡāna on the south, separated by mountains which formed the border. Evidently the name was then extended to the lands on the right bank of the Oxus. This new usage probably resulted from the acquisition of lands and influence north of the Oxus by the local princes of Badakšān; it took root in the nomenclature of modern political geography as a result of the action of the Soviet government, which in 1925 created the Autonomous Region of Gorno-Badakshan (Mountain-Badakšān) within the Socialist Soviet Republic of Tajikistan. Although the existence of this political unit is intended primarily to give recognition to the ethnic and religious distinctiveness of the Pamir and Wākān peoples, its name evokes a definite historical tradition with memories of the past expansion of the Özbek states and peoples of the north into more or less all the Oxus right bank lands. European and American geographers and historians often speak of "Badakšān in the proper sense," meaning the area south of the Oxus (e.g., W. Barthold in EI^{1-2}). Badakšān's limits to the south, unlike the north, have long been firmly fixed on the crestline of the Hindu Kush (*Bābor-nāma*, tr. Beveridge, pp. 46, 204), which separate it from the Kabul country and Nūrestān (Kāferestān). In the eighteenth and nineteenth centuries, the Özbek princes of Badakšān achieved a considerable westward expansion and temporarily held sway over Qaṭaḡān and Kondūz. A relic of those days survived in the former administrative divisions of Afghanistan, Badakšān being a "minor" province subordinate to the neighboring "major" province of Qaṭaḡān until the reorganization in 1964.

Natural environment. The heart of Badakšān is the upper valley of the Amu Darya (Oxus), known here as the Panǰ and in its highest reach in Afghan territory as the Wākān. In the frontier demarcation at the end of the nineteenth century, a long corridor adjoining the Wākān river and extending to the Chinese frontier was left in Afghanistan so that the British Indian empire and the Russian-controlled Central Asian territories might be kept apart. The deep valleys of the Oxus and its tributaries, on the left bank (the Kokča) and on the right bank (the Pāmīr river which forms the Soviet-Afghan frontier in the east of the Wākān corridor, the Gunt [Ghund] which is named ʿAlīšūr in its upper course, and the Bārtang which is named Morḡāb further upstream and Oksu in its highest reach), lie embedded between blocks of the Pamir plateau, the great orographic node where the Hindu Kush, Karakoram, and Kunlun Shan converge. In structure the Pamir node is complex, the orogenesis being Hercynian in the north, Cimmerian and Alpine in the South where the Gondwanan and Asiatic plates come into contact. Fragments of pre-Cambrian basement rock and granite masses of various ages are interspersed among overlying mesozoic formations. The whole surface has been raised to altitudes averaging between 3,000 and 4,000 m, above which tower lofty ice-covered blocks averaging between 5,000 and 6,000 m. Some peaks in the north exceed 7,000 m. (Communism Peak 7,495 m, in the Academy of Science range; Lenin Peak 7,134 m, in the Trans-Alai range). The Hindu Kush also exceeds 7,000 m on the Pakistani-Afghan frontier (Kūh-e Nawšāk 7,485 m). Access from the Kokča basin to Nūrestān and the Panjšīr valley is only possible over very steep passes (Anǰoman pass to Panjšīr, 4,400 m; several passes to Nūrestān, ca. 4,500 m).

This highland has an extremely harsh climate. On the

Pamir plateaux average temperatures are estimated at -20° C in January and 10° to 12° C in July, while the winter minima can fall to about -50° C. The annual rainfall, which can be as much as 800 to 1,500 mm on west-facing and northwest-facing massifs, falls to less than 200 mm on sheltered plateaux in the Pamir and less than 100 mm in the Oksu basin, with the result that these areas are highland deserts. In the bottom of the Oxus valley at altitudes of 300 to 400 m, and likewise in the tributary valleys, warm semi-desert or steppe conditions prevail. Moderate temperatures combined with relatively ample rainfall are found in the middle stretches of the valleys; at Fayżābād, the chief town of Afghan Badakšān, average temperatures are 0.1° in January and 26.4° in July and annual rainfall is 521 mm. Between the warm steppe of the valley bottoms and the cold desert of the high ground, there is a belt of natural forest, consisting mainly of junipers (*Juniperus seravschanica, Junipersus polycarpos*); its breadth in the west is around 1,000 m, and its floor is 1,500 m in the Kokča valley and progressively higher to the east; in the upper Wāḵān valley and the Pamir it disappears on account of the aridity. The primitive forest, however, has almost everywhere been cut down. In this environment, agricultural activity is concentrated in the valleys where glacier-fed streams provide means of irrigation, while pastoral activity can be pursued on high ground in the Pamir up to 3,000-3,500 m.

Population groups and lifestyles. As a highland region, generally remote from centers of urban civilization and only traversed by the very arduous Oxus valley route of the trans-Asiatic "silk road," Badakšān has served as a refuge for peoples of ancient stock who still live there side by side with descendants of peoples who have arrived more recently. Seen as a whole, it is a veritable ethno-linguistic museum.

1. The highland peasants. The great majority of the population consists of Persian-speaking Tajiks, who predominate in the Kokča basin, the Darvāz (or Nesay) area on the Afghan side of the northward bend of the Oxus, and in general throughout Afghan Badakšān. Also present are remnants of more ancient peoples known to the Russians as "Mountain (Gornye) Tajiks" or "Pamir (Pamirskie or Pripamirskie) Tajiks" and to their Tajik neighbors as "Ḡalča." They speak East Iranian languages and are split into several groups: The Šoḡnī people in the Gunt basin and at Khorog (Khoruk), the Rūšānī people in the Rūšān district adjoining the Oxus, and the Bārtang people in the Bārtang valley speak closely interrelated dialects and together constitute the largest group, perhaps three quarters of the total of the Ḡalčas, in the Soviet territory, The Wāḵī people of the Wāḵān valley amount to about one-fifth of the total, roughly half of them being domiciled in Afghanistan. The Yāzḡolāmī people, numbering a few thousand, live in thirteen villages in the valley of the same name north of Rūšān in the Soviet territory. The Eškāšemī people, who together with the related Zēbākī and Sanglēčī groups also number a few thousand, live for the most part in Afghanistan near the

Oxus bend at the entrance to the Wāḵān corridor. The Wānčī people, who live in the Wānč valley in the far north of the Soviet territory, ceased to speak their own language about a century ago and are now assimilated to their Tajik neighbors, the Monjī people live in the Monjān (upper Kokča) valley in Afghanistan).

The separateness of the Pamir peoples as regards language is coupled with religious nonconformity. Most of them remain faithful to Ismaʿilite Shiʿism, to which their ancestors were converted by the great Ismaʿilite poet Nāṣer(-e) Ḵosrow (1004-72), and to the Nezārī sect; but the Wānčī and Yāzḡolāmī peoples reverted to Sunnism at the end of the nineteenth century and are now rapidly fusing with the Tajiks. A small minority of the Bārtang is also Sunnite. None of the Pamir languages is fixed in writing. An attempt by the Soviet authorities to make Šoḡnī a literary language failed to gain acceptance. The language of civilization is Tajik, i.e., Persian (written in Cyrillic script in the Soviet territory). Among the Pamir languages, Wāḵī seems the most resistant.

No real differences exist between the Pamir Tajiks (Ḡalča) and the Tajiks properly so called in fields such as life-style, material culture, and social organization (Kussmaul, pp. 97-99). Basically they are all sedentary peasants, dependent for their livelihood on irrigated and usually terraced fields in the valley bottoms. Arboriculture (nuts, apples, mulberries, etc.) is one of their main activities. They also practice rain-fed cultivation on suitable slopes and breed flocks which they take to nearby mountain pastures on short-distance migrations.

2. The immigrant groups. Side by side with this long-established peasantry live the descendants of successive immigrant groups. From the sixteenth century onward, bands of Özbeks moved across the Oxus and established themselves in low-lying areas of the present Afghan Badakšān (the western and northwestern sectors adjoining Qaṭaḡan and the Oxus plain). Ḡelzay Paštūns have come to the same areas in small numbers since the start of the nineteenth century. The Özbeks and the Paštūns appear to be still mostly nomadic or semi-nomadic, migrating over much longer distances than do the Tajiks. The summer pastures in the basin of Lake Šēva (altitude 3,400 m) attract nomads and semi-nomads from far afield, apparently quite often from regions south of the Hindu Kush.

The high plateaux of the Pamir, which until the seventeenth century were uninhabited and only penetrated by hunting parties, have since then been occupied, at first seasonally, later permanently, by Kirghiz shepherds belonging to a Turkic people with a long tradition of nomadism. Today those living in the Soviet territory are more or less settled as workers in large pastoral establishments, within whose boundaries regular transhumance is still practiced; those living in Afghanistan are still pure nomads with widely separate seasonal abodes. The latter, who had found refuge in Afghanistan from the Russian revolution, were somewhat over 3,000 strong before most of them moved to

Pakistan after the installation of the communist régime at Kabul in 1979, now also to Turkey. All the Kirghiz and Hanafite Sunnis.

3. Population. According to the first returns of the Afghan census of 1979, the province of Badaḵšān had 497,758 inhabitants. It is very difficult to appraise the exact proportions of the different ethnic groups in this total. The population of the Autonomous Region of Gorno-Badakhshan at that time was 127,000 including 115,000 Tajiks and Pamir Tajiks (not distinguished since the census of 1959), 8,500 Kirghiz, and 1,780 Russians. Since 38,000 Pamir Tajiks and 42,000 persons able to speak the various Pamir languages were recorded in the census of 1939, their present number may be reckoned at anything between 60,000 and 100,000 (see also BADAḴŠĀN ii, below).

4. Modern economy. This mountainous country has not yet been opened to modern economic development of any importance. In Afghan Badaḵšān the motorable road goes no further than Fayżābād. In the Soviet territory an "East Pamir highway" (Vostochno-pamirskiĭ trakt) from Khorog via Morḡāb and Karaart to Osh in Farḡāna has been constructed for strategic reasons; it is joined at Tuzkul' by a frontier road which ascends the Oxus valley above Khorog and then runs along the Pamir river. Nevertheless the economy of Soviet Badakhshan remains purely agricultural and pastoral, aside from some small food-processing and building material industries at Khorog. The only outward-oriented economic activity worthy of note in Afghan Badaḵšān is the working of the lapis lazuli mines. Badaḵšān is the sole supplier of this semi-precious stone to world markets. (Lapis lazuli is known to have been used in ancient Mesopotamia as early as the third millennium B.C. and to have been exported as far as Mauritania; its importance in the middle ages is attested by Marco Polo.) The deposits lie in a synclinal trough of marble embedded in gneiss at an altitude of 2,500-2,600 m on the left side of the Kokča valley, above the village of Sar-e Sang 70 km from Jorm. The annual output, produced by some thirty miners, was on the order of two to four tons, and the price in 1971 was 265 U.S. dollars per kg. Only two settlements in Badaḵšān deserve to be ranked as towns: Fayżābād in the Afghan territory and Khorog in the Soviet territory.

Bibliography: 1. General studies and descriptions. (a) General: W. Barthold, "Badakhshān," in *EI*[1−2] (mainly historical). T. G. Abaeva, *Ocherki istorii Badakhshana*, Tashkent, 1964 (economic and political history until the end of the 19th century, with geohistorical data in chapter 1; important Russian bibliography). (b) Afghan Badaḵšān: Mawlawī Borhān-al-Dīn Khan Koškakī, *Rāhnamā-ye Qaṭaḡān wa Badaḵšān*, Kabul, 1302 Š./1923 (lithograph); Russian tr. by A. A. Semenov, *Kattagan i Badakhshan*, Tashkent, 1926; new ed. with French tr., introd., and notes by M. Reut, *Qataghan et Badakhshan*, 3 vols., Paris, 1979. *Gazetteer of Afghanistan* I, 1972. (c) Soviet Badaḵšān: A. Bennigsen and H. Carrère d'Encausse, "Autonomous Region of Soviet Gorno-

Badakhshān," in *EI²*, s.v. *Badakhshān* (basic data on population and ethnic composition; important bibliography, mainly Russian, up to 1958); idem and C. Lemercier-Quelquejay, *Les musulmans oubliés. L'Islam en Union Soviétique*, Paris, 1981, pp. 164-65 (updates the article in *EI²*). N. A. Kislyakov and A. K. Pisarchik, *Tadzhiki Karategina i Darvaza* (ethnography, but mainly concerned with a border district). I. K. Narzikulov and K. V. Stanyukovich, eds., *Atlas Tadzhikskoĭ SSR*, Dushambe and Moscow, 1968 (essential for the physical and economic geography).

2. Monographs and travel accounts concerning particular districts (except the Pamir and Wāḵān). (a) Afghan Badaḵšān. i. Studies: F. Kussmaul, "Badaxšan und seine Taǧiken," *Tribus* 2, August, 1965, pp. 11-99 (fundamental on means of subsistence, material culture, spiritual life). P. Snoy, "Nuristan und Munǧan," ibid., pp. 101-48. E. Grötzbach, *Kulturgeographischer Wandel in Nordost-Afghanistan seit dem 19. Jahrhundert*, Afghanische Studien 4, Meisenheim am Glan, 1972 (mainly about Qaṭaḡān). W. Rauning, "Einige Bemerkungen zu Verkehr- und Handelstendenzen in der afghanischen Provinz Badakhshan," in J. Schneider, ed., *Wirtschaftskräfte und Wirtschaftswege (Festschrift H. Kellenbenz)*, Cotta, 1978, pp. 549-83. E. Huwyler and I. von Moos, "Über den Steinbock in der Vorstellungswelt der Bewohner des Munjan-Tales," *Afghanistan Journal*, 1979, pp. 131-43. I. von Moos, *Die wirtschaftlichen Verhältnisse im Munjan-tal und der Opiumgebrauch der Bevölkerung*, Listal, 1980 (Bibliotheca Afghanica, Schriftenreihe 1). ii. Travel accounts: J. Wood, *A Personal Narrative of a Journey to the Source of the River Oxus by . . . Badakhshan*, London, 1841 (Afghan Badaḵšān and Wāḵān). E. F. Fox, *Travels in Afghanistan, 1937-38*, New York, 1943 (esp. pp. 25-127). O. Rudston de Baer, *Afghan Interlude*, London, 1957 (esp. pp. 117-81). M. Eiselin, *Wilder Hindukusch*, Zurich, 1963, P. Levi, *The Light Gardens of the Angel King. Journeys in Afghanistan*, London, 1972 (esp. pp. 164-80). iii. Lapis Lazuli mines: J. Wood, op. cit., pp. 262-67 (the earliest description). J. Blaise and F. Cesbron, "Données minéralogiques et pétrographiques sur le gisement de Sar-e Sang, Hindou Kouch, Afghanistan," *Bulletin de la Société française de minéralogie et cristallographie*, 1966, pp. 333-48. G. Hermann, "Lapis-lazuli: the Early Phases of its Trade," *Iraq* 30, 1, 1968, pp. 21-57. J. Wyart, P. Bariand, and J. Filippi, "Le lapis-lazuli de Sar-e Sang (Badakhshan, Afghanistan)," *Revue de géographie physique et de géologie dynamique*, 1972, pp. 443-48. H. Kulke, "Die lapislazuli Lagerstätte Sare Sang (Badakhshan). Geologie, Entstehung, Kulturgeschichte und Bergbau," *Afghanistan Journal*, 1976, pp. 43-56. P. Bernard, "Les mines de lapis-lazuli du Badakshan," pp. 49-51, 95-97 in P. Bernard and H. F. Francfort, *Etudes de géographie historique sur la plaine d'Aï Khanoum (Afghanistan)*, Paris, 1978. (b) Pamir and Wāḵān. i. General: M.

Veniukoff (= Veniukov), *The Pamir and the Sources of the Amu Daria*, tr. J. Michell, London, 1866. H. Yule, "An Essay on the Geography and History of the Regions on the Upper Waters of the River Oxus," pp. xxi-cv in J. Wood, op. cit., new ed., London, 1872. M. Veniukov, *Opyt voennogo obozreniya russkikh granits v Azii*, St. Petersburg, 1875. J. B. Paquier, *Le Pamir, étude de géographie physique et historique sur l'Asie Centrale*, Paris, 1876. N. Severtzow, "Etude de géographie historique sur les anciens itinéraires à travers le Pamir," *Bulletin de la Société de géographie*, 1896, pp. 417-67, 553-610. G. N. Curzon, *The Pamirs and the Source of the Oxus*, London, 1896 (also published in *Geographical Journal*, July-August/ September, 1896). A. Hermann, *Das Land der Seide und Tibet im Lichte der Antike*, Leipzig, 1938 (pp. 101-53 on the historical geography of the Pamir and the upper Oxus). A. N. Zelinskiy, "Ancient Routes through the Pamirs," *Central Asiatic Review*, 1965, pp. 44-54. ii. Travel accounts: T. E. Gordon, The *Roof of the World*, Edinburgh, 1876. G. Bonvalot, *Du Caucase aux Indes à travers le Pamir*, Paris, 1889. G. Capus, *Le toit du monde*, Paris, 1890. F. E. Younghusband, *The Heart of a Continent*, London, 1896. G. Morgan, *Ney Elias, Explorer and Envoy Extraordinary in High Asia*, London, 1971 (pp. 156-214 on the Russian and Afghan Pamir). (c) The Afghan Wāḵān and Pamir: J. B. Shor, *After You, Marco Polo*, New York, 1955 (French tr., Paris, 1956). P. Mirwald and H. Roemer, "Beobachtungen in Wakhan (NO Afghanistan)," *Erdkunde*, 1967, pp. 48-57. R. and S. Michaud, "Winter Caravan to the Roof of the World," *National Geographic Magazine*, 1972, pp. 435-65. K. Gratzl, ed., *Hindu-Kusch. Österreichische Forschungsexpedition in den Wakhan 1970*, Graz, 1972. K. Gratzl and R. Senarclens de Grancy, "Materielle und geistige Struktur einer Siedlung am Oberlauf des Amu Darya," *Ethnologische Zeitschrift*, 1973, pp. 54-105. C. Naumann and J. Niethammer, "Zur Säugetierfauna des Afghanischen Pamir und des Wakhan," *Bonner zoologische Beiträge*, 1973, pp. 237-48. R. Dor, *Contribution à l'étude des Kirghiz du Pamir afghan*, Paris, 1975 (Cahiers Turcica 1). W. Raunig, *Menschen im Wakhan, afghanischen Pamir*, Zurich, 1976, R. Dor, "Lithoglyphes du Wakhan et du Pamir," *Afghanistan Journal*, 1976, pp. 122-29. R. and S. Michaud, *Caravanes de Tartarie*, Paris, 1977 (remarkable photographs). R. Senarclens de Grancy and R. Kostka, eds., *Grosser Pamir. Österreichisches*

Table 5

POPULATION OF BADAKŠĀN PROVINCE, AFGHANISTAN (1978-79)

Name of district	1 Area (km^2)	2 Total sedentary population (1979)	3 Density (Inhab./km^2)	4 Urban population(%)	5 Number of tents in summer 1978 (3): Paštūn	5 Number of tents in summer 1978 (3): Non-Paštūn
Fayżābād (center of province)	3,014	140,300	47	6	265	—
Woloswālī:						
Bahārak (1)	2,860	46,100	16	—	1,184	870
Darwāz	4,094	51,800	13	—	—	270
Eškāšem	4,296	7,300	2	—	—	—
Jorm	3,581	50,200	14	2	—	—
Kešm	3,021	73,200	24	—	265	—
Rāḡ (2)	2,089	62,200	30	—	1,663	888
Šeḡnān (1)	3,782	18,200	5	—	285	1,137
Wāḵān	11,766	9,200	1	—	—	—(4)
ʿAlāqadārī:						
Korān-o-Monjān	4,305	5,600	1	—	—	—
Šahr-e Bozorg	894	29,000	32	—	—	—
Zēbāk	3,691	4,600	1	—	—	—
Total of province	47,393	497,700	11	2	3,662	3,165

Sources: Columns 1 to 4, *Natāyej-e moqaddamātī-e noḵostīn saršomārī-e nofūs*, Kabul, 1359 Š./1981. Figures have been rounded. Column 5, D. Balland and A. de Benoist, *Nomades et semi-nomades d'Afghanistan*, forthcoming. Notes: (1) Two *ʿalāqadārī*, the Bahārak and Šeḡnān districts, were raised to the *woloswālī* level in 1361 Š./1982 and 1363 Š./1984 respectively. (2) Since 1358 Š./1979 the *woloswālī* of Rāḡ has incorporated the former *ʿalāqadārī* of Ḵʷāhān (777 km^2). (3) All recorded tents, except 20 Özbek, belong to nomads (2,218) and semi-nomads (4,589) wintering in other provinces, as shown in Table 6. (4) The Kirghiz (q.v.) nomads of the Wāḵān corridor were not included in the survey.

Forschungsunternehmen 1975 in den Wakhan-Pamir/Afghanistan, Graz, 1978. R. Dor and C. M. Naumann, *Die Kirghizen des Afghanischen Pamir*, Graz, 1978. M. N. Shahrani, *The Kirghiz and Wakhi of Afghanistan. Adaptation to Closed Frontiers*, Seattle and London, 1979. R. Dor, "Nouvel exil pour les Kirghiz?" *Afghanistan Journal*, 1979, pp. 24-27.

3. The Soviet Pamir and Wākān: W. Geiger, *Die Pamir-Gebiete: eine geographische Monographie*, Vienna, 1887 (Geographische Abhandlungen II, 1). F. de Rocca, *De l'Alaï à l'Amou-Daria*, Paris, 1896. N. de Poncins, *Chasses et explorations dans la région des Pamirs*, Paris, 1897. O. Olufsen, *Through the Unknown Pamirs. The Second Danish Pamir Expedition, 1898-1899*, London, 1904. Prince Louis of Orleans and Bragança, *A travers l'Hindu-Kush*, Paris, 1906. Commandant de Bouillane de Lacoste, *Autour de l'Afghanistan*, Paris, 1908. A. Schultz, *Landeskundliche Forschungen im Pamir*, Hamburg, 1916 (Abhandlungen des Hamburgischen Kolonialinstituts 33). O. Paulsen, *Studies in the Vegetation of the Pamir*, Copenhagen, 1920. E. Toeplitz-Mroszowska, *La prima spedizione italiana attraverso i Pamiri*, Rome, 1930.

(X. DE PLANHOL)

ii. MODERN PROVINCE

Badakšān is a province (*welāyat*) of northeastern Afghanistan which covers 47,393 km². It is presently (1363 Š./1984) divided into eight districts (*woloswālī*) and three subdistricts (*ʿalāqadārī*). The main town and

Table 6

GEOGRAPHICAL ORIGIN OF NOMADS AND SEMI-NOMADS SUMMERING IN BADAKŠĀN (IN TENTS)

	Badakšān	Takār	Baḡlān	Kondūz	Samangān	Total
Paštūn						
nomads	—	150	43	860	370	1,423
semi-nomads	—	188	53	1,998	—	2,239
Non-Paštūn						
nomads	—	—	445	150	200	795
semi-nomads	20	86	867	1,307	90	2,370
Total	20	424	1,408	4,315	660	6,827

Table 7

LAND USE IN BADAKŠĀN PROVINCE, AFGHANISTAN (1967)

Name of district	Cultivated lands (ha)			Forests (ha)	% of irrigated land under			Water Mills (Units)
	Irrigated (*ābī*)	Non-irrigated (*lalmī*)	Fallow		Canals	Springs	Wells	
Fayżābād	5,880	24,336	13,344	12,850	80	18	2	152
Woloswālī:								
Bahārak	6,096	1,500	1,970	5,534	98	2	—	73
Darwāz	8,176	30,932	17,100	12,280	98	2	—	70
Eškāšem	690	1,120	698	—	100	—	—	40
Jorm	4,804	—	960	16,448	94	6	—	49
Kešm	4,800	27,168	14,544	6,166	93	7	—	96
Rāḡ	4,224	18,012	9,850	10,782	90	10	—	94
Šeḡnān	1,040	1,556	986	5,000	90	10	—	41
Wākān	16,554	2,264	5,186	—	100	—	—	28
ʿAlāqadārī:								
Korān-o-Monjān	3,832	9,536	5,534	9,660	100	—	—	30
Šahr-e Bozorg	3,212	3,360	2,322	7,710	60	40	—	38
Zēbāk	2,452	376	678	3,570	100	—	—	19
Total of province	61,760	120,160	73,172	90,000	93.6	6.2	0.2	730

Source: *Natāyej-e eḥṣāʾīyagīrī sarwē-ye moqaddamātī-e zerāʿatī sāl-e 1346 Š.*, Kabul, n.d., 7 vols. The figures are only very rough estimates and the reliability of some of them may be questionable.

provincial center is Fayżābād (q.v.) and Jorm is the only other locality with urban status within the province.

Although first attempts to erect Afghan Badakšān into a province seem to date back to Amir ʿAbd-al-Raḥmān's reign (H. K. Kakar, *Government and Society in Afghanistan. The Reign of Amir ʿAbd al-Rahman Khan*, Austin, 1979, p. 49), the area long remained merged with adjacent Qaṭaḡān (q.v.) to make up the province of Qaṭaḡān and Badakšān. Under King Amān-Allāh, Badakšān was a *ḥokūmat-e kalān* within that province and its subdivisions included four districts (*ḥokūmatī*) and six subdistricts (*ʿalāqa*) (*Neẓām-nāma-ye taqsīmāt-e molkīya-ye Afḡānestān*, Kabul, 1300 Š./1921, p. 21; a slightly different picture, which may suggest local administrative reorganization, is given by B. K. Koškakī, *Rāhnamā-ye Qaṭaḡān wa Badakšān*, Kabul, 1302 Š./1923, p. 21; French translation by M. Reut, *Qataghan et Badakhshân*, Paris, 1979, p. 14). In 1324 Š./1945 Badakšān was made a separate province of second rank (*ḥokūmat-e aʿlā*) and the general administrative reform of 1343 Š./1964 had it finally promoted to full provincial status.

See Tables 5, 6, and 7 for compilation of the main available data about the present population and land use in the province, districts, and subdistricts.

(D. BALLAND)

iii. THE NAME

The area's ancient name is not known. Its later name Badakšān is derived from the Sasanian official title *bēdaxš* or *badaxš*, Pahlavi *bythš* in Parthian inscriptions, *bthšy* in Middle Persian inscriptions; Greek *bidix, pitiaxou/pituaxou* (genitive); Armenian *bdeašx*; Syriac *pəṭaḥšā, afṭaḥšā*, from the root of which the Arabic *mofatteš*, meaning "inspector," probably stems. This could well have been the original meaning of a likely etymon **pati-axša* (see also BIDAXŠ.)

The patronymic suffix *-ān* indicates that the country belonged, or had been assigned as a fief, to a person holding the high rank of a *badaxš*. In this respect, Badakšān resembles other names of countries (or later of cities) based on a personal name or an official title or function, such as Azerbaijan, Isfahan, Kermānšāhān, Tehran, etc. (for details, see W. Eilers, *Onoma* 21, 1977, p. 286).

Badakšān was from early ancient times onward the source of the Near Eastern world's supply of lapis lazuli (Sumerian *za-gìn*, Akkadian *uqnûm*, in the Islamic languages *lājvard*). This beautiful blue stone was highly valued, the beards of gods were often carved from it, and the chips hewn away in the carving were made into a paste for decorative painting of stone and ceramic objects (Wulff, *Crafts*, pp. 147-48). Since the only lapis lazuli deposits in the ancient world were those in Badakšān, the finds of lapis lazuli artifacts give positive evidence of the great antiquity of east-west caravan traffic (along the later "silk road").

Badakšān was also famous as a source of rubies. The French "balais" and English "balas," specifying a variety of ruby (spinel), are traceable to *badaxš*, *d* being changed to *l* in some East Iranian languages.

It has been suggested that Bałasakan, the Armenian name of a district in Caucasia, might correspond to Badakšān (J. Markwart, *Ērānšahr*, pp. 17, 279); but the name given to this district in the Sasanian inscriptions on the Kaʿba-ye Zardošt is Balāsakān. In the trilingual inscription of Šāpūr at the same site, *Bythškn* (Parth. = Mid. Pers. *Bthškn* = Greek *Pitixigan*) appears as the patronymic of a certain Ardašīr, no doubt taken from his father's or grandfather's official title.

Bibliography: For a detailed discussion, see W. Eilers, *IIJ* 5, 1961, pp. 209ff., 309. A different explanation of the title is given by H. S. Nyberg in *Eranos* 44, 1946, p. 237, n. 2, and *Manual of Pahlavi* II, 1974, pp. 47f. R. N. Frye, *Orientalia* 15, 1962, p. 354, and W.-P. Schmid, in W. Hinz, ed., *Altiranische Funde und Forschungen*, 1969, p. 153, n. 22, argue for **bitīya'xšāyaθiya* (Parth.) = **dvitīya'xšāya-* (Mid. Pers.), which would mean "second ruler," i.e., a high-ranking minister. See also O. Szemerényi, in *Monumentum H. S. Nyberg* II, Acta Iranica 5, Tehran and Liège, 1975, pp. 363-65.

(W. EILERS)

BADAKŠĪ, MOLLĀ SHAH (also known as Shah Moḥammad), a mystic and writer of the Qāderī order, given both to the rigorous practice of asceticism and to the ecstatic proclamation of theopathic sentiment. Born in 990/1582 to a *qāżī* in the village of Araksā in the Rostāq area of Badakšān, Mollā Shah received his initial religious training in Balk. After a residence of three years in Kashmir followed by wanderings that took him as far as Agra, he came to Lahore to join the following of Shaikh Mīānmīr (or Mīānjīv), a Qāderī saint of Egyptian origin. Initially rebuffed by Mīānmīr, Mollā Shah won his respect and acceptance by feats of great self-denial. Thereafter Mollā Shah's spiritual progress was swift; reportedly he soon became able totally to dispense with sleep and to spend every night in communion with the prophets and saints. When Mīānmīr pronounced his training complete, Mollā Shah returned to Kashmir to escape the heat of Lahore and spent there most of the rest of his life. Although he generally shunned all company, living enclosed in a narrow cell, he attracted a large following and sporadically turned his attention to the training of disciples. Among his adepts were two members of the Mughal family, Dārā Šekōh and Jahānārā, who left accounts of their relations with Mollā Shah in *Sakīnat al-awlīā* and *Resāla-ye ṣāḥebīya* respectively. Despite these ties with the ruling dynasty, he was repeatedly threatened with persecution because of his proclamation of the doctrine of *waḥdat al-wojūd* in Ḥallājian terms that aroused the hostility of certain exoterists. (For example, he said in one of his verses: "When the intelligent one comes to know himself, he becomes God, O friend!"). It is said that only Dārā Šekōh's intervention with his father, Šāhjahān, saved Mollā Shah from execution by the governor of Kashmir. Likewise, when Awrangzēb came to the throne in 1068/1658, Mollā Shah's other royal disciple, Jahānārā, found it necessary to intercede on behalf of her master. Three years later, Mollā Shah died in Lahore, where he was buried next to Mīānmīr in a shrine constructed by Jahānārā.

The chief successor of Mollā Shah was a certain Walī Rām. From him descended an initiatic line, characterized by an extreme emphasis on *waḥdat al-wojūd*, that persisted in the Punjab until the thirteenth/nineteenth century. The last heir of Mollā Shah appears to have been Qayṣar Shah (d. 1281/1864).

Mollā Shah's literary fame is based chiefly on his Persian poetry, which includes quatrains as well as a number of *maṯnawīs*. He also composed some technical treatises on Sufism, including *Resāla-ye šāhīya*, an exposition of *waḥdat al-wojūd* written for Dārā Šekōh and Jahānārā, and a commentary (known as *Tafsīr-e Šāh* or *Šāh-e tafāsīr*) on the first, second, third, and twelfth suras of the Koran.

Bibliography: (1) Accounts by Mollā Shah's disciples: Dārā Šekōh, *Sakīnat al-awlīā*, ed. T. Čand and M.-R. Jalālī-Nā'īnī, Tehran, 1344 Š./1965, pp. 152-204. Jahānārā Bēgom, *Resāla-ye ṣāḥebīya* (Pers. original unpublished; Urdu tr., Lucknow, 1316/1898). Tawakkol Beg, *Nosḵa-ye aḥwāl-e Šāhī*, ms. BM Rieu supp. 130. (2) Secondary accounts: Alfred de Kremer, "Mollâ Shâh et le spiritualisme oriental," *JA* 13, 1869, pp. 105-69 (based largely on *Nosḵa-ye aḥwāl-e Šāhī*). F. Meier, *Abū Sa'īd-i Abū l-Ḫayr*, Acta Iranica 11, Tehran and Liège, 1976, pp. 492-94. Ḡolām Sarvar Lāhūrī, *Ḵazīnat al-awlīā*, Lucknow, 1320/1902, I, pp. 173-74. Idem, *Ḥadīqat al-awlīā*, ed. M. E. Mojadeddi, Lahore, 1396/1976, pp. 56-57. S. A. A. Rizvi, *A History of Sufism in India* 11, Delhi, 1983, pp. 115-26. M. Usman, *The Life and Teachings of Mulla Shah*, unpublished doctoral dissertation, University of the Punjab, Lahore, 1953. Amirbek Habibov, *Ganj-i Badakšon*, Dushanbe, 1972, pp. 98-102. Annemarie Schimmel, *Islamic Literatures of India*, Wiesbaden, 1973, p. 41. (3) Discussion of Mollā Shah's writings: Ẓohūr-al-Dīn, *Pākistān mēn fārsī adab kī tārīḵ*, Lahore, 1974, pp. 124-63 (with full synopses of all his works). Storey-Bregel, I, pp. 146-47 (mentions only the *tafsīr*). M. Ṭofayl, "'Olamā-ye Panjāb kī tafsīrī ḵadamāt ('arabī zabān mēn)," *Fekr o naẓar* 22/2, 1984, pp. 87-100.

(H. ALGAR)

BADAḴŠĪ SAMARQANDĪ, the poet laureate (*malek-al-šo'arā'*) of the Timurid Mīrzā Uluḡ Beg (murdered 853/1449). Dawlatšāh Samarqandī, Ḵᵛāndamīr, and Āḏar Bīgdelī all say that he was the foremost poet at Samarqand and that Uluḡ Beg and the courtiers held him in high esteem, particularly admiring his odes (*qaṣīdas*), but none of them gives his personal name or the date of his death. He may, however, be identical with Mawlānā Moḥammad Badaḵšī, whom Ḵ'āndamīr (IV, p. 347) mentions as an associate of Mīr 'Alī-Šīr Navā'ī (d. 906/1500) for thirty years and as an expert and author of books on riddle composition. Since Mīr 'Alī-Šīr Navā'ī spent several years in Transoxiana (Ṣafā, *Adabīyāt* IV, p. 283) before his move to Herat in 862/1457, it seems quite likely that his associate for thirty years was Badaḵšī, the *malek-al-šo'arā'*.

Bibliography: See also Ḵ'āndamīr, *Ḥabīb al-sīar* (Tehran) IV, p. 38. Dawlatšāh, ed. Browne, p. 420. Āḏar, *Ātaškada*, Bombay, 1277/1860-61, p. 320. Mīr 'Alī-Šīr Navā'ī, *Majāles al-nafā'es*, pp. 19, 193, Ḵayyāmpūr, *Soḵanvarān*, p. 79.

(Z. SAFA)

BADAL. See PAŠTŪNWĀLĪ.

BĀDĀM "almond."
i. *General.*
ii. *As food.*

i. GENERAL

Biogeography of natural occurrences of almond trees. The genus *Amygdalus* is very common in Iran and Afghanistan and throughout the Turco-Iranian area. Iran and Anatolia were the center in which its various species evolved and from which they were diffused. It is probably now represented in Iran by nine species, several endemic (Zohary, 1973, p. 373). Most often they have the form of small, thorny bushes (sub-genus *Lycioides*, whose diversification appears to have begun in Iran) or of taller, tree-like shrubs which grow in colonies (sub-genus *Spartioides*). The last examples of the latter are the colonies of *Amygdalus scoparia* on the southwestern flank of the Zagros. Also widespread is the sub-genus *Eu-Amygdalus*, to which the cultivated almond tree (*Amygdalus communis* L.) belongs, the commonest wild species being the *Amygdalus orientalis* and the *Amygdalus korschinskii*. Several of these species enter into most plant associations in the arid interior of Iran and Afghanistan. They are found as underbrush in the oak woodlands of the Zagros, the dry juniper forest on the southern slopes of the Alborz and the Khorasan mountains, and even in the semi-humid forest of the Qaradāḡ, as well as in low-lying (*garmsīr*) districts. Stands of *Amygdalus spartioides* in association with pistachio trees are particularly widespread in the interior basins of Iran, where they form the dominant element of the vegetational cover in wooded steppe areas between forest and true steppe. This pistachio-almond association (termed "Junipero-Pistacietea" by M. Zohary, "Bergmandel-Pistazien Baumflur" by H. Bobek) has its lower limit at 700 m around Herat and the Harīrūd valley in eastern Khorasan, 1,100-1,200 m east of the Dašt-e Kavīr, 1,300 m around the Lūt, 1,500 m in the Sarḥadd of Baluchistan; its upper limit is ca. 2,500 m in central Kūhestān east of the Lūt, ca. 3,000 m on the flanks of the Kūh-e Taftān, ca. 3,000-3,200 m in the Kermān mountains. The maximum width of this belt corresponds to the isohyets of 150-300 m annual rainfall.

Human use of almonds and almond trees. The *Amyg-*

dalus communis (or *Prunus amygdalus*), though undoubtedly native to the Iranian land-mass, is seldom found in natural stands there today. Indeed it is possible that the descriptions of wild types may be based on specimens of the cultivated type which have reverted to nature. The sweet-fruited variety is certainly a mutant of the bitter-fruited variety, developed by grafting of the latter onto many different wild species, in particular the closely related *Amygdalus korschinskii*. In any case, almonds were already important in Iranian agriculture and diet in ancient times. Strabo (11.13.11) states that the Medes made a sort of bread out of roasted almonds. Together with pistachio nuts, acorns, and wild pears, almonds must have formed part of the diet of the young Persians whose initiation into manhood was a spell of open-air life in the wooded steppe (Strabo, 15.3.18). A prescribed quantity of dried sweet almonds had to be delivered daily for the table of the Persian kings (Polyaenus, *Strategica* 4.32). In the Pahlavi literature, there is a mention of these wholesome nuts in chapter 27 of the *Bundahišn*. They still play an important part in Iranian and Afghan arboriculture and diet. Cultivated almond trees are found up to the altitude of 2,365 m in the mountains of Afghanistan. In Iran the average annual production in the 1970s was reckoned to be 50,000 tons; for Afghanistan no trustworthy figures are available, but estimates of the country's annual exports (mainly to India) in the 1950s ranged from 2,500 to 4,000 tons.

In addition to its value as a food source, the almond tree has had and still has other uses in Iranian daily life. Thus it used to be peeled and pounded and its oil extracted by pressing the resulting paste in one's fists. The oil was used as a laxative like that of castor beans (*karčak*). The wood of the wild almond (particularly *Amygdalus scoparii*) is reputed to make the best charcoal and to be excellent firewood (Schlimmer). In the nineteenth century walking sticks made from the wood of the *Amygdalus orientalis* were very fashionable. *Mollā*s in Afghanistan often carry an almond-wood wand as a sort of amulet. The wood is also used to make handles of whips for defending oneself against snakes (Aitchison). In Iran an eye-shaped gold or silver object, called a *bādāma*, is attached to an infant's bonnet to ward off the evil eye.

Bibliography: J. E. T. Aitchison, "Notes to Assist in a Further Knowledge of the Products of Western Afghanistan and of North-Eastern Persia," *Transactions of the Botanical Society*, Edinburgh, 1891, pp. 1-223 (esp. p. 164). H. Bobek, *Die natürlichen Wälder und Gehölzfluren Irans*, Bonner Geographische Abhandlungen 8, Bonn, 1951, esp. pp. 34-37. J. Humlum, *La géographie de l'Afghanistan*, Copenhagen, 1959, pp. 185, 187-88, 347. S. Kitamura, *Flora of Afghanistan*, Kyoto, 1960, p. 177. B. Laufer, *Sino-Iranica*, Field Museum of Natural History, Publication 201, Anthropological Series, XV, 3 Chicago, 1919, pp. 193, 405-09. H. Massé, *Croyances et coutumes persanes*, 2 vols., Paris, 1937. J. L. Schlimmer, *Terminologie médico-pharmaceutique et anthropologique française-persane*, Tehran, 1874 (lithograph), repr. Tehran, 1970, pp. 32-33. N. Vavilov and D. D. Bukinich, *Zemledel'cheskiĭ Afganistan*, Leningrad, 1929, pp. 225, 455-57. M. Zohary, "On the Geobotanical Structure of Iran," *Bulletin of the Research Council of Israel, Section D, Botany*, vol. II D, Supplement, March, 1963, passim, esp. pp. 35-38. Idem, *Geobotanical Foundations of the Middle East*, 2 vols., Stuttgart and Amsterdam, 1973, pp. 373-74, 585-88, 629.

(X. de Planhol)

ii. As Food

Almonds are consumed both fresh and, more commonly, dried. In the early spring, when the nut is young and tender fresh fuzzy, green almonds, called *čaḡāla-bādām* are crunchy and edible. They are sold by vendors on street corners, after having been dipped in salted water. They are also cooked into a stewed lamb dish, *ḵorešt-e čaḡāla-bādām*, an infrequent delicacy, since the almonds are edible in this form for only a very short time each year. This dish incorporates chunks of sautéed lamb with finely chopped mint and parsley. It is flavored with sour-grape juice, simmered slowly for several hours, and served with rice.

Dried almonds are served frequently between meals, roasted, salted, and mixed with shelled hazelnuts and pistachios, and unshelled pumpkin and watermelon seeds. This mixture is called *ājīl* (q.v.).

Dried almonds are used extensively in Persian cuisine, particularly to embellish and flavor rice dishes, such as a variation of *ʿadas-polow* (lentil pilaf) which calls for the addition of slivered almonds and currants or raisins. *Moraṣṣaʿ-polow* (jewel-studded rice), derives its name from the nuts which decorate this festive dish, including almonds, pistachios, and hazelnuts. Another popular rice dish, *šīrīn-polow* (sweet pilaf) is often prepared with a combination of slivered almonds and pistachios sprinkled throughout the rice, which is further flavored with sweetened orange-peel slivers and chunks of boned, cooked chicken.

Dried almonds are used extensively in preparing baked goods, such as *nān-e bādāmī*, a cookie made with beaten egg whites, sugar, cardamom, and ground almonds, or *qoṭṭāb*, an almond-filled, deep-fried cake. A popular pastry which can be prepared with almonds is *bāqlavā* (q.v.), made with filo dough, butter, sugar, cardamom, and either coarsely ground almonds or a combination of almonds and pistachios. A popular method of flavoring the almonds is to immerse them in narcissus petals in a tightly covered tin for several days, replacing the petals with fresh ones every day until the almonds have absorbed their fragrance. A popular confection made with slivered almonds is *sowhān-e ʿasalī*, made with sugar, honey, butter, and almonds, and flavored with saffron.

(N. Ramazani)

BĀDĀN B. **SĀSĀN.** See ABNĀ'.

BĀDĀN PĪRŪZ. See ARDABĪL.

BADAŠT, small village of about 1,000 inhabitants, 7 km east of Šāhrūd, Khorasan, site of a Babi conference in late Rajab–early Šaʿbān, 1264/late June–early July, 1848, convened on the instructions of the Bāb. Physical arrangements were undertaken by Mīrzā Ḥosayn-ʿAlī Nūrī, who during the conference took on the title of Bahā' and in later years became better known as Bahā'-Allāh (q.v.). Also during the conference the title Qoddūs was given to Mollā Moḥammad-ʿAlī Bārforūšī and Ṭāhera to Qorrat-al-ʿAyn, who were both members of the earliest group of the Bāb's disciples, the *ḥorūf-e ḥayy* (Letters of the Living; q.v.). Bahā'-Allāh rented two gardens in the vicinity of Badašt for their use and a third for himself.

The conference marks a critical turning point in the development of the Babi movement. Up to this time, although the Bāb had implicitly claimed the station of a Messenger (*rasūl*) of God, he had instructed his followers to keep to the Islamic *Šarīʿa*. Then, in late 1847-early 1848, the Bāb wrote the *Bayān-e fārsī* (q.v.) in which he laid out the fundamentals of the Babi *Šarīʿa* and, in Spring, 1264/1848, he issued a call for his followers to gather in Khorasan. The primary purpose of the resulting conference was to announce the abrogation of the Islamic *Šarīʿa* and the inauguration of a new Babi *Šarīʿa*. A subsidiary purpose of the conference was to discuss ways of releasing the Bāb from his imprisonment at Mākū.

Accounts of the proceedings of the conference are not completely in agreement. There was a clash between Bārforūšī and Ṭāhera with the former adopting a conservative position with regard to the break with the Islamic past and the latter taking up a radical position. In the end, Ṭāhera won the debate but the two protagonists ended the conference amicably. Indeed one source states that this confrontation was pre-arranged in conjunction with Bahā'-Allāh so as to prepare the Babis for and mitigate the impact of the break with the Islamic *Šarīʿa* (see Nabīl, p. 294 n.). But, despite this, there was a great deal of consternation among those attending, particularly when Ṭāhera underlined this break by appearing in public unveiled. Some left the Babi movement after the conference. Babi and Bahai exegesis identifies the whole episode as *al-Qīāma* "the Resurrection" (Koran 75) and *al-Wāqeʿa* " the Event" (Koran 65).

Some Babi and Bahai sources (e.g., Nabīl, p. 298) appear to confirm the accusation of the *Nāsek al-tawārīk* (III, pp. 238-39) that there was some immorality among the Babis at the conference following the abrogation of the Islamic *Šarīʿa* (but see denial of this in *Noqṭat al-kāf*, p. 152). The lengthy passage in the *Noqṭat al-kāf* (pp. 144-52) that Ivanov (pp. 80-85) considers to be a socially-radical speech (stating that property is usurpation) by Qoddūs at Badašt needs careful appraisal. It is more likely a digression by the author.

After the conference, the majority of the participants set off towards Māzandarān but were attacked by the villagers of Nīālā and dispersed.

Bibliography: Moḥammad Nabīl Zarandī, *The Dawn-Breakers: Nabīl's Narrative of the Early Days of the Bahā'ī Revelation*, tr. and ed. Shoghi Effendi, Wilmette, 1962, pp. 291-300. *Ketāb-e noqṭat al-kāf*, ed. E. G. Browne, *Kitāb-i Nuqṭatu'l-Kāf* (attributed to Ḥājī Mīrzā Jānī), Leyden and London, 1910, pp. 144-54. Lesān-al-Molk Moḥammad-Taqī Khan Sepehr, *Nāsek al-tawārīk*, ed. M. B. Behbūdī, Tehran, 1353 Š./1974, III, pp. 238-39. M. S. Ivanov, *Babidskie vosstaniya v Irane (1848-1852)*, Moscow, 1939, pp. 80-85, 136-37 (reviewed by V. Minorsky in *BSOAS* 11, 1946, pp. 878-80). A.-L.-M. Nicolas, *Seyyed Ali Mohammed dit le Bāb*, Paris, 1905, pp. 279-87. Razmārā, *Farhang* III, p. 44.

(M. MOMEN)

BADĀ'ŪNĪ, 'ABD-AL-QĀDER B. MOLŪKSĀH B. ḤĀMED, polyglott man of letters, historian, and translator of Arabic and Sanskrit works into Persian who flourished during the reign of Akbar.

Life. Badā'ūnī was born at Toda Bhim in the former princely state of Jaypur on 17 Rabīʿ II 947/21 August 1540 (*Montakab al-tawārīk*, Calcutta, I, p. 363). At the age of eighteen he was taken to Sanbhal to study under Shaikh Ḥāṭema Sanbhalī (I, p. 425, III, pp. 2, 66). In 966/1558-59 he went to Agra (II, p. 32), the then center of learning, where he studied for some years under Shaikh Mobārak Nāgawrī (III, pp. 67, 74). After his father died at Agra in 969/156 (II, p. 53) he moved to Badā'ūn (Badā'ōn), where he married in 975/1567-68 for the second time (II, p. 105); about his first marriage we know nothing. In 973/1565-66, leaving Badā'ūn, he became the *ṣadr* (highest justice officer) of Ḥosayn Khan (II, pp. 86-87, 222), the *jāgīrdār* (land grant holder) of Paṭiālī (not Paṭiālā as in *EI*[1], p. 856), and moved with him to Lucknow and Gānt-u-Gōlā (the place is still unidentified). In 981/1574 he left the service of Ḥosayn Khan following a quarrel and went to Agra where he was presented to Akbar (II, p. 172). Impressed by his ability Akbar appointed him in 983/1575-76 as one of the seven court imams to lead the Wednesday prayers (II, p. 226). In the same year 1,000 *bīgas* of land were granted to him as a *madad-e maʿāš* (income supplement) at Basāwar and after this he took a prominent part in literary activities. (In 997/1588-89 the grant was transferred to Badā'ūn; II, p. 368.)

At about the same time as Badā'ūnī, Abu'l-Fażl, son of Badā'ūnī's old teacher Nāgawrī, also came to the court and he and his brother Fayżī gradually became Akbar's favorites: they led an increasingly unorthodox, syncretistic, esoteric movement at the court, which culminated in the famous Dīn-e Elāhī, Akbar's private religious sect. Badā'ūnī, a strict and conservative Sunni, lost Akbar's favor and never won it back. The date of his death ranges from 1000 to 1024 (according to Storey, II/2, p. 1309, 1024/1615 may be nearest to the truth). His grave is according to Baktāvar Singh's Urdu

Tārīḵ-e Badāyūn (Bareilly, 1285/1668) at 'Aṭāpūr near Badā'ūn.

Works. Badā'ūnī's fame rests mainly on his Persian *Montaḵab al-tawārīḵ*, also called *Tārīḵ-e Badā'ūnī*, a general history of India from Soboktegīn (r. 366-387/977-97) up to the year 1004/1595-96, which he began in 999/1590. The first volume starts with the Ghaznavids and ends with the death of Homāyūn, the second covers the first forty years of Akbar's reign, and the third consists of a *taḏkera* or biographical anthology of saints, physicians, and men of letters of the time. One of the sources used by Badā'ūnī was Neẓām-al-Dīn Aḥmad's *Ṭabaqāt-e akbarī*. The *Montaḵab al-tawārīḵ* was not published during the lifetime of its author. He deliberately kept it secret as it contained critical remarks about Akbar's religious policies such as prohibiting the call for prayers in the imperial palace, the slaughter of cows, and the establishing of a brothel in the city while wine was kept running 24 hours a day, etc.

Badā'ūnī was also a poet with the penname "Qāderī," but none of his poetry has come down to us. Other works of Badā'ūnī, most of them commissioned by Akbar, comprise the no longer extant *Ketāb al-aḥādīṯ* (989/1581), a collection of forty Hadiths on the merits of holy war (*jehād*), and the *Najāt al-Rašīd*, a Sufi ethical treatise containing interesting historical anecdotes, controversial discussions, and an account of the Mahdawī movement (ed. Lahore, 1972). In 999/1590 he collaborated on a no longer extant Persian translation of Yāqūt's *Mo'jam al-boldān*. Translations from Sanskrit include the following: *Nāma-ye ḵeradafzā*, composed in 989/1581 and partly in 1003/1595, a translation of a famous Sanskrit story collection about Rāja Vikramāditya called in Hindi *Singhāsan battīsī* (The thirty-two [tales] of the throne); several Persian translations of this work exist but none of them can be definitely identified as that of Badā'ūnī. While he was only a collaborator on a translation of the *Mahābhārata* (Persian title *Razm-nāma*; 990/1582), he alone completed the translation of the *Rāmāyaṇa* (*Tarjama-ye Ketāb-e Rāmāyan*; 992-97/1584-89). In 983/1575-76 he took part in the translation of *Atharvaveda*, but this was not completed (*Montaḵab* II, p. 212). In 1003/1595 he was ordered to complete the *Baḥr al-Asmār*, a translation of some story (possibly the *Kathāsaritsāgara*) made for Sultan Zayn-al-'Ābedīn of Kashmir. His *Tarjama-ye Tārīḵ-e Kašmīr* (999/1590-91) is a revised and abridged translation of a history of Kashmir, probably the *Rāja-taranginī*, of which a translation had previously been made by Mollā Shah Moḥammad Šāhbādī.

In 1000/1591-92 he was instructed by Akbar to epitomize the Arabic portion of the *Jāme' al-tawārīḵ* (*Montaḵab* II, p. 84). Finally, he assisted in the compilation of *Tārīḵ-e alfī*, a general history of Islam down to the 1000th year, of which the first two volumes were revised by Badā'ūnī.

Bibliography: Badā'ūnī, *Montaḵab al-tawārīḵ*, ed. A.-'A. Kabīr-al-Dīn Aḥmad and W. Nassau Lees, Bib. Ind., 2 vols., Calcutta, 1864-69; Lucknow, 1868; Eng. tr., Calcutta: I, G. S. A. Ranking, 1898; II, W. H. Lowe, 1884; III, W. Haig, 1925; repr. Patna, 1973, Neẓām-al-Dīn Aḥmad, *Ṭabaqāt-e akbarī*, Bib. Ind., Calcutta, 1913-, II, p. 468. 'Alī Aḥmad Khan "Asīr," *Ḥayāt Abu'l-Qāder Badāyūnī*, ms., *Badāyūn*, special issue of *Ḏu'l-Qarnayn*, April, 1956. Baḵtāwar Singh, *Tārīḵ-e Badāyūn*, Bareilly, 1285/1868. T. W. Beale, *An Oriental Biographical Dictionary*, repr. Lahore, 1975, p. 4b. Ḡolām-'Alī Āzād Belgrāmī, *Ḵezāna-ye 'āmera*, Cawnpore, 1871, p. 323, no. 79. H. Blochmann, "Badáoní and his Works," *JASB* 38, 1869, vol. 1, pt. 1, pp. 105-44. H. M. Elliot, *Bibliographical Index*, Calcutta, 1849, pp. 227-58. H. M. Elliot and J. Dowson, *History of India as Told by its own Historians* V, pp. 485-549. *EI*² I, pp. 856-57. H. Mukhia, *Historians and Historiography during the Reign of Akbar*, New Delhi, 1976. Raḥmān-'Alī, *Taḏkera-ye 'olamā'-e Hend*, Cawnpore, 1894, p. 130. E. Rehatsek, *Akbar Shah's Divine Monotheism*, Bombay, 1866. Storey, *Persian Literature* II/1, pp. 435-440. H. H. Wilson, "Account of the Religious Innovations Attempted by Akbar," *Quarterly Oriental Magazine* 1/1, Calcutta, 1824, pp. 49-62.

(A. S. BAZMEE ANSARI)

BĀDĀVARD (wind fall), the name of one of the seven treasures of Ḵosrow Parvēz in the *Šāh-nāma* (Moscow ed., IX, p. 236 vv. 3790f.). The treasures of Ḵosrow Parvēz, including the *bādāvard*, are also mentioned by Ṯa'ālebī (*Ḡorar*, pp. 700f.), Gardīzī (ed. Ḥabībī, p. 36), and the *Mojmal* (p. 81). As for the origin of the *bādāvard*, according to Ṯa'ālebī when Ḵosrow Parvēz learned that the East Romans had rebelled against his father-in-law Mauricius and installed another emperor, he sent his general Šahrbarāz to the aid of Mauricius. Šahrbarāz based himself at Alexandria and prepared to attack Constantinople. Fear of an attack by Šahrbarāz daunted the new emperor so much that he had all the valuables in the Roman treasure-stores laden on a ship and then fled, but the wind drove the ship to Alexandria and all the valuables fell into the hands of Šahrbarāz, who took them with him to Iran. Ḵosrow Parvēz thanked God for sending the favorable wind and named the treasure *bādāvard* (lit., brought by the wind). This story, which is also given by Jāḥeẓ (*Ketāb al-tāj*, ed. A. Zéki Pacha, Cairo, 1914, pp. 180ff.) and Mas'ūdī (*Morūj*, ed. Pellat, I, p. 311) and repeated by Ḥamd-Allāh Mostawfī (*Tārīḵ-e gozīda*, ed. 'A. Navā'ī, Tehran, 1339 Š./1960, p. 122) and Ḵ'āndamīr (*Ḥabīb al-sīar*, lithograph, Tehran, 1271/1855, p. 122), is a fiction invented to explain the name *bādāvard*. In the *Šāh-nāma* (V, p. 400 vv. 2796f.), Ḵosrow Parvēz's treasures are said to have previously belonged to the past kings of Iran, and some of them, including the *bādāvard*, are said to have been first acquired by Kay Ḵosrow. The mentions of royal treasures, like those of exploits such as dragon-slaying, of occurrences of miracles, and of possession of divine fortune (*farr*, q.v.) and distinctive bodily marks, must all be seen as arguments for the legitimacy of rulers. In the ideology of Iranian kingship, this was a matter of great importance (see

Khaleghi-Motlagh, "Farāmarz-nāma," *Īrān-nāma* 1/1, 1361 Š./1982, p. 43 n. 23).

The names of K̲osrow Parvēz's treasures were also applied to musical modes and melodies. One of the melodies ascribed to Bārbad, the chief minstrel in K̲osrow Parvēz's reign, bore the name *bādāvard* and is mentioned by several poets, among others by Neẓāmī Ganjavī (*K̲osrow o Šīrīn*, Baku, 1960, p. 332, v. 4) and Manūčehrī (*Dīvān*, ed. Moḥammad Dabīrsīāqī, 2nd ed., Tehran, 1338 Š./1959, p. 19, v. 281).

Bibliography: See also Mehrī Bāqerī, "Afdīhā-ye haždahgāna-ye K̲osrow-e Parvīz," *NDA Tabrīz*, 1357 Š./1978, no. 125, pp. 91-115.

(DJ. KHALEGHI-MOTLAGH)

BADĀYEʿ, a collection of *ḡazal*s by Saʿdī. See SAʿDĪ.

BADĀYEʿNEGĀR, ĀQĀ **MOḤAMMAD-EBRĀHĪM.** See NAWWĀB-E TEHRĀNĪ.

BAD̲D̲ or BAD̲D̲AYN (perhaps two places), a mountainous region (*kūra*) in Azerbaijan and a center of K̲orramīs (Ebn al-Nadīm, ed. Tajaddod, pp. 406-07). There was located the castle of Bad̲d̲, which became the residence and headquarters of Bābak-e K̲orramī (q.v.) during his revolt against the ʿAbbasid caliphate (201/816-222/837). Bad̲d̲ was located between Azerbaijan and Arrān, close to the river Aras (Masʿūdī, *Morūj* II, p. 75; VI, p. 187; VII, pp. 62-63, 123-24; Abū Dolaf, p. 6; Yāqūt, I, p. 529), one parasang from Ardabīl (Ebn K̲ordād̲beh, p. 121; Nafīsī, p. 37: 21 parasangs). Its sunless and foggy climate is mentioned by Abū Dolaf and Yāqūt (loc. cit.). The remains of Bad̲d̲, currently known as Qalʿa-ye Jomhūr (probably named after the neighboring Jomhūr mountains), according to the report of the Archeological Mission (summer 1345 Š./1966) lie 50 km from Ahar on a western branch of the Qarasū river, 3 km southwest of Kalībar. The remaining building is composed of a castle and a palace on the top of a mountain, 2,300-2,600 meters above sea level, surrounded by 400-600 meter deep valleys. There is only a narrow and arduous path to the castle, which made it inaccessible during Bābak's revolt. The position of the castle, the watch-towers, the furnaces, and its solid building show the military importance of Bad̲d̲ (see the illustrations in Kāmbak̲š-e Fard). The castle was conquered and ruined by Afšīn's army on 9 Ramażān 222/15 August 837. It has been mentioned and described by Arab poets such as Ḥosayn b. Żaḥḥāk Bāhelī, Abū Tammām, and Boḥtorī (Ṭabarī, III, p. 1256; Ebn K̲ordād̲beh, p. 121; Masʿūdī, *Tanbīh*, pp. 93, 160; Yāqūt, loc. cit.). Abū Dolaf (loc. cit.) saw K̲orramīs in Bad̲d̲ in the middle of the 4th/10th century expecting the Mahdī.

Bibliography: Abū Dolaf Mesʿar b. Mohalhel K̲azrajī, *al-Resāla al-t̲ānīa*, ed. V. Minorsky, Cairo, 1955, p. 6; Pers. tr. S. A. Ṭabāṭabāʾī, Tehran, 1354 Š./1975, pp. 46-47. Ebn K̲ordād̲beh, pp. 120-21. G. Flügel, "Bābek, seine Abstammung und erstes Auftreten," *ZDMG* 23, 1869, p. 539 n. 1. S. Kāmbak̲š-e Fard, "Qalʿa-ye Jomhūr yā dež-e Bad̲d̲," *Honar o mardom* 50, Ād̲ar, 1345 Š./December, 1966, pp. 2-6. Idem, *Barrasīhā-ye tārīk̲ī* 1/4, Dey, 1345 Š./January, 1967, pp. 6-28. A. Kasrawī, *Šahrīārān-e gomnām*, 3rd ed., Tehran, 1353 Š./1974, p. 153. M. J. Maškūr, *Naẓar-ī be tārīk̲-e Ād̲arbāyjān*, Tehran, 1349 Š./1970, pp. 149, 401-02. Masʿūdī, *Morūj* II, p. 95, VI, p. 187, VII, pp. 62-63, 123-24, 468; idem, *Tanbīh*, Beirut, 1981, pp. 93, 160. S. Nafīsī, *Bābak-e K̲orramdīn*, 2nd ed., Tehran, 1342 Š./1963, pp. 37-39. Gh. Sadighi, *Les mouvements religieux iraniens au IIe et au IIIe siècle de l'hégire*, Paris, 1938, pp. 242-43, 274, 277-78. S. J. Torābī Ṭabāṭabāʾī, *Āt̲ār-e bāstānī-e Ād̲arbāyjān*, Tehran, 1355 Š./1976, pp. 466-71. Yāqūt, *Boldān* I, pp. 528-30.

(Ḡ.-Ḥ. YŪSOFĪ)

BĀDENJĀN "eggplant, aubergine."

i. *The plant.*
ii. *Uses in cooking.*

i. THE PLANT

Bādenjān (or Bādemjān), the eggplant or aubergine, *Solanum melogena* L. of the Solanaceae family. Persian terms which perhaps denote particular varieties of the eggplant, e.g., *kahparak* (*Borhān-e qāṭeʿ*; *Farhang-e Nafīsī*), *kahlam* (*Borhān-e qāṭeʿ*; Steingass), and some borrowed Arabic terms, e.g., *ʿanab* (Vullers; *Farhang-e Nafīsī*; Steingass), *majd* (Steingass; ʿĪsā Bey) which in both Persian and Arabic also means mandrake, *wajd* (Abū Ḥanīfa; Steingass; ʿĪsā Bey), and *ḥadaq* (Bīrūnī, p. 69; Abū Ḥanīfa, pp. 21, 66) from the Arabic root *ḥdq* signifying "to be round." *Bādenjān-e barrī* (wild eggplant) is the name given to the Indian plant, *Solanum xanthocarpum* Schradl. and Wendl.

Botanical aspects. The species *Solanum melongena* L. has numerous varieties, and is capable of being crossed with other Indian species of *Solanum*, particularly *Solanum incanum* L. to which it is closely related, and also, in certain conditions, with *Solanum indicum* L. and *Solanum xanthocarpum* Schradl. and Wendl., with which it produces fertile hybrids (Choudhury in Simmonds). This raises the question whether all the species are really distinct.

History and geography of eggplant use. The plant is native to South Asia and was domesticated in India. It was brought to the Iranian lands at a very early but indeterminable date. In ancient times Iranian and Arab sailors carried it to East Africa, as shown by the presence of a number of specific terms for it in Ethiopia. It did not reach the Eastern Mediterranean lands, however, until a relatively late period, probably after the Arab conquest of Iran (Chodury, ibid.). The conquering Turks got to know the plant in Iran. The spread of the word *bādenjān* can be traced in the Eastern Turkish *patingen*, Turkish and Russian *patinjan*, Georgian *badnjan*, Astrakhan Tatar *badarjan* or *badijan*, and westward in some European languages. In Christian western Europe, however, with the exception of parts of Spain and southern Italy which had once been under Moslem rule, the eggplant only became known after the renaissance.

Cultivation. Though native to tropical regions where it is perennial, the eggplant can accommodate itself to colder climates where it becomes annual. This facility explains why so many varieties of the species *Solanum melongena* L. are found in Iran. These have fruit which ranges in color from a more or less deep purple to a bright yellow almost like egg yolk, which may be long, round, or ovoid in shape and from ca. 10 to ca. 40 cm long. Although the medieval Iranian botanists have left little information on these matters, it may be taken for certain that the dark purple eggplant was widely cultivated in the 3rd/9th century because Rāzī uses its color as a reference in the chapter on dental diseases in his *Ketāb al-ḥāwī fi'l-ṭebb* (III, pp. 94, 137).

Writing at the end of the 6th/12th century, the Andalusian botanist Ebn al-ʿAwwām states in his *Ketāb al-felāḥa*, on the authority of Abu'l-Ḵayr Ešbīlī, that four varieties were cultivated: the Egyptian with white fruit, the Syrian with purple fruit, a dark red variety found at Seville, and a more brown-colored variety found at Cordoba. He then quotes a passage from Ebn Waḥšīya's book on Nabataean agriculture (written or compiled probably in the 3rd/9th century) in which six varieties are noted, but he gives no further particulars. He mentions spring fruit and autumn fruit, but only with the qualification that they ought not to be eaten, presumably because they would not be fully ripe; it may therefore be surmised that in warm temperate regions planting or flowering took place twice a year, in January-February and in August. Ebn al-ʿAwwām explains in detail the method of cultivation, which required plenty of water to make the fruit more juicy and less bitter, though the plant could tolerate poor soils. This description tallies with the forms of eggplant cultivation found in Iran. Its importance in Iran is confirmed by Abu'l-Fażl ʿAllāmī, who states in his work the *Āʾīn-e akbarī* (I, p. 72) that "this vegetable is on sale in the markets in Iran all the year round and in such abundance that it is sold for 1.5 *dām* per *sīr*" (75 grams—a low price for those days).

Health aspects. All the leading medieval Iranian writers on medicine and botany urge caution in use of the eggplant. Special steps must be taken to avert harmful effects of its acidity and bitterness. It must only be eaten when ripe and cooked (Rāzī, *De simplicibus*; Māsargūya, cited by Ebn Sīnā, *Qānūn* II; Bīrūnī, *Ketāb al-ṣaydana fi'l-ṭebb*. Ebn al-Bayṭār, *Ketāb al-jāmeʿ le'l-mofradāt*). These writers consider the eggplant to be a cause of heat and dryness of the second degree. Its harmful effects are not only internal but also external; it makes the complexion swarthy or sallow, gives rise to pimples on the face, causes ophthalmia, ulcers, impetigo, leprosy, and elephantiasis, aggravates hemorrhoids, etc. Internally it causes constriction and blockage, making the blood become thick and black, and giving rise to insomnia, epilepsy, enlargement of the liver, and excess of black bile with resultant depression. But if the salt in it is removed or if it is cooked with oil or vinegar, it acquires beneficial qualities, as it then neutralizes the bile and is useful in the treatment of ear diseases (Edrīsī, cited by Ebn al-Bayṭār, Ar. ed., I, p. 80; tr., I, p. 191), hemorrhoids, and nausea. Eggplant seeds are still used at Tehran as an expectorant for relief of asthma and catarrh (Hooper, p. 173).

In popular belief likewise, the eggplant is considered rather dangerous. When washing a fruit to remove the salt, a cook in Tehran will say that the poison must be taken out. From Ebn Waḥšīya (quoted by Ebn al-ʿAwwām) we have an amusing account of notions held about this plant at the time when it first became known in the Eastern Mediterranean lands. Fantastic tales were then told to the effect that it would vanish and reappear 3,000 years later under the influence of the moon and the stars.

Etymology of bādenjān. Persian *bādenjān* is an early loan from the Pali *vātingana* (Turner), as evidenced by the numerous dialect forms of the word, e.g., *bāḏenjān* (Golius in Mesgnien-Meninski), *bādengān*, *bādeljān*, *bādlejān*, and popular *pātlejān* (Mesgnien-Meninski), *badenjūn* in Yarani (Christensen, 1930, p. 286), *pātešgā*, *pātengā* (*Farhang-e Nafīsī*; Steingass), *våyæmjun* Farīzandi (Christensen, 1930, p. 286), *väŋgūn* in Semnāni, and *vaŋgum* in Sangesari (Christensen, 1935, p. 182).

Bibliography: Abu'l-Fażl ʿAllāmī, *Āʾīn-e akbarī*, ed. Blochmann, I, p. 72; tr. Blochmann end Jarret, I, p. 67. Abū Ḥanīfa Dīnavarī, *Ketāb al-nabāt*, ed. B. Lewin, *The Book of Plants of Abû Hanîfa al-Dînawarî. Parts of the Alphabetical Section*, Uppsala, 1953, pp. 21, 66. Bīrūnī, *Ketāb al-ṣaydana fi'l-ṭebb*, ed. and tr. Ḥakīm Moḥammad Saʿīd, Karachi, 1973, p. 69. A. Christensen, *Contributions à la dialectologie iranienne*, 2 vols., Copenhagen, 1930, 1935. Ebn al-ʿAwwām, *Ketāb al-falāḥa*, tr. J. Clément-Mullet, Paris, 2 vols., 1846-67, II, pp. 236-41. Ebn-al-Bayṭār, *Ketāb al-jāmeʿ le-l'mofradāt*, 4 bks. in 2 vols., Cairo, 1974-75; tr. L. Leclerc, 3 vols., *Le traité des simples*, Paris, 1877-83, I, p. 191. Ebn Sīnā, *al-Qānūn fi'l-ṭebb*, 3 vols., Baghdad, I, p. 272. *Farhang-e Nafīsī*, Tehran, 4 vols., 1317-18 Š./1938-39. A. G. Haudricourt and L. Hedin, *L'homme et les plantes cultivées*, Paris, 1934, pp. 142, 151. D. Hooper, *Plants and Drugs of Iran and Iraq*, Chicago, 1937, p. 173. A. Isa Bey, *Dictionnaire des noms de plantes*, Cairo, 1930. F. Mesgnien-Meninski, *Lexicon Arabico-Persico-Turcico*, 4 vols., Vienna, 1780. Rāzī, *Ketāb al-ḥāwī fi'l-ṭebb*, 17 vols., Hyderabad, 1955-64, III, pp. 94, 137. Idem, *De simplicibus*, Argentorati (Strasburg), 1531, p. 3. N. W. Simmonds, ed., *Evolution of Crop Plants*, New York, 1976. F. Steingass, *A Comprehensive Persian-English Dictionary*, 1st ed., London, 1892. R. L. Turner, A *Comparative Dictionary of Indo-Aryan Languages*, 2 vols., London, 1965. I. A. Vullers, *Lexicon Persico-Latinum*, 3 vols., 1864. A. M. Watson, *Agriculture Innovation in Early Islamic World*, London and New York, 1983.

(F. AUBAILE-SALLENAVE)

ii. Uses in Cooking

Eggplant has been used in Persian cuisine in a variety of ways: as a basic ingredient of appetizers (*mazas*) served before meals or with drinks, in main courses, and pickled in vinegar. One of the first references to the culinary aspects of the plant occurs in a medieval Persian medical treatise, which describes its medicinal value and methods of preparation (E. Jorjānī, *Ḏaḵīra-ye ḵ˘ārazmšāhī*, ed. J. Moṣṭafawī, Tehran, 1352 Š./1973, III/1, pp. 122, 154).

Two kinds of eggplants are common in Iran: the conventional *bādenjān-e rasmī*, which is long and thin, and the more ample *dolma'ī*, which was imported from abroad. In Persian cuisine, choice eggplants are straight, long, firm, and black. Eggplants are among the foods that are preserved and stored for winter in Iranian homes (*qorma-ye bādenjān*). Selected in the last month of summer when they are most abundant, eggplants are preserved in two ways: 1. After peeling, they are cut, salted, and left to "sweat," thereby losing their biliousness (*zardāb, talḵāb, sawdā'*); then they are hung on a line to dehydrate in the sun (the dried eggplants are rehydrated twenty-four hours before use); 2. the peeled eggplants are browned in a great deal of oil, placed in a copper pot, and then covered with a thick layer of hot oil which congeals to seal them.

In Persian cuisine, unlike that of Turkey, Greece, and the countries of North Africa, eggplants are cooked peeled and generally seasoned with cinnamon or turmeric, the latter being more to Iranian taste. Most eggplant dishes are classified *nānḵ˘orešī* (eaten with bread) and served as appetizers consumed with alcoholic beverages.

An early eggplant dish mentioned by the 8th/14th-century poet Bosḥāq Aṭʿema (q.v.) is *būrānī-e bādenjān*, chopped eggplant sautéed with onions and turmeric, slowly cooked, and then mixed with yogurt (Āšpazbāšī, *Sofra-ye aṭʿema*, p. 46; Bosḥāq Aṭʿema, *Dīvān*, ed. Mīrzā Ḥabīb Šīrāzī, Istanbul, 1303/1885-86, p. 104). Popular in Iranian cuisine is the combination of *kašk* (condensed whey) and eggplant, which is found in the dish *āš-e kašk o bādenjān*, layered sautéed eggplant, grilled onions, and red beans covered by whey seasoned with turmeric (Mosīū Rīšahr Khan, *Ṭabbāḵī*, p. 27). A variant of the ubiquitous Persian stew and soup *āb-gūšt* (q.v.) contains eggplant, meat, *ḡūra* (unripe grapes), potatoes, tomatoes, and split peas. Similarly, a variety of *kūkū*, the traditional Persian vegetable soufflé, *kūkū-ye bādenjān*, calls for mashed, grilled eggplant, eggs, parsley, walnuts, and onions (M. R. Ghanoonparvar, *Persian Cuisine*, Lexington, 1982, I, p. 134). Another traditional recipe, *māst o bādenjān*, which combines eggplant, yogurt, and dry mint, is called *nāzḵātūn* by Tehranis (cf. Ghanoonparvar, *Persian Cuisine* II, p. 150, whose recipe calls for pomegranate juice). In Persian stews (*ḵ˘orešes*), eggplant is cooked with chicken and *ḡūra* or pomegranate juice in a dish called *mosammā-ye* (or *mosamman-e*) *bādenjān* (Āšpazbāšī, *Sofra-ye aṭʿema*, pp. 23-24; *Farhang-e fārsī* III, p. 4,119) and with lamb in *ḵ˘oreš-e bādenjān* (N. Ramazani, *Persian Cooking*, n.p., 1974, p. 138). Among other dishes prepared with eggplants are: *āš-e darhamjūš, kotla-ye bādenjān* (cutlet of *bādenjān*), *fesenjān-e bādenjān, yaḵnī-e bādenjān, bādenjān-e sorḵ-karda, ḥalīm(-e) bādenjān, kašk o bādenjān, eškana-ye bādenjān*. The introduction of the ampler American *bādenjān* has allowed cooks to prepare such stuffed eggplant dishes as *dolma-ye bādenjān* (Ramazani, *Persian Cooking*, pp. 50-51).

Eggplants also figure in the regional cooking of Iran. *Bādenjān-polow*, which combines a paste of chopped, sautéed eggplant, chopped meat, and assorted spices with white rice, is prepared mainly in Fārs and Kermān. *Bādenjān-e qāsemī* or *mīrzā qāsemī*, a casserole of grilled eggplants, garlic, tomatoes, and eggs, is a specialty of northern Iran (Ghanoonparvar, *Persian Cuisine* I, p. 140).

The rise of the domestic canning and jarring industry during the last two decades in Iran, has added to the number of preserved eggplant products on the market. Consumers can purchase an eggplant preserve made from *bādenjān-e rasmī*, heavy syrup, cloves, and cardamom. Also widely available is an array of pickled eggplant and vegetable preparations.

Bibliography: Given in the text. See also Ḥājī Moḥammad-ʿAlī Bāvarčī, *Kār-nāma dar bāb-e ṭabbāḵī o ṣanʿat-e ān*, in *Āšpazī dar dawra-ye ṣafawī*, ed. Ī. Afšār, Tehran, 1360 Š./1981, pp. 83, 85, 86, 156, 157, 238. Mīrzā ʿAlī-Akbar Khan Āšpazbāšī, *Sofra-ye aṭʿema*, Tehran, 1353 Š./1974, pp. 20, 29, 30-31, 33, 39, 40, 42, 44, 53, 54, 57, 60, 61, 66. *Dastūr-e ṭabbāḵī o tadbīr-e manzel barā-ye dabīrestānhā-ye doḵtarān*, Tehran, 1331 Š./1952, pp. 44, 49, 50, 53, 76, 77, 107, 117, 139, 144, 167. Mosīū Rīšahr Khan Mo'addeb-al-Molk, *Ṭabḵ-e īrānī o farangī o šīrīnpazī*, 4th ed., Tehran, 1311 Š./1933, pp. 28, 35, 54, 55, 70, 76, 101, 102, 123. B. Bāmdād, *Ṭabbāḵī-e īrānī, farangī, torkī*, Tehran, 1312 Š./1933, pp. 9, 17, 129, 130.

(ʿE. Elāhī)

BĀDGĪR (wind-tower), literally "windcatcher," a traditional structure used for passive airconditioning of buildings. Windcatchers are found throughout the Middle East, from Pakistan to North Africa (Coles and Jackson, "A Wind-Tower House in Dubai," pp. 1-25; idem, "Bastakia Wind-Tower Houses," pp. 51-53) where they have been built since antiquity. In construction and design they exhibit a great deal of regional variety but they all perform a similar function (Badawy, pp. 122-28): channeling prevailing winds trapped in vents above the roofs of buildings down to cool and ventilate the rooms below. Windcatchers are built in many regions of Iran, predominantly on houses in areas with a hot arid climate. In Bandar-e ʿAbbās and other ports along the Persian Gulf they are normally square towers built on the roofs with vents on one side open to the sea-breezes. Light bamboo screens are often placed across the vents over which water may be thrown on summer afternoons to cool by evaporation the air

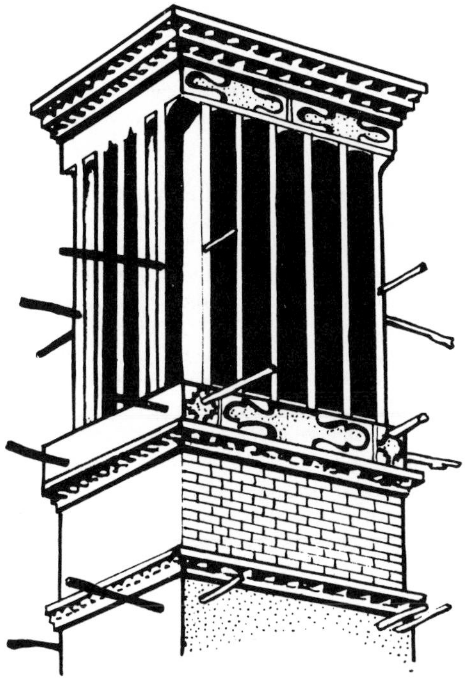

Figure 7. A wind tower in Yazd with projecting timber poles to which scaffolding is attached for maintenence

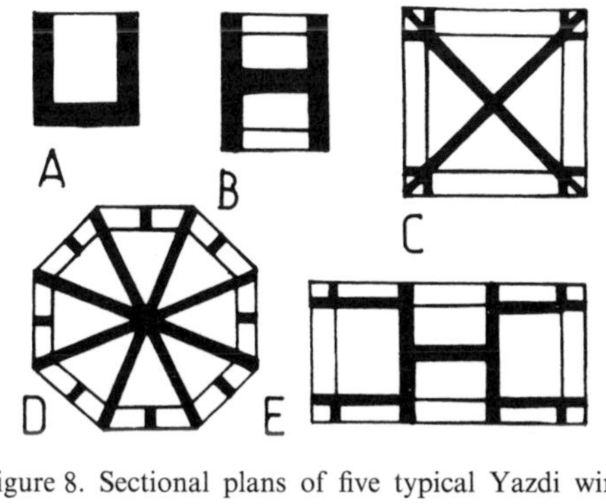

Figure 8. Sectional plans of five typical Yazdi wind tower types at vent level. A. Unidirectional B. Two directional C. Four directional D. Octagonal with two vents on each side E. Four directional with two "false" vents on two opposite sides

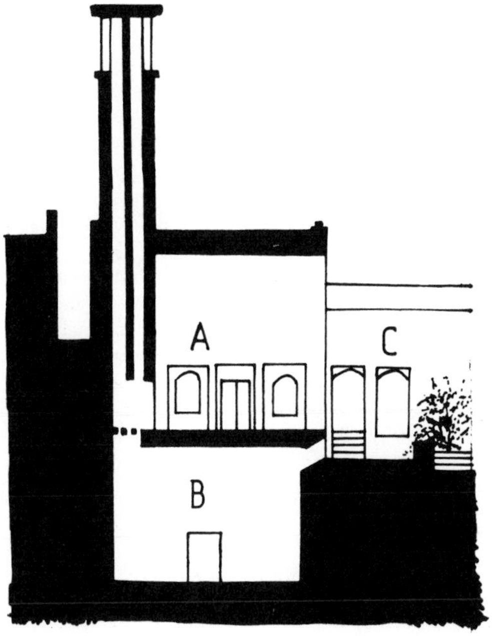

Figure 9. Cross section through a windcatcher serving the main summer rooms of a house in Yazd. A. *Ṭālār* B. Basement C. Courtyard with pool

passing down into the rooms below (Roaf, 1983, pp. 257-68). In Khorasan and Sistan, rooms have simple unidirectional vaulted vents over them called locally *mehna* (Tavassoli, p. 49). In the Sīrjān region, houses have distinctive unidirectional barrel-vaulted vents with slatted openings. Khuzistan has many fine windcatchers which serve the basements for which towns like Ahvāz are famous. Windcatchers are also built in Shiraz, Isfahan, Tehran, Qom, Semnān, and Dāmḡān but they are most widely used in the cities, towns, and villages to the south of the central desert in the Kāšān, Nā'īn, Yazd, Kermān, and Ṭabas regions. Yazd is known as "*šahr-e bādgīrhā*" (the city of windcatchers) and is renowned for the number and variety of its windcatchers, some of which date from the Timurid period (Figure 7) (O'Kane, p. 85). Windcatchers here are brick towers which generally rise from between 30 cm to 5 m above the roof although the tallest *bādgīr* in the world, built at Bāḡ-e Dawlatābād in Yazd, rises 33.35 m above the roof of the garden pavilion it serves. Windcatchers have vents at the top in one, two, or up to 8 sides (Figure 8) and these vents were decorated in brick, mud plaster or ornately carved lime plaster.

The most common use of windcatchers is to cool and ventilate summer living rooms on the ground and basement floors of houses (Roaf, 1982, pp. 57-70); air trapped in the vents of the tower is cooled as it descends and in turn cools the occupants of the rooms below by convection and evaporation (Figure 9). When there is little or no wind, air rises up the tower, the walls of which are heated by the sun, so drawing cool humid air from the courtyard and basement through the summer rooms (Bahadori, pp. 144-54). Ventilation by windcatchers is particularly important in basements which are slept in on summer afternoons and nights. Windcatchers are also built onto the living quarters of caravanserais, over prayer halls of mosques, and on water cisterns where they efficiently chill stored water by evaporative cooling.

Bibliography: A. Badawy, "Architectural Provision against Heat in the Orient," *JNES* 17, 1958, pp. 122-28. M. N. Bahadori, "Passive Cooling Systems in Iranian Architecture," *Scientific American* 239, 2, February, 1978, pp. 144-54. A. Coles and P. Jackson, "A Wind-Tower House in Dubai," *Art and Architectural Research Papers*, 1975, pp. 1-25. Idem, "Bastakia Wind-Tower Houses," *The Architectural Review*, July, 1975, pp. 51-53. B. O'Kane, "The Madrasa al-Ghiyāṯiyya at Khargird," *Iran* 14, 1976, p. 85. S. Roaf, "Windcatchers," in *Living with the Desert*, ed. E. Beazley and M. Harverson, Aris and Phillips, 1982, pp. 57-70 Eadem, "Windcatchers in the Middle East," *Islamic Architecture and Urbanism*, selected papers from a symposium organized by the College of Architecture and Planning, King Faisal University, Dammam, 1983, pp. 257-68. M. Tavassoli, *Architecture in the Hot Arid Zone*, Tehran, 1975, p. 49.

(S. Roaf)

BĀḎḠĪS, also BĀDḠĪS, region in eastern Khorasan, between Herat and the middle course of the Harīrūd in the south, and Marv al-Rūḏ and the headwaters of the Morḡāb in the north; the southern part now falls administratively into the Herat and Bādḡīsāt provinces of northwestern Afghanistan, and the northern part into the southernmost part of the Turkmenistan SSR.

i. *General and the early period.*

ii. *Modern province.*

i. General and the Early Period

The region of Bāḏḡīs is bisected in an east-west direction by the Paropamisus mountains, which rise towards the east to 11,791 ft/5,535 m; the southern slopes drain towards the Harīrūd, and the rather gentler northern ones into the Morḡāb basin via such streams as the Kūšk and Kāšān. The medieval geographers describe Bāḏḡīs as being considerably wooded and a noted source for pistachios (see, e.g., *Nozhat al-qolūb*, ed. p. 153, tr. p. 151); some of the woodland still survives, with extensive pistachio, juniper, and mulberry trees. It also comprised much pasture land, where sheep in particular were raised (see below). The present population of the region includes a substantial proportion of the Iranian Jamšīdīs of the Čahār Aymāq group, with Iranized Turco-Mongol Qalʿa-ye Now Hazāras in the eastern part (see J. Humlum et al., *La géographie de l'Afghanistan. Étude d'un pays aride*, Copenhagen, 1959, pp. 67-68, 85-86, 147-48, 185).

Yāqūt (*Moʿjam al-boldān*, Beirut, 1374-76/1955-57, I, p. 318) gives a popular etymology for the name, *bād-ḵīz* "place where the wind arises," from the region's windiness. In fact, the name Bāḏḡīs goes back to Avestan Vāitigaēsa, later appearing in Armenian geographical sources as Watagēs, Watgēs, according to Markwart (Marquart), *Ērānšahr*, p. 77.

History. During Sasanian times, Bāḏḡīs was substantially held by the Hephthalite people of the Kadisheans (the name surviving into early Islamic times as a place name Qādes). There was a Nestorian Christian population here; in the Synod of Išōʿyab in 588, a bishop of Bāḏḡīs and Qadīšastān, suffragan of the Metropolitan of Herat, is mentioned (Markwart, op. cit., pp. 64, 77-78).

During the first century of Islam, Bāḏḡīs passed into Arab hands, together with Herat and Pūšang, around 32/652-53, under the caliph ʿOṯmān for already in that year there is mentioned a rebellion against the Arabs by an Iranian noble Qāren (Ebn al-Aṯīr, Beirut, 1385-87/1965-67, III, p. 135), followed by further unrest in these regions in 41/661-62. The main references to Bāḏḡīs in the sources over the next three centuries are indeed largely in connection with various revolts against Arab-Islamic domination, often with sectarian religious elements prominent. In the mid-Omayyad period, Bāḏḡīs was a stronghold of the Arabs' most strenuous opponent in the East, the northern Hephthalite ruler Ṭarḵān Nīzak, finally subdued by the governor Qotayba b. Moslem al-Bāhelī in 91/710; Yāqūt, loc. cit., calls Bāḏḡīs "the headquarters of the Hephthalites," *dār mamlakat al-Hayāṭela*, and it was here that his principal fortress had lain, captured in 84/703 by Yazīd b. Mohallab (Ṭabarī, II, pp. 1129-31). It was a center for the would-be prophet Behāfarīd, and he was captured in Bāḏḡīs by Abū Moslem in 131/749. Shortly afterwards, during al-Manṣūr's caliphate, Ostāḏsīs appeared there (Gh. H. Sadighi, *Les mouvements religieux iraniens au IIe et au IIIe siècle de l'hégire*, Paris, 1938, pp. 128, 157-58; B. Scarcia Amoretti, in *Camb. Hist. Iran* IV, pp. 489-90, 497-98). The town of Karūḵ, on the southern fringes of Bāḏḡīs and lying to the northeast of Herat, was in the 3rd/9th century a major center of the Kharijites, who survived in Khorasan and Sīstān after their suppression in the west; the Saffarid amir Yaʿqūb. b. Layṯ had to cope with a rising of them under their own "Commander of the Faithful," immediately after his capture in 259/873 of Khorasan from the Taherids (see C. E. Bosworth, "The Armies of the Ṣaffārids," *BSOAS* 31, 1978, pp. 543-44). A century later, Moqaddasī (Maqdesī), p. 323, still describes Kharijites as surviving there, but the geographers state that by then, Bāḏḡīs was substantially orthodox, and Samʿānī, *Ansāb*, Hyderabad, 1382-1402/1962-82, II, pp. 21-22, mentions some *ʿolamāʾ* from there. On the cultural plane, mention should be made of a local poet in New Persian of the Taherid period, Hanẓala of Bāḏḡīs, a few of whose verses survive (G. Lazard, *Les premiers poètes persans (IXe-Xe siècles)*, Paris and Tehran, 1964, I, pp. 17-18, 53, II, p. 12).

The medieval geographers of the 3rd-4th/9th-10th centuries describe Bāḏḡīs as essentially rural and agricultural, with no large cities. According to the *Ḥodūd al-ʿālam*, pars. 23-24 = tr. Minorsky, p. 104, comm., p. 327, Bāḏḡīs had 300 villages. The northern part of the region was known as Ganj Rostāq, with three main settlements lying on the road connecting Herat with Marv al-Rūḏ: Baban (q.v.) or Babna (the most populous of the three, and residence of the local governor), Bağšūr (a flourishing town, of fair size, on the desert fringes of the Morḡāb, and apparently near the modern Qalʿat Mawr on the railway branch from Marv to Kūška, a site marked by a mound and considerable ruins; it relied on wells for its drinking water), and Kīf. In southern Bāḏḡīs, Moqaddasī and Ebn Ḥawqal mention eight settlements: Kūḡānābāḏ or Kūh Ḡūnābāḏ (where the residence of the local governor was), Dehestān (larger and more prosperous than the former, with houses built of mud brick and its water supply from *qanāt*s; this probably corresponds to the modern shrine of Ḵˇāja Dehestān to the northeast of Herat, and must of course be distinguished from the Dehestān to the east of the Caspian Sea), Kūfā, Bost, Jāḏāvā, Kābarūn, Kālavūn, and Jabal al-Feżża "the mountain of silver," *Ḥodūd al-ʿālam*'s Kūh-e Sīm (where silver-mining had, however, ceased, through lack of fuel for smelting, by the 4th/10th century). Most of these settlements of Bāḏḡīs depended on rainwater for their agricultural lands and wells for drinking water, the streams flowing down to the Morḡāb providing too little water for extensive irrigation. See Ebn Ḥawqal, ed. Kramers, II,

Table 8

POPULATION OF BĀDḠĪS PROVINCE, AFGHANISTAN (1978-79)

Name of district	1 Area (km²)	2 Total sedentary population (1979)	3 Density (Inhab./km²)	4 Urban Population (percent)	5 Wintering nomads (tents)[1]	6 Number of tents in summer 1978[2] Paṣ̌tūn	 Others
Qalʿa-ye Now (Center of province)	3,794	66,700	18	8	1,805	450	1,040
Woloswālī:							
Ḡōrmāč	2,326	27,100	12	—	525	1,235	—
Jawand	6,411	37,000	6	—	205	1,395	2,830
Morḡāb	4,196	35,000	8	—	1,622	800	550
Qādes	3,339	43,700	13	—	823	780	360
Total of province	20,066	209,500	10	3	4,980	4,660	4,780

Sources: Columns 1 to 4, *Natāyej-e moqaddamātī-e nokostīn saršomārī-e nofūs*, Kabul, 1359 Š./1981. Figures have been rounded and are mere estimates since no record of census for Bādḡīs province have reached Kabul. Columns 5 to 6, D. Balland and A. de Benoist, *Nomades et semi-nomades d'Afghanistan* (forthcoming).

Notes: (1) All wintering nomads except 100 Turk tents are Paṣ̌tūn. Nearly half of the total (i.e., 2, 365 tents) are short-range nomads remaining within the province in summer. (2) Among the nomads (2,565 tents) and semi-nomads (6,875 tents) spending summer in Bādḡīs, 85 percent and 96 percent respectively are short-range migrants living permanently within the limits of the province.

Table 9

LAND USE IN BĀDḠĪS PROVINCE, AFGHANISTAN (1967)

Name of district	Cultivated lands (ha) Irrigated (*ābī*)	 Non-irrigated (*lalmī*)	 Fallow	Forests (ha)	Percent of irrigated land under Canals	 Springs	 *Kārēz*	Water mills (units)
Qalʿa-ye Now	5,682	32,044	17,158	14,706	64	22	14	90
Woloswālī:								
Ḡōrmāč	5,364	16,326	9,234	10,530	66	34	—	30
Jawand	3,774	19,408	10,344	2,440	76	24	—	106
Morḡāb	9,024	14,966	9,386	99,602	70	30	—	106
Qādes	5,340	18,476	10,306	22,282	26	29	45	116
Total of province	29,184	101,220	56,428	149,560	61	28	11	448

Source: *Natāyej-e eḥṣāʾīyagīrī sarwē-ye moqaddamātī-e zerāʿatī sāl-e 1346 Š.*, Kabul; n.d., 7 vols. The figures are only very rough estimates; the reliability of some of them may be questionable.

pp. 440-41, tr. Wiet, II, pp. 426-27; Moqaddasī, pp. 298, 308; Mostawfī, loc. cit.; Barbier de Meynard, *Dictionnaire géographique, historique et littéraire de la Perse*, Paris, 1861, p. 75; Le Strange, *Lands*, pp. 412-15; Barthold, *An Historical Geography of Iran*, Princeton, 1984, pp. 47-49.

In later times, there is little specific mention of Bāḏḡīs under that name, but its pastures were naturally sought after by the various nomadic powers of the eastern Islamic world, and the war of 668/1270 between the Chaghatayid Mongol ruler of Central Asia, Baraq, and the Il-khanid ruler of Iran, Abāqā, arose from quarrels over these pasture grounds. Their lushness remained famous over the ensuing centuries, and a nineteenth-century traveler like J. P. Ferrier (1845-46) describes those of the Hazāras of Qalʿa-ye Now, with their flocks of sheep, goats, camels, and buffaloes, as the best in all Asia (*Caravan Journeys and Wanderings in Persia, Afghanistan, Turkistan, and Beloochistan*, London, 1856, p. 192).

Bibliography: Given in the text.

(C. E. Bosworth)

ii. Modern Province

Bāḏḡīs is a province (*welāyat*) of northwestern Afghanistan created in 1343 Š./1964 out of the former province of Herat (q.v.). Since the recent loss of the Košk-e Kohna *ʿalāqadārī*, transferred back to Herat province, Bāḏḡīs province covers 20,066 km^2 and is presently (1363 Š./1984) divided into four districts (*woloswālī*). The only locality with urban status is the provincial center, Qalʿa-ye Now (q.v.).

See Tables 8 and 9 for compilation of main available data about present population and land use in the province and districts.

(D. Balland)

BADĪʿ, rhetorical embellishment. The Arabic word *badīʿ* refers in general to the concept of novelty. In the Koran the Creator is named *badīʿ al-samawāt wa'l-arż* (2:117; 6:101), which implies that the act of creation was without precedent and not dependent on any model. As an adjective with a passive meaning, the word may be rendered in English by "new, novel, unusual," or synonyms indicating that the thing thus qualified makes a startling impression on account of its novelty. During the early Islamic period it developed into a technical term through its use in discussions about Arabic poetry and ornate prose. According to Jāḥeẓ (d. 255/868-69), the transmitters of Arabic poems (*rowāt*) applied it to figurative expressions like *sāʿed al-dahr*, "the forearm of fate" (*al-Bayān wa'l-tabyīn*, Cairo, 1948, IV, pp. 55-56). The term *al-badīʿ* became especially associated with the style of the *moḥdaṯūn*, the poets of the early ʿAbbasid period. One of them, Moslem b. Walīd (d. 181/803), is said to have introduced its technical use. Ebn al-Moʿtazz (d. 296/908), another prominent representative of this school of poetry, gave it a permanent place in the terminology of Arabic literary theory. He adopted it in his *Ketāb al-badīʿ* (ed. I. Kratchkovsky, London, 1935) as a covering term for a set of rhetorical figures, considered to be characteristic of the poetry of the *moḥdaṯūn*. From this time onwards, *badīʿ* became established as a collective noun denoting rhetorical embellishment. The figures of speech are known under several other names used plurally, such as *badāyeʿ*, *ṣanāyeʿ* or *ṣenāʿāt* (artifices), and *maḥāsen* (beauties). Since the 7th/13th century the *ʿelm al-badīʿ* was recognized as a branch of the science of rhetoric (*ʿelm al-balāḡa*). The use of rhetorical devices as an embellishment of speech was, in the words of Ḵaṭīb Demašq Qazvīnī, permissible as long as it was appropriate and not harmful to the clarity of expression (*baʿd reʿāyat taṭbīqeh ʿalā moqtażāʾ al-ḥāl wa wożūḥ al-dalāla*; see *Īżāḥ*, ed. Būlāq, 1317-19/1899-1901, IV, p. 283). Although *badīʿ* was, in the view of Jāḥeẓ, exclusively a characteristic of Arabic, the concept was in the course of time also applied to other Muslim literatures, in particular those of the Persians and the Turks.

Ebn al-Moʿtazz wrote his treatise on the figures of speech with the aim of demonstrating that the startling features of the style adopted by the *moḥdaṯūn* were not as novel as they appeared to conservative critics, but could be found already in the earliest works of Arabic literature. Most of his examples were drawn from the Koran, the *ḥadīṯ nabawī* (sayings of the prophets), and other early prose as well as from the ancient poetry of the Arabs. He criticized, on the other hand, the excessive use of rhetorical figures, for which the poetry of Abū Tammām (d. ca. 231/845-46) had become notorious in his days. Under the heading of *badīʿ*, Ebn al-Moʿtazz discussed five figures: *esteʿāra* (metaphor), *tajnīs* (paronomasia), *moṭābaqa* (antithesis), *radd al-aʿjāz ʿalā mā taqaddamahā* (the repetition of words in different places), and *al-madhab al-kalāmī* (the use of argumentation as a rhetorical device). To this he added twelve other figures which he called *maḥāsen al-kalām wa'l-šeʿr*. The reason of this terminological differentiation is not known. It was not taken over by later writers. The importance of the *Ketāb-al-badīʿ* to the history of Arabic rhetoric lies in the fact that for the first time the various terms current in discussions of style were united into a single framework. This provided a model to later textbooks, which very much increased the number of the rhetorical figures dealt with.

The method of defining figures and demonstrating their use by means of a collection of examples, which thus became predominant in Arabic literary theory, could serve various purposes. In the *Ketāb naqd al-šeʿr* (ed. S. A. Bonebakker, Leiden, 1956), written in the early 4th/10th century, Qodāma b. Jaʿfar tried to establish a systematic approach to the criticism of poetry. Without mentioning the term *badīʿ*, he based his argumentation largely on discussions about rhetorical figures and introduced several new terms. His influence on later writers about rhetorical subjects equals the impact made by Ebn al-Moʿtazz.

Another application was concerned with the study of the Koran. Already Ebn Qotayba (d. 276/889) had shown the importance of rhetoric to the understanding of the Koranic text in his *Ketāb taʾwīl moškel al-Qorʾān* (ed. A. Ṣaqr, Cairo, 1954). The doctrine of the inimitability of the Holy Book (*eʿjāz*) was not only founded on its contents but also on the qualities of its style. The study of the latter was pursued by many writers. One of them was Bāqellānī (d. 403/1013) whose work has been examined by G. E. von Grunebaum (*A Tenth-Century Document of Arab Literary Theory and Criticism*, Chicago, 1950).

The possibility that the rhetorical theory of the Arabs was derived from, or at least influenced by, the corresponding tradition of the antique world has often been discussed. The two works by Aristotle which deal with the subject, the *Rhetoric* and the *Poetics*, were known to medieval Muslim civilization, but they appear not to have been widely read outside the limited circle of the philosophers. They remained beyond the sphere of interest of the people who wrote on *badīʿ*. The Hispano-Arab Qarṭājannī (d. 684/1285) made an attempt to harmonize the rhetoric of the Arabs with Greek theory, but this was an isolated instance (cf. W. Heinrichs, *Arabische Dichtung und griechische Poetik*, Beirut, 1969).

It cannot be denied, however, that there are many similarities between the Arabic figures of speech and those which have been current in the West as part of the classical legacy. A common background might be found in the educational system of late antiquity. Rhetoric belonged to the *artes liberales* taught in the Hellenistic schools which existed in the Middle East before the Islamic period. It is possible therefore that the development of Arabic rhetoric was influenced along this way, but it is difficult to find confirmation of this in the written sources (see W. Heinrichs, "Literary Theory," pp. 32f., with further references).

The study of literary art, pursued assiduously by the Arab philologists, was extended to several other subjects besides the figures of speech. The full range of its interests about the 5th/11th century is shown in encyclopedic works such as *Ketāb al-ṣenāʿatayn* by Abū Helāl ʿAskarī (d. after 400/1009-10) and *Ketāb al-ʿomda* by Ebn Rašīq (d. 456/1063-64 or 463/1070-71); see also the anthology *Arabic Poetics in the Golden Age* by V. Cantarino (Leiden, 1975). The most original contributions were made by ʿAbd-al-Qāher Jorjānī (d. 471/1078, q.v.). He wrote two works which changed the course of literary theory, although they did not themselves circulate very widely. In *Dalāʾel al-eʿjāz*, Jorjānī enlarged the discussion concerning the unique style of the Koran to an analysis of the rhetorical values inherent in the syntax of Arabic (cf. the digest of its contents by M. Weisweiler, "ʿAbdalqāhir al-Curcānī's Werk über die Unnachahmlichkeit des Korans und seine syntaktisch-stylistischen Lehren," *Oriens* 11, 1958, pp. 77-121). His *Asrār al-balāḡa* (ed. H. Ritter, Istanbul, 1954; tr. idem, *Die Geheimnisse der Wortkunst*, Wiesbaden, 1959) contains an extremely subtle, though not very systematic, study of the use of imagery. Jorjānī treats separately simile (*tašbīh*), metaphor (*esteʿāra*), analogy (*tamṯīl*), and other kinds of tropes which until that time had been included in the lists of *badīʿ* figures. The new ideas put forward by Jorjānī were cast into a more scholastic form by later writers and so provided the substance of the rhetorical doctrine which gained authority in Muslim education. The most important chain of transmission ran through the compendium *Meftāḥ al-ʿolūm* by Sakkākī (d. 626/1229) and the various digests, commentaries and marginal notes based on the *Meftāḥ*. To these texts belong the *Talḵīṣ al-Meftāḥ* and the more extensive *Īżāḥ fiʾl-maʿānī waʾl-bayān* by Ḵaṭīb Demašq Qazvīnī (d. 739/1338), and the *Moṭawwal* and *Moḵtaṣar* by Saʿd-al-Dīn Taftazānī (d. ca. 791/1389).

The science of rhetoric consisted in this tradition of three disciplines. The *ʿelm al-maʿānī* continued the line of research which Jorjānī had begun in his book on *eʿjāz*, and studied the semantic aspects of syntax. The second discipline, the *ʿelm al-bayān*, was concerned with the study of trope (*majāz*) and its subdivisions. The remaining figures of speech were left to the *ʿelm al-badīʿ*, where the figures based on phonetic features (*badīʿ lafẓī*) were further distinguished from those based on meaning (*badīʿ maʿnawī*). For educational purposes the exposition of rhetorical figures often was given the form of a *qaṣīda badīʿīya*. A well-known poem of this kind was composed by Ṣafī-al-Dīn Ḥellī (d. 749/1349). To Western readers, the contents of classical Arabic *badīʿ* became accessible through A. F. Mehren's *Die Rhetorik der Araber*, Copenhagen and Vienna, 1853.

The first attempts to develop a literary theory applicable to Persian texts date from the beginning of the 5th/11th century. During the early Ghaznavid period a few treatises on the prosody of Persian poems are known to have been written, though none of them have survived. An adaptation of the Arabic theory of *badīʿ* is not on record until the later part of that century. If earlier poets make mention of rhetorical terms occasionally, they probably derived them from Arabic textbooks. No other were available yet to Kayqāvūs b. Eskandar who in his *Andarz-nāma* (written in 475/1082-83, q.v.) gave a list of "artifices as they are employed by the poets" and especially recommended the use of metaphor in panegyrics (ed. Ḡ.-Ḥ. Yūsofī, Tehran, 1345 Š./1967, pp. 189f.).

Moḥammad b.ʿOmar Rādūyānī, writing between 481/1088 and 507/1114, claimed to be the first who took up the subject of Persian rhetoric. He did not, however, create an entirely new branch of literary scholarship. His book, the *Tarjomān al-balāḡa* (ed. with a facsimile of the unique manuscript by A. Ateş, Istanbul, 1949) was modeled on an Arabic work of the early 5th/11th century: *Ketāb al-maḥāsen fiʾl-naẓm waʾl-naṯr* by Abuʾl-Ḥasan Naṣr Marḡīnānī. Both writers, about whose lives very little is known, must have lived in Transoxania. Their books are simple textbooks on *badīʿ*, but Rādūyānī made considerable additions to the work of his predecessor. He not only supplied more complete definitions; the number of terms dealt with is also more than doubled (cf. Ateş, op. cit., s.v. *giriş*, pp. 39ff.). The examples are all drawn from Persian poetry, although he addresses himself in his commentary both to the writer of official prose (*dabīr*) and to the poet. His favorite model of good style is the poetry of ʿOnṣorī (d. 431/1039-40; q.v.) the poet laureate of the Ghaznavid court. The technical terms retained their Arabic forms, as they did throughout the history of Persian rhetorical theory. Rādūyānī made, however, an effort to provide Persian equivalents in his definitions.

The *Tarjomān al-balāḡa* was regarded as lost until the discovery of a manuscript in a Turkish library in 1948. It had in the course of time been falsely attributed to the poet Farroḵī. In spite of the fact that the work must have fallen into oblivion already quite soon, it remained accessible to later generations in a completely recast form made by Amīr Rašīd-al-Dīn Moḥammad ʿOmarī, better known as Rašīd(-e) Vaṭvāṭ (d. 578/1182-83), the *Ḥadāʾeq al-seḥr fī daqāʾeq al-šeʿr* (ed. ʿA. Eqbāl, Tehran, 1308 Š./1929-30). This work became the standard textbook on *badīʿ* as far as the Persian tradition was concerned. The most striking difference with the *Tarjomān al-balāḡa* is the introduction by Rašīd Vaṭvāṭ of examples from Arabic prose and poetry, which always precede the Persian quotations. The *Ḥadāʾeq al-seḥr* participates on account of this also in the Arabic study of rhetoric. Many of the Persian lines quoted by Rādūyānī, which were taken from Samanid and early Ghaznavid poetry, were replaced by specimens of the work of more recent poets. The list of figures treated by Rašīd Vaṭvāṭ does not differ very much from that of his predecessor, but the definitions of the terms are often more adequate in the revised text.

The success of the *Ḥadāʾeq al-seḥr* inspired many writers to produce books of the same kind. They usually restricted themselves to a discussion of Persian materials. The most prominent among them are: Šaraf-al-Dīn Ḥasan Rāmī (fl. second half of the 8th/14th century), *Ḥadāʾeq al-ḥaqāʾeq*; ʿAlī b. Moḥammad Tāj Ḥalāwī (fl. 8th/14th century), *Daqāʾeq al-šeʿr* (ed. Sayyed Moḥammad-Kāẓem Emām, Tehran, 1341 Š./1962); Mīr Sayyed Borhān-al-Dīn ʿAṭāʾ-Allāh (d. 919/1513-14), *Badāʾeʿ al-ṣanāʾeʿ* and *Takmīl al-ṣenāʿa*. A commentary on the *Ḥadāʾeq al-seḥr* was compiled in 1297/1879-80 by Mīrzā Abu'l-Qāsem Farhang Šīrāzī (see further Eqbāl's introd. to *Ḥadāʾeq al-seḥr*, pp. *sh* ff.).

The use of the *qaṣīda* for presentations of figures of speech was also popular in the Persian tradition from an early date onwards. Among the first specimens known to us is the poem entitled *Badāʾeʿ al-asḥār fī ṣanāʾeʿ al-ašʿār* by Faḵr-al-Dīn Qewāmī Moṭarrezī of Ganja (fl. end of the 6th/12th century). It demonstrates most of the currently used figures. E. G. Browne provided a rhetorical commentary to this *qaṣīda-ye maṣnūʿa*, including a comparison with an English textbook of the sixteenth century, in *Lit. Hist. Persia* II, pp. 46-76. Similar poems were made by Badr Jājarmī (d. 687/1288, q.v.), Salmān Sāvajī (d. 778/1376-77), Ahlī Šīrāzī (d. 942/1535-36), and many others (cf. Eqbāl, op. cit.).

The most distinguished work in the history of Persian literary theory is undoubtedly *al-Moʿjam fī maʿāyīr ašʿār al-ʿajam* (ed. M. Qazvīnī, London, 1909, M.-T. Modarres Rażawī, Tehran, 1314 Š./1935-36, 2nd ed., 1338 Š./1959), which was completed about 630/1232-33 by Šams-al-Dīn Moḥammad b. Qays Rāzī, or Šams-e Qays. Although it certainly was not as widely read as the *Ḥadāʾeq al-seḥr*, the *Moʿjam* surpassed it both in scope and richness of contents. It was in fact the first complete poetics dealing with Persian poetry. The two sections of the book treat respectively metrics (*ʿarūż*) and the theory of rhyme and the criticism of poetry (*qāfīat wa naqd-e šeʿr*). An epilogue contains observations on the practice of poetry (*šāʿerī*) and plagiarism (*sareqāt-e šeʿr*). Šams-e Qays assigned the rhetorical figures a place in the second section. This indicates that he considered them to be tools of the literary critic in the first place. The influence of Rašīd Vaṭvāṭ on this part of his work is obvious, but the list of figures examined in the *Moʿjam* contains several terms which cannot be found earlier in the Persian tradition. Some of these terms can be retraced to the *Naqd al-šeʿr* of Qodāma b. Jaʿfar, though they may have been borrowed through later sources (cf. Bonebakker, op. cit., introduction, p. 59). Šams-e Qays, who originally wrote his poetics in Arabic, was also in many other ways dependent on Arabic literary theory, but the distinction between the *ʿelm al-bayān* and the *ʿelm al-badīʿ*, which was introduced by his contemporary Sakkākī, was not yet known to him. His examples are almost exclusively Persian, the most frequently quoted poet being Anwarī (q.v.). In his description of the types of poetry (*ajnās-e šeʿr wa anwāʿ-e naẓm*) he pays some attention to the forms which are specifically Persian, but his approach remains inadequate because of its subservience to the categories of Arabic poetics. Yet, Šams-e Qays went further into the direction of an unbiased examination of the phenomena of Persian poetry than any other rhetorician of the traditional school.

The extent to which the catalogues of rhetorical figures increased in volume can be measured from some of the later textbooks which have been digested by Western scholars. The ancient type of *badīʿ* collections, which continued to treat the tropes amongst the other figures of speech, is found in the *Majmaʿ al-ṣanāʾeʿ* by Neẓām-al-Dīn Aḥmad b. Moḥammad Ṣāleḥ, written in 1060/1650; this was the source of Francis Gladwin's *Dissertations of the Rhetoric, Prosody and Rhyme of the Persians* (Calcutta, 1801). To the same category belongs the list of about one hundred terms, divided into *lafẓī* figures (based on phonetic characteristics and *maʿnawī* figures (based on semantic aspects), included in the dictionary *Haft qolzom*, compiled by Qabūl Moḥammad (ed. Lucknow, 1822), which was translated by Fr. Rückert and W. Pertsch, *Grammatik, Poetik und Rhetorik der Perser*, Gotha, 1874 (originally published in *Wiener Jahrbücher* 40-44, 1827-28).

The scholastic approach to rhetoric which developed under the influence of Jorjānī and Sakkākī did not, however, fail to penetrate Persian literary theory as well. This tendency is represented by the *Ḥadāʾeq al-balāḡa*, a work dealing with tropes apart from the *badīʿ* figures, written by Šams-al-Dīn Faqīr Dehlavī (d. 1183/1769-70). It provided the materials for Joseph Garcin de Tassy, *Rhétorique et prosodie des langues de l'orient musulman* (Paris, 1873; repr. Amsterdam, 1970).

An adaptation of traditional rhetorical theory to the requirements of modern education in Iran was made by Jalāl-al-Dīn Homāʾī in *Fonūn-e balāḡat wa ṣenāʿāt-e adabī* (Tehran, 1354 Š./1975-76). It is based on the *Moʿjam* of Šams-e Qays as well as on more recent works.

The Persian textbooks of *badīʿ* were primarily practical tools, both for writers and poets. Embellishment of style was as important to the historiographer, the government official, and the writer of mystical treatises as it was to the poet of the court. They all had to consider the prevailing literary taste, which demanded a high degree of ornamentation. The contents of the textbooks were never quite similar. In the course of time the number of figures increased considerably. Yet, a corpus of basic figures, arranged in roughly the same order, can be found in most instances. Only some of the most important of these figures can be mentioned here. The term *tajnīs*, paronomasia, denotes several types of assonance and of similarities based on the Arabic script. The complete form is called *tajnīs-e tāmm*, homonymy or wordplay. Other figures referring to the phonetic aspect (*lafẓ*) of words are *takrār* (also *takrīr*, *mokarrar*), repetition; *qalb* or *maqlūb*, anagram; *radd al-ʿajoz ʿalaʾl-ṣadr*, repeating the last word of a hemistich at the beginning of the next. More comprehensive terms are *tarṣīʿ*, parallelism of cadence and rhyme between two hemistichs; *sajʿ*, the use of prosodic elements in ornate prose; and *eʿnāt* or *lozūm mā lā yalzam*, the imposition of certain extra obligations on the composition of a poem, such as the use of the same word in a number of lines or even in an entire poem (e.g., in the case of the Persian *radīf* rhyme).

The figures based on meaning (*maʿnī*) are primarily those which can be categorized as tropes. The most general term is *majāz*, figurative speech, the opposite to *ḥaqīqat*, direct speech. The tropes are further distinguished into *tašbīh*, simile, with a great number of subdivisions; *esteʿāra*, metaphor; *tamṯīl*, analogy; and *kenāya*, allusion. The semantic relationship between more than one theme or image can be constructed as a *motażādd*, antithesis. To the arrangement of themes within a line of verse or a sentence pertain *jamʿ*, combination; *tafrīq*, separation; and *taqsīm*, division. Other aspects of meaning are involved in figures like *īhām*, amphibology, and *madḥ šabīh ba ḏamm*, praise which seems to be blame, resp. its reverse *ḏamm šabīh ba madḥ*.

Besides the *lafẓī* and *maʿnawī* figures the categories of *badīʿ* also include terms referring to modes of presentation, for instance, *soʾāl o jawāb*, question and answer, or to the articulation of a discourse, such as *eltefāt*, apostrophe. The best way (*ḥosn*) to deal with the main parts of a panegyrical poem is demonstrated in sections on the *maṭlaʿ*, the opening line, *maqṭaʿ* the closing line, *taḵalloṣ*, turning from the introductory section to praise, and *ṭalab*, asking for reward. Genres like *loḡaz*, enigma, and *moʿammā*, riddle, are usually included as well, but they became the subject of separate monographs in the 9th/15th century. In the *Moʿjam* of Šams-e Qays a number of general stylistic prescriptions are given which are not normally found in other Persian textbooks: e.g., *tafwīf*, elegance, correctness, and simplicity in the use of meter and rhyme and in the choice of words and expressions, as well as the avoidance of rare and archaic vocabulary (p. 329); *talmīḥ* and *ījāz*, both prescribing conciseness of style; *mosāwāt*, "equalizing" words and meanings.

Many of the terms defined in the *ʿelm al-badīʿ* have parallels in Greek and Latin terminology (cf. Browne, *Lit. Hist. Persia* II, pp. 46-76; *Asrār al-balāḡa*, ed. Ritter, 1954, p. 4). There are nonetheless dissimilarities on essential points between the classical and the Islamic traditions of rhetorical theory. The former was throughout its history mainly concerned with oratory, the latter with literature. Some divergencies are related to this difference in outlook: The Greek figure *homoioteleuton* corresponds to an entire branch of Muslim literary scholarship, the study of rhyme; others reveal a dissimilarity as far as the terminological framework is concerned: The terms *alliteratio* and *anaphora* do not have precise parallels in *badīʿ*, but the figures which they denote were frequently used in the literatures of the Muslims.

The dependence of Persian rhetorics upon its Arabic predecessor reflects the complicated cultural situation in Iran since the coming of Islam. Even after the rise of a national literature, the Iranians continued to write in Arabic, both in scholarly works and in creative writings. The *ʿelm al-badīʿ* was by origin a critical counterpart to the revolt of the *moḥdaṯūn* poets against the conventions of classical Arabic poetry. The early Persian poets borrowed a great deal from this new school of Arabic poetry. In literary criticism the awareness of the interrelation of the two literatures became an obstacle to the development of an adequate theory of Persian poetry. As a consequence, references to Persian features are few and usually marginal in Persian rhetorics. Paradoxically, the most profound analyses relevant to Persian poetry must be sought in Jorjānī's *Asrār al-balāḡa*, a book written in Arabic by an Iranian, who only discusses Arabic poems (ed. Ritter, pp. 19ff.; *Die Geheimnisse*, pp. 1*f.).

The ideosyncrasies of Persian rhetoric appear most clearly in the realm of tropes, which has been investigated by Ritter (*Bildersprache*) and, in much greater detail, by B. Reinert (*Ḫāqānī*; see also his article "Probleme der vormongolischen arabisch-persischen Poesiegemeinschaft und ihr Reflex in der Poetik," in G. E. von Grunebaum, ed., *Arabic Poetry: Theory and Development*, Wiesbaden, 1973, pp. 71-105). Both writers have pointed to the growing importance of metaphor as against the predominance of explicit similes in ancient Arabic poetry. The poetic language became saturated with imagery, and complex forms of metaphorical expression came into use. The figure *tanāsob*, also called *morāʿāt al-naẓīr*, denotes the use of a "harmonious imagery," which may encompass more than one line. Amphibology is often also involved (*īhām-e tanāsob*). As the functions of themes and images were frequently inversed, such extended metaphors could easily become independent poetical elements: The poets conjured imaginative scenes in which the individual images were brought into a causal relationship to each other by means of "phantastic etiologies" (*ḥosn-e taʿlīl*). This procedure was applied especially to the descriptions of nature which were inserted into romantic *maṯnawī* poems, notably into the works of Neẓāmī. In panegyric poetry the hyperbole (*mobālaḡa*) was used in extreme forms, for instance, through the projection of macrocosmic qualities into the personality of an earthly patron of the poet. In many metaphorical expressions, exemplified by *Jorjānī* in the metaphor "the hand of the northern wind" (cf. *Asrār*, p. 43; *Geheimnisse*, p. 64), a personification of non-human themes is implied. All these features have found their fullest development in Persian poetry, although they can be met with also in non-classical Arabic poems.

Bibliography: Studies on the history of Arabic literary theory are contained in the works of G. E. von Grunebaum, H. Ritter, and S. A. Bonebakker mentioned in the article as well as in: Amjad Trabulsi, *La critique poétique des Arabes jusqu'au Ve siècle de l'Hégire*, Damascus, 1956; S. A. Bonebakker, "Reflections on the *Kitāb al-badīʿ* of Ibn al-Muʿtazz," in *Atti del Terzo Congresso di Studi Arabi i Islami*, Ravello, 1966, Naples, 1967, pp. 191-209; idem, "Poets and Critics in the Third Century A. H.," in *Logic in Classical Islamic Culture*, ed. G. E. von Grunebaum, Wiesbaden, 1970, pp. 85-111; idem, "Aspects of the History of Literary Rhetoric and Poetics in Arabic Literature," *Viator. Medieval and Renaissance Studies* 1, 1970, pp. 75-95; W. Heinrichs, "Literary Theory : The Problem of its Efficiency," in *Arabic Poetry. Theory and Development*, ed. G. E. von Grunebaum, Wiesbaden, 1973, pp. 19-69; G. J. H. van Gelder, *Beyond the Line*, Leiden, 1982, esp. pp. 1-22. See also *EI*², s.vv. "Badīʿ," "Balāg̲ha," "Iʿdjāz," "Madjāz," and "al-Maʿānī wa'l-bayān." Many works on Persian rhetoric are still unpublished. Surveys of the extant texts are given in Monzawī, III, pp. 2124-52, and Storey, *Persian Literature* III/1 C, Leiden, 1984, pp. 176-206. The catalogues of Persian manuscripts should also be consulted. Modern studies on aspects of the Persian theory of literature are rare. The most important are Hellmut Ritter, *Über die Bildersprache Nizāmīs*, Berlin and Leipzig, 1927 (a study of metaphor and simile in epic poetry, largely independent of the traditional approach); Jan Rypka, "Ḫāqānīs Madā'in-Qaṣīde rhetorisch beleuchtet," *Archív orientální* 27, 1959, pp. 199-205 (an analysis of the use of *badīʿ* figures); Benedikt Reinert, *Ḫāqānī als Dichter. Poetische Logik und Phantasie*, Berlin and New York, 1972 (an investigation of the functioning of several figures of speech from the point of view of formal logic).

(J. T. P DE BRUIJN)

BADĪʿ, designation of the calendar system of Babism and Bahaism (q.v.), originally introduced by the Bāb (q.v.) in several works, including his Persian *Bayān* (5:3, pp. 152-54). It is based on a solar year of nineteen months, each of nineteen days, together with four or five intercalary days (whose positioning is a matter of disagreement between Azalī Babis and Bahais). There are also cycles (*wāḥed*) of nineteen years, each year of which has a particular name: Each such cycle constitutes a *koll šayʾ*. The months and days of the week have Babi names. The year begins on the vernal equinox, which is celebrated as Nowrūz. The Bāb himself did not appoint any other festivals than this (although he did mention "days of glory and sadness" on which sermons were to be read; Arabic *Bayān* 7:11, p. 30), but a total of eleven days are held sacred by the Bahais in commemoration of events in the history of the sect; work is suspended on nine of these (*Bahāʾī World*, pp. 688-89). The last month of the year (ʿAlā) replaces Ramażān as that of the fast, observed, as in Islam, from sunrise to sunset. Friday is reserved by the Bāb, not as a day of congregational prayer, but as a time for listening to sermons (Arabic *Bayān* 9:9, p. 42). Bahais date the commencement of the Badīʿ era from the Nowrūz preceding the announcement of the Bāb's mission in Jomādā I, 1260/May, 1844 (Browne, *Traveller's Narrative*, p. 425), but there are indications that the Bāb himself intended it to begin in the sixth year after that event (Miller, *Bahāʾī Faith*, p. 63; cf. Bāb, *Haykal al-dīn*, pp. 5-6).

Bibliography: Sayyed ʿAlī-Moḥammad Šīrāzī (the Bāb), *Bayān-e fārsī*, Tehran, n.d. Idem, *al-Bayān al-ʿarabī* and *Ketāb-e haykal al-dīn*, published in one volume, Tehran, n.d. E. G. Browne, ed. and tr., *A Traveller's Narrative Written to Illustrate the Episode of the Bāb*, 2 vols., Cambridge, 1891, II, pp. 412-25. W. McE. Miller, *The Bahāʾī Faith: Its History and Teachings*, South Pasadena, California, 1974. *The Bahāʾī World* 16, Haifa, 1976, pp. 688-91 (also earlier volumes). *Principles of Bahāʾī Administration*, 3rd ed., London, 1973, pp. 53-57.

(D. M. MACEOIN)

BADĪʿ, ĀQĀ BOZORG, son of Ḥāji ʿAbd-al-Majīd of Nīšāpūr, a young Bahai martyr who has gained a certain distinction in Bahai lore on account of his carrying a letter from Bahāʾ-Allāh to Nāṣer-al-Dīn Shah and his subsequent execution (July, 1869).

Bibliography: Fāżel Māzandarānī, *Ẓohūr al-Ḥaqq* VI (private ms.), fols. 30-32. H. M. Balyuzi, *Bahāʾu'llāh, the King of Glory*, Oxford, 1980, pp. 293-314 (see in particular the account of the arrest and execution of Badīʿ by Moḥammad Walī(y) Khan Sepahdār-e Aʿẓam, pp. 303-09). M. Momen, *The Bābī and Bahāʾī Religions. 1844-1944: Some Con-*

temporary Western Accounts, Oxford, 1981, pp. 254-55.

(M. MOMEN)

BADĪʿ BALḴĪ, ABŪ MOḤAMMAD BADĪʿ B. MOḤAMMAD B. MAḤMŪD BALḴĪ, poet of the 4th/10th century, contemporary and panegyrist of Abū Yaḥyā Ṭāher b. Fażl b. Moḥammad Čaḡānī (d. 381/991), one of the rulers of the Čaḡānīān district in Transoxiana. Some verses by him are quoted in the *Lobāb al-albāb* of ʿAwfī (Tehran, pp. 260-61), who also gives the name and lineage of his patron. Hedāyat (*Majmaʿ al-foṣaḥāʾ* I, pp. 456-62) attributed Badīʿ's verses to Badāyeʿī Balḵī (q.v.), the poet of the 5th/11th century who wrote the didactic poem *Pand-nāma-ye Nōšīravān* or *Rāḥat al-ensān*; in fact he had mistaken the former's name for the latter's pen-name and mixed up their writings.

Bibliography: Nafīsī, *Naẓm o naṯr*, p. 23. Ṣafā, *Adabīyāt* I, 5th ed., Tehran 1363 Š./1984, pp. 422-23. Ḵayyāmpūr, *Soḵanvarān*, p. 81.

(Z. SAFA)

BADĪʿ-AL-ZAMĀN B. ḤOSAYN BĀYQARĀ, Timurid prince (*mīrzā*) of the line of ʿOmar Šayḵ. He was the eldest son of Sultan Ḥosayn Bāyqarā (r. Herat 873-911/1469-1506, q.v.) and Begā Solṭān Begīm, the daughter of Sultan Moʿezz-al-Dīn Sanjar of Marv (*Ḥabīb al-sīar* (Tehran) IV, p. 320). His father had originally entrusted him with the government of Jorjān and Astarābād, but after joining his father in a successful war against Ḥeṣār, he was named ruler of Balḵ (*Ḥabīb al-sīar* IV, p. 198). Badīʿ-al-Zamān then asked Ḥosayn Bāyqarā to confirm his son, Moḥammad Moʾmen Mīrzā, as ruler of Astarābād, arguing that he had assigned it to him at the time of his circumcision (Bābor, fol. 41). Ḥosayn Bāyqarā, however, decided to give Astarābād to his own favorite son, Moẓaffar Ḥosayn Mīrzā, while, according to Bābor, he gave Badīʿ-al-Zamān Balḵ "in the interests of Transoxania" (Bābor, fol. 36). This incident became the cause of enmity between father and son and, according to Bābor, resulted in the rebellion of Ḥosayn Bāyqarā's other sons against him (Bābor, fol. 166).

Badīʿ-al-Zamān eventually allied himself with the powerful amirs, Ḵosrow Shah and Šojāʿ-al-Dīn Ḏu'l-Nūn Arḡūn, against his father (*Ḥabīb al-sīar* IV, p. 207). His first battle against his father took place at Pol-e Čerāḡ in Šaʿbān, 902/May, 1497, and ended in Badīʿ-al-Zamān's defeat and narrow escape (Bābor, fol. 416). The next day, Moḥammad Moʾmen, who was holding Astarābād, was captured after a battle against his uncle, Moẓaffar Ḥosayn, and sent to Herat where he was imprisoned in Ṣafar, 903/September, 1497. As a result of an intrigue on the part of Moẓaffar Ḥosayn's mother, Ḵadīja Bīkī Āḡā, who was also Sultan Ḥosayn Bāyqarā's most influential wife, and the powerful vizer, Neẓām-al-Molk, Ḥosayn Bāyqarā was induced to sign the death warrant of his young and popular grandson, Moḥammad Moʾmen (*Ḥabīb al-sīar* IV, p. 214).

Badīʿ-al-Zamān was defeated by his father a second time at Alang Nešīn in Šawwāl, 903/June, 1498, and was then persuaded to make peace with his father in 904/1498 by the latter's foster-brother and confidant, Mīr ʿAlī-Šīr, who often acted as mediator in the frequent disputes between the two. Badīʿ-al-Zamān now asked to be granted the government of Balḵ again, but acquiesced in his father's offer of Farāh and Sīstān (*Ḥabīb al-sīar* IV, pp. 237-38).

After the death of Ḥosayn Bāyqarā in 911/1506, Badīʿ-al-Zamān and his brother, Moẓaffar Ḥosayn, ruled together as co-regents in Herat until the city was taken by the Uzbek Moḥammad Šaybānī Khan in 913/1507, at which time Badīʿ-al-Zamān fled, leaving his harem and treasure behind (*Ḥabīb al-sīar* IV, pp. 363-76; Bābor, fols. 183, 205b). After a long period of peregrination which included a year's stay in India, Badīʿ-al-Zamān returned to Khorasan, now under Safavid rule, in 919/1513. He was allowed to live in Azerbaijan and was sent 1,000 dinars daily from Tabrīz as a stipend from Shah Esmāʿīl (*Ḥabīb al-sīar* IV, p. 394). When the Ottoman sultan, Selīm, conquered Tabrīz in 920/1514, he treated Badīʿ-al-Zamān with great respect and took him back with him to Istanbul where, according to the *Ḥabīb al-sīar*, he died a few months later of the plague (see also Loṭfī, p. 236; Sām Mīrzā, p. 13, says he died 14 months later). He was survived by a son, Moḥammad Zamān Mīrzā. Like his fellow Timurid princes, Badīʿ-al-Zamān was a poet, who wrote under the pen-name Badīʿī (Faḵrī Heravī, pp. 46-47).

Bibliography: Primary sources: Bābor, *Bābor-nāma*, ed. A. S. Beveridge, *The Bābur-nāma*, Leiden, 1905. Solṭān Moḥammad Faḵrī Heravī, *Taḏkera-ye rawżat al-salāṭīn*, ed. ʿA. Ḵayyāmpūr, Tabrīz, 1345 Š./1966. *Ḥabīb al-sīar* IV, Tehran, 1333 Š./1954. Loṭfī Pasha, *Tawārīḵ-e āl-e ʿOṯmān*, Istanbul, 1341/1923. Sām Mīrzā Ṣafawī, *Toḥfa-ye sāmī*, ed. Waḥīd Dastgerdī, Tehran, 1314 Š./1935. Secondary sources: V. V. Bartol'd, "Mir Ali-Shir i politicheskaya zhizn'," in his *Sochineniya* II/2, Moscow, 1964, pp. 249-53; German tr. W. Hinz, *Herāt unter Ḥusein Baiqara dem Timuriden*, Leipzig, 1938; Eng. tr., V. and T. Minorsky, *Four Studies on the History of Central Asia* III, Leiden, 1962.

(M. E. SUBTELNY)

BADĪʿ-AL-ZAMĀN HAMADĀNĪ, ABU'L-FAŻL AḤMAD B. ḤOSAYN B. YAḤYĀ (b. Hamadān 358/968, d. Herat 398/1008), Arabic belle-lettrist and inventor of the *maqāma* genre.

Abu'l-Fażl Aḥmad, known as Badīʿ-al-Zamān (Wonder of the age), studied in Hamadān with the great Arab philologist, Ebn Fāres (d. 395/1004). In 380/990-91 he went to Ray, where he benefited from the presence at the court of the famous Buyid minister and literary patron, Ṣāḥeb b. ʿAbbād. Thence, Badīʿ-al-Zamān traveled to Jorjān (Gorgān), where he lived among the Ismaʿilis. The biographical sources are not completely clear about Hamadānī's religious affiliations. Some, cite the historian of Hamadān, Sīrawayh, to the effect that Hamadānī was a Sunni and learned in Hadith but

Ṣafadī notes that Badīʿ-al-Zamān was accused of Ashʿarism. However, Monroe's conclusion (pp. 52-55, based partly on Hamadānī's own writings) that Badīʿ-al-Zamān converted to Shiʿism and then later reverted to Sunnism is probably correct.

Badīʿ-al-Zamān arrived in Nīšāpūr in 382/992 (Ṯaʿālebī, *Yatīma* IV, p. 257) or in 392/1001 (Yāqūt, *Odabāʾ* I, p. 96). It was here that his rivalry with the noted Arabic littérateur Abū Bakr K̲ˇārazmī (d. 383/993) took root, a rivalry said to have contributed to the latter's demise. According to Ṯaʿālebī (*Yatīma* IV, p. 258), who apparently knew Hamadānī personally, the latter traveled so widely in Khorasan, Sīstān, and Ḡazna that there was not a single place he did not visit and benefit from. He finally settled in Herat, where he died in 398/1008, at age forty. Hamadānī is said to have gone mad towards the end of his life (Yāqūt, *Eršād* I, p. 95; Ṣafadī, *al-Wāfī* VI, p. 355). Both Ṣafadī (*al-Wāfī* VI, p. 358) and Ebn K̲allekān (*Wafayāt* I, p. 129) give the same two variants of the death of Badīʿ-al-Zamān. According to the first he died from poisoning. According to the second he suffered a stroke and was quickly buried. Then he awoke in his grave and his voice was heard in the night. But when people opened the grave, he was found dead, his hand clutching his beard.

Hamadānī had a pleasant countenance, was good company, lofty of spirit, a good person to befriend, but, at the same time, someone who was bitter when it came to his enemies. The biographers note his prodigious memory, which seems to have been photographic. He could apparently glance quickly at several pages of a book he did not know and then reproduce their contents. Hamadānī was also quite skilled in spontaneous composition. If someone suggested to him that he compose a *qaṣīda* (ode) or an epistle on an unusual subject, he would do so immediately and without hesitation. Hamadānī's linguistic skills are worthy of note as well. He was able to easily translate Persian poetry rich with unusual expressions into Arabic verse.

Perhaps even more significant for Hamadānī as creator of the *maqāmāt* was his sense of humor and play. Ṣafadī (*al-Wāfī* VI, pp. 357-58), for example, recounts an encounter between K̲ˇārazmī and Hamadānī, in which the latter declined a word incorrectly. When K̲ˇārazmī chided him for it, he replied with a word play based on the misdeclined word. On another occasion, with the same K̲ˇārazmī, Badīʿ-al-Zamān showed his linguistic skills by a series of verbal stunts based on words ending with the same consonants.

But Badīʿ-al-Zamān owes his fame to the new literary genre he created, the *maqāma* genre, one of the few totally new, yet lasting, genres created in medieval Arabic literature. The *maqāmāt* of Hamadānī are a set of adventures narrated in rhymed prose (*sajʿ*), but also including original poetry. They revolve around a rogue hero, Abu'l-Fatḥ Eskandarī, and a narrator, ʿĪsā b. Hešām. The most common (though by no means the only) structural pattern in the *maqāmāt* is one in which ʿĪsā finds himself in one of the cities of the Islamic world and happens upon a swindler who is invariably cheating his audience. After much verbal display, usually on the part of the rogue hero, ʿĪsā discovers that he has indeed been witnessing a disguised Abu'l-Fatḥ in action. After this process of recognition, the two bid each other adieu, until the next *maqāma*. But, the literary role of ʿĪsā b. Hešām in Hamadānī's *Maqāmāt* is not restricted to that of narrator. He performs tricks of his own, like those of Abu'l-Fatḥ (e.g., in the *maqāma* of Baghdad).

Holding the text together, thus, are not only the repeated narrative structures of the *Maqāmāt* but also the interplay of the two central characters. Abu'l-Fatḥ is a hero who lives by his wits (mostly verbal) and who often takes advantage of the gullibility of his audience. Furthermore, in a certain sense, he initiates ʿĪsā b. Hešām (and the reader) into the art of roguery.

According to the sources, Hamadānī wrote four hundred *maqāmāt*, though only fifty-two have come down to us. Apparently, as well, they were written in the earlier part of his life. Badīʿ-al-Zamān is also credited with the authorship of a number of epistles.

Ḥarīrī (d. 516/1122), who was Hamadānī's most important continuator in the *maqāma* genre, clearly attributed the creation of this new form to Badīʿ-al-Zamān (Šarīšī, *Šarḥ maqāmāt al-Ḥarīrī* I, p. 21). However, Ḥoṣrī (d. 413/1022), in his *Zahr al-ādāb* (I, pp. 305-06), claimed that the *Maqāmāt* of Hamadānī were written to counter a set of stories invented by Ebn Dorayd (d. 321/933) and written in unusual language. This claim has caused much ink to be spilled over the question of origins, and has set scholars searching for stories which might have served as prototypes for the *maqāmāt*. What is important is not that a specific story from an earlier literary work inspired Hamadānī or even served as a model for him, but that the entire earlier Arabic literary (and specifically *adab*) corpus was there for Badīʿ-al-Zamān to draw upon and that the rogue hero he devised has antecedents in other *adab* character types, like the *ṭofaylī* (or party crasher). Badīʿ-al-Zamān's innovation consists in the creation of a set of texts all employing the same distinctive discourse, revolving around the same characters and characteristic plots, and whose setting traveled from one location to the next.

Most intriguing from a literary historical and biographical point of view is the relationship of Badīʿ-al-Zamān to his rogue hero. Abu'l-Fatḥ, like his creator, is widely traveled, has a sense of humor, and, perhaps most important, is able to manipulate the Arabic language and its traditions with virtuosity. Badīʿ-al-Zamān has left his mark on Arabic letters not only through his own qualities but through their reflection in the literary hero he created, Abu'l-Fatḥ Eskandarī, and the genre which embodies both.

Bibliography: Editions of Hamadānī's works: *Maqāmāt*, ed. Moḥammad ʿAbdoh, 6th ed., Beirut, 1968. *The Maqāmāt of Badīʿ al-Zamān al-Hamadhānī*, tr. with an introd. and notes, W. J. Prendergast, London, 1915. *Kašf al-maʿānī wa'l-bayān ʿan rasāʾel Badīʿ-al-Zamān*, Beirut, n.d.

For the most important primary sources on the life of Hamadānī and the origins of the *Maqāmāt* see Ebn

K̲allekān (Beirut), I, pp. 127-29. Ṣafadī, *Ketāb al-wāfī be'l-wafayāt* VI, ed. S. Dedering, Wiesbaden, 1972, pp. 355-58. T̲aʿālebī, *Yatīma* (Cairo) IV, pp. 256-301. Yāqūt, *Odabāʾ* I, pp. 94-118. Ḥoṣrī, *Zahr al-ādāb wa t̲amar al-albāb*, ed. Moḥammad Moḥyī-al-Dīn ʿAbd-al-Ḥamīd, Beirut, 1977. Šarīšī, *Šarḥ maqāmāt al-Ḥarīrī* I, ed. Moḥammad Abu'l-Fażl Ebrāhīm, Cairo, 1969.

On Hamadānī and his *Maqāmāt*, see also Mārūn ʿAbbūd, *Badīʿ-al-Zamān al-Hamad̲ānī*, Cairo, 1980. A. F. L. Beeston, "The Genesis of the *Maqāmāt* Genre," *Journal of Arabic Literature* 2, 1971, pp. 1-12. Šawqī Żayf, *al-Maqāma*, Cairo, 1980. Moḥammad Rošdī Ḥasan, *At̲ār al-maqāma fī našʾat al-qeṣṣa al-meṣrīya al-ḥadīt̲a*, Cairo, 1974. A. F. Kilito, "Le genre 'Séance': Une introduction," *Stud. Isl.* 43, 1976, pp. 25-51. Idem, *Les Séances: Récits et codes culturels chez Hamadhānī et Harīrī*, Paris, 1983. Fedwa Malti-Douglas, "*Maqāmāt* and *Adab*: 'Al-Maqāma al-Mad̲īriyya' of al-Hamadhānī," *JAOS* 105/2, 1985, pp. 247-58. James T. Monroe, *The Art of Badīʿ az-Zamān al-Hamadhānī as Picaresque Narrative*, Beirut, 1983.

(F. Malti-Douglas)

BADĪʿ-AL-ZAMĀN MĪRZĀ, by most accounts the last of the Chaghatay/Timurid rulers of Badak̲šān. He was either the grandson (by a daughter) of Solaymān Mīrzā (or Solaymān Shah) (*Baḥr*, f. 70b; *Selselat al-salāṭīn*, f. 167a), who was a cousin of Bābor and a direct descendant of Tīmūr (Lowick, 1965, p. 222), or the grandson (*az aḥfād-e*) (again by a daughter of Moḥammad Ḥakīm Mīrzā (*Baḥr*, f. 69a) and died or was killed on or about 12 Šawwāl 1011/25 March 1603.

Despite the expulsion of the Timurids from Transoxania and Khorasan during the first decade of the sixteenth century, Badak̲šān remained a stronghold of Chaghatay/Timurid sentiment until the early seventeenth century, first under Solaymān Mīrzā (920/1514-997/1589), then under another grandson and often rival, Šāhrok̲ Mīrzā b. Ebrāhīm (r. 983/1575-992/1584) (Lowick, 1972, p. 285). In 992/1584, the Shaybanid khan, ʿAbd-Allāh (Khan) b. Eskandar (q.v.) took Badak̲šān and its chief city, Qondūz, from Šāhrok̲ but sometime not long thereafter, the region was again in Timurid hands.

According to *Tārīk̲-e rāqemī* (f. 202a), Badīʿ-al-Zamān Mīrzā seized Qondūz and Badak̲šān from Šāhrok̲ and killed him (but according to Abu'l-Fażl ʿAllāmī, *Akbar-nāma* III, p. 423, cited by Lowick, 1972, p. 285 the latter died peacefully in 1016/1607). When the Toghay-Timurids succeeded the Shaybanids in Transoxiana and Balk̲ during 1007-09/1599-1601, Badīʿ-al-Zamān Mīrzā at first accepted their sovereignty but then in 1011/1603, while the Toghay-Timurids were coping with a Safavid invasion of Balk̲ led by Shah ʿAbbās, he opened negotiations with Shah Jahāngīr (*Baḥr*, f. 69a). After the Safavid defeat and withdrawal (and apparent inconclusive outcome of the negotiations with Jahāngīr), Badīʿ-al-Zamān Mīrzā was forced to confront a Toghay-Timurid army alone and was killed shortly after his fortress at Qondūz fell (*Baḥr*, f. 70b; *Tarīk̲-e rāqemī*, f. 202a; *Selselat al-salāṭīn*, f. 167a).

There is some evidence that Badīʿ-al-Zamān Mīrzā was not the last Timurid and that the strength of Badak̲šāni loyalty to that dynasty had not waned. According to one source, the Toghay-Timurid army leader named another Timurid, Mīrzā Moḥammad Zamān, a son of Šāhrok̲, to govern Badak̲šān. He survived about one year and then was killed by a Shaybanid pretender seeking refuge after defeat at the hands of the Toghay-Timurids (*Selselat al-salāṭīn*: *Tārīk̲-e rāqemī*, loc. cit.).

Bibliography: N. S. Lowick, "Coins of Sulaiman Mirza of Badakhshan," *Numismatic Chronicle*, Ser. 7, 5, 1965, pp. 221-29. Idem, "More on Sulaiman Mirza and his Contemporaries," ibid., 12, 1972. Maḥmūd b. Amīr Wālī, *Baḥr al-asrār fī manāqeb al-ak̲yār*, ms., India Office Library, no. 575. Mollā Šaraf-al-Dīn b. Nūr-al-Dīn Andejānī, *Tārīk̲-e rāqemī*, ms., Royal Asiatic Society, no. 166. Ḥājī Mīr Moḥammad Salīm, *Selselat al-salāṭīn*, ms., Bodleian Library, no. 169.

(R. D. McChesney)

BADĪʿ-AL-ZAMĀN NAṬANZĪ. See ADĪB NAṬANZĪ.

BADĪʿ KĀTEB JOVAYNĪ, MOḤAMMAD. See KĀTEB JOVAYNĪ.

BADĪHA-SARĀʾĪ, composition and utterance of something improvised (*badīh*), usually in verse.

Among the Arabs, poetic improvisation (*ertejāl*, a term used in Persian also) was practiced and admired from pre-Islamic times (Nicholson, pp. 75, 418, 436). Among the Iranians, it has been a mark of poetical talent and skill. It has long been customary to declaim poems at official ceremonies, private celebrations such as wedding feasts, and in modern times school speech days and also mourning assemblies. For these occasions, appropriate poems are composed or improvised and pieces from the classics are recited. The custom has added excessive bulk to the *dīvān*s of many poets. Neẓāmī ʿArūżī in his *Čahār maqāla* (written ca. 550/1155) calls it the "highest pillar" (*rokn-e aʿlā*) of poetical skill, which every poet should master (p. 57). He quotes *robāʿī*s by ʿOnṣorī, Moʿezzī and Azraqī, and a *qeṭʿa* by Rašīdī, which those poets extemporized, as well as five *bayt*s which he himself wrote and uttered before the wine bowl had been passed around twice (pp. 57, 68-69, 71, 74, 85; Browne, *Lit. Hist. Persia* II, pp. 37-39, 336, 339-40). The epigrammatic *robāʿī* and the *qeṭʿa* in one of the *mosaddas* meters are most often used, but more difficult forms and meters are attempted. In the 1970s, the Shah ʿAbbās Hotel at Isfahan employed a poet who could in minutes produce a *qaṣīda* for an occasion or guest. At the Eighth Congress of Iranian Studies at Kermān 25-30 Šahrīvar 1356/16-21 September 1977, a *mošāʿara* (poetic contest) was held in which the contestants improvised even quite long poems. Political and social verse, which in the twentieth century has sometimes swayed public opinion, was for the most part written for newspapers and periodicals (notably the humorous *Tawfīq* 1317 Š./1938-1352 Š./1973), but was also improvised at meetings.

In both classical and folk music, singers have freedom to improvise the lyric (*taṣnīf*) and the melody within the appropriate *dastgāh* (musical mode), although in the past few decades they have generally chosen *taṣnīf*s composed by others. ʿĀref Qazvīnī (q.v.) composed *taṣnīf*s which echo his own and his audience's feelings about topics of the day. These were either composed at short notice or improvised.

Bibliography: Neẓāmī ʿArūżī, *Čahār maqāla*, ed. M. Qazvīnī and M. Moʿīn, 3rd ed., Tehran, 1333 Š./1954. R. A. Nicholson, *A Literary History of the Arabs*, London, 1907, repr. Cambridge, 1930 and 1953. E. G. Browne, *The Press and Poetry of Modern Persia*, Cambridge, 1914. Rūḥ-Allāh Ḵāleqī, *Naẓar-ī be musīqī*, Tehran, 1316 Š./1937. Ella Zonis, *Classical Persian Music*, Cambridge, Massachusetts, 1973. ʿĀref Qazvīnī, *Kollīyāt-e dīvān-e Mīrzā Abu'l-Qāsem ʿĀref Qazvīnī*, Tehran, 1337 Š./1958.

(F. R. C. BAGLEY)

BADĪLĪ, SHAIKH AḤMAD, a Sufi shaikh in 6th/12th-century Sabzavār, renowned for his mastery of the exoteric as well as the esoteric science. The designation Badīlī—which was also his *taḵalloṣ*—appears to have arisen from the belief that he was a *badīl* (substitute), one of a seven or, more commonly, forty-member class of *awlīāʾ* (q.v.). In 582/1186-87, Sultan Shah b. Īl Arslān besieged Sabzavār in the course of his battles against ʿAlāʾ-al-Dīn Tekeš Ḵᵛārazmšāh, and when the siege became protracted, the people of the city begged Shaikh Aḥmad Badīlī to intercede on their behalf. Accordingly he went out to the camp of Sultan Shah who received him with great respect and promised not to harm the Sabzavāris if they opened their gates to his army. The gates of the city were then opened, and Sultan Shah kept his promise.

Badīlī is said to have written poems, both *ḡazal*s and quatrains, on mystical themes, as well as treatises; none of his writings are known to have survived except for a quatrain preserved by Jovaynī.

Bibliography: Jovaynī, II, pp. 24-25. *Ḥabīb al-sīar* (Tehran) II, p. 636.

(H. ALGAR)

BĀDKŪBA. See BAKU.

BĀDPĀYĀN. See ARTHROPODS.

BADR ČĀČĪ, a Persian poet of the 8th/14th century, born in the town or district of Čāč (also written Šāš) in Transoxiana, which had been a frontier fortress and was destroyed before the Mongol invasion in the wars of the Ḵᵛārazmšāh, Sultan Moḥammad (596/1200-617-1220; ruins still exist at its site not far from Tashkent.

The poet, who acquired the titles Badr-al-Zamān and Faḵr-al-Dīn and used the pen-name Badr or Badr Čāčī, evidently migrated in early manhood from his homeland to India and obtained a position in the service of the sultan of Delhi, Abu'l-Maḥāmed Ḡīāṯ-al-Dīn Moḥammad b. Ḡāzī Malek Toḡloq (725/1324-752/1351). He has left a large number of odes (*qaṣīdas*) in praise of this ruler, who held him in high esteem, giving him a place at the royal table and honoring him with the title Faḵr-al-Dīn. In 745/1344 the sultan sent him on a diplomatic mission to Deogir (Dawlatābād) in the Deccan.

With few exceptions, Badr Čāčī's poems consist of praise of the Sultan Moḥammad b. Toḡloq or description of his own experiences and feelings. He collected them into a *dīvān* in 745/1344 and recorded the date in a chronogram (a verse containing the words *dawlat-e šah* which have the numerical value 745 in the *abjad* notation). He took Anwarī and Ḵāqānī as his models in the art of *qaṣīda*-writing and used material from the odes of both. His poetry is full of verbal and intellectual artifices and erudite expressions. Structurally his style is characterized by an exuberance of speech and imagery, particularly in the use of elaborate similes and metaphors, which recalls the language of the poets of the later part of the 6th/12th century.

Badr Čāčī's poems did not become well-known in Iran but won great fame in India. E. G. Browne (*Lit. Hist. Persia* III, p. 106) noted that Badr Čāčī came next to Amīr Ḵosrow and Ḥasan Dehlavī in Indian esteem and that many Indian-trained scholars of Persian literature considered these three to be surpassed only by Saʿdī and Mawlawī Rūmī.

In several *taḏkera*s (biographical anthologies), including the *Maḵzan al-ḡarāʾeb* of Aḥmad-ʿAlī Khan Hāšemī Sendīlavī, this poet is confused with Badr Jājarmī (d. 686/1287) and wrongly described as a pupil of Majd Hamgar and eulogist of the Ṣāḥeb-e Dīvān Jovaynī. In the *Ḵolāṣat al-ašʿār* of Taqī-al-Dīn Kāšī, another surname, Šervānī, is added to his name Badr Šāšī and he is confused with Badr Šervānī (d. 854/1450).

Edgar Blochet (*Cat. Bib. Nat.* II, pp. 206-07) ascribes to Badr Čāčī a narrative poem in *motaqāreb* (the meter of Ferdowsī's *Šāh-nāma*) about the reign of Moḥammad b. Toḡloq and states that he completed it in 745/1344. Ṣafā, however (*Adabīyāt* III, p. 856), thinks that since Badr Čāčī's only known poems are those in the *dīvān*, Blochet's reading of the verses in which Badr Čāčī recorded the compilation of the *dīvān* and gave the date 745 in the chronogram *dawlat-e šah* must have caused him to imagine that Badr Čāčī also wrote a narrative poem in the style of the *Šāh-nāma*.

Since no sultan or amir other than Moḥammad b. Toḡloq receives praise in Badr Čāčī's odes, it seems likely that the poet's death took place at some date between 745/1344 (the year in which he compiled his *dīvān* and was sent to Deogir) and 752/1351 (the year in which Moḥammad b. Toḡloq died).

Only one edition of Badr Čāčī's *dīvān* has been printed (ed. Mawlawī Moḥammad, Kanpur,

1307/1889), but numerous manuscripts have been preserved (Monzawī, *Noskahā* III, pp. 2247-48).

Bibliography: Āqā Bozorg Ṭehrānī, *al-Darīʿa* 9/1, p. 128. Šādān Belgerāmī, "Awlād-e Ḥosayn; Kalām-e Badr-e Čāč," *Oriental College Magazine* (Urdu) 9/3, 1927, pp. 1-20. Ḵayyāmpūr, *Soḵanvarān*, p. 80. Nafīsī, *Naẓm o naṯr* I, pp. 203-04. Ṣafā, *Adabīyāt* III/2, pp. 852-68.

(M. Dabīrsīāqī)

BADR-al-**DĪN EBRĀHĪMĪ,** author of the Persian dictionary *Farhang-e zafāngūyā wa jahānpūyā* (The eloquent and world-seeking dictionary) composed in India in the late 8th/14th or early 9th/15th century. There is no information about his life and other works. The work is divided into seven parts (*baḵš*), each of which is a separate dictionary individually titled by the author and divided into alphabetically arranged chapters (*gūna*). Each chapter contains explanations of words beginning with the same letter and is divided into sections (*bahr*) according to the last letter of the word explained. The *Zafāngūyā* is one of the first Persian dictionaries to cover a comparatively large lexicographical field (5170 words), the first to use the principle of alphabetization, and the earliest attempt in Persian lexicography at compiling a multilingual dictionary. In it we have a consistent, explicit statistic of the foreign loanwords in Persian and the first attempt at classifying them.

The first three parts are devoted to the Persian lexicon and are arranged according to the formation of the words: simple words (part 1), complex words (part 2), and Persian, mostly old, infinitives (part 3; infinitives are seldom found in earlier dictionaries). In an appendix to the dictionary, the author has gathered Persian expressions and compounds with strange meanings. The Arabic lexicon constitutes part 4; the "mixed lexicon" (i.e., Arabic-Nabatean-Persian) part 5; the "Roman" lexicon (i.e., words of Greek, Latin, or Syriac provenience) part 6; the Turkic lexicon part 7. For some of the words Badr-al-Dīn quotes Indian equivalents (*hendovī*).

Badr-al-Dīn was the first to list phraseological elements separately. In the preface to the dictionary he explains the tasks of his lexicographical work and the principles for the presentation of the material. He introduces an innovation into the very composition of a lexical article. He gives a descriptive characterization of the reading of the word to be explained, sometimes noting variant readings, and marking *maʿrūf* and *majhūl* vowels. To a greater extent than his predecessors he quotes dialectal vocabulary, mentioning words from Shiraz, Gīlān, Bukhara, Farḡāna, and Transoxiana. He also strives to adapt his dictionary to the reading of a variety of written texts, and to a certain degree for direct dealings with the foreign-speaking population. He uses older dictionaries such as *Loḡat-e fors* by Asadī Ṭūsī, the *Farhang-nāma* by Faḵrī Ḡawwās, the *Resāla-ye Naṣīr-e Aḥmad* (before 822/1419), and the *Farhang-e Ferdowsī* (before 822/1419), to which the text contains frequent references. Badr-al-Dīn's dictionary served as an authoritative source for later lexicographers, such as Ebrāhīm Fārūqī (*Farhang-e ebrāhīmī*, comp. 878/1473), Maḥmūd b. Żīāʾ-al-Dīn (*Tohfat al-saʿāda*, comp. 916/1510), Shaikh Moḥammadzād (*Moʾayyed al-fożalāʾ*, comp. 925/1519), Sorūrī (*Majmaʿ al-fors*, comp. 1008/1600), Jamāl-al-Dīn Ḥosayn Enjū (*Farhang-e jahāngīrī*, comp. 1017/1608), etc.

For a long time the *Farhang-e zafāngūyā* was counted as lost, but at the beginning of the 1960s the discovery of two manuscripts was reported: One, in the Orientalist Library of Patna (India), is a complete copy of the dictionary, but defective at the edges, written in the 9th/15th century. The second manuscript was identified by S. I. Baevskiĭ in an incomplete copy of an unidentified dictionary in the library of the State University of Tashkent, written in 1123/1711. Baevskiĭ used this copy as the basis for an edition of the dictionary, comparing the Indian manuscript. In 1978, he published a report of the discovery of a third (incomplete) manuscript of the dictionary (wr. 998/1590) in the catalogue of the Ketāb-ḵāna-ye Senā (the Senate Library; no. 527), Tehran, which had until then been known in scholarly literature as the *Farhang-e panj-baḵšī*.

In 1986 Baevskiĭ identified a fourth manuscript. The manuscript, described in W. Pertsch, *Verzeichniss der persischen Handschriften* (Berlin, 1888, p. 142, no. 74) is dated 921/1515 but does not name itself. It contains a complete copy of the *Farhang-e zafāngūyā*, closely resembling the Tehran copy in its redaction.

Bibliography: Badr-al-Dīn Ebrāhīmī, *Farhang-e zafāngūyā wa jahānpūyā*, ed. S. I. Baevskiĭ (facsimile, text, translation, index), Moscow, 1974. Idem "Unikalʾnaya rukopisʾ persidskogo tolkovogo slovarya 'Farkhang-i Zafanguya va dzhakhanpuya'," *Narody Azii i Afriki* 3, 1965, pp. 118-21. Idem, "Rukopisʾ 'Slovarya Pandzhbakhshi'/'Pyatichastnogo slovarya'," in *Pisʾmennye pamyatniki i problemy istorii kulʾtury narodov Vostoka*, Moscow, 1979, I, pp. 15-21. Idem, "Identifikatsiya neopoznannoĭ rukopisi persidskogo farkhanga v 'Kataloge persidskikh rukopiseĭ' sobraniya Korolevskoĭ Biblioteki v Berline," *Narody Azii i Afriki*, 1987, I, pp. 104-05.

(S. I. Baevskiĭ)

BADR-al-**DĪN** b. shaikh ebrāhīm **SERHENDĪ,** a Sufi author, translator, and disciple of the celebrated Aḥmad Serhendī (q.v.). He was probably born in or around 1002/1593-94 (see Maḥbūb Elāhī, in the preface to *Ḥażarāt-al-qods*, pp. 9-10); for seventeen years he was associated with Aḥmad Serhendī (ibid., p. 157), who addressed to him a number of letters included in his *Maktūbāt* (ed. Lucknow, 1877, I, pp. 395-98, 428-29; II, pp. 67-68; III, pp. 57-59). At some time, probably after Aḥmad Serhendī's death, Badr-al-Dīn also had connections with Dārā Šokūh (Šukōh), upon whose request he translated into Persian a number of Arabic works concerning the life and thought of ʿAbd-al-Qāder Jīlānī (Gīlānī) (Storey, I, p. 1002; *Ḥażarāt al-qods*, pp. 158-59). This connection between Dārā Šokūh and one of Aḥmad Serhendī's disciples is noteworthy, and its further investigation may throw interesting light on the relationship between Dārā Šokūh and the Naqšbandīya.

Badr-al-Dīn's chief importance lies in his contribution to Naqšbandī hagiography. His *Sanawāt al-atqīā'* (ms., India Office, D.P. 672) consists of a *moqaddema* (fols. 2b-21b), which deals mainly with Biblical figures accepted into Islamic tradition, and of eleven chapters (fols. 21b-337a) which describe the lives of important Sufis and persons venerated by the Sufis in the first eleven centuries of the Islamic era. His other major work, the *Ḥażarāt al-qods*, deals in its first part with the *ḵolafā' rāšedūn*, a number of Sufis of the classical period, and the Naqšbandī saints until Ḵ˅āja Bāqībellāh and his disciples. The second and greater part of the book is devoted to the life, teachings, and miracles of Aḥmad Serhendī, as well as of his sons and successors. The book is most valuable as a reflection of the image of Serhendī among his disciples, but must be used cautiously as a source of factual information about him.

Bibliography: Badr-al-Dīn Serhendī, *Ḥażarāt al-qods*, Urdu tr. (of the first part) by Ḵ˅āja Aḥmad Ḥosayn, Lahore, 1922; ms., India Office, D.P. 630 (second part only); edition of the second part by Maḥbūb Elāhī, Lahore, 1971 (using three mss. found in Sufi *ḵānqāhs* in the subcontinent, but not the D.P. 630 or the other mss. mentioned by Storey; see p. 413 of the edition). Amīn Aḥmad Rāzī (*Haft eqlīm*, ms., India Office, Ethé, *Cat. India Office Library*, 727, fol. 140a. Storey, I, pp. 1001-03. Y. Friedmann, *Shaykh Aḥmad Sirhindī. An Outline of his Thought and a Study of his Image in the Eyes of Posterity*, Montreal and London, 1971, pp. 10, 92-94, and passim.

(Y. FRIEDMANN)

BADR-AL-DĪN TABRĪZĪ, architect and savant active in Konya in Anatolia during the third quarter of the thirteenth century. He is described by Aflākī (I, p. 389) as the architect (*me'mār*) of the tomb of the great mystic poet Jalāl-al-Dīn Rūmī (d. 1273). He came to Anatolia probably as one of those Iranian craftsmen and men of learning who sought refuge in Asia Minor after the Mongol invasion of Iran in the middle of the thirteenth century. The *Manāqeb al-ʿārefīn* states that Badr-al-Dīn possessed, in addition to skills as an architect, knowledge of astrology, mathematics, geometry, spells and magic, alchemy, philosophy, and the cultivation of citrus (I, p. 141). A disciple (*morīd*) of Rūmī, Aflākī (I, p. 387) lauds him as "the second Socrates and Greek Plato." After Rūmī's death, he is said to have been charged by the Saljuq amir, ʿAlam-al-Dīn Qayṣar, with the construction of a tomb for the saint, apparently of the *ayvān* type, which is known today as the Yešil Qubbe (Green Dome) because of the addition of a turquoise-faience revetted tower over the original structure during the Qaramanid period (800/1397-98).

Bibliography: Šams-al-Dīn Aḥmad Aflākī, *Manāqeb al-ʿārefīn*, ed. T. Yazıcı, Ankara, 1976, I, pp. 141, 193-94, 387-89. H. Karamağaralı, "Mevlana'nın türbesi," *Türk etnografya dergisi* 7-8, 1964-65, pp. 38-42. L. A. Mayer, *Islamic Architects and their Works*, Geneva, 1958, p. 57.

(H. CRANE)

BADR JĀJARMĪ, MALEK-AL-ŠOʿARĀ' BADR-AL-DĪN B. ʿOMAR, a 7th/13th-century poet who enjoyed renown in his own time. Born in Jājarm, Khorasan, he received his education in *adab* in that province and later moved to Isfahan where he entered the service of Ḵ˅āja Bahā'-al-Dīn b. Šams-al-Dīn Moḥammad Jovaynī, the governor of Isfahan and ʿErāq-e ʿAjam. At Isfahan he met and made friends with the poets Majd Hamgar and Emāmī Heravī. He learned much from Majd Hamgar, who was his senior in years and standing; this probably explains why compilers of *taḏkera*s (biographical anthologies) have described him as Majd Hamgar's pupil.

Jājarmī was Ḵ˅āja Bahā'-al-Dīn's panegyrist and also wrote poems in honor of the latter's father, the *ṣāḥeb-e dīvān*, Ḵ˅āja Šams-al-Dīn Moḥammad Jovaynī, and uncle, the historian ʿAṭā-Malek Jovaynī. It seems that he spent almost all his life as a poet in the service of the Jovaynī family. He died on 29 Jomādā II 686/11 August 1287, shortly after Majd Hamgar and Emāmī. A *marṯīa* (elegy) written by Badr Jājarmī on the death of Saʿd-al-Dīn Ḥamawī in 650/1252 contains expressions of devotion which suggest that he may have been a disciple of that shaikh.

Of Jājarmī's poetry, estimated by Nafīsī (*Naẓm o naṯr* I, p. 162) at 4,000 verses, a large number is quoted in various *taḏkera*s, mostly in the *Mo'nes al-aḥrār* (comp. 741/1340) of his son Moḥammad b. Badr Jājarmī. Altogether this work contains 1,122 verses by him, including 201 from a treatise on limb spasms (*eḵtelājāt-e aʿżā'*) which he wrote and 32 about powers (*eḵtīārāt*, i.e., astrological influences) of the moon, the rest being *qaṣīda*s, *ḡazal*s, *qeṭʿa*s, *mosammaṭ*s and *robāʿī*s and other quatrains.

In content, Jājarmī's oeuvre comprises eulogies, elegies, chronograms, oaths, and jests. It is mediocre poetry for the most part, displaying some sort of poetic artifice, such as the question and answer form, the repeated word-play (*tajnīs-e mokarrar*), the acrostic (*tawšīḥ*), the divided metaphor (*taqsīm*), the use of words consisting solely of undotted letters throughout a poem, etc. All these frills attest to his bent for rhetoric, of which he was indeed the foremost contemporary master. Worthy of mention is his Persian verse rendering of a well-known Arabic *qaṣīda* by Abu'l-Fatḥ Bostī.

Bibliography: *Al-Ḏarīʿa* IX/1, p. 128. Dawlatšāh, ed. Browne, pp. 26, 105, 174, 219-21. Faḵr-al-Dīn Ṣafī, *Laṭā'ef al-ṭawā'ef*, ed. A. Golčīn-e Maʿānī, Tehran, 1336 Š./1957, p. 288. Ḵayyāmpūr, *Soḵanvarān*, p. 80. *Majmaʿ al-foṣaḥā'* I, pp. 633-34. Moḥammad b. Badr Jājarmī, *Mo'nes al-aḥrār*, 2 vols., ed. Mīr Ṣāleḥ Ṭabībī, 1337 Š./1958, and 1350 Š./1971, passim. Moḥammad-ʿAlī Modarresī, *Rayḥānat al-adab*, 3rd ed., Tabrīz, 1346 Š./1967, I, p. 376. Ṣafā, *Adabīyāt* III/1, 1358 Š./1979, pp. 558-67. Šams-al-

Dīn Sāmī, *Qāmūs al-aʿlām* (in Turkish), Istanbul, 1316/1898, II, p. 1254.

(M. Dabīrsīāqī)

BADR KHAN. See BEDIR KHAN.

BADR ŠĪRVĀNĪ, 9th/15th-century poet (b. 789/1387 in the town of Šamāḵī/Shemaha in Šervān district of Caucasia, d. 19 Šawwāl 854/26 November 1450) and one of the most outstanding representatives of Azerbaijani poetry. Little is known about his childhood and education except that he studied at his birthplace, was badly treated by his father Ḥājī Šams-al-Dīn and his stepmother, and suffered from poverty. Though deeply attached to his own country he had to travel extensively in search of daily bread for his family. In addition to his difficult life the ravages of local wars and invasions and the occupation of his native land by the Qara Qoyunlū profoundly influenced his artistic development. He expressed strong feelings against those who waged war, yet had to compose odes praising amirs and men of wealth and power to gain a living.

Badr Šīrvānī began writing poetry at the age of 10-11. His *dīvān* was published in 1985 in Moscow based on the only known manuscript, preserved in the library of the Institute of Oriental Studies in Uzbekistan SSR Academy of Sciences. It contains 824 verses (12,437 *bayt*s [couplets]), composed in almost all genres and forms of classical Persian poetry, though *ḡazal*s and *qaṣīda*s predominate. In addition to Persian, Badr Šīrvānī wrote poetry in his mother tongue Azeri, Arabic, and in a dialect of Persian he calls *zabān-e kenār-e āb* (the coastline tongue).

Badr Šīrvānī was a contemporary of Fażl-Allāh Naʿīmī and Sayyed Yaḥyā Šīrvānī (Bākūʾī), leaders of the Ḥorūfī (q.v.) and Ḵalwatī movements, but sympathized with neither of them.

Bibliography: *Catalogue of Oriental Manuscripts of Uzbekistan SSR Academy of Sciences* V/2, Tashkent, 1954, p. 156. Badr Šīrvānī, *Dīvān*, ed. A. H. Rahimov with introd. and index, Moscow, 1985. Dawlatšāh Samarqandī, *Taḏkerat al-šoʿarāʾ*, ed. M. ʿAbbāsī, Tehran, 1337 Š./1958-59, p. 424. Taqī-al-Dīn Kāšānī, *Ḵolāṣat al-ašʿār wa zobdat al-afkār*, ms., no. 321, fols. 120a. and 120b. in B. Dorn, *Catalogue des manuscrits et xylographes orientaux de la Bibliothèque Impériale Publique de St. Pétersbourg*, St. Petersburg, 1852. India Office ms. no. 677, fols. 683b-691a. A. H. Rahimov, "Bädr Širvaninin gäbäläyä häsr etdiyi šeʿr" (Badr Šīrvānī's verse devoted to Gabala), *Izvestii Akademii Nauk Azerbaĭdzhanskoĭ SSR* 2, 1973, pp. 48-53. Idem, "Bädr Širvaninin ʿMiratus-säfa'ye namäʿlum näziräsi vä Xagani haggïnda bäʿzi geydläri (Badr Šīrvānī's unknown imitation (*naẓīra*) to *Merʾāt al-ṣafā* and some notes about Ḵāqānī), *Izvestii Akademii Nauk Azerbaĭdzhanskoĭ SSR*, 1976, pp. 3-10. Idem, "Bädr Širvaninin Därbändin hakimi Ämir Isfändiyar vä gälʿädarï Ämir Iftixara häsr etdiyi gäsidälär haggïnda" (About Badr Šīrvānī's *qaṣīda*s devoted to the Derbent ruler Amir Esfandīār and the commandant Amir Efteḵār), *Izvestii Akademii Nauk Azerbaĭdzhanskoĭ SSR* 1, 1978, pp. 53-60. Idem, "Bädr Širvaninin yazdïǧï maddeyi-tarixlär" (Chronograms written by Badr-e Šīrvānī), *Izvestii Akademii Nauk Azerbaĭdzhanskoĭ SSR* 1983, 1, pp. 50-56; 2, pp. 46-51.

(A. H. Rahimov)

BĀDRANG. See BĀLANG; CITRUS FRUITS.

BADRĪ KAŠMĪRĪ, BADR-AL-DĪN ʿABD-AL-SALĀM B. EBRĀHĪM ḤOSAYNĪ, a Persian poet in India in the second half of the 10th/16th century. He was an adherent of the Naqšbandī order and a disciple of one of its masters, Ḵʷāja Moḥammad Eslām, at whose instance he composed most of his poems. In the ornate prose preface of his versified story of Alexander (*Qeṣṣa-ye Ḏu'l-qarnayn*), he states that in the years 976/1568-988/1580 he had written *maṯnawī*s, *qaṣīda*s, *ḡazal*s, and prose works entitled *Meʿrāj al-kāmelīn*, *Rawżat al-jamāl*, and *Serāj al-ṣāleḥīn*, that he had compiled a *dīvān* of his *qaṣīda*s and *ḡazal*s, and that subsequently in 988/1580 he had planned a collection of seven narrative poems in *maṯnawī* verse, namely *Manbaʿ al-ašʿār* on the model of Neẓāmī's *Maḵzan al-asrār*, *Mātam-sarā* on that of ʿAṭṭār's *Manṭeq al-ṭayr*, *Zohra o Ḵʷoršīd* on that of Sanāʾī's *Ḥadīqat al-ḥaqīqa*, *Šamʿ-e delafrūz* on that of Amīr Ḵosrow's *Ḵosrow o Šīrīn*, *Maṭlaʿ al-fajr* on that of Jāmī's *Sobḥat al-abrār*, *Laylī o Majnūn* on that of Hātefī's *Laylī o Majnūn*, and *Rosol-nāma* on that of Saʿdī's *Būstān*; the collection was entitled *Baḥr al-awzān*, and he had completed the seventh piece (i.e., the *Rosol-nāma*) in 989/1581, using the *motaqāreb* meter and drawing materials from different historical sources such as the annals of Ṭabarī, the history of Ebn Aʿṯam Kūfī, the *Jāmeʿ al-tawārīḵ* of Rašīd-al-Dīn Fażl-Allāh, the *Tārīḵ-e gozīda* of Ḥamd-Allāh Mostawfī, the *Żafar-nāma* of Šaraf-al-Dīn Yazdī, etc. Badrī Kašmīrī's *Qeṣṣa-ye Ḏu'l-qarnayn* or *Eskandar-nāma* runs to 7,000 verses and is dedicated to the Uzbek ruler ʿAbd-Allāh II (991/1583-1006/1597); it is a mediocre work of little substance, being limited to rapid recitation of events with none of the artistic coloring or attention to scenes and moods usually to be found in Persian narrative poems.

Bibliography: Badr-al-Dīn Kašmīrī, *Qeṣṣa-ye Ḏu'l-qarnayn*, the poet's preface, ms., Bibliothèque Nationale, Paris, Suppl. 501. E. Blochet, *Cat. Bib. Nat.* III, pp. 352-54, s.v. *Eskandar-nāma.* Nafīsī, *Naẓm o naṯr* I, pp. 444-45. Ṣafā, *Adabīyāt* V/2, Tehran, 1364 Š./1985, pp. 713-17.

(Z. Safa)

BĀDRŪDI, one of the local dialects of the Kāšān region, spoken in Bādrūd, a *dehestān* (rural district) of Naṭanz (q.v.). Locally the dialect is called *ozun dei* 'village language'. The material for Bādrūdi was collected in Bād, the center of the *dehestān*, in August of 1969. Other villages in Bādrūd which speak the dialect are Erīsmān. ʿAbbāsābād, Ḵāledābād, Dehābād, Famī,

Matīnābād, and Sar-āsiā, all in the *dehestān* of Naṭanz.

The village of Bād. Bād is a rather large village, some 74 km southeast of Kāšān (via Hanjan Bridge), situated at the edge of the salt desert (Dašt-e Kavīr) in the *garmsīr* (hot zone), south of Abūzaydābād (q.v.). Its population was about 4,500 (about 6,000 with its farms) when the writer visited it in 1969. It had seven quarters and six mosques. Drinking water was obtained from a deep well about 6 km from the village. Irrigation water came from a *qanāt* and four deep wells. The orchards (*bāḡs*, said to be around 2,000) and the fields belonged to small owners. The main produce were wheat and barely as winter crops (*šatawī*) and tobacco, melon, watermelon, cucumber as summer crops (*ṣayfī*); also fruits were grown, chiefly pomegranates, figs, grapes, and some dates. Of late the village had been exporting grass seed for lawns. It had about 1,000 carpet looms engaged principally in weaving rugs (*qālīča*). Some 150 belonged to the state-run Iranian carpet company, Šerkat-e Farš-e Īrān. (See also Razmārā, *Farhang* I, p. 30.)

The dialect. Phonology. The vowels are *i, e, a, ü, u, ö,* (*o*), *ā*; *ā* becomes somewhat rounded before the nasals and *o* appears to be an allophone of *ā*, but my material is too limited to allow a detailed phonological analysis. (In the examples below inconsistencies in the recorded material have not been corrected.) The consonants are the same as in Persian. In phonology Bādrūdi, like other Kāšāni dialects exhibits the general features of northwestern Iranian (cf. ABYĀNA'Ī): *y-* < *y-*; *sp* < Proto-Iranian **tsu̯* < IE. **k̑u̯* (> Av. *sp*, OPers. *s*); *b-* < *du̯-*; *z* < OIr. *z* < IE. palatal *ĝ*(*h*) (> OPers. *d*); *j-* < OIr. *j* < IE. velar *g*(*h*); examples *ya* 'barly', *öšpöš* 'louse', *bar* 'door', *ezze* 'yesterday', *jen* 'woman' (but *zanda* 'alive', from NPers.). Noteworthy features of phonological development of Bādrūdi include: *l* < *rt* in *vā-gel-* 'to return' and *mālá* 'mother' (also *mo*); intervocalic *č* > *č* in *pič-* 'to cook' (but *rij-* 'to pour'); loss of dentals, *r*, and *h* in word-final position (often with compensatory lengthening of the preceding vowel, e.g, *pe:* 'father', *ša:* 'town'); loss of *x* initially before *r* (e.g., *rin-/ri-* 'to buy', *rus* 'rooster') and before *t* in past stems (e.g., *vot-* 'said', *batta* 'is asleep').

Morphology. The nominal system is based on two numbers, one case, and one grammatical gender, and is therefore simpler than that found in most Kāšāni dialects (cf. ABŪZAYDĀBĀDĪ and ABYĀNA'Ī).

The plural is formed by adding the plural marker *-e* to the singular, e.g. *bāl-e ama na-mer* 'do not break our spades'; *böz-e ama az ošksāli be-mard-en* 'our goats died of drought'. In ergative constructions when the logical direct object is plural sometimes the verb (in fact the past participle) also takes the plural marker, e.g., *dözz-e sarbāz-e-šun dar-kos-e* 'the thieves hit (past tense) the soldiers'; *tura b-ame xiār-e hamö-š ba-xard-e* '[a] jackal came [and] ate all the cucumbers'. More often, however, the verb is put in the singular, e.g., *vacc-e* (plur. of *vacca*) *bāl-e-šun ar-get* 'the children picked up the spades'. Often the singular is used for the plural when the verb or a referring pronoun indicates the plural number, e.g., *sarbāz ö döz da:vā-šun be-ka* 'the soldiers and the thieves quarreled'. Nouns in *-a* add the glide *-y-* before the plural marker (*zumā-y-e* 'bridegrooms'). Plurals in *-un* occur rarely and appear not to be genuine at this stage of the language (my informant's son who did not know the dialect as well as his father, used it more often). The dialect does not seem to have any special device for expressing definition.

Personal pronouns have two cases, direct case: *a, tö, nön/nen* (this/that), *ama, šama, nü/nan* (those/these); and oblique (possessive) case: *men, ta, nön/nen, ama, šama, nuin/nömin.* The direct forms are used as the subject of verbs (in the past tenses of transitive verbs if the agent is expressed also by a personal pronoun). My limited material has oblique forms only as genitive in *eżāfa* constructions, but judging by other Kāšāni dialects it was probably also used as object of verbs in non-ergative constructions and governed by pre- and postpositions. Examples: *tö ba-št-i* 'you went', *nü ba-šun xard* 'they ate', *böz-e men-eš ba-köšt* 'he killed my goat', *dass-e ta nāgir-un* 'I do not take your hand'. The enclitic pronouns are *-m, -d, -š, -mun, -dun, -šun.* They are used as possessive pronouns and as direct and indirect object, e.g. *raxt-em dar-em-puš* 'I put on my clothes', *ba-š-raysin* 'make him dance!'. In the ergative construction of the past tenses of transitive verbs, the agent is indicated by enclitic pronouns instead of personal endings. In verbs with a preverb and in compound verbs, the enclitic pronoun follows the preverb or the nominal complement; otherwise it is normally, but not necessarily, attached to the word immediately preceding the verb.

The verbal system is based on two stems, present and past, six persons, and two 'modal' prefixes, namely *ba-/be-* for the imperative, the subjunctive, the preterit, and the periphrastic tenses (perfect, pluperfect, and perfect subjunctive), provided that the stem has no preverb or nominal complement ("plain" stem); and *a-* (durative or progressive tense marker) for the present/future and the imperfect. The personal endings are *-un, -e, -e, -im, -id, -en* for the tenses built on the present stem, i.e., present, subjunctive, and imperative, except that the ending of the 2nd pers. sing. imperative is *nil*; and *-un, -i, nil, -im, -id, -en* for the past tenses of intransitive verbs (the 2nd pers. sing. *-e* is sometimes narrowed into *-i*, and the 3rd pers. *-e* is sometimes opened into *-a*). The perfect stem is formed from the past stem by prefixing *be-/ba-* if the stem is plain and adding the perfect marker *-a*. The pluperfect is formed with the perfect stem and the preterit of 'to be'. In the subjunctive perfect the auxiliary is the subjunctive of 'to be'.

The negative and prohibitive prefix is *na-*, which, joined with the durative marker, produces *nā-*.

Examples of verb forms and constructions: Imperative: *ba-fes, ba-fes-id* 'throw!' (irregular: *bure* [sing.], *ba-id* [plur.] 'come!'); *vā-gel* 'return!', *dāy-ne* 'open!'. Present/future: *a-ters-un, a-ters-e*, etc. 'I fear, you fear, etc.', *a-šun* 'I go, am going, shall go'. Present subjunctive: *ba-tar-sid* '(that) you fear', *age dar-ke* 'if he falls' (the subjunctive is used also for the conditional).

Past tenses of intransitive verbs: Imperfect: *a-šd-un* 'I used to go', *a-tersā(-w)-un* 'I used to fear'. Preterite: *ba-šö* 'he went', *ba-št-im* 'we went', *var-gelā* 'he returned', *ba-tarsā-v-i* 'you feared' (*-v-* or *-w-* are used as connective consonantal glides after back vowels). Perfect: *mö men se passā ba-št-a Karbalā* 'my mother has gone three times to K.', *ba-ško-v-a* 'has dried', *vacca batt-a* 'the child has gone to sleep', *ba-tarso-w-a* 'has feared'. Pluperfect: *ba-tarsā bö* 'had feared'. Perfect subjunctive: *ba-vot-a bu* 'should have said'. Past tenses of transitive verbs: Imperfect: *dar-m-a-puš* 'I was putting on [clothes]'. Preterit: *bāl-e men-eš ba-mart* 'he broke my spades'. Perfect: *do sāat a raxt-em dar-em-pušt-a* 'it is two hours since I put on my clothes' (the agent being *-m-*). Pluperfect: *dar-em-pušd-e bö* 'I had put on [clothes]'.

A secondary past stem is made by adding *-ā* to the present stem. The causative stem is formed by adding *-in* to the present stem (past stem *-in-ā*), e.g., *ba-vez* 'run!', *ba-š-vez-in* 'make him run', *ba-m-rays-in-ā* 'I made him dance'. The passive is formed by adding *-i* to the present stem (past stem *-i-ā*), e.g., *nā-pec-i-a* 'it does not get cooked' (*nā-* <*na-* + *a-*), *dar-nā-bend-i-a* 'it does not congeal' (lit. 'it is not bound'). The infinitive is obtained by prefixing *ba-* and adding *-an* to the past stem, e.g., *ba-šd-an ve az ba-med-an a* 'to go is better than to come'.

For 'to want to' the auxiliary *pia* (past *piā*) is used with the present subjunctive. The agent is expressed by the enclitic pronouns, even in the present tenses. The enclitic pronouns are attached to the durative marker *a-* and precede *pia* (*piā*), e.g., *a-d-pia ba-še ša:* 'you want to go to the town (i.e., Kāšān)', *ama sāl-e bi a-mun-pia ba-šim Karbalā* 'next year we want to go to Karbalā', *ezze a-m-piā ba-šun ša:, na-gelā* 'yesterday I wanted to go to Kāšān [but] it did not turn [out possible]. For 'must' the frozen form *apia* is employed with the present subjunctive, but the agent is expressed by the direct personal pronouns, e.g., *tö apia de temen ā-da* 'you must give two tumans', *a nāpia* 'I must not', *Hasan apia ār-da* 'Ḥasan must give'.

The base *h-* is used for 'to exist'; *xodā ha, šaytun na-ha* 'God exists, the devil does not', *a hun tā b-ay* 'I stay (lit. am) until you come'. The 3rd sing. copula is *a*.

Lexicon. Following are some characteristic Bādrūdi words: *pe:*, *bābā* 'father', *mo*/*mālá* 'mother', *xo* 'sister', *pür* 'son', *jen* 'woman', *bāysura* 'wife's father', *xasrü* 'wife's mother', *mali* 'cat', *kua* 'dog', *maš* 'fly', *karg* 'hen', *gorg* 'wolf', *guja* 'calf', *düm* 'face', *börma* 'weeping', *katta* 'wooden shovel', *ruj* 'day', *sabā* 'tomorrow', *perā* 'day after tomorrow', *pišim* 'noon', *diar* 'afternoon', *uz* 'walnut', *tüm* 'seed', *venow* 'ash tree', *yört* 'room', *kada* 'house', *asejan* 'broom', *mārenju* 'sparrow', *dale* 'a little', *bi* 'other, next', *eten* 'now', *ru* 'in', *ba-ver* 'tear!', *vā-derz-*/*vā-dešt* 'to sew', *ba-ve* weave!', *jen-*/*jet* 'to strike, play (an instrument)', *kod-*/*kos* 'to hit'.

Bibliography: For comparison with related dialects see Christensen, *Contributions* I, pp. 124ff.; E. Yarshater, "The Jewish Communities of Iran and their Dialects," in *Mémorial Jean de Menasce*, ed. Ph. Gignoux and A. Tafazzoli, Paris, 1974, pp. 458ff.; idem "Distinction of Grammatical Gender in the Dialects of Kashan Province and the Adjoining Areas," in *Papers in Honour of Professor Mary Boyce* II, Acta Iranica 25, Leiden, 1985, pp. 727ff.; V. A. Zhukovskiĭ, *Materialy dlya izucheniya persidskikh" narêchiĭ* I, St. Petersburg, 1888 (dialects of the region of Kāšān, etc.).

(E. YARSHATER)

BĀDŪSPĀN or BĀDŪSBĀN, FĀDŪSBĀN, mountainous district of northern Iran on the Caspian side of the Alborz mountains, in Ṭabarestān (Māzandarān), known to the medieval geographers. It lay one day's march to the south of Sārīya (Sārī), had no towns or Friday mosques, but numerous villages. The chief villages were Manṣūra and Ūram Ḵāst where the lord resided.

Bibliography: Eṣṭaḵrī, pp. 205-06 (Qādūsīān). Ebn Ḥawqal, tr. Kramers, pp. 316-18. Yāqūt, I, p. 216. Le Strange, *Lands*, pp. 372-73.

(X. DE PLANHOL)

BADUSPANIDS, a dynasty ruling Rūyān and Rostamdār from the late 5th/11th to the 10th/16th century with the title of *ostandār*s and later of kings. It is named after Bādūspān (Pādūspān), son of Gīl Gīlān Gawbāra, who according to legend came to rule Rūyān when his brother Dābūya succeeded Gawbāra on the throne of Gīlān. The claim of the rulers of Rūyān to be descended from this Bādūspān is reflected in the *Tārīḵ-e Rūyān* of Awlīā'-Allāh Āmolī (writing around 760/1359) who gives a pedigree of the contemporary ruler Jalāl-al-Dawla Eskandar going back to Bādūspān. This pedigree is in its earlier part entirely fictitious. Ẓahīr-al-Dīn Marʿašī (d. 892/1487) adds accounts of the reigns of early rulers allegedly descended from Bādūspān; some of these are known from Ebn Esfandīār's account to be Qarenid *espahbad*s of Lāfūr. Modern reconstructions of a Baduspanid dynasty ruling Rūyān continuously since Sasanid times are based on Marʿašī. *Ostandār*s ruling Rūyān are known from the 4th/10th century (see RŪYĀN; S. M. Stern, "The Coinage of Āmul," in *NC*, 7th ser., vol. 7, 1967, pp. 231, 233; *Camb. Hist. Iran* IV, pp. 218-19). Their kingdom is named in contemporary Arabic sources al-Ostandārīya from which the Persian name Rostamdār is derived. In the 5th/11th century Rūyān was mostly under the domination of Zaydī ʿAlids, and there is no mention of *ostandār*s in this period. The *ostandār*s of the 4th/10th century do not appear in the pedigree of the rulers of the 6th/12th century. There is no evidence that they claimed descent from Bādūspān. It will thus be appropriate to confine the name Baduspanids to the later dynasty.

The first *ostandār* of this dynasty known is named Nāṣer-al-Dawla Šaraf-al-Dīn Naṣr b. Šahrīvaš on coins minted in Rūyān and Kajū in 502/1108-09 and 504/1110-11 on which the overlordship of the Saljuq sultan Moḥammad Ṭapar is acknowledged. More doubtful is his mention on two coins on which Sultan Maḥmūd b. Moḥammad (511-23/1118-31) is acknowledged as overlord. Naṣr b. Šahrīvaš is not mentioned in the literary sources and does not appear in Ẓahīr-al-Dīn's list of *ostandārs*. It seems likely, however, that he belonged to the same family as the later rulers. (Information kindly provided by A. H. Morton. See at present his article "Trois Dinars de l-Ustundār Naṣr," *RN*, 6th ser., vol. 16, 1974, pp. 10ff. Some of the results of this article will be modified by a forthcoming article of the same author.) In Ebn Esfandīār's *Tārīḵ-e Ṭabarestān* *ostandārs* of Rūyān appear slightly later as vassals of the Bavandid kings of Māzandarān. The first one mentioned is Šahrīvaš(n) (Ẓahīr-al-Dīn has Šahrnūš) b. Hazārasf who was persuaded by the Bavandid ʿAlāʾ-al-Dawla ʿAlī not to aid the amir ʿAbbās of Ray when the latter occupied Āmol ca. 534/1140. After ʿAlāʾ-al-Dawla's death and the succession of Šāh-Ḡāzī Rostam, Šahrīvaš first joined the latter's brother and rival Tāj-al-Molūk Mardāvīj who with the backing of Sultan Sanjar made war on Šāh-Ḡāzī. Later Šahrīvaš changed sides and was rewarded by Šāh-Ḡāzī with the hand of his sister or daughter and his possessions in Nātel and Pāydašt as her dowry. Šahrīvaš died about 553/1168. His brother Kaykāʾūs b. Hazārasf had fled from him in his youth and joined the service of Šāh-Ḡāzī at first as a mere foot soldier. His mother was a sister of the ʿAlid Kīā Bozorg al-Dāʿī ela'l-Ḥaqq al-Reżā b. al-Hādī, known as "king of Daylamān" (not of the Ismaʿili chief Kīā Bozorgommīd of Alamūt as has been held). Kīā Bozorg, who had a strong following of Zaydī Daylamites, was a major vassal of Šāh-Ḡāzī holding Rūdbast in fief from him and leader of the struggle against the Ismaʿilis in Daylamān. Šāh-Ḡāzī made Kaykāʾūs a knight and after the death of Kīā Bozorg (ca. 551/1156) put him in charge of his land holdings and the war against the Ismaʿilis. After the death of Šahrīvaš he also gained possession of Rūyān after seizing Nāmāvar b. Bīsotūn, a kinsman who had claimed the succession. Later he revolted against Šāh-Ḡāzī jointly with Faḵr-al-Dawla Garšāsf, lord of Golpāyegān. He inflicted a severe defeat on Šāh-Ḡāzī's son Šaraf-al-Molūk Ḥasan but then was subdued and pardoned by Šāh-Ḡāzī. Šaraf-al-Molūk after his accession (560/1165) gave him ownership of the land which he had held as a tax-paying fief (*be-żamān*) from Šāh-Ḡāzī. Šaraf-al-Molūk's son and successor Šāh-Ardašīr at first also honored him but later decided to take back ownership of Šāh-Ḡāzī's land in Rūyān and Daylamān and appointed Mobārez-al-Dīn Arjāsf b. Faḵr-al-Dawla Garšāsf as *esfahsālār* in Āmol, who harassed Kaykāʾūs. The latter resisted advice of his vassals that he should revolt. When his only son Jostān died, Šāh-Ardašīr agreed to his request that he should take charge of his one-year-old grandson and later give him his daughter in marriage and return his ancestral reign to him. Shortly afterwards he died (ca. 580/1184). According to Ebn Esfandīār Kaykāʾūs was, like his ancestors and many of his subjects, an adherent of the school of the Zaydī imam al-Moʾayyad be'llāh (d. 411/1020).

After Kaykāʾūs his nephew Hazārasf b. Šahrīvaš gained recognition in Rūyān. He alienated his most powerful vassals by killing some of their relatives and making peace with the Ismaʿilis. They deserted to Šāh-Ardašīr who, after vainly warning Hazārasf, permitted Arjāsf to invade Rūyān. Hazārasf was forced to seek refuge with the Ismaʿilis. Šāh-Ardašīr now gave the former kingdom of Kīā Bozorg Dāʿī b. Hādī in Daylamān to an ʿAlid. When Hazārasf killed him in a surprise attack, Šāh-Ardašīr personally led a campaign against him and gave the reign of Rūyān to Hezabr-al-Dīn Ḵᵛoršīd. Hazārasf and his brother Ḵalīl sought refuge with the Saljuq sultan Ṭoḡrel in Hamadān (ca. 581/1185) but failed to get his backing. They were more successful in Ray with the amir Sarāj-al-Dīn Qāymāz who gave Hazārasf his daughter in marriage and an army to reconquer his country. Hazārasf was defeated, however, by Hezabr-al-Dīn. He and his brother then came to Kajū secretly but failed to gain support among the people. Hazārasf surrendered to Šāh-Ardašīr seeking his pardon, and his brother died. He was soon imprisoned by Šāh-Ardašīr at the instigation of his enemies and murdered by Hezabr-al-Dīn who was afraid that Šāh-Ardašīr might return the reign of Rūyān to him. Qāymāz sought permission of his overlord Atābak Moḥammad Pahlavān to avenge his son-in-law's murder but was removed from the governorship of Ray by him (581/1186).

When the grandson of Kaykāʾūs had grown up (ca. 595/1199), Šāh-Ardašīr brought him from Ray with his tutor to Nātel intending to give the reign of Rūyān and Daylamān to him. His plans met opposition in Rūyān, however, and a group of rebels killed his governor Pādešāh-ʿAlī and the prince's tutor and put Bīsotūn b. Nāmāvar (b. Bīsotūn?) on the throne in Kajū. Šāh-Ardašīr suppressed the revolt (ca. 596/1200), and Bīsotūn sought refuge with the Ismaʿilis.

The detailed account of Ebn Esfandīār ends here, and the further history of the dynasty until the middle of the 8th/14th century is known only from the summary and poor account of Awlīāʾ-Allāh Āmolī. The dates of events and reigns given by him must generally be taken with reserve. According to him, Šāh-Ardašīr installed the grandson of Kaykāʾūs, Zarrīnkamar b. Jostān, as ruler of Rūyān, and the latter died in 610/1213-14 after the lapse of the Bavandid reign. His son and successor Bīsotūn undertook a counteroffensive against the rulers of Gīlān, who had expanded into Daylamān, and established his residence for some time in the mountains of Lāhījān. He died in 620/1223. His son Faḵr-al-Dawla Nāmāvar cannot yet have reached adulthood at that time. He is said to have served the Ḵᵛārazmšāh Jalāl-al-Dīn for a year, presumably toward the end of the latter's reign (617-28/1220-31). Returning to his homeland, he brought Rūyān and Daylamān under his control. According to Awlīāʾ-Allāh, he died in 640/1242-43; the date given by Marʿašī, 666/1267-68, is certainly too late. After him his eldest son Ḥosām-al-Dawla Ardašīr ruled Daylamān, while another son, Eskandar, reigned in Nātel in Rūyān. When Ardašīr died (still in 640/1242-43), he was succeeded by a third brother, Šahrāgīm b. Nāmāvar. He was pushed out of Gīlān by an offensive of the local rulers. A final peace agreement established by Namakāvarūd as the border which remained in effect for centuries.

As the Bavandid kingdom of Māzandarān was restored, close ties, strengthened by frequent marriage alliances, were resumed between the *ostandārs* and the kings of Māzandarān. The relation was now, however, more equal, and gradually the Baduspanids gained ascendancy in power as Rūyān was less affected by Mongol interference and control than Māzandarān. Šahrāgīm and the Bavandid king Šams-al-Molūk, his son-in-law, were ordered by the il-khan Abāqā (663-80/1265-82) to join the siege of the Isma'ili stronghold of Gerdkūh. When they deserted, Māzandarān was invaded by Ḡāzān Bahādor. Šahrāgīm surrendered to him, was pardoned, and again joined the siege of Gerdkūh until its seizure in 669/1270. Later he revolted against the Mongol Qotloboḡā and thus provoked the execution of his ally Šams-al-Molūk and a punitive Mongol campaign to Rūyān in which the country was ravaged as never before. He then submitted to the il-khan and recovered his kingdom. His death date is given as 671/1272-73. Nothing remarkable is reported about the reign of his son and successor Faḵr-al-Dawla Nāmāvar Šāh-Ḡāzī who died in 701/1301-02 and was succeeded by his brother Kay Ḵosrow. The latter is said to have had nearly a hundred children and died in 712/1312-13. His son Šams-al-Molūk Moḥammad was a pious ruler who sought the company of religious scholars and founded numerous mosques and *ḵānaqāh*s in Rūyān. He died in 717/1317 and was succeeded by his brother Naṣīr-al-Dīn Šahrīār. The latter built the palace, town, and bazaar of Korkū in Kalārrostāq and carried out three campaigns to Eškevar bringing Daylamān and Garjīān as far as Tīmjān under his sway. He refused all contact with the Il-khanid court and gave aid to the Bavandid Rokn-al-Dawla Šāh-Kay Ḵosrow, his brother-in-law, against the Mongol Amir Mo'men and his son Qotloḡšāh, who had occupied Āmol, and against the powerful Kīā Jalālī family established in Sārī. In 725/1325 he was murdered by his nephew Eskandar at the instigation of his brother Tāj-al-Dawla Zīār b. Šāh-Kay Ḵosrow, who took over the reign giving the rule of Kalārrostāq to Eskandar. His brother 'Ezz-al-Dawla opposed him seeking Il-khanid backing but was defeated. Tāj-al-Dawla died in 734/1333-34 in Kavīr and was succeeded by his son Jalāl-al-Dawla Eskandar, who gave his brother Faḵr-al-Dawla Šāh-Ḡāzī the rule of Nātelrostāq. The disintegration of the Il-khanid empire after the death of Abū Sa'īd in 736/1335 gave him the opportunity to expand to the southern Alborz mountains and to bring the area from Qazvīn to Semnān under his control. He backed the Bavandid Faḵr-al-Dawla Ḥasan in resisting the attempt of Mas'ūd Sarbadār to establish his suzerainty over Māzandarān. When Mas'ūd advanced from Āmol into Rostamdār he was captured and brought before Eskandar who had him executed in 745/1344. In 746/1346 he founded the town of Kojūr as his capital near the ruins of the former town of Kajū (earlier Kajja), which had been destroyed in the early Mongol invasions. He settled many people from Qazvīn and prominent Turkish and Mongol clans from Ray and Šahrīār in different quarters of the town and fortified it with the castle of Šāhdez and a wall. After the murder of his ally, the Bavandid Faḵr-al-Dawla, by the sons of Kīā Afrāsīāb Čalābī in 750/1349, he gave shelter to the Bavandid's minor sons. His attempts to restore them ended in defeat of his army outside Āmol. In 761/1360 he was by mistake wounded by a bodyguard after a commotion at a drinking party and died three days later.

His brother Faḵr-al-Dawla Šāh-Ḡāzī now succeeded to the rule. Ẓahīr-al-Dīn Mar'ašī's information that he continued the feud with the Čalābī Kīās seems anachronistic since Sayyed Qewām-al-Dīn Mar'ašī had killed Kīā Afrāsīāb and expelled his family from Āmol in 760/1359. Faḵr-al-Dawla died in 781/1379 and was succeeded by his son 'Ażod-al-Dawla Qobād. At this time the Mar'ašī *sayyeds* ruling Māzandarān decided to bring Rūyān under their sway and accused the kings of Rostamdār of lack of cooperation and of mistreating the dervishes of their order. In 782/1380 Sayyed Faḵr-al-Dīn b. Qewām-al-Dīn inflicted a defeat on Qobād and seized the coastal plains of Rūyān. In the following year Qobād was killed in a battle at Laktor, and Faḵr-al-Dīn occupied Kojūr which became his permanent residence. The dates given may be some years too late since Ẓahīr-al-Dīn in his further account dates the death of Sayyed Qewām-al-Dīn, who was still alive at the time of these events, in 781/1379. The Mar'ašī *sayyed*s intended to keep Rūyān. However, when Tīmūr's plans to conquer Māzandarān became known in 792/1390, they decided to put the Baduspanid Sa'd-al-Dawla Ṭūs b. Zīār on the throne there in the hope that he would side with them against Eskandar Šayḵī, son of Kīā Afrāsīāb, who accompanied Tīmūr and incited him against the Mar'ašī *sayyed*s. Ṭūs secretly corresponded with Eskandar Šayḵī, however, and in 794/1392 joined the army of Tīmūr in Astarābād. After Tīmūr's conquest of Māzandarān in 795/1393, he successfully pleaded for mercy for the captured *sayyed*s. They were deported, and Eskandar Šayḵī was appointed governor in Āmol by Tīmūr. Ṭūs was, according to Ẓahīr-al-Dīn, murdered by his nephew Eskandar b. Gostahm b. Zīār in 796/1394. It is unknown whether Eskandar succeeded him in the reign. Ẓahīr-al-Dīn elsewhere describes Kayūmarṯ b. Bīsotun b. Gostahm b. Zīār as the immediate successor of Ṭūs, but he must have been too young at this time.

When Eskandar Šayḵī joined Tīmūr's campaign to Azerbaijan in 802/1399-1400, and Tīmūr put his own men in control of most of Rūyān, Kayūmarṯ b. Bīsotūn was left in possession of the castle of Nūr. Eskandar Šayḵī later returned to the fortress of Fīrūzkūh where he revolted against Tīmūr (ca. 804/1802). The leaders of the army sent against him by Tīmūr asked Kayūmarṯ to join them since he was known to be an enemy of Eskandar. They put him in fetters, however, and sent him to Eskandar in the hope of persuading the latter to submit. Eskandar immediately released Kayūmarṯ who went to Šīrāz to the court of Tīmūr's son, where he was well received. After the death of Tīmūr in 807/1405 he was arrested. A few months later he escaped and traveled disguised in a group of *qalandar*s to Nūr. There he killed the Timurid commander of the castle and, with the help of the native populace, gained quickly control over all of Rūyān and Rostamdār. Tīmūr's son Šāhrok̲, who conquered Māzandarān in 809/1407, evidently confirmed his reign and later showed him much favor. During his fifty years' reign he restored the dynasty once more to a role of prominence on the Caspian scene. He converted to Twelver Shi'ism and induced most of his subjects to follow his example. This meant politically a closer association with the Mar'ašī *sayyed*s ruling Māzandarān. Early during his reign (ca. 812/1409) he gave military aid to Sayyed G̲īāt̲-al-Dīn against Sayyed 'Alī Sārī, the chief of the *sayyed*s recognized by Šāhrok̲, and then gave him shelter after his defeat. In 816/1413 he provided G̲īāt̲-al-Dīn's ally Sayyed 'Alī Āmolī, who had been expelled from Āmol by Sayyed 'Alī Sārī, with an army to recover the town. After 'Alī Sārī's death in 820/1417, however, he recognized the latter's son Sayyed Mortażā, concluding an agreement with him. Sayyed Mortażā's son Sayyed Moḥammad married his daughter while his own son Malek Kā'ūs was given the daughter of Sayyed Qewām-al-Dīn Āmolī in marriage. Kayūmart̲ received some border land. In 823/1420 he sent an army at the request of Sayyed Mortażā to aid him against a revolt of Sayyed Naṣīr-al-Dīn. South of the Alborz mountains he raided the territories of Elyās K̲ˇāja, amir of Qom and a powerful vassal of Šāhrok̲, seizing the fortress of Ṭabarak near Ray and attacking Besṭām and Semnān. He neutralized the complaints of Elyās to Šāhrok̲ by repeatedly sending one of his sons with lavish gifts to the latter. Šāhrok̲ eventually sent 'Abd-al-'Alī Bakāvlī with an army to warn Kayūmart̲ and back Elyās if necessary. He was killed in an attack of the army of Rostamdār near Šamīrān. Kayūmart̲ immediately released the son of Elyās, who had been captured in the battle, and other captives with his apology. He also begged Šāhrok̲, who dispatched another army, for pardon and was forgiven on a promise of future restraint. In the west he interfered in the territory of the Kīā'ī *sayyeds* of eastern Gīlān. He seized Alamūt after a brief siege from the Isma'ili imam K̲odāvand Moḥammad and held it for over a year when it was taken by Kīā Moḥammad b. Mahdī Kīā of Lāhījān. In 830/1427 he renewed his raids to Tonakābon and Alamūt. In the following year the army of Gīlān raided and devastated his territories of Ṭāleqān and Qaṣrān. After its withdrawal Kayūmart̲ invaded Tonakābon, burned the residence of its ruler sayyed Dā'ūd Kīā, and killed many of his men including two *sayyed*s of his family. The latter offence in particular gave Kīā Moḥammad cause to seek an alliance with Sayyed Mortażā of Sārī and Elyās K̲ˇāja of Qom for common action against Kayūmart̲. In 832/1429 the latter was attacked from three sides. Routed by the army of Gīlān and wounded, he fled first to Kojūr and Nātel. His territories were divided by the victors between his relatives Malek Nowzar, a grandson of Ṭūs, and Malek Ḥosayn, great-grandson of Jalāl-al-Dawla Eskandar, whose fathers had been killed by him. He now sought refuge with Šāhrok̲ in Herat and persuaded him to intervene for him. On Šāhrok̲'s instruction Kīā Moḥammad returned his land to him except for Ṭāleqān and the fortress of Fālīs. They were given back to him later in 845/1441-42 by Kīā Moḥammad's son Mahdī Kīā when he sought his backing against his brother Nāṣer Kīa. In 840/1436-37 Kayūmart̲ became once more involved in the rivalry among the Mar'ašī *sayyed*s backing Sayyed Ẓahīr-al-Dīn, the author of the history of Māzandarān, in his attempt to wrest the reign of Sārī from Sayyed Mortażā's son Sayyed Moḥammad. When Ẓahīr-al-Dīn and his ally Sayyed Kamāl-al-Dīn Āmolī were defeated by Moḥammad in alliance with Amir Hendkā, Šāhrok̲'s governor of Astarābād, he gave them shelter but soon concluded an agreement with Moḥammad under which he received Mīānrūd in return for a promise not to aid the rebels. After Kamāl-al-Dīn gained control of Āmol and the acquiescence of Moḥammad, Kayūmart̲ aided Kamāl-al-Dīn's rival Sayyed Mortażā and entered Āmol with him. He was forced to flee, however, as the army of Kamāl-al-Dīn counterattacked. He sheltered Sayyed Mortażā until he gained the throne of Āmol after the death of Kamāl-al-Dīn in 849/1445. Kayūmart̲ died in 857/1453.

At first the youngest son of Kayūmart̲, Malek Mozaffar, tried to claim the succession in Kojūr. The eldest surviving son, Malek Kā'ūs, then gained general allegiance. Because of his despotic rule many members of the family soon turned to support another brother, Malek Eskandar. Kā'ūs subdued the revolt with the help of a Gilite army sent by Kīā Moḥammad and exacted a pledge of loyalty from Eskandar. A few months later Mozaffar and another brother, Malek Īraj, again revolted in favor of Eskandar. In spite of some support from Kīā Moḥammad, Kā'ūs was forced to seek refuge with Sayyed 'Abd-al-Karīm Sārī, ruler of Māzandarān. Eskandar sent gifts and pledges of loyalty to the Qara Qoyunlū Jahānšāh in Tabrīz, whose suzerainty was now recognized in Gīlān and Māzandarān. Jahānšāh invested him with the rule of Rostamdār and instructed Kīā Moḥammad to back him. The latter now concluded an alliance with him. When Jahānšāh, however, came on a campaign to Khorasan, 'Abd-al-Karīm joined his army and praised the merits of Kā'ūs so effectively to him that he decided to invest Kā'ūs with the reign. When Jahānšāh returned from his campaign to Astarābād, Mozaffar, sent by Eskandar and the people of Rostamdār, and a messenger of Kīā Moḥammad urged him to change his mind again. Jahānšāh now ordered that the crown land should be equally divided between the brothers and each brother should keep the land he inherited. Kā'ūs returned to Nūr which he had personally inherited and in addition held the castle of Lavāsān in the south. He engaged in a feud with Eskandar who in addition to the former capital controlled most of the father's territories. Faithful to his treaty with Eskandar, Kīā Moḥammad sent Ẓahīr-al-Dīn Mar'ašī three times (860/1456, 865/1461,

867-68/1472-73) with a Gilite army to back him against Kā'ūs. The latter received some ineffective aid from Sayyed Asad-Allāh of Āmol. Kā'ūs finally was forced to send an envoy to Jahāngīr in Tabrīz to seek his intervention. The latter firmly instructed Kīā Moḥammad to bring about a peace settlement between the brothers on the basis of a division of the crown land everywhere leaving Kojūr and Nātel to Eskandar. Kā'ūs died in 871/1467.

His eldest son, Malek Jahāngīr, succeeded and immediately went to Tabrīz to secure the confirmation of the Qara Qoyunlū Jahāngīr leaving his brother Šāhrok̲ as his deputy. Šāhrok̲ was murdered a few months later by one of his own men, and his brother Kay K̲osrow took charge until the return of Jahāngīr. The feud with Eskandar continued off and on until both went to Qom to the court of the Āq Qoyunlū ruler Uzun Ḥasan whose suzerainty was recognized in Gīlān and Māzandarān since 873/1469. Uzun Ḥasan reaffirmed the division of the crown land. Jahāngīr obtained Nātelrostāq in addition to Nūr and Lavāsān, and the other members of the family were given the choice of vassalage to either of the two rulers. In 880/1475 there was renewed strife, and Ẓahīr-al-Dīn was once more sent by Kīā Moḥammad with a Gilite army to aid Eskandar, but a settlement was reached without fighting. Eskandar died in 881/1476. (For a firman of Eskandar dated 21 Rabīʿ II 878/17 October 1473 concerning the endowment of the sanctuary of Shaikh Majd-al-Dīn Kīā Āmolī see Ḥ. Modarresī Ṭabāṭabā'ī, "Haft fermān-e dīgar az pādešāhān-e Torkomān," *Barrasīhā-ye tārīk̲ī* 11/2, 1355 Š./1976, pp. 113-17).

Rostamdār remained divided into the two kingdoms of Kojūr and Nūr ruled by the descendants of Eskandar and Kā'ūs respectively until the Safavid Shah ʿAbbās put an end to both dynasties. Both dynasties were weakened by the division, and the Kīā'ī rulers of Gīlān were able to maintain a protectorate over Rostamdār exacting military allegiance which was later overshadowed by Safavid power. They usually had close relations with and backed the rulers of Kojūr, who as the principal line claimed the title of *malek-al-molūk*, while the rulers of Nūr offered an aggressive opposition and were often allied to the Marʿašī *sayyed*s of Māzandarān. The dynasty of Kojūr continued after Eskandar as follows:

1. Malek Tāj-al-Dawla b. Eskandar (881-97/1476-92). In 892/1487 he obeyed the instructions of the Āq Qoyunlū Yaʿqūb, who was present in Daylamān, to prevent the Marʿašī Sayyed ʿAbd-al-Karīm of Sārī from passing through Rostamdār to return to Māzandarān and was rewarded with the allegiance of Malek Shah G̱āzī, lord of Kalārrostāq, who had previously been a vassal of Malek Jahāngīr of Nūr.

2. Malek Ašraf b. Tāj-al-Dawla (897-915/1492-1509). In 897/1492 he joined the army sent by the Kīā'ī ruler of Gīlān, Mīrzā ʿAlī, to Māzandarān in support of the Marʿašī Mīr ʿAbd-al-Karīm against Mīr Šams-al-Dīn of Sārī. After initial success the campaign of Mīrzā ʿAlī's army ended in disaster. He also participated in the second Gīlāni campaign to Māzandarān in 899/1494 which was more successful. About 903/1497-98 he was with the Gīlāni army dispatched by Mīrzā ʿAlī which vainly besieged the fortress of Ṭārom. About 910/1504 Malek Bīsotūn of Nūr opened a new offensive against the rival dynasty seizing most of Rostamdār and laying siege to Kojūr which was defended by Ašraf's son Kā'ūs. In 913/1507 Ašraf and his brother Malek Abū Saʿīd came to Sultan Aḥmad Khan, the new Kīā'ī ruler of Gīlān, to request his help against Bīsotūn. With a Gīlāni army they laid siege to Bīsotūn's castle of Harsī. The castle surrendered after arrival of the news of Bīsotūn's murder in Nūr and the succession of his son Bahman. Aḥmad Khan gave Harsī to Ašraf and Barār, another castle belonging to Bīsotūn, to Abū Saʿīd. Shortly afterwards Aḥmad Khan received Kā'ūs b. Ašraf in Lammasar and, at the request of Ašraf, recognized him as heir apparent and concluded a treaty with him. Ašraf soon quarreled with his son, who refused to relinquish Kojūr to him. In 915/1509 Kā'ūs imprisoned Ašraf and won the approval of Aḥmad Khan who at the same time agreed to the request of Malek Bahman for the return of the castle of Harsī to him. A year later Ašraf escaped and found refuge with Āqā Rostam Rūzafzūn, ruler of Māzandarān. Kā'ūs requested help from Aḥmad Khan who, however, was unable to respond as he was on the way to the Safavid court in Qazvīn. Before he returned Ašraf had taken possession of Lārejān. Nothing further is known about his fate until his death in 921/1515.

3. Malek Kā'ūs b. Ašraf (915-50/1509-43). His relations with Aḥmad Khan were close, and in 920/1514 marriage ties were established between them. In 921/1515 the truce which Aḥmad Khan had arranged between Kā'ūs and Bahman was broken by the latter. Aḥmad Khan offered to mediate but received an insolent answer from Bahman. Only when Kā'ūs laid siege to Harsī, Bahman apologized to Aḥmad Khan. The latter bade both kings to his court and arranged a reconciliation. In 929/1523 both kings joined Mīr ʿAbd-al-Karīm Marʿašī of Sārī for a visit to the court of Shah Esmāʿīl. According to Nūr-Allāh Šoštarī he was perhaps poisoned by his son Kayūmart̲, who had been imprisoned by him for eighteen years.

4. Malek Kayūmart̲ b. Kā'ūs (950-63/1543-56). He reigned at first, in his father's lifetime, in Lārejān. At this time he invaded western Māzandarān in support of Mīr Sultan Morād Marʿašī when he tried to establish his ruler there. Later he came to the court of Mīr ʿAbd-Allāh Marʿašī in Sārī and cooperated with him in the murder of Sayyed ʿAzīz Bābolkānī. After the death of his father Kā'ūs, his uncle Bīsotūn b. Ašraf at first succeeded him in Kojūr. As he had earlier killed his brother Eskandar and now killed his own son Jahāngīr, the people revolted against him in favor of Kayūmart̲. When Mīr Qewām-al-Dīn Marʿašī after the murder of his brother Zayn-al-ʿĀbedīn by Mīr ʿAbd-Allāh sought refuge in Kojūr, Kayūmart̲ established close ties with him giving him his daughter in marriage. (For a *fatḥ-nāma* addressed to him by the Safavid Shah Ṭahmāsb in Moḥarram, 956/February, 1549 see ʿAbd-al-Ḥosayn

Navā'ī, *Šāh Ṭahmāsb Ṣafawī*, Tehran, 1350 Š./1971, pp. 173-87).

5. Malek Jahāngīr b. Kā'ūs (963-75/1556-68). He reigned in Kojūr while his nephew Bahman b. Kayūmarṯ ruled Lārejān which became independent of Kojūr. Jahāngīr was married to an aunt of Khan Aḥmad Khan b. Ḥasan Khan of Gīlān.

6. Malek Sultan Moḥammad b. Jahāngīr (975-98/1568-90). He became an adherent of the Noqṭawī heresy and was accused of claiming divinity. According to Shaikh 'Alī Gīlānī he abolished prayer and fasting in Rostamdār, and his subjects "drank his urine." He was at odds with Khan Aḥmad Khan of Gīlān, his maternal cousin, concerning the rule of Tonakābon, and about 992/1584 routed a Gīlāni army sent by him. (For two letters exchanged between Moḥammad and Khan Aḥmad see Navā'ī, *Šāh Ṭahmāsb Ṣafawī*, pp. 113-17). In 985/1577 he received and entertained Mīr 'Alī Khan b. Qewām-al-Dīn Mar'ašī, his paternal cousin, who was engaged in a struggle for the reign of Māzandarān with Mīrzā Moḥammad Khan b. Morād Khan. After the death of 'Alī Khan, who had become ruler of Māzandarān, in 989/1581, he interfered in Māzandarān in competition with his cousin Malek Bahman of Lārejān. He seized and pillaged Sārī but withdrew after learning of the approach of Mīr Ḥosayn Khan b. Ḥasan Mar'ašī who had been appointed by the Safavid Shah Moḥammad to govern Māzandarān. After Mīr Ḥosayn's murder in 992/1584 he again invaded Māzandarān initially invited by Bahman who, however, became apprehensive about his aims and left as he approached. Moḥammad brought Māzandarān under his sway burning and looting everywhere. About 994/1586 he also captured Nūr putting its ruler Malek 'Azīz with most of his family to death and seized the castle which Bahman had built for himself in Āmol. Before his death he gradually lost control of Māzandarān as his general Ḵ᷾āja Ḡarībšāh was killed and a fortress he built in Bārforūšdeh fell.

7. Malek Jahāngīr b. Moḥammad. In 1002/1593 he came to the court of Shah 'Abbās and became a favorite boon companion of his. In 1003/1594 he murdered two prominent men from Gīlān at the shah's signal during a drinking party in Qazvīn. He was forced to flee and entrenched himself in the castle of Kojūr. According to one account he was besieged there in 1004/1595, escaped, and was captured after forty days of hiding. Shah 'Abbās ordered Malek Ḥasan Lavāsānī, a Baduspanid loyal to the shah, to kill him on 22 Jomādā I 1004/23 January 1596. According to another account the siege of Kojūr took place in 1006/1598-99. Jahāngīr escaped to some other castles and was eventually captured and killed in the same year together with his brothers Malek Kā'ūs and Malek Ašraf.

Malek Bahman of Lārejān was closely associated with Mīr 'Alī Mar'ašī, his nephew, during his reign in Māzandarān (985-89/1577-81) and spent much time at his court. He vainly incited him to revolt against the Qezelbāš and Safavid rule. Later he betrayed him together with some Māzandarāni opponents of the Mar'ašī *sayyeds*. He continued interfering in Māzandarān during the reign of Mīr Ḥosayn Khan who was murdered in 992/1584 by Bahman's allies. As Malek Moḥammad of Kojūr gained control of much of Māzandarān, Bahman's influence was reduced and he lost the castle he had built for himself in Āmol to his nephew. After the latter's death (998/1590) he recovered it and continued to cause trouble in Māzandarān even after he had been graciously received by Shah 'Abbās. When the shah's general Farhād Khan occupied Māzandarān in 1005/1596-97, he met some resistence at the castle of Āmol and, after its surrender, was ordered to proceed against Bahman in Lārejān. Bahman surrendered after a brief siege on a promise of safety. Shah 'Abbās kept him first in Isfahan and then handed him over to Ḥosayn Lavāsānī in Qazvīn who killed him in 1006/1597-98 in revenge for his earlier attack on Lavāsān and his murder of Ḥosayn's brother Ḥasan Lavāsānī. Bahman's seventeen-year-old son Kay Ḵosrow now surrendered the fortress of Samankūr. Shah 'Abbās handed him and his brothers and family to Ḥosayn Lavāsānī who killed all of them.

The rulers of Nūr, descendants of Kā'ūs, b. Kayūmarṯ, were:

1. Malek Jahāngīr b. Kā'ūs (871-904/1467-99). He refused to join the Gīlāni campaign to Māzandarān in 897/1492 and shortly afterwards sent an army to aid an invader of the territories of Mīrzā 'Alī of Gīlān at Lammasar. In retaliation Mīrzā 'Alī ordered four punitive campaigns to Nātel and Nūr which ravaged Jahāngīr's territories and besieged him in Nūr (901-03/1496-98). He was finally forced to sue for peace, and his son Kā'ūs came to the court of Mīrzā 'Alī to conclude the treaty.

2. Malek Bīsotūn b. Jahāngīr (904-13/1499-1507). Jahāngīr had appointed his son Kā'ūs as his successor but he was opposed by his brother Bīsotūn. Kā'ūs asked Mīrzā 'Alī for support in accordance with their treaty of friendship. A joint army besieged Bīsotūn in the castle of Dārnā. The siege ended in failure because of disunity among the allies, and Kā'ūs was captured and killed by Bīsotūn. A second attack on Dārnā by Mīrzā 'Alī's army also failed. Bīsotūn's successful offensive against Malek Ašraf of Kojūr has been described. He was widely hated and feared for his brutality and was murdered while drunk by one of his wives whose family he had killed.

3. Malek Bahman b. Bīsotūn (913-57/1507-50). He was put on the throne by his family after his father's murder. In 915/1509 he sent an envoy to Sultan Aḥmad Khan seeking an end to the long hostility between the rulers of Gīlān and Nūr. A treaty of friendship was concluded and Aḥmad Khan returned the fortress of Harsī to him. Bahman married a sister of Aḥmad Khan. He was also married to a milk-sister of Sayyed 'Abd-al-Karīm Mar'ašī, ruler of Māzandarān, and had a treaty of alliance with him. In 917/1511 he sent an army to back him in subduing Sārī. In 929/1532 he joined him for a visit of the court of Shah Esmā'īl. His quarrel with Malek Kā'ūs of Kojūr in 921/1515 has been mentioned

His sister was married to Mīr Sultan Maḥmud, son of Mīr ʿAbd-al-Karīm, who came to Nūr seeking his support after ʿAbd-al-Karīm's death in 932/1526 against Maḥmūd's brother Mīr Šāhī, who succeeded to the rule in Sārī. As Maḥmūd died soon, Bahman gave his son Mīr ʿAbd-Allāh, his own nephew, some ineffective help to gain control of Māzandarān. Later after Mīr ʿAbd-Allāh had been established as ruler of Māzandarān, he counseled him and sent some of his men to assist him in the murder of Sayyed Mīr Zayn-al-ʿĀbedīn whose popularity Mīr ʿAbd-Allāh feared. Bahman is said to have killed nearly forty members of his own family.

4. Malek Kayūmarṯ b. Bahman. He received his cousin Mīr ʿAbd-Allāh Marʿašī when he was on his way to the Safavid court after surrendering Māzandarān to Mīr Sultan Morād about 967/1560. When Morād after murdering ʿAbd-Allāh in 968/1561 decided to send the latter's daughter, who was to become the mother of Shah ʿAbbās, to the Safavid court, Kayūmarṯ went to Māzandarān to protest, warning that her marriage to a Safavid prince might result in a claim of their son to Māzandarān and Rostamdār. Soon afterwards he sheltered ʿAbd-Allāh's son ʿAbd-al-Karīm after the latter had vainly tried to establish himself in Āmol against Morād. He assisted ʿAbd-al-Karīm in a second attempt, invaded Māzandarān and defeated Morād in Savādkūh. ʿAbd-al-Karīm ruled western Māzandarān for some time, but in 973/1565-66 Morād expelled him and regained control. He now established close relations with Kayūmarṯ; his daughter was married to Malek Bahman, eldest son of Kayūmarṯ, and his son, Mīrzā Moḥammad Khan, married a daughter of Kayūmarṯ. The latter received Mīrzā Moḥammad after he had revolted against his father and brought about a reconciliation. In 983/1575 Morād visited him after Malek Bahman had been killed by one of his own men. Morād's daughter, widow of Bahman, now was married to his brother Malek ʿAzīz. Kayūmarṯ also visited Mīrzā Moḥammad Khan after his succession to the rule of Māzandarān in 984/1576. He probably died soon afterwards. He is said to have repeatedly visited the court of Shah Ṭahmāsb.

5. Malek Sultan ʿAzīz b. Kayūmarṯ. About 990/1582 Mīr Šams-al-Dīn b. Mīr Ebrāhīm, a nephew of Mīr Morād Khan, came to him from Qazvīn seeking his aid on the basis of his blood relationship. ʿAzīz provided him with an army led by Malek Bīsotūn of Kalārrostāq. They were defeated, however, in Māzandarān, and Šams-al-Dīn was killed by Malek Bahman of Lārejān. ʿAzīz was killed together with five sons, a brother, and a nephew by Moḥammad b. Jahāngīr of Kojūr when the latter seized Nūr about 994/1586.

6. Malek Jahāngīr b. ʿAzīz. He came in 1002/1593-94 to the court of Shah ʿAbbās and voluntarily surrendered his possession to him. Shah ʿAbbās gave him an estate near Sāva where he remained until his death.

Bibliography: Ebn Esfandīār. Awlīāʾ-Allāh Āmolī, *Tārīḵ-e Rūyān*, ed. M. Sotūda, (Tehran) 1348 Š./1969. Ẓahīr-al-Dīn Marʿašī, *Tārīḵ-e Gīlān*, ed. M. Sotūda, (Tehran) 1347 Š./1968. Idem, *Tārīḵ-e Ṭabarestān wa Rūyān wa Māzandarān*. ʿAlī b. Šams-al-Dīn, *Tārīḵ-e Ḵānī*. ʿAbd-al-Fattāḥ Fūmanī, *Tārīḵ-e Gīlān*. Eskandar Monšī, *Tārīḵ-e ʿālamārā-ye ʿabbāsī*. The last four in B. Dorn, *Muhammedanische Quellen zur Geschichte der südlichen Küstenländer des kaspischen Meeres*, vols. 1-4, St. Petersburg, 1850-58, or subsequent editions. Nūr-Allāh Šoštarī, *Majāles al-moʾmenīn*, Tehran, 1352 Š./1973, II, pp. 390-95. Mollā Shaikh ʿAlī Gīlānī, *Tārīḵ-e Māzandarān*, ed. M. Sotūda, Tehran, 1352 Š./1973, pp. 80-90. Mīr Tīmūr Marʿašī, *Tārīḵ-e ḵāndān-e Marʿašī-e Māzandarān*, ed. M. Sotūda, [Tehran, 1977]. H. L. Rabino, "Les dynasties du Mazandaran," *JA* 228, 1936, pp. 443-74.

(W. Madelung)

BĀFQ, a small oasis town of central Iran (altitude 3,293 feet/1,004 m) on the southern fringe of the Dašt-e Kavīr, 62 miles/100 km southeast of Yazd in the direction of Kermān. Brackish water is supplied from *qanāt*s and springs, and the main local activities are agriculture and weaving; some well-known iron deposits lie to the north of the town. It is now the administrative center of a *baḵš* of the same name in the province of Yazd; about 1950 the population of the *baḵš* was 14,273 and of the town of Bāfq 6,228.

The early Islamic history of Bāfq is obscure, and the greater events of Iranian history passed it by, lying as it does to the north of the main Yazd-Kermān highway. The medieval Arabic and Persian geographers mention a Bāft of Bāfd, but this must clearly be the small place in Kermān province between Kermān town and Sīrjān: thus in the *Ḥodūd al-ʿālam*, tr. Minorsky, p. 124, Bāft and Ḵīr, are placed between Sīrjān and Jīroft, and in Yāqūt, *Boldān*, (Beirut) I, p. 326, Bāft, and II, pp. 344, 346, Ḵabq and Babq are in the Ḵabīṣ district (cf. Schwarz, *Iran*, pp. 227-28, 252, and for the modern town of Bāft, Razmārā, *Farhang* VIII, pp. 39-40).

Nevertheless, the more northerly Bāfq near Yazd undoubtedly existed in the Saljuq period, for it is several times mentioned, in contexts where its geographical position is certain (see Moḥammad b. Ebrāhīm's *Tārīḵ-e Saljūqīān-e Kermān*, ed. M.-E. Bāstānī Pārīzī, Tehran, 1343 Š./1964, e.g., pp. 40, 109, 180 [mentioned with Kūhbanān, Rāvar, and Behābād as places handed over to the atabeg of Yazd in the time of the Oghuz ruler in Kermān in the second half of the 6th/12th century, Malek Dīnār], 181 [the latter's military operations there]). In the reign of Shah ʿAbbās, musketeers (*tofangčīān*) from the Bāfq district are mentioned as distinguishing themselves in warfare with the Ottomans in Transcaucasia in 1016/1607-08 (Aḥmad-ʿAlī Khan Wazīrī, *Tārīḵ-e Kermān* [*Sālārīya*], ed. Bāstānī Pārīzī, Tehran, 1340 Š./1961, p. 281).

Bibliography: See also Le Strange, *Lands*, p. 310. Razmārā, *Farhang* X, pp. 34-35. Dehḵodā, letter *bāʾ*, pp. 492-93.

(C. E. Bosworth)

BĀFQĪ, AYATOLLAH **MOḤAMMAD-TAQĪ** (1292-1365/1875-1946), a religious scholar known for his forthright opposition to Reżā Shah Pahlavī. Born to a merchant, Ḥājj Moḥammad Bāqer, in the small town of Bāfq near Yazd, Bāfqī, began his religious studies at the age of 14 when he went to Yazd to study *feqh* and *oṣūl* with Ḥājj Mīrzā Sayyed ʿAlī Labḵandaqī. Fourteen years later, he proceeded to Najaf, completing his study of those subjects with such masters as Āḵūnd Moḥammad Kāẓem Ḵorāsānī and Āḵūnd Moḥammad Kāẓem Yazdī and studying Hadith with the great traditionist, Ḥājj Mīrzā Ḥosayn Nūrī. After seventeen years in Najaf, he went to Karbalā to study ethics with Ḥājj Sayyed Aḥmad Mūsawī Karbalāʾī before returning to Iran in 1336/1917-18 or 1337/1918-19. He settled in Qom, taking up residence in the Bāḡ-e Panba quarter, and began attempts to revive the religious teaching institution (*ḥawża*) of the city, in collaboration with Shaikh Abu'l-Qāsem Kabīr and Ayatollah Fayż.

These efforts bore fruit in 1340/1922, when Shaikh ʿAbd-al-Karīm Ḥāʾerī arrived in Qom and was persuaded by a number of *ʿolamāʾ*, headed by Bāfqī, to remain there and devote himself to the revival of the *ḥawża*. Bāfqī became one of Ḥāʾerī's chief aides, with particular responsibility for providing the growing number of *ṭollāb* with clothing. In addition, he presided over the building of three new mosques, sometimes participating himself in the labor of construction. He also made his presence felt in Qom by engaging energetically in *amr be maʿrūf wa nahy az monkar* (commanding the good and forbidding the evil); he was able, for example, to exact from the barbers of Qom an undertaking not to shave anyone's beard (beardlessness being traditionally regarded as reprehensible, particularly for religious students and scholars). At one point, the government attempted to prohibit such activity on the part of Bāfqī and other *ʿolamāʾ*, but when he responded with an angry sermon denouncing Reżā Shah as comparable to the pharaohs, the government temporarily retreated. Not content with such oral condemnation, Bāfqī is said to have written to the monarch several times, demanding that he change policies viewed by the *ʿolamāʾ* as incompatible with Islam.

The conflict between Bāfqī and Reżā Shah came to a head in 1346/1928 when a party of women from the court came bareheaded to the shrine in Qom to watch the Nowrūz ceremonies of that year. Informed of their presence, Bāfqī—who was preaching in the shrine courtyard at the time—sent the women a message objecting to their presence in the shrine in that state and demanding their withdrawal. News of the incident was telegraphed to Tehran, and Reżā Shah came immediately to Qom, together with an armored unit led by Teymūrtāš, minister of the court. The shrine was surrounded, and Teymūrtāš was sent inside, still wearing his boots, to drag Bāfqī down from the pulpit and arrest him. Reżā Shah personally kicked and reviled him, and he was sent off to prison in Tehran. After a few months he was released, but compelled to reside in the shrine of Shah ʿAbd-al-ʿAẓīm in southern Tehran. However, he was able to visit Mašhad in 1353/1935-36.

Bāfqī regained his freedom of movement with the deposition of Reżā Shah in 1941. Returning briefly to Qom, he was instrumental in preventing the opening of a liquor store in the city. From Qom he proceeded to the shrine cities of Iraq for a stay of eleven months, but it was in Shah ʿAbd-al-ʿAẓīm that he spent the last years of his life. He died on 12 Jomādā I, 1365/3 August 1946, and was buried in Qom next to Shaikh ʿAbd-al-Karīm Ḥāʾerī.

Bāfqī's angry response to the presence of bareheaded women in the shrine at Qom in 1928 is held by some to have helped delay for some eight years the unveiling of women. In general, his fearlessness in confronting Reżā Shah made a considerable impact on the *ḥawza* in Qom; thus Ayatollah Ḵomeynī, in the lectures on ethics he gave there in the 1930s, would hold up Bāfqī as an example to be emulated.

Bibliography: Āqā Bozorg Ṭehrānī, *Ṭabaqāt aʿlām al-šīʿa*, Najaf, 1373/1954, I/1, pp. 248-49. Sh. Akhavi, *Religion and Politics in Contemporary Iran*, Albany, NY, 1980, pp. 41-42. P. W. Avery, *Modern Iran*, London, 1965, p. 288 (Avery's account of Bāfqī's clash with the court women is garbled, and places it in the wrong year). ʿA. Davānī, *Nehżat-e rūḥānīyūn-e Īrān*, Qom, 1360 Š./1981, II, pp. 156-57. Michael M. J. Fischer, *Iran: From religious Dispute to Revolution*, Cambridge, Mass., 1980, pp. 112, 129 (Fischer also gives a wrong date for the incident with the court women). ʿA. Rabbānī Ḵalḵālī, *Šohadā-ye rūḥānīyat-e šīʿa dar yek ṣad sāl-e aḵīr*, Qom, 1402/1982, pp. 154-57. M. Šarīf Rāzī, *Āṯār al-ḥojja*, Qom, 1332 Š./1953, I, pp. 31-36. Idem, *Ganjīna-ye dānešmandān*, Tehran, 1352 Š./1973, I, pp. 286-87.

(H. ALGAR)

BĀḠ "garden."

i. *Etymology.*
ii. *General.*
iii. *InPersian literature.*
iv. *In Afghanistan.*
(For *Bāḡ in Persian art*, see GARDEN.)

i. ETYMOLOGY

Bāḡ, the Middle and New Persian word for "garden," as also the Sogdian *βāγ*, strictly meant "piece" or "patch of land," corresponding to the Gathic Avestan neuter noun *bāga-* "share," "lot" (*Y.* 51.1; see Ch. Bartholomae, *Altiranisches Wörterbuch*, Strassburg, 1904, col. 952) and to the Old Indian masculine noun *bhāgá-* "share," "possession," "lot," which appears in Kauṭilya's *Arthaśāstra* with the similar connotation of a share in landed properties. Comparable semantic development is shown by the Hebrew *ḥēleq* "share," which came to mean 'field" (not to be confused with the Akkadian *eqlum* and Arabic *ḥaql* "field") and by the Greek *ho klḗros* and *tò méros*. In the Talmud the aramaicized word *bāḡā* has the meaning "common land" (G. Dalman, *Aramäisch-Neuhebräisches Wörterbuch*, Frankfurt, 1901, p. 45). On account of the chaotic state of the text at the end of chapter 2 of the *Frahang ī pahlavīk*, evidence of a Pahlavi ideogram is lacking (W. Eilers, *ZDMG* 90, 1936, p. 164 n. 3. G. R. Driver, *Aramaic Documents of the Fifth Century B.C.*, Oxford, 1954, p. 110).

The diminutive *bāḡča* means "small garden" or "vegetable patch." In the northwestern dialects of today, as also in earlier periods, *bāḡ* has had a rival in the New and Middle Persian *raz* "vineyard." This word is written with the ideogram KARMĀ in the *Frahang ī pahlavīk* and also appears in the Awroman and Nisa documents (W. Eilers and M. Mayrhofer, "Kurdisch *būz* und die indogermanische 'Buchen'-Sippe...," *Mitteilungen für die Anthropologische Gesellschaft Wien* 92, 1962, p.92. W. Eilers and U. Schapka, *Mitteliranische Mundarten aus der Sammlung W. Eilers* I: *Die Mundart von Chunsar*, Wiesbaden, 1976, p. 379.

The old word for "garden" *paridaiza-* (Old Persian **paridayda-*), literally "walled" (whence *pardēz*, Greek *hò parádeisos* "park for animals," "paradise," Arabic *ferdaws*) survives in the New Persian *pālīz* "vegetable garden," "melon bed," though today this most often denotes an unenclosed patch.

Other words for "garden" are the New Persian *būstān* (from *bōδistān*, whence the Armenian *burastan*), literally "place of perfume," Arabic *bostān* (plur. *basātīn*), and *golestān* "rose garden" or "flower garden." (On the relationship to the Arabic words, see W. Eilers, *Die vergleichend-semasiologische Methode in der Orientalistik*, Abh. der Mainzer Akademie der Wissenschaften, Mainz, 1974, pp. 24f.).

In toponymy, *bāḡ* occurs frequently in either the fore or the rear position, e.g., Bāḡ-e Amīr, Bāḡ-e Now, or Kārīzbāḡ, Nowbāḡ. In Turcophone areas, the same suffixed form is sometimes found, e.g., Qarābāḡ, but less frequently than the compound ending, e.g., Malekbāḡī, Morādbāḡī, which also appears in Kurdish toponyms and tribal names, e.g., Gelbāḡī (explained by folk etymology in the *Šaraf-nāma* as "come into the garden!"). Derivatives such as *bāḡča*, *bāḡestān*, *bāḡū(k)* also enter into place-names.

The long duration of the rivalry between *bāḡ* and *raz* is shown by the use of Dadbaka-bag side by side with Dadbaka-ras as names of cultivable lands in the Greek Awroman documents (q.v.).

(W. EILERS)

ii. GENERAL

In Iranian agriculture, the word *bāḡ*, though usually translated as "garden," means more precisely an enclosed area bearing permanent cultures—i.e., all kinds of cultivated trees and shrubs, as opposed to fields under annual crops (*zamīn-e zīr-e kešt* or *kešt-e sālāna*)—in land-use statistics (the *Village Gazetteer* of 1966) as well as in everyday speech. It includes orchards (*bāḡ-e mīva*) vineyards (*bāḡ-e mow*), olivegroves (*bāḡ-e zeytūn*), tea plantations (*bāḡ-e čāy*), but not vegetable gardens (*sabzīkārī* or *ṣayfīkārī*).

The most conspicuous and best-known form is the irrigated gardens of old sedentary settlements (piedmont oases and mountain villages) in interior Iran and Afghanistan (Planhol, 1964, p. 96). Whatever the water source may be (*qanāt*, *nahr* diverted from a stream, spring or well), the gardens are usually clustered together close to the head-race of the irrigation network, around the village or just below it (examples in English, 1966, pp. 53-54; Berthaud, 1968, p. 300; Balland, 1974, p. 177; Bazin, 1974, p. 45 etc.). This location allows to irrigate them as frequently as possible, every six to twelve days in the hot season, whereas the fields lying underneath are much less often irrigated. The small or large plots are generally enclosed with high mud walls, or terraced in hilly areas, and served by a dense network of footpaths and irrigation channels. Most gardens are not cultivated between the trees, but some are sown with grass or alfalfa or include small patches of vegetables. Wheat and other staple crops are sown in gardens only in mountain settlements having too scarce cropland. Temporary dwellings may be built in remote gardens (Balland, 1974, pp. 178-79).

Gardens of arid Iran and Afghanistan can be divided into three climatic levels (called *Höhenstufen* by Ehlers, 1980a, p. 225): 1. Hot lands of the *garmsīr*, within the limit of date-palm cultivation, where the main crops are dates and citrus fruit, as in Bam and Narmāšīr (Fecharaki, 1976). 2. Still warm lands of the piedmonts and interior basins, up to about 1500 meters high, as around Qom (Bazin, 1974) or Kermān (English, 1966), with pomegranate and figs, pistachio in the dryest places, vineyards in better watered areas, and olive trees in a quite limited district around Rūdbār and Manjīl (Bazin, 1980, II, pp. 113-15). 3. Colder level (*sardsīr*) of valleys and intramontane basins, e.g., in central Alborz (Hourcade and Tual, 1979, pp. 59-61 and map 19), or West and East Azerbaijan (respectively Berthaud, 1968, pp. 315-17, and Bazin, 1980, II, pp. 98-101). The proportion of cultivable land devoted to gardens is low on average: about 10 percent around Kermān (English, 1966), but varies considerably, both regionally and locally. The highest proportion occurs in villages or districts having the best water resources, such as the central part of the Isfahan oasis (Planhol, 1969, p. 394).

Settlements of newly sedentarized nomads can often be recognized by the lack of or the very small size of their gardens, e.g., the Paštūn villages south of Ḡaznī (Balland, 1974, pp. 176-77).

A quite different pattern occurs in the Caspian provinces of Iran (Ehlers, 1971): there the low-lying irrigable lands are exclusively devoted to rice cultivation, and the gardens, always rainfed, appear to be a part of the "pluvial lands" (Bazin, 1980, I, p. 146) stretching on foothills or alluvial embankments (see aerial photographs nos. 1 and 2 in Sahami, 1965). These pluvial lands are a mosaic of small plots surrounded by hedges, where gardens intermingle with scattered houses, wheat and tobacco fields, meadows, and remnants of forests. Besides all kinds of temperate fruit

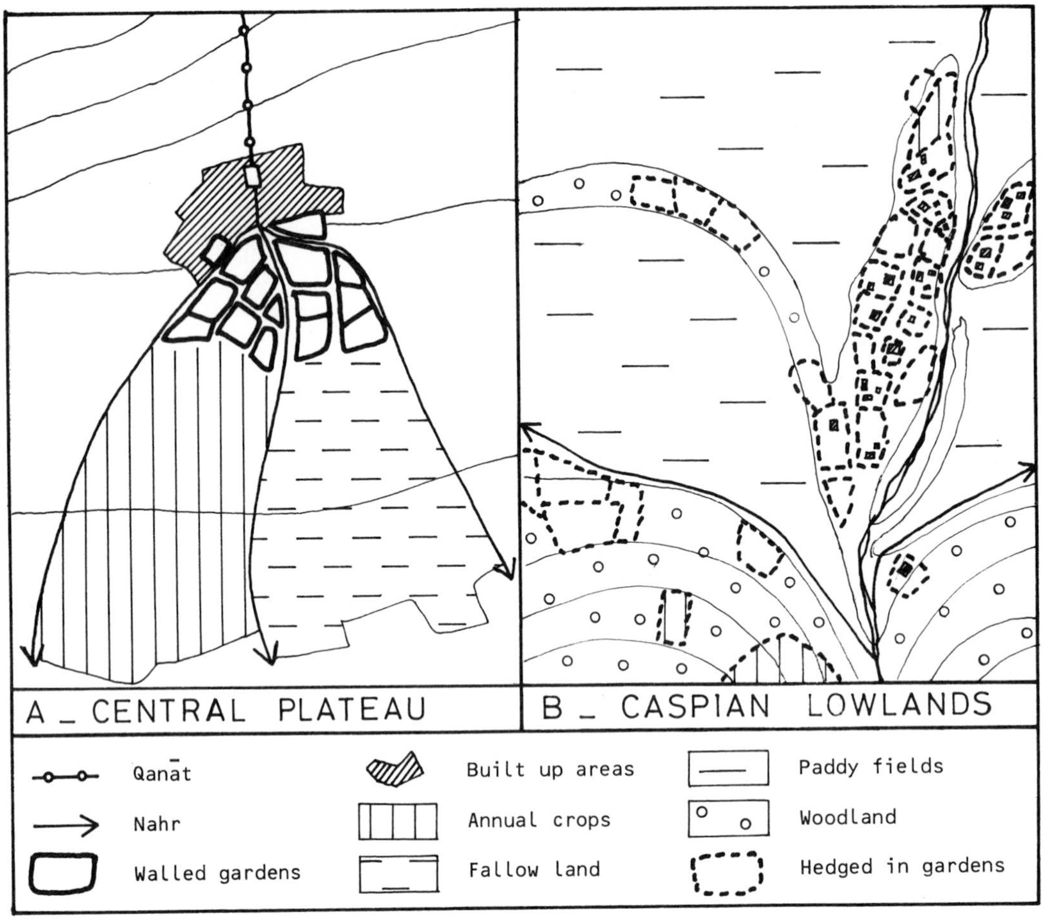

Figure 10. The two types of garden location in Iran

species, three more specific crops occupy extensive areas in some specialized districts: mulberry trees (the leaves of which are gathered to breed silkworms) in western and eastern Gīlān; tea in Fūmanāt and especially south of Lāhījān (Ehlers, 1971); citrus fruit in easternmost Gīlān and western Māzandarān (Asif, 1977).

Gardens differ also from fields with respect to their socio-economic status. In the traditional feudal-like agrarian society, the landlords could exploit their *bāğs* in several ways (Lambton, 1953, pp. 323-25): they could be worked by the same sharecroppers as the fields, but the tenants often paid a heavier share to the landlord, for instance 3/4 instead of 2/3 in some villages around Qom (Bazin, 1974, p. 56), and generally paid it in cash and not in kind; other gardens were given to specialized gardeners (*bāğdār* or *bāğbān*), with whom either the produce or the trees were shared by half (Lambton, 1969, pp. 197-98); some were directly cultivated by the landlord hiring wage laborers (*rūz mozd*), or leased to a third person, particularly around large cities. In some cases, a peasant might have planted trees that became his own property (*aʿyān*), with rights distinct from the land (*ʿarṣa*) belonging to the landlord (Lambton, 1969, p. 26) or even possess a small garden in full property.

The gardens were mostly excluded from expropriation in the three successive stages of the Iranian land reform (Lambton, 1969, pp. 68 and 221; Ehlers, 1979, pp. 444-45), unless the peasants possessed the *aʿyān*. In many oases of central Iran, all the landlords' interests and efforts focused upon gardens, something which led to a more intensive exploitation of existing gardens, while the surrounding fields distributed to their former tenants fell into decay, owing to an insufficient supply of water (Ehlers, 1980b). On the other hand, the large agro-business estates created after 1970, often in connection with dams and large irrigation schemes, paid little attention to gardening, except for a few mulberry plantations in the Caspian lowlands. More and more inhabitants of large cities such as Tehran have bought gardens in order to build summer dwellings or tourist accommodations in a pleasant environment (Hourcade, 1979, p. 132).

Bibliography: M. I. Asif, "Growing citrus in Iran," *World Crops and Livestock* 29/4, 1977, pp. 165-

67. D. Balland, "Vieux sédentaires tadjik et immigrants pachtoun dans le sillon de Ghazni (Afghanistan oriental)," *Bulletin de l'Association de géographes français* 417-18, 1974, pp. 171-80. M. Bazin, *La vie rurale dans la région de Qom*, Paris, 1974. Idem, *Le Tâlech, une région ethnique au nord de l'Iran*, Paris, 1980, 2 vols. E. Berthaud, "La vie rurale dans quelques villages chrétiens de l'Azerbaidjan occidental," *Revue de géographie de Lyon* 43/3, 1968, pp. 291-331. E. Ehlers, "Die Teelandschaft von Lahidjan/Nordiran," in *Beiträge zur Geographie der Tropen und Subtropen*, Tübinger Geographische Schriften 34, Tübingen, 1970, pp. 229-42. Idem, "Nordpersische Agrarlandschaft. Landnutzung und Sozialstruktur in Ghilan und Mazanderan," *Geographische Rundschau* 23/9, 1971, pp. 329-42. Idem, "Die iranische Agrarreform. Voraussetzungen, Ziele und Ergebnisse," in H. Elsenhans, ed., *Agrarreform in der Dritten Welt*, Frankfurt and New York, 1979, pp. 433-70. Idem, *Iran. Grundzüge einer geographischen Landeskunde*, Darmstadt, 1980a. Idem, "The dying oases of central Iran—A Few Remarks on Causes and Consequences," in W. Meckelein, ed., *Desertification in Extremely Arid Environments*, Stuttgarter Geographische Studien 95, Stuttgart, 1980, pp. 65-71. P. W. English, *City and Village in Iran. Settlement and Economy in the Kirman Basin*, Madison, Milwaukee, and London, 1966. P. Fecharaki, "Les oasis des plaines de la région de Bam et du Narmâchir (Lut méridional, Iran)," *Cahiers d'Outre-Mer* 29, 1976, pp. 70-101. P. Gentelle, "L'oasis de Khulm," *Bulletin de l'Association de géographes français* 370, 1969, pp. 383-93. B. Hourcade, "Réforme agraire et spéculation foncière dans la région de Tehran," in G. Schweizer, ed., *Interdisziplinäre Iran-Forschung*, Beihefte zum Tübinger Atlas des Vorderen Orients, Reihe B, Nr. 40, Wiesbaden, 1979, pp. 131-39. B. Hourcade and A. Tual, *Documents pour l'étude de la répartition de quelques traits culturels dans la région de Téhéran* I: *Alborz central*, Paris, 1979. A. K. S. Lambton, *Landlord and Peasant in Persia*, Oxford, 1953. Idem, *The Persian Land Reform 1962-1966*, Oxford, 1969. X. de Planhol, "Traits généraux de l'utilisation du sol en Perse," in *Land Use in Semi-Arid Mediterranean Climates. UNESCO/IGU Symposium Iraklion (Greece), 19-26 Sept. 1962*, UNESCO, Arid Zone Research, XXVI, Paris, 1964, pp. 95-99. Idem, "L'oasis d'Isfahan d'après P. Fesharaki," *Revue géographique de l'Est* 9/3-4, 1969, pp. 391-96. C. Sahami, *L'économie rurale et la vie paysanne dans la province sud-caspienne de l'Iran. Le Guilân*, Publications de la Faculté de Lettres et Sciences Humaines de l'Université de Clermont-Ferrand, fasc. 22, Clermont-Ferrand, 1965. *Farhang-e ābādīhā-ye kešvar* (*Village Gazetteer*), Tehran, Markaz-e Āmār-e Īrān, 1968-70 (one or two vols. for every *ostān*).

(M. BAZIN)

iii. IN PERSIAN LITERATURE

Bāḡ appears both as an object of description and as the prime source of nature imagery in Persian literature. As a poetic image, *bāḡ* stands for order and beauty, and the link between man and nature. In modern poetry it can be a locus for social criticism. It is also a source of book titles and musical modes (e.g., *čahār-bāḡ*). Under the influence of mystical thought, *bāḡ* becomes a symbol of Paradise. Finally, *bāḡ* as conventionalized in literature summarizes the Persian attitude toward nature.

Actual gardens are frequently mentioned in literature, and the building of a new garden is often the occasion for a poem celebrating the event. Descriptions of gardens, however, are so conventionalized that they are non-distinctive, the only specific detail being the date of the event expressed in a chronogram (*mādda-ye tārīḵ*). Gardens are the setting for parties and revelry, seasonal celebrations such as Nowrūz and Mehragān, festivities connected with the end of Ramażān, or any other public or private occasion. They are also thought of as places of private retreat, and as examples of royal pomp and magnificence.

Although gardens are always described in conventional terms, many of the specific flowers and trees common to them on the Iranian plateau and the Indian subcontinent are found in the poetry about gardens. Certain other physical features, such as the surrounding wall, are hardly ever mentioned. The pattern for this sort of description was set by the Ghaznavid poets Farroḵī and Manūčehrī, and continued to the twentieth century. In spring the garden was at its most beautiful, and the spring flowers and indeed the garden as a whole quickly became images for all that is beautiful, especially the poet's beloved. From here it was only a short step to personifying the garden, and making possible rich clusters of images, such as Farroḵī's (*Dīvān*, ed. Dabīrsīāqī, Tehran, 1335 Š./1956-57, p. 11) of spring drinking wine from the cup (the blooming red rose) held by the garden (the leaves of the *čenār*, plane tree, are likened to human hands), or Manūčehrī's mythic narrative of two lovers, the cloud and the garden (*Dīvān*, ed. Dabīrsīāqī, Tehran, 1338 Š./1959-60, pp. 188-90).

Persian poets never hesitated to mix images of paganism with images of Islam. The profusion of colorful flowers and the glittering surface of the watercourses were often likened to jewels, and this image was extended by the Ghaznavid poets to make the garden into an idol temple, an idea reinforced, no doubt, by Sultan Maḥmūd's expeditions to India in search of treasure. Farroḵī, celebrating spring, says "The garden became an idol temple and the rose bush, the idol; the rose-worshipping shaman [i.e., the nightingale] was drinking wine" (op. cit., p. 307).

More complex however, are the images of the garden as Paradise. It is likely that the form of Persian gardens was influenced by descriptions of the archetypical garden of Paradise in the Koran, which stress its green color, shade, fruits, fountains of running water, and cool pavilions where the inhabitants may drink a wine that does not intoxicate. A *qaṣīda* by Moʿezzī praising a royal garden and probably dedicated to the Saljuq Malekšāh, contains many of the features of the garden of Paradise: the king like the sun and his throne raised to the seventh heaven, the presence of Reżwān, fruit trees, streams of water, and houris (*Dīvān*, ed. ʿA. Eqbāl, Tehran, 1318 Š./1939-40, p. 315). The idea of an earthly Paradise captured the imagination of Persian poets, and the image was so powerful that it appears as late as the nineteenth century in a *qaṣīda* of the Qajar poet Fatḥ-ʿAlī Khan Ṣabā, and the great nineteenth-century garden in Shiraz was called Bāḡ-e Eram (q.v.), after the earthly rival of Paradise.

From the image of the garden as an earthly Paradise, mystical poets and prose writers extended it to symbolize Paradise itself. Again the Koranic passages provided the model, and features of the actual garden such as the watercourses and cypress trees corresponded to the divine archetype. The cypress tree, for example, is likened to the Ṭūbā, and then, in a line from Ḥāfeẓ, associated with his beloved: "You think about the Ṭūbā tree and I about my beloved's stature; everyone thinks according to his aspiration" (*Dīvān*, ed. M. M. Qazvīnī and Q. Ḡanī, Tehran, 1330 Š./1951-52, p. 40). The beloved was frequently described as one of the houris who were promised to the faithful for their enjoyment. In this regard, the 7th/13th-century mystic Rūzbehān Baqlī "draws our attention to the alleged prophetic tradition that one should find spiritual recreation by looking at three things: water, greenery, and a lovely face" (A. Schimmel, 1976, p. 23). For Jalāl-al-Dīn Rūmī, the garden becomes a symbol of divine beauty which both displays and conceals the eternal beauty of the archetypal gardener, God. The mystical lover and his divine beloved are like a rose and its thorn. When the lover becomes one with the beloved, the rose becomes one with the thorn and all duality is resolved.

In modern poetry, the garden continues to be a prominent image, but now it often appears in contexts of social criticism as well as of love. In 1932 Abu'l-Qāsem Lāhūtī wrote a poem entitled "Bāḡbān" (The gardener) in which he compares Stalin to a wise gardener who knows best what to prune in the garden and what to encourage. More recently, Forūḡ Farroḵzād in "Del-am barā-ye bāḡča mīsūzad" (My heart bleeds for the garden) used a withered and dying garden at the back of her house as a symbol of Iranian culture and society in her time. She remembers the garden as flourishing when she was a child, and now that she is an adult she finds that people are filled with self-concern but nobody cares for the garden. In a different vein, in her poem "Fatḥ-e bāḡ" (The victory of the garden) is a joyful love poem set in a garden, using garden imagery to express her feelings.

The garden is not always an image of happiness and beauty, however. In classical poetry, autumn in the garden was a time of sadness and nostalgia, when cold winds take the place of warm breezes and black and white are the predominant colors (crows and snow). A modern poet has used the garden as the central image in a poem consoling a friend on the death of his child: "Ḵadīv my friend, truly death's hand is fickle. It always plucks the rose and never sees the thorns and twigs. Instead of the brush and thorns, it carries the rose from the garden: what a sinister gardener, what a fearful pruning" (M. Aḵawān Ṯāleṯ, "al-Salām yā sayyednā al-Ḵadīv," *Negīn* 9, no. 99, 1352 Š./1973-74, p. 10).

As conceptualized in literature, the garden comes to symbolize man's relation to nature in Persian culture. The garden's life cycle parallels that of man: Each has its youth and spring and its autumn and decline. However, the stylized, idealized idea of the garden presented in poetry represents a stark contrast with what lies outside the garden wall: the desert. Hot, dry, dangerous, and inhospitable, the desert is always a threat to life, and the wall serves to keep the desert out as it keeps the garden in. Within the wall, nature is controlled and made to serve the purposes of man: The chaos and danger of nature outside are changed to order and security. In this small Paradise man, not nature, is dominant, and nature can be enjoyed on man's terms.

Bibliography: C.-H. de Fouchécour, *La description de la nature dans la poésie lyrique persane du XIe siècle*, Paris, 1969. William Hanaway, "Paradise on Earth: The Terrestrial Garden in Persian Literature," in *The Islamic Garden*, ed. R. Ettinghausen, Washington, D. C., 1976, pp. 43-67. Annemarie Schimmel, "The Celestial Garden in Islam," ibid., pp. 11-39. D. N. Wilber, *Persian Gardens and Garden Pavilions*, Rutland, Vermont, 1962.

(W. L. HANAWAY)

iv. IN AFGHANISTAN

Much of Afghanistan consists of treeless craggy mountains, dry sandy deserts, or semi-desert plains. The people inhabiting this land have consequently cherished all forms of gardens, which have become an integral part of Afghan culture. Villagers hold meetings and socialize in their orchards, middle-class urbanites delight in visiting outlying gardens, and the wealthy most often have large gardens inside their walled compounds. Some maintain gardens outside the cities, with or without structures, to which they repair on weekends and holidays.

Pre-Mughal gardens. Since the time the Achaemenids began their eastward expansion in the sixth century B.C., the Afghan area has periodically come under the rule of empires originating in Iran, Central Asia, and India, all of which nurtured garden traditions. Because these earliest gardens were destroyed by the passage of conquering armies one must turn to descriptions by ancient writers or the findings of archeologists in order to glean any information about them. For instance, in 1151 A.D. ʿAlāʾ-al-Dīn Ḡūrī destroyed the garden-palaces of the Ghaznavids (977/1186) in Ḡaznī (see the summary report on the Italian Archeological Mission in Afghanistan by A. Bombaci and U. Scerrato in *East and West*, N. S. 10, 1959, pp. 3-56) as well as those at Bost and Laškarī Bāzār (D. Schlumberger, "Lashkari Bazar," in *MDAFA* 18, 1963, p. 80). The armies of Jengiz Khan (1220) and Tīmūr (Tamerlane; 1281) wrought much havoc (Klaus Fischer, *Nimruz*, Bonn, I, 1976; II, 1974), but their Timurid and Mughal successors, ruling at Herat and Kabul, initiated a cultural renaissance which touched the entire Indo-Iranian region. Gardens were celebrated components of this florescence.

In Herat, the gardens at Gāzargāh tended by Tīmūr's son, Šāhrok̲ (d. 1447) and those at Tak̲t-e Safar created by the grandson of Tīmūr's son ʿOmar, Sultan Ḥosayn Bāyqarā (d. 1506), have lost all semblance to their original Persian garden forms but their names remain, recalling a golden age.

Mughal gardens. Kabul was taken in 1504 by a young fugitive from Farḡāna, a descendant of both Jengiz Khan and Tīmūr who was destined to become the emperor Bābor (r. 1526-30), founder of the Mughal empire of India (1526-1857). The adornment of Kabul and its environs became his lifelong passion. In his memoirs, the *Bābor-nāma* (tr. A. Beveridge, London, 1917), Babur writes that scarcely a year after his takeover he purchased a garden with "great plane (*čenār*) trees" at Estālef, a hillside village 34 miles north of Kabul. Here he built a *tak̲t* under the *čenār* and made the "zig-zag" water channels "straight and orderly" to conform to the ideals of a Persian garden (p. 216). Just below this garden he enclosed the spring of K̲ᵛāja Seh Yārān (Three friends) in mortared stone-work so as to better admire the *arḡavān* (Judas tree or red bud; p. 217). The *tak̲t* with its *čenār* and the spring with its *arḡavān* continued to be popular picnic spots up until the end of the 1970s when war ravaged the area.

Bābor mentions over twelve gardens outside the walled city of Kabul where he met envoys and distributed robes of honor (Čenār-bāḡ, p. 401), cavorted with friends at all-night, all-day wine-drinking parties (Bāḡ-e Banafša [Violet garden]; pp. 395, 414), or recuperated (Čār-bāḡ; p. 254). In India he remembered the gardens fondly and continued to send letters concerning their upkeep until the time of his death (p. 645).

Bābor's will directed that his body be returned to a garden in Kabul, but the original name is unknown. The emperor Jahāngīr's (r. 1569-1627) memoirs, the *Tūzok-e jahāngīrī* (tr. A. Rogers, London, 1914) lists seven famous Kabul gardens he "perambulated" in 1607 (p. 106), but gives no name to the garden where he visited Bābor's tomb and distributed alms (p. 110). The *Pādšāh-nāma* lists ten gardens in Kabul at the time of Shah Jahān's (r. 1627-58) visit in 1638, and gives details of the orders he gave for embellishing the tomb site, but no name of the garden is specified (appendix V in *Baburnama*, tr.).

Nevertheless, this account describes the garden as being 500 yards long with 15 terraces 30 yards apart, and 12 waterfalls cascading into marbled reservoirs on the tenth and ninth terraces, and at the entrance at the bottom of the slope. Shah Jahān ordered the tomb on the fourteenth terrace to be surrounded by a pierced-marble screen and a marble mosque built on the terrace below. It was completed in 1640 (inscription).

This fits the configuration of Bāḡ-e Bābor today, but only the general form, the terraces, three venerable *čenār*, the mosque and tomb are recognizable. In 1883 when Amir ʿAbd-al-Raḥmān gave up residence in the old city of Kabul (Fayż Moḥammad, *Serāj al-tawārīk̲*, Kabul, 1915, p. 379), he constructed a pavilion with a wooden-pillared verandah over the reservoir on the tenth terrace, and a large *ḥaram-sarāy* nearby. The gardens then gradually assumed the form of an English garden much favored by later royal families. Ladies' *mēlas* (fairs) and other festive occasions were held here, including the coronation of Amir Ḥabīb-Allāh (r. 1901-19; K. Seraj and N. H. Dupree, *The KES Collection of Vintage Photographs*, New York, 1979, nos. 90-93).

The pavilion and the *ḥaram-sarāy* were later used as residences for foreigners (A. Hamilton, *Afghanistan*, London, 1906, pp. 354, 375) and embassies (O. von Niedermayer, *Afghanistan*, Leipzig, 1925, pp. 31-32; E. Trinkler, *Through the Heart of Afghanistan*, tr. B. Featherston, London, 1928, p. 176). Finally, Bāḡ-e Bābor became a public park and swimming pools were added, but the complex was increasingly neglected during the 1960s when the pavilion became a hospital and the *ḥaram-sarāy* a boarding school for tribal boys. The Italian archeological mission (IsMEO) began the restoration of the mosque in 1964 and in 1970 a survey considered the possibility of reconstructing the gardens in the Mughal style (M. Parpagliolo, *Kabul: The Bagh-i-Babur*, Rome, 1972). These plans were never implemented.

The only Mughal garden in Afghanistan retaining any of its original appearance is the garden at Nemla, 26 miles west of Jalālābād on the old road to Kabul. Local lore credits Nūr Jahān, wife of Emperor Jahāngīr who was renowned for her gardens, with its creation. In his memoirs the emperor speaks of creating the Jahānārā (World-adorning) garden in Kabul in 1607 (p. 106), but makes no mention of a garden at Nemla although he describes a grand hunt in its vicinity on their way back to India (p. 125). Architectural details suggest a date between the end of the sixteenth and the beginning of the seventeenth centuries, however (M. Parpagliolo, p. 2, n. 3).

The enclosed garden is 400 square yards and contains many classic Mughal elements including an orderly grid pattern of intersecting water channels lined with cypress interspersed with poplar and fruit trees. One waterfall wall is honeycombed with deep niches in which candles were placed behind the cascade, a favorite detail of the period. The bungalow now at its center was built by Amir Ḥabīb-Allāh (r. 1901-19).

Post-Mughal gardens. The next period of extensive garden building began at the end of the nineteenth century under Amir ʿAbd-al-Raḥmān (r. 1880-1901) whose palaces were set in walled parklike gardens about which he writes movingly in his autobiography (*The Life of Abdur Rahman: Amir of Afghanistan*, ed. Sultan

Mahomed Khan, London, 1900, II, p. 104). The amir retained an English gardener from Yorkshire named Wild (J. A. Gray, *At the Court of the Amir*, London, 1895, p. 482) to oversee these gardens filled with trellises, arbors, reflecting pools, sculptured fountains, and tall gas lamps, features which became prominent in subsequent periods (K. Seraj, no. 89, dated 1900).

Outside the walled city of Kabul, west of the river, the amir built a massive 500-yard square citadel (Arg; ca. 1882) with "a garden nearly as large as the whole city of Kabul around it" (*The Life of Abdur Rahman* II, p. 61). Spacious courtyard gardens were planted throughout the complex, and the amir's private pavilion, the Kot-e Bāḡča (House of the Little Garden), was surrounded with fragrant flowers (Hamilton, p. 350). The Arg continues to be the seat of government, but buildings have encroached on most of the outer garden space. The amir was proud of his building program (ibid., p. 68) and many of his palaces are still in use, although somewhat altered. Bāḡ-e Šāhī with its adjoing *ḥaram-sarāy* in Bāḡ-e Kawkab (Star garden; begun 1300/1883, completed 1303/1887, Fayż Moḥammad, pp. 424, 489) in the eastern town of Jalālābād, the winter capital, has been in continuous use and the eleven acres of lush gardens at Bāḡ-e Šāhī were meticulously maintained. It has rarely been open to the public. Manzel-bāḡ (begun 1300/1883, completed 1302/1884; Fayż Moḥammad, p. 417) in a 20-acre walled garden one stage (*manzel*) east of the southern city of Kandahar, has served variously as a hotel, a cinema, and a tractor depot so the gardens are largely depleted but still retain vestiges of their former state. The massive Bāḡ-e Jahānārā palace at Ḵolm (begun 1307/1889, completed 1309/1892; Fayż Moḥammad, p. 784) in the north was highlighted by stately firs, fruit trees, terraced gardens, and a reflecting pool. Restored in 1975 as a museum, it was rendered uninhabitable by an earthquake in 1976.

In Kabul, the 30-acre garden surrounding the Čehel-sotūn (Forty pillars) palace (1880; inscription) are still well-maintained. Outside the south gate of the Arg there were two garden-sarais, Būstān (Garden) and Golestān (Rose-garden). Named after works by the renowned thirteenth-century poet, Saʿdī, often quoted by Bābor, these sarais had once belonged to Oloḡ Beg Kābolī, an uncle of Bābor's who ruled Kabul and Ḡaznī from ca. 1464-1501 (*Baburnama*, pp. 95, 251). Here Amir ʿAbd-al-Raḥmān built a palace with adjoining *ḥaram-sarāy* (1893; inscription). The amir's palace in the Būstān-sarāy eventually became his mausoleum, and in 1964 the surrounding walls were removed to create Kabul's newest public garden called Zarnegār (Adorned with gold).

The many-domed and arcuated palace at Bāḡ-e Bālā (1893; Gray, p. 498) located on a high, vine-covered hill some 2.5 miles west of Kabul best represents the amir's garden-palaces. It has been accessible to the public since it became a fashionable restaurant after restoration in 1966. The plan, clearly derived from the Central Asian Islamic tradition, utilizes a square with two spacious high-domed halls at the center and four small-domed rooms at each corner connected by wide colonnaded verandahs.

The exterior is finished in gleaming white gypsum plaster. The whitewashed interior ornamentation, in both impressed and carved plasterwork, is classically Islamic, depicting arabesques and a variety of floral patterns; patera painted in bold colors are set with mirrors. Arched openings between rooms were hung with embroidered hangings in place of doors, and the rooms were provided with such novelties as wall-fireplaces, wall-lighting fixtures, and massive imported crystal chandeliers. A Mughal-style fountain originally in the entrance hall was not included in the restoration, but the reflecting pool occupying a high terrace on the east was retained. The amir presided over *darbār*s from a window overlooking the pool (*The Life of Abdur Rahman* II, frontispiece) and died in the same room at midnight on 2 October 1901.

ʿAbd-al-Raḥmān's son, Amir Ḥabīb-Allāh, built lavish palaces largely in British colonial style, but the next garden-building surge occurred under his son, King Amān-Allāh (r. 1919-29). The garden landscaping at the center of Dār al-Amān (1923), a new city six miles south of Kabul, caused some western visitors to "gasp" (J. Fleming, *Asia* 29/4, p. 328). Amān-Allāh advocated tearing down garden walls and opened the first public garden, Bāḡ-e ʿOmūmī, at the site of Bābor's Čār-bāḡ along the Kabul river. It gradually gave way to buildings, but the landscaped complex of terraces forming Amān-Allāh's Bāḡ-e ʿOmūmī in the hill resort of Paḡmān, 12 miles west of Kabul, continued to be popular until the current hostilities erupted in 1979. It was furnished with fountains, a café, a band stand, a cinema/theater, and an amphitheater forming the core of an ambitious building program carefully regulated by the *Neẓām-nāma-ye taʿmīrāt-e Paḡmān* (July, 1922). Article 4 of this building code required all structures to be fronted with "gardens of willows, *čenār*s, and other flowering shrubs" so that the entire town might resemble a garden. The last Afghan monarch, Moḥammad Ẓāhir Shah (r. 1922-73) was an avid horticulturist and continually embellished the more formal public gardens at the Tapa (King's garden), also in Paḡmān.

Bibliography: See also S. Crowe et al., *The Gardens of Mughul India*, London, 1972. N. H. Dupree, "Early Twentieth Century Afghan Adaptations of European Architecture," *Art and Archaeology Research Papers* 11, London, 1977, pp. 15-21. Idem, "A Building Boom in the Hindukush," *Lotus International* 26, Milan, 1980, pp. 114-21. Gul-badan Begum, *Humayun-nama*, tr. H. Beveridge, London, 1902. F. Martin, *Under the Absolute Amir*, London, 1907. C. Masson, *Narratives of Various Journeys in Balochistan, Afghanistan, the Punjab and Kalat*, London, 1844 (on Bāḡ-e Bābor, see II, p. 239). E. and A. Thornton, *Leaves from an Afghan Scrapbook*, London, 1910. D. N. Wilber, *Persian Gardens and Garden Pavilions*, Tokyo, 1962.

(N. H. Dupree)

BĀḠ-E BĀLĀ. See BĀḠ iv.

BĀḠ-E ERAM, a famous and beautiful garden at Shiraz. Its site close to the embankment of the Rūdḵāna-ye Ḵošk was formerly on the northwestern fringe of the city but is now well inside the greatly expanded urban area. The present garden and mansion are not very old but, like the other famous gardens of Shiraz, may well have replaced an earlier foundation. D. N. Wilber surmised that its antecedent may have been the Bāḡ-e Šāh mentioned in accounts of the Safavid period, but the present writer, after studying the sketches of Shiraz which have come down from that period, particularly those made by Chardin, considers that the Bāḡ-e Šāh must have been opposite the former city gate called Darvāza-ye Bāḡ-e Šāh, probably on the grounds now occupied by the Saʿdī and Namāzī hospitals.

Bāḡ-e Eram, originally a foundation of a Qašqāʾī chief (see below) as his city residence, lay at a distance of one mile to the northwest of Shiraz. It had an area which, if sown with wheat, would require 290 maunds of seed (Fasāʾī, II, p. 164).

Forṣat Šīrāzī, a contemporary of Fasāʾī, praised the Bāḡ-e Eram for its beautiful flowers, refreshing air, tall cypresses (a stately, beautiful cypress tree there known as *sarv-e nāz* has long been a major tourist attraction), fragrent myrtles, flowing watercourses, and numerous cascades. The garden contained a fine mansion, which according to Fasāʾī (loc. cit.) was erected by Jānī Khan (d. 1239/1823-24), the paramount chief (*īlḵānī*) of the Qašqāʾī tribe under the late Zands, but Forṣat attributes its foundation to the *īlḵānī* Moḥammadqolī Khan, the fourth son of Jānī Khan. The Bāḡ-e Eram was subsequently purchased by Ḥājī Naṣīr-al-Molk, who ordered the construction of a new mansion (the one still standing), entrusting the work to the architect Ḥājī Moḥammad-Ḥasan Meʿmār (*Āṯār-e ʿAjam*, p. 511). Forṣat describes this mansion as consisting of a reception hall (*tālār*), which was a roof supported by two massive pillars and received light through sash windows (*orosī*), and two storeys of side rooms. Another garden was added, containing an orangery (*nāranjestān*) together with a stable (*bārband*) and a pavilion (*kūšk*). An inscription on the stone plinth of the facade of the mansion consists of verses by Shirazi poets such as Faṣīḥ-al-Molk Šūrīda (1274/1857-1345/1926). The verses include the date 1339/1921 as well as descriptions of the constructional work and praises of the then owner Naṣīr-al-Molk.

After the coup d'état of 1332 Š./1953 and the exile of the Qašqāʾī brothers, who in the meantime had regained ownership of the Bāḡ-e Eram, the government confiscated the garden and later on gave it to Pahlavi University (now the University of Shiraz).

During this period the former mud walls were replaced with iron railings, old trees were cut down to make room for lawns, and a broad street named Eram Boulevard was laid out on the northwest side.

Early during the revolution of 1357 Š./1978-79, the Qašqāʾīs repossessed the garden; shortly afterward its owner Ḵosrow Khan dedicated it to the people of Shiraz. The garden has now been made into a botanical garden and the mansion has been assigned to the Faculty of Law of the university.

Bibliography: Moḥammad-Naṣīr Forṣat Šīrāzī, *Āṯār-e ʿAjam*, Bombay, 1313/1895, repr. 1353/1934. D. N. Wilber, *Persian Gardens and Garden Pavilions*, Tokyo, 1962; tr. Mahīndoḵt Ṣabā, *Bāghā-ye Īrān o kūškhā-ye ān*, Tehran, 1348 Š./1969. R. Pechère, "Etude de jardins historiques," in UNESCO, *Iran*, March, 1973. Moḥammad-Taqī Moṣṭafawī, *Eqlīm-e Pārs*, Tehran, 1343 Š./1964; tr. R. N. Sharp, *The Land of Pars*, Chippenham, England, 1978, p. 315.

(K. AFSAR)

BĀḠ-E FĪN, known also as Bāḡ-e Šāh-e Kāšān and Bāḡ-e Šāh-e Fīn, a royal garden at about one parasang to the southwest of the city of Kāšān, where subterranean waters from the Dandāna and Haft Kotal mountains emerge to form the Fīn springs (Sohayl Kāšānī, p. 49). More than 22,608 m^2 (Moṣṭafawī), Fīn Gardens contain an ornate, tiled pool which is the source of cold artesian waters that feed the park's system of basins and water channels and that ultimately irrigate the two small villages of upper and lower Fīn. Above the central pool is a two-story pavilion of carved ornamental stone containing four alcoves (*šāhnešīn*) and daises. At one time, over the pavilion was a one- (Sohayl Kāšānī, p. 50) or two- (Īzadyār, p. 272) story, bowler-shaped extension built of iron and wood that survived until the mid-Qajar period. The two-story pavilion, a rectangular reflecting pool fronting it, and a walkway that connects the pavilion to the garden entryway form the basic layout of Bāḡ-e Fīn.

The Safavid Shah Ṣafī (r. 1038-52/1629-42) is credited with the original construction of Fīn Gardens (Sohayl Kāšānī, p. 49; Hedāyat, VIII, p. 463); the site was evidently next to or above the ruins of a Mongol-era structure (Meškātī, p. 11). Ṣafī was not the first Safavid king to use the springs of Fīn; ʿAbbās I built a garden, no trace of which has survived (Sohayl Kāšānī, p. 51) and Shah Esmāʿīl I once gave a royal audience there (Narāqī, 1345 Š./1966, p. 96). Shah Ṭahmāsb is also credited with the foundation of this garden. During the reign of Shah Solaymān (1077-1105/1666-94) a partitioned pool was built outside the garden where the springs emerged from the ground; this pool, known as Čašma-ye Solaymānī, was repaired and rebuilt "ca. thirty years ago" (Moṣṭafawī). The Safavid kings would also generally stop and rest at Fīn Gardens while passing through Kāšān (Hedāyat, VIII, p. 482; Narāqī, p. 141).

During the Qajar period, in 1220/1805, Fatḥ-ʿAlī Shah ordered damage done to the garden by an 1190/1776 earthquake to be repaired (Narāqī, 1345 Š./1966, p. 9). His reign also saw the erection of a gatehouse, the pavilion known as Ṣoffa-ye Fatḥ-ʿalīšāhī, under which a turquoise, tiled pool and numerous fountains were installed (Hedāyat, X, p. 137; Šīrvānī,

p. 457), several buildings flanking the pavilion including a small *ḥammām* in which Amīr(-e) Kabīr (q.v.) was murdered (Sohayl Kāšānī, pp. 51-52); the pavilion's cupolas and arched ceilings were adorned with portraits of the shah and Qajar princes. A chronogrammatic poem by Ḵāvarī inscribed on the building in raised *nastaʿlīq* puts the date of the pavilion's completion at 1226/1811 (Meškātī, p. 11; Šīrvānī, p. 457). During the reign of Moḥammad Shah (r. 1250-64/1834-48) another pool with several small fountains was erected. The Qajar kings maintained Fīn Garden, using it as a base camp on journeys to their hunting grounds around Kāšān (Moṣṭafawī, loc. cit.; Īzadyār, p. 272); toward the end of the Qajar era, some of the rulers of Kāšān would use it as their residences and seats of government (Sohayl Kāšānī, p. 77; Narāqī, pp. 4, 11, 21). During the rebellion of Nāyeb Ḥosayn Kāšī, the *nāyeb*'s son Māšāʾallāh Khan dislodged some of the marble and tiles from the residence and used them in his own palace (Narāqī, 1345 Š./1966, pp. 248, 257; Īzadyār, p. 273); Bāğ-e Fīn was later declared an historical landmark and the damage was repaired (Moṣṭafawī).

Bāğ-e Fīn owes most of its notoriety to the fact that from 8 Ṣafar 1268/3 December 1851 it served as the exile home of the deposed Prime Minister Mīrzā Taqī Khan Amīr Kabīr (Ādamīyat, p. 707), who on 17 Rabīʿ I 1268/10 January 1852 was assassinated in its small *ḥammām* (Ādamīyat, p. 726). Fīn Gardens then fell into disrepair until Prince Jalāl-al-Dīn Mīrzā Eḥtešām-al-Molk became governor of Kāšān (Afšār, p. 105) repaired the structure and made it his official residence (Sohayl Kāšānī, p. 51).

Bibliography: F. Ādamīyat, *Amīr Kabīr o Īrān*, 3rd ed., Tehran, 1354 Š./1975. Reżāqolī Khan Hedāyat, *Rawżat al-ṣafā*, Qom, 1339 Š./1960. Īzadyār, "Bāğ-e Šāh-e Fīn-e Kāšān," *Armağān* 23, 1327 Š./1948, pp. 272-76. N. Meškātī, "Bāğ-e tāriḵī-e Fīn-e Kāšān," *Īrān-e emrūz* 3/11, 1320 Š./1942, pp. 10-14. M.-T. Moṣṭafawī, "Yak gūša az behešt dar kenār-e kavīr-e Lūt," *Eṭṭelāʿāt-e māhāna* 7/5, 1333 Š./1954, pp. 12-13. Ḥ. Narāqī, *Kāšān dar jonbeš-e mašrūṭa-ye Īrān*, Tehran, 2535 = 1355 Š./1976. Idem, *Tārīḵ-e ejtemāʿī-e Kāšān*, Tehran, 1345 Š./1966. Z. Šīrvānī, *Bostān al-sīāḥat*, Tehran, 1338 Š./1959. ʿAbd-al-Raḥīm Kalāntar Żarrābī Sohayl Kāšānī, *Merʾāt Qāsān*, ed. Ī. Afšār, *FIZ* 3, 1334 Š./1955, pp. 105-261; 2nd ed. published under the title *Tārīḵ-e Kāšān*, ed. Ī. Afšār, Tehran, 1341 Š./1962. See also R. G. Watson, *History of Persia*, London, 1866, pp. 398-406.

(ʿA.-A. SAʿĪDĪ SĪRJĀNĪ)

BĀĞ-E GOLESTĀN. See GOLESTĀN PALACE.

BĀĞ-E JAHĀNNAMĀ. See SHIRAZ.

BAG NASK, one of the Avestan *nask*s of the *gāhānīg* group, i.e., texts connected with the *Gāθā*s, now lost almost in its entirety (see AVESTA). This *nask* is listed in the survey of the Avesta in *Dēnkard* 8.1.9, is briefly described in 8.4, and its contents are resumed in *Dēnkard* 9.47-68 (also in the *Persian Rivayats*; see the bibliography). It consisted of twenty-two *fragard*s (twenty-one according to the *Persian Rivayats*, p. 3), the first three of which are extant as *Y.* 19-21. These contain a commentary on the three holy prayers which precede the *Gāθā*s: the *Ahuna vairiia*, *Aṣ̌əm vohū*, and *Yeŋ̇he hātąm*. The rest of the *Bag nask*, now lost, contained a commentary on the *Gāθā*s and the prayer *Airiiə̄mā išiiō*, which closes the *Gāθā* collection. Like the Pahlavi version of the *Gāθā*s themselves, the Pahlavi version of the commentary is of little or no help for understanding the Avestan text of the *Gāθā*s though it may afford some insight into the development of Zoroastrian doctrine.

In the manuscripts of the Avesta, *Y.* 19-21 are called *Bagān yašt* rather than *Bag nask*, which is likely to cause some confusion since in the *Dēnkard* the name *Bagān* (or *Bayān*) *yašt* (*nask*) is given to that part of the Avesta which contained the *Yašt*s. However, while the second *bagān*/*bayān* is the plural of *bag*/*bay* (for Av. *baγa-*) "god," the first *bagān* is probably for *baγąm*, accusative of *baγā-*, which is found in the final verses of all three prayers: *Baγąm Ahunahe vairiiehe*/*Aṣ̌ahe vahištahe yazamaidē*, *Baγąm Yeŋ̇he.hātąm hufraiiaštąm aṣ̌aonīm yazamaidē* "we worship the *baγā-* (consisting) of (or: called) *Ahuna Vairiia*/*Aṣ̌əm vohū*/ the well-worshipped, truthful *Yeŋ̇he.hātąm*." Note also that *Yasna* 19 calls itself *baγa* ... *Ahunahe vairiiehe* and that the *Šāyest nē-šāyest* (13.1, see below) also quotes the form *baγąm*. The term *baγā-* (different from *baγa-* "god") is usually translated as "part, piece" (e.g., *AirWb.*, col. 922; Darmesteter preferred "divine prayer," p. 165 n. 17). It is rendered in the Pahlavi version of the *Yasna* as *baxtārīh*, literally "distributorship." In *Y.* 55.7 the *Staota yesniia* is referred to as *baγąm*, but these texts make up the *nask* called *Stōd yašt*. The three *Aṣ̌əm vohū*s at the end of *Y.* 11.15 are called *baγąm* in the *Šāyest nē-šāyest* (13.1) and may have belonged to the *Bag nask* (Kotwal, pp. 40f., 100).

Yasna 19-21 contain the only remnants in Avestan language of a once extensive commentary on the holy *Gāθā*s of Zaraθuštra and related texts, somewhat comparable to the Old Indian commentaries on the Rig-veda. Of the three commentaries the first, on the *Ahuna Vairiia*, is by far the longest, twenty-one paragraphs against five for each of the other two. The technical vocabulary of these commentaries has not yet received the study it deserves. We may note here the use of nominal derivation, as in *vacō yaṯ ahumaṯ yaṯ ratumaṯ* "the utterance containing the words '*ahu*' and '*ratu*'" (19.8) and *uštatāt-* "being '*uštā*'" (21.4), and technical terms such as *kāraiia-* "to *point to, *refer to" (*AirWb.*, col. 448) and *cinasti* and *para.cinasti* "to *assign" (what is spoken of to somebody; see Narten, esp. pp. 86ff.).

All three commentaries contain interesting doctrinal matters, of which we may note the following. Of the three prayers, the *Ahuna vairiia* and *Aṣ̌əm vohū* are said to be the words of Ahura Mazdā, but the *Yeŋ̇he hātąm* to have been spoken by Zaraθuštra and addressed to the Aməṣ̌a Spəntas. Boyce (*Zoroastrianism* I, p. 263 n. 52) argues against ascribing the composition of the *Yeŋhe hātąm* to Zaraθuštra—in contrast to the *Gāθās* and the *Ahunwar*—on the basis of its "syntactical awkwardness," perhaps rightly, though the lack of consensus regarding the syntax of these old Avestan prayers recommends caution in passing this kind of judgement. The *Ahuna vairiia*, we are told, was created by Ahura Mazdā before anything else in the material universe and before the creation of the demons (*Y.* 19.1-4) but after the Aməša Spəṇtas (19.8). When the evil one first appeared Ahura Mazdā recited the *Ahuna vairiia* and a passage from the *Gāθās* (*Y.* 45.2). These points were elaborated in the cosmological Pahlavi texts (perhaps already in lost Avestan texts); in the *Bundahišn* it is said that the *Ahunwar* was the manifestation of the "fire-shape" (*āsrō-kirb*) which Ohrmazd in the beginning fashioned from the "endless lights" (*anagrān rōšnān*) and which was needed to repel the initial attack of Ahriman (see AHUNWAR [i, p. 683] and Zaehner, p. 479 index s.v. *Ahunvar*).

The social divisions are said in *Y.* 19.16-18 to be dependent on the word of Ahura Mazdā (i.e., the *Ahuna Vairiia*), which "has four classes, five masters" (*caθru.pištra panca.ratu*), namely (1) the priest (*āθrauuan*), the warrior (*raθaēštar*), the agriculturer (*vāstriiō.fšuiiant*), and the artisan (*hūiti*, only mentioned here in the Avesta; Pahl. *hutuxš*); and (2) the masters of the house, the village, the tribe, the country (*māniia, vīsiia, zantuma, daxiiuma*), and Zaraθuštra.

Bibliography: The passages in the *Dēnkard* and *Persian Rivayats* are: (1) *Dēnkard* 8.1.9: Dresden, pp. 305.20-306.2, Madan, p. 678.3, tr. West, pp. 7, 418; (2) *Dēnkard* 8.4: Dresden, pp. 302.13-20, Madan, p. 681; tr. West, pp. 13, 420, 429, 439; (3) *Dēnkard* 9.47-68: Dresden, pp. 151.19-149 end, 240-194.4; Madan, pp. 873-936, DH (*The Codex DH, Being a Facsimile Edition of Bondahesh, Zand-e Vohuman Yasht, and Parts of Denkard*, Tehran, [1971-72]), pp. 237.7-end [the ms. breaks off in the 17th *fragard*]; tr. West, pp. 303-84. The passages from the *Persian Rivayats* were translated by West, pp. 418-47 and were not repeated by Dhabhar in his translation (see *Persian Rivayats*, p. 4.). See also Darmesteter, *Zend-Avesta* I-III, esp, I, pp. 160-77 (text), III, pp. x-xi, xvi. B. N. Dhabhar, ed., *The Persian Rivayats of Hormazyar Framarz and Others*, Bombay, 1932. M. Dresden, ed., *Dēnkart, a Pahlavi Text. Facsimile Edition of the Manuscript B of the K. R. Cama Oriental Institute Bombay*, Wiesbaden, 1966. F. M. P. Kotwal, *The Supplementary Texts to the Šāyest nē-šāyest*, Copenhagen, 1969. J. Narten, "Avestisch *CIŠ*," in *Monumentum H. S. Nyberg*, Acta Iranica 5, Tehran and Liège, 1975, pp. 81-92. H. Reichelt, *Avesta Reader*, Strassburg, 1911, repr. Berlin, 1968, pp. 73-75, 174-76 (*Y.* 19 text and commentary). M. R. Unvala, *Dârâb Hormazyâr's Rivâyat* I, Bombay, 1922. W. E. West, *Pahlavi Texts* IV: *Contents of the Nasks*, SBE 37, Oxford, 1892, repr. Delhi, etc., 1965. F. Wolff, *Avesta, die heiligen Bücher der Parsen*, Strassburg, 1910, repr. Berlin, 1960, pp. 49-54. R. C. Zaehner, *Zurvan. A Zoroastrian Dilemma*, Oxford, 1955, repr. New York, 1972.

(P. O. SKJÆRVØ)

BĀĞ-E PĪRŪZĪ (or Fīrūzī), literally "Garden of Triumph," a royal garden in Ğazna lying beside the Fīrūzī palace and the ʿArūs-al-Falak mosque, founded and built by Sultan Maḥmūd of Ğazna. Maḥmūd was a great builder and possessed palaces and gardens in every important city (see Šabānkāra'ī, pp. 68, 70; Nāẓim, pp. 166-67; Bosworth, *Ghaznavids*, pp. 139ff.) but he especially loved this garden and was buried there on Thursday, 23 Rabīʿ II 421/30 April 1030, according to his own will and the common practice of the Ghaznavids (Bayhaqī, pp. 13, 335; Šabānkāra'ī, p. 66; Jīlānī Jalālī, p. 217). Two days after his arrival in Ğazna on 8 Jomādā II 422/2 June 1031, Sultan Masʿūd visited his father's tomb and ordered a *rebāṭ* to be built there. He also insisted on consuming its legacies as they were indicated, then forbade anyone to come to the garden for pleasure. Farrokī Sīstānī in his elegy for Sultan Maḥmūd says that he can never again see the flowered Bāğ-e Fīrūzī without Maḥmūd (*Dīvān*, p. 91). Bayhaqī (p. 890) mentions that when he wrote his book (probably in 451/1059, see S. Naficy [Nafīsī] in *EI*[2] I, p. 1131), the building of the garden and its central square (*meydān*) has been changed and dilapidated. During Masʿūd's reign some ceremonies took place in the garden, particularly army reviews (Bayhaqī, pp. 526, 654, 702, 736-37, 890, in the years 425/1033-34, 427/1035-36, 429/1037-38, 430/1038-39, 432/1040-41). The lawn (*każrā*') of the garden was the temporary jail of Amir Moḥammad's four sons in 432/1040-41 (Bayhaqī, pp. 893-94).

The Bāğ-e Pīrūzī has now been completely destroyed but the extant tomb of Maḥmūd, which is situated in a little village named Rawża-ye Solṭān (The sultan's tomb) about two miles to the north of the present town of Ğazna (Nāẓim, p. 167; S. Flury, *Syria* 6, 1925, pp. 61-90), shows where it was located (see Bombaci and Scerrato, p. 19).

Bibliography: A. Bombaci and U. Scerrato, "Summary Report on the Italian Archaeological Mission in Afghanistan," *East and West*, n.s. 10/1-2, 1959, pp. 3-55. Bosworth, *Ghaznavids*, pp. 139-41, 286 n. 29. Farrokī Sīstānī, *Dīvān*, ed. M. Dabīrsīāqī, 3rd ed., Tehran, 1363 Š./1984. Ğ. Jīlānī Jalālī, *Ğazna wa ğaznavīān*, Kabul, 1351 Š./1972, pp. 187, 217. K. Kalīlī, "Āṯār-e bāstānī-e šahr-e Ğaznī," *Akbār-e Dānešgāh-e Mašhad* 2/5, 1339 Š./1960. Idem, *Dīvān*, ed. M.-H. Omīdvār Harātī, Tehran, 1341 Š./1962, pp. 228-41. Dehkodā, s.v. M. A. Madadī, *Važʿ-e ejtemāʿī-e dawra-ye ğaznavīān*, Kabul, 1356 Š./1977, pp. 509-15. M. Nāẓim, *The Life and Times of Sulṭān Maḥmūd of Ghazna*, Cambridge, 1931, pp. 166-67. Moḥammad b. ʿAlī b. Moḥammad Šabānkāra'ī, *Majmaʿ al-ansāb*, ed. M. Ḥ. Moḥaddeṯ, Tehran, 1363 Š./1984. G. T. Vigne, *A Personal Narrative of a Visit to Ghuzni, Kabol, and Afghanistan*, London, 1840. D. N. Wilber, *Afghanistan*, New Haven, 1956,

p. 373. Ḡ.-Ḥ. Yūsofī, *Farrokī Sīstānī, šarḥ-e aḥwāl o rūzgār o šeʿr-e ū*, Mašhad, 1341 Š./1962, pp. 229-32.

(Ḡ.-Ḥ. Yūsofī)

BĀḠ-E ŠĀH (the king's garden), currently the name of a garrison (*pādgān*) in the western part of present-day Tehran. In the mid-Qajar period, the site was a broad, circular field about 1000 m in diameter situated on the outskirts of the city near one of its west gates and devoted to horseback riding and racing (ʿA. Mostawfī, *Šarḥ-e zendagānī-e man*, 2nd ed., Tehran, 1343 Š./1964, I, pp. 366-67). Adjoining the gate and abutting the racetrack was a crescent-shaped structure, from the second story of which the shah, his family, and his retainers would watch the races; the royal butlery occupied the lower story (M.-Ḥ. Eʿtemād-al-Salṭana, *Rūz-nāma-ye kāṭerāt*, ed. Ī. Afšār, 2nd ed., Tehran, 2536 = 1356 Š./1977, p. 197). In 1299/1882, Nāṣer-al-Dīn Shah ordered his treasurer and customs minister Amīn-al-Solṭān to oversee the digging of a *qanāt* which would convert the field into a formal park (Eʿtemād-al-Salṭana, *Tārīk-e montaẓam-e nāṣerī*, Tehran, 1298-1300/1881-83, III, p. 381). Water, at a volume of six *sang*s, borne by the *qanāt* fed numerous channels and more than 400 fountains and filled a large central pond adorned by eighty fountains (Dūst-ʿAlī Khan Moʿayyer-al-Mamālek, *Yāddāšthā-ī az zendagānī-e koṣūṣī-e Nāṣer-al-Dīn Šāh*, Tehran, 1361 Š./1982-83, p. 47) and a central island, on which a statue of the shah on horseback was erected. Apparently when the statue was unveiled, state dignitaries present at the ceremony bowed reverently before it. Branding such reverence a kind of idolatry, the people of Tehran rose up to protest, which is why no other statues of the shah were attempted. Several fine buildings and kiosks were constructed and a small zoo was set up in the southern section of the park at a total cost of 30,000 tomans (Eʿtemād-al-Salṭana, *Čehel sāl tārīk-e Īrān dar dawra-ye pādšāhī-e Nāṣer-al-Dīn Šāh: al-Maʾāṯer wa'l-āṯār* I, ed. Ī. Afšār, Tehran, 1363 Š./1984, p. 85; idem, *Kāṭerāt*, pp. 166, 437; Mostawfī, I, p. 366; S. ʿA. Ḥosaynī Balāḡī, *Tārīk-e Tehrān: Qesmat-e markazī wa możāfāt*, Qom, 1350/1931, p. 116). A tower-shaped building "Borj-e Manẓar," overlooking Tehran and fields adjacent to it, was erected in one corner of the park (Moʿayyer-al-Mamālek, p. 48); another building in the shape of a caleche was built near the lake (Balāḡī, *Tārīk-e Tehrān*, p. 116).

They called the park Bāḡ-e Šāh, by which name the nearby city gate also became famous. The race course was moved to Dūšān Tappa in the eastern part of Tehran (Mostawfī, I, p. 366). Bāḡ-e Šāh soon became a home away from home for Nāṣer-al-Dīn Shah, who, while on outings to his Dalīčāy hunting grounds near Qazvīn, would spend the night there (Eʿtemād-al-Salṭana, *Merʾāt al-boldān*, Tehran, 1294/1877, p. 39).

Moẓaffar-al-Dīn Shah (r. 1313-24/1896-1907), continued the tradition of his predecessor by using Bāḡ-e Šāh as the royal summer residence (*yeylāq*). Moreover, during his reign, because of its proximity to Tehran's western gate, Bāḡ-e Šāh also became the place where foreign dignitaries and ambassadors were received before entering the city (ʿA. Ẓahīr-al-Dawla, *Kāṭerāt o asnād*, ed. Ī. Afšār, Tehran, 1351 Š./1973, p. 21). It was also during the reign of Moẓaffar-al-Dīn Shah that Bāḡ-e Šāh achieved historical significance. According to Nāẓem-al-Eslām Kermānī, in the beginning of Rabīʿ I, 1324/May, 1906, when popular demand for implementing the royal edict establishing the *ʿAdālat-kāna* (House of Justice) peaked, Prime Minister ʿAyn-al-Dawla (q.v.) convened the *Šūrā-ye Dawlatī* (State Council) in Bāḡ-e Šāh, hoping to forestall the *ʿAdālat-kāna* (M. Nāẓem-al-Eslām Kermānī, *Tārīk-e bīdārī-e Īrānīān*, ed. ʿA.-A. Saʿīdī Sīrjānī, 4th ed., Tehran, 1362 Š./1983, I, pp. 380-92).

Bāḡ-e Šāh gained true notoriety as the site where a number of leaders of the Constitutional Revolution were executed by Moḥammad-ʿAlī Shah. When the breach between Moḥammad-ʿAlī Shah and the first Majles became irreparable, on 4 Jomādā I 1326/3 June 1908 the shah moved in full force to Bāḡ-e Šāh, to which his private quarters and state apparatus were also transferred (M.-M. Šarīf Kāšānī, *Wāqeʿāt-e ettefāqīya dar rūzgār*, Tehran, 1362 Š.1983, p. 177; Mostawfī, II, p. 261; Ẓahīr-al-Dawla, p. 329). Nineteen days later (23 Jomādā I 1326/23 June 1908), imperial troops bombarded the Majles, and a number of well-known deputies, such as Sayyed Moḥammad Ṭabāṭabāʾī, Sayyed ʿAbd-Allāh Behbahānī, Ḥājī Mīrzā Naṣr-Allāh Beheštī Malek-al-Motakallemīn, and Mīrzā Jahāngīr Khan Ṣūr-e Esrāfīl (qq.v.) were captured, dragged off in chains to Bāḡ-e Šāh, and, the next day, either executed or imprisoned (Nāẓem-al-Eslām, II, pp. 151-60, 270).

Fearful of public outrage in Tehran, Moḥammad-ʿAlī decided to make the easily defended Bāḡ-e Šāh his permanent residence, and it was there that he convened gatherings attended by his court and royalist clerics. He also met there with a group of anti-Majles divines lead by Shaikh Fażl-Allāh Nūrī, who made his way from the city in the royal carriage (Nāẓem-al-Eslām, II, p. 169). On 12 Šawwāl 1326/7 November 1908, Bāḡ-e Šāh was the site of a meeting of monarchist clerics and members of court held to fulfill a promise the shah had made to foreign diplomats to reconvene the Majles. The participants unanimously condemned the Majles and the renewal of constitutional government as detrimental to Islam and against the *Šarīʿa* and declared that they would leave the country if the shah reopened parliament (Nāẓem-al-Eslām, II, p. 237).

Fearing the advance of nationalist troops from the provinces, Moḥammad-ʿAlī eventually left Bāḡ-e Šāh for the Salṭanatābād palace on 24 Rabīʿ II 1327/16 May 1909. Finally, after Constitutionalist forces had gained control of Tehran, on 27 Jomādā II/16 July of the same year, the shah, his attendants, and about 500 of his soldiers and attendants took refuge in the Russian Legation at Zarganda (Nāẓem-al-Eslām, II, pp. 493-94; E. G. Browne, *The Persian Revolution of 1905-1909*, London, 1966, p. 321).

Bāḡ-e Šāh became historically important again in

1911, when W. Morgan Shuster was invited to Iran as treasurer-general. Shuster, whose mission was to straighten out the country's finances, proposed that a five-company battalion of Treasury Gendarmerie be formed. His proposal was approved by the Majles and Bāğ-e Šāh became battalion headquarters. Two years later, when the Treasury Gendarmerie became a national gendarmerie under the command of the Swedish colonel Hjalmarsen, it remained headquartered in Bāğ-e Šāh. In 1340/1921, the gendarmerie was merged with the cossack division, and Bāğ-e Šāh became an official garrison (J. Šahrī, *Gūša-ī az tārīk-e ejtemā'ī-e Tehrān-e qadīm*, Tehran, 1357 Š./1978, I, p. 178; P. Afsar *Tārīk-e žāndārmerī-e Īrān*, Qom, 1332 Š./1953, pp. 46, 48, 278).

After the revolution of 1357 Š./1978-79, the garrison at Bāğ-e Šāh became the Lāhūtī garrison (after a leader of the revolution who died in a car accident) and later was renamed Pādgān-e Ḥorr after the martyr of Karbalā Ḥorr b. Yazīd Tamīmī.

Bibliography: Given in the text.

('A.-A. SA'ĪDĪ SĪRJĀNĪ)

BĀĞ-E SALṬANATĀBĀD. See SALṬANATĀBĀD.

BAGA, an Old Iranian term for "god," sometimes designating a specific god.

i. *General.*
ii. *In Old and Middle Iranian.*
iii. *The use of* baga *in names.*

i. GENERAL

Baga- is attested in early and late Iranian with two meanings (1) agent noun "disributor," glossed by Parsi Sanskrit *vibhaktar-* and (2) noun of action and result "portion." Beside the noun, the verb *bag-* "give or receive portions" is in frequent use: *bag-*, present *baj-* and *baxš-*, participle *baxta-*, and nominal derivative *bāga-*. The cognate words are cited in full in *Dictionary of Khotan Saka*, p. 300: Avestan *baž-*, *baxta-*, *bāga-*; Sogdian *βaxš-*, *βxt-*, *βyn-*; Zoroastrian Pahlavi *baxš-*, *baxt*, Khotan Saka *būṣṣ-*, *būta-*; Old Indian (Sanskrit) *bhájatiṃ bhaktá-*, *bhága-*, *bhāgá*, traced in Indo-European in J. Pokorny, *Indogermanisches etymologisches Wörterbuch*, Bern and Munich, 1959, p. 107 s.v. *bhag-*.

The agent noun *baga-* "distributor" was adopted as a name for "god" and "gods." In Old Persian *baga-* occurs beside *maθišta bagānām* "greatest of gods" for Ahuramazdā. It renders the Akkadian Semitic *ilu* "god."

In the Avesta the word *yazata-* "worshipful" was preferred, the later Zor. Pahl. *yazd* and Ossetic *izäd*, in Greek script *isdi-* in the name Isdigerdēs, Yazdkirt, Armenian Yazkert. The other word of divinity, *dai-* "shine," is retained once in the Avestan word *dyaoš* "from the sky" (genitive from *dyau-*) and in *daiva-* of the Avestan phrase *daēvāiš-ca mašyāiš-ca* "with gods and men." Normally this word for the ancient gods was developed to "devils" in the Zoroastrian tradition. The North Iranian Khotan Saka also had developed *dyūva-* "devil" from *daiva*. A trace of the older "god" can be seen in the name *Dēv-dād* "created by god." Xerxes in a Persepolis inscription reported *daivadānam viyakanam* "I destroyed the house of devils" (*XPh* 37).

In the later Zoroastrian books Pahlavi and Pāzand *baga-* became *bay* (*bk'*, *by'*, Pāzand *bay*) and occurs associated with *yazata-* in the phrase *yazdān bayān* "gods" (*bk'n*, *by'n*). A lost *nask* "book" of the Avesta (a word preserved in its earlier non-technical sense in Caucasian Georgian *nask'-v-i* "knot," verbal *nask'-va*) was called *Bay* (*bk'*) and *Bayān*. The Avestan *bayō.baxtā-* can be rendered either "bestowed as a portion" or "distributed by the gods," the second meaning can be supported by the compound (*Dēnkard*, ed. Madan, p. 603.6) *bay-tāšīt* "created by gods." The Aramaic ALHA "god" was interpreted by *bay*; it is used in the Ḥājjīābād inscription and in the inscription of *Šāpūr* I, Parthian line 1 *mzdyzn ALHA*, **mazdēzn bay*, Greek MASDAASNĒS THEOS. The king Kosrow I is called *im bay* "his present Majesty" (*Dēnkard*, p. 413.9). Šāpūr son of Ohrmazd is quoted in *Škand-gumānīk Vičār* (ed. P. J. de Menasce, Fribourg, 1945, pp. 118-19, 10.70) *ōi bay šāhpūr i šāhą šāh i hōrməzdą* "the god Šāpūr king of kings son of Ohrmazd." The *bay yazdkart* is cited in *Dēnkard*, p. 949, 21. The word *baya-* gave Sogdian *βγ-* (in Arabic script this *β-* was expressed by the letter *f* with three dots on it, which in normal Arabic could be replaced by *f*). The Buddhist Sogdian employed *βγ-* of the Buddha P 2.1137-45 *βγ'n βγtm pwty* "the most godlike of gods Buddha." The Khotan Saka had preferred *gyastānu gyastä* "god of gods" from *yazata-*. Sogdian had the plural *βγ'yšt*, **βayišt*, gen. plural *βγ'n*, **βayān*, and *βγ'ysť n*, **βayastān* for "paradise."

The Kušan *bagapouro* (from *baga-puθra-*) is represented in Turfan Parthian *bγpwhr* and New Persian *fayfūr*, and found in Armenian *čen-bakour*, the Chinese imperial title *t'ien-tsï* "son of heaven," to which the Old Indian word was *deva-putra-*. Manichean and Christian texts use this same word for "son of god."

Turfan Parthian had *bg*, **bay* with plural *bayān* and adjective *bayānīy*. Turfan Persian had developed *-y-* from *-γ-* in *by*, **bay*, plural *ba'ān* (*b''n*) and adjective *bayānīy*. This *bai* is found in New Persian *bē-doxt*, *bē-loft* "from **baga-duxtā* "daughter of god" for the planet Venus. About A.D. 800 Iranian *bay* is present in Kirkut (Qiryiz) *bai*, written by the Chinese sign *buâi* (Mathews, *Chinese-English Dictionary*, no. 4991, modern *pei*) cited in *JA*, 1950, p. 298. The Kirkut adopted the Turkish language only in the 7th-8th centuries.

Khotan Saka has *be'ga-*, *ba'ga-*, and *be-* in the title *be'garakä*, *ba'garakä*, and *berakä* for Turkish *bägräk*.

From Turkish, in proper names Ossetic has *bī* "prince," as in *Baras-bī* "tiger, prince."

Turkish took the title *bäg*, *beg*, and later *bey*; in early Turkish in Brāhmī script it was *bhek*, and in Byzantine Greek the Khazar title was written *mékh*. The form *bägräk* occurs in a Turfan Manichean source. In Arabic script the Turkish title was *bag*, *bak*, and *bāk*.

The sacred fire called *farn-bay* "the distributor (god) of *farn*" (*farn* was equated with Aramaic GDH "fortune") was located at Kārīān in Fārs. The Pāzand read the name as *farō-bag* and in Armenian it probably gave *hour-bak*.

In Kushan inscriptions this *baga-* is *vaka-* and *vvaga-* in the name Vaka-mihira and Vvaga-mihira "the god Miθra." The *v-* and *vv-* are an attempt to express the fricative *β*. The Kushan *bakana-pati-* "temple official" is *βγn-pt* in Sogdian. Armenian has *bagin* (q.v.) "shrine, altar" from Parthian.

Choresmian from Toprak-kala has *βγy* for the sixteenth day of the month corresponding to *mtr* "Miθra," as Bīrūnī gave *fγy*, **βaγ*, from *βaγi* for the same day.

The word *baga-* occurs in many proper names in ancient Persia. In Greek these names are written with Baga- and Mega-. The name *bg-srw*, **baga-srava-* occurs in an Aramaic papyrus from Egypt.

Two toponyms contain the word *baga-* in Persia, others are in Armenia. The rock of *Behistūn*, Bīsotūn is on *tò Bagístanon óros*. The *Bundahišn* cites *Baγ-dāt ī baγān-dāt* "Baghdad which is created by the god(s)" (TD_2, p. 205.12).

In the sense of "portion" Gathic Avestan has *baga-*, beside later *baγa-* and *baγā-*, which is glossed by Zor. Pahl. *baγ*, *bažišn*, and *baxtārīh*.

The derivative *baxta-* "distributed, allotted" also is frequent later. The Avestan phrase in *Vištāsp yašt* 38, *baxta-ca nivaxta-ca*, is explained to mean *pat nēvakīh ut frazandān* "possessed of good things and children" where "possessed" is Pahlavi *baxtadār* (*baxtiyār*). The *baxt* "fortune" takes the form of a *varrak ī vazurg* "great ram" mounted behind Artaxšaθr (Ardašīr) in his flight from Artapān (Ardavān).

The noun derivative *bāga-* is also important in connexion with *baga-*. A later form is attested in Khotan Saka *haṃbāya-* (sing. *haṃbā*, plural *haṃbāya*) "portion" corresponding to Turfan Parthian *'mb'g*, **ambāγ*, Turfan Persian *hmb'w*, **hambāv*, "rival," Zor. Pahl. *hambāγ*, Pāzand *hambāi*, *hambāe* "companion." Through connexion with "possessions" the Iranian *bāγ* gave Turkish *bai* "rich," whence Mongol *bayan* "rich." In Ossetic the Turkish *bai-* occurs in the personal family name *Bai-tuγantä* "rich" and "bird of prey." As a "portion of land" New Persian has *bāγ* "garden" and Pāzand has *bāγastą i vahəšt* "garden of Paradise," that is Garōδamān, and *vahišt* is in Zor. Pahlavi *bōδastān* "garden as place of perfumes." From Alanian (that is older Ossetic) Caucasian Čečen has (with many other words of Alanian origin) the word *bai* "meadow, lawn," plural *beš*, with Inguš *bai*, plural *bäš* (the plural suffix is *-aš* and *-š-*).

This *bāγ* "rich" is also found in the Finno-Ugrian Ostyak *way*.

(H. W. Bailey)

ii. In Old and Middle Iranian

The old IE. term for the heavenly gods, the cognate of OInd. *devá-*, Lat. *deus*, etc., was generally devalued in Iranian to "false or evil god" and ultimately "demon" (Av. *daēva-*, Old Pers. *daiva-*, Mid. Pers. *dēw*, etc.). In the sense "god," this word was replaced either by *yazata-* "(a being) worthy of worship" (Av. *yazata-*, Mid. Pers. *yaz(a)d*, NPers. *īzad*, etc.) or by *baga-*.

It is not likely that OIr. *baga-* derives from a word meaning "god" in IE., despite the occurrence of *bogŭ* "god" in the Slavonic languages (probably as a result of Iranian influence). Etymologically, *baga-* "god" belongs to the verbal root *bag* "to distribute, allot" and may be equated with OInd. *bhága-*, a divine epithet probably meaning "dispenser; generous one," beside which there exists also a second noun *bhága-* "distribution, allotted portion" equivalent to Av. *baγa-* "portion, lot," Slavonic **bogŭ* in derivatives such as *ubogŭ* "poor" (from "*portionless"). It is this latter word which is personified in the Rigveda as the minor deity Bhaga (one of the Ādityas, a group headed by Varuṇa and Mitra). (See P. Thieme in B. Schlerath, ed., *Zarathustra*, Darmstadt, 1970, p. 401.)

Av. *baga-* occurs only once in the *Gāθās*, in a much-debated passage (*Y.* 32.8) where it possibly means "portion" or "distribution." In the later Avestan texts *baγa-* occurs occasionally as a title of divinities (Ahura Mazdā, Māh, Mithra), but it is debatable whether it should still be understood in the earlier sense of "dispenser" (cf. OInd. *bhága-*) or already as "god." The development of the latter meaning is securely attested in Old Persian, where *baga-*, translated by words meaning "god" in Babylonian and Elamite, is the only generic term for the divinities worshipped by the Achaemenids.

There is no certain trace of *baga-* in the Mid. Ir. Saka dialects, where forms derived from *yazata-* (Khot. *gyasta-*, Tumshuqese *jezda-*) are used instead, while Islamic Choresmian has adopted Ar. *'llh* for "God" (but cf. Chor. (')*βγ(y)k* "doll" from **baga-ka-*). All other attested Mid. Ir. languages retain forms derived from *baga-* in the sense "god": Mid. Pers. *bay* (plur. *bayān*, *ba'ān*), Parth. *baγ*, Bactr. *bago*, Sogd. *βγ-*. All these forms are used as honorific titles, not only of gods but also of kings and other men of high rank, in which case the translation "lord" is usually appropriate, e.g., Bactr. *i bago šao Kanēški* "the lord king Kanishka." In Zoroastrian Pahl. *im bay* "this lord" and *ōy bay* "that lord" mean "His (present) Majesty" and "His late Majesty" respectively. A peculiar use of the plur. form to refer to the monarch is found in the Sasanian inscriptions (and perhaps in the Sogd. "Ancient letters," see W. B. Henning, "Soghdisch *βγ''n-*," *ZDMG* 90, 1936, pp. 197-99), e.g., Inscr. Parth. *LKM 'LHYN* (*išmāh bayān*) "Your Majesty." A derivation of the Turk. lordly title *bäg*, later *bey*, from Iranian is superficially attractive but quite uncertain (see G. Doerfer, *Türkische und mongolische Elemente im Neupersischen* II, Wiesbaden, 1965, pp. 402-06).

It is probable that *baga-* "god" sometimes designates a specific deity as "the god" *par excellence*. Various attempts have been made to identify "the god" so referred to, as Ahura Mazdā, as Mithra, or as an Iranian equivalent of the Vedic Varuṇa (see M. Boyce,

"Varuna the Baga," further identifying Varuṇa with the Av. Apąm Napāt [q.v.]), but no basis has ever been stated for the assumption that *baga-* "the god" in a personal name such as **Baga-dāta-* "given by (the) god" must refer to the same divinity at all periods and in all parts of the Iranian world. However, strong evidence that Baga was sometimes used as a by-name of Mithra is provided by calendrical data first exploited by J. Marquart (Markwart), *Untersuchungen zur Geschichte von Eran* I, Göttingen, 1896, pp. 63-65; II, Leipzig, 1905, pp. 129, 132-34 (see also V. A. Livshits, "The Khwarezmian Calendar and the Eras of Ancient Chorasmia," *Acta Antiqua Academiae Scientiarum Hungaricae* 16, 1968, pp. 444-46, for Chor. data). Thus, the seventh month of the year is named after Mithra in Mid. Pers. *Mihr māh*, Arm. *Mehekan*, early Chor. *mtr*, but after Baga in Old Pers. **Bāgayādiya* (attested in El. transcription) and *Bāgayādi(š)* (q.v.), Sogd. *βγk'n(c)* (cf. the similar formations used to name the ninth month: Mid. Pers. *Ādur māh*, Arm. *Ahekan*, early Chor. *'trw*, Old Pers. *Āçiyādiya* (q.v.) and **Āçiyādi(š)*). Likewise, the sixteenth day of the month is known as *Mihr rōz* in Mid. Pers., *mtr* in early Chor., *myš* in the Sogd. calendar given by Bīrūnī, etc., but as *fγy* (for **βγy*) in Bīrūnī's Chor. calendar, *βγy-rwc* in a Sogd. document from Mount Mug, *bgy* in a Chor. inscription.

A different interpretation of these facts was proposed by W. B. Henning, "A Sogdian God," *BSOAS* 28, 1965, pp. 242-54. Chiefly on the basis of an etymology of Sogd. *βγ'ny-pš-kt'kw* "wedding" as "making of a Baga-union" and a reference to *βγy*, apparently as a god distinct from *myδr'* "Mithra," in a Sogd. marriage contract, he identifies Baga with the Vedic Bhaga: both in India and in Iran, B(h)aga would be a god with a "special interest in marriage" and closely associated (but not identical) with Mit(h)ra. This theory has been supported with onomastic data by P. Gignoux, "Le dieu Baga en Iran," *Acta Antiqua Academiae Scientiarum Hungaricae* 25, 1977 (1980), pp. 119-27, but it has also been strongly challenged, see especially A. Dietz, "Baga and Miθra in Sogdiana," in *Études mithriaques*, Acta Iranica 17, Tehran and Liège, 1978, pp. 111-14, and S. Zimmer, "Iran. *baga*—ein Gottesname?," *MSS* 43, 1984, pp. 187-215, and cannot be regarded as proven.

Bibliography: The article by S. Zimmer just cited includes a useful discussion of most problems concerning *baga-*, while the Old and Mid. Ir. usage is surveyed by M. Boyce, "Varuna the Baga," in *Monumentum Georg Morgenstierne*, Acta Iranica 21, Leiden, 1981, pp. 59-73, esp. 61-65. On the relationship between OIr. *baga-* and OInd. *bhága-*, Slavonic *bogŭ* see M. Mayrhofer, *Kurzgefasstes etymologisches Wörterbuch des Altindischen* II, Heidelberg, 1963, pp. 457-59. Regarding H. W. Bailey's suggested reading and interpretation of Khot. **vvūvayau* as a royal title derived from **baga-yauna-* (e.g., in *The Culture of the Sakas in Ancient Iranian Khotan*, Col. Lect. Ser. 1, Delmar, 1982, p. 11) see R. E. Emmerick in *Studies in the Vocabulary of Khotanese* II, ed. R. E. Emmerick and P. O. Skjærvø, Vienna, 1987, pp. 132-34.

(N. SIMS-WILLIAMS)

iii. THE USE OF BAGA IN NAMES

Baga- as a name element occurs in names of towns, e.g., *Bagadāta-*, modern Baghdad "given by *baga*" or "established by *baga*," **Bagadāna-* "temple (?) of (the) god(s)," Old Armenian *Bagaran*, a town and a village (see Hübschmann), with derivative suffix *-ka-* Bactrian *bagolaggo* "altar" (or proper name "The Sanctuary"), today *Baḡlān*, name of the region (see Henning), *Bagastāna-* in Media "place of the gods," so named after the nearby Bīsotūn carvings and inscriptions, *Bag(e)is* in Lydia; rivers, e.g., *Bagrades*, today Nābendrūd, *Bagossala*, probably modern Bug, Ukraina; and mountains, e.g., *tò Bagístanon óros* at Bagastāna, see above, *Bagôon óros* between Areia and Drangiana (see Pauly-Wissowa, II, 2, cols. 2765-74; S. I, col. 237). Most of the names, however, are personal names and exclusively men's names. All three Indo-European name types are attested, namely, one-stem-names ("short names"), derivatives (mostly hypocoristica), and compound names. Short names are seldom (e.g., *Baga* inscription of Priene 1st cent. A.D., perhaps *Vaga*, "Indoscythian" stratega inscription ca. 20 A.D.). The hypocoristica (e.g., *Bagaios*, *Bagauka-*) have been treated in many articles by R. Schmitt (see Schmitt, 1982 and "Indogermanische Chronik"). Of compound names, *Bagabigna-* and *Bagabuxša-* are attested in the Old Persian inscriptions (see *IPNB*), but more than 60 other Old Iranian names are found from the sixth or even eighth century B.C. in Aramaic, Armenian, Babylonian, Egyptian, Elamite, Greek, Hebrew, Indo-Arian, Latin, Lydian, and Lykian tradition, see Schmitt, 1982 with references, also to the studies on the phonetic shape of Old Iranian *baga-* in these languages respectively. The Middle Iranian names are only partially published, see Gignoux, 1980a, 1980b, and forthcoming parts of *Iranisches Personennamenbuch*. At present, four *baga* names are known from epigraphical Middle Persian: 'twrbg, bg'twr, bg'whrm[zd], plnbgy (this itself part of compounds), and one from Sogdian: βγyfrn. On the linguistic classification and interpretation of these compound names, see Schmitt, 1981, and Zimmer, 1984.

Contrary to the opinion of Gignoux, 1980a and b, these names do not provide any evidence for the existence of an Iranian deity "Baga." See the detailed analysis of the arguments in Zimmer, 1984. Old Iranian *baga-*, from Indo-Iranian **bhaga-*, means "allotment, distribution," later also "god" [but see also BAGA i, above], and in Middle Iranian *bag/bay* "god, lord" as a mode of address of gods and noble men. Nowhere in Iranian is this word a name. Only in India did the concept of "allotment, distribution" become the Āditya Bhaga.

Mayrhofer's suggestion (*Etymological Sanskrit Dictionary* II, p. 457) that *baga-* in Iranian names replaces the old **daiva-* whose meaning had been changed to "evil deity" by Zarathustra, is quite attractive, but hard to prove.

The Old Persian month name *Bāgayādi-* (q.v.) is interpreted by R. Schmitt as "(month of) worship of the god," against Henning's suggestion "(month of) fertilizing (?) the fields" (comparing Middle and Modern Persian *bāḡ* "garden" [q.v.]). This interpretation is supported by the parallel formation *Açiyādiya/*Açiyādiš* (Elamite) "(month of) fire-worship" (cf. the Middle Persian month *Ādur*, Armenian *Ahekan*; see i, above). This could imply a special worship of Miθra (?) in one month, and of Ātar in the other, perhaps because of some major feasts celebrated in these months.

For place and personal names containing Baga-, see, e.g., BAGARAN; BAGAWAN; BAGAYARIČ; BAGAZUŠTA; BAGHDAD; BAGRATIDS.

Bibliography: Ph. Gignoux, "Le dieux Baga en Iran," *Acta Antiqua Academiae Scientiarum Hungaricae* 25, 1977 [1980], pp. 119-27 (1980a). Idem, "Les noms propres en moyen-perse épigraphique," *Pad nām ī yazdān*, Université de la Sorbonne Nouvelle, Travaux de l'Institut d'Études Iraniennes 9, 1979 [1980], pp. 35-100 (1980b). W. B. Henning, "Surkh Kotal," *BSOAS* 18, 1956, pp. 366-67, Acta Iranica 15, 1977, pp. 503-04. W. Hinz, *Altiranisches Sprachgut der Nebenüberlieferungen*, Wiesbaden, 1975. H. Hübschmann, "Die Altarmenischen Ortsnamen," *Indogermanische Forschungen* 16, 1904, pp. 410-11. M. Mayrhofer, *A Concise Etymological Sanskrit Dictionary* (*Kurzgefasstes Etymologisches Wörterbuch des Altindischen*), Heidelberg, 1965-80. Idem, *Onomastica Persepolitana*, Vienna, 1973, esp. 8.184-8.244. M. Mayrhofer and R. Schmitt, eds., *Iranisches Personennamenbuch*, Vienna, 1977ff. (*IPNB*). R. Schmitt, "Altpersisch-Forschung in den Siebzigerjahren," *Kratylos* 25, 1980 [1982], pp. 1-66. Idem, "Indogermanische Chronik, chap. V c 3," *Die Sprache*, Vienna, twice yearly. Idem, review of Gignoux, 1980b, *Studia Iranica* 10, 1981, pp. 154-59. St. Zimmer, "Iran. baga- —ein Gottesname?" *MSS* 43, 1984, pp. 187-215 (with further references). R. Zwanziger, *Studien zur Nebenüberlieferung iranischer Personennamen in den griechischen Inschriften Kleinasiens*, Ph.D. dissertation, Vienna, 1973.

(ST. ZIMMER)

BAGABUXŠA. See MEGABYZUS.

BAGĀN YAŠT (1) one of the *dādīg* (legal) *nasks* of the Avesta; (2) name of *Y.* 19-21 (see BAG NASK). The *Bagān yašt* (the *Dēnkard* has *yast* for *yašt* or *yasn*; the *Persian Rivayats* have *Bağān yašt* and *Bayān yašt*), according to the brief account of it in the *Dēnkard* (8.15), contained descriptions of Ahura Mazdā, highest of all the gods (**wisp* [ms. *yst'*] *bayān abardom*), and the remaining invisible and visible gods in the world (*abārīg apaydāg ud paydāg gētīgān-iz yazdān*) (*Dēnkard*, Dresden, p. 105 [82]; Madan, p. 692; tr. West, pp. 34f.; the *Persian Rivayats* in West, pp. 418, 426, 431, 436). It is generally assumed that at least some of the known *yašt*s plus the *Hōm yašt* (*Y.* 9-11) and the *Srōš yašt* (*Y.* 57) belonged to this *nask*. According to the *Persian Rivayats* (p. 4) it had seventeen sections and one *rivayat* enumerates sixteen *yašt*s belonging to the *Bagān yašt*: the nineteen known *yašt*s less *Yt.* 2, 3, 6 (West, p. xlv n. 1; Darmesteter, II, pp. xxvi-xxviii). The old *yašt* manuscript F numbers the six last *yašt*s (*Yt.* 14-19) as 11-16, which may be based upon an old tradition (Darmesteter, ibid.).

The reason for the lack of any substantial information about this *nask* in the *Dēnkard* is no doubt due to the fact that the Pahlavi version of the *yašt*s had been lost by the time the *Dēnkard* was compiled. A few quotations from the *Bagān yašt* not found in the *yašt* collection may have survived (see West, pp. 470-71).

Bibliography: Darmesteter, *Zend-Avesta* II, pp. xxvi-xxviii; III, pp. x-xi, xvi. B. N. Dhabhar, ed., *The Persian Rivayats of Hormazyar Framarz and Others*, Bombay, 1932. M. R. Unvala, *Dârâb Hormazyâr's Rivâyat* I, Bombay, 1922. W. E. West, *Pahlavi Texts* IV: *Contents of the Nasks*, SBE 37, Oxford, 1892, repr. Delhi, etc., 1965. (H. W. Bailey's emendation to **Bagān* of an unreadable word in a Pahlavi text dealing with the history of the Avesta is quite hypothetical; *Zoroastrian Problems in the Ninth-Century Books*, Oxford, 1943, 2nd ed., 1971, pp. 160f.)

(P. O. SKJÆRVØ)

BAGARAN (Turk. Pakran), a town and fortress of the Armenian principality of Aršarunikʻ (40° 12′ north latitude, 43° 39′ east longitude) 5 km (3 miles) west of the right bank of the Axurean river (Arpaçai). Bagaran, lit. "the god's place," was founded at the end of the third century B. C. by the Armenian King Orontes (Eruand) II (ca. 212-ca. 200 B.C.) to house the images of the gods and the royal ancestors brought from the earlier holy city of Armavir (q.v.). Orontes established his brother Eruaz there as high priest of the Armenian pantheon (Moses of Khorene, 2.40; tr. Thomson, p. 182) and during the king's reign Bagaran became the religious center and holy city of Orontid Armenia. In the time of Artaxias (Artašēs) I (189-ca. 161 B.C.) the idols of Bagaran were transferred to the new capital Artaxata (Artašat, ibid., 2.49) but Bagaran remained an important cult center until the conversion of Armenia to Christianity (ca. 314).

When the Bagratids acquired Aršarunikʻ in the ninth century Bagaran was only briefly its first capital but in the period of the Bagratid kingdom (884-1045), the town flourished as a stop on the transit trade route from the later Bagratid capital, Ani, to the west.

Bagaran was noted for the fine church of St. Theodore (erected 624-31), now totally destroyed. Bagaran was destroyed in the Mongol period but its remains were still visible in the early twentieth century.

Bibliography: L. Ališan, *Ayrarat*, Venice, 1890. J. Dimitrokalis, "Kʻnnakan xrher" and S. Milani, "Satiroykʻ čartarapetutʻyan ew vałmiǰnadaryan k'arakonk' ekłec'ineri cagman harc'eri šurj," in *Sovetakan Arvest*, Erevan, 1970, no. 5. S. T. Eremyan, *Hayastanə əst "Ašxarhac'oyc'"-i*, Erevan, 1963, p. 42. T. X. Hakobyan, *Hayastani patmakan ašxarhagrut'iwnə*, 2nd ed., Erevan, 1968, pp. 132-33. S. Manuč'aryan and H. Xalp'axc'yan "Bagaran," *Hayastani sovetakan hanragitaran* II, Erevan, 1976, p. 197. N. Sargsyan, *Tełagrut'iwnk'i P'ok'r ew i Mec Hayastan*, Venice, 1864. T. T'oramanyan, *Nyut'er haykakan čartarapetut'yan patmut'yan*, pts. 1-2, Erevan, 1942-48. C. Toumanoff, *Studies in Christian Caucasian History*, Washington, 1963, pp. 302, 306, 310, 319, 320.

(R. H. HEWSEN)

BAḠAVĪ, ABU'L-ḤASAN 'ALĪ B. 'ABD-AL-'AZĪZ B. MARZBĀN B. SĀBŪR, traditionist (*moḥaddeṯ*) and philologist in the 3rd/9th century. He came from Bağšūr, a town near Marv-al-Rūḏ. Since he was more than ninety years old when he died in 286/899 or 287/900, his birth can be placed in the last decade of the second century A. H. Little is known about his life except that he certainly studied in Iraq and then settled at Mecca, where he remained until his death. He was considered reliable by some well-known authorities on Hadith such as Dāraqoṭnī and Ebn Abī Ḥātem, but because poverty forced him to take fees for his lectures, he was rejected by the eminent traditionist Abū 'Abd-al-Raḥmān Nasā'ī.

Baḡavī is mentioned as the compiler of a *mosnad* (collection arranged under the sources of transmission). Foremost among his teachers was Abū 'Obayd Qāsem b. Sallām Heravī, a theologian, philologist, and jurist who died at Mecca probably in 224/838-39. The latter's books *Ḡarīb al-ḥadīṯ*, *al-Ḥayż*, and *al-Ṭahāra* were transcribed and passed on by Baḡavī; a section entitled *Joz' fīhi men ḥadīṯ 'Alī b. 'Abd-al-'Azīz 'an Abī 'Obayd al-Qāsem b. Sallām* still survives in manuscript (Sezgin, *GAS* I, p. 161). Among Baḡavī's other teachers were Fażl b. Dokayn Abū No'aym Taymī (d. 219/834) and 'Affān b. Moslem Abū 'Oṯmān Ṣaffār (d. probably 220/835). His most distinguished pupil was his nephew 'Abd-Allāh b. Moḥammad b. 'Abd-al-'Azīz Abu'l-Qāsem Baḡavī known as Ebn bent Aḥmad b. Manī' (d. 317/929). Another pupil, Solaymān b. Aḥmad Abu'l-Qāsem Ṭabarānī (d. 360/971) also gained some repute.

Bibliography: Ebn Abī Ḥātem, *al-Jarḥ wa'l-ta'dīl* III, 1, Hyderabad (Deccan), 1360/1941, p. 196. Ebn al-Nadīm, *al-Fehrest*, ed. G. Flügel, Leipzig, 1871, p. 72. Yāqūt, *Eršād al-arīb 'alā ma'refat al-adīb* V, ed. D. S. Margoliouth, Leiden and London, 1911 (GMS 64), pp. 247-49. Moḥammad Ḏahabī, *Taḏkerat al-ḥoffāẓ*, 3rd ed., II, Hyderabad (Deccan), 1376/1956, pp. 622-23. Idem, *Mīzān al-e'tedāl* II, Cairo, 1325/1907, p. 232. Idem, *al-'Ebar fī ḵabar man ḡabar* II, Kuwait, 1961, p. 77. Ebn Ḥajar 'Asqalānī, *Tahḏīb al-tahḏīb* VII, Hyderabad (Deccan), 1326/1908, pp. 362-63. Idem, *Lesān al-mīzān* IV, Hyderabad (Deccan), 1330/1912, p. 241. Ḵayr-al-Dīn Zereklī, *al-A'lām*, 2nd ed., V, Cairo, 1374/1955, p. 113. 'Omar Reżā Kaḥḥāla, *Mo'jam al-mo'allefīn* VII, Damascus, 1378/1959, p. 124.

(H. SCHÜTZINGER)

BAGAWAN (Baguan or At'ši Bagawan), a district of the land of Kaspianē (Arm. *Kasp'k'*, later *P'aytakaran*) lying along the right bank of the Araxes river and corresponding to the northeastern part of Iranian Azerbaijan. Here was located the town of Bagaran or At'ši Bagawan (Ar. and Pers. Bāgarvān or Bājarvān) now Badcharvan (Bājarvān), a village in Prishib *raion* in Soviet Azerbaijan of the district center of the same name. Nearby flows the Bagarwan river, now Bazarchaĭ (Bazarčāy) but still called the Bagaru by the Armenians and the local Iranian-speaking Ṭāleš. In the seventeenth century the district was still called Bejirwan, while the name At'ši (presumably from Mid. Pers. *ātaš* "fire") suggests that the town may once have been a center of Zoroastrian worship (Eremyan, p. 42).

Bibliography: See also the anonymous seventh-century Armenian geography *Ašxarhac'oyc'*, in A. Abrahamyan, *Anania Širakac'u matenagrut'yunə*, Erevan, 1944. Łewond Erec', *Patmut'iwn Hayoc'*, St. Petersburg, 1887, p. 101. H. Hübschmann, *Die altarmenischen Ortsnamen*, Strassburg, 1904, repr. Amsterdam, 1969, p. 351. S. T. Eremyan, *Hayastanə əst "Ašxarhac'oyc'"-i*, Erevan, 1963.

(H. R. HEWSEN)

BAGAWAN, an ancient locality in central Armenia situated at the foot of Mount Npat (Gk. Niphates, Turk. Tapa-seyd) in the principality of Bagrewand west of modern Diyadin. The name means literally "town of the gods." It is attested in Greek as Sakauana (for *Bagauana) in Ptolemy (*Geography* 5.12.7). Agathangelos (par. 817) explains it as *dic'-awan* "town of the gods," but Moses of Khorene as *bagnac'n awan* "town of altars" (see Hübschmann, p. 411). Bagawan was one of the chief shrines of pagan Armenia and a perpetual fire was kept burning there (Moses of Khorene, 2.77, tr. Thomson, p. 225); the New Year's festival on the first day of the month of Nawasard was celebrated by the royal family at Bagawan (Agathangelos, par. 836; ed. and tr. Thomson, pp. 371f.). The account of Moses of Khorene (2.56) of the altar erected by Bagawan by the "last Tigran" and his attribution of the establishment of this festival to King Valarsaces (Vałaršak) are probably his own inventions (cf. Moses of Khorene, tr. Thomson, pp. 493-94 notes). After the conversion of Armenia to Christianity (ca. 314), it is here that King Tiridates (Trdat) the Great and his court are said to have been baptized by St. Gregory the Illuminator in the Euphrates (Agathangelos, par. 832), whose southern arm (Muratsu) takes its source nearby. St. Gregory is said to have founded the important monastery of St. John the Baptist here from which the town received its Turkish name Üç Kilise "the three churches." According to Moses of Ḵhorene (3.67; tr. Thomson, p. 347) Shah

Yazdegerd (Yazkert) II of Iran camped at Bagawan during his invasion of Armenia in 439.

The church of St. John the Baptist at Bagawan was erected on the left bank of the Euphrates in 631-39. It was surrounded by a high wall flanked with towers which protected the monastic buildings within. The monastery was pillaged by the Kurds in 1877 and was totally destroyed after 1915.

Bibliography: L. Ališan, *Ayrarat*, Venice, 1890. S. T. Eremyan, *Hayastanə əst "Ašxarhac'oyc'"-i*, Erevan, 1963, p. 42. T. X. Hakobyan, *Hayastani patmakan ašxarhagrut'iwn*, 2nd ed., Erevan, 1968, pp. 90, 135, 136, 371. Idem et al., "Bagavan," in *Haykakan sovetakan hanragitaran* II, Erevan, 1976, p. 196. H. Hübschmann, *Die altarmenischen Ortsnamen*, Strassburg, 1904, repr. Amsterdam, 1969, pp. 380, 411. H. T. Tozer, *Turkish Armenia and Eastern Asia Minor*, London, 1881, pp. 392-94. C. Toumanoff, *Studies in Christian Caucasian History*, Washington, 1963, pp. 319-20.

(R. H. HEWSEN)

BĀGAYĀDIŠ (*b-a-g-y-a-di-i-š*, attested only in gen. °*yādaiš*/°*y-a-d-i-š*), name of the seventh month (September-October) of the Old Persian calendar, mentioned in Darius I's Behistun inscription 1.55 (see Kent, *Old Persian*, p. 161a). It is equivalent to Akkadian Tašrītu and Elamite Manšarki (several attestations only in the Persepolis tablets; see R. T. Hallock, *Persepolis Fortification Tablets*, Chicago, 1969, pp. 74, 724a). In the Persepolis tablets the Old Persian name is often rendered as Elamite Bakeyatiš (with numerous variants; see ibid., p. 673b), which indicates an Old Persian by-form *Bāgayādya- (see W. Hinz, *Neue Wege im Altpersischen*, Wiesbaden, 1973, pp. 67f.). The etymological interpretation of the name Bāgayādiš is disputed: The form is best understood as "(month of) worship of the god" (perhaps Mithra), since *bāga-yādi-* "pertaining to **baga-yāda-* 'worship of the god(s)'" represents a common Indo-Iranian compound type (see J. Wackernagel and A. Debrunner, *Altindische Grammatik* II/2, Göttingen, 1954, p. 303, par. 190a). The interpretation of the name as "fertilizing the farmland" or "irrigation of the gardens" (thus W. B. Henning, *JRAS*, 1944, p. 134 = *Selected Papers* II, Acta Iranica 15, Tehran and Liège, 1977, p. 140), based only upon NPers. *bāḡ* "garden," seems less probable.

See also BAGA.

Bibliography: Given in the text. See also W. Brandenstein and M. Mayrhofer, *Handbuch des Altpersischen*, Wiesbaden, 1964, p. 110, s.v. W. Eilers, *Der alte Name des persischen Neujahrsfestes*, Mainz and Wiesbaden, 1953, passim.

(R. SCHMITT)

BAGAYAŘIČ, also BAGAŘIČ or BAGAŘINČ; Gk. *Bagaris (Strabo, 11.14.14). Basgoidariza (ibid., 12.3.28), and *Bagarizaka (Ptolemy, 5.13.4); Turk. Pekeric; a locality in the district of Daranałi in northwestern Armenia, about 91.6 km (55 miles) west of Erzerum 40° 53′ north latitude, 40° 13′ east longitude) Bagayařič lay on the main road through northern Armenia linking Sebastea (Sīvās) in the Roman Empire with Ecbatana (Hamadān) in Media via Satala, Bagayařič, Karin (Erzerum) and Artaxata (Artašat).

Bagayařič was celebrated as the site of the great temple of Mihr (Mithras, one of the eight principal pagan shrines of pre-Christian Armenia), traditionally built by Tigranes II the Great (r. B.C. 95-56). It is possible that all of the surrounding district of Daranałi formed the domain of this temple for after its destruction at the time of the conversion of Armenia to Christianity (ca. A.D. 314), Daranałi became the property of the Armenian church. At the turn of the twentieth century, Bagayařič consisted of two adjoining villages Verin "upper" and Nerkin "lower" Bagařič, consisting respectively of 80 and 130 homes, half of which were inhabited by Armenians and the rest by local Muslims, the two together forming the larger village in the *caza* (district) of Derǰan. Ruins of the temple and an old castle could still be seen at Bagařič at that time.

Bibliography: L. Ališan, *Ayrarat*, Venice, 1890. S. T. Eremyan, *Hayastanə əst "Ašxarhac'oyc'"-i*, Erevan, 1963, p. 42. T. X. Hakobyan, *Hayastani patmakan ašxarhagrut'iwnə*, 2nd ed., Erevan, 1968, pp. 221, 226. Idem, "Bagařič," in *Haykakan sovetakan hanragitaran* II, Erevan, 1976, p. 196. H. Hübschmann, *Armenische Grammatik*, Leipzig, 1897, p. 113. Idem, *Die altarmenischen Ortsnamen*, Strassburg, 1904, repr. Amsterdam, 1969, pp. 284, 287, 379. I. A. Orbeli, *Izbrannye trudy*, Erevan, 1963. A. Perikhanyan, *Khramovye ob"edineniya Maloĭ Azii i Armenii*, Moscow, 1959.

(R. H. HEWSEN)

BAGAZUŠTA, Old Iranian personal name. **Baga-zušta-* "beloved of the god(s)" is the Median counterpart of Old Persian **baga-dušta-*, which is attested in Elamite Ba-ka-du-iš-da and Greek Megadóstes (Benveniste, *Titres et noms propres en iranien ancien*, Paris, 1966, p. 117; Hinz, *Altiranisches Sprachgut der Nebenüberlieferungen*, Wiesbaden, 1975, p. 55).

1. The manufacturer of a plate in a Persepolis text of 467/66 B.C. (R. A. Bowman, *Aramaic Ritual Texts from Persepolis*, Chicago, 1970, no. 18.2: *bgpšt*, to be corrected to *bgzšt* according to M. N. Bogolyubov, *Izvestiya Akademii Nauk SSSR. Seriya literatury i yazyka* 32, 1973, p. 177).

2. A "Caspian" from Elephantine island, son of Bāzu (P. Grelot, *Semitica* 21, 1971, p. 108) and husband of Ūbīl, in Aramaic documents of 437, 434 and 401 (402?) B.C. (E. G. Kraeling, *The Brooklyn Museum Aramaic Papyri*, New Haven, 1953, nos. 3.2ff. and 12.4ff. [*bgzšt*]; no. 4.3 [*bgzwšt*]).

3. A Persian dignitary of unknown rank (Ba-ga-zu-uš-tu_4/tú) in a Babylonian deed of Xerxes' reign (Amherst 258:4.12; A. Ungnad, *Archiv für Orientforschung* 19, 1959-60, pp. 80ff.; M. A. Dandamayev, "Vavilonskiĭ

dokument o drevnikh irantsakh," in *Voprosy iranskoĭ i obshcheĭ filologii*, Tiflis, 1977, pp. 93-97).

4. A foreman (*šaknu*) of Indians, son of Bagapâtu, in Babylonian documents of 423 to 417 B.C. (*BE* X 53:24, Lo.E.; 70:6. 9, R. [Ba-ga-ʾ-zu-uš-tu_4]; *PBS* II/1, 4:17; 16:17, L.E.; 135:25, L.E.; 137:15 [Ba-ga-ʾ-zu-uš-tu_4]; *TMHC* 190:14 [Ba-ga-ʾ-zu-uš-tu_4]).

5. Another such foreman, son of Parurê (Ba-ga-zu-uš-tu_4), in a deed of 425 B.C. (*BE* IX 76:11).

6. The son of a certain Bagadâtu (Ba-ga-zu-uš-tu_4) in a document of 422 B.C. (*PBS* II/1, 192:18, U.E.).

7. A Lycian from Telmessus (Megasústas) in two Greek honorary inscriptions (*TAM* II/1, 15 II 3; 15 III/IV 5; 16, 2) from Roman times.

Bibliography: See also R. Schmitt, *BNF*, N. F. 6, 1971, pp. 25-27, and *Die Sprache* 17, 1971, pp. 177f. L. Zgusta, *Kleinasiatische Personennamen*, Prague, 1964, p. 307, par. 886c.

(R. SCHMITT)

BAĠDĀD. See BAGHDAD.

BAĠDĀDĪ, ʿABD-AL-QĀHER B. ṬĀHER ŠĀFEʿĪ TAMĪMĪ, (ca. 350/961-429/1038) mathematician, Shafiʿite jurist and Ashʿarite theologian. He was born in Baghdad, the son of a wealthy merchant by the name of Ṭāher b. Moḥammad b. ʿAbd-Allāh b. Ebrāhīm (cf. *Taʾrīḵ Baġdād* IX, p. 358 n. 4923; Sobkī, *Ṭabaqāt*² V, pp. 51ff.). Early on his father left the capital and settled in Nīšāpūr; there he spent much of his money for scholarly purposes and by that acquired some recognition among the educated circles of the town. The son had wide interests; he was said later on to master seventeen different disciplines. As early as 370/980-81, he took part, as he reports himself (*Farq bayn al-feraq*, ed. Badr, p. 213.10ff.), in a discussion with a Karrāmī theologian in the presence of Nāṣer-al-Dawla Moḥammad b. Ebrāhīm Sīmjūr, the military commander of the Samanids. Yet we do not know anything about his career during the next forty years. We suspect that his theological activities were possibly hampered by the growing influence the Karrāmīya acquired in Nīšāpūr. Sübüktigin (d. 387/997) who had taken the place of the Simjurids as supporter of the declining Samanid suzerainty was impressed by the asceticism of Abū Yaʿqūb Esḥāq b. Maḥmašāḏ, a Karrāmī living in Nīšāpūr; his son Maḥmūd (of Ġazna) supported Abū Yaʿqūb's son Moḥammad b. Esḥāq and made him *raʾīs* of the town in 398/1007. We may assume that it was during this period that ʿAbd-al-Qāher wrote his (lost) *Ketāb fażāʾeḥ al-Karrāmīya*. The Karrāmī *raʾīs* was deposed in 410/1019, but the opposition that got the better of him was directed by a Hanafite, the *qāżī* Ṣāʿed b. Moḥammad Ostowāʾī, whereas ʿAbd-al-Qāher was a Shafiʿite. Only in 411/1220, when profiting from the new intellectual climate the Shafiʿite jurist and Ashʿarite theologian Abū Esḥāq Ebrāhīm b. Moḥammad Esfarāʾīnī started lecturing in the ʿAqīl mosque in Nīšāpūr, did the tide seem to turn in his favor. He attended Esfarāʾīnī's courses and, after the latter's death in 418/1027, took over his chair. He was then in his late sixties and universally known as Shaikh Abū Manṣūr or Abū Manṣūr-al-Motakallem. His prestige was, however, rather short-lived, for when the Saljuqs appeared on the horizon one decade later he left for Esfarāʾīn. Toḡrel entered Nīšāpūr in Šawwāl, 429/July, 1038; ʿAbd-al-Qāher died in Esfarāʾīn in the same year. He seems to have had relations with this town long before; perhaps he studied there with Esfarāʾīnī before 411. Esfarāʾīn was a stronghold of Shafiʿism; moreover, ʿAbd-al-Qāher's tribe, the Tamīm, had settled there. His daughter may have been the mother of Šāhfūr b. Ṭāher Esfarāʾīnī (d. 471/1079).

Since we do not hear of any official position held by ʿAbd-al-Qāher it is quite possible that, besides spending his father's great fortune, he gained his living as a mathematician and geometer. As such he is mentioned by Neẓāmī ʿArūżī in the beginning of the third chapter of his *Čahār maqāla* (ed. Qazvīnī, p. 61.14f.), as the author of a *Ketāb al-takmela* on arithmetic which was highly praised. The only trace of his activity in this field is his *Ketāb al-īżāḥ ʿan oṣūl ṣenāʿat al-massāḥ*, a treatise on the art of surveying (i.e., mostly on plain geometry) which is preserved in its Arabic original and a Persian translation of the sixth century (facsimile edition of both texts by Aḥmad Golčīn-e Maʿānī, Tehran, 1347 Š./1968).

In theology and jurisprudence he was strong in disputation; this may have cost him some sympathies. As a Shafiʿite, he composed verses against Abū Ḥanīfa (cf. Sobkī, *Ṭabaqāt*² V, p. 142.3ff.) and started a protracted controversy with a Hanafite jurist who had defended the superiority of his *maḏhab* (for the contents cf. Sobkī, pp. 145ff., n. 4, according to the *Ṭabaqāt al-wosṭā*). He wrote *Manāqeb al-emām al-Šāfeʿī* and fought for Šāfeʿī's doctrine that the Koran may not be abrogated by the Sunna (ibid., pp. 136f., n. 4). He composed a commentary on the *Meftāḥ fī forūʿ al-Šāfeʿīya* by Ebn al-Qāṣṣ Ṭabarī (d. 335/946; cf. *Kašf al-ẓonūn* (Istanbul), p. 1769.20f.). In theology, he retains, together with his teacher Esfarāʾīnī and Ebn Fūrak (d. 406/1015), the responsibility for the spread of Ashʿarism in Nīšāpūr and obviously also Esfarāʾīn. Like the two others, he adjusted the doctrine to the requirements of anti-Karrāmī polemics; thus, in contrast to Ašʿarī's or Bāqellānī's approach, he used metaphorical language in the explanation of the divine attributes in order to avoid Karrāmī anthropomorphism. His *Ketāb oṣūl al-dīn* (Istanbul, 1346/1928) which, for each problem of scholastic theology, defines the "orthodox" Ashʿarite position after having enumerated the "sectarian" aberrations, was certainly intended as a kind of catechism for the general reader.

In Europe, ʿAbd-al-Qāher has been mainly known as a heresiographer. His *Ketāb al-farq bayn al-feraq* which heavily leans on older sources but furnishes some original information, was edited three times (by Moḥammad Badr, Cairo, 1328/1910; by Moḥammad Zāhed Kawṯarī, Cairo, 1367/1948; by Moḥyī-al-Dīn ʿAbd-al-Ḥamīd, Cairo, [1964]). There is an English translation (in two parts: part 1 by K. Chambers Seelye, New York, 1920; part 2 by A. S. Halkin, Tel Aviv, 1935) and a Persian one (by Moḥammad Jawād Maškūr, Tehran, 2nd ed., 1344 Š./1965). ʿAbd-al-Qāher's grandson (?) Šāhfūr b. Ṭāher used the book in his courses and published an adapted version under the title *al-Tabṣīr fi'l-dīn* (ed. Kawṯarī, Cairo, 1374/1955). The Hanbalite scholar ʿAbd-al-Razzāq Rasʿanī (d. 661/1263) shortened it into a *moḵtaṣar* (ed. Ph. Hitti, Cairo, 1924). ʿAbd-al-Qāher had used most of the material contained in the book in his *Ketāb al-melal wa'l-neḥal* (ed. A. N. Nader, Beirut, 1970).

He seems to have been positive toward Sufism. He wrote a treatise about the superiority of a patient poor man over a grateful rich one (*Kašf al-ẓonūn*, Istanbul, p. 462, last line). Qošayrī was among his pupils.

Bibliography: The main biographical notice is ʿAbd-al-Ḡāfer Fāresī, *Sīāq taʾrīḵ Naysābūr*, ed. R. N. Frye, in *Histories of Nishapur*, Cambridge, Mass., 1966, text II, fol. 55a. 15ff.; slightly shortened version in Ṣarīfīnī, *Moḵtaṣar*, ed. Frye, ibid., text III, fol. 105a.4ff. (= ed. M. Kāẓem-al-Maḥmūdī, Tehran, 1403/1983, pp. 545f.). It is used in all later accounts, cf. Ebn ʿAsāker, *Tabyīn kaḏeb al-moftarī*, Damascus, 1347/1928-29, pp. 253f. Qefṭī, *Enbāh al-rowāt*, Cairo, 1950ff., II, pp. 185f., no. 400. Ebn Ḵallekān III, p. 203, no. 392. Kotobī, *Fawāt al-wafayāt* II, Beirut, 1973, pp. 370ff. Sobkī, *Ṭabaqāt*[1] III, pp. 238ff.; *Ṭabaqāt*[2] V, pp. 136ff. (with additions from the *Ṭabaqāt al-wosṭā*). Asnawī, *Ṭabaqāt al-šāfeʿīya* I, Baghdad, 1391/1971, pp. 194ff., no. 169. Ebn Kaṯīr, *al-Bedāya*, Cairo, 1351-/1932-, XII, p. 44. Soyūṭī, *Boḡyat al-woʿāt*, ed. M. Abu'l-Fażl Ebrāhīm, Cairo, 1384/1964, II, p. 105, no. 1555. Yāfeʿī, *Merʾāt al-janān* III, Hyderabad, 1337-/1918-, III, p. 52 Bağdatlı Paşa, *Hadyat al-ʿārefīn* I, Istanbul, 1951, p. 606.7ff. Cf. also *GAL* I, p. 482; S. I. pp. 666f. H. Laoust, in *REI* 29, 1961, pp. 19ff. M. Allard *Le problème des attributs divins*, Beirut, 1965, pp. 316ff. and 329ff. H. Halm, *Die Ausbreitung der šāfiʿitischen Rechtsschule*, Wiesbaden, 1974, pp. 52f. and 82. D. Gimaret, *Théories de l'acte humain*, Paris, 1980, pp. 119f. There is a *Ketāb al-nāseḵ wa'l-mansūḵ* of his preserved in the ms. Berlin, Ahlwardt 478.

(J. van Ess)

BAḠDĀDĪ, BAHĀʾ-al-DĪN. See bahāʾ-al-dīn baḡdādī.

BAḠDĀDĪ, ABU'L-FAŻL (d. 550/1155), sixth/twelfth century Sufi whose name appears in the initiatic chain of the Neʿmatallāhī order. Together with Shaikh Abu'l-Najīb ʿAbd-al-Qāher Sohrawardī (d. 563/1168), he is said to have been a *morīd* of the celebrated mystic and writer, Aḥmad Ḡazālī (d. 520/1126). In his versified account of the Neʿmatallāhī *selsela*, Shah Neʿmat-Allāh Walī (d. 834/1431), describes Abu'l-Fażl Baḡdādī as "the most accomplished of the accomplished" (*afżal-e fāżelān*), and regards him as the tenth link in the initiatic chain (quoted in Maʿṣūm-ʿAlīšāh, *Ṭarāʾeq al-ḥaqāʾeq*, ed. Moḥammad-Jaʿfar Maḥjūb, Tehran, 1339 Š./1960, I, p. 458 and II, p. 326). Apart from the fact that Baḡdādī was known for his extreme asceticism, and that his successor was a certain Abu'l-Barakāt (d. 570/1174), little else is known of him. The great Neʿmatallāhī encyclopedist, Maʿṣūm-ʿAlīšāh, has stated that Abu'l-Fażl Baḡdādī is also to be found in the Refāʿī *selsela* (*Ṭarāʾeq al-ḥaqāeq* II, p. 351), but this is doubtful. Various accounts of the Refāʿī *selsela* do mention a certain Abu'l-Fażl b. Kāmel (or Kāmeḵ) as living two generations before Shaikh Aḥmad Refāʿī, but the *moršed* of this Abu'l-Fażl was ʿAlī Qareʾ Wāseṭī, not Aḥmad Ḡazālī (see Asʿad Madanī, *al-Mosalsal*, Istanbul, n.d., p. 13, and introduction by Ḥosayn Nāẓem Helwānī to Shaikh Aḥmad Refāʿī, *al-Borhān al-moʾayyad*, Damascus, n.d., p. 13).

Bibliography: Maʿṣūm-ʿAlīšāh, *Ṭarāʾeq al-ḥaqāʾeq* II, pp. 283-85. R. Gramlich, *Die Schiitischen Derwischorden Persiens; erster Teil: die Affiliationen*, AKM 36, 1, pp. 8, 9, 29. J. Nurbakhsh, *Masters of the Path*, New York, 1980, pp. 32-33.

(H. Algar)

BAḠDĀDĪ, mawlānā ḴĀLED ŻĪĀʾ-al-DĪN (1193-1242/1779-1827), the founder of a significant branch of the Naqšbandī Sufi order—named Ḵāledī after him—that has had a profound impact not only on his native Kurdistan but also on many other regions of the western Islamic world. Mawlānā Ḵāled apparently acquired the *nesba* Baḡdādī through his repeated stays in Baghdad, for it was in the Kurdish town of Qarādāḡ, about five miles distant from Solaymānīya, that he was born in 1193/1779. His father was a Sufi (probably of the Qāderī order), who was popularly known as Pīr Mīkāʾīl Šeš-angošt, and his mother also came from a celebrated Sufi family of Kurdistan. For many years, however, Mawlānā Ḵāled's interests were focused exclusively on *ʿelm*, the formal traditions of religious learning, and his later, somewhat abrupt, turning to Sufism is highly reminiscent of the pattern found in many a classic Sufi biography.

His studies began in Qarādāḡ, with the memorization of the Koran, the assimilation of basic works of Shafiʿite *feqh*, and the learning of elementary logic. He then traveled to other centers of religious study in Kurdistan, concentrating on logic and *kalām*. Foremost among his teachers were two brothers, Shaikh ʿAbd-al-Raḥīm and Shaikh ʿAbd-al-Karīm Barzanjī. Next he came to Baghdad, where he astounded the established *ʿolamāʾ* with his learning and worsted them in debate on many topics (at least according to Ḵāledī hagiographical sources). Such was his precocious mastery of the traditional religious sciences that the governor of Bābān proposed him a post as *modarres*, but he modestly refused. However, when ʿAbd-al-Karīm Barzanjī died of the plague in 1213/1798-99, Mawlānā Ḵāled assumed responsibility for the *madrasa* in Solaymānīya he had founded. There Mawlānā Ḵāled remained for about seven years, distinguished as yet only by his great learning and a high degree of asceticism that caused him to shun the company of secular authority.

In 1220/1805, Mawlānā Ḵāled conceived a desire to perform the hajj, and the journey he undertook as a result turned his aspirations to Sufism. Traveling by way of Mosul, Diyarbekir, Aleppo, and Damascus, he stopped for a few days in Medina before continuing to Mecca. There he encountered an anonymous, saintly Yemeni, who prophetically warned not to condemn hastily anything he might see in Mecca apparently contradicting the *Šarīʿa*. Once arrived in Mecca, Mawlānā Ḵāled went forthwith to the Kaʿba, where he saw a man sitting with his back to the sacred structure and facing him. Forgetting the admonition he had heard in Medina, Mawlānā Ḵāled inwardly reproved the man, who immediately divined his thoughts and said, "do you not know that the worth of the believer is greater in God's eyes than the worth of the Kaʿba?" Penitent and overwhelmed, Mawlānā Ḵāled asked for forgiveness and begged the stranger to accept him as disciple. He refused, telling Mawlānā Ḵāled that his master awaited him in India. After the hajj, he returned to Solaymānīya and his duties at the *madrasa* but was inwardly agitated by the desire to find his destined master. Finally, in 1224/1809, an Indian dervish by the name of Mīrzā Raḥīm-Allāh ʿAẓīmābādī chanced to visit Solaymānīya, and he recommended to Mawlānā Ḵāled that he travel to India and seek initiation from a Naqšbandī shaikh of Delhi, Shah ʿAbd-Allāh (also known as Shah Ḡolām-ʿAlī) Dehlavī. Mawlānā Ḵāled departed immediately.

He traveled overland to India, through Iran and Afghanistan. There are indications in Mawlānā Ḵāled's poetry that the journey was harsh and unpleasant, partly, no doubt, because of his insistence on doing vigorous sectarian debate with the various Shiʿite *ʿolamāʾ* he encountered, especially Shaikh Esmāʿīl Kāšī, a *mojtahed* of Tehran. He reached Delhi about a year after leaving Solaymānīya, and was immediately initiated into the Naqšbandī order by Shah ʿAbd-Allāh. It is said that in five months he completed all the stages of spiritual wayfaring laid down in the Naqšbandī order, and that in a year he attained the highest degree of sainthood (*al-welāya al-kobrā*). He was then sent back to Solaymānīya by Shah ʿAbd-Allāh, with full authority to act as his *ḵalīfa* in western Asia and to grant initiation not only in the Naqšbandī but also in the Qāderī, Sohrawardī, Kobrawī, and Češtī orders.

The return journey—again punctuated by hostile debate with Shiʿite *ʿolamāʾ*—took about fifty days and saw Mawlānā Ḵāled in Muscat, Yazd, Shiraz, Isfahan, Hamadān, and Sanandaj. Soon after his return, he came for a brief period to Baghdad, preaching the Naqšbandī way with considerable success. In Solaymānīya, however, rival shaikhs, of the Qāderī order, resented his popularity and tried to enlist the authority of the governor of the city against him. In 1228/1813, he therefore left prudently for another stay in Baghdad, where he took possession of a delapidated *madrasa* and turned it into a Naqšbandī hospice and began recruiting numerous and often influential *morīds*. When one of his enemies from Solaymānīya sent a letter to Saʿīd Pasha, the governor of Baghdad, accusing Mawlānā Ḵāled of heresy in the hope of destroying his success, the maneuver failed: Saʿīd Pasha remained convinced of Mawlānā Ḵāled's rectitude and had the celebrated Hanafite *faqīh*, Moḥammad Amīn b. ʿĀbedīn, compose a refutation of the charges raised against Mawlānā Ḵāled. He was thus able to make a triumphant return visit to Solaymānīya, where a *zāwīa* was built for him by Maḥmūd Pasha, governor of the city. He chose, however, to continue residing in Baghdad, and began to organize his ever-increasing following in the Ottoman lands by appointing *ḵalīfa*s for different areas. Among those he sent out from Baghdad was Shaikh Aḥmad Kaṭīb Erbīlī, his *ḵalīfa* for Damascus. Erbīlī succeeded in recruiting the *moftī* of Damascus, Ḥosayn Efendi Morādī, into Mawlānā Ḵāled's branch of the Naqšbandī order, and in 1238/1823 Morādī was able to persuade Mawlānā Ḵāled to move from Baghdad to Damascus.

He remained in Damascus for the remaining years of his life, leaving only to visit Jerusalem, where an impressive welcome was organized for him by his *ḵalīfa* for the city, Shaikh ʿAbd-Allāh Fardī, and to perform the hajj once again. In 1241/1826, the plague struck Damascus. He foresaw that he would die of the infection and after making meticulous provision for the place and manner of his burial, and appointing Shaikh Esmāʿīl Anārānī as his chief *ḵalīfa*, he died on 14 Ḏu'l-qaʿda 1242/8 June 1827 and was buried on one of the foothills of Jabal Qāsīyūn, on the edge of the Kurdish quarter of Damascus. Later a building was erected over the tomb, comprising a *zāwīa* and a library; it is still frequented.

Mawlānā Ḵāled established a new branch of an existing Sufi order; he did not originate a completely new one. Much of his significance lies, then, in his giving renewed emphasis to traditional tenets and practices of the Naqšbandī order, notably adherence to the *Šarīʿa* and the *sonna* and avoidance of vocal for silent *ḏekr*. Nonetheless, there were elements in his teaching that were novel and controversial, even among other Naqšbandīs. Foremost among these was his interpretation of the practice known as *rābeṭa*—the linking, in the imagination, of the heart of the *morīd* with that of the preceptor. In the only formal treatise he wrote on Sufi matters, Mawlānā Ḵāled defined it in novel fashion as "an imaginary fixing of the form of the shaikh between the eyes of the *morīd*," and he proclaimed that *rābeṭa* was to be practised exclusively with reference to himself, even after his death (*Resālat al-rābeṭa*, contained in *Majmūʿa ʿaẓīma fī asrār al-ṭarīq*, Istanbul, n.d., p. 20).

Equally important for the identity of the Ḵāledī branch of the Naqšbandī order was its political orientation: a pronounced loyalty to the Ottoman state as focus of Muslim unity and strength, and a concomitant hostility to the imperialist powers of Europe. Almost everywhere the Ḵāledīya went, from Daghestan to Sumatra, its members stood out through their militant attitudes and activities.

The diffusion of his following was extremely wide, reaching from the Balkans and the Crimea to South-East Asia just one generation after his death. His principal following was, however, in the Islamic heartlands, the Arab, Turkish, and Kurdish provinces of the Ottoman state and the Kurdish-inhabited areas of Iran. He gained many followers among the Ottoman learned hierarchy; not only Ebn ʿĀbedīn, but also Maḥmūd al-Alūsī, author of the important *tafsīr Rūḥ al-maʿānī*, and Makkīzāda Moṣṭafā ʿĀṣem Efendi, *šayḵ-al-eslām* under Maḥmūd II, were his *morīd*s. Almost everywhere in Anatolia as well as in the capital itself, the Ḵāledī branch of the Naqšbandī order came to supersede branches of more ancient origin, and in Syria, Palestine, and Iraq, the Naqšbandīs assumed an important place in the ranks of the Sufis for the first time.

Mawlānā Ḵāled had a special impact on the religious life of his homeland, Kurdistan. For the Kurds, the practice of Islam had been traditionally connected with membership in a Sufi order, and the Qāderī order had predominated in most Kurdish-inhabited areas. With the emergence of the Ḵāledīya, matters were changed: the Qāderīya lost their preeminence to the Naqšbandīya, and many shaikhly families switched their allegiance from the former to the latter. Kurdish identity became to a degree associated with the Ḵāledī branch of the Naqšbandī order, and this fact, together with the hereditary form that the leadership of the order assumed in Kurdistan, accounts for the prominence of various Naqšbandī families in Kurdistan down to the present.

It is also worth remarking that Mawlānā Ḵāled harbored a distinct enmity to the Shiʿites; he concludes his treatise on the *rābeṭa*, for example, with an imprecation against "the apostate Persians" as well as "the cursed Christians." His spiritual descendants in Kurdistan fully assimilated these attitudes, so that the revolt of the Naqšbandī Shaikh ʿObayd-Allāh in the Orūmīa (Urmia) region in 1880 was not only a rebellion against Iranian rule but also a war against Shiʿism.

Mawlānā Ḵāled influenced his contemporaries mostly by means of his teaching, and posterity by means of the many lines of descent that go forth from him; he is certainly not among the most prolific of Sufi writers. Nonetheless, he left behind a number of writings in both poetry and prose. His *Dīvān* (first published at Būlāq in 1260/1844) consists of poems written in Persian, Arabic, and Gūrānī Kurdish, mostly the first. Some of the Persian *ğazal*s—all written under the influence of Indo-Persian masters such as Bīdel and Mīr Dard—show delicacy and imagination, but the general level of his verse is mediocre, and its chief interest lies in the biographical information that can be culled from it. His letters, in both Arabic and Persian, were collected and published after his death, and they attest to the widespread influence he enjoyed. Finally, there are the treatise he composed on the *rābeṭa*, and other brief pieces relating to various theological questions.

Bibliography: The chief source on the life of Mawlānā Ḵāled Baḡdādī is Ebrāhīm Faṣīḥ Ḥaydarī, *al-Majd al-tāled fī manāqeb al-šayḵ Ḵāled*, Istanbul, 1292/1874. A briefer account, drawing on earlier sources, is contained in ʿAbd-al-Majīd al-Ḵānī, *al-Ḥadāʾeq al-wardīya fī ḥaqāʾeq ajellāʾ al-Naqšbandīya*, Cairo, 1306/1889, pp. 224-28, which also lists his main successors in the Ottoman lands (pp. 259-61). Concerning the transmission of the Ḵāledīya to South East Asia, see Aboebakar Atjeh, *Pengantar Ilmu Tarekat* (*Uraian Tentang Mystik*), Bandung, 1964, pp. 334-37. The history of the Ḵāledīya in Kurdistan has been discussed by Martin van Bruinessen in *Agha, Shaikh and State*: *On the Social and Political Organization of Kurdistan*, Utrecht, 1978, pp. 281-96, and Moḥammad-Rāʾūf Tawakkolī in *Tārīḵ-e taṣawwof dar Kordestān*, Tehran, n.d., pp. 196-225. The collected works of Mawlānā Ḵāled, in Persian, Arabic, and Kurdish, have been reprinted in a single volume by Mollā ʿAbd-al-Karīm Modarres, together with a lengthy biographical introduction in Kurdish, under the title *Yād-e mardān*: *Mawlānā Ḵāled-e Naqšbandī*, Baghdad, 1979. The only study of Mawlānā Ḵāled in a Western language is Albert Hourani, "Shaikh Khalid and the Naqshbandi Order," *Islamic Philosophy and the Classical Tradition*, ed. S. M. Stern, A. Hourani, and V. Brown, Oxford, 1972, pp. 89-103.

(H. ALGAR)

BAGHDAD, Iranian connection.

i. *Before the Mongol invasion.*

(*From the Mongol invasion to the Ottoman occupation*, see Supplement.)

i. BEFORE THE MONGOL INVASION

Baghdad, whose official name was originally Madīnat-al-Salām, the City of Peace, was founded in 145/762 by the second ʿAbbasid caliph, Abū Jaʿfar al-Manṣūr as his official capital. From this time until the sack of the city in 656/1258 by the Mongols, apart from a brief period in the third/ninth century, Baghdad was the home of the ʿAbbasid caliphs. Until the end of the fourth/tenth century it was the most important center of Arabic culture and letters and was almost certainly the biggest city in the Muslim world. It remained throughout an Arabic-speaking city but partly because of its metropolitan status, and partly because of its geographical position, there were considerable Persian elements in its population and urban environment.

Although it was founded near the ancient Sasanian capital of Ctesiphon, known to the Arabs as Madāʾen, in an area which had been under Persian rule at least since the fourth century, there does not seem to have been extensive Persian settlement in the little village of Baghdad or any of the small neighboring communities which were later swallowed up by the great city. (For the distribution of the Persian population in Sasanian Iraq, see Morony, pp. 181-213). While the name of the city may have been derived from two Old Persian words, *bag* "god" (see BAGA iii) and *dād* "given," the probability is that most of the inhabitants were Aramaic-speaking Nabateans. Persian elements came after the foundation of the city and took four main forms: architectural influence on the original design, Persian military settlement in the early years of the city, later rule by dynasts of Persian origin, notably the Buyids, and the continuing settlement of Persian scholars and intellectuals.

The most important feature of the architecture of early Baghdad was the celebrated round city, whose walls encircled the caliph's official residence and the first great mosque. While it is impossible to cite any direct influence, there were a number of examples of round cities from pre-islamic Persia which may have provided inspiration. Ctesiphon was surrounded by oval ramparts, although this may have reflected the natural growth of the city rather than deliberate planning. Clearer parallels can be found in the Sasanian round cities at Dārābgerd and Fīrūzābād, which like Baghdad had four main gates, in Fārs, and at the very striking Parthian and Sasanian ritual center at Taḵt-e Solaymān in Media.

Persian influence also seems to have been evident in the building techniques, although we are dependent on literary sources for our information as none of the original structures survive. The great mosque was built with brick walls and a hypostyle prayer-hall with wooden columns supporting a flat roof, making it the inheritor of an Iranian architectural tradition which stretched back to the great Achaemenid *apadāna* (q.v.) at Persepolis. The caliph's palace boasted a typically Persian *ayvān* with a dome-chamber immediately behind it; the *ayvān* can be traced to the nearby Sasanian palace at Ctesiphon, while the palaces at Fīrūzābād and Sarvestān, also of Sasanian date, had the combination of *ayvān* and dome-chamber. Building materials, on the other hand (brick sometimes strengthened by reeds) naturally owed more to the Mesopotamian tradition and resources than to the Iranian pattern of building in rubble masonry.

The peopling of the new city was a reflection of the reasons for its foundation. The inhabitants can be divided into two groups, the military settled by the caliph and those who flocked to the new city to take advantage of the economic opportunities offered. Although many of the leaders of the ʿAbbasid army were, or at least claimed to be, of Arab descent, it is clear that most of the rank and file were of Persian origin. There were also a number of families of Iranian notables, the Barmakids of Balḵ for example, and the Sulid family, descendents of the native princes of Gorgān. These military groups were settled in certain defined areas of the city, mostly in the district to the northwest of the round city which came to be known as the Ḥarbīya and the names of the different groups give us a clear idea of their geographical origins. As might be expected, the vast majority of them came from Khorasan and Transoxania, where the ʿAbbasid armies had been recruited, rather than from western Iran or Azerbaijan. We find numerous individuals of Persian origin who were assigned plots of land for themselves and their followers but also areas given to people from different districts; the Marvrūdīya (from Marvrūd) in the round city itself, a suburb (*rabaż*) of the Persians (Fors, which may imply people of Fārs, rather than Persians in general), a suburb of the Khwarezmians, and a mosque of the people of Bukhara, all in the Ḥarbīya. A second wave of Persian military settlers came in 151/768 when the future caliph al-Mahdī, then heir apparent, came from Ray, where he had been based for ten years as governor of Khorasan and established a new city on the east bank of the Tigris. It was in these eastern quarters that the Barmakids acquired their main properties.

The children of these Persian settlers' families took the name of *abnāʾ*, said to have been short for *abnāʾ al-dawla* (sons of the state) but also an echo of the title *abnāʾ* (q.v.) taken by those Persians in the Yemen who had acknowledged Moḥammad's authority in the early days of Islam. In this way they proclaimed both their loyalty to the dynasty and their Persian identity, and at least until the civil war which followed the death of Hārūn al-Rašīd in 193/809, they retained close links with their homeland.

These Persian settlers were probably greatly outnumbered by settlers of the second group, the Arabs and local Nabateans from the Sawād of Kūfa. Thus despite the strong Persian element in the population, Arabic was the vernacular language of the city and it seems that by the early 3rd/9th century, fifty years after its foundation, these Persians had become completely acculturated and lost any connection with their country of origin.

The year 204/819 saw the entry of al-Maʾmūn, and his Khorasani supporters into Baghdad and once again there was an influx of Persian soldiers and administrators into Baghdad, but its effect on the city was short-lived. Al-Maʾmūn's chief adviser had been Fażl b. Sahl, a Persian of Iraqi origin whose openly expressed aim it had been to restore the influence of the Persian land-owners (*dehqāns*) and make the ʿAbbasid caliphs the true heirs of the Sasanian tradition; but he was assassinated in 202/818, and when al-Maʾmūn did reach Baghdad, he was obliged to make compromises with the local people which left the Arab nature of the city virtually intact.

The essentially Arab character of Baghdad was preserved in part because of the move of the caliphal court to Samarrāʾ in the reign of the caliph al-Moʿtaṣem (218-227/833-842), since the new administrative and military establishments, in which Persian elements were pronounced, were based in the new city. Baghdad was effectively ruled by a branch of the Taherid family, but they do not seem to have promoted Persian influence in the city.

There was, however, another development at this time which led to a new wave of Persian settlers of a very different sort. The study of Muslim tradition (*ḥadīṯ*) was established in Baghdad in early ʿAbbasid times but it was given renewed impetus by the opposition of many Baghdadis to the government of al-Maʾmūn and al-

Mo'taṣem and the Mu'tazilite doctrine they espoused. They expressed their opposition by a firm commitment to the traditions of the Prophet whose study became the most important of the religious sciences. This meant that scholars from Persia who wished to acquire expertise in this field flocked to Baghdad. This trend was reinforced by the fact that Baghdad lay on the *ḥajj* (pilgrimage) route from Iran to Mecca and Medina. In this way numerous religious figures passed through the city and many stayed on to become permanent residents. For this reason, Persians came to form a much larger element among the clergy (*'olamā'*) of Baghdad than Syrians, Egyptians, or North Africans. An interesting example of how this worked in practice can be seen in the career of the historian and traditionist Ṭabarī (d. 310/923). Originally, as his name suggests, from Ṭabarestān in northern Iran, he came to Baghdad in search of traditions and in the end took up permanent residence there. He continued to be supported by revenues from his family estates in Ṭabarestān which were brought to him by pilgrims from his native province passing through the city. In this way he, and numerous other Persians, contributed not just to the intellectual life of the city, but to its economic survival as well. They did not, however, import Persian culture to Baghdad: they had come to immerse themselves in Islamic learning whose language was Arabic, and they seem to have taken on the language and customs of their adopted home.

The return of the caliphate to Baghdad in 278/892 led to a renewed building campaign, this time largely confined to the east bank of the Tigris, where the palaces of caliphs and military leaders in the Mok̲arram quarter, came to form the core of modern Baghdad. It seems likely that the 'Abbasid court of this period was strongly influenced by Persian ideas of royal splendor, and from this period we have tales of elaborate court ceremonial, of vast and opulent palaces and golden birds singing in silver trees which were alien to early Islamic styles of monarchy. That Persian influence played its part is suggested by the fact that the caliph al-Mo'tażed (279-89/892-902) gave two of his new palaces the typically Persian names of Ferdows (paradise) and Tāj (crown) but we have neither detailed enough descriptions of the architecture nor archeological evidence to show how far this Persian influence extended.

Persian influence was greatly increased under the rule of the Buyids. They were themselves of Persian origin, from Deylam on the southwestern shores of the Caspian Sea. They adopted many of the styles of Sasanian monarchy, including the use of the title *šāhanšāh* along with their Muslim titulature. They were also Shi'ites and some of them certainly patronized Shi'ite shrines in the city; but the great movements of Persian pilgrims to the Shi'ite shrines of Iraq, which led to so much Persian influence in the area, did not begin until much later. This was partly because Shi'ism did not become the established faith of Persia until Safavid times, but partly too because the main Shi'ite shrine of Baghdad, at Kāẓemayn, the old cemetery of the Qorayš, was venerated as much by Sunnis as by Shi'ites in this period.

The first Buyid sovereign of Baghdad, Mo'ezz-al-Dawla Aḥmad (334-56/945-67), relied on Turkish soldiers and locally recruited bureaucrats, although he did employ workers from Ahvāz and Isfahan on his new palace. The chaos which ensued under the rule of his son 'Ezz-al-Dīn Bak̲tīār, led to the conquest of Iraq by the greatest of the Buyids, Ażod-al-Dawla (q.v.) in 367/978. Ażod-al-Dawla's political power was based in Fārs, the old Sasanian homeland, and he brought with him bureaucrats from there, some with ancient Iranian names like Sābūr (Šāpūr) b. Ardašīr, who founded an important educational establishment in the city; he even imported plants from Fārs to revive the ruined gardens of Baghdad. He spent lavishly on building, mostly on palaces but also on his celebrated hospital (*bīmārestān*, the Persian word is used), the 'Ażodīya. This set a pattern for the Persian patronage of charitable institutions which was continued under the Saljuqs. Ażod-al-Dawla's activities were brought to a premature end by his death in 372/983, and his Buyid successors lacked the resources to continue them. While the Buyids did bring Persian elements to Baghdad, in personnel, resources and royal styles, they did not make Baghdad a Persian capital and the language of court and administration remained Arabic.

The same seems to have remained true for Saljuq Baghdad after 447/1055, a period which saw the foundation of the greatest of the Baghdad schools, the Neẓāmīya, founded by the Persian vizier K̲ᵛāja Neẓām-al-Molk in 457/1065. Indeed the movement which saw the foundation of numerous *madrasas* in Baghdad in this period was largely of Persian inspiration. After 552/1157 the Saljuq hold on Baghdad effectively disappeared, and the last century before the Mongol conquest saw the city under the rule of the 'Abbasid caliphs and the political links with Persia broken.

There were other ways in which Baghdadi lifestyles were influenced by Persian elements. In dress the high *qalansowa* (a tall conical hat) which became fashionable in the 3rd/9th century was an example. Persian festivals were celebrated by the caliphs, especially Now Rūz, which became a major event in the city from the time of the caliph al-Motawwakel (232-47/847-61). Many common dishes in Baghdad cuisine, *bezmaverd* and *sīkbāj* for example, had Persian names, and from the time of Hārūn al-Rašīd (170-93/786-809), the typically Persian game of polo became a favorite pastime at court. If we add to this, the vast influx of Persian material goods, textiles, ceramics, and metalwork, attracted by the high-spending court, a picture emerges of an upper-class culture strongly influenced by Persian practice. All this, however, did not make Baghdad a Persian city and the Persian elements were pervasive but never overwhelming; only in the Jalayerid period, after the departure of the 'Abbasids, did Baghdad come near to being a Persian capital.

Bibliography: M. M. Ahsan, *Social Life under the Abbasids*, London and New York, 1979. G.

Makdisi, "Muslim Institutions of Learning in Eleventh Century Baghdad," *BSOAS* 24, 1961, pp. 1-56. K. A. C. Creswell, *Early Muslim Architecture*, 2 vols., Oxford, 1940. A. A. Duri, "Baghdad," *EI*². H. Kennedy, *The Prophet and the Age of the Caliphates*, London, 1986. J. Lassner, *The Topography of Baghdad in the Early Middle Ages*, Detroit, 1970. G. Le Strange, *Baghdad during the Abbasid Caliphate*, London, 1900. M. Morony, *Iraq after the Muslim Conquest*, Princeton, 1984. D. Sourdel, *Le vizirat abbaside*, 2 vols., Damascus, 1959-60, passim.

(H. KENNEDY)

BAGHDAD PACT, popular name for the 1955 pro-Western defense alliance between Turkey, Iraq, Iran, Pakistan, and the United Kingdom. At the height of the Cold War, the Middle East, with strategic bases bordering the Soviet Union, vital communications links, and significant oil wealth, represented a valuable region for Western interests. Initial attempts to align the emerging states in the area to Britain and the United States having failed (Anglo-Egyptian Treaty of 1936 and Anglo-Iraqi Treaty of 1930), London and Washington initiated a sequence of well-known agreements, including the treaty of "friendship and cooperation for security" between Turkey and Pakistan (2 April 1954); the "military assistance" understanding between Iraq and the U.S. (21 April 1954); the Turkish-Iraqi "mutual cooperation pact" (24 February 1955); the special agreement between Iraq and Britain (5 April 1955) which amalgamated the political-military bloc of pro-Western regimes into the Baghdad Pact (Khadduri, pp. 309-24).

The Pact's purpose was the "maintenance of peace and security in the Middle East region" (Preamble) and called on member-states to "cooperate for their security and defense" (Article 1) and to "refrain from any interference whatsoever in each other's internal affairs" (Article 3). "Open for accession to any member of the Arab League or any other state actively concerned with the security and peace in this region" (Article 5), the American-engineered alliance was intended to satisfy several objectives (Europa, p. 102). It appealed to its members for very different reasons although the rising influence of the Soviet Union and that of Arab nationalism, were widely shared. By agreeing to this treaty, Turkey improved its relations with Western powers and Iraq strengthened its position vis-à-vis Egypt (Gallman, pp. 21-65). Iraq, as the original opponent of Arab nationalism, goaded Cairo to stand in the way of the pro-Western alliance. Yet, London's membership, intended to replace its 1930 preferential treaty which was about to expire, disappointed many Arab leaders, especially Gamal ʿAbd-al-Nāṣer, who hoped for a neutral Arab bloc between the West and the USSR. Nāṣer opposed the Pact because he perceived it as a threat to his foreign policy objectives and as a tool geared to serve Western political and economic interests. Cairo also feared that such an alliance would isolate Egypt and strengthen the pro-British regime of Nūrī al-Saʿīd in Baghdad. Egyptian-instigated agitations against contemplated membership by Jordan and Lebanon were partially responsible for the disturbances in both countries in 1956 and 1957 leading the U.S. and Britain to intervene militarily. The Iraqi premier considered the Pact as a vindication of his source of power and to demonstrate his allegiance to the West broke diplomatic relations with Moscow in January, 1955. For Pakistan, the Pact was intended to balance relations with India and help it benefit from Western economic largesse. Iran, having abandoned its tradition of third-power policy and having disregarded Prime Minister Moṣaddeq's experiment with a neutralist approach, wished to align itself with the West. Yet, despite the shah's unquestionable sense of Soviet and Communist danger, he saw a unique opportunity in the alliance for the preservation of his throne (Ramazani, 1975, p. 276).

After the application of the Eisenhower Doctrine in 1958, opposition to the alliance in the Northern Tier emerged among indigenous nationalist groups. The U.S., having joined the Pact as an Associate member in 1956, exercised great influence in the Economic and Counter-Subversion Committees but received a severe jolt when, in July, 1958, a bloody army revolt overthrew the pro-Western Hashemite monarchy of Fayṣal II, bringing into power the revolutionary Qāsem regime. The Shah of Iran was shaken, fearing a similar fate for himself and viewing the upheaval in Baghdad as a "clear and imminent" source of threats to regional stability (Ramazani, 1975, p. 281). Iraq's consequent withdrawal from the Pact, henceforth the Central Treaty Organization (CENTO, q.v.), led to the transfer of the International Secretariat from Baghdad to Ankara, Turkey. In the wake of the Pact's demise, the U.S. signed several defense treaties with Iran, Turkey, and Pakistan, guaranteeing their security against foreign aggression.

Bibliography: *The Baghdad Pact: Origins and Political Setting*, London, 1956. *Europa-The Middle East, 1960*, London, 1960, pp. 99-102. Waldemar J. Gallman, *Iraq under General Nuri*, Baltimore, 1964, pp. 66-87. Majid Khadduri, *Independent Iraq, 1932-1958: A Study of Iraqi Politics*, London, 1960, pp. 307-50. R. K. Ramazani, *The Northern Tier: Afghanistan, Iran, and Turkey*, New York, 1966, pp. 117-23. Idem, *Iran's Foreign Policy, 1941-1973: A Study of Foreign Policy in Modernizing Nations*, Charlottesville, 1975, pp. 274-78.

(J. A. KECHICHIAN)

BAGINA, BAGINAPATI, reconstructed Old-Iranian words. The first designates a temple housing a cult image (from *baga-* "god," "image of a god" + suffix *-ina-* "belonging to"); the second, the master of such a temple.

The form and meaning of both words are obvious from their descendants in various Middle-Iranian languages: Parthian (loanword in Armenian) *bagin* "pagan sanctuary" (the early Arm. historians list seven *bagink*ʿ,

two of which stood in Bagaran and Bagawan; in a Christian context; also "altar set before a pagan image"), *bagnapet* "chief of the temple"; Pahlavi *bašnbed*, "idol-priest" (once in a Manichean polemical text); Bactrian **βaγənpat* (in Middle-Indian inscriptions from Mathura: *bakanapati-*, *vakanapati-*, designating an official in charge of an image-temple established by the Kushan emperors); Sogdian *vaγn* (*βγn-*) "temple housing statues of gods," in Christian context "altar"), *vaγnpat* (*βγnpt-*) "priest" and in a Buddhist context "sorcerer" (hence *βγnpt'nch-* "sorceress").

In Sasanian Iran these words fell into disuse, no doubt as a result of the policy of the State church to impose fire-worship as the only lawful form of the Zoroastrian cult.

This development did not take place in Sogdiana, where at the time of the Arab conquest *vaγnpat* and *muγpat* "magus" are still attested as distinct offices, as shown by the archive documents found at Mt Mugh. This duality is confirmed by the accounts of the conquest, which mention side by side "idol-temples" and "fire-temples." Judging from the place-names ending in *-fağn* or *-bağn* which can be gathered from the Medieval sources, image-sanctuaries had been widespread in Sogdiana as well as in neighboring Ustrushana, Farğāna, and Čāč, including in rural areas. The first element of the toponyms seldom provides a clue to the identification of the gods once worshipped in the temples (Smirnova's attempts [1971] must be used with caution). It can be assumed that most of them belonged to the Iranian pantheon; but Shaivite intrusions or influences are also to be considered, and one place-name, *Sanjarfağn* (next to Samarqand), shows that the name *vağn* was eventually applied to Buddhist cult-places also (*sanjar* < Sanskrit *saṃghārāma* "Buddhist monastery"), despite the pejorative use of cognate words in Sogdian Buddhist literature.

Bibliography: H. W. Bailey, *BSOAS* 14, 1952, pp. 420-23. V. V. Barthold, *Turkestan down to the Mongol Invasion*³, London, 1968, pp. 120-33. Idem, "Istoriya kul'turnoĭ zhizni Turkestana," 1927, repr. in *Sochineniya* II/1, Moscow, 1963, p. 215. M. Boyce in *Studies in Judaism in Late Antiquity* 12 (= *Studies for Morton Smith at Sixty*), Leiden, 1975, IV, p. 99. Idem, *Zoroastrianism* II, Leiden and Cologne, 1982, pp. 227-29. F. Grenet, *Abstracta Iranica* 7, 1984, no. 129. W. B. Henning, *BSOS* 8, 1936, pp. 583-85. Idem, *BSOAS* 28, 1965, pp. 250-52. V. A. Livshits, *Sogdiĭskie dokumenty s Gory Mug* II: *Yuridicheskie dokumenty i pis'ma*, Moscow, 1962, pp. 111-13, 170-71. N. Sims-Williams, *The Christian Sogdian Manuscript C2*, Berliner Turfantexte 12, Berlin, 1985, pp. 61-62. O. I. Smirnova, *Strany i narody Vostoka* 10, Moscow, 1971, pp. 90-108.

(F. Grenet)

BAĠLĀN, place name in northeastern Afghanistan.

i. *Kushan period.*
ii. *Modern province.*
iii. *Modern town.*

i. Kushan Period

The name originally derives from the Bactrian *bagolango* "image-temple" (< OIr. **baga-dānaka-*), a term used in the inscription of Nokonzoko (SK4) from the archeological site of Surkh (Sorḵ) Kotal in Afghanistan. In this text, the temple-complex excavated by the Délégation Archéologique Française en Afghanistan from 1951-63, is named as *Kanēško oanindo bagolango*, probably to be understood as "Kanishka-Victory-Temple." Though since the word *oanindo* represents both the name of an astral deity of victory, depicted winged and thus named on the Kushan gold coinage, and as an adjective "victorious," some scholars have taken it as an epithet referring to Kanishka.

The temple excavated at this site appeared to be a fire-temple of dynastic character, dedicated for the rulers of the Kushan dynasty. It was founded perhaps early in the reign of Kanishka (according to the unfinished inscription SK2 in the year 289 of an unstated era which is most probably a Greco-Bactrian era of about 155 B.C., thus fixing the date of construction to about A.D. 124), and restored in the year 31 of a different era, probably of Kanishka I's own enthronement, perhaps thus equivalent to A.D. $125 + 31 = 156$ or shortly after. The complex contained a *cella*, an attached subsidiary fire-temple piled with fine ashes, statues of at least two Kushan emperors, one of which seems identical with a coin-portrait of Huvishka, and a stone orthostat in poorly preserved state which appears to show an enthroned ruler in the presence of a trophy (for another theory see Fussman, p. 123).

The temple site is some 15 km northwest of Pol-e Ḵomrī in northern Afghanistan on the road to Balḵ, and about the same distance from the modern administrative center of Baġlān, a straggling settlement on the opposite (east) bank of the Qondūz River beside the road from Pol-e Ḵomrī to Qondūz. The meaning and original location of the name were evidently forgotten during the Middle Ages, so that it attached vaguely to the district as a whole, and ultimately to its modern center. The region was no doubt closely connected with the Kushan dynasty, and it bore in the Islamic period the name Ṭoḵārestān which derives from that of the Tocharoi, the ancient horde of which they became the rulers.

See also BACTRIA; SORḴ KOTAL.

Bibliography: D. Schlumberger, M. Le Berre, and G. Fussman, *Surkh Kotal en Bactriane*, MDAFA 25, Paris, 1983, 2 vols. Besides the excavation reports there listed on p. viii, see especially W. B. Henning, "Surkh Kotal," *BSOAS* 18, 1956, pp. 366-67; idem, "The Bactrian Inscription," *BSOAS* 33, 1960, pp. 47-55; also I. Gershevitch, "The Well of Baghlan," *Asia Major* 12, 1961, pp. 90-109; idem, "Bactrian Inscriptions and Manuscripts," *IF* 72, 1967, pp. 27-57; A. D. H. Bivar, "The Kaniska Dating from Surkh Kotal," *BSOAS* 26, 1963, pp. 498-502.

(A. D. H. Bivar)

ii. Modern Province

Bāḡlān is a province (*welāyat*) of northeastern Afghanistan which covers 17,106 km^2. It is presently (1363 Š./1984) divided into five districts (*woloswālī*) and four subdistricts (*ʿalāqadārī*). The main town and provincial center is Baḡlān and three more localities within the province have urban status (Pol-e Ḵomrī, Nahrīn, and Dahān-e Ḡōrī, recently renamed Šahīd Nyāz Gol).

The province of Baḡlān was created in 1343 Š./1964 out of the former province of Qaṭaḡan.

See Tables 10 and 11 for compilation of main available data about present population and land use in the province, districts, and subdistricts.

(D. Balland)

iii. Modern town

Baḡlān is a district and town of Afghanistan, in the upper valley of the Sorḵāb (Qondūz) river on the northern slope of the Hindu Kush range. At the end of the nineteenth century, the district had a population estimated at 1,000 Paṧtūn and Tajik families with its own governor (*ḥākem*), who resided at the village of Qešlāq-e Qāżī (a little to the north of the present industrial town), but was subordinate to the governor of the adjacent (southward) district of Ḡorī. Some time in the first third of the nineteenth century, the administrative headquarters had been moved to another site five km to the north, i.e., the old town (Šahr-e Kohna), where a twice-weekly bazaar had long been held.

Urban growth in the district began in the 1930s when the opening of the motorable road from Kabul to Qondūz over the Šebar pass made the Sorḵāb valley an important line of communication. Three main urban nuclei, each bearing the name Baḡlān, came successively into being. (1) Old Baḡlān, mentioned above, had a still mainly rural appearance and a bazaar which, in the early 1970s, comprised some seventy shops and teahouses (*čāy-ḵānas*) but only became really busy in the autumn when villagers from the surrounding plain came to sell their cotton. (2) New Baḡlān (Šahr-e Jadīd), about four km to the south, was founded in 1937 as a new chief town for the province of Qaṭaḡan and became the headquarters of the province of Baḡlān under the territorial reorganization of 1964. Thanks to this administrative role, the town grew rapidly. In 1973 its bazaar comprised some six hundred shops, for the most part only open on market days (Mondays and Fridays). The shopkeepers consist of a Tajik group, mainly from the Parvān district, of an immigrant Paṧtūn element

Table 10

POPULATION OF BAḠLĀN PROVINCE, AFGHANISTAN (1978-79)

Name of district	1 Area (km^2)	2 Total sedentary population (1979)	3 Density (Inhab./km^2)	4 Urban Population (percent)	5 Wintering nomads (tents) (3)	6 Number of tents in summer 1978[4] Paṣtūn	 Others
Baḡlān (center of province)	1,644	109,800	67	36	1,233	30	40
Woloswālī:							
Andarāb	2,344	49,300	21	—	35	440	1,140
Dōšī	1,735	37,600	22	—	—	—	1,135
Ḵōst-o-Fereng (1)	2,552	46,700	18	—	—	140	1,000
Nahrīn	1,583	48,900	31	7	—	120	465
Pol-e Ḵomrī	671	98,100	146	32	52	—	60
ʿAlāqadārī:							
Borka	842	34,300	41	—	—	—	190
Ḵenjān	988	16,800	17	—	—	245	71
Šahīd Nyāz Gol (2)	1,795	38,000	21	4	—	115	1,018
Tāla-o-Barfak	2,952	14,400	5	—	—	110	550
Total of province	17,106	493,900	29	15	1,320	1,200	5,669

Sources: Columns 1 to 4, *Natāyej-e moqaddamātī-e noḵostīn saršomārī-e nofūs*, Kabul, 1359 Š./1981. Figures have been rounded. Columns 5 to 6, D. Balland and A. de Benoist, *Nomades et semi-nomades d'Afghanistan*, forthcoming. Notes: (1) This district was detached from Taḵār province about 1974. (2) From 1358 Š./1979 this is the new official name of Dahān-e Ḡōrī district and town (Nyāz Gol was a martyr of the Ṯawr Revolution).(3) Wintering nomads of Baḡlān province are of various ethnic stocks, the Paṣtūn (230 tents) coming third to the Tīmūrī (540 tents) and Moḡol (310 tents). (4) All nomads (625 tents) and semi-nomads (6, 244 tents) recorded come from within the province. Main groups are Hazāra (2,173 tents, semi-nomads) in the west Tajik (1,506 tents, semi-nomads) in the east, these two groups amounting to more than 50 percent of the migrating population.

Table 11

LAND USE IN BAḠLĀN PROVINCE, AFGHANISTAN (1967)

Name of district	Cultivated lands (ha) Irrigated (*ābī*)	Non-irrigated (*lalmī*)	Fallow	Forests (ha)	% of irrigated land under Canals	Springs	Water mills (units)
Baḡlān	26,668	3,618	7,142	118	100	—	82
Woloswālī:							
Andarāb	4,558	3,010	2,416	67,880	99	1	104
Dōšī	4,258	4,686	3,194	2,246	100	—	75
Ḵōst-o-Fereng	6,540	48,858	28,102	10,020	70	30	80
Nahrīn	11,872	57,788	31,268	5,084	99.9	0.1	99
Pol-e Ḵomrī	23,234	30,134	19,714	204	100	—	80
ʿAlāqadārī:							
Borka	1,920	24,790	12,780	—	99	1	28
Ḵenjān	1,040	40	228	6,452	97	3	54
Šahīd Nyāz Gol	4,504	25,296	13,548	5,304	99	1	?
Tāla-o-Barfak	2,124	288	586	252	99.6	0.4	43
Total of province	86,718	198,508	118,978	97,560	98	2	645

Source: *Natāyej-e eḥṣāʾīyagīrī sarwē-ye moqaddamātī-e zerāʿatī sāl-e 1346 Š./1967*, Kabul, n.d., 7 vols. The figures are only very rough estimates; the reliability of some of them may be questionable.

from Qandahār and the Nangrahār district, and of some others from Mazār-e Šarīf and Tašqorḡān. The town is split into two parts by the main road; the original nucleus with the grain and fruit markets lies in the western part, but the craftsmen's shops and the restaurants and *čāy-ḵānas*, frequented mainly on market days, are all in the eastern part. The town was spaciously laid out and has kept a verdant appearance. It possesses some superior institutional buildings (secondary schools and a hospital) and comfortable residential sections. (3) The Industrial town (Baḡlān -e Ṣanʿatī), eight km to the south, took shape around the sugar refinery built in 1938-40 by the Škoda company of Czechoslovakia. The refinery was owned by a private firm, though eighty-five percent of the capital belonged to the National Bank of Afghanistan. With a capacity to treat 60,000 tons of beet and produce 7,000-8,000 tons of sugar per annum, the refinery employed 140 permanent staff and 1,000-1,200 seasonal workers. In addition, a modern silk factory was established in the town in 1951. The sugar company owned roughly one sixth of the 340 shops in the bazaar and a large proportion of the dwellings, which it built to house its employees. The houses were more modern than those of the other agglomeration and had the benefits of water and electricity, which the company supplied to them as well as providing a special hospital and schools. The town is also the seat of the provincial Agriculture Department, whose installations and staff houses are located here. The fact that some of the bazaar shops were being used as dwellings indicates that the bazaar had been made too large and that the main commercial activities were still centered in the administrative town.

It may be asked whether the three agglomerations, which had a total population of 39,228 according to the preliminary report of the 1979 census, really form one town. The answer is certainly affirmative in the case of Old Baḡlān and New Baḡlān, as the old settlement depends on the new town for all modern-type services. The industrial town, however, seems on the whole to be an independent entity, and in fact has a separate municipal administration. At the same time the brisk traffic of two-wheeled cabs (*gādīs*) and motor vehicles on the road to the new town shows that contact between the two centers is very close.

Bibliography: L. W. Adamec, *Gazetteer of Afghanistan* I, Graz, 1972, pp. 40-41. E. Grötzbach, *Kulturgeographischer Wandel in Nordost-Afghanistan seit dem 19. Jahrhundert*, Afghanische Studien 4, Meisenheim am Glan, 1972, passim. Idem, *Städte und Basare in Afghanistan. Eine stadtgeographische Untersuchung*, Beihefte zum Tübinger Atlas des Vorderen Orients, Reihe B, 16, Wiesbaden 1979, pp. 82-84. The Baḡlān sugar refinery was the subject of several articles in the Kabul periodical *Eqteṣād* in 1318 Š./1939 and thereafter, particularly in a special issue, no. 225 of 1319 Š./1940.

(X. de Planhol)

BAGŌAS, the Greek name of two eunuchs from the Achaemenid period.

1. The chief eunuch and general under Artaxerxes III. He played a prominent role in court affairs, being the most trusted friend of Artaxerxes III (Diodorus Siculus, 16.47.4). During the reconquest of the rebellious Egypt in 343 B.C. Bagōas and Mentor of Rhodes

commanded the main body of the Persian army and Greek mercenaries who took the border fortress Pelusium and then occupied the country. At the sack of the Egyptian city Bubastis the Greek mercenaries imprisoned Bagōas who was soon rescued by Mentor (Diodorus, 16.50.1-6). Then Artaxerxes III sent Bagōas to put the upper satrapies in order, giving him supreme power over them (Diodorus, 15.50.8).

At the end of 338 B.C. Bagōas poisoned Artaxerxes III and murdered all his sons, except the youngest, Arses (Diodorus, 17.5.3-4; cf. also Aelianus, *Varia Historia* 6.8). Though Bagōas attained supreme power, he could not ascend the throne himself and instead made Arses a puppet king. In the summer of 336 B.C. Arses and all his children were murdered by Bagōas, who presented the throne to Darius III, a distant member of the Achaemenid family Codomannus (Strabo, 15.3.24; Curtius, 6.3.12). When Bagōas attempted to poison Darius III himself, the king compelled him to drink a cup of deadly poison.

Bagōas possessed famous gardens near Babylon (Theophrastus, *Plant-researches* 2.6.7) and a palace in Susa which Alexander the Great gave to Parmenion for residence (Plutarch, *Alexander* 39). See also F. Cauer, "Bagoas," in Pauly-Wissowa II, cols. 277f.; A. T. Olmstead, *History of the Persian Empire*, Chicago, 1948, pp. 437 and 489f.; J. M. Cook, *The Persian Empire*, London, 1983, pp. 224f.

2. A Persian eunuch who was a favorite of Darius III and Alexander the Great (Curtius, 6.5.23 and 10.1.25-27; Plutarch, *Alexander* 67). His life was fictionalized by M. Renault in *The Persian Boy* (1972).

(M. DANDAMAYEV)

BAGRATIDS, THE, possibly the most important princely dynasty of Caucasia (Bagratuni in Armenia, Bagrationi in Georgia), attaining to the kingly status in the ninth century and retaining it in Georgia to the nineteenth. Like the House of Artsruni they were an offshoot of the Orontids, Achaemenian satraps and, later, kings of Armenia (ca. 400-ca. 200 B.C.), originally appanaged in the old Orontid fief of Bagrevand (ca. 5,000 km^2) in Ayrarat, in north-central Armenia, and, like the Orontids, they claimed descent from a solar deity. On Armenia's conversion to Christianity in 314, this claim was abandoned in favor of a descent, together with the majority of the Armenian princes, from the once-divine (astral), but now merely heroic, mythical primogenitor of the Armenians, Hayk‘. Later still, under biblical influences, the Bagratids claimed a Hebrew origin, which was further elaborated by the end of the eighth century as the celebrated legend of their descent from King David of Israel. Bagadates (Bagadāta; in some MSS Magadates), strategus of Tigranes the Great of Armenia and his viceroy of Syria and Cilicia in 83-69 B.C. (Appian, *Syriaca* 11.8.48-49; cf. Toumanoff, 1963, pp. 320-21), appears to have been the earliest-known member of this house; it is not impossible that both the family's chief patronymic and its Hebrew legend may have been connected with the memory of this renowned ancestor.

Historically, the Bagratids appear in 314 reigning, no longer in Bagrevand, but in Sper (ca. 6,000 km^2) with the great castle of Bayberd (modern Bayburt) in the valley of the C‘oruh, in northwestern Armenia; their history has continued to the present day and their uninterrupted genealogy dates from ca. 555. Subsequently they reigned also in Kogovit, east of Bagrevand, dominated by the castle of Dariunk‘ (modern Doğu-Bayazıt), and in Tmorik in the southernmost part of Vaspurakan, in southern Armenia. They also held the hereditary offices of Coronant (*t‘agadir*) of the kings of Armenia and of Guardian of the Caucasian (Moschic) Mountains and bore in addition the gentilitial title of *aspet* (see ASPBED ii), whence their other short-lived name of Aspetuni. The political weight of this house is evidenced by its military potential: a force of 1,000 horse was the feudal aid the Bagratids owed to their suzerain, the King of Armenia.

The partition of Armenia in 387 into an Iranian and a Roman vassal state, then the annexation of the Western kingdom by the Empire, and finally the abolition of the East Armenian Monarchy in 428, which ended the perennial tension between the Armenian Crown and the insubordinate dynastic princes who were its vassals, placed these princes in the necessity of choosing between the two rival imperial allegiances. The Bagratids proved successful in maneuvering between the two powers. They were immediate vassals of the emperor in Sper, in the years 387-532 (before Justinian I annexed it), whereas, in their Persarmenian princedoms, they were, from 428, like the rest of the East Armenian princes free at last from the local king's overlordship, immediate vassals, under the supervision of an Iranian viceroy (*marzpan*), of the distant Great King. Partition and annexation did not, however, save Armenia from tension. In West Armenia, the princes, who chafed under Byzantine bureaucratism and espoused anti-Byzantine theological views, flirted with the court of Ctesiphon; while those East Armenian princes who took their Christianity seriously looked, despite theological divergencies, to the court of Constantinople for aid, when resisting recurrent Iranian outbursts of an anti-Christian policy.

In this field of tension, the Bagratids chose to remain prudently non-committal. Accordingly, they abstained from taking part in the heroic insurrection of the princes, led by the Mamikonid dynasty, against Iranian religious aggression in 451. In fact, Tiroc‘ I, prince of the Bagratids (to give him the official title of the heads of the house) actually adhered to the policy of collaboration promoted by Vasak I, Prince of Siunia. Yet, during the next insurrection, in 482, Isaac II Bagratuni joined the Mamikonids, was even chosen by the princes to be viceroy of Armenia, and lost his life in a battle. Most often, though, the politic Bagratids succeeded in combining the two allegiances. Of this Smbat IV presents an outstanding example. At first, together with his Mamikonid confrère, he led Armenian troops as auxiliaries in Emperor Maurice's European wars; and at the imperial court knew both disgrace and favor: the Emperor, in sign of suzerainty, adopted him (Eusebius, chap. 10). But next he appeared as a favorite at the court of Ctesiphon: he was appointed to be *marzpan* of Gorgān (Hyrcania) in the years 595-602, was decorated with the epithet of *xosrō-šnūm* (joy of Ḵosrow), and led Iranian troops in the defence of the eastern frontier. His son and successor, Varaz-Tiroc̣ II, in his youth a cup-bearer to the great king and recipient, in his turn, of the epithet of *javitian-xosrō* (eternal Ḵosrow), was named to be *marzpan* of Armenia in the years 629-ca. 631. But soon thereafter he passed to the side of the emperor, became involved in palace conspiracies at Constantinople, was pardoned and made presiding prince of Armenia in 645, when, after Heraclius's war on Iran, the empire came to control practically the entire country.

Imperial control of Armenia meant that, in lieu of the former Iranian viceroy, one of the local princes was appointed to preside over the others as ruler of the country for the emperor. Thus was born the office of presiding prince. However, within a quarter of a century, the rising caliphate destroyed the weakened Sasanian monarchy and, becoming largely its successor, proceeded to supplant the empire in the exercise of suzerainty over that perennial apple of discord. This was the first instance of a Christian vassal state of the Islamic empire. The office of presiding prince of Armenia (or its equivalent: ruling high constable) was maintained, in the gift of the caliph. But the empire did not abandon its claims to Armenia, and the country continued, as before, to be a battle-ground of its imperial neighbors. Thus its presiding princes were now the caliph's vassals, now the emperor's. Those who obeyed the latter would receive the Byzantine dignity of patrician or even the higher one of curopalate (reserved at that time for the emperors' brothers and nephews), while those of the caliph's were called *baṭrīq*, an Arabic rendering of "patrician."

During this period of Armenian history, while the rival Mamikonids began to decline, the power and importance of the Bagratids waxed. Though on the whole pro-Arab, they occasionally resorted to their traditional policy of interchangeable allegiances. Thus, Smbat VI was presiding prince for the emperor, with the dignity of patrician, in 691-97; then for the caliph in 697-700; and finally again for the emperor, with the dignity of curopalate, in 700-11. During the period of the principate, twelve Bagratid princes held the office of presiding prince (or its equivalent), three with the dignity of curopalate. Only once did the dynasty exchange its policy of prudence for one of heroism, and quite disastrously for itself. In 774-75, the Armenian princes, still led by the Mamikonids, rose in revolt against the caliph; and Smbat VII Bagratuni, the then ruling high constable, joined them. The result was defeat and again death in battle of the Bagratid (see *Histoire des arméniens*, ed. G. Dédéyan, Toulouse, 1982, p. 194). Along with the other insurgents the Bagratids suffered territorial losses, as Kogovit, Tmorik, and the momentarily controlled territory of

Vaspurakan passed to the more consistently prudent Arcrunis. However, on the imperial frontier, the Bagratids still held Sper, with its silver mines; and this proved a source of wealth and power. Then, the recent insurrection having broken the might of the Mamikonids, the Bagratids possessed themselves of their principalities of Taraun, southern Tayk̒, Bznunik̒ and, subsequently, Bagrevand, which had once been their own; later they purchased from the Kamsarakans (q.v.) those of Aršarunik̒ and Širak with the cities of Bagavan and Ani (which became, successively, Bagratid capitals); and they also acquired that of Mokk̒ (Moxoene), though it soon passed to the Arcrunis. Within less than a century after the disaster of 775, they regained and increased their political importance, and then reigned over a powerful and consolidated west-central Armenian state. Since this disaster had ruined and weakened many princely houses, which were reduced to dependence on a few others, the might of those few who had survived the ruin was vastly increased. Armenia thus came to be divided into only just three big political formations: the Arcrunid state in the south, the Siunid state in the east, and the Bagratid state which proved the most successful. Cautiously maneuvering, as they had always done, between, on the one hand, the caliphate, which was on the decline now and breaking up into a number of succession states, and, on the other, the empire, which was concentrating upon a struggle with these, the Bagratids monopolized the office of presiding prince and then, in 884, converted it into kingship. Recognition was easily obtained from caliph and emperor. The Armenian monarchy, abolished in 428, had been restored.

With this, Bagratid family history becomes the history of the restored kingdom of Armenia. There followed a period of greatness, cultural and economic, no less than political, a "Bagratid renascence." Yet it contained seeds of decay. Disintegration soon set in resulting in weakness, which, in turn, proved an invitation to external foes to put an end to it. The Bagratids had largely themselves contributed to the ruin of Armenia. They failed to keep their state consolidated by apportioning it among their several branches. Next to the kings of Armenia at Ani (bearing the title of king of kings), there thus arose the kings of Kars (962-1064) and the kings of Loṙi (982, surviving until ca. 1101); there were the princes of Taraun (826-966/7), dispossessed by the Byzantines, but continuing in the empire as the houses of the Taronitae and the Tornicii. Not to be outdone, the rival, but hitherto dependent, Arcrunis and Siunis proceeded to assume, in their turn, the royal style.

The invitation this dissolution provided was soon accepted. Saljuq Turks began attacking Armenia from the east early in the 1000s. The terrorized Arcrunid king of Vaspurakan soon ceded his state to the empire, in 1021-22. Then, in 1045, the last king of Armenia, Gagik II, was inveigled into Constantinople and there bullied into abdicating in favor of the emperor, his host. He was given lands in Cappadocia, a palace in the capital, the dignity of magistros, and was murdered by the Byzantines in 1079-80. In 1064, the king of Kars ceded his state to the emperor. Most of Armenia lost independence becoming part of the empire. This was followed by the emigration of a number of princes, followed by their vassals, either to Georgia or to the empire itself, especially to Cilicia. The country was left quite leaderless and, owing to the then Byzantine policy of disarmament, quite undefended. A void was created which the Saljuqs soon filled. The Byzantine attempt to counter ended in the defeat at Manjikert in 1071, after which not only Armenia, but also Anatolia were lost to the empire.

The Armenian Bagratids (of the house of Loṙi) disappear from history in the thirteenth century; the Byzantine Bagratids (Taronitae), in the fourteenth. The still flourishing Georgian line of the Bagratids is descended from Vasak, younger brother of Smbat VII, who passed to Georgia after 775. The Georgian Bagratids were kings of Central Georgia from 888, of United Georgia from 1008, partitioned in their turn the country into three kingdoms at the end of the fifteenth century, and were dispossessed through the Russian annexations in the nineteenth century. The history of this line is inextricably bound with that of Georgia.

The Bagratids contributed largely to the cultural aspect of the "Bagratid renascence" of Armenia. Their capital of Ani, a great economic no less than political center, acquired in the ninth and tenth centuries also an imprint of this cultural activity. A city of "40 gates and 1001 churches," with a population of possibly 50,000, it contained many splendid edifices, including the Bagratid palace-fortress (reared upon the Kamsarakan foundations), the magnificent cathedral (built in 998-1000) and the round church of Gagik I (ca. 1005-10), both built by the celebrated architect Trdat (Tiridates). The Bagratids founded the abbeys of Hałbat and Sanahin that were to become important centers of learning; and they raised the great castle of Amberd, later enlarged by the Kamsarakan-Pahlavunis (q.v.) to mention but a few examples of their building activity.

Table 12

BAGRATID KINGS OF ARMENIA

Ašot I the Great	884-90
Smbat I the Martyr	890-913
Ašot II the Iron (King of Kings)	913-28
Ašot anti-king	921-36
Abas I	928-52
Ašot III the Merciful	952-77
Smbat II the Conqueror	977-89
Gagik I	989-1020
John-Smbat III	1020-41
Ašot IV the Valiant co-king in one half of the realm	1021-39/40
Abas co-king	
Gagik II (abdicates)	1041/42-45
Byzantine annexation	1045

They, moreover, were patrons of the letters, and the historians Eusebius (Sebēos) in the seventh century, Ps. Moses of Khorene, and Leontius (Łevond) in the eighth, and Šapuh Bagratuni (d. 912, himself a member of the dynasty, a son of King Ašot I, whose work has not reached us) were their adherents and protégés. The Georgian Bagratids, on their part, contributed, even more than their Armenian kinsmen, to the flowering of civilization in their own country of Georgia.

Bibliography: I. Sources. a. Armenian. Aristaces of Lastivert (Aristakēs Lastivertc‘i), *History of Armenia*: *Patmut‘iwn Aristakeay vardapeti Lastivertc‘woy*, in (the collection) Łukasean Matenadaran 6, Tiflis, 1912, pp. 2, 10 (written at the end of the 10th cent. and covers the period from ca. 1000-71). Cyriacus of Ganja (Kirakos Ganjakec‘i), *History of Armenia*: *Patmut‘iwn Hayoc‘ arareal Kirakosi vardapeti Ganjakec‘woy*, in Łukasean Matenadaran 3, Tiflis, 1909, passim (covers the period from the 4th cent. to 1265). Eliseus (Eḷišē), *History of the Vardanians*: *Eḷišēi patmut‘iwn Vardananc‘*, in *Łukasean Matenadaran* 11, Tiflis, 1913, pp. 3, 4 (history of the Armenian insurrection of 451, according to the tradition written in the 5th cent.). Eusebius (Sebēos), *History of Heraclius*: *Patmut‘iwn Sebeosi episkoposi i Herakln*, in Łukasean Matenadaran 7, Tiflis, 1913, pp. 10, 11, 14-19, 28, 29, 32, 33, 34 (7th cent. work covering the period from ca. 590 to ca. 661, traditionally ascribed by some to a Xosrovik, also of the 7th cent.). Faustus (P‘awstos) Buzand, *History of Armenia*: *P‘awstosi Buzandac‘woy patmut‘iwn Hayoc‘*, Venice, 1933, passim (probably written in the 5th cent. though it has been thought that Faustus wrote before the invention of the Armenian alphabet and so in Greek or Syriac and that the present text is a translation; most important despite a detrimental textual tradition; only bks. 3-5 survive, covering the period from 314 to 367). The Gregorian cycle: 1st recension or *The Agathangelus*: A. Armenian Agathangelus, *Agat‘angełay patmut‘iwn Hayoc‘*, in Łukasean Matenadaran 15, Tiflis, 1914, pp. 112/795, 126/873. B. Greek Agathangelus, ed. V. Langlois in *Collection des historiens anciens et modernes de l'Arménie* I, Paris, 1867, pp. 136, 165 (history of the conversion of Armenia by St. Gregory in 314, traditionally ascribed to Tiridates the Great's secretary of that name. The Greek Agathangelus appears to have been translated from the Armenian in 464-68.). 2nd recension of *Life of St. Gregory*: A. Greek Life, ed. G. Garitte, *Documents pour l'étude du livre d'Agathange*, Studi e Testi 127, Vatican City, 1946, p. 98. B. Arabic Life, ed. N. Marr in *Zapiski vostochnago otdeleniya Imperatorskago Russkago Arkheologicheskago Obshchestva* 16, St. Petersburg, 1905, p. 86. The Arabic Life does not appear to be earlier than the 9th cent. The Greek life may be more ancient than recension 1). John VI, Katholikos of Armenia, or John of Draskhanakert (Yovhannēs Drasxanakertec‘i), *History of Armenia*: *Yovhannu Drasxanakertec‘woy patmut‘iwn Hayoc‘*, in

Łukasean Matenadaran 5, Tiflis, 1912, passim (chief prelate of Armenia [897-925/30], the author brings his history to 923-24, having taken an active part in the events described in it). Lazarus of P'arpi (Łazar P'arpec'i), *History of Armenia*: *Łazaray P'arpec'woy patmut'iwn Hayoc'*, in Łukasean Matenadaran 2, Tiflis, 1907, passim (a continuation of Faustus from 387 to 485, written at the end of the 5th or the beginning of the 6th cent.). Leontius (Łevond), *History of Armenia*: ed. I. Ezeanc', *Patmut'iwn Łewondeay meci vardapeti Hayoc'*, St. Petersburg, 1887, pp. 5, 6, 8, 10, 21, 22, 25, 26, 28, 33, 34 (written at the end of the 8th cent. and covering the period from the 740s to 788). Mathew of Edessa (Matt'eos Uřhayec'i), *Chronicle*: *Patmut'iwn Matt'eosi Uřhayec'woy*, Jerusalem, 1869, I, pp. 5, 8-10, 14, 53, 56-61, 65-66; II, p. 119. Moses of Kałankaytuk' or of Daskhuren (Movsēs Kałankatuac'i or Dasxuranc'i), *History of Albania*: ed. M. Emin, *Movsēsi Kałankatuac'woy patmut'iwn Ałuanic' ašxarhi*, in Łukasean Matenadaran 8, Tiflis, 1912, passim ("[Caucasian] Albanian antiquites" ascribed to the above, compiled, as it appears, at the end of the 10th cent., not, as used to be held, in the 12th cent.). Ps. Moses of Khorene (Movsēs Xorenac'i), *History of Armenia*: *Srboy hōrn meroy Movsēsi Xorenac'woy patmut'iwn Hayoc'*, in Łukasean Matenadaran 10, Tiflis, 1913, passim ("Armenian antiquities," the final composition of which belongs to the latter part of the 8th cent., but which contains valuable historical tradition, which may have been first set to writing in the 5th, the alleged *floruit* of Moses). Stephen (Step'annos Asołik), *Universal History*: ed. S. Malxaseanc', *Step'annosi Tarōnc'woy Asołkan patmut'iwn tiezarakan*, in Hratarakut'iwn T'ip'lisiənk. Hayerēn grkert hrat 20, St. Petersburg, 1885, passim. Vardan, *Universal History*: *Howakumn patmut'ean Vardanay vardapeti lusabaneal*, Venice, 1862, passim (based on a number of sources now lost, this late-13th-cent. work is brought to 1267.).

b. Byzantine. George Cedrenus, *Historiarum compendium*, in *Corpus scriptorum historiae byzantinae*, Bonn, 1838, II, pp. 556-59. Constantine Porphyrogenitus, *De administrando imperio*, ed. G. Moravcsik, Budapest, 1949, pp. 43, 45, 46. Idem, *De cerimoniis*, ed. J. P. Migne, *Patrologiae cursus completus*, p. 112, 2.48. Theophanes, *Chronographia*, ed. J. P. Migne, *Patrologiae cursus completus*, pp. 108, 744. Theophylactus Simocatta, *Historiae*, ed. C. de Boor, Leipzig, 1887, 3.8.6.

2. Modern works. N. Adontz, *Armenia in the Period of Justinian*, tr. and revised by N. Garsoïan, Lisbon, 1970, pp. 228, 237, 241-42, 311, 319-21, 339, 344, 369 and passim. Idem, "Les Taronites en Arménie et à Byzance," *Byzantion*, 1934, 1935, 1936, and "La généalogie des Taronites," *Byzantion*, 1939, repr. in *Études arméno-byzantines*, Lisbon, 1965, pp. 197-263, 339-45. S. Der Nersessian, *L'art arménien*, Paris, 1977, pp. 81-122. R. Grousset, *Histoire de l'Arménie*, Paris, 1947, pp. 123, 130, 146, 161, 168, 199, 202, 217-22, 259-65, 282-86, 291-92, 298-99, 307-11, 313-14 and passim. *Hakhpat*, Documenti di Architettura Armenia 1, publ. by Facoltà di architettura del politecnico di Milano and Accademia delle Scienze dell'Armenia Sovietica, Milan, 1968. Justi, *Namenbuch*, pp. 406-11, 417-18, 436-38, 467-69. J. Laurent, *L'Arménie entre Byzance et l'Islam*, Paris, 1919, pp. 83-86 and passim. J. Markwart (Marquart), *Osteuropäische und ostasiatische Streifzüge*, Leipzig, 1903, Exkurs IV: "Der Ursprung der iberischen Bagratiden." Idem, "Die Genealogie der Bagratiden und das Zeitalter des Mar Abas und Ps. Moses Xorenac'i," *Caucasica* 6/2, Leipzig, 1930. Idem, *Südarmenien und die Tigrisquellen*, Vienna, 1930, pp. 495-500. L. Movsēsean, "Loři et l'histoire de la famille bagratide Kurikian," *Revue des études arméniennes* 7/2, 1927, pp. 209-66. *Sanahin*, Documenti di Architettura Armenia 3, Milan, 1970. C. Toumanoff, *Studies in Christian Caucasian History*, Georgetown, 1963, pp. 132, 201-03, 223-52, 277-354. Idem, *Manuel de généalogie et chronologie pour l'histoire de la Caucasie chrétienne*, Rome, 1976, pp. 96-178, 516, 519, 522-23, 526, 534-35, 552, 588. Idem, "Armenia and Georgia," *Cambridge Medieval History* IV, 1966, pp. 593-620. Idem, "Caucasia and Byzantium," *Traditio* 27, 1971, pp. 121-30.

(C. TOUMANOFF)

BAHĀ'-ALLĀH, MĪRZĀ ḤOSAYN-ʿALĪ NŪRĪ (1233-1309/1817-92). Iranian notable and founder of the Bahai religion or Bahaism (q.v.). He was born 2 Moḥarram 1233/12 November 1817 in Tehran into the household of a notable family from Māzandarān. His father, Mīrzā ʿAbbās Nūrī (d. 1839), known as Mīrzā Bozorg, served the court of Fatḥ-ʿAlī Shah Qājār (1797-1834) (q.v.) in several capacities. He was appointed vizier to the shah's twelfth son, the il-khan of the Qajar tribe. He grew close to First Minister Mīrzā Abu'l-Qāsem Qā'emmaqām, and in 1834 he was appointed governor and tax-farmer of Borūjerd and Luristan (Lorestān). But in 1835 the new monarch Moḥammad Shah (1834-48) had Qā'emmaqām executed, and the new first minister, Ḥājī Mīrzā Āqāsī, removed Mīrzā Bozorg from his posts and stopped his salary (Bāmdād, *Rejāl* VI, pp. 126-29). The family retained lands around its ancestral village of Takor on the Nūr district of Māzandarān.

In his youth Mīrzā Ḥosayn-ʿAlī demonstrated pacifist tendencies, and was disturbed when he read an account of the early Muslim execution of the Banū Qorayẓa in Medina (Bahā'-Allāh, in Ešrāq Ḵāvarī, ed., *Mā'eda-ye āsmānī* VII, p. 136). At the wedding of one of his brothers he received a lesson about the world's ephemerality when he saw that, after a puppet show about a royal court, all the pomp was packed into trunks at the end (Bahā'-Allāh, "Lawḥ-e ra'īs," in *Majmūʿa-ye maṭbūʿa*, pp. 107-10). Mīrzā Ḥosayn-ʿAlī, the future Bahā'-Allāh, was just reaching adulthood when his father fell from power and the experience may have further disillusioned him with worldly politics and predisposed him to a meditative spirituality, and, later, the adoption of the radical religion of Babism (q.v.). Bahāʾ-Allāh wrote, late in his life, that Moḥammad Shah committed two "heinous deeds," the banishment of the Bāb to Azerbaijan and the murder of Qāʾemmaqām, and this consideration appears to have partially underpinned his advocacy from the 1870s of constitutional constraints on the monarchy ("Kalemāt-e ferdowsīya," in *Majmūʿa-ī az alwāḥ*, pp. 35-36; tr. Taherzadeh, p. 65). Indeed, many of Mīrzā Bozorg's children reacted against the orthodoxies of Qajar Shiʿism. Of Mīrzā Bozorg's thirteen children by four wives and three concubines, at least one adopted Shaikhism (q.v.) and at least six others Babism.

The new first minister, Āqāsī, offered Mīrzā Ḥosayn-ʿAlī his patronage, despite his being the son of an enemy, but the young Nūrī proved uninterested, and the two later fell out when Mīrzā Ḥosayn-ʿAlī refused to sell some land and villages to the rapacious Āqāsī. (Moḥammad "Nabīl-e Aʿẓam" Zarandī, *Maṭāleʿ al-anwār*, MS. International Bahá'í Archives, Haifa; partial Eng. tr. Shoghi [Šawqī] Effendi Rabbani [q.v.], *The Dawn-Breakers*, New York, 1932; repr. Wilmette, 1974, pp. 120-22.) Mīrzā Ḥosayn-ʿAlī was in contact with Shaikhis from Nūr and from Tehran, a natural development given the popularity of esoteric Shaikhism with Qajar-era notables and his own speculative bent. When Mollā Ḥosayn Bošrūʾī came to Tehran in 1844 to spread the new beliefs of Babism, centered on Sayyed ʿAlī-Moḥammad Šīrāzī the Bāb (q.v.), he met with local Shaikhis. One of them, Mollā Moḥammad Moʿallem Nūrī, became a Babi and consented to contact Mīrzā Ḥosayn-ʿAlī for Bošrūʾī. Mīrzā Ḥosayn-ʿAlī in this manner accepted the Bāb's claims to religious authority as the gate of the Twelfth Imam. Soon thereafter, late in 1844 or in 1845, Mīrzā Ḥosayn-ʿAlī returned to his village of Takor, where he endeavored to spread Babism in Nūr and in Māzandarān. His prestige as a local notable gave him many openings, and this missionary journey met with some success, even among some members of the religious class. Through him, as well, his brothers Mīrzā Yaḥyā (whom Mīrzā Ḥosayn-ʿAlī raised, aged 14 in 1844) and Mīrzā Mūsā became Babis (*Ketāb-e noqṭat al-kāf*, ed. E. G. Browne, E. J. W. Gibb Memorial Series 15, 1910, pp. 239-40; Zarandī, *Maṭāleʿ*, tr. pp. 102-20; ʿAbd-al-Bahāʾ *Maqāla-ye šaḵṣ-ī sayyāḥ*, E. G. Browne, ed. and tr. as *A Traveller's Narrative*, Cambridge, 1891, pp. 72-78, tr. pp. 56-62).

Mīrzā Ḥosayn-ʿAlī used his position and his contacts in Tehran, not only to spread Babism, but to protect his coreligionists. He did so at some risk, however, since the aid he gave the poet Qorrat-al-ʿAyn and other Babis after they were accused in the slaying (actually by a Shaikhi) of Mollā Taqī Baragānī caused him to suffer temporary imprisonment in Tehran. In 1847 the government exiled the Bāb to imprisonment in Azerbaijan. In the summer of 1848 eighty-one prominent Babis gathered for twenty-two days in Khorasan in the village of Badašt. Mīrzā Ḥosayn-ʿAlī and his young brother Mīrzā Yaḥyā both attended. Mīrzā Ḥosayn-ʿAlī played a low-key role, renting gardens for Qorrat-al-ʿAyn and others, and suggesting theophanic names for some of the Babis, whom the Bāb had encouraged to glorify God by adopting divine names. From this point Mīrzā Ḥosayn-ʿAlī adopted the name Bahāʾ (the glory, [of God]). Mīrzā Yaḥyā became Ṣobḥ-e Azal (The morn of eternity). In the conflict at the conference between those who wanted to retain the Islamic law (*Šarīʿa*) and those who knew of the Bāb's recent announcement that he was the messianic Mahdī or Qāʾem, empowered to begin another dispensation, Bahāʾ-Allāh took the side of the pro-change group, who won out (*Noqṭat al-kāf*, pp. 145-54, 240-41; for Bahāʾ-Allāh's role see Zarandī, *Maṭāleʿ*, tr. pp. 278-300; 459-61, 584-85).

Violence broke out between the Babis and the Qajar government in the second half of 1848, and Bahāʾ-Allāh and several companions, including his half-brother Yaḥyā (then aged 17 or 18), set out from Nūr to help the besieged Babis at Šayḵ Ṭabarsī near Bābol, Māzandarān, in early December, 1848, but they were arrested and imprisoned in Āmol (*Noqṭat al-kāf*, pp. 242-43; Zarandī, *Maṭāleʿ*, tr. pp. 368-77, 461-62, 583-84; Mīrzā Ḥosayn Hamadānī, *Tārīḵ-e jadīd* ms., Cambridge University Library, Browne Or. F. 55/9, tr. E. G. Browne, *The New History of Mīrzā ʿAlī Muḥammed, the Bāb*, Cambridge, 1893; repr. Amsterdam, 1975, pp. 64-65). The following three years witnessed a series of disasters for the Babis, whom government troops besieged and then massacred in Māzandarān, Nayrīz, and Zanjān. On 9 July 1850 the government had the Bāb executed, but only after he had declared himself an independent manifestation of God (*maẓhar-e elāhī*) and had written a book of laws, the *Bayān-e fārsī* for the new religion he founded.

The Bāb had been in correspondence with the Nūrī brothers from his prison, and after the death of many prominent disciples in 1848-50, they emerged as the most likely leaders. Bahāʾ-Allāh, then aged thirty-three and a well-known notable, might have been expected to become the leading Babi. But surprisingly, the Bāb appears to have indicated for Mīrzā Yaḥyā Ṣobḥ-e Azal (then around nineteen) a high station or leadership position, at least nominally, in Babism. The young Azal, however, seems to have possessed little widespread authority or legitimacy, and the 1850s saw the Babi community splinter into a number a regional sects headed by various claimants to theophanic status. The Bāb's works emphasized that another messianic figure, "He whom God shall make manifest (*man yoẓheroh Allāh*)" would appear. More important, the disheartened Babis seem to have been looking for charismatic leaders to replace the Bāb. Azal at first refused to denounce these rivals outright, rather incorporating them into a "theophanic field" with himself at the apex. Later in the 1850s Azal became more intolerant of rivals. Bahāʾ-Allāh, on the other hand, attempted to deflate Babi "manifestations" (*ẓohūrāt*) even in early 1951, asserting his own high station. He snubbed the Babi disciple Sayyed Baṣīr-e Hendī of Multan when he came to visit Nūr, because the Indian made grandiose claims. Finally, Bahāʾ-Allāh "took pity on him and manifested upon that temple of servitude, [Sayyed Baṣīr] the effulgences of divinity, [*tajallīyāt-e robūbīyat*] from that glory of paradise (*Bahāʾ al-reżwān*, [i.e., Bahāʾ-Allāh])." (*Noqṭat al-kāf*, p. 258; see also pp. 238-61).

In June, 1851, Bahāʾ-Allāh left Tehran for Karbalāʾ in Iraq at the suggestion of First Minister Amīr Neẓām Taqī Khan (later Amīr[-e] Kabīr), who attempted to coopt him by offering him a government post whenever he should return. Bahāʾ-Allāh refused the post, but took the hint that he should leave Iran for a while. Bahāʾ-Allāh found Babis in Karbalāʾ following a Sayyed ʿOloww, who claimed to be a divine incarnation until Bahāʾ-Allāh's greater prestige caused him to renounce his pretensions. While in Karbalāʾ in 1851, according to his companion Shaikh Ḥasan Zonūzī, Bahāʾ-Allāh said he was himself the return of Imam Ḥosayn (whom many expected to appear after the Mahdī, whom Babis identified with the Bāb), though he kept this "messianic secret" from most of his associates. In public, Bahāʾ-Allāh supported Azal, in the interests of unity, and worked to spread Babism in Karbalāʾ (Zarandī, *Maṭāleʿ*, tr. pp. 32, 587, 593-94).

The fall of Amīr Kabīr and the rise of Mīrzā Āqā Khan Nūrī Eʿtemād-al-Dawla as first minister under Nāṣer-al-Dīn Shah had the potential for changing Bahāʾ-Allāh's political fortunes. The first minister wanted a rapprochement with Bahāʾ-Allāh, a relative from his region of the country, and with the Babis. He wrote Bahāʾ-Allāh asking him to return to Tehran, and the latter complied. The first minister's brother lavished hospitality on Bahāʾ-Allāh in Tehran for a month, after which the Babi notable retired to a summer house in Šemrān. On the way, he met briefly with Shaikh ʿAlī ʿAẓīm, learning that ʿAẓīm and other radical Babi leaders in the capital had planned the assassination of the shah in retaliation for the execution of the Bāb. Bahāʾ-Allāh condemned the plan. On August 15, 1852, Babis did attempt to assassinate the shah, but failed. (Zarandī, *Maṭāleʿ*, tr. pp. 595-602; Ḥasan Fasāʾī, *Fārs-nāma-ye nāṣerī*, tr. H. Busse, *History of Persia under Qajar Rule*, New York, 1972, pp. 302-04; Sheil to Malmsbury, correspondence August 1852, FO 60/171 in M. Momen, *The Bābī and Bahāʾī Religions, 1844-1944: Some Contemporary Western Accounts*, Oxford, 1981, pp. 128-46.)

Though he knew suspicion would fall on him, Bahāʾ-Allāh declined to go into hiding. He went to Zarganda, staying with his brother-in-law, Mīrzā Majīd, who acted as secretary to the Russian ambassador. His presence was reported to the shah by Ḥājī ʿAlī Khan Ḥājeb-al-Dawla. Nāṣer-al-Dīn Shah demanded that the Russian legation hand Bahāʾ-Allāh over, but the ambassador insisted on delivering him to Mīrzā Āqā Khan Nūrī, who sympathized with Bahāʾ-Allāh. Mīrzā Āqā Khan, however, proved unable to protect Bahāʾ-Allāh when anti-Babi riots broke out in Tehran, and Bahāʾ-Allāh was arrested and made to walk in chains to the Sīāh Čāl (black pit) dungeon. At length he was found innocent. His stay in the crowded, filthy dungeon, where he watched several Babi friends being executed, proved important for Bahāʾ-Allāh's spiritual development. He later wrote that he at that point decided to "undertake, with the utmost vigor, the task of regenerating" the Babi community (Bahāʾ-Allāh, *Lawḥ-e Šayḵ*, pp. 14-16; tr. Shoghi Effendi, pp. 20-22). He had several mystical experiences and dreams of a visionary nature while in prison. Despite having found him innocent, the government exiled Bahāʾ-Allāh, who chose to return to Iraq in the Ottoman empire, arriving in Baghdad on 12 January 1853. In Iran, the aftermath of the attempt on the shah's life saw widespread massacres of suspected Babis, and pillaging of the Nūrīs' property in Takor (Zarandī, *Maṭāleʿ*, tr. pp. 602-50; Moḥammad-Ḥasan Khan Eʿtemād-al-Salṭana [*Rūz-nāma-ye ḵāṭerāt*, ed. Ī. Afšār, Tehran, 1350 Š./1971, p. 957] asserts that Mīrzā Āqā Khan Nūrī, who remained in power until 1858, offered his resignation over the issue of Bahāʾ-Allāh's imprisonment).

A small number of other Babis chose to follow Bahāʾ-Allāh into exile in Iraq, including his half-brother Mīrzā Yaḥyā Ṣobḥ-e Azal, who arrived a few months later. Azal tended to distance himself from the community, spending his time in disguise and dealing with affairs through proxies, including Bahāʾ-Allāh, who publicly deferred to his brother. In Baghdad during 1853 differences arose between Bahāʾ-Allāh, and Azal and his close disciples. A close companion, Dahajī, wrote that Bahāʾ-Allāh disagreed with Azal's policy of remaining incognito, and left Baghdad in order to distance himself from Azal. He retired for two years (1854-56) to Kurdistan, living the life of a Sufi dervish. Azal's continued attempts to assassinate the shah, of which Bahāʾ-Allāh disapproved, may have been another source of contention. Prominent Babis in Baghdad, feeling a need for Bahāʾ-Allāh's stabilizing influence, pleaded with him to return from Sulaimaniya, which he did in 1856 (Mīrzā Mehdī Dahajī, "Resāla," ms., Cambridge University Library, Browne Or. F. 57, p. 48; Mīrzā Javād Qazvīnī, "Resāla," ms., Cambridge University Library, Browne Or. F. 26, tr. E. G. Browne in *Materials for the Study of the Babi Religion*, Cambridge, 1918, pp. 7-9; Bahāʾ-Allāh wrote an important mystical poem while staying with the Ḵāledī Naqšbandīs in Sulaimaniya, that mentions his "mission" [*beʿṯatī*], "al-Qaṣīda al-warqāʾīya," *Āṯār* III, pp. 196-215).

From 1856 to 1863 Bahāʾ-Allāh lived in Baghdad, building up an increasingly loyal following in Iran through his elegant mystical aphorisms and crisp doctrinal treatises in Persian or Arabic such as the *Kalemāt-e maknūna* (Hidden words), *Haft wādī* (Seven valleys), and *Ketāb-e īqān* (Book of certitude). He took very seriously a widely believed Muslim prophecy that the Mahdī or Jesus Christ would appear in 1280/1863-64, and put off making any public announcement until then, though evidence abounds that he kept a "messianic secret" for years before (for the wave of millenarianism that swept the Muslims of Arabia and India in the years just before 1280, see O. Pearson, *Islamic Reform and Revival in Nineteenth Century India: the Tariqah-i Muhammadiyyah*, Ph.D. dissertation, Duke University, 1979, pp. 211-12). Bahāʾ-Allāh replaced the disastrous militancy of the Babis to which leaders like Azal were still committed with an emphasis on internal personal transformation similar to Sufi ethics and mysticism.

In the 1860s, Bahāʾ-Allāh's gatherings attracted many local notables and Iranian pilgrims, lending him greater influence in Iran as well as in Baghdad. Despite his emphasis on communal harmony, however, sporadic communal violence broke out between Shiʿites and Babis, and among factions of Babis, especially among unruly tradesmen and religious students, and Ottoman and Persian officials often laid this violence at his door. Bahāʾ-Allāh's influence worried his enemies in the Iranian government and among the Shiʿite clerics, and he narrowly escaped assassination at the hands of a man hired by the Iranian consul in Baghdad, Mīrzā Bozorg Khan. Mollā ʿAbd-al-Ḥosayn Ṭehrānī, Nāṣer-al-Dīn Shah's religious envoy to the shrine cities, cooperated with the consul, and began a major Shiʿite drive against Bahāʾ-Allāh and the fifty or so Babis in Iraq that lost steam when Shaikh Mortażā Anṣārī (q.v.), the leading *marjaʿ-e taqlīd*, refused to join in on the grounds that he knew nothing about the Babis. (Bahāʾ-Allāh, *Ketāb-e īqān*, pp. 210-12; tr. Shoghi Effendi, pp. 249-53; ʿAbd-al-Bahāʾ, *Maqāla*, pp. 107-18, tr. pp. 82-88; Dahajī, "Resāla," pp. 81-82; Ostād Moḥammad-ʿAlī Salmānī, *Ḵāṭerāt*, ms., International Bahá'í Archives, Haifa; Eng. tr. M. Gail, *My Memories of Bahāʾullāh*, Los Angeles, 1982, pp. 15-20; Mīrzā Abu'l-Fażl Golpāyegānī, "Resāla be Aleksandr Tumanskii," R. Mehrābḵānī, ed., *Rasāʾel wa raqāʾem*, Tehran, 1978, pp. 65-76; tr. J. Cole, *Letters and Essays 1886-1913*, Los Angeles, 1985; "Two State Papers of 1862," in Browne, *Materials*, pp. 270-81.)

Alarmed at the revival of Babi activity under Bahāʾ-Allāh's de facto leadership, and at the easy access to Iranians enjoyed by the Babi leaders situated so near the Shiʿite shrine cities, Mīrzā Ḥosayn Khan Mošīr-al-Dawla (q.v.), the Iranian consul in Istanbul who at that point considered the Babis subversive, pressured the Ottomans to exile Bahāʾ-Allāh farther from Iran. The Ottomans complied, calling Bahāʾ-Allāh to Istanbul in the spring of 1863. Before he left Baghdad, Bahāʾ-Allāh camped for twelve days at the Garden of Necip Paşa, where a large number of friends came to bid him farewell. During these days, to intimates, "he would speak of the Bāb's Cause and declare his own" (Salmānī, *Ḵāṭerāt*, tr. p. 22; see also Dahajī, "Resāla," pp. 65-70, 153-54; Qazvīnī, "Resāla," p. 16). In late April, 1863, Bahāʾ-Allāh declared himself, to a handful of close followers, the promised one foretold by the Bāb. Perhaps because the year 1280 had not yet begun, he delayed any written declaration for almost a year.

After a four-month journey overland, Bahāʾ-Allāh and his entourage arrived in Istanbul. He had chosen twenty Babis to accompany him, in addition to his own family and muleteers; these were often men he thought might make trouble if left to themselves. Azal voluntarily accompanied his older brother, traveling incognito. Bahāʾ-Allāh met with a few Ottoman officials who came to visit him, but refused to seek audiences with the sultan or first minister. In Istanbul in 1863 he first gave evidence of thinking about the global social reforms that he advocated in later years. He told former First Minister Kemal Pasha that the Ottomans, and the world, should adopt a universal auxiliary language to be taught alongside local languages in every nation, so that "the whole earth would come to be regarded as one country" (Bahāʾ-Allāh, *Lawḥ-e šayḵ*, p. 90, tr. p. 38.) Because he refused to build alliances with Ottoman politicians, Bahāʾ-Allāh had no means of resisting Mošīr-al-Dawla's pressure on the sultan to exile him still farther away. Sultan ʿAbdülaziz (ʿAbd-al-ʿAzīz) commanded that Bahāʾ-Allāh be banished to Edirne in Rumelia, a common site for the exile of political prisoners. Bahāʾ-Allāh at first refused to leave Istanbul, and wanted to make a stand against the Ottomans, seeking either to overturn the sultan's edict or to attain martyrdom when troops came to arrest the Babis. But such a plan required unanimity, and when Azal declined to go along it fell through (Salmānī, *Ḵāṭerāt*, tr. p. 39-41, Qazvīnī, "Resāla," tr. pp. 18-19). Bahāʾ-Allāh and his entourage, as well as Azal and his, lived in Edirne from 12 December 1863 to 12 August 1868. They received an Ottoman stipend for their support. In the winter and spring of 1864/1280, Bahāʾ-Allāh gradually began announcing himself to friends in Iran. In the "Sūrat Damm" (Sura of blood), written twenty years after the Bāb's declaration (1260/1844) for Mollā Moḥammad "Nabīl" Zarandī, then in Iran, Bahāʾ-Allāh said he was the return (*rajʿa*) of the Bāb, that is, "He whom God would make manifest" (*Āṯār* IV, pp. 1-15). Close disciples of Bahāʾ-Allāh in Iran like Mīrzā Ḥaydar-ʿAlī Eṣfahānī received such letters and began increasingly passing them on to other Babis. For his followers, Bahāʾ-Allāh's assertion that he was an independent manifestation of God able to found a new dispensation made Azal's position as head of the old Babi religion irrelevant. Bahāʾ-Allāh and his supporters in any case held that the Bāb's appointment of Azal had been a ruse to draw the fire of Iranian officials from Bahāʾ-Allāh. In spring of 1866 Bahāʾ-Allāh moved to a separate house from that of Azal, saying that Azal had attempted to have him killed, and, meeting with failure, had then imputed similar plots to his older brother. Bahāʾ-Allāh began more openly proclaiming his status as an independent prophet, writing suras he said were divine revelation (*waḥy*). In September, 1867, he decisively broke with Yaḥyā, addressing to him a letter in which he set forth his station and demanded his brother's obedience. Yaḥyā refused, challenging Bahāʾ-Allāh to a test of the divine will (*mobāhela*) at the mosque of Sultan Selim, but Azal lost face when he changed his mind and did not appear (Bahāʾ-Allāh, "Lawḥ-e Naṣīr," in *Majmūʿa-ye maṭbūʿa*, pp. 166-202; see Bahāʾ-Allāh's many Edirne-period works in *Āṯār*, vol. 4; Dahajī, "Resāla," pp. 35-38, 283-85; Salmānī, *K̲āṭerāt*, tr. pp. 42-48, 93-105; Qazvīnī, "Resāla," tr. pp. 19-27).

From 1866 Bahāʾ-Allāh began addressing a series of letters to world leaders, announcing his advent as the promised one of all religions. His first was a long general letter of moral exhortations, the *Sūrat al-molūk* (Sura of the kings, 1866). Specific individuals therein addressed were Sultan ʿAbd-al-ʿAzīz and the Iranian ambassador, Mošīr-al-Dawla. In 1868 he wrote a long letter (*Lawḥ-e solṭān*) to Nāṣer-al-Dīn Shah, saying Babis under his leadership were not militant, and requesting an end to their persecution in Iran. The shah had Bahāʾ-Allāh's emissary bearing this letter tortured and killed. Bahāʾ-Allāh also wrote Napoleon III, elliptically proclaiming himself the return of Christ (Bahāʾ-Allāh, *Alwāḥ-e nāzela k̲eṭāb be molūk*, pp. 3-70, 91-117, 143-201; for Western diplomatic correspondence on Bahāʾ-Allāh in the Edirne period, see Momen, *The Bābī and Bahāʾi Religions*, pp. 185-200).

In 1868 the Ottoman government exiled the Babis once more. Bahāʾ-Allāh and his followers, along with a few Azalīs, were sent to the prison city of ʿAkkā on the coast of Palestine, while Azal, his companions, and a few Bahais were sent to Famagusta, Cyprus. Bahāʾ-Allāh was imprisoned in the citadel for over two years, where some of his followers died from the unsanitary conditions. There he continued his proclamation to world leaders, including Queen Victoria, Tsar Aleksander II, and Pope Pius IX. From 1870 to 1877 Bahāʾ-Allāh was kept under house arrest in the old city of ʿAkkā. In the late 1860s and early 1870s most Babis in Iran went over to Bahāʾ-Allāh, becoming Bahais. These believers in a new revelation asked for a new code of religious and ritual law. Around 1873 Bahāʾ-Allāh in ʿAkkā set down a new book of law and ritual, the *Ketāb-e aqdas*, which he said derived from divine revelation, meant to replace both the Koran and the *Bayān* (Aleksandr Tumanskiĭ, *Kitabe akdes*, Mémoires de l'Académie impériale des sciences de St. Petersbourg, 8th ser., vol. 3, no. 6, 1899; Dahajī, "Resāla," pp. 154-56; Qazvīnī, "Resāla," tr. pp. 27-52).

His improving relations with local officials were only disturbed once, when some of the rougher of his followers in ʿAkkā, unbeknownst to Bahāʾ-Allāh, plotted and carried out the murder of several Azalīs who had been spying on the Bahais for the Ottomans and stirring up local inhabitants against them. Bahāʾ-Allāh denounced the murderers in no uncertain terms, but the incident revived restrictions on his movements. In 1877, however, the Pasha gave him permission to live in a mansion outside ʿAkkā, at Mazraʿa till 1879, then at Bahjī until his death in 1892. His advocacy of social reforms in the 1870s won him new respect from old foes like Mošīr-al-Dawla. Bahāʾ-Allāh gradually convinced many Qajar notables that he represented no political threat (Eʿtemād-al-Salṭana wrote in 1892 in his *Rūz-nāma-ye k̲āṭerāt*, 1st ed., p. 957: "Mīrzā Ḥosayn-ʿAlī, an old man, was no assassin"). In the ʿAkkā period his financial support probably came from believers' contributions as well as from the Ottoman stipend. Bahāʾ-Allāh married three times, once in Iran (Āsīa "Nawwāb" K̲ānom), once in Baghdad, a cousin (Mahd-e ʿOlyā) whose family had been martyred, and once in ʿAkkā (Gowhar K̲ānom). In accordance with Babi law, he had only two wives at any one time (Bahai law later required monogamy). He had fourteen children, four of them girls; five sons predeceased him (Qazvīnī, "Resāla," tr. Browne, pp. 45-65; Dahajī, "Resāla," pp. 285-91; Western primary accounts of ʿAkkā period in Momen, *Bābī and Bahāʾi Religions*, pp. 201-40). Before his death Bahāʾ-Allāh appointed his eldest son, ʿAbd-al-Bahāʾ ʿAbbās Effendi (q.v.) to head the Bahai faith after him ("Ketāb ʿAhdī," in *Majmūʿa-ī az alwāḥ*, pp. 134-38).

Religious doctrines. Bahāʾ-Allāh taught a theological *via negativa*, writing that God's essence is unknowable, and he is simply the absolute truth (*al-ḥaqq*, *al-ʿamāʾ*). Following the theology of Muʿtazilism and Shaikhism, Bahāʾ-Allāh teaches that God's essential attributes (*ṣefāt al-d̲āt*) are identical to his essence ("Lawḥ madīnat al-tawḥīd," *Māʾeda-ye āsmānī* IV, p. 321). According to Bahāʾ-Allāh, both God and the universal matter have always existed temporally, though God is essentially prior to matter, which is essentially originated (*moḥdaṯ d̲ātī*: Bahāʾ-Allāh, "Lawḥ al-ḥekma," *Majmūʿa-ye maṭbūʿa*, p. 40; this is Avicennian). He rejected the Sufi doctrine of existential monism or *waḥdat al-wojūd*, and denied that God becomes incarnate (*ḥolūl*) in the world, or manifests (*ẓohūr*) his essence corporeally (Bahāʾ-Allāh, *Haft wādī*, *Āṯār-e qalam-e aʿlā* 3:114-15; *Ketāb-e īqān*, p. 79; "Lawḥ-e Salmān," *Majmūʿa-ye maṭbūʿa*, pp. 140-42).

The transcendent essence of God and the originated material world are bridged in Bahāʾ-Allāh's thought by the Word of God (*kalemat Allāh*, *kalām Allāh*; also called *ketāb Allāh* and *amr* or divine command), a temporally preexistent principle whereby God created composite creatures. The Word of God manifests (*ẓa-hara*) itself in human form, in the shape of prophets and messengers ("Lawḥ al-ẓohūr," ms. AB 201, Bahāʾī World Centre, Haifa; "Lawḥ al-ḥekma," pp. 41-42; "Lawḥ Ašraf," *Majmūʿa-ye maṭbūʿa*, p. 212; "Sūrat al-raʾīs," *Majmūʿa-ye mobāraka*, p. 87). Bahāʾ-Allāh distinguished between prophets (sing. *nabī*[*y*]) who simply came with a mission to their people and "prophets endowed with constancy" (*anbīāʾ olu'l-azm*), who revealed new religious legislation abrogating that of the previous dispensation. He wrote of the Zoroastrian, Mosaic, Christian, Islamic, and Babi dispensations, recognizing all of them as divinely-ordained religions progressively leading up to his own (he did not exclude other world religions, and his son ʿAbd-al-Bahāʾ later incorporated Buddha and Krishna into the schema). He taught the sinlessness (*al-ʿesma al-kobrā*) of the legislating prophets, though he wrote that their human souls could progress and be purified. The purpose of the advent of prophets is to transmit God's grace and educate souls for their own spiritual advance in this world and in the afterlife (Bahāʾ-Allāh, "Ešrāqāt," in

Čand lawḥ, pp. 54-59; "al-Qaṣīda al-warqā'īya," *Āṯār* 3: 198; *Ketāb-e aqdas*, Bombay, n.d., p. 51; *Ketāb-e īqān*, pp. 82-83).

Bahā'-Allāh's doctrine of prophets is theophanic. He held that prophets manifest the active attributes (*ẓohūr-e asmā' wa ṣefāt*) of God into the material world, though he denied that God's essence (*ḏāt*) itself could ever be manifested, differing in this regard from Druze and other Shi'ite esotericists. In neo-Platonic fashion, he sometimes refers to the totality of God's active attributes as the "self" (*nafs*) of God. Only through the prophets and messengers of God, he wrote, could human beings attain a knowledge of God's attributes, which his envoys mirror forth. He said that prophets have a two-fold nature (*do 'onṣor*), one physical and the other divine (*elāhī*), Corresponding to two stations (*maqām*), the human, and the station wherein his voice is the voice of God. The doctrine of the divinity (*olūhīyat*) of all the prophets does not imply incarnation, but refers to the manifestation of the active attributes of God. Explaining his own station, he compared God's manifestation in him to the divine effulgence in the burning bush of Moses, and wrote of divinity, "This station is the station in which one dies to himself (*fanā'*) and lives to God. Divinity, whenever I mention it, indicates my complete and absolute self-effacement." (*Lawḥ-e šayḵ*, p. 30; see also *Majmū'a-ye maṭbū'a*, p. 340; "Tajallīyāt," in *Čand lawḥ*, pp. 203-05). Because all prophets manifest the same divine attributes, in Bahā'-Allāh's doctrine they are all metaphysically identical, though their human personalities differed. Thus, each is a "return" of the previous prophets (but this does not imply reincarnation of the human soul, a doctrine Bahā'-Allāh rejected).

Social teachings. Bahā'-Allāh's enunciation of steps for social reform dates to his arrival in the Turkish-speaking provinces of the Ottoman empire in the mid-1860s, and continued during his Palestine exile 1868-92. He was in Edirne during some of the Ottoman debate on constitutionalism, and around 1868 wrote Queen Victoria that the parliamentarian form of constitutional monarchy she presided over was the best type of government. In 1866 he had denounced the international arms race, urging that the money poured into it be instead spent on the poor. Later in 'Akkā he advocated the convening of an international parliament that would guarantee peace through the principle of collective security. He urged the adoption of one universal language throughout the world, and of uniform weights, measures, and currency. He forbade religious and racial prejudice, and discouraged nationalist chauvinism ("Glory not in this that you love your country, glory in this that you love mankind"). He urged universal education of children, and his insistence that daughters be educated along with sons is only one of many indications that he supported an improved status for women. He advocated the adoption of modern technology in the Middle East, arguing that it was only an extension of Greek science and philosophy, which Middle Easterners had long accepted ("Lawḥ maleka Vīktūrīa," *Alwāḥ-e nāzela*, p. 133; "Sūrat al-molūk," ibid.; *Ketāb-e aqdas*, pp. 52-53; other quotes and points in "Lawḥ al-ḥekma," *Majmū'a-ī az alwāḥ* and tr. Taherzadeh; this entire volume has these reformist emphases).

Bibliography: Most of the major primary sources have been cited in the course of the article. Several thousands of Bahā'-Allāh's letters and writings are preserved by Bahais in private archives in Iran and at the "International Bahá'í Archives" in Haifa, Israel. The best primary sources for Bahā'-Allāh's life, the chronicle by Mollā Moḥammad "Nabīl" Zarandī, the memoirs of Āqā Ḥosayn Āščī, and those of Āqā Reżā Qannād Šīrāzī, all close companions of Bahā'-Allāh in Iran and during his exile, remain in ms. in Haifa; these have been summarized by H. M. Balyuzi, *Bahá'u'lláh*, Oxford, 1980. The first part of Zarandī was translated, as noted above. A reliable but slightly abridged English translation of memoirs by another companion, Salmānī, has appeared recently (op. cit.). The *Noqṭat al-kāf* contains primary material for the Babi movement in the 1840s and early 1850s, despite lingering questions about possible late interpolations in the recension published by Browne. The "Resāla"s of Sayyed Mehdī Dahajī and Mīrzā Javād Qazvīnī, companions of Bahā'-Allāh, are also valuable (microfilms of these and other Cambridge University Library Browne mss. are in the Library of Congress and the University of Michigan, British Manuscript Project). Bahā'-Allāh's eldest son, 'Abd-al-Bahā', wrote a valuable chronicle, cited above, translated by Browne as *A Traveller's Narrative*. Some important details are in Mīrzā Ḥaydar-'Alī Eṣfahānī, *Bahjat al-Ṣodūr*, Bombay, 1331/1912-13, a small portion of which was translated by A. Faizi, *Stories from the Delight of Hearts*, Los Angeles, 1980. Primary biographies of Bahā'-Allāh's major disciples in Iran are in Kāẓem Samandar, *Tārīḵ-e Samandar wa molḥaqāt*. Tehran, 131 *Badī'*/1974. Momen's collection of Western documentary sources is useful, though neither the Ottoman nor the Iranian archives have been intensively explored for Bahā'-Allāh's biography (see Moḥammad-'Alī Mowaḥḥed, "Asnād-ī az āršīv-e dawlatī-e Estānbūl," *Rāhnamā-ye ketāb* 6, 1342 Š./1963, pp. 102-10). Because of his access to family history and private manuscripts as Bahā'-Allāh's great-grandson, Shoghi Effendi's *God Passes By* (Wilmette, Ill., 1944) is also useful. Many Azalī sources exist, some of them primary, but they are hard to collate with sources originating with Bahā'-Allāh and his supporters, because they are so hostile and contradictory. Of note here are Mollā Rajab-'Alī Qāher, "Ketāb," ms. Cambridge University Library, Browne Or. F. 24; and 'Ezzīya Ḵānom, "Tanbīh al-nā'emīn," ms. Cambridge University Library, Browne Or. F. 60.

Most of Bahā'-Allāh's major works have been published, though no scientific editions have been prepared. Multivolume collections of his writings include *Āṯār-e qalam-e aʿlā*, 8 vols., Tehran, 1963-76? and ʿAbd-al-Ḥamīd Ešrāq Ḵāvarī, ed., *Māʾeda-ye āsmānī*, 10 vols., Tehran, 1971-73; repr. New Delhi, 1985. Facsimiles of many documents by or relating to the Bāb and Bahā'-Allāh were privately published in the 1970s by the Iran National Bahai Archives (INBA) in 100 volumes. Important works by Bahā'-Allāh from the 1850s and early 1860s are in *Āṯār*, vol. 3, including *Jawāher al-asrār*, *Haft wādī* and *Čahār wādī*; for Eng. tr. of the latter two see *The Seven Valleys and the Four Valleys*, tr. Ali Kuli Khan and Marzieh Gail, Wilmette, Ill., rev. ed. 1952. *Kalemāt-e maknūna*, from the late 1850s, is in *Majmūʿa-ye maṭbūʿa-ye alwāḥ-e mobāraka*, Cairo, 1920, repr. Wilmette, Ill., 1978, tr. Shoghi Effendi, *The Hidden Words*, London, 1949. Works from the 1850s and early 1860s can also be found in INBA, vol. 36, and in *Māʾeda-ye āsmānī*, vol. 4. One of Bahā'-Allāh's more important theological and eschatological works, written in 1862 for an uncle of the Bāb, is *Ketāb-e īqān*, Cairo, 1902, Eng. tr. Shoghi Effendi, *The Kitáb-i-Íqán*: *The Book of Certitude*, Wilmette, 1931, 1970, Fr. tr. Hyppolyte Dreyfus et Mīrzā Habibullāh Chirazi, *Le livre de la certitude*, Paris, 1904. Other tablets of the mid-1860s can be found in the section on Reżwān in ʿA. Ešrāq Ḵāvarī, ed., *Ayyām-e tesʿa*, Tehran, n.d., including the *Lawḥ-e ṣabr*, set down on April 21, 1863. Many of Bahā'-Allāh's Arabic letters to Iran declaring his independent prophethood in 1864-68 are in *Āṯār*, vol. 4, including the *Sūrat damm*, and the *Sūrat al-aṣḥāb*. His epistles to the world's rulers written in 1866-69 are in *Alwāḥ-e nāzela ketāb be molūk wa roʾasā-ye arż*, Tehran, 124 *Badīʿ*/1968; partial tr., Shoghi Effendi, *Proclamation of Bahā'u'llāh to the Kings and Leaders of the World*, Haifa, 1967. Persian writings from the Edirne period and many significant essays from the ʿAkkā period, 1868-92, are in *Majmūʿa-ye maṭbūʿa*. Bahā'-Allāh's most important opus, the *Ketāb-e aqdas* (1873) was published at the Dutt Prashad Press: *al-Ketāb al-aqdas wa nabża-ī men alwāḥ Bahāʾ-Allāh*, Bombay, 1890. A poor translation of the *Ketāb-e aqdas* with fundamentalist Christian commentary was unaccountably published by the Royal Asiatic Society: E. Elder and W. Miller, tr. and ed., *Al-Kitab al-Aqdas or the Most Holy Book*, Oriental Translation Fund, N.S., vol. 38, London, 1961; the contemporary official Bahai approach to this book of laws can be seen in *A Synopsis and Codification of the Kitáb-i-Aqdas, the Most Holy Book of Bahá'u'lláh*, Haifa, 1973. Several collections have been published of Bahā'-Allāh's tablets on global social reform and world government written from 1877 to 1892, including *Alwāḥ-e mobāraka-ye hażrat-e Bahāʾ-Allāh šāmel-e ešrāqāt wa čand lawḥ-e dīgar*, Tehran, n.d.; and *Majmūʿa-ī az alwāḥ ke baʿd az Ketāb-e aqdas nāzel šodand*, Hofheim-Langenhain, 1980, pp. 35-36, Eng. tr. H. Taherzadeh et al., *Tablets of Bahá'u'lláh Revealed after the Kitáb-i-Aqdas*, Haifa, 1978. Bahā'-Allāh's last major book, which contains many passages of autobiography, is *Lawḥ-e mobārak ketāb ba Šayk Moḥammad Taqī Mojtahed*, Hofheim-Langenhain, 1982, pp. 14-16, Eng. tr. Shoghi Effendi Rabbānī, *Epistle to the Son of the Wolf*, Wilmette, 1971, Fr. tr. H. Dreyfus, *L'épitre au fils du loup*, Paris, 1913. Translations into other European languages have for the most part followed the English rather than the original languages. Important translations in addition to those noted above are *Gleanings from the Writings of Bahā'u'llāh*, tr. Shoghi Effendi, Wilmette, Ill., 1939; and *Prayers and Meditations*, tr. Shoghi Effendi, London, 1957.

Most of the Arabic and Persian originals were published in the twentieth century by the Bahai Publishing Trust in Tehran, destroyed in 1979, but many have been recently reprinted in the original languages at the Bahai Publishing Trusts at Hofheim-Langenhain in West Germany, in Wilmette, Ill., and in New Delhi. For rare nineteenth-century editions of Bahā'-Allāh's works see *Alwāḥ-e Bahāʾ-Allāh moštamel bar sūrat-e haykal... wa ḡayroh*, Bombay, 1890 and *Alwāḥ-e Bahāʾ-Allāh*, Bombay, 1893; see also Baron Victor Rosen, *Collections scientifiques de l'institut des langues orientales du ministère des affaires étrangères*, St. Petersburg, vol. 1: *Manuscrits arabes*, 1877, pp. 179-212; vol. 3: *Manuscrits persans*, 1886, pp. 1-51; vol. 6: *Manuscrits arabes*, 1891, pp. 141-225; Rosen, ed., *al-Majmūʿ al-awwal men rasāʾel al-šayk al-bābī Bahāʾ-Allāh*, (Historico-Philological Section of the Imperial Academy of St. Petersburg, 1908); and Aleksandr Tumanskiĭ, ed., *Ketāb ʿahdī wa lawḥ-e bešārāt*, in *Zapiski* of the Russian Oriental Society 7, 1892, pp. 183-92, 193-203, as well as his edition of the *Ketāb-e aqdas*, cited above. A brief survey of Bahā'-Allāh's major works is ʿA. Ešrāq Ḵāvarī, *Ganj-e šāyegān*, Tehran, 123 *Badīʿ*/1966) A traditional Bahai commentary in English on a large number of these works in A. Taherzadeh, *The Revelation of Bahá'u'lláh*, 3 vols., Oxford, 1974.

No modern, academic biography of Bahā'-Allāh has yet been written, though Balyuzi uses some critical apparatus. Early relevant Western scholarship includes: E. G. Browne, "The Babis of Persia," *JRAS* 21, 1889, pp. 485-526, 881-1009; "Some Remarks on the Babi Texts Edited by Baron Victor Rosen," *JRAS* 24, 1892, pp. 259-332; "A Catalogue and Description of 27 Babi Manuscripts," *JRAS* 24, 1892, pp. 433-99, 637-710; and "Babiism," in *The Religious Systems of the World*, ed., London, 1905, (other works by Browne are cited in the text); and Hermann Roemer, *Die Babi-Baha'i*, Potsdam, 1911). A short biographical notice is Bāmdād, *Rejāl* I, pp. 434-42. Modern academic works bearing on Bahā'-Allāh's life are A. Bausani, *Persia Religiosa da Zoroaster a Bahâ'u'llâh*, Milan, 1959; idem, "Bahā'-īs," *EI*[2]; M. Bayat, *Mysticism and Dissent*: *Socioreligious Thought in Qajar Iran*, Syracuse, 1982; D. MacEoin, *From Shaykhism to Babism*, Ph.D. dissertation, Cambridge University, 1979; A. Amanat, *The*

Early Years of the Babi Movement, Ph.D. dissertation, Oxford University, 1981; and for the Bahai religion see P. Smith, *The Bābī and Bahāʾī Religions: From Messianic Shīʿism to a World Religion* (forthcoming). For the 1850s see J. Cole, "Bahā'u'llāh and the Naqshbandī Sufis in Iraq, 1854-1856," in J. Cole and M. Momen, eds., *From Iran East and West: Studies in Bábí and Bahá'í History* II, Los Angeles, 1984, pp. 1-28; and K. Kazemzadeh and F. Kazemzadeh, "Bahā'u'llāh's Prison Sentence: The Official Account," *World Order* 13, Winter 1978-79, pp. 11-13. Recent academic works of interest include the following articles in *Bahāʾī Studies Bulletin* (*BSB*), on offset publication (ed. S. Lambden, Department of Religion, University of Newcastle-upon-Tyne, England): K. Beveridge and D. MacEoin, "Seven Manuscripts Attributed to Bahā'u'llāh," *BSB* 1/4, 1983, pp. 33-56; articles by S. Lambden: "A Tablet of Bahā'u'llāh to Georg David Hardegg: The "Lawḥ-i Hirtīq," *BSB* 2/1, 1983, pp. 32-62; "A Tablet of Bahā'u'llāh in the Late Baghdad Period," *BSB* 2/3, 1983, pp. 107-12; "A Tablet of Mīrzā Ḥusayn ʿAlī Bahā'u'llāh of the Early Iraq Period: The Tablet of All Food," *BSB* 3/1, 1984, pp. 4-67; "An Early Poem of Mīrzā Ḥusayn ʿAlī Bahā'u'llāh: The Sprinkling of the Cloud of Unknowing (*Rashḥ-i ʿAmāʾ*)," *BSB* 3/2, 1984, pp. 4-114; M. Momen, "The Bahāʾī Influence on the Reform Movements of the Islamic World in the 1860s and 1870s," *BSB* 2/2, 1983, pp. 47-65.

(J. R. I. Cole)

BAHĀʾ-AL-DAWLA, ABŪ NAṢR **FĪRŪZ.** See BUYIDS.

BAHĀʾ-AL-DAWLA, ʿALĪ B. MASʿŪD. See ʿALĪ B. MASʿŪD.

BAHĀʾ-AL-DĪN ʿĀMELĪ, SHAIKH MOḤAMMAD B. ḤOSAYN BAHĀʾĪ, also known as Shaikh Bahāʾī, Imami scholar and author born near Baalbek on 27 Ḏu'l-ḥejja 953/18 February 1547 (other dates are also given). He moved with the rest of his family to Isfahan and from there to Qazvīn after the execution in 966/1558 of al-Šahīd al-Ṯānī, who had been his father's mentor; reports that Bahāʾī was taken to Khorasan already at the age of seven are probably incorrect. Bahāʾī's father was appointed by Shah Ṭahmāsb I (r. 930/1524-984/1576) to serve as *šayḵ-al-eslām* in several important cities to propagate Twelver Shiʿism among the populace. According to some authorities, Bahāʾī accompanied his father throughout these years; others maintain that he remained in Qazvīn to pursue his studies. Uncertainty also surrounds Bahāʾī's whereabouts after his father relinquished his post to go on the hajj. According to one version, Bahāʾī accompanied him to Mecca and to Bahrain where he stayed until his father's death in 984/1576-77, and only then returned to Iran to take up the post in Herat that had once been his father's. A second version has it that Shah Ṭahmāsb refused to let Bahāʾī leave the country and ordered him instead to replace his father as *šayḵ-al-eslām* in Herat. The existence of a letter sent to Bahāʾī from his father in Bahrain argues in favor of the second version.

Bahāʾī's erudition won him the admiration of Shah ʿAbbās I (r. 996/1588-1038/1639), who appointed him *šayḵ-al-eslām* of Isfahan after the death of the previous incumbent, Bahāʾī's father-in-law Zayn-al-Dīn ʿAlī Menšār ʿĀmelī (from whom Bahāʾī inherited a particularly rich library). During his years in Isfahan he befriended Mīr Dāmād and counted among his many students Mollā Ṣadrā and Moḥsen al-Fayż. He was known for his charitable deeds, which included turning his home into a refuge for orphans, widows, and the poor. Bahāʾī was active in the service of the Safavid state and advocated the expansion of the powers of the *ʿolamāʾ*. He resigned his post after a brief period, perhaps in reaction to attacks by rival clerics.

Bahāʾī spent a number of years traveling outside Iran. After performing the hajj he went to Egypt (where he is known to have been in 992/1584, associating with Shaikh Moḥammad b. Abi'l-Ḥasan Ṣeddīqī Šāfeʿī, d. 993/1585), to Jerusalem (where he spent much of his time at the Masjed al-Aqṣā) and Syria. Reports that he only returned to Iran after thirty years are, however, contradicted by his own testimony. He is thus known to have visited Tabrīz in 993/1585, Qazvīn in 1001/1592-93, Mašhad in 1007/1598-99 (or 1008/1599-1600, and Azerbaijan in 1015/1606, the latter two places in the company of Shah ʿAbbās. It is likely that Bahāʾī did not leave Iran after 1019/1610. He spent his last years in Isfahan, and died there on 12 Šawwāl 1030/30 August 1621 (or 12 Šawwāl 1031/20 August 1622). He was buried in Ṭūs.

Bahāʾī was a prolific writer, composing perhaps as many as one hundred works in both Arabic and in Persian. Among the best known are the two anthologies, *Kaškūl* (written in Egypt) and the earlier *Meḵlāt*, both consisting of morsels of information on divers subjects in typical *adab* fashion. He composed works on *tafsīr*, *ḥadīṯ*, grammar, and *feqh* (such as the *Jāmeʿ-e ʿabbāsī* and the epistle prohibiting the consumption of meat slaughtered by the *ahl al-ketāb*). His interest in the sciences is evident in works such as the astronomical treatise *Fī tašrīḥ al-aflāk* (Anatomy of the heavens) and the summa of arithmetic, *Ḵolāṣat al-ḥesāb* (of which a German translation by G. H. L. Nesselmann was published as early as 1843). In addition, he wrote a book of divination (*Fāl-nāma*) and other works on the occult sciences. Bahāʾī was also a poet, and is best remembered for his two allegorical *maṯnawīs*, *Nān o ḥalwā* and *Šīr o šakar* (both published, together with other works, in Cairo [1347/1928-29] and later in Tehran [ed. Ḡolām-Ḥosayn Jawāherī, 1341 Š./1962] under the title *Kollīyāt-e ašʿār wa āṯār-e fārsī-e Šayḵ Bahāʾ-al-Dīn Moḥammad al-ʿĀmelī mašhūr be Šayḵ Bahāʾī*).

In Imami circles, Bahāʾī is regarded as one of the leading lights of his age, and as the *mojadded* of the eleventh/seventeenth century. It is thus noteworthy that certain Sunni scholars wish to see in him one of their own. Their attitude is apparently based on a misunderstanding of Bahā'ī's behavior: since he moved between Ottoman and Safavid territories, probably he felt constrained to suit his public utterances to the circumstances. The actions surrounding his visit to Syria are a case in point: before entering the country, he changed the introduction to a *tafsīr* originally dedicated to Shah ʿAbbās and instead dedicated the work to the Ottoman Sultan Morād III (r. 982/1574-1003/1595). During his stay in Ḥalab he professed his allegiance to Shafiʿite Sunnism and his love of the Ṣaḥāba, and claimed that his apparent Shiʿism had been forced on him by the Safavid ruler; and he left Ḥalab in haste when he heard that people from his home area of Jabal ʿĀmel were about to visit him (thus exposing him as a Shiʿite. There is in fact no doubt that Bahā'ī was, by both upbringing and conviction, a dedicated Imami, as witness his frequent pilgrimages to the tombs of the imams, his poem in praise of the Twelfth Imam, his verses defending the practice of vilifying Abū Bakr and ʿOmar, and especially his proselytizing efforts among non-Shiʿite Iranians. In composing commentaries on Sunni works (such as the *tafsīrs* of Zamaḵšarī and Bayżāwī) Bahā'ī was continuing a tradition established by previous Imami authors.

Despite the subsequent apologetics of some Imami scholars, it is clear that Bahā'ī had distinct Sufi leanings, for which he was severely criticized by Moḥammad Bāqer Majlesī. In fact, Bahā'ī appears in the chain of both the Nūrbaḵšī and Neʿmatallāhī spiritual genealogies (Maʿṣūm-ʿAlīšāh, *Ṭarā'eq al-ḥaqā'*eq ed. M. J. Maḥjūb, Tehran, 1339 Š./1960, I, pp. 183, 254, II, p. 322). During his travels he dressed as a dervish and frequented Sufi circles. In his *Resāla fi'l-waḥda al-wojūdīya* (ed. Cairo, 1328/1910), Bahā'ī speaks of the Sufis as true believers, calls for an unbiased assessment of their utterances, and refers to his own mystical experiences. His Persian verses, too, are replete with mystical allusions. At the same time Bahā'ī called for strict adherence to the *šarīʿa* as a prerequisite for embarking on the *ṭarīqa*, and condemned pantheistic and antinomian mysticism.

Bibliography: Ḥorr ʿĀmelī, *Amal al-āmel*, ed. Aḥmad Ḥosaynī, Najaf, 1385/1965-66, I, pp. 155-60. Aḥmad Amīnī Najafī, *al-Ḡadīr* XI, Beirut, 1397/1977, pp. 244-84. S. A. Arjomand, "Religious Extremists (Ghuluww), Ṣūfism and Sunnism in Safavid Iran: 1501-1722," *Journal of Asian History* 15, 1981, pp. 16, 25-27. Yūsof Baḥrānī, *Lo'lo'at al-baḥrayn*, ed. Moḥammad Ṣādeq Baḥr-al-ʿOlūm, Najaf, 1386/1966, pp. 16-23. A Bausani, in *Proceedings of the Ninth Congress of the UEAI*, Leiden, 1981, pp. 23ff. Brockelmann, *GAL* II, pp. 414-15; S. I, pp. 76, 741; S. II, pp. 595-97. Browne, *Lit. Hist. Persia* IV, pp. 253, 407, 426-28. Ebn Maʿṣūm Madanī, *Solāfat al-ʿaṣr*, Cairo, 1324/1906-07, pp. 289-302. Eskandar Beg Monšī, *Tārīḵ-e ʿālamārā-ye ʿabbāsī*, Tehran, 1350 Š./1971, pp. 155-57, 761. E. Glassen, *Der Islam* 48, 1972, p. 265. I. Goldziher, "Beiträge zur Literaturgeschichte der Šîʿa und der sunnitischen Politik," *Sb.d. Königl. Akad. d. Wiss.* 78, Vienna, 1874, pp. 458-67 (= *Gesammelte Schriften*, Hildesheim, 1967ff., I, pp. 280-89). Ḡ.-M. Jawāherī, ed., *Kollīyāt-e ašʿār o āṯār-e fārsī-e Šayḵ Bahā'-al-Dīn Moḥammad al-ʿĀmelī mašhūr ba Šayḵ Bahā'ī*, Tehran, [1341 Š./1962], pp. 1-24. Kaḥḥāla, IX, pp. 242-43. Moḥammad-Bāqer Ḵᵛānsārī, *Rawżāt al-jannāt*, ed. A. Esmāʿīlīān, Qom, 1390-92/1970-72, VII, pp. 56-84. Maʿṣūm-ʿAlīšāh, *Ṭarā'eq al-ḥaqā'eq* I, pp. 254-67. Moḥammad-ʿAlī Tabrīzī Modarres, *Rayḥānat al-adab* II, Tehran, 1364-73/1944-53, pp. 382-98. Moḥebbī, *Ḵolāṣat al-aṯar*, Cairo, 1284/1867-68, III, pp. 440-55. Moḥsen al-Amīn, *Aʿyān al-šīʿa* XXVI, pp. 231-35, 239-44. Saʿīd Nafīsī, *Aḥwāl o ašʿār-e fārsī-e Šayḵ Bahā'ī*, Tehran, 1316 Š./1937. ʿAbbās Qomī, *Fawā'ed al-rażawīya*, Tehran, 1327 Š./1948, pp. 139, 502-21. Zereklī, *Aʿlām* VI, Beirut, 1980, p. 102. [See Addenda and Corrigenda.]

(E. Kohlberg)

BAHĀ'-AL-DĪN BAḠDĀDĪ, MOḤAMMAD B. MO'AYYAD BAḠDĀDĪ (or BAḠDĀDAKĪ) ḴᵛĀRAZMĪ, a master of the art of Persian letter-writing (*tarassol*) in the 6th/12th century (d. after 688/1289). He was from Baḡdādak, a place in Ḵᵛārazm. According to the *Tārīḵ-e gozīda* (apud M. Qazvīnī in ʿAwfī, *Lobāb* I, pp. 349-50), he was the younger brother of Shaikh Majd-al-Dīn Abū Saʿīd b. Mo'ayyad Baḡdādī (Baḡdādakī), Ḵᵛārazmī, a well-known mystic in the period around the turn of the 6th/12th and 7th/13th centuries. Nothing else is known about his background and early life. His rise to fame began when he took charge of the *dīvān-e enšā'* (chancellery) of the Ḵᵛārazmšāh ʿAlā'-al-Dīn Tekeš b. Īl Arslān (r. 568/1172-596/1200). In the *Haft eqlim* (I, p. 106) he is said to have also been the secretary of the next Ḵᵛārazmšāh, Sultan Moḥammad (596/1199-617/1220), but this is hard to verity.

Bahā'-al-Dīn's connection with the Khwarazmian court twice landed him in prison: once after a disagreement with Tekeš's vizier Neẓām-al-Molk Šams-al-Dīn Masʿūd Heravī (d. 596/1199-1200), and for a much longer time, from 582/1186 to 585/1189, when he was detained at Marv by Tekeš's brother and rival for the throne, Solṭānšāh Moḥammad b. Īl Arslān (d. 589/1193). He was set free when the two brothers made peace (Jovaynī, II, p. 23). During this second spell he wrote his *Resāla-ye ḥabsīya* (Message from prison), a fine specimen of Persian prose. After his release he reentered the service of ʿAlā'-al-Dīn Tekeš. There are mentions of him from then until the year 588/1192 (ibid., p. 28). Rāzī's statement (*Haft eqlīm* I, p. 106), followed by Hedāyat's *Majmaʿ al-foṣaḥā'* (I, p. 443) that he died in 545/1150 is therefore incorrect.

Bahā'-al-Dīn won fame in his own lifetime for the excellence of his prose writings and the cogency of his poems. The collection of his official letters named *al-Tawassol ela'l-tarassol* (Guide to letter-writing; q.v.) receives high praise among contemporary litterateurs such as ʿAwfī (*Lobāb* I, p. 139) and Saʿd-al-Dīn Varāvīnī, the author of the *Marzbān-nāma*. He excelled in writing ornate Persian prose, usually laden with

Arabic words and phrases. In the history of Persian prose he stands among the foremost pioneers of this style.

Bahāʾ-al-Dīn's *al-Tawassol ela'l-tarassol* was printed together with his *Resāla-ye ḥabsīya* at Tehran in 1315 Š./1936. A complete *qaṣīda* (in praise of ʿAlāʾ-al-Dīn Tekeš) and eleven other verses from his pen are quoted in ʿAwfī's *Lobāb al-albāb*; they are enough to show that he was a skillful writer of poetry in the style prevalent in the 6th/12th century.

Bibliography: See also Bahāʾ-al-Dīn Moḥammad b. Moʾayyad Baḡdādī, *al-Tawassol ela'l-tarassol*, ed. Aḥmad Bahmanyār, Tehran, 1315 Š./1936. ʿAwfī, *Lobāb* I, pp. 139-42, 328-30; ed. Nafīsī, pp. 121-25 and notes, esp. pp. 592-93. Nafīsī, *Naẓm o naṯr* I, pp. 86, 94, 115, 120. M. Qazvīnī, *Bīst maqāla-ye Qazvīnī* II, Tehran, 1332 Š./1953, pp. 252-56. Ḏ. Ṣafā, *Adabīyāt* II, 5th ed., Tehran, 2536 = 1356 Š./1977, pp. 973-77. Idem, *Ganjīna-ye soḵan* III, Tehran, 1353 Š./1974, pp. 50f.

(Z. SAFA)

BAHĀʾ-AL-DĪN JOVAYNĪ, MOḤAMMAD B. ʿALĪ. See JOVAYNĪ, MOḤAMMAD B. ʿALĪ.

BAHĀʾ-AL-DĪN JOVAYNĪ, MOḤAMMAD B. ŠAMS-AL-DĪN. See JOVAYNĪ, MOḤAMMAD B. ŠAMS-AL-DĪN.

BAHĀʾ-AL-DĪN ABŪ BAKR MOḤAMMAD B. AḤMAD B. ABĪ BEŠR **ḴARAQĪ** (MARVAZĪ) was born in a village named Ḵaraq near the city of Marv, where he apparently spent his professional life and where he died in 533/1138-39. His name is sometimes given as Abū Moḥammad ʿAbd-al-Jabbār b. ʿAbd-al-Jabbār b. Moḥammad; and he is sometimes identified with Bahāʾ-al-Dīn Abū Moḥammad Ḵaraqī, a philosopher and expert on the mathematical sciences of whom a biography is given by Bayhaqī (Wiedemann, pp. 72-73 [*Aufsätze* I, pp. 654-55]).

Bahāʾ-al-Dīn's most important work was on astronomy, geography, and chronology, the *Montaha'l-edrāk fī taqāsīm al-aflāk* (The limit of the reachable concerning the division of the spheres) *Kašf al-ẓonūn* (Leipzig), VI, no. 13124). This consists of three *maqālāt*, of which the first, on the arrangement of the celestial spheres, supports the theory of Abū Jaʿfar al-Ḵāzen and of Ebn al-Hayṯam that the planets are carried by physically solid spheres; in it Ḵaraqī gives the coordinates of 83 fixed stars and the longitudes of the apogees of the planets for the year 1444 of "Alexander," which began on 1 October 1132 (Nallino, I, pp. lxvi-lxvii), and gives the common Islamic values for the obliquity of the ecliptic (23;35°; Nallino, I, p. 159) and the precession of the equinoxes (1° in 66 years; Nallino, I, p. 292). The second *maqāla* describes the earth, including the computation of the local oblique ascensions and ascendants. Its second *bāb*, on the oceans and seas, which is based on the lost work of Jayhānī, has been edited, translated into Latin, and compared to Battānī and Ebn Rosta (Nallino, I, pp. 167-75; II, p. xxiii). And a passage from this *maqāla* concerning the terrestrial path of the equator and the "cupola" of the earth has been edited and translated into French (Ferrand, pp. 4-6, 17-20). The third and last *maqāla* discusses chronology (Nallino, I, p. 245), including the astrological concepts of Jupiter-Saturn conjunctions and of cycles. The introduction of the *Montaha'l-edrāk* has been translated into German (Wiedemann and Kohl, pp. 205-09 [*Aufsätze* II, pp. 630-34]).

Ḵaraqī himself composed a summary of the *Montaha'l-edrāk* in two books. He entitled this the *Tabṣera fi'l-hayʾa* (Instruction concerning astronomy) (*Kašf al-ẓonūn*, III, no. 2379) and dedicated it to Sanjar's vizier Abu'l-Ḥosayn ʿAlī b. Naṣīr-al-Dīn. The introduction to this work has also been translated into German (Wiedemann and Kohl, pp. 209-11 [*Aufsätze* II, pp. 634-36]). The *Tabṣera* was extremely popular as can be judged from the large number of extant manuscripts and from the fact that commentaries on it were composed by Moḥammad b. Mobārakšāh Boḵārī in 733/1332-33 (Brockelmann, p. 863) and by Aḥmad b. ʿOṯmān Jūzjānī, who died in 744/1343-44 (Suter, p. 164).

Bibliography: C. Brockelmann, *GAL* S. I, Leiden, 1937. G. Ferrand, "Notes de géographie orientale," *JA* 202, 1923, pp. 1-35. C. A. Nallino, *Al-Battānī sive Albatenii Opus astronomicum*, 3 vols., Milan, 1899-1907. H. Suter, *Die Mathematiker und Astronomen der Araber und ihre Werke*, Leipzig, 1900. E. Wiedemann, "Einige Biographien nach *al-Baihaqī*," *Sb. Phys.-Med. Soz. Erlangen* 42, 1910, pp. 59-77 (= idem, *Aufsätze zur Arabischen Wissenschaftsgeschichte*, 2 vols., Hildesheim and New York, 1970, I, pp. 641-59). E. Wiedemann and K. Kohl, "Einleitung zu Werken von *al Charaqī*," *Sb. Phys.-Med. Soz. Erlangen* 58-59, 1926-27, pp. 203-11 (*Aufsätze* II, pp. 628-36).

(D. PINGREE)

BAHĀʾ-AL-DĪN MOḤAMMAD WALAD B. ḤOSAYN B. AḤMAD ḴAṬĪB BALḴĪ (546-628/1151-1231), father of Mawlānā Jalāl-al-Dīn Rūmī (q.v.), the great Sufi poet and eponym of the Mevlevî order, with reference to whom he became posthumously known as *Mawlānā-ye bozorg* (the elder Mawlānā). In his lifetime he was generally known as Bahāʾ-e Walad, and often referred to in addition by the title *solṭān al-ʿolamāʾ* (king of the scholars). According to his grandson, Solṭān Walad (d. 632/1235), the title originated with a dream seen on the same night by all the muftis of Balḵ in which the Prophet himself designated Bahāʾ-al-Dīn as *solṭān al-ʿolamāʾ*; when they awoke, they hastened to pay homage to him (*Walad-nāma*, ed. J. Homāʾī, Tehran, 1315 Š./1936, p. 188, see also Ferīdūn Sepahsālār, *Resāla-ye Sepahsālār*, Kanpur, 1319/1910, p. 7 and Šams-al-Dīn Aḥmad Aflākī, *Manāqeb al-ʿārefīn*, ed. T. Yazıcı, Ankara, 1959, I, p. 7). Bahāʾ-e Walad himself records that the title *solṭān al-ʿolamāʾ* was given him in a dream by an old man of luminous visage, and thereafter he insisted on using the title when singing the *fatwā*s he issued (*Ma'āref*, ed. B. Forūzānfar, Tehran, 1333 Š./1954, I, pp. 188-89).

Bahā'-e Walad says that he was approaching the age of 55 on 1 Ramażān 600/3 March 1203 (*Ma'āref* I, p. 354); he must therefore have been born in 546/1151-52. His father was a scholar and ascetic of great eminence in Balḵ, the offspring of a family that had been settled in Khorasan for many generations. According to many writers, they were descended from the caliph Abū Bakr (*Resāla-ye Sepahsālār*, p. 6; *Manāqeb al-'ārefīn* I, p. 7; Jāmī, *Nafaḥāt*, p. 457). Sepahsālār does not provide a complete genealogy and the six, seven, or eight generations mentioned by other authors are clearly too few to bridge the six centuries that elapsed between Abū Bakr and Bahā'-e Walad (see B. Forūzānfar, *Resāla dar taḥqīq-e aḥwāl wa zendagānī-e Mawlānā Jalāl-al-Dīn Moḥammad*, Tehran, 1315 Š./1936, p. 4). The two lines found in some copies of the *Walad-nāma* that attribute Bakri descent to Bahā'-e Walad were probably inserted in the text by a copyist (see A. Gölpınarlı's footnote to his translation of *Walad-nāma* under the title *İbtida-name*, Ankara, 1976, p. 237). There is no reference to such descent in the works of Bahā'-e Walad and Mawlānā Jalāl-al-Dīn or in the inscriptions on their sarcophagi. The attribution may have arisen from confusion between the caliph and another Abū Bakr, Šams-al-A'emma Abū Bakr Saraḵsī (d. 483/1090), the well-known Hanafite jurist, whose daughter, Ferdows Ḵātūn, was the mother of Aḥmad Ḵaṭīb, Bahā'-e Walad's grandfather (see Forūzānfar, *Resāla*, p. 6).

Tradition also links Bahā'-e Walad's lineage to the Ḵ ̆ārazmšāh dynasty. His mother is said to have been the daughter of 'Alā'-al-Dīn Moḥammad Ḵ ̆ārazmšāh (d. 596/1200), but this appears to be excluded for chronological reasons (Forūzānfar, *Resāla*, p. 7).

Bahā'-e Walad followed the profession of preacher and mufti in Balḵ, adhering to the example of his ancestors. Throughout his life he gave great importance to his identity as *'ālem*, wearing the garb of the *'olamā'* and insisting that he be accommodated in *madrasa*s, not *ḵānaqāh*s, during his travels (*Resāla-ye Sepahsālār*, pp. 6, 19; *Manāqeb al-'ārefīn* I, p. 17). Nonetheless, elements of Sufism are discernible in his recorded discourses, and two Sufi lineages have been attributed to him. The first connects him, by way of his grandfather, with Aḥmad Ḡazālī (d. 520/1126; see *Resāla-ye Sepahsālār*, p. 6, and *Manāqeb al-'ārefīn* II, p. 998), and the second makes him a disciple of Najm-al-Dīn Kobrā (d. 617/1220; see Jāmī, *Nafaḥāt*, p. 457, and *Tārīḵ-e gozīda*, p. 789). The latter affiliation is dubious and is reported with some reserve by Jāmī. No mention of Kobrā or sign of concern with the distinctive themes of the Kobrawī order is to be found in Bahā'-e Walad's discourses. All sources are agreed that Bahā'-e Walad's principal disciple, in the Sufi sense, was Sayyed Borhān-al-Dīn Moḥaqqeq Termeḏī (d. 638/1240).

Bahā'-e Walad had in common with the Kobrawīs marked hostility to 'Alā'-al-Dīn Moḥammad Ḵ ̆ārazmšāh. This hostility was due to the prominence at his court of the philosopher-theologian Faḵr-al-Dīn Rāzī (d. 606/1210). Bahā'-e Walad publicly denounced Rāzī, together with his royal patron, as religious "innovator" (*ahl-e bed'at*) who had "taken refuge in two or three dark corners while abandoning the numerous miracles and proofs [of positive religion]" (*Ma'āref* I, p. 82). Bahā'-e Walad also had other enemies in the realm of the Ḵ ̆ārazmšāh, men such as Qāżī Zayn-al-Dīn Farāzī, 'Amīd Marvazī and Rašīd-al-Dīn Ḵānī, whose hostility Aflākī attributed, in typical hagiographical fashion, to jealousy and the illusions fostered by excessive formal learning (*Manāqeb al-'ārefīn* I, p. 11). A supplementary reason for Bahā'-e Walad's discomfort in Balḵ may have been the Ḵ ̆ārazmšāh's conflict with the 'Abbasids and his proclamation of 'Alā'-al-Molk, a *sayyed* from Termeḏ, as caliph (Jovaynī, III, pp. 244-45). Finally, fear of the impending Mongol cataclysm may also have persuaded Bahā'-e Walad to migrate westwards.

The exact date and circumstances of Bahā'-e Walad's departure from Transoxiana are difficult to establish. Mawlānā Jalāl-al-Dīn relates that he was present with his father at the conquest of Samarkand by the Ḵ ̆ārazmšāh in 604/1207-08 (*Fīhi mā fīh*, ed. B. Forūzānfar, Tehran, 5th ed., 1362 Š./1983, p. 173), so their westward journey must have begun some time thereafter. Sepahsālār's account of Bahā'-e Walad's migration, which ascribes a decisive role to intrigues by Faḵr-al-Dīn Rāzī, is replete with implausible details (*Resāla-ye Sepahsālār*, p. 8). It is in any event probable that Bahā'-e Walad's departure from the territory of the Ḵ ̆ārazmšāh came after the death of Rāzī, since he appears to have been in Vaḵš until 607/1211 (see Forūzānfar, introd. to *Ma'āref* I, p. xxxvii). Ḥamd-Allāh Mostawfī gives 618/1221 as the date of his departure (*Tārīḵ-e gozīda*, p. 791), but a review of all the evidence led Forūzānfar to choose 610/1214 as the most likely date (*Resāla*, p. 14).

According to a tradition found in Dawlatšāh (ed. Browne, p. 193), Bahā'-e Walad and his party passed through Nīšāpūr on their journey to the west, where they were deferentially received by the great Sufi poet Farīd-al-Dīn 'Aṭṭār (d. 617/1220). On arriving in Baghdad, Bahā'-e Walad heard of the destruction of Balḵ by the Mongols. It is said that they were respectfully greeted in Baghdad by Shaikh Šehāb-al-Dīn Sohravardī (d. 631/1234) and lodged in the Mostanṣerīya *madrasa* (*Resāla-ye Sepahsālār*, p. 18). At least the latter detail must be false, since the Mostanṣerīya was not completed until 631/1234, some three years after the death of Bahā'-e Walad (Foruzānfār, *Resāla*, p. 18). The party proceeded from Baghdad by way of Kūfa to the Hejaz, and after performing the hajj traveled through Syria to Anatolia, where their first stopping-place was Malatya. Jāmī's claim that they next spent four years in Erzincan (Arzenjān) (*Nafaḥāt*, p. 458) is contradicted by Aflākī's assertion that Bahā'-e Walad refused even to enter the city, because of the evil nature of its people (*Manāqeb al-'ārefīn* I, p. 22). Before finally settling in Konya, Bahā'-e Walad is said also to have stayed in Akşehir for one year (*Resāla-ye Sepahsālār*, p. 9) or four years (*Manāqeb al-ʿārefīn* I, p. 25) and in Larende (present-day Karaman) for at least seven years (*Manāqeb al-ʿārefīn* I, p. 25). One of Bahāʾ-e Walad's wives, Amīna Ḵātūn, and a son, ʿAlāʾ-al-Dīn, died and were buried in Larende, which points to a fairly protracted residence there.

Bahāʾ-e Walad finally arrived in Konya in about 626/1229. The story found in both Sepahsālār and Aflākī that the Saljuq ruler ʿAlāʾ-al-Dīn Kayqobād (d. 634/1237) went out to escort him into the city must be dismissed in view of the more sober account found in the *Walad-nāma* (p. 191). It remains true that Kayqobād, together with many of the notables of Konya, swiftly became sincere devotees of Bahāʾ-e Walad. Kayqobād wished to lodge him in the precincts of his palace, but he insisted on residing at the Altūnīya *madrasa*. Only two years after his arrival in Konya, Bahāʾ-e Walad died, after a brief illness on 18 Rabīʿ II 628/23 February 1231. Kayqobād was much grieved by his passing and proclaimed seven days' public mourning (*Walad-nāma*, p. 193). He had an enclosure built around his tomb, which was later surmounted with a dome by Amir Badr-al-Dīn Gawhartāš, the *lālā* of Kayqobād (I. H. Konyalı, *Konya tarihi*, Konya, 1964, p. 632).

As his sole literary monument, Bahāʾ-e Walad left behind the *Maʿāref*, a collection of his discourses recorded and gathered by his disciples. They consist chiefly of explanations of Koranic verses and traditions of the Prophet and of answers to theological and legal questions; from them emerges the picture of a powerful, perceptive and often irascible preacher whose chief concern was the supremacy of the *šarīʿa* or the holy law. The *Maʿāref* had a considerable influence on Mawlānā Jalāl-al-Dīn Rūmī: he read the book regularly, lectured on it to his own disciples, and may have written glosses on its fourth part. It is not, then, surprising that numerous echoes of the *Maʿāref* are to be found in the *Maṯnawī* (see Forūzānfar, introd. to *Maʿāref* I, pp. xiv-xxix).

Bibliography: The first volume of Bahāʾ-e Walad's *Maʿāref*, containing the first three books, was published by B. Forūzānfar in Tehran in 1333 Š./1954. The second volume, containing the fourth book—which may have been in part a draft for some sections of the first three books—followed in 1338 Š./1959. Both volumes were reprinted in 1352 Š./1973.

(H. ALGAR)

BAHĀʾ-AL-DĪN NAQŠBAND, Ḵ ͮāja Moḥammad b. Moḥammad Boḵārī (718-91/1318-91), eponym of the Naqšbandīya, one of the most vigorous and widespread Sufi orders. In the tradition of the order, especially in Turkey, he is known as Šāh-e Naqšband. The earliest Naqšbandī texts do not explain the meaning of the sobriquet Naqšband or how Bahāʾ-al-Dīn came to acquire it. It was later interpreted, quasi-unanimously, as referring to the imprint (*naqš*) of the Divine Name *Allāh* that is fixed in the heart through constant and silent invocation (see, for example, ʿAbd-al-Majīd Ḵānī, *al-Ḥadāʾeq al-wardīya*, Cairo, 1306/1888, p. 9). In the usage of Bukhara—the city of which he became virtually the patron saint—Bahāʾ-al-Dīn was often called Ḵ ͮāja Balā-gardān (the averter of disaster), with reference to the protective powers bestowed on him by one of his preceptors, Bābā Moḥammad Sammāsī (Jāmī, *Nafaḥāt*, p. 385).

Bahāʾ-al-Dīn was born in Moḥarram, 718/March, 1318, in the hamlet of Qaṣr-e Hendovān, one *farsaḵ* from Bukhara. Accounts that attribute to him descent from the Prophet, by way of Imam Jaʿfar al-Ṣādeq, are to be treated with reserve (see Ḡolām Sarvar Lāhūrī, *Ḵazīnat al-aṣfīāʾ*, Bombay, 1290/1873, I, p. 545). The earliest sources make no mention of such ancestry, although they too indicate that Amīr Kolāl, Bahāʾ-al-Dīn's principal teacher on the path, was a Ḥosaynī *sayyed* (Faḵr-al-Dīn ʿAlī Ṣafī, *Rašaḥāt ʿayn al-ḥayāt*, Tashkent, 1329/1911, p. 43). It may be that Bahāʾ-al-Dīn's initiatic *selsela*, which does include Jaʿfar al-Ṣādeq, was confused with his genealogy.

Three days after his birth, Bahāʾ-al-Dīn was adopted as spiritual progeny by Bābā Moḥammad Sammāsī (q.v.), a master to whom his paternal grandfather owed allegiance. Sammāsī assigned his future training on the path to Amīr Kolāl, his most prominent disciple. The chronology of Bahāʾ-al-Dīn's relations with Sammāsī and Amīr Kolāl is unclear, since the principal sources on his life are simple assemblages of anecdotes, unconnected by narrative thread. Bahāʾ-al-Dīn may not have seen Sammāsī again until it was time for him to marry, and his grandfather sent him to Sammāsī for the choice of bride to be ratified (Jāmī, *Nafaḥāt*, p. 381). As for Amīr Kolāl, it is said that Bahāʾ-al-Dīn had from him the link of companionship (*nesbat-e ṣoḥbat*), instruction in the customs of the path (*taʿlīm-e ādāb-e ṭarīqat*), and the inculcation of *ḏekr* (*talqīn-e ḏekr*) (Jāmī, *Nafaḥāt*, p. 382). Bahāʾ-al-Dīn spent many years with Amīr Kolāl, being often upbraided for complacency with his still imperfect state and assigned, by way of chastisement, to menial tasks such as fetching the water for his master's ablutions (Mawlānā Šehāb-al-Dīn, *Manāqeb-e Amīr Kolāl*, ms. Zeytinoğlu [Tavşanlı] 169, ff. 40a-b, 49a).

It was during his association with Amīr Kolāl that Bahāʾ-al-Dīn had a vision resulting in a new and significant affiliation. The vision amounted to a second initiation, at the hands of the spiritual being (*rūḥānīyat*) of Ḵ ͮāja ʿAbd-al-Ḵāleq Ḡojdawānī (d. 617/1220), thus earning Bahāʾ-al-Dīn the additional epithet of Owaysī, with reference to the remote but powerful link between the Prophet and his Yemeni companion, Oways Qaranī. Wandering among the graves of Bukhara, Bahāʾ-al-Dīn saw his predecessors in the *selsela*, from the recently deceased Bābā Moḥammad Sammāsī to Ḡojdavānī, Ḵ ͮāja ʿAbd-al-Ḵāleq told him, with great emphasis, that he should adhere narrowly to the *šarīʿa*, avoiding *roḵṣat* (dispensation) in favor of rigorous obedience (*ʿazīmat*).

The chief consequence of this command was that

Bahā'-al-Dīn began restricting himself to silent *d̲ekr* (*d̲ekr-e k̲afī* or *k̲ofya*), withdrawing from the circle of Amīr Kolāl whenever the dervishes began engaging in vocal *d̲ekr* (*d̲ekr-e jalī* or *jahrī*) (*Rašaḥāt*, p. 55). This led to resentment among them, but Bahā'-al-Dīn continued to treat Amīr Kolāl with the utmost reverence and enjoyed his increasing favor. On the occasion of the building of a mosque in his native village of Sūk̲ārī, Amīr Kolāl rebuked his disciples for their hostility to Bahā'-al-Dīn and praised him as one whom God Himself had favored above the rest (*Rašaḥāt*, p. 55).

Bahā'-al-Dīn's next association was with Mawlānā ʿĀref Dīkgarānī, another disciple of Amīr Kolāl, in whose company he sought out the practitioners of silent *d̲ekr* (*Rašaḥāt*, p. 49). He then spent time with two Turkish masters, both belonging to the Yasawī order which had in common with the line of Sammāsī and Amīr Kolāl spiritual descent from K̲ᵛāja Yūsof Hamadānī (q.v.). His association with the first of these two, Qotam Šayk̲, was relatively brief, but with the second, K̲alīl Atā, he spent as much as twelve years. K̲alīl Atā appears to be identical with a certain Qażān (or Ḡazān) Khan, who ruled over the Chaghatay Khanate from 735/1335 to 748/1347 (see Zeki Velidi Togan, *Umumi türk tarihine giriş*, Istanbul, 1981, p. 63). According to the *Manāqeb-e Amīr Kolāl* (ff. 34b-35a), Bahā'-al-Dīn acted as the executioner for this particularly savage ruler until he was overthrown by a military rebellion. One is tempted to see in this association an early instance of the Naqšbandī predilection for influencing rulers in the direction of implementing the *šarīʿa*, as has, indeed, been suggested by Togan ("Gazan-Han Halil ve Hoca Bahaeddin Nakşbend," *Necati Lugal armağanı*, Ankara, 1968, pp. 775-84), but nothing in the evidence available permits such a conclusion. It seems rather that Bahā'-al-Dīn's time with Qażān represented a hiatus in his spiritual career.

His prolonged and varied apprenticeship completed, Bahā'-al-Dīn began the training of his own disciples, residing again in his birthplace of Qaṣr-e Hendovān. He left the region of Bukhara only three times thereafter. Two of these journeys were undertaken to perform the *ḥajj*; on the second of them he stayed three days in Herat to visit Shaikh Zayn-al-Dīn Abū Bakr Ṭayyābādī (d. 791/1389). On the third journey he again visited Herat, this time at the invitation of its ruler, Moʿezz-al-Dīn Ḥosayn, to whom he explained the principles of his path while behaving with exemplary ascetic detachment (Jāmī, *Nafaḥāt*, p. 386).

Bahā'-al-Dīn Naqšband died on 3 Rabīʿ I 791/2 March 1389, in Qaṣr-e Hendovān, which was now renamed, out of deference to him, Qaṣr-e ʿĀrefān. At a later point that cannot be exactly determined, the place acquired its present designation of Bāvaddīn (Bahā'-al-Dīn according to the colloquial pronunciation of the Bukharans). As the Naqšbandī order grew and Bahā'-al-Dīn's posthumous fame grew, a vast complex of buildings grew up around his tomb (K. Bendrikov, *Ocherki po istorii narodnogo obrazovaniya v Turkestane*, Moscow, 1960, p. 29). More generally, the spiritual presence of Bahā'-al-Dīn was a principal factor in Bukhara's status as a center of learning and sanctity for all the Muslim regions of Inner Asia.

A number of poems and treatises have been attributed to Bahā'-al-Dīn Naqšband, almost certainly without justification. On the other hand, the litany that bears his name, *Awrād-e bahāʾīya*, may indeed have been composed by him, although there is no reference to it in the early Naqšbandī texts and its recitation has never been a pillar of regular Naqšbandī practice (there are numerous printings of the *Awrād*; see, for example, that in Aḥmad Żīā'-al-Dīn Kumušk̲ānawī, *Majmūʿat al-aḥzāb*, Istanbul, 1311/1893, II, pp. 2-14, with the commentary of Shaikh Moḥammad Saʿīd K̲ādemī). The verbal legacy of Bahā'-al-Dīn consists chiefly in the sayings recorded anecdotally in books of hagiography such as the *Rašaḥāt*, the *Nafaḥāt*, and Ṣalāḥ-al-Dīn Bok̲ārī's *Anīs al-ṭālebīn* (q.v.) and, more fully and systematically, by K̲ᵛāja Moḥammad Pārsā, together with commentary and elucidation, in *Resāla-ye qodsīya* (numerous editions; the best is that of Aḥmad Ṭāherī-ʿErāqī, Tehran, 1354 Š./1975).

Pārsā (d. 822/1420), a leading scholar of Bukhara, was one of the principal successors of Bahā'-al-Dīn, and it seems even that he was designated as his main *k̲alīfa* during one of the pilgrimages to Mecca. According to certain accounts, Bahā'-al-Dīn confirmed this nomination on his deathbed (*Rašaḥāt*, p. 57), but it was K̲ᵛāja ʿAlā'-al-Dīn ʿAṭṭār Bok̲ārī (q.v.), already favored by Bahā'-al-Dīn through being married to his daughter, that emerged in the end as the main successor. More significant for the perpetuation of the Naqšbandī line was, however, a third *k̲alīfa*, Mawlānā Yaʿqūb Čarkī (d. 851/1448); he initiated K̲ᵛāja ʿObayd-Allāh Aḥrār (q.v.), under whose auspices the Naqšbandīya became supreme among the Sufi orders of Central Asia and began its expansion in other areas of the Muslim world.

Precisely why K̲ᵛāja Bahā'-al-Dīn should be seen as a central link in the *selsela* of which he is a part, rather than figures preceding or following him, is difficult to establish. According to a retrospective periodization of the *selsela*, it was known from the time of K̲ᵛāja Yūsof Hamadānī until that of Bahā'-al-Dīn as *ṭarīq-e k̲ᵛājagān* (the path of the masters), with reference to the title *k̲ᵛāja* that Hamadānī and his successors bore; and from then on as *ṭarīq-e naqšbandī* (Moḥammad b. Solaymān Baḡdādī, *al-Ḥadīqat al-nadīya fi'l-ṭarīqa al-naqšabandīya*, n.p., n.d., p. 22). However, more than a century after the death of Bahā'-al-Dīn, ʿAbd-al-Raḥmān Jāmī saw fit to entitle his brief treatise on the principles of the path *Sar-rešta-ye ṭarīq-e k̲ᵛājagān* (ed. ʿA.-Ḥ. Ḥabībī, Kabul, 1343 Š./1964). In one sense, the origins of the Naqšbandī path are traceable to K̲ᵛāja ʿAbd-al-K̲āleq Ḡojdawānī, who formulated its main principles in eight succinct Persian phrases known as *kalemāt-e qodsīya* (sacred words) and who is often referred to as *sar-ḥalqa-ye selsela-ye k̲ᵛājagān* (the chief in the line of masters; *Rašaḥāt*, p. 20). Bahā'-al-Dīn's Owaysī initiation at the hands of Ḡojdawānī serves, in fact, to confirm his pre-eminence. It appears to have been Bahāʾ-al-Dīn's insistence on silent *ḏekr*—practised only sporadically by earlier links in the *selsela*—that was crucial for the identity of the line descended from him and for the unique permanence of his imprint upon it. Later "renewers" of the Naqšbandīya such as Shaikh Aḥmad Serhendī (d. 1034/1624) and Mawlānā K̲āled Baḡdādī (d. 1242/1827) (qq.v.) were seen only as originating branches of the Naqšbandī order, not as founding new and autonomous orders.

Closely linked to Bahāʾ-al-Dīn's exclusive observance of silent *ḏekr* was his repudiation of music (*samāʿ*) and retreat (*k̲alwa*) as means of spiritual progress (Jāmī, *Nafaḥāt*, p. 386). Likewise, his denial that adherence to a *selsela* is in itself meritorious; his deprecation of charismatic feats (*karāmāt*); his shunning of a distinctive form of dress for himself and his followers; his dislike for the practice of residing in a hospice (*k̲ānaqāh*)—in short, his rejection of most of the customary appurtenances of Sufism—are all highly reminiscent of the Malāmatī movement of 4th/10th-century Nīšāpūr. Pārsā claimed, indeed, that "whatever holds true of the Malāmatīs holds true of our masters (*k̲ʷājagān*) also" (*Faṣl al-k̲eṭāb*, quoted by Saʿīd Nafīsī, *Sar-češma-ye taṣawwof dar Īrān*, Tehran, 1345 Š./1964, p. 180). This permits us to identify Bahāʾ-al-Dīn Naqšband as an heir not only of the figures mentioned in his *selsela* but also, in a more diffuse sense, of the Malāmatīs.

The original Naqšbandīya has accordingly sometimes been described as specifically Iranian or Khorasanian in its orientation (see, for example, Fuad Köprülü, *Türk edebiyatında ilk mutasavvıflar*, 2nd ed., Ankara, 1966, p. 93). This is justified in that the companions of Bahāʾ-al-Dīn were overwhelmingly Tajik-speaking urban dwellers, and the masters of the Yasawī order were contrastingly known as "the Turkish shaikhs" (*mašāyek̲-e Tork*; see Zeki Velidi Togan, "Yeseviliğe dair bazı yeni malumat," in *Fuad Köprülü armağanı*, Istanbul, 1953, p. 523). There was, however, a Yasawī—and hence Turkish—contribution to the spiritual formation of Bahāʾ-al-Dīn, and within three generations after his death the Naqšbandīya began spreading among the Turkish peoples of Central Asia, thereby demonstrating a universal appeal.

The hypothesis of Mahāyāna Buddhist influence on the origins of the Naqšbandīya (advanced by Aziz Ahmad, *An Intellectual History of Islam in India*, Edinburgh, 1969, p. 40) must be discounted for lack of evidence.

Bibliography: H. Algar, "The Naqshbandī Order: a Preliminary Survey of its History and Significance," *Stud. Isl.* 44, 1976, pp. 123-52. Ṣalāḥ-al-Dīn Bok̲ārī, *Anīs al-ṭālebīn* (unpublished; for information on mss., see "Anīs al-ṭālebīn," *EIr.* II, pp. 76f.). V. A. Gordlevskiĭ, "Bakhauddin Nakshbend Bukharskiĭ," *Izbrannye Sochineniya*, Moscow, 1962, III, pp. 369-86. Jāmī, *Nafaḥāt*, pp. 384-88. Abu'l-Ḥasan Moḥammad Bāqer b. Moḥammad ʿAlī, *Maqāmāt-e Šāh-e Naqšband*, Bukhara, 1327/1909. M. Molé, "Autour du Daré Mansour: l'apprentissage mystique de Bahāʾ al-Dīn Naqshband," *REI*, 1959, pp. 35-66. Naṣrullāh Efendi, *Risāle-i bahāiye*, Istanbul, 1328/1910. K̲ʷāja Moḥammad Pārsā, *Resāla-ye qodsīya*, ed. M.-Ṭ. ʿErāqī, Tehran, 1354 Š./1975. Moḥammad al-Rak̲āwī, *al-Anwār al-qodsīya fī manāqeb sādāt al-naqšabandīya*, Cairo, 1344/1925, pp. 126-42. Fak̲r-al-Dīn ʿAlī Ṣafī, *Rašaḥāt ʿAyn al-ḥayāt*, Tashkent, 1329/1911, pp. 54-58. Zeki Velidi Togan, "Gazan-Han Halil ve Hoca Bahaeddin Nakşbend," *Necati Lugal armağanı*, Ankara, 1968, pp. 775-84. Tahsin Yazıcı, "Nakşbend," in *İA*.

(H. ALGAR)

BAHĀʾ-AL-DĪN SOLṬĀN WALAD, MOḤAMMAD, 7th-8th/13th-14th-century Sufi shaikh and poet, son and eventual successor of Mawlānā Jalāl-al-Dīn Rūmī (Mawlawī). Bahāʾ-al-Dīn was born on 25 Rabīʿ II 623/24 April 1226 to Gowhar K̲ātūn at Lāranda (modern Karaman), where Jalāl-al-Dīn's father Bahāʾ-al-Dīn Walad, and later Jalāl-al-Dīn himself, were *madrasa* professors. The family moved to Konya when Bahāʾ-al-Dīn was three years old and there he spent most of his life. Bahāʾ-al-Dīn grew up amidst scholars and Sufis, consciously modeling himself upon his father and also much influenced by the latter's mentor Borhān-al-Dīn Moḥaqqeq Termeḏī (*Walad-nāma*, pp. 3-4, 179). By the age of twenty he was a key member of the fraternity, and may already have acquired the honorific name of Solṭān Walad. He faithfully served Rūmī's three closest intimates, Šams-al-Dīn Tabrīzī, Ṣalāḥ-al-Dīn Zarkūb, and Ḥosām-al-Dīn Čalabī, until they died. Solṭān Walad brought back Šams-al-Dīn after he had been driven from Konya in 644/1246 (*Walad-nāma*, pp. 47-50). After Šams's disappearance the following year, Jalāl-al-Dīn instructed Solṭān Walad to take Ṣalāḥ-al-Dīn Zarkūb as shaikh; Walad followed him exclusively (*Walad-nāma*, pp. 97-98) until Zarkūb's death in 657/1258. He married Zarkūb's daughter Fāṭema, and later two other wives, named Noṣrat and Sonbola. Altogether Solṭān Walad had four sons (including Jalāl-al-Dīn Amīr ʿĀref, his successor as shaikh) and two daughters. When Rūmī himself died in 672/1273, Ḥosām-al-Dīn Čalabī, who had succeeded Ṣalāḥ-al-Dīn as Rūmī's successor (*k̲alīfa*), urged Solṭān Walad to take his father's place but was persuaded by him to assume this position (*Walad-nāma*, pp. 122-24). Acclaimed once more as rightful head of the Order on the death in 683/1284 of Ḥosām-al-Dīn, the humble Solṭān Walad finally accepted, but still regarded Karīm-al-Dīn Baktamūr (d. 690/1291) as his master.

Under the leadership of Solṭān Walad, the Order was for the first time formed into an organized group like other Sufi fraternities. One part of the ritual *samāʿ* later became known as the *dawr-e waladī*, but the precise extent of Solṭān Walad's role in formalizing the Mawlawīya rites and institutions is unknown. While lacking Jalāl-al-Dīn's unique visionary genius, Solṭān Walad possessed not only saintliness but also practical abilities, energy, and a clear sense of purpose. He found it necessary to cultivate good relations with the Saljuq and Mongol rulers and other notables. In his *Rabāb-nāma* (ed. ʿAlī Solṭānī Gerdfarāmarzī, Tehran, 1359 Š./1980, pp. 35-38), Walad recounts how he defended himself against a disciple's criticism for composing verse in praise of such unworthy men. Authorized representatives were sent to numerous parts of Asia Minor and elsewhere to propagate and establish the brotherhood (*Walad-nāma*, pp. 155-56). By the time of his death on 12 Rajab 712/13 November 1312, Solṭān Walad had set on secure foundations the Mawlawīya, which was to become one of the major Sufi orders.

Solṭān Walad followed his father in composing *ḡazal*s and longer poems as well as giving discourses. Aware that many disciples had difficulty in understanding Rūmī's writings, he re-interpreted them in simpler language. Walad's writing lacks intensity, fluency, or new ideas and modes of expression; but its simple didactic clarity is some compensation. In another respect, however, Solṭān Walad is an innovative and important poet. He was the first in Asia Minor to compose a considerable body of verse in Turkish: 129 *bayts* in the Persian *Dīvān*, 162 in the *Rabāb-nāma*, and 80 in the *Walad-nāma* (studies are listed in T. Yazıcı, "Sultan Veled," in *İA* XI, pp. 28-32).

Works. Not all of Solṭān Walad's writings have been published. For mss., see M. Önder et al., *Mevlâna bibliyografyası* II, Ankara, 1974, pp. 304-24 and H. Ritter, "Philologika XI: Maulānā Ǧalāluddīn Rūmī und sein Kreis," *Der Islam* 26, 1942, pp. 229-38. His extant works are: 1. *Dīvān*, comprising over 12,700 verses. Many poems are *naẓīra*s in emulation of *ḡazal*s by Rūmī; as in the latter's *Dīvān*, no fewer than 29 meters are used. Besides the Turkish *bayts*, there are a few *molammaʿāt* (poems in which more than one language is used), and verses in Greek. Editions are: *Dīvān-e Solṭān Walad* (Persian), ed. F. N. Uzluk, Istanbul, 1941, ed. with introduction S. Nafīsī, Tehran, 1338 Š./1959. *Dīvān-e torkī-e Solṭān Walad* (Turkish verses), ed. Kilisli R. Bilge, Istanbul, 1341/1922. M. Mansuroğlu, *Sultan Veled'in Türkçe manzûmeleri* (superior ed.), Istanbul, 1958. 2. *Walad-nāma* (ed. J. Homāʾī, Tehran, 1315 Š./1936), also known as *Ebtedā-nāma* or *Maṯnawī-e waladī*, in about 10,000 *bayts*. Begun and completed in 690/1291, this poem contains a wealth of biographical and other information about Rūmī and his circle, as well as teachings on Sufism. 3. *Rabāb-nāma*, a *maṯnawī*, written in 700-01/1301, is largely didactic and elucidates diverse aspects of Sufism and some passages from Rūmī's works. 4. *Entehā-nāma* (in ms.), Solṭān Walad's last *maṯnawī*, is devoted to teachings on Sufi doctrine and practice. Like the *Rabāb-nāma*, it comprises about 8,000 verses. 5. *Maʿāref*, a compilation of Solṭān Walad's discourses. In their written form, at least, these are far more structured and less spontaneous than those preserved in the *Fīhi mā fīhi* of Rūmī or the *Maʿāref* of Bahāʾ-al-Dīn Walad. A French translation by E. de Vitray-Meyerovitch has been published (*Maître et disciple: Kitab al-maʿarif*, Paris, 1982).

Bibliography: Primary sources: Sources on Solṭān Walad's life and work are relatively copious. They include his own writings, particularly *Walad-nāma*. Contemporary and generally reliable is Farīdūn b. Aḥmad Sepahsālār's *Resāla dar aḥwāl-e Mawlānā Jalāl-al-Dīn Mawlawī*, ed. Saʿīd Nafīsī, Tehran, 1325 Š./1946. More hagiography than history, but still significant, is Aḥmad Aflākī's *Manāqeb al-ʿārefīn*, ed. T. Yazıcı, 2 vols., Ankara, 1976, II, pp. 784-824.

Secondary sources. The best general study on Solṭān Walad's life and work is in Turkish: A. Gölpınarlı, *Mevlânâ'dan sonra Mevlevîlik*, Istanbul, 1953, pp. 29-64. On the Turkish verses and their importance, see: E. J. W. Gibb, *A History of Ottoman Poetry* I, London, 1900, pp. 151-63 and M. F. Köprülü, *Türk edebiyatında ilk mutasavvıflar*, 2nd ed., Ankara, 1966, pp. 197-206. Browne, *Lit. Hist. Persia* III, pp. 155-56. B. Forūzānfar, *Taḥqīq-e aḥwāl o zendagānī-e Mawlānā Jalāl-al-Dīn Moḥammad mašhūr be Mawlawī*, 2nd ed., Tehran, 1332 Š./1953. Ḵayyāmpūr, *Soḵanvarān*, p. 274. Nafīsī, *Naẓm o naṯr* I, pp. 160, 199; II, p. 760. Rypka, *Hist. Iran Lit.*, pp. 180, 242. Ṣafā, *Adabīyāt* III/2, pp. 705-12 and index.

(M. I. WALEY)

BAHĀDOR, a Turco-Mongol honorific title, attached to a personal name, signifying "hero, valiant warrior." In the form *bağatur* (from which *bahādor* derives) the term was in use among the steppe peoples to the north and west of China as early as the seventh century, according to the history of the Sui dynasty (589-619), and it is found as Old Turkish *batur* a century later in the Köktürk khanate. Further to the west, the Proto-Bulgars used *bağatur* in the ninth century. As an honorific formally conferred upon an individual by the ruler, *bağatur* (also *ba'atur*) was given currency by Jengiz (Čengīz) Khan (whose father was called Yesügei Bağatur), who awarded this designation to those members, reportedly one thousand in number, of his personal forces whom he wished to recognize for outstanding valor and service. This use of *bağatur*/*bahādor* was continued in the Mongol successor states. In the Ulus Chaghatay (Čağatāy), for example, according to the *Tārīḵ-e rašīdī*, the chief figures of state around the khan included, alongside the great tribal chieftans, a large group of *bahādor*s, men with no following of their own who were yet recognized by the khan for their personal qualities and achievements; and in the Indo-Timurid state established by Bābor the title was commonly conferred upon major men of state whose ties were primarily to the dynasty rather than to their own kin groups. *Bahādor* remained in use in India even under British rule.

Bahādor was also adopted as a regnal title by Muslim Mongol and Turkman dynasts. The first to do so was the il-khan Abū Saʿīd (716-36/1316-35), who had himself styled "al-solṭān al-ʿādel Abū Saʿīd bahādor ḵān" in official documents. This regnal usage was followed by the dynasts of the Jalayerid, Timurid, Qara Qoyunlū, Āq Qoyunlū, Safavid, Indo-Timurid, and, most particularly, Özbek states.

Bibliography: Doerfer, *Türkische und Mongolische Elemente im Neupersischen* II, Wiesbaden, 1965, pp. 366-77. M. Fuad Köprülü, "Bahadır," in *İA* II, pp. 216-19. Denis Sinor, "Bahādur," in *EI*², p. 913. B. Vladimirtsov, *Le régime social des mongols*, Paris, 1948, pp. 93, 95, 111, 114, 118, 119, 121.

(C. FLEISCHER)

BAHĀDOR KHAN. See ABŪ ḠĀZĪ.

BAHĀDOR SHAH I, II. See MUGHALS.

AMIR **BAHĀDOR JANG,** ḤOSAYN PASHA KHAN, the head of the royal guards (*kešīkčībāšī*) and minister of court under Moẓaffar-al-Dīn Shah. (r. 1313-24/1896-1307) and the head of the royal guards and minister of war (*sepahsālār-e aʿẓam*) under Moḥammad-ʿAlī Shah Qājār (r. 1324-27/1907-09). Born (ca. 1271/1855) into a family of military tradition in Azerbaijan, he was the son of Moḥammad-Ṣādeq Khan Qarābāḡī Ājūdānbāšī (*adjudant-en-chef*) and a descendant of Ḥājj Kāẓem Khan Tofangdār (Māfī, *Ḵāṭerāt* I, p. 205). Having entered the service of the crown prince Moẓaffar-al-Dīn Mīrzā in Tabrīz, in 1301/1884 he became *yūzbāšī* (in charge of 100 servants); in 1303/1886 he was promoted to the rank of *qūllar-āqāsībāšī* (head of all servants); retaining the latter title, in 1309/1891-92 he also became *ājūdānbāšī* (q.v.) to the crown prince in his capacity as *sartīp-e awwal* and was called *ājūdānbāšī-e Āḏarbāyjān*. In 1310/1892-93 he acquired the title Amir Bahādor(-e) Jang (Bāmdād, *Rejāl* I, p. 384).

During Moẓaffar-al-Dīn Shah's reign he first replaced ʿAbd-Allāh Khan Qājār Nāẓem-al-Salṭana as *Kešīkčībāšī* (1314/1896-97) and was also put in charge of guarding the royal residence. In 1321/1903 he was promoted to the rank of *sardār* and later replaced Mīrzā Maḥmūd Khan Ḥakīm-al-Molk as the Minister of Court. Under the army reorganization plan (late 1322/early 1905) he was given the command of about 9,000 men stationed chiefly in Kermān, Isfahan, and Fārs. In the *bast* (q.v.) held in the Shah ʿAbd-al-ʿAẓīm sanctuary south of Tehran in Šawwāl, 1323/December, 1905, which included prominent clergy and merchants who requested from the shah the dismissal of Solṭān ʿAbd-al-Majīd Mīrzā ʿAyn-al-Dawla (q.v.), the prime minister, Amir Bahādor was sent with a large cavalry in an unsuccessful mission to appease the protestors. The *bast* resulted in further consolidation of the opposing party and added to their demands the removal of the Belgian citizen M. Naus from the control of the Persian customs, and more importantly the establishment of an *ʿadālat-ḵāna* (house of justice); it was also a prelude to the oncoming Constitutional movement. Moẓaffar-al-Dīn Shah had immense confidence in Amir Bahādor who as a result became very influential at court, and amassed a great fortune; he also accompanied the shah on his three visits to Europe (1900, 1902, and 1905; Churchill, no. 46).

After Moḥammad-ʿAlī Shah's accession, Amir Bahādor was at first ignored by the new shah, but their common anti-Constitutionalist zeal soon drew them together and he was reappointed to command the royal bodyguard. His oath of allegiance to the Majles (22 Šaʿbān 1325/1 October 1907) did not alter his highly unpopular image with the Constitutionalists who later attributed the shah's abortive coup d'etat of Ḏu'l-qaʿda, 1325/December, 1907, to his influence. By the early 1326/early 1908 Amir Bahādor gained full control over the notorious Sīlāḵor regiment, stationed in and around the palace. Moḥammad-ʿAlī Shah, like his father, fully trusted this regiment and regarded it as his sole protection (Moḡīṯ-al-Salṭana, *Nāmahā*, pp. 194-95). A series of demonstrations towards the end of Rabīʿ II, 326/late May, 1908 called for Amir Bahādor's removal, and the shah reluctantly complied on 2 Jomādā I/2 June. In the meantime, while conspiring secretly with the shah against the Constitutionalists, Amir Bahādor took refuge in the summer residence of the Russian legation in Zarganda north of Tehran, and remained there until 7 Jomādā I/7 June. On the 15th of Jomādā I/15 June it became known that Amir Bahādor was given control of the royal artillery (*tūp-ḵāna*), which itself had already mobilized a contingent of some 200 strong including certain provincial forces and elements of urban thugs (*Tārīḵ-e bīdārī* II, p. 151). This additional force was stationed in the Bāḡ-e Šāh (q.v.) garison which had recently become the headquarters of the shah, the Russian cossack brigade, and other anti-Constitutionalist factions. Following the coup d'etat of 23 Jomādā 1326/23 June 1908, Amir Bahādor was made Sepahsālār-e aʿẓam (9 Jomādā II 1326/9 July 1908) and held the office of minister of war in the third and fourth cabinets, of Mīrzā Aḥmad Khan Mošīr-al-Salṭana (1326/1908; Bāmdād, *Rejāl* I, p. 385; Kasrawī, *Mašrūṭa*, p. 623). In this period of counter-revolutionary turmoil he was a powerful figure and had a strong influence on the shah, to such an extent that he was described as "virtually dictator of Persia" (Mr. Marling to Sir Edward Grey, Browne, *The Persian Revolution*, p. 261 n. 2. In the following year after strong pressure on the shah by the British and Russian legations, Amir Bahādor was removed from office but remained within the court circle. Realizing the imminent victory of the Constitutionalists, he unsuccessfully applied to the *ʿolamāʾ* of Najaf for asylum in the *ʿAtabāt* (*Tārīḵ-e bīdārī* II, p. 437). Upon the conquest of Tehran by the Constitutionalists, Amir Bahādor followed the dethroned Moḥammad-ʿAlī to Zarganda under joint Russian and British protection (28 Jomādā II 1327/17 July 1909); and because of his staunch anti-Constitutionalist stance, he was excluded from the general amnesty of 15 Šaʿbān 1327/1 September 1909; and was soon to accompany the deposed shah into exile (23 Šaʿbān 1327/9 September 1909) first to Russia and later to various places in Europe, assisting him in gathering forces (see, e.g., Browne, *Press and Poetry*,

p. 327). When on 20 Rajab 1329/17 July 1911 Moḥammad-ʿAlī Shah launched a futile come-back, Amir Bahādor was in his company (Kasrawī, *Āḏarbāy-jān*, pp. 172-73). Later he separated from Moḥammad-ʿAlī Mīrzā and lived in Vienna. Finally some years later he managed to obtain permission from the government to return to Tehran, where he died around 1336/1918.

In contrast to the widely-held harsh image of him, Amir Bahādor was reportedly unsophisticated and quite keen on observing religious rites (see, e.g., Šarīf Kāšānī, *Wāqeʿāt* I, p. 257; Dawlatābādī, *Ḥayāt-e Yaḥyā* I, pp. 150-51, 210; Kasrawī, *Mašrūṭa*, Tehran, 1356 Š./1977, p. 27; Moẓaffar-al-Dīn Shah, *Safar-nāma*, p. 33; Tāj-al-Salṭana, *Ḵāṭerāt*, p. 94; Mostawfī, *Šarḥ-e zendagānī*, pp. 138, 151). He had great affection for Ferdowsī's *Šāh-nāma*, and could recite appropriate verses when the occasion arose (Bāmdād, *Rejāl* I, p. 386; Bozorg-Omīd, *Az mā-st*, pp. 130-31), and would privately perform certain episodes of the epic (Rošdīya, *Sawāneḥ*, p. 139). He also sponsored the publication of a large and finely made lithograph edition of that book, popularly known as the *Šāh-nāma-ye amīr-bahādorī* (Tehran, 1322/1904). When he was minister of court, and following a recommendation by the prime minister ʿAyn-al-Dawla, Amir Bahādor also sponsored the publication of the three volumes of *Tafṣīl wasāʾel al-šīʿa* of Ḥorr ʿĀmelī (Tehran, 1323-24/1905-06).

What had remained of Amir Bahādor's luxurious residence in Tehran was later purchased by the government (1346 Š./1967) and allocated to the Anjoman-e Āṯār-e Mellī (q.v.; M.-Ṭ. Moṣṭafawī, *Āṯār-e tārīḵī-e Ṭehrān* I: *Amāken-e motabarraka*, ed. M.-Ḥ. Moḥaddeṯ, Tehran, 1361 Š./1982, pp. 451-73).

Bibliography: Scattered references to Amir Bahādor are found in sources dealing with the Constitutional period but no detailed biography has yet been published. Biographical sketches are found in Bāmdād, *Rejāl* I, pp. 384-86, and G. P. Churchill, *Biographical Notices of Persian Statesmen and Notables, August 1905*, Calcutta, 1906. Sources referred to in the text: A. Bozorg-Omīd, *Az mā-st ka bar māst*, 2nd ed., Tehran, 1363 Š./1984. E. G. Browne, *The Press and Poetry of Modern Persia*, Cambridge, 1914. Idem, *The Persian Revolution of 1905-1909*, London, 1966. Y. Dawlatābādī, *Tārīḵ-e moʿāṣer yā ḥayāt-e Yaḥyā* I, 2nd ed., Tehran, 1361 Š./1982. Neẓām-al-Salṭana Māfī, *Ḵāṭerāt wa asnād-e Ḥosaynqolī Ḵān Neẓām-al-Salṭana Māfī* I: *Ḵāṭerāt*, ed. M. Neẓām Māfī et al., Tehran, 1361 Š./1982. Y. Moḡīṯ-al-Salṭana, *Nāmahā-ye Yūsof Moḡīṯ-al-Salṭana (1320-1334)*, ed. M. Neẓām Māfī, Tehran, 1362 Š./1983. Foreign Office, *Blue Book* (Cd. 4581): *Correspondence Respecting the Affairs of Persia, December 1906 to November 1908, Persia no. 1, 1909*, London, 1909. M. Nāẓem-al-Eslām Kermānī, *Tārīḵ-e bīdārī-e īrānīān*, 3 vols., new ed. ʿA.-A. Saʿīdī Sīrjānī, Tehran, 1346-49 Š./1967-70. Moẓaffar-al-Dīn Shah Qājār, *Safar-nāma-ye mobāraka-ye šāhanšāhī*, Tehran, 1319/1901. S. Rošdīya, *Sawāneḥ-e ʿomr*, Tehran, 1362 Š./1983. M.-M. Šarīf Kāšānī, *Wāqeʿāt-e ettefāqīya dar rūzgār*, ed. M. Etteḥādīya (Neẓām Māfī) and S. Saʿdvandīān, I, Tehran, 1362 Š./1983. T. Tāj-al-Salṭana, *Ḵāṭerāt-e Tāj-al-Salṭana*, ed. M. Etteḥādīya (Neẓām Māfī) and S. Saʿdvandīān, Tehran, 1361 Š./1982.

(A. GHEISSARI)

BAHAI FAITH or **BAHAISM,** a religion founded in the nineteenth century by the Iranian notable Bahāʾ-Allāh (q.v.; commonly Bahá'ulláh or Bahā'ullāh in Western works) that grew out of the Iranian messianic movement of Babism (q.v.) and developed into a world religion with internationalist and pacifist emphases.

i. *The faith.*
ii. *Bahai calendar and festivals.*
iii. *Bahai and Babi schisms.*
iv. *The Bahai communities.*
v. *The Bahai community in Iran.*
vi. *The Bahai community of Ashkhabad.*
vii. *Bahai persecutions.*
viii. *Bahai shrines.*
ix. *Bahai temples.*
x. *Bahai schools.*
xi. *Bahai conventions.*
xii. *Bahai literature.*

i. THE FAITH

History. Bahaism as a religion had as its background two earlier and much different movements in nineteenth-century Shiʿite Shaikhism (following Shaikh Aḥmad Aḥsāʾī [q.v.]) and Babism. Shaikhism centered on theosophical doctrines and believed that a perfect Shiʿite existed on earth at all times, and many Shaikhis (as well as other Shiʿites) expected the return of the hidden Twelfth Imam in 1260/1844. Shaikhis in particular joined the messianic Babi movement of the 1840s, which shook Iran as Sayyed ʿAlī-Moḥammad Šīrāzī proclaimed himself, first the *bāb* or "gate" of the Twelfth Imam, and then the return of the imam himself. As the new creed spread, violence broke out between Shiʿites and Babis, ending when Qajar government troops intervened to besiege and massacre the Babis. The government executed the Bāb in 1850. Some Babi leaders in Tehran plotted, in revenge, the death of Nāṣer-al-Dīn Shah, but the assassination failed and large numbers of suspected Babis were tortured and killed.

An Iranian notable and important Babi figure, Mīrzā Ḥosayn-ʿAlī Nūrī, "Bahāʾ-Allāh" was imprisoned but found innocent after the attempted assassination. He was exiled to Iraq, in the Ottoman empire, then to Istanbul and Edirne in Turkey. He was accompanied by his younger half-brother, Mīrzā Yaḥyā Ṣobḥ-e Azal, whom the Bāb appears to have pointed to in 1850 as leader of the Babi community. The Bāb had also spoken of the advent of another messianic figure, "he whom God shall make manifest (*man yoẓheroh Allāh*)," and in 1863 in the garden of Necip Paşa in Baghdad Bahāʾ-

Allāh informed a handful of close followers that he was the messianic figure promised by the Bāb (Ostād Moḥammad-ʿAlī Salmānī, *Ḵāṭerāt*, ms., International Bahā'i Archives, Haifa; Eng. tr. M. Gail, *My Memories of Bahā'u'llāh*, Los Angeles, 1982, p. 22). While in Edirne (1863-68) Bahā'-Allāh wrote letters to Babi followers in Iran openly proclaiming himself to be the spiritual "return" (*rajʿa*) of the Bāb. During the Edirne period relations between Bahā'-Allāh and Ṣobḥ-e Azal became increasingly strained, and in 1867 Bahā'-Allāh sent his younger brother a missive demanding his obedience to the new revelation, which Azal rejected. Babis in Iran were then forced to choose between Bahā'-Allāh and Azal. The vast majority accepted the assertions in Bahā'-Allāh's writings that he was a manifestation of God (*maẓhar-e elāhī*) bearing a new revelation, rejecting Azal's form of Babism. Although the Bahais date the inception of their religion from Bahā'-Allāh's 1863 private declaration in Baghdad, the Bahai community only gradually came into being in the late 1860s, and most Babis did not become Bahais in earnest until after 1867, though many may have been partisans of Bahā'-Allāh earlier (Bahā'-Allāh, "Sūrat damm," *Āṯār-e qalam-e aʿlā* IV, Tehran, 125 *Badīʿ*/1968, pp. 1-15; "Lawḥ-e Naṣīr," *Majmūʿa-ye maṭbūʿa-ye alwāḥ*, Cairo, 1920, pp. 166-202; Salmānī, *Ḵāṭerāt*, tr. pp. 42-48, 93-105).

In 1868 Bahā'-Allāh and some close followers were exiled to ʿAkkā, in Palestine, by the Ottomans, and Azal and his partisans were sent to Cyprus. The vast majority of Babis lived in Iran, and Bahā'-Allāh found ways to continue to send epistles and tablets (sing. *lawḥ*) to them. In 1873, while under house arrest in the old city of ʿAkkā, Bahā'-Allāh, in response to requests by the Bahai community in Iran for a new book of laws to accompany his new revelation, set down the *Aqdas* (*al-Ketāb al-aqdas, Ketāb-e aqdas* "Most holy Book" [q.v.]), meant to supersede the Koran and the Bāb's book of laws, the *Bayān*.

One of the problems facing the Babis in the 1850s and 1960s was that of religious authority. With the execution of the Bāb and the massacre of many prominent Babi disciples, the original leadership of the religion was mown down. Regional sects developed within Babism, with local claimants to high station competing for allegiance. Azal, who followed a policy of keeping himself incognito, provided little effective leadership. Bahā'-Allāh won out partially because he solved these problems of legitimacy and organization. The *Aqdas* prescribes that in every locality a Bahai steering committee (termed *bayt al-ʿadl* "house of justice" [q.v.]) should be set up to administer the affairs of the religion. In addition, Bahā'-Allāh provided active leadership through his letters from exile, and through his close companions (called *moballeḡīn* "teachers") who were sent back to Iran to implement his policies (*al-Ketāb al-aqdas*, Bombay, n.d., pp. 30-31; ʿAbd-al-Bahā', *Taḏkerat al-wafā'*, Haifa, 1924; Kāẓem Samandarī, *Tārīḵ-e Samandar wa molḥaqāt*, Tehran, 131 *Badīʿ*/1974; Mīrzā Ḥaydar-ʿAlī Eṣfahānī, *Bahjat al-ṣodūr*, Bombay, 1913).

After 1873 the Bahais in Iran began to organize themselves in accordance with the *Aqdas* and gradually began to follow its laws. For example, because of that book's emphasis on the education of children of both sexes, informal Bahai schools were set up. The Christian missionary Bruce noted in 1874 in Isfahan the rapid increase in Bahais (letter of Reverend Bruce, 19 November 1874, in M. Momen, ed., *The Bábí and Bahá'í Religions, 1844-1944: Some Contemporary Western Accounts*, Oxford, 1981, p. 244). J. D. Rees of the Indian civil service found in 1885 evidence of substantial Bahai followings among the merchant class in Qazvīn, and among townsmen in Hamadān, Ābāda, and Mašhad (J. Rees, "The Bab and Babism," *Nineteenth Century* 40, 1896, pp. 56-66, quoted in Momen, *Babi and Bahá'í Religions*, p. 245). The government and the Shiʿite *ʿolamā'* carried out periodic persecution of the new religion, as in Isfahan in 1874 and 1880, in Tehran in 1882-83, and Yazd in 1891 (see missionary and consular reports in Momen, *Bábí and Bahá'í Religions*, pp. 251-305). Bahaism spread in this period, not only among Iranian Shiʿites but also among the Zoroastrians in Yazd and Jews in Kāšān and Hamadān (see the letters to the Zoroastrians by Mīrzā Abu'l-Fażl Golpāyeganī (q.v.) in his *Rasā'el wa raqā'em*, ed. R. Mehrābḵānī, Tehran, 1978, pp. 463-511). Internationally, Bahaism spread from the late 1860s to 1892 in Iraq, Turkey, Ottoman Syria, Egypt, Sudan, the Caucasus, Turkish Central Asia, India, and Burma.

Bahā'-Allāh appointed his eldest son ʿAbbās Effendi ʿAbd-al-Bahā' (q.v.) to head up Bahaism after him. ʿAbd-al-Bahā' assumed the leadership of the religion in 1892 upon his father's death, and was accepted by almost all Bahais as the perfect exemplar of his father's teachings. Some of his younger half-brothers, led by Moḥammad-ʿAlī, joined a handful of Bahai "teachers" in opposing ʿAbd-al-Bahā''s authority, but this small group eventually died out. From 1892 to 1921, under ʿAbd-al-Bahā''s leadership, Bahaism spread to Tunisia, Arabia, North America, Europe, China, Japan, South Africa, Brazil, and Australia, as well as making further progress in countries where it had earlier been established, such as India. The well-organized Bahai community of the United States was particularly active in spreading the religion, and was encouraged to do so by ʿAbd-al-Bahā' in such of his writings as the *Alwāḥ-e tablīḡī-e Amrīkā* (in ʿAbd-al-Bahā', *Makātīb* III, Cairo, 1921; tr., *Unveiling the Divine Plan*, New York, 1919).

In Iran Bahais continued to be active, and to spread their religion. They faced several waves of major persecutions. The 1896 assassination of Nāṣer-al-Dīn Shah by Mīrzā Reżā Kermānī (q.v.) a follower of Sayyed Jamāl-al-Dīn "Afḡānī" (q.v.) was widely blamed on Babis or Bahais at first. Pogroms against Bahais were undertaken in 1903 in Rašt, Isfahan, and especially Yazd (Moḥammad-Ṭāher Malmīrī, *Tārīḵ-e šohadā'-e Yazd*, Cairo, 1926; diplomatic correspondence in Momen, *Bábí and Bahá'í Religions*, pp. 373-404). They were caught in the middle of the Constitutional Revolution of 1905-11. Despite the support for constitutionalism in Bahā'-Allāh's writings, Bahai leaders were careful not to take sides too openly, primarily, it seems, in order to avoid provoking their opponents in the opposing camps thus endangering their vulnerable community, but probably also out of concern that their very identification with the cause might undermine it in Iran. Nevertheless, 'Abd-al-Bahā' around 1906 urged Bahais to attempt to elect two *ayādī-e amr Allāh* "Hands of the cause of God" (q.v.) to parliament (copies of ms. letters in the author's possession). He later became disillusioned with the Majles and urged Bahais to dissociate themselves from politics ('Abd-al-Bahā', *Resāla-ye sīāsīya*, Tehran, 1913), a policy which gradually became frozen into a Bahai principle. Anti-Bahai attacks increased again at times of political unrest, and the early 1920s prelude to Reżā Khan's coup also saw numerous pogroms (diplomatic correspondence in Momen, *Bábí and Bahá'í Religions*, pp. 405-52).

'Abd-al-Bahā' further refined the Bahai administrative apparatus, calling for elections of local Houses of Justice or Spiritual Assemblies (*maḥfel-e rūḥānī-e maḥallī*) by majority vote, and preparing for the election of national Spiritual Assemblies (*maḥfel-e mellī*) and of an international House of Justice (*bayt al-'adl-e bayn al-melalī*). Also in his will and testament (*Alwāḥ-e waṣāyā*, in 'Abd-al-Ḥamīd Ešrāq Ḵāvarī, ed., *Resāla-ye ayyām-e tes'a*, Tehran, 103 *Badī'*/1947, repr. 129 *Badī'*/1973, pp. 456-84; tr. Shoghi Effendi, *Will and Testament of 'Abdu'l-Baha*, New York, 1925) he appointed his grandson Shoghi (Šawqī) Effendi Rabbānī (q.v.) leader of Bahaism after him as *walī-e amr Allāh* (Guardian of the cause of god). He stipulated that Shoghi Effendi should appoint the next guardian from among his children or close cousins. Some Bahais, like Ruth White, refused to accept Shoghi Effendi, others, like Aḥmad Sohrāb thought him too authoritarian. Only a miniscule number of Bahais, however, followed them, and Shoghi Effendi's vigorous leadership and administrative abilities led to a great expansion in the number of Bahais world-wide. In his first decade of leadership he presided over the election of Bahai national Spiritual Assemblies in the British Isles (1923), Germany (1923), India (1923), Egypt (1924), the United States of America (1925), and Iraq (1931) (Shoghi Effendi, *God Passes By*, Wilmette, I11., 1944, 1970, pp. 323-401; Ruḥíyyih [Mary Maxwell] Rabbānī, *The Priceless Pearl*, London, 1969).

After 1925 many Iranian Bahais began refusing to be identified by their family's ancestral religion on their passports and other official papers, and Bahai institutions began issuing marriage certificates in accordance with the laws of the *Aqdas*. In 1927 Bahais convened their first national conference of delegates from the nine provinces of Iran, and planned to begin annual national conventions like those held in the United States. Bahais organized for the establishment of primary schools, the improvement of the status of women, and the propagation of their religion. The secularism of the Reżā Shah government in the late 1920s at first helped the Bahais, who built a Bahai center (*ḥaẓīrat al-qods*) in Tehran, and began holding public meetings. There, eighty-four of the ninety-five delegates to the national convention gathered to elect the first national Spiritual Assembly in 1934 in accordance with the by-laws translated from those of the national Spiritual Assembly of the United States. Walī-Allāh Khan Warqā was elected chairman, 'Alī-Akbar Forūtan became secretary. National committees were set up for children's education, women's progress, and the establishment of a Bahai house of worship (*mašreq al-aḏkār*) on a tract of land near Tehran ("Report Prepared by the National Spiritual Assembly of the Bahā'īs of Iran," *The Bahá'í World: A Biennial International Record* 6, Wilmette, I11., 1937, repr. 1980, pp. 94-108; "Bahā'ī Administrative Divisions in Iran," *Bahá'í World* 7, Wilmette, I11., 1939, pp. 571-75).

From 1934, however, the Reżā Shah period was not a particularly happy one for the Iranian Bahai community, though violence against them occurred much less frequently because of better security and less influence over affairs by the Shi'ite *'olamā'*. Reżā Shah's autocratic rule meant he brooked no independence and uncontrolled activity from any social or religious institutions, including Bahaism. The rise of the Bahai administrative order was perceived as a challenge to this central policy, and therefore all schools belonging to the Bahai community were closed (see BAHAI SCHOOLS) throughout Iran. Moreover, his government refused to recognize the validity of Bahai marriage certificates, banned the printing and circulation of Bahai literature, closed some local Bahai centers, confiscated Bahai ballot boxes at district conventions in some localities, forbade Bahais to communicate with their coreligionists outside Iran, dismissed some Bahai government employees, and demoted some Bahais in the military. Elections of the national Spiritual Assembly had to be held by mail (Knatchbull-Hugessen to Simon, no. 554, 15 December 1934, FO 371/17917, quoted in Momen, *Bábí and Bahá'í Religions*, pp. 477-78, see also pp. 462-81; National Spiritual Assembly of the Bahais of Iran, "Annual Report," *Bahá'í World* 7, Wilmette, I11., 1939, pp. 133-45).

The installation of Moḥammad Reżā Pahlavī as shah in the 1940s signaled no change in the legal status of Bahaism. Looser government authority in that decade allowed an increase in major mob attacks on Bahais, such as those at Ābāda in May of 1944, and at Šāhrūd in July-August of 1944. In 1946-50 the national Spiritual Assembly of the Bahais of Iran adopted a six-point plan for spreading Bahaism and for improving the status of women. For the first time, women were elected to Bahai assemblies in Iran (they had served on them in the West much before), and women's adult education and literacy classes were set up (*Shiraz Diary*, no. 91, 15-31 May 1944, FO 371/40162 in Momen, *The Bábí and Bahá'í Religions*, pp. 479-80; "Report from Persia," ed. and tr. M. Gail, *Bahá'í World* 10, Wilmette, I11., 1949, pp. 35-48; Horace Holley, "International Survey of Current Bahā'ī Activities," *Bahá'í World* 11, Wilmette, I11., 1951, pp. 34-36).

In 1955, in a move which seems to have done as much for the appeasement of *'olamā'* as to divert the attention of the general populace from unpopular policies, including the forging of a US-British-sponsored military alliance (the Baghdad Pact, q.v.), the shah's military destroyed the dome of the Bahai center in Tehran, Ayatollah Behbahānī (a pro-court clergyman, q.v.) sent congratulatory telegrams to the shah and to Ayatollah Borūjerdī the chief Shi'ite clergyman in Qom. The *'olamā'* and pro-clerical deputies in the docile parliament took the opportunity to voice support for the complete outlawing of the Bahai faith, the jailing of all avowed Bahais, and the sequestration of all Bahai property. During this campaign some Bahai shops and farms were damaged by mob attacks, and a number of Bahais were assaulted. The government ultimately gave up the move, but the campaign did strengthen the hand of the *'olamā'* with the government until the late 1950s (S. Akhavi, *Religion and Politics in Contemporary Iran*, Albany, N.Y., 1980, pp. 76-87).

In the 1950s Shoghi Effendi appointed a large number of Hands of the Cause, and constituted some of them as an International Bahai Council, in preparation for the election of the Universal House of Justice. In 1953 he launched a global campaign of peaceful proselytizing for Bahaism, the "Ten-year World Crusade (*jehād*)," which sought with some success to spread the religion even to remote areas and islands. Shoghi Effendi did not live to see the end of the project, dying in London in 1957. Because he died childless, and the actions of his eligible relatives had forced him to excommunicate them, he had found it impossible to appoint a Guardian to succeed him. In 1963 the International Bahai Council convened in London a global congress and the first Universal House of Justice was elected. It included five American members, two from Britain, and two Iranians. Almost all Bahais accepted its authority, though a small number followed Hand of the Cause Mason Remey, who declared himself the Guardian despite 'Abd-al-Bahā''s stipulation of descent from Bahā'-Allāh. The Remey movement remained tiny. The Universal House of Justice was thereafter elected every five years by members of the world's national Spiritual Assemblies. Its seat, like that of 'Abd-al-Bahā' and Shoghi Effendi Rabbānī, is in Haifa, now Israel, near the shrines of the Bāb and Bahā'-Allāh. After 1957 Bahaism became a mass movement in some parts of the Third World, in Africa, South Asia, and South America. Some of the first mass conversions occurred in Uganda, India, and Bolivia. (P. Haney, "The Institution of the Hands of the Cause;" letters issued by the Hands of the Cause 1957-63; and M. Hofman, "International Survey of Current Bahā'ī Activities," in *Bahā'í World* 13, Haifa, 1970, pp. 245-309, 333-94; B. Ashton, "The Most Great Jubilee" and "The Universal House of Justice," *Bahā'í World* 14, Haifa, 1974, pp. 57-80, 425-43; Universal House of Justice, *Wellspring of Guidance*, Wilmette, Ill., 1969; V. Johnson. "An Historical Analysis of Critical Transformations in the Evolution of the Bahā'ī World Faith," Ph.D. dissertation, Baylor University, 1974, pp. 330-90.)

In the 1960s and early 1970s the lot of Bahais in Iran improved somewhat, though they still continued to labor under many legal and latent social disabilities. In 1964 Iran had 530 local Spiritual Assemblies. In 1975 Bahais feared for their safety when Moḥammad-Reżā Shah insisted that all Iranians join his *Rastāḵīz* party. The national Spiritual Assembly of the Bahais of Iran informed the shah that although Bahais were law-abiding citizens, they could not join his party, given the non-political nature of Bahaism. In the 1970s Bahais were often watched and harassed by the shah's security apparatus, SAVAK, and the Bahai Publishing Trust in Tehran was forced to offset rather than print books and to limit the number of books it circulated in order to avoid sanctions.

A number of Bahais, such as Ḥabīb Ṯābet, Hożabr Yazdānī, and 'Abd-al-Karīm Ayādī, grew extremely rich and powerful under the Pahlavīs, and helped form a general public impression of Bahais as a bourgeois group supportive of the unpopular policies of the regime and close to the shah or the royal family. This rekindled dormant prejudices and provoked anger and resentment towards the Bahai community as a whole but the Babi and Bahai religions were mass movements, encompassing villagers and peasants, artisans and tradesman, and working class people in the large cities, who formed the vast majority of the country's three to four hundred thousand Bahais (P. Smith, "A Note on Bābī and Bahā'ī Numbers in Iran," *Iranian Studies* 15, 2-3, 1984, pp. 295-301) and who had no desire for or interest in siding with unpopular policies and alienating the majority. That these ordinary Bahais were forbidden by their national Spiritual Assembly from joining any political party, and even from voting (unlike their coreligionists in the West, who may vote if they can do so without joining a party) made their political preferences a private matter which, in normal circumstances, should have been viewed as irrelevant to the political process.

Since its inception in 1979, the Islamic Republic of Iran has, despite denials and explanations, demonstrated every intention of destroying the Bahai community altogether. It has gradually and systematically confiscated all Bahai properties and investment companies, fired Bahai civil servants, dissolved all Bahai national and local Spiritual Assemblies, and executed nearly two hundred of the country's most active and prominent Bahais. It has harassed, detained, and persecuted many others on various pretexts, ranging from violation of Islamic laws, to conspiracy with and spying for international Zionism and imperialism. Since the Islamic Republic considers the performance of Bahai marriage ceremonies heretical and illegitimate, local Spiritual Assembly members who performed them have been tried on charges of promoting prostitution. Bahais who went on visitation to shrines in Israel or sent monetary contributions to the Bahai world center in Haifa came under suspicion of supporting

Zionism or spying for it, even though the establishment of ʿAkkā and Haifa as Bahai centers dated from the nineteenth century, long before the founding of Israel. Hundreds of recantations have appeared in newspapers, the circumstances of their procurement being highly suspicious. The parliament has made it illegal for parents to pass Bahaism on to their children, has refused admittance of Bahai children to schools, and denies Bahais ration cards. The government's confiscation of membership records at the National Bahai Center in Tehran allows it to identify Bahais throughout the country (Human Rights Commission of the Federation of Protestant Churches in Switzerland, "Declaration on the State of Religious Minorities in Iran," *World Order* 13, no. 4, 1979, pp. 15-20; Amnesty International U.S.A., "Under Penalty of Death: In Iran a Campaign of Terror against Bahā'is," *Matchbox*, October, 1983, p. 11).

Administrative apparatus. Bahai administration evolved gradually, but this overview will discuss current practice. Bahaism possesses no clergy formally trained to administer rituals. Rather, the administration both of religious observances and of community affairs rests with elected officials. At the level of villages, towns, cities, or counties, these officials constitute the local Spiritual Assembly, consisting of nine members elected annually on the eve of April 21 by universal adult suffrage and by secret ballot. Women as well as men serve on the local and national Spiritual Assemblies (*Aqdas*, pp. 30-31; ʿAbd-al-Bahā' in ʿA. Ešrāq Ḵāvarī, ed., *Ganjīna-ye ḥodūd wa aḥkām*, New Delhi, 1980, pp. 57-67; Shoghi Effendi, *Bahá'í Administration*, Wilmette, Ill., 1986, pp. 20-24; "The Local Spiritual Assembly," *Bahá'í World* 14, pp. 511-30).

In addition to their own, usually closed administrative meetings, every nineteen days local Spiritual Assemblies sponsor the Bahai feast (*żīāfat*) for the entire community, consisting of three parts. In the first part local lay believers read from Bahai writings first, and then often from scriptures of other religions, as well. In the second part community affairs are discussed. Committees of the local Spiritual Assembly and its officers give reports on their activities. Suggestions may be made from the floor for the local Spiritual Assembly to consider at its next meeting. The third part consists of friendly conversation over refreshments. Because the feast partially has the character of a community business meeting, only registered members of Bahaism may attend. (Bahā'-Allāh, *Aqdas*, pp. 30-31, 61; ʿAbd-al-Bahā', quoted in Ešrāq Ḵāvarī, ed., *Ganjīna*, pp. 156-58; National Spiritual Assembly of the Bahā'is of the British Isles, comp., *Principles of Bahá'í Administration*, London, 1950, pp. 51-53.)

Bahai communities are also apportioned among larger districts for the purpose of electing delegates to an annual national convention. The district conventions, held in the autumn, elect a number of delegates, based on the size of the local Bahai population, and send with them local concerns they want raised at the national convention. The national convention takes place again in April and elects nine members to the national Spiritual Assembly. Campaigning is not allowed at these elections, though discussion of issues is encouraged (Shoghi Effendi, *Bahá'í Administration*, pp. 65, 79, 89, 91). The national Spiritual Assembly, an institution created by ʿAbd-al-Bahā' (Bahā'-Allāh had spoken only of the local Houses of Justice and of the Universal House of Justice), has the responsibility of administering the affairs of the national Bahai community and of propagating the religion in its country (Shoghi Effendi, *Bahá'í Administration*, passim).

Every five years members of all the Bahai national Spiritual Assemblies in the world send their ballots to or gather at an international convention to elect nine persons to the Universal House of Justice. Of this body Bahā'-Allāh wrote, "It is incumbent upon the Trustees of the House of Justice to take counsel together regarding those things which have not outwardly been revealed in the Book, and to enforce that which is agreeable to them" ("Kalemāt-e ferdowsīya," *Majmūʿa-ī az alwāḥ ka baʿd az Ketāb-e aqdas nāzel šodand*, Hofheim-Langenhain, 1980, p. 37; tr., p. 68; cf. "Ešrāqāt," *Majmūʿa-ī az alwāḥ*, pp. 75-76; tr. pp. 128-29). All these elected institutions make their decisions by majority vote, though unanimity is preferred, after long discussions called consultation (*mašwerat*), in which members are urged not to become attached to their own suggestions, but to consider each motion dispassionately.

This administrative structure is complemented by appointed institutions of the "learned" (*ʿolamā' fi'l-Bahā'*) (Bahā'-Allāh, *Aqdas*, pp. 170-71). The first body of the learned were the Hands of the Cause of God appointed by Bahā'-Allāh and by Shoghi Effendi. Since only the Guardian could appoint Hands of the Cause, according to ʿAbd-al-Bahā', the lapsing of the institution of the guardianship after 1957 meant that the institution of the Hands also lapsed. The Universal House of Justice has attempted to compensate by creating a new institution of counselors (*mošāwerīn*) who are appointed to five-year terms. They have the functions of protecting Bahaism from internal threats to its integrity such as schism, and of spreading the religion. The counselors appoint, with the consent of the Universal House of Justice, auxiliary board members with either of the specific functions of protection and propagation. The auxiliary board members appoint assistants, again with approval from their superiors. Members of these appointed institutions of the learned have no executive power, and can only advise the elected institutions ("The Institution of the Hands of the Cause," *Bahá'í World* 14, 459-74; Universal House of Justice, *Wellspring of Guidance*). Since no Bahai seminaries or full-time clerical offices exist, the institutions of the learned are filled by active laymen, often teachers, librarians, or other intellectuals.

Theology. Bahai theology posits several metaphysical levels of reality. The highest of these is the divine realm of unicity (*aḥadīya*), wherein only God's essence and his essential attributes exist. In this station (*maqām*), God's knowledge is his essence and his essence is his knowledge; God is unmanifest and alone, and completely inconceivable. In the second station God manifests himself by his essence to his essence, bringing into existence the Word of God (*kalemat Allāh*) or divine manifestation (*ẓohūr-e elāhī*). This primal manifestation of God then dawns forth on the world of contingency (*emkān*) with all the names and attributes of God, causing the new creation to come into being. Each being can reflect an attribute of God, but only human beings can spiritually advance to the point where they can reflect all the attributes of God. They can do so only with the help of prophets and messengers, called generally manifestations of God (*maẓhar-e elāhī*), who perfectly show forth the names and attributes of God in the human realm. Unlike similar Sufi schemas, in the Bahai system metaphysical realms are absolutely separate; Bahai thought rejects the Sufi theory of *waḥdat al-wojūd* or existential monism ('Abd-al-Bahā', "Tafsīr-e konto kanzan makẖfīan," *Makāteb-e 'Abd-al-Bahā'* II, Cairo, 1330/1911-12, pp. 2-55; Bahā'-Allāh, *Majmū'a-ye maṭbū'a*, pp. 339, 346).

Bahai psychology accepts a basically Aristotelian view of the various types of soul or spirit, positing a vegetative spirit with its faculty of spatial growth, the animal spirit with its sensitive and locomotive faculties, and the immortal human spirit or rational soul (*nafs-e nāṭeqa*), with its faculty of intellectual investigation. But two further spirits are posited. The spirit of faith is a moral and ethical faculty whereby the human soul acquires the perfections of God. Finally, the holy spirit (*rūḥ al-qods*) pertains only to the prophets and messengers, or manifestations of God. Prophets possess all of these spirits, from the bodily ones through the rational soul, and including the holy spirit ('Abd-al-Bahā', *al-Nūr al-abhā fī mofāważāt 'Abd-al-Bahā': goft-o-gū bar sar-e nāhār*, Leiden, 1908, pp. 108-10, 114-17, 154).

The universal intellect (*'aql-e koll*) or word of God (*kalemat Allāh*), the first, preexistent emanation of God, perceives the universe directly and intuitively. It emanates this knowledge upon the prophets, allowing them to found systems of religious law which are appropriate to the conditions of society. They know the necessary connections that relate all entities in the world, and their laws are aimed at regulating and balancing this world-system. God has been sending manifestations of God, whether prophets or messengers, since the inception of the human race, and will continue to do so in the future. Bahā'-Allāh's writings recognized all the Judaic prophets, Zoroaster, Jesus Christ, Moḥammad, the Bāb, and Bahā'-Allāh himself as historical manifestations of God, and 'Abd-al-Bahā' recognized such South Asian figures as Krishna and Buddha, as well. The Bahai conception of progressive revelation, which sees successive manifestations of God as having brought increasingly sophisticated religious teachings over time, allows Bahais to incorporate local religious traditions throughout the world into their schema. An essential Bahai teaching is the ultimate unity of all the great prophets and founders of the world religions. Indeed, despite their individuality and differences in station, each manifestation of God can be seen as a "return" (*raj'a*) of his predecessors, not in the sense of reincarnation but in that of the return of spiritual attributes (Bahā'-Allāh, "Jawāher al-asrār," *Āṯār-e qalam-e a'lā* III, Tehran, 129 *Badī'*/1972-73, pp. 33-37; Bahā'-Allāh, *Ketāb-e īqān*, Cairo, 1900, pp. 127-29, 147-48; 'Abd-al-Bahā', *Mofāważāt*, pp. 119-20, 123-24, 164-66).

Bahai anthropology sees human beings as burdened with the passions of an animal nature, which can be overcome only through special training and effort. The teacher in this enterprise of spiritual education is the manifestation of God. 'Abd-al-Bahā' spoke of three kinds of education. The first is education for the welfare of the body. The second is education for the welfare of human society, including policy, administration, commerce, industry, sciences, and arts. This is an education for civilization and progress. The third is education for a sound character and the acquisition of divine perfections. The educator is perfect in all respects and by his teachings organizes the world, brings nations and religions together, and delivers man from vices ('Abd-al-Bahā', *Mofāważāt*, pp. 6-7).

In the Bahai interpretation, human history has been dominated by spiritual cycles (sing. *dawr*) initiated by the periodic advent of a new prophet. Bahā'-Allāh interprets Koranic references to the resurrection day (*qīāma*) and the attainment of the presence of God (*leqā' Allāh*; see Koran 29:33, 18:110, 13:2, 2:46, 2:49) as symbolic allusions to the advent of a new manifestation of God (Bahā'-Allāh, *Ketāb-e īqān*, pp. 115-19). 'Abd-al-Bahā' taught that a great cycle in human religious history is characterized by three periods. The first is a series of manifestations of God which prepare for a universal theophany. The second period starts when the universal manifestation of God arrives and begins his dispensation. The third period within the great cycle is that of manifestations of God that succeed the universal manifestation. Although they can reveal new laws and abrogate his ordinances, they remain under his spiritual shadow. Adam (whom Bahais do not consider the first man) began the current cycle, in which the first, preparatory period extended from his time until the Bāb. Bahā'-Allāh was the universal manifestation for this cycle. After no less than a thousand years, further manifestations of God may arise, but their spiritual themes will start from Bahā'-Allāh's principles of the political and religious unification of the earth for human welfare ('Abd-al-Bahā', *Mofāważāt*, pp. 120-22; Bahā'-Allāh, *Aqdas*, pp. 38-39).

Social principles. Bahaism sees itself as primarily preaching the unity of mankind, and criticizes nationalist chauvinism and jingoism as productive of war. Bahā'-Allāh wrote, "The earth is but one country (*waṭan*), and mankind its citizens (*ahl-e ān*)" ("Lawḥ-e maqṣūd," in *Majmū'a-ī az alwāḥ*, p. 101; tr. p. 167). To unite the world Bahais advocate the adoption of a universal language, to be chosen by the leaders of the world ("Bešārāt," no. 3, "Kalemāt-e ferdowsīya," no. 8, *Majmū'a-ī az alwāḥ*, pp. 11, 37-38). Bahā'-Allāh charged the Universal House of Justice with promoting peace among the secular powers to avert exorbitant defense expenditures ("Lawḥ-e donyā" in *Majmūʿa-ī az alwāḥ*, p. 50; tr. p. 89). He urged the establishment of a world assembly of rulers to discuss peace and to prevent wars through collective security ("Lawḥ-e maqṣūd," in *Majmūʿa-ī az alwāḥ*, p. 99, tr. p. 165). Bahāʾ-Allāh apparently did not mean this internationalism to detract from loyalty to national governments, since he commanded obedience to government and attempted to make the Babi community less radical ("Bešārāt," nos. 4, 5 in *Majmūʿa-ī az alwāḥ*, pp. 11-12). Bahāʾ-Allāh did not, however, simply approve of the governments in power; despite both Ottoman and Qajar opposition to the principle, he advocated constitutional monarchy on the British model as a means of restraining tyranny ("Bešārāt," no. 15, pp. 13-14).

ʿAbd-al-Bahāʾ in his journeys to Europe and North America 1910-13 often listed the basic principles of Bahaism. A typical listing is (1) the independent investigation of reality (*taḥarrī-e ḥaqīqat*, the opposite of *taqlīd* or blind imitation), (2) the unity of mankind, (3) religion must be a source of unity and harmony, otherwise a lack of religion would be preferable, (4) religion and science complement one another, (5) religious, racial, political, and nationalist prejudices are destructive of human society, (6) equal rights for all human beings, (7) greater equality of income distribution (*taʿdīl-e maʿīšat*) so that none would be needy, (8) world peace through the foundation of an international court of arbitration that would settle disputes, (9) the separation of religion from politics, (10) education and advancement for women, (11) the inculcation of spiritual virtues and ethics to complement material civilization (ʿAbd-al-Bahāʾ, *Keṭābāt ḥażrat ʿAbd-al-Bahāʾ fī Awrobbā wa Amrīkā* I, Cairo, 1921, repr. Karachi, 1980, pp. 30-32). Shoghi Effendi elaborated at length on the Bahai conception of world government in his letters of the 1930s, published as *World Order of Bahā'u'llāh* (2nd, rev. ed., Wilmette, Ill., 1974).

Laws and ethics. The basic book of laws in Bahaism is the Arabic *al-Ketāb al-aqdas*, though it is supplemented by a number of other works. Laws of ritual pollution are abolished, and peoples of other religions are decreed ritually pure, unlike the case in Twelver Shiʿism (*Aqdas*, pp. 79-81). Believers are commanded to consort with the followers of all religions with amity and concord (p. 144). If someone shows anger to a Bahai and torments him, the Bahai must respond with kindness and lack of opposition (p. 152). Believers are forbidden to carry arms except when necessary (p. 157). The *Aqdas* makes it incumbent on believers to engage in productive work, interdicting begging (pp. 32-33). It insists on meticulous cleanliness and polite manners (*laṭāfa*; pp. 50-51). Slander and backbiting are forbidden (pp. 22). It is mandatory for parents to arrange for the education of both male and female children (pp. 52-53). Repentance for misdeeds is commended, but only in private and not before a clergyman (p. 53; Bahāʾ-Allāh, "Bešārāt," in *Majmūʿa-ī az alwāḥ*, p. 12). Listening to music is allowed, and is recommended as a means of spiritual advance (*Aqdas*, pp. 53-54). Holy war (*jehād*) is forbidden ("Bešārāt," p. 10).

The *Aqdas* forbids the imbibing of intoxicants and use of opium, as well as gambling (pp. 120, 153-54). It prohibits murder and adultery (p. 22). It prescribes banishment and imprisonment for theft, and the tattooing of an identifying mark on the forehead of third-time offenders (pp. 48-49). Wounding or striking another person is punishable by a set of fines, depending on the severity of the injury (p. 60). There is also a fine (*dīa*) to be paid to the victim's family for manslaughter (p. 185). The minimum penalty for arson and first-degree murder is life imprisonment; the maximum for arson is to be burned, the maximum for murder is execution (pp. 64-64). Slavery is forbidden (p. 75). All believers must leave a will (p. 111).

Marriage is enjoined; the *Aqdas* permits two wives, but recommends only one and ʿAbd-al-Bahāʾ later interpreted this verse to allow only one wife. The consent of both individuals and the permission of all four parents is required, as is the payment of a limited dowry by the man (pp. 64-67). It is permitted to marry non-Bahais (Bahāʾ-Allāh, *Resāla-ye soʾāl o jawāb*, Iran National Bahai Archives, no. 63, Tehran, n.d., p. 36). Adultery is punishable by a fine which doubles with each offense, payable to the house of justice (*Aqdas*, p. 53). Divorce is allowed but only after a year of patience is waited out during which no conjugal relations take place. Remarriage is permitted (pp. 70-73). It is forbidden to marry one's father's widow, and homosexuality is prohibited (pp. 110-11).

Believers are to pay a nineteen-percent religious tax on gold and on profits beyond expenses, called the *ḥoqūq Allāh* (the right of God; pp. 100-01). In addition, *zakāt*, another religious tax, is to be paid, in accordance with the laws of the Koran (p. 145).

Religious rituals and observances. Like Bahai administration, Bahai religious observances have evolved over time. For the sake of brevity, these will be discussed in terms of twentieth-century practice, and only widely practiced or central rituals will be surveyed. There are four basic sorts of daily ritual. The *Aqdas* prescribes the private recitation by individuals of verses revealed by Bahāʾ-Allāh every morning and evening (p. 149; *Soʾāl o jawāb*, p. 30). In addition, believers are to go to a central place of worship (*mašreq al-aḏkār*) between dawn and two hours after sunrise to recite and listen to prayers (*monājāt*; *Aqdas*, p. 116; *Soʾāl o jawāb*, pp. 7-8). Aside from these supplicatory prayers, believers are to pray an obligatory prayer (*ṣalāt*, *namāz*) after ablutions (*wożūʾ*). Bahāʾ-Allāh set down three different obligatory prayers, a long one with prostrations to be said once in twenty-four hours, a middle prayer to be said three times a day, and a short prayer to be said once a day. Believers may choose any one of these to say individually. Congregational *ṣalāt* is forbidden, as are pulpits (sing. *menbar*). The believer must face the *qebla* (point of adoration) while performing the obligatory prayer, which is fixed as Bahāʾ-Allāh's resting place. It is not necessary to face the *qebla* when saying other sorts of prayer (*Aqdas*, pp. 152-53, *So'āl o jawāb*, pp. 29-30; Ešrāq Ḵāvarī, ed., *Ganjīna*, pp. 11-33). Finally, once a day believers should seat themselves facing the *qelba* and repeat the greatest name of God, *Allāho abhā*, ninety-five times (*Aqdas*, pp. 21-22). Another important ritual prayer is the *ṣalāt* for the dead, which is the only sort of *ṣalāt* Bahā'-Allāh permitted to be said in congregation; it is almost identical with that set down by the Bāb in the *Bayān* (*wāḥed* 5, *bāb* 11) (Ešrāq Ḵāvarī, ed., *Ganjīna*, pp. 136-41).

The Bahai calendar (*Badīʿ*, q.v.), originating with the Bāb, consists of nineteen months of nineteen days each, in addition to a short intercalary period. At the beginning of each Bahai month, Bahais are to gather in the nineteen day feast (*żīāfat-e nūzdah rūza*), discussed above under administration, where the only approximation to a ritual is the reading by lay believers of passages from scripture. The *Aqdas* instructed that the intercalary days be placed just before the last month, the month of fasting (*ʿAlāʾ*). Bahais are to fast (*ṣīām*) from the age of maturity (15), from sunrise to sunset for nineteen days. Since the Bahai calendar is a solar one, the fasting month always falls just before the vernal equinox. The intercalary days (*ayyām-e hā*) are set aside as a time of gift giving and feasting. The fast usually ends on 20 March, and the vernal equinox (Nowrūz) starts the new year (pp. 18-21, 126). Nowrūz is one of nine Bahai holy days on which work must be suspended. Bahais hold festive gatherings on these days. They include the anniversaries of the birth of the Bāb and of Bahā'-Allāh (celebrated on 1 and 2 Moḥarram in the Middle East, and on 20 October and 12 November in the rest of the world), and the first, ninth, and twelfth days of Reżwān, the twelve-day (April 21-May 2) festival celebrating Bahā'-Allāh's declaration of his mission in Baghdad (pp. 112-15; *So'āl o jawāb*, pp. 1-2). The other holy days are the declaration of the Bāb, the martyrdom of the Bāb, and the "ascension" (*ṣoʿūd*) of Bahā'-Allāh (texts relating to these holy days have been collected by Ešrāq Ḵāvarī in *Resāla-ye ayyām-e tesʿa*).

Pilgrimage (hajj) is required of financially able male believers once in a lifetime either to the house of the Bāb in Shiraz or the house of Bahā'-Allāh in Baghdad (*Aqdas*, p. 32; *So'āl o jawāb*, p. 15; Ešrāq-Ḵāvarī, ed., *Ganjīna*, pp. 67-71). Even before setting down the *Aqdas*, Bahā'-Allāh wrote out tablets containing instructions for the performance of the pilgrimage, and had Moḥammad "Nabīl" Zarandī perform the rites at the house of the Bāb. These include the paring of nails, ablutions, the recitation of special verses, and circumambulation. But problems of security prevented subsequent performance of the rites. At present, the pilgrimage is not undertaken, given the persecution of Bahais in Iraq and the destruction of the house of the Bāb by the revolutionary government in Iran in 1979. Visitation (*zīārat*) often psychologically took its place, many believers simply visiting the house of the Bāb in Shiraz, the house of Bahā'-Allāh in Baghdad, or the Bahai properties in Edirne, Turkey, and Haifa and ʿAkkā (now in Israel). A nine-day visitation to the Bahai shrines in Haifa and ʿAkkā has become common among Bahais who can afford it.

Bibliography: Most of the published primary sources for Bahaism are cited in the article. A large number of community histories of Bahais in various parts of Iran are in mss. in Iranian archives and at the International Bahā'i Archives in Haifa. An important biographical dictionary of Iranian Bahais is ʿAzīz-Allāh Solaymānī, *Maṣābīḥ-e hedāyat*, 8 vols., Tehran, 1964-68?. For the relatives of the Bāb who became Bahais see Moḥammad-ʿAlī Fayżī, *Ḵāndān-e afnān*, Tehran, 127 *Badīʿ*/1970. For Bahai doctrines see ʿA. Ešrāq Ḵāvarī, *Moḥāżerāt*, Tehran, 120 *Badīʿ*/1963. Much primary material was printed in the English-Persian periodical, *Star of the West*, Chicago and Washington, D.C., 1910-33. Volumes of the official Bahai yearbooks, *The Bahá'í World*, cited above, often contain documents of a primary nature. An important Western travel account of the Bahais in nineteenth-century Iran is E. G. Browne, *A Year Amongst the Persians*, London, 1893, and other material (mostly hostile) relating to Bahai history is in Browne's *Materials for the Study of the Bábí Religion*, Cambridge, 1918. Diplomatic and missionary documents have been published in Momen, *The Bábí and Bahá'í Religions*, cited above.

A glossary of Bahai terms is Mīrzā Asad-Allāh Fāżel Māzandarānī, *Asrār al-āṯār*, 5 vols., Tehran, 1967-72. Some material for Bahai history is also in the same author's *Tārīḵ-e żohūr al-ḥaqq*, vol. 8, pts. 1 and 2, Tehran, 131-32 *Badīʿ*/1975-76. General histories of the Babi and Bahai movements are Mīrzā Abu'l-Fażl Golpāyeganī and Mīrzā Mehdī Golpāyeganī, *Kašf al-ḡeṭāʾ*, Tashkent, 1919?; and ʿAbd-al-Ḥosayn Avāra, *al-Kawākeb al-dorrīya*, 2 vols., Cairo, 1923. See also for expositions of Bahai doctrine Mīrzā Abu'l-Fażl Golpāyeganī, *Ketāb al-farāʾeż*, Cairo, 1898, and *al-Dorar al-bahīya*, Cairo, 1900, tr. J. Cole, *Miracles and Metaphors*, Los Angeles, 1982; idem, *al-Ḥojaj al-bahīya*, Cairo, n.d., tr. ʿAlīqolī Khan, *Bahāʾī Proofs*, Chicago, 1914; Wilmette, Ill., 1984; Golpāyeganī's letters, cited above, are a primary source.

Academic work on the general history and global growth of Bahaism includes A. Bausani, "Bahā'īs," in *EI*[2], and idem, *Persia Religiosa da Zoroaster a Bahâ'u'llâh*, Milan, 1959; P. Smith, *The Bābī and Bahāʾī Religions: from Messianic Shīʿism to a World Religion*, Cambridge (forthcoming); P. Berger, "From Sect to Church: A Sociological Interpretation of the Bahai Movement," Ph.D. dissertation, New School for Social Research, New York, 1954; idem, "Motif messianique et processus social dans le Bahaisme," *Archives de sociologie des religions* 4, 1957, pp. 93-107; A. Hampson, "The Growth and Spread of the Bahā'i Faith," Ph.D. dissertation, University of Hawaii, 1980; V. Johnson, "An Historical Analysis of Critical Transformations" (cited above).

Further academic work on the history of Bahaism includes articles in M. Momen, ed., *Studies in Bábí and Bahá'í History* I, Los Angeles, 1982, and J. Cole and M. Momen, eds., *From Iran East and West: Studies in Bábí and Bahá'í History* II, Los Angeles, 1984, a continuing series of books: For the period 1863-92, see M. Momen, "Early Relations between Christian Missionaries and the Bábí and Bahā'í Communities," in *Studies* I, pp. 49-84; J. Cole, "Bahā'u'llāh and the Naqshbandī Sufis in Iraq, 1854-1856," ibid., II, pp. 1-30; M. Caton, "Bahā'í Influences on Mīrzā ʿAbdu'llāh, Qajar Court Musician and Master of the *Radīf*," ibid., II, pp. 31-66; S. Stiles, "Early Zoroastrian Conversions to the Bahā'ī Faith in Yazd, Iran," ibid., II, pp. 67-134; for the life of Bahā'-Allāh see H. M. Balyuzi, *Bahā'u'llāh*, Oxford, 1980. For ʿAbd-al-Bahā' see A. Bausani and D. MacEoin, "ʿAbd-al-Bahā'," in *EIr*. I, pp. 103-04; and H. M. Balyuzi, *ʿAbdu'l-Bahā': The Centre of the Covenant of Bahā'u'llāh*, Oxford, 1971. For Egypt in this period see J. Cole, "Rashid Rida on the Baha'i Faith: A Utilitarian Theory of the Spread of Religions," *Arab Studies Quarterly* 5, 1983, pp. 276-91. Academic work on the American Bahai community includes: W. Collins, "Kenosha 1893-1912: History of an Early Bahā'ī Community in the United States," in Momen, ed., *Studies SBBH* I, pp. 225-54; R. Hollinger, "Ibrahim George Kheiralla and the Bahā'ī Faith in America," ibid., II, pp. 95-134; P. Smith, "The American Bahā'ī Community, 1894-1917: A Preliminary Survey," ibid., I, pp. 85-224; P. Smith, "*Reality* Magazine: Editorship and Ownership of an American Bahā'ī Periodical," ibid., II, pp. 95-134; R. Stockman, *The Bahā'ī Faith in America 1892-1900*, Wilmette, Ill., 1985. For the Shoghi Effendi period see L. Bramson-Lerche, "Some Aspects of the Development of the Bahā'ī Administrative Order in America, 1922-1936," in Momen, ed., *Studies* I, pp. 255-300; and ʿA. Ešrāq K̲āvarī, *Raḥīq-e mak̲tūm*, 2 vols., Tehran, 103 *Badīʿ*/1946. For comments on Bahais in modern Yazd, Iran, see M. Fischer, "Zoroastrian Iran: Between Myth and Praxis," Ph.D. dissertation, University of Chicago, 1973. For Bahaism in India see W. Garlington, "The Bahai Faith in Malwa," in G. A. Oddie, ed., *Religion in South Asia*, Delhi, 1977; idem, "Bahā'i Conversions in Malwa, Central India," in Momen, ed., *Studies* II, pp. 157-88; idem, "The Bahá'í Faith in Malwa: The Study of a Contemporary Religious Movement," Ph.D. dissertation, Australian National University, 1975; and S. Garrigues, "The Bahá'í Faith in Malwa: Identity and Change Among the Urban Bahā'īs of Central India," Ph.D. dissertation, University of Lucknow, 1975. For the Bahai faith in West Africa see Anthony Lee, Ph.D. in progress, Univ. of California, Los Angeles. For Bahai religious observances see D. MacEoin, "Ritual and Semi-Ritual Observances in Bābism and Bahā'ism," paper presented at the 1980 Lancaster Conference on the Babi and Bahai faiths, Lancaster University, England.

There is a voluminous tertiary literature on Bahaism. Impartial writing about the Bahais in the Middle East is rare. Significant works, though critical, are ʿAbd-al-Razzāq Ḥasanī, *al-Bābīyūn wa'l-Bahā'īyūn fī mażāhem wa hāżerehem*, Sidon, 1957; and Aḥmad Kasrawī, *Bahā'īgarī*, Tehran, 1322 Š./1943. Christian polemics against Bahaism are W. Miller, *The Bahā'ī Faith: Its History and Teachings*, South Pasadena, CA, 1974; J. R. Richards, *The Religion of the Bahā'īs*, London, 1932; and S. G. Wilson, *Bahā'ism and its Claims*, New York, 1915, 1970. Intelligent surveys of Bahaism by Western converts with little training in Middle East studies include J. Esslemont, *Bahá'u'lláh and the New Era*, London, 1923; J. Ferraby, *All Things Made New*, London, 1957; and W. Hatcher and D. Martin, *The Bahá'í Faith: The Emerging Global Religion*, San Francisco, 1984.

(J. COLE)

ii. BAHAI CALENDAR AND FESTIVALS

The notion of renewal of time, implicit in most religious dispensations, is made explicit in the writings of the Bāb (q.v.) and Bahā'-Allāh (q.v.). To give this spiritual metaphor a concrete frame and to signalize the importance of the dispensation which he came to herald, the Bāb inaugurated a new calendar. In a significant break with the Islamic system, he abandoned the lunar month and adopted the solar year, commencing with the astronomically fixed vernal equinox (March 21), the ancient Persian new year festival of Now Rūz (q.v.; Persian *Bayān* 6:14). Bahā'-Allāh confirmed this calendar in *al-Ketāb al-aqdas* (40:258-60; see AQDAS), and ʿAbd-al-Bahā' (q.v.) set the final number of Bahai holy days, i.e., festivals and commemorative days on which work is suspended, at nine per year. The Bahai year (see BADĪʿ) consists of 19 months of 19 days each, i.e., 361 days, with the addition of four intercalary days (five in leap years) between the 18th and the 19th months in order to adjust the calendar to the solar year. The Bāb named the months after the attributes of God. The original Arabic names and their accepted English equivalents and correspondence dates to the Gregorian calendar are as follows:

Month	Arabic name	Translation	First days
1st	Bahā'	Splendor	March 21
2nd	Jalāl	Glory	April 9
3rd	Jamāl	Beauty	April 28
4th	ʿAẓamat	Grandeur	May 27
5th	Nūr	Light	June 5
6th	Raḥmat	Mercy	June 24
7th	Kalemāt	Words	July 13
8th	Kamāl	Perfection	August 1
9th	Asmā'	Names	August 29
10th	ʿEzzat	Might	September 8
11th	Mašīyat	Will	September 27
12th	ʿElm	Knowledge	October 16
13th	Qodrat	Power	November 4
14th	Qawl	Speech	November 23
15th	Masā'el	Questions	December 12
16th	Šaraf	Honor	December 31
17th	Solṭān	Sovereignty	January 19th
18th	Molk	Dominion	February 7th
19th	ʿOlā	Loftiness	March 2nd

The intercalary days are February 26 to March 1 inclusive. The 19th month is designated as the month of fasting.

The nine holy days are: (1) festival of Now Rūz (New Year), March 21; (2) 1st day of the festival of Reżwān (Declaration of Bahā'-Allāh) April 21; (3) 9th day of the festival of Reżwān, April 29; (4) 12th day of the festival of Reżwān, May 2; (5) declaration of the Bāb, May 23; (6) ascension of Bahā'-Allāh, May 29; (7) martyrdom of the Bāb, July 9; (8) birth of the Bāb, October 20; (9) birth of Bahā'-Allāh, November 12.

Bibliography: The Bāb, *Bayān-e fārsī*, n.d., n.p. Bahā'-Allāh, *Ketāb-e aqdas*, Bombay, 1908. Shoghi Effendi, *God Passes By*, Willmette, Ill., 1944. 'Abd-al-Ḥamīd Ešrāq Ḵāvarī, *Ayyām-e tes'a*, Tehran, 1947.

(A. Banani)

iii. Bahai and Babi Schisms

Although it never developed much beyond the stage of a sectarian movement within Shi'ite Islam, Babism experienced a number of minor but interesting divisions, particularly in its early phase. The first of these involved the defection of three of the earliest converts of the Bāb, led by Mollā Javād Valīānī, who transferred their allegiance to Mollā Moḥammad Karīm Khan Kermānī (q.v.) as the authentic head of the Shaikhi school (q.v.). Although the scale of this defection was small, it did have repercussions on the Babi community at Karbalā', whose leader, Fāṭema Baragānī (Qorrat-al-'Ayn; q.v.), a maternal cousin of Valīānī, wrote a refutation of his allegations against the Bāb. Valīānī's concern centered on what he perceived as the Bāb's break with the more conservative wing of Shaikhism. By thus distancing themselves from the Bāb's claims, he and those who supported him helped sharpen the growing sense of division within the Shaikhi ranks and encouraged the Bāb and his followers to demonstrate a clearer identity for themselves. (See MacEoin, "From Shaykhism," pp. 199-203.)

A more serious split occurred soon after this at Karbalā' itself, where Qorrat-al-'Ayn and a probable majority of the Babis of the region came into conflict with Mollā Aḥmad Ḵorāsānī and his supporters. The issues involved in this dispute were complex (and are dealt with in contemporary materials written by the chief participants), but the central point of contention appears to have been the status accorded Qorrat-al-'Ayn and other Letters of the Living (*ḥorūf al-ḥayy*; see BABISM). As with Valīānī, Ḵorāsānī's principal worry was that the Bāb and his chief followers were claiming (or, in the case of the former, having claimed for him) a quasi-divine status out of keeping with a more conservative Shi'ite interpretation. This quarrel appears not to have been fully resolved before Qorrat-al-'Ayn was forced to leave Karbalā' for Baghdad and, eventually, Iran. (See MacEoin, "From Shaykhism," pp. 203-07.)

Apart from her dispute with Ḵorāsānī, Qorrat-al-'Ayn came into conflict with other Babis over her radical interpretations of doctrine, in particular her tendency to push for the abolition of the Islamic religious Law (*šarī'a*). Something of this division seems to have surfaced during the famous Babi conclave held at Badašt in Māzandarān in the summer of 1847, when Qorrat-al-'Ayn led an abolitionist party in opposition to a poorly-defined group who resisted such a radical development. There are indications that a wider split occurred between the radicals at Badašt and the followers of Mollā Ḥosayn Bošrū'ī (q.v.) at Shaikh Ṭabarsī (see *Noqṭat al-kāf*, pp. 153-54, 155).

After the Bāb's death in 1850 and the death or dispersal of most of the Babi leadership, divisions of a more complex nature occurred within the surviving community. In Iran and in Baghdad, where a core of sect members took up residence under the leadership of Mīrzā Yaḥyā Nūrī Ṣobḥ-e Azal (q.v.), over twenty individuals made separate claims to some form of divine inspiration, usually based on the ability to compose verses (*āyāt*). Most notable among these was the Azerbaijan-based Mīrzā Asad-Allāh Ḵo'ī Dayyān, whose followers became known as Dayyānīs. His movement was short-lived, however, ending after his assassination in 1856. The divisions of this period culminated in the increasingly bitter dispute between Ṣobḥ-e Azal and his half-brother Mīrzā Ḥosayn-'Alī Bahā'-Allāh (q.v.). From about 1866, this leadership quarrel hardened into a permanent division between Azalī and Bahai Babis. (See MacEoin, "Divisions and Authority Claims.")

The history of Bahaism as a distinct movement is punctuated by divisions of varying severity, usually occurring as responses to the death of one of the religion's leaders. It has become an article of faith in modern Bahai circles that the religion is protected from schism by the Covenant system of authoritative succession (see below). This has led to a strong emphasis on orthodoxy, with a tendency to play down or even ignore present or past divisions. Thus, "There are no Bahá'í sects. There never can be" (Hofman, *Renewal*, p. 110). At the same time, it should be stressed that there is a high degree of cohesion within the movement and that the authority of the mainstream Bahai leadership is seldom challenged.

Following the death of Bahā'-Allāh in Palestine in 1892, a serious clash took place between his two oldest sons, 'Abbās (see 'ABD-AL-BAHĀ') and Mīrzā Moḥammad-'Ali. It was accepted that, in his will, Bahā'-Allāh had appointed 'Abbās his successor and interpreter of the holy text, in keeping with traditional Shi'ite notions of vicegerency (*weṣāya*). But Moḥammad-'Alī and his partisans accused 'Abd-al-Bahā' of making excessive claims for himself. Since 'Abd-al-Bahā''s real claims seem to have been quite limited, it is likely that his opponents were really objecting to his somewhat radical interpretations of Bahai doctrine, particularly his social and political theories. Moḥammad-'Alī and his supporters (who included most of Bahā'-Allāh's family) termed themselves Ahl al-tawḥīd or Mowaḥḥedūn and were dominant for some time in Syria. 'Abd-al-Bahā' drew his support chiefly from Bahais in Iran and, increasingly from the late 1890s, from the growing community in the United States, where a cult based on his personality was developed. His eventual success is attributed by Berger to his ability to sustain charismatic appeal within the new movement ("Motif messianique," p. 102; conflicting versions of the quarrel may be found in Browne, *Materials*, pp. 72-112 and Balyuzi, *'Abdu'l-Bahā*, pp. 50-61).

The split did, however, extend into America eventually, following the defection to Moḥammad-ʿAlī of Ibrahim George Kheiralla, the first Bahai missionary to that country. By 1899, the American Bahai community was divided into two factions: a majority of those loyal to ʿAbd-al-Bahāʾ and a minority of "Behaists." In 1900, Kheiralla founded a Society of Behaists, with himself as its Chief Spiritual Guide and with Churches of the Manifestation in Chicago and Kenosha. The Behaist faction was later reorganized as the National Association of the Universal Religion, but the number of its adherents dwindled rapidly, particularly after the successful visits to North America made by ʿAbd-al-Bahāʾ between 1911 and 1913. In Palestine, the followers of Moḥammad-ʿAlī continued as a small group of families opposed to the Bahai leadership in Haifa; they have now been almost wholly re-assimilated into Muslim society (see Cohen, "Bahá'í Community of Acre").

Mainstream Bahaism, as represented by ʿAbd-al-Bahāʾ and his followers, responded to the challenge of factionalism by emphasizing the doctrinal ideal of a Covenant (*ʿahd, mīṯāq*) designating a single individual head of the faith *markaz al-mīṯāq* "Center of the Covenant"), to whom all believers were to render unquestioning obedience. The centrality of the Covenant system first became apparent in 1917-18 in the course of the Chicago Reading Room Affair, during which a group of dissenting Bahais in Chicago were expelled from the main body. (See Smith, "American Baha'i Community," pp. 189-94.)

Under the leadership of Shoghi Effendi (q.v., 1921-1957), the Bahai movement underwent radical structural changes with the creation of a tightly-controlled administrative organization modeled on modern Western management systems. Challenges to Shoghi Effendi's authority or that of the bodies under him were in numerous cases met by the excommunication of groups or individuals as Covenant-Breakers (*nāqeżu'l-mīṯāq*). The only significant breakaway groups to emerge during this period, however, were the New History Society based in New York around the anti-organization views of Ahmad Sohrab and Julie Chanler (see Johnson, "Historical Analysis," pp. 311-18), and the German Bahai World Union which re-emerged after World War II as the World Union for Universal Religion and Universal Peace and the Free Bahais of Stuttgart. In the East, dissent tended to be even more individual, taking the form of personal defections from the movement rather than organized groupings. Faeg's Scientific Society founded in Egypt about 1923 was atypical. Since all of the schismatic groups of this period found their raison d'être in the rejection of religious organization, it was inevitable that they should be short-lived and restricted in their influence.

The death of Shoghi Effendi in 1957 presented the movement with a potential crisis of major proportions, but also allowed the administrative system established by him to demonstrate its widespread acceptance within the community at large. Between 1957 and 1963 (when a universal House of Justice, *bayt al-ʿadl-e aʿẓam* [q.v.], was elected), the religion had no leader. Shoghi had had no children, had excommunicated his entire family, and had failed to designate any other successor. From about 1958, Charles Mason Remey, President of the International Baha'i Council, began to oppose the notion that there could be no successor to the Bahai Guardianship (*welāya*), and in 1960 he declared himself to be the second Guardian of the Bahai Faith. Under Remey's leadership, a minority group organized themselves successively as the Bahais under the Guardianship, Bahais under the Hereditary Guardianship, and the Orthodox Abha World Faith, with its headquarters in Santa Fe (see Johnson, pp. 342-80). Remey died in 1974, having appointed a third Guardian, but the number of adherents to the Orthodox faction remains extremely small. Although successful in Pakistan, the Remeyites seem to have attracted no followers in Iran. Other small groups have broken away from the main body from time to time, but none of these has attracted a sizeable following.

Bibliography: H. M. Balyuzi, *'Abdu'l-Bahá*, London, 1971. P. Berger, *From Sect to Church: A Sociological Interpretation of the Baha'i Movement*, Ph.D. dissertation, New School for Social Research, 1954. Idem, "Motif messianique et processus social dans le Baha'isme," *Archives de sociologie des religions* 4, 1957, pp. 93-107. E. G. Browne, ed., *Materials for the Study of the Bábí Religion*, Cambridge, 1918. E. Cohen, "The Bahá'í Community of Acre," *Folklore Research Center Studies* 3, Jerusalem, 1972, pp. 119-41. D. Hofman, *The Renewal of Civilization*, London, 1960. R. Hollinger, "Ibrahim George Kheiralla and the Bahá'í Faith in America," in J. Cole and M. Momen, eds., *From Iran East and West: Studies in Bábí and Bahá'í History* II, Los Angeles, 1984, pp. 95-133. V. E. Johnson, *An Historical Analysis of Critical Transformations in the Evolution of the Baha'i World Faith*, Ph.D. dissertation, Baylor University, 1974, esp. pp. 241-51, 306-21, 342-80, 410-15.

Ḥājī Mīrzā Jānī Kāšānī, *Ketāb-e Noqṭat al-Kāf*, ed. E. G. Browne, Leiden and London, 1910. D. MacEoin, *From Shaykhism to Babism: A Study in Charismatic Renewal in Shiʿi Islam*, Ph.D. dissertation, Cambridge University, 1979. Idem, "Divisions and Authority Claims in the Bābī Community, 1850-1866," unpublished paper. W. McE. Miller, *The Baha'i Faith: Its History and Teachings*, South Pasadena, 1974, pp. 173-85, 198-201, 260-68, 274-77, 310-23. P. Smith, *A Sociological Study of the Babi and Baha'i Religions*, Ph.D. dissertation, Lancaster University, 1982, pp. 285-86, 313-16, 321-25, 330-38, 343-48. Idem, "The American Bahá'í Community, 1894-1917: A Preliminary Survey," in M. Momen, ed., *Studies in Bábí and Bahá'í History* I, Los Angeles, 1982, pp. 85-223. A. Sohrab, *Broken Silence*, New York, 1942. Idem, *Abdul Baha's Grandson: Story of a Twentieth Century Excommunication*, New York, 1943. R. White, *The Bahai Religion and its Enemy, the Bahai Organization*, Rutland, Vt., 1929.

(D. M. MacEoin)

iv. The Bahai Communities

The development of the Bahai faith (q.v.) has been accompanied by a massive transformation of the religion's social base. From being a religion predominantly composed of those of Iranian Shiʿite background, it has become a worldwide movement comprising people of a multitude of religious and national backgrounds. Of the contemporary Bahai population, probably fewer than one in ten are Iranians.

Overall pattern of Bahai expansion. A distinctive Bahai community may be said to have come into being during the 1860s and 1870s following the open rupture between the leaders of the Babi movement. Mīrzā Ḥosayn-ʿAlī Nūrī Bahāʾ-Allāh (1817-92) had already begun to successfully reanimate and coordinate the various Babi communities in Iran and Iraq. When he laid claim to be the promised one of Babism (1866), his message was widely accepted. Most Babis became Bahais, only a minority siding with Bahāʾ-Allāh's half-brother, Ṣobḥ-e Azal (see azali babism). Well coordinated, the emerging Iranian Bahai community possessed considerable dynamism. Successful missionary activity was soon undertaken, not only amongst Iran's Shiʿite majority, but also amongst the Jewish and Zoroastrian minorities (from the 1880s). Further afield, small Bahai communities were established in Turkey, Syria, Egypt, India, and Asiatic Russia, mostly amongst expatriate Iranians.

Bahai expansion beyond the Middle East and the Iranian diaspora only began after the passing of Bahāʾ-Allāh (1892) and the succession of his son, ʿAbd-al-Bahāʾ (1844-1921), as leader. In the 1890s, an active community developed in North America, Americans in turn establishing Bahai groups in England, France, Germany, Hawaii, and Japan. Groups were also later established in Australia and New Zealand. Western Bahais also traveled widely in the Middle East, India, and Latin America, significantly contributing to the sense of the world community among the Bahais.

Plans for a systematic global expansion of the Bahai religion had been outlined by ʿAbd-al-Bahāʾ, most clearly in his *Tablets of the Divine Plan* (1916-17). However, it was only under the leadership of his grandson, Shoghi Effendi Rabbani (1897-1957), that such plans were actually implemented on any large scale. Devoting the early years of his ministry to consolidating and standardizing the system of Bahai administration (1922-early 1930s), Shoghi Effendi then employed this administration as a means of securing systematic expansion, at first only in selected countries, through a series of national and regional Bahai plans (1937-53), and then globally in an international Ten Year Crusade (1953-63). This approach has been continued since Shoghi Effendi's death (1957), with a series of Nine, Five, Seven, and Six Year Plans (1964-73; 1974-79; 1979-86; 1986-92). The resultant expansion has led to Bahai communities being established in most countries of the world.

Expansion and distribution. Some indication of the extent of Bahai expansion can be gained from the statistics in Table 13. These figures indicate a slow rate of expansion during the 1928-52 period, rapid growth only occurring after 1952 and the introduction of international teaching plans. Other indices of expansion include the growth in the number of languages in which Bahai literature is produced, from 8 or so in 1928, to 70 in 1953, and 757 in 1986, and in the number of tribal and ethnic groups represented in the community, from 42 in 1952 to over 2,100 in 1986 (see *Bahá'í World* II, pp. 193-210; XII, pp. 775-827); Shoghi Effendi, *The Bahá'í Faith, 1844-1952*; and Universal House of Justice, Department of Statistics, *The Seven Year Plan, Statistical Report, Riḍván 1986*).

In terms of total numbers, the official Bahai estimate in April, 1985, was that there were in the region of 4.7 million Bahais worldwide. In terms of distribution, fifty-nine percent of the Bahai world total live in Asia, twenty percent in Africa, eighteen percent in the Americas, 1.6 percent in Australasia and 0.5 percent in Europe. There are relatively few Bahais in the Communist world and little organized activity is permitted. (See Table 14.)

The areas of Bahai expansion can be divided into three separate "worlds": the Islamic heartland in which the religion first developed (the Middle East, North Africa, and Asiatic Russia); the West (North America, Western Europe, Australia, and New Zealand); and the Bahai "Third World" (including the Far East; Smith, *Bábí and Bahá'í Religions*, pp. 162-71). In these terms, there has been a marked change in the distribution of Bahais during the present century. Taking the distribution of local Bahai Spiritual Assemblies as a measure of change, in 1945, out of a total of 505 Assemblies, the majority, sixty-one percent, were in the Islamic heartland (mostly in Iran), twenty-nine percent were in the West (mostly in the U.S.A.), and only ten percent were in the Bahai Third World (mostly in India and Latin America). By 1983, however, out of a total of 24,714 Assemblies, the figures were respectively two, eleven, and seventy-eight percent (calculated from *Bahá'í World* X, pp. 551-82; and Universal House of Justice, Department of Statistics, *The Seven Year Plan, 1979-1986, Statistical Report 1983*). Although the Assembly distribution figures underrepresent the larger local Bahai communities (such as those in Iran), the overall trend is clear. As a consequence of the international teaching plans of the last thirty years, the Bahai Faith has become a predominantly non-Islamic Third World religion.

Table 13

SELECTED BAHAI STATISTICS, 1928-1986

Year	1928	1952	1964	1986
Bahai localities	579	2,425	15,186	116,707
Local Spiritual Assemblies	102	611	4,566	32,854
National Spiritual Assemblies	9	9	56	148

Sources: *Bahá'í World* II, pp. 189-91; Shoghi Effendi, *The Bahá'í Faith, 1844-1952: Information Statistical and Comparative* (London: Bahá'í Publishing Trust, 1953); Universal House of Justice, *The Bahá'í Faith: Statistical Information, 1844-1968* (Haifa: Bahá'í World Centre, 1968); Universal House of Justice, Department of Statistics, *The Seven Year Plan, 1977-1986: Statistical Report, Riḍván 1986* (Haifa: Bahá'í World Centre, 1986), pp. 37, 38, 45.

Table 14

SELECTED BAHAI STATISTICS, APRIL 1986

Total numbers (in 1,000s)	World Total 4,739	Africa 969	Americas 857	Asia 2,807	Australasia 84	Europe 22
National Spiritual Assemblies	148	43	41	27	17	20
Countries where the Bahai Faith is established:						
—Independent countries	166	51	35	37	11	32
—Dependent territories or overseas departments	48	6	16	3	13	10
Local Spiritual Assemblies	32,854	7,258	6,500	17,524	857	715
Localities where Bahais reside	116,707	35,657	26,570	48,730	2,902	2,848

Sources: Department of Statistics, *The Seven Year Plan, Statistical Report, Riḍván 1986* (Haifa: Bahá'í World Centre, 1986), pp. 37, 38, 41, 45, 49.

The Bahai communities of the Islamic heartland: 1. Iran. During the years of their initial expansion, the Babis had succeeded in establishing a widespread network of groups in most Iranian cities and in rural areas in several different regions, but after the Bāb's execution (1850), the Babi groups and network had become fragmented. Bahā'-Allāh's recoordination of these groups during the late 1850s and the 1860s provided the basis for the emergence of the Bahai religion as a social entity. Utilizing itinerant Bahai couriers and teachers, Bahā'-Allāh and ʿAbd-al-Bahā' (acting increasingly as chief organizer for his father) created a viable Iranian Bahai community, whilst the efficient and widespread distribution of Bahā'-Allāh's major writings provided the basis for doctrinal unity.

Commitment to missionary expansion was strong. Bahai groups were established in areas such as Gīlān and the Persian Gulf coast which the Babis had not reached. New converts were gained among the Shiʿite population, including men of considerable ability and prominence such as Mīrzā Abu'l-Fażl Golpāyegānī (q.v.), converted in 1876. Contacts were established with members of the Jewish and Zoroastrian minorities, and significant numbers of conversions made from the 1880s onwards, particularly in Hamadān and Yazd. Of major population groups, only the nomadic tribes and the Sunni and Christian minorities remained effectively beyond the reach of Bahai missions.

In terms of social class, both the existing "Babi" membership and the new converts represented a wide-ranging diversity. European observers noted the particular success which the Bahai missionaries enjoyed among the educated classes, but craftsmen, urban workers, and peasants were also well-represented. In contrast to Babism, relatively few clerics were converted: The *ʿolamā'* now had a well-defined and negative image of the Babi-Bahai movement, and were thus more resistant to its message. Correspondingly, Bahai merchants assumed greater prominence in the leadership of the movement within Iran; Bahai *ʿolamā'*, however, remained important. Bahai women also assumed importance within the community, the successful "familialization" of the religion providing a major basis for its social consolidation.

Reflecting the activity of the Bahai community, there was a recrudescence of persecution. Thus, throughout the Qajar period, there were sporadic attacks on the Bahais, a number being killed, and many more being despoiled of their property. Religious animosity towards the Bahais as unbelievers was an important motivation here, particularly for the clerics who led most of the attacks. Other factors were also involved, however. Thus, whilst increasing numbers of the Qajar elite perceived that the universalistic and pacific policies of Bahā'-Allāh contrasted sharply with the militancy of the Babis, there was an understandable tendency to confuse the two movements, and hence to regard the Bahais as potentially seditious. (For an indication of changing attitudes amongst later Qajar officials, see Amīn-al-Solṭān's statement in Momen, *Bábí and Bahá'í Religions*, pp. 358-59). Again, certain local clerical and civil leaders readily used persecution of Bahais to secure their own financial or political advantage. The execution in 1879 of two Bahai merchants who were creditors to Mīr Moḥammad-Ḥosayn, Imam Jom'a of Isfahan, assumed particular notoriety in this regard (Momen, ibid., pp. 274-77). Persecutions increased as popular agitation against the Qajar regime mounted, a widespread series of attacks occurring in 1903 (ibid., pp. 373-404).

Bahai expansion within Iran appears to have reached its peak in the early decades of the present century. Thereafter, it has had to rely increasingly on natural increase, so that whilst the number of Bahais in Iran has recently been in the region of 300-350,000, this represents less than one percent of the total population. At the beginning of the century, by contrast, the percentage may have been as high as 2.5 (Smith, "Bábí and Bahá'í Numbers in Iran," pp. 296-98). Lack of research precludes a proper analysis of this decline.

Overt persecution of the Bahais during the Pahlavi period (1925-79) was limited, outbreaks occurring in 1926, 1944, and 1955, in this later case with the government's active support. At the same time, Bahais were denied full civil rights. They were unable to contract legal marriage, freely publish literature, or publicly defend themselves against the well-organized propaganda campaign which their opponents mounted against them. The Bahai schools, as the schools of other religious minorities, were closed in 1934.

Under the Islamic Republic (from 1979), the Bahai situation has markedly worsened. Regarding the Bahais as heretics, Zionist agents, and anti-revolutionary subversives, the regime has actively pursued persecution of the Bahais. Over 200 have been killed; hundreds have been imprisoned; thousands have been purged from government employment. Bahai students and school children have been expelled from educational institutions. Community and individual properties and assets have been seized. All Bahai organizations have been disbanded. And all Bahai activities have been forbidden. The situation is bleak. (For sources on the current wave of persecution see the bibliography.)

2. Turkestan and Caucasia. The consolidation of Russian rule in Turkestan (Transcaspia) and its consequent economic development encouraged Iranian immigration during the 1880s. Bahais were amongst these immigrants, and by 1890, there were about one thousand of them in the new provincial capital of Ashkhabad (Lee, "Bahá'í Community of 'Ishqábád," pp. 1-13). In 1889, Shi'ite militants murdered a prominent Bahai. The Russian authorities' trial and imprisonment of the assailants was hailed by the Bahais as the first occasion on which judicial punishment had been meted out to their persecutors. Henceforth the Bahai community in Turkestan flourished, Ashkhabad providing a convenient refuge from persecution in Iran. Increasingly prosperous, the Bahais were able to establish their own meeting hall, kindergartens, elementary schools, clinic, libraries, and public reading rooms. A magazine, *K̲ᵛoršīd-e k̲āvar* (Sun of the East), and printing presses were also established, and, in 1902, work began on a Bahai house of worship, the Mašreq al-Adkār, the first ever to be built. As in Iran, Spiritual Assemblies were established to coordinate the affairs of the local Bahai communities, the central Assembly in Ashkhabad exercising authority over the Bahais in the various other cities of Turkestan. Bahai immigrants were also amongst those Iranians who moved to Caucasia, particularly Russian Azerbaijan, and a second Bahai community developed there, centered in Baku.

The Russian Revolutions of 1917 initially created very favorable conditions for the Bahais, who came to enjoy even greater freedom of expression and organization. Teaching activity was extended to ethnic Russians, a number of whom joined the community. Indeed, for a time, the Bahai youth organization was able to provide serious competition for recruits to the Communist Komsomol (Kolarz, *Religion in the Soviet Union*, p. 471). However, the situation rapidly deteriorated from 1928 onwards, with a build-up of anti-Bahai activity, including the arrest and exile of leading Bahais and the closure or expropriation of Bahai institutions, including the Mašreq al-Ad̲kār. There was a further wave of mass arrests, exiles and deportations (mainly to Iran) in 1938, and the Bahai communities of Asiatic Russia were all but destroyed. Following earthquake damage, the Mašreq al-Ad̲kār was later demolished.

3. Syria, Palestine, and Israel. Bahā'-Allāh was exiled to 'Akkā in Ottoman Syria in 1868. With him were some seventy or so of his family and disciples. These formed the core of a Bahai colony which grew, mostly through immigration from Iran, as the conditions of confinement were eased. Groups of Bahais also moved to Beirut and Haifa, and to the Galilee, where a Bahai agricultural settlement was established.

'Akkā, and after 1909, the neighboring town of Haifa, served as the administrative and spiritual headquarters of the Bahai religion, the burial places of Bahā'-Allāh, the Bāb, and 'Abd-al-Bahā' becoming its major places of pilgrimage. To avoid any threat to this status, the Bahai leaders discouraged or even prohibited any proselytism amongst the local population, a policy which was continued from the Ottoman period through to the present day, both under the British Palestine Mandate and the State of Israel. During the 1940s, Shoghi Effendi drastically reduced the size of the local Bahai community, instructing all Bahais who were not involved in the tasks of the "Bahai World Center" to leave Palestine. This policy still obtains, so that only Bahais involved in the faith's international administration or the maintenance of its shrines and other properties are allowed to reside in the Holy Land.

4. Egypt and other Arab countries. Next to Iran, the

most important Middle Eastern Bahai community has been Egypt. Founded in the 1960s by expatriate Iranians, the community came to include native Sunni Muslim and Christian converts. The distinguished Bahai scholar, Mīrzā Abu'l-Fażl Golpāyegānī, provided the community with intellectual leadership during the 1890s and 1900s, and taught for a while at al-Azhar. Bahai Assemblies were also formed, translations of Bahai writings into Arabic were made, and books and pamphlets were printed. Though limited in scale, Bahai activities naturally provoked the opposition of many orthodox Muslims. There were several local disturbances against the Bahais, but more significant were a series of declarations by the religious courts (from 1925) that Bahais were not Muslims and that Muslim converts were apostates. Nevertheless, Bahais attained a degree of official recognition, and were able to continue their activities until 1960, when all Bahai activities were banned by Presidential decree, and a number of Bahais were arrested (*Bahā'ī World* XVII, p. 78).

Elsewhere in the Arab world, the longest established Bahai community is that of Iraq, which effectively dates from the time of Bahā'-Allāh's exile there in the 1850s. Though subject to sporadic attacks by Shi'ite militants, the community was gradually able to expand its activities and even to elect a Bahai national Spiritual Assembly in 1934. As in Egypt, in recent years, all Bahai activities have been banned (from 1970). Indeed, in general, the position of the Bahais in the Middle East has become more difficult in the post-war years, the growth of modern Arab nationalism and the location of the Bahai headquarters in what has become the State of Israel leading to the Bahais coming to be regarded as a suspect minority, and not just as a heretical sect. Apart from Iran, all Bahai communities in the Middle East are very small.

The Bahai communities in the West: *1. North America.* The Bahai teachings were first introduced to the West by a Syrian Christian convert, Ibrahim George Kheiralla. Establishing himself in Chicago, he gained his first converts in 1894. With a circle of enthusiastic followers, Bahai groups were soon established in other centers, notably New York City. In 1898-99, Kheiralla visited 'Abd-al-Bahā' in 'Akkā, and, after disagreeing with him over matters of doctrine, eventually became a partisan of 'Abd-al-Bahā''s half-brother, Mīrzā Moḥammad-'Alī. Most of the American Bahais, however, tended to side with 'Abd-al-Bahā', and an energetic campaign of activities was soon resumed. American Bahai teachers traveled to various parts of the United States, Canada, and Europe. There was an extensive publication of Bahai literature, including several translations of scripture, pilgrims' accounts of visits to 'Abd-al-Bahā', and a number of expositions of Bahai teachings by Westerners. Local and national organizations were established—though not without controversy, many American Bahais were plainly antipathetic to organized religion. Plans were made for the construction of a Bahai Mašreq al-Aḏkār near Chicago (actually completed in 1953). And contacts were established with the Bahais of Iran and the East, several Americans visiting Iran in connection with medical and education projects. By the time of 'Abd-al-Bahā''s tour of the United States and Canada (April-December, 1912) there were several thousand American Bahais, and these were already beginning to have a considerable impact on the overall development of the religion.

In the 1920s Shoghi Effendi initiated his policy of standardizing and strengthening the system of Bahai administration. He received enthusiastic support from the North American National Spiritual Assembly, particularly from its long-time secretary, Horace Holley. In prosecuting their plans, the American Assembly encountered considerable initial resistance from those Bahais who were suspicious of religious organization. Two distinct opposition movements emerged, headed respectively by Ruth White and Ahmad Sohrab, but the majority of the Bahais were gradually persuaded of the need for centralized organization. By the late 1920s, the new administrative system was consolidated, and from 1937 onwards a definite series of expansion plans was undertaken. Success was modest in terms of total numbers, and by the early 1960s there were still only eleven thousand Bahais in North America. A policy of widespread diffusion was very successful, however, and through pioneer moves, the Bahais established themselves in all American states and Canadian provinces. The achievement of separate National Assembly status for Canada (1948) and Alaska (1957), provided a major spur to expansion in those territories.

The Bahai situation in North America changed dramatically in the late 1960s and early 1970s. In common with most other Western countries and as part of a significant general change in attitudes towards religion, the community experienced a great boom of youth conversions. A second wave of conversions followed as the American Bahais successfully made contact with rural Afro-Americans in the southern states. The combined impact of these two developments was considerable. In terms of total numbers, the Bahai population was greatly increased, so that now there are in the region of one hundred thousand Bahais in the USA. In terms of social composition, there was also a major change. The community had always been ethnically diverse, but had tended towards a predominantly urban and middle class membership. The new and very large southern constituency, by contrast, was often poor, or poorly educated. Again, the influx of youth had a major impact on the range of cultural styles within the community, young Bahais often taking a leading role in the further propagation and administration of the religion.

2. Europe. The first groups of Bahais in Europe were formed as a result of contacts with American Bahais: Britain and France from 1899 and Germany from 1905. The British and French groups remained particularly small, with fewer than a hundred members in each until the 1930s. The German community was more dynamic, but nowhere in Europe was there a response comparable to that in the United States. 'Abd-al-Bahā' visited the European Bahais twice (August–December, 1911; December, 1912–June, 1913), but was unable to engender much more than generalized sympathy for the Bahai cause.

After the First World War (1914-18), there was an increasing pace of activity, particularly in Germany, where many new Bahai groups were established, and there was extensive publishing activity, including a German Bahai magazine (*Sonne der Wahrheit*). There was also extensive contact with the Esperanto movement. Administrative development proceeded more slowly than in America, but National Assemblies were formed in both Britain and Germany in 1923. In 1937, all Bahai activities and institutions in Germany were banned by order of the Gestapo because of the religion's "international and pacifist" teachings. A number of Bahais were later imprisoned, and after the outbreak of the war (1939), Bahai activities came to an end throughout occupied Europe. The British Bahais, by contrast, became increasingly active, their community remaining the largest in Europe until the present.

In the aftermath of the Second World War, the American Bahais undertook a major teaching campaign in much of Western Europe, local Bahai communities being established in all of the countries outside the communist block. As in America, the European Bahais gained a lot of youthful converts from the late 1960s onwards. Even so, there are still only in the region of 22,000 Bahais in Europe, the lowest concentration in relationship to the general population in any world region outside of the communist block. (Universal House of Justice, Department of Statistics, *The Seven Year Plan, Statistical Report, Riḍván 1986*, Haifa: Bahá'í World Centre, 1986, pp. 48-49). There is a Mašreq al-Aḏkār near Frankfurt.

3. The "Anglo-Pacific." A Bahai group was established in Hawaii in 1902. Communities were established in Australia and New Zealand during the 1920s. Growth remained limited in these areas until after the Second World War, despite the formation of a joint National Bahai Assembly for Australia and New Zealand in 1934. Growth has been far more marked in recent years. A Mašreq al-Aḏkār was dedicated in Sydney in 1961.

The Bahai "Third World": 1. Latin America and the Caribbean. Bahai teachers from the United States visited Latin America even before the First World War, but sustained activity only began in the inter-war period, particularly after the start of the first American Seven Year Plan (1937-44), which aimed to establish Bahai Local Assemblies in all the mainland republics. Regional National Assemblies, one each for Central and South America, were established in 1951. Initially, the Latin American communities drew much of their membership from amongst the urban middle classes, but from the 1950s onwards, increasing contacts were made with the Amerindians, particularly in the Andean countries. Poorer social groups now predominate in most of the region, and many of the Bahai communities have become increasingly involved in fostering educational and development programs. A Mašreq al-Aḏkār was dedicated in Panama in 1972.

2. Africa. Apart from the Arab Bahai communities of North Africa, there were very few Bahais in the continent until the 1950s. Development thereafter was rapid, particularly in East Africa. There are now reported to be some 969,000 Bahais in the whole continent (Universal House of Justice, Department of Statistics, *Statistical Report, Riḍván 1986*, p. 48). There is a Mašreq al-Aḏkār in Kampala.

3. Southern Asia. The Bahai community of the Indian subcontinent dates back to the 1870s, the Bahai teacher, Jamal Effendi, undertaking an extensive tour at Bahā'-Allāh's direction (1872-78). Most of the early Bahais were either of Iranian extraction or were Persianized Indians. Little contact was made with the Hindu masses. Nevertheless, the Bahai community embarked on an energetic campaign to propagate the Bahai teachings, and an extensive Bahai literature in the main Indian languages was developed.

By concentrating their efforts on the urban lecture-going population, the Bahais greatly limited their chances of success, and even as late as 1961, there were still less than nine hundred Bahais in the whole of India (*Bahá'í World* XIII, p. 299). The decisive breakthrough was the determined attempt to present the Bahai teachings to the rural masses. When this was done (from 1961), the whole character of the community was changed, and large numbers of people became Bahais, most of them Hindu by background. By 1973, there were close to 400,000 Bahais in India (Garlington, "The Baha'i Faith in Malwa," p. 104), and there are now said to be approaching two million. A Mašreq al-Aḏkār has recently been dedicated in New Delhi (1986). Active and expanding Bahai communities have also developed in the other countries of the subcontinent. There are many educational and development projects.

4. The Far East, Southeast Asia and the Pacific. There were Iranian Bahai traders in China at an early date, but the earliest indigenous Bahai group to be established in the Far East was in Japan (1914). This community has remained small, however, and Bahai teachers have experienced more success in Korea.

In Southeast Asia, the earliest community was in Burma, as an outgrowth of activities in India (from 1870s). Elsewhere, a few Bahai groups were established during the inter-war period, but large-scale expansion only began in the 1950s. Until its reunification and the disbanding of the Bahai administration under the new communist government, the largest and most prominent Southeast Asian community was in South Vietnam. Bahai activities are also restricted in Indonesia, but there are active communities in most other countries of the region.

The development of Bahai groups in the Pacific region has occurred mostly since the Second World War. Although small in numbers, several of these communities, because of the small population base, now have some of the highest concentrations of Bahais in the world. A Mašreq al-Aḏkār was recently opened in Western Samoa (1984).

The role of Iranians in the present-day Bahai community. Although Iranians now constitute fewer than one-tenth of the total Bahai population, they remain a significant presence within the Bahai world community. In many Asian countries, Iranian Bahais were the original "pioneer-teachers" whose missionary endeavors did much to establish the first Bahai groups. Iranian pioneers were also an important element in the establishment of Bahai communities in several African countries, and there are small groups of Iranian Bahais in many other countries.

In general, the number of expatriate Iranian Bahais has greatly increased since the Islamic revolution. It is not yet possible to quantify this diaspora, but it is clear that many thousands of Bahais have left Iran, the majority eventually emigrating to North America or Europe. Given the relatively small size of the indigenous Bahai communities in Europe, this Iranian influx has had a major impact on their demographic composition, several European Bahai communities now including a very large proportion of Iranians (certainly in several cases, well over a third). A similar situation has developed in some parts of North America (e.g., southern California).

Iranian Bahais also remain a significant presence in the international administration of the Bahai Faith. At the present time, two of the members of the Universal House of Justice (the supreme Bahai ruling body) are of Iranian background, as are 20 out of 72 Continental Counsellors. There are also Iranian members on many Bahai national Spiritual Assemblies.

Bibliography: General. As yet, the only general account of the history of the Bahai communities is P. Smith, *The Bábí and Bahá'í Religions: From Messianic Shi'ism to a World Religion* (Cambridge, 1986). See also A. Hampson, *The Growth and Spread of the Bahá'í Faith* (Ph.D. dissertation, University of Hawaii, 1980) and P. Smith, *A Sociological Study of the Bábí and Bahá'í Religions* (Ph.D. dissertation, University of Lancaster, 1982). Valuable sources of information are the *Bahá'í Yearbook*, New York, 1926; the successive volumes of *Bahá'í World*, Wilmette, 1928-56; Haifa, 1970-; Shoghi Effendi, *God Passes By*, Wilmette, 1944; and the series *Studies in Bábí and Bahá'í History*, Los Angeles, 1982-. Besides *Bahá'í World*, sources of statistical information include Shoghi Effendi, *The Bahá'í Faith, 1844-1952: Information Statistical and Comparative*, London, 1953; Universal House of Justice, *The Bahá'í Faith: Statistical Information, 1844-1968*, Haifa, 1968; and idem, Department of Statistics, *The Seven Year Plan, 1979-1986: Statistical Report, Riḍván 1983*, Haifa, 1983, and *Statistical Report, Riḍván 1986*, Haifa, 1986.

Iran. There is no general account of the Iranian Bahai community. Useful references in addition to those above include M. Momen, *The Bábí and Bahá'í Religions, 1844-1944: Some Contemporary Western Accounts*, Oxford, 1981: P. Smith, "A Note on Bábí and Bahá'í Numbers in Iran," *Iranian Studies* 17, 1984, pp. 295-301; S. Stiles, *Zoroastrian Conversions to the Bahá'í Faith in Yazd, Iran* (M.A. thesis, University of Arizona, 1983) and idem, "Early Zoroastrian Conversions to the Bahá'í Faith in Yazd, Iran," in *From Iran East and West. Studies in Bábí and Bahá'í History* II, ed. J. R. Cole and M. Momen, Los Angeles, 1984, pp. 67-93. On the current wave of persecutions see Bahá'í International Community, *The Bahá'ís of Iran: A Report on the Persecution of a Religious Minority*, rev. ed., New York, 1982. R. Cooper, *The Bahá'ís of Iran*, rev. ed., London, 1985. More generally, see D. Martin, "The Persecution of the Bahá'ís of Iran, 1844-1984," *Bahá'í Studies* 12-13, 1984.

Turkestan. W. Kolarz, *Religion in the Soviet Union*, London, 1961, pp. 470-73; A. A. Lee, "The Rise of the Bahá'í Community of 'Ishqábád," *Bahá'í Studies* 5, 1979, pp. 1-13.

North America. P. Smith, "The American Bahá'í Community, 1984-1917: A Preliminary Survey," in *Studies in Bábí and Bahá'í History* I, ed. M. Momen, Los Angeles, 1982, pp. 85-223; R. Stockman, *The Bahá'í Faith in America* I, Wilmette, 1985.

India. W. N. Garlington, *The Bahá'í Faith in Malwa: A Study of a Contemporary Religious Movement* (Ph.D. dissertation, Australian National University, 1975); idem, "The Bahá'í Faith in Malwa," in *Religion in South Asia*, ed. G. A. Odie, London, 1977, pp. 101-17; S. L. Garrigues, *The Bahá'ís of Malwa: Identity and Change Among the Urban Bahá'ís of Central India*, (Ph.D. dissertation, University of Lucknow, 1976).

(P. SMITH)

v. THE BAHAI COMMUNITY OF IRAN

Origins. With the Declaration of the Bāb in 1260/1844, followed by his being accepted as the promised Qā'em (the Hidden Imam) by a handful of early believers, the first Babi community was born in the city of Shiraz. As his claims spread and the missionary journeys of his earliest believers, known as Letters of the Living (*Ḥorūf al-ḥayy*), and other disciples intensified, more communities were formed, chiefly along the route taken by Mollā Ḥosayn Bošrū'ī (d. 1849) from Shiraz in the south, to Tehran in the north, and several locations in his home province, Khorasan. Qoddūs (d. 1849) and Moqaddas's (d. 1889) activities in Kermān, Yazd, and other central cities, Bahā'-Allāh's (d. 1892) visit to Māzandarān, and Ṭāhera's (d. 1852) journeys from Karbalā' to Qazvīn, through western provinces, made enough converts to establish communities in all those provinces. The Bāb's own journey from Shiraz towards the north (to Kolayn, several kilometers south of Tehran), and then to Tabrīz, via Qazvīn and Zanjān, strengthened, consolidated, and enlarged the communities that had already been established in those areas.

By July, 1850, when the Bāb was executed in Tabrīz, there was no province in the entire country in which from a few up to ten Babi communities had not been established. These early Babi communities of Muslim converts, who were generally from Shaikhi background, had come from various strata of Persian society, although a few Jews and Zoroastrians had also joined the movement (*Māzandarānī*, 1943, p. 395; *Samandar*, p. 348).

The Bāb proclaimed the absolute truth of religious evolution, asserted the continuity of revelation, as opposed to its finality, a doctrine dogmatically held by the Muslims, brought a new Book and laid down laws and ordinances for a new religious order. He provided his believers with a motivation towards new standards of living, longing for advancement, and desire for change in their outlook. The spirit of the new day and order, enshrined in the writings of the Bāb, was sufficient to energize the communities to work in a collective unity for the creation of change towards improved private and social conditions.

The formation of the Babi communities in Iran was a direct result of intensified missionary activities of individual believers who attracted people to their cause. The conversion of a nobleman, a landlord, or a learned cleric provided an element of encouragement for large-scale conversion in some localities, while a sympathetic attitude on the part of some officials and religious authorities helped the rapid expansion of the community. A distinguishing feature of the early Babi communities was their eagerness to hold dawn prayers, listen to sermons, and attend study groups to read and discuss the writings of the faith. Meetings with non-believers to discuss religious matters, aimed at attracting them to the faith, and meetings with traveling teachers or passing believers were the most common social activities of the early communities. The strongest Babi communities in the rural areas, in terms of population and stability, were formed in Sangsar near Semnān, Najafābād near Isfahan, and Saysān near Tabrīz; however, numerous towns and cities also had large communities. The social life of the early communities was characterized by continuous interaction with the non-Babi populace, which was naturally hostile to the emergence of a new religion. The result, almost everywhere in the entire country, was social and religious conflict; persecution, restriction, banishment, and execution of the Babis.

The emergence of Bahā'-Allāh (q.v.) as a religious leader of the Babi community and the proclamation of his claim to be the fulfillment of the Bāb's prophecies of the advent of *man yoẓheroh Allāh* (he whom God will make manifest) attracted the vast majority of the Babis to his call. Some, however, remained Babis, and some followed Ṣobḥ-e Azal (q.v.), half-brother of Bahā'-Allāh, who claimed the leadership of the Babi community. Through his writings to the individual leading Babis and by sending his devoted followers to various communities, Bahā'-Allāh gradually increased the number of his followers, who became known as Bahais. During his ministry (1853-92), the Bahai communities grew in size and number, and performance of the duties prescribed in his writings became an essential mark of membership in the community. Communal activities, such as attending the Holy Day meetings, prayer sessions, sermons, and other religious activities increased.

Towards the end of Bahā'-Allāh's stay in Adrianople (1863-68), a number of religious, theological and social principles were expounded in his writings which found progressive development in the private and collective life of the Bahais. At his passing (1892), he left approximately 50,000 believers scattered in Iran and other Middle Eastern countries ('Abd-al-Bahā', *Majmū'a-ye makātīb*, Tehran, 1975, no. 13, photocopied ms., p. 3).

During the ministries of 'Abd-al-Bahā' (1892-1921), Bahā'-Allāh's son and successor, and Shoghi Effendi (1921-57), 'Abd-al-Bahā''s grandson and Guardian of the Faith, the local Bahai communities developed substantially, Bahai laws and ordinances were put into action, Bahai administrative institutions, particularly from the early 1930s, were slowly and steadily established. The institution of the Nineteen Day Feast (*Żīāfat-e Nūzdah-rūza*), prescribed in the *Aqdas* (q.v.), came into full function as a vital pillar in the socio-religious life of the communities, and in various aspects of the faith several other developments, which deserve closer study, took place.

Bahai administration. From the early days of the faith to the closing years of the nineteenth century (1844-97), the religious and social affairs of the communities were conducted through the non-institutionalized consultation and arbitration of the leading Bahais in each locality. The Hands of the Cause of God (*Ayādī-e Amr Allāh*, q.v.) appointed by Bahā'-Allāh ('Alā'ī, pp. 369-493), were charged with the responsibility of organizing teaching campaigns, protecting the faith and, to a lesser extent, being involved in all the major developments of the communities. At the instructions of 'Abd-al-Bahā', they began forming local Bahai councils (*Mahfel-e šawr*) in Azerbaijan, which gradually extended into other provinces. In 1314/1897, the Council of Tehran was formed and six years later, in 1320/1903, it was officially constituted of four Hands and five others who were chosen by the Hands to serve on it. This was the first local Spiritual Assembly of Tehran which prepared its constitution and held weekly meetings to conduct the affairs of the community (Māzandarānī, *Ẓohūr al-Ḥaqq*, ms., Bahá'í Archives, Haifa, MD16-3, vol. 7, pp. 153-54).

Following the pattern set in Tehran, local Spiritual Assemblies were gradually formed in other parts of Iran until the 1920s when the principles of Bahai election were slowly adopted in the formation of the Spiritual Assemblies and their legal and administrative roles and rights in conducting the affairs of the communities were established and recognized by believers. Statistical reports for Iran show a significant growth since 1950 in the number of Spiritual Assemblies and localities where

Bahais resided; while in that year the number of local Spiritual Assemblies was 280, and that of localities 712, in 1968 the number of Spiritual Assemblies reached 560 and of localities 1541. In 1979, 679 Spiritual Assemblies and 1699 localities were reported (Department of Statistics, Bahá'í World Centre, Haifa, Statistical Reports).

At the first national convention of the Bahais of Iran, held in Tehran over a period of eight days beginning on April 26, 1934, the first national Spiritual Assembly (*maḥfel-e rūḥānī-e mellī*) of the Bahais of Iran, a milestone in the history of the Bahai community, with its seat in Tehran, was elected (*The Bahá'í World* 6, pp. 22-23). The social and religious affairs of the national community of the Bahais of Iran, which, prior to 1934 had been directed by the former Central Assembly of Tehran, were transferred to the new body. Following the formation of the national Spiritual Assembly, the by-laws of the national Spiritual Assembly of the United States were translated into Persian and adopted with modifications by the Persian national Spiritual Assembly. Also national committees were appointed to help the national Spiritual Assembly with specific tasks (*The Bahá'í World* 6, p. 94). The establishment of the Bahai Administrative Order in Iran called for adherence to discipline, and soon it was found that sanctions had to be applied suited to the offense, from conscious and flagrant disregard of fundamental Bahai precepts and laws to disobedience to the head of the faith.

The first National Plan for the expansion and consolidation of the faith in Iran and adjoining lands came into effect on October 11, 1946 and lasted for 45 months ending on July 9, 1950. The objectives of the plan included the consolidation of all local Bahai communities; the re-establishment of 62 dissolved Spiritual Assemblies; the formation of 22 new groups and the creation of 13 new centers (*The Bahá'í World* 4, pp. 34-35). Following the first plan, the Persian Bahai community was assigned certain goals and objectives in the Ten Year Crusade (1953-63), the Nine Year Plan (1964-73), the Five Year Plan (1974-79), and the Seven Year Plan (1979-86). The detailed goals and achievements of the community are found in the volumes of *Aḵbār-e amrī* for the respective periods.

Bahai women. In the early years of the 1930s Bahai women joined the movement of discarding the veil and gradually abandoned the traditional veiling practice. This development opened new fields of service for women and made possible their fuller participation in the social and administrative activities of the communities. A central women's progress committee was formed in 1944 to organize women's activities throughout the country. Some of the fundamental tasks accomplished by this committee and its supportive bodies in various localities included holding the first convention of Anjoman-e Tarraqī-e Neswān (Society for the Advancement of women) in 1947 in Tehran (*The Bahá'í World* 11, p. 563), following which local and regional conferences, educational gatherings, and regular classes for illiterate women were conducted. As a result of continued effort and educational training, particularly during the Four Year Plan for the Bahai Persian women (1946-50) (*The Bahá'í World* 12, p. 65), they were enabled to acquire sufficient self-confidence and social recognition to fill elective and appointive offices in the community. Bahai women were elected to membership of the Spiritual Assemblies for the first time in 1954 (*Āhang-e Badīʿ* 10/2-3, 1334 Š./1955). By April 1973, illiteracy among Bahai women under the age of 40 was eradicated throughout the country (*The Bahá'í World* 15, p. 248). In recent years, prior to 1979, the Bahai women of Iran were participating in various fields of Bahai activities. Since 1979 scores of them who played effective roles in both rural and urban Bahai communities were imprisoned and more than twenty have been executed.

Bahai youth. Bahai youth of Iran, too, have played a role in the secular and spiritual destiny of the community throughout its history, but organized activities of youth date back to the establishment of a youth group in Tehran in 1929 which was soon followed by the formation of other youth groups in all the major Bahai centers in the country. In 1949-50, a total of 207 Bahai youth committees (*lajna-ye javānān*) existed in Iran to organize youth activities which included holding regular classes and conferences to deepen young people's knowledge of the faith; establishing and operating libraries and clubs; conducting literacy classes; teaching in children's education classes; holding exhibitions of fine arts and crafts; and spreading the message of the faith to non-Bahais. Starting from year 103 *Badīʿ*/1946, national Bahai youth conventions (*kānvenšan-e mellī-e javānān*) were held in Iran to plan, activate, and coordinate youth activities. A report shows that within a few years between the late 1960s and early 1970s more than 1500 Bahai youth pioneered to homefront goals and more than 100 pioneers settled in foreign goal areas (*The Bahá'í World* 15, p. 249). The number and efficiency of the local youth committees were increased in the years immediately prior to the 1979 revolution. They were guided and supervised by the National Youth Committee (Lajna-ye Mellī-e Javānān) based in Tehran.

Education. An achievement in which dozens of Bahai communities invested their financial and intellectual efforts was the establishment of Bahai schools (q.v.) in tens of cities, towns, and villages to educate Bahai and non-Bahai children. They were closed by order of the government in 1934 (*The Bahá'í World* 6, pp. 26-30).

An educational, devotional, and recreational institution which originated in America in 1927 and was established in Iran in the summer of 1939 was the Bahai Summer School. The first Persian Summer School, held in Ḥājīābād, some 40 kilometers northeast of Tehran, consisted of three sessions of ten days in which a total number of 214 Bahais participated (*The Bahá'í World* 8, p. 78). As circumstances permitted, summer schools were held for many years in various localities in Tehran and other provinces. The permanent seat of the summer schools, run under the aegis of the national Spiritual Assembly, was in Ḥadīqa, an estate on the slopes of Mount Alborz to the northeast of the capital (see below), which attracted several hundred participants each summer.

Since 1315/1898 Bahai "Character Training Classes" (*Kelāshā-ye dars-e ak̲lāq*) have been conducted in Tehran and other Bahai centers. In recent years a good deal of attention and expertise has been given to the advancement of Bahai child education and a considerable amount of children's literature has been produced in Iran.

Publications. Since the establishment of the Bahai faith in Iran thousands of believers have received letters from its central figures: the Bāb, Bahā'-Allāh, and 'Abd-al-Bahā'. These letters (*makātīb, alwāḥ*), which are scattered among the families of the recipients, form a substantial portion of the Bahai sacred texts, and their collection, preservation, and transcription have always ranked high in the list of responsibilities of local and national Spiritual Assemblies in Iran; thus far, more than thirty volumes of these letters have been published.

One of the achievements of the community was the establishment of the Bahai Publishing Trust in 1959 (*The Bahá'í World* 12, p. 292). Since 1316/1899, Bahai sacred texts have been hectographed and mimeographed by Mīrzā 'Alī-Akbar Rūḥānī (known as Moḥebb-al-Solṭān) (*Māzandarānī*, 1974, p. 483) and others. Although the restrictive laws of the country prohibited the Bahais from printing their literature by letterpress, through the establishment of the trust, Bahai literature was regularly and systematically published in typewritten or calligraphic form until 1979 when the trust was closed under the Islamic régime. Between 1959 and 1979, several hundred titles were produced and distributed. The trust was also responsible for the publication of circulars, newsletters, pamphlets, and magazines. In 1975 alone, it produced 181,390 copies of books and pamphlets totaling 31 million pages (*The Bahá'í World* 16, p. 263). In the early 1970s an audio-visual center was established in Iran which made rapid growth during the few years of its existence. A report shows that in the mid-1970s the center produced 27 cassette programs containing prayers, songs, and speeches amounting to 40,000 copies, and 28 reels of film (ibid.). The Persian Bahai community also published several periodicals. One of the most popular, aiming at the educational and intellectual training of Bahai youth, the *Āhang-e badī'*, was established in Iran in 102 *Badī'*/1945 as a publication of the Tehran Bahai Youth Committee and then became a national magazine which gained the support of 1,200 subscribers in the early 1950s (*The Bahá'í World* 12, p. 570). Suspended for five years (112-117 B./1955-60) due to intensified restrictions by the Government, *Āhang-e badī'* was published for more than three decades until it was stopped by the onset of the Islamic régime.

Beginning in 1300 Š./1921 the Bahai community published a magazine called *Ak̲bār-e amrī*. Containing the holy writings of the Bahai faith, domestic and foreign Bahai news, official announcements of Bahai administrative bodies, and articles on various aspects of the faith, the magazine became a vital means of communication and a register of the main historical events for six decades until its closing in 1980. Starting in 105 B./1948, the Bahai women of Iran published a monthly magazine, called *Tarāna-ye omīd*, to educate and entertain Bahai families, with special attention to women's affairs. After some years of suspension, it reappeared in 130 B./1973 to function for several more years until 1979 (*Ak̲bār-e amrī* 52/11, September, 1973, pp. 332-34).

The year 124 B./1967 witnessed the publication of a magazine for the Bahai children of Iran. Named *Varqā*, the magazine was regularly published each month until 1979 and was supported by subscribers all over the country and abroad. This magazine played a significant role in the educational and intellectual life of Persian Bahai children for more than a decade. After the 1979 revolution, the magazine has continued to be published in India. To these major national periodicals, *Našrīya*, a news bulletin of the local Spiritual Assembly of Tehran, should be added. Distributed free of charge to each Bahai family in Tehran every 19 days, *Našrīya* functioned for a dozen years and kept its readers informed of the major news and developments in the Bahai community of Tehran.

Endowments and properties. The acquisition, preservation, and maintenance of the places directly associated with the history of the Bahai faith have been among the goals of the community since its early years. The places consisted of houses and sites associated with the principal figures of the faith, burial places of Bahai saints, places where the martyrdoms of believers took place, prisons, fortresses, and defense centers of heroes and renowned Bahais. The fact that these places were located throughout the country made their care a major undertaking for various committees at local and national levels. The work included the registration, description, and photographing of the sites in addition to their regular maintenance and restoration. In the late 1960s more than 124 holy places belonged to the faith in various localities throughout the country. To this should be added more than 200 national and 452 local endowments consisting of Bahai centers, cemeteries, hostels, and public baths (Department of Statistics, Bahá'í World Centre, Haifa, "Persia – Nine Year Plan File," 14 January 1969).

To fulfill a commandment of Bahā'-Allāh to build a House of Worship (Mašreq al-ad̲kār) the Bahais of Iran acquired 3.58 square kilometers (*The Bahá'í World* 10, p. 48) of land on the slopes of Mount Alborz, named Ḥadīqa, in northeast Tehran, for the eventual construction of their first temple. Although the temple has yet to be built, a complex of buildings was erected there to serve as the seat of Bahai summer schools and other social and administrative activities.

Cemeteries. Since the Bahais have always been prohibited from burying their dead in Muslim cemeteries, the acquisition of burial grounds, termed *Golestān-e*

Jāvīd (Eternal garden) in the Persian literature of the faith, has been a major goal of the Bahai communities throughout the country. From the earliest days, Bahai dead have been buried in their own private properties, in plots of land donated by individual Bahais to the community as local endowments, or, where possible, in the community-owned cemeteries obtained by collective financial contributions of individual Bahais. A systematic process of acquiring separate Bahai cemeteries, however, was inaugurated in most Bahai communities in the 1920s and continued in later decades. Prior to the 1979 revolution, most of the principal Bahai centers had their own cemeteries run under the supervision of the local Spiritual Assembly. After the revolution most of them have been destroyed and desecrated.

Economic and social institutions. Through the donations of individual Bahais, the first Bahai fund (*Šerkat-e ḵayrīya*) was established in Tehran in 1907 to financially support Bahai teachers, facilitate the education of Bahai children, provide sufficient care of Bahai orphans, the aged and handicapped, and be of assistance to students of higher education (*Māzandarānī*, VII, p. 259). In 1917 a Children's Savings Company, which later was registered as Šerkat-e Now-nahālān, was founded in Qazvīn. On 23 November 1919 'Abd-al-Bahā' wrote a prayer in which he sought God's blessing for its success and durability (*Māzandarānī*, op. cit., p. 322). He also donated two gold coins of five rubles each to its capital. The company had about 9,000 shareholders with approximately 120 million rials (about $1,700,000) in assets in 1967, half a century after its establishment. (*Yādgār-e jašn-e panjāhomīn sāl-e ta'sīs-e šerkat-e sahāmī-e now-nahālān*, Tehran, 1967, pp. 1-2.)

In 1940 'Abd-al-Mīṯāq Mīṯāqīya, a well-known Bahai of Tehran, built a hospital and donated it to the Bahai community. The hospital rapidly developed to employ highly respected physicians, and to obtain advanced equipment. It became known as one of the best medical centers in Tehran. In the early 1970s a nursing school, affiliated with the hospital, was inaugurated and the hospital itself opened medical clinics in Boir Aḥmad (*The Bahá'í World* 16, p. 264). In 1940 an institution for Bahai orphans was founded (*The Bahá'í World* 9, p. 251) which served the community for many years. On a more general level, an achievement of the Bahai communities in Iran was the establishment of modern public baths in most of the major populated towns and villages throughout the country to replace the unhygenic traditional baths. Some of the baths were built and donated to the community by individual Bahais and some were established through the collective financial participation of the members of the community.

Outstanding figures. Among the outstanding individuals in the first century of the faith was Abu'l-Fażl Golpāyegānī (q.v.), who accepted the Bahai Faith in 1293/1876 and became a distinguished believer, particularly active in the propagation of its principles. He spent several years in prison due to his Bahai activities, then traveled extensively before settling in Egypt, where he died in 1914. Among his works are *Borhān-e lāme'*, translated and published as *The Brilliant Proof* (1912), *al-Ḥojaj al-bahīya*, translated and published as *Miracles and Metaphors* (1981). A selection of his shorter works, entitled *Letters and Essays* (1985), is also available in English. His other works such as *al-Farā'ed*, *Šarḥ-e Āyāt-e Mowarraḵa*, *Kašf al-ḡeṭā'*, and a few collections of his shorter works exist in Arabic and Persian.

Mīrzā Ḥasan Ṭālaqānī, son of Mīrzā Moḥammad-Taqī, known as Adīb (q.v.) al-'Olamā' and Adīb-e Ayādī, was born in Šawwāl 1264 (September 1848) in Karkabūd near Ṭālaqān. He received his elementary education in that city and traveled to Tehran and Isfahan for further education. The depth and range of his knowledge in Islamic studies, history, and Arabic and Persian literature gained him enough scholarly prestige to be invited to work as one of the co-writers of the *Nāma-ye dānešvarān*, a voluminous biographical work initiated under 'Alīqolī Mīrzā E'teżād-al-Salṭana. He also participated in the preparation of the *Qamqām-e Zakkār* written by Mo'tamed-al-Dawla Farhād Mīrzā during 1303-05 (1886-88). Adīb was distinguished as a writer, poet, and educator. He passed away on 6 Ḏu'l-qa'da 1337 (4 August 1919) in Tehran.

An outstanding historian of the Bahai faith, Asad-Allāh Fāżel Māzandarānī (d. 1957), is the author of a nine-volume work covering the history of the first Bahai century (1844-1944). The work, volumes three and eight of which have so far been published (in 1943 and 1974-75), records the full biographies of the Bāb, Bahā'-Allāh, and 'Abd-al-Bahā', the faith's leading disciples and learned members, poets, martyrs, and other prominent personalities. It covers the history of the persecutions of the Bahais; discusses the internal crises of the faith and, more significantly, contains excerpts from the holy writings and includes documentation and a considerable number of pictures. Other works of Fāżel include his dictionary of commonly used proper terms and titles in Bahai literature, *Asrār al-āṯār*, which was published in five volumes (1967-72) of more than 1,600 pages. Fāżel's other major work, *Amr wa ḵalq*, contains hundreds of selections from the Bahai holy writings grouped under topics related to philosophical, theological, religious, and administrative matters. The work was published in Iran (1954-74) in four volumes. Among the other outstanding figures of the Bahai faith, was 'Azīz-Allāh Meṣbāḥ (d. 1945), a well-educated writer and poet who served the community as an educator in the Tarbīat school for a quarter of a century, taught in Bahai classes and summer schools, and left poetry and other works. The remarkable achievement of 'Abd-al-Ḥamīd Ešrāq Ḵāvarī (d. 1972) in writing and compiling more than 40 books and dozens of articles in every major field of Bahai studies also deserves to be mentioned.

Persian Bahais in international Bahai fields. The Persian Bahai community, as the oldest and wealthiest Bahai community in the world, both culturally and materially, has played a vital role in almost every major accomplishment of the Bahai world community. The earliest Bahai communities in the Middle East, and southern Russia were without exception formed through the pioneering activities of the Persian Bahais. In later periods they traveled and settled in different parts of the world to propagate the faith (*The Bahá'í World* 13, pp. 291-92). During the Ten Year World Crusade (1953-63) and subsequent global activities, the Persian community contributed substantial manpower and financial support. During 1968-73 alone, as a partial goal of the international Nine Year Plan (1964-73), 3,500 Persian Bahais were relocated in goal areas, both domestic and international, and some five thousand individuals, often using their own resources, served as missionaries abroad (*The Bahá'í World* 15, p. 247).

When in 1951-53 and again in 1957, Shoghi Effendi proclaimed the appointment of thirty-one Bahais as Hands of the Cause of God, eleven were Persians. In the first election of the Bayt al-ʿAdl-e Aʿẓam (the Universal House of Justice, April, 1963) three out of nine were Persians. At the present time, twenty-one Persians (out of 72) are members of the continental boards of counselors, supreme bodies responsible for the expansion and protection of the faith (*Bahá'í News*, no. 657, December, 1985, p. 1), and more than 250 Persians serve as members of 148 national Spiritual Assemblies throughout the world (Department of Statistics, Bahá'í World Centre, Haifa, "Annual Election Reports," April, 1986).

Internal crises and external persecutions. It would be impossible to study the Bahai community without taking into consideration the internal crises and external persecutions that have affected the entire Bahai community throughout its history; personal desire to achieve leadership appears to have been the prime source of internal crises, particularly in the periods of transition of authority. The sanctions which are imposed on offenders range from warnings to deprivation of one's right of voting in Bahai elections, and to excommunication in the severest case, which is termed covenant-breaking (*naqż-e ʿahd*). The authority for punishment, expulsion, and reinstatement is vested in the Center of the Faith (*markaz-e mīṯāq*) and its institutions. Although the internal crises have not caused sectarianism in the community, they have been sufficiently powerful to mobilize the unifying forces of the faith to counter them. The negative effects of the crises, however, are negligible when compared with the destructive consequences of external persecutions.

The history of the Bahai faith in Iran during the past fifteen decades has been one of joy resulting from the faith's progress, and of bitter suffering, resulting from successive waves of persecution. Since its inception, the Bahai community of Iran has longed to spread the message of the faith, to enforce the laws and ordinances prescribed in its holy writings, to establish its religious and administrative institutions, and to function as a free community, loyal to the laws and constitution of the land, whose government would recognize the faith's fundamental right of existence. Against these aspirations, the secular and religious forces of the country not only stood firm, denying its right as a religious community, restricting its basic freedoms, and belittling its teachings and doctrines, but also rose to uproot its very being from the land of its birth. The persecution of the Bahai faith which dates back to the confinement of the Bāb and his early followers in Shiraz, has continued uninterruptedly to the present time. Although in the history of the persecution, there are short intervals of relative ease in the general condition of the community, it is, nonetheless, impossible to cite a single year in which one sort of persecution or another did not take place (see BAHAI FAITH, vii).

The establishment of the Islamic Republic of Iran in 1979 put an end to the organized, systematic activities of the Bahai faith in that country. By order of the new government all Bahai holy places, endowments, and properties were confiscated; Bahai institutions at the national and local levels ceased to function; thousands of Bahais, virtually in each major town and city, were arrested, tortured, and imprisoned, and more than 180 of them were executed. This number does not include dozens of Bahais who have been kidnapped or have disappeared without a trace. Since 1979 thousands of Bahais have been driven from their homeland by these unrelenting persecutions. A good number of them, still homeless, are classified as "refugees" in various countries around the world.

Bibliography: In addition to the sources cited in the article the following references deal with various aspects of the Bahai community in Iran. The main source of information for events and developments, however, is the *Akbār-e amrī*, a national Persian Bahai news magazine published with few interruptions from 1921 to 1980.

Collection and publication of Bahai holy texts, books and periodicals: *The Bahá'í World* III, 1928-30, p. 33; IV, 1930-32, p. 82; V, 1932-34, p. 117; IX, 1940-44, p. 30; X, 1944-46, p. 47; XII, 1950-54, p. 570; XIII, 1954-63, p. 292; XV, 1968-73, p. 248; XVI, 1973-76, pp. 262-63.

History of the faith in Iran, including chronological history, local history and the history of eminent Bahais: *Āhang-e badīʿ* 23/1-2, 1968, pp. 29-32; 29/3-4, 1974, pp. 11-25; ʿAbd-al-ʿAlī ʿAlāʾī, *Moʾassesa-ye Ayādī-e Amr Allāh*, Tehran, 1973; H. M. Balyuzi, *Eminent Bahāʾīs*, Oxford, 1985; E. G. Browne, *A Year Amongst the Persians*, New York, 1926 (lengthy references to the Bahai faith, see index); Neʿmat-Allāh Ḏokāʾī Bayżāʾī, *Taḏkera-ye šoʿarā-ye qarn-e awwal-e bahāʾī*, Tehran, 1964-72, 4 vols.; G. N. Curzon, *Persian and the Persian Question*, London, 1892, 2 vols. (numerous references to the Babi faith, see index); ʿAbd-al-Ḥamīd Ešrāq Ḵāvarī, *Nūrayn-e nayyerayn*, Tehran, 1966; idem, *Taqwīm-e tārīḵ*, Tehran, 1969; Moḥammad-ʿAlī Fayżī, *Ḵānedān-e Afnān*, Tehran, 1970; idem, *Neyrīz-e moškbīz*, Tehran, 1972; J. R. Hinnells, *A Handbook of Living*

Religions, U.K., 1984, pp. 475-98; Nikki R. Keddie, *Iran, Religion, Politics and Society*, London, 1980, pp. 15-23, 94-96; Moḥammad-ʿAlī Malek Ḵosrovī, *Eqlīm-e nūr*, Tehran, 1961; idem, *Tārīḵ-e šohadāʾ-e amr*, Tehran, 1973, 3 vols.; D. M. MacEoin, *From Shaykhism to Babism*, Ph.D. thesis, Cambridge University 1979; Moḥammad-Ṭāher Mālmīrī, *Tārīḵ-e šohadāʾ-e Yazd*, Cairo, 1924; Moḥammad Ṭabīb-e Manšādī, *Šarh-e šohadāʾ-e manšād*, Tehran, 1970; Asad-Allāh Fāżel Māzandarānī, *Ẓohūr al-Ḥaqq*, Tehran, [1943], III; 1974-75, VIII, 2 parts; Rūḥ-Allāh Mehrābḵānī, *Šarḥ-e aḥwāl-e Janāb-e Mīrzā Abu'l-Fażāʾel Golpāyegān*, Tehran, 1974; Naṣr-Allāh Rastegār, *Tārīḵ-e ḥażrat-e Ṣadr al-Ṣodūr*, Tehran, 1945; Moḥammad Šafīʿ Rūḥānī, *Lamaʿāt al-anwār*, Tehran, 1975, 2 vols.; Kāẓem Samandar, *Tārīḵ-e Samandar*, Tehran, 1974; ʿAzīz-Allāh Solaymānī, *Maṣābīḥ-e Hedāyat*, Tehran, 1964-75, 9 vols.; Moḥammad-Nabīl Zarandī, *The Dawn-Breakers*, tr. Shoghi Effendi, Wilmette, 1974.

Local and national Spiritual Assemblies, conventions, and other administrative bodies: *Āhang-e badīʿ* 32/9-10, 1977, pp. 62-66; *The Baháʾí World* II, 1926-28, pp. 187-90; III, 1928-30, pp. 32-34; IV, 1930-32, p. 82; V, 1932-34, pp. 116-19; VI, 1934-36, pp. 22-23, 94; XI, 1946-50, p. 36; XV, 1968-73, p. 247.

Persecution: *The Baháʾí World* II, 1926-28, pp. 287-294; III, 1928-30, p. 32; V, 1932-34, p. 118; VI, 1934-36, pp. 96-99; VII, 1936-38, pp. 88, 136-140; VIII, 1938-40, pp. 73-75, 185-88; IX, 1940-44, pp. 97-102; X, 1944-46, pp. 35-43; XI, 1946-50, pp. 35-36; XIII, 1954-63, pp. 292-96; XVII, 1976-79, pp. 79-80; XVIII, 1979-83, pp. 380-92; Douglas Martin, *The Persecution of the Bahá'ís of Iran 1844-1984*, Ottawa, 1984.

Plans for the expansion and consolidation of the faith: *Āhang-e badīʿ* 15/8-10, 1960, pp. 290-94; 17/10, 1963, pp. 217-18; 18/3-6, 1963, pp. 135-48; 20/11-12, 1966, pp. 391-92; 25/9-10, 1970, pp. 280-81; 27/1-2, 1972, pp. 7-8; 29/3-4, 1974, pp. 3-10; 29/5-6, 1974, pp. 5-16; 31/11-12, 1977, pp. 6-10; 32/9-10, 1975, pp. 5-6; *The Bahá'í World* XI, 1946-50, pp. 34-35; XIII, 1954-63, pp. 291-92; XIV, 1963-68, p. 101; see also relevant pages and tables in *The Bahá'í Faith, 1844-1963, Ramat Gan* (Israel), n.d.; *The Nine Year Plan 1964-1973*, Haifa, 1973; *The Five Year Plan 1974-1979*, Haifa, 1979; *The Seven Year Plan 1979-1986*, Haifa, 1986.

Post-1979 persecutions: *Die Bahá'í im Iran—Dokumentation der Verfolgung einer religiösen Minderheit*, Langenhain, 1985; *The Bahá'ís in Iran—a Report on the Persecution of a Religious Minority*, New York, 1981; *The Bahá'í World* XVIII, 1979-83, pp. 249-368, for a partial bibliography of references see pp. 369-79; *Persecution of the Bahá'ís in Iran 1979-1985*, New York, 1985; Roger Cooper, *The Baha'is of Iran*, London, 1985; Margit Warburg, *Iranske dokumenter*, Copenhagen, 1985.

Properties, holy places, endowments: *Āhang-e badīʿ* 22/2-3, 1967, pp. 73-75; 23/3-4, 1968, pp. 94-96; *The Bahá'í World* III, 1928-30, p. 33; IV, 1930-32, pp. 80-81; V, 1932-34, p. 116, 119; VI, 1934-36, p. 25; VII, 1936-38, p. 88; VIII, 1938-40, p. 79, 191; X, 1944-46, pp. 47-48; XII, 1950-54, pp. 64-65.

Socio-educational institutions: *Āhang-e badīʿ* 23/5-6, 1968, pp. 126-37; *The Baháʾí World* III, 1928-30, p. 33; V, 1932-34, pp. 116-17; VI, 1934-36, pp. 26-30; VIII, 1938-40, p. 78; IX, 1940-44, p. 521; XIII, 1954-63, p. 33; XVI, 1973-76, p. 264.

Women: *Āhang-e badīʿ* 4/2, 1949, pp. 17-18; 10/2-3, 1955 (special issue entirely devoted to Bahai women); *The Bahá'í World* III, 1928-30, p. 33; V, 1932-34, p. 121; VI, 1934-36, p. 31; X, 1944-46, p. 48; XI, 1946-50, p. 36, 563; XII, 1950-54, p. 65; XV, 1968-73, p. 248; Forūḡ Arbāb, *Aḵtarān-e Tābān*, Tehran, 1975.

Youth: *Āhang-e badīʿ* 1/1, 1945, pp. 14-16; 1/2, 1945, p. 9; 5/18, 1950, pp. 383-87; 7/7, 1952, pp. 11-14; 16/6, 1961, p. 158; 17/7, 1962, pp. 155-58; 18/9, 1963, pp. 356-58; 19/8, 1964, pp. 285-87; 20/7, 1965, pp. 280-82; 271/11-12, 1973, pp. 27-31; 32/5-6, 1977, pp. 87-96; *The Bahá'í World* V, 1932-34, p. 120; VIII, 1938-40, p. 189; XII, 1950-54, pp. 566, 570, 573; XIII, 1954-63, p. 759; XV, 1968-73, p. 249; XVI, 1973-76, p. 262; see also *Sāl-nāma-ye javānān-e bahāʾī-e Īrān* (Persian Bahai Youth's Year Book) devoted to youth affairs, in several vols., Tehran, 1949-65.

(V. RAFATI)

vi. THE BAHAI COMMUNITY OF ASHKHABAD (ʿEŠQĀBĀD)

Attracted by religious freedom and economic opportunities unavailable to them in Iran, Iranian Bahais began to settle in Ashkhabad around 1884; the community prospered and reached its peak during the period 1917-28.

The first Bahai settlement in Ashkhabad dates back to 1300/1882 when Moḥammad-Reżā Arbāb b. Moḥammad Kāẓem Eṣfahānī and Ḥājī ʿAbd-al-Rasūl Yazdī b. Moḥammad-ʿAlī Yazdī made their way there from Iran. During the next two years, they were followed by Ostād ʿAlī-Akbar Bannāʾ Yazdī, Ostād Moḥammad-Reżā Ḵorramšāhī, members of their families, their friends and others. The early Bahai settlers of Ashkhabad were principally contractors and traders; also present, but fewer in number, were craftsmen, artisans, and simple laborers.

The community's early years were marked by rapid physical and economic growth and religious tolerance on the part of Ashkhabad's non-Bahai inhabitants. The arrival of the respected Bahai scholar Mīrzā Abu'l-Fażl Golpāyeganī on 15 July 1889 greatly enhanced the intellectual life of the community (R. Mehrābḵānī, *Šarḥ-e aḥwāl-e Abu'l-Fażāʾel Golpāyeganī*, Tehran, 1974, p. 161).

An event that affected the early history of the community occurred on 12 Moḥarram 1307/8 September 1889 when a well-known Bahai leader, the seventy-year-old Ḥājī Moḥammad-Reżā Eṣfahānī, was stabbed to death in the Ashkhabad *bāzār*. His murder was engineered by fanatical Shiʿites who could not tolerate the increasing prosperity of the Bahai community. Immediately after Ḥājī Moḥammad-Reżā's murder, the conspirators were arrested, and a special court was convened. The court sentenced two of the Shiʿite assassins to death and five others to exile and/or imprisonment for terms ranging from sixteen months to fifteen years; but, through the intercession of the Bahai community, the sentences were commuted. This act of forgiveness enhanced the prestige of the Bahais and earned them, for the first time, government recognition and protection (A. ʿAlīzād, *Tārīḵ-e amr-e mobārak dar madīna-ye ʿEšqābād*, ms., Haifa: Bahai International Archives, MR 2403, I, pp. 32-34).

The community continued to grow and to form social and religious organizations during the years immediately after Ḥājī Moḥammad-Reżā's assassination. In 1313/1895, the first local Spiritual Assembly was founded (A. Māzandarānī, *Ẓohūr al-ḥaqq*, Tehran, 1974-75, VIII, p. 981). A Bahai school for boys was begun, regular gatherings to observe holy days were held, committees were formed to conduct community affairs and, by 1319/1901, the Bahai population of Ashkhabad topped 1000 (Māzandarānī, p. 983). From Ashkhabad, which served as the center of Bahai activities, the faith made its way to Tashkent, Marv, and Samarkand.

The community's most outstanding achievement, however, was the erection of the first Bahai temple (Mašreq al-Aḏkār) in the world. The temple had been planned during the ministry of Bahāʾ-Allāh (q.v.; Shoghi Effendi, *God Passes By*, Wilmette, 1970, p. 300) and was designed, under the direct supervision of ʿAbd-al-Bahāʾ (q.v.), by Ostād ʿAlī-Akbar Bannāʾ, during his visit to ʿAkkā in 1311/1893 (Māzandarānī, p. 995). The temple was started in 1902 and officially inaugurated in 1919.

From 1917 to 1928, the Bahai community flourished. In 1335/1917, the journal *Ḵ'oršīd-e ḵāvar* began publication (ʿAlīzād, I, p. 69); in 1336/1918, the Bahai Youth League was formed and established a public library, published a Bahai calendar for ten years, arranged seminars, produced a wall-mounted bulletin, *Fekr-e javān* for young people, and offered music classes and literacy courses for adults (ʿAlīzād, I, pp. 71-84). In 1338/1920, the local Spiritual Assembly of Ashkhabad was officially recognized by the government (Māzandarānī, p. 990), regular gatherings were held to acquaint non-Bahais with the faith, two kindergartens were founded and various institutions such as the pilgrim house, the meeting hall, the medical clinic and two Bahai schools operated at full capacity.

Around the middle of 1928, the Bahais of Ashkhabad, conspicuous by their activities and influence, became the special victims of a general Soviet campaign against all religions. The Soviets appropriated the temple in 1928 and rented it to the Bahais for a five-year period which was extended for another five years. Bahai activities and institutions were curtailed or abolished, and leading members of the community were imprisoned or deported to Iran. During the early 1930s, the government-imposed economic hardships became so severe that many Bahai families, on the point of actual starvation, were forced to emigrate to Iran.

In the mid-1930s, the Bahai community was able to regain its freedom and revitalize its administrative organization; however, this brief renascence was cut short by fresh waves of persecution that began in the early months of 1938. In February, 1938, several hundred Bahais were arrested, houses were searched and literature and relics were confiscated; those arrested were charged with "working to the advantage of foreigners" (*Bahá'í World* VIII, 1938-40, p. 88). During their confinement, which lasted more than fifteen months and, in some cases, twenty-one months (ʿAlīzād, I, pp. 134-36), several Bahai prisoners died, and the rest were gradually exiled to Siberia. About 600 old men, women, and children were deported to Iran (*Bahá'í World* VIII, p. 89). The temple was converted to an art gallery in 1938 and was severely damaged in an earthquake ten years later. In 1963, it was demolished by the authorities and replaced by a public park.

Unauthenticated reports suggest that around 200 Bahais continue to live in and around Ashkhabad but do not have any organization or religious activities.

Bibliography: ʿAbd-al-Bahāʾ, *Memorials of the Faithful*, Wilmette, 1971, tr. M. Gail, p. 128. ʿA. Āvāra, *Kawākeb al-dorrīyah*, Cairo, 1924, II, pp. 55-58. *Bahá'í World*, Wilmette, repr., 1980-81, I (1925-26), pp. 79-81; III (1928-30), pp. 168-69; VII (1936-38), pp. 100-02; VIII (1938-40), pp. 87-90, 525-32; XIV (1963-68); England: Universal House of Justice, 1974, pp. 479-81. ʿA. Bannāʾ, *Tārīḵ-e ʿEšqābād*, Tehran, 1976, no. 94. ʿA. Ešrāq Ḵāvarī, *Moḥāżarāt*, Tehran, 1963, I, pp. 424-28. Idem, *Raḥīq-e maḵtūm*, Tehran, I, pp. 580-84. M. Fayżī, *Ḵānadān-e Afnān*, Tehran, 1970, pp. 107-09. Idem, *Laʾālī-e deraḵšān*, Tehran, 1966, pp. 213-17. ʿA. Forūtan, *Ḥekāyat-e del*, Oxford, 1981, pp. 15-30. A. Lee, "The Rise of the Bahai Community of ʿIshqābād," *Baha'i Studies* 5, 1979, pp. 1-13. M. Momen, *The Bábí and Bahá'í Religions*, Oxford, 1981, pp. 296-300 and passim. F. Ṣahbāʾ, "Moqaddama-ī bar šarḥ-e aḥwāl-e Fāżel Jalīl Āqā Sayyed Mehdī Golpāyegānī," *Āhang-e badīʿ* 26/4-5, 1350 Š./1971, pp. 128-33, 148-50, 152-53, 156-60. F. Šahīdī, "Yāddāšthā-ye tārīḵī rājeʿ be amr-e bahāʾī dar ʿEšqābād," *Āhang-e badīʿ* 27/3-4, 1351 Š./1972, pp. 7-11. S. Effendi, *Tawqīʿāt-e mobāraka*, Tehran, 1972, I (1922-26), pp. 32-38; II (1927-39), pp. 103-04. ʿA. Solaymānī, *Maṣābīḥ-e hedāyat*, Tehran, III, 1966, pp. 15-39, 256-60, 579-83; VI, 1968, pp. 407-20. *Star of the West* 14/1, 1923-24, pp. 23-24; 14/5, p. 154. M. Ṯābet Marāḡaʾī, *Dar ḵedmat-e dūst*, Tehran, 1975, pp. 440, 442-45, 453-57.

(V. RAFATI)

vii. BAHAI PERSECUTIONS

Bahai persecutions were a pattern of continuing discriminatory measures against adherents and institutions of the Bahai religion, punctuated by outbreaks of both random and organized violence against individuals and property. Although Bahai accounts conflate earlier episodes involving Babis (see BABI EXECUTIONS AND UPRISINGS) with those concerned with Bahais in the proper sense, there are good grounds for avoiding this approach in analyzing what are really quite distinct phenomena. At the same time, it is worth observing that much of the original animus against Bahais was rooted in fears roused by Babi militancy between 1848 and 1853.

Persecution in the late 19th and 20th centuries was ostensibly motivated and justified by religious considerations, whereas in recent decades anti-Bahai polemic has become heavily politicized, even under the Islamic Republic. Nevertheless, social and economic factors cannot be discounted in the earlier period any more than simple religious prejudice in the later. The earliest anti-Bahai activities were essentially continuations of previous attacks on Babis and took the form of isolated beatings, expulsions, lootings, or killings; such incidents were almost always initiated by individual *ʿolamāʾ* or local government officials for whom they were expedient. From the 1920s, however, physical attacks gave way on the whole to general civil and religious discrimination, representing a broader consensus of anti-Bahai feeling at all levels of society. Even then, the potential for actual violence was never far beneath the surface, as demonstrated by the events of 1955 and the 1980s.

The main accusations leveled against the Bahais may be found in the extensive anti-Bahai polemical literature published in Iran since the last century (see the bibliography). Religiously, Bahais are considered *koffār* (unbelievers) in that they claim a book and prophet chronologically posterior to the Koran and Moḥammad, regard the Islamic *šarīʿa* (canonical law) as abrogated and replaced by that of their own faith, and seek to convert Muslims to their beliefs. More recently, however, it has become customary to condemn Bahaism precisely because it is "not a religion" but a political movement working in conjunction with royalist, Zionist, American, British, or other agencies for the subversion of Islam and the Iranian nation. It is perhaps worth placing on record here that no convincing evidence has ever been presented for Bahai involvement with British, Israeli, or American intelligence or with SAVAK (the state security agency): the real reasons for Bahai unpopularity must be sought on deeper social and psychological levels.

Among incidents in the Qajar period, the following may be noted: the execution of three Bahais in Tabrīz in 1283/1867, following the murder of an Azalī Babi by one of the accused; several outbreaks of trouble in the Isfahan region, including a wave of arrests in 1291/1874, the executions of two wealthy Bahai merchants in 1296/1879, and mass expulsions in Najafābād and Sedeh in 1306/1889—in these and other incidents, major roles were played by Shaikh Moḥammad-Bāqer Eṣfahānī, his son Shaikh Moḥammad-Taqī (Āqā Najafī, q.v.), Mīr Sayyed Moḥammad, the *emām-e jomʿa* of Isfahan, and Solṭān-Masʿūd Mīrzā Ẓell-al-Solṭān (q.v.); the arrest of some 50 Bahais, including several leaders of the movement, in Tehran in 1300/1883; the murder of 5 Bahais in Torbat-e Ḥaydarī in 1314/1896; the murder of Ḥājī Moḥammad Tabrīzī in Mašhad in 1315/1898, leading to a prolonged wrangle between the prime minister (Amīn-al-Dawla) and the authorities in Mašhad; further disturbances in Najafābād in 1316-17/1897, involving a *bast* (seeking the protection of an inviolate location) of some 300 people at the British telegraph office; the execution of 7 Bahais in Yazd in 1308/1901, on the orders of Solṭān-Ḥosayn Mīrzā Jalāl-al-Dawla; and a series of disturbances in 1321/1903, in Rašt, Isfahan (where 3 Bahais were killed and some 4000 sought *bast* in the Russian consulate), and Yazd (where about 100 Bahais were put to death). (For details of these and other incidents, see in particular Momen, *Bábí and Baháʾí Religions*; Nicolas, *Massacres*; Browne, *Materials*, chap. 7; Shoghi Effendi, *God Passes By*, pp. 198-203, 296-99).

In the course of these and other outrages against Bahais, frequent representations were made to the Iranian government by the British and Russian legations, but at no time were serious measures taken to proceed against the guilty parties or to prevent further outbreaks. The Bahai incidents may thus be considered as particular foci for foreign concern about issues of civil liberties and the enforcement of law and order in Iran at this period.

During the period of the Constitutional Revolution, both royalists and constitutionalists were accused by their opponents of being "Babis," usually without any distinctions between Azalīs (q.v.) and Bahais. Although the Bahais claimed to be neutral and did not, for the most part, engage in overt political activity, this was not always clear to the general public. Their Azalī rivals, with whom they were frequently confused, certainly did number among their ranks several prominent reformers. At the same time, the Bahais were well represented in court and government circles, and writings of the Bahai leadership of the period express support for the shah and disapproval of constitutionalist activities (see MacEoin, "Religious Heterodoxy;" Roemer, *Bābī-Behāʾī*, pp. 153-60). Although direct attacks on Bahais at this time were limited, it seems certain that the sect's long-term failure to win the sympathy of anti-traditionalist elements in Iranian society dates from this period.

In the Pahlavi era, anti-Bahai feeling entered a new phase. From about 1342/1926, "the moves against the Baha'is assumed a more subtle, pseudo-legal nature" (Momen, *Bábí and Baháʾí Religions*, p. 462). A pogrom in Jahrom in that year, which was instigated for political motives by Esmāʿīl Khan Ṣawlat-al-Dawla and in which eight individuals died, was to be the last outbreak on that scale until 1955. A major factor in the decline of violent attacks was undoubtedly the weakness of the *ʿolamāʾ* under Reżā Shah, but this did not prevent discrimination against Bahais taking other forms. Denied official recognition in the 1906 Constitution or subsequent legislation, the Bahais were unable to secure basic rights as a religious community on a par with those accorded to Jews, Christians, or Zoroastrians, whose civil recognition depended on their status as *ahl al-ketāb* (peoples of a [sacred] book). Bahai institutions were unable to register as corporate bodies in law (as they were doing in other countries at that time); Bahai marriages were not legally recognized; the printing, circulation, and import of Bahai literature was banned (although Bahai books and journals did continue to be published in typewritten or lithographed format); Bahai centers were often closed and meetings prohibited or disrupted; Bahais in government employ (including army officers) were occasionally dismissed or demoted. One of the most serious setbacks suffered by the Bahai community was the closure in May, 1934, of the prestigious Tarbīat school in Tehran, followed by other Bahai schools throughout the country on the grounds that these institutions had closed on Bahai holy days in the previous year. Although this last measure has to be set in the context of the broader policy towards foreign and religious minority schools in general, it had a particularly severe effect on the Bahais, whose schools, attended by many non-Bahai children from the upper and new middle classes, represented the only acceptable presence of the sect within society at large.

During this period, the Bahai community of Iran grew substantially in numbers. From an estimated 100,000 adherents in the 1880s (between 1.25 and 2.00 percent of the population), it rose to nearly 200,000 by the 1950s, by which point the Bahais were probably the largest religious minority in the country (for details, see Smith, "Babi and Baha'i Numbers"). In spite of this, Bahaism was unable to make the transition from the status of a "sect" (sociologically defined) to that of a "church" or recognized independent religious body. Bahais (including women) were generally well educated, disproportionately represented in the professional and entrepreneurial classes, included large numbers of converts from the Jewish and Zoroastrian (but not, as a rule, the Christian) communities, and had active ties with converts to their faith in Europe, North America, and elsewhere. From about 1909, American Bahai teachers and doctors lived and worked in Iran, winning the respect of liberal elements, but identifying Bahaism with foreign interests in the eyes of the more conservative (as demonstrated in the incident in 1342/1924, when the American vice-consul in Tehran, Robert Imbrie, was killed by a mob which mistakenly believed him to be a Bahai; see Momen, *Bábí and Bahá'í Religions*, pp. 462-65). Bahais themselves emphasized their support for Reżā Shah's attacks on the clergy and for his various programs of modernization (e.g., Shoghi Effendi, *Bahá'í Administration*, pp. 171-73), but this failed to win them sympathy from either the shah or secular modernists, while it served further to alienate conservative and religious elements. This was to prove disastrous for the Bahais in later years, as the Pahlavi reforms came to be more widely criticized and they found themselves identified (as they had identified themselves) as bearers of Western values within an Islamic context. In this sense, the Bahais' own optimism about the pace and direction of change was, in the long term, to prove their own worst enemy once "progress" itself became charged with negative connotations; at the same time, the identification of the Bahais with secularizing reform, anti-clericalism, and support for the monarchy cannot be overlooked as, in itself, a strong factor in turning public opinion against those things.

In 1374/1955, following a series of anti-Bahai speeches by Shaikh Moḥammad-Taqī Falsafī, which were broadcast throughout Iran during the month of Ramażān/April-May, the national Bahai headquarters in Tehran was occupied by the army, after which the Minister of the Interior announced in the Majles that orders had been issued for the suppression of Bahaism. With official sanction, a brutal pogrom followed across the country, in the course of which many Bahais were murdered, property (including holy sites) confiscated and destroyed, women raped, Bahais in government employ dismissed, and numerous other measures taken to harass the Bahais individually and collectively. The Bahai movement, which by this date had a widespread international following, mounted a campaign—which included an appeal to the United Nations—to bring foreign pressure to bear on the Iranian government to stop the outrages, and by 1957 the situation had returned to one of strained "normality." Various explanations have been advanced to account for the 1955 pogrom, of which Fischer's seems most plausible: that the government was trying to "buy off" the right-wing Islamic opposition of Kāšānī and the Fedā'īān-e Eslām (Fischer, *Iran*, p. 187). Other factors are discussed by Akhavi (*Religion and Politics*, p. 77).

During the 1950s, Shaikh Maḥmūd Ḥalabī's Ḥojjatīya organization was established with the express aim of conducting campaigns against the Bahais. Both the Ḥojjatīya and the Tablīgāt-e Eslāmī (Islamic propaganda) group actively worked against Bahai interests during the 1960s and 70s, disrupting meetings, intimidating sect members and would-be converts, publishing and disseminating often scurrilous anti-Bahai literature. There is even evidence of collaboration between the Tablīgāt-e Eslāmī and SAVAK in the organization of anti-Bahai activities, including extensive surveillance of sect members (Nash, *Secret Pogrom*, p. 51; Anonymous, *Bahaism*, pp. 37-54).

Since the revolution of 1979, the situation for Iranian Bahais has deteriorated seriously. During the first seven years of the new regime, some 200 Bahais, including a large proportion of the national leadership, were executed, many more imprisoned, property confiscated and destroyed on a large scale, thousands dismissed from their employment, the funds of Bahai-owned companies sequestered, and the community generally harassed as "enemies of Islam," agents of foreign powers, or supporters of the shah's regime. As a result of these measures, large numbers of Bahais have fled Iran, acquiring the status of religious refugees in several countries. In spite of intense international condemnation by the United Nations, human rights groups, and some national parliaments, the Iranian government has refused to modify its position on the Bahai issue, leaving fears that members of the sect will remain scapegoats for the foreseeable future.

Bahai sources regularly inflate the numbers of individuals killed in persecutions, usually citing the figure of over 20,000. This often involves conflation with the figures for Babi martyrs, but even so 20,000 is highly exaggerated. In all, it is estimated that 300 to 400 Bahais have died in the course of incidents in Iran from the inception of the movement (see MacEoin, "From Babism to Baha'ism," pp. 236-37, and idem, "A Note on the Numbers").

Analyses of anti-Bahai prejudice, which extends from the religious right to the political left of Iranian society, have so far been limited. The standard polemical works are grossly distorted and cannot be relied on for information about the real causes of conflict, although they do permit valuable insights into the psychological factors at work. Bahai accounts are generally more accurate but prone to oversimplification and exaggeration (see MacEoin, "Iran's Troubled Minority"). MacEoin has attempted to develop an analysis based on the parallel between Western and Bahai perceptions of Bahaism as a positive bearer of Western, "progressive" values on the one hand and Iranian perceptions of the faith as a negative bearer of foreign, anti-Islamic influences on the other ("The Baha'is of Iran"). Future analyses may use as their model sociological work on the controversiality of new religious movements carried out in recent years in Europe and North America.

Bibliography: Accounts of specific incidents: M. Momen, *The Bábí and Bahá'í Religions 1844-1944: Some Contemporary Western Accounts*, Oxford, 1981, chaps. 14, 17, 18, 20, 26, 27, 28, 29, 30, 32. Shoghi Effendi, *God Passes By*, Wilmette, 1944, pp. 198-203, 296-99, 362-63. A. L. M. Nicolas, *Massacres de Babis en Perse*, Paris, 1936; E. G. Browne, ed., *Materials for the Study of the Bábí Religion*, Cambridge, 1918, pp. 35-43, 289-308. Ḥājī Moḥammad-Ṭāher Mālmīrī, *Tārīḵ-e šohadā-ye Yazd*, Cairo, 1342/1924. Sayyed Moḥammad Ṭabīb Manšādī, *Šarḥ-e šahādat-e šohadā-ye Manšād*, Tehran, 127 B. (*Badīʿ*)/1970-71. Moḥammad Labīb, *The Seven Martyrs of Hurmuzak*, tr. M. Momen, Oxford, 1981. Moḥammad-ʿAlī Fayżī, *Neyrīz-e moškbīz*, Tehran, 129 B./1972-73, pp. 142-75. Moḥammad Šafīʿ Rūḥānī Neyrīzī, *Lamaʿāt al-anwār* II, Tehran, 132 B./1975-76. Moḥammad-ʿAlī Malek-Ḵosravī, *Tārīḵ-e šohadā-ye amr* III, Tehran, 130 B./1973-74, pp. 335-588. *The Baha'i World: An International Record* XIII, 1954-63, Haifa, 1970, pp. 291-96. Baha'i International Community, *The Bahá'ís in Iran, a Report on the Persecution of a Religious Minority*, New York, June, 1981 (Supplement, September, 1981). Idem, *Chronological Summary of Individual Acts of Persecution against Bahá'ís in Iran*, New York, 1981.

General accounts: Roger Cooper, *The Baha'is of Iran*, Minority Rights Group Report 51, London, 1982. Geoffrey Nash, *Iran's Secret Pogrom*, Sudbury, 1982. Christine Hakim, *Les Bahá'ís ou victoire sur la violence*, Lausanne, 1982. D. MacEoin, "The Baha'is of Iran: the Roots of Controversy," in *BRISMES Proceedings of the 1986 International Conference on Middle Eastern Studies*, Oxford, 1986, pp. 207-15. Idem, "Iran's Troubled Minority," *Gazelle Review of Literature on the Middle East* 11, 1985, pp. 44-49. Idem, "From Babism to Baha'ism: Problems of Militancy, Quietism, and Conflation in the Construction of a Religion," *Religion* 13, 1983, pp. 219-55, esp. pp. 225-27, 235-38. Idem, "A Note on the Numbers of Babi and Baha'i Martyrs in Iran," *Baha'i Studies Bulletin* 2/2, 1983, pp. 84-88. Idem, "Religious Heterodoxy and Qajar Politics," *IJMES* (forthcoming). Peter Smith, "A Note on Babi and Baha'i Numbers in Iran," *Iranian Studies* 17/2-3, 1984, pp. 295-301. S. Akhavi, *Religion and Politics in Contemporary Iran*, Albany, 1980, pp. 33, 76-87.

Anti-Bahai literature: Sayyed Ḥasan Kīāʾī, *Bahāʾī: az kojā wa čegūna paydā šoda?*, Tehran, 1349 Š./1970. Sayyed Moḥammad Bāqer Najafī, *Bahāʾīān*, Tehran, 1357 Š./1979. A. Mūsawī, *Noqṭa-ye Ūlā, Jamāl-e Abhā, Markaz-e Mīṯāq*, Tehran, 1348 Š./1969. Yūsof Fażāʾī, *Taḥqīq dar tārīḵ wa falsafa-ye Bābīgarī, Bahāʾīgarī, wa Kasrawīgarāʾī*, Tehran, 1354 Š./1974-75. Aḥmad Kasrawī, *Bahāʾī-garī*, Tehran, 1321 Š./1942. ʿAlī Amīrpūr, *Ḵātemīyat wa pāsoḵ be-sāḵtahā-ye Bahāʾīyat*, Tehran, 1340 Š./1961. Mīrzā Moḥammad-Mahdī Khan Zaʿīm-al-Dawla, *Taʾrīḵ al-Bābīya aw meftāḥ bāb al-abwāb*, Cairo, 1321/1903; Pers. tr. Shaikh Ḥasan Farīd Golpāyegānī, *Meftāḥ bāb al-abwāb yā tārīḵ-e Bāb wa Bahāʾ*, Tehran, 1346 Š./1967. Dr. H. M. T., *Moḥākama wa barrasī dar tārīḵ wa ʿaqāʾed wa aḥkām-e Bāb wa Bahāʾ*, 3rd ed., 3 vols., Tehran, 1344 Š./1965. Anonymous, *Baha'ism: Its Origins and Its Role*, Našr-e Farhang-e Enqelāb-e Eslāmī, the Hague, 1983 (?). Mīrzā Abū Torāb Hodāʾī ʿErāqī, *Bahāʾīyat dīn nīst*, Tehran, ca. 1370/1950. Mīrzā Fatḥ-Allāh b. ʿAbd-al-Raḥīm Yazdī, *Bāb o Bahāʾrā be-šenāsīd*, Hyderabad, 1371/1951-52. Anonymous, *Eʿterāfāt-e sīāsī yā yāddāšthā-ye Kenyāz Dālgorūkī*, in 1943 ed. of the *Khorasan Yearbook* and numerous subsequent editions. See also M. Fischer, *Iran: From Religious Dispute to Revolution*, Cambridge and London, 1980, p. 187. H. Roemer, *Die Bābī-Behāʾī*, Potsdam, 1912, pp. 153-60. Shoghi Effendi, *Bahá'í Administration*, Wilmette, 1960, pp. 93, 104-08, 117-20, 133-34, 149-50, 159, 170-73. S. Akhavi, *Religion and Politics in Contemporary Iran*, Albany, 1980, p. 187.

(D. M. MacEoin)

viii. Bahai Shrines

Of the Bahai sites of pilgrimage and visitation, the most important are the tombs of Bahāʾ-Allāh and the Bāb in Israel and the houses of the Bāb and Bahāʾ-Allāh in Shiraz and Baghdad.

Shrines and holy places in Israel. Since Bahā'-Allāh's exile to Palestine in 1868, the Bahai world spiritual and administrative center has been in the Acre ('Akkā) Haifa area. The most important Bahai holy places there are: (1) The shrine of the Bāb, halfway up Mt. Carmel in Haifa. 'Abd-al-Bahā' had the Bāb's remains secretly brought from Iran in 1899 and built a stone building in traditional Levantine style in 1909, where the Bāb's remains were placed. 'Abd-al-Bahā' himself was buried there in 1921. In 1948-53 Shoghi Effendi added a white marble superstructure, consisting of a columned arcade topped by a drum and gold dome, designed by the Canadian Bahai architect William Sutherland Maxwell (1874-1952). The Shrine of the Bāb is surrounded by extensive gardens. (2) The Monument Gardens, also in the area of the shrine, are the white marble tombs of several members of 'Abd-al-Bahā''s family: his sister Bahā'īya (Bahīya) K̲ānom (q.v.), his brother Mīrzā Mahdī, his mother Nawwāb, and his wife Monīra. Each tomb is in the form of a small dome supported by columns. (3) The International Bahai Archives, built above the shrine of the Bāb by Shoghi Effendi in 1954-57 to exhibit historic relics and documents. It is constructed of white marble in the style of a Greek temple. (4) The seat of the Universal House of Justice, a large columned white marble building of classical style completed in 1983. (5) The mansion of Mazra'a, a house used by Bahā'-Allāh in 1877-79. This was a summer house of 'Abd-Allāh Pasha about 6 km north of Acre that 'Abd-al-Bahā' rented for Bahā'-Allāh once the authorities no longer insisted on his close confinement in the city. A stone house set amid the fields and orchards of the coastal plain, it was leased by the Bahais in 1950 and purchased in 1973. (6) The mansion of Bahjī, a large house 2 km northwest of Acre, built by 'Abd-Allāh Pasha for his mother in 1821. Bahā'-Allāh moved to the house in 1879 and remained there the rest of his life. After Bahā'-Allāh's death the house fell into disrepair. Shoghi Effendi gained custody of the house in 1929 and restored it. He eventually acquired large parcels of land around the house, which have gradually been developed into a circular park. (7) The shrine of Bahā'-Allāh, a small stone building next to the mansion of Bahjī. Bahā'-Allāh was buried in a house used by his son-in-law adjacent to Bahjī. Eventually a monumental superstructure is planned for this shrine as well, which is the Bahai *qebla*.

A number of other historic sites are owned or controlled by the Bahais in the Acre/Haifa area. These include the cell in the prison barracks where Bahā'-Allāh was confined, the houses of 'Abbūd and 'Abd-Allāh Pasha in Acre, the house of 'Abd-al-Bahā' in Haifa, and several gardens near Acre used by Bahā'-Allāh. For the most part these have been restored and are visited by Bahai pilgrims.

The two other sites of Bahai pilgrimage are no longer in Bahai hands. The house of Bahā'-Allāh in the Kark̲ district of Baghdad was seized by the Iraqi government in 1925. This was the house Bahā'-Allāh lived in for most of his stay in Iraq. Bahā'-Allāh declared it a site of pilgrimage in his book of laws, the *al-Ketāb al-aqdas* (*Ketāb-e aqdas*). The house of the Bāb in Shiraz—a beautifully preserved nineteenth-century middle-class home in the old part of the city—was seized by the authorities and demolished in 1980. This was ordained to be a place of pilgrimage both by the Bāb in the *Bayān* and by Bahā'-Allāh.

Bahais also consider a number of historic sites elsewhere to be holy places—places visited by the Bāb, Bahā'-Allāh, or 'Abd-al-Bahā'; sites of martyrdoms; and tombs of martyrs and important believers. These include a number of places in the West visited by 'Abd-al-Bahā' and a large number of places in Iran—notably the houses of Bahā'-Allāh in Tehran and Māzandarān; houses associated with the Bāb in Shiraz, Būšehr (Bushire), Isfahan, and Urmia; the site of the conference of Badašt; and the cell where Bahā'-Allāh was imprisoned in 1852-53. These were expropriated following the revolution in 1979.

A Bahai who is able is obligated to make a pilgrimage once in his lifetime to pray at the shrine of Bahā'-Allāh or at the house of the Bāb in Shiraz or the house of Bahā'-Allāh in Baghdad. In addition, it is considered spiritually uplifting to visit places associated with holy souls and martyrs. There is little ritual associated with visiting the Bahai shrines. Visitors are expected to remove their shoes and maintain an atmosphere of quiet reverence but are otherwise free to do as they wish. Bahais commonly wear their national dress on formal occasions while on pilgrimage.

Bibliography: D. S. Ruhe, *Door of Hope: A Century of the Bahá'í Faith in the Holy Land*, Oxford, 1983, is a meticulously researched account of the Bahai holy places in Israel, mainly written for the use of pilgrims. E. Braun and H. E. Chance, *A Crown of Beauty*, Oxford, 1982, is a similar work written for visitors. R. Rabbani, *The Priceless Pearl*, London, 1969, esp. pp. 228-66, is a biography of Shoghi Effendi with a great deal of information on the development of the Bahai shrines. U. Giachery, *Shoghi Effendi: Recollections*, Oxford, 1973, contains much information about the architecture of the shrines. *A Synopsis and Codification of the Kitáb-i-Aqdas*, Haifa, 1973, p. 61, n. 26, summarizes Bahai law concerning pilgrimages and visits to holy places.

(J. Walbridge)

ix. Bahai Temples

The Bahai temple, designated in Bahā'-Allāh's *Ketāb al-aqdas* (Most holy book) as Mašreq al-ad̲kār (lit. Dawning place of the mention of [God]), is known usually in the West as "House of Worship." Although the faith originated in Iran, no Bahai temple was ever built in that country, due to local antagonism. The history of the faith, however, shows that since the time of Bahā'-Allāh until the present, the Bahais of Iran have gathered in private Bahai homes to pray and to read the writings of the faith.

Although the basic spiritual and physical characteristics of the Bahai temple were described in the writings of Bahā'-Allāh (q.v.), their details were gradually elaborated on numerous occasions in the writings of his son and successor, 'Abd-al-Bahā' (d. 1921, q.v.). It was during the latter's ministry that the atmosphere of religious tolerance in Ashkhabad ('Ešqābād) inspired the Bahais to build the world's first Bahai temple under the personal guidance and close attention of 'Abd-al-Bahā'. While in the Chicago area in 1912 he also laid in Wilmette the corner-stone of the second Bahai temple.

During the ministry of 'Abd-al-Bahā''s grandson and successor, Shoghi Effendi (1921-57), purchasing land for the construction of future temples became an important goal for many Bahai communities and the construction of the temples in Germany (Europe), Uganda (Africa), and Sydney (Australia) were assigned to the Bahais of these countries. Since 1963 the Universal House of Justice, the supreme elected governing body of the Bahais of the world, has called for the construction of three additional temples in Panama City (Latin America), Samoa (Pacific Ocean), and New Delhi (India).

Bahai laws prescribe that a temple be built with the utmost possible perfection in each town and village, and emphasize that its doors be open to all regardless of religion, race, color, nationality, sex, or other distinction; that only the holy scriptures, of Bahai or other religions, be read or chanted therein, in any language; that no musical instruments be played although readings and prayers set to music may be sung by choirs; that no pictures, statues, or images be displayed within the temple walls; that no sermons be delivered and no ritualistic ceremonies practised; and that no pulpits or altars be erected as an incorporated architectural feature, although readers may stand behind a simple, portable lectern. There being no clergy in the Bahai faith, readers are selected from the community, none serving as a permanent reader. The architect of a Bahai temple could be a Bahai or not, and the submission of designs by the public is permissible. The spirit of the Bahai laws emphasizes that a Bahai temple is a gathering place where the followers of all faiths may worship God without the imposition of denominational practices or restrictions. Since the act of worship is deemed to be purely individual in character, rigidity and uniformity are avoided in Bahai temples.

As stipulated by 'Abd-al-Bahā', the essential architectural character of the temple requires a nine-sided, circular shape. Although a dome has so far been a feature of all Bahai temples, it is not regarded as an essential part of their structure. It has been advanced that the number nine, as the largest single digit representing comprehensiveness and unity, stands as the numerical value of the Arabic word "Bahā'," from which the words Bahā'-Allāh and Bahai have been derived. Existing Bahai temples, surrounded by gardens and often referred to as "silent teachers," have played an important role in familiarizing the public with Bahai history and teachings, and because of their unique designs reflecting the indigenous cultural, social, and environmental elements of their locations, they continue to attract large numbers of the public.

The Bahai temple, as one of the outstanding institutions conceived by Bahā'-Allāh, is surrounded by a complex of humanitarian, educational, and charitable institutions such as a hospital, an orphanage, a school, a university, a hostel, etc. It belongs to the international Bahai community which is governed by the Universal House of Justice. The cost of constructing temples has been met by voluntary contributions made by Bahais throughout the world, they being explicitly forbidden to accept donations for the advancement of the faith from non-Bahais, a stricture rigorously upheld. Houses of Worship are maintained and administered by the national Spiritual Assembly of the Bahais of the country in which they are located.

The structural design of the first Bahai temple in Ashkhabad was prepared by Ostād 'Alī-Akbar Bannā' and work, which was started in 1902 and supervised by Ḥājī Mīrzā Moḥammad-Taqī, the Wakīl-al-Dawla, was completed in 1919. The temple, which served the community for two decades was expropriated by the government and converted into an art gallery in 1938. Ten years later, violent earthquakes seriously damaged the building and the heavy rains of the following years weakened the structure to the point that the Soviet authorities decided to demolish the remaining edifice and convert the site into a public park.

The temple in Wilmette, near Chicago, on Lake Michigan was designed by Louis J. Bourgeois in 1919, while the corner-stone had already been laid on 1 May 1912 by 'Abd-al-Bahā'. Dedicated in 1953, it is the most ornate Bahai temple in the world and can seat 1,191 people. It is 191 feet from the lowest level to the pinnacle of the dome ribs, and the diameter of the exterior of the dome is 90 feet.

The construction of the temple near Kampala, Uganda, designed by Charles Mason Remey, started in May, 1957 and the temple was opened to the public on 15 January 1961. The height of the building is 124 feet, and the diameter of its dome is 44 feet. It has seating capacity of 800.

The fourth Bahai temple, with a seating capacity of 600, also designed by Remey, was officially dedicated on 16 September 1961 at Ingleside, near Sydney, Australia. It is located in a seven-acre property and the height from its basement floor to the top of the spire is 130 feet.

The fifth Bahai temple was constructed at Langenhain, in the Taunus Hills near Frankfurt-am-Main, West Germany. Designed and built by Teuto Rocholl, a non-Bahai architect, the temple seats about 500 persons, measures 158 feet in diameter at its base, and 92 feet in height from base to the top of the dome. Twenty-seven pillars support the dome in the interior. The central rotunda is brightened by the reflection of the sun on 570 glass panels. The temple was dedicated on 4 July 1964.

The corner-stone of the sixth Bahai temple was laid atop Cerro Sonsonate, seven miles north of Panama

City, Panama, on 8 October 1967. It was designed by the English architect, Peter Tillotson. Construction started on 1 December 1969 and the temple was dedicated on 29 April 1972. Its seating capacity is 550; its diameter at base is 200 feet, and its overall height is 92 feet.

The seventh temple, which was designed by Hossein Amanat (Ḥosayn Amānat), was built in Western Samoa, in the Pacific Ocean. An area of approximately 17 acres surrounds it, and it can seat 700. The construction of the temple was commenced in 1979 and it was dedicated on 1 September 1984. The building is 102 feet high and is located at Tiapapata, in the hills behind Apia.

The eighth Bahai temple, near Nehru Place, at Bahapur, in New Delhi, India, and known as the Lotus Temple because of its shape, was dedicated on 24 December 1986. Designed by Fariburz Sahba (Farīborz Ṣahbā), the temple stands in an area of 26.7 acres and has an overall height of 40.8 meters and is 70 meters in diameter. The temple contains 1,200 fixed seats, expandable to 2,500.

The Bahais of Iran acquired an area of 3,580,000 square meters on the slopes of Mount Alborz, named Ḥadīqa, in northeastern Tehran, for the eventual construction of the first temple in that land. Although the design was prepared and preliminary studies were undertaken, hostile circumstances prevented its construction. A complex of buildings, however, was erected on the site in the 1960s and dedicated to educational and administrative activities.

Of a total of 148 national Bahai communities around the world, 84 have acquired sites for the future construction of temples; the remainder are in the process of securing them. In many cases the lands acquired have, in the meantime, been put to agricultural uses, or buildings devoted to the education of children, etc., have been erected on them.

Bibliography: General work and articles regarding the significance and purpose of the Bahai temples. ʿAbd-al-Bahāʾ, *The Promulgation of Universal Peace*, Wilmette, 1982, pp. 65-66, 71-72. Idem, *Selections from the Writings of ʿAbduʾl-Bahá*, Haifa, 1978, pp. 95-100. *Baháʾí Year Book* 1, 1925-26, pp. 59-64. ʿA. Ešrāq Ḵāvarī, *Ganjīna-ye ḥodūd wa aḥkām*, Tehran, 1350 Š./1971, pp. 230-40. A. Fāżel Māzandarānī, *Amr wa ḵalq*, Langenhain, 1986, IV, pp. 147-53. W. S. Hatcher and J. D. Martin, *The Baháʾí Faith—The Emerging Global Religion*, San Francisco, 1984, pp. 169-71. H. Holley, *The Meaning of Worship—The Purpose of the Baháʾí House of Worship*, Wilmette, 1980. H. Hornby, *Lights of Guidance*, New Delhi, 1983, pp. 487-90. A. Taherzadeh, *The Revelation of Baháʾuʾlláh*, Oxford, 1983, III, pp. 343-48. A. Vail, "The Baháʾí Temple of Universal Peace," *The Open Court* (*Chicago*) 45/7, July, 1931, pp. 411-17, R. Weinberg, "The Dawning Place," *World Faiths Insight*, N.S. 12, February, 1986, pp. 26-29. Specific articles and progress reports on individual temples listed chronologically by date of completion. Ashkhabad (Russia): A. Bakšandagī, *Mašreq al-aḏkār-e ʿEšqābād*, MS., Haifa, Baháʾí World Centre Library, 1985. *Baháʾí Year Book* 1, 1925-26, pp. 79-81. *The Baháʾí World* 2, 1926-28, pp. 121-22; 3, 1928-30, pp. 168-69; 14, 1963-68, pp. 479-81. M. Momen, *The Bábí and Baháʾí Religions, 1844-1944*, Oxford, 1981, pp. 442-43. Wilmette: H. Dahl, "Baháʾí Temple Gardens: The Landscape Setting of a Unique Architectural Monument," *Landscape Architecture* 43/14, July, 1953, pp. 144-49. A. McDaniel, *The Spell of the Temple*, New York, 1953. P. Murphy, "It Couldn't Be Done Today," *Modern Concrete* 42/12, April, 1979, pp. 40-45. Shoghi Effendi, *God Passes By*, Wilmette, 1987, pp. 348-53. B. Whitmore, *The Dawning Place: The Building of a Temple*, Wilmette, 1984. *Baháʾí Year Book* 1, 1925-26, pp. 64-78. *The Baháʾí World* 2, 1926-28, pp. 116-20; 3, 1928-30, pp. 142-67; 4, 1930-32, pp. 189-216; 5, 1932-34, pp. 267-321; 6, 1934-36, pp. 397-416; 7, 1936-38, pp. 429-46; 8, 1938-40, pp. 516-34; 9, 1940-44, pp. 485-502; 10, 1944-46, pp. 411-24; 12, 1950-54, pp. 524-47; 13, 1954-63, pp. 743-48; 17, 1976-79, pp. 375-76. Kampala: *The Baháʾí World* 13, 1954-63, pp. 705-19. Sydney: "Baháʾí Temple, Third in the World, Being Built on Mona Vale Hilltop, Sydney," *Building, Lighting, Engineering*, 24 September 1958, pp. 38-39. *The Baháʾí World* 13, 1954-63, pp. 721-32. Frankfurt: *The Baháʾí World* 13, 1954-63, pp. 733-41; 14, 1963-68, pp. 483-88. Panama City: P. Tillotson, "Nine Gateways to God: British Design for a Temple in Panama," *Concrete* 6/11, November, 1972, pp. 22-24. *The Baháʾí World* 14, 1963-68, pp. 493-94; 15, 1968-73, pp. 632-49. Samoa: M. Day, "A Beacon of Unity," *Tusitala*, Autumn, 1985, pp. 32-33. *The Baháʾí World* 16, 1973-76, pp. 488-89; 17, 1976-79, pp. 371-74. New Delhi: R. Sabikhi, "Temple Like 'A Lotus Bud, Its Petals Slowly Unfolding'," *Architecture*, September, 1987, pp. 72-75. F. Sahba, "The Baháʾí House of Worship, New Delhi," *IABSE Symposium, Paris-Versailles 1987: Concrete Structures for the Future*, France, 1987, pp. 579-84. *The Baháʾí World* 16, 1973-76, pp. 486-87; 17, 1976-79, pp. 368-70.

(V. RAFATI AND F. SAHBA)

X. BAHAI SCHOOLS

The Bahai schools were a series of government-recognized educational institutions established, owned, and controlled by the Bahai community in various centers of Iran and Ashkhabad and conducted on Bahai principles from 1897 until 1929 in Ashkhabad and until 1934 in Iran.

Despite the significance of child education, both general and religious, as explicitly propounded in the writings of Bahāʾ-Allāh, who made the education of both boys and girls an obligation of the parents (see *Baháʾí Education*, pp. 4-6), and further elaborated by his son and successor, ʿAbd-al-Bahāʾ (d. 1340/1921; ibid., pp. 11-53), the prolonged and severe persecution of the Bahai community which started with the inception of the Babi faith in Iran in 1260/1844 and continued throughout the period of Bahā'-Allāh's ministry (d. 1309/1892), had prevented the process of formal education of Bahai children from unfolding until about 1897. Before then, only informal elementary classes could be offered by individual believers at private homes on a tutorial basis. These classes were designed primarily to provide fundamental courses on the Persian and Arabic languages and literatures, and the history and writings of the Bahai faith. They were held in early Bahai communities such as Russian Turkmenistan, Burma, and various places in Iran like Najafābād near Isfahan.

Under the guidance of 'Abd-al-Bahā' more than thirty Bahai schools were gradually established as circumstances permitted throughout Iran and several places in India, Egypt, Turkey, Palestine, and southern Russia.

Established, controlled, and funded through the support of the Bahai community, the earliest Bahai schools began in Tehran and Ashkhabad (q.v.), now in Russian Turkmenistan, and were followed by the erection of the Tawakkol school in Qazvīn, the Ta'yīd and the Mawhebat (for girls) in Hamadān, the Waḥdat-e Bašar in Kāšān, the Ma'refat in Ārān (near Kāšān), the Taraqqī in Šahmīrzād (near Semnān), the Mīṯāqīya in Neyrīz, and a number of similar schools in Ābāda, Qomrūd (near Kāšān), Najafābād, Bahnamīr (near Sārī), Maryamābād and Mehdīābād (near Yazd), Bārforūš, Sārī, Bošrūya (in Khorasan), Eštehārd (near Karaj), and several other schools outside Iran such as Tashkent, Marv, İskenderun (Turkey), and Daidanaw (Burma). Bahai schools not only attracted the children of Bahai background but soon gained enough educational strength and reliability to attract children of various religious and social backgrounds.

The Tarbīat school was established in Tehran in 1315/1897 and two years later became officially recognized by the government. Founded by Ḥājī Mīrzā Ḥasan Adīb Ayādī (d. 1337/1918), the Tarbīat became one of the best known schools in Iran by virtue of the devotion of its teachers, the advanced quality of its curriculum, and its high standard of order and discipline (*Ṯābet*, pp. 94-95; *Bahá'í News* 1/7, 1910, p. 5). During the first few years of its existence the Tarbīat was supported by financial contributions from individual Bahais, but, as it expanded in subsequent years, the local Spiritual Assembly of Tehran formed a management committee. Among its earliest members were Dr. 'Aṭā'-Allāh Bakšāyeš (d. 1363/1944) and Dr. Moḥammad Monajjem (d. 1338/1920). Following Adīb, Monajjem and Bakšāyeš, 'Azīz-Allāh Meṣbāḥ (d. 1363/1945) and 'Alī-Akbar Forūtan became the principals of the school. A statistical report shows that the school in 1330/1911 had a total of 371 students in 8 grades (in 11 classes), 18 faculty members, and 4 staff (ms., International Bahá'í Archives, Haifa, MR 1402). By 1932 the school offered 6 preparatory grades and 4 intermediate grades; of the 26 teachers, 20 were Bahais, and of the 541 students, 339 were Bahais, 175 Muslims, 21 Christians, 4 Jews, and 2 Zoroastrians (*The Bahá'í World* V, p. 117).

The foundation of the Tarbīat school for girls in Tehran was in response to 'Abd-al-Bahā''s emphasis on the education of women as a matter of necessity. Established in the name of Dr. 'Aṭā'-Allāh Bakšāyeš in 1329/1911 (*Solaymānī*, 1973, p. 23), a few American Bahais such as Miss Lillian Kappes (d. 1338/1920), Dr. Susan Moody (d. 1353/1934), Dr. Genevieve Coy (d. 1382/1963), and Miss Adelaide Sharp (d. 1396/1976) served in the school in close cooperation with their Persian Bahai and non-Bahai colleagues. Starting with 6 grades for children and offering special courses for girls up to the age of 20 (*Ṯābet*, p. 104), the school could accommodate 400 students around 1919 (*Āvāra*, p. 73) and a decade later was advanced enough to offer 11 grades to 719 students, of whom 359 were Bahais, 352 Muslims, and 8 Jews. (*The Bahá'í World* V, p. 117).

Outside Iran, the private informal education of the Bahai children of Ashkhabad, which had started with the establishment of the Bahai community in that land in 1301/1883 (*Tārīḵ-e moḵtaṣar-e ta'sīs wa baqā-ye madrasa-ye pesarāna wa doḵtarāna-ye bahā'īān-e 'Ešqābād 1897-1927*, ms., International Bahá'í Archives, Haifa, M1678), received official governmental recognition in 1315/1897 through the unfailing efforts of its founders Sayyed Mehdī Golpāyegānī (d. 1346/1928) and Ḥājī Mīrzā Ḥosayn Mo'allem Yazdī (d. 1346/1928) who erected a new building for the school and hired Bahai and non-Bahai teachers (*Solaymānī*, 1968, pp. 407-17). By 1907, the increasing number of girl students required a separate girls' school of seven grades. Both schools (ca. 1927) had 462 students (237 boys and 225 girls), 62 of whom were non-Bahais; 20 percent of the students were exempted from paying the tuition and 46 percent would pay part of it (*Tārīḵ-e moḵtaṣar*). These Bahai schools were the first educational institutions to be conducted along modern pedagogical lines in the region (*Hoonaard*, p. 109). The schools were confiscated by the Bolshevik government in 1929 (*Māzandarānī*, 1975, p. 1041). Following the foundation of Bahai schools in Tehran and Ashkhabad, numerous other schools were opened in almost every major Bahai community. To refer to just a few leading ones, in Qazvīn, the first Bahai school, called the Tawakkol, was opened in 1324/1908 as a result of the encouragement and financial support of the leading Bahais of the city such as Mīrzā Mūsā Ḥakīmbāšī (Ḥakīm Elāhī) and Mīrzā Reżā Khan Taslīmī under the management of Ḥājī Ebrāhīm Wā'eẓ.

In 1327/1909 the Ta'yīd school for boys and the Mawhebat school for girls were officially opened in Hamadān (*Ešrāq Ḵāvarī*, p. 139), through the efforts of Mīrzā Āqā Jān Ṭabīb b. Hārūn, and in 1331/1913 were officially recognized by the government (*Ṯābet*, p. 39). The name Mawhebat was given the school by 'Abd-al-Bahā', who continued to encourage it ('Abd-al-Bahā', pp. 13-14, 25, 83-84, 183-85).

The Bahai school in Kāšān, which was formed in 1316/1898 through the efforts of Ḵ'āja Rabī' (d.

1336/1917) received official governmental recognition in 1328/1910 under the name of Waḥdat-e Bašar, given also by ʿAbd-al-Bahāʾ. The school started with 6 grades and in 1332/1913, the seventh grade was added (*Māzandarānī*, 1972, p. 283).

The local Spiritual Assembly of the Bahais of Najafābād, in about 1328/1910, hired a private teacher to conduct necessary classes for the Bahai children of the village. These classes, which lasted for two years, were the predecessors of a school which was inaugurated in 1330/1912 as a branch of the Tehran Tarbīat school, to offer four grades under the management of Moḥammad-ʿAlī Šāʾeq. In 1337/1919 the school continued its services under a new name, Saʿādat, and in 1344/1926 developed to a six-grade school and was officially recognized by the government in 1349/1931 in the name of Aḥmad Šahīdī, its principal. It continued until 1352/1934 when, with about 127 students, it was closed by order of the government.

In the same village the Saʿādat school for girls occupied its own building in 1346/1928 to accommodate classes in three grades and was officially recognized in 1347/1929. In 1348/1930 it expanded to a six-grade school and in the last three years of its services (1350-52/1932-34) all 24 girls who graduated from the sixth grade passed the final Ministry examinations. The school was closed by order of the government in 1352/1934 (*The History of the Saʿādat Schools in Najafābād*, ms., Bahá'í International Archives, Haifa, M1741). Subsequent to the establishment of these schools, the Saʿādat school in Bārforūš, in 1331/1912, a Bahai school in Ardestān in 1332/1913 (*Ṯābet*, pp. 39-40), and many others in other centers came into being.

As Bahai institutions, the daily operation of these schools was in conformity with Bahai teachings and principles. Schools were free for the children of poor families and others would pay a sum in proportion to the financial means of the family. The total tuition paid by the students, however, in most cases, was not sufficient to run the school, and the balance had to be paid by the local Spiritual Assembly of the city or be met through private contributions of individual Bahais.

In 1313 Š./1935 the Deputy Minister of Education under Reżā Shah issued an official order to the effect that since the Tarbīat school had been closed on Thursday, 15 Āḏar 1313 Š./6 December 1934 (the commemoration day of the martyrdom of the Bāb), it could no longer operate (*Martin*, p. 17; *The Bahá'í World* VI, p. 27). The closing of the Tarbīat school was followed by the closing of all other Bahai schools in the country. Since then they have remained closed and the efforts of the Bahais to have the order rescinded have been of no avail.

In addition to the regular, recognized Bahai schools, in 1315/1898 Sayyed Ḥasan Hāšemīzāda (known as Motawajjeh) (d. 1335 Š./1956) gathered a group of Bahai children of south Tehran and inaugurated Bahai classes which became known as "Character Training Classes" (Kelāshā-ye dars-e aḵlāq) and soon were formed in all parts of the city and gradually were instituted in the whole country on Friday mornings (Solaymānī, 1968, pp. 40-45). At the outset the curriculum of these classes consisted of the memorization of prayers and short excerpts from Bahai and other sacred texts. Later the *Dorūs al-dīyāna*, written by Moḥammad-ʿAlī Qāʾenī (d. 1303 Š./1924) and published in Ashkhabad in 1329/1911, was used and the study of selections from Bahāʾ-Allāh's *Ketāb-e īqān* (The book of certitude) and *Aqdas* (The most holy book, q.v.), ʿAbd-al-Bahāʾ's (q.v.) *Maqāla-ye šaḵṣ-ī sayyāḥ* (A traveler's narrative) and *Mofāważāt* (Some answered questions), and the Persian translation of J. E. Esslemont's *Bahá'u'lláh and the New Era*, formed the curriculum.

As the classes extended, management committees both at the local and national levels were formed to conduct and supervise the classes. The children of each community were grouped according to their age to form classes from grades one to twelve. To fulfill the academic need of the various classes ʿAlī-Akbar Forūtan (in 1933) compiled a series of special textbooks for various grades which became basic standard books and were widely studied throughout the country. The series consisted of Bahai history, laws, ordinances, and administrative principles. Depending on the mutual interest of the teachers and the students, other materials, in addition to the text books, were also taught in the classes. No salary was paid to the teachers and no tuition fees were charged.

Bahai children's classes are currently held throughout the Bahai world in 165 countries or territories (*The Seven Year Plan: 1979-1986*, Haifa, 1986, p. 75) and the curriculum is prepared by the national and/or local committees in charge of the classes. Many are attended by non-Bahai students, as well.

Bahai seasonal schools, mostly summer and winter schools, are also held around the world to foster association and a spirit of fellowship among the Bahais, provide intellectual training, and offer courses on the history, tenets, and administration of the faith as well as fundamental courses on the history and teachings of other religions, to deepen their understanding of different aspects of the faith. Courses are usually conducted in lecture form and are accompanied by study classes, seminars, and workshops.

Originated in America in 1927 (*Shoghi Effendi*, 1970, p. 340) for the primary use of the Bahais, Bahai summer schools were adopted by other Bahai communities around the world and are open to non-Bahais who wish to learn about the faith and the social life of the Bahai community. Bahai seasonal schools as national institutions function under the direct supervision of the national Spiritual Assembly in each country and every member of the Bahai community is encouraged to attend one of the schools each year.

The first Bahai summer school in Iran was instituted in 1939 on the estate of a Bahai in Ḥājīābād, some 40 kilometers northeast of Tehran, and as circumstances permitted continued functioning in various locations until 1979, when the Bahai institutions were closed by the Islamic government.

The latest statistical report shows that 128 national Assemblies, 86 percent of the national communities in the world, held seasonal schools by April, 1968 (*The Seven Year Plan*, p. 100). For detailed reports on Bahai seasonal schools see the "Survey of Current Bahá'í Activities" in volumes of *The Bahá'í World*.

Bibliography (including references on the Bahai views on education): ʿAbd-al-Bahāʾ, *Makātīb-e ʿAbd-al-Bahāʾ*, Tehran, 121 B. (*Badīʿ*)/1964, IV, pp. 13-14, 25, 48-49, 83-84, 93, 95, 143-44, 183-85. ʿAbd-al-ʿAlī ʿAlāʾī, *Moʾassesa-ye Ayādī-e AmrAllāh*, Tehran, 130 B./1973, pp. 455-56. ʿAbd-al-Ḥosayn Āvāra, *al-Kawākeb al-dorrīya*, Cairo, 1924, II, pp. 73-76. *Bahá'í Education: A Compilation*, Wilmette, 1977. *Bahá'í News*, Chicago, I, 1910, 6, pp. 6-7; 7, pp. 3-7. *The Bahá'í World*, Wilmette, repr., 1980-81: IV, 1930-32, p. 82; V, 1932-34, p. 117; VI, 1934-36, pp. 26-28, 30, 96-97, 485; XIV, 1963-68, Haifa, 1974, p. 327. ʿAbd-al-Ḥamīd Ešrāq Ḵāvarī, *Taqwīm-e tārīḵ*, Tehran, 126 B./1969, pp. 125, 139-40, 155. ʿAlī-Akbar Forūtan, "A Short History of the Tarbiyat Schools of Tihran, Iran," *Glory* 8/2, May-June 1976, pp. 3-5. Will C. van den Hoonaard, "A Pattern of Development: An Historical Study of Bahá'í Communities in International Development," *Bahá'í Studies Notebook*, Ottawa, Ont., 3/3-4, February, 1984, pp. 109-14. Douglas Martin, *The Persecution of the Bahá'ís of Iran 1844-1984*, Ottawa, 1984. Asad-Allāh Māzandarānī, *Asrār al-āṯār*, Tehran, 129 B./1972, V, p. 283, Idem, *Ẓohūr al-ḥaqq*, Tehran, 132 B./1975, VIII, 2 pts., p. 982. Shoghi Effendi, *God Passes By*, Wilmette, 1970, pp. 299, 363, 371-72. Idem, *Tawqīʿāt-e mobāraka*, Tehran, 105 B./1948, pp. 370-79. ʿAzīz-Allāh Solaymānī *Maṣābīḥ-e hedāyat*, Tehran, II, 121 B./1964, pp. 557-59; VI, 125 B./1968, pp. 407-17; VIII, 130 B./1973, pp. 22-25, 347-49. *Star of the West*, Chicago, 5/5, 1914-15, p. 74; 11/13, 1920-21, p. 226; 19, pp. 324-26; 12/7, 1921-22, p. 141. ʿAbbās Ṯābet, *Tārīḵča-ye madrasa-ye Tarbīat-e banīn-e Tehrān*, ms., Bahai International Library, Haifa, Pam 142-284.

(V. Rafati)

xi. Bahai Conventions

Bahai conventions occur at the national and international level for the primary purpose of electing the national Spiritual Assemblies and the Universal House of Justice (see MAḤFEL-E RŪḤĀNĪ and BAYT AL-ʿADL).

The first Bahai convention in the world was probably the meeting convened by the Chicago Spiritual Assembly on 26 November 1907 for the purpose of choosing a site for the House of Worship (Mašreq al-Aḏkār) that was to be built. Thereafter, conventions were held annually in the United States and, from 1910, on ʿAbd-al-Bahāʾ's instructions, were held each year during the Bahai festival of Reżwān (21 April-2 May). In 1909, with the approval of ʿAbd-al-Bahāʾ, the convention decided to set up a formal national body to be called the Bahai Temple Unity, the precursor of the national Spiritual Assembly in the United States.

In some countries, Bahai conventions antedate the establishment of the national Spiritual Assembly since there were national Bahai institutions that were precursors of that body. In Iran, for example, the first national convention was held in 1927 to elect the "Central Spiritual Assembly" although the national Spiritual Assembly was not formally set up until 1934. In other countries, the holding of national conventions postdated the establishment of national Spiritual Assemblies which were elected by postal ballots until then. This occurred in the British Isles where the national Spiritual Assembly was elected in 1923, but the first convention was not held until 1927. In general, however, the development of Bahai conventions lagged behind in the East compared with the West because of the difficulties of holding large meetings.

Currently, Bahais in electoral districts elect delegates to the national convention. The Universal House of Justice decides the total number of delegates depending on the number of Bahais in that country. The lowest number of delegates is nine and the numbers can then rise in multiples of five, nine and nineteen. The highest number of delegates is currently 171. Each national Spiritual Assembly then distributes the delegates among the electoral districts in proportion to the number of Bahais in each district.

The national convention is held annually, although this may be changed in the future by the Universal House of Justice. It has two main functions: Firstly to elect the new national Spiritual Assembly—each delegate votes for nine persons from among the whole adult Bahai community of that country; secondly, the National Convention may consult on any subject it wishes and can make resolutions to be passed on to the national Spiritual Assembly. However, the national Spiritual Assembly has no obligation to act on these resolutions, only to consider them.

The international convention is at present held every five years in Haifa to elect the Universal House of Justice. All national Spiritual Assembly members are eligible to attend and vote.

Both national and international conventions are usually held during the Reżwān period (see above). The convention elects its own chairman and secretary. Bahai elections are by secret ballot; there are no electioneering or canvassing of votes and no nominations of candidates.

Bibliography: *Principles of Bahaʾi Administration*, London, 1950, pp. 61-72. *National Spiritual Assembly*, no. 5 of a series of compilations issued by the Universal House of Justice, London, 2nd ed., 1973, pp. 10-16.

(M. Momen)

xii. Bahai Literature

Bahai literature is a large body of writing in Persian and Arabic produced by leaders and adherents of the Bahai religion in Iran from the 1860s to the present. This article is concerned primarily with poetry and belles lettres rather than apologetic, didactic, historiographical, liturgical, or scriptural materials, except insofar as the last-mentioned exhibit characteristics of literary interest.

The immediate antecedents of Bahai literature are the various scriptural and apologetic writings produced in the 1260s/1840s by the Bāb (q.v., and see BAYĀN) and some of his leading followers. Babism was primarily a literate and elitist movement among a section of the Shi'ite *'olamā'*, but from its outset conventional learning and scholarly writing were, if not wholly rejected, relegated to a status much inferior to that enjoyed by the products of "innate knowledge" and "inspired" composition or "revelation," in which the speed of writing was regarded as a sign of divine activity. In the later phase of the movement (roughly 1264/1848 to 1283/1866), the ability to write or utter "divinely-inspired" verses became the chief criterion whereby claimants to religious authority might be judged. Several individuals regarded as *ommī* (in this case unlearned (but not illiterate) began to write in this manner, but apart from works by the Bāb and Mīrzā Yaḥyā Nūrī Ṣobḥ-e Azal (q.v.), very little of this material has survived. Nevertheless, those writings we do possess, together with letters and fragments by other members of the Babi hierarchy (all of them *'olamā'*, like Mollā Moḥammad-'Alī Bārforūšī Qoddūs (q.v.), Qorrat-al-'Ayn Ṭāhera (q.v.), Sayyed Yaḥyā Dārābī (q.v.), and Sayyed Ḥosayn Yazdī) share certain important characteristics (see MacEoin, *Babi Doctrine and History*, chap. 4). There is a tendency toward esotericism, obscurantism, idiosyncrasy in matters of style, grammar, and subject, and the use of extended doxological and invocatory formulae (particularly in elaborate perorations based on the divine names). Free association and stream-of-consciousness-style composition are marked features of some works, e.g., the Bāb's *Ketāb al-asmā'* and *Ketāb-e panj ša'n* or Ṣobḥ-e Azal's *Mer'āt al-bayān, Ṣaḥā'ef al-Azal, Laḥaẓāt*, etc.

These characteristics are retained in the later writings of Ṣobḥ-e Azal (which include a great deal of poetry), but otherwise the Azalī branch of Babism has been almost bereft of literary productions of any kind, in spite of the existence of Azalī literateurs such as Mīrzā Āqā Khan Kermānī (q.v.), Shaikh Aḥmad Rūḥī Kermānī (q.v.), and Mīrzā Yaḥyā Dawlatābādī (q.v.). Mīrzā Ḥosayn-'Alī Nūrī Bahā'-Allāh (q.v.), whose Bahai version of the original Babi movement rapidly ousted its Azalī rival throughout Iran, first came to prominence as one of the unlearned revealers of inspired verses in Baghdad during the 1850s and then as the de facto head of the faith in the 1860s. His early writings represent a significant departure from most previous Babi writing (except for the poetical works of Qorrat-al-'Ayn, with whom he was associated) in that they are, for the most part, couched in straightforward prose or verse. Although he was later to take a marked aversion to such matters, Bahā'-Allāh was at this period markedly influenced by Sufi writing and even spent a two-year period (1270-72/1854-56) living as a dervish in Kurdistan (see Cole, "Baha'u'llah and the Naqshbandi Sufis"). Sufi influences are particularly at work in a small number of poems composed in Baghdad, Kurdistan, and Istanbul, several of which bear the pen name (*taḵalloṣ*) "Darvīš." The most important of these are: 1) a Persian *ḡazal* entitled *Rašḥ-e 'amā*, generally considered his earliest extant work; 2) an Arabic *qaṣīda* of 127 distichs (*bayt*s) entitled *al-Qaṣīda al-warqā'īya*, modeled on 'Omar ebn al-Fāreż's famous *Naẓm al-solūk*; 3) a Persian *maṯnawī* of 318 *bayt*s entitled *Maṯnawī-e mobārak*, written in Istanbul and probably the last of Bahā'-Allāh's works in verse. Perhaps the most noticeable feature of these poems, which are written in an elegant yet uncomplicated style and possess considerable freshness, is the complete absence of identifiably Babi elements.

This is also largely true of some of Bahā'-Allāh's earliest prose works, several of which are of real literary merit. Notable among these are: 1) *Haft wādī* and 2) *Čahār wādī*, two Persian mystical treatises along the lines of 'Aṭṭār's *Manṭeq al-ṭayr*; 3) *Kalemāt-e maknūna*, a collection of Persian and Arabic aphoristic statements, mostly of an ethical nature; 4) the *Ḥorūfāt-e 'ālīn*, a short Arabic disquisition on death, which also exists in a Persian translation by the author; 5) the *Ketāb-e īqān*, one of his very few full-length works, being a book of apologetic and exegesis written in a lucid and original Persian style; 6) the *Jawāher al-asrār*, an Arabic treatise along similar lines written about the same time; and 7) a series of brief Persian and Arabic poems and prose pieces, largely mystical in nature, including "Lawḥ-e mallāḥ al-qods" and "Lawḥ-e nāqūs," all in prose, and the poems "Lawḥ-e ḥūrīya," "Lawḥ-e šakar-šakan," "Lawḥ-e ḡolām al-ḵold," "Lawḥ-e halhala yā bešārāt," "Sāqī az ḡayb-e baqā'," "Bāz ā wa be-deh jām-ī," and "Az bāḡ-e elāhī."

Although Bahā'-Allāh continued to write extensively in Edirne (1280-85/1863-68) and Palestine (1285-1309/1868-92), his later work is, with only a few exceptions, increasingly turgid, repetitive, and visibly lacking in the linguistic brilliance and poetic energy that characterize his early output. The contents of some of these later writings reveal an acquaintance with European ideas, but the style and format remain Persian. Divorced from its earlier mysticism, Bahā'-Allāh's prose becomes less elegant and even archaic. Perhaps the best products of this period are a series of proclamatory letters to several kings and rulers in Asia and Europe, some of which exhibit a polished epistolatory style. His last major work, a book-length Persian letter to the famous *mojtahed* of Isfahan Āqā Najafī, is a rambling patchwork of quotations from earlier works tied together with personal reminiscences and historical allusions. The need to produce "inspired" verses at great speed in response to the stream of letters and petitions arriving from Iran and elsewhere led him to rely more and more on established formulae in order to keep up with the demand.

By contrast, the works of Bahā'-Allāh's eldest son 'Abbās ('Abd-al-Bahā', q.v.) exhibit the mannered characteristics of an urbane and well-educated litterateur in touch with modern currents of thought and behavior and with some European writing. Whereas his father's Arabic was heavily Persianized, simple, and frequently ungrammatical, that of 'Abd-al-Bahā' is polished, careful, and more Arab than Iranian in its manner. His earliest work, a commentary on the Hadith "*konto kanzan makfīyan*" written in his late teens in Edirne for 'Alī Ševket Pasha, shows close familiarity with the ideas and exegetical methods of philosophical Sufism. These and related themes occur in several other works which appear to be from roughly the same period, including *tafsīr*s on the *Sūrat al-fāteḥa* and the words *ḡolebat al-Rūm* (Koran 30:1). Other issues begin to emerge in later works, however, among which social and political questions come increasingly to the fore. The most detailed and interesting of these works is a Persian treatise entitled *al-Resāla al-madanīya* (or *Ketāb asrār al-ḡaybīya le-asbāb al-madanīya* [sic]), written in 1292/1875 and published anonymously in Bombay (1310/1892-93) and Cairo (1329/1911), and later translated twice into English. This work, which makes general proposals for reform in Iran and the Islamic world as a whole, deserves to be more seriously regarded as a contribution to the reformist literature of the period. Much slighter and rather more conservative in tone is the *Resāla-ye sīāsīya* (1893), also published anonymously. Of less interest are his *Maqāla-ye šaksī sayyāḥ* (A traveler's narrative), a brief anonymous history of Babism written about 1303/1886 and later published together with a translation by E. G. Browne; and the *Tadkerat al-wafā'*, a collection of meager hagiographies given as table-talks in 1915 and published posthumously in Haifa in 1343/1924. Until his death in 1340/1921, 'Abd-al-Bahā' kept up a vast correspondence with Bahais in Iran, Europe, and the United States, and his collected "tablets" (*alwāḥ*; *tawqī'āt*) contain numerous examples of his mature literary style. Of interest too are his many public addresses delivered in Europe and North America, his table-talks collected under the title *al-Nūr al-abhā fī mofāważāt ḥażrat 'Abd-al-Bahā'*, and his numerous Persian prayers (*monājāt*). The latter are often extremely beautiful, with a fine feeling for the rhymes and cadences of the language; some are even written in verse.

'Abd-al-Bahā''s grandson and successor, Šawqī (Shoghi Effendi, q.v., d. 1377/1957), wrote principally in English, all his major works being translated later into Persian; but he also penned large quantities of letters in the latter language, as well as some in Arabic. His baroque and mannered style, with its extended periods, archaisms, and at times contrived vocabulary, had a marked effect on Bahai writing in this century, encouraging it to be florid, hyperbolic, and out of step with general changes in modern Persian letters (a phenomenon paralleled by Bahai writing in English during the same period). At the same time, Šawqī's elegant and sensitive translations of Bahai scriptural writings (largely works by Bahā'-Allāh) deserve to be mentioned here.

Bahai writing in general has concentrated on apologetics and historiography, and includes very few works of real literary merit or wider interest, with the partial exceptions of the writings of Mīrzā Abu'l-Fażl Golpāyegānī (q.v.), some autobiographical works (notably Mīrzā Ḥaydar-'Alī Eṣfahānī's *Behjat al-ṣodūr*, Yūnes Khan Afrūkta's *Kāṭerāt-e noh-sāla*, and Dr. Ḥabīb Mo'ayyad's *Kāṭerāt-e Ḥabīb*), and a few collections of hagiographical biography in the tradition of Islamic *rejāl* literature (notably Solaymānī's *Maṣābīḥ-e hedāyat* and Bayżā'ī's *Tadkera-ye šo'arā'*).

There is, however, a substantial body of poetry written by Iranian adherents of the faith, some of which is of an exceptionally high standard, although it remains for the most part unknown outside Bahai circles. Bahai poetry is essentially a continuation of classical Persian and Arabic religious verse, although it has its own themes and conventions. Much of it is didactic or apologetic in nature, and most of it makes for dull reading, but this is more than compensated for by the vigor and freshness of the better examples.

A number of early Babis wrote poetry, among them Ḥājj Solaymān Khan Tabrīzī and Karīm Khan Māfī (Behjat Qazvīnī), but little of their work has survived. Of much greater importance is the verse of Qorrat-al-'Ayn Ṭāhera, which has remained popular with Bahais and has even gained a well-deserved reputation with a wider public in Iran and India. Born in Qazvīn 1229/1814 into a family of '*olamā*', she received training as an '*ālema* and became a leading exponent of the Shaikhi (q.v.) school. An early convert of the Bāb's, she dominated the Iraqi branch of the Babi movement until 1263/1847, when she returned to Iran. Her influence on the formulation of Babi doctrine was considerable, and the numerous apologetics she wrote on behalf of the sect helped provide the impetus for the break with Islam in 1264/1848. Imprisoned for several years in Tehran, she was executed following the attempt on the life of Nāṣer-al-Dīn Shah in 1268/1852. Her reputation among modern Bahais rests largely on the belief that she was an early champion of women's rights, something which has no foundation in fact. Nevertheless, her legendary stature combined with the genuine beauty of many of the poems she composed has given her work a firm place in Bahai literature. Only a small number of her poems (as well as several falsely attributed to her) have been published, but the present writer has discovered several manuscripts of what appear to be authentic works by her, from which a scholarly edition of her poetry may eventually be prepared.

The existence of poetry by Qorrat-al-'Ayn and Bahā'-Allāh gave the writing of verse an acceptable place in the Bahai movement, even when the marked anti-Sufism of Bahā'-Allāh and 'Abd-al-Bahā' (see, e.g. Bahā'-

Allāh, *Alwāḥ-e mobāraka*, pp. 184-88; ʿAbd-al-Bahāʾ, *Makātīb* I, p. 346) rendered many of the classical models unacceptable and blocked the possibility of a spontaneous development of mystical verse within the religion. Although ʿAbd-al-Bahāʾ spoke disparagingly of the poets of the past (*Makātīb* I, p. 451), he did express approval of poetry written on Bahai religious themes and included versified passages in some of his letters (e.g., ibid., pp. 414, 421, 439; II, pp. 54-55). Since both singing and instrumental music were permitted in *al-Ketāb al-aqdas* (see AQDAS), poetry became a natural extension of liturgical recitation and a useful vehicle for the expression of numinous feelings and didactic intentions.

The earliest Bahai poet of merit was Mollā Yār-Moḥammad Zarandī Nabīl (1247-1310/1831-92), better known as the author of the history translated into English by Shoghi Effendi as *The Dawn-Breakers* or *Nabil's Narrative*. Converted to Babism at an early age, Zarandī was among the Babis who took up residence in Baghdad in the 1850s. Having failed to attract a following for theophanic claims advanced by himself, he became one of the earliest proponents of belief in Bahāʾ-Allāh as the Babi messiah. After journeys which took him to Iran, Iraq, Turkey, and Egypt, he finally settled in Palestine, where the Bahai exile community was located from 1285/1868. His history was begun in 1305/1886 and completed shortly before his suicide in 1310/1892, following the death of Bahāʾ-Allāh.

Very little of Nabīl's poetry has been published. A lengthy poem in couplet form (*maṯnawī*) providing details of Babi and Bahai history was printed in Cairo in 1342/1923-24, but copies of it are extremely rare and it has not been reissued since then; another historical *maṯnawī*, entitled *Hejr o weṣāl* (Separation and union) has not so far found its way into print. Several examples of the shorter poems, including two fine *qaṣīdas*, each with the refrain *Bahāʾ, Bahāʾ*, have been published by Browne (*JRAS* 24, 1892, pp. 323-25; *Materials*, pp. 351-57) and Bayżāʾī (*Taḏkera* III, pp. 421-35). Nabīl does appear, however, to have been a prolific writer: Bayżāʾī states that he has seen a collection of his poems amounting to 10,000 *bayts*, the bulk being made up of *maṯnawīs* (*Taḏkera* III, p. 418). Apart from the vigor of style in his non-historical poems, the chief characteristic of Nabīl's work is its use of hyperbole in reference to the claims and person of Bahāʾ-Allāh.

Of great literary merit is the work of Zarandī's younger contemporary, Āqā Mīrzā ʿAlī-Ašraf Lāhījānī, known as ʿAndalīb (ca. 1270/1853-54—1335/1917), whose *dīvān* runs to over 750 pages. Originally a Shaikhi, ʿAndalīb was converted to Bahaism in his twenties, after which he became widely known in Lāhījān for his convictions. In 1300/1883, he was arrested along with several others in the vicinity of Rašt and imprisoned there for almost two years; it was during this period that he completed his *dīvān* of *ḡazals*, amounting to over 300 poems. He later took up residence in Shiraz, where he remained, apart from several journeys (including two to Palestine), until his death.

ʿAndalīb's *ḡazals*, written in the classical style, are notable for the absence of overt references to Bahai beliefs or figures, and have undeservedly been neglected by non-Bahai anthologists. His other poetry is unqualifiedly Bahai in inspiration, consisting largely of poems in praise of Bahāʾ-Allāh and ʿAbd-al-Bahāʾ or on various Bahai festivals, particularly that of Reżwān (see ʿĪD-E REŻWAN). He also wrote a lengthy *maṯnawī* on the martyrdoms of two Bahai brothers in Isfahan in 1296/1879 (*Dīvān*, pp. 433-70) and another in reply to criticisms of Bahai belief. Apart from his fame as a poet, ʿAndalīb enjoyed a reputation as one of the leading controversialists of the Bahai movement in his day. A lively account of his technique is given by E. G. Browne in *A Year Amongst the Persian* (pp. 401-02, 433-35, 436-38, 438-40, 442-43). At least one prose work in defence of Bahaism (an *estedlālīya* in reply too Shaikh Bahāʾī Lāhījānī) is extant but unpublished.

The writing of apologetic was a particular concern of another Bahai poet of the same period, Mīrzā Moḥammad Sedehī, known as Naʿīm (1272-1334/1856-1916), whose most popular work, *Aḥsan al-taqwīm* or *Jannat al-naʿīm*, is an extended poetical apology for Bahaism. Of peasant stock, Naʿīm had a limited education but wrote poetry from an early age and formed part of a small literary circle in the village complex of Sedeh. This small group, which included the poets Āqā Sayyed Moḥammad Nayyer and Āqā Sayyed Esmāʿīl Sīnā, was converted to Bahaism in 1298/1881. Arrested and expelled from the Isfahan area, Naʿīm settled in Tehran, where he taught Persian at the British embassy and established a class for young Bahai missionaries, which he ran until his death.

Apart from the *Aḥsan al-taqwīm*, which has been published in several editions, including an annotated recension by ʿAbd-al-Ḥamīd Ešrāq Ḵāvarī, Naʿīm is well known in Bahai circles for his *Qaṣīda-ye nūnīya* (published in full but without title, with a translation by E. G. Browne in his *Literary History of Persia* IV, pp. 198-220), a *Bahārīya* (or *Sayfīya*) modeled on that of Mīrzā Ḥabīb Qāʾānī, and a *morabbaʿ* entitled *Manẓūma-ye bīst o noh ḥorūf*. Naʿīm also wrote several prose works, some of which have been published; these include two Bahai apologies (*estedlālīya*), a refutation of the Persian introduction to the *Ketāb-e noqṭat al-kāf*, and a collection of passages from the Persian *Bayān* (q.v.). The apologetic and didactic character of so much of Naʿīm's verse makes it rather forced and often turgid, although one cannot deny the ingenuity with which he incorporates textual references and quotations into the first part of his *Aḥsan al-taqwīm*. Where his poetry is freed from these restraints, however, it does reveal considerable charm.

In contrast to the overtly sectarian character of the above writers, the work of Abu'l-Ḥasan Mīrzā Shaikh al-Raʾīs (1264-1336/1848-1918) is for the most part concerned with broader issues. A son of Moḥammad-Taqī Mīrzā Ḥesām-al-Salṭana, Abu'l-Ḥasan trained as an *ʿālem* and acquired a reputation as a preacher and a constitutionalist. He appears to have been converted to

Bahaism at an early age, either by his mother or by Mīrzā ʿAlī-Reżā Sabzavārī Mostašār-al-Molk. Although Shaikh al-Raʾīs never openly proclaimed his Bahai allegiance, his connection with the faith did become known and proved a spur for controversy on more than one occasion. Under the sobriquet of Ḥayrat, Shaikh al-Raʾīs wrote a small amount of poetry, most of which has been collected in the compilation entitled *Montaḵab-e nafīs*. There are also several poems by him on Bahai themes, some of which have been published by Bayżāʾī (*Taḏkera* I, pp. 282-90). His prose works include the *Resāla-ye etteḥād-e Eslām*, written for Sultan ʿAbd-al-Ḥamīd, and the *Resālat al-abrār*, an Arabic diatribe against Ḡolām Aḥmad Qādīānī.

Mīrzā Moḥammad Ardestānī, known as Nāṭeq (1298-1355/1880-1936), also started life as an *ʿālem*, but abandoned his clerical calling following his conversion in 1325/1907. He was for eleven years Director of the Bahai Waḥdat-e Bašar school in Kāšān and later taught at the Taʾyīd school in Hamadān before becoming a full-time Bahai missionary. His *dīvān* of almost 400 pages was published posthumously by the Bahais in Tehran. Although they show little originality, Nāṭeq's poems at least take a somewhat broader view than those of most Bahai poets. Several prose works by him remain unpublished.

There are numerous other Bahai poets, most of whom have been made known thanks to the assiduous researches of Neʿmat-Allāh Ḏokāʾī Bayżāʾī, whose 4-volume *Taḏkera-ye šoʿarā-ye qarn-e awwal-e bahāʾī* contains biographies and samples of the work of no fewer than 134 individuals. Not very many of these are of much literary merit, of course, since Bayżāʾī's criterion for inclusion appears to have been that someone be a Bahai and write poetry. Nevertheless, his collection does serve to draw attention to the work of several individuals previously unknown and possibly worth further notice. It is worth observing that a reasonable number of female poets appear in this collection, several of whom were active in the Babi and early Bahai periods.

Bibliography: Neʿmat-Allāh Ḏokāʾī Bayżāʾī, *Taḏkera-ye šoʿarā-ye qarn-e awwal-e bahāʾī*, 4 vols., Tehran, 127-29 B. (*Badīʿ*)/1970-73. ʿAzīz-Allāh Solaymānī, *Maṣābīḥ-e hedāyat*, 9 vols., Tehran, 121-132 B./1964-76, I: Nayyer, Sīnā, Warqāʾ, Fāżel-e Qāʾenī; II: Abu'l-Fażl Golpāyegānī, *Mawzūn*, Meṣbāḥ; III: Naʿīm, Nāṭeq; VII: ʿAndalīb, Shaikh al-Raʾīs. ʿAlī-Ašraf Lāhījānī, *Dīvān-e ʿAndalīb*, Tehran, 126 B./1969-70. Mīrzā Moḥammad Sedehī, *Aḥsan al-taqwīm yā jannāt al-naʿīm* (with other works), ed. Mehrabān Šahrīār-Sorūš Maryāmābādī Yazdī, Bombay, 1306 Š./1927; ed. ʿAbd-al-Ḥosayn Naʿīmī, Delhi, 117 B./1960-61. ʿAbd-al-Ḥamīd Ešrāq Ḵāvarī, ed., *Jannāt-e Naʿīm*, 2 vols., Tehran, 130-31 B./1973-75. Mīrzā Moḥammad Nāṭeq, *Dīvān-e Nāṭeq*, Tehran, 124 B./1967-68. ʿAzīz-Allāh Meṣbāḥ, *Dīvān-e ašʿār-e Meṣbāḥ*, Tehran, 122 B./1965-66. Abu'l-Ḥasan Mīrzā Shaikh al-Raʾīs, *Montaḵab al-nafīs*, Tehran, 1312/1894-95. Ostād Moḥammad-ʿAlī Salmānī, *My Memories of Bahá'u'lláh*, tr. Marzieh Gail, Los Angeles, 1982 (includes translations of several odes by Salmānī). E. G. Browne, *A Literary History of Persia* IV, Cambridge, 1924, pp. 198-220. Idem, *Materials for the Study of the Bábí Religion*, Cambridge, 1918, pp. 343-58. Idem, *A Year Amongst the Persians*, 3rd ed., London, 1950. A. Taherzadeh, *The Revelation of Bahá'u'lláh*, 3 vols., Oxford, 1974-83. ʿAbd-al-Ḥamīd Ešrāq Ḵāvarī, *Ganj-e šāyegān*, Tehran, 124 B./1967-68 (on the works of Bahāʾ-Allāh). Mīrzā Ḥosayn-ʿAlī Nūrī Bahāʾ-Allāh, *Āṯār-e qalam-e aʿlā* III, Tehran, 129 B./1972-73 (contains *Jawāher al-asrār*, *Haft wādī*, *Čahār wādī*, *Maṯnawī-e mobārak*, *Qaṣīda-ye warqāʾīya*). Idem, *Māʾeda-ye āsmānī*, ed. ʿAbd-al-Ḥamīd Ešrāq Ḵāvarī, IV, Tehran, 129 B./1972-73, pp. 176-211 (poems of Bahāʾ-Allāh). Idem, *Kalemāt-e maknūna*, Tehran, 128 B./1971-72 (and numerous other editions, including an illuminated ed., Frankfurt, n.d. [ca. 1974]). Idem, *The Hidden Words of Bahā'u'llāh*, tr. Shoghi Effendi, London, 1929. Idem, *Ketāb-e īqān*, Cairo, 1352/1933; tr. Ali Kuli Khan, *The Book of Assurance* (*The Book of Ighan*), New York, n.d.; tr. Shoghi Effendi, *The Kitáb-i-Íqán. The Book of Certitude*, New York, 1931. Idem, *The Seven Valleys and the Four Valleys*, tr. Ali-Kuli Khan, New York, 1945. Idem, *Alwāḥ-e mobāraka-ye Ḥażrat Bahāʾ-Allāh* [Bombay], n.d. ʿAbd-al-Bahāʾ ʿAbbās Effendi, *al-Resāla al-madanīya*, Bombay, 1310/1892-93; Cairo, 1329/1911. Idem, *Mysterious Forces of Civilization*, tr. Johanna Dawud, London, 1910. Idem, *The Secret of Divine Civilization*, tr. Marzieh Gail, Wilmette, 1957. Idem, *Makātīb Ḥażrat ʿAbd-al-Bahāʾ*, 3 vols., Cairo, 1328-40/1910-1921. Idem, *Taḏkerat al-wafāʾ*, Haifa, 1924. Idem, *Memorials of the Faithful*, tr. Marzieh Gail, Wilmette, 1971. Idem, *al-Nūr al-abhā fī mofāważāt ʿAbd-al-Bahāʾ*, ed. Laura Clifford Barney, London, 1908. Idem, *Some Answered Questions*, ed. and tr. Laura Clifford Barney, London, 1908. Idem, *Monājāthā-ye Ḥażrat ʿAbd-al-Bahāʾ*, Bombay, n.d. Idem, *Majmūʿa-ye monājāt*, Tehran, 129 B./1971-72. A Banani, "The Writings of Abdal-Baha," in *Bahá'í World* XV, 1968-73, Haifa, 1976, pp. 780-84. Anonymous, *Ba yād-e ṣadomīn sāl-e šahādat-e nābega-ye dūrān, Qorrat-al-ʿAyn*, Tehran, 1368/1949. Ḥesām Noqabāʾī, *Ṭāhera Qorrat-al-ʿAyn*, Tehran, 128 B./1971-72. Martha Root, *Tahirih the Pure, Iran's Greatest Woman*, Karachi, 1938, repr. Los Angeles, 1981 (contains some original Persian poems). D. MacEoin, *Early Babi Doctrine and History: A Survey of Source Materials* (forthcoming). L. P. Elwell-Sutton and D. MacEoin, "Ḳurrat al-ʿAyn," in *EI*². J. R. Cole, "Bahá'u'lláh and the Naqshbandí Sufis in Iraq, 1854-1856," in J. R. Cole and M. Momen, eds., *From Iran East and West: Studies in Bábí and Bahá'í History Volume 2*, Los Angeles, 1984, pp. 1-28. Mīrzā Ḥaydar-ʿAlī Eṣfahānī, *Behjat al-ṣodūr*, Bombay, 1913. Idem, *Stories from the Delight of Hearts*, tr. and abridged A. Q. Faizi,

Los Angeles, 1980; Yūnes Khan Afrūḵta, *Ḵāṭerāt-e noh-sāla*, Tehran, 124 B./1967-68. Ḥabīb Mo'ayyad, *Ḵāṭerāt-e Ḥabīb*, 2 vols., Tehran, 118, 129 B./1961-62, 1972-73. Mīrzā Abu'l-Fażl Golpāyegānī, *Majmūʿa-ye rasāʾel-e Ḥażrat Abi'l-Fażāʾel*, Cairo, 1339/1920. Idem, *Rasāʾel wa raqāʾem*, ed. R. Mehrābḵānī, Tehran, 134 B./1977. Idem, *Miracles and Metaphors*, tr. J. Cole, Los Angeles, 1982. Idem, *Letters and Essays 1886-1913*, tr. J. Cole, Los Angeles, 1985.

(D. M. MacEoin)

BAHĀ'ĪYA ḴĀNOM (b. 1262/1846, Tehran), eldest daughter of Bahā'-Allāh (q.v.) and considered by Bahais as the "outstanding heroine of the Bahai Dispensation" (Shoghi Effendi, *God Passes By*, Wilmette, 1965, p. 108). She was named Fāṭema but is better known by her titles of Bahā'īya Ḵānom, Bahīya Ḵānom and Ḥażrat-e Waraqa-ye ʿOlyā (usually translated as the Greatest Holy Leaf). From the age of seven, she accompanied her father and family in the successive stages of their exile (Baghdad, Istanbul, Edirne, and finally ʿAkkā). During these years, she refused to marry and dedicated herself to the service of her father and the organization of the household. When Bahā'-Allāh died in 1892 and most of his family turned against ʿAbd-al-Bahā', she remained loyal to her brother.

Bahā'īya Ḵānom's most important contributions were however reserved for her advanced years, when she occupied an increasingly important position, complementing her brother's role, and later nurturing and supporting Shoghi Effendi in the early years of his ministry. She also met Bahais who came to Haifa as pilgrims, maintained an extensive correspondence, and acted as custodian of relics and archives. She was put in charge of affairs during ʿAbd-al-Bahā''s travels, 1911-14, and on several occasions during Shoghi Effendi's absences from Haifa. Those who met her describe her as possessing a quiet, self-effacing nature, a remarkable combination of outward frailty and inner strength. She died in Haifa on 15 July 1932.

According to Bahai teaching, there is in each religious dispensation one woman (the Virgin Mary, Fāṭema the daughter of Moḥammad, and, in the Babi dispensation, Qorrat-al-ʿAyn Ṭāhera, q.v.) who outshines all others and becomes an embodiment of feminine virtues and even a symbol of the feminine aspects of the Divine. Bahā'īya Ḵānom fills this role in the Bahai dispensation.

Bibliography: A commemorative volume entitled *Bahīyyih Khānum, the Greatest Holy Leaf*, Haifa, 1982, was published on the 50th anniversary of her death. It contains many translations of her previously unpublished writings and also passages written about her by Bahā'-Allāh, ʿAbd-al-Bahā', and Shoghi Effendi. It also has an appendix listing all significant references to her in English-language Bahai publications. Her spoken reminiscences are in Lady [Sara] Blomfield, *The Chosen Highway*, Wilmette, 1967, pp. 37-69, and M. H. Phelps, *Life and Teachings of Abbas Effendi*, New York and London, 1903, pp. 12-94 (the relevant sections has been reprinted as *The Master in ʿAkkā*, Los Angeles, 1985). See also M. Gail, *Khānum, the Greatest Holy Leaf*, Oxford, 1982. J. Savi, *Bahīyyih Khānum, ancella di Bahā*, Rome, 1983. For a Bahai assessment of her spiritual and symbolic significance, see B. Nakhjavani, *Response*, Oxford, 1981, pp. 30-35, 40-41.

(M. Momen)

BAHĀR, a Persian literary, scientific, political, and social affairs monthly founded by Mīrzā Yūsof Khan Āštīānī, called Eʿteṣām-e Daftar and Eʿteṣām-al-Molk (q.v.; 1291-1356/1874-75–1937-38). Mīrzā Yūsof was the son of Mīrzā Ebrāhīm Khan and the father of the poetess Parvīn Eʿtesāmī. He was a deputy in the second Majles, and later its chief librarian and a member of the Education Commission (Komīsīūn-e Maʿāref). *Bahār* was founded in Tehran and was published over two periods: 1. from Rabīʿ II, 1328/April, 1910 to Ḏu'l-qaʿda, 1329/October, 1911, and 2. from Šaʿbān, 1339/April, 1921 to Jomādā I, 1341/December, 1922. Each issue comprised sixty-four pages and was distributed at an affordable price. In the first issue, Eʿteṣāmī wrote, "the purpose of *Bahār* is to provide a proper and an appealing forum for various significant topics of scientific, literary, ethical, historical, and artistic interest to people of understanding and to acquaint the public with valuable information..." Most of the material published in *Bahār* was written or translated by Eʿteṣām-al-Molk himself. During the first period of its publication, Mīrzā Reżā Khan Modabber-al-Mamālek (later editor of *Tamaddon*, Šawwāl, 1338 June, 1920) was *Bahār*'s managing editor, and for the second period ʿAbbās Ḵalīlī (later editor of *Eqdām*, 1299 Š./1921) assumed the editorship. The style of the journal remained uniform over both periods and the journal itself faithful to its stated purpose. During the second period of publication, the literary section was expanded and translations from the works of such French writers as Hugo and Rousseau appeared with greater frequency. The broad range of *Bahār*'s contents can be gauged from a reprint of the journal which was edited by Abu'l-Fatḥ Eʿteṣāmī (Tehran, 1321 Š./1943) and arranged under seventeen different topics.

Bahār represented a departure from traditional Persian journalism; readers found its willingness to discuss contemporary literature and literary criticism a refreshing change. The journal's emphasis on educating the public about developments in European science and technology seems to have struck a responsive chord among the Persian reading public, who were hungry for new ideas. To E. G. Browne, *Bahār* appeared "very modern and European in tone" (*Lit. Hist. Persia* IV, p. 489; cf. Āryanpūr, *Az Ṣabā tā Nīmā* II, p. 115). Eʿteṣām-al-Molk himself remarked in an article (2/12, 1341/1922, p. 705) "some have objected that the contents of the journal are predominately European in orientation." One must attribute this emphasis on the modern world to Eʿteṣām-al-Molk himself, who, though fluent in Arabic and well-versed in the culture of Islamic Iran, felt it his duty to inform the public about

European literature and culture and about new forms of learning. *Bahār* also stressed the education of women and often introduced model women of note to its readers.

Though, according to Āryanpūr (II, p. 114), most of the European literature published in *Bahār* came via Turkish and Arabic translations which Eʿteṣām-al-Molk retranslated into Persian, I suspect that, in addition to his foraging in Arabic and Turkish journals, Eʿteṣām-al-Molk also found some of his material in French writings of the time. His clear and simple Persian prose was well suited to translate the ideas of European culture into terms the ordinary reader would appreciate. For its style and content *Bahār* won praise among such Persian writers as Moḥammad-Żīāʾ Haštrūdī (p. 11) and the poet laureate Moḥammad-Taqī Bahār (*Dāneškada*, founded 1297 Š./1919, nos. 11-12).

Bibliography: Ch. Balaÿ and M. Cuypress, *Aux sources de la nouvelle persane*, Paris, 1983, pp. 15, 31, 48. E. G. Browne, *The Press and Poetry of Modern Persia*, Cambridge, 1914, pp. xiv, xvi, 15, 24. ʿA.-A. Dehḵodā, "Tārīḵča-ye zendagānī-e Yūsof Eʿteṣāmī (Eʿteṣām-al-Molk)," *Bahār* 1, 2nd ed., Tehran, 1321 Š./1943, pp. b-v. P. Eʿteṣāmī, *A Nightingale's Lament*, tr. H. Moayyad, Lexington, 1985, p. xi. M.-Ż. Haštrūdī, *Montaḵabāt-e āṯār*, Tehran, 1342/1923-24. M. Qazvīnī, "Wafayāt-e moʿāṣerīn, Eʿteṣāmī," *Yādgār* 3, 1325 Š./1946, p. 35. J. Rypka, *Hist. Iran. Lit.*, pp. 382, 387, 388. M. Ṣadr Hāšemī, *Tārīḵ-e jarāyed wa majallāt-e Īrān* II, Isfahan, 1332 Š./1954, pp. 26-30.

(Ḡ.-Ḥ. YŪSOFĪ)

BAHĀR, the name of several minor Persian magazines and newspapers.

1. A weekly, later daily, newspaper founded in Mašhad in 1336/1917-18 by Shaikh Aḥmad Bahār, a relative of Moḥammad-Taqī Malek-al-Šoʿarāʾ Bahār (q.v.). It was published irregularly, but continued at least until the end of 1311 Š./1932. It was concerned mainly with local news and announcements.

2. A newspaper published in Tehran in Farvardīn, 1321 Š./March, 1942, as the organ of the Peykār party, a middle-of-the-road group opposed to the Tūda (Tudeh) party. The editor was Ḵosrow Eqbāl, and on the editorial board was Maḥmūd Tafażżolī, who later became the editor of *Īrān-e mā*, a lively and somewhat left-of-center periodical.

3. On page xvi of Browne's *The Press and Poetry*, there is a brief biographical note provided by Mīrzā Ḥosayn Kāẓemzāda on Malek-al-Šoʿarāʾ, in which it is stated that "during the latter period of the constitution he founded the newspaper Bahār at Mashhad." No further details are given, and the newspaper is not listed in the register of publications that forms the first half of Browne's book. Probably the reference is to *Now-bahār* (and its substitute *Tāza-bahār*), which was founded by Bahār in Mašhad in 1328/1910.

Bibliography: E. G. Browne, *The Press and Poetry of Modern Iran*, Cambridge, 1914, p. xiv. M. Ṣadr Hāšemī, *Tārīḵ-e jarāyed wa majallāt-e Īrān*, 4 vols., Isfahan, 1327-32 Š./1948-53, II, p. 29. L. P. Elwell-Sutton, "Iranian Press 1941-47," *Iran* 6, 1968, p. 81.

(L. P. ELWELL SUTTON)

BAHĀR, MOḤAMMAD-TAQĪ **MALEK** AL-**ŠOʿARĀʾ**, 20th-century poet, scholar, journalist, politician, and historian (1265-1330 Š./1886-1951).

 i. *Life and work.*
 ii. *Bahār as a poet.*

i. LIFE AND WORK

Bahār may have taken his *taḵalloṣ* Bahār after the poet Mīrzā Naṣr-Allāh Bahār Šīrvānī, who had died on a visit to the house of Moḥammad-Taqī's father in 1300/1882-83 ('Erfānī, p. 36; Āryanpūr, II, p. 124). Bahār himself does not comment upon his pen-name in his autobiographical note ("Maktūb," *Ārmān*, quoted in M. Golbon, ed., *Bahār wa adab-e fārsī*, Tehran, 2535 = 1355 Š./1976, II, pp. 195-96). His father, Mīrza Moḥammad Kāẓem Ṣabūrī, was the official poet laureate (Malek-al-Šoʿarāʾ) at the shrine in Mašhad.

Life. Bahār's father was his first teacher. By the time he started formal education at the age of six he was already proficient in reading Persian and the Koran, and he wrote his first poem at the age of ten. Among his later teachers was Adīb Nīšāpūrī (q.v.), a traditional poet and scholar in literary sciences (Kāvarī, pp. 40ff., 234ff.), who cultivated the style of the ancient poets of Khorasan in the tradition of the *bāzgašt-e adabī* (q.v.).

Bahār's studies were interrupted at fifteen when his father apprenticed him to his uncle, a glass seller ('Erfānī, pp. 41, 94 n.). Ṣabūrī died in 1322/1904, and Bahār returned to his studies, particularly Arabic which led him to recent books and periodicals from Egypt and eventually drew his attention towards Western ideas of science and progress ('Erfānī, p. 43; Āryanpūr, p. 124). Having sent a congratulatory *qaṣīda* to Moẓaffar-al-Dīn Shah on his accession (*Dīvān* I, p. 3), he was rewarded with his father's title of Malek-al-Šoʿarāʾ, and thus became a government employee at the shrine of Mašhad. For his stipend he wrote and recited poems on official occasions ('Erfānī, p. 45). Already familiar with the ideas of freedom and constitution, he joined the constitutionalists in Mašhad at the age of twenty when the constitution was granted in 1324/1906. Later he joined Anjoman-e Saʿādat in Mašhad. During the period known as Estebdād-e Ṣaḡīr (Jomādā I 1326-Rajab 1327/June 1908-August 1909) he helped publish the clandestine paper *Ḵorāsān* under the pseudonym Raʾīs al-Ṭollāb; there, his first political poems were printed (Bahār, *Tārīḵ-e moḵtaṣar-e aḥzāb-e sīāsī* I, Tehran, 1357 Š./1978, p. b; Browne, p. 21; Āryanpūr, pp. 124, 128-30). He also began writing articles for *Ḥabl al-matīn* of Calcutta for which he had to develop a new prose style suitable for modern needs (*Tārīḵ-e moḵtaṣar* I, pp. d-h; 'Erfānī, pp. 191-92).

In 1328/1910, Bahār helped organize the Democratic

Party of Mašhad, assisted by Ḥaydar Khan ʿAm(ū)oḡlī. He began his own publication *Now-bahār*, but his anti-Russian policy led to a series of suppressions which included the closing down of *Now-bahār*; Bahār was ordered to Tehran just as the Majles was closed (1330/1911) by troops (*Tārīḵ-e moḵtaṣar*, pp. *h*, 11-12; Browne, p. 334). On his way he met Ḥaydar Khan ʿAmoḡlī for the last time (ʿErfānī, pp. 63-64). After a listless year in Tehran, spent in writing for *Ḥabl al-matīn* and some literary articles, he returned to Mašhad. Politics were dangerous, but he was able to publish articles on female emancipation, the evils of polygamy, and superstition among the *ʿolamāʾ* in a revived *Now-bahār* (*Tārīḵ-e moḵtaṣar* I, p. *z*). Having been elected to the third Majles in 1332/1914 he moved to Tehran where he published *Now-bahār* (*Tārīḵ-e moḵtaṣar* I, p. *z*; Āryanpūr, p. 332). In Ḏuʾl-ḥejja, 1333/November, 1915, the advance of a Russian force from Qazvīn to Tehran provoked a "migration" to Qom, during which, returning from a mission, he suffered a broken arm in an accident (*Tārīḵ-e moḵtaṣar* I, pp. 17-20, 22). He was returned to Tehran for treatment and banished to Bojnūrd in 1334/May, 1916. The revolution in Russia removed the pressure on Persia, and Bahār cooperated in reorganizing the Democratic Party. Now his attention was claimed more by literature; he founded a literary society, *Dānēškada*, and a journal of the same name was published between April, 1918 and April, 1919 (Ṣadr Hāšemī, II, pp. 270-72).

Bahār was elected to the fourth Majles, which, however, did not convene until Tīr, 1300 Š./June, 1921. In the meantime a coup d'etat took place in Esfand, 1299 Š./February, 1921, and its leader Sayyed Żīāʾ-al-Dīn became the prime minister. Though acquainted with Sayyed Żīāʾ-al-Dīn, he was surprised by the coup and declined an offer from him to cooperate. He was soon arrested and detained until the fall of Sayyed Żīāʾ-al-Dīn three months after the coup (*Tārīḵ-e moḵtaṣar*, pp. 91-92, 116-17). Finally released, he took up his Majles seat, but declined to resume the editorship of the paper *Īrān*, which he had been editing before his arrest, and avoided political journalism (*Tārīḵ-e moḵtaṣar* I, p. 129).

As a member of the fifth Majles, Bahār opposed the movement of Reżā Khan (the military leader of the coup and the future Reżā Shah) towards dictatorship and despite threats sided with Sayyed Ḥasan Modarres, the leading figure of the opposition (*Dīvān* I, p. 398). He actually became the target of an assassination attempt following a debate in the Majles (8 Ābān 1304 Š./30 October 1925) but instead of Bahār, Wāʿeẓ Qazvīnī, a journalist who had a striking resemblance to him but who had nothing to do with the issues involved, was brutally murdered in front of the Majles (*Tārīḵ-e moḵtaṣar* II, Tehran, 1363 Š./1984 [a detailed account of Bahār's political activities during the period], pp. 299ff.). Afterwards he took no part in the debates. He was elected from Tehran to the sixth Majles (1305 Š./1926), but avoided politics and occupied himself with scholarship. In 1927, he studied Pahlavi with the German archeologist E. Herzfeld, then visiting Tehran.

In 1308 Š./1929, he was suddenly imprisoned for a year. On release, his attempt to publish his *dīvān* was censored, and on Nowrūz 1312 Š./1933 he was again imprisoned until the summer, then exiled to Isfahan. His enforced leisure enabled him to study and write a great deal. On his return to Tehran, he was appointed to the Faculty of Letters at the University of Tehran. He took part in the Ferdowsī millenary celebrations in 1313 Š./1934, and managed to live and work in peace till Reżā Shah's abdication in 1320 Š./1941.

The Anglo-Russian invasion of 1941 awakened his political conscience. He republished *Now-bahār* and in 1323 Š./1945 published the first volume of his history of political parties (*Tārīḵ-e moḵtaṣar-e aḥzāb-e sīāsī*). In 1945 he was invited to Baku for the 25th anniversary of the establishment of Soviet Azerbaijan and elected to the 14th Majles on his return. He was appointed as minister of education when Qawām-al-Salṭana formed his cabinet in January, 1946, but resigned after a few months. He headed the Democrats in the 15th Majles but was already ill. In 1947 he went to the hospital in Leysin, Switzerland. By April, 1949, consumption was confirmed and he returned home to die in April, 1951. He was buried in the Ẓahīr-al-Dawla cemetery in Šemīrān.

Works. Bahār's literary production was prodigious. Both in his own mind and in the recognition of his countrymen he was first and last a poet. His *dīvān* was published posthumously by his brother Moḥammad Malekzāda in two volumes (I, Tehran, 1335 Š./1956, 2nd ed. 1344 Š./1965; II, Tehran, 1336 Š./1957). Though delicate considerations kept a few poems out of the printed *dīvān*, these two volumes present a complete sweep of the poet's production from his youth to his death-bed. Malekzāda's annotations are very helpful if sometimes inaccurate in details.

Bahār's earliest poems are the threnodies for his father, which demonstrate a craft already well learned. His position as poet of the Mašhad shrine led to panegyrics both religious and personal. He owes much to his father's example in his religious poems, while most of his poems are exercises in traditional forms modeled after classical masters. One *mosammaṭ* (*Dīvān* I, p. 12), modeled on one by Manūčehrī, may be Bahār's earliest use of a form he exploited later in his political verse. His poetry charts his growing awareness of social and political ideas. His first important political poem, which won him recognition, was a *mostazād* (*Dīvān* I, p. 145; *Tārīḵ-e moḵtaṣar* I, pp. *b-j*), modeled on one by Ašraf Gīlānī (q.v.) and published in the newspaper *Ḵorāsān* in Jomādā I, 1327/May-June, 1909 (Browne, pp. 185-86, 260-61). While still in Mašhad, he had to consider the different elements of local society in his public poems, but in Tehran the pressure on him to write formal poems decreased. His poetry now recorded his personal reactions to political events, his style ranging from emulations (*esteqbāl*) of the old masters (e.g., *Dīvān* I, p. 284), to the use of colloquial language (*Dīvān* I, p. 285).

Bahār's literary education advanced with his association in the *Dāneškada* group with writers familiar with European languages. Bahār was able to make Persian versions of their translations from European poetry (e.g., *Dīvān* II, p. 317, from La Fontaine, *Fables*, book 5, IX). These and original poems in a similar vein contributed to the growing number of the poet's "private" poems. At the same time, Bahār continued to write "public" poetry, attacking many aspects of life and politics as well as his political enemies. Such poems reached a climax with the events of 1925, after which the public poems were addressed to the suspicious new monarch, while the private poems became increasingly intimate, restricted to the ears of the poet's immediate circle. Bahār's experiences, in prison and exile, as a teacher of literature, were all inspiration for his poetry. The scholarship that was his refuge in the difficult years between 1925 and 1941 is manifest in his verse of the period. Reżā Shah's abdication is barely mentioned, but other events inspired poems for the rest of Bahār's life. Several, including some beautiful *ḡazal*s, express his pain and isolation during his illness; one *qaṣīda*, written in his Swiss hospital bed (*Dīvān* I, p. 774), is an excellent example of Bahār's use of tradition for contemporary, personal purposes.

Throughout his life, Bahār wrote poems in all the traditional forms; he experimented a few times with stanza forms of foreign type, but he rejected totally new forms of verse and returned, even at the end of his life, to the old tradition. Yet his subjects, and often his diction, are unmistakably modern.

Bahār's scholarly works include: *Sabk-šenāsī* (3 vols., Tehran, 1321 Š./1942, repr. 1337 Š./1958), a detailed standard history of Persian prose illustrated by many examples; *Tārīḵ-e moḵtaṣar-e aḥzāb-e sīāsī* (I, Tehran, 1323 Š./1944, 1337 Š./1958; II, Tehran, 1363 Š./1984), a personal view of political developments of the time, important both as a primary historical source and for Bahār's biography; and *Tārīḵ-e taṭawwor-e šeʿr-e fārsī* (ed. M.-T. Bīneš, Mašhad, 1334 Š./1955, ed. ʿA. Maḥmūdī Baḵtīārī, Tehran, 1342 Š./1963), a work on poetry originally intended to be similar to his *Sabk-šenāsī*; only a few sections of this book were written before illness prevented him from working. His papers and miscellaneous works have been published by M. Golbon in *Ferdowsī-nāma-ye Bahār* (Tehran, 1345 Š./1966), *Tarjama-ye čand matn-e pahlavī* (Tehran, 1347 Š./1968), and *Bahār o adab-e fārsī* (2 vols., Tehran, 1351 Š./1972 with the third volume in preparation). Bahār also composed a number of songs (*taṣnīf*s), some of which are still quite popular (e.g., N. Ḥaddādī, *Čehel o do tarāna-ye qadīmī*, Tehran, 2536 = 1356 Š./1977, pp. 26-40, 108-13). He published scholarly editions of *Tārīḵ-e Sīstān* (Tehran, 1314 Š./1935), *Mojmal al-tawārīḵ wa'l-qeṣaṣ* (Tehran, 1318 Š./1939), part of ʿAwfī's *Jawāmeʿ al-ḥekāyāt wa lawāmeʿ al-rewāyāt* (Tehran, 1324 Š./1945), and Balʿamī's *Tārīḵ* (published posthumously by M. Parvīn Gonābādī, vol. I, Tehran, 1341 Š./1962).

Bibliography: B. ʿAlawī, "Ḵazān-e Bahār," *Payām-e now* 4/11-12, pp. 1-13. Y. Āryanpūr, *Az Ṣabā tā Nīmā*, 2 vols., Tehran, 1351 Š./1972, II, pp. 123-37, 332-49. M. Bahār, "Bahār o ḵāna o ḵānavāda," *Āyanda* 10/2-3, 1363 Š./1984, pp. 94-100. E. Browne, *Press and Poetry in Modern Persia*, Cambridge, 1914, pp. 260-89. ʿA. ʿErfānī, *Šarḥ-e aḥwāl o āṯār-e Malek al-Šoʿarāʾ Moḥammad-Taqī Bahār*, Tehran, 1335 Š./1956. M. Esḥāq, *Soḵanvarān-e Īrān dar ʿaṣr-e ḥāżer* I, Delhi, 1351/1932-33, pp. 358-403. M.-ʿE. Eslāmī Nadūšan, "Be yād-e dahomīn sāl-e dargoḏašt-e Malek-al-Šoʿarāʾ Bahār," *Payām-e novīn* III/10, 1340 Š./1961, pp. 1-10. Idem, "Dahomīn sāl-e marg-e Bahār," *Yaḡmā* 14, 1340 Š./1961, pp. 145-52. M. Golbon, "Sālšomār o gozīda-ye ketāb-šenāsī-e Bahār," *Āyanda* 10/2-3, 1363 Š./1984, pp. 107-12. *Īrān-nāma* 5/4, 1987. Ḥ. Ḵaṭībī, "Sabk-e ašʿār-e Bahār," *Yaḡmā* 4, 1330 Š./1951, pp. 454-61, 496-500. ʿA.-Ḥ. Ešrāq Ḵāvarī, "Adīb Nīšābūrī," *Armaḡān* 7, 1304 Š./1925, pp. 234-45. Ḵayyāmpūr, *Soḵanvarān*, p. 90. M. B. Loraine, "A Memoir on the Life and Poetical Works of Maliku'l Schuʿarāʾ Bahār," *IJMES*, 1972, pp. 140-68. Idem, "Bahār in the Context of the Persian Constitutional Revolution," *Iranian Studies* 5/2-3, 1972, pp. 79-87. F. Machalski, "Muhammad Taqi Bahar as a Painter of Nature," *Iran Society Silver Jubilee Souvenir 1949-69*, Calcutta, 1970, pp. 233-37. S. M. Moḥīṭ Ṭabāṭabāʾī, "Ḵāṭerāt-ī čand az Malek-al-Šoʿarāʾ Bahār," *Āyanda* 10/2-3, 1363 Š./1984, pp. 101-06. A. Nīkūḥemmat, *Zendagī o āṯār-e Bahār* I, Tehran, n.d.; II, Kermān, 1334 Š./1955. L. S. Peĭsikov, "M. Bakhar kak uchonyĭ filolog," *Kratkie soobshcheniya Instituta vostokovedeniya* 36, Moscow, 1959, pp. 9-22. Rypka, *Hist. Iran. Lit.*, pp. 373-74 and index. M. Ṣadr Hāšemī, *Tārīḵ-e jarāʾed wa majallāt-e Īrān*, 4 vols., Isfahan, 1327-32 Š./1948-53, I, p. 313; II, pp. 98-99, 243-45; IV, pp. 313-16. M. ʿA. Sepānlū, "Javānī-e Bahār," *Naqd-e āgāh*, Tehran, 1363 Š./1984, pp. 5-29. M.-R. Šafīʿī Kadkanī, "Šeʿr-e Bahār," *Āyanda* 10/10-11, 1363 Š./1984, pp. 635-42. R. Yāsamī, *Adabīyāt-e moʿāṣer-e Īrān*, Tehran, 1316 Š./1937, pp. 30-32. Ḡ.-Ḥ. Yūsofī, "Ostād Bahār šāʿer-ī mellī wa honarmand-ī wāqeʿī būd," *Nāma-ye farhang* 1, 1330 Š./1951, pp. 78-81, 123-25. Idem, "Naẓar-ī be Sabk-šenāsī-e Ostād Bahār," *Āyanda* 10/2-3, 1363 Š./1984, pp. 84-93. B. N. Zakhoder, "Bakhar 1886-1951," *Kratkie soobshcheniya Instituta vostokovedeniya* 36, Moscow, 1959. ʿA. Zarrīnkūb, "Šeʿr-e Bahār," *Soḵan* 8, 1336 Š./1957, pp. 840-46, 953-60. Idem, "Bahār, setāyešgar-e āzādī," in *Bā kārvān-e ḥolla*, Tehran, 1343 Š./1964, pp. 309-24.

(M. B. LORAINE)

ii. BAHĀR AS A POET

Bahār is probably the most significant writer of *qaṣīda*s since the end of the 6th/12th century, and no doubt the last great poet of this genre. His masterful manipulation of Persian language and dexterity and ingeniousness in molding it into eloquent expressions for treating a wide variety of subjects and themes (social, philosophical, political, personal, etc.) are surely unmatched by any other writer of *qaṣīdas* in the 20th century. His style has the unmistakable imprint of the 4th-5th/10th-11th-century masters, yet it exhibits a certain modernity of thought and expression which makes his poetry more than an imitation of past masters, and he convincingly (*Bahār wa adab-e fārsī* II, pp. 195-96) refuted A. Kasrawī's accusations that he in his early career had plagiarized Bahār Šīrvānī's *qaṣīdas* (J. Matīnī, *Īrān-nāma* 5/4, p. 557).

Bahār was directly involved in the political events of his time and his poetry often turns into a vehicle for conveying personal opinions on political and social issues. Despite his generally lofty style, he was hardly shy of using popular and "unpoetical" expressions in his poetry; even loanwords of European origin were not foreign to him and he used them with the same mastery that he showed in reviving archaic and obsolete words. On the whole he adhered to the Khorasanian style (q.v.) but also believed that young poets should be free to experiment with new and unconventional modes of poetical expressions, including free verse (*Nok̲ostīn kongra*, p. 302). Bahār can justifiably be called the poet who, while himself advocating and practicing classical-style poetry, did much to help advance new genres and expand the horizon of Persian poetry, thus contributing to the eventual emergence of modernist poetry.

Bibliography: R. Barāhenī, *Ṭelā dar mes*, 3rd ed., Tehran, 1358 Š./1979, pp. 201-05, 269. ʿA.-ʿA. Dastḡayb, *Sāya-rowšan-e šeʿr-e now-e fārsī*, Tehran, 1348 Š./1969, p. 131. J. Homāʾī, "Takmīl-e šarḥ-e ḥāl-e Bahār be qalam-e negāranda-ye 'Malek-al-Šoʿarāʾ Bahār'," appended to *Ak̲bār-e Dānešgāh-e Tehrān* 5/9. *Nok̲ostīn kongra-ye nevīsandagān-e Īrān*, Tehran, 1326 Š./1947, pp. 7, 9, 302. M. Parvīn Gonābādī, "Panjomīn sāl-e dargod̲ašt-e Bahār," *Sok̲an* 6, 1334, pp. 351-53. D̲. Ṣafā, *Ganj-e sok̲an*, 4th ed., III, Tehran, 1348 Š./1969, pp. 327-29. M. Šafīʿī Kadkanī, *Edāma-ye šeʿr-e fārsī (az Mašrūṭīyat tā soqūṭ-e salṭanat)*, Tehran, 1359 Š./1980, pp. 36-38. Ḡ.-Ḥ. Yūsofī, "Yādgār-e Bahār," *Bahār wa adab-e fārsī*, ed. M. Golbon, I, Tehran, 2535 = 1355 Š./1976, pp. xv-xl. ʿA.-Ḥ. Zarrīnkūb, *Šeʿr-e bī-dorūḡ šeʿr-e bī-neqāb*, 3rd. ed., Tehran, 2536 = 1356 Š./1977, pp. 36-38. *Īrān-nāma* 5/4, 1366 Š./1987, was dedicated to Bahār on the occasion of the 100th anniversary of his birthday; it includes two letters by him, articles by J. Matīnī, Ḥ Moʾayyad, D̲. Ṣafā, M. Bahār, and P. Bahār, and comments by Persian scholars and litterateurs.

(J. Matīnī)

BAHĀR-e KESRĀ "The spring of K̲osrow" (Ṭabarī), Farš-e zamestānī "Winter carpet" (Balʿamī), or *Bahārestān* "Spring garden" (*Ḥabīb al-sīar*), a huge, late Sasanian royal carpet. The carpet measured 60 cubits (*araš*, *d̲erāʿ*) square (ca. 27 m × 27 m), that may have covered the floor of the great audience hall (Ayvān-e Kesrā) at the winter capital of Madāʾen. Representations of paths and streams were embroidered on it with gems against a ground of gold. Its border was embroidered with emeralds to represent a cultivated green field in which were flowering spring plants with fruit embroidered with different colored gems on stalks of gold with gold and silver flowers and silk foliage. It was used as a place to drink, as if in gardens, when the winter winds blew. The *Ḥabīb al-sīar* explains that when one sat on it in winter, it was as if it was spring.

When Madāʾen fell to the Muslims in 16/637 this carpet was too heavy for the Persians to carry away so it was taken with the other booty. The Muslims called it *al-qeṭf* "the picked" and, since it was left over after Saʿd b. Abī Waqqāṣ divided the booty, he sent it to ʿOmar in Medina. Although the assembly agreed that ʿOmar should use his own judgment in disposing of it, ʿAlī was concerned lest someone be deprived of a rightful share in the future; so ʿOmar cut it up and divided it among the Muslims. Although ʿAlī did not receive one of the best pieces, he sold his for 20,000 dirhams.

Bibliography: Ṭabarī, I, pp. 2452-54. Balʿamī, *Tārīk̲*, Tehran, 1337 Š./1958, pp. 304-05; facs. ed., Tehran, 1344 Š./1966, p. 17 (description). Idem, tr. Zotenberg, *Chronique* III, pp. 417-18. Ebn al-At̲īr (repr.), II, p. 518. *Ḥabīb al-sīar*, Tehran, I, p. 483. *Survey of Persian Art* VI, pp. 2274-75.

(M. G. Morony)

BAHĀRESTĀN (Spring garden, Abode of spring, and similar renderings in various languages), occasionally referred to as *Rawżat al-ak̲yār wa toḥfat al-abrār* (Garden of the virtuous and rare gift of the pious), is an anecdotal and moralistic work of belles-lettres in prose (both plain and rhythmic-rhyming) and verse, by ʿAbd-al-Raḥmān Jāmī (q.v.), composed in the poet's old age, in 892/1487, and dedicated to the Timurid Sultan Ḥosayn Bāyqarā (r. 875-912/1470-1506). Like many other works in this genre, it is written in professed imitation of Saʿdī's Golestān (q.v.), which the author had notionally used in teaching his son. These two works have been widely employed as text books, which has led to a great proliferation of manuscripts, editions, and translations—all of widely varying quality.

The main body of the *Bahārestān* is divided into eight so-called gardens (*rawża*), the same number of chapters (*bābs* "gates") as in the *Golestān*, but it often diverges considerably from the latter in themes, content, treatment, and style. These gardens, to paraphrase summarily their rather elaborate and fanciful titles, are concerned with: 1. words and deeds of the mystics; 2. wisdom of the sages; 3. justice and statecraft; 4. munificence and generosity; 5. love (of various kinds); 6. jest and merriment (some obscence and acerbic material here); 7. poetic composition (with plentiful examples and criticism); and 8. animal fables. The work is of modest size, of comparable length with the *Golestān*, though this is probably as much a typical feature of the genre as a conscious imitation.

Jāmī is commonly seen as a gifted and versatile, but somewhat unoriginal reworker of old themes (e.g., *Laylī o Majnūn*, *Yūsof o Zolayḵā*), old genres, and old styles. This is certainly the case with the *Bahārestān* though in the Epilogue Jāmī claims (not always with full justice) originality for the stories themselves. It is a clever work, but the work of a man in his seventies, and an inadequate indication of his characteristic skill and periodic profundity. It must also go without saying that—coming, as it did, over two centuries later than the *Golestān*—it could not hope to achieve the freshness and spontaneity of that work. With all this, however, the book has still attained for itself a distinctive place in Persian literature.

Certain characteristics of Jāmī's professional posture can be seen in the *Bahārestān*. There is, for example, an enormous self-assurance and a sense of his own worthiness; if he does sometimes write here as a mystic, it is with singular coolness and self-control. He is above all a scholar and an artist, with a linguistic sense that is both erudite and delicate, and usually unforced. One quality he does seem to share with Saʿdī is a feeling for humanity, and particularly for its less fortunate majority, though it is not easy to relate this significantly to his own high and affluent social standing.

Bibliography: The potential bibliography is large, but most of it is of little value and nearly all of it is long since out of print. The first and major "edition" is that of Baron O. M. von Schlechta-Wssehrd, Vienna, 1846. It is accompanied by a German translation which is for the most part painfully "faithful," but which omits matter judged to be excessively scabrous. An English version (full, but likewise unsatisfactory), attributed to E. Rehatsek, was published anonymously, and allegedly at Benares, by the so-called Kama Shastra Society in 1887. C. E. Wilson's *Persian Wit and Humour* (London, 1883) includes an attempt to deal with the notorious Garden VI by a measure of boldness, certain omissions, and a little Latinity. A sensitive and intelligent French version is that of Henri Massé, Paris, 1925. See also A. J. Arberry, *Classical Persian Literature*, London, 1958, pp. 430-32. Browne, *Lit. Hist. Persia* III, p. 515. J. Rypka, *Hist. Iran. Lit.*, pp. 287, 788. Ṣafā, *Adabīyāt* IV, Tehran, 2536 = 1356 Š./1977, pp. 514-15.

(G. M. Wickens)

BAHĀRESTĀN, the name of a garden, public square, and complex of buildings in central Tehran, the main part of which presently forms the headquarters of an Islamic revolution militia, the Central Committee of the Islamic Revolution (Komīta-ye Markazī-e Enqelāb-e Eslāmī); the southern section houses the Majles library.

The site was originally the property of Moḥammad-Ḥasan Khan Sardār Īravānī and was purchased by Ḥājī ʿAlī Khan Eʿtemād-al-Salṭana. Toward the end of his life (1293/1896), Mīrzā Ḥosayn Khan Mošīr-al-Dawla Sepahsālār purchased the property, intending to construct a mansion, a mosque, and a grand *madrasa* on it (Momtaḥen-al-Dawla, *Ḵāṭerāt*, ed. Ḥ. Ḵānšaqāqī, Tehran, 1352 Š./1973, p. 234; the *madrasa*, Madrasa-ye ʿĀlī-e Sepahsālār, a center for theological studies, has, since the revolution of 1357 Š./1978-79, been renamed Madrasa-ye Šahīd Moṭahharī). When Sepahsālār died without an heir in 1298/1881-82, Nāṣer-al-Dīn Shah seized the property and its buildings. In imitation of the name of the nearby Negārestān palace (the site of Fatḥ-ʿĀlī Shah's private quarters), the shah dubbed the property "Bahārestān" (J. Šahrī, *Gūša-ī az tārīḵ*, Tehran, n.d., p. 204). The spacious public square fronting the site also came to be known as the Bahārestān (ʿA. Mostawfī, *Šarḥ-e zendaganī-e man*, 2nd ed., Tehran, 1343 Š./1964, I, p. 499).

The Bahārestān building has been the scene of many historical events. Sepahsālār, a reformer and an admirer of European culture and law, is said to have hoped that the building and the *madrasa* would perhaps one day become a place where the nation's deputies could meet. A statement attributed to Ẓell-al-Solṭān seems to confirm this report: "I visited [Sepahsālār] while he was on his way to Khorasan. As he was at prayer, I spoke with my aunt [Sepahsālār's wife]... His prayers completed, Mīrzā Ḥosayn turned to my aunt and said, 'Your brother has taken my house and school from me, but I hope that the day will come when this same house will be a house of parliament where representatives will meet and that parliament will uproot the Qajar tyranny'" (M. Nāẓem-al-Eslām Kermānī, *Tārīḵ-e bīdārī-e Īrānīān*, 4th ed., ed. ʿA.-A. Saʿīdī Sīrjānī, Tehran, 1362 Š./1983, I, p. 142). These statements seem apocryphal, since Sepahsālār's death preceded Nāṣer-al-Dīn's confiscation of his property. Sepahsālār may have been referring to the fact that the Qajar ruler had driven him from his home and exiled him to Khorasan (Ḵ. M. Sāsānī, *Sīāsatgarān-e dawra-ye Qājār*, Tehran, 1346-52 Š./1967-73, I, p. 92); such sentiment would be understandable in a man who visited Europe several times and realized the advantages of its legal systems, and who was also aware of the corruption of the Qajar court.

The Bahārestān garden and buildings were completed in 1296/1879 (the date 1288/1871 given by Bāmdād [*Rejāl* II, p. 322 n. 3] is evidently wrong); the date is celebrated in a chronogramatic ode by Ḥājī Mīrzā Ḥasan Eṣfahānī Ṣafī ʿAlīšāh with which the calligrapher Moḥammad-Ebrāhīm Badāyeʿnegār adorned the architrave of the inner building in the east wing of the garden. This architrave was later transferred to the new structure built to house the Majles library in the south wing.

The Bahārestān consisted of two structures, an outer quarter (*bīrūnī*) and an inner one (*andarūnī*, qq.v.) located in the eastern part of the garden. After Nāṣer-al-Dīn Shah confiscated the property, the inner quarter became the residence of Malījak, ʿAzīz-al-Solṭān (q.v.) and his wife, the shah's daughter; thus it came to be known as the ʿAzīzīya (M.-Ḥ. Eʿtemād-al-Salṭana, *Rūz-nāma-ye ḵāṭerāt*, ed. Ī. Afšār, 2nd ed., Tehran, 1350 Š./1971, p. 961). During Nāṣer-al-Dīn Shah's reign, the outer quarter, which contains a spacious hall and luxurious rooms, was used to receive important foreign visitors and on occasion served as the crown prince's temporary residence in Tehran (Mostawfī, I, p. 499).

After the edict of constitutional government of 25 Jomādā II 1324/17 August 1906, Prime Minister Mošīr-al-Dawla ordered that the outer building become the site of the new parliament; but the representatives, especially the clerics, objected on grounds that the Bahārestān was not centrally located and that a share of the land was still in dispute (Nāẓem-al-Eslām, I, p. 573). Therefore the first college of electors (clerics, ministers, and courtiers charged with arranging the election of the first deputies) met at the Madrasa-ye Neẓām (Nāẓem-al-Eslām, I, p. 574). But three weeks after the elections, when the Madrasa-ye Neẓām was found to be too small to hold all the elected deputies, the meetings of the National Assembly were transferred to the building and grounds of the Bahārestān (M. M. Šarīf Kāšānī, *Wāqeʿāt-e ettefāqīya dar rūzgār*, Tehran, 1362 Š./1983, p. 106; Bāmdād, *Rejāl* II, p. 322 n. 3). To commemorate the event, a gold plaque inscribed with the words *dār al-šūrā-ye mellī* (national assembly house) and *ʿadl-e moẓaffar* (justice triumphant; an ambiguous phrase referring also to Moẓaffar-al-Dīn Shah), the numerical value of which is the date 1324/1906, was placed over the entrance to the garden (Nāẓem-al-Eslām, II, p. 8; cf. M. Hedāyat, *Ḵāṭerāt o ḵaṭarāt*, 2nd ed., Tehran, 1344 Š./1965, p. 144, who mistakenly attributes the calligraphy to Reżā Kalhor [d. 1310/1892-93]).

During the first session of the Majles, the deputies sat on the floor of the great hall arranged in a four-row square (Ḥ. Taqīzāda, *Maqālāt*, ed. Ī. Afšār, Tehran, 2536 = 1356 Š./1978, IX, p. 215). At that time, various opportunistic, special interest groups would congregate in the guise of *anjoman*s (leagues) in the Bahārestān garden and in the Sepahsālār *madrasa*, from which they would disrupt the Majles with their provocative demonstrations and speeches (A. Majd-al-Eslām Kermānī, *Tārīḵ-e enḥelāl-e majles*, ed. Ḵalīlpūr, Isfahan, 1351 Š./1972). With the shah and the Majles at loggerheads, the shah took refuge in the Bāḡ-e Šāh (q.v.), and imperial troops terrorized the people. Threatened by this, the lightly-armed Constitutionalists took cover in the Bahārestān and the adjacent buildings. On 23 Jomādā I 1326/4 July 1908, imperial troops commanded by Amīr Bahādor surrounded the Bahārestān garden and shelled the Majles building. Eight hours later, after a number had been killed, some of the deputies fled, others were taken prisoner, and Cossacks, imperial troops, and the rabble of Tehran looted the Bahārestān down to its curtains, doors, and windows (Nāẓem-al-Eslām, *Tārīḵ-e bīdārī* II, p. 156).

A year later (24 Jomādā II 1327/13 July 1909), after the leaders of the Constitutional movement had defeated the shah and entered Tehran in triumph, the Bahārestān garden was the site of a grand celebration. On the same site three days later, a high commission deposed Moḥammad-ʿAlī Shah and arranged the accession of his son Aḥmad Mīrzā (Nāẓem-al-Eslām, II, p. 494).

The Bahārestān building was eventually repaired and once again became the home of the National Assembly. In later years, the hall and the rooms were furnished, and the ʿAzīzīya was converted into the library of the National Assembly.

In 1312 Š./1933, a statue was purchased for the Assembly from the estate of Sardār Asʿad Jaʿfarqolī Khan Baḵtīārī for the Bahārestān garden grounds. Known as the "angel of freedom," the statue is of a winged figure spearing a vanquished devil of tyranny. The heirs of Sardār Asʿad later returned the money used to purchase the statue and presented it as a gift to the Assembly (ʿA. Balāḡī, *Tārīḵ-e qesmathā-ye ḡarbī wa jonūbī wa šarqī-e Tehrān*, Qom, n.d., p. 94).

The original Bahārestān building, with a few cosmetic changes, still exists, but the Majles library was moved to new quarters in the south corner of the garden. The Bahārestān garden was expanded northward and eastward, and a new National Assembly building was erected in that section of the garden. With the advent of the 1979 revolution, the name and venue of the National Assembly have changed: the Islamic Assembly (Majles-e Šūrā-ye Eslāmī) now meets in what was formerly the Senate building. The Bahārestān buildings and garden now house the "Central Committee of the Islamic Revolution."

Bibliography: Given in the text.

(ʿA.-A. SAʿĪDĪ SĪRJĀNĪ)

BAHĀRESTĀN-E ḠAYBĪ, a detailed history in Persian of Bengal and Orissa for the period 1017-34/1608-24 composed by Mīrzā Nathan ʿAlāʾ-al-Dīn Eṣfahānī. ʿAlāʾ-al-Dīn's father, Malek ʿAlī Ehtemām Khan, a Persian immigrant who had served as the castellan (*kūtvāl*) of Agra under Akbar, was promoted by Jahāngīr to the rank of 1,000 *dat* (personnel) and 300 *savār*s (horsemen) in 1607 and sent to Bengal as *mīr baḥr* (chief of artillery and flotilla; see *Tūzok-e jahāngīrī*, p. 68; *Bahārestān-e ḡaybī*, ms., fol. 2b). In Bengal ʿAlāʾ-al-Dīn served in the contingent of his father and got closer to Eslām Khan Češtī, the governor general of Bengal, Bihar, and Orissa. On Ehtemām Khan's death in 1021/1612, ʿAlāʾ-al-Dīn entered the imperial service with the military rank of 500 *dat* and 250 *savārs* (*Bahārestān*, fol. 97b), later receiving the title of Šetāb Khan.

Bahārestān-e ḡaybī, composed in 1034/1624, is ʿAlāʾ-al-Dīn's only literary work and contains his memoirs. It is a significant historical work, written in a simple, inornate style, but containing a first-hand, detailed account of the military, political, and social events of Bengal and Orissa in the first quarter of the seventeenth century. It provides detailed information about the military strength of the Nuhani and Karrani Afghans in eastern Bengal, the Pani Afghans in Orissa, and the Mughal relations with the non-Muslim rulers of Kooch Behar, Assam, Orissa, Tippera, and Arracan (cf. *Bahārestān*, fols. 78b, 97b, 104b, 211a-212b). Oddly enough, the work does not seem to have gained much attention; no later Mughal historians quote it as a source of information. The reason for this may be the non-literary style of the work as well as the author's desire to portray his father and himself as the heroes of every military campaign in which they took part.

The work is divided into four *daftars* (books), each of which is further divided into *dāstāns* (narratives). The first part, entitled *Eslām-nāma*, deals with the events that took place in Bengal, Bihar, and Orissa during the governorship of Eslām Khan Češtī; the second *daftar*, untitled, covers the governorship of Qāsem Khan; the third is entitled *Ebrāhīm-nāma* after the governor Ebrāhīm Khan Fīrūz Jang; the fourth, entitled *Wāqeʿāt-e jahānšāhī* describes the arrival of the rebel prince Šāh-Jahān in Bengal and his usurpation of authority. *Bahārestān* exists in a single manuscript made during the lifetime of the author and preserved in the Bibliothèque Nationale, Paris. A rotograph copy of this manuscript is kept in the Decca University Library. A summary translation into English was made by M. I. Bohrah (*A History of the Mughal Wars in Assam, Cooch Behar, Bengal, Behar and Orissa during the Reigns of Jahāngīr and Shāhjahān*, Gauhati, 1936).

Bibliography: Qeyam U'ddin Ahmad, "Mirza Nathan–A Memoirist of the 17th Century," in *Historians of Medieval India*, ed. Mohibbul Hasan, New Delhi, 1968. S. N. Bhattacharya, "Conquests of Islam Khan (1600-1613)," in Sarkar, *History of Bengal* II, pp. 247-72, esp. p. 247 n. 1. Blochet, *Cat. Bib. Nat.* I, p. 617. Nūr-al-Dīn Moḥammad Jahāngīr, *Tūzok-e jahāngīrī*, Calcutta, 1864. Moʿtamed Khan, *Eqbāl-nāma-ye jahāngīrī*, Calcutta, 1865. Ḵᵛāja Neʿmat-Allāh Hervī, *Tārīḵ-e ḵān-jahānī*, ed. S. M. Emām-al-Dīn, II, Dacca, 1962. J. N. Sarkar, *History of Bengal* II, Dacca, 1948, preface, p. x. S.R. Sharma, *Bibliography of Mughal India*, Bombay, 1938, repr. Philadelphia, 1977, pp. 69-70. Storey, I/2, p. 714.

(I. H. SIDDIQUI)

BAHĀRLŪ, a Turkic tribe of Azerbaijan, Khorasan, Kermān, and Fārs. According to J. Malcolm, it was originally a branch of the Šāmlūs (q.v.), "who were brought into Persia from Syria by Timur" (*The History of Persia*, London, 1829, I, p. 237). Also of this opinion was A. Houtum-Schindler, who added that "in Fars, they are generally known as Arabs, probably on account of their having come from Syria" (*Eastern Persian Irak*, London, 1896, p. 48). But neither of these authorities provided any documentary evidence to back up his claim, and it could be argued that if the Bahārlūs of Fārs are often called Arabs it is because of their association with the Arab tribe in the Ḵamsa (q.v.) tribal confederacy. On the other hand, a close connection does exist between the Bahārlū tribe and the Qarāgozlū (q.v.) tribe, which is known to have been a branch of the Šāmlū tribe (see F. Sümer, "Ḳarā Gözlü," in *EI*[2] IV, pp. 577-78). There is a village by the name of Qarāgozlū 25 km northwest of Mīāndoāb (Razmārā, *Farhang* IV, p. 365), which is very near the area inhabited by Bahārlūs, northwest of Marāḡa; there are villages by the name of Bahārlū and Qarāgozlū west of Hamadān (ibid., V, pp. 60 and 321); and there is a clan of the Bahārlūs of Fārs by the name of Qarāgozlū (personal interviews with Ebrāhīm Khan Bahārlū and Amīr Āqā Khan Bahārlū, Shiraz, 1957).

V. Minorsky believed that Bahārlū was another name for the Barānī (or Bārānlū) tribe, which was the tribe of the Qara Qoyunlū ruling dynasty, and that the tribe was an offshoot of the Īvā (q.v.) tribe, which was one of the basic Oghuz divisions ("The Clan of the Qara-Qoyunlu Rulers," in *Mélanges Fuad Köprülü*, Istanbul, 1955, p. 391; idem, "Bahārlū," in *EI*[2] I, p. 919). However, F. Sümer has shown that there is no concrete evidence to substantiate the claim that the names Bahārlū and Barānī refer to the same tribe (*Kara Koyunlular* I, Ankara, 1967, pp. 23-24). At the time of the Qara Qoyunlūs, the Bahārlūs lived in the vicinity of Hamadān, a fact which prompted Minorsky to suggest that the name was derived from that of the fortress of Bahār, 14 km northwest of that city ("The Clan," p. 392; "Bahārlū," p. 919). But the fact that in the eighteenth century there was a tribe by the name of Bahārlū in central Anatolia (C. Niebuhr, *Reisenbeschreibung nach Arabien und andern umliegenden Ländern*, Copenhagen, 1774, II, p. 415) suggests that part of the tribe stayed behind when the ancestors of the Bahārlūs of Iran moved to the Hamadān region and that the name existed already before that event took place.

From all the information available, it appears that the Bahārlū tribe joined the Qara Qoyunlū tribal confederacy only after the latter had already been formed, most probably following the conquest of Hamadān by Qarā Yūsof in 1408. In any case, it was not until the reign of Jahānšāh (r. 841-72/1438-67) that the Bahārlū leaders reached any degree of prominence. During that period, the chief of the tribe was ʿAlī Šakar Beg, of the Balāl, or Būlāllū, clan. According to ʿAbd-al-Bāqī Nehāvandī, he was one of the ablest of the Qara Qoyunlū commanders and was responsible for the conquest of most of western and southwestern Iran in 861/1457 (*Maʾāṯer-e raḥīmī*, Calcutta, 1924, I, pp. 46-49). ʿAlī Šakar Beg established marital ties with the Qara Qoyunlū ruling family, but their exact nature is still debated. According to Bābor, Jahānšāh married ʿAlī Šakar Beg's daughter, Pāšā Begom (A. S. Beveridge, *The Bābur-nāma in English*, London, 1969, p. 49). But according to Fażl-Allāh b. Rūzbehān, it was Jahānšāh's son, Moḥammad Mīrzā, who married her (V. Minorsky, *Persia in A.D. 1478-1490*, London, 1957, p. 42).

ʿAlī Šakar Beg's son, Pīr-ʿAlī Beg (who is also sometimes called Šīr-ʿAlī Beg), succeeded him as chief of the Bahārlū tribe. He was one of Jahānšāh's officers, and when that ruler was defeated by Uzun Ḥasan Āq Qoyunlū (q.v.) in 872/1467, he took refuge with the Timurids in Khorasan, along with Ebrāhīm Beg, Jahānšāh's grandson, and four or five thousand families of Bahārlūs. There, the exiled leaders entered the service of Abū Saʿīd (q.v.), the last Timurid ruler who tried to restore Tīmūr's empire from Kāšḡar to Transcaucasia

(*Bābur-nāma*, p. 49). When Abū Saʿīd was, in turn, defeated by Uzun Ḥasan in 1469, Pīr-ʿAlī Beg and Ebrāhīm Beg joined Sultan Ḥosayn Bāyqarā, the Timurid ruler of Khorasan (875-912/1470-1506). Uzun Ḥasan repeatedly wrote to Ḥosayn Bāyqarā, demanding the extradition of the exiled leaders (one of these messages has been preserved in Istanbul (Nuruosmaniye Kütüphanesi 4031, no. 51, münşeât mecmuası 3b-7b). When he received no answer, he dispatched no less than three armies to Khorasan (Mīrḵᵛānd, *Rawżat al-ṣafāʾ*, Lucknow, 1874, VII, pp. 16-17; John E. Woods, *The Aqqoyunlu: Clan, Confederation, Empire*, Minneapolis, 1976, p. 125). Later, Pīr-ʿAlī Beg broke with Ḥosayn Bāyqarā and entered the service of Sultan Maḥmūd, Abū Saʿīd's third son, who had established himself in Ḥeṣār-e Šādmān (in today's Tajikistan). There, Pāšā Begom, who had become widowed and had followed her brother, Pīr-ʿAlī Beg, into exile, was married to Sultan Maḥmūd (*Bābur-nāma*, p. 49; Minorsky, *Persia*, p. 42).

When Uzun Ḥasan died in 882/1472, Pīr-ʿAlī Beg attempted to recapture his former power base in Iran. Together with his brother Bayrām Beg and a brother of Sultan Maḥmūd by the name of Abū Bakr, he led a combined force of Bahārlūs and Čaḡatāys into Kermān province by way of Sīstān and Bam. This tribal army seized both Kermān and Sīrjān, which were poorly defended, and then headed for Fārs. But it was routed by an expeditionary force dispatched by the new Āq Qoyunlū ruler, Sultan Yaʿqūb (r. 883-96/1478-90; q.v.). Pīr-ʿAlī Beg, Bayrām Beg, and Abū Bakr, abandoning their families in Sīrjān, fled to Gorgān. There, a force sent by Ḥosayn Bāyqarā attacked them. Abū Bakr was killed and the Bahārlū leaders were captured. Pīr-ʿAlī Beg was then blinded and Bayrām Beg was executed (Minorsky, *Persia*, pp. 42-43).

Pīr-ʿAlī Beg's successor as chief of the Bahārlūs of Khorasan was his son Jān-ʿAlī Beg (who was erroneously called Yār-ʿAlī by Bābor). He settled down in Badaḵšān and, by the late 900s/1490s, had entered the service of Bābor (*Bābur-nāma*, p. 91). While fighting for Bābor in the Andījān area in 1499, he received such a blow on the head that it had to be trepanned (ibid., p. 109). However, in spite of these injuries, he continued to serve Bābor, following him to Kabul and then to India (ibid., p. 546).

Jān-ʿAlī Beg's son, Sayf-ʿAlī Beg, also served Bābor. When Bābor died, he entered the service of Homāyūn (937-63/1530-56) and, at the time of his own death, was governor of Ḡaznī. Sayf-ʿAlī Beg's son, Bayrām Khan (d. 968/1561), became a famous statesman of Mughal India. He was Akbar's *ḵānbābā* (guardian) and first *ḵān-e ḵānān* (chief minister). He was also a distinguished scholar, poet, and patron of the arts (A. S. Bazmee Ansari, "Bayrām Khan," in *EI*² I, pp. 1135-37).

Solṭānqolī Qoṭb-al-Molk, the Turkic adventurer who founded the Qoṭbšāhī dynasty at Golconda, in the Deccan, in 901/1496 was also a Bahārlū (Moḥammad Qāsem Hendūšāh Astarābādī, *Tārīḵ-e Forešta*, Cawnpore, 1884, p. 167). During its rule of nearly two centuries (901-1098/1496-1687), this dynasty produced a distinctive Indo-Muslim culture (R. M. Eaton, "Ḳuṭb Shāhī," in *EI*² V, pp. 549-50).

During the period following the collapse of the Qara Qoyunlū empire, the Bahārlūs who had remained in Western Iran gradually settled down in Azerbaijan, together with several other Qara Qoyunlū tribes. These seem to have collaborated with the Āq Qoyunlūs, for we hear of a certain Ḥasan Beg Šakaroḡlū who was an ally of the Āq Qoyunlū ruler Alvand b. Yūsof when the latter was attacked by Shah Esmāʿīl Ṣafawī at Naḵjavān in 907/1501-02 (Ḥasan Rūmlū, II, pp. 25-26; *Ḥabīb al-sīar* IV, p. 463).

The Bahārlūs did not play an important role during the Safavid period. Although Malcolm claims that the Bahārlū tribe was one of the seven tribes which constituted the mainstay of the early Safavid rulers (*History of Persia* I, p. 326), this is not confirmed by any reliable source. Ḥasan Rūmlū (pp. 78, 202) mentions only two Bahārlūs of note during that period, namely Moḥammad Bahārlū, who was commander of the fortress at Balḵ in 922/1516, and Walī Beg Bahārlū who, along with many other Qezelbāš leaders, supported Esmāʿīl Mīrzā in his quest for the throne following the death of Shah Ṭahmāsp in 984/1576. Moreover, Monajjembāšī's list of the eight principal Qezelbāš tribes does not include the Bahārlūs (*Taḏkerat al-molūk*, p. 194).

Today, there are traces or fragments of the Bahārlū tribe in Turkey, the USSR, and Iran. There is a village by the name of Bahārlū in the province (*vilayet*) of Dīārbakr in eastern Anatolia (*Gazetteer No. 46: Turkey*, Washington, D.C., 1960, p. 69). There are Bahārlūs in the districts of Shusha and Zengezur in Russian Azerbaijan (M. H. Valili Baharlu, *Azerbaycan, coğrafi, tabii, etnografi ve iktisadi mülâhazât*, Baku, 1921, p. 61). There are also three villages by the name of Bahārlū in Russian Azerbaijan (*Gazetteer No. 42: U.S.S.R.*, 2nd ed., Washington, D.C., 1970, I, p. 283). Another group of Bahārlūs is to be found in Iranian Azerbaijan. While visiting the province in 1906, the French scholar, Eugène Aubin, found the plain of the Dīzajrūd, northeast of Marāḡa, inhabited by Bahārlūs (*La Perse d'aujourd'hui*, Paris, 1908, p. 101). It must be the group which M. L. Sheil had earlier estimated at 2,000 families (*Glimpses of Life and Manners in Persia*, London, 1856, p. 396). Today, these Bahārlūs have lost their tribal identity and are included in no current list of the tribes of Azerbaijan. But the area in which they dwell nevertheless contains villages with highly suggestive names, e.g., Būlāllū, the name of the principal Bahārlū clan during the 9th/15th and 10th/16th centuries, and Āḡač Erī, the name of another Qara Qoyunlū tribe. Nearby are villages by the names of Ālpāvot and Bārānlū, two more Qara Qoyunlū tribes (Razmārā, *Farhang* IV, pp. 37, 41, 72, 99). Further south, there is the aforementioned village by the name of Bahārlū in the Sanandaj region (Razmārā, *Farhang* V, p. 60).

To the east, some Bahārlūs live in the village of Bahārmarz, 12 km south of Darmīān, near the Afghan border, in southern Khorasan. There is also a village by the name of Balāl, 3 km northwest of Bošrūya, in the same province (Razmārā, *Farhang* IX, pp. 60, 65). Then, according to Ḥasan Fasā'ī (II, p. 310), there is a tribe by the name of Bahārlū in K̲ᵛārazm (K̲īva).

In Kermān province, there is a small tribe by the name of Bar-e Bahārlū. It dwells between Rābor and Bezenjān and, in late Qajar times, consisted of about forty families (H. Field, *Contributions to the Anthropology of Iran*, Chicago, 1939, p. 235).

Finally, there is a Bahārlū tribe in Fārs. According to tribal tradition, these Bahārlūs came from northwestern Iran (personal interviews with Ebrāhīm Khan Bahārlū and Amīr Āqā Khan Bahārlū, Shiraz, 1957). But the fact that one of their *tīra*s (clans) is called Mašhadlū suggests that they were among those Bahārlūs who fled to Khorasan following the collapse of the Qara Qoyunlū state. Field claims that they settled in Fārs in the 12th/18th and 13th/19th centuries (ibid., p. 216). But this could not be the case if they came from Khorasan. One is tempted to believe that both the Bar-e Bahārlūs of Kermān and the Bahārlūs of Fārs are descendants of the Bahārlūs who were abandoned in Sīrjān when Pīr-ʿAlī Beg and his brother Bayrām Beg were defeated by Sultan Yaʿqūb Āq Qoyunlū in 1478, for the Bar-e Bahārlūs have settled down in Sīrjān and the Bahārlūs of Fārs have established themselves in an area immediately to the southwest of that region.

Until the 1280s/1860s, the Bahārlūs of Fārs were fully nomadic. Their summer quarters were in the districts of Rāmjerd, Marvdašt, and Kamīn, north of Shiraz, and their winter quarters were around Dārāb and Īzadk̲ᵛāst, in southeastern Fārs (Fasā'ī, II, p. 310). M. L. Sheil estimated their number at 1,230 families in 1849 (*Glimpses*, p. 399); K. E. Abbott at 2,000 families in 1850 ("Notes Taken on a Journey Eastwards from Shiráz... in 1850," *JRGS* 27, 1857, p. 153). Their last important leader was Mollā Aḥmad Khan Bozorgī of the Aḥmadlū clan, who ruled between 1268/1851-52 and 1275/1858-59 (Fasā'ī, II, pp. 310-11). Upon his death, a fierce struggle for power ensued. Massacre followed massacre. So great were the losses in human life that the tribe was never again able to recover its former strength and the tribesmen decided that they were no longer numerous enough to participate in the lengthy seasonal migrations to which they were accustomed. The remaining Bahārlūs settled down in their winter quarters and eked out a living from a mixture of agriculture and pastoralism, as well as from the proceeds of banditry. L. Pelly, who visited them in the early 1860s, wrote that they "are very mischievous and a set of robbers, who by killing each other have put an end to themselves and their ketkhodas, and all that remains of them are some horsemen, who wander about plundering everyone that comes in their way" ("Brief Account of the Province of Fārs," *Transactions of the Bombay Geographical Society* 17, 1963, p. 183). Similar observations were made by H. B. Vaughan ("A Journey Through Persia, 1887-88," *Royal Geographical Society; Supplementary Papers* III/2, 1892, p. 97), A. T. Wilson (*South West Persia... 1907-1914*, London, 1941, p. 47), G. Demorgny ("Les réformes administrative en Perse," pt. 1, *RMM* 12, March, 1913, p. 103), P. M. Sykes (*A History of Persia*, 3rd ed., London, 1951, II, p. 479), and others. Their exploits as bandits are also described in *Waqāyeʿ-e ettefāqīya*.

In 1278/1861-62, the tribe was absorbed into the K̲amsa tribal confederacy, which was formed by the governor-general of Fārs, Solṭān Morād Mīrzā, in an endeavor to check the growing influence of the Qašqā'ī tribal confederacy (P. Oberling, *The Qashqā'i Nomads of Fārs*, The Hague, 1974, p. 65).

In 1311 Š./1933 the Bahārlū tribe of Fārs comprised 8,000 families forming twenty *tīra*s: Ebrāhīmk̲ānī, Aḥmadlū, Esmāʿīlk̲ānī, Būrbūr, Bakla, Jāmbozorgī, Jarga, Jūqa, Ḥājītarlū, Ḥājīʿaṭṭārlū, Ḥaydarlū, Rasūlk̲ānī, Saqqez, Ṣafīk̲ānī, ʿĪsābīglū, Karīmlū Kolāhpūstī, Mašhadlū, Nāṣerbīglū, Waraṯa (Kayhān, *Jog̲rāfīā* II, p. 86).

Since World War II, the Bahārlūs have become completely sedentary, living the year round in the *dehestān*s (subdistricts) of Fasārūd, K̲osūya and Qarīat-al-K̲ayr in the *bak̲š* (district) of Dārāb (Razmārā, *Farhang* VII, pp. 88, 165, 171). O. Garrod, a British physician who visited Fārs toward the end of the war, noted that the Bahārlūs were "fast losing their tribal organization and characteristics" ("The Nomadic Tribes of Persia To-Day," *Journal of the Central Asian Society* 33, 1946, p. 44) and concluded: "The Baharlus, once the foremost horsemen and more feared warriors and bandits of Eastern Fārs, have sadly degenerated from the effects of Malaria and the diseases bred in the cumulative filth of their settlements" (ibid.).

By 1336 Š./1957, the tribe's population had dwindled to a mere 4,000 individuals (personal interview with Amīr Āqā Khan Bahārlū).

Bibliography: See also Ḥasan Fasā'ī, *History of Persia Under Qājār Rule*, tr. H. Busse, New York, 1972, pp. 208ff., 219, 221, 307, 336, 340ff., 360ff., 363ff., 387, 388 n., 390, 391 n., 418. M. S. Ivanov *Plemena Farsa*, Moscow, 1961, pp. 50-52. ʿA.-A. Saʿīdī Sīrjānī, ed., *Waqāyeʿ-e ettefāqīya: Majmūʿa-ye gozārešhā-ye k̲ofyanevīsān-e Engelīs dar welāyāt-e jonūbī-e Īrān az sāl-e 1291 tā 1322 qamarī*, 2nd ed., Tehran, 1362 Š./1983, index, s.v. Bahārlū. Abū Bakr Ṭehrānī, *Ketāb dīārbakrīya*, ed. N. Lugal and F. Sümer, 2nd ed., Tehran, 2536 = 1356 Š./1977.

(P. Oberling)

BAHĀRVAND, a Lur tribe now living mostly in the *dehestān*s (districts) of Kargāh and Bālā Garīva, south and southwest of K̲orramābād. It forms a part of the Dīrakvand tribal confederacy. According to oral tradition, the connection between the Bahārvands and the Dīrakvands was established toward the end of the 10th/16th century, when a man named Bahār moved to the village of Dara-ye Naṣab, south of K̲orramābād, from the village of Robāṭ, north of that town, and married a certain Dīrak, who was the leader of the

Dīrakvand tribe (S. Amanollahi-Baharvand, *The Baharvand, Former Pastoralists of Iran*, Ph.D. thesis, Rice University, May, 1975, p. 43).

Under Bahār's grandsons, Morād-ʿAlī and Kord-ʿAlī, the Bahārvand tribe was divided into two clans, Morād-ʿAlīvand and Kord-ʿAlīvand. For a long time, the tribe had its summer quarters around Dara-ye Naṣab and its winter quarters further south, toward Dezfūl. But at the end of the 11th/17th century, for reasons that are still unknown, it was forced to dwell the year round in its winter quarters in the Korkī region, where it eked out a living from both agriculture and animal husbandry (ibid.).

Owing to dynamic leadership and a growing population, the tribe, starting in 1830, underwent a period of expansion, as a result of which it became "one of the most powerful tribes of Luristan with substantial holdings of land" (ibid., p. 44). It defeated the Sagvand tribe, which had encroached upon its territory, taking over the Čenāra mountains, as well as the plains of Reżā, Čīn-e Zāl and Bīdrūba. Toward the end of the 13th/19th century, it moved northward, routing the Mīr tribe and occupying the Ṭāʾī valley. Then, in 1321/1903, it defeated the Pāpī tribe, reoccupying the Dara-ye Naṣab valley and annexing the nearby Ṭāf valley (ibid., pp. 44-49). A. T. Wilson, who visited Luristan in 1329/1911, described the Bahārvand tribe as the strongest of the Dīrakvand tribes. According to him, it contained some 1,000 families (the same figure is given by Kayhān [*Jogrāfīā* II, p. 66] for 1311 Š./1932) with a fighting force of 1,000 men, 500 of whom were armed with rifles, and possessed large flocks of sheep and goats, many mares and a number of mules (*Luristan*, Simla, 1912, p. 19). In 1332/1914, the Bahārvand tribe allied itself with the Mīr tribe and conquered the Kargāh (K̲orramābād) valley (Amanollahi-Baharvand, op. cit., p. 49).

The Bahārvand tribe, like other tribes of the Pīš(-e) Kūh, suffered greatly from the harsh measures taken by General Aḥmad Amīr Aḥmadī to quell tribal unrest in the region in 1923 and from Reżā Shah's forced settlement policy. Ḥosayn Khan, the leader of the tribe, and his brother were both arrested in 1929 and kept in confinement for twelve years (ibid., p. 51).

Today, the Bahārvands are completely sedentary. According to a list of the tribes of Iran published in 1963, it then comprised 5,000 families (J. Behruz, *Iran Almanach*, 3rd ed., Tehran, 1963, p. 424).

Bibliography: See also Ḥ. Īzadpanāh, *Āt̲ār-e bāstānī o tārīk̲ī-e Lorestān*, K̲orramābād, 2535 = 1355 Š./1976, table facing p. 4.

(P. OBERLING)

BAHDĪNĀN (Kurdish Bādīnān), name of a Kurdish region, river, dialect group, and amirate. The region comprises roughly the largely mountainous northern *qażā*s of Mowṣel *lewā* of Iraq (according to the pre-1973 administrative division) including ʿAmādīya, ʿAqra, Dahōk, Zāk̲ū, Zībār (divided between Arbīl and Mowṣel *lewā*s in 1944), and Šayk̲ān. The first four *qażā*s were regrouped into a new administrative division, Dahōk *moḥāfaẓa*, in 1973. The majority of the population are Kurds (see figures in Edmonds, p. 439) and speak Kurmanji, the major Kurdish dialect group, also called Bādīnānī (see, among others, Jardine and Blau). The dominant religion is Islam (Shafiʿite Sunni), although the area, especially Šayk̲ān and Jabal Senjār, has been the stronghold of the minority religion Yazīdī. Other sizable, but declining, minorities are Christians (Chaldean/Assyrian) and Jews. The Zēy Bādīnān river is a stretch of the Great Zab River (*Times Atlas*, pl. 34) between its two tributaries, K̲āzer River and Rūbār-ī Rawāndez. It forms the eastern boundary of Bahdīnān territory.

The Bahdīnān amirate, one of the more powerful and enduring Kurdish principalities, was founded by the eponymous Bahāʾ-al-Dīn, originally from Šams-al-Dīnān (q.v.; Kurd. Šamzīnān, region now forming part of Hakkari province in Turkey), who established his hereditary rule in the town of ʿAmādīya (Bedlīsī, pp. 145-46) in the wake of the decline of Zangid power (7th-8th/13th-14th centuries). Threatened by the expansionist and centralizing efforts of the Ottoman and Safavid empires, Bahdīnān princes were drawn into prolonged confrontations with these two rival powers. Inseparably linked with these external wars was the endless conflict with other Kurdish principalities, tribal chiefs, and religious and ethnic minorities. In spite of these upheavals, Bahdīnān survived until the mid-13th/mid-19th century when Moḥammad Pasha of Rawāndūz, the conqueror amir of the neighboring Soran principality captured ʿAqra and ʿAmādīya and deposed the rulers Esmāʿīl Pasha and Moḥammad Saʿīd Pasha (1248/1832). Bahdīnān authority was, however, restored under Esmāʿīl Pasha soon after the Ottoman government succeeded in defeating the Soran amir and putting an end to this principality in 1834. Pursuing their protracted centralization policy, the Ottomans were able to overthrow the Bahdīnān amirate in 1842 (Yaḥyā, no. 43, p. 157; Jwaideh).

Bibliography: Maḥfūẓ ʿOmar ʿAbbāsī, *Amārat Bahdīnān al-ʿabbāsīya*, Mosul, 1969. Amīr Šaraf Khan Bedlīsī, *Šaraf-nāma*, ed. M. ʿAbbāsī, Tehran, 1343 Š./1964, pp. 145-56. J. Blau, *Le Kurde de ʿAmādiya et de Djabal Sindjar: Analyse linguistique, textes folkloriques, glossaires*, Paris, 1975. Ṣ. Damlūjī, *Amārat Bahdīnān al-kordīya*, Mosul, 1952. C. J. Edmonds, *Kurds, Turks and Arabs*, London, 1957, p. 439. R. F. Jardine, *Bahdinan Kurmanji: A Grammar of the Kurmanji of the Kurds of Mosul Division and Surrounding Districts*, Baghdad, 1922. W. Jwaideh, *The Kurdish Nationalist Movement: Its Origins and Development*, Ph.D. dissertation, Syracuse University, 1960, pp. 165-68, 173-75. Anwar Māʾī, *al-Akrād fī Bahdīnān*, Mosul, 1960. *The Times Atlas of the World*, 7th ed., New York, 1985, pl. 34. ʿAbd-al-Fattāḥ ʿAlī Yaḥyā, "al-Mollā Yaḥyā al-Mezūrī wa soqūṭ amārat Bādīnān," *Kārvān* (Arbīl) 4, 1986, no. 41, pp. 149-59; no. 42, pp. 147-55; no. 43, pp. 149-60.

(A. HASSANPOUR)

BAḤĪRĪ, a major Shafiʿite family of Nishapur in the eleventh century. The family's eponym is Baḥīr b. Nūḥ b. Ḥayyān b. Moḵtār about whom nothing concrete is known. The names are recorded of several family members who lived in the early tenth century, but Abū ʿAmr Moḥammad b. Aḥmad b. Moḥammad b. Jaʿfar b. Baḥīr is the first Baḥīrī to be more than just a name. He held the post of *mozakkī* in Nishapur which gave him the authority to place people on the official list of court witnesses. Witnesses functioned as bailiffs and notaries, and only men of unimpeachable honesty and social standing could be appointed. Abū ʿAmr was also a prominent teacher of *ḥadīṯ* (tradition).

Abū Naṣr ʿAbd-al-Raḥmān, the eldest of Abū ʿAmr's four sons, inherited the post of *mozakkī*, which then passed to his brother Abū ʿAbd-al-Raḥmān ʿAmr when he died only three years after his father in 399/1009. ʿAmr also taught *ḥadīṯ* in the Old Congregational Mosque in Nishapur, a stronghold of the city's Hanafite faction, during the period when the Hanafites supported the persecution of the Shafiʿite-Ashʿarite faction launched by the vizier ʿAmīd-al-Molk Kondorī. This may indicate that the Baḥīrīs were Shafiʿites but not Ashʿarites. Another brother, Abū ʿOṯmān Saʿīd Mūlqābādī (named for the part of Nishapur the family lived in), served with distinction in the army of Maḥmūd of Ghazna during his invasions of India.

Several Baḥīrīs served as *mozakkīs* or other functionaries of the qadi's court in the next generation. The most remarkable was Abū Saʿīd Esmāʿīl who was born in 419/1028 and died in 501-02/1108. An Ashʿarite, unlike earlier family members, he was closely associated with the family of the noted Shafiʿite Sufi Abu'l-Qāsem Qošayrī. Unspecified financial misfortune forced him to sell the last of his family's estates, but subsequent success as a merchant enabled him to become a landowner again. In later life he was considered an important scholar and teacher of *ḥadīṯ*.

Little is known about later members of the family, including one Abū Saʿd Moḥammad who is described as being pure of heart but strange and savage of nature. The last known figure is Abū Bakr ʿAbd-al-Raḥmān, who studied under Qošayrī in his youth and died at the age of 87 in 539-40/1145.

Bibliography: R. W. Bulliet, *The Patricians of Nishapur*, Cambridge, Mass., 1972, chap. 12, with full references to the mss. ed. in facs. by R. N. Frye, *The Histories of Nishapur*, The Hague, 1965. See also Habib Jaouiche, *The Histories of Nishapur. Register der Personen- und Ortsnamen*, Wiesbaden, 1984.

(R. W. BULLIET)

BAHMAʾĪ, a Lur tribe of the Kohgīlūya (Kūh[-e] Gīlūya). Until well into the second half of the 13th/19th century, it was one of the largest and most powerful tribes of the Behbahān region. According to Layard, who visited the Bahmaʾīs in 1840, they comprised some 3,000 families, and had a fighting force of "about 2,000 excellent matchlock-men and a small but very efficient body of horsemen" ("A Description of the Province of Khuzistan," *JRGS* 16, 1846, p. 23). According to C. A. de Bode, who was in the Kohgīlūya at the same time as Layard, the tribe comprised only some 2,000 families (*Travels in Luristan and Arabistan*, London, 1845, I, p. 280). But both travelers were equally impressed by the Bahmaʾīs' refractoriness and energy as raiders (see e.g., Layard, "A Description," p. 23). De Bode called them "the wildest and most unruly tribe among the mountaineers of Fārs" (p. 280).

The last important leader of the Bahmaʾīs was Ḵalīl Khan, who ruled the tribe from his fortress, the Qalʿa-ye Aʿlā (sometimes spelled Qalʿa ʿAlāʾ), 53 km northwest of Behbahān. He appears to have been a picturesque bandit in the manner of Fra Diavolo (see descriptions by Layard, p. 23, and De Bode, p. 280). During Ḵalīl Khan's lifetime, his eldest son, Jaʿfar Khan, built the two strongholds of Qalʿa-ye Aʿlā and Dīšmūk, 20 km east of the Qalʿa-ye Aʿlā and since then the tribe became divided into the Garmsīrī, with headquarters at Qalʿa-ye ʿAlā, and Sardsīrī, with headquarters at Dīšmūk (M. Żarrābī, "Ṭawāyef-e Kohgīlūya," *FIZ* 9, 1340 Š./1961-62, p. 291).

After the death of Ḵalīl Khan, which occurred late in the nineteenth century, there was a struggle for the succession between his sons and the sons of his brother, Moḥammad-Ḥosayn Khan. In the course of this contest for leadership, Moḥammad-ʿAlī Khan, a son of Moḥammad-Ḥosayn Khan, slew Jaʿfar Khan and declared himself the new chief of the tribe. But forty days later, Moḥammad-ʿAlī Khan was, in turn, killed by a son of Jaʿfar Khan. These two murders and the feud that ensued led to the division of the Bahmaʾī tribe into two separate tribes, the Bahmaʾī Moḥammadī and the Bahmaʾī Aḥmadī tribes (*Żarrābī*, pp. 291-93). But in spite of this the Bahmaʾīs continued their raids, retaining their warlike reputation, and, writing in the mid-1890s, Ḥasan Fasāʾī could still say that ten Bahmaʾī riflemen were worth a hundred Baḵtīārīs (*Fārs-nāma* II, p. 275).

Fasāʾī (ibid.), G. Demorgny ("Les réformes administratives en Perse: Les tribus du Fars," pt. 1, *RMM* 22, March, 1913, pp. 117-18) and M. Kayhān (*Jogrāfīā* II, p. 89) all estimated the number of Bahmaʾīs at 3,000 families. Today, the Bahmaʾīs are scattered over a wide area covering three adjacent *dehestān*s, Bahmaʾī Sarḥaddī, Bahmaʾī Sardsīr, and Bahmaʾī Garmsīr, northwest of Behbahān (Razmārā, *Farhang* VI, pp. 64-65). Because they have thoroughly blended in with the local population, it is no longer possible to give an accurate estimate of their population.

Bibliography: Given in text. See also M. Bāver, *Kūhgīlūya wa īlāt-e ān*, Gačsārān, 1324 Š./1945, pp. 120-29. N. Afšār-e Nāderī, *Monogerāfī-e īl-e Bahmaʾī*, Tehran, 1347 Š./1968.

(P. OBERLING)

BAHMAN "avalanche." See BARF.

BAHMAN, author of Qeṣṣa-ye Sanjān, q.v.

BAHMAN, the New Persian name of the Avestic Vohu Manah (Good Thought) and Pahlavi Wahman.

i. *In the Avesta.*

ii. *In the Pahlavi texts.*

i. In the Avesta

Vohu Manah (Good Thought) is one of the divine beings to whom the name Aməša Spenta is given in the post-Gathic parts of the Avesta. As with all these beings, an originally abstract idea has been personified and deified. (On ideas and their personifications in Zoroaster's thinking, see Thieme, *Die vedischen Āditya*, pp. 404f.). In many contexts it is unclear whether *vohu manah* (good thought) or *vahišta manah* (best thought) means the abstract idea or the divine being, but as in the case of the other personifications, a synergy of the idea and the being is apparent. (Such is the view of Boyce, *Zoroastrianism* I, pp. 212f., and Humbach, *Die Gathas*, p. 55. On the other hand, Nyberg, *Religionen*, p. 121, and Duchesne-Guillemin, *Zoroastre*, pp. 205ff., and *The Western Response*, pp. 227ff., consider *vohu manah* to be in all respects a being, while Insler, *The Gathas*, pp. 25ff., reckons him to be wholly an idea).

Vohu manah means literally the good moral state of a person's mind which alone enables him to perform his duties, whether these be worship of Ahura Mazda or care of cows, which in the *Gāθās* is deemed particularly important. For example, it is said of Ahura Mazdā's dominion that mankind "will augment it by good thought" (*Y.*31.6), while righteous believers are described as persons "who through their practice of good thought are in the community of the milch cow" (*Y.*34.14).

As a being, Vohu Manah appears in the *Gāθās* mainly in association with Ahura Mazdā and other beings, e.g., "I too shall praise you, O Truth, as never before, (you) and Good Thought and the Wise Lords" (*Y.* 28.3; cf. *Y.* 28.9, and *Y.* 33.11). In the abode where Ahura Mazdā dwells, Vohu Manah is present together with the souls of the truthful (*Y.* 49.10). One of the designations of the next world is "Abode of Good Thought" (*Y.* 32.15). Vohu Manah is presented as one of the basic facts of the creation (*Y.* 44.4). Ahura Mazdā is named as his father (*Y.* 31.8; 45.4), but this relationship, which other divine beings also enjoy, is not pictured in clearly anthropomorphic terms. Just as Ahura Mazdā is related to Vohu Manah (*Y.* 32.2), so too does man strive for partnership with him (*Y.* 49.3, 5). One characteristic function of Vohu Manah is that of an adviser (*Y.* 44.8, 13; 47.3). Man ought to follow the "Ways of Good Thought" (*Y.* 34.12, 13; 51.16). Anyone who does good to a truthful person—among other things by tending cows—will have a place "on the meadow of Truth and Good Thought" (*Y.* 33.3).

Vohu Manah, the being, also acts as a protector of man and his animals, but is not the only performer of this function. "Who could be found to be the protector of my cattle, of myself, (who) other than Truth, than you, O Wise Lord, and Best Thought?" (*Y.* 50.1). Conversely the herdsman, charged with the care of cows, is described as "Good Thought's supporter" (*Y.* 31.10). There is probably also an allusion to Vohu Manah's role in the sentence "Whom do you appoint, O Wise One, to be a keeper for one like me . . ., (whom) other than your Fire and your Thought?" (*Y.* 46.7).

It has often been assumed (e.g., by Lommel, *Die Religion*, pp. 123ff., and Boyce, *Zoroastrianism* I, pp. 209ff.) that a special relationship between Vohu Manah, the being, and animals, particularly the cow as representative of the animals, is already manifest in the *Gāθās*; but there is no clear evidence of such a relationship in the texts (cf. Narten, *Die Aməṣ̌a Spəṇtas*, pp. 107ff.).

In line with the dualistic world view, *vohu manah* is opposed by *aka manah* (bad thought) or *acišta manah* (worst thought). Here again tendencies to personification appear in some contexts: the *daēvas* are "seeds from Worst Thought" (*Y.* 32.3), hell is called the "abode of Worst Thought" (*Y.* 32.13), the deceiver dwells "with Worst Thought" (*Y.* 47.5). (On the conflict between Good Thought and Bad Thought, visualized as beings, see Lommel, *Die Religion*, pp. 37f.).

The importance given in the *Gāθās* to the idea and personification of *vohu manah* is probably a specifically Zoroastrian feature. In the Vedas there is no instance of a compound of the abstract noun *mánas* and the adjective *vásu* with an ethical connotation. The word *sumati*, cited by Geiger (*Die Aməša Spəntas*, p. 241) can hardly, in view of its different etymology, prove anything relevant to the Indo-Iranian period. (See Lommel, *Die Elemente*, pp. 380f., who thinks it improbable that Vohu Manah is from the Indo-Iranian period. For a different explanation of Vohu Manah, see Duchesne-Guillemin, *La religion*, pp. 200ff.).

In the Younger Avesta there are few references to *vohu manah* the abstract idea, but many invocations and mentions of Vohu Manah the divine being. In general, however, these give no indications of the being's special attributes and functions (see Lommel, *Die Religion*, p. 38). Even so, it is significant that wherever the Aməša Spəntas are mentioned by name, and despite differences in the order of mention, the first rank after Ahura Mazdā is always held by Vohu Manah, whereas in the *Gāθās* Aša appears more important and closest to Ahura Mazdā. Also important is Vohu Manah's role as the victorious opponent of Aka Manah: "Bad Thought will be vanquished, Good Thought will be the victor" (*Yt.* 19.96). In another context Vohu Manah reappears in the role of protector: "When the Evil Spirit assailed the creation of Good Truth, Good Thought and Fire intervened" (*Yt.* 13.77). In the race and combat for the light of good fortune, Vohu Manah takes part, together with Aša Vahišta (Best truth) and Fire, as a champion of Spənta Mainyu (most Beneficent Spirit), but only Fire is mentioned as an actual combatant. Finally Vohu Manah appears as the being who will welcome the truthful man's soul in the afterworld (*Y.* 32.15 and *Y.* 49.10 quoted above, *Vd.* 19). This, by the way, is the only setting where the portrayal is at all graphic: "Good Thought rises from his throne made of gold, Good

Thought proclaims... (*Vd.* 19.31), but on the whole Vohu Manah as presented in the Younger Avesta is rather colorless—a being of some importance, but without distinctive attributes.

The second day of the month is dedicated to Vohu Manah, which is consistent with the order of precedence which places Vohu Manah second after Ahura Mazdā. The eleventh month is also sacred to Vohu Manah.

Bibliography: M. Boyce, *Zoroastrianism* I, Leiden and Cologne, 1975. J. Duchesne-Guillemin, *Zoroastre*, Paris, 1948. Idem, "The Western Response to Zoroaster," Ratanbai Katrak Lectures, Oxford, 1956, repr. in B. Schlerath, ed., *Zarathustra*, 1970. Idem, *La religion de l'Iran ancien*, Paris, 1962. B. Geiger, *Die Aməša Spəntas. Ihr Wesen und ihre ursprüngliche Bedeutung*, Vienna, 1916 (Sb. Kais. Akademie der Wissenschaften in Wien 176, 7). H. Humbach, *Die Gathas des Zarathustra* I, Heidelberg, 1959. S. Insler, *The Gāthās of Zarathustra*, Tehran and Liège, 1975. H. Lommel, *Die Religion Zarathustras*, Tübingen, 1930, repr. Hildesheim and New York, 1971. Idem, "Die Elemente im Verhältnis zu den Ameša Spentas," in *Festschrift für Ad. E. Jensen* I, Munich, 1964, repr. in Schlerath, ed., *Zarathustra*. J. Narten, *Die Aməṣ̌a Spəṇtas im Avesta*, Wiesbaden, 1982. H. S. Nyberg, *Die Religionen des alten Iran*, Leipzig, 1938, repr. Osnabrück, 1966. B. Schlerath, ed., *Zarathustra*, Wege der Forschung 169, Darmstadt, 1970. P. Thieme, "Die vedischen Āditya und die zarathustrischen Aməša Spənta," in Schlerath, ed., *Zarathustra*.

(J. NARTEN)

ii. IN THE PAHLAVI TEXTS

In the Zoroastrian tradition Bahman is the first of the Aməša Spəntas and the protector of cattle. In the Pahlavi writings, with their strong dualist perspective, he has the arch-demon Akōman as his adversary. Both in the Younger Avesta and in the Pahlavi literature he acts as Ohrmazd's auxiliary in the work of creation.

Bahman, as his name indicates, has two essential qualities, goodness (*wehīh*) and thought (*menišn*). He therefore, according to the exegesis of the *Dādestān ī dēnīg* (2.15-16), differs from Srōš, who exists in speech (*gōwišn*), and from Ard (Aša), who exists in action (*kunišn*); but according to another tradition, Bahman dwells in the intelligence (*axw*), Srōš in thought (*menišn*), and Spandarmad in the spirit (*vārom*; *Dēnkard*, p. 49.16). Although Bahman remains the protector of cattle and the embodiment of their five species (*Zātspram* 23.2), the literature lays much greater stress on his relationship to mankind. He plays an important part in mankind's destiny, both here below and in the beyond. In the present world, he does thrice-daily counts of the good and bad thoughts, words, and deeds of every human being (*Dādestān ī dēnīg* 13.2-3); but he is not the sole account-keeper (*āmārgar*), as Mihr, Srōš, and Rašn are also charged with the task, particularly at the final judgment of each individual. Bahman acts as the guide of souls, but the *Ardā Wīrāz-nāmag* (chap. 11.163) explains that he only intervenes at the last stage of the soul's journey, by accompanying it to the abode of Ohrmazd where he himself resides. Finally it is stated that during the Renewal at the end of time, Bahman will be consulted about everything (*Dēnkard*, p. 824. 12-13).

The Pahlavi texts contain legendary accounts describing Bahman's involvement with Zoroaster's birth (see the texts in Molé, *La légende*). Zoroaster was laughing when he was born because Bahman was dwelling in him (*Dēnkard*, bk. 5.2.5), Bahman being the *mēnōg* who brings happiness (*Zātspram* 8.15). Bahman's opposition to Akōman is illustrated with examples from Zoroaster's tribulations in infancy; it is Bahman who, accompanied by Srōš, brings a ewe to Zoroaster to nourish him (*Zātspram* 10.11; *Dēnkard*, bk. 7.3.17). Since Bahman is so close to Ohrmazd, it is not surprising that he played a part in the plan to create Zoroaster, being required to carry the sacred *hōm* from which Zoroaster's body was made (*Dēnkard*, bk. 7.2.17-25), or that he escorted Zoroaster to his interviews with Ohrmazd. Similarly he appears as a messenger sent to Vištāsp to dispel his doubts and as a guide (*parwānag*) summoned by Tištar to make rain fall (*Zātspram* 3.8).

No Avestan *yašt* is specifically dedicated to Bahman. The frequently expressed opinion that the substance of a lost *Bahman yašt* (q.v.) has been preserved in the Pahlavi book *Zand ī Wahman Yasn* does not rest on any solid foundation. The *yašt*s dedicated to the Aməša Spəntas are not old (see Boyce, *Textual Sources*, p. 91) but are all late fabrications, as Darmesteter first noted. Internal analysis of the *Zand ī Wahman Yasn* reveals no resemblance in either substance or form to the ancient *yašt*s. The arguments from the language put forward by G. Widengren and other Swedish scholars are weak and unconvincing. Even the title of *Bahman yašt* was invented by modern scholars (see A. Hultgård, in Hellholm, ed., *Apocalypticism*, p. 388), but Bahman does not enter into the *Zand ī Wahman Yasn* at all. In reality the book is a late compilation of myths and apocalyptic speculations.

Bahman's name does not often appear in onomastics, being much less widely used than Mithra or Ādur as a component of personal names. This is surprising for a divine being so closely concerned with mankind.

See also AMƏŠA SPƏNTA; APOCALYPTIC.

Bibliography: B. T. Anklesaria, ed., *Zand-í Vohûman Yasn and two Pahlavi Fragments*, Bombay, 1957. M. Boyce, *Textual Sources for the Study of Zoroastrianism*, Manchester, 1984. Ph. Gignoux, *Le livre d'Ardā Vīrāz*, Paris, 1984. Idem, "Sur l'inexistence d'un Bahman Yasht avestique," *Journal of Asian and African Studies* 32, Tokyo, 1986, pp. 53-64. D. Hellholm, ed., *Apocalypticism in the Mediterranean World and the Near East*, Tübingen, 1983. J. de Menasce, *Le troisième livre du Dēnkart*, Paris, 1973. M. Molé, *La légende de Zoroastre d'après les livres pehlevis*, Paris, 1967 (*Dēnkard*, bks. 5 and 7). G. Widengren, *The Great Vohu Manah and the Apostle of God*, Uppsala, 1945).

(PH. GIGNOUX)

BAHMAN son of ESFANDĪĀR, a Kayanian king of Iran in the national epic. This king does not appear in the Avesta but is mentioned as one of the Kayanian kings in the *Dēnkard* (ed. Sanjana, VII, p. 6.4), *Bundahišn* (36.9), and *Bahman yašt* (3.20-29). Various Pahlavi, Arabic, and Persian sources give his name in forms such as Wahman (*Bundahišn*), Bahman (*Šāh-nāma*; Masʿūdī, *Morūj*, ed. Pellat, p. 272; Dīnavarī, pp. 28, 29), Ardašīr Bahman (*Bahman yašt*; Ṭabarī, I, p. 686; Ebn Balḵī, p. 52; Ebn al-Aṯīr, repr., I, p. 278), Kay Ardašīr (Ḥamza, pp. 25, 37; Bīrūnī, *Āṯār al-bāqīa*, p. 105), Kay Bahman, and add the epithet "long-handed" (*al-ṭawīl al-bāʿ*, *derāzdast*); they thus identify him with Artaxerxes I (r. 465-25 B.C.), who was surnamed Macrocheir in Greek and Longimanus in Latin. In the accounts of historians such as Ṭabarī (I, p. 688) and Masʿūdī (loc. cit.), his mother is said to have been from the Children of Israel and to have borne the name Astūrīā (i.e., Esther of the Old Testament). Ṭabarī (I, p. 651), Masʿūdī (loc. cit.), and most of the other historians (e.g., Dīnavarī and Ebn al-Balḵī) attribute to him the overthrow of Boḵt Naṣṣar (Nebuchadnezzar) and the return of the Children of Israel to their homeland; and some, such as Masʿūdī and Ebn al-Balḵī, add that Bahman appointed Kūroš (i.e., Cyrus the Great) to perform this task. Bahman is thus identified not only with the Achaemenid Artaxerxes I but also with Cyrus. (On the intermixture of various traditions concerning Bahman, see E. Yarshater, "Were the Sassanians Heirs to the Achaemenids?" in *La Persia nel medioevo*, Rome, 1971, pp. 521f.). Although traces of the careers of Achaemenid kings can be found here and there in the stories of Kayanian kings before Bahman, this influence only becomes fully apparent when the reigns of Bahman and his successors Dārā and Dārā b. Dārā are reached. Bahman is described in the *Bahman yašt* and the *Dēnkard* as one of the greatest Mazdayasnian kings of Iran (*Camb. Hist. Iran* III/1, pp. 470f.), but he is not one of the Kayanian kings named in the Avesta. It is therefore better to regard him as not a Kayanian king but as basically a mixture of Cyrus and Artaxerxes I.

In the *Šāh-nāma* it is stated that after the death of Bahman's father Esfandīār in combat with Rostam, Bahman invaded Sīstān with a large army, devastated that region, and slew Rostam's descendants; but since Rostam, according to the *Šāh-nāma*, had already been treacherously killed by his half-brother Šaḡād before the start of the campaign, Bahman only slew Rostam's son Farāmarz and imprisoned Rostam's father Zāl, whom he later released at the request of his own paternal uncle Pašūtan (*Šāh-nāma*, Moscow, VI, p. 345 vv. 36f.). The accounts of the historians differ. According to Ṭabarī (I, p. 687), Masʿūdī, (loc. cit.), and Ebn al-Aṯīr (loc. cit.), Bahman slew Rostam, Zāl, Farāmarz, and Zavāra; according to Ebn al-Balḵī, he slew Zāl and Farāmarz. The *Bundahišn* (loc. cit.) and most of the Arabic and Persian sources give the length of Bahman's reign as 112 years, but some say 120 and others 80 years (Ṭabarī, I, p. 688; *Šāh-nāma* VI, p. 343; Masʿūdī, loc. cit.; Bīrūnī, *Āṯār al-bāqīa*, p. 105; *Mojmal*, p. 53; Ebn al-Aṯīr, loc. cit.). They all praise him as a righteous king. The importance attached to Bahman's reign in Zoroastrian literature can be seen in a passage in the *Bahman yašt* where the reigns of the kings are likened to tree branches made of seven metals. The branches, listed in order of importance and in the main also historical sequence, are the golden reign of Goštāsp, the silver reign of Bahman, the brass reign of Ardašīr Pāpakān, the bronze reign of the Arsacid Balāš, the tin reign of Bahrām Gōr, and the steel reign of Ḵosrow I Anōšīravān, together with the branch of impure iron which symbolizes the rule of the shaggy-haired demons (*dēws*) born of the seed of anger, probably referring to the rule of the Arabs.

Arabic and Persian sources (e.g., Ṭabarī, Ebn Balḵī) state that Bahman had five children—two sons named Dārā and Sāsān and three daughters, one named Ḵomānī or Homāy and entitled Čehrāzād, the others named Bahmandoḵt and Farnak; that Bahman married his own daughter Homāy on account of her incomparable beauty; that Homāy was the mother of his son Dārā; and that on his deathbed he designated his daughter-wife Homāy, who was then pregnant by him, to be his successor. According to the *Šāh-nāma* (VI, p. 351 vv. 164f.), Bahman's other son Sāsān, being resentful of his father's choice of Homāy to succeed him, went to Nīšāpūr, took a wife there, and had a son to whom they gave the paternal name Sāsān; this second Sāsān was the grandfather of Ardašīr Pāpakān (q.v.), the founder of the Sasanian empire. Later in the *Šāh-nāma* (VII, p. 116 vv. 69f.), another story, different from the above but consistent with the account in the *Kār-nāmag*, is told in explanation of Ardašīr's ancestry: after the death of Dārā in the war with Alexander, Dārā's son, who was named Sāsān, fled to India where he took a wife, and his descendants down to the fourth generation were all named Sāsān, his great-great-grandson being the father of Ardašīr Pāpakān. Thus Ardašīr's lineage, according to the second story, went back to Bahman through Homāy, not through Bahman's son Sāsān. The accounts of Ardašīr Pāpakān's lineage in the *Bundahišn* (35.36) and in Ṭabarī (I, pp. 813f.) give different lists of Bahman's descendants down to Ardašīr, but concur with the first *Šāh-nāma* story in relating Ardašīr to Bahman through Sāsān, not through Homāy. In any case all these stories were obviously fabricated in the Sasanian period to provide evidence for the legitimacy of Ardašīr and his descendants.

A different account of Bahman's career has also come down. The Persian prose version of this is lost, but a versified rendering by Īrānšāh b. Abi'l-Ḵayr, with the title *Bahman-nāma*, survives in a manuscript in the British Library (Or. 2780), and a summary is included in the *Mojmal* (pp. 53-54). For further details see BAHMAN-NĀMA.

According to the *Bahman-nāma*, Bahman was killed by a dragon when out hunting (ms. Or. 2780, fols. 134-87). With regard to the manner of Bahman's death, it should be noted that this is the only instance of the killing of a legitimate ruler by a dragon. The episode, if not wholly fictitious, may perhaps symbolize the conquest of the Iranian crown and throne by a foreigner.

Wise sayings ascribed to Bahman are quoted in a chapter of Ebn Meskūya's (Meskawayh's) *al-Ḥekma al-ḵāleda* (ed. ʿAbd-al-Raḥmān Badawī, Cairo, 1952, pp. 61f.) and in Taqī-al-Dīn Moḥammad Šūštarī's *Jāvīdān ḵerad* (ed. Behrūz Ṯarvatīān, Tehran, 2535 = 1355 Š./1976, pp. 111ff.). In some sources (e.g., Ṭabarī, I, p. 687) he is also credited with the foundation of the town Bahman-Ardašīr (q.v.).

Bibliography: See also A. Christensen, *Les Kayanides*, Copenhagen, 1932, s.v. Vahman.

(DJ. KHALEGHI-MOTLAGH)

BAHMAN JĀDŪYA (or Jāḏōē), Sasanian general engaged in the defense of the Sawād of ʿErāq during the Muslim conquest in the 630s. He belonged to the Median or Pahlavik faction led by Rostam at Madāʾen and had a reputation for being anti-Arab. Because of his bushy eyebrows he was called Ḏu'l-Ḥājeb (owner of bushy eyebrows) as was Mardānšāh. During Ḵāled b. Walīd's raid in 12/633 he was sent with an army to back up the forces of Andarzağar, who had gone to oppose Ḵāled in the territory of Kaskar. When Ḵāled defeated Andarzağar at Walaja the survivors joined Bahman Jādūya, who left Jābān in charge of local defense in the western Sawād and returned to Madāʾen. During the rest of Ḵāled's campaign he camped with the vanguard outside Madāʾen.

During Abū ʿObayd b. Masʿūd Ṯaqafī's campaign in the Sawād in 13/634, Rostam sent Bahman Jādūya against him with a force which included elephants and the royal leopard-skin standard (Derafš-e Kāvīān). He turned the Muslims back at Bābel west of the Tigris, drove them across the Euphrates, and camped at Qoss al-Nāṭef on the east bank. Abū ʿObayd camped at Marwaḥa across the river, and when he crossed the Euphrates on a floating bridge and attacked the Persians, Bahman Jādūya caught the Muslims with their backs to the river and inflicted a serious defeat on them in the battle of the Bridge (*yawm al-Jesr*) in the fall of 13/634. Abū ʿObayd was trampled to death by an elephant, the bridge was broken by an Arab, and some 4,000 Arabs perished by drowning. Moṯannā b. Ḥāreṯa Šaybānī managed to retie the bridge and rallied 3,000 Arab survivors, although some of them returned to Madīna. Bahman Jādūya was unable to follow up this victory because, as his army was about to cross the river, news came that the faction of the people of Fārs under Fīrūzān at Madāʾen had overthrown Rostam-e Farroḵzād and his faction, and Bahman Jādūya was dismissed and recalled to the capital.

Bahman Jādūya also fought in the center of the Sasanian army under Rostam-e Farroḵzād at the battle of Qādesīya in 16/637, where he was killed by Qaʿqāʿ b. ʿAmr Tamīmī in revenge for the death of Abū ʿObayd and the others killed at the Battle of the Bridge. The claim that he fought and was killed at the battle of Nehāvand is due to confusing him with Mardānšāh.

Bibliography: Balāḏorī, *Fotūḥ*, pp. 251-52, 255. Ebn al-Aṯīr (repr.), II, pp. 387f., 393f., 438-41, 461, 472, 474. Justi, *Namenbuch*, pp. 107, 374. Masʿūdī, *Morūj* IV, pp. 212-13. Ṭabarī, I, pp. 2030, 2032, 2053, 2060, 2174-77, 2179f., 2182, 2258, 2260, 2300, 2306, 2309, 2618.

(M. MORONY)

BAHMAN MĪRZĀ (fl. 1225/1810-1301/1883-84), the fourth son of ʿAbbās Mīrzā (q.v.) and brother of Moḥammad Shah (r. 1250-64/1834-48). After Moḥammad Mīrzā succeeded Fatḥ-ʿAlī Shah, he appointed Bahman Mīrzā (at the time governor of Ardabīl) governor of Tehran (19 Šaʿbān 1250/21 December 1834). Later Bahman Mīrzā became the governor of Hamadān and, when his uterine brother Qahramān Mīrzā died, succeeded him as governor of Azerbaijan.

During the last years of Moḥammad Shah's reign, Iran was in a state of political and social turmoil. Debilitated by gout, the shah had turned the government over to his grand vizier Ḥājī Mīrzā Āqāsī (q.v.). While Ḥājī Mīrzā Āqāsī was taking control of the kingdom, in Khorasan Moḥammad Shah's maternal uncle Allāhyār Khan Āṣaf-al-Dawla was plotting against the shah and grand vizier. Apparently the plot was to proceed as follows: Āṣaf-al-Dawla's son Moḥammad-Ḥasan Khan Sālār, with the help of his brothers was to wrest control of Khorasan from Moḥammad Shah and to gather a large force of cavalry and infantry to march on Tehran. After they had taken the capital, they were to replace Moḥammad Shah with Bahman Mīrzā (Eʿtemād-al-Salṭana, *Montaẓam-e nāṣerī*, 1300/1883, III, p. 188). Ḥājī Mīrzā Āqāsī got wind of the conspiracy and moved to stop it. Though Āṣaf-al-Dawla used the pretext of going on pilgrimage to escape the country through Azerbaijan, the *sālār* and his brothers went ahead with their revolt, effectively taking control of Khorasan and declaring their independence from the central government (Bāmdād, *Rejāl* I, p. 196). Bahman Mīrzā, who may have known of and have been an accomplice in his uncle's plot, learned that Ḵosrow Khan Gorjī had been dispatched to Kurdistan to subdue a revolt by Reżāqolī Khan Ardalān (a grandson of Fatḥ-ʿAlī Shah). This report was particularly ominous for Bahman Mīrzā, who had heard that Ḵosrow Khan's route was to take him through Zanjān for the purpose of arresting him. Well aware of Ḵosrow Khan's reputation for cruelty, Bahman Mīrzā made his way by a byroad to Tehran. Apparently unsure about Bahman Mīrzā's intentions, Ḥājī Mīrzā Āqāsī ordered Ḵosrow Khan to travel to Zanjān to force the prince into a rash act, which is what happened (Nāder Mīrzā, *Tārīḵ o joğrāfīā-ye Dār-al-salṭana-ye Tabrīz*, Tehran, 1323/1905, p. 196). In Tehran, Bahman Mīrzā tried to see Ḥājī Mīrzā Āqāsī at the ʿAbbāsābād fort, but the grand vizier would not admit him as he was one of the conspirators. Though Moḥammad Shah eventually gave Bahman Mīrzā sanctuary, his behavior toward him was anything but friendly, and the prince still felt threatened by the machinations of the grand vizier; thus, one day while out riding, he took refuge in the Russian embassy.

The Czarist government, which saw harboring a Persian prince as an important element in its foreign policy toward Iran, granted Bahman Mīrzā asylum, and several days later the prince left Iran for Tiflis accompanied by his wives, children, secretaries, and servants. After a little more than three years in Tiflis, Bahman Mīrzā took up residence in Šūšī (capital of Qarābāḡ) where he spent the rest of his exile and died in 1301/1883-84. Throughout this relatively long exile, he enjoyed the protection and support of the Czarist government, which stipulated for him a yearly stipend of 30,000 silver rubles (= 15,000 *tomans*) and each year gave him another princely sum under another heading (Nāder Mīrzā, loc. cit.; M. T. Sepehr, *Nāseḵ al-tawārīḵ* (*Tārīḵ-e Qājārīya*), Tehran, 1385/1965, III, p. 118).

Nāder Mīrzā (loc. cit) considers Bahman Mīrzā innocent of the charge of plotting against Moḥammad Shah (for which he blames Ḥājī Mīrzā Āqāsī) and attributes the accounts of Bahman Mīrzā's ambition by Reżāqolī Khan Hedāyat (*Rawżat al-ṣafā-ye nāṣerī* X, Tehran, 1339 Š./1960, pp. 341f.) and M.T. Sepehr (*Nāseḵ* III, pp. 118-23) to the authors' desire to please the monarch. Nāder Mīrzā describes Bahman Mīrzā as "dignified and reserved, a man of means and leisure," and quite astute in amassing wealth. According to him Bahman Mīrzā's good government in Tabrīz brought peace and security to Azerbaijan and earned him popularity.

Bahman Mīrzā had more than 100 children and grandchildren, and his sons and grandsons continued to serve the Czarist government and army. One of them, Dārāb Mīrzā, even tried to capture Zanjān the year that the Russians occupied northern Iran (1909), but was repulsed by Constitutionalist forces ('A. Navā'ī, *Fatḥ-e Tehrān*, Tehran, 1356 Š./1977, pp. 223-40).

Bahman Mīrzā's residence in Czarist territory gave the Russian government new incentive to meddle in the internal affairs of Iran. On one occasion, at the beginning of the reign of Nāṣer-al-Dīn Shah after three designated crown princes had died in childhood, the Russians insisted that their own royal retainer be installed as Nāyeb-al-Salṭana ('A. Navā'ī, "Walī'ahd-hā-ye Nāṣer-al-Dīn Shah," *Yādgār* 3/10, 1326 Š./1947, pp. 54-67; the words of Mīrzā Āqā Khan Nūrī cited by Count de Gobineau (report dated 3 Šawwāl 1273/7 June 1857 in vol. 28 of the documents relating to Iran in the French Foreign Office) explicitly refer to this meddling: "A crown prince must be declared as soon as possible, for the Russian chargé has been to see the shah several times to insist on behalf of his government that Bahman Mīrzā be named Nāyeb-al-Salṭana" (Bāmdād, *Rejāl* I, p. 197).

Bahman Mīrzā was a man of letters and a patron of literature; authors and translators dedicated many works to him. Always amiable and generous in his dealings with others, he gave scholars, poets, and artists a special place of honor. While residing in Tabrīz, he asked Mollā 'Abd-al-Laṭīf Tasūjī and Mīrzā Moḥammad-'Alī Khan Šams-al-Šo'arā' Sorūš Eṣfahānī, to translate the *Alf layla wa layla* (q.v.) into Persian. Tasūjī rendered the tales into elegant Persian prose, while Sorūš culled the works of classical Persian poets to find, as best he could, analogues to the original Arabic verse. Where he failed to do so, he would translate the Arabic into Persian verse himself (M. Qazvīnī, "Wafayāt-e mo'āṣerīn," *Yādgār* 3/4, 1946, p. 8).

An avid reader and bibliophile, Bahman Mīrzā possessed a magnificent library. At the suggestion of his brother Moḥammad Mīrzā, he compiled a *taḏkera* and named it *Taḏkera-ye moḥammadšāhī* after him. He began the work in 1249/1833 while governor of Ardabīl and enlarged it in 1256/1841 after stints as governor of Tehran and Tabrīz gave him access to more and better sources. *Taḏkera-ye moḥammadšāhī* is divided into three *reštas*; the first deals with 123 past poets, the second with the poetry of the king, his offspring, and two other poets (13 poets), and the third with fifty-seven contemporary poets. The book is of little value for biographical information but is replete with extensive selections of poetry (e.g., 4,500 verses from Ferdowsī alone; see Golčīn-e Ma'ānī, *Taḏkerahā* I, pp. 330-38).

Bibliography: M.-J. Nā'īnī, *Jāme'-e ja'farī*, ed. Ī. Afšār, Tehran, 1353 Š./1974, p. 99. On British efforts to repatriate Bahman Mīrzā, see F. Ādamīyat, *Amīr Kabīr o Īrān*, 4th ed., Tehran, 1354 Š./1975, pp. 200-02, 235, 465. On the *Taḏkera-ye moḥammadšāhī*, see also Storey, I/2, pp. 893-95.

('A. Navā'ī)

BAHMAN MĪRZĀ, BAHĀ'-AL-DAWLA, the thirty-seventh son of Fatḥ-'Alī Shah, born 26 Šawwāl 1226/13 November 1811 of Golbadan Bājī, originally a (Georgian?) slave girl of Fatḥ-'Alī Shah's mother Mahd-e 'Olyā (Aḥmad Mīrzā 'Ażod-al-Dawla, *Tārīḵ-e 'ażodī*, ed. 'A. Navā'ī, Tehran, 1355 Š./1976, p. 22). Bahman Mīrzā's mother came to prominence after Mahd-e 'Olyā's death, when she was chosen as head of the household pursestrings, a task she performed with efficiency and fidelity (*Tārīḵ-e 'ażodī*, pp. 22-24). When the shah married her she received the title Ḵāzen al-dawla (treasurer of the state).

A prince of the realm, Bahman Mīrzā was entitled to participate in the government of Iran, however, as the shah's thirty-seventh son his power was limited. In 1252/1836, he replaced 'Abbāsqolī Khan Javānšīr as governor of Kāšān and in 1256/1840 became the governor of Yazd. As governor, he lead an expedition against the Isma'ili Āqā Khan I Maḥallātī (q.v.), but was defeated and fled ignominiously back to Yazd (Reżāqolī Khan Hedāyat, *Tārīḵ-e rawżat al-ṣafā-ye nāṣerī*, Tehran, 1339 Š./1960, pp. 250-51).

Bahman Mīrzā appears to have been interested in books. A manuscript purchased by E. G. Browne (*Lit. Hist. Persia* IV, p. 450 n. 2) had been copied for him.

Bahman Mīrzā also wrote a diary which contains notes on Qajar history (Monzawī, *Nosḵahā* VI, p. 4329).

Bibliography: Given in the text. See also Yaḡmā Jandaqī, *Majmūʿa-ye āṯār*, ed. S. ʿA. Āl-e Dāwūd, Tehran, 1362 Š./1983, II, pp. 123, 229-30.

(ʿA. NAVĀʾĪ)

BAHMAN YAŠT, Middle Persian apocalyptical text preserved in a Middle Persian version in Pahlavi script, a Pāzand (i.e., Middle Persian in Avestan script) transliteration containing supplementary material, and a garbled New Persian translation made in 1496 (see West, *Sacred Books of the East*, Oxford, 1880, V, pp. lvi-lviii; not 1497 as stated by J. C. Tavadia, p. 122). The designation *Bahman yašt* stems from Anquetil du Perron, the pioneer of Zoroastrian studies in Europe (A. H. Anquetil-Duperron, *Zend-Avesta, ouvrage de Zoroastre...*, Paris, 1771, I/2, pp. xviii-xix), and is an abbreviation of *Zand ī Wahman yašt*, the title of the Middle Persian and Pāzand versions. In chapter 3.1 of the Pahlavi text, the source of the work is named as *Zand ī Wahman yasn* (which West unwarrantedly emended to *yašt*). This must have been the Middle Persian translation of an Avestan text. Almost certainly no part of the Avestan original has been preserved, because even if there is truth in the tradition that *Yašt* 1.24-32, is a remnant of the lost *Bahman yašt* (J. Darmesteter, *Le Zend-Avesta* II, Paris, 1892-93, repr. 1960, p. 331), this section has nothing in common with the well-attested *Bahman yašt* texts. According to Ph. Gignoux an Avestan original never did exist ("Sur l'inexistence d'un Bahman Yasht avestique," *Journal of Asian and African Studies* 32, Tokyo, 1986, pp. 53-64).

Contents of the Middle Persian version. Chapter 1, modeled on the *Stūdgar* (*sic*, i.e. *Sūdgar*) *nask*, recounts Ohrmazd's revelation to Zarathustra and describes a tree with four branches, of gold, silver, steel, and "mixed" iron, symbolizing four periods to come after the millennium of Zarathustra.

Chapter 2 tells how, in the time of Mazdak, Ḵosrow I (531-79) ordered that the *Bahman yašt* and other Avestan texts should be made public but their *zand*s (i.e., Pahlavi commentary) should be reserved for the students among the clergy.

Chapter 3, modeled on the *Zand ī Wahman yasn*, repeats chapter 1 in greater detail and describes, among other things, a tree with seven branches, of gold, silver, copper, bronze, tin, and "mixed" iron.

Chapters 4 and 5 tell how calamities which will befall Iran at the end of the tenth millennium when enemy nations—Arabs, Byzantines, Turks, Chionites, Hephthalites (?), Tibetans, Chinese (see H. W. Bailey, "Iranian Studies," *BSOS* 6, 1932, pp. 945-53), and others, will push almost as far as Padašxwārgar and conquer Iran, causing decay of religion, breakdown of social order, debasement of law and morality, and degeneration of nature.

Chapter 6 is another account of events at the end of the millennium of Zarathustra: domination by Roman Christians, Turks, and Arabs, escape of Iranian fugitives to Padašxwārgar.

Chapters 7 and 8 describe events of the eleventh millennium, that of Ušēdar. Before and during this time, the warrior Wahrām Warzāwand and Wištāsp's immortal son, Pišyōtan the Priest, combine to overcome the hostile armies and restore Iran and its religion. Finally the god Mihr (Mithra) intervenes on Pišyōtan's side in the struggle against the demons, who have exceeded their term of rule by 1000 years, and defeats the demon Xešm, whereupon he and his followers flee back to hell.

Chapter 9 begins with a statement that Ušēdar will appear in the year 1800 (variant reading: 1600; after the start of the millennium of Zarathustra?) and Pišyōtan at the end of the millennium. This is followed by a sketch of conditions in the millennium of Ušēdarmāh, an account of the unloosing of Až ī Dahāk (see AŽDAHĀ) and the great harm done to the world by this monster before his death at the hands of Karšāsp, and finally a portrayal of the final deliverance by Sōšyāns.

Importance for the history of religion. The *Bahman yašt* is the most important apocalyptic work in Zoroastrian literature, primarily because its vision of the tree (in chapter 3, and in an older form in chapter 1) is obviously comparable with Nebuchadnezzar's vision of the image of the world empires (in *Daniel* 2: 27-45; see also *Daniel* 7). Until recently the hypothesis of Irano-Babylonian influence was accepted by most scholars (see A. Hultgård, "Das Judentum in der hellenistisch-römischen Zeit und die iranische Religion," in *Aufstieg und Niedergang der römischen Welt* II: *Prinzipat* XIX/1, ed. W. Haase, Berlin and New York, 1979, p. 525, nn. 59 and 60; T. Olsson, "The Apocalyptic Activity. The Case of Jāmāsp Nāmag," in D. Hellholm, ed., *Apocalypticism in the Mediterranean World and the Near East*, Tübingen, 1983, pp. 26-27). This hypothesis implies that the Iranian apocalyptic concepts were a source of the Judeo-Christian concepts. Against it, arguments for the direct dependence of the Iranian on the Jewish tradition have now been advanced by E. Bickerman (*Four Strange Books of the Bible, Jonah, Daniel, Koheleth, Esther*, New York, 1967, pp. 68, 117) and J. Duchesne-Guillemin ("Apocalypse juive et apocalypse iranienne," in U. Bianchi and M. J. Vermaseren, *La soteriologia dei culti orientali nell'Impero Romano*, Leiden, 1982, pp. 758-59). (For earlier opinions to this effect, see Olsson, op. cit., p. 26 n. 34). The text does not, however, support Bickerman's and Duchesne-Guillemin's interpretation of "mixed iron" as "iron and clay." M. Boyce ("On the Antiquity of Zoroastrian Apocalyptic," *BSOAS* 47, 1984, pp. 70-72) suspects borrowing from Greek sources in western Iran in the late fourth century B.C. and dependence of the *Daniel* apocalypse on the Iranian apocalypse. Her interpretation of the difficult words *āhan* (*ī*) *abar gumēxt* as "iron ore" is also problematic. (For an explanation of these words as being corrupted from *āhan xāk abar gumēxt* "iron mixed with earth," see Ph. Gignoux, "Nouveaux regards sur l'apocalyptique iranienne," *Comptes rendus de l'Académie des inscriptions et belles-lettres*, Paris,

1986, pp. 334-46.) A Hultgård (op. cit., pp. 524-26), while stressing the originality of the Iranian imagery, concludes that the author of the *Book of Daniel* took over an Iranian concept of successive world empires, which had been passed on by the Seleucids, together with a Zoroastrian picture of four world eras. Weight is lent to this opinion by the fact that the presentation of the four ages in the *Sūdgar nask* (*Dēnkard* 9.8, ed. Madan, p. 792; West, *Sacred Books of the East* XXXVII, Oxford, 1892, pp. 180-81) gives the impression of having been revised and updated rather than conceived in the Sasanian period. On the other hand it is possible that the metal symbolism in the *Book of Daniel* may have been thought up first; if so, this would be an argument for early dependence of the Iranian tradition on the Jewish tradition.

There are also some similarities between the *Bahman yašt* and the "Oracles of Hystaspes" (1st century B.C.). On the strength of them F. Cumont and G. Widengren have judged the oracle to be dependent on an Iranian source, while J. Duchesne-Guillemin has come to the reverse conclusion (F. Cumont, "La fin du monde selon les sages orientaux," *RHR* 52, 1931, pp. 64-93; J. Bidez and F. Cumont, *Les mages hellénisés* II, Paris, 1938, pp. 361-76; G. Widengren, "Leitende Ideen und Quellen der iranischen Apocalyptic," in D. Hellholm, op. cit., pp. 121-26. J. Duchesne-Guillemin, op. cit., pp. 757-58). The fact that the prospective enemies are called "girdle-wearers" in the Egyptian potter's oracle as well as in the *Bahman yašt* has recently been discussed, but Iranian origin denied (L. Koenen, "Die Adaptation ägyptischer Königsideologie am Ptolemäerhof," in E. van't Dack, P. van Dessel, and W. van Gucht, *Egypt and the Hellenistic World*, Louvain, 1981, pp. 181-83).

Source material and elaboration. Being a literary work, the *Bahman yašt* should not be simply equated with the transmitted material which it contains. E. W. West surmised that the extant texts are versions of an 11th- or 12th-century "epitome" of a Middle Persian *Zand ī Wahman yasn* written at the end of the 7th century (*Sacred Books of the East* V, pp. liii-lvi, p. 194 n. 4), and that the Avestan text was probably a compilation of older source material made under the early Sasanians (pp. liv-lv). M. Boyce (op. cit., p. 68) thinks that the original may have been a late Avestan text dating from the troubled time of the Macedonian conquest, and S. K. Eddy attempted to reconstruct such an "original version of Hellenistic date" (*The King is Dead*, Lincoln, 1861, pp. 343-49). G. Widengren (op. cit., pp. 105-19) inferred from an analysis of chapters 7-9 that the Middle Persian text may be based on a Parthian zurvanistic adaptation of a zoroastrianized *yašt* (which in that case cannot have been *Bahman yašt*). On several points, however, different perceptions are also possible. West had already cited the linguistic evidence for an Avestan origin of the Middle Persian text, but had also acknowledged that the typical style of the Avesta might have been imitated in the Middle Persian text.

When the title *Bahman yašt* seemingly promises information about Bahman, Vohu Manah of the Avesta, who escorted Zarathustra to the presence of Ohrmazd, the fact that Bahman does not enter into the work at all is bound to cause surprise. It indicates that the naming and perhaps also (as suggested by West) the literary recension were secondary developments. This certainly seems true of the tree simile drawn in chapter 1 and redrawn in chapter 3, which is ascribed to the *Stūdgar nask* although in the epitome of the *Sūdgar nask* in the *Dēnkard* the same theme is presented without the tree imagery.

Both the existence of an Avestan substratum (Widengren, op. cit., pp. 112-17; Boyce, op. cit., p. 69) and the occurrence of repeated revisions (Widengren, op. cit., p. 118) may be taken as proved. Also discernible are some secondary borrowings from old traditional sources (Olsson, op. cit., pp. 38-46) and even, in chapter 9, some responses to the undue delay of the appearance of Ušēdar (West, op. cit., p. 231 n. 1). The pretensions to apocalyptic knowledge in the *Bahman yašt* were what prompted its continual revision and elaboration. The result is an often contradictory mixture of various layers of tradition (West, pp. lv-lvi), which are all the harder to differentiate because of the poor state of preservation of the text. The extant versions give the impression of being a work of elaboration and supplementation rather than an epitome. The probably original component appears to begin with chapter 3, where the *Zand ī Wahman yasn* is mentioned by name, and to end with the last section of chapter 5, which is a Middle Persian translation of the *Yeŋhē hātąm*, the prayer at the close of most parts of the *yasna*. If this is so, the original subject matter would have been concerned solely with the tenth millennium, i.e., the time-span of the tree vision.

See also APOCALYPTIC i: IN ZOROASTRIANISM.

Bibliography: Editions and translations. E. W. West, tr., *Bahman Yasht*, in *Sacred Books of the East* V, pp. 189-235 (the first complete translation of the Middle Persian version). K. A. D. Nosherwân, ed. and tr., *The Text of the Pahlvi Zand-î-Vôhûman Yasht*, Bombay, 1903 (Middle Persian text with Gujarati translation). E. T. Anklesaria, ed. and tr., *Zand-î Vohûman Yasn and Two Pahlavi Fragments*, Bombay, 1957 (Middle Persian text with English translation; the references in the present article are to this edition). The Pāzand text is included in *Pāzend Texts*, ed. and collated by E. E.K. Antiâ, Bombay, 1909, pp. 339-48. The New Persian version has been printed in E. M. R. Unvâlâ, ed., *Dârâb Hormazyâr's Rivâyat* II, Bombay, 1922, pp. 86-101, Eng. tr. E. B. N. Dhabhar, ed., *The Persian Rivayats of Hormazyar Framarz and Others*, Bombay, 1932, pp. 457-81. See also J. C. Tavadia, *Die mittelpersische Sprache und Literatur der Zarathustrier*, pp. 121-24, and M. Boyce, "Middle Persian Literature," pp. 49-50, n. 8, and idem, "The Poems of the Persian Sibyl and the Zand ī Vahman Yašt," in *Mélanges Lazard*, Paris (forthcoming).

(W. SUNDERMANN)

BAHMANAGĀN. See BAHMANJANA.

BAHMAN-ARDAŠĪR (or Forāt Maysān), town and subdistrict in Maysān in lower Iraq. The town of Forāt is known from the first century A.D. as a fortified terminus for caravan trade on the left bank of the lower Tigris, eleven or twelve miles downstream from Charax. Formerly identified with the town of Tanūma, opposite ʿAššār (Obolla), Forāt has been located by Hansman at Maḡlūb, 17.4 km (10.8 miles) southeast of Jabal K̲īāber (Charax). Called Pᵉrat̲ d̲ᵉ Mayšan in Syriac, this town was the see of the metropolitan bishop of Mayšān by 310.

According to Ḥamza and Ebn al-Faqīh, Bahman-Ardašīr was founded or rebuilt by the Sasanian Ardašīr I (r. 226/7-245). Some sources (Ṭabarī, I, p. 687; T̲aʿālebī, Ḡorar, p. 378, cf. p. 485; *Mojmal*, p. 54) attribute its foundations to Bahman son of Esfandīār (q.v.), but the earliest attested use of this name is in 544 when the Nestorian bishop of Vahman-Ardašīr is called the metropolitan of Mayšan. Bahman-Ardašīr is also named as one of the four subdistricts (*ṭasāsīj*) of the *kūra/ostān* of Šād̲-Bahman (Maysān, Kūra Dejla) by Ebn K̲ordād̲beh, Qodāma, and Yāqūt, although Yāqūt also identifies Bahman-Ardašīr as the entire *kūra* of Forāt al-Baṣra. The contraction, Bahmanšīr (q.v.), was used both for the town and for the lower Tigris estuary. The PR mintmark on Sasanian coins may not stand for Forāt as is often claimed, because that was not the official Sasanian name and it has not been found on Arab-Sasanian coins, although Forāt was a mint for post-reform Islamic dirhams from 81/700 until 96/714-15.

After the conquest of Forāt by ʿOtba b. Ḡazwān in 14/635, it remained a center of local Muslim administration and was involved in revolts by the Zanj in 70/689-90, 75/695 and during the 3rd/9th century. By the 7th/13th century Forāt was in ruins.

Bibliography: For ancient Forāt see Pliny, *Natural History* 6.32; S. N. Nodelman, "A Preliminary History of Characene," *Berytus* 13, 1960, p. 102; J. Hansman, "Charax and the Karkheh," *Iranica Antiqua* 7, 1967, pp. 25, 46, 52. For the Nestorian bishopric see J. B. Chabot, *Synodicon Orientale*, Paris, 1902, pp. 71, 89, 94, 321, 350, 321; J. M. Fiey, *Assyrie chrétienne*, Beirut, 1968, III, pp. 263-64. For Bahman-Ardašīr as a town and subdistrict see Ebn K̲ordād̲beh, p. 7; Qodāma b. Jaʿfar, *Ketāb k̲arāj*, Leiden, 1889, p. 235; Ebn al-Faqīh, p. 198; Ḥamza, pp. 38, 46; Ebn Qotayba, *al-Maʿāref*, ed. T̲. ʿAkkāša, Beirut, 1960, p. 654; Yāqūt, I, p. 770, III, pp. 227, 861-62; J. Markwart, Ērānšahr, p. 41; M. Morony, "Continuity and Change in the Administrative Geography of Late Sasanian and Early Islamic al-ʿIraq," *Iran* 20, 1982, p. 35; idem, *Iraq after the Muslim Conquest*, Princeton, 1984, pp. 159-60. On coins see F. Paruck, "Mint-marks on Sasanian and Arab-Sasanian Coins," *Journal of the Numismatic Society of India* 6 1944, p. 118; R. Göbl in F. Altheim and R. Stiehl, eds., *Ein Asiatischer Staat*, Wiesbaden, 1954, pp. 87-88; idem, *Sasanidische Numismatik*, Brunswick, 1968, p. 84; A. Bivar, "A Sasanian Hoard from Hilla," *Numismatic Chronicle*, 1963, p. 168; J. Walker, *A Catalogue of the Arab-Sasanian Coins*, London, 1941, pp. cxxxiii-cxxxiv, cxli. For the Muslim conquest of Forāt see Ṭabarī, I, p. 2379; Yāqūt, IV, p. 468. For the Zanj at Forāt see Balād̲orī, *Ansāb al-ašrāf*, Greifswald, 1883, XI, pp. 304-05, 308; Wakīʿ, *Ak̲bār al-qożāt*, Cairo, 1366/1945, II, p. 57; Ṭabarī, III, pp. 1757-64; Ebn al-At̲īr (repr.), I, p. 384; H. Halm, *Die Traditionen über den Aufstand Ali ibn Muhammad des "Herrn der Zanj"*, Bonn, 1967, pp. 59-60, 72-74.

(M. MORONY)

BAHMANID DYNASTY, a dynasty founded in 748/1347 in the Deccan (Sanskrit Dakṣiṇa, lit. right hand; Prakrit Dakkhin, lit. south; Persian Dakan), the table-land region in India situated south of the Narbadā River and the Vindhyāchal range and north of the Mysore Plateau and the Tungbhadra River, by ʿAlāʾ-al-Dīn Ḥasan Bahman Shah, who with other *ṣadah* nobles rose in revolt against Toḡloq rule at Delhi. The dynasty ruled until 934/1528, finally disintegrating into the five independent Muslim kingdoms of the ʿEmādšāhīs of Berār, the Neẓāmšāhīs of Ahmadnagar (q.v.), the Barīdšāhīs (q.v.) of Bīdar (q.v.), the ʿĀdelšāhīs (q.v.) of Bījāpūr (q.v.), and the Qoṭbšāhīs of Golconda (Hyderabad). The Bahmanid kingdom with its fluctuating boundaries, stretched at its zenith from the Arabian Sea in the west to the Bay of Bengal in the east and from Berār and the Vindhyāchal range in the north to the Tungbhadra River in South India. The first eight Bahmanid kings who ruled from their capital at Gulbarga (Aḥsanābād) were: ʿAlāʾ-al-Dīn Ḥasan Bahman Shah (Jomādā I, 748-Rabī I, 759/August, 1347-February, 1358); Moḥammad I (until D̲u'l-qaʿda, 776/April, 1375); ʿAlāʾ-al-Dīn Mojāhed (until Moḥarram, 780/April, 1378); Dāʾūd I (until Ṣafar, 780/May, 1378); Moḥammad II (until Šaʿbān, 799/April, 1397); Ḡīāt̲-al-Dīn Tahmtan (until Šawwāl, 799/June, 1397); Šams-al-Dīn Dāʾūd II (until Rabīʿ I, 800/November, 1397); and Tāj-al-Dīn Fīrūz (until Šawwāl, 825/September, 1422). The last ten kings who ruled from their capital at Bīdar (Moḥammadābād) were: Šehāb-al-Dīn Aḥmad I (until Šawwāl, 839/April, 1436); ʿAlāʾ-al-Dīn Aḥmad II (until Rajab, 862/May, 1458); ʿAlāʾ-al-Dīn Homāyūn (until D̲u'l-ḥejja, 865/September, 1461); Neẓām-al-Dīn Aḥmad III (until Šawwāl, 867/July, 1463); Šams-al-Dīn Moḥammad III (until Ṣafar, 887/March, 1482); Šehāb-al-Dīn Maḥmūd (until D̲u'l-ḥejja, 924/December, 1518); Aḥmad IV (until Moḥarram, 927/December, 1520); ʿAlāʾ-al-Dīn Shah (until Jomādā II, 929/March, 1523); Walī-Allāh (until 931/1526), and Kalīm-Allāh (until 934/1528); for the political history of the Bahmanids see Korešta, I, pp. 273-376; Ṭabāṭabā, pp. 11ff.; and ʿEṣāmī, pp. 421ff.).

The Bahmanids claimed descent from the legendary king of Iran, Bahman b. Esfandīār. According to Ferešta (pp. 273-74) the founder of the dynasty, ʿAlāʾ-al-Dīn Ḥasan, adopted Gangū (Kānkūy) Bahman as part of his name because while at Delhi he served Gangū, a Brahman whose blessings led him to kingship. Others have read the names Gangū or Kānkūy as Kākūya, suggesting his link to the Kākūya of Isfahan (Šērwānī, 1985, p. 35).

The Bahmanid kingdom was not only the first independent Muslim kingdom in South India, but it was also one of the greatest centers of Iranian culture in the sub-continent. The Bahmanid elite consisted mainly of Iranian, Turk, Dakanī, or Muslim migrants from northern India, in addition to the local Hindu population; however, the Iranians along with the Turks and Afghans dominated Bahmanid society and to a large extent shaped its destiny. Its two most powerful ministers, Fażl-Allāh Īnjū and Maḥmūd Gāwān, like many other Iranian nobles and officials, played a vital role in the expansion of the Bahmanid domain. They also cultivated Persian poets, writers, and scholars.

The Bahmanid kings and princes also took a deep interest in Persian, some of them becoming well-versed in Persian language and literature. Mojāhed Shah spoke fluent Persian and Turkish, as did Moḥammad II and ʿAlāʾ-al-Dīn Aḥmad II (Ferešta, pp. 296, 301, 338). Fīrūz Shah, whose reign is regarded as the golden period of the Bahmanid rule, had a passion for languages; he married a number of Iranians, Arabs, and Indians to practice speaking their own languages with them. In addition Fīrūz is said to have known several Indian languages (Ferešta, p. 308; Siddiqi, 1952, p. 98). He composed Persian verses under the pennames of Fīrūzī and ʿOrūjī (Besṭāmī, p. 83).

The active interest which the Bahmanid rulers took in Iranian culture and Persian, might be attributed, among other factors, to their eminent Iranian teachers, one of whom, Fażl-Allāh (Ferešta, p. 302) later rose to the position of prime minister (Šērwānī, 1985, p. 106). Himself a student of the great Iranian savant Mollā Saʿd-al-Dīn Taftāzānī (d. 792/1390), Fażl-Allāh was in charge of teaching the Bahmanid princes, including Fīrūz, under Moḥammad II. Another Iranian teacher was Šaraf-al-Dīn Ṣadr(-e) Jahān of Šūštar who was subsequently appointed as the chief magistrate of the kingdom. (For Gāwān's letter to the magistrate see Gāwān's, p. 185.) He was entrusted to educate the young king Moḥammad III whom Ferešta (p. 347) calls the most accomplished Bahmanid king after Fīrūz.

Many scholars from Iran, Arabia, and Central Asia assembled at the Bahmanid capital. Fīrūz used to send ships to Iran and Arabia to bring Persian and Arabic scholars, and himself taught important Persian and Arabic classics three days a week (Ferešta, p. 308). He had an observatory built which was supervised by Sayyed Maḥmūd Garzūnī and Ḥakīm Ḥasan of Gīlān (Šērwānī, 1985, p. 100). Fīrūz visited the scholars in the *madrasa* and, despite the disapproval of Mollā Esḥāq Sarhendī, would engage in free conversation with them (Ferešta, p. 307). He was also fond of listening to the *Šāh-nāma* (Besṭāmī, p. 80).

The spread of education was instrumental in the wide knowledge of Persian. Several *madrasa*s were established in various parts of the kingdom where Persian, Arabic, and Islamic studies were taught. Among them the *madrasa* founded by Maḥmūd Gāwān at Bīdar in 876/1471 was known for its academic excellence. Writing in 1023/1614, Ferešta praises the fine building of the *madrasa* (p. 385), which consisted of one thousand rooms for the students and teachers and a grand library housing rare Persian and Arabic manuscripts. Among the scholars invited by Gāwān to teach in the *madrasa* were the celebrated Persian poet ʿAbd-al-Raḥmān Jāmī (d. 898/1492), Jālāl-al-Dīn Davānī (908/1502), and Shaikh Ṣadr-al-Dīn ʿAbd-al-Raḥmān Rawwāsī (d. 871/1466; Šērwānī, 1985, p. 203; Gāwān, pp. 14, 152, 172).

The origins of Indian Sufism were in Iran; many of the great Indian Sufis traced their ancestry to Iran, and the Bahmanids held Sufis in great esteem. ʿAlāʾ-al-Dīn Ḥasan, while at Delhi, visited Neẓām-al-Dīn Awlīā (d. 725/1325), the spiritual guide of Amīr Ḵosrow (d. 725/1325), who prophesied his kingship (Ferešta, p. 274). His and his two successors' coronations were performed by the noted Sufi Shaikh Serāj Jonaydī (670-781/1271-1380; Šērwānī, 1985, pp. 33, 82). However, the greatest Sufi of the Bahmanid reign was Sayyed Moḥammad Bandanavāz Gīsūdarāz (d. 825/1422), a renowned poet and writer of Persian whose tomb at Gulbarga still attracts more devotees than any other shrine, Muslim and non-Muslim alike. These Sufis exerted moral influence on the kings and nobles. For instance, it was at the displeasure of Shaikh Zayn-al-Dīn of Shiraz (d. 771/1369) that Moḥammad I gave up drinking. When the shaikh gave shelter to Bahrām Khan of Māzandarān who had rebelled against Moḥammad I, the king ordered the exile of the saint but he took refuge in the mausoleum of his spiritual guide Borhān-al-Dīn Ḡarīb (d. 738/1337) at Ḵoldābād. Ultimately the king had to apoloigize to the saint (Ferešta, p. 294; Ṭabāṭabā, p. 33).

Other Sufis, delivering their discourses generally in Persian, often would quote Persian verses from the great mystic poets of Iran. Disciples recorded these discourses and compiled them in the form of books, which eventually endeared Persian to the seekers of truth. *Aḥsan al-aqwāl*, a collection of Borhān-al-Dīn Ḡarīb's sayings, was compiled by Ḥamīd Qalandar (Aʿẓamī, p. 63). The *Jawāmeʿ al-kalem* is a compilation of Gīsūdarāz's sayings. *Qawwālī* (mystical song recital) was a regular feature of the assemblies of these Sufis where Persian *ḡazal*s were generally sung. Moḥammad I was so fond of *qawwālī* that he invited a number of *qawwāl*s (singers) and musicians from Delhi who sang the *ḡazal*s of Amīr Ḵosrow and Amīr Ḥasan Sejzī (d. 737/1356) who is known as the "Saʿdī of India" (Ferešta, p. 288). It was out of the Bahmanid devotion to Sufism that Aḥmad I, who shifted the capital from Gulbarga to Bīdar, invited the great Iranian mystic Šāh

Ne‘mat-Allāh Walī (d. 834/1431) to Bīdar through his two emissaries Shaikh Ḥabīb-Allāh Jonaydī and Mīr Šams-al-Dīn of Qom. The saint sent a letter written in his own hand and a green cap of twelve scallops (*tark*) to the king along with his disciples Qoṭb-al-Dīn of Kermān, who was received by Aḥmad I with all reverence. Not satisfied with this, the king again despatched K̲ᵛāja ‘Emād-al-Dīn of Semnān and Sayf-Allāh to the saint with the request that if he could not come himself to India, he might kindly send one of his sons. But since Šāh Ne‘mat-Allāh had only one son, K̲alīl-Allāh, he sent his grandson Nūr-Allāh who was received by the Bahmanid officials, including Mīr Abu'l-Qāsem of Gorgān at the Čāl Port and escorted to Bīdar. Aḥmad I himself went out of the capital to receive Nūr-Allāh, and they met at Ne‘matābād, so called because of the king's devotion to Šāh Ne‘mat-Allāh. The site practically assumed the status of the Bahmanid capital. Later on, we find Maḥmūd K̲aljī, the king of Mālwa, searching for the treasure of the saint's family at Ne‘matābād. (Kermānī, p. 97). Nūr-Allāh was given the title of *malek-al-mašā'ek̲*.

After the death of Šāh Ne‘mat-Allāh in 834/1431, his son K̲alīl-Allāh came to Bīdar along with his two sons Ḥabīb-Allāh and Moḥebb-Allāh. Both Nūr-Allāh and Ḥabīb-Allāh were married to daughters of Aḥmad I while Moḥebb-Allāh was married to the grand-daughter of the king, the daughter of Prince ‘Alā'-al-Dīn Aḥmad II (Ferešta, pp. 328-29; Ṭabāṭabā, p. 65; Šērwānī, 1985, p. 152; Šāh Ne‘mat-Allāh Walī, introd.). The marriage relations between the two families continued in the subsequent years, which shows that the Bahmanids set store by family relations with the Iranian elite. The third daughter of Aḥmad I was married to Jalāl-al-Dīn, a grandson of the Sufi Sayyed Jalāl of Bukhara. Another daughter of Aḥmad II was married to a Mongol prince, Šāhqolī (Šērwānī, 1985, p. 152). The grandsons of Šāh Ne‘mat-Allāh Walī played crucial roles in the Bahmanid politics, occasionally siding with the anti-king factions. Thus, Ḥabib-Allāh lent his support to Ḥasan Khan who had rebelled against his brother, King Homāyūn, and he was killed in 863/1459. His death was mourned by Shah Ṭāher of Astarābād in a versified chronogram (Ferešta, p. 342). Moḥebb-Allāh retained his saintly position, as a result of which successive kings paid great reverence to him as well as to his successors (Ṭabāṭabā, pp. 88, 96, 107; Ferešta, p. 366; Šērwānī, 1985, p. 250). K̲alīl-Allāh is buried at Bīdar; his domeless tomb bears the finest specimens of *tolt̲* calligraphy written by Mog̲īt̲ of Shiraz (Šērwānī, 1985, p. 154; Ṭabāṭabā, p. 81).

The mausoleum at the tomb of Šāh Ne‘mat-Allāh at Māhān in Kermān was built by Aḥmad I; however, it was completed a little after his death in Moḥarram, 840/July, 1436 (Šāh Ne‘mat-Allāh Walī, introd., pp. xviii, xix). The king was so devoted to the saint that when he fed the poor and the pious at the first anniversary of the saint's death, he himself stood up to wash the hands of the guests (Ṭabāṭabā, p. 68; Šērwānī, 1985, p. 134). Aḥmad I is himself known as *walī* (saint), which may be a reference to his devotion to Šāh Ne‘mat-Allāh Walī. The anniversary of his death is celebrated by both Hindus and Muslims, on the 20th of the Muslim lunar month coinciding with the Hindu festival of Holi (Šērwānī, 1985, p. 135; for Aḥmad I, see Ẓahīr-al-Dīn Aḥmad, 1940). Another Iranian Sufi who was equally revered at the Bahmanid court was Sayyed Ḥanīf of Gīlān (d. 900/1494). We find him along with Šāh K̲alīl-Allāh and Moḥebb-Allāh performing the coronation of Aḥmad II, Aḥmad III, and Moḥammad III (Ṭabāṭabā, pp. 75, 96, 107; Šērwānī, 1985, p. 158, no. 13).

The Bahmanids also cultivated poets and writers of Persian. Among these poets was Shaikh Fak̲r-al-Dīn Ād̲arī of Esfarā'en, famous for, among other works, the *Bahman-nāma*, a versified history of the Bahmanids till the time of Homāyūn, composed at the instance of Aḥmad I. Later, he went back to Khorasan with a huge gift from the king, but continued to update his work until his death in 866/1462. The work was continued by two other poets of the Bahmanid court, Naẓīrī and Sāme‘ī, who brought it up to the fall of the dynasty (Ṣafā, *Adabīyāt* IV, p. 323). The poet was held in great esteem by the Bahmanids; Aḥmad II gave up drinking under the influence of a didactic poem (*naṣīḥat-nāma*), which Ād̲arī had addressed to him in 855/1451 (Siddiqi, 1952, p. 125). The couplets composed by Ād̲arī in praise of the new royal palace at Bīdar were beautifully calligraphed by Šaraf-al-Dīn of Māzandarān, a disciple of Ne‘mat-Allāh Walī and engraved artistically by the stone-cutters of the Deccan (Ferešta, pp. 325-26; Ṭabāṭabā, p. 71). Sāme‘ī was patronized by Maḥmūd Gāwān, for whose *madrasa* built in 876/1471 he had versified a chronogram (Ferešta, p. 358; Ṭabāṭabā, p. 119, ascribes the chronogram to Maḥmūd Badr of Shiraz). The poet was alive at least until 887/1482 when he mourned the death of Moḥammad III in a versified chronogram conveyed by the key-phrase *k̲arābī-e Dakan* (ruin of Deccan; Ferešta, p. 361; Ṭabāṭabā, p. 134); subsequent events proved the phrase to be true. Gāwān was killed by Moḥammad III and Sāme‘ī along with other poets mourned his death (Ferešta, pp. 357-58).

Another poet who continued Ād̲arī's *Bahman-nāma*, Naẓīrī of Ṭūs, whose *dīvān* is extant, was attached to Shah Ḥabīb-Allāh and was imprisoned along with him by Homāyūn while he was crushing the rebellion of his brother, Ḥasan Shah. The prisoners were later on released forcibly by Ḥasan Tork. Naẓīrī must have been greatly relieved at the death of Homāyūn as is evident from his pungent and satirical chronogram composed on the occasion (Ṭabāṭabā, p. 95; Rieu, II, p. 642). ‘Eṣāmī's *Fotūḥ al-salāṭīn* is another important historical Persian *mat̲nawī* of this period and is aptly described as the "*Šāh-nāma* of India" as it contains, in about 12,000 couplets, the accounts of Muslim India from the reign of Maḥmūd of Ḡazna to that of the first Bahmanid ruler ‘Alā'-al-Dīn Ḥasan. ‘Eṣāmī, whose forefathers held ministerial positions under the Slave Kings of Delhi, had to migrate to Dawlatābād in 727/1327 at the age of sixteen, under the order of Moḥammad b. Toḡloq (725-52/1324-51). He started composing the *Fotūḥ* on 27 Ramażān 750/10 December 1349 and completed it on 6 Rabīʿ I 751/14 May 1350. The work is the only extant contemporary history of the Bahmanids and, being written by an eye-witness to the events, which are mostly described without poetic exaggeration, can be considered quite authentic (*Fotūḥ al-salāṭīn*, preface).

Sayyed Moḥammad Ḥosaynī known as Bandanavāz Gīsūdarāz (720-825/1320-1422), a Češtī saint whose ancestors belonged to Herat, was not only the great spiritual guide of the Bahmanids but also a noted Persian poet and writer. His poems, especially the *ḡazal*s, were compiled under the title of *Anīs al-ʿoššāq* by one of his disciples. True to the Iranian Sufi traditions, Gīsūdarāz sings of his deep love for the Divine Being. In his mystical poetry he seems to be under the impact of Amīr Ḵosrow, Amīr Ḥasan Sejzī, Shaikh Aḥmad Jām, and Saʿdī. Gīsūdarāz is also credited with a large number of prose works, including a collection of sixty-six letters; however, the authenticity of some of his works is doubtful. Like other Češtī saints of India, Gīsūdarāz was given to *samāʿ* (song) where Persian *ḡazal*s were performed. He observed that Hindi poetry does not carry the deep spiritual appeal of Persian poetry. The most notable prose works of Gīsūdarāz is *Jawāmeʿ al-kalem*, a collection of his sayings compiled by his son Moḥammad Akbar in 803/1400. It is regarded as one of the best collections of Sufi sayings, on a par with such works as *Fīh mā fīh, Asrār al-tawḥīd*, and *Fawāʾed al-fowād*. (For his life and works see Ḥ. Ṣeddīqī, *Ḥażrat Gīsūdarāz*, Hyderabad, n.d.; *Jawāmeʿ al-kalem*, Hyderabad, 1356/1937; *Anīs al-ʿoššāq*, Hyderabad, 1360/1941; *Ḥadāʾeq al-ons*, Hyderabad, n.d.

Maḥmūd Gāwān, the celebrated vizier, is considered the greatest prose stylist of the Bahmanid period, although he composed poetry as well. Gāwān hailed from Gīlān and came to Bīdar as a merchant; he was awarded the title of *malek al-tojjār*. Later on, Homāyūn made him prime minister. He expanded the Bahmanid kingdom with his strategy and statesmanship and introduced a series of reforms in administration; unfortunately his tenure was cut short when he was put to death by Moḥammad III in Ṣafar, 886/April, 1481, and buried at Bīdar. His death was mourned by a number of poets including ʿAbd-al-Karīm of Hamadān and Mollā Sāmeʿī, whom he had patronized (Ferešta, pp. 357-58; Ṭabāṭabā, p. 132; for his life see Šērwānī, 1942; Ṣafā, *Adabīyāt* IV, pp. 499ff.). Maḥmūd Gāwān's extant works are: *Rīāż al-enšāʾ* and *Manāẓer al-enšāʾ*; both in Persian, the former is a collection of his personal as well as official letters, 148 in number, which he wrote to the kings, rulers, nobles, viziers, scholars, and poets of his day as well as his relatives. His correspondents include ʿAbd-al-Raḥmān Jāmī, Šaraf-al-Dīn ʿAlī Yazdī, Jalāl-al-Dīn Davānī, Ḵᵛāja ʿObayd-Allāh Aḥrār (d. 896/1490), Sultan Abū Saʿīd Gūrkānī, Sultan Ḥosayn Bāyqarā, Moḥammad II, the Ottoman sultan, ʿAlāʾ-al-Dīn Gīlānī, the king of Gīlān, etc. The author wrote a preface to this collection which he entitled *Rīāż al-enšāʾ*. Though the letters are written in a very flowery, ornate style and are profusely interspersed with Arabic verses and quotations, they contain valuable information on the social, cultural, and political life of the Bahmanids (*Rīāż al-enšāʾ*, introd.). In his other surviving work, *Manāẓer al-enšāʾ*, which deals with the art of *enšāʾ* or letter writing and allied subjects, Gāwān maintains that a *monšī* (secretary) is superior to a poet, but a real *monšī* is not easily available. He also explains the various kinds of official letters such as *manšūr*, *farmān*, *ʿarīża*, *roqʿa*, *meṯāl*, etc. (S. H. Askari, "Manāzir-ul-Insha of Mahmud Gāwān," *Bayāż* 1/2-3, 1977, pp. 126-41).

Another Bahmanid scholar, Shaikh ʿAyn-al-Dīn of Bījāpūr (d. 795/1392) known as *Ganj-al-ʿOlūm*, wrote a supplement to the *Ṭabaqāt-e nāṣerī* of Menhāj b. Serāj. His tomb at Bījāpūr was built by Maḥmūd Gāwān (Šērwānī, 1985, p. 75). Shaikh Ebrāhīm of Multan (d. 900/1494) compiled a sort of encyclopedia called *Maʿāref al-ʿolūm* in the reign of Aḥmad II. Sayf-al-Dīn Ḡūrī, prime minister under ʿAlāʾ-al-Dīn Ḥasan and the successive kings, wrote *Naṣāʾeḥ al-molūk* on the art of politics and administration but the work does not seem to be extant (Šērwānī, 1985, p. 55). Ḡūrī reminds one of Neẓām-al-Molk, and he might have been prompted to compose *Naṣāʾeḥ al-molūk* on the pattern of the *Sīāsat-nāma*. Qāżī Šehāb-al-Dīn ʿOmar of Dawlatābād, a great scholar of Arabic and Persian during this period, is the author of numerous works among which *al-Baḥr al-mawwāj* is said to be a Persian commentary on the Koran in several volumes (Siddiqi, 1952, p. 112). Among no longer extant Persian and Arabic works composed under Fīrūz Shah are historical works by Mollā Dāʾūd of Bīdar (Ferešta, I, p. 277), Mollā Moḥammad Lārī (Besṭāmī, pp. 75, 79), and Mollā ʿAbd-al-Karīm of Hamadān (Šērwānī, 1985, p. 237).

Bahmanid architecture shows the influence of the Iranian style and is quite different from the Muslim architecture of North India. The outward decorations, especially calligraphic embellishments, are all deeply marked by the influence of Iranian architecture. It is significant to note that some of the important official buildings of the Bahmanids were constructed under the supervision of Rafīʿ b. Šams, a master architect of Qazvīn who built a unique mosque in the Gulbarga Fort in 769/1367 (Šērwānī, 1985, p. 59). The great mausoleums of Gīsūdarāz at Gulbarga represent the height of Iranian-Bahmanid architecture (Šērwānī, 1985, p. 126). The tombs of the Bahmanid kings at Gulbarga and Bīdar also reflect Iranian influence in their domes and arches, use of colored tiles, calligraphy, and plaster decorations. The tomb of Aḥmad I at Bīdar bears beautiful specimens of Persian calligraphy depicting two *šajara*s (genealogical trees) of Šāh Neʿmat-Allāh Walī. The calligrapher Moḡīṯ of Shiraz had written there the names of the Prophet Moḥammad and ʿAlī in various calligraphic hands: *kūfī*, *ṭoḡrā*, *nasḵ*, etc., a masterpiece of Iranian calligraphy as hardly seen in other Bahmanid buildings (Šērwānī, 1985, p. 131). The

Iranian insignia of a lion with a rising sun behind it is carved on a royal palace in Bīdar (Šērwānī, 1985, p. 130).

The large number of the Iranian nobles and officials —as well as Turks. Afghans, and Arabs who had embraced the Iranian culture—at the Bahmanid court must have made considerable impact on the social customs of the elite and the masses. The Bahmanid rulers celebrated the Iranian festival of Nowrūz. When Moḥammad I was presented the famous Fīrūza throne, he ascended it on Nowrūz (Ferešta, p. 288). Sayf-al-Dīn Ḡūrī, Fażl-Allāh Īnjū, and Maḥmūd Gāwān all served the Bahmanids as prime ministers. Ṣafdār Khan of Sīstān helped Moḥammad and Mojāhed in their wars and his son Moqarrab Khan was in charge of the Bahmanid artillery (Šērwānī, 1985, p. 57), while another son, Ṣalābat Khan, was appointed governor of Berār with the title of *majles-e ʿālī*. Bahrām Khan of Māzandarān, who revolted against Moḥammad I and saved himself by taking shelter in the monastery of Shaikh Zayn-al-Dīn. Aḥmad Beg of Qazvīn was appointed *pēšvā* (deputy prime minister) by Ḡīāṯ-al-Dīn Tahmtan (Ferešta, p. 304). Fīrūz sent Taqī-al-Dīn Īnjū, the son-in-law of Fażl-Allāh Īnjū along with Mawlānā Fażl-Allāh Sabzavārī as his envoy to Tīmūr, who favored the Bahmanid king by accepting his suzerainty over the Deccan, Gujarat, and Mālwa (Ferešta, p. 312). Ḵalaf-e Ḥasan of Baṣra received the title of *malek al-tojjār* from Aḥmad I and the position of *wakīl-e moṭlaq* (prime minister). Later on, Maḥmūd Gāwān also became *malek al-tojjār*. Gord-ʿAlī of Sīstān, Mīr-ʿAlī Kāferkoš, and Efteḵār-al-Molk of Hamadān were some of the generals of Ḥasan Baṣrī (Ferešta, pp. 320-21). Both Ḥasan and Gāwān are said to have favored Iranians over the local Muslims. Gāwān seems to have employed a number of officers from Gīlān; one of his close associates, Saʿīd Gīlānī, was killed with him (Ferešta, p. 357).

The death of Gāwān put a halt to the growing Iranian influence in the Bahmanid kingdom and provided an opportunity for the rise of the local nobles. However, some of the Iranian nobles took advantage of the weakening Bahmanid kingdom and declared themselves independent. Thus, Yūsof ʿĀdel Khan established the ʿĀdelšāhī kingdom at Bījāpūr and Qoṭb-al-Molk of Hamadān founded the Qoṭbšāhī dynasty at Golkonda (Hyderabad).

Bahādor of Gīlān, who was in the service of Maḥmūd Gāwān, was entrusted with the administration of Konkan, Goa, and the western coast. He assembled an army consisting mostly of the soldiers from Gīlān, Māzandarān, Iraq, and Khorasan and declared himself independent. Maḥmūd Bahmanī marched against him, and after several skirmishes, Bahādor pleaded for peace through the mediation of Ḵᵛāja Neʿmat-Allāh of Tabrīz. It was however a short-lived respite. Bahādor was ultimately killed by the Bahmanid forces in 899/1493 (Ferešta, p. 368, Siddiqi, 1952, pp. 177-80, Ṭabāṭabā, p. 177, Šērwānī 1985, p. 255).

While the Bahmanids inherited their administrative system from the Toḡloqs at Delhi with Persian as the official language, they introduced several reforms and changes in the government and consequently many new terms found their way into Persian. The kingdom was divided into a number of *ṭaraf*s (plur. *aṭrāf*, provinces) and the governor was called *ṭarafdār*. The *ṭarafdār*s were known by their special titles; thus the *ṭarafdār* of Berār was titled *majles-e ʿālī* and that of Dawlatābād *masnad-e ʿālī*. The *ṭarafdār*s of Bīdar and Gulbarga were called respectively *aʿẓam-e homāyūn* and *malek nāʾeb*. The *wakīl-e moṭlaq* or *wakīl al-salṭanat* (prime minister) was assisted by a minister designated as *pēšvā*. The officers who mobilized the irregular army were known as *bārbardār*s. The king was guarded by his special body guards known as *ḵāṣṣa ḵayl* and the king's personal armament were kept by *yakka javānān* (see Siddiqi, 1935, pp. 463ff.).

Bibliography: ʿAbd-al-Jabbār, *Taḏkera-ye awlīāʾ-e Dakan* I, Hyderabad, 1328/1921-22. Idem, *Taḏkera-ye salāṭīn-e Dakan*, Hyderabad, 1328/1921-22. Ẓahīr-al-Dīn Aḥmad, *Aḥmad Šāh Walī Bahmanī*, Hyderabad, 1940. Idem, *Maḥmūd Gāwān*, Hyderabad, 1927. Šoʿayb Aʿẓamī, *Fārsī adab be ʿahd-e Toḡloq*, Delhi, 1985. ʿAlī b. Ṭayfūr Besṭāmī, *Ḥadāʾeq al-salāṭīn fī kalām al-ḵawāqīn*, ed. Š. Anṣārī, Hyderabad, n.d. Percy Brown, *Indian Architecture (Islamic Period)*, chap. XIII. ʿAbd-Allāh Čaḡatāy, "Bānī-e salṭanat-e Bahmanīya," *Borhān* (Delhi), April, 1941. U. N. Day, *Medieval Malwa*, Delhi, 1965, pp. 147ff. ʿEṣāmī, *Fotūḥ al-salāṭīn*, ed. A. S. Usha, Madras, 1948. Moḥammad Qāsem Hendūšāh Astarābādī Ferešta, *Golšan-e ebrāhīmī*, Lucknow, 1321/1903-04, I, *maqāla* iii, pp. 273-376. J. Fergusson, *History of Indian and Eastern Architecture*, London, 1910. Maḥmūd Gāwān, *Rīāż al-enšāʾ*, ed. Shaikh Chand, Hyderabad, 1948. T. W. Haig, *Hyderabad Archaeological Department Report*, 1915-16; 1918-20; 1925-26; 1928-29; 1929-30; 1931-32; 1937-40. Idem, "Inscriptions at Gulbarga," *Epigraphica Indo-Moslemica*, 1907-08. Idem, "Some Notes on the Bahmany Dynasty," *JASB* 73/1, extra no. 1904, pp. 463ff. Naṣīr-al-Dīn Hāšemī, *Dakanī kalčar* (Dakani culture). Lahore, 1963. Šehāb-al-Dīn Kermānī, *Maʿāṯer-e maḥmūdšāhī*, ed. N. H. Anṣārī (Ansari), Delhi, 1968. J. S. King, *History of the Bahmani Dynasty*, London, 1900. John Marshall, "The Monuments of Muslim India," in *Cambridge History of India*, Cambridge, 1928, pp. 630ff. Idem in *Proceedings of the Indian History Congress*, 1943, pp. 238ff. Maʿṣūm-ʿAlīšāh Šīrāzī, *Ṭarāʾeq al-ḥaqāʾeq*, Tehran, 1318/1900-01. Rafīʿ-al-Dīn Šīrāzī, *Taḏkerat al-molūk*, MS *tārīḵ* no. 1081, Asafiya Library. H. K. Šērwānī (Sherwani), *The Bahmanis of the Deccan*, Delhi, 1985, Urdu tr. Raḥm-ʿAlī Hāšemī, *Dakan-kē bahmanī salāṭīn*, New Delhi, 1978. Idem, *Dakani Culture*, Delhi, 1971. Idem, "Gangu Bahmani," *Journal of Indian History* 20/1, 1941, pp. 95ff. Idem, *Mahmud Gawan, the Great Bahmani Wazir*, Allahabad, 1942. A. M. Siddiqi, *Bahmanī Salṭanat*, Hyderabad, 1952. Idem, "Malik Saifuddin Ghori," *Indian History Congress*, Calcutta,

1939, pp. 701ff. Idem, "Organization of the Central and Provincial Governments of the Deccan and the Bahmanis," in *Proceedings of the All India Oriental Conference*, Mysore, 1935, pp. 463ff. Idem, *Tārīḵ-e Golkonda*, Hyderabad, 2nd ed., 1964. Moḥammad Solṭān, *Armaḡān-e Solṭānī*, Hyderabad, 1903. E. E. Speight, "Coins of the Bahmani Kings of the Deccan," *Islamic Culture* 9, 1935, pp. 269ff. Sayyed 'Alī Ṭabāṭabā, *Borhān-e ma'āṯer*, ed. Sayyed Hāšemī, Hyderabad, 1936. Šāh Ne'mat-Allāh Walī Kermānī, *Kollīyāt-e dīvān-e Šāh Ne'mat-Allāh*, ed. M. 'Abbāsī, Tehran, 1362 Š./1983. G. Yazdani, *Bidar, Its History and Monuments*, Hyderabad, 1947.

(N. H. Ansari)

BAHMANJANA (Arabicized form of Mid. Pers. Bahmanagān; forms such as Bahmanča or Bahmančena are also found). Each day of the thirty-day months of the Zoroastrian calendar had its own name. The second day of the month was named Bahman's day (Bahmanrūz). The eleventh month also bore Bahman's name. Days which had the same name as the month in which they fell were festivals, and the Middle Persian names of these were formed by addition of the suffix *agān* to the day-name. One of them was Bahmanagān, which fell on the second day of the month of Bahman. Bahmanjana is a later modified form of Bahmanagān.

This was one of the Zoroastrian festivals which Muslim Iranians maintained in the Islamic period, right down to the Mongol invasion in 616/1219. Festivities to celebrate the day took place among all classes of the people as well as at royal courts. The author of *Farhang-e Ānandrāj* (I, p. 816) wrongly identified it with Sada, another festival held in the month of Bahman.

Although the description of Bahmanjana by Asadī (*Loḡat-e fors*, ed. Dabīrsīāqī, p. 158) implies that it was an obsolete festival at his time (5th/11th century), the poet Anwarī, who lived somewhat more than a century after Asadī (*Majma' al-foṣaḥā'* I, p. 407) speaks of its popularity in his time, i.e., the later part of the 6th/12th century. Given that Asadī compiled his dictionary while in exile in Azerbaijan, it may be that the practice of celebrating this festival was more widespread in eastern than in western Iran.

In Khorasan, according to Bīrūnī (p. 257) and Gardīzī (ed. Ḥabībī, p. 246) an assortment of meat and all sorts of grain, vegetables, and fruits were cooked together in a pot (*dīg-e Bahmanjana*); people treated each other to the dish thus prepared and which was widely sold in the market. In one of the panegyrics of Manūčehrī (*Majma' al-foṣaḥā'* III, p. 1261) addressed to the Ghaznavid sultan Mas'ūd (r. 421-32/1030-41) on the day of Bahmanjana, the poet mentions the pot and refers to the singing of "Bahman" and "Qayṣarān" songs in the festivities.

It was usual to wear new clothes for this festival and eat flowers of the *bahman* plant, which were sprinkled on food, added to the ingredients in the pot, and also eaten with sugar; they were supposed to strengthen the memory. The *bahman* plant is known to have been the same as the *zardak-e ṣaḥrā'ī* (a wild carrot), which flowers in the month of Bahman (January-February) and has a red or white root. Being counted a medicinal plant, it is mentioned in Arabic texts, whence it passed into Latin and in the form *béhen* into French. Two varieties, *béhen rouge* and *béhen blanc*, are found and still used in medicine. Also eaten on the day were leaves of the wild rue (*sepand*) mixed with milk, likewise for strengthening the memory. According to *Borhān-e qāṭe'* (ed. Mo'īn, I, pp. 328-29) the day was believed to be specially auspicious for digging up medicinal plants and roots and for extracting oils and making perfumes. The day was also recommended for cutting and wearing new clothes, paring the nails, and trimming the hair.

These customs stemmed from beliefs of the Zoroastrians that each of their sacred days had a special character making it appropriate for the performance of a particular task. Today, however, the detailed observances of the festival have lapsed even among Zoroastrians, although the monthly Bahmanrūz continues to be an especially holy day for them (see Boyce, pp. 89-90).

As long as the celebration of Bahmanjana remained customary at royal courts, congratulatory odes for the occasion were addressed to rulers and dignitaries by court poets. The dictionaries cite verses from such poems by Farroḵī, Manūčehrī, 'Oṯmān Moḵtārī, Anwarī, and other pre-Mongol poets.

Bibliography: Abū Rayḥān Bīrūnī, *al-Tafhīm le-awā'el ṣenā'at al-tanjīm*, 2nd ed., Tehran, n.d. M. Boyce, *A Persian Stronghold of Zoroastrianism*, Oxford, 1977. Faḵr-al-Dīn Mobārakšāh Ḡaznavī, *Farhang-e Qawwās*, ed. Naḏīr Aḥmad, Tehran, 1353 Š./1974 (where Bahmanjana is wrongly identified with the first day of Bahman; see the editor's notes). Moḥammad Pādšāh Šād, *Farhang-e Ānandrāj*, ed. M. Dabīrsīāqī, I, Tehran, 1335 Š./1956, p. 816 (Bahmančena). *Dā'erat al-ma'āraf-e fārsī*, ed. Ḡ.-Ḥ. Moṣāḥeb, I, Tehran, 1345 Š./1966, p. 480. *Yašthā*, ed. E. Pūr-Dāwūd, Tehran, 2536 = 1356 Š./1977, pp. 89-90. Ḏ. Ṣafā, *Gāhšomārī o jašnhā-ye mellī-e īrānīān*, Tehran, 1356 Š./1977, pp. 127-28.

(Z. Safa)

BAHMAN-NĀMA, epic poem of about 9,500 lines recounting the adventures of Bahman son of Esfandīār (q.v.). The earliest mention of *Bahman-nāma* is in *Mojmal al-tawārīḵ* (ed. M.-T. Bahār, Tehran, 1318 Š./1939) which gives the author as Īrānšān b. Abi'l-Ḵayr (pp. 92, 463). The name is difficult to read and Bahār suggests the alternative form Īrānšāh, which has been accepted by most scholars. *Mojmal al-tawārīḵ* (p. 2) also mentions an *Aḵbār(-e) Bahman* which may be a different version of this tale. *Majma' al-foṣaḥā* (I, pp. 110, 494) mentions a *Bahman-nāma* by Jamālī Mehrījerdī, a contemporary of Lāme'ī Gorgānī (b. ca. 414/1023-24) but only a few scattered verses of this remain (see S. Nafīsī, "Jamālī Mehrījerdī," *Āyanda* 1,

1304 Š./1925, pp. 589-95). From references to historical events, and dedications to both Nāṣer-al-Dīn Maḥmūd b. Malekšāh and Ḡīāṯ-al-Dīn Moḥammad b. Malekšāh, it seems highly likely that Īrānšāh b. Abi'l-Ḵayr wrote and revised *Bahman-nāma* between 485/1092-93 and 501/1107-08. Summaries of the story of Bahman can be found in *Mojmal al-tawārīḵ*, pp. 53-54, and in Malekšāh Ḥosayn Sīstānī, *Eḥyāʾ al-molūk* (ed. M. Sotūda, Tehran, 1344 Š./1966), pp. 40-45. The earliest known manuscript is in the British Museum (C. Rieu, *Supplement to the Catalogue of Persian Manuscripts in the British Museum*, London, 1895, no. 201, dated 800/1397-98). Other manuscripts are in the Bodleian (*Cat. Bodleian*, no. 2544, undated), the Bibliothèque Nationale (Blochet, *Cat. Bib. Nat.*, nos. 1192-93, 10th/17th cent.), and the British Museum (Rieu, *Supplement*, no. 197, dated 1252/1836-37). A lithographed edition was published in Bombay in 1325/1907-08.

The story, in summary, is as follows: Bahman, at the behest of Rostam, marries Katāyūn (or Kasāyūn), daughter of the king of Kashmir. Katāyūn is accompanied by a youth Lo'lo' who is secretly her lover. She persuades Bahman to place Lo'lo' in charge of the army and the treasury, whereupon Lo'lo' bribes the army to revolt against Bahman. Bahman flees to Egypt where he marries Homāy, daughter of the king of Egypt, raises an army, and returns to Iran. There he regains his kingdom and banishes Lo'lo'. Meanwhile, Rostam and his brother Zavāra have been killed by the king of Kabul. Bahman mourns Rostam's death and then sets out for Sīstān to take vengeance on Rostam's descendents.

Bahman and Farāmarz, who is now the ruler of Sīstān, fight three times and Bahman is defeated each time. Bahman wins the fourth battle and Farāmarz flees. Bahman conquers Sīstān, takes Zāl prisoner, and pursues Bānū Gošasp and Zar Bānū (daughters of Rostam) to Kashmir where he captures them. Farāmarz is killed in India and Bahman gains control of all the lands that Farāmarz formerly held. At this point, he sets out to destroy the tombs of Rostam and his ancestors. Āḏar Borzīn son of Farāmarz appears with an army to fight Bahman, and is captured. Bahman visits the tombs of Garšāsp, Narīmān, Sām, and Rostam, and at each tomb he receives a precious gift and a message from the deceased urging him to be merciful. As a result he proceeds to Sīstān where he forgives Zāl, frees him and Rostam's daughters, and rebuilds the palaces and cities there. He sends Āḏar Borzīn to the north of Iran.

In the north, Āḏar Borzīn meets Rostam-e Ṭūr, known also as Rostam-e Yak-dast (Malekšāh Ḥosayn Sīstānī, *Eḥyāʾ al-molūk*, ed. M. Sotūda, Tehran, 1344 Š./1966, p. 43), Rostam-e Ṭūr Ṭabarī (ibid., p. 44), and Rostam-e Ṭūr Gīlī (*Mojmal*, p. 54). Together they raise an army to challenge Bahman. Bahman sends a daughter of Rostam to fight Āḏar Borzīn. After a series of battles Bahman and Āḏar Borzīn make peace. At the end of the story Bahman installs his daughter Homāy on the throne and he himself is devoured by a dragon while on a hunting expedition.

The present *Bahman-nāma* should not be confused with a *Bahman-nāma* written by Nūr-al-Dīn Ḥamza b. ʿAbd-al-Malek Āḏarī Ṭūsī (d. 866/1461-62), which is a versified history of the Bahmanid sultans of the Deccan.

Bibliography: Ḏ. Ṣafā discusses the date of composition of *Bahman-nāma* in his "Bahman-nāma," *Āmūzeš wa parvareš* 14, 1323 Š./1944, pp. 136-43. For discussions of *Bahman-nāma* in the context of Persian epic poetry, see Ḏ. Ṣafā, *Ḥamāsasarāʾī dar Īrān*, Tehran, 1333 Š./1954, pp. 289-94, 538-42. Idem, *Adabīyāt* II, Tehran, 1339 Š./1960, pp. 363-64. M. Molé, "L'épopée iranienne après Firdōsī," *La Nouvelle Clio* 5, 1953, pp. 377-93. Rypka, *Hist. Iran. Lit.*, pp. 162-66. R. ʿAfīfī, "Bahman-nāma," *Āyanda* 8, 1361 Š./1982, pp. 773-79.

(W. L. HANAWAY, JR.)

BAHMANŠĪR (less commonly Bahmešīr, Bahmānšīr, or Baḥr al-Mašīr), the name of the distributary which branches off the left bank of the Kārūn river in the Ḵūzestān plain a short distance above Ḵorramšahr, and of a *dehestān* near this town. Approximately 70 km (43.5 miles) long, the Bahmanšīr runs parallel with the Šaṭṭ-al-ʿArab (Arvandrūd), from which it is separated by Ābādān island, and flows into a different estuary called Ḵor-e Bahmanšīr. At the turn of the century the banks of the Bahmanšīr were lined with villages and date-palms down to within 16 km of the Persian Gulf. It has a minimum depth of about three meters at low tide and increasing depths toward the estuary. Thus in the nineteenth century some small British ships were able to sail up or down the Bahmanšīr creek (Major Eastcourt's ship the "Euphrates" in the expedition of 1836; Lieutenant Selby's boat in 1841). The Bahmanšīr was sounded by the British for navigation in 1888 and 1890. At the end of the century there was talk of deepening the creek and draining the marshes so that Iran might have a direct river access to the Persian Gulf independent of the Šaṭṭ-al-ʿArab, but nothing was done then or later. Its impracticability for the use of ocean liners was demonstrated in 1890 (Wilson, p. 282).

According to Masʿūdī (*Tanbīh*, p. 52) Bahmanšīr was the Persian name of the lower stretch of the Tigris extending from Maftaḥ to Obolla and ʿAbbādān (Ābādān). The name Dahana-ye Šīr found in *Ḥodūd al-ʿālam* seems to refer to Bahmanšīr (tr. Minorsky, pp. 74, 214). The Kārūn then reached the sea by a course which lay further east (today known as the Kārūn-e Aʿma "Blind Kārūn"). At some unknown time, but certainly not later than the early ʿAbbasid period, the Kārūn was joined to the Šaṭṭ-al-ʿArab by an artificial channel. The name Ḥaffār (Digger) is given to this channel in Western sources and may be taken as a reference to its artificial origin but locally the channel was called Bahmanšīr according to Lorimer (pp. 209-10). The channel cuts across the Bahmanšīr creek, making it the recipient of part of the Kārūn's waters.

The name Bahmanšīr is thought to be a contraction of Bahman Ardašīr I, referring to the Sasanian king Ardašīr I, who is traditionally credited with many public works (Ḥamza, p. 46; Yāqūt, I, p. 770).

See also KĀRŪN.

Bibliography: William Francis Ainsworth, *A Personal Narrative of the Euphrates Expedition*, 2 vols., London, 1888, II, pp. 132-33. G. N. Curzon, "The Karun River and the Commercial Geography of South-West Persia," *Proceedings of the Royal Geographical Society*, 1890, pp. 509-32, esp. 516-17. Idem, *Persia and the Persian Question*, 2 vols., London. 1892, II, pp. 341-42. "Kārūn," in *EI*² IV. J. G. Lorimer, *Gazetteer of the Persian Gulf, ʿOman and Central Arabia* II/1, repr. Farnborough, England, 1970, pp. 4-5, 209-11. Kayhān, *Jog̱rāfīā* II, p. 77. *Persian Gulf Pilot*, 9th ed., London, 1942, pp. 255. Razmārā, *Farhang* VI, p. 65. Sir A. T. Wilson, *The Persian Gulf*, Oxford, 1928.

(X. DE PLANHOL)

BAHMANYĀR AḤMAD (DEHQĀN), scholar, educator, and man of letters, b. 1301/1884 in Kermān, d. 1334 Š./1955 in Tehran. Bahmanyār received his first education from his father Āqā Moḥammad-ʿAlī, himself a scholar, and from his brother. He soon became proficient in Arabic and Persian literature and at sixteen could teach Arabic grammar and literature and write a commentary on one of his father's scholarly works.

Two periods can be distinguished in his life. During the first one (1289-1308 Š./1910-29) he joined the Constitutional Movement of 1285 Š./1906, published the weekly paper *Dehqān* in Kermān (1st issue Šawwāl, 1329/October, 1911) and the *Fekr-e āzād* in Mašhad (1301-02 Š./1922-23) and Tehran (1303 Š./1924). In 1294 Š./1915, due to his political involvements, he was exiled by the British from Kermān to Fārs, where he was jailed for more than fourteen months. While in jail he learned Ottoman Turkish and translated a few Turkish poems into Persian. He also studied astronomy with a fellow prisoner. Upon his release he went to Tehran where he was in bad financial straits. Finally he entered the government service, serving the Ministries of Finance, Education, and Justice in a number of cities for about nine years. During the second period (from 1308 Š./1929 until his death in 1334 Š./1955), Bahmanyār became a high-school teacher in Tehran (1308 Š./1929), a faculty member at the Dār al-Moʿallemīn (Teachers' college; 1310 Š./1931), professor of Arabic and Persian at Tehran University (1314 Š./1935), and a permanent member of the Farhangestān-e Īrān (Academy of Iran; 1321 Š./1942).

His work is characterized by clarity and simplicity of language. It includes *Toḥfa-ye aḥmadīya*, a two-volume commentary on the *Alfīya* of Ebn Mālek (Kermān, 1330/1912), a biography of Ṣāḥeb b. ʿAbbād (Tehran, 1344 Š./1965), *Dāstān-nāma-ye bahmanyārī* (Tehran, 1357 Š./1978), and critical editions of Moḥammad b. Monawwar's *Asrār al-tawḥīd* (Tehran, 1314 Š./1935), Bahāʾ-al-Dīn Moḥammad Bag̱dādī's *al-Tawassol ela'l-tarassol* (Tehran, 1315 Š./1936), Ebn Fondoq's *Tārīḵ-e Bayhaq* (Tehran, 1317 Š./1938), Abū Manṣūr's *Ketāb al-abnīa ʿan ḥaqāʾeq al-adwīa* (Tehran, 1346 Š./1967), some *resālas* by Ḥājj Moḥammad-Karīm Kermānī, and a number of articles. His *Majmaʿ al-amṯāl* is yet to be published. Bahmanyār also wrote some poetry, all along traditional lines. He seems to have left a memoir, a part of which ("Yāddāšt-e ayyām-e āvāragī") was used by Bāstānī Pārīzī (p. 109).

Bibliography: Ī. Afšār, "Aḥmad Bahmanyār," *FIZ* 3, 1334 Š./1955, pp. 293-95. J. Homāʾī, "Dargoḏašt-e marḥūm Aḥmad Bahmanyār," *MDAT* 3/2, 1334 Š./1955, pp. 52-80. M. Ṣadr Hāšemī, *Tārīḵ-e jarāʾed o majallāt-e Īrān*, 4 vols., Isfahan, 1327-32 Š./1948-53, II, pp. 308-10; IV, pp. 82-84. M. Moʿīn, *Farhang-e fārsī* V, Tehran, 1345 Š./1966, p. 306. M.-E. Bāstānī Pārīzī, "Dāstān-nāma-ye bahmanyārī," in his *Jāmeʿ al-moqaddamāt*, Tehran, 1363 Š./1984, pp. 61-141.

(J. MATĪNĪ)

BAHMANYĀR, KĪĀ RAʾĪS ABU'L-ḤASAN B. MARZBĀN AʿJAMĪ ĀḎARBĀYJĀNĪ (d. 458/1066), one of Ebn Sīnā's pupils during his stay in Hamadān (405/1015-415/1024) and Isfahan (415/1024-428/1037). Very little is known about his life. Originally a Zoroastrian converted to Islam, his knowledge of Arabic was not perfect (*g̱ayr māher fī kalām al-ʿarab*; see Bayhaqī, p. 97 end; Ḵ ͮānsārī, II, pp. 157.18f., 160.16). Bahmanyār is known mainly as a commentator and transmitter of Ebn Sīnā's philosophy. His main work, the *Ketāb al-taḥṣīl* (see the Bibliography) was compiled in Isfahan between 415/1024 and 428/1037 for his uncle, the Zoroastrian Abū Manṣūr b. Bahrām b. Ḵ ͮoršīd b. Yazdyār. It offers the quintessence of Ebn Sīnā's logic, physics, and metaphysics according to his *Šefāʾ*, *Najāt*, and *Ešārāt wa'l-tanbīhāt*, and also contains, as he informs us (*Ketāb al-taḥṣīl*, p. 1.7), results of his discussions with Ebn Sīnā. This book, which follows Ebn Sīnā's *Dāneš-nāma-ye ʿalāʾī* in structure, is said to have been translated into Persian (Ḵ ͮānsārī, II, p. 157.19f.) and summarized (Ebn Abī Oṣaybeʿa, II, p. 204.5f) by ʿAbd-al-Laṭīf Bag̱dādī (d. 629/1231-32). The preserved manuscripts of the *Taḥṣīl* differ in length; see Anawati, p. 19; further mss. Ragıp Paşa 880, copied 1118/1706; B.M., add. 16.659, fols. 201r(197r)-228v(224v).

The discussions between Ebn Sīnā and Bahmanyār during the time of ʿAlāʾ-al-Dawla (cf. Neẓāmī ʿArūżī, *Čahār maqāla*, tr. Browne, pp. 126f.) also resulted in a collection of answers by Ebn Sīnā on questions by his pupils, mainly by Bahmanyār. In this collection, called *Mobāḥaṯāt* (Gohlman, pp. 100f.; Ebn Abī Oṣaybeʿa, II, p. 19.20), Ebn Sīnā comments on difficulties of his *Šefāʾ*, *Ešārāt wa'l-tanbīhāt*, and *Enṣāf*. The text is transmitted in different versions; the only available edition (see Bibliography) does not include all manuscripts and versions, some of which contain answers on questions by other pupils of Ebn Sīnā, namely Abū Manṣūr b. Zayla and Abū Jaʿfar Moḥammad b. Ḥosayn b. Marzbān (Mahdawī, p. 202). On the varying manuscripts see Mahdawī, pp. 202-12; Anawati, pp. 82-85; further mss.: B.M., 8069 [18th-19th cent.], fols. 17v-21);

Feyzullah Efendi, 2188, fols. 211r-220r (starts with nr. 5 of Mahdawī, p. 210). Two letters by Ebn Sīnā appended to the manuscript preserved in Egypt are written to a person addressed as *Šayḵ al-fāżel* which apparently means Bahmanyār (*Čahār maqāla*, ed. Qazvīnī and Moʿīn, p. 446 n. 5).

Akin to the above-mentioned texts is a collection of notes (*Taʿlīqāt*) on fundamental terms of metaphysics, physics, and logic taken by Bahmanyār from explanations given by Ebn Sīnā. It is not yet clear whether the *Taʿlīqāt* are the result of Bahmanyār's discussions with Ebn Sīnā in Hamadān (Gohlman, pp. 54f.) during the reign of Šams-al-Dawla (so Badawī in his edition, p. 6) or have been compiled later in Isfahan during the reign of ʿAlāʾ-al-Dawla. On mss. see Mahdawī, pp. 60-64; Anawati, pp. 19-21. An excerpt of the text appears under the name of Fārābī (v. Michot, *MIDEO* 15, 1982, pp. 231-50).

Three more treatises are attributed to Bahmanyār. They too follow Ebn Sīnā and contain short descriptions of metaphysics (*Resāla fī mawżūʿ ʿelm mā baʿd al-ṭabīʿ*), of the degrees of beings (*Resāla fī marāteb al-mawjūdāt*), and of the perceiving powers of the soul according to Peripatetic philosophy (*Maqāla fī ārāʾ al-maššāʾīn fī omūr al-nafs wa qowāhā*). The fact that Bahmanyār's books in the first place aim at explicating and summarizing ideas of his teacher Ebn Sīnā and that they to some extent may be based on notes taken from his master's lectures makes it difficult to differentiate between the writings of Ebn Sīnā and those of his pupils, and explains why the above-mentioned summary of metaphysics (following the *Šefāʾ*) has often been attributed in manuscripts to Ebn Sīnā (also called *Eṯbāt al-mabdaʾ al-awwal*; cf. Mahdawī, pp. 259f.; Anawati, pp. 235f.). In an analogous manner we can explain why the above-mentioned *Resāla fī marāteb al-mawjūdāt* has also been attributed at least in one case (ms. Berlin 3058), under the title of *Resāla fī eṯbāt al-mofāraqāt*, to another pupil of Ebn Sīnā, namely to Abū ʿAbd-Allāh Maʿṣūmī. Two manuscripts have ascribed the text to Bahmanyār (Anawati, p. 19), as well as a third, incomplete manuscript (Köprülü, Istanbul 1604; see Anawati, p. 19) which has the title *Faṣl men Ketāb fī eṯbāt al-ʿoqūl al-faʿʿāla wa'l-dalāla ʿalā ʿadadehā wa eṯbāt al-nofūs al-samāwīya*. However, to make matters more complicated, the *Resāla fī eṯbāt al-mofāraqāt*, which is identical with the *Resāla fī marāteb al-mawjūdāt* is ascribed to Fārābī in numerous manuscripts and publications (Ḥosayn-ʿAlī Maḥfūẓ and Jaʿfar Āl Yāsīn, *Moʾallafāt al-Fārābī*, Baghdad, 1395/1975, p. 309).

A more autonomous treatise is Bahmanyār's *Maqāla fī ārāʾ al-maššāʾīn fī omūr al-nafs wa qowāhā* (ms. Nafiz Paşa, Istanbul, 1350, fols. 54v-57r). It is a supplementary treatise on what has been said by Ebn Sīnā in his *Šefāʾ* (*Ṭabīʿīyāt, Nafs*; ed. Anawati and Saʿīd Zāyed, Cairo, 1395/1975, pp. 27ff., esp. 50ff.) and deals mainly with the perception (*edrāk*) of the souls of man and stars.

Further writings by Bahmanyār which seem to be lost include: *Ketāb al-bahja fī manṭeq wa'l-ṭabīʿī wa'l-elāhī* (Baḡdādī, I, p. 244; Ḵʷānsārī, II, p. 157) = (?) *Ketāb al-rotba fi'l-manṭeq* (Bayhaqī, p. 98.3) = *Ketāb al-zīna fi'l-manṭeq* (Šahrazūrī, II, p. 38, 11); a fragment of the *Ketāb al-bahja* on God's (*al-wājeb*) knowledge of himself has been preserved by Ḵʷānsārī, II, p. 158.15-18); *Ketāb al-saʿāda* (Ḵʷānsārī, II, p. 157 end; Baḡdādī, I, p. 244); *Ketāb fi'l-mūsīqā* (Bayhaqī, p. 98.4 = Šahrazūrī, II, p. 38.11). Several gnomological sayings are ascribed to Bahmanyār in Bayhaqī, pp. 98.5-99.2 (taken over, with omissions, by Šahrazūrī, II, pp. 38.12-39.2 and Ḵʷānsārī, II, p. 158.19-21).

Bahmanyār's extant works give the impression that he was very much interested in Ebn Sīnā's Neoplatonic teaching of the divine uncaused, self-sufficing, and necessary first cause and the creation caused by it through emanations (*fayż*). Moreover, he paid much attention to the soul of man and stars, its perceiving powers and afterlife. According to one report (Ḵʷānsārī II, p. 158) Bahmanyār differed from Ebn Sīnā in his teaching of the soul; contrary to Ebn Sīnā he maintains that the soul is not unchanged in its afterlife—as plants and living beings change in the course of time—but is similar (*šebh, naẓīr*) to what it has been before. This difference between Bahmanyār and Ebn Sīnā can not modify our view that Bahmanyār stands in the shadow of his great master. He has become known to posterity as commentator of Ebn Sīnā, but seems not to have had much influence; we only hear that Bahmanyār's pupil Abu'l-ʿAbbās Lawkarī has taken care for the propagation of his ideas and thus of Ebn Sīnā's philosophy in Khorasan (Bayhaqī, p. 126.10f.; Ḵʷānsārī, VI, p. 314.12).

Bibliography: Printed works by Bahmanyār: *Resāla fī marāteb al-mawjūdāt*, ed. and tr. S. Poper, in *Behmenjär Ben El-Marzubān, der persische Aristoteliker aus Avicenna's Schule: Zwei metaphysische Abhandlungen von ihm Arabisch und Deutsch mit Anmerkungen*, Leipzig, 1851, pp. 17-28 (tr. pp. 24-47), ed. ʿAbd-al-Jalīl Saʿd in *Bahmanyār, mā baʿd al-ṭabīʿa*, Cairo, 1329/1911, pp. 12-19. *Resāla fī mawżūʿ ʿelm mā baʿd al-ṭabīʿa*, ed. and tr. S. Poper, ibid., pp. 2-16 (tr. pp. 1-23) = ed. Saʿd, pp. 2-11. *Al-Mobāḥaṯāt* (with answers by Ebn Sīnā), ed. ʿAbd-al-Raḥmān Badawī, in *Aresṭū ʿend al-ʿarab* I, Cairo, 1947 (2nd ed., Kuwait, 1978), pp. 119-246. *Taḥṣīl*, Cairo, 1329/1911; new ed. by Mortażā Moṭahharī, Tehran, 1349 Š./1970; partial Russ. tr. A.V. Sagadeeva, *Kniga pervaya. Perevod s arabskogo, vvodnaya stat'ya i kommentarii*, Baku, 1983. *Taʿlīqāt* (compilation of Ebn Sīnā's text in the recension of ʿAbd-al-Razzāq), ed. ʿAbd-al-Raḥmān Badawī, Cairo, 1392/1973; an excerpt of this text (ed. Badawī, pp. 16.2-193-19) is ascribed to Fārābī (ed. Hyderabad, 1346/1927).

Primary sources: Esmāʿīl Pasha Baḡdādī, *Hadīyat al-ʿārefīn* I, Istanbul, 1951, col. 244. Moḥammad Bāqer Ḵʷānsārī, *Rawżāt al-jannāt fī aḥwāl al-ʿolamāʾ wa'l-sādāt* II, Tehran and Qom, 1392/1972, pp. 157-61. Ebn Abī Oṣaybeʿa, *ʿOyūn al-anbāʾ fī ṭabaqāt al-aṭebbāʾ*, ed. A. Mueller, Koenigsberg, 1884, repr. 1972. Ẓahīr-al-Dīn Bayhaqī known as Ebn Fondoq,

Tatemmat ṣewān al-ḥekma = *Taʾrīḵ ḥokamāʾ al-eslām*, ed. Moḥammad Kord ʿAlī, Damascus, 1946, pp. 97-99. Abū ʿObayd Jūzjānī, *Sīrat al-Šayḵ al-Raʾīs*; *Fehrest kotob Ebn Sīnā*, ed. and tr. W. E. Gohlman, *The Life of Ibn Sina*, Albany, New York, 1974; the text has been used by Qefṭī, *Taʾrīḵ al-ḥokamāʾ*, ed. J. Lippert, Leipzig, 1903, pp. 413ff. Neẓāmī ʿArūżī, *Čahār maqāla*, ed. Moḥammad Qazvīnī, rev. Moḥammad Moʿīn, 3rd ed., Tehran, 1333 Š./1954, text p. 124, notes pp. 444-47; Eng. tr. E. G. Browne, London, 1921, 2nd ed., 1978. Šams-al-Dīn Moḥammad b. Maḥmūd Šahrazūrī, *Nozhat al-arwāḥ wa rawżat al-afrāḥ*, Hyderabad, 1396/1976, II, pp. 38f.

Secondary sources: S. M. Afnan, *Avicenna, His Life and Works*, London, 1958, pp. 233f. G. C. Anawati, *Moʾallafāt Ebn Sīnā*, Cairo, 1950. T. J. de Boer, *The History of Philosophy in Islam*, tr. E. R. Jones, 2nd ed., New York, 1967, pp. 146f. Brockelmann, *GAL* I, p. 458, S. I, p. 828. *EI*[2] I, p. 926. ʿAlī-Aṣḡar Ḥalabī, *Tārīḵ-e falāsefa-ye īrānī az āḡāz-e eslām tā emrūz*, Tehran, 1351 Š./1972, pp. 365-68. Kaḥḥāla, III, Beirut, 1376/1957, p. 81. Yaḥyā Mahdawī, *Fehrest-e noskahā-ye moṣannafāt-e Ebn Sīnā*, Tehran, 1333 Š./1954. ʿAbd-Allāh Naʿema, *Falāsefat al-Šīʿa: Ḥayātohom wa ārāʾohom*, Beirut, ca. 1960, p. 263. Ṣafā, *Adabīyāt* I, pp. 318-19. Umarbek Sultonov, *Muosiri Abuali ibni Sina* [*Moʿāṣerān-e Abū ʿAlī Ebn-e Sīnā*], Dushanbe, 1980, pp. 64-66.

(H. DAIBER)

BAḤR. See ʿARŪŻ; BAḤR-E ṬAWĪL.

BAḤR-E ḴAZAR. See CASPIAN SEA.

BAḤR-E Ḵᵛ ĀRAZM. See ARAL SEA.

BAḤR-E ʿOMĀN. See DARYĀ-YE ʿOMĀN.

BAḤR-E ṬAWĪL, a type of Persian verse generally consisting of the repetition of a whole foot (*rokn*) of the meter *hazaj* (⏑ – – –) or of a whole foot of the meter *ramal* (– ⏑ – –) or of permissible variations of the two. The difference between *baḥr-e ṭawīl* and other metrical poetry, such as the *robāʿī* (quatrain), *qaṣīda* (ode), *ḡazal* (lyric), *mosammaṭ* (stanzaic verse), *maṯnawī* (rhymed couplets), etc., is that in the latter types, the poet is permitted to use four or six or at most eight feet per line, while a line of *baḥr-e ṭawīl* can contain up to twenty or even more feet. Another basic difference is that the number of feet in *baḥr-e ṭawīl* varies from line to line of a particular poem, whereas in other forms of rhythmic verse the number of feet in the first line has to be maintained throughout the entire poem. There is some disagreement among prosodists as to whether both defining characteristics, namely, hypermetricality and variation in the number of feet per line, have to be met before a poem is classified *baḥr-e ṭawīl*. Some would exclude a poem by ʿAbd-al-Wāseʿ Jabalī (q.v.) on grounds that it fails to meet the second condition, i.e., a foot of *hazaj-e makfūf* (⏑ – – ⏑) and one of *ramal-e maqṣūr* (– ⏑ – ⏑) recur twice in each line. The poem begins:

ayā sāqī al-modām marā bāda deh tamām
samanbūy o lālafām ke tā man dar-īn maqām
zanam yak nafas be kām ke kas-rā ze ḵāṣ o ʿām
dar īn manzel ay ḡolām omīd-e qarār nīst

(*Dīvān-e ʿAbd-al-Wāseʿ Jabalī*, 2 vols., ed. Ḏ. Ṣafā, Tehran, 1339-41 Š./1960-62, II, pp. 639-40).

Another characteristic that distinguishes *baḥr-e ṭawīl* from other metrical verse is that each line ordinarily culminates in a word ending in a syllable containing the long vowel *ā*, a *qāfīa* (rhyme), and a *radīf* (refrain) of *rā*. Of course, *baḥr-e ṭawīl*s exist that rhyme in a different manner and that lack a *radīf*. Internal rhyme also sets *baḥr-e ṭawīl* apart; often within a line one finds mono- and polysyllabic rhyme schemes as well as secondary *qāfīa* or *qāfīa* and *radīf*.

The diction used in *baḥr-e ṭawīl* poems is simple and direct as a rule. Because it does not force the poet to complete his thought within the confines of a hemistich or a line and allows as much metrical space as necessary to express a point, *baḥr-e ṭawīl* became popular on all levels of society. Moreover, with its successive internal rhymes, *baḥr-e ṭawīl*, when recited, produces the kind of inviting and prolonged melody in the reciter that listeners find engaging.

Baḥr-e ṭawīl is not as old as other verse forms; the earliest extant specimens date back to the Timurid period (9th/15th century) (P. N. Ḵānlarī, "Qadīmtarīn baḥr-e ṭawīl," *Soḵan* 22/11-12, 1352 Š./1973, pp. 1140-41). It is likely that *baḥr-e ṭawīl* was introduced for recreation and novelty of form, and as a forum for the poet's virtuosity, the same factors which had motivated such master poets as Manūčehrī Dāmḡānī (d. 432/1040) to create the *mosammaṭ* and Masʿūd-e Saʿd-e Salmān (438-515/1046-1121) the *mostazād*. *Baḥr-e ṭawīl*'s special features, which were elaborated by Safavid poets, made it a popular medium among professional story tellers (*naqqālān, maʿrakagīrān*) who used it to stir the emotions of their audiences. An example of *baḥr-e ṭawīl* is found in the Safavid period romance *Amīr Ḥamza-ye Ṣāḥebqerān* (Tehran University, Central Library ms. no. 2612) in which a foot of *ramal-e maḵbūn* (⏑ ⏑ – –/⏑ ⏑ – –) recurs (*ṣanam-ī lāla-ʿeḏār-ī, be raveš bād-e bahārī, be negah āhū-ye čīnī o be qad sarv-e ḵarāmān o be-roḵ čūn mah-e tābān o dahan ḡonča-ye ḵandān o lab-aš laʿl-e Badaḵšān o zanaḵdān čo namakdān o*. . .). During the Qajar period, the form served the purposes of reciters of Shiʿite martyrologies and passion plays (*taʿzīa*), thereby bringing new life to their calling (e.g., M. Honarī, *Taʿzīa dar ḵūr*, Tehran, 1354 Š./1975, pp. 148-54). Since the Constitutional era, *baḥr-e ṭawīl* has become a popular vehicle for experimentation with political and social themes; taking advantage of the form's capacity to arouse interest, satirists would cloak their warnings about the state of Persian society in wit and occasional mild ribaldry (see, e.g., various issues of the weekly paper *Tawfīq* and A. Ḥālat, *Baḥr-e ṭawīlhā-ye Hodhod Mīrzā*, Tehran, 1354 Š./1975).

Specimens of Arabic *baḥr-e ṭawīl* (adapted from Persian) date back to the 11th/17th century when Iraqi poets produced what they called *band*.

Baḥr-e ṭawīl is also the designation of a meter in Arabic prosody (⏑ – – ⏑ – – –) hardly ever used by Persian poets. Šams-al-Dīn Moḥammad b. Qays Rāzī, who quotes three Persian lines in this meter, observes that they are mere imitations of Arabic poetry since the meter does not suit "sound poetic taste" (*ṭabʿ-e salīm*) in Persian (*al-Moʿjam fī maʿāyīr ašʿār al-ʿajam*, ed. M. Qazvīnī, rev. M.-T. Modarres Rażawī, Tehran, 1336 Š./1957, pp. 71-72).

Bibliography: Given in the text. See also M. Akawān Ṯāleṯ, "Taḥqīq-ī dar bāra-ye baḥr-e ṭawīl-e pārsī," *Māh-nāma-ye farhang* 3, 1340 Š./1961, pp. 33-42. M.-E. Bāstānī Pārīzī, "Sayyed Bonederakṯī," *Gowhar* 1/11-12, 1352 Š./1973, pp. 1028-34. *Dīvān-e ʿEṣmat Bokārāʾī*, British Museum ms. Or 864/1. M. Darakšān, "Kohantarīn baḥr-e ṭawīl," *Āyanda* 11/4-5, 1364 Š./1985, pp. 280-86. L. P. Elwell-Sutton, *The Persian Metres*, London, New York, and Melbourne, 1976, pp. 192-93. P. N. Kānlarī, "Past o boland-e šeʿr-e now," *Sokan* 13/2, 1341 Š./1962, pp. 141-51. Ẓahīr al-Dīn Marʿašī, *Tārīk-e Ṭabarestān o Royān o Māzandarān*, ed. M. Tasbīḥī, Tehran, 1345 Š./1976, pp. 330-33. M. Moḥīṭ Ṭabāṭabāʾī, "Baḥr-e ṭawīl-e Mīr ʿAbd-al-ʿAẓīm Marʿašī," *Gowhar* 2/1, 1353 Š./1974, pp. 21-27. M.-Ḥ. Tasbīḥī, "Taẓmīn-e ġazal-e Ḥāfeẓ dar baḥr-e ṭawīl," *Waḥīd* 11, 1353 Š./1974.

(M. Dabīrsīāqī)

BAḤR-AL-ʿOLŪM, SAYYED MOḤAMMAD MAHDĪ (1155/1742-1212/1797), a Shiʿite scholar who exercised great influence both in Iraq and in Iran through the numerous students he trained. He began his studies in Karbalā, first with his father, Sayyed Mortażā, a descendant of the Majlesī family, and then with Shaikh Yūsof Baḥrānī. Later he proceeded to Najaf to study with Shaikh Moḥammad-Mahdī Fotūnī (d. 1183/1769) and Shaikh Moḥammad-Taqī Dawvaraqī (d. 1187/1773), who became his two chief teachers. He returned to Karbalā only briefly to study under the celebrated Moḥammad-Bāqer Behbahānī (q.v.) before settling definitively in Najaf to embark on his own career of teaching. Great polemical skills are attributed to Baḥr-al-ʿOlūm: he is said to have converted many Jews to Shiʿite Islam by his arguments, and such was the mastery of Sunni *feqh* that he acquired in debate with Sunni *ʿolamāʾ* that he taught the subject in Mecca for two years without his Shiʿite identity being detected. By contrast with many of his colleagues, he was not, however, unconditionally hostile to Sufism, for he refused to declare the celebrated Neʿmatallāhī Sufi, Nūr-ʿAlīšāh, an unbeliever, and he even facilitated his safe departure from Karbalā at a time of danger. Baḥr-al-ʿOlūm's biographers report that he was favored by miraculous communication with the Prophet and the imams, especially the Twelfth Imam. He wrote little of substance, but was so highly regarded for his learning that he became the leading scholar in the whole Shiʿite world after the death of Behbahānī. His posthumous influence was also great, especially in Iran, where pupils of his such as Mollā Aḥmad Narāqī, Moḥammad-Bāqer Raštī and Ḥājj Ebrāhīm Kalbāsī were often able to impose their will on secular authority.

Bibliography: Moḥammad b. Solaymān Tonokābonī, *Qeṣaṣ al-ʿolamāʾ*, Tehran , n.d., pp. 168-74. Moḥammad-Bāqer Ḵʷānsārī, *Rawżāt al-jannāt fī aḥwāl al-ʿolamāʾ wa'l-sādāt*, Tehran, 1304/1887, p. 677. Ḥājj Mīrzā Ḥosayn Nūrī, *Mostadrak al-wasāʾel*, Tehran, 1321/1903, III, p. 384. Moḥammad-ʿAlī Modarres, *Rayḥānat al-adab*, Tabriz, n.d., I, pp. 234-35. Moḥammad Ḥerz-al-Dīn, *Maʿāref al-rejāl fī tarājem al-ʿolamāʾ wa'l-odabāʾ*, Najaf, 1384/1964 (see index, III, p. 396 under "Moḥammad-Mahdī Baḥr-al-ʿOlūm" for references to his students). Javād Nūrbakš, introduction to Nūr-ʿAlīšāh, *Jannāt al-weṣāl*, Tehran, 1348 Š./1969, pp. v-vi; Hamid Algar, *Religion and State in Iran, 1785-1906: The Role of the Ulama in the Qajar Period*, Berkeley and Los Angeles, 1969, pp. 57, 59, 66, 69. A treatise on mysticism attributed to Baḥr-al-ʿOlūm has been published under the title *Resāla-ye sayr o solūk-e mansūb be Baḥr-al-ʿOlūm*, ed. S. M.-Ḥ. Ṭehrānī, Tehran, 1360 Š./1981.

(H. Algar)

BAHRA, a term meaning "share," "gain," or "profit," used within the economic context of Islamic Iran to mean "return on investment or production." This holds true for the various uses of the term: (1) as a fiscal term meaning "tithe," or as "economic rent," especially in agricultural relationship, and (2) as "interest."

Bahra *as a fiscal and agricultural term. Bahra* as a technical fiscal term has been in use since Mongol times in the same sense as the terms *moqāsema* or *karāj*, which meant land tax or more specifically the government's share or crop (Petrushevski, p. 724). This is also brought out by the use of the term *bahra* as a synonym of *māl wa motawajjehāt*, probably meaning land tax(es) (ibid.). The use of the terms *bahra-ye mazrūʿāt* or *bahra-ye maḥṣūlāt wa ertefāʿāt* (share of the crop; share of the harvest and usufruct) was frequent as well (Nakjavānī, I, pp. 198, 332; II, p. 140). As opposed to the government's share, for which we also find the use of the term *bahra-ye dīvānī*, there existed the term *bahra-ye mālekāna* or the landlord's share. The term *bahra* also occurred with a diminutive ending *bahrača* (Papaziyan, pp. 195, 226, 295; Nakjavānī, I/2, p. 372). In a document relating to the Jalayerid period it is stated that the tax-collectors (*motaṣarref*) had to take twenty percent of the crop yield (*dah do*), in some provinces, while in others they had to take twenty-five percent (*čahār yak*; Nakjavānī, II, p. 140). The last term survived in the form of *čerek* in Azerbaijan where it was still used as late as the beginning of the twentieth century (Alizade, p. 239). The term *bahra* was still in use in early Safavid times in a fiscal sense. In Qajar times, however, the term appears to have lost its specificity. We find the term *bahra-ye amlāk* used in some parts of ʿErāq-e ʿAjam to denote villages that have become ruined and do not pay taxes anymore (FO 60/144, Sheil to Palmerston, 29/1/1849, app., unfoliated). In the Caucasus area the term *bahragāna* was used to denote a system of sharecropping, in which the peasants participated as a community. As such it was a variation of the *boníča* system (q.v.). The *bahrakār* system was followed in the rich agricultural lands, while on less favorable lands the *yārīkār* system prevailed, each characterized by a special tax rate (Bournoutian, pp. 118, 119, 128). In general, however, in Qajar times the term occurred more frequently as *bahra-ye mālekāna* to denote the landlord's share of the crop (Lambton, p. 140).

Bahra *as interest*. The term *bahra* meaning interest is a recent innovation. Prior to the 1930s the word was not applied in this sense. For example, in a basic textbook like Moṣṭafā Fāteḥ's *Pūl wa bānkdārī*, *bahra* implies profit (pp. 230, 232) while the term *rebḥ* is used to denote interest. It is only in the 1940s that economic textbooks and essays drop the traditional term *rebḥ* and take up *bahra* to refer to interest (see for example Ḵosrowpūr, pp. 98, 100). In that sense the term *bahra* is a fixed or predetermined return on the use of money.

As such it is synonymous with the religious technical term *rebā* or usury which, according to various Koranic verses, is forbidden in Islam. Notwithstanding the latter usage *bahra* is not always used as a synonym for *rebā*. This is clearly demonstrated for example in the 1979 constitution of the Islamic Republic of Iran (articles 43.1.5 and 49).

Lending and borrowing at interest (*bahra*) are topics separate from, but related to, banking (q.v.). While non-bank loans (e.g., from and to bazaar merchants) are an important feature in Iranian finance, this article will focus on the policies and practices of banks because they can be more easily observed, are more readily controlled by the government, and have been the subject of government regulations.

The leaders of the Islamic Republic have universally understood the Koranic ban on *rebā* as applying to all kinds of interests, that is, to any return earned on a transaction in which the capital provided by the lender was not at stake. The exegesis on the ban in interest has focused on the professed goals of Islam of social justice and appropriate income and wealth distribution. The widely cited work by Moḥammad-Bāqer Ṣadr, *Eqteṣādonā* (pp. 626-27), argues that income should come from contributions to production of direct and indirect labor and money-lending makes no such contribution. Sayyed Maḥmūd Ṭāleqānī, (pp. 170-85) makes the same point, but goes on to suggest that interest is evil primarily because it encourages the unbridled pursuit of material wealth to the exclusion of other goals. (See also M.-B. Ṣadr's *Bank al-lā rabawī fi'l-Eslām*.) The collective work *The Philosophy of Islam* emphasizes instead that interest "is grave injustice" that "makes the rich, richer and the poor, poorer" (p. 627).

Under the Islamic Republic, interest policy has not been a major issue of discussion nor an area in which change has been rapid. The 1979 constitution contains only two passing references to interest. Interest charges were replaced in 1981 by service fees which amounted to much the same thing. The interest-free banking law *Qanūn-e ʿamalīyāt-e bānkī-e bedūn-e bahra*, introduced in March, 1982, and passed on August 30, 1983, was relatively uncontroversial, unlike some other economic issues that sparked much debate in the Majles and disagreement between the Majles and Šūrā-ye Negahbān (Council of Guardians). Establishment of new interest-free accounts was permitted through March 21, 1984, and existing acounts did not have to be converted to an interest-free basis until March 21, 1985.

The interest-free system has features similar to the previous banking system. Under a *fatwā* (religious ruling) permitting lending at interest between father and son, the Central Bank (Bānk-e Markazī-e Īrān) continues to charge interest to the government, which is by far the largest borrower in the country. Under the regulations set by the Central Bank of the Islamic Republic (Bānk-e Markazī-e Jomhūrī-e Eslāmī), all banks pay depositors the same rate of return, which in 1982 was 7.2 percent for short-term deposits and 9.0 percent for long-term, compared to the old system's rates of 7.0 and 8.5 percent. Since no bank can increase the rate paid to its depositors in order to attract more funds, the economic incentive for the bank managers is to assure security rather than to seek out more profitable use for the bank's funds. As a result, funds tend, under the new system as under the old, to be directed toward more established enterprises rather than to new ventures.

The interest-free system also has major new features. Rather than making loans at interest, banks use their funds primarily for capital participation (*możāraba*), partnership (*mošāraka*), or installment sales (*ejāra*), as well as for some interest-free loans on which the service charge is 2.5 percent. The returns earned by banks are closely governed by Central Bank regulations, which has led to statements that the new system is much like interest-charging banking. Interest-free banking in Iran is not entirely the same as in other countries, much as interest-charging systems differ among countries. Descriptions of interest-free finance based on experience elsewhere—e.g., Pakistan, Sudan, Bangladesh, Egypt, Denmark, or Luxemburg—should not be assumed to apply fully to Iran.

See also BANKING, ISLAMIC.

Bibliography: A. A. Alizade, *Sosyalnoekonomicheskaya i politicheskaya istoria Azerbaĭdzhana XIII-XIV vv.*, Baku, 1956. G. A. Bournoutian, *Eastern Armenia in the Last Decade of the Persian Rule 1807-1828*, Malibu, 1982. Moṣṭafā Fāteḥ, *Pūl wa bānkdārī*, Tehran, 1309 Š./1930. ʿA.-A. Ḵosrowpūr, *Bānkdārī*, Tehran, 1325 Š./1946. A. K. S. Lambton, *Landlord and Peasant in Persia*, London, 1953. Moḥammad b. Hendūšāh Naḵjavānī, *Dastūr al-kāteb*, ed. A. A. Alizade, Moscow, 1971. A. D. Papaziyan, *Persidskii dokumenty Matenadarana*, Erevan, 1956. I. P. Petrushevski, *Kešāvarzī wa monāsebāt-e arżī dar Īrān-e ʿahd-e Moḡol* II, Tehran, 1357 Š./1978. Moḥammad-Bāqer Ṣadr, *Eqteṣādonā*, Najaf, 1960. Idem, *Bank al-lā rabawī fi'l-Eslām*, Najaf, n.d. *The Philosophy of Islam*, Karachi, 1982, a collective work attributed to Moḥammad Ḥosaynī Beheštī and Javād Bāhonar. Sayyed Maḥmūd Ṭāleqānī, *Eslām wa mālekīyat*, Tehran, 1344 Š./1965, repr., 1357 Š./1978.

(P. CLAWSON and W. FLOOR)

BAHRAIN, Ar. Baḥrayn, lit. "two seas," the name originally applied to the area of the northeastern Arabian peninsula now known as Ḥasā (Aḥsā').

i. *Geography*.
ii. *Shiʿite elements in Bahrain*.
iii. *History of political relations with Iran*.
(For *Carmathians in Bahrain* see CARMATHIANS.)

i. GEOGRAPHY

Several interpretations of the name Bahrain, both popular and learned, have been put forward. The most probable (Oestrup) explains it by the presence of the promontory and archipelago extending eastward from the mainland in the direction of the Qaṭar peninsula, which divide into two parts the waters in this section of the upper Persian Gulf. The name now refers exclusively to the archipelago (composed of thirty-six islands, with a total area of 622 km^2) and to the independent state located there, or sometimes only to its largest island, formerly called Owāl or Awāl, popularly Samak (the fish), which extends almost 40 km from north to south and 15 km from west to east at its widest points. The other important islands are Moḥarraq, Nabīh Ṣāleḥ, and Setra northeast of the main island; Ḥawār to the southeast; and Omm Naʿsān to the west. The north-south axis passing through the main island coincides with a massive anticlinal dome of Jurassic and Cretaceous limestones that belongs to the family of marginal folds along the northeastern edge of the Arabian plateau. Carved out in the center by relief inversion, it reaches its highest point in the crest of the Jabal Doḵān, at an altitude of 124 meters.

Bahrain possesses a desert climate. Precipitation (annual mean: 95 mm), which falls only between January and May, is carried by rare cyclonic lows originating in the Mediterranean and penetrating as far as the Persian Gulf and is completely inadequate to support a rural population. But the island, like the northeastern coast of the mainland, possesses an important underground aquifer originating in the heights of central Arabia, which gushes forth here in large springs, in the form of natural artesian wells (some of them under the sea bed) along the entire northern perimeter of the main island. The aquifer can also be tapped along the full length of this coast by means of very shallow wells (the water level has, however, dropped recently because of overexploitation). In the interior of the island underground drainage channels funnel the waters from the piedmont. Irrigation crops of cereals, fruits, and legumes, sheltered by date palms, are thus widespread along the entire northern periphery of the island.

It is not surprising then that this site, so favorable for human habitation and located halfway between the head of the Persian Gulf and the straits of Hormoz (Hormuz), played an important role in the trade and life of the gulf at a very early period. The island's freshwater resources made it a valuable provisioning station for ships. It has been demonstrated that Bahrain must be identified with the Dilmun of the Assyro-Babylonian texts, an important staging point in the maritime commerce between Mesopotamia and the cities of the Indus during the third and second millennia B.C., and with Tylos of the Classical Latin and Greek texts (see the history and survey of this subject in Bibby). In the Islamic Middle Ages there was already an important city located on the site of present-day Manāma, a busy center of transit trade and the hub of pearl fishing in the entire gulf (Edrīsī, tr. Jaubert, I, pp. 372-73; Ebn Baṭṭūṭa, II, p. 246). This maritime activity reached its peak at the end of the nineteenth and the beginning of the twentieth century. At that time Bahrain possessed about 1,500 ships in its own right and served as the embarkation point for 3,000-4,000 ships a year; it was a center of pearl fishing and trade and was visited especially by numerous Indian merchants. The decline began, however, after World War I, owing to competition from Japanese cultured pearls. There were 400 pearl-fishing boats in Bahrain in about 1930, 250 still on the eve of World War II, but only 150 in 1946. Today there is hardly anything more than a small shrimp-fishing industry (Fougerouse, pp. 100-01).

A new economic phase began with the discovery in 1932 of a petroleum field in the center of the island, which was brought into production in 1934. Production of crude oil, topping 1 million tons a year after 1935 and stabilized at about 1.5 million tons between 1948 and 1956, steadily increased thereafter to a maximum of 3.8 million tons in 1970. A large refinery (present capacity: 13 million tons), established in the northeastern part of the island near Setra, processes, in addition to the crude from Bahrain, oil coming from Saudi Arabia by underwater pipeline. On the other hand, between the island and the mainland there is an offshore oil field the production from which is managed by Saudi Arabia, though the revenues are divided between it and Bahrain. Finally, a rich field of natural gas, in two superimposed strata, the reserves of which are estimated at 150 billion m^3, has been under exploitation since the end of the 1970s at a rate of 4.5 billion m^3 a year. Downstream from the petroleum refinery a petrochemical complex has been constructed and operating since 1985, producing ammonia and methanol. Plans for an important new refinery that would process heavy crude oil from Saudi Arabia into light petroleum products at the rate of 80,000 barrels a day are also underway.

Local oil production has, however, declined since 1972. In 1980 it amounted to only 2.8 million tons, and the oil field will doubtless be exhausted by 1995. So

Bahrain is currently orienting its economy more and more toward a broadly diversified industry, based for the present on local gas and in the future on the important gas resources of the neighboring region. A large aluminum smelting plant (capacity 165,000 tons a year) processes ore coming from Australia. An aluminum rolling mill was opened in 1984, and three other factories make finished products. A factory for the initial smelting of iron ore (capacity 4 million tons annually) has just opened on an artificial island east of the port of Manāma. Four desalination plants furnish the water necessary for these installations and for the population, for whose needs the natural springs are now quite insufficient. Extensive shipyards for repair and overhaul, the most important in the Persian Gulf, were opened in 1977, also on an artificial island. In addition, there are a cement plant and numerous small industries of various kinds. Finally, in its post-petroleum phase Bahrain is coming to function as a sort of service center for the entire gulf. It has become a hub of international communications and telecommunications; a very busy commercial arena for "exempt" multinational companies; and finally—and most important—a world banking center, with 178 "offshore" establishments in 1983, serving the entire international community and especially Saudi Arabia, playing a role comparable to that of Beirut before the Lebanese civil war and benefiting from the decline of the latter city.

All this activity has attracted to Bahrain a considerable foreign population, especially during the fifteen years that followed the declaration of independence in 1971. The indigenous population, which in 1941 comprised 90,000 inhabitants, of whom 16,000 were foreigners, and in 1971 216,000 people, of whom 38,000 were foreigners, had reached, by the time of the 1981 census, 350,000 people, of whom 112,000 (32 percent) were foreigners. The foreign population had thus tripled in ten years. This foreign population provided most of the labor force: 81,000 (74,000 men and 7,000 women) compared to 64,000 working persons (57,000 men and 7,000 women) of Bahraini nationality. Four-fifths of this foreign population (87,000 people) consisted of non-Arab Asians, especially Indians and Pakistanis (in domestic employment and other service occupations), Thais, South Koreans, and Filipinos (in construction and industrial jobs). Bahrain also counted a European and North American colony of more than 5,000 people. Iranians are numerous (certainly several thousand) but are not distinguished in the census, so that their exact number is unknown. The capital, Manāma, on the northeastern side of the main island, and the port of Moḥarraq, on a small neighboring island linked to the capital by a causeway, contain the majority of the population.

Bibliography: See the following article.

(X. de Planhol)

ii. Shiʿism in Bahrain

Bahrain came into the Iranian sphere of influence for the first time in the Sasanian period. After the Portuguese occupation (1521-1602), it again fell under Persian domination for nearly two centuries, despite several Omani invasions, in 1718 and 1738, which caused major devastation and the abandonment of villages, mentioned by Niebuhr in the 1760s (II, p. 188). In 1753 the island was reoccupied by the Persians, who remained until 1783, when it was conquered by the Arab dynasty of Āl Ḵalīfa, of mainland Bedouin stock descended from the Banū ʿOtba of Qaṭar. Iranian claims to the island were renewed several times subsequently, however, notably at the time of the 1861 and 1871 treaties establishing the British protectorate in Bahrain and at the Turkish conquest of the Ḥasā in 1871 (see Esmaʿīli; Adamiyat; Tadjbakhche). They were officially abandoned only after a mission of mediation by the United Nations Organization in 1971, at the moment when the emirate achieved its independence. Obviously Persian domination has been reflected in a degree of cultural influence, which, however, should certainly not be exaggerated, for the agents of Iranian power have often been the Howala or other Arab chieftains established in the eighteenth century in the region of Būšehr on the Iranian coast of the gulf (Rentz and Mulligan, p. 942).

The question is particularly relevant in connection with Shiʿism. The island actually contains two quite distinct cultural and religious strata. The urban population, concentrated around the Āl Ḵalīfa dynasty in the two cities of Manāma and Moḥarraq, is Sunnite, primarily of the Malikite rite, with a very few Hanbalite elements reflecting Wahhābī influence. The rural population is Shiʿite. It is generally estimated at about half the indigenous population, perhaps even 55 to 60 percent (no precision is possible, for sectarian affiliation is not recorded in the censuses). This rural Shiʿite population calls itself by the name Baḥārna, Baḥārena, or Beḥārna (sing. Baḥrānī; Hansen, 1968, p. 22) and readily claims not to be Arab, in order to distinguish itself from the population of Bedouin origin that revolves around the dynasty. It is certainly this attitude that has given rise to the rumor—obviously without foundation but repeated frequently in Iranian publications or those reflecting Iranian political views on the archipelago (Tadjbakhche, pp. 14, 223) and sometimes reported in survey works (Aubry, p. 453)—according to which these people are supposed to be of Persian origin and to speak Persian among themselves, at least part of the time. But to what extent did the Shiʿism of the pre-Bedouin population of Bahrain owe its origin to Persian influence and to the period of Persian domination in the island? The answer to this question must be categorically negative. Shiʿism, in various forms, is very old on the northeastern coast of Arabia and Bahrain, connected with the Carmathian movement and in geographical proximity to the great Shiʿite province of southern Iraq, where it has continued uninterrupted since the Buyid period. Twelver Shiʿism was deeply rooted in the Ḥasā at the beginning of the fourteenth century (Ebn Baṭṭūṭa, II, p. 247). During the Persian domination in the seventeenth and eighteenth centuries, religious influence seems to have flowed mainly from Bahrain to Iran, rather than the reverse. Niebuhr (II, p. 189) states very clearly that Persian clerics traveled to the shaikhs of Bahrain, considered "the university of the Shi'ites," to acquire the Arab culture that they required.

This symbiotic period, however, did allow the introduction of a certain number of Persian elements into the material and spiritual culture of the island. It has been shown, for example, that female costume, notably the veil (*čādor*) and the garments worn during the pilgrimage, include elements that are manifestly Persian (Hansen, 1968, pp. 71ff., 166), whereas male costume does not differ from the Arab type common in the region. Equally, however, some differences must be noted. Pious images, which are frequent among Iranian Shi'ites, are very rare in Bahrain (ibid., p. 149). Their diffusion among the lower classes in Iran seems to have occurred mainly in the Qajar period, and their absence from Bahrain is obviously to be explained by the much less active cultural relations after the Arab conquest of 1783. In the same way the new elements developed in Iran during the Pahlavi period (for example, the solar calendar) have never spread to Bahrain. In fact, the essential element continues to be the emotional attachment of the Shi'ites of Bahrain to Iran, which they regard as their spiritual home (ibid., p. 185). In order to determine more precisely the ultimate role of Iran in the Shi'ite culture of the island, a comparative study of this culture and that of the Ḥasā, on the neighboring mainland, would be necessary, but no such study has yet been undertaken.

Other elements in the material culture of Bahrain are just as certainly of Persian origin. The underground drainage channels, for example, are known on Bahrain as *qanāt* (Hansen, 1968, p. 85; Bibby, passim), the term used in western and southern Iran, rather than as *falaj*, the term used in Oman. But Persian terminology on this subject reaches as far as central Arabia (Naval Intelligence, p. 34) and is not specific to Bahrain. In sum, it does not appear possible, at least in the present state of knowledge, to define clearly an Iranian cultural stratum on Bahrain.

Bibliography: F. Adamiyat, *Bahrein Islands*, New York, 1955. A. Aubry, "Bahrain," in P. Bonnenfant, ed., *La péninsule arabique aujourd'hui* II, Paris, 1982, pp. 453-71. C. D. Belgrave, "Pearl Diving in Bahrain," *Journal of the Royal Central Asian Society*, 1934, pp. 450-52. Idem, "The Portuguese in the Bahrain Islands 1521-1602," ibid., 1935, pp. 617-30. Idem, *Personal Column*, London, 1960. J. H. D. Belgrave, *Welcome to Bahrain*, 9th ed., Manama, 1975. J. T. Bent, "The Bahrain Islands in the Persian Gulf," *Proceedings of the Royal Geographical Society*, 1890, pp. 1-19. G. Bibby, *Looking for Dilmun*, New York, 1969; French tr., *Dilmoun, La découverte de la plus ancienne civilisation*, Paris, 1972. M. Malek Esmaïli, *Le golfe Persique et les îles de Bahrein*, Paris, 1936. M. Fougerouse, *Bahrain, un exemple d'économie post-pétrolière au Moyen-Orient*, Paris, 1983. H. H. Hansen, "The Pattern of Women's Seclusion and Veiling in a Shī'a Village. Field Research in Bahrain," *Folk* 3, 1961, pp. 23-42. Idem, "Growing Up in Two Different Muslim Areas. Field Research in Iraqi Kurdistan and in Bahrain," ibid., 5, 1963, pp. 143-56. Idem, *Investigations in a Shī'a Village in Bahrain*, Publications of the National Museum, Ethnographical Series 12, Copenhagen, 1968. L. Lockhart, *Nadir Shah*, London, 1938. S. Nafīsī, *Baḥrayn*, Tehran, 1333 Š./1954. E. A. Nakhleh. *Bahrain. Political Development in a Modernizing Society*, Lexington, Mass., 1976. Naval Intelligence Division, *Iraq and the Persian Gulf*, Geographical Handbook Series, Oxford, 1946, esp. pp. 142-45. C. Niebuhr, *Description de l'Arabie*, 2 vols., Paris, 1779. J. Oestrup, "Al-Baḥrayn," in *EI*[1]. G. Rentz and W. E. Mulligan, "Al-Baḥrayn," in *EI*[2]. M. G. Rumaihi, *Bahrain, Social and Political Change since the First World War*, The Centre for Middle Eastern and Islamic Studies of the University of Durham 5, London and New York, 1976. A. W. Stiffe, "Ancient Trading Centres of the Persian Gulf VII: Bahrein," *Geographical Journal* 18, 1901, pp. 291-94. G.-R. Tadjbakhche, *La question des îles Bahrein*, Publications de la Revue générale de droit international public, N.S. 1, Paris, 1960. A. T. Wilson, *The Persian Gulf*, London, 1928, esp. pp. 83-91, 244-49, and passim. F. Wüstenfeld, *Bahreïn und Jemama nach arabischen Geographen beschrieben*, Göttingen, 1874. [J. Cole, "Rival Empires of Trade and Imami Shi'ism in Eastern Arabia, 1300-1800," *International Journal of Middle East Studies* 19, 1987, pp. 177-203.]

(X. de Planhol)

iii. History of Political Relations with Iran

Up to 1970, Iran claimed that "Bahrain had always and uninterruptedly formed part of Persia in past centuries, except during the Portuguese occupation from 1507 to 1622, in which year the Persian Government resumed possession of this territory" (Ramazani, 1966, p. 248). Yet, even though the Portuguese were driven out of Bahrain in 1622 by the Safavid Shah 'Abbās, Persian rule over the island did not become effective until 1753, when Shaikh Naṣīr of Būšehr sent an expeditionary force to conquer the archipelago from the Arab Howayla tribe. In 1783, Bahrain was reconquered by the Arab al-'Otūb tribe led by Aḥmad al-Ḵalīfa. The British government, which had entered into treaty relations with al-Ḵalīfa in 1820, formalized its ties through treaties signed in 1847, 1856, 1861, and the Executive Agreements of 1880 and 1892 establishing "exclusive" control over Bahrain's foreign relations (Lorimer, pp. 836-999, passim), and questioned the validity of the Iranian claim. Relations between Manāma and Tehran were consequently affected by the rise of British hegemonic influence in the area challenging Iran's posture.

Iran disclosed its claim to Bahrain on November 22, 1927, when "the Persian Acting Minister for Foreign Affairs addressed a sharp letter to Sir Robert Clive, the

British Minister at Tehran, in which he reiterated that Bahrain was incontestably in Persian possession" (Adamiyat, p. 194). In that letter, a copy of which was sent to the League of Nations, the Iranian government protested against the May 20, 1927, treaty concluded between Britain and Saudi Arabia. Article 6 of the Treaty of Jiddah stated that the King of Hijaz and of Najd and their dependencies "undertakes to maintain friendly and peaceful relations with the territories of Koweit and Bahrain and with the shaikhs of Qatar and the Oman coast who are in special treaty relations with His Britannic Majesty's Government" (Adamiyat, p. 194). London rejected this protest in a letter dated January 18, 1928, from Sir Austen Chamberlain, the British Foreign Secretary, to Hovhannes Khan Mossaed (Mosāʿed), the Persian chargé d'affaires in London. The British denied that "any valid grounds" existed upon which Iran could claim sovereignty over Bahrain (Khadduri, p. 633), and stressed that not only was the shaikh of Bahrain an "independent" ruler but that the island and its inhabitants were under British protection.

The Iranian claim was renewed in 1952 and 1956 to no avail. But on November 12, 1957, Tehran decided to officially integrate Bahrain as the fourteenth Iranian province in the administrative divisions of the country, drawing strong protests from Britain and the League of Arab States. Addressing the Majles, the Iranian foreign minister responded by declaring: "Our Arab brothers should know that Bahrain is part of our body and the question of Bahrain is of vital interest to Iran" (Ramazani, 1972a, p. 46). Bahrain's politico-strategic significance increased when it became a British stronghold east of Suez after the People's Democratic Republic of Yemen achieved independence. Its strategic appeal to Iran was further heightened when Britain announced its intention to withdraw its troops from throughout the Gulf before the end of 1971 and to terminate the treaties binding it to the Gulf shaikhdoms. Moreover, London encouraged the Arab shaikhdoms to unite into a federation. Bahrain, Qatar, and the seven Amirates of the Trucial Coast opened negotiations in February, 1968, which drew sharp criticisms from the shah. Tehran announced its opposition to the project on July 8, 1968, when the foreign minister released a strongly worded communiqué stating that "the creation of a so-called confederation of Persian Gulf emirates embracing the Bahrain islands is absolutely unacceptable to Iran" (Ramazani, 1972a, p. 48). The K̲alīfa turned to Britain and Saudi Arabia for support and, following the Bahraini ruler's visit to Saudi Arabia, King Faysal declared that the Arabs must fill the vacuum created by the British withdrawal. In response, the shah cancelled his scheduled state visit to Saudi Arabia but hinted on January 4, 1969, in a New Delhi press conference, that his country and Riyadh considered the future of the Persian Gulf to be the concern of the bordering countries alone. On this occasion, he softened his attitude toward Bahrain, and suggested that the indigenous population should voice freely its wishes through a United Nations supervised referendum. Shaikh ʿĪsā b. Salmān al-K̲alīfa, fearing that such a referendum would create tension between Persians and Arabs in the Gulf area, rejected this suggestion, drawing a strong threat from the shah on September 9, 1969, who declared that Iran would not recognize Bahrain as an independent state, and if it was admitted to the United Nations Iran would leave that organization (Ramazani, 1972a, p. 51).

After several months of secret negotiations the problem was resolved. During 1969, Shaikh ʿĪsā visited London and Washington. The shah also clarified his intentions and took the initiative on March 9, 1970, by formally requesting the good offices of the Secretary General to send an emissary, so that the true wishes of the people of Bahrain with respect to the future status of the Islands of Bahrain could be ascertained (Ramazani, 1972b, p. 4). Britain accepted the proposal and Secretary General U Thant's personal representative, Vittoria Winspeare Guicciardi, headed a five-member delegation to Bahrain from March 29 to April 18, 1970. Foreign minister Ardašīr Zāhedī revealed that Iran would only accept the recommendations of the mission if they were ratified by the Security Council, and Shaikh ʿĪsā stressed that Bahrain's acceptance of the UN mission in no way implied that it recognized the Iranian claim as legitimate.

The Guicciardi delegation interviewed civic and religious officials and ordinary individuals and representatives in a wide variety of organizations, institutions, and professional groups, asking them to choose either union with Iran, or status as a British protectorate, or independence. The mission found that Bahrainis "virtually unanimously" wanted a "fully independent sovereign state" and the great majority insisted that it should be an Arab state (Ramazani, 1972a, p. 135). The report was endorsed by the Security Council on April 30 and Iran indicated its acceptance of the Bahrain settlement. Prime Minister Hoveyda introduced a resolution to the Majles and the Senate and the government's action was approved by the Majles on May 14 by 184 votes to 4 and unanimously by the Senate on May 18 (Ramazani, 1972a, p. 53). But the complications associated with the British-sponsored federation of Persian Gulf Amirates encouraged both Iran and Bahrain to contemplate the emergence of an independent state. Manāma declared its independence on August 14, 1971, and Tehran reportedly was the first nation to extend diplomatic recognition.

The Iranian-Bahraini rapprochement throughout the 1970s was sealed by high level visits and the 1971 agreement delineating the continental shelf between the two countries. Cooperation in the economic and cultural spheres culminated with the official *Pārs* news agency agreement in 1977 to exchange cultural programs and information. Yet, political relations between Iran and Bahrain soured on the issue of Persian Gulf security. The shah, for example, did not welcome the 23 December 1971 Jufair Agreement which legalized the U.S. Navy's presence in Bahrain. The shah declared that, as before, Iran did not want any foreign presence in the Gulf, be it England, the United States, or China (Ramazani, 1975, p. 435). The Iranian invasion of Abū Mūsā and the Tonbs (30 November 1971), and the shah's proposed Gulf Security Pact, in the form of an Iranian-led military alliance, further aggravated the situation. Saudi reservations, Iran's lopsided military predominance in the Gulf, and the Iranian revolution contributed to the abandonment of the contemplated alliance. Bahrain aligned itself with the Saudi position while trying to maintain friendly relations with Iran. In June, 1978, during an official visit to Tehran, Shaikh ʿĪsā praised Iran's role as a "regional power," and hailed the shah's efforts to take measures against the dangers threatening the region.

In December, 1978, Shaikh ʿĪsā expressed serious concern over events in Iran, which, he predicted, would inevitably affect the security and stability of the Persian Gulf. Manāma felt directly threatened by the sequels to the Iranian Revolution within Bahrain itself, as more than half of Bahrain's population is Shiʿite. Demonstrations supporting Iran did indeed take place in Bahrain in 1979 when Ayatollah Ṣādeq Rūḥānī revived the old Iranian territorial claim to the Amirate, accusing the ruler of oppressing his people, declaring that the Iranian Majles that had renounced claims to the archipelago in 1970 had been illegal, and announcing that Iran still regarded Bahrain as its 14th Province, pending the decision of the future National Assembly on the matter. Iranian Foreign Minister Ebrāhīm Yazdī dismissed Rūḥānī's pronouncements as personal opinion. Despite this denial, Bahraini Prime Minister Shaikh K̲alīfa vehemently denounced the Iranian claim, and stressed that Manāma sought to establish cordial relations with the new Iranian regime on a basis of mutual trust and that they would not allow anyone to divide the two peoples. On September 24, Rūḥānī returned to the offensive threatening to "annex" Bahrain unless its rulers adopted "an Islamic form of government similar to the one established in Iran" (Ramazani, 1986, p. 49). Prime Minister Mehdī Bāzargān officially denied that his country had any expansionist designs in the Persian Gulf region, claiming that Rūḥānī's pronouncements were unauthorized and worthless. Bāzargān's ambassador to Riyadh, Moḥammad Javād Rażawī, declared that Iran respected other nations' sovereignty and had no claims or ambitions on any part of the Persian Gulf. Shortly thereafter, Bāzargān's deputy, Ṣādeq Ṭabāṭabāʾī, went to Bahrain to ease the mounting tension (Ramazani, 1986, p. 49). The normalization of relations between Bahrain and Iran was sealed by the visit of Iranian Foreign Minister Ṣādeq Qoṭbzāda to Manāma in 1980.

On 13 December 1981, however, Bahrain announced that it had arrested a group of "saboteurs" allegedly trained in Iran. The Bahraini interior minister then charged that the group had planned to assassinate Bahraini officials and that it belonged to the Islamic Front for the Liberation of Bahrain, which had its headquarter in Tehran, adding that its "sixty" members were all Shiʿites (Ramazani, 1986, p. 50). Yet, despite the fact that not a single Iranian was arrested in connection with the coup plot, Bahraini officials blamed the revolutionary regime for organizing the incident. Political relations between the two countries further deteriorated as the conservative Arab monarchies on the Persian Gulf, joined in the Gulf Cooperation Council since 1981, implicitly extended their support to Baghdad in the Iran-Iraq War (q.v.).

Bibliography: Fereydoun Adamiyat, *Bahrain Islands: A Legal and Diplomatic Study of the British-Iranian Controversy*, New York, 1955, pp. 155-203. Maurice Fougerouse, *Bahrein: Un exemple d'économie post-pétrolière au Moyen-Orient*, Paris, 1983, pp. 21-58. M. A. Manshur Garakani, *Sīāsat-e Englīs dar K̲alīj-e Fārs wa tārīk̲ wa joḡrāfīā-ye Jazāʾer-e Bahrain*, Tehran, n.d. J. B. Kelly, "The Persian Claim to Bahrain," *International Affairs* 33/1, January, 1977, pp. 51-70. Majid Khadduri, "Iran's Claim to the Sovereignty of Bahrayn," *The American Journal of International Law* 45/4, October, 1951, pp. 631-47. J. G. Lorimer, *Gazetteer of the Persian Gulf, Oman, and Central Arabia*, pp. 836-999. Saʿīd Nafīsī, *Baḥrayn. Ḥoqūq-e 1700-sala-ye Īrān*, Tehran, 1333 Š./1954-55. Jahāngīr Qāʾemmaqāmī, *Baḥrayn wa masāʾel-e K̲alīj-e Fārs*, Tehran, 1341 Š./1962-63. Rouhollah K. Ramazani, *Iran's Foreign Policy 1941-1973: A Study of Foreign Policy in Modernizing Nations*, Charlottesville, 1975, pp. 411-27. Idem, *The Foreign Policy of Iran, 1500-1941: A Developing Nation in World Affairs*, Charlottesville, 1966, pp. 247-50. Idem, *The Persian Gulf: Iran's Role*, Charlottesville, 1972a, pp. 45-56, 125-39. Idem, *Revolutionary Iran: Challenge and Response in the Middle East*, Baltimore, 1986, pp. 48-53, 131-33. Idem, "The Settlement of the Bahrain Dispute," *Indian Journal of International Law* 12/1, 1972b, pp. 1-14. ʿAlī Zarrīn-qalam, *Sar-zamīn-e Baḥrayn: Az Dawrān-e bāstān ta emrūz*, Tehran, 1337 Š./1958-59, pp. 85-104, 332-34.

(J. A. Kechichian)

BAHRĀM, the Old Iranian god of victory, Avestan Vərəθraγna, Middle Persian Warahrān, Wahrān.

i. *In Old and Middle Iranian texts.*
ii. *Representation in Iranian art.*

i. In Old and Middle Iranian Texts

BAHRĀM, original meaning "smiting of resistance;" not found in Old Persian; Middle Persian *Warahrān*, frequently used in the proper names of persons of the male sex, the hypostasis of "victory" and one of the principal figures in the Zoroastrian pantheon. His alter ego in the Avesta is *Dāmōiš Upamana* (*Yt.* 10.9), which I. Gershevitch (*The Avestan Hymn to Mithra*, Cambridge, 1959, p. 169) interprets as "Likeness of Ahura's creature," a probable synonym of **ahuraδātahe upamana-*. Together with Čistā, he is one of the principal companions of Miθra (*Yt.*10.70).

Bahrām is the great warrior god of Zoroastrianism, but his figure also contains a wealth of archaic, pre-Zoroastrian elements which clearly point to an Indo-Iranian era (P. Thieme, "The 'Aryan' Gods of the Mitanni Treaties," *JAOS* 80, 1960, pp. 312-14). His Avestan epithets are: *amavant-* "strong, endowed with attacking might," *ahuraδāta-* "created by Ahura," *barō.xᵛarəna-* "bearing *xᵛarənah-*," *hvāxšta-* "possessing good peace," *hvāyaona-* "possessing a good place," *aršō.kara-* "conferring virility," *maršō.kara-* "rendering decrepit," *frašō.kara-* "making wonderful." The epithets *hvāxšta-* and *hvāyaona-* associate him with Čistā (É. Benveniste and L. Renou, *Vṛtra et Vṛθragna. Étude de mythologie indo-iranienne*, Paris, 1934, pp. 58ff.) while *aršō.kara-*, *maršō.kara-*, and *frašō.kara-* relate him to Zurwān (H. S. Nyberg, "Questions de cosmogonie et de cosmologie mazdéennes," *JA* 219, 1931, pp. 86ff.).

In the Avesta, Vərəθraγna has all the characteristics of an ancient warrior god, the personification of a force that shatters and overcomes any resistance or defense, an irresistible offensive force which displays its strength in attack. For this reason he is associated with *Vanaintī Uparatāt* "Conquering Superiority" (*Yt.* 14.0, 64) and is venerated as *yazatanąm zayō.təmō* "the most highly armed of the gods" (*Yt.* 14.1), *amavastəmō* "the most endowed with attacking might" (*Yt.* 14.3), *xᵛarənaŋuhastəmō* "the most endowed with *xᵛarənah-*" (*Yt.* 14.3). He is represented as being in constant battle against his enemies, men and demons (*daēva*s), wizards (*yātu*s) and *pairikā*s, *kavi*s and *karapan*s (*Yt.* 14.4, 62).

Bahrām yašt (*Yt.* 14), dedicated to Vərəθraγna, belongs to the most ancient sections of the Younger Avesta or, at least, contains many archaic elements (A. Christensen, *Études sur le zoroastrisme de la Perse antique*, Copenhagen, 1928, pp. 7-8; M. Boyce, *Zoroastrianism* I, p. 63). *Bahrām yašt* is not one of the better preserved *yašt*s, yet it gives us a vivid and exhaustive picture of the divinity. It first enumerates the ten incarnations, in both animal and human form, of Vərəθraγna. These recall, although exact correspondences are lacking, the *avatāra*s of Viṣṇu in Purāṇic literature, or the ten incarnations of Indra (J. Charpentier, *Kleine Beiträge zur indoiranischen Mythologie*, Uppsala, 1911, pp. 25-68): an impetuous wind (*Yt.* 14.2-5); a bull with horns of gold (v. 7); a white horse with ears and muzzle of gold (v. 9); a camel in heat (vv. 11-13); a boar (v. 15); a youth at the ideal age of fifteen (v. 17); a falcon or bird of prey, *vārəγna-* (vv. 19-21); a ram (v. 23); a wild goat (v. 25); and an armed warrior (v. 27). It is interesting to note that the Avesta also attributed some of these metamorphoses to Tištrya (*Yt.* 8.13, 16, 20): the youth of fifteen, the bull with the horns of gold and the white horse; to Xᵛarənah (*Yt.* 19.35): the bird *vārəγna-*, and to Vayu: the camel (*Dēnkard*, ed Sanjana, IX, 23.2-3; Benveniste and Renou, pp. 35f.). The first metamorphosis, the impetuous wind, also links the god of victory to Vāta (Vayu), another divinity endowed with warlike virtues in Iranian mythology (H. S. Nyberg, *Die Religionen des alten Iran*, Leipzig, 1938, p. 75; S. Wikander, *Vayu* I, Lund, 1942; G. Widengren, *Les religions de l'Iran*, Paris, 1968, pp. 33ff.).

After the description of the incarnations of the god, the *Bahrām yašt* goes on to list the favors and gifts bestowed by Vərəθraγna on Zaraθuštra and on those who worship him according to the cult. These gifts are victory in thought, in word, and in action, as well as in declamatory speech and in retort, in conformity with a conception dating back to the Indo-Iranian practice of verbal contest (F. B. J. Kuiper, "The Ancient Aryan Verbal Contest," *IIJ* 4, 1960, pp. 243, 246). This evident Zoroastrianization of the cult of Vərəθraγna, which is reflected in *Yt.* 14.28-33, is coupled with a more popular image of the god, one in which he is more closely linked to magical elements and practices of exorcism which find parallels in India (B. Geiger, *Die Aməša Spəntas. Ihr Wesen und ihre ursprüngliche Bedeutung*, Vienna, 1916, pp. 66ff.; H. Lommel, *Die Yäšt's des Awesta*, Göttingen, 1927, pp. 134-35; Benveniste and Renou, pp. 30-31). These were principally a matter of the so-called "magic of the feather," i.e., oracles based on the falling or flying of a falcon's feather, and so on (vv. 34-46). The rest of the *yašt* (vv. 47-64) is a hymn of praise to the god. The power of the god and the strength which this transmits to the Airyas are such as to confound all their enemies. On the other hand, the Vyāmburas (an unknown people), whom the *Bahrām yašt* describes as those who shed blood, burn prohibited wood, and make forbidden animal sacrifices (see Benveniste and Renou, pp. 37-38) follow other ritual practices in the cult of the god, which the faithful worshipers of Mazdā must stay away from (vv. 54-56).

The *Bahrām yašt* appears to be something of a patchwork, and in many passages recalls other Avestan texts. Christensen (pp. 7-8) notes these passages, comparing *Yt.* 14.15 with *Yt.* 10.70, *Yt.* 14.28-33 with *Yt.* 16.6-13, and *Yt.* 14.48-53 with *Yt.* 8.56-61, and prudently declares his inability to decide whether the passages in question belonged originally to one *yašt* or the other. In some cases, however, it is possible to say that *Yt.* 14 has borrowed from other *yašt*s (in the case of *Yt.* 14.62 and *Yt.* 10.35-36 for example) while in others the opposite seems to be true (as in the case of *Yt.* 8.56-61 and *Yt.* 14.48-53; Benveniste and Renou, p. 38).

Evolution of Bahrām. Our knowledge of Vərəθraγna indicates that the god's functions were not limited to war and physical or military victory. He has other epithets and other characteristics which make him a more complex figure, one connected also with virility and sexual potency as well as health and physical integrity. He is defined as the one who gives man the "spring of the testicles," *ərəzōiš xå* (*Yt.* 14.29) and as the one who is *baēšazyō.təmō*, "the most gifted with healing" or healing powers (*Yt.* 14.3). In modern times, Bahrām is particularly worshipped as a divinity protecting those who undertake journeys (Boyce, *Zoroastrianism* I, p. 62 and n. 267). In fact, the Zoroastrian reform must have had a great influence on the evolution of this divine figure. This can also be inferred from the roles of Warahrān and Bahrām in later religious writings, from the Pahlavi texts of the ninth century to those of Parsism (see below). The principal evolution of Vərəθraγna in Zoroastrianism is without doubt to his role as the god of victory over the forces of evil in an intellectual and moral sense. The evolution of Vərəθraγna/Warahrān/Bahrām can not be understood outside the context of a radical revolution in traditional ethical and religious values. This has been pointed out by G. Dumézil, among others, (*Heur et malheur du guerrier*, Paris, 1985², pp. 179ff.).

The name. The interpretation of the god is one of the classic points for comparative analysis in the Indo-Iranian field and, at the same time, one of the most widely debated subjects. In the Avestan language we have, besides the name of the god, a neuter noun, *vərəθraγna-* "smiting of resistance," and an adjective *vərəθraγan-* "victorious." This adjective is applied to various divine entities, to the hero Θraētaona and to the Zoroastrian *saošyant*s and has a corresponding Vedic term, *vṛtrahán*, a well-known epithet of Indra, one of whose many feats was the slaying of the dragon *Vṛtra*. On this basis it has been thought that there existed in Indo-Iranian times an Indra *vṛtrahán*, warrior god and slayer of a dragon, echoes of whom, purified by the Zoroastrian reform, were to be found in Iran in Vərəθraγna, stripped of his dragon-slaying functions, and in the *daēva* Indra, demonized in the new religion. According to J. P. de Menasce ("La promotion de Vahrām," *RHR* 133, 1947-48, pp. 5-18), Iran is also supposed to have conserved traces, only preserved in the Armenian *Vahagn*, of a myth of Vərəθraγna dragon slayer. However, this characteristic of Vahagn has been seen by others as secondary or due to local elements (Benveniste and Renou, p. 80). According to the supporters of another theory, there were originally both an Indo-Iranian god, **Vṛtraghan*, and a dragon-slaying hero: While Iran conserved the ancient divine figure, India is thought to have made an innovation, promoting Indra to the rank of god and attributing to him the characteristics and functions of *Vṛtraghan. Of the two theories, the first is, in part at least, the more probable, as long as it is recognized that the principal function of the divinity was not necessarily to slay a dragon, but rather to destroy an obstacle, *vərəθra-*, such as that blocking the flow of the waters, in order to fulfill a cosmogonic task. In fact, what remains certainly valid in the theory of Benveniste and Renou is their demonstration of the secondary nature of the dragon/demon Vṛtra compared to the original Indo-Iranian source. However, it can not be denied that Indra was a god right from the beginning, and not a hero. This is demonstrated by the mention of him in the famous Mitanni treaty of the fourteenth century B.C. (J. Duchesne-Guillemin, *La religion de l'Iran ancien*, Paris, 1962, pp. 177f., and cf. Widengren, pp. 33f., 59f.).

Besides being frequently applied to gods or men, the adjective *vərəθraγan-* was probably also an epithet of fire. The *vərəθraγan ātar*, the "Victorious Fire," is in all probability the ancestor of the *ādur ī warahrān* (q.v.) of the inscriptions of Kerdēr (3rd cent. A.D.) and of the *Ātaš Bahrām* of more modern times, later interpreted, after the Sasanian era, as the "Fire of Vərəθraγna" owing to a natural confusion of the adjective with the name of the god of victory (Boyce, *Zoroastrianism* II, pp. 222ff.). The so-called "Fire of Bahrām" would therefore be a later creation and have no direct link with the ancient god: It would have become so in the minds of the faithful because of a natural misunderstanding, abetted in Islamic times by a progressive decay in Zoroastrian priestly teaching as regards the tradition of religious beliefs and practices.

The cult. Vərəθraγna was one of the principal gods of the ancient Iranian pantheon and his cult was spread throughout the Iranian and Iranianized world, probably from the beginning of the Achaemenid era. This was due both to the survival of an ancient pre-Zoroastrian cult and to the high position given to the god in the new religion. As the divinity of war and victory, he was the protector of his people in arms and accorded well with the bellicose character and expansionistic aims of the Iranian military aristocracy.

As regards the cult of Vərəθraγna among the peoples of the Iranian Plateau, the prestige which Ares enjoyed with the Karmanians, who worshipped him as their only god, is noteworthy (Strabo, 15.2.14). In all probability, behind this piece of information, which probably goes back to Nearchus, there must in fact have been the cult of the great Iranian divinity of war and victory (Benveniste and Renou, p. 87). This type of divinity was, in any case, common to other Iranian peoples who were not from the plateau, such as the Scythians. Let it suffice to recall the particular cult which, according to Herodotus (4.59.62), they reserved for Ares (with regard to the Scythian Ares, cf. G. Dumézil, *Romans de Scythie et d'alentours*, Paris, 1978, pp. 19ff.).

In the Seleucid and Parthian era, i.e., under the influence of Hellenism, Vərəθraγna was interpreted in Greek fashion as Ares and as Herakles, who also passed on to him certain iconographical features. The traces of this syncretism are widely attested to (cf. E. Bickerman, in *Camb. Hist. Iran* III/1, p. 14, and D. M. Lang, ibid., pp. 532, 535), and the inscription of King Antiochus I of Commagene (1st cent. B.C.) in the famous sanctuary of Nimrud Dagh provides explicit evidence of this in the sequence of the three divine names: Artagnes (Vərəθraγna), Herakles, Ares (cf. J. Duchesne-Guillemin, "Iran und Griechenland in der Kommagene," *Xenia* 12, Constance, 1984).

The identification of Vərəθraγna with Ares was also echoed in astrology, which had been introduced into Iran through Greco-Babylonian influence. The Pahlavi texts give the planet Mars the name *Wahrām* (for the relevant passage of the *Bundahišn*, cf. D. N. MacKenzie, "Zoroastrian Astrology in the *Bundahišn*," *BSOAS* 27, 1964, p. 513) so that we have the following correspondences for the names of the planets: Greek Ares, Babylonian Nergal, Iranian Vərəθraγna/Warahrān/Wahrām/Bahrām (for astrology in Zoroastrian Iran cf. R. C. Zaehner, *Zurvan. A Zoroastrian Dilemma*, Oxford, 1955, pp. 147ff.). The

Greco-Babylonian-Iranian religious syncretism, which was also reflected by the spreading of astrological doctrines, something originally extraneous to Zoroastrianism, thus codified the correspondences Vərəθraγna-Nergal-Ares and transfused them into the great syncretistic phenomenon of the Mysteries of Mithra, in which the identification of Vərəθraγna with Herakles was also iconographically reflected (F. Cumont, *Les mystères de Mithra*, Brussels, 1902², pp. 18, 185; and, on the problems concerning the Iranian background of the religion of the Mithraic Mysteries, G. Widengren, "The Mithraic Mysteries in the Greco-Roman World with Special Regard to their Iranian Background," in *La Persia e il mondo greco-romano*, Accademia Nazionale dei Lincei, Roma, 1966, pp. 433-55).

Armenia. From the Iranian world proper, Vərəθraγna also spread to the Iranianized world, both east and west, or to the parts of the world most strongly influenced by Iranianism. Armenia is the most conspicuous example. In fact, in Armenia (H. Hübschmann, *Armen. Etymologie*, pp. 75-78, 508f.), which was profoundly influenced by Parthian Iranianism, Vərəθraγna, identified with Herakles, was one of the three principal divinities of Iranian origin (the other two were Ahura Mazdā- Aramazd and Anāhitā-Anahit "the strangler of dragons," *višapak'ał/drakontopniktēs*. With him were associated two female divinities, Anahit herself and his concubine Astłik, identified with the Greek Aphrodite (M. L. Chaumont, *Recherches sur l'histoire d'Arménie de l'avènement des Sassanides à la conversion du royaume*, Paris, 1969, pp. 73, 151). The views held by certain scholars (Benveniste and Renou, pp. 75-80) on the extra-Iranian origin of the Armenian Vahagn are without a doubt exaggerated and, for the most part, erroneous (G. Widengren, *Stand und Aufgaben der iranischen Religionsgeschichte*, Leiden, 1955, pp. 38f.).

Eastern Iran. To the east of the Iranian world, Vərəθraγna, in the form ORLAGNO (A. Maricq, "La grande inscription de Kaniska et l'étéo-tokharien, l'ancienne langue de la Bactriane," *JA* 246, 1958, p. 426), appears in the monetary pantheon of the Kushans, where the god is represented with a winged headdress, a characteristic motif in Iranian symbolism, which likens him to Xᵛarənah, i.e., to the FARRO of the Kushans (J. M. Rosenfield, *The Dynastic Arts of the Kushans*, Berkeley and Los Angeles, 1967, pp. 95f.). The Avestan idea of the bird *vārəγna-* (see above), the incarnation both of Vərəθraγna and of Xᵛarənah, is likely to have been behind this symbolism (cf. F. Grenet, "Notes sur le panthéon iranien des Kouchans," *Studia Iranica* 13, 1984, p. 256).

Also to the east of the Iranian world, the Sogdian pantheon contained a Wšγn, corresponding to the ancient divinity (W. B. Henning, "A Sogdian God," *BSOAS* 28, 1965, p. 252), and Sogdian Manicheism gave the name Wšγn to the hero Adamas (E. Waldschmidt and W. Lentz, *Manichäische Dogmatik aus chinesischen und iranischen Texten, SPAW*, Phil.-hist. Kl., 1933, Berlin, 1933, pp. 510, 565). Without going outside eastern Iran, Bīrūnī has conserved the names of the days of the Sogdian and Choresmian calendars: the names of the twentieth day of the month have been explained by tracing them back to Vərəθraγna (Benveniste and Renou, pp. 83f.), the divinity to whom the same day was dedicated in the Avestan calendar (*Sīrōza* 1.20; 2.20).

Middle Persian Wahrām. In the Pahlavi texts Wahrām is especially associated with Mihr yazd, Rašn ī rēstag, Way ī weh, Aštād yazd, and Xwarrah ī dēn ī weh ī mazdēsnān (*Ardā Wīrāz-nāmag* 5.3). During the first three days after death, until the fourth dawn of the deceased, he accompanies and guides the soul on its journey into the beyond (*Mēnōg ī xrad*, chap. 2) together with Srōš and Way ī weh. His association with Mihr, Rašn, and Srōš is a reflection of doctrines already present in the Avesta (cf. Gershevitch, *Avestan Hymn*, pp. 193f.). Furthermore, as has been noted by J. P. de Menasce (see above), Wahrām enjoyed a special "promotion" within the Zoroastrian pantheon, becoming the seventh of the Amahraspandān, the "victorious" (*pērōzgar*) because he had managed to drive Ahriman back into hell (cf. Dumézil, *Heur et malheur*, pp. 183ff.).

The popularity of Bahrām has always been great among the Zoroastrian communities, even after the Sasanian era. Bahrām has always, in fact, conserved his outstanding position, thanks both to the late association with *vərəθraγan- ātar*, the *ādūr ī warahrān* or the *Ātaš Bahrām* (see above) and to his role as the protector of wayfarers and travelers (M. Boyce, *Zoroastrians. Their Religious Beliefs and Practices*, London, 1979, pp. 89, 218).

See also AŽDAHĀ.

Bibliography: Given in the text. See also Gray, *Foundations*, pp. 117-19. H. Lommel, *Der arische Kriegsgott*, Frankfurt, 1939. J. Duchesne-Guillemin, *Zoroastre. Étude critique avec une traduction commentée des Gâthâ*, Paris, 1948, pp. 43-46.

(G. GNOLI)

ii. REPRESENTATION IN IRANIAN ART

Art representations of Bahrām, the god of victory, reflect the perception of his being as understood through religious and mythological data of various periods. He is represented in different forms throughout the centuries of Iranian art according to prevailing norms and art styles of each period. During the Seleucid, Parthian, and early Sasanian periods he is depicted as the Greek Herakles, a naked male figure holding a club manifesting physical strength. Later in the Sasanian period, the deity is pictured as the victorious fire of the Sasanians, *ātaš ī Wahrām* (see ĀTAŠ) on seals and coins and as different animal incarnations enumerated in *Yašt* 14 and represented in Sasanian art.

The life-size rock sculpture of Herakles carved beside the main east-west highway at Bīsotūn near Kermānšāh may reflect the fact that the Iranian god was the patron divinity of travelers. He is there shown in a reclining position holding a goblet in his left hand; his club is by his feet, and a lion skin is outlined on the rock below. An inscription dates the sculpture to 163 of the Seleucid era, i.e., 148 B.C. (Georgina Herrmann, *The Iranian Revival*, Oxford, 1977, p. 31; M. Boyce, "Iconoclasm among the Zoroastrians," in *Christianity, Judaism and other Greco-Roman Cults: Studies for Morton Smith at Sixty*, ed. J. Neusner, Leiden, 1975, p. 100). A shrine of Herakles has been identified at Masjed(-e) Solaymān and a stone statue found there shows the god grasping the Nemean lion (Roman Ghirshman, "La terrace sacrée de Masjid-i-Solaiman," *Comptes rendus de l'Académie des inscriptions et belles-lettres*, 1969, p. 484). Figurines of Herakles have been found in the ruins of Seleucia on the Tigris (W. Von Ingen, *Figurines from Seleucia on the Tigris*, Ann Arbor, 1939, pp. 106-08, pl. XVIII), at Susa (Herrmann, op. cit., p. 39), sculptures at Palmyra and Dura-Europos (S. Downey, *The Excavations at Dura-Europos*, Final Report, III/1, fasc, 1: *The Heracles Sculpture*, New York, 1969), and stele of Assur (W. Andrae, *Das wiedererstandene Assur*, Leipzig, 1938, p. 175, pl. 80d). At the site of Nimrud Dagh, Bahrām is equated with Herakles in sculptures and inscriptions of Mithradates Kallinikos and in those of his son Antiochus, dated to the first century B.C. Figures of syncretistic Iranian and Greek gods are represented next to the figure of Antiochus on each side of his funerary mound. One of the gods is identified by an inscription as Artagnes-Herakles-Ares (Helmut Waldmann, *Die kommagenischen Kultreformen unter König Mithradates I. Kallinikos und seinem Sohn Antiochus I*, Leiden, 1973, pp. 8ff., 36ff.). An image of Herakles has been noted next to a row of figures on a rock in the Šīmbār valley in Elymais, dated to A.D. 100 (M.A.R. Colledge, *Parthian Art*, New York, 1977, p. 92).

In the early Sasanian period Bahrām is still represented as the Greek Herakles. In the investiture relief of Ardašīr I at Naqš-e Rajab III, one of the two small figures facing each other inserted between the figures of Ahura Mazdā and the king is Bahrām. He is represented in the nude and holding a club in his right hand and a lion's skin in his left hand (Louis Vanden Berghe, *Reliefs rupestres de l'Iran ancien*, Brussels, 1984, pp. 126-27, fig. 9). Perhaps Bahrām the god is the patron deity of the future Sasanian king Bahrām I, the other small figure in the relief pictured as facing him and paying homage to him. It is significant that five Sasanian kings were named after this deity.

It is during the Sasanian period that *wahrām* is noted as the generic name of the principal fires. According to J. Duchesne-Guillemin it may be the Bahrām fire that is represented by the throne-altar seen on the reverse of certain coins, and by the head in the altar flames of others ("Zoroastrian Religion," *Camb. Hist. Iran* III/2, p. 903). In the *Dādistān ī dēnīg* 31.7 it is stated that Bahrām is seen in the fire (E. W. West, *Pahlavi Texts*, SBE 18, Delhi, 1965, p. 65).

The bird on an altar depicted on a Sasanian intaglio (*Survey of Persian Art*, 2nd ed., Tokyo, 1964, pl. 255T) represents Bahrām, for the falcon is his bird (J. Duchesne-Guillemin, op. cit., p. 903). Moreover wings on the crowns of Sasanian kings derive from a bird of prey associated with Bahrām. This emblem signified the special relationship between the king and his patron deity Bahrām. It is first seen on the crown of Bahrām II who bears the god's name and is later copied by King Pērōz whose name means victorious, as well as King K̲osrow Parwēz also bearing victory in his name (Kurt Erdmann, "Die Entwicklung der sasanidischen Krone," *Ars Islamica* 5, 1951, p. 87 n. 4).

Boar and eagle heads on the caps of crown princes also symbolize this deity (R. Göbl, "Sasanian Coins," *Camb. Hist. Iran* III/1, pp. 326-27). Boar figures are widespread in Sasanian art and occur in stucco and on silver, textiles, and seals (Kurt Erdmann, "Eberdarstellung und Ebersymbolik in Iran," *Bonner Jahrbücher* 147, 1942, pp. 345-83). It has been argued that this figure represents Bahrām in his most ferocious aspect, for in this form he accompanies Mithra in *Yašt* 10.70; and in his own *Yašt* 14.15 his strength as a powerful attacking boar is well emphasized (E. Benveniste et L. Renou, *Vṛtra et Vṛθragna*, Paris, 1934, pp. 34ff.). Probably the boar motif on the seal which is stated by Moses of Kałankatouc' and by Faustus of Byzantium to constitute the seal of the state is a figuration of Bahrām (M. K. Patkanian, "Essai d'une histoire de la dynastie des Sassanides d'après les renseignements fournis par les historiens arméniens," *JA* 7, 1866, p. 113). Other animal motifs on Sasanian seals have also been identified as possible avatars of Bahrām (Christopher J. Brunner, *Sasanian Stamp Seals in the Metropolitan Museum of Art*, New York, 1978, pp. 78, 92, 102, 104).

Bibliography: Given in the text. See also the general works Christensen, *Iran Sass*. R. Ghirshman, *Iran, Parthians and Sasanians*, London, 1962. R. Göbl, *Sasanidische Numismatik*, Brunswick, 1968. E. Herzfeld, *Iran in the Ancient East*, Oxford, 1941. J. Kröger, *Sasanidischer Stückdekor*, Mainz, 1982. V. Lukonin, *Persia* II, London, 1971.

(P. JAMZADEH)

BAHRĀM, the name of six Sasanian kings and of several notables of the Sasanian and later periods. The name derives from Old Iranian Vṛθragna, Avestan Vərəθraγna, the god of victory (see above), Middle Persian Warahrān, Wahrām (most often spelled wlhl'n), Parthian *Warθagn, borrowed into Armenian as Vahagn, and Wa(r)hrām (spelled wryhrm), borrowed into Armenian as Vṙam. See also Justi, *Namenbuch*, pp. 361-65; H. Humbach and P. O. Skjærvø, *The Sassanian Inscription of Paikuli* III/1, Wiesbaden, 1983, pp. 130-31; *Iranisches Personennamenbuch* II/2, p. 171.

i. *Bahrām I, son of Šāpūr I.*
ii. *Bahrām II, son of Bahrām I.*
iii. *Bahrām III, son of Bahrām II.*
iv. *Bahrām IV, son of Bahrām III(?).*
v. *Bahrām V Gōr, son of Yazdegerd I.*
vi. *Bahrām V Gōr in Persian legend and literature.*
vii. *Bahrām VI Čōbīn.*

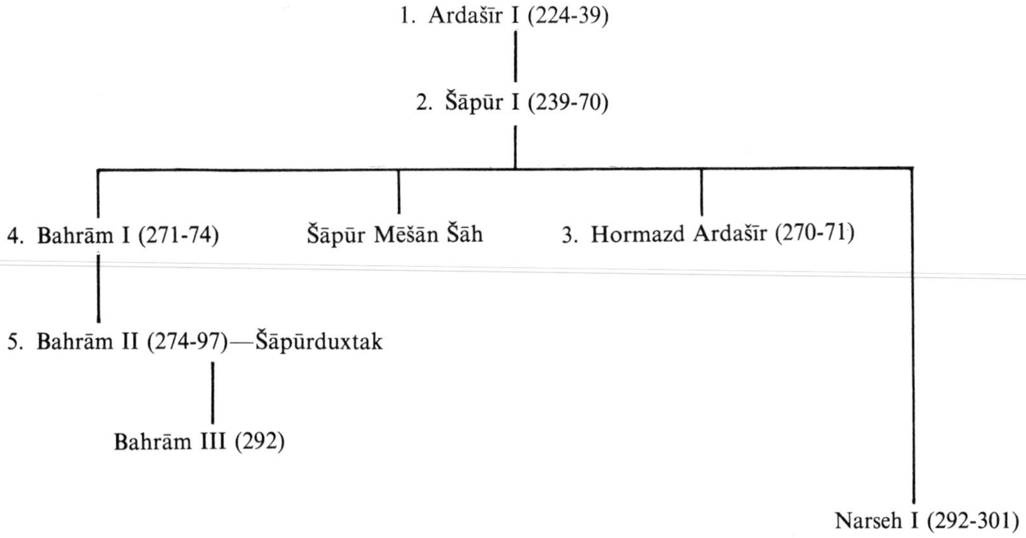

Figure11. The order of succession of the early Sasanian kings

i. Bahrām I

Bahrām I, the fourth Sasanian king and son of Šāpūr I, succeeded Hormozd (Ohrmezd) I and ruled from June, 271 until September, 274 (for the chronology of the early Sasanians, the findings of W. B. Henning, *Asia Major*, 1957, p. 116, are followed here). Four of Šāpūr's sons are named in his Kaʿba-ye Zardošt inscription (A. Maricq, *Classica et Orientalia*, Paris, 1965, pp. 61-62): Bahrām Gēlān Šāh, Šāpūr Mēšān Šāh (King of Mesene), Hormozd (Ohrmezd) Ardašīr, Wuzurg Šāh ī Arminān (Great King of Armenia), and Narseh Sakān Šāh (King of the Sakas, exceptionally honored later in the inscription, Maricq, ibid., p. 58, as "the noble Mazdā-worshipping Narseh, King of Sind, Sakastān, and Tūrān to the edge of the sea"). The order shows that Bahrām was the eldest son (Henning, "Notes on the Great Inscription of Šāpūr I," in *Professor Jackson Memorial Volume*, Bombay, 1954, p. 419 n. 6), and indeed, the prince is shown on the Naqš-e Rajab investiture relief of Ardašīr I, facing his name-deity Bahrām, who is figured in the Hellenistic guise of Herakles, nude and club in hand (W. Hinz, *Altiranische Funde und Forschungen*, Berlin, 1969, p. 124 with pl. 59). However, despite Bahrām's age and Narseh's exalted position, the succession of Šāpūr had been decided in favor of Hormozd Ardašīr, who, however, reigned for only just over a year. Then Bahrām ascended the throne, probably with the help of the influential priest, Kardēr. Narseh probably looked upon Bahrām as a usurper (see BAHRĀM, iii), but had to settle for the second rank in the empire, becoming "Great King of Armenia" (V. Lukonin, "Varakhran i Narse," in *VDI* I, 1964, pp. 48ff.; H. Humbach and P.O. Skjærvø, *The Sassanian Inscription of Paikuli* III/1, Wiesbaden, 1983, pp. 66ff.).

Bahrām was fond of fighting, hunting, and feasting, which he regarded as virtues (Henning, "Mani's Last Journey," *BSOS* 10, 1942, p. 951), and Sasanian-based sources praised him as a benevolent and worthy king. This was no doubt partly due to his reversal of Šāpūr's policy of religious tolerance, which enabled the clergy led by Kardēr to proceed with the establishment of a Zoroastrian state church. In 274, he ordered the imprisonment and subsequent execution of Mani, and the persecution of his followers (Henning, ibid., pp. 949ff.). Otherwise Bahrām's short reign was uneventful. His coins show him wearing the characteristic crown of Mithra: a headgear adorned with ray-shaped spikes (K. Erdmann, "Die Entwicklung der sasanidischen Krone," *Ars Islamica* 15-16, 1951, p. 96; R. Göbl, *Sasanian Numismatics*, Brunswick, 1971, p. 43, pl. 3 nos. 40-47). The lost Book of the Portraits of Sasanian Kings (Ḥamza, p. 50) depicted Bahrām I as standing, holding a lance in the right hand and leaning upon a sword held in the left, and wearing red gown and trousers and a gold crown topped with a sky-blue globe (Erdmann, op. cit., p. 96 n. 3). Following Ardašīr and Šāpūr, Bahrām I symbolized his accession in a rock-relief (Bīšāpūr IV) showing him on horseback, receiving the diadem of royalty from Ohrmezd, also shown mounted. The relief is accompanied by a Mid. Pers. inscription. The dignified spirituality of the king, the sweeping gesture of the god, the finely balanced composition, and the proportionate, majestic figures of the horses make this monument "artistically the most appealing example of Sasanian rock sculpture" (E. F. Schmidt, *Persepolis* III: *The Royal Tombs and Other Monuments*, Chicago, 1970, p. 129. See further F. Sarre and E. Herzfeld, *Iranische Felsreliefs*, Berlin, 1910, pp. 215ff.; G. Herrmann and R. Howell, *The Sasanian Rock Reliefs at Bishapur*, pt. 2, Iranische Denkmäler, Lief. 10, Berlin,

1981). Later, Narseh tampered with this sculpture and substituted his own name for that of Bahrām (see Schmidt, op. cit., p. 129 n. 71 for reference).

Bibliography: See also Ṭabarī, tr. Nöldeke, *Geschichte der Perser*, pp. 47-48. Other Oriental, Greek, and Syriac sources are listed by Justi, *Namenbuch*, p. 361 no. 7. The identification of Bahrām I with Bahrām Kūšān Šāh, who on his coins wears a crown adorned with a pair of ram's horns and who is known also from a Sasanian silver plate now in the Hermitage (K. Erdmann, "Die sasanidischen Jagdschalen," in *Jahrb. d. preuss. Kunstsammlung* LIX, 1930, p. 190 with references) must be rejected on the evidence of the Kaʿba-ye Zardošt inscription which specifies that Bahrām was King of Gēlān. On Bahrām's religious policy see further W. Hinz, "Mani and Kardēr," in *La Persia nel medioevo*, Rome, 1971, pp. 485ff.

(A. Sh. Shahbazi)

ii. Bahrām II

Bahrām II, the fifth Sasanian king, succeeded his father Bahrām I in September, 274 (cf. W. B. Henning, *Asia Major*, 1957, p. 116) and reigned for 17¼ years (Nöldeke, *Geschichte der Perser*, p. 415), i.e., till the end of 291. He regarded the high priest Kardēr as his mentor and bestowed on him many honors and the new title "savior of Bahrām's soul," promoted him to the rank of noble (*wuzurg*), appointed him the custodian of the dynastic shrine of Ādur Anāhīd at Eṣṭaḵr, and the supreme judge of the empire. Under the influence and leadership of Kardēr, the consolidation of the state religion continued and non-Zoroastrians, such as the Manicheans and Christians, were persecuted (J. Duchesne-Guillemin, in *CHI* III/2, 1983, pp. 881ff. with literature). Bahrām himself showed a special devotion to his name-deity by naming his son Bahrām and choosing the wings of the god's bird, Av. *vārəγna*, as the main element of his crown (E. Herzfeld, *AMI* 9, 1938, pp. 110ff.; K. Erdmann, "Die Entwicklung der sasanidischen Krone," *Ars Islamica* 15-16, 1951, pp. 97ff.). In the political arena, Bahrām II faced substantial difficulties. Vopiscus (*Vita Cari* 8, in *Scriptores Historiae Augustae*) reports that the Romans under Emperor Carus invaded Mesopotamia while the Persians were engaged in civil war. Claudius Mamertinus adds that Bahrām's brother Ormies (Hormazd) rebelled and was supported by the Saccis (Sakastanians), Gellis (Gēlān/Gēls), and Ruffis. The last name was amended by Markwart (*Ērānšahr*, p. 36) into Cussis "Kūšāns," and on this emended form Herzfeld based a case for the identification of the rebel Hormozd with an eastern king who styled himself on his coins Ohromoz Kūšān Šāhān Šāh (*Paikuli* I, Berlin, 1924, pp. 42ff., and more fully in *Kushano-Sasanian Coins*, Calcutta, 1930, pp. 7ff.). However, the Latin form for the Kūšāns being *Cusenis*, the emendation is unsatisfactory, and Hormozd Kūšān Šāhān Šāh may well have been a vassal of Šāpūr II (J. M. Rosenfield, *The Dynastic Arts of the Kushans*, Berkeley and Los Angeles, 1967, pp. 117ff. with literature). The rebellion of Hormozd was, in any event, centered on Sakastān, and lasted for several years. It was finally crushed, and, as Agathias reports (4.24), Bahrām II conquered the people of Sakastān and made his son, Bahrām, governor of that region with the title Sakān Šāh (*Sagestanōn basileus*). The Romans meanwhile took advantage of Bahrām's preoccupation in the east, and advanced on Ctesiphon without meeting much resistance, but suddenly withrew upon the death in mysterious circumstances of Emperor Carus. Bahrām then regained Mesopotamia and arranged a peace treaty with Emperor Diocletian (Vopiscus, *Vita Probus* 17, explained by Nöldeke, *Geschichte der Perser*, p. 94 n. 1; Zonaras 12.30; W. Ensslin, "Zur Ostpolitik des Kaisers Diokletian," *Sb. der bayer. Ak. der Wiss.*, 1942, p. 9).

Under Bahrām II Sasanian art achieved a high degree of excellence especially in the representations of the king and his courtiers. The lost Book of Portraits of Sasanian Kings (Ḥamza, p. 50) depicted Bahrām II as enthroned, holding a bow with an arrow by its string in the right hand (cf. the seated archer on Arsacid coins), and wearing a red gown, green trousers, and a crown adorned with a sky-blue globe (Erdmann, art. cit., p. 96 n. 35). He is better known from his coin portraits and rock reliefs. The coins are of four types (V. Lukonin, *Iran v III veke/Iran in the Third Century*, Moscow, 1979, pp. 155ff.; R. Göbl, *Sasanian Numismatics*, Brunswick, 1971, pp. 43ff.). One type shows Bahrām alone; another with his wife (Šāpūrduxtak, a daughter of Šāpūr Mēšān Šāh, hence the king's cousin: V. Lukonin, *Kul'tura sasanidskogo Irana*, Moscow, 1969, p. 112; W. Hinz, *Altiranische Funde und Forschungen*, Berlin, 1969, p. 194); a third one with his heir, Bahrām Sakān Šāh (depicted as a youth facing the king); and a fourth—and more usual—type figures the king and the queen facing the crown prince. The reverse of the coins often shows Bahrām and his queen flanking a fire altar, and in one series the latter personage is identified as "Šāpūrduxtak, Queen of Queens" (Lukonin, op. cit., p. 116). The detailed coin imagery is reflected in the ornamentation of a silver cup discovered at Sargveshi, Georgia, and now in the Hermitage (P. O. Harper, "Sasanian Medallion Bowls with Human Busts," in D. K. Kouymjian, ed., *Near Eastern Numismatics, Iconography, Epigraphy and History. Studies in Honor of George C. Miles*, Beirut, 1975, pp. 63ff., with literature). It bears four circular medallions: two enclose the bust of Bahrām, the third that of Šāpūrduxtak, and the fourth that of Bahrām Sakān Šāh. Of the rock reliefs, one at Gūyom, 27 km northwest of Shiraz, shows Bahrām II standing alone (E. F. Schmidt, *Persepolis* III: *The Royal Tombs and other Monuments*, Chicago, 1969, p. 134). Another at Sar Mašhad south of Kāzerūn, is carved directly above an inscription by Kardēr, and depicts Bahrām as a hunter who has killed a lion and is dispatching a second one with his sword; he holds the right hand of his queen in a gesture of protection while Kardēr and a fourth figure, probably a prince, look on

(E. Herzfeld, "Reisebericht," *ZDMG* 80, 1928, pp. 256ff.; Hinz, op. cit., pp. 215-16; L. Trümpelmann, *Das sasanidische Felsrelief von Sarmashad*, Iranische Denkmäler, Lief. 9, Berlin, 1975). The scene has been given various symbolic and allegorical interpretations, but it best affords the simple explanation as a royal show of courage in a real-life hunt (cf. more recently P. Calmeyer and H. Gaube in *Papers in Honour of Mary Boyce*, Acta Iranica 24, Leiden, 1985, pp. 43-49; P. O. Skjærvø, *AMI* 16, 1983, pp. 269ff.). A third rock relief, at Naqš-e Bahrām, near Nūrābād, 40 km north of Bīšāpūr, represents Bahrām II seated in full front view, flanked by Kardēr and Pāpak, satrap of Georgia, on his left and two other dignitaries on his right. A fourth sculptured scene (Bīšāpūr V) illustrates Bahrām, figured as a horseman, facing a Persian dignitary who is leading a delegation of six men resembling Arabs in their attire, who bring—perhaps as tribute—horses and dromedaries (Schmidt, loc. cit., with literature; and G. Herrmann and R. Howell, *The Sasanian Rock Reliefs at Bishapur*, pt. 2, Iranische Denkmäler, Lief. 10, Berlin, 1981). But the historical context of this monument is uncertain. A fifth relief, at Naqš-e Rostam (carved over an erased Elamite sculptured scene), illustrates Bahrām II—standing in full regalia—among his family and courtiers: to the left are shown the busts of the queen, a senior prince, the crown prince Bahrām Sakān Šāh, Kardēr, and Prince Narseh; on the right are depicted the busts of Pāpak, satrap of Georgia, and two other dignitaries (description in F. Sarre and E. Herzfeld, *Iranische Felsreliefs*, Berlin, 1910, pp. 71-73; Schmidt, op. cit., pp. 129-30; interpretation in Hinz, op. cit., pp. 191ff.). A sixth relief, also sculptured at Naqš-e Rostam (below the tomb of Darius the Great), pictures an equestrian combat commemorating Bahrām's victory over two unidentified foes, one of whom is prostrate under the king's horse, and the other is being unhorsed by a blow from the king's lance. Directly above this relief is carved another equestrian combat where a prince, probably Bahrām Sakān Šāh, is depicted as victor over two adversaries, one already fallen and the other being unhorsed. The two reliefs have been interpreted as illustrating, allegorically, Bahrām's wars with Emperor Carus and Hormozd Kūšān Šāhān Šāh (A. D. H. Bivar, "Cavalry Equipment and Tactics on the Euphrates Frontier," *Dumbarton Oaks Papers* 26, 1972, pp. 279ff.). However, while the reference to the Romans may well be accepted, Hormozd Kūšān Šāhān Šāh must be excluded on account of chronology and the fact that Hormozd, the younger brother of Bahrām II, was not king of the Kūšāns (see above). Finally, there are two pairs of figures carved at Barm-e Delak (q.v.), 10 km southeast of Shiraz, one showing Bahrām II standing and facing Kardēr, the other representing a princess and an unidentified dignitary (Erdmann, "Die sasanidischen Felsreliefs von Barmi Dilak," *ZDMG* 99, 1949, pp. 50ff.; Schmidt, op. cit., p. 133; Hinz, op. cit., pp. 217ff.), but the context is not certain.

Bibliography: Oriental sources are listed in Justi, *Namenbuch*, p. 362 no. 9, but their data are inaccurate and insufficient. For silver-works attributable to Bahrām II see K. Erdmann, *Ars Islamica* 15-16, 1951, p. 97. Bahrām II's rock reliefs have been stylistically studied by G. Herrmann, "The Sculptures of Bahram II," *JRAS* 1970, pp. 165-71.

(A. Sh. Shahbazi)

iii. Bahrām III

Bahrām III, Sakān Šāh (corrupt orthography: Šāhanšāh), the sixth Sasanian king, son of Bahrām II (less likely of Hormozd I, see Nöldeke, *Geschichte der Perser*, p. 49 n. 1, p. 436a n. 3), ruled for four months. He was proclaimed king (despite his reluctance, it is claimed, see E. Herzfeld, *Paikuli* I, Berlin, 1924, p. 171 with reference) in Fārs, by a group of nobles led by Wahnām, son of Tatrus, and supported by Ādurfarrōbay, king of Mēšān. But an assembly of many nobles, including the heads of great families as well as the high priest Kardēr, challenged the succession and swore allegiance to Bahrām's grand-uncle, Narseh, "Great King of Armenia," inviting him to come from Armenia to Ctesiphon and ascend the throne. In a swift campaign, Wahnām was captured and executed, but the fate of Bahrām is not recorded. Narseh then tampered with the investiture relief of Bahrām I at Bīšāpūr, substituted his own name for that of the former, and added the prostrate figure of a fallen enemy under the king's horse (symbolizing Wahnām or, less likely, Bahrām III). Bahrām himself does not seem to have left any monument. A number of coins showing a king with a fluted crown were formerly attributed to him but are now assigned to Narseh (see especially R. Göbl, "Narsē und nicht Bahrām," *Numismatische Zeitschrift* 78, 1959, pp. 5-13). Also, a fragmentary silver plate ornamented with a figure wearing the fluted crown and identified in an accompanying Mid. Pers. inscription as "Bahrām, King of Kings of Iran and Non-Iran" (see S. Eilenberg, "A Sasanian Silver Medallion of Bahrām III," *Ars Orientalis* 2, 1957, pp. 487f.) is considered suspect (Göbl, op. cit., p. 5).

Bibliography: Oriental sources are listed in Justi, *Namenbuch*, p. 362 no. 10. The account given here is based on the bilingual (Mid. Pers. and Parthian) inscription of Narseh at Paikuli, now restudied and published with restored text and commentary by H. Humbach and P. O. Skjærvø, *The Sassanian Inscription of Paikuli* III/1, Wiesbaden, 1983, pp. 28ff.; cf. R. N. Frye, *The History of Ancient Iran*, Munich, 1983, pp. 375-77. For Narseh's addition of the fallen figure to the reclaimed relief of Bahrām I, see A. A. Sarfarāz, *Iran*, 13, 1975, p. 171 pls. iii, iv; and G. Herrmann, *The Sasanian Rock Relief at Bishapur*, pt. 2, Iranische Denkmäler, Lief. 10, Berlin, 1981, pp. 19-20.

(O. Klíma)

iv. Bahrām IV

Bahrām IV succeeded Šāpūr III and ruled 388-99. Ṭabarī (tr. Nöldeke, *Geschichte der Perser*, p. 71) calls him a son of Šāpūr II, but, according to Agathias (4.26), Ḥamza (p. 20), *Šāh-nāma* (Moscow, VII, p. 262) and others, he was a son of Šāpūr III, which is more likely (Nöldeke, op. cit., p. 71 n. 2). Prior to his accession, Bahrām was governor of Kermān and bore the title Kermān Šāh (a name which may linger in that of Kermānšāh(ān), a town in western Iran; Nöldeke, ibid., n. 3). An amethyst intaglio in the British Museum displays a masterly engraved bust of this prince as wearing a pearl-rimmed diademed cap and identified by a Pahlavi inscription: Wahrān Kermān Šāh, son of the Mazdā-worshipping Lord Šāpūr, king of kings of Iran and non-Iran, who is a scion of lords (see E. Herzfeld, *Paikuli* I, Berlin, 1924, p. 78).

Bahrām negotiated with emperor Theodosius I over Armenia in 389, and they divided that land between their empires. But when Bahrām's appointee over the larger Persian section (called Persarmenia) went over to his co-religionist Romans in 394, he was replaced by Bahrām's brother Wahrānšāpūr (Bahrāmšāpūr, Arm. Vramšapuh). A year later a horde of Huns swept from North Caucasus into the south and were defeated and repulsed only on Mesopotamian soil (Nöldeke, op. cit., p. 72 with references). A weak ruler, Bahrām fell victim to a conspiracy by powerful nobles and lost his life. A magnificently cut chalcedony intaglio in the British Museum represents this king, recognizable from his falcon-shaped crown (on which see R. Göbl, *Sasanian Numismatics*, Brunswick, 1971, p. 48), javelin in hand and trampling the body of an unidentified fallen enemy (see A. D. H. Bivar, *Catalogue of the Western Asiatic Seals in the British Museum*: *Stamp Seals* II: *The Sassanian Dynasty*, London, 1969, p. 56, pl. 4: BCl).

Bibliography: Sources are listed in Justi, *Namenbuch*, p. 362, no. 12. See further K. E. Güterbock, *Byzanz und Persien*, Berlin, 1906, p. 128; J. H. Schmidt, *Syria*, 1934, p. 22; Christensen, *Iran Sass.*, pp. 253f.

(O. Klíma)

v. Bahrām v Gōr

Bahrām V Gōr, son and successor of Yazdegerd I, reigned from 420 to 438. His mother was said to have been Šōšanduxt, a daughter of the Jewish exilarch (Markwart, *Provincial Capitals*, par. 74). As a youth he was brought up at the court of the Lakhmid kings of Ḥīra, Noʿmān and his son Monḏer (he had probably been banished thither upon some disagreement with his father, see Nöldeke, *Geschichte der Perser*, p. 90 n. 2). Since the death of Šāpūr II in 379, nobles and priests had increased their prestige and power at the expense of central authority, electing, deposing and killing kings (among them Yazdegerd I) at will; and they now intended to exclude Yazdegerd's sons from the succession (Christensen, *Iran Sass.*, pp. 253ff.). The eldest son, Šāpūr, governor of Persarmenia, hurried to Ctesiphon to seize the throne but was murdered by the nobles, who elected a prince of Sasanian descent, Ḵosrow by name, as king (Nöldeke, op. cit., p. 91 n. 4). Bahrām asked and received military assistance from Monḏer, and marched on the capital. Alarmed, the nobles negotiated with him and accepted his claim after exacting from him the promise that he would right his father's misrule. According to the Persian tradition celebrated in the *Šāh-nāma* (Moscow, VII, pp. 296-303) and other Sasanian-based sources, Bahrām opted for an ordeal, suggesting that the royal crown and garb be placed between two lions, and whoever could retrieve them by killing the beasts should be acknowledged as the divinely favored king; and while Ḵosrow withdrew, Bahrām underwent the ordeal and won the throne. He left the task of administration to his father's officials, especially to Mihr Narseh, grand minister (*wuzurg framadār*) of the empire. He also remitted taxes and public debts at festive occasions, promoted musicians to higher rank and brought thousands of Indian minstrels (*lūrīs*) into Iran to amuse his subjects, and he himself indulged in pleasure-loving activities, particularly hunting (his memorable shooting of a wonderful onager, *gōr*, is said to have given origin to his nickname Gōr "Onager [hunter]"). These measures made Bahrām one of the most popular kings in Iranian history. Right after his accession, he proved himself in battle against the White Huns (the Hephthalites) who had invaded eastern Iran. Leaving his brother Narseh as regent, Bahrām took the road from Nisa via Marv to Kušmēhan, where he fell upon the enemy, won a resounding victory, and obtained precious booty from which he made rich offerings to the fire temple of Ādur Gušnasp. On his return, he appointed Narseh governor of Khorasan. However, on the western front, Bahrām was less successful. Many Armenian Christians had appealed or defected to the Romans, and the refusal to surrender them resulted in open hostility in 421. Mihr Narseh led the Persian forces but engagements were indecisive, and finally a treaty was signed giving freedom of religion to the Christians in Iran and Zoroastrians in the Byzantine empire, and obliging the Romans to contribute financially to the defense of the Caucasus passes against the Huns. Bahrām then deposed the Armenian king, Artašeš (Ardašīr), son of Bahrāmšāpūr (Vramšapuh), and replaced him with a margrave (*marzbān*).

Bahrām V is exceedingly popular in Iranian literature and art (see below). His coins show him as wearing a crown with three-step crenellations and a large crescent of the moon; they also introduce certain novelties such as the appearance of the crowned king's bust within the flames of the fire altar on the reverse (R. Göbl, *Sasanian Numismatics*, Brunswick, 1971, p. 49, pl. 9 nos. 153-58). No monument has survived of Bahrām V. His death is said in one tradition to have occurred during a hunt; according to another version, he died a natural death (summer of 438).

Bibliography: The main Sasanian-based account is given by Ṭabarī, tr. Nöldeke, pp. 85-112. See also Dīnavarī, pp. 53ff.; *Šāh-nāma*, Moscow, VII, pp. 266ff.; *Nehāyat al-erab* apud E.G. Browne, *JRAS*, 1900, pp. 222ff.; Masʿūdī, *Morūj* II, pp. 157ff.,

191; Ṯaʿālebī, *Ḡorar*, pp. 553ff. For chronology see Nöldeke, op. cit., pp. 419ff. Concerning Bahrām's love for music and the role of the minstrels see M. Boyce, "The Parthian *gōsān* and Iranian Minstrel Tradition," *JRAS*, 1957, pp. 11, 30f. Armenian, Syriac, and Byzantine references to Bahrām are listed in Justi, *Namenbuch*, p. 362 no. 14, and used by Nöldeke in his notes on Ṭabarī. Bahrām's relations with the Christians are discussed by J. Labourt, *Le christianisme dans l'empire perse*, Paris, 1904, pp. 117ff.

(O. KLÍMA)

vi. BAHRĀM V GŌR IN IN PERSIAN LEGEND AND LITERATURE

The growth of legends around prominent figures is familiar in Persian literature, and the case of Bahrām V is an excellent example of this. The relatively colorless and straightforward accounts by the early historians (Ṭabarī, Dīnavarī, Balʿamī, Ebn Balḵī), which emphasize Bahrām's military prowess and his efforts to rule well, contain small hints of the way the legends will develop. Ferdowsī's and Ṯaʿālebī's accounts contain many of the characteristics of popular romances: a childless king (Yazdegerd I) who eventually fathers a son, the boy's auspicious horoscope, his precocious physical and intellectual development, his education in the three areas of letters, manly arts, and kingship, and a life devoted to military and amorous adventures and the chase. His sobriquet *gōr* (wild ass) is said to have been inspired by a spectacular hunting feat where he killed a lion and an onager with one arrow, or in later accounts, by his love of hunting wild asses.

The major versions of the romance of Bahrām Gōr are in Ferdowsī's *Šāh-nāma*, Neẓāmī's *Haft peykar*, and Amīr(-e) Ḵosrow's *Hašt behešt*. In each case the framework of the story is the same, but the emphasis and details differ considerably. Ferdowsī's is the most balanced, and presents the life of Bahrām in an exemplary fashion, many of his adventures giving him the opportunity to display qualities admired in Persian kings. Neẓāmī's and Amīr Ḵosrow's are psychologically more subtle, but also more erotic and symbolic. In the latter two the account is dominated by an elaborate framed story, focused on seven princesses whom Bahrām marries and the stories that each one tells him as he visits them on successive days of the week. The symbolism of planets, colors, and the number seven pervades the romance.

One of the most remarkable differences among the various versions of the story is the manner of Bahrām's death. Ferdowsī's version has Bahrām die in his sleep, while in *Haft peykar* and *Hašt behešt* he chases an onager into a cave and disappears. Versions of the legend by early historians have him sink into a swamp, fall into a deep pit, or drown. Most of these variants appear to be local legends. For a discussion of this question, see M.-J. Maḥjūb, "Gūr-e Bahrām Gōr," *Īrān-nāma* 1, 1361 Š./1983, pp. 147-63.

Bahrām Gōr is mentioned in early literary sources as the first person to write poetry in Persian. ʿAwfī, *Lobāb* I, pp. 19-20, quotes Arabic and Persian verses attributed to him, but the Persian ones are obviously of a later date.

The homonyms *gūr* "onager," and *gūr* "grave" have led to many puns in classical Persian poetry, such as in this line from Ḥāfeẓ: *Kamand-e ṣayd-e bahrāmī be-afkan jām-e Jam bar dār/ke man peymūdam īn ṣaḥrā na Bahrām ast o na gūraš* (Throw down Bahram's hunting lasso and take up Jamshid's cup/I have crossed this plain and there is neither Bahrām nor his onager, or: his grave; *Dīvān*, ed. Qazvīnī and Ḡanī, Tehran, 1320 Š./1941-42, p. 188).

The adventures of Bahrām Gōr are a favorite subject for manuscript illustrations. J. Norgren and E. Davis in their *Preliminary Index of Shah-Nameh Illustrations* (Ann Arbor, 1969) list thirty-two scenes showing Bahrām Gōr, the most popular of which are "Bahrām Gōr hunting in the company of Āzāda," "Bahrām snatching the crown from between two lions," and "Bahrām kills a dragon." Manuscripts of the *Haft Peykar* and *Hašt behešt* are also frequently illustrated.

Bibliography: P. J. Chelkowski, *Mirror of the Invisible World*, New York, 1975 (includes a prose translation of *Haft peykar*). L. N. Dodkhudoeva, *Poemy Nezami srednovekovoĭ miniatyurnoĭ zhivopisi*, Moscow, 1985. R. Ettinghausen, "Bahram Gur's Hunting Feats or the Problem of Identification," *Iran* 17, 1979, pp. 25-31. M.-J. Maḥjūb, "Hašt behešt wa Haft peykar," *Īrān-Nāma* 1, 1362 Š./1983, pp. 346-87. M. Moʿīn, *Taḥlīl-e Haft peykar-e Neẓāmī*, Tehran, 1338 Š./1959-60. M. S. Simpson, "Narrative Allusion and Metaphor in the Decoration of Medieval Islamic Objects," in H. L. Kessler and M. S. Simpson, eds., *The Pictorial Narrative in Antiquity and the Middle Ages*, Studies in Art History 16, Washington, D.C., 1985, pp. 131-50.

(W. L. HANAWAY, JR.)

vii. BAHRĀM VI ČŌBĪN

Bahrām VI Čōbīn, chief commander under the Sasanian Hormozd IV and king of Iran in 590-91, was a son of Bahrāmgošnasp, of the family of Mehrān, one of the seven great houses of the Sasanian period (Justi, *Namenbuch*, p. 363 no. 23). First mentioned in Šāpūr's Kaʿba-ye Zardošt inscription ("Arštāt, the Mehrān, from Ray," see W. B. Henning, *BSOAS* 14, 1952, p. 510), the family remained the hereditary margraves of Ray and produced notable generals (Nöldeke, *Geschichte der Perser*, p. 139 n. 3). Bahrām was called Mehrbandak (Arm. Mehrevandak; Justi, loc. cit.), but his tall and slender physique earned him the nickname Čōbīn(a), var. Šōpēn "Javelin-like" (*Šāh-nāma*, Moscow, VIII, p. 377; cf. V. Minorsky, *JRAS*, 1933, p. 108). Bahrām started as margrave of Ray (Masʿūdī, *Morūj* II, p. 213), commanded a cavalry force which captured Dārā in 572 (Theophylactos Simocatta, 3.18.10f.), became Spahbaḏ of the North (i.e., satrap of Azerbaijan and Greater Media) under Hormozd IV, and fought a

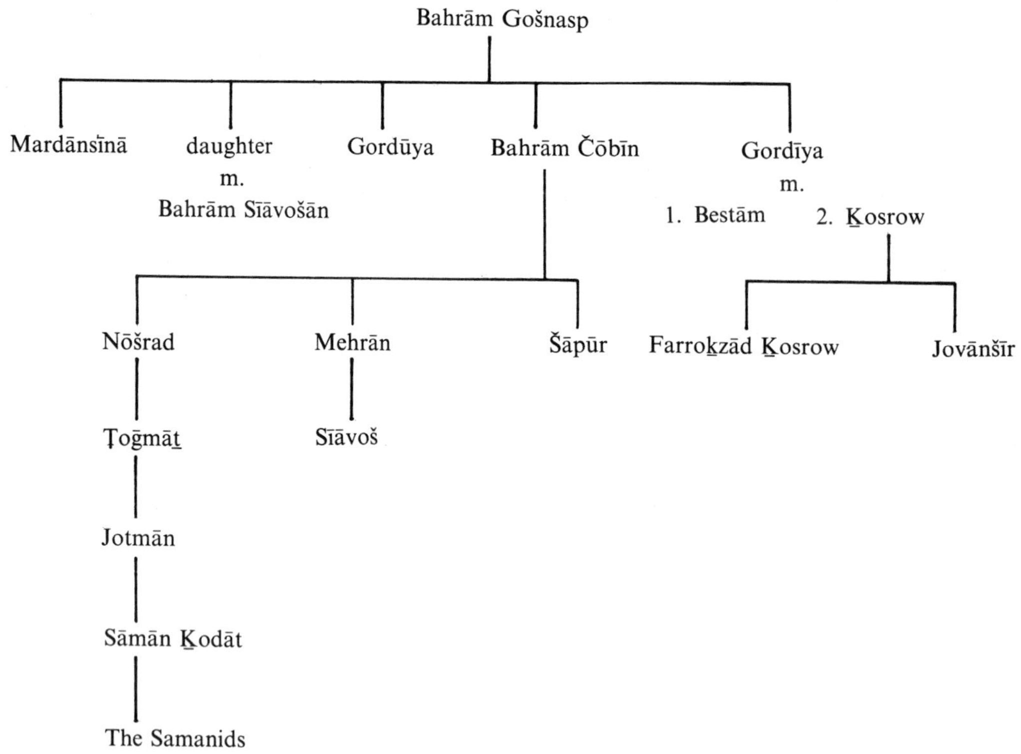

Figure12. Descent of the Samanids from Bahrām Čōbīn. (For the Samanids, see Bīrūnī, *Chronology*, p. 89; for Šāpūr, see *Syrische Kronik*, p. 9; see also Justi, *Namenbuch*, s.vv.)

long but indecisive campaign against the Byzantines in northern Mesopotamia (Dīnavarī, p. 94; cf. *Šāh-nāma*, Moscow, VIII, p. 388. For the campaign see M. J. Higgins, *The Persian War of Emperor Maurice*, Washington, 1939, pp. 35ff.). Late in 588, a horde of the Hephthalites, subjects of the Western Turks since 558, invaded eastern provinces of the Persian empire, and with the sanction and support of their overlords, reached Bādgīs and Herat. In a council of war, Bahrām was elected commander-in-chief of the Iranian army and satrap of Khorasan, furnished with a trained force, reportedly of 12,000 picked horsemen, and sent against the invaders whom Sasanian-based sources (as well as Theophylactos, 3.6) call Turks. Marching with remarkable speed, Bahrām first engaged and defeated the Western Turks and took the city of Balḵ. He then occupied the land of the Hephthalites, and crossing the Oxus won a resounding victory over the Eastern Turks, personally slaying their Great Ḵāqān (Ču-lo-hóu in Chinese records; J. Marquart, "Historische Glossen zu den alttürkischen Inschriften," *WZKM* 12, 1898, pp. 189-90, and E. Chavannes, *Documents sur les Toukiue* [*Turcs*] *occidentaux*, St. Petersburg, 1903, pp. 242ff.; falsely called Šāwa/Sāva/Sāba in Sasanian-based sources, see under Bendōy and Bestām) with an arrowshot which became as proverbial as that of Āraš (q.v.). Finally, he advanced to the famous Dež-e Rōyēn "Brazen Hold," at Baykand near Bukhara (Dīnavarī, pp. 81ff.; Balʿamī, *Tārīḵ*, pp. 1074ff.; *Šāh-nāma*, Moscow, VIII, pp. 331ff.; Ṯaʿālebī, *Ḡorar*, pp. 642ff.; Ṭabarī, tr. Nöldeke, pp. 268ff.; *Nehāyat al-erab fī aḵbār al-Fors wa'l-ʿArab*, apud E.G. Browne, *JRAS*, 1900, pp. 233ff. These Sasanian-based sources must be corrected by the account by [Pseudo-]Sebeos, tr. in Markwart, *Ērānšahr*, p. 83, and elucidated by him in *Wehrōt und Ārang*, Leiden, 1938, pp. 137ff., and K. Czeglédy, "Bahrām Čōbīn and the Persian Apocalyptic Literature," *Acta Orientalia Hungarica* 8, 1958, pp. 21ff.).

Meanwhile Hormozd had alienated the magnates by imprisoning and executing many renowned men, reducing the size of the cavalry force, and decreasing the army's pay by 10 percent (Theophylactos, 3.13.16; Ṭabarī, tr. Nöldeke, pp. 264-68). Distrustful of Bahrām even before the eastern expedition (Yaʿqūbī, I, p. 188), Hormozd could not tolerate the popularity of his own general, and giving out that Bahrām's reserving of a few choice items of the booty for himself was an indication of rebellion, he removed the victor from his posts, and sent him a chain and a spindle to show that he regarded him as a low slave "as ungrateful as a woman" (Dīnavarī, pp. 84ff.; see also *Šāh-nāma*, Moscow, VIII, pp. 397-98; Theophylactos, 3.6-8, says that Bahrām was again sent to the Roman front and was defeated in Albania, whereupon Hormozd disgraced him; Nöldeke, op. cit., p. 272 n. 3, favored this version in 1879, but one of the best non-Iranian sources, discovered ten years later, *Die von Guidi herausgegebene syrische Chronik*, tr. Th. Nöldeke, Vienna, 1893, p. 5, confirms that Bahrām rose in arms while still in the east). Bahrām's noble descent, his cultured manners and generosity, his military accomplishments and leadership skills, and his daring and shrewdness had earned him so elevated a position among his devoted troops and the public (A. Christensen, *Romanen om Bahram Tschobin, et Rekonstruktionsforsøg*, Copenhagen, 1907) that their rebellion against the ungrateful king followed naturally. Having settled his quarrel with the Turks, Bahrām appointed a satrap for Khorasan (Ṯaʿālebī, op. cit., p. 658; *Šāh-nāma*, Moscow, VIII, pp. 418f.), then marched on Ctesiphon via Ray, and was joined by many veterans from the western front (Theophylactos, 4.1). To forestall his supremacy, the nobles in the capital seized power, and led by Bendōy and Bestām (q.v.) and supported by Prince Ḵosrow, they slew Hormozd and put his son on the throne. On Bahrām's approach, however, they fled toward Azerbaijan but were intercepted and defeated, many of their troops deserting to Bahrām. Ḵosrow succeeded, through the heroic self-sacrifice of Bendōy, in escaping into Byzantine territory (*Syrische Chronik*, pp. 5ff.; Theophylactos, 4.9; Nöldeke, *Geschichte der Perser*, pp. 272ff., 418-19, 434; Dīnavarī, pp. 89ff.; Balʿamī, op. cit., pp. 1079ff.; *Nehāya*, apud Browne, *JRAS*, 1900, pp. 237f.; Ṯaʿālebī, op. cit., pp. 657ff.; Yaʿqūbī, I, pp. 190f.; Ebn Balḵī, p. 100; [Ps.-]Sebeos, tr. M. K. Patkanian, *Essai d'une histoire de la dynastie des Sasanides*, Paris, 1866, pp. 87ff. [= *JA*, 1866, pp. 187ff.]).

Bahrām entered Ctesiphon and proclaimed himself king of kings (summer, 590), claiming that Ardašīr, the upstart son of Sāsān the shepherd, had usurped the throne of the Arsacids, and now he was reestablishing their right (*Šāh-nāma*, Moscow, IX, pp. 29-32; Yaʿqūbī, I, p. 192; the humble origin of Ardašīr was already noted by Agathias, 2.27). He tried to support his cause with the following apocalyptic belief then current: The Sasanians had identified the Seleucid era (312 B.C.) with the era of Zoroaster (H. Lewy, *JAOS* 64, 1944, pp. 197ff.; S. H. Taqizadeh, *JRAS*, 1947, pp. 33ff.), thereby placing Ardašīr some 500 years after the prophet and leaving 500 years for the duration of their own dynasty (*Šāh-nāma*, Moscow, VII, pp. 90-91). The close of Zoroaster's millennium was to witness chaos and destructive wars with the Xyōns (Hephthalites/Huns) and Romans, followed by the appearance of a savior (details and references in Czeglédy, op. cit., pp. 35ff.). And Bahrām had risen some 500 years after Ardašīr (so *Šāh-nāma*, Moscow, IX, p. 30), and had saved Iran from chaos, the Xyōns and the Romans; he therefore claimed to be and was hailed by many as the promised savior, Kay Bahrām Varjāvand (Czeglédy, op. cit., pp. 36-39). He was to restore the Arsacid empire and commence a millennium of dynastic rule (*Šāh-nāma*, Moscow, IX, pp. 60-62). He issued coins in his own name. They represent him as a majestic figure, bearded and wearing a crenellated crown adorned with two crescents of the moon; and they are dated to year 1 and 2 (R. Göbl, *Sasanian Numismatics*, Brunswick, 1971, p. 52).

Bahrām's hopes were unfulfilled. Many nobles and priests preferred to side with the inexperienced and less imposing Ḵosrow, who, in return for territorial concessions, had obtained a Byzantine force of 40,000 (*Chronicle of Seʿert*, in *Patrologia Orientalis* XIII/4, p. 466), and was now marching toward Azerbaijan, where an army of over 12,000 Armenians under Mūšel (cf. Dīnavarī, p. 94) and 8,000 Iranians gathered and led by Bendōy and Bestām ([Ps.-]Sebeos, tr. Patkanian, op. cit., p. 93) awaited him. Hoping to prevent a union of those forces, Bahrām left Ctesiphon with a much smaller army, but arrived too late. The two sides fought for three days in a plain near Lake Urmia, and on the eve of the fourth, Bendōy won over Bahrām's men by pledging, in the name of Ḵosrow, their pardon and safety. In spite of his bravery and superb generalship, Bahrām was defeated, and his camp, children, and wives were captured. He himself left the battlefield, accompanied by 4,000 men, and since Ḵosrow had in the meantime sent a force to Ctesiphon and had secured it, the only road open was eastward. Bahrām marched to Nīšāpūr, defeating a pursuing royalist force and an army of a local noble of the Kārēn family at Qūmeš. Ceaselessly troubled, Bahrām finally crossed the Oxus, and was received honorably by the Ḵāqān of the Turks, entered his service and achieved heroic feats against his adversaries. Ḵosrow could not feel secure as long as Bahrām lived, and he succeeded in having him assassinated. The remainder of his troops returned to northern Iran and joined the rebellion of Bestām (*Syrische Chronik*, pp. 5-7; Theophylactos, 4ff.; [Ps.-] Sebeos apud Patkanian, op. cit., pp. 92ff.; Yaʿqūbī, I, pp. 192ff.; Dīnavarī, pp. 90-105; Ṭabarī, tr. Nöldeke, pp. 275-89; *Nehāya*, pp. 238-42; Balʿamī, op. cit., pp. 1083ff.; Higgins, op. cit., chaps. II and III; L. N. Gumilev, "Bakhram Chubin," in *Problemy vostokovedeniya* III, 1960, pp. 228-41).

Given time and opportunity to deal with internal problems, Bahrām would have probably achieved no less than Ardašīr I had done, but he was faced with too many odds. It was not Ḵosrow but his superior Byzantine mercenaries who defeated Bahrām (Theophylactos, loc. cit.). The betrayal by his own brother, Gordōy, and the capture of his family severely limited his maneuvering ability. He was handicapped by the lack of cooperation from the bureaucrats, and the animosity of nobles unwilling to serve one of their own equals (Dīnavarī, p. 99; Theophylactos, 4.12; Ṯaʿālebī, op. cit., pp. 660f.). His own chivalry in letting Ḵosrow's supporters leave the realm unmolested (Dīnavarī, p. 94), and in ignoring the escape of the resolute Bendōy, turned against him by giving his enemies the possibility to unite. His religious tolerance (see G. Widengren,

Iranica Antiqua 1, 1961, pp. 146-47) alienated the powerful clergy (Theophylactos, 4.12f.; Ṭabarī, tr. Nöldeke, p. 282). Even the apocalyptic belief he put to use was masterfully turned against him when Ḵosrow employed the following propaganda devices. He initially remitted one half of the annual poll-tax (Dīnavarī, p. 102), and bestowed riches on great fire temples (cf. *Šāh-nāma*, Moscow, IX, pp. 104f., 136). He then ordered his secretaries to publish an account of the events from the rise of Bahrām to the restoration of Ḵosrow (Bayhaqī, *al-Maḥāsen wa'l-masāwī*, ed. F. Schwally, Giessen, 1902, p. 481) wherein Bahrām was pictured as a soldier of fortune and an evil usurper. Finally, Ḵosrow circulated a modified version of the apocalyptic prophecy according to which the end of Zoroaster's millennium was to witness the arrival with a vast army of a lowly false pretender from Khorasan, his usurpation of the throne, and his swift disappearance, followed by a short period of foreign rule over Iran and the restoration of peace and prosperity by a "victorious king" (*aparvēž xvatāy*) who would even take many cities from the Romans; and since Ḵosrow had restored the kingdom and destroyed the lowly usurper Bahrām, he now claimed to be the true savior of Iran, and assumed the title Aparvēž, Parvēz (Czeglédy, op. cit., pp. 32ff.). However, Bahrām's memory was immortalized in a masterfully composed Pahlavi romance, the *Bahrām Čōbīn-nāma* (Mas'ūdī, *Morūj* II, p. 223; *Fehrest*, p. 305; Bal'amī, op. cit., p. 1081), which was translated by Jabala b. Sālem (*Fehrest*, loc. cit.), and found its way—intermingled with another account, favorable to Ḵosrow Parvēz—into the works of Dīnavarī (pp. 81-104), Ferdowsī (*Šāh-nāma*, Moscow, VIII, pp. 331-430 and IX, pp. 10-178), Bal'amī (op. cit., pp. 1073ff.), and the *Nehāya* (pp. 233ff.). The picture of Bahrām in the romance is that of an illustrious knight of kingly origins and noble disposition, a superb, highly educated and disciplinarian general, and a witty, just, and wise king. He is the best archer, and comes from the family of Mēlād (Mithridates/Mehrdād) the Arsacid, himself of the line of Kay Āraš (q.v.), son of Kay Qobād (who is here confused with the famous archer: J. Marquart, *ZDMG* 69, 1895, pp. 633-35). When Iran is simultaneously attacked by the Romans, the Ḵazars, the Arabs, and the Turks, he saves the empire by crushing the most dangerous enemy, the Turks; and he takes action against Hormazd who had unjustly disgraced him, only after his troops and an assembly of nobles urge him to do so. His accession to the throne is sanctioned by the nobles, and he fights for his right with gallantry and pluck. Above all, he is a man of his word, devoted to his men and his fatherland. The novel describes details of his life, thoughts and deeds with such vividness and moving affection that its reflection in the *Šāh-nāma* counts as one of the masterpieces of Persian literature (Nöldeke, *Geschichte der Perser*, pp. 474-78). It clearly was published while Bahrām's memory was still very much alive, and its form and main features have been restored by Arthur Christensen (op. cit.).

Bahrām is credited with the writing of a manual on archery (*Fehrest*, p. 304). He was survived by three sons: Šāpūr, who supported Bestām's rebellion and was executed (*Syrische Chronik*, p. 9); Mehrān, whose own son, Sīāvoš, King of Ray, fell fighting the Arabs in 643 (Justi, *Namenbuch*, p. 300 no. 9); and Nōšrad, the ancestor of the Samanids (Bīrūnī, *Chronology*, p. 48). The popularity of Bahrām persisted in Iranian nationalist circles long after his death. Thus, Senbād could claim that Abū Moslem (q.v.) had not died but was staying with the Savior (Mahdī) in a "Brazen Hold" (i.e., Bahrām's residence in Turkistan), and will soon return (Czeglédy, op. cit., pp. 40-41 citing Neẓām al-molk, *Sīar al-molūk* [*Sīāsat-nāma*], ed. H. Darke, 1347 Š./1968, p. 280).

Bibliography: Given in the text.

(A. Sh. Shahbazi)

BAHRĀM, newspaper founded in Tehran in Bahman, 1321 Š./February, 1943 by 'Abd-al-Raḥmān Farāmarzī, a journalist of note and himself editor of the daily *Keyhān* (q.v.). The editor was Parvīz Ḵaṭībī. It had a somewhat checkered career, first appearing as a substitute for the newspaper *Keyhān*, which at that time was a left-leaning publication. During 1323 Š./1944, it became temporarily the organ of the middle-of-the-road party 'Adālat, with which 'Alī Daštī, Ebrāhīm Ḵ'āja Nūrī and others were associated. Later in the year, however, its politics had once again moved leftward, and its name was included in the ranks of the Freedom Front, the group that opposed Prime Minister Sā'ed's policies. Although for some time thereafter it had no independent existence, it appeared once in 1325 Š./1946 as a substitute for the pro-Soviet Tūda party newspaper *Ẓafar*. In Ābān, 1325 Š./November, 1946, it began a new lease of life as an evening paper published by the secretariat of Aḥmad Qawām's (Qawām-al-Salṭana) Ḥezb-e Demokrāt-e Īrān (Democratic Party of Iran), with Aḥmad Ārāmeš as editor. The relationship, however, seems not to have been an entirely happy one, and toward the end of 1325 Š./early 1947, it ceased publication for the last time.

Bibliography: L. P. Elwell-Sutton, "Iranian Press 1941-47," *Iran* 6, 1968, p. 81. Ḡ.-Ḥ. Ṣāleḥyār, *Čehra-ye maṭbū'āt-e mo'āṣer*, Tehran, 1351 Š./1973, p. 260.

(L. P. Elwell-Sutton)

BAHRĀM son of Gōdarz, a hero in the reigns of Kay Kāōs and Kay Ḵosrow, renowned for his valiant service in all the wars (*Šāh-nāma*, Moscow, II-IV). During Sīāvoš's war with Afrāsīāb (q.v.), Bahrām and Zanga-ye Šavarān become Sīāvoš's counselors after Rostam is sent back from the battlefield. After Sīāvoš's flight to Tūrān, Bahrām is put in cammand of the Iranian army until the arrival of Ṭōs. The most memorable episode involving Bahrām is in the story of Ferōd. Halfway along the route of the march against Tūrān, Ṭōs orders Bahrām to go and capture a mounted warrior, whose presence on a hill overlooking the

Iranian army has made Ṭōs anxious. On coming face to face with the young warrior, Bahrām recognizes him to be Ferōd, a son of Sīāvoš and a half-brother of Kay Ḵosrow. Ferōd has resolved to go over to the Iranians so that he may join with them in avenging his father's blood. Bahrām goes back to Ṭōs, but Ṭōs rejects Bahrām's excuse for not having carried out his order and sends others to do the task. Ferōd is eventually slain by Bīžan and Rahhām. Bahrām considers the killing of Ferōd to be a wrong for which the Iranians deserve punishment by God. The subsequent loss of many Iranian troops, who are caught in the snow, and further defeats at the hands of the Turanians seem to him to be divine retribution for the shedding of Ferōd's blood. Seeing himself as somehow to blame for Ferōd's death, he no longer cares for his own life. Later on in the same campaign, he loses his whip in a battle. He takes the dropping of the whip which had his name on the handle to be a bad omen, and fears that the enemy may find it and make false boasts. Against the advice of his father and brother, Bahrām rides to the battlefield at night in search of the whip. After binding the wounds of an Iranian soldier who has been presumed dead, he finds the whip and dismounts to pick it up; but just at that moment his horse hears some mares neighing and bolts. Bahrām runs to catch it, but finds himself surrounded by foes. He refuses to surrender, but is overwhelmed by the Turanians and killed by Tažāv.

According to the *Mojmal* (p. 91), Bahrām was the master of ceremonies (*amīr-e majles*) in Kay Ḵosrow's reign.

(DJ. KHALEGHI-MOTLAGH)

BAHRĀM O GOLANDĀM. See KĀTEBĪ.

BAHRĀM B. MARDĀNŠĀH, a Zoroastrian priest (*mōbed*) of the town of Šāpūr in Fārs, mentioned in several Arabic and Persian sources as a translator of the *Xwadāy-nāmag* from Pahlavi into Arabic (Ḥamza, pp. 9, 23-24; Bīrūnī, *Āṯār al-bāqīa*, p. 99; *Fehrest*, p. 245; "Moqaddama-ye qadīm-e Šāh-nāma," in M. Qazvīnī, *Bīst maqāla* II, Tehran, 1332 Š./1953, pp. 55, 60; Balʿamī, *Tārīḵ*, 2nd ed., Tehran, 1353 Š./1974, p. 126; *Mojmal*, pp. 2, 21, 39, 58, 65, 83, 84).

Ḥamza gives the title of Bahrām's translation as *Ketāb taʾrīḵ molūk Banī Sāsān* (History of the Sasanian kings). He states (p. 24) that Bahrām referred in it to the existence of numerous *Šāh-nāma* manuscripts and great differences between them, and consulted more than twenty manuscripts for his own translation. To judge from the quotations given by Ḥamza, Bīrūnī, and the compiler of the *Mojmal*, Bahrām's translation differed greatly from Ebn al-Moqaffaʿ's lost Arabic version and from Ferdowsī's *Šāh-nāma*. For example, in Bahrām's book, Gayōmarṯ was the first man, not the first king. This suggests that Bahrām's translation was based on the texts of the *Xwadāy-nāmag*, which, in some passages, closely followed the Avesta and must therefore have been compiled by Zoroastrian priests rather than court historians. The supposition is consistent with the report that Bahrām was himself a *mōbed*.

Bibliography: Given in the text. On the *Xwadāy-nāmag* see also M. Boyce, "Middle Persian Literature," pp. 57-59.

(DJ. KHALEGHI-MOTLAGH)

BAHRĀM MĪRZĀ (923-57/1517-49), youngest son of Shah Esmāʿīl by a Mowsullū Turkman wife and full brother of Shah Ṭahmāsb; he is remembered for achievements in two areas: military and cultural. Shah Tahmāsb relied on his brother's loyalty and military valor for assistance against both his internal and external enemies. As was customary among the Safavids, Bahrām was made the governor of various provinces with the assistance of a guardian (*lālā*) who was the effective head of the local administration. In 936/1529-30 Bahrām and his guardian Ḡāzī Khan Takkalū were given responsibility for the province of Khorasan and stationed in Herat, where they had to face a siege by the Uzbeks under ʿObayd Khan from the spring of 938/1532 until Rabīʿ I, 940/October, 1533. The ability of the Safavid garrison to withstand this prolonged siege was due principally to the fact that Uzbeks antagonistic to ʿObayd Khan supplied them with food, so that eventually ʿObayd Khan raised the siege and retreated. This Uzbek retreat was closely followed by the arrival of Shah Ṭahmāsb in November, 1533, when the administration of Ḡāzī Khan and Bahrām Mīrzā was replaced by that of Aḡzīvar Khan Šāmlū and Sām Mīrzā. For the next few years Bahrām Mīrzā was active in campaigns against the Ottomans who had invaded Iran. In the fall of 941/1534, he participated in battles in Azerbaijan and in the following year harassed the Ottoman forces that were trying to regain control of the Iranian territory they had held briefly the year before. In 943/1536-37, after the conclusion of these campaigns, Bahrām Mīrzā served briefly as governor of Lāhījān with Ḥasan Āḡā as his guardian but was unable to deal with the local problems effectively. Subsequently, perhaps sometime between 953-56/1546-49, he was given responsibility for Hamadān with Čarāḡ Solṭān Gerāmpā Ostājlū as his guardian. During this period there was another Ottoman invasion in which the Safavid prince Alqās Mīrzā collaborated with the invaders by leading an army of irregular troops that attacked Hamadān and seized Bahrām Mīrzā's wives and children. They were taken to Baghdad, but eventually were returned when Alqās Mīrzā died and his rebellion was suppressed. Bahrām had three sons: Solṭān Ḥosayn Mīrzā, who became governor of Kandahār; Ebrāhīm Mīrzā, the governor of Mašhad; and Badīʿ-al-Zamān Mīrzā, the governor of Sīstān. The latter two were killed on the orders of Shah Esmāʿīl II in 978/1570-71.

In addition to his political and military activities, Bahrām Mīrzā was skilled as a calligrapher, painter, poet, and musician. He is also remembered as an important patron of the arts. His taste appears to have closely paralleled that of his brother Shah Ṭahmāsb because some of the same painters and calligraphers worked for both brothers. Rostam-ʿAlī Ḵorāsānī, a nephew of the renowned Behzād (q.v.), was Bahrām's chief calligrapher. Two important Safavid court painters, Āqā Mīrak Eṣfahānī and Mīr Moṣawwer executed figural wall paintings in a garden pavilion constructed for Bahrām Mīrzā. The only surviving example of Bahrām's patronage is an album now in the Topkapı Sarayı Library, Istanbul (Hazine 2154), which contains examples of both calligraphy and paintings, including samples by Bahrām Mīrzā and his associates.

Bibliography: M. Bayānī, *K̠ošnevīsān*, pp. 103-04, 188-203, 207-08. L. Binyon, J. V. S. Wilkinson, and B. Gray, *Persian Miniature Painting*, London, 1933, pp. 139, 183-89. Dūst Moḥammad, *A Treatise on Calligraphists and Miniaturists*, ed. M. A. Chaghtai, Lahore, 1936. Eskandar Beg, 1350 Š./1971, pp. 44, 58, 60, 67, 72-74, 79, 99, 110, 136-37, 478, 961; tr. Savory, pp. 74, 96, 98, 100, 111-12, 114-15, 120-21, 163, 182-83. Qāżī Aḥmad, tr. Minorsky, pp. 60, 75, 91, 147, 183. K. M. Röhrborn, *Provinzen und Zentralgewalt Persiens im 16. und 17. Jahrhundert*, Berlin, 1966, pp. 41, 43, 46, 100ff., 146.

(P. SOUCEK)

BAHRĀM MĪRZĀ, MOʿEZZ-AL-DAWLA, the second son of the crown prince ʿAbbās Mīrzā. Bahrām Mīrzā began his service to the court as governor of K̠oy in 1243/1828, the year his father retreated before the Russian advance. When the Russians besieged K̠oy, ʿAbbās Mīrzā withdrew his son and replaced him with Amir Aṣlān Khan Donbolī (Bāmdād, *Rejāl* I, p. 192).

At the time of Fatḥ-ʿAlī Shah's death (1250/1834), Bahrām Mīrzā was with his older brother, the crown prince Moḥammad Mīrzā, in Tabrīz. When Moḥammad Mīrzā acceded to the throne, several of Fatḥ-ʿAlī's sons and grandsons rebelled against him. The new shah ordered Bahrām Mīrzā to take control of Kermānšāh, K̠ūzestān, and Lorestān from the rebellious Moḥammad-Ḥosayn Mīrzā Ḥešmat-al-Dawla, the son of Moḥammad-ʿAlī Mīrzā Dawlatšāh, and his brothers Asad-Allāh Mīrzā and Naṣr-Allāh Mīrzā. To avoid confrontation with Bahrām Mīrzā, Moḥammad-Ḥosayn Mīrzā traveled on side roads to reach Tehran; however, he was soon arrested along with a number of princes opposed to Moḥammad Shah and imprisoned in Ardabīl. Having taken control of the southwest region, Bahrām Mīrzā captured Asad-Allāh Mīrzā and Naṣr-Allāh Mīrzā and sent them to Tehran. He then summoned his brother Farhād Mīrzā from Tabrīz and made him governor of Lorestān.

In 1253/1837-38, accompanied by Major H. C. Rawlinson, a British military adviser sent to Iran as a drill instructor, Bahrām Mīrzā set out for Šūštar to put down the Bak̠tīārī chief Moḥammad-Taqī Khan Čahār Lang (G. Rawlinson, *A Memoir of Major-General Sir Henry Creswicke Rawlinson*, New York, 1898, pp. 59-64).

Early in 1837, due to complaints by the people of Kermānšāh, Bahrām Mīrzā was recalled to Tehran (Rawlinson, p. 66). In 1267/1850, Bahrām Mīrzā became Nāyeb-al-Īāla (deputy governor) of Tehran in the absence of Nāṣer-al-Dīn Shah and his prime minister Mīrzā Taqī Khan Amīr(-e) Kabīr, who were on a tour of Isfahan. In the same year he published a military drill manual called *Neẓām-e nāṣerī*, in the introduction of which Bahrām Mīrzā mentions that 400 copies were published in Tehran (M. Dehqān, "Neẓām-e nāṣerī," *Barrasīhā-ye tārīk̠ī* 4/4, 1348 Š./1969, p. 149). The official gazette of Iran *Waqāyeʿ-e ettefāqīya* describes the manual as "well done and carefully written" (F. Ādamīyat, *Amīr Kabīr o Īrān*, p. 382).

In 1275/1858, after the dismissal of Prime Minister Mīrzā Āqā Khan Nūrī (q.v.), Bahrām Mīrzā was given the title Moʿezz-al-Dawla and appointed governor of Azerbaijan. He was governor in name only, however, having turned the entire administration over to his vizier ʿAzīz Khan Mokrī (q.v.). In 1277/1860, Nāṣer-al-Dīn Shah appointed his son, Crown Prince Moẓaffar-al-Dīn Mīrzā, governor of Azerbaijan, and Bahrām Mīrzā was summoned to Tehran. He spent the next decade as head of the bureau of military justice (Majles-e Taḥqīq wa Dīvān-e Neẓām; 1282-85/1865-68) and as governor of K̠ūzestān and Lorestān (1285-87/1865-69). After a brief tenure of nearly one year as governor of Māzandarān (1289-90/1873-74), he was again appointed as governor of K̠ūzestān and Lorestān and in 1295/1878 became the Minister of Justice. He suffered a heart attack and died on 8 D̠u'l-ḥejja 1299/21 October 1882.

Among Nāder Mīrzā's biographies of the governors of Tabrīz, Bahrām Mīrzā receives only the briefest of notices (*Tārīk̠ o joğrāfīā-ye dār al-salṭana-ye Tabrīz*, Tehran, 1323/1905, pp. 193-94), which indicates that but for soldiering he had no true interests. He seems to have been oblivious of the social welfare of the people he governed. The frequency with which Bahrām Mīrzā's provincial gubernatorial assignments changed bespeaks a mercilessness in his methods of amassing wealth, which eventually incurred the people's anger and caused his own dismissal.

Bibliography: Given in the text. See also F. Ādamīyat, *Amīr Kabīr o Īrān*, Tehran, 1354 Š./1975, pp. 292, 355, 469, 522. For a description of Bahrām Mīrzā's library, see Q. Ḡanī, *Yāddāšthā-ye Doktor Qāsem Ḡanī*, London, 1984, IX, p. 481.

(ʿA. NAVĀʾĪ)

BAHRĀM(-E) PAŽDŪ, Parsi poet of the 7th/13th century and father of the famous Parsi poet Zardošt(-e) Bahrām (2nd half of 7th/13th century, author of the *Zardošt-nāma*). Zardošt mentions his departed father in his versified Persian *Ardā Wīrāf-nāma* (ed. ʿAfīfī, p. 20 v. 389) as a man of letters (*adīb*; variant reading *ṭabīb* "physician"), *hērbad*, astrologer, and well versed in the Dari and Pahlavi languages. Bahrām's only surviving work is a Persian poem of 330 distichs in the *hazaj* meter entitled *Bahārīyat*, completed 14 Esfandārmad 626 *yazdegerdī* (655/1257). It contains a description of the beauty of spring and Nowrūz and a praise of the kings who had propagated the Zoroastrian religion and of its leaders, the righteous deceased, the prophet Zoroaster, as well as those who remember the poet and copy his poem. However, it has little literary merit and is poorly composed.

The only surviving manuscript of the *Bahārīyat* is included in a codex in the Public Library, Leningrad (see Rosenberg, introd., pp. iii and ix). The codex contains 512 folios and was copied between 1064-66/1653-55. The *Bahārīyat* covers fols. 219v-223v (being preceded by the *Ardā Wīrāf-nāma*) and bears the date 1065/1654.

Bibliography: Zardošt Bahrām Paždū, *Ardā Werāf-nāma-ye manẓūm*, ed. R. ʿAfīfī, Mašhad, 1343 Š./1965. Fr. Rosenberg, *Le livre de Zoroastre*, St. Petersburg, 1904. Dr. L. Smirnova kindly provided copies of some folios of the manuscript.

(Ž. Āmūzgār)

BAHRĀM SĪĀVOŠĀN (i.e., Bahrām son of Sīāvoš) was a supporter of Bahrām Čōpīn or Čōbīn (q.v.), the general in the reigns of Hormozd IV (578-90) and his son Ḵosrow II Parvēz (590-628). According to the account in the *Šāh-nāma*, he took part in Bahrām Čōpīn's campaign against the Turks (Moscow ed., VIII, p. 369 vv. 912f.) and supported Bahrām Čōpīn's subsequent revolt against Hormozd (ibid., v. 1528). Later he was commissioned by Bahrām Čōpīn to lead a force in pursuit of Ḵosrow after his flight to Byzantine territory. Reports of what then happened are given by Ṭabarī (I, pp. 998-99), Dīnavarī (pp. 9-95), Ebn al-Aṯīr (repr., I, pp. 473-74), Balʿamī (*Tārīḵ*, pp. 1082-83), Ferdowsī, the compiler of the *Mojmal al-tawārīḵ* (pp. 77-78) and the Christian historian Eutychius (10th century; *Annals* I, pp. 213-14). The fullest reports are those in the *Šāh-nāma* (IX, p. 50 vv. 676f.) and Dīnavarī's. Bahrām Sīāvošān and his troops overtook Ḵosrow, who was spending the night in a monastery, but Ḵosrow's maternal uncle Bendōy (see BESṬĀM AND BENDŌY) appeared in Ḵosrow's clothes on the monastery roof and tricked Bahrām into delaying the surrender until the morning and thus letting Ḵosrow escape during the night. When Bahrām Sīāvošān found out, he arrested Bendōy and took him to Bahrām Čōpīn. Despite Bahrām Čōpīn's order that Bendōy should be kept as a prisoner in Bahrām Sīāvošān's custody, Bendōy joined in Bahrām Sīāvošān's night-time carousals and contrived with promises and threats to turn him against Bahrām Čōpīn. Bahrām Sīāvošān thought of a plan to kill Bahrām Čōpīn by going to the polo field with a sword hidden under his coat, but Bahrām Čōpīn got word of the plan from Bahrām Sīāvošān's wife. (According to Ferdowsī, this woman was in love with Bahrām Čōpīn; according to Dīnavarī, she was the daughter of Bāhrām Čōpīn's sister; according to Eutychius, Bahrām Sīāvošān was the husband of Bahrām Čōpīn's sister). After the arrival of the players at the polo field, Bahrām Čōpīn proceeded to tap each one on the back with his stick in a feigned gesture of good will. When Bahrām Sīāvošān's turn came, Bahrām Čōpīn heard the knock of the polo- stick on the sword fastened under his cloak, and swiftly drew his own sword and killed him.

Bibliography: Given in the text. See also Nöldeke, *Geschichte der Perser*, pp. 281f.

(Dj. Khaleghi-Motlagh)

BAHRĀMĪ, FARAJ-ALLĀH, DABĪR AʿẒAM (1878/79?-1951), Reżā Shah's personal secretary and an early supporter who played a key role in Reżā Shah's control of absolute power. A well educated son of a bureaucrat, he held the position of the chef de cabinet of the Ministry of War during the fourth Majles (June, 1921-June, 1924) where he served as a prudent adviser in parliamentary affairs. When in October 1922 Reżā Khan came under attack by the press and in the Majles for his disregard for law and the constitution, Bahrāmī managed to dissuade the enthusiastic army officers from taking extreme measures such as military take-over of the Majles and suppression of the opposition press and advocated instead the use of parliamentary maneuvers (Bahār, *Tārīḵ*, pp. 226-43).

In 1924, possibly with the help of the army, he was elected to the fifth Majles (February, 1924-February, 1926) where, according to one observer, he used "cunning diplomatic maneuvers" to help put together the majority which eventually voted for the establishment of the Pahlavī dynasty ("Jomhūrī-nāma," cited in Bahār's *Dīvān*, pp. 359-66). Among Bahrāmī's political activities in this period was membership of a certain *komīta-ye taḥawwol wa enqelāb* (committee for reform and revolution). This group consisted of a handful of Majles deputies and supporters of Reżā Khan who had made a special personal allegiance to the leader. They regularly met Reżā Khan in his house to discuss strategy for the final overthrow of Qajar rule.

As a close aide, Bahrāmī accompanied Reżā Khan in his victorious expeditions, most notably, the one that ended Ḵazʿal's separatist claims in Khuzistan in December, 1924. On this occasion, Bahrāmī wrote on behalf of Reżā Khan the account of the achievements of the new patriotic hero thereby maximizing the latter's propaganda gains (Pahlavī, *Safar-nāma*, cited in Makkī, *Tārīḵ* III, pp. 182-290). This document is an articulate statement expressing Reżā Khan's case for a secure and independent Iran free from bandits and corrupt officials.

By 1925 Bahrāmī was close enough to the new shah to be expected to become his first court minister. Instead he was given the post of the head of the royal secretariat, a position which allowed him to maintain his personal contact with the shah. Bahrāmī was also a member of the inner circle of scholars who met the shah regularly in his early years as monarch in order to familiarize him with various aspects of Persian history and culture. Instructions were at times emotional and centered around nationalistic themes such as the glories of the past Iranian kings (Makkī, *Tārīḵ* VI, pp. 175-81).

In July, 1927, Bahrāmī joined Teymūrtāš, Dāvar, Yazdānpanāh and Fīrūz to form the short-lived, anticlerical and nationalistic Īrān-e Now (New Iran) party in an attempt to form a single party system. (Wilber, *Riza Shah*, p. 122; F.O. 248/1383, No. 409 Cline to

Chamberlin). For unknown reasons, he fell out of favor with the shah and never regained the close relationship he once enjoyed as a member of the court's inner circle. After spending some time in Europe, he returned to Iran and served as the governor general of Isfahan and Fārs. While in Shiraz, he formed a cultural society to promote new and innovative trends in arts and literature (Ḡanī, *Yāddāšthā* V, pp. 150-51). In March, 1932, he became the minister of post and telegraph (F.O. 371/16967, 1932 *Annual Report*, p. 56), and in 1933 he became the governor general of Khorasan, where he supervised the planning of Ferdowsī's one-thousandth birthday celebrations. He was dismissed in the middle of 1934 apparently over disagreements with the shah (Daštī, *Ayyām*, p. 249). The Shah's growing distrust eventually led to Bahrāmī's arrest and imprisonment in the spring of 1935, allegedly for plotting to put restraints on the shah's power (ibid.; Wilber, *Riza Shah*, p. 164). He was released and sent to internal exile on the intercession of Mahdīqolī Hedāyat, to whom the shah pledged not to kill Bahrāmī (Hedāyat, *K̲āṭerāt*, p. 412). Aside from brief intervals in the 1940s when Bahrāmī served as the governor general of Isfahan or the minister of the interior, he generally withdrew from politics and pursued his literary and scholarly interests for the rest of his life.

Bahrāmī served Reżā Shah as a parliamentarian, a skillful secretary, speech writer, and adviser. He organized political coalitions, helped create a proper image for the emerging Reżā Shah and articulated a reform program. As an educator, he helped communicate the nationalist ideas popular among many intellectuals to the new monarch. His downfall was not unusual among those early supporters of Reżā Shah who tried to get too close to the power they had helped to create.

Bibliography: M.-T. Bahār (Malek-al-Šoʿarāʾ), *Dīvān*, Tehran, 1335 Š./1956-57. Idem, *Tārīk̲-e mok̲taṣar-e aḥzāb-e sīāsī*, Tehran, 1323 Š./1944-45. British Foreign Office Archives: F.O. 371, F.O. 248. ʿA. Daštī, *Ayyām-e maḥbas*, Tehran, 1339 Š./1960. Q. Ḡanī, *Yāddāšthā-ye Doktor Qāsem Ḡanī* I, V, XI, London, 1980-84. M. Hedāyat, *K̲āṭerāt wa k̲aṭarāt*, 2nd ed., Tehran, 1344 Š./1965-66. E. K̲ʿājanūrī, *Bāzīgarān-e ʿaṣr-e ṭelāʾī*, Tehran, 1357 Š./1979. Ḥ. Makkī, *Tārīk̲-e bīst-sāla-ye Īrān* I-VI, Tehran, 1357 Š./1978-79–1362/1983-84. ʿA. Sāmī, *Šīrāz*, Tehran, 1337 Š./1958. N. Šīfta, *Rejāl-e maʿrūf-e Īrān*, Tehran, 1324 Š./1945. D. Wilber, *Riza Shah Pahlavi: The Resurrection and Reconstruction of Iran*, New York, 1975.

(M. AMĀNAT)

BAHRĀMĪ SARAK̲SĪ, ABU'L-ḤASAN ʿALĪ,

Persian poet and leading literary scholar of the early 5th/11th century. He was one of the many poets who gained access to the court at Ḡazna in the reigns of Sultan Maḥmūd b. Sübüktegin (388/998-421/1030) and his sons Moḥammad and Masʿūd and composed odes (*qaṣīdas*) in their honor; a line preserved in *Loḡat-e fors* (ed. Dabīrsīāqī, p. 158) seems to refer to Maḥmūd's successful raids into India. ʿAwfī, in his *Lobāb al-albāb*, first mentions Bahrāmī as one of this group (II, pp. 55-57) and later (II, p. 68) places him at the head of the section on poets of the Saljuqs. If these statements are correct, it must have been after the conquest of Khorasan by the Saljuqs that Bahrāmī, like his better-known contemporary ʿAsjadī (q.v.), began writing praises of prominent men of that dynasty. The date of Bahrāmī's death is not known. The date 500/1106 given in *Majmaʿ al-foṣaḥāʾ* (I, p. 449) is quite unlikely.

Bahrāmī's surviving poems are *qaṣīdas*, *ḡazals*, and graceful *qeṭʿas* in the style of the poets of the Samanid and early Ghaznavid periods. He also wrote on literary subjects. Neẓāmī ʿArūżī (*Čahār maqāla*, text, p. 48) ascribes to Bahrāmī two books with the titles *Ḡāyat al-ʿarūżayn* (The ultimate on the two prosodies), or *ʿarūżīyīn* according to Rāzī (*Moʿjam*, p. 182), and *Kanz al-qāfīa* (The treasure-store of rhyme); in his opinion, study of the two books was essential for acquisition of poetic skills. Both are lost. The title of the first book indicates that it dealt with Arabic as well as Persian prosody. The third title, *K̲ojasta-nāma*, mentioned by ʿAwfī (II, p. 56) and described by him as unequaled in its field, may well be the Persian title of *Ḡāyat al-ʿarūżayn*. Bahrāmī is twice mentioned by Rāzī, who acknowledges his debt to Bahrāmī in the composition of his own treatise on prosody, *Moʿjam* (pp. 174, 182).

Bibliography: Neẓāmī ʿArūżī, *Čahār maqāla*, ed. M. Qazvīnī and M. Moʿīn, 3rd ed., Tehran, 1333 Š./1954, nn. pp. 98-99. ʿAwfī, *Lobāb* (Tehran), nn. pp. 677-78. Browne, *Lit. Hist. Persia* II, pp. 20, 115, 116, 156-57. B. Forūzānfar, *Sok̲an o sok̲anvarān*, 2nd ed., Tehran, 1350 Š./1971, p. 1530. K̲ayyāmpūr, *Sok̲anvarān*, p. 93. Šams-al-Dīn Moḥammad b. Qays Rāzī, *al-Moʿjam fī maʿāyīr ašʿār al-ʿAjam*, ed. M. Qazvīnī and M.-T. Modarres Rażawī, Tehran, 1336 Š./1957. *Haft eqlīm* II, p. 40. S. Nafīsī, *Aḥwāl o ašʿār-e Rūdakī*, 3 vols., Tehran, 1309 Š./1930-1319 Š./1940, pp. 17, 1307. Rypka, *Hist. Iran. Lit.*, p. 432 Ḏ. Ṣafā, ed., *Ganj-e sok̲an* I, 5th ed., Tehran, 1354 Š./1975, p. 146. Idem, *Adabīyāt* I, 5th ed., pp. 567-68.

(Z. SAFA)

BAHRĀMŠĀH B. MASʿŪD III B. EBRĀHĪM, ABU'L-MOẒAFFAR,

Ghaznavid sultan in eastern Afghanistan and northwestern India with the favored honorific title (among many) of Yamīn-al-Dawla wa Amīn-al-Mella, reigned 511-?552/1117-?1157. Bahrāmšāh was one of Masʿūd III's several sons, though probably not by the latter's wife Jawhar K̲ātūn, daughter of Malekšāh, the Mahd-e ʿErāq, mother of his short-reigned predecessor Arslānšāh (q.v.).

When Masʿūd III died in 508/1115, a struggle for the succession ensued among his sons, with the throne passing briefly to the dead sultan's second and third sons Šīrzīl and Arslānšāh. Bahrāmšāh escaped imprisonment by the latter through being fortunately away from Ḡazna in Zamīndāvar at the time of his father's death. He failed to assert his claim militarily at Tīgīnābād in the vicinity of modern Kandahār, hence fled via Sistan to the court of the Saljuq sultan of the east, Sanjar. Sanjar (who was impressed by Bahrāmšāh's skill with the spear and bow, according to an anecdote of Fak̲r-e Modabber's) provided military help for the Ghaznavid claimant, and a joint Saljuq–Saffarid army defeated Arslānšāh outside Ḡazna in 510/1117 and placed Bahrāmšāh on the throne there. Bahrāmšāh nevertheless had to flee when Arslānšāh returned with an army from India, but the return of a Saljuq force enabled Bahrāmšāh to secure his position once more and to dispose of Arslānšāh once and for all (512/1118).

Bahrāmšāh now began an undisputed reign of some four decades, almost as lengthy as that of his grandfather Ebrāhīm b. Mas'ūd I (q.v.), remaining, except for one brief episode, the faithful vassal of Sanjar and the Saljuqs, a dependence expressed in the inclusion of Sanjar's name, together with that of the 'Abbasid caliph, on the coinage which Bahrāmšāh minted for use in eastern Afghanistan. Also, the Ghaznavid had to despatch his eldest son Dawlatšāh to the Saljuq court at Marv as a hostage and to pay a heavy tribute to Sanjar. Only once did Bahrāmšāh's restiveness at this last requirement break out into positive action, when in 529/1135 he renounced allegiance and the payment of tribute to Sanjar; but the advent of a Saljuq army, which plundered Ḡazna and drove Bahrāmšāh temporarily into India, brought him to heel again, and it is possible that he fought alongside other dependent princes of the Saljuqs in Sanjar's army in 536/1141 at the battle of the Qaṭvān Steppe against the Qarā K̲etāy.

The money to pay this tribute doubtless stemmed mainly from the plunder of India, which continued, as in earlier Ghaznavid times, to serve as a milch cow for the sultans, although precise details of the Ghaznavid campaigns there are lacking in both the Islamic and the indigenous Indian sources. We do, however, know about Bahrāmšāh's expedition into India during the early years of his reign in order to supress a rebellion by the general Moḥammad b. 'Alī Bāhālīmī (see BŪ ḤALĪM) and his son Mo'taṣem in the western Panjab.

Bahrāmšāh's later years were clouded by threats from the rising power of the Šansabānī family of Ḡūr in central Afghanistan (see GHURIDS). Bahrāmšāh's attempts to extend the traditional suzerainty of his house over the Ghurids brought a riposte from the latter. Sayf-al-Dīn Sūrī, Bahā'-al-Dīn Sūrī and 'Alā'-al-Dīn Ḥosayn (q.v.) captured Ḡazna in 543/1148, but the next year Bahrāmšāh reappeared from the Indian frontier lands and took his vengeance on the Ghurid leaders and those in Ḡazna who had collaborated with them. These measures provoked 'Alā'-al-Dīn Ḥosayn's second expedition against Ḡazna, which led to its destruction as an imperial capital and center of art and culture for the eastern Islamic world and earned for the Ghurid the unenviable nickname of Jahānsūz "world-incendiary" (these events are probably to be placed in 544 or 545/1150). The sumptuous buildings erected by the Ghaznavids from the spoils of India and the rich libraries assembled there were now destroyed or dispersed, and on his march back to Ḡūr 'Alā'-al-Dīn further devastated Ghaznavid palaces at Bost and probably also at Laškarī Bāzār (qq.v.).

Bahrāmšāh only dared to return from India to Ḡazna after 'Alā'-al-Dīn had been rash enough to provoke Sanjar and to suffer a defeat from the latter near Herat (547/1152). The date of Bahrāmšāh's death is uncertain, but indirect evidence from the sources would seem to place it in 552/1157. He was succeeded by his son K̲osrowšāh, under whom the Ghaznavid empire entered it final phase of being reduced to its northwest Indian provinces before the Ghurids dealt it its death-blow in 586/1186.

The Ghaznavid empire, dependent as it was on the Saljuqs and increasingly threatened by the Ghurids, was in Bahrāmšāh's reign only a shadow of what it had been in the previous century. Yet from the literary and cultural point of view, his reign was one of autumnal splendor, for his court was adorned by such outstanding figures of Persian literature as 'Ot̲mān Mok̲tārī and Mas'ūd-e Sa'd-e Salmān (qq.v.) in the early years of his sultanate, and Sanā'ī, Sayyed Ḥasan and Abu'l-Ma'ālī Naṣr-Allāh (qq.v.) in the main part of his reign.

Bibliography: The main primary sources are Jūzjānī, *Ṭabaqāt-e nāṣerī*, ed. Ḥabībī, 2nd ed., I, pp. 241-43, 336-45, tr. Raverty, I, pp. 108-11, 340-61, and Ebn al-At̲īr, years 508, 529, 532, 541, 543, 547, to which details can be added from the sources for Saljuq history (Bondārī, Ḥosaynī) and from later Persian and Indo-Muslim sources like Mostawfī, Mīrk̲ᵛānd, and Ferešta. In the absence of more extensive purely historical sources, the supplementary details which can be gleaned from *adab* works like Fak̲r-e Modabber's *Ādāb al-ḥarb wa'l-šajā'a* and 'Awfī's *Jawāme' al-ḥekāyāt*, and from the *dīvāns* of contemporary poets, are of special significance. These sources are utilized by Gulam Mustafa Khan, "A History of Bahrām Shāh of Ghaznīn," *Islamic Culture* 23, 1949, pp. 62-91, 199-235 (also published separately), and by Bosworth, *The Later Ghaznavids*, pp. 91-120, and idem in *Camb. Hist. Iran* V, pp. 158-61.

(C. E. BOSWORTH)

BAHRĀMŠĀH B. ṬOḠRELŠĀH. See SALJUQS OF KERMĀN.

BAHRAMŠĀH SHROFF. See BEHRAMSHAH SHROFF

BAḤRĀNĪ, AḤMAD B. MOḤAMMAD B. YŪSOF B. ṢĀLEḤ, described as the leading representative in his generation of Imami Shi'ite scholarship in Bahrain. His family descended from the coastal al-K̲aṭṭ, but he himself was born and brought up in the village of Maqāba, near the northwestern corner of Bahrain (cf. J. G. Lorimer, *Gazetteer of the Persian Gulf, 'Oman, and Central Arabia* IIA, Calcutta, 1908, p. 224); hence his *nesbas* K̲aṭṭī Maqābī. Baḥrānī spent some years in Isfahan, receiving an *ejāza* from Moḥammad-Bāqer

Majlesī (q.v.; d. 1110/1698-99) and joining Moḥammad-Bāqer Sabzavārī (q.v.; d. 1090/1679) for study sessions. He died of the plague in 1102/1690-91, together with his brothers Yūsof and Ḥasan, while on a pilgrimage to Kāẓemayn, and was buried there. He was probably not very old at his death, since his father survived him by one year.

Most of the meager information on Baḥrānī derives from the biographical notices of his pupil Solaymān b. ʿAbd-Allāh Māḥūzī (d. 1121/1709), according to whom Baḥrānī excelled in both *oṣūl* and *forūʿ*, possessed an eloquent Arabic style, and was also a fine poet. Of his *Ketāb rīāż al-dalāʾel* only part of the section on *ṭahāra* was known to later generations. In addition to further works on *feqh*, Baḥrānī was also the author of two epistles on logic and of several theological tractates. In the *Resāla fī wojūb al-jomʿa ʿaynan* (also known as the *Resāla fī ʿaynīyat ṣalāt al-jomʿa*), written in refutation of an epistle by his pupil Solaymān b. ʿAlī Šāḵūrī (d. 1101/1689-90), Baḥrānī argued that the full Friday service was incumbent on believers even during the occultation of the twelfth imam. None of Baḥrānī's works has been printed, and at present it is not even clear which (if any) are preserved in manuscript form.

Bibliography: Yūsof b. Aḥmad Baḥrānī, *Loʾloʾat al-baḥrayn*, ed. Moḥammad-Ṣādeq Baḥr-al-ʿOlūm, Najaf, 1386/1966, pp. 36-39. Ḥorr ʿĀmelī, *Amal al-āmel*, ed. Aḥmad Ḥosaynī, Najaf, 1385/1965, II, pp. 28-29. ʿAbd-Allāh Efendī, *Rīāż al-ʿolamāʾ*, Qom, 1401/1980-81, I, pp. 68-69. Ḵᵛānsārī, *Rawżāt al-jannāt*, ed. A. Esmāʿīlīān, Qom, 1390-92/1970-73, pp. 87-88. ʿAbbās Qomī, *Fawāʾed al-rażawīya*, Tehran, 1367/1947-48, pp. 36-37. *Aʿyān al-šīʿa* X, pp. 205-10.

(E. KOHLBERG)

BAḤRĀNĪ, HĀŠEM B. SOLAYMĀN B. ESMĀʿĪL B. ʿABD-AL-JAWĀD B. ʿALĪ B. SOLAYMĀN B. NĀṢER ḤOSAYNĪ KATKĀNĪ TŪBLĪ, Imami scholar and author. He was a sayyed descended from the Šarīf Mortażā and Imam Mūsā al-Kāẓem and came from the village of Katkān in Tūblī on the main island of Bahrain. He also referred to himself as Qārūnī Baḥrānī. Since the date of completion of one of his books is mentioned to be 1070/1659-60, he was most likely born not later than about 1050/1640. His studies took him to Mašhad, where he received the general *ejāza* of Sayyed ʿAbd-al-ʿAẓīm b. ʿAbbās Astarābādī, an Aḵbārī scholar and pupil of Shaikh Bahāʾ-al-Dīn ʿĀmelī. This was before 1074/1664 since he used Shaikh Ṭūsī's *Tahḏīb* with ʿAbd-al-ʿAẓīm's *ejāza* in writing his *Tartīb al-tahḏīb* begun in or before that year. In Najaf he received the *ejāza* of Faḵr-al-Dīn b. Moḥammad b. Ṭarīḥ Rammāḥī Najafī (d. 1087/1676). After the death of Shaikh Moḥammad b. Mājed Māḥūzī in 1105/1693-94, he was put by the Safavid authorities in charge of the judgeship and censorship of public morals (*omūr ḥesbīya*) in Bahrain. He died in 1107/1695-96 or 1109/1697-98 in the village of Noʿaym in the house of his wife's family. He was buried in Tūblī, where his tomb remained well known. Among his students and transmitters of his works are mentioned his son ʿĪsā, ʿAlī b. ʿAbd-Allāh b. Rāšed Baḥrānī Maqābī, and Solaymān b. ʿAbd-Allāh Setrāwī Māḥūzī.

The number of his books and treatises is said to have approached seventy-five, most of them on religious subjects. Some were, however, in the possession of those for whom they were composed and thus available only in Bahrain. Most of his books were compilations quoting a wide range of Shiʿite sources some of which had not been available to Majlesī for his encyclopedia *Beḥār al-anwār*. Yūsof Baḥrānī admits not having seen a single work containing a *fatwā* of his. Mīrzā ʿAbd-Allāh Efandī, however, mentions a large *Ketāb al-tanbīhāt* (apparently lost) containing his deductions of legal rules in all chapters of *feqh*. The following of his works have been published: 1. *Al-Borhān fī tafsīr al-Qorʾān*, a commentary on the Koran dedicated to the Safavid Shah Solaymān and completed in 1097/1686. It consists mostly of relevant quotations of the imams and occasionally of Sunnite sources favorable to the Shiʿite point of view without any interpretations of the author (*al-Ḏarīʿa* III, p. 94). 2. *Tartīb al-tahḏīb*, a rearrangement of the legal traditions contained in Ṭūsī's *Tahḏīb al-aḥkām* according to subject matter with some corrections of the *esnāds* in five volumes completed in 1079/1669 (*al-Ḏarīʿa* IV, pp. 64-65). 3. *Maʿālem al-zolfā fī maʿāref al-našʾa al-ūlā wa'l-oḵrā*, on the states of men in this world, death, the grave, the resurrection, paradise, and hell (*al-Ḏarīʿa* XXI, pp. 199-200). 4. *Nozhat al-abrār wa-manār al-afkār fī ḵalq al-janna wa'l-nār*, containing 251 traditions which confirm that paradise and hell are already created (*al-Ḏarīʿa* XXIV, p. 107). 5. *Manāqeb Amīr al-Moʾmenīn*, on the merits of ʿAlī b. Abī Ṭāleb quoting Sunnite sources with some explanatory comments. The identity of the author, concealed in the book, is known through the quotations of Aḥmad b. Solaymān Baḥrānī in his *ʿEqd al-leʾāl fī manāqeb al-nabī wa'l-āl* (*al-Ḏarīʿa* XXII pp. 322-23). 6. *Madīnat maʿājez al-aʾemma al-eṯnay ʿašar wa dalāʾel al-ḥojaj ʿala'l-bašar*, on the miracles of the twelve imams. Completed in 1090/1679 (*al-Ḏarīʿa* XX, p. 253). 7. *Ḡāyat al-marām wa ḥojjat al-ḵeṣām fī taʿyīn al-emām men ṭarīq al-ḵaṣṣ wa'l-ʿāmm*, containing Shiʿite and Sunnite traditions about the virtues of ʿAlī b. Abī Ṭāleb and the imams and texts supporting their imamate. Completed in 1103/1692. A Persian translation entitled *Kefāyat al-ḵeṣām fī fażāʾel al-emām*, containing some additional traditions, was prepared on the order of Nāṣer-al-Dīn Shah by the Mollābāšī Moḥammad-Taqī b. ʿAlī Dezfūlī and was published in 1277/1860-61 (*al-Ḏarīʿa* XVI, pp. 21-22). 8. *Tabṣerat al-walī fī man raʾā al-mahdī ʿalayh al-salām fī zamān abīh aw fī ḡaybateh al-ṣoḡrā aw al-kobrā*, about 76 persons who saw the Twelfth Imam down to the year 664/1265-66. Completed in 1099/1688 (*al-Ḏarīʿa* III, pp. 326). 9. *Al-Maḥajja fī mā nazal men al-Qorʾān fi'l-qāʾem al-ḥojja*, about 120 verses of the Koran alluding to the twelfth imam. Completed in 1097/1686 (*al-Ḏarīʿa* XX, p. 144).

Bibliography: Ḥorr ʿĀmelī, *Amal al-āmel*, ed.

Sayyed Aḥmad Ḥosaynī, Baghdad, 1385/1965, II, p. 341. Mīrzā 'Abd-Allāh Efandī, *Rīāż al-'olamā'*, ed. Sayyed Aḥmad Ḥosaynī, Qom, 1401/1980-81, V, pp. 298-304. Yūsof Baḥrānī, *Lo'lo'at al-Baḥrayn*, ed. Moḥammad-Ṣādeq Baḥr-al-'Olūm, Najaf, 1386/1966, pp. 63-66. K̲ʷānsārī, *Rawżāt al-jannāt* n.p., 1347/1928-29, pp. 736-37. 'Alī b. Ḥasan Baḥrānī, *Anwār al-badrayn*, Najaf, 1377/1957-58, pp. 136-40. Edition of Hāšem b. Solaymān, *Ketāb al-borhān*, Qom, 1394/1974, IV, pp. 552-56. Brockelmann, *GAL, S.* II, pp. 506, 533.

(W. MADELUNG)

BAḤRĀNĪ, JAMĀL-AL-DĪN (also KAMĀL-AL-DĪN) 'ALĪ B. SOLAYMĀN SETRĀWĪ, Imami scholar and philosopher inclining to mysticism of the first half of the 7th/13th century. Ḥaydar Āmolī counts him among the scholars who ranked the Sufi gnosis above all other knowledge (*Jāme' al-abrār wa-manba' al-asrār*, ed H. Corbin and O. Yaḥyā, Tehran and Paris, 1969, p. 498). Very little is known about his life. He evidently studied and taught in the town of Setra on a minor island of Bahrain, where his tomb was still known centuries after his death. His only known teacher was Kamāl-al-Dīn Aḥmad b. 'Alī b. Sa'īd b. Sa'āda Baḥrānī, like him an Imami theologian and philosopher who was also buried in Setra. From him he transmitted Shi'ite traditions with an *esnād* leading back to Ṭūsī (Ebn Abī Jomhūr Aḥsā'ī, *Ḡawālī al-la'ālī*, ed. Mojtabā 'Erāqī, Qom, 1403/1983, I, p. 12). He also submitted to him twenty-four questions on the divine attribute of knowledge. After Ebn Sa'āda's death he sent these questions with Ebn Sa'āda's summary answers and his own critical remarks to Naṣīr-al-Dīn Ṭūsī, presumably after the latter's departure from Alamūt in 654/1257. Ṭūsī's comments on the questions and answers are extant (M.-T. Dānešpažūh, *Fehrest-e Ketābḵāna-ye... Meškāt...*, Tehran, 1330-35 Š./1951-56, pp. 180-81, 2561-62; Moḥammad Modarresī Zanjānī, *Sargoḏašt o 'aqāyed-e K̲ʷāja Naṣīr-al-Dīn Ṭūsī*, Tehran, 1335 Š./1956, pp. 225-29). 'Alī b. Solaymān was the teacher of Kamāl-al-Dīn Mīṯam b. 'Alī Baḥrānī (d. after 681/1282). His works were transmitted by his son Ḥosayn to 'Allāma Ḥellī.

The following of his works are known: 1. *Al-Ešārāt*, about the secrets of existence, prophethood, and sainthood (*welāya*). It seems to be the same as *Ešārāt al-wāṣelīn elā 'olūm al-'amyān wa tanbīhāt ahl al-'eyān men arbāb al-bayān*, a supplement to the author's *Kašf al-asrār al-īmānīya wa hatk asrār al-keṭābīya* (*al-Ḏarī'a* II, pp. 96, 98). 'Alī b. Solaymān's pupil Mīṯam Baḥrānī wrote a commentary on it (*al-Ḏarī'a* XIII, p. 91; Modarres Rażawī, *Aḥwāl o āṯār-e... K̲ʷāja Naṣīr-al-Dīn Ṭūsī*, Tehran, 1334 Š./1955, p. 114). 2. *Me'rāj al-salāma wa menhāj al-karāma*, in which he explained the doctrine of an anonymous contemporary scholar on the existence of the Necessary Being (*wojūd wājeb al-wojūd*; Dānešpažūh, *Fehrest* III, p. 362). 3. *Al-Nahj al-mostaqīm 'alā ṭarīqat al-ḥakīm*, a commentary on Ebn Sīnā's mystical *'Aynīya* poem on the soul. It has also been ascribed, probably falsely, to Mīṯam Baḥrānī (*al-Ḏarī'a* XXIV, pp. 424-25). 4. *Meftāḥ al-ḵayr fī šarḥ resālat al-ṭayr*, a commentary on the introduction (*dībāja*) of Ebn Sīnā's mystical *Resālat al-ṭayr* (*al-Ḏarī'a* XXI, p. 329). 5. *Qeṣṣat Salamān wa Absāl*, selected from Ḥonayn b. Esḥāq's version of the story with some omissions and additions. It has been published at the margin of Ṭūsī's *Šarḥ al-ešārāt* (Tehran, 1305/1887-88, *namaṭ* 9) without mention of the author (Dānešpažūh, *Fehrest* III, pp. 260-62).

Bibliography: Majlesī, *Beḥār al-anwār*, Tehran, 1376-1405/1957-85, CVII, p. 65. Ḥorr 'Āmelī, *Amal-al-āmel*, ed. Sayyed Aḥmad Ḥosaynī, Baghdad, 1385/1965-66 II, p. 189. Mīrzā 'Abd-Allāh Effendī, *Rīāż al-'olamā'*, ed. Sayyed Ḥosaynī, Qom, 1401/1980-81, IV, pp. 101-02. Yūsof Baḥrānī, *Lo'lo'at al-Baḥrayn*, ed. Moḥammad Ṣādeq Baḥr-al-'Olūm, Najaf, 1386/1966, pp. 253, 164-65. Nūrī Ṭabarsī, *Mostadrak al-wasā'el*, Tehran, 1318-21/1900-04, III, p. 462. 'Alī b. Ḥasan Baḥrānī, *Anwār al-badrayn*, Najaf, 1377/1957-58, pp. 61-62. *A'yān al-šī'a* XLI, p. 273.

(W. MADELUNG)

BAḤRĀNĪ, YŪSOF B. AḤMAD B. EBRĀHĪM DERĀZĪ, Imami author and jurisprudent. He was born in 1107/1695-96 to a merchant family in the Baḥrānī village of Māḥūz. In the wake of Bahrain's occupation by the imam of 'Oman in 1129/1717, the family fled to the mainland, settling in Qatif (Katif). After his father's death in 22 Ṣafar 1131/14 January 1719, Yūsof took charge of the family affairs and commuted between Qatif and Bahrain while pursuing his studies. He finally left Bahrain for Iran soon after the abdication in 1135/1722 of the last Safavid shah Solṭān Ḥosayn. He went first to Kermān and then to Shiraz, where he enjoyed the patronage of its ruler Moḥammad-Taqī Khan. Baḥrānī lived in Shiraz longer than is usually assumed: his *Masā'el šīrāzīya, Kašf al-qenā'* (both completed in 1149/1737) and *Resāla moḥammadīya* (written for his brother in 1155/1742) were all composed in that city. He then moved to Fasā, where he likewise benefited from his close connection with the governor, one Moḥammad-'Alī, who exempted him from taxes on his investments in agriculture. In Fasā Baḥrānī began his monumental legal work *al-Ḥadā'eq al-nāżera* which, though it occupied him for the rest of his life, remained uncompleted. During disturbances in 1163/1750 Baḥrānī's home was attacked and many of his books and other possessions were looted. He fled with his family to the countryside, and then proceeded to Karbalā'. There he soon became one of the foremost religious authorities: he had a large circle of pupils, and also composed numerous *fatwās* in response to questions reaching him from various places. He died in 4 Rabī' I 1186/5 June 1772 at the height of the plague which ravaged Iraq, though it is not stated that his death was caused by it.

Baḥrānī is a pivotal figure in the Aḵbārī-Oṣūlī dispute in the 18th century. He originally adhered to the Aḵbārī position, in opposition to his father's Oṣūlī views. Later he adopted a modified Aḵbārī stance, accusing the hard-line Ak̲bārīs of dividing the ranks of the Imamites, and praising Majlesī for taking a middle course (*ṭarīq wosṭā*) between the two camps. In his *Dorar najafīya* (completed in D̲u'l-qa'da, 1177/May, 1764) Baḥrānī rejects the extremist Ak̲bārī view that all believers are *moqalledūn*. He defines *taqlīd* as the acceptance of someone else's view without that view being accompanied by a proof text (*dalīl*). This practice, he maintains, only existed during the period of the presence (*ḥożūr*) of the imams. In his own times, says Baḥrānī, the *'āmmī* expects each *fatwā* to be based on the sources, and the scholar, of course, uses his judgment. Thus the Ak̲bārīs engage in *ejtehād* no less than the Oṣūlīs, and only avoid using this term because they regard it as pejorative. In his *Ḥadā'eq* Baḥrānī reverts to a more traditional Ak̲bārī position; yet his overall conclusion is that both Ak̲bārīs and Oṣūlīs are devoted followers of the imams, and that even if individuals from either camp veer from the path of truth out of ignorance or inadvertence, this is no reason to heap abuse on the group as a whole.

Baḥrānī's moderate views were not shared by all his colleagues and students: some were fiercely anti-Oṣūlī while others, in contrast, forsook the Ak̲bārī school altogether in favor of the Oṣūlīs. Baḥrānī himself engaged in disputations with the leading exponent of Oṣūlī Shi'ism, Moḥammad-Bāqer Behbahānī (d. 1205/1790); however, relations between the two appear to have been civil, and Behbahānī, led the prayers at Baḥrānī's funeral.

Many of Baḥrānī's works have survived. These include (in addition to those already referred to) the *Lo'lo'at al-Baḥrayn*, comprising biographies of leading Imamite scholars from Baḥrayn and elsewhere, and the *Kaškūl* (also known as *Jalīs al-ḥāżer wa anīs al-mosāfer*), a compilation of edifying stories, anecdotes and poems of a typical *adab* type. His *al-Nafaḥāt al-malakūtīya fi'l-radd 'ala'l-ṣūfīya*, which may no longer be extant, included an attack on the more extreme aspects of popular Sufism.

Bibliography: Baḥrānī, *Lo'lo'at al-Baḥrayn*, Najaf, 1386/1966, pp. 442-51 (an autobiographical notice). Abū 'Alī Ḥā'erī, *Montaha'l-maqāl*, [Tehran], 1300/1882-83, pp. 334-35. K̲'ānsārī, *Rawżāt al-jannāt*, ed. A. Esmā'īlīān, Qom, 1390-92/1970-72, VIII, pp. 203-08. Nūrī Ṭabarsī, *Mostadrak al-wasā'el*, Tehran, 1382-84/1962-64, III, pp. 387-88. Tonakābonī, *Qeṣaṣ al-'olamā'*, n.p., 1304/1886-87, pp. 203-06. Modarres, *Rayḥānat al-adab*, [Tehran], 1364-73/1945-54, II, pp. 421-22. 'Abbās Qomī, *Fawā'ed al-rażawīya*, Tehran, 1367/1948, pp. 713-16. G. Scarcia, "Intorno alle controversie tra Aḥbārī e Uṣūlī presso gli Imāmiti di Persia," *RSO* 33, 1958, p. 224. *A'yān al-šī'a* LII, Beirut, 1381/1961, pp. 71-74. Ḥ. Modarresī Ṭabāṭabā'ī, *An Introduction to Shī'ī Law*, London, 1984, pp. 55-56. J. Cole, "Shi'i Clerics in Iraq and Iran, 1722-1780: The Akhbari-Usuli Conflict Reconsidered," *Iranian Studies* 18, 1985, pp. 14-15, 19. E. Kohlberg, "Aspects of Akhbārī Thought in the Seventeenth and Eighteenth Centuries," in *Eighteenth Century Renewal and Reform Movements in Islam*, ed. N. Levtzion and J. Voll, Syracuse (forthcoming).

(E. KOHLBERG)

BAḤRAYN. See BAHRAIN.

BAḤRĪ, MAḤMŪD B. BĀQER QĀDERĪ, Sufi and poet of the Deccan who flourished in the late 11/17th century. The son of a provincial qadi, Baḥrī spent his first twenty years in his native Gogi, a small town in the 'Ādelšāhī kingdom of Bijapur (895/1490-1097/1686). There he studied Sufism with a certain Shah Bāqer and developed ties with the Češtī order. During the reign of Sultan Sekandar 'Ādelšāh (1083/1672-1097/1686) Baḥrī settled in the capital city Bijapur; after the collapse of the dynasty in 1097/1686 at the hand of Awrangzēb, he moved to Hyderabad, and then back to Gogi, where he died in 1130/1717-18.

From the time he took up residence in Bijapur, Baḥrī adopted the life of a Sufi recluse and an anti-establishment poet, a style that he maintained for the remainder of his life. Much of his lyrical poetry reflects the outlook of an ecstatic Sufi. Notable in this respect is his Dakhnī poem *Man lagan*, translated by the author into Persian as *'Arūs-e 'erfān*, which in point of its combination of anecdotes, short stories, and didactic verses, recalls the *Golestān* of Sa'dī. Another such work is his *Bangāb-nāma*, a Dakhnī poem of a dozen cups (*jām*) which eulogizes *bangāb*, a greenish drink made from milk and *bang* (hemp, q.v.). The poet's advocacy of the narcotic drink seems to have been both allegorical and literal, for he identified its use with those ecstatic Sufi dervishes with whose values and lifestyles he openly sympathized. On the other hand, the poet scorned the urban establishment of Sufis who had accommodated themselves comfortably with orthodox Islam, citing their low literary standards, their concern merely with expanding their circles of Sufi clients, and their compromises with the court—although he himself eulogized Awrangzēb in his poetry—and the men of the world (*ahl-e donyā*). Living in a climate of political instability and religious conservatism, Baḥrī thus emerges as a social critic as well as a Sufi. In fact, he even compared Bijapur of his own day with the Baghdad of Ḥosayn b. Manṣūr Ḥallāj, probably hinting that he himself would suffer Ḥallāj's fate should he be placed at the hands of the authorities of Bijapur. He is also the author of a *maṯnawī* in Dakhnī and a short Persian commentary on the poems of Nāṣer(-e) K̲osrow (*Šarḥ-e ğazal-e Ḥakīm Nāṣer-e K̲osrow*). His *dīvān* contains *ğazal*s and *qaṣīda*s.

Bibliography: Maḥmūd Baḥrī, *'Arūs-e 'erfān*. Hyderabad, Salar Jang Museum, Tasawwuf no. 114, Calcutta, Asiatic Society, Pers. MS. 1283. M. Hafiz Syed, ed., *Kollīyāt-e Baḥrī*, Lucknow, 1339. Richard M. Eaton, *Sufis of Bijapur*, Princeton, 1978. Marshall, *Mughals*, pp. 100-01.

(R. M. EATON)

BAIDU. See BĀYDŪ.

BAIEV, GAPPO. See BAYATI̱, GAPPO.

BĀJ, a principal Zoroastrian observance meaning primarily "utterance of consecration;" reference to *bāj* has been current in Mazdean literature since at least Sasanian times, spelt in Book Pahlavi *wʾc*, Middle Persian *wāz*, Parthian *wāj*, and variously *wāj, wāž, bāj, bāž, bāz* in New Persian. Boyce and Kotwal, in their exhaustive studies of *bāj*, explain the term as deriving from Old Iranian *wā̆k-* "word, speech" and follow Tavadia's definition of *bāj* as a "particular essential formula" which precedes, accompanies, or follows an action (J. C. Tavadia, in *Dinshah Irani Memorial Volume*, pt. 2; Boyce and Kotwal, I, p. 57). Always recited in Avestan language, *bāj* serves to frame ritual actions with a symbolic boundary of sacred speech (just as the physical boundary of the *karš* "furrow" known as *pāvi* is drawn around the actual location of a religious ritual). A *bāj* must be recited without faltering, and only the prescribed actions (and none other) may be performed under the protection of that *bāj*. The major Zoroastrian liturgical rite, the *yasna*, is held to be so powerful in itself that its initial and concluding *bāj* are simply one recitation of the prayer *ašəm vohū*, by each priest, before and after the ceremony. Integral parts of the *yasna* ritual, however, have their own *bāj*, when the two celebrant priests "give" and "take" *bāj* between themselves to maintain the utmost cooperation, "so that their full ritual power (*ʿamal*) may be concentrated in order to make more effective the rite about to be performed" (Boyce and Kotwal I, p. 60). A shorter form of the *yasna* ceremony (*yašt ī keh*) contains a *bāj* which is called *yašt ī drōn* "service of the *drōn*" (because there it encloses the ritual tastings of the *drōn* "sacred portion [of bread]"). The *yašt ī drōn* was said as a service in its own right as a *bāj ī nān xwardan* "*bāj* for eating bread," i.e., as a grace for eating food at normal daily meals. Just as in temple services after the initial *bāj* was spoken no words other than those of the accompanying *bāj* might be pronounced, so with *bāj ī nān xwardan* silence was maintained until the concluding *bāj* was spoken after the meal. In liturgical and domestic contexts, if any other speech was necessary it was uttered *bista* "with closed [lips]" (New Persian *basta*, cf. Middle Persian *māwāg* "inarticulate[ly]"). Nowadays in Iran only priests eat with *bāj*, as also in India where Parsi priests do so only when maintaining high states of ritual purity and for festivals. *Yašt ī drōn*, which is known by the generic term *bāj* among Parsi Zoroastrians, is said as a powerful prophylactic prayer for many actions in daily life; such a *bāj* is dedicated to the *yazad* whose protection is believed to be strongest for the particular action. E.g., Srōš is invoked to protect against decay and death (for funerary and purification rites, etc.). Forms of *bāj* have functioned as frames for the highest religious and also the most personal human actions, and as such they have exerted a force of discipline and control upon Zoroastrian community and individual.

Bibliography: M. Boyce and F. M. Kotwal, "Zoroastrian *bāj* and *drōn* I, II," *BSOAS* 34, 1971, pp. 56-73, 299-313. J. J. Modi, *Religious Ceremonies and Customs of the Parsis*, Bombay, 2nd ed., 1937, chap. XV. T. D. Anklesaria and S. D. Bharucha, *Dādestān-e dīnī*, Bombay, 1926, pp. 48-54. J. C. Tavadia, ed., *Šāyast nē-šāyast*, Hamburg, 1930, passim.

(A. V. WILLIAMS)

BĀJ, a term denoting tribute to be paid by vassals to their overlord, in which sense it is also used as a generic term "tax," or as referring to road tolls. Its original meaning may have been "portion, share" (from the root *bag* "to apportion," *AirWb.*, col. 921). The term *bāji* is first encountered in an Old Persian inscription by Darius at Persepolis (ca. 500 B.C.): ". . . those are the countries that fear me and bring me tribute (*bājim*)" (DPe 1.9; Kent, *Old Persian*, p. 136). In Old Persian the tax collector was **bājikāra* (Frye, p. 139). In Middle Iranian times we find Parthian *bāž* (*bʾz*) in the inscription of Šāpūr I on the Kaʿba-ye Zardošt at Naqš-e Rostam in which Šāpūr, after enumerating the parts of his empire, says, "all these lands (*šahr*) and kings (*šahrdār*) stood (or: were placed) in tribute and servitude (*pad bāž ud bandagīf*) to Us;" and about the vanquished Caesar Philippus the Arab he states that Philippus paid ransom money and "stood in tribute to Us" (ŠKZ 11.3-4; Gk. version 1.9 *eis phorous*). Early New Persian has the forms *bāz* (*Ḥodūd al-ʿālam*), *bāž* (*Šāh-nāma* and the Ghaznavid poet Bahrāmī Saraḵsī), and *bāj* (*Šāh-nāma* and Dawlatšāh Samarqandī [p. 49] when he records that Maḥmūd of Ḡazna demanded tribute *bāj o ḵarāj*, from the ruler of Deylam). The word is often found in compounds such as *bāžbān, bāžḵᵛāh, bāždār* "tax collector," and *bāžgāh* "tax collection office" (Wolff, *Glossar*).

The earliest mention of *bāj* in Islamic times is found in the *Ḥodūd al-ʿālam* (tr. Minorsky, p. 120), according to which in the town of Dār-e Torbat "there live Muslims who levy the toll (*bāz*) and keep watch on the road." Ferdowsī used the word to mean "tribute," as is clear from the phrase *bāž o sāv* "tribute and tax" and from the term *bāž-e Rūm*, the tribute paid by the Romans to the victorious Sasanians.

Since Samanid times *bāj* most probably also designated road tolls, as evidenced from the *Ḥodūd al-ʿālam*. This is also true of the Saljuq era. Under Sanjar, *bāj(-e masālek)*, or road tax, was levied to ensure safety on the roads (Horst, p. 78). This usage is also borne out by Nāṣer(-e) Ḵosrow, who calls Aleppo a *bājgāh* "customs house." This use of the term is also borne out by a number of lexicographers. In the *Loḡat-e fors* (ed. Dabīrsīāqī) the word is defined as *ḵarāj* (p. 55), while ʿAbd-al-Qāder (ed. Salemann) explains it as customs duties, tithe, and tax. *Borhān-e qāṭeʿ* defines *bāj* as money taken from travelers on the road.

In Mongol times *bāj* was used as a synonym for *rāhdārī* (road tax). Rašīd-al-Dīn speaks about *bāj* taken from travelers at fixed stations on the road, at a specific rate (ed. Jahn, pp. 289ff.). Under the Jalayerids and the Timurids the word was used as meaning both road tax and tax. Nak̲javānī (pp. 167-69) uses the terms *bājgāh* and *bājdār* "road guards" and *bājdārī* "road tax," and indicates that *bāj* was levied at a specific rate, namely, one cow: nine dinars; one donkey: eight dinars; one pack animal: seven dinars; one mule: six dinars; one camel: five dinars. Šaraf-al-Dīn Yazdī (p. 378) uses it in a generic sense of "tax, impost," as do contemporary texts (Aubin, p. 94; Asfezārī, p. 393). K̲ʷāndamīr (p. 463) also uses it in a generic sense along with *tamḡā*, taken from merchants, *zakāt*, and *k̲arāj*. In Āq Qoyunlū and Qara Qoyunlū times *bāj* was used both for road and merchandise tax, as well as being a generic term. In a decree issued by Yaʿqūb Qara Qoyunlū the word is used synonymously with *tamḡačīān wa bājdārān wa mostaḥfeẓīn-e ṭoroq-e dīvānī* (Modarres Ṭabāṭabāʾī, pp. 89-90). In the Ottoman fiscal *qānūn*s for eastern Anatolia (formerly subject to the Āq Qoyunlū), which are slightly changed Āq Qoyunlū laws, the word *bāj* is used both for tax and road tax. The term *bāj-e tamḡā* refers to a tax levied on all kinds of goods bought and sold in the city, while *bāj-e bozorg* was the customs duties levied on goods in transit or imported into the country (Barkan). According to Efendiev (p. 46) the levying of *bāj* under the Āq Qoyunlūs was heavy and one of the causes of the ruinous state of Iran. Under the Safavids the term is encountered less than in the preceding periods. Ḥasan Rūmlū (p. 337) uses it to denote tribute which neighboring tribes had paid for a long time to Herat. The unknown author of the *ʿĀlamārā-ye ṣafawī* (pp. 137, 309, 343, 473, 478, 539, 542, 596) writing around 1675 uses the phrase *bāj o k̲arāj* in the sense of tribute that was paid every year by vassals (*bājgoḏār*) to their suzerain. Eskandar Beg (ed. Afšār, 2nd ed., I, pp. 35, 492, 519) uses *bāj o k̲arāj* in the general sense of tax.

In the eighteenth century Maḥmūd Ḥosaynī Monšī (fols. 305a, 360b, 660a) uses the phrase *bāj o k̲arāj* several times to designate tax in general. Moḥammad-Hāšem Rostam-al-Ḥokamāʾ (p. 180) refers to Nāder Shah as *bājgīr-e kešvarsetān* "the tax-levying conqueror."

In Qajar times *bāj* is more frequently used, mainly with reference to merchandise or road tax. In Mašhad the city gate toll around 1840 was referred to as *bāj* (Ferrier, p. 117), while terms like *bāj-e rāh* (road tax), *bāj-e namak* (salt tax), *bāj o k̲arāj-e k̲oškbār* (dried fruit tax), *bāj-e fīlī* (elephant tax), and *bāj-e Šemrān* (Šemrān tax) are also found (*Majalla-ye mālīa wa eqteṣād* 1/2, Tehran, 1303 Š./1924, p. 4; *Qānūn-e elḡā-ye mālīāt-e ṣanʿatī wa mālīāt-e šomārī*, 30 Āḏar 1305 Š./1926; Taḥwīldār, p. 123; *Qānūn-e 19 Bahman 1304 Š./1926; Qānūn-e 3 Rabīʿ I 1328/1909*; Kasrawī, *Mašrūṭa*, p. 39; Baladīya-ye Ṭehrān, *Dovvomīn sāl-nāma-ye eḥṣāʾī-e šahr-e Ṭehrān*, Tehran, 1310 Š./1929, p. 193). However, the term is also used in the meaning of tribute; e.g., when the Qarabāḡ ruler Ebrāhīm K̲alīl Khan Javānšīr was defeated by the Qajars, he offered to pay *bāj o k̲arāj* and to give hostages (Fasāʾī, *Fārs-nāma*, p. 240). It is also used in the general sense of tax, as in the firman by Nāṣer-al-Dīn Shah granting the bakers and butchers of Iran exemption from taxes in 1896 (Afżal-al-Molk, p. 20). The word is still used today, albeit with a rather negative connotation.

Bibliography: Ḡolām-Ḥosayn Afżal-al-Molk, *Afżal-al-tawārīk̲*, ed. M. Etteḥādīya, Tehran, 1361 Š./1982. Moʿīn-al-Dīn Moḥammad Zamčī Asfezārī, *Rawżat al-jannāt fī awṣāf madīnat Herāt*, ed. Moḥammad-Kāẓem Emām, Tehran, 1338 Š./1959. ʿAbd-al-Qāder Baḡdādī, ed. Salemann, *Abdulqadiri Bagdadensis lexicon Shahnamaianum*, St. Petersburg, 1895. *ʿĀlamārā-ye ṣafawī*, ed. Yad-Allāh Šokrī, Tehran, 1350 Š./1971. J. Aubin, *Deux sayyids de Bam au XVe siècle*, Wiesbaden, 1956. Ömer Lûtfi Barkan, "Osmanlı devrinde Akkoyunlu hükümdarı Uzun Hasan Bey'e ait kanunlar," *Tarihî vesikalar dergisi* 1/2, 1943, pp. 91-106, 1/3, 1943, pp. 184-97. Dawlatšāh Samarqandī, *Taḏkerat al-šoʿarāʾ*, Tehran, n.d. O. A. Efendiev, *Obrazovanie azerbaĭdzhanskogo gosudarstva Sefevidov v nachale XVI veka*, Baku, 1961. J. P. Ferrier, *Caravan Journeys in Persia...*, London, 1857. R. N. Frye, *The Heritage of Persia*, Chicago, 1966. H. Horst, *Die Staatsverwaltung der Grosselǧūqen und die Ḫōrazmšāhs*, Wiesbaden, 1964. K̲ʷāndamīr, *Dastūr al-wozarāʾ*, ed. Saʿīd Nafīsī, Tehran, 1317 Š./1938. Maḥmūd Ḥosaynī Monšī, *Tārīk̲-e aḥmadšāhī*, Moscow, 1974. Nak̲javānī, *Dastūr al-kāteb* II, Moscow, 1971. Nāṣer(-e) K̲osrow, *Safar-nāma*, ed. M. Ḡanīzāda, Tehran, n.d. Rašīd-al-Dīn, *Tārīk̲-e mobārak-e Ḡāzānī*, ed. K. Jahn, London, 1940. Moḥammad-Hāšem Rostam-al-Ḥokamāʾ, *Rostam al-tawārīk̲*, ed. Moḥammad Mošīrī, Tehran, 1348 Š./1969. Ḥasan Rūmlū, *Aḥsan al-tawārīk̲*, ed. C. N. Seddon, Baroda, 1931, vol. 1. Šāpūr I, inscription on the Kaʿba-ye Zardošt, ed. M. Back, *Die Sassanidischen Staatsinschriften*, Acta Iranica 18, Tehran and Liège, 1978, pp. 284-371. Modarres Ṭabāṭabāʾī, ed., *Farmānhā-ye torkmān-e Qara Qoyunlū wa Āq Qoyunlū*, Qom, 1352 Š./1973. Moḥammad-Ḥosayn Khan Taḥwīldār. *Joḡrāfīā-ye Eṣfahān*, Tehran, 1342 Š./1963. Šaraf-al-Dīn Yazdī. *Ẓafar-nāma*, Calcutta, 1888, vol. 2.

(W. Floor)

BĀJALĀN, a Kurdish tribe which has settled in the *dehestān*s of Qūratū, Ḏohāb and Jagarlū in the *šahrestān* of Qaṣr-e Šīrīn, on the Iraqi border (Kayhān, *Joḡrāfīā* II, p. 60). According to H. C. Rawlinson, the tribe moved from the Mosul area to the Ḏohāb area in the eighteenth century ("Notes on a March from Zoháb... to Kirmánsháh," *JRGS* 9, 1839, p. 107). Its link to the Mosul area is confirmed by the existence of a group of Bājalān villages a few miles northeast of that city (C. J. Edmonds, *Kurds, Turks and Arabs*, London, 1957, p. 10, n. 1).

One of the most prominent leaders of the Bājalāns was ʿAbd-Allāh Khan, who served as pasha of Ḏohāb for the Ottoman government during the mid-1700s. In the spring of 1167/1754, he fought against Moḥammad

Khan Zand when the latter occupied the Kermānšāh region (J. R. Perry, *Karim Khan Zand*, Chicago, 1979, pp. 55, 184). In late 1188/early 1775, Naẓar-ʿAlī Khan Zand, who had been dispatched by Karīm Khan to reestablish Zand hegemony over Kurdistan, defeated ʿAbd-Allāh Khan near Ḵānaqīn, slaughtering 2,000 of his men and seizing 120,000 head of livestock (ibid., p. 187). The Bājalāns became embroiled in the civil wars which were unleashed by the death of Karīm Khan Zand in 1779, but played only a marginally important role in them (see E. Beer, ed., *Das Târîkh-i Zendîje des Ibn ʿAbd el-Kerîm ʿAlî Riẑâ von Šîrâz*, Leiden, 1888, p. 19; Nāmī Eṣfahānī, *Tārīḵ-e Gītīgošā*, Tehran, 1317 Š./1938-39, p. 242; H. J. Brydges, *The Dynasty of the Kajars*, London, 1833, pp. 48, 58, 141).

The Bājalān lands became a permanent part of Iranian territory when Moḥammad-ʿAlī Mīrzā, the governor of Kermānšāh, occupied the Ḏohāb region in 1222/1807-08 (Rawlinson, op. cit., p. 26). The last notable leader of the Bājalān tribe was ʿAzīz Khan Šojāʿ-al-Mamālek, who reached the peak of his influence during the last two decades of the nineteenth century. Around 1882, he was summoned to Isfahan by Ẓell-al-Solṭān and was entrusted with the mission of guarding the marches in the vicinity of Qaṣr-e Šīrīn. Upon his return to western Iran, he built a fort at Qūratū on the Ḏohāb river and established several villages for his sons and other relatives. Toward the end of his rule, a feud erupted between his family and the family of his brother, Ḵalīfa Aʿẓam Khan, in which two of the sons of each were killed. As a result of this feud, the tribe rapidly disintegrated following ʿAzīz Khan's death in November, 1903 (H. L. Rabino, "Kermanchah," *RMM* 38, 1920, p. 20).

The Bājalān population was estimated at 2,000 families by Rawlinson (op. cit., p. 107), at 600 families by Rabino (op. cit., p. 20) and at 1,300 families by M. Mardūḵ (*Tārīḵ-e Mardūḵ*, Tehran, n.d, I, p. 78). According to Mardūḵ, some 70 families of Bājalāns have migrated to the Qazvīn region.

The Bājalān tribe is composed of the following branches (*tīras*): Jomūr, Qāzānlū, Šīrāvand, Ḥājīlār Ḡarībāvand, and Dandāvand (E. B. Soane, *To Mesopotamia and Kurdistan in Disguise*, London, 1912, p. 407). According to Mardūḵ, the Jomūrs and Qāzānlūs are of Lak origin (op. cit., p. 78).

The Bājalāni dialect belongs to the Gūrāni (q.v.) group.

Bibliography: Given in the text. See also D. N. MacKenzie in *EI²* I, pp. 887-88.

(P. Oberling)

BĀJARVĀN, a town in the medieval Islamic province of Mūḡān (q.v.), i.e., the area southwest of the Caspian Sea and south of the Kor (Kura) and Aras (Araxes; qq.v.) rivers. Its site is unknown, but it must have lain in what is now the extreme northeastern tip of the modern Iranian province of Azerbaijan, to the south of the Aras (the modern frontier with the Azerbaijan SSR) and in the Ḵorūslūdāḡ region, for the medieval geographers place it 20 *farsaḵs* north of Ardabīl and 4 *farsaḵs* north of Barzand, the other main town of Mūḡān.

It was apparently the chief town of Mūḡān, if Maqdesī's (Moqaddasī's) *madīnat Mūḡān*, which he says was verdant and fertile, is to be identified with Bājarvān; but by Mostawfī's time (8th/14th century) both Bājarvān and Barzand were mere villages. Bājarvān seems to have played little part in history, except that in 112/730, during Hešām's caliphate, the invading Khazars besieged it, but were repulsed by the Arab general Saʿīd b. ʿAmr Ḥarašī (Ebn al-Aṯīr, V, pp. 161-62; D. M. Dunlop, *History of the Jewish Khazars*, Princeton, 1954, pp. 72-74); and it must have witnessed fighting during the movement of Bābak and the Ḵorramīya (qq.v.), whose fortress of Baḏḏ (q.v.) lay very near. Bājarvān did, however, have a place in popular legend, which identified it with the village (*qarya*) mentioned in the Koran (18:77), where Moses and the "Green Prophet" Ḵeżr (or Ḵażer) were refused food during their journey to the confluence of the two seas and where the "Water of Life," *ʿayn al-ḥayāt*, was located (Yāqūt, *Boldān* I, p. 454).

Bibliography: Maqdesī (Moqaddasī), p. 378. *Nozhat al-qolūb*, p. 90; tr. Le Strange, pp. 91-92. Le Strange, *Lands*, pp. 175-76, 230-31.

(C. E. Bosworth)

BĀḴARZ or Govāḵarz, a district of the medieval Islamic province of Qūhestān/Qohestān (q.v.) in Khorasan, lying to the west of the middle, northerly-flowing course of the Harīrūd, with Ḵᵛāf on its west, Jām on its north, Pūšang on its east and the desert on its south. A popular etymology derived its name from *bād-harza* "place where the wind blows."

The medieval geographers describe Bāḵarz as a fertile region, mainly irrigated by *qanāts*, producing fruit, cereals, and a famed variety of fruit syrup. Its chief urban center was Mālīn (local pronunciation, Mālān), noted for a special type of "long," presumably ellipsoid, melon, and possibly to be identified with the modern Šahr-e Now in the district of the Khorasan *ostān* still known as Bāḵarz today.

In the period of the Arab conquests, when Yazdegerd III was being pursued to his final fate, ʿAbd-Allāh b. ʿĀmer b. Korayz (q.v.) deputed ʿOmayr b. Aḥmad Yaškorī to occupy Qūhestān (31/651-52); but according to Balāḏorī, it was actually Yazīd Jorašī who conquered by force Zām or Jām, Bāḵarz, and Jovayn of Nīšāpūr. The garrisons of both Qūhestān and Sīstān to its south were certainly subsequently manned mainly by Arab tribesmen of Bakr b. Wāʾel (of which Yaškor were a component; Balāḏorī, *Fotūḥ*, p. 403, tr. P. K. Hitti, and F. C. Murgotten, *The Origins of the Islamic State*, Columbia Studies in History, Economics and Public Law 68/1-2, New York, 1916-24, pt. 2, p. 160; Ebn al-Aṯīr (repr.), III, p. 124). In the early ʿAbbasid period, Bāḵarz, like Khorasan in general, was badly affected by the prolonged Kharijite revolt of Ḥamza b. Āḏarak (q.v.), and at one point, in 181/797, the son of the governor of Khorasan ʿAlī b. ʿĪsā b. Māhān (q.v.) managed to inflict a defeat, only however temporary in its effects, on Ḥamza at Bāḵarz (Ebn al-Aṯīr, VI, pp. 150-51). Bāḵarz is mentioned sporadically in the sources up to the Mongol invasions and beyond. Thus, in the warfare between the Ḵᵛārazmšāh Tekeš and his brother Solṭān-šāh over possession of Khorasan, the former at one point, in 583/1187, made over possession of Jām, Bāḵarz and Zīr-e Pol (unidentified) to Solṭānšāh (Jovaynī, tr. Boyle, I, p. 298). Bāḵarz is still described as a flourishing area under the Timurids. Thereafter it is less frequently mentioned, although Curzon mentions the districts of Jām, Bāḵarz, and Ḵᵛāf as being under the governorship of a magnate of Arab descent, one Noṣrat-al-Molk toward the end of the nineteenth century (*Persian Question* I, p. 199).

Medieval Bāḵarz was notable also in that it produced the Saljuq official and noted literary anthologist ʿAlī b. Ḥasan Bāḵarzī (d. 462/1075; q.v.) and the Sufi Shaikh Sayf-al-Dīn Bāḵarzī (d. 646/1248 or shortly thereafter).

Bibliography: See also Maqdesī (Moqaddasī), p. 319 n. *c*. Yāqūt, *Boldān* (Beirut) I, p. 316, V, p. 44. *Nozhat al-qolūb*, p. 153; tr. Le Strange, p. 151. Le Strange, *Lands*, p. 357. D. Krawulsky, *Iran. Das Reich der Īlḫāne: Eine topographisch-historische Studie*, Wiesbaden, 1978, p. 70. Eadem, *Ḫorāsān zur Timuridenzeit nach dem Tārīḫ-e Ḥāfeẓ-e Abrū (verf. 817-823 h.)* I: *Edition und Einleitung*, Wiesbaden, 1982, pp. 37-38.

(C. E. Bosworth)

BĀḴARZĪ ḴORĀSĀNĪ, RAʾĪS **ABUʾL-QĀSEM ʿALĪ** B. ḤASAN B. ABIʾL-ṬAYYEB, an Iranian littérateur of the 5th/11th century who composed poems in both Persian and Arabic and won a name for skill in the art of letter-writing (*tarassol*). After preliminary studies at Bāḵarz, his birthplace in Khorasan, he went to Nīšāpūr and received instruction in legal (*šarʿī*) subjects from Shaikh Abū Moḥammad ʿAbd-Allāh b. Yūsof Jovaynī, the father of Emām-al-Ḥaramayn Jovaynī. His friendship with ʿAmīd-al-Molk Abū Naṣr Kondorī began when they were fellow-pupils of this teacher. Despite his profound knowledge of religious subjects, particularly Shafiʿite jurisprudence, he chose not to work in that field, preferring to concentrate on Persian and Arabic literature. He soon acquired great skill in the arts of Persian and Arabic prose and verse composition. After ʿAmīd-al-Molk Kondorī had become the vizier of the Saljuq sultan Ṭoḡrel Beg, he invited Bāḵarzī, who had already spent some time in governmental service at Basra, to come to Baghdad, and appointed him a secretary. Bāḵarzī stayed only a few years at Baghdad before he resigned and went back to Khorasan. There he remained until he was murdered, while hosting a convivial party, at Nīšāpūr in 467/1074.

Bāḵarzī won a reputation for eloquence in Persian and Arabic alike. In ʿAwfī's reckoning, he excelled with both languages and in both poetry and prose. ʿAwfī saw his *dīvān* entitled *al-Aḥsan fī šeʿr ʿAlī b. al-Ḥasan* and quotes some verses from it in *Lobāb al-albāb*. No copy of this *dīvān* has survived, but excerpts under the same title *al-Aḥsan* are preserved in a manuscript in the British Library. Some specimens of his poetry have been printed in the Aleppo edition of the *Domyat al-qaṣr*. ʿAwfī in his *Lobāb al-albāb* quotes twenty-two verses by Bāḵarzī and tells of seeing a collection of Bāḵarzī's quatrains (*robāʿīs*), entitled *Ṭarab-nāma* and arranged in the order of the dotted letters, from which he quotes seven *robāʿīs*. Amīn Rāzī quotes seven Persian verses by Bāḵarzī in his *Haft eqlīm*.

The best-known work of Bāḵarzī is his *Domyat al-qaṣr wa ʿoṣrat ahl al-ʿaṣr*, designed as a supplement to Ṯaʿālebī's *Yatīmat al-dahr*. It is a *taḏkera* (biographical anthology) in seven parts, presenting Arabic poets of the Beduin tribes, the Hejāz, Syria, Dīār Bakr, Azerbaijan, the Jazīra, Maḡreb, Iraq, Ray and Jebāl, Jorjān, Astarābād, Dehestān, Qūmes, Ḵᵛārazm, Transoxiana, Khorasan, Qūhestān, Sīstān, and Ḡazna. In addition, some prose pieces by writers of belles-lettres are included. This list is enough to show that the *Domyat al-qaṣr* is an important source of information on Arabic poets and writers in various Islamic territories up to Bāḵarzī's lifetime. Also preserved is a book of selections from the *Domyat al-qaṣr*, made by ʿEmād-al-Dīn Moḥammad b. Moḥammad Eṣfahānī under the title *Zobdat al-noṣra wa noḵbat al-ʿoṣra*.

Bibliography: Bāḵarzī, *Domyat al-qaṣr wa ʿoṣrat ahl al-ʿaṣr*, Aleppo, 1349/1930. ʿEmād-al-Dīn Moḥammad Eṣfahānī, *Zobdat al-noṣra wa noḵbat al-ʿoṣra*, Leiden, 1889. ʿAwfī, *Lobāb*, ed. Nafīsī, pp. 66-69, and notes, especially pp. 625-26. *Haft eqlīm* I, pp. 166-68.

(Z. Safa)

BAKHSHIEV MISHI (Baxşijəv Mişi in the Judeo-Tat Roman alphabet used in 1929-38; 1910, Derbent–1972, Makhach-Qalʿa), Judeo-Tat author. A shoemaker's apprentice at the age of 11 and afterwards a fisherman, he was sent in 1928 as a komsomol (communist youth union) activist to study at a *rabfak* (pre-higher school for workers) in Krasnodar and then at the Moscow Institute for Land Utilization. Back in Daghestan, upon his graduation in 1936, he was entrusted in a short period with several minor posts in the local party-administration apparatus and accordingly settled in Daghestan's capital Makhach-Qalʿa. In 1941 shortly after the outbreak of the Soviet-German war, he joined the army as a front-line correspondent. Discharged in 1953 with the rank of lieutenant-colonel, he was given the post of deputy-head of the propaganda department of the Daghestani party apparatus and in 1956 became the head of the Party Life department of the main Daghestani Russian-language newspaper *Dagestanskaya Pravda* and in a short time its deputy editor-in-chief. He remained in this position until 1969 when he had to retire officially because of his poor health but reportedly since it was decided that a Jew could not hold such a high post in a Muslim republic in the aftermath of the 1967 Arab-Israel war.

Bakhshiev began to publish in the early 1930s, while studying in Moscow, first as a poet (collection of poems *Əri Komsomol* "To the Communist Youth Union," 1932). His poems of the 1930s are on the average level of the Judeo-Tat poetry of the time both formally (almost complete rejection of traditional folk-lore forms in favor of those adapted from the Russian poetry) and topically (the nexus of topics reflecting the crisis of the traditional life structure of Mountain Jews tackled mainly as proofs of their becoming rooted in the Soviet reality). Bakhshiev's first major prose work was the novella *Puşorəhuj tozə zindəguni* (Towards the new life, 1932). Patterned after Azarbaijani Soviet models, its plot unfolds against the background of the prerevolutionary and early postrevolutionary years. His second novel *Vətəḡəciho* (The fishermen, 1933) is set among the Jewish fishermen of his native town. Though impaired by straightforward didacticism, both novellas are distinguished by a skillful portrayal of the heroes. In the mid-1930s Bakhshiev debuted as a playwright too. His *Bəsḡuni igidho* (The victory of the heroes, 1936), which dealt with the Civil War in Daghestan, was the first heroic drama in Judeo-Tat. The drama *Xori* (Earth, 1939) delineated the unification of Mountain-Jewish kolkhozes with non-Jewish ones and the struggle of "retrograde elements" against it. The play in verse *Şoh Abbas vəhombol* (King ʿAbbās and the porter, 1940) was based on folk-lore motifs. From the early 1930s on Bakhshiev was also engaged in literary translating from Russian. While with the army, Bakhshiev began to publish in Russian and it remained the second language of his writings for the years to come. However, he wrote in Russian only prose (collections: *Rasskazy o moikh zemlyakakh*, 1956; *Prostye lyudi*, 1958; *Zashumyat sady*, 1962; *Pust' uznayut lyudi*, 1970). Still in active service Bakhshiev published in 1950 his first post-war book *Odomohoj jəki* (Kith and kin), a collection of poems, stories and plays. His book *Odomihoj vatanmə* (People of my homeland, 1960) contained alongside eight stories and two pre-war plays the drama *Ḡismət mərdə nəmərd nixuru* (The lot of a [real] man is not to be taken by a villain), a preliminary tackling of one of the plots of his magnum opus, the first Judeo-Tat multi-plotted novel *Xuşəhoj ongur* (Bunches of grapes, 1963). Its main plot—a clash between the innovator in viticulture and those favoring old methods—is typical of the so-called "kolkhoz novel," widespread in literatures of the USSR in the 1950s-early 1960s. This plot is interwoven with several others: a family saga, a war plot, a picaresque plot, and the life story of the Judeo-Tat writer ʿAso'il Binaev (1882-1958) told mainly by means of flashbacks. The last theme contains criticism, though hesitant and indicating self-censorship, of aspects of the Stalin era. Bakhshiev's post World War II poetry (collected posthumously in *Mə xosdənym vəsalə* "I love the spring-time," 1976) largely remained on the same artistic level as his poetry of the 1930s. Topically it is characterized by a shift from Mountain Jewish to general Daghestani themes. His late drama *Dy dədəj* (Two mothers, published in *Vatan Sov timu* annual, 1965) which centers on a confrontation between a natural mother, a Russian Ashkenazi Jewess, and an adoptive one, a Mountain Jewess, is evidently the best Judeo-Tat play of the post-World War II period.

Both the poetical and prose style of Bakhshiev is lucid and relatively simple. Hebraisms are present both in his prose and poetry. Though Bakhshiev tries to avoid Russianisms in his poetry, Russian loan-words and calques from Russian are present and, at times, abundant in the language of his prose.

Bibliography: M. Amaev and S. Tumanov, *Pisateli Sovetskogo Dagestana (Spravochnik)*, Makhachkala, 1964, pp. 30-31. H. Anisimov, "Əçərgəhoj zindəho" (Amidst the living), *Vatan Sov timu*, 1975, pp. 66-70. H. Avsalumov, "Hyrmətly pisatel xəlḡimu" (Esteemed writer of our people), in Mişi Baxşijev, *Mə xosdənym vəsalə*, pp. 3-10. M. Zand, "The Literature of the Mountain Jews of the Caucasus," *Soviet Jewish Affairs* 15, 1985, no. 2, pp. 3-22; 16, 1986, no. 1, pp. 35-51.

(M. Zand)

BAKŠĪ, a Buddhist lama or scholar, in particular during Mongol hegemony in Iran; subsequently, by extension, any kind of scribe or secretary. The word, which is Turkish, is derived from Chinese *po-shih* (man of learning) and not, as once believed, from Sanskrit *bhikṣu*, which itself denotes a Buddhist lama. Jovaynī, I, pp. 10, 44 (tr. Boyle, pp. 14, 59-60), employs the term *tūyīn* (Chinese *tao-jen* "man of the path"), the original of the *tuin* of his contemporary, the Flemish missionary William of Rubruck (*Itinerarium*, ed. A. van den Wyngaert, *Sinica Franciscana* I, Quaracchi and Florence, 1929, pp. 227-32, 294-97). The word *bakšī* appears only later, in the writings of Rašīd-al-Dīn Fażl-Allāh and Waṣṣāf. The period covered by these authors, that of the il-khan Hülegü (Hūlāgū) and his successors, witnessed the brief emergence of Buddhism, for the last time, as a major religion in Iran; it was facilitated by the tolerant attitude of the Mongol rulers towards the representatives of all religious groups and sects, and by the fiscal exemptions granted to them. If he did not actually embrace the Buddhist faith, as his elder brother the Great Khan Qubilai did, Hülegü at least inclined towards it during his last years (Kirakos, pp. 237-38). His son Abaqa appears to have been partial to the *bakšīs* and entrusted them with the care of his grandson, the future il-khan Ḡāzān (Rašīd-al-Dīn, III, text pp. 295, 373, tr. pp. 165-66, 209). After a temporary setback under the Muslim Aḥmad-Tegüder (Takūdār), came the heyday of the *bakšīs*, coinciding with the reign of Ḡāzān's father Arḡūn (683/1284-690/1291), who may actually have become a Buddhist and who showered favors upon them. During his final illness, which had apparently resulted from a life-prolonging drug prescribed by a *bakšī* from India, only two Mongol amirs, his chief minister Saʿd-al-Dawla, and the *bakšīs* were allowed into his presence (ibid., text pp. 223-24, tr. pp. 128-29). After his adoption of Islam in 694/1295, however,

Ḡāzān, in contrast with Aḥmad-Tegüder, began to enforce Islam as the state religion. Although he had been reared by *baḵšīs* and, while governor of Khorasan for his father, had built a Buddhist temple in Ḵabūšān (Qūčān; ibid., text p. 373, tr. p. 209), Ḡāzān set about destroying Buddhist foundations, some of which were converted into mosques, and imposed Islam on the lamas (Waṣṣāf, p. 324). Once it became evident, however, that many were using Islam merely as a cloak for the practice of their old faith, they were given leave to depart from Iran and return to their original homes in Kashmir, India, and Tibet (Rašīd al-Dīn, III, text pp. 396-97, tr. p. 224).

The growth and termination of Buddhist influence in Mongol Iran, a phenomenon that doubtless extended very little outside the court, is an obscure process. What appear to be the remains of cave-temples from this period have been excavated in Azerbaijan; but we lack any Buddhist written sources and are dependent on those emanating from Muslim and Christian writers. One difficulty is that *baḵšīān* are sometimes linked with *qāmān* (i.e., shamans) and possibly, therefore, confused with them. The *baḵšīs*, for example, who strove to induce Ḡāzān's brother and successor Öljeitü (Ūljāytū), himself likewise at one time a Buddhist, to abandon Islam in 707/1307-8 (Kāšānī, *Tārīḵ-e Ūljāytū Solṭān*, ed. M. Hambly, Tehran, 1348 Š./1969, pp. 98-99) were most probably shamans rather than lamas (see Boyle in *Camb. Hist. Iran* V, p. 402). Nevertheless, a lama named Kamālaśrī, who apparently came from Kashmir, was in Iran at the beginning of the 8th/14th century, assisting Rašīd-al-Dīn with the composition of the Indian section of his great historical encyclopedia (*Die Indiengeschichte des Rašīd-al-dīn*, ed. and tr. K. Jahn, Vienna, 1980, introd., pp. 10-12).

After the suppression and eclipse of Buddhism in Iran, the term *baḵšī* came to denote a scribe who drafted Turkish or Mongol documents (e.g., Barthold, *Turkestan*³, p. 55 n. 4), and was thus synonymous with *bitikčī*. In time it was applied to any master, including quacks and sorcerers, and even, among the Anatolian Turkmen of the 15th-16th centuries, a wandering minstrel. The connection with the military officer entitled *baḵšī* in Mughal India, and with the Anglo-Indian term *buxee* derived from it (Sir Henry Yule and A. C. Burnell, *Hobson-Jobson: A Glossary of Anglo-Indian Words and Phrases*, new ed. W. Crooke, London, 1903, s.v.), is regarded as somewhat tenuous.

Bibliography: Primary sources: Kirakos Ganjakecʿi, tr. L. A. Khanlaryan, Moscow, 1976, pp. 225, 237-38. Marco Polo, ed. and tr. A. C. Moule and P. Pelliot, *The Description of the World*, London, 1938, I, pp. 188-90. Rašīd-al-Dīn, *Jāmeʿ al-tawārīḵ*, Baku, III, passim. Ricoldo of Monte Croce, *Liber peregrinationis*, ed. J. C. M. Laurent, *Peregrinatores Medii Aevi Quatuor*², Leipzig, 1873, p. 117. Waṣṣāf, *Tajzīat al-amṣār wa tazjīat al-aʿṣār*, lithograph ed., Bombay, 1269/1853, passim. See also A. Bausani, "Religion under the Mongols," in *Camb. Hist. Iran* V, pp. 540-43. G. Doerfer, *Türkische und mongolische Elemente im Neupersischen*, Wiesbaden, 1959-75, II, pp. 271-77. B. Karlgren, *Grammata Serica Recensa*, Stockholm, 1972, pp. 204 no. 771a, 256 no. 970a. B. Laufer, "Loan-Words in Tibetan," *T'oung Pao* 17, 1916, pp. 485-87. *Matthews' Chinese-English Dictionary*, nos. 5322, 5776. P. Pelliot, *Notes on Marco Polo*, Paris, 1959-73, I, p. 63. E. Quatremère, ed., *Histoire des Mongols de la Perse*, Paris, 1836, pp. 184-99 n. 51. B. Spuler, "*Bakhshī*," in *EI*². Idem, *Mongolen*³, pp. 178-87, 191. For the archeological evidence, see W. Ball, "The Imamzadeh Maʿsum at Vardjovi: A Rock-cut Il-khanid Complex near Maragheh," *AMI* 12, 1979, pp. 329-40. For the relations of the lamas with the Mongol imperial family in general, see H. Franke, "Tibetans in Yüan China," in *China under Mongol Rule*, ed. J. D. Langlois, Jr., Princeton, 1981, pp. 296-328. L. Petech, "Tibetan Relations with Sung China and with the Mongols," in *China among Equals*, ed. M. Rossabi, Berkeley and Los Angeles, 1983, pp. 173-203.

(P. JACKSON)

BAḴT "fate, destiny."
i. *The term.*
ii. *The concept.*

i. THE TERM

BAḴT (Middle and New Persian) "fate, lot," often with the positive sense of "good luck" (*ḵᵛošbaḵtī*), though the related NPers. verb *bāḵtan* means "to lose" (as opposed to *bordan* "to win") in a game or gamble. The Avestan passive past participle *baxta*, from Aryan *bhag-* "to allot" (Old Indian *bhajati* "divides," *bhakta* "apportioned") appears as a neuter noun meaning "allotted destiny" or "fate's decree" (*Vd.* 5.8, 21.1), mainly with the negative sense of "misfortune, doom, perdition" (*Y.* 8.23; *AirWb.*, col. 928). The Iranian word accordingly fits the concept of fate as the prealloted share, held by all nations and expressed in words such as Greek *hē aîsa* and *ho oîtos* "destiny" corresponding to the Avestan masculine noun *aēta* "part" (Indo-Germanic *ai-to-*; see Pokorny, p. 10, and Güntert, *Kalypso*, p. 248²) as well as *hē moîra* "goddess of fate" and *tò méros* "part" (IE. *smer-*); Hittite *henkan* "fate, plague, death," properly "apportionment" (*henk* "to apportion"); Russian *dólya* and *dolyúshka* "share, lot, destiny," nouns related to the verb *delit'* "to divide." From the Muslim Arabs has come the universally known "kismet" (Arabic *qesma* "fate" and *qesm* "part;" see Eilers, "Schöpfergott," in *Ex Orbe Religionum, Studia Geo Widengren Oblata*, Leiden, 1972, II, p. 400). Syriac likewise has *ḥelqā* "fate" from *ḥəlaq* "to divide, to allot" (whence the Pahlavi ideogram *HLKWN-* for the semantically identical Mid. Pers. *baxtan/baxš*).

Typical Persian idioms are *baḵt-e bīdār* "wide-awake luck," *baḵt-e javān* or *now* "young" or "new luck," *baḵt-e sabz* "green luck," all meaning good fortune in contrast to *baḵt-e ḵofta* "sleeping luck," *baḵt-e bargašta* "reversed" or "dwindling luck," i.e., ill-fortune.

A compound which deserves note is Mid. Pers. *baḡ(ō)baxt* "God-given destiny" from Avestan *baγō-bakta* "decided by God" (*Y*. 8.35; see *AirWb*., col. 922); it appears in the *Bundahišn* as an epithet of the Alborz range. In the modern language there are compounds meaning "fortunate" such as *baxtāvar* and *baxtūr* (from *baxt-āβar*), Baktīār (from *baxta-dāra-*), a man's name, whence Baktīārī, the name of the tribe in western Iran, as well as *kᵛošbakt, javānbakt, nowbakt*; likewise *bakt-āzmā'ī* (lit., "testing one's luck") "lottery." There are also personal names such as Āzādbakt, Nēkbakt, Šādbakt (Justi, *Namenbuch*, pp. 487f.). The name of the Baktagān salt lake west of Neyrīz is probably a patronymic derived from a shortened form of such a man's name.

More doubtful is the relationship of *bakt* "fate" to *baktak* "nightmare" (Eilers, *Die Al, ein persisches Kindbettgespenst*, Munich, 1979, pp. 44.16, 45.18, 48.5) and to *baktū* "thunder" (fate's utterance of threats?). *Baktū* is also a name of mountains (A. Gabriel, *Durch Persiens Wüsten*, Stuttgart, 1935, p. 203), but probably then refers to water partings; cf. Kūh-e Bakt-āb (S. Hedin, *Eine Routenaufnahme durch Ostpersien* I, Stockholm, 1918, p. 57).

Formed from *bhag-* with a suffixed *š* is the Mid. Pers. and NPers. *bakš* "part." The derived verb *bakšīdan* "to divide" or "give" ought to be distinguished from the homophonous *bakšīdan* "to forgive" (Man. Mid. Pers. *aβa-xšāy-*, Parth. *aβa-xšāh-*). Another form *bāš* is probably the source of the NPers. stem *pāš* (East Persian *fāš* from *βāš*) found in *pāšīdan* 'to scatter, sprinkle," *ābpāš* "watering can," and the place names Ābpāšān and Bāšgāh given to water-distribution points (Eilers, *Geographische Namengebung*, Munich, 1982, p. 40).

Also related to *bhag-* 'to divide, allot" are the Avestan neuter noun *baxəδra* "part," Mid. Pers. and NPers. *bahr* "share," and with metathesis NPers. *bark* "part" (*AirWb*., col. 923; Nyberg, *Manual* II, p. 43a).

Further derivatives of the same fruitful root are Mid. Pers. *baḡ* and NPers. *foḡ* (East Iranian, with labial vowel), from Old Persian *baga* (q.v.) "God" (as distributor, cf. Arabic *al-Qāsem*), or, in poetry, "idol;" Mid. Pers. and NPers. *bāḡ* (q.v.) "garden," properly "piece of land;" NPers. *bāj* or *bāž* "tribute, toll," from the Old Persian masculine noun *bāji;* and finally the place name Balk, derived through a form Bahl/Baxl from Old Persian Baxtriš, the name of the province, which must have been connected with water distribution (cf. *bāš/pāš* above; Eilers, *Geographische Namengebung*, pp. 23f., 40). For the Bactrian camel (the two-humped draft animal), the term is *boktī* with labial vowel.

Still to be mentioned are NPers. *bāzī* "game" and the numerous compounds of *bāz* such as *asbbāz* "jockey," *gūybāz* "polo player," *'ešqbāz* "philanderer," *kabūtar-bāz* "pigeon fancier," *lajjbāz* "nagger," *šamšīrbāz* "fencer," *tanābbāz* "tightrope walker," *waraqbāz* "card player," *zanbāz* "seducer," etc.; also *sarbāz* "soldier,"

literally one who gambles with his head, and *jānbāz* "life-risker," e.g. dare-devil acrobat.

The question whether the Arabs borrowed their word *waqt* "time" from *bakt* or an East Iranian form thereof remains uncertain. *Waqt* (pronounced *vakt, voket*, or the like) is not of Semitic origin, and the concepts of time and fate are not far apart (cf. Arabic *dahr* which means both).

Bibliography: Given in the text.

(W. Eilers)

ii. The Concept

The Middle Persian and New Persian term *bakt*, which designates "lot, share, fortune," is derived from the root *bag-* "to distribute, allot," from which is derived also one of the most common Indo-Iranian terms for a deity, *baga-* (q.v.). As *bakt* is, strictly speaking, a passive participle meaning "distributed, allotted," its primary meaning was "that which is allotted to man." Like the modern English "lot, share," to which other modern languages have corresponding terms, and like certain Semitic terms which have the same basic sense, the Iranian term developed from the sense of "share" to that of "fortune."

In meaning, this term forms part of a whole group of Iranian words which refer to the effect of superior forces on the destinies of people. Such words are the terms which designate "time," like Middle Persian *zamān* or *zamānag* (NPers. *zamāna*), *rōzgār* (NPers. *rūzgār*); or words which refer to the heavenly sphere, to the sky and to the heavenly bodies, such as NPers. *sepehr, āsmān, axtar*, etc.; and in the Islamic period a number of terms borrowed from Arabic (e.g., *qażā' qadar*).

In Sasanian Zoroastrianism the power of fate, or the notion of the destiny allotted to man, is quite prominent, and numerous literary allusions to this idea can be quoted. In a sense this idea is part of the wider conception of predestination, the idea that most human fortunes are determined before the birth of the individual, perhaps even as early as the creation of the world. This idea does not necessarily have a bearing on the somewhat complicated question of the freedom of the will or of the possible existence of ethical determinism in Zoroastrianism; at least the wording of the *Gāθās* seems to indicate that Zoroaster regarded good and evil as being the outcome of the free and individual decision of the two primordial spirits and of mankind, and it goes without saying that there is full human responsibility for the actions done by the individual (see, for example, H. Lommel, *Die Religion Zarathustras nach dem Awesta dargestellt*, Tübingen, 1930, pp. 22f.).

It is clear, however, that in the Sasanian view man's life is dominated to a very large extent by the intervention of fate. Fate (*baxt, brēh, brīhēnišn*, which seem to be interchangeable) is never clearly defined. Sometimes the terms indicating it refer to divine decree, but often one has the impression that the power of fate is independent and is subordinate neither to Ohrmazd nor to Ahreman. When it acts on its own, its intervention is never explained as motivated by ethical or religious considerations, and one may be led to the conclusion that this power is morally indifferent and that its decree is arbitrary, which is why it appears in such unexpected and unpredictable a manner. A typical term, synonymous with *baxt*, which indicates its mode of action is *jahišn*, from the verb *jastan* "to jump, to come about without previous warning." The Pahlavi treatise *Mēnōg ī xrad* distinguishes between two separate concepts, *baxt* and *bagōbaxt*. The former is defined as "that which was allotted from the beginning," and the latter as "that which they allot again" (*Mēnōg ī xrad*, 23.6-7). This has been interpreted as the contrast between fate and divine providence (by E. W. West in his translation in *Sacred Books of the East* XXIV, Oxford, 1885, p. 55), but the concepts are not clear. The power of fate was described by the same composition as capable of causing the wise man to be deluded in his actions, and the ignorant to be intelligent in his action, etc. (chap. 22).

Sasanian thinkers sought to define and explain the scope of the effectiveness of the intervention of fate in human life. One often quoted definition says: "The material world (*gētīg*) is (governed) by fate (*baxt*), the spiritual world (*mēnōg*) by action" (Pahlavi *Vidēvdād*, 5.9), which indicates that things belonging to the sphere of religious activity are the responsibility of man, and it is only in mundane matters that fate can have its way and man is powerless. It has been suggested that this formula reflects a borrowing from a Neoplatonic source (cf. J. Duchesne-Guillemin in *Hommages à Georges Dumézil*, Collection Latomus 45, 1960, pp. 102-03). Another text defines the relationship between "fate" (*baxt*) and "action" (*kunišn*) as complementary, resembling the interdependence of body and soul (*Pahlavi Texts*, p. 94). In another text they are compared to two bales on the back of a mule. An elaborate scheme dividing the spheres of human existence among the various elements which make it up is found quoted in several places in Pahlavi literature (cf. *Dēnkard*, bk. 6, D1a, and parallels, references in S. Shaked, *Wisdom of the Sasanian Sages*). According to that scheme, "fate" (called *brēh*) governs "living, wife, children, authority, and wealth," while the other sections of human endeavor are allocated to four other areas, called action, habit, substance, and heritage. Fate does not change things radically, it is specified in a number of instances, but it creates the necessary conditions so that an action should be effective.

Some scholars have tended to regard all expressions of the power of fate over human destinies as connected to the Zurvanite brand of Zoroastrianism, but this seems too one-sided and takes out of the domain of "orthodox" Zoroastrianism many works which have always been regarded by Zoroastrians as part of their own literature. It may be argued that orthodox Zoroastrians were not much less given to faith in the overwhelming dominion of fate in the world than those who adopted the Zurvanite myth. It seems, indeed, that the term for fate was venerated as a deity among Zoroastrians, for we have in Sasanian onomastics a name such as Baxt-āfrīd, which means "created by Fortune," and among carriers of this name there is one prominent Zoroastrian sage of the Sasanian period (see Shaked in *Wisdom of the Sasanian Sages*, p. 283).

Much the same range of ideas about fate and human power is present in the early Islamic literature in Persian, with the variation that the delicate relationship between fate and the divine is here often expressed in Islamic terms. Both the astronomical terms and those relating to decree and predestination are very commonly employed, especially in works which reflect the influences of pre-Islamic Iran. It is emphasized that man's will and effort turn to nothing against the power of fate. The poetic compositions of Ferdowsī (*Šāh-nāma*) and Gorgānī (*Vīs o Rāmin*) continue the themes and ambiguities of Sasanian literature as far as this topic is concerned. The Iranian Muslim thinker Meskawayh (Meskūya; d. 421/1030) mentions the matters which are obtained through "*baxt* and fortune (*jadd*)" as pertaining to the happiness of the body, which is part of the happiness of the person, although he mentions that this is denied by "profound philosophers" (Meskawayh, *Tahdīb al-aḵlāq wa taṭhīr al-aʿrāq*, ed. Ebn al-Ḵaṭīb, Cairo, 1398, p. 92).

Bibliography: L.-C. Casartelli, *La philosophie religieuse du mazdéisme sous les sassanides*, Paris, Bonn, and London, 1884, pp. 28f. A. V. W. Jackson, *Zoroastrian Studies*, New York, 1928, pp. 219-44 (on the Zoroastrian doctrine of the freedom of the will). J. C. Tavadia, "Pahlavi Passages on Fate and Free Will," *ZII* 8, 1931, pp. 119-32. Rašīd Yāsemī, "Eʿteqād-e Ferdowsī dar bāb-e kūšeš wa taqdīr," in *Hazāra-ye Ferdowsī*, Tehran, 1944, pp. 173-78. Helmer Ringgren, *Fatalism in Persian epics* (Uppsala Universitets Årsskrift 1952, no. 13), Uppsala and Wiesbaden, 1952. J. Duchesne-Guillemin, *La religion de l'Iran ancien*, Paris, 1962, pp. 130ff. R. C. Zaehner, *The Dawn and Twilight of Zoroastrianism*, London, 1961, pp. 243ff. Āturpāt-i Ēmētān, *The Wisdom of the Sasanian Sages*, tr. S. Shaked, Boulder, Colorado, 1979, pp. xliff.

(S. SHAKED)

BAḴTAGAN LAKE, part of the Lake Nīrīz basin situated about 1,525 m above sea level in the province of Fārs, approximately 50 km east of Shiraz. Originally identical with the Nīrīz lake itself, it has been repeatedly mentioned by medieval geographers (e.g., Eṣṭaḵrī, pp. 100, 101, 102; Ebn Ḥawqal, pp. 263, 265, 276, 277; Moqaddasī, p. 446). At the present, it is common to divide the basin of the Nīrīz into a northern portion (*daryāča-ye Ṭašk*) and a larger southern part (*daryāča-ye Baḵtagān*). The basin, surrounded in the northwest and south by high mountains, is fed by the Kor river and other smaller streams all of which are oligohaline or mesohaline in character. In wet years the whole basin is covered by a single water-surface, covering an area of approx. 1,000 to 1,500 km² and reaching a depth of 1 m to 1.10 m. Normally, however, there are two intermittent lakes, separated at their western ends by the delta of the Kor river. Due to considerable fluctuations of the lake level within a few years, reports on the existence of one lake, of two lakes, or no lake at all are rather confusing. Due to high salt contents of the lakes, salt is harvested as soon as the water-level lowers and the salt deposits are exposed on the surface.

See also NĪRĪZ.

Bibliography: Kayhān, *Jog̲rāfīā* I, pp. 89-92. D. B. Krinsley, *A Geomorphological and Paleoclimatological Study of the Playas of Iran*, Washington, D.C. (Geological Survey, United States Dept. of the Interior: Contract no. PRO CP 70-800; Project No. 7628), 1970, 2 vols., esp. vol. 1, pp. 236-44. H. Löffler, *Beiträge zur Kenntnis der iranischen Binnengewässer* I: *Der Niriz-See und sein Einzugsgebiet, Internationale Revue Ges. Hydrobiologie und Hydrographie* 44, 1959, pp. 227-76. H. L. Wells, "Surveying Tours in Southern Persia," *Proc. Royal Geographical Society*, London, N.S. 5, 1883, pp. 138-63.

(E. EHLERS)

BAK̲TAK, a folkloric she-creature of horrible shape, personifying a nightmare. Bak̲tak was believed to have been one of Alexander's slave girls who accompanied him on his expedition in search of the water of life (*āb-e ḥayāt*; see ĀB, ii). According to the legend, after the water was found, it was poured into a goatskin; but, before it could be carried away, a crow punctured the skin with its beak, spilling the contents onto the ground. Bak̲tak then quickly scooped the water into her hands and drank it; thus both she and the crow are said to have become immortal. Alexander, enraged, ordered her nose cut off and replaced with a nose of clay.

Bak̲tak is reputed to know where all the treasures of the earth are hidden. A nightmare occurs when Bak̲tak throws herself upon the sleeper who, in the dark, must try to grab the creature's nose. Lest she lose her nose, Bak̲tak will reveal one of the treasures to him; but, if the sleeper wants to stop the nightmare and make Bak̲tak go away, he must wiggle his finger (Ṣ. Hedāyat, *Neyrangestān*, Tehran, 2536 = 1356 Š./1977, pp. 123-24; cf. H. Massé, *Croyances et coutumes persanes*, Paris, 1938, II, pp. 366-67). Bak̲tak has also been described as a massive, perspiring black bundle which falls upon the sleeper and tries to suffocate him. She also answers to *Bīnīgelī* (clay-nosed) or *Ġūl* (Donaldson, *The Wild Rue*, London, 1938, pp. 175-76). Other names include: Bark̲afj, Būšāsb, Estanba, Faranjak, Gūšāsb, K̲ork̲ojīvan (M. Moʿin, *Farhang-e fārsī* III, p. 2778 s.v. *Kābūs*).

Bak̲tak resembles the Āl (q.v.), another "female devil" of Iranian folklore "whose attack can be neutralized by grabbing its nose." Other Bak̲tak-like creatures, which appear in local folklore, are: *Taptapo* (in the Rāmhormoz region) who has a necklace (*nābanda*) which it hangs on a nail or a tree; *Ševlī* (in the Arāk region) "which weighs like a mountain on the chest of the sleeper and prevents him from moving or shouting;" and *Šavah* (in the K̲omeyn region, probably a variant of the word *šabaḥ*, ghost), who like *Taptapo* has a necklace (*galūband*) on which its life depends and which, before throwing itself on the hapless sleeper, it hangs on a drain spout (Archives of the Markaz-e Farhang-e Mardom, Tehran, communication from A. Enjavī).

The name Bak̲tak also appears in the Safavid period romance *Romūz-e Ḥamza*, as K̲osrow II Anōšīravān's evil vizier. M. J. Maḥjūb believes Bak̲tak in this context to be a misreading of Bok̲tag or Bok̲tak, the father of Bozorgmehr, K̲osrow's wise counselor (M. J. Maḥjūb, oral communication).

Bibliography: Given in the text.

(F. GAFFARY)

BĀK̲TAR, designation of the "west" in Modern Persian, but its Pahlavi equivalent *abāxtar* means "north," probably borrowed from Parthian (cf. Man. Parth. *abāxtar*, see M. Boyce, *A Reader in Manichean Middle Persian and Parthian*, pp. 115-16); the Manichean Middle Persian word for "north" is *abarag* (ibid., pp. 62, 65, text *y* 4.14). It is derived from Av. *apāxtara* "north." In the Zoroastrian cosmogonical division, the northern part (*nēmag/kanārag* "side") is called *abāxtar*, which is under the superintendence of the star Haptōrang "Ursa Major" (*Bundahišn* 2.7). The Zoroastrians also supposed hell to be located in the north, where Ahreman and the demons reside (*Vd.* 7.2, 8.16, 19.1; *Hādōxt nask* 2.25; *Bundahišn*, loc. cit.; *Dēnkard* 7.4.36, 7.6.7, *Dādestān ī dēnīg* 33.5, etc.). It is, therefore, maintained that during the religious ceremonies one should not point the tips of the *barsom*-twigs toward the north (*Šāyest nē šāyest*, ed. Kotwal, 14.2 and p. 107); no one is allowed to throw any food or flower or to pour out water or wine to the north during the night (*Šāyest nē šāyest*, ed. Tavadia, 10.7, and ed. Kotwal, 12.18; *Ṣad dar-e nat̲r*, ed. Dhabhar, 30; *Dēnkard* 9.19.2).

According to the Pahlavi and Arabo-Persian books and the geography of Moses of Khorene, the Iranian empire was divided, on the pattern of the four cardinal points, into four parts or sides (*kustag, sōg, kanārag, nēmag, pāygōs*; see Christensen, *Iran Sass.*, pp. 352, 370ff.; V. G. Lukonin in *Camb. Hist. Iran* 3/2, pp. 732; C. Brunner, ibid., pp. 747ff.). This division seems to be more mythological and mental rather than real and administrative (see Gignoux, *AION* 44, 1984, pp. 555ff.). Whatever the case, the northern part in this division is called *abāxtar* in Pahlavi (*Mādayān ī čatrang* 26, in *Pahl. Texts*, p. 118), *bāxtar/βāxtar* in Arabic sources (Masʿūdi, *Tanbīh*, p. 31; Ebn Rosta, p. 103). As the north was believed by the Zoroastrians to be the abode of the Evil Spirit (Ahreman), the word *abāxtar* was generally replaced by the name Ādurbādagān, Arab. Ād̲arbāyajān, the most famous province of the northern part of the empire (*Šahrīhā ī Ērān*, ed. Markwart, par. 58; Gardīzī, p. 21, K̲ᵛārazmī, *Mafātīḥ*, p. 115; Ebn K̲ordād̲beh, *Masālek*, p. 118), or by Kapkoh 'Caucasus' (Moses of Khorene, see Markwart, *Ērānšahr*, pp. 17, 94). The same religious belief probably motivated the author or the scribe of the Pahlavi treatise *Sūr saxwan*, par. 12 (ed. Tavadia, *Journal of the K. M. Cama Oriental Institute* 29, 1935, pp. 33, 64, 65) to delete the title *abāxtar spāhbad* "commander-in-chief of the north," when enumerating the four commanders in chief of the Sasanian empire.

There is a confusion as to the usage of *bāḵtar* in the early New Persian literature. It is rarely used in its original meaning "north" (*Tārīḵ-e Sīstān*, p. 23; *Šāh-nāma*, Moscow, V, p. 157 v. 1271; IX, p. 195 v. 3131, p. 204 v. 3271), but generally signifies "east" (*Moqaddama-ye Šāh-nāma-ye abū-manṣūrī* in *Hazāra-ye Ferdowsī*, Tehran, 1944, p. 139; *Šāh-nāma* III, p. 197 v. 3008; V, p. 285 v. 832; VII, p. 84 v. 1421) or "west" (*Šāh-nāma* I, p. 18 v. 78; VI, p. 177 v. 191, p. 188 v. 376; VII, p. 224 v. 89, p. 232 v. 232 etc.). There is a unique example recorded by Bīrūnī (*Āṯār*, p. 217, 1.72), quoting Zādūya as his source, in which *abāxtar* (written *afāhtar* i.e. *aβāxtar*) is used in the sense of "south." It is apparently a lapsus either by Bīrūnī or by the author of his source. The above-mentioned variety of usage may be due to the different literary and geographical traditions. After the northern region of Iran had ceased to be called *abāxtar* and *ḵʷarāsān* (Pahl. *xwarāsān*) "east" became the name of the eastern province in the early Islamic period, the word *bāḵtar* was gradually used for the "east" and later on for the "west."

Bibliography: See also K. Inostrantsev, "Arabisch-persische Miszellen zur Bedeutung der Himmelsgegenden," *WZKM* 25, 1911, pp. 91-97. A. Kasrawī, "Čār sū," *Peymān*, 1312 Š./1933, pp. 1-2, repr. in Y. Ḏokāʾ, ed., *Kārvand-e Kasrawī*, Tehran, 1352 Š./1973, pp. 391-99. E. Pūr-e Dāvūd, "Čār sū," in *Hormazd-nāma*, Tehran, 1331 Š./1953, pp. 389-402. D. Monchi-Zadeh, *Topographisch-historische Studien zum Iranischen Nationalepos*, Wiesbaden, 1975, pp. 164ff.

(A. TAFAŻŻOLĪ)

BĀḴTAR, the name of (1) a Persian educational magazine published at Isfahan in 1312 Š./1933-1314 Š./1935 and (2) a Persian political newspaper published at Isfahan and Tehran from 1314 Š./1935 to 1324 Š./1945. (On the word *bāḵtar* see above.)

(1) The educational magazine was launched at Isfahan in Āḏar, 1312 Š./November, 1933. The publication license was held by Naṣr-Allāh Sayfpūr Fāṭemī, and the editorship was entrusted to Amīrqolī Amīnī, then editor of the newspaper *Aḵgar*. Technical and administrative assistance was provided by *Aḵgar* and literary and scholarly advice was given by the eminent poet Moḥammad-Taqī Bahār (Malek-al-Šoʿarāʾ), who was then living in internal exile at Isfahan. Some of Bahār's poems were published for the first time in *Bāḵtar*. He also contributed scholarly articles, including a series headed "Ferdowsī" about recent research on the *Šāh-nāma* and its author and one headed "Bāḵtar Means North." In addition to Bahār, a number of other writers, scholars, and poets, mostly resident at Tehran, sent articles or pieces to Isfahan for publication in *Bāḵtar* (Ṣadr Hāšemī, no. 267). Reports of world scientific advances were also included in Bāḵtar, and political aspects were not neglected. The magazine supported Reżā Shah Pahlavī and his policies and invariably had the slogan "God, Shah, Country" printed on the back of the cover.

Bāḵtar usually had 82 pages measuring 18 × 33 cm with one column per page. Illustrations and advertisements filled part of the space. The annual subscription rate was 40 rials, with a 25 percent reduction for military personnel, students, and subscribers to *Aḵgar*. Altogether 31 issues were brought out, the last one being dated Mehr, 1314 Š./October, 1935. Sets are preserved in libraries in Iran, and some copies are held in the library of the School of Oriental and African Studies of the University of London.

(2) After closing down the educational magazine, Naṣr-Allāh Sayfpūr Fāṭemī launched a journal of news and political comment at Isfahan under the same title *Bāḵtar*. The editor was his brother Ḥosayn Fāṭemī. Initially it was printed once a week, later three times a week, at Isfahan; but from 10 Tīr 1321 Š./1 July 1942 onward it was printed at Tehran, and soon after that date it was transformed into an afternoon daily. In this last period the licensee ceased to involve himself directly or regularly in the management of the newspaper and left all its business in the hands of the editor, Ḥosayn Fāṭemī (the future Minister of Foreign Affairs in Dr. Moḥammad Moṣaddeq's cabinet). Beside home and foreign news and comments on current affairs, *Bāḵtar* carried items on a wide range of subjects. Politically it did not follow a definite line but frequently changed course.

Publication of *Bāḵtar* came to a halt in Farvardīn, 1324 Š./April, 1945, because most of the editorial staff were away on long journeys abroad. In Ḵordād/June of the same year some issues were brought out as substitutes for another Tehran newspaper, *Āzād*. Four years later Ḥosayn Fāṭemī started the much better known newspaper *Bāḵtar-e emrūz* under a separate publication license. An issue of *Bāḵtar-e emrūz* was published under the title *Bāḵtar* in Mordād, 1329 Š./August, 1950, when *Bāḵtar-e emrūz* was subject to a ban.

The newspaper *Bāḵtar* had four pages measuring 35 × 48 cm with four columns per page. Its price was thirty *šāhīs* at the start and one rial in the last year. Sets are preserved in the Majles Library, the Central Library of Tehran University, and the University and Municipal Libraries at Isfahan. The Library of Congress in Washington holds an incomplete set.

Bibliography: M. Ṣadr Hāšemī, *Tārīḵ-e jarāʾed wa majallāt-e Īrān*, Isfahan, 1327 Š./1948-1332 Š./1953, nos. 267-68. R. Lescot, "Notes sur la presse iranienne," *REI* 2-3, 1939, p. 273. L. P. Elwell-Sutton, "The Iranian Press, 1941-1947," *Iran* 6, 1968, no. 97.

(N. PARVĪN)

BĀḴTAR-E EMRŪZ (Today's West), daily evening newspaper published in Tehran from 8 Mordād 1328 to 28 Mordād 1332 Š./9 August 1949 to 19 August 1953. It was founded by its editor-publisher Ḥosayn Fāṭemī (1917-54, q.v.), one of the principal associates of

Dr. Moḥammad Moṣaddeq (q.v.) in the National Front (Jebha-ye Mellī; q.v.). Its editorial board included Moḥammad Moḥīṭ Ṭabāṭabāʾī, Jalālī Nāʾīnī, Raḥmat Moṣṭafawī, Sepehr Zabīḥ, Nāṣer Amīnī, and Esmāʿīl Pūrvālī, some being journalists of stature; Naṣr-Allāh Šīfta and Saʿīd Fāṭemī were associate editors. In format it was slightly larger than tabloid (32 × 52 cm); it consisted of four, six, and occasionally eight pages, and was devoted to national as well as international news. It carried pictures, usually on its first page, and featured commentary. The name, *Bāḵtar-e emrūz*, was a combination of the names of two earlier publications—*Bāḵtar* and *Mard-e emrūz* (q.v.) that Ḥosayn Fāṭemī had been associated with.

The rousing daily editorials penned by Fāṭemī himself were exhortative commentary on the day's events and energetic exposition of the National Front's views and positions. *Bāḵtar-e emrūz* as an "unofficial" spokesman of the National Front advocated and led a public opinion campaign for the nationalization of the Anglo-Iranian Oil Company, a platform whose initial concept and suggestion was posthumously credited to Fāṭemī by Moṣaddeq.

Bāḵtar-e emrūz was banned several times and was replaced by *Sargoḏašt* and *Bāḵtar* on two occasions; once during the premiership of General Ḥ-ʿA. Razmārā (q.v.), who opposed the nationalization legislation, Fāṭemī was also imprisoned. Subsequent to the approval by the Majles on 20 March 1951 of the Nationalization Act, Moṣaddeq became prime minister on May 10 and appointed Fāṭemī as his deputy and government spokesman. Thenceforth, *Bāḵtar-e emrūz*, which had reached a daily circulation of more than thirty thousand (a record for Iran at the time), gained substantially in political status; both in Iran and abroad its views were construed as reflecting inner thinking of the government leaders. On 16 February 1951, Fāṭemī was the target of an assassination attempt by a youthful member of Fedāʾīān-e Eslām (q.v.) while delivering a memorial speech at the tomb of Moḥammad Masʿūd (q.v.), the assassinated editor of *Mard-e emrūz*. Narrowly escaping death, he was hospitalized for several months, during which period he ceased his direct supervision of *Bāḵtar-e emrūz* and occasionally even missed his daily column. On 30 September 1952, he was appointed foreign minister, a position that he held until 19 August 1953, when the Moṣaddeq government was overthrown by a CIA-engineered coups d'etat. On the same day, *Baḵtar-e emrūz* offices and printing house were ransacked and that day's issue never reached the newsstand.

Almost a decade later, the name *Bāḵtar-e emrūz* was temporarily revived when a group of National Front supporters living in exile in Europe and America attempted to reorganize themselves under the banner of this newspaper. In April, 1962, a regular weekly publication of what was called *dawra-ye jadīd* (new series) in a bulletin-size format under the direction of Ḵosrow Qašqāʾī and the editorship of Moḥammad ʿĀṣemī began in Munich. There was very little resemblance in format or content between the original and this revived version, which was said to have been under the influence of the Tudeh party and its supporters. After two years, this period of publication came to an end. Between the years 1964 and 1966 supporters of the National Front in the United States, under the leadership of ʿAlī Šāyegān, a former close associate of Dr. Moṣaddeq, chose *Bāḵtar-e emrūz* as the name of their official publication. In this period there were about ten irregular issues published.

The African and Middle Eastern Division of the U.S. Library of Congress is in possession of a set of *Bāḵtar-e emrūz* containing the 22 February to 28 July and 30 July 1950 to 26 July 1952 issues.

Bibliography: B. Afrāsīābī *Moṣaddeq wa tārīḵ*, Tehran, 1360 Š./1981, pp. 348-77. ʿA. Jānzāda, *Moṣaddeq*, Tehran, 1979, pp. 119-220. Ḵ. Malekī, *Ḵāṭerāt-e sīāsī*, Tehran, 1361 Š./1982, pp. 104-11. Ḡ. Moṣawwer-e Raḥmānī, *Ḵāṭerāt-e sīāsī*, Tehran, 1363 Š./1984, pp. 131-56, 217-77. N. Šīfta, *Doktor Fāṭemī*, Tehran, 1364 Š./1985.

(ʿA. M. Š. FĀṬEMĪ)

BAḴTĀVAR KHAN, MOḤAMMAD (1029?-96/1620?-85), historian and official at the court of the Mughal emperor Awrangzēb (1068-1118/1658-1707) and a patron of literature. A eunuch, he joined the service of Prince Awrangzēb in 1065/1654, initially as a presenter of petitions (*ḵedmat-e ʿarāyeż*); but during the war of succession between Awrangzēb and his brothers in 1067-68/1657-58, he became the prince's personal attendant (Bakhtāwar, I, pp. 25, 62, 101, 130). At the second coronation of Awrangzēb in Ramażān, 1069/June, 1659, Baḵtāvar served as a whisk bearer, and in August of the same year he received the title of khan (ibid., pp. 152, 165). In 1076/1666 he was given the *manṣab* of 1,150 *savārs* (ibid., p. 338), and four years later he became *dārūḡa-ye ḵawāṣṣān*. He died at Aḥmadnagar on 15 Rabīʿ I 1096/19 February 1685 and was buried at Baḵtāvarpūra (now Bastī Nabī Karīm) near Delhi.

Baḵtāvar's first work, *Āʾīna-ye baḵt* or *Čahār āʾīna* (comp. 1068/1658), describes the four battles Awrangzēb fought against his brothers in his bid for the throne. His *Bayāż*, completed in 1084/1673-74, comprises selections from the poetry of well-known Persian mystical poets such as Sanāʾī, ʿAṭṭār, and Rūmī. *Rīāż al-awlīāʾ*, a *taḏkera* of Sufis and *ʿolamāʾ* from the classical period to Awrangzēb's reign, and is an important source for the religious personages of the period. His epitome *Merʾāt al-ʿālam* is a compendium of history divided into an introduction (*moqaddema*), seven parts (*ārāyeš*), an appendix (*afzāyeš*), and a conclusion (*ḵātema*). The book is famous for its seventh part, which is subdivided into three sections (*pīrāyeš*); it is one of the most important primary sources for the political history of the first ten years of Awrangzēb's period as well as for the intellectual and cultural history of the era. Written in simple Persian, the *Merʾāt* is not an official history of Awrangzēb's reign but complements the official chronicle *ʿĀlamgīr-nāma* of Monšī Moḥammad

Kāẓem by providing additional details of certain events and personalities (for details, see ibid., introd., pp. 23-45). Another significant contribution of this work lies in the sections devoted to the *mašāʾeḵ* and the *ʿolamāʾ* (part seven), calligraphers (appendix), and the poets of Awrangzēb's period (conclusion). Elliot and other scholars have attributed *Merʾāt al-ʿālam* and other works by Baḵtāvar to Moḥammad Baqā, Baḵtāvar's contemporary and author of *Merʾāt-e jahānnomā*. However, from the contemporary and near-contemporary sources it is established that Baḵtāvar was indeed the author and compiler of the works attributed to him above (for details, see ibid., introd., pp. 14-16).

Baḵtāvar was interested in art and literature and was the patron of a number of Persian poets, facilitating the entry of numerous poets, writers, and *ʿolamāʾ* into the imperial court (ibid., introd., pp. 18-19). He also took an active interest in public building activities such as mosques, *sarāy*s, and a township near Delhi (ibid., II, pp. 519-24), and had a mausoleum constructed for himself.

Bibliography: S. S. Alvi, "The Historians of Awrangzeb: A Comparative Study of Three Primary Sources," *Essays on Islamic Civilization*, ed. D. P. Little, Leiden, 1976, pp. 57-73. Bakhtāwar Khān, *Mirʾāt al-ʿĀlam*: *History of Emperor Awrangzeb ʿĀlamgīr*, ed. S. S. Alvi, I-II, Lahore, 1979. H. M. Elliot, *The History of India as Told by Its Own Historians*, ed. J. Dowson, London, 1877, VIII, pp. 150-53. Mostaʿed Khan, *Maʾāṯer-e ʿālamgīrī*, Eng. tr. Jadunath Sarkar, Calcutta, 1947, pp. 59, 61, 142, 155. Moḥammad-Afżal Sarḵoš, *Kalemāt al-šoʿarāʾ*, Lahore, n.d., pp. 25-26. *EI*[2] I, p. 954. Rieu, *Pers. Man.* I, pp. 124-27; III, pp. 890-91, 975. Storey, I, pp. 132-33, 517, 1012.

(S. S. ALVI)

BAḴTĪĀR, ABŪ ḤARB B. MOḤAMMAD, the patron of the poet Manūčehrī (d. 432/1040-41) who praised his bravery, nobility, magnanimity, learning, and eloquence in three *qaṣīda*s and one *mosammaṭ* on the occasion of the ancient Iranian festivals of Sada (*Dīvān*, pp. 21-22), Mehragān (pp. 90-95), and Nowrūz (pp. 114-16, 169-73). The choice of these festivals may indicate that Baḵtīār belonged to a noble family of Iranian origin.

In my annotations to the *Dīvān* of Manūčehrī I had suggested that Baḵtīār might be identical with Abū Ḥarb b. ʿAlāʾ-al-Dawla Abū Jaʿfar Moḥammad b. Došmanzīār, the governor of Naṭanz, but the publication of three extant inscriptions of his (see Bibliography) has revealed his full identity as Abū Ḥarb Baḵtīār the son of Ḥājeb Abū Jaʿfar Moḥammad b. Ebrāhīm, one of the amirs of Semnān and Dāmḡān (old Qūmes). He was a vassal of the Ziyarid amirs and a contemporary of Falak-al-Maʿālī Manūčehr b. Qābūs (r. 402-23/1012-32) and his successors. The inscriptions are in chronological order: 1. in Dāmḡān, in the palace of his father, known as Pīr-e ʿAlamdār, dated 417/1026, when his father was already dead; 2. in Dāmḡān, on the minaret of the Tārī-ḵāna mosque of Dāmḡān during the reign of Falak al-Maʿālī; this must have been written between 417/1026 and 423/1032, when Baḵtīār had the position of *ḥājeb* at the court of this king; 3. in Semnān, on the minaret of the Friday mosque, which was built during his governorship between the years 417/1026 and 426/1035.

Bibliography: *Dīvān-e Manūčehrī*, ed. M. Dabīrsīāqī, 3rd ed., Tehran, 1347 Š./1968-69; 5th ed., Tehran, 1363 Š./1984, nn. pp. 244, 245. Ch. Adle and A. S. Melikian-Chirvani, "Les monuments du XIe siècle du Dâmqân," *Studia Iranica* 1/2, 1972, pp. 229-97. Ch. Adle, "Le minaret du Masjed-e Jâmeʿ de Semnân. *Circa* 421-25/1030-34," ibid., 4/2, 1975, pp. 177-86.

(M. DABĪRSĪĀQĪ)

BAḴTĪĀR, TEYMŪR, Iranian general born in 1914, the son of Sardār Moʿaẓẓam Baḵtīārī. At the age of fourteen, he was sent to Beirut where he studied at a French high school until he was nineteen. Upon graduation he was accepted at St. Cyr military academy, where he studied between 1930-35. On his return to Iran, he was sent to Zāhedān, Baluchistan, with the rank of 1st lieutenant. He was married first to Īrān Khanom the daughter of Sardār(-e) Ẓafar, a well-known Baḵtīārī chieftain. That marriage produced a daughter and a son who died in early childhood. His second wife was Qodrat Ḵānom, who bore him two sons.

During the Moṣaddeq era, Baḵtīār was the commander of several provincial garrisons including Kermānšāh on the Iran-Iraq border. The shah's second wife, Ṯorayyā (Sorayya) Esfandīārī, was of the same tribe and cemented the bond of loyalty of the general to the royal family. His meteoric rise to power began after the fall of Moṣaddeq in August, 1953, when he was called to Tehran, promoted to brigadier general, and put in charge of Tehran's military governorship. In that position he waged a vigorous campaign to eradicate the Tudeh (Tūda) party, the Fedāʾīān-e Eslām, and to a lesser extent remnants of the pro-Moṣaddeq National Front. In 1954, he uncovered the Tudeh military organization (*Ketāb-e sīāh*) and a year later he arrested Nawwāb Ṣafawī, the leader of Fedāʾīān-e Eslām. Twenty-four ringleaders of the Tudeh military organization, Nawwāb Ṣafawī, and Ḵalīl Ṭahmāsebī, the assassin of the late Premier General Ḥājī-ʿAlī Razmārā, were executed after having been convicted by a military tribunal. In February 1958, he was appointed as the first chief of SAVAK (State Security and Intelligence Organization). Four years earlier at the age of 40 he had become the youngest three-star general in recognition of his successful, anti-communist and anti-Islamic fundamentalist campaign.

In 1961, when Dr. ʿAlī Amīnī was made prime minister, he convinced the shah that the more moderate general Pākravān should replace Baḵtīār. The shah, who had become somewhat concerned about Baḵtīār's ambitions and reported contact with President Kennedy in Washington D.C., consented. The general soon turned into a sworn enemy of the shah. First in Europe and then in Lebanon and Iraq, he contacted every known opponent of the regime. In retaliation, he was cashiered as an officer and a warrant for his arrest and extradition from Lebanon was issued. While in Iraq, he met not only Ayatollah Komeynī but also Dr. Reżā Rādmaneš, the general secretary of the Tudeh party, and Maḥmūd Panāhīān, the war minister in the short-lived Ādarbāyjān Republic of 1945-46. SAVAK was instructed by the shah to eliminate Baktīār at all costs. In a carefully organized plot, SAVAK agents managed to cultivate his trust. On August 12, 1970, his trusted driver, sent two years earlier from Tehran, shot him as he was lured to an area near the Iranian border ostensibly for hunting. Half a dozen Iranian agents were arrested and promptly executed for bringing an end to the life of the colorful general at the age of fifty-six.

Bibliography: *Ketāb-e sīāh*, 1954. Records in the Documentary Center, Iran Liberation Army, Paris 1982. G. de Villiers, *L'irrésistible ascension de Moḥammad Reza Shah d'Iran*, Paris, 1975. *Iranian Oral History Project*, Harvard University, Cambridge, 1986. Some of the information in this article was obtained in interviews with members of the Iran Liberation Army.

(S. ZABIH)

BAKTĪĀRĪ, a *gūša*. See HOMĀYŪN.

BAKTĪĀRĪ, the *nesba* of a number of Baktīārī chiefs.

Abu'l-Fatḥ Khan. See Abu'l-Fatḥ Khan Baktīārī.

Ḥājī **ʿAlīqolī** Khan **Sardār Asʿad**, one of two military commanders who marched on Tehran, deposed Moḥammad-ʿAlī Shah, and revived the aborted movement for constitutional government in Iran.

ʿAlīqolī, a member of the Haft Lang branch of the Baktīārī tribe and the fourth son of Ḥosaynqolī Khan Īlkānī (Sepehr, p. 576; Moʿayyer-al-Mamālek, p. 68), was born in 1274/1857-58, when the tribe was at its winter encampment. He completed his elementary education with the tribe and, after accompanying his mother on a pilgrimage to Mecca, received the title of Ḥājī (*Sepehr*, pp. 576-77). On 27 Rajab 1299/14 June 1882, the powerful governor of Isfahan and the southern provinces of Iran, Masʿūd Mīrzā Ẓell-al-Solṭān, acting on his father Nāṣer-al-Dīn Shah's instructions (Ẓell-al-Solṭān, p. 309; Eʿtemād-al-Salṭana, p. 210), garrotted Ḥosaynqolī Īlkānī, who had come to Isfahan at the governor's invitation. Ẓell-al-Solṭān also imprisoned Ḥosaynqolī's two sons, Esfandīār Khan and the twenty-five-year-old ʿAlīqolī Khan (Sepehr, p. 579; Bāmdād, *Rejāl* II, p. 449), who served the governor as brigadier (*sartīp*) and colonel (*sarhang*) respectively (ʿOkkāša, p. 183). A year later, however, as a result of Prime Minister ʿAlī-Aṣḡar Khan Amīn-al-Solṭān's intercession, ʿAlīqolī Khan was released from prison (Sepehr, pp. 177, 579) and brought to Tehran with the rank of brigadier (ibid., p. 593). In the role of honored hostage, he took command of the hundred-man brigade of Baktīārī horsemen that formed the prime minister's elite guard (Sepehr, p. 579; Owżan, *Waḥīd* 3/11, p. 92; Bāmdād, *Rejāl* II, p. 450) and that served fifty men at a time (Ẓell-al-Solṭān, p. 241). ʿAlīqolī's brother Esfandīār remained in prison until 1305/1887-88, when Ẓell-al-Solṭān was removed from office (Sepehr, pp. 171, 569; ʿOkkāša, p. 252), and with the title Sardār(-e) Asʿad became deputy chief (*īlbegī*) of the Baktīārī tribe. Upon Esfandīār's death in 1321/1903 (Bāmdād, *Rejāl* II, p. 448; or 1322/1904-05 [Sepehr, p. 593]), the title Sardār Asʿad was conferred upon ʿAlīqolī Khan (Sepehr, p. 594). During the more than forty-day interval between Nāṣer-al-Dīn Shah's assassination (17 Ḏu'l-qaʿda 1313/1 May 1896) and Moẓaffar-al-Dīn Shah's arrival in the capital, ʿAlīqolī Khan and his horsemen protected the life of Amīn-al-Solṭān, who had taken up residence in the Golestān palace and was directing affairs of state during that critical period (ibid., p. 175; Bāmdād, *Rejāl* II, p. 450). After the accession of Moẓaffar-al-Dīn Shah, with Amīn-al-Solṭān removed from office and exiled to Qom (1314/1896), Sardār Asʿad left Tehran to join his tribe. He returned to the capital in 1316/1898, during Amīn-al-Solṭān's second term as prime minister (Moʿayyer-al-Mamālek, p. 71). In 1318/1900-01, Sardār Asʿad visited several European capitals via India and Egypt, and, after a little more than two years residence in the advanced Europe of those days, having taken part in the funeral of the Queen of England and having become a Freemason in Paris, he returned to Iran (Sepehr, pp. 176, 580). Though, because of his close association with Amīn-al-Solṭān and with other important personages at the court of Moẓaffar-al-Dīn Shah he was considered a man of influence (Neẓām-al-Salṭana, I, pp. 206, 213), Sardār Asʿad did not remain in Tehran long. After Amīn-al-Solṭān was removed from office a second time (1321/1903), Sardār Asʿad, unwilling to serve as the commander of the guard protecting the new prime minister ʿAyn-al-Dawla (Moʿayyer-al-Mamālek, p. 71) and believing that a person must either live in civilized countries such as those of Europe or in the mountains (Sepehr, p. 176), rejoined his tribe. Sardār Asʿad returned to Tehran, but, finding the political atmosphere of the capital intolerable, in 1324/1906, during the first months after the issuing of the constitutional edict (*farmān-e mašrūṭīyat*) and about the time of the accession of Moḥammad-ʿAlī Shah, who preferred Sardār Asʿad's rival Amīr(-e) Mofakkam and treated the sons of Ḥosaynqolī Khan with indifference (ʿOkkāša, p. 555), he once again made his way to Europe, seeking treatment for his eyes (Sepehr, p. 581). It was during this three-year sojourn that Sardār Asʿad received word in Paris of the shelling of the Bahārestān (q.v.) and the arrest of the Constitutionalists. He contacted a group of exiles who had been driven from Iran by the tyranny of Moḥammad-ʿAlī Shah and who often gathered in Paris, and thanks to the financial resources at his disposal, turned his house into a meeting place for those opposed to Qajar despotism (Mokber-al-Salṭana, p. 181; Afšār, pp. 430-31; Sepehr, p. 581; Qazvīnī, p. 100). Having heard that the Qajar king had appealed to the Baktīārī tribe for help in putting down Constitutionalist forces and that several Baktīārī leaders had gone to Tehran and been ordered to quash the uprising in Tabrīz, he wrote admonishing letters to his relatives (Malekzāda, pp. 1080, 1082; Dānešvar ʿAlawī [p. 20] writes that he made a secret trip to Isfahan incognito and, residing in the house of an Armenian of Jolfā, met with Ḥājī Āqā Nūr-Allāh, an influential cleric from Isfahan and the brother of Āqā Najafī, and several other supporters of the Constitution to plan a revolt and then returned to Paris; however, there is no mention of this trip in the other sources, and it is probably apocryphal). As news of the general uprising in Iran filtered back to Europe, Sardār Asʿad met with the British ambassador in Paris (Moʿāṣer, p. 991) and Deputy Minister of Foreign Affairs Sir Charles Hardinge in London (Bāmdād, *Rejāl* II, p. 450; Navāʾī, p. 7; Mokber-al-Salṭana, p. 181). His discussions with British authorities made him confident that they would not stand in the way of the reestablishment of Iranian constitutional government (Malekzāda, p. 1028) and, in fact, would welcome his intervention at this juncture—as he was in any event a supporter of Britain. (The British did not want to see the credit of opposing the despotic monarch go only to the Azerbaijani fighters and their allies from the Caucasus, whose victory would have increased the Russian influence in Iran). He then felt free to dispatch messengers and messages urging his older brother Najafqolī Khan Ṣamṣām-al-Salṭana Īlkānī Baktīārī to amass troops and occupy Isfahan (Nāẓem-al-Eslām, II, p. 274; ʿOkkāša, p. 592). Eventually Sardār Asʿad himself, accompanied by his younger brother Yūsof Khan Amīr(-e) Mojāhed and his nephew Mortażāqolī Khan, the son of Ṣamṣām-al-Salṭana, traveled to southern Iran by sea. En route he was greeted by Muslim and Parsi Iranians living in Aden and Bombay (Sayyāḥ, p. 613). Toward the end of Ṣafar, 1327/March, 1909, two and a half months after Baktīārī horsemen had attacked Isfahan and Ṣamṣām-al-Salṭana had taken complete control of the city, ousting the state-appointed governor, Sardār Asʿad disembarked at Moḥammara (Korramšahr; Moʿāṣer, p. 1055). There he was enthusiastically greeted by the British-installed ruler of Kūzestān Shaikh Kazʿal (Sayyāḥ, p. 613). Together they prepared a telegram demanding a return to constitutional government and expressing their loyalty to the monarchy and sent it via Ażod-al-Dawla. Their telegram also contained this ultimatum: "If by the second month, a warrant (*dastkaṭṭ*) for the return of constitutional government is not issued, we shall resort to force" (Mostašār-al-Dawla, p. 233; Moʿāṣer, p. 1061). In the meantime, Shaikh Kazʿal, who was certain of British approval (Navāʾī, p. 7), sent a 10,000-toman draft to Ṣamṣām-al-Salṭana in Isfahan (Sepehr, p. 599).

Sardār Asʿad sent his brother Amīr Mojāhed to Tehran to meet with and advise Baktīārī chiefs loyal to the shah (Malekzāda, p. 1094), and he himself traveled through Kuzestān to the Baktīārī region. He went directly to Jāneqān, where he delegated two of his relatives to raise an army (Sayyāḥ, p. 614). Finally on 23 Rabīʿ II 1327/14 May 1909 (Sayyāḥ, p. 628), at the head of an army of 1,500 horsemen and infantry, Sardār Asʿad entered Isfahan and joined forces with Ṣamṣām-al-Salṭana's 1,500 troops. The resulting 3,000-man army staged outside of Isfahan to prepare to march on Tehran (Dawlatābādī, III, p. 104). Several days earlier (11 Rabīʿ II 1327/2 May 1909), the two brothers had sent a telegram via the Austrian ambassador, the ranking diplomat in Tehran, to the representatives of other foreign countries, declaring that, since the Constitutionalists' repeated demands had gone unanswered, they were going to Tehran to submit their entreaties to the shah in person and that because they feared that base and corrupt elements would try to prevent them, the aggrieved parties, from entering the capital, they had assembled what forces they could to accompany them to Tehran. They would not tolerate, whatever the pretext, the introduction of foreign troops into Iran and therefore requested the representatives of the great powers to maintain their neutrality and not to engage in any form of intervention (Sepehr, p. 560).

Already troubled by the revolt in the provinces and the movement of forces from Tabrīz and Rašt under the command of Sepahdār Tonokābonī, the shah's anxiety grew upon hearing of Sardār Asʿad's preparations. As a result of repeated visits by Russian and British diplomats, on 14 Rabīʿ II 1327/5 May 1909 he issued a proclamation concerning the renewal of elections and the opening of parliament (Nāẓem-al-Eslām, II, p. 439). This proclamation was greeted with popular rejoicing and festivities. Advised by the Russian and British consuls-general that marching on Tehran was now pointless, Sardār Asʿad had no choice but to return to Isfahan and disband his troops (Dawlatābādī, III, p. 104).

But a month later, when the shah's promises proved false, Sardār Asʿad, after meetings with British Consul-General Grahame (Navāʾī, p. 7), on 27 Jomādā I/16 June, set forth from Isfahan with 700 cavalrymen (Navāʾī, p. 13) and a number of Baktīārī khans and leaders (Malekzāda, p. 1096). After Ṣamṣām-al-Salṭana's rebellion and with Farmānfarmā having elected not to go to Isfahan to confront him (Nāẓem-al-Eslām, II, p. 285), the shah used false promises to get Amīr Mofakkam Baktīārī and the horsemen under his command to undertake the mission. As Amīr Mofakkam remained camped at Kāšān for nearly seven months, awaiting necessary supplies and provisions (Sepehr, p. 573), Sardār Asʿad, aware of the tribal warfare and feelings of revenge that would be provoked by a confrontation with his kinsmen and fellow Baktīārīs, decided to avoid the city. He traveled instead through Neyzār to Qom (Nāẓem-al-Eslām, II, p. 468; Navāʾī, p. 13). The advance battalion of the Sardār's forces, composed of 200 cavalry under the command of his son Sardār(-e) Bahādor and two of the Sardār's nephews, entered Qom on 6 Jomādā II/25 June (Nāẓem-al-Eslām, II, p. 468) and were welcomed by its chief administrator of religious property (*motawallībāšī*), who previously had had a taste of the Constitutionalists' vengeance. They occupied the city and, in an unprecedented display of discipline, prevented any form of savagery. The next day Sardār Asʿad entered the city with the remainder of his troops (Dawlatābādī, III, p. 105; Nāẓem-al-Eslām, II, p. 469).

On 4 Jomādā II/23 June, British Secretary of State for Foreign Affairs Sir Edward Grey, who saw Sardār Asʿad's movements as counter to his own strategy, sent a telegram to his envoy in Tehran, Sir George Barclay, telling him in effect that serious steps must be taken to stop Sardār Asʿad from reaching Tehran and that it would be wise of him to give the Sardār the details of the program of reform promulgated by the two powers (*Ketāb-e ābī* III, p. 582).

As news of Sardār Asʿad's arrival in Qom spread, the anxiety felt by the royalists increased. With Premier Saʿd-al-Dawla demanding action, on Barclay's suggestion and with the approval of Sir Edward Grey, the Russian and British consuls-general were delegated to go to Qom and dissuade Sardār Asʿad from continuing his march on Tehran (*Ketāb-e ābī* III, p. 580; Nāẓem-al-Eslām, II, p. 456). The Sardār, however, did not accept their advice, saying, "The two embassies have been deceived; the shah does not have the slightest intention of establishing constitutional government" (8 Jomādā II/27 June; *Ketāb-e ābī* III, pp. 583, 637). During secret meetings with the British consul-general in Isfahan, Grahame, the Sardār said in effect: to stop now would be impossible; a great deal of money has been spent—besides I could not hope to receive a pardon from the shah (Barclay's telegram, dated 6 Jomādā II 1327/25 June 1909; Moʿāṣer, pp. 1135, 1137).

A group of Ḵalaj freedom fighters (*mojāhed*) joined Sardār Asʿad's troops in Qom (Nāẓem-al-Eslām, II, p. 519), and finally on 13 Jomādā II/2 July, he left Qom for Tehran (Moʿāṣer, p. 1146). Previously having cajoled a number of royalist Baḵtīārī leaders and mounted troops, e.g., Ḵosrow Khan Sardār Ẓafar, into joining him (ʿOkkāša, p. 595; Sayyāḥ, p. 619; Malekzāda, p. 1094), Sardār Asʿad again tried to avoid a confrontation with Amīr Mofaḵḵam by sending him a message stating that, if he did not stand in his way and, instead of battling his fellow Baḵtīārī, would fight the army in the north, he (Sardār Asʿad) was prepared to cede him all the wealth he possessed and to accept him as the permanent chief of the Baḵtīārī tribe. Amīr Mofaḵḵam did not accept his offer (ʿOkkāša, p. 596; Sayyāḥ, p. 642) and marched to Ḥasanābād to block Sardār Asʿad's path. The Sardār reacted to this news by changing his route and going through Rebāṭ-e Karīm; there he held secret discussions with Amīr Mofaḵḵam but was unable to disabuse him of his loyalty to the shah (Sepehr, p. 181). Sardār Asʿad in turn rejected the arguments of G. Churchill and Major Stokes, representatives of the two powers, who were sent to dissuade him from attacking Tehran (*Ketāb-e ābī* III, p. 608) and traveled to Qarātappa. At the same time Sepahdār Tonokābonī, with whom Ṣamṣām-al-Salṭana and Sardār Asʿad had been corresponding and had reached an understanding, decamped with a force of 750 *mojāheds* (Šarīf Kāšānī, pp. 392, 395) at Yengī-emām. Sardār Asʿad, whose army was a *farsaḵ* away, went to meet him personally (Sepehr, p. 182), and the two Constitutionalist commanders prepared their plan of attack on Tehran.

As the two armies, one from the north and the other from the south, were nearing one another around Qandīšāh, eight Baḵtīārī chiefs and relatives of the Sardār were mistakenly killed by some of Yeprem's (Ephraim Saʿīd's) *mojāheds*. As soon as he learned of the incident, Sardār Asʿad wisely decided to stop the Baḵtīārīs from avenging the murder and accepted the apologies of the *mojāheds*, thereby avoiding war between the two armies (Šarīf Kāšānī, p. 399; Navāʾī, p. 71; Malekzāda, p. 1181). The armies merged at Bādāmak (Sepehr, p. 581) and on 21 Jomādā II/17 July, engaged government forces commanded by Amīr Mofaḵḵam (Šarīf Kāšānī, p. 401). After three days of inconclusive fighting, the two Constitutionalist commanders, having formed a plan, set out for the capital by night (ʿOkkāša, p. 601). On 24 Jomādā/20 July (Sepehr, p. 581; Nāẓem-al-Eslām, II, p. 487), they entered Tehran through the Bahjatābād gate without encountering serious resistance from the Iranian officers of the cossack brigade and settled in the Bahārestān buildings (Nāẓem-al-Eslām, II, p. 499; Moʿāṣer, p. 1143).

With the ousted shah having fled to the Russian legation and after a group of prominent Constitutionalist leaders had met in an extraordinary session of the assembly, Sardār Asʿad was chosen as minister of interior and Sepahdār Tonokābonī as minister of war (Bāmdād, *Rejāl* II, p. 451) in the new cabinet that was formed without a premier (28 Jomādā II 1327/24 July 1909). This was done despite the fact that most Constitutionalist statesmen and those with the country's best interests at heart opposed having the two Constitutionalist military commanders in administrative posts of government (Mostašār-al-Dawla, p. 256; Šarīf Kāšānī, pp. 245, 445; Dawlatābādī, III, p. 122; Moḵber-al-Salṭana, p. 194). Be that as it may, Sardār Asʿad was apparently not inclined to accept the post, and had to be persuaded by Sepahdār Tonokābonī who insisted that he take it (Sepahsālār, p. 295; Moḵber-al-Salṭana, p. 194). Around ten months later, during the middle of Rabīʿ II, 1328/April, 1910 (Sepehr, p. 587), the Majles, at the insistence of Nāṣer-al-Molk (Dawlatābādī, III, p. 126), selected Sardār Asʿad as minister of war in the cabinet of Sepahdār Tonokābonī; but on 4 Rajab 1328/12 July 1910, with the formation of the Mostawfī-al-Mamālek cabinet, the two conquerors of Tehran left their cabinet posts and, with the consent of the Majles (which at this time had discretion over filling its empty seats), became deputies in the National Assembly. At this crucial juncture, with rebellion brewing in every corner of Iran and power struggles rife, the Baḵtīārī army under Sardār Asʿad's general command and led by his son Sardār Bahādor (Jaʿfarqolī Khan who later received the title Sardār Asʿad from his father) in conjunction with Yeprem Khan and his army, distinguished themselves in putting down the rebels and claimants (such as Raḥīm Khan Čelpīānlū, Sālār-al-Dawla, and Sardār Aršad-al-Dawla); more important, they eliminated the difficulty posed by the transgressions of *mojāhed*s who entered Tehran with Sattār Khan and Bāqer Khan (qq.v.; Sepehr, pp. 743-45).

In Ṣafar, 1329/February, 1911, Mostawfī-al-Mamālek's cabinet fell and Sepahdār Tonokābonī became premier again; however, Sardār Asʿad was not prepared to accept a cabinet post. Two months later, when he was awarded the medal *nešān-e qods* and the sum of 6,000 tomans, he returned the medal to the state and gave the money to the Ministry of Sciences to spend on education (Sepehr, p. 590). Vexed by the unsettled state of affairs in Iran, on 1 Jomādā II 1329/3 June 1911 (ibid., pp. 590, 746), the Sardār traveled to Europe to continue treatment for his eyes. Even during his treatments, he engaged in discussions designed to place himself in the position of vice-regent or to replace the then vice-regent Nāṣer-al-Molk with Saʿd-al-Dawla, who was living in Switzerland at the time (Dawlatābādī, p. 215). Sardār Asʿad returned to Iran at the start of winter of that year (1329/1912; Sepehr, p. 746), and, in the absence of Vice-Regent Nāṣer-al-Molk (in Europe on the pretext that he was ill) and with Sepahdār Tonokābonī appointed governor of Azerbaijan as a result of a Russian ultimatum and incursion into northern Iran, became an influential figure in the country during Ṣamṣām-al-Salṭana's premiership (Dawlatābādī, II, pp. 215-17). However less than a year after he returned to Tehran, Sardār Asʿad lost his sight and strength in his limbs (Sepehr, pp. 747, 766) and retired to his home. He spent his remaining years, which coincided with the beginning of World War I, in dictating various books and in educational activities (ibid., p. 766); his house was always open to scholars and littérateurs. Sardār Asʿad died on 7 Moḥarram 1336/23 October 1917 at the age of sixty-three (Qazvīnī, p. 99; most of the available sources give the second half of Moḥarram as the date of his death. This mistake is probably due to the interval between his death in Tehran and his burial in Isfahan). The people of Tehran paid fitting tribute to his memory by closing schools and offices during the funeral procession (Moʿayyer-al-Mamālek, p. 72; Owžan, *Waḥīd* 4, p. 264), which brought the Sardār's body to Isfahan for burial at the Takīa-ye Mīr (Sardār Ẓafar, 4, p. 950) of the Takt-e Fūlād cemetery (Moʿayyer-al-Mamālek, p. 72; Bāmdād, *Rejāl* II, p. 451).

Some Iranian historians who have tried to attribute the early 20th-century movement for constitutional government in Iran solely to British instruction and instigation insist that Sardār Asʿad was carrying out the policy of a foreign power during the affair (Bāmdād, *Rejāl* II, p. 451), without actually believing in popular government himself. Several facts can be cited which sustain this view: 1. the special relations the Baktīārī khans enjoyed with the British government and the services rendered by Esfandīār Khan in policing the roads of Kuzestān and the awards he received from Queen Victoria for his services; 2. more significantly, the agreement of Sardār Asʿad, Ṣamṣām-al-Salṭana, and the other Baktīārī khans to a 3-percent instead of a 10-percent share of the oil company of the south (Owžan, *Waḥīd* 4, pp. 175, 176; Bāmdād, *Rejāl* II, p. 450); 3. the patriarchal tradition among the Baktīārī and the inviolable authority invested in the khan (Sayyāḥ, p. 625); 4. the British interest in and active encouragement of establishing a constitutional government and ending the absolute power of the shah, whose guarantor was the Russian czar; this was especially evident after the dissolution of the first Majles, when disturbances broke out in Azerbaijan and Russian influence among the leaders of the *mojāhed*s of Tabrīz and Gīlān was likely and when the British were searching for a solution that would both bring peace to the country and also allow the monarchy to remain in the Qajar family (thereby eliminating the possibility of the Russians' using the Treaty of Torkamānčāy to intervene). Despite these facts, study of Sardār Asʿad's life makes it clear that he was not solely an agent of British policy; he was also a man devoted to popular government and the advancement of the nation. He was the product of an environment which was exceptional for Iran of that era; his father, Ḥosaynqolī Khan, in the face of all the prevailing tribal violence and cruelty, remained a man of poetic sensibility (he was the author of many verses in the Baktīārī dialect) and was respected by a reform-minded, progressive premier like Mīrzā Ḥosayn Khan Sepahsālār (Ẓell-al-Solṭān, p. 243). ʿAlīqolī Khan was himself also enthused about learning and possessed an inquiring mind and a spirit that sought reform and that was not polluted by many of the prejudices of the time (Major Stokes quoted in Sepehr, p. 642). Raised in an environment in which, because of the Baktīārī khans' close ties to British officials and travelers (Wright, pp. 43-44; Sepehr p. 639), Sardār Asʿad met many Europeans in his youth, his desire to see Europe ultimately impelled him to travel there and made him a devoted admirer of European order and advancement. It is no wonder then that a man with such a background, who had direct experience with and bitter memories of Nāṣer-al-Dīn's tyranny and the bloodshed and power of Ẓell-al-Solṭān, who witnessed firsthand the raids on the treasury made by Moẓaffar-al-Dīn Shah's comrades, and who saw how greedy clerics kept the people in ignorance and superstition, would turn to the secret of European advancement in viewing the expansion of modern schools as the key to his country's awakening and would join his voice to those of respected and progressive men who were calling for creation of schools and libraries before the announcement of the Constitution. It was during his second trip to Europe and his association with a group of the outstanding refugee intellectuals and reformers, who also resided in Paris and were often his guests, that he heard news of the remonstrations of Shaikh Fażl-Allāh Nūrī and like-minded clerics who supported the tyranny of Moḥammad-ʿAlī Shah in the name of the

Koran and Islam and of the unleashing of bands of ruthless troops on the people, that he conceived a passion for constitutional government and the rule of law. It was Sardār Asʿad's respect for law and order that restrained the Baktīārī tribe, long-accustomed to robbing and pillaging, from any form of such crimes after their conquests of Qom and Tehran.

Other historians view Sardār Asʿad's basic motive as a desire to gain the crown for himself. While such ambition on his part is not out of the question, Sardār Asʿad was not uninformed; he knew of the Russian pledge to maintain the monarchy for the descendants of the vice-regent ʿAbbās Mīrzā (q.v.), and he also had seen evidence of the coordination of Russian and British policy on Iran in that era. Moreover, his behavior after the conquest of Tehran suggests that he refrained from accepting the vice-regency (Owžan, *Waḥīd* 4, p. 217) and even had to be persuaded by Sepahdār Tonokābonī and other well-intentioned men to take the foreign affairs portfolio (Sepahsālār, p. 295). He took the post of minister of war at the insistence of Nāṣer-al-Molk (Dawlatābādī, III, pp. 126-27) but a year after Tehran was taken withdrew from public life altogether. Sardār Asʿad was apparently one of the few people who knew what the Constitutional revolution was all about. Thus, when the Armenian commander Yeprem Khan was chosen to be the head of the police force and Sepahdār Tonokābonī objected on the basis of his religion, Sardār Asʿad pointed out that under constitutional government the majority must rule (Šarīf Kāšānī, p. 409). For the same reason, after Tehran fell, he joined the so-called *enqelābī* group, the "democrats," and sided more with such statesmen as Mošīr-al-Dawla, Moʾtaman-al-Molk, Ṣanīʿ-al-Dawla, Woṯūq-al-Dawla, and Taqīzāda, who favored the freedom and civilization of Europe (Šarīf Kāšānī, p. 409), unlike Sepahdār Tonokābonī, who joined the group known as *eʿtedālī*s with Sayyed ʿAbd-Allāh Behbahānī and sided with Sardār Moḥyī, Żarḡām-al-Salṭana, Bāqer Khan, and Sattār Khan (Dawlatābādī, III, pp. 127-40; Owžan, *Waḥīd* 4, p. 230).

Sardār Asʿad's behavior was tempered by moderation (Qazvīnī, pp. 100-01) and was free of malice and revenge. When he was at the height of his power, he was humane in his treatment of his father's murderer Ẓell-al-Solṭān and of Amīr Mofakkam, who never wavered in his opposition to the Sardār (Malekzāda, pp. 1077, 1313; ʿOkkāša, p. 601; Owžan, *Waḥīd* 4, p. 214). During the first days after the conquest of Tehran, in response to Sepahdār Tonokābonī who decried the return of fugitive members of the first Majles, Sardār Asʿad brought calm by promising "Wait until we dethrone Moḥammad-ʿAlī, then we will think of something; it is too early now" (Sepahsālār, p. 295). After Colonel Liakhoff, commander of Moḥammad-ʿAlī Shah's cossack brigade, swore his allegiance to constitutional government, Sardār Asʿad allowed him to continue in his post (Mostašār-al-Dawla, p. 98).

So devoted to maintaining constitutional government was Sardār Asʿad that he personally confronted the rebellions of Sattār Khan and Bāqer Khan, who, while national heroes and the people's favorites, were supported by armed *mojāhed*s who were fomenting riots at the instigation of Sardār Moḥyī (Dawlatābādī, III, pp. 127-40). When these armed supporters refused to lay down their arms, despite all the proof of their complicity and the binding vote of the Majles, Sardār Asʿad sent his son Amir Bahādor along with Yeprem Khan to disarm them (Sepahsālār, p. 286; Sepehr, p. 744). He also sent his son and relatives with Baktīārī cavalry to fight rebels wherever they raised their heads ibid., p. 576; Shuster, pp. 90, 127; Owžan, p. 209). After hearing rumors of Sepahdār Tonokābonī's secret dealings with the deposed shah (Shuster, p. 90), he sent him a reproachful telegram warning, "After having his share of life and fame, how could a man destroy his good name?" (Malekzāda, p. 1378).

While Sepahdār Tonokābonī was an emotional man, quick to anger and mercurial, Sardār Asʿad was the picture of virtue, steadfast, forgiving, farsighted, and a promoter of education (Bāmdād, *Rejāl* II, p. 451). More than anything else he focused on training the nation and the expansion of existing educational facilities. With his encouragement and resources, and occasionally under his own direction, several books written in European languages were translated into Persian and published (Qazvīnī, p. 99; Sepehr, pp. 44, 593; Bāmdād, *Rejāl* II, p. 451). Using his own funds he sent a number of young Baktīārīs, who had been educated in schools established by him (Rāʾīn, p. 26; Malekzāda, p. 1079; Sepehr, pp. 44, 593), to Europe for further education (Qazvīnī, p. 100; Bāmdād, *Rejāl* II, p. 451). He was a man beloved by the people, just, and uncorrupted by the graft-taking that was customary at the time (Mostašār-al-Dawla, p. 98; Bāmdād, *Rejāl* II, p. 451). He was also free of the boasting and immune to the kind of toadyism that was practiced in his day.

These qualities notwithstanding, after the initial uproar of the Constitutional movement died down and after Sardār Asʿad's gradual withdrawal from public life, the Baktīārī chiefs reverted to their old nature, i.e., cupidity, and made forays into the already bankrupt public treasury (Shuster, pp. 122, 206; Sepahsālār, p. 299). These forays went so far, after Sardār Asʿad lost his sight and retired to his home, that the Baktīārī khans, who were often provincial rulers, vied with one another in possessing their own personal armies. In addition to official forces provided by the state, each ruling khan also maintained a number of Baktīārī horsemen, which sometimes reached 200 and whose pay was borne by the state treasury (Mostawfī, II, p. 368).

Bibliography: Ī. Afšār, *Awrāq-e tāzayāb-e mašrūṭīyat wa naqš-e Taqīzāda*, Tehran, 1359 Š./1980. N. Dānešvar ʿAlawī, *Tārīḵ-e mašrūṭīyat-e Īrān wa jonbeš-e waṭanparastān-e Eṣfahān wa Baḵtīārī*, Tehran, 1337 Š./1958. Dawlatābādī, *Ḥayāt-e Yaḥyā*. M.-Ḥ. Eʿtemād-al-Salṭana, *Rūz-nāma-ye ḵāṭerāt*. *Ketāb-e ābī: Goḏāreš-e maḥramāna-ye wezārat-e omūr-e ḵāreja-ye Englīs dar bāra-ye enqelāb-e Īrān*, ed. A. Bašīrī, Tehran, 1363 Š./1984. M. Malekzāda,

Tārīk-e mašrūṭīyat-e Īrān, 2nd ed., Tehran, 1363 Š./1984. Ḥ. Mo'āṣer, *Tārīk-e esteqrār-e mašrūṭīyat dar Īrān*, Tehran, 1347 Š./1968. D. Mo'ayyer-al-Mamālek, "Rejāl-e 'aṣr-e nāṣerī," *Yaḡmā* 11, 1337 Š./1958. M. Mokber-al-Salṭana Hedāyat, *Kāṭerāt o kaṭarāt*, 2nd ed., Tehran, 1344 Š./1965. Ṣ. Mostašār-al-Dawla, *Kāṭerāt wa asnād*, ed. Ī. Afšār, Tehran, 1362 Š./1983. 'A. Mostawfī, *Šarḥ-e zendagānī-e man*, 2nd ed., Tehran, 1343 Š./1964. 'A.-Ḥ. Navā'ī, *Fatḥ-e Tehrān*, 2536 = 1356 Š./1977. M. Nāẓem-al-Eslām Kermānī, *Tārīk-e bīdārī-e īrānīān*, ed. 'A.-A. Sa'īdī Sīrjānī, Tehran, 1362 Š./1983. Ḥ. Neẓām-al-Salṭana Māfī, *Kāṭerāt o asnād*, Tehran, 1361 Š./1982. E. Żayḡam-al-Salṭana 'Okkāša, *Tārīk-e īl-e Baktīārī*, ed. F. Morādī, Tehran, 1365 Š./1986. A. Owžan, "Tārīk-e Baktīārī," *Waḥīd* 3-4, 1345-46 Š./1966-67. M. Qazvīnī, *Yādgār* 5/1-2. E. Rā'īn, *Anjomanhā-ye serrī dar enqelāb-e mašrūṭīyat*, Tehran, 1345 Š./1966. E. Ṣafā'ī, *Asnād-e bargozīda-ye dawrān-e Qājārīya*, Tehran, 2535 = 1355 Š./1976. Ḥ.-K. Sardār Ẓafar, "Kāṭerāt-e Sardār Ẓafar Baktīārī," *Waḥīd* 4. M.-M. Šarīf Kāšānī, *Wāqe'at-e ettefāqīya dar rūzgār*, Tehran, 1362 Š./1983. M.-'A. Ḥājj Sayyāḥ, *Kāṭerāt*, ed. Ḥ. Sayyāḥ, Tehran, 1364 Š./1985. M.-W. Sepahsālār Tonokābonī, *Yaddāšthā-ye parākanda*, comp. A.-'A. Kal'atbarī, ed. M. Tafażżolī, Tehran, 1362 Š./1983. W. M. Shuster, *The Strangling of Persia*, New York, 1912. 'Abd-al-Ḥosayn Lesān-al-Salṭana Sepehr, *Tārīk-e baktīārī*, Tehran, 1361 Š./1982. D. Wright, *The English amongst the Persians*, London, 1977. S. M. Ẓell-al-Solṭan, *Tārīk-e sargodašt-e mas'ūdī*, Tehran, 1362 Š./1983.

('A.-A. Sa'īdī Sīrjānī)

Ḡolām-Ḥosayn Khan **Šehāb-**al-**Salṭana**, then **Sardār**(-e) **Moḥtašam** (1866?-1950), one of the few Baktīārī chiefs who played a national role after the Constitutional revolution (1324-27/1906-09). He was the sixth son of Emāmqolī Khan, known as Ḥājī Īlkānī, founder of the younger branch of the Haft Lang, whose chiefs were titled *kawānīn-e bozorg* (great khans). After seven years in the service of Moḥammad Shah while still a prince, he was twice *īlbegī* and twice *īlkānī* of the Baktīārī tribe between 1905 and 1921, and occupied a government position 1911-13, when the government was dominated by the Baktīārī chiefs. He was one of the few members of his family who was not arrested and executed in 1933. He died in Tehran in 1950 and is remembered as a pensive, courageous and extremely honest man.

Bibliography: J.-P. Digard, "Jeux de structures. Segmentarité et pouvoir chez les nomades Baxtyâri d'Iran," *L'homme* 102 (27/2), 1987, pp. 12-53. G. R. Garthwaite, *Khans and Shahs: A Documentary Analysis of the Bakhtiyari in Iran*, Cambridge, 1983, passim.

(J.-P. Digard)

Ḥosaynqolī Khan, the son of Ja'farqolī Khan, from the Dūrakī clan of the Haft Lang, the first credible Baktīārī *īlkān*. After his father was killed in 1252 Š./1836-37, he was adopted for a time by his paternal uncle and then entered the service of Manūčehr Khan Mo'tamed-al-Dawla (q.v.). After Mo'tamed-al-Dawla defeated and sent Moḥammad-Taqī Kanūrsī of the Čahār Lang (q.v.) into hiding, Ḥosaynqolī Khan prospered. As a reward for his services to Manūčehr Khan in this campaign, he was appointed deputy governor (*nāyeb al-ḥokūma*) of the Baktīārī region and gradually brought the other Baktīārī Khans under his authority. He was ruthless in suppressing and executing his opponents; he ruled as the *īlkān* of the entire Baktīārī region for close to forty years.

The length of Ḥosaynqolī Khan's tenure and the spread of his influence began to concern Nāṣer-al-Dīn Shah; he was especially worried by the Baktīārī *īlkān*'s dealings with the British and the Grey-Mackenzie company. The shah was also troubled by the ever-increasing power of Ẓell-al-Solṭān in the central and southern parts of Iran; he thus dispatched Ḥājī Mīrzā 'Abd-al-Ḡaffār Khan Najm-al-Molk to the Baktīārī regions on the pretext of estimating the costs of building the Ahvāz dam, but in actuality to gather intelligence on the size and strength of Ḥosaynqolī Khan's forces. In the course of his detailed report to the shah on the extent of the *īlkān*'s power and influence among the tribes of the south, Najm-al-Molk indicated that Ḥosaynqolī Khan possessed more than 1,000 mares, each of which was worth between 100 and 800 tomans. He concluded "his intentions are not honest, and these sentiments are deeply rooted among the Baktīārī." Najm-al-Molk's report confirms previous reports that Farhād Mīrzā Mo'tamed-al-Dawla, the ruler of Fārs, had prepared for the shah. Nāṣer-al-Dīn was therefore persuaded to have the *īlkān* executed; he instructed his son Ẓell-al-Solṭān, the ruler of Isfahan, to put an end to the *īlkān*. Ẓell-al-Solṭān invited the *īlkān* to Isfahan, and the *īlkān* complied, taking part in ceremonies to review his host's troops. At the end of the ceremonies, his comment "One hundred Baktīārī horsemen are the equal of one thousand of such troops" provided greater impetus for Ẓell-al-Solṭān to carry out his plan. With the ceremonies over, Ẓell-al-Solṭān brought the *īlkān* and his two sons, Esfandīār Khan and 'Alīqolī Khan (qq.v.) to government house for discussions; after separating him from his sons and imprisoning them, Ẓell-al-Solṭān issued the order to execute the *īlkān*, which his agents carried out that night (27 Rajab 1299/14 June 1882). In addition to the ruthlessness and bravery requisite in the life and position of an *īlkān*, Ḥosaynqolī was also a man of sensitivity and refined taste, who was famous for his Baktīārī dialect poetry.

Bibliography: S. Ẓ. Baktīārī, *Yāddāšthā wa kāṭerāt*, Tehran, 1362 Š./1983. Bāmdād, *Rejāl* I, p. 442. G. N. Curzon, *Persia and the Persian Question* II, London, 1892. G. R. Garthwaite, *Khans and Shahs: A Documentary Analysis of the Bakhtiari in Iran*, Cambridge, 1983. Ḥ. S. Maḥallātī, *Safar-nāma*, Tehran, 1356 Š./1977, pp. 279-80. 'A.-Ḡ. Najm-al-Molk, *Safar-nāma*, ed. M. Dabīrsīāqī, Tehran, 1341 Š./1962, pp. 24, 47, 53, 76. Ḥ. Sa'ādat Nūrī, *Ẓell-al-*

Solṭān, Tehran, 1347 Š./1968, pp. 156-203. M. M. Ẓell-al-Solṭān, *Tārīk̲-e mas'ūdī*, Tehran, 1362 Š./1983, pp. 286-311.

Ja'farqolī Khan **Sardār(-e) As'ad III,** the eldest son of Ḥājī 'Alīqolī Khan Sardār As'ad II, born 1296/1878-79. In 1327/1909, he accompanied his father and the army of the south in their conquest of Tehran. After Moḥammad-'Alī Shah was removed and after the convening of the extraordinary session of the Majles to run the country, Ja'farqolī Khan was appointed to the ten-member revolutionary court, in which several opponents of constitutional government were tried and condemned to death. During this time, followers of the deposed Moḥammad-'Alī Shah were fomenting rebellion and attacking the property, persons, and wives of the populace throughout Azerbaijan, especially in the districts of Ardabīl and Arasbārān. The second Majles considered the creation of a force to suppress these rebellions a necessity. The leader of this force was Yaprim Khan who was accompanied on his campaigns by Ja'farqolī Khan and the Bak̲tīārī cavalry. The successful quelling of the revolts added to Ja'farqolī's popularity.

Until 1336/1917-18, Ja'farqolī was titled Sardār(-e) Bahādor; after the death of his father, he received the title Sardār As'ad. In 1338/1919-20, he was appointed governor of Kermān and a short time thereafter became governor of Khorasan. With the advent of Reżā Shah, Ja'farqolī cooperated sincerely with the new shah and, after Teymūrtāš was removed from office and imprisoned, his closeness to and standing with Reżā Shah increased. However, at the outset of Ādar, 1312 Š./November, 1933, when he was minister of war in the Forūg̲ī cabinet, Ja'farqolī was arrested by the order of Reżā Shah as he accompanied him on a tour of Māzandarān. He was arrested and several months later, on 13 Farvardīn 1313 Š./2 April 1934, word spread that Sardār As'ad had died in jail. It was rumored that he was poisoned or executed in prison; he was not more than fifty-five when he died. Mok̲ber-al-Salṭana Hedāyat writes: "Sardār As'ad was not tried, though it was said that the Bak̲tīārī had been secretly supplied with weapons. Later, in meetings with the shah I heard [him say], 'Yes, they want to bring Moḥammad-Ḥasan Mīrzā; there can be no more licentiousness than this.' The shah said no more, but it was clear that he was referring to Sardār As'ad. For my part, I have seen nothing but sincere devotion to the Pahlavī ruler by Sardār As'ad, and I have my doubts about how he was characterized."

Bibliography: Bāmdād, *Rejāl* I, pp. 245-46. M. Mok̲ber-al-Salṭana Hedāyat, *K̲āṭerāt wa k̲aṭarāt*, Tehran, 1344 Š./1965, pp. 199, 403. 'A. Mostawfī, *Šarḥ-e zendagānī-e man*, Tehran, 1325 Š./1946. W. M. Shuster, *The Strangling of Persia*, New York, 1912.

('A.-Ḥ. NAVĀ'Ī)

Loṭf-'Alī Khan **Šojā'-al-Solṭān,** then **Amīr-e Mofak̲k̲am,** Bak̲tīārī chief (1862-1946), fourth son of Emāmqolī Khan, known as Ḥājī Īlk̲ānī. As chief of the personal guard of Moḥammad-'Alī Shah Qājār, he was opposed to the march of the Bak̲tīārīs on Tehran in July, 1909, and was one of the few Bak̲tīārī chiefs not to participate in it. He was *īlk̲ānī* of the Bak̲tīārī tribe 1930-33.

Moḥammad-Reżā Khan **Sardār-e Fāteḥ** (1885-1934), the ninth son of Emāmqolī Khan, known as Ḥājī Īlk̲ānī, founder of the younger branch of the Haft Lang, whose chiefs were titled *kawānīn-e bozorg* (great khans). He married a daughter of his paternal uncle Najafqolī Khan Ṣamṣām-al-Salṭana (q.v.) and was the father of Šāpūr Bak̲tīār (b. 1914 in Beirut), the last prime minister of Moḥammad-Reżā Shah Pahlavī (r. 1320-51 Š./1941-78). Sardār-e Fāteḥ received his title at the order of another paternal uncle, Ḥājī 'Alīqolī Khan Sardār As'ad II (q.v.), during the march of the Bak̲tīārīs on Tehran in July, 1909. He was governor of Yazd in 1914 and of Isfahan in 1921, then *īlbegī* of the Bak̲tīārī tribe in 1930. He retired to Tehran in 1930, was arrested in 1933 together with several other members of his family, and was executed in prison in 1934.

Moḥammad-Taqī Khan, the last and most famous of the great Khans from the Čahār Lang faction of the Bak̲tīārī tribe (d. 1851 in prison). Working for the political unity of the Bak̲tīārīs, Moḥammad-Taqī Khan was arrested by Farhād Mīrzā Mo'tamed-al-Dawla, governor of Isfahan, in 1841, leaving the field open for his rival Ḥosaynqolī Khan (q.v.) of the Haft Lang fraction. The year 1841 marks the end of the Čahār Lang supremacy over the Bak̲tīārī tribe.

Mortażāqolī Khan (1876?-1961), one of the last Bak̲tīārī chiefs to have played an important political role. The only son of Najafqolī Khan Ṣamṣām-al-Salṭana (q.v.) and grandson of Emāmqolī Khan, known as Ḥājī Īlk̲ānī, he was *īlbegī*, *īlk̲ānī*, and *ḥākem* of the Bak̲tīārī tribe from 1925 to 1945. During this period he was a witness to all the stages of the transformation of the administration of the tribe: the abolition of the titles *īlbegī* and *īlk̲ānī* in 1933, the division of the territory of the tribe between the two provinces of Isfahan and K̲ūzestān in 1936, and the creation of the governorate of Čahār Maḥāl and Bak̲tīārī in 1943. In 1946, Mortażāqolī Khan, who had married a daughter of the Qašqā'ī chief Ṣawlat-al-Dawla, was together with the Qašqā'ī brothers one of the leaders of the tribal uprising in Fārs (1325 Š./1946), the so-called "southern movement" (*nahżat-e jonūb*). This was fomented by the English in order to organize the secession of the southern tribal provinces and led to the reorganization of the cabinet by Prime Minister Aḥmad Qawām (Qawām-al-Salṭana; cf. Homayounpour, pp. 20, 165). Ousted by his cousin and rival Abu'l-Qāsem Khan of the Īlk̲ānī branch, Mortażāqolī Khan then ceased to play any political role.

Bibliography: Bāmdād, *Rejāl* III, p. 181 (Loṭf-'Alī Khan). J.-P. Digard, "Jeux de structures. Segmentarité et pouvoir chez les nomades Baxtyâri d'Iran," *L'homme* 102 (27/2), 1987, pp. 12-53. G. R. Garthwaite, *Khans and Shahs: A Documentary Analysis of the Bakhtiyari in Iran*, Cambridge, 1983, passim. P. Homayounpour, *L'affaire d'Azarbaïdjan*, Lausanne, 1967 (Mortażāqolī Khan). A. H. Layard, "A Description of the Province of Khúzistán," *JRGS* 16, 1846, pp. 1-105; idem, *Early Adventures in Persia*. . . , London, 1887 (Moḥammad-Taqī Khan).

(J.-P. DIGARD)

Najafqolī Khan **Ṣamṣām**-al-**Salṭana,** an *īlk̲ān* of the Bak̲tīārī tribe and prime minister of Iran after Moḥammad-ʿAlī Shah was deposed. The second son of Ḥosaynqolī Khan Īlk̲ānī, Najafqolī was born in 1270/1853-54 and was educated to the point of literacy while with the tribe. After his father was killed by Ẓell-al-Solṭān, the reigns of Bak̲tīārī government fell into the hands of Najafqolī's paternal uncles. When Ẓell-al-Solṭān was removed from the governorate of Isfahan in 1305/1887-88 and Najafqolī's elder brother Esfandīār Khan was released from prison and made *īlk̲ān*, Najafqolī became his deputy (*īlbegī*). With his brother's death in 1331/1913, Najafqolī assumed the office of *īlk̲ān* with the title Ṣamṣām-al-Salṭana (the "sword of the sultanate") and was given the governorate of the Čahār Maḥāl of the Bak̲tīārī region.

After the bombardment of the Majles building, Mīrzā Moḥammad Khan Kāšī was appointed governor of Isfahan by Moḥammad-ʿAlī Shah; the new governor ended Ṣamṣām-al-Salṭana's short tenure as ruler of the Čahār Maḥāl region. It was not long, however, before the people of Isfahan, who had had their fill of the shah's tyranny, were emboldened by news of the successful resistance against royal forces in Tabrīz. In Jomādā I, 1327/May-June, 1909, acting on the instructions of his younger brother, ʿAlīqolī Khan, who was in Europe at the time and in contact with expatriate liberationist circles, and after obtaining the agreement of Ḥājī Āqā Nūr-Allāh, an influential Isfahani *mojtahed* (spiritual leader) and supporter of constitutional liberty, and assurance of support from his paternal cousin Ḥājī Ebrāhīm Khan Żarḡām-al-Salṭana, Ṣamṣām-al-Salṭana attacked and took Isfahan with a force of Bak̲tīārī cavalry. The Qajar governor having fled without resisting, Ṣamṣām-al-Salṭana became the governor of the province. After learning of the fall of Isfahan, Moḥammad-ʿAlī Shah first delegated Farmānfarmā to confront Ṣamṣām-al-Salṭana; however, when Farmānfarmā declined, the shah turned to several loyal Bak̲tīārī khans residing in the capital, among them Amir Mofak̲kam Sardār Ẓafar, and ultimately appointed Sardār Ašjaʿ to go to Isfahan. The loyalist khans started out for Isfahan, but, on the pretext of not having the necessary supplies, stopped near Kāšān. In the meantime, Sardār Asʿad ʿAlīqolī Khan, who had returned from Europe via Moḥammara, was sending messages to the Bak̲tīārī khans asking them to refrain from familial warfare. He went to Bak̲tīārī territory to gather forces and entered Isfahan. Around the time the army of the north was making for Tehran, Sardār Asʿad left Isfahan, also headed for the capital, and accompanied by Ṣamṣām-al-Salṭana's cavalry. The two armies finally took Tehran and forced the shah's resignation.

Sometime later, with rumors rife in Tehran that Moḥammad-ʿAlī Shah was preparing to attack Iran, the cabinet of Sepahdār fell and Constitutionalist leaders, who needed Bak̲tīārī cavalry to repel the shah's impending invasion and put down other rebellions, chose Ṣamṣām-al-Salṭana as prime minister with the portfolio of minister of war. With the help of the Majles, Ṣamṣām-al-Salṭana announced a 100,000-toman reward for the capture of Moḥammad-ʿAlī Shah. The American financial agent W. Morgan Shuster (q.v.) also greatly aided the effort to finance the war and military preparations. Finally, with the killing of Aršad-al-Dawla and with Moḥammad-ʿAlī Shah's attack neutralized, the Russians, using the pretext that Shuster's efforts ran counter to the financial and nonmaterial interests of the Czarist state, sent a note of protest to Iran and moved their troops from Rašt to Qazvīn. Foreign Minister Wot̲ūq-al-Dawla visited the Russian embassy to apologize; however, the Russians told him that another ultimatum was in the offing. They demanded that Shuster and his colleagues leave Iran within forty-eight hours, stating that Iran had no right to hire foreign agents without the approval of the Russian and British governments. The British government sided with the Russians; however, the nation of Iran to a person stood up against this presumption, and the Majles rejected the ultimatum. The terrified Regent (*nāyeb-al-salṭana*) Nāṣer-al-Molk and Prime Minister Ṣamṣām-al-Salṭana, however, accepted it and dissolved the second Majles (2 Moḥarram 1330/23 December 1911); as a result, Ṣamṣām-al-Salṭana gained absolute control of the government and Bak̲tīārī influence spread on all levels. During this period, the Russians bombarded the cupola of the Emām Reżā shrine and massacred people in Rašt, Tabrīz, and Urmia. In the south, the British, for their part, were eroding the rights of the people and the interests of the Iranian state. A year and a half later in Ṣafar, 1331/January, 1913, the government of Ṣamṣām-al-Salṭana fell; he retired to his home until Jomādā II, 1337/March, 1918, when he again became prime minister. Four months later, however, because he was unable to cope with a severe famine and restore order in the country, Aḥmad Shah asked him to resign. When he declined, the shah removed him from office and asked Wot̲ūq-al-Dawla to form a new cabinet; Ṣamṣām-al-Salṭana, though confined to his home, continued to assert that he was prime minister.

Two years later he was appointed governor of Khorasan in the government of Qawām-al-Salṭana; however, because of the revolt of Colonel Moḥammad-Taqī Khan Pesyān in Mašhad against Qawām-al-Salṭana and Ṣamṣām-al-Salṭana's devotion to Moḥammad-Taqī Khan, he refused to go to Khorasan (K̲ordād, 1300 Š./May-June, 1921). Ṣamṣām-al-Salṭana spent the last years of his life in Čahār Maḥāl of the Bak̲tīārī region and died there in 1309 Š./1930 at the age of 82. He was buried with military honors in the Takt-e Pūlād cemetery in Isfahan.

Ṣamṣām-al-Salṭana was a sincere man, passionately devoted to the cause of constitutional government. However, true to his tribal background, he ruled the government as a chief; he was also a generous and forgiving man. During his prime-ministership, a commercial council composed of six merchants and six representatives of the state was formed and the gendarmerie of Iran was created by Swedish officers.

Bibliography: Bāmdād, *Rejāl* I, p. 331. G. R. Garthwaite, *Khans and Shahs: A Documentary Analysis of the Bakhtiari in Iran*, Cambridge, 1983. Mostawfī, *Šarḥ-e zendagānī* II, pp. 388-89. ʿA.-Ḥ. Navāʾī, *Dawlathā-ye Īrān az āğāz-e mašrūṭa tā ūltīmātom*, Tehran, 1356 Š./1977. E. Ṣafāʾī, *Rahbarān-e mašrūṭa* I, Tehran, 1362 Š./1983, pp. 223-56. W. M. Shuster, *The Strangling of Persia*, New York, 1912.

(ʿA.-Ḥ. NAVĀʾĪ)

Naṣīr Khan **Ṣārem-**al-**Molk,** then **Sardār-e Jang** (1864-1932), Baktīārī chief, fifth son of Emāmqolī Khan, known as Ḥājī Īlkānī. As commander of the cavalry regiment stationed in Tehran at the outbreak of the Constitutional revolution, he was one of the few Baktīārī chiefs who remained favorable to the Qajars. He was *īlkānī* during World War I. In the eyes of the Baktīārīs, he remains a legendary figure as a fierce warrior of indomitable courage.

Bibliography: J.-P. Digard, "Jeux de structures. Segmentarité et pouvoir chez les nomades Baxtyâri d'Iran," *L'homme* 102 (27/2), 1987, pp. 12-53. G. R. Garthwaite, *Khans and Shahs: A Documentary Analysis of the Bakhtiyari in Iran*, Cambridge, 1983, passim.

(J.-P. DIGARD)

BAKTĪĀRĪ MOUNTAINS, central part of the Zagros mountain range, more or less identical to the settlement area of the Baktīārī nomads. The Baktīārī mountains, also known under the name Baktīārī-Zagros, cover an area limited by the following natural boundaries: The Sezār river, the northwestern tributary to the Dez river (see ĀB-E DEZ), forms the boundary against Lorestān; the Kārūn Vanak, Kersān, and Mārūn delineate the boundary between the Baktīārī mountains and the Kūhgīlūya part of the Zagros. The watershed between the endorheic basins of central Iran and the gulf tributaries may be considered as the eastern margin, while the mountain front of the Zagros between the Dez and Mārūn rivers forms a natural boundary to the west.

Within these boundaries, the Baktīārī mountains represent not only the central, but also the highest part of the whole Zagros system, a number of crests exceeding 12,000 ft for many miles and some peaks reaching above 14,000 ft. Zardkūh, at 4,548 m/14,920 ft is the highest peak of the entire Zagros range. "The gradual rise from the northwest and southeast toward the Bakhtiari Mountains merely reflects the longitudinal structure of the Central Zagros, and appears to be related to broad warping of the fold surface, which may still be in progress" (Oberlander, 1965, pp. 12-13).

The impressive basin-range-structure of the Baktīārī mountains, a result of the geological development of the Zagros system since late Cretaceous time and culminating in the orogenesis of Tertiary upfolding, is accentuated by the complicated and unique drainage system, which itself is the result of geology and topography. The Baktīārī mountains sensu stricto are part of the Folded Zagros and, as such, characterized by extensive north-northwest to south-southeast running ridges (anticlinal axes) and deeply incised valleys, connected with each other by numerous transverse gorges (*tang*). The vertical differences between some crest elevations and valley bottoms amount to more than 2,000 m; some of the narrow and extremely incised transverse gorges are more than 1,500 m deep. On the whole, the Baktīārī mountains represent the most intensively folded part of the Zagros system and thus are characterized by the most pronounced topography of any Iranian mountain range. This is also the reason for the past inaccessibility of the whole area, which only recently was penetrated by highways and railways. It also explains the preservation of an extremely well-developed cultural unity and identity in the mountain complex, which is today inhabited almost entirely by the Baktīārī nomads. As far as we know, the development of a specific highland way of life may date back to prehistoric times (cf. Zagarell, 1982).

Climatically, the Baktīārī mountains may be described as part of a comparatively humid and mesothermal climate. Its main characteristics are a pronounced seasonality in annual precipitation and cold and snowy winters. Šahr(-e) Kord, e.g., a town 60 km east of Isfahan and situated 2,066 m above sea level, is considered to be one of the coldest places in Iran; its average January mean temperature in the period between 1956 and 1971 was −1.7 °C, the annual average amounting to 12.0 °C. Almost each winter, absolute minima of less than −20 °C are recorded, the absolute minimum temperature during the mentioned period showing −28.5°C. Average elevation and exposure of the Baktīārī mountains to the moist west-winds of winter are the reasons for considerable precipitation, which amounts almost everywhere to more than 1,000 mm. In extremely exposed areas there may be even more than 2,000 mm, while, on the other hand, certain basins and valleys in the rain shadows of high ranges may receive considerably less. The predominantly winter precipitation is the reason for the existence of recent small cirque glaciers and numerous perennial firn patches, especially in the surroundings of the Zardkūh (cf. Grunert et al., 1978). The almost ubiquitous presence of large cirques in the highest parts of the Baktīārī mountains (Desio, 1934; Falcon, 1946; McQuillan, 1969) proves a considerable glaciation during the Pleistocene era.

Topography and climate are the basis of a natural vegetation which, in its original state, may be described as a "semi-humid oak forest" (Bobek, 1951) with

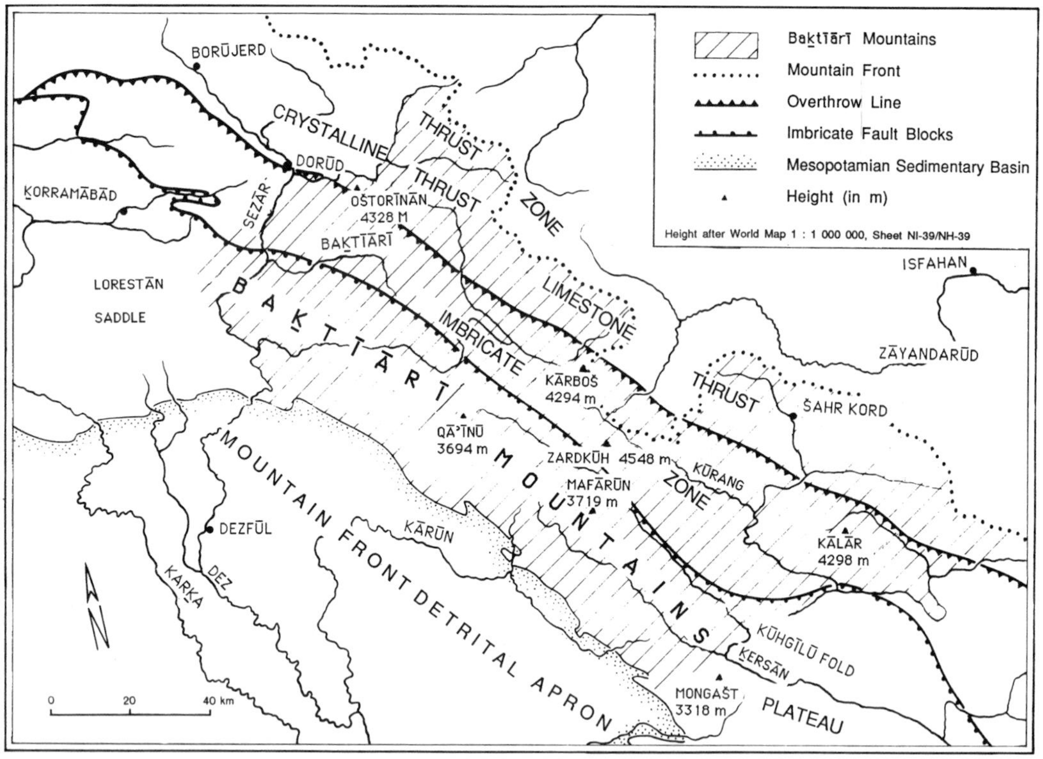

Figure 13. Location of the Baḵtīārī mountains (after Oberlander, 1965)

Quercus Brantii as the dominant tree. On the whole, the original vegetation of the Baḵtīārī mountains is that of "a somewhat dry, cold-resistant, and deciduous forest with broad-leaved, summer green oaks as its dominant members" (Bobek, 1968, p. 285). These forests remained more or less intact until the 13th/19th century, when rising demand for charcoal, increasing population pressure, and improved accessibility caused their rapid destruction (de Planhol, 1969). Today, tree cover is limited to steep slopes and backward areas, while brushes, shrubs, and steppe-like grass vegetation predominate.

The present-day economy of the Baḵtīārī mountains, dating back to the opening up of the region by the construction of the so-called Lynch road in the 13th/19th century (Ehmann, 1974; Zagarell, 1975), is characterized by a combination of agriculture and various forms of nomadism. Agriculture is concentrated in the basins of the different mountain ranges and along the irrigable terraces of the many perennial rivers. Wherever irrigation is possible, it is the basis of an intensive cultivation of various grains, grapes, vegetables (particularly onions), and fruit trees; in the basins rain-fed agriculture is widespread. The hills and the slopes of the different mountain ranges offer excellent pastures for summer grazing. Carpet weaving is one of the major sources of additional income, both in rural and tribal areas.

Due to the exceptional climatic position of the Baḵtīārī mountains and their richness in perennial rivers, which has caused their characterization as "an island of moisture" in comparison to both their forelands (Oberlander, 1965, p. 15), the mountains have developed since 1960 as a center of major dam construction projects. Dez, Kārūn, and Mārūn have been or will be equipped with dams for irrigation projects and energy generation. Moreover, the divide between the endorheic basins of central Iran and the exorheic basins of the gulf tributaries has recently been penetrated by a 3 km-long tunnel near Kūhrang (broken through?), in order to divert water from the headwaters of the Kārūn to the upper reaches of the Zāyandarūd, thus stabilizing the water supply of Isfahan and its environs.

The Baḵtīārī mountains were first penetrated by the construction of the Lynch road in 1899. Since that time the region has developed as one of the main thoroughfares between central Iran and the southwest, especially Ḵūzestān (Ehmann, 1974). The Trans-Iranian railway also partly follows the valleys of the Baḵtīārī mountains. In connection with highway and railway construction such major towns as Alīgūrdaz and Aznā came into existence. On the whole, however, the entire region is still sparsely populated, with the population concentrated in the basins and the narrow valley bottoms.

See also BAḴTĪĀRĪ TRIBE.

Bibliography: I. Bishop. "The Upper Karun Region and the Bakhtiyari Lurs," *The Scottish Geographical Magazine* 8, 1891, pp. 1-14. H. Bobek, "Die natürlichen Wälder und Gehölzfluren Irans," *Bonner Geographische Abhandlungen* 8, Bonn, 1951. Idem, "Vegetation," in *Camb. Hist. Iran* I, pp. 280-93. C. A. de Bode, "Travels in Luristan and Arabistan," 2 vols., London, 1845. R. Burn, "The Bakhtiari Hills: An Itinerary of the Road from Isfahan to Shushtar," *Journal of the Asiatic Society of Bengal* 65/2, 1897, pp. 170-79. A. Desio, "Appunti geografici et geologici sulla catena dello Zardeh-Kuh in Persia," *Memorie geologiche e geografiche di Dainelli* 4, 1934, pp. 141-67. D. Ehmann, "Verkehrsentwicklung und Kulturlandschaftswandel in Bakhtiyari (Mittlerer Zagros)," *Sociologus*, N.S. 24, 1974, pp. 137-47. N. L. Falcon, "The Bakhtiari Mountains of South-West Persia," *The Alpine Journal* 46, 1934, pp. 351-59. Idem, "The Evidence for a Former Glaciation in the S. W. Persian Mountain Belt," *Geographical Journal* 107, 1946, pp. 146-47. J. Grunert et al., "Rezente Vergletscherungsspuren in zentraliranischen Hochgebirgen," *Eiszeitalter und Gegenwart* 28, 1978, pp. 148-66. J. V. Harrison, "The Bakhtiari Country, South-Western Persia," *Geographical Journal* 80, 1932, pp. 193-210. A. H. Layard, "Ancient Sites among the Bakhtiyari Mountains: Extracted from a Communication by A. H. Layard, Esq. With Remarks on the Rivers of Susiana, and the Site of Susa, by Prof. V. P. Long," *JRGS* 12, 1842, pp. 102-09. H. F. Mac Millian, "The Flora of the Bakhtiary Country. With Some Hints on Collecting and Drying Specimens," *The Naft. Anglo-Persian Oil Company Magazine* 4, 1928, 22, pp. 20-23. H. McQuillan, "Small Glacier on Zardeh Kuh, Zagros Mountains, Iran," *Geographical Journal* 135, 1969, p. 639. T. M. Oberlander, "The Zagros Streams: A New Interpretation of Transverse Drainage in an Organic Zone," *Syracuse Geographical Series* 1, 1965. Idem, "The Origin of the Zagros Defiles," in *Camb. Hist. Iran* I, pp. 195-211. X. de Planhol, "Le déboisement de l'Iran," *Annales de géographie* 430, 1969, pp. 625-35. H. C. Rawlinson, "Notes on a March from Zohab, at the Foot of Zagros, along the Mountains of Khuzistan (Susiana), and from Thence through the Province of Luristan to Kirmanshah, in the Year 1836," *JRGS* 9, 1839, pp. 26-116. H. A. Sawyer, "The Bakhtiyari Mountains und Upper Elam," *Geographical Journal* 4, 1894, pp. 481-505. A. Zagarell, "Nomad and Settled in the Bakhtiari Mountains," *Sociologus*, N.S. 25, 1975, pp. 127-38. Idem, *The Prehistory of the Northeast Baḫtiyari Mountains, Iran: The Rise of a Highland Way of Life*, Beiheft zum Tübinger Atlas des Vorderen Orients, Series B (Geisteswissenschaften), no. 42., Wiesbaden, 1982. See also *Camb. Hist. Iran* I, index, p. 768.

(E. EHLERS)

BAKTĪĀRĪ TRIBE

i. *Ethnography.*
ii. *The Baktīārī dialect.*
iii. *Baktīārī carpets.*

i. ETHNOGRAPHY

Territory and way of life. The Baktīārī tribe (*īl*) is one of the the two biggest in Iran, the other being the Qašqā'ī. In the 1970s, the Baktīārīs numbered in all approximately 600,000, and about one third of them were nomadic. They are Twelver Shi'ites and speak a Lori dialect. Sedentarized Baktīārīs live in towns and in many villages in Čahār Maḥāl, in the Farīdan district down to Isfahan, and in Kūzestān (Khuzistan) down to Ahvāz. The nomads and some sedentary people live in the tribal territory, called the "Baktīārī country" (*kāk-e īl-e baktīārī*), an area of roughly 75,000 km^2 stretching from the Dez river, Šūštar, and Rām Hormoz on the west to Dārān and the outskirts of Šahr-e Kord on the east (see Figure 14).

The traditional Baktīārī way of life is typical of the long-distance nomadism which evolved in the Zagros highlands from the thirteenth century onward, at first under the impact of the Mongol invasions, and probably attained its present form during the eighteenth century, in a defensive reaction against increasing fiscal and administrative pressures experienced under successive Iranian régimes.

The Baktīārī nomads move between a summer abode (*yeylāq*) in the high mountains (summit, Zardakūh 4,548 m) and a winter abode (*garmsīr*) in the western foothills adjoining the Kūzestān plain. The ecological boundary between the two zones coincides roughly with the course of the Āb-e Bāzoft. Thus the Baktīārī country falls into two different administrative provinces: Čahār Maḥāl, where the summer quarters lie, and Kūzestān, in which the winter quarters are included. The seasonal migrations (called *bār*) made by different sections of the tribe vary in length and can reach 300 km. The migration into the mountains takes place in springtime when the weather and the vegetation are at their best; it lasts longer (15 to 45 days) than the reverse migration (8 to 30 days). The migration routes are seldom, if ever, changed, because in this region there are only five or at best seven cols over which the Zagros ranges can be crossed; they lead to campsites (*javārgāh*) which are likewise almost always the same, being fixed by longstanding conventions. As is well known, these routes are extremely arduous. The nomads suffer frequent accidents and losses of livestock when they clamber over snow-covered cols and through rock-encumbered gorges and when they either swim or float on rafts held up with inflated goatskins across the Kārūn and other raging rivers at the time of the snow-melt. Despite all these difficulties, seasonal migration is necessary because of the prevalence of cold and snow in the *yeylāq* from October to April and heat and drought in the *garmsīr* from May to September, and often also the exhaustion of the pastures after several months of

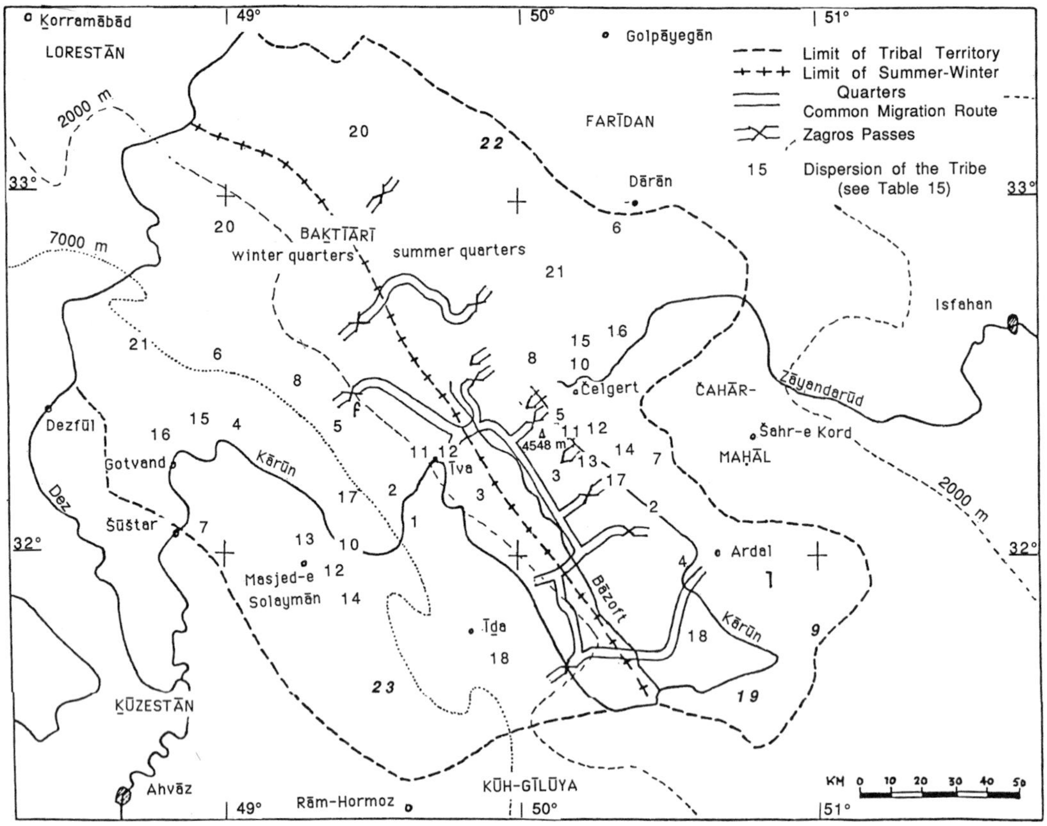

Figure 14. Baktīārī territory

intensive use. Other possible ways to solve the problem have been suggested, for example to combine sheep folding with fodder crop cultivation and short-range transhumance; but for the time being, in the absence of any satisfactory alternative, nomadism remains the only feasible technique for efficient pursuit of livestock raising in this region.

Economy and material culture. The tribe's main economic activities are determined by the migration cycle. The Baktīārī are primarily breeders of sheep and goats, which provide most of their cash income (from sale of lambs for slaughter and to a lesser extent clarified butter), much of their food (milk and milk products and on rare occasions meat), and raw materials (wool, goat-hair, and leather) for their handicrafts. The lambs and kids are born in or around February in the *garmsīr* and sold in the autumn after being fattened on highland pastures. The ewes, after the lambing, are milked for human consumption until June. Shearing is done in the spring, soon after the migration. The Baktīārī also breed asses, mules, and a small number of cattle for load-carrying, riding, and draft purposes (ploughing and threshing). Some groups belonging to the tribe who are of Arab descent (the ʿArab-Kamarī) specialize in the breeding of buffalos; now sedentarized, they formerly took these animals on the treks for sale to Armenian villagers in Čahār Maḥāl and Farīdan, who used them for agricultural tasks. The only camels to be seen in the Baktīārī country are dromedaries belonging to Turkish groups, not affiliated to the tribe, who practice transhumance into the Zagros from Čahār Maḥāl (Larakīs from around Gandomān) and even from the Isfahan area (villagers from Čālšotor, Rīz, Ḡolāmkᵛāst). Many Baktīārīs now cultivate wheat, which in the form of bread is their staple diet, and barley, which in poor seasons can be used as supplementary fodder for livestock. Their farming system, like their pastoral system, is tied to the migration cycle. In the *yeylāq*, the nomads sow at the beginning of September, shortly before their autumn trek, and reap and thresh in July of the following year after their return. In the *garmsīr*, they sow at the end of October and complete the harvesting at the end of their stay, the crops being precocious cereals which reach maturity in five months.

Supplementary items are obtained by hunting (gazelles in the *garmsīr*, ibexes in the *yeylāq*, partridges, pheasants, etc.) and by gathering wild plants and vegetable substances such as berries and mushrooms for food and others for use as dyestuffs and craft materials; some of them, e.g., manna (*gaz*) and gum tragacanth

Table 15

THE PRINCIPAL SUBDIVISIONS OF THE BAK̠TĪĀRĪ TRIBE

īl	*bak̠š/qesmat*	*bāb/bolūk*	*ṭā'efa*	
Bak̠tīārī	Haft Lang	Dūrakī	Zarāsvand	1
			Gandalī	2
			Mowrī	3
			Osīvand	4
			Bāmadī	5
			Asterekī-Čārbūrī	6
			Sohonī (Hamule)	7
		Bābādī Bāb	Bābādī 'Alī-Anvar	8
			Bābādī 'Akkāša	*9*
			Rökī	10
			Molmolī	11
			Šehnī	12
			Madmolīl	13
			Gomar-Naser	14
			Pepdīnī	15
			Galla	16
		Behdārvand (Monjezī)		17
		Dīnāronī		18
		Jānakī		*19*
	Čār Lang	Mamīvand		20
		Mamsāla		21
		Mogū'ī		*22*
		Kīānersī		*23*

Note: The figures in the right-hand column refer to Figure 14; those in italic denote wholly sedentarized groups (Digard, 1979, pp. 134-35)

(*zīdī*) are in commercial demand. The Bak̠tīārīs are passionately fond of hunting. For each of these activities there is a proper time and place in the migration cycle. Taken as a whole, they show how well the Bak̠tīārī community has adapted its way of life to the peculiar environmental conditions of the Central Zagros.

The principal handicraft of the Bak̠tīārīs is weaving, on horizontal looms with single rows of warp-threads or on looms with perforated cards. The wool and hair which they use come from their own sheep and goats. This activity, which is pursued solely by the women, produces a wide range of goods of high quality as regards both robustness and artistic merit: ropes, straps, sacks, saddle-bags (*k̠oržīn, k̠orjīn*) for carriage and storage of belongings, and tunics (*čūqā*) in natural white wool with vertical indigo stripes which, together with the tall skull-cap (*kolāh-e k̠osravī*) and wide, black trousers (*tombūn, tonbān*), form the typical male attire of the Bak̠tīārīs. Another product is the black goat-skin sheet used for making the shed-like tents (*bohon*) which are the ordinary homes of the nomads, though some also have stone houses (*līr*), mud or mud-brick houses (*tū*), or brushwood huts (*kapar, lowka*). The Bak̠tīārī carpets, famous under the trade name Bībībāf, were woven by ladies (*bībī*) of the tribal aristocracy until production ceased in the 1930s as a result of political upheavals (see below); it has now been resumed, though at a less high standard of quality, in certain villages near Isfahan such as Ḡolāmk̠ᵛāst.

All other goods and services which the Bak̠tīārīs require are supplied by shopkeepers (*dokondār, dokkāndār*) from nearby villages and towns, such as Ardal, Čehelgert, Īḏa, Lālī, Gotvand, Masjed-e Solaymān, or by craft specialists, who do not belong to the tribe but move to its different locations, such as shoemakers (*gīvakaš*), felt makers (*nemetmāl, namadmāl*), blacksmiths (*āhangar*), joiners (*tak̠tkaš*), "gypsies" (*kowlī*) who make sieves, carding combs, spindles, etc., and may perhaps really be of Indian origin, musicians (*tūšmāl*), barber-circumcisers (*dallāk*), tailors (*k̠ayyāṭ*). All these tradespeople, and in particular the *kowlī*s, are held in low esteem by the *Bak̠tīārīs*, who describe them generically as *ḡorbatī* (homeless people).

Social organization. One of the peculiarities of Bak̠tīārī social organization is the existence of numerous interlocked social units within the tribe, reflecting an exceptionally high degree of lineal segmentation at different levels. Each tent is the home of a nuclear family (*k̠ānvāda*). An encampment (*māl*), comprising three to twelve tents, corresponds to the extended family (*tāš* or *awlād*). During the treks, kindred encampments join together in migration units (*tīra*) with strengths of the order of one hundred persons. The *tīra*s themselves are combined in clans (*ṭā'efa*), the biggest of which (the Mowrī, Bābādī, Gandalī) run to 25,000 persons, and the *ṭāʾefa*s in sections (*bāb* or *bolūk*). Finally these sections belong to one or the other of the two parts (*baḵš* or *qesmat*), namely the Haft Lang and the Čār (Čahār) Lang, which make up the Baḵtīārī tribe (*īl*).

It is often supposed that this elaborate structure rests wholly on patrilineal descent. In the tribe's actual functioning, however, the groups corresponding to these different levels of segmentation do not all play equally important roles. The basic social units are the kin groups, from the tent to the *tīra*, which may be described as "joint families" because membership in them is determined by three main principles: (1) a rule of patrilineal descent, whereby membership is transmitted in the male line or, in other words, a person must belong to the same group as his father and to that group alone; (2) a preference for marriage between patrilineal cousins begotten by two brothers, i.e., marriage of a man to his father's brother's daughter (*tātazā*), though actual implementation of this preference was found to range from 18 percent to 43 percent in different Baḵtīārī groups; (3) a rule of residence, whereby the wife is required to move after marriage from her father's home to her husband's home (virilocality) or to her husband's father's home (patrilocality). The so-defined social units are the settings within which real solidarity is maintained, not only in cases of conflict with other groups but also in the daily tasks of productive work. Flock tending, sowing, and reaping are done jointly by the agnate members of each encampment or, during the treks, by those of each *tīra*. At this level, "joint families" and "corporate groups" wholly coincide. In short, the encampments and the *tīra*s are autonomous units living in different places. This dispersion, which enables the Baḵtīārīs to avoid overcrowding at watering places and overgrazing of pastures, is essential for their survival as a community.

The large units, from the *ṭāʾefa* to the *īl*, have in some respects the opposite role. Kinship figures prominently in their definition but is not directly relevant to their function. At these levels of segmentation the genealogies are fictitious, reflecting the concern of the Baḵtīārīs to justify past facts such as adoptions, regroupings, and political alliances by explaining them in terms of filial relationship. These large units only act as solidarity groups in very exceptional circumstances, for example in the event of a serious conflict when a special relationship between two or more of them imposes an obligation of mutual support. (The term for such a relationship is *hīn-čū*, "blood on the stick," which refers to the Lorī saying *hīn ze čū pöy nīemon* "the blood never comes off the stick," Digard, 1987). On the other hand, the large units have a permanent importance insofar as they integrate the basic units, most often on territorial lines. The autonomy and dispersion of the encampments and *tīra*s must in practice be coupled with the flexibility which becomes necessary when pasture lands or migration routes have to be changed on account of overgrazing or overcrowding. This flexibility is attainable thanks to the existence of large social units with authority over wide areas, which are held collectively or indivisibly while the rights of use are apportioned among the several kin groups.

Political organization. Another peculiarity of the Baḵtīārī tribal organization is the political power structure, which shows a degree of hierarchic centralization generally thought to be unusual in kinship-based systems. Until the 1950s, authority was concentrated in the hands of an *īl-ḵān* (supreme head of the tribe) and an *īl-beg* (his assistant) and then apportioned, at different levels of the pyramid of segmentation, among the *kalāntar*s (headmen) of the *ṭāʾefa*s, *kadḵodā*s (masters) of the *tīra*s, and *rīš-safīd*s (elders) of the *tāš* or *awlād*. These functionaries maintained order, administered justice, and acted as intermediaries between the tribesfolk and the outside world; but their most important task, as regards impact on the ordinary life of the Baḵtīārīs, was that of coordinating migrations and settling disputes about overused pasturelands and watering places. Originally a service rendered to the tribespeople, this function became a source of economic and social privilege (access to the best pastures, ability to attract clienteles, etc.). The result was the emergence of a class of chiefs (khans) sharply marked off from the simple nomads (*lor*s—a term not to be confused with the same word used as the name of the tribes of Lorestān). In like manner the tribe's top political leadership went beyond its original coordinating function and gradually assumed an exploitative and authoritarian role, imposing taxes, levying troops, and mustering political factions (*basta*) to work for the interests of the khans.

Factors extraneous to the tribe also favored the evolution of the Baḵtīārī political leadership on these lines. One of the most important was the grant of crown (*ḵāleṣa*) lands to individual khans in reward for military or other services—a practice dating from the Middle Ages. Such lands, unlike those in the tribal territory proper, became private property and could therefore be cultivated. This undoubtedly explains why the leading khans for a long time held a near-monopoly of agricultural production, on which many of the nomads were dependent, sometimes even for essential food. The economic grip on the tribe given to the khans by their ownership of agricultural estates was reinforced by the demographic factor which from time to time compels a nomadic society to get rid of surplus manpower. Shepherds forced by ruinous losses to accept exile and sedentarization could in the last resort find employment on these estates, while landowning khans could obtain in this way ample numbers of inexpensive and more than usually docile agricultural laborers (*raʿīyat*, i.e., subjects or peasants, as opposed to *lor* in the sense of nomads). These sedentary people are the poor relations of the nomads—victims of a process which is a necessary requirement for the viability of the nomadic pastoral system.

A second factor which helped to make the Baḵtīārī leadership all-powerful and unaccountable was the direct intervention by Iranian governments in appointments and dismissals of tribal chiefs. This began in the eighteenth century and became a regular practice under the Qajars, who sought to control the tribes and the neighboring areas through a system of indirect rule based mainly on the tribal chiefs. The authority of the khans was officially recognized and enhanced with new powers to maintain order in their areas, collect taxes, mobilize troops on behalf of the shah, and the like. Loyalty to the shah was profusely rewarded with honors and titles, but the slightest lapse was ruthlessly punished. After such an incident the last great Čār Lang (Čahār Lang) chief, ʿAlī Mardān Khan, was declared an outlaw (*yāḡī*) and taken prisoner in 1841, and the way was opened for his Haft Lang rivals. Ḥosaynqolī Khan Haft Lang was appointed superintendent (*nāẓem*) of the Baḵtīārīs by the shah in 1862 and head of the tribe (*īl-ḵān*) in 1867. He was the first recipient of this title, and in the tribe he became known by the surname Īlḵānī. In 1882 the shah caused him to be murdered and replaced by his brother Emāmqolī Khan, surnamed Ḥājī Īlḵānī. From then almost without interruption until the abolition of the title khan in 1956, the successive heads of the tribe were descendants of one or the other of the two brothers. As a result of the murder, the Baḵtīārīs were divided into partisans (*bastagān*) of the Īlḵānīs and of the Ḥājī Īlḵānīs, but it would be more correct to interpret this division as a means to preserve the tribe's unity in the face of the central government's machinations. In reality the composition of these factions was determined by agreements reached between the two branches of the family of the khans in 1894 and 1912, whereby their respective strengths were periodically reviewed to ensure that no imbalance should arise and their members were not organized as two opposing sides but were recruited equally from within each line. In short the *basta* factions served a double purpose: to keep power in the family of the "great khans" (*ḵawānīn-e bozorg*), and to prevent either branch of the family from prevailing over the other. This peculiar type of factionalism is certainly one of the oddest aspects of Baḵtīārī social organization. Nothing quite equivalent to it has been observed in any other community in the world.

A third and more recent factor which further strengthened the power of the Baḵtīārī khans was the presence of British firms in Ḵūzestān from the end of the nineteenth century onward. The opening of the Lynch road through the south of the Baḵtīārī country via Īḏa and Ardal in 1897 was followed by the discovery and extraction of petroleum at Masjed-e Solaymān and later at other places in the tribe's *garmsīr*. These developments deprived several thousand nomads of traditional pastures but brought a bonanza to the *ḵawānīn-e bozorg*. For their undertaking to maintain the security of the oil installations, these khans were rewarded with 5 percent of the shares of the First Exploration Company, and as a result became entitled to part of the Anglo-Iranian Oil Company's profits for twenty-five years and to substantial compensation after the company's withdrawal. Being beholden to the British for these economic benefits, the Baḵtīārī chiefs could occasionally be manipulated against the central government in case of need.

Thanks to this double legitimation by external authorities and to the privileges and gains accruing therefrom, the Baḵtīārī khans were in a position both to tighten their grip on the tribe and to acquire a foothold in the central government apparatus. If trouble with the shah should arise, they controlled a formidable body of troops which they were ready to throw into action, as they did in 1909 during the struggle for constitutional government. Military ventures enhanced the prestige of the khans among the tribesmen and at the same time gave them chances to appropriate further lands at the expense of neighboring peasant communities. In the early years of the nineteenth century, the Baḵtīārīs were indeed a state within the state.

Recent changes. The first attempt to deal with the situation which has just been described was made by Reżā Shah in the 1930s. Against the tribes, particularly the Baḵtīārīs, whose organization, power, and way of life he considered incompatible with national modernization on Western lines, the new ruler unrelentingly pursued a threefold policy of: (1) forcible sedentarization of the nomads, both in Ḵūzestān and in Čahār Maḥāl, through posting of troops on the migration routes to prevent access; (2) detribalization, through detention and execution or expropriation of the leading khans and replacement of these khans with army officers, who were put in charge of the tribe's affairs and the territorial administration; (3) deculturation by various means, including vexatious measures such as the prohibition of beards and obligation to wear Western-style suits and the Pahlavī hat (képi) instead of the traditional costume, to which the Baḵtīārīs are deeply attached. On balance this policy proved unsuccessful (from the viewpoint of its promoters), because the events of the second world war disrupted the Iranian state apparatus, and the majority of the Baḵtīārīs then resumed their traditional migrations and way of life. Nevertheless Reżā Shah's policy had lasting consequences insofar as it polarized social antagonisms within the tribe. The removal of power from the hands of the *ḵawānīn-e bozorg* only cut off the top of the social pyramid, leaving intact an intermediate layer of *kalāntar*s and *kadḵodā*s whose number ran to several hundred. These men were appointees of the khans and may be said to have constituted the tribe's officer corps. Being unsure of their position after the sudden disappearance of their superiors, they were reluctant to act in any way that might involve risk of harsh repression. Moreover, their traditional functions such as administration of justice had been taken from them and given to government officials or army officers. For all these reasons, the *kalāntar*s and *kadḵodā*s tended to lose interest in tribal affairs and to concern themselves solely with managing their own properties. This was hardly surprising, because the khans had always treated them well in order to make sure of their loyalty and had been particularly generous in granting them agricultural lands. At the other pole, the rank and file of the nomads, who owned no land but only possessed livestock, were hit much harder by the compulsory sedentarization imposed on the tribe for ten years. Their losses of livestock in the period have been estimated at 60 percent. The few foreign travelers who saw the Baḵtīārīs at that time speak only of their distress and impoverishment.

In Moḥammad Reżā Shah's reign, no radical decision on policy toward nomadism appears to have been taken until about 1339 Š./1960. After the war and in the 1950s, the tribes, including the Baḵtīārīs, were still politically powerful and active, as they showed during the premiership of Moḥammad Moṣaddeq. Being unable to ignore them, the successive cabinets wavered between cooperation and repression. Among the conciliatory measures were the restitution of properties to the khans in 1945, the Koenig mission and plan in 1947-48, the conference of the tribes in September, 1948, and the establishment of a civilian High Council of the Tribes in 1953. For the Baḵtīārīs, the shah's marriage in February, 1951, to Ṯorayyā Esfandīārī, a great-granddaughter of an Īlḵānī, was a sign of favor. In 1957 compensation was paid to the Baḵtīārī khans for their losses due to oil nationalization. Among the repressive measures were the exiling of the family of the Qašqā'ī khans in 1954, the establishment of a branch of the General Staff and a corps of specially trained officers to handle tribal affairs in 1956, the abolition of the title khan in the same year, and the decision, taken in 1957, that all the tribes should be disarmed. Ultimately the unfavorable attitude prevailed.

After the long period in which the Iranian authorities had alternately warred and bargained with the tribes, the new policy was to feign ignorance of their existence. This was made manifest in the Land Reform law of January, 1962, and the additional clauses of January, 1963, neither of which contains any mention of nomads or tribes. Only after the new laws had been enforced did their repercussions become apparent. The limitation on large landownership evidently affected some of the nomadic tribal areas more than others; it made little difference to the Baḵtīārīs because most of the big estates owned by the khans lay outside the tribal territory. Much more momentous was the law for the nationalization of pasturelands, which in the case of the Baḵtīārīs had the following practical results: (1) uncultivated lands were confiscated and registered as state property; (2) such lands could not be exploited or used in any way without official graziers' permits (*javāz-e 'alafčar*), which were granted to individuals; (3) each permit conferred on a grazier the right to use a measured lot of pastureland, the area of which was calculated, after weighting for the quality of the natural vegetation, on the basis of either the size of the recipient's flock if less than the equivalent of 100 head of "small cattle" (i.e., sheep and goats), or maximum of 100 head no matter how much his flock exceeded that limit; (4) graziers who obtained such permits and thus became the sole authorized users of such pasturelands were required to pay for the privilege by contributing an annual tax of 15 rials per head of sheep, 30 rials per head of bovine cattle, and no less than 150 rials per goat.

The first consequence of these measures was a substantial reduction of the area in pastoral use. The total area fell because, as soon as the rules were announced, many of the Baḵtīārī nomads hastened to plow up whole tracts in order to place them beyond the scope of the law. The areas used by individuals showed a decline because they were calculated from incorrect figures based on the assumed maximum holding of 100 animals per grazier. The degree of this underestimation of the Baḵtīārī flocks became evident when the authorities permitted certain large breeders in Kermān province to send their animals to graze in the Baḵtīārī tribal territory. Although the proclaimed purpose of the nationalization law was to protect the vegetational cover, its implementation led to worse overgrazing in several places than under the traditional system. At the same time the grant of the grazing rights to individuals swept away some of the tribe's best institutions, particularly those conducive to collective management of natural resources. Last but not least, the freezing of flock ownership by individuals, at either the number held on the date of the law's enforcement or 100 in the case of previously larger holdings, frustrated the natural ambition of every animal-breeder to increase his stock and therewith his wealth. By the mid-1970s, these measures had made many Baḵtīārīs lose heart and had also caused the tribe to lose a considerable number of members—those overtaken by the nationalization law before they could increase their flock to a viable minimum (around 60 sheep).

Seemingly a technical measure, the pasturelands nationalization law had much wider repercussions than could have been anticipated. It contributed to the profound transformation of production systems and social relationships then in progress in Iran. In the case of the Baḵtīārīs, it quickened an exodus of poorer tribesmen into low-grade jobs in the petroleum and agro-industrial sectors in Ḵūzestān and the steelworks at Āryāšahr near Isfahan. Not all the Baḵtīārīs, however, were equally affected. Some of them, particularly *kalāntar*s and *kadḵodā*s untouched by the successive forays against their superiors, the khans, fared rather well in the changing circumstances. The prestige and authority of these intermediate chiefs were put to use in the new system, and alternatives to stockbreeding were opened to them. Some became labor supply contractors—a lucrative business, as they were the initial recipients of the wages of the laborers whom they recruited. Their zeal in this role served the interests of large companies and state agencies but endangered the stockbreeding and the very existence of their own tribe.

The events of 1979 did not kindle any real revolutionary fervor among the Baḵtīārīs but gave opportunities to settle old scores. The freedom prevailing in the months immediately after the insurrection, together with a strong demand for meat in local markets deprived of imported supplies, prompted a resurgence of nomadic pastoralism, but this did not last long. At the instigation of the revolutionary guards (_pāsdārān_), tribal councils (_šūrā-ye ʿašāʾerī_) took shape in every _tīra_, giving the _lor_s and above all the youths scope to perform roles and turn the tables on their former tribal superiors. The _kalāntar_s and _kadḵodā_s were not removed, but ceased to be heeded and withdrew more than ever into their own shells. Before long, men of the "construction crusade" (_jehād-e sāzandagī_) arrived in all parts of the Baḵtīārī country and began to build roads, bridges, silos, schools, and houses, to bring electricity and telephone lines to villages, and to set up a network of producer and consumer cooperatives. For the first time the Baḵtīārī nomads were offered incentives for voluntary sedentarization on relatively favorable terms. Many actually took the plunge, finally acknowledging that "the plow and the ewe are in the same place" (_kīš o mīš yek jā'st_).

Thus the conditions in which the Baḵtīārīs live appear to have changed more in the first six years of the Islamic Republic than in the half-century of the Pahlavī regime. Is this remarkable turn irreversible? Are the Baḵtīārīs going to acquire the mentality of public assistance recipients? Is their stockbreeding bound to decline and their tribal identity to disappear? The future will answer these questions.

Bibliography: D. Brooks, "The Enemy Within: Limitations on Leadership in the Bakhtiari," in R. Tapper, ed., _The Conflict of Tribe and State in Iran and Afghanistan_, London and New York, 1983, pp. 337-63. M. C. Cooper, _Grass_, New York and London, 1925. G. N. Curzon, _Persia and the Persian Question_, London, 1892, II, pp. 330-87. J.-P. Digard, "Histoire et anthropologie des sociétés nomades: le cas d'une tribu d'Iran," _Annales: Economies, Sociétés Civilisations_ 28/6, 1973, pp. 1423-35. Idem, "De la nécessité et des inconvénients, pour un Baxtyâri, d'être Baxtyâri. Communauté, territoire et inégalité chez des pasteurs nomades d'Iran," in Equipe écologie et anthropologie des sociétés pastorales, ed., _Pastoral Production and Society/Production pastorale et société_, Cambridge and Paris, 1979, pp. 127-39. Idem, "Les nomades et l'Etat central en Iran: quelques enseignements d'un long passé d'ʿhostilité réglementée'," _Peuples mediterranéens/Mediterranean Peoples_ 7, 1979, pp. 37-53. Idem, _Techniques des nomades Baxtyâri d'Iran_, Cambridge and Paris, 1981. Idem, "Jeux de structure. Segmentarité et pouvoir chez les nomades Baxtyâri d'Iran," _L'homme_ 27/2, 1987. D. Ehmann, _Bahtiyaren. Persische Bergnomaden im Wandel der Zeit_, Wiesbaden, 1975 (Beihefte zum Tübinger Atlas des Vorderen Orients, B/2). G. R. Garthwaite, _Khans and Shahs. A Documentary Analysis of the Bakhtiyari in Iran_, Cambridge, 1983. ʿA. Karīmī, "Neẓām-e mālekīyat-e aržī dar īl-e Baḵtīārī" (The landownership system in the Baḵtīārī tribe), _Honar o mardom_ 189-90, 2537 = 1357 Š./1978, pp. 67-83. A. H. Layard, "A Description of the Province of Khúzistán," _JRAS_ 16, 1846, pp. 1-105. Idem, _Early Adventures in Persia, Susiana and Babylonia, Including a Residence Among the Bakhtiyáris and Other Wild Tribes, Before the Discovery of Niniveh_, 2 vols., New York and London, 1887. A. Rosman and P. G. Rubel, "Nomad-sedentary Interethnic Relations in Iran and Afghanistan," _IJMES_ 7/4, 1976, pp. 545-70. V. V. Trubetskoĭ, _Bakhtiary. Osedlokochevye plemena Irana_, Moscow, 1966. P. Varjāvand et al., _Bāmādī, ṭāʾefa-ī az Baḵtīārī_, Tehran, 1346 Š./1967. H. Wright, ed., _Archaeological Investigations in Northeastern Khuzistan_, Ann Arbor, 1979. A. Zagarell, _The Prehistory of the Northeast Bakhtiyari Mountains, Iran. The Rise of a Highland Way of Life_, Wiesbaden, 1982 (Beihefte zum Tübinger Atlas des Vorderen Orients, B/42).

(J.-P. DIGARD)

ii. THE BAḴTĪĀRĪ DIALECT

Baḵtīārī, the dialect and subdialects of the Baḵtīārs in southwestern Iran (between 31° and 34° north latitudes and 48° and 52° east longitudes), is very closely related to the dialects of the Boir-Aḥmadī, Kohgīlūya, and the Mamasanī to the south (population: Baḵtīārī 570,000, B.-A. 120,000, K. 110,000, M. 90,000). These, together with Lorī to the west and north, constitute the "Perside" southern Zagros group, as opposed to Kurdish dialects in the northern Zagros, with which Baḵtīārī shares a number of lexical and morphological items and phonological features, e.g., _piā_ "man," _korr_ "boy," _bard_ "stone," _mul_ "neck"; the topicalizer and vocative marker _ak(ū)_; the "Zagros-_d_," i.e., the intervocalic lenisation, or loss, of _d_ (see below). Other typical items, most shared with Fārs dialects, include: _tē_ "eye," _seil_ "watching," _(h)ars_ "tear," _nift_ "nose," _hauš_ "courtyard," _tū_ "room, house," _g(y)er_ "cliff, rock," _van/vand_ "throw," _uft/wast_ "fall," _kip/kipist_ "fall down."

Phonology. Consonants show some of the typical "Southwest" Iranian changes from Old to New Iranian: 1. initial _*w > b_, _*waita > bēd_ "willow;" 2. initial _*wi/*wr̥ > gu_, _*wi-raica > gurūs_ "flee," _*wr̥ka > gurg_ "wolf;" 3. initial _*y > j_, _*yāmaka > jūwa_ "shirt, suit;" 4. initial _*dw > d_, _*dwar > der_ "door;" 5. _*k̑ > h_, _*ak̑aina > āhan_ "iron;" 6. _*ĝ > d_, _*ĝāmātar > dūwā_ "son-in-law;" 7. _*k̑w > s_, _*gau k̑wanta > gusind_ "sheep;" 8. _*ĝw > z_, _*ĝwan- > zuūn/zōn_ "tongue;" 9. _*θr > s_, _*āθrya-āp- > āsiāu_ "mill."

Among the main later changes, two are typically Baḵtīārī: 1. intervocalic _*m > w_, e.g., _dāmād > dūwā_ "son-in-law," _dāman > dūwan_ "skirt," _jāma > jūwa_ "dress, shirt," _āmad > oweid_ "came;" and 2. _š > s_ in the 3rd sing. and plur. personal suffixes _-š/-šūn > -s/-sūn_, and in _īšā > īsā_ "you" (plur.), and other words, e.g., _angušt > angust_ "finger." Other changes are: Initial _x > h_, _xār > hār_ "thorn," Arabic _xabar > hawar_ "message." (Note sporadic _x > q_ and _q > x_: _xurōs > qurūs_ "rooster," Arabic _qahr > xahr_ "anger.") Initial _xw > h_ before mid and high vowels, _xwēš > hēs_ "self, own;" but _xw > x_ elsewhere, _xwafs > xous_ "sleep," _xwar > xar_ "eat." Preconsonantal _x > h_, _taxl > tahl_ "bitter," _tuxm > tuhm > tōm_ "seed." _f_ before _t > h_, _raft > raht > rahd_ "went," _guft > guht > guhd_ "said" (not in Persian loans like *baft* "weft"), but > *u* before strident, *xwafs* > *xous* "sleep," Arabic *kafš* > *kouš* "shoe." Postfricative voiceless stops, mainly *t*, tend to become voiced, *haštād* > *hašdād* "80," *tariste* > *tarisde* "could;" thus *ft/xt* > *fd/xd* > *hd*, *raft* > *rahd* "went," *suxt* > *suhd* "burnt." Voiced stops, in final position: *b* > *v*, *jēb* > *jēv* "pocket," *d* is generally lost after long high vowel, *bēd/beḏ* "willow," but *zī* "soon;" intervocalic position, *b* > *w*, *bi-bur* > *buwur* "cut!" *g* > *y*, *tē-gal* > *tī-yel* "eyes," while *d* > *y* or is lost, *mādīyān* > *māyūn* "mare," *duxtar* > *duhdar* > *du(w)ar* "daughter, girl." Geminate *rr/ll* tend to be aspirated > *hr/hl*, **dar-n* > *darr-* > *dahr* "tear," **br-n* > *burr* > *buhr* "break" (intransitive).

The main developments of the vowels are as follows: Long **ē* generally remains *ĕ*, indefinite suffix *-ē*, *lēs* "lick," *xwēš* > *hēš*. (Note *ī* > *ē* in several Arabic loans, *taqsīr* > *tasxēr* "fault.") Long **ō* tends to remain unchanged, *durōq* > *durō* "lie," *kōh* > *kō* "mountain," but is raised to *ū* before dentals and palatals, *dōst* > *dūst* "friend," *dōz* > *dūz* "sew." Baktīārī *ū* changed further to *ī* before non-strident dentals, *mōd* > *mūd* > *mī* "hair," *zūd* > *zī* "soon," *xūn* > *hīn* "blood." Long **ā* tends to be quite rounded in Baktīārī and is raised to *ō* before Baktiari *ī/y*, *bādū* > *bāhū* > *bōhī* "arm," *xāya* > *hōya* "egg;" pre-nasal *ā* is raised to *ō/ū*, e.g., *xāna* > *hōna* "house," *šām* > *šōm* "dinner," especially in frequent suffixes, e.g., *asp-ūn* "horses," and the 3rd plural suffix *-šōn* > *-sūn*. *Ā* is sporadically changed to *a(h)*, *šāh* > *sah* "black," *mān* > *mahn* "remain."

Baktīārī *ah*, *ih*, *uh* (from preconsonantal *ā*, *x*, *ft*, and *rr/ll*) tend to be lowered to *ē*, *ē*, *ō*. This change, together with the change *ft/xt* > *hd* and the intervocalic loss of *d*, results in characteristic contracted verb forms, *rahd-um bī/rē-m bī* "I had gone," *girihd-um/girē-m* "I took," *suhd-um/sō-m* "I burnt." Hiatus is avoided by the insertion of *n* before: 1. forms of the substantive verb, *dast-e kē-n-i* "In whose hand is it?" 2. personal suffixes, *dād-e-n-um* "He has given to me" (*dād-e* 3rd sing. perf.); 3. the direct/indirect object marker *a*, *alī-n-a* "(to) Ali"; 4. the *ē* preceding relative clauses, *tāzī-n-ē ke*... "the hunting dog who ...." Vocalic verb stems insert a *h*-like glide before endings, *bū-h-e/bū-'-e* "that he be."

Grammar. The plural has three markers: inanimate *ā*, human *ūn* and *gal*, animals all three. Of these, *gal* appears to imply the notion of collective set; e.g., *māl-ā* "tents, houses," *ded-ūn/dedū-yel* "sisters," *gā-w-ūn/gā-h-ā* "cows," *guar-gal* "calves." The specific direct/indirect object is marked by *a*, *har dī gyāgū-n-a kušden* "They killed both brothers," *daftarī-n-a qam neid* "For D. there is no sorrow." Indefiniteness is marked by *ē*, *ya kār-ē* "a task." Topicalizer/endearment *ak*, *yār-ak-um* "my friend," *dā-k-e pīr-um* "my old mother." (Note *ak* after pronouns in *be mun-ak ci tovūn* "What strength is there to me?") Vocative: *ey* and *ak*, *dūst-ey/dūst-ak* "o friend!" (*Ak* is to be distinguished from optional *k* after *ā*, e.g., *pā-m/pā-k-um* "my foot.") Dependent nominals are connected to their head noun by *i* (often elided after vowel), *gul-i bustūn* "the rose of the fragrant garden." Frequent prepositions: *wā* "with, to," *we/bi* "to" (note *we bā-t* "with you"), *wur* "on, in(to)," *sī* "for, to," *tēy* "before, to," *ze* "from," *men(-i)* "in," *cī* "like."

The pronouns, personal suffixes, verbal endings, and the present and past of "to be" are as follows:

	Pronoun	Suffix	Ending	'am'	'was'
I	*mu*	*um*	*um*	*hum*	*bīdum*
you (sing.)	*tu*	*et*	*ī*	*hī*	*bīdī*
(s)he/this, that one	*yō*				
that one	*hō*				
		es	*e*	*he/hed*	*bīd*
that	*ū*				
this	*ī*				
we	*īmā*	*mūn*	*īm*	*hīm*	*bīdīm*
you (plur.)	*īsā*	*tūn*	*īn*	*hīn*	*bīdīn*
they/those	*yōnūn*				
these	*hōnūn*				
		sūn	*en*	*hen*	*bīden*
those	*ūnūn/ōnā*				
these	*īnūn*				

The direct/indirect object forms add *(n)-a*. *Yō* is the general referential pronoun, but 'this one' when in contrast with *hō* 'that one'. *Yō/hō* only occur independently, *yō gul-e bustūn-e u hō šounam-es-e* "This one is the rose of the fragrant garden and that one is its dew," *dāng ye-n-en* "the complaints are this," *yō ke*... "this one who...," *hō ce bīd* "Who was that?" *Ū/ī* occur both independently and before nouns, *ū bard* "that stone," *ī piā* "this man;" *ī* may occur before the substantive verb and relative clause, *ī-n-um/in-ūn-īm* "Here I am/we are!" *na ī-n-e* "Isn't it this one?" The plurals of *ī/ū* occur rarely, *ce hesāw-e ze īnūn īxōī* "What reckoning do you want from these?" *ūnūn kē bīd-en* "Who were those people?"

The personal suffixes have the following functions: 1. possessor, *dast-um* "my hand" (the independent possessive is expressed by pronoun + "to be," *hama kas-emū tu-n-īm* "We all are yours"); 2. direct object, *bexared-um/bexare-m* "that he eat me," *burd-es-e* "He has taken it;" 3. indirect object, *šou īyām tu-n-a* "Tonight I come for/to you;" 4. object of prepositions, *sī-t* "for you," *wur-s* "on it." Note the use of the direct object function to express existence, *tā zinde-t-e* "As long as you are alive," *neid-et* "You are not here" (compare colloquial Persian 3rd sing. *nist-eš* "He isn't here"). Similarly, the direct object is used, *tā tu-n-a hest* "as long as you are here" (German 'Solange es *dich* gibt').

The verb system is typically West Iranian. In the present "to be" has non-emphatic enclitic forms, as indicated in the table above, distinguished from the emphatic forms based on *hest*, *hed-/neid-*, *du mō diyer hedum* "I will be here two more months." Note the frequent use of *na* separated from the verb, *na hō-n-i* "Isn't it that one?" The regular verbal paradigm may be shown as follows (verb *kun/kerd* "do," 1st sing.; traditional terms added):

Present	ī-kun-um	Present Subj.	be-kun-um
General Pres.	kun-um	Optative	kun-ā-m
Imperfect	ī-kerd-um	Counterfactual	ī-kerd-um
Past	kerd-um	Past	kerd-um
Perfect	kerd-um-e	Perfect Subj.	kerd b-um
Past Perfect	kerd-um bī	Past Counterfactual	kerd-um bī

The aspectual, modal, and negative prefixes are as follows: non-general imperfective aspect ī, neg. n-ī; present subjunctive, be/neg. na; imperative, be/neg. ma. The optative suffix is ā. In addition, the 3rd sing. of the past may prefix be, be-kard "he did it." These precede the directional-locational prefixes wā, wā-b "become," wer, wer-ār "bring forth," der, der-ār "bring out:" be-wer-isde "he has stood up," n-ī-wer-isde "he was not standing (up)."

As opposed to the progressive/inchoative present, the general present expresses general habitual action, ze šūmī tā dam-a suv vazan-um zane šūr "From nightfall to morning my Vazan wanders about." The optative expresses wishes, tu-n-a (be-)bīn-a-m "Oh, may I see you." Stative forms are distinguished from perfect forms by adding the endings after bīd, [nišeste bī]-m "I was sitting" vs. [nišest]-um bī "I had sat down."

The causative suffix is n/ūn, sūz-n "burn (something)," pīc-ūn "twist (something)." The intransitive past ending is ist, buhr-isd "it broke" vs. bur-īd "broke it," xam-isd-e "it is (has) bent over." (Pseudo-) passive is expressed by the perfect participle ending in -é + (wā-) b "become," beste bīd-um "I was tied." Modal verbs (all followed by the subjunctive) are: tar/tarisd "can," ke tare z-es berūhe "Who can go away from her?;" wā/wāstī "must," amšou wā duhdar-a bedīn bi mu "Tonight you must give your daughter to me;" xā(h)/xāst "want," īxōm ruvum bi šahr "I want to go to the city."

Syntax and conjunctions. 1. cūn "because;" 2. ayer/ar "if;" general condition with general present, ar kunī, xarj makun "If you make it (i.e., a loan), do not spend it;" factual condition with present indicative, ar har neidī, īfamī "If you are not an ass, you will understand," ar bi xou ībīnum-es, makun-um z-ī xou bēyār "When I am seeing her in my dream, do not wake me up from that sleep;" pre-condition to other action with past, ar duhdar-i tu bi fulūn kasūn nadādī, duhdar-et īmīre "If you do not give your daughter to so-and-so, your daughter will die;" 3. tā, temporal clauses, tā tari "as long as you can;" 4. ki, temporal clauses, tu ki rahdī "when you went," final clauses, muntazir bī ki jēv-i hō-n-a buwure "He was waiting for him to pick his pockets," object clauses, dīd-um ki neid "I saw that he was not there;" relative clause, har ki mandīr-i homsā-s-e, šou be šōm xouse "Whoever waits for his neighbor, will sleep without dinner," tāzī-n-ē ke bi zūr fešnen šekāl, šekāl nīkone "The hunting dog whom they send to hunt by force will not hunt."

Sample verses: ayer mu bāl dāšt-um/ī-perīd-um//zi dīn-i parīrū/ī-daunīd-um///zi ī sīna-ispēd/yār-i Fāyiz//bi har qīmat ī-fruhd/ī-xerīd-um///Persian: agar man bāl dāštam/mīparīdam//az dombāl-e parī-rū/mīdavīdam/// az īn sīna-safīd/yār-e Fāyeż//be har qeymat

mīforūkt/mīkarīdam/// "If I had wings, I would fly. I would run after the fairy-faced girl. From this white-bosomed girl, the beloved of Fāyeż, I would buy at whatever price she would sell."

Bibliography: D. Afsar Baḵtīārī, Montakabāt-ī az ašʿār-e šāʿer-e farzāna Dārāb Afsar Baḵtīārī, ed. A. Sepantā, Tehran, 1344 Š./1965. B. Dāvarī, Żarb al-matalhā-ye Baḵtīārī, Tehran, 1343 Š./1964. A. Houtum-Schindler, "Beiträge zum kurdischen Wortschatze," ZDMG 38, 1884, pp. 43-116; 42, 1888, pp. 73-79. D. L. R. Lorimer, The Phonology of the Bakhtiari, Badakhshani, and Madaglashti Dialects of Modern Persian, London, 1922. Idem, "A Bakhtiari Prose Text," JRAS, 1930, pp. 347-64. Idem, "The Popular Verse of the Bakhtiari of Southwestern Persia, I, II, III," BSOAS 16, 1954, pp. 542-55; 17, 1955, pp. 92-110; 26, 1963, pp. 55-68. Idem, "A Bakhtiari Persian Text," in Indo-Iranica, Mélanges Georg Morgenstierne, ed. G. Redard, Wiesbaden, 1964, pp. 129-33. O. Mann, "Skizze der Lurdialekte," SPAW, phil.-hist. Kl., Berlin, 1904, pp. 1173-93. Idem, Kurdisch-persische Forschungen II: Die Mundarten der Lurstämme im südwestlichen Persien, Berlin, 1910. J. N. Marr, "Obrazets bakhtiarskoĭ literatury" (Specimens of Baḵtīārī literature), Doklady Akademiya Nauk, Ser. B, vol. 4, 1927, pp. 53-58. V. A. Zhukovskiĭ, Materialy dlya izucheniya persidskikh" narechiĭ, pt. 3: Narechie bakhtiyarov" cheharlang" i kheftleng" [Materials for the study of Persian dialects, pt. 3: The dialect of the Čahārleng and Haftleng Baḵtīārs], ed. S. F. Ol'denburg, St. Petersburg, 1923.

(G. L. WINDFUHR)

iii. BAḴTĪĀRĪ CARPETS

"Baḵtīārī" is a label generally applied, in both the trade and literature, to a wide range of flat-woven and knotted pile carpets from southwestern Iran. As such, the term must be considered a territorial, rather than an ethnic, designation, since it may refer not only to the weaving of pastoral nomads, but also to that of the region's sedentary agriculturalists, and each group includes both Baḵtīārī and non-Baḵtīārī elements.

Flat-woven Rugs. Although the manufacture of a variety of flat-woven objects such as weft-wrapped decorated saltbags (namakdān), saddlebags (korjīn, korzīn), and warp-faced tablet-woven straps and bands (malband, tang) by the nomadic Baḵtīārī is well documented in publications by anthropologists, ethnologists, geographers, commercial travelers, and others, whether flatwoven rugs (gelīm) are produced by this group, or by the region's sedentary population, is controversial. There is, however, a type of gelīm classified, in both the trade and recent literature, as Baḵtīārī which is distinguished by its double-interlocked tapestry structure. In this type of weft-faced weave, wefts of adjoining color areas are looped through each other, backward and forward, at each passage, creating two parellel ridges at each join on the back. While this structure is not reversible, it is far stronger than the double-faced slit-tapestry weave more commonly seen in Persian *gelīms*.

Woollen warps and wefts are characteristic of the "Baḵtīārī" *gelīms*; side finishes may include either wool or goat hair. Undyed cotton yarns may be included as design highlights.

Motifs frequently seen in "Baḵtīārī" *gelīms* include highly stylized double-headed bird forms, horned animals, *būta*, and swastikas. It must be noted that, as these motifs also occur in flat-weaves attributed to other groups, particularly the Lurs, basing provenance solely upon them is problematic.

Knotted pile carpets. Although the label Baḵtīārī has traditionally been applied to any pile carpet thought to have been woven in that so-called region, recently writers have tried to distinguish rugs made by the area's nomads from those produced by its sedentary population, on the bases of structure and design. Accordingly, double-wefted, symmetrically knotted carpets with woollen foundations are classified as "tribal," or nomadic, Baḵtīārī products. In contrast, single-wefted carpets with cotton foundations are considered indicative of Baḵtīārī "village" manufacture; these rugs are generally termed "Čahār Maḥāl(l)" after the district near Isfahan where the bulk of such carpets are thought to originate. This method of classification cannot be considered absolute, as there are variations in numbers of weft passes, knotting density, and types of knot in both categories. Moreover, Digard has documented the employment of cotton warps and wefts by nomadic weavers in the manufacture of their woollen pile carpets.

Differentiating Baḵtīārī pile carpets according to design is also difficult. As with flat-weaves, many of the designs seen in "tribal" Baḵtīārī carpets, such as the offset repeat of cypress trees also appear in carpets attributed to the Lurs. Others, including what is probably the best-known Baḵtīārī design, the so-called garden or brick (*kešt*) design, in which the field is divided into square compartments, each containing a flowering plant or tree, is produced by both Čahār Maḥāl and nomadic weavers. Other designs are more specifically associated with Čahār Maḥāl. These include medallion (*toranj*) and corner (*lačak*); prayer niche and figural designs; notable in the latter category is a group with heraldic lions. Čahār Maḥāl attributions are supported by published pieces with these designs which bear inscriptions stating that they are products of specific villages in that district, e.g., *ʿAmal-e Šalamzār-e Baḵtīārī*.

Rugs attributed to Čahār Maḥāl manufacture are generally considered to be commercial products; as Edwards indicates, at least one major Western firm exported carpets from several of that district's villages from the early twentieth century onward. Moreover, even prior to that time, as Mrs. Bishop noted, at least some of the nomadic Baḵtīārī were engaged in weaving for the market. In the trade, the most finely woven Baḵtīārī carpets are termed *bībībāf* (see Digard, 1975); to this category belong a group of carpets which contain presentation and commission formulae and the names and titles of various Baḵtīārī khans.

Dyes. Although Edwards noted the use of natural dyestuffs in at least some of the Čahār Maḥāl villages, today it has become more usual for both nomadic and settled weavers to entrust the dyeing of yarns for weaving to sedentary dyers who employ artificial colorants. Traditionally, dyes were derived from locally available substances, the most common of these being indigo (*nīl*) and madder (*rūnās*), for various shades of blue and red, respectively. *Gandal*, from the herb *gandalāš*, produces the mustard yellow and, in conjunction with madder, yellow-orange colors considered distinctive of both pile and flat weaves from the Baḵtīārī region; interestingly, *gandal* does not seem to have been extensively used as a dye in other parts of Iran.

Bibliography: H. R. d'Allemagne, *Du Khorassan au pays des Bachtiaris. Trois mois de voyage en Perse*, Paris, 1911, I, p. 91; VI, pp. 151-202. S. Āzādī, *Farš-e Īrān*, Hamburg, 1977, pp. 64-65. M. S. Bell, "Kum to Isfahan," *Blackwood's Edinburgh Magazine* 145, June, 1889, pp. 843-64. I. B. Bishop, *Journeys in Persia and Kurdistan*, 2 vols., London, 1891. M. C. Cooper, *Grass*, New York, 1925. G. N. Curzon, *Persia and the Persian Question*, London, 1892, II, pp. 273-303. J.-P. Digard, "Campements Baxtyari. Observations d'un ethnologue sur des matériaux intéressants d'archéologue," *Studia Iranica* 4/I, 1975, pp. 117-29, pls. xxii-xxiii. Idem, *Techniques des Nomades baxtyari d'Iran*, Paris, 1981, pp. 116-33. A. C. Edwards, *The Persian Carpet*, London, 1953, pp. 307, 310-12, pls. 354-64. A. de Franchis, and J. T. Wertime, *Lori and Bakhtiyari Flatweaves*, Tehran, 1976. G. R. Garthwaite, "The Bakhtiyari Khans, the Government of Iran and the British, 1846-1915," *IJMES* 3/1, 1972, pp. 24-44. J. Housego, *Tribal Rugs*, London, 1978, pp. 13, 14, 22, 23, pls. 52, 54-59, 64, 88-89. A. H. Layard, "A Description of the Province of Khuzistan," *JRGS* 16, 1856, pp. 1-105. Idem, *Early Adventures in Persia, Susiana, and Babylonia*, 2 vols., London, 1887. Idem, *The Layard Papers*, British Museum mss. Add. 39064 no. 3, fols. 189-227. G. S. Nasseri, *Perserteppiche/Tapis Persans*, Wiesbaden, 1971, nos. 42, 46. I. Neff and C. V. Maggs, *Dictionary of Oriental Rugs*, London and Johannesburg, 1977, pp. 59-60. K. A. Ḥ. Nīkzād, *Šenāḵtan-e sarzamīn-e Čahār Maḥāl*, Isfahan, 1357 Š./1978, pp. 238-50. Y. Petsoupolis, *Kilims*, New York, 1979, pp. 19, 311-19. H. Rawlinson, "Notes on a March from Zohab . . . to Kirmanshah, in the Year 1836," *JRGS* 9, 1839, pp. 26-109. J. H. Stocqueler, *15 Months Pilgrimage through Untrodden Tracts of Khuzistan and Persia, in a Journey from India to England*, London, 1832, II, pp. 94-118. P. Tanavoli, *Lion Rugs*, Basel, 1985, pp. 30-35, 64; nos. 1, 49-51. J. T. Wertime, "The Lors and Bakhtiyaris," in *Yörük*, ed. A. N. Landreau, Pittsburgh, 1978, pp. 49-50. H. E. Wulff, *The Traditional Crafts of Persia*, Cambridge, Mass., 1966, p. 191.

(A. Ittig)

BAKTĪĀRĪS of AFGHANISTAN. Two small Paštō-speaking groups in the eastern part of the Irano-Afghan area bear the name Baktīārī or Baktīār. There is nothing in the scanty information about them to show that they have any connection with the Baktīārī tribes of the Zagros region, whose eastward spread under the aegis of Nāder Shah Afšār appears to have ended with his death in 1160/1747.

1. A group Baktīār(ān), Baktīārī, or Baktīārkēl (the first form being the commonest) lives in the southeast of Afghanistan. They were allied to the Mīānkēl, a Paštūn tribe, and finally were adopted into its genealogical structure (Šēr-Moḥammad Khan, *Tawārīk-e Kᵛoršīd-e Jahān*, Lahore, 1311/1894, p. 227; J. A. Robinson, *Notes on Nomad Tribes of Eastern Afghanistan*, New Delhi, 1935, repr. Quetta, 1978, p. 175). In the nineteenth century they were nomads, migrating with Mīānkēl tribesmen between the middle Indus valley and the Afghan highlands and reputedly specializing in the horse trade (A. Hamilton, *Afghanistan*, London, 1906, p. 204). When they lost control of their winter grazing grounds as the result of a conflict with the Ganḍāpūr tribe (Šēr-Moḥammad Khan, loc. cit.), several lineages turned to sedentary life in their old summer quarters in southeastern Afghanistan (one hundred families in the estimate of J. A. Robinson, op. cit., p. 176). They have thus given their name to several localities between Ḡaznī and Qandahār (L. W. Adamec, *Gazetteer of Afghanistan* V: *Kandahar and South-Central Afghanistan*, Graz, 1980, p. 78, s.v. Bakhtiar. M. H. Nāhež, ed., *Qāmūs-e joḡrāfīā'ī-e Afḡānestān* I, Kabul, 1335 Š./1956, p. 225, s.v. Baktīār; *Aṭlas-e qaryahā-ye Afḡānestān, A Provisional Gazetteer of Afghanistan*, Kabul, 1353 Š./1975, I, pp. 230, 239, 273, and III, p. 1320). It is unlikely, however, that there is any connection between this group and two places, named Qal'a-ye Baktīār and Baktīārān, which lie close to Kabul, in the city's southern and northeastern outskirts respectively; Baktīārān is known to have been settled by Ḡelzī people at the end of the nineteenth century (*Gazetteer of Afghanistan* VI: *Kabul and Southeastern Afghanistan*, p. 57).

The origin of this tribal group is obscure. Although they are probably not indigenous, the theory of their transplantation from western Iran at the time of Nāder's campaign (which still has supporters, e.g. V. V. Trubetskoĭ, *Bakhtiary*, Moscow, 1966, p. 15; D. Ehmann, *Baḫtiyaren. Persische Bergnomaden im Wandel der Zeit*, Wiesbaden, 1975, p. 50) stems from a rash identification made by M. Elphinstone (*An Account of the Kingdom of Caubul*, London, 1815, repr. Graz, 1969, p. 376) and amplified by H. Field, who did not hesitate to make them descendants of a Baktīārī garrison purportedly left at Peshawar by Nāder Shah (*An Anthropological Reconnaissance in the Near East, 1950*, Cambridge, Mass., 1956, p. 31); the theory must be rejected because there is evidence that Baktīār nomads were already living in the Solaymān mountains and foothills in the early years of the seventeenth century (Kᵛāja Ne'mat-Allāh, *Makzan-e Afḡānī*, tr. B. Dorn, *History of the Afghans*, pt. 2, London, 1836, repr. London, 1965, and Karachi, 1976, pp. 55-56). A local tradition makes them members of a saintly lineage (*stāna*) of the Šērānī tribe who acquired the apotropaic name Baktīār "fortunate," and claims that their ultimate ancestor, Sayyed Esḥāq, came from Iraq (Kᵛāja Ne'mat-Allāh, tr. Dorn, loc. cit.; H. G. Raverty, *Notes on Afghanistan and Part of Baluchistan*, London, 1880-88, repr. Lahore, 1976, pp. 429, 525f.). The genealogical tree of the tribe presented by Moḥammad Ḥayāt Khan (*Afghanistan and Its Inhabitants*, tr. from the "Hayat-i-Afghan" by H. Priestley, Lahore, 1874, repr. Lahore, 1981, p. 280), though far from complete, contains data which complement those given by Kᵛāja Ne'mat-Allāh and Šēr-Moḥammad Khan (op. cit., p. 274).

2. There are also nomads and seminomads named Baktīārī who spend the winter in various places in the southern Bactrian plain and the summer in the central highlands of Afghanistan. Their total number in the 1970s exceeded eight hundred families. The most important group has winter campsites near Ḥażrat-e Solṭān in the Province of Samangān, where the village of Qarya-ye Baktīārī bears their name. Others are reported in the Āqča oasis (35 percent of the total) and in the Fāryāb province (5 percent). Also mentioned are some forty sedentary families in the village of Ḥasan Bolāq, north of Maymana. Although the literature contains some scattered allusions, the first full proof of the existence of Baktīārī communities in northern Afghanistan was obtained by the Afghan Nomadic Survey of 1357 Š./1978 (D. Balland and A. de Benoist, *Nomades et semi-nomades d'Afghanistan*, forthcoming). It should be added that there may be some more settlements which escaped the notice of the survey teams. The real ethnic status and origin of these people can only be conjectured. Some describe themselves as Tājīk, Paštūn, or *sayyed*, But most say only that they are Baktīārī. This suggests that they were involved in the restructuring processes which have taken place throughout northern Afghanistan since the nineteenth century. They all speak Paštō, but in general are bilingual, using Persian for their second language as Paštō-speakers in the Bactrian region frequently do. Moreover, the only lineage name found among them, that of the 'Abd-Allāh-kēl near Āqča, is typically Paštūn. These characteristically Paštūn features suggest that they are late-comers in the region. The supposition that they stem from Baktīārān families displaced from southeastern Afghanistan seems highly probable.

A compact colony of Baktīārī Fārsīwān and Tājīk has been recorded in the southwestern part of the Herāt oasis. It was estimated at about 925 families in the 1880s (Mirza Muhammad Takki Khan, *Report on the City and Province of Herat*, tr. W. R. H. Merk, ca. 1886, India Office Records, London; see also L. W. Adamec, ed., *Gazetteer of Afghanistan* III: *Herat and Northwestern Afghanistan*, Graz, 1975, p. 53, s.v. Birinji) but seems never to have been mentioned again since then.

Bibliography: Given in the text.

(D. BALLAND)

BAKTĪĀR-NĀMA, an example of early New Persian prose fiction in the form of a frame story and nine included tales, the earliest version of which seems to be by Šams-al-Dīn Moḥammad Daqāyeqī Marvazī, the late 6th/12th-early 7th/13th-century author. The frame story is briefly as follows: King Āzādbakt of Nīmrūz (i.e., Sīstān) marries his general's daughter against her father's will. The angry general overthrows Āzādbakt, who flees with his pregnant wife. She bears a son whom they abandon in the desert.

The baby is found and brought up by a robber chief. One day while robbing a caravan he is captured and taken to the city. Āzādbakt, who has regained his kingdom, notices the youth and takes him into his service without recognizing him as his son. Renamed Baktīār, the youth rises quickly in the court. His rapid promotion arouses the jealousy of the king's ten viziers. One day Baktīār inadvertently angers the king and is imprisoned. The chief vizier forces the queen to accuse Baktīār falsely of making improper advances to her. The king condemns Baktīār to death, but he pleads innocence and tells a story which catches the king's interest. On each of the succeeding eight days Baktīār tells a tale that postpones his execution, while each day another vizier tries to persuade the king to execute him. On the tenth day Baktīār is ordered to the scaffold, but the robber chief who had brought him up steps forward from the crowd and identifies him. The king and queen recognize their son from a token they had given him. Reconciled with Baktīār, the king abdicates the throne and crowns his son.

Each of the nine (ten in some Arabic versions) tales told by Baktīār relates to his situation, either from his own point of view by stressing the unfortunate results of actions which are ill-considered or based on malicious advice or from the viewpoint of the narrator by stressing the theme of the failure of a father and son to recognize each other. The queen and viziers tell no counter-tales, but merely call for Baktīār's death.

Clouston, Nöldeke, and Ethé have asserted that the *Baktīār-nāma* derives from or imitates the *Sendbād-nāma*, but there is no evidence for this claim other than their similar formal structures and the motif of a youth falsely accused by a disappointed woman. The fact that both are frame stories relates them generically, but the motif of the falsely accused youth is too widespread geographically and chronologically to be evidence of derivation or imitation. Furthermore, the two plots are quite different.

In the same context, some commentators claim that the *Baktīār-nāma* derives ultimately from an Indian text. This is unlikely in the light of Perry's argument that the *Sendbād-nāma* is of Iranian origin, and the fact that no convincing connection has been made between the *Baktīār-nāma* and an Indian prototype. Nor is there any evidence that the *Baktīār-nāma*, as we know it, derives from a Middle Persian original. *Tārīk-e Sīstān* (pp. 8-9) mentions a *Baktīār* who was *jahān-pahlavān* (chief hero) during the reign of Kosrow II Parvēz, traces his lineage through Rostam back to Garšāsp, and says that his story can be read in the *Baktīār-nāma*. *Eḥyāʾ al-molūk* (pp. 47-48) repeats this account with some additions. The story appears nowhere else, and there is no reason to identify this *Baktīār* with the maligned prince of the *Baktīār-nāma*.

The earliest known example of *Baktīār-nāma* is an Arabic version entitled *ʿAjāʾeb al-bakt fī qeṣṣat al-eḥday ʿašar wazīran mā jarā lahom maʿ Ebn al-Molk Āzādbakt*, dated A.D. 1000 (published in Egypt, 1886; repr. by D. Ṣafā, Tehran, 1347 Š./1968). The earliest known Persian version is dated 663/1265 (Bib. Nat. ms. 2035; see *Cat. Bib. Nat.* IV, pp. 14-15). Almost identical with this is Leyden Codex 593 dated 695/1295-96, discussed by Nöldeke. A summary of *Baktīār-nāma* appears in an anonymous *Eskandar-nāma* of the 12th-14th century A.D. (ed. Ī. Afšār, Tehran, 1343 Š./1964, pp. 198-99). An Uighur version dated 838/1434-35 is described by Jaubert. Versions of the *Baktīār-nāma* appear in some manuscripts of *Alf layla wa layla* (see Chauvin for details).

Internal evidence, the prose style, and statements by ʿAwfī (*Lobāb* I, p. 212) make it most likely that Bib. Nat. ms. 2035 is the work of Šams-al-Dīn Moḥammad Daqāyeqī Marvazī. Little is known of Daqāyeqī, a contemporary of ʿAwfī (q.v.), who is said also to have written a *Sendbād-nāma* in prose. Daqāyeqī's *Baktīār-nāma* was edited and published by D. Ṣafā under the title *Rāḥat al-arwāḥ fī sorūr al-mefrāḥ* (Tehran, 1345 Š./1966). Together with *ʿAjāʾeb al-bakt*, Ṣafā also published an edition of Bib. Nat. ms. 2036 (*Cat. Bib. Nat.* IV, pp. 15-16) dated 809/1406 under the title *Baktīār-nāma*.

Bibliography: See also Ī. Afšār, "Tarjama-ye fārsī-e *Baktīār-nāma*," *Jahān-e now* 6, 1330 Š./1951, pp. 246-47. A. J. Arberry, *Classical Persian Literature*, London, 1958, pp. 170-79 (discusses various translations of *Baktīār-nāma* and gives a lengthy selection in English). V. Chauvin, *Bibliographie des ouvrages arabes ou relatifs aux arabes publiés dans l'Europe chrétienne de 1800 à 1885* VIII: *Syntipas*, Liège, 1904, pp. 13-17, 78-89 (a useful guide to Arabic versions of the *Baktīār-nāma*). H. Ethé, "Neupersische Litteratur," in Geiger and Kuhn, *Grundr. Ir. Phil.* II, pp. 323-25. A Jaubert, "Notice et extrait de la version turque du *Bakhtiar-naméh* d'après le manuscrit en caractères ouïgours que possède la Bibliothèque Bodléïenne d'Oxford," *JA* 10, 1827, pp. 146-67. Malekšāh Ḥosayn Sīstānī, *Eḥyāʾ al-molūk*, ed. M. Sotūda, Tehran, 1344 Š./1965. Th. Nöldeke, "Ueber die Texte des Buches von den zehn Veziren, besonders über ein alte persische Recension desselben," *ZDMG* 45, 1891, pp. 97-143 (discusses and gives lengthy selections from Leyden Codex 593). W. Ouseley, *The Bakhtyār Nama*, ed. W. A. Clouston, London, 1883 (an English translation, with introduction and notes). B. E. Perry, *The Origin of the Book of Sindbad*, Berlin, 1960. M. Rowšan, "Rāḥat al-arwāḥ," *Rāhnamā-ye ketāb* 9, 1345 Š./1966, pp. 503-07 (a review of Ṣafā's edition).

(W. L. HANAWAY, JR.)

BAKTOḠDĪ. See BEKTOḠDĪ.

BAKU (Pers. Bādkūba), capital city of the Azerbaijan Soviet Socialist Republic and one of the chief ports on the Caspian sea.

i. *General.*

ii. *History in the 19-20th centuries.*

i. GENERAL

Name and origin. The form Bākū, used both in literary Persian (see Dehḵodā, s.v.) and in European languages, goes back to medieval Islamic sources where it existed alongside the forms Bākūya, Bākūh, and Bākoh (Sara Ashurbeĭli, *Ocherk srednevekovogo Baku*, Baku, 1964, pp. 35-37). The colloquial Persian form Bādkūba, which popular etymology suggests to be the original name derived from the natural conditions of the site ("wind-beaten"), appears to be of relatively recent date (ibid., pp. 37-38, mentioning texts from the 17th century onward). Finally the local Turkish-speaking population pronounces the word as Bakï, a form that became official with the adoption of Azeri Turkish as the literary language of the republic.

The etymology of the word Bākū, like the antiquity of the settled site itself, is unclear; the country later known as Šervān, an area of which Baku was the port and eventually the capital, lay to the east of Arrān, the classical Caucasian Albania (q.v.), of which it was sometimes considered to be a part and the easternmost extension; the original population of Arrān was of non-Iranian and non-Turkic stock; in Šervān, however, there was considerable Sasanian influence and political control, especially along the coastal strip through Baku to Darband (for the purpose of defense against invasions from the north), so that theories such as that linking Baku to the form Bagawān = "God's Place" (possibly due to a fire temple on one of the petroleum sites) are not implausible (ibid., pp. 39-41).

History. In written sources, Baku first appears as a distinct, inhabited place only in the Islamic period, when the 10th-century geographers and travelers mention its two principal assets: petroleum and position on the coast with a natural harbor that favored both fishing and merchant shipping. These qualities made Baku one of the targets of Varangian-type maritime raids by the Rūs of Tmutorokan mentioned by Masʿūdī (*Morūj* II, p. 21, for the year 301/913-14).

Politically, Baku was throughout the Islamic Middle Ages part of the province of Šervān and, with Šamāḵī, one of the two residences of the long-lasting dynasty of the Šervānšāhs. While petroleum was the single most remarkable article of Baku's consumption and export, the city also benefited from its role as a hub of long-distance maritime as well as caravan trade. Silk and silk-products, carpets, salt, and saffron are, after petroleum, among the articles most frequently mentioned as passing through its port and gates. These circumstances as well as Baku's role as the later capital of the Šervānšāhs, when the political center of gravity shifted there after the damage suffered by Šamāḵī from earthquakes, also spurred a lively local manufacturing industry (especially carpets); and civil and religious building carried out chiefly by the rulers, local or suzerain (such as the city walls, the celebrated palace of the Šervānšāhs, the formidable Borj-e Doḵtar [Maiden's tower], or the intriguing *ḵānaqāh*-type structure in the bay of Baku usually referred to as "Bailov rocks"; see A. S. Bretanitskiĭ, *Zodchestvo Azerbaĭdzhana XII-XV vv. i ego mesto v arkhitekture Perednego Vostoka*, Moscow, 1966, pp. 78-90, 215-46 and passim).

The prosperity of medieval Baku as a busy port and trading and manufacturing center as well as a residence of the Šervānšāhs has been mentioned by a number of contemporary sources; these also reveal the position of Persian and Arabic as the dominant vehicles of political and cultural expression. Thus the 12th-century poet Ḵāqānī, in a panegyric to the Šervānšāh Aḵsetān b. Manūčehr, praises Baku as a great city collecting customs from Persia and the Khazars (*Dīvān*, Tehran, 1978, p. 34). A description of Baku as a busy oil-exporting port has been left by one of its natives, ʿAbd-al-Rašīd Bākovī (fl. 1403), in his *Ketāb talḵīṣ al-āṯār wa ʿajāʾeb al-malek al-qahhār* written in Arabic (ed. Z. M. Bunyatov, Moscow, 1971, pp. 120-22 [Ar. text] and 89-90 [Russ. tr.]; an abridged French tr. by De Guignes, in *Notices et extraits* II, Paris, 1789). Bākovī mentions, among other things, an oil well producing over two hundred camel-loads a day, and another, producing a special white petroleum, whose [daily] lease brought [the ruler] a revenue of 1,000 dirhams; a curious animal addition to this mineral oil was that obtained from seals which the people of Baku hunted on a nearby island (the present-day island of Zhiloĭ); they also used the skins of these seals to pack the mineral oil and export it. On the religious front, Bākovī states that the people of Baku were Sunni Muslims of the Shafiʿite creed, while there were some Christian villages in the countryside.

Throughout this period Šervān, like the rest of former Arrān, continued to be distinct from medieval Azerbaijan, whose territory's northern limit was the rivers Aras and Kor. We can infer that the population of Baku continued to speak for some time the indigenous language mentioned by Arab authors as the original idiom of Arrān. With the spread of the Saljuq Turks in the 5th/11th century and their suzerainty over the Šervānšāhs, there began a process of Turkicization that brought a common linguistic denominator to both the paleo-Caucasian population of Šervān and the Iranian population of Azerbaijan.

Baku, like the entire principality of Šervān, was annexed to Iran by the Safavids in several stages during the 10th/16th century, so that the long reign of the Šervānšāhs, along with the region's independence, came to an end. Persian rule was briefly replaced by the Ottoman one (1578-1607), and then continued until the middle of the 12th/18th century when a weakening of central control made possible, in the Caucasian provinces, the formation of several smaller khanates, among them that of Baku.

In the meantime the growing strength and proximity of the Russian empire began to affect Baku as well. This is already palpable in the account of the 11th/17th-century Turkish traveler Evliya Çelebi (Awlīā' Čalabī), who stresses Baku's importance as the Persian shahs' bulwark against the "King of Moscow"; he also mentions the attacks of Russian Cossacks raiding the area of Baku with their boats from bases in the Volga estuary—a noteworthy analogy to the 4th/10th-century raids by the Rūs. At the same time, however, the Turkish traveler's account reveals that the participation of Russians in Baku's long-distance trade rose to a privileged position: Russian merchants brought sable and grey squirrel skins, walrus tusks, and Russian leather, mostly to be re-exported to Persia, and bought petroleum, salt, saffron, and silk (*Sīāḥat-nāma*, Istanbul 1314/1896-97, II, pp. 300-02).

An expedition led by Peter the Great in 1723 led to a temporary Russian occupation of Baku; this occupation ended in 1735 with the treaty of Ganja. Definitive Russian annexation, carried out in October, 1806, was ratified in 1813 by the Treaty of Golestān (q.v.). The first decades of Russian rule changed little in the traditional physiognomy of Baku, but a dramatic growth set in from the middle of the century onward: This was caused by a rapid modernization of both the technological and commercial exploitation of its high quality petroleum, and by the designation of Baku as the capital of the *guberniya* (principal administrative unit in Tsarist Russia) of the same name in 1859. Thus Baku, a town inhabited by some 3,000 people in 1806, had 222,000 inhabitants in 1909; by 1901, the region's oil fields produced over one-half of the world's output of petroleum.

The upheavals of the October Revolution in 1917 led to a collapse of Russian rule and, by September, 1918, to the establishment of a republic dominated by the Turkish-speaking majority of the area. This republic, with Baku as its capital, assumed the name of Azerbaijan, until then used only for territories south of the Kor and Aras. The fragility of this political formation, made precarious also by the presence of large minorities (chiefly Armenian and Russian, each of whom formed one third of the population of Baku), was demonstrated in April, 1920, when the Soviet forces put an end to its existence. Soviet administration, however, retained the Turkish linguistic identity of the region's majority population and in this sense also the aspirations of the short-lived independent republic, a step that removed it even further from the Persian cultural orbit of which Šervān had been a part throughout the Middle Ages. Since 1936, Baku has been the capital of one of the sixteen constituent republics of the Soviet Union, and a modern city of over 1,700,000 inhabitants (in 1985), with Azeri Turkish and Russian as the two official languages.

Bibliography: Classical sources: Eṣṭaḵrī, p. 190. Masʿūdī, *Tanbīh*, p. 60. *Ḥodūd al-ʿālam*, tr. Minorsky, p. 145. Moqaddasī, p. 376. Abū Dolaf, *al-Resāla al-ṯānīa*, facs. ed. and Russ. tr. P. G. Bulgakov and A. B. Khalidov, Moscow, 1960, fol. 184b and p. 36; ed. and tr. V. Minorsky, *Abū Dulaf Misʿar b. al-Muhalhil's Travels in Iran*, Cairo, 1955, pp. 35 and 72. Studies: Sara Ashurbeĭli, *Gosudarstvo Shirvanshakhov*, Baku, 1983, passim. W. Barthold, tr. S. Soucek, *An Historical Geography of Iran*, Princeton, 1984, pp. 227-28, 236. *EI*², s.v. "Bākū," *Azärbaijan Sovet Ensiklopedijasy* I, Baku, 1976, pp. 550-57.

(S. SOUCEK)

ii. HISTORY IN THE 19TH-20TH CENTURIES.

In the first decades of the nineteenth century, the Russian autocrat Alexander I (1801-25) used both diplomatic pressure and military force to bring the semi-independent principalities and khanates of Transcaucasia under Russian suzerainty. After the annexation of Eastern Georgia in 1801 and the establishment of a permanent Russian presence south of the Caucasus, the commander of Russian troops, General Tsitsianov, began a series of campaigns into Caucasian Azerbaijan, taking Ganja in 1804, Karabakh (Qarabāḡ) and Šervān in 1805, before being killed outside Baku early in 1806. That fall Baku was captured by General Bulgakov, and Iran later gave up its claims to Baku, as well as to Georgia, Šervān, Karabakh, and Ganja, in the Treaty of Golestān (12 October 1813). The city was placed under the Russian military governor in Derbent, and the oil lands, salt ponds, and fish industries were taken over by the state. Much of the Persian system of landholding and peasant-landlord relations was maintained by the tsarist authorities, though the Russian treasury appropriated the lands of the former khans and of the *dīvān*. The peasantry was divided into state peasants and landlord serfs, with the latter a distinct minority.

After the conclusion of the second Russo-Persian War in 1828 (Treaty of Torkamānčāy), Baku and eastern Transcaucasia enjoyed nearly a century of peace. The local economy revived, and Baku emerged as the most important Caucasian trading port on the Caspian. At the beginning of the 1830s, the variety of currencies left by the khanates was replaced by a single Russian monetary system, and a decade later the imperial Russian standards of weights and measures were introduced. The first secular Russian school was opened in Baku in 1832, and instruction was carried on in both Russian and Azeri. At first the oil industry developed slowly, as lands were leased by the state to local entrepreneurs. In 1848, so Soviet sources claim, a Russian technician, F. A. Semenov, drilled the first oil well in the world. But it was only in the last thirty years of the century that the rapid expansion of drilling, refining, and shipping of oil products helped create an upper class of oil industrialists. Foreign entrepreneurs like the Swedish brothers Ludwig and Robert Nobel were instrumental in making Baku the world's leading producer of oil by the beginning of the twentieth century.

Military governance of Transcaucasia ended in

1841, and the territory was divided into two provinces: the Georgian-Imeretian *guberniya* and the Caspian *oblast'*. But this division was short-lived, and, with the appointment of Prince Mikhail Vorontsov as Viceroy of the Caucasus (1844), four provinces were created (1846) with Baku and much of Caucasian Azerbaijan falling into Shemakh province. As part of his policy to attract local elites to supporting Russian rule, Vorontsov convinced Nicholas I (1825-55) to legitimize the landholding structure in Muslim Transcaucasia, and in 1846-47 the hereditary rights of Muslim landlords over their lands and peasants were recognized in law. Even after the Emancipation Decree of 1861 was extended to Caucasian Muslim areas in 1870, the landlords retained much of their authority over both peasants and properties.

Baku became the administrative center of the province (renamed Baku province) after an earthquake devastated Shemakh in 1859. The municipal reform of 1864 was applied to Baku in 1878, and a duma and a mayor, elected by the urban propertied class, were permitted to administer local affairs within strict limits. While ultimate authority in the city remained in the hands of appointed governors and police officials, the upper middle class of industrialists and merchants gained considerable influence by the end of the century. The few Azerbaijani magnates, like Tagiev and Topchibashev, competed for dominance both in the economy and in local politics with the well-placed Armenian and Russian bourgeoisie. The Russian state often gave preferential treatment to the Christian population, and in 1892 the non-Christian representation in the Baku duma was limited to one-third of the membership.

At the other end of Baku society the oil industry had spawned a multinational working class, which by the early twentieth century was engaging in strikes and demonstrations, organizing illegal trade unions, and responding positively to Social Democratic appeals. In 1904 Baku oil workers and their Marxist leaders negotiated the first general labor contract in Russian history. During Russia's first revolution (1905), Baku workers formed a soviet of workers' deputies but restricted much of their activity to economic, rather than political, concerns. Relations between Armenians and Azerbaijanis in the city degenerated into riots and massacres while tsarist officials either sat passively or encouraged the inter-ethnic bloodletting. For his apparent involvement in the events the governor of the city, Prince Nakashidze, was assassinated by Armenian revolutionaries.

Even with the restoration of a harsh political order in 1907-08, the oil economy did not regain its earlier levels, and on the eve of World War I workers again launched massive strikes. Three years later revolution ended tsarist rule, and the resurrected Baku soviet became the de facto governing institution in the city for almost two years. From April through July, 1918, the Bolsheviks under the leadership of Stepan Shahumian held power in the city (the Baku Commune) and initiated a series of social reforms. But this brief experiment ended by summer, and in September Turkish troops occupied the city. Baku was declared the capital of independent Azerbaijan, and a nationalist government moved there from Ganja. Turkish occupation was replaced by British at the end of the World War, and the fragile Musavatist (Mosāwātī) regime tried to maneuver between the Allied Powers, from whom it hoped for recognition; Soviet Russia, whose Bolshevik loyalists threatened the government's existence from both within and outside; and the independent Armenian state with which Azerbaijan had conflicting territorial ambitions. Once the British evacuated (August, 1919), the enthusiasm of many Baku workers for Soviet power and the presence of the Red Army on the border became irresistible. On 28 April 1920, Baku became the capital of the Soviet Socialist Republic of Azerbaijan. That year it hosted the famous Congress of the Peoples of the East.

Baku underwent a rapid and far-reaching transformation under Soviet rule. Its population grew from 439,100 in 1926 to 1,022,000 in 1979, and the central parts of the city were modernized to look like a Western municipality. At first governed by Bolsheviks of Russian, Armenian, as well as Azerbaijani nationality, by the 1930s the leading cadres of Baku and Azerbaijan were almost entirely Azerbaijani. During the Stalinist period an associate of Lavrenti Beria, M. Bagirov, dominated party and state in Azerbaijan, presiding over the economic development of Baku and the political demise of the older generation of Soviet leaders. In the quarter-century since the death of Stalin (1953), Baku has developed into the seventh largest city in the Soviet Union, a major industrial center, and the cultural crucible for the Azerbaijani people.

Bibliography: A. Altstadt-Mirhadi, "The Azerbaijani Bourgeoisie and the Cultural-Enlightenment Movement in Baku: First Steps Toward Nationalism," in R. G. Suny, ed., *Nationalism and Social Change in Transcaucasia: Essays in the History of Armenia, Azerbaijan, and Georgia*, Ann Arbor, 1983, pp. 197-208. I. A. Guseĭnov, et al., *Istoriya Azerbaĭdzhana* II, Baku, 1960. J. D. Henry, *Baku: An Eventful History*, London, 1905. A. Mil'man, *Politicheskiĭ stroĭ Azerbaĭdzhana v XIX-nachale XX vekov*, Baku, 1966. A. Novikov, "Zapiski gorodskogo golovy," *Obrazovanie*, 1904, no. 9, pp. 94-146; no. 10, pp. 65-126; no. 11, pp. 131-64; no. 12, pp. 45-71. R. G. Suny, *The Baku Commune, 1917-1918: Class and Nationality in the Russian Revolution*, Princeton, 1972. T. Swietochowski, "National Consciousness and Political Orientations in Azerbaijan, 1905-1920," in R. G. Suny, op. cit., pp. 209-32. Idem, *Russian Azerbaijan, 1905-1920: The Shaping of National Identity in a Muslim Community*, Cambridge, 1985.

(R. G. SUNY)

BAKWĀ, DAŠT-E, an extensive piedmont alluvial plain in the southwest of Afghanistan. Lying at about

700-750 m above sea level, it is drained by one of the Sīstān rivers, the Ḵospāsrūd, which may perhaps have taken over an old bed of the Ḵāšrūd (J. Pias, *Formations superficielles et sols d'Afghanistan*, Paris, 1976, pp. 118f.). On the north the Dašt-e Bakwā is bordered by mountains of the Sīāhband range; on the south it merges with the Dašt-e Mārgō, of which it forms, so to speak, the antechamber; on the west it is separated from the Farāh oasis by hills of the Ḵormāleq chain; on the east, beyond the Ḵāš river, it abuts on the higher platform of the Wāšēr piedmont. With a scanty but not insignificant annual average precipitation of about 100 mm, the Dašt-e Bakwā is a semi-desert dotted with clumps of tamarisk shrubs (*gaz*). In the 13th/19th century it sustained an abundant fauna of wild herbivores (antelopes, onagers) and birds (partridges, bustards), but since then they appear to have undergone severe decline due to human reoccupation.

For agriculture the Bakwā plain offers real potentialities. In past times it enjoyed a measure of prosperity based on *qanāt* irrigation. Remains of several hundred long-abandoned *qanāt*s show what a large area was once in use. The fact that only some sixty *qanāt*s are still in working order bears witness to an outright abandonment of cultivation, which cannot easily be dated but seems to have culminated in the 13th/19th century when the area was a frontier zone in dispute between the rival principalities of Herat and Qandahār. Reports from that time speak of chronic insecurity and constant pillage of oases and caravans by both the Paṣ̌tūn Dorrānī nomads and the much-feared Baluchis, who rode swift dromedaries and did not hesitate to raid the plain from their bases far to the south ("Itinerary from Yezd to Herat" [no author], *J(R)ASB* 13/2, 1844, p. 841, repr. in G. W. Forrest, ed., *Selections from the Travels and Journals Preserved in the Bombay Secretariat*, Bombay, 1906, p. 11. J. P. Ferrier, *Caravan Journeys and Wanderings in Persia, Afghanistan, Turkistan and Beloochistan*, London, 1857, repr. Westmead, 1971, pp. 274, 280, 282 n., 399ff.). The virtually deserted plain then became a vast winter camping ground in the control of the Paṣ̌tūn Nūrzī nomads; it had a reputation for its wealth of herbage (C. E. Yate, *Khurasan and Sistan*, Edinburgh, 1900, repr. Nendeln, 1977, p. 11).

Despite the restoration of order, symbolized by the first establishment of a garrison in Amir Ḥabīb-Allāh's reign (r. 1319-37/1901-19; L. W. Adamec, ed., *Historical and Political Gazetteer of Afghanistan* II: *Farah and Southwestern Afghanistan*, Graz, 1973, p. 30), the Dašt-e Bakwā remained thinly populated until the 1950s (M. H. Nāhez̤, ed., *Qāmūs-e joḡrāfīā'ī-e Afḡānestān* I, Kabul, 1335 Š./1956, pp. 246ff.). The authorities then resolved to promote its agricultural recolonization, for which the prerequisite was a new irrigation system. After an ambitious project to divert water from the Helmand river had been discarded as too costly (A. A. Michel, *The Kabul, Kunduz and Helmand Valleys and the National Economy of Afghanistan*, Ph.D. thesis, Columbia University, New York, 1959, p. 205), it was decided to have recourse to private capital. A policy of systematic sale of uncultivated state lands enabled bourgeois purchasers from Kabul and Qandahār to acquire ownership of vast tracts, which they began to bring under extensive cereal cultivation (winter wheat and barley). This required heavy investment in wells (which reach the water-table at depths of 15 to 20 m and show maximum yields of 45 liters per second each) and in motor-driven pumps, tractors, and related agricultural equipment. Loans provided by the Agricultural Development Bank gave a strong impetus to the spread of irrigated and mechanized cultivation from 1349 Š./1970 onward. In order to guide and coordinate this activity, the Ministry of Agriculture embarked in 1353 Š./1974 on a special program for the district comprising dissemination of knowledge, surveys of water and soil resources, and establishment of an experimental farm to test possibilities of making the agricultural system more intensive through introduction of summer crops such as maize, cotton, sunflower, and vegetables (*Prōža-ye ābyārī-e Dašt-e Bakwā*, Kabul, Ministry of Agriculture, 1354 Š./1975). In this context, typical of neo-capitalist agrarian development more or less aided and controlled by the state, the Bakwā plain became one of the most dynamic outposts of agricultural pioneering in Afghanistan. The sedentary population of the administrative district (*woloswālī*) of Bakwā (2,078 km^2, part of the province of Farāh) more than doubled in a decade, rising from about 6,000 around 1350 Š./1971 (M. W. Jalmay, *Kandahār. Tārīḵ, joḡrāfīā, koltūr*, Kabul, 1351 Š./1972) to 13,800 at the census of 1358 Š./1979. Concomitantly, the number of nomad families wintering in the district, mainly Nūrzī (Dorrānī but also some Esḥāqzī (Dorrānī), Nāṣerī (*Ḡelzī*), and Zūrī (non-Paṣ̌tūn), fell to fewer than 600 families against an estimated strength of 3,000 families in 1893 (Adamec, loc. cit.).

The town of Bakwā (population 1,500) lies in the middle of the plain and is surrounded by a small oasis irrigated from three *qanāt*s. Also known as Solṭān Bakwā, it is renowned for its old and impressive Islamic cemetery (P. Zestovsky, "L'oasis de Sultan Bakva," *Afghanistan* 6/3, 1950, pp. 41-51). In the 13th/19th century it was only a "small collection of huts and tents" (H. C. Marsh, *A Ride through Islam*, London, 1877, p. 160). Although its role as a caravan station on the old route from Qandahār to Herat via Farāh ceased when the modern concrete-paved highway was built on a line 30 km to the north, its *bāzār* escaped decline, thanks mainly to the presence of the district administrative offices. In 1357 Š./1978 the *bāzār* had some fifty shops and showed real animation as the mart of an area in course of transformation (cf. S. Radojicic, *Report on Possible Provision of Drinking Water for the Places of Gereshk, Qala-i-Kah, Anardar, Khake Safed, Fararod, Gulestan, Bakwa, Kohsan and Obe*, Kabul UNICEF, 1978, p. 9).

Bibliography: Given in the text.

(D. BALLAND)

BĀLĀBĀN, a cylindrical-bore, double-reed wind instrument about 35 cm long with seven finger holes and one thumb hole, played in eastern Azerbaijan in Iran and Soviet Azerbaijan (where it is also called *düdük*). This instrument can be made of mulberry or other harder woods, such as walnut. The bore through the instrument is about one and a half cm in diameter. The double reed is made out of a single tube of cane about six cm long and pressed flat at one end. The performer uses air stored in his cheeks to keep playing the *bālābān* while he inhales air into his lungs. This "circular" breathing technique is commonly used with all the double-reed instruments in the Middle East.

(CH. ALBRIGHT)

BALADĪYA (Municipality), the name or part of the name of several municipal newspapers and journals published in Iran and Afghanistan ca. 1907-39. They include, in order of their dates of publication:

1. *Qāsem al-akbār-e baladīya*, a weekly, one-page Persian newspaper lithographed in Tehran and edited by Mīrzā Abu'l-Qāsem Khan Hamadānī, the licensee and editor of *Baladīya* (see below; Browne, *Press and Poetry*, pp. 124-25). The paper appears to have started late in Rabīʿ I, 1325 (early May, 1907); it contained cartoons and social criticism. For holdings see U. Sims-Williams, *Union Catalogue of Persian Serials and Newspapers in British Libraries*, London, 1985, p. 107; R. Mach and R. D. McChesney, *A List of Persian Serials in the Princeton University Library*, Princeton, 1971; M. Solṭānī, *Fehrest-e rūz-nāmahā-ye fārsī dar majmūʿa-ye Ketāb-kāna-ye Markazī wa Markaz-e Asnād-e Dānešgāh-e Tehran* I, Tehran, 1354 Š./1975, p. 122.

2. *Baladīya* (Tehran, 1907) appeared forty days before the passage of the Qānūn-e Baladīya (Municipality Act) of 20 Rabīʿ II 1325/2 June 1907. Its first licensees and editors were Mortażā Mūsawī Dezfūlī and Mīrzā Abu'l-Qāsem Hamadānī; the latter took full control after the seventh issue (Ṣadr Hāšemī, *Jarāʾed o majallāt* II, pp. 17-19). In addition to news about the municipality, *Baladīya* also contained articles on foreign affairs and, after the founding of the Anjoman-e Baladī (Municipal Council), carried the minutes of council meetings. The paper ranged from four to eight pages, 17 × 29.50 cm, and a subscription cost eighteen *qerān*s in Tehran, twenty-three elsewhere in Iran, and twelve French francs in Europe. For holdings see Browne, *Press and Poetry*, p. 56; R. Mach and R. D. McChesney, *A List of Persian Serials in the Princeton University Library*, Princeton, 1971; U. Sims-Williams, *Union Catalogue of Persian Serials and Newspapers in British Libraries*, London, 1985, p. 20; M. Solṭānī, *Fehrest-e rūz-nāmahā-ye fārsī dar majmūʿa-ye Ketāb-kāna-ye Markazī wa Markaz-e Asnād-e Dānešgāh-e Tehrān* I, Tehran, 1354 Š./1975, p. 29. Some issues of the newspaper are also kept in the Majles Library and the Bibliothèque Nationale.

3. *Šūrā-ye baladī*, a Persian newspaper lithographed in Tehran four times weekly in 1907 and edited by Moʿtamed-al-Eslām Raštī, who was also the publisher of *Yādgār-e enqelāb*, Tehran and Qazvīn, 1909. *Šūrā-ye baladī* was solely devoted to publishing the minutes of the Tehran municipal council. Eight issues were published from Jomādā II–Šaʿbān, 1325/July-September, 1907; the yearly subscription rate was thirty-six *qerān*s in Tehran, forty-six elsewhere in Iran, and twenty-one francs abroad. Some issues of *Šūrā-ye baladī* are kept in the Tehran University and Majles libraries and in the Bibliothèque Nationale. For holdings see Browne, *The Press and Poetry*, p. 112; R. Mach and R. D. McChesney, *A List of Persian Serials in the Princeton University Library*, Princeton, 1971.

4. *Anjoman-e baladīya-ye Eṣfahān* (Isfahan, 1907-08) began as *Faraj baʿd az šeddat* on 5 Šawwāl 1325/12 November 1907, but shortly underwent an identity change to reflect its semi-official status. It was established and edited by the celebrated Isfahani *wāʿeẓ* Āqā Mīrzā Nūr-al-Dīn Majlesī and appeared three times monthly (Ṣadr Hāšemī, *Jarāʾed* I, pp. 293-97). The paper's four lithographed pages (21.5 × 34.5 cm) contained articles on social and municipal affairs written in an ornate prose style. A yearly subscription cost twelve *qerān*s in Isfahan, fifteen in other parts of Iran, and eight francs abroad (Browne, *Press and Poetry*, p. 47). Some issues of the newspaper are kept in the Majles Library, the libraries of the University of Isfahan, and the Isfahan office of Arts and Cultures; elsewhere some copies are preserved in the Cambridge University Library and Bibliothèque Nationale.

5. *Baladīya-ye Eṣfahān* (Isfahan, 1908) was a biweekly successor to the previous entry that began 4 Ḏu'l-ḥejja 1325/9 January 1908 and ceased in Moḥarram, 1326/March, 1908 (Browne, *Press*, p. 56). It was edited by Mīrzā ʿAbbās Khan Čahārmaḥālī, who gained fame as a poet pen-named *Šeydā* (Ṣadr Hāšemī, *Jarāʾed* II, pp. 20-22); he also published *majalla-ye farhangī-e Dāneškada-ye Eṣfahān* in 1303 Š./1925. In addition to the municipal council minutes, *Baladīya-ye Eṣfahān* devoted its four, 22 × 35 cm pages to articles on literature and society. A yearly subscription was twenty-five *qerān*s in Isfahan, thirty elsewhere in Iran, and thirty-three abroad. For holdings see U. Sims-Williams, *Union Catalogue of Persian Serials and Newspapers in British Libraries*, London, 1985, p. 87. Issues of the journal are also kept in the University of Isfahan, Art and Culture, and Majles Libraries.

6. *Baladīya* (Tabrīz, 1909) was a biweekly newspaper lithographed in Tabrīz from 8 Moḥarram 1327/31 January 1909 under the editorship of Aḥmad Mīrzā (Browne, *Press*, p. 56; Ṣadr Hāšemī, *Jarāʾed* II, p. 20). Specimens of the paper held in the Ketāb-kāna-ye Tarbīat in Tabrīz contain eight two-column pages, measuring 22 × 35 cm. An issue cost 200 *dīnār*s in Tabrīz and five *šāhī*s elsewhere.

7. *Balad al-amīn* (Mašhad, 1910) was published weekly from Moḥarram/January-February until 24 Jomādā II 1328/2 July 1910 and was edited by Mīrzā Moḥammad-Ṣādeq (Browne, *Press*, p. 55). It was lithographed on paper measuring 19 × 32 cm and cost ten *qerān*s in Mašhad and fifteen elsewhere in Iran (Ṣadr

Hāšemī, *Jarāʾed* II, p. 17). For holdings see Sims-Williams, *Union Catalogue*, p. 19.

8. *Baladīya* (Rašt, 1919) was published towards the end of the year 1337 (summer, 1919) under the editorship of Nāder Mīrzā Ārāsta (Ṣadr Hāšemī, *Jarāʾed* II, p. 20).

9. *Baladīya* (Tehran, 1921-36) was at first a bimonthly and then a monthly journal published from 19 Jawzā 1300/9 June 1921 until Esfand, 1314 Š./February, 1936 when it was renamed *Šahrdārī*. The editorship of the journal was held consecutively by ʿAbbās Ḵalīlī, Abu'l-Ḥasan Maʿdančī, Mahdī Māfī, Reżā Šahrzād, and Kāẓem Šarīfī. The size varied from eighteen to one hundred pages measuring 21 × 27 cm initially and 16 × 22.5 cm after the journal's tenth year. *Baladīya* was illustrated and contained advertisements in Persian and French. It cost sixteen *šāhīs* initially and increased to fifty *qerāns* in its eleventh year (Ṣadr Hāšemī, *Jarāʾed* II, p. 20). Series of the newspaper are kept in major libraries in Iran.

10. *Baladīya* (Rašt, 1929) was published (apparently only once) in Esfand, 1307 Š./February, 1929 under the editorship of Amīr Eršād. It contained thirty-two two-column pages, measuring 21 × 28.5 cm. It is kept in the National Library of Rašt and the Central Library of Tehran University.

11. *Baladīya-ye Eṣfahān* (Isfahan, 1930-31) was founded in Ābān, 1309 Š./October, 1930, by the noted pianist Colonel Ḥabīb-Allāh Khan Šahrdār, mayor of Isfahan, and was edited by the poet Moḥammad-ʿAlī Mokrem (Ṣadr Hāšemī, *Jarāʾed* II, pp. 22-23), who was to become founder and publisher of several newspapers and magazines in Isfahan. The journal was illustrated and contained articles on the city and public health. Its twenty to twenty-four two-column pages measured 17 × 22 cm; a yearly subscription cost twelve *qerāns* in Isfahan, fifteen elsewhere in Iran, and twenty abroad.

12. *Baladīya-ye Herāt* (Herāt, 1933-39) began on 11 Ḥūt 1311 Š./2 March 1933 under the editorship of Mīrzā ʿAbd-Allāh Aḥrārī and was later edited by Ṣafar-ʿAlī Amnī. It contained twenty-eight pages measuring 17 × 22 cm and contained articles on history, medicine, and public health; a yearly subscription cost six *afḡānīs* locally, seven elsewhere in Afghanistan, and seven shillings abroad.

See also ANJOMAN-E EṢFAHĀN.

(N. PARVĪN)

BALĀḎORĪ, ABU'L-ḤASAN or ABŪ BAKR AḤMAD B. YAḤYĀ B. JĀBER, leading Arab historian of the 3rd/9th century, whose *Ketāb fotūḥ al-boldān*, in particular, contains much original and indispensable information on the Arab conquests of Iran.

Life. The exact details of Balāḏorī's life are shadowy, but he was probably born at, and spent most of his life in, Baghdad and Iraq, though his grandfather Jāber b. Dāwūd had been a secretary in the government administration in Egypt. He studied in Syria, including at Damascus, Antioch, and Ḥoms, and whilst in Iraq he derived knowledge, directly from lectures and also from their writings, from such historians as Moḥammad b. Saʿd (d. 230/845), Madāʾenī (d. 235/850), and Moṣʿab Zobayrī (d. 233/848), and from the grammarian and Koranic scholar Abū ʿObayd Qāsem b. Sallām (d. 224/838). His own birth date must, accordingly, have fallen at some point within the first three decades of the ninth century A.D. The unusual *nesba* of Balāḏorī apparently stems from his grandfather's inadvertent use of, and reported death from, the stimulant to the mind and memory made from the marking-nut tree, *Semecarpus anacardium* L. (Arabic *Balāḏor*, from Skr. *bhallātaka*; see B. Laufer, *Sino-Iranica, Chinese Contributions to the History of Civilization in Ancient Iran*..., Chicago, 1919, repr. Taipei, Taiwan, 1967, pp. 482, 582). Balāḏorī himself seems to have been closely connected with the ʿAbbasid court, as a boon-companion (*nadīm*) of the caliph al-Motawakkel (r. 232-47/847-61), and enjoying close relations with subsequent rulers like al-Mostaʿīn (r. 248-52/862-66) and al-Moʿtazz (r. 252-55/866-69), deriving personal information from members of the ruling family, including from Hebat-Allāh b. Ebrāhīm b. Mahdī (*Ansāb al-ašrāf*, fol. 355a-b) and from al-Motawakkel himself (*Fotūḥ al-boldān*, p. 146.6, on a point concerning the history of Aleppo); but the statement that he acted as tutor for al-Moʿtazz's son, the future poet Ebn al-Moʿtazz (Margoliouth, p. 116; Brockelmann, *GAL* I, p. 147) seems to be based on a misconception. Balāḏorī seems to have become less persona grata with al-Moʿtamed than with his predecessors, and he probably died at the end of the latter's caliphate or at the opening of al-Moʿtażed's one, in about 279/892.

Ebn al-Nadīm, (*Fehrest*, p. 113; [Tehran], pp. 125-26), followed by Yāqūt, (*Odabāʾ* II, p. 131), lists a metrical Arabic translation of a *Ketāb ʿahd Ardašīr*, not otherwise known, and further mentions that Balāḏorī was known as a translator from Persian to Arabic. He seems also to have had some reputation as a poet and satirist, verses of his being quoted by Yāqūt in his biography of Balāḏorī (*Odabāʾ* II, pp. 127-32).

Works. If the details of Balāḏorī's life are obscure, his two major works have an importance as sources for early Islamic history second only to the history of Ṭabarī (q.v.). The lengthier one, his *Ansāb al-ašrāf*, is a history based on genealogical principles, clearly influenced by the *ṭabaqāt* method of arrangement adopted by his master Ebn Saʿd. His immediate models for the work were doubtless Hešām b. Moḥammad Kalbī's *Jamharat al-nasab* (extant) and Hayṯam b. ʿAdī's *Ketāb taʾrīḵ al-ašrāf* (lost). The *Ansāb al-ašrāf* (*ašrāf* here = "leading men in the state," those entitled to *šaraf al-ʿaṭāʾ*, stipends from the *Dīvān* at the highest rate) is conceived on a mammoth scale. The surviving complete manuscript, Istanbul Aşır Efendi (= Reis-ül-küttâb) 597-98, comprises 1,227 folios, and is thus almost as long as Ṭabarī's *Taʾrīḵ* (table of contents by M. Hamidullah, "Le 'Livre des généalogies' d'al-Balāḏurīy," *Bulletin d'études orientales* 14, Damascus, 1952-54, pp. 197-211, also prefixed by him to volume I of the edition, see below). It is primarily a biographical and genealogical record (but also provides, within the biography of a caliph, a continuous history of his times), beginning with the Prophet Moḥammad, his kinsmen of the Banū Hāšem, including the ʿAbbasid and the ʿAlids; continuing on to the Banū ʿAbd Šams, with especial detail on the Omayyads, and the rest of the clans of Qorayš, including those of Abū Bakr and ʿOmar, the latter's biography already distinctly hagiographical in character; and ending with the other tribes of Możar, including the whole of Qays, with Ṯaqīf at the very last. The other North Arab branch, Rabīʿa, and the South Arabs, Yaman, are not treated; Ḥājī Ḵalīfa, (*Kašf al-ẓonūn*, Leipzig, I, p. 274) states that Balāḏorī died before he could finish the work. Notable in Balāḏorī's general approach is the fact that, although a courtier of the ʿAbbasids, he devoted over one-third of his book to the Omayyads, treating them objectively and even sympathetically; Goitein has suggested (introd. to vol. V, pp. 15-16) that the ʿAbbasid caliphs viewed the history of their predecessors not invariably as that of enemies but also as valuable precedents for statecraft and sound administration. Whilst mainly focussed on events in the Syria-Iraq-Arabia heartland, the *Ansāb al-ašrāf* also provides information on events which affected Iran such as the activities of governors of the East like Zīād b. Abīhi, the ravages of the Kharijites in Iran, and the factional strife of the Arab tribes there; the present writer has used it for the events in Sīstān and Zābolestān which preceded the great revolt of the so-called Peacock Army (*Jayš al-Ṭawāwīs*) under ʿAbd-al-Raḥmān b. al-Ašʿaṯ which nearly toppled the caliphate of ʿAbd-al-Malek (see Bosworth, "ʿUbaidallāh b. Abī Bakra and the 'Army of Destruction' in Zābulistān (79/698)," *Der Islam* 50, 1973, pp. 268-83, repr. in *The Medieval History of Iran, Afghanistan and Central Asia*, London, 1977, art. XIX).

The following sections of the *Ansāb al-ašrāf* have been published: I, ed. M. Ḥamīd-Allāh, Cairo, 1959; II, ed. Moḥammad Bāqer Maḥmūdī, Beirut, 1394/1974; III, ed. ʿAbd-al-ʿAzīz Dūrī, Beirut, 1398/1978; IV-V: *The Ansāb al-Ashrāf of al-Balādhurī*: IVa, ed. M. Schloessinger and M. J. Kister, Jerusalem, 1971; IVb, ed. Schloessinger, Jerusalem, 1938 (the two preceding volumes, plus the early part of V, also ed. Eḥsān ʿAbbās, Beirut and Wiesbaden, 1979); V, ed. S. D. F. Goitein, Jerusalem, 1936; XI, ed. W. Ahlwardt as *Anonyme arabische Chronik*, Greifswald, 1883.

Balāḏorī's other major work, the *Ketāb fotūḥ al-boldān* [*al-ṣaḡīr*], survives as the shorter version of what was apparently a larger and fuller work on the same subject. In it, Balāḏorī gives a continuous narrative of the Arab conquest for each province of the Islamic empire, deriving his material from works of the historians of these various regions, supplemented by his own personal travels, as far as possible, and enquiries on the spot for material. He then sifted the accounts and produced a balanced narrative, usually (though not invariably) refraining from citing parallel, or contradictory, accounts of the same events. The editio princeps of this work was made by M. J. de Goeje, as *Liber expugnationis regionum auctore ... el-Belâdsorî*, Leiden, 1866 (repr. Leiden, 1968), with numerous subsequent Middle Eastern prints, e.g., ed. Ṣalāḥ-al-Dīn Monajjed, Cairo, 1956-60. O. Rescher published a German translation of as far as p. 239 of de Goeje's edition, Leipzig, 1917-23, and a complete English translation was made by P. K. Hitti and F. C. Murgotten, *The Origins of the Islamic State*, Columbia Studies in History, Economics and Public Law 68/1-2, New York, 1916-24 (pt. 1 repr. Beirut, 1966); sections dealing with the conquest of Iran have been translated into Persian by Ā. Āḏarnūš (Tehran, 1346 Š./1967).

The *Fotūḥ al-boldān* is of the highest importance for the Islamic conquest of Iran and the adjacent parts of the Caucasus, Afghanistan, and Central Asia, supplementing, but often adding fresh material, the annalistically-arranged information of Ṭabarī. Separate sections are devoted to the Arabs' overrunning of Iraq, Jebāl, Ray and Qūmes, Azerbaijan, Gorgān and Ṭabarestān, Ahvāz, Fārs, Kermān, Sīstān and Kabul, Khorasan and Transoxania (especially detailed), and Makrān and Sind. One of his prime sources was the philologist Abū ʿObayda Maʿmar b. Moṯannā (q.v.), who provided information not found in other sources, e.g., that the Arabs first crossed the Oxus as early as ʿOṯmān's caliphate during the governorship in Khorasan of ʿAbd-Allāh b. ʿĀmer b. Korayz (q.v.) (p. 408). But interspersed with the accounts of military raids and battles is much material on social and cultural affairs, e.g., on the change from Persian to Arabic (*naql al-dīwān*) in the government departments under the Omayyads; the colonization of Azerbaijan by the Arabs; the rallying of the Persian cavalry of the Sasanians, the *asāwera* (q.v.), to the Arabs; etc.

Bibliography: Given in the text. See also Barthold, *Turkestan*³, p. 6. D. S. Margoliouth, *Lectures on Arabic Historians*, Calcutta, 1930, pp. 116-19. Brockelmann, *GAL* I, pp. 147-48, S. I, p. 216. Sezgin, *GAS* I, pp. 320-21 (with further bibliography). C. F. Becker and F. Rosenthal, "al-Balādhurī," in *EI*² I, pp. 971-72. Rosenthal, *A History of Muslim Historiography*, 2nd ed., Leiden, 1968, index, s.v. A. A. Duri, *The Rise of Historical Writing among the Arabs*, ed. and tr. L. I. Conrad, Princeton, 1983, pp. 61-64.

(C. E. Bosworth)

BALĀḠAT (Arabic *balāḡa*), one of the most general terms to denote eloquence in speech and writing. Its etymology is usually based on the meaning "to reach" of the verb *balaḡa*. Therefore *baloḡa* "to be eloquent" is taken to mean: to be able "to convey" the intended meaning effectively, and in an attractive manner, to the mind of a listener or a reader. A person of whom this can be said is called *balīḡ* (plur. *bolaḡāʾ*). This predicate is more properly used to qualify speech (*kalām*) but, according to the classical theory, only at the level of syntactic units. To single words the cognate concept of *faṣāḥat* (purity of language) should be applied. The delimitation of *balāḡat* and *faṣāḥat* was often discussed in Arabic literary theory. Sometimes they were regarded as synonyms or at least as largely overlapping concepts. The prevailing opinion was, however, that the latter referred to the wording (*lafẓ*) and the former to the semantics (*maʿnā*) of speech. Nevertheless the two remained closely related to each other: an utterance could never be said to be *balīḡ* if it was not at the same time *faṣīḥ*, i.e., free from any faults of pronunciation, grammar, or lexicon.

In pre-Islamic Arab Society, eloquence was important to the orator (*kaṭīb*) as well as to the oral Bedouin poet. Early *adab* works reflect this emphasis on the good style of the spoken word. One of the points discussed was whether the orator might use gesticulations to add force to his words or not. At the same time eloquence was recognized as an ideal familiar to other nations as well. Foreign traditions—of the Persians, the ancient Greeks, the Byzantines, and the Indians—provided some of the many definitions which became current in Muslim literature. Jāḥeẓ even quotes prescriptions concerning eloquence from a *ṣaḥīfa* which was brought to Bahgdad by Indian scholars during the vizierate of the Barmakid Yaḥyā b. Ḵāled (*Bayān* I, pp. 92-93).

In the Arabic works on literary theory, eloquence was mainly discussed with regard to written works, both in prose and in poetry. A justification for the study of *balāḡat* was found in the doctrine of the *eʿjāz*, (inimitability) of the Koran. The text of the Koran was considered to possess the characteristics of *eʿjāz* in the most perfect form. To be familiar with their rules was therefore a prerequisite to the understanding of the meaning of the Revelation in the Koran. The eminent place of the study of good style in Muslim education, as well as its close link with the study of the Arabic language, were also based on this doctrine.

Various definitions of *balāḡat* were attempted but none of them can be said to have reached the status of a standard formulation. It remained a rather vague notion which lent itself to many applications. One finds, for instance, under the heading of ʿAbd-al-Qāher Jorjānī's *Asrār al-balāḡa* (The secrets of eloquence) a treatise on imagery and the figurative use of language, but in the Persian textbook *Tarjomān al-balāḡa* of Rādūyānī it encompasses all figures of speech and is used as an equivalent of *badīʿ*. Abu'l-Ḥasan Rommānī (d. 384/994), an early writer on *eʿjāz*, drew up an inventory of ten parts (*aqsām*) of *balāḡat* which comprises besides the use of various types of figurative speech a number of general stylistic criteria ("Nokat," p. 70). The notion of concision (*ījāz*), under the condition of clarity of expression, is often mentioned as a basic rule of *balāḡat*. It has a counterpart in the ability to expand without tediousness. Other aspects of eloquence are conformity to the circumstances (*entehāz al-forṣa*) and attention to the proper arguments (*al-baṣar fī'l-ḥojja*).

Eventually the branches of literary criticism which developed within Muslim civilization became known collectively as the science (*ʿelm*) or art (*ṣenāʿa*) of *balāḡat*. In this usage it comprises primarily two disciplines: the *ʿelm al-maʿānī*, studying the role of syntax in literatury style, and the *ʿelm al-bayān* (qq.v.) which deals with the theory of similes, metaphors, and tropes. Their rules provide the foundation for the use of rhetorical embellishment, which is the subject of a third discipline, the *ʿelm al-badīʿ* (q.v.). This classification of literary theory became prevalent in the eastern part of the Muslim world from the 8th/14th century onwards as far as Arabic literature was concerned.

Although Iranians (especially Abd-al-Qāher Jorjānī and Abū Bakr Yūsof Sakkākī Ḵᵛārazmī) made important contributions to the scholastic study of Arabic eloquence, most Persian textbooks are no more than practical guides to the use of figures of speech in the ancient tradition of *badīʿ*. Šams-al-Dīn Moḥammad b. Qays however enters briefly upon the general principles of eloquence. He stresses the preference of concision over expansion and relates the following definition: "the critics have said: *balāḡat* is good words with the right meanings, and *faṣāḥat* means that the words are free from difficulty. *Balāḡat* appears in three kinds of expression: concision (*ījāz*), balance (*mosāwāt*), and expansion (*basṭ*)." (*Moʿjam*, p. 370).

Bibliography: From the many works dealing with aspects of *balāḡat* only a few can be mentioned here: Abū ʿOṯmān ʿAmr b. Baḥr Jāḥeẓ, *Ketāb al-bayān wa'l-tabyīn*, Cairo, 1367/1948, I, pp. 88-97. Abu'l-Ḥasan ʿAlī b. ʿĪsā Rommānī, "Nokat fī eʿjāz al-Qor'ān," in *Ṯalāṯ rasā'el fī eʿjāz al-Qor'ān*, Cairo, 1955, pp. 69-104. Abū Helāl ʿAskarī, *Ketāb al-ṣenāʿatayn*, Cairo, 1371/1952, pp. 6-54. Ebn Rašīq, *al-ʿOmda fī maḥāsen al-šeʿr wa ādābeh wa naqdeh*, Cairo, 1374/1955, I, pp. 241-50. M. Fešārakī, "Īstā'ī o taqlīd o enteḥāl dar ta'līf-e kotob-e balāḡī," *Āyanda* 12/9-10, 1365 Š./1986-87, pp. 570-78. Ḵaṭīb Demašq Qazvīnī, *Talḵīṣ al-Meftāḥ* (with commentaries by Taftāzānī and others), Būlāq 1317/1899, I, pp. 70ff. Moḥammad b. ʿOmar Rādūyānī, *Tarjomān al-balāḡa*, Istanbul, 1949. Šams-al-Dīn Moḥammad b. Qays Rāzī, *al-Moʿjam fī maʿāyīr ašʿār al-ʿajam*, ed. M. Qazvīnī, rev. M.-T. Modarres Rażawī, Tehran, 1334 Š./1955. Jalāl-al-Dīn Homā'ī, *Fonūn-e balāḡat wa ṣenāʿat-e adabī*, Tehran, 1354 Š./1975, pp. 9-26. G. J. van Gelder, "Brevity: The Long and the Short of It in Classical Arabic Literary Theory," in *Proceedings of the Ninth Congress of the U.E.A.I.*, Leiden, 1981, pp. 78-88. *EI*², s.vv. "Balāgha," "Faṣāḥa," "Iʿdjāz," and "al-Maʿānī wa'l-bayān."

(J. T. P. de Bruijn)

BALĀĠĪ, MOḤAMMAD-JAWĀD B. ḤASAN B. ṬĀLEB B. ʿABBĀS RABAʿĪ NAJAFĪ, Imami author, poet, and polemicist. Born in Najaf in 1282/1865-66 (or, less probably, in 1285/1868-69 or 1280/1863-64) to a well-known family of scholars, he spent his early years at his birthplace (except for a sojourn in Kāẓemayn between 1306/1888-89 and 1312/1894-95), before departing in 1326/1908 for Samarra, where he lived for ten years. Following the British occupation of the city he moved back to Kāẓemayn and supported circles seeking independence for Iraq. Two years later he returned to Najaf, and devoted his time to teaching and writing. He was admired by many for his modesty and piety. In this last years he suffered from ill-health; he died of pleurisy on Sunday, 22 Šaʿbān 1352/10 December 1933.

Balāġī was versed not only in the traditional Islamic sciences, but was also acquainted with some Western Biblical and Orientalist publications, and knew English, Hebrew (which he acquired mainly from Baghdadi Jews), and Persian. He was thus well equipped for the task which he had set himself in many of his forty-eight works (and which earned him the honorific *al-mojāhed*), proving the superiority of Islam to other faiths. In his two major works, *al-Hodā elā dīn al-moṣṭafā* and the more popular *al-Reḥla al-madrasīya* (both written in response to Christian missionary books), Balāġī analyses passages from the Old and New Testaments with a view to proving that these are replete with inconsistencies, contradictions, linguistic errors, and blasphemous expressions, and that the Bible as we have it today (*al-rāʾej*) preserves little of the original book (*al-ḥaqīqī*). His opposition to Bahaism was particularly vehement, and he was actively involved in the successful campaign to deny the Bahais possession of the house in Baghdad in which Bahāʾ-Allāh had lived during his Iraqi exile, and which had become a Bahai shrine (cf. Shoghi Effendi, *God Passes By*, Wilmette, 1944, pp. 356-60).

In addition to his polemical writings, Balāġī wrote extensively on Imami *oṣūl* and *forūʿ*. His strong commitment to Imami Shiʿism was expressed in various ways: he composed a poem defending the belief in the Hidden Imam, and is also credited with reviving the *ʿāšūrāʾ* mourning ceremonies at Karbalāʾ.

Bibliography: Brockelman, *GAL*, S. II, p. 804. *Aʿyān al-šīʿa* XVII, pp. 67-104. *Aʿlām al-šīʿa* I, pp. 323-26. Jaʿfar Bāqer Āl Maḥbūba, *Māżī al-Najaf wa-ḥāżerohā*, Najaf, I, 1378/1958, pp. 377-78 (including Balāġī's photo), II, 1374/1955, pp. 61-66. Zereklī, *Aʿlām* VI, Beirut, 1980, p. 740. Kaḥḥāla, IX, p. 163. Aḥmad Ḥosaynī, preface to Balāġī's *al-Reḥla*, Najaf, 1382/1963, pp. 3-16. Tawfīq Fokaykī, preface to Balāġī's *al-Hodā*, Najaf, 1385/1965, pp. 6-21.

(E. Kohlberg)

BALʿAMĪ, ABŪ ʿALĪ MOḤAMMAD b. MOḤAMMAD.

See AMĪRAK BALʿAMĪ.

BALʿAMĪ, ABU'L-FAŻL MOḤAMMAD b. ʿOBAYD-ALLĀH b. MOḤAMMAD BALʿAMĪ TAMĪMĪ,

vizier to the Samanid amir Naṣr b. Aḥmad, father of the vizier and historian Abū ʿAlī Moḥammad b. Moḥammad Balʿamī (see AMĪRAK BALʿAMĪ) and thus member of a distinguished family in the service of the rulers of Transoxania and Khorasan. The unusual *nesba* Balʿamī is explained by Samʿānī, *Ketāb al-ansāb* (Leiden, fol. 90a = ed. Hyderabad, II, pp. 313-14) as either from Balʿam, a place in Anatolia which the Omayyad general Maslama b. ʿAbd-al-Malek raided and occupied, or else from Balʿamān, a village of the Marv oasis where the vizier's forebears had settled since the time of Qotayba b. Moslem (q.v.). Whatever the family's origins—and it is unknown whether they were of pure Arab blood or had been non-Arab, presumably Iranian, *mawālī* or clients of the Arab tribe of Tamīm—they moved to Bukhara where, Samʿānī states, Balʿamīs were still living in his own time (6th/12th century).

Samʿānī's information here that Abu'l-Fażl Moḥammad first served Amīr Esmāʿīl b. Aḥmad (r. 279-95/892-907; q.v.) is uncorroborated in the historical sources. He only appears in the reign of Esmāʿīl's grandson Naṣr II b. Aḥmad (r. 301-31/913-42; q.v.). At some unknown date, but probably about 309/921, he became vizier to Naṣr in succession to Abu'l-Fażl b. Yaʿqūb Nīšāpūrī (Maqdesī, p. 337), and from now onwards, he is sporadically mentioned in the sources (Gardīzī, Ebn al-Aṯīr) as involved in military and diplomatic activities. Already in 309/921 he was with the Samanid forces suppressing in a battle near Ṭūs the revolt of Daylamite Laylī b. Noʿmān on behalf of the Zaydī ʿAlid al-Dāʿī ela'l-Ḥaqq Ḥasan b. Qāsem; in the next year, he combined with the Turkish commander of the Samanids Sīmjūr Dawātī in Ṭabarestān against the Daylamite Mākān b. Kākī (q.v.); and in 321/933 he was with Amir Naṣr in Gorgān conducting operations against the Daylamite ruler of Jebāl and Ray, Mardāvīj b. Zīār (q.v.).

Balʿamī also interceded for the release from jail of the commander Abū ʿAlī Moḥammad b. Elyās (see ĀL-E ELYĀS), who subsequently established for himself a virtually autonomous principality in Kermān; and for the general Ḥosayn b. ʿAlī Marvazī or Marv-al-rūḏī, who seems to have been caught up in the Ismaʿili Shiʿite movement in Transoxania during the last years of Naṣr b. Aḥmad's reign (see for this episode, Barthold, *Turkestan*², pp. 242-44). Ṯaʿālebī quotes verses of thanks by Ḥosayn addressed to Balʿamī after his release from imprisonment in the citadel of Herat (*Yatīma* [Cairo] IV, p. 85, French tr. C. Barbier de Meynard, in *JA*, series 5, 1, 1853, p. 204). Balʿamī also played a decisive role in the crisis of the popular revolt in Bukhara, at some date between 317/929 and 320/932, led by the baker Abū Bakr. The amir's brothers, eager for power, were released from prison, and Naṣr himself was absent at Nīšāpūr. By coming to terms with the son of Ḥosayn b. ʿAlī Marvazī, Balʿamī was able to secure the amir's crossing of the Oxus, his return to the capital, and the quelling of the rebellion.

Balʿamī was clearly, together with Jayhānī, the driving force during what seems to have been the reign of a weak and impressionable ruler. He is further praised, e.g., by Samʿānī, as a maecenas and encourager of poets and scholars, including of the poet Rūdakī (q.v.), and public buildings erected by him at Marv and Bukhara are mentioned. Not surprisingly, Neẓām-al-Molk praises the Balʿamīs as the viziers par excellence of the Samanids (*Sīāsat-nāma*, ed. Darke¹, 1347 Š./1968, p. 218, tr. idem, London, 1968, p. 178). A collection of royal decrees (*tawqīʿāt*) drafted by Balʿamī is mentioned by Neẓāmī ʿArūżī (*Čahār maqāla*, ed. M. Qazvīnī, rev. M. Moʿīn, Tehran, 1333 Š./1954, text, p. 22, notes, pp. 23-24, 469). His vizierate endured until 326/938, according to Ebn al-Aṯīr, when he was succeeded in that office by Abū 'Alī Moḥammad Jayhānī. Bal'amī died on the night of 10 Ṣafar 329/13-14 November 940, according to Sam'ānī.

Bibliography: Primary sources: Gardīzī, ed. Nazim, pp. 30, 32. Ebn al-Aṯīr (repr.), VIII, pp. 125, 132, 263, 278, 378. Nāṣer-al-Dīn Monšī Kermānī, *Nasā'em al-asḥār*, ed. Jalāl-al-Dīn Ormavī, Tehran, 1338 Š./1959, p. 35, reproduced in Sayf-al-Dīn 'Oqaylī, *Āṯār al-wozarā'*, ed. Ormavī, Tehran, 1337 Š./1959, pp. 146-47 (brief, uninformative and inaccurate). Eṣṭaḵrī, pp. 260, 307. Moqaddasī (Maqdesī), p. 317. Studies: Barthold, *Turkestan*², pp. 241ff. D. M. Dunlop, "Bal'amī," in *EI*² I, p. 984.

(C. E. BOSWORTH)

BĀLANG, citron, the fruit of a species of citrus tree (*Citrus medica cedrata*). The candied unripe fruit is an article of commerce under various names; in Europe it is used as a flavoring in cakes, particularly Christmas cakes. In modern Iran, chiefly in Gīlān and Māzandarān, a tasty jam called *morabbā-ye bālang* is made from the ripe fruit.

The word *bālang* (also, in vulgar speech, incorrectly *pālang*) appears to be derived, through a putative metathesis *bārdang*, from *bādrang* which in turn is derived from Middle Persian *vātrang*. No explanation has yet been found for the Aramaic ideogram BYLBWŠY' (or something similar) given as the lexigraphic symbol for *vātrang* in the *Frahang ī Pahlavīk*.

This plainly Iranian word passed by way of Aramaic into Arabic as *toronj*, *otronj*, *otrojj* (Pers. *toranj*, *otroj*). It is found in the Talmud as *eṯrōḡ* (Hebrew) and *eṯrōḡā* or *eṯrūḡā* (Aramaic), and likewise in Syriac, perhaps reflecting a putative *vaθrāng*/*vaθrāγ* with change of the *v* to '. For the Jews, the *eṯrōḡ* or "apple of paradise" is one of the four plants of the festive bunch of flowers in the Feast of Tabernacles (Succoth).

The same word *bālang*/*bādrang* is also a name of the sweet basil (usually called *rayḥān*) and appears to have been wrongly applied to some other plants. It enters into compounds such as *bādrangbū(ya)*, *bālengū*, *palangmešk* or *palangmūš* (varieties of calamint) and probably also *bādrū*, *bādrūj*, *bādrūz*, *bādrūča*, and the like (a variety of basil).

As regards the etymology of the Middle Persian *vātrang*, the word is probably to be explained as a compound of *vāt* (New Persian *bād*) "wind" with the connotation of "scent" plus *rang* "color" or "variety," thus meaning scented (cf. *rayḥān*, the Arabic word for sweet basil, from *rīḥ* "wind" with the connotation of scent). Another possibility, however, is that it might be a popular adaptation of a foreign, perhaps Eastern loanword; the ending *ang* could be derived from an old form *an-(a)k*.

Unrelated to the above are the homonymous words *pālang* (oxhide shoe worn by peasants), *pālang*/*pālank* or *palang*/*palank* (bed), *peleng*, *pelengak* (filliping, snapping of finger) in the dialect of Shiraz, also *pālang* (small window) and *palang*/*palank* = *peleng* (width of a gate), which may be from *pā(y)* (foot) plus *leng* (leg, also step as a measure of length).

See also CITRUS FRUITS.

Bibliography: Immanuel Low, *Aramäische Pflanzennamen*, Leipzig, 1881, p. 46, nos. 17, 18. Siegmund Fraenkel, *Die aramäischen Fremdwörter im Arabischen*, Leiden, 1886, p. 139. Victor Hehn, *Kulturpflanzen und Haustiere in ihrem Übergang aus Asien*..., 8th ed., Berlin, 1911, pp. 450f. Esmā'īl Zāhedī, *Vāža-nāma-ye gīāhī*, Tehran, 1337 Š./1959, p. 62, no. 335.

(W. EILERS)

BALĀŠ, the name of a number of kings and several dignitaries and notables during the Parthian and Sasanian periods.

The Parthian form of the name, the oldest, is Walagaš. In Middle Persian it is Wardāxš, in Pahlavi Walāxš. The forms Walāš, Balāš, and even Golāš, attested especially in New Persian and in Arabic, are later. Armenian has Vałarš, which seems to be a borrowing from Middle Persian. The Syriac forms Walgāš, Walgēš, and Wologēš are borrowings from Parthian. The name occurs most often, however, in Greek, where it is spelled in quite varied ways: Vologaisos, Vologesos (or Vologeses), Bologaisos, Bologesos, Olagasos, Ologasos, and so on. In the later Greek authors one finds Balas, Blasēs or Blassēs, and Blasos or Blassos, forms that correspond to Walāš or Balāš. In Latin the spellings Vologaesus, Vologessus, Vologeses, etc. are attested (on the variants of this name cf. Nöldeke, *ZDMG* 28, 1874, pp. 94ff.; Justi, *Namenbuch*, pp. 344ff.; and Hübschmann, *Armenische Grammatik*, p. 79). We also note that, in the trilingual inscription of Šāpūr I on the Ka'ba-ye Zardošt, the Greek Oualas(s)ou (ll. 60, 64), the genitive of Oualassēs or Oualassos (cf. Maricq, *Syria* 35, 1958, pp. 327, 329 = *Classica et Orientalia*, Paris, 1965, pp. 69, 71), corresponds to Middle Persian Wrd'hšy and to Parthian Wlgšy.

The etymology of the name is uncertain. Starting with Walagaš, which seems to be the original form, Justi (pp. 346, 495) proposes the meaning "strength" (Av. *varəda*) for the first element in the compound, while he relates the second element to Modern Persian *gaš* or *geš* "handsome" (see also Pott, *ZDMG* 13, 1859, p. 391). These interpretations are debatable.

(M. L. CHAUMONT)

Balāš I, reigned ca. 51- ca. 76-80. He was a son of Vonones, king of Atropatene (Media), who was a brother of Artabanus II. Balāš I's reign was remarkably long for a Parthian king, but fraught with internal and external difficulties. His attempt to obtain the throne of Armenia for his brother Tiridates in 53 inevitably gave concern to the Romans. (On Roman-Parthian conflicts over Armenia, see M. L. Chaumont, 1976, pp. 71ff.). The Roman-backed Armenian king Mithridates had been murdered in 52 by his nephew Radamistus, a son of Pharasmanes, king of Iberia, and the Parthians, taking advantage of the resultant disorder, marched into Armenia and placed Tiridates on the throne. The Romans at first had no choice except to negotiate, because their troops were then in a disorganized state, but the tide turned in their favor when civil war broke out among the Parthians. A revolt against Balāš I was launched in 55, or perhaps 54, by a prince who may have been a son of Vardanes I (opinion of Hanslik, col. 1841) or one of Balāš I's own sons named Vardanes (opinion of Debevoise, p. 180, and many other scholars). Shortly after this, a rebellion in Hyrcania flared up. It seems likely that the two uprisings were connected; Vardanes may well have launched his revolt from Hyrcania. Balāš I consequently had to withdraw his troops from Armenia for action in Hyrcania. At the same time he accepted the Roman demands for peace and hostages. By delivering some Parthian princes as hostages to the Romans, he conveniently got rid of several potential rivals.

The chronology of the subsequent fighting over Armenia cannot be worked out with any precision, because Tacitus, our principal source, reports the events in four different passages in his *Annals* (13.34-41, 14.23-26, 16.1-17 and 24-31), each covering the events of several years, while the later historian Dio Cassius (80.19-23) gives only a general review of what happened. The Roman march into Armenia began not before the year 58. After conquering Artaxata, the capital, and later also Tigranokerta, and compelling Tiridates to flee, the Romans placed Tigranes V, a great-uncle of Archelaus, the last king of Cappadocia, on the Armenian throne. Before long, Tigranes invaded the adjacent principality of Adiabene, which was under Parthian suzerainty. It was now Balāš I's turn to have to negotiate. An attack on a vassal of the Parthians by the Roman-appointed Tigranes was virtually an attack by the Romans themselves, and although Balāš's adversary Vardanes had disappeared from the scene sometime around 58, the Hyrcanians maintained their formidable resistance. Balāš I therefore made peace with Hyrcania, which in effect meant that this province ceased to belong to the Parthian empire.

In any case Balāš was now in a position to intervene in Armenia itself. Military operations by both sides, with several breaks for parleys, ended in a success for Balāš. The Roman force, then under Cesennius Paeta who had taken over the command of the Armenian campaign from Corbulo, was surrounded by Balāš's troops in its winter camp near Rhandeia on the Arsanias (Muratsu, a tributary of the Euphrates) and eventually had to capitulate at the end of the year 62. In the summer of 63, however, the Romans, who had in the meantime assembled another large force, again marched into Armenia. Recognizing the unlikelihood of Parthian victory in the war, Balāš I sent emissaries with peace proposals. The Romans advised him to apply to Nero at Rome for the grant of the Armenian throne to his brother Tiridates as a Roman vassal. Long delays followed before Tiridates finally set out in 66 on his famous journey to Rome, where he received his investiture as king of Armenia from Nero in a grandiose ceremony (described by Dio Cassius, 62, 63.5.2). The arrangement satisfied both sides. The Parthians were the real masters in Armenia but recognized the validity of the Roman claim to suzerainty over the kingdom (on the legal aspect of the arrangement, see Ziegler, p. 75).

Relations remained friendly until Nero's death in 68, and Balāš strove thereafter to maintain peace. During the subsequent Roman civil wars, he proposed to send 40,000 mounted archers in support of Vespasian, but the latter gratefully declined the offer. The first discord arose after an invasion of the Parthian empire by Alan nomads, which began in 72. Balāš asked Vespasian for help against them in 75, but received the chilly response that "it would not be proper for the emperor to interfere in other people's affairs" (Dio Cassius, 65, 66.15.3).

Balāš I died not long afterward, certainly not later than 80 (McDowell, pp. 119ff., 230), possibly as early as 76/77 (Le Rider, *Suse*, pp. 174-75) or 78 (Sellwood, p. 220). In this as in several other cases, the dating depends on the question to which Parthian king a small number of coins should be attributed.

Coins minted at Seleucia at the end of Balāš I's reign bear not only the figure of Balāš but also that of a young man, the king Pacorus II (77-78; Le Rider, p. 175). This Pacorus appears to have been a son of Balāš; whether he was appointed co-regent or (as so often in Parthian history) came forth as a counter-king is uncertain. In any case the course of events in the following decades is impenetrably obscure.

In the Parthian context, Balāš I's long reign deserves a measure of credit. The judgements of Kahrstedt (pp. 82-83) are too negative, those of Hanslik (col. 1847) and Keall (pp. 624ff.) are more positive. Balāš's long tenure is in itself evidence of his diplomatic skill. Unlike many other Parthian rulers, he did not eliminate his kinsmen but gave them high offices and honors. The dispute over Armenia, always a bone of contention between the Romans and the Parthians, was settled on terms by no means unfavorable to Parthia. Balāš also found time to establish a new commercial center, Vologaisias, which evidently became an important town (Koshelenko, pp. 761ff.); identification of its site has not yet been possible, and the question whether the frequently mentioned town-names Vologaisias and Vologesocerta refer to one and the same place (Maricq, pp. 264ff.) or two different places (Chaumont, 1974, pp. 77ff.) also remains unsolved.

Bibliography: M. L. Chaumont, "L'Arménie entre Rome et l'Iran," in *Aufstieg und Niedergang der römischen Welt: Geschichte und Kultur Roms im Spiegel der neueren Forschung. 2. Principat*, ed. H. Temporini and W. Haase, II, 9, 1, Berlin, 1976, pp. 71-194. Idem, "Etudes d'histoire parthe III. Les villes fondées par les Vologèse," *Syria* 51, 1974, pp. 75-89. N. C. Debevoise, *A Political History of Parthia*, Chicago, 1938. R. Hanslik, "Vologaeses I," in Pauly-Wissowa, Suppl., IX, cols. 1839-47. U.

Kahrstedt, *Artabanos III. und seine Erben*, Bern, 1950. E. J. Keall, "Parthian Nippur and Vologases' Southern Strategy: an Hypothesis," *JAOS* 95/4, 1975, pp. 620-32. G. A. Koshelenko, "La politique commerciale des Arsacides et les villes grecques," in *Studi in onore di Edoardo Volterra* I, Milan, 1971, pp. 761-65. A. Maricq, "Vologésias, l'emporium de Ctésiphon," *Syria* 36, 1959, pp. 264-76 (repr. in *Classica et Orientalia*, Paris, 1965, pp. 113-25). R. H. McDowell, *Coins from Seleucia on the Tigris*, Ann Arbor, 1975. G. Le Rider, *Suse sous les séleucides et les parthes*, MDAFI 38, 1965. K. Schippmann, *Grundzüge der parthischen Geschichte*, Darmstadt, 1980. D. G. Sellwood, *An Introduction to the Coinage of Parthia*, London, 1971. K. H. Ziegler, *Die Beziehungen zwischen Rom und dem Partherreich*, Wiesbaden, 1964, p. 75. See also *Camb. Hist. Iran* III, pp. 79-86, 295, 447, 758, 1153.

Balāš II, a son or grandson of Balāš I, appears to have reigned, with some interruptions, from 77/8 to 89/90. The question again depends on coin attribution. His accession took place some time after the death of Balāš I. As mentioned above, coins from the end of Balāš I's reign also bear the figure of Pacorus II. The latter was soon challenged, however, by rival throne claimants, namely Balāš II and Osroes, a brother or brother-in-law of Pacorus II. It has not been possible to determine the attributions of coins from this period, and so the surmises offered by scholars differ widely. Sellwood (pp. 226, 229) thinks that Balāš II first appeared as a rival of Pacorus II, but McDowell (pp. 119ff.) thinks that the coins attributed to Balāš II are coins of Balāš I and that Balāš II's reign did not begin until 105/06. Hanslik (col. 1847) places Balāš II's reign as late as 128-47. Le Rider (p. 174) has proposed a different solution to the problem of the apparent great length of Balāš II's reign, which on the evidence of certain coins could have lasted from 77/8 to 146/7; he postulates the existence of a third king named Balāš and attributes the coins minted in 77/8, 89/90 and 106-08 to Balāš II, making Balāš III king from 111/2 onward (instead of Balāš II as previously supposed). The present writer finds this hypothesis acceptable.

It is not known whether the three rival throne claimants had operational bases in particular regions, but the fact that the coins of all three were minted at Seleucia indicates that the city frequently changed hands. Balāš II was apparently driven out first, as no coins of his later than 89/90 are known. Thereafter only two contestants were in the field; if Le Rider's hypothesis is accepted, they were Osroes and Balāš III. At the start of Trajan's Parthian war, the Parthian throne was probably held by Osroes, as it is he who is mentioned as the adversary of the Romans.

Bibliography: R. Hanslik, in Pauly-Wissowa, Suppl., IX, cols. 1847-48. R. H. McDowell, *Coins from Seleucia on the Tigris*, Ann Arbor, 1975. G. Le Rider, *Suse sous les séleucides et les parthes*, MDAFI 38, 1965. D. G. Sellwood, *An Introduction to the Coinage of Parthia*, London, 1971. See also *Camb. Hist. Iran* III, pp. 87-88, 94, 295-96, 692.

Balāš III, king from 129 to 146/8 (according to Le Rider; cf. Hanslik, col. 1847, under Vologaeses II). The struggle between Osroes and Balāš III appears to have continued after, perhaps even during, Trajan's Parthian war. Balāš III finally prevailed in 127/8 or in any case not later than 129. The minting of coins of Osroes at Seleucia cease from 127/8 onward, but Osroes is known to have met the emperor Hadrian during the latter's tour of the East in 129 and to have obtained the release of his daughter, whom the Romans had captured in 116.

Balāš III soon came up against the usual "Parthian problem" of a pretender's revolt. This particular counter-king, Mithridates IV, seems only to have controlled provinces on the Iranian plateau (Debevoise, p. 244 n. 15; Sellwood, p. 262). Roman-Parthian relations having been trouble-free in the first part of Balāš III's reign, and the Roman historians being uninterested in Parthia's internal affairs, information about the course of events is lacking. All that can be said is that Mithridates's venture did not bring him any lasting success.

A much graver threat to Balāš III's rule came from the invasion by Alan nomads in the years 134-36. They penetrated into Albania, Media, Armenia, and also Cappadocia, and were only driven out with great difficulty and doubtless heavy financial expense. In the reign of Hadrian's successor Antoninus Pius (138-61), trouble over Armenia again flared up, but details of the events, which probably took place between 140 and 144, are lacking. All that is known is that the Romans installed a new king in Armenia. Balāš III made no countermove, either because he did not feel strong enough or perhaps because he did not wish to endanger the flourishing long-distance trade, from which the Parthians drew large profits (see Chaumont, pp. 146-47; Ziegler, pp. 110-11).

Bibliography: M. L. Chaumont, "L'Arménie entre Rome et l'Iran," in *Aufstieg und Niedergang der römischen Welt: Geschichte und Kultur Roms im Spiegel der neueren Forschung, 2. Principat*, ed. H. Temporini and W. Haase, II, 9, 1, Berlin, 1976, pp. 71-194. R. Hanslik, in Pauly-Wissowa, Suppl., IX, cols. 1848-51. K. H. Ziegler, *Die Beziehungen zwischen Rom und dem Partherreich*, Wiesbaden, 1964. See also *Camb. Hist. Iran* III, pp. 93, 296-97, 450, 1153.

Balāš IV reigned from ca. 147/8 to 190/1 or 192/3. In the first part of this king's reign, Roman-Parthian relations remained peaceful. Balāš IV, however, was probably waiting for a chance to settle the Armenian problem on terms more favorable to Parthia. When the imperial throne passed to Marcus Aurelius in 161, Balāš saw the time as ripe. For the first (and last) time, the Parthians declared war on the Romans. No precise information on the reasons for this step has come down. Ziegler (p. 112) may perhaps be right in his surmise that

Balāš IV had long been unwilling to drop the Parthian claim to influence in Armenia. Initial successes appeared to justify Balāš's calculation. A Roman army was defeated at Elegeia on the Euphrates in 161, and Armenia was occupied and placed by Balāš under a new king named Pacorus (Chaumont, pp. 147-48). At the same time, the Parthians invaded Syria. The Romans, however, despite their initially precarious situation, soon began to counterattack. Lucius Verus, then co-emperor with Marcus Aurelius, took over their supreme command and had the support of the able generals C. Avidius Cassius, M. Statius Priscus, and P. Martius Verus. In 163 they overran Armenia and installed a new king, Sohaemus (Chaumont, pp. 149-50). After expelling the Parthians from Syria, they began to penetrate into Mesopotamia in 164/5. Dura Europos fell to them after hard fighting and thenceforth remained in Roman hands. At this juncture many of the Parthian vassals and their troops deserted Balāš (again showing how much the Parthian great kings depended on the local rulers within the empire: see Wolski, pp. 379ff., 385-86). As a result, Seleucia was captured by the Romans some time after December, 165. Whether the city was then really destroyed, as scholars relying on ancient authors often assert, seems doubtful because coins were again being minted at Seleucia in November, 166 (Hopkins, p. 161; Debevoise, p. 251, n. 58). The nearby royal capital, Ctesiphon, was also taken, and Balāš IV's palace was demolished. Only the outbreak of a plague saved the Parthians from crushing defeat and forced the Romans to withdraw. It is not clear from the sources whether the two sides concluded a formal peace treaty (Ziegler, p. 114, and Schur, col. 2025, assume that they did, while Debevoise, pp. 252-53 says nothing to the contrary). Rome's new eastern frontier ran from Dura Europos northward along the Ḵābūr river, and the region west of this line, including not only Edessa but also Carrhae and Nisibis, belonged to the Roman empire. (The exact line is uncertain, and there is disagreement on the question whether these cities and Singara were annexed in the reign of Marcus Aurelius or not until that of Septimius Severus. See Ziegler, p. 114, n. 131; Magie, pp. 15, 44; Oates, p. 72; Bertinelli, pp. 41ff.).

In the following decades peace between the two empires prevailed. An opportunity for the Parthians to cause trouble for the Romans on their eastern frontier arose early in the year 175 when Avidius Cassius, the victor of Ctesiphon, proclaimed himself emperor in Syria. It is not known whether Balāš contemplated intervention in the prospective civil war between this pretender and Marcus Aurelius, but if so, he failed to act in time, because Avidius Cassius was put to death by his own troops a few months later. Soon afterward Marcus Aurelius traveled to the East and confirmed the state of peace between Rome and Parthia in talks with Balāš IV's envoys at Antioch in the summer of 176. The peace endured throughout the reign of Marcus Aurelius and his son and successor Commodus (180-92).

Balāš IV died in 190/1 or 192/3. (Le Rider, p. 461, and Sellwood, p. 267, give the earlier date, but McDowell, p. 235, and Hanslik, col. 1851, state that coins of Balāš IV were minted as late as 193, and Debevoise, p. 255, accepts the later date.) Since coins of Balāš V dated 191 also exist, it is possible that Balāš IV had made his son co-regent (surmise of Hanslik, loc. cit.) or that a civil war between the father and the son had broken out (surmise of Debevoise, loc. cit.). There are also some coins from ca. 190 minted for a king who (according to Sellwood, p. 281) bore the name Osroes (previously often misread as Artabanos); apart from the coins, nothing about him is known.

Balāš IV managed to hold the Parthian throne for more than forty years. He suffered defeats at the hands of the Romans but did not have to deal with the usual internal troubles due to revolts of pretenders and resultant civil wars (unless the surmise of a civil war with his son Balāš V is correct).

Bibliography: M. G. A. Bertinelli, " I Romani oltre l'Eufrate nel 11 secolo d.C. (le province di Assiria, di Mesopotamia e di Osroene)," in *Aufstieg und Niedergang der römischen Welt*: *Geschichte und Kultur Roms im Spiegel der neueren Forschung*, *2. Principat*, ed. H. Temporini and W. Haase, II, 9, 1, Berlin, 1976, pp. 3-45. M. L. Chaumont, "L'Arménie entre Rome et l'Iran," ibid., pp. 71-194. N. C. Debevoise, *A Political History of Parthia*, Chicago, 1938. R. Hanslik, in Pauly-Wissowa, Suppl., IX, cols. 1851-52. C. Hopkins, *Topography and Architecture of Seleucia on the Tigris*, Ann Arbor, 1972. R. H. McDowell, *Coins from Seleucia on the Tigris*, Ann Arbor, 1975. D. Magie, *Roman Rule in Asia Minor* II, Princeton, 1950. D. Oates, *Northern Iraq*, London, 1968. G. Le Rider, *Suse sous les Séleucides et les Parthes*, MDAFI 38, 1965. W. Schur, "Parthia II B," in Pauly-Wissowa, XVIII/4, 1949, cols. 1987-2029. D. G. Sellwood, *An Introduction to the Coinage of Parthia*, London, 1971. J. Wolski, in Deutsche Historische Gesellschaft, *Neue Beiträge zur Geschichte der Alten Welt* I, ed. E. C. Weiskopf: *Alter Orient und Griechenland*, Berlin, 1964, pp. 379-84. K. H. Ziegler, *Die Beziehungen zwischen Rom und dem Partherreich*, Wiesbaden, 1964, p. 75. See also *Camb. Hist. Iran* III, pp. 93, 117-18, 297, 484.

Balāš V succeeded his father in 190/1 or 193 and reigned until 207/8. During these years the Roman empire was itself afflicted with the "Parthian" malady. After the murder of Commodus in 192, three rival army commanders set their sights on the throne. Later two of them, Pescennius Niger and Septimius Severus, remained to fight it out. The Parthians gave some help, but not much, to Pescennius Niger who commanded the legions in Syria. The historian Herodian (3.1, pp. 1-3) implies that the Parthian great king could only urge his vassals to send troops. It would therefore appear that the great king did not have a large force at his own disposal. On the other hand Balāš V may have supported the rebels in the Roman-ruled territory of Osrhoene who, together with the army of the Parthian vassal-state of Adiabene, laid siege to the Roman-held city of Nisibis (Hanslik, col. 1851, and Debevoise, p. 256, reckon that he did, but Ziegler, p. 130, holds that the siege was an independent venture by the king of Adiabene, not a deliberate treaty breach by Balāš V).

In 194 Septimius Severus finally achieved victory in the Roman civil war, and in the following year he marched into western Mesopotamia with the aim of recovering the lost territories (see Hasebroek, pp. 73ff.). The course of events cannot be traced with precision, mainly because it is not known whether various incidents took place in this campaign or in Severus's second compaign which began in 197. In any case Osrhoene and Nisibis were reconquered. The only uncertain point is whether it was at this time that Osrhoene was made a Roman province and that a new province of Mesopotamia comprising areas east of Osrhoene was constituted. (This is the opinion of Ziegler, p. 131, and Bertinelli, p. 39; but see Magie, II, pp. 1543-54.) Adiabene also was conquered or at least was the scene of a victory, and another victory was won over some Arabs, as indicated by Severus's assumption of the titles "Parthicus Adiabenicus" and "Parthicus Arabus." The prospects for the Parthians were far from favorable when the emperor had to call off his campaign and return home to deal with the army commander in Gaul, Clodius Albinus, who set himself up as counter-emperor. After defeating Albinus near Lugdunum (Lyon) early in 197, Septimius Severus resumed his war with the Parthians. In the meantime Balāš V had suppressed revolts in Iran and defeated the pro-Roman king Narses of Adiabene. He then marched into Mesopotamia and besieged but failed to capture Nisibis. When Roman reinforcements arrived, the Parthians gave up the siege. The Romans then took the offensive, advancing down the Euphrates to Seleucia and Babylon, which they occupied without resistance, though they had to fight hard before Ctesiphon fell to them, probably late in the year 198 (Bertinelli, pp. 37ff.). The emperor now assumed the title "Parthicus Maximus." The Romans were unable, however, to hold onto their gains. Difficulties in obtaining adequate food supplies and reinforcements obliged them to withdraw. On the way back, Septimius Severus attempted to seize Hatra, but like Trajan was unsuccessful. The Roman troops probably spent the winter in northern Mesopotamia, and in the spring of 199 they made a second attempt on Hatra but were again repulsed and suffered heavy losses. They then finally withdrew to Syria. It seems likely that a peace treaty between the two powers was concluded in 199, though the ancient sources are silent on the subject. While Septimius Severus had not been able to make any large and lasting gains, he at least obtained a secure frontier with the Parthian empire. Two new Roman provinces were now constituted, namely Osrhoene (less a small area including the capital Edessa, which apparently continued to be a vassal kingdom) and Mesopotamia, and three new legions (I-III Parthicae) were mustered to garrison and defend these provinces. Recent archeological investigations (see Bertinelli, pp. 41ff.) have made it possible to trace parts of the Roman defense line. This *limes* ran through Alaina (Tell Hayal), Singara (Balad Senjar) and further east through sites at Zagurae (Ain Sinu) to Vicat (Tell Ibra); the finds do not show whether the frontier ran to Ad Flumen Tigris (Mosul), which would have been its rational terminus.

Roman-Parthian relations remained peaceful in the rest of the reigns of Balāš V, who died in 206/7, and Septimius Severus, who died in 211. Only after the accession of the latter's son Commodus did things change.

Bibliography: M. G. A. Bertinelli, "I Romani oltre l'Eufrate nel II secolo d.C. (le province di Assiria, di Mesopotamia e di Osroene)," in *Aufstieg und Niedergang der römischen Welt*: *Geschichte und Kultur Roms im Spiegel der neueren Forschung*, *2. Principat*, ed. H. Temporini and W. Haase, II, 9, 1, Berlin, 1976, pp. 3-45. N. C. Debevoise, *A Political History of Parthia*, Chicago, 1938. R. Hanslik, in Pauly-Wissowa, Suppl., IX, cols. 1852-53. I. Hasebroek, *Untersuchungen zur Geschichte des Kaisers Septimius Severus*, Heidelberg, 1921. Herodian, *Ab excessu divi Marci*, ed. K. Stavenhagen, Leipzig, 1922. D. Magie, *Roman Rule in Asia Minor* II, Princeton, 1950. K. H. Ziegler, *Die Beziehungen zwischen Rom und dem Partherreich*, Wiesbaden, 1964, p. 75. See also *Camb. Hist. Iran* III, pp. 94, 297.

Balāš VI succeeded his father Balāš V in 207/8. Not many years passed before his authority was challenged by his brother Artabanus IV (still often mentioned as Artabanus V; the new numbering is used here for the reasons given in ARTABANUS, q.v.). Fighting between the two probably began ca. 213. Artabanus appears to have succeeded in taking over large parts of the empire. The fact that many of his coins are probably from Ecbatana indicates that he controlled Media, and the inscription on a stele found at Susa shows that he held that city. On the other hand coin-finds show that Seleucia remained in Balāš VI's possession (McDowell, p. 200).

No doubt the internecine strife among the Parthians encouraged the Romans to embark on an "active" course. In 213/4 Caracalla invited the king of Osrhoene, Abgar IX, to Rome and then flung him into jail, and later he attempted to play the same trick on the king of Armenia (name unknown). In revulsion against the imprisonment of the king of Osrhoene, an anti-Roman rebellion broke out (for details, see Chaumont, pp. 134ff.; Maricq, pp. 297ff.).

By this time the emperor Caracalla was probably already planning to start a new Parthian war. In search of a pretext, he sent a demand to Balāš VI for the delivery of two fugitives, a philosopher named Antiochus and a certain Tiridates (whether the latter was an Armenian prince or a brother of Balāš V who had gone over to Septimius Severus in his second Parthian campaign is uncertain; see Chaumont, p. 155). Surprisingly, Balāš VI delivered the two hostages, thus depriving Caracalla of his pretext. Instead Caracalla began with an expedition against Armenia. He gave the command to a former slave and theater-dancer named Theocritus. The venture was a fiasco.

Before long, Caracalla concocted another pretext for war against the Parthians. In 216 he sent a request to Artabanus IV for the hand of his daughter in marriage, and Artabanus refused. Opinions differ on the question whether this proposal was genuine (Ziegler, p. 133) or not meant seriously (Schur, col. 2028). Caracalla then set out on "his" war in the summer of 216. The fact that the Roman emperor addressed the request for a bride to Artabanus IV is generally seen as evidence that Artabanus IV had finally won the contest with his brother Balāš VI (Debevoise, p. 265; Chaumont, p. 155); but, against this, coins of Balāš VI are known to have been minted at Seleucia until at least 221/2 (Le Rider, p. 461; Sellwood, p. 290; until 222/3 according to McDowell, pp. 200, 237). It is even possible that a silver tetradrachm from the year 228 should be attributed to Balāš VI (opinion of Sellwood, p. 290). If so, there would be reason to suppose that, after the last decisive battle in 224 or thereabouts when the Sasanian beat the Parthians and killed Artabanus IV, Balāš VI kept the resistance against them going for some time, mainly in Mesopotamia.

Bibliography: M. L. Chaumont, "L'Arménie entre Rome et l'Iran," in *Aufstieg und Niedergang der römischen Welt*: *Geschichte und Kultur Roms im Spiegel der neueren Forschung*, *2. Principat*, ed. H. Temporini and W. Haase, II, 9, 1, Berlin, 1976, pp. 71-194. N. C. Debevoise, *A Political History of Parthia*, Chicago, 1938. R. Hanslik, in Pauly-Wissowa, Suppl., IX, col. 1852. G. Le Rider, *Suse sous les Séleucides et les Parthes*, MDAFI 38, 1965. R. H. McDowell, *Coins from Seleucia on the Tigris*, Ann Arbor, 1975. K. Schippmann, *Grundzüge der parthischen Geschichte*, Darmstadt, 1980. W. Schur, "Parthia II B," in Pauly-Wissowa, XVIII/4, 1949, cols. 1987-2029. D. G. Sellwood, *An Introduction to the Coinage of Parthia*, London, 1971. B. Simonetta, "Note di numismatica partica. Vologese V, Artabanos V e Artavasde: una revisione di fatti e di ipotesi," *Numismatica* 19-20, Rome, 1953-54, pp. 19-22. K. H. Ziegler, *Die Beziehungen zwischen Rom und dem Partherreich*, Wiesbaden, 1964. See also *Camb. Hist. Iran* III, pp. 94, 96, 297.

(K. SCHIPPMANN)

Balāš, Sasanian king of kings (484-88) (Gk. Balas, Blasēs, Blassos, Valas, etc.). Balāš, son of Yazdegerd II (r. 438-57), was chosen by the magnates of the kingdom—of whom the most influential at that time were Zarmehr Sōḵrā and Šāpūr Mehrān—to succeed his brother Pērōz (r. 459-84) after the latter had been defeated and killed in an expedition against the Hephthalites (Huns) in A.D. 484 (Łazar P'arpec'i, Venice, pp. 544-47, par. 87; Langlois, II, p. 352; Procopius, 1.5.2; according to Ṭabarī, I, p. 882, and Ya'qūbī, *Ta'rīḵ*, I, p. 185, Balās was Pērōz's son). Balāš, who was of a pacific and conciliatory temperament, made peace with Vahan Mamikonean, leader of the Armenian rebellion (P'arpec'i, pp. 547ff., pars. 88-97; Langlois, II, pp. 353ff.). As a result of this agreement, Balāš received the aid of Vahan Mamikonean against his brother Zarer or Zareh, who had put himself forward as claimant to the throne. Thanks to the Armenian cavalry, Zarer was defeated and killed (P'arpec'i, pp. 589-95, pars. 93-95; Langlois, II, pp. 360-61). Thereafter Vahan was welcomed with great pomp by Balāš, who named him at first *hazarapet* and later *marzbān* of Armenia (P'arpec'i, pp. 597-620 pars. 95-99; Langlois, II, pp. 361-65). Balāš wished to be humane and benevolent. The legend engraved on the obverse of his coins, *hwkd wld'hš* (the good prince Walāxš), is significant (see Göbl, I, p. 51, table XV, pl. 11, nos. 178-79) and according to a tradition of the Islamic period, he took great care of the welfare of his humblest subjects (Nöldeke, *Geschichte der Perser*, p. 134). Balāš showed favor to Christians. At the opening of the synod that took place at Seleucia in A.D. 486, presided over by the catholicos Acacius, he was saluted as the "good and amiable Walāš, King of Kings" (*Synodicon Orientale*, p. 53, tr. p. 299). It seems that he even sent Acacius as his ambassador to the emperor Zeno in 485 or 486 (*Synodicon Orientale*, p. 527, tr. p. 553; cf. pp. 300, n. 3, and 533, n. 6). In another action, he ordered Barṣaumā, bishop of Nisibis, together with the *marzbān* Kardag Naḵwergān, to carry out the demarcation of the frontiers between the Sasanian and Roman empires (*Synodicon orientale*, pp. 529-30, tr., pp. 536-37). On the other hand, Balāš incurred the disapproval of the Magians because he wished to endow the cities with public baths in the Roman manner (Wright, p. 12). Equally he displeased his troops (ibid.) and he was no more successful in satisfying the notables, who, probably urged on by Zarmehr Sōḵrā, deposed him after four years of his reign in order to replace him with his nephew Qobād/Kavād (Theodorus Lector, *Historia ecclesiastica* 2.51 = *Patrologia graeca* LXXXVI, p. 209). The foundation of Balāšābād (Walāxšābād), near Seleucia on the Tigris, has been attributed to Balāš (Nöldeke, *Geschichte der Perser*, p. 134) through an anachronism. It has already been demonstrated that the true founder of this city was the Arsacid Balāš I (see above).

Bibliography: R. Göbl, *Sasanidische Numismatik*, Braunschweig, 1968. Christensen, *Iran Sass.*, pp. 295-97, 388. *Šāh-nāma*, Borūḵīm ed., VII-VIII, pp. 227ff. *Synodicon Orientale*, ed. J. B. Chabot, Paris, 1902. W. Wright, ed., *The Chronicle of (Pseudo) Joshua the Stylite* II, Cambridge, 1882.

Dynasts of Hatra.

1. Walgaš (2nd cent.), son of Naṣrū, at first "lord" (*mr'*), then "king (*mlk'*) of 'Arab(s) (of Hatra)" (inscriptions 140, 193, 286; A. Caquot, *Syria* 41, 1964, pp. 259-68; B. Aggoula, *Syria* 52, 1975, pp. 184-85 and 63, 1986, pp. 356, 363, nos. 348, 366). This is probably a dynast of Hatra and its dependent territory under Parthian suzerainty. The new evidence of Hatra inscription no.

348 proves that the Walgaš in question is son of Naṣrū: *ṣlm' dy Wlgš br Nṣrw mry'* "statue of Walgaš the lord, son of Naṣrū" (Aggoula, 1986, p. 356). Thus Walgaš must have been the brother of Sanaṭrūq I. Naṣrū ruled in 137/8 and Sanaṭrūq 1 in 161/2 so Walgaš must have ruled between these two dates (Aggoula, *Mélanges de l'Université St Joseph* 17, 1972, pp. 54, 60-61; 1986, p. 363) and was thus a contemporary of the Arsacid King Valagaš/Balāš IV (III). The new evidence disproves earlier attempts to place this Walgaš about 150 or 200, i.e., between Worōd and Naṣrū (J. T. Milik, *Recherches d'épigraphie proche-orientale*, 1972, p. 364) or before 138 (H. J. W. Drijvers, in *ANRW* II/8, pp. 824-25).

2. A prince or king of Hatra, represented dressed in Parthian fashion on a great lintel discovered near the remains of a sanctuary at Hatra, with the inscription *nṣr blgš* "victory of Walgaš" (Caquot, *Syria*, 1953, p. 238 no. 33). The identification of this Walgaš with the Arsacid Balāš I suggested by F. Safar (Caquot, p. 239) is based on too scanty evidence.

3. Walgaš son of Walgaš, known from inscription no. 366, engraved on a column commemorating the erection of a statue: *ṣlm' dy Wlgš br Wlgš* "statue of Walgaš, son of Walgaš" (Aggoula, 1986, p. 363). It is not certain that this is the son of King Walgaš above.

Bibliography: Given in the text.

Lesser Notables.

1. King of Kermān (210?), defeated by Ardašīr I, who took him prisoner and took possession of his capital (Nöldeke, *Geschichte der Perser*, p. 10; Christensen, *Iran Sass.*, p. 87). He was probably a vassal dynast who by some authors was erroneously identified with the Arsacid Balāš VI (V).

2. A prince, son of Pāpak and presumably brother of Ardašīr I, listed in the fifth rank of notables in the inscription of Šāpūr I (242-70) on the Kaʿba-ye Zardošt (Maricq, p. 327 [69]). His name is spelled Mid. Pers. Wrd'hš, Parth. Wlgšy, Gk. genitive OUALASSOU).

3. Son of Selōk (Seleucus), listed in the 33rd rank of notables in the inscription of Šāpūr I (Maricq, p. 329 [71]). His name is spelled like that of no. 2.

4. Vałarš, an Armenian prince of Anjit (Anzitene), *hazarapet* "chiliarch" at the accession of King Tiran of Armenia (ca. 338?; Faustus, 3.12, Venice, 1933, p. 40 = Langlois, *Historiens* I, pp. 221, 222; *Genealogy of St Gregory* 3 = Langlois, *Historiens* II, p. 24).

5. A *marzbān* of Bēṯ ʿArbāyē (?) under Šāpūr II (309-79) (Hoffmann, p. 29).

6. A bishop of Nisibis (d. 361?) who succeeded Babu between 346 and 350 (Justi, p. 345 s.v. Walagaš no. 6; W. Ensslin in Pauly-Wissowa, VII A/2, col. 2091 s.v. Walagasch no. 2; Fiey, pp. 23, 29-33). The *Chronicon Paschale* (ed. L. Dindorf, Bonn, 1832, I, p. 539) attributes to him a letter on the third siege of Nisibis by Šāpūr II in 350. He was a contemporary of St Ephrem, who mentions him in a flattering manner in *Carmina Nisibena* (ed. G. Bickell, Leipzig, 1886, index, p. 234 s.v. Vologeses). An inscription discovered at Nisibis commemorates the erection of a baptistery by this bishop (Sarre and Herzfeld, II, pp. 336-46).

7. A student at the Persian school in Edessa in about 450 (Martin, p. 26; Labourt, p. 257).

8. The leader of a troop of Massagete (Hunnish) cavalry under the orders of Belisarius (532) (Procopius, *De bello vandalico* 1.11.12; Theophanes, *Chronographia* I, anno 6026, ed. J. Classen and I. Bekker, Bonn, 1839, p. 292; Justi, p. 345, s.v. Walagaš no. 12; Ensslin, s.v. Walagasch no. 6).

9. The son of Dādmehr and grandson of Zarmehr, governor of Ṭabarestān from 575-600 (Dorn, pp. 42, 319; Justi, p. 345, s.v. Walagaš no. 13).

10. The grandson of Āḏarwalāš, murderer of Bāw (679; Dorn, pp. 42, 46, 206, 323; Justi, p. 346, s.v. Walagaš no. 14).

Bibliography: Ẓahīr-al-Dīn Marʿašī, *Tārīḵ-e Ṭabarestān o Rūyān o Māzandarān*, ed. B. Dorn, *Geschichte von Tabaristan, Rujan und Mazanderan*, St. Petersburg, 1850. W. Ensslin in Pauly-Wissowa, VIIA/2, col. 1948. J. M. Fiey, *Nisibe, métropole syriaque orientale*, CSCO 388 (Subsidia 54), Louvain, 1977. G. Hoffmann, *Auszüge aus syrischen Akten persischer Martyrer*, Leipzig, 1880. J. Labourt, *Le christianisme dans l'empire perse sous la dynastie sassanide*, Paris, 1904. A. Maricq, "Res Gestae Divi Saporis," *Syria* 35, 1958, pp. 295-360 (repr. in *Classica et Orientalia*, Paris, 1965, pp. 37-101). J. P. P. Martin, *Le Pseudo-Synode connu sous le nom de Brigandage d'Éphèse*, Paris, 1875. F. Sarre and E. Herzfeld, *Archäologische Reise im Euphrat- und Tigrisgebiet*, Berlin, 1911-20.

(M. L. Chaumont)

BALĀSAGĀN, (Ar. Balāsajān, Balāšajān; Armenian Bałasakan) an Iranian toponym in *-agān* (*-akān*) "country of the Balās)," designating a region located for the most part south of the lower course of the rivers Kor (Kura, Gk. Kyros, Lat. Cyrus) and the Aras (Araxes), bordered on the south by Atropatene and on the east by the Caspian Sea.

i. *In pre-Islamic times.*
ii. *In Islamic times.*

i. In Pre-Islamic Times

The country and its inhabitants. The heart of this country was the *dašt i-Bałasakan* "Balāsagān plain," which the Armenian *Geography* of Pseudo-Moses of Khorene (Adontz, p. 124*) places in Albania and which is virtually identical with the Moḡān (Mūḡān) steppe. According to Ebn Ḵordāḏbeh (p. 121), this plain was located on the road from Barzand to Varṯān (Vartanakert). It is extremely doubtful that in the Sasanian period Balāsagān extended as far as the Caucasus range and the Darband pass, as Maricq believes (Honigmann and Maricq, pp. 81-82).

We must agree with Trever (p. 75) that Balāsagān was partially identical with the region that Aelianus (*De natura animalium* 17.7), citing Amyntas, an author of the fourth century B.C., called "land of the Caspians" (see AELIANUS), a region also known in the Hellenistic period under the name Caspiana (which had been taken from the Medes of Atropatene by the Armenians at the beginning of the second century B.C.). Given that Caspiana was for the most part included in the later province of P'aitakaran in the *Geography* of Pseudo-Moses (see Hübschmann, pp. 4, 267ff., 351-52), it follows that Balāsagān corresponds to the part of the territory of that province that was situated south of the Kor.

The ethnic term Bałasčik', attested only in Armenian, was formed from Bałasakan (cf. Markwart, *Ērānšahr*, p. 120; Hübschmann, p. 412). The fact that Ełišē (*Histoire d'Arménie* 7.30, Venice, pp. 262-64; Langlois, II, p. 227) designates one king of Balāsagān as a Hun must not be taken literally and does not by any means permit the conclusion of a Hunnish origin for the inhabitants of Balāsagān.

Balāsagān in the Sasanian empire. It is in the trilingual inscription of Šāpūr I, carved a little after A.D. 260, that Balāsagān is attested for the first time (Mid. Pers. l. 2: *Bl'sk'n*; Parth. l. 2: *Bl'skn*; Gk., l. 3: *Balasagene* [?], see Maricq, p. 49). The fact that, in this inscription, this country is mentioned independently of Albania in the list of provinces of the Sasanian empire could mean that at the time of its conquest by Ardašīr I or Šāpūr I it formed a sort of political entity, even if it was more or less subject to the kingdom of Albania. On the other hand, Ebn Kordādbeh (p. 18) mentions the king of Balāsagān (Balāšajān Shah) among the dynasts who received the title of king from Ardašīr (cf. Adontz, p. 170). This would indicate that the king of Balāsagān had made an act of submission and allegiance to Ardašīr (or to Šāpūr), of whom he became, by the same act, a vassal.

Faustus reports that, under the reign of the king of Armenia Kosrow II, Gregory, catholicos of Iberia and Albania, attempted to convert the kingdom of Sanesan (the same one that Pseudo-Moses of Khorene, 3.3, knew under the name Sanatruk). This Sanesan, king of the Massagetes (Alans), also ruled over other peoples, among whom figured the Bałasčik'. Having invaded Armenia, the army of the king of the Massagetes was cut to pieces by the Armenians; the survivors fell back toward the country of the Bałasčik' (*ašxarhn bałačik'*; Faustus, 3.7; Langlois, II, pp. 215-16). It would seem then that, toward A.D. 335-36, the Massagete Sanesan occupied a part of Balāsagān, where he recruited troops, all the while recognizing, at least nominally, the suzerainty of the king of kings. At the beginning of the following century, Saint Mesrob, in the course of his evangelistic mission, preached in Balāsagān, a country that, according to Koriun, then belonged to Albania (11.5, p. 34). This situation could be explained by a kind of dependence (vassalage) of Balāsagān in relation to Albania.

Balāsagān is mentioned in connection with the revolt of the Armenians against the Persians under Yazdegerd II. Thus, in a battle that took place near the Lop'nas river, some Armenian lords attacked the king of Balāsagān and his troops (Ełišē, 4.59, pp. 147-48; Langlois, II, p. 208; Movsēs Kałankatuac'i, 2.2, p. 67). The context leaves no doubt that the forces of Balāsagān were at that time fighting on the side of the Persians. But the king of the country, Heŕan, called Hun by Ełišē, was not slow to revolt against his Sasanian overlord. In fact, we learn that he subsequently massacred a Persian army in Albania, after which he was killed on the orders of Yazdegerd II (Ełišē, 7.30, pp. 263-64; Langlois, II, pp. 147-48).

It is probably to the Sasanian administration that the creation of districts called in Armenian Spanderanperož, Ormizdperož, At'sibagawan, and, probably, Alewan, all located south of the Kor, were created (cf. Hübschmann, p. 352). The two first-named, in Middle Persian Spandarān-Pērōz and Hormizd-Pērōz, are obviously names of Sasanian origin.

The Christianization of Balāsagān and Iranian survivals in local paganism in the late period. There were two attempts at conversion of Balāsagān: first, that of Gregory, which must have ended in his martyrdom, then that of Saint Mesrob. We do not know the results of these missions and whether or not conversion of this country was pursued subsequently. One fact is certain: In the third quarter of the sixth century a bishop of Balāsagān by the name of Timothy figured, with other bishops, among those named in a letter addressed by the catholicos John II of Armenia to the catholicos of Albania (*Livre des lettres*, p. 21: Movsēs Kałankatuac'i, 2.7, p. 72). Besides, a Sasanian seal published recently (Gignoux, II, p. 64, cf. p. 5) is inscribed in Pahlavi in the name "of the great catholicos of Hlb'n and of Balāsagān;" Hlb'n in this context could very well be the Middle Persian name of the city called Alewan in Armenian (perhaps identical with Ptolemy's city of Albana, 5.11.2), capital of the district of the same name situated in Balāsagān.

It is nevertheless true that toward the year A.D. 800 the region of Moğān remained still unconverted. The bishop Eliya, appointed to preach the Gospel in that country, which was no longer called Balāsagān, found there a population given to the worship of a God by the name of Yazd, who resided in an oak tree called "king of the forest;" the bushes that surrounded this tree were called "children of Yazd." The local population claimed to have received this god from its ancestors (Thomas de Marga, II, pp. 509-512; cf. Fiey, pp. 340-41). In Pahlavi *yazd* is the ordinary term denoting a god. The cult that Bishop Eliya had to combat was manifestly a borrowing from the beliefs of Mazdaism, a borrowing that must have originated in the Sasanian period and been amalgamated with a very different indigenous cult of the sacred trees.

Bibliography: N. Adontz, *Armenia in the Period of Justinian*, tr. by N. G. Garsoïan, Lisbon, 1970. Ełišē, *Histoire d'Arménie*, Venice, 1950. J. M. Fiey, *Parole de l'Orient* 2/2, 1971. Ph. Gignoux, *Catalogue de sceaux, camées et bulles sassanides*, Paris, 1978. E. Honigmann and A. Maricq, *Recherches sur les Res*

Gestae Divi Saporis, Mémoires in 8° de l'Académie royale de Belgique, Classe des lettres 47, 4, Brussels, 1953. H. Hübschmann, *Die altarmenischen Ortsnamen*, Indogermanische Forschungen 16, Strasbourg, 1904. Movsēs Kałankatuacʻi, *Histoire de l'Albanie*, tr. C. J. E. Dowsett, *The History of the Caucasian Albanians by Movsēs Dasxurançi*, London and New York, 1961. Koriun, *Vie de S. Maštocʻ*, ed. Akinian, Venice, 1952. V. Langlois, *Collection des historiens de l'Arménie*, 2 vols., Paris, 1867-69. *Livre des lettres*, Tiflis, 1901. Thomas de Marga, *The Book of Governors*, tr. by E. A. W. Budge, London, 1893. A. Maricq, "Res Gestae Divi Saporis," in *Classica et Orientalia*, Paris, 1965. K. V. Trever, *Ocherki po istorii i kul'ture kavkazskoĭ Albanii* (Essay on the history and culture of Albania in the Caucasus), Moscow and Leningrad, 1959.

(M. L. CHAUMONT)

ii. IN THE ISLAMIC PERIOD

In Islamic times, Balāsagān spanned the plain extending across the lower course of the Aras (Araxes) river (q.v.), from Barḏaʿa through Baylaqān (qq.v.) to Varṯān, Bājarvān (q.v.), and Barzand. It included the provinces of Arrān and Mūḡān (q.v.), though as Minorsky noted, the name is common in Armenian sources but rare in Islamic ones. Nevertheless, we find it mentioned by Balāḏorī, who says that in about 24/645 the caliph ʿOṯmān sent Salmān b. Rabīʿa Bāhelī to Arrān, and after the surrender of Baylaqān, Barḏaʿa, etc., he summoned the Kurds of Balāsagān to Islam and imposed the *jezya* on some of them; similarly, when Ḥoḏayfa b. Yamān made a peace treaty with the *marzbān* of Azerbaijan, one of the provisions was that the Arabs should not expose the local people to the depredations of the Kurds of Balāsajān and the Sabalān mountains (*Fotūḥ*, pp. 203, 326, tr. P. K. Hitti and F. C. Murgotten, *The Origins of the Islamic State* I, New York, 1916, p. 319, II, New York, 1924, p. 20; cf. Schwarz, *Iran*, pp. 998, 1156-57, 1248). The classical Arabic geographers rarely mention Balāsagān under that name, but the 4th/10th-century traveler Abū Dolaf (q.v.) says in his *al-Resāla al-ṯānīa* that he traversed the plain, noting the ruins of 5,000 (*sic*) villages there; he adds that popular legend located there the *Aṣḥāb al-rass* "People of the ditch" of Koran 25:40, 50:12 or else the host of Goliath, who was allegedly killed and buried at Urmia (V. Minorsky, *Abū-Dulaf Misʿar Ibn Muhalhil's Travels in Iran (circa A.D. 950)*, Cairo, 1955, sec. 16, tr. p. 36, comm. p. 75).

Bibliography: Given in the text.

(C. E. BOSWORTH)

BALĀSĀḠŪN, a town of Central Asia, in early Islamic times the main settlement of the region known as Yeti-su or Semirechye "the land of the seven rivers," now coming mainly within the eastern part of the Soviet Kazakhstan. The exact site of Balāsāḡūn is uncertain. Barthold, followed by subsequent Soviet scholars, suggested that its site is modern Aq-peshin near Frunze on the northern edge of the Kirgiz SSR, whilst O. I. Smirnova places it 15 miles/24 km to the southwest of Toqmaq (see Jovaynī, tr. Boyle, I, p. 58 n. 21). The early Islamic sources clearly locate it in the valley of the Ču river, but only Moqaddasī (Maqdesī), p. 275, gives any description of it; he calls Valāsakūn large, populous, and prosperous. It must have been a Sogdian foundation, and in Maḥmūd Kāšḡarī's time (second half of the 5th/11th century), Sogdian was still spoken there, together with Turkish; he states that the town also had the Turkish names of Quz-Ordu and Quz-Uluš (*Dīvān loḡāt al-Tork*, tr. Besim Atalay, Ankara, 1939-41, I, pp. 30, 62, 64).

Balāsāḡūn is first mentioned by Muslim historians towards the end of the Samanid Amir Naṣr b. Aḥmad's (q.v.) reign, i.e., ca. 330-31/942-43, when it was overrun by infidel Turks and its Muslim inhabitants (probably trading elements operating from there, since Balāsāḡūn at this time lay well outside the *Dār al-Eslām*) appealed to Bukhara for help (Neẓām-al-Molk, *Sīāsat-nāma*, chap. 46, ed. H. Darke, Tehran, 1340 Š./1961, pp. 290, 295, tr. idem, London, 1960, pp. 220, 224). These Turks were probably the Qarluq founders, some decades later, of the Qarakhanid (q.v.) tribal confederation, who, from a military base at Balāsāḡūn, succeeded to the Samanid heritage in Transoxania; both Balāsāḡūn and the nearby town in Farḡāna of Ūzgand (Özgend) were to be important centers for the Qarakhanids, held by various members of the ruling family, such as Aḥmad Ṭoḡān Khan b. Hārūn Boḡrā Khan, brother of ʿAlītigin (q.v.), who was in 416/1025 driven out of Balāsāḡūn by his other brother and rival Yūsof Qadïr Khan of Kāšḡar and Ḵotan (Bayhaqī, cited in Barthold, *Turkestan*[3], pp. 285, 294), so that henceforth, it seems to have fallen within the eastern Qarakhanid khanate. It was still only just within the boundaries of Islamic lands, and Ebn al-Aṯīr, ed. Tornberg, IX, pp. 355-56, ed. Beirut, IX, 520, records in 435/1043-44 the conversion of 10,000 tents of Turkish nomads who spent the summer in Bolḡār on the Volga and the winter around Balāsāḡūn, and who had been harrying the Muslims in Balāsāḡūn and Kāšḡar. The region played a significant cultural role amongst the Qarakhanids. The lexicographer Maḥmūd Kāšḡarī came from the nearby town of Barsḵān (q.v.), and the Turkish language which he describes in his dictionary is essentially that of the local Čegel, akin to the Qarluq; and Yūsof Ḵāṣṣ Ḥājeb, author of the pioneer Turkish Mirror for Princes, the *Qutadḡu bilig*, was actually a native of Balāsāḡūn and presented his book to the Qarakhanid ruler of Kāšḡar.

In 531/1137 the Gūr Khan of the Qara Khitays (q.v.) conquered Balāsāḡūn from the Qarakhanids and set up his army camp, the Ḵosun-ordu (lit., strong ordu) in the Ču valley near the town (Jovaynī, tr. Boyle, I, p. 355; Barthold, *Four Studies on the History of Central Asia*, tr. V. and T. Minorsky, Leiden, 1962, I, pp. 102-03). In the fighting between the Qarakhanids and the Ḵᵛārazmšāh Sultan ʿAlāʾ-al-Dīn Moḥammad (q.v.) in the opening years of the 7th/13th century, the Gūr Khan reconquered Balāsāḡūn with great slaughter in 607/1210, according to Jovaynī (tr. Boyle, I, p. 360; Barthold, *Turkestan*[3], pp. 326, 367); but shortly afterwards, it passed into the hands of Jengiz Khan's Mongols as they advanced against the Nāymān Mongol rival commander Küčlüg, although the sources give no explicit details of the process (*pace* Barthold, ibid., p. 402, cf. Boyle, "Balāsāghūn," in *EI*[2]). Whether Balāsāḡūn was destroyed at this time or not, it certainly did not flourish under the Mongols, and it now disappears from historical mention.

Bibliography: Given in the text. See also Le Strange, *Lands*, p. 487. *Ḥodud al-ʿālam*, tr. Minorsky, pp. 280, 291. E. Bretschneider, *Mediaeval Researches from Eastern Asiatic Sources*, London, 1910, I, pp. 226-28. Sir Henry Yule and H. Cordier, *Cathay and the Way Thither*, London, 1914-15, repr. Taipei, 1966, IV, pp. 163-64.

(C. E. BOSWORTH)

BALĀSĀNĪ, MAJD-AL-MOLK ABU'L-FAŻL ASʿAD B. MOḤAMMAD QOMĪ, *mostawfī* or financial intendant to the Saljuq sultan Berk-yaruq (Barkīāroq) b. Malekšāh [q.v.] in the early years of the latter's reign and then, from 490/1097 till his death in 492/1099, vizier to that monarch. The *nesba* also appears in the form Barāvestānī, from the name of a village in the region of Qom.

Majd-al-Molk had been *mostawfī*, in succession to Šaraf-al-Molk K͟ʷārazmī, during Malekšāh's sultanate, but once Berk-yaruq came to the throne, he became the real power in the state. With the support of his patron, the sultan's mother Zobayda K͟ātūn, he managed in 488/1095 to secure the dismissal from the vizierate of the capable Mo'ayyed-al-Molk b. Neẓām-al-Molk and the appointment of his less capable brother Fak͟r-al-Molk, estranged from Mo'ayyed-al-Molk through a quarrel over their father's inheritance. His influence, exercised through Fak͟r-al-Molk, was now high, and two years later (490/1097) he became vizier in name also; but he came up against the jealousy of the Turkish military commanders, whose support for the struggle against his half-brother Moḥammad Tapar (q.v.) was vital to Berk-yaruq. The amir Öner was provoked into a fruitless rebellion at Ray and killed there in 492/1099, but others of the amirs, led by Zangī, Aq-Böri, and the sons of Bursuq, took advantage of the assassination of the amir Bursuq by the Ismaʿilis to present the sultan with an ultimatum: the price of their future support was to be the head of Majd-al-Molk, now accused, because of his Shiʿite leanings, of complicity in the killing. According to Rāvandī, Berk-yaruq refused; according to Ebn al-At͟īr, he reluctantly agreed to hand him over, on condition that his life was spared, but before this handing-over took place, the amirs murdered Majd-al-Molk on 18 Šawwāl 492/7 September 1099.

Among the poets, Moʿezzī (ca. 440/1048-ca. 520/1126) praised Majd-al-Molk, and the sources speak of his piety, modesty, and extensive charities, above all to the ʿAlids and to the descendants of ancient houses. He was a moderate Shiʿite who was buried at Karbalā' and who made benefactions to the Shiʿite shrines, but who also gave money to the Ḥaramayn and restored the cover over ʿOt͟mān's tomb in Medina.

Bibliography: The main primary sources are Rāvandī, *Rāḥat al-ṣodūr*, ed. M. Iqbál, London, 1921, pp. 145-46. Bondārī, *Ẓobdat al-noṣra wa nok͟bat al-ʿoṣra*, ed. M. Th. Houtsma in *Recueil de textes relatifs à l'histoire des Seldjoucides* II, Leiden, 1889, pp. 87-88. Ebn al-At͟īr, Beirut, 1385-87/1965-67, X, pp. 252-53, 282, 289-91. Of secondary studies, see M. F. Sanaullah, *The Decline of the Saljūqid Empire*, Calcutta, 1938, pp. 42-43, 98. ʿAbbās Eqbāl, *Wezārat dar ʿahd-e salāṭīn-e bozorg-e saljūqī*, Tehran, 1338 Š./1959, pp. 109-14. *Cambridge History of Iran* V, pp. 108-09, 248, 260-63, 267-68. C. L. Klausner, *The Seljuk Vezirate, A Study of Civil Administration 1055-1194*, Cambridge, Mass., 1973, pp. 42, 46-48, 92, 105-06.

(C. E. BOSWORTH)

BĀLĀSARĪ, term popularly used to distinguish ordinary Shiʿites from members of the Shaikhi sect. The distinction is sometimes expressed by the alternative formulae of "Shaikhi/Motašarreʿ" and "Shaikhi/Oṣūlī," the latter example implying a continuity between Ak͟bārī Shiʿism and Shaikhism (qq.v.). The Shaikhi school itself was also known in the early period by the name "Kašfīya" in reference to the principle of *kašf* or the revelation of knowledge by supernatural means (Raštī, *Dalīl*, p. 9; cf. Čahārdehī, *Šayk͟īgarī*, pp. 51-52). The term "Bālāsarī" was applied to other Shiʿites by the Shaikhis on the grounds that, when in the shrine of the Imam Ḥosayn at Karbalā', the former advanced to a position above the head of the imam in order to pray, whereas the Shaikhis, in imitation of their founder, Shaikh Aḥmad Aḥsā'ī (d. 1241/1826; q.v.), remained below the head out of respect for the imam (Kermānī, *Hedāyat*, p. 83; Zarandī, *Dawn-Breakers*, pp. 84-85).

Disputes between Shaikhis and Bālāsarīs began with the excommunication (*takfīr*) of Aḥsā'ī by Mollā Moḥammad-Taqī Baraḡānī (q.v.) and other *ʿolamā'* around 1238/1822 and intensified during the leadership of Aḥsā'ī's successor, Sayyed Kāẓem Raštī (d. 1259/1844; q.v.; see MacEoin, *From Shaykhism*, pp. 75-81, 105-15). Both Aḥsā'ī and Raštī insisted on the essential orthodoxy of their teaching, a position which was maintained by the two main branches of the school after Raštī's death, those of Azerbaijan and Kermān. Broadly expressed, the Shaikhi position was that differences between them and their Bālāsarī opponents lay in the area of subsidiary religious matters (*forūʿ*) rather than basic principles (*oṣūl*) or that the two groups were divided by temperament (*mašrab*) rather than religion (*mad͟hab*) (Kermānī, *Hedāyat*; Jalālī, *Šayk͟īya*, p. 126). Shaikhi *ʿolamā'* often held important posts within the religious establishment, and it was not always easy or useful to draw clear lines between them and other Shiʿites.

In Azerbaijan, the Shaikhi community was led by Ḥājī Mīrzā Šafīʿ Ṯeqat-al-Eslām Tabrīzī (ca. 1218/1803-1301/1884; q.v.) and Ḥojjat-al-Eslām Mollā Moḥammad Mamaqānī (d. 1268/1851-52 or 1269/1852-53; q.v.) and included numbers of influential individuals among the *ʿolamāʾ*, merchants (*tojjār*), government officials, and nobility (see Čahārdehī, pp. 175-98). Although the Shaikhi establishment in Tabrīz asserted its orthodoxy by playing a central role in the condemnation and execution of Sayyed ʿAlī-Moḥammad the Bāb (q.v.) in 1264/1848 and 1266/1850 (see MacEoin, *From Shaykhism*, pp. 130-31), this did not result in an immediate resolution of the issue between the two parties. In 1266/1850, Mīrzā Aḥmad Tabrīzī declared *takfīr* against the Shaikhis and issued a *fatwā* banning them from the public baths. An altercation ensued and was followed by serious rioting throughout the city (Čahārdehī, pp. 49-50). Another outbreak of violence occurred in 1285/1868-69 following the death of Mamaqānī (Bāmdād, *Rejāl* VI, p. 83). In general, the Shaikhi and Bālāsarī communities remained religiously and socially divided, with separate mosques and baths, a ban on intermarriage, and restricted social relations. Efforts to reconcile the two groups were made by Mīrzā ʿAlī Ṯeqat-al-Eslām (1277/1860-1330/1912; q.v.), a Shaikhi leader whose involvement in the Constitutional movement and death at the hands of the Russians were major factors in the reintegration of the Shaikhis into the orthodox community in the post-Constitutional period.

The situation in Kermān was equally complicated by political and social factors. The first head of the Shaikhi community there, Ḥājj Moḥammad-Karīm Khan Kermānī (1225/1810-1288/1870; q.v.), was the most successful of the claimants to overall leadership of the school in Iraq and Iran. Kermānī's father, Ebrāhīm Khan Ẓahīr-al-Dawla (q.v.), was a cousin and son-in-law of Fatḥ-ʿAlī Shah and served as governor of Kermān from 1218/1803 until his death in 1240/1824-25 (Aḥmadī, *Farmāndehān*, pp. 50-55). Ẓahīr-al-Dawla's descendants, known as the Ebrāhīmīs, remained one of the most important families in the region and were closely linked to the Shaikhi school through Karīm Khan, whose control over much of his father's inheritance gave him considerable influence within the family. During the period of Karīm Khan's leadership, relations between Shaikhis and non-Shaikhis in Kermān were relaxed, but conditions deteriorated after his death and the succession of his second son, Ḥājj Moḥammad Khan (1263/1846-1324/1906).

In 1294/1877, there was general unrest in Kermān following a rise in bread prices. At one point, attacks were made by a mob on houses belonging to Shaikhis (Scarcia, p. 223). Some months after the death of the town's leading *mojtahed*, Ḥājj Āqā Aḥmad Rafsanjānī, in the following year, trouble broke out between his son, Ḥājj Shaikh Abū Jaʿfar, and Moḥammad-Raḥīm Khan, the older brother of the Shaikhi leader, Moḥammad Khan. According to Mostawfī, a group of Shaikhis initiated the violence that followed by launching an attack on the house of Shaikh Abū Jaʿfar (Jalali, pp. 187-88). The dispute was only settled when Nāṣer-al-Dīn Shah summoned both Abū Jaʿfar and Moḥammad-Raḥīm Khan to Tehran.

During the next thirty years or so, Moḥammad Khan remained the most influential religious figure in Kermān, combining spiritual authority with immense wealth and close links with the ruling dynasty. Although the total number of Shaikhis in Iran at this point was only about 50,000, of whom 7000 lived in Kermān province (Sykes, *Ten Thousand Miles*, p. 197), the sect's influence was considerable. Moẓaffar-al-Dīn Mīrzā (shah from 1896) was known to have become a Shaikhi while living in Tabrīz (Bāmdād, *Rejāl* IV, p. 121), while many other Qajar notables were attached with varying degrees of closeness to the school and its leadership. Scarcia describes Shaikhism as "a sort of bland, innocuous, and quasi-snobbish type of anti-clerical movement of the court" ("Kerman 1905," p. 201).

In Kermān itself, the influence of the Ebrāhīmī family was challenged by that of the Wakīlīs, descendants of Moḥammad-Esmāʿīl Khan Wakīl-al-Molk I (governor of Kermān from 1277/1860 to 1284/1868), many of whom held important posts in the local administration. The first sign of wider opposition to Ebrāhīmī/Shaikhi dominance came in the form of demonstrations against Moḥammad Khan in Torbat-e Ḥaydarīya and Mašhad during a pilgrimage made by him to the latter town in 1319/1901 (Jalali, p. 191). Moḥammad Khan's unpopularity seems to have had less to do with religious animosity than with his role as a Qajar notable and his expressed disapproval of constitutionalism (Bayat, *Mysticism and Dissent*, p. 182), a position which contrasted markedly with that of Azerbaijani Shaikhis such as Ṯeqat-al-Eslām.

Matters reached a head in the Shaikhi-Bālāsarī "war" of 1323/1905, which has been described by some writers as "the spark that first set the fire of the Constitutional Revolution" (ibid., p. 183). Trouble began in 1321/1903 under the governorship of Sardār ʿAzīz-Allāh Mīrzā Ẓafar-al-Salṭana (q.v.), when protests about a rise in the price of bread were followed by attacks on the houses of the rich and on the Shaikhi *madrasa* (Scarcia, p. 224). Ẓafar-al-Salṭana was dismissed in Rabīʿ I, 1322/May-June, 1904, and replaced by ʿAlī-Naqī Mīrzā Rokn-al-Dawla, who quickly alienated much of the populace. The new governor entrusted the tax administration of the province to the Ebrāhīmī family, thereby intensifying opposition, particularly on the part of the Wakīlīs (Kermānī, *Bīdārī*, p. 69). A sectarian dimension was introduced when a preacher from Mašhad, Shaikh Šamšīrī Barīnī, arrived in Kermān and, after agitating against Zoroastrians and Hindus, began to issue public condemnations of the Shaikhis. Barīnī was soon joined in his attacks by Ḥājj Mīrzā Moḥammad-Reżā, the son of the above-mentioned Shaikh Abū Jaʿfar, who arrived in Kermān in Rabīʿ I, 1323/May, 1905, after a fourteen-year absence and quickly allied himself with the Wakīlī family (ibid., pp. 70-71). Fighting broke out in Jomādā I, 1323/July, 1905, when an attempt was made to take control of the Shaikhi Bāzār-e Šāh mosque. The authorities in Tehran responded by dismissing Rokn-al-Dawla and replacing him by Ẓafar-al-Salṭana (ibid., pp. 72-73; Scarcia, pp. 228-29).

In Šaʿbān/October, Mīrzā Moḥammad-Reżā incurred the new governor's displeasure by provoking attacks on Jewish homes. An attempt to control the situation was met by a declaration of *jehād* against the Shaikhis and the Qajars. Brief fighting was followed by the arrest, bastinado, and expulsion of Moḥammad-Reżā and some of his colleagues. This led in turn to a boycott of the mosques by all of the town's *ʿolamāʾ* except for Moḥammad Khan (Scarcia, pp. 230-31). At this point, however, the Shaikhi/Bālāsarī element took a back seat as leading *ʿolamāʾ* in Tehran reacted to the bastinado of Mīrzā Moḥammad-Reżā. What had started as a local sectarian squabble now acquired a wider dimension as a factor in the agitation for a constitution (Kermānī, *Bīdārī*, pp. 78ff.). Moḥammad Khan's death in Moḥarram, 1324/February, 1906, served to reduce further the religious aspect of the quarrel, and with the end of the Qajar hegemony, Shaikhi influence on local politics diminished considerably. Anti-Shaikhi feeling has re-emerged occasionally in the modern period (Scarcia, pp. 236-37), but with none of its former intensity. The murder of the Shaikhi leader Abu'l-Qāsem Ebrāhīmī (q.v.) in 1979 led to the transfer of the school's leadership to Iraq, but otherwise the position of the Shaikhi communities of Iran appears to be little changed.

See also SHAIKHISM.

Bibliography: The main elements of the Shaikhi/Bālāsarī controversy can be traced in the following works: Sayyed Kāẓem Raštī, *Dalīl al-motaḥayyerīn*, n.p., 1276/1859-60. Ḥājj Moḥammad-Karīm Khan Kermānī, *Hedāyat al-ṭālebīn*, 2nd ed., Kermān, 1380/1960. Idem, *Resāla dar jawāb-e Ḥājj Mollā Maḥmūd Neẓām-al-ʿOlamāʾ*, Kermān, 1350/1931. Ḥājj Moḥammad Khan Kermānī, *Resāla-ye behbahānīya*, Kermān, 1351/1932. Ḥājj Abu'l-Qāsem Khan Kermānī, *Resāla-ye falsafīya*, Kermān, 1350 Š./1971. Mīrzā Moḥammad-Bāqer Hamadānī, *Ketāb al-ejtenāb*, n.p., 1308/1891. Idem, *Resāla-ye naʿl-e ḥāżera*, in one volume with above. Accounts of the disputes in Tabrīz and Kermān may be found in the following: G. Scarcia, "Kerman 1905: La 'guerra tra Šeiḫī e Bālāsarī'," *Annali del Istituto Universitario Orientale di Napoli*, N.S. 13, 1963, pp. 195-238. Moḥammad Hāšemī Kermānī, "Naẓar-ī be-eḵtelāfāt wa entеḵābāt-e Kermān," *Etteḥād-e mellī* 11, nos. 318-66, 18 Ḵordād 1333 Š./8 June 1954-26 Ordībehešt 1334 Š./16 May 1955). Moṣṭafā Khan Mostawfī, *Jang-e Šayḵī wa Bālāsarī dar Kermān*, MS in the library of Moḥammad Hāšemī Kermānī. Nāẓem-al-Eslām Kermānī, *Tārīḵ-e bīdārī-e Īrānīān*, ed. ʿA.-A. Saʿīdī Sīrjānī, I, Tehran, 1346 Š./1967, pp. 69-84. Kasrawī, *Mašrūṭa*, 1344 Š./1965, pp. 52-54, 130-35. Mortażā Modarresī Čahārdehī, *Šayḵīgarī, Bābīgarī*, 2nd ed., Tehran, 1351 Š./1972-73, pp. 175-98, 247-58. Aḥmad-ʿAlī Khan Wazīrī Kermānī, *Tārīḵ-e Kermān*, ed. M.-E. Bāstānī Pārīzī, Tehran, 1340 Š./1961, pp. 440-44 note (synopsis of Kermānī, *Bīdārī*). Shaikh Yaḥyā Aḥmadī, *Farmāndehān-e Kermān*, ed. M.-E. Bāstānī Pārīzī, Tehran, 1354 Š./1975-76, introd., pp. 20-22, 190-97 (synopsis of Kermānī, *Bīdārī*). Aflaton Jalali, "The Shaykhīya of Ḥājjī Muḥammad Karīm Khān in Kirmān," unpub. MS, 1982, pp. 180-211. H. Algar, *Religion and State in Iran 1785-1906*, Berkeley and Los Angeles, 1969, pp. 243-44. M. Bayat, *Mysticism and Dissent. Socioreligious Thought in Qajar Iran*, Syracuse, 1982, pp. 181-83. Percy M. Sykes, *Ten Thousand Miles in Persia or Eight Years in Iran*, London, 1902, p. 197. D. M. MacEoin, *From Shaykhism to Babism: A Study in Charismatic Authority in Shīʿī Islam*, Ph.D. thesis, Cambridge University, 1979.

(D. M. MACEOIN)

BĀLAVĪ. See BĀLAWĪ.

BALAWASTE, a ruin site in the eastern part of the Khotan oasis, near the village of Domoko.

Fragments of manuscripts (given the signature DK = Domoko), pottery, and plaster were found at this site by Sir Mark Aurel Stein on his first and second expeditions in 1900 and 1906. On his third expedition in 1916, dealers in the local *bāzār* offered him pieces of a mural painting which, they said, had been removed by local treasure-hunters from the walls of a temple at Balawaste. The best pieces had been sold shortly before to Vice-Consul Colonel H. J. Harding. These and the pieces acquired by Stein passed into the possession of the New Delhi Museum. Other pieces were purchased by C. P. Skrine for the British Museum and by E. Trinkler for the Übersee-Museum at Bremen. The Metropolitan Museum in New York and the Academy for Oriental Culture at Tokyo also possess some fragments. It is uncertain whether all these pieces come from the same temple and whether the temple lay at the Balawaste site visited by Stein.

Approximately 94 pieces can be combined to form a sequence of life-size Buddhas, Bodhisattvas, divine beings, and *lokapāla*s with their *parivāra* (retinue). A fragment now in Bremen depicting the *lokapāla* Vaiśravaṇa is particularly important because it bears the inscription of the donor Śūraputra in Khotanese. The main scene probably consisted of five groups each made up of a sitting Jina Buddha attended by two standing Bodhisattvas. The picture of Vairocana (now in Delhi) is renowned for the painting of the upper part of the body; his attendants (like those in the fragment at Bremen) are clad only in loin-cloths. Also belonging to the series is a picture (parts now in London and Bremen) of a sitting four-armed deity, probably to be identified as the "silk god" seen by Stein on painted wooden tablets from Dandan Öilik. Possibly this god, being the tutelary deity of Khotan, was accompanied by the rulers of the five regions of the world. All the gods are sitting on lotus flowers in a pool, surrounded by smaller Buddhas, Bodhisattvas, and divine beings. In view of the artistic style and the type of the clothing, the picture can be dated ca. 600 A.D. It is the most important surviving specimen of Khotanese art. The Tibetan art of the thirteenth century is in a related style. The picture also explains the lists of gods in certain Khotanese manuscripts as being descriptions of pictures in famous temples. Some sixty fragments with representations of the "Thousand Buddhas" come from the outer walls of the same or another temple; they too were said by the dealers to have been taken from the ruins at Balawaste.

Bibliography: G. Gropp and R. E. Emmerick, *Archäologische Funde aus Khotan*, Bremen, 1974, pp. 105ff., 362ff. J. Williams, "The Iconography of Khotanese Painting," *East and West* 23, 1973, pp. 109-54.

(G. GROPP)

BĀLAWĪ, prominent Nīšāpūr family of the 4th/10th and 5th/11th centuries. Aḥmad b. ʿAbd-Allāh b. Aḥmad b. Bālūya (whence the family name Bālawī) had five sons all named Moḥammad but with different *konya*s. What little is recorded about them establishes that their social origins were commercial. They are called brokers and clothing dealers, but Abū Bakr Moḥammad is also said to be from an old and wealthy family so the family's commercial origins may have been a generation or more earlier. Abū Naṣr Moḥammad was a courtier of the Samanid that ruled Khorasan from Bukhara. The last brother died in 374/984 at the age of ninety-four. Two members of a collateral line of Bālawīs are also known in this generation.

In the next generation the Bālawīs became noted more for scholarship and involvement with Islamic legal matters than commerce. Abū Moḥammad ʿAbd-al-Raḥmān held the office of *mozakkī*, which maintained the list of legal witnesses who served as bailiffs and notaries. He was patronized by the more noted *mozakkī* Abū ʿAmr Baḥīrī, who arranged for him to hold *ḥadīṯ* classes, the ultimate sign of acceptance into the religious and scholarly elite. A similar indication of acceptance may be seen in the marriage between a cousin and the daughter of Abū Bakr Aḥmad Ḥarašī Ḥīrī, who was also called ʿOṯmānī because of his descent on his mother's side from the caliph ʿOṯmān. Ḥarašī was a leading Shafiʿite legal scholar. He served both as *mozakkī* and later as judge (*qāżī*), being the last Shafiʿite to hold the normally Hanafite-dominated post.

The Bālawī family continued for two more generations, and some members were called *mozakkī*. But little is known about them. One branch of the family acquired the additional name Kayyālī (grain measurer) through intermarriage with a little-known family that appears to have similarly advanced from commercial origins to positions of wealth, land ownership, and acceptance by other elite or patrician families.

Bibliography: R. W. Bulliet, *The Patricians of Nishapur*, chap. 7, with full references to the mss. ed. in facs. by R. N. Frye, *The Histories of Nishapur*, The Hague, 1965.

(R. W. BULLIET)

BALDARČĪN. See BELḎERČĪN.

BĀLEḠ, an Arabic term meaning full age, adult, mature, in contrast to the term *ṣaḡīr* (minor). According to various schools of Islamic law, including the Shiʿite school, there is a clear distinction between girls and boys attaining the age of majority. Presuming sanity, the age of *bolūḡ* (majority) for boys is said to be between thirteen to fifteen (some have said ten for boys and nine for girls). The only undisputed traditional criterion for majority is either on reaching orgasm or growing pubic hairs (in male or female). Reference is usually made to Koran 24:58 which indicates that the children attain the age of puberty by having venereal (wet) dreams. No reference is made to manipulated ejaculation by the youth, as masturbation is a major sin in Islam. Koran 4:5 commands to take care of orphans until they reach the age of marriage. Shaikh Faḵr-al-Dīn Ṭorayḥī (d. 1085/1674-75) in *Majmaʿ al-baḥrayn* states that majority is attained by anyone who (a) has grown rough pubic hairs or, (b) has reached orgasm, or (c) has reached the age of nine for girls or ten to fifteen for boys. Šams-al-Dīn Abū ʿAbd-Allāh Moḥammad b. Makkī ʿĀmelī Šāmī, known as the First Šahīd, executed in Damascus in 786/1384 (*al-Lomʿa al-demašqīya*), Shaikh Bahāʾ-al-Dīn Moḥammad ʿĀmelī known as Shaikh Bahāʾī, (*Jāmeʿ-e ʿabbāsī*, Tehran, 1363 Š./1984, pp. 164-65), and Sayyed Moḥammad-Kāẓem Yazdī (*ʿOrwat al-woṯqā*) and others record the consensus that the age of majority for girls is nine. Moḥaqqeq Ḥellī (d. 676/1277-78) in his most authoritative *Šarāyeʿ al-Eslām* says that the age of majority for boys is prima facie fifteen or any one of the other two physical criteria as recorded before, whichever occurs first. Ḥājj Mollā Hādī Sabzavārī in *Šarḥ-e Nebrās* writes that adulthood in either male or female is established by either "having venereal dreams," or having rough pubic hairs, or alternatively reaching the age of nine for girls and the age of fifteen for boys. Any one of these criteria is sufficient. Sabzavārī then goes on to philosophize and justify why women become mature under Islamic law earlier than men. His grounds of justification inter alia are: The figure of nine is a perfect figure and the Almighty knows that women are much fairer and weaker than men and die earlier, thus the Almighty has compensated women by granting them an earlier status of majority than men. Ayatollah Ḵomeynī (*Tawżīḥ al-masāʾel*, question 2252) states three criteria for reaching the full age: growing rough pubic hairs, ejaculation, and the completion of fifteen lunar years of age for boys and nine lunar years for girls. Notably Ayatollah Ḵomeynī regards the first two criteria common to both sexes whereas other Shiʿite jurists have expressed different views. For instance, Ayatollah Moḥammad Waḥīdī (*Tawżīḥ al-masāʾel*, question 2260) considers the completion of the age of nine lunar years the only criterion of *bolūḡ* in women, whereas for men he states the following three: completing the age of fifteen lunar years, growing rough pubic hairs, and having wet dreams.

Those who have not attained the age of *bolūḡ*, as in Roman law, are divided into two categories: 1. Those younger children who can be termed as pupils and have no power to enter into any contract whatsoever and 2. young persons under the age of *bolūḡ* who can be termed minors and who have the capacity to be a party to a contract from which they benefit, e.g. by accepting an offer of gift gratuitously (article 1212 of the Iranian Civil Code). Apart from this distinction pupils and minors have no contractual capacity under Shiʿite law. Thus any contract which purports to have been made by a pupil or minor is, as a rule, void and therefore unenforceable with the possible exception that if necessities are supplied to a pupil or a minor, he or his guardian must pay a reasonable price for them. Article 212 of the Iranian Civil Code states that a contract made by a person who had not reached the age of *bolūḡ* is void. Nevertheless, a minor's estate, but not a pupil's, is liable for tort (ʿA. Šāyegān *Ḥoqūq-e madanī-e Īrān*, 3rd ed., Tehran, 1324 Š./1945-46 p. 225).

Usually the age of majority is discussed by Shiʿite jurists for four purposes. First, and most importantly, for the sake of *taklīf*, i.e., full capacity in the eyes of God for performing all *wājeb*s (ritual obligations such as saying daily prayers and keeping fast in Ramażān). Secondly for purposes of entering into contractual obligations and in particular the contract of marriage (cf. Koran 4:5, which states that orphans should be looked after until they reach the age of marriage; then if they are mentally mature one is to give them all their estate. Thirdly, for purposes of criminal responsibility as there is a presumption in Islamic law that a pupil is incapable of committing crime; thus *bolūḡ* is a major criterion in the definition of a criminal under Islamic law. Under the 1982 Iranian Law of Retribution (pars. 138-58), children below the age of *bolūḡ* who engage in adultery or sodomy cannot be punished. Lastly, a person who has not reached the age of *bolūḡ* cannot sue or be sued, although a minor (not a pupil) can sue his guardian for failure in the provision of support (article 96 of the Iranian Law on Guardianship).

Orthodox Islamic law imposes no age qualification whatever for marriage, and there is thus no bar to the marriage of minors concluded by their guardians. Indeed the father's permission is considered essential for the marriage of any bride by many Emāmī jurists (including Ayatollah Ḵomeynī) as well as under article 1042 and 1043 of the Iranian Civil Code 1313-14, although the latter article allows the registration of civil marriage by a female without her guardian's approval if the guardian having been given notice of the proposed marriage fails to satisfy the registrar why the marriage should not be registered. However, as stated by Sayyed Moḥammad-Kāẓem Yazdī (d. 1337/1918-19), it is prohibited to consummate the marriage with a minor wife under the age of nine whether she is "free, a slave, permanent wife, or temporary wife" (*ʿOrwat al-woṯqā*, 2nd ed., 1392/1972, p. 99). Such an "arranged marriage" can be set aside by the husband only after he reaches *bolūḡ*. Thus Āqā Sayyed ʿAlī Ṭabāṭabāʾī (d. 1231/1815-16) states that divorce by a youth is not valid until he has had a venereal dream (*Rīāż al-masāʾel*).

The age of majority under secular, civil law (Articles 1208-10 of the Iranian Civil Code) which was in force in Iran prior to the revolution of 1358 Š./1979 was eighteen for both men and women. Articles 1209 and 1210 of the Iranian Civil Code imply that anybody, male or female, who is under the age of eighteen years, is a minor under Iranian law and as such lacks any legal capacity to administer his own estate by Article 1207 (S. Ḥ. Emāmī, *Ḥoqūq-e madanī* I, Tehran, 1333 Š./1954-55, pp. 166).

Under article 1180 of the Iranian Civil Code, a minor is subject to the legal authority of the father and paternal grandfather. Article 1041 of the Iranian Civil Code disallowed the marriage of girls below the age of fifteen and boys below the age of eighteen, but authorized the court to grant exemption from this age limit in exceptional circumstances to girls over thirteen and boys over fifteen. Under article 1168-72 of the Civil Code the custody of the children rests with the father but the mother has priority to take custody of male children less than two years old and of female children under the age of seven. By the Custody of Children Act 1982, children whose fathers died were allowed to remain under the custody of their mothers.

Bibliography: Shiʿite law: Shaikh Abu'l-Qāsem Najm-al-Dīn Jaʿfar Moḥaqqeq Ḥellī, *Šarāyeʿ al-Eslām fī masāʾel al-ḥalāl wa'l-ḥarām*, ed. ʿAbd-al-Raḥīm, n.p., 1928. Abū ʿAbd-Allāh Moḥammad Šahīd, *al-Lomʿa al-demašqīya*, ed. M. A. Āqā Rafīʿī, 2 vols., Tehran, 1961. Sayyed ʿAlī Ṭabāṭabāʾī, *Rīāż al-masāʾel*, n.p., n.d. Sayyed Moḥammad-Kāẓem Yazdī, *ʿOrwat al-woṯqā*, n.p., n.d. Ayatollah Rūḥ-Allāh Ḵomeynī, *Tawżīḥ al-masāʾel*, Tehran, n.d. Iranian civil law: S. H. Amin, *Middle East Legal Systems*, Glasgow, 1985. Idem, *Commercial Law of Iran*, Tehran, 1986. Idem, *Islamic Law in the Contemporary World*, Tehran, 1985.

(S. H. AMIN)

BALḴ, a town and province in northern Afghanistan.

i. *Geography.*
ii. *From the Arab conquest to the Mongols.*
iii. *From the Mongols to modern times.*
iv. *Modern town.*
v. *Modern province.*
vi. *Monuments.*

(For the ancient history of Balḵ see BACTRIA.)

i. GEOGRAPHY

The city of Bactra, later Balḵ, owed its importance to its position at the crossing of major routes: the west-east route along the foot of the Khorasan and Hindu Kush mountains from Iran to Central Asia and China, and the route by left bank tributaries of the Oxus and passes through the mountains of central Afghanistan to northwestern India. The river of Balk̲ (Balk̲āb, q.v.) gives easy access by the valley of its tributary the Dara-ye Ṣūf and the Qarā Kotal pass to the Bāmīān basin and thence to Kabul. This route has the advantage of being the westernmost of the roads over the Hindu Kush and thus the shortest for travelers from the west, as well as one of the easiest. Its existence must have been the main reason why a great city arose in the area where the Balk̲āb debouches into the plain.

Within this area and on the irrigated alluvial fan, at a distance of about 12 km from the mountains, the city was built on a site (the Bālā Ḥeṣār of today) which was probably coextensive with a slight rise in the plain and perhaps adjacent to an old arm of the river. This is only a supposition, because adequate archeological exploration has not yet been carried out. In any case, the site subsequently grew higher through the gradual accumulation of the debris left by successive human occupants.

Bibliography: A Foucher, *La vieille route de l'Inde de Bactres à Taxila*, MDAFA 1, 2 vols., Paris 1942-47.

(X. de PLANHOL)

ii. HISTORY FROM THE ARAB CONQUEST TO THE MONGOLS

Information on the process of the Arab conquest of Balk̲ is somewhat vague. According to Balāḏorī (*Fotūḥ*, p. 408), Aḥnaf b. Qays raided Balk̲ and Ṭok̲ārestān in ʿAbd-Allāh b. ʿĀmer b. Korayz's governorship of Khorasan during the caliphate of ʿOṯmān (32/653), but further attempts at controlling the city were not possible until Moʿāwīa had restored a measure of peace and stability to the troubled Arab empire. In 42/662-63 ʿAbd-Allāh b. ʿĀmer nominated Qays b. Hayṯam over Khorasan, who in turn sent ʿAbd-al-Raḥmān b. Samora into Khorasan and Sīstān, conquering Balk̲ and, allegedly, Kabul. But the people of Balk̲ renounced their peace agreement with the Arabs, and in 51/671, Rabīʿ b. Zīād had to reappear at Balk̲; it is clear that no firm or enduring Arab control over the city was ever established in the early Omayyad period. It was, however, during these raids under ʿOṯmān and Moʿāwīa that the great Buddhist shrine of Nowbahār, situated in the *rabaż* (suburb) of the city according to the classical Arabic geographers, was despoiled and destroyed, although it long remained a sacred site; the northern Hephthalite prince Ṭark̲ān Nīzak (q.v.) went to pray there and to derive blessing when he rebelled in Gūzgān and lower Ṭok̲ārestān against the Arab governor Qotayba b. Moslem Bāhelī (q.v.) in 90/709 (Ṭabarī, I, p. 1205), necessitating Qotayba's despatching 12,000 men to Balk̲.

From its strenuous opposition to the Arabs on various occasions, and the latter's vengeful reprisals, Balk̲ is described as being largely ruinous in the mid-Omayyad period, so that the Arabs built for themselves a new military encampment two *farsak̲s* away, called Barūqān, where what was normally a comparatively small Arab garrison (at least in comparison with that of Marv) was installed, until in 107/725, after an outbreak of feuding amongst the Arab troops at Barūqān (represented in such sources as Ṭabarī, perhaps misleadingly, as a tribal clash of Qays and Yaman), the governor Asad b. ʿAbd-Allāh Qasrī (q.v.) restored Balk̲ on its former site, employing as his agent for this Barmak, the somewhat shadowy father of the early ʿAbbasid minister K̲āled Barmakī (Ṭabarī, II, pp. 1490-91); Barūqān now drops out of mention. A few years later, Asad temporarily transferred the capital of Khorasan from Marv to Balk̲, giving the latter city an access of prosperity.

The last Omayyad governor in Khorasan, Naṣr b. Sayyār Kenānī (q.v.), built Balk̲ up into a significant military base. In 116/734, according to Ṭabarī, II, pp. 1566-67, he had there an army of 10,000 men, composed of the Arab tribesmen of Khorasan and also probably of Syrian forces, which he used against the rebel Ḥāreṯ b. Sorayj. During the ʿAbbasid *daʿwa* in Khorasan led by Abū Moslem (q.v.), Balk̲ was strongly defended for Naṣr and the Omayyads by Zīād b. ʿAbd-Allāh Qošayrī. Abū Moslem sent against him and against other loyal government forces of Ṭok̲ārestān, including the local Iranian princes, his lieutenant Abū Dāwūd K̲āled b. Ebrāhīm Bakrī. Possession of the city oscillated between the Omayyad defenders and Abū Moslem's commanders Abū Dāwūd and ʿOṯmān b. Kermānī, until it was secured for the revolutionaries at the third attempt (130/747-48). See for this early period of the consolidation of Arab control and of islamization, Markwart, *Ērānšahr*, index s.v.; J. Wellhausen, *The Arab Kingdom and Its Fall*, Eng. tr., Calcutta, 1927, index s.v.; P. Schwarz, "Bemerkungen zu den arabischen Nachrichten über Balkh," in *Oriental Studies in Honour of Cursetji Erachji Pavry*, London, 1933, pp. 434-43; M. A. Shaban, *The ʿAbbāsid Revolution*, Cambridge, 1970, index s.v.

Little is heard of Balk̲ during the early ʿAbbasid period, but it was a base for Hārūn al-Rašīd's commander ʿAlī b. ʿĪsā b. Māhān in the operations against the rebel Rāfeʿ b. Layṯ b. Naṣr b. Sayyār, and the fact that Balk̲ suffered from a violent earthquake in 203/818-19 is mentioned. Soon afterwards, it came within the vast governorship of the East held by the Taherid family from the ʿAbbasid caliphs. But with the seat of the Taherids' power at Nīšāpūr, 500 miles to the west, Balk̲ seems to have been left, according to the general pattern of Taherid overlordship in the east, to local princes. These were from the Abu Dawudid or Banijurid family, most probably of Iranian stock. Dāwūd b. ʿAbbās b. Hāšem b. Banījūr was governor in Balk̲ from 233/847-48 onwards, in succession to his father, and was the builder of the village and castle of Nowšād or Nowšār near Balk̲. He was still there when the Saffarid Yaʿqūb b. Layṯ destroyed Nowšād and temporarily captured Balk̲ before going on to Kabul (in 256/870 according to

Gardīzī, ed. Nazim, p. 11, in 257/871 according to Ebn al-Aṯīr, ed. Beirut, VII, p. 247). Dāwūd fled to the Samanids in Samarqand, returning to Balk̲ and retaking it soon afterwards and dying there in 259/873. His kinsman (nephew ?) Abū Dāwūd Moḥammad b. Aḥmad ruled in Balk̲ from 260/874, and was involved in the complex power struggle between rival condottieri for control of Khorasan after the Taherids' loss of Nīšāpūr to the Saffarids in 259/873. Abū Dāwūd was immediately besieged in Balk̲ by 5,000 troops under Abū Ḥafṣ Yaʿmar b. Šarkab, and then soon afterwards was again attacked by Abū Ḥafṣ's brother Abū Ṭalḥa Manṣūr after the latter had been expelled from Nīšāpūr (see Ebn al-Aṯīr, VII, pp. 296, 300, giving the data for the second attack as 265/878-79 or 266/879-80). This Abū Dāwūd also controlled Andarāb and Panjhīr (qq.v.) in Badak̲šān (q.v.), where he minted coins from the local silver, and was still ruling in Balk̲ in 285/898 or 286/899, when the Saffarid ʿAmr b. Layṯ summoned him and the other local potentates of northern Khorasan and Transoxania to obedience. ʿAmr's plans of extending his control to these regions were of course speedily dashed by his defeat near Balk̲, after fortifying that city with a moat and rampart, at the hands of the Samanid Esmāʿīl b. Aḥmad (q.v.) (287/900). See for these events, Gardīzī, ed. Nazim, pp. 11-19; Naršak̲ī, *Tārīk̲-e Bok̲ārā*, tr. Frye, pp. 87ff.; Markwart, *Ērānšahr*, pp. 301-02; Barthold, *Turkestan*³, pp. 77-78, 224-25; C. E. Bosworth "Banīdjūrids," in *EI*², Suppl.

The late 3rd/9th- and 4th/10th-century geographers expatiate with enthusiasm on the amenities and the flourishing state of Balk̲ at that time, calling it *Omm al-belād* "the greatest of the cities of Khorasan" from the populousness of the region (Yaʿqūbī, *Boldān*, p. 287; tr. Wiet, p. 100) and *Balk̲ al-bahīya* "Splendid Balk̲" (cf. Moqaddasī, p. 302); it was equal in size to Marv and Herat, and according to Moqaddasī again, rivaled Bukhara in size. It stood on a river, the Balk̲āb (or as Ebn Ḥawqal, ed. Kramers, p. 448, names it, the Dah-ās "[turning] ten mills"), which came down from the Hindu Kush but which did not, in Islamic times, actually reach the Oxus, petering out in the sands. The Balk̲āb divided at the city into twelve branches to irrigate the surrounding countryside; among the products of this agricultural area are mentioned citrons, oranges, water-lilies, and grapes, in sufficient quantities for export, whilst the nearby open steppes were used for rearing an excellent strain of Bactrian camels. Outside these domains, however, lay salt marshes and deserts. The ruins of Nowbahār were apparently still impressive, and the author of the *Ḥodūd al-ʿālam* (372/982) mentions wall-paintings and other wonders there; by his time, construction of the original building was attributed to the Sasanian emperors. Balk̲ had the usual tripartite plan of an inner citadel (*qohandez*), an inner city (*madīna* or *šahrestān*), and an outer city or suburb (*rabaż* or *bīrūn*). There were mud brick walls (mud brick being also the normal material for the houses of Balk̲) around both the *madīna* and the *rabaż*, with a ditch beyond the outer wall; in earlier times, there had been a wall twelve *farsak̲s* long, with twelve gates, enclosing both the city and adjacent villages, as a protection from nomads and other marauders, but by the 3rd/9th century this no longer existed. In the next century, the *rabaż* seems to have had seven gates and the *madīna* four, the latter a number characteristic of a number of other Persian cities. The seven *rabaż* gates included the Bāb Hendovān, attesting the presence nearby of a colony of Indian traders, and the Bāb al-Yahūd, showing the existence of a Jewish community also (both these groups were still of significance in Balk̲ at the end of the nineteenth century, despite the complete eclipse of Balk̲ as a trading center; see C. E. Yate, *Northern Afghanistan or Letters from the Afghan Boundary Commission*, Edinburgh and London, 1888, p. 256). The *Ḥodūd al-ʿālam*, indeed, describes Balk̲ as the emporium (*bārkad̲a*) of India. The markets were mainly situated in the *madīna*, where stood the main Friday mosque; according to Yaʿqūbī, there were forty-seven mosques with *menbars* in the moderate-sized towns of the Balk̲ region. See for the information of the Arab geographers, Le Strange, *Lands*, pp. 420-22, to which should be added the Persian *Ḥodūd al-ʿālam*, tr. Minorsky, p. 108; Barthold, "*Istoriko-geograficheskiĭ obzor Irana*," in his *Sochineniya* VII, Moscow, 1971, pp. 41-44, 47-49, tr. S. Soucek, *Historical-Geographical Survey of Iran*, Princeton, 1983, pp. 25-26; Barthold, *Turkestan*³, pp. 76-79.

This commercial and economic prosperity was reflected in Balk̲'s role in nurturing ulema (*ʿolamāʾ*) and other scholars, whom Samʿānī, *Ansāb*, ed. Hyderabad, II, pp. 303-35, describes as innumerable. In fact, these included such figures as the early Sufi Abū Esḥāq Ebrāhīm b. Adham (d. 161/778), who stemmed from Balk̲ before he went westwards to Syria (cf. Ebn al-Aṯīr, VI, p. 56), the geographer and astronomer Abū Zayd Aḥmad Balk̲ī (d. 322/934), and the Muʿtazilite philosopher Abu'l-Qāsem ʿAbd-Allāh Balk̲ī (d. 319/931). Scholars like these, and especially traditionists, theologians, and religious lawyers, were surveyed and classified in the local histories and *ṭabaqāt* books on the notable men of Balk̲, one of which, a *Ketāb fażāʾel Balk̲*, was apparently written by Abū Zayd Balk̲ī himself (see Bibliography).

Thus under the Samanids, Balk̲ was especially flourishing, although the warfare of rival military factions in the last decades of the emirate affected it on certain occasions. The Ḥājeb Fāʾeq K̲āṣṣa was governor there during the ascendancy of the Sīmjūrīs in the 370s/980s, and in 381/991 he was besieged in Balk̲ by Abu'l-Ḥasan Ṭāher b. Fażl, of the Muhtajid family of Čaḡānīān; the latter was, however, killed, and Fāʾeq was confirmed in the governorship of Balk̲ and Termed̲ in 382/992 by the Qarakhanid invader of Transoxania, Boḡra Khan Hārūn. When Maḥmūd of Ḡazna and the Qarakhanids partitioned the Samanid empire between themselves, the lands north of the Oxus fell to the former, although the Qarakhanids for long coveted also northern Khorasan. Hence in 396/1006 the Ilig Khan Naṣr sent his general Čaḡritigin or Jaʿfartigin into Ṭok̲ārestān. The population of Balḵ resisted fiercely, and the city was plundered before Čaḡritigin was forced to retreat to Termeḏ on Maḥmūd's return from India, the Ilig's ambitions here being finally quelled by Maḥmūd's overwhelming victory at Katar, 12 miles from Balḵ, in 398/1008. It was during Čaḡritigin's occupations of Balḵ that the Bāzār-e ʿĀšeqān or "Lovers' market" built there by the sultan himself was destroyed; Maḥmūd later censured the people for resisting the enemy and so causing the loss of his lucrative property. We have other information about Ghaznavid constructions in the city, including mention of a fine garden laid out by Maḥmūd, whose upkeep was a burden on the local people until the sultan grudgingly transferred the onus to the local Jewish community. We also learn that the *raʾīs* or civic head of Balḵ, Abū Esḥāq Moḥammad b. Ḥosayn, supplied money to Maḥmūd for his campaigns when the flow of taxation revenues from Khorasan dried up after the exactions of the vizier Esfarāʾenī; doubtless these subventions were made by the Balḵ merchant community as a whole. See on this period, Barthold, *Turkestan*[3], pp. 253-54, 259, 272, 276, 280, 288-89, 291; M. Nāẓim, *The Life and Times of Sulṭān Maḥmūd of Ghazna*, Cambridge, 1931, pp. 31, 39, 42-43, 48-50, 154, 166; Bosworth, *Ghaznavids*, index s.v. Balkh.

Although threatened by the incursions of the Saljuqs during the latter years of Masʿūd of Ḡazna's reign, Balḵ did not, like Nīšāpūr and Marv, fall immediately into the Turkmen's hands, even after Masʿūd's disastrous defeat at Dandānqān (q.v.) in 431/1040. There seems nevertheless to have been a disaffected element in the city's population who probably wished to reach an accommodation with the Saljuqs, for Masʿūd's vizier reported the presence of large numbers of "corrupt persons, evil-wishers and malevolently-inclined people" there, and at one point it was in fact briefly occupied and plundered by the Turkmen. But Balḵ was a key point in the Ghaznavid defence system for northern Afghanistan, protecting the capital Ḡazna itself, and resistance there was organized against Čaḡri Beg Dāwūd by the local *ṣāḥeb-e barīd* Abu'l-Ḥasan Aḥmad ʿAnbarī, called Amīrak Bayhaqī (q.v.).

Despite his efforts, Balḵ seems to have passed definitely to the Saljuqs early in Mawdūd of Ḡazna's reign, for in 435/1043-44 Čaḡri Beg's son Alp Arslān, based on Balḵ, fended off a Ghaznavid attempt to reconquer northern Afghanistan. Alp Arslān was now formally invested with the governorship of all northeastern Khorasan, including Balḵ and Ṭoḵārestān, as far as the Oxus headwaters, the day-to-day running of administration here falling to Čaḡri Beg's vizier Abū ʿAlī Šāḏān; and on his accession in 451/1059 the sultan Ebrāhīm b. Masʿūd of Ḡazna made a peace treaty with Čaḡri Beg at last recognizing Saljuq control of these regions. During Alp Arslān's reign, the governor here was the sultan's son Ayāz, who was momentarily ejected from Balḵ in 456/1072 by the Qarakhanids when his father died and was soon afterwards succeeded by the new Saljuq sultan's other brother Tekiš (466/1073-74). The allocation of this northeastern corner of the Saljuq empire to princes of the ruling family not infrequently led ambitious princes into rebellion against the sultan in distant western Iran. Thus in 490/1097 Berk-Yaruq (Barkīāroq) had to spend seven months at Balḵ suppressing the outbreak of a Saljuq claimant, Moḥammad b. Solaymān b. Čaḡri Beg, called Amīr-e Amīrān, whose father had at one time been governor of Balḵ and who had received military help from the Ghaznavids.

During the first half of the 6th/12th century, Balḵ came within the extensive sultanate of the east held by Sanjar (q.v.). The city remained flourishing, not least intellectually; a Neẓāmīya *madrasa* had been built there, either by the great vizier Neẓām-al-Molk himself or with his encouragement, and in the later part of the century, the poet Anwarī (q.v.; d. 585/1189-90?) spent his last decades there. Towards the end of Sanjar's reign, however, Saljuq power in Khorasan was challenged by external rivals such as the Ḵᵛārazmšāhs and the Ghurids, and by the internal malcontent element of the Oghuz nomads who pastured their flocks in the upper Oxus region and who chafed under the heavy hand of Saljuq taxation and officialdom, including that of Sanjar's governor in Balḵ, ʿEmād-al-Dīn Qamāč. In 547/1152 the Ghurid ʿAlāʾ-al-Dīn Ḥosayn occupied Balḵ for a while with Oghuz help. In the next year the Oghuz offered conciliatory terms to Qamāč, which he shortsightedly rejected; he attacked them outside Balḵ, but was routed by them and had to flee to Sanjar's capital at Marv, leaving Balḵ to be plundered by the Oghuz, with considerable destruction of public buildings. The Oghuz now installed themselves at Balḵ, offering their obedience to Sanjar's nephew, the Qarakhanid Maḥmūd Khan, and held the city for several years. Later, suzerainty over it passed to the Qarā Ḵetāy of Transoxania, until in 594/1198 the Ghurid Bahāʾ-al-Dīn Sām b. Moḥammad of Bāmīān occupied it when its Turkish governor, a vassal of the Qarā Ḵetāy, had died, and incorporated it briefly into the Ghurid empire. Yet within a decade, Balḵ and Termeḏ passed to the Ghurids' rival, the Ḵᵛārazmšāh ʿAlāʾ-al-Dīn Moḥammad, who seized it in 602/1205-06 and appointed as governor there a Turkish commander, Čaḡri or Jaʿfar.

In summer of 617/1220 the Mongols first appeared at Balḵ. It seems that the city surrendered peacefully to the incomers, but in spring 618/1221 Jengiz Khan himself arrived there, and Balḵ was subjected to a frightful sacking, conceivably after a revolt of the populace against the Mongol garrison. Whether Balḵ did indeed have a population of 200,000 before the Mongol massacres, which last involved a large part of the populace, is unconfirmed, but certainly the agricultural and commercial activities on the eve of the invasion described by Yāqūt (*Moʿjam al-boldān* I, p. 713), when Balḵ supplied produce to Khorasan and Ḵᵛārazm, was dealt a severe blow, from which the city did not recover till Timurid times. See, for the Saljuq period and after, the standard sources for Saljuq and Mongol history (Bondārī, Rāvandī, Ebn al-Aṯīr,

Jovaynī, etc.); of secondary literature see Barthold, *Turkestan*; Bosworth and Boyle, in *Camb. Hist. Iran*, V; and Bosworth, *Later Ghaznavids*.

Bibliography: This is substantially given in the article. It should be noted that Balk̲, like other cities of Khorasan, seems to have had a lively genre of local histories and works on the excellencies and merits of the city, many of these being biographical in approach. Virtually all of these are apparently lost, but material from several of them was used by the Šayk̲-al-Eslām Abū Bakr ʿAbd-Allāh b. ʿOmar Balk̲ī for his *Ketāb fażāʾel Balk̲* (610/1214), of which a Persian translation by ʿAbd-Allāh b. Moḥammad Ḥosaynī was made at Balk̲ in 676/1278 (ed. ʿAbd-al-Ḥayy Ḥabībī, *Fażāʾel-e Balk̲*, Tehran, 1350 Š./1971; cf. Storey, I, pp. 1296-97).

(C. E. Bosworth)

iii. From the Mongols to Modern Times

The medieval and modern history of Balk̲, which has been filled with breaks and recoveries, offers a prime opportunity for a new approach to the study of the post-Mongol period in arid Central Asia. The political history and ethnic evolution of the Balk̲ oasis have essentially shared with Mā Warāʾ al-Nahr (Transoxania) frontier and population movements that can be traced until the middle of the nineteenth century. The final integration of Balk̲ into the Afghan domain was then hastened by the Anglo-Russian accord of 1873, which established the Amu Darya as the boundary between the zones of influence of the two empires.

Balk̲ belonged to the Mongol Empire after its surrender to Jengiz Khan in 617/1220 and, with Bactria, formed the southern part of what became the khanate of Chaghatay. The destruction resulting from the Mongol conquests was very severe at Balk̲, and the city remained in ruins for more than a century (Ebn Baṭṭūṭa, p. 299); for some time, however, hypotheses about the long-term consequences of this destruction have been debatable, for Balk̲ did recover some prosperity in the course of the eighth/fourteenth century. Subsequently it was a valued appanage in the territorial system of the different Jengizid ruling houses until the twelfth/eighteenth century. Thus a long period of conflicts began, on the background of the disputes over the succession and revolving around real or nominal control of these appanages. In this way the Mongol princes of the khanate of Chaghatay vied with one another, whether directly or indirectly through the intermediary of local dynasts, like the Kart rulers (*maleks*) of Herat, who were involved on several occasions.

The territorial changes brought about by the formation of Tīmūr's (Tamerlane's) empire initiated long periods of stability, which, however, began with the devastation caused by the Balk̲ campaign in 771/1369. The city was included successively in Tīmūr's, Šāhrok̲'s, and Olog̲ Beg's possessions, then, after more than twenty years of internal struggle, belonged to Sultan Ḥosayn Bāyqarā, who ruled southern Turkestan between 872/1468 and 911/1506 and established his brother Bāyqarā at Balk̲. The former died in combat against the Uzbek, who were ultimately victorious, after the short reigns of two of his sons, and established themselves permanently as far as the Hindu Kush. The period of Tīmūr and his descendants, the Timurids, was recognized from the beginning as favorable to the development of urban civilization (Clavijo, pp. 141-48).

The subsequent Uzbek period lasted three centuries, the longest in the post-Mongol history of Balk̲. The establishment of the Uzbeks was reflected in major construction activity at Balk̲ (Mukhtarov, pp. 17-97), which became the third or fourth most important city of their empire. The written reports on Shaibanid and Janid Balk̲ are quite numerous, and many contemporary authors came from this center of power or lived there (Akhmedov, pp. 3-14; Mukhtarov, pp. 8-16). The position of Balk̲ in relation to Bukhara improved in the eleventh/seventeenth century: It became the second most important city in the Bukharan domain and the capital of the heirs to the Janid throne. This important position, however, attracted invaders and led to redefinition of international frontiers in the region.

From the west the Safavids installed themselves in Khorasan; the Uzbeks recaptured Balk̲ from them in 922/1516. From the southeast came the Mughals; their occupation of Balk̲, from 1051/1641 to 1057/1647, under the command from 1056/1646 of Awrangzēb, who then became emperor, represented a last attempt to restore the old domain of Bābor. The episode of Nāder Shah a hundred years later was equally transitory. On the other hand, the birth of Dorrānī Afghanistan turned the Amu Darya into a frontier, where first *atalīks*, then Mangit amirs of Bukhara struggled with the Sadōzay and Moḥammadzay rulers of Afghanistan for a century. In 1164/1751 Aḥmad Shah incorporated Balk̲ into a political entity unconnected with Mā Warāʾ al-Nahr for the first time since the Mongol conquest. In 1257/1841 the Afghans permanently recaptured the city from the Bukharans, who had reestablished themselves there in 1241/1826 (Ivanov, pp. 107ff.). The suzerainty of the latter did not come to an end, however, until Bukhara itself lost its sovereignty in 1285/1868. Balk̲, which had shrunk to a large village during the twelfth/eighteenth century, finally lost its status as an administrative center in 1282/1866, in favor of Mazār-e Šarīf. Reduced to 500 households by the beginning of the twentieth century, the population of Balk̲ has since increased but is still only one tenth that of its neighbor.

The conditions of recent decline at Balk̲ show that standard explanations of the frequent periods of crisis in the history of the Central Asian oases must often be revised. At Balk̲, both the population and the number of canals have diminished since the twelfth/eighteenth century, the latter dropping from eighteen to eleven. These facts, along with the importance of nomads around Balk̲ and the supposed drying up of the Balk̲āb (q.v.), could all be taken as evidence of the evolution of a typical post-Mongol Central Asian city. "It is only within the last 750 years that Balkh has fallen on evil days" (Toynbee, p. 95). The decline of Balḵ in favor of Mazār-e Šarīf must be viewed aside from the question of the so-called tomb of ʿAlī, within the framework of solidarities resulting from the irrigation networks: The two cities form part of the same oasis and depend on the same supply line through the canals from the Balḵāb. It thus seems more significant for the history of the development of the oasis to emphasize the migration of urban population from there to Mazār-e Šarīf, via Taḵta Pol, rather than contrast the modern village with the large ancient city. In fact, with about 30,000 inhabitants in 1295/1878 and 100,000 today, Mazār-e Šarīf demonstrates the capacity of the irrigation system in the oasis, where present population density is between 30 and 100 inhabitants per square kilometer (*Tübinger Atlas*, A VIII 3), to continue to support the largest city in Afghan Turkestan, as it has done in the past.

The cultural character of the Balḵ oasis today reflects the ethnic and political shifts in its post-Mongol history. The Turkish populations, especially the Uzbeks but also the Turkmen, predominate over the Tajiks. There are also colonies of Pashtun, though fewer than in the Maymana and Tāšqorḡān oases; one Jewish community; and some Arabic-speaking villages (*Tübinger Atlas*, A VIII 16). The linguistic picture is differentiated, including an important component of the Fārsī of Balḵ, but it corroborates the profound Uzbekization of the region (*Tübinger Atlas*, A VIII 11).

See also BALḴĀB.

Bibliography: An initial attempt to make use of the Arabic geographers to follow the continuous course of the history of Balḵ was that of V. V. Barthold, *Istoriko-geograficheskiĭ obzor Irana* I: *Baktriya, Balkh i Tokharistan*, Sochineniya 7, Moscow, 1971, pp. 39-59. In this article Barthold throws doubt on the assertion that in antiquity the Balḵāb flowed into the Oxus. For a history of Balḵ on the eve of the Mongol conquest see Abū Bakr Wāʿeẓ Balḵī, *Fażāʾel-e Balḵ*, Pers. tr. ʿAbd-Allāh Moḥammad Ḥosaynī Balḵī, ed. ʿA. Ḥabībī, Tehran, 1351 Š./1972. The situation of Balḵ after the Mongol conquest is described by *Ebn Baṭṭūṭa* (Paris) II, pp. 299. The ruling dynasties of the khanate of Chaghatay have been reconstructed from the Chinese and Islamic lists by L. Hambis, "Le chapitre VII du Yuan Che," *T'oung Pao* 38, supplement, 1945, pp. 57-64. A report on the prosperity of Timurid Balḵ is furnished by Ruy Gonzalez de Clavijo, *Embajada a Tamorlan*, ed. by F. Lopez Estrada, Madrid, 1943, pp. 141-48. A history of the Timurid period is the *Maṭlaʿ-e saʿdayn*, by ʿAbd-al-Razzāq Samarqandī. Since the first great Uzbek chronicles were published by A. A. Semenov, more and more works of commentary and editions of Shaibanid and Janid texts have been issued. Particularly noteworthy is *Baḥr al-asrār fī manāqeb al-akyār*, a work by Maḥmūd b. Amīr Walī, prepared on the orders of the Janid governor of the town, Nāder-Moḥammad, translated by Riazul Islam, Karachi, 1980; and the publication of part of the eighteenth-century *Tarīḵ-e raḥīmī*, of which only two of the many manuscripts, mss. D. 710 and C. 1683, contain the list of the eighteen medieval and modern irrigation canals; cf. M. A. Salakhetdinova, "K istoricheskoĭ toponomike Balkhskoĭ oblasti," *Palestinskiĭ sbornik* 21/84, 1970, pp. 222-28; the most recent bibliographies of the published and unpublished Timurid, Uzbek, and Afghan sources on Balḵ can be found in B. A. Akhmedov, *Istoriya Balkha*, Tashkent, 1982, and A. Mukhtarov, *Pozdnesrednevekovyĭ Balkh*, Dushanbe, 1980. The former work also represents the most thorough study on the Uzbek khanate of Balḵ and the latter provides the most complete description of the evolving topography of the city and the transition from the Timurid to the Uzbek period; it also gives a list of the eighteen *nahr* and the *jūy* connected with each, cf. pp. 99-109. For the entire Uzbek period in central Asia, see I. P. Ivanov, *Ocherki po istorii Sredneĭ Azii*, Moscow, 1958. For the historical ethnography and Uzbekization of the area, see B. K. Karmysheva, *Ocherki etnicheskoĭ istorii yuzhnykh rayonov Tadzhikistana i Uzbekistana*, Moscow, 1976. For geography, see J. Humlum, *La géographie de l'Afghanistan*, Copenhagen, 1959; and *Tübinger Atlas des Vorderen Orients*, Section 9, Series A, Wiesbaden, 1984. See also A. Toynbee, *Between Oxus and Jamna*, London, 1961.

(V. FOURNIAU)

iv. MODERN TOWN

The crisis in Balḵ's urban evolution came in the mid-13/19th century. Great damage was done to the town and the surrounding area in the troubled times following its destruction by the amir of Bukhara in 1840 and its recapture by the Afghans of Dōst Moḥammad in 1850, which gave rise to an exodus of many of its Uzbek inhabitants. A further cause of decline was lack of maintenance of the irrigation canals. One of the results was that Balḵ became a very unhealthy place, and it is therefore not surprising that the Afghans, when again in control after 1850, preferred to base their governorate of Turkestan at Taḵta Pol near Mazār-e Šarīf, later at Mazār-e Šarīf itself. The exact date of the move from Balḵ is uncertain (in 1866, according to Barthold, *EI*[1] III, p. 430; during Moḥammad-Afżal Khan's governorship of Afghan Turkestan, according to Peacocke, in *Gazetteer of Afghanistan* IV, p. 110; after 1878, according to Grodekoff, *Ride from Samarcand to Harat*, London, 1880, p. 80, quoted by Centlivres, p. 124). It may be that at first only a temporary move was intended. In any case the transference was complete and final when the British frontier delimitation commission passed through in 1886. Balḵ's population was then reckoned to be some 600 families of Tājīks, Uzbeks, and Arabs, of whom 100 were old local families, together with 40 Jewish families and a community of 20 Hindu families originally from Shikarpur in Sind. All lived in the southeastern quarter of the old town inside the wall. The *bāzār* then had 60 shops. In addition to the permanent inhabitants, there was a floating population of about 1000 Pashtun families in the town and outside the wall. Another source, however, speaks of only 200 Tājīk families (*Gazetteer of Afghanistan* IV, p. 112; cf. C. E. Yate, *Northern Afghanistan*, Edinburgh and London, 1888, pp. 255ff.). The decline continued in the following decades. The sketches of Balk̲ in the first world war by Niedermayer (p. 48) and in 1924 by Foucher (I, p. 59) depict a mean village of hovels situated to the south of the citadel with a still existing Jewish quarter to the west.

A new phase set in when work on the construction of a new town began in 1934. It was laid out geometrically in concentric circles around a central square with eight radial arteries. The initial plan was overambitious, providing for 1,270 houses together with a large *bāzār* of some 400 shops and 32 *sarāy*s (K. Ziemke, *Als deutscher Gesandter in Afghanistan*, Berlin, 1939, p. 229). Actual achievement fell far short; in 1973 (according to Grötzbach, p. 105) only 430 houses had been built and demand for them was weak, the attraction of Mazār-e Šarīf still being dominant throughout the region. According to the preliminary returns of the 1979 census, Balk̲ then had only 7,242 inhabitants (communication from D. Balland). Even so, its economic role was by no means negligible. It became an important market for agricultural produce (cotton, melons, almonds, karakul pelts). Buyers from Mazār-e Šarīf came on the market days (Monday and Thursdays) to take advantage of the lower prices, and two-way business with Mazār-e Šarīf grew after the start of a regular bus service. Four cotton firms, two of which had ginneries, were located in Balk̲ and its outskirts. After the opening of the asphalted Mazār-e Šarīf-Šeberḡān highway with a 2 km branch to Balk̲ in 1970, Balk̲ began to attract tourists. From 1972 onward it had the benefit of electricity generated by gas from fields in the region. It also possessed a good primary school and a small hospital. Though only 20 km from Mazār-e Šarīf, Balk̲ ranked as a small independent center.

Bibliography: L. W. Adamec, ed., *Gazetteer of Afghanistan* IV, 1979, pp. 98-112. O. von Niedermayer and E. Diez, *Afghanistan*, Leipzig, 1924. A. Foucher, *La vieille route de l'Inde de Bactres à Taxila*, MDAFA 1, 2 vols., Paris, 1942-47. M. Le Berre and D. Schlumberger, "Observations sur les remparts de Bactres," in B. Dagens et al., *Monuments préislamiques d'Afghanistan*, MDAFA 19, Paris, 1964, pp. 61-105. P. Centlivres, "Structure et évolution des bazars du Nord Afghan," in E. Grötzbach, ed., *Aktuelle Probleme der Regionalentwicklung und Stadtgeographie Afghanistans*, Afghanische Studien 14, Meisenheim am Glan, 1976. E. Grötzbach, *Städte und Basare in Afghanistan: Eine stadtgeographische Untersuchung*, Beihefte zum Tübinger Atlas des Vorderen Orients, series B, no. 16, Wiesbaden, 1979. A. Mukhtarov, *Pozdnesrednevekovyĭ Balkh* (*Materialy k istoriciheskoĭ topografii goroda v XVI-XVIII vv.*), Dushanbe, 1980. B. A. Akhmedov, *Istoriya Balkha* (*XVI-pervaya golovnia XVIII v.*), Tashkent, 1982.

(X. de Planhol)

Table 16

POPULATION OF BALK̲ PROVINCE, AFGHANISTAN (1978-79)

Name of district	1 Area (km²)	2 Total sedentary population (1979)	3 Density (Inhab./km²)	4 Urban population (percent)	5 Wintering nomads (tents)	6 Number of tents in summer 1978 (all semi-nomads)
Mazār-e Šarīf (center of province)	48	103,400	2,154	100	—	—
Woloswālī:						
Balk̲	481	70,000	145	10	—	283
Čārbōlak	511	45,500	89	—	—	—
Čemtāl	1,732	50,000	29	—	28	1,070
Dawlatābād	864	65,400	76	9	—	—
Nahr-e Šāhī (1)	1,771	32,000	18	—	45	—
Šōlgara	1,663	73,300	44	8	110	1,095
Šōrtapa	1,284	25,000	19	—	—	—
ʿAlāqadārī:						
Čārkent	1,445	29,500	20	—	—	—
Deh Dādī	233	32,500	140	—	—	—
Kešendeh	1,801	42,700	24	—	—	1,135
Total of province	11,833	569,300	48	22	183 (2)	3,583 (3)

Sources: Columns 1 to 4, *Natāyej-e moqaddamātī-e nok̲ostīn saršomārī-e nofūs*, Kabul, 1359 Š./1981. Figures have been rounded. Columns 5 to 6, D. Balland and A. de Benoist, *Nomades et semi-nomades d'Afghanistan*, forthcoming. Notes: (1) In 1363 Š./1984 this *woloswālī* was shrunk by the establishment of the Mārmol *ʿalāqadārī* for which no statistics are available. (2) These nomads spend summer in northern Hazārajāt (q.v.). (3) Local migrants; most claim to be Uzbek (1, 180 tents, i.e., 33, percent), Arab (1,040 tents: 29 percent) or Hazāra (820 tents: 23 percent). Only 140 tents claim a Pashtun descent.

Table 17

LAND USE IN BALḴ PROVINCE, AFGHANISTAN (1967)

Name of district	Cultivated lands (ha)			Forests (ha)	Percent of irrigated land under				Water mills (units)
	Irrigated (*ābī*)	Non-irrigated (*lalmī*)	Fallow		Canals	Springs	*Kārēz*	Wells	
Mazār-e Šarīf	—	—	—	—	—	—	—	—	—
Woloswālī:									
Balḵ	40,186	—	8,038	—	100	—	—	—	69
Čārbōlak	47,706	—	9,592	—	100	—	—	—	54
Čemtāl	30,810	6,858	9,540	—	100	—	—	—	45
Dawlatābād	62,584	—	12,516	—	100	—	—	—	121
Nahr-e Šāhī	21,858	3,778	6,262	11,492	99.8	0.2	—	—	160
Šōlgara	6,098	19,074	10,752	58,592	99.7	0.1	—	0.2	139
Šōrtapa	2,572	—	514	126	100	—	—	—	56
ʿAlāqadārī:									
Čārkent	18	26,516	13,262	234	67	22	11	—	90
Deh Dādī	11,368	1,388	2,968	—	98.8	1	—	0.2	133
Kešendeh	1,300	31,072	15,796	456	99.9	0.1	—	—	45
Total of province	224,500	88,686	89,240	70,900	99.9	0.1	<0.1	<0.1	912

Source: *Natāyej-e eḥṣāʾīyagīrī sarwē-ye moqaddamātī-e zerāʿatī sāl-e 1346 Š.*, Kabul, n.d., 7 vols. The figures are only very rough estimates; the reliability of some of them may be questionable.

v. Modern Province

Balḵ is a province (*welāyat*) of northern Afghanistan which covers 11,833 km². In 1363 Š./1984 it was divided into seven districts (*woloswālī*) and four subdistricts (*ʿalāqadārī*). The main town and provincial capital is Mazār-e Šarīf (q.v.) and three more localities within the province have urban status (Balḵ, Dawlatābād and Šōlgara or Boynaqara).

Balḵ province was created in 1343 Š./1964 out of the former and much larger province of Mazār-e Šarīf.

See Tables 16 and 17 for compilation of main available data about population and land use in the province, districts, and subdistricts.

(D. Balland)

vi. Monuments of Balḵ

The successive city-walls. The mud ramparts of Balḵ which still survive, superimposed one upon the other, at an impressive length and height, more than 20 m at the citadel (Bālā-Ḥeṣār) and on the southern side, are the most substantial remains of the ancient periods of the "Mother of Cities." Archeological examination of these ramparts has provided the key to the successive stages of the topographical development of the town (see Le Berre and Schlumberger). The initial limit is represented by the Bālā-Ḥeṣār ("Balḵ I"); its circular plan is probably inherited from the Achaemenian period, while its present Timurid circuit-wall largely reuses the massive Greek rampart which, in 208-06 B.C., withstood the attack of the Seleucid Antiochus III. From the Greek period also dates a gigantic wall built against the nomadic incursions along the northern edge of the oasis, where its remains have been traced for a length of 60 km (Kruglikova; Pugachenkova, 1976); it is mentioned as still in use by Yaʿqūbī (fl. 276/889), and it sheltered other important towns, mainly Delbarjīn (Greek-Kushan period) and Zādīān-Dawlatābād (Saljuq period).

The development of a southern suburb of Balḵ along the caravan-road to India led to a first extension of the walled city ("Balḵ IA": late Greek or Kushan period). At some time between the Kushans and the Islamic conquest it was further enlarged to the east ("Balḵ II"). These walls with square towers remained in use until Balḵ was thoroughly destroyed in 617/1220 by the Mongols of Jengiz Khan.

In 765/1363 the Bālā-Ḥeṣār was reoccupied by Amir Ḥosayn, after which Tīmūr and his successors completely refortified the whole city while slightly moving it to the west, probably because the eastern part had become marshy after the destruction of the irrigation system. This last rampart (Balḵ III), made of heterogeneous materials extracted from the ruins left by the Mongols, had semi-circular towers, and was adorned at its southern side by the monumental Bābā-Kōh gate (or Nowbahār gate; now destroyed) and by the Borj-e ʿAyyārān, an eight-arched belvedere (Foucher, p. 164, pl. VI; Mukhtarov, pp. 21-42).

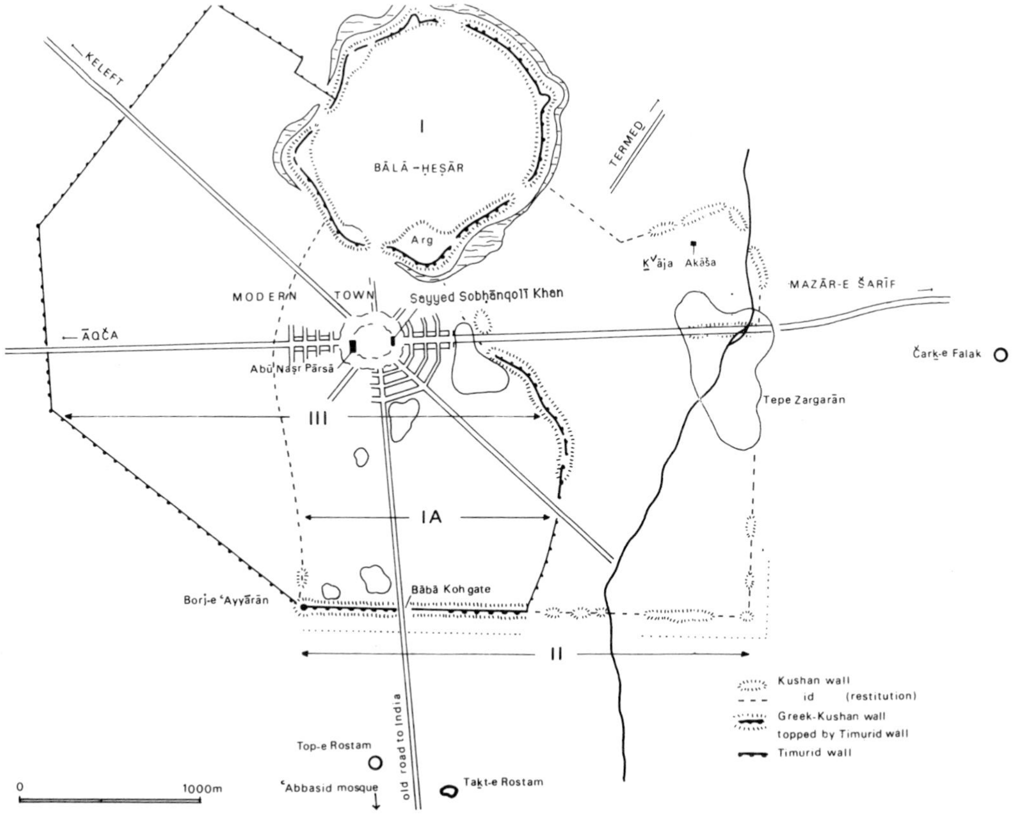

Figure 15. Monuments of Balk̲

The Buddhistic remains. Apart from the ramparts, the only monuments which have survived from pre-Islamic Balk̲ are Buddhistic *stūpa*s, which owed their preservation to the massivity of their mud-brick masonry. Four, all standing along the roads on the outskirts of the city, were identified by A. Foucher in 1924-25; the Top-e Rostam, in the south, was the only one he excavated. Although greatly ruined and stripped of all its decoration, it can be reconstructed as the most monumental *stūpa* witnessed north of the Hindu Kush (dimensions: square platform 54 × 54 m, cylindrical dome 47 m in diameter, total height probably ca. 60 m). Its location and size correspond to those of the "New Monastery" described in the 7th century by the Chinese pilgrim Hsüan-tsang (Th. Watton, *On Yuan Chwang's Travels in India* I, London, 1904, pp. 108-09); otherwise known as the Nowbahār (from Sanskrit *nava-vihāra*), it is renowned in the Islamic sources because the Buddhist ancestors of the Barmakids had been its administrators. But the neighboring Tak̲t-e Rostam, a steep mound sometimes considered the remains of the convent itself, looks rather like the mud platform of an early medieval manor (*kōšk*). Two other *stūpa*s, the Čark̲-e Falak and the Āsīā-ye Kohnak, have mosques grafted onto their remains, a clear indication of the continuity of cult-places (Foucher, pp. 83-98, 168-69, pls. XIX-XXII; Mélikian-Chirvani, 1974).

Pre-Mongol Islamic monuments. A building of outstanding interest is an ʿAbbasid suburban mosque known locally as Noh Gombad or Ḥājī Pīād, which was discovered in 1966, at a short distance south of the Top-e Rostam. Built of baked bricks, it consists of four round pillars standing in the center of a square (20 × 20 m) formed by three curtain walls and an open façade which is articulated on two more pillars; the pillars were linked to each other and to coupled columns attached to the walls by perpendicular arcades, the inner space being thereby divided into nine equal squares, each of which originally supported a dome. A deeply carved stucco ornamentation still covers the capitals, imposts, and bases of the pillars, as well as the spandrels and soffits of the arches; the motifs include grape leaves, freely moving vine-scrolls, fir-cones, palmettes, rosettes, set in interlacing straps and thickly packed so as to fill up the panels almost entirely. Neither the architectural composition nor the decoration have their direct origin in the Central-Asian tradition (which, for example, ignored the open arcatures); they rather represent the direct transposition of a model which took shape in the heart of the ʿAbbasid empire and from there spread both east and west (where the clearest examples now surviving are to be found, especially some religious monuments of Tulunid Egypt). The stucco ornament has its closest parallels in the styles A and B of Samarra, which indicates the first half of the 9th century as the most probable date of construction (Pugachenkova, 1968; Golombek; differently Mélikian-Chirvani, 1969).

The only other monument which can be ascribed to the pre-Mongol Islamic period is the plain, single-chambered, domed mausoleum known as Bābā Rōšnay (at the southwest of the Bālā-Ḥeṣār; first half of the 11th century; Pugachenkova, 1978, pp. 31-32).

Timurid and Ashtarkhanid monuments. 3 kms to the east of the outer wall stands the mausoleum locally known as Mīr-e Rūzadār, surrounded by ornamented brick burial enclosures. The mausoleum preserves an elaborate interior decoration (angular interlacing ribbed design on the dome and niches, enhanced by painting); but the outer dome and exterior facing are lacking, which has led to the supposition that the monument remained unfinished because of the political troubles of the 1440s (Pugachenkova, 1978, pp. 33-35; Mukhtarov, pp. 75-83). Its architectural composition expresses the Timurid taste for the octagonal tomb-chamber, with external vaulted niches hollowed in the facets and angles, and projection entrance-room. The same composition is repeated, with variations, at the later mausoleums of Ḵᵛāja Bajgāhī (eastern edge of the town; 17th cent.) and Ḵᵛāja Akāša; it is also to be found, in a more sophisticated form, at the funerary mosque of Ḵᵛāja Abū Naṣr Pārsā, perhaps the most famous monument of Balḵ. It was erected in 867/1462-63, shortly after the death of the theologian, who is buried in the platform which lies in front. The usual entrance-room is replaced here by a tall *pēštāq* flanked by two minarets, each of which is preceded by slender corkscrew pillars. The whole of the façade and the fluted outer dome were veneered in *kāšī* whose predominant tint is a cold silvery blue; their manufacture was of the best quality, but due to an inadequate mode of fixation large surfaces have collapsed. The interior, lighted by sixteen lattice openings at the basis of the drum, is richly ornamented by a well-preserved angular interlace of stucco, completed by painted floral motives (Pugachenkova, 1970). Together with the contemporary mosque at Anau (Turkmenistan), this monument represents one of the finest examples of late Timurid memorial architecture.

Balḵ had a late flourish under the Ashtarkhanid dynasty, when it formed the apanage of the heirs to the throne of Bukhara (1007-1164/1599-1751). From this time dates the *madrasa* built by the Sayyed Sobḥānqolī Khan in the last years of the 11th/17th century; only the tiled entrance *ayvān* remains, facing the mosque of Abū Naṣr Pārsā in the garden which is now the center of the town. The ruins of the governor's palace, including a small mosque, which were excavated by Foucher in the Arg of the Bālā-Heṣār, cannot be precisely dated but obviously belong to the late Islamic period also (Foucher, pp. 98-112, 165-66, pls. XI-XVIII).

Bibliography: The successive phases of the archeological exploration of Balḵ are described in: O. von Niedermayer and E. Diez, *Afghanistan*, Leipzig, 1924, pp. 204-05 (brief description of the main Islamic monuments); A. Foucher, *La vieille route de l'Inde de Bactres à Taxila*, MDAFA 1, vol. 1, Paris, 1942, pp. 55-121, 163-70, pls. V-XXVI (general survey; excavations at the Top-e Rostam and at the citadel); M. Le Berre and D. Schlumberger, "Observations sur les remparts de Bactres," in *Monuments préislamiques d'Afghanistan*, MDAFA 19, Paris, 1964, pp. 61-105 pl. XXXII-XLV, figs, 10-19 (study of the successive city-walls; supersedes R.S. Young, "The South Wall of Balkh-Bactra," *American Journal of Archaeology* 59, 1955, pp. 267-76; completed by J. Cl. Gardin, *Céramiques de Bactres*, MDAFA 15, Paris, 1957). The wall of the oasis is studied by I. T. Kruglikova, *Dil'berdzhin* [I], Moscow, 1974, pp. 9-15, and by G. A. Pugachenkova, "K poznaniyu antichnoĭ i rannesrednevekovoĭ arkhitektury Severnogo Afganistana," in *Drevnyaya Baktriya* I, ed. I. T. Kruglikova, Moscow, 1976, pp. 137-41. On the Nowbahār/Top-e Rostam see also A. S. Mélikian-Chirvani, "L'évocation littéraire du bouddhisme dans l'Iran musulman," *Le monde iranien et l'Islam* 2, Geneva and Paris, 1974, pp. 10-23 (discusses the Islamic sources); K. Fischer, Indische Baukunst islamischer Zeit, Baden-Baden, 1976, p. 131. The Islamic monuments have been seriously studied for 20 years only. On the 'Abbasid mosque: G. A. Pugachenkova (Pougatchenkova), "Les monuments peu connus de l' architecture médiévale de l'Afghanistan," *Afghanistan* 21/1, 1968, pp. 17-27; A. S. Mélikian-Chirvani, "La plus ancienne mosquée de Balkh," *Arts Asiatiques* 20, 1969, pp. 3-19; L. Golombek, "Abbasid Mosque at Balkh," *Oriental Art* 25, 1969, pp. 173-89. On the mosque of Abū Naṣr Pārsā: G. A. Pugachenkova, "A l'étude des monuments timourides d'Afghanistan," *Afghanistan* 23/3, 1970, pp. 33-37; eadem, *Zodchestvo Tsentral'noĭ Azii XV vek*, Tashkent, 1976, pp. 30 and 61. On other monuments recently discovered: Eadem, "Little Known Monuments of the Balkh Area," *Art and Archaeology Research Papers*, London, June, 1978, pp. 31-40. A. Mukhtarov, *Pozdnesrednevekovyĭ Balkh*, Dushanbe, 1980.

(F. GRENET)

BALḴĀB (Bactros of the classical authors), the river of Balḵ (locally pronounced Balḵaw). This perennial river is a major feature of the geography of northern Afghanistan. The 4th/10th-century geographers Eṣṭaḵrī (p. 278) and Ebn Ḥawqal (p. 488, tr. Kramers, p. 433) call it the Dah-ās (ten-mills) river, because a total of ten mills were driven by its waters. The name Dah-ās was still in use in the 13th/19th century (J. P. Ferrier, *Caravan Journeys and Wanderings in Persia, Afghanistan, Turkistan, and Beloochistan*, London, 1857, repr. Westmead, 1971 and Karachi, 1976, p. 224), though apparently then given only to one of its delta branches. It is called the "river of Balk" by the author of *Ḥodūd al-ʿālam* (pp. 38, 43, tr. Minorsky, pp. 70, 73, 336), a name often applied to the Oxus (Jeyḥūn) by early Muslim geographers (e.g., Eṣṭakrī, pp. 6, 12, 143; Moqaddasī, pp. 19, 23). It passed by the towns Madr and Rebāṭ-e Karvān in the regions of Andarāb and Gūzgānān before it reached the plain of Balk where it passed by the Nowbahār Gate of the city, branched off into twelve irrigation canals, and finally reached Sīāhgerd on the road to Termed in the north. Its water was all used for irrigation (Eṣṭakrī, p. 278; Ebn Ḥawqal, p. 488; *Ḥodūd al-ʿālam*, p. 99, tr. Minorsky, p. 108).

The Balkāb is 471 km long, and the area which it drains has been estimated at 19,250 km^2, for the most part mountainous country. Its course starts at the point, about 2,880 m above sea level, where the cascade-like outlets of the Band-e Amīr (q.v.) lakes in the Kūh-e Bābā converge. For this reason the upper course is called the Band-e Amīr River. The use of this name has also been extended to reaches further downstream (C. E. Yate, *Northern Afghanistan*, Edinburgh, 1888, repr. Lahore, 1976, p. 255). Flowing initially in a southwestward direction, the Balkāb pierces the ridges of the Kūh-e Bābā and its northern outliers (known as the Kūh-e Balkāb) in a series of narrow defiles and sharp bends before finally taking a northward direction. After leaving the final gorge of Kūh-e Alborz the Balkāb debouches onto the Bactrian piedmont. Here it has formed a huge alluvial fan of more than 2,000 km^2, on which it splits into divergent arms so as to form a real inland delta. Along its very twisty lower course of about 100 km, which runs at an oblique angle to the westernmost generatrix of the alluvial fan, successive distributaries branch off between Pol-e Emām Bokrī at the head of the fan, where six separate channels diverge, and a place called Seh Darak 12 km upstream from Āqča (q.v.), where the Balkāb splits into three arms and loses its distinct identity.

Any water left over at the end of each distributary is now lost when it reaches the sands of the Afghan Kara Kum, which separate the Bactrian piedmont from the valley of the Āmū Daryā (Oxus). On the other hand, traces of old branches running well beyond the present forward limit of the delta have recently been discovered by Soviet archeologists (A. V. Vinogradov, "Issledovaniya pamyatnikov kamennogo veka v severnom Afganistane," in *Drevnyaya Baktriya* II, Moscow, 1979, pp. 7-62, esp. p. 14). Moreover, the distribution of the archeological sites from different period and the lie of the ancient great wall built to protect the Balkāb oasis attest to a crucial phase of delta retreat sometime between the Achaemenid and the Kushan periods (I.T. Kruglikova and V. I. Sarianidi, "Pyat'. let raboty sovetsko-afganskoĭ arkheologicheskoĭ ekspeditsii," ibid., I, 1976, pp. 3-20, see map p. 16). It is suggested that some undetermined natural factor (neotectonic movement, change of course following an exceptional flood?) may have caused this retreat, which is greatest in the center of the deltaic structure, reaching 10-12 km in the vicinity of Dalberjīn and Dašlī as against 4-5 km in that of Nečka and Altin Tepe to the east (V. I. Sarianidi, *Drevnie zemledel'tsy Afganistana*, Moscow, 1977, pp. 28-30). The delta has thus acquired its present bilobate front. Its moribund parts are mainly occupied by expanses of uncultivable salt-encrusted clay.

The Balkāb throughout its course has a regime typical of snow-fed mountain rivers. High water occurs in May and June when the snow on the Kūh-e Bābā is melting. At Rebāṭ-e Bālā, where the river enters the lowland, its average discharge in that season is approximately 100 m^3 per second. A peak of 531 m^3 per second was recorded on 29 May 1977. The low water season normally shows a somewhat greater drop in winter, when the snow lies on the ground, than in summer and autumn, when rain is rare. The lowest discharge recorded at Rebāṭ-e Bālā was 16.7 m^3 per second on 12 July 1971. The lakes in the upper part of the Balkāb basin perform a remarkably effective regulatory function in moderating seasonal and annual fluctuations of the discharge, as Table 18 shows.

Up to the point where the river enters the Bactrian lowland, the discharge shows a constant increase. This is due to the fact that in the mountains it receives many tributaries and its valleys being narrow, little water is diverted for irrigation, except in the small plains of Nayak (Yakāwlang) on the upper course and Boynaqara (Šōlgara) lower down. Thanks to the resultant

Table 18

DISCHARGE OF THE BALKĀB RIVER AT SELECTED STATIONS

Gauging station (with altitude)	Period of record	Mean discharge (m^3/sec)	Specific discharge (l/sec/km^2)	Ratio of maximum to minimum mean monthly discharge	Ratio of maximum to minimum annual discharge
Below Band-e Amīr (2,882 m)	1969-76	1.4	3.3	2.5	1.5
Nayak (2,580 m)	1969-78	5.4	3.7	3.9	1.9
Rebāṭ-e Bālā (432 m)	1964-78	49.4	2.7	2.9	2.6

abundance of the available water, the Balḵāb's alluvial fan is the biggest oasis in central Bactria. It is usually called the Balḵ oasis though it stretches without interruption from Mazār-e Šarīf to Āqča. An appropriate name for it would be Balḵāb oasis.

The irrigation network is very old, the first communities of oasis cultivators having come into being in the Bronze Age (e.g., at Dašlī), and its development has been complex. Some of the canals are mere natural distributaries which were fixed and brought under control. Others are wholly man-made and fed by means of diversion dams such as the Band-e Sūḵta southwest of Balḵ. The *Ḥodūd al-ʿālam* (p. 99, tr. Minorsky, p. 108) gives the number of the principal irrigation canals in the 4th/10th century as twelve. Modern sources, while differing as to the names of the canals, generally agree in putting their number at eighteen, which accords with the name Haždah Nahr often given to the whole oasis area (A. Mukhtarov, *Pozdnesrednevekovyĭ Balkh*, Dushanbe, 1980, pp. 101ff.; L. W. Adamec, ed., *Gazetteer of Afghanistan* IV, 1979, pp. 249-64). In a recent but unreliable report, the total is given as only eleven (Asian Development Bank, *Technical Assistance to the Government of Afghanistan for the Balkh River Irrigation Project*, n.p., 1971).

In the 19th century, when the local rural depopulation was at its height, the volume of the unused water was great enough to generate extensive marshes around Āqča (C. E. Yate, op. cit., pp. 255, 267) and even in the heart of the oasis (F. E. Ross, ed., *Central Asia: Personal Narrative of General Josiah Harlan 1823-1841*, London, 1939, p. 26). Since then, cultivation in the oasis has been considerably expanded. Water losses, however, are still substantial as a result of seasonal fluctuations in the discharge of the Balḵāb. With a view to better management of the water, a contract with the Soviet government for construction of a reservoir dam at Čašma-ye Šafā in the Kūh-e Alborz gorge was signed in 1355 Š./1976. The contract also provided for a hydroelectric generating station and remodeling of the irrigation network in the oasis. Preliminary studies were undertaken before the revolution of 1357 Š./1978 but, so far as is known, constructional work has not yet been started.

Balḵāb is also the name of a district (*ʿalāqadārī*) in the province of Jawzjān. It covers 2,476 km² in the middle part of the basin of the river of the same name. The census of 1358 Š./1979 recorded its population as 27,900. Its administrative center is Tarḵō, also called Tarḵōj (altitude 1,750 m).

Bibliography: Given in the text. See also Markwart, *Ērānšahr*, p. 230; idem, *Wehrot und Arang*, Leiden, 1938, pp. 3f.; Pauly-Wissowa, II/2, col. 2814; and the following hydrological reports: V. L. Shul'ts, *Reki Afganistana*, Moscow, 1968; Ministry of Water and Power, *Hydrological Yearbook 1964-1975, Part IV-9 to 13* (*Murghab, Shirintagab, Sarepul, Balkh and Khulm River Basins*, Kabul n.d.); idem, *Hydrological Yearbook 1976-1978, Part IV* (*North Flowing Rivers*), Kabul, 1980.

(D. BALLAND)

BALḴĪ, ABŪ ʿALĪ ʿABD-ALLĀH B. MOḤAMMAD B. ʿALĪ, a traditionist (*moḥaddeṯ*) and author. The date of his birth is not known, but may be placed around 220/835-225/840 because one of his teachers, Qotayba b. Saʿīd Abū Rajāʾ Ṯaqafī Balḵī, died at Baḡlān near Balḵ in 240/854. Also mentioned as Abū ʿAlī Balḵī's teachers are ʿAlī b. Ḥojr Abu'l-Ḥasan Marvazī (d. 244/858) and Moḥammad b. Yaḥyā Abū ʿAbd-Allāh Ḏohlī Nīsābūrī (d. 258/272). Little is known about his life. He resided for a time at Nīšāpūr, where his pupil Aḥmad b. Moḥammad Abū Ḥāmed Šarqī Nīsābūrī (d. 325/937) probably studied with him, and in his later years at Baghdad, where he taught his best known pupils Moḥammad b. Maḵlad Abū ʿAbd-Allāh Dūrī (d. 331/943), ʿAbd-al-Bāqī b. Qāneʿ Abu'l-Ḥosayn Omawī (d. 351/962), Moḥammad b. ʿAbd-Allāh Abū Bakr Šāfeʿī (d. 354/965), and Moḥammad b. ʿOmar Abū Bakr Jeʿābī (d. 355/966). Finally he returned to his homeland Balḵ. He was murdered at Balḵ by Qarmaṭī assassins late in 295/907-08. Two works, now lost, are attributed to him; *Ketāb-al-taʾrīḵ* on history and *Ketāb al-ʿelal* on flaws in Hadith transmission.

Bibliography: *Taʾrīḵ Baḡdād* X, pp. 93-94. Ebn al-Jawzī, *al-Montaẓam fī taʾrīḵ al-molūk wa'l-omam* VI, Hyderabad, 1357/1938, p. 79. Ḏahabī, *Ḥoffāẓ*³ II, Hyderabad, 1376/1956, p. 690. Idem, *al-ʿEbar fī ḵabar man ḡabar* II, Kuwait, 1961, p. 102. ʿAbd-Allāh Yāfeʿī, *Merʾāt al-janān* II, Hyderabad, 1338/1919-20, p. 223. Zereklī, *Aʿlām*² IV, Cairo, 1374/1954, p. 261. Kaḥḥāla, VI, p. 132.

(H. SCHÜTZINGER)

BALḴĪ, ABŪ ʿALĪ MOḤAMMAD B. AḤMAD. See ABŪ ʿALĪ-MOḤAMMAD B. AḤMAD BALḴĪ.

BALḴĪ, ABU'L-QĀSEM ʿABD-ALLĀH B. AḤMAD. See ABU'L-QĀSEM KAʿBĪ.

BALḴĪ, ḤAMĪD-AL-DĪN ABŪ BAKR ʿOMAR. See ḤAMĪD-AL-DĪN ABŪ BAKR ʿOMAR BALḴĪ.

BALUCHISTAN

i. *Geography, history, and ethnography.*
ii. *Archaeology.*
iii. *Baluchi language and literature.*
iv. *Music of Baluchistan.*
v. *Baluch carpets.*

i. GEOGRAPHY, HISTORY, AND ETHNOGRAPHY

This article is divided into the following sections: 1. introductory review of problems in the history and ethnography of the Baluch, i.e., the present-day inhabitants of Baluchistan; 2. geography; 3. the origins of the Balōč, i.e., the people who brought the name into the area; 4. the early history of the area between Iran and

India (Baluchistan); 5. the eastward migrations of the Balōč; 6. the establishment of the khanate in Kalat; 7. the autonomous khanate, 1666-1839; 8. the period of British dominance, 1839-1947; 9. the Baluch in Pakistan, Iran, and Afghanistan since 1947; 10. the diaspora; 11. ethnography. [Note: place names in Pakistan have not been transliterated.]

1. Introduction.

The total number of Baluch in Baluchistan (in Afghanistan, Iran, and Pakistan), the Arab states of the Persian Gulf, and elsewhere in Asia and Africa is variously estimated at between three and five million. Their history up to the time when they were drawn into Western colonial history in the 19th century is poorly known. A copious literature has been produced on them since then, especially in English, but also in Persian and several other European and regional languages. But so far there has been no attempt to synthesize and interpret all the available material.

Baluchistan is generally understood by the Baluch and their neighbors to comprise an area of over half a million square kilometres in the southeastern part of the Iranian plateau, south of the central deserts and the Helmand river, and in the arid coastal lowlands between the Iranian plateau and the Gulf of Oman. Its boundaries are vague and not consistent with modern provincial boundaries. It appears to have been divided throughout history between Iranian (highland) and Indian (lowland) spheres of influence, and since 1870 it has been formally divided among Afghanistan, Iran, and India (later Pakistan). It is unclear when the name Baluchistan came into general use. It may date only from the 12th/18th century when Naṣīr Khan I of Kalat during his long reign in the second half of the 12th/18th century became the first indigenous ruler to establish autonomous control over a large part of the area.

The origins of the Balōč and of their name are similarly unclear. They appear to have lived in the northwestern part of the area (southeast of Kermān) at the time of the Arab conquest. But their activities may even at that time have extended a considerable distance to the east. They appear to have migrated farther east, and beyond Makrān, beginning around the time of the arrival of the Saljuqs in Kermān in the 5th/11th century, and continuing intermittently for the next five centuries, up to the spread of Safavid power in the 10th/16th century, with major movements probably in the 6th/12th and 9th/15th centuries.

How and when the Balōč arrived in the region of Kermān is unknown. Their claim (in their epic poetry; see BALUCHISTAN iii, below) to be Arabs who migrated from Aleppo after fighting at Karbalā' cannot be taken at face value. The various inconclusive theories concerning their origins are reviewed by Dames (1904, pp. 7-16).

The scanty evidence for them between the Arab conquest and the arrival of the Saljuqs is also difficult to evaluate, partly because of the authors' characteristic urban prejudice against nomadic tribes. But it suggests that they numbered in the tens of thousands at most; that they were pastoralists, herding sheep and goats; and that, like other Middle Eastern pastoralists, they were highly mobile, if not entirely nomadic, living in tribal communities (in the sense that they construed their social relations according to genealogical—patrilineal—criteria); and that they were poorly integrated into the settled polity, which they continually harassed.

In terms of general cultural values and world view, the Baluch in recent times resemble neighboring Muslim tribal populations in both the historical and the ethnographic records. What has emerged as distinctively Baluch, beside the language, Baluchi, is the structure of their social and political relations. But this structure is more likely to be a product of their recent pluralist experience in Baluchistan than a heritage of their earlier history. (It has not yet been changed significantly by their incorporation into modern state structures.) Baluch identity in Baluchistan has been closely tied to the use of the Baluchi language in intertribal relations. Modern Baluchi has a clear pedigree, with a number of grammatical features and vocabulary of the "Northwest" Iranian type (see BALUCHISTAN, iii, below). But Baluch ethnicity today cannot be so clearly defined. On the one hand, many communities generally recognized as Baluch by themselves and by others are of alien origin and have been assimilated over the last four centuries. On the other hand, there is no evidence that all the considerable number of scattered communities known as Baluch in other parts of Iran, Afghanistan, and Soviet Turkmenistan (most of which are not presently Baluchi-speaking) are in fact historically related, or, if they are related, that they separated from each other in Baluchistan.

Within Baluchistan the population is not ethnically homogeneous. Some communities are identified (by themselves and others) as Balōč (see 10 below), with the implication that they are descended from those who entered the area as Balōč; while others, though considered members of Baluch society now and identifying as Baluch in relation to the outside world, are known within Baluch society by other tribal (e.g., Nowšērvānī, Gīčkī, Bārakzay) and subethnic (e.g., Brahui, Dehwār, *ġolām*, Jaḏgāl, Mēd) designations, with the implication that they have adopted Baluch identity relatively recently—but not that they are for that reason in any way outsiders. Some of these "Baluch" predate the arrival of the Balōč. Others (e.g., the Bārakzay, q.v., who are of recent Afghan origin) postdate them. There are also remnants of what were (under autonomous Baluch rule, as well as under the British, 1666-1947) larger non-Muslim communities, mostly Hindu, Sikh, Isma'ili, or Bahai traders, who are not considered Baluch. The Baluchi language was the language of interethnic as well as intertribal relations. Although participation in Baluchi intercourse generally seems to have led to assimilation, being Muslim appears to have been a necessary precondition. However, the Baluch in the Makrān who became Ḏekrī (Zikri) in the 10/16th century did not for that reason cease to be Baluch. The Baluch generally claim that all Baluch are Hanafite Muslims, although, apart from the Ḏekrīs (who are known but rarely discussed), there are some small Shiʿite communities on the northwestern fringes of Iranian Baluchistan, a fact which is unknown farther east.

The vast territory of greater Baluchistan has been divided historically into a number of areas, among which Makrān (in the south), Sarḥadd (in the northwest), and the area known earlier as Tūrān that includes the modern towns of Kalat and Khuzdar (Qoṣdār/Qozdār; in the east), have been the most significant. Stronger Iranian and Indian political centers to the west, north, and east (particularly, Kermān, Sīstān, Qandahār, Delhi, Karachi), and even the sultan of Oman to the south, have intermittently claimed suzerainty over parts of these areas, and considered them as their legitimate hinterland. The idea of one Baluch community in a politically unified Baluchistan may have originated in Naṣīr Khan's successes in the 12th/18th century. His successors were unable to maintain control of the part of the area he claimed to rule as khan, let alone continue to pursue what appear to have been his ambitions to incorporate all the Baluch into one nation. But the policy of indirect rule pursued by the British, who began to encroach in the area during the following generation, and maintained the khan irrespective of internal processes that would either have destroyed or transformed the khanate, kept alive the idea of a unified Baluchistan—against considerable odds—at least up to the borders that the British negotiated with the Qajar government in Iran, and the Afghan government in Kabul in the second half of the 13th/19th century. By 1947, the idea of Baluchistan was too firmly established to be superseded or transcended by the new concept of Pakistan. The political activities of the Baluch in Pakistan (who constitute probably two thirds of the total Baluch population) reinforce and confirm Baluch identity in Iran, Afghanistan, and elsewhere.

The Balōč appear to have become culturally dominant in the area in the late medieval period, along with the spread of Baluchi as a lingua franca—though the details and causes of each process are unclear. It was not until much later that the majority of the population of the area came to identify themselves as Baluch, probably as a result partly of the success of Naṣīr Khan's policies, and partly because of the later British administrative classification. The assimilation of almost the whole population to Baluch identity and the dominance of Baluchi (at least for public, political purposes) is difficult to explain, since the tribesmen who established the khanate of Kalat (and therefore also the political autonomy and identity of the area) in the mid-11th/17th century spoke not Baluchi, but Brahui, and conducted their administration in Persian by means of a bureaucracy recruited among the Dehwār, who were Tajik peasants. Immigrant Baluchi speakers (Balōč) were probably not numerically dominant except in non-agricultural parts of the area.

Baluchistan remains a palimpsest of cultural and linguistic discontinuities. Although the existing literature is much greater than for other comparable tribal areas of the Iranian world, the underlying heterogeneity raises a number of problems for any systematic account of Baluchistan and the Baluch. These problems cannot yet be definitively treated. Far more historical and ethnographic research is needed. What follows is only a preliminary synthesis.

2. Geography.

Baluchistan has received relatively little attention from geographers. Apart from the initial descriptions provided by scholars like Vredenberg for the Gazetteers, and by Harrison for the Admiralty Handbook (Persia), Snead worked along the Makrān coast in 1959-60, and Vita-Finzi worked in western Makrān in the mid-1970s—both geomorphologists—and Scholz, a cultural geographer, conducted short studies from Quetta. The standard work on the geography of Afghanistan (Humlum) devotes a few pages to the Baluch areas in the southwest of the country. The following description is based mainly on the Gazetteers and the author's field notes.

Throughout most of Baluchistan the topography is extremely broken and mountainous, varying in altitude from 1,500-2,000 m (the steppe on the edge of the Iranian plateau, at the base of mountains) to over 3,500 m in the north and northeast and to sea level on the coastal plain. In the part that is now southwestern Afghanistan, and here and there in the 500 km wide zone between the Afghan border with Pakistan and the coast, the land opens out into vast expanses of featureless semidesert and desert. Temperatures are continental in the highlands with bitterly cold winters and extreme diurnal and seasonal ranges; the lowlands and coastal areas are subtropical. Extremes of summer heat (with high humidity during the monsoon) occur at low altitudes away from the coast in the Kacchi-Sibi plain and the larger Makrān valleys. High winds are also regularly recorded, related to the well known *bād-e sad o bīst rūz* phenomenon in Sīstān.

Rainfall varies mainly according to altitude. Though rare in summer on the Iranian plateau, it may come at any season, but may fail altogether for several years in succession, especially at the lower altitudes. The highlands and high mountains in the east and northeast receive up to 400 mm, even more in places on the eastern escarpment. Most of the rest sees an average of 100 mm or less—though averages are misleading because of wide annual fluctuations. Rain falls mostly in winter (as snow at high altitudes). The monsoon brings summer humidity and occasionally significant rain to the coast and lowlands. For example, in 1964 it rained heavily every day for two weeks in August over a large area of Makrān (see below, on *baš*). Sometimes such weather edges up the escarpments and marginally affects the Iranian plateau. Summer rain can be torrential and in the mountains flash floods may cause sensational damage. Heavy rain turns the coastal plain into a morass of clayey mud, impassible for human, animal, or motorized traffic until it dries out, possibly as much as a week. In the southern mountains some rivers flow continuously for stretches; elsewhere occasional pools often last till the next flood. In the Nahang and Sarbāz rivers some of the deeper pools contain crocodiles. (Game generally has become scarce except for ibex in the higher mountains, and the ubiquitous partridge and smaller game birds, such as chikara, sisi, pigeon, and some sandgrouse and quail. Wild sheep, deer, black bear, wild pig, wolf, jackal, hyena, fox, and porcupine also occur.) Here and there pools provide a trickle of water to irrigate a nomad's garden plot. Water is nowhere abundant or (with few exceptions) perennial, but in the mountains soil is the limiting factor for agriculture. On the coastal plain on the other hand, the soil is often good but there is no water except from rain or runoff, and the ports have no reliable water supply.

The history of settlement in Baluchistan is reflected in its toponymy. Place names fall into three categories: Names that are of Baluchi origin, or have been Baluchized, are used for most minor natural features: rivers, streams, rocks, mountains; old settlements and major natural features tend to have pre-Baluch names; and new settlements, dating from the middle of the last century in Iran, and the middle of this century in Pakistan generally have Persian or Urdu names. Urban settlement in Baluchistan today is all the result of Persian and Pakistani administrative and (more recently) development activity. The Baluch have never developed an urban way of life, and though many now live in towns, the towns are essentially non-Baluch (Iranian or Pakistani) in character. Most of the major Baluch agricultural settlements, however, have developed on the sites of pre-Baluch towns, known from the time of premedieval prosperity, that was based on investment in agriculture, as well as trade. Since the medieval period, both before and since the Baluch became dominant, up to the beginning of modern development, agricultural settlement has been dependent on the protection of rulers who lived in forts. A few traders clustered around the forts. But the cultural center of gravity of Baluch life was among the nomads who controlled the vast areas between the settlements.

Within the geographical and cultural diversity of Baluchistan a number of districts have emerged historically, each with its own distinctive geographical features. Starting from the Iranian plateau in the north, the following are the significant natural and cultural divisions of Baluchistan (the modern administrative divisions are almost identical): the Sarḥadd, the Māškīd (Maškēl) depression, the Māškīd drainage are of Sarāvān-Panjgur, the northeast highlands of Quetta, Pishin, Zhob, Loralai, and Sibi, the Mari-Bugti hills, the eastern highlands of Sarawan-Jahlawan, the Jāz Mūrīān depression, Makrān, the Kacchi-Sibi lowlands, and the coastal plain including Las Bela and Daštīārī.

"Sarḥadd" appears to have come into use in the medieval period for the southern "borderlands" of Sīstān. It is a high plateau, averaging 1,500-2,000 m in altitude and dominated by the two volcano massifs, Kūh-e Taftān (4,042 m) and Kūh-e Bazmān (3,489 m). Although it is now thought of as coterminous with the *šahrestān* of Zāhedān, its historical boundaries were not strictly defined and usage of the term varied according to fluctuation in the relative strength of local rulers: It was sometimes considered to extend into the northeastern part of the Jāz Mūrīān depression and into the Māškīd drainage of Sarāvān, and westward through southern Nēmrōz and Helmand provinces and Chagai and even into Kharan. It is characterized by cold winters and moderate summers, with precipitation concentrated in the winters, as snow on the higher ground. There are large areas of sand on either side of the border with Afghanistan. Apart from the general steppe vegetation, there are relict stands of wild almond and pistachio on the plains, especially between K̲āš (also K̲ʿāš, Bal. Vāšt) and Gošt (Gwašt), and juniper in the mountains. The area is characterized by isolated hills and depressions that function as internal drainage basins. The larger depressions, *hāmūn*, are generally saline; the smaller ones, *navār*, in some cases contain sweet water. Traces of old *band*s (q.v.) are evident on the plain southwest of Taftān and elsewhere. The only significant agricultural settlement of any antiquity is K̲āš, which lies to the south of Taftān. A few old villages nestle at the foot of the mountain, mainly on the eastern side. The most notable are Lādīz and Sangān. K̲āš depends upon irrigation from *qanāt*s, which though probably ancient were redeveloped by entrepreneurs from Yazd under Reżā Shah. There are also a few *qanāt*s across the border in Chagai.

Since the medieval period the Sarḥadd has been divided among a number of tribes. The most important are the Esmāʿīlzay (renamed Šahbak̲š under Reżā Shah), Mīr-Balūčzay, Rīgī, Yār-Moḥammadzay (renamed Šāhnavāzī under Reżā Shah), Gamšādzay, Nārūʾī, and Gūrgēč. Across the modern borders in Afghanistan and Pakistan the major tribes are Sanjarānī, Jamāl-al-Dīnī, Bādīnī, Moḥammad-Ḥasanī, and the Brahui-speaking Mengal. Some ten thousand out of the estimated ninety thousand Baluch in Afghanistan, especially the Nārūʾī, Rīgī, Sanjarānī, and Gūrgēč tribes, are closely related to the groups across the border in Iran and Pakistan. Most Afghan Baluch are presently refugees in the neighboring part of Pakistan.

The *hāmūn* of the Māškīd river lies on the southwestern side of a large depression of some 15,000 square miles that, although geographically an extension of the Sarḥadd, has generally been controlled separately from a fort on its northeastern side, known as Kharan. In the British period Kharan was a separate principality under Kalat. Earlier it had been dependent on Qandahār. It is mostly desert and includes a large area of sand dunes on the southern side. It is bounded on the north by the range of Ra'skoh which divides it from Chagai, and on the south by the Siahan range which separates it from Panjgur and Makrān. There is a large area of thick tamarisk forest downstream from the seat of the principality (Kharan-Kalat) on a river that was once

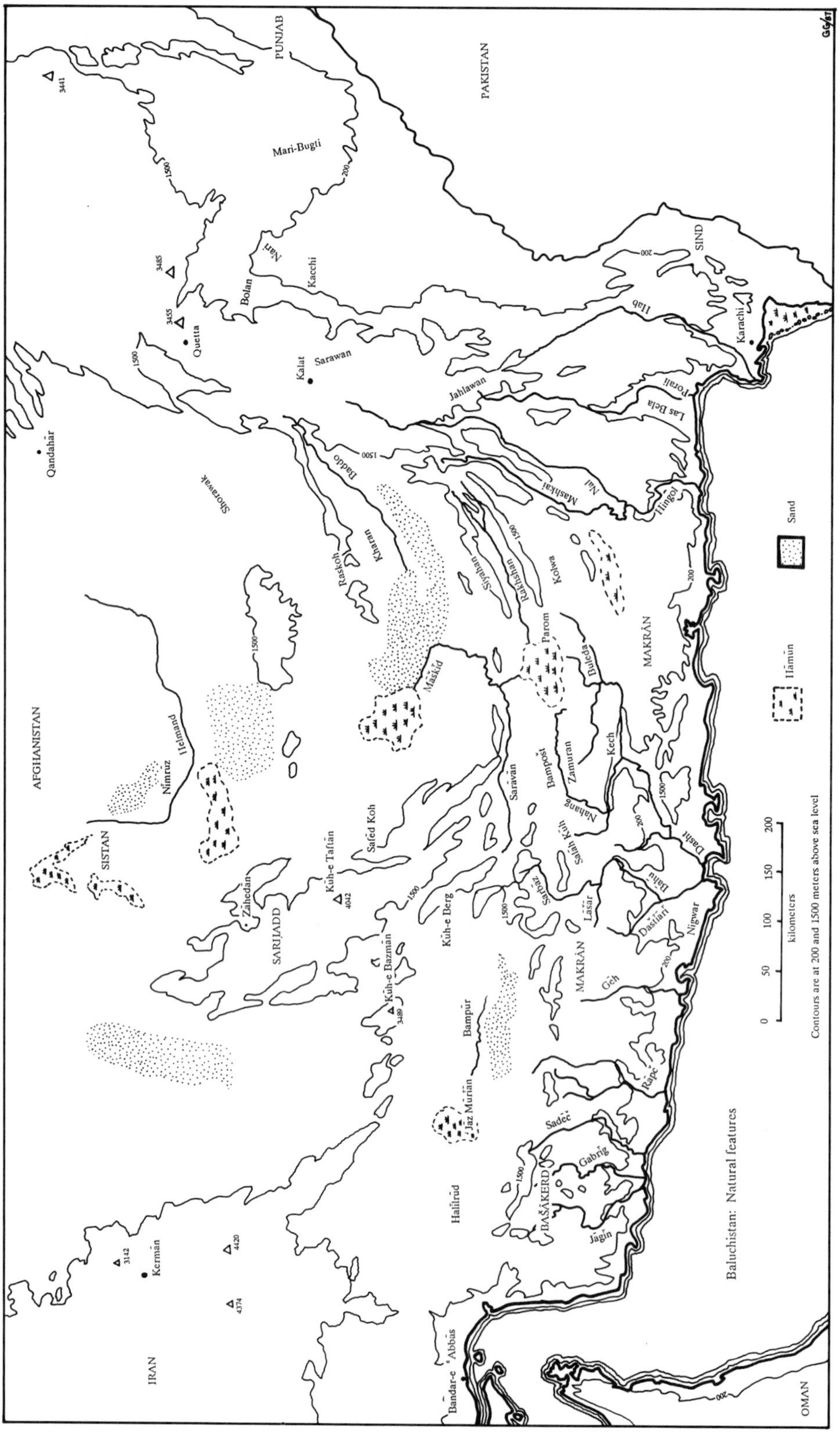

Figure 16. Baluchistan: Natural features

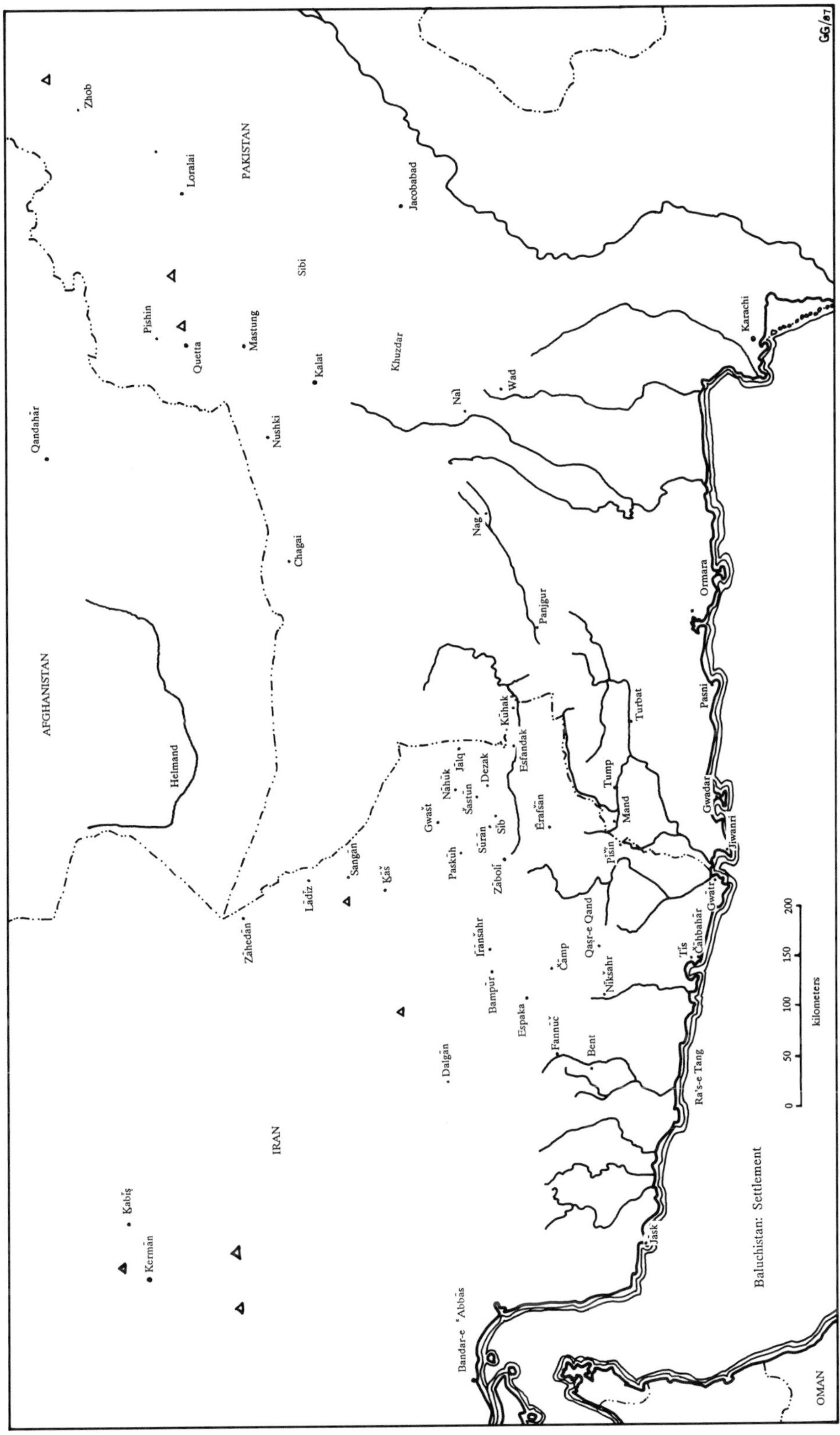

Figure 17. Baluchistan: Settlement

dammed and supports annual cultivation. On the western side of the Māškīd *hāmūn* there is a large area of rather poor quality date palms which have been important in the ecology of some of the Sarḥadd tribes to the west in Iran. A number of massive stone dams, now known in the archeological literature as *gabar-bands*, appear to have supported terraced fields in the hills bordering the main depression (Stein, pp. 7, 15-34, 145-47; Raikes, 1965). This type of engineering continues to be practiced on a small scale throughout Baluchistan (and in other parts of Afghanistan, Iran, and Pakistan; see below and ĀBYĀRĪ). It was probably more important in earlier periods.

The ruling tribe in Kharan are the Nowšērvānī, who claim Persian origin. Other important tribes are the Rak̲šānī, Moḥammad-Ḥasanī, and the Brahui-speaking Sāsolī and Samalārī.

South of Kūh-e Taftān the plateau drops away to below 1,000 m along the course of the Māškīd river and its tributaries, forming the districts of Sarāvān and Panjgur, before it turns back north into Kharan. Presently the river carries water only after rain. The ecology is transitional with elements from both the temperate plateau and the subtropical south. Where the main tributaries join, the river flows through a deeply eroded gravel plain and peneplain, completely barren except for clumps of *pīš* (*Nanorrhops ritchiana*) in the occasional wadis. Kūh-e Berg, a narrow 2,500 m ridge which runs 150 km northwest to southeast, divides Sarāvān from the Jāz Mūrīān depression. Magas (renamed Zābolī under Reżā Shah) at over 1,200 m below the southern end of Kūh-e Berg grows the best quality dates on the Iranian side of the border. East of it two long parallel valleys contain the old agricultural settlements of Paskūh, Sūrān and Sīb in the first, and Gošt, Šastūn (the modern town of Sarāvān), and Dezak (renamed Dāvarpanāh under Reżā Shah) in the second. Other old settlements lie farther downstream and in the mountains on either side: Kallagān, Esfandak, Kūhak, Nāhūk, Jālq, Kant, Hīdūč, Āšār, Afšān, Ērafšān. Bampošt, which is one of the major areas of mountain nomadism and *āp-band* (*āb-band*; see below) farming, lies to the south of the Māškīd. Both districts depend upon *qanāt*s and settled populations have probably predominated over nomads throughout the historical period. A large proportion of the cultivators of Sarāvān and Sīb-Sūrān are Dehwār. Other tribes include the Bārakzay, most recently the dominant group, their predecessors in power the Bozorgzāda (of whom one branch, the Mīr-Morādzay, held the forts in Sīb, Sūrān, Paskūh, Kant, Gašt, Hūšak; while another branch, Neʿmat-Allāhī, controlled Jālq and Dezak), Nowšērvānī (in Nāhūk, Kūhak, Esfandak), Ṣāḥebzāda (who are *sayyeds*), Malekzāda, Lorī, Nātūzay, Sepāhī (who formed the militia of the Bozorgzāda), Arbāb (who are smallholders), Balōč tribes known as Sīāhbor, Čākarbor, ʿAbdolzay, Čārīzay, Dorrazay (in Bampošt and Hīdūč), Kord (in Magas); the Balōč in Salāhkoh and the neighboring mountains are Āskānī, Porkī, Sēpādak; the *šahrī* in Ērafšān are Raʾīs and Watkār.

In Panjgur, which in many ways is a mirror image of Sarāvān across the border in Pakistan, settlement is more restricted. The Rak̲šān has a course of over 150 miles but from Nāg at the northeastern end of the valley down to the confluence with the Māškīd close to the Iranian border (although there are large areas of flood farming) it supports irrigation (either directly or by *qanāt*) only around Panjgur itself. Remains of a dam dating from the pre-Balōč period were still visible a hundred years ago at a place called Bonestān below Panjgur. Sarāvān has been most closely associated with the Sarḥadd and Bampūr. Panjgur has generally been most closely associated with Kech and therefore considered part of Makrān, but the influence of Makrān has always been disputed by Kharan, which has managed to remain dominant in the border area in Esfandak and Kūhak.

The districts of Zhob, Loralai, Pishin, Quetta in the northeast are based on river valleys that drain out of the mountains around Quetta, which include two peaks over 3,400 m. Until two hundred years ago they had been more closely related to Qandahār than Kalat, and they became part of Baluchistan as a result of the political relationship between Kalat and Qandahār, a situation that was later reinforced by British border interests. Except for Loralai these districts were never settled by Balōč and their population remains mainly Pashtun, unassimilated to Baluch identity. Although they enjoy relatively high rainfall they remained mainly pastoral until the recent commercial development of fruit growing. Important areas of forest survive in the mountains, especially juniper (*Juniperus excelsus*) between 2,000-3,000 m and wild olive (*Olea cuspidata*). Major earthquakes were recorded in 1888, 1892, 1900, 1902 (*Gazetteer* V, pp. 30-31), and again the 1936. The major Pashtun tribes are the Kākaṛ, Tarīn, Panī, Acakzay. The Baluch tribes in Loralai are the Buzdār, Lēgarī and Gōrčānī. In Quetta-Pishin there are only few Baluch pastoralists, mostly Rind (*Gazetteer* V, p. 77). There are now migrants from many Baluch tribes in the vicinity of Quetta.

South of Quetta a tongue of highland and mountain extends almost to the coast, dividing the lower Indus valley from Makrān. The main rivers are the Hingol, Porali, Baddo, and Hab. This was the medieval Tūrān, and as Sarawan and Jahlawan it has provided the center stage of Baluch history. Sarawan is literally the "above-land" and Jahlawan is the "(be)low-land" (Jahlawan becomes Jhalawan in Pakistani Urdu nomenclature), but the terms derive not from the topography but from the two divisions of the largely Brahui-speaking confederation living there. Kalat is the seat of Sarawan and Khuzdar of Jahlawan. Nal and Wad are other important tribal centers. The 1936 earthquake destroyed the Aḥmadzay fort (Mīrī) in Kalat as well as the city of Quetta (Baluch, 1975, p. 121). Although these districts have slightly higher rainfall than most of Baluchistan south and west of Quetta, they were mainly pastoral and nomadic until the recent extension into them of the national power grid, which encouraged investment in wells and pumps and settled agriculture and led to neglect of the traditional *qanāt* and *band* technology (see below). Pastoral transhumance to the lowlands of Kacchi on the west, which was the basis of the political preeminence of the area, remains important. The major tribes are the Ra'īsānī, Šahvānī, Bangalzay, Lēhrī, Langaw, Rostamzay, Mengal, Bīzenjō, Kambarānī (Qambarānī), Mīrwarī, Gorgnārī, Ničatī, Sāsolī, K̲edrānī, Zārakzay, and the Zēhrī (of which only the last is Baluchi-speaking).

East of Sarawan and Jahlawan the terrain drops almost to sea level within some 20 km. This is the piedmont plain of Kacchi (the northern part of it belongs to the district of Sibi that extends up the valleys into the high mountains east of Quetta). Kacchi is about 2,000 km^2, sloping from an elevation of about 150 m at Sibi in the north to 50 m at Jacobabad in the south. Since the introduction of a canal from the Indus in the 1930s the southern part has become the most productive agricultural part of Baluchistan. The majority of the year-round population are Jats. Cultivation in Kacchi depends on harnessing the floods that arrive in July and August from the monsoon on the hills—there is less than 100 mm of rain on the plain. The main rivers are the Bolan and the Nari. Seasonal river discharge onto the agricultural land of Sibi, Kacchi, Las Bela, Bāhū, and Bampūr was traditionally managed in the same way (though on a smaller scale than) the discharge of the Helmand into the delta lands of Sīstān. (The annual rebuilding of the barrages in Sīstān is described in Tate, 1909, pp. 224-226.) It was the most important event of the year, using all available labor. Crops include sorghum, pulses, and sesame. There is a *nā'eb* for each village, appointed by the khan. The Jats construct huge embankments across the dry riverbeds to catch and divert the torrential floods. As the fields are flooded, they break one dam and let the water rush down to the next. The Nari has more than fifteen such dams. Most of them require repair or reconstruction during winter, for which the labor is provided by the nomads. Nomads also provide the labor for harvesting. The traditional organization has been modified recently by administrative changes (N. Swidler, p. 102). The major tribes are the Rind, Magasī, Dumbkī, Omrānī, Bulēdī, K̲ōsa, Jātōī, Kēbārī, Mugārī, Dīnārī, Čālgrī, Marī, and Būgṯī.

South of Loralai an isolated area of hill country extends southward to the banks of the Indus, bounded on the east by the southern end of the Sulaiman range. These are the Mari-Bugti hills, called after the tribes that have controlled them with a considerable degree of autonomy into the modern period. They consist chiefly of narrow parallel ridges of closely packed hills, which form the gradual descent from the Sulaiman plateau into the plains, intersected by numerous ravines and generally barren and inhospitable. But here and there are good patches of grazing, and a few valleys which have been brought under cultivation. The Marī are the largest Baluch tribe and were estimated at 60,000 (Pehrson, p. 2). They are Baluchi-speaking and identify strongly as Baluch, claiming to be descended from a branch of the Rind tribe. But they speak a distinct dialect of Baluchi, and have always jealously guarded their autonomy from the larger Baluch polity, especially as represented by Kalat. In their political organization they display features that are reminiscent of their Pashtun neighbors, such as tribal councils.

To the northwest the historical boundary between Baluchistan and Kermān is a vague no-man's land in the Jāz Mūrīān depression. The Jāz Mūrīān is a large *hāmūn*, about 300 km long and 70,000 km^2 in area, into which the Bampūr river drains from the east and the Halīlrūd from the west. A low range separates it from Narmāšīr and the Dašt-e Lūt to the north. A large area of dunes impedes communication on the southeast side, and there is a thickly wooded area, mainly tamarisk, along the banks of the Bampūr river below Bampūr. Most of the rest, except for a varying amount of shallow water in the center, is flat desert, with high summer temperatures, but an open gateway to Kermān in the winter. There is a score of rich agricultural villages around Īrānšahr (previously Fahraj, Baluchi Pahra) and Bampūr (of which the largest is Aptar) depending partly on *qanāt*s and partly on a dam above Bampūr, which is the site of the largest fort in western Baluchistan. The agricultural population is mainly low-status tribesmen and *ḡolām*s. 100 km west of Bampūr, on the northeast edge of the central depression, is the center of the Bāmerī tribe, who breed the best fast riding camels. They engage in a small amount of cultivation based on shallow wells from which they raise the water by means of long counterbalanced poles (Arabic *šādūf*).

South of the Jāz Mūrīān and Sarāvān the Makrān mountains extend in a 150-220 km wide zone from Bašākerd in the west to Mashkai in Jahlawan in the east. There is a number of parallel east-west ranges and valleys that resemble steps from the Iranian plateau down to the coast. They are rugged and difficult to traverse, though the peaks rarely exceed 2,000 m. The most important rivers are the Jāgīn, Gabrīg, Sadēč, Rāpč, Sarbāz, Kech, and its tributary Nahang. The western rivers cut through the mountains in deep gorges, of which Sarbāz is the most spectacular. In the east the major river is the Kech, which runs 150 km due west between two ranges before joining the Nahang and turning south through a gap to the sea. Rainfall is scanty and irregular, and summer temperatures are high, but the monsoon brings humidity and occasional rain that reduces the temperature and resuscitates the vegetation. The Makrān mountains are the home of Balōč nomadic pastoralists. Natural vegetation is sparse, and they divide their time between their animals (mainly goats) and their *āp-band*. Where valleys open out and contain soil but no water, a *band* is built round a terrace of good alluvial soil to catch occasional rain, or water channeled from the river after flood. The few permanent settlements are riverine and small. Most are situated in the sweep of a bend or where a river issues onto desert plains. The main centers are Bent, Fannūj,

Geh (renamed Nīkšahr under Reżā Shah), Qaṣr-e Qand, Bog, Rāsk, Čāmp, and Lāšār, Espaka, Mand, and Tump. There are over 50 villages on either side of a long gorge in the Sarbāz river, and an almost continuous string of oases lining the banks of the Kech river with fields and date plantations irrigated from both *kārīz* and cuts (Bal. *kawr-jō*; *kawr* is Baluchi for "river") taking off from large pools in the river bed. Tump and Mand enjoy similar conditions. Kolwa is an 80-mile natural continuation of the Kech valley to the east separated by an almost imperceptible watershed. It contains by far the greatest dry crop area of the Makrān. The Dasht valley carries the united Kech-Nahang through the coastal range to the sea, irrigating important agricultural land on either side. The Buleda valley north of Turbat has some agriculture, as do some spring-irrigated areas in the Zamuran hills north of the Nahang river. Otherwise, apart from Parom and Balgattar which are saline flats, Makrān supports only pastoralism. The crops in the mountains are rice and dates, though a wide range of fruits and vegetables are grown in small quantities, and mangoes deserve special mention. Dates are par excellence the crop of the Makrān; 109 cultivated (*nasabī*) varieties are listed in the Makrān *Gazetteer*, apart from wild (*kurōč*) varieties. *Pīš* is the most typical of all Makrān plants. It grows on rocky ground up to 1,000 m, and provides a famine food, as well as fiber. The main tribes of the Makrān mountains are the Gīčkī, Bulēdī, Hōt, Bīzenjō, Nowšērvānī, Mīrwārī, Rind, Ra'īs, Lāndī, Kattawār, Kēnagīzay, Mullāzay, Šīrānī, Mubārakī, Lāšārī, Āhurānī, Jadgāl, Sardārzay. The Šīrānī hold Geh, Fannūj, and Bent; the Mubārakī, who are a branch of the Šīrānī, hold Čāmp and Lāšār. The Bulēdī held forts in Rāsk, Qaṣr-e Qand, Bog, and Hīt and their warrior *zāt* was the Bar. Katrī and Bāpārī are non-Baluch merchants. The cultivators in Makrān are mostly landless.

The coastal plain varies in width from almost zero to as much as 100 km in Daštīārī and more in Las Bela. It contains no reliable supplies of fresh water, but supports considerable forest and woodland of *Prosopis*, *Zyziphus*, and *Acacia spp*. The coastline is deeply indented with bays, which provide good anchorages for Čāhbahār (formerly Tīs, a little to the north of it) and Gwadar, among other ports. In the west the plain is mostly low and swampy or sandy, but farther east there are hills near the coast and headlands. Bare sandstone has weathered into fantastic shapes. At their seaward base some of them have deteriorated into badlands and are difficult to traverse. The main rivers, which only flow after heavy rain, pass between the sandstone massifs, providing the only passages inland. A line of mud volcanoes extends along the coast, of which the largest, Napag (10 miles north of Ras Tank/Ra's Tang), has a cone built up to 50 m by constant eruptions of greenish mud (*Persia*, p. 141). There are extensive mangrove swamps intersected by creeks in the Gwatar bay and the rivers to the west. The rivers contain quicksands. The soil in Daštīārī and Bela, like Kacchi and some parts of Makrān such as Parom and along the Dasht river, has unusual moisture-retaining capability. After one good rain it will hold water long enough to obtain a crop of sorghum. Daštīārī relied on the Kājūkawr and Bāhū on the Mazankawr (the continuation of the Sarbāz river) for irrigation. But about a hundred years ago both of these rivers cut back so that except in exceptional floods the water was out of reach of the agricultural land. In both Daštīārī and Las Bela dams were built seasonally from earth and trees, as in Kacchi. Small fishing communities of Mēd live here and there on the beach. Scattered along the plain are mobile villages and camps of Balōč who are mainly pastoral, but practice a little cultivation after rain. All these populations have traditionally depended on rain and rain-filled ponds as the only source of water.

3. The origins of the Baluch.

The earliest extant source (*Šahristānīhā ī Ērān-šahr*, a Pahlavi text written in the 2nd/8th century, though probably representing a pre-Islamic compilation; see Markwart, *Provincial Capitals*, pp. 5, 15, 74-76) lists the Balōč as one of seven autonomous mountain communities (*kōfyār*). Arabic writers in the 3rd/9th and 4th/10th centuries (especially Ebn Ḵordāḏbeh, Mas'ūdī, Eṣṭaḵrī, Moqaddasī) mention them, usually as Balūṣ, in association with other tribal populations in the area between Kermān, Khorasan, Sīstān, and Makrān. All these tribes (of which only the Balōč survive in name) were feared by the settled population. The sources also add some detail, but the implications are unclear. The Balōč appear to have had a separate district of Kermān, but they also lived in two districts of Sīstān (Eṣṭaḵrī) and appeared in a tract some distance to the east of Fahraj (the eastern border of Kermān), probably modern Kharan (Ḵārān) or Chagai (Ebn Ḵordāḏbeh). Eṣṭaḵrī also records them as peaceful, though Moqaddasī claims they were more troublesome than the Kūč, with whom they are often paired (for references see Dames, 1904b, pp. 26-33, who also provides a more detailed discussion).

The Balōč are generally considered to have arrived in Kermān from the north (e.g., Dames, 1904b, pp. 29-30). The evidence for this assumption depends on two arguments: the classification of Baluchi as a "Northwest Iranian" language and the fact that in Ferdowsī's *Šāh-nāma* (composed at the beginning of the 4th/10th century on the basis of earlier works now lost) they are mentioned in conjunction with Gīlān. According to Ferdowsī (see, e.g., Dehḵodā, s.v. Balōč) the Sasanian kings Ardašīr and Ḵosrow I Anōšīravān fought the Balōč and the Balōč fought for several other Sasanian kings. It has also been argued that the Balōč left traces of their language in the oases of the central deserts of the Iranian plateau as they migrated south (Minorsky, 1957; Frye, 1961). Some of this evidence (e.g., place names), if pertinent, could be the result of later raiding activities on the part of small numbers of Baluchi-speakers. (Such activities have been recorded as late as the 13th/19th and early 14th/20th centuries.) There is no other evidence that could be used either to date or to corroborate the theory of a southward migration by the Balōč.

It is clear that the desert areas east and southeast of Kermān have been generally insecure throughout much of the historical period. The early Muslim writers were preoccupied with the unpredictability of populations not controlled by the government, and by the danger to travelers. Their descriptions tell us little more about the populations of these areas than we might expect. They kept flocks and lived in goat-hair tents. Their native language was not Persian. They seem to have been concentrated in the more fertile mountains southeast of Kermān and to have plundered intermittently on the desert routes to the north and northeast.

The situation with regard to the security of travel apparently deteriorated, because in 361/971-72 the Buyid ʿAżod-al-Dawla (q.v.) considered it worthwhile to conduct a campaign against them. The Balōč were defeated, but they continued to be troublesome under the Ghaznavids and the Saljuqs. When they robbed Maḥmūd's ambassador in the desert north of Kermān between Ṭabas and K̲abīṣ, Maḥmūd sent his son, Masʿūd, against them (Dames, 1904b, pp. 32-33). Although the eastward migration of the Balōč appears to have intensified soon after this, there are still Balōč in eastern Kermān province.

It is important to note that the sources do not mention any leaders. It is likely that the Balōč at this period were a series of tribal communities not sharing any feelings of common ethnicity. In fact, the name Balōč (Balūč) appears to have been a name used by the settled (and especially the urban) population for a number of outlaw tribal groups over a very large area. The etymology is unclear, as is that of Kūč (also written as *Kūfeč*, *Kōfč* or—arabized—*Qofṣ*), a name generally taken to refer to a comparable neighboring tribal community in the early Islamic period. The common pairing of Kūč with Balūč in Ferdowsī (see, e.g., Dehk̲oda, s.vv.) suggests a kind of rhyming combination or even duplication, such as is common in Persian and historically related languages (cf. *tār o mār*). The Balōč may have entered the historical record as the settled writers' generic nomads. Because of the significance of their activities at this period they would gradually have become recognized as the nomads par excellence in this particular part of the Islamic world. It is possible, for example, that Balūč, along with Kūč, were terms applied to particular populations which were beyond the control of settled governments; that these populations came to accept the appellation and to see themselves in the cultural terms of the larger, more organized society that was established in the major agricultural territories; but they remained, then as now, a congeries of tribal communities of various origins. There is also ethnographic evidence to suggest that Balūč, irrespective of its etymology, may be applied to nomadic groups by the settled population as a generic appellation in other parts of eastern and southern Iran. The other tribal populations recorded in southeastern Kermān in the early Islamic period, which did not survive in name, may have assimilated to the Baluch identity. An important feature of the history of the Baluch up to the 14th/20th century has been their ability to assimilate numerous and diverse elements. Their history may have begun in the area east and southeast of Kermān around the time of the Arab conquest and their ethnogenesis may have been a product of the insecurity of a vast desert area which the governments of the period did not care to control despite their need for secure communications across it. It must be remembered, however, that such a theory of the origin of the Baluch leaves open the question of how and when the language spread to become the lingua franca (though not the mother tongue) of all assimilated Baluch.

4. The early history of the area.

Throughout its history the area between Iran and India has been strongly affected by influences from the more fertile areas surrounding it, particularly Kermān, Sīstān, Qandahār, Punjab, Sind, and Oman. Sea traffic connected it to the Indian Ocean and the Persian Gulf. Little historical research has yet been focused on it, and the relevant syntheses so far available derive coincidentally from the pursuit of answers to questions arising from primary interests in the civilizations to the east and west.

What is now Baluchistan has long interested scholars as the hinterland of the settled societies of the Indus valley, the Iranian plateau, and Mesopotamia. A number of important archeological sites have yielded evidence of human occupation extending back to the fourth millennium (see BALUCHISTAN ii, below). Archeologists and philologists have sought evidence of overland connections between the early civilizations of the Indus valley and Mesopotamia. Between 3000 and 2000 B.C. Sumerian and Akkadian records indicate trade relations between the Tigris-Euphrates valley and places called Dilmun, Makan, and Melukhkha, which, though their exact location has been a matter for debate, were obviously situated down the Persian Gulf and beyond. Makan is generally assumed to be related to Makrān which in later historical periods is the name of the southern half of the area, the coast, and its hinterland (Eilers, Hansman). Whether or not Makan always included this area, in the early periods the name seems to have applied mainly to the southern shores of the Gulf of Oman. This connection is significant, since it has continued into the present (though in more recent times the close relationship between the populations of what are now Baluchistan and Oman has been reduced by the apparatus of modern nation-states).

From the mid-1st millennium onward the area was divided into named provinces of the Persian empires. Maka and Zra^{n}ka appear in the inscriptions of Darius at Bīsotūn and Persepolis. Maka here is certainly modern Makrān (the southern half of Baluchistan), and Zra^{n}ka (NPers. Zarang), the Zarangai of Herodotus, Drangiane of Arrian, etc., was Sīstān, which appears then and later to have included most of the northern parts of the area and sometimes even to have extended into Makrān. More specific information is provided by Greek authors who began to be interested in the Persian Gulf as a result of the Persian wars (Herodotus, 3.93). Alexander's expeditions beyond the Persian empire late in the 4th century generated more detailed writing. This was further encouraged by commercial interest in the sources of various luxury commodities, mainly spices and dyestuffs, which were already reaching the eastern Mediterranean from the Indian Ocean.

The province Alexander traversed on his return to Iran from India was named Gedrosia. The experience of his army and fleet given by Arrian is interesting because it suggests that (contrary to the assessments of modern ecologists) the natural conditions of Baluchistan have not changed significantly over the past 2,300 years. There were ports in Sonmiani Bay, northwest of modern Karachi, and at Gwadar (Badara) and Tīs (Tesa; earlier Talmena). Population was generally sparse, partly Indian, including the Arbies and Oreitae, partly Iranian, including the Myci (assumed to be related to Maka). Water and provisions were difficult to find without good guides. In the inland valleys agriculture was facilitated by sophisticated engineering of small-scale irrigation, based mainly on the yield from summer rains. The most fertile area was the Kech valley, which was densely settled. A highway to the Indus ran from the capital Pura, probably modern Bampūr, which is the largest area of fertile watered land, though it could have been in Kech, the next largest, or possibly even in one of the narrower river valleys, such as the Sarbāz. Indians, both Hindu and Buddhist, lived in Pura; through it both land and sea trade could pass onto the arterial route to Kermān.

Alexander founded an Alexandria at the principal settlement of the Oreitae in modern Las Bela. As he proceeded westward he was forced to strike inland by the difficulty of the coastal terrain. Between Bela and Pasni was the worst stretch of the whole expedition. Apart from intolerable heat and lack of food, water, and firewood, at one point a flash flood swept away most of the women and children following the army and all the royal equipment and the surviving transport animals. From Pasni they proceeded along the flat coastal plain to Gwadar, then inland to Pura. The experience of the fleet under Nearchos was similar. The daily search for food and water rarely produced more than fish meal and dates, sometimes nothing. Along the beach they found communities of Ichthyophagi (fish eaters), hairy people with wooden spears who caught fish in the shallows with palm bark nets and ate them raw or dried them in the sun and ground them into meal, wore fish skins, and built huts of shells and bones of stranded whales (Arrian, *Anabasis* 21-26, *Indica* 23-33).

The next significant information comes from the Sasanian period, when the area was once again integrated into a provincial administration. A king of Makrān paid homage to Narseh (son of the Sasanian Šāpūr I) at Narseh's accession, who during the reign of his father bore the honorific (?) title of "king of Sakastān, Tūristān, and Hind up to the shore of the sea," and later Bahrām's son is called King of Sakas in the Paikuli inscription, which suggests that it was a not insignificant province (Skjærvø, III/2, pp. 10-11). Šāpūr I named four administrative entities within the area—Tugrān (later Tūrān, and presently Sarawan or Kalat), Pāradān (probably modern Kharan), and Hind (presumably Sind, or the land watered by the Indus), as well as Makrān—as appendages of Sakastān (Sīstān). The eastern boundary of the Sasanian province of Kermān was set at the port of Tīs on the coast, and at *Pohlpahraj (Fahraj), modern Īrānšahr, just beyond Bampūr at the far side of the irrigable area of the Jāz Mūrīān depression. Beyond that the kingdom of Makrān stretched along the coast to the port of Daibul at the mouth of the Indus. The kingdom of Pāradān stretched eastward from Bampūr to Tūrān. The kingdom of Tugrān probably extended from Kīzkānān (modern Kalat) and the Bolan pass (that connected Walishtan, modern Quetta, with the Sibi and Kacchi lowlands) through the Budahah district and the Pab and Kirthar ranges to a vague border with Makrān and Hind near Daibul. It appears to have been well populated by people who spoke a non-Iranian language, possibly Brahui as today. The main town was called Bauterna (modern Khuzdar). (For references and more detailed discussion see Brunner, pp. 772-77; Chaumont, pp. 130-37.)

Toward the end of the caliphate of ʿOmar, Makrān was invaded by the Arabs (23/644), who found it as unattractive as most outsiders appear to have done both before and since. After defeating the local ruler and marching almost to the Indus, they reported back to ʿOmar that it was an unattractive region, with the result that ʿOmar ordered that the Arabs should not cross the Indus. A similar sentiment is attributed to another commander: that the water in Makrān was scanty, the dates poor in quality; that a small army would be swallowed up in the deserts and a large one would die of hunger (Bosworth, 1968, pp. 1-25).

After the Arab conquest most of the area soon returned to its more characteristic condition of internal autonomy under alien hegemony. In particular it continued to serve as a refuge for people who had been displaced from the more fertile conditions of Iran and India. Especially, in the next few centuries, since Sīstān was a major center of Kharijite sentiment, many Kharijites found their way into Makrān (Bosworth, 1968, pp. 37-41).

In the early 5th/11th century the Ghaznavid empire established a pattern which has continued into more recent history. The geopolitical interests of the Ghaznavids, centered to the northeast of the area, complemented the decline of Sīstān, and brought Qoṣdār (Khuzdar), and through it much of Makrān, into dependency on Qandahār. Since then, although the governments of the western plateau (modern Iran) continued (until the establishment of Zāhedān as the administrative capital of the Iranian province of Baluchistan under Reżā Shah) to see Makrān as an extension of Kermān, governments on the eastern plateau (modern Afghanistan) have seen it as a southward extension from Qandahār.

Over the next three centuries, when first the Saljuqs and then the Mongols ruled in Iran, Iranian influence did not extend very far beyond Kermān, and Makrān became relatively autonomous again. In the 7th/13th century Marco Polo calls it Kesmacoran (Kech-Makrān), suggesting that the agricultural settlements along the Kech river were the most flourishing part of the area. Food was abundant and good (he mentions the full range of staples: rice and wheat, meat and milk). Kech had its own ruler (*malek*), and the people, who included non-Muslims and lived by commerce as much as agriculture, trading both overland and by sea in all directions, spoke a language Polo did not recognize. It is also worth noting that he identified the kingdom of Kesmacoran as the last in India, rather than the first in Iran (II, pp. 401-03). During this period Balōč migration intensified and the area began to take on the character of Baluchistan, absorbing a succession of immigrant groups, of which the Balōč were neither the first nor the last. But the history of the area cannot be understood as a refuge area or backwater. It is a borderland between India and Iran and a bridge between the Iranian plateau and the Arabian peninsula. Political and economic influences from both Iran (including what later became Afghanistan) and India continually affected the political economy, and local leaders have generally looked in both directions for potential sources of external support in their internal conflicts.

5. The eastward migrations of the Balōč.

Although many Balōč moved into and through Makrān starting in the 5th/11th century, others were probably already present in the general area east of Kermān. Evidence for the migration is sparse. There are two major types: the corpus of traditional Baluchi poetry and later Mughal histories.

The poems claim that the Balōč are descended from Mīr Ḥamza (Mīr is a Baluchi title for leaders, Arabic *amīr*), the uncle of the Prophet; that they fought with the sons of ʿAlī at Karbalāʾ, whence they migrated to Baluchistan. There are two possible interpretations of this epic history. First, tribal populations in the Muslim world have typically traced their genealogies back to the time of the Prophet as a way of legitimizing their Islam in their own tribal (i.e., genealogical) terms. Second, there are a number of ways in which Arab groups could have found their way into the heterogeneous tribal population that eventually assimilated Baluch identity east of Kermān, whether or not their forebears had fought at Karbalāʾ. Some of the original Arab invaders may have remained in the area, and there is evidence of migration across the Persian Gulf from Arabia into the Kermān region in the early centuries of Islam.

The poems tell of arrival in Sīstān and of the hospitality of a king named Šams-al-Dīn. A ruler (*malek*) by that name claiming descent from the Saffarids is known to have died in 559/1164. After a time another ruler called Badr-al-Dīn (of whom we have no independent record, unless he was a Ghurid) persecuted them and drove them out. Little else of any significance is identifiable, except the occasional place name in Makrān (see discussion in Dames, 1904b, pp. 35-36). It seems likely that this sort of eastward progress was determined by the use that various minor rulers may have had for a mercenary force.

The first record of movement into Sind is from the 7-8th/13-14th centuries. The main divisions of the Balōč tribes described in the poems presumably reflect events during this period. According to the poems a Mīr Jalāl Khan who was leader of all the Balōč left four sons, Rind, Lāšār, Hōt, and Kōraī, and a daughter named Jātō, who married his nephew Morād. These five became the eponymous founders of the five main tribes of the poems, the Rind, Lāšārī, Hōt, Kōraī and Jātōī. The poems tell of forty-four tribes (called *tuman* or *bōlak*), of which forty were Balōč, and four were servile tribes dependent on them. Other important names that have survived to the present are Drīšak, Mazārī, Dumbkī, Khōsā. The Hōt seem to have been in the area earlier than the others. It may be significant that some names are derived from known place names in Baluchistan. Many of the prominent tribes of today are not mentioned in the poems, such as Būgṭī, Bulēdī, Buzdār, Kasrānī, Lēgarī, Lund, Marī. Since these tribes were probably there in the 9th/15th century, the absence of their names in the poems suggests that either they are later branches of the old tribes, or they were not then Balōč and have been assimilated since.

In the 9th/15th century another wave carried the Balōč into southern Punjab. This was the period of Mīr Čākar (Čākor) Rind, the greatest of Baluchistan heroes. Some groups from the Rind tribe migrated from Sibi to Punjab, and spread up the valleys of the Chenab, Ravi, and Satlej rivers. Meanwhile, the Dōdaī (probably a Sindhi tribe assimilated during the previous 200 years) and Hōt moved up the Indus and the Jhelam. Bābor, the first Mughal emperor, found Balōč in Punjab in 925/1519. He hired them, as did his successor, Homāyūn. The first actual settlement of Balōč in Punjab appears to have been made in the reign of Shah Ḥosayn in Multan 874-908/1469-70–1502, who gave them a *jāgīr* (probably in return for military service)–an act which attracted more Balōč into the area. In Punjab many Balōč turned to settled agriculture in the 10th/16th century. (The references for this period are listed and discussed in more detail by Dames, 1904b, pp. 34-43.)

Although large numbers of Balōč moved into the Indus valley, there has never been any question of moving the boundaries of Baluchistan eastward to incorporate them. Balōč who settled in the lowlands, with the exception of Kacchi, tended to assimilate linguistically with the surrounding population, and lose their ties with kin in the highlands, though many (we cannot know what proportion) have retained their Balōč identity.

6. Events leading to the establishment of the Baluch khanate of Kalat.

The 10th/16th century saw the rise of Safavid power in Iran and of Mughal power in India, and the arrival of European ships in the Sea of Oman and the Persian Gulf. The interests and conflicts of these three outside powers could not fail to affect the internal politics of the Balōč and other communities that lay between them. The major events that form the basis of Baluchi epic poetry, remembered as the wars between the Rind and Lāšārī tribes, occurred during this period and were obviously conditioned by the opportunities and incentives afforded by the larger geopolitical context.

The Safavids reestablished some Iranian control in Makrān, mainly from Bampūr, Dezak, and Sīstān (Röhrborn, pp. 12, 74, 82-83). In 1515, Shah Esmāʿīl (who had no navy) was forced to accept the Portuguese occupation of Hormoz, and concluded a treaty with the admiral, Alfonso de Albuquerque (q.v.), on terms that included the provision that the Portuguese would assist the shah in suppressing a revolt in Makrān. However, this collaboration, which would have been the first of its type with a European force in the area, proved abortive because of Albuquerque's death. In 1581, for reasons that are unclear, the Portuguese destroyed the ports of Gwadar and Tīs (Lorimer, I/1A, pp. 7-8).

The Dutch arrived in Hormoz at the beginning of the 11th/17th century and the British appeared soon afterward. In 1613 Sir Robert Sherley, who stopped at Gwadar on his way to Isfahan as ambassador, was nearly killed when a group of Baluch made a surprise attack on his ship. But afterward he wrote to the East India Company (established in 1600) in London recommending that they set up a factory in Gwadar, because it was autonomous, tributary to Iran, safe from the Portuguese, and promised "the richest traffic in the world." In 1650 a Baluch guard defended Muscat (Masqaṭ) on behalf of the Portuguese (though the Imam of Muscat ousted the Portuguese later in the same year; see Lorimer, I/1A, p. 39). All the Europeans readily took on various groups of Baluch as guards and mercenaries. The Baluch did not display any solidarity in relation to these non-Muslim aliens. Baluch and foreigner cooperated or fought, according to local interests and animosities.

At this time the overland traffic was still taxed by the ruler (*malek*) of Kech, who also controlled Gwadar, and according to Pietro della Valle was on friendly terms with the Persian government. But around 1029/1620 Kech was taken over by the Bulēdī tribe, who appear to have been followers of the Ḏekrī (Zikri) heresy (see 11 below: *ethnography*), and dominated the whole of Makrān up to Jāsk until 1740 (Lorimer, 1/2, pp. 2150-51).

The prevalence of heresy in Makrān during this period may have separated it more than usual from the events of the highlands. Qandahār and the Quetta-Pishin area to the north changed hands between the Safavids and Mughals more than once, but although the Safavids eventually retained Qandahār and claimed the highlands down to Kalat (Röhrborn, p. 13), the Mughal influence was more significant in the history of the Baluch. Homāyūn is reputed to have given Shal (Quetta) and Mastung to a Baluch named Lawang Khan (*Gazetteer* V, p. 34). A Mīr Qambarānī (Kambarānī) used Mughal support to drive out the Jats from the Jahlawan district to the south, though his son, Mīr ʿOmar, was confronted with the Arḡūns of Qandahār. When Bābor took Qandahār (1522), Shah Bēg Arḡūn had moved to Sind, and Mīr ʿOmar seized an opportunity to take Kalat. He was driven out and killed by Rind and Lāšārī Balōč from Makrān, who included the figures celebrated in the heroic ballads, Mīr Šayhak Rind, his son Mīr Čākar Rind, and Mīr Gwahrām Lāšārī. But the Baluch did not stay; they moved on to Kacchi, leaving Mīr Čākar's father-in-law, Mīr Mandō, in Kalat. Mīr Čākar appears to have remained in the area of Sibi and the Bolan Pass. In 1556 shortly before he died he is said to have acknowledged the suzerainty of the Mughals. In Kalat Mandō was soon overpowered by Brahui tribesmen under Mīr Bijjar, the son of ʿOmar. After Mīr Bijjar, Kalat was again taken by the Mughals, though they never managed to control the surrounding tribes. But with the loss of Qandahār the Mughal hold on the highlands weakened and the Brahui under Mīr Ebrāhīm Khan Mīrwārī managed to regain Kalat. Mīr Ebrāhīm declined to rule, and the khanate was offered to Mīr Ḥasan, his brother-in-law. Mīr Ḥasan was the first "khan of the Balōč." The term Baluch (as used in this article) applies to participants in the polity that developed under his rule and that of his successors.

Mīr Ḥasan died without issue shortly after acceding to the title, the government passed to Mīr Aḥmad Khan Qambarānī, who became the eponymous founder of the Aḥmadzay dynasty of the State of Kalat (Baluch, pp. 69-75; Rooman, pp. 28-29).

7. The Aḥmadzay khanate of Kalat up to the intrusion of British power (1666-1839).

The major factors in the history of Kalat in this period (before the encroachment of the British and the reawakening of Persian interest in the area) were the expansion of Kalat territory under the early khans, the effects of Nāder Shah's activities with regard to India, and the Persian Gulf; the power of Nāder Shah's successor in Qandahār, Aḥmad Shah Abdālī; the decline of the khanate after the death of Mīr Naṣīr Khan I in 1795; the ambitions of Moḥammad Shah Qājār, and the development of British interest. The uplands and the lowlands continued to have distinct political histories, though the success of Naṣīr Khan I in the second half of the 12th/18th century integrated them to some extent for the duration of his reign. From this period onward the history of the area has been seen in relatively exlusive terms as the history of Baluchistan (though its exact boundaries were often vague). Outside interest in the area, such as that of Oman (in Gwadar) and of Afghanistan (in "Pashtunistan"), have been seen as intrusive. However, a deeper historical perspective makes it clear that up until this period the area was neither an exclusive nor an integrated political or cultural unit; rather it formed part of a larger area that included Qandahār and Sīstān to the north and Oman to the south, and lay between the political poles of Iran and India. Within Kalat the highlands and lowlands were only loosely related: The lowlands were closely related to Oman, and the highlands were an extension of Qandahār. The subsequent history of the area is easier to follow when seen in these larger geopolitical terms. (This section is based on the more detailed discussions in Baluch, Lockhart, Rooman, the *Gazetteers*, and the author's unpublished ethnohistorical research.)

Continuity of authority in Kalat dates from the accession of Mīr Aḥmad Qambarānī in 1666. Mīr Aḥmad ruled for thirty years and became an ally of the Mughal emperor Awrangzīb ʿĀlamgīr I. He spent his life fighting the Bārōzay Afghans to the north and the Kalhora rulers of Sind to the south in order to preserve and expand his territory. He finally succeeded in controlling both Sibi and the Quetta-Pishin area. But his son, Mīr Meḥrāb Khan I, was still obliged to fight the Kalhoras. He defeated them in 1695, though he died in the battle. Mīr Samandar Khan, Meḥrāb's brother's son and successor, continued to keep the Kalhora family in check and also defeated a military expedition from Iran under Ṭahmāsb Bēg, who planned to annex western Baluchistan to Iran. Samandar was rewarded for these services by the Mughals with the port of Karachi and other gifts.

The acquisition of power by a local leader, who was able to establish the framework for dynastic succession in Kalat, transformed the political economy of the area, and set the scene for the later development of Baluch society. During the two centuries up to the time when the British took over the affairs of Kalat the general pattern of the khan's external relations was accommodation with the political power in Qandahār and in Delhi, hostilities with Sind, and disorder in relations with Kermān. Baluch tribes in western Makrān and the Sarḥadd often raided into Iran—especially during the reign of Shah Sultan Ḥosayn, the last Safavid monarch 1105-35/1694-1722 (Lorimer, I/2, p. 2152). In 1721 the British and Dutch factories at Bandar-e ʿAbbās (q.v.) were attacked by a force of four thousand Baluch on horseback, who (apparently encouraged by the Afghan invasion of Persia) overran the province of Kermān and raided westward into Lārestān.

The rise of the Ḡelzay under Mīr Ways in Qandahār early in the 12th/18th century changed the political climate in Baluchistan. Quetta and Pishin were reattached to Qandahār in 1709. Mīr Aḥmad Khan II, the son of Mīr Meḥrāb Khan, whose profligacy displeased the Baluch sardars, was killed by his younger brother Mīr ʿAbd-Allāh Khan who then succeeded him. ʿAbd-Allāh (r. 1714-34), who was known as Qah(h)ār Khan, was one of the stronger Aḥmadzay rulers, and remained relatively free to pursue his military and political ambitions during the period immediately preceding Nāder Shah's appearance at Qandahār. He managed to conquer Kacchi in the south, Harand and Dajil in the northeast, Panjgur, Kech, and even Bandar-e ʿAbbās to the west, and Shorawak in the northwest. The last brought him into more direct conflict with Shah Ḥosayn K̲aljī (r. 1725-38) of Qandahār, who joined forces with the Kalhoras in Sind in an attempt to defeat him. They were successful, and the khan tried to punish the Kalhoras again, but was defeated and killed in Kacchi.

Though the Aḥmadzay's alliance with the Mughals had served them well, their enforced accommodation with the highland power of Nāder Shah and his successor in Qandahār, Aḥmad Shah Abdālī, served them even better. The conflict between Nāder Shah and the Mughals allowed the Aḥmadzay to establish themselves to the point where the British would later decide to rule through them, despite their declining abilities.

In concentrating his attention on the south, Mīr ʿAbd-Allāh Khan had served the Mughals too well and incurred the wrath of Nāder Shah. Nāder had named ʿAbd-Allāh his governor of Baluchistan and required him to move against the ʿAbdālīs in Qandahār from the south, while he, Nāder, moved in from the west. Owing to his entanglement with the Kalhoras, which led to his death in battle, ʿAbd-Allāh had failed to respond. Before Nāder was able to punish Kalat, ʿAbd-Allāh's son, Mīr Moḥabbat Khan, was found unsatisfactory by the Baluch sardars, and replaced by his brother Mīr Ahltāz Khan. However, the sardars soon found Mīr Ahltāz no better and reinstated Moḥabbat (though Ahltāz seems to have retained some power among the Dehwār in Mastung). Nāder sent Pīr Moḥammad, the *beglarbegī* of Herāt, against Kalat. In 1149/1736, rather than fight, both Moḥabbat and Ahltāz went to Qandahār and submitted to Nāder Shah, who took the elder, Moḥabbat, into his service and appointed him governor of Baluchistan including Makrān. Nāder also gave them the lowland plains of Kacchi (then ruled by the Kalhoras of Sind) as blood compensation for the death of Mīr ʿAbd-Allāh Khan. As a result the khanate now controlled both highland and lowland grazing and more land for cultivation throughout the year. Their resource base was greatly increased and the stage was set for further internal political development.

Following the assassination of Nāder Shah in 1160/1747, Aḥmad Shah Abdālī, later known as Dorrānī, who was heir to Nāder Shah's paramountcy over Kalat, deposed Moḥabbat and put in his place another younger brother, Mīr Naṣīr Khan, who with his mother had been a hostage in Nāder's camp since 1737. Naṣīr was historically the most significant of the Aḥmadzay rulers. He ruled for nearly half a century, and established the organization of the state of Kalat for the remainder of its existence. He was the only khan who successfully transcended tribal loyalties.

Of the land that had accrued to the state of Kalat up to this time half was reserved for the Aḥmadzay as crown land and the other half was divided among the tribes that made up the fighting force from Sarawan and Jahlawan. The khan allocated land to the tribes in two categories: *ḡam* lands and *jāgīr* lands. *Ḡam* lands were allocated according to the number of fighting men supplied by each tribe, with the stipulation that the land be used to raise crops to support the fighting force in the field. Since it was communal property of each tribe, it could not be alienated. One-twelfth of the income was gathered by the leader of each tribe and submitted to the khan as revenue. Unlike the *jāgīr* this land could be confiscated by the khan if the tribe failed in its obligations. It is interesting to note that this communal tenure originated with the khan and was not generated by the tribal community itself, as is often assumed. The khan's crown lands were worked by Dehwār, whereas the tribes used Jat cultivators.

Naṣīr set about building his fighting force in three "regiments": the Sarawan regiment, the Jahlawan regiment, and a special regiment directly under his own command. He chose one tribe each from Sarawan and Jahlawan (which may have laid the basis of the later ranking of the tribes) to lead and to be responsible for recruitment from their respective areas. He also formed a bureaucracy, by creating offices of government: a *wazīr* was given charge of internal and foreign affairs; a *wakīl* was made responsible for the collection of tribute and blood compensation, and the revenue from crown lands; a *dārōğa* was put in charge of the organization of the Dehwār cultivators on crown lands, and worked through Brahui *nāʾebs* (deputies). Finally, a *šāh-(ā)qāsī* (after Nāder's *ešīk-āqāsī*) was given direction of *darbārs* and the seating arrangement for leaders according to their rank. Beside these officers, he created two councils. Membership in one of the councils (*majles-e moṣāḥebīn*) was by his own nomination, and primarily from among his close kinsmen, but it also included the two leaders of the tribes of Sarawan and Jahlawan. The second was a council of sardars (*majles-e mošāwarat*). Members of the first council, or their representatives, had to remain at Kalat continuously along with one-twelfth the number of soldiers raised by each tribe (*ğamē paškar*). Judicial powers were vested in the sardars who were subject to guidance by *qāżīs* (judges) according to the religious law (*Šarīʿa*), except that local custom took precedence in matters of adultery and murder. The written language for state business was Persian, and bureaucratic positions were recruited from the Persian-speaking Dehwār peasant community.

Quetta had come under Nāder Shah when he took Qandahār, and he assigned it to Naṣīr and his mother during the time that Mīr Moḥabbat Khan held Kalat. Aḥmad Shah is said to have finally given it to Kalat after receiving assistance from Naṣīr in a campaign in eastern Iran in 1751—as a kind of *šāl* (lit. present of a shawl) for his mother, Bībī Maryam. But Pishin remained under the Dorrānīs.

Kalat was still subordinate to the Abdālī court of Qandahār. The treaty between them called for an annual payment of Rs 2,000 from Kalat to Qandahār, and the provision and maintenance of 1,000 soldiers in Qandahār. An apparent act of insubordination on the part of Naṣīr, who failed to respond when summoned to Qandahār, led to the negotiation of a new treaty after Aḥmad Shah Abdālī failed to defeat him outright. Because Aḥmad Shah needed Naṣīr's support elsewhere, the new treaty was more equal. The khanate no longer paid tribute or maintained a force at Qandahār. Instead, Kalat provided a fighting force only when the Afghans fought outside their kingdom, and then the khan would be provided with money and ammunition. The new treaty was sealed by a pledge of loyalty to Qandahār and the marriage of the khan's niece to Aḥmad Shah Abdālī's son. In the settlement with Qandahār the final accommodation was that the shah gave Naṣīr the title of *beglarbegī* while the khan recognized him as suzerain.

With the security and freedom of action afforded by the new treaty with Qandahār and the resulting stabilization of the northern and eastern border, Naṣīr was able to move against the neighboring territories of Kharan, Makrān, and Las Bela. The Gīčkī (who had become dominant in Makrān in 1740) and most of the Bulēdī were Ḏekrī. Naṣīr made nine expeditions against them. The struggle was ended, apparently before 1778, by a compromise under which the revenues of the country were divided equally between the Gīčkī leaders and the khan, with the direct administration remaining in the hands of the Gīčkī, who were divided into two branches, a senior branch in Panjgur and a junior one in Kech and Gwadar.

Naṣīr led some twenty-five military expeditions during his rule. Beside the Gīčkī in Makrān, he fought against Las Bela, Kharan, the Marī, and the Baluch Tālpūr family that had succeeded the Kalhoras in Sind. All these accepted his suzerainty. He also fought with the Sikhs of Punjab and with ʿAlī Mardān Khan of Tūn and Ṭabas in eastern Iran. At the end of his rule his authority extended over an area not very different from the later Pakistani province of Baluchistan, though it did not extend so far to the north or northeast, and only the central parts were directly administered.

Meanwhile, the course of events in the Makrān lowlands had been changed by activities in Oman and by the interest Nāder Shah had taken in the Persian Gulf—although Nāder's officers were incompetent and corrupt and were defeated by the Gīčkī. The imam of Oman continued a practice, possibly originated by the Portuguese, of recruiting Baluch from Makrān into his service. At least one exclusively Baluch community on the Omani coast today dates from this period. In 1740 Aḥmad b. Saʿīd, governor of Sohar, conducted a coup and founded the Āl Bū Saʿīd dynasty. Being a merchant and shipowner, he was unable to rely on tribal connections and was obliged to recruit Baluch and African slaves as mercenaries. In 1784 a pretender to the government of Oman, named Sayyed Solṭān b. Aḥmad, sought refuge in Makrān. According to local traditions Solṭān came first to Zik, a fortified village of the Mīrwārī tribe in Kolwa, and thence, having been joined by Dād-Karīm Mīrwārī, proceeded to Kharan, where his cause was espoused by Mīr Jahāngīr, a Nowšērwānī leader. The group then paid their respects to Mīr Naṣīr Khan at Kalat. Naṣīr at first seems to have undertaken to help the supplicant to establish himself in Oman, but in the end only gave him Gwadar. At the time Gwadar had declined in prosperity and was an insignificant fishing village. There is no record of Naṣīr's intention. He appears to have given no thought to the interests of the Gīčkī. Later Oman claimed that the gift was intended to be in perpetuity—which later khans denied but were generally unable to contest. The situation was contested by the Gīčkīs, who argued that Naṣīr could alienate only his own half of the revenue, not the half that belonged to them. Until 1792, when Solṭān finally became ruler of Oman, he appears to have made Gwadar a base for expeditions against the Omani coast. After establishing himself in Oman he made Gwadar a dependency and sent a representative with troops to occupy it and build a fort. He then sent a force to Čāhbahār, which (with the aid of the Isma'ili merchant community) entered the harbor under the pretext of fishing, and then took the town by surprise. Čāhbahār had been under a Bulēdī, named Šafīʿ Moḥammad, who paid a quarter of his revenue to Mīr Sobḥān, the Jadgāl ruler at Bahu, though he had for some time also paid another quarter to Oman. Čāhbahār seems to have been lost to Oman on the death of Solṭān in 1804, but to have been recovered again after a short interval. Its revenue in 1809 was Rs 5,000 per year, which still went entirely to the Sultan of Oman. Little more is known of Gwadar and Čāhbahār until the encroachment of the British attracted the interest of the Persian government in the 1860s, except that it rapidly overtook the neighboring ports, Pasni and Jiwanri, in prosperity. The rulers of the major Makrān settlements were in continuous contact with Oman with regard to the status and security of the ports.

Mīr Naṣīr Khan was a strict Muslim. He protected the Hindu traders in his territory, and felt an obligation to combat the heresy of the Ḏekrīs (Zikris) in Makrān. The half-century of political stability he provided had significant economic results. Both agriculture and trade increased. Some sections of the Nārūʾī in Kharan, Chagai, and southern Sīstān turned to agriculture. But after Naṣīr's death the decline was rapid. He was succeeded by his eldest son, Maḥmūd, who was still a minor aged seven. Almost immediately the influence of Kalat ceased to be felt in Makrān and the area became divided among the local leaders. The circumstances of the succession are unclear. But it appears that it was disputed by a grandson of Moḥabbat, called Bahrām. Bahrām took Karachi, but was defeated by the regent acting in the name of Maḥmūd, with assistance from Shah Zamān, the ruler of Qandahār.

When he came of age, Maḥmūd proved inadequate to the task of rebuilding his father's state. Seeing his lack of aptitude for the position, the peripheral territories all reasserted their independence. In 1810 Henry Pottinger, one of the first English travelers to visit Baluchistan, found the sardars acting independently. Maḥmūd's son, Mīr Meḥrāb Khan II, stopped the decline for a while. He regained Kech, but had trouble with his ministers, which caused him losses in the north and east.

For this period immediately preceding British intervention in the area, there is for the first time some relatively detailed economic data. The khan had crown lands in most of the provinces of the state, but most of the revenue was consumed by the agents who collected it. Most of his income was drawn from Kacchi, which was the most productive of his provinces. His revenue from this source was estimated at Rs 300,000 per annum. Kalat had earlier (as Kīzkānān) been an important entrepot for merchandise from Khorasan, Qandahār, Kabul, and India, but by the 1820s its trade was insignificant (Waaltyer, II, p. 528; Masson, II, pp. 122-23). The entire income of Baluchistan and its dependencies in 1810 was estimated at no more than Rs 200,000 (Schefer, p. 7). Ḥājī ʿAbd-al-Nabī (who according to Leech undertook a secret reconnaissance of Makrān in 1838) traveled part of the way from Mastung toward Panjgur with the khan's *šāh-qāsī*, who was on his way to collect the revenue with a body of 300 horse, foot, and camelry. The revenue is later stated to be 2,000 Kashani rupees, plus a proportion of the crop. The same traveler reported that at Kharan, which was independent of Kalat and under the suzerainty of Qandahār, there were five or six ironsmiths, one Hindu trader, many carpenters, and sixty weavers. At Dezak in the west he found at least 1,000 cotton weavers and fabrics exported in all directions, and a hundred Hindu traders. He continues to give figures for many of the settlements of the Sarḥadd and the Makrān, with many interesting political and economic details and accounts of his adventures. Beyond the authority of the khan of Kalat and the sultan of Oman the territory—most of what is now Baluchistan within Iran—was generally divided into miniature republics based on forts in the agricultural settlements. Pottinger in 1810 found that Persian authority was held in contempt by the ruler of Bampūr. The Persian claim to the whole of Baluchistan up to India had continued since the Achaemenids, though in the medieval period only Nāder Shah Afšār sought to enforce it. It was finally the activity of the rebellious Āqā Khan (q.v.) between 1838 and 1844 that led Moḥammad Shah Qājār to send forces into the area.

During the same period the eastern part of Baluchistan appears to have had more trade. We are told that Bela had about 300 houses, one third occupied by Hindus. Wad in Jahlawan was a small town, comprising two groups of mud houses about 100 yards apart, the western group containing about 50 houses mainly inhabited by Hindu traders, the eastern group containing 25-30 houses of Muslims including sardars of the Mengal tribe, ʿĪsā and Walī Moḥammad. Nal, the seat of the Bīzenjō tribe, 15 miles to the west, was roughly the same size but had a fort. Khuzdar had a ruined fort and several small hamlets of 2-3 houses each, perhaps 60 houses altogether, only three of Hindus, though there had formerly been 30. Kalat itself had as many as 800 houses, many inhabited by Hindus, and two outlying settlements inhabited by the Bābī tribe of Afghans in exile (Masson, II, pp. 121-23).

Early in the 19th century the British in India began to take a more serious interest in the interior because of their concern about their northwestern frontier. In 1809, when the first Englishman, a Captain Grant, set out to explore whether a European army might enter India from that direction, the British resident in Muscat (Captain Seton) advised him that the whole area was unsettled. Gwat(a)r, where Grant landed, belonged to Mīr Sobḥān, a Jadgāl leader who ruled from Daštīārī and Bāhū and was the strongest ruler in Makrān (Lorimer, I/II, p. 2154). From there he marched to Čāhbahār, then to Nigwar, the coastal plain to the east of Čāhbahār, where he met Mīr Sobḥān and was well received. At the end of February he reached Qaṣr-e Qand, where he found an independent ruler, Shaikh Samandar. He waited there for Moḥammad Khan, the ruler of Geh (now Nīkšahr), under whose protection he was to travel into the interior. Geh was second only to Kech in local power. From Geh he marched to Bampūr. The ruler in Bampūr was unreliable, and Grant returned to Qaṣr-e Qand, Geh, and Čāhbahār, and then along the coast to Jāsk, and on to Bandar-e ʿAbbās. Grant reported that his journey was possible only because of the letters of introduction he carried from the British resident in Muscat to Mīr Sobḥān. Grant also carried letters of credit from Muscat, and there was plenty of trade between Muscat and Čāhbahār. He traveled in European clothes and found everyone "more civil and hospitable than they had been represented." Like Pottinger, he found no Persian influence in Makrān.

In 1839 the failure of a British diplomatic mission to Kabul and the arrival there of a Russian envoy led to the British viceroy's decision to invade Afghanistan and reinstall Shah Šojāʿ in Kabul (see ANGLO-AFGHAN WARS, i). In order to ensure safe passage of the army to Qandahār, it was necessary to control Baluchistan. Leech, the first Englishman formally despatched to conclude an agreement with the khan, failed. Later Sir Alexander Burnes was sent and an agreement was arrived at in March, 1839, which guaranteed the sovereignty and borders of Kalat and made the khan responsible for the safe passage and provisioning of the British troops in return for Rs 15,000 in addition to the cost of provisions (Aitchison, XI, p. 209). This agreement marked the end of the autonomy of Baluchistan.

8. The British period, 1839-1947.

The next hundred years saw an explosion of publications on the Baluch and Baluchistan. The information was produced through the interest of the neighboring powers, who finally achieved a definitive division of the area into three separate provinces of the adjacent nation-states.

Early in the 19th century the British set about gathering and organizing information on the whole of India, which they eventually published in the form of district gazetteers. The district gazetteer series for Baluchistan (1906-08) comprises eight volumes. Each gazetteer deals with an administrative district or group of districts and is organized into four chapters: basic geographical description, including an historical review of the social situation; a statement on the economic condition (agriculture, rents, labor and prices, weights and measures, forests and other natural resources, trade and transportation); an account of the administration (revenue, justice, police, public works); and finally miniature gazetteers describing individual settlements. The Baluchistan series is an extraordinary compendium of information, and ranks among the best of all the Indian gazetteers (Scholberg, p. 49) as well as other literature of the same type. This section is based on information taken from the gazetteers, the Persian syntheses by Taqīzāda and Jahānbānī, and the author's unpublished ethnohistorical research except where otherwise noted.

The extension of British interest westward through Makrān stimulated Persian interest in pursuing ancient claims to the area. As they sought to reestablish their authority the Persians also began to gather information. Early efforts resulted from the interest of governors-general of Kermān under Nāṣer-al-Dīn Shah (see Farmānfarmā, Wazīrī, Sepehr). Later and more detailed efforts followed on the pacification of the area under Reżā Shah (see Jahānbānī, Kayhān, Razmārā, Taqīzāda). The Russians began to explore Persian Baluchistan around the turn of the century (see Rittikh, Zarudnyĭ). Other Europeans, especially Germans, also took an interest (e.g., the Austrian Gasteiger), though they published little new information.

From 1839 to 1947 the greater part of Baluchistan was—formally or informally—under the British Empire, whose interest was essentially in securing and protecting its North-West Frontier Province from both Afghanistan and Iran. At a particular stage in this endeavor the British negotiated formal international borders through the territories of Baluch tribes with both Iran and Afghanistan, roughly according to the effective sphere of influence of the khan of Kalat, but with some attention to the interests of local leaders. They then sought to control the administration of the state of Kalat, at first through the khan, later in the name of the khan, and they gradually took on the direct administration of buffer areas between them and Afghanistan as well as some other especially troublesome areas such as the eastern districts of the Marī and Būgṭī tribes. The British intervened in the life of the Baluch mainly in order to bolster the authority of the khan and the subsidiary rulers in Makrān, as a means of maintaining peace and internal security, to establish the frontier, to lay the telegraph line, and (after some delay) finally to abolish the slave trade. The government of Afghanistan paid little attention to its Baluch population. But the Persian government sought to control as much as possible of Baluchistan by exploiting the ambitions and animosities of the local rulers; it did not establish a functioning administrative structure for the area until later.

The agreement between the British and Mīr Meḥrāb Khan in 1839 soon ran into trouble. Many of the sardars opposed it, and some of them sabotaged it by waylaying Burnes on his way back from Quetta, stealing the document and making out that they were acting on the instructions of the khan. The British were deceived, and resolved to punish the khan. In November of the same year they invaded Baluchistan and attacked Kalat. Mīr Meḥrāb Khan was killed in the action. Determined to control the route into Afghanistan, the British then installed in Kalat a great grandson of Mīr Moḥabbat Khan, the fourteen-year-old Mīr Šahnavāz Khan, with a Lieutenant Loveday as regent, and dismembered the khan's dominions. Mastung and Quetta were given to Shah Šojāʿ, though the British continued to control them in his name. Kacchi was placed under the political agent for Western Sind. However, Meḥrāb's son, whom he had named Mīr Naṣīr Khan II, was able to rally the tribes and retake Kalat in the following year (Rooman, pp. 41-43). Benefiting from a wave of popular support Naṣīr was able soon after to regain Quetta, Mastung, and Kacchi. Local skirmishes continued till 1842, when the British retired from Baluchistan because of more pressing problems in Afghanistan and elsewhere. As a condition of their withdrawal, Sibi remained under the British and Pishin was reoccupied by the Afghans, though Quetta remained with Kalat. The British undertook to help Naṣīr in case of outside attack, while Naṣīr accepted Shah Šojāʿ and the East India Company as suzerain powers who could station their forces anywhere in Kalat in emergency. The khan further agreed to act under British advice, refrain from any engagement without their previous sanction and to fix a pension for Mīr Šahnavāz and his family (Aitchison, XI, pp. 210-11). Essentially, the khan had secured British support for local Baluch autonomy under conditions similar to his historical relationship to the Afghans. The new ingredient was the role the British now played in Afghan interests. Shortly afterward the British also contrived to control the Marī through the khan, though the relationship did not last. The British annexed Sind in 1843, and Punjab in 1849. In 1854 the situation was formalized by a treaty in Khangarh (later Jacobabad) which included an annual subsidy to the khan of Rs 50,000 (Rooman, p. 44).

The state of Kalat was now incorporated into the British colonial system. Even the Baluch who were not controlled by Kalat were deeply influenced by the British connection. The khan was essentially a paid official, an intermediary between the British and the sardars (who continued until recently to hold real authority with the tribes). As a result the khan gradually lost his authority with the sardars (N. Swidler, p. 49), and the British were obliged to an increasing extent to work directly with, and to subsidize, each sardar. This practice was later extended into western Baluchistan (Iran) with the construction of the telegraph in the 1860s.

Naṣīr was succeeded in 1857, on his death, by his step-brother Mīr Ḵodādād Khan, aged sixteen. Ḵodādād ruled until 1893—a period marked by serious conflicts with the sardars. Ḵodādād appears not to have understood the significance of the colonial power, which continually frustrated his efforts to rule, while not only he but many of the sardars were dependent on British subsidies. For a while the British were content simply to contain events through diplomacy and subsidies. But in 1875 in response to the Russian advance into Turkestan they decided to construct a railway and a telegraph link to Baluchistan. They sent Captain Robert Sandeman to Kalat to develop the basis for a more positive "forward" policy. Sandeman succeeded in composing outstanding disputes between the khan and the sardars, and designed a way of administering the tribes through their own chiefs in accordance with tribal custom but under British supervision, which later became well known as the Sandeman system of indirect rule (Thornton). In the following year Sandeman concluded the Mastung Settlement, according to which the Treaty of 1854 was renewed and enhanced: the khan was to have no independent foreign relations, a permanent British garrison was to be posted in Kalat, the khan was to send a representative to the government of India, the British were to be the sole arbiters in disputes between the khan and the sardars, and the projected railway and telegraph were to be protected in the interests of both parties. The khan's annuity was raised to Rs 100,000, beside Rs 25,000 for the construction of more outposts and for ensuring the security of transport and communications. The trade rights of the khan with Afghanistan and India were also transferred to the British for another Rs 30,000 per year (Aitchison, XI, pp. 215-18).

The subsidies paid to the sardars were contingent upon their loyalty to the khan and the maintenance of internal peace. The sardars were still encouraged to settle disputes by traditional procedures, through sardar circles for intratribal cases, and jirgas when disputes were intertribal. However, all jirga decisions were subject to review by the British political agent. In general, the British system seemed to fit the tribal system well (N. Swidler, p. 53). The sardars and the British agents understood each other's conception of authority and were able to work together. But in the long term the British system had the effect of dividing the Baluch into numerous personal fiefdoms based on individual sardars, and elevated the khan to an exclusively ceremonial status.

In 1877 Sandeman occupied Quetta, and with the khan's consent established the administrative center of the Baluchistan Agency. Quetta was used as a base for the second Afghan War (q.v.) in 1878 (brought on by increasing British fear of Russian influence in Afghanistan). The war was concluded by the Treaty of Gandamak in 1879, which ceded Pishin to the British. One after another all the districts along the border with Afghanistan were leased to the British in return for an annual payment and incorporated into the province of British Baluchistan. Kalat was sealed off from all territories that were of strategic interest to the British. The Quetta cantonment soon surpassed Kalat and Mastung both as an administrative and as a commercial center. Although Baluchistan remained a relatively isolated area, peripheral to the Indian economy, the social effects of British investment should not be underestimated. Cash crops were introduced close to the major routes. A certain amount of sedentarization took place as new villages were built. Some sardars were knighted, and British Indian dress and pomp began to appear in Baluchistan (N. Swidler, p. 51).

Mīr Ḵodādād Khan did not accommodate to the changing situation. Gradually his position became untenable, and in 1893 he was forced to abdicate. He was succeeded by Mīr Maḥmūd Khan II, who ruled until 1931. Maḥmūd identified himself with British interests and received strong British support, but at the price of continued erosion of the power of the khanate. In 1899 a treaty was signed which leased out Nushki in perpetuity for Rs 9,000 per year (Aitchison, XI, pp. 224-25). Another treaty in 1903 added the perpetual lease of Nasirabad for Rs 115,000. In 1912, as one of a series of bureaucratic reforms, a state treasury was established with branches at Mastung, Khuzdar, and other provincial centers. A veterinary hospital was opened at Kalat. A road was built to Wad and to Panjgur, and some schools were opened. The khan also made a nominal contribution to the British war effort, but the sardars were beginning to react to his subservience and the British were forced to intervene more than once to put down a revolt.

After the death of Maḥmūd in 1931, Mīr Aʿẓam Jān, the third son of Ḵodādād, who ruled for two years, showed some sympathy for local anti-British sentiments. He was succeeded in 1933 by Mīr Aḥmad-Yār Khan, who ruled for the remainder of the British period. On the accession of Mīr Aḥmad-Yār Khan the state of Kalat was comprised of Sarawan and Jahlawan, Kacchi, with Kharan, Las Bela, and Makrān as client principalities. Chagai, Nushki, Nasırabad, Zhob and Loralai and the Mari-Bugti district constituted the British province of Baluchistan under British political agents; Dera Ghazi Khan was part of Punjab, and Jacobabad was in Sind.

Although not entirely unaffected by British influences from the east, the western Baluch had fared very differently. After the death of Nāder Shah in 1160/1747, what is now Persian Baluchistan had for a time been under the Dorrānī rulers of Afghanistan, but after 1795 it was divided among local rulers. Although for a short time the khans of Kalat, and especially Mīr Naṣīr Khan I, were able to extend their hegemony into parts of it, the rulers of the small agricultural settlements scattered throughout the area, and of the nomadic groups, continually rebelled against any imposition of taxes or other exaction, and even relationships based on marriage alliance were never reliable for long. There was always a tendency to play off one leader against another, and Qandahār competed with Kalat for the allegiance of local leaders.

Persian interest was rearoused in 1838 when the Āqā Khan (q.v.), head of the Ismaʿili sect, fled to India after rebelling against Tehran. In 1843 he was given asylum by the British in Karachi, which they had recently occupied. At the end of the same year, his brother, Sardār Khan, took 200 horsemen with him by land to Čāhbahār, where the small Ismaʿili community provided a base from which he was able by intrigue to gain possession of Bampūr. He was soon defeated by the governor-general of Kermān on orders from Tehran. But from then on the Persians took a more serious interest in Makrān, and began to pursue a policy of encouraging the local rulers to compete for formal titles in return for the obligation to levy and remit annual taxes (Lorimer, I/2, p. 2157). A garrison was established at Bampūr (which has always been the major agricultural district in western Baluchistan) and military expeditions were mounted periodically toward the east and southeast. Bampūr was occupied on a permanent basis in 1850, and one by one the local rulers of Dezak, Sarbāz, Geh, and Qaṣr-e Qand acknowledged the obligation to pay taxes to the governor, Ebrāhīm Khan (Taqīzāda). In 1856 Moḥammadšāh Khan of Sīb rebelled, trusting in the impregnability of his fort, which (judging by the almost contemporary description given by Sepehr, and what could still be seen in 1965) was probably at least as high and strong, if not as large as the Bampūr fort. But the Sīb fort was taken by a force from Kermān.

The British telegraph project changed the geopolitical balance of relations in the area (Saldanha). A report to Bombay in 1861 by a Rev. G. P. Badger (who had experience as British chaplain and interpreter in Persia and the Persian Gulf) explained clearly the British problem of having to deal with both the local chiefs, the sultan of Oman, and the Persian government. They dealt with the problem by respecting the authority of each wherever they found it in force, and resolving conflicts among them as and when they arose. They made agreements for the passage and protection of the line with Kalat, Las Bela, Pasni, and Kech. When construction began in 1863 Ebrāhīm Khan, the governor in Bampūr, threatened the Omani representatives in the ports, and incited Rind tribesmen to harry communities on the outskirts of Gwadar, though he did not molest the telegraph working parties. Tehran actually repudiated his efforts, though official communications continued to emphasize that both Gwadar and Čāhbahār were part of Persia. British plans to build the telegraph had reawakened in the Persians their ancient territorial consciousness and determined them initially to claim the whole of Makrān up to the British frontier in Sind. At the same time they desired the security of a formal agreement. They therefore bargained hard and actively from a position of relative weakness. The Persian envoy who visited Kalat in 1862 declared that Persia had no designs on Kech or Makrān, and requested negotiation of the boundary. Similarly, Ebrāhīm Khan, the governor of Bampūr, wrote to the political agent at Muscat in April, 1863, saying that Gwadar was not under his authority. The British meditated on the problem for two years and finally demurred; they had nothing to gain, and they stood to lose the good will of the local rulers without gaining the protection of the Persian government (Lorimer, I/2,

p. 2163). The Persian government continued its policy of playing off the local rulers one against another with the aim of reducing their authority and establishing its own as far as possible, and gave out that they were planning an attack on Kech (ibid., p. 2157). During this period the principal rulers in western Makrān were Mīr ʿAbd-Allāh Bulēdī of Geh who controlled the coast from Jāsk to Čāhbahār, and Dīn-Moḥammad Sardārzay in Bāhū who beside Daštīārī controlled the coast from Čāhbahār to Gwadar. They were related by marriage, but they were potential rivals, since both accepted payment from the sultan of Oman to protect the ports. (Protection was essential both against local disorder and against the claims of Kalat: In 1847 Faqīr Moḥammad, the khan's *nāʾeb* in Kech and the principal power in eastern Makrān, had attacked Gwadar with 1,000 men in order to extort from Saʿīd Ṯowaynī, the regent of Oman, a supposedly customary annual present which had been withheld for two years in succession, but was unsuccessful. The khan of Kalat continued to claim Gwadar, and periodically sent similar expeditions). ʿAbd-Allāh and Dīn-Moḥammad had both acknowledged Persian suzerainty, but now that the telegraph was coming they let it be known that they would work with the British. Around 1866 Shaikh ʿAbd-Allāh who ruled Qaṣr-e Qand and Sarbāz had recently been murdered, and the Persians had recognized his son as ruler of Qaṣr-e Qand, but had given Sarbāz to the head of another family, who was devoted to the Persian interest.

The telegraph line was finally continued in 1869 to Jāsk and Hanjām Island, and in 1870 the British were obliged to set up a tripartite commission (with representatives of Persia, Kalat, and Britain) for the definition of the frontier (Lorimer, I/2, p. 2034). From 1863 a British assistant political agent was stationed at Gwadar, and from 1879 a native agent took his place. They reported to the director of Persian Gulf Telegraphs in Karachi. Beginning in the 1870s yearly subsidies for the protection of the Indo-European Telegraph line were paid by the British to the khan of Geh (Rs 1,000), to eleven elders of the Baluch communities of the oasis of Geh (Rs 1,600), to the leader of the Nārū'ī tribe (Rs 600), to the sardar of Daštīārī (Rs 600), to three elders of Baluch communities of the oasis of Daštīārī (Rs 400 each), to the sardar of Bāhū Kalāt (Rs 100), among others (Pikulin, p. 123). The subsidy to the ruler of Geh was reduced from Rs 3,000 to Rs 1,000 in 1899, the remainder being distributed among minor chiefs along the line; Daštīārī and Bāhū then received Rs 1,000 each. In 1864 the protection of Čāhbahār devolved upon two local chiefs, Dīn-Moḥammad Jaḏgāl of Daštīārī, and Mīr ʿAbd-Allāh of Geh, who received Rs 900 and 200 respectively per year from the revenue of 7,000. In 1868 or 1869 Dīn-Moḥammad quietly occupied it, and it was never recovered for Oman. But a period of struggle and negotiation ensued between Oman, Dīn-Moḥammad, and Persia, in the course of which the Persian governor-general of Kermān appeared in Qaṣr-e Qand. In 1869 Ebrāhīm Khan occupied Čāhbahār, but in 1871 the Persians waived all claim to Gwadar (ibid.). In 1872 Ebrāhīm Khan annexed Čāhbahār permanently to Persia, initially under the protection of Ḥosayn Khan of Geh. Its thriving commercial community soon dispersed apparently with the encouragement of Ebrāhīm Khan, much of it to Gwadar (Lorimer, loc. cit.; Goldsmid, p. lii). Despite Ebrāhīm Khan's efforts the British Sandeman system of indirect rule with the aid of subsidies had extended into western Makrān, and when he died it was the major power in the area.

In the meantime, a division of influence between Kalat, Afghanistan, and Persia had been worked out and legitimized for the time being by the boundary commissions. But the Persians (working through Ebrāhīm Khan) both preempted and disputed some details of the commission's findings. They took Pīšīn (east of Rāsk; not to be confused with Pishin north of Quetta) in 1870, and Esfandak and Kūhak in 1871—directly after the commission had awarded it to Kalat. In the north Ebrāhīm Khan also defeated Sayyed Khan Kord, known as sardar of the Sarḥadd, in Ḵāš (Sykes, 1902, p. 106). From then on Ebrāhīm controlled most of the settlements of the Sarḥadd and Makrān up to the present border by a combination of force, threats, and the posting of minor officials, but he was not able to control the tribes of the Sarḥadd (see Pikulin, p. 122; Zarudnyĭ, p. 164; Galindo, p. 251), and Baluch raiding remained a problem on both sides of the Iran-Afghanistan border (Ferrier). Ebrāhīm Khan was the son of a baker from Bam, and had achieved almost total subjugation of western Baluchistan. He died in 1884, after three decades in the position. His son died a few months later, and Zayn-al-ʿĀbedīn, his son-in-law, became governor, but in 1887 he was replaced by Abu'l-Fatḥ Khan, a Turk. Abu'l-Fatḥ Khan was, however, dismissed, and Zayn-al-ʿĀbedīn Khan reappointed.

During the remainder of Nāṣer-al-Dīn Shah's reign the pattern of Persian exactions continued unchanged, with consequent hostilities between competing chiefs. Around 1883 ʿAbdī Khan Sardārzay, son of Mīr Dīn-Moḥammad was put in charge of Gwatar. In 1886 the population of Gwatar moved across the frontier to avoid his exactions, but returned in 1887 on the death of Mīr Hōtī in Geh. In 1896 it was reported that 2,000 people had emigrated from the district, and the British Indian traders of Čāhbahār who had reestablished themselves complained that their trade was ruined. Nāṣer-al-Dīn Shah agreed to a new Perso-Baluch boundary commission because of unrest on the border (Sykes, 1902, p. 225). Minor revisions were made to both the Persian and the Afghan borders in the mid-1890s.

During this period the Bampūr governors had been encouraged in their aggressive treatment of the local Baluch rulers by the governors-general in Kermān who made frequent winter visits to Bampūr. In 1891, after an absence of two years, the governor-general revisited the district, making solemn promises that he would imprison nobody, but the promises were broken, and several Baluch leaders were seized and detained for several years (Sykes, 1902, p. 106).

After the death of Nāṣer-al-Dīn Shah in 1313/1896, the Baluch thought there was no new shah, and the absence of a Persian force fostered this delusion. Because of fear of the Kermān governor-general (Farmānfarmā) there was no rebellion until he left Kermān. But in 1897 the Acting Superintendent in the Indo-European Telegraph Department at Jāsk was robbed and murdered while camping on an annual tour of inspection near the Rāpč river east of Jāsk. In the same year Sardār Ḥosayn Khan attacked Fahraj (Sykes, p. 132; Zarudnyĭ, p. 200) and led a general rebellion against the Persian government in the Sarḥadd, Sarāvān, and Bampūr, demanding reduction of taxes. This was refused and the revolt spread to Sarbāz, Dezak, Lāšār, and Bampošt. Ḥosayn Khan occupied Bampūr, Fahraj, and Bazmān and other places which had small Iranian garrisons, and controlled most of the northern part of the province, and several Baluch groups which had hitherto remained neutral in troubles between ruling families and the "Qajars" (as the Baluch now called Persians) joined him. A large Persian force sent from Kermān to restore order in 1897 was defeated. The uprising lasted about three years and finished only when Ḥosayn Khan was given the governorship—a major precedent. Now a Baluch leader, the head of a principal family, officially had the right and duty to collect the taxes of the whole of Baluchistan within Iran. In return for the added legitimacy of a title a Baluch leader had acknowledged all Persia's claims. Up to this time the Baluch seem not to have acknowledged such claims, though they expected to have to deal continually with the claims of outside powers, including Persia, Oman, Qandahār, and Delhi. On the other hand, in this new arrangement the Persian government appeared to acknowledge the local autonomy of the Baluch. It might be expected that in this situation unless there was a strong governor in Kermān no taxes would leave Baluchistan, and in fact from this time until 1928 Persian control of Baluchistan was once again only nominal (Pikulin, pp. 123–26).

In January, 1898, in consequence of the murder of Graves and the generally unsettled state of the country, 150 rifles of the Bombay Marine Battalion under two British officers, of whom 100 were to be located at Čāhbahār and 50 at Jāsk, were dispatched from India. No objection was made by the Persian government. In April the Čāhbahār detachment was reduced to 50 rifles and Indian officers replaced the British. As the presence of these guards had an excellent effect in giving confidence at both places, they were maintained after the troubles subsided, and permanent barracks were built at Jāsk and Čāhbahār. However, away from the ports there were other difficulties. In 1903 two despised communities, one of Mēds (fishermen) on the coast and another of Lattis (mixed farmers) inland, were driven out of Bāhū. They moved across the border to Jiwanri and Paleri. Around the same time Moḥammad Khan Gīčkī of Kech had fled across the border in the other direction when his uncle, Shaikh 'Omar, was expelled from the fort of Turbat by the khan of Kalat's *nāʾeb* in Kech. Increasing disorder in Makrān, along with Russian and French activity in the Persian Gulf, caused anxiety among the British, who by now were concerned to protect Indian trade interests in the Persian Gulf, as well as the telegraph, beside their general interest in border security. The Persian government was unable or unwilling to meet the British halfway by matching British power on their side of the border. The British, therefore, tried to protect their interests unilaterally. In 1901 they asked permission to set up a vice-consulate at Bampūr for the protection of British subjects. Persia opposed it, but allowed them to set one up in Bam instead. Later Persia allowed the British to lead a punitive expedition against Magas and Ērafšān.

On the death of Ḥosayn Khan, Saʿīd Khan, his son, succeeded to the forts of Geh, Bent, and the ports. He also inherited Qaṣr-e Qand from his mother. He decided to expand, and took Sarbāz. Next, he joined up with Bahrām Khan Bārānzay (from a tribal group also known as Bārakzay, apparently from the Afghan Bārakzay [see BĀRAKZĪ], who had entered the area from Afghanistan early in the 19th century, though by this time they were fully assimilated as a Baluch and Baluchi-speaking) who ruled Dezak, and they took over Bampūr and Fahraj in 1907 when there was no governor in residence. An army was sent against them from Kermān in 1910. Saʿīd submitted. But Bahrām resisted. Saʿīd was made governor of Baluchistan, but the real power in the province remained with Bahrām Khan (Jahānbānī, pp. 35-38).

Early in 1916 German agents extended their activities to the Sarḥadd and endeavored to raise the tribes there against the British. Seeing their supply lines in danger, the British sent a Colonel R. E. H. Dyer to organize the Chagai levies. At this time the Gamšādzay under Halīl (Ḵalīl) Khan held the area around Jālq and Safēdkoh. West of them were the Yār-Moḥammadzay under Jīānd Khan (an elderly man who had been informal overlord of the Sarḥadd for many years). West of Ḵāš were the Esmāʿīlzay under Jomʿa Khan. Each tribe had around a thousand families, or one to two thousand fighting men each. Dyer succeeded in his task with the help of a small local tribe, the Rīgī, and the conventional British strategy of subsidizing the local leaders for their efforts to enforce order.

Mīr Bahrām Khan died in Bampūr in 1921. Having no son, he was succeeded by his nephew, Dūst-Moḥammad Khan. The Bārakzay family had become the most powerful government in Persian Baluchistan, by virtue of personal control over both Fahraj-Bampūr and Sarāvān and marriage alliances with the rulers of the major settlements of Makrān. Dūst-Moḥammad made considerable progress in consolidating the power of his predecessor, mainly through more strategic marriage alliances.

In March, 1924, the control of the tribes of the Sarḥadd district of Persian Baluchistan (who had enjoyed conventional British subsidies since the occupation of the country in 1915-16 under Dyer) was formally surrendered by the British to the Persian government, which undertook to continue the payments. Not surprisingly, the Persians failed to keep this undertaking, and disturbances broke out in the Sarḥadd during the summer of 1925 and again in 1926, owing partly to the high-handed methods of certain of the military officials and partly to discontent due to loss of the subsidies. The disturbances were quelled, without serious fighting, after further assurances had been given by the Persian government (Aitchison, XIII, p. 37; cf. Pikulin, p. 200).

In 1928, however, the new Pahlavī government of Iran was sufficiently well established to turn its attention to Baluchistan. Dūst-Moḥammad Khan refused to submit, trusting in the network of alliances he had built up over the whole of the province south of the Sarḥadd. However, as soon as Reżā Shah's army under General Amīr Amān-Allāh Jahānbānī arrived in the area, the alliances dissolved. Dūst-Moḥammad Khan was left with a relatively small force and few allies of any consequence. The Persian army had little difficulty in defeating him. Once again Baluch political unity proved highly brittle. Dūst-Moḥammad eventually surrendered and was pardoned on condition he live in Tehran. After a year, he escaped while on a hunting trip. In due course he was recaptured, and having killed his guard in the escape was hanged for murder. In the meantime the rest of the Bārakzay family sought refuge in British territory, and the leading members of the family were given allowances there so long as they remained. The Persians continued to govern through local rulers. They recognized Jān-Moḥammad Bulēdī as sardar of Qaṣr-e Qand; Meḥrāb Khan Bozorgzāda as sardar of Jālq, returning to him the property which he had lost to Dūst-Moḥammad Khan; Moḥammadšāh Mīr-Morādzay as sardar of Sīb; and Šahbāz Khan Bozorgzāda as sardar of Dezak (Baluchistan, pp. 30-33).

Intermittent outbreaks of disorder continued in Baluchistan throughout the remainder of Reżā Shah's reign. They were due to a number of factors, including the zealousness or corruption of Persian officials, and Baluch inability to understand why the Persian officials should be interfering in their affairs. Major examples were the rebellion of Jomʿa Khan Esmāʿīlzay in the Sarḥadd in 1931, who was subdued and exiled to Shiraz; and a rebellion of a number of tribes in Kūhak in 1938, demanding reduction of customs duty on livestock, in which 74 were shot under orders from General Alborz (Jahānbānī; Pikulin, p. 140).

No account of this period would be complete without some mention of slavery (see BARDA AND BARDADĀRĪ), which was allowed to continue in Baluchistan (as in other parts of the Persian Gulf) long after it had been prohibited internationally. In the mid-13th/19th century along the Makrān coast there appears to have been both an export trade and an import trade in slaves. Unsuspecting Baluch tribesmen (probably from the despised groups such as the Mēd) were picked up in raids along the coast and sold to merchants, who shipped them from isolated western coastal settlements, such as Galag and Sadēč. It is not clear how late African slaves were still arriving in Makrān. Gwadar and Čāhbahār were excluded from the British agreement with Oman for limiting the slave trade in 1839, when Pasni was set as the western limit of prohibition. Baluch tribesmen were still indignant in the 1960s about the prohibition on slavery. On several occasions between the 1880s and 1930s groups of Rind tribesmen at Mand caused trouble over British attempts to restrict their use of slaves (Lorimer, I/2, p. 2475). Slavery was abolished officially in Persian Baluchistan in 1929 (Pikulin, p. 144), but the status of black slaves in western Makrān barely changed until well into the second half of this century.

9. The modern period.

Since the end of World War II great changes have occurred for all Baluch throughout Baluchistan—gradually at first, accelerating since 1970 because of the changed political economy of the Persian Gulf. At the same time Baluch history has diverged. Since the state of Kalat became an integral part of the new independent state of Pakistan, three separate national governments, none of which included Baluch representation, have sought to integrate and assimilate them into national life at minimum cost. In Afghanistan the major factors affecting the Baluch have been the Helmand river development schemes, the government's Pashtunistan policy, and (most recently and drastically) the Soviet occupation of Afghanistan. In Iran the successive Pahlavi governments attempted to neutralize the sardars and at the same time suppress any activity among the Baluch that could lead to ethnic consciousness or solidarity. Their tactics were similar to those of the Qajars, and the tactics of the Islamic Republic since 1979 have not differed significantly. However, the significance of these tactics and the relative power of the government of Iran to control the area have changed in important ways. In Pakistan, where ethnic awareness has been most developed, the political discourse has revolved around the general objective of reestablishing the autonomous Baluch polity, the khanate, in something resembling its mid-13th/19th-century form, independent of Afghan (local Pathans or Pashtuns), Persian, or Punjabi (in the guise of Pakistani bureaucracy) interference, though probably connected in some form of federation with Pakistan. Failure to achieve this objective led to fighting with the Pakistan army in 1973-74 and isolated guerrilla activity before and since. Overall, as a result of increased literacy and access to the outside world, this period has seen the growth of ethnic and cultural awareness among all Baluch, which should be evaluated in the context of similar phenomena in other parts of the world during the same period.

The Baluch in Afghanistan have received the least attention from their national government. The main effect on their lives of the Helmand project that began in 1948 and continued in various forms until the end of the Dāwūd regime in 1978, was that it brought a steady stream of outsiders into an otherwise isolated part of the country. The declaration of the Afghan government for a "Pashtunistan," which (though left purposely vague) was inspired by the idea of restoring to Afghan rule the areas lost to Kalat and the British which were ruled from Qandahār in some cases as late as the mid-13th/19th century, similarly barely affected them. Until 1978 many Baluch in Afghanistan related more closely to their kin in Iran and Pakistan than to the rest of Afghanistan.

Soon after the coup in April, 1978, however, officials of the new government entered the area and attempted to reconstruct community life in accordance with Marxist principles. The Baluch reacted strongly, especially to measures that interfered with their ideas of gender relations, property, and authority. Since the Soviet occupation in 1980, most of the estimated ninety thousand Afghan Baluch have moved into Iran or Pakistan. A relatively small number are engaged in resistance activity inside Afghanistan, with medical and other support from relatives mainly in Iran. Generally, the great majority of the Baluch of all three countries have avoided commitment either for or against the Kabul regime, because of their rivalry with the Pashtuns and the Punjabis in Pakistan and with the national government in Iran.

One policy of the Ḵalq regime in Afghanistan (1978-79) deserves special notice. Immediately after the coup, Baluchi (along with Uzbek, Turkman, Nūrestānī) was added to Pashto and Darī in the list of official languages of Afghanistan. Baluchi, therefore, became a language of publication and education in Afghanistan. However, there is currently no evidence that the policy continues, or that books or periodicals in Baluchi continue to be published.

In Iran the Baluch were barely the majority of the population in the province of Balūčestān o Sīstān. There were no institutions that could serve as a focus for the development of a Baluch ethnic or cultural awareness. Publication in Baluchi was illegal. Education was in Persian only. Baluch dress was not allowed to be worn in school or in any official activity.

The Bārakzay, who returned to Iran after the departure of the British, campaigned successfully for the return of the *ḵāleṣa* lands which had been their main support up to 1928. Government policy was to provide a livelihood for the old ruling families throughout the province in order to make them dependent and coopt them into the national system. They also used them for local positions such as town mayors. The policy worked in the long term, and with few exceptions in the short term as well. On the other hand, the province was barely touched by the economic and social reforms that were carried out at the national level. For example, no Baluch owned enough land to be affected by the land reform law. The province was still not entirely quiet, but serious incidents were rare. Minor revisions were made to the border with Pakistan in 1958.

Several members of the old ruling families, especially the Bārakzay and the Sardārzay in Sarāvān, Sarbāz, Qaṣr-e Qand, and Daštīārī, showed an interest in a Free Baluchistan movement beginning in the 1960s. They had a small but loyal following among the nomads in the Makrān mountains and connections with Baluch of a similar mind in the émigré communities across the Persian Gulf. Through these connections they developed contacts with the government of Iraq, which was always ready to stir up Baluch in Iran in retaliation for the shah's interference among the Kurds in Iraq. Mīr ʿAbdī Khan Sardārzay was the major figure in this movement, but he eventually submitted and was pardoned by the shah on condition he live the rest of his life in Tehran, which he did. Another figure in the movement was Amān-Allāh Bārakzay, who took up the cause again after the revolution of 1357 Š./1978-79.

The most significant events in Baluch history since the departure of the British have occurred, as might be expected, in the area they vacated. They left behind a significant degree of confusion about the status of the princely states, such as Kalat, in relation to the successor governments of India and Pakistan. Kalat, in addition, had made it clear that its position was different from that of other princely states, because it was not "Indian." On August 15, 1947, the day after the creation of Pakistan, the khan accordingly declared the independence of Kalat. But he offered to negotiate a special relationship with Pakistan in matters of defense, foreign affairs, and communications. His offer was rejected. The strategy pursued by the government of Pakistan in the following decades was conditioned partly by Afghanistan's Pashtunistan policy and partly by the imperative need to build a viable state. We still do not know to what extent international interests in the stability of the region, especially on the part of the British and the Americans, may have played a role. In March, 1948, the khan was persuaded by Mohammad Ali Jinnah (the founder of Pakistan; 1876-1948) to bring Baluchistan into Pakistan, despite the fact that the sardars had not agreed to the move. Less than a month later the Pakistani army annexed Baluchistan (Baluch, *Inside Baluchistan*, pp. 150-66).

A major factor in the opposition of the Baluch sardars to straightforward accession to Pakistan was the fact that Pakistan had insisted on perpetuating the separate status of the three "leased" Baluch territories (Las Bela, Kharan, and Makrān) that had been detached by the British (Harrison, p. 24). But the use of coercion was mitigated by its action a few years later in constituting the Baluchistan States Union within West Pakistan (1952-55), which provided for substantial autonomy and postponed final integration (Wirsing, p. 10). The final blow to Baluch aims came in 1955 when Baluchistan along with all the other provinces of West Pakistan were incorporated into One Unit. (Gwadar remained with Oman until it was purchased by Pakistan for £3 million sterling [$8,400,000] in 1958.)

To begin with, the biggest problem of the Baluch was lack of strong leadership. As resistance built up during the One Unit period (1955-70), three men gradually began to stand out as potential modern leaders. These were Khair Bux Marri (Ḵayrbaḵš Marī), Ghaus Bux

Bizenjo (Qawsbaḵš Bīzenjō), and Ataullah (ʿAṭāʾ-Allāh) Mengal (Harrison, pp. 40-69). When the One Unit was dissolved in 1970 the Baluch reacted cautiously. In the following general election, Bhutto's Pakistan People's Party (PPP) won no seats in Baluchistan, only 2 percent of the vote, and no seats in the provincial assembly. The National Awami Party (NAP) emerged with three seats in the National Assembly and eight seats in the Baluchistan provincial assembly. The NAP was headed by Khan Abdul Wali (ʿAbd-al-Walī) Khan, a Pashtun who was the son of the veteran Pashtun nationalist Khan Abdul Ghaffar (ʿAbd-al-Ḡaffār) Khan, and was basically a regionalist alliance of Baluch and Pathans. It had been founded in 1957 and was to some extent a descendant of a pre-independence anti-partition movement. Within days of the election Bhutto attempted to set aside the results by appointing one of his own supporters among the Baluch, Ghaus Bux Raisani (Qawsbaḵš Raʾīsānī), as governor of Baluchistan. Under pressure, however, he agreed to let the NAP, in coalition with the conservative Jamiat-ul-Islam (Jamʿīyat-al-Eslām) party (JUI), form a government. Mir Ghaus Bux Bizenjo was appointed governor of Baluchistan in April, 1972. The NAP-JUI parliamentary coalition in the Baluchistan Provincial Assembly elected Sardar Ataullah Khan Mengal as its leader, who thus became chief minister of the province. In February, 1973, Bhutto replaced both governors, and dismissed the government of Baluchistan on the pretext that the NAP-JUI government had allowed and even encouraged the spread of lawlessness and violence throughout the province, and that it aimed at independence. A cache of Soviet arms was discovered in the Iraqi embassy, supposedly destined for Baluchistan. Bhutto then appointed Akbar Khan Bugti, the leader of the Būgṭī tribe and hostile to NAP, as governor. But Bugti was forced to resign in less than a year, and the disorder and violence spread. Ghaus Bux Bizenjo and Ataullah Khan Mengal, as well as Khair Bux Marri, who was the president of NAP in Baluchistan, were arrested. Between 1973 and 1977 eastern Baluchistan became the scene of a major tribal rebellion against the government of Pakistan. At its height in 1974 an estimated 55,000 Baluch were engaged, mainly from the Mengal and Marī tribes. The number of Pakistani troups has been estimated at 70,000. Iran, which continued to fear Baluch separatism, sent a number of helicopters. Many Baluch fled to Afghanistan. As many as 10,000 Marī remained there in 1986. The major part of the fighting was over in 1974, when the government of Pakistan published its view of what had happened in a white paper, but hostilities continued intermittently until the end of Bhutto's regime in 1977. In April, 1976, Bhutto announced the abolition of the "sardari system" in a speech in Quetta, making illegal the traditional tribal system of social control and revenue. (Ayyub Khan had already attempted to abolish it, without success.) In 1977 the martial law administration released the NAP leaders and hostilities ceased (Wirsing, p. 11).

Meanwhile, in Pakistan Baluchi had been given the status of an official language for both publication and education. Two academies were established for the promotion of Baluchi and Brahui languages and cultures. (It was in the government's interest to see Brahui develop as a distinct identity, which would weaken Baluchistan solidarity.) Quetta radio became the major producer of programs in Baluchi. (Radio Zāhedān and Radio Kabul had less than ten hours a week each.) Baluch writers published magazines and books in Baluchi, English, and Urdu. Beginning in the 1960s an increasing number of Baluch writers have published on the history and culture of the Baluch.

In Pakistan Baluch nationalism continues to be a political factor at the national level. It has been suggested that the idea of Baluch nationalism began with Dūst-Moḥammad Khan's resistance to Reżā Shah in Iran in 1928 (Harrison, p. 3). But it is doubtful whether the combination of general ethnic awareness, interest in political unity, and potential for strong leadership, which are necessary for a successful nationalist movement, existed in a significant proportion of the Baluch anywhere before the 1960s at the earliest. Since then it has motivated an increasing number of young Baluch in Pakistan, Iran, and the Persian Gulf. In February, 1981, Khair Bux Marri and Ataullah Mengal were persuaded to help create a London-based coalition of Baluch émigré groups called the World Baluch Organization, the purpose of which is to raise money for the Baluch cause.

10. The diaspora.

Beside the Pakistani province of Baluchistan, the Iranian province of Balūčestān o Sīstān, and the neighboring corner of Afghanistan, Baluch communities extend into neighboring areas in each country—Sind and Punjab in Pakistan, Farāh, Herat, Bādgīs, Fāryāb, Jūzjān (Jawzjān) in Afghanistan, and Kermān, Khorasan, Semnān, and Gorgān in Iran. They also extend into neighboring countries—Soviet Turkmenistan, India, the countries of the Persian Gulf, Oman, Kenya, and Tanzania (especially Zanzibar).

Very little has been published about these diaspora communities, and it is difficult to obtain reliable information about them. They tend not to be encouraged to develop their ethnic identity. In Iran, those in Gorgān moved in from Sīstān as migrant labor in the 1960s. Others, in Khorasan and Semnān, have been there longer, in some cases much longer. Many of them have lost their language, some within living memory. Those to the north of Baluchistan are all pastoralists, or have been until recently. As for the carpets that are known as Baluch in international trade see BALUCHISTAN V, BALUCH CARPETS, below. The best Baluch rugs were made before the middle of this century in Baluch communities living among Turkmen on either side of the current border between Afghanistan and Soviet Turkmenistan. Their handicraft is derivative of the Turkmen product, though distinctive in both design and texture. The Baluch in

Soviet Turkmenistan include Shiʿites. They all came from Sīstān, some from the Afghan and some from the Iranian side of the border. There were three main waves of migration. The first arrived in the late 19th century; the second between 1917 and 1920; and the last and largest between 1923 and 1928. In 1959 they numbered 7,842, but had increased to 18,997 in 1979 by natural fertility. They live in the Mary oblast' on kolkhoz and sovkhoz. There are also small groups of Baluch in Tajikistan but these have already assimilated linguistically to the Tajik. Small groups of Brahui in Turkmenistan still speak Brahui but are rapidly assimilating to Baluchi. The Soviets seem to favor the ethnic survival of the Baluch (Bennigsen, pp. 120-21), probably for reasons similar to the Pakistani encouragement of the Brahui. The Baluch of Ḏahīra in Oman have been there so long that they are now classed as an Omani tribe. They retain no direct connection with the Baluch on the Bātena coast or elsewhere in Oman. Another group is located some ninety miles to the south of Boraymī in the interior. In Zanzibar the Baluch had established themselves in the service of the Muscadine empire. After the coup in 1963 they lost their privileged status and, in order to avoid being ruled by an African government which did not respect their separate identity, some of them wrote letters to distant relatives in Makrān, attempting to make arrangements to return. In 1965 a Baluch from Kenya enrolled as a foreign student at Tehran University.

There are records of migration out of Makrān since about 1800, and most of the diaspora seems to have occurred in the 12th/18th and 13th/19th centuries. But some moved out as early as the 9th/15th century, while others may have followed different itineraries from earlier points of dispersal in Iran, and may hold clues relevant to some of the problems treated in the first section of this article. They moved mainly for economic reasons, and worked in the pearl industry before the oil industry. They have wandered as soldiers of fortune possibly since Sasanian times. Many of the émigré communities have assimilated in language and other respects to the surrounding society, but still retain their identity. Many more may have assimilated and lost their identity. It is characteristic of areas of low biological productivity such as Makrān that they are net producers of people.

11. Ethnography.

The gazetteers provided a data base for the study of the habitat and society of British Baluchistan, and the states of Kalat, Las Bela, Kharan, and Makrān, which is unique for the Iranian area. Since the middle of this century a handful of contemporary scholars have sought to build on this base by applying modern theoretical approaches in new field studies, often asking new questions.

Modern ethnographic work began with Pehrson, who worked among the Marī for six months before he died in 1955. Barth visited the same group briefly in 1960 while editing Pehrson's work for publication. Pehrson's work deals mainly with the social relationships of everyday life in herding communities, including gender relations. From 1963 to 1965 N. and W. Swidler worked among Brahui-speakers in Sarawan and Kacchi. W. Swidler established the connection between ecological conditions, the technological requirements of herding and pastoral production, and the social dynamics of camp and herding groups. N. Swidler reconstructed the political development of the khanate on the basis of a combination of ethnographic observation and a reading of the historical sources. In 1963-67 Spooner conducted a series of studies in Sarāvān and Makrān (Iran). He also worked briefly in the Baluch areas of Afghanistan in 1965, and later in 1982-83 he was able to make several brief tours of Pakistani Baluchistan. He focused on the ecology of pastoralism and the dynamics of leadership in what was effectively a mixed, pluralist society, especially the function of the *ḥākom* (Ar. *ḥākem*). His main concern was to work out to what extent ecological explanations might illuminate the history of the Baluch. Salzman worked among the Yār-Moḥammadzay (renamed Šahnavāzī under Reżā Shah) of the Sarḥadd (Iran) in 1967-68, 1972-73, and 1976. He showed how nomads may rely not only on pastoralism but on a variety of unrelated resources and use their mobility to exploit each geographically separate resource at the appropriate season. He has also explored the relationship between ecological adaptation and political organization and the conditions under which nomads might modify their ecological adaptation and become settled farmers, and he applied an evolutionary approach to the analysis of variation in political organization, and investigated under what circumstances a state structure might develop out of tribes and settled life out of nomadism. In addition to pursuing similar interests C. and S. Pastner also investigated gender relations in Panjgur in 1969 and in a Baluch coastal village outside Karachi in 1976. In 1976 also Bestor described a community of Kord during a brief stay at the foot of Kūh-e Taftān in the Sarḥadd (Iran), and Orywal worked for a season among the Baluch in Afghanistan in 1976-77. This final section gives basic information on traditional Baluch society, culture, economy, and habitat, based on the works of the above scholars and the unpublished field notes of the author.

Baluch society is stratified. There are four social classes, which are essentially hereditary and occupational: *ḥākomzāt*, Balōč, *šahrī*, and *ḡolām*; convenient glosses for these terms are aristocracy, nomads, cultivators, and slaves. *Ḥākom* is the Baluchi pronunciation of *ḥākem*, the Qajar term for ruler; *ḥākomzāt* are the extended families of sardars who were able to establish a direct relationship with the governor in Bampūr or otherwise usurp that status. (Nawab and sardar carry similar connotations in Pakistani Baluchistan.) Balōč are those nomads, or descendants from nomadic tribes, who are considered to have been the original Balōč who brought the name and the language into Baluchistan. *Šahrī* (from Baluchi *šahr* "cultivated area") signifies settled cultivator. *Ḡolām* entered Baluch society as slaves (other terms are also found, such as *darzāda, naqīb*). Although there were slaves of various origins, physiognomies, and skin color, since abolition only those of African origin are unable to manage any change in their social status. They are now free according to the law of each country, but at least through the 1960s their status and options within Baluch society had changed little. Apart from African *ḡolām*, mobility across class boundaries is possible but it is relatively uncommon.

Secondary distinctions are also made within these classes on the basis of tribe (*zāt*), and the relative status of a Balōč and a *šahrī* varies in practice according to tribal affiliation and the experience of particular communities, since a *šahrī* community may accumulate wealth and cultivate honor over generations, and a Balōč community may lose its honor. There is a wide range of status within the *šahrī* category. Some are equivalent to helots. Many are probably descendents of pre-Balōč communities, and have retained relatively large holdings. Although all are now spoken of in tribal terms, it is very likely that this idiom derives from the cultural dominance of the tribally organized Balōč, and that before the Baluchization of the area the population was not tribal. Tribalism seems to have become the pervasive idiom of social organization with the arrival of the Balōč, whose leading families were able to take over some of the settlements and acquire a new basis of power (though they lost some of them to later immigrants). If this interpretation is valid, recent assessments of Makrān as a detribalized part of Baluchistan may be misinterpretations: it is possible that tribalism was always weak or nonexistent in communities that were originally not tribal but only adapted their discourse to the tribalism of their masters. But the tribal ideology, which is implicitly associated with the Balōč, pervades all communication.

Baluch tribal organization is not uniform. Some tribes follow a strict patrilineal reckoning of descent, give no inheritance to daughters, and in assessing social status ascribe little importance to the origin of the mother, while others reckon descent bilineally, give equal inheritance shares (of land) to sons and daughters, and ascribe equal importance to the origin of the mother in questions of social status. (Unlike Persian, Baluchi makes no terminological distinction between matrilateral and patrilateral kin.) The model of patrilineal genealogy is used to model links between groups and to represent political affiliation and legitimacy, and as a means of relating historical events to the present. Where the father is an important leader and it is likely that the eldest son will take his place, it is usual for the father to set aside an extra portion for him before the general division of the inheritance. This must be done with the consent of the other sons and daughters, and is known as *mīrwandī*.

The tribal ideology extends throughout Baluchistan and beyond, but each family belongs to one or another small community, whose size and stability is related to the local conditions of pastoralism or agriculture. These primary groupings are strung together in chains of hierarchical relations, which integrate the various types of larger grouping. Each community is encapsulated in an asymmetrical model of the larger society, which is rationalized in tribal terms. It may have little or no interest in lineage or genealogy to provide a framework for everyday social relations.

Each individual is identified by membership in a tribal group, and each tribal group belongs to one or other of the four classes. Many tribes, though now accepted as Baluch, are of known recent alien origin—from Iran (e.g., the Nowšērvānī), Afghanistan (e.g., the Bārakzay), Muscat (possibly the Bulēdī), or the Indus valley (the Gīčkī). Most tribes are small, a few hundred or at most a thousand or so families. (The Marī with a population of 60,000 are by far the largest.) Each is generally known as belonging to one of the four classes, and each family has a place in a chain of allegiance or fealty relationships which cut across class categories. Marriage between classes occurs (especially in the few cases where a tribe which is Balōč or *šahrī* has a branch which has become *ḥākomzāt*), but a woman should not marry down. In the case of mixed parentage the lowest status prevails. The settled and nomadic communities are closely interrelated economically, and interdependent. Names of the major tribes in each district of Baluchistan are given in the geographical section above. A fuller list may be found at the end of Baloch (1974) and Jahānbānī (1957).

The tribes of the khanate were ranked in two distinct groupings, one of Sarawan and one Jahlawan. The rank was symbolized in a number of ways: Seats in the khan's council (*majles, dīvān*) were assigned. Those nearest the khan had the greatest prestige. The Sarawan sardar ranked first and sat on his right; the Jahlawan sardar sat on his left. Then the sardars from Sarawan and Jahlawan alternated according to rank. The presents given by the khan upon the succession of a new sardar also varied according to the position the tribe held in the rank order. The khan would formally recognize a new Zarakzay sardar by conferring on him a Kashmir shawl, a length of brocade, a horse with a silver harness, and a dagger with a golden hilt. A new Mengal sardar would receive the same with the exception of the dagger. A Bīzenjō sardar would receive only the shawl and brocade, plus a broadcloth coat. Similarly, the sum of money given by the khan at the death of a sardar or a member of a sardar's family also varied according to rank. When a high-ranking sardar died, the khan would personally visit the bereaved family. The death of a middle-rank sardar called for a visit by the khan's son or brother. For minor sardars the khan would send one of his officials (*Gazetteer* VI/B, p. 112).

Beside the classes there are other categories of tribe, such as Kord, Brahui, Dehwār, Jat (Jaṭṭ), Jaḍgāl, Lāsī, Lorī, Mēd. In some sense these categories were and are both Baluch and not Baluch, depending on the context, and some were high status while others were low. All these categories, however, as distinct from others that will be discussed briefly below, were essentially within Baluch society because they were incorporated into the political structure of the Baluch polity. While there is presently a tendency to emphasize the ethnicity of these terms, historically their meaning has probably fluctuated and there is some evidence that they have been somewhat elastic categories. It has been assumed generally that the Kord have migrated from Kurdistan, and the Kord themselves currently make the same assumption (for which there seems to be no evidence). The Kūfeč or Kūč of the early Islamic period were considered to be a kind of Kurds (Ebn Ḥawqal, p. 221.1). They are found today in two areas: around Kūh-e Taftān in the Iranian Sarḥadd, and in Sarawan (Pakistan). In status they are equivalent to Balōč. The Brahui are distinguished only by their language, which shares a large amount of vocabulary with Baluchi (which most Brahui also speak). The core of Brahui-speaking areas are Sarawan-Jahlawan, but scattered Brahui-speakers are also to be found in most of the northern districts, including Sīstān and Soviet Turkmenistan. The Dehwār speak a form of Persian, close to Darī and Tajik. They appear to have been the agricultural community of the plateau, in Mastung and Iranian Sarāvān, and could be the descendants of the pre-Islamic agricultural community, when these areas were controlled by the provincial ruler of Sīstān. They have been important in recent history as the *ūlūs* (Baluchi *olos*) of the khan, forming both his peasantry on the plateau and his bureaucracy. (*Ūlūs*, which has been used as the name of a Baluchi magazine, also includes Baluch who for one or another reason have lost their tribal connections.) The relationship between the khan and his *ūlūs* differs from that between a sardar and his tribesmen. In the latter case both are members of the same *kawm* (Arabic *qawm*), related by ties of kinship and the obligation to share in the common weal and woe (*šādī-ḡam*). No idiom of kinship or shared honor obtains between the khan and his *ūlūs* (N. Swidler, p. 151), and they were not subject to military service. Under the khan, therefore, the Dehwār had a separate non-Baluch status. Their status under the Bārakzay in Iranian Sarāvān may have been similar, but currently among the Iranian Baluch they enjoy a status similar to *šahrī*. Jat, Jaḏgāl, and Lāsī (assumed to be related to the Jats of India) all speak related forms of Sindhi. The Lāsī are the peasants (*ūlūs*) of the *jām* (hereditary ruler) of Las Bela. The Jaḏgāl are the population of Daštīārī. The Jat are the peasants (again, the khan's *ūlūs*) of Kacchi. The Lāsī and Jat have a relatively low status within the *ūlūs* of the khan and the *jām*, but the Jaḏgāl of Daštīārī enjoy a higher status because of their local autonomy under their own *ḥākom*. Finally, the Lorī and the Mēd are despised and barely differentiated from the *ḡolām*. The Lorī are gypsies who wander throughout Baluchistan, entertaining and performing other services. The Mēd are the small fishing communities that live on the beaches of Makrān. There is some evidence that these subethnic identities are not absolute even where they involve the use of different languages. Morgenstierne (p. 9) first noticed the evidence suggesting that some communities had switched back and forth between Baluchi and Brahui (a Dravidian language) at least once. In seems likely on linguistic grounds that the original Brahui probably migrated from south India around a thousand years ago (J. Bloch apud Morgenstierne, pp. 5-6, and Elfenbein, personal communication). Baluch and Brahui were not mutually exclusive identities (as has been claimed by some both among the Brahui and among writers such as Rooman). Similarly, we should not assume that the Jaḏgāl are necessarily descended from the Jat or Lāsī because of their language. The Mēd probably represent a pre-Islamic population that may be descended from the Ichthyophagi encountered by Alexander's fleet. The Jat and Jaḏgāl (literally "Jaṭṭ-speakers"), and the Zott (referred to in early Islamic sources), could be descendents of the Yutiya or Outii of the Achaemenian empire, and represent an earlier settled population of Indian origin (cf. Brunner, p. 772). The remaining *ḡolām* were brought in through the Muscadine trade mainly in the 13th/19th and early14th/20th centuries.

The relationship between the Baluch and the Pashtuns also deserves some attention. Pashtuns constitute a very large minority in the Pakistani province of Baluchistan. Most of them live in the northern districts, which were never occupied by Baluch, but there are also Pashtun entrepreneurs and traders elsewhere in the province. In the northeast there is some evidence that the Baluch-Pashtun relationship also is less absolute than at first appears. Barth (1964) explains the relationship by contrasting the structures of the two societies, Baluch and Pashtun. He shows that the cultural border between Baluch and Pashtuns in northeast Baluchistan (Pakistan) has moved slowly and intermittently northward at the expense of the Pashtuns, without any associated movement of population. Groups known to have been formerly Pashtuns and Pashto-speaking were, when he was there in 1960, Baluchi-speaking and fully accepted by themselves and others as Baluch. Others have suggested that the Marī may be of Pashtun origin because of similarities in their tribal organization. Although several factors suggest that the border would move in the opposite direction (e.g., relative population growth rates, comparative affluence and aggressiveness), this Baluch assimilation of Pashtuns could have been predicted on the basis of a comparison of the ways their social and political relations are organized. The structure of Baluchi-speaking society is better adapted to the problems of incorporating refugees. Owing to the disorder that had been chronic in the area for over a century before its incorporation into India, many whole communities disintegrated into bands of refugees. The model for the whole Pashtun system might be characterized as a group of brothers, each of which expects to be equal with the others. But Baluch society, though ostensibly derived from the same concepts of kinship and descent, is not based on an egalitarian council. Defense of honor is important among the Baluch, but the essential model for their society is the relationship between a father and his sons. In Baluch society, everyone knows implicitly where he stands in relation to everyone else—in terms of authority and loyalty, status and honor. Equality of authority and honor do not have to be upheld in every interaction. Refugees in Baluch society find a secure position by operating in Baluchi. By speaking and doing Baluchi they come to be assimilated into the Baluch polity. (Other explanations of the apparent assimilation of Pashtuns by Baluch are of course possible. For example, Pashtuns could have become Baluch simply as a result of being isolated from their main polity. The phenomenon of change of identity and its relation to change of language and change of social status requires more careful investigation.)

There are also other groups that live in Baluchistan and are not considered to be part of Baluch society or capable of assimilation. The most significant of these are Hindus, Sikhs, Parsis, Isma'ilis, and Bahais, who have traditionally formed small trading communities around the forts of sardars and in the ports. In what is now Pakistan these were encouraged and protected by the British as well as the sardars. Partition saw a significant decline in these communities on the Pakistan side. In Iran the Bahais have been generally free from persecution in Baluchistan. There are also communities of Hazāras, especially in Quetta, who migrated from Afghanistan in the late 13th/19th and early 14th/20th centuries. Finally there are Persians (mainly Yazdis) and Pakistanis (mainly Punjabis) who moved to Baluchistan as civil servants and bought land and stayed.

The most important event in the life of a Baluch is marriage. Even in the relatively small number of cases where a man marries more than once, the first marriage is the most important socially. It gives him a new set of relatives, or (if the marriage is to a close cousin) rearranges his existing kin ties and establishes his social position for the rest of his (and her) life. The main prestation associated with the event is the Islamic *mahr*, which is high. It was rials 10,000 (about $130,00) for poor Baluch nomads in eastern Iranian Makrān in 1964. For *ḥākomzāt* it was reckoned as 75 percent of the expected patrimony of the groom, as a way of ensuring that at least three quarters of his property would be inherited by the bride's children. However, in most Baluch communities divorce is rare.

Weddings are the classic celebrations among the Baluch (see Gabriel, 1935, pp. 233-61 for an example). Details vary from place to place but the following are standard practice for relatively affluent Baluch. The rite and the celebration take place in the bride's community and are accompanied by music and dancing; by *tās-gardēn*, passing round the bowl to collect toward the expenses; by ceremonial washing of bride and groom, separately, the groom preceded by dancing musicians to a convenient stream; by *ḥannā-gardēn*, circulating the henna (with which the nails of the bride are tinted) for a collection for the bride's nurse; by *čam-dīdukānī*, literally "eye-seeing," a toll taken by the bride's old nurse from the groom for the right to see his bride's face as he enters the *ḥejla* (bridal chamber). (For examples of songs sung at each stage, see Morgenstierne, 1948, p. 278.)

Much of Baluch culture is not unfamiliar to students of other tribal populations in the Iranian world, but there are a number of distinguishing features. One of the more obvious distinguishing features of Baluch society is the high respect accorded to status and authority and especially to the authority of the sardar or *ḥākom*. Marī talk about the *pāg-wāja* (Pehrson, p. 26), the "turban-chief," and to confirm a man in the position of sardar is to tie the turban on him. A sardar (and even more so a *ḥākom* or *na(w)wāb*, or the khan himself, who had managed to establish a supratribal status for themselves) was based in a fort in the main agricultural center under his control. His income depended more on what he could control than on what he owned. It consisted of the produce of land personally owned by him (worked by *ḡolām* who received their keep, or local *šahrī* who took a share of the harvest or some other compensation such as use of the *ḥākom*'s water for their own land); a tithe (*dah-yak*) on all agricultural produce of the *šahrī* whom he controlled (this included all in his center plus a hinterland which varied according to his strength and prestige); service (Baluchi *srēnbandī*) from all Balōč who acknowledged his position; tax (*mālīyāt*) from both *šahrī* and Balōč (originally tax due to Qajar, khan, or British representatives). These are Baluch revenue concepts—practice varied from place to place. Basically the *ḥākom* relied on the labor of his subject peasant population for income and on the allegiance of nomadic pastoralists for physical strength. The sardar is obliged to make himself available to his tribesmen, to hear disputes and petitions when they are brought to him. Informants talk about this in terms of *mardomdārī*. Each person has the right of direct appeal, and a good portion of each day the sardar is in residence is spent holding court (Swidler, 1977, p. 113). One of the more common words in Baluch usage is *kamāš*, which denotes senior. In any social situation someone is implicitly recognized as *kamāš* (whether inter pares or not), and there is never any doubt about who it is (except in cases of open conflict). The rulers of agricultural settlements vie with each other for the allegiance of the nomads. In their forts in the agricultural settlements they are able to store grain, which they can then use to finance a militia. Such militias were used to impose a tithe and other contributions on the agricultural or pastoral populations they could control. The nomads are egalitarian, but they are encapsulated in a hierarchical system.

The overwhelming majority of Baluch are Hanafite Muslims. Although there is wide variation in the degree of religiosity, being Muslim is for these an essential component of being Baluch. There are, however, two important non-Hanafite communities. The first of these is the Bāmerī community centered on Dalgān west of Bampūr, who are Shi'ite—probably as a result of their location, which put them in close contact with the Qajar authorities. (However, it is not known when they became Shi'ite, and it should be remembered that some of the early Islamic sources suggest that some of the Baluch were Shiʿite.) The second was in the 12th-13th/18th-19th centuries a relatively large community in Makrān, Māškay, and the coast of Las Bela, who called themselves Ḏekrī (Zikri, Bal. Zigrī). Zikrism appears to have begun as a branch of the Mahdawī sect which was established late in the 9th/15th century by Sayyed Moḥammad Kāẓemī Jawnpūrī (847-910/1443-1505, q.v.), who proclaimed himself mahdī. The leaders of the sect in Makrān are said to have books, including *Ṣafā-nāma-ye Mahdī* and *Tardīd-e mahdawīyat*. Moḥammad Jawnpūrī was expelled from Jawnpūr; went to Deccan where he converted the ruler, but on the outbreak of a religious rebellion he was driven out. Eventually with a small group of followers he arrived in Sind. Again he was expelled. He went to Qandahār, where Shah Bēg Argūn, son of Ḏu'l-Nūn Bēg is said to have become his disciple. But the people and mullas demonstrated against him there as well. Next he went to Farāh, where according to the *Tardīd* he died. However, the Makrān Ḏekrīs allege that he disappeared from Farāh and after visiting Mecca, Medina, Aleppo, and other parts of Syria traveled through Persia by way of Lār to Kech, where he settled on the Kūh-e Morād outside Torbat. He preached there for ten years, converted all Makrān and died. The sect appears to be the remnant of the Mahdawī movement which assumed a definite shape in India at the end of the 9th/15th century through the teaching of Sayyed Moḥammad but died out early in the 11th/17th century. It was most probably introduced into Makrān by his disciples. As noted above, there seems to have been some connection between the success of Zikrism and rise of Bulēdī power. At the beginning of the eighteenth century when Mollā Morād Gīčkī (who has a special place in Ḏekrī history) ousted the Bulēdī, Zikrism was advanced again. (There is no evidence of any connection between this and the supposed Sikh origin of the Gīčkī tribe in Makrān.) Mollā Morād may have introduced the idea of Kūh-e Morād as substitute for the Kaʿba, and he may have dug the well known as *čāh-e zamzam* in front of the Torbat fort. Naṣīr Khan I sought to wipe out the heresy, and attacked and defeated Makrān partly for that purpose during the rule of Malek Dīnār, the son of Mollā Morād.

The principal doctrines of Zikrism are: that the dispensation of the Prophet has come to an end and is superseded by the Mahdī; that the Prophet's mission was to preach and spread the doctrines of the Koran in their literal sense, but that it remained for the Mahdī to put new constructions on their meaning (the Mahdī is *ṣāḥeb-e taʾwīl*); *ḏekr* replaces *namāz* (ritual prayer); the fast of Ramażān is not necessary; the *šahāda* (confession of faith) is changed to "lā elāh ella'llāh wa Moḥammad Mahdī rasūl Allāh;" *zakāt* (alms tax) is replaced by *ʿošr* (tithe); and, finally, this world and the goods of this world should be avoided. Religious observance takes the form of *ḏekr* and *keštī*. *Ḏekr* is performed at stipulated times throughout the day, similarly to *namāz* which it replaces, and *keštī* is performed on specific dates. *Ḏekr* is repeated in two ways: *ḏekr-e jalī*, the formula spoken aloud and the *ḏekr-e ḵafī* formula is said silently. The *ḏekrs* are numerous, and each consists of ten or twelve lines. They are said six times a day: before dawn, early dawn, midday, before sunset, early night, and midnight. *Keštī* is held any Friday night which falls on the 14th of the month, and during the first ten nights of the month Ḏu'l-ḥejja, and the day following the *ʿĪd al-żoḥā*. Principal *keštī* is held on the 9th night of Ḏu'l-ḥejja. It is also performed at births, circumcisions, and marriages, and in pursuance of vows. Performers form a circle, as for a typical Baluch dance. One or more women with good voices stand in the center, while the men circle round. The women sing songs praising the Mahdī and the men repeat the chorus. The ceremonies continue into the night. *Ḏekr* is held in places set apart as *ḏekrāna*. In settled communities the men and women are segregated, but not among nomads. There is no burial service. The Ḏekrī are said to hold their mullas in greater respect than Muslims (*Gazetteer*, VII, pp. 116-20). Since Naṣīr Khan's crusades in the 12th/18th century, and more especially since the increased association of Islam with the ideas both of Baluch autonomy and of Pakistan, the number of adherents appears to have declined. The practice of *taqīya* makes it difficult to assess the number of adherents. In Iran it may have died out completely, but it appears still to be significant in Pakistani Makrān.

A number of factors seem to have led to an increase in Islamic consciousness among the Baluch in recent decades. The power of the sardars has suffered at the hands of the state in all three countries. The *mawlawī* (religious authorities educated in India) have taken the place of secular sardar authority in many communities—especially in Iran, where they also represent Baluch Sunni Islam, as distinct from the Persian Shiʿism. With the increase in Islamic awareness there has been an increase in the practice of secluding women among the higher classes in settled communities. However, the type of religious interest that made many Baluch susceptible to Zikrism is still in evidence in the widespread use of shrines (which may be developed out of graves or simply from natural features such as trees or hills), and the attention given to wandering dervishes (religious mendicants). It may be significant that dervishes wear their hair long, and it appears that it was customary earlier for all Baluch to wear long hair (see two photographs of Mīr Ḵodādād Khan, the tenth khan of the Baluch who ruled 1857-93 in Baluch, 1975, after p. 108).

The primary values of Baluch society are those of the pastoral Balōč, and Islamic precepts tend to be suppressed where they conflict. The Baluch are proud of their code of honor, which embodies the following principles: to avenge blood with blood; to defend to the death anyone who takes refuge in one's dwelling; similarly to defend any article of property that is entrusted to one's safekeeping; to extend unquestioning hospitality to any that seek it and to defend one's guest with one's life so long as he chooses to stay, escorting him to one's borders (if necessary) when he chooses to leave (however, a guest who chooses to stay more than three days becomes a client and is required to explain his situation); never to kill a woman, a minor, or a non-Muslim; in a case of homicide or injury, to accept the intercession of a woman of the offender's family; never to kill within the *ḥaram* of a shrine; to stop fighting if a mulla, a *sayyed*, or a woman carrying the Koran on the head intervenes; to kill an adulterer. None of these principles differs essentially from the similar code held by the Pashtuns and by other tribal societies in southwest Asia. They are obviously not the principles of a society with a centralized system of social control.

Other values which are prominent in Baluch discourse about the ideal Baluch society include the principle that Baluch do not engage in trade and especially that though they may sell grain and meat that they produce, they would not sell fruit or vegetables. It is the right of any traveler to sate his hunger on growing crops as he passes by. The underlying principle of the relationship of the Baluch to his land is that this territory (that all outsiders despise as waterless mountain and desert) is the ideal country, and it is up to the Baluch to adapt themselves to it, to know its resources and enjoy them. The Baluch is first and foremost a warrior and a pastoralist, and serves his community by being unquestioningly loyal to his sardar; though he may take up many other activities, he does not forget what makes him Baluch. Many writers have remarked on Baluch inattention to matters of hygiene and prophylaxis—an attitude that may derive from these principles.

The idea that Baluch society is a society of travelers is highlighted by the importance given to the institution known as *ḥāl*. This is a ritual of greeting and exchange of information that is enacted in various degrees of formality whenever two or more Baluch meet, whether as host and guest or away from village and camp. In the classic case, two groups of riders whose paths cross in the desert, first dismount, shake hands, and sit facing each other. Then they determine who is *kamāš*, who ranks senior among them. Usually this is obvious to all, or can be accomplished by a nod. The *kamāš* then "takes the news"—presides over a session in which each asks after the health of the others and their families and recounts what is newsworthy in their recent experience. The ritual may or may not include real or important news. It is carried out even if both sides have met recently. It is often done in Baluchi, even by travelers who have another native language. Most of the phrases are stereotyped and given in a peculiar intonation. The right to take the news is the test of social rank in Makrān.

The code along with these other related values constitutes the ideal against which Baluch-ness is measured. In practice there is much deviation. In the case of vengeance killing it is interesting to see how some of those interested in establishing some degree of centralized authority in Baluch society (not only the khan) modified the code. The Marī tribal council recognized a graded scale of blood compensation for men: sardar or other member of ruling lineage, Rs 8,000; *wadēra* (leader of a section of the tribe), *mukaddam* (Ar. *moqaddam*, leader of a community), and other prominent men (*mu'tabarē mard*), Rs 4-7,000; *kawmī mard* (commoners), *seyyāl* (other Baluch, Pathans), Rs 2,000; women and non-Baluch, Rs 1,000. In western Baluchistan there was a traditional blood price alternative to vengeance killing, which varied from tribe to tribe, generally between twelve and eighteen thousand rupees earlier in this century. For instance, for the Rind it was Rs 12,000: if a Rind were killed by a man from another tribe Rs 12,000 would have to be paid to the dead man's family to settle the feud. However, it was not usually paid in cash, and the interpretation in kind varied according to circumstances. Furthermore, before settlement could be made the two parties had to be brought together, which would be difficult unless both parties acknowledged the same sardar. If they did, the sardar would exact a fine from the offender (say 500 rupees) and attempt to bring them to agreement. For instance, in an area where donkeys were valued, a good donkey might be accepted as the first Rs 1,000. If the settlement was earnestly desired by the injured party, Rs 100 might be accepted for another thousand, and so on. If agreement could not be reached, the close relatives of the dead man (father, brother, son, uncle, or cousin, according to age and means) would seek to kill the killer, or, in some cases a comparable man from the same tribe. Such a second killing again would require settlement in the same way and negotiations would reopen. Once the settlement was made the offending party might give a woman (of suitable social status) in marriage to a close relative of the dead man to seal it. Alternatively, the killer would go to the home of the killed according to the refugee principle in the code of honor. But he would be likely to do this only if the killing had been accidental, or if he very much regretted it. He would normally take with him a shaikh (religious man) or other *kamāš*. The Bārakzay, who aspired to create a centralized Baluch state, claim that they had no *hūn* (Persian *ḵūn* "blood"); they would either kill or forgive.

The material culture and technology of the Baluch also differ little from those of their neighbors. The dress of men is wide baggy trousers drawn in at the ankle and tied at the waist, a long shirt, and turban. But women's dress is distinctive—a full shift with a deep front center pocket. The women's dress still (and the men's dress previously) is distinguished by embroidery. It is not clear to what extent the ornateness of men's dress until recently was a function of the pomp that developed around the khan of Kalat under the British, and may have been derived from India. But although they are generally geometrical (like, for example, those of the Turkmen) it is difficult to trace the designs of women's embroidery to non-Baluch origins. Carpets (see v, below) do not appear to have been woven in Baluchistan until very recently. The only textiles of any significance produced traditionally in Baluchistan, other than clothing, were a coarse thick one-sided flatweave, and the dhurrie that was woven in Las Bela. Other handicrafts that deserve mention are the products of the ubiquitous *pīš*. Nomads weave the dried leaves into matting and elaborate basketry and even spoons and water pipes; they twist them into rope from which they make sandals (Baluchi *sawās*) and harnesses. There is also local pottery made by specialists in a few village communities. The subject of dwelling construction requires a special note. Beside goat-hair (black) and *pīš*-matting tents and mud-brick and adobe houses, there are a number of dwelling types in Makrān that are less mobile than tents and less permanent than mud. One of these is a frame constructed of date-palm leaf stems tied with *pīš* rope and covered with *pīš* matting in the shape of an egg cut lengthwise. Another type is domed; the dome is covered with *pīš* stems, the walls built of reeds or date palm stems, covered with mats and sometimes rough-cast with mud, resembling a yurt. There are also flat-roofed shelters without walls (Baluchi *kāpar*, Persian *kapar*), and the water-cooled *ḵār-ḵāna*, in which an opening on the windward side is packed densely with camel thorn (*Alhagi camelorum*) and kept wet. Most of these types are also found elsewhere in southern Iran (see Gershevitch, 1959, passim, with illustrations).

The material culture and technology of Baluch pastoralism emphasize accommodation to the variation in natural conditions. Apart from their seasonal movement between pastures, and their movement from camp to camp in the continual reshuffling of camp-communities, nomadic Baluch are always on the move. They need to travel widely in order to cultivate small plots of land, to find stray animals, to keep up visiting obligations, to purchase grain and other nonpastoral commodities, to make pilgrimages, and to cultivate political connections. They live in a *mētag* or *halk* (*ḵalq* "camp"); typically they cooperate with kin and affines in the management of one or more flocks; they cultivate small plots which provide fruit and vegetables and sometimes a little grain or a fodder crop, and they have a reciprocal relationship with a farming community which allows them to participate in the date harvest in return for sharing their milk and dairy products in the spring. In the summer of 1964 a typical area for Makrān mountain nomads (Salāhkoh) contained 72 tents in an area of some 400 square miles. They were distributed in twelve encampments of two to nine tents each. The camps move irregularly according to rainfall. Rains produce various effects: a slow steady rain resuscitates the range, but does not produce runoff to irrigate a crop; a flash flood often alters the configuration and depth of a torrent bed and the subsequent availability of surface water, and affects rights to agricultural land. Beside different combinations of agriculture and pastoralism, the Baloč run varying numbers of camels, sheep, goats, cattle, and even water buffalo, with the addition of donkeys for transport, and in some parts mules or horses for prestige riding. Their nomadism allows them the flexibility not only to exploit the best pasture within reach, but to integrate other resources into their annual cycle. They think of their society in terms of a community of camps rather than a collection of separate camp communities. Although there has been a tendency toward sedentarization since the 1960s, it has been stronger in the Sarḥadd, Sarawan-Jahlawan, and the northeast than Makrān, where it continues to be possible for nomads to offset drought years with earnings in the Persian Gulf states.

The main fixed point around which the annual cycle revolves is *āmēn* (Persian *hāmīn*), the date harvest, when all (except a minimum number of shepherds who remain behind with the flocks) move off to the vicinity of a large date-growing area. For while the greater part of the date crop is probably grown by *šahrī* settlements, dates are of no less importance to the Balōč than to the *šahrī*. *Āmēn* is looked forward to as the axis of the annual cycle. Prophesies are made of the exact day when the dates will turn color (which happens a month before ripening). Everyone talks about how much fruit the palms will bear this year, and later how the season is progressing, and takes samples from community to community for comparison. There are no other essential agricultural or pastoral tasks. *Āmēn* is the season for visiting and all forms of celebration that do not have to be held at another time of the year.

Many nomads spend a disproportionate amount of their time on *band* cultivation. A *band* maximizes the use of irregular and ephemeral stream flow or runoff and at the same time accumulates and evens out soil deposits in mountainous or undulating terrain, where either soil or soil moisture would otherwise be insufficient for cultivation. It is a dry stone or earthen structure built across the course of drainage in order to hold the water while it drops its silt and sinks slowly through the accumulated deposit. As a low investment technology in isolated mountainous areas with sparse population such as Baluchistan, and especially Makrān, it provides them with the capability of raising small quantities of fruit and vegetables and supplementary crops of grain. It may have been more important in pre-Balōč times (Raikes, 1965).

Throughout most of Baluchistan direct rainfall is of negligible value for agriculture, but one of the most important sources of water for irrigation is the runoff and wadi flooding which are the immediate results of rainfall. With little assistance the runoff from a whole catchment is gathered by the nature of the terrain itself and directed onto prepared fields, along with its invaluable sediment. However, although a considerable volume of water is thus made available, the supply is extremely irregular, and will not generally support permanent settlement. In some parts wells are used, operated by hand by means of counterpoised water-lifts (see ĀBYĀRĪ). The most important example is probably in the Dalgān, west of Bampūr. In places where there is a shallow water table with a large catchment these can be reasonably reliable, but nevertheless do not provide enough water to justify permanent agricultural settlement. In the mountain ranges which cross the southern part of the area many of the larger river beds retain flowing water in parts throughout the year. Staple crops include wheat, barley, millet, sorghum, rice, beans, onions, and dates, but pomegranates, bananas, papaw, mango, and many other fruits and vegetables are also grown.

The conditions of irrigated agriculture in settled communities in Baluchistan are very different from the cultivation of nomads. Communities vary between a few hundred and a few thousand, but conform mostly to a recognizable pattern: The cultivation is done largely by serfs or helotized smallholders; in the center is a fort—often high and imposing; the fort was traditionally occupied by a ruler, who by means of various forms of taxation or ownership effectively commanded the greater part of the agricultural production, and used his position to build and rebuild networks of alliances with similar agricultural centers and with the nomads who controlled the expanses of mountain and desert between the settlements. Although most holdings in Baluchistan were small compared to the more fertile part of the plateau, some sardars accumulated considerable estates. The most significant were those of Mīr Aḥmad-Yār Khan Aḥmadzay, Ataullah Khan Mengal (the sardar of one of the largest tribes), Qaws Bux Bizenjo, Qaws Bux Raisani, Dōdā Khan Zārakzay, Nabī-bakš Zehrī. Similarly, in Kharan the Nowšērvānī, especially Ḡolām Moṣṭafā Nowšērvānī; in Makrān the Gīčkī; in Sibi the Būgṭī, especially Nawab Moḥammad Akbar Khan Būgṭī, and the Marī, especially Nawab Khair Bux Mari, and in Chagai and Afghanistan the Sanjarānī, Jamāldīnī, and Bādīnī. In Iran the Bārakzay had by far the largest holdings, but the Bozorgzāda, Bulēdī, Sardārzay, and Šīrānī were also wealthy.

Despite these large holdings, Baluchistan is extremely arid, and for the most part suited to only the most extensive forms of resource use, such as goat or camel husbandry. Perennial irrigation on any significant scale has until recently been available only at Bampūr. Other historically important agricultural areas are Kolwa, Dasht, Las Bela, Daštīārī, and Kacchi (the last three of which have been developed recently to varying extents); but these depended traditionally on seasonal flood diversion and were less reliable. Otherwise, reliable cultivation is supported only in a certain number of well-defined locations, where cultivable soil and an accessible supply of water suitable for irrigation coincide, mostly in river valleys, especially the valleys of the Māškīd and its tributaries, the Kech and the Sarbāz. Investment in *qanāt*s (Baluchi *kahn*; the standard term in Pakistan otherwise is *kārēz*) irrigation, which has always been important in the Māškīd and Kech basins, possibly from the earliest times, began to be expanded in the last century. Since the middle of this century irrigation has expanded again as a result of the availability of cheap energy for pumping ground water—diesel in Iran and the national electricity grid which has been extended into Sarawan in Pakistan. *Kārēz* building is being expanded again in Makrān, financed by remittances from the Persian Gulf.

Final remarks. Compared to most of the other tribal or ethnic minorities of the Iranian world the Baluch (in Iran, Afghanistan, and Pakistan) are probably more linguistically diverse and stratified and pluralistic. The nature of the topography has made communication difficult and the paucity and sparseness of natural resources have limited the size of settlements. Potential leaders have been unable to build up large confederacies or otherwise extend their authority beyond their immediate constituencies. Pashtuns, Punjabis, Sindhis, Bashkardis, Sistanis all experience natural conditions similar to those of their nearest Baluch neighbors. Apart from the use of Baluchi as a lingua franca and a particular hierarchical type of political structure, most Baluch cultural features are also shared by their neighbors. Similarly, the history of most parts of the world is to some extent a function of interference from outside. The geography and ecology are directly related to the settlement pattern, which places special constraints on political development and offers particular opportunities to outside influence. The structural factors are a function of both the settlement pattern and the cultural history of the populations that came to the area. The final result could not have come about if the history of Iran and India had not led to particular types of interference and withdrawal at particular times. What distinguishes the Baluch (as distinct from the Balōč) from their neighbors is presumably, therefore, the peculiar combination of their geography, culture, and dependency which has led them to subscribe to a common language and set of political ideas.

Bibliography: Given its historical marginality, the size of the literature on Baluchistan is remarkable. But this is due to the interest of the neighboring and other powers that competed to control it as their hinterland—the Persians, Greeks, Arabs, Afghans, British and other colonial powers, Pakistanis, and finally in recent decades the Baluch themselves. The sources therefore fall into the following general categories: (1) pre-Islamic sources; (2) works by Muslim (Arab, Persian, and Mughal) historians and travelers before the arrival of the British in India; (3) works by British administrators, scholars, and travelers; (4) official publications of the government of India; (5) official publications of the government of Pakistan; (6) works by Pakistani scholars; (7) works by Western and Soviet scholars since 1947; (8) reports generated by U.N. and other international and bilateral development projects since 1950; (9) works by Baluch scholars since 1950. What follows is an alphabetical listing of the more significant and accessible sources, including those which have served as the basis of the present article.

Ḥājī ʿAbd-al-Nabī (Hajee Abdun Nabee), ed. Major Robert Leech (see below). C. U. Aitchison, *A Collection of Treaties, Agreements and Sanads Relating to India and Neighbouring Countries* XI, XIII,

Calcutta, 1933. Abu'l-Fażl ʿAllāmī, *Āʾīn-e akbarī*, ed. Blochmann. Arrian, *Anabasis and Indica*, ed. and tr. P.A. Brunt, London, 1983. Ẓahīr-al-Dīn Moḥammad Bābor, *Bābor-nāma*, tr. A. S. Beveridge, London, 1922 (repr. New Delhi, 1970). Mir Khudabux Bijarani Marri Baloch, *The Balochis through Centuries. History versus Legend*, Quetta, 1965. Idem, *Searchlights on Baloches and Balochistan*, Karachi, 1974. Mir Ahmad Yar Khan Baluch, *Inside Baluchistan: A Political Autobiography of His Highness Baigi: Khan-e-Azam-XIII*, Karachi, 1975. Muhammad Sardar Khan Baluch, *History of the Baluch Race and Baluchistan*, Quetta, 1962 (repr. 1977). *Baluchistan: List of Leading Personages in Baluchistan*, Government of India Central Publication Branch, Calcutta, 1932. F. Barth, "Ethnic Processes on the Pathan-Baluch Boundary," in *Indo-Iranica. Mélanges présentés à G. Morgenstierne*, Wiesbaden, 1964, pp. 13-20. Idem, "Competition and Symbiosis in North-East Baluchistan," *Folk* 6, 1964, pp. 15-22. A. Bennigsen and S. Enders Wimbush, *Muslims of the Soviet Empire*, London, 1985. Zulfikar Ali Bhutto, *Prime Minister Zulfikar Ali Bhutto Abolishes Sardari System*, from his speech at Quetta, 8 April 1976. N. M. Billimoria, *Bibliography of Publications Relating to Sind and Baluchistan*, Lahore, 1930 (revised 1977). W. T. Blanford, *Note on the Geological Formations Seen Along the Coasts of Baluchistan, etc.*, Records of the Geological Survey of India, Calcutta, 1872. E. Blatter and P. F. Halberg, "Flora of Persian Baluchistan and Makran," *Journal of the Bombay Natural Historical Society* 24, 1910. H. Bobek, "Beiträge zur klimaökologischen Gliederung Irans," *Erdkunde* 6, 1952, pp. 65-84. C. E. Bosworth, *Sistan under the Arabs, from the Islamic Conquest to the Rise of the Saffarids (30-250/651-864)*, Rome, 1968. Idem, "The Kūfichīs or Qufṣ in Persian history," *Iran* 14, 1976, pp. 9-17. C. E. Bosworth, R. M. Burrel, K. McLachlan, and R. M. Savory, eds., *The Persian Gulf States. A General Survey*, Baltimore, 1980. D. Bray, *Life-History of a Brahui*, London, 1913. Idem, "The Jat of Baluchistan," *Indian Antiquary* 54, 1925, pp. 30-33. C. Brunner, "Geographical and Administrative Divisions: Settlements and Economy," in *Camb. Hist. Iran* III/2, pp. 747-77. *Cambridge History of India*, Delhi, 1958-63. M. L. Chaumont, "États vassaux dans l'empire des premiers Sassanides," in *Monumentum H. S. Nyberg* I, Acta Iranica 4, Tehran and Liège, 1975, pp. 133-46. G. B. Castiglioni, "Appunti geografici sul Balucistan Iraniano," *Rivista geographica italiana* 67, 1960, pp. 109-52, 268-301. B. D. Clark, "Tribes of the Persian Gulf," in Bosworth et al., pp. 485-509. G. F. Dales, *The Role of Natural Forces in the Ancient Indus Valley and Baluchistan*, Anthropological Papers 62, University of Utah, 1962. Idem, "Harappan Outposts on the Makran Coast," *Antiquity* 36/142, 1962, pp. 86-93. M. L. Dames, *Popular Poetry of the Baloches*, 2 vols., London 1904a. Idem, *The Baloch Race*, Asiatic Society Monographs 4, London, 1904b (quoting Elliot, *History of India*). J. Dresch, "Bassins arides iraniens," *Bulletin de l'Association des géographes français* 430, 1975, pp. 337-51. Idem, "Cuvettes iranaises comparées: Djaz Murian et Lut," *Geography* (Tehran) 1, 1976, pp. 8-19. R. E. H. Dyer, *Raiders of the Sarhad, Being an Account of a Campaign of Arms and Bluff against the Brigands of the Persian-Baluchi Border*, London, 1921. W. Eilers, "Das Volk der Maka vor und nach der Achämeniden," in *Kunst, Kultur und Geschichte der Achämenidenzeit und ihr Fortleben*, ed. H. Koch and D. N. Mackenzie, Berlin, 1983, pp. 101-22. J. Elfenbein, *A Baluchi Miscellanea of Erotica and Poetry: Codex Oriental Additional 24048 of the British Library*, AIUON 43/2, Suppl. no. 35, Napoli, 1983. Mountstuart Elphistone, *An Account of the Kingdom of Caubul*, London, 1815. A. T. Embree, ed., *Pakistan's Western Borderlands*, Durham, 1977, W. A. Fairservis, *Preliminary Report on the Pre-Historic Archaeology of the Afghan Baluchi Areas*, American Museum Novitates, American Museum of Natural History, New York, 1952. Fīrūz Mīrzā Farmānfarmā, *Safar-nāma-ye Kermān o Balūčestān*, ed. M. Neẓām Māfī, Tehran, 1342 Š./1963. K. Ferdinand, "The Baluchistan Barrel-Vaulted Tent," *Folk* 2, 1960, pp. 33-50. *Ferešta*, tr. Briggs. J. P. Ferrier, *Caravan Journeys and Wanderings in Persia, Afghanistan, Turkestan and Beloochistan*, London, 1857. H. Field, *An Anthropological Reconnaissance in West Pakistan 1955*, Peabody Museum, New York, 1959. E. A. Floyer, *Unexplored Baluchistan. A Survey with Observations Astronomical, Geographical, Botanical, etc., of a Route through Mekran, Bashkurd, Persia, Kurdistan and Turkey*, London, 1882. R. N. Frye, "Notes on a Trip to Biyabanak, Sistan and Baluchistan in the Winter 1951-2," *Indo-Iranica* 6, 1952, pp. 1-6. Idem, "Remarks on Baluchi History," *Central Asiatic Journal* 6, 1961, pp. 44-50. A. Gabriel, *Durch Persiens Wüsten*, Stuttgart, 1935. Idem, "The Southern Lut and Iranian Balutschistan," *Geographical Journal* 92, 1938, pp. 193-211. Idem, *Aus den Einsamkeiten Irans*, Stuttgart, 1939, E. G. Gafferberg, *Beludzhi Turkmenskoĭ SSR*, Institut Etnografii Miklukho Maklai, Leningrad, 1969. R. E. Galindo, *A Record of Two Years Wanderings in Eastern Persia and Baluchistan*, Simla, 1890. Y. Gankowsky, "Social Structure of Pakistan's Brahui-Baluchi Population," *Journal of South Asian and Middle Eastern Studies* 5/4, 1982, pp. 57-73. A. Gansser, "The Taftan Volcano (SE Iran)," *Ecologae Geologicae Helvetiae* 64, 1971, pp. 319-44. A. Gasteiger, *Von Teheran nach Belutschistan. Reise-Skizzen*, Innsbruck, 1881. *Gazetteer*, Baluchistan District Series, ed. R. Hughes-Buller and C. F. Minchin, Bombay, 1906-08. I. Gershevitch, "Travels in Bashkardia," *Royal Central Asiatic Society Journal* 46/3-4, 1959, pp. 213-25. F. J. Goldsmid, ed., *Eastern Persia. An Account of the Persian Boundary Commission 1870-1872*, London, 1876. Government of Pakistan, *White Paper on Pakistan*,

Quetta, 1974. N. P. Grant, "Journal of a Route through the Western Parts of Makran," *JRAS* 5, 1839, pp. 328-42. W. Haig, draft of unpublished book concerning the period 1913-1918 in Persia including Baluchistan, in *Collection of Private Papers*, St. Anthony's College, Oxford. J. Hansman, "A Periplus of Magan and Meluhha," *BSOAS* 36, 1973, pp. 553-86. J. V. Harrison, "Coastal Makran," *Geographical Journal* 97, 1941, pp. 1-17. Idem, "The Jaz Murian Depression, Persian Baluchistan," ibid., 101, 1943, pp. 206-25. S. S. Harrison, *In Afghanistan's Shadow: Baluch Nationalism and Soviet Temptations*, Carnegie Endowment for International Peace, New York, 1981. R. B. Hetu Ram, *Tārīḵ-e Balūčestān*, Quetta, 1907. A. Houtum-Schindler, "Notes on Persian Baluchistan. From the Persian of Mirza Mehdi Khan," *JRAS* 7, 1877, pp. 147-54. A. Jahānbānī, *ʿAmalīyāt-e qošūn dar Balūčestān az Mordād tā Bahman 1307*, Tehran, 1336 Š./1957. Idem, *Sargoḏašt-e Balūčestān*, Tehran, 1338 Š./1959. Kayhān, *Joḡrāfīā*. Kent, *Old Persian*. N. de Khanikoff, *Mémoire sur la partie méridionale de l'Asie Centrale*, Paris, 1864. J. H. Lace, "A Sketch of the Vegetation of British Baluchistan," *Journal of the Linnaean Society* 28, 1897, pp. 228-327. Lambton, *Landlord and Peasant*. R. Leech, "Brief History of Kalat Brought down to the Disposition and Death of Nawab Khan Braho-ee," *JASB* 12, 1843, pp. 473-512. Idem, "Notes Taken on a Tour through Parts of Baloochisthan, in 1838 and 1839, by Hajee Abdun Nubee, of Kabul, Arranged and Translated by Major Robert Leech," ibid., 13, 1844, pp. 667-706, 786-826. L. Lockhart, *Nadir Shah. A Critical Study Based Mainly upon Contemporary Sources*, London, 1938. Lorimer, *Gazetteer*. Markwart, *Provincial Capitals*. M. Maroth, "Sistan nach den arabischen geographischen Quellen," in *Studies in the Sources on the History of Pre-Islamic Central Asia*, ed. J. Harmatta, Budapest, 1979, pp. 145-51. C. Masson, *Narrative of Various Journeys in Balochistan, Afghanistan and the Panjab*, London, 1842. S. B. Miles, *The Countries and Tribes of the Persian Gulf*, London, 1919 (repr. 1966). V. Minorsky, "Mongol Placenames in Mukri Kurdistan (Mongolica 4)," *BSOAS* 19, 1957, p. 81. G. Morgenstierne, *Report on a Linguistic Mission to North-Western India*, Oslo, 1932. Erwin Orywal, *Die Baluc in Afghanisch-Sistan*, Kölner Ethnologische Studien 4, Berlin, 1982. C. McC. Pastner, "A Social, Structural and Historical Analysis of Honor, Shame and Purdah," *Anthropological Quarterly* 45/4, 1972, pp. 248-61. Idem, "Cousin Marriage among the Zikri Baluch of Coastal Pakistan," *Ethnology* 18, 1979, pp. 31-47. C. McC. Pastner and S. Pastner, "Agriculture, Kinship and Politics in Southern Baluchistan," *Man* 7/1, 1972, pp. 128-36. R. N. Pehrson, *The Social Organization of the Marri Baluch*, ed. F. Barth, Viking Fund Publications in Anthropology 43, New York, 1966. *Persia*, Geographical Handbook Series, Naval Intelligence Division, London, 1945. M. Pikulin, *Beludzhi*, Moscow, 1959. Marco Polo, *The Book of Ser Marco Polo, the Venitian, Concerning the Kingdoms and Marvels of the East*, tr. H. Yule, rev. and enl. H. Cordier, London, 1926. H. Pottinger, *Travels in Beloochistan and Sinde; Accompanied by a Geographical and Historical Account of Those Countries with a Map*, London, 1816 (repr. Westmead, 1972). R. B. Diwan Jamiat Rai, *The Domiciled Hindus*, ed. Denys Bray, Delhi, 1913. R. L. Raikes, "The Ancient Ghabarbands of Baluchistan," *East and West*, N.S. 15/1-2, 1964-65, pp. 26-35. H. G. Raverty, *Notes on Afghanistan and Baluchistan*, Lahore, 1878. Razmārā, *Farhang*. P. A. Rittikh, "Poezdka v Persiyu i Persidskiĭ Beludzhistan 1900," *Izvestiya Russkogo geograficheskogo obshchestva* 38, 1902. K. M. Röhrborn, *Provinzen und Zentralgewalt Persiens im 16 und 17 J.*, Studien zur Sprache, Geschichte und Kultur des Islamischen Orients, Berlin, 1966. A. Rooman, *The Brahuis of Quetta-Kalat Region*, Pakistan Historical Society, Memoir 3, Karachi, 1960. E. C. Ross, "Memorandum of Notes on Mekran, together with Report on a Visit to Kej and Route through Mekran from Gwadur to Kurrachie," *Bombay Geographical Society* 18, 1867, pp. 36-77. J. P. Rumsey, "Some Notes on Leadership in Marri Baloch Society," *Anthropology Tomorrow* (University of Chicago) 5, 1957, pp. 122-26. J. Saldanha, *Official History of the Mekran Telegraph Line from Karachi to Jask*, n.p., 1895. P. C. Salzman, "Adaptation and Political Organization in Iranian Baluchistan," *Ethnology* 10/4, 1971, pp. 433-44. Idem, "Multi-Resource Nomadism in Iranian Baluchistan," *Journal of Asian and African Studies* 7, 1972, pp. 60-68 (also published in W. Irons and N. Dyson-Hudson, eds., *Perspectives on Nomadism*, Leiden, 1972). Idem, "The Proto-State in Iranian Baluchistan," in *Origins of the State: The Anthropology of Political Evolution*, ed. R. Cohen and E. R. Service, Philadelphia, 1978, pp. 125-40. Idem, ed., *When Nomads Settle, Processes of Sedentarization as Adaptation and Response*, New York, 1980. C. Schefer, tr., *Histoire de l'Asie Centrale par Mir Abdoul Kerim Bouchary*, Paris, 1876. W. H. Schoff, tr., *Periplus of the Erythraean Sea: Travel and Trade in the Indian Ocean by a Merchant of the First Century*, New York, 1912. H. Scholberg, *The District Gazetteers of India. A Bibliography*, Inter Documentation Company AG ZUG, Switzerland, 1970. F. Scholz, *Belutschistan (Pakistan). Eine sozialgeographische Studie des Wandels in einem Nomadenland seit Beginn der Kolonialzeit*, Göttinger Geographische Abhandlungen 63, 1964. H. P. Schurmann, *The Mongols of Afghanistan*, The Hague, 1962. Schwarz, *Iran*, pp. 260ff. Mīrzā Moḥammad-Taqī Lesān-al-Molk Sepehr, *Nāseḵ al-tawārīḵ*, ed. J. Qāʾemmaqāmī, Tehran, 1337 Š./1958. E. A. Shteĭnberg, "Vosstaniya v Beludzhistane i Khuzistane," *Novyĭ Vostok* 25, 1921. H. Humbach and P. O. Skjærvø, *The Sassanian Inscription of Paikuli* III/1: *Restored Text and Translation*, III/2: *Commentary*, Wiesbaden, 1983. C. P. Skrine, "The Highlands of Persian Baluchistan," *Geographical Journal* 78, 1931, pp. 321-40. Idem, "The Quetta Earthquake," ibid., 88, 1936, pp. 414-30. R. E. Snead, "Active Mud Volcanoes of Baluchistan, West Pakistan," *Geographical Review* 54, 1964, pp. 546-60. Idem, *Physical Geography of the Makran Coastal Plain of Iran*, Albuquerque, New Mexico, 1970. B. Spooner, *Religious and Political Leadership in Persian Baluchistan*, Ph.D. thesis, Oxford University, 1967. Idem, "Politics, Kinship and Ecology in South-East Persia," *Ethnology* 8/2, 1969, pp. 139-52. Idem, "Notes on the Toponymy of the Persian Makran," in *Iran and Islam*, ed. C. E. Bosworth, Edinburgh, 1971, pp. 517-33. Idem, "Nomadism in Baluchistan," in *Pastoralists and Nomads in South-East Asia*, ed. L. S. Leshnik and G. D. Sontheimer, Wiesbaden, 1975, pp. 171-82. Idem, "Who are the Baluch?" in *Qajar Iran*, ed. C. E. Bosworth and C. Hillenbrand, Edinburgh, 1984, pp. 93-112. Idem, "Weavers and Dealers: The Authenticity of an Oriental Carpet," in *The Social Life of Things: Commodities in Cultural Perspective*, ed. A. Appadurai, Cambridge, 1986, pp. 195-235. Sir A. Stein, *An Archaeological Tour to Gedrosia*, New Delhi, 1931 (repr. 1982). A. W. Stiffe, "Mudcraters and Geological Structures of the Makran Coast," *Quarterly Journal of the Geological Society*, 1874. N. B. Swidler, "Brahui Political Organization and the National State," in Embree, 1977, pp. 108-25. Idem, *The Political Structure of a Tribal Federation: The Brahui of Baluchistan*, Ph.D. dissertation, Columbia University, New York, 1969. W. W. Swidler, *Technology and Social Structure in Baluchistan, West Pakistan*, Ph.D. dissertation, Columbia University, New York, 1968. Idem, "Economic Change in Baluchistan: Processes of Integration in the Larger Economy of Pakistan," in Embree, 1977, pp. 85-108. P. Sykes, "Some Notes on Journeys in Southern and South-Eastern Persia," *Journal of the Manchester Geographical Society* 21, 1905, pp. 1-12. Idem, *Ten Thousand Miles in Persia or Eight Years in Iran*, London, 1902. Ḥ. Taqīzāda, in Jahānbānī, 1957, historical chapter. G. P. Tate, *Kalat*, Calcutta, 1896. Idem, *The Frontiers of Baluchistan*, London, 1909. T. H. Thornton, *Colonel Sir Robert Sandeman: His Life and Work on Our Indian Frontier*, London, 1895 (Quetta, 1977). W. Tomaschek, "Zur historischen Topographie von Persien," *Sb. Wiener (Österreichischen) Akademie der Wissenschaften* 102, 1883, pp. 145-231, 561-99. Y. R. Vinnikov, *Beludzhi Turkmenskoĭ SSR*, Sovetskaya ètnografiya, 1952, no. 1. L. Virsa, *Dera Ghazi Khan Field Staff Report*, Islamabad, 1984. C. Vita-Finzi, "Quaternary Deposits in the Iranian Makran," *Geographical Journal* 141, 1975, pp. 415-20. E. W. Vredenburg, "A Geographical Sketch of the Baluchistan Desert and Parts of Eastern Persia," *Memoirs of the Geological Survey of India* 31/2, 1901, pp. 179-302. Idem, "Geology of Sarawan, Jhalawan, Mekran and the State of Las Bela," *Records of the Geological Survey of India* 38, 1909, pp. 189-215. W. H. Waaltyer, *A Geographical Statistical and Historical Description of Hindostan and the Adjacent Countries*, London, 1820. Aḥmad-ʿAlī Khan Wazīrī Kermānī, *Tārīḵ-e Kermān*, ed. M.-E. Bāstānī Pārīzī, Tehran, 1340 Š./1961. Idem, *Jog̲rāfīā-ye mamlakat-e Kermān*, ed. M.-E. Bāstānī Pārīzī, Tehran, 1346-47 Š./1967-68. A. T. Wilson, *The Persian Gulf*, London, 1928. R. G. Wirsing, *The Baluchis and Pathans*, London, 1981. N. Zarudnyĭ, "Tret'ya èkskursiya po vostochnoĭ Persii," *Zapiski Russkogo geograficheskogo obshchestva* 50, 1916, pp. 1-448.

(B. Spooner)

ii. Archeology

The archeological record of Iranian Baluchistan, in the southeastern corner of Iran, is very limited. Although early travelers often described the region's antiquities, the first significant archeological research was done by Sir Mark Aurel Stein during the early 1930s. His efforts focused on the Bampūr valley, where he recorded numerous sites and conducted a few, limited excavations. Stein's research confirmed that Baluchistan had been inhabited during prehistoric times by groups believed to have cultural affiliations with those in western Iran. Until recently, Stein's research constituted the extent of archeological knowledge about Baluchistan.

In 1966 Beatrice de Cardi conducted limited excavations at Bampūr (q.v.) to clarify the region's prehistoric sequence. While limited in scope, these excavations revealed a sequence which remains the basic reference for the prehistory of Iranian Baluchistan. Gary W. Hume surveyed the Sarhad (Sarḥadd) plateau region in 1966-67 looking especially for Paleolithic sites and also discovered a few later prehistoric sites. The pottery from these sites was studied by Judith T. Marucheck who later conducted a systematic archeological survey of that region (see Miragliuolo, 1979) in 1975. The only other archeological research completed to date was Maurizio Tosi's study of the Damin grave goods in 1970.

Baluchistan may have been inhabited first during the Pleistocene as proposed by Hume (1976), based on Paleolithic sites found in the Ladiz valley. The most important were three locations which yielded simple stone tools such as choppers, flakes, and flake tools. These tools stylistically resemble those associated with the Lower Paleolithic period in areas outside of Iran. Precise dating of these materials is debated, but the finds suggest a potential for other Paleolithic research in this region.

There is little other evidence of subsequent human settlement in Baluchistan until the late fourth millennium B.C. Based on her Bampūr excavations de Cardi (pp. 257-68) thought these early settlements, Periods I-IV, had close cultural affiliations with contemporary settlements in Kermān Province and that, as a group, they may have had ultimately some type of indirect cultural affiliation with developments occurring farther to the west. Using more recent data Tosi (1970) and

Lamberg-Karlovsky (1972; Lamberg-Karlovsky and Tosi, 1973) have argued that the Bampūr data reflect an extension of basically indigenous cultural developments which occurred in Turkmenistan, eastern Iran, especially Šahr-e Sūḵta, and southern Afghanistan. The number and size of these archeological sites which date between ca. 3200-2000 B.C. are very modest and appear to reflect the activities of village agriculturalists and pastoral nomads. At the same time, several scholars (Dales, 1977; Kohl, 1978; Lamberg-Karlovsky and Tosi, 1973; Potts, 1978) contend that these communities were also involved in extensive trade networks which linked such areas as Turkmenistan, Sīstān, Pakistani Baluchistan, the Persian Gulf, and the Indus valley. These same scholars, as well as de Cardı, feel that after 2500 B.C., Bampūr Periods V-VI, this area became increasingly involved with a Persian Gulf trading network linking Mesopotamia, southeastern Iran, Oman, Bahrain, and the Indus valley. Despite the possibility of involvement in such extensive trading networks, the extent and intensity of which may be debated (Shaffer, 1982), cultural developments in Iranian Baluchistan remained modest by comparison with surrounding regions.

Early in the second millennium B.C. many of these settlements were abandoned, suggesting a population decrease or, perhaps, a shift to increased pastoral nomadism. These changes are often attributed to the impact of the Indo-Aryan invasions and/or a long period of drought. During the first millennium B.C. and especially in the Parthian and Sasanian periods, the situation altered and there was a population increase suggested by a larger number of archeological sites. One important factor in this increase was the introduction of *qanāt* (q.v.) irrigation which allowed the first major settlement of lowland plain areas. Consequently both agricultural and pastoral nomadic elements of the economy expanded. This expansion continued into the latter half of the first millennium A.D., resulting in the increasing use of ever more marginal agricultural lands and a decreasing ability of the region to meet subsistence and surplus production requirements. Population increases and competition over resources ultimately required stronger political controls reflected in the appearence of early fortifications. The problems of increasing population combined with a decreasing carrying capacity of the land, due to overgrazing and soil exhaustion, continued into the medieval period. Ultimately these insurmountable problems of ecological decline resulted in another widespread abandonment of the region until the Baluchis arrived in approximately the seventeenth century.

Bibliography: F. G. Dales, "Shifting Trade Patterns between the Iranian Plateau and the Indus Valley in the Third Millennium B.C.," in *Le plateau iranien et l'Asie Centrale des origines à la conquête islamique*, ed. J. Deshayes, Centre National de la Recherche Scientifique, Paris, 1977, pp. 67-68. B. de Cardi, "Excavations at Bampur: A Third Millennium Settlement in Persian Baluchistan, 1966," *Anthropological Papers of the American Museum of Natural History* 51, 1970, pp. 233-355. G. W. Hume, *The Ladizian: An Industry of the Asian Chopper-Chopping Tool Complex in Iranian Baluchistan*, Philadelphia, 1976. P. Kohl, "Western Asian Trade in the Third Millennium B.C.," *Current Anthropology* 19, 1978, pp. 463-92. C. C. Lamberg-Karlovsky, "Trade Mechanisms in Indus-Mesopotamian Interrelations," *JAOS* 92, 1972, pp. 222-29. Idem and M. Tosi, "Shahr-i Sokhta and Tepe Yahya: Tracks on the Earliest History of the Iranian Plateau," *East and West* 23, 1973, pp. 21-53. J. T. Marucheck, *A Technological and Comparative Analysis of Pottery from Iranian Baluchistan*, M. A. thesis, 1972, Department of Anthropology, The American University, Washington, D. C. J. T. Miragliuolo, *Non-Urban Sites and Mobile Settlement Patterns: A Survey of an Unknown Corner of Baluchistan*, Ph.D. dissertation, 1979, Department of Anthropology, The American University, Washington, D. C. D. Potts, "Towards an Integrated History of Culture Change in the Arabian Gulf Area: Notes on Dilmun, Makkan and the Economy of Ancient Sumer," *Journal of Oman Studies* 4, 1978, pp. 29-51. J. G. Shaffer, "Harappan Commerce: An Alternative Perspective," in *Anthropology in Pakistan*, ed. S. Pastner and L. Flam, South Asia Occasional Papers and Theses no. 8, Ithaca, 1982, pp. 166-210. Sir M. Aurel Stein, *An Archaeological Tour in Gedrosia*, Memoirs of the Archaeological Survey of India, no. 43, New Delhi, 1931. Idem, *Archaeological Reconnaissance in Northwestern India and Southeastern Iran*, London, 1937. M. Tosi, "A Tomb from Damin and the Problem of the Bampur Sequence in the Third Millennium B. C.," *East and West* 20, 1970, pp. 9-50.

(J. G. SHAFFER)

iii. BALUCHI LANGUAGE AND LITERATURE

Baluchi (Balōčī), the language of the Baluch (Balōč), is a member of the Western Iranian group of languages, bearing affinities to both main representatives of Western Middle Iranian: Middle Persian and Parthian. Baluchi has, however, a marked individuality of its own, and differs from both of these languages in important respects (see below).

I. The Baluchi language.

The name. Concerning the name Balōč, despite the great deal that has been written, there is still no general agreement on either its linguistic connections or its meaning (see Dames, in *EI*[1]; Pikulin, 1959). If the word is Iranian, H. W. Bailey's suggestion (apud Hansman, 1973) that it might represent Old Iranian **u̯adrau̯atī* "Gedrosia, the land of underground water channels" could explain why the people are unknown prior to their arrival in the southeast Iranian area more than a thousand years ago from the central Caspian region: in their original homeland they would have had another name, and their identification with any of the tribes living there in Sasanian times or earlier, mentioned by classical writers, is necessarily very difficult.

The name is first recorded in Arabic as *blwṣ* and in Persian as *blwj*, in the *Ḥodūd al-ʿālam* (comp. 982), both spellings representing *blwč*. Their earliest reliable geographical location occurs in Masʿūdī (fl. 943; see Bailey, art. cit., p. 586), who couples the Balōč with the Kōfič, locating the former in the deserts, and the latter in the mountains of eastern Persia. Moqaddasī (fl. 985; Bailey, ibid.) states that both western and eastern Makrān (present-day southeast Persian Baluchistan and Pakistani Baluchistan) were united and inhabited by the *blwṣy*, with a capital town at "bnnjbwr" (Bannajbūr), perhaps the Panjgur oasis in present day Pakistani Makrān.

Ṭabarī, enumerating the enemies of the Sasanian king Ḵosrow I Anōšīravān (531-79), does not mention the Baluch, and hence the reference to them in the same connection in the *Šāh-nāma* (comp. ca. 1020; "Kōč and Balōč") cannot be historical, since Ferdowsī's historical sources are known to be the same as those used by Ṭabarī. It seems likely that Ferdowsī has replaced another name, perhaps *blnjr* (*balangar*?) with what was by his time a stereotyped phrase denoting bandits or marauding freebooters.

Thus the Baluch tradition of a migration to their present habitat from the west in the 7th-8th centuries A.D. has an echo of history in it, strengthened by the linguistic connections of Baluchi, and one is led to the assignment of the original home of the Baluch to somewhere just east or southeast of the central Caspian region, the meeting point of Middle Persian and Parthian, and which then probably extended northward into present-day Soviet Turkmenistan.

It seems entirely likely that the first migrations eastward started much earlier, in late Sasanian times, initiated perhaps by the generally prevailing unsettled conditions in the Caspian area. These migrations most probably took place in several independent waves and over several centuries, some considerably antedating the Saljuq arrival in Kermān ca. 1060. Indeed, many areas of Kermān and Sīstān may have been at least partially occupied by Baluch migrants by the 8th century, for at the time of the Arab conquest of Kermān in 644, it is stated by later geographers that they came into contact with large numbers of *Qwfṣ* and *Blwṣ*, "Kōč and Balōč," in the mountains of eastern Persia (see C. E. Bosworth, "The Kūfichīs or Qufṣ in Persian History," *Iran* 14, 1976, p. 10, who quotes Tomaschek and Markwart; see also Le Strange, *Lands*, pp. 322f.).

Records of the Baluch are much more plentiful from the time of Maḥmūd of Ḡazna, as well as more circumstantial, and it is very likely that they were settled in their present-day habitat well before the 15th century (see Dames in *EI*[1] I, pp. 625-40; Frye in *EI*[2] I, pp. 1005-06).

Geographical distribution. Baluchi is the principal language of an area extending from the Marv (Mary) oasis in Soviet Turkmenistan southward to the Persian Gulf, from Persian Sīstān eastward along the Helmand valley in Afghanistan, throughout Pakistani Makrān eastward nearly to the Indus river, including in the south the city of Karachi, with a large and growing salient in the hills east and northeast of Quetta. There are also large populations of Baluchi speakers in the United Arab Emirates and in Kuwait.

Between the Marv region and about 100 km south of Bīrjand in Persia, colonies of Baluchi speakers are scattered and few. Baluchi becomes the principal local language at about 32° north latitude, extending westward to about 59° east longitude, and southward over the province of Sīstān o Balūčestān to the Persian Gulf.

In Afghanistan, Baluchi is the principal language of the Nīmrūz province. There are also colonies of Baluchi speakers scattered throughout the western part of the country, as far north as the Soviet frontier; but Baluchi is the principal local language only from Čaḵānsūr southward. It extends past Zaranj, the provincial capital, along the Helmand valley eastward to about 64° east longitude, and southward of the river to the Pakistan frontier in Chagai. (It is to be noted that in the middle Helmand region, Brahui enjoys equal status with Baluchi, most speakers being bilingual.) Baluchi is the main language of the whole of Pakistani Makrān as for east as a north-south line through Nushki (ca. 66° east longitude), where it meets Brahui. The latter extends northwest and south of Nushki in Pakistan over much of Sarawan and Jahlawan as far south as Las Bela, thus separating a large group of Baluchi speakers in the hills east and northeast of Quetta (the Marī-Būgṯī territory), concerning which see below (*Dialects*). This territory extends north as far as Dera Ismail Khan (ca. 36° north latitude).

Most Baluchi speakers are Baluch tribesmen, the only substantial non-Baluch group to speak it being Brahui tribesmen; the status of Baluchi is higher, if only marginally so. Until recently Baluchi has had no official status in the four countries in which it is spoken, and as a consequence many Baluchi speakers are bi- or trilingual. In 1978, however, it was given the status of "national language" in Afghanistan. As a written language it has a short history: three manuscripts in the British Museum (see Elfenbein, 1960 and 1983) were written in the first half of the 19th century and represent the oldest datable monuments in the language known at present. (There have been reports of 19th-century manuscripts from Kalat in Pakistan, perhaps written at the court.)

Written literary cultivation began in earnest only about 1950 in Pakistan (see below), and at the present time Baluchi is printed only there, although a small amount has been printed in some other Middle Eastern countries and in India. In 1979 a modest start in Baluchi printing was made in Iran and in Kabul (see below).

It is not easy to give reliable estimates for the number of speakers of Baluchi, due to the lack of appropriate census material. The following figures are probably all rather conservative: In the Marv Oasis in Soviet Turkmenistan (mainly emigrants from Afghanistan from the late 19th century; Pikulin, 1959, p. 35 [quoting Ya. R. Vinnikov, *Beludzhi Turkmenskoĭ SSR*, n.d.], gives 40,000; but Gafferberg, 1969, gives 10,000; Vinnikov is more likely to be closer to the facts): 40,000.

In Afghanistan (from Čaḵānsūr in the west, eastward along the Helmand river to Landī Moḥammad Āmīn Ḵān, ca. 64° east longitude: L. Dupree, *Afghanistan*, Princeton, New Jersey, 1973, p. 63, gives 100,000 Baluch and ca. 200,000 Brahuis: the figures seem to have been reversed); 200,000.

In Iran (mainly in the province Sīstān o Balūčestān, westward to a line ca. 59° east longitude, and from approximately Zābol in the north to the Gulf of Oman in the south, with colonies elsewhere as far north as the Soviet frontier; estimates vary from 500,000 [Spooner, 1971] to 750,000 [W. E. Griffith, "Iran's Foreign Policy in the Pahlavi Era," in G. Lenczowski, *Iran under the Pahlavis*, Palo Alto, 1978, p. 383, quoted in R. G. Wirsing, *The Baluchis and Pathans*, Minority Rights Groups Report no. 48, London, 1981, p. 17, n. 14]; both of these figures are probably underestimated): 750,000.

In the Arabian Peninsula (mainly in Oman, the United Arab Emirates and Kuwait; mainly emigrants from India [Pakistan] since Mughal times, as laborers and in the local armed forces; various estimates from local sources since 1979): 500,000.

In Pakistan (mainly in the provinces Baluchistan and Sind, excluding the Brahui strip between ca. 65°-67° east longitude; from the Pakistan censuses of 1961 and 1981): 750,000 in Sind, mainly in Karachi; and 1,500,000 in Baluchistan: total, 2,500,000; grand total ca. 3,600,000. It is very likely in fact somewhat more. (These figures are probably more reliable than those given by Elfenbein, 1983, p. 491.).

Three non-Baluchi languages are spoken within the mainly Baluchi-speaking area, namely Brahui (q.v.) and two Indo-Aryan languages: Jaḍgālī, spoken by the Jaṭṭ, immigrants from Sind, who inhabit Daštīārī, the extreme southeast corner of Persian Makrān, and Khetrani, spoken by Baluch in the extreme east of the Baluchi-speaking area, east of Dera Ghazi Khan.

Linguistic position. Baluchi is in all essentials a "northwestern" Iranian language, closely related to the Middle Iranian Parthian language and modern Kurdish, Tati, Ṭāleši, and other dialects (see MacKenzie on the dialectology of "southwestern" and "northwestern" Iranian). The following survey provides a picture of the ancestry of Baluchi.

1. Phonology. Baluchi ranges itself with Parthian against Middle Persian in the following cases: it has *s* and *z* from IE. **k̂* and **ĝ(h)*, e.g., *asin* 'iron', *kasān* 'small', *zāmāt* 'bridegroom', *zān-* 'know', *zir* 'sea', corresponding to Parth. *'swn, ks, z'm'd, zān-, zyrh*, Mid. Pers. *'hwn, kyh, d'm'd, d'n-, dry'b*; it has preserved OIr. intervocalic *d* and *g*, e.g., *ōdā* 'there', *pād* 'foot', *nigōš-* 'listen', Parth. *'wwd, p'd, ngwš-*, Mid. Pers. *'wy, p'y, nywš-*; OIr. initial *j*, e.g., *jan-* 'strike', Parth. *jn-*, Mid. Pers. *zn-*; OIr. *rd*, e.g., *zird* 'heart', Parth. *zyrd*, Mid. Pers. *dyl*. Note also *p(i)tī* 'other', from **bidī*, Parth. *bdyg*, Mid. Pers. *dwdyg*, NPers. *dī(gar)*.

Baluchi agrees with (Middle) Persian against Parthian in the following cases: It has *j* from OIr. initial *y*, e.g., *jitā*, Pers. *jodā*, Parth. *ywd*; *s* from OIr. *θr*, e.g., *se* 'three', *pusag* 'son,' Mid. Pers. *sh* (Pers. *se*), *pws*, Parth. *hry*, *pwhr*; note also *ās* 'fire' (in all dialects except Raḵšāni, which has *āč* from NPers. *ātaš*).

Baluchi differs from most other modern West Iranian languages in the following cases: It has preserved OIr. intervocalic stops *p, t, k*, and *č* and *j*, e.g., *āp* 'water', *būta* 'was', *hūk* 'swine', *brāt* 'brother', *rōč* 'day', *drāj* 'long', and has changed OIr. fricatives *f, θ, x*, into stops, *p, t, k*, e.g., *kopag* 'shoulder', cf. Av. *kaofa-*, OPers. *kaufa*; *gūt* 'excrement', Av. *gūθa-*; *kar* 'ass', Av. *xara-*; *kānī* 'well', spring', Parth., Pers. *xān*; note also (with metathesis) *patka* 'cooked' < **paxta-*, *ātka* 'came' < **āxta* < **āgata-*. Baluchi has *gwa-* (or *g-*) from OIr. *w-*; *w-* or *h-* from OIr. *xw-*; *mm* and *nn* from OIr. *šm* and *šn*; and *ša-* < OIr. *fra*; e.g., *gwāt* 'wind', Av. *vāta-*, *gīst* 'twenty', Av. *vīsati*; *war-* 'eat', Parth. *wxr-*, Mid. Pers. *xwr-*; *wasp-* 'to sleep', Pahl. *xwafs-*; *wašš* 'pleasant', Parth. *wxš*, Mid. Pers. *xwš*; but *hēd* 'sweat', Av. *x'aēδa-*; *čamm* 'eye', Av. *čašman-*; *tunnag* 'thirsty', Mid. Pers. *tyšng*; *šawašk-* 'sell', Mid. Pers. *prwxš-*, Pers. *forūš-*. Some of these sound changes are found in other dialects as well. Thus *w* > *g(w)* in the Central dialect of Ḵūr (in the Dašt-e Kavīr) and in the "Southeast Iranian" languages Parāčī and Ōrmuṛī (see AFGHANISTAN v. LANGUAGES and vii. PARĀČĪ); a relative chronology for this sound change is provided by the loanwords *gwahr* 'cold' from Khetrāni *vahor*, and *gwač* 'calf' from Sindhi *vachʰ* which show that Baluchi still had *w-* on its first contact with these Indian languages. The change of *xw* > *w* is also found in Gōrāni (*war-* 'eat') and *šm* > *hm* in Ōrmuṛī (*čim* 'eye') and Baškardi (*čehm* 'eye'). Baluchi *šiš* 'louse' agrees with Baškardi *šōš* against forms from **spiša-* in most other Iranian languages (Pers. *šepeš*).

2. Morphology. Baluchi, like most West Iranian languages (not Kurdish, Zāzā, Tāti, Sangesari) has lost the Old Iranian gender distinctions.

The commonest Baluchi ending for the oblique plural of nouns is *-ān*, characteristic of Western Iranian languages. Similarly, the originally collective suffix *-gal*, now used as a plural suffix (most frequently in Eastern Hill Baluchi), is found in Kurdish, Fārs dialects, and some Central dialects.

In the first person pronouns the old stem distinction between direct and oblique cases (Av. *azəm*, gen. *mana*, etc.) has been lost in Baluchi as in Persian and most other Western Iranian languages, except, e.g., Kurdish and Zāzā.

The present endings of the Baluchi verb, like those, e.g., of Parthian go back to Old Iranian forms in *-aya-*, cf. 1 sing. *-īn* (some dialects *-ān*, from the old subjunctive), 3 sing. *-īt*, e.g., *gušīn*, *gušīt* 'I say', 'he says'. Some *n*-stems have short forms, e.g., *kant* 'he does', *zānt* 'he knows', but *wānīt* 'he reads' (on the short forms see Gershevitch, in M. Boyce and I. Gershevitch, eds., *W. B. Henning Memorial Volume*, London, 1970, pp. 161-74). Persian, on the contrary, has a mixture of forms from Old Iranian *-a-* and *-aya-* (see W. B.

Henning, "Das Verbum des Mittelpersischen der Turfanfragmente," *ZII* 9, 1933, p. 232 [= *Acta Iranica* 14, p. 139], Ghilain, *Essai sur la langue parthe*, Louvain, 1939, p. 112). The infinitive ends in *-ag* < MIr. *-ak* as in some East Iranian languages, including Parāčī and Ōrmuṛī. The Rak̲šāni dialect, however, has *-tin*, possibly borrowed from Persian. The present tense durative prefix is *a-* in all dialects (also in Baškardi and Lārestāni), but this prefix is often without value. The prefix *de-* is heard sporadically in Rak̲šāni (*dede*).

3. Syntax. The *eżāfa* construction characteristic of Persian and other (south)western Iranian languages, including Kurdish, is not used in Baluchi, except occasionally (as in most modern Iranian languages) in some types of formal poetry and in stereotyped phrases borrowed from Persian. Characteristic of most Baluchi dialects except Rak̲šāni is the common Iranian passive (also called ergative) construction of past transitive verbs. Rak̲šāni is the only dialect to have adopted the active construction, probably from Persian. North Rak̲šāni is the only dialect to use exclusively the active construction; Central and Southern Rak̲šāni (and all other dialects) use "ergative" constructions, either partly or entirely.

4. Lexicon. The Iranian lexicon of Baluchi contains a number of East Iranian "substrate" words, of which the following is a selection:

Baluchi *nagan* 'bread', Sogd. *nγn*, Pashto *naγan*, Par. *naγōn* (but Mid. Pers. *n'n*, Pers. *nān*); *saγan* 'dung', Par. *saγōn*, Wakhi *səgīn*, Orm. *skan* (Khot. *satana-*) (but Pahl. *sargēn*, Pers. *sargīn*); *gwanḍ* 'short', Khot. *vanda-* 'small', Par. *γanōkō*; *gud* 'cloth, clothes', cf. Par. *āγun* 'to dress', Pashto *āγund-* (but Man. Mid. Pers. *pymwč-*, Man. Parth. *pdmwč-*, Pers. *pōš-*); *gar* 'cliff', Wakhi, Pashto *γar*, Orm. *grī* 'mountain; *zāhg* 'son', Par. *zāγa*, Sogd. *z''k*; but Parth., Mid. Pers. *zhg* (cf. Mid. Pers. *pws*, *pwsr*, Pers. *pesar*); *šarr* 'good', Sogd. *šyr*, Pashto *ṣ̌ə*, Orm. *širr*, Khot. *śśära-* (but Mid. Pers., Pers. *xūb*).

In other respects the vocabulary of Baluchi is typically "southwestern," e.g., *mūd* 'hair', *bard* 'spade', *sōčaq* 'burn', *rōč* 'day', *šōdag* 'wash'.

On the whole, however, the linguistic position of Baluchi is obscured by its numerous borrowings, principally lexical (though there are some syntactic ones as well; see below on *Syntax*); there are also certainly substrate influences from languages spoken in areas in which Baluch have dwelt for long periods during their migrations, or with whom they have had close contact. All Baluchi dialects possess numerous loanwords from several different Indo-Aryan languages, which may be the result of independent Baluch migrations at different times.

Dialects. Six major dialects can be distinguished, differing from each other in phonology, morphology, syntax, and lexicon. Of these, Rak̲šāni is by far the most widely spoken, and can itself be subdivided into three regional varieties. The other five dialects are fairly uniform. The first comprehensive survey of all Baluchi dialects was Elfenbein's *The Baluchi Language* (1966), and the dialect description given there is now in need of correction in the light of fuller knowledge; the dialect name Lāšāri is to be preferred to Loṭūni.

It is important to realize that Baluchi is a very conservative language, and its dialects, in spite of the vastness of the area in which they are spoken, are quite remarkably similar; with the exception of Eastern Hill Baluchi (see below), speakers from all areas readily understand one another. Proceeding roughly from north to south the dialects are:

(1) Rak̲šāni, extending from Marv in Soviet Turkmenistan southward in Persia and Afghanistan through Sīstān to ca. 28° north latitude, southward of K̲āš (Bal. Hwāš), and as far to the west of these areas as Baluchi is spoken. There are three subdialects: (a) Kalati, in Pakistan from Las Bela northward throughout Jahlawan and Sarawan (where the main language is Brahui), up to just south of Quetta where it meets Pashto; (b) Panjguri, in Pakistani Makrān, including most of K̲ārān from Kolwa in the east to Kech in the west; its southern boundary is just north of the Kech valley, whence it spreads approximately to the Rak̲šān river in the north; (c) Sarḥaddi, over by far the largest area, including Pakistani Chagai from Nushki in the east, westward along the Persian frontier as far as Baluchi is spoken, about 59° east longitude; southward approximately to 28° north latitude where, in Pakistan, it meets Panjguri in K̲ārān, and in Persia, Sarāvāni north of Īrānšahr; northward it includes all the parts of Afghanistan where Baluchi is spoken, along the Helmand river from ca. 64° east longitude westward to Čak̲ānsūr and across the Persian frontier with all parts of Sīstān where Baluchi is spoken, and thence northward in both Afghanistan and Persia to Marv in Soviet Turkmenistan. Its north-south extension is thus nearly 10° of latitude, and its east-west extension nearly 6° of longitude. Sarḥaddi is the principal dialect used for radio broadcasts in both Quetta and Kabul.

(2) Sarāvāni, a dialect enjoying considerable prestige in Persia, is centered on the village of Sarāvān (ca. 62° east longitude, 27° north latitude) roughly 150 km southeast of K̲āš. The main dialect of Baluchi radio broadcasts from Zāhedān, it extends from Gašt (Bal. Gōšt) some 60 km north of K̲ās to Kūhak (Bal. Kūwag) on the Persia-Pakistan frontier. It crosses the frontier into Pakistan, but its principal territory lies in Persia. Southward it extends nearly as far as Rāsk, and thence northward it includes most villages up to ca. 30 km north of Īrānšahr. Both the towns Bampūr and Īrānšahr are in the Sarāvāni area, although Sarḥaddi is as often heard in Īrānšahr as is Sarāvāni, as is to be expected, since Īrānšahr is the largest town in the province south of Zāhedān.

(3) Lāšāri, centered on the village of Lāšār, ca. 120 km south of Īrānšahr by road. It is a very conservative dialect, whose boundaries and Espaka in the north, southward through Pīp nearly to Nīkšahr and Qaṣr-e Qand in the east, and Fanūč (Bal. Pannūč) in the west, where Baluchi meets Persian and Baškardi.

(4) Kechi, spoken principally in the Kech valley of Pakistani Makrān, south of the central Makrān range;

it extends from Hirōk westward to Tump, excluding the village of Mand, but including the villages to the north of the Giš river.

(5) Coastal dialects, spoken from Bīābān in Persia eastward along the coast to Čāhbahār, and extending northward to include Nīkšahr, Qaṣr-e Qand, and Hūdar; in Pakistan Mand, Dašt, and the coastal strip from the Persian frontier eastward to include Gwādar, Pasnī, and Ormāṛa; in Karachi there live more than 700,000 Baluchi speakers, with no one dialect predominant.

(6) Eastern Hill Baluchi, spoken almost entirely in the hilly tribal area east of Quetta mainly by members of the Marī and Bugṭī tribes, extending from somewhat north of Jacobabad in the Upper Sind Frontier northward to Dera Ghazi Khan, and from Sibi in the west nearly to the Indus river in the east. The area is almost entirely Baluchi-speaking, although other languages coexist with it. Fingers of Baluchi are probing northward, mainly at the expense of Pashto, and at present the area between Dera Ghazi Khan and Dera Ismail Khan is dominated by Baluchi. This dialect has played a dominant role in early published descriptions of the language, due to its location in former British India (Pakistani Makrān was in Kalat State), a role disproportionate to its real importance.

Writing. The oldest written Baluchi is represented by a manuscript in the British Museum (see Elfenbein, 1961, 1983), dating from early in the 19th century. There was little literary cultivation in the language during the rest of the century; it was not until the 1930s that a few individuals, led by Moḥammad Ḥosayn "ʿAnqā," began to write for a public in Baluchi, producing a short-lived weekly paper *Bōlān*. The impetus to write for publication in the language continued, however, and after the creation of Pakistan in 1947, Baluchi academies were established in Karachi in 1956 and Quetta in 1959 for the purpose of encouraging publication of Baluchi literature. The academy in Karachi ceased to exist in the late 1950s, but the Baluchi Academy in Quetta is still (1987) flourishing. The efforts of these enthusiasts have, however, met with little response outside Pakistan, and only in 1978 were the first stirrings of effort to publish in Baluchi elsewhere to be felt: These took the form of a magazine *Sōb* (Victory) from Kabul and a short-lived newspaper from Persia. The Baluch cultural center remains at Quetta. (For details see *Literature* below.)

The script commonly used (except in Kabul, where Pashto script is employed) to write Baluchi is a modified Urdu script, with the retroflex consonants *ṭ, ḍ, ṛ, ṇ* marked by a superscript *ṭā* and nasalized final vowels indicated by *nūn* without the diacritic point following the vowel, when the writer wishes to do so. There is less agreement in writing the morphemes of the language, where more divergence from Urdu writing customs is necessary: Endings are sometimes written in a "phonetic" style, using *hamza* to separate them from the nominal or verbal stem; sometimes the endings are joined to the stems without *hamza*; often both systems are used together. Some conventions from Arabic used to be employed, such as *tanwīn*, which was used in very early writing to indicate the ending *-ēn*. *Tašdīd* is used very occasionally, but vowels and diphthongs are very haphazardly indicated: short *a, i, u* usually not at all, but long *ā, ī, ū* usually in Perso-Urdu style, with no distinction made between internal *ē* and *ī*, or between *ō* and *ū*, all four of which are separate phonemes in Baluchi. Final *-ē* and *-ī* are distinguished as in Urdu. *Sokūn* is seldom used, and the diphthongs *ay* and *aw* are indicated, or not, according to the whim of the writer, so that a printed text is very difficult to read accurately.

All Pakistani dialects are represented in writing (a northern Rakšāni in Kabul), no standard written language having as yet evolved, and most writers mix dialects freely, using theoretical forms from other dialects, so that very often a wholly artificial written language results. Sarḥaddi speakers especially tend to use Coastal forms, real and imagined, at whim. The Coastal dialect retains a particular prestige as that in which much of the extensive traditional literature is preserved, and its forms easily penetrate other dialects.

Linguistic description. 1. Phonology. Baluchi has a particularly simple phonemic structure: Vowels, *a, i, u, ā, ī, ū, ē, ō*; diphthongs *ay, aw*. Consonants: stops *p, t, k, b, d, g, ṭ, ḍ*; affricates *č, j*; sibilants *s, z, š, ž*; continuants *w, y, l, m, n, r, ṛ, ṇ*; the spirants *f, x, γ* are common in loanwords in all dialects, but tend rapidly to *p, k, g* respectively as the words become naturalized. Eastern Hill Baluchi, uniquely, keeps them, and in addition has also developed *θ* and *δ* from postvocalic *t* and *d*; and intervocalic *b* tends to become *v*.

2. Morphology. The following grammatical outline is based on the Coastal dialect, with Rakšāni forms given in parentheses.

Noun declension. There is no nominal gender, all nouns being declined alike in a three-case system, singular and plural. A suffixed, unstressed *-ē* functions as indefinite article, cf. Persian *-ī*.

	Singular	Plural
Nom.	*lōg (gis)*	*lōg (gis)*
Gen.	*lōgē (gisay, gisē)*	*lōgānī (gisānī)*
Obl.	*lōgā (gisā, gisayā)*	*lōgān (gisān, gisānā)*

Pronouns are treated differently depending on whether or not the dialect construes the past transitive verbs passively. Pronominal declension is perhaps the most economically described by means of a four-case system, except in Rakšāni, which, lacking the passive (ergative) construction, has a three-case system.

Personal Pronouns

	Singular	Plural
	1st person	
Nom.	*man (man)*	*mā (ammā)*
Gen.	*manī (manī, mnī)*	*māī (ammē)*
Dat./acc.	*manā (manā, mnā)*	*mā (ammā)*
Obl.	*man (mnīyā)*	*mā (--)*

	2nd person	
Nom.	*taw* (*ta*)	*šumā* (*šumā*)
Gen.	*taī* (*tay*, *tī*)	*šumāī* (*šumē*)
Dat./acc.	*tarā* (*trā*)	*šumārā* (*šumārā*)
Obl.	*taw* (--)	*šumā* (--)
	3rd person	
Nom.	*āy* (*ā*)	*āhān* (*āwān*)
Gen.	*āyē* (*āy*, *āyī*)	*āhānī* (*āwānī*)
Dat./acc.	*āyā* (*āyrā*)	*āhān*(*rā*) (*āwānā*)
Obl.	*āyā* (*āy*)	*āhān* (*āwān*)

The Rak̲šāni form *mnīyā* is only used in northern Rak̲šāni, after prepositions. Note the difference between the nominative and oblique forms of the Rak̲šāni 3rd person pronoun in the singular.

By far the most commonly used suffixed pronouns are the 3rd sing. *-ī*/*ē*, 3rd plur. *-iš* (often interchanged, the plural being used for the singular, and vice versa); suffixed to nouns they mean 'his, their; for him, for them'; suffixed to the endings of verbs, 'him, them; for him, for them'; as agent for the past transitives, often suffixed to the preceding word, 'he/by him, they/by them'. The pronominal suffixes for the other persons and numbers are less used in most dialects (except in poetry) but are still common is spoken Kechi, Sarāvāni, and Lāšāri.

Demonstrative Pronouns

	'this'	
	Singular	Plural
Nom.	*ē*, *ēš*	*ēšān* (*ēšiyān*)
Gen.	*ēši*	*ēšānī* (*ēšiyānī*)
Obl.	*ēšā* (*ēšiyā*)	*ēšān* (*ēšiyān*)
	'that'	
Nom.	*ā*	*āhān* (*āwān*)
Gen.	*āyē*	*āhānī* (*āwānī*)
Obl.	*āyā*	*āhān* (*āwān*)

These pronouns are also used adjectivally. The forms of 'that' are often mixed with those of the 3rd person pronoun by many speakers.

The interrogative pronouns are *kay* 'who?', gen. *kay*, *kayī*, obl. *kayā*; and *čē* 'what?', gen. *čē*, obl. *čēā* (*čēwā*).

Conjugation. The suffixed substantive verb (copula) and the present/future endings are as follows:

	Copula		
	Present	Past	Present/Future
	Singular:		
1	*-ān* (*-un*)	*-atān* (*-atun*)	*-ān* (*-īn*)
2	*-ē* (*ay*)	*-atē* (*-atay*)	*-ē* (*-ay*, *-ē*)
3	*-in*(*t*) (*-int*)	*-at* (*-at*)	*-īt*, *-t* (*-īt*, *-t*)
	Plural:		
1	*-ēn* (*-an*)	*-atēn* (*-atan*)	*-in*, *-ēn* (*-an*)
2	*-it* (*-it*)	*-atit* (*-atit*)	*-it* (*-it*)
3	*-ant* (*-ant*)	*-atant* (*-atant*)	*-ant* (*-ant*)

Past tense transitives have no ending in the singular and *-ant* in the plural, where the agreement (only in number) is with the "grammatical subject" ("ergative" construction). Some Rak̲šāni dialects, however, have adopted the New Persian construction. Past intransitives take the full set of endings in all dialects. There is, however, much "mixed construction," especially in Sarāvāni, and in most Rak̲šāni.

There is a durative-continuative prefix *a-* (cf. Pers. *mī-*) which has, however, lost its semantic function in many dialects, and *k-* is prefixed to the present/future stems of some verbs with an initial vowel (often to the past as well). This prefix also has a durative meaning (see below on semantics). All verbs are inflected alike, but this simple system is complicated by an involved set of periphrastic constructions, and the large number of irregular verbs, whose past stems are not formed with *-ita* suffixed to the present stem.

A verbal noun (infinitive) is formed by the suffix *-ag* joined to the present verbal stem (except in Rak̲šāni, which usually prefers *-tin* joined to the past stem). Examples of periphrastic constructions are:

man rawagī-ān (*raw-* 'go')	'I ought to go'
manā rawagī-int	'I must go'
man kār a-kanān (*kan* 'do')	'I am doing work'
man kār kanagā-hān	'I am doing work'
man kār kanagā bān	'I shall be working'
man kār kanagā bītān (Rak̲š. *būtun*)	'I was working'
man kār kut (Rak̲š. *kurt*/*kurtun*)	'I worked'
man kār kuta(*g*) (Rak̲š. *kurta*)	'I have worked'
man kār kanagā-atān (*-atun*)	'I had been working'
man kār kanagā-atatān (*-atatun*)	'I must have been working'
man kār kanag bibān (*bibīn*)	'I may be working'
man kār kanag bītatān (*būtatun*)	'I had already been working'
manā(*rā*) *kār kanagā-int*	'work is being done for me'
man kār kanān-ān	'I am continuously working'
man kār kut kanān (*kurt kanīn*)	'I can work'
man kār kut kuta (*kurt kurta*)	'I could work, I was able to work'
ē kār kanag bīt kant (*būt kant*)	'this work can be done'

The sufix *-ōk* is freely productive, joined to present verbal stems it means 'one who does...', joined to nouns 'one who is...': *nindōk* 'a sitter', *kanōk* 'a doer', *barōk* 'a carryer', *ārōk* 'a bringer', *kušōk* 'a killer'; it can also be attached to nouns, e.g., *sarōk* 'president', *watanōk* 'patriot'.

Semantics. There is a continuative verbal form *man gušagā-hān* (*man gušagā-un*) 'I am speaking', formed on Urdu models, and common in all dialects spoken in Pakistan, and not unknown elsewhere. The simple verbal form with prefixed *a-*, e.g., *man a-gušān* (*man a-gušīn*) has the same meaning, cf. Rak̲š. *man a-gušīn trā* 'I'm telling you', vs. *man gušīn ki* 'I say that...', *kēčī man a-*

gušt 'I was saying', vs. *man gušt* 'I said' (note the passive construction). Also *man edā kōštīn* 'I'm standing here', *man edā kōštun* 'I was standing here', vs. *man edā ōštātun* 'I stood here'. The *a-* prefix is present in nearly all dialects regularly, but seems to have lost its significance except in Rakšāni, where its use is semantically significant. It is hardly ever indicated in native writing now; older writers suffixed *alef* to a preceding word.

The *irrealis* construction is formed by prefixing *bi-* to the past stem of the verb, to which is then suffixed *-ēn* and the copula in Rakš.: *aga man drōg bibastēnun, tō ā manī sarā patt na kurt* 'If I had lied, then he would not have trusted me'; *age ā manī haddā biyātkēn, tō man ayrā hamē gappā guštun* 'If he had come to my place, then I would have told him this matter'. In dialects with the 'ergative' construction we get: *aga man drōg bibastēn, tō āyā manī sarā patt nakut; aga āy manī haddā biyātkēn, tō man āyrā hame gapp gwašt.* Examples containing 1st and 2nd plural pronouns: *āyā mā (šumā) jatant, āy mārā (šumārā) jatant*, or *mā jatant-ī* (the last in only one dialect) 'he struck us (you)'; one also hears *āyā mā jat* or *mā jat-ī.*

There is also an important causative formation, for the most part by means of the suffix *-ēn* added to the present stems of verbs, which are then conjugated like verbs in *-ēnag*: *man trā rasēnīn-ī* 'I'll send it to you'; but there are many irregular formations.

Syntax. The main differences from Persian syntax are the following:

(a) The *eżāfa* construction is absent; Pers. *sar-e man* 'my head' is expressed by *manī sar*; Pers. *asb-e dūst-e šomā* 'your friend's horse' by *šumē dōstē asp*.

(b) The past tenses of transitive verbs are construed passively in all dialects except in some Rakšāni dialects, where the Persian active construction is more common. Examples: Coastal *man gūnī zurtant o šutān* 'I took the sacks and went'; *zī manī brātān gwašt-iš ki, ēdā bnind, mā kayēn* 'yesterday my brothers said, wait here, we shall come'; active construction: Rakš. *tay piss manī sundukān pāč kurt* 'thy father opened my boxes'; *ta watī lingān prōštay* 'thou hast broken thy legs'; but also, in the same dialect, *ta watī lingān prošt; ḍrēwar lārīā āwurt* 'the driver brought the lorry', cf. *ḍrēwarā lārī āwurt* 'the lorry brought the driver': both these sentences are ambiguous, and each could mean the other. To be certain, one has to say *ḍrēwarārā lārī āwurt* 'the lorry brought the driver', or *ā ḍrēwar-int, ki lārī āyā (āwā) āwurt* 'that is the driver whom the lorry brought'.

(c) Prepositions are uncommon and usually occur in conjunction with postpositions, as in Pashto. Postpositions require the genitive of the governed noun: *kitāb mēzē sarā-int* 'the book is on the table', *dračk gisay dēmā-int* 'the tree is in front of the house', *biyā gōn man pajā* 'come along with me', *man šutun pa Ahmadē randā* 'I went after Ahmad', *ča ēšī guḍā, man hiččī na dīt* (*dīst, dīstun*) 'after this, I saw nothing'.

(d) The use of nominal case endings in conjunction with the absence of the *eżāfa* construction make syntactical constructions and word order much freer in Baluchi than they are in Persian, as the following examples of prose narrative illustrate.

An account, in ordinary Rakšāni colloquial style:

Aga kassē aš watī badīgānī dastā bitačīt, ō yakk Balōčēay bāhōṭ bibīt, tō balōčī riwājā āyī nigādārī parz-int. Balōč watī bāhōṭā hičč bar badīgānī dastā na dayant, ō ayī nang-ō-mālā a-sambant. Bāz barān Balōč pa bāhōṭā jang ham kanant, ō āyī nangā pān-ant. Walē gēštir hamē ki bāhōṭā watī haddā dārant, tānki ā wat diga jāgāē ma-rot. [From Barker and Mangal I, pp. 425-26.] 'If anyone flees from the hands of his enemies and becomes the refugee of a Baluch, then by Baluchi tribal law his protector-duty is (i.e., it is the duty of a Baluch to act as his protector). The Baluch never deliver their refugees into the hands of their enemies, and protect their honor and property. Many times the Baluch will also fight for a refugee, and are guardians of his honor. But most often (those who keep a refugee) will keep a refugee in their place (only), until he himself goes to another place.'

Literary and formal style:

Ča drustēn jawān ō dēmātirēn adabē zāntkārānī ṭōlīyē xayālē padā, adabārā bāyd-int ki zindagīyē ādēnk bibīt, zindagīyē drustēn rang-ō-dāng, kad-ō-bālād hamē ādēnkē tahā yakk-pa-yakkā sāf-zāhir bibant; aga zindagī bēḍawl ō badrang-int, adabārā bāyd-int ki āyārā hamā rangā pēš bidārīt, āyī habarē pardāhā ma-kant, ki čārōkānā zindagī badrang gindagā kāyt, har paym ki zindagīyē rang-ō-drōšum-int, ča āyā mūdē kisāsā ham pad-kinzag ma-bīt. Aga zindagī hōn-ō-rēm-ō-gandagīyē mazanēn kumbē, ō adīb wašš-zēmulēn ši'rānī pirr-bandag, ō širkinēn labzānī tarrēnag-ō-tāb dayagā, yakk ṭūhēn durōgē bandīt o gušīt ki "na! ā yakk sarsabz ō prāh-dāmānēn malguzārē," guḍā ē yakk hančēn radē, ki zindagī wat āyā hičč bar na bakšīt. Hamē rangēn adīb zūt yā dēr juhlēn kōr-čātēyā kapīt, ō hančō gār-ō-gumsār bīt ki diga barē kasse āyī sōjā ham na-dant." [From the Preface to *Mistāg*, by 'Abd-Allāhjān Jamāldīnī, Karachi, 1959, one of the earliest literary publications. Arabic words are written in their Arabic spelling in the original publication, the usual practice. The above extract indicates actual pronunciation.] "According to the thought of all sections of the better and forward-looking scholars of literature, literature has to be a mirror of life; all of life's sorts and sizes must each individually, clean and clear, be seen in the mirror; if life is confused and wicked, literature must show it so; it must not draw a veil over the fact that to some observers of it, life comes wicked to the sight; whatever the features of life may appear to be, there is to be no flinching from it, not even by a hair's breadth. If life is really a great pool of blood, pus, and filth, and the writer is a composer of pleasing melodic verses, a giver of sweet twists and turns to words, he tells a huge lie, and says, 'No! It is a greensward and a broad mountain pasture'—then he is so mistaken that life itself will never forgive him. This sort of writer will sooner or later fall into a deep blind well, and will be so lost and forgotten that nobody will ever give news of him again."

Loanwords. The main source of loanwords is Persian, through which most of the Arabic loanwords also come.

This Persian source has been until quite recently the eastern, Afghani, variety, and many words such as *zūt* 'quickly' which seem Baluchi because of the final voiceless stop, can just as well be loanwords from Afghani Persian, which devoices final stops. Many Baluchi words are old Persian loanwords now lost to the original language, e.g., *ēr* 'under, down' (Mid. Pers. *ēr*, cf. NPers. *z-īr* 'under'), *gudar* 'crossing' (Pers. *goḏar*).

Another rich source for borrowings has been Indian languages and to a lesser extent the language of the Brahui, with whom the Baluch have been for centuries in close contact. The Indian languages concerned are in the main Sindhi and Lahndā, and now latterly Urdu.

II. Baluchi literature.

The literature of Baluchi—until quite recently entirely oral and still largely so—consists of a large amount of history and occasional balladry (epic poetry), stories and legends, romantic ballads, and religious and didactic poetry, of which there is an extensive corpus; in addition there is a large variety of domestic verse: work songs, lullabies, and riddles. Possibly the first modest attempt to collect some of this extensive literature is represented by the manuscript BM Cod. Add. 24048 (Elfenbein, 1982). In any case it is quite certain that no systematic attempts were made to collect and reduce to written form any sizeable part of this literature prior to the European (mainly British) interest in it in the 19th century. Of these collections, the earliest of note was made by A. Lewis in 1855; the next important one was by T. J. L. Mayer in 1900. By far the most important and systematic, however, are those by M. Longworth Dames, in 1891, 1907, and 1909. Unfortunately all of these works deal with material which came only from one small area, and in Eastern Hill Baluchi only, thus giving a misleadingly restricted picture of the real extent and variety of this literature, and an inflated estimate of the importance of the dialect in which it was collected. The language of classical Baluchi poetry is traditionally in three dialects (in order of their status and importance): Coastal, Eastern Hill Baluchi, and Kechi.

Historical ballads. The oldest historical ballads (called *daptar šāʾirī* "ballads of origins") deal with the first emigrations of the Baluch from Aleppo, their traditional (and legendary) home. There are many of these ballads, only a few of which have been collected (a poor example of one in *Linguistic Survey of India*; see Grierson, 1927). Some of these ballads may go back to the 16th century. They all agree that the Baluch are the sons of Mīr Ḥamza, and rose up in Aleppo, where they sided with Ḥosayn in his struggle with Caliph Yazīd, fighting at Karbalā, (The "history" up to this point is of course quite imaginary.) There are two main tribes, the Rind and the Lāšārī, with one chief of chiefs, Šayhakk, as well as many subtribes and several inferior slave tribes. They depart after the battle, and the next centuries are passed over in silence. We next hear that they have reached Sīstān, settling in the region of Rūdbār, "where they live for a time in relative peace, until a change in ruler from "Šams-al-Dīn" (perhaps Šams-al-Dīn Moḥammad Kort, ruler of Herat 1246-77, see ĀL-E KART), who is friendly to them, to "Badr-al-Dīn," who is not, causes them to separate. Some go southeastward to Makrān, while most go southwestward toward Lār, Pahrā (now Īrānšahr), and Bampūr, where they wander for three years looking for a place to settle. Thereafter, under the leadership of Mīr Jalāl Khan, the main body enters Makrān, passing Mand, Kech, as far as Kolwa, wandering one further year. At Āšal in Kolwa, Mīr Čākur, son of Šayhakk, is born, perhaps in the middle of the 15th century.

Most accounts describe this part of Makrān as very uncongenial to the Baluch, barren and waterless as it is, and it is not until they reach the more eastern portions near Kalat that they begin to settle, perhaps meeting there earlier settlers from a previous wave.

Heroic ballads. It is at this point that the principal cycles of classical Baluchi heroic balladry begin. The first and most important of them can be conveniently called the Čākur cycle, which comprises the numerous ballads concerning Mīr Čākur, the leading hero of Baluchi legend altogether. Most of these ballads are concerned with a long and destructive thirty years' war between the Rind and the Lāšārī, and comprise some very fine epic poetry. While it is true that the events described in these ballads are not to be found in other sources for the history of the region, poor as they are, still it is possible from internal evidence to estimate the dates to lie between the years 1475-1525 with some degree of likelihood.

Relations between the Rind and the Lāšārī were never easy, and after the descent through the Bolān pass into the Indus valley and the settlement of the Sibi and Kacchi region, the overall chief Šayhakk died, and the two tribes could no longer contain their differences. Mīr Čākur, son of Šayhakk, became the leader of the Rind, while his rival Mīr Gwaharām, the son of Nōdbandag (another venerated chief) became the leader of the Lāšārī. Dealings between the two tribes were plagued by jealousy and distrust, and to add to their difficulties both leaders conceived a passion for the same lady, the Lāšārī Gōhar, who for her part preferred the Rind chief Mīr Čākur. Several small events, each the subject of ballads, set the stage for an explosion which, when it came, resulted in a long and pitilessly destructive struggle, which tradition states to have lasted thirty years. The various events are celebrated in many poems, some said to be written by Bībarg, a lieutenant of Mīr Čākur. Although defeated in the first battles, the Rind were finally victorious. An alliance with "the Turk" (perhaps Ḏu'l-Nūn Beg Argūn of Qandahār, ca. 1480) by the Rind so strengthened their final attack on the Lāšārī that the latter were virtually wiped out and ceased to play much part in subsequent Baluchi history. Gwaharām is said to have escaped south into Sind with a few followers. The Rind settled at first mainly around Sibi and then spread northward and southward. Some traveled as far south as the coast, thence spreading out westward toward Persia, eventually settling the whole

Makrān coast as far as Bīābān. These coastal Baluch, together with those settled in the Upper Sind Frontier in the "Tribal Areas" constitute the oldest settlements today, and speak the most archaic dialects, often called "Rindī."

There are ballads describing their participation in various adventures as freebooters in battles with the "Turks," i.e., the Mughals, in India in particular in the campaign of Emperor Homāyūn in 1555 against Delhi. Mīr Čākur is said to have had a palace at Sibi, and to have engaged in campaigns in Multan and Punjab; he is buried at Saṭgarh in the Multan district, in what was an impressive tomb.

The Dōdā-Bālāč cycle. Perhaps the most important cycle after the Čākur cycle is what can be called the Dōdā-Bālāč cycle. The lady Sammī and her husband, both Bulēdī, take refuge with Dōdā the chief of the Gorgēj Rind. Upon the death of Sammī's husband there is a dispute about the inheritance, in which Sammī withholds from the heirs of her dead husband a small part of the herd of cattle which is her own private property (allowed by tribal law). In some versions, Bībarg, the Bulēdī chief, organizes a raid in which the disputed cattle are carried off by force, while Dōdā is asleep in the sun. The raid thus takes place, exceptionally, in full daylight, and is thus all the greater insult to the Gorgēj and to Dōdā who has given Sammī refuge. Dōdā is rudely awakened by two women, variously described as his mother-in-law, sister-in-law, neighbors, or other relations, who tell him what has happened. Dōdā is at first reluctant to pursue and punish the raiders, but after taunts and jibes by the women, who accuse him of cowardice and lawbreaking, he gathers together a few companions and sallies forth to meet the Bulēdī at the Garmāp pass (near Sangsilā in Bugṭī country) and is killed.

For his attempt Dōdā is highly regarded in Baluchi legend, and by some is considered a hero comparable even to Čākur or Nōdbandag. The parallel to the war of the Rind and Lāšārī is explicit in many versions of the subsequent events. The Bulēdī, emboldened by their initial successes, continue to raid, and the Gorgēj to defend themselves even though numerically and otherwise weaker, until they are nearly exterminated; in some versions only Bālāč, the son (in some versions the brother) of Dōdā, and his half-brother Nakīb are left alive among the Gorgēj.

Nakīb, whose mother was a slave girl, is the more mettlesome of the two. Though described as "black" and a slave (slaves in Baluchi legend are always "black," often in fact negroid), he is very courageous, while Bālāč is dilatory like his father. For three years Nakīb exhorts the "lazy, cowardly, unworthy" Bālāč to act, but it is not until the latter has a dream in which he attacks the Bulēdī alone and wins revenge for his father that he at last decides to take action. He and Nakīb proceed alone to harry the Bulēdī over the whole of their territory, slaying threescore-and-one Bulēdī in one famous encounter. Bībarg is also slain, and the Bulēdī retreat to settle in the southern plains of Sind.

Bībarg's taunts of cowardice and indecision, Bālāč's agony of shame, fury, and doubt, Nakīb's urgings to action are the subject of a large ballad literature, some of it of as fine an epic quality as is to be found, in which the conditions of life in all their stark bleakness are described for a Baluch who dedicates himself to do his duty. Some of it has been collected and published.

The Mazārī cycle. The wars of the Mazārī also form a cycle. In the early years of the 19th century, when Bahrām Khan was chief, a band of Mazārī raided the cattle of Gol Moḥammad Brāhōī, of the Jamālī Brāhōī, and subsequently, after negotiations, refused to return more than twenty-four female camels. The original causes of the raid lay, as so often, in disputed ownership of grazing grounds, and Gol Moḥammad decided to attack the Mazārī in force. He was at first driven off, but in a second engagement he succeeded in capturing a whole camel herd. Threescore Mazārīs pursued; all dismounted at Jarōpošt and fought hand to hand. Gol Moḥammad and fourscore of his men were killed.

Other literature. Mīr Hammal Jīhand "Sultan of Kalmat" is the subject of several ballads. A ruler of Makrān in the 16th century, he was often engaged with the Portuguese, who frequently raided the coast during this time, burning Gwādar and Pasnī in 1581. Mīr Hammal boasted that he could easily drive them away, but in a naval battle he was decisively beaten, captured alive by the Portuguese, and taken to south India (in some versions to Portugal), where he was imprisoned. Efforts to ransom him failed, whereupon the Portuguese tried to persuade him to settle and take as wife one of them. Mīr Hammal refused to marry a "*kafīr*" woman, and eventually died in prison. He is reputed to have written a history of his years in captivity and to have sent it to Kalmat, but no trace of it has been found. The ballads about him also describe the local custom women since adopted of mourning for him by binding their hair on Saturdays.

There is beside this particular literature of Baluch concerns, an extensive literature regarding many of the famous Islamic stories common to all Muslim peoples: stories of *parīs*, of ʿĪsā and Bārī, Laylā and Majnūn, Farhād and Šīrēn. More especially Baluch is the ballad of Dōstēn and Šīrēn, and those about Šēh (Shaikh) Morīd. Modern poets, foremost among them Gol Khan Naṣīr, have written new versions of these legends.

The time has not yet arrived for a comprehensive survey of Baluchi literature, for which the material at hand is as yet far too incomplete.

Many of the actors in events are themselves held to be bards (Bībarg, Bālāč, Qabīl Jaṭ, Gwaharām), many individual ballads being attributed to them. Some of these "attributed" classical poems were collected by Dames in 1909 and by Šēr Moḥammad Marī in 1970, but neither their age nor authenticity can be verified.

The earliest important poet for whom definite information is available is Jām Durrak, court poet at the court of Naṣīr Khan I of Kalat (1749-95), whose love poetry is still remembered and recited. Some of it has been collected and published (see the bibliography).

The 19th century saw a large literary flowering, and nearly every event of public or private importance (battles, celebrations, political events) saw the composition of a ballad to commemorate it, often by poets whose names and localities are known. In the western Kech valley, the town of Mand was of special importance, the home of Mollā Fażl and Mollā Qasīm, both in the first part of the century. Also important are ʿEzzat Lalla from Panjgur, Bālāč from Sibi, Nūr Moḥammad Bamapoštī from Bampošt in Persian Baluchistan, Mollā Balnāma Ḥassān from Bāhō Kalāt in the same area.

In the latter half of the 19th century and the first part of the 20th century there have also been major poets: Faqīr Šēr Jān of Nushki, Mollā ʿEsmāʿīl of Tump (Kech), Ostā Ḥassān Zargar also of Kech, Mollā Ğolām Nabī Ḵārānī of Kolwa, among others, all writers of narrative ballads as well as romantic ones on important themes of the day.

The British Afghan wars were productive of, among other things, some important historical narrative ballads: one describes the expedition of General Willshire against Kalat in 1839, and there are many descriptions of the prevailing state of tribal unrest in Kalat State and in British Baluchistan, a state which continued until Sir Robert Sandeman in 1867 established a measure of control over the anarchic tribes by negotiating treaties, the first such ever concluded with them; as a result Baluch tribes kept the peace during the Second Afghan War in 1878, itself the subject of balladry. Sandeman himself became a legend, and there are many poems about Sanman Sāhb.

Modern literature. After the turn of the century, and particularly at the end of the first World War (for which Marī Baluch had refused to recruit soldiers for the Indian Army), a new national consciousness among Baluch generally produced a generation of writers who by the 1930s created an entirely new Baluchi cultural scene—one in which the printed word began to play a role for the first time. While it was nominally mainly literary in character, politics played an important role from the start, and one of the purposes of many writers was the awakening of a national consciousness, in which the mother tongue of course played a major part.

The first of this new generation of writers to become widely known was Moḥammad Ḥosayn "ʿAnqā" (b. 1909, d. 1977) whose weekly newspaper in Baluchi, *Bōlān*, was the first of its kind; it survived, remarkably, for several years at Mach near Quetta until the end of the 1930s. Groups of enthusiasts were not lacking, however, to continue such efforts, and a bewildering variety of newspapers and "little magazines" have been born and died in the past 50 years, the first after *Bōlān* of the 1930s being *Ōmān*, ed. by Maulvī (Mawlawī) Ḵayr Moḥammad Nadvī in Karachi in the early 1950s. These literary activities have usually had a marked political content, so that relationships with central governments have never been easy. Other early writers include ʿAbd-al-ʿAzīz Kūrd (d. ca. 1970), Sayyed Hašīmī (d. 1980), Raḥm-ʿAlī Marī (d. ca. 1940). Probably the most important single events were the foundation of Baluchi academies for the publication of all types of written material (in Karachi ca. 1956 by Sayyed Hašīmī), and in Quetta in 1959, the latter being preceded there by the Balūčī Zubānē Diwān in 1950 (ʿAbd-Allāhān Jamāldīnī, b. 1922, Gol Khan Naṣīr, 1914-84, and Ğolām Moḥammad Šāhwānī, d. ca. 1957). While the academy in Karachi lasted only a few years, it did important work; the academy in Quetta, on the other hand, is still flourishing, with some 60 titles to its credit, many of which are still in print. Gol Khan Naṣīr's *Gulbāng* (Balūčī Zubānē Diwān, Quetta, 1952), a collection of poems, was one of the first publications. Gol Khan was the leading poet of the years after 1950, with many works published by the Baluchi Academy in Quetta, including four large volumes of poetry, written for the most part in traditional Baluchi styles. By contrast, ʿAṭā Šād (b. ca. 1940) is a leading poet in new, nontraditional styles, including free verse. Other leading poets in the classical and modern style are Mīr ʿĪsā Qomī (b. ca. 1915) of Torbat, and ʿAbd-al-Waḥīd Āzāt Jamāldīnī (1915-81) of Nūški. Āzāt founded the monthly *Balōčī* (Karachi, 1956-69; Quetta, 1969-) and was its editor until his death.

See also BRAHUI.

Bibliography: Older (pre-1889) works. The only works still worth consulting are C. E. Gladstone, *Biluchi Handbook*, Lahore, 1874; E. W. Marston, *Grammar and Vocabulary of the Mekranee Beloochee Dialect*, Bombay, 1877; Major E. Mockler, *A Grammer of the Baloochee Language, as it is Spoken in Makrān, in the Persi-Arabic Character*, London, 1877; E. Pierce, "A Description of the Mekranee-Beloochee Dialect," *JRAS Bombay* 11, pp. 1-98 (fairly accurate descriptions, mainly of the Coastal dialect but phonologically very hard to follow and differing dialect forms are mixed without discrimination); A. Lewis, *The Gospel According to St. Matthew*, Allahabad, 1884; idem, *Balochi Stories, as Spoken by the Nomad Tribes of the Sulaiman Hills*, Allahabad, 1855 (accurate and quite reliable; Eastern Hill Baluchi).

Early work (1889-1920). The first scientific and comparative studies of the phonology, history, and etymology of Baluchi by an authority on the subject are the following works by W. Geiger: "Dialektspaltung in Balūčī," *Sb. Bayr. Akad. d. Wiss.* 1, Munich, 1889, pp. 65-92; "Balūčische Texte mit Übersetzung I, II," *ZDMG* 43, 1889, pp. 579-89, 47, 1893, pp. 440-49; "Etymologie des Balūčī," *Abh. Bayr. Akad. d. Wiss.* 19, 1890, pp. 107-53; "Lautlehre des Balūčī," ibid., pp. 399-443 (most of this is still useful but it must be remembered that Geiger had little other Middle Iranian material than the older Pahlavi studies at his disposal), culminating in his classical account of the language from the standpoint of Iranian philology: "Die Sprache der Balūtschen," in *Grundriss* I, pp. 231-48 and 417-23. By M. L. Dames we have the following important works: *A Textbook of the Balochi Language*, Lahore, 1891; *Balochi Tales*, London,

I-II, 1892, III-IV, 1893, V, 1897; *The Baloch Race*, London, 1904; *Popular Poetry of the Baloches*, London, 1907 (the most ambitious and comprehensive collection of Baluchi ballads ever published, containing Baluchi texts with English translation; unfortunately marred by many inaccuracies in the Baluchi text and far too free English translations); "Balōčistān, Language and Literature," in *EI*[1], 1913, pp. 633-34 (useful particularly for the historical and ethnographic survey). Usable but inaccurate, with many misprints, are the two works by J. L. Mayer (Eastern Hill Baluchi): *Biluch Classics*, Fort Munro-Agra, 1901; *English-Biluchi Dictionary*, Lahore, 1909 (the earliest and in many ways most interesting of such dictionaries).

Modern works (1920-). H. W. Bailey, "Maka," *JRAS*, 1982, pp. 10-13. M. Barker and A. Kh. Mengal, *A Course in Baluchi*, 2 vols., Montreal, 1969 (modern language course in Rak̲šāni Baluchi, laden with "drills" and exercises; the most thorough description to date of any Baluchi dialect; texts and glossaries; painstaking and accurate). A. Bausani, "La letteratura Beluci," in O. Botto, *Storia delle letterature orientali*, Milan, 1969, II, pp. 643-48 (poorish summaries of a few tales taken from Dames, *Popular Poetry*; Jām Dorrak is also mentioned). G. Buddruss, "Buttern in Baluchistan," in *Wort und Wirklichkeit. Studien zur Afrikanistik und Orientalistik Eugen Ludwig Rapp zum 70. Geburtstag*, ed. B. Benzing, O. Böcher, and G. Mayer, II, Meisenheim am Glan, 1978, pp. 1-16 (an interesting specimen of Afghani Baluchi, with notes and tr.). N. A. Collett, *A Grammar, Phrase Book and Vocabulary of Baluchi* (*As Spoken in the Sultanate of Oman*), 1983, 2nd ed., 1986, Abingdon, Kent (Kēči dialect used by Balōč recruits from Pakistan in the Omani forces; the vocabulary includes occasional Rak̲šāni and Coastal forms, and some words unrecorded in Baluchi so far). W. Eilers, "Das Volk der Maka vor und nach den Achaemeniden," in H. Koch and D. N. MacKenzie, eds., *Kunst, Kultur, und Geschichte der Achaemenidenzeit und ihr Fortleben*, AMI, Ergänzungsband 10, Berlin, 1983, pp. 101-19. J. Elfenbein, "Baluchistan, Language," in *EI*[2], 1960, pp. 1006-07 (in the historical part read "northwestern" for "eastern" and "southwestern" for "western"; the dialect geography is completely revised in the text above). Idem, "Baluchi Mss. in the British Museum," in *Trudy XXV Mezhdunarodnogo Kongressa Vostokovedov* II, Moscow, 1960, pp. 364-66 (preliminary discussion of the three mss.). Idem, "A Balūčī Text, with Translation and Notes," *BSOAS* 24, 1961, pp. 86-103 (ed., tr. of one story with notes from the most interesting of the three mss). Idem, *A Vocabulary of Marw Baluchi*, Naples, 1963 (etymological vocabulary of all Marv Baluchi texts). Idem, *The Baluchi Language, a Dialectology with Texts*, London, 1966 (a first attempt at a comprehensive first-hand account of all Baluchi dialects, with some texts and a small, poor word list; mainly descriptive, with a few historical notes on the development of dialects; for the most part still valid). Idem, "Report on a Linguistic Mission to Helmand and Nīmrūz," *Journal of Afghan Studies* 2, 1979, pp. 39-44 (dialectology of Afghani Baluchi). Idem, *A Baluchi Miscellanea of Erotica and Poetry: Codex Oriental Additional 24048 of the British Library*, AION 43/2, Supp. 35, Naples, 1983 (the oldest of the three mss. in the British Library, perhaps written ca. 1820 at the request of H. H. Wilson, 1786-1860, professor of Sanskrit at Oxford University, whose wife donated the ms. to the British Library in 1861; the dialect is an unusual variety of Coastal Baluchi, probably from Kalmat in present-day Pakistani Makrān). Idem, "Notes on the Balochī-Brāhūī Linguistic Commensality," *TPS*, 1982, pp. 77-98 (description of some important phonological and morphological borrowings by Brahui from Baluchi). Idem, "Balochi from Khotan," *Studia Iranica* 14, 1985, pp. 223-38 (176 Baluchi words noted in H. W. Bailey, *Dictionary of Khotan Saka*, with corrections and comments). Idem, "Mythologie der Balutschen," in Klett and Cotta, *Wörterbuch der Mythologie*, 2nd ed., H. W. Haussig, Stuttgart, 1983-, pp. 491-507. V. A. Frolova, *Beludzhskiĭ yazyk*, Moscow, 1960 (no history or dialectology). R. N. Frye, "Remarks on Baluchi History," *Central Asiatic Journal* 6, 1961, pp. 44-50 (Baluchi history in Islamic sources). E. G. Gafferberg, *Beludzhi Turkmenskoĭ SSR*, Moscow, 1969. G. W. Gilbertson, *English-Balochi Colloquial Dictionary* I-II, Hertford, 1925. Sir G. A. Grierson, "Balōchī," in *Linguistic Survey of India* X: *Eranian Family*, Calcutta, 1921, pp. 327-421 (useful summary of phonology and grammar, with many texts and list of words). J. Hansman, "A Periplus of Magan and Meluhha," *BSOAS* 36, 1973, pp. 554-84, with an annex by H. W. Bailey, pp. 584-87. V. A. Livshits, "Beludzhskiĭ yazyk," in *Narody Sredneĭ Azii i Kazakhstana*, Moscow, 1962, pp. 157-58. D. N. MacKenzie, "Origins of Kurdish," *TPS*, 1961, pp. 68-86 (on the dialectology of western Iranian languages). G. Morgenstierne, *Report on a Linguistic Mission to North-Western India*, Oslo, 1932, pp. 4-25. Idem, "Notes on Balochi Etymology," *NTS* 5, 1932, pp. 37-53 (with important new material). Idem, "Balochi Miscellanea," *Acta Orientalia* 20, 1948, pp. 253-92 (remarks on phonology; historical and etymological notes). Idem, "Neu-Iranische Sprachen," in *HO* I, IV/1, Leiden and Cologne, 1958, pp. 169-70. I. M. Oranskiĭ, "Beludzhskiĭ yazyk," in *Iranskie yazyki*, Moscow, 1963, pp. 141-45, 170-71, tr. J. Blau, Paris, 1977, pp. 146-50, 196 (fairly complete survey of published material). M. G. Pikulin, *Beludzhi*, Moscow, 1959 (summary of material published abroad). V. S. Rastorgueva, "Beludzhskiĭ yazyk," in *Yazyki narodov SSSR* I, Moscow, 1966, pp. 323-41. G. Redard, "Balōčī," in *Current Trends in Linguistics* VI, The Hague, 1970, pp. 107-08 (state of the art and bibliography). S. N. Sokolov, *Grammaticheskiĭ ocherk yazyka beludzheĭ Sovetskogo Soyuza*, Trudy Instituta

Yazykoznaniya 6, Moscow, 1956, pp. 57-91 (detailed grammatical description of the Zarubin texts). V. S. Sokolova, *Beludzhskiĭ yazyk*, Novye svedenie fonetiki iranskikh yazykov II/6, Moscow and Leningrad, 1950 (first Russian sketch). Idem, *Beludzhskiĭ yazyk*, Ocherki po fonetike iranskikh yazykov I, Moscow and Leningrad, 1953 (detailed phonological analysis; some word lists and texts). Idem, "Beludzhskiĭ yazyk," in *Sovremennyĭ Iran*, Moscow, 1957, pp. 83-93 (brief sketch). B. Spooner, "Notes on Baluchī spoken in Persian Baluchistan," *Iran* 5, 1967, pp. 51-71 (short description and word list; Sarḥaddi and "Makrāni" Baluchi by an anthropologist; inaccurate phonology; unselective bibliography). I. I. Zarubin, "K izucheniya beludzhskogo yazyka i folklora," *Zapiski Kollegii Vostokovedov* 5, Leningrad, 1932, pp. 653-79 (the first Baluchi text with good Russian translation; useful). Idem, *Beludzhskie skazki*, Leningrad, I, 1932, II, 1949 (a huge collection of prose stories in the Marv dialect with Russian translation; accurate and reliable).

Modern literary Baluchi texts: Bašīr Aḥmad Balōč, ed., *Durrčīn*, Quetta, 1963 (some of the work of Jām Dorrak). A. J. Jamāldīnī, ed., *Mistāg*, Karachi, 1959 (an early and fairly representative collection of new Baluchi poetry). Miṭha Khan Marī, *Raḥm-ʿAlī Marī*, Quetta, 1978 (poetry of an important poet). Šer-Moḥammad Marī, ed., *Balōčī kōhnēn šāḥirī*, Quetta, 1970 (the first collection of classical Baluchi ballads since Dames, 1907; Eastern Hill Baluchi in Sindhi script; introd. and notes in Baluchi; many printing errors). Gol Khan Naṣīr, *Gulbāng*, Quetta, 1952 (one of the first indigenous publications). Idem, *Šap girōk*, Quetta, 1973: *Grand*, Quetta, 1975; *Dōstēn o Šīrēn*, Quetta, 1977 (collections of poetry; the last a lengthy recast of a classical Baluchi story of two lovers).

(J. Elfenbein)

iv. Music of Baluchistan

Melodies in the music of Baluchistan are usually connected with particular ceremonies (*marāsem*), usually religious rites, festivals, or holidays. The principal religious rites are exorcism (*gwātī*), ecstasy (*māled-e pīr-e patar*), and mourning (*majāles-e tarḥīm*); the most important festivals and holidays are weddings, childbirth, circumcision, date harvesting (*hāmīn*), and wheat harvesting. The relationships between melodies and particular ceremonies are reflected in their names.

Līkō and Zahīrōk. These are vocal forms (*āvāzī*) and are sung when one is away from close relatives, friends, a beloved, and even from one's country. In the beginning Zahīrōk was only sung by two groups of women, who in the course of their daily work would exchange melodies. This method of performance is not common today; in practice Zahīrōk is sung by male singers accompanied by a short-necked fiddle (*sorūd*, also *surōz*, or *kēčak*, Pers. *qeyčak*).

The Līkō and Zahīrōk, which contain similar texts, differ in that each is common to a particular area of Baluchistan and that each has different melodic characteristics. Līkō is most common in Sarḥadd-zamīn and Zahīrōk in Mokrān (Makurān). Among the characteristics of the Sarḥaddi style is the repetition of hemistichs which are performed in one period, usually composed of two sentences or two melodic figures. The first sentence or figure of the period has an unfinished quality, while the second sentence or figure evokes a feeling of completion.

Kordī (Kurdī). The text of Kordī, like Līkō and Zahīrōk, evokes the suffering arising from distance and separation, but in Līkō and Zahīrōk the suffering is real, while in Kordī there is only remembrance of separation. The text is usually in the dialect of Rūdbār and the region between Īrānšahr and Bampūr. Kordī was also initially sung by women when working with stone handmills used for making wheat flour; however, this is no longer the custom. Kordī, like Līkō and Zahīrōk, has free meter. The name Kordī may suggest that this *āvāz* was associated with a branch of the Kurds in Baluchistan.

Mōtk or Mowtk. These are for the ceremonies of *tarḥīm*, the assembly convened for the blessing of the dead and mourning. The text of this *āvāz* describes the virtues of the deceased and the sorrow of mourning. On this basis Mōtk can be counted as a type of elegy (*marṯīa*). Mōtk is usually performed by a group of women without instrumental accompaniment. The verses (*bayt*) and refrains (*tarjīʿband*) are sung alternately by two groups of singers or by soloist and group. This way of performing appears to be no longer customary. Mōtk, like Līkō, Zahīrōk, and Kordī, is not strictly metrical.

Šayr (*Šeʿr*). This is an *āvāz* with poetic text consisting of epic stories, romance, historical events, social narrative, advice, etc. The poet (*šāʿer*), also called *pālavān* (*pahlavān*), performs Šayr with instrument and voice. Baluchi *pālavān*s sing of historical events, thereby preserving the history of Baluchistan orally. Šayr is usually sung in gatherings of important people or khans; on rare occasions it can also be performed at wedding ceremonies. The instruments accompanying the performance are the plucked, long-necked lute (Bal. *dambūra*, Pers. *tanbīra*) providing a rhythmic drone, and the *sorūd* (*qeyčak*). The most important and well-known Šayrs current in Baluchistan are epic Šayr, including *Mīr Qanbar*, *Čākur wa Gwaharām*, *Ḥażrat Adham*, and *Moḥammad Ḥanīfa*; historical Šayr, including *Jīhand Khan* and *Dādšāh*; love Šayr, including *ʿEzzat wa Mehrōk*, and *Še* (*Šayḵ*) *Morīd wa Hānī*; social narrative, including *Mīr Pasond Khan* and *Morād Khan* (see also on Baluchi literature above).

Gwātī. This term, literally "windy" or "windiness," is also used to designate depression believed to be caused by an evil spirit disturbing the psychosomatic equilibrium, for which another term is *jenn-zadagī* (spirit possession). The use of *gwātī* as a musical term arises from the belief that only music is able to rid the possessed body of unclean spirits and restore it to health by means of a trance. Belief in unclean spirits is found both in

Baluchistan, in particular in its coastal regions, and on most of the Persian Gulf coast. The most important types of evil spirits are the *zār*s (for the names of which see Rīāḥī, pp. 4-5), *dīv*s, *gwāt*s, and *jenn*s, further distinguished by gender and creed (Muslim or non-Muslim). Different instruments are used to exorcise different spirits, e.g., for a *zār* only drums (*lēvā*) are used, but *gwātī* ceremonies (*le'eb*) use all of the instruments current in Baluchistan, mainly *sorūd* and double flute *dōnelī* performing a specific repertory of songs and instrumental pieces. The word *mūkām* (*maqām*: mode) in Baluchistan is attributed to instruments that participate in the customs of *gwātī*. A kind of dance, or stirring, not unlike that of the dervishes, is an indispensible part of the *gwātī* ritual. When the participants are men, the dance is called *damāl* and the leader is always a man, called *ḵalīfa*. Female *gwātī* dance may be led by a man or a woman. The generic term for the leader of the ceremonies is *gwātīe māt* (lit. the mother of *gwātī*), whether a man or a woman (today most often a man). The most famous *gwātīe māt* was a woman from Mesqaṭ by the name of Zaynab. In deference to her, the *ḵalīfa* and the instrumentalists sing the following line at the beginning of each *gwātī*: *Zaynab gwātīe māt-int, ḥalwā na wārta Zaynabā* (Zaynab is the mother of *gwātī*, Zaynab has not eaten *ḥalwā*). The *gwātīe māt* first diagnoses the existence of *gwāt* and then fixes the precise stages of the patient's convalescence (*daraja-ye kopār*), choosing the music used in the ceremonies. The ritual is performed every night from three to seven or even fourteen nights, depending on the type and severity of the disease, and ends with a sacrifice. The text of the *āvāz* of the Gwātī includes praises (*madḥ*) dedicated to the mystics La'l Šahbāz Qalandar, buried in Sehwān (Sind), and 'Abd-al-Qāder Jēlānī (Jeylānī, Gīlānī; qq.v.)

Māled (*Mawlūd*) *pīr-e paṭar*. The ceremonies of *māled*, which last only two to three hours, are most common in the coastal regions of Baluchistan, but are now gradually being forgotten. In *māled* the *āvāz* is accompanied only by the drums called *ṭabl* and *daf* (single skin frame drum, called *samā'* or *māled*); only in exceptional cases is the oboe (*sūrnā*) also used. The leader of the *māled* ceremony, who sometimes plays the *samā'* himself, is called *ḵalīfa*. The ceremonies of *māled* are in one sense parallel to those performed at the Qāderī meetings of Kurdistan. Reaching ecstatic states during the *ḏekr*, some participants of *māled* (called *mastān* "the drunk ones") insert swords, knives, and daggers into their bodies.

The following *āvāz* are used in marriage and childbirth ceremonies:

Nāzēnk. This term means "worship" or "praise" (verb *nāzēnag*) and in the first place designates praise of the bride, groom, and newborn baby, but also of God. Nāzēnk is sung at the following times: when the groom is taken to the bath, after returning from the bath, when the bride and groom are seated on the "throne," and during the first six nights after childbirth.

Lāḏō and Hālō. Like Nāzēnk, Lāḏō (Laylō, Laylarī) and Hālō are particular to marriage ceremonies. Both Lāḏō and Hālō are performed before and during the groom's bath, but in addition Hālō is used during the *ḥanā-bandān* ceremony on the eve of the wedding day. Lāḏō is named after its refrain: *lāḏō lī lāḏō*.

Šaptākī (also Sepat). This is an unaccompanied *āvāz* with poetry praising God, his Prophet, and the great religious figures recited by relatives and friends gathering in the room of the mother during the night after childbirth. The ceremony lasts from six to forty nights, depending upon the family's finances. The *āvāz* is usually performed by two groups of singers who alternate singing verses and refrains.

Sepat, *Wazbat*, *and Nāt* (*Na't*). Sepat is also sung during childbirth ceremonies in honor of the mother. The text of Sepat or Wazbat is also devoted to the praise of God, saints, and great religious figures. Nāt is performed chorally during Šaptākī ceremonies and like Šaptākī is an *āvāz* with lyrics that extol and eulogize the Prophet, his descendants, and the other prominent figures of Islam.

Sawt (*ṣawt*). This term is applied to many melodies in the music of Baluchistan, accompanied by any of the instruments current there. Its lyrics are about love or joy and are called *šayyānī sawt*. The performers of Sawt, called *sawtī*, perform in engagement, marriage, and circumcision ceremonies and other celebrations and holidays. (The term is also applied to short poems, not necessarily intended for singing.)

Bibliography: L. Mobaššerī, *Āhanghā-ye maḥallī-e manāṭeq-e jonūbī-e Īrān* I, Tehran, 1335 Š./1956. 'A. M. Aḥmadīān, "Mūsīqī dar Balūčestān," *Majalla-ye honar o mardom* 183, 1356 Š./1977, pp. 57-65. M. A. Barker and A. K. Mengal, *A Course in Baluchi*, Montreal, 1969, II, pp. 263-349 (contains samples of poetry and metrical analysis). J. During, *Musique d'extase et de guérison du Baloutchistan. Anthologie de la musique traditionelle iranienne*, Paris, 1981 (a record with a notice on the *gwātī*s). Idem, *Musique et mystique en Iran*, Ph.D. dissertation, Strasbourg, 1985, pp. 166-370. J. Kuckertz and M. T. Massoudieh, *Volkgesänge aus Iran*, Bässler Archiv 23, 1975. M. T. Massoudieh, "Hochzeitslieder aus Balūčestān," *Jahrbuch für musikalische Volks- und Völkerkunde*, Berlin and New York, 1973, pp. 59-69. Idem, *Mūsīqī-e Balūčestān*, Tehran, 1364 Š./1985. Idem, *Tajzīa wa taḥlīl-e 14 tarāna-ye maḥallī-e Īrān*, Tehran, 1353 Š./1974. 'A. Rīāḥī, *Zār o bād o balūč*, Tehran, 1356 Š./1977. Qureshi and Burckhardt, "Pakistan," in *The New Grove's Dictionary of Music*, London, 1980.

(M. T. MASSOUDIEH)

v. BALUCH CARPETS, RUGS, AND OTHER PRODUCTS

A distinct group of carpets, woven by Baluch tribes in the northeastern Iranian province of Khorasan and the Sīstān area, is known as Baluch carpets (Edwards, p. 185). These carpets were not, as is frequently erroneously assumed, made in Makrān, where the main body of the Baluch tribes live (Wegner, 1980, pp. 57, 59).

In addition to the Baluch, many other ethnic groups in Khorasan weave carpets that look like the Baluch carpets and are designated as such. The tribes that make such carpets in the same region are the Tīmūrī, the Kurd, the Arab, the Brahui, the Jamšīdī, and the Barbarī (Azadi and Besim, pp. 15, 16). The main characteristics of carpets in the Baluch tradition are the following:

Colors. The use of dark colors like dark blue or blue-black, dark brownish red, dark reddish brown, dark brown verging on black (mainly for outlines), dark purplish brown, dark brownish violet, and occasionally some ivory is characteristic. Because of the almost black outlines the dark colors appear even darker. These carpets thus possess a somber charm that appeals to many connoisseurs and collectors.

Camel hair is sometimes woven into the niches (*meḥrāb*) of Baluch prayer carpets. These rugs are less somber, even occasionally light in ground color. The idea that this material is actually wool dyed with walnut husks (Edwards, p. 186) is incorrect; it is undyed camel hair.

Occasionally a few old carpets are found with ivory fields; most of them come from the Qā'enāt and Sīstān areas. They sometimes seem more colorful than the normal Baluch carpets.

Ornament. Because of the prevalence of ornaments like rectangles, hexagons, and octagons, Baluch carpets belong to the geometric category of nomad carpets. Repeated or alternating lozenges and medallions, in regular or offset rows, play an extremely important role in the design of these carpets. Frequently the rows create a honeycomb pattern, so that the ground color of the field is no longer distinguishable. Indeed, this feature is characteristic of Baluch carpets. Plant motifs also occur in the Baluch repertoire of forms, but they have been rendered angular and geometric.

The nomenclature and meaning of Baluch motifs are not very well known. Statements in the carpet literature that the craftsmen did not understand what they were weaving are incorrect. Such statements are a sign of retreat before the extraordinarily difficult problems of research in this area. Such complex questions cannot be understood or explained through quick investigations. Rather, they require years of arduous study in the field, which have not yet taken place.

Technique. Baluch carpets are all knotted with the asymmetrical knot, that is, the so-called "Persian or Senna knot," open to the left. In traditional pieces the warp (*tār*) always consists of two-ply wool, Z-spun and S-twisted (*čap-o-rāst rīsīda*), and is light in color. In newer pieces the warp can also be of cotton. The weft (*pūd*) of Baluch carpets consists of two sinuous brown or dark brown shoots, contrary to C. A. Edwards' opinion that all Baluch carpets are single-wefted (p. 186). On rare occasions the first weft is drawn taut, thus creating a difference in levels, as for example in the Kurd Baluch. The weft is usually two-ply, Z-spun, and loosely twisted. Frequently, however, the weft can be a single strand.

The pile is also two-ply, Z-spun and loosely twisted. Many Baluch carpets, for example, the Sālār-ḵānī from the area of Torbat-e Ḥaydarī, include some silk in the pile of wedding and dowry carpets. This material is extremely expensive for the Baluch and represents the ultimate in luxury. They must buy or barter for the silk because they do not themselves manufacture it.

Selvedges. One of the most notable characteristics of Baluch carpets is the way in which their selvedges are handled. These can be up to 2 cm wide; the material is dark brown or black goat hair. In rare instances the selvedges may be worked in a form of braiding with supplementary wefts. Usually, however, they are produced by passing the supplementary wefts over and under groups of four or more warps two, three, or four times, thus creating respectively double-, triple-, or quadruple-corded selvedges.

Uses. The Baluch, like many other nomads, manufacture a number of objects in pile or flat-woven technique, which serve different functions. Such products include double saddlebags (*ḵorjīn, asb-jol*); cushion covers (*bāleš*); saddle covers (*rūzīnī*); horse blankets (*rū-asbī*); ground covers on which meals are served (*sofra*); weavings for catching flour as it comes from the mill (*sofra-ye ārd*); bags for special purposes (*dārāk*); donkey chest bands (*gūr-band*); blinders for donkeys, horses, and camels (*čašm-bandān*); etc.

Although we have general knowledge of the characteristics mentioned, it is nevertheless extremely difficult to attribute carpets to specific makers (tribes, subtribes, clans, etc.) and regions (Khorasan and Sīstān, Saraḵs, Torbat-e Ḥaydarī, etc.). The main reason is that there are almost no detailed publications on Baluch carpets, in contrast, for example, to Turkman carpets, on which there are many Russian field studies. Besides, it is still not known even which tribes and subtribes produce carpets at all. The single published monograph (Azadi and Besim, pp. 28-29) includes only the second attempt (the first being Edwards, p. 185) to provide a list of tribes that manufacture knotted-pile carpets. These tribes are as follows: 'Alī Akbar-ḵānī from the Qā'enāt region; 'Abd-al-Sorḵ from the area around Saraḵs, Nīšāpūr, and Sabzavār; 'Alī Mīrzā'ī, from the Saraḵs area; Bahlūlī (or Bahlūrī) from the vicinity of Ḵ˘āf, Jangal, and Torbat-e Ḥaydarī; the Bāyazīdī from around Maḥvalāt and Torbat-e Ḥaydarī; the Jān-Begī from the area of Rošḵ˘ar and Torbat-e Ḥaydarī; the Jān-Mīrzā'ī from the Torbat-e Ḥaydarī district; the Fatḥ-Allāhī (Fatollāhī) from the northern Zābol area; the Ḥasanzā'ī found dispersed throughout the entire region; the Qarā'ī, who belong with the Sālār-ḵānī, from Torbat-e Ḥaydarī; the Ḵānzā'ī from the Saraḵs area; the Kolāh-derāzī from the neighborhood of Kāšmar and Torbat-e Ḥaydarī; the Kūrḵa-īlī or Sālār-ḵānī in the area of Jangal and Torbat-e Ḥaydarī; the Kurd from around Saraḵs; the Lāḵī from the area of Saraḵs and Qā'enāt; the Madad-ḵānī from the region of Zābol and Qā'enāt; the Narīmānī from the area of Torbat-e Jām and Mašhad; the Raḥīm-ḵānī from the Saraḵs and Torbat-e Ḥaydarī area; the Sarbandī from

Sīstān; the Šāhzā'ī from around Torbat-e Jām; the Tūḵī subtribes Jamālzā'ī and Sūrānī from the area south of Nehbandān and the Sīstān region; the Vāḵerī in the neighborhood of Seydābād in the Mašhad district.

Bibliography: S. Azadi, *Persian Carpets* I: *Inauguration of the Carpet Museum in Teheran/Iran*, Hamburg and Tehran, 1977. Idem, "Einige Teppiche in Belutschtradition," *Weltkunst* 48/8, 1978. Idem and A. Besim, *Carpets in the Baluch Tradition*, Munich, 1986. R. Barberie, *Geknüpfte und gewebte Arbeiten der Belutsch-Nomaden*, Vienna, 1982. P. Bausback, *Alte Knupfarbeiten der Belutschen*, Mannheim, 1980. I. Bennett, "Three Baluch Rugs," *Halı* 1/4, 1978, pp. 399-400. D. Black, *Rugs of the Wandering Baluchi*, London, 1976. J. W. Boucher, "Baluchi Weaving of the 19th Century," *Halı* 1/3, 1978, pp. 284-87. M. Craycraft, *Belouch Prayer Rugs*, Point Reyes Station, Calif., 1982, M. L. Dames, *The Baloche Race*, London, 1904. A. C. Edwards, *The Persian Carpet*, London, 1953, 1960, 1975. J. Elfenbein, "Balūčistān," in *EI*[2] I. M. E. Enay and Azadi, *Einhundert Jahre Orientteppich-Literatur*, Hanover, 1977. W. Geiger, *Ethymologie des Baluči*, in Abh. Königlich Bayerischen Akademie der Wissenschaften, 1. Kl., 19, Munich, 1899. S. A. Hilhofer, *Die Teppiche Zentralasiens*, Hanover, 1968. W. Ivanov, "Notes on the Ethnology of Khurassan," *The Geographical Journal* 67/1, 1926, p. 143. A. Janata, "Die Bevölkerung von Ghor," *Archiv für Völkerkunde* 17-18, 1962-63, pp. 73-156. Idem, "Völkerkundliche Forschungen in West-Afghanistan 1969," *Bustan* 2-3, 1970, pp. 50-65. Idem, "Flachgewebe aus West-Afghanistan," *Heimtex* 3, 1979, pp. 72-92. H. M. Jones and J. W. Boucher, *Baluchi Rugs*, Washington, D.C., 1974. M. G. Konieczny, *Textiles of Baluchistan*, London, 1979. P. W. Meister and S. Azadi, *Persische Teppiche*, Hamburg and Frankfurt am Main, 1971. Pakistan-American Cultural Centre, ed., *Folk Craft of Baluchistan and Sind*, Karachi, 1968. D. Schletzer, *Alte und antike Teppiche der Belutsch und Ersari*, Hamburg, 1974. W. Stanzer, "Balutsch-Teppiche Werden Salonfähig," *Afghanistan Journal* 9/4, 1982, p. 146. B. and D. H. G. Wegner, "Stickereien in Afghanistan," *Textilhandwerk in Afghanistan* [Bibliotheca Afghanica 3], Liestal, 1983, pp. 133-57. D. H. G. Wegner, "Nomaden- und Bauernteppiche in Afghanistan," *Baessler Archiv*, N.S. 12, 1964, pp. 141-77. D. H. G. Wegner, "Some Notes on the Rugs of Baluchi Nomads and Related Weavers," *Halı*, 1/3, 1978, pp. 287-93. D. H. G. Wegner, "Der Knüpfteppich bei Belutschen und ihren Nachbarn," *Tribus* 29, 1980, pp. 57-105. J. Zick-Nissen, *Nomadenkunst aus Belutchistan*, Berlin, 1968.

(S. AZADI)

BALŪHAR O BŪDĀSAF. See BARLAAM AND IOSAPH.

BALŪṬ (Middle Persian *balūt* and Arabic *ballūṭ* from Aram. *bālot/belūṭa*; see Mashkour, p. 82), common designation in New Persian both for acorn and oak, *Quercus* L.

Geobotany. Botanists-pharmacologists of the Islamic era (in Persia and in Arab lands), like their Greek predecessors Dioscorides and Galen, display scant, if any, information about the great variety of oaks and their habitats, though they know much about the medicinal virtues of oaks and "oak-apples" (see below). Ebn Sīnā (d. 428/1037) even deals with the oak and the chestnut tree under one and the same heading, *ballūṭ* (*Qānūn* II [Pers. tr.]. pp. 99-100). The most comprehensive overall description is to be found in Tonokābonī's *Toḥfat al-mo'menīn* (written in Persian in the reign of the Safavid Solaymān I, 1078-1105/1667-94), pp. 177-79, where, after indicating that *balūṭ* is called *dār-māzī* in the vernacular of Ṭabarestān and *bālūṭ* in Persian, he comments on a threefold distinction based on the form of the fruits, which he quotes from Ebn al-Kabīr's *Mā lā yasaʿ al-ṭabīb jahlah* (compiled in 711/1311-12): "one kind with roundish fruits, and that is *šāh-balūṭ* [chestnut]; two kinds with oblong fruits one with sweet edible acorns, and the other with bitter inedible ones, as observed in Deylam and Ṭabarestān."

Only in the past few decades have a number of botanists endeavored to clear up the confused mass of imperfect data about the genus *Quercus* L. in Iran. Ḥ. Ṯābetī (1976, pp. 573-603), availing himself mainly of the findings of A. Camus (1936-39), M. Zohary (1961-63), K. Djavanshir (1967), and K. Browicz and G. L. Menitsky (1971), and employing the latest terminology, presents the following species, subspecies, or varieties:

1. *Quercus Atropatana* Schwarz. General habitat: Caspian forests from Arasbārān and Ṭavāleš to Gorgān and Katūl. Local names: *pālīt/pālet* (in Arasbārān), *kar-māzū* (in Rāmsar, Kalārdašt, Kojūr, Katūl).

2. *Q. Brantii* Lindl. General habitat: Zagros highlands in W. Azerbaijan, Kermānšāh, Kurdistan, Luristan, Baḵtīārī, and Fārs. Local names: *balūt* or *palīt* (in Kermānšāhān, Baḵtīārī, Fārs, etc.), *māzū* (in Luristan, etc.), *balū/balī/barū*, *barū-dār* or *māzī* (in Sardašt, Kurdistan). There are three varieties: a) *Q. Brantii* Lindl. var. *Belangeri* (DC.) Zohary = *Q. persica* J. & Sp. var. *Belangeri* DC.; b) *Q. Brantii* Lindl. var. *Brantii* Browicz; c) *Q. Brantii* Lindl. var. *persica* (J. & Sp.) Zohary = *Q. Persica* J. & Sp. (this last synonym, now discarded, is the source of designations such as *balūṭ-e īrānī* "Iranian oak," or *balūṭ-e ḡarb* "western oak," by which *Q. Brantii* is usually referred to in current Persian literature on the subject).

3. *Q. carduchorum* C. Koch. Habitat: Mīrābād (in Sardašt).

4. *Q. castaneaefolia* C.A.M. ssp. *castaneaefolia* Browicz & Menitsky. General habitat: Caspian and Caucasian forests; in Iran, from Āstārā to Golīdāḡ and Golestān (easternmost points in the so-called Hyrcanian floristic region). Local names: *boland-māzū* (in ʿAmmārlū, Lāhījān, Deylamān), *māzū/mūzī/meyzī* (in Gīlān, Māzandarān, Gorgān), *pālūt* (in Āstārā), *māyzū* (in Ṭavāleš), *ešpar/īšbar* (around Rašt), *sīā(h)-māzū* (in Kojūr).

5. *Q. cedrorum* Ky. (= *Q. sessiliflora* Ky. = *Q. iberica* Stev.). Habitat: Pesān Valley (in Urmia), Sardašt, Kurdistan.

6. *Q. infectoria* Oliv. Three subspecies: a) ssp. *Boissieri* (Reut.) Schwarz; habitat: Kurdistan and Sardašt; b) ssp. *latifolia* Schwarz; habitat: Kurdistan and Sardašt; c) ssp. *petiolaris* Schwarz; habitat: Kurdistan and Sardašt. Local names: *dār-māzū, māzū-dār, māzū.*

7. *Q. Komarovii* Camus. Habitat: K̲oy, Sardašt. Local name: *āq-pālīt.*

8. *Q. Libani* Oliv. Habitat: Urmia, Sardašt, Kurdistan. Local names: *yavol/vovol*, and for var. *pinnata* Hd.-Mz.: *vayval/vahval.*

9. *Q. longipes* Stev. Habitat: K̲oy and Oskū (in Azerbaijan). Local names: *pālīt, oskūpālītī.*

10. *Q. macranthera* Fisch. & Mey. Habitat: high Caspian forests from Arasbārān to Gorgān. Local names: *pālet* (in Arasbārān), *ūrī* (in Dorfak, Javaherdašt, Rāmsar), *kūrī* (in Rāmsar), *pāča-māzū* (in Lāhījān), *dambel-mūzī* (in Savādkūh), *torš-e māzū* (in Katūl).

11. *Q. magnosquamata* Djav. Habitat: Sardašt, Kurdistan. Local names: *vahel, vovol.*

12. *Q. mannifera* Lindl. Habitat: Sardašt, Kurdistan. Common name: *(derak̲t-e) gaz-e ʿalafī.*

13. *Q. ovicarpa* Djav. Habitat: west Azerbaijan, Sardašt, Kurdistan.

14. *Q. Petraea* L. ssp. *iberica* (Stev.) Krasslin (= *Q. iberica* Stev.). Habitat: Caspian forests from Gīlān to Gorgān, especially in Tālār, Čālūs, and Harzevīl valleys. Local names: *kar-māzū, sefīd-māzū, sefīd-balūt.*

15. *Q. polynervata* Djav. Habitat: Sardašt, Kurdistan. Local name: *yovol.*

16. *Q. robur* L. Habitat: Azerbaijan, Kurdistan. The ssp. *pedunculiflora* (C. Koch) Menitsky is found in west Azerbaijan and, reportedly, in Mašhad.

17. *Q. vesca* Ky. Habitat: Sardašt (from Zamzīrān to Pīrānšahr) and probably, Kurdistan.

Note that cork oak, *balūṭ-e čūb-pamba(ʾī), Quercus suber* L., first introduced into Iran in 1957-58, has been naturalized at some points along the Caspian littoral.

Area. In west and southwest Iran, where well-defined stands of oak exist, their total surface area has been estimated at 3,448,000 hectares, divided into two main areas: a *Q. infectoria* and *Q. Libani* association, ca. 598,000 hectares, in west Kurdistan and in the Sardašt region, and a *Q. Brantii* var. *persica* association, ca. 2,850,000 hectares, mainly on southwestern slopes of the Zagros (M. Moḥammadī, on the authority of V. Tregubov, 1970).

Uses. Eating acorns, either roasted whole or ground and baked into bread, is probably the oldest use of oaks in Iran. Bīrūnī, *Ketāb al-ṣaydana*, pp. 97-98 (Ar. text), quotes from Rāzī the following appreciation, which, he suspects, is related by the latter from the Greek physician Oribasios (ca. 325-ca. 400 A.D.): "*Ballūṭ*'s nutritional value is superior to that of [other] fruits, and even approximates that of the grains with which bread is made; and in the past, people used to live on *ballūṭ* alone." But Anṭākī (d. 1008/1599), *Tad̲kera* I, remarks that "the acorn bread, made in time of famine, is coarse, difficult to digest, and produces black bile." Even in our times, "in years of distress and food shortage, Lurs and Kurds feed on *balūṭ*" (Nāẓem-al-Aṭebbāʾ ʿA.-A. Nafīsī, *Farhang-e Nafīsī*, Tehran, 1318 Š./1940, s.v.). Normally the principal consumers of acorns are domestic and wild animals in the area.

Oak timber, especially that from *Q. castaneaefolia* and *Q. Libani*, being hard, durable, and waterproof, is used in Iran for making boats, casks, outdoor rice depots, slabs and planks for rural houses (in the rainy Caspian region), furniture, doors, windows, agricultural implements, etc. *Q. castaneaefolia* timber is also an export article. Oak wood is valued as firewood and for making charcoal. The bark, with its considerable tannin (*māzūj*) content, is used in tannery.

Gall-nuts from *Q. Brantii* var. *persica* or from *Q. infectoria*, variously called *barā-māzīj/-māzū, māzūj, māzū-rūskā, qolqāf/golgāv, zešga, k̲arnūk, qeča, sečak* etc., rich in tannin, are used in tannery and dyeing; they are exported, too (see also their medicinal use below). A persistent belief about the origin of "oak-apples" (Arabic *ʿafṣ*) in Islamic medico-botanical works—a belief that goes back to Theophrastos according to Bīrūnī (loc. cit.), or to Galen according to Ebn al-Telmīd̲ (d. 560/1165; as related by Tonokābonī, loc. cit.)—is that they are also the fruits of the oak, which produces alternatively acorns one year and galls the next (see also another explanation of galls in Bīrūnī, loc. cit., and in ʿAqīlī K̲orāsānī, *Mak̲zan al-adwīa*, p. 124).

The sweetish manna commonly called *gaz-e ʿalafī* (or sometimes erroneously *gaz-angabīn*, which, properly, is tamarisk manna; see Schlimmer, *Terminologie*, p. 358), resulting from the sting of a certain small insect on the young leaves and twigs of *Q. mannifera*, is used in confectionery (especially in making the sweetmeat *bāsloq* or as a cheaper substitute for *gaz-angabīn* in making the delicacy called *gaz*).

Medicinal uses. Early in the Islamic era, all parts of the oak (and above all, *joft-e balūṭ*, i.e., the exocarp of acorn kernels) were acknowledged as astringent and dessicative, and consequently various preparations thereof have been prescribed for checking different morbid discharges of blood, etc. (e.g. hemoptysis, dysentery intestinal ulcers, menorrhagia, spermatorrhea), or for dressing various sores and wounds (for further information about these and other uses of the oak, see Tonokābonī and ʿAqīlī K̲orāsānī, loc. cit., who reflect and embody mainly the traditional Greco-Islamic medicinal botany). The *gaz-e ʿalafī* manna, however, should be dealt with apart, because, although it is an oak product, it is free of the astringent tannin and is used in popular medicine in the same cases as tamarisk manna, i.e., as an aperient (especially for children, who are enticed by its taste) and as an expectorant and demulcent.

Bibliography: Dāwūd Anṭākī, *Tad̲kera*, 2 vols., Cairo, 1308-09/1890-91. Moḥammad-Ḥosayn ʿAqīlī K̲orāsānī, *Mak̲zan al-adwīa*; offset repr. Tehran, 1349 Š./1970?, from the litho ed., Tehran, 1276/1859-60.

Abū Rayḥān Bīrūni, *Ketāb al-ṣaydana*, ed. with English tr. by Hakim Mohammad Said, Karachi, 1973. Karim Djavanshir, *Atlas of Woody Plants of Iran*, Tehran, 1976. Ebn Sīnā, *Qānūn dar ṭebb* II; Pers. tr. by ʿAbd-al-Raḥmān Šarafkandī, Tehran, 1362 Š./1983. M. J. Mashkour, *A Comparative Dictionary of Arabic, Persian and the Semitic Languages*, Tehran, 1978. Manṣūr Moḥammadī, *Barrasī-e manābeʿ-e ṭabīʿī-e tajdīd-šavanda-ye manṭaqa-ye Zāgros wa naḥwa-ye modīrīyat-e ān dar āyanda* (21 pp.; in the 1st vol. of a collection of mimeographed articles and reports, variously paged, presented at a seminar on the same general subject, held in Yāsūj in 1364 Š./1985). Ḥabīb-Allāh Ṯābetī, *Jangalhā, deraḵtān o deraḵtčahā-ye Īrān*, Tehran, 1976. Moḥammad-Mo'men Ḥosaynī Tonokābonī, *Toḥfat al-mo'menīn* [*Toḥfa-ye Ḥakīm Mo'men*], Tehran, 1360 Š./1981?

(H. Aʿlam)

BALYSA- (Khotan Saka), *bārza-* (Tumšuq Saka), a word adapted to Buddhist use for the transcendental Buddha. In pronunciation, *b* was bilabial *v* and *ys* was voiced sibilant *z*, for which Tumšuq Saka had a new sign *za*. The Tumšuq Saka, older *bārsa-* and later *bārza-*, has kept the older *rz*, replaced in Khotan Saka by *lys* /*lz*/.

The base alternates in ablaut *barz-*: *braz-*. In Old Persian *braz-* is represented by *brazmaniya* of which the precise meaning is not assured (see Aša). Outside Iranian, Old Indian has *brah-* alternating with *bṛh-* (with *h* from IE. *ĝh*) in the words *brahmán* (masc.), *bráhman-* (neut.), *brāhmaṇa-*, *bṛh-*, *bṛhas-pati-* with still unsettled meaning. The later Buddhist Sanskrit has *brahma-* in a good sense (as in *brahma-svara-* of the Buddha's voice) and the name of a supernatural being *mahā-brahmāṇa-*.

In Khotan Saka texts *balysa-* translates Buddhist Sanskrit *buddha-* (often *gyasta- balysa-* "*deva* Buddha" or *gyastānu gyasta- balysa-* "Buddha, *deva* of *devas*"), but *balysa-* also renders *brahman-*, *bhagavant-* "lord," *tathāgata*, *sarvajña-* "omniscient," epithets of the Buddha. The compound *balysa-bajāṣṣa-* translates *brahma-svara-* "the Buddha voice." To *balysa-* the adjectives are *balysāna-* and *balysūña-*. The abstract *balysūsti-* renders *bodhi-* "transcendental knowledge" and *sarvajña-tattva-* "the essence of all knowledge." The compound *balysūñavūysaa-* "seeker after bodhi" renders the Buddhist *bodhisattva*.

The religion of Khotan was therefore Barzaic (as Zoroastrian *mazdayazna-* was Mazdaic). The word *balysa-* was not an isolated relic from the Old Iranian Mazdaic religion. Other older Iranian religious terms were carried over into the Buddhist vocabulary of Khotan as well. Thus the Zoroastrian Avestan *spənta Ārmaitiš* was kept in the dialectal *śśandrāmatā-*, but equated with Buddhist *śrī-* "fortune" and the goddess Śrī. The world mountain Buddhist *Sumeru* is replaced by *ttaira haraysa* near to the Avestan *taēra-* "peak" and *harā bərəz* "lofty Harā," modern *Alborz*. The word *phārra-*, older *farnah-* (Av. *xᵛarnah-*, So. *prn-*), is used of the stages of the Buddhist religious career. (From Sogdian it was borrowed into Tokhara of Kuci as *perne*, rendering Buddhist Sanskrit *lakṣmī* "fortune.") Further *urmaysdān-*, nom. *urmaysde*, from older *ahura-mazdān-* is used for the sun. The old *daiva-* "demon" and *yazata-* "worshiped being" became *dyūva-* and *gyasta-* (Tumšuq *jezda-*) "god," with *balysa-* as title of the Buddha.

Bibliography: H. W. Bailey, *Khotanese Texts* VI, Cambridge, 1967, pp. 225-30, Idem, *Dictionary of Khotan Saka*, 1978, pp. 133, 272, 467.

(H. W. Bailey)

BĀLYŪZĪ, ḤASAN MOWAQQAR (b. Shiraz, 1908; d. London, 12 February 1980), Bahai author and administrator, the son of ʿAlī-Moḥammad Khan Mowaqqar-al-Dawla and member of the Afnān family (q.v.). He was educated at the American University, Beirut, and the London School of Economics. He founded with Mojtabā Mīnovī the Persian service of the British Broadcasting Corporation. Bālyūzī was elected member of the national Spiritual Assembly of the Bahais of Great Britain and Ireland, 1933-60, and chairman, 1942-60. Shoghi Effendi appointed him as one of the Hands of the Cause of God (Ayādī-e Amr Allāh, q.v.), 1957. He was elected as one of the Hands resident in Haifa, 1958-59. In the last twenty years of his life, when ill health prevented public activity, Bālyūzī concentrated on writing a number of histories of the Bahai faith, which have come to be regarded among the Bahais as standard works on the subject.

Bibliography: Principal works of Ḥ. M. Bālyūzī: *Bahā'u'llāh*, London, 1938. *A Guide to the Administrative Order of Baha'u'llah*, London, 1941. *Edward Granville Browne and the Bahā'ī Faith*, London, 1970. *ʿAbdu'l-Bahā, the Centre of the Covenant of Bahā'u'llāh*, London, 1971. *The Bāb, the Herald of the Day of Days*, Oxford, 1973. *Bahā'u'llah, the King of Glory*, Oxford, 1980. *Ḵhadijih Bagum, the Wife of the Bāb*, Oxford, 1981. *Eminent Baha'is in the Time of Baha'u'llah*, Oxford, 1985.

(M. Momen)

BAM (also written *bām*) "bass," the lowest-pitched string in music. The seventeenth-century dictionary *Borhān-e qāṭeʿ* states s.v. *bām* that "people also say *tār-e bām* (the low string), which is the thick string set in musical instruments." The New Persian word *bam* has been borrowed in Arabic as *bamm* and in Armenian as *bamb*. The contrary of *bam* is *zīr* (variant *zīl*) "treble."

The explanation given by the present writer (and offered by him for discussion several years ago) is that the two terms refer to the way in which the performer's fingers pluck the strings—from below for a high note and from above for a low note. NPers. *zīr* is derived from Mid. Pers. *az ēr* and OPers. **hača adari* "from below." NPers *bam* is from Mid. Pers. **apam* < OPers. **upama* "highest." Likewise in ancient Greek music *hē hypatē* (*chordē*) "the highest (string)" designated the lowest-pitched string, and conversely *hē neatē* or *netē* "the last" or "deepest" designated the highest-pitched string (W. Eilers, *Die vergleichend-semasiologische*

Methode in der Orientalistik, Abh. Mainzer Akad. Wiss., 1973, pp. 62f.).

There are grounds to suppose that *bam* keeps its original meaning of "high" or "highest" in many names of places in the southeast of Iran. The following list is taken from Razmārā, *Farhang* VIII and IX: Bam, Bampūr/Bambūr, Bambūyān, Bam-moḡān (see Eilers, *Das Volk der Makā*, *AMI* Ergänzungsband 10, Berlin, 1983, p. 114), Bamrūd, and, with *bam* as the suffix, Āhūbam, Dehnowbam, Salūbam. There are also some place-names with the lengthened form *bām*: Kalātabām, Bām-čenār, Bām(a)kān (in the province of Yazd). All are settlements or localities in mountainous country.

NPers. *bām* "roof" is generally thought to be derived from OPers. **pāna* "shelter," but the Mid. Pers. form *bān* "roof" (e.g., in the *Frahang ī Pahlavīk*) has initial *b* and could well be a variant of *bām* "high." Just as *bam* "lowest-pitched string" has the attested variant *bām*, so might OPers. **upama* have had a lengthened form **upāma* (cf. OInd. *katama* "which" and NPers. *kodām*). The form *bān* found in Pahlavi and some dialects might thus be a secondary offshoot of *bām*.

The word *bām* under discussion here must not be confused with *bām* "radiance" found in NPers. *bāmdād* "dawn, morning," in Mid. Pers. *bāmī* "glowing" (root *bhā*-), and in geographical names such as Bāmīān "belonging to radiant (Balḵ)" and the widespread mountain name Kūh-e Bāmū, which (like Kūh-e Ṣabā) means "mountain in the sunrise," i.e., in the east.

(W. Eilers)

BAM (in Arabic, Bamm), a town in southeastern Iran, located on the southwestern rim of the Dašt-e Lūt basin at an altitude of 1,100 m.

i. *History and modern town.*

ii. *Ruins of the old town.*

i. History and Modern Town

Bam is a large oasis that owes its existence to the runoff from the Jabal Bārez mountains; during the wet season rivers such as the Tahrūd, which traverses the town, provide enough flow to run the mills. However, since the dry season lasts most of the year, particularly important to the town's survival is its system of twenty-five *qanāt*s. Though Bam, at 1,100 m altitude, is generally considered *garmsīr* (hot region), it is known for a variety of *sardsīr* (cold region) produce.

The town may owe its name to the term "vahma" (prayer, glorification; W. Tomaschek, "Zur historischen Topographie von Persien II," Sb. Kaiserl. Akad. Wiss., Phil.-hist. Kl. 108, 1885, p. 585). Whatever the case, Bam, which appears for the first time in 9th/10th-century Arab geographies, was founded by the Sasanians during their settlement of Kermān and southeastern Iran. It seems to have been a walled stronghold in a region plagued by repeated incursions and banditry; Eṣṭaḵrī (p. 166) characterizes the citadel as impregnable. Aside from date farming, Bam's economy was chiefly based on cotton, which sustained a prosperous artisan class. Durable and prized cotton fabric, embroidered veils, cloaks, kerchiefs, and fine turbans were produced in Bam and exported to Khorasan, Mesopotamia, and even as far as Egypt (Ebn Ḥawqal, p. 223; cf. *Ḥodūd al-ʿālam*, tr. Minorsky, p. 125). In addition to its citadel, Bam also boasted three Friday mosques, two of which served the orthodox community, the other the small but well-off Kharijites. Moqaddasī (p. 465) mentions Bam's foul-tasting water and notes that *qanāt*s provided the principal supply. The accounts of Arab geographers are repeated more or less by subsequent authors (cf. *Nozhat al-qolūb*, ed. Le Strange, p. 72; tr. p. 139), and it is not until 1810, when Lieutenant Henry Pottinger (1789-1856) visited the town, that an original description of Bam appeared. During the entire intervening period, the town was a strategically important projection of Iranian power, serving first as an Il-khanid and later a Safavid outpost in Baluchistan.

In the 18th century, Bam's role as a frontier fortress became paramount. After being occupied by Afghans twice in 1719 and during the period 1721-30, Bam emerged as the forward Iranian position vis-à-vis the Ḡelzay tribe, which probably with Nāder Shah Afšār's authorization had established itself in neighboring Narmāšīr. The Shiʿite Ḡelzays seemed to have been on friendly terms with the Zands, for Loṭf-ʿAlī Khan Zand fled in their direction after the fall of Kermān (1794). In 1795, the governor of Bam captured Loṭf-ʿAlī Khan and turned him over to the founder of the Qajar dynasty, Āqā Moḥammad Khan, who, to commemorate his victory over the last of his Zand rivals, erected a pyramid of their skulls (still visible to Pottinger some nineteen years later, *Travels in Beloochistan and Sinde*, London, 1816, p. 202). The Ḡelzays were driven out from Narmāšīr in 1801 and replaced by Baluchi tribes, but the town was strongly fortified in 1810 and remained so during the first half of the 19th century due to the insecurity of the region.

Bam was occupied once again by Āqā Khan Maḥallātī (q.v.) during his 1840-41 insurrection and remained in an unsettled state until around 1855 (A. Gasteiger, *Von Teheran nach Beludschistan*, Innsbruck, 1881, p. 77). The restoration of peace allowed the town to grow beyond its walls, and a new settlement was founded along the river in enclosed gardens and date groves 1,000 m to the southwest.

Unfettered by walls and fear of invasion, Bam expanded rapidly at the end of the 19th and beginning of the 20th century. In 1881, though Bam lost its status as Baluchistan's governor's seat, the governor, who normally resided in Bampūr, preferred the milder summers there. Population estimates vary from E. Smith's eight to nine thousand (F. Goldsmid, *Eastern Persia: An Account of the Journey of the Persian Boundary Commission of 1870-72*, London, 1876, p. 244) to O. B. St John's two thousand families (ibid., p. 86) to Gasteiger's six thousand in 1881 (*Von Teheran*, p. 78). In 1895, P. M. Sykes estimated the population to be thirteen thousand (*Ten Thousand Miles in Persia*,

London, 1902, p. 217), and the same figure was cited by A. Gabriel in 1928 (*Im weltfernen Orient*, Munich, 1929, p. 195). Commercial activity also grew apace during this period; Bam's *bāzār*, considered "small and poor" by O. B. St John (Goldsmid, *Eastern Persia*, p. 85), "miserably small and insignificant" by E. Smith in 1872 (ibid., p. 196), and "little" by E. Sykes in 1895 (*Through Persia on a Sidesaddle*, 2nd ed., London, 1901, p. 195), seemed bustling to A. Gabriel in 1928 (*Im weltfernen Orient*, p. 195). The covered *bāzār* consisted of two distinct parts and of a separate Zoroastrian section occupied by some fifty Parsi merchants (according to the 1966 census, Bam had 156 Zoroastrian inhabitants). The site of felt hat (*kolāh*) and sandal (*mal(e)kī*) manufacturing, the *bāzār* also served as a central distribution point for the region's agricultural products and handicrafts. Henna, indigo, rice, and dates were exported to Kermān, and from Bam objects made by artisans in Yazd and Kermān reached the rest of Iranian Baluchistan.

Today Bam remains an important commercial hub and has an enhanced administrative role as the seat of its own *šahrestān*. As of 1973, the *bāzār* contained 576 commercial establishments, 105 itinerant merchants, and several small-scale building-material factories and produce-processing plants (primarily dates and citrus fruits). The overall population has grown from 15,737 in 1956, to 21,761 a decade later, and in 1976 reached 30,422, most of whom were engaged in agriculture. In contrast to Narmāšīr with its highly diversified agriculture, over the last quarter century Bam agriculture has come to be virtually dominated by date and citrus farming, the produce of which is marketed mainly in Tehran. In recent years, however, certain grains and alfalfa have been cultivated among the fruit trees, providing many yearly harvests of winter feed necessary for livestock (principally sheep and goats).

Bibliography: General: L. Lockhart, "Bam," in *EI²* I, p. 1008. H. Gaube, *Iranian Cities*, New York, 1979. Schwarz, *Iran* III, pp. 236-38. Le Strange, *Lands*, p. 312. 19th-century travelogues and descriptions other than those mentioned in the text: K. E. Abbott, "Geographical Notes Taken during a Journey in Persia in 1849 and 1859," *JRGS* 25, 1855, pp. 1-78, esp. pp. 42-43. F. Farmānfarmā, *Safar-nāma-ye Kermān wa Balūčestān*, ed. M. Neẓām Māfī, Tehran, 1342 Š./1963, pp. 6-8. G. Curzon, *Persia and the Persian Question*, London, 1892, II, p. 252-54. P. M. Sykes, *Ten Thousand Miles in Persia*, London, 1902, esp. pp. 216-18. Contemporary descriptions: E. Ehlers, "Die Stadt Bam und ihr Oasen-Umland," *Erdkunde*, 1975, pp. 38-52. Great Britain Naval Intelligence Geographical Handbook Series, *Persia*, Oxford, 1945, pp. 44, 106; pls. 8, 71, 73, 75, 76, 100. P. Fešārakī, *Ābādīhā-ye ḥawża-ye ābgīr-e lūt-e jonūbī*, Tehran, 2536 = 1356 Š./1978. Idem, "Les oasis des plaines de la région de Bam et du Narmachir," *Les Cahiers d'Outre-Mer*, 1976, pp. 70-101. *Āmār-nāma-ye ostān-e Kermān, 1356*, Tehran, 1359 Š./1980, pp. 3, 4, and passim. Razmārā, *Farhang* VIII, pp. 51-53.

(X. de Planhol)

ii. Ruins of the Old Town

The Citadel of Bam (*arg-e Bam*), the ruins of a once large settlement built on a hill at a maximum height of about 200 m and a radius of about 1.5 km was, until a century ago, the principal residence of the inhabitants of Bam. Surrounding the citadel was a deep moat which is partially intact. Inside the moat are the citadel's first wall and ramparts, behind which are the ruins of buildings that were evidently where the middle class and the citadel's guards made their homes. Next comes a second wall behind which were the homes of the aristocracy and the wealthy, and finally, protected by a third wall, on the highest point in the citadel, were the seat of government and the residences of its leaders.

Of the three walls and battlements, the third, which defends the citadel's highest point, has seen the least damage; it is also apparently the oldest part, for it is constructed of bricks that date back to the Sasanian era. Remains of the second round of walls can still be seen, especially its several gates. The outer walls have suffered the most damage because of the spillover of rain from the citadel's higher points and particularly because local farmers used the ancient earthworks as a source of fertilizer.

A building with four open corner rooms (*čahār faṣl*) stands at the highest point in the citadel, and next to it are the remains of a watchtower (this tower apparently once consisted of seven stories, three of which Fīrūz Mīrzā destroyed during the Qajar period [p. 8]). The tower was used to send signals with fire by night and smoke by day to the surrounding countryside, and thus came to be known as the "fire tower" (*ātaš-ḵāna*). The name may also be related to a fire temple and a place where a sacred flame was tended.

The *čahār faṣl* and the mosque adjoining it have been repaired several times, once some thirty years ago (Bāstānī, *Wādī-e Haftvād*). Surrounding this building are several caved-in ruins which presumably were a stable, a government storehouse, and the quarters of officials and those affiliated with the government.

At its midpoint, the width of the citadel's outer wall is fourteen *ḏar*ʿ, while its ramparts are ten *ḏar*ʿ wide; it is built from a hard clay which is so durable that, according to Eʿtemād-al-Salṭana (p. 293), "no matter how hard one struck it with a pick, from morning until night, not even one *ḏar*ʿ would be damaged."

The moat around the citadel was quite deep; when it was under siege, the defenders would feed water from the Abāreq river into it. Once. during the Saljuq period, the inhabitants of Bam brought water from as far away as twenty *farsang*s (ca. 120 km) to fill the moat, but this precipitated the ruin of the *rabaż* and the city wall (Ḵabīṣī, p. 103). The present city of Bam is located to the south of the citadel; apparently, its development took place during the last century when security provided by the a strong central government in Iran made the sanctuary of the citadel's thick walls unnecessary.

Local legend has it that the citadel of Bam was the capital of Haftvād of Kermān (q.v.). It is also said that Haftvād resided in Kermān's Qal'a-ye Doḵtar and built the present city of Kermān with the riches that he acquired because of the Kerm ("Worm"; S. M. Hāšemī, in *Našrīya-ye farhang-e Bam*, p. 53; Bāstānī Pārīzī, *Rāhnamā-ye āṯār-e tārīḵī-e Kermān*, p. 6). If Haftvād was indeed the citadel's founder, then the earliest record of it dates back to around A.D. 224. At that time Ardašīr Bābakān, by conquering Kermān, put an end to the rule of Haftvād, who was an historical figure whose minted coins are extant (Pīrnīā, p. 2680).

Above the citadel is a place still famous as "Kot-e Kerm"; Wazīrī (*Tārīḵ*, p. 263) refers to the gate of "Kot-e Kerm"; *Kot* in local parlance means "hole or refuge." Ḥamd-Allāh Mostawfī (*Nozhat al-qolūb*, p. 140) relates "Bam was the place where the Haftvād burst." Near Kot-e Kerm is a gate, through which one enters a second citadel.

The gates to the citadel were of course limited in number, consisting of the Kot-e Kerm, Šāhnešīn, Qūrḵāna, and Ḡolām-ḵāna gates, the names of which go back to Qajar times. Moqaddasī (p. 465) speaks of four gates: the Narmāsīr, which undoubtedly faced east; the Kūsakān; the Esbīkān, which probably faced the famous city Espehka of Baluchistan to the southeast; and the Kūrjīn. Unlike citadels in wetter regions, in which reservoirs were used to provide water, at Bam water was supplied by means of an underground channel known as a *šotorgalū*, for its curving course (Sayf-al-Dīnī, in *Našrīya-ye farhang-e Bam*, p. 35). There were also wells on the grounds of the citadel that could be tapped during emergencies. According to Wazīrī (*Joḡrāfīā*, p. 92), above the fort there was a well more than 200 *ḏar'* deep, which contained the most appetizing water. Quoting the now apparently lost *Bam-nāma* of Šams-al-Dīn Bamī, Wazīrī attributes the digging of the well to the prophet Solomon (*Tārīḵ*, p. 246). In an account contemporary with Wazīrī's E'temād-al-Salṭana, who devotes more scrutiny to the matter, wrote (p. 293) that the well was 40 *gaz* deep and that a second well, at a lower level, was 30 *ḏar'*, and a third was 27 *ḏar'*; water was brought up from these wells with buckets weighing 135 kg (45 *man-e tabrīzī*), which, though used a thousand times daily, would not show defect or wear. Sykes (p. 250) curiously puts the depth of the second well at only 54 m. More accurate than these sources are local reports that state that drinking water was extracted from these wells by means of a water wheel which supplied the needs of the citadel's inhabitants at a flow rate of two *sangs*. In 1258/1842, 'Abbāsqolī Khan Javānšīr reexcavated one of the wells that had silted up (Bāstānī Pārīzī, *Farmānfarmā-ye 'ālem*, p. 363).

Situated above the citadel was a windmill that ground grain for the populace; this mill continued to function until about a century ago (Wazīrī, *Joḡrāfīā*, p. 94). Owing to the region's perpetually strong north wind, the mill was always in operation. According to E'temād-al-Salṭana, the mill was last repaired in the time of Ebrāhīm Khan Sarhang As'ad-al-Salṭana by Moḥammad-Qāsem Khan Bamī. The millstones were about 10 *ḏar'* (ca. 3 m) in diameter and about 75 cm thick (*Mer'āt al-boldān*, p. 293).

The citadel contains a relatively small enclosure which was probably a monastic retreat or a school or a place where religious ceremonies were held (*takīa*). There is also a pavilion that housed a gymnasium (*zūrḵāna*) whose exercise pit was sunk 1.5 m below the surface of the fort. The Mīrzā Na'īm *takīa*, which may also have served as a religious school is located in the citadel next to a small mosque. This mosque, which is not the citadel's principal one, may have been built in Safavid times. The bathhouse, which also may be Safavid in origin, was located behind the citadel's large west tower; the remains of the bath's two reservoirs are still discernible. The *bāzār* is situated where the citadel's entry gate begins and at the end of an open space, in which, in addition to commercial sites, were places for religious ceremonies and public mourning. The dimensions of the shops and merchants' compartments (*ḥojras*) located at the beginning of the *bāzār* differ from those found at the end of it. In the center of the *bāzār* was an intersection (*čahār sūq*) in which the (*dārūḡa*) quarters of the police official and a bakery are discernible. The roof of the *bāzār* no longer exists.

The building of the citadel's mosque is attributed to 'Abd-Allāh b. 'Āmer, who captured Bam in 29/650. He reportedly blessed the mosque by placing in its sanctuary a piece of the tree under which the pladge at Ḥodaybīya had been made. According to Wazīrī (*Tārīḵ*, p. 280), the mosque, known as Masjed-e Ḥażrat-e Rasūl, still stood, in good shape, outside the citadel in 1291/1874. According to the *Bam-nāma* (in Wazīrī, loc. cit.), 'Abd-Allāh built a second mosque inside the town, using a donation by an old woman who had converted to Islam, but no trace of this mosque remained in Wazīrī's time. The *Ḥodūd al-'ālam* (ed. Sotūda, p. 128) states that there were three congregational mosques in Bam: one for the Kharijites, one for the Muslims, and the other within the walls. If the temple converted to a mosque was indeed that of Ebn 'Āmer, then that mosque must have been within the walls; however, if the mosque, which is known today as the Masjed-e Rasūl is meant, then it was outside the walls of the citadel. (See also *Survey of Persian Art* II, p. 930.)

A group of Kharijites, who were hounded out of Iraq by Ḥajjāj b. Yūsof Ṯaqafī, found refuge in the deserts around Kermān, especially in Bam and Jīroft. For years they resisted Ḥajjāj under the leadership of a certain Qaṭarī, who was killed around Jīroft in 75/694. The Kharijites remained in Bam, maintaining a mosque and practicing their rite, until Ya'qūb b. Layṯ Ṣaffār fought and defeated their leader Esmā'īl b. Mūsā in 254/868, when they were completely wiped out (Bāstānī Pārīzī, *Ya'qūb Layṯ*, p. 211). Around this time the citadel of Bam fell into the hands of Ya'qūb Layṯ, who was also in the process of subduing the Bārez and Qofṣ tribes and captured the Qofṣ chief, holding him hostage in the citadel (Afżal Kermānī, *'Eqd al-'olā*, p. 123). The citadel appears in the Saljuq-era sources when it was controlled by princes or such men of the first rank and viziers as

Abu'l-Mafāker Żīā'-al-Dīn (Afżal Kermānī, *Badāye'*, p. 41). One of the amirs who lived at the close of the Saljuq era in Kermān, Sābeq-al-Dīn (*'Eqd al-'olā*: Šāyeq-al-Dīn), was partly able to check an invasion of Ḡozz by holding the Bam citadel (Moḥammad b. Ebrāhīm, pp. 90ff.). He was the citadel keeper (*kūtvāl*) of Moḥammad Shah b. Bahrām Shah, the eleventh king of the Qāvordīān (Kabīṣī, p. 91).

The Qarākatā'īān (Qara Khitay) also strove continually to make Bam the stronghold in the east and southeast regions of their holdings. The citadel was also the focus of wars fought between Możaffar-al-Dīn Moḥammad Shah Qarākatā'ī and the Sīstānis, which were prolonged principally by the citadel's sturdiness (Monšī Kermānī, p. 82). Akī Šojā'-al-Dīn, an *'ayyār* (q.v.) and a *ṣo'lūk*, was able to hold out against Amir Moḥammad Możaffarī in the citadel. Finally in 743/1342, after Amir Moḥammad diverted a river into a channel aimed at the base of the walls and the ramparts of the citadel fell, Akī Šojā'-al-Dīn emerged with his sword and shroud draped about his neck (Wazīrī, *Tārīk*, p. 485; Kotobī, p. 34). At the end of his life Amir Moḥammad Możaffarī was arrested by his sons, blinded, and imprisoned in the citadels of Ṭabarak in Isfahan, Qal'a-ye Sang in Sīrjān, and finally of Bam, where he passed away in 765/1364. His body was carried to Meybod for burial (Wazīrī, *Tārīk*, pp. 485, 516).

During the time of Tīmūr's successors, Prince Abā Bakr ruled over Bam and became involved in hostilities with Sultan Oways Tīmūrī. Abā Bakr wished to rebuild the citadel's tower and ramparts; however, Sayyed Šams-al-Dīn Bamī, one of Bam's noted gnostics, persuaded him not to do so, as it would keep the people from their farms (*Maqāmāt*, p. 180). This caused Abā Bakr to be defeated by Sultan Oways, who, after his victory, ordered the citadel to be repaired. He then rounded up the survivors in the citadel and had his opponents killed; over the ruins of their homes within the walls, the victors planted barley (*Našrīya-ye farhang-e Kermān*, p. 42; Wazīrī, *Tārīk*, p. 568). Oways's repair of the citadel is mentioned in an inscription on the mosque dated 810/1407. E. Schröder (*Survey of Persian Art* II, pp. 943f.) believes this mosque to be Saffarid in origin; however, it seems more likely that it was built over the foundation of a fire temple. The citadel continued to serve as a center of resistance: Pīr Moḥammad, a rebellious Timurid amir, held the fort for many years (*Maqāmāt*, p. 124), ultimately yielding to the authority of Mīrzā Alvand Beg.

During the Safavid era, the citadel served as a staging area and headquarters for the army of Ganj-'Alī Khan, whose incursions into Baluchistan during the reign of Shah 'Abbās I form a full chapter in the history of Kermān (Bāstānī Pārīzī, *Ganj-'Alī Kān*, p. 42). During the time of Karīm Khan Zand, the citadel fell into the hands of Sīstānī and Owḡānī tribesmen; A'ẓam Khan Owḡānī and Moḥammad-Ḥosayn Khan Sīstānī with their many sons held sway over the fort and the eastern territories for a long period. The ruler of Kermān's attempt to oust them at Dīvār-e Boland came to naught (Bāstānī Pārīzī, *Wādī-e Haftvād*, p. 171). When Āqā Moḥammad Khan Qājār conquered Kermān, Loṭf-'Alī Khan Zand made it to Bam, where the Sīstānis allowed him to stay outside the walls of the citadel. They finally turned him over to Āqā Moḥammad Khan, thus temporarily strengthening their position in Bam (Bāstānī Pārīzī, *Āsīā-ye haft sang*, p. 220).

The English traveler Pottinger, who passed through Bam during the time of Fatḥ-'Alī Shah (ca. 1231/1816) on his way to India, visited the citadel, which he describes in some detail.

During the reign of Moḥammad Shah, Āqā Khan Maḥallātī's (q.v.) taking refuge in the citadel and his familial ties with the Sīstāni rulers of Bam caused Fīrūz Mīrzā to lead an army there and besiege the citadel. After resisting the attackers for a time, Āqā Khan surrendered and emerged from the citadel with a Koran and his sword draped around his neck and was sent to Tehran (1254/1838; Aḥmadī, p. 77). Several years later Āqā Khan revolted once more and went to Kermān and Bam. Driven from Bam by Fażl-'Alī Khan Qarabāḡī and Amir Ḥabīb-Allāh Khan Tūpkāna, he escaped to India. From that time it was forbidden to reside in the citadel, which was converted into a garrison (Bāstānī Pārīzī, *Farmānfarmā-ye 'ālem*, p. 315). Wazīrī, who visited the citadel a year later wrote, "now but for two platoons of soldiers, an officer, a few cannoneers, two artillery pieces with their attendants, and about fifty cavalry whom the provincial government of Kermān has ordered to protect it, the citadel is deserted" (*Jofrāfīā*, p. 94). Fīrūz Mīrzā Noṣrat-al-Dawla, who revisited Bam forty years after his first incursion, wrote in his travel diary (*Safar-nāma*, p. 7), "the fort's garrison, arsenal, and armory are still in place; however, the city [i.e., the citadel's settlement] is completely destroyed . . . the engineering aspects of the citadel are astonishing . . . the walls are wide enough to accommodate two artillery pieces. It has a considerable moat. The city walls have been built on a height which even at a gallop is not easily climbed." Immediately after the defeat of Āqā Khan in 1259/1843, minor repairs were made on the fort by 'Abbāsqolī Khan Kord Jehān-Bīglū (Hedāyat, X, p. 273).

Percy Sykes, the British officer who was successful in forming the South Persia Rifles Brigade in southern Iran, visited Bam in 1320/1902. At the time the city had but 13,000 people, two gates, and a *bāzār* 600 *ḏar'* long.

In recent years (1337 Š./1958), the National Monument Council of Iran (Anjoman-e Āṯār-e Mellī) instituted repairs on the citadel's pavilion (*Rūz-nāma-ye Haftvād* 90, 1337 Š./1958). The entire citadel was placed on the historical monuments list and was protected from further destruction. Throughout its history, the citadel was protected by the collective efforts of the people of every class; each person who had a residence and property outside of the fort was also required to maintain his own special room within the walls. Both before and after wars, villagers and city folk always undertook the repair and reconstruction of the citadel;

farmers, laborers, and builders would come from all around and work on the structure. During times of siege, the inhabitants of the town would repair to their rooms within the walls, bearing their precious possessions, and bolt the doors. Until recently, it was proverbial among the people of Kermān that one did not give his daughter in marriage to someone who did not have a room within the citadel.

Bibliography: Afżal Kermānī, *ʿEqd al-ʿolā le'l-mawqaf al-aʿlā*, ed. ʿA.-M. ʿĀmerī, 2nd ed., 1356 Š./1977. Idem, *Badāyeʿ al-zamān fī waqāʾeʿ Kermān*, ed. M. Bayānī, Tehran, 1326 Š./1947. Shaikh Yaḥyā Aḥmadī, *Farmāndehān-e Kermān*, ed. M.-E. Bāstānī Pārīzī, 2nd ed., Tehran, 1354 Š./1975. M.-E. Bāstānī Pārīzī, *Āsīā-ye haft sang*, 5th ed., Tehran, 1364 Š./1985. Idem, *Aždahā-ye haft sar*, 2nd ed., Tehran, 1363 Š./1984. Idem, *Farmānfarmā-ye ʿālam*, Tehran, 1364 Š./1985. Idem, *Ganj-ʿAlī Ḵān*, 2nd ed., Tehran, 1362 Š./1983. Idem, in *Našrīya-ye Farhang-e Bam*, 1335 Š./1956; 1337 Š./1958. Idem, *Rāhnamā-ye āṯār-e tārīḵī-e Kermān*, n.p., 1335 Š./1956. Idem, *Wādī-e Haftvād*, Tehran, 1355 Š./1976. Idem, *Yaʿqūb-e Layṯ*, 3rd ed., Tehran, 1363 Š./1984. M. Ḥ. Eʿtemād-al-Salṭana, *Merʾāt al-boldān*, Tehran, 1294/1877. Fīrūz Mīrzā, *Safar-nāma*, ed. M. Neẓām Māfī, Tehran, 1342 Š./1963. Reżāqolī Khan Hedāyat, *Rawżat al-ṣafā-ye nāṣerī*, Tehran, 1339 Š./1960. M.-E. Ḵabīṣī, *Saljūqīān wa Ḡozz dar Kermān*, ed. M.-E. Bāstānī Pārīzī, Tehran, 1343 Š./1964. Maḥmūd Kotobī, *Tārīḵ-e Āl-e Moẓaffar*, ed. ʿA.-Ḥ. Navāʾī, Tehran, 1335 Š./1956. Moḥammad b. Ebrāhīm (?), in Houtsma, *Recueil*. Nāṣer-al-Dīn Monšī Kermānī, *Semṭ al-ʿolā le'l-hażrat al-ʿolyā*, ed. ʿA. Eqbāl Āštīānī, Tehran, 1328 Š./1949. Ḥ. Nūrbaḵš et al., *Arg-e Bam*, Tehran, 1355 Š./1974. Ḥ Pīrnīā, *Īrān-e bāstān*, n.p., 1313 Š./1934. H. Pottinger, *Travels in Baloochistan and Sinde*, London, 1816. *Maqāmāt-e Ṭāher-al-Dīn Moḥammad wa Šams-al-Dīn Ebrāhīm*, ed. J. Aubin, in *FIZ* 2, 1333 Š./1954. *Rūz-nāma-ye Haftvad*, 1337 Š./1958. P. M. Sykes, *Ten Thousand Miles in Persia or Eight Years in Iran*, London, 1902. A. ʿA. Ḵ. Wazīrī, *Jog̲rāfīā-ye Kermān*, ed. M.-E. Bāstānī Pārīzī, 2nd ed., Tehran, 1353 Š./1974. Idem, *Tārīḵ-e Kermān*, 3rd ed. [Tehran], 1364 Š./1985. See especially H. Gaube, *Iranian Cities*, New York, 1979, pp. 99-132 (richly illustrated; references to Western sources).

(M.-E. Bāstānī Pārīzī)

BĀMDĀD, a weekly Persian newspaper published in Tehran from Šawwāl, 1325/November, 1907, by Anjoman-e Etteḥādīya-ye Markazī-e Aṣnāf (Council of the central league of guilds). It was edited by Ḡolām-ʿAlī Khan Qājār Qezel Ayāḡ (later editor of the newspaper *Ṣerāṭ al-ṣanāyeʿ*); however, its manager and principal columnist was the noted reformist, constitutionalist politician and Majles deputy Mīrzā Yaḥyā Dawlatābādī (1863-1938; q.v.), who signed his articles "Yaḥyā al-Ḥosaynī." *Bāmdād* was published concurrently with another guild publication, *Anjoman-e aṣnāf*, in which Mīrzā Yaḥyā held similar responsibilities (Ṣadr Hāšemī, *Jarāʾed o majallāt* II, p. 5). *Bāmdād* showed a liberal bent and professed to have set the awakening of all Iranians, particularly guild members, as its goal. It contained four three-column pages measuring 28.5 × 41 cm; a yearly subscription cost one toman in Iran and five French francs abroad.

Bibliography: Browne, *Press and Poetry*, p. 54. M. Solṭānī, *Fehrest-e rūz-nāmahā-ye fārsī dar majmūʿa-ye Ketāb-ḵāna-ye Markazī wa Markaz-e Asnād-e Dānešgāh-e Tehrān* I, Tehran, 1354 Š./1975, pp. 27-28. U. Sims-Williams, *Union Catalogue of Persian Serials and Newspapers in British Libraries*, London, 1985, p. 20.

(N. Parvīn)

BĀMDĀD, MAHDĪ (d. 1352 Š./1973), the son of Rafīʿ Ḵorāsānī (titled Rafīʿ-al-Mamālek). Bāmdād made a career in the civil service and was one of the assistants to the prime minister in the cabinet of Ḥakīm-al-Molk from Ābān to Bahman, 1324 Š./October, 1945-February, 1946, but is best known as the author of *Šarḥ-e ḥāl-e rejāl-e Īrān dar qorūn-e 12 wa 13 wa 14 hejrī* (Biographies of [notable] personages of Iran in the 12th, 13th, and 14th/18th, 19th, and 20th centuries), Tehran, 6 vols., 1347-51 Š./1968-72 (see below). His only other published work is the *Āṯār-e tārīḵī-e Kalāt o Saraḵs* (Historical monuments of Kalāt and Saraḵs), a lecture delivered on 2 Ābān 1333 Š./24 October 1954 to the Anjoman-e Āṯār-e Mellī-e Īrān (q.v.) and published that year by the society (publication no. 30) in Tehran and again in 1344 Š./1965. In the introduction to that work, Bāmdād explains that in 1332 Š./1953, he spent several months traveling in eastern Iran, Afghanistan, and Pakistan for the purpose of observing communities in those areas and comparing toponyms that appear in classical geographies and the *Šāh-nāma* with their modern forms. During his travels in the north of Khorasan, he examined the archeological remains of Kalāt and Saraḵs and made notes on them. According to the introduction to his *Rejāl*, Bāmdād also wrote *Ḵāṭerāt-e man* (My memoirs), *Čehel sāl kārmand-e dawlat* (Forty years as a civil servant), and *Sīāḥat-e 23 mamlakat yā safar-nāma-ye Orūpā wa Efrīqā* (Travels to twenty-three countries or a travelogue of Europe and Africa), but these works were never published.

Bāmdād's *Rejāl*, originally planned to cover ten volumes, was published with many illustrations during the years 1347-51 Š./1968-72 in Tehran, volumes five and six being independent supplements to the previous four. The work is based on a variety of sources; however, not all sources available to him were exhausted nor was the information found in the ones he did consult critically examined. Among the principal sources for many of the biographies of the statesmen, politicians, litterateurs, and cultural and religious figures found in the work are Maʿṣūm-ʿAlīšāh's *Ṭarāyeq al-ḥaqāyeq*, Ḥasan Fasāʾī's *Fārs-nāma-ye nāṣerī*, Modarres's *Rayḥānat al-adab*, Eʿtemād al-Salṭana's *Rūz-nāma-ye ḵāṭerāt* (his main source of information) and *al-Maʾāṯer wa'l-āṯār*, Sepehr's *Nāsek̲ al-tawārīk̲*, *Nāma-ye dāneš-varān*, Mo'allem Ḥabībābādī's *Makārem al-āṯār*, and the newspapers *Šaraf* and *Šarāfat*. He also used works by European authors, particularly E. G. Browne, G. N. Curzon, and Count de Gobineau.

Though Bāmdād's work is the most complete biographical survey of the last two and a half centuries currently available, nevertheless it suffers from serious omissions, both as regards certain periods and certain social groups. The *Rejāl* does not include figures from the Nāder Shah and Zand periods and relatively few from the Qajar period outside of Nāṣer-al-Dīn Shah's reign. The chief reason for these omissions is that Bāmdād's principal source, the *Rūz-nāma-ye k̲āṭerāt*, is the diary of Moḥammad-Ḥasan Khan E'temād-al-Salṭana, the director of government publications under Nāṣer-al-Dīn Shah, which covers only the years 1292-1313/1875-96. The contents of *Rejāl* have to some extent been skewed by its author's exaggerated reliance on the *Rūz-nāma*: he sometimes treats figures outside of the realms of government, letters, and learning as well as tangential issues merely because they are mentioned in the diary for one reason or another (e.g., Esmā'īl Khan Jalāyer [VI, p. 41], Moḥammad-Taqī [VI, p. 21], Akbar Mīrzā [VI, p. 44], 'Alī-Akbar Šowharī [V, p. 159], and Moḥammadqolī Khan [V, p. 257]), while the biography of an important figure like Moḥammad Moṣaddeq is missing. Social groups, such as women, scholars, poets, and mystics of the period apparently held little interest for Bāmdād. His work is devoted to men (*rejāl*), and such important women as Qorrat-al-'Ayn (I, p. 204), Fak̲r-al-Dawla (III, p. 199), and Amīna Aqdas (III, p. 317) are only marginally mentioned, while many others, such as Parvīn E'teṣāmī and Qamr-al-Molūk Wazīrī (qq.v.), were completely ignored. Among male authors and poets the biography of Mīrzā Abu'l-Ḥasan Khan Ṭabīb is treated in one page (VI, p. 8), without mentioning his works, and in the biography of Mīrzā Moḥammad-'Alī Naqīb-al-Mamālek there is no reference to his *Amīr Arslān Rūmī* (q.v.), the most widely read Persian story of the last part of the Qajar period. Most men of learning are not mentioned at all, only a few receive brief notices, e.g., Forṣat Šīrāzī, Moḥammad Qazvīnī, 'Abbās Eqbāl Āštīānī (whose works Bāmdād made liberal use of without quoting his source, cf. Eqbāl's biography of Yaḥyā Khan Mošīr-al-Dawla in *Yādgār* 1/3 with *Rejāl* IV, p. 441), and Moḥammad Mo'īn (III, p. 237, IV, pp. 15, 203, V, p. 131). Bāmdād demonstrates that he had no ear or liking for poetry (VI, p. 12) by quoting fourteen lines of insipid poetry by Moḥammad-Nabī Khan (V, pp. 271-72) and six pages of the poetry of Ḥājj Sayyed Naṣr-Allāh Taqawī (III, p. 118), while not a single line from the poetry of the poet laureate Maḥmūd Khan is quoted in his biography (V, p. 282).

Though Bāmdād's professed aim was to "present figures in a realistic manner" (I, p. 1) his work is far from being objective and to the point. He frequently criticizes the political figures he writes about but his criticism is rarely concerned with their roles in society, most often it is directed at their moral acts and intentions and their private lives (e.g., their addiction to opium, drink, or gambling). He strongly disliked demagogues and "religious charlatans" and opposed the clerical class and reciters of passions (*rawża-k̲ᵛān*; V, p. 297, VI, pp. 18, 20). His lack of complete objectivity is also seen in such generalizations as "since he was a poet and a man of this country, he used everything" (V, p. 141) or "all in all, Īraj Mīrzā's character was like that of the rest of the poets of his era" (I, p. 175), and occasionally falls prey to emotionalism, e.g., on the *ṣandūq-e 'adālat* (II, p. 440), and in the biography of Mīrzā Āqā Khan Nūrī (IV, pp. 370f.), during which (pp. 371-72) he quotes two pages on cholera from the travelogue of Count de Gobineau. Occasionally his criticism seems to have been partially prompted by personal vendettas, as in the case of Badī'-al-Zamān Forūzānfar (V, p. 37) and 'Alī-Akbar Bāṣer-al-Salṭana (V, p. 161).

Bāmdād saw the hand of non-Iranians (especially the Russians and the British) behind events in Iran. He states that most of the prime ministers and viziers of the Qajar and Constitutional periods came to power with the help of foreign embassies (IV, p. 368), that all of Iran's leaders were cut from the same cloth (V, p. 128), that one could not find a court physician who was not in league with or the agent of foreigners (III, p. 278), that the factions and religions found in Iran were all created by outsiders (III, p. 18) and, finally, that the bombardment of the Majles in 1326/1908 by Moḥammad-'Alī Shah was only a facade (III, p. 6) and that after his fall a governing body was formed by "those invisible hands" (*az mā behtarān*) for Iranians (VI, p. 293).

A major shortcoming of *Rejāl* is its lack of proportion in the length of the biographies. Four pages are devoted to the life of Nāṣer-al-Dīn Shah's illiterate saddle master (III, p. 415) and even more to that of a fugitive thief (III, p. 163), while such significant figures in the political and the cultural history of Iran as Āk̲ūnd Mollā Moḥammad-Kāẓem K̲orāsānī (q.v.; I, p. 4), Sayyed Kāẓem Raštī (III, p. 137), and Sayyed Moḥammad Ṭabāṭabā'ī (III, p. 279), were treated in less than a page or even just a few lines. Bāmdād's exaggerated reliance on E'temād-al-Salṭana's *Rūz-nāma-ye k̲āṭerāt* caused him to include in the *Rejāl* many details of little or no significance or relevance that E'temād-al-Salṭana had jotted down as personal notes about courtiers and his acquaintances, thus sometimes resulting in lengthy, tedious, and even incoherent articles (e.g., III, pp. 20ff., IV, pp. 246ff.).

Negligence in giving the date of birth and often even the date of death of his contemporaries (e.g., Moḥammad-'Alī Khan Dargāhī [II, p. 242], Naẓar-'Alī Khan Lor [VI, p. 283], 'Alī-Akbar Dāvar [II, p. 427], and 'Alī Sohaylī [II, p. 380]) and lack of or incomplete references to his sources, whether quoted or not (e.g., V, p. 244), somewhat detract from the usefulness of the work; moreover occasional mis-information and errors (e.g., see BAK̲TĪĀRĪ, 'ALĪQOLĪ KHAN SARDĀR AS'AD) requires it to be used with great caution. Numerous technical shortcomings bespeak a rushed publication that left no time for the author to reread and edit his work, e.g., repetition of biographies in III, p. 125 and V, p. 178, and in IV, p. 15 and VI, p. 282; flawed sentences, e.g., I, p. 3; ambiguous wording (e.g., in V, p. 178, it is unclear whether Mīrzā Qāsem Khan was the minister of construction or his father Mīrzā Ḥasan Khan or Mīrzā Asad-Allāh Khan; see also I, p. 3), and lapses in the recording of dates (e.g., "altogether ʿAbd-al-Bahā"'s travels were from Ramażān, 1327 [. . .] to Moḥarram, 1332 [. . .] two years, three months, and some odd days" (II, pp. 202).

The biographies are listed by first names, e.g., the biography of Mīrzā Āqā Khan Nūrī appears under Naṣr-Allāh. The indexes at the end of each volume are unfortunately incomplete.

Despite these numerous shortcomings, Bāmdād's work is important as a pioneering effort for compiling a national biography of Iran and especially for the photographs that it contains (esp. vols. V and VI).

Bibliography: For a critical review of the *Rejāl* see Ḥ. Maḥbūbī Ardakānī, *Rāh-namā-ye ketāb* 12/7-8, 1348 Š./1969, pp. 538-43; 13/10-12, 1349 Š./1971, pp. 771-78.

(ʿA.-A. SAʿĪDĪ SĪRJĀNĪ)

BĀMBIŠN. See BĀNBIŠN.

BĀMDĀD-E ROWŠAN, a Persian journal of news and political comment published in Tehran from 16 Rabīʿ I 1339/1 February 1915 until 2 Ramażān 1341/19 April 1924. The journal was edited by the poet and reformer Mīrzā Moḥammad-ʿAlī Khan Ḵorāsānī, later Bāmdād (1885-1951; Ṣadr Hāšemī, *Jarāʾed o majallāt* II, pp. 5-6). Mīrzā Moḥammad, a Constitutional movement activist and political agitator in Khorasan, Tehran, and Maḥāl(l)-e Baḵtīārī, who later changed his family name to Bāmdād, survived a death sentence to become a member of the sixth session of the Majles and one of the founders of the Ḥezb-e Īrān (Bāmdād, *Rejāl* III, pp. 420-22). The editorship of the journal was entrusted to Āqā Mīrzā Ḥosayn Qazvīnī in 1301 Š./1922 (ibid., p. 6). *Bāmdād-e rowšan* championed the cause of Islamic unity and an independent Iran, and was suppressed in 1919 for, among other reasons, its opposition to the foreign policy of Prime Minister Mīrzā Ḥasan Woṯūq-al-Dawla. During World War I, it favored Germany and Turkey. *Bāmdād-e rowšan* was a four-page, five-column paper measuring 43 x 59 cm; a yearly subscription cost fifty *qerān*s in Tehran, fifty-five elsewhere in Iran, and eighty abroad. Series of *Bāmdād-e rowšan* are kept in major libraries of Iran and the Cambridge University Library.

Bibliography: M. Bāmdād, *Adab čīst wa adīb kīst?*, Tehran, 1343 Š./1964. U. Sims-Williams, *Union Catalogue of Persian Serials and Newspapers in British Libraries*, London, 1985, p. 20. M. Solṭānī, *Fehrest-e rūz-nāmahā-ye fārsī dar majmūʿa-ye Ketāb-ḵāna-ye Markazī wa Markaz-e Asnād-e Dānešgāh-e Tehrān* I, Tehran, 1354 Š./1975, p. 28. *Fehrest-e rūz-nāmahā-ye mawjūd dar Ketāb-ḵāna-ye Mellī-e Īrān*, Tehran, 2536 = 1356 Š./1977, p. 55. R. Mach and R. D. McChesney, *A List of Persian Serials in the Princeton University Library*, Princeton, 1971.

(N. PARVĪN)

BĀMĪA (or Bāmīā), okra, the edible unripe seed-pods of *hibiscus esculentus* of the genus *Malvaceae* or mallows.

i. *The plant.*
ii. *In cooking.*
iii. *The sweet.*

i. THE PLANT

A native of Africa, okra has long been naturalized and extensively cultivated in some countries neighboring Iran, especially in Turkey, Iraq, and the Indian subcontinent; but, as stated by J. L. Schlimmer, *Terminologie*, p. 7, it was introduced into the culinary art of Persians by Arabs from Baghdad in the 19th century. The mucilaginous, bland okra pods do not seem to have ever been very popular in Iran; the same author, writing in A.D. 1874, ibid., already points out this relative unpopularity, saying that "the fruits of *Abelmoschus esculenta* [*sic*; i.e., *A. esculentus* = *Hibiscus esculentus*] are sought for as a vegetable only by [resident] Europeans and by Arabs settled in Persia." Even nowadays it is grown and eaten mostly in Iranian Azerbaijan (both East and West) and in Kurdistan, although its cultivation has been extended in recent times to other regions such as Isfahan and Mašhad.

In Afghanistan, it grows precociously in abundance in warm regions such as Qandahār and Nangrahār.

The earliest, and unique, mention of okra as a medicinal vegetable in Arabic sources on materia medica in the Islamic era is found in Ebn al-Bayṭār (d. 646/1248), I, p. 81, who quotes his teacher the Sevillian botanist Abu'l-ʿAbbās Aḥmad surnamed Ebn al-Rūmīya (561-637/1165-1239) as having written, in addition to a description of the whole plant: "*Bāmīa* is [found] in Egypt [. . .] and Egyptians eat it with meat, that is, the capsules of the fruits while they are tender [. . .]." As to its pharmacological properties, Ebn al-Bayṭār quotes "somebody else": "By nature it is 'cold' and 'moist',—the 'moistest' of all vegetables. The blood produced from it is bad. It is of little nutritive value. It is said to agree with people with a hot temperament. Its harmful effects are averted if it be eaten with a lot of hot spices." Ebn al-Bayṭār's quotations first reappeared (in translation) in Persian medico-pharmacological works in ʿAqīlī Ḵorāsānī's *Maḵzan al-adwīa*, p. 107, compiled in 1183/1769-70, and thence down to modern works in Persian, e.g., A. Nafīsī, *Ḵawāṣṣ-e ḵʷordanīhā*, pp. 165-66.

Bibliography: Moḥammad-Ḥosayn ʿAqīlī Ḵorāsānī, *Maḵzan al-adwīa*, offset reprint, Tehran, 1349 Š./1970?, from the lithographic ed., Tehran, 1276/1859-60. *Dāʾerat al-maʿāref-e Āriānā*, Kabul, 1328-Š./1949-. Ebn al-Bayṭār, *al-Jāmeʿ le mofradāt al-adwīa wa'l-aḡḏīa*, 4 vols., Bulaq, 1291/1874. Abū Torāb Nafīsī, *Ḵawāṣṣ-e ḵʷordanīhā o āšāmīdanīhā ṭayy-e qorūn o aʿṣār*..., Isfahan, 1362 Š./1983. J. L. Schlimmer, *Terminologie médico-pharmaceutique et anthropologique française-persane*..., Tehran, 1874. Moḥammad Ṭabāṭabāʾī, *Applied Botany for Agriculture and Natural Resources* I: *Plants for Extensive Cultivation* (in Persian; mimeographed text now in press).

(H. Aʿlam)

ii. In Cooking

The unripe fruit of *bāmīa*, which has a large amount of mucilage, is used in preparing certain dishes, including stews and casseroles. The fruit, or pod (12-15 cm long), is dark green, conical, tapered at one end, and contains numerous dark-colored seeds. Among Persian dishes that utilize *bāmīa*, are the following: *ḵʷorāk-e bāmīa bā morḡ* (okra with chicken), *ḵʷorāk-e bāmīa bā qeyma* (okra with ground beef), *ḵʷorāk-e bāmīa bā gūšt* (okra and lamb casserole), and *ḵʷorešt-e bāmīa* (stewed lamb with okra). In preparing these dishes, the *bāmīa* is always first soaked in vinegar and salt water.

Bibliography: N. Ramazani, *Persian Cooking*, Charlottesville, Virginia, 1982, pp. 153-54, 171, 180-81. G. Watt, *A Dictionary of the Economic Products of India*, London, 1889-1906, vol. 4.

(N. Ramazani)

iii. The Sweet

Bāmīa is a sweet, sticky confection made with a deep-fried dough shaped like finger-length buns, coated with a treacly syrup, often dyed pink or gold. As with most Iranian confections it is served principally between meals, with afternoon tea, or any time of the day when visitors might drop in. In addition, it is strongly associated with Ramażān, the Muslim month of fasting, when there is a great deal of visiting among relatives, and when special sweetmeats are served at *efṭār*, the breaking of the daily fast at sundown. Traditionally, sweet delicacies are served at this time, before the evening meal, providing a quick surge of energy, a much-needed lift at the end of a day of alimentary abstinence.

A less well-known variety of *bāmīa* is *bāmīa-ye pīčī*, dark in color, very thin, and shaped like a conical spiral coil. It is usually sold in street-corner stalls in provincial towns or in the poorer sections of big cities. A popular game among children is to vie with each other to lift and uncoil as large a piece of the brittle confection as possible before it breaks, the broken piece of *bāmīa* being the reward.

Bāmīa is not usually prepared at home. However, a recipe for doing so may be found in N. Ramazani, *Persian Cooking*, Charlottesville, Virginia, 1982, pp. 231-32.

(N. Ramazani)

BĀMĪĀN, town in central Afghanistan, important prehistoric and Buddhist site.

i. *The Bāmīān basin.*
ii. *History and monuments.*
iii. *Modern town and district.*
iv. *Modern province.*

i. The Bāmīān Basin

The town of Bāmīān owes its rise to the presence of a tectonic depression, the Bāmīān basin, in the central highlands of Afghanistan and to the facilities for communication which this provides. The basin, 50 km long and at the most 15 km wide, has a roughly west-east trend and is flanked on the north by the Kūh-e Sang-e Časpān (4,400 m), the westernmost extension of the Hindu Kush, on the south by the Kūh-e Bābā (5,135 m). It is one of a number of intramontane basins aligned along a major tectonic fracture (the Herat fault). The Ḡūrband basin to the east and Yakāōlang basin to the west are continuations of the same depression.

Sedimentation of the Bāmīān basin began early in the Cenozoic era (mid-Eocene "Dokani formation" of lacustrine limestones, on average 50 m thick). The basin was derived from the post-Cretaceous erosion surface to which belong the highest parts of central Afghanistan. In the main, the basin is filled with Oligocene sediments ("Zohāk formation" of sandstones and conglomerates 1,000 m thick, followed by the fluvio-eolian "Buddhas formation" 70 m thick and the concomitant "Qalʿaja formation" of volcanic and sedimentary material) and with miocene sediments stripped from the adjacent mountain ranges ("Ḡolḡola formation" of fluvio-paludal conglomerates and limestones). Compression in the Ponto-Pliocene period has left traces, mainly in the east of the basin, in the form of extrusions of the pre-Cenozoic basement marked off by "piano-key" faults. The whole basin was later reshaped, in the Quaternary era, into a series of levels carved in the Cenozoic formations. The highest levels are piedmont glacis formed by erosion during climatic oscillations which facilitated lateral "planation." The lowest levels are solely alluvial terraces of climatic origin formed in phases of ice-cap expansion on the surrounding mountains.

The Bāmīān basin is thus a morphologically and structurally complex unit. Its altitude ranges from 2,500 m to 3,000 m. The alluvial bottom (called the Tagāō) is no more than a narrow strip with a length of some 20 km and a width which varies between 1 km and 2 km. Since the upthrust of the Kūh-e Bābā was greater and probably took longer than that of the Hindu Kush, while the line of greatest subsidence gradually shifted northward, the basin is remarkably unsymmetrical in its morphology and structure, having a long slope on the south side and a much shorter slope on the north (Hindu Kush) side. The present river system is similarly unsymmetrical, with longer and more copious streams on the south side because the north-facing slope of the Kūh-e Bābā is better watered than the south-facing slope of the Hindu Kush.

As for the climate, the bottom of the basin appears (from observations taken over three years only) to have a régime of the continental high-altitude type, with severe winters (January average -5.6°C, July average 17.4°C) and semi-arid characteristics (annual average precipitation, 148 mm; maximum in one year, 194 mm, minimum 88 mm; rainiest season, spring). Dry farming is pursued on the mountain sides but is not feasible in the bottom of the basin, where irrigation is essential for plant and crop growth (wheat, alfalfa, potatoes, also some apricot and apple orchards, poplar and willow plantations, etc.).

The rise of a town in this harsh environment was not due to agricultural prosperity but resulted from the value of the communication facilities. Bāmīān is a key point for control of the roads and passes through the Afghan mountains linking Bactria to the Kabul basin and northwestern India. To the east, the Šebar pass (2,985 m) gives easy access to the Ḡūrband troughs which lead to the Panjšīr valley and the northern part of the Kabul basin. To the north, the Bāmīān basin is drained by the Sorḵāb (upper course of the Kondūz river), but its narrow gorges do not provide easy passage. The traditional and always busiest road takes a more easterly route through valleys of transverse tributaries of the Sorḵāb and then over the Āq Rebāṭ, Dandānšekan, and Qara Kotal passes (3,100, 2,7000, and 2,850 m), after which the old road follows the upper valley of the Balḵ river while the modern road follows the Ḵolm river by way of Haybak (in Samangān province). The traditional Šebar pass road was made fit for automobiles in the 1920s and continued to be the busiest route over the Hindu Kush until the construction of the Sālang tunnel in 1964 shifted the traffic to a route usable in winter. Bāmīān's position midway between Bactria and Peshawar at the approach to the most difficult passes and the resultant opportunities to purvey provisions and accommodation for caravans explain why it became a particularly important stopping place and a chosen site for monumental religious sanctuaries. In recent times several other routes beside the ancient highway have come into use, making Bāmīān a regional road hub. To the southeast, a shorter route to Kabul is provided by a new road over the Ḥājīgak and Onay passes (3,700 m and 3,350 m), with a steep descent between them into the upper Helmand (Hīrmand) valley (traditionally avoided by caravans). To the west, a road of purely local importance gives access to the Yakāōlang basin, whence there is a link to the motorable direct road through the central mountains and the upper Harīrūd valley to Herat.

Bibliography: J. Lang and J. Pias, "Morphogénèse dunaire et pédogénèse dans le bassin intramontagneux de Bamian (Afghanistan)," *Revue de géographie physique et de géologie dynamique*, 1971, pp. 359-68. J. Lang, "Bassins intramontagneux néogènes de l'Afghanistan central," ibid., 1972, pp. 415-25. V. Balland and J. Lang, "Les rapports géomorphologiques quaternaires et actuels du bassin de Bamiyan et de ses bordures montagneuses (Afghanistan central)," ibid., 1974, pp. 327-50. J. Lang, *Un modèle de sédimentation molassique continentale en climate semi-aride: Bassins intramontagneux cénozoiques de l'Afghanistan central*, unpublished thesis, Université Pierre et Marie Curie, 3 vols., Paris, 1975.

Description and history of routes: E. Trinkler, *Afghanistan, eine landeskundliche Studie*, Petermanns Mitteilungen, Ergänzungsheft 196, Gotha, 1928, pp. 57-74. A. Foucher, *La vieille route de l'Inde, de Bactres à Taxila*, 2 vols., MDAFA 1, Paris, 1942-47, pp. 17-28, 45-49. C. Rathjens, Jr., "Karawanenwege und Pässe im Kulturlandschaftswandel Afghanistans seit dem 19. Jahrhundert," *Herrmann von Wissmann Festschrift*, Tübingen, 1962, pp. 209-21.

(X. de Planhol)

ii. History and Monuments

Bāmīān is celebrated for the beauty of its landscape and for the presence of two colossal statues of the Buddha. In the past it was a caravan halt and a renowned artistic center, as well as a center for the propagation of Buddhism.

Early History. Situated 2,500 meters above sea level and enclosed between the high mountains of Ḵ᷾ājaḡar (an extension of the western Hindu Kush) on the north and Kūh-e Bābā on the south, the valley of Bāmīān provided the necessary sheltered corridor permitting passage of one of the main ancient routes linking India and China.

The name Bāmīān, according to P. Pelliot, is from Middle Persian Bāmīkān (*Bundahišn*, TD_2, p. 88.2; Bamikan in the *Geography* of (Pseudo-)Moses of Khorene; Marquart, *Ērānšahr*, p. 92). From the fifth century onward it appears in the Chinese texts in different forms: Fan-yang, Fan-yan, Fang-yan, and Fan-yen-na (see Marquart, p. 215). These texts are of two kinds; on one hand, there are texts dealing with Bāmīān when it was included in the great Chinese administrative reorganization connected with the western countries, and, on the other, travelers' reports. The celebrated Chinese pilgrim Xuanzang, who visited Bāmīān between 629 and 645, left a very important description of its monuments and of the social and religious life of its inhabitants (tr. Beal, I, pp. 49-53). Nearly a century later, the Korean monk Huichao, who passed through Bāmīān in 727, described it as an independent and powerful kingdom, despite the presence of the Arab armies to the north and south of the region.

The Islamization of the population of the valley took place gradually. Instead of being brutally suppressed, most of the princes of Bāmīān, who bore the title *šēr* ("king," translated incorrectly as "lion" by Yaʿqūbī in *Boldān*, p. 289), were named to important posts at the court in Baghdad or elsewhere. Ṭabarī (III, p. 1335) reported that a *šēr* of Bāmīān had been named governor of Yemen in 229/844. Yaʿqūb the Saffarid destroyed a great temple and sent the idols to Baghdad (Ṭabarī, III, p. 1851), but this did not signal the end of the pre-Islamic life of Bāmīān.

PLATE IV

The 55-meter Buddha statue at Bāmīān (photo Z. Tarzi)

Not until the Ghaznavids did the non-Muslim indigenous dynasty of Bāmīān succumb. Under the Ghurids Bāmīān was for almost a century (550-609/1155-1212) the capital of a great kingdom extending to the north of the Oxus (Amu Darya). The valley was part of the kingdom of the K̠ʷārazmšāhs in 618/1221, when Jengiz (Čengīz) Khan, in order to avenge the death of his grandson, totally razed the city and massacred its inhabitants.

Under the Mughals the name of Bāmīān is mentioned again, especially in connection with Awrangzēb, whose depredations there included using the large Buddha of 55 meters as a target for his cannons.

In the nineteenth century several European travelers visited the Bāmīān valley (Godard et al.), but not until the Délégation Archéologique Française en Afghanistan (DAFA) has studied the archeological remains, between 1922 and 1930, did the site become accessible to tourists.

Monuments. As an important center of Buddhism, Bāmīān received numerous bequests and donations, which allowed erection of important cult monuments. On the northern slope of the Bāmīān valley there is a cliff which contains two statues of standing Buddhas, the one to the east 38 meters high, the other, to the west, 55 meters high. Both are sheltered under trilobed arches decorated with wall paintings and are surrounded by dozens of artificial caves in different forms, varying in plan from circular to polygonal and from square to rectangular. These caves are ornamented with wall paintings and architectural elements executed in relief. It is believed that the smaller standing Buddha and the surrounding caves (the group A-G) are the oldest works at Bāmīān. Traces of later restorations and alterations have also been discovered.

The 55-meter statue and the adjacent caves (numbered from I to XV) form a more coherent complex, influenced by the art of Gandhara and that of the Guptas of India; this influence can be seen in the graceful proportions of the statue itself and also in the wall paintings in its niche, all executed between the fifth and sixth centuries A.D.

Situated in the central part of the cliff, between the two Buddhas, are other cave groups (e.g., E, H, I, J, and K). They consist either of trilobed niches that at one time sheltered seated Buddhas (E, H, and I) or of grottos (J and K), the wall paintings of which are the artistic apogee of Bāmīān. Here various influences commingled gradually, giving birth to a unique art, one of the principal characteristics of which is the use of primary colors like the lapis blue of the bodhisattva in group E or the red ocher of the bodhisattva in group K. The wall paintings of Folādī and the fragments at Kakrak should be linked to this phase of the school of Bāmīān (sixth-eighth centuries).

A large reclining Buddha in *parinirvāṇa* 1,000 feet (ca. 300 meters) long has not yet been excavated (Pelliot in Godard et al.).

We have only fragmentary information on the royal city and on two large Buddhist monasteries built not far from the cliff. On the other hand, two important ruins of the Islamic period are still standing: The first, to the southeast of the cliff, is called Šahr-e Ḡolḡola; the second, Šahr-e Żoḥāk, or the Red City, is situated farther east of Bāmīān on a rocky spur at the intersection of the roads leading to Kabul.

The "Irano-Buddhist" art of Bāmīān, thanks to the valley's geographical position, thus functioned as a link in the long chain running from India and Gandhara to Bactria and Sogdia, eventually reaching Chinese Central Asia and finally Tun-huang.

Bibliography: L. Bachhofer, review of B. Rowland, *The Wall-Paintings...*, in *Art Bulletin* 20, 1938, pp. 230ff. A. Foucher, "Rapport A. Foucher" (a letter addressed to E. Senart about the antiquities of Bāmīān), *JA*, April-June, 1923, pp. 354-68. Idem, *La vieille route de l'Inde de Bactres à Taxila*, MDAFA 1, 2 vols., Paris, 1942-47. J. Godard, Y. Godard and J. Hackin, *Les antiquités bouddhiques de Bāmiyān*, MDAFA 2, Paris and Brussels, 1928. J. Hackin and J. Carl, *Nouvelles recherches archéologiques à Bāmiyān*, MDAFA 3, Paris, 1933. J. Hackin, J. Carl, and J. Meunié, *Diverses recherches archéologiques en Afghanistan (1933-1940)*, MDAFA 8, Paris, 1959. T. Higuchi, *Bāmiyān: Art and Archaeological Research on the Buddhist Cave Temple in Afghanistan 1970-1978*, 4 vols., Kyoto, 1983 (in Japanese). Huichao (Huei-ch'ao), tr. W. Fuchs, *Huei-ch'aos Pilgerreise durch Nordwest-Indien und Zentralasien um 726*, APAW, Phil-hist. Kl., Berlin, 1928. T. Kodera, M. Maeda, and A. Miyaji, *Bāmiyān*, Nagoya, 1971 (in Japanese). B. Rowland, *The Wall-Paintings of India, Central Asia and Ceylon*, Boston, 1938. Z. Tarzi, *L'architecture et le décor rupestre des grottes de Bāmiyān*, 2 vols., Paris, 1977. Idem, "La grotte K3 de Bāmiyān," *Arts asiatiques* 38, 1983, pp. 20ff. Xuanzang (Hsüan-tsang, tr. S. Beal, *Si-yu-ki. Buddhist Records of the Western World*, 2 vols. in one, London, n.d.

(Z. Tarzi)

iii. Modern Town and District

Bāmīān was destroyed by Jengiz Khan's troops and did not recover quickly. The place was still desolate forty years later when Jovaynī wrote his history. Nevertheless the importance of its geographical position ensured that it would be repopulated. From the Timurid period onward a town reappeared, and Bābor several times mentions it as an interesting place and the headquarters of a district; but the general decline of the transcontinental caravan trade prevented it from growing again to the size of the pre-Mongol city. The first foreign travelers who passed through Bāmīān (Moorcroft, 1823; Masson, Burnes, and Mohan Lal, 1832; Wood, 1837) describe it as a small town (Mohan Lal, p. 89: a village) enclosed within a wall and divided into several quarters, with two-story but low-built houses, lying in the bottom of the valley opposite the cliff of the Buddhas. The pre-Mongol dwelling sites on the top of cliff had not been reoccupied. The alluvial bottomlands were well tilled and dotted with fortified houses. There was also a considerable number of dwellers in caves dug out of the cliffs. While the revenue from the district was not large, taxes on goods in transit yielded 70,000 rupees annually. Trade was active, and the place depended on it. Then and later, Bāmīān appears to have been a stronghold of the Afghan monarchy in the central mountains. The district, however, was still claimed by the Uzbek amirs of the north, who continued to levy tribute, payable mainly in the form of slaves, on the Hazāra tribes of the mountains (Wood, pp. 200-01, 206) and sometimes raided as far as Bāmīān. The town was raided by Morād Beg, the amir of Kondoz, in 1836 (C. T. Vigne, *A Personal Narrative of a Visit to Ghuzni, Kabul and Afghanistan*, London, 1843, p. 329) but in 1841 Morād Beg's domain only extended to the Āq Rebāṭ pass (Wood, p. 205). The Afghan grip evidently gave rise to the present ethnic and sectarian make-up of the town, which stands as a Sunnite Tajik and Pashtun island in the midst of mountains inhabited by Isma'ili and Twelver Shi'ite Hazāras. This ethnic transformation was already complete in the early 19th century (Mohan Lal, p. 89); there are no grounds for holding that Bāmīān was still Shi'ite at that time (as stated by Canfield, p. 98, who misunderstood the facts reported by Wood, p. 206). The submission of the Hazāras at the end of the 19th century confirmed this situation.

Since then, Bāmīān's principal role has been that of a regional center. This has clearly been the case since the town was raised to the rank of headquarters of a province in the administrative reorganization of 1964, which exactly coincided with the opening of the Sālang tunnel and road and the consequent ending of Bāmīān's activities in trans-Hindu Kush commerce. On the other hand, agriculture in the Bāmīān valley became strongly commercialized and outward-looking, and was distinctly more advanced than in the neighboring mountains. Wheat, eggs, potatoes, dried yoghurt (*qorūt*), and also poplar wood were supplied to the Kabul market. The town had a busy *bāzār* of 300-400 shops and a much frequented twice-weekly market (on Mondays and Thursdays). Built along the line of the main street, Bāmīān was growing rapidly but suffering from the lack of a town plan. The preliminary returns of the 1979 census recorded 7,355 inhabitants in the town and 268,517 in the province, which comprises the whole western part of the Hazārajāt including the Yakāōlang basin, the upper valley of the Kondoz river, the Kūh-e Bābā, and the upper Helmand valley.

Bibliography: *Bābur-nāma*, tr. A. S. Beveridge, London, 1921, pp. 96, 205, 311, 351, 409. W. Moorcroft and G. Trebeck, *Travels in Hindustan..., Kabul, Kunduz and Bokhara*, 2 vols., London, 1841, II, pp. 386f. C. Masson, *Narrative of Various Journeys in Baloochistan, Afghanistan and the Panjab*, 3 vols., London, 1842, II, pp. 378-395. A. Burnes, *Travels into Bokhara*, 3 vols., London, 1834, I, pp. 182-88. Mohan Lal, *Travels in the Panjab, Afghanistan, and Turkestan, to Balkh, Bokhara, and Herat...*, London, 1846, pp. 86-90. J. Wood, *A Personal Narrative of a Journey to the Source of the River Oxus...*, London, 1841, pp. 198-207. Ḡ. 'O. Rasūlī, *Eqteṣādīyāt-e Bāmīān*, Kabul, 1351 Š./1972. R. L. Canfield, *Faction and Conversion in a Plural Society: Religious Alignments in the Hindu Kush*, Anthropological Papers, Museum of Anthropology, University of Michigan 50, Ann Arbor, 1973.

(X. de Planhol)

iv. Modern Province

Bāmīān province (*welāyat*) of central Afghanistan covers 17,411 km². It is presently (1363 Š./1984) divided into four districts (*woloswālī*) and one subdistrict (*'alāqadārī*). The only locality with urban status is the provincial center, Bāmīān (see above). The province of Bāmīān was created in 1343 Š./1964 out of the former provinces of Kabul and Parvān (= Šamālī).

Tables 19-21 contain the main available data about present population and land use in the province, districts, and subdistrict.

(D. Balland)

Table 19

POPULATION OF BĀMĪĀN PROVINCE, AFGHANISTAN (1978-79)

Name of district	1 Area (km²)	2 Total sedentary population (1979)	3 Density (Inhab./km²)	4 Urban population (percent)	5 Number of tents in summer 1978 Pashtun	Non-Pashtun
Bāmīān (center of province)	2,152	46,800	22	16	235	30
Woloswālī:						
Kahmard (1)	3,253	32,300	10	—	41	70
Panjaw	1,537	45,700	30	—	1,034	—
Waraṯ	2,823	69,700	25	—	1,117	—
Yakāōlang	6,575	55,600	8	—	496	650
ʿAlāqādārī:						
Šebar	1,071	18,400	17	—	514	—
Total of province	17,411	268,500	15	3	3,437 (2)	750 (3)

Sources: Columns 1 to 4, *Natāyej-e moqaddamātī-e nok̲ostīn saršomārī-e nofūs*, Kabul, 1359 Š./1981. Figures have been rounded. Column 5, D. Balland and A. de Benoist, *Nomades et semi-nomades d'Afghanistan*, forthcoming. Notes: (1) Since 1358 Š./1979 this *woloswālī* includes the former *ʿalāqadārī* of Sayḡān (1,652 km²). (2) Most of them are nomads (56%) and the others seminomads. (3). Most of them are seminomads (64%) and the main group is Balūč (440 tents). Nomads and seminomads spending the summer in Bāmīān province come from a very large area, as shown in Table 20.

Table 20

GEOGRAPHICAL ORIGIN OF NOMADS AND SEMINOMADS SUMMERING IN BĀMĪĀN PROVINCE (IN TENTS)

	Ḡaznī	Paktīā	Nangrahār	Laḡmān	Konar	Baḡlān	Samangān	Balk̲	Helmand	Total
Pashtun nomads	350	519	743	65	90	25	29	93	4	1,918
seminomads	—	—	580	—	—	20	19	900	—	1,519
Non-Pashtun nomads	—	—	—	—	—	—	180	80	10	270
seminomads	—	—	—	—	—	—	70	410	—	480
Total	350	519	1,323	65	90	45	298	1,483	14	4,187

Table 21

LAND USE IN BĀMĪĀN PROVINCE, AFGHANISTAN (1967)

Name of district	Cultivated lands (ha) Irrigated (*ābī*)	Non-irrigated (*lalmī*)	Fallow	Forests (ha)	Percent of irrigated land under Canals	Springs	Wells	Water mills (units)
Bāmīān	3,874	556	932	46	80	20	—	105
Woloswālī:								
Kahmard	2,476	946	612	24	63	37	—	69
Panjaw	4,866	—	1,614	492	59	41	—	121
Waraṯ	7,486	3,404	3,336	1,852	91	9	—	255
Yakāōlang	3,428	1,172	1,086	748	76	16	8	37
ʿAlāqadārī:								
Šebar	1,028	672	432	38	28	45	27	64
Total of province	23,158	6,750	8,012	3,200	75	23	2	651

Source: *Natāyej-e eḥṣāʾīyagīrī sarwē-ye moqaddamātī-e zerāʿatī sāl-e 1346 Š.*, Kabul, n.d., 7 vols. The figures are only very rough estimates; the reliability of some of them may be questionable.

BAMPŪR

i. *Prehistoric Site*
ii. *In Modern Times*

i. Prehistoric Site

The position of Bampūr near a river and major routes explains the presence there of prehistoric and later settlements at the foot of a fortress on a high mound. While the mound has not been excavated, Sir Aurel Stein carried out sondages nearby during reconnaissance in the Bampūr valley in 1932 (1937, pp. 104-31). In 1966 Beatrice de Cardi initiated further excavations to establish a ceramic sequence for the region, trenches Y and Z producing consistent results within six successive occupational phases designated Periods I-VI (de Cardi, 1967; 1968; 1970).

The earliest occupation contained no material like that known farther west at Čāh-Ḥosaynī or Yaḥyā V a-c (Lamberg-Karlovsky, 1970, p. 95). While its absence does not preclude such deposits elsewhere on the site, no firm date was assigned to Period I, though links with Yaḥyā IVC suggest a settlement existed by the late 4th millennium (Lamberg-Karlovsky, 1972, p. 97). The range of gray and cream-slipped wheel-made wares and associated objects from the mud-brick building comprising Bampūr I-IV reflected strong ties with the Helmand culture as exemplified at Shahr-i Sokhta (Šahr-e Sūḵta) from late II-III and in Mundigak IV 1-2 (Tosi, 1970, p. 13; 1974, p. 32) and is of relevance to the concept of interaction spheres in and around the Indo-Iranian borderlands (Lamberg-Karlovsky, 1972, p. 99).

New ceramics appeared at the end of Bampūr IV, suggesting contact with Fārs, Makrān, and Oman. Buff and red-slipped wares became dominant in Periods V-VI, when streak-burnished, black-on gray and incised gray wares like those in Shahr-i Sokhta IV (ca. 2200-1800 B.C.) were introduced. Both gray wares occur also in collective burials of the Umm an-Nar (Omm al-Nār) culture of Oman (cf. de Cardi, 1970, figs. 38 and 42; During Caspers, 1970, figs. 45-46, pp. 319-25; de Cardi et al., 1976, figs. 15 and 17, pp. 118-23), and though few of them can be closely dated Hili North Tomb A is ascribed to the last quarter of the 3rd millennium (Cleuziou and Vogt, 1983, p. 43).

While the evidence from Sīstān and Oman points to a terminal date for Bampūr VI in the late 3rd millennium, radiocarbon determinations for Yaḥyā IVB (Lamberg-Karlovsky, 1971, p. 94) suggest an earlier dating and the matter remains unresolved.

Bibliography: R. Biscione, "The Burnt Building of Period Shahr-i Sokhta IV. An Attempt of Functional Analysis from the Distribution of Pottery Types," in G. Gnoli and A. V. Rossi, eds., *Iranica*, Naples, 1979, pp. 291-306. S. Cleuziou and B. Vogt, "Umm an Nar Burial Customs. New Evidence from Tomb A at Hili North," *Proceedings of the Seminar for Arabian Studies* 13, London, 1983, pp. 37-52. B. de Cardi, "The Bampur Sequence in the Third Millennium B.C.," *Antiquity* 41, 1967, pp. 33-41. Idem, "Excavations at Bampur, South-East Iran: A Brief Report," *Iran* 6, 1968, pp. 135-55. Idem, "Excavations at Bampur, a Third Millennium Settlement in Persian Baluchistan, 1966," *Anthropological Papers of the American Museum of Natural History, New York* 51/3, 1970, pp. 233-355. B. de Cardi, S. Collier, and D. B. Doe, "Excavations and Survey in Oman," *Journal of Oman Studies* 2, Oman, 1976, pp. 101-75. E. C. L. During Caspers, "A Note on the Carved Stone Vases and Incised Grey-ware," apud de Cardi, 1970, pp. 319-25. C. C. Lamberg-Karlovsky, "Excavations at Tepe Yahya, Iran, 1967-1969, Progress Report 1," *Bulletin of the American School of Prehistoric Research* 27, Peabody Museum, Harvard University, 1970, pp. 1-134. Idem, "Tepe Yahya 1971 Mesopotamia and the Indo-Iranian Borderlands," *Iran* 10, 1972, pp. 89-100. C. C. Lamberg-Karlovsky and D. Schmandt-Besserat, "An Evaluation of the Bampur, Khurab and Chah Husseini Collections in the Peabody Museum and Relations with Tepe Yahya," *Bibliotheca Mesopotamica* 7, Malibu, 1977, pp. 113-34. C. C. Lamberg-Karlovsky and M. Tosi, "Shahr-i Sokhta and Tepe Yahya: Tracks on the Earliest History of the Iranian Plateau," *East and West*, N.S. 23/1-2, 1973, pp. 21-53. Sir Aurel Stein, *Archaeological Reconnaissances in North-Western India and South-Eastern Iran*, London, 1937. M. Tosi, "Excavations at Shahr-i Sokhta, a Chalcolithic Settlement in the Iranian Sistan: Preliminary Report on the First Campaign, October-December 1967," *East and West*, N.S. 18/1-2, 1968, pp. 9-66. Idem, "Excavations at Shahr-i Sokhta. Preliminary Report on the Second Campaign, September-December 1968," *East and West*, N.S. 19/3-4, 1969, pp. 283-386. Idem, "A Tomb from Damin and the Problem of the Bampur Sequence in the Third Millennium B.C.," *East and West*, N.S. 20/1-2, 1970, pp. 9-50. Idem, "Bampur: A Problem of Isolation," *East and West*, N.S. 24/1-2, 1974, pp. 29-49. Idem, "The Dating of the Umm an-Nar Culture and a Proposed Sequence for Oman in the Third Millennium B.C.," *Journal of Oman Studies* 2, Oman, 1976, pp. 81-92.

(B. de Cardi)

ii. In Modern Times

Bampūr, a *bakš* and *qaṣaba* (borough) in the *šahrestān* of *Īrānšahr* in the province of Balūčestān o Sīstān, bounded by the *bakš*es of Bazmān to the north, Sarbāz to the east, Nīkšahr and Qaṣr-e Qand to the south, and Kahnūj (*šahrestān* of Jīroft) to the west. The plain of Bampūr is encircled by several high mountains: Jebāl-e Bārez and Kūh-e Bazmān to the north, the mountains of Bašākerd, Fannūj, and Čāmp to the south, the mountains of Esfandeqa to the west, and Zardkūh, Espīdān, and Sīāhband to the east. For this reason the spring floods flow through riverbeds that are dry or almost dry during the rest of the year (e.g., Šahābrūd,

Kūskīnrūd, and the Kahūr and Lāšār rivers) onto the plain of Bampūr. The Bampūr river, originating in the northeastern mountains of Īrānšahr, is fed by the Konārakī, Dāmen, and Kārvāndar rivers and waters most of the arable land of Bampūr before flowing into the Hāmūn-e Jāz-e Mūrīān 50 km to the west. The river is never dry and other streams that flow underground in sandy terrain also feed it. Earthen dams divide the Bampūr into eight branches, which permit irrigation of 12 villages (1,300 ha). Arable land that lies too far from the river is irrigated by *qanāt*s and, more recently, deep wells. Modern agricultural technology, like machinery and chemical fertilizers, has been little exploited in this district, and production is therefore lower than in comparable areas in central and southern Iran. Thanks, however, to plentiful and relatively good water and mild weather, the plain of Bampūr is one of the most productive agricultural regions of Baluchistan. The main products are wheat, barley, corn, and dates (which are not exported because packing facilities are lacking). The land is partly state-owned and partly belongs to small landowners. In the 1960s state land yielded about 1,500 tons of wheat and 600 tons of corn yearly, most of which was exported across the southeastern borders of Iran (Nāṣeḥ, p. 166). Owing to good pastureland in the valleys around Bampūr, dairy products are also important. In 1336 Š./1957, 2,000 cows, 6,000 sheep, 4,000 camels, and 400 donkeys were counted in the area (ibid., p. 162), in 1360 Š./1981, 1,180 cows and calves and 34,280 sheep, goats, and kids (Āmārgīrī-e Rūstā'ī-e Jehād-e Sāzandagī, year 1360 Š./1981-82).

The *baḵš* of Bampūr is divided into two sections: the mountainous area, including the *dehestān* of Čānf, which is situated in the valleys of the Āhūrān range, and the plain including the *dehestān*s of Ḥūma and Maskūtān. The lowest point in the plain lies 900 m above sea level; the highest mountain peak is the volcanic Kūh-e Bazmān (2,500 m).

Bampūr, like other *baḵš*es of the province, has a mild and relatively humid climate. In June and July the temperature often rises to 48°C; in winter it falls to 2°C. Annual rainfall in the center of the *baḵš* is about 120 mm (*Našrīya-ye Dā'era-ye Jogrāfīā'ī-e Setād-e Arteš-e Jomhūrī-e Eslāmī-e Irān. Ostān-e Sīstān o Balūčestān*, Tehran, 1364 Š./1985, p. 12). Until a few years ago the entire population of Bampūr retreated to *ḵārḵānas* (q.v.) in the hot season, and most inhabitants still do.

The *baḵš* of Bampūr includes the following *dehestān*s: Ḥūma, Maskūtān, Lāšār, Čānf, Fannūj, Bent, and Malūrān, comprising 160 villages and more than 500 settlements (Afšār Sīstānī, pp. 293-340). The total population in 1335 Š./1956, was 40,041 (Jahānbānī, p. 74); in 1345 Š./1966 it was reported as 51,606 for the *baḵš* and 15,686 for the *dehestān* (Afšār, pp. 301-40). The population is mostly Baluch, belonging to the two tribes of Mobārakī and Šīrānī, and follows the Hanafite school. It speaks Baluchi and its entire lifestyle is Baluchi (Nāṣeḥ, p. 165).

The administrative center of the *baḵš* is situated at 60°7′15″ E, 27°11′35″ N (Afšār, p. 294). It lies on the Čāhbahār highway 25 km west of Īrānšahr, 363 km from Čāhbahār, and 392 km from Zāhedān. A 350-km asphalt road connects Nōkjūb 4 km east of Bampūr to the city of Bam (Āmārgīrī-e Rūstā'ī, p. 13). The central *dehestān* of Bampūr includes 29 villages and 7 farms and has a total population of 4,182, housed in 3,881 dwellings (mostly reed huts). Drinking water is supplied through pipelines from a deep well in the vicinity of the Bampūr dam. Electricity is supplied from Īrānšahr. The *dehestān* has eight public baths, six infirmaries, twenty-three elementary schools, seven intermediate schools (*rāhnamā'ī*), one high school, eighteen mosques and *ḥosaynīya*s, five post offices, and a telegraph office. There are 2,500 ha of arable land, irrigated by the Bampūr river, three *qanāt* systems, and thirteen deep and medium wells (Āmārgīrī-e rūstā'ī, 1360).

Old Bampūr was situated 500 m from the main street of the modern town of Bampūr, on the top of a hill, where its remains are still visible. The hill rises about 80 m above the surrounding area; because of its strategic position, it was the site of the residence of the governor of Baluchistan until the end of the 13th/19th century. As the frontier army in this area was also garrisoned there, it was one of the most developed parts of the province. It was often demolished and rebuilt during the rebellion of the Baluch chieftains in the last century and also during the rise of Āqā Khan (1257/1841) and his brother Abu'l-Ḥasan Khan in 1260/1844 (Fīrūz Mīrzā, p. 30, quoting *Nāseḵ al-tawārīḵ*; Afšār, p. 236). But the unfavorable climate, the unhealthy drinking water, which had to be carried from the river, and also the wind called *lawār* blowing from the Lūt desert caused a high death rate among the soldiers assigned to this post from other towns in Kermān. This is quite apparent from the large numbers of soldiers' tombs surrounding the fortress (Fīrūz Mīrzā, pp. 29, 39). Finally, in 1297/1880, Fīrūz Mīrzā Noṣrat-al-Dawla, the governor of Kermān and Makrān, made a trip to Baluchistan and transferred the army garrison from the half-ruined fortress of Bampūr to the village of Fahraj (now Īrānšahr) four parasangs away, where the climate was more favorable. Since then Bampūr has lost its former importance (Fīrūz Mīrzā, pp. 32, 36, 38; Afšār, p. 295).

Bibliography: Ī. Afšār Sīstānī, *Negāh-ī be Sīstān o Balūčestān*, Tehran, 1363 Š./1984. Fīrūz Mīrzā Farmānfarmā Noṣrat-al-Dawla, *Safar-nāma-ye Kermān o Balūčestān*, ed. M. Neẓām Māfī, Tehran, 1342 Š./1963. A. Jahānbānī, *Sargoḏašt-e Balūčestān o marzhā-ye ān*, Tehran, 1338 Š./1959. Ḏ. Nāṣeḥ, *Balūčestān*, Tehran, 1345 Š./1966.

('A.-A. SA'ĪDĪ SĪRJĀNĪ)

BĀMŠĀD, a musician at the court of the Sasanian king Ḵosrow II Parvēz (A.D. 591-628) whose name is mentioned together with that of Bārbad (q.v.) in a poem by the Persian poet Manūčehrī (*Dīvān*, ed. M. Dabīrsīāqī, 3rd ed., Tehran, 1347 Š./1968, p. 19 v. 280). The Persian lexicons state that he was a famous musician equal to Bārbad (Dehḵodā, *Loḡat-nāma*, s.v. Bāmšād).

(A. TAFAŻŻOLĪ)

BĀMŠĀD, a Persian newspaper and a news and public affairs magazine published in Tehran 1956-68. Its licensee and chief editor was Esmāʿīl Pūrwālī (b. 1301 Š./1922 in Mašhad), a professional journalist whose career began in 1319 Š./1940 and includes stints as the editor of the newspaper *Īrān-e mā* (Tehran, 1943-47), Paris correspondent of National Iranian Radio and Television (1971-76), and editor of the magazine *Rūzgār-e now* currently published in Paris. The weekly *Bāmšād* was first brought out as a publication of the newspaper *Īrān-e mā*, but, after three issues, became an independent weekly magazine. Popular for its illustrations and its diverse contents, *Bāmšād* ranged from 72 to 84 pages, measured 12 × 18.5 cm, and cost five rials. In the fall of 1335 Š./1956, an independent newspaper *Bāmšād* began publishing simultaneously with the magazine; it was a four-page, seven-column paper with an average measurement of 32 × 44.5 cm and contained a separate, humor supplement called *Mašhadī Bābā*. In the summer of 1336 Š./1957, the publication of a line from Ḥāfeẓ construed to have a slightly satirical flavor as a caption to a childhood picture of Moḥammad-Reżā Shah led to the suppression of both the newspaper and the magazine and to Pūrwālī's arrest. Though the satire proved to be unintentional, *Bāmšād* magazine remained censored until its editor was released from prison. The magazine was at its most popular during the tenure of Prime Minister ʿAlī Amīnī. At the outset of 1343 Š./1964, *Bāmšād* was published in the form of a weekly news magazine of twenty, seven-column pages, measuring 29 × 42 cm; its illustrations were seasoned with political cartoons signed by Moḥsen Davallū. It assumed the shape of an *Express* or *Newsweek*-style news and public affairs magazine from 8 Ābān 1345 Š./30 October 1966 until 1347 Š./1969, when political and financial constraints forced it to stop publication. During this period, it contained between 48 and 114 three-column pages, measuring 21 × 28.5 cm, and cost ten rials. It was well-illustrated and sported eye-catching Davallū caricatures on the cover; interior caricatures were drawn by Laṭīfī. Well-known contributors to *Bāmšād* included: Ḥasan Arsanjānī, Moḥammad-Reżā ʿAskarī, Parvīz Āzādī, Tūraj Farāzmand, Šāʾallāh Nāẓerīān, Īraj Nabawī, and Dāryūš Homāyūn. After the revolution of 1979, Pūrwālī published *Bāmšād* in a smaller format, but, after two issues, discontinued publication and emigrated to Paris. In the fall of 1360 Š./1981, he began the Persian magazine *Rūzgār-e now*. Incomplete sets of *Bāmšād* are kept in major libraries of Iran.

Bibliography: *Fehrest-e rūz-nāmahā-ye mawjūd dar Ketāb-ḵāna-ye Mellī-e Īrān*, Tehran, 2536 = 1356 Š./1977, p. 53. K. Amīr Nūrī, *Fehrest-e našrīyāt-e mawjūd dar Ketāb-ḵāna-ye Markaz-e Madārek-e Farhangī-e Enqelāb-e Eslāmī*, Tehran, 1362 Š./1983, p. 27. R. Mach and R. D. McChesney, *A List of Persian Serials in the Princeton University Library*, Princeton, 1971. [See Addenda and Corrigenda.]

(N. PARVĪN)

BAN-E SORMA, a necropolis of the Early Bronze Age, excavated in 1967 by the Belgian Mission in Iran. It lies along the banks of the Laškān river, at 3.5 km from the village of Čavār in the district Īlām, province of Pošt-e Kūh, Īlām, western Luristan (Lorestān). This necropolis extends over a wide plateau divided by depressions into three zones: areas A, B, and C. The tombs are scattered, except in the southwest corner of area A, where a group of eleven tombs was discovered together. The funeral vaults are impressive for their size. Most measure from 8 to 16 m in length and are 1.70 to 3 m wide and 1.50 to 2.10 m deep. They were closed by enormous covering stone slabs. Pebbles were placed around each slab and the entire tomb was edged with solid counterweights. Inside, the walls of thick limestone ashlars are arranged in regular horizontal courses, but in such a way that the top opening is narrower than the bottom. These vault burials are family or collective sepulchers, containing several bodies, but only rare fragments of bone were preserved.

The graves contained funerary furnishings, consisting mostly of pottery, metal objects, and engraved cylinder seals. Pottery included coarse unpainted and painted monochrome or polychrome ware. The polychrome ware is decorated with wide zoomorphic bands over the whole surface of the vessel, painted in brownish-black and reddish-orange on a buff ground. This pottery is related to the "Diyala Ware" from Mesopotamia. Metal objects are made of copper or bronze. The artisans used for this copper alloy, lead, antimony, and arsenic. Tin was not commonly used.

Among the metal objects there are tools and weapons (knives, daggers, spearheads, socketed spears, flat axes, socketed axes, chisels, awls), personal items (needles, pins, rings, bracelets, belt-buckles, tweezers, cosmetic implements), and vessels. Silver was frequent for hair spirals, earrings, and rings. Necklaces were made of

PLATE V

Ban-e Sorma, Area A

beads from fossil opercles and dentalia and snail shells. Stones were also used: lapis-lazuli, azurite, diorite, alabaster, and obsidian. The cylinder seals, made of calcite or serpentine, are engraved with diagonal scenes of animal fights (caprids, lions, panthers, dragons, androcephalous bulls), often in the presence of personages, and mythical scenes representing the god in a boat with a prow in the form of the bust of another god.

By analogy with the funeral furnishing from the Old Elamite period at Susa IV (= Susa Dc-Dd) and with those from the Old Sumerian Period in Mesopotamia—Ur (Royal Tombs), Mari, Kish, Lagash, Khafajah, Tell Asmar—the collective tombs from Ban-e Sorma must be situated in the Early Dynastic III period about 2600-2400 B.C. Since written sources are lacking, it is difficult to determine which population occupied this necropolis. Most probably the tombs at Ban-e Sorma should be attributed to the Elamites. The graveyard at Ban-e Sorma (and others of the same kind, e.g., Qalʿa-ye Neṣār, Dar-e Tanhā) are interesting in that they show that, from about 2600 B.C., the tribes from Pošt-e Kūh, Luristan, played an important part in the formation of the bronze civilization in Luristan.

Bibliography: L. Vanden Berghe, "Luristan, la nécropole de Bani Surmah," *Archéologia* 24, Paris, 1968, pp. 53-62. Idem, "Excavation Report," *Iran* 7, 1969, pp. 170, 71.

(L. Vanden Berghe)

BĀNA, a *šahrestān* in the province of Kurdistan, located in a mountainous, well-forested region of western Iran at 35° 59′ north latitude and 45° 53′ east longitude, 1,529 m above sea level, with an area of 794 km^2. The *šahrestān* of Bāna consists of one town of the same name and seven rural districts (*dehestān*): i.e., Alūt, Poštarbabā, Pahlavīdež, Dašta Tāl, Sabadlū, Ševī, and Namašīr. It is bordered on the east by Saqez and Marīvān, on the west by Sardašt, on the south by Iraq, and on the north by Saqez and the Gaworg region (a dependency of Mahābād). Bāna is 260 km from Sanandaj and 21 km from the Iraqi border. Animal husbandry is the principal occupation of the inhabitants of Bāna, and tobacco and wild fruit gathered from nearby forests are its main crops. Most of the inhabitants are Muslims who follow the Sunnite (Shafiʿite) rite; they speak the dialect of south Kurmanji (Sōrānī) Kurdish.

Part of Kurdistan for centuries, Bāna owed its political and strategic importance to its common border with the Ottomans and its location among the three large Kurdish tribal confederations, namely, the Ardalān, the Bābān, and the Mokrīān.

Old Bāna consists of two citadels, Barožakūn and Ševī, and the area of Bāna. The government of the region was generally in the hands of the Ek̲tīār-al-Dīn family, who along with secular power also maintained religious authority. During the Safavid period, members of this family were held in high esteem and received the title of sultan. The first virtually independent ruler of the area was Mīrzā Beg b. Mīr Moḥammad, who was the son-in-law of Bega Beg (1494-1535), the ruler of Ardalān. Protection of the border areas between Iran and the Ottomans from K̲oy to Kermānšāh was generally the responsibility of the rulers of Bāna. Until the death of Nāder Shah Afšār in 1747, the rulers of Bāna governed under the direct supervision of the kings of Iran with relatively broad discretionary powers. After Nāder's death, during the time of K̲osrow Khan Bozorg Wālī-e Ardalān (1754-91), Bāna's rulers came under the supervision of the *wālī*s of Ardalān; by order of the kings of Iran the two groups were always to be united by marital ties (*Šarḥ-e ḥālāt*, p. 21).

In the 18th and 19th centuries, plague epidemics wiped out a considerable proportion of Bāna's inhabitants. In 1944 the entire region was embroiled in the turmoil caused by the revolt of Moḥammad-Rašīd Khan Dārūk̲ānī. More recently, during the Iran-Iraq conflict, many in Bāna have fallen victim to the aerial bombardment of both sides; much of the region has been destroyed, and its inhabitants have become refugees, most taking refuge in Iraq. For this reason it is very difficult to estimate Bāna's present population; however, according to the 1976 census (*Saršomārī-e nofūs wa maskan* CXXI, p. 2), the town of Bāna had 15,552 inhabitants.

Bibliography: Šaraf-al-Dīn Bedlīsī, *Šaraf-nāma* I, Petersburg, 1860, pp. 320-22. Shaikh Moḥammad Mardūk̲ Kordestānī, *Tārīk̲-e Mardūk̲* II, Tehran, 1323 Š./1944, pp. 67-70. Razmārā, *Farhang* V, pp. 44-46. Mīrzā Šokr-Allāh Fak̲r-al-Kottāb Sanandajī, *Toḥfa-ye nāṣerīya*, ms. dated 1318/1900, Ketāb-k̲āna-ye Ḥājj Ḥosayn Āqā Malek, Tehran, pp. 49-52. *Šarḥ-e ḥālāt-e Amīr Solaymān Bīg wa salāṭīn-e Bāna wa ḥokmrānī-e ānhā*, ms. Cambridge University Library (prepared for publication by the author). Moḥammad-Raʾūf Tawakkolī, *Jog̲rāfīā wa tārīk̲-e Bāna*, Tehran, 1358 Š./1980. Idem, 2nd ed., Tehran, 1363 Š./1984. Mīrzā ʿAlī-Akbar Monšī Waqāyeʿnegār, *Ḥadīqa-ye nāṣerīya*, ms. dated 1309/1891, Ketāb-k̲āna-ye Mellī-e Tehran, Kāk̲-e Golestān, etc., pp. 19-22.

(ʿA. Mardūk̲)

BANAFŠA (Mid. Pers. *wanafšag*, arabicized as *banafsaj*; cf. the cognate Kurd. *wanawša*, Māzandarāni *vanūše*, Semnāni *benowša*, etc., and the Armenian loanword *manušak*), common name for the genus *Viola* L. in New Persian.

Of the very large group of violas distributed in temperate regions of the northern hemisphere, A. Parsa, *Flore* I, "Violaceae," pp. 956-70, lists and describes the following 16 species as native to Iran: 1. *Viola alba* Besser.; 2. *V. armena* Boiss. & Huet; 3. *V. cinera* Boiss.; 4. *ebracteola* Fenzl (= *V. modesta* Fenzl var. *parviflora* Fenzl); 5. *V. hymettia* Boiss. & Heldr.; 6. *V. kitaibelina* Roem. & Shult (= *V. tricolor* L. var. *kitaibelina* Ledeb.); 7. *V. modesta* Fenzl; 8. *V. occulta* Lehm.; 9. *V. odorata* L.; 10. *V. pachyrrhiza* Boiss. & Hoh.; 11. *V. riviniana* Reich.; 12. *V. silvestris* (Lam.) Reichb. (= *V. caspica* Freyn., and the var. *mesenderana*

Freyn. & Sint); 13. *V. sintenisii* W. Bckr; 14. *V. spathulata* Willd.; 15. *V. suavis* M.B. (= *V. odorata* L. var. *suavis* Boiss.); 16. *V. tricolor* L. var. *arvensis* Murr. (In the 7 published vols. of A. Ghahreman's *Flore de l'Iran*, vol. I, no. 40, a new variety, *V. spathulata* Willd. var. *latifolia* Ghahreman, and vol. VI, no. 748, the species *V. stockssi* Boiss. are also found.) Details about these species and varieties may be found in these works. In this article only the *V. odorata* L. and the *V. tricolor* L. will be discussed.

The *Viola odorata* (or some other odoriferous species and varieties popularly assimilated to it), called simply *banafša* or sometimes *banafša-ye īrānī* "Iranian violet" (in contradistinction to *banafša(-ye) farangī* "European violet." i.e., pansy; see below) or *banafša-ye moʿaṭṭar/ʿaṭr* "the fragrant violet," grows wild in Iran, typically in out-of-the-way shady cool spots both on high and low lands almost everywhere climatic conditions are favorable, but, reportedly, it is particularly abundant in Rostamābād (in Gīlān), in Kandavān valley (near Čālūs), in the forest around Rāmsar, and in the woods in Gorgān (for Gorgān, see A. Ḵalīqī, p. 365; cf. *banafša-ye ṭabarī* "the violet native to Ṭabarestān," sometimes used in classical Persian poetry to designate it). An old favorite in Iran, this violet is already mentioned in the *Bundahišn* (tr. Anklesaria, 16.13, pp. 148-49) among plants having sweet-scented blossoms and (16A.2, pp. 152-53) is said to belong to [the Īzad] Tīr. In the text *King Xusraw and His Boy* (par. 82) it is said that the scent of violets is like the scent of girls.

Violets, whether *Viola odorata* or others, are not necessarily violet in color: hues ranging from white to deep, blackish purple (including yellow, blue, lilac, dark blue [*kabūd*], violet, etc.) have been reported. Some earlier historical evidence to this effect can be found in Persian literature and in some works on materia medica: a white violet is attested in the poetry of Manūčehrī Dāmḡānī (d. 432/1040-41; *Dīvān*, ed. M. Dabīrsīāqī, 5th ed., Tehran, 1363 Š./1984, p. 207); the (dark) blue vault of heaven has been qualified by some as *banafšagūn* "violet-colored," and Bīrūnī (362-440/973-1048) quotes Būlos (i.e., Paulus Aeginata, fl. 640) as having written, "Some people use the oil from the purple [*banafsaj*], some that from the saffron-colored one, and some that from the white one" (*Ṣaydana*, p. 102; see also below on the color implications in reference to the hair on the head and the down on the face of poets' sweethearts).

From certain botanical features of violas there have developed some violet-based similes and metaphors in classical Persian literature. The pecular corollas of violets or, perhaps, a bunch of these suggest ringlets, disheveled or curly hair, or a loose lock of hair. This feature plus the blackish purple color of some varieties, with or without the idea of fragrance, have formed the basis for such a metaphor as *banafša*: hair, and for such similes as *banafša-mūy/zolf* "having violety hair," referring to the hair of some poets' sweethearts). The poet Qā'ānī Šīrāzī (d. 1270/1853), in the opening distich of a picturesque *mosammaṭ* (*Dīvān*, Tehran, 1363 Š./1984, pp. 669-71), has this further heightened comparison for violets: "Violets have grown on brooksides as if the houries of Paradise had loosened their hair" (*gosasta ḥūr-e ʿīn ze zolf-e ḵ īš tārhā*). The bluish gray hue of some other varieties has resulted in similes such as *banafša-ʿārež/ʿeḏār* "having violety cheeks/face," referring to the grayish nascent down on the cheeks and upper lip of the poet's (imaginary) adolescent inamorato (these similes are often chromatically enhanced by a contrast to the color of the cheeks/face compared to *lāla* "[rosy] tulip" or *saman* "[white] jasmine").

Also typically, violets are low-growing plants with inconspicuous, humble, pensive-looking (cf. the etymology of *pansy*, *Viola tricolor*, in English) flowers which, in some species, slightly bend on their stalks, as if looking down for shame. Further, they seem to prefer secluded, shady spots (underbrush, hedges, cracks in alpine rocks, etc.), almost overshadowed by neighboring vegetation. A certain combination of these features has given rise in Persian litterature to three romantic associations of ideas: (1) modesty, bashfulness, humility; (2) neglectfulness; (3) neglect, regret, sorrowfulness, mournfulness (an Arab author quoted by Šehāb-al-Dīn Aḥmad Nowayrī, 677-733/1278-1332, *Nehāyat al-arab* XI, p. 229, even compares the sweet violet to "a forsaken lover, resting his head [in grief] on his knee,"—a motif also found in the Persian poet Ḵāqānī, d. 595/1199: "like the violet, I am laying may head on my knees, while these are a thousand times more violetish [i.e., bruised] than my lips").

Wild sweet-smelling violets may also be naturalized as garden plants. As early as 921/1515-16, the agriculturist Abū Naṣrī Heravī (*Eršād al-zerāʿa*, pp. 207-08) provides instructions for the cultivation of *banafša* (in the Herat area), of which he mentions three varieties: "dark blue, both double (*sad-barg*, lit., "centipetalous") and ordinary (*rasmī*), purple, and white." Eʿtemād-al-Salṭana, in his *al-Ma'āṯer wa'l-āṯār* I (ed. Ī. Afšār, Tehran, 1363 Š./1984, p. 136), which records all the innovations and achievements during the first forty years of the Qajar Nāṣer-al-Dīn Shah's reign (1264-1313/1848-96), mentions the cultivation of "three hues of double [*por-par*] Iranian violets" as well as the introduction of "three varieties of pansies [*banafša-ye farangī*]" in city gardens in Tehran. Incidentally, Abū Naṣrī Heravī (op. cit., p. 223) also mentions a *banafša-ye kūhī*, lit., "mountain violet," "whose plant grows up to half a cubit high, and whose flowers are purple and fragrant."

Wild pansy, *V. tricolor* L. var. *arvensis* Murr., grows in woods and meadows in the north, northwest, and west of Iran as well as in the Alborz and Tehran regions (see Ghahreman, op. cit., VI, no. 749). In contrast to its fragrant relative, *V. odorata*, it is scentless (this may account for its local Māzandarāni name *vasnī-benafše*, mentioned by Ghahreman, ibid., lit., "violet of the *vasnī* [i.e., the co-wife]"). The cultivated, hybridized pansy, *V. tricolor* var. *hortensis*, generally called *banafša-ye farangī* "European violet," as indicated by its Persian epithet and by Eʿtemād-al-Salṭana (see above), is a rather new addition to garden flowers in Iran. Although scentless like its wild parent, it has become very popular, because it blooms early in spring and is associated with the Iranian Nowrūz festivities, all the more so as the strange markings on the blooms make them look somewhat like jovial human faces, an anthropomorphism appealing particularly to the Persian imagination.

Phytotherapists or physicians of the Islamic era, generally indifferent to the botanical diversity of native species of *Viola*, have recognized numerous medicinal properties in *banafša/banafsaj* (occasionally called *forfīr/ferfīr* in some Arabic sources; from Gk. *porphyra* "purple color") in general, an account of which will be found in most works on traditional materia medica (e.g., in Arabic, Ebn al-Bayṭār, *al-Jāmeʿ* I, pp. 114-15, and, in Persian, ʿAqīlī Ḵorāsānī, *Makzan al-adwīa*, pp. 127). The earliest reference in Persian works to *Viola* varieties from a medicinal viewpoint probably is that by Mowaffaq-al-Dīn ʿAlī Heravī, author of the oldest extant independent Persian treatise on materia medica, *K. al-abnīa* (probably compiled in 339/950?), ed. A. Bahmanyār and Ḥ. Maḥbūbī Ardakānī, p. 67: "The best is [first] *banafša-ye kūhī* [mountain violet], and then *banafša-ye eṣbahānī* [Isfahan violet], and the more fragrant [they are, the better]" (on "Isfahan violet," see also below). Aḵawaynī Boḵārī (d. ca. 373/983?), author of the oldest extant medical text in Persian, *Hedāyat al-motaʿallemīn*, mentions the following uses for *banafša*, some of which, absent in previous works, probably are from his personal experiences. He uses it as part of an enema against quinsy (p. 308); in a pectoral poultice against a kind of "dry" cough (p. 318); in an emollient enema against pleurisy (p. 328); in an enema against ileus (p. 429); in a hepatic poultice against jaundice (p. 467); in a dorsal (or lumbar) poultice against nephritis, and in a concoction "to be poured" on the patient's back in case of suppurative nephritis (p. 482); in an ointment against vesical inflammation (p. 503); in an infusion to be used as a sitz-bath against uterine cancer (p. 538); in a poultice against sciatica (p. 572); in an infusion "to be poured" on the patient's head in case of fever caused by sunstroke (p. 649); in a sitz-bath against fever caused by grief and preoccupation (p. 654); in baths against hectic fever (pp. 665, 667), etc. The internal uses of *banafša* and of *banafša-ye eṣbahānī* (the difference between the two is not specified by the author) are: (*banafša*) in a mixture (with some other simples) against headache of bilious origin (p. 225); (*banafša* preserve) in *kašk-āb* against vesical inflammation (p. 501); in a linctus against pleurisy (p. 329); in a laxative infusion against anorexia (p. 357); (*banafša-ye-eṣbahānī*) in an electuary against colic (p. 434); in a drink with rosewater against hepatic dysfunction (p. 437); with sugar against tertian fever, etc. Nowadays, in popular or traditional therapeutics, dried violet blossoms are sometimes used by themselves in infusion as febrifuge, but usually with some other vegetable simples, the best-known combination of

which is the *č(ah)ār-gol* ("the four flowers," i.e., violets, water lilies, mallows and squash/pumpkin flowers) in a concoction indicated as febrifuge, "coolant," emollient, or pectoral.

Bibliography: Given in the text. See also Qāsem b. Yūsof Abū Naṣrī Heravī, *Eršād al-zerāʿa*, ed. M. Mošīrī, Tehran, 1346 Š./1967. Abū Bakr Rabīʿ b. Aḥmad Aḵawaynī Boḵārī, *Hedāyat al-motaʿallemīn fiʾl-ṭebb*, ed. J. Matīnī, Mašhad, 1344 Š./1965. M.-Ḥ. ʿAqīlī Ḵorāsānī, *Makzan al-adwīa*, offset reprint, Tehran, 1349 Š./1970?, from the litho. ed., Tehran, 1276/1859-60. Abū Rayḥān Bīrūnī, *K. al-ṣaydana fiʾl-ṭebb*, ed. Mohammed Said and Rana Ehsan Elahie, *Al-Bīrūnī's Book on Pharmacy and Materia Medica*, Karachi, 1973 (p. 102 n. on etymology from Skt. *vana-puṣpa* "wood flower" is proposed). Ebn al-Bayṭār, *al-Jāmeʿ le mofradāt al-adwīa waʾl-aḡḏīa*, 4 pts. in 2 vols., Bulaq, 1291/1874. A. Ghahreman, *Flore de l'Iran en couleur naturelle*, Tehran, 1978-. Horn, *Etymologie*, p. 53. Aḥmad Kalīqī, *Golkārī: Parvareš-e gīāhān-e zīnatī-e Īrān*, Tehran, 1364 Š./1985-86. Mowaffaq-al-Dīn Abū Manṣūr ʿAlī Heravī, *Ketāb al-abnīa ʿan haqāʾeq al-adwīa*, ed. A. Bahmanyār and Ḥ. Maḥbūbī Ardakānī, Tehran, 1346 Š./1967-68. Šehāb-al-Dīn Aḥmad Nowayrī, *Nehāyat al-arab fī fonūn al-adab*, 16 vols., n.p., n.d. A. Parsa, *Flore de l'Iran*, Tehran, I/1, 1951. J. M. Unvala, *The Pahlavi Text "King Husrav and His Boy*," Paris, n.d.

(H. AʿLAM)

BANĀʾĪ HERAVĪ, KAMĀL-AL-DĪN ŠĪR-ʿALĪ, son of Ostād Moḥammad Sabz Meʿmār, poet and musicologist (857-918/1453-1512). The son of an architect and master builder (*meʿmār*), he chose the pen name Banāʾī; the frequently given reading Bannāʾī (e.g., Browne, *Lit. Hist. Persia* III, p. 457; *Cat. Bib. Nat.* III, p. 318) is incorrect, because in each verse where the poet's name occurs the meter requires that it should be read Banāʾī. Although he changed his pen name to Ḥālī in his later years, he is best known under his original pen name. Banāʾī was born and educated in Herat, where he acquired a wide knowledge of literature, science, calligraphy, and music, and a reputation for proficiency in all. He then turned his attention to Sufism and began to lead an ascetic life. After traveling to central Iran in search of a spiritual guide, he made his way to Fārs and there became a disciple of Shaikh Šams-al-Dīn Moḥammad Lāhījī, the head of the Nūrbaḵšī order of Shiraz (Ṣafā, *Adabīyāt* IV, pp. 397-98), whom he praises in some of his odes (*qaṣīda*s). He stayed in Shiraz until, at the invitation of the Āq Qoyunlū sultan Yaʿqūb (r. 883-96/1478-90), he moved to Tabrīz, where he rose to high rank in the sultan's service. He dedicated his narrative, didactic poem *Bahrām o Behrūz* (or *Bāḡ-e eram*) to Yaʿqūb and also composed *qaṣīda*s for him and for the Šervānšāh Farroḵyasār. He stayed in Azerbaijan until Yaʿqūb's death (896/1490) and then returned to Herat, but discord with Amir ʿAlī- Šīr Navāʾī again forced him to leave his native Herat and go to Samarkand. For some time he was a eulogist of Solṭān ʿAlī Mīrzā, a grandson of the Timurid sultan Abū Saʿīd, and of Badīʿ-al-Zamān Mīrzā, the son and successor of Ḥosayn Bāyqarā, the sultan of Herat. Later he gained admittance, with the rank of poet laureate (*malek-al-šoʿarā'*) to the court of the Uzbek ruler, Moḥammad Šaybānī (Šaybak) Khan. During the Uzbek invasion of Khorasan, he accompanied Šaybānī Khan when the latter entered Herat. Thereafter he remained in Khorasan until Šaybānī Khan's defeat and death at the hands of Shah Esmāʿīl Ṣafawī in 916/1510, when he returned to Transoxiana in the retinue of Tīmūr Solṭān, a son of Šaybānī Khan. He met his death in the massacre of the Sunnis at Qaršī (918/1512) carried out by Shah Esmāʿīl's general and chief minister, Amir Najm Yār Aḥmad Eṣfahānī, known as Ṯānī.

Banā'ī is generally judged to be one of the most accomplished and eloquent poets of the Timurid period. Like earlier masters of the craft, he began to write poetry after he had acquired a solid grounding in prose composition and conventional sciences. He thus combined breadth of knowledge with sharpness of mind and flair for eloquence. His fidelity to the poetic traditions of the old masters is apparent throughout his work and has left a strong imprint on his language, which is notable for its precision and clarity. He liked the poetry of the earlier periods better than that of his own; his study of the *dīvān*s of other poets prompted him to quote from and reply to their best-known *qaṣīda*s and *ḡazal*s. Thus he compiled two *dīvān*s, one of the *qaṣīda*s, *ḡazal*s, *qeṭʿa*s, and *robāʿī*s written under the pen name Banā'ī, the other of the replies to *ḡazal*s of Saʿdī and Ḥāfeẓ, written under the pen name Ḥālī. Taqī-al-Dīn Kāšī, the author of the *taḏkera Ḵolāṣat al-ašʿār*, estimates the number of verses in the first *dīvān* at 6,000 and in the second *dīvān* at 3,000. It is significant that, following Banā'ī, several poets of the Safavid period composed whole *dīvān*s in reply to Saʿdī, Ḥāfeẓ, Feḡānī, and others. Banā'ī is also the author of *Šaybānī-nāma*, an account of the important events in central Asia from the rise of Šaybānī Khan to the disintegration of the Timurid sultanates (Storey, I, p. 372).

There is a manuscript of the *dīvān* of Banā'ī in the Bibliothèque Nationale (*Cat. Bib. Nat.* III, p. 318), and a large number of his poems under both pen names are quoted in Taqī-al-Dīn Kāšī's *Ḵolāṣat al-ašʿār*.

Banā'ī is not to be confused with another user of the pen name Ḥālī, Dūst Moḥammad, known as Qaṣīdagū, who died in 939/1532. The latter is also mentioned, and some examples of his *qaṣīda*s are quoted, in the *Ḵolāṣat al-ašʿār*.

Bibliography: Moḥammad Qodrat-Allāh Gōpāmavī Hendī, *Taḏkera-ye natā'ej al-afkār*, Bombay, 1336/1918, pp. 99-100. Mīr ʿAbd-al-Razzāq Ḵˇāfī, *Bahārestān-e soḵan*, Madras, 1958, pp. 383-85. ʿAlī-Ebrāhīm Khan Ḵalīl, *Ṣoḥof-e ebrāhīmī*, ms. 663 (W. Pertsch, *Verzeichniss der persischen Handschriften der königlichen Bibliothek zu Berlin*, Berlin, 1888; a photostatic copy, no. 2976, is in the Central Library of the University of Tehran). Ḵˇāndamīr, *Ḥabīb al-sīar* IV, pp. 348-49. Mīr Taqī-al-Dīn Kāšī, *Ḵolāṣat al-ašʿār wa zobdat al-afkār*, ms. Ḵayyāmpūr, *Soḵanvarān*, p. 89. Ḥājj Moḥammad Maʿṣūm Šīrāzī, *Ṭarā'eq al-ḥaqā'eq*, Tehran, 1316-19/1898-1901, III, pp. 50, 59. S. Nafīsī, *Naẓm o naṯr*, pp. 310-11. ʿAlī-Šīr Navā'ī, *Majāles al-nafā'es*, pp. 60, 232. M. A. Rāzī, *Haft eqlīm* II, pp. 152-54. Ṣafā, *Adabīyāt* IV, pp. 393-411. Sām Mīrzā Ṣafawī, *Toḥfa-ye sāmī*, Tehran, 1314 Š./1935, pp. 95-100. Nūr-Allāh Šūštarī, *Majāles al-mo'menīn*, Tehran, n.d., p. 307. Storey, I/1, pp. 301-03.

(Z. SAFA)

BANĀKAṮ, BENĀKAṮ (in Jovaynī, Fanākat), the main town of the medieval Transoxanian province of Šāš or Čāč, to be distinguished from the nearby town of Benkaṯ, another name of the town of Šāš, later Tashkent. Banākaṯ flourished in early Islamic times and almost certainly had a pre-Islamic history as a center of the Sogdians. According to Markwart, *Wehrot und Arang*, Leiden, 1938, pp. 162-63 n., the name derives from Mid. Pers *bon* "base, foundation" plus *kaṯ* "town," hence "chief town, capital." The town lay at the confluence of the Syr Darya or Jaxartes (which Jovaynī apparently calls "the River of Fanākat") with its right-bank tributary the Āhangarān or Angren (medieval Nahr Īlāq) and at the mouth of the Gijigen valley, hence to the southwest of modern Tashkent; both the ruins of old Banākaṯ and of its replacement Šāhroḵīya (see below) have been noted by Russian archeologists from 1896 onwards (Barthold, *Turkestan*[3], p. 169).

We do not possess information about the coming of Islam to Banākaṯ but local Iranian princes seem to have persisted there into Samanid times, and we have a detailed description in Moqaddesī, pp. 277, 335, of the town in the second half of the 4th/10th century. He calls it the capital of Šāš, with an orthodox Sunni but quarrelsome and turbulent population. There was a citadel (*qohandez*) with gates opening on to the inner town (*madīna*) and on to the inner one of the two outer towns (*rabaż*), where the majority of *bāzār*s lay; the Friday mosque was up against the city wall. The town had extensive gardens and orchards and produced "Turkestan" cloth and bows. Four stages to the north lay Asfījāb (q.v.) and the beginning of the Turkish steppes. It was apparently a place of some importance under the Qarakhanids, and coins were minted there under these princes (see E. von Zambaur, *Die Münzprägungen des Islams, zeitlich und örtlich geordnet* I, Wiesbaden, 1968, p. 79). When Jengiz Khan's hordes appeared in Transoxania, the Qanglï Turkish garrison under the Ḵˇārazmšāh's commander Iletgü Malek defended Banākaṯ for four days against 5,000 Mongol troops under Alaq Noyon, Sögetü, and Taqāy. On its surrender, there was a general massacre of the garrison, whilst the male population was impressed into the Mongol forces (Jovaynī, tr. Boyle, I, pp. 91-92).

Barthold doubted that it was this event specifically which caused the town's destruction, but opined that it probably fell into ruin in the later 7th/13th century. At any rate, in 794/1392 (year of the monkey), it was rebuilt by Tīmūr and named Šāhroḵīya after his son and successor Šāhroḵ (Šaraf-al-Dīn ʿAlī Yazdī, *Ẓafar-nāma*, Calcutta, 1885-88, II, p. 636). As such, it is mentioned by other authors such as Ebn ʿArabšāh, Moḥammad Ḥaydar Doḡlāt, and Bābor, the latter writing that in his time (opening of the 10th/16th century), Šāhroḵīya came within the territories of the Chaghatayid Khans; it apparently had a strong fortress and played a role in military operations up to the 12th/18th century (see Moḥammad-Ḥaydar Doḡlāt, *Tārīḵ-e rašīdī*, tr. N. Elias and E. D. Ross, London, 1895, pp. 112, 289; *Bābor-nāma*, tr. A. S. Beveridge, London, 1922, pp. 7, 23-24, 54, 151). Chinese accounts of the Timurid and Uzbek periods name it as Sa-lu-hai-ya (E. Bretschneider, *Mediaeval Researches from Eastern Asiatic Sources*, London, 1888, II, pp. 253-55). Finally, it sank into total decay, although the ruins still bear the name "Šarqīya" as a degenerate form of "Šāhroḵīya."

Bibliography: Given in the text. See also *Ḥodūd al-ʿālam*, tr. Minorsky, p. 118 par. 25.83. Le Strange, *Lands*, p. 482. Barthold, *Turkestan*[3], pp. 169, 407, 416-18.

(C. E. Bosworth)

BANĀKATĪ, Abū Solaymān Dāwūd b. Abi'l-Fażl Moḥammad (d. 730/1329-30), poet and historian. Nothing is known of his early career, except that he was presumably a native of Banākaṯ (q.v.), the later Šāhroḵīya in Transoxania. His general history from Adam to the beginning of the reign of the il-khan Abū Saʿīd (q.v.), the *Rawżat ūli'l-albāb fī maʿrefat al-tawārīḵ* (or *fī tawārīḵ al-akāber*) *wa'l-ansāb*, was completed on 25 Šawwāl 717/31 December 1317 (*Rawżat*, p. 2; cf. p. 479, with the month alone): although toward the end of the work he refers to Abū Saʿīd's enthronement at Solṭānīya in Rabīʿ II, 718/June, 1318 (p. 478), this event is known to have taken place in the previous year. The work is for the most part an abridgment of the *Jāmeʿ al-tawārīḵ*, the vast historical encyclopedia of Rašīd-al-Dīn, whom Banākatī admits he was attempting to emulate (*Rawżat*, p. 1), and is divided into nine *qesms*: (1) the prophets and patriarchs; (2) the ancient kings of Persia; (3) Moḥammad and the caliphs; (4) Persian dynasties contemporary with the ʿAbbasids; (5) the Jews; (6) the Christians and the Franks; (7) the Indians; (8) the Chinese; and (9) the Mongols. Only the final section of the ninth *qesm*, covering the years 703-17/1304-17, has any original value, and constitutes in fact our earliest source for the reign of the il-khan Ūljāytū (Öljeitü). At Ūjān, toward the end of Ḏu'l-qaʿda, 701/July-August, 1302, Banākatī had been awarded the title of *malek-al-šoʿarā* by Ūljāytū's predecessor Ḡāzān (*Rawża*, p. 465). Some specimens of his poetry are preserved in the *Rawża*, and one by Dawlatšāh (p. 227), who describes him as "learned and accomplished" (*mard-e dānešmand o fāżel*) and gives him the *laqab* of Faḵr-al-Dīn; otherwise he supplies scant detail.

Bibliography: *Rawża*, ed. Jaʿfar Šeʿār, Tehran, 1348 Š./1969. Dawlatšāh, ed. Browne, p. 227. Storey, I, pp. 79-80 (q.v. for further references). Browne, *Lit. Hist Persia* III, pp. 100-03. *EI*[2] I, p. 1011.

(P. Jackson)

BANĀN, ḠOLĀM-ḤOSAYN (b. Tehran, Ordībehešt, 1290 Š./May, 1911, d. Tehran, 10 Esfand 1364 Š./29 February 1986) one of the foremost Persian singers of the twentieth century. He was known for the quality of his voice, vast knowledge of *āvāz* repertory, exactness of style, ability to match poetry with music, and expressive interpretation of Persian poetry.

Banān was born in Tehran into a prominent family with a background in government service. His father, Karīm Khan Banān-al-Dawla, son of Moḥammad-Taqī Mīrzā Fażl-Allāh Khan Mostawfī Nūrī, appreciated traditional music. His mother was the daughter of Moḥammad-Taqī Mīrzā Roknī (Rokn-al-Dawla), a brother of Nāṣer-al-Dīn Shah (*Majalla-ye mūsīqī-e rādīo-ye Īrān*, p. 13). Banān's home environment fostered artistic development. His father sang and played the *tār* (long-necked lute; Abu'l-Ḥasan Varzī apud Farrahī), his mother played the piano, and his maternal aunt played the *ney* (end-blown flute). Once a week friends of his father would attend an informal party to which well-known musicians of the day were also invited (Mallāḥ, p. 3).

Banān received the education customary in the families of bureaucrats, with emphasis on penmanship and Persian literature, in both of which he excelled at school. His handwriting was of calligraphic quality, and he knew many poems by heart (Yarshater). He was known then and throughout his life for his prodigious memory, his ability to pick up accents and to mimic the gestures and diction of others (Mallāḥ, pp. 4-5). Banān learned to play the piano from his mother and would sing and accompany himself (*Majalla-ye mūsīqī-e radīo-ye Īrān*, p. 13). He also listened to and imitated recordings of his father's voice. His sisters studied the *tār* with Mortażā Ney-Dāvūd. Banān was present during his sisters' *tār* lessons, and would learn and memorize the pieces to help them remember their lessons. Ney-Dāvūd recognized his talent and persuaded Banān's father to let him study voice with him (Mallāḥ, pp. 3-4). He began working with Ney-Dāvūd at the age of eleven and later began his main vocal studies with the religious singer Żīāʾ-al-Ḏākerīn (a *rawża-ḵ*ᵛ*ān*, or reciter of Shiʿite passions), one of the favorite singers of Banān's father (Mallāḥ, pp. 5-6; Behrūzī). Later he also studied voice with Nāṣer Sayf, who used to sing at the Anjoman-e Oḵowwat (q.v.).

Banān was influenced by a number of other vocalists and instrumentalists. As a young man he listened to and imitated the voice of Janāb Damāvandī, whose voice was high-pitched, but also soft and very relaxed. He was later impressed by Adīb Ḵᵛānsārī, who was known to him through his recordings. Other singers who indirectly influenced his style were Reżāqolī Mīrzā Ẓellī, Ṭāherzāda, Tāj Eṣfahānī, and Amīr Qāsemī (on these, see Ḵāleqī, vol. I, index).

Although there was no systematic vocal *radīf* (repertoire) during the period of Banān's apprenticeship, there were different regional schools, among which the schools of Isfahan and Shiraz were of note. Banān's style was a combination of those found in Isfahan and Tehran (Varzī). His singing was also influenced by the violin style of Abu'l Ḥasan Ṣabā (q.v.), whose written repertoire was formulated in conjunction with Żīā'-al-Ḏākerīn (Varzī).

In 1923 ʿAlī-Naqī Wazīrī (q.v.) the celebrated composer and performer, returned from a five-year stay in Europe and set out to reform the traditional music by his new compositions, his introduction of Western orchestration and notation, and the founding of a music conservatory and, a little later, a musical club, where regular concerts were scheduled by his ensemble. Ruḥ-Allāh Ḵāleqī, a student and assistant of Wazīrī and his eventual successor as the director of the National Conservatory of Music (Madrasa-ye Mūsīqī-e Mellī), recognized Banān's exceptional voice and persuaded him to join his programs, and Banān gradually became the major vocal performer of the concerts arranged by Ḵāleqī in the Wazīrī style (Yarshater). It was his acquaintance with the works of Wazīrī and the association with Ḵāleqī which impressed upon him the importance of clarity of singing, expressive rendering of the lyrics, and careful matching of the meaning of classical lyrics with appropriate melodic materials (*gūšas*) of traditional modes (*dastgāhs*). It was also Ḵāleqī, the founder of the National Music Society (Anjoman-e Mūsīqī-e Mellī), who encouraged him to sing more frequently rhythmic vocal compositions accompanied by an orchestra.

Banān began working as a young man for the Department of Agriculture in 1936 and later for the Īrānbār Company in Ahvāz. In 1943 he returned to Tehran to work for the Ministry of Food and eventually became responsible for distribution of bread coupons for the Department of Grain and Bread (Edāra-ye Ḡalla wa Nān; Mallāḥ, p. 8). He began singing for Radio Tehran in 1942. He first performed with Abu'l-Ḥasan Ṣabā's ensemble, which included both Western and Persian instruments. These programs were broadcast live one or two evenings a week. Banān also performed regularly with the National Music Society (Anjoman-e Musīqī-e Mellī), which performed once or twice a month. The music society primarily performed the compositions of Wazīrī and Ḵāleqī, which were largely long vocal compositions performed by a soloist accompanied by a large orchestra of Persian and Western instruments. Banān was first interested only in performing *āvāz* (traditional singing; q.v.); but Ḵāleqī, impressed by Banān's voice, persuaded him to sing these new compositions with the orchestra. Although Banān did not read music, his ability to memorize allowed him to learn these pieces easily; he would write the name of the *gūšas*, rhythm, rests, and orchestral interludes in the margin of the lyrics (Mallāḥ, p. 11).

Banān performed regularly at both formal and informal gatherings. He paid careful attention to his choice of poetry and the accompanying music and would plan what to sing by going over his notebook at the beginning of an evening. At informal parties, he would often first entertain by telling stories and singing popular and comic songs, saving serious performances for late in the evening. Often at these gathering he would improvise rhythmic (*żarbī*) pieces, accompanying himself on a drum.

His preference for singing eventually led him to pursue a career in music exclusively. The National Music Society had by then divided into two organizations, the National Conservatory of Music (Honarestān-e Mūsīqī-e Mellī) and the "Flowers Program" (Barnāma-ye Golhā, begun in 1955 and ably directed by Dāwūd Pīrnīā; Varzī). In 1953 he became one of the first teachers at the Conservatory (Mallāḥ, p. 9), although this was secondary to his performing career. He taught instrumentalists and vocalists using the traditional oral method of instruction (Mallāḥ, p. 12).

Banān continued to work for the radio two or three times a week, performing fifteen minute segments that included *āvāz* and a short *taṣnīf*. He performed songs in the style of the day as well as more classical pieces. These song compositions included works by ʿAlī-Naqī Wazīrī, Rūḥ-Allāh Ḵāleqī, Naṣr-Allāh Zarrīnpanja, Mortażā Maḥjūbī, Akbar Moḥsenī, and ʿAlī Tajwīdī. Lyricists for these pieces included Rahī Moʿayyerī and Nawwāb Ṣafā. He became the most prominent singer to perform for the programs "Multi-colored Flowers" (*Golhā-ye rangārang*) and "Eternal Flowers" (*Golhā-ye jāvīdān*). These programs were a continuation of Ḵāleqī's efforts to revitalize Persian music. They were arrangements and orchestrations of traditional Persian music, along with newer compositions that utilized basically Persian melodies with Western orchestration, harmonies, and interludes.

In 1958 as the result of a car accident, Banān lost vision in his right eye, which had a noticeable impact on his singing. Not only did he take his work more seriously, but from that time he also began to sing more rhythmic pieces that had popular appeal (Mallāḥ, pp. 13-15). Banān retired from active singing around 1967, although he continued to sing occasionally at private parties.

Banān was careful and exact in his own performance and worked daily to improve his singing (*Majalla-ye rādīo-ye Īrān* 14, 1336 Š./1957, p. 20). He did not perform for television, preferring to sing for a live audience. Since he also did not perform in nightclubs or concerts, the majority of people knew him only through the sound of his voice on radio and recordings. He led a relatively simple life, and was never well off. He had four marriages and two children. His first wife, Maryam Wazīrī, was a sister of ʿAlī-Naqī Wazīrī (communication by Mallāḥ); his last wife was Parī Āvar, who survives him.

Banān's vocal style. Banān was known for the quality of his voice as well as for his style of singing. He had a relatively lowpitched, soft, and relaxed vocal style. His

Tables 22 and 23 contain a nearly complete listing of performances by Banān recorded on tape. They are based on a list compiled by Mr. Karīm ʿAbd-al-Rasūlī.

For the radio programs in which the pieces were performed the following abbreviations have been used: G. J. = Golhā-ye Jāvīdān; G.R. = Golhā-ye Rangārang; G.T. = Golhā-ye Tāza; B.S. = Barg-e Sabz; Š.G. = Yak Šāḵ-e Gol; M.R. = Music on the Radio; M.C. = Tehran Conservatory of Music. In each table the pieces are arranged alphabetically by *dastgāh* and within each *dastgāh* by program in the above order. Pieces for which no program number or program is known are listed alphabetically by the title of the piece. By comparing the two tables it can be easily seen which of the songs (*taṣnīfs*, *tarānas*, etc.) listed in Table 23 were performed in conjunction with the *āvāz*es listed in Table 22 and who were the accompanyists.

Table 22

BANĀN: ĀVĀZ

Program	Lyrics	Accompanyist
	ABŪ ʿAṬĀ	
G.J. 98	*Az har-če mīravad soḵan-e dūst ḵᵛoštar ast* (Saʿdī)	L. Majd (tār)
G.J. 118		Orchestra
G.R. 201	*Yak rūz dar āḡūš-e to ārām gereftam*	M. Maḥjūbī (piano), ʿA. Tajwīdī (violin)
	Man pas az ʿešq-e to bar ʿešq-e jahān mīḵandam	
	AFŠĀRĪ	
G.J. 136 (see Šūr)		
G.R. 134	*Goftam āhan-delī konam čandī*	M. Maḥjūbī (piano), A. Ṣabā (violin), R. Varzanda (santūr), Ḥ. Ṭehrānī (tombak)
G.R. 143	*Ey ḵeradmand ze mā dūr ke mā mastān-īm*	M. Ḵāledī and A. Ṣabā (violin), M. Maḥjūbī (piano)
G.T. 18		M. Maḥjūbī (piano)
G.R. 228	*Ze eštīāq-e to jān-am be-lab rasīd kojā-ī?*	
B.S. 31	*Ey sāqī-e ātaš-rū mast az mey-e nāb-am kon*	
Š.G. 142[a]		
	BAYĀT-E EṢFAHĀN	
G.J. 131	*Raftī o hamčonān be ḵīāl-e man andar-ī* (Saʿdī)	
G.R. 224	*Ḵīālangīz o jānparvar čo būy-e gol sarāpā-ī* (R. Moʿayyerī)	
G.R. 224-Ṯ	*Āmad ammā dar negāh-aš ān nevāzeshā nabūd* (A. Varzī)	J. Maʿrūfī (piano)
G.R. 252	*Dānī ke čīst dawlat dīdār-e yār dīdan* (Ḥāfeẓ) *Hamrāh-e ḵᵛod nasīm-e ṣabā mībarad marā*	
G.R. 254	*Sīna mālāmāl-e dard ast ey darīḡā marḥam-ī* (Ḥāfeẓ)	
B.S. 63	*Ey del mabāš ḵālī yak dam ze ʿešq o mastī* (Ḥāfeẓ)	Ḥ. Badīʿī (violin), J. Šahnāz (tār)
B.S. 107	*Hamčo nūr az čašm-am raftī o namīāʾī*	Ḥ. Badīʿī (violin), A. ʿEbādī (setār)
M.R.	*Mā nām-e ḵᵛod ze ṣafḥa-ye delhā setorda-īm* (Ṣāʾeb Tabrīzī) *Man ḵᵛod ey sāqī az īn šawq ke dāram mast-am* (Saʿdī) *Har ke šod maḥram-e del dar ḥaram-e yār bemānd* (Ḥāfeẓ)	A. Ṣabā (violin)

Table 22 (Contd.)

Program	Lyrics	Accompanyist
	BAYĀT-E ZAND/TORK	
G.J. 92	*Marā čo qebla to bāšī namāz nag'zār-am*	A. ʿEbādī (setār), Ḥ. Kasāʾī (ney)
G.J. 138	*Man namīgūyam ke ʿāqel bāš yā dīvāna bāš*	Yāḥaqqī (violin)
G.R. 252	*Hamrāh-e k̲ᵛod nasīm-e ṣabā mībarad marā*	M. Maḥjūbī (piano)
	ČAHĀRGĀH	
G.J. 137	*ʿĀšeq-e rūy-e jānfazā-ye to-īm*	M. Maḥjūbī (piano), ʿA. Tajwīdī (violin)
G.J. 139	*Šekofta šod gol-e ḥamrā o gašt bolbol mast* (Ḥāfeẓ)	A. ʿEbādī (setār), M. Maḥjūbī (piano), Yāḥaqqī (violin)
B.S. 86	*Ḥasb-e ḥāl-ī naneveštīm o šod ayyām-ī čand* (Ḥāfeẓ)	M. Maḥjūbī (piano)
M.C.	*Ḥasb-e ḥāl-ī naneveštīm o šod ayyām-ī čand* (Ḥāfeẓ)	M. Meftāḥ (qānūn)
	DAŠTĪ	
G.R. 103	*Raftī az īn dīār o nadādī k̲abar marā*	Ḥ. Kasāʾī (ney), M. K̲āledī (violin), R. Varzanda (santūr), A. ʿEbādī (setār)
G.R. 149	*Če k̲alāf sar zad az mā ke dar-e sarāy bastī* (Saʿdī)	Tajwīdī (violin), R. Varzanda (santūr)
G.R. 176	*Ze eštīāq-e to jān-am be-lab rasīd kojā-ī?*	
G.R. 217[b]	*Deylamān: Čonān dar qayd-e mehr-at pāyband-am*	orchestra
G.R. 230	*To sūz-e āh-e man ey morḡ-e šab če mīdānī* (R. Moʿayyerī?)	M. Maḥjūbī (piano)
G.R. 232	*K̲abar-at hast ke bī rū-ye to ārām-am nīst* (Saʿdī)	Ḥ. Kasāʾī (ney), M. Maḥjūbī (piano)
G.R. 232-B	*Mat̲nawī: Ey ney-e maḥzūn navā-ī sāz kon* (Nāẓerzāda Kermānī)	J. Maʿrūfī (piano), Wazīrītabār (clarinet)
G.R. 234 (Daštī + Māhūr)	*Tāb-e banafša mīdahad ṭorra-ye mošksā-ye to* (Ḥāfeẓ)	J. Maʿrūfī (piano)
G.R. 250	*Dād ḥosn-at be-to taʿlīm k̲ᵛodārāʾī-rā* (ʿĀref)	M. Maḥjūbī (piano)
Š.G. 403[c]		
M.R.	*Bak̲t-e āʾīna nadāram ke dar ū mīnegarī* (Saʿdī)	
M.C.	*Na tanhā man gereftār-am be-dām-e zolf-e zībāʾ-ī*	
M.C.	*Tā k̲abar dāram az ū bī-k̲abar az k̲ᵛīštan-am*	
	Dīvāna-ye moḥabbat-e jānāna-am hanūz	J. Maʿrūfī (piano), A. Ṣabā (violin), Wazīrītabār (clarinet)
	Ḡam-at dar nehān-k̲āna-ye del nešīnad (Ṭabīb Eṣfahānī)	
	Raftī az īn dīār o nadādī k̲abar marā	R. Varzanda (santūr)
	Tā ke dar selsela-e zolf-e to āvīk̲ta-īm (Olfat)	
	Tā raft ān negār-e ʿazīz az kenār-e man	
	HOMĀYŪN	
G.R. 222-B	*Čašm-e mast-at če konad bā man-e bīmār emšab*	J. Maʿrūfī (piano)
G.R. 245	*K̲ᵛāham ey gol k̲ār gardam tā be-dāmān-at nešīnam* (Šeydā)	L. Majd (tār), P. Yāḥaqqī (violin)

Table 22 (Contd.)

Program	Lyrics	Accompanyist
G.R. 251	Baḵtīārī: *Meṯl-e pīštarā...*	
B.S. 145	*Gar bovad ʿomr be-mey-ḵāna ravam bār-e degar* (Ḥāfeẓ)	R. Varzanda (santūr), Yāḥaqqī (violin)
M.R.	*Bā ʿazīzān dar nayāmīzad del-e dīvāna-am*	
M.R.	*Mast-īm o ʿāšeq-īm o be golzār mīravīm*	M. Maḥjūbī (piano)
	Āmad ammā dar negāh-aš ān navāzešhā nabūd (A. Varzī)	J. Maʿrūfī (piano)
	Bīdād	Ṭāṭāʾī (violin)
	Har laḥẓa dar bar-am del az andīša ḵūn šavad	L. Majd (tār)
	Mā dar-e ḵalwat be-rūy-e ǧayr bebastīm (Saʿdī)	M. Maḥjūbī (piano), L. Majd (tār), J. Šahnāz (tār), ʿA. Tajwīdī (violin)
	MĀHŪR	
G.J. 91	*Farroḵ ṣabāḥ-e ān ke to bar vey goḏar konī*	
G.J. 130	*Agar na rūy-e del andar barābar-at dāram* (Saʿdī)	A. ʿEbādī (setār), J. Šahnāz (tār)
G.J. 131	*Raftī o hamčonān be-ḵīāl-e man andar-ī* (Saʿdī)	L. Majd (tār)
G.R. 234 (Daštī and Māhūr, see Daštī)		
G.R. 237	*Hama ʿomr bar nadāram sar az īn ḵomār-e mastī*	J. Maʿrūfī (piano)
M.R.	*Dūš ān parī ke raḵna be-delhā nomūd o raft*	J. Maʿrūfī (piano)
M.R.	*Mardān-e ḵodā parda-ye pendār darīdand*	J. Maʿrūfī (piano)
M.C.	*Alā yā ayyoha'l-sāqī* (Ḥāfeẓ)	
M.C.	*Del mīravad ze dast-am ṣāḥeb-delān Ḵodā-rā* (Ḥāfeẓ)	
M.C.	*Del sarā-parda-ye moḥabbat-e ūst* (Ḥāfeẓ)	L. Majd (tār)
M.C.	*Man ḵᵛod ey sāqī az īn šawq ke dāram mastam* (Saʿdī)	
	NAVĀ	
	Kāškī čūn to kas-ī dāštamī (Ḵāqānī)	M. Maḥjūbī (piano)
	ʿOŠŠĀQ AND BŪSALĪK	
G.R. 210	*Āmadī jān-am be qorbān-at walī ḥālā čerā* (Šahrīār)	
	SEGĀH	
G.J. 128	*Māhrūyā dar jahān āvāza-ye āvāz-e to'st*	
G.J. 131	*Raftī o hamčonān be-ḵīāl-e man andar-ī* (Saʿdī)	A. ʿEbādī (setār), Ḥ. Kasāʾī (ney), L. Majd (tār)
G.J. 132	*Del-ī dāram ḵarīdār-e moḥabbat* (Ḥāfeẓ)	R. Varzanda (santūr)
G.J. 139	*Šekofta šod gol-e ḥamrā o gašt bolbol mast* (Ḥāfeẓ)	
G.R. 46	*Az dar dar āmadī o man az ḵᵛod be-dar šodam*	Ḥ Badīʿī (violin), Ḥ. Kasāʾī (ney), J. Šahnāz (tār)
G.R. 109	*Sawdā-ye ʿešq ʿāqel o dīvāna sūḵta* (Nāẓerzāda Kermānī)	

Table 22 (Contd.)

Program	Lyrics	Accompanyist
G.R. 136	*Če karda-am ke marā mobtalā-ye ḡam kardī*	L. Majd (tar), A. Ṣabā (violin), R. Varzanda (santūr)
G.R. 174	*Yād ān šab ke ṣabā bar sar-e mā gol mīrīḵt* (M.-E. Bāstānī Pārīzī)	
G.R. 190	*Sar-e kūy-e dūst ʿomr-ī qadam az wafā zadam man*	L. Majd (tār), ʿA. Tajwīdī (violin)
G.R. 211	*ʿAzm-e ān dāram ke emšab nīm-mast*	
G.R. 216-B/Š.G. 90	*Bīār bāda ke mā-rā be hīč ḥāl emšab; yā be-nazd-e ḵ̌īštan rāh-am bedeh* (ʿErāqī)	A. ʿEbādī (setār)
G.R. 370		
B.S. 27	*Ḵ̌ošā kas-ī ke ze ʿešq-aš dam-ī rahāʾī nīst*	M. Maḥjūbī (piano), ʿA. Tajwīdī (violin)
B.S. 83	*Ṭarīq-e ʿešq-e jānān bī-balā nīst*	M. Maḥjūbī (piano), F. Šarīf (tār), A. Tajwīdī (violin)
M.C.	*Hazār jahd bekardam ke serr-e ʿešq bepūšam* (Saʿdī) *Be-qaṣd-e morḡ-e rūḥ-am delrobā-ī dāna mīrīzad*	J. Maʿrūfī (piano), Wazīrītabār (clarinet)
	ŠŪR	
G.J. 136 (also Afšārī)	*Čo čašm-e šūḵ az Farhād dīdī*	Ḥ. Badīʿī (violin), Ḥ. Kasāʾī (ney), M. Maḥjūbī (piano)
G.J. 145	*Sāqī-e farroḵ roḵ-e man jām-e čo golnār bedeh*	A. ʿEbādī (setār), J. Šahnāz (tār), R. Varzanda (santūr), Yāḥaqqī (violin)
G.J. 156	*Gar-am qabūl konī w'ar berānī az dar-e ḵ̌īš* (Saʿdī)	
G.R. 172-B/B.S. 89	*Konūn ke ṣāḥeb-e možgān-e šūḵ o čašm-e sīāh-ī* (Forūḡī Basṭāmī)	A. ʿEbādī (setār), M. Maḥjūbī (piano), F. Šarīf (tār), Yāḥaqqī (violin)
G.R. 219	*Ḵ̌ošā dard-ī ke darmān-aš to bāšī* (Ḥāfeẓ)	
G.R. 242	*Dūstān waqt-e gol ān beh ke be-ʿešrat kūšīm* (Ḥāfeẓ)	Ḥ. Badīʿī (violin), M. Maḥjūbī (piano), J. Šahnāz (tār)
G.R. 249	*Gadā-ye ʿešq-am o solṭān-e ḥosn šāh-e man-ast* (ʿĀref)	M. Maḥjūbī (piano)
G.R. 256	*Man-am ke dīda be-dīdār-e dūst kardam bāz* (Ḥāfeẓ)	M. Maḥjūbī (piano)
M.R.	*To ān na-ī ke del az ṣoḥbat-e to bar gīrand*	
M.C.	*Bī-del o ḵasta dar īn šahr-am o deldār-ī nīst* (Homā Šīrāzī)	M. Maḥjūbī (piano)
Be-yād-e Šīrāz	*Bārhā gofta-am o bār-e degar mīgūyam* (Ḥāfeẓ) *Āb-e ḥayāt-e man-ast ḵāk-e sar-e kūy-e dūst* (Saʿdī) *Ān-rā ke ḡam-ī čūn ḡam-e man nīst če dānad* *Na qarār dāda būdī ke šab-ī be ḵalwat āyī* (Nezārī Qohestānī)	R. Varzanda (santūr)

[a]About Moʾayyad Ṯābetī
[b]In memory of Reżā Maḥjūbī
[c]In memory of Rūḥ-Allāh Ḵāleqī

Table 23

BANĀN: TARĀNA, TAṢNĪF, ŻARBĪ

Program and/or *āvāz*	Lyrics	Composer
	ABŪ ʿAṬĀ	
G.J. 118	*Emrūz mahā k͟ᵛīš ze bīgāna nadānīm*	M. Maḥjūbī
G.R. 201	*Dāram ḡam-e jānkāh-ī*	
	Moštāq o parīšān: Āmadī vah ke če moštāq o parīšān būdam (Saʿdī)	ʿA. N. Wazīrī
	AFŠĀRĪ	
G.R. 143	*Dīšab ke to dar k͟āna-ye mā āmada būdī*	
G.R. 205/G.T. 18/ Š.G. 142	*Ātašīn lāla: Ey ātašīn lāla* (R. Moʿayyerī)	
G.R. 228	*Tan-am dar kūra-ye tab sūzad emšab*	R. K͟āleqī
	Dok͟tar-e fālbīn: Nāzanīn dok͟tarak-ī	
	Mastāna: Sāqī bīā k'az ʿaql o dīn bīgāna-am bīgāna	R. K͟āleqī
	Partow-e ʿešq: Partow-e ʿešq-e to ey šamʿ-e forūzān-am	
	BAYĀT-E EṢFAHĀN	
G.R. 224	*Bahār-e delnešīn: Tā bahār-e delnešīn āmada ṭarf-e čaman*	R. K͟āleqī
G.R. 224-T͟	*Hastī če bovad qeṣṣa-ye por ranj o malāl-ī*	Ḥ.-ʿA. Mallāḥ
G.R. 254	*Čang-e Rūdakī: Būy-e jūy-e mowlīān āyad hamī* (Rūdakī)	R. K͟āleqī
B.S. 107	*Če mīk͟ᵛāhī: Marā ze čašm-at afkandī degar če mīk͟ᵛāhī*	
M.C.	*Man ke farzand-e īn sarzamīn-am*	R. K͟āleqī
Šomā o radio	*Dīšab mah-e man to hamdam-e ke būdī*	
	Be-k͟āṭer-e to: Bar mā tīr-e balā mībārad az negah-ī	
	Bīā sāqī: Bīā ey sāqī ze hejr-at gela dāram	
	Mey-e nāb: Dīšab be seyl-e ašk rah-e k͟ᵛāb mīzadam (Ḥāfeẓ)	R. K͟āleqī
	Raqṣ-e mastāna: Dar sīna-am del be-yād-e to mastāna raqṣad	
	Šab: Bovad mah čūn safīna-ye zar	
	Sawdāzada: Sawdāzada o mastāna āmad šab-ī az mey-k͟āna	
	ČAHĀRGĀH	
	Bar čehra-ye gol nasīm-e nowrūz k͟ᵛoš ast	
	Mastī-e ʿāšeqān: Tā to ey sāqī	R. K͟aleqī
	Raqṣ-e dard: Mastāna bezan čūn gol be čaman	
	DAŠTĪ	
G.R. 103	*Tanhā to-ī tanhā to-ī dar k͟alwat-e tanhā'ī-am* (M. Atābakī (Zohra))	
G.R. 176	*Ramīdī o raftī: Dīdī ey mah ke nāgahān ramīdī o raftī*	
G.R. 217	*Kāravān: Hama šab nālam čūn ney* (R. Moʿayyerī)	
G.R. 230	*Morḡ-e ḥaqq: Morḡ-e ḥaqq nālad har dam dar del-e šab ey māh* (R. Moʿayyerī)	M. Maʿrūfī
G.R. 232/G.R. 232-B	*Navā-ye ney: Čonān-am bāng-e ney ātaš bar jān zad* (R. Moʿayyerī)	

Table 23 (*Contd.*)

Program and/or *āvāz*	Lyrics	Composer
G.R. 250	*Gerya kon: Gerya kon ke gar k̲ūn gerī t̲amar nadārad* (ʿĀref Qazvīnī)	ʿĀref Qazvīnī
M.R. *Bak̲t-e āʾīna*	*Āh-e saḥar: Yak šab āk̲er dāman-e āh-e saḥar k̲^{v}āham gereft* (Forūḡī Basṭāmī)	
M.R.	*Bolbol-e mast: Be har golbon-ī bolbol-e mast* (Gol-e Golāb)	ʿA. N. Wazīrī
M.R.	*Delšekan: Če begūyam ke če karda ḡam-e to marā*	
M.R.	*Dok̲tar-e rāmešgar: Ey dok̲tar-e rāmešgar če zībā-ī*	
M.R.	*Naḡma ye nowrūzī: Gol-e man bostān gašta čūn rūy-at*	R. K̲āleqī
M.R.	*Nāmahā-ye gom-šoda: Čūn seyl ašk az dīda rīzam*	
M.R.	*Rāz-e negāh: To hamčo māh-ī māh-e derak̲šān*	
M.C. *Na tanhā*	*Partow-e mehr: Dīdam gīāh-ī dar čaman*	Zarrīnpanja
M.C. *Tā k̲abar*	*Čašm-e ātašīn: Ey do čašm-e k̲ūnfešān-am*	
M.R. *Dīvāna-ye*	*Elāha-ye nāz: Bāz ey elāha-ye nāz bā del-e man besāz*	A. Moḥsenī
Ḡam-at	*Afsūn-e sok̲an*	
	Če šabhā: Če šabhā ke az dūrī-at nak̲oftam	
	Dānī ke čīst dawlat dīdār-e yār dīdan (Ḥāfeẓ)	
	HOMĀYŪN	
G.R. 222-B/M.R. *Mast-īm*	*Nadānam-at be ke mānī ke āfat-e del o jān-ī*	M. Maʿrūfī
G.R. 245/M.R. *Bā ʿazīzān*	*Šab-e javānī: Tā be key az īn del-āzārīhā*	
M.R.	*Dar ārzū-ye to: Del-ī be k̲ūn nešasta dāram*	
M.R.	*Rāz-e negāh: Čašm-e fattān-aš bā negāh-ī*	
M.C. *Har laḥẓa*	*Honar-e to: Morḡ-e del-am har dam mīšod ṣayd-e qafas-ī*	Ḥ. Yāḥaqqī
M.C.	*Bād-e now-bahārī: Mey agar-aš šūrafkan at̲ar-ī'st*	
	Tūša-ye ʿomr: Čūn bālā-ye to ravān	
	Ze mā ey-gol če dīdī	
	MĀHŪR	
G.R. 234	*Šāk̲a-ye gol-e šekasta: Gar-če zešt-am zībā bovad serešt-am*	Zarrīnpanja
G.R. 237	*Na del maftūn-e delband-ī na jān madhūš-e delk̲^{v}āh-ī* (R. Moʿayyerī)	
G.R. 370[a]	*Borow ey šab ke če ḡamparvar-ī*	
M.R. *Dūš*	*Ḡam-e jahān: Bar k̲īz o mak̲^{v}or ḡam-e jahān-e god̲arān* (ʿOmar K̲ayyām); *Ze to sarmast o k̲omār-am k̲abar az k̲^{v}īš nadāram*	Ḥ.-ʿA. Mallāḥ
M.R. *Mardān-e*	*K̲^{v}odpasand: Če k̲^{v}odpasand-ī ey del be dīgarān bengar*	
M.C. *Del sarāparda*	*K̲arīdār-e to: Na to goftī ke be-jāy āram o goftam ke nayārī* (Saʿdī)	
M.C. *Man k̲^{v}od*	*Gūšanešīn*	
M.C.	*K̲arīdār: Man-e bīmāya ke bāšam ke k̲arīdār-e to bāšam* (Saʿdī)	
	Az yād rafta: Dīgar az mā yād-ī nakonī	
	Če šabhā: Če šabhā ke az dūrī-at nak̲oftam	
	Man agar ze jahān be to rū nakonam če konam	
	Rah-e ʿešq: ʿĀref gūyad ke dalq-e pašmīna-ye man	ʿA. N. Wazīrī
	Sāqī	

Table 23 (Contd.)

Program and/or *āvāz*	Lyrics	Composer
	'OŠŠĀQ O BŪSALĪK	
G.R. 210-b	*Āmadī jān-am be qorbān-at walī ḥālā čerā* (Šahrīār)	R. Ḵāleqī
	SEGĀH	
G.J. 128	*Ey dīdan-e to ḥayāt-e jān-am*	
G.R. 136	*Man-e bīdel sāqī be-negāh-ī mast-am* (R. Mo'ayyerī)	
G.R. 174[b]	*Ṣabā raft*	M. Ḵāledī
G.R. 190	*Marā 'āšeq-ī šeydā to kardī* (M. Ṭohā)	
G.R. 211	*Ḥayrān-am ḥayrān-am*	
G.R. 216-B/Š.G. 90	*Rūz-e azal: Man az rūz-e azal dīvāna būdam*	M. Maḥjūbī
M.C. *Hazār jahd*	*Ārzū-ye del: Bā ū nešastan be-kām*	
M.C.	*Nā-omīd: Ḵ[v]oš ān zamān-ī ke del bar to bastam*	
Be-qaṣd-e	*Zāhed-e pašīmān: Waqt-rā ḡanīmat dān ān-qadar ke bet'vānī* (Ḥāfeẓ)	Ḥ.-'A. Mallāḥ
	Čūn ḵazān-am: Now-bahār-e marā čonān ḵazān karda-ī	
	Jām-e jahānbīn: Sālhā del ṭalab-e jām-e Jam az mā mīkard (Ḥāfeẓ)	R. Ḵāleqī
	Mey-kada-ye ārzū: Borow ey šab ke če ḡamparvar-ī	
	Namānda raftī: Āmadī ranj-e marā afzūda raftī	
	Partow-e mehr: Ey del ze jān-am če ḵ[v]āhī	
	ŠŪR	
G.J. 156	*Har ke šod maḥram-e del dar ḥaram-e yār bemānd* (Ḥāfeẓ)	
G.R. 172-B (B.S. 89)	*Ey omīd-e del-e man kojā-ī*	
G.R. 242	*Ḵodāyā 'ešq-ī ḵ[v]āham čūn šarār sūzān*	
G.R. 249	*Če šūrhā ke man be-pā* ('Āref Qazvīnī)	'Āref Qazvīnī
G.R. 256	*Āḏarābādagān: Ey qebla-ye āzādagān*	
M.R. *Kojā ravand*	*Bīā bīā ey gol-e man sarḵ[v]oš-am ze būy-at*	
M.C. *Bī-del*	*Gerya-ye šam': Ze ašk-am šo'lahā ḵīzad*	Zarrīnpanja
M.C.	*Payām-e 'āšeq: Ey šāna agar dīdī šekanj-e zolf-aš-rā*	E. Manṣūrī
M.C.	*Baḵt-e bīdār: Bāz ā bāz ā to gol-e zībā-ye man-ī*	
M.C.	*Būsa-ye ārzū: Čo košad partow-e mah abr-e sīah-parda be šabhā*	
Na qarār	*Wa'da-ye weṣāl*	
	Gol be dāmān kard ṣaḥrā	
	Payām-e nasīm: Az nasīm-e now-bahārān bešanīdam payām-e šādī	
	Soḵan-e negāh: Ze negāh-at mastī rīzad	

[a]Also in Segāh
[b]In memory of Abu'l-Ḥasan Ṣabā

facial expression and singing style were also relaxed. The ideal vocal quality of his time had been high-pitched and intense, possibly due to the tendency of religious singers to project for their large audiences. His modulations (*taḥrīr*) and vocal ornamentations were soft, effortless, clear, and well-placed in the context of his singing (Yarshater). Ḵāleqī has likened his *taḥrīr* to the sound of pearls dropped on a marble floor (*Varzī*). His use of these vocal ornaments was systematic in type, length, direction, and place. His use of rests was also systematic. He knew how much and where to put a pause in order to create and resolve suspense for the listeners.

Banān had knowledge of both Persian music and poetry. In selecting music for a poem, he was careful to choose the *gūšas* that fit the meaning of the poetry. He was also careful to match the melody and ornaments to the poetry and was attentive to poetic interpretation (Mallāḥ, p. 8). He had great control and musical skill and was able to express whatever meaning or feeling was in the poetry, varying vocal quality, intensity, and timing. He planned the essential outline and direction of his performance shortly before he performed. At times he would modify the traditional order of the *gūšas* to fit the poetry. He would also choose specific lines of a *ḡazal* and at times would vary their order. He then developed his musical expression and improvisation according to poetic interpretation. Banān developed a style that was uniquely his own, drawing from a number of influences. He worked on his style in private; experimenting, innovating, and perfecting it. His favorite accompanists, Reżā Varzanda on the *santūr* (hammered dulcimer) and Loṭf-Allāh Majd on the *tār*, had developed the ability to play and to follow him according to this style. He also enjoyed working with the pianist Mortażā Maḥjūbī and with the violinists Mahdī Ḵāledī, Maḥmūd Tājbaḵš, and Parvīz Yāḥaqqī (Varzī; Ṣafā, p. 193).

Banān's place in Persian music. Banān's voice appealed to and was respected by a wide variety of people. Although he was primarily a performer of traditional *āvāz* and was trained in the *dastgāh* (q.v.) system of Persian music, he adapted to the musical trends of his day and performed the more Westernized compositions of Wazīrī, Ḵāleqī, and others. He also performed popular songs that appealed to people that did not have a background in classical Persian music. In addition to being technically skilled in both poetic interpretation and musical expression, he was extremely versatile and innovative. He carefully crafted his performances, ever developing and perfecting his style. Beyond the expertise of his craft, Banān had great power of emotional expression and communication. He could take people out of themselves, refreshing and transforming them spiritually. The ability to place people easily into a transcendent state (*ḥāl*) is considered a unique gift, and for this Banān became almost legendary as a supreme interpreter of Persian poetry and music.

Bibliography: Ḵosrow Behrūzī "Ḵāṭera-ī az kūdakī-e Banān, "Rādīo Īrān, interview with Banān, Tehran. Margaret Caton "*The Classical Taṣnif: A Genre of Persian Vocal Music*, Ph.D. Dissertation, University of California, Los Angeles, California, 1983, pp. 92, 274-301, 397-400, 490-92, 515-18. Farhang Farrahī, interview with Abu'l-Ḥasan Varzī, Mortażā Varzī, and Ḥasan Šahbāz, Rādīo Īrān, Los Angeles, California, 7 March 1986. Rūḥ-Allāh Ḵāleqī *Sargodašt-e musīqī-e Īrān* I, Tehran, 1956, pp. 358, 432. Ḥosayn-ʿAlī Mallāḥ, "Ǧolām-Ḥosayn Banān," *Payām-e novīn* 1/11-12, 1338 Š./1959, pp. 1-15. *Majalla-ye mūsīqī-e rādīo-ye Īrān* 13, 1337 Š./1959, pp. 13, 22. *Majalla-ye rādīo-ye Īrān* 14, 1336 Š./1957, pp. 20, 28. Nawwāb Ṣafa "Banān-ī ke man mīšenāḵtam," *Rahāvard* 3/10, 1986, pp. 190-96. Mortażā Varzī, interview, Los Angeles, California, 25 September 1986. E. Yarshater, personal communication and "Ǧolām-Ḥosayn Banān," *Īrān-nāma* 6/1, 1987, pp. 25-30.

(M. CATON)

BĀNBIŠN, Middle Persian "queen." The Pahlavi ideogram for *bānbišn* is *MLKTA* (see *Frahang ī pahlavīk*, chap. 12, l. 4, where the variant *b'nbwšn, bānbušn*, is listed). In Manichean Middle Persian the word is spelled *b'nbyšn* and it was borrowed into Armenian as *bambišn* (Hübschmann, *Armenische Grammatik*, pp. 116f.). A substandard form *bāmbušt* was borrowed into Sogdian (Gershevitch, pars. 1246, 1518) and from there found its way into Uigur and Chinese (Henning, 1940, pp. 17f.). The Old Persian ancestor of *bānbišn* is not attested but must have been **māna-pašnī*, corresponding to Avestan *dəmąnō.paθnī* "mistress (of the house)," from Old Iranian **dmāna-paθnī* (see *AirWb.*, col. 1093; Kent, *Old Persian*, p. 32; Tedesco, pp. 64-66; Benveniste, 1954, p. 301). The genuine Sogdian form is *δvāmban* "lady" (variously spelled, see Gershevitch, pars. 14, 43, 304, 449, 466, cf. also Skjærvø, p. 70 n. 14). The initial *b-* of *bānbišn* is likely to be due to analogy with *bānūk* "lady," attested from Old Persian times as a loanword in Elamite *ba-nu-qa(-na-be)* (Hinz, p. 423).

In the Sasanian inscriptions, *bānbišn* (written MPers. *MLKTA*, Parth. *MLKTE*) "queen" matches *šāh* "king" (*MLKA*). The title is found in Šāpūr I's inscription on the Kaʿba-ye Zardošt, dating from 262/3 (Greek *basílissa*), as the title of a certain Dēnak. Corresponding to *šāhān šāh* (MPers. *MLKAn MLKA*, Parth. *MLKYN MLKA*) we have **bānbišnān bānbišn* (*MLKTAn MLKTA*) as the title of Šāpūr I's daughter Ādur-Anāhīd and Pāpak's daughter Dēnak. There are also Xwarranzēm, the *šahr bānbišn* "queen of the empire" (MPers. l. 25), Šābuhrduxtag, the *Sagān bānbišn* "queen of Sakas" (l. 25), Stahryād "the queen" (l. 26), and Dēnak, the *Mēšān bānbišn* "queen of Mesene" (l. 30) (see Henning, 1954, pp. 43f.; Gignoux, *Glossaire*, pp. 28, 57; on Sthly't see Gignoux, in *Iranisches Personennamenbuch*, p. 160; differently Lukonin, pp. 16ff.).

The title *MLKTAn MLKTA* is found on a Sasanian coin, applied to Wahrām II's spouse (Lukonin, pp. 11, 39, 48), and on a Sasanian seal, where it is again applied to a certain Dēnak (Herzfeld. p. 75).

In Manichean Middle Persian and Parthian texts we find a *Sagān bānbišn* (MPers., M 3 R 17-18; Henning, 1942, pp. 949, 951 n. 4), a *'šk'n b'nbyšn* "the Arsacid queen" (MPers., Sundermann, 1973, p. 47, l. 856), and *[šhr]d'r b'nbyšn Xwdws* "the sovereign's queen Xudōs" (Parth., Henning, 1943, pp. 73-74). The last occurrence suggests that the Middle Persian form *bānbišn* was used also in Parthian.

Sogdian *p'mpwšt* is found as the title of the queens of Abaršahr (Sogdian, Sundermann, 1981, p. 41, l. 436); in other Sogdian texts the same title symbolizes the virtue of patience: "and a queen from whom crowned sons are born" (*'ty p'mpwšṯ ckn'c δyδymβrṯ "jwn "jyynd*, M 133 V II 14-16, and *'ṯy pcm'k p'mpwšṯ kyy δyδymβr wyšpšṯ zndy*, IB 4981 e 3-4, both texts unpublished).

Bibliography: E. Benveniste, "Éléments perses en araméen d'Égypte," *JA* 242, 1954, pp. 297-310. Idem, *Titres et noms propres en Iran ancien*, Paris, 1966, pp. 27-34. I. Gershevitch, *A Grammar of Mani-*

chean Sogdian, Oxford, 1954. W. B. Henning, *Sogdica*, London, 1940. Idem, "Mani's Last Journey," *BSOAS* 10, 1942, pp. 941-53. Idem, "The Book of the Giants," *BSOAS* 11, 1943, pp. 52-74. Idem, "Notes on the Great Inscription of Šāpūr I," in *Prof. Jackson Memorial Volume*, Bombay, 1954, pp. 40-54. E. Herzfeld, *Paikuli* I, Berlin, 1924. W. Hinz, "Die elamischen Buchungstäfelchen der Darius-Zeit," *Orientalia* 39, 1970. H. F. J. Junker, ed., *Frahang ī pahlavīk*, Heidelberg, 1912. V. G. Lukonin, *Iran v III veke*, Moscow, 1979, esp. pp. 9-58. P. O. Skjærvø, "Khotanese *v*- < Old Iranian **dw*-," *BSOAS* 48, 1985, pp. 453-67. W. Sundermann, *Mittelpersische und parthische kosmogonische und Parabeltexte der manichäer*, Berlin, 1973. Idem, *Mitteliranische manichäische Texte kirchengeschichtlichen Inhalts*, Berlin, 1981. P. Tedesco, "Perse bānbišn," *BSL* 26, 1925, pp. 64-66.

(W. Sundermann)

BAND "dam." *General remarks.* The word means something that factually or figuratively binds, ties, or restricts (cf. Av. *banda-* "bond," Eng. *bond*). In geographical nomenclature it is applied to ranges (mainly in Afghanistan, e.g., Band-e Torkestān), passes (*darband*) and, above all, old dams and barrages built to store or divert water for irrigational use and urban consumption (the term for a modern dam is *sadd*).

The word *band* passed from Persian into Turkish (modern spelling *bent*). In particular it is applied to the reservoirs in the forest of Belgrade, north of Istanbul, which were built in Byzantine times to store water for the city and were renovated and extended in the 16th century.

Dam construction techniques were developed in early phases of the history of the lands of Iranian civilization: weirs under the Achaemenids, weirs with sluice gates under the Sasanians. Construction of arched dams began in the Mongol period (ca. 1250-1350), e.g., the Kebār dam 25 km south of Qom, the Koreyt dam 28 km west of the oasis of that name which lies 18 km south of Ṭabas, and the Kalāt-e Nāderī dam in the mountains of Khorasan. The word *band* also appears in many names of villages, referring to preserved or vanished dams, and of places close by.

Exploration and cataloguing of dam remains is still far from complete; those more or less adequately described are listed below by region:

Fārs. It appears, in the present state of our knowledge, that the earliest big dams were built on the Kor river and its tributaries, which water the Marvdašt (Persepolis) plain, the old homeland of the Achaemenids. (1) Situated above the river's entry into the plain are the probably Sasanian remains of the Band-e Doḵtar, or Sang-e Doḵtar, and downstream therefrom the almost certainly Achaemenid remains of the Band-e Borīdān. These served to irrigate the districts of Kāmfīrūz and Rāmjerd. The Band-e Borīdān is mentioned by Ebn al-Balḵī (p. 151) under the name Band-e Rāmjerd; it was an ancient structure and after its restoration in the 6th/12th century by the *atābak* Faḵr-al-Dawla Čāvlī (Čawlī) it acquired the name Faḵrestān and was the principal dam in this sector; in the Mongol period it again fell into ruin, and in the Safavid period it appears to have been only temporarily repaired. In the 13th/19th century it was replaced by a new structure named Band-e Nāṣerī after the reigning Nāṣer-al-Dīn Shah. The modern Dorūdzan dam (Sadd-e Dāryūš-e Kabīr) is located not far from this site. (2) Below the confluence of the Kor and the Polvār, the district of Korbāl is irrigated by means of a series of barrages named, in descending order, Band-e Amīr (q.v.), Band-e Fayżābād, Band-e Tīlakān (or Band-e Maymūn), Band-e Mavān, Band-e Ḥasanābād, and Band-e Jahānābād. Medieval sources credit the Buyid ruler ʿAżod-al-Dawla (r. 338-72/949-83) with the construction of the Band-e Amīr. The Band-e Fayżābād, however, is undoubtedly the oldest (Achaemenid and Sasanian); it must be identical with the Band-e Qaṣṣār (dam of the fullers) which was once repaired by the *atābak* Čawlī (Ebn al-Balḵī, p. 152). Since he only knew of the Band-e Amīr, the Band-e Qaṣṣār, and the Band-e Rāmjerd, it can be inferred that the other dams are more recent (probably Safavid or Zand). (3) On the Māyen, a left-bank tributary of the Kor, about 5 km upstream from the confluence, an old dam named the Band-e Ḥājī Moʾaḏḏen is intact and still in use. It commands a canal which in March, 1971, had a flow of 1.5 m^3 per second and now irrigates 400 hectares. Vestiges of a much bigger canal are visible. G. Kortum (p. 117) holds that this was another work of ʿAżod-al-Dawla, undertaken initially to supply water for the city of Eṣṭaḵr, later abandoned, and again brought into use in a quite recent period. Another noteworthy weir in Fārs, probably of pre-Islamic origin, is Band-e Bahman (q.v.) across the river Qara Āḡāj.

Ḵuzestān. Several large dams were built as a result of Šāpūr I's victory over the Roman emperor Valerian in A.D. 260. According to the traditional account, the captive Romans were put to work on building bridges over the Karḵa, Kārūn, and Dez rivers, which would provide better communication with the newly reconquered western provinces. The idea then came up that these huge bridges might be made to serve also as irrigation barrages by means of sluice gates. The bridge-barrage known as the Band-e Qayṣar (i.e., Valerian's bridge), or Šādorvān-e Tostar, on the Kārūn above Šūštar was originally 550 m long, but since its final rupture in 1885 only 28 arches on the left bank and 7 on the right bank now remain. It is not wholly straight, because rock ledges in the river were used as foundations for the piers. Two other Sasanian barrages are to be seen near Šūštar on a diversion canal dug in the Sasanian period, known today as the Āb-e Gargar and mentioned in medieval texts under the name Mašroqān; these are the Band-e Gargar and, some way upstream, the Band-e Mīān, also called Band-e Moḥammad-ʿAlī Mīrzā because it was restored in the 19th century by a son of Fatḥ-ʿAlī Shah with that name. At the point 40 km downstream from Šūštar where the Āb-e Gargar rejoins the Kārūn, ruins of another barrage, the Band-e Qīr (bitumen dam), still stand.

The mountains south of Kāšān. Remains of several dams built to supply the town and district with water can still be seen. Among them are the Band-e Kavār, the Band-e Fer'awnī, the Band-e Qamṣar and the Band-e Qohrūd, the biggest, which was a gravity dam made of rubble; the last three are described as being very old ('Abd-al-Raḥīm Kalāntar Żarrābī [Sohayl Kāšānī], *Tārīḵ-e Kāšān*, ed. Ī. Afšār, 2nd ed., Tehran, 1341 Š./1962, pp. 20, 26, 60-62; Comte de Sercey, *La Perse en 1839-1840*, Paris, 1928, pp. 229-30; Goblot, 1973, p. 16).

The Ḡaznī district in Afghanistan. Within a radius of two or three dozen km from Ḡaznī there are three important dams which were built early in the 4th/11th century at the sultan Maḥmūd's behest to supply the town and its rural outskirts with water and have recently been rebuilt or restored. (1) The Band-e Solṭān (sometimes named Band-e Maḥmūdī in literary texts), a curved gravity dam 23 km north of Ḡaznī, restored in the second quarter of the 10th/16th century by command of Bābor (*Bābor-nāma*, tr. A. S. Beveridge, London, 1922, p. 219), was still in working order in 1836 (G. T. Vigne, *A Personal Narrative of a Visit to Ghazni, Kabul and Afghanistan...*, 2nd ed., London, 1843, p. 138). In the years 1910-20 a new dam was built from the same footing on the east bank but on a line slightly downstream from that of the old one. Its capacity is 20 million m^3. For a time it was officially renamed Band-e Serāj after a title of the amir Ḥabīb-Allāh, and in recent publications it is sometimes designated Band-e Ḡaznī, but among the people it continues to be known as the Band-e Solṭān. (2) The Band-e Zanaḵān in the valley of the same name 20 km northeast of Ḡaznī, already ruined in the 10th/16th century (*Bābor-nāma*, loc. cit.), reconstructed between 1935 and 1957. It provides water for irrigation in the intramontane Keyvān plain. (3) The Band-e Sardeh on the middle course of the Jelga river 37 km southeast of Ḡaznī, still in use in Bābor's time but in ruins in 1839 (J. S. Broadfoot, "Reports on Parts of the Ghilzi Country...," *Royal Geographical Society, Supplementary Papers* 1, 1885, pp. 346-47). Between 1961 and 1967 it was rebuilt with Soviet aid on an overambitious scale. Having a designed capacity of 164 million m^3, it ought in principle to irrigate more than 17,000 hectares, but the inflow from the river proved to be less than expected, and the ancillary work made slow progress.

The Helmand basin. (1) The name Band-e Tīmūr is given to an irrigated area about 15 km long on the left bank of the Arḡandāb (q.v.) some 30 km downstream from its confluence with the Tarnak, but no trace of a barrage remains (L. W. Adamec, ed., *Historical and Political Gazetteer of Afghanistan* V, p. 86). (2) The Band-e Kūhak or Band-e Sīstān at the head of the Helmand delta in the Sīstān plain is a simple diversion barrage constructed of makeshift materials (ibid., p. 126).

Bibliography: Given in text. See also 1. Techniques: H. E. Wulff, *The Traditional Crafts of Persia*, Cambridge, Mass., 1966, pp. 246-48. H. Goblot, "Kebar en Iran, sans doute le plus ancien des barrages-voûtes (1300 environ)," *Arts et manufactures* 154, June, 1965, pp. 43-49. Idem, "Sur quelques barrages anciens et la genèse des barrages-voûtes," *Revue d'histoire des sciences* 20, 1967, pp. 109-40. Idem, "Du nouveau sur les barrages iraniens de l'époque mongole (première moitié du XIVe siècle)," *Arts et manufactures* 239, April, 1973, pp. 14-20. Idem, "Essai d'une histoire des techniques de l'eau sur le plateau iranien," *Persica* 8, 1979, pp. 117-26. 2. Kor valley: Le Strange, *Lands*, pp. 277-78 (with references to Arabic sources). A. Houtum-Schindler, "Note on the Kur River in Fars, Its Sources and Dams, and the Districts It Irrigates," *Proceedings of the Royal Geographical Society*, 1891, pp. 287-91. K. Bergner, "Bericht über unbekannte achaemenidische Ruinen in der Ebene von Persepolis," *AMI* 8, 1936-37, pp. 2-4. M. B. Nicol, "Rescue Excavation near Dorudzan," *East and West*, 1970, pp. 245-85. G. Kortum, *Die Marvdasht-Ebene in Fars: Grundlagen und Entwicklung einer alten iranischen Bewässerungslandschaft*, Kieler geographische Schriften 44, Kiel, 1976, pp. 94-105, 115-18. 3. Ḵūzestān: M. Dieulafoy, *L'art antique de la Perse* V, Paris, 1885, pp. 105-12, fig. 97. Le Strange, *Lands*, pp. 235-37. Guide Bleu, *Moyen-Orient*, Paris, 1956, pp. 718-21. 4. Ḡaznī district: D. Balland, "Passé et présent d'une politique des barrages dans la région de Ghazni, *Studia Iranica* 5, 1976, pp. 239-53.

(X. DE PLANHOL)

BAND-E AMĪR (the amir's dike) or Band-e 'Ażodī, a dam or weir constructed across the Kor river at the southeast end of the Marvdašt plain in Fārs, approximately 15 km south of the town of Marvdašt and 20 km northeast of Shiraz. It takes its name from the Daylamite ruler 'Ażod-al-Dawla (r. 338-72/949-83; q.v.), who is credited with its construction in 356/975 to provide water to the district of Upper Korbāl. According to 4th/10th-century A.D. accounts, the region originally was a desert plain without water. 'Ażod-al-Dawla's weir raised the waters of the Kor to form an extensive reservoir. Ten waterwheels along the reservoir raised the waters to a higher level and so irrigated the three hundred villages in the area.

Built of stone blocks set in cement, the weir's foundations were laid in masonry with lead joints. Its upper portion served as a bridge, supported by thirteen pointed arches and measuring 350 feet long and 18 feet wide. The structure was acclaimed in the contemporary account of Moqaddasī as "one of the wonders of Fārs" (Le Strange, *Lands*, p. 277). Ebn al-Balḵī considered the weir so well built that "even an iron tool could not scratch it and it never would burst asunder" (pp. 151-52). Writing over a hundred years later, Mostawfī found it a mightier weir than that of the Sasanian Šāpūr II at Šūštar (*Nozhat al-qolūb*, p. 109). It seems to have remained in good repair well into the 11th/17th century, when it was described by French and English travelers to Iran. Yet in 1821, Claudius Rich found it in a ruined condition (*Journey to Persepolis*, p. 261). It was apparently restored some time after and still remains in use.

A village of the same name has existed on the western side of the weir since at least the early 13th/19th century. A number of mounds in the immediate vicinity cover the remains of the medieval village and possibly pre-Islamic structures. Band-e Amīr figures in Thomas Moore's orientalist poem, "Lalla Rookh" (1817): "There's a bower of roses by Bendemeer's stream, and the nightingale sings round it all the day long."

Bibliography: Given in the text. See also C. Barbier de Maynard, *Dictionnaire géographique, historique et littéraire de la Perse, extrait du Modjem al-Bouldan de Yaqout*, Paris, 1861, p. 313. Fasāʾī, II, p. 257. Forṣat Šīrāzī, *Āṯār-e ʿajam*, Bombay, 1354/1935, pp. 251, 253-57 and illustration no. 37. T. Herbert, *Travels in Persia, 1627-1929*, ed. E. Denison Ross and E. Power, New York, 1929, pp. 84, 87, 110, J. J. Morier, *A Second Journey through Persia... between the Years 1810 and 1816*, London, 1818, p. 73 and illustration facing p. 74. M.-T. Moṣṭafawī, *Eqlīm-e Pārs*, Tehran, 1343 Š./1964, p. 47 and picture no. 96. W. G. Ouseley, *Travels into Various Countries of the East* II, London, 1821, pp. 180-85. C. J. Rich, *Journey to Persepolis*, London, 1821. A. B. Tilia, *Studies and Restorations at Persepolis and Other Sites of Fars* II, Rome, 1978, p. 85.

(J. LERNER)

BAND-E AMĪR, the chain of natural lakes 90 km west of Bāmīān in Afghanistan (30° 12′ north latitude and 66° 30′ east longitude).

Physiography. The lakes lie in beds of Cretaceous clay and limestone at 2,900 m altitude on the course of small rivers coming from the east (the headwaters of the Balḵāb, q.v.). After flowing through gorges, the rivers are dammed at several points by natural barriers of travertine. The lakes cover a total area of 5,985 km^2. From east to west there are eight main lacustrine units with widely different degrees of sedimentation, ranging from a dry lake bed (no. 7) and some very shallow pools (nos. 1, 2, 3, 5) to large lakes tens of meters deep (nos. 4, 6, 8; lake no. 4 has an area of 4,875 km^2 and a depth of 28 m). The natural dams occur at sharp drops in the streambeds, travertine being deposited where the water flow ceases to be calm and becomes turbulent. Vegetal organisms (cyanophytes, chlorophytes, mosses, algae, etc.) play an essential role in the precipitation of the dissolved calcium compounds. No traces of hydrothermal activity have been found. The Band-e Amīr travertine fits the definition "continental lacustrine deposit of several compounds precipitated by biological activity of vegetal organisms rather than by purely chemical processes" (Lang and Lucas, 1970). Formation of the travertine deposits took place in interglacial phases (the evidence pointing to two glacial Quaternary phases) and continues in the present postglacial phase. During these phases the water outlets have cut steep-walled channels through the dams.

The lakes in popular imagination and daily life. The spectacular aspect of the natural dams has prompted belief in their miraculous origin. They are said to have been built by the Prophet's son-in-law ʿAlī. The names of the successive dams and the lakes which they impound are Band-e Ḏu'l-feqār (dam of ʿAlī's sword), Band-e Pūdena (of the mint plants), Band-e Panīr (of the cheese), Band-e Ḵaybat (of the magic), Band-e Qanbar (of Qanbar, ʿAlī's groom), Band-e Ḡolāmān (of the slaves). All relate to episodes of a legend which has come down in two closely similar versions (one outlined by Leech apud Burnes, the other by Foucher and again by Hackin and Kohzad). It seems likely (as suggested by Bernard) that ʿAlī's exploits have a wider geographical reference and are to be interpreted as an etiological legend about use of rivers from the Hindu Kush for irrigation. A small sanctuary (*zīārat*) in honor of ʿAlī was built at a quite recent date (in 1332/1914 according to Hackin and Kohzad, in 1324/1906 according to Caspani and Cagnacci). The Hazāra people of the district catch fish in the lakes and use the cascades to turn water mills. After the construction of a motor track from Bāmīān and a small hotel, the extraordinary scenery of these turquoise-hued lakes in their setting of almost white-colored bare mountains began to attract tourists.

Bibliography: 1. General descriptions: W. R. Hay, "Band-i-Amir," *Geographical Journal* 87, 1936, pp. 348-50. R. Dollot, *L'Afghanistan*, Paris, 1937, pp. 130-32. E. Caspani and E. Cagnacci, *Afghanistan, Crocevia dell'Asia*, Milan, 1951, pp. 233-34. H. Caillemer, *Islam blanc sur le toit du monde*, Paris, 1969, pp. 168-69. 2. Physical geography: A. F. de Lapparent, "Les dépôts de travertin des montagnes afghanes à l'ouest de Kaboul," *Revue de géographie physique et de géologie dynamique*, 1966, pp. 351-57. J. Lang and G. Lucas, "Contribution à l'étude de biohermes continentaux: Barrages des lacs de Band-e-Amir (Afghanistan central)," *Bulletin de la Société géologique de France*, 1970, pp. 834-42 (2 figs., 2 plates). U. Jux and E. K. Kempf, "Stauseen durch Travertinabsatz im zentralafghanischen Hochgebirge," *Zeitschrift für Geomorphologie*, N.S., supp. 12, 1971, pp. 107-37. 3. The legend, its forms, and its interpretation: A. Burnes, *Cabool*, London, 1842, pp. 232-33. Hay, loc. cit. Dollot, loc. cit. A. Foucher, *La vieille route de l'Inde, de Bactres à Taxila*, 2 vols., MDAFA 1, Paris, 1942, I, pp. 130-32. R. Hackin and A. A. Kohzad, *Légendes et coutumes afghanes*, Paris, 1953, pp. 11-15. P. Bernard, "Aï Khanoum 'la barbare'," in P. Bernard and H. P. Francfort, *Études de géographie historique sur la plaine d'Aï Khanoum (Afghanistan)*, Paris, 1978, pp. 17-25. 4. Photographs of the lakes: Hay, op. cit., p. 349. Caspani and Cagnacci, op. cit., p. 224. A. and M. Delapraz, *Afghanistan*, Neuenburg, 1964, p. 31 (in color). R. Klass, *Land of the High Flags*, New York, 1964, photo XV. M. Klimburg, *Afghanistan*, Vienna, 1966, p. 272. L. Fischer, *Afghanistan, eine geographisch-*

medizinische Landeskunde, Berlin, 1968, p. 154. Caillemer, op. cit., p. 206. R. Michaud, *Afghanistan*, Paris, 1970, folders 4 and 8 (the latter exceptional, being of winter scenes; in color). Jux and Kempf, op. cit., pp. 126-30.

(X. DE PLANHOL)

BAND-E BAHMAN, an ancient dam built on the Qara Āḡāj river nearly sixty km south of Shiraz. The river, known in classical sources as the Zakān, is the longest river in Fārs, beginning in the mountains west of Shiraz and, after sprouting several tributaries, ending near the Persian Gulf port of Kangān as the Mond or Mand river. Though Band-e Bahman is an ancient monument of considerable size, it has been ignored by all but a few classical writers. According to Mostawfī (*Nozhat al-qolūb* I, p. 119), "Bahman b. Esfandīār built a dam across this river to raise its waters for the irrigation of the villages of Kavār." The most detailed description of Band-e Bahman comes in *Āṯār-e ʿajam* (pp. 15-16), which places the dam "nine *farsaḵs* south of Shiraz and one *farsaḵ* west of the village of Kavār" and gives its length as "twenty-five *zarʿ*s" and its width as "3 1/2 *zarʿ*s." Also according to this description, "the height of the dam varies from four to five *zarʿs* owing to the repairs made on it over the years... but the river behind the dam is only about one *zarʿ* deep. In the middle of the dam, there is a sluice (*kalʿ-e āb*) with two gates... Two water channels have been dug, one old, the other new, behind the dam to irrigate the cultivated lands of Kavār. The mountain to the rear of the dam is known as Kūh-e Bahman and a half *farsaḵ* to the southwest in a pass there is a mound of stones in which Bahman is said to be buried." It is not known when Band-e Bahman was constructed, but the name alone would suggest that it is of great antiquity, perhaps originating in Achaemenid times. Whatever the case, the base of the dam is certainly pre-Islamic. It is still in use, providing water to farmland in the Kavār district.

Bibliography: Forṣat Šīrāzī, *Āṯār-e ʿajam*, Bombay, 1354/1935. G. Kuros, *The Art of Irrigation in Ancient Iran*, Tehran, 1348 Š./1969, p. 228.

(K. AFSAR)

BAND-E TORKESTĀN (boundary wall of Turkistan), or less commonly Tīrband-e Torkestān, the mountain range in northwestern Afghanistan which runs in a west-east direction for 200 km between the upper valley of the Morḡāb to the south and the plains of the Āmū Daryā to the north. It is a horst of continental Jurassic schists and sandstones, generally dark in color, thrust up in a spectacular way between relatively low-lying plateaus of whitish Cretaceous limestones and calciferous clays. The western part of the north slope borders directly on the Neocene sediments and Quaternary loess deposits of Turkistan. The summits are truncated, having been reduced in probably pre-Miocene times to an erosion surface (3,200-3,300 m; highest point 3,481 m); they perhaps conserve elements of a pre-Cretaceous abrasion surface. The range is severely denuded, but contains sparse colonies of junipers. It has scarcely any permanent human population, but is frequented in summer by inhabitants of nearby villages, mainly Uzbeks on the north slope and Fīrūzkūhīs on the south slope, and by a few Pashtun groups.

Bibliography: L. W. Adamec, ed., *Historical and Political Gazetteer of Afghanistan* IV: *Mazar-i-sharif and North-Central Afghanistan*, pp. 126-27. A. F. de Lapparent and J. Stöcklin, "Sur le Jurassique et le Crétacé du Band-e Turkestan (Afghanistan du Nord-Ouest)," *Bulletin de la Sociéte géologique de France*, 1972, pp. 159-64.

(X. DE PLANHOL)

BANDA "servant."

i. *The term.*

ii. *Old Persian* bandaka.

i. THE TERM

Banda (NPers.) and its precursors *bandak/bandag* (Mid. Pers.) and *bandaka* (OPers.) meant "henchman, (loyal) servant, vassal," but not "slave" (for which see BARDA AND BARDADĀRĪ). Occurrences of the word *ba^{n}daka* in the inscription of Darius I at Bīsotūn (DB) provide the earliest evidence.

The New Babylonian rendering of *bandaka* is ^{lú}*qal-la-a* "subordinate," and the Elamite rendering is ^{m}*ú li-ba-ru-ri*, i.e. *lipar-ú-ri* (*ú* meaning "I") "my henchman" or "servant." It should be noted that in the Akkadian version the word for "subjects" in section 7 (corresponding to DB 1.19) is not *qallu* (cf. Arabic *qalīl* "little," base QLL) but ^{lú}*ir*^{pl} = *ardū*, which is the Old Babylonian word *wardum* (root *wrd* "to be under"). In the Elamite version the concept is expressed by an abstract noun: *li-ba-me* ^{m}*ú-ni-na hu-ud-da-iš* "they rendered service to me" (cf. NPers. *bandagī kardand*).

Extensions of nouns designating persons and professions by means of the suffix *ka* occur frequently in the Aryan languages. Thus OPers. *bandaka* is from *banda* (cf. the Old Indian masculine noun *bandha* "bond, fetter") from the Indo-European root *bhendh*, also the source of English "bind, band, bond." OPers. *bandaka* thus has a meaning similar to that of English "bondsman." OInd. *bandhaka*, however, came to mean "one who binds with fetters" or "captures," having undergone a semantic evolution different from that of OPers. *bandaka* to NPers. *banda*.

C. Bartholomae went astray in interpreting the word literally as "one who wears fetters." NPers. *banda*, plur. *bandagān* (Pahlavi *bandakān*) and its long-attested doublet *bastagān* (a passive participle from the same root) mean "dependent" or "relative" and are synonymous with *ḵ̌īšān* and *ḵ̌īšāvandān*. NPers. *ḵ̌īšāvand*, a compound of *ḵ̌ēš* and *ā-vand* (from °*βant*), has much the same meaning of "own folk" as *qawm-e ḵ̌īš*, *ahl-e ḵ̌īš*, *ḵ̌īšān* or *familiares* among the Romans and *oikeîoi/oikétai* among the Greeks. In addition to the meaning of relatives by blood or marriage, all these words carry a connotation of duty to serve (more explicitly conveyed in NPers. *k̲ānazād*). In the modern language, the human relationship of "binding" and "being bound" is expressed in many uses of the verb *bastan/band* and its derivatives and in locations into which they enter.

In Middle Iranian, *bandag* (*bndk/g*) is found in Pahlavi and has the same meaning of "(loyal) servant" as in Achaemenid and modern times. The same is true of the Sogdian *βantak*. In the Turfan fragments *bandag* has become *bannag* through a process of assimilation also seen in the main dialect of Persis (Southwestern Mid. Pers. *bng* as against Northwestern, i.e. Parthian *bndg*). Although the *Frahang ī pahlavīk* (beginning of chapter 13) does not clearly vouch for *ʿbd* (*ab̲dīn*?) as the ideogram for *bandak* (*bavandak*?), the Aramaic *ʿab̲d(ā)* with the phonetic suffix *ak*, meaning "servant," is well attested in Sasanian inscriptions, where the abstract noun for "service" also is found in the Mid. Pers. form *bandakīh* (written *OBDkyhy*) and the Parth. form *bandakīf* (written *OBDkpy*). The Pahlavi Psalter has *OBDk* for *bandak*. In line 16 of the Apsʾy inscription at Bīšāpūr there is a mention of "menservants and maid-servants," *bandak ut kanīsak* (written *OBDk W knysky*, the latter word having an anomalous *s* instead of *ṣ* = *č*).

The word occurs as a patronymic in the list of dignitaries in Šāpūr I's inscription on the Kaʿba-ye Zardošt at Naqš-e Rostam: Bandagān (Mid. Pers. Bndkʾn, Parth. Bndkn, Greek Bandigan) father of Zurvāndāt.

Compounds of *banda(k)* occur frequently as personal names but otherwise are uncommon. The word *k̲ar-banda*, meaning (1) "ass keeper" or "ass driver" (taken into Syriac in the Sasanian period as *ḥarəb̲andəqā*) and (2) "mule," probably began as a compound ending in the stem of the verb *bastan* "to bind," like *dīvband* "exorciser," *kārband* "industrious, docile."

Among the many examples of men's names with the component *banda(k)* are Āturbandak "Servant of the Fire" (Justi, *Namenbuch*, pp. 51a, 488), Barāzbanda "Servant of the Wild Boar," i.e., Bahrām (Justi, p. 349b), Jošnaspbanda (= Gošnāspbanda) "Servant of the Fire of the Stallion" (Justi, p. 355a), Hazārbanda "Servant of the Thousand" (scil., *yazata*s), or simply "He who has a thousand servants" (Justi, p. 128a), Māhbandak "Servant of the moon" (but see Justi, pp. 185b, 490), Mihrevandak (with *v* from *β*) "Servant of the god Mithra," an Iranian general whom the Armenians defeated in A.D. 571 (Justi, p. 214b), Šāh-banda (Safavid period; Justi, p. 274a), Otrārbanda "toward (the place) Otrār" (A.D. 810-11; Justi, pp. 336f.).

K̲odābanda (= Banda-ye K̲odā) "Servant of God" has been a name of rulers and dignitaries from medieval to modern times. It accords with an age-old formula which goes back to Akkadian *Warad-ilim* and can be traced through Old Testament Hebrew ʿAb̲dəʾēl/ʿAb̲diʾēl and Syriac ʿAbdallāhā to Arabic ʿAbd-Allāh. It reappears in Christian calques such as Greek Theódoulos and German Gottschalk and finally in Turkish names with suffixed *qolī*.

Also to be placed in this category (notwithstanding the contrary opinion of W. B. Henning and H. S. Nyberg) are the personal names with the suffix *vand* (from *βand/t*) peculiar to chiefs of the Zagros region in the Middle Ages, such as ʿAbbāsvand, Aḥmadā-vand, Jalāl(ā)vand, Jalīlvand, Ḥamavand (= Mo-hammadvand), Ḥasanāvand, etc. Many of these have subsequently become names of tribes or places. In the toponymy of southwestern Iran, some of the names which evolved in this way (man's name → tribe's name → place name) have kept the *b* of *band*, e.g., Farrāšband and Esmāʿīlband west of Fīrūzābād in Fārs. The word formation is analogous to that of *k̲ʾīšāvand* "relative, dependent" (discussed above) and has no connection with the OPers. and Aryan suffix *vant*.

In the polite speech of modern times, *banda* "(your) servant" is used as a substitute for *man* "I" and therefore takes the first person of the verb (e.g., *banda ānjā būdam* "I was there"). Conversely *sarkār* or *ḥażrat/janāb-e ʿālī* "(your) excellency" replaces *šomā* "you" and takes the second person. The locution has ancient oriental precedents in Akkadian *waradka* (fem. *waradkī*) and Old Testament Hebrew *ʿab̲dək̲ā* "your servant," polite for "I," and fem. *ămāt̲ək̲ā* "your maid," but these take the third person. Expressions such as *kamtarīn banda* "(your) most humble servant" are still used today in letter endings. In progressive circles, however, such styles and likewise the use of *banda* for "I" are now generally avoided.

Bibliography: *AirWb.*, col. 924. W. Brandenstein and M. Mayrhofer, *Handbuch des Altpersischen*, Wiesbaden, 1964, p. 110. W. Eilers, "Damawend," *Archiv Orientální* 22, 1954, 24, 1956, 37, 1969, pp. 185, 271ff., 315f., 326. Idem, *Westiranische Mundarten aus der Sammlung W. Eilers* III: *Die Mundart von Sīvänd*, Wiesbaden, 1988, pp. 15f. Gignoux, *Glossaire*, pp. 19, 20, 48, 49. Idem, *Iranisches Personennamenbuch* II/2, p. 55 no. 184 and reverse index p. 209b. W. Hinz, *Altpersischer Wortschatz*, *AKM* 27/1, Leipzig, 1942, pp. 70f. Justi, *Namenbuch*, pp. 488, 516, and elsewhere. Kent, *Old Persian*, pp. 17 par. 39, 30 par. 75 III, 39 par. 111, 42 par. 122, 46 par. 132 I, 51 par. 146 II. Mayrhofer, *Dictionary* II, p. 407.

(W. EILERS)

ii. OLD PERSIAN BANDAKA

The OPers. occurrences of *bandaka* are all in the Bīsotūn inscription, where it is an epithet of men of high rank whom Darius had chosen to be his generals against the "rebels": Vidarna, Vindafarnā, and Gaubaruva (members of the seven great noble families), Dādṛši the Persian and Vivāna (satraps), Vaumisa and Artavardiya (of whom we know only that they were Persians), Dādṛši the Armenian, and Taxmaspāda the Mede. All Darius's generals except his father Vištāspa were his *bandaka*s. The word here means a nobleman "bound" to the king in a relationship which, though subordinate, was freely accepted and probably sealed with an oath. The relationship was symbolized by a girdle, worn by all Persians including the king in the Achaemenid period and throughout the history of ancient Iran.

Undoubtedly a similar relationship existed between the Sasanian king Narseh (r. 292-302) and "the greatest, the best, and the noblest subjects in our possessions" (Paikuli inscription, sections 16, 50, 95). These were all princes with distinguished titles who had rallied to Narseh and become his *bandags*.

The word *bandaka/bandag* was used not only with reference to dignitaries but also with the meaning of "servant," i.e., any person whose relationship to another is one of obedience and/or dependence. Thus in DB 1.19 the conquered countries are said to be Darius's "servants" (*bandakā*). The Aramaic word *ʿlym* "lad, servant" (cf. Latin *puer*), which is used to translate OPers. *bandaka*, is used in Aramaic documents found in Egypt as the term for "dependent" or "employee": e.g., a bailiff employed by Aršām (Arsames), the Persian satrap of Egypt, his groom whose son received an estate, some workers, and a sculptor, as well as a freed slave who, given the change of his status, could not be reduced to servitude again. The conventional form of opening address in letters in Imperial Aramaic is "To A. from Y., his servant" (*ʿlym*; Cowley, p. 135, Driver, docs. nos. 2, 6, 8, 9). This formula reappears in Sogdian letters of the 8th century A.D., where the writer, being socially inferior to the addressee, declares himself to be the latter's *bandag* (Freiman, passim). Selōk, the author of an inscription at Persepolis, similarly calls himself the *bandag* of his king Šāpūr Sakānšāh (Back, p. 496).

Although these facts seem to justify the conclusion that *bandaka/bandag* never meant "slave," the problem presents difficulties. There is no evidence that *bandaka* ever meant "war captive." Several other facts must also be taken into account. In Akkadian there are two possible equivalents of *bandaka*, namely *ardu*, which means either "slave" in the legal sense or "inferior" in any way (even the king being inferior to his god), and *qallu*, which means "slave, servant" or the like (see also i, above). Then again the choice of *doulos* for the Greek translation of *bandaka* (attested in literary texts such as Darius's letter to Gadatas) can only be explained if *bandaka* was taken to signify, literally or figuratively, "slave." The semantics of Mid. Pers. *bandag* are equally complex. In the Bīšāpūr inscription (ŠVŠ 16) it may perhaps denote slaves offered together with other possessions by Šāpūr to Aps'y, but in Mid. Pers. legal texts the only term denoting "slave" appears to be *anšahrīk*. The "slave and master" (*bandag–xwatāy*) antithesis found in the Manichean texts and in the *Dēnkard* (VI, E43 a-e, advice to a *bandag* on ways to attain a better position; Shaked, p. 211) demonstrates the inferiority of the *bandag* but no more.

In both the Achaemenid and the Sasanian periods, *bandaka/bandag* definitely referred to the fact that all individuals were subject to the king and that some were also dependent on men of higher rank. At the same time, the status of the humblest was always depicted, in the vivid language of military-political metaphor, as being like that of the captive and the slave.

The subordination of the *bandag* was not solely political and economic, as the word was also used to denote the relationship between a worshiper and his god: the expression "slave to the gods" is found in the *Dēnkard* (Shaked, p. 177). Likewise in religious writings the word *bandag* is widely used with the meaning of "God's creatures." There, too, the girdle (*kostī*) worn by the initiated Zoroastrian is the symbol of his obedience as a faithful follower of the Good Religion (see, e.g., chap. 18 of the *Vīdēvdād*).

The relationship which the word *bandaka* implies probably stems from a prehistoric rank differentiation in tribal élites and in the military retinue of the chief or "king," already changed in Darius I's time, when also a non-Persian was able to be his *bandaka*.

Curiously enough, the word has been adduced in support of diametrically opposed historical interpretations. N. Pigulevskaya (pp. 141-58) saw it as proof of a "slavery-based mode of production" in Parthian and Sasanian Iran, while G. Widengren (1969, pp. 21-44) made use of it for his depiction of "feudalism" in pre-Islamic Iran. For opposite ideological reasons, each writer ignores the "Asiatic mode of production" or "Asiatic despotism." From an objective viewpoint, it can hardly be maintained that the *bandaka* relationship was the basis of feudalism in ancient Iran, for many other factors must have been present: the breakup of communal landownership, the diversification of war techniques, and the increasing use of coins for money, to mention only a few. One certain fact, however, is that "despotism" in ancient Iran had a peculiar and remarkable capacity to incorporate great noble families, which were not only powerful but also stable. Feudalism did not enter the scene until after the disappearance of these great families and their replacement by local gentry (*dehqāns*) in the reign of K̲osrow I Anōšīravān (531-79). Only then and subsequently did the words *bandag* and *banda* perhaps refer to feudal relationships.

See also BARDA AND BARDADĀRĪ; ḠOLĀM.

Bibliography: M. Back, *Die Sassanidischen Staatsinschriften*, Acta Iranica 18, 1978. A. Cowley, *Aramaic Papyri of the Fifth Century B.C.*, Oxford, 1923. J. Greenfield, "Some Notes on the Arsham Letters," in *Irano-Judaica*, ed. S. Shaked, Jerusalem, 1982, p. 11. H. Humbach and P. O. Skjærvø, *The Sassanian Inscription of Paikuli* III, Wiesbaden, 1983. O. Klíma, "Zur Problematik der Sklaverei im alten Iran," *Altorientalische Forschungen* 5, 1977, pp. 91-96. M. Macuch, *Das Sasanidische Rechtsbuch "Mâtakdân i hazār dātistān,"* Wiesbaden, 1981, pp. 79-84. A. Perikhanian, "Iranian Society and Law," in *Camb. Hist. Iran* III/2, pp. 627-80. N. Pigulevskaya, *Les villes de l'état iranien aux époques parthe et sassanide*, Paris, 1963. S. Shaked, *Wisdom of the Sassanian Sages*, New York, 1979. G. Widengren, *Der Feodalismus im alten Iran*, 1969. Idem, "Le symbolisme de la ceinture," *Iranica Antiqua* 8, 1968, pp. 133-55.

(C. Herrenschmidt)

BANDAR "harbor, seaport; commercial town." The word is presumably derived from the root *band* "to bind" (Pers. *bastan*), but probably not in the sense of "binding," i.e., "mooring" (ships) but rather as the enclosed (bound up) area of the harbor, like Ar. *sadd* "jetty, mole." Vullers (*Lexicon Persico-Latinum* I, p. 267) suggests that *bandar* may be from *band-dar* "gateway of the jetty/mole." The word for harbor has not yet been found in Middle Persian.

The concept of *bandar* probably continues an old Oriental tradition. Its double meaning of "harbor" on a river or a sea and "town, center of commerce and communications" (also in the inland) agrees well with that of Akkadian *kārum* from Sumerian *kar* "fortification (of a harbor), break-water." The *kārum* of Kāniš in Anatolia, the present ruin of Kültepe near Kayseri, was famous. At this site thousands of Old Assyrian cuneiform business documents from the the 2nd millennium B.C. have been found (see W. F. Leemans, "The Importance of Trade," *Iraq* 39, 1977, pp. 1-10). Note also that in Thessalian Greek, the word *limēn* "harbor" has also acquired the meaning of "market."

In Neo-Syriac *šā(h)-bandar*, lit. "harbor king," is used as a title meaning "(Turkish) consul" while in Arabic it is still used as a family name. Both title and office resemble the Arabic *malek-al-tojjār* "king of merchants," i.e., head of the merchants' guild and its official representative at a market place. This title recalls the Old Babylonian office of *wakil tamkāri* (cf. Ar. *wakīl* "representative").

(W. Eilers)

BANDAR-E ʿABBĀS(Ī), a port city in the *ostān* of Hormozgān, on the Persian Gulf, 16 km northwest of Hormoz island and 85 km from the coast of Oman.

Geographical situation and historical background. At the entrance to the Persian Gulf, Bandar-e ʿAbbās extends about 2 km along the shallow Clarence (K̲ūrān) strait between Qešm island and the mainland; its lack of a natural harbor obliges vessels to use tenders to handle cargo, a hazardous operation in winter. The risks are mitigated somewhat by the extensive, sheltered anchorage in the waters between the nearby islands of Qešm, Lārak, and Hormoz (qq.v.). The town has a great strategic and commercial importance as a link between the Gulf and the Irano-Afghan hinterland with easy passes, through the Zagros mountains, to Kermān, Yazd, and Shiraz. Bandar-e ʿAbbās has little to offer its inhabitants: a semi-arid climate, very hot in summer with afternoon temperatures exceeding 40 °C (104 °F) and, nevertheless, oppressively humid. Cisterns are insufficient to supply drinking water, which has to be piped in from ʿEsīn some 16 km to the northwest. Despite these repulsive elements, the location is extremely favorable to the maritime relations of Iran with the outside world.

Bandar-e ʿAbbās is the successor to the emporium of old Hormoz, the seaport of Kermān and Sejestān, near present-day Mīnāb 80 km to the east (Le Strange, *Lands*, p. 318). Around 1300, old Hormoz was moved to the island of Jarūn which changed its name to accommodate the move. At that time, Bandar-e ʿAbbās, which was known as Šahrū (Eṣṭak̲rī, p. 67) and Sūrū (Ebn Ḥawqal, p. 220; Sūrū is the name of a village located southeast of the present-day port, where tradesmen of the town, at the end of the 19th century, owned country houses; see Floyer, p. 139), was a fishing village and ferry terminal for Hormoz island. It was also known as Sīrū (Moqaddasī, p. 454) and Šahrūvā (*Ḥodūd al-ʿālam*, tr. Minorsky, p. 124). The form "Tūsar" given by Mostawfī, *Nozhat al-qolūb*, (trans. pp. 137-38) is certainly the result of misreadings.

When new Hormoz became an important trading center, Šahrū, some 20 km away, at the foot of the continental highlands, benefited in turn as a source of the island's provisions and as its principal outlet to the mainland. Shortly after they took Hormoz in 1507, the Portuguese built a fort at Šahrū, which then came to be known by a variety of names: Gomrū, Kombrū, Gombarū in Oriental sources; Cambarão and Comorão in Portuguese writings; Combru (P. Della Valle, *Les fameux voyages* III, Paris, 1663-65, pp. 576-80) and Gombroon, Gambron, Camoron, Comoran, etc., in other European sources. Lockhart (*EI*²) proposed a derivation from the old name of Jarūn (other forms: Zarūn, Garaon, etc.), transferred to the mainland after the island became Hormoz, but Gombroon is probably a corruption of *gomrok*, the common term for "customs house," derived via Turkish from the modern Greek *komérki* (from Italian *commercio*; Le Strange, *Lands*, p. 319). Obviously it was there that goods from Hormoz landed on the continent.

The Safavid harbor. In 1615, the Portuguese fort passed into the hands of the Safavid Shah ʿAbbās I (q.v.), who with the help of the British navy was also able to take Hormoz some seven years later. Shah ʿAbbās then decided to bring the port to the mainland and renamed the site of Šahru after himself. To reward his British allies, he exempted them from all duties, granted them half of the customs revenues of the new port, provided that they operate two vessels in the Gulf to protect their shipping. The town prospered quickly; in 1622, Della Valle characterized Combru as "more of an emporium than a town, where people from all nations disembark," especially many Jews and Indians, but also noted that "the shops were poorly stocked." In 1628 Thomas Herbert confirmed the lively, cosmopolitan nature of the new port, where he reports seeing English, Dutch, Danish, Portuguese, Armenian, Georgian, Muscovite, Turkish, Arab, Indian, and Jewish merchants (*Travels in Persia*, London, 1928, pp. 41-49). Numerous travelogues and sources such as the British East India Company's *Gombroon Diary* (India Office Library, *Persia and the Persian Gulf Records* I-VI) give a detailed picture of life in Bandar-e ʿAbbās for the rest of the 17th century.

Despite its status as the chief Safavid port, Bandar-e 'Abbās's growth was modest. To Tavernier, who visited several times during the decade 1645-55, it was "good-sized" (*Les six voyages*, Utrecht, 1712, p. 768); however, Thévenot, who stopped in Bandar-e 'Abbās in 1667, judged it "very small," and not the equal of a good-sized village" (*Suite du voyage de Levant*, Paris, 1674, pp. 265-66). Chardin, who was a frequent visitor during the period 1667-77, estimated the number of houses between 1,400 and 1,500, a third of which belonged to Indians and fifty to Jews (*Voyages* XVII, Paris, 1830, pp. 123-29). The physician Engelbert Kaempfer, who lived in Bandar-e 'Abbās from 1685 to 1688, reckoned the Indians constituted the majority of the population (*Amoenitatum exoticarum*... V, Lengovia, 1712, pp. 716-17; English tr. *Journey into Persia and other Oriental Countries*, London, 1736), which is certainly explained by the fact that Europeans found the climate too unhealthy for long-term residence. In summer, most of the inhabitants would retire to the neighboring hills. Though Shah 'Abbās I had a large cistern (*āb-anbār*) built, only the lower classes made use of it; the wealthier residents drew their water from a nearby spring. Europeans sought refuge not only from the foul water but also from homesickness and the dangers of the climate in a large variety of alcoholic concoctions, especially in "punch," which owes its name to a combination of five (*panj*) basic ingredients: *araq*, lemon juice, sugar, nutmeg, and water. Johann van Mandelslo mentions "palepunzen," a corruption of "bowl of punch" (*De Gedenkwaardige Zee en Landt Reyse deur Parsien en Indien*, Amsterdam, 1658, p. 24) and his fellow countryman Jean Struys, who visited Bandar-e 'Abbās in 1672, warned of the dangers of overconsumption (*Les voyages... en Moscovie, en Tartarie, en Perse*, Amsterdam, 1681, pp. 329-32). In this desolate and semi-desert place, haunted by the howls of jackals (Herbert), food was generally imported from abroad; fruits and vegetables were supplied from Qešm. Local staples consisted of dates and fish, the heads and entrails of which were fed to the livestock, giving to milk and milk products a particularly disagreeable taste. From the middle of the century wells were dug around the town, which allowed some gardens and orchards to be grown (Tavernier).

Despite its inhospitable conditions and deadly climate, Bandar-e 'Abbās developed into a thriving commercial center. John Fryer (*A New Account of East India and Persia... 1672-1681* II, London, 1909, pp. 158-64) lists British imports of fabric from England, cotton and cotton cloth from India, indigo, ores, and steel. Purchases included wool from Kermān, raw and woven silk, carpets, brocades, saffron, rhubarb, rosewater, dates, goats and horses for India. The Dutch, whose trade Fryer estimates to be the most important, primarily sold spices (pepper, nutmeg, cloves), sugar, copper, and Indian cloth and bought silk, carpets, and velvets; they also took payment in silver and gold coin. There was, in addition, a lively trade in pearls from the Gulf.

The decay. The Omani period. Bandar-e 'Abbās was not immune to the decline of Iran that culminated in the Afghan invasion of 1722. In 1727, 4,000 Baluchi horsemen sacked all but the fortified British and Dutch factories (trading stations; A. Hamilton, *A New Account of the East Indies*, Edinburgh, 1727, pp. 108-09). Nor did Bandar-e 'Abbās benefit from the restoration of national order under Nāder Shah Afšār; in 1736, he commandeered all of the port's pack animals from an East India Company caravan loaded with Kermān wool (L. Lockhart, *Nadir Shah*, London, 1938, p. 113). Though in 1741 Bandar-e 'Abbās gained a cannon foundry out of Nāder Shah's overall strategic policy in the Persian Gulf, he put an end to the port's vitality by levying punitive taxes on commerce and by designating Būšehr (q.v.), much closer to Shiraz and Isfahan, as his principal outpost on the Gulf. The consequences of his policies were quick to follow; in 1750, Bartholomew Plaisted recorded that only one out of every ten of the port's houses was occupied (*Journal from Calcutta*, London, 1758, p. 11), but in 1758, the British physician E. Ives noted that the Dutch and English factories were still in operation (*A Voyage from England to India*, London, 1773, pp. 197-202). However, in 1759, a French squadron burned the British factory, and in 1762 first the British and then the Dutch abandoned Bandar-e 'Abbās for Būšehr.

Not surprisingly Iranian government indifference to the fate of the town went hand in hand with the economic decline. Control of the region passed into the hands of Arab tribal chiefs whose allegiance to Persian authority was more nominal than real. A Persian firman of 1793 recognized the Sultan of Muscat's influence over a coastal strip extending 150 km between Mīnāb in the east and Kamīr in the west as well as the islands of Qešm and Hormoz. Five years later, the Sultan signed a treaty that allowed the British East India Company to enter Bandar-e 'Abbās once again. According to James Morier, in 1811 the Sultan maintained a garrison of 120 Nubians and eighty Arabs to protect the port against pirates (*A Second Journey through Persia*, London, 1818, app. B). The Qajar government at times tried to reestablish its hold over Bandar-e 'Abbās, but it was not until 1855 that it reached an accord with the Omanis that limited the term of their lease to twenty years in exchange for an annual payment of 16,000 tomans. Taking advantage of trouble in Muscat, the Qajars gained final control of the port in 1868.

Bandar-e 'Abbās's Omani period was marked by profound physical change. With the exception of the Dutch factory, refurbished to house the Omani governor, the port's older homes had been largely abandoned, and a new settlement composed of flimsily built huts established. But, owing to the insecurity of the waters around Būšehr, commerce did not stop entirely in Bandar-e 'Abbās. In 1830, J. R. Wellsted estimated the population to be between 4,000 and 5,000 (*Travels to the City of the Caliphs* I, London, 1840, p. 75). At the end of the Omani period, Pelly estimated it at between 8,000 and 9,000, the difference probably to be explained by the fact that most of the population left town for the summer.

Persian recovery. The stagnation (1868-1964). The end of the Omani period brought a modest renewal of activity. In 1871, Evan Smith noted that though the town, having just been decimated by cholera and famine, was in a sorry state, cotton, opium, asafetida, and henna from Yazd and Kermān were being exported from Bandar-e 'Abbās; the customs duties leased to a British agent were estimated at 25,000 tomans ("The Persian-Afghan Mission, 1871," *Eastern Persia* I, ed. F. J. Goldsmid, London, 1876, pp. 296-98). There were four Europeans and a number of Indian merchants. By 1889, a wide range of products was being transshipped through Bandar-e 'Abbās; exports included opium, cotton, dates, salt, wool, pistachios, almonds; imported were cotton fabric, thread, copper, iron, tin, spices, indigo, sugar, tea, glassware, and porcelain (G. N. Curzon *Persia and the Persian Question* II, London, 1892, p. 426). Nine-tenths of the imports were from Great Britain and India, one half of the exports to India. The British reopened their consulate in 1900.

Though one found merchants from as far away as Kabul in Bandar-e 'Abbās and tea and indigo from India went to Bukhara this way, the port had for Iran, at that time, only a regional function restricted to eastern and southeastern parts of the country. The roads and railways that were constructed during the first half of the twentieth century in other parts of the country bypassed Bandar-e 'Abbās. In 1928, Alfons Gabriel characterized port trade as mediocre; exports: wool, carpets, nuts, pistachios, and dry fruit; imports: fabrics, thread, rice, sugar, and wood (*Im weltfernen Orient*, Munich, 1929, pp. 66-71). As late as 1961, Bandar-e 'Abbās only handled 42,000 tons of cargo (two-thirds exports, some local oil transport). The only notable economic developments during this period were the spinning mill and a fish-canning plant (tuna and sardines) built under Reżā Shah. The latter, built in 1947 with a total capacity of 4 million cans per year, remained dormant for fifteen years, but during the period 1957-63 produced an average of 400,000 cans yearly and in 1968 600,000.

Bandar-e 'Abbās's stagnation kept population growth at a stable level; in 1928, it was estimated at 10,000 (Gabriel, op. cit., p. 66); in 1937, 15,000 by the Great Britain Naval Intelligence (Geographical Handbook Series, *Persia*, Oxford, 1945, p. 500) but 11,400 by L. Lockhart (*Persian Cities*, London, 1960, p. 175); and in 1956, still only 17,710 (*Saršomārī-e 'omūmī, 1335 Š.*). After 1928 the population became almost exclusively Persian, including the fishermen, which is unusual in the Gulf and explains later difficulties in supplying the cannery. There were also a few Arab and Baluch; some thirty families of K̠ᵛājas from Hyderabad; Jats, whose women were employed as water carriers; and some Portuguese-Indians from Goa. The last non-Muslim Indians returned to India during World War II. Shi'ites constituted the majority of the population, but a Sunnite minority resided in the western part of the town. Although as part of Reżā Shah's modernization broad thoroughfares and open squares were cut into the city, Bandar-e 'Abbās retained its traditional character: a small *bāzār*, mud-brick houses sometimes built on coral foundations, and a forest of both simple and ornate *bādgīrs*, the *bādgīr-e 'arab*, open toward the sea, and the *bādgīr-e lūla*, open on all four sides.

The rebirth of Bandar-e 'Abbās. With the decision in 1964 to build a new deep-water port in a well-sheltered area some 8 km southwest of the center of town, Bandar-e 'Abbās changed markedly. Opened in 1967, the port can accommodate vessels with 10-m displacements and has an annual capacity of 1.5 million tons of cargo. It is primarily (90 percent) devoted to exports of chromite ore mined in a region 160 km to the northeast; ocher from Hormoz is also shipped from the new port. In 1968, 220,000 tons of cargo, 165,000 of which were imports, passed through the harbor, and by 1972-73, total tonnage reached 300,000. At the same time the fishing fleet was revitalized, and canning output hit 2.5 million (60 percent of capacity). The renascence of the port was further enhanced when Iranian naval headquarters in the Persian Gulf was transferred there from K̠orramšahr in 1973, and when a Bandar-e 'Abbās-Kermān highway was constructed to end the port's isolation from the country's hinterland.

The recent, rapid economic development of Bandar-e 'Abbās has led to a corresponding increase in population; censuses taken in 1966 and 1976 put the population at 34,627 and 89,103 respectively, making the region second only to the Tehran metropolitan area in growth. Bandar-e 'Abbās's population has quite recently swelled with refugees from the Iran-Iraq war; in summer 1984, the municipality estimated that 185,850 people resided in the city (private communication).

Bibliography: Given in the text. Other general studies: L. Lockhart, in *EI*² I, pp. 1044-45. G. Schweizer, *Bandar 'Abbas und Hormoz, Schicksal und Zukunft einer iranischen Hafenstadt am Persischen Golf*, Wiesbaden, 1972. A. W. Stiffe, "Ancient Trading Centres of the Persian Gulf," *Geographical Journal* 16, 1900, pp. 211-15. On Šahrū, see Schwarz, *Iran*, pp. 255, 275, 287. For a bibliography of travelogues mentioning Bandar-e 'Abbās, see A. Gabriel, *Die Erforschung Persiens*, Vienna, 1952. See also E. A. Floyer, *Unexplored Baluchistan*, London, 1882, pp. 139-40. M.-'A. Sadīd-al-Salṭana, *Safar-nāma*, ed. A. Eqtedārī, Tehran, 1362 Š./1983, index. J. de Morgan, *Mission scientifique en Perse* II, Paris, 1895, pp. 211-15. On the modern period see W. H. Keddie, "Fish and Futility in Iranian Development," *The Journal of Developing Areas* 6, 1971, pp. 9-28. H. Velsink, "Iran's New Port of Bandar Abbas," *The Dock and Harbour Authority* 49, 1969, pp. 339-45. G. Kortum, "Hafenprobleme Irans im nördlichen Persischen Golf," *Geographische Rundschau* 23, 1971, pp. 354-62. U. Gerke and H. Mehner, *Iran*, Tübingen, 1975, pp. 268, 392, 426. *Iran: A Country Study*, ed. R. F. Nyrop, Washington, D.C., 1978, index.

(X. de Planhol)

BANDAR-E GAZ, a port on the southern shore of the Astarābād (q.v.) bay in the southeastern Caspian Sea, a few kilometers from a group of nine hamlets known collectively as Gaz. In the mid-nineteenth century, this shoreline (called Kenāra, cf. Curzon, I, p. 185 and Rabino, p. 66; and Kenār Gaz, cf. O'Donovan, I, p. 297) was uninhabited, but the installation of Russians on the Āšūrāda (q.v.) islands after 1837 made it very important strategically. The site, at the mouth of a small stream, opposite the tip of the Mīānqāla peninsula and at the entrance of the bay, is doubly favored in that it is both sheltered from sea winds and easily accessible by sea. Russians built a trading post at the port in 1845 (Marvin, p. 331), but were prevented from establishing themselves further by the creation of a Persian post in 1867.

For about fifteen years, Bandar-e Gaz was the major port in the southeastern Caspian, a place from which muleteers could carry Russian merchandise to Astarābād, northeastern Iran, Khorasan, and even Herāt. The town comprised wooden shanties, a few customs buildings, solidly built houses for Russian and British agents, and a large caravansary. Port installations were limited to a precarious wooden pier built on piles. In 1881, imports (cloth, tea, sugar, metal, and hardware) amounted to 287,640 pounds sterling; and exports (wool and skins, silk, cotton, boxwood, gallnuts and dried fruits), to 86,280 pounds sterling. Nearly all trade was in the hands of Armenian merchants. When the Trans-Caspian Rail road reached ʿEšqābād (Ashkhabad (q.v.), in 1881, opening a much shorter route toward Mašhad, port traffic slackened considerably; a decade later, trade had fallen off to 51,900 pounds sterling of imports and about 20,000 pounds sterling of exports (Curzon). The town stagnated until the 1930s, when it was superseded by the newly developed Bandar-e Šāh. In 1942, vessels with a draft of ten feet could use the approximately one-kilometer long jetty; and the port's capacity was about 35,000 tons a year. Estimated at about 4,000 inhabitants in 1940 (*Persia*, p. 513), the population was put at 6,100 in 1966.

Bibliography: G. N. Curzon, *Persia and the Persian Question*, London, 1892, I, pp. 184-85; II, pp. 568-69. Ç. M. MacGregor, *Narrative of a Journey through the Province of Khorasan in 1875*, London, 1879, II, pp. 164-72. C. Marvin, *The Russians at Merv and Herat*, London, 1883, pp. 331-32, 336-51. Naval Intelligence Division, *Persia*, Oxford, 1945, p. 513. E. O'Donovan, *The Merv Oasis*, London, 1882, I, pp. 297-305. H. L. Rabino, *Mazandaran and Astarabad*, London, 1928, p. 66. N. von Seidlitz, "Handel und Wandel an der kaspischen Südküste," *Petermanns Mitteilungen*, 1869, pp. 98-103, 255-68.

(X. DE PLANHOL)

BANDAR-E MĀHŠAHR (Bandar-e Maʿšūr), a port at the western end of the Persian Gulf, on the northern bank of the K̲or-e Mūsā tideway, which forms the lower course of the Jar(r)āḥī river. At the end of the 19th century, Bandar-e Māhšahr was a small port used exclusively by native boats that hauled goods for neighboring Arab tribes (cloth and dates were imported; wheat, rice, barley, clarified butter, and wool exported). After the development of Bandar-e Šāhpūr (q.v.), petroleum reservoirs were built at Bandar-e Māhšahr, as it was situated on the railway that was constructed in 1943 to join Bandar-e Šāhpūr with the oil fields of Āḡā Jārī. Furthermore, since 1945, a pipeline that carries oil from the Āḡā Jārī fields to the refinery at Ābādān has passed through Bandar-e Māhšahr. With oil production on the rise, in 1948 the town became a port for exporting crude oil. Bandar-e Māhšar could be used by ships of up to 40,000 tons. It remained the major outlet for Iranian petroleum with annual traffic amounting to more than forty million tons, until installations at K̲ārg, which were accessible to supertankers that could carry loads of 100,000 tons, were started up in 1960. Thereafter, crude oil was no longer exported; however, refined products from Ābādān, which no longer has an active port, were exported through Bandar-e Māhšahr. During the period 1956-66, the town's population rose modestly from 15,694 to 16,594. After this relative stagnation, Bandar-e Māhšahr began to grow again as home to part of the labor force from the important petrochemical complex in nearby Bandar-e Šāhpūr. The population reached 30,000 in 1976.

Bibliography: British Naval Intelligence, *Persia*, Oxford, 1945, pp. 501-02. G. N. Curzon, *Persia and the Persian Question*, London, 1892, II, p. 400. I. Djazani, *Wirtschaft und Bevölkerung im Khuzistan und ihr Wandel unter dem Einfluss des Erdöls*, Tübingen, 1963. E. Ehlers, *Iran*, Darmstadt, 1980, pp. 304, 465-66. A. Melamid, "The Geographical Pattern of Iranian Oil Development," *Economic Geography* 35, 1959, pp. 199-218.

(X. DE PLANHOL)

BANDAR-E PAHLAVĪ. See ANZALĪ.

BANDAR-E ŠĀH (now Bandar-e Torkaman), a port on the southeastern Caspian Sea at the entrance of the Astarābād bay and about eight km south of the mouth of the Atrak. It was constructed from scratch during the 1930s at the terminus of the trans-Iranian railroad and consisted of a 200-meter-long jetty and a 12-kilometer-long channel. Four or five berths were provided for ships with displacements of a thousand tons. In 1935-36, total exports amounted to 48,000 tons and imports to 2,000. By 1941, however, there was so much silt in the channel that regular dredging was abandoned. Though the port had a theoretical daily capacity of 200 tons, traffic for all of 1940 reached only 970 tons. The town of Bandar-e Šāh comprised port buildings and a few houses for employees. In 1941, the Russians deepened the channel to fourteen feet, and the port's capacity increased to 1,200-1,500 tons a day. But with wartime activities over, and as the level of the Caspian Sea grew steadily lower and silt continued to accumulate, port traffic all but disappeared and did not revive despite development plans dating from the early 1970s. The port's bay still served as a place for fishing sturgeon; however the real reason behind its prosperity and rapid growth was its position as a railhead and an outlet for the Turkestan steppes, where agriculture was burgeoning during the 1950s and 1960s. When the railroad was extended to Gorgān in 1961, Bandar-e Šāh lost some of its importance. In 1966, there were 13,081 inhabitants. Since the Islamic Revolution of 1357 Š./1978-79, the town has been known as Bandar-e Torkaman.

Bibliography: H. Kopp. "Städte im östlichen iranischen Kaspitiefland," *Erlanger Geographische Arbeiten* 33, 1973, p. 151. Naval Intelligence Division, *Persia*, Oxford, 1945, pp. 510-11. P. Somerville-Large, *Caviar Coast*, London, 1968, pp. 36-37, 41-42.

(X. de Planhol)

BANDAR-e ŠĀHPŪR (Bandar-e Emām Ḵomeyni since the revolution of 1979), a port at the far end of the Persian Gulf, at the terminus of the trans-Iranian railroad. The town is located at about 70 km from the Gulf on poorly reinforced alluvium along the northern shore of the Ḵor Mūsā, the outlet of the Jarāḥī river, which flows down from the Zagros mountains. At low tide, vessels that draw 24 feet can enter the Ḵor Mūsā; and at high tide 29.5 feet. In the 1930s, Reżā Shah chose this site, about 12 km below the small traditional port of Bandar-e Māhšahr, as the site for Iran's own railroad terminus on the Gulf at a distance from Šaṭṭ al-ʿArab. Declared open in 1932, the port had a pier a thousand feet long. After a second pier 1,800 feet long was built in 1941, the port's capacity reached about a thousand tons a day. However there were still fewer than a thousand inhabitants. During a second phase of development begun in 1943, a 65 km-long narrow-gauge railroad was laid from the port to the Āḡā Jārī oil fields. When a large port for the oil industry was opened at Bandar-e Māhšahr in 1948, Bandar-e Šāhpūr was reduced to competing for traffic in general merchandise with Ḵorramšahr, which was hooked up to the trans-Iranian railroad. The population was 3,726 in 1956 and 6,013 in 1966. Local development took off with the construction, just east of the town, of a major petrochemical complex, Shahpur Chemical Company (Šerkat-e Sehāmī-e Šīmīā'ī-e Šāhpūr, which, mostly producing ammonified fertilizers, employed about 2,000 persons when it opened in 1973. Since it was turned toward the domestic market, it was difficult to justify its peripheral location at a port, which was strongly criticized. The building, in association with Japanese capital, of another industrial complex, the Iran Chemical Development Company, specialized in olefins (560,000 tons a year) and aromatics (860,000 tons a year), was finished in 1979 at the time of the revolution. According to forecasts, this complex should lead to the development of a city of 50,000 inhabitants.

Bibliography: Naval Intelligence Division, *Persia*, Geographical Handbook Series, Oxford, 1945, pp. 501-02. A. Melamid, "The Geographical Pattern of Iranian Oil Development," *Economic Geography* 35, 1959, pp. 199-218. Razmārā, *Farhang* IV, p. 51.

(X. de Planhol)

BANG (Middle and New Persian; in Book Pahlavi also *mang*, Arabicized *banj*), a kind of narcotic plant. In older Arabic and Persian sources *banj* is applied to three different plants: hemp (*Cannabis sativa* or *indica*), henbane (*Hyoseyamus niger* etc.), and jimsonweed (*Datura stramonium*). The effects of these three narcotic plants vary, something which may explain the widely differing descriptions of *bang* in the Middle Persian texts. In modern Persian *bang* is hashish.

i. *In ancient Iran.*
ii. *In modern Iran.*

i. In Ancient Iran

In the Middle Persian texts *bang* (*mang*) is described sometimes as a lethal and sometimes as a hallucinogenic drug. Thus, when Ahrimen attacked the creation, Ohrmazd gave the primordial bull a "medicinal" *mang* (*mang bēšaz*) to lessen its injury. The bull immediately became feeble and sick and passed away (*Bundahišn*, tr. chap. 4.20). However, *bang* was also an ingredient of the "illuminating drink" (*rōšngar xwarišn*) that allowed Wištāsp to see the "great *xwarrah*" and the "great mystery." This *mang ī wištāspān* (Pahlavi *Vd.* 15.14; *Ardā Wirāz-nāmag* 2.15) was mixed with *hōm* (*Dēnkard* 7.4.85) or wine (*Pahlavi Rivayat* 47.27). It was an integral part of the ecstatic practice aimed at opening the "eye of the soul" (*gyān čašm*; Gnoli, pp. 414ff., 435ff.) and was therefore drunk by Ardā Wirāz (*Ardā Wirāz-nāmag* 1.20, 2.9, 15, 16) before his journey into the other world (Gignoux, p. 152 n. 4; cf. Vahman, p. 14 n. 9).

The word must be etymologically related to Avestan *baŋha*/*bangha* (*Air Wb.*, col. 925, in compounds: *abaŋha*, *Pouru*, *baŋha*, *vībaŋha*, see *Air Wb.*, cols. 87, 901, 1447) and further to OInd. (Atharvavedic) *bhaṅga*. This etymological connection was challenged by Henning (pp. 33f.), but unconvincingly (see Widengren, 1955, pp. 66ff.; Boyce, *Zoroastrianism* I, pp. 231 n. 11, 280 with n. 14; Belardi, p. 117).

Bibliography: H. W. Bailey, "Ambages Indoiranicae," *AION-L*1, 1959, pp. 113-46. W. Belardi, *The Pahlavi Book of the Righteous Viraz*, Rome, 1979. Ph. Gignoux, *Le livre d'Ardā Vīrāz*, Paris, 1984. G. Gnoli, "Ašavan," in *Iranica*, ed. G. Gnoli, Naples, 1979, pp. 387-452. W. B. Henning, *Zoroaster, Politician or Witch-doctor?*, London, 1951. H. S. Nyberg, *Die Religionen des alten Iran*, Germ. tr. H. H. Schaeder, Leipzig, 1938, pp. 177f., 290f., 341f. Idem, *A Manual of Pahlavi* II, Wiesbaden, 1974, p. 125. F. Vahman, *Ardā Wirāz Nāmag*, London and Malmö, 1986. G. Widengren, "Stand und Aufgaben der iranischen Religionsgeschichte," *Numen* 2, 1955, pp. 47-132. Idem, *Die Religionen Irans*, Stuttgart, 1965, pp. 70ff. Idem, "Révélation et prédication dans les Gāthās," in *Iranica*, ed. G. Gnoli, Naples, 1979, pp. 339-64. Idem,

Göttingische Gelehrte Anzeigen 231, 1/2, 1979, pp. 56ff. (review of B. Schlerath, ed., *Zarathustra*, Darmstadt, 1970, with reference to K. Rudolph, "Zarathuštra-Priester und Prophet," ibid., pp. 270-313, reprinted from *Numen* 8, 1961, pp. 81-116).

(G. Gnoli)

ii. In Modern Iran

Hemp cultivation and hashish production flourish in dry and sunny regions that are 1,500-2,000 m above sea level; thus hashish produced in Afghanistan is the most prized variety, and places most hospitable to hemp growing in the Tehran province and adjacent area are Sāva, Qāsemābād-e Qandīšāh in Šahrīār. The plant requires a great deal of water and is usually grown along streams; where this is not possible, fields must be watered daily during the first two months of growth, every other day in the third and fourth months, and every third day thereafter.

The height achieved by the mature plant depends on the soil and the type of fertilizer used; plants generally grow to a height of 0.5 m-2 m; however, in areas such as Shiraz, the use of chemical fertilizers has increased vertical growth to more than 3 m. The planting season depends on the local climate; it generally runs from March to April; the harvest goes from the end of August to the end of November, the best time being two or three days after the first autumnal chill when the plant stalks begin to redden. After the plant reaches full maturity, but before it flowers, the male flowers must be weeded from the fields to prevent them from pollinating the females (otherwise the delicate female buds will be turned to hemp). After the male flowers are eliminated, females are weeded in such a way as to space them 0.5 m-1 m apart (depending on climatic conditions and the suitability of the ground to plant growth). Harvest time comes with the first cold spell when the old leaves at the base of the plant stalk start to yellow. Methods of producing *bang* and hashish vary from place to place; some of the most common can be summarized as follows.

Production of superior-quality hashish. When the plants have budded and a thick, sticky, dust-like paste appears under the delicate leaves of the bud, the delicate leaves at the top of the stalks and the buds are gathered together and kept in the dark until they dry. They are then spread out on a heavy cloth of thick weave (such as the woolen floor coverings known as *gelīm*s and *jājīm*s). They are rolled up in the rug and the rug is pressed and rubbed the way a fuller would press felt. As a result of the rubbing, the paste from the leaves and buds adheres to the rug; the rug is then beaten over a smooth type of fabric (such as calico or nylon or leather) so that the female flowers that adhere to it fall to the fabric. The brownish flowers, which are greasy and sticky, are rolled into pellets and consumed as hashish or *čars*. In place of a thick woolen rug, to knead the dry leaves one can also use muslin (*karbās*), placing the leaves 0.5 cm apart on it. The cloth is then folded five or six times and then rolled up so that the leaves can be kneaded.

Production of ordinary-quality hashish. In the fall plants are gathered, branches are separated from the stalks and bound together to look like old-fashioned whisk brooms. They are then kept in a dark room so that the leaves dry. The branches are shaken so that the dry leaves fall to the ground; the leaves are then kneaded in the manner described above. If the volume of leaves is great, they are placed on a hard surface such as asphalt or brick and a horse wearing blinkers tramples them to soften them up. The pliable greenish substance obtained is then placed on a thick woven rug and kneaded as described above. The slightly oily brownish paste that sticks to the rug is extracted and shaped into pellets or cubes to be consumed as second-grade hashish. The crushed leaves that do not adhere to the rug are moistened and shaped into pellets that tend to be green in color, and not very potent. These pellets are called "horse-hoof hashish" (*ḥašīš-e somm-e asbī*) and evidently form the kind of hashish that was called *bang* in days gone by; however, contemporary Iranian parlance does not distinguish among *bang*, hashish, and *čars*. Other names for this narcotic are *asrār*, *sabza*, *sabzak*, and *waraq al-ḵīāl*.

Another form of hashish that has become popular recently, being favored by Iranians who have returned from the United States, is produced by separating the branches from the stalk without extracting the buds and the delicate leaves. These then are bound together into a "broom" and allowed to dry: then the buds within the bundle, which are still soft, moist, and yellowish, are separated as "marijuana" and rubbed together. The rest of the plant material, which is lower in quality, is kneaded in the manner described above and turned into bang.

To produce hashish oil (*rowḡan-e bang*), the most delicate leaves and buds are separated from the plant, dried, and rubbed and pressed. The resulting dust-like substance is placed in a pot of tepid water; the pot is then heated over a medium flame and the solution is brought to a near-boil. The globules of hashish oil that appear on the surface of the water are skimmed off and placed in a bottle.

Hashish is typically consumed in a water pipe, a long-stemmed pipe know as a *čopoq*, or a cigarette. To increase the oily hashish's combustibility, it is mixed with tobacco; in the *čopoq*, for example, a layer of hashish is covered with a layer of tobacco and packed on top of them is another, thin layer of hashish—this is called a "two-story *čopoq*" (*čopoq-e do-ṭabaqa*). Hashish is sometimes mixed with opium and smoked in an opium pipe; the mixture is called the "fairies' spirit" (*rūḥ al-ajenna*). Hashish oil is generally consumed by thoroughly mixing a drop of it with a liter of *dūḡ* (a drink made from yogurt), and drinking the resulting mixture. This mixture, which is extremely potent and dangerous, is called *dūḡ-e waḥdat* (the *dūḡ* of annihilation): overconsumption of this drink can cause severe palpitations which, if not immediately counteracted by the consumption of a great deal of animal fat, can be fatal.

Though it has been written that the use of hashish and *bang* does not cause physical dependency, when intoxicated, those who have used the narcotic for years are subject to tremors. The psychological dependency, as shown by the impatience and depression that the user displays when unable to obtain hashish, however, is undeniable. One of the general signs of hashish intoxication is a false appetite, which if not checked by others can cause the intoxicated to indulge in painful overeating. Other general aspects of hashish intoxication are a kind of forgetfulness and unawareness of reality and of life's aggravations, induced by a strengthening of the power of imagination and the realization of repressed desires in the world of make-believe. Hashish also distorts the vision; the ability to judge depth and distance is so changed that the intoxicated occasionally imagines a puddle of water a boundless ocean, a sparrow in a tree the mythical bird Sīmorḡ or a giant airplane, or a ray of light shining through a crack heaven itself. This condition is occasionally accompanied by uncontrollable fear and terror of imaginary visions and of reified chimera along with a dream-filled sleep in which the user traverses the earth, flies to the farthest reaches of the heavens, jaunts about the Milky Way, and sees all of his unfulfilled dreams and impossible desires realized. Some hashish users become silent and introspective, while others are subject to pointless fits of uncontrollable laughter and an unnatural euphoria.

Continued use of hashish generally causes lapses of memory, pronounced mental dysfunction, engenders in the user a condition similar to retardation and idiocy and may eventually lead to manic-depressive psychosis.

The sale, purchase, and use of the narcotic products of the hemp plant are illegal in Iran, and they are not that popular among its present-day inhabitants. Their use was evidently greater during the Safavid and Qajar periods; however, the euphoria-seekers of today's Iran turn more to opiates and alcohol. Hashish is more widely consumed on the Indian subcontinent, in Afghanistan, Turkey, and the Arab countries, especially Egypt and Syria; those familiar with the smell can readily identify the hashish smoke coming from the many water pipes in most of the coffee houses of Cairo. In Iran the traditional methods of consuming *bang* and *čars* in a water pipe or a *čopoq* (q.v.) or in the *dūḡ-e waḥdat* (q.v.) are carried on mostly by itinerant dervishes and by those affecting the ways of Sufis; consumption of hashish and marijuana in cigarettes is generally favored by the limited number of elite euphoria-seekers who have returned from the West.

(The information in this article is based on local investigations and interviews.)

(ʿA.-A. Saʿīdī Sīrjānī)

BANG KAUP, JOHANN WILHELM MAX JULIUS (known as Willy), German orientalist, b. 9 August 1869, d. 8 October 1934; son of Heinrich Bang, judge of the court martial of the fortress at Wesel and later mayor of the town, and his spouse Auguste née Kaup.

Having been persuaded through an exchange of letters with the orientalist H. L. Fleischer to choose a university course in Oriental Studies, Bang Kaup entered the field at an early age. He studied Old Persian, Avestan, Manchu, and Mongol with Charles de Harlez. As early as 1889 he wrote articles on the Avesta and the Old Persian inscriptions. Together with H. Weissbach he prepared a new edition of the inscriptions, bringing out the first fascicle in 1893 and the second in 1909. During this time both wrote detailed essays which greatly added to the understanding of the inscriptions.

Another of Bang Kaup's interests was English literature. Between 1896 and 1914 he published some important studies in this field and was responsible, as editor, for the collective work *Materialien zur Kunde des älteren englischen Dramas*.

From 1893 onward Bang Kaup also devoted time to research in the promising area of the Old Turkish stone inscriptions. The way had been opened by the success of the Danish linguist V. Thomsen in deciphering the runic script. Bang Kaup applied himself to the interpretation of the contents of the inscriptions, keeping to the strictest criteria of comparative linguistics and using data from all Turkish dialects. He thus made a major contribution to the development of Turcology into an independent discipline. His work in this field, begun in 1893, increasingly absorbed him after 1917. Together with J. Markwart he succeeded in solving the chronological riddle of the Old Turkish inscriptions through the discovery that the juxtaposition of the numerals in Old Turkish is based on counting within the highest order of magnitude (e.g., *iki otuz* "two thirty" = 22). Between 1910 and 1914 he worked on the Codex Cumanicus and drew attention through his writings to the inadequacies of the previous work on the text; he himself published exemplary partial editions. He then turned to the Old Turkish manuscripts found in the Turfan oasis. After his appointment to the University of Berlin in 1918, he concentrated on the study of the Turfan texts. His profound analyses of the manuscript fragments edited by A. von Le Coq were published in articles which have provided guidelines for scholars ever since. This research, together with his very wide knowledge of Turkic languages and dialects, enabled him to achieve new insights, particularly into the Manichean-Turkish and Christian texts (e.g., in his articles "Manichäische Laienbeichtspiegel," "Manichäische Hymnen," "Bruchstücke einer nestorianischen Georgspassion," all in *Le Muséon*). In collaboration with Annemarie von Gabain he elucidated further texts (*Türkische Turfan-Texte* I-VI, *SPAW*, 1929-34), and they brought out the first glossary (*Analytischer Index*, *SPAW*, 1931).

In several articles Bang Kaup discussed problems in the historical grammar of the Turkish languages ("Vom Köktürkischen zum Osmanischen," "Monographien zur türkischen Sprachgeschichte"). His "Turkologische Briefe aus dem Berliner Ungarischen Institut" (in *Ungarische Jahrbücher*, 1925-34) attest not only his perspicacity and erudition but also his insistence on caution. His correspondence forms part of his scholarly legacy. He exerted a particularly strong and long-lasting influence on Turcology during the productive years of his service at the Ungarisches Institut in Berlin. He founded a school there and had many foreign students who subsequently carried on work with his methods in their own countries. To his students, as von Gabain has warmly testified, he gave unfailing help and encouragement to persevere in constructive effort for the development of Turcology. Friendship and mutual respect marked his relations with scholars in other Oriental disciplines, particularly Iranian studies. His writings are notable for their clarity and lively style as well as their content.

Bibliography: H. H. Schaeder, "Zu W. Bang's sechzigstem Geburtstag," *Ungarische Jahrbücher* 9, 1929, pp. 181-87. H. de Vocht, "Bibliographie der Arbeiten von Professor W. Bang Kaup," *Ungarische Jahrbücher* 9, 1929, pp. 188-95. A. von Gabain, "W. Bang Kaup 1869-1934," *Ungarische Jahrbücher* 14, 1934, pp. 335-40 (additions to the *Bibliographie* on p. 140). Idem, "Persönliche Erinnerungen an W. Bang Kaup," in *Sprache, Geschichte und Kultur der altaischen Völker*, Berlin, 1974, pp. 51-55. Idem, "Bang Kaup," in *Neue Deutsche Bibliographie* I, Berlin, 1953, p. 576. A. N. Kononov, "W. Bang-Kaup. Zum hundertsten Geburtstag," in *Sprache, Geschichte und Kultur der altaischen Völker*, Berlin, 1974, pp. 47-49. S. Khassankhanova, *Zur Geschichte der Berliner Turkologie in der ersten Hälfte des 20. Jahrhunderts. Die Erschliessung der alttürkischen Turfan-Texte. W. Bang-Kaup und seine sprachwissenschaftliche Schule*, unpublished dissertation, Berlin, 1979.

(P. Zieme)

BANGĀLA. See BENGAL.

BANGAŞ, on of the least-known Pashtun tribes in the Solaymān range, Pakistan, and one of the few that are not named after eponymous ancestors. The origin of the name is obscure since, as Raverty (p. 387 n.) pointed out, the folk etymology from *bon-kaš* (Persian for "root-drawer") is not acceptable.

The tribe is a combination of lineages from various origins. Evidence of this comes from both the lineage names (e.g., Lağmānī and J̌amšēdī) and the mythical descent of the tribe from a man named Esmāʿīl, who moved from Persia to the Solaymān mountains but whose eleventh-generation ancestor was the famous Arab general Ḵāled b. Walīd and whose wife was a Formolī (a local Iranian ethnic group; Š.-M. Khan, pp. 311f.). At this point, nothing—apart from distant kinship through the same Arab ancestor—relates the Bangaş to the Pashtun genealogical megastructure, wherein they are nowadays incorporated through the Karlāni branch, which comprises several Solaymāni tribes that have been genealogically adopted and more or less culturally pashtunized. This incorporation, which is never clearly formulated in terms of filiation or even of adoption, may have originated in a military alliance between the Bangaş and Ḵaṭak (q.v.) in the 9th/15th century.

The tribe is formed around two fractions Gār(ī) and Sāmel(zī), whose names supposedly derive from those of Esmāʿīl's two sons. Interestingly, Gār and Sāmel also designate the two rival political leagues between which the Solaymāni tribes have been traditionally divided. Following M.-Ḥ. Khan (p. 297), some authors have concluded that this pan-Pashtun political cleavage first took place among the Bangaş and then gradually passed among neighboring tribes. According to another hypothesis (Bellew, p. 106), the Bangaş's genealogy metaphorically transposes a long-standing political (or other) duality that existed before the tribe was formed. In any case, the decomposition of traditional political structures since, at least, the last century has generated much discordance between the genealogical status of lineages and their declared political affiliations (see Table 24).

The Bangaş also stand out among the Pashtun because the majority are Shiʿite and a minority Sunni. It has often been said (e.g., Caroe, pp. 202ff.) that Shiʿism among the Pashtun—in fact only among the Bangaş, the Tūrī (q.v.), and a small part of the Ōrakzī (q.v.)—is but the modern avatar of religious dissent going back to the Rōšānī heresy (q.v.). As regards the Bangaş, Bellew (p. 105) has suggested that the tribe, given the name of its putative ancestor, might have formed around the preaching of Ismaʿili missionaries. Surprisingly, the details of Bangaş myths fit in with this hypothesis in ways that had not previously been suspected. Before settling in the Solaymān range, Esmāʿīl, it is said, abode in Mūltān, a town over which he was appointed governor (*Gazetteer*, p. 30). Using his genealogy to make a quick calculation, this event can be placed in the 4th/10th century (and not in the 7th/13th as indicated in the *Gazetteer*), in other words, during the very period when Mūltān was the center of a short-lived Ismaʿili state. The ultimate episode in the myth, which has to do with Esmāʿīl's arrival in the Solaymān mountains (specifically in the Gardīz region which was then an active center of the Kharijite movement), is historically grounded in the religious persecution that followed the Mūltān takeover by Sultan Maḥmūd of Ḡaznī (on three successive occasions during 396-401/1006-10; A. N. Khan, pp. 44ff.). All evidence leads to considering Esmāʿīl to be a metaphor for either a *dāʿī* or a small Ismaʿili community and to seeking for the origins of Shiʿism among the Pashtun in the Ismaʿili *daʿwa* activities in Khorasan during the early centuries of the emergence of the sect. This conclusion is reinforced by Raverty's remark (p. 389) that the Pashtun Shiʿites recognize the Agha Khan's authority.

The ethnogenesis of the Bangaş, therefore, seems both to be religious and to be located in the Gardīz region during the Ghaznavid period. The myth has transposed these origins in terms of Esmāʿīl's marriage with a woman from Formol (= Orgūn), a district just south of Gardīz. Later on the Bangaş, who were then

Table 24
THE BANGAŞ TRIBE

Main Bangaş lineages	Genealogical descent	Political affiliation	Religion
Bā'īzī	Gār	Gār	Sunni
Mīrānzī	Gār	Gār + Sāmel minority	Sunni + Shi'ite
Sāmelzī	Sāmel	Gār + Sāmel minority	Shi'ite + Sunni minority

expelled from their mountain den by the Ḡelzī during Tīmūr's invasions, crossed the Paywār pass and progressively moved into the upper Korram basin on the eastern slopes of the Solaymān mountains. There they met the hostility of the Ōrakzī who were eventually, owing to the Bangaş's tactical alliance with the K̲aṭak who were moving into the same area, pushed back into the Safīdkūh (Spīngar) foothills. The Bangaş could then occupy the whole area that, just south of the Safīdkūh, was called the Bangaş district in the 10th/16th century (Beveridge, p. 220), whence the name. Even today, they are mainly settled along the major route between Afghanistan and India that passes through the Mīrānzay and Kōhāt valleys. Though forced to cede most of the upper Korram valley to the Tūrī in the 12th/18th century, the Bangaş still have a few isolated villages there, in particular Šalozān which, near the Afghanistan border, is the westernmost point that they still inhabit.

Like the other tribes in the Solaymān range, the Bangaş have provided mercenaries to India during the Mughal and British periods. In the early 14th/20th century, about 1,500 Bangaş were serving in the Indian army and militias (Ridgway, pp. 76f.). In 1125/1713, one of these mercenaries, a member of the Sāmelzay lineage, managed to be granted an important principality in the Gangetic Doab and founded the dynasty of the nawabs of Farrok̲ābād, from the name of the capital he built there (Irvine, 1878, pp. 259-383; 1879, pp. 49-170; Rašīd, I, pp. 272ff.). The last Bangaş nawab was exiled to Mecca in 1859 because of his involvement in the Sepoy Mutiny of 1857 (Raverty, p. 387 n.).

The number of Bangaş in the Northwest Frontier Province was estimated at 7,925 men in the 1901 census (Ridgway). Although they apparently used to lead a seminomadic life (*Gazetteer*, p. 31), they are now settled farmers (Dichter, p. 125). In the late 13th/19th century, there were still indications that *wēš* (the periodic redistribution of land) was practiced (*Gazetteer*, pp. 85ff.). The Bangaş have a few matrimonial customs peculiar to themselves with, it seems, traces of matrilocality (Rose, II, pp. 58ff.).

Bibliography: There is no monograph about the Bangaş. More general sources about the Pashtun tribes must be consulted even though they mostly repeat each other without adding much information. Only those providing original information are cited here. The most detailed accounts of the tribe's lineage structure are found in Š.-M. Khan and M.-Ḥ. Khan; the latter, however contains errors in transcriptions. The fullest reports about the geographical distribution of lineages and sublineages are given in Ridgway and *Frontier*. Ẕahīr-al-Dīn Bābor, *Bābor-nāma*, tr. A. S. Beveridge, *The Bābur-nāma in English*, London, 1922, repr. London, 1969. D. Balland, "Du mythe à l'histoire: aux origines du chiisme chez les Pashtun" (forthcoming). H. W. Bellew, *An Inquiry into the Ethnography of Afghanistan*, Woking, 1891, repr. Graz, 1973. O. Caroe, *The Pathans*, London, 1958. D. Dichter, *The North-West Frontier of West Pakistan: A Study in Regional Geography*, Oxford, 1967. *Frontier and Overseas Expeditions from India*, Calcutta, 1908, repr., Quetta, 1979, II, pp. 310ff. *Gazetteer of the Kohat District 1883-4*, Calcutta, n.d. W. Irvine, "The Bangash Nawābs of Farrukhabad, a Chronicle (1713-1857)," *Journal of the Asiatic Society of Bengal* 47/1, 1878; 48/1, 1879. A. N. Khan, *Multan, History and Architecture*, Islamabad, 1403/1983. M.-Ḥ. Khan, *Ḥayāt-e Afḡān*, tr. H. Priestley, *Afghanistan and Its Inhabitants*, Lahore, 1874, repr. Lahore, 1981. Š.-M. Khan, *Tawārīk̲-e k̲ʷoršīd-e jahān*, Lahore, 1311/1894. S. Abdur Rashid, *History of the Muslims of Indo-Pakistan Sub-continent*, Lahore, 1978. H. G. Raverty, *Notes on Afghanistan and Part of Baluchistan*, London, 1880-88, repr. Lahore, 1976. R. T. I. Ridgway, *Pathans*, Calcutta, 1910. H. A. Rose, *A Glossary of the Tribes and Castes of the Punjab and North-West Frontier Province*, Lahore, 1919, repr. Lahore, 1978.

(D. BALLAND)

BANĪ ARDALĀN, a Kurdish tribe of northwestern Iran, now dispersed in Sanandaj (Senna) and surrounding villages. V. Minorsky believed that the name Ardalān was derived from a Turkish rank (*Tad̲kerat al-molūk*, p. 113 n.). The ruling family of this tribe claimed descent from Saladin (Ṣalāḥ-al-Dīn) (B. Nikitine, *Les Kurdes*, Paris, 1956, p. 167). Other tribal legends made them originate in Sasanian or early 'Abbasid times (V. Minorsky, "Senna," in *EI*[1] IV, p. 227). According to Šaraf-al-Dīn, the earliest known leader of the tribe, Bābā Ardalān, was a descendant of Aḥmad b. Marwān, who ruled in Dīārbakr. He settled down among the Gūrāns in Kurdistan and toward the end of the Mongol period took over the Šahr-e Zūr region, where he established himself as an absolute ruler (Šaraf-al-Dīn Khan Bedlīsī, *Šaraf-nāma*, tr. F. B. Charmoy, St. Petersburg, 1868-75, II, pp. 106-07). When he visited Sanandaj in 1820, C. J. Rich was told that the

Ardalāns were from the Māmū'ī clan of the Gūrān tribe (*Narrative of a Residence in Koordistan*, London, 1836, II, p. 214).

It is not known when the Ardalāns established themselves in Sanandaj, but it was probably in the 14th century. Using that town as their capital, they ruled over a large Kurdish principality, the area of which corresponded roughly to that of the present-day *šahrestān* (sub-province) of Sanandaj. This region included several Kurdish tribes, besides the Ardalāns' own tribe, the Banī Ardalān, namely the Jāfs, the Kalhors, the Mandamīs and the Shaikh Esmā'īlīs (Rich, *Narrative*, p. 217). The Ardalān state was completely independent until it was incorporated into Safavid Iran as a semi-autonomous frontier province by the name of Ardalān. At that time the khans of the tribe were given the title of *wālī*, or amir of the marches, by the Iranian government (Nikitine, *Les Kurdes*, pp. 167-70). Nearly all the *wālīs* of Ardalān from then on were Ardalāns. The only exceptions were *wālīs* who were imposed upon the province by the Iranian government when the latter was trying to impose its will upon a recalcitrant khan.

During the Safavid period, the Ardalāns were deeply involved in the struggles between the Iranian and Ottoman empires and, whenever it suited them, they shifted their allegiance to the Ottoman government (Minorsky, "Senna," p. 227). Among the amirs of note who served Shah Ṭahmāsb I (r. 1524-76) was one Tīmūr Khan Ardalān, whom Eskandar Monšī identified as "governor of Ḥasanābād and Palangān," both of which were districts of Ardalān (*Eskandar Beg*, tr. Savory, p. 227). Another leader of the tribe, Khan Aḥmad Khan, was raised at the court of Shah 'Abbās I (r. 1588-1629) and then was sent by him to Sanandaj in 1615 to take over the governorship of that province from his ailing father (ibid., pp. 1081, 1144).

Sobḥānverdī Khan, the Ardalan *wālī* at the beginning and at the end of Nāder Shah's rule (1736-47), was a particularly successful and popular leader. But, in 1155/1742-43, he was temporarily replaced by his son Aḥmad Khan, who had accompanied Nāder on his conquest of India (1738-39). Aḥmad Khan was made governor of a region stretching all the way from Hamadān to the confines of Mosul. However, he almost immediately ran afoul of the Afšār ruler by distributing among his own famished people stores of wheat which were intended for the Iranian army. He was forced to flee for his life, ending up in Istanbul, where he was warmly received (Nikitine, "Les valis d'Ardelan," *RMM* 49, 1922, pp. 88-89; J. R. Perry, *Karim Khan Zand*, Chicago, 1979, p. 25).

Another distinguished Ardalān *wālī* was Ḵosrow Khan Bozorgī (r. Moḥarram, 1168–1203/1754–88-89). He was a staunch supporter of Karīm Khan Zand (r. 1750-79). In April, 1777, he was defeated in a clash with Ottoman forces, but later that year he participated in a victorious campaign against the Turks launched by Karīm Khan (Perry, *Karim Khan Zand*, pp. 184-85, 190-91; Ṣādeq Eṣfahānī, *Tārīḵ-e gītīgošā*, Tehran, 1317 Š./1938-39, pp. 282, 293-95). During the period of anarchy which followed the death of Karīm Khan, Ḵosrow Khan defeated two of the pretenders to the throne, first Allāhqolī Khan Zangena at the Gardana-ye Bagān pass, near Sanandaj, and then Ja'far Khan Zand at Bahār, near Hamadān. He conquered a vast area, which included Malāyer and Golpāyegān, and, when he realized that Āqā Moḥammad Khan Qājār (r. 1203–12/1789–99) was the strongest contender for the crown, he threw his support behind him. In the 1760s, Ḵosrow Khan began the construction of a large palace, which he called Ḵosrovīya, in Sanandaj (Nikitine, "Les valis," pp. 191-94).

The last important Ardalān *wālī* was Amān-Allāh Khan Bozorgī (r. 1214–40/1799-80–1824-25). During his long, productive rule, he purchased land, stimulated agricultural production, planted gardens, built fortifications and entertained on a lavish, regal scale, which greatly impressed his foreign visitors (see J. Malcolm, *Sketches of Persia*, London, 1845, pp. 283-87; J. Macdonald Kinneir, *A Geographical Memoir of the Persian Empire*, London, 1813, pp. 144-45; R. K. Porter, *Travels in Georgia, Persia, etc.*, London, 1822, II, pp. 566-68; Rich, *Narrative*, pp. 206-20). Fatḥ-'Alī Shah (r. 1797-1834) valued his services so highly that he arranged for one of his daughters to marry one of the khan's sons (Nikitine, "Les valis," p. 96). On the other hand, Nāṣer-al-Dīn Shah (r. 1848-96) was determined to undermine the power and influence of the Ardalāns. He first interfered in the affairs of the province in 1851 (see E. I. Chirikov, *Putevoĭ zhurnal*, St. Petersburg, 1875, pp. 323-35, 524-27). Then, in 1284/1867-68, he terminated Ardalān's special status as a semi-autonomous frontier province (which it shared with Arabistan [Ḵūzestān] and the Pošt-e Kūh) and named his own uncle, Farhād Mīrzā Mo'tamad-al-Dawla, as *ḥākem* (governor) of what had become simply the province of Kurdistan, thus putting an end to the Ardalān dynasty (Nikitine, "Les valis," pp. 101-03).

In the 1860s, the number of Banī Ardalāns was estimated at 5,000 families or approximately 25,000 individuals (F. B. Charmoy's notes to *Šaraf-nāma* I, p. 43). By now, they have become too scattered to permit a reliable estimate.

In 1941 the Banī Ardalāns participated in the first Kurdish revolt in Iran during World War II (H. Arfa, *The Kurds*, London, 1966, p. 68). However, they were not involved in the establishment of the Kurdish Republic at Mahābād in 1946, and the territory of that short-lived secessionist state did not include Sanandaj (see W. Eagleton, *The Kurdish Republic of 1946*, London, 1963, p. 127).

Bibliography: Given in the text. See also M. Mardūḵ Kordestānī, *Tārīḵ-e kord wa Kordestān*, Tehran, 1358 Š./1979, I, pp. 76-77, II, pp. 10-48. Storey, I, pp. 369, 1300. E. B. Soane, *To Mesopotamia and Kurdistan in Disguise*, London, 1912, pp. 376-79. H. L. Rabino, *Report on Kurdistan*, Simla, 1911.

(P. OBERLING)

BANĪ ḤARDĀN, a Shi'ite Arab tribe of Howayza

(Ḥawīza) district in Ḵūzestān. Small in number (they were estimated at 2,500 persons early in the century, and at 500 families, i.e., roughly the same number, in the 1930s), their range is comparatively extensive: north of Ahvāz, west of Ahvāz to Howayza, between the Kārūn and the Karḵa rivers, and inland from the left bank of the Āb-e Gargar. Their main centers are Kūt Nahr Hāšem, Dūb-e Ḥardān, and Čārṭāq. Formerly predominantly nomadic (Lorimer, II, p. 120, noted only 100 persons settled), they have progressively sedentarized, cultivating wheat and barley and raising sheep. They are organized into six sections.

Bibliography: (Great Britain) Admiralty, *Persia*, Geographical Handbook Series, Oxford, 1945, p. 380. Henry Field, *Contributions to the Anthropology of Iran*, Chicago, 1939, pp. 192-93. J. G. Lorimer, *Gazetteer* II, p. 637-38. M. F. von Oppenheim, *Die Beduinen*, ed. W. Caskel, 4 vols., Wiesbaden, 1967, IV, pp. 35-36.

(J. PERRY)

BANĪ LĀM, a numerous and historically important Shiʿite Arab tribe of northwestern Ḵūzestān, southern Lorestān, and adjacent parts of Iraq. Their range extends from the foothills of the Pošt-e Kūh south to the Tigris at ʿAmāra, and east to the Karḵa south of Šūš. Once nomadic pastoralists, the Banī Lām are now mainly sedentary, growing a range of cereals (except rice) and raising sheep. Nomadic sections used regularly to cross the frontier, some moving south to ʿAmāra district and others north to the foothills in summer. Their total numbers were estimated at 45,000 ca. 1910, and their population in Iran at 5,700 families in 1934, rising to 10,650 in 1945 (Lorimer, *Gazetteer* II, p. 1084; Field, pp. 195-96; *Persia*, pp. 378-79). They are organized in four divisions and sixteen sections, and are predominantly Shiʿite. A number of later tribes and tribal sections of Ḵūzestān (e.g., of the Āl-e Kaṯīr, q.v.) are said to be of Lām origin (Field, pp. 195-96).

Their eponym was one Lām b. Ḥāreṯa, a chief of the Qaḥṭān in the Hejaz. Until the late 4th/10th century they were part of the Ṭayye' tribe, but when this disintegrated the Banī Lām made a name for themselves raiding the pilgrim route between Basra and Medina. Pushed out of northern Hejaz in the 9th/15th century, they moved to the lower Tigris-Euphrates region about 950/1550 (Oppenheim, II, pp. 320, 324; III, pp. 18-19). Late in the 10th/16th century they migrated to the east bank of the Tigris, taking territory from the Banī Rabīʿa, whose chief was provincial governor (*wālī*) of Ḥowayza for the Safavids. Subjected to punitive raids by the Mamluk pashas of Baghdad throughout the 11th/17th and 12th/18th centuries, they at times joined with the Montafeq Arabs, or their Lor neighbors, or Iranian armies, in attacks on Baghdad and Basra, as during Nāder Shah's sieges of Baghdad in 1145/1733 and of Basra in 1156/1743 (Longrigg, pp. 93-94, 124-26; Lockhart, p. 68). During the troubled 1750s, before the establishment of Zand rule in southwestern Iran, they joined with the Mošaʿšaʿīān (q.v.) against the Āl-e Kaṯīr in almost continuous war (Kasrawī, pp. 142-50).

In the 13th/19th century both Ottoman and Iranian governments intervened periodically to chastise the turbulent Banī Lām and their neighbors, without appreciable effect; inter- and intratribal feuding continued, as did raids on road and river traffic. During World War I the Banī Lām under Shaikh Ḡażbān answered the Turks' call for a *jehād* and harassed the British forces holding the line of the Karḵa to protect the oil pipeline (Oppenheim, III, pp. 200-04). In the 1920s frequent disputes flared between the *wālī* of Pošt-e Kūh and the Banī Lām when they moved in from Iraq for the summer grazing, but during the next decade Reżā Shah's government troops effectively reduced the scale of migration and accelerated sedentarization.

Bibliography: (Great Britain) Admiralty, *Persia*, Geographical Handbook Series, Oxford, 1945. ʿA. ʿAzzāwī, *ʿAšāʾer al-ʿErāq*, 4 vols., Baghdad, 1947, IV, pp. 174, 177. *EI*[2] V, pp. 645-46 H. Field, *Contributions to the Anthropology of Iran*, Chicago, 1939. A. Kasrawī, *Tārīḵ-e pānṣad-sāla-ye Ḵūzestān*, Tehran, 1330 Š./1951. L. Lockhart, *Nadir Shah*, London, 1938. S. H. Longrigg, *Four Centuries of Modern Iraq*, Oxford, 1925. Manūčehr Żarābī, "Ṭawāyef-e Mīānāb," *FIZ* 10, 1341 Š./1962, pp. 394-407.

(J. PERRY)

BANĪ SĀLA (not to be confused with the Āl Bū Ṣāleḥ of southern Iraq), a Shiʿite Arab tribe of Howayza (Ḥawīza) district in Ḵūzestān. Their territory, centered on Šowayb, extends some 25 miles along the banks of the Karḵa river southwest of Ahvāz as far as Šeyḵ Moḥammad and into the Tigris-Karḵa marshes (*Persia*, pp. 378-79). Their numbers were estimated earlier this century at 15,000 (Lorimer, *Gazetteer* II, pp. 123, 1654-55) or 2,100 families (Field, p. 199). Once camel breeders, they are now mostly settled cultivators and stockbreeders, but include marsh men (*meʿdān*; notably the Ḥalāf section, ca. 800 huts) and nomads (esp. the Ḥamūdī section, 400 tents). The latter spend winter and spring on the plains away from the river. The Banī Sāla originated from the Ṭayye' tribe, or by other accounts from Tamīm (ʿAzzāwī, IV, pp. 194), and in the 12th/18th and 13th/19th centuries were subjects of the Montafeq confederacy (Oppenheim, IV, pp. 34).

Bibliography: (Great Britain) Admiralty, *Persia*, Geographical Handbook Series, Oxford, 1945. ʿA. ʿAzzāwī, *ʿAšāʾer al-ʿErāq*, 4 vols., Baghdad, 1947. H. Field, *Contributions to the Anthropology of Iran*, Chicago, 1939. M. F. von Oppenheim, *Die Beduinen*, ed. W. Caskel, 4 vols., Wiesbaden 1967.

(J. PERRY)

BANĪ TAMĪM, an Arab tribe of western Ḵūzestān, both settled and nomadic, raising sheep and camels. Their range lies between Howayza and Ahvāz, where they are also known as the Banī Mālek (*Persia*, pp. 378, 380; Field, pp. 198-99). Their numbers were estimated at 10,000 persons before World War I, when they also extended south on the Kārūn as far as Qājārīya

(Lorimer, *Gazetteer* II, pp. 123, 1858), and in the 1940s at 2,200 families (Oppenheim, IV, p. 25). They are Shiʿite, and organized in sixteen sections.

Their earlier history, and in particular their relation to the classical tribe of Tamīm, some of whom had emigrated to Ḵūzestān even before Islam (*EI*² I, p. 528b), and to the several groups of Tamīm in present-day Iraq, is not clear. Some Banī Tamīm occupied Dawraq early in the 10th/16th century, but were ousted ca. 1000/1591-92 by Sayyed Mobārak, the Mošaʿšaʿī *wālī* of ʿArabestān (Ḵūzestān); in the 1760s they were identified as subjects to the Montafeq confederacy of southern Iraq (Niebuhr, p. 388; Oppenheim, IV, pp. 45-47).

There are also groups of Banī Tamīm along the Gulf littoral, in the *dehestān*s of Ḥayāt Dāwūd, Šabānkāra, Rūd Ḥella, and Angalī (Fasāʾī, II, pp. 81, 82).

Bibliography: (Great Britain) Admiralty, *Persia*, Geographical Handbook Series, Oxford, 1945. H. Field, *Contributions to the Anthropology of Iran*, Chicago, 1939. C. Niebuhr, *Beschreibung von Arabien*, Copenhagen, 1772. M. Freiherr von Oppenheim, *Die Beduinen*, ed. W. Caskel, 4 vols., Wiesbaden, 1967.

(J. PERRY)

BANĪ ṬOROF (Banu Turuf), a large Shiʿite Arab tribe of Howayza (Ḥawīza) district in Ḵūzestān, mostly sedentary, centered north of Howayza between Sūsangerd and Bostān (Besaytīn). In the early years of this century their population was put at 20,000 (Lorimer, *Gazetteer* II, p. 119), and in the 1930s at 8,000 families. They are organized in two sections, the slightly larger Bayt Saʿīd and the Bayt Ṣayyāḥ, a division which tradition attributes to a feud between brothers (Oppenheim, IV, pp. 24, 27-38; *Persia*, pp. 378-79; Field, p. 199). They trace their lineage to the Ṭayyeʾ tribe, and are related to the Banī Ṭorof of Hendīya (near Najaf) in Iraq.

Their history is obscure until the 1850s, when they are mentioned as a small group of *meʿdān* (marsh Arabs) under the patronage of the Banī Lām (q.v.). Later in the century they were flourishing northeast of the Hawr al-Ḥawīza, along the new course of the Karḵa as far as Sūsangerd, still living partly as *meʿdān*, raising buffalo, cows, and sheep, cultivating rice, barley, and wheat, and attracting clients. By the 1890s the Banī Ṭorof had grown strong enough to throw off the rule of the Shaikh of Howayza and deal directly with the government of Nāṣer-al-Dīn Shah. In 1906 it took an Iranian army to force them to pay taxes. During the Constitutional Revolution, Shaikh Ḵazʿal of the Banī Kaʿb acquired the right to their taxes and drew on their manpower to advance his own ambitions (Oppenheim, IV, pp. 39-40; Kasrawī, pp. 139, 233, 235; ʿAzzāwī, IV, pp. 190-91). During World War I they joined the Turks against the British forces occupying Ahvāz, and suffered when the Ottoman army withdrew and the British delivered them to Ḵazʿal. In 1924, when Ḵazʿal broke with Tehran, the Ṭorof rebelled against him and all other authority; in 1928 they stormed the tax office in Howayza, killed the director, and demanded the removal of Iranian officials. They were finally dispersed by government forces using aircraft.

Thereafter, some Banī Ṭorof emigrated to twelve new villages centered on Ḥamīdīya in the Nahr Hāšem district, where for some time they exercised a hegemony over the Banī Kaʿb and Banī Lām residents before being absorbed by them (Oppenheim, IV, pp. 40-41).

Bibliography: (Great Britain) Admiralty, *Persia*, Geographical Handbook Series, Oxford, 1945. ʿA. ʿAzzāwī, *ʿAšāʾer al-ʿErāq*, 4 vols., Baghdad, 1947. H. Field, *Contributions to the Anthropology of Iran*, Chicago, 1939. A. Kasrawī, *Tārīḵ-e pānṣad-sāla-ye Ḵūzestān*, Tehran, 1330 Š./1951. M. F. von Oppenheim, *Die Beduinen*, ed. W. Caskel, 4 vols., Wiesbaden, 1967.

(J. PERRY)

BĀNK-E MARKAZĪ-E ĪRĀN (Central Bank of Iran), a bank established under the Iranian Banking and Monetary Act of 7 Ḵordād 1339 Š./28 May 1960 to undertake the central banking activities in the country. Its functions and powers were expanded and consolidated by the Monetary and Banking Law of 18 Tīr 1351 Š./9 July 1972 and were further revised by the Usury-Free Banking Law of 8 Šahrīvar 1362 Š./30 August 1983. The latter law also modified its name to the Bānk-e Markazī-e Jomhūrī-e Eslāmī-e Īrān.

Central banking activities in Iran grew gradually in line with the development of modern financial institutions and practices. The first major step taken by the government in this area was the granting of exclusive right of issuing bank notes, for sixty years, to the Bānk-e Šāhanšāhī-e Īrān (Imperial Bank of Persia, later Iran)—a British company—founded in 1889 (Issawi, *The Economic History*, p. 346). In addition, the Bank was used as banker for the government and delivered silver bars to the mint for coinage.

The Iranian Constitution of 1906 had provided for the creation of a state-owned bank. Such a bank, called Bānk-e Mellī-e Īrān (National Bank of Iran), was established on 8 September 1928, with an initial capital of 20 million rials, under an act of Parliament (Majles), passed on 4 May 1927. Bānk-e Mellī was to assume the role of both a commercial and a central bank and, under an agreement signed on 30 May 1930, took over the central banking functions of the Imperial Bank, including the right of note issue, in return for payment of 200,000 British pounds. Twenty-five years later, a board was set up within Bānk-e Mellī, under the first comprehensive banking act of 1955, in order to supervise the activities of the growing banking system (Bānk-e Mellī-e Īrān, *Tārīḵča*).

The dual banking function of Bānk-e Mellī, however, brought about a conflict within the Iranian banking system, and this in turn led to the splitting up of Bānk-e Mellī and the creation of Bānk-e Markazī-e Īrān in 1339 Š./1960, as an autonomous body, with an initial capital of 3.6 billion *rīāl*s (Amuzegar, *Iran*, p. 131). Bānk-e

Markazī's main objectives, which have changed very little under the successive banking acts, consist of maintaining the value of the currency and equilibrium in the balance of payments, facilitating commercial transactions, and assisting the attainment of economic goals, policies and programs of the government.

For the purpose of achieving these objectives, Bānk-e Markazī was charged with formulation and implementation of monetary and credit policies within the framework of overall economic policies of the government. The Bank's other functions included the issuance of currency for circulation, supervision of banks and credit institutions, formulation and administration of foreign exchange policies and regulations, and control of gold and capital flows. In addition, as banker to the government, Bānk-e Markazī became responsible for keeping the accounts of the public sector, handling its banking transactions, acting as the government's agent for sale of government bonds and treasury bills and their redemption, maintaining the country's foreign exchange and gold reserves, acting as custodian of the crown jewels, representing the country in the International Monetary Fund, and concluding payments agreements in implementation of economic agreements reached between Iran and other countries (Bānk-e Mellī-e Īrān; *Qānūn-e bānkī*, articles 31-32, pp. 12-13).

The powers granted to Bānk-e Markazī at its creation were expanded substantially under the law of 1972 to include inter alia: conducting open market operations; establishing rediscount rates; fixing interest rates and other charges and commissions paid and received by banks; determining reserve requirements, liquidity ratios, minimum capital requirements, reserve-deposit ratios, and interest payment on banks' legal reserves; setting up credit ceilings and terms and conditions governing bank loans; limiting bank activities to specific areas or sectors; and licensing new banks and bank branches (Bānk-e Markazī-e Īrān, *The Monetary and Banking Law of Iran*, article 14, pp. 8-9).

The functions and powers of Bānk-e Markazī were revised following the Islamic Revolution of February, 1979, which led to the nationalization of private banking, consolidation of existing banks, and elimination of usury (interest) in the banking system. In early 1979, there were 36 banks (excluding Bānk-e Markazī) operating in the country, with 8,189 branches at home and 86 branches abroad. Twenty-eight of these banks, including thirteen joint ventures with foreign banks, were privately owned and accounted for nearly one half of banking operations in the country. These private banks were nationalized according to a decision taken by the Islamic Revolutionary Council on 17 Ḵordād 1358 Š./7 June 1980 and subsequently were consolidated, together with eleven government-owned banks, into ten banks, of which six engaged in commercial and four in specialized banking (Bānk-e Markazī-e Jomhūrī-e Eslāmī-e Īrān, *Bānkdārī*, pp. 57-58). These measures were followed by the adoption of the Law of Usury (Interest)-Free Banking in August, 1983, in order to bring Iranian banking practices into line with the requirements of Islamic principles.

While the Law prohibited payment and receipt of interest in banking operations, it provided for payment of non-fixed bonuses and distribution of profits, arising from banking operations, to depositors. Banks were allowed to use their funds, with a view to earn profits, through such arrangements with their customers as: *mošārakat* (equity-sharing), *możāraba* (capital-cum-labor contract), *ejāra be šarṭ-e tamlīk* (lease-purchase contract), *moʿāmalāt-e aqsāṭī* (installment contract), *mozāraʿa* and *mosāqāt* (agricultural contracts), direct investment, *salaf* (pre-purchase) dealings, and *joʿāla* (commission contracts). In addition, the banks were obliged to earmark a part of their resources for interest-free loans (*qarż al-ḥasana*) to their customers (Bānk-e Markazī-e Jomhūrī-e Eslāmī-e Īrān, *The Law for Usury-Free Banking*, articles 7-17, pp. 4-6).

Bānk-e Markazī's policy instruments were also changed. The short-term credit policies and facilities are now decided by the Council of Ministers upon the recommendations by the Bank's General Assembly, and long-term credit policies and facilities are decided by the Majles. In order to implement the monetary and banking policies of the country, Bānk-e Markazī is now empowered to fix the minimum and maximum rates of return and banks' fees and other charges for different types of transaction arrangements, to identify areas for direct investment and *mošārakat* by banks, to determine limits of banks' participation in various transactions as well as maximum facility to each customer, and to determine types, amounts, and minimum/maximum bonuses given to depositors (ibid., article 20, pp. 6-7; see also idem, *Āʾīn-nāmahā*).

Institutionally, Bānk-e Markazī is an autonomous agency of the government, managed by a governor who is appointed for five years by the Council of Ministers, upon the recommendation of the Minister of Economic Affairs and Finance. The report and accounts of the Bank's activities are submitted annually for approval to a general meeting of its shareholders, composed of three ministers representing the government as the sole shareholder, and chaired by the Minister of Economic Affairs and Finance. The general meeting also receives the report of an independent supervisory board which is charged with overseeing the accounts and the balance sheet of the Bank and with ensuring their conformity to the laws (Bānk-e Markazī-e Īrān, ibid., articles 16-23, pp. 9-16).

The Currency and Credit Council, which is composed of eleven members from various sectors and headed by the Bank's governor, provides advice to the Bank on general policy matters and decides on a number of issues pertaining to its supervisory role on monetary and banking regulations, under the banking laws. The governor is also assisted, in the day-to-day operational and administrative issues of the Bank, by an Executive Board comprising, in addition to himself as the chairman, the deputy governor, vice-governors, and the secretary-general of the Currency and Credit Council.

Furthermore, the Note Reserve Control Board has the task of controlling the issue of currency and its withdrawal from circulation (ibid.).

The assets and liabilities of Bānk-e Markazī amounted to 5,984 billion *rīāls* ($70.8 billion) on 20 March 1983, and it had earned a gross income of 144.2 billion *rīāls* ($1.7 billion) during the year ending on the foregoing date (Bānk-e Markazī-e Jomhūrī-e Eslāmī-e Īrān, *Economic Report*, pt. 2, the Balance-sheet).

Bibliography: Jahangir Amuzegar, *Iran: An Economic Profile*, Washington, D.C., 1977. Bānk-e Markazī-e Īrān, *Annual Report and Balance-Sheet*, Tehran, published annually 1962-78. Idem, *The Monetary and Banking Law of Iran*, approved on 18 Tīr 1351 Š./9 July 1972, Tehran, n.d. Bānk-e Markazī-e Jomhūrī-e Eslāmī-e Īrān, *Āʾīn-nāmahā wa dastūr al-ʿamalhā-ye ejrāʾī-e qānūn-e ʿamalīyāt-e bānkī-e bedūn-e rebā*, Tehran, 1984 (unpublished). Idem, *Bānkdārī wa sīāsathā-ye pūlī wa eʿtebārī*, Tehran, 1984 (unpublished). Idem, *Economic Report and Balance-Sheet*, Tehran, published annually 1959-84. Idem, *The Law for Usury-Free Banking*, approved on 30 August 1983, Tehran, 1983. Bānk-e Mellī-e Īrān, *Qānūn-e bānkī wa pūlī-e kešvar*, 7 Ḵordād 1339, Tehran, n.d. Idem, *Tārīḵča-ye sī-sāla-ye Bānk-e Mellī-e Īrān*, Tehran, n.d. Moṣṭafā Fāteḥ, *Pūl wa bānkdārī*, Tehran, 1309 Š./1930. L. E. Frechtling, "The Reuter Concession in Persia," *Asiatic Review*, London, 1938. Charles Issawi, *The Economic History of Iran, 1800-1914*, Chicago, 1971. Esfandiar Yaganegi, *Recent Financial and Monetary History of Persia*, New York, 1934.

(M. YEGANEH)

BANKING IN IRAN.

i. *History of banking in Iran.*
ii. *Banking in the Islamic Republic of Iran.*

i. HISTORY OF BANKING IN IRAN

Introduction. This article traces the historical development of banking in Iran, from the establishment of the first modern banks, by foreign concerns in the late 1880s, to the nationalization and consolidation of banks in 1979. It follows the growth of the banking system in the context of Iran's economic development in the same period and attempts to highlight the role of particular banks and the evolving banking system in Iran's economic development process, despite the theoretical debate as to the relationship of banking and economic development in general (see Basseer, 1981, pp. 1-80). (The names of Persian banks are given in their Persian form, the names of some of the major banks also in their English or anglicized form.)

Introduction of modern banking. The first modern bank to start operations in Iran was the British-owned New Oriental Bank which in 1888 opened branches and established agencies in Tehran, Mašhad, Tabrīz, Rašt, Isfahan, Shiraz, and Būšehr (Curzon, I, p. 474). The New Oriental Bank was shortly replaced by another British-owned bank, the Imperial Bank of Persia (1889), which was to remain as a major financial institution in the country for more than six decades.

Prior to the introduction of modern banks, such banking operations as extending loans, discounting and collecting bills of exchange (*bījak*), acceptance of deposits, and transfer of funds were carried out by reputable merchants. The major merchant-bankers of the late nineteenth century included Ḥājī Moḥammad-Ḥasan Amīn-al-Żarb (q.v.), Tūmānīān Brothers, and Jahānīān Brothers (Bank Melli Iran, 1958, pp. 40-44). In addition, a number of money dealers, or *ṣarrāf*, lent money, mostly at 24-36 percent per annum. Among the merchant-bankers of his time, Amīn-al-Żarb was a leading businessman who operated a trading company throughout the key cities in Iran and abroad. He attempted to establish a modern bank in Iran, but as in many other instances, this indigenous effort was frustrated by the ruling Qajar shahs (Abdullaev, cited in Issawi, pp. 42-48).

Other efforts to establish a bank in Iran, notably a joint venture among English, French, Turkish, and Persian interests, namely, "Banque de Perse et d'Afghanistan" was also aborted (ibid.). However, the first bank actually to open branches in Iran was the New Oriental Bank Corporation in 1888. It operated less than two years in Iran, but was relatively successful in its short life span. It paid annual interest of 2.5 percent on current accounts and 4 percent on accounts running for more than 6 months. Its lending rates centered around 12 percent, although it charged a lower 6-8 percent to the shah (Curzon, I, p. 474). Significantly, the bank introduced a form of paper money, in the shape of cashier orders, for sums from five krans (*qerān*) upward, payable to the bearer, which enjoyed relative acceptance in the capital (ibid.).

However, in 1889, as a result of the grant of an exclusive bank concession by Nāṣer-al-Dīn Shah to Julius de Reuter (q.v.), the New Oriental Bank closed its operations and sold its assets for £20,000 to the resulting Imperial Bank of Persia (Bank Melli Iran, 1958, p. 55).

Although all indications show that the New Oriental Bank was successful in Iran, that bank did not enjoy a favorable reputation in London. Despite the fact that in 1887 the bank's world-wide profits were £31,730 with equity capital of approximately £500,000 and paid 6 shillings dividends on £5.00 book value shares (*Times*, June 16, 1888, p. 8), it "suspended payment" in 1892 and was liquidated in 1893 (*Bankers Almanac*, 1974, p. 61131).

Bānk-e Šāhī (Imperial Bank of Persia). Article 1 of the all-embracing Reuter concession (see Kazemzadeh, pp. 100-47) called for the establishment of a state bank. The bank was given the exclusive right to issue bank notes (article 3) and it was exempted from any taxation (article 5). It was also to provide the Persian government with individually negotiated loans. In return, the Persian government was assigned 6 percent of the bank's net profits, or £4,000, whichever was larger.

Table 25

IMPERIAL BANK OF PERSIA TOTAL ASSETS AND NUMBER OF BRANCHES SELECTED YEARS, 1890-1951

Year	Assets (in million £)	Branches	
		Iran	Abroad
1890	1.8	8	2
1891	2.1	8	2
1895	1.4	8	1
1910	2.8	15	0
1920	8.3	17	3
1928	14.3	24	5
1929	13.1	25	4
1930	10.2	24	3
1935	7.4	18	2
1940	9.3	13	2
1945	29.7	14	4
1950	38.9	11	12
1951	51.5	9	13

Source: Imperial Bank of Persia, *Balance Sheet*, London, 1890-1951, after Bharier, 1971, pp. 238, 240.

Initially, the nominal equity capital of the bank was set at £4 million, with £1 million paid in at the outset. The bank was legally formed in London, under a British royal charter of incorporation. The shares were issued on a subscription basis and, as a result of the attractiveness of the concession, within a few hours it was "subscribed fifteen times over" (Curzon, I, p. 475).

In a very short time the Imperial Bank was operational and after purchasing the branches and the goodwill of the New Oriental Bank offered a wide range of banking services. Furthermore, in 1890 the Imperial Bank introduced the first bank notes in Persia. The notes ranged from 1 toman (*tūmān*) to 1,000 tomans. At the outset it circulated £28,000 worth of notes. Within six months of its existence, the bank was able to attract double the deposits previously made with the New Oriental Bank, and by the end of 1890 these deposits reached £113,000. Table 25 shows total assets and number of branches of the Imperial Bank for selected years up to 1951, the last full year of its operations in Iran.

The bank's activities were not always successful and recurrently met with commercial and public resistance. Although the merchants were previously familiar with *bījak*s and foreign bank notes they resisted the acceptance of the Imperial Bank notes. In Tabrīz for example, *bījak*s comprised 60 percent of the mode of transactions by 1919 (Bank Markazi, *Bulletin* 1/1, 1962, p. 1).

A major deterrent to the acceptability of the notes was the fact that they were only convertible to silver kran, in the city where they were issued. The bank, well aware of the public distrust of its notes, had adopted that policy to avoid runs in any one city. The other reason, of course, was that the bank earned substantial profits from transferring money from one city to another. In 1911 the bank charged a commission of as high as 8 percent for transferring funds from one city to another (Shuster, p. 270).

In 1899, the merchant-bankers of the time finally concerted their efforts and formed a joint company called 'Omūmī (public) to compete with the Imperial Bank. The company was formed by 17 of the most influential of the merchants, including Tūmānīān Brothers, Ḥājī Loṭf-'Alī Etteḥād, Ḥājī Bāqer and the famed Malek-al-Tojjār (Issawi, p. 45). Although the company was formed with 1 million tomans (£20,000) capital, and had the support of the public, it could not compete with the larger resources of the Imperial Bank. The latter not only drove 'Omūmī bankrupt, but proceeded to drive a number of the top merchant-bankers, notably the Tūmānīān Brothers, out of business (Bank Melli Iran, 1958, pp. 40-45).

In 1892, the Imperial Bank extended the first major foreign loan to the government of Iran, for £500,000 at 6 percent per annum (Browne, p. 31), which added to its leverage against the Persian government. The bank, although privately owned, continued to remain as a semi-political institution. Its shareholders' meetings were often a podium for declaring British foreign economic policy in Persia, and for interfering with internal Persian politics (see, e.g., *Times*, December 13, 1904, p. 15, and *Times*, December 14, 1905, p. 14).

The Imperial Bank tended to finance primarily business concerns linked with Britain, notably Sassoon and the Anglo-Iranian Oil Company. On the whole it adopted a policy of refraining from extending credit to Iranian nationals (Bharier, 1967, p. 297). As a state bank the Imperial Bank did very little to foster indigenous capital formation or support the Iranian currency. Between 1890 and 1904, for example, the kran devalued by more than 50 percent (Yaganegi, pp. 52-87).

With the establishment of indigenous banks starting in 1929, the Imperial Bank gradually lost two-thirds of its deposits to these banks and was replaced as the "state" bank by Bānk-e Mellī-e Īrān (see below). It remained as a profitable enterprise and paid an average dividend of 9 percent per annum of its paid-up capital. However, starting in 1948, as a result of stringent reserve and other requirements, its fortunes dwindled in Iran. In the following years it changed its name to the British Bank of Iran and the Middle East (Bānk-e Īrān o Ḵāvar-e Mīāna) and diversified its operations in the neighboring countries, while curtailing its operations in Iran.

By 1952, as a result of the Iranian strife with Britain, after having lost most of its deposits, the Imperial Bank closed its operations in Iran (*Times*, 1 August, 1952, p. 5). The ensuing British Bank of Iran and the Middle East resumed its activity as a joint-venture bank with majority Iranian ownership in 1959. It operated as a purely commercial bank until the revolution of 1979, when along with all other private banks it was nationalized.

Bānk-e Esteqrāżī-e Rūs (Russian loan bank) and other

foreign banks. Subsequent to the Reuter bank concession, the Russian government, spearheaded by Yakov Polyakov, an entrepreneur who had extensive commercial interests in Iran, demanded, among other concessions, establishment of a Russian bank in Iran. In 1890, Polyakov received a 75-year concession to establish a loan bank, which later became variously known as Russian Loan Bank, Iranian Loan Company, Banque des Prêts, and Banque d'Escompte de Perse. Formed as a private company, the bank was capitalized with 2 million French francs, half of which were spent "on the concession" (Kazemzadeh, pp. 272-73).

By 1898, partially due to an initial lack of success as a business enterprise, the shares of the bank were formally transferred to the Russian Ministry of Finance. The management of the bank fell under the jurisdiction of the Russian embassy in Iran; and in fact the Russian commercial attaché at times acted as the formal manager of the bank (Bank Melli Iran, 1958, p. 39). In practice it operated as a branch of the Russian State Bank until 1921, when it was finally turned over to Iran by the Soviet government.

The Loan Bank acted as a quasi-commercial bank, accepting deposits and lending to merchants, officials, and the Iranian government. In its commercial activities it naturally specialized in financing trade with Russia and other East European countries. As a lender to the Iranian government, it notably undertook the 1900 loan of Rbs 2.5 million (ca. £2.3 million). This loan, which was to replace an existing loan from the Imperial Bank of Persia, was aimed at reducing the power of the rival British banking institution (Yaganegi, p. 25).

There are few indications whether the Russian Loan Bank was ever profitable. Its mission, although commercial in appearance, was more of a political nature. For example, it subsidized the Cossack Brigade, a mercenary force in Iran (Shuster, *Persia*, p. 290). On the whole, like its British competitor, it did very little to finance indigenous economic activity in Iran.

Three years after the closing of the Loan Bank the Soviet Government established the Bānk-e Īrān o Rūs, which was to remain as a small wholly foreign-owned bank, serving Iran's bilateral trade with the Soviet Union.

The only other foreign-owned bank operating in Iran, prior to the late 1950s, was the Ottoman Bank. This British- (later French-) owned institution, which was already active in the Middle East, opened a branch in Iran in 1919 (Wilson, p. 269). Although by 1930 it had four branches in the country it remained a relatively small commercial enterprise until 1948, when it closed its Iranian branches. It returned to Iran in 1958, but only as a minority shareholder in a joint-venture bank (Bānk-e Eʿtebārāt).

The establishment of Iranian banks. One of the first items on the agenda of the first Iranian parliament (Majles) was the establishment of an indigenous national bank. The move was naturally aimed at reducing the foreign financial domination. In 1907, the Majles approved the establishment of a national bank and its charter was formally signed (*Times*, February 7, 1907, p. 3).

However, despite the public enthusiasm, due to the politico-economic conditions of the time, the move failed to materialize (Bank Melli Iran, 1958, p. 66). Iranian-owned banks were not formed until Reżā Shah's reign, almost two decades later.

The first Iranian-owned bank to operate in Iran was Bānk-e Sepah, which was establish in 1925. It was capitalized with the army pension fund and operated only as a semi-commercial bank. The first National Bank in Iran, Bānk-e Mellī-e Īrān, was formed on August 19, 1928, and was to become Iran's leading bank and later among the top fifty banks in the world. It started operations with the small paid-up capital of 8 million krans (£162,000), wholly owned by the government of Iran. Its charter was conceived by the Majles as a profit-making joint-stock company to "deal in all monetary transactions and endeavor to promote trade, industry and agriculture" (Ministry of Finance of Iran, *Announcement* no. 899, August 19, 1928).

Within three years Bānk-e Mellī attracted half of the deposits in the country and embarked upon the implementation of socially desirable government policies. It was instrumental in mobilizing the monetary resources of the country during Reżā Shah's reign. The following are some of the key financial innovations which this bank introduced in its early years of operations: (1) Branch banking. From its outset, Bānk-e Mellī adopted an expansionary policy in branch banking, opening fifteen branches in its first year of operation and reaching eighty-nine branches by 1940 (see Table 26). In contrast, the Imperial Bank never had more than twenty-five branches in Iran. Bānk-e Mellī's branch expansion policy helped to monetize the savings of the population in a large number of provincial cities and towns. (2) National bank notes. After purchasing the bank note issuing rights from the Imperial Bank, Bānk-e Mellī adopted a uniform national bank note policy, abolishing multiple regional ones. It also reduced fund transfer charges within the country. These measures were instrumental in easing interregional trade barriers

Table 26

BANK MELLI IRAN, SELECTED DATA*

	1928	1940
Authorized capital	20	300
Paid-up capital	8	235
Debtors	40	2,577
Savings and time deposits	55	795
Demand deposits	183	1,784
Notes in circulation	0	1,215
Net profits	0	134
Total assets	277	4,643
Number of branches	15	89

*Sums in million rials. Source: Bank Melli Iran, 1958, p. 185.

Table 27

FINANCIAL AGGREGATES AND COST OF LIVING INDEX
SELECTED YEARS, 1941-53

Year ending March 21	Currency in circulation	Sight deposits	Money supply	Savings and time deposits	Credits to public sector	Credits to private sector	Cost of living index (1935 = 100)
	(in billion rials)						
1941	1.2	3.4	4.5	0.6	3.0	1.5	251
1944	6.0	5.8	11.8	0.4	4.7	1.3	1,085
1946	6.9	6.8	13.7	0.8	5.8	2.3	877
1949	6.7	8.2	14.9	0.8	4.5	4.4	996
1951	7.3	9.1	16.4	1.1	7.7	5.3	893
1953	8.8	11.2	20.0	1.2	12.8	5.4	1,045

Sources: Bank Melli Iran, 1958, pp. 28, 187, 192, 193, 196, 217, 227. Bharier, 1971, pp. 43, 81, 243. Murray, 1950.

in the country. (3) Government lending. In the 1930s Bānk-e Mellī became the main source of borrowing for the public sector. It financed most of the short and medium term needs of the government for its vast developmental efforts. This policy put a limit on credits to the private sector. For example, by 1940 the total of loans to the public sector reached Rls 1,985 million, comprising more than two-thirds of the bank's credit allocation to the nonfinancial sector (Murray, p. 271). (4) Gold standard. Bānk-e Mellī was instrumental in placing Iran's currency on the gold standard by changing the official currency from the silver-based krans to the gold-based rials. The secular depreciation of silver prices in the world markets, plus a sharp decline following the Wall Street crash of 1929, had caused the kran to devalue along with silver, reducing Iran's foreign exchange reserves drastically. During the period of 1928-31, the world price of silver dropped by 33 percent, which, along with the deterioration of Iran's balance of trade, caused a 50 percent devaluation of the Iranian currency. However, the change to a dual, gold and silver, standard later contributed to maintaining Iran's currency parity vis-à-vis European ones in the late 1930s. (5) Development banks. Bānk-e Mellī was also instrumental in starting Iran's first two development banks in this period. Two departments of Bānk-e Mellī were expanded to become two autonomous development banks namely Bānk-e Rahnī-e Īrān (mortgage bank) and Bānk-e Kešāvarzī (agricultural bank). Although at their infancy these two special banks did not have a major impact on the agricultural sector or on the construction activity (Bharier, 1967, p. 297), a number of years later they became the leading special banks in servicing those sectors (see below).

In short, Bānk-e Mellī's policies in the 1930s laid the financial foundation for Reżā Shah's reforms and development efforts. However, most of those development efforts were halted with the advent of war and the occupation of Iran.

Banking conditions 1941-53. During the occupation years (1941-45), the huge Allied expenditures, the deterioration of the state's fiscal machinery, and the lack of public confidence in the banking sector pressed the government, through the Šūrā-ye Neẓārat-e Ḏaḵīra-ye Eskenās (note reserve control board), to rely inordinately on the expansion of money supply. It was the case of a desperate government merely printing money to finance not only its own deficits, but also to provide local currency for the Allied armies' extremely large expenditures. The public, on the other hand, tended to hoard money due to a lack of confidence in the banking sector.

In the three years 1941-44, the notes and coins in circulation increased fivefold (see Table 27). The huge infusion of currency in circulation into the money supply, however, resulted in only a 24 percent increase in sight deposits, and savings and time deposits in fact decreased by 50 percent (Table 27), reflecting substantial hoarding at that time and a lack of financial intermediation growth. The credits to the public sector, although increased, were not allocated for development purposes. The result was over 332 percent inflation in three years which, coupled with stagnant productivity, eroded much of the development achieved in the previous decades and almost destroyed the infant indigenous banks.

As a direct result the rial was devalued by 50 percent in 1941, and its convertibility to precious metals was repealed in 1942. The cover of bank notes (i.e., the precious-metals backing for the issuance of currency) was reduced to 60 percent in 1941 and was maintained in that fashion until 1944.

After the occupation years a degree of normalcy prevailed and monetary order was reinstated by increasingly nationalistic governments. In late 1944 the rial cover was increased to 100 percent. Symbolically the crown jewels, the state's collection of precious jewels, were revalued to Rls 1.7 billion and were placed with Bānk-e Mellī as a backing for the currency. The remaining cover was comprised of gold, silver, and foreign exchange (Bank Melli Iran, *Bulletin*, Spring, 1945, p. 10). These measures, as symbolically introduced as they were, were aimed at increasing the public confidence in the currency and at decreasing the practice of hoarding.

The first reserve requirement for banks was imposed in 1946, by which the banks were required to deposit 15 percent of their sight deposits and 6 percent of their fixed deposits with Bānk-e Mellī. This normal central banking requirement was regarded as a major sovereign move to control foreign banks. It paved the way for the 1948 decree by the council of ministers to levy stringent requirements on foreign banks in order to curtail and heavily regulate their activities. Significantly, the 1948 decree required the foreign banks to convert their subscribed capital into local currency, an action which they had evaded up to that time.

The above decrees, although probably aimed at foreign banks, had a stabilizing effect on the monetary sector as a whole. With other stabilizing developments, they caused a gradual fall in prices. The cost of living index had shown a steady decrease up to 1948, and relative stability in the succeeding years (see Table 27) despite adverse developments. The nonfinancial reasons for the deflation were the increased supply of goods after World War II and the large accumulated reserves of the government.

Nevertheless, a major disruption to the financial sector occurred subsequent to the actions of the Bank of England, which held most of Iran's foreign exchange reserves. As a result of the nationalization of the Anglo-Iranian Oil Company, the Bank of England in 1952 imposed severe restrictions on the conversion of Iran's sterling holdings and in essence froze the bulk of Iranian financial assets abroad (Mahdavi, pp. 441-42). This measure plus the drop in oil revenues led to an immediate devaluation of the rial.

Despite the major blow to Iran's economic activity resulting from the drop in oil exports, the banking sector on the whole maintained relative stability. Monetary authorities and Bānk-e Mellī's management during the Moṣaddeq period did not resort to inordinate expansion of money supply. The Banking Decree of 1948 also paved the way for the establishment of the first privately owned Iranian commercial banks.

As a result of Dr. Moṣaddeq's nationalistic measures, both as a Majles deputy and as the prime minister, the foreign banks truncated their operations and, as noted above, the two British banks finally closed offices. The only remaining foreign bank, Bānk-e Īrān o Rūs, adopted a low profile policy, which it retained during the following decades. The decline in foreign bank activity opened the market for indigenous private banks. In 1949 Bānk-e Bāzargānī, the first indigenous private bank, was established. In 1952 five private banks (Bānk-e Pārs, Ṣāderāt, Tehrān, Bīma-ye Bāzargānān, and Aṣnāf) and one associated with the Pahlavi Foundation (Bānk-e ʿOmrān) were established. In addition, Bānk-e Mellī's powers were expanded by the passage of Iran's first banking law (1952), formally granting it central banking powers.

The introduction of private banks was subsequently a major impetus to the extension of credits to the private sector, and to private capital formation in general. Dr. Moṣaddeq's nationalistic policies, although short-lived, paved the way for the later expansion of indigenous private sector economic activity in the decades to follow.

Banking conditions 1954-78. (a) The establishment of Bānk-e Markazī-e Īrān (Central Bank of Iran). With the formation of the indigenous commercial banks in the 1950s, the degree of government control and regulation of the banking structure increased gradually and substantially. The 1952 banking law was revised in 1955 and called for the establishment of the banks' supervisory board, associated with Bānk-e Mellī, to regulate the activities of all banks in Iran. The latter revision also paved the way for the formation of joint-venture banks with foreign participation. The 1955 banking act soon proved inadequate. It had bestowed upon Bānk-e Mellī supervisory functions which at times were contradictory with its position as the largest profit-making commercial bank in the country (Bank Markazi Iran, *Bulletin* 2/10, 1963, p. 489). This development plus the growth of banking activity as a whole warranted the establishment of a relatively independent central bank. As a result, with the passing of the 1960 monetary and banking law, Bānk-e Markazī-e Īrān (q.v.) was established. Following a number of revisions and refinements in the law, notably in 1972, the Bānk-e Markazī was empowered to set monetary policy and perform all central banking functions within the framework of Iran's overall economic policy. It was the first bank designated to compile and publish national accounting data on a systematic basis.

(b) Commercial banks. In this period commercial banks were formed mostly in two intervals, during the years 1958-59 and 1973-75. The first interval marks a period of relatively high economic growth, a surge in foreign trade and investments and a large increase (45 percent annual rate) in money supply. The years 1958-59 also mark a period of increasing westernization of the Iranian economy and the passing of the "law for the attraction and protection of foreign investments" (*qānūn-e jalb o ḥemāyat-e sarmāyagoḏārī-e ḵārejī*; 1959). Out of the twelve commercial banks formed in 1958-59, one was government-owned (Bānk-e Bīma-ye Īrān), and out of the remaining eleven private banks, eight were joint-venture banks with majority local and minority foreign ownership. Of the three purely private indigenous banks, Bānk-e Īrānīān later became a joint-venture bank between the American First National City Bank and local concerns (1968). In 1961, the government established Bānk-e Refāh-e Kārgarān (workers' welfare bank).

The first joint-venture bank established in Iran was Bānk-e Eʿtebārāt-e Īrān, which was formed with the equity participation of the French Crédit Lyonnais, Crédit Industriel et Commercial, and Ottoman Bank. Of the first eight joint-venture banks two had previously operated in Iran, one as a purely indigenous bank (Bank of Tehran) and the other as a purely foreign one (Bank

Table 28

COMMERCIAL BANKS IN IRAN, SELECTED DATA AS OF 20 MARCH 1976

	Year of establishment	Paid-in capital	Percent foreign share	Deposits non-bank	Total assets	Profit before taxes
		(in billion rials)				
Joint-venture and foreign banks:						
Dāryūš (Darioush)	1974	1.0	35	2.8	10.7	0.20
E'tebārāt	1958	1.5	35	17.6	63.1	0.46
Foreign Trade[1]	1958	1.0	40	10.3	37.9	0.70
International[1]	1975	1.0	35	3.4	13.3	0.04
Iran and Japan	1959	1.5	32	14.3	36.2	0.52
Iran and Middle East	1959	1.0	35	9.9	14.4	0.21
Iran and Holland	1959	1.5	35	11.2	47.8	0.46
Iran and Arab	1975	1.0	33	0.3	3.5	0.03
Iranians'	1975	1.0	35	6.9	25.5	0.37
Irano-British	1958	1.0	35	9.1	15.5	0.20
Īrān o Rūs	1924	1.3	100	1.0	15.8	0.10
Tehran	1952	3.0	30	66.3	119.5	0.61
		15.8		153.6	403.2	3.90
Private Iranian[2]:						
Bāzargānī-e Īrān	1949	2.1		48.6	69.8	0.55
Ta'āwonī wa Tawzī'	1959	1.0		14.0	19.3	0.06
Īrānšahr	1975	3.0		9.8	24.7	—
Kār	1958	3.1		12.3	55.2	0.64
Pārs	1952	1.0		18.9	34.6	0.23
Ṣāderāt	1952	8.0		238.9	348.1	4.03
Ṣanāye'	1973	5.0		11.8	79.8	2.14
Šahrīār[1]	1973	3.8		8.1	39.8	0.85
		27.0		362.4	671.1	8.50
Total private		42.8		516.0	1,074.3	12.40
Pahlavi Foundation:						
'Omrān:	1952	2.0		46.2	57.6	0.37
Government banks:						
Bīma-ye Īrān	1958	0.9		8.4	14.1	0.25
Mellī-e Īrān	1928	16.0		305.6	545.6	6.42
Refāh-e Kārgarān	1961	5.0		40.6	52.5	0.73
Sepah	1925	3.0		118.3	166.4	1.14
		24.9		472.9	776.6	8.54
Total commercial		69.7		1,035.1	1,908.5	21.31

Source: Iranian Bankers Association, 1977. Notes:

1. Majority private, minority government ownership.
2. Does not include Bānk-e Aṣnāf (established 1952) and Bīma-ye Bāzargānān (established 1953), which were dissolved by the Bānk-e Markazī-e Īrān.

of Iran and the Middle East, the former Imperial Bank of Persia; see above). The total capital formation in the joint-venture banks by the end of 1959 was approximately Rls 1.6 billion ($21 million), or 60 percent of all private-bank capital in that year (see Basseer, 1982, p. 261). Table 28 contains a list of all commercial banks, types of ownership, dates of establishment, and key operating data (in 1976).

The second interval of banking expansion was in 1973-75. With the dramatic increase in oil revenues, in this interval, the government intensified its Western-oriented economic strategy and once again launched liberalized financial and investment policies. Out of the five relatively large private banks formed in the 1973-75 interval, three were joint-venture banks. With the two exceptions cited above, all commercial banks established in the 1954-78 period were formed with majority private capital. Upon establishment the private banks, and especially the purely indigenous private banks, embarked upon a high degree of competition in opening branches and tapping the rising savings of the population. In the period 1954-78, the number of banking units (branches) in Iran grew from 285 or approximately 15 units per million of population to 7,919 or 226 per million (Bank Markazi Iran, *Annual Report*, 1978, p. 106). By 1978, almost all provinces in Iran were covered by the banking network. In Tehran alone there were approximately 500 banking units per million.

The largest number of banking units belonged to Bānk-e Ṣāderāt, a rapidly growing private bank, which was partially owned by its employees. By 1978, of all the banking units in existence, approximately half belonged to Bānk-e Ṣāderāt. The larger and older Bānk-e Mellī held roughly one-fifth of the banking units.

In addition to domestic branch expansion, by 1978 the larger Iranian banks had established a total of thirty-four branches and representative offices abroad (see Armfield, p. 1315). The foreign branches served to facilitate Iran's rapidly increasing foreign trade and disbursements abroad.

Expansion of the banking network helped to mobilize the country's growing financial resources. The attraction of deposits by the banking sector provided a valuable pool of loanable funds to be utilized by both the private and the public sectors. The availability of credits along with the rising national income helped the enormous expansion of private sector economic activity in the 1954-78 period. The government in this period greatly encouraged the expansion of private financial intermediation. Moreover, through the regulations of the banking sector the state kept the cost of finance relatively low. In the period of 1954-78 aggregate private deposits at constant prices rose twenty-sixfold and credits to the private sector at constant prices rose over fiftyfold, outpacing by far the nineteenfold estimated increase of the GNP in the 1954-78 period (see Basseer, 1982, p. 276). Table 29 shows aggregate financial data for selected years during this period.

By 1978, commercial banks provided 69.9 percent of the banking credits to the private sector, the rest emanating from special banks (Bank Markazi Iran, *Annual Report*, p. 279). As can be seen from Table 29 the interest rates charged by commercial banks on credits to the private sectors were in the 8 to 14 percent range. Considering the rate of inflation, especially in the 1970s, the high rates of return on investments and the 20 to 26 percent interest rates in the *bāzār*, or the "curb market" (see Basseer, 1982, pp. 194-98), the bank lending rates were relatively low.

By and large the commercial banks provided short-term working capital financing at relatively low cost for domestic firms. They also facilitated Iran's fast-growing domestic and foreign trade. The task of institutional financing of capital investments was largely left to the special banks.

Shortly after the fall of the shah private commercial banks along with special banks, insurance companies, and many other firms were nationalized by the revolutionary council (May 28, 1979). Only Bānk-e Īrān o Rūs was not nationalized in that year. By October, 1979, the plan for merging and consolidation of banks was approved. According to this plan, the banks with similar activities were merged. Thus five new consolidated banks were created. The new banks were Bānk-e Maʿdan wa Ṣanʿat (industrial and mining bank), Bānk-e Maskan (housing bank), Bānk-e Kešāvarzī (agricultural bank), Bānk-e Tejārat (mercantile bank), and Bānk-e Mellat (people's bank). Of the existing banks, Bānk-e Mellī, Bānk-e Sepah, Bānk-e Refāh-e Kārgarān, and Bānk-e Ṣaderāt continued their operations under government control (Bank Markazi Iran, *Annual Report*, 1980, published in 1982, pp. 81-82). Furthermore, in 1983 the law for Islamization of the banking sector and abolition of interest rates was passed (idem, 1983), setting the ground for launching of ensuing Islamic banking practices. (See also below, BANKING IN THE ISLAMIC REPUBLIC OF IRAN.)

(c) Special banks. Special banks, either by law or charter, were established to supply credits for the development of specific sectors of the Iranian economy. These special or development banks were intended to extend the types of credit which the commercial banks had traditionally refrained from supplying. The areas of specialization of the development banks were industry, agriculture, and housing, which all required medium and long term credits. Table 30 shows the list of special banks by areas of specialization and indicates the dates of establishment, types of ownership, and key operating data for those banks in 1976.

Of the ten special banks in existence two (industrial) banks were privately owned, four (industrial, construction) banks were mixed enterprises with majority private ownership, and the rest were government enterprises. The government special banks all originated before 1958, whereas special banks with private share capital were established after 1958, along with the aforementioned financial liberalization policy of the government. Nevertheless, by 1978 approximately 83 percent of the equity capital of special banks was owned by the government. Among the special banks only two

Table 29

SELECTED FINANCIAL INDICATORS, SELECTED YEARS, 1954-78

Year ending March 21	Money supply	Savings and time deposits	Total credits to private sector	Total credits to public sector	Average lending rate at Bank Melli (percent)	Cost of living index (1970 = 100)	Inflation rate (percent)
	(in billion rials)						
1954	24	1	8	10	8.0	52.3	10.0
1958	43	3	15	21	10.0	70.1	4.5
1960	40	11	31	26	13.0	80.0	13.0
1962	40	16	51	29	9.4	87.7	1.6
1966	60	45	102	46	8.6	93.5	0.2
1970	90	115	199	155	9.7	100.0	3.5
1972	117	179	278	176	11.0	107.1	5.5
1974	203	313	489	298	12.2	126.5	11.1
1976	446	699	1,068	625	13.0	160.5	10.0
1978	790	1,306	1,862	1,039	14.0	234.0	25.1

Sources: For 1954, 1958 data: Bank Melli Iran, *Annual Report*, 1954, 1958. For all other years: Bank Markazi Iran, *Annual Report*, 1960-78.

Table 30

SPECIAL BANKS IN IRAN, SELECTED DATA AS OF 20 MARCH 1976

	Paid-in capital	Percent foreign share	Type of ownership	Total assets	Private savings and time deposits	Profit before taxes
	(in billions rials)					
Industrial:						
Industrial and Mining Development Bank of Iran	7.0	13.48	Private	106.5	—	1.04
Industrial Credit Bank	7.1	—	Government	79.5	—	1.04
Development and Investment Bank of Iran	2.0	20.62	Private	13.4	—	0.35
Azarbaijan Development Bank	0.5	—	Mixed	0.6	—	0.02
Ḵazar Development Bank	0.5	—	Mixed	0.5	—	0.02
Ḵūzestān Development Bank	0.5	—	Mixed	0.5	—	0.02
	17.6			201.0	—	2.49
Agricultural:						
Agricultural Development Bank of Iran	8.1	—	Government	35.2	—	0.21
Agricultural Cooperative Bank of Iran	36.8	—	Government	72.4	2.8	1.13
	44.9			107.6	2.8	1.34
Housing and Construction:						
Bānk-e Rahnī-e Īrān	7.2	—	Government	57.4	34.3	0.85
Bānk-e Sāḵtemān	3.0	—	Mixed	13.8	0.3	0.49
	10.2			71.2	34.6	1.34
Total Special	72.7			379.8	37.4	5.17

Source: Iranian Bankers Association, *Iran Banking Almanac*, 1977.

(industrial) banks had (minority) foreign share ownership. Foreign equity investment contributed only 2 percent of the total equity capital of special banks (Table 30).

Among the special banks, as seen from Table 30, industrial development banks had the largest assets. In the latter group, the government-owned Bānk-e Eʿtebārāt-e Ṣanʿatī (industrial credit bank) and the privately owned Bānk-e Tawseʿa-ye Ṣanʿatī wa Maʿdanī (industrial and mining development bank) were instrumental in starting and/or expanding hundreds of the leading private industrial concerns. The government's Bānk-e Eʿtebārāt operated under Iran's Plan Organization and in late 1978 started to go public. However, it was nationalized in 1979 along with all other banks. Bānk-e Tawseʿa, on the other hand, began as a private joint-venture bank. It was established with the assistance of the International Bank for Reconstruction and Development (IBRD) and was formed with 60 percent publicly owned Iranian capital, and 40 percent foreign subscribed by a syndicate of international financial institutions, led by Lazard Frères and Chase Manhattan Trust Corporation. The initial paid-in-equity capital of this bank was Rls 400 million. However, the government of Iran along with the IBRD and the USAID all committed long-term loans, totaling another Rls 1,100 million, to the bank at the time of its establishment (Benedick, p. 120). Subsequently, Bānk-e Tawseʿa was highly successful not only in financing a number of major industrial and mining firms but also in helping to start the Tehran stock exchange (1967), the specialized Bānk-e Sāḵtemān, and the regional development banks.

The industrial banks supplied approximately half of the institutional credits to the non-oil industrial sector; the rest were provided by commercial banks. The supply of credits by the banking system as a whole to the private industrial sector had a major impact in that sector's remarkable growth rate (estimated 11 percent per annum on average) in the 1954-78 period.

The second group of special banks in terms of size of assets were the two government-owned agricultural banks. The older Bānk-e Taʿāwon-e Kešāvarzī-e Īrān (agricultural cooperative bank of Iran, previously Bānk-e Kešāvarzī) extended mostly small-scale loans to a large number of farmers and farming cooperatives. However, Bānk-e Tawseʿa-ye Kešāvarzī (agricultural development bank of Iran, previously Ṣandūq-e Tawseʿa-ye Kešāvarzī-e Īrān [agricultural development fund]) specialized in making larger loans to a small number of agro-business concerns. Together the two agricultural banks supplied approximately 80 percent of the country's institutional credits to the agricultural sector (Aresvik, pp. 169-74). Nevertheless, despite the activities of the above banks, the agricultural sector, which employed approximately half of the work force by 1977, obtained only 9 percent of the total credits in that year (Basseer, 1982, pp. 301-02). By and large the Iranian farmers had to rely on self-financing and trade credit to finance a great portion of their needs. It is not surprising that the agricultural sector in the 1954-78 period had a slow, albeit steady, growth rate of 2-3 percent per annum.

The third group of special banks were the construction and mortgage banks. Of these the leading Bānk-e Rahnī-e Īrān specialized in extending housing mortgage and construction loans. Owned jointly by the Ministry of Housing and City Planning and Bānk-e Mellī, Bānk-e Rahnī also acted as a state regulatory agency for housing credits and savings and loan associations. It helped establish a number of privately owned savings and loan associations in the major cities of Iran, beginning in 1972. Both it and the savings and loan associations offered contractual savings-loan schemes, which required potential homeowners to make fixed deposits for periods of six to 36 months, in exchange for the ability to borrow one to six times the amount of the deposits (see Basseer, 1974). Despite the activities of the special as well as the commercial banks, by and large, the supply of residential and construction credits was relatively small in Iran, at least up to the early 1970s.

On the whole, the special banks served to allocate government-sanctioned credits to designated sectors. The government not only allocated a part of its annual budget to special banks—particularly industrial and agricultural banks—but also increasingly channeled Bānk-e Markazī's funds to special banks. The government provided approximately one-third of the non-capital source of funds of special banks, the rest emanating from domestic and foreign sources. The government also set relatively low rates of interest on special banks' lending rates, especially to industry and agriculture. These rates were generally two to six percent lower than the commercial bank rates. In real terms (adjusted for inflation), these rates were almost consistently negative throughout the 1970s.

In short, the special banks partially fulfilled the allocative function of providing long-term finance to the key sectors of Iran's economy, a function which the commercial banks did not deem profitable to perform. The non-housing special banks generally favored financing capital intensive projects, which met the licensing and indicative guidelines of the government.

Summary and conclusion. Modern banking in Iran was introduced and dominated by foreign banks up to the late 1920s. The foreign banks, despite their early contribution in introducing many financial innovations, did little to foster indigenous economic development. They replaced Iran's traditional banker-merchants and their restrictive policies tended to limit the growth of the nascent urban private sector. With the establishment of state-owned banks in the late 1920s, the banking system provided a growing source of funds for the public sector's rapidly increasing development expenditures. The availability of internal credits helped reduce the country's reliance on foreign borrowings. However, the predominant absorption of credits by the public sector up to the early 1950s was made at the expense of the private sector. The result was relatively slow expansion of private investments and a slow rate of capitalistic transformation.

However, with the establishment of private indigenous and joint-venture banks in the 1950s, the banking sector increasingly helped to monetize Iran's growing private savings and provided a larger supply of finance capital for the private sector as well as for the public sector. Furthermore, the rental price of capital and the interest rates charged to the private entrepreneurs were kept low in real terms. The availability and the low cost of borrowing on the one hand and the rising national income on the other tended to encourage private sector economic activity.

The state, especially in the 1960s and 1970s, as a part of its Western-oriented and indicative economic planning, increasingly utilized the banking system to expand private capital formation in general and in designated enterprises in particular. The guided expansion of private enterprise resulted in the rapid growth of the urban-based mercantile and industrial sectors. The latter sectors also enjoyed the largest share of the supply of credits from the banking system. The state, along with a number of other measures, notably the land reform, used the banking system in order to break away from Iran's precapitalistic economic conditions. Nourished by the vital flow of oil revenues the overall result was a rapid rate of Western-oriented economic growth and capitalistic transformation.

The rate of transformation of the Iranian economy and accompanying financial expansion was especially accelerated after 1973, when the oil revenues increased dramatically. However, when the rate of economic and financial expansion proved unsustainable, particularly in the light of stagnating oil revenues in 1978, various economic brakes were applied. In 1978, for the first time, the gross national product in real terms dropped by 8.7 percent (Bank Markazi Iran, *Annual Report*, 1978). Nevertheless, interestingly, the banking system during the 1978-79 revolution kept its resilience and despite many institutional disruptions for the most part operated normally. Aggregate demand and savings deposits increased dramatically. Bānk-e Markazī, by and large, bailed out the banking system in the face of huge capital flight and imminent bankruptcies (see its *Annual Report*, 1980, pp. 73-83).

Thus, the revolution put an end to nine decades of Western-oriented banking expansion. In 1979, immediately after the establishment of the provisional government, all banks along with a number of other financial and industrial establishments were nationalized, and the governor of the Bānk-e Markazī was executed. The nationalization and the subsequent consolidation of the banks paved the way for the launching of Islamic banking.

Bibliography: Sharif Adib-Soltani, "Private Investments in Iran, 1937-1959," Tehran, Plan Organization, 1962. Oddvar Aresvik, *The Agricultural Development in Iran*, New York, 1976. J. W. Armfield, "Iranian Banks Knock on London's Door," *Banker*, November, 1975. Ahmad Ashraf, "Historical Obstacles to the Development of a Bourgeoisie in Iran," in *Studies in the Economic History of the Middle East*, ed. M. A. Cook, London, 1970, p. 327. George B. Baldwin, *Planning and Development in Iran*, Baltimore, 1967. Shaul Bakhash, "Rapid Branch Expansion Continues in Iran," World Banking XXV, *The Financial Times*, 19 May 1969, p. 21, col. 5. Amin Banani, *The Modernization of Iran, 1921-1941*, Stanford, 1961. Bank Markazi Iran, *Annual Report and Balance Sheet*, Tehran, 1960-80. Idem, *Bulletin*, Tehran, 1962-78 (includes the following unsigned articles: "Banking In Iran," 1/1, 1962; "Experience in Estimating National Income and Product of Iran," 1/4, 1962; "Some Observations on Problems of Banking in Iran," 2/10, 1963. Idem, *Circular*, Tehran, from 1961. Idem, *Investors Guide to Iran*, Tehran, 1966. Idem, *Monetary and Banking Act, July 1972*, Tehran, 1972. Idem, *National Income of Iran, 1338-50 (1959-72)*, Tehran, 1975. Idem, *The Law of Usury Free Banking*, Tehran, August, 1983. Bank Melli Iran, *Balance Sheet*, Tehran, 1948-78. Idem, *Thirty Years History of Bank Melli Iran, 1928-1958* (Tārīḵ-e sī-sāla-ye Bānk-e Mellī-e Īrān, 1307-1337), Tehran, 1958. *Bankers Almanac and Yearbook, 1973-1974*, London, 1974, p. G1131. Potkin Basseer, *The Case of Bank Rahni Iran*, Tehran, 1974. Idem, *A Note on the Tehran Stock Exchange*, Tehran, 1973. Idem, *The Role of Financial Intermediaries in Economic Development: The Case of Iran, 1888-1978*, Doctoral dissertation, the George Washington University, 1982. Richard E. Benedick, *Industrial Finance in Iran*, Boston, 1964. Julian Bharier, "Banking and Economic Development in Iran," *Bankers Magazine*, 1967. Idem, *Economic Development in Iran 1900-1970*, London, 1971. Edward G. Browne, *The Persian Revolution of 1905-1909*, Cambridge, 1910. The Chase Manhattan Bank, *A Capital Market Study of Iran*, New York, 1975. George N. Curzon, *Persia and the Persian Question*, 2 vols., London, 1892. M. Ḥejāzī, *Mīhan-e mā*, Tehran, 1328 Š./1949, pp. 753-57. Industrial and Mining Development Bank of Iran, *Annual Report and Balance Sheet*, Tehran, 1960-77. Idem, "Articles of Association," Tehran, 1959. Iranian Bankers Association, *Iran Banking Almanac*, Tehran, 1973-78. "Iran: Nationalization Trend Continues," *Business Week* 25, June, 1979, p. 28. "Iran's Miracle That Was," *Economist*, 20 December 1975, pp. 68, 28-32. Iran-U.S. Business Council, *Iran-U.S. Finance Conference: A Report*, Washington, D.C., 1976, pp. 119-21. Charles Issawi, *The Economic History of Iran: 1800-1914*, New York, 1973. Firuz Kazemzadeh, *Russia and Britain in Persia, 1864-1914: A Study in Imperialism*, New Haven, 1968. Ḥ. Maḥbūbī Ardakānī, *Tārīḵ-e mo'assasāt-e tamaddonī-e jadīd dar Īrān*, 2 vols., Tehran, 2537 = 1357 Š./1978, II, index pp. 432-33. H. Mahdavi, "The Patterns and Problems of Economic Development in Rentier States: The Case of Iran," in H. A. Cook, ed., *Studies in the Economic Development of the Middle East*, London,

1970. J. Murray, *Iran Today, An Economic and Descriptive Survey*, Tehran, 1950. "Persia To Have a Bank," *New York Times*, 13 October 1889, p. 11. W. M. Shuster, *The Strangling of Persia*, New York, 1912. The Statistical Center of Iran, *Bayān-e āmārī*, Tehran, 1977. *Times* (London), 16 June 1888, p. 8; 2 December 1890, p. 5; 11 December 1890, p. 11; 19 December 1906, p. 14; 7 February 1907, p. 3; 12 February 1907, p. 10; 1 January 1952, p. 3; 17 July 1952, p. 10. A. T. Wilson, *Persia*, London, 1932. Esfandiar B. Yaganegi, *Recent Financial and Monetary History of Persia*, New York, 1934.

(P. Basseer)

ii. Banking in the Islamic Republic of Iran

Islamic banking is based on the principle of profit-earning on equity participation, the earning of interest (*bahra*, q.v.) being forbidden. The merits of such a system compared to the system more common in the West (fixed interest rates and guaranteed value of deposits) is a matter of debate among economists. On the one hand, the Islamic system has certain disadvantages compared to the Western system: The equity investment principle makes Islamic banks less liquid and therefore perhaps not as flexible; the profit-sharing concept requires businessmen to share more information with banks than they may be prepared to do; banks must devote much effort to analyzing businesses because their capital is at risk; and Islamic banking is not well suited for financing consumer purchases or government deficits. For these reasons among others, pre-twentieth-century efforts to implement Islamic banking were not particularly successful.

On the other hand, some economists have argued that an equity-based system is better suited to adjust to shocks and to avoid banking crises precisely because it excludes predetermined interest rates and does not guarantee the value of deposits. Indeed, the Islamic banking system bears a striking resemblance to proposals made in the 1930s and 1940s by eminent economists for reform of the U.S. banking system (Fisher, Simons, Friedman). Furthermore, it may be suggested that Islamic banking permits the payment of a high return on capital which is economically justified in less developed countries but which would be unacceptable to regulators who set interest rates under a Western-style banking system.

On the deposit side, banks accept two basic sorts of deposits: *qarż al-ḥasana* and term investment deposits. In theory, the principal in *qarż al-ḥasana* deposits is guaranteed but the account earns no profit, while the term deposits do not have a guaranteed principal but earn profit. In practice, however, banks offer bonuses and prizes for *qarż al-ḥasana* savings deposits (but not for *qarż al-ḥasana* current deposits), and banks insure at their own expense the principal in term investment deposits (Bānk-e Markazī-e Jomhūrī-e Eslāmī-e Īrān, 1986a). Furthermore, the Bānk-e Markazī (Central Bank) sets one uniform rate which all banks pay on term investment deposits. As practiced in Iran, therefore, Islamic banking involves a guaranteed rate of return, without funds being at risk—which makes the system rather similar to Western banking.

On the lending side, the Law on Interest-Free Banking authorizes a variety of transactions, and the Central Bank closely regulates distribution of credit among the categories and by borrower type (e.g., various industries and types of agriculture). On 20 March 1986 Islamic transactions accounted for 1,833,038 million rials outstanding from the commercial banks to the private sector, while 3,005,792 million rials were outstanding to the private sector on facilities under the previous system (Bānk-e Markazī-e Jomhūrī-e Eslāmī-e Īrān, "The Practical Aspects of Islamic Commercial Banking," paper presented at the International Islamic Banking Seminar, Tehran, 1986). On the Islamic side, the facilities and their share in the total were: 1. *qarż al-ḥasana* (10.9%): provision of a sum to a borrower who is to pay back the same sum at a later date; 2. civil partnership or *mošāraka* (13.3%): contribution of capital by several persons to a common pool on a joint-ownership basis; 3. legal partnership and direct investment (11.0%): ownership of stock in joint-stock companies or direct ownership by banks; 4. *możāreba* (16.0%): the bank provides the funds utilized by the borrower in trading, with profits split between the two; 5. forward delivery transactions (3.1%): advance cash purchase of products at a fixed price; 6. installment sales (of equipment or materials for production or of housing) (32.1%): the borrower makes payments over time sufficient to allow the bank to recover the cost and to make a profit; 7. hire purchase (0.9%): the borrower leases a good owned by the bank with the stipulation that the leaseholder will ultimately receive title; 8. *jeʿāla*, either as *ʿāmel* or as *jāʿel* (1.3%): one party (*jāʿel*) pays another party (*ʿāmel*) to perform a service; 10. *możāraʿa* (not available): the bank turns land over to the borrower for a fixed period for farming in return for a specified share of the harvest; 11. *mosāqā* (not available): the banks turns over trees to the borrower for a specified share of the produce; 12. purchase of debt (10.2%): banks may discount debt documents and commercial papers.

In practice, the profit rate to be earned from each activity is tightly regulated by the Bānk-e Markazī, which sets minimum and maximum profit rates by industry. Furthermore, failure to repay a loan on time results in a penalty which is calculated in the same manner as interest. The Bānk-e Markazī also closely regulates the distribution of credit; for instance, the *qarż al-ḥasana* transactions (on which the banks make no profit) are essentially all at its direction. In sum, Islamic banking in Iran involves lending at rates that are largely set in advance, with additional payment required if funds are kept longer—which makes the system rather similar to Western banking.

To some extent, the similarities between Islamic banking in Iran and Western banking reflect the problems in the transition to the new system; e.g., personnel had to be trained in new skills and techniques, and the confidence of the public in the new system had to be ensured. Furthermore, the Islamic banking system was introduced at a difficult moment, when the banking system was suffering from bad debts extended just before the 1979 revolution and when Iran was in the midst of a deep recession.

More important, however, the characteristics of Iran's Islamic banking system have been shaped by the need to finance a large government deficit. Islamic banking theory provides little guidance on how a government can finance its deficit. The technique used in Iran has been to require banks to lend large sums to the government, both by buying government bonds and by depositing reserves in the central bank for on-lending to the government. In the first eleven months of 1364 Š.(1985-86), these two forms of lending to the government absorbed 58% of the increase in private sector deposits (478.2 billion rials out of 827.6 billion rials; Bānk-e Markazī-e Jomhūrī-e Eslāmī-ē Īrān, 1986b). In order that banks could continue to pay rates of profit sufficient to attract deposits when so much of their funds was tied up in loans to the government, the government has paid interest on its borrowing. This has been justified on the basis of a religious ruling (*fatwā*, q.v.) that it is permissible to pay interest to oneself and that the government and the nationalized banks are all one corporate person.

Bibliography: Bānk-e Markazī-e Jomhūrī-e Eslāmī-e Īrān, "Mobilization of Resources and Granting of Facilities," paper presented at the International Islamic Banking Seminar, Tehran, 1986a. Idem, "Report on the Banking System During 1363-1364," paper presented at the International Islamic Banking Seminar, Tehran, 1986b. R. Cooper, "A Calculator in One Hand and the Koran in the Other," *Euromoney*, November, 1981. I. Fisher, *100% Money*, New Haven, 1945. M. Friedman, "The Monetary Theory and Policy of Henry Simons," in his *The Optimum Quantity of Money and Other Essays*, Chicago, 1969. Mohsin Khan, "Islamic Interest-Free Banking," *International Monetary Fund Staff Papers* 33/1, March, 1986 (this publication has an extensive bibliography on Islamic banking theory). H. Simons, *Economic Policy for a Free Society*, Chicago, 1948.

(P. CLAWSON AND W. FLOOR)

BANNĀʾĪ (construction). Though the subject of monumental architecture in Iran has been the focus of a number of studies and analyses (see, for example, ARCHITECTURE), popular building crafts have received considerably less scholarly attention. The treatment of "domestic architecture," which is accorded a mere ten pages in *A Survey of Persian Art* (III, pp. 900-12), is indicative of the indifference endemic among orientalists and art historians to anonymous buildings. On the subject there are but a few monographs and studies on regional building crafts and even fewer works on construction in the area as a whole (see Wulff, *Crafts*, pp. 102-35). While the term *bannāʾī* covers the entire construction field, in this brief study domestic building techniques, in particular, which are more or less part of the traditional crafts, and the recent evolution of popular housing will be emphasized. Monumental architecture, the organization of interior spaces, and portable housing such as tents, huts, etc., which form the subjects of separate entries, will not be discussed.

The word *bannāʾī*, used to refer to the construction of buildings, is derived from *bannāʾ* "mason"; however, because of the rarity of wood on the Persian plateau, construction materials are almost exclusively of mineral origin (stone, gypsum, and especially mud), and the master builder (*meʿmārbāšī, ostād*) is the mason. Only in the Caspian provinces, which enjoy abundant supplies of wood, does the carpenter (*najjār*) play a predominant role in construction (Bromberger, 1986, p. 79). As for the rest of the country, it is in the use of inorganic materials (like bricks) that traditional Iranian architecture has made its most important contributions to the arts of building: construction of barrel vaults (*ṭāq-e żarbī*) without centering and of corbeled brick domes (*gonbad*; Creswell, pp. 245, 321; Beazley and Harverson, pp. 23-26; Wulff, pp. 102-05).

Principal traditional construction methods. Though in the country as a whole and especially between the Caspian sea and the Iranian plateau, these are quite varied, it is possible to extrapolate several predominant architectural formulas, ranging from foundations to roofing systems.

The first operation consists of marking out the future building by tracing the lines of the walls with powdered lime (*āhak*) or gypsum (*gač*); for an ordinary structure the form and area are agreed upon between the mason and the client, without the need for plans. The foundations (*pey*) are laid in trenches (*šālūda*) measuring 20 to 100 cm deep and consist of layers of stone rubble alternating with layers of a mixture of mud, water, and burnt lime (*šefta*). The only exceptions to this formula are types of underground dwellings called *lu* in the Kavīr or caves (see, e.g., Gabriel, p. 175; Wulff, pp. 102-03)—or houses in specific regions, like the elevated structures of the Caspian provinces, which are raised on stilts to protect them from the damp soil (see Bromberger, 1986, pp. 60-64; Bazin and Bromberger, p. 42 and map 21).

For the construction of walls (*dīvār*, in dialects also *tīfāl*) different materials are used, depending upon the region and the purpose of the building.

1. *Kāh-gel* is a mixture of levigated earth, water, and chopped straw, which is vigorously kneaded with the bare feet, then formed into chunks, which are arranged in courses (*mohra*) about 50 cm high. When one course is finished, the builder levels it with a trowel (*māla*), then allows it to dry for two or three days before resuming work: "Otherwise the wall will collapse under its own weight" (Beazley and Harverson, p. 17). These mud walls generally have a slight batter and, for protection from the rain, are capped with baked bricks

or thorny brushwood "weighed down with a course of a mixture of loam and lime that sets and becomes water resistant" (Wulff, p. 109). Chunks of *kāh-gel* are used especially in the construction of walls surrounding orchards, courtyards, and even icehouses.

2. Unbaked bricks (*k̲ešt*) shaped in wooden molds (*qāleb*) are the most common material used in the construction of the walls of traditional peasant houses. These bricks generally measure 20-25 cm square by 4-8 cm thick and are laid with mud mortar (*melāṭ*). The surface of the wall is usually coated with a fine mixture of clay and wheat chaff (*gel-e pīl*), applied with a trowel, which gives it a smooth and regular appearance. Exterior walls, which support the roof and also serve an insulating function, are very thick (60-90 cm), whereas interior walls are often built of only single thicknesses of brick.

3. Baked brick (*ājor*) is a material traditionally reserved for important buildings (notables' houses, caravansaries, mosques, and so on) but the use of which has become considerably more popular in the last three decades. The mortar used with these bricks is a mixture of slaked lime and sand (*šen-āhak*), to which in modern construction procedures cement is added. For structures that will be in contact with water, like reservoirs (*āb-anbār*) or the central basins in domestic courtyards, a particularly resistant mortar (*sārūj*) composed of sand, lime, ashes, husks and straw, or goat hair (Wulff, p. 113) is necessary.

4. Stone (*sang*) is used for footings and foundations, rarely for construction of walls except in certain provinces like Fārs or in well-defined types of buildings (e.g. mountain caravansaries, q.v.; see Siroux, pp. 35-43). This material, which was more commonly used for construction in ancient Iran, was progressively displaced by baked brick, particularly after the 7th/13th century (*Survey of Persian Art* III, p. 899).

5. Wood (*čūb*) forms the skeletons of walls only in the Caspian provinces. A *dīvār-e čūbī* consists either of stacked logs (*verjīn*) or of timber frames constructed from poles (*zigəl*). The interstices are filled with mud tempered with rice straw (*kuləš-ə-gəl*); the structure of the wall, whether of logs or poles, is then coated with plaster. Only in the mountain chalets of Alburz herdsmen are the logs or poles of the skeletons allowed to show (Bromberger, 1986, pp. 66-67; Bromberger, 1974, 41-45; Bazin, I, 165).

The other essential phase of the construction process is completion of the roof, of which four principal types can be enumerated.

1. The flat roof (*bām, pošt-e bām, rūbūn*) is the most common type, particularly in the piedmont areas (the dry slopes of the Alburz and the Zagros). It is constructed of large joists (*tīr*), which rest on the main walls; boards (*pardū, dastak*) are laid on (and sometimes nailed to) these joists and are then covered with cane matting (*ḥaṣīr*), reeds, or even a thick layer of brush. Next several thin layers of mud (*kāh-gel*) are applied and compacted by means of a stone roller (*ḡaltabān*). This type of roof, which provides the inhabitants with excellent insulation, requires periodic maintenance and repairs. Each year a 2-3 centimeter layer of *kāh-gel* must be added, and after each rainfall the stone roller must be used or the main fissures and cracks repaired.

2. The barrel vault (*ṭāq-e żarbī*) is used to roof rectangular buildings in areas where wood is rare, notably in central Iran. A remarkable feature is that these vaults are constructed without the aid of centering. Most often the unbaked bricks are laid up obliquely in successive laminae through the length of the building and leaning against a vertical wall at the back (Christensen, pp. 100-101; Desmet and Fontaine). The vault may also include a semidome at one end or may be built from each end and finished in the middle with courses of bricks laid perpendicular to the preceding ones. These bricks are very carefully mortared with a mixture of mud and lime.

3. The dome (*gonbad*), either spherical or conical, is used in the same regions for roofing buildings on a square plan. Squinches, i.e., vertical arches constructed at the upper corners of the building, ensure the transition between the square plan of the base and the circular plan of the dome (see photographs and drawing in Beazley and Harverson, p. 25; Wulff, p. 105; for the origin of this technique in the Iranian world, see Godard, pp. 209-10). The bricks are most often laid and mortared in corbeled courses, that is, each course projecting beyond the preceding one, from the bottom to the apex of the dome.

The barrel vault and dome are plastered with mud on the interior as well as on the exterior, so that their structures are rarely visible; such a roof is sometimes even completely hidden from view on the exterior by a second, flat roof constructed above it as protection against deterioration caused by rain and snow and as a useful space for sleeping during the summer.

4. The sloping roof constructed on a wood frame is characteristic of the architecture of the Caspian provinces (Bromberger, pp. 68-79) but is also known sporadically in other regions of the country, especially mountainous ones: for example, Kurdistan (Christensen, pp. 126-27). The simplest form is the gabled roof with two symmetrical inclines. The hipped roof is the most common type in the Caspian region, corresponding to a rectangular building plan, the characteristic module of vernacular architecture. The roof with four equal sides covers buildings on a square plan. Roofing materials offer a certain variety: rice straw (*kuləš*) in the Caspian provinces; cane (*gālī*), wooden planks (*tak̲ta*), or shingles (*lata*) on the piedmont and the Alburz heights; and tiles (*sofāl*) fastened on their convex faces to the battens in northwest Gīlān province.

Recent developments. In most rural regions of Iran the sequence of construction operations has changed profoundly during the last thirty years; traditionally materials were manufactured and prepared in situ, whereas today they are purchased in industrial production centers that are sometimes quite distant. Baked bricks and cement have become the predominant construction materials, almost completely displacing unbaked mud. The growth of cement production, in response to strong demand in both urban and rural markets, has been particularly spectacular: 54,000 tons in 1950, 668,000 tons in 1962-63, and 3.7 million tons in 1973 (Issawi, pp. 381-82; *Iran Almanac 1972*, pp. 330-31). In 1971-72 the number of bricks manufactured annually at Tehran was estimated at 2.43 billion, that is, 6 million a day, supplying not only the market in the capital but also the northern and southern regions of the country (*Iran Almanac 1972*, p. 331). In some instances these technical changes have brought with them a complete modification in the building trades: In the Gīlān plain, for example, the cement-block layer (*bulok*; from French *bloc*) has replaced the carpenter, who was the traditional builder, and the layer of galvanized iron (*ḥalabsāz*) has replaced the thatcher (*gālīsāz*) as the roofer.

At the same time these rapid technical changes, combined with the overall development of society, have shattered the customary framework for the organization of work and the transmission of skills. Traditionally a mason began his career as an apprentice (*šāgerd*) to a master craftsman (*ostād*). In the city such master craftsmen generally belonged to a guild (*ṣenf*), which fulfilled several functions: mutual assistance and support, collection of taxes to be paid to the government, transmission of skills, candidacy examinations for apprentices seeking to become masters (for the seventeenth and eighteenth centuries, see Keyvani, pp. 141-49; for the early nineteenth century, see Kuznetsova, pp. 285-92). The masons' guilds were well represented in Iranian cities. To cite one example, that of Erevan at the beginning of the nineteenth century consisted of twenty-five masters, employing seventy apprentices and eighteen journeymen (*kārgar*) paid by the day; in number of members it ranked fourth among the eleven guilds listed (Kuznetsova, p. 289), which is still a long way, however, from the 12,000 architects (*meʿmār*) and builders (*bannāʾ*) supposed to have been active at Isfahan in the Safavid period (Keyvani, p. 56).

In rural areas traditional construction linked the mason, assisted by several helpers (*šāgerd, kārgar*), on one hand, and the family and friends of the client, on the other. These last took care of the less specialized work, such as transport and preparation of certain materials, leveling the ground before construction, digging the foundation trenches, and so on, whereas the mason performed the more skilled tasks, such as raising the walls and constructing the vaults.

In fact, the development of construction since the 1950s is a good indicator of the changes that have affected Iranian society during the last three decades: the demographic explosion and swelling of the urban population, westernization of technology, and disappearance of traditional skills. In 1940 the number of workers in the urban construction sector was estimated at 60,000 (Floor, p. 28); in 1966 this number was four times greater for Iran as a whole. The building trades thus represented 5.7 percent of the total work force; in 1976, during a "building boom," this percentage had more than doubled (to 13.5 percent, that is, 1.2 million people, usually employed by small businesses, out of a total work force of 8.8. million). The majority of these new masons, often immigrants from rural areas, have no specific training, nor have they the competence that was formerly acquired through apprenticeship or family tradition. That is one of the reasons for the mediocre quality of recent constructions. More basically, the construction crisis was one of the most acute symptoms of the larger prerevolutionary crisis: insufficient housing, real-estate speculation, doubling of the average price per square meter at Tehran between 1974 and 1977. The collapse of the Pahlavi state has led to a spectacular increase in private construction, carried on without licensing: The number of buildings completed at Tehran thus tripled in three years (Hourcade and Khosrokhavar, pp. 62-83). In 1982 steps were taken to limit high-rise construction in Tehran, with the aim of preventing erection of buildings more than three stories tall. These measures, combined with the economic crisis, poverty, and the high cost of construction materials, have brought a recession to this key sector of the country's economy.

Bibliography: A. A. Bakhtiar and R. Hillenbrand, "Domestic Architecture in Nineteenth Century Iran: the Manzil-i Sartîp Sidihî Near Isfahan," in E. Bosworth and C. Hillenbrand, eds., *Qajar Iran: Political, Social and Cultural Change 1800-1925*, Edinburgh, 1983, pp. 383-93. M. Bazin, *Le Tâlech: Une région ethnique au nord de l'Iran*, Paris, 1980. M. Bazin and C. Bromberger, *Gilân et Azarbâyjân oriental. Cartes et documents ethnographiques*, Paris, 1982. E. Beazley and M. Harverson, *Living with the Desert: Working Buildings of the Iranian Plateau*, Warminster, 1982. C. Bromberger, *Habitat, architecture et société rurale dans la plaine du Gilân*, Paris, 1986. Idem, "Habitations du Gilân," *Objets et mondes* 14/1, 1974, pp. 3-56. N. Christensen, "Haustypen und Gehöftbildung in Westpersien," *Anthropos* 62/1-2, 1967, pp. 89-138. K. A. C. Creswell, *A Short Account of Early Muslim Architecture*, London, 1958. H. Desmet and P. Fontaine, *La région d'Arāk et de Hamadān. Cartes et documents ethnographiques*, Paris (forthcoming). W. Floor, *Industrialization in Iran, 1900-1941*, Durham, 1984. A. Gabriel, *Durch Persiens Wüsten*, Stuttgart, 1935. A. Godard, *L'art de l'Iran*, Paris, 1962. *Iran Almanac 1972*, Tehran, 1972. B. Hourcade and F. Khosrokhavar, "L'Habitat révolutionnaire' à Téhéran, 1977-1981," *Hérodote* 31, 1981, pp. 61-83. C. Issawi, ed., *The Economic History of Iran 1800-1914*, Chicago, 1971. M. Keyvani, *Artisans and Guild Life in the Later Safavid Period: Contributions to the Social-Economic History of Persia*, Berlin, 1982. N. A. Kuznetsova, "Guild Organization. Early Ninteenth Century," in Issawi, 1971, pp. 285-92. G. Petherbridge, "The House and Society," in *The Architecture of the Islamic World*, ed. G. Michell, New York, 1978, pp. 193-208. F. Raḥīmī Lārījānī, "Sāḵtemānhā-ye azajī dar tārīḵ-e meʿmārī-e Īrān," *Āyanda*, 1361 Š./1982, nos. 3-4, pp. 168-75, 5, pp. 317-26. R. Rainer, *Traditional Building in Iran*, Graz, 1977. W. Simpson, "Mud Architecture: Notes Made in Persia and Other Countries," *Transactions of the Royal Institute of British Architecture*, N.S. 3, 1887, pp. 570-80. M. Siroux, *Caravansérails et petites constructions routières en Iran*, Cairo, 1949. G. Zander, "Observations sur l'architecture civile d'Ispahan," *Iranian Studies* 7/1-2, 1974, pp. 294-319.

(C. Bromberger)

BANNERS (*'alam, derafš*). In the earliest surviving Persian lexicon, the *Loḡat-e fors* (ed. Dabīrsīāqī, p. 70), Asadī Ṭūsī glosses the word *derafš*, or banner, as a signaling or guiding device (*'alāmat*). Jamālī Yazdī, the author of a popular encyclopedia entitled *Farroḵ-nāma* (ed. Ī. Afšār, Tehran, 1344 Š./1965, p. 318) more explicitly states in 580/1184-85 that the *derafš* is "an ensign at which the whole army keeps looking in the battlefield. That is called the center." The meaning remained unchanged in the 8th/14th century. Ebn Hendūšāh (*Seḥāḥ al-fors*, ed. 'A. Ṭā'atī, Tehran, 2535 = 1355 Š./1976, p. 151) understands *derafš* as "an ensign and a shining standard," while in 744/1343-44, Šams-e Faḵrī simply enters it with the gloss *'alam* in his *Me'yār-e jamālī* (*Vāža-nāma-ye fārsī, Bakš-e čahārom-e Me'yār-e jamālī*, ed. Ṣ. Kīā, Tehran, 1337 Š./1958, p. 213).

The sheen or gleam of the *derafš*, a notion conveyed by its etymology (see Horn, *Etymologie*, p. 123), is no mere ornamental characteristic but one linked with its very purpose: to serve as a guiding device or, to put it in military language, as a rallying point. This is borne out by the glosses provided for *'alam* by the 6th/12th-century Arab lexicographer Ebn Manẓūr (*Lesān al-'Arab*, Cairo, 1955, 15 vols.; repr. Beirut, n.d., XII (letter *mīm*). He enters *'alam* with the gloss *manār* "lighthouse." As a second meaning, Ebn Manẓūr notes that *'alāma* and *'alam* are devices "stuck in deserts that those who go astray may be guided by them." A third meaning is "mountain." Indeed the fundamental meaning of a guiding device, which is therefore shiny and as high as possible, is implicit in Persian literary usage from the earliest times.

Countless references in epic literature as well as in chronicles show that, in the clouds of dust that enveloped troops as they fought in sandy land, the glitter of the banner was the only way that warriors had of following the moves of their commanders or of identifying the enemy. As Afrāsīāb leads his army to confront the Iranians under Rostam, Gorāza sees "an army that was like a black cloud... A banner emerged from the azure blue [mass]" (*Šāh-nāma*, ed. Mohl, II, p. 54 1.597).

Colors seem to have been used specifically by certain groups at certain times. In the *Šāh-nāma*, for example, the banner of the Turanians is black (*Šāh-nāma*, Mohl, I, p. 414 1.381). The colors selected for banners would seem to have been those used for any type of emblem by a given group. "His banner is black and black is his surcoat," Zāl warns his son Rostam as the latter is about to confront Afrāsīāb, the king of Tūrān (*Šāh-nāma* I, p. 466 1.36 A). In the next line, he adds that "A black banner is attached on top of his helmet." This important verse demonstrates that the small banners stuck into small spiky openings on top of helmets that we know from 9th/15th and 10th/16th-century miniature painting hark back to a distant past. They are certainly not later than the Samanid period, as proven by Ferdowsī's mention, and might conceivably go back to Sasanian times. The line moreover leaves no doubt that the banner was an emblem which warriors were keen to display. On the other hand, there is evidence that a variety of colors could be used for the banners displayed by an army following guidelines that are as yet unclear. In the *Šāh-nāma*, for example, there is frequent reference to banners that are red, purple, and yellow. Sometimes, even additional colors are mentioned. When Ṭōs leads his troops into Torkestān, the shimmering Derafš-e Kāvīān makes "the atmosphere red, yellow, blue, purple" (*Šāh-nāma* II, p. 592, 1.402).

The material of banners was often silk, the shimmering fabric par excellence. Thus space may become like purple silk (*parand*) and the banners glitter (*Šāh-nāma* III, p. 588 1.2104). *Parnīānī derafš* "silken banner" is a recurring phrase. Different royal emblems could be used concurrently. Describing the advance of the Iranian army, a couple of distichs below the verses that have just been quoted, Ferdowsī goes on: "Behind each banner, there followed another banner—some with dragons, others with the image of the eagle" (1.2107). Miniature painting bears out the evidence of poetry. Early illuminated manuscripts have not come down to us even though literary sources clearly show that *Šāh-nāma* manuscripts were already being illustrated by the early 6th/12th century, contrary to a widely held belief (A. S. Melikian-Chirvani, "Le *Shāh-Nāme*, Miroir du Destin," *Stud. Ir.* 17, 1988, pp. 43-44). From the 8th/14th century on, such representations are not uncommon. In the earliest illuminated Persian manuscripts preserved in nearly original condition banners are represented without figural emblems. For example, in a miniature from an early 8th/14th-century copy of Rašīd-al-Dīn's *Jāme' al-tawārīḵ*, the banner of the king of India is a vertical rectangle filled with green cross-hatching. Three small elongated triangular red streamers, a longer one flanked by two shorter ones, are attached to its side. His enemy Sultan Maḥmūd holds a long spear tilted at a 45-degree angle and with a small triangular green streamer fastened to the shaft about one third of the way down (D. T. Rice and B. Gray, *The Illustrations of the "World History" of Rashīd al-Dīn*, Edinburgh, 1976, pl. 56, pp. 150-51). All the streamers are crosshatched. Identical banners occur in scenes featuring Iranians (e.g., p. 148, pl. 55, showing the Ziyarid Qābūs confronted with the Buyid army). These were therefore standard formats at the time of the manuscript. Both types were still being used around Ṣafar, 731/November, 1330, when the copyist of a *Šāh-nāma* generally considered to be of the Shiraz school completed his task (J. M. Rogers, F. Çağman, Z. Tanındı, *The Topkapı Saray*,

The Albums and Illustrated Manuscripts, London, 1986, p. 51). Done in a crude manner, they provide the earliest securely dated examples of banners with figural emblems. In one miniature (pl. 36), a banner consists of a vertical rectangle or possibly a square of scarlet with a narrow gold border; it is prolonged by two triangular streamers of ocher. On the scarlet patch is the image of a flying bird among cloud bands stylized in the Chinese manner. The bird and clouds are gilt, suggesting brocaded silk. In a miniature from the fourth feat (*k̲ᵛān*) of Esfandīār (pl. 33), large triangular banners carried by horsemen stand about three times the height of the horses. A red banner carries the golden or ocher image of a dragon, a green banner the golden image of a bird. A third banner is of plain rusty ocher. One miniature from a dispersed *Šāh-nāma* manuscript probably executed in the late 8th/14th century shows an interesting variant (B. Gray, *Persian Painting*, Geneva, 1961, p. 43). The subject is Manučehr's victory over Tūr. In the Iranian camp a horseman stands at one end of a line that also includes a rider beating on heavy war drums and two other horsemen sounding long, straight trumpets. The first horseman, who may be characterized as the royal standard-bearer, steadies with both hands a long red shaft, again about three times the height of his horse. It is crowned by an ensign, probably of brass and consisting of a series of axial elements flanked by confronted dragon heads. Immediately below a hairy tassel or tail flutters in the wind. Below that is a tall rectangular banner with a single streamer attached to its upper rim. Along the upper section of the rectangle is a short band of *nask̲ī* calligraphy in gold on a deep blue ground between two gold fillets. It consists of two titles that normally introduce the royal protocol on objets d'art of that period, *ʿezza le-Mawlānā al-So[l]ṭān* "Might/glory to our lord the sultan" (cf. A. S. Melikian-Chirvani, *Islamic Metalwork from the Iranian World 8-18th Centuries*, London, 1982, pp. 214a [top inscription] 22lb, 222b all on brass bowls from Fārs, the first two probably contemporary with the manuscript). The remaining portion of the banner, which is about four times as high as it is wide, is divided into two panels. In the upper panel the golden figure of an angel, apparently in flight, his left hand raised, is depicted on a vermilion ground. The figure wears a crown and may represent the archangel Gabriel. The lower panel is filled with a herringbone pattern in gold on a scarlet ground. The same abstract pattern recurs on the streamer. The rigidity of the fabric, contrasting with the undulating movement of the "tassel" above, suggests heavy brocade with thick gold threads. In the fight scene, one of the riders pierces his foe on a long spear of proportions identical to the flagpole. Near the spearhead a small rectangular strip of fabric, which in real life would have been about ten inches long, is prolonged at its lower edge by a very narrow strip of red fabric while, slightly above the miniature banner, two similar strips flutter in the air. Such a spear, with its attached miniature banner, may have been the early inspiration for the very principle of a large banner.

A double-page miniature from the same manuscript shows two facing armies, each massed against the outer frame of one page (M. Ş. Ipşiroğlu, *Masterpieces from the Topkapı Museum: Paintings and Miniatures*, pl. 19). In the open space, two horsemen are engaged in single combat under the watchful eye of a third horseman. Taken in conjunction with the previous page, this miniature is of the utmost importance. It shows how the royal standard-bearers stood in proper battle order. On each side five horsemen stand near the center of the troops close behind the front lines; they hold banners that by convention are clustered in the top corner. The four farthest banners, of which only portions are visible, are of the type already described, identifiable from the gold script on blue at the tops and portions of the angel below. The inscriptions taken together can be read: *ʿEzza le-mawlānā al-malek al-aʿdal al-aʿl[am] al-moʾayyed al-moẓaffar...* "glory to our lord the most just and wise king, the supported [by heaven], the victorious." This protocol identifies these four banners as royal standards, presumably of the type prevalent in Fārs and perhaps elsewhere as well. The association of the angel suggests that it must also have have been a royal emblem. The nearest banner on each side consists of a large elongated triangle; in a trapezoidal panel near the shaft a lion passant is represented in gold on a vermilion ground. The remainder of the triangle is filled with herringbone pattern.

The concurrent use of the triangular banner with a lion effigy suggests that the two types, each with its specific iconography, had different purposes. These have yet to be elucidated. Banners with lion effigies are repeatedly mentioned in Persian literature in royal or quasi-royal contexts. Azraqī Heravī writes in the 5th/11th century: "And because the black lion is the image on his standard, the black lion becomes more valiant in combat" (*Divān*, ed. S. Nafīsī, Tehran, 1336 Š./1957, p. 89). ʿAbd-al-Wāseʿ Ḡarjestānī Jabalī, who died in 555/1160, writes in a panegyric to a prince: "And if by you the lion of the forest is threatened when you are angry, your threat renders him more helpless than the lion on the banner" (*Divān*, ed. Ḏ. Ṣafā, Tehran, 1339 S./1960, p. 269: helpless because lifeless). Elsewhere (p. 273) Jabalī conjures the image of "the lion in the sky (= Leo)," agitated like "the lion on the banner when the wind blows."

Two other emblems of royal character recur in 9th/15th- and 10th/16th-century miniatures, echoing Ferdowsī's line quoted above. One is a bird with flame-like tail and wings like those of an eagle, which is the mythical Sīmorḡ. It occurs in a *Šāh-nāma* of Bāysonḡor (q.v.), commissioned in 833/1429-30. The miniature depicts the army led by Rostam confronting the troops of the K̲āqān of Čīn (L. Binyon, J. V. S. Wilkinson, and B. Gray, *Persian Miniature Painting*, London, 1933, pl. XLVIIIA, pp. 69-70). On a standard held upright by a standard-bearer in Rostam's army, the Sīmorḡ is very clearly depicted on the vertical rectangular section prolonged by a long triangular streamer. Dragons also occur, invariably in a royal or princely context.

Such a dragon may be seen in a manuscript of Neẓāmī's *Ḵamsa* which was completed in Šawwāl, 850/20 December 1446-17 January 1447 and was illuminated by Solṭān-ʿAlī Bāvardī (I. Stchoukine, "Sultân ʿAlî al-Bâvardî," *Syria* 44/3-4, 1967, pl. XXIV/2). The standard appears behind the imperial parasol, held above Alexander as he watches the wall being built against Gog and Magog. On the vertical rectangular panel of the standard, basically similar to those of the much earlier *Jāmeʿ al-tawārīḵ*, a dragon rises threateningly, its spiked tongue lashing out. Above it an epigraphic band carries the Arabic words "the supreme sultan" [*al-solṭān al-aʿẓam*], extracted from the usual imperial protocol, which explicitly identifies the banner as a royal emblem. A dragon is also to be seen on a standard in the *Šāh-nāma* manuscript executed around that time, possibly about 843/1440, for Moḥammad Jūkī, the brother of prince Bāysonḡor (color plate in R. H. Pinder Wilson, *Persian Painting of the Fifteenth Century*, London, 1958, p. 11, pl. 4). It appears in a miniature illustrating the slaying of Zarasp, son of Ṭōs, son of the king Nōdar, at the hands of Ferōd. The standard of Zarasp is of a type related to the previous example. In the upper panel of a vertical rectangle (proportionally shorter than the corresponding panel in the *Ḵamsa*) a yellow dragon is depicted on a green ground. Above it is a royal-blue band without an inscription. The lower panel is lavender, as is the triangular streamer attached to the side at the top.

From the 9th/15th century on, religious inscriptions seem to have played an increasing role, although caution must be exercised in view of the limited number of surviving illuminated manuscripts of the 14th century. An important miniature with regard to the history of banners occurs in a manuscript of the *Ḵamsa* dated (according to Rogers, Çağman, and Tanındı, op. cit., p. 113, pl. 71), 880/1475-76 and Moḥarram, 886/March, 1481. It was copied by a calligrapher attached to Sultan Yaʿqūb. In the miniature representing the armies of Ḵosrow Parvēz and Bahrām Čōbīn, Ḵosrow's five royal standard-bearers appear in a row in the top left corner. Each banner consists of a horizontal rectangle of rigid material, to which is attached an undulating triangular banner of a lighter color. The rigid panels, alternately green and azure, carry polylobed escutcheons in gold with the triple invocation to God, Moḥammad, and ʿAlī. The same invocation occurs on the standards of the enemy.

Smaller banners, more elongated and devoid of epigraphy, are carried by various officers. Very small triangular streamers of the same shape as the latter are attached just below the spearheads of the warriors, a reminder of the fundamental nature of the banner: a streamer attached to a weapon. Longer inscriptions become more common in the 10th/16th century. In the manuscript of the *Šāh-nāma* commissioned by Shah Ṭahmāsb, which survived intact into the 20th century, when it was torn apart and dispersed by Arthur Houghton Sr. in the early 1970s, Koranic inscriptions occur on royal standards.

The miniature depicting Qāren defeating Bārmān (S. C. Welch, *A King's Book of Kings*, New York, 1976, pl. on p. 137) shows sections of two royal standards, one red, the other green, on the far left. The inscription on the red standard reproduces Koran 61:13 ("Victory comes from God and triumph is near; tell the tidings of joy to the Believers, oh Moḥammad"). The scribe has daringly added "oh ʿAlī." Traditional invocations also occur in the manuscript. In the miniature illustrating the killing of Kalbād at the hands of Farīborz (ibid., pl. on p. 165) the banner of Farīborz, son of Kay Kāʾūs, is stuck in the ground at right. The large triangular pink banner carries an elongated cartouche with the triple invocation in gold lettering on black: "Oh God! Oh Moḥammad! Oh ʿAlī!" It is noteworthy that on the banner of Kalbād, symmetrically planted in the ground at the left, no inscription is visible amid the ornamental motifs. Similarly, the miniature banner set in the spike atop Farīborz's helmet carries the triple invocation, in gold letters on a vermilion ground, but no inscription is visible on the miniature red banner that has fallen from Kalbād's helmet. [See Addenda and corrigenda.]

See also ʿALAM WA ʿALĀMAT.

Bibliography: Given in the text.

(A. S. MELIKIAN-CHIRVANI)

BĀNŪ, originally "lady," now also in common use as an alternative to *ḵānom* "Madam, Mrs." (from Turkish *xan-ım* "my lord"). The Middle Persian form of the word was *bānūk* (*bānūg*). Compounds with *bānū* include *kad-bānū* "mistress of the house" (Pahl. *katak-bānūk*) and *šāh-bānū* "shah's wife, queen," the latter introduced under the Pahlavi dynasty to replace Arabic *maleka*. *Bānū* is found as a component in women's names such as Arjomandbānū (d. 1630, wife of the Mughal emperor Šāh Jahān; Justi, *Namenbuch*, p. 22b), Bahravarbānū (Justi, p. 60b), Gowharbānū (Justi, p. 112b), Jahānzēbbānū (d. 1705, grand-daughter of Šāh Jahān; Justi, p. 115b), Kadbānūya (Justi, p. 150b; cf. the numerous Southeast Iranian place names in -*ūya*), Mehrbānū (Justi, p. 205a), Parībānū (name of a fairy in *Thousand and One Nights*; Justi, p. 246b), Šahrbānū ("mistress of the empire;" Justi, p. 276b; Eilers and Schapka, I, p. 233.8, II, pp. 284.7, 285.11), Tājbānū (Justi, p. 318b), Zarbānū (Justi, p. 381b). It is not always clear in these cases whether *bānū* is part of the name or a title.

Alone or as the first component of names are Bānū (cf. Bʾnwky on the intaglio of a Sasanian seal, Ph. Gignoux, *IPNB* II/2, p. 55 no. 185), Bānūdoḵt (?), the mother of Ḵosrow I, and Bānū-Gōšasp (cf. Gōšasp-bānū), the daughter of Rostam (Justi, pp. 62f.).

Armenian *banuk* shows that the Mid. Pers. pronunciation was *bānūk*, not *bānōk*. Nevertheless, the word appears to belong to the large group of hypocoristic names in -*ōk*. The Pahlavi ideogram for *bānūk* given in the *Frahang ī pahlavīk* is *MRTA*, from Aramaic *martā*, cf. the name Martha in the New Testament. In the Nisa documents and the Sasanian inscriptions, *bānūk* is represented by the ideograms *MROTA* (Mid. Pers.) and

MRATY (Parth.), in which the *ʿayin* and the *aleph* are graphic intrusions. Similarly, the masculine counterparts Mid. Pers. *xwadāy* and Parth. *xwadāw* are represented by *MROḤ(Y)* (Mid. Pers.) and *MRAY* (Nisa), originally perhaps from Aramaic *marʾēh* and *marʾī* "his/my master" (see, e.g., Henning, "Mitteliranisch," p. 36).

In the inscription of Narseh I at Paikuli (Mid. Pers. l. 9, Parth. l. 8: Humbach and Skjærvø, p. 35) the goddess Anāhīt is called "the lady," just as Ištar was known among the Babylonians and Assyrians as *Bēltum* or *Bēlit* "lady," or *Bēltī* "my lady."

No precursor of *bānū* is found in Old Iranian. Most probably it is a hypocoristic abbreviation of Mid. Pers. *bānbišn* (q.v.) "queen," originally "mistress of the house" (cf. Av. *dəmanō/nmānō.paθnī*, Pashto *mērman[a]*, Morgenstierne, pp. 44, 47; ideogram Mid. Pers. *MLKTA*, Parth. *MLKTH*, Aram. *malkəṯā*). The second element of *bānbišn* has been dropped in the same way as, for instance, in the name Šahrū from Šahrbānū. The etymology proposed by Dehḵodā (*Loḡat-nāma*, s.v. *Bānū*), deriving *bānū* from *bān* "protector, possessor" is untenable.

Modern dialects have forms deriving from Persian *kadbānū* in the sense of "mistress of the house," thus Baḵtīārī *kaivenū* or *kēivenū* and Kurdish *kaivānū* (Lorimer, p. 106b).

Bibliography: W. Eilers and U. Schapka, *Westiranische Mundarten aus der Sammlung Wilhelm Eilers I: Die Mundart von Chunsar*, Wiesbaden, 1976, II: *Die Mundart von Gäz*, Wiesbaden, 1979. Horn, *Etymologie*, p. 41 no. 178. H. Hübschmann, *Armen. Etymologie*, pp. 116 no. 98, 117 no. 100. Idem, *Persische Studien*, 1895, p. 25 no. 178. H. Humbach and P. O. Skjærvø, *The Sassanian Inscription of Paikuli* III/1, Wiesbaden, 1983. D. L. R. Lorimer, *The Phonology of the Bakhtiari, Badakhshani and Madaglashti Dialects of Modern Persian*, London, 1922. G. Morgenstierne, *An Etymological Vocabulary of Pashto*, Oslo, 1927. P. Tedesco, *BSL* 26, 1925, p. 64.

(W. Eilers)

BANŪ AMĀJŪR (or **MĀJŪR**), ABU'L-QĀSEM ʿABD-ALLĀH (ʿAlī according to Ebn Yūnes) b. (A)Mājūr Torkī and his son Abu'l-Ḥasan ʿAlī, astronomers. The descendants of a Turk from Farḡāna named Amājūr or Mājūr, Abu'l-Qāsem and his son came from Herāt. The suggestion made by A. Sayılı (pp. 101-03) that they were connected with the family of Amājūr, an amir of Damascus who died in 264/877-78, is possibly correct but does not contradict their eastern origins. Abu'l-Ḥasan made a series of at least six observations of the planets, apparently at Shiraz, between 26 Rabīʿ I 272/10 September 885 and 1 Moḥarram 297/20 September 909 (Ebn Yūnes, pp. 174-79); the third observation, on 18 Šawwāl 288/6 October 901, is specifically stated to have taken place in Shiraz, while the dates of the first, fourth, and fifth are given in both the Arab and Persian calendars. The family seems to have been in Baghdad, however, when Abu'l-Ḥasan observed the planets again between Moḥarram and Rajab of 306/June, 918-January, 919 and compared his results with computations made with the tables of Ḥabaš and Ptolemy (Ebn Yūnes, pp. 120-27); in the same year, 306 *hejrī*/288 *yazdegerdī* (these years overlap from 6 April to 2 June 919) the Banū Amājūr observed Regulus and determined the rate of progression to be Ptolemy's 1° in 100 years (Ebn Yūnes, pp. 166-69). Abu'l-Qāsem, Abu'l-Ḥasan, and the latter's freedman Mofleḥ b. Yūsof further calculated a series of five lunar and two solar eclipses between 12 Safar 311/1 June 923 and 14 Ḏu'l-qaʿda 321/5 November 933 and compared these calculations with their observations of the events themselves (Ebn Yūnes, pp. 128-41). Finally the same trio observed the sun and determined the parameters of its motions, though those accepted by the Banū Amājūr in their *Zīj al-badīʿ* differ from those adopted by Mofleḥ (Ebn Yūnes, pp. 150-53).

From Ebn Yūnes' reports of their observations it is clear that the Banū Amājūr were particularly concerned with an attempt to correct the tables of Ḥabaš on the basis of new data, and that they also considered the relation of Ptolemy's parameters to their own. It is known that Abu'l-Qāsem had personal contact with the astronomer Ebn al-Adamī, who died in 308/920-21, but nothing further concerning their personal lives appears in the Islamic biographical tradition (Ebn al-Nadīm, ed. Flügel, p. 280; Ebn al-Qeftī, p. 220-21, 231, 234). Those sources do, however, give a list of their writings, ascribed to Abu'l-Qāsem: 1. *Ketāb al-qenn* (?) (Book of the slave?), only in Ebn al-Nadīm. 2. *Ketāb al-zīj al-ḵāleṣ* (The pure astronomical tables), Kennedy, p. 135 no. 78. 3. *Ketāb zād al-mosāfer* (Book of provisions for the traveler). 4. *Ketāb al-zīj al-mozannar* (The girdled astronomical tables), Kennedy, p. 135 no. 79. 5. *Ketāb al-zīj al-badīʿ* (The amazing astronomical tables), Kennedy, p. 125 no. 8; this is the only *zīj* specifically named by Ebn Yūnes and may be the source of all the observation reports that he records. 6. *Ketāb zīj al-sendhend* (Astronomical tables of the Sendhend), Kennedy, p. 135 no. 90; this is presumably a reworking of the *zīj al-Sendhend* of Abū Jaʿfar Moḥammad Ḵʷārazmī. 7. *Ketāb zīj al-mamarrāt* (Astronomical tables of transits), Kennedy, p. 134 no. 67. 8. *Ketāb zīj al-Merrīḵ ʿala'l-taʾrīḵ al-fāresī* (Astronomical tables of Mars according to the Persian calendar), only in Ebn al-Qeftī.

None of the above-mentioned works is extant, but there does exist in manuscripts at Paris a *Zīj al-ṭaylasān* ascribed to Abu'l-Qāsem ʿAlī b. Mājūr; it is perhaps of the type described by Goldstein, that is, cowl-shaped or triangular. There is also preserved in manuscripts at Paris and Leiden a *Jawāmeʿ aḥkām al-kosūfāt (kosūfayn) wa qerān al-kawākeb (kawkabayn)* (Collection of judgments from eclipses and planetary conjunctions). This is said to contain a reference to a conjunction that took place in 699/1299-1300 (Brockelmann, p. 397), though in fact no significant conjunction occurred during that year. The authenticity of this astrological text is yet to be established.

Bibliography: Brockelmann, *GAL*, S. I, p. 397. B. R. Goldstein, "A Medieval Table for Reckoning Time from Solar Altitude," *Scripta Mathematica* 27, 1962, pp. 61-66. Ebn al-Qefṭī, *Taʾrīḵ al-ḥokamāʾ*, ed. J. Lippert, Leipzig, 1903. Ebn Yūnes, *Zīj al-kabīr al-ḥākemī*, in Caussin de Perceval, "Le livre de la grande table Hakémite," *Notices et extraits des manuscrits* 7, year 12, pp. 16-240. *EI*² III, pp. 702-03. E. S. Kennedy, *A Survey of Islamic Astronomical Tables*, Philadelphia, 1956. A. Sayılı, *The Observatory in Islam*, Ankara, 1960. F. Sezgin, *GAS* V, p. 282. Suter, *Mathematiker*, pp. 49-50.

(D. Pingree)

BANŪ ʿABBĀS. See ʿABBASIDS.

BANŪ ʿANNĀZ. See ʿANNAZIDS.

BANŪ LAḴM. See LAKHMIDS.

BANŪ MĀJŪR. See BANŪ AMĀJŪR.

BANŪ MONAJJEM, a family of intellectuals, closely connected to the caliphs of the 3rd-4th/9th-10th centuries and claiming descent from an ancient Iranian lineage. Their genealogy is given by Ebn al-Nadīm (ed. Flügel, pp. 143-44), from whom it is in part copied and supplemented by Ebn Ḵallekān (tr. de Slane, IV, pp. 84-88). Ebn al-Nadīm learned of this genealogy from the family history composed by one of its members, Abu'l-Ḥasan Aḥmad b. Yaḥyā, and directly from another, Abu'l-Ḥasan ʿAlī b. Hārūn, who began without finishing a genealogy of the family but whom Ebn al-Nadīm knew personally.

The most distinguished members of the family were Yaḥyā b. Abī Manṣūr, an astronomer who worked for al-Maʾmūn (r. 198-218/813-33) and was the first of the family to be a Muslim; his son ʿAlī (d. 275/888-89), a close companion of al-Motawakkel (r. 232-47/847-61); and the latter's son, the theologian Yaḥyā (241–13 Rabīʿ I 300/855-56–26 October 912), who was a companion of al-Mowaffaq, the powerful brother of al-Moʿtamed (r. 256-79/870-92), as well as of succeeding caliphs. The interests of the family members lay in astronomy (including the Persian calendar), astrology, poetry, music (especially singing), theology, and law.

In the genealogical stemma (Figure 18), I have followed Justi in interpreting the Arabic forms of the Persian names in Ebn al-Nadīm since, as Ebn Ḵallekān also realized, they are very corrupt. Note that, since there are eight generations between Yazdegerd and Abū Manṣūr (who lived in the late 2nd/8th century), the founder of the family cannot be identical with the last Sasanian monarch but must have lived a century or so before him.

Yazdejerd
|
Mehr-Jošnas
|
Aštād
|
Farroḵdād
|
Mehānīdād-Jošnas
|
Kād
|
Warīd
|
Abān-Jošnas, known as Abū Manṣūr Monajjem
|
Yaḥyā b. Abī Manṣūr
|
Moḥammad — ʿAlī (d. 275/888–89) — Saʿīd — Ḥasan

Sons of ʿAlī: Aḥmad — ʿAbd-Allāh — Yaḥyā (241/855-56 –300/912) — Hārūn (d. 288/901)
|
ʿAlī (277/890–91 –352/963–64)
|
Hārūn

Figure 18. Banū Monajjem

(D. Pingree)

BANŪ MŪSĀ, the name applied to three brothers, ʿAbbasid astronomers whose father was Mūsā b. Šāker, said to have been a robber in his youth in Khorasan and who became an astronomer (*monajjem*) and companion of the caliph al-Maʾmūn while the latter was still in Marv, before becoming caliph in 198/813. When Mūsā died he left his three sons, Moḥammad, Aḥmad, and Ḥasan, in the care of al-Maʾmūn, who in turn entrusted them to Esḥāq b. Ebrāhīm Mosaʿbī. They were trained by Yaḥyā b. Abī Manṣūr in the Academy of Science (*bayt al-ḥekma*) in Baghdad, where they seem to have spent the rest of their lives. In connection with their interests in the exact sciences, however, they sent scholars to Byzantium to seek out Greek scientific manuscripts and worked closely with several of the translators from Greek into Arabic, notably Ṯābet b. Qorrā and Ḥonayn b. Esḥāq. Moḥammad, in fact, is said to have discovered Ṯābet, who was then a money-changer in Ḥarrān, on his way back from a trip to Byzantium, and to have brought him to Baghdad, where he taught him astronomy (Ebn al-Nadīm, ed. Flügel, p. 272). It was perhaps on this trip that Moḥammad saw the place of the Seven Sleepers at Ephesus (Bīrūnī, *al-Āṯār al-bāqīa*, p. 290, tr. Sachau, p. 285).

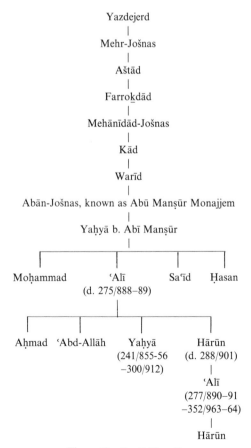

The three brothers were commissioned by al-Maʾmūn to measure the length of a degree of latitude and therefrom the circumference of the earth; they carried this task out successfully in the desert plain near Senjār in northern Mesopotamia (Nallino, pp. 420-35). They also made astronomical observations together at Baghdad. The solar parameters that they established following the *zīj al-momtaḥan* are reported by Ebn Yūnes (pp. 149, 151); the sun's mean motion in a Persian year there given agrees with the statement made by Bīrūnī (p. 52, tr. p. 61) that Moḥammad and Aḥmad had determined that a solar year was 365 days and less than 6 hours long. Aḥmad is said by Ebn Yūnes (pp. 151, 153) to have independently determined a similar set of solar parameters in 220 *Yazdegerdī*/851-52. The three brothers also observed the longitude of Regulus from their house on a bridge in Baghdad in 209 Y./840-41, 216 Y./847-48, and 219 Y./850-51 according to Ebn Yūnes (pp. 163, 165), who also refers to their observation of Sirius (p. 165). Bīrūnī (pp. 151-54, tr. pp. 147-49) used the lunar parameters resulting from their observations in his computations of the nativities (*mawleds*) of the years.

From Ṭabarī, we know that Moḥammad and Aḥmad were employed as civil engineers by the caliph al-Motawwakel (232-47/847-61), and that Moḥammad was deeply involved in the politics surrounding the caliphate of al-Mosta'īn (248-52/862-66; Hill, p. 5). Moḥammad died in Rabī' I, 259/January, 873 (Ebn al-Nadīm, p. 271).

The three brothers together were responsible not only for astronomical observations and the lost *zīj* that reported them but also for the *Ketāb ma'refat mesāḥat al-aškāl al-basīṭa wa'l-korīya* (Book of knowing the measurement of plane and spherical figures), as it is entitled in the redaction (*taḥrīr*) made by Naṣīr-al-Dīn Ṭūsī (Sezgin, *GAS* V, pp. 251-52); this *taḥrīr* has been published in the *Majmū' al-rasā'el* of Ṭūsī (II, sec. 1). The original was translated into Latin by Gerard of Cremona in the twelfth century as the *Verba Filiorum Moysi Filii Sekir*. An edition of the Latin text with an English translation is given by Clagett (pp. 223-367), who has also summarized the enormous impact that this treatise had on medieval Latin geometry in the thirteenth and fourteenth centuries. Apparently the three brothers together also joined in writing a no longer extant *Ketāb fi'l-qarasṭūn* (Book concerning the balance) according to Ebn al-Nadīm (p. 271). And they wrote an exposition of astrology entitled *Ketāb al-darajāt* (Book of the degrees; Sezgin, *GAS* VII, pp. 129-30).

The oldest brother, Moḥammad, was also the most productive, though only one of his many works is still extant. This is the *Ketāb ḥarakat al-falak al-ūlā* (Book of the first motion of the celestial sphere), which is a lengthy treatise on Ptolemaic astronomy (Sezgin, *GAS* VI, p. 147). There also survives one manuscript of a work depending on one of his that is lost, the *Ro'yat al-helāl 'alā ra'y Abī Ja'far Moḥammad b. Mūsā b. Šāker* (The Sighting of the new moon according to the opinion of Abū Ja'far Moḥammad b. Mūsā b. Šāker; ibid.). Ebn al-Nadīm (p. 271) ascribes to Moḥammad four other mathematical works and one on linguistics.

The only surviving work of the second brother, Aḥmad, is his *Ketāb al-ḥīal* (Book of ingenious devices), which describes various hydraulic automata operated by pneumatics. It has recently been edited and translated by Hill. Ebn Yūnes, as indicated above, knows of a *zīj* by Aḥmad. Ebn al-Nadīm (p. 271) ascribes to the two brothers two cosmographical works that no longer exist: one by Moḥammad on the beginning of the world, the other by Aḥmad denying the existence of a ninth celestial sphere beyond that of the fixed stars. The same bibliographer mentions two treatises concerning a discussion between Aḥmad and Sanad b. 'Alī, perhaps concerning the difficulties that the Banū Mūsā faced because of the failure of their agent, Farḡānī, to construct the Ja'farīya canal properly.

To the third brother, Ḥasan, is attributed only one work (*Ketāb al-šakl al-modawwar al-mostaṭīl*), now lost, on the ellipse.

Bibliography: M. Clagett, *Archimedes in the Middle Ages* I, Madison, 1964. Ebn al-Qefṭī, *Ta'rīḵ al-ḥokamā'*, ed. J. Lippert, Leipzig, 1903, pp. 441-43. Ebn Yūnes, *al-Zīj al-kabīr al-ḥākemī*, in Caussin de Perceval, "Le livre de la grande table Hakémite," *Notices et extraits* 7, year 12, pp. 16-240. D. R. Hill, *The Book of Ingenious Devices*, Dordrecht, 1979. C. A. Nallino, "Il valore metrico del grado di meridiano secondo i geografi arabi," in his *Raccolta di scritti editi e inediti* V, Rome, 1944, pp. 408-57. Naṣīr-al-Dīn Ṭūsī, *Majmū' al-rasā'el*, 2 vols., Hyderabad, 1358-59/1939-40.

(D. PINGREE)

BANŪ OMAYYA. See OMMAYADS.

BĀNŪ PĀRS, "Lady of Pārs," the name of a Zoroastrian shrine in the mountains at the northern end of the Yazd plain. The sacred rock is on a natural platform above a riverbed, usually dry but filled in rainy seasons with flood waters off the mountains. Two other river courses join it just below the shrine, a fourth a little lower down. Then a mountain ridge blocks their path and forces the waters, when in spate, to swing round and churn their way past it to reach the plain. Both sight and sound are tremendous; and even when the channels are dry, their deep boulder-strewn courses bear witness to the force and abundance of the waters in their season. By the shrine itself a never-failing spring fills a small pool.

The shrine appears to have been dedicated originally to Ardwīsūr Anāhīd (q.v.), who had the cult title Bānū (see ibid.), and whose veneration in the Yazd area is attested by the popularity there of the girl's name Āb-Nāhīd (q.v.). The characteristic sacrifice to Bānū-Pārs was that of cows, made annually at the shrine by local Zoroastrians until the late 13th/19th century. The cow is known to have been the sacrifice proper of old to Anāhīd (Plutarch, *Life of Lucullus* 24; cf. *Nīrangistān*, chaps. 70-71, ed. A. Waag, Leipzig, 1941, p. 81).

In Islamic times a new belief evolved as to the identity of the "Lady" of the shrine, embodied in the following legend: When Yazdegerd III was fleeing from the invading Arabs, his family took refuge in Yazd. Their pursuers catching up with them there, they scattered. A princess made her way northward on foot. She begged a peasant for a drink, and he milked his cow for her, but the animal kicked over the bowl, and she had to press on, parched. The annual cow sacrifice was said to be a punishment for this one beast's wayward act. Followed by Arab soldiers, the princess struggled as far as the sacred rock, where, exhausted, she cried out to Ohrmazd for help; the rock opened, and she passed alive into it. (A similar legend attaches to the Muslim shrine to Šahrbānū, reputedly another daughter of Yazdegerd III, at Ray.)

In pre-Muslim times the sacred rock was probably not enclosed. Thereafter a tiny mud-brick cell was built over it, which in 1962 was replaced by a small, elegant brick building, with domed sanctuary. The annual pilgrimage, lasting five days, now takes place in July. The earliest literary reference to the shrine is from A.D. 1626, when a Parsi emissary is recorded to have "rendered homage to K̲ātūn Bānū Pārs, which is a place of pilgrimage" (M. R. Unvala, ed., *Dârâb Hormazyâr's Rivâyat*, Bombay, 1922, II, p. 159 l. 3; B. N. Dhabhar, tr., *The Persian Rivayats of Hormazyar Framarz and Others*, Bombay, 1932, p. 593). K̲ātūn, a Turkish rendering of Bānū, is used in the shrine legend as the princess's proper name, but has no popular currency.

Bibliography: Given in the text. See also P. M. Sykes, *Ten Thousand Miles in Persia*, London, 1902, p. 156. M. Boyce, "Bībī Shahrbānū and the Lady of Pārs," *BSOAS* 30, 1967, pp. 30-44. Idem, *A Persian Stronghold of Zoroastrianism*, Oxford, 1977, pp. 248-55.

(M. Boyce)

BANŪ SĀJ, more correctly Āl Abi'l-Sāj, a family named after its ancestor Abu'l-Sāj which served the ʿAbbasid caliphate from the reign of al-Ma'mūn or al-Moʿtaṣem and later ruled Azerbaijan (279-317/892-929). It originated from two neighboring villages, Jankākaṯ and Sūydak, in Ošrūsana (Ebn Ḥawqal, p. 506) and was probably, as suggested by V. Minorsky (*Studies in Caucasian History*, London, 1953, p. 111) on the basis of the name of the founder, of Sogdian, rather than Turkish, origin.

1. Abu'l-Sāj Dīvdād b. Dīvdast Ošrūsanī was evidently enlisted by Afšīn (q.v.), prince of Ošrūsana, in the army which he raised for the caliph al-Ma'mūn. He is first mentioned in the reign of al-Moʿtaṣem as a prominent commander in Afšīn's army besieging the K̲orramī rebel Bābak in Bad̲d̲ (qq.v.) in 222/837. He delivered Bābak, after the latter was surrendered by the Armenians, to Afšīn in Barzand on 10 Šawwāl/15 September. In 224/839 al-Moʿtaṣem sent him with an army to Lārez and Donbāvand in the war against Māzyār. Probably still in the same year, or early in 225/840, Afšīn, according to Yaʿqūbī (*Tārīḵ* II, p. 583), dispatched him with a strong army to Azerbaijan, ostensibly to subdue Mankjūr, Afšīn's seditious lieutenant there. Afšīn was accused, however, of having encouraged Mankjūr, his cousin, to revolt and to have sent Abu'l-Sāj to aid him. Al-Moʿtaṣem now sent the Turk Boḡā Kabīr who seized Mankjūr. If the accusation was sound, Abu'l-Sāj seems to have escaped punishment. In 242/856, according to Ṭabarī (III, p. 1436), or in 244/859, according to others, the caliph al-Motawakkel put him in charge of the road from Baghdad to Mecca. It was probably at this time that he seized the rebel Hasanid Moḥammad b. Ṣāleḥ and destroyed his base at Sowayqa, a village near Medina belonging to the ʿAlids (Yāqūt, *Boldān* III, p. 198). About 249/863, under al-Mostaʿīn, he was sent to northern Syria to subdue a revolt among the Tanūḵ in the region of Qennasrīn. He was recalled from Arabia to Baghdad in 251/865 and robes of honor were bestowed on him by al-Mostaʿīn, whose position now was threatened by a revolt of Turkish commanders in Samarra in favor of al-Moʿtazz. Moḥammad b. ʿAbd-Allāh b. Ṭāher who was still loyal to al-Mostaʿīn sent Abu'l-Sāj to defend Madā'en. He inflicted two defeats on the Turks at Jarjarāyā but could not prevent their penetrating into Madā'en. In Moḥarram, 252/February, 866, after Moʿtazz had been recognized as caliph by Ebn Ṭāher and al-Mostaʿīn, he returned to Baghdad and was appointed by Ebn Ṭāher to govern the regions of the Sawād irrigated by the Euphrates. He proceeded to Qaṣr Ebn Hobayra and then to Kūfa after his lieutenent had arrested a rebel ʿAlid there. Still in the same year he was again put in charge of the road to Mecca, and the rebel Hasanid Moḥammad b. Yūsof fled before him from the Hejaz to Yamāma where he founded the reign of the Banu'l-Oḵayżer. In 254/868 Abu'l-Sāj was appointed governor of Dīār Możar, Qennasrīn, and ʿAwāṣem. In 261/875 he was put in charge of Ahvāz and the war against the Zanj rebels. When his brother-in-law ʿAbd-al-Raḥmān was, however, defeated and killed by the Zanj near Dūlāb, Abu'l-Sāj retreated to ʿAskar Mokram and the Zanj entered Ahvāz. Soon thereafter he was dismissed from the government of Ahvāz, but remained in the province. A report of the *Tārīḵ-e Sīstān* (p. 230, with the emendation of the editor) that Yaʿqūb b. Layṯ Ṣaffār deposited with him the treasures captured in the castle of Ebn Wāṣel in Fārs in Šawwāl, 261/July, 875 (Ṭabarī, III, p. 1889) seems unreliable. According to Ṭabarī (III, p. 1891) Abu'l-Sāj received Moḥammad b. Zaydūya, a deserter from Yaʿqūb's army, in Ahvāz later in this year. He joined Yaʿqūb, however, as the latter passed through ʿAskar Mokram, and was well received and honored by him. He appears to have been present at the defeat of Yaʿqūb at Dayr al-ʿĀqūl in Rajab, 262/April, 876, and afterward criticized Yaʿqūb's conduct of the war (Ebn K̲allekān, ed. ʿAbbās, VI, p. 415). Al-Mowaffaq, brother and coregent of the caliph al-Moʿtamed, confiscated his estates and property after the battle. Upon Yaʿqūb's death in 265/879, Abu'l-Sāj joined his brother and successor ʿAmr. When the latter made peace with the caliph, Abu'l-Sāj took leave from him in Fārs to go to Baghdad. On his way he

died in Gondēšāpūr in Rabīʿ II, 266/November-December, 879.

2. Abū ʿObayd-Allāh Moḥammad b. Abi'l-Sāj. After the death of Abu'l-Sāj, ʿAmr b. Lay̱t gave his son Moḥammad charge of the Holy Cities in the Hejaz and of the Baghdad-Mecca road. Moḥammad entered Mecca after expelling Abu'l-Moḡīra Maḵzūmī, an ally of the Zanj, on 8 Ḏu'l-ḥejja 266/2 July 880. During the next three years he secured the Baghdad-Mecca road, defeating Hayṣam ʿEjlī, chief of the Banū ʿEjl, who controlled the region of Kūfa (Šawwāl, 267/May, 881), killing Moḥammad b. ʿAli Yaškorī near Wāseṭ (268/881-82) and capturing a convoy of money and weapons of Maḵzūmī near Ṭā'ef (269/882-83). In Jomādā II, 269/December, 882-January, 883, he was given by Hārūn b. Mowaffaq, the later caliph al-Moʿtażed, control of Anbār, the Baghdad-Euphrates road, and Raḥbat Ṭawq. On 29 Šawwāl 269/11 May 883 he entered Raḥbat Ṭawq after expelling Aḥmad b. Mālek b. Ṭawq and then proceeded to Qarqīsīā driving off Ebn Ṣafwān ʿOqaylī. When Mowaffaq, after the death of Aḥmad b. Ṭūlūn in 270/884, decided to take the offensive against the latter's son Ḵomārawayh, Moḥammad jointly with Ebn Kondāj, governor of Mosul (Mawṣel), took Aleppo (Ḥalab) in 271/884, and al-Mowaffaq appointed Moḥammad governor of it. He stayed there and refused to join the campaign of Hārūn b. Mowaffaq against Ḵomārawayh, since Hārūn had offended him by accusing him of cowardice. After Hārūn withdrew from Syria, Moḥammad quarreled with Ebn Kondāj and in 273/875-76 recognized the suzerainty of Ḵomārawayh as the latter started a counteroffensive to regain Syria. He sent his son Dīvdād to Ḵomārawayh as a hostage for his loyalty and repeatedly defeated Ebn Kondāj seizing all of Jazīra and Mosul. In 274/887, however, he broke with Ḵomārawayh causing havoc in northern Syria. The latter defeated him at Ṯanīa near Damascus and then, though generously releasing his son Dīvdād, drove him out of Syria as far as Mosul. Ebn Kondāj now allied himself with Ḵomārawayh and took the offensive against Moḥammad. The latter initially won a surprise victory near Mosul and pursued Ebn Kondāj to Raqqa. While he gained the backing of al-Mowaffaq, Ebn Kondāj in Syria was aided by Ḵomārawayh. After a defeat by Ebn Kondāj near Raqqa, Moḥammad fled first to Mosul and in Rabīʿ I, 276/September, 889, joined Mowaffaq in Baghdad and accompanied him on his campaign to Jabal, Karaj, and Isfahan, from which he returned to Baghdad in Ṣafar, 278/May, 891.

Ebn al-Aṯīr's report (VII, p. 436) that Moḥammad was appointed by Mowaffaq governor of Azerbaijan in 276/889 is almost certainly mistaken since he neither took up his position nor sent a deputy there at this time. It has been commonly accepted, however, by historians of Armenia who are inclined to date the coronation of Sempad (Sanbāṭ) I, Bagratid king of Armenia, in 891 (see Thopdschian, p. 166 n. 2). As governor of Azerbaijan Moḥammad claimed suzerainty over part of Armenia and sent Sempad a crown and presents in the name of the caliph. This event must evidently be dated not before 279/892. According to Ebn Ẓāfer (p. 34) Moḥammad was appointed governor of Azerbaijan by al-Moʿtamed in 279/892. He left Baghdad after marrying his daughter to Badr, the *ḡolām* of al-Moʿtażed, most likely after al-Moʿtażed's succession to the caliphate and his appointment of Badr as police chief in Rajab, 279/October, 892 (the daughter was transferred to Badr only in 280/893; Masʿūdī, *Morūj* VIII, p. 144). In Rabīʿ I, 380/May, 893, he took Marāḡa, overcoming fierce resistence by ʿAbd-Allāh b. Ḥasan, chief of the Hamdān in the province. He confiscated ʿAbd-Allāh's property and put him to death. Though he chose Marāḡa as his capital, he later resided mostly in Bardaʿa. After an invasion of Georgia and Albania by Sempad in 895, he occupied Naḵjavān (Nakhichevan) and Dabīl (Dvin) but suffered a defeat and made peace with the king. He began acting more and more independently toward the caliphal government. It was perhaps at this time that he assumed the traditional title of the kings of Osrūšana, Afšīn, which appears on a coin minted in Bardaʿa in 285/898. His assumption of the title may well be related to the overthrow of the last Afšīn of Osrūšana by the Samanids in 280/893. In 285/898 he submitted again to the caliph al-Moʿtażed, was formally invested by him with the rule of Azerbaijan and Armenia, and sent his son Abu'l-Mosāfer Fatḥ as a hostage to Baghdad. At the same time he resumed his offensive against Armenia, penetrating to Kars (Qārṣ) and capturing the wife of Sempad. He established his son Dīvdād in Dabīl and then invaded Vaspurakan, forcing its ruler, the Arcrunid Sargis Ašot, to submission. Next he occupied Tiflis. In 287/900 his loyalty to the caliph came again under doubt as his eunuch commander Waṣīf ostensibly revolted and invaded Ṯoḡūr. Informed that Waṣīf was in fact acting in concert with his master who was plotting to bring Dīār Możar under his sway, al-Moʿtażed was forced to lead a campaign against Waṣīf and captured him. Moḥammad carried out a further invasion of Vaspurakan and was preparing for a new compaign against Sempad when he died in Bardaʿa during an epidemic in Rabīʿ I, 288/March, 901 (Ebn Ḵallekān, Beirut, II, p. 250).

3. Dīvdād b. Moḥammad b. Abi'l-Sāj. He was put on the throne by the army after his father's death but was overthrown by his uncle Yūsof a few months later. Refusing his uncle's offer to stay with him he arrived in Baghdad in Ramażān, 288/October, 901. Nothing is known about his further life.

4. Abu'l-Qāsem Yūsof b. Abi'l-Sāj, born in 250/864. He is first mentioned in 271/885 as governor of Mecca, when he attacked and chained the official leader of the pilgrims, a *ḡolām* of the governor of Medina. He was himself seized by some soldiers aided by the pilgrims and carried off to Baghdad. In 280/893 he captured a group of Kharijites in the region of Mosul and sent them to Baghdad. In 282/895 he was sent from Baghdad to Ṣaymara to participate in a campaign. He used the occasion, however, to escape to his brother Moḥammad in Azerbaijan and on the way seized some money

belonging to the caliphal government. He seems to have stayed in Azerbaijan until, after Moḥammad's death, he seized the reign from his nephew. During his reign he moved the capital to Ardabīl and razed the walls of Marāġa. King Sempad sought to escape the Sajid overlordship by entering into immediate vassalage to the caliph al-Moktafī. As he refused a summons of Yūsof, the latter invaded Armenia. In 290/903 a settlement was reached as Sempad accepted a crown from Yūsof, thus acknowledging his overlordship. Yūsof had never gained recognition by al-Moktafī, and in 295/908 an army was sent from Baghdad against him. Only after al-Moqtader's succession to the caliphate was an agreement negotiated, and in 296/909 Yūsof was invested with the government of Azerbaijan and Armenia. The vizier Ebn al-Forāt was evidently instrumental in the settlement, and Yūsof considered him thereafter as his protector at the caliphal court and had him regularly named on his own coinage. The minor principalities of Transcaucasia were evidently also put under his overlordship. In 296/908 he brought Tiflis under his control, and about this time also came to Darband (Bāb), capital of the Hāšemī dynasty, and, on the instruction of Ebn al-Forāt, rebuilt the walls of the town (Helāl, pp. 217-18; Minorsky's dating of the visit [1958, p. 70] cannot be correct). Soon thereafter Yūsof resumed his war against King Sempad, who had been encouraged by the caliph to arm against him. He found an ally in Gagik, the prince of Vaspurakan. In lengthy campaigns he first captured and poisoned the king's son Musheł and later seized the king himself. After holding him a prisoner for a year, he tortured and beheaded him (about 301/914) in sight of the fortress of Erenjak, hoping to demoralize its garrison. The unprecedented brutality of Yūsof's treatment of the Armenians in this war is noted by Ebn Ḥawqal (p. 343) who mentions that the people of Baghdad refused to buy Armenian slaves knowing that they were *ahl ḏemma*. Yūsof initially also maintained a hostile attitude toward Sempad's son and successor Ašot II (Ašūd), but after Gagik refused to cooperate further with him and Ašot gained general backing in Armenia he recognized him (about 304/917). His attention was at this time turning to a new conflict with the caliph al-Moqtader. After the dismissal of his protector Ebn al-Forāt from the vizierate in 299/912, he had begun to withhold part of his annual tribute to the caliphate. In 303/915-16 he imprisoned an envoy of the caliph but later released him and sent him back with presents and money. When Ebn al-Forāt was reappointed vizier in 304/917, Yūsof seized Zanjān, Abhar, Qazvīn, and Ray from the Samanid governor Moḥammad b. ʿAlī Ṣoʿlūk, who had usurped the governorship, and claimed that the previous vizier, ʿAlī b. ʿĪsā, had invested him with the governorship. Most sources suggest that Yūsof's claim was entirely false and that he was hoping that Ebn al-Forāt would be able to protect him. According to ʿArīb (p. 67), however, ʿAlī b. ʿĪsā admitted that he had ordered Yūsof to fight Ṣoʿlūk with the caliph's approval, though without appointing him governor. Al-Moqtader was, in any case, thoroughly incensed and rejected all overtures from Yūsof. The latter defeated an army sent against him near Ray. In 305/919 Mo'nes, the ʿAbbasid commander-in-chief, marched against him, and he withdrew to Azerbaijan. Mo'nes pursued him and was defeated in a first battle. Yūsof generously did not press his advantage to capture him. About this time ʿAbd al-Malek b. Hāšem b. Sorāqa, the Hāšemī ruler of Darband, who had been overthrown by his nephew, sought refuge with Yūsof. The latter confirmed him in his governorship and gave him an army, which restored him to power. In Ṣafar, 307/July, 919, Mo'nes routed and captured Yūsof near Ardabīl together with his nephew, probably Abu'l-Mosāfer Fatḥ. He was carried to Baghdad and imprisoned by al-Moqtader for three years. In Moḥarram, 310/May, 922, he was released on the intercession of Mo'nes and invested with the governorship of Ray, Qazvīn, Abhar, Zanjān, and Azerbaijan. He first proceeded to Azerbaijan, which had remained under the control of his *ḡolām* Sobok. Toward the end of 311/March, 924, he defeated and killed Aḥmad b. ʿAlī, the brother of Ṣoʿlūk, who was in control of Jebāl, between Abhar and Zanjān and entered Ray. In 313/925 he left for Hamadān where he stayed five months and then returned to Ray and Azerbaijan. In 314/926 he was, against his objections, called to Iraq to take charge of the war with the Qarmaṭīs and came with his army to Wāseṭ. A year later he was heavily defeated by the Qarmaṭī leader Abū Ṭāher Jannābī near Kūfa on 9 Šawwāl 315/8 December 927. He was captured and, during an abortive attempt by caliphal troops to free him, killed by two brothers of Abū Ṭāher in Ḏu'l-qaʿda, 315/January, 928. His troops were integrated into the caliphal army and became known as the Sājīya.

5. Abu'l-Mosāfer Fatḥ b. Moḥammad b. Abi'l-Sāj. He was appointed governor of Azerbaijan by al-Moqtader in Ḏu'l-ḥejja, 315/February, 928, and was murdered by a *ḡolām* of his in Aradabīl in Šaʿbān, 517/September-October, 929. According to another account he was besieged in Marāġa by mutinous troops and killed by them. A son of his, Abu'l-Faraj, became a commander in the caliphal army and a companion of Amīr al-Omarā' Ebn Rā'eq.

Bibliography: Yaʿqūbī, *Ta'rīḵ* II, pp. 583, 608, 619. Ṭabarī. Masʿūdī, *Morūj* VII, pp. 395, 403; VII, pp. 144, 200, 275, 284-86. Idem, *Tanbīh*, pp. 82-83. Abu'l-Faraj Eṣfahānī, *Maqātel al-ṭālebīyīn*, ed. A. Ṣaqr, Cairo, 1368/1949, index s.v. Abu'l-Sāj. Idem, *Aḡānī*[1] XV, pp. 89, 94; XVI, pp. 360-61, 371. ʿArīb b. Saʿd Kāteb Qorṭobī, *Ṣelat ta'rīḵ al-Ṭabarī*, ed. M. J. de Goeje, Leiden, 1897. Ebn Meskawayh, *Tajāreb*. Helāl Ṣābe', *Ta'rīḵ al-wozarā'*, ed. H. Amedroz, Beirut, 1904. Hamaḏānī, *Takmelat ta'rīḵ al-Ṭabarī*, ed. A. Y. Kanʿān, Beirut, 1961. Anonymous, *al-ʿOyūn wa'l-ḥadā'eq* IV, ed. Omar Saïdi, Damascus, 1972-73. Ebn al-Aṯīr. Ebn al-ʿAdīm, *Zobdat al-ḥalab men ta'rīḵ Ḥalab*, ed. S. al-Dahhān, I, Damascus, 1951, pp. 74, 80-84. Ebn Ẓāfer, "al-Dowal al-monqaṭeʿa," in G. W. Freytag, *Locmani Fabulae*, Bonn, 1823, pp. 34-40. Armenian sources: Hovhannes Catholicos, *Histoire d'Arménie par le patriarche Jean VI*, tr. M. J. Saint-Martin, Paris, 1841, index s.v. Afschin and Youssouf. Thomas Ardzruni, *Histoire des Ardzrouni*, tr. M. Brosset, in *Collections d'historiens arméniens* I, St. Petersburg, 1874. Stepanos Asołik, *Des Stephanos von Taron armenische Geschichte*, tr. H. Gelzer and A. Burckhardt, Leipzig, 1907, pp. 118-23. Stepanos Orbelian, *Histoire de la Siounie*, tr. M. Brosset, I, St. Petersburg, 1864, pp. 108, 112-21. M. Defrémery, "Mémoire sur la famille des Sadjides," *JA*, 4th ser., 9, 1847, pp. 409-46, 10, 1848, pp. 396-436. H. Thopdschian, "Politische und Kirchengeschichte Armeniens unter Ašot I. und Smbat I.," *Mitteilungen des Seminars für Orientalische Sprachen, Westasiatische Abt.* 8, 1905, pp. 166-207. R. R. Vasmer, "O monetakh Sadzhidov," in *Izvestiya obshchestva obsledovaniya i izucheniya Azerbaĭdzhana* V, Baku, 1927. H. Bowen, *The Life and Times of ʿAlī ibn ʿĪsā*, Cambridge, 1928, index. V. Minorsky, *Studies in Caucasian History*, London, 1953, pp. 104, 111, 118-19. Idem, *A History of Sharvan and Darband*, Cambridge, 1958, pp. 19, 43, 58-60, 70, 152. W. Madelung in *Camb. Hist. Iran* IV, pp. 228-32, 244-45. A. Ter-Ghewonyan, *The Arab Emirates in Bagratid Armenia*, tr. N. G. Garsoïan, Lisbon, 1976, index.

(W. MADELUNG)

BANŪ SĀSĀN, a name frequently applied in medieval Islam to beggars, rogues, charlatans, and tricksters of all kinds, allegedly so called because they stemmed from a legendary Shaikh Sāsān. A story frequently found in the sources, from Ebn al-Moqaffaʿ (q.v.) onward, states that Sāsān was the son of the ancient Persian ruler Bahman b. Esfandīār, but, being displaced from the succession, took to a wandering life and gathered round him other vagabonds, thus forming the "sons of Sāsān." Another explanation says that the Persian nation as a whole took to begging and vagabondage after the Arab conquest of the 1st/7th century and excited pity by claiming to be descendants of the dispossessed Sasanian house, and the process whereby the name of a fallen dynasty is satirically or ironically applied to a subsequent group seems psychologically possible. Further etymologies have been sought in Sanskrit and in Persian itself (see Bosworth, I, pp. 22-24).

The Banū Sāsān, as depicted for us in such works of Arab *adab* literature as those of Jāḥeẓ, Ebrāhīm b. Moḥammad Bayhaqī, Abū Dolaf, and the *maqāmāt* of Badīʿ-al-Zamān Hamaḏānī and Ḥarīrī, must have ranged—whether in groups or as individuals—all over the Islamic lands and as far as the borders of India. Specifically in regard to the Iranian lands, the beggar leader Ḵāled b. Yazīd in Jāḥeẓ's *Ketāb al-boḵalāʾ* boasts that he has in the course of his life headed bands of robbers and desperadoes from the outlaws and bandits of Jebāl, of the Baṭṭ river region in Ḵūzestān, of the Kūfečīs (q.v.) of Kermān and Baluchistan, and the pirates of Qīqān of the Makrān coast. In almost all the literature relevant to the Banū Sāsān, the Kurds are singled out as the nation of predators and brigands par excellence, and Ḵāled b. Yazīd in his enumeration of the beggar leaders mentions Jaʿfar Kordī among various others with Persian names, such as Banjawayh, Ḥammawayh, Sahrām, Saʿdawayh, Mardawayh, etc. From Abū Dolaf's poem (see below), it emerges that the Kābolis (or perhaps in this context, the Indians in general) were especially famed as jugglers and conjurors (see Jāḥeẓ, *Boḵalāʾ*, ed. Ṭaha Ḥājerī, Cairo, 1958, pp. 46, 50, tr. Ch. Pellat, *Le livre des avares*, Paris, 1951, pp. 66, 71; Bosworth, I, pp. 34ff., 93-94, 171).

Regarding the ethnic composition of these beggars and rogues, doubtless representatives of all the Middle Eastern peoples were to be found within their ranks, while from the social aspect we can only surmise, in the absence of firm documentation, that the greater part of them may have been misfits in society or déracinés and were probably from the lowest strata of the population. It is clear that they should be differentiated from such groups in medieval Iranian society as the *ʿayyārs* (q.v.), who seem to have been primarily urban and rural vigilantes, at times paramilitary groups, and the *šoṭṭār* or urban mobsters and rowdies, and from such bodies in more recent Iranian society as the urban *lūṭīs* (q.v.)

The medieval Arabic literature, as well as giving us the names of beggar chiefs and their groups, also provides us with the texts of two lengthy poems written in the jargon or argot of the Banū Sāsān, i.e., the *qaṣīda sāsānīyas* of the traveler and littérateur Abū Dolaf Ḵazrajī (q.v.) (4th/10th century) and of the Iraqi poet Ṣafī-al-Dīn Ḥellī (8th/14th century). The first of these poems was actually written for the great vizier of the Buyids, the Ṣāḥeb Esmāʿīl b. ʿAbbād (q.v.) (Ṯaʿālebī, *Yatīmat al-dahr*, ed. Moḥammad Moḥyi'l-Dīn ʿAbd-al-Ḥamīd, Cairo, 1375-77/1956-58, III, pp. 356-57, cf. Bosworth, I, pp. 76ff.). In this jargon, the so-called *monākāt* or *monāḡāt Banī Sāsān*, while the general basis is clearly Arabic, many loan words appear, including some from Persian. Thus in Abū Dolaf's *qaṣīda*, we have *boštadārīyūn* "porters," from Persian *pošt-dārī* "one who carries something on his back" (v. 90; Bosworth, II, p. 259); *ḵ*ᵛ*ošbūyī* "drugged stew," from Persian *ḵ*ᵛ*oš-būy* "fragrant, having a savory smell" (v. 116; Bosworth, II, pp. 268-69); and *kors* "fasting, hunger," from Persian *gors, gorosnagī* "hunger" (vv. 79, 116; Bosworth, II, p. 253). In that of Ṣafī-al-Dīn—which was written for one of the Turkmen Artoqid rulers of Dīārbakr, at whose court Persian cultural influence was strong—we find rather more Persian elements, such as *boštadārī*, here "slave boy," also in *boštakānī ḵorda* "peddler of trashy, insignificant goods," with the second element also Persian (vv. 7, 46; Bosworth, II, pp. 305, 332); *hankām* "assembly, circle" and verb *hankama* "to gather round," from Persian *hangām(a)* "assembly, crowd of traders, players, etc.," → "noise, commotion"; *jarraḵa* "to dance," perhaps from Persian *čarḵ* "wheel" → "a turning circle of dancers" (v. 54; Bosworth, II, p. 336); and *ḵandaja* "to laugh," from Persian *ḵandagī* "laughter" (v. 55; Bosworth, II, p. 337).

One should finally note traces of the persistence of the Banū Sāsān and their jargon on the far eastern fringes of the Iranian world as attested in an anonymous *Ketāb-e sāsīān-e bā-kamāl* (Book of the most consummate beggars), possibly dating from the 8th/14th century and preserved at Tashkent, which contains a jargon vocabulary with Persian equivalents (the form *sāsī* for *sāsānī* is not infrequent in Persian contexts; cf. Dehḵodā, s.v.). This has been thoroughly investigated by A. L. Troitskaya in her "Abdoltili. Argo tsekha artistov i muzikantov Sredneĭ Azii," *Sovetskoe vostokovedenie* 5, 1948, pp. 251-74, where she notes the persistence of several of these jargon terms (some in turn traceable back to Abū Dolaf's time) up to the 14th/20th century among the guilds (*mehterlik*) of artists and musicians in what is now Soviet Uzbekistan (cf. Bosworth, I, pp. 171-76).

See also BEGGING i.

Bibliography: See in general C. E. Bosworth, *The Mediaeval Islamic Underworld. The Banū Sāsān In Arabic Society and Literature*, 2 vols., Leiden, 1976, to be supplemented by idem, "Jewish Elements in the Banū Sāsān," *Bibliotheca Orientalis* 33/5-6, September-November, 1976, pp. 289-94.

(C. E. BOSWORTH)

BAQĀ' WA FANĀ', Sufi term signifying "subsistence and passing away." The Sufi teaching of passing away from worldly reality and being made subsistent in divine reality describes the apex of mystic experience and union with God. As a correlative pair of notions, in which *fanā'* logically precedes *baqā'*, it is applied to two levels of meaning, the passing away of human consciousness in the divine and the obliteration of imperfect qualities of the soul by substitution of new, divinely bestowed attributes. Of the two terms, *fanā'* is the more significant concept in Sufi writings and occasionally implies connotations expressed by its counterpart. Though possibly similar in its meaning to the Buddhist *nirvāṇa*, *fanā'* does not denote the extinction of individual life. The link of *baqā' wa fanā'* with ideas of *ekstasis* prevalent in Hellenistic culture appears to be tenuous as well.

In his ascetic struggle, the mystic of Iranian Sufism strives to abandon this world (*donyā*) before it leaves him and to slay his carnal soul (*nafs*) before it breathes its last, because he experiences physical existence—including the body, the senses, and the lower self—as existence alienated from God. In mystic vision on the other hand, he professes and actually realizes oneness of God (*tawḥīd*), the eternal and true reality, one without partners, beside whom the mystic's temporal existence has no claim to reality and his self no right to selfhood. In realizing *tawḥīd*, the mystic has to pass away from any trace of individual self-consciousness so that his self is blotted out in actual non-existence and God alone exists and in truth subsists (*al-fanā' fi'l-tawḥīd*). The teaching of Abu'l-Ḥasan Ḵaraqānī (d. 425/1033; q.v.), "One is a Sufi who is not. The Sufi is a day that has no need of sun, a night that needs neither moon nor star, and a non-existence that needs no existence" (Jāmī, *Nafaḥāt*, p. 298) expands Jonayd's insight that the mystic's existence is his greatest sin ('Aṭṭār, II, p. 7; Ebn Ḵallekān, I, p. 374), and Abū Bakr Wāseṭī's statement that non-existence is the mystic's *qebla* while existence his falling into *kofr* ('Aṭṭār, II, p. 273).

This non-existence, however, equals the state of original existence humanity possessed in the presence of God at the primordial covenant of *alast* prior to creation (Koran 7:172). Originally conceived by Abu'l-Fayż Ḏu'l-Nūn (d. 245/860), developed by Sahl b. 'Abd-Allāh Tostarī (d. 283/896), spread in Sufi circles by Abu'l-Qāsem Jonayd (d. 298/910), publicly proclaimed by Ḥosayn b. Manṣūr Ḥallāj (d. 309/922), and enigmatically articulated by Abū Bakr Šeblī (d. 334/945), this original standing of man (*waqfa*) before God at the primordial covenant, when man received his own intellect in and through his profession of God's oneness, is reactualized by the Sufi in his dying to worldly existence and his returning to his original, primal state in the presence of God (Böwering, pp. 153-57, 185-207). Returning to his non-existence, which actually is his only true existence, the mystic "is as he was, when he was before he was" (Ḏu'l-Nūn, quoted by Kalābāḏī, p. 105) or has reached his goal of "returning to the beginning" (Jonayd, quoted by Anṣārī, p. 168), so to speak "being the way he was at the moment he was not as yet" (Šeblī, quoted by 'Aṭṭār, II, p. 175).

The fundamental experience of passing away from actual existence and subsisting in primordial existence was couched in the language of *fanā'* and *baqā'* by the Sufi Abū Sa'īd Ḵarrāz (d. 286/899; *ennaho awwal man takallama fī 'elm al-fanā' wa'l-baqā'*, Solamī, p. 228; cf. Hojvīrī, p. 180) and adopted in the short epistle, *Ketāb al-fanā'*, attributed to Jonayd (Abdel-Kader, p. 31-39; for questions of authenticity cf. Reinert, p. 132). There is no proof for the views advanced by Zaehner that the Sufi teaching of *fanā'* derives from Hindu philosophy or, even more temerariously, adopts the Upanishadic *tat tvam asi* (*Hindu and Muslim Mysticism*, London, 1960, pp. 94-97, and *Indo-Iranian Journal* 1, 1957, pp. 286-301). It is an erroneous claim as well that Bāyazīd Besṭāmī (q.v.) was the first to have introduced the term *fanā'* into Sufism, as assumed by Hartmann (p. 64) and apparently also Ritter (1954, p. 231). The connection of the teaching of *fanā'* and *baqā'* in Sufi *tafsīr* literature with the sole Koranic passage (55:26-27) citing the roots of both terms together ("All that dwells upon the earth is perishing [*fānen*], yet still abides [*yabqā*] the Face of thy Lord, majestic, splendid") is a reading of Sufi views into Koranic language rather than an organic terminological development out of Koranic roots.

The transition from existence to non-existence or primordial existence is not a total annihilation, since the Sufi's self is not reduced to pure nothingness. Rather, it is purification of the Sufi's self which is drawn to higher forms of being and ultimately absorbed in God. Ebn al-'Arabī defined the matter in categorical terms: "There is no passing away (*fanāʾ*) except from such and such as there also is no subsisting (*baqāʾ*) except through such and such and with this and that. The from-away belongs necessarily to *fanāʾ* (*fa-ʿan le'l-fanāʾ lā bodd menh*). According to the Sufis, however, passing away on the mystic path means always passing away from the lower (state by being absorbed) in the higher" (II, p. 512). At an advanced stage of perfection the mystic puts on divine attributes, in Abu'l-Ḥosayn Nūrī's words, "being fashioned in the attributes of God" (*al-takalloq be-aklāq Allāh*, ʿAṭṭār, II, pp. 54-55), and in Najm-al-Dīn Kobrā's view, becoming the subject of divine attributes and capable of "creating, bringing forth, giving life, causing death, having mercy, punishing and other things that belong to the divine attributes of bounty and justice" (*Fawāʾeḥ*, ed. Meier, p. 29). In its perfect form, the experience of *fanāʾ* and *baqāʾ* is understood in Sufism as *al-fanāʾ ʿan al-nafs* and *al-baqāʾ be'llāh*, and ultimately as *al-fanāʾ fe'llāh*, but not as *al-fanāʾ ʿan Allāh*.

The crucial point of passing away is reached when the Sufi's own self is stripped off, like a snake shedding its skin, and the mystic's own self-identity is obliterated. In shedding the self of ordinary self-perception—the self that is identifiable by a person's name—the mystic reaches his true self that is ultimately and profoundly one with God. This is illustrated by Šeblī's saying, "It has been my life-long desire to be alone with God, without that Šeblī was there at this being alone," and Šehāb-al-Dīn Yaḥyā Sohravardī's description of the Sufi's ascent from the Muslim creed, "no god save God," through the stages of "no he save He," "no thou save Thou," and "no I save I" to the stage where there is but the One (*Resāla-ye safīr-e sīmorḡ*, in Spies and Khatak, pp. 27-29).

The mystic's true self is discovered in the depth of his personality as the divine secret of God's own I-ness taking the place of the mystic's self and overcoming the duality of subject and object in their identity. Realizing this secret, the *Bīsar-nāma* of pseudo-ʿAṭṭār exclaims, "I am God, I am God, am God" (*man kodā-yam, man kodā-yam, man kodā*), and Nasīmī's *Dīvān* takes up a theme of Rūmī's *Maṯnawī* (bk. 5, vv. 2022-23), "I beheld that I am God from top to toe" (*sar tā ba-qadam wojūd-e kᵛod ḥaq dīdam*; cf. Ritter, 1955, p. 590). Rūmī catches this secret in the image of a ruby permeated by the rays of the sun and transformed as if into sunlight. As long as the ruby is ruby, there are as yet two, ruby and sunlight, but when the penetration of sunlight is complete there is only one brilliance (bk. 5, vv. 2025-35). The old "I" (*ana*) has become the "no" (*lā*) that is denied by the new "I": *man man nī-am* ("I am not I") as Rūmī says (bk. 1, vv. 3124-26).

As the mystic loses the identity with his own self, he experiences identity with God, as illustrated by Besṭāmī's famous utterance, "I shed my own self as a snake shed its skin; then I beheld my own essence (*ḏāt*), and lo, I was He (*ana howa*)" (Sahlajī, pp. 77, 118), and in Abū Saʿīd b. Abi'l-Kayr's exclamation: "When you see me you see Him, and when you see Him you see me" (Ebn Monawwar, p. 259). The certainty that God has become the mystic's I-ness, being the "this-ness" (*annīa*) not the "where-ness" (*aynīya*) of his individual self—a distinction recorded in Bīrūnī's *Taḥqīq mā le'l-Hend* (p. 66, quoted by Gramlich, p. 328)—induces the mystic to pronounce theopathic utterances (*šaṭaḥāt*), such as Besṭāmī's *sobḥānī*, Ḥallāj's *ana'l-Ḥaqq* and others (cf. e.g., Rūzbehān Baqlī, *Šarḥ-e šaṭḥīyāt*). These ecstatic expressions of Sufi experiences of *fanāʾ* and *baqāʾ* are rooted in the old Sufi conviction that only God can truly say "I" (Sarrāj, p. 32) and inspired by typical Sufi interpretations of Koranic verses, e.g., God's word to Moses, "I am your Lord" (*ennī ana rabboka*; 20:12), and Pharaoh's claim, "I am your Lord Most High" (*ana rabbokom al-aʿlā*; 79:24) (see Nwyia, pp. 178-83, and Böwering, pp. 190-97).

The consciousness of absorption in God induced some Iranian mystics to lay claim to divine self-consciousness. Asked about the contradiction of his description of the true mystic as one able to lift the earth and the seven heavens with a single eyelash, while he had defined him earlier as unable to carry the weight of a fly, Šeblī answered, " at that time I was I, now I am He" (*āngāh mā mā būdīm aknūn mā ūʾst*; cf. ʿAṭṭār, II, p. 176). According to ʿAṭṭār's account, Karaqānī believed that he could fill the seven heavens and the earth by himself, span the distance between the earth and the divine throne with one giant step, cause a deluge with one drop of his heart's blood, move heaven and earth, and engulf all of creation with his knowledge (II, pp. 212-15). He even is said to have claimed, "I am the Chosen of the age, I am God of the age" (*moṣṭafā-ye waqt-am wa kodā-ye waqt-am*; ibid., II, p. 211). Claims ascribed to Besṭāmī, e.g., "I am I; there is no god save I; so worship me" (Sahlajī, p. 122), and, "Moses desired to see God. I do not desire to see God—He desires to see me" (Ebn al-Jawzī, p. 333), even more vividly depict the mixing of human and divine consciousness in mystic speech uttered in the experience of *fanāʾ* and *baqāʾ*. The speaker of the utterance may be either God or the mystic, God speaking with the tongue of the mystic, or the mystic speaking out of the experience of divine consciousness within himself.

Bibliography: The chapters on *fanāʾ* and *baqāʾ* in the Sufi handbooks and A. H. Abdel-Kader, *The Life, Personality and Writings of Al-Junayd*, London, 1962. Farīd-al-Dīn ʿAṭṭār, *Taḏkerat al-awlīāʾ*, ed. R. A. Nicholson, 2 vols., London, 1905-07. Kᵛāja ʿAbd-Allāh Anṣārī, *Ṭabaqāt al-ṣūfīya*, ed. ʿA. Ḥabībī, Kabul, 1340 Š./1961. Abū Rayḥān Bīrūnī, *Taḥqīq mā le'l-Hend*, Hyderabad, 1377/1958. G. Böwering, *The Mystical Vision of Existence in Classical Islam*, Berlin, 1980. Ebn al-ʿArabī, *al-Fotūḥāt al-makkīya*, 4 vols., Cairo, 1329/1911. Ebn al-Jawzī, *Talbīs Eblīs*, Cairo, n.d. Ebn Kallekān, *Wafayāt al-aʿyān*, ed. E. ʿAbbās, Beirut, n.d. Moḥammad b. Monawwar, *Asrār al-tawḥīd*, ed. Ḏ. Ṣafā, Tehran, 1332 Š./1953. R. Gramlich, *Die schiitischen Derwischorden Persiens. Zweiter Teil: Glaube und Lehre*, Wiesbaden, 1976, esp. pp. 313-35 (a thorough treatment of the topic). R. Hartmann, "Zur Frage nach der Herkunft und den Anfängen des Sufitums," *Der Islam* 6, 1916, pp. 31-70. ʿAlī b. ʿOṯmān Hojvīrī, *Kašf al-maḥjūb*, ed. V. Žukowsky, repr. Tehran, 1336 Š./1957. Abū Bakr Kalābāḏī, *Ketāb al-taʿarrof*, ed. A. J. Arberry, Cairo, 1933. F. Meier, *Die Fawāʾiḥ al-ǧamāl wa-fawātiḥ al-ǧalāl des Naǧm ad-dīn al-Kubrā*, Wiesbaden, 1957. R. A. Nicholson, *The Mystics of Islam*, London, 1914. P. Nwyia, *Exégèse coranique et langage mystique*, Beirut, 1970. B. Reinert, *Die Lehre vom* tawakkul *in der klassischen Sūfik*, Berlin, 1968. H. Ritter, "Die Aussprüche des Bāyezīd Bisṭāmī," *Westöstliche Abhandlungen*, ed. F. Meier, Wiesbaden, 1954, pp. 231-43. Idem, *Des Meer der Seele*, Leiden, 1955. Jalāl-al-Dīn Rūmī, *Maṯnawī-e maʿnawī*, ed. R. A. Nicholson, 8 vols., London, 1925-40. Rūzbehān Baqlī, *Šarḥ-e šaṭḥīyāt*, ed. H. Corbin, Tehran, 1344 Š./1965. Sahlajī, *al-Nūr men kalemāt Abī Ṭayfūr*, in *Šaṭaḥāt al-ṣūfīya*, ed. ʿA. Badawī, Cairo, 1949. Abū Naṣr Sarrāj, ed. R. A. Nicholson, *The Kitāb al-lumaʿ fiʾl-taṣawwuf*, London, 1914. Abū ʿAbd-al-Raḥmān Solamī, *Ṭabaqāt al-ṣūfīya*, ed. N. Šorayba, Cairo, 1372/1952. O. Spies and S. K. Khatak, *Three Treatises on Mysticism*, Stuttgart, 1935. R. C. Zaehner, "Abū Yazīd of Bisṭām—a Turning Point in Islamic Mysticism," *IIJ* 1, 1957, pp. 286-301. Idem, *Hindu and Muslim Mysticism*, London, 1960.

(G. BÖWERING)

BĀQELĀ (also pronounced *bāqālā* or *bāqālī*; in Arabic texts, *bāqellā*[ʾ], broad beans, i.e., the grains of *Vicia faba* L. Older Iranian dialectal names recorded by Abū Bakr b. ʿAlī Kāsānī in his Persian version of Bīrūnī's *Ṣaydana* (1st half of the 8th/15th century), I, p. 116: Sajzī (= Sīstanī) *kālūsak* and Bosti *kūsak*.

One of the oldest crops in the Old World, *bāqelā* seems to have always been grown in the Near and Middle East wherever climatic conditions are favorable to its cultivation. In Iran, it is grown rather extensively in the Caspian provinces (especially in Gīlān and Māzandarān) and, to a lesser extent, in the south and southwest. Qāsem Abūnaṣrī Heravī, *Eršād*, pp. 91-92, mentions the cultivation of two varieties of it (namely, *rasmī* "standard" and *mīrzāʾī* also called *baḡdādī* "from Baghdad" in the Herat area in 921/1515-16. Nowadays two main indigenous varieties are grown in Iran: the common one (sometimes referred to as *māzandarānī* "native of Māzandarān"), in varying sizes according to cultivars, and the local variety called *pāča bāqlā* in Gīlān, with slender seedpods looking like French beans (*lūbīā*) and containing small tender grains, which are never eaten raw or cooked by themselves, but as the main ingredient of the popular Gīlāni dish *bāqlā-qātoq* (see below).

Eating fresh raw *māzandarānī* broad beans is common in Gīlān and Māzandarān, either alone or (as in Gīlān) with cooled *kata* (undrained boiled rice), salted fish eggs, etc.; but selling and enjoying (especially by people of the lower classes) of hot cooked broad beans (*bāqelā-garmak*) sprinkled with salt and pow-

dered Persian marjoram (*golpar*) are not an uncommon street scene in cold weather almost everywhere in Iran. Broad beans, either fresh or (when out of season) dried, form the specific ingredient of a number of dishes: *bāqelā-polow* (pilaw cooked with green beans and dill and customarily eaten with meat or chicken, *ḵ'oreš-e bāqelā* (a kind of stew with *bāqelā*, meat, dill, and, occasionally, scrambled eggs), *kūfta bāqelā* (ground-meat balls with green *bāqelā*), *dampoḵtak* or *damī* (*kata*, yellow dried *bāqelā*, fried onion, turmeric), the Gīlāni dish *bāqlā-qātoq* (*pāča bāqlā* cooked with dill, garlic, and turmeric, into which eggs are emptied at the end), etc. After the harvest *bāqelā* pods and plants are used as cattle fodder.

The popularity of *bāqelā* in Iran is only marred by the eventuality of favism, many severe and even fatal cases of which are annually reported from Gīlān and Māzandarān in some predisposed individuals who have ingested fresh raw Māzandarānī broad beans (the variety *pāča bāqlā* reportedly does not cause favism) and who even have just inhaled the pollen from *bāqelā* flowers in or near *bāqelā* fields (for statistics on favism in Iran, see Jalāl Jamālīān, *Fāvīsm o rābeṭa-ye ān bā bāqelā*, Shiraz, 1355 Š./1976-77). Although classical authors of Arabic materia medica in the Islamic era (see bibliography) have noted some harmful side effects of ingesting raw fresh *bāqelā* (e.g., it produces a lot of winds, i.e. flatulence, noxious thick "humors," flabby flesh, debilitates the mind, causes headache, vertigo, sadness, and depression, prevents one from having "divinatory dreams"), Abūnaṣrī Heravī seems to be the first Islamic author to refer to this mysterious favism when he says (ibid.): "If someone goes into a place where broad beans are in bloom, he runs the risk of falling sick, because blooming broad beans, infectious as they are, will affect [him] deeply."

The numerous medicinal virtues and uses indicated for *bāqelā* (also called *fūl* in Arabic) by "laic" physicians and pharmacologists of the Islamic era (as found, e.g., in Ebn al-Bayṭār's *Jāmeʿ* I, pp. 76-78, and Ebn Sīnā's *Qānūn* II [Persian tr.], pp. 101-02) are derived mainly from Dioscorides and Galen (an exhaustive inventory in Persian is found in M.-Ḥ. Aqīlī Ḵorāsānī, *Maḵzan al-adwīa*, compiled in 1183/1769-70, p. 106); but the earliest genuinely Islamic references to the virtues of broad beans are to be found in religious (Shiʿite) sources, namely those references transmitted by Aḥmad b. Moḥammad Barqī Qomī (d. 274/887?), *Ketāb al-maḥāsen*, p. 506, from Imam Jaʿfar al-Ṣādeq (d. 148/765) as having said: "Broad beans increase the marrow in shinbones, and the brain; they produce fresh blood and, if eaten with their husks, they 'tan' the stomach."

Bibliography: Qāsem b. Yūsof Abūnaṣrī Heravī, *Eršād al-zerāʿa*, ed. M. Mošīrī, Tehran, 1346 Š./1967. Moḥammad-Ḥosayn ʿAqīlī Ḵorāsānī, *Maḵzan al-adwīa*, offset reprint, Tehran, 1349 Š./1970?, from the lithographed ed., Tehran, 1276/1859-60. Abū Jaʿfar Aḥmad b. Moḥammad Barqī Qomī, *Ketāb al-maḥāsen*, ed. Jalāl-al-Dīn Ḥosaynī Ormavī, 2nd ed.,

Qom, 1331 Š./1952? Ebn al-Bayṭār, *al-Jāmeʿ le-mofradāt al-adwīa wa'l-aḡdīa*, 4 vols., Bulaq, 1291/1874. Ebn Sīnā, *Qānūn dar ṭebb*, Persian tr. ʿAbd-al-Raḥmān Šarafkandī, Tehran, bk. 2, 1362 Š./1983. Abū Bakr b. ʿAlī Kāsānī, *Ṣaydana*, Persian version (8th/15th century) originally based on Abū Rayḥān Bīrūnī's *Ketāb al-Ṣaydana* in Arabic, ed. M. Sotūda and Ī. Afšār. 2 vols., Tehran, 1979.

(H. AʿLAM)

AL-**BĀQER, ABŪ JAʿFAR MOḤAMMAD** b. ʿAlī b. Ḥosayn b. ʿAlī b. Abī Ṭāleb, the fifth imam of the Twelver Shiʿites. His mother was Omm ʿAbd-Allāh Fāṭema, Ḥasan b. ʿAlī's daughter, who is described as a saintly woman. His honorary name al-Bāqer is commonly held to refer to his "splitting open knowledge (*bāqer al-ʿelm*)," signifying his erudition in the religious sciences. It was said that the Prophet Moḥammad named him so when he predicted the birth of his great-great-grandson and charged the long-lived companion Jāber Anṣārī (d. 73/692) with conveying his salutations to him. According to most Shiʿite sources, he was born in Medina in 57/677 and died there in 114/732 at the age of 57. The preference for these dates seems to rest partly on the parallelism of 57. According to another Shiʿite report, he predicted correctly his death at 58 years, just as his ancestors ʿAlī, Ḥosayn, and ʿAlī b. Ḥosayn had all been killed, or died, at 58. According to Wāqedī, he died in 117/735 and, according to Ḵalīfa b. Ḵayyāṭ, in 118/736 (*Ta'rīḵ Ḵalīfa b. al-Ḵayyāṭ*, ed. A. Ḍ. ʿOmarī, Beirut, 1397/1977, p. 349). These dates seem more likely since the reports about the rising of his brother Zayd in 120-22/738-40 suggest that he had died only recently so that the question of the succession was still open among his Kufan followers. The death date mentioned by Masʿūdī (*Morūj* VI, p. 17), 125-26/743-44, is definitely too late. Equally unacceptable is the birth date 44/664 implied by Wāqedī, since his father is known to have been 23 years old at the battle of Karbalā' in 61/680. Other dates given for al-Bāqer's birth are 54/676 and 59/678-79. Most of his life he stayed in Medina. As an infant he was present at the battle of Karbalā'. According to Madā'enī (*Aḡānī* I, p. 13), his father sent him and his brother ʿAbd-Allāh together with the wife and family of Marwān b. Ḥakam to Ṭā'ef just before the siege of Medina under Yazīd in 63/683. This was done for the safety of his sons, who were still minor children, and of Marwān's wife as is evident from the parallel report of Abū Meḵnaf (Ṭabarī, II, pp. 410, 420) where, however, only ʿAbd-Allāh, without al-Bāqer, is mentioned. According to Shiʿite reports, al-Bāqer was briefly summoned by the caliph Hešām (105-25/724-43) to Damascus where he confounded Christians in debate. He attended the funeral of the Shiʿite poet Koṯayyer ʿAzza in Medina in 105/723 and rewarded Komayt, another Shiʿite poet, when the latter recited a poem before him, and he gave him permission to eulogize the Omayyads. The reports in some late Sunni sources that he died at Ḥomayma, the seat of the ʿAbbasids in Palestine, probably rest on a confusion with the ʿAbbasid Moḥammad b. ʿAlī and are unreliable. He was buried in Medina in the cemetery of Baqīʿ al-Ḡarqad.

Sunni and Shiʿite sources agree in describing him as an eminent religious scholar. They sharply contrast, however, in their reports about his scholarly activity and views. In the Sunni sources he appears as a member of the conservative orthodox aristocracy of Medina transmitting mostly from, and to, well-known Sunni authorities. He is quoted as declaring his loyalty to Abū Bakr and ʿOmar, calling them imams of right guidance and dissociating himself from their enemies. He called Abū Bakr the Truthful (*ṣeddīq*) and, when questioned about it, jumped up to repeat it three times adding that whoever did not call him so, his word would not be accepted by God on earth and in the hereafter. He reported that ʿAlī had followed the practice of Abū Bakr and ʿOmar with regard to the share of the Prophet and his relatives in the booty explaining that ʿAlī did not wish to be charged with contravening their practice. He cursed Moḵtār, the avenger of Ḥosayn, as a liar and declared his dissociation from the extremist Shiʿites Moḡīra b. Saʿd and Bayān. He denied that he or anyone of the family of the Prophet had ever upheld the doctrine of *rajʿa* (q.v.) or considered any offense as equivalent to polytheism. He affirmed that his father and he prayed behind "them" (the representatives of the Omayyad caliphate) "without practicing religious dissimulation (*fī ḡayr taqīya*)" (Ebn Saʿd, V, p. 158). He denied being the Mahdi and affirmed that the Mahdi would be of ʿAbd Šams adding that in his view he was none other than the later caliph ʿOmar II (Ebn Saʿd, V, p. 245). When later the Khorasanian leaders Qaḥṭaba and Solaymān b. Kaṯīr asked him about the identity of the rightful imam, he referred them to the ʿAbbasid Moḥammad b. ʿAlī in Syria.

Ṭabarī quotes Bāqer in his history frequently about details of the life of Moḥammad and ʿAlī and cites a lengthy report of his about the events leading up to the death of Ḥosayn at Karbalā'. He is invariably considered a trustworthy transmitter by the Sunni *ḥadīṯ* experts. Nasā'ī mentions him as one of the early legal scholars (*foqahā'*) of Medina. Abū Dāwūd included a *ḥadīṯ* transmitted by him in his *Sonan*. Numerous edifying sayings of his were narrated in Sufi circles.

In Shiʿite tradition al-Bāqer appears as the inaugurator of the religious and legal teaching that was further elaborated by his son Jaʿfar al-Ṣādeq and formed the basis of Imami Shiʿism. Here he stood within the tradition of the radical wing of the Shiʿites, repudiating the caliphate of Abū Bakr, ʿOmar, and ʿOṯmān and endowing the ʿAlid imams with supernatural qualities and knowledge. From the Kaysānīya, the main representatives of radical Shiʿism in his time, he seems to have adopted doctrines like *badā'* (q.v.) and *rajʿa*, the return of some of the dead before the resurrection for retaliation. He shunned, however, revolutionary activity and espoused the principle of *taqīya*, precautionary dissimulation. He is quoted as stating: "*Taqīya* is part of my religion and the religion of my fathers. Whoever has no *taqīya* has no faith." The systematic practice of *taqīya* no doubt explains the contrast between the Sunni and Shiʿite reports about his teaching. Neither of the two aspects presented by them should be considered as basically fictitious.

Al-Bāqer's views on legal and ritual questions are frequently quoted in Imami and Zaydī works. It is clear that some of the basic characteristics and specific rules of Twelver Shiʿite law, like the permission for the temporary marriage (*motʿa*) and the prohibition of the ritual wiping of the shoes (*masḥ ʿala'l-koffayn*), go back to him. A commentary on the Koran attributed to al-Bāqer was transmitted by his disciple Abu'l-Jārūd Zīād b. Monder and is quoted frequently in the *Tafsīr* of ʿAlī b. Ebrāhīm Qomī. It reflects a strictly predestinarian theology (see W. Madelung, "The Shiite and Khārijite Contribution to pre-Ashʿarite *Kalām*," in P. Morewedge, ed., *Islamic Philosophical Theology*, Albany, 1979, pp. 136-37 n. 51). Al-Bāqer appears often as the author of apocalyptic prophecies, transmitted from him mostly by the Shiʿite traditionist Jāber Joʿfī. In spite of their Shiʿite character, such prophecies were taken over and transmitted by Sunni traditionists. Although some elements of this material may go back to al-Bāqer, most of it consists of later elaborations posterior even to Jāber (see Madelung, "The Sufyānī between Tradition and History," *Stud. Isl.* 63, 1986, esp. pp. 10-11, 34-35).

The Shiʿite biographical sources narrate numerous stories of a legendary character about al-Bāqer's debates with religious leaders and scholars like Ṭāwūs, Qatāda b. Deʿāma, Moḥammad b. Monkader, Abū Ḥanīfa, ʿAmr b. ʿObayd, Nāfeʿ b. Azraq and his son ʿAbd-Allāh b. Nāfeʿ, whom he stunned by his religious learning. They ascribe many miracles to him, like his conversing with ring-turtledoves and a wolf, his answering questions of jinnis on religious law and his being served by a jinni, his being visited by Keżr and the prophet Elias, his restoring youth to the aged Ḥabbāba Wālebīya and giving temporary eyesight to the blind Abu'l-Baṣīr, and his causing an earthquake by lightly moving a thread brought by the angel Gabriel from heaven. According to some anachronistic stories he died poisoned, either involuntarily by the caliph ʿAbd-al-Malek (d. 86/705) with a poisoned saddle during a quarrel between al-Bāqer and Zayd b. Ḥasan about the inheritence of the Prophet or by the caliph Ebrāhīm b. Walīd (ruling in 127/745).

Bibliography: Ebn Saʿd, V. pp. 235-38. Balādorī, *Ansāb al-ašrāb* III, ed. ʿAbd-al-ʿAzīz Dūrī, Beirut, 1398/1978, p. 116. Yaʿqūbī, *Ta'rīk*, pp. 365-66, 384-85. Anonymous, *Akbār al-dawla al-ʿabbāsīya*, ed. ʿAbd-al-ʿAzīz Dūrī and A. Moṭallebī, Beirut, 1971, pp. 132, 169, 184-85, 204-05. Nawbaktī, *Feraq al-šīʿa*, ed. H. Ritter, Istanbul, 1931, pp. 52-55 and index. Ṭabarī, index s.v. Moḥammad b. ʿAlī b. al-Ḥosayn. Abū Jaʿfar Moḥammad Kolaynī, *al-Oṣūl men al-kāfī*, ed. ʿAlī-Akbar Ḡaffārī, Tehran, 1388/1968-69, I, pp. 303-04, 469-72: *Aḡānī*[1] I, p. 13; VIII, p. 43; XV, pp. 123, 126; XVI, p. 88; XX, p. 147. Abū ʿAbd-Allāh Moḥammad Mofīd, *al-Eršād*, ed. Kāẓem Mūsawī Mīāmavī, Tehran, 1377/1957-58, pp. 245-54, tr. I. K. A. Howard, London, 1981, pp. 393-407. Abū Noʿaym Eṣfahānī, *Ḥelyat al-awlīā'*, Cairo, 1932-38, III, pp. 180-92. Abū ʿAlī Fażl b. Ḥasan Ṭabresī, *Eʿlām al-warā be-aʿlam al-hodā*, ed. ʿAlī Akbar Ḡaffārī, Beirut, 1399/1979, pp. 259-65. Abu'l-Faraj b. al-Jawzī, *Ṣefat al-ṣafwa*, Hyderabad, 1389/1969, II, pp. 60-63. Ebn Kallekān (Beirut), IV, p. 174. Erbelī, *Kašf al-ḡomma fī maʿrefat al-a'emma*, Qom, 1381/1961, II, pp. 329-66. Abū ʿAbd-Allāh Moḥammad Dahabī, *Sīar aʿlām al-nobalā'* IV, ed. Ma'mūn Ṣāgerjī, Beirut, 1401/1981, pp. 401-09. Ṣalāh-al-Dīn Kalīl Ṣafadī, *al-Wāfī be'l-wafayāt* IV, ed. S. Dedering, Wiesbaden, 1394/1974, pp. 102-03. Ebn Ḥajar ʿAsqalānī, *Tahdīb al-tahdīb*, Hyderabad, 1325-27/1907-09, IX, pp. 350-52. Moḥammad-Bāqer Majlesī, *Beḥār al-anwār*, Tehran, 1376-1405/1956-85, XCVI, pp. 212-367. *Aʿyān al-šīʿa* IV/2, pp. 3-28. D. M. Donaldson, *The Shiite Religion*, London, 1933, pp. 112-19. M. G. S. Hodgson, "How Did the Early Shiʿa Become Sectarian?" *JAOS* 75, 1955, pp. 10-13. S. H. M. Jafri, *Origins and Development of Shīʿa Islam*, London, 1979, index s.v. Muḥammad al-Bāqir.

(W. MADELUNG)

BĀQER KHAN SĀLĀR-E MELLĪ, one of the popular heroes of the Constitutional Revolution during the defense of Tabrīz in the period of the Lesser Autocracy (*estebdād-e ṣaḡīr*, Jomādā I, 1326–Rabīʿ II, 1327/June, 1908–July, 1909). Son of Ḥājī Reżā, he was born in Tabrīz in the 1870s and was a bricklayer by profession before emerging as the chief *lūṭī* of the Kīābān quarter, one of the largest in Tabrīz, located in the extreme east of the city and home of some middle rank pro-Constitution *ʿolamā'*. Being himself from an orthodox (*motašarreʿ*) background but with an inclination to the pro-Constitution Shaikhi leader Teqat al-Eslām, he joined the ranks of the revolutionary militia (*mojāhedīn*) no later than Rabīʿ I, 1325/May, 1907. During the earliest rounds of clashes between the supporters of the Anjoman-e Ayālatī (provincial assembly) of Tabrīz and their local opponents, he led a small band from his own quarter as a semi-independent force only partially under the control of the Anjoman. Later, like his fellow citizen Sattār Khan Sardār-e Mellī (q.v.) he was recruited into the newly organized police force in an effort to check the urban disturbances and repel the royalist-inspired raids of the Šāhsevan chief Raḥīm Khan Čalabīānlū.

In the following months he rose to some prominence as a result of some internal developments of which the most significant were the increasing insecurity and the threat of the local tribal khans; the final polarization of the city quarters into pro- and anti-constitution groupings—partly but not wholly on traditional sectarian lines—with the Anjoman representing the Kīābān, Amīrkīz, and southeastern quarters, and the rival Eslāmīya prevalent in Šotorbān (Devečī), Sorkāb, and Bāgmīša (see "La carte de Tauris pendant la révolution," in E. G. Browne, *The Persian Revolution of*

1905-1909, London, 1910, pp. 248-49); the further consolidation of the *mojāhedīn* and the inner struggle for the control of the Anjoman between the Caucasian faction directed by the Markaz-e Ḡaybī (Secret center) and the native faction supported by most merchants and pro-Constitution *ʿolamāʾ*, with which Ḵīābān was associated; and finally the difficulties in supplying provisions to the city. These elements provided a suitable climate for the chief *lūṭīs* like Nāʾeb Bāqer to gain supremacy, as the trouble-ridden Anjoman and the city authorities were dependent on them for maintaining order.

The intensification of the struggle against Moḥammad-ʿAlī Shah and the Constitutionalists' resistance to the reimposition of the despotic rule turned Bāqer Khan in the eye of the public into a local hero. What added a crucial boost to Bāqer Khan's popularity was his commitment to the ideals of *Mašrūṭa*—as he understood them—which was largely lacking among the *lūṭīs* of the rival quarters. As the tension between Moḥammad-ʿAlī Shah and the Majles reached its apex, the Constitutionalists of Tabrīz dispatched Bāqer Khan, Sattār Khan, and other *mojāhedīn* to Bāsmenj (12 miles southeast of Tabrīz) to recruit a force of 300 and march to Tehran in defense of the Majles (17 Jomādā I 1326/17 June 1908), but soon the disappointing news from the capital and the impending danger of attacks on Tabrīz made Bāqer Khan return to the barricades of his own quarter and prepare for a defense which lasted ten months. The fighting started immediately in Tabrīz after the fall of the Majles (23 Jomādā I 1326/23 June 1908) when, along with the coup in Tehran, Moḥammad-ʿAlī ordered an assault on the Constitutionalists' position in the southeastern wing of the city. Bāqer Khan resisted the joint forces of Eslāmīya and Qarajadāḡi horsemen and soon was able to inflict heavy casualties on them. But in less than two weeks the government advances frustrated his hopes, and made him cede to Russian pressure and signal his surrender by hoisting a white flag over his quarter (3 Jomādā II 1326/4 July 1908). However, the stiff resistance and persuasion of Sattār Khan, who reminded Bāqer Khan of their earlier pledge, made him resume the fighting. Bāqer Khan remained overshadowed for the rest of the engagements, however, by the more adventurous Sattār Khan as the core of the resistance was gradually moved to Amīrḵīz. In the months prior to Šaʿbān, 1326/August, 1908, when the reinforced government troops under the command of the newly appointed governor ʿAyn-al-Dawla started a new offensive, the coalition of the two leaders effectively reduced the danger of Eslāmīya, pushed Raḥīm Khan's forces out of the city, reorganized the *mojāhedīn*, unified most quarters in their defensive strategy, and defeated the Mākū regiment.

In the next prolonged phase of the conflict (Šaʿbān, 1326–Rabīʿ I, 1327/August, 1908-May, 1909), Bāqer Khan's skill in street battles was further extended to open-field combat; in the major battle of Sārīdāḡ (29 Ṣafar 1327/22 March 1909), one of the highlights of his career, he led the *mojāhedīn* forces to capture the positions overlooking Tabrīz and tried, though suffering high casualties, to open the supply routes to the starving city. The outcome of the fighting remained inconclusive, yet resistance led by Bāqer Khan and Sattār Khan exhausted the government troops and forced ʿAyn-al-Dawla to negotiate for lifting the siege. Furthermore, for some months Tabrīz demonstrated the only effective opposition to Moḥammad-ʿAlī Shah and remained a source of encouragement for the formation of other centers of resistance. But the weakening position of the shah made the Russians intervene, and the starvation and shortages gave them the necessary pretext to bring a small contingent into Tabrīz, thus frustrating the short-lived hopes of an imminent victory and forcing Bāqer Khan and Sattār Khan to seek refuge in the Ottoman consulate (8 Rabīʿ II 1327/29 April 1909). Yet despite the Russian's threatening gestures, Moḥammad-ʿAlī's position was irredeemable, and soon after his abdication (27 Jomādā II 1327/16 July 1909) Bāqer Khan felt safe enough to return to the scene, though only to encounter a mixed reception.

In the course of the next year, though his personal popularity as the hero of the resistance was hardly ever tarnished by the excesses of his supporters or by his unsuccessful campaign around the province, both the provincial governor Moḵber-al-Salṭana, who showed some anxiety over the alleged disturbances and intervention of the *mojāhedīn*, and the Russian consul, who became exceedingly apprehensive of the potential danger posed by Bāqer Khan, were critical of his presence. Their combined pressure, blessed with British approval, compelled the central government to arrange for the forced departure of Bāqer Khan and Sattār Khan for Tehran. Though in appearence it was a half-hearted invitation to show gratitude for their efforts to reestablish the Constitution, in reality it was an exile from which they never returned (7 Rabī I 1328/19 March 1910). The effusive welcome at Tehran, ephemeral and ironic as it appears, was still an acknowledgment of their popularity and the role they played in the restoration of the Constitution. But soon the bitter power struggle between the rival Constitutionalist factions made the recently arrived heroes of Tabrīz side with political groupings about whom they knew very little. Bāqer Khan nominally allied himself with the Moderates (*eʿtedālīyūn*) and tried in vain to secure some place for himself within the exclusive circle of influential statesmen, but soon, following Sattār Khan, he joined with ʿAbd-al-Ḥosayn Khan Moʿezz-al-Solṭān Sardār Moḥyī, a revolutionary leader from Gīlān who shared the same grievances and disappointments with the Tabrīzi leaders. In less than four months, despite widespread support and popularity, Bāqer Khan and his partners become politically isolated. They enjoyed neither the support of the Baḵtīārī–Armenian coalition (under the co-leadership of Sardār Asʿad [q.v.] and Yeprem [q.v.] who both were on good terms with the Democrats) nor that of the Moderates headed by

Moḥammad-Walī Khan Sepahdār. The wave of assassinations and feuding quickly culminated in a showdown in Pārk-e Atābak, the residence of Sattār Khan and the center for the *mojāhedīn*. After a brief resistance Sattār Khan and Bāqer Khan had to surrender with humiliation when their supporters who ignored the Majles ultimatum for disarmament were crushed by government troops (30 Rajab 1328/7 August 1910). This was probably a plot sponsored by the Democrats to get rid of the Azerbaijani *mojāhedīn* and subject their leaders to isolation and despair.

After five years of obscurity in Tehran and living on a government pension, in the summer of the 1915 and on the occasion of Mohājarat (immigration) and the formation of a nationalist government in exile, Bāqer Khan joined the Committee for National Defense and together with remnants of the Tabrīz resistance participated in skirmishes with Russian forces before retreating to Kermānšāh and later to Karkūk and Mawṣel as the Ottoman forces were withdrawing from western Iran. Though disillusioned and in despair, Bāqer Khan preferred to remain on the Kurdistan border rather than retreat to Turkey. In Moḥarram, 1335/November, 1916, in the confused days just before the British advance in northern Iraq, while wandering in the border villages near Qaṣr-e Šīrīn, he was offered overnight shelter by the Kurdish bandit Moḥammad-Amīn Ṭālebānī who on the same night murdered him and all his party and dumped their bodies nearby.

Bāqer Khan was said to be a bold and short-tempered patriot, a good example of the popular hero with loyalties not only to his own quarter and city, but to the whole of the Constitutional ideals. He was politically unsophisticated, however, and was susceptible to easy manipulation. He hardly ever escaped from what might be called the *lūṭī* mentality. Time and again he was deceived and ignored because of errors in judgment, when, for instance, he gave in to the persuasions of the Russian agent in Tabrīz or made his plans public in the battle of Sārīdāğ or miscalculated the Russian military move or underestimated the rival political factions in Tehran. He was typical of those Constitutionalists whose sincere hopes and aspirations were repeatedly frustrated by the vested interests of the dominant groups. Bāqer Khan was helplessly caught up in a complex political situation, yet he emerged as the symbol of a momentary resistance and was acknowledged as such when many other figures of the Constitutional period disappeared in the twilight of the post-Constitutional politics.

Bibliography: F. Ādamīyat, *Fekr-e demokrāsī-e ejtemāʿī dar nahżat-e mašrūṭīyat-e Īrān*, Tehran, 1354 Š./1975, pp. 130-46. E. Amīrḵīzī, *Qīām-e Āḏarbāyjān wa Sattār Ḵān*, Tabrīz, 1339 Š./1950 (see the index). Bāmdād, *Rejāl* I, pp. 179-81. E. G. Browne, *The Persian Revolution of 1905-1909*, London, 1910, chaps. 8-9, pp. 441-42 n. 22. Y. Dawlatābādī, *Ḥayāt-e Yaḥyā*, 4 vols., Tehran, 1330-31 Š./1951-52, III, p. 135. N. Fatḥī, *Zendagī-nāma-ye šahīd-e nīknām Ṯeqat-al-Eslām Tabrīzī*, Tehran, 1354 Š./1975 (see the index). D. Fraser, *Persia and Turkey in Revolt*, London, 1910, pp. 64-82. M. Hedāyat, *Ḵāṭerāt wa ḵaṭarāt*, 2nd ed., Tehran, 1344 Š./1965, pp. 176-200. A. Kasrawī *Āḏarbāyjān*, 8th ed., Tehran, 1356 Š./1977, chaps. 6-17. Idem, *Mašrūṭa*, 13th ed., Tehran, 1356 Š./1977, chaps. 6-15. M. Malekzāda, *Tārīḵ-e enqelāb-e mašrūṭīyat-e Īrān*, 7 vols., Tehran, 1328-33 Š./1949-54, V, pp. 9-62, 205-44, VI, pp. 188-239. Ḥ. Moʿāṣer, ed., *Tārīḵ-e esteqrār-e mašrūṭīyat dar Īrān*, Tehran, 1347 Š./1968, chaps. 22-24. *Parliamentary Papers (Blue Book), Persia*, 1909-12. E. Rāʾīn, *Yeprem Ḵān Sardār*, Tehran, 1350 Š./1971 (see the index). E. Reżwānī, *Enqelāb-e mašrūṭīyat-e Īrān*, Tehran, 1345 Š./1966, chap. 5. E. Ṣafāʾī, *Asnād-e sīāsī-e dawrān-e qājārīya*, Tehran, 1346 Š./1967, pp. 425-26. Idem, *Rahbarān-e mašrūṭa*, 2 vols., Tehran, 1344 Š./1965, I, pp. 386-412. K. Ṭāherzāda Behzād, *Qīām-e Āḏarbāyjān dar enqelāb-e mašrūṭīyat-e Īrān*, Tehran, 1334 Š./1955 (see the index). M. B. Vījūya, *Balvā-ye Tabrīz (Tārīḵ-e enqelāb-e Āḏarbāyjān)*, ed. ʿA. Kātebī, 3rd ed., Tehran, 1355 Š./1976 (see the index).

(A. Amanat)

BĀQĪBELLĀH NAQŠBANDĪ, ḴᵛĀJA ABU'L-MOʾAYYAD RAŻĪ-AL-DĪN OWAYSĪ, born in Kabul in 971/1563-64 or 972/1564-65 as a son of the *qāżī* of that city, ʿAbd-al-Salām; studied the traditional theological sciences under Ṣādeq Ḥalwāʾī whom he followed to Transoxiana. Already at an early age he seems to have mastered very thoroughly these sciences, but at the same time he felt attracted toward the mystical life. His passionate search for a suitable *pīr* (elder) brought him to many *ḵānaqāh*s in Transoxiana where he received a first introduction to the Naqšbandī order, but unable to find a satisfying fulfillment of his spiritual need he turned to India (Lahore) and afterward to Kashmir, where he stayed with Shaikh Bābā Walī. After Bābā Walī's death in 1000/1591-92 he returned to Transoxiana, where he was formally initiated into the Naqšbandī order by Mawlānā Ḵᵛājagī Moḥammad Amkanagī (son and disciple of Mawlānā Darvīš, who was a *ḵalīfa* of Mawlānā Moḥammad Zāhed Vaḵšī, one of the principal *ḵalīfa*s [successors] of Ḵᵛāja ʿObayd-Allāh Aḥrār). Besides Bāqībellāh claims to have received a spiritual initiation from Ḵᵛāja Bahāʾ-al-Dīn Naqšband. Sent as a *ḵalīfa* to India in order to propagate the Naqšbandī order there he first stayed for a year in Lahore and in 1007/1598-99 settled down permanently in Delhi's Fīrūzābād, where he died 25 Jomādā II 1012/30 November 1603. He had two sons, Ḵᵛāja ʿObayd-Allāh (Ḵᵛāja-ye Kalān) and Ḵᵛāja Moḥammad ʿAbd-Allāh (Ḵᵛāja-ye Ḵᵛord), both born (of different mothers) in 1010/1601-02. He wrote several short treatises (*rasāʾel*) on the exegesis of certain chapters of verses of the Koran, on certain traditions, and on mystical subjects (e.g., *Nūr-e waḥdat*, on monism); they are cited rather extensively in the *Zobdat al-maqāmāt* and have been published in the *Ḥayāt-e bāqīa*. His poetical writings (*maṯnawī*s, chronograms, a *sāqī-*

nāma, quatrains, and separate verses) have been published in the *ʿErfānīyāt-e bāqī*, and, together with his letters to devotees and disciples, in his *kollīyāt*. He is perhaps best known for his *Selselat al-aḥrār*, which contains quatrains accompanied by his own commentary; this work, in which he upholds the doctrine of the *waḥdat-e wojūd*, was later commented upon by his disciple Aḥmad Serhendī in the latter's *Šarḥ-e robāʿīyāt*, upon which a supercommentary was written by Shah Walī-Allāh Dehlavī. One of his disciples, Mīr Moḥammad Jān, wrote down Bāqībellāh's sayings (*malfūẓāt*) uttered during sessions (*majāles*) held in Delhi. They have been published in the *Ḥayāt-e bāqīa*. Finally A. A. Rizvi mentions a *Kalemāt-e ṭayyebāt*, discourses of Bāqībellāh. As a Naqšbandī, Bāqībellāh represents the sober type of Sufi, meticulously adhering to the Islamic law (*šarīʿa*) and averse to ecstatic mystical experiences, but on the other hand his sympathetic attitude toward Ebn al-ʿArabī shows that he was not rigid and dogmatic in his ideas. This, together with his warm personality, accounts for his high reputation in Delhi, with the common man and the noble alike. Despite his bad health and early death he contributed much to the propagation of the Naqšbandī order in India. His type of mysticism, which seems to have found its purest continuation in his two sons, breathes a spirit different from that of his well-known disciple Aḥmad Serhendī, whose Naqšbandī-Mojaddedī line, however, came more to the fore in India.

Bibliography: Moḥammad ʿAbd-al-Ḡaffār, ed., *Ḥayāt-e bāqīa*, Delhi, 1323/1905-06. Rašīd Aḥmad Aršad, *Ḥayāt-e Bāqī*, Karachi, 1969. A. S. Bazmee Ansari, "Bāḳī bi'llāh," in *EI*² I, p. 957 (with further bibliography). Abu'l-Ḥasan Zayd Fārūqī and Borhān Aḥmad Fārūqī, eds., *Kollīyāt-e Bāqībellāh*, Lahore, n.d. Neẓām-al-Dīn Aḥmad Kāẓemī, ed., *ʿErfānīyāt-e Bāqī*, Delhi, 1970. Moḥammad-Hāšem Kešmī, *Zobdat al-maqāmāt*, Delhi, 1307/1889-90. A. A. Rizvi, *Muslim Revivalist Movements in Northern India in the Sixteenth and Seventeenth Centuries*, Agra, 1965, pp. 185-93. Idem, *A History of Sufism in India*, pt. 2, Delhi, 1983, pp. 185-86. Badr-al-Dīn Serhendī, *Ḥażarāt al-qods*, pt. 1 (Urdu tr.), Lahore, 1923. Storey, 1/2, p. 989.

(J. G. J. TER HAAR)

BĀQLAVĀ (or Baqlavā)

i. *The word.*
ii. *The sweet.*

i. THE WORD

The etymology of the word *bāqlavā*, found in Arabic (*baqlāwa*), Turkish (*baklava*), and Greek (*mpaklabâs*), has not yet been determined. According to G. Doerfer (p. 255), the word does not seem to be from Turkish. A Persian origin is suggested by the suffix *-vā*, perhaps the Persian suffix *-vā*/*-bā* found in terms for food and cuisine and deriving from *-βāy* < *pāk*, cf. *poḵtan* "to cook" (cf. *Grundriss* I/2, p. 79; and *EIr.*, s.v. ĀŠ); however, the first element of the word is of unknown origin (a derivation from *balg*, a common dialect form of *barg* "leaf," or from Ar. *baql* "herb" is unlikely).

(W. EILERS)

ii. THE SWEET

Bāqlavā is a sweet pastry known throughout the Middle East which in Iran is commonly made with almonds, (*bādām*), less frequently with pistachios (*pesta*), and, in the past, with lentils (*ʿadas*). In Turkey and Greece it is made with walnuts and covered with a kind of dough which forms a harder surface than that of the Persian *bāqlavā*. The Turkish *bāqlavā* is the one commonly used in the West. The pistachio *bāqlavā* is considered more elegant than the other kind. The finest quality *bāqlavā* in Iran is reputed to be that which is made in Yazd, where it is packed in tins and prepared for sale throughout the country. Tins of *bāqlavā* are frequently given to friends and relatives as gifts at Nowrūz.

In Iran the almonds and sugar are pounded or ground together, then mixed with melted butter or fine quality shortening, and flavored with cardamom (*hel*) before being spread over layers of very thin filo dough (*nān-e lavāš* or *nān-e tonok*). Alternate layers are then built up, the top sprinkled with slivered almonds or pistachios; it is then baked until golden. When cool, it is cut into lozenge-shaped pieces. A sweet syrup made with boiled sugar and water, frequently flavored with rose water (*golāb*), is then poured over the pastry.

Traditionally, *bāqlavā* is not made in the home, but in bakeries and special factories. In recent years, as ovens and baking facilities have become more prevalent in Iran, increasing numbers of women have taken to preparing *bāqlavā* at home, particularly for special occasions such as weddings.

Although traditionally *bāqlavā* is lozenge-shaped, when made at home it is sometimes cut into squares, and sometimes rolled into individual, cigarette-shaped rolls.

Bibliography: N. Ramazani, *Persian Cooking*, Charlottesville, 1982, pp. 219-21. C. Roden, *A Book of Middle Eastern Food*, New York, 1972, pp. 397-98.

(N. RAMAZANI)

BAQLĪ, SHAIKH RŪZBEHĀN. See RŪZBEHĀN.

BAQQĀL-BĀZĪ (lit. grocer play), a form of improvised, popular slapstick comedy, the origins of which can be traced to buffoons who performed at the courts of kings, to such merry, grotesque pageants as the *bar nešastan-e kūsa* (beardless man's mount) and the *mīr-e nowrūzī* (prince of the New Year) from the Sasanian period (Gaffary, pp. 362-63), or possibly to the extravagant goat-costumed dances under the Safavids (ibid., pp. 363-64). *Baqqāl-bāzī* is distinguished among the various forms of popular comedy in Iran by its own set of rules. It is performed at teahouses (*qahwa-ḵāna*) or private residences during weddings, or birth or circumcision parties. The principal characters in this genre were a rich miserly grocer and his lazy, absent-minded servant who was inclined to do the opposite of his master's bidding, thus provoking a comic response from the audience (Bayżā'ī, p. 170). The servant was generally played by an actor in blackface (*sīāh*), who would tease and make fun of people and things. The plays were about bullies who stole goods, particularly yogurt from the grocer's stall, and hit one another in the face with it. Other *baqqāl-bāzī* characters were the *māstī* (or *māssī*, yogurt seller, in winter processionals performed in Arāk; Enjavī, pp. 67-71), the *čordakī*, and the *rīšakī* (ibid.). Travelers in Iran in 1812 report seeing a comedy from a house terrace, which must have been a *baqqāl-bāzī* (Freygang, pp. 328-39, quoted in Rezvani, p. 114). In it the yogurt seller was approached by a character wearing different disguises in each scene, pretending to buy yogurt but in fact stealing it each time. The yogurt seller is not only a victim of theft but also ends up with his face covered in yogurt.

In *baqqāl-bāzī*, as in the Commedia dell'Arte, there was no written script but a series of improvisations on a given plot. Gobineau, who stayed in Iran twice between the years of 1855 and 1863, says (p. 404) that *baqqāl-bāzīs* were crude farces or "beggars' plays," likely to evolve into solid comedies of the Goldini variety, for instance. The valuable text from 1294/1877, Ḥosayn Khan's *Joḡrāfīā-ye Eṣfahān* (pp. 86-87), gives first-hand information on a company of buffoons that performed in *baqqāl-bāzī*. He states that such plays were originally created out of public necessity and that, although they appeared entertaining, in fact they contained precious indications of the rules of social behavior and served as a moral guide to those who refused to be influenced by sermons or moral injunctions, human errors and shortcomings and their consequences being the subject matter of the plays. Like all jests, *baqqāl-bāzī* on occasion helped to redress an injustice. Ḥosayn Khan tells the story of one of Isfahan's acting groups' good deeds. When one of the Persian kings (presumably Fatḥ-ʿAlī Shah, in Šaʿbān, 1240/April, 1824, cf. Fasā'ī, pp. 170-72) launched a punitive expedition against Isfahan's troublemakers, his soldiers and civil servants committed serious offenses. No one dared speak of their exactions to him. At the time a *baqqāl-bāzī* troupe was due to perform before the king; the company had the courage to act out the king's officers' and tax collectors' misdeeds. After the performance, the king had all those who were wrongly arrested released and rehabilitated. Ḥosayn Khan is of the opinion that the dialogues carried on by the actors in Isfahan, who were in fact pious people, were worth recording. Most of these people emigrated to Tehran and other cities.

Nāṣer-al-Dīn Shah (r. 1264-1313/1848-96) was interested in Iranian traditional theater (both passion plays, *taʿzīa*, and improvised comedy). He maintained several skillful court jesters, among whom was the well-known Karīm Šīra'ī. A play called *Baqqāl-bāzī dar ḥożūr* (*baqqāl-bāzī* in the presence [of the king]; text in B. Mo'menī, *Tīātr-e Karīm Šīra'ī* and J. Malekpūr, I, pp. 279-301) has been wrongly attributed to Karīm Šīra'ī, who could not have written it because, despite the buffoon's relative freedom and the king's appreciation of the way he would ridicule some of his courtiers and statesmen, he could not tolerate the use of such strong language or social criticism (especially when directed at the royal family) at court. The play was probably written around 1872-73 by a liberal-minded opponent to the king and his rule; parts of it could have been added during the following 20 years. This unique text (with its characters like *čordakī*, *reškī*, and *māstī*) contains, however, valuable information on the genre's acting, costumes, makeup, and props. The other famous entertainer under Nāṣer-al-Dīn Shah was Esmāʿīl Bazzāz, a draper by trade, who in his performances changed the *baqqāl* (grocer) of the traditional plays into other characters such as a court physician, a colonel, and even the Tehran chief of police in 1300/1883, the last mentioned of whom reacted angrily and had the performer beaten. The comedian was avenged, however, after he complained of his punishment to the shah (Eʿtemād-al-Salṭana, p. 231). Esmāʿīl Bazzāz retired in 1310/1892 (idem, p. 836, and Bektāš, p. 37).

M. Rezvani reports having seen *baqqāl-bāzī* in the early 1920s in the Caucasus and in Iran (pp. 112-14). In Azerbaijan it was called *bagkal-oyunu*, and one of its characters used a stick (*čomāq*), similar to Arlecchino's bat in the Commedia dell'Arte, to beat people. Rezvani recalls a play he saw at Astarābād in 1923, called Nowrūz-ʿAlī after the grocer's servant, whose prodigious laziness provides the comedic material of the play.

Baqqāl-bāzī has contributed an idiom to colloquial Persian: *baqqāl-bāzī dar āvardan* "to make a scandal." Other forms of Persian comedy are called: *kačalak-bāzī*, *maskara-bāzī*, *rūḥawżī*, *sīāh-bāzī*, *takta-ḥawżī*, *tamāšā*, *taqlīd*.

See also DALQAK.

Bibliography: M. Bektāš, *Faṣl-nāma-ye tīātr*, Tehran, 1357 Š./1978, no. 5. B. Bayżā'ī, *Nemāyeš dar Īrān*, Tehran, 1344 Š./1965. J. Chardin, *Voyages en Perse*, Paris, 1811. A.-Q. Enjavī, *Jašnhā wa ādāb-e zamestān*, Tehran, 1352 Š./1973. M.-Ḥ. Eʿtemād-al-Salṭana, *Rūz-nāma-ye kāṭerāt*. Fasā'ī, *Fārs-nāma-ye nāṣerī*, tr. Busse. F. and W. Freygang, *Lettres sur le Caucase et la Géorgie, suivies d'un voyage en Perse en 1812*, Hamburg, 1816; tr. *Letters from the Caucasus and Georgia*, London, 1823. F. Gaffary, "Evolution of Rituals and Theatre in Iran," *Iranian Studies* 17/4, 1984, pp. 361-89. A. de Gobineau, *Religions et philosophies dans l'Asie Centrale*, Paris, 1865; repr. 1957. Ḥosayn Khan, *Joḡrāfīā-ye Eṣfahān*, ed. M. Sotūda, Tehran, 1342 Š./1963. J. Malekpūr, *Adabīyāt-e nemāyešī dar Īrān*, Tehran, 1363 Š./1984. B. Mo'menī, *Tīātr-e Karīm Šīra'ī*, Tehran, 2537 = 1357 Š./1978. M. Rezvani, *Le théatre et la danse en Iran*, Paris, 1962.

(F. GAFFARY)

BĀR (audience). The royal audience was one of the most important and enduring of the court ceremonies practiced in Iran. Initially it was influenced, in certain details of the ceremonial, by similar Egyptian and Assyrian practices, and subsequently it in turn influenced the practices of imperial Rome, medieval Europe, and above all the caliphate and the Indian empire (Walser, pp. 19ff., 22ff.). In Iran the audience ceremony endured without significant change until the 20th century.

i. *From the Achaemenid through the Safavid period.*
ii. *The Qajar and Pahlavi periods.*

i. From the Achaemenid through the Safavid Period

Reliefs on stone from the Achaemenid period, particularly the relief found at the treasury site at Persepolis in the excavations by the American archeological mission in 1936, depict an audience given by Darius (521-485 B.C.), and the Greek historians supply further information. The formalities were as follows. The audience seeker addressed his request and stated his reasons to the head of protocol, who explained the procedure to him and on the appointed day escorted him to the king's presence. The king in full regalia sat erect on a high-backed chair, wearing a tall hat called *kidaris* and holding a long scepter in his right hand and a lotus flower in his left hand. Behind the king stood his personal servants and his bodyguard (Ghirshman, fig. 255). In the relief depicting Darius's audience, the heir apparent Xerxes appears in equally fine array, standing at his father's right side and also holding a lotus leaf in his left hand, while his right hand is raised as a signal that he is about to speak.

In later periods, high-ranking officers, officials, and nobles also attended royal audiences. Each had a preallotted place, and the nearness of his place to the king marked the importance of his rank. Likewise, being seated was rated higher than standing, and being on the king's right higher than being on his left (*Šāh-nāma*, ed. Mohl, IV, p. 612 vv. 3007ff.). If anybody was put in a place lower than one befitting his rank, it was a sign that he had incurred the royal displeasure (Bayhaqī, pp. 32ff.). In the Sasanian period, the king sat on cushions on a golden throne, and the crown was hung on a chain in such a position that it seemed that the king was wearing it when he sat down. These practices remained in vogue under the first Islamic dynasties in Iran, who took the Sasanians as their model. At the Sasanian court, a curtain was kept hanging between the king and the audience seeker until the latter reached his place, when it was drawn aside. This custom was maintained, likewise in imitation of the Sasanians, at the Omayyad and ʿAbbasid caliphal courts but is not mentioned in accounts of the courts of the Islamic dynasties in Iran. As soon as the audience seeker saw the monarch, he was required to kiss the ground. In later periods, kissing the king's throne or his hand and signet ring was also customary. At the caliphal court, kissing the ground was not at first required, as it was thought sufficient that the person being received in audience should say "Peace upon you, O Prince of the Believers, and God's mercy and blessings!" In later times, however, this was superseded by ground kissing, and, although initially the heir apparent, sons of the caliph, Hashemites, judges, theologians, ascetics, and Koran reciters were exempted, ultimately they too had to conform to the originally Iranian custom (Ṣābe', p. 31; Jāḥeẓ, *Tāj*, p. 7; von Kremer, II, pp. 246ff.).

After kissing the ground, the person being received was bidden by the king to stand. He then waited for the king to question him. In the Sasanian period he commenced his reply with the words "May you live for ever" (*anōšag bawēd*), sometimes adding "and attain success!" (*ō kāmag rasēd*). In later times also, it was usual to express such a wish, e.g., "May the king's life be long!" (*Kār-nāmag*, ed. Sanjana, 9.16.20, 10.7.9, 12.13, 13.9.15; *Šāh-nāma* I, p. 318 v. 1289; VII, p. 362 v. 81; Ṭabarī, I, pp. 824, 1048; Bayhaqī, 2nd ed., pp. 63, 65, 73, 75).

In Achaemenid times, the person being received had to hold his hand in front of his mouth while speaking to the king, in Sasanian times a handkerchief (Ṭabarī, I, p. 1036; *Šāh-nāma* VII, p. 362 v. 88; Nöldeke, *Geschichte der Perser*, pp. 343, 367; Christensen, *Iran Sass.*, p. 400). He stood to attention with his arms crossed while the king was speaking (*Šāh-nāma* IV, p. 218 v. 2528; VII, p. 362 vv. 80, 87).

In addition to these formalities, there were several precise rules which had to be observed by the person being received and others attending an audience. One was that nobody might speak except in answer to a question from the king. Anyone bidden to speak must speak slowly and briefly and not repeat himself. Correcting the king's words, mentioning adverse omens, exaggeration, backbiting, laughing, spitting, and blowing the nose were not permitted. All those present had to observe the rule of silence and, as far as possible, refrain from coughing and sneezing. Those who were to come close to the king ought to have previously used the toothpick so as to have good breath, but ought not to use strong scent. At the ʿAbbasid court, the person being received was required to wear black, the color of the ʿAbbasid flag, but nobody might wear red shoes because red was the color of the caliph's shoes. It was also impermissible to drink water at the caliphal court. Other courts, however, were less exacting; visitors to the Buyid, Il-khanid, Timurid, and Safavid courts were allowed to sip water, and special cups for this purpose were placed in the audience hall. On leaving the king's presence, the person who had been received had to walk backward for some distance to avoid turning his back on the king. Furthermore, nobody could enter the palace precincts on horseback unless the king had previously authorized him to do so. When audiences were granted to persons who had come from abroad and did not know the language of the country, an interpreter was summoned (Plutarch, *Themistocles*, pp. 27ff.; *Kār-nāmag*, 10.7.9-13, 12.4.13; *Šāh-nāma* I, pp. 98 v. 355, 144 vv. 369f., 146 v. 375, 172 vv. 687f., 302

vv. 1084f., 315 vv. 1288f., 324 vv. 1365f., 488 vv. 22ff.; IV, pp. 218 vv. 2526ff., 532 v. 2059; V, p. 170 v. 827; VI, p. 24 vv. 230ff., 652 vv. 1308ff.; VII, p. 282 vv. 3340f.; Ṭabarī, I, p. 859; III, p. 59; Ṣābe', pp. 32, 33f., 35f., 52, 57, 59, 68, 74f.; Jāḥeẓ, *Tāj*, pp. 7, 28, 69, 112, 125f.; Mas'ūdī, *Morūj*, ed. Pellat, I, p. 288; Yāqūt, *Odabā'* V, pp. 349, 355; Gardīzī, ed. Ḥabībī, p. 136; Nöldeke, *Geschichte der Perser*, p. 93).

In pre-Islamic times, women had the right to seek and attend audiences (*Šāh-nāma* I, p. 315 vv. 1281ff.). The king's spouse is seen beside him in pictures on vessels which have survived from the Sasanian period (Ghirshman, *Iran, Parthians and Sassanians*, figs. 244, 259). Likewise at the courts of the Mongol Il-khans and Tīmūr, the monarch's mother, wives, and daughters took part in audiences, sitting or standing beside or behind him in positions determined by the rank of each; furthermore they themselves gave audiences, at which they received not only women and male relatives but also unrelated men (Carpini, IX, 13. vi, 14. viii; *Nachtrag*, 7, 8. Ebn Baṭṭūṭa, II, pp. 387f., 406; Jovaynī III, plate facing p. 101; Clavijo, pp. 244f., 268). But at the courts of the caliphs and other dynasties in Iran in the early Islamic period, no women were present at audiences except dancing girls.

In order to reach the royal presence, the audience seeker of whatever rank or sex had first to obtain permission from the head of protocol. This official was usually a military man of noble birth, sometimes a close relative of the ruler (Jāḥeẓ, *Tāj*, p. 28; Mas'ūdī, *Morūj* I, p. 288; *Šāh-nāma* I, p. 172 v. 687). The Samanids and Ghaznavids, however, appointed Turks, and Maḥmūd Ḡaznavī even chose good-looking young slave soldiers who from time to time took his fancy (Bayhaqī, pp. 134, 159f., 329f.).

In the Achaemenid period this office was held by the *hazārapati* (Greek *chiliarchos*), i.e., the commander of the royal bodyguard. In the Sasanian period the holder was called the *handēmāngarān sālār* (Christensen, *Iran Sass.*, pp. 113, 394f.). In the *Šāh-nāma* he is mentioned as the *sālār-e bār* (head of protocol) and *pardadār* (keeper of the curtain). The corresponding official at the 'Abbasid court was the *ḥājeb al-ḥojjāb* (head chamberlain), who had a large staff of chamberlains under him. Since *ḥājeb* is the Arabic translation of *pardadār*, it may be inferred that at the Sasanian court the *sālār-e bār* had likewise been in command of the chamberlains. In the Samanid and Ghaznavid periods the chamberlains were designated *ḥājeb* and their chief *ḥājeb-e bozorg*, and under the Saljuqs these terms remained in use together with *bārbeg* for the former and *amīr-e bār* or *olOḡ bārbeg* for the latter (Rāvandī, pp. 128, 367, 390). Under the Il-khans officers of the bodyguard (*kezīk-kešīk*) held positions similar to those of the *ḥājeb*s of earlier times and were headed by the *amīr-e kezīk* (Rašīd-al-Dīn, pp. 543, 908, 958). At Tīmūr's court the function was performed by three royal princes, who were called *mīrzā* (short for *amīrzāda*, son of the *amīr*). In the Safavid period all matters relating to royal audiences were handled by an official named the *īšīk āqāsī bāšī*, who was assisted in his task of keeping order at such gatherings by guards known as *yasāvolān-e soḥbat* (macebearers in attendance; *Taḏkerat al-molūk*, ed. Minorsky, p. 64; Anṣārī, p. 51). The designation *īšīk āqāsī bāšī* endured throughout the Qajar period; under the Pahlavi dynasty it was changed to *ra'īs-e tašrīfāt-e darbār* (head of court protocol). In all periods of Iranian history, holders of this office enjoyed high status and great influence. Not infrequently they were privy to conspiracies, which led in some cases to the deposition or murder of the ruler and sometimes also to their own rise to higher rank (Diodorus Siculus, *Bibliotheca Historica*, chap. 69; Ṣābe', p. 71; Jāḥeẓ, *Rasā'el*, pp. 159f.; Gardīzī, pp. 136, 160f.; Jorfādaqānī, pp. 40, 92f., 127, 157; Bayhaqī, pp. 12, 33, 58, 325f., 433, 865f.; Rāvandī, pp. 159f., 233, 235, 254f., 264; Jovaynī, II, pp. 211f., 258f.; Rašīd-al-Dīn, pp. 543, 546f., 908, 919, 1065f.; Qāšānī, p. 124; Clavijo, pp. 283f.).

Throughout the history of Iran, it was always customary that the person being received should bring gifts for the king and accept gifts from him. For governors of provinces and envoys from other kings, this was essential. Under the Il-khans and Tīmūr the practice was considered so important that anyone who had failed to bring a gift could not hope to gain access to the khan. The expressions *tegšīmīšī* and *uljāmīšī* (*kardan/yāftan*), which were in use in the Mongol period, meant "to bring gifts and be received in audience" (Jovaynī, I, p. 213; III, p. 46; Rašīd-al-Dīn, pp. 542, 543, 809, 831, 879, 881, 891, 896; Qāšānī, p. 54, etc.). If the donor was a man of importance, the gifts were laid out on the audience day in the presence of the person being received and displayed publicly before they were carried to the king in the audience hall. Carriers of such gifts are portrayed in the reliefs flanking the steps of the Apadāna at Persepolis (*Šāh-nāma* I, p. 318 vv. 1290f.; II, p. 268 vv. 872f.; V, p. 242 vv. 1692f.; VI, p. 234 vv. 1987f.; Bayhaqī, pp. 52, 53, 471, 474; Carpini, IX, 12. v.; Clavijo, pp. 159, 168, 218f., 243f., 327f.; *'Ālamārā-ye ṣafawī*, p. 449; Moḥammad Rafī' Anṣārī, pp. 51f.; *Taḏkerat al-molūk*, pp. 14, 96; Kaempfer, pp. 24, 66, 106, 271, 276f.; Tavernier, pp. 130, 146).

Audiences were normally held in a hall in the palace, but in spring and summer sometimes in the palace garden, in which case the crown and throne were carried to the garden and a parasol was erected. In Achaemenid times the hall of the Apadāna was used for audience ceremonies, in late Sasanian times halls in Ḵosrow's palace. Rulers in Islamic times held their audiences in buildings specially constructed for the purpose. The great khans of the Mongols were still tent dwellers and therefore gave audience in tents, but under the Il-khans reception in the palace gradually again became customary. From Tīmūr's reign there are reports of audiences in both palaces and tents. In the Safavid period use of tents finally ceased, and as in old times the royal audience, now called the *majles*, took place in a palace —at first at Qazvīn, later at one of many fine edifices such as the ʿĀlī Qāpū (q.v.), Čehel Sotūn, Kāḵ-e Bāḡ-e Golestān, Kāḵ-e Bāḡ-e Bolbol, and others at Isfahan. For an audience day, the floor of the hall was laid with carpets, and its walls were adorned with colorful screens, pictures of battles and feasts, and portraits of kings; the hall was embellished with flowers, lamps, censers, and artificial trees bearing jewel-studded leaves, fruits, and birds; the pools were beautified with floating flowers and fruits, and the *jets d'eau* were put into play. Armed guards wearing splendid uniforms and gold or silver belts stood in rows inside the hall and outside. Sometimes animals tethered with golden chains, such as lions, leopards, tigers, camels, elephants, and horses were put on display in front of the palace. For special audiences, such as those held on Nowrūz and Mehragān festival days or for reception of envoys from foreign courts, the pageantry was greatly increased (Christensen, p. 397). Envoys arriving from abroad normally spent several days in the capital before they were received in audience; sometimes, particularly in the Safavid period, they were guests of the government during the whole of their stay in the country (*Šāh-nāma* I, pp. 144 v. 366, 172 vv. 684f.; III, p. 364 vv. 844f.; VI, p. 146 vv. 277ff.; Ṣābeʾ, pp. 14f., 79; Gardīzī, p. 200; Bayhaqī, pp. 48f., 50, 380, 470f., 655, 713f.; Jorfādaqānī, p. 132; Jovaynī, III, pp. 98, 101; Rašīd-al-Dīn, pp. 947f.; Banākatī, pp. 464f.; Qāšānī, pp. 45f., 133; Clavijo, pp. 206ff., 237ff., 241, 269ff.; *ʿĀlamārā-ye Ṣafawī*, p. 593; Ḥasan Rūmlū, pp. 88, 92, 482, 484, 487; Qāżī Aḥmad, pp. 6, 63, 85, 89; Olearius, pp. 130f.; Tavernier, pp. 123f.; Kaempfer, pp. 206ff., 252ff.; Christensen, *Iran Sass.*, p. 397).

Royal audiences fell into two categories: (1) the private audience (*bār-e ḵāṣṣ*) for reception of dignitaries of the kingdom and foreign princes and envoys or for consideration of state business, (2) the public audience (*bār-e ʿāmm*) for reception of members of the public. Nowrūz and Mehragān audiences were similarly divided into celebrations for the élite (*ḵāṣṣa*) and the public (*ʿāmma*). On the first five days of each festival the king held public audiences for commoners, and on the sixth day he began a series of private audiences for dignitaries, nobles, and members of the royal family. Members of the nobility were not allowed to attend the public audiences (Bīrūnī, *al-Āṯār al-bāqīa*, pp. 218f.; idem, *Tafhīm*, p. 253; Neẓām-al-Molk, p. 60; Masʿūdī, *Morūj* I, p. 311).

In ancient Iran, the royal audience formed such an important part of the system of government that the audience and the monarchy were thought to be inseparable; if ever the audiences ceased, the monarchy too would cease (*Šāh-nāma* V, p. 176 v. 912; VII, p. 12 vv. 88f.). For this reason instruction in the rules of the audience ceremony was part of the education of royal princes (*Šāh-nāma* II, pp. 200 v. 88, 218 v. 190; IV, p. 684 v. 3865).

At both public and private audiences one of the king's principal duties was to hear complaints. For this reason the term "(hearing of) grievances" (*maẓālem*) was sometimes used instead of "audience" (*bār*) in the Islamic period. Every ruler vowed at the start of his reign that he would sit to hear grievances once or twice a week on prescribed days (*Šāh-nāma* V, pp. 102 v. 35f., 232 v. 11; VI, pp. 162 v. 33f., 180 vv. 25ff.; Bayhaqī, pp. 195, 472, 675; Ebn al-Aṯīr, X, p. 459; Bondārī, p. 7). From the viewpoint of members of the public, the king sitting in audience was their last legal resort, as he had power to give redress to those whose rights had been violated by his officials and courtiers. The king could also grant pardons. If an offender was admitted to an audience, this was taken to mean that he would probably be pardoned. Therefore, in the popular view, the measure of a king's justice was his willingness to sit in audience. A king who was *farāḵbār*, i.e., held audiences frequently, was thought to be a just ruler, while one who was *tangbār*, i.e., did so seldom, was considered unjust. The people did not forgive a king who neglected to hold audiences on the prescribed days unless there were compelling reasons such as a journey, war, sickness, death of a relative, receipt of bad news (*Šāh-nāma* I, p. 162 v. 586; III, p. 8 v. 50; IV, p. 220 vv. 256ff.; VI, pp. 4 vv. 8ff., 222 v. 752, 702 v. 1899; VII, p. 278 v. 3298; Bayhaqī, pp. 199, 703, 747; Ṭabarī, I, p. 871; Rāvandī, pp. 254, 277; Nöldeke, *Geschichte der Perser*, p. 113; idem, *Aufsätze*, p. 106).

Even so, there was always the risk that chamberlains might abuse their power or that courtiers might contrive to prevent commoners from gaining access to the king (*Šāh-nāma* VI, p. 162 vv. 33f.). Various precautions against this danger are mentioned; for example, the king might get rid of suspected chamberlains, or he might hold public audiences in a field outside the palace precincts after giving instructions that petitioners should wear red clothes so as to catch the king's eye. Such precautions were evidently more theoretical than practical, and, although certain kings are reported to have observed them, the reports often have a fabulous aspect like the story of Anōšīravān's "chain of justice" (*Tārīḵ-e Sīstān*, p. 265; Neẓām-al-Molk, pp. 13, 55f.; Rāvandī, p. 131). On the other hand, there are many recorded instances of deception by kings who summoned men to audiences and arrested or even killed them as soon as they arrived. The best-known case is the murder of Abū Moslem (q.v.) in 137/755 by order of the perfidious caliph al-Manṣūr; having obeyed a summons to an audience, he was escorted to the audience hall and killed by the caliph's guards right there. Similar foul play was not uncommon in later times, notably under the Samanids, Ghaznavids, and Saljuqs (Gardīzī, pp. 160f.; Bayhaqī, pp. 66, 68f., 97, 99; Rāvandī, pp. 259f.).

In the long run, however, such abuses and crimes did not detract from the prestige of the royal audience. At all times the audience was an important part of both court ceremonial and governmental administration.

See also DARBĀR; SALĀM.

Bibliography: 1. Achaemenid period. A. Erman, *Die Literatur der Ägypter*, Leipzig, 1923, pp. 53ff. R. Ghirshman, *Persia. From the Origins to Alexander the Great*, London, 1964, figs. 160-65, 246, 254, 255.

W. Hinz, *Altiranische Funde und Forschungen*, Berlin, 1969, pp. 63ff. A. Parrot, *Assur. Die mesopotamische Kunst vom 13. vorchristlichen Jahrhundert bis zum Tode Alexanders des Grossen*, Munich, 1961, figs. 112, 113, 115-17. E. F. Schmidt, *Persepolis* I, Chicago, 1953, pp. 162ff. P. E. Schramm, *Kaiser, Rom und Renovatio*, Leipzig and Berlin, 1929. W. von Soden, *Herrscher im alten Orient*, Berlin, 1954, pp. 90ff. G. Walser, *Audienz beim persischen Grosskönig*, Zurich, 1965. A. Wiedersich, *Prosopographie der Griechen beim Perserkönig*, Breslau, 1922.

2. From the Sasanians to the Saljuqs. A. Alföldi, "Die Geschichte des Throntabernakels," *La Nouvelle Clio*, 1949-50, pp. 536-66. Bayhaqī, 2nd ed., pp. 618f., 655, 657 ('Amr b. Layṯ's audiences), 713f. Abū Rayḥān Bīrūnī, *Tafhīm*, ed. J. Homā'ī, Tehran, 1316 Š./1937. Fatḥ b. 'Alī b. Moḥammad Bondārī Eṣfahānī, *Tawārīḵ Āl Saljūq*, in Houtsma, *Recueil*. J. Ch. Bürgel, *Die Hofkorrespondenz 'Aḍud ad-Daulas und ihr Verhältnis zu anderen historischen Quellen der frühen Buyiden*, Wiesbaden, 1965, p. 78. H. Busse, *Chalif und Grosskönig*, Beirut, 1969, pp. 203-22. Idem, "Thron, Kosmos und Lebensbaum im Schāhnāma," in *Festgabe deutscher Iranisten zur 2500. Jahrfeier Irans*, Stuttgart, 1971, pp. 8ff. A. Christensen, *Iran Sass.*, pp. 66ff., 466ff. Ebn al-Aṯīr (repr.), VIII, p. 196 (Mardāvīj's throne, crown, and audiences). Ebn al-Balḵī, *Fārs-nāma*, repr. 1968, p. 97 (the throne, the assigned places at audiences). Ebn al-Jawzī, *Montaẓam*, pt. 7, pp. 7, 99f. (Buyid audiences). Ebn Meskawayh, *Tajāreb* I, pp. 317f. (Mardāvīj's throne, crown, and audiences). 'A.-A. Faqīhī, *Āl-e Būya wa awżā'-e zamān-e īšān bā namūdār-ī az zendagī-e mardom-e ān 'aṣr*, n.p., 1357 Š./1978, pp. 328-39, 343. Gardīzī, ed. Ḥabībī, p. 200 (Mas'ūd Ḡaznavī's throne, crown, and audience hall). R. Ghirshman, *Iran. Parthians and Sassanians*, London, 1962, figs. 214, 225-26, 242, 244-46, 259. Ḥamza (Kāvīānī Press), Berlin, n.d., p. 34 (royal dress and regalia). Helāl al-Ṣābe', *Rosūm Dār-al-Ḵelāfa*, ed. M. 'Awād, Baghdad, 1964, pp. 14f. (Buyid audiences). Jāḥeẓ, *Rasā'el*, ed. 'A. M. Hārūn, Cairo, 1965. Idem, *Ketāb al-tāj fī aḵlāq al-molūk*, ed. A. Zakī Bāšā, Cairo, 1322/1914, pp. 27 (the royal fan and fly whisk), 28 (Ḵorrambāš). Abu'l-Šaraf Nāṣeḥ Jorfādaqānī, *Tarjama-ye tārīḵ-e yamīnī*, ed. J. Še'ār, Tehran, 2537 = 1357 Š./1978. A. von Kremer, *Culturgeschichte des Orients* II, Vienna, 1877. Mas'ūdī, *Morūj*, ed. Pellat, I, pp. 228 (story of the Sasanian throne), 288 (Ḵorrambāš), 295; V, pp. 112 (Ya'qūb b. Layṯ's audiences), 270 (Mardāvīj's throne). Idem, *Tanbīh*, ed. 'A. E. Ṣāwī, Cairo, 1938, p. 93 (royal dress and regalia). Moḥammad b. 'Alī Rāvandī, *Rāḥat al-ṣodūr wa āyat al-sorūr*, ed. M. Eqbāl, London, 1921. Naršaḵī, pp. 12f. (audiences given by the ruler of Bukhara's wife before 656/1276). Ḵ'āja Neẓām-al-Molk Ṭūsī, *Sīāsat-nāma*, ed. J. Še'ār, Tehran, 1348 Š./1969. Th. Nöldeke, *Geschichte der Perser*, pp. 221f., 453f. Idem, *Aufsätze zur persischen Geschichte*, Leipzig, 1887, repr. Graz, 1974. Ẓahīr-al-Dīn Abū Šojā' Rūḏravārī, *Ḏayl tajāreb al-omam*, ed. H. F. Amedroz, Cairo, 1914-16, pp. 17f., 111 (Buyid audiences). *Šāh-nāma*, ed. Mohl, I, p. 172 vv. 682-83 (royal regalia and positions assigned to participants in audiences); II, p. 268 v. 868 (the throne); IV, pp. 226 vv. 2620f. (the curtain in audiences), 612 v. 3015 (the king holding a citron in his hand); VI, pp. 24 vv. 242 and 247 (the throne), 282 vv. 1467ff. (positions of participants); VII, pp. 306 vv. 3634ff. (the Ṭāqdīs throne), 314 vv. 3723ff. (bribing the head of protocol), 326 v. 3864 (suspension of the crown on a chain), 362 vv. 90ff. (the throne and its ornamentation), 362 vv. 93ff. (the king's hand). J. Sauvaget, *La mosquée omeyyade de Médine*, Paris, 1947, pp. 129ff. Spuler, *Iran*, pp. 344ff., 363ff. Ṯa'ālebī, *Ḡorar*, pp. 698f. (the Ṭāqdīs throne). Ṭabarī, I, p. 946 (suspension of the crown). *Tārīḵ-e Sīstān*, pp. 222f., 265f. (Ya'qūb b. Layṯ's audiences), 317f. (Naṣr b. Aḥmad Sāmānī's audiences), 378f. (audience given by Tāj-al-Dīn Abu'l-Fażl Naṣr b. Aḥmad, the amir of Sīstān, in 448/1054). Wolff, *Glossar*.

3. Mongol period. Abu'l-Qāsem 'Abd-Allāh b. Moḥammad Qāšānī, *Tārīḵ-e Ūljāytū*, ed. M. Hambly, Tehran, 1348 Š./1969. Faḵr-al-Dīn Abū Solaymān Dāwūd Banākatī, *Tārīḵ-e Banākatī*, ed. J. Še'ār, Tehran, 1348 Š./1969. C. R. Beazley, *The Text and Versions of John de Plano Carpini and William de Rubruquis*, London, 1903. Doerfer, I, sec. 50 (audiences among the Mongols). Ebn Baṭṭūṭa, II, Paris, 1854, pp. 346, 383f., 387f., 406. Rašīd-al-Dīn, *Jāme' al-tawārīḵ*, ed. B. Karīmī, vols. 1-2, Tehran, 1338 Š./1959. Johann de Plano Carpini, *Geschichte der Mongolen und Reisebericht 1245-47*, tr. and explained by F. Risch, Leipzig, 1930. F. Risch, *Wilhelm von Rubruck: Reise zu den Mongolen 1253-55*, Leipzig, 1934. Spuler, *Mongolen*², pp. 261ff.

4. Tīmūr and the Timurids. Clavijo, *Embassy to Tamerlane*, tr. from Spanish by G. Le Strange, London, 1929. Abū Ṭāleb Ḥosaynī Torbatī, *Tozūkāt-e tīmūrī. Institutes, Political and Military. Written by the Great Timour*, with Eng. tr. by Major Davy, publ. Joseph White, Oxford, 1783; 2nd ed. of the text, Tehran, 1343 Š./1964, pp. 326ff.

5. Safavid period. Anonymous, *'Ālamārā-ye ṣafawī*, ed. Y. Šokrī, Tehran, 1350 Š./1971. Moḥammad-Rafī' Anṣārī Mostawfī-al-Mamālek, *Dostūr al-molūk*, ed. M. T. Dānešpažūh, appendix to MDAT 16/5-6, 1346 Š./1967. Englebert Kaempfer, *Am Hofe des persischen Grosskönigs* (*1684–85*), ed. W. Hinz, Tübingen and Basel, 1977. Adam Olearius, *Die erste deutsche Expedition nach Persien* (*1635–39*), ed. from the original by H. von Staden, Leipzig, 1927. Qāżī Aḥmad Qomī, *Ḵolāṣat al-tawārīḵ*, ed. with German tr. H. Müller, *Die Chronik*..., Wiesbaden, 1964. J.-B. Tavernier, *Voyages en Perse*, Geneva, 1970.

See also J. Ḵāleqī Moṭlaq, "Bār o āyīn-e ān dar Īrān," *Īrān-nāma* 5/3, 1366 Š./1987, pp. 392-438; 6/1, 1366 Š./1987, pp. 34-75 (covering all periods).

(DJ. KHALEGHI-MOTLAGH)

ii. Qajar and Pahlavi Periods

The first Qajar shah was mostly engaged in foreign wars or struggles over the succession and paid little attention to formulating a detailed protocol for the royal audience (usually called *salām* in this period). In fact, it was not until the long reign of Nāṣer-al-Dīn Shah, during which Iran enjoyed a certain degree of political stability, that such a protocol was developed; it remained generally in force until the end of the dynasty. Until 1299/1881-82 Nāṣer-al-Dīn Shah regularly held public audience in the hall of the Taḵt-e Marmar (marble throne) on Nowrūz (new year); after that time the newly built Tālār-e Mūza (museum hall), later renamed Tālār-e Tājgoḏārī (coronation hall), was used for this purpose. At these ceremonies princes, ministers, and military and civil dignitaries were arrayed in order of rank (though this order was not always strictly observed). Palace cooks and eunuchs could be seen standing beside viziers and generals (Eʿtemād-al-Salṭana, p. 422). The shah would then appear in a military uniform studded with diamonds and other precious stones, carrying the diamond-studded sword (*šamšīr-e jahāngošā*) of Fatḥ-ʿAlī Shah and wearing the royal crown with a jeweled plume.

At the earlier *bār*s each guest would receive a purse containing 150 silver *šāhī* and five gold *do-hezārī* coins; in later times, however, the number of *šāhī*s declined, and the gold coins were omitted completely. The shah also received handsome gifts for himself (ibid., pp. 945-46). At first the diplomatic corps was received as a unit, the senior diplomat wishing the monarch a happy new year on behalf of his colleagues; the shah would then make a brief response through his interpreter. After the *bār*s had been moved to the Tālār-e Mūza, representatives of foreign governments were received individually by the shah, while the minister of foreign affairs and the royal interpreter stood at his right and left respectively. The *bār* at Nowrūz was customarily followed by displays of athletic skills, including gymnastics and wrestling bouts; the shah would reward the participants by throwing handfuls of gold coins. When Nowrūz coincided with days of solemn religious observance, however (as in 1312/1894, when it fell on 23 Ramażān), the *bār* was not held.

Beside Nowrūz there were other occasions for *bār*s. One such occasion was Nāṣer-al-Dīn Shah's return from his European tour. A general audience was held at the Taḵt-e Marmar on 24 Ṣafar 1308/25 October 1890. Military and civil grandees, as well as representatives from all classes of society, were stationed in the garden facing the open hall from the south. Military officers wore tall lambskin hats and blue broadcloth vests with shoulder straps indicating their ranks, the religious leaders their customary long cloaks and turbans, and judges tall cylindrical hats wrapped in cashmere shawls to match their cashmere robes. The shah appeared at the bottom of the garden and passed along the line, as the guests greeted him with bows, until he reached the throne, which was covered with a superb Persian rug and furnished with a pearl-studded cushion for him to lean against. As soon as he was seated, an attendant handed him a cup of coffee and a narghileh adorned with turquoise stones. He then spoke briefly of his satisfaction with the administration of the country during his absence. In response there were two orations on the happy occasion of his return and a program of choral music in his praise. The shah remained seated on the throne throughout these ceremonies, which lasted for about an hour, then left for the Golestān palace through a corridor to his left (Feuvrier, pp. 120-21).

The first major modification to the protocol of the *bār* under the Pahlavis was replacement of the long cashmere cloak (*jobba-ye terma*) and cylindrical hat by full formal dress (*lebās-e rasmī*) on the European model.

Two types of *bār*, or *salām*, were regularly held under the Pahlavis (1304-57 Š./1925-79). The first was the general audience (*salām-e ʿāmm*) held on four official festivals: the shah's birthday (24 Esfand/15 March for Reżā Shah and 4 Ābān/26 October for Moḥammad-Reżā Shah); Nowrūz (1 Farvardīn/21 or 22 March); ʿĪd-e Mabʿaṯ (27 Rajab), the day the Prophet was charged to recite the word of God; and ʿĪd-e Ḡadīr-e Ḵomm (18 Ḏu'l-ḥejja, q.v.), the day on which, according to the Shiʿites, Moḥammad nominated ʿAlī as his successor. The second was the special audience (*salām-e ḵāṣṣ*) held on the ʿĪd-e Feṭr (1 Šawwāl), the celebration at the end of Ramażān.

Under Moḥammad-Reżā Shah the general *bār* usually lasted from 8:00 a.m. to 1:00 p.m. in the grand audience hall of the Golestān Palace, known as Tālār-e Tājgoḏārī. Groups composed of members of the cabinet and parliament, ranking representatives of foreign states, directors of institutions and government agencies, and community leaders were received separately by the shah, according to a preestablished timetable. The master of royal ceremonies usually informed each group of its scheduled time at least one week in advance. Members of the group arrived at the palace half an hour before the appointed hour and were greeted by the master of ceremonies, who then conducted them into the audience hall, where they arranged themselves in order of rank to await the arrival of the monarch. The shah was announced by the master of royal ceremonies and entered in the full uniform of commander in chief, to be greeted with bows by the assembled notables. The leader of the group expressed on behalf of his colleagues good wishes on the auspicious occasion and received a brief reply from the monarch, who then proceeded past the line and left the hall through the doorway by which he had entered.

Separate audiences were granted in the following order: 1) Representatives of the clergy were received by the shah seated in his private office, rather than in the Tālār-e Tājgoḏārī. Only a few (at most five) men from the Tehran area attended these audiences, dressed in clerical robes and turbans; the religious leaders of Qom and Mašhad, the two most important Islamic centers in Iran, rarely if ever participated. 2) The second group included the minister of court, the shah's military and civil adjutants, department heads from the Ministry of the Court, and the directors of subordinate agencies like the Pahlavi Foundation, the Royal Bureau of Social Services (Sāzmān-e Šāhanšāhī-e Ḵadamāt-e Ejtemāʿī), and the Institute for the Protection of Mothers and Infants (Bongāh-e Ḥemāyat-e Mādarān o Kūdakān). 3). Members of the cabinet and their deputies came next, with the ministers aligned behind the prime minister in order of seniority of service, then of age. Former prime ministers and speakers of the Majles, as well as those who had received the Homāyūn or Tāj decorations, were considered senior to their colleagues, regardless of their tenure in office. 4) Senators and deputies of the Majles were received in two separate groups. 5) Next came ranking government officials, heads of state agencies (selected for the occasion by their respective departments), and judges of the supreme court (Dīvān-e ʿĀlī-e Kešvar). In the early 1320s Š./1940s ministers were ranked as follows, according to the official manual of protocol (*Dastūr-e tašrīfāt*, pp. 4-5): Foreign Affairs (Omūr-e Ḵāreja), Finance (Dārāʾī), Justice (Dādgostarī), Interior (Kešvar), Education (Farhang), Roads (Rāh), Industry and Commerce (Pīša o Honar o Bāzargānī), Communications (Post o Telegrāf o Telefon), Agriculture (Kešāvarzī), and Health (Behdārī). 6) Officials and faculty of the University of Tehran and other institutions of higher learning, who were arrayed in order of seniority of service. 7) The foreign diplomatic corps, including ambassadors, ministers plenipotentiary, and chargés d'affaires in that order, attended only on the occasion of Nowrūz and the shah's birthday. They dressed according to the customs and protocol of their respective countries. Representatives of some Islamic states also participated in the audience on the ʿĪd-e Mabʿaṯ, when they were received by the shah in his private office. 8) Former ministers, ambassadors, and provincial governors formed a separate group. 9) Next the president of the National Oil Company, trustees of government-controlled banks and insurance companies, members of the chamber of commerce, publishers of major Tehran newspapers, and representatives of the bar association (Kānūn-e Wokalā-ye Dādgostarī) were received. 10) The succeeding group included ranking municipal authorities of Tehran, like the mayor, members of the city council, and other high officials, as well as community leaders and guild chiefs (*roʾasā-ye aṣnāf*). 11) Ranking officers of the armed forces (from colonel up, *Dastūr-e tašrīfāt*, p. 2), the police, and the gendarmerie were the last group presented.

The state dress prescribed for court officials, ministers, and their deputies was frock coat, trousers, and bicorn hat, all of black broadcloth; black patent-leather boots; and white gloves. The frock coat had gold-embroidered cuffs, a high closed collar, and seven gilt buttons bearing the Persian lion and sun. A long sword with a golden hilt was worn on the left side, and the side seams of the trousers were trimmed with gold braid 10 cm wide. Ministers had panels of gold embroidery on the front and back of the coat; in addition, the prime minister wore a braided gold belt and tassel. Deputy ministers had panels of embroidery on the back but not the front. Dignitaries lower than the rank of deputy minister had no embroidery on either the fronts or backs of their frock coats. The bicorn hat was creased in the middle and ornamented with white feathers and gold braid clasped in the center by a circle in the three colors of the Iranian flag: red, white, and green. (According to *Dastūr-e tašrīfāt*, p. 19, other forms of official dress were permitted in the Persian Gulf area in summer.)

University and college professors attended the *bār* dressed in hexagonal caps with tassels and long black robes with wide bands sewn onto the shoulders in the colors of the schools or institutions they represented. Judges appeared in black robes with white lace on the collars and shoulders and tall cylindrical hats. Other groups wore black jackets, trousers striped in charcoal and light gray, neckies, white shirts, black patent-leather boots, and tall cylindrical hats. Decorations and medals were worn on the left side of the chest or as pendants.

The *salām-e ḵāṣṣ* was held at Saʿdābād Palace when ʿĪd-e Feṭr fell in summer and at Nīāvarān palace when it fell in winter. The shah customarily received members of the cabinet, the presiding officers of the Majles and the Senate, the commander of the armed forces, the chief of the Iranian intelligence agency SAVAK, and representatives of Muslim countries.

In addition to these regularly scheduled *bār*s or *salām*s, ambassadors and ministers plenipotentiary assigned to Tehran were granted royal audience to present their credentials. On the appointed date the representative would be met at his embassy by the master of ceremonies of the Ministry of Foreign Affairs, who would personally conduct him and the ranking members of his staff to the court, where they would be greeted at the gate with their national anthem played by a military band. Then they would be conducted to the anteroom, where the master of royal ceremonies would greet them. The latter would then conduct the ambassador or minister plenipotentiary and his counterpart from the Ministry of Foreign Affairs to an audience with the shah. The minister of court, military and civil heads of the court departments, and the minister of foreign affairs would also be present. The foreign representative would submit his credentials and ask permission for his colleagues, who had remained behind in the waiting room, to be introduced to the monarch. After these ceremonies the foreign delegation would be ushered out of the palace in exactly the same manner in which it had arrived.

In an effort to keep all important national matters under his close personal control, Moḥammad-Reżā Shah received in audience (*šarafyābī*) the prime minister twice a week; the president of the Senate, the speaker of the Majles, the president of the National Oil Company, the head of SAVAK, the commanders of the various branches of the armed forces, the chief of the military staff, and the head of police reported to him once a week. According to *Dastūr-e tašrīfāt* (p. 6), black jackets and top hats were required dress for such meetings. All ministers, except for those of war and foreign affairs, reported through the office of the prime minister unless they were specifically summoned by the shah or had something particularly significant to report to him directly. The minister of foreign affairs often met with him at the end of each day. The master of royal ceremonies oversaw the general management of the official audiences with the shah, and the adjutants made sure that daily court routines proceeded smoothly and on schedule.

The *šarafyābīs* were held in the Kāk̲-e Marmar (marble palace) and in the Kāk̲-e Mak̲ṣūṣ (private palace) and in summer in Saʿdābād Palace. When, after the assassination attempt on the shah at the Marble Palace 10 April 1965, Nīāvarān Palace (Kāk̲-e Nīāvarān) was built, most audiences were transferred to it. The new palace incorporated the Jahān-namā, a Qajar construction, which was used for morning audiences; the Kāk̲-e Mak̲ṣūṣ-e Nīāvarān was used in the afternoon.

At such meetings the shah received his vistors seated. They greeted him with a bow and bowed again when taking their leave. If the shah honored them by stretching forth his hand, they would normally kiss it. As none of his adjutants attended such meetings, the monarch's instructions were conveyed through his visitors, who submitted them in writing to the royal chancery.

Audiences with the queen were requested and granted through her office, and a similar protocol was followed.

For further details see COURT.

Bibliography: E. Aubin, *La Perse d'aujourd'hui. Iran-Mésopotamie*, Paris, 1908, pp. 133ff. *Dastūr-e tašrīfāt*, Tehran, 1321 Š./1942. Eʿtemād-al-Salṭana, *Rūz-nāma-ye k̲āṭerāt*. J. B. Feuvrier, *Trois ans à la cour de Perse*, Paris, 1906. Mahdīqolī Hedāyat Mok̲ber-al-Salṭana, *K̲āṭerāt o k̲aṭarāt*, Tehran, 1329 Š./1950, pp. 121-23. W. Litten, *Persische Flitterwochen*, Berlin, 1925. J. Polak, *Persien. Das Land und seine Bewohner*, Leipzig, 1865, I, pp. 379ff. C. Serena, *Hommes et choses en Perse (1877-78)*, Paris, 1883, pp. 231ff.

(Ḥ. FARHŪDĪ)

BAR HEBRAEUS. See EBN ʿEBRĪ.

BAR KŌNAY, THEODORE (Kēwānay = Saturninus, not Kōnī, according to Cambridge University Library ms. Add. 1998; cf. Burkitt, p. 14 n. 1), an 8th–9th-century Nestorian teacher (doctor, *malfānā*, in a ms. from Mosul; Pognon, p. 105) and writer from Kaškar in Mesopotamia (Babylonia; cf. Alfaric, p. 24 n. 7), not to be confused with his namesake, an uncle ordained as Bishop of Lāšōm in 893 (Baumstark, 1922, p. 218; Ortiz de Urbina, p. 202, with references; Pognon, p. 105; mistaken by Duval, p. 214). Theodore Bar Kōnay is referred to as the author of a number of funeral orations and a church history (Baumstark, op. cit., p. 219), but is above all known as the author of the *Book of Scholia* (*kᵉṯāḇā deskōlyōn*), composed in 791-92 and dedicated to his "brother" Yōḥannān. The work is an impressive mixture of fantastic and remarkably sound pieces of information in "11 *mēmrē* (discourses) with a thematic treatment of the entire Bible accompanied by a logical-grammatical, speculative-theological, and anti-heretical commentary, including in particular an apology presented in the form of a catechism for Christian teaching and a valuable overview of such heretical dogmas as Chaldean, Greek, and Persian forms of paganism; this was supplemented by objective exegesis of selected biblical passages from each book supported by exact contributions to lexicology" (Baumstark, 1922, pp. 218f.). Of special importance for Iranian studies is book 11, dealing with heretical sects and religions, Christian as well as non-Christian, e.g., Simon Magus (cf. Acts 8), Menandros, Basilides, the Carpocrates, the Ebionites, Valentinos, the Ophites, Tatian, the Montanists, Alchasai (with important, but imprecisely placed details; see ALCHASAI), Bardesanes, Arius, Origen, the Mandeans, the Zoroastrians, and, first and foremost, the Manicheans (see Baumstark, 1954, pp. 188f., for further references). The most important extracts of book 11 were published and translated by Pognon, and the whole text was edited by Addai Scher (*CSCO, Scriptores Syri* 65-66, Paris and Leipzig, 1912; on his manuscripts, including M.-A. Kugener's collation of the Berlin ms. Orient. Quart. 871 [Cumont, app. III, pp. 76-80], see vol. 66, pp. 1-2).

The Book of Scholia is not an entirely independent piece of work; Bar Kōnay's primary source is Epiphanius of Salamis (4th cent.), not the *Panarion* ("Medicine basket," i.e., against all heresies), but the summary of this work, the *Anakephalaiōsis*, and, no doubt, only in a Syriac translation (Pognon, pp. 106-07). Among his other sources are the *Apology* falsely attributed to Meliton of Sardes (2nd cent.) and, directly or indirectly, the Nestorian Theodore of Mopsuestia (ca. 360-428; his now lost *Perì tēs en Persídi magikēs* [On the teaching of the Magians in Persia], the original text of which was still known by Photios [9th cent.]), both well-known in Syriac tradition (Baumstark, 1922, pp. 27, 103).

The section on Zarathustra (*ʿl zrdwšt mgwšʾ*), "this impure one" (*hnʾ ṭnpʾ*), and his teachings (Pognon, pp. 111ff., 161ff.) has been thoroughly examined by Benveniste. While the biography is filled with legendary details taken from non-Zoroastrian sources, Theodore Bar Kōnay's survey of the teachings pretends to be based on a writing by Zarathustra himself ("*he says that*," "*about* x *he says*") (Benveniste, pp. 175ff.). It contains inter alia the story of Zurvān's giving birth to Ohrmazd and Ahriman, of which three further versions are preserved (another Syriac version and two in Armenian), and allusions in Manichean, Syriac, and Arabic texts (cf. R. C. Zaehner, *Zurvan. A Zoroastrian Dilemma*, Oxford, 1955, pp. 418ff.) and in this connection also the epitheta of Zurvān (*ʾšwqr, pršqr, zrwqr, zrwn*, Pognon, p. 111, line 10 from the bottom; cf.

Benveniste, p. 176; Zaehner, pp. 435, 439, 441; and *EIr.* I, p. 430).

Most significant in the *Book of Scholia*, however, is the section on Manichean cosmogony, as it gives direct quotations from Mani and thus forms an obvious contrast to Theodore's own more or less fantastic notes on the biography of Mani. In quoting Mani, Theodore reveals that his own Syriac language, far from being the language of Edessa, is closely related to the Aramaic of Mani himself, so in the important rendering of the name of the Great Builder as Bān Rabbā (Mandaic *ban*, "official" Syriac *banāya*, Arabic *al-bannā'*, thus understood by Th. Nöldeke, *ZDMG* 43, 1889, p. 546; cf. Adam p. 17 n. 22, with a reference to *Kephalaia*, p. 49, line 24; and especially H. J. Polotsky, "Manichäismus," in Pauly-Wissowa, Suppl. VI, 1935, col. 242 [= *Collected Papers*, Jerusalem, 1971, p. 699]).

Beside the translation of Pognon both translations and commentaries have been published by Cumont, Schaeder, Jackson, Adam, and Böhlig. As a contribution to the understanding of essential parts of the teaching of Mani, the *Book of Scholia* is of primary value. According to Schaeder (p. 245), "only Theod. B. K. had the insight to fathom the insoluble interrelationship between cosmology and soteriology in Mani." But riddles still remain, e.g., the "Angel (*malakā*), whose name is Nḥšbṭ" (Pognon, p. 127, lines 20-21, and pp. 185-86; see Jackson, p. 225; the latest attempt at interpreting the word is Hermann Stocks, "Manichäische Miszellen IV, Nahaschbat," *Zeitschrift für Religions- und Geistesgeschichte* 4, 1952, pp. 77f.).

Bibliography: A. Adam, *Texte zum Manichäismus*, Berlin, 1954. P. Alfaric, *Les écritures manichéennes* I, Paris, 1918, pp. 118-19. A. Baumstark, *Geschichte der syrischen Literatur mit Ausschluss der christlich-palästinensischen Texte*, Bonn, 1922. Idem and A. Rücker, "Die syrische Literatur," in *HO* 3/2-3 Leiden, 1954. E. Benveniste, "Le témoignage de Théodore bar Kōnay sur le zoroastrisme," *Le monde oriental* 26-27, 1932-35, pp. 170-215. A. Böhlig with the collaboration of J. P. Asmussen, *Die Gnosis* III: *Der Manichäismus*, Zurich and Munich, 1980. F. C. Burkitt, *The Religion of the Manichees*, Cambridge, 1925. F. Cumont, *Recherches sur le manichéisme* I: *La cosmogonie manichéenne d'après Théodore bar Khôni*, Brussels, 1908. R. Duval, *Anciennes littératures chrétiennes* II: *La littérature syriaque*, Paris, 1899. A. V. W. Jackson, *Researches in Manichaeism*, New York, 1932, pp. 221-54. Th. Nöldeke, "Bar Chōnī über Homer, Hesiod und Orpheus," *ZDMG* 53, 1899, pp. 501-07. I. Ortiz de Urbina, *Patrologia Syriaca*, Rome, 1958; 2nd ed., 1965. H. Pognon, *Inscriptions mandaïtes des coupes de Khouabir* II, Paris, 1899. H.-C. Puech, *Le manichéisme. Son fondateur, sa doctrine*, Paris, 1949. H. H. Schaeder, "Iranische Lehren," in R. Reitzenstein and H. H. Schaeder eds., *Studien zum antiken Synkretismus aus Iran und Griechenland*, Leipzig and Berlin, 1926, repr. Darmstadt, 1965, pp. 203ff..

(J. P. ASMUSSEN)

BAR-E MEHR, a fire temple in Yazd. See DAR-E MEHR

BARĀ'A, an Imami theological term denoting dissociation from the enemies of the imams. During the conflict between ʿAlī and Moʿāwīa, formulas of dissociation were used by both parties, and this practice was continued by both Omayyads and ʿAlids throughout the Omayyad period. At this stage the ʿAlids only dissociated from those who had fought ʿAlī while he was in power. With the emergence (during the first half of the 2nd/8th century) of an Imami doctrine of the imamate based on allegiance (*walāya*) to the imams and enmity (*ʿadāwa*) toward their enemies, *barāʾa* was broadened to include both the usurpers who had deprived ʿAlī of his God-given rights and those who had supported these usurpers. It thus applied to the majority of the *ṣaḥāba*, and in particular to the first three caliphs.

As a religious duty, *barāʾa* is either subsumed within *walāya* or is regarded as a necessary complement to it (as in ʿAlī al-Reżā's letter to al-Ma'mūn, in Ebn Bābawayh, *ʿOyūn akbār al-Reżā*, Najaf, 1390/1970, II, pp. 123, 124-25). The duty of dissociating from four male and four female idols is mentioned in two creeds of Ebn Bābawayh, the *Resālat al-eʿteqādāt* (tr. A. A. A. Fyzee, *A Shīʿite Creed*, London, 1942, p. 109) and the *Hedāya* (Tehran, 1377/1957-58, pp. 8f.). The reference to the idols is probably an instance of *taqīya*, those who are in fact meant being Abū Bakr, ʿOmar, ʿOṯmān, and Moʿāwīa, ʿĀ'eša, Ḥafṣa, Hend, and Omm Ḥakam (Moʿāwīa's sister) (cf. Majlesī, *Beḥār al-anwār* XVIII/2, p. 434). In contrast, dissociation from an imam is considered a heinous crime, and it is a moot point whether the believer may resort to it so as to save his life.

In the period preceding the Greater Occultation (see ḠAYBA), dissociation was implemented by a public declaration of the imam or by a message sent privately to the person concerned. The message might be oral or written; the former was preferred by the earlier imams, and the latter by those imams who spent much of their lives in prison, as well as by the *safīrs*. The *safīrs* showed a predilection for formal documents which were distributed among the community. With the start of the Greater Occultation the right to pronounce *barāʾa* devolved naturally on the scholars and lawyers.

In times of danger, *barāʾa* could often be pronounced only within a circle of trusted friends; at other times it could not be pronounced at all and had to be kept in the heart, in which case it is referred to as "that which is concealed" (*al-możmar*) (Ebn Bābawayh, *Creed*, p. 116).

Barāʾa is often accompanied by imprecations which are uttered during supererogatory prayers (*qonūt*), on the occasion of the Ḡadīr Ḵomm festival, or when standing over the grave of an enemy. Where the believer enjoys freedom of action (*ekṯīār*), dissociation also takes the form of social ostracism: The believer must not give the adversaries alms tax or help them in any other way; he may not allow them to perform the pilgrimage on his behalf; he may neither pray behind them nor accept their testimony as valid (Ebn Bābawayh, *Hedāya*, p. 9).

While *barā'a* was directed primarily against non-Imami enemies of the imams, it was also used against other categories of opponents. These included Imamis who did not toe the official line on certain doctrinal or theological issues (e.g., Zorāra b. Aʿyan and Yūnos b. ʿAbd-al-Raḥmān); deviant members of an imam's family (e.g., ʿAbd-Allāh, the son of Jaʿfar al-Ṣādeq); erstwhile Imamis who abandoned the Emāmīya as a result of disagreements over the identity of the imam; and extremist Shiʿites (*ḡolāt*), regardless of whether these had at some point belonged to the Emāmīya (Kohlberg, pp. 158-67). At the same time the imams (as well as Imami scholars) were keenly aware of the danger of *barā'a*'s being abused through application to all who deviated from rigidly held principles (a habit of which the Kharijites were accused). Hence traditions in which the believers are exhorted to define faith in as broad a manner as possible, so as to accommodate within its bounds Imamis guilty of various sins or lapses. In one case at least, a tradition of this kind is entitled *al-nahy ʿan al-barā'a* "prohibiting dissociation" (*Ketāb Jaʿfar al-Ḥazramī*, ms. Tehran University no. 962, fol. 41b).

Bibliography: Given in the text. See also Koleynī, *ʿOṣūl al-kāfī*, Tehran, 1375-77/1955-57, II, pp. 22-23, 42-45, 124-27, 221, 405. Ebn Abi'l-Ḥadīd, *Šarḥ nahj al-balāḡa*, Cairo, 1959-64, IV, pp. 54, 113-16. Moḥammad-Bāqer Majlesī, *Beḥār al-anwār*, n.p., 1305-15/1887-97, IV, pp. 175-76; VII, pp. 368-71; IX, pp. 416-21; XVIII/2, pp. 383, 396-98. E. Kohlberg, "*Barā'a* in Shīʿī Doctrine," *Jerusalem Studies in Arabic and Islam* 7, 1986, pp. 139-75.

(E. KOHLBERG)

BARĀDŪST (Kurdish Brādōst), name of Kurdish tribe, region, mountain range, river, and amirate.

The tribe, mostly settled now, lives in Barādūst *nāḥīa* of Rawāndūz *qażā* in Arbil *lewā/moḥāfaẓa*, Iraq. They are Shafiʿite Sunnis and speak the Kurmanji dialect of Kurdish mixed with the neighboring Sorani dialects (see the folklore material collected by K̲ōšnāw). According to the information provided by the earliest available account (Bedlīsī, pp. 382-88), the tribe (*ʿašīrat-e Barādūst*, p. 385) or, rather, the conglomerate of Barādūst tribes (*ʿašīrat wa aqwām*, p. 386), must have been much larger, occupying the entire region to the west of Lake Urmia.

The region comprised, in the early 11th/late 16th century, several *nāḥīa*s including Targavar, Margavar, Dol, Ṣūmāy, and Urmia (Bedlīsī, pp. 382-88). The Ottoman-Persian frontier of 1639, which survived until World War I and forms the present boundary of Iran with Turkey and Iraq, divided Barādūst territory into two parts. In the late 13th/19th-century administrative division of the Ottoman empire, Barādūst was a *nāḥīa* of Rawāndūz *qażā*, Šahrezūr *sanjaq*, Mosul *welāyat* (Cuinet, II, p. 846). Following the disintegration of the Ottoman Empire, this *nāḥīa* was officially incorporated into Iraq in 1925, where it had 108 villages with a population of 5,185 in 1957 (Iraq Republic, pp. 238-42). Under the Qajar dynasty, the western limits of Margavar, Dašt, Targavar, Barādūst, and Ṣūmāy formed part of the often disputed Ottoman-Persian frontier (Mohandesbāšī, p. 150). In the administrative redivision of Iran under the Pahlavīs, the boundaries of the traditional *nāḥīa*s or *maḥāl*s of Barādūst, Targavar, Margavar, Dol, and Ṣūmāy were left more or less intact forming *dehestān*s of Urmia (*Ketāb-e asāmī-e dehāt-e kešvar*, pp. 460-73). The decennial census of 1335 Š./1956 counted 63 villages with a population of 7,302 in Barādūst *dehestān* (Iran Government, p. 37).

Barādūstdāḡ or Čīā-y Nīwak̲ēn, a mountain range over 5,000 feet above sea level and about 25 miles long, stretches northwest from the Rawāndūz river opposite the town of Rawāndūz in Iraq to Rūbārī Rūkūčūk, a tributary of the Great Zab (Naval Intelligence Division, p. 109 and fig. 27 facing p. 103). The snow-fed Barādūst river rises in the peaks of the mountain range along the Iran-Turkey border, flows through Barādūst territory, and, joined by other headwaters, forms Nāzlūčāy, which discharges into Lake Urmia to the northeast of the city of Urmia (*Times Atlas*, pl. 37; *Gazetteer of Iran* I, map I-11-B).

The formation of Barādūst amirate was part of the process of the rise of Kurdish political power in the form of small dynasties and numerous (semi-) independent amirates that appeared all over Kurdistan in the 10th-11th/15th-16th centuries (see Bedlīsī for an early account of the principalities until 1005/1597). Bedlīsī (p. 382) related the founders of the principalities to the Hasanwayhid dynasty (348-406/959-1015, q.v.) and divided them into two lines—the amirs of Ṣūmāy and those of Targavar and Qalʿa-ye Dāwūd (pp. 384-88). At the climax of its power, the amirate's domain extended from the western shores of Lake Urmia to parts of the *welāyat*s of Arbil, Baghdad, and Diyarbakır (ibid., p. 383).

The hereditary rule of Barādūst, like that of other amirates, was, however, soon threatened by the centralizing and expansionist policies of the Ottoman and Safavid empires, which turned Kurdistan into a battlefield for more than three centuries. To protect their sovereignty, Barādūst princes put up continued resistance to both empires though they often relied on one against the other. Thus, after initial opposition to Shah Esmāʿīl's efforts to establish his authority over the area, the powerful Barādūst amir Ḡazī Qerān rallied to the Safavids (Bedlīsī, pp. 382-83). However, after the famous Ottoman-Safavid battle of Čālderān (q.v.) (920/1514), the principality switched allegiance to the victorious Ottoman side.

Shah ʿAbbās I (996-1038/1588-1629, q.v.) initially recognized the hereditary rule of Barādūst princes though relations deteriorated and Amir Khan Barādūst (K̲ānī Lapzērīn, "The Gold-Hand Khan") revolted against the shah in the fortress of Demdem (Kurd. Dimdim) in 1017/1608. The neighboring Mokrī (q.v.) principality joined forces with the Barādūst throughout the revolt, which has become a major theme of Kurdish folklore and literature (Dzhalilov) and is also described in an eyewitness report by the shah's chronicler Eskandar Beg (pp. 791-801, 807-11).

To undermine the growing power of the Kurdish element, the Safavid and Qajar monarchs sent numerous punitive expeditions to the area, massacred the population of Mokrī principality (Eskandar Monšī, pp. 811-14), transferred thousands of Kurds (Perry, pp. 205, 208, 209) from the western lake area, and resettled there the Turkish tribes of Afšār (q.v.; see also Mīrzā Rašīd, pp. 49-55) and Qarapāpāḵ (q.v.).

By the late 13th/mid-19th century, when Qajar and Ottoman state power was extended to all parts of Kurdistan, the principality had already disintegrated. Conflicts with the central government continued, however, and once more the entire territory of West Azerbaijan came under the rule of the Šakār (Kurd. Šikāk) tribe led by Esmāʿīl Āḡā Simkō, "Semītqū" (see Arfa; van Bruinessen). Princely families and tribal organization have largely disappeared since World War II, giving way to modern party organization of Kurdish nationalism (e.g., the autonomist Kurdish Republic established in West Azerbaijan in 1946 and the autonomist war that began in August, 1970).

See BOUNDARIES i.

Bibliography: G. H. Arfa, *Under Five Shahs*, Edinburgh, 1964, s.v. Simko. Amir Šaraf Khan Bedlīsī, *Šaraf-nāma*, ed. M. ʿAbbāsī, Tehran, 1343 Š./1964. M. van Bruinessen, "Kurdish Tribes and the State of Iran: The Case of Simko's Revolt," in *The Conflict of Tribe and State in Iran and Afghanistan*, ed. R. Tapper, New York, 1983, pp. 364-400. V. Cuinet, *La Turquie d'Asie* II, Paris, 1892, p. 846. D. Dzh. Dzhalilov, *Kurdskiĭ geroicheskiĭ èpos "Zlatorukiĭ Khan,"* Moscow, 1967. Eskandar Monšī Torkmān, *Tārīḵ-e ʿālamārā-ye ʿabbāsī*, Tehran, 1350 Š./1971-72. *Gazetteer of Iran* I, p. 105, map I-II-B. Ghilan, "Les Kurdes persans et l'invasion ottomane," *Revue du monde musulman* 2/5, May, 1908, pp. 1-22; 2/10, October, 1908, pp. 193-210. Iran Government, Ministry of Interior, Public Statistics, National and Province Statistics of the First Census of Iran, Nov., 1956, I, *Number and Distribution of the Inhabitants for Iran and the Census Provinces*, Tehran, August, 1961, p. 37. Iraq Republic, Wezārat al-Dāḵelīya, Modīrīyat al-Nofūs al-ʿĀmma, *al-Majmūʿa al-eḥṣāʾīya le-tasjīl ʿamm 1957; Sokkān al-qorā le-alwīat al-Mūṣel wa'l- Solaymānīya wa Arbīl wa Karkūk wa Dīālā*, Baghdad, 1961, pp. 234-42. *Ketāb-e asāmī-e dehāt-e kešvar*, Wezārat-e Kešvar, Edāra-ye Koll-e Āmār wa Ṯabt-e Aḥwāl, vol. 1, 1329 Š./1950, pp. 460-73. S. Ḵōšnāw, "Bašēkī dīš la gōrānīī foḷklōrī kurdī la nāwčay Brādōst dā" (Kurdish folk songs in the Brādōst region, pt. 2), *Karwan* (Arbil), 4/39, December, 1985, pp. 101-05. V. Minorsky, "Ṣōmāi," in *EI*[1] IV, p. 193. Idem, "Shakāk," ibid., p. 290. Idem, "Urmiya," ibid., pp. 1032-36. Mīrzā Rašīd Adīb-al-Šoʿarāʾ, *Tārīḵ-e Afšār*, ed. P. Šahrīār Afšār and M. Rāmīān, Tabrīz, 1346 Š./1967 (numerous accounts of Barādūst/Afšār encounters). Jaʿfar Khan Mohandes-bāšī Mošīr-al-Dawla, *Resāla-ye taḥqīqāt-e sarḥad-dīya*, Tehran, 1348 Š./1969, pp. 150-66. Naval Intelligence Division (Great Britain), *Iraq and the Persian Gulf*, September, 1944, p. 109 and fig. 27 facing p. 103. B. Nikitine, "Barādūst," in *EI*[2] I, pp. 1030-31. Idem, "Rawāndiz Ruiyndiz," in *EI*[1] III, pp. 1130-32. J. Perry, "Forced Migration in Iran during the Seventeenth and Eighteenth Centuries," *Iranian Studies* 8/4, 1975, pp. 199-215. Razmārā, *Farhang* IV, p. 85. *The Times Atlas of the World*, 7th ed., New York, 1985, pl. 37.

(A. HASSANPOUR)

BARAḠĀNĪ MOLLĀ **MOḤAMMAD-TAQĪ,** QAZVĪNĪ, ŠAHĪD-E ṮĀLEṮ, an important Shiʿite *ʿālem* of Qazvīn (d. 1263/1847). Baraḡānī was the first cleric to declare *takfīr* (ca. 1238/1822) against Shaikh Aḥmad Aḥsāʾī (q.v.), and subsequently became the leading opponent of Shaikhism in Iran. He studied in Iran and Iraq, and accompanied his teacher, Moḥammad-ʿAlī Ṭabāṭabāʾī, on the 1242/1826 jihad against Russia. After a disagreement in Tehran with Fatḥ-ʿAlī Shah, he returned to Qazvīn, where he acquired a reputation as one of the best preachers of his day. His best-known work is the *Majāles al-mottaqīn* on the sufferings of the imams. His brother, Moḥammad Ṣāleḥ, wrote numerous works on this theme. His niece, Fāṭema (Qorrat-al-ʿAyn), became famous as a Babi leader but Moḥammad-Taqī's own opposition to Shaikhism and Babism increased and led to his murder in the mosque he had built in Qazvīn (Jāmeʿ-e Ṣaḡīr) on 15 Ḏu'l-qaʿda 1263/25 October 1847, apparently the work of three Babis. The title *šahīd-e ṯāleṯ* (the third martyr) was subsequently conferred on him, and his tomb remains prominent in Qazvīn.

Bibliography: Moḥammad b. Solaymān Tonokābonī, *Qeṣaṣ al-ʿolamāʾ*, Tehran, n.d., pp. 19-66 (with numerous digressions). Āḡā Bozorg Ṭehrānī *Ṭabaqāt aʿlām al-šīʿa* II, Najaf, 1956, pp. 226-28. Mollā Mīrzā Moḥammad-ʿAlī Kašmīrī *Nojūm al-samāʾ*, Lucknow, 1303/1885-86, pp. 407-11. Bāmdād, *Rejāl* I, pp. 203-04. Moḥammad-Taqī Baraḡānī *Majāles al-mottaqīn*, Tehran, 1280/1863-64, and other editions. Moḥammad Šarīf Rāzī, *Ganjīna-ye dānešmandān* VI, Tehran, 1354 Š./1975, pp. 162-63.

(D. M. MACEOIN)

BARAK, a kind of firm and durable woven cloth used for coats, overcoats (*labbāda*), shawls (in Afghanistan), *čūḵa*s (surcoats for shepherds) and leggings (locally *peytowa*). It seems that in the past it was mainly used to make hats and gowns (*qabā*) for dervishes (see *Ānand Rāj* I, p. 678, quoting a poem of Saʿdī). According to the *Borhān-e qāṭeʿ* (ed. Moʿīn, I, p. 260) *barak* designated a kind of short dress worn by the people of the marshes (*mardom-e dār al-marz*).

Barak is rare; the main center of fabrication is Bošrūya in Khorasan, a town situated about 107 km southwest of Šahr-e Ferdows (formerly Tūn). Good quality *barak* is made from the underhair of goats (*kork*, i.e., mohair), inferior quality from camel hair. The wool is gathered in late spring and must be separated from the top hair by means of special wooden combs (cf. Wulff, pp. 177, 180-82). The quality of *barak* is determined by the purity of the mohair. It may be beaten to make it fluffier and easy to spin. By means of a spindle (*tongol* or *dūk* in the local dialects) the pure soft wool is spun into long strands (locally *farat*). These strands must be very fine to produce high-quality *barak*. The weaver, usually a woman, sits with her feet in a pit; at one end the warps (*tūn*) are attached to a wall and at the other to a beam (called *navard* in Khorasan) in the pit. Using her left and right foot alternately, the weaver separates two warps and passes the soft wool weft (*tāb*) between them. The finished *barak* is a long, narrow piece of cloth, which is then kneaded in the bath to tighten the weave. Finally, it is ironed and readied for market. *Barak* has the natural colors white, milk white, brown, dark brown, and black; pieces of inferior quality may be dyed with madder (*rūnās*).

Well known kinds of *barak* are made by the Barbarī tribe of Hazāra (*barak-e hazārī*) and in Bošrūya and Kermān province. The sale of *barak* was an important and profitable business in the past. Numerous family names such as Barakčī, Barakčīān, Barakforūš, point to past or present engagement in the trade. Mašhad is now the center of *barak* sales. There are *barak* shops on all sides of the holy shrine of Imam Reżā. The main trading center used to be in the great *bāzār*, but now it is located in the Bāzār-e Reżā and small sarais (*tīmča*).

Barak is usually sold by the *čūb* (an ancient measure of length); one piece (*qawāra*) of *barak* measures eighteen *čūb*s (ca. 3.5 or 4.5 yards).

Bibliography: Moḥammad Pādšāh, *Farhang-e Ānand Rāj*, ed. M. Dabīrsīāqī, Tehran, 1335 Š./1956. H. E. Wulff, *The Traditional Crafts of Persia*, Cambridge, Mass., 1966.

(T. BĪNEŠ)

BARAKĪ BARAK, an inhabited locality in the province of Lōgar in Afghanistan (*Afghanistan*, p. 15) 33°58′ north latitude, 68°58′ east longitude), made up of three component parts: 1. a large village of the Tajik type with rows of houses sandwiched between narrow alleys leading to squares—a compact layout suitable for defense in a region of chronic insecurity; 2. a settlement of the Pashtun type consisting of about ten fortified farmhouses (*qalʿa*s) with high walls, corner towers, and a gateway surmounted by an upper room (*bālā-ḵāna*; see Kieffer, 1986); 3. a *bāzār*, separated from the village by a gap of 500 meters, with a rest house (*sarāy*) for travelers and some governmental buildings. Prior to 1979, the total population was between 3000 and 4000. On most British maps from the 19th century the only place shown is Barakī Rājān (*Afghanistan*, p. 15: 33° 56′ north latitude, 68° 55′ east longitude), which formerly was the seat of a governor and had an important *bāzār*, now for the most part in ruins. Barakī Barak, situated on the link road joining the main Kabul-Ḡaznī and Kabul-Gardēz routes, became the governor's seat sometime in the mid-19th century and remained so until ca. 1970, when the local administration was moved to Pol-e ʿAlam on the Kabul-Gardēz highway. Under the new configuration Barakī Barak is also the name of a whole district in Lōgar province (*Gazetteer of Afghanistan* VI, pp. 91-92), with an area of 329 km² and a pre-1979 population of between 30,000 and 40,000.

The importance of the village lies in its being the abode of the Ōrmuṛ people of Afghanistan. The country's last Ōrmuṛī speakers live in the nearby *qalʿa*s (Kieffer, *Grammaire de l'ōrmuṛī*; idem, *Le multilinguisme*, pp. 115-26; Morgenstierne, pp. 307-414). Ōrmuṛī together with Parāčī constitutes the Southeast Iranian language group; it is spoken by the Ōrmuṛ people, who use it as their clan language, at Barakī Barak in Lōgar province and also at Kāṇīgrām in Pakistani Waziristan. The name Ōrmuṛ appears to mean literally "fire quenched." Both in Afghanistan and in Pakistan, however, they call themselves Barakī, Bīrkī, Brakī, or the like—an ethnonym obviously related to the toponym Barakī Barak but of uncertain etymology, all the attempted explanations being mere conjecture (Kieffer, *Grammaire de l'ōrmuṛī*). The Ōrmuṛī speakers of Barakī Barak call the place Grām, an Indo-Aryan word meaning "village," as in Kāṇī-grām which means "fire village," cf. Sanskrit *grāma*. With few exceptions, the Ōrmuṛ people of Barakī Barak are now assimilated to the persophone Tajiks. Definitely of the Tajik ethnic group are the inhabitants of Barakī Rājān; there is no evidence to suggest that they were ever related to the Ōrmuṛ people.

The earliest references to the "Barakīs" are found in the *Bābor-nāma* (Bīrkī on p. 207, but Barakistān on p. 220) and in the works of Elphinstone (Burrukees on p. 315) and Leech (Baraky).

Bibliography: *Afghanistan. Official Standard Names Gazetteer*, U.S. Board on Geographic Names 15, Washington, 1971. *Bābor-nāma*, tr. A. S. Beveridge, 1922, repr. 1969, pp. 207, 220. M. Elphinstone, *An Account of the Kingdom of Caubul and Its Dependencies in Persia, Tartary, and India*, 1st ed., London, 1815, repr. with notes by A. Janata, Graz, 1969. C. M. Kieffer, *Grammaire de l'ōrmuṛī* (forthcoming). Idem, "Le multilinguisme des Ormuṛs de Baraki-Barak (Afghanistan). Note sur des contacts de dialects: ōrmuṛī, paṣ̌tō et persan kāboli," *Studia Iranica* 1, 1972, pp. 115-26. Idem, "La maintenance de l'identité ethnique chez les Arabes arabophones, les Ōrmuṛ et les Parāčī en Afghanistan," in Erwin Orywal, *Die ethnischen Gruppen Afghanistans. Fallestudien zu Identität und Intergruppenbeziehungen*, Wiesbaden, 1986, 101-39. R. Leech, "A Vocabulary of the Baraky Language," *Journal of the Royal Asiatic Society of Bengal* 7, 1838, pp. 727-31. G. Morgenstierne, *Indo-Iranian Frontier Languages* I, Oslo, 1929. *A Provisional Gazetteer of Afghanistan* I, Kabul, 1975. *Qāmūs-e joḡrāfīā-ye Afḡānestān* I, Kabul, 1335 Š./1956.

(C. M. KIEFFER)

BĀRAKZAY DYNASTY. See AFGHANISTAN x; and DORRĀNĪ.

BĀRAKZĪ (singular Bārakzay), an ethnic name common in the entire eastern portion of Iran and Afghanistan, where it is found both among the Pashtun of Afghanistan and Pakistan and the Baluch of southeastern Iran (in the region of Bampūr). It is formed on a common classical model: the name of an eponymous ancestor, Bārak, plus the suffix *-zī* (the plural of Pashto *zay* "descendant").

In the detailed Pashtun genealogies there are no fewer than seven instances of the ethnic name Bārakzī, at very different levels of tribal segmentation. Six of them designate simple lineages within six different tribes located in the Solaymān mountains or adjacent lands: the Baṛēc (q.v.; Ḥayāt Khan, p. 81), the Jamand of Haštnagar (Šēr-Moḥammad Khan, p. 199), the Kākaṛ (q.v.; idem, p. 241), the K̲aṭak (q.v.; idem, p. 183; Rose, II, p. 527), the Mūsāk̲ēl (q.v.; *Dictionary of the Pathan Tribes*, p. 34), and the Šērānī (q.v.; ibid.; Rose, III, p. 408). The seventh instance, on the other hand, designates one of the most important Pashtun tribes in numbers and historic role, part of the Zīrak branch of the Dorrānay confederation (q.v.). The presence of Bārakzī of indeterminate ethnic identity has also been reported in the Panjšēr valley northeast of Kabul (Adamec, *Gazetteer* VI, p. 93, forty houses; Balland and Benoist, thirty seminomadic families).

Other ethnic names derived from Bārak also occur among the Tarakī (Bārakk̲ēl; Šēr-Moḥammad Khan, p. 216) and the Wazīr Otmānzī (Bārakk̲ēl; idem, p. 252), as well as in less clearly identifiable forms among the K̲ōgyānī (idem, p. 249), the Lōdī (idem, p. 224), and the Moḥmand (q.v.; Ḥayāt Khan, p. 132).

The homonymy of these different groups is naturally not sufficient to establish any relationship among them. Nevertheless, some Baluch authors use it as an argument for claiming a Pashtun origin for the Baluch Bārakzī of Bampūr (Sardar Khan Baluch, n.d., p. 82). In the absence of the slightest historical confirmation, it is preferable to interpret these homonyms as an instance of onomastic convergence linked to the wide diffusion of the personal name Bārak. In fact, other examples of such ethnonymic convergence abound among the Pashtun and the Baluch, though they generally involve tribal names derived from personal names of Arabic origin (Moḥammad, Aḥmad, ʿAlī, Ḥasan, and the like), the spread of which followed the path of Islamicization. That is not the case with Bārak. Furthermore, as the word is not attested in Pashto except in ethnic names (and a modern borrowing of English "barrack"), its origin is puzzling. The theory of H. W. Bellew (p. 163), who attempted to derive it from Barakī/Bərkī, the vernacular name of the Ōrmuṛ (see BARAKĪ BARAK), is unacceptable for philological reasons. More convincing is the connection that can be established with Turkish *baraq/barak* ("very furry, hairy"; also the name of a breed of long-haired dog, an excellent courser and hunter), which is found both as a personal name, notably in the princely genealogies of the Jengizids (*EI*² I, p. 1031, Bosworth, pp. 146, 153), and as an ethnic name from the fifth century (name of a tribe of the Tabḡač confederation in northern China, according to Bazin, p. 272) down to our own time (among the Uzbeks on both banks of the Āmū Daryā; Jarring, pp. 23, 57; Karmysheva, pp. 90, 105; in Anatolia: Tanyol).

Of all the groups having a Bārak as eponymous ancestor, the Bārakzay tribe of the Dorrānay confederation is the only one about which there is ample, though not always precise, information. That is true, for example, of its numbers, for which the following estimates are available; at least 30,000 families at the beginning of the nineteenth century (Elphinstone, p. 398), 50,000 families a century later under the reign of Amān-Allāh (Ḥayāt-Allāh Khan, p. 122), 300,000 individuals in the middle of the twentieth century (Aslanov, p. 57; Aslanov et al., p. 14). There is thus agreement among the authors that the tribe is one of the two principal components of the Dorrānay confederation and apparently has been so since the formation of the latter.

Genealogical traditions, as reported in learned Afghan historiography, suggest that in this instance the eponymous ancestor Bārak could have lived in the eighth/fourteenth century and perhaps could have been a contemporary of Tamerlane (according to Fōfalzāy, tables between pp. 9-10 and 242-43). The name of the tribe itself is attested only from the Safavid period, when one of its notables, Moḥammad Khan (not Aḥmad, as Malcolm, II, p. 410, erroneously reported), was sent on a mission to the court of Shah ʿAbbās I (Ferrier, 1858, p. 68). Moḥammad Khan is the eponymous ancestor of the Moḥammadzay section of the Bārakzay tribe, which has played a leading role in the modern history of Afghanistan. It was almost at the same period that the Ḡelzay tribes took over the Abdālī (that is, the Dorrānay) tribes' control of the Qandahār region and obliged the latter to retreat westward into eastern Khorasan and the Herat region (Lockhart, p. 95). Only after the reconquest of Qandahār by Nāder Shah Afšār, with whom they were allied, in 1150/1738 were they able to regain a foothold in that part of Afghanistan (Bok̲ārī, p. 15). In the allotment of lands that ensued the Bārakzī were awarded extensive tracts in the lower Arḡestān valley on the southern perimeter of the Qandahār oasis (Singh, p. 18; Rawlinson, p. 825).

Since the emergence of Afghanistan as an independent state (1160/1747), the Bārakzī have played a major political role. At first they entered the service of the young Sadōzay dynasty, which their *sardārs* had helped to place on the throne and to whose army they furnished a contingent of 907 cavalry in Aḥmad Shah's time (Elphinstone, p. 398; Rawlinson, p. 826). But this alliance did not survive the test of time. Superior in numbers, led by ambitious chiefs, and encouraged by the internal decay of Sadōzay power, the Bārakzī were not slow to aspire to political primacy within the Dorrānay confederation and thus within Afghanistan.

After 1235/1819 the real power passed to their most influential section the Moḥammadzī. For the details of this development see AFGHANISTAN X. POLITICAL HISTORY. Here it must be noted that the new Bārakzay dynasty was in its turn rapidly weakened by internal rivalries. Two Moḥammadzay lineages thus succeeded each other on the throne at Kabul. Following the usage of English authors of the nineteenth century, they are commonly designated by the respective names of the cities where they had risen to power. The lineage of the *sardārs* of Kabul, descended from the first Bārakzay amir, Dōst-Moḥammad Khan (q.v.), reigned from 1235/1819 to 1307 Š./1929, with a brief interruption during the Sadōzay restoration in 1255-59/1839-43. The rival *sardārs* of Peshawar, descended from Sultan Moḥammad "Ṭelā'ī," half-brother of Dōst-Moḥammad, were known also by the neologism Moṣāḥebān because of the favored position (*moṣāḥeb-e ḵāṣṣ*) that its chiefs occupied at the court of the amir Ḥabīb-Allāh; it succeeded the Kabul branch in 1308 Š./1929, lasting until 1352 Š./1973, and managed to keep control of power after the fall of the monarchy throughout the span of the first Afghan republic (1352-57 Š./1973-78).

The political hegemony of the Bārakzī thus lasted a total of a century and a half. In this period, characterized from beginning to end by the practice of systematic tribal nepotism, the entire tribe, and more particularly its Moḥammadzay section, occupied a privileged position in the high civil and military administration of the Afghan state (examples are given in Kakar, pp. 24, 113, and Schinasi, pp. 111ff.; cf. Adamec, *Who's Who*). As a result, important modifications occurred in the geographical distribution of the Bārakzī, notably the establishment of important colonies at Kabul and in the principal provincial seats of power.

The present geographical distribution of the Bārakzī is not well known in detail, being characterized by broad diffusion. Following the pattern of most Dorrānay tribes, they can be divided schematically into three major settlement areas.

1. The oldest is situated in western Afghanistan between Herat and the approaches to the Helmand valley. It was there that the tribe retreated in the Safavid period, but some elements may have been established there several centuries earlier (Stack, pp. 51ff.). Today the Bārakzay population there is residual and very scattered. Any attempt at sketching the whole must be based on the punctilious observations made at the end of the nineteenth century, which, though very precise, are filled with gaps (see *Records of Intelligence Party* I, preferable to the much more summary information in Adamec, *Gazetteer* II, pp. 35, 237, 300, and III, p. 49). In 1885 the number of Bārakzī in the province of Herat alone was put at 1,264 families, of which 845 were in the nine *bolūk*s into which the Herat oasis itself was divided and 150 (probably an underestimate) were nomadic (Moḥammad Takkī Khan). Nomadism was still common among this population in 1978. The *Afghan Nomad Survey* counted 696 Bārakzay nomad families, scattered among fourteen different winter camps dotted along the Harīrūd valley between Ōbē and Ḡōrīān, around Adraskān, and along the middle Farāhrūd. The majority of these nomads summered in the mountains of southern Ḡōr. Those on the Harīrūd nevertheless stood somewhat apart because of their extreme poverty, which severely limited their mobility, and because of their general shift from the Pashto to the Persian language.

2. The second area of Bārakzay population encompasses the two large oases of Qandahār and the middle Helmand, on either side of its confluence with the Arḡandāb. This was the great tribal resettlement area in the eighteenth century, and it is still today the principal Bārakzay center. Estimated at 21 percent of the sedentary population, between 70,000 and 100,000 people, the Bārakzī were thus the most important tribal group in Helmand province at the end of the 1970s. They predominated in extensive areas around Gerešk and Laškargāh, as well as in the modern irrigation area of Šamalān, on the right bank of the Helmand, accounting for almost half the population of each of these three districts, whereas their relative importance did not surpass 11 percent in the Nowzād district north of Gerešk and they were very lightly represented in the rest of the province (according to a 1975 census based on a random sample of 4 per cent of families, U.S.A.I.D., pp. 18ff.; see also Scott, 1980, pp. 4ff., which, though based on the same data, gives slightly different estimates). The importance of the tribe in the composition of the Qandahāri population, though apparent in the fact that a central quarter of the old city bears its name (Wiebe, p. 142), cannot be established exactly, except by returning to nineteenth-century estimates, according to which it constituted between 10 and 25 percent of the total population of the city (according to Bellew, cited in MacGregor, p. 493, and Ferrier, 1857, p. 321, respectively). The Bārakzī of the Qandahār oasis, especially numerous in the southern part, are today entirely settled, though it seems they were still largely nomadic at the beginning of the nineteenth century (Elphinstone, p. 398). On the other hand, a small nucleus of Bārakzay nomads (eighty-five families in 1978) still exists in Helmand province.

3. The third area of Bārakzay diffusion encompasses all of northern Afghanistan. The tribe entered this region at the end of the nineteenth century as a result of the transfer of nomadic groups from the south, which was intended to populate the territory along the northern frontier. The Bārakzī who were thus established in the Golrān region in 1886 (Tapper, p. 65; repr., p. 243) seem to have left. On the contrary, those who arrived in Bādḡīs during the summer of the same year and encountered there the hostility of the Fīrōzkōhī (Kakar, p. 132) gave rise to the most important Bārakzay colony in all of Afghan Turkestan. The principal settlements at present are located north of Bālā Morḡāb, as well as to the west and north of Maymana, around Qaysār and Jalāyer (see Adamec, *Gazetteer* IV, pp. 289ff., for the Bārakzī of the Qaysār *woloswālī*). Many of these newcomers have preserved a pastoral

way of life: 330 nomadic families and 840 seminomadic families were counted there in 1978, but, of this total of 1,170 families, a quarter (30 and 260 families respectively) no longer made more than a short migration in spring and were mainly engaged in agriculture. The majority (880 families in all) still passed the summers in the mountain pastures of the Safēdkōh and Band-e Torkestān; ten families from Jalāyer even summered on the distant pastures of western Hazārajāt. A secondary center of Bārakzay population exists in the Qaṭaḡan, where in 1978 fourteen seminomadic families were counted east of Kondoz (Nawābād), whereas ten nomadic and eighty seminomadic families were recorded northeast of Baḡlān (Dašt-e Bāy Saqāl). The summer pastures of the first group are located in the Dašt-e Šēwa (Badaḵšān); the second group migrates to the mountain pastures of the upper Andarāb and Fereng (central Hindu Kush). Finally, one more northern center, consisting of only twenty seminomadic families, is located in the region of the middle Balḵāb. There was thus a total of 1,294 Bārakzay families, both nomadic and seminomadic, living in northern Afghanistan in 1978, that is, a number larger than that of their nomadic fellow tribesmen living in the southwestern part of the country. An indeterminate number of settled families must undoubtedly be added.

According to Šēr-Moḥammad Khan (p. 183), the genealogical structure of the Bārakzī is articulated in five major subtribes: the ʿAbd-Allāhzī, the Bāʾīzī, the Naṣratzī (Nāṣerzī), the Nūr-al-Dīnzī, and the Rokn-al-Dīnzī. The Nūr-al-Dīnzī seem to be the most important of them, for it is from their midst that both the Moḥammadzay clan—thus the most recent of the reigning Afghan dynasties—and the Acəkzay tribe (q.v.) sprang; all the historical traditions of the latter point to its being an old Bārakzay section that was elevated to the status of an independent tribe by Aḥmad Shah in the eighteenth century (Elphinstone, p. 398). A total of seventeen names of living lineages was collected by R. B. Scott (1971, p. 8 bis) and the 1978 Afghan Nomad Survey. The fact that several of them (Ḵānōzay, Šakarzay) are common to other Dorrānay tribes, especially the Alēkōzī, is an argument supporting the thesis of the instability of tribal configurations within a confederation of this type.

In Iranian Baluchistan the name Bārakzay is borne by one of the numerous *ḥākomzāt* lineages, which shared in political power within traditional Baluch society (Spooner). It controlled the Bampūr oasis and the region around it. Virtually independent of the central government during the Qajar period, it gradually extended its political influence over a great part of southeastern Persia and the neighboring regions of Indian Baluchistan, seeking to establish there a true Baluch confederation. It was in order to break this burgeoning regional power that Reżā Shah Pahlavī launched a two-pronged military offensive on land and in the air in 1307 Š./1928, followed by savage repression, the principal victim of which was Dōst-Moḥammad Khan, the Bārakzay *ḥākom* (i.e., *ḥākem*, governor) of Bampūr, who was hanged at Tehran and is regarded today as a martyr in the cause of Baluch nationalism (Jahānbānī; Sardar Khan Baluch, 1977, pp. 260ff., where the name of the lineage has unfortunately been distorted). This episode ended with the effective incorporation of the region into the territory of Iran; nevertheless a Baluch nationalist movement still exists, and the Bārakzay lineage continues to play an important role within it (Harrison, pp. 17, 118f.).

Bibliography: Despite its wide geographic distribution, the Bārakzay tribe has not been the object of a specific study. Its historical importance is such, however, that all general works and a number of regional studies of Afghanistan treat it to a greater or lesser extent. Cited here are those that provide basic data. All information relating to nomadism among the Bārakzī has been taken from Balland and Benoist.

Afghan Nomad Survey, 1978, unpublished. L. W. Adamec, ed., *Gazetteer of Afghanistan*, 6 vols., Graz, 1973-85. Idem, *Historical and Political Who's Who of Afghanistan*, Graz, 1975. M. G. Aslanov, "Afgantsy," in N. A. Kislyakov and A. I. Pershits, *Narody Peredneĭ Azii*, Moscow, 1957. Idem et al., "Ethnography of Afghanistan," in G. Grassmuck, L. W. Adamec, and F. H. Irwin, eds., *Afghanistan. Some New Approaches*, Ann Arbor, 1969 (a partial and sometimes defective translation of Aslanov, 1957). D. Balland and A. de Benoist, *Nomades et semi-nomades d'Afghanistan*, forthcoming. L. Bazin, "Recherches sur les parlers t'o-pa," *T'oung Pao* 39/4-5, 1950, pp. 228-329. H. W. Bellew, *An Inquiry into the Ethnography of Afghanistan*, Woking, 1981, repr. Graz, 1973. ʿAbd-al-Karīm Boḵārī. C. E. Bosworth, *The Islamic Dynasties*, Edinburgh, 1967. R. Dankoff, "Baraq and Burāq," *Central Asiatic Journal* 15/2, 1971, pp. 102-17 (suggests etymological connection with So. *β'r'k*, Khot. *bārgya-* "rider;" pp. 111f.). *A Dictionary of the Pathan Tribes on the North-West Frontier of India*, Calcutta, 1899. M. Elphinstone, *An Account of the Kingdom of Caubul and Its Dependencies in Persia, Tartary, and India*, London, 1815, repr. Graz, 1969. J. P. Ferrier, *Caravan Journeys and Wanderings in Persia, Afghanistan, Turkistan, and Beloochistan*, London, 1857, repr. Westmead, 1971. Idem, *History of the Afghans*, London, 1858. ʿA. Wakīlī Fōfalzāy, *Dorrat al-zamān fī taʾrīḵ Šāh Zamān*, Kabul, 1337 Š./1958. S. S. Harrison, *In Afghanistan's Shadow: Baluch Nationalism and Soviet Temptations*, New York, 1981. Moḥammad Ḥayāt Khan, *Ḥayāt-e Afḡān*, tr. H. Priestley, *Afghanistan and Its Inhabitants*, Lahore, 1874, repr. 1981. Ḥayāt-Allāh Khan, *Jōḡrāfīā-ye Afḡānestān*, Kabul, n.d. A. Jahānbānī, *ʿAmalīyāt-e qošūn dar Balūčestān az Mordād tā Bahman 1307 Š.*, 2nd ed., Tehran, 1336 Š./1957. G. Jarring, *On the Distribution of Turk Tribes in Afghanistan*, Lunds Universitets Årsskrift, N. F. Avd. 1, 35, No. 4, Lund, 1939. H. K. Kakar, *Government and Society in Afghanistan: The Reign of Amir ʿAbd al-Rahman Khan*, Austin, 1979. B. K. Karmysheva, *Ocherki ètnicheskoĭ istorii yuzhnykh* raĭonov Tadzhikistana i Uzbekistana, Moscow, 1976. L. Lockhart, *The Fall of the Safavi Dynasty and the Afghan Occupation of Persia*, Cambridge, 1958. C. M. MacGregor, *Central Asia*, pt. 2: *A Contribution Towards the Better Knowledge of the Topography, Ethnology, Resources, and History of Afghānistān*, Calcutta, 1871. J. Malcolm, *Histoire de la Perse depuis les temps les plus anciens jusqu'à l'époque actuelle*, 4 vols., Paris, 1821. H. C. Rawlinson, "Report on the Dooranee Tribes Dated 19th April 1841," in MacGregor, 1871, pp. 823-69 (a fundamental text; it is better to consult this version than the very defective new edition published in Adamec, *Gazetteer* V, pp. 509-77). *Records of Intelligence Party, Afghan Boundary Commission* I: *Diary of Major Maitland*, Simla, 1888. H. A. Rose, *A Glossary of the Tribes and Castes of the Punjab and North-West Frontier Province*, Lahore, 1919, repr. 1978. M. Sardar Khan Baluch, *The Great Baluch*, Quetta, n.d. Idem, *History of Baluch Race and Baluchistan*, 2nd ed., Quetta, 1977. M. Schinasi, *Afghanistan at the Beginning of the Twentieth Century*, Naples, 1979. R. B. Scott, *The North Shamalan: A Survey of Land and People*, U.S.A.I.D., Kabul, 1971. Idem, *Tribal and Ethnic Groups in the Helmand Valley*, Occasional Paper of the Afghanistan Council of the Asia Society 21, New York, 1980. Šēr-Moḥammad Khan, *Tawārīḵ-e Ḵᵛoršīd-e Jahān*, Lahore, 1311/1894. G. Singh, *Ahmed Shah Durrani, Father of Modern Afghanistan*, Bombay, 1959, repr. Quetta, 1977. B. Spooner, "Politics, Kinship, and Ecology in Southeast Persia," *Ethnology* 8/2, 1969, pp. 139-52. S. C. Stack, *Herat: A Political and Social Study*, Ph.D. dissertation, University of California, Los Angeles, 1975. Mīrzā Moḥammad Takkī Khan, *Report on the City and Province of Herat*, tr. by W. R. H. Merk, London, n.d. (ca. 1886), ms. in India Office records; C. Tanyol, "Baraklarda örf ve adet araştımaları," *Sosyologi dergisi* 7, 1952, pp. 71-108; 8, 1953, pp. 126-35; 9, 1954, pp. 67-96. N. Tapper, "The Advent of Pashtun *Māldārs* in North-Western Afghanistan," *BSOAS* 36/1, 1973, pp. 55-79, reprinted with emendations as "Abd al-Rahman's North West Frontier: The Pashtun Colonisation of Afghan Turkistan," in R. Tapper, ed., *The Conflict of Tribe and State in Iran and Afghanistan*, London, 1983, pp. 233-61. U.S.A.I.D., *1975 Farm Economic Survey of the Helmand Valley*, Kabul, n.d. [1978]. D. Wiebe, "Die räumliche Gestalt der Altstadt von Kandahar," *Afghanistan Journal* 3/4, 1975, pp. 132-46.

(D. BALLAND)

BARĀMEKA. See BARMAKIDS.

BĀRĀN "rain." The words for "rain" and "to rain" in Iranian languages are all derived from the OIran. root *wār-*, though the stem formation of the noun varies. The thematic form **wāra-* is found both in Old Iranian: Avestan *vāra-*, Middle Iranian: Khotanese *bāra-*, Sogdian *w'r*, and in modern Iranian: Parachi *ḡār*, Sanglichi *bōr*, and Wakhi *wïr* (also *boronrawī*); a derived form in *-iš* is found in many dialectal variants of NPers., *bāreš*, and in Baluchi, *gwāriš* (beside *gwārag*); a derived form in *-ān* is found in Mid. Pers. *wārān*, NPers. *bārān*, Munji and Ishkashmi *boron* (from Pers.? Ishkashmi also *urnaduk*); cf. also Ossetic Digor *warun*, Iron *war̲in* (= infinitive); forms derived from stems in *aka* are found in Baluchi *gwārag* (= infinitive), Yidgha *wärīḡo*, Pashto *(w)oryā* or *(w)əryā*, and Shughni *warɛyj*. Ōrmuṛi has only the Persian loanword *bārān*, but has preserved the verb *ḡōr-* (Barakī Barak), *ḡwar-* (Kāṇīgrām). (See, e.g., Bailey, *Dictionary*, p. 278.)

It is interesting to note that in modern Iranian languages violent and dangerous rainfall events are often designated by borrowings from Arabic (*ṭūfān* for typhoon, *barq* for lightning, *raʿd* for thunder, *sayl* for sudden deluge), whereas for phenomena considered beneficial a terminology of Iranian origin has been preserved: Rain is described as beneficent in the *Dādestān ī dēnīg* 37.31; and hail, Persian *žāla*, Pashto *žaləy*, despite the damage that it can cause to crops, particularly after the blossoming of fruit trees in the spring, enjoys a favorable reputation, doubtless because it does not run off on the ground and thus saturates the earth with moisture. In the Iranian-speaking world, Pashto is unique in having an abundant vocabulary of Indian origin for the different, typically tropical rainfall manifestations that occur in the eastern portion of Irano-Afghan territory (*paršakāl* "summer rain, monsoon," also called *wasə* and *bāresāt*; *šēba* "deluge"; *pūna* "drizzle"; and so on).

Although lying between the fortieth and twenty-fifth parallels north, the Irano-Afghan area is far from presenting the regular decrease in precipitation from north to south that characterizes the Mediterranean zone: Ahvāz (31° 20′N) and Mazār-e Šarīf (36° 42′N) receive exactly the same annual rainfall (187 mm); Bandar-e ʿAbbās (27° 11′N) is hardly less well watered (139 mm) than Saraḵs (157 mm at 36° 32′N). The topography, on one hand, and the presence of marine expanses, on the other, are responsible for these anomalies. They are the principal geographic factors in the territorial distribution of precipitation.

1. Geographical factors in the distribution of precipitation.

The influence of the mountains on the distribution of precipitation has less to do with altitude than with their orientation in relation to the prevailing middle-latitude westerly cyclonic movements, which bring the greater part of the annual rainfall. The presence of the oblique Zagros and Hindu Kush ranges at the western and eastern extremes of Irano-Afghan territory introduces great contrasts between the relatively humid piedmonts and slopes exposed to the winds, on one hand, and the much more arid piedmonts and slopes of the sheltered sides, on the other. Dezfūl (143 m above sea level), on the western piedmont of the central Zagros, thus receives 358 mm, whereas Isfahan (1,570 m), on the eastern piedmont, receives only 108 mm, though both cities lie in the same latitude, which is also that of

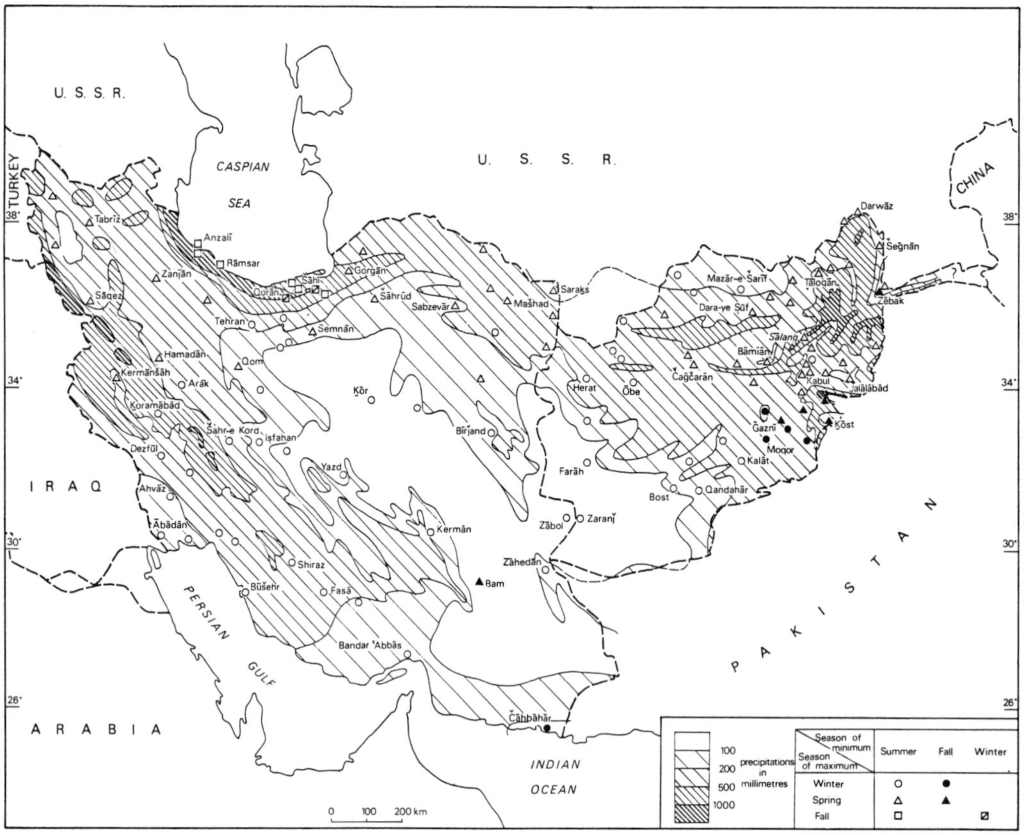

Figure 19. Mean annual precipitation in Iran and Afghanistan and the seasonal patterns at selected localities

Ghardaïa in the Algerian Sahara. The highest peaks of the two ranges receive about 1,000 mm (982 and 1,018 mm respectively, falling in 100 days at North Sālang and South Sālang in the central Hindu Kush, the only permanent meteorological stations located at altitudes higher than 3,000 m). At their low points, the intramontane basins are islands of relative aridity, growing progressively drier the farther to the east they are located: Whereas in the Azerbaijan and Fārs basins 300 mm or more are recorded (Urmia, 360 mm in 93 days; Shiraz, 304 mm), those of the Hindu Kush receive less than 300 mm (Bāmīān, 138 mm in only 37 days; Zēbak, 125 mm; see Figure 19).

That the broad saddle extending between the Zagros and the Hindu Kush does not present a zonal organization in bands of decreasing rainfall toward the south is owing to modifications introduced into the regional atmospheric circulation by the presence of the Indian Ocean to the south and the Caspian Sea to the north. These two marine expanses have a humidifying influence, which can be correctly understood only if its two components are clearly distinguished. On one hand, they ensure the formation of new fronts within the turbulent air currents that cross them from west to east, which explains the abnormally high humidity of their eastern shores, which is much greater on the Caspian (Gorgān, 696 mm) than on the Persian Gulf (Būšehr, 221 mm) because of the decreasing frequency of cyclonic circulation toward the south. On the other hand, the seas moisten some of the convergent winds that are generated by every cyclonic event. On the Persian Gulf the process affects southwesterly winds coming from Arabia but nevertheless carrying some humidity to the Iranian coast. On the Caspian the northeasterly winds account for the superabundant rainfall on the southern Caspian shore and the northern slopes of the Alborz. Rainfall increases steadily from east to west, proportional to the maritime reach of the northeasterly winds striking the coast (Šāhī, 761 mm; Rāmsar, 1,212 mm in 136 days; Anzalī, 1,810 mm in 138 days). It seems to reach its maximum (doubtless more than 2,000 mm) at the level of the medium-altitude beech forests on the Alborz, at about 1,500 m.

This exceptionally high humidity makes the Caspian provinces, especially Gīlān (q.v.), which is the best watered among them, unique in a country as generally arid as Iran. Aridity is obviously greatest in the center of the great inland basins, which combine all possible handicaps: low altitude, position sheltered from the dominant winds, continentality. Mean annual precipitation there is always below 100 mm (Zaranj, 53 mm in only nine days; K̲ūr, 36 mm; and doubtless even less in

Table 31

SEASONAL PATTERNS OF PRECIPITATION IN IRAN AND AFGHANISTAN

Key station	Mean annual precipitation (mm)	Percentage of mean annual precipitation falling in				Synthetic precipitation formula
		Winter (W)	Spring (S)	Summer (s)	Fall (F)	
Mašhad	240	32	55	2	11	SWFs
Ḡaznī	297	41	47	7	5	SWsF
Bandar-e ʿAbbās	139	72	18	1	9	WSFs
Čāhbahār	92	72	15	9	4	WSsF
Rašt	1,349	32	19	12	37	FWSs
Ḵōst	476	21	35	34	10	SsWF

Table 32

SYNOPTIC ORIGIN OF PRECIPITATION DAYS IN SOME REGIONS OF IRAN (1965-69)

Regions	Westerly disturbances (both frontal, or superficial, and upper tropospheric)	Thermodynamic instability (1)	Maritime air advection (1)	Indeterminable
Gīlān	57.5%	9%	13%	20.5%
Azerbaijan	69	9.5	—	21.5
Ḵūzestān	84	4	—	12
Khorasan	79	4.5	—	16.5
Baluchistan	70	11	—	19
Iran as a whole	74.5	6.6	2.1	16.8

(1) These factors are to some extent underestimated because multiple-cause precipitation days have been ascribed to westerly disturbances only. Adapted from Alijani and Harman, 1985.

the center of the Dašt-e Lūt, considered unable to support life). It is more difficult to define the upper limits of aridity. It can be assumed that they coincide with the lower limits of rainfall agriculture. It has thus been shown that dry-farmed winter wheat disappears when annual precipitation is below 210 mm in southern Iran and below 230 mm in northern Iran—a difference that arises from the lateness of the growing season caused by intense winter cold in the north (Perrin de Brichambaut and Wallén, p. 15). The 230-mm limit can be extended to the greater part of Afghanistan, where research into agricultural climatology is less advanced but where continentality is at least equal to that of northern Iran. At this level of analysis, then, nearly two-thirds of the Irano-Afghan area are unsuitable for unirrigated agriculture because of excessive aridity. Nevertheless, it should be noted immediately that even the remaining third offers very uneven conditions, because the seasonal distribution of precipitation is far from homogeneous.

2. Rainfall patterns.

The seasons of maximum and minimum rainfall, and sometimes also the frequency of such extremes within the year, show important regional variations, which, however, follow a relatively simple pattern (Figure 19 and Table 31).

In general maximum precipitation occurs in winter south of latitude 34°N and in spring north of it. This [major] boundary line is breached at only two points, on the Tehran piedmont and in northwestern Afghanistan, where the winter maximum prevails as far north as 36° and 37°N respectively. More specifically the average monthly maximum south of 34°N falls in January and north of it in April, although in the latter instance it sometimes occurs in March (in the eastern Alborz, Bādḡīs, and Bactria) or in May (at some intramontane stations in Azerbaijan and the Hindu Kush). A part of the cold season precipitation falls in the form of hail and especially snow (in the Hindu Kush the number of days with snowfall exceeds the number of rainy days at elevations above 2,700 m; see BARF).

The general determinants of winter and spring rainfalls are those of the middle latitudes, with polar disturbances and Mediterranean frontal depressions playing the major role (Table 32). The southernmost advance of the former and the path of circulation followed by the latter are both determined by the latitude of the subtropical jet stream. In the last analysis, then, it is seasonal latitudinal shifts in the jet stream that account for the contrast between patterns with maximum winter rainfall and those with maximum spring rainfall.

Furthermore, all else being equal and within the limits already defined, conditions are more favorable

Table 33

PRECIPITATION AND RAIN-FED AGRICULTURE (*LALMĪ*) IN NORTHERN (N) AND SOUTHERN (S) AFGHANISTAN

Station	Mean annual precipitation (mm)	Season of maximum: Date	Season of maximum: % of total precipitation	% of total precipitation falling in May	% of *lalmī* land in the total cultivated area of surrounding district (1)
I. Darwāz (N)	437	Spring	44	12	79
Pag̱mān (S)	422	Spring	45	8	11
II. Dara-ye Ṣūf (N)	281	Spring	52	13	97
Moqor (S)	287	Winter	51	3	45
Kalāt (S)	286	Winter	62	1	28

(1) Very rough estimates from *Natāyej-e ehsāʾīyagīrī sarwē-ye moqaddamatī-e zerāʿatī sāl-e 1346 Š.*, Kabul, n.d., vol. 2. Although their reliability may be doubtful, it is assumed that this does not affect interdistrict comparisons, especially when figures show great differences.

Table 34

ANNUAL PRECIPITATION VARIABILITY IN IRAN AND AFGHANISTAN

Class of mean annual precipitation	Number of stations	Mean index of absolute variability (Max/Min)	Key station: Name (with number of years on record)	Precipitation (mm): Mean	Precipitation (mm): Maximum recorded	Precipitation (mm): Minimum recorded	Max/Min
Less than 100 mm	9	8.4	Zābol (14)	61	128	12	10.7
100-200 mm	26	5.3	Sarak̲s (10)	157	364	65	5.6
200-500 mm	63	3.1	Zanjān (19)	320	481	142	3.4
500-1000 mm	8	2.6	Gorgān (18)	696	1,583	529	3
More than 1000 mm	6	2.1	Rašt (19)	1,349	2,048	958	2.1
Whole area	112	3	Kabul (27)	312	524	176	3

Source: Personal elaboration of available precipitation data. For Iran the tables of Alex, 1985 (pp. 187-248), have been relied upon. For Afghanistan the author's own compilations from the archives and yearbooks of the Afghan Meteorological Institute, Kābul, have been used.

for dry farming of cereals when maximum precipitation occurs later in the year. Regions with predominant spring rainfall are more favorable than those with the maximum in winter, and among the former those with the maximum in April (or better still in May) are more favorable than those with the maximum in March. In Afghanistan, where the length and intensity of winter cold over the greater part of the territory impose rainfall cultivation of spring wheat sown in April and harvested in September, instead of winter wheat, the preferred growing zone is thus north, rather than south, of the Hindu Kush, despite annual rainfall totals that hardly differ (Table 33 and Figure 20D). Misunderstanding of the fundamental role of seasonal precipitation patterns in the geography of dry farming has often led to incorrect paleoclimatological reconstructions, especially by archeologists (e.g., Jaguttis-Emden, 1981).

The Caspian climate is an exception here, too. Maximum precipitation falls in the autumn (October). It is linked to strong cyclonic activity over the Caspian Sea at that season, reinforced by the fact that at the same time the waters reach their highest temperature and consequently their maximum potential for humidifying the overlying air masses. During that period it rains, on the average, more than two days out of five. On the other hand, spring, the other season of intense cyclonic activity in the Caspian latitudes, is only third in rainfall, after winter, for there is very little evaporation from the cool sea.

Minimum precipitation uniformly falls in the summer, the season during which the Irano-Afghan latitudes experience tropical high-pressure cells, which are stable and dry. Precipitation then is slight (less than 5 percent of the annual total) and often totally absent for several months, from June to September-October in the north, from April to November in the south. There is thus a very simple overall pattern, with a single dry season in summer, which means that the Iranian environment is part of the Mediterranean bioclimatic area.

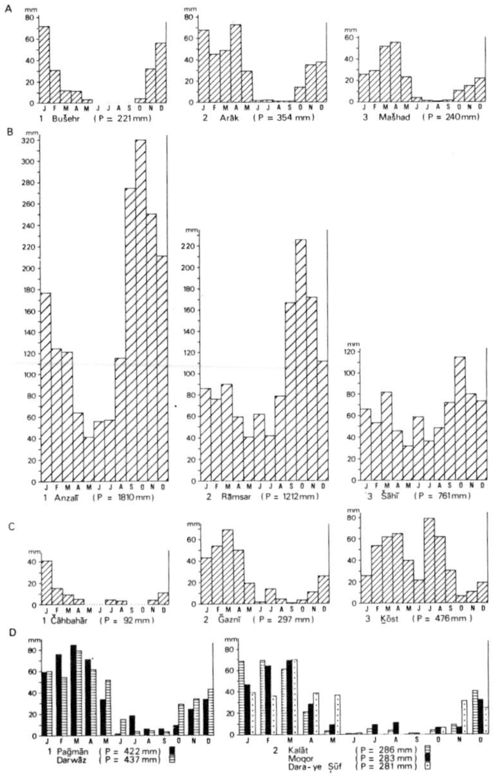

Figure 20. Main contrasts in the monthly distribution of precipitation in the Irano-Afghan area (see Figure 19 for localization of the selected stations). A. South-north alteration in semiarid Iran. B. West-east alteration in the Caspian provinces of Iran. C. The originality of monsoon-influenced southeastern Iran and Afghanistan. D. Examples of unequally favorable distribution of precipitation in rain-fed agriculture areas of eastern Afghanistan

The Caspian region and the Pakistani borders are nevertheless exceptions to this rule. In the first instance, the particular conditions of atmospheric circulation above the Caspian Sea ensure that the summer minimum, though always marked, is still quite substantial (more than 10 percent of annual precipitation), sufficient, for example, to jeopardize the drying of the harvest. The Caspian climate thus does not include a dry season.

In the east westward penetration of the Indian summer monsoon current under the ridge of barometric high pressure causes a rainy season between mid-June and the beginning of September. Although this thin layer of humid eastern tropical air can move north across the crest of the Hindu Kush (e.g., the September, 1972, rains at Bāmīān; Rathjens, 1978, p. 24) or advance west as far as Fārs, it is strong and regular only in three limited areas: upper Badaḵšān around Zēbak, southeastern Afghanistan south of the Spīnḡar, and Iranian Baluchistan (Figure 19). Only in those areas do

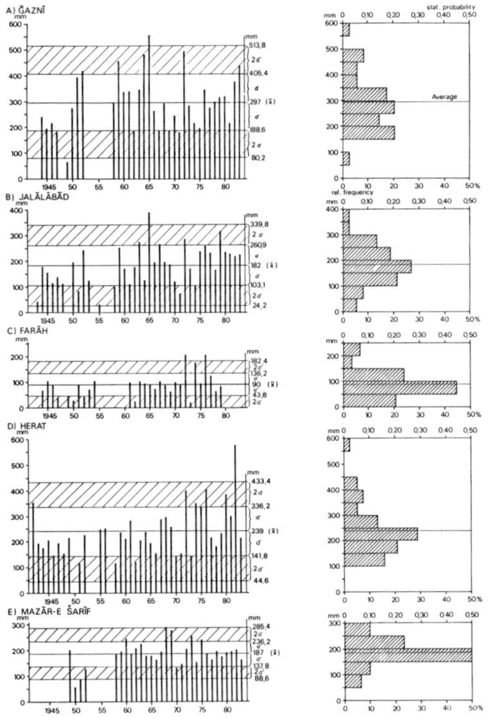

Figure 21. Rainfall variability at five Afghan stations (1942-83). [$\bar{x}$ = average, σ = standard deviation]

clearly defined bimodal rainfall patterns occur, characterized by a primary maximum in the cold season (a Mediterranean feature), a secondary maximum in the summer (a tropical feature), and displacement of the primary minimum toward autumn. Summer rainfall, which decreases from east to west, reflecting the thinning out and drying up of the monsoon current, is on the average insufficient (only 20-30 mm in eastern Afghanistan, about 10 mm in Iranian Baluchistan) to interrupt the bioclimatic aridity of summer. Only in the extreme east, in the Ḵōst basin (Paktīā province), is the summer wet enough to produce a climate with two dry seasons, characterized not only by an almost perfect balance between spring and summer rainfalls (35 and 34 percent respectively of the 476 mm that fall at Ḵōst in sixty-three days) but also by a significant reversal of monthly rhythms, with the primary maximum occurring in July (79 mm in eight days) and a secondary maximum in April (65 mm in nine days; averages calculated over a twenty-year period). This very special situation, in which both subtropical (or western) and tropical (or eastern) climatic influences operate, explains the finely differentiated mosaic of precipitation patterns on the Solaymān mountains and their approaches, in contrast to the great monotony of such patterns over the rest of the Irano-Afghan area. The mean that can be established among these conflicting influences nevertheless masks an extremely changeable reality: Sometimes the monsoon rains are almost entirely absent (less than

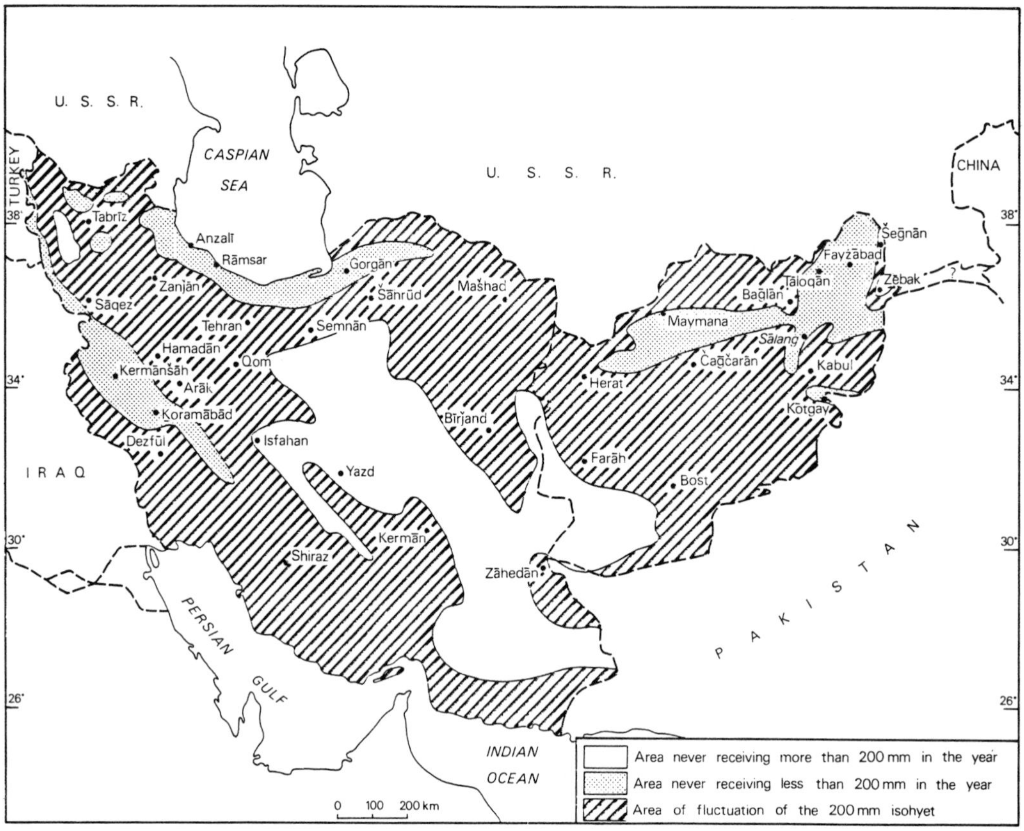

Figure 22. Fluctuations of the 200-mm isohyet in the Irano-Afghan area

40 mm was received at K̲ōst during the whole summer in 1968 and 1969); sometimes they are torrential (more than 250 mm in the summers of 1964, 1973, and 1979). Sometimes the Mediterranean rains are deficient (1970); sometimes they are overabundant (1965, 1972).

Variability from year to year is, in fact, a fundamental feature of precipitation in the entire Irano-Afghan area. It affects both the amount and the pattern of rainfall.

3. Variability of precipitation.

This variability can be measured on several scales, the first of which is that of annual totals. Calculated on the basis of data from 112 stations scattered over the entire territory studied, the average index of absolute annual variability (i.e., relation between the annual maximum and minimum registered) is 3. That means that, from one year to the next, the amount of precipitation can vary from one to three times. In fact, normally, the lower the average rainfall, the greater the variability (Table 34).

Taking into account the fact that at best available rainfall data cover only a few decades, secular variability is doubtless always higher than the estimates. Very informative in this respect are the Persian Gulf stations, for which we have an almost continuous series of data since the nineteenth century, thanks to the diligence of British consular officials in the region. For example, in the period 1955-74 Būšehr registered annual extremes of 79 and 412 mm, providing an index of variability of 5.2, yet earlier clues suggest that there was a much greater range of variation, from absolute aridity (0 mm) in the year 1877 to the 676 mm experienced in 1894 (Bobek, 1951, p. 11).

Figure 22 represents the irregularity in annual precipitation cartographically; it is based on fluctuations of the 200 mm isohyet, considered the absolute lower limit for dry farming. It shows a clear three-part division of the area: an arid core, where rainfall is always less than 200 mm and in which agriculture can be conducted only by means of irrigation, in oases; scattered humid areas on the periphery, which always receive more than 200 mm and are thus to be considered prima facie safe for rainfall agriculture (the western slopes of the central Zagros, the northern slopes of the Alborz, the Caspian plain, and the northern slopes of the mountains of Afghan Turkistan and the Hindu Kush); and, finally, a semiarid transitional zone, which straddles the 200-mm isohyet and thus falls into the arid zone in some years and into the humid category in others. Obviously it is in this last zone, by far the largest of the three, that agricultural risks are greatest and variations in rainfall the most fraught with consequences.

Detailed examination of annual rainfall data from thirty-one Afghan stations, each having been in operation for more than ten years, sheds further light on the

Table 35

MONTHLY FREQUENCY (IN PERCENT) OF ALL ANNUAL RAINFALL MAXIMA RECORDED FOR SELECTED STATIONS IN AFGHANISTAN

Stations	J	F	M	A	My	J	Jy	A	S	O	N	D	Total (100%) = Number of years on record
Kabul	7	19	37	33	—	—	—	—	—	—	—	4	27
Ǧaznī	15	20	33	20	3	—	9	—	—	—	—	—	34
Gardēz	3	37	27	14	3	—	3	3	—	3	—	7	30
Ḵōst	5	15	10	20	5	—	30	15	—	—	—	—	20
Jalālābād	5	8	35	29	8	—	3	3	3	—	3	3	37
Qandahār	35	30	15	5	—	—	—	—	—	—	5	10	20
Farāh	30	37	20	3	—	—	—	—	—	—	—	10	30
Herat	34	18	32	2.5	2.5	—	—	—	—	—	—	11	38
Maymana	8	12	48	16	4	—	—	—	—	—	—	8	25
Mazār-e Šarīf	3.5	30	40	13	—	—	—	—	—	—	3.5	10	30
Fayżābād	—	11	28	33	22	—	—	—	—	—	—	6	18

Note: The underlined figure indicates the date of the mean monthly rainfall maximum.
Source: The author's own tabulation from archives and yearbooks of the Afghan Meteorological Institute, Kabul.

nature, magnitude, and significance of annual variations in the recent period. Of a cumulative total of 645 recorded years, 341 have fallen below the local average (53 percent) and 304 above it. Following the usual hydroclimatological definition, which designates as abnormal any year that shows a deviation from the average exceeding one standard deviation, only ninety-five instances of abnormal aridity and ninety-two instances of abnormal humidity can be identified. And, if only years deviating from the mean by a value greater than two standard deviations are taken into account, only seven instances of severe aridity can be identified, versus twenty-two instances of really superabundant humidity. The conclusion is, then, that very wet years have been more frequent than very dry years but that a moderately dry year is the most frequent anomaly (Figure 21). A further regional analysis of the data clearly demonstrates that stations situated north of the Hindu Kush diverge from those in the far south in recording relatively moderate annual variability (their average index does not surpass 2.3) and a slight predominance of wet years over dry years. This kind of climate, with relatively moderate variability and prevalence of wet years over dry years, doubtless favors dry farming and must be taken into account in explaining the remarkable extent of such farming north of the Hindu Kush.

Variability in total precipitation from year to year is in fact only a result of variability in short-term rhythms—whether seasonal, monthly, or daily—which are more crucial for the peasant. At this level, for example, a very large fluctuation in the date of maximum precipitation can be observed (Table 35). Except in the narrow zone of monsoon influence, the only truly stable feature is the summer dryness. Without pushing analysis of the data farther, it appears that there is a fundamental distinction between two types of precipitation hazard, the effects of which are of different magnitude both in duration and in extent of the area affected.

Droughts correspond to absence of rainfall during the usual rainy season. They can thus be viewed as extensions of the normal summer dryness to the greater part of the year, even to the entire year. The inhibitory mechanisms capable of thus blocking normal precipitation rhythms are linked to global, or at least supra-regional, meteorological events. For example, an abnormal cyclonic wave may push the subtropical jet stream too far north, or, conversely, an unusual anticyclonic surge may oppose the penetration of the westerlies. In either instance the area affected is large: Droughts are never local, and their consequences are proportionally broad, sometimes dramatically so. A series of rather dry winters triggered a great famine in Iran in 1870-72, sparing only the northwestern and western regions of the country. A century later the drought of 1970-71 in Afghanistan brought an 18 percent decline in cereal production, the loss of forty-two percent of the herds, and a rise in human mortality from famine that is impossible to measure. Its reverberations were such that it might be considered the indirect cause of the fall of the monarchy in 1973. Not all precipitation deficits reach this magnitude. But an early cessation in rainfall during the cold season is sufficient to curtail the subsequent harvest to some extent. Variability in precipitation directly determines the levels of national agricultural production. It thus has considerable economic impact.

Aside from widespread and long-lasting disasters like droughts, which always have deferred effects, there is a second type of precipitation disaster that is brutal and short-lived. It consists of heavy rainstorms, some of which approach or even surpass 100 mm in twenty-four hours. Various weather conditions, generally quite localized, can cause them: There can be sharp thermo-convectional instability following prolonged heating of the ground, a strong surge in the summer monsoon, or even the vertical superposition of a cold upper tropospheric trough on a surface frontal depression; the last is by far the most frequent. It is in the coastal and subcoastal areas, which are bathed in warm, humid, and thus very unstable air, that the heaviest deluges are experienced. Of ten Iranian stations having recorded daily rainfalls above 100 mm during recent decades, five are located near the Persian Gulf and four in the Caspian provinces. In the first region, the rainstorms typically occur in winter, and the measured maximums do not exceed 200 mm (196 mm at K̲ārg and Gačsārān, 121 mm at Dezfūl). In the second, they can occur in any season except spring; in frequency and violence—both aggravated by the formidable barrier of the Alborz—they are unequaled elsewhere (353 mm in twenty-four hours were recorded at Anzalī, 260 at Rāmsar). In a continental environment, on the other hand, this type of torrential rainfall is much rarer and less severe and tends to be concentrated in the spring. In Afghanistan, for example, the daily maximum recorded up to the present is only 96 mm (at Darwāz, on March 24, 1973). In the zone of influence of the summer monsoon it does not exceed 64 mm (at Sardeh, near Ḡaznī, on July 6, 1978, and August 7, 1983.

Whatever the regional deviations may be, everywhere torrential rains cause damage, both direct (diffuse rainwash erosion on the slopes and sheet flooding on the piedmonts, destruction of buildings) and indirect (flash floods). In extreme instances they can be fatal. A recent example is furnished by the exceptional monsoon of the summer of 1978 in eastern Afghanistan: Two rainy episodes (on July 5-6 and August 17-19), as short-lived as they were violent, caused the death of 173 people and several thousand head of livestock and the destruction of some 2,000 houses, several dozen nomad camps, and more than 400 underground channels (*kārēz*). Furthermore, several thousand hectares of agricultural land were washed away. This catastrophe has had many historical precedents, some of which have been even more devastating, for example, the floods at Qom (spring, 1636), Qazvīn (April, 1851), Shiraz (January, 1908), and Rafsanjān (March, 1910; Melville, pp. 140ff.). Because the areas affected are always rather limited, this type of event, however spectacular it may be, does not really have an impact equal to that of a drought. But, whereas the death-dealing effects of the latter have been mitigated (in Afghanistan) or eliminated (in Iran as governments have set up apparatus for rapid and effective relief (communications networks, food stockpiles) while conducting prevention policies based mainly on development of irrigation, rainstorms continue to be as dangerous to human life as ever.

Whether prolonged or sudden, spectacular or insidious, these natural precipitation catastrophes are an aspect of regional climatic normality that is too often little understood. They are not indicators of climatic change but merely recurrent events, the retrospective study of which, though still in its infancy, has already led to recognition of a frequency ranging between five and fifteen years (all rainfall hazards included), as well as of the role of social and political context in determining the magnitude of famines.

Paleoclimatic variations, particularly studied in Iran by geomorphologists and archeologists, have been the subject of contradictory observations and interpretations. The main difficulty in such reconstructions in fact is to determine whether a well-attested arid phase has resulted from a decrease in rainfall or from a rise in temperature that causes evaporation to increase and, conversely, whether a "rainy" phase has resulted from heavy precipitation or from a decrease in temperature and evaporation. The possibility that such variations have not occurred simultaneously over the whole of the Irano-Afghan territory cannot be excluded and would partly explain some of the contradictions among researchers.

Bibliography: The basic data are furnished by the national climatic yearbooks published regularly at Tehran and Kabul. The most significant of them (extending through 1974 for sixty-two Iranian stations and through 1977 for forty-two Afghan stations) have been conveniently brought together in M. Alex, *Klimadaten ausgewählter Stationen des Vorderen Orients*, TAVO, Beiheft A14, Wiesbaden, 1985. The basic data on Iran used in the present article have been drawn from this work. As for Afghanistan, where in general the meteorological network has been more recently established, the archives and yearbooks of the Meteorological Institute of Kabul through 1983 have also been consulted.

The records are not always as precise and consistent as one could wish. It must be emphasized, first of all, that the observation periods are of very unequal length for the different stations; rarely does any of them approach the thirty-year span necessary for calculating climatological "norms." Many have been in operation for only a few years, especially in Afghanistan, where, after a remarkable expansion in the 1970s, the meteorological network was severely curtailed in the 1980s. Second, the figures systematically combine rainfall and snowfall, which is why total precipitation, rather than rainfall proper, has been discussed in this article. Finally, the recording of rainy days (understood here as those days that receive 0.1 mm or more) has been rigorous only in Afghanistan. In Iran often only days receiving at least 1 mm are recorded. Any systematic treatment of this important aspect of rainfall is thus impossible.

The principal studies dealing with precipitation in Iran are H. Bobek, "Beiträge zur klima-ökologischen Gliederung Irans," *Erdkunde* 6/2-3, 1952, pp. 65-84; Ch. Djavadi, *Climats de l'Iran*, Monographies de la Météorologie Nationale 54, Paris, 1966; M. H. Ganji, "Climates of Iran," *Bulletin de la Société de Géographie d'Égypte* 28, 1955, pp. 195-299; and idem, Climate," in *Camb. Hist. Iran* I, pp. 212-49. For Afghanistan, the basic works are H. M. Herman, *Le climat de l'Afghanistan*, Monographies de la Météorologie Nationale 52, Paris, 1965; V. I. Titov, *Klimaticheskie usloviya Afganistana*, Moscow,

1976; and ʿA. Wāḥed and ʿA.-Ḥ. Ğaffārī, *Režīm-e bārandagī dar sāḥa-ye jomhūrī-e demōkrātīk-e Afgānestān*, Kabul, Rīāsat-e hawāšenāsī, 1360 Š./1981; these recent titles do not at all supersede the pioneering publication of H.-E. Iven, *Das Klima von Kabul*, Geographische Wochenschrift, Beiheft 5, Breslau, 1933; and especially those of E. Stenz, the virtual originator of the Afghan meteorological service: "The Climate of Afghanistan: Its Aridity, Dryness and Divisions," *Bulletin of the Polish Institute of Arts and Science in America* 4, 1946, pp. 1-16; and "Precipitation, Evaporation and Aridity in Afghanistan," *Acta Geophysica Polonica* 5/4, 1957, pp. 245-66.

Detailed cartographic representations of precipitation (corrected here on several points) can be found in Ganji, ed., *Climatic Atlas of Iran*, Tehran, 1965; P. Lalande et al., *Cartes climatiques de l'Afghanistan*, Publications of the Meteorological Institute 4, Kabul, 1974; and in Maps A IV 4 ("Mean Annual Rainfall and Variability, 1984") and A IV 5-6 ("Rainfall Reliability and Seasonal Rainfall Patterns 1985"), both by Alex, op. cit.

Daily rhythms, especially the occurrence of heavy rains, have attracted the attention of some researchers: A. H. Gordon and J. G. Lockwood, "Maximum One-Day Falls of Precipitation in Tehran," *Weather* 25/1, 1970, pp. 2-8; and C. Rathjens, "Hohe Tagessummen des Niederschlags in Afghanistan," *Afghanistan Journal* 5/1, 1978, pp. 22-25.

Synoptic aspects have been dealt with in B. Alijani and J. R. Harman, "Synoptic Climatology of Precipitation in Iran," *Annals of the Association of American Geographers* 75/3, 1985, pp. 404-16 (a study that would have been more instructive had its authors taken into account the precipitation totals instead of drawing conclusions entirely from the number of rainy days); A. Khalili, "Precipitation Patterns of Central Elburz," *Archiv für Meteorologie, Geophysik und Bioklimatologie*, Ser. B., 21, 1973, pp. 215-32; C. De Rycke and V. Balland, "Une région de contact climatique majeur: Les confins indo-afghans," in P. Pagney and S. Nieuwolt, eds., *Études de climatologie tropicale*, Paris, 1986, pp. 103-21; T. R. Sivall, "Synoptic-Climatological Study of the Asian Summer Monsoon in Afghanistan," *Geografiska Annaler* 59A, 1-2, 1977, pp. 67-87.

Study of the relation between precipitation and rainfall agriculture should begin with Bobek, "Verbreitung des Regenfeldbaus in Iran," in *Geographische Studien: Festschrift für J. Sölch*, Vienna, 1951, pp. 9-30; and C. Jentsch, "Grundlagen und Möglichkeiten des Regenfeldbaus in Afghanistan," in *Tagungsbericht und wissenschaftliche Abhandlungen des 38. deutschen Geographentages Erlangen-Nürnberg 1971*, Wiesbaden, 1972, pp. 371-79. On a more general level see G. Perrin de Brichambaut and C. C. Wallén, *A Study of Agroclimatology in Semi-Arid and Arid Zones of the Near East*, World Meteorological Organization, Technical Note 56, Geneva, 1964. An example of archeological extrapolation from abridged contemporary observations is found in M. Jaguttis-Emden, "Zum Problem der Klimaabhängigkeit früher Ackerbaugesellschaften im westlichen Zagros," in W. Frey and H.-P. Uerpmann, eds., *Beiträge zur Umweltgeschichte des Vorderen Orients*, TAVO, Beihefte, A8, Wiesbaden, 1981, pp. 257-74.

Recent rainfall disasters and some of their human and economic consequences have been the subject of special analyses. On the drought of 1970-71 in Afghanistan see D. Balland and C. M. Kieffer, "Nomadisme et sécheresse en Afghanistan: L'exemple des nomades Paštun du Dašt-e Nāwor," in Équipe Écologie et Anthropologie des Sociétés Pastorales, ed., *Pastoral Production and Society*, Cambridge and Paris, 1979, pp. 75-90 (Persian translation in *Īlāt wa ʿašāyer*, Majmūʿa-ye ketāb-e āgāh, Tehran, 1362 Š./1983, pp. 303-19, without the bibliography); N. T. Clark, "Some Probable Effects of Drought on Flock Structure and Production Parameters in Northwestern Afghanistan," *Nomadic Peoples* 15, 1984, pp. 67-74; and Rathjens, "Witterungsbedingte Schwankungen der Ernährungsbasis in Afghanistan," *Erdkunde* 29/3, 1975, pp. 182-88. On the exceptional importance of the 1978 monsoon rains in the same country, see De Rycke, "Étude climatologique d'une invasion de mousson en Afghanistan central et oriental en juillet 1978," in *Climatologie tropicale et établissements humains/Tropical Climatology and Human Settlements*, Acts of Symposium 23 of the 25th International Congress of Geography, Dijon, 1984, pp. 89-101.

Paleoclimatic variations have been treated in several publications, which cannot all be enumerated here. For the Pleistocene, an attempt at synthesis has been presented in Ganji, "Post-Glacial Climatic Changes on the Iranian Plateau," in W. C. Brice, ed., *The Environmental History of the Near and Middle East Since the Last Ice Age*, London, 1978, pp. 149-63. An excellent survey of the various conflicting theories can be found in E. Ehlers, *Iran: Grundzüge einer geographischen Landeskunde*, Darmstadt, 1980, pp. 125-27.

Historical climatology, for a long time ignored, has been the subject of an initial survey of sources from the Islamic period in C. Melville, "Meteorological Hazards and Disasters in Iran: A Preliminary Survey to 1950," *Iran* 22, 1984, pp. 113-50 (which also deals with Afghanistan, though marginally).

See also ĀB, iii; and BARF.

(D. BALLAND)

BARANĪ, ŻĪĀʾ-AL-DĪN B. MOʾAYYED-AL-MOLK, (ca. 684-758/1285-1357), Indian-born Muslim historian who wrote in the period of the Delhi sultanate. Related by descent and marriage to middle-ranking Muslim service families (his father was *nāʾeb* of Baran and his uncle was *kūtwāl* of Delhi), Baranī spent his maturity as courtier and sometimes boon campanion (*nadīm*) of Sultan Moḥammad Toḡloq (r. 725-52/1324-51); earlier, Baranī had been an attendant (*ḵādem*) upon the *češtī* shaikh Neẓām-al-Dīn Awlīā' (636-725/1238-1325). Loss of royal favor and temporary internment in the Punjab fort of Bhatnēr under Moḥammad Toḡloq's successor Fīrūz Shah (r. 752-790/1351-88) turned Baranī toward writing. Baranī may have been adjudged guilty of association with the raising at Delhi of a rival to Fīrūz Shah, following Moḥammad Toḡloq's death near Thatta in Sind. Aḥmad Ayāz, Moḥammad Toḡloq's appointed deputy at the capital, unaware that the army with Moḥammad Toḡloq had accepted Fīrūz as sultan, put a young lad on the throne (alleging him to be the late sultan's son), with the support or acquiescence of some officers and notables at Delhi.

Baranī's extant works are: *Na't-e moḥammadī, Akbār-e Barmakīān, Fatāwā-ye jahāndārī*, and *Tārīk-e fīrūzšāhī.* Written with the *Yawm al-ḥesāb* in mind, the *Fatāwā-ye jahāndārī* and the *Tārīk-e fīrūzšāhī* respectively imbue and are imbued by an ideal of Islamic rulership expressed in part through symbols and motifs which express Baranī's understanding and representation of pre-Islamic Iranian monarchical tradition. Baranī's *Fatāwā-ye jahāndārī* does more than cite apothegms and anecdotes of old Persian kings, viziers, and sages along with traditions from the prophet Moḥammad and memorabilia of the early Arab and 'Abbasid caliphs (cf. Ḡazālī's *Naṣīḥat al-molūk*); Baranī islamizes yet further the Zoroastrian maxim that "religion and rulership are twin brothers"—he proclaims that, given the deterioration in human behavior in his age and the fading force of the ascetic example of the Prophet and the first four Sunni caliphs, pious Muslim kings should employ the force, generate the awe, and display the ostentation of the royal descendants of Cyrus (*Fatāwā-ye jahāndārī*, pp. 139-42). Kings must maintain their authority, even at the cost of killing Muslims for non-*ḥadd* offenses, but seek their peace with God by using authority thus protected to uphold the *Šarī'a*, curb heresy, and abase the infidel in India. In thus serving Islam, Muslim rulers must be advised by viziers and served by functionaries of high birth and character. Hostile to the promotion under the Delhi sultanate of Hindu converts, Baranī appealed to Iranian traditions to deny that high moral and intellectual attainment could accompany low birth (see, e.g., *Fatāwā-ye jahāndārī*, fols. 211b-213a, pp. 288-91; *Tārīk-e fīrūzšāhī*, pp. 36-37). His *Tārīk-e fīrūzšāhī* was a subtle assessment, according to his criteria, of the performances of seven sultans of Delhi. Baranī's experience in India prompted his judgments, but he looked to Iran as a cultural region for their nourishment.

Bibliography: *Tārīk-e fīrūzšāhī*, ed. Sayyed Aḥmad Khan, Calcutta, 1862. *Fatāwā-ye jahāndārī*, ed. Afsar Salīm Khan, Lahore, 1972. *Tārīk-e Āl-e Barmakīān*, Bombay, 1889. Moḥammad Ḥabīb and Afsar Salīm Khan, *The Political Theory of the Delhi Sultanate*, Allahabad, n.d. P. Hardy, *Historians of Medieval India*, 1st ed., London, 1960, pp. 20-39. Idem, "Baranī," *EI*² I, pp. 1036-37. Idem "Didactic Historical Writing in Indian Islam: Żiyā al-Dīn Baranī's Treatment of the Reign of Sultan Muhammad Tughluq," in *South Asia*, ed. Y. Friedmann, Jerusalem and Boulder, 1984, pp. 38-59 (= vol. 1 of *Islam in Asia*). S. Nurul Hasan, "Sahifa-i-Na't-i-Muhammadi of Zia-ud-din Barani," *Medieval Indian Quarterly* 1/3-4, Aligarh, 1953, pp. 100-05. K. A. Niẓāmī, *On History and Historians of Medieval India*, Delhi, 1983, pp. 124-40. Storey, I/1, pp. 505-08, 2, p. 1082.

(P. HARDY)

BARĀQ BĀBĀ (655-707/1257-58–1307-08), a crypto-shamanic Anatolian Turkman dervish close to two of the Mongol rulers of Iran. The name Barāq means "hairless dog" in Qipchaq Turkish, this being the title of honor given him by his master Sarï Saltūq when he eagerly swallowed a morsel his master had expectorated (Köprülü, 1929, p. 15). According to certain legends, Barāq Bābā was a son of 'Ezz-al-Dīn Keykā'ūs II, a Saljuq who took refuge with the Byzantines; adopted by the patriarch of Byzantium, he grew up a Christian until restored to Islam by Sarï Saltūq (Wittek, 1952, pp. 658-59). In fact he was born in a village near Tokat (Ṭūqād) in central Anatolia where his father worked the land. Although Barāq Bābā has been listed as one of the principal successors of Ḥājī Bektāš (d. 669/1271?; see Gölpinarlı, ed., 1958, pp. 81, 90), this is chronologically impossible. He was rather a *morīd* of Sarï Saltūq, a semilegendary warrior saint who propagated Islam in the Crimea and the Dobruja.

At a date that cannot be determined, Barāq Bābā left Sarï Saltūq and traveled to the Il-khanid court, probably because of a reverse his master's forces had suffered. When Barāq Bābā came into the presence of Ḡāzān Khan in Tabrīz, a tiger (or, according to some accounts, a lion) was unleashed on him to test his occult powers; a cry from him was sufficient to halt it in its tracks. Thereafter he enjoyed the trust both of Ḡāzān and of his successor, Moḥammad Kodā-banda Oljāytū (Öljeytü), who appears to have used him on several diplomatic (or possibly espionage) missions.

In 706/1306 Barāq Bābā arrived in Damascus, carrying the Il-khanid banner and a letter of appointment. His outlandish appearance aroused both disgust and amusement: He was naked except for a red loincloth (*fūṭa*) and extremely filthy, wearing a kind of felt turban to which cowhorns were attached on his head. His companions were similarly dressed and carried with them an assortment of bones and bells, to the accompaniment of which Barāq Bābā would dance, imitating the antics of monkeys and bears ('Asqalanī, 1385/1966, I, p. 6). Afram, the governor of Damascus, tested Barāq Bābā by confronting him with a wild ostrich, which he is said instantly to have tamed. After an unsuccessful attempt to enter Egypt, Barāq Bābā and his party traveled back and forth between Damascus and Jerusalem before returning to Iran.

The following year, when the inhabitants of Gīlān revolted against Il-khanid rule, Barāq Bābā was sent to assist in restoring order. A party of Gīlānis intercepted him and a group of his followers near Lāhījān. Addressing him as "shaikh of the Mongols" (*šayk-e Moḡolān*), they upbraided him for serving "the enemies of the

Muslims" and butchered him. Those of his followers who survived the attack gathered his bones and took them back for burial at Solṭānīya (Dorn, 1858, IV, pp. 148-51).

Barāq Bābā's influence outlived him, both in Solṭānīya and in Anatolia. Oljāytū had a hospice constructed for his followers in Solṭānīya, to which he assigned a daily expenditure of fifty dinars; Barāq Bābā's descendants presided over this hospice. In Anatolia, Geyiklī Bābā, who had ties with the Ottoman sultan Orḵān, and Tapdūq Emre, the preceptor of the celebrated mystical poet Yūnos Emre, were both regarded as Barāq Bābā's successors, and, more generally, a class of dervishes known as Barāqīyūn seems also to have existed (Gölpınarlı, 1961, p. 43).

Barāq Bābā left behind a brief *resāla* comprising laconic and enigmatic sayings in Qipchaq Turkish; about fifty years after his death, a learned commentary was written on it, in elegant Persian and with copious quotations from Persian Sufi poets, by a certain Qoṭb-al-ʿAlawī (for a facsimile of the autograph text of the commentary, see Gölpınarlı, 1961, pp. 457-72). Noteworthy in the text of the *resāla* are the claim to have served "the sultan" (presumably Oljāytū) as a loyal soldier and the concluding prayer which calls for the Byzantine rulers of Constantinople and Trebizond to be defeated and thrown in the sea.

Qoṭb-al-ʿAlawī's interpretation of the ecstatic utterances contained in the *resāla* in conformity with the classical Sufism of Iran suggests that no clear line of demarcation separated the crypto-shamanic Sufism of Barāq Bābā and his peers from its established and orthodox counterpart. Barāq Bābā is said, indeed, to have been one of those whom Ḡāzān Khan consulted concerning the life and teachings of Mawlānā Jalāl-al-Dīn Rūmī; it is possible that Barāq Bābā may have met him early in life (Aflākī, 1953, II, p. 848). Olo ʿĀref Čelebi (d. 710/1320), head of the Mawlawī (Mevlevi) order, visited the Barāqī hospice at Solṭānīya, where he was hospitably received by Ḥayrān Amīrjī, a descendant of Barāq Bābā. Ḥayrān Amīrjī later paid a return visit to Konya (Aflākī, 1953, II, p. 860).

Barāq Bābā is said to have believed that ʿAlī was a divine incarnation and that he in turn had reappeared in the person of Moḥammad Ḵodā-banda (who did indeed come to profess Shiʿism; see Sümer, 1976, p. 210). If this is true, it is possible to see in Barāq Bābā an early exponent of the potent mixture of Turkic shamanism, Sufism, and *ḡolāt*-Shiʿism that some two centuries later brought the Safavids to power.

Bibliography: Šams-al-Dīn Aḥmad Aflākī, *Manāqeb al-ʿārefīn*, ed. T. Yazıcı, Ankara, 1953, II, pp. 848, 860. Ebn Ḥajar ʿAsqalānī, *al-Dorar al-kāmena fī aʿyān al-meʾa al-ṯāmena*, ed. M. S. Jādd-al-Ḥaqq, Cairo, 1385/1966, II, pp. 5-6. Claude Cahen, *Pre-Ottoman Turkey*, New York, 1968, pp. 354-55. Haydar-Ali Diriöz, "Kutb-ul-Alevi'nin Barak Baba risalesi," *Türkiyat mecmuası* 9, 1946-51, pp. 167-70. Bernard Dorn, *Muhammedanische Quellen zur Geschichte der südlichen Küste des kaspischen Meeres*, St. Petersburg, 1859, IV, pp. 148-51. Mircea Eliade, *Shamanism: Archaic Techniques of Ecstasy*, Princeton, 1972, pp. 402-03. Ziyaeddin Fahri, "Barak Baba risalesi," *Hayat* 2/29, June 16, 1927, p. 55. Abdülbaki Gölpınarlı, ed., *Vilâyet-Nâme: Manakib-i Hacı Bektas-i Veli*, Istanbul, 1958, pp. 81, 90. Idem, *Mevlânâ'dan sonra Mevlevilik*, new ed., Istanbul, 1983, pp. 11, 13, 70, 72, 83, 94. Idem, *Yunus Emre ve tasavvuf*, Istanbul, 1961, pp. 17-26, 255-75, 457-72. Fuad Köprülü, "Anadolu'da İslamiyet," *Darülfunun Edebiyat Fakültesi mecmuası* 2, 1338/1919-20, pp. 392-94. Idem, *Influence du chamanisme turco-mongol sur les ordres mystiques musulmans*, Istanbul, 1929, pp. 14-19. Idem, *Türk edebiyatında ilk Mutasavvıflar*, new ed., Ankara, 1966, pp. 179-80. Bernard Lewis, "Barāḳ Bābā," in *EI*². Ahmet Yaşar Ocak, *Bektaşî Menakıbnamelerinde İslam öncesi inanç motifleri*, Istanbul, 1983, p. 108. Faruk Sümer, *Safevi devletinin kuruluşu ve gelişmesinde Anadolu türklerinin rolu*, Ankara, 1976, p. 210. Zeki Velidi Togan, *Umumi türk tarihine giriş*, 3rd ed., Istanbul, 1981, pp. 270-71, 334-35. Osman Turan, "Selcuk Türkiyesi din tarihine dair bar kaynak," *Köprülü armağanı*, Istanbul, 1953, p. 548. Idem, *Selcuklular zamanında Türkiye tarihi*, 2nd ed., Istanbul, 1984, pp. 425, 581, 596. Paul Wittek, "Yazijioghlu ʿAli on the Christian Turks of the Dobruja," *BSOAS* 45, 1952, pp. 650, 658-59. Hilmi Ziya (Ülken), "Anadolu tarihinde dini ruhiyat müşahedeleri," *Mihrab* 1/13, Haziran, 1340/June-July, 1924, pp. 438-44.

(H. Algar)

BARĀQ KHAN. See NOWRŪZ AḤMAD KHAN.

BARAQĪ, ḴᵛĀJA ʿABD-ALLĀH, first of the successors appointed by Ḵᵛāja Yūsof Hamadānī (d. 555/1160, q.v.) to exercise spiritual authority after his passing. He is said to have originated in Ḵᵛārazm and joined the circle of Hamadānī in Bukhara in his early youth, although, according to another account, it was his great-grandfather who made the move from Ḵᵛārazm to Bukhara, establishing there a respected family of Hanafite *foqahāʾ*. The name Baraqī has been taken either as a *nesba*, referring to the town of Baraq, slightly to the north of Gorganj, or as being derived from an arabicized form of *bara* (sheep), Ḵᵛāja ʿAbd-Allāh's ancestors supposedly having been shepherds. He was buried in the cemetery on the Šārestān hill of Bukhara, close to Abū Bakr Kalābāḏī, author of the *Ketāb al-taʿarrof*, although by the 9th/15th century the precise location of his tomb had become obscured. Baraqī appears not to have nominated any successors of his own, and it was two other successors of Hamadānī, Ḵᵛāja Aḥmad Yasawī and Ḵᵛāja ʿAbd-al-Ḵāleq Gojdovānī (q.v.), who perpetuated the distinctly central Asian line of Sufi affiliation that Hamadānī had inaugurated.

Bibliography: Jāmī, *Nafaḥāt*, p. 377. Aḥmad b. Maḥmūd Moʿīn-al-Foqarā, *Tārīḵ-e Mollāzāda dar ḏekr-e mazārāt-e Boḵārā*, ed. Aḥmad Golčīn-e Maʿānī, Tehran, 1339 Š./1960, p. 66. Ḡolām Sarvar Lāhūrī, *Ḵazīnat al-asfīāʾ*, Lucknow, 1320/1902, I,

p. 531. Fak̲r-al-Dīn ʿAlī Ṣafī, *Rašahat ʿayn al-ḥayāt*, Tashkent, 1329/1911, p. 7. Ebn al-At̲īr, *al-Lobāb fī tahd̲īb al-ansāb*, ed. Moṣṭafā ʿAbd-al-Wāḥed, Cairo, 1971, I, p. 158.

(H. ALGAR)

BARAŠNOM, the chief Zoroastrian purification rite, consisting of a triple cleansing, with *gōmēz* (cow's urine), dust, and water, followed by nine nights' seclusion, during which three simpler cleansings take place. The rite is administered by a "purifier," Av. *yaoždāθrya-*, Pahl. *yōjdāhragar*. The cleansings are from head to foot, hence its Pahl./Persian name, from *Av. barəšnu-*, "head"; but, as this is true also of lesser purifications, the rite's full, distinctive name is *barašnom-e nō-šaba* (Darī *nō-šwa*) "*barašnom* of the nine nights." The Parsis term it *barašnom-nāhn* "the *barašnom* washing," or simply *nāhn*.

The rite is described in detail (but not named) in *Vd.* 8.37-72, more briefly in *Vd.* 9.1-37, its expressed purpose there being to cleanse those polluted by contact with *nasā*, carrion. It was administered on clean, barren ground, 30 paces from fire, water, and the *barəsman* (see BARSOM). Nine shallow pits, *maya-*, were dug in a straight line from north to south, so that the polluted person (Pers. *rīmanī*) moved from the direction of hell to that of heaven (*Pahl. Vd.* 9.32). The first six pits were a pace apart, but a gap of three paces separated them from the last three. A furrow, *karšā-*, was drawn round all nine pits, and twelve more furrows, in sets of three, inside it, the last three pits being again somewhat separated by this means. (For a plan see J. Darmesteter, *Le Zend-Avesta* II, opposite p. 102.) Stones, clods, potsherds, or pieces of wood were placed within the outer furrow before the first pit, and after the ninth, and also in the gap between the sixth and seventh pits, so that the *rīmanī*'s feet never touched the good earth (*Vd.* 9.11). The *yaoždāθrya* stood outside the furrows, reciting Avesta, beginning with *Y.* 49.10.3. First he poured *gōmēz* into a metal pot fixed to the end of a rod with nine "knots," Pahl. *nō-grih*, and reached this to the *rīmanī*, who rubbed his hands with it and then every part of his body, from head to foot, finally reciting the *Ahunwar* (q.v.) and *Kəm-nā Mazdā* (*Vd.* 9.27). This process was repeated in the next five pits, with a dog being shown the *rīmanī* after each cleansing, evidently to aid the expulsion of evil. Between the sixth and seventh pits the *rīmanī* dried his body with fifteen applications of dust, then in the last three pits the *yaoždāθrya* handed water to him, with which he rubbed himself all over, once in the seventh pit, twice in the eighth, thrice in the ninth (*Vd.* 9.31). Finally, on the stones beyond the ninth pit the *yaoždāθrya* censed him, and putting on fresh clothes he retired to a place of seclusion (Pahl. *armēšt-gāh*, Persian *barašnom-k̲āna*, Parsi *nāhn-k̲āna*). There on the fourth, seventh, and tenth mornings he bathed body and clothes with *gōmēz* and water, regaining thereby full purity.

In the ninth century A. D. Zādspram, *mōbad* of Serkān in Fārs, sought to substitute for this rite a simpler one described in *Vd.* 8.99-103; but his brother Manuščihr, the Persian high priest, suppressed this attempted innovation. (See *The Epistles of Manuščihr*, ed. B. N. Dhabhar, Bombay, 1912; tr. E. W. West, *SBE* XVIII, pp. 279-366, with appendices IV and V, pp. 431-58.) Detailed descriptions in the *Persian Rivayats* show the rite being administered thereafter in close accord with the *Vendidad* prescriptions (ed. Unvala, I, pp. 586-88, 594-99; tr. Dhabhar, pp. 360, 369-77). The most notable changes were that the pits had been replaced by sets of stones (in fives and threes), laid on the ground; and the arrangement of the twelve inner furrows was slightly altered. (For a plan see *Persian Rivayats*, ed. Unvala, I, p. 587; tr. West, *SBE* XVIII, p. 435.) A walled, round enclosure was now used, the *barašnom-gāh*, Parsi *barsingō* (see A. V. W. Jackson, *Persia Past and Present*, New York, 1906, p. 383; M. Boyce, *Zoroastrianism* I, p. 314 n. 114; *A Persian Stronghold of Zoroastrianism*, Oxford, 1977, pp. 112-13, 118). Among the Parsis the arrangement of the stones differs again slightly (for plans see *Persian Rivayats*, ed. Unvala, I, pp. 588, 600), and they are aligned west to east (see P. K. Anklesaria, "The Direction of the Arrangement of Stones in the *Barašnūm-gāh* in Iran and India," in *Sir J. J. Zarthoshti Madressa Centenary Volume*, Bombay, 1967, pp. 162-64). Nowadays the Parsi *barsingō* is usually a rectangular yard within the precinct of a fire temple.

The *Persian Rivayats* and other Zoroastrian Persian writings indicate extensive use of the *barašnom*. Every member of the community was required to undergo the rite at least once, to cleanse the pollutions of birth (*Ṣad dar nat̲r*, chap. 36.1-2, and *Ṣad dar Bondaheš*, chap. 72, ed. B. N. Dhabhar, Bombay, 1909; cf. *Vd.* 19.33); and this was general practice in the Iranian community down to the early twentieth century (see Boyce, *Persian Stronghold*, pp. 111-12, 113, and cf. pp. 125, 126-27). For women the rite was administered by women of priestly family, with a priest reciting the Avestan prayers within earshot. Contact with *nasā* and other forms of pollution necessitated the rite, and it was part of the preparation required of converts (*Persian Rivayats*, ed. Unvala, I, p. 282; tr. Dhabhar, p. 276). Every priest had to undergo *barašnom* before being initiated *hērbad* and *mōbad*, and again before solemnizing the highest rituals. This remains the custom today; but in India the Bhagarias (q.v.) of Bombay began for some reason withholding the rite from the laity there in the mid-eighteenth century. Yet nearly a hundred years later, a Parsi recorded, "it was not rare to see [lay] persons, both male and female, themselves going through the ceremony" (J. J. Modi, *Persian Farziāt Nāmeh . . . of Dastur Darab Pahlan*, Bombay, 1924, p. 16 n. 2). Nowadays in India it is almost entirely restricted to priests, who undergo it both for their own purity, and vicariously for lay persons. In Iran it remains theoretically available to all, but there is now a shortage of qualified *yōjdāhragar*s. Reformists in both communities reject the rite.

Bibliography: Given in the text. See also H. Anquetil-Duperron, *Zend-Avesta*, Paris, 1771, II, pp. 545-48. J. J. Modi, *Ceremonies and Customs of the*

Parsis, 2nd ed., Bombay, 1932, pp. 102-41. D. Menant, "Sacerdoce zoroastrien à Nausari," *Annales du Musée Guimet* 36, 1912, pp. 221-89, with photographs of the ritual, one of which was reproduced by M. Molé, *L'Iran ancien*, Paris, 1965, following p. 97, and by J. Bauer, *Symbolik des Parsismus*, Tafelband, Stuttgart, 1973, p. 123. For further photographs see S. S. Hartmann, *Parsism; The Religion of Zoroaster*, Leiden, 1980, pls. xix-xx.

(M. Boyce)

BĀRBAD, minstrel-poet of the court of the Sasanian king Ḵosrow II Parvēz (r. 591-628 A.D.). His name is recorded as Fahl(a)bad/ḏ, Bahl(a)bad/ḏ, Fahl(a)wad/ḏ, Fahr(a)bad/ḏ, Bahr(a)bad/ḏ, or Bārbad/ḏ in the Arabic sources and as Bārbad/ḏ in the Persian sources. As to the original form, Nöldeke (p. 42 n. 2) thought that the arabicized forms such as Fahl(a)bad/ḏ represented Pahlavi Pahr-/Pahlbad, and the form Bārbad (or rather *Pārbad) was due to the ambiguity of the Pahlavi character *h*, which could equally represent the sound *ā̆*. Christensen (*Iran. Sass.*, p. 484 n. 2), on the other hand, considered Bārbad the correct form. On the evidence of the oldest attestation of the name in Arabic, namely Bahr-/Bahlbad in a poem of Ḵāled b. Fayyāż (d. ca. 718, see Yāqūt, III, p. 252; Qazvīnī, p. 230) and the other arabicized forms, it is more likely that the original form was Pahr-/Pahlbad (with *-hr-*/*-hl-* < OIr. *-rθ-* or *-θr-*?), from which *Pārbad and later Bārbad developed (for the development of *-ahr* to *-ār*, cf. Pahl. *šahr*, Pers. *šār*, beside *šahr* "city") with assimilation of $p-b>b-b$ (cf. Pahl. Pābak/g, NPers. Bābak). This explanation is strengthened by the attestation of Pahr-/Pahlbad, probably a proper name, on a Sasanian seal (see Gignoux and Gyselen, p. 112; cf. *phlp't* on another seal, ibid., p. 101).

Only scant information, mostly of a legendary nature, is preserved about Bārbad in the Arabic and Persian sources. According to these, he was the most distinguished and talented minstrel-poet of his epoch. According to the older sources, he was a native of Marv (Ebn Ḵordāḏbeh, *Ketāb al-lahw*, p. 16; Eṣṭaḵrī, p. 262; Ps. Jāḥeẓ, p. 363; Ṯaʿālebī, *Ḡorar*, p. 694; *Nozhat al qolūb*, p. 157), whereas later sources (Šams-al-Dīn Rāzī, p. 193, *Farhang-e jahāngīrī*, *Borhān-e qāteʿ*, etc.; see Dehḵodā, *Loḡat-nāma*, s.v. Bārbad) mention Jahrom in Fārs as his hometown. The latter assumption was probably inspired by a verse of Ferdowsī (*Šah-nāma* [Moscow] IX, p. 277 v. 376), according to which Bārbad, after having been informed of the murder of Ḵosrow, traveled from Jahrom to Tīsfūn (Ctesiphon).

His first meeting with the king is related in a legend recorded by Ferdowsī (ibid., pp. 266ff.) and Ṯaʿālebī (pp. 694ff.), according to which Bārbad, being a young talented musician, aspired to become one of Ḵosrow's court minstrels, but Sargīs (or Sarkaš), the chief court minstrel, jealously kept him away from the court. Bārbad therefore concealed himself among the leaves of a tree in the king's garden, where a banquet was being held, and sang three songs to his *barbaṭ*, the first called *Dād-āfrīd* (an abbreviated form of *dādār-āfrīd* "created by god" according to *Šāh-nāma*, p. 228 v. 3644; Ṯaʿālebī has *Yazdān-āfrīd*); the second *Peykār-e gord* "battle of the hero" according to *Šāh-nāma*, v. 3652, but *Partow-e Farkār* "splendor of Farkār" according to Ṯaʿālebī; and the third *Sabz dar sabz* "green in the green" (*Šāh-nāma*, v. 3659; Ṯaʿālebī has *Sabz andar sabz*). The king was highly delighted by his minstrel's talent, gave him audience, and made him his chief minstrel (*Šāh-nāma*, v. 3676).

The legends related by Islamic authors clearly show Bārbad's influence with the king. According to one legend, the oldest version of which is in Arabic verse by Ḵāled b. Fayyāż (see above), when the king's favorite horse, Šabdēz, died, neither the master of the horse nor any other courtier dared for fear of death to notify the king. Bārbad, however, was able to save the life of the master of the horse by composing a poem and singing it for the king to the accompaniment of his instrument. The same story is retold in other sources (Ṯaʿālebī, pp. 703f.; Ps. Jāḥeẓ, p. 364; Qazvīnī, p. 230). Ḵosrow's favor toward Bārbad motivated the courtiers to appeal to him to mediate with the king whenever one of them was the object of disfavor. They also presented their requests through him to the king (Ps. Jāḥeẓ, pp. 363-64; Qazvīnī, p. 156). Even Šīrīn, the king's favorite wife, is said to have once asked Bārbad, through his singing and playing, to remind the king of his promise to build her a castle. For this service the queen gave the minstrel an estate near Isfahan, in which he settled his family (Ebn al-Faqīh, pp. 158f.; Qazvīnī, p. 296; Yāqūt, IV, p. 113; Ṭūsī, p. 210). According to another story (Neẓām-al-Molk, pp. 174f.), a courtier, having incurred the king's disfavor, was put in prison and nobody dared to visit him except Bārbad. When the king reproached him for this, he responded with a witty remark and thus avoided the king's anger.

Islamic sources abound in stories about Bārbad's minstrel skill and talent. According to one of them (*Aḡānī* V, p. 58), a musician who together with Bārbad was present at a royal banquet, instigated by jealousy, took advantage of the latter's temporary absence from the banquet and disordered the strings of his lute. On his return to the banquet, Bārbad, unaware that his instrument was out of tune, started to play. As kings did not approve of musicians' tuning their instruments in their presence, he continued his performance so dexterously that nobody noticed the defect of his instrument. It was only after the banquet that the king was informed of it.

Bārbad was a poet-musician of panegyric as well as elegy. He used to compose verses and sing them to his own accompaniment on various occasions, e.g., in the great Iranian festivals, especially Nowrūz and Mehragān, at state banquets, etc. He also versified victories and current events (Ps. Jāḥeẓ, pp. 363ff.). He is related to have composed, at the request of the workmen, a melody called *Bāḡ-e naḵjīrān* "garden of the game" on the occasion of the completion of the great gardens at Qaṣr-e Šīrīn (Ebn al-Faqīh, pp. 158ff.; Yāqūt, IV, pp. 112-13). Neẓāmī (*Ḵosrow o Šīrīn*, pp. 190-94) mentions the names of the thirty airs composed by Bārbad for each day of the month. These names, with some variations, are also recorded in some Persian dictionaries such as *Borhān-e qāṭeʿ* (see Christensen, 1918, pp. 368-77, and *Iran. Sass.*, pp. 485f.). He is also said to have composed for the banquet of the king 360 melodies, one of which he used to sing each day (*Tārīḵ-e gozīda*, p. 123). Ṯaʿālebī (p. 698) attributes to him the authorship of the royal modes (*ḵosravānī*), apparently the same as the seven royal modes (*ṭoroq al-molūkīya*) mentioned by Masʿūdī (*Morūj*, ed. Pellat, V, pp. 127-28; cf. also Ebn Ḵordāḏbeh, *Lahw*, p. 15). The only surviving piece of his poetry in Middle Persian, though in Arabic script, is a panegyric in three hemistichs quoted by Ebn Ḵordāḏbeh (p. 16; see Tafazzoli, p. 338).

The end of Bārbad's life is also related in a legendary way. According to the *Šāh-nāma* ([Moscow] IX, p. 277 vv. 374-413), after Ḵosrow's death Bārbad hurried from Jahrom to Tīsfūn, where he recited some elegies about his master's death, cut his four fingers, and burned his instruments. According to another tradition (Ṯaʿālebī, *Ḡorar*, pp. 704f.), Bārbad was poisoned by his rival Sarjas (Sargīs, Sarkaš). But Ebn Qotayba (*ʿOyūn al-aḵbār* I, p. 98) and Ebn ʿAbd Rabbeh (*ʿEqd al-farīd* II, p. 182) attribute this murder to a musician called *Yošt (or *Zīwešt[?] or Rošk[?] in Jāḥeẓ, *Ḥayawān* VII, p. 113, and *Rabūst[?] by Ṭūsī, *ʿAjāyeb*, p. 546). According to Ebn Ḵordāḏbeh (p. 17), on the other hand, it was Bārbad who killed his pupil Šarkās (probably *Sarkēs or Sargīs, etc.), but the murderer's witty remark earned him the pardon of the king, who did not want to lose both his minstrels.

Bibliography: A. Christensen in *Dastur Hoshang Memorial Volume*, Bombay, 1918. Ebn ʿAbd Rabbeh, *ʿEqd al-farīd* II, Cairo, 1956. Ebn Ḵordāḏbeh, *Ketāb al-lahw*, ed. Aḡnāṭīūs, Beirut, 1961. E. G. Browne, "The Sources of Dawlatshāh, with Some Remarks on the Materials Available for a Literary History of Persia and an Excursus on Bārbad and Rūdagī," *JRAS*, 1899, pp. 54ff. Ebn Qotayba Dīnavarī, *ʿOyūn al-aḵbār* I, Cairo, 1963. Ph. Gignoux and R. Gyselen, *Sceaux sasanides*, Louvain, 1982. Jāḥeẓ, *Ḥayawān*, ed. Moḥammad Hārūn, VII, Cairo, 1945. Ps. Jāḥeẓ, *al-Maḥāsen wa'l-ażdād*, ed. G. van Vloten, Leiden, 1894-1932. Neẓāmī Ganjavī, *Ḵosrow o Šīrīn*, ed. Waḥīd Dastgerdī, Tehran, 1333 Š./1954. Ḥamd-Allāh Mostawfī, *Tārīḵ-e gozīda*, ed. ʿA.-Ḥ. Navāʾī, Tehran, 1339 Š./1960. Th. Nöldeke, *Iranisches Nationalepos*, 2nd ed., Leipzig, 1920. Zakarīyāʾ Qazvīnī, *Āṯār al-belād*, ed. Wüstenfeld, Göttingen, 1848. Šams-al-Dīn Rāzī, *Moʿjam*, pp. 192-93. Ḵᵛāja Neẓām-al-Molk Ṭūsī, *Sīar al-molūk* (*Sīāsat-nāma*), ed. H. Darke, Tehran, 1347 Š./1968. A. Tafazzoli, "Some Middle-Persian Quotations in Classical Arabic and Persian Texts," in *Mémorial Jean de Menasce*, ed. Ph. Gignoux and A. Tafazzoli, Tehran and Liège, 1974, pp. 337-49. Moḥammad b. Maḥmūd Ṭūsī, *ʿAjāʾeb al-maḵlūqāt wa qarāʾeb al-mawjūdāt*, ed. M. Sotūda, Tehran, 1345 Š./1966.

(A. TAFAŻŻOLĪ)

BARBARO, GIOSAFAT, Venetian merchant, traveler, and diplomat (Venice, 1413-94). He was appointed Venetian ambassador to Persia (1473-78) in order to solicit its Āq Qoyunlū sovereign Uzun Ḥasan ("il signor Assambei;" d. Šawwāl, 882/January, 1478) to wage war upon the increasingly menacing power of the Ottoman Turks; but in the end he realized that Uzun Ḥasan "had not the slightest intention of going against the Ottomans." Barbaro's travel book, written in 1487 and divided into two parts (Tana or Azov and surrounding countries and Persia) is somewhat lacunary and discontinuous; nevertheless it contains noteworthy historical information. The Persian section of the narrative concerns the figure of Uzun Ḥasan, his diplomatic and military activity, his court and camp, riches, feasts (dances, wrestling, exotic animals); the Persian trading routes and economy (goods, paper money, *qanāts*); the towns of Tabrīz, Solṭānīya, Isfahan (where Barbaro met A. Contarini, another Venetian envoy to Persia), Shiraz, Kāšān, Qom, Yazd, Lār, Hormoz, Darband, Astarābād, Baku, and their *bāzārs* and monuments; the remains of "Cilmynar" (Čehel-menār, i.e., Persepolis), the reliefs at Naqš-e Rostam, and the tomb of Cyrus; curious customs, manners of sufis, *qalandars*, and dervishes.

Bibliography: Lord S. of Alderly, ed., *Travels to Tana and Persia by losafa Barbaro and Ambrogio Contarini*, London, 1873. R. Almagià in *Dizionario biografico degli Italiani*, Rome, 1964, VI, pp. 106-09. L. Lockhart, R. Morozzo della Rocca, and M. F. Tiepolo, eds., *I viaggi degli ambasciatori veneti Barbaro e Contarini*, Rome, 1973.

(A. M. PIEMONTESE)

BARBAṬ, the prototype of a family of short-necked lutes characterized by a rather flat, pear-shaped sound box which was carved with the neck out of a single piece of wood and covered by a wooden soundboard or table that came to have two holes either in the shape of a "3" or an "S." Held in place on a bridge which was glued to the table, the strings of the *barbaṭ* were fastened to pegs placed on both sides of the head, which jutted out at right angles to the neck. The *barbaṭ*'s frets and four silk or gut strings (from three to seven in the Indian form; according to other sources [Mallāḥ, p. 94], the original had three strings to which a fourth was added) were plucked with a wooden plectrum and tuned in fourths, reaching a range of two octaves. During the Islamic period, the four strings were given the names *bam*, *maṯlan*, *maṯlaṯ*, and *zīr*, which suggests that the prototype *barbaṭ*, perhaps inspired by the *ṭanbūr*, had only two strings (Pers. *bam* and *zīr*) and that two others were interposed between the original strings, later followed by a fifth string. The tuning, fretting, and fingering of the *barbaṭ* constitute the basics of what is known about musical theory in Islamic culture.

Ḵᵛārazmī (p. 238) derives *barbaṭ* from *bar* "chest" and *baṭ* "duck"; indeed the profile of the instrument resembles a duck, the back forming the belly and the neck the head. A debatable etymology considers *barbaṭ*

(Pahl. *barbut* or *barbud*) to be derived from the Greek *barbitos*, but, apart from their both being stringed instruments, there is no significant resemblance between the two. It is also said that *ud* in *barbud* became Arabic *ʿūd* (wood), which term may refer to the evolution of the old types of lutes with skin sound board into the new one with wooden sound table.

The *barbaṭ*, probably originated in central Asia (Marcel-Dubois, 1942, p. 205; Vyzgo, pl. XXVII). The oldest pictorial representations of this instrument are found at the first-century B.C. site (Vyzgo, pl. XIX; others date it to the first century A.D.) of Ḵalčayān in North Bactria (present-day South Uzbekistan). While doubts remain about the dating of the "bas-relief" representing a *barbaṭ* (ibid., pl. XXVII), the terra-cotta statuette from Dal'verzin Tepe (ibid., pl. XIX) seems to belong to the oldest strata (1st cent. B.C.) and is at the moment the oldest evidence of the existence of the *barbaṭ*. Farmer (*EI*[1] IV, p. 985) cites a *barbaṭ* in an Indian sculpture of the second century B.C., which seems to appear in northwest India only during the 1st century A.D. (ibid.); however, the dating is open to question. More clear-cut is the evidence provided by the existence of a very similar form of the *barbaṭ* ("luth échancré"), found in a Gandhara sculpture from the 2nd-4th centuries A.D. (Marcel-Dubois, p. 88). The instrument may well have been introduced by the Kushan aristocracy, whose influence is attested in Gandharan art. This form of *barbaṭ* was probably adopted in Persia a few decades later; it is said to have appeared during the reign of Bahrām Gōr, when, according to the *Šāh-nāma* (ed. Borūḵīm, VII-VIII, p. 2259), 10,000 Lōrīs arrived from India, "all excelling in the art of the *barbaṭ*." (This suggests that the instrument was imported to Iran via north India.) Used widely throughout the Middle East and central Asia, the *barbaṭ* was adopted around 600 A.D. by the Arabs of Ḥīra, but was later supplanted by an improved modification, the *ʿūd* (attributed to Zaryāb, 8-9th cent.; Farmer, loc. cit.), which originally had four, then five double gut strings, a deeper and rounder sound box made of wood strips, and a neck that was independent from the body. For some time the new lute retained such features of the old *barbaṭ* as simple, as opposed to double, strings and seven frets that divided the fingerboard; nevertheless, double-stringed and non-fretted lutes also existed. It seems that the term *barbaṭ* disappeared sooner than the instrument itself, which was replaced by the *ʿūd*. While Kendī (p. 21) only mentions the five-string *ʿūd*, other early theoreticians (Ḵᵛārazmī, see Manik, p. 38, and Ebn Sīnā: *barbaṭ* in the *Najāt*, *ʿūd* in the *Šefāʾ*; see Manil, p. 48) use the terms *barbaṭ* and *ʿūd* synonymously. Iranian iconography attests to the instrument's use until the 4th/10th century, but the term *ʿūd-e qadīm* used by later authors (Marāḡī, p. 125) is probably a reference to the obsolete *barbaṭ* or to a variant with four double strings, smaller than the *ʿūd-e kāmel* with its five double strings. The *barbaṭ* survived for centuries in classical poetry as a trope that evoked Iranian music's golden age, in which such artists as Bārbad, the famous *barbaṭ* player and singer, performed for Ḵosrow II Parvēz.

A *barbaṭ* is pictured in the 13th-century Spanish illustrated musical manuscript *Cantigas de Santa Maria* (Farmer, *EI*[1] IV, p. 986). A kind of *barbaṭ*, quite similar to the original form, is still found in China; legend has it that Emperor Wu-ti (140-87 B.C.) created it, but its use is only attested from the early third century under the sinicized Persian name *pi'pa* (referred to by Marāḡī, p. 126). It has also been adopted in Japan as the *biwa* (derived from the Persian), as well as in other Asian nations like Vietnam, Korea, and Cambodia.

Bibliography: Moḥammad-ʿAlī Emām Šūštarī, *Īrān: gāhvāra-ye dāneš o honar*, Tehran, 1348 Š./1969, pp. 137-40. H. G. Farmer, "ʿŪd," in *EI*[1]. Idem, *Islam, Musikgeschichte in Bildern* III, Leipzig, n.d. Idem, "Ud," in *New Grove's Dictionary of Music and Musicians*, London, 1980. Yaʿqūb b. Esḥāq Kendī, *Resāla fī ḵobr taʾlīf al-alḥān*, ed. R. Lachmann and M. el-Hefni, Leipzig, 1931. Abū ʿAbd-Allāh Moḥammad Ḵᵛārazmī, *Mafātīḥ al-ʿolūm*, ed. G. van Vloten, Leiden, 1895. Ḥosayn-ʿAlī Mallāḥ, *Manūčehrī Dāmḡānī wa mūsīqī*, Tehran, 1363 Š./1984, pp. 94-100. L. Manik, *Das arabische Tonsystem im Mittelalter*, Leiden, 1969. ʿAbd-al-Qāder b. Ḡaybī Marāḡī, *Maqāṣed al-alḥān*, ed. T. Bīneš, Tehran, 2536 = 1356 Š./1978. C. Marcel-Dubois, *Les instruments de musique de l'Inde ancienne*, Paris, pp. 89, 205. T. S. Vyzgo, *Muzykal'nye instrumenty Sredneĭ Azii* (Musical Instruments of Central Asia), Moscow, 1980.

(J. DURING)

BARBERRY (*zerešk; Berberis* spp., family Berberidaceae). Species of this genus are found in the northern, eastern, and southeastern highlands of Iran (Alborz, Qaradāḡ in Azerbaijan, ranges of Khorasan, Bārez mountain in Kermān). They reach heights of 1 to 3 m, seldom reaching 4 m, and have long branches, copious thorns, denticulate leaves, and red berries which form in clusters on the outer branches in midspring, after the yellow flowers have shed their petals, and ripen in midsummer. Dried berries of *Berberis integerrima* Dunge have culinary and pharmaceutical uses. The shrub and the berries are both called *zerešk* in most of Iran, *zārj* or *zārč* in parts of the south (in northern Iran *zerešk* usually designates the species *Berberis vulgaris* L., in other parts *Berberis integerrima* Bunge). In Persian medical books the terms *anbarbārīs* (Ebn Boṭlān, p. 86; Jorjānī, p. 471.9ff.), *anbarbīrīs, zerešk* (Heravī, p. 13 and n.), *zerek* (Aḵawaynī, p. 119), *zartak, zarak* (Amīrī, p. 40), *barbārīs*, and *ambarbārīs* (Dehḵodā, s.vv.) are often used (*barbārīs*, etc., may be of Syriac origin; Amīrī, loc. cit.).

In cookery, barberries (especially from *Berberis integerrima*) are added as a flavoring to soups, polows, and chicken stuffings. A refreshing sherbet made from water drained from barberries and sugar is thought to be useful for getting rid of bile, i.e., curing biliousness. To make *zerešk-polow* washed barberries are sprinkled on strained boiled rice, more rice is poured on top, and the dish is then simmered. Addition of barberries to various sorts of soups imparts pleasant tartness. Cleaned chickens are stuffed with barberries and rice, walnuts, or other ingredients before being roasted or cooked.

In traditional medicine, barberries are classed as a cold, dry substance and thought to possess the properties that check diarrhea; strengthen the stomach, liver, and heart; eliminate excess bile; relieve thirst; and cool stomach heat, internal inflammations, and blood ebullition. Mixtures of barberries with hot drugs are considered useful for relief of blockages of the liver, bowels, and intestines; for cure of dysentery caused by coldness and weakness of the liver and bowels; and generally for the treatment of patients afflicted with cold (*mabrūdīn*). A barberry-wormwood mixture is thought to improve digestion, and barberry juice to prevent vomiting and fainting. The berries are said to cure stomach ulcers and dysentery due to bowel weakness and barberry poultices to relieve acute abscesses. A mixture of barberry, apple, and lemon juices with sugar is believed to counteract dangerous poisons and to cure snakebite, palpitations, vomiting, and loss of appetite. Eating barberries, however, is thought to cause flatulence (remediable with cloves) and dryness and constipation (remediable with sugar and sweets). The bark from the bush's stem, called *ʿūd al-rīḥ* in Arabic and *ārgīs* in Persian medical books, has similar medicinal properties. A drink made by infusion of the bark in hot water is thought to have a tonic effect on the liver when it is afflicted by cold, and rinsing the mouth with this liquid is thought to heal gumboils, strengthen the gums, and ease toothache. A concentrated decoction of the bark is used in the form of drops to relieve chronic eye diseases and as an enema to cleanse the liver and heal intestinal ulcers. From the wood and bark is extracted a yellow dye called berberine, used for dyeing wool for carpets and tanning leather.

In Persian literature, teardrops (*serešk*) are likened to barberries (*zerešk*). In modern colloquial usage, when somebody gets unduly nervous or excited, those present will bid him or her to calm down by saying "*Zerešk*!" or "*Āb(-e) zerešk*!" This idiom evidently refers to the supposed antibilious and antimelancholic properties of barberries and their juice.

Bibliography: Abū Bakr Akawaynī Bokārī, *Hedāyat al-motaʿallemīn fi'l-ṭebb*, ed. J. Matīnī, Mašhad, 1344 Š./1965. M. Amīrī, *Farhang-e dārūhā wa vāžahā-ye došvār*, Tehran, 1353 Š./1974. K. Browicz and I. Zelienski, "Berberidaceae," in K. H. Rechinger, ed., *Flora Iranica*, Graz, 1975, p. 111. Dehkodā, s.v. *zerešk* (q.v. for poetic citations). Ebn Boṭlān, *Taqwīm al-ṣeḥḥa*, Pers. tr., ed. Ḡ.-Ḥ. Yūsofī, Tehran, 1350 Š./1971. Abū Manṣūr Mowaffaq Heravī, *Ketāb al-abnīa ʿan ḥaqāʾeq al-adwīa*, ed. A. Bahmanyār and Ḥ. Maḥbūbī Ardakānī, Tehran, 1344 Š./1965. Moḥammad Moʾmen Ḥosaynī, *Toḥfa-ye Ḥakīm Moʾmen*, n.p., n.d., pp. 108-09. Sayyed Esmāʿīl Jorjānī, *Ḏakīra-ye kᵛārazmšāhī*, ed. ʿA-A. Saʿīdī Sīrjānī, Tehran, 1355 Š./1976. Sayyed Moḥammad-Ḥosayn ʿOqaylī ʿAlawī Korāsānī Šīrāzī, *Qarābādīn-e kabīr*, Tehran, n.d., pp. 734-37. Ḥ. Ṯābetī, *Jangalhā, derakthā, wa deraktčahā-ye Īrān*, 2nd ed., Tehran, 1355 Š./1976. ʿAlī Zargarī, *Gīāhā-ye dārūʾī*, 3rd ed., Tehran, 1340 Š./1961, I, p. 55.

(*EIr*.)

BARBIER DE MEYNARD, CHARLES ADRIEN CASIMIR, French orientalist (1826-1908). He was born at sea on a voyage from Istanbul to Marseilles on 8 February 1826. His maternal grandfather was a doctor practicing medicine at Istanbul, and his mother came from Therapia (Tarabya); about the rest of his family nothing is known. After winning a scholarship to pursue his secondary education at the Collège Royal de Louis le Grand in Paris, he took the college's training course in Arabic, Turkish, and Persian for "jeunes de langues," i.e., prospective dragomans.

In 1850 he was appointed dragoman and head of the chancellery at Jerusalem, but in the following year he was forced by ill health to return to France. He did not remain idle, however, but soon began to write articles for the *Journal Asiatique*, the organ of the Société Asiatique, of which he became a member in 1850 (and was ultimately elected chairman, in succession to Ernest Renan after the latter's death in 1892). This journal published his first important article, "Tableau littéraire du Khorassan et de la Transoxiane au IVe. siècle de l'hégire," in 1853 (pp. 169-239) and 1854 (pp. 291-361), and his last research report, "Surnoms et sobriquets dans la littérature arabe," in 1907 (9, pp. 173-244, 365-428; 10, pp. 55-118, 192-273); he is said to have corrected the proofs of this report on his deathbed.

In 1854 Barbier de Meynard was attached to the French mission in Iran, the secretary of which was Count de Gobineau. He resided in Tehran for a year or so, and took the opportunity to amplify the knowledge of Persian literature and history which he had acquired in Paris. Among other things, he embarked on the preparation of *Dictionnaire géographique, historique, et littéraire de la Perse et des contrées adjacentes, extrait de Moʿjem el-Bouldân de Yaqout*, which he brought out in 1861. This was also the year in which he and his collaborator Pavet de Courteille began to publish the work for which he is most widely remembered, the nine volumes of the text, translation, and index of Masʿūdī's *Morūj al-ḏahab* (*Les prairies d'or*; Paris, 1861-77). Between 1856 and 1863, he studied with Jules Mohl, the Persian scholar engaged in the monumental task of editing and translating Ferdowsī's *Šāh-nāma*. He was greatly influenced by this master. After Mohl's death in 1876, Barbier de Meynard prepared his handwritten material for publication.

Barbier de Meynard's Persian studies did not prevent him from finding time for a sojourn in Istanbul prior to his appointment as professor of Turkish at the Ecole des Langues Orientales in 1863. He held this post for the rest of his life, combining it with the professorship of Persian at the Collège de France, to which he was appointed in succession to Mohl. In 1878, he was elected member of the Académie des Inscriptions et Belles-

Lettres, at whose request he took part in the compilation of several volumes of *Recueil des Historiens des Croisades, Historiens Orientaux*, namely, volumes II, III, and IV, the last of which, published in 1896, contains the history of the reigns of Nūr-al-Dīn and Ṣalāḥ-al-Dīn from *al-Rawżatayn fī ak̲bār al-dawlatayn* of Abū Šāma. Part of his time was spent in compiling and seeing through the press the two volumes of his *Dictionnaire turc-français*, which came out in 1881 and 1886 and which may be considered his most important scientific work. In 1885 the Collège de France transferred him, at his own request, to the chair of Arabic left vacant by the death of Stanislas Guyard. In addition he became the administrator of the Ecole des Langues Orientales in 1898.

After 1903 declining health compelled him to give up part of his teaching; but he continued to receive students in his room during his terminal illness. He died in Paris on the night of 30-31 March 1908.

The published works of Barbier de Meynard are relatively numerous; in the obituary written by P. Girard, thirty-six are listed. Several remain valuable and are still consulted, particularly his editions and translations of texts, though the *Morūj* requires some emendation to take account of 20th-century advances in Arabic studies. Although most of his works are in the Arabic field, the above-mentioned *Tableau littéraire du Khorassan* and *Dictionnaire géographique* attest the excellence of his Persian scholarship. He also published the first French translation of Saʿdi's *Būstān* in 1877 and contributed several articles on Iran to *Journal Asiatique*.

Bibliography: Paul Girard, "Notice sur la vie et les travaux de Barbier de Meynard," in *Comptes rendus des séances de l'Académie des Inscriptions et Belles-Lettres*, Paris, 1909.

(Ch. Pellat)

BARD-e BAL, a necropolis excavated in 1969-70 by the Belgian archeological mission in Iran, along the banks of the Garāb river one km northwest of the ruined village of Čenārbāšī, and 54 km southeast of Īlām, province of Pošt-e Kūh. Seventy tombs, dating from the end of Iron Age I and Iron Age II, were found on the site. These were generally cist tombs which were sometimes fitted with large stone-slab doors. Despite their small size, they were mostly not individual tombs; graves of Iron Age I were often reused in Iron Age II. The pottery is an unpainted buff ware, occasionally with incised decoration and applied buttons. In Iron Age I almost all metal objects are made of bronze; in Iron Age II we find that weapons are still made of bronze whereas personal ornaments are made of iron. The Bard-e Bal necropolis is important because it provides an archeological context by which to approximate the date (12th-10th centuries B.C.) of the typical Luristan bronzes, such as spike-butted axes, whetstone handles in the form of crouched caprids, and finials with upright standing ibexes, that were discovered there.

Bibliography: L. Vanden Berghe, "La nécropole de Bard-i Bal au Luristan," *Archeologia* 43, 1971, pp. 14-23. Idem, "Excavations in Pusht-i Kuh. Tombs Provide Evidence on Dating Typical Luristan Bronzes," *Archaeology* 24, 1971, pp. 263-71 (especially pp. 268-71, figs. 12-20). Idem, "Recherches archéologiques dans le Luristan, sixième campagne 1970: Fouilles à Bard-i Bal et Pay-i Kal," *Iranica Antiqua* 10, 1973, pp. 1-55.

(L. Vanden Berghe)

BARD-e BOT. See ELYMAIS.

BARD-e NEŠĀNDA, a complex of ancient ruins in K̲ūzestān, situated 18 km northwest of the town of Masjed-e Solaymān (where similar ruins exist) at 675 m altitude on the edge of the Bak̲tīārī mountains. The name means "erected stone." The earliest mention of this site is in a brief statement by J. M. Unvala in *Revue d'Assyriologie* 25, 1928, p. 86. R. Ghirshman visited it in 1947; he began excavations in 1964 and continued in 1965 and 1966. The complex is 700 m long and 250 m wide. Ghirshman describes it as made up of three parts: a "castle" (château) which was the ruler's residence, a terrace 250 m to the east which was used for religious rituals, and a village or "lower town" 100 m to the north (R. Ghirshman, *MDAFI* 45, 1976, pp. 9-10). The "castle" is a building 29.80 m long and 18.60-19 m wide with a central courtyard or hall measuring 9.70 × 6.75 m, around which large chambers are grouped. Ghirshman, who could only devote five days to excavation of the "castle," found evidence that it had been constructed in three phases. In this reckoning, the first phase was contemporaneous with the start of the terrace construction, which he placed in the pre-Achaemenid period, and the last phase extended into the early Islamic period. As regards the village, a plan was published (op. cit., fig. 2), but not a report.

Throughout the excavations, the principal aim was to explore the great terrace. Finding differences in the methods of construction, Ghirshman distinguished a "lower terrace" and an "upper terrace." A sloping roadway ca. 150 m long gives access to the lower terrace. The total length of the two terraces is 157.20 m. The upper terrace is the oldest structure in the complex. The excavators noted two different constructional phases. From phase 1 there are only a small "podium" and an "annex" of roughly the same size. Ghirshman thought that religious ceremonies in honor of Ahura Mazdā were performed around a fire altar which existed on the podium (op. cit., p. 50). In the light of certain finds of small artifacts, Ghirshman felt able to place the commencement of the podium in the 7th-6th century B.C. (op. cit., p. 28; in another context, on p. 50, he speaks of the 8th-7th century). It remains questionable, however, whether these finds provide adequate evidence for such an early dating. The phase 1 part of the terrace must have been still in existence in the Hellenistic period (op. cit., p. 39). This upper terrace was later extended, probably during the reign of Camniscires I, king of Elymais in the mid-2nd century B.C. (op. cit., p. 36 n. 1, p. 39). Finally the whole structure was again greatly enlarged, increasing its length to 157.20 m. The most important building in this part of the terrace is a four-pillared room, the "tetrastyle temple" (op. cit., pp. 39ff.). Two reliefs on pillars of the portico fronting this temple are thought by Ghirshman to represent Anāhitā and Miθra. He therefore infers that the temple was dedicated to these two deities, and he places the date of construction in the 1st-2nd century A.D. (op. cit., p. 225). The whole complex, in his opinion (p. 50), probably remained in use up to the mid-4th century A.D.

The ruins of Bard-e Nešānda, together with those at Masjed-e Solaymān, provide important clues for identification of temples in Elymais mentioned by ancient Greek and Roman writers (see Schippmann and Vanden Berghe, *Reliefs rupestres*, pp. 16ff., 20). The temple of Ahura Mazdā at Bard-e Nešānda may well be the same as the temple of Bēl (the Semitic equivalent of Ahura Mazdā) at which Antiochus III met his death in 187 B.C. while attempting to plunder its treasure (Strabo 16.1.18). The temple of Anāhitā and Miθra at Bard-e Nešānda might likewise be viewed as the precursor of the temple of Artemis-Nanaia which Antiochus IV (175-64 B.C.) attempted to plunder (Polybius, 31.9), but such an identification would not accord with Ghirshman's dating of the construction in the 1st-2nd century A.D. Also mentioned in the sources (Justin, 41.6.8; Strabo, 16.1.18) is a temple of Artemis, called Ta Azara by Strabo, which lay somewhere in Elymais and was plundered by Mithridates I after his conquest of Susa in 139-38 B.C. Anāhitā is simply an Iranian name for Artemis-Nanaia.

Bibliography: C. Augé, R. Curiel, and G. Le Rider, *Terrasses sacrées de Bard-è Néchandeh et Masjid-e Solaiman. Les trouvailles monétaires*, MDAFI 44, 1979. R. Ghirshman, *Terrasses sacrées de Bard-è Néchandeh et Masjid-e Solaiman*, MDAFI 45, 1976. K. Schippmann, *Die iranischen Feuerheiligtümer*, Berlin and New York, 1971, pp. 251ff. Idem and L. Vanden Berghe, *Les reliefs rupestres d'Elymaïs (Iran) de l'époque parthe*, Iranica Antiqua, Suppl. 3, Ghent, 1985, pp. 16ff., 20. L. Vanden Berghe, *Bibliographie analytique de l'archéologie de l'Iran ancien*, Leiden, 1979, nos. 1110-25.

(K. SCHIPPMANN)

BARDA and **BARDADĀRĪ**, slaves and slavery. The word *barda* is from Old Iranian **u̯arta-* "captive, enslaved," Avestan *varəta-* (*AirWb.*, col. 1368; note especially *varətəm az-* "to lead away in captivity," cf. Mid. Pers., Parth. *wardāz*, see ii, below), whence Mid. Pers. *wardag* "captive, prisoner" and *wardagīh* "captivity." In the Pahlavi texts slaves are usually denoted by the terms *anšahrīg* or *banda* (q.v.).

i. *In the Achaemenid period.*
ii. *In the Sasanian period.*
iii. *In the Islamic period up to the Mongol invasion.*
iv. *From the Mongols to the abolition of slavery.*
v. *Military slavery in Islamic Iran.*
vi. *Regulations governing slavery in Islamic jurisprudence.*

i. In the Achaemenid Period

At the beginning of the Achaemenid period, the institution of slavery was still poorly developed in Iran. In Media a custom existed whereby a poor man could place himself at the disposal of a rich person if the latter agreed to feed him. The position of such a man was similar to that of a slave. However, he could at any time leave his master if he was poorly fed (see I. M. D'yakonov [Diakonoff], *Istoriya Midii*, Moscow and Leningrad, 1956, pp. 334-35). By the time their own state had emerged (the first half of the 6th cent. B.C.), the Persians knew only of such primitive slavery, and slave labor was not yet economically significant.

The most common term to designate slaves in ancient Iran was the word *bandaka-*, a derivative of *banda-* "bond, fetter" (see BANDA and Kent, *Old Persian*, p. 199). This word was utilized not only to designate actual slaves, but also to express general dependence. For instance, in the Behistun [Bīsotūn] inscription, Darius I calls his satraps and generals his *bandakas* (in the Babylonian version *qallu* "slave"). Likewise Darius I calls Gadates, his governor in Ionia, his slave (*doulos*; see W. Dittenberger, *Sylloge Inscriptionum Graecarum* I, Leipzig, 1915, no. 22), just as in many countries of the ancient East, all the subjects of the king, including even the highest-ranking officials, were considered slaves of the king. Therefore the Greek authors wrote that, with the exception of the king, the entire Persian people were a crowd of slaves (see, e.g., Herodotus, 7.135; Xenophon, *Anabasis* 2.5.38). In the same way, the authority of the heads of patriarchal families over members of their own families was tyrannical and they could treat their children as slaves (see Aristotle, *Ethica Nicomachea* 9.12).

One of the Old Iranian terms to designate slaves was **gr̥da-* the original meaning of which was "household slave(s)." This term is attested in the Aramaic letters of Aršām, the satrap of Egypt in the 5th century B.C., in Babylonian texts of the Achaemenid period in the form *garda/u*, and in Elamite documents from Persepolis as *kurtaš* (see G. R. Driver, *Aramaic Documents of the Fifth Century B.C.*, Oxford, 1957, p. 63). These persons were workers of the royal household and of the households of Persian nobility in Iran, as well as in Babylonia and Egypt. The overwhelming majority of *kurtaš* consisted of foreigners. In terms of their composition and legal status, the *kurtaš* were not homogeneous. In all probability, there were among them a significant number of slaves who were prisoners of war, a few free people who worked voluntarily for wages, and some individuals who were temporarily working off their labor service. Thus, with the passage of time the word *kurtaš* acquired the broader meaning "worker."

In the Elamite version of the Behistun inscription *kurtaš* is the equivalent of Old Persian *māniya-* (in the Babylonian version it is rendered with a term meaning "hired laborers"). *Māniya-* probably meant "household slave(s)" (see Kent, *Old Persian*, p. 202).

As a result of the far-flung conquests of the

Achaemenids there occurred a sharp change in the royal household and in the households of the Persian nobility from primitive patriarchal slavery to intensive utilization of the labor of foreign workers in agriculture and partly in crafts. A portion of these foreigners were exploited as slaves, while the remainder were treated as semi-free people and were settled on royal land. Usually they were prisoners of war recruited from those who had rebelled against Persian rule or put up resistance to the Persian army (see M. Dandamayev, "Foreign Slaves on the Estates of the Achaemenid Kings and their Nobles," in *Trudy dvadtsat' pyatogo mezhdunarodnogo kongressa vostokovedov* II, Moscow, 1963, pp. 151-52).

A substantial number of slaves who performed domestic work for the Achaemenids and Persian nobility (bakers, cooks, cupbearers, eunuchs, etc.) were also recruited from among the representatives of vanquished peoples. Babylonia alone was obliged to supply the Persian king for these purposes an annual tribute of 500 boys (Herodotus, 3.92). A certain number of such slaves were purchased by Persians on the slave market as well (Herodotus, 8.105).

Our information on privately owned slaves in Iran is scanty and haphazard. A Babylonian slave sale contract from Persepolis has been preserved and dated to the reign of Darius I. However, the contracting parties as well as the slave himself were Babylonians (see M. W. Stolper, "The Neo-Babylonian Text from the Persepolis Fortification," *JNES* 43, 1984, pp. 299-303). In 523 B.C. a certain Razamarma, son of Razamumarga, and Aspumetana, son of Asputatika, sold their slave women Kardara and Patiza to a Babylonian for 2 2/3 minas of silver (J. N. Strassmaier, *Inschriften von Cambyses, König von Babylon*, Leipzig, 1890, no. 384). The contract was drafted in Babylonian at Humadēšu (Uvādaicaya in the Old Persian version of the Behistun inscription), a city in the Persepolis area (see R. Zadok, "On the Connections between Iran and Babylonia in the Sixth Century B.C.," *Iran* 14, 1976, p. 74; Stolper, art. cit., p. 306). The sellers and the slave women, judging from their names, were of Iranian descent, but the buyer was a Babylonian. In 528 B.C. a slave woman who had been purchased in Elam was sold in the Babylonian city Opis (Strassmaier, op. cit., no. 143). In 508 B.C. there was among the slaves of the Egibi business house in Babylon a slave woman from Gandara (J. N. Strassmaier, *Inschriften von Darius, König von Babylon*, Leipzig, 1897, no. 379, line 44). In 511 B.C. one Babylonian sold "his slave woman, a Bactrian" in Sippar (see for references M. A. Dandamaev, *Slavery in Babylonia*, DeKalb, 1984, p. 108; cf. ibid., p. 111, on a slave with the Iranian name Patiridāta). These slaves apparently were prisoners of war (the "booty of the bow").

Under the Achaemenids in Babylonia and other conquered countries Persian nobles became large slave owners (see for references Dandamaev, op. cit., p. 111). According to some documents, Iranians sold their slaves in Babylonia (see, e.g., H. G. Stigers, "Neo- and Late Babylonian Business Documents," *Journal of Cuneiform Studies* 28, 1976, no. 22).

On the whole, there was only a small number of slaves in relation to the number of free persons even in the most developed countries of the Achaemenid empire, and slave labor was in no position to supplant the labor of free workers. The basis of agriculture was the labor of free farmers and tenants and in handicrafts the labor of free artisans, whose occupation was usually inherited within the family, likewise predominated. In these countries of the empire, slavery had already undergone important changes by the time of the emergence of the Persian state. Debt slavery was no longer common. The practice of pledging one's person for debt, not to mention self-sale, had totally disappeared by the Persian period. In the case of nonpayment of a debt by the appointed deadline, the creditor could turn the children of the debtor into slaves. A creditor could arrest an insolvent debtor and confine him to debtor's prison. However, the creditor could not sell a debtor into slavery to a third party. Usually the debtor paid off the loan by free work for the creditor, thereby retaining his freedom.

Judging from Babylonian documents and Aramaic papyri of the Achaemenid period, slaves were sometimes set free with the stipulation that they continue to serve the master or provide him with food and clothes as long as the latter was alive (see Dandamaev, op. cit., pp. 438-55).

In Babylonia, the slaves often worked on their own and paid a certain quitrent from the *peculium* they possessed. The size of the quitrent on the average when calculated in monetary terms amounted to 12 shekels of silver a year. Such a sum was also what the average annual payment of a hired adult employee amounted to, regardless of whether he was free or a slave. The slave himself cost around 60-90 shekels of silver, and for 1 shekel it was possible to purchase 180 liters of barley or dates.

Bibliography: Given in the text.

(M. A. DANDAMAYEV)

ii. In the Sasanian Period

The word *wardag* is first attested in the Sasanian inscriptions of the third century in the meaning of "slave" or "captive." Describing the campaigns of King Šāpūr I, the high priest Kirdēr (Kartir) tells how the army enslaved, burned, and devastated (*u-š wardag ud ādursōxt ud awērān kard*) wherever it went but that he himself then by the order of the king of kings (re)established (*winnārišn kard*) the Magians and fires in those areas. Thus he did not allow harm to come to them or let them be enslaved, and those that had become enslaved, those he took and sent them back to their own lands (inscription of Kirdēr on the Kaʿba-ye Zardošt at Naqš-e Rostam, lines 12-13; M. Back, *Die sassanidischen Staatsinschriften*, Acta Iranica 18, Tehran and Liège, 1978, pp. 426-29).

The related Middle Persian and Parthian word

wardāz "captivity" is found in a similar context in the inscription of Šāpūr I on the Kaʿba-ye Zardošt (Mid. Pers. 1.15, Parth. 11.5, 12; Gk. 1.26 has *ēkhmalōtisamen* "We took prisoner [of war]": Back, pp. 296, 315).

The main source of information on institutions of the Sasanian period, which also provides valuable material on the legal and social status of slaves, is the Pahlavi law book *Mādayān ī hazār dādestān*, a compilation of law cases collected by Farroxmard ī Wahrāmān in the sixth century A.D. Although only part of the chapter on slaves (*Mādayān*, pt. 1, 1.1-17) has come down to us in an unique manuscript of the *Mādayān*, the discussion of different legal aspects of slavery in chapters actually dedicated to other matters enables us to reconstruct to a certain extent the main features and even many important details of the institution. Later Pahlavi sources, especially book VIII of the *Dēnkard*, the *Pahlavi Rivayat Accompanying the Dādestān ī Dēnīg*, and the *Ērbadestān*, supply additional information, which also helps us understand certain complicated passages on slavery in the *Mādayān*. Another legal compilation made for the Christians in Sasanian Iran, the law book of Īšōʿboxt—extant only in a Syriac translation of the Persian original—provides material on the status of slaves in the Christian communities of Iran, in which Sasanian legal norms had been adapted insofar as they were compatible with Christian religious views.

The most commonly used expressions designating slaves in the Middle Persian sources are *anšahrīg*, literally "foreigner," and *bandag*, literally "bound." The latter term does not exclusively designate the slave (in the sense of an unfree person having no or only limited legal and civic rights), but is used of every subject of the sovereign, regardless of his social rank and standing in the phrase *šāhān šāh bandag* "subject of the king of kings." This use of the word, which calls attention to the fact that each subject was absolutely submitted to the will of the sovereign, is well known in Old Persian (cf. Darius's *manā ba^{n}daka* in the Behistun [Bīsotūn] inscription). Similarly the *ātaxš-bandag* or *ādurān-bandag* "slave of a fire temple" was not a slave in the real sense of the word, but a free person dedicated to the service of a Zoroastrian fire temple, and who had—unlike the slave—complete citizen's rights.

Another expression of an ambiguous nature, *tan*, lit. "body," is used in the *Mādayān* to designate a person who is given for a certain time as security for a debt to the creditor and kept by him in bondage for the arranged period of time. The person given as security could be a relative of the debtor (pt. 1, 57.15; the son is named) or a warrantor (*pāyēnān/pāyandān*), who assumed personal, lit. "physical," liability (*pad tan* "with his body") for the debt and could be enslaved by the creditor if the debtor failed to discharge the loan. It is not quite clear whether the term *tan* was also used in general to designate the slave, e.g., in the *Dēnkard* passage (Madan, p. 719.13) *abar girān wināhīh ī tan (ī) ēr ō anēr abespurdan* "On the grave offense of delivering an Iranian 'body' (= slave?) to a non-Iranian." A similar statement occurs in the *Mādayān* (pt. 1, 1.13-15) with the unambiguous *anšahrīg*: *anšahrīg ō ag-dēnān frōxt nē pādixšāy* "One is not entitled to sell a slave to infidels." Despite the similarity between the two passages, it is not unlikely that the expression *tan* was used in the *Dēnkard* sentence in the general sense of "person" or, as elsewhere in the *Mādayān*, in the narrow sense of a person having only limited legal capacity, which could apply not only to slaves, but also to women and minors. It is not certain, whether other terms of an ambiguous nature, such as *rahīg* "youth, young man, servant" (cf. NPers. *rahī* "slave") and *wīšag* "people, plebs," lit. "belonging to a *vis*" (cf. Khotan-Saka *bīsa-* "servant, slave") were also used in the special sense of "slave." The context in which these two expressions occur in the *Mādayān* (pt. 1, 92.10 and pt. 2, 40.3, 5) gives no clue as to their exact meaning.

As in other societies of antiquity, the original source of slaves was probably war, which is apparent in the most commonly used expression *anšahrīg* "outlander." The *Mādayān* also mentions other sources, such as the sale of children by their fathers (pt. 1, 33.13-17) and the enslavement of persons given as security for a debt to the creditor for a limited period of time, as already described above (pt. 1, 57.12-58.3). Descent from a slave was another factor, which could—but did not invariably—lead to slavery. In a short and unfortunately not very precisely formulated article (pt. 1, 1.2-4) we are informed that "up to the reign of Wahrām" only children whose fathers were slaves had the status of slaves, not those whose mothers were kept in bondage, i.e., the offspring of slave women and free men had the status of free persons. (There were altogether five rulers named Wahrām. The last one reigned from 420 to 439. Since the compilation of the *Mādayān* must have been completed after the reign of K̲osrow Anōšīravān, i.e., after 579, any one of the rulers named Wahrām could be meant. Although there are no clues in the text as to which sovereign is referred to, it seems probable that the compiler meant the ruler closest to his own time, i.e., the last Wahrām.) The article continues with an explanation of this regulation by quoting the words of the well-known Avesta commentator and jurist Sōšāns (second half of the third century), who declared that "the child belongs to the father" (*waččag pid xwēš*) and therefore receives the status of the father. Obviously juridical opinion as to the status of slave children changed after the reign of the above-mentioned Wahrām and at the time of the compilation of the law book, since the sentence ends with the statement "now they (i.e., the jurists) say that (the child belongs to) the mother" (*ud nūn gōwēnd kū mād*). From this last passage we may conclude that in this period, as opposed to "up to the reign of Wahrām," children whose mothers were slaves also had the status of slaves, even if they were the offspring of union with free men.

Although the slave was regarded in Sasanian law mainly as an object of right, he could be to a certain limited extent also a subject of right. In this respect Sasanian legal praxis did not differ substantially from that of other societies of antiquity. Though the slave was defined as a "thing" (*xwāstag*), it could not be easily ignored that he possessed human faculties, which set him apart from other objects or animals. The human nature of the slave, his possession of reason and speech, made it difficult to place him completely into the category of "things," especially since the slave's capacities could be and were used to the master's advantage. The same double standard in legal thinking is reflected in the juridical norms of all societies of antiquity: the slave was incontestably looked upon as a possession; however, he belonged to the special category of "animated possession," as Aristotle defined it and was thus also regarded as a person. In Sasanian law limited legal capacity could be conceded to the slave, while he remained at the same time an object of right.

Several cases in the *Mādayān* illustrate the double status of the slave, as object and person, while others deal with him exclusively as a possession. Two articles explicitly designate the slave as a "thing" (pt. 1, 64.9-14; 69.3-9); many others describe him as an object of transactions on the part of the owner: He could be sold, leased, and given away as a gift. He could also serve as security for a loan and be given to the creditor as a pawn (*graw*, pt. 1, 39.2-5, 5-9). Different grades of slave ownership were possible: The slave could belong wholly to one master or be the joint property of two or more persons, each of whom as co-proprietor (*bahr-xwēš*) was entitled to dispose of him according to his theoretical share. Ownership of a slave could also be transferred to another man for an arranged period of time, for example, every second year, the formula for which is given in the law book as "I give this slave to Mihrēn (i.e., such-and-such a person) (to own) for one year every second year" (*kū-m ēn anšahrīg har dō sāl ēw sāl ō Mihrēn dād*; cf. pt. 1, 69.3-6). The slave's income (*windišn*) belonged to the master, who could dispose of it according to his will and also transfer it separately from his slave to a third party (pt. 2, 2.11-14). Slaves are also mentioned who had the status of *glebae adscripti*, who were bound to the soil and were alienated together with the land (*dastkard*) on which they worked (pt. 1, 18.9-10; pt. 2, 36.16-37.1).

Although in all these cases the slave is described as a "thing," the legal rights of the slave owner in respect to the treatment of this "thing" were restricted, which placed the slave on a somewhat different level from other objects or animals in the lawful ownership (*xwēšīh*) of his master. Sasanian law prescribed a penalty (*tāwān*) for cruel treatment and mutilation of slaves (and incidentally women, who were dealt with as subordinate persons with only very limited legal rights), thus protecting them to a certain extent from arbitrary acts on the part of the owners (pt. 1, 1.4-6). It was also forbidden to sell a Zoroastrian slave, whose right to practice his religion was ensured by law, to an infidel. In this case both parties involved in the transaction, the slave owner and the purchaser, were treated as thieves and received the punishment prescribed for theft (*drōš*, pt. 1, 1.13-15). A slave converted to Zoroastrianism could leave his infidel owner and become a "subject of the king of kings," i.e., a free citizen, after having compensated his previous master. An important passage in the *Ērbadestān* indicates that even a loan (*abām*) was granted (probably by a religious institution) to the slave for this purpose (ed. Kotwal and Boyd, 12v. 11-15).

The slave's human faculties were fully allowed in litigation: He could appear in court not only as a witness, but also as a plaintiff or a defendant in civil suits, particularly those involving disputes over ownership of the slave himself. The double status of the slave as object and subject of right is perfectly illustrated in several articles, which leave no doubt that the slave was accepted as a legal person in court, while remaining at the same time in the category of things. For example, in one law case (pt. 1, 107.9-12) the plaintiff (*pēšēmār*) declares that the defendant (*pasēmār*) against whom he addresses his suit is his slave, i.e., he brings action for the return of his property by suing the thing itself. The slave in this case does not claim to have been manumitted, but declares that he is the property of another man. Although the slave is a party to the suit and therefore a subject, recognized as a legal person in court, his unfree status notwithstanding, he appears at the same time by his own declaration as the property of a third party, i.e., as an object.

Limited legal capacity could also be conceded to the slave by his master. It was possible for the slave owner to assign to his slave the right of disposal over his own income (*pad windišn pādixšāy kard*), i.e., to grant him a peculium, thus also enabling him to receive gifts from a third party (pt. 2, 3.6-13). Normally the slave had no capacity for acquisition; a gift from a third party could only be handed to a slave when his master renounced his right of ownership (pt. 1, 106.1-4). Unfortunately it is not made clear whether the power of disposal over his income enabled the slave to undertake obligations in his own right with or without further authorization on the part of the master. An article in the law book of ʿĪšōboxt confirms the legal right of the slave to dispose of his peculium according to his will. However, law in the Christian communities may have differed in this respect from Zoroastrian law (cf. Sachau, p. 139, par. 16). Even if it were possible for the slave to receive active legal capacity in relation to his peculium, it still remains uncertain whether he had the unrestricted right to enjoy the fruit. In the case cited above (*Mādayān*, pt. 2, 3.6-13) a slave who belongs to two masters is granted the power of disposal over his income by one of the masters, hence also the right to acquire one-half of a gift transferred to him by a third party. The other half belongs to the master, who has not authorized the slave. However, if the title (*nāmag*) to the gift results in opening a new source of income for the slave, the latter master is fully entitled to dispose of the profits.

A slave could receive his freedom from his master by the legal act of manumission. He could be completely liberated, or receive only partial liberation, i.e., be freed to a certain extent (one-half, one-third, one-tenth), which was usually the case when the slave was the joint property of several masters one (or more) of whom gave the slave freedom in relation to his theoretical share. However, it was also possible for one master to whom the slave wholly belonged to manumit him to a limited extent (pt. 1, 103.4-6). Children of a slave who was partially liberated were also free to the same extent as their parent (pt. 1, 1.6-7). A slave who converted to Zoroastrianism and had a non-Zoroastrian master had the right to buy his freedom on his own initiative, as already mentioned above. On the other hand, if a slave embraced Zoroastrianism after his infidel master had already converted, he lost his legal right to manumission once and for all (pt. 1, 1.16-17). After being given a certificate of manumission (*āzād-hišt*), the slave became a free man, a "subject of the king of kings." Legal authorities had different opinions on the possibility of re-enslaving a freedman. Unfortunately the article in which they are presented (pt. 1, 20.7-10 = 31.15-32.1) gives no clue as to the circumstances: In the opinion of the jurist Rad-Ohrmazd, a return to slavery was possible.

Slaves who were dedicated to a Zoroastrian fire temple were divided into two categories in the Sasanian law book: (a) the *anšahrīg ī ātaxš*, who was—as we may deduce from the very sparse information on temple slavery—a slave in the true sense of the word, i.e., a person with no (or only very limited) legal rights, whose labor was probably mainly used on the temple estates, and (b) the *ātaxš-bandag* or *ādurān-bandag*, who was a free person, even of noble origin, and only a "slave" in the metaphorical sense of the word, insofar as he was religiously "bound" to the fire. One of the most prominent figures in Sasanian history, the grand vizier (*wuzurg-framādār*) Mihr-Narseh, was given by King Wahrām V (421-39) to the fire temple of Ardwahišt and that of Afzōn-Ardašīr, where he served as an *ātaxš-bandag* for several years. During the reign of Yazdegerd II (439-57) he was punished for an offense he committed in his capacity as "fire slave" by being transferred to the royal estates (*ōstān*), where he worked up to the reign of Pērōz (459-84), who in his turn—after conferring with the *mōbedān mōbed* Mardbūd and other persons in his council—gave him to the service of the fire temple of Ohrmazd-Pērōz (pt. 2, 39.11-17). However, not all "fire slaves" were of most noble origin; a freedman could also be given to the *ātaxš-* or *ādurān-bandagīh*, i.e., religious service of a fire temple by his master, who had liberated him previously for this purpose. A partially manumitted slave could only serve as an *ātaxš-bandag* to the extent in which he was set free (pt. 1, 103.4-6). A man could also dedicate his wife and children to the service of a sacred fire, as we learn from the above-named Mihr-Narseh (pt. 2, 40.3-6).

Bibliography: M. Macuch, *Das sasanidische Rechtsbuch "Mātakdān-i Hazār Dātistān" (Teil II)*, Wiesbaden, 1981. A. Perikhanian, *Sasanidskiĭ sudebnik*, Erevan, 1973. Idem, "Iranian Society and Law," in *Camb. Hist. Iran* III/2, pp. 635-40. E. Sachau, *Syrische Rechtsbücher* III: *Corpus juris des persischen Erzbischofs Jesubocht*, Berlin, 1914. *Ērbadīstān ud Nirangistān. Facsimile Edition of the Manuscript TD*, ed. F. M. Kotwal and J. W. Boyd, Cambridge, Mass., and London, 1980.

(M. Macuch)

iii. In the Islamic Period up to the Mongol Invasion

Early Islamic society was essentially a slave-holding one, and it seems likely that Iranian society of the time exhibited two of the types of slavery known elsewhere in the pre-modern Old World—agricultural/industrial slavery and domestic slavery—certainly together with a third type, whose development from the 3rd/9th century onward seems to have been peculiar to the Islamic world, namely military slavery. For a consideration of this last, see v, below, but it should meanwhile be noted here that the institution of military slavery was to have a special significance for Iranian history in that, from the end of the 4th/10th century onward, dynasties of Turkish military slave origin began to arise within the Iranian lands, starting with the Ghaznavids (q.v.) in eastern Iran and Afghanistan, who stemmed from Sebüktigin, military slave of the Samanids (q.v.), and continuing through the numerous lines of *atābaks* (q.v.) in later Saljuq Iran to the sultans of Delhi and other provinces of the culturally Iranized realm of Muslim northern India.

In this section, what might be viewed as slavery in a civilian context will alone be treated. That the first type of slavery, the agricultural/industrial, existed in early Islamic Iran has largely to be inferred. One might tentatively assume that the agricultural servitude characteristic of lower Iraq in the first four centuries or so of Islam, involving such nonindigenous races as the black African Zanj and the Indian Zoṭṭ, a slavery fairly well documented for us in the historical sources on account of the periodic rebellions of these despised and exploited groups, was also practiced in the almost identical habitat and climate of the adjacent Iranian province of Ahvāz, where such crops as sugarcane and rice were grown, crops which lent themselves to larger-scale agricultural organization and for which it was not always easy to find free cultivators. Evidence is, however, regrettably sparse for this and for agricultural slavery elsewhere in the oasis economies of Iran, Transoxania, and K̲ᵛārazm. The large estates of the hydraulic society of pre-Arab conquest K̲ᵛārazm, whose existence has been revealed by Soviet archeologists, may well have required serf laborers then and up to the disappearance of the Afrighid K̲ᵛārazmšāhs (see Āl-e Afrīḡ; S. P. Tolstov, *Auf den Spuren der altchoresmischen Kultur*, Berlin, 1953, pp. 207ff.). We do have an item of information from Ebn Meskawayh, who (*Tajāreb* I, p. 289; tr. IV, p. 337) mentions that the *mamālīk al-tonnā'*, presumably agricultural slaves of local landowners, helped defend Shiraz against the incoming Daylamite troops of ʿAlī b. Būya (the later ʿEmād-al-Dawla) in 322/934.

Domestic slavery in Iran was of the kind familiar in the rest of the Islamic world at that time. Slaves were used as domestic servants and attendants, including in the women's quarters or harem. For this last function, eunuchs were of course preferred, or if intact males were used, then it was recommended that they should be dark-skinned, physically unprepossessing, and as a result unattractive to women (thus according to Kaykāvūs b. Eskandar, *Qābūs-nāma*, ed. Ḡ.-Ḥ. Yūsofī, 3rd ed., Tehran, 1364 Š./1985, p. 114; tr. R. Levy, *A Mirror for Princes*, London, 1951, p. 102). The total social and physical inferiority of the eunuch also meant that in pre-Saljuq times he might on occasion be employed in the office of market inspector or *moḥtaseb*, since he had no respect for anyone and no obligations toward them (Neẓām-al-Molk, *Sīāsat-nāma*, chap. VI, ed. M. M. Qazvīnī and M. M. Čahārdehī, Tehran, 1334 Š./1956, p. 56; tr. H. Darke, *The Book of Government or Rules for Kings*, London, 1960, p. 47). Slave girls were favored as concubines, and certain of the wives of ʿAbbasid caliphs who gave birth to princes and future caliphs, being of the status of *omm walad*, are mentioned as being Iranian, e.g., Marājel, the concubine of Hārūn-al-Rašīd, said to be from Bāḏḡīs in northwestern Afghanistan, and the mother of the future caliph al-Ma'mūn, born in 170/787 (Ebn Qotayba Dīnavarī, *Maʿāref*, ed. T. ʿOkkāša, Cairo, 1960, pp. 383, 387; Yaʿqūbī, *Ta'rīḵ* II, p. 538; Ṭabarī, III, p. 758); and also Māreda, born in Kufa but of Sogdian stock, slave of Hārūn al-Rašīd, who bore him the future caliph al-Moʿtaṣem, born in 179/795 or 180/796 (Ṭabarī, III, pp. 758, 1329; N. Abbott, *Two Queens of Baghdad*, Chicago, 1946, pp. 141-42). Slave girls were also trained for use as singers and dancers, and might be found in the *majāles* or court sessions of governors in Iran like those of the Taherids (q.v.) at Nīšāpūr in the 3rd/9th century.

The characteristics of various types of slave and the need for the careful purchaser to keep in mind his specific needs when bargaining for a slave are well set forth in the special chapter of Kaykāvūs's *Qābūs-nāma* on the buying of slaves (chap. 23, pp. 111-19; tr. pp. 99-108). The desiderata for harem attendants have been mentioned above; also discussed in detail by Kaykāvūs are the desiderata regarding slaves to be employed in secretarial and financial duties, as musicians, as soldiers, as tenders of farm animals and horses, and as domestics and cooks.

Concerning the provenance of slaves in Iran, we have a reasonable amount of information. In early Islamic times, parts of Iran itself remained unislamized, and these infidel regions could be raided for slaves. This was the case with Daylam (q.v.) in northwestern Iran up to the time of the appearance there of the ʿAlid *dāʿī* Ḥasan b. Zayd b. Moḥammad (second half of the 3rd/9th century; Eṣṭaḵrī, p. 205; Ebn Ḥawqal, p. 377, tr. Kramers, p. 366); while slaves were captured from the mountainous region of Ḡūr (q.v.) in central Afghanistan, a pagan enclave there till the early Ghaznavid period (*Ḥodūd al-ʿālam*, tr. Minorsky, pp. 109-10; C. E. Bosworth, "The Early Islamic History of Ghūr," *Central Asian Journal* 6, 1961, p. 122; repr. in *The Medieval History of Iran, Afghanistan and Central Asia*, London, 1977, chap. 9). But it was above all the Turks who, from their hardy steppe background, were regarded as supremely suitable for military service and were accordingly praised for this aptitude by authors like the 3rd/9th century author Jāḥeẓ (q.v.) in his epistle on the excellences of the Turks (*Resāla fī manāqeb al-Tork wa-ʿāmmat jond al-ḵelāfa*, ed. G. van Vloten in *Tria opuscula auctore . . . al-Djahiz*, Leiden, 1903, pp. 1-56, tr. C. T. Harley-Walker, "Jahiz of Basra to al-Fath ibn Khaqan on the 'Exploits of the Turks and the Army of the Khalifate in General'," *JRAS*, 1915, pp. 631-97; analyzed by F. Gabrieli, in *Rivista degli studi orientali* 32, 1957, pp. 477-83). But their loyalty and single-minded devotion to their masters—since they were, like all slaves brought from distant lands, déracinés, and with no ties or vested interests within their new home country—made them equally favored for palace and domestic service. The Turkish slave cupbearer or *sāqī* is a familiar figure in Persian poetry, and such personalities as Sultan Maḥmūd of Ḡazna's cupbearer and favorite Ayāz b. Aymaq (q.v.) not only played what seems to have been at the time a certain political role at the Ghaznavid court but in later ages became elaborated into a significant literary figure (see, e.g., G. Spiess, *Maḥmūd von Ġazna bei Farīdu'd-dīn ʿAṭṭār*, Basel, 1959, pp. 46-95). Of course, beardless boys and young men like Ayāz must often have been used by their masters as catamites.

Such Turkish slaves entered Iran through the two land corridors connecting the lands of ancient Middle Eastern civilization with the inner Asian and eastern European steppes, namely a northwestern corridor through southern Russia and the Caucasus into Azerbaijan, and a northeastern one through Ḵᵛarazm and Transoxania into Khorasan. Slaves came into the Iranian world as captives of war from the Arab campaigns in the Caucasus against the Ḵazars (q.v.) and from the campaigns in central Asia against the local Iranian peoples and the Turks of the steppes beyond, from the end of the 1st/7th century onward. Thus Naršaḵī (p. 62, tr. R. N. Frye, pp. 44-45) mentions how in 87/706 the Arab governor Qotayba b. Moslem (q.v.) slew all the males in the town of Baykand in Sogdia and enslaved all the women and children. Eighty hostages of noble birth taken from the *ḵātūn* or queen of Bukhara in 56/676 by the governor of Khorasan Saʿīd b. ʿOṯmān were transported, against Saʿīd's pledge to the contrary, to Medina and set to work there as agricultural slaves, a process which was so demeaning for them that, one day, they all entered Saʿīd's house, killed him, and then committed mass suicide (Naršaḵī, pp. 54, 56-57, tr. pp. 40-41; cf. H. A. R. Gibb, *The Arab Conquests in Central Asia*, London, 1923, pp. 19-20). Subsequently, Turkish slaves captured in the course of Muslim raids into infidel territory (*dār al-ḥarb*) were supplemented by a steady flow of Turks brought to slave markets in such places as Darband, Samarqand, Bukhara, Kīš, and Naḵšab (Nasaf), victims of internecine Turkish warfare in the steppes (as was the case of Sebüktigin) or even deliberately sold by their own families.

The Samanid amirate in Khorasan and Transoxania dominated the corridor into northeastern Iran during the 3rd-4th/9th-10th centuries, and owed much of its economic prosperity, stressed by contemporary geographers, to the important trade in Turkish slaves. Slaves regularly formed a part of the land tax of Khorasan sent by governors there like the Taherids to Baghdad and of the tribute forwarded to the caliphs by the Samanids from Transoxania and by the Saffarid brothers Ya'qūb and 'Amr b. Layṯ from their conquests in eastern Afghanistan and the fringes of India. The geographer Maqdesī ([Moqaddasī] ca. 375/985) states that in his time the annual levy (*ḵarāj*) of Khorasan included, among other things, 1,020 slaves. The Samanid amirs regulated the transit trade in slaves across their territories, requiring a license (*jawāz*) for each slave boy and a fee of 70-100 dirhams, the same fee but no license for each slave girl, and a lesser fee, 20-30 dirhams, for each mature woman (pp. 340-41). Commenting on the superlativeness of Turkish slaves, Maqdesī's near-contemporary Ebn Ḥawqal states that he had more than once seen a slave sold in Khorasan for as much as 3,000 dinars (p. 353, tr. p. 346); the average rate for a Turkish slave in Taherid times was, however, around 300 dirhams (Barthold, *Turkestan*², p. 240).

For northwestern Iran, a similar stream of slaves was imported from the Caucasus and beyond, comprising Turks, again through the intermediary of the Ḵazars, but also non-Turkish peoples of the Caucasus and eastern Europe such as the Alans, the Rūs, and the Ṣaqāleba (these peoples and their characteristics as slaves are mentioned by Kaykāvūs; the fair-skinned Ṣaqāleba probably included, as well as Slavs, Finno-Ugrian peoples of eastern Russia like the Burṭās or Mordvins; cf. A. Z. V. Togan, "Die Schwerter der Germanen, nach arabischen Berichten des 9-11. Jts.," *ZDMG* 90, 1936, p. 22). The endemic *ḡazw* conducted by the Muslims in the Caucasus region must also have brought in a steady flow of Christians as slaves, comprising Greeks, Armenians, and Georgians, the first two groups again mentioned by Kaykāvūs (*Qābūs-nāma*, pp. 115-16, tr. p. 104). Illustrating the volume of trade passing through the northwestern corridor into Iran, Ebn Ḥawqal, p. 353, tr. p. 346, mentions that the tax farm (*moqāṭa'a*) of the customs post at Ḵūnaj on the road running from Ardabīl in Azerbaijan to Zanjān in Jebāl was generally rented out annually for 100,000 dinars, in some years going up to one million dirhams; the dues (*lawāzem*) levied here included those on the transit of slaves.

Finally, we should note that the Saffarids' campaigns in eastern Afghanistan and then the Ghaznavids' ones into the plains of northern India opened up the Indian world as a source of slave manpower, for the eastern Iranian lands at least. A single campaign of Maḥmūd of Ḡazna in 409/1018, that to Qanawj in the Ganges valley, yielded 53,000 captives, causing the price of slaves in the market at Ḡazna to fall as low as 2-10 dirhams a head (C. E. Bosworth, *Ghaznavids*, p. 102); and by the end of the 5th/11th century, Indian slaves were sufficiently known in Iran at large for Kaykāvūs to discuss the various aptitudes of different Indian social groups and castes for employment as slaves (*Qābūs-nāma*, p. 116; tr. pp. 104-05).

Bibliography: Given in the text. See also Spuler, *Iran*, pp. 439-40.

(C. E. BOSWORTH)

iv. FROM THE MONGOLS TO THE ABOLITION OF SLAVERY

1. The Il-khanid, Timurid, Safavid, and Zand periods (1300-1800). Male slaves were referred to as *ḡolām* (in Arabic lit. a youth) or *zar-ḵarīd* (lit. bought by gold), while black slaves also were commonly called *kākā sīāh*. Female slaves were referred to as *kanīz(ak)* (Polak, I pp. 248, 258; Mostawfī, I, p. 213 n.; Naḵjavānī, II, pp. 67, 68, 70).

Sources of supply. After the Mongol period, the manner in which white slaves were obtained basically remained unchanged, i.e., warfare and raids continued to be the main slave-producing activities. Tīmūr, for example, "had as many as a thousand captives, who were skilful workmen, and laboured all the year round at making head pieces, and bows and arrows" (Clavijo, p. 172). Of course prisoners of war (*asīr*) could be ransomed as happened to the Portuguese captured after the conquest of Hormuz (Anonymous, I, p. 218 n. 1). Poor parents who sold their children were a small source of supply of slaves. Slaves were also imported from India: Herbert (p. 110) in 1628 observed that on the ships that sailed with his from Surat to Bandar-e 'Abbās there were "above three hundred slaves whom the Persians bought in India: Persees, Ientews (gentiles [i.e. Hindus]) Bannaras [Bhandaris?], and others," Black slaves, of course, continued to be supplied from East Africa by sea (for depictions of a black slave girl and a black *ḡolām* see de Bruijn, pls. 89-90). Major upheavals were especially fertile in providing slaves; during the Afghan occupation (1722-30), for example, thousands were enslaved. The regular Baluch incursions in southeastern Iran and those of the Uzbek in northeastern Iran also led to the captivity and enslavement of thousands of people. In these cases, Sunni Muslims enslaved both fellow Sunnis and Shi'ites. In the Caucasus, Christians were the principal victims. In 1768, peasants and tribesmen of the Naḵjavān khanate petitioned Karīm Khan Zand to prohibit the Bīrzāda tribe from enslaving them (Perry, p. 212).

In addition to violence and outright purchase, gifts were another means of obtaining slaves. The shah both bought slaves and received them as gifts, e.g., on the occasion of Nowrūz (Anonymous, I, p. 48; Kaempfer, p. 128). The Armenians, who had to give tribute to their Iranian overlords inter alia in the form of maidens and youths, refused to do so around 1780 (Perry, p. 213). The shahs also presented others with slaves. Shah

Yaʿqūb Āq Qoyunlū, for example, bestowed handmaidens (*jawārī*) and slave girls (*savārīd*) on the *ʿolamāʾ* (Minorsky, 1957, p. 52). When Georgian ambassadors visited Shah Esmāʿīl I, "a damsel was given them as a present" an Italian traveler noted (*Narrative*, pp. 207, 217; cf. Ebn Baṭṭūṭa II, p. 337).

Employment of slaves. Slaves were used for many purposes, mainly for domestic service and pleasure. In the *bāzār* of Tabrīz, Ebn Baṭṭūṭa (II, p. 344) saw a richly dressed beautiful slave boy showing precious stones in front of the jewelers' shops to attract buyers. Young slave boys were used for acts of sodomy, while beautiful girls also served as sex objects (Barbaro and Contarini, p. 207). Slave girls also were prostituted by their owners (Nakjavānī, II, p. 289). All dignitaries had large households with many slaves for display (Kaempfer, p. 136), and Europeans in Iran also kept a few slaves.

Eunuchs. A special and influential category of slaves were the eunuchs or *kᵛājas*, who were castrated at a young age (between 7-10 years) before being sold to their ultimate owners. They were mainly dark-skinned, though white ones also occurred; Ebn Baṭṭūṭa (II, p. 338) mentions a Greek eunuch. However, under the Safavids there were no white eunuchs until Shah ʿAbbās I, who himself performed the operation of castration several times; the chief eunuch (*kᵛājabāšī*) was the senior black eunuch (*rīšsafīd*) of the harem. According to Chardin (VI, p. 42), the majority of the dark-skinned eunuchs were not Africans, but Indians, mainly from Malabar and Bengal, who were lighter skinned than African blacks. Around 1590, however, 100 Georgian *ḡolām*s were castrated; the most esteemed among them was appointed as their chief or *yūzbāšī* (commander of a hundred). At the same time, a *yūzbāšī* was appointed over the black eunuchs. Thenceforth power was shared between the chiefs of the black and white eunuchs. The shah was the only one allowed to own white eunuchs. Depending on their ages (usually 8-16) and levels of education, eunuchs sold at the very high prices of between 1,000 and 2,000 francs; Shah ʿAbbās II nevertheless owned some 3,000 eunuchs. Elite families, depending on their wealth, usually owned between two and eight eunuchs (*Taḏkerat al-molūk*, pp. 56, 127; Chardin, VI, pp. 41-43). It would seem that white eunuchs suffered only the loss of their testicles, while black eunuchs had all their genitalia removed. If they wished to urinate they made use of a quill, which they were compelled to carry with them (Elgood, p. 180). Reports from state officials were passed on to the shah via the chief eunuch (*īšek-āḡāsībāšī*) of the harem, who had his own quarters within the complex. He also returned the shah's reply to these state officials. A eunuch was also the keeper of the treasury, while his deputy, a black eunuch as well, was the keeper of the keys to the treasury. Only the black eunuchs had free access to the harem, which they seldom left. They did light housework, as well as guarding the shah's women. It was believed that their blackness made them safe, because it was considered ugly and unattractive. White eunuchs could enter the harem only on the specific instructions of the shah. White eunuchs served as the shah's bodyguards and guarded the royal palace, accompanying the shah wherever he went. The chief of the white eunuchs was called *mehtar* or "senior." The latter was always with the shah; he lived in a palace of his own and was very influential (Chardin, V, p. 378; Thévenot, II, p. 102). The shah, always surrounded and served by eunuchs, "has some 50 male slaves, who take care of his menial needs, such as being dressed. They also have charge of the drapery, and the buttery" (Anonymous, I, p. 48). During public audiences "nine to ten small eunuchs of 10 to 14 years old are arranged behind the Shah; they are the most beautiful children whom one has seen, they are richly dressed, and form a semi-circle behind him; they seem to be marble statues such is their immobility, having their hands on their stomach, their heads high and their eyes straight" (Chardin, V, p. 470). When serving the shah they knelt down.

Slave soldiers. The slave soldiers (*ḡolām*), who disappeared during the Mongol period, became important again in the time of Ḡāzān Khan (A.D. 1295-1304). Rašīd-al-Dīn (Jahn, p. 308) reports that a military *eqṭāʿ* whose holder died without heirs was to be given to one of his old *ḡolām*s. Ebn Baṭṭūṭa (II, pp. 302, 343) mentions the presence of *mamlūk*s, i.e., slaves, in the Il-khanid court of Abū Saʿīd. *Ḡolām*s are also mentioned by Nakjavānī (I, pp. 228, 234-35), who says that they were inter alia used to protect caravans. One of the Sarbadār leaders, Wajīh-al-Dīn (ca. 1350), also recruited a bodyguard of Turkic *ḡolām*s (Dawlatšāh, ed. Browne, p. 280). With the decline of the Il-khanids the *ḡolām*s again began to achieve prominence under the Chubanids (Aharī, pp. 70-74). The early Safavids, like their Qara Qoyunlū and Āq Qoyunlū predecessors, did not employ slave soldiers. The Safavid *ḡolām* corps was only created around 998/1590 as a result of Shah ʿAbbās I's problems with the Qezelbāš amirs (q.v.). The corps was headed by the *qūllar-āḡāsībāšī* and was composed of *ḡolām*s, keepers of the armory (*yasāvolān-e qūr*), and *jārčī*s armed with *jazāʾerī* (large-caliber muskets) and served under *yūzbāšī*s (*Taḏkerat al-molūk*, p. 73). At the same time, a seperate vizier and finance officer (*mostawfī*) for the corps were appointed (Röhrborn, p. 32). The former was in charge of keeping records of their employment, their performance, and the manner and level of payment. The latter was in charge of the records of the *ḡolām*s. "He faithfully kept the individual files, mentioning dates of issue of *raqam*s of employment, amount of salary, grants, *toyūl, hama-sāla*, claims and (periods of) absence from, and presence of duty." (*Taḏkerat al-molūk*, p. 73). The *mostawfī* also kept records of dismissals and deaths, as well as all financial records.

The education of the young *ḡolām*s (both castrates and non-castrates) in reading and court etiquette was institutionalized under the shah. As long as the *ḡolām*s were beardless they had a special tutor. When they reached puberty, they entered the military and were placed under the *qūllar-aḡāsībāšī*. The young *ḡolāms* were housed in a small palace called *ḵāna-ye gāv* (cow's house; Chardin, VIII, pp. 38-39). According to Thévenot (II, p. 101) there were about 1,400 *ḡolāms*, while Chardin (V, p. 308) says there were 1,200. Under Šāhroḵ Shah (about 1750 A.D.) the *ḡolām* corps numbered at least 1,500 men (Ḥosaynī Monšī, I, fols. 95a, 96b).

Influence of slaves. *Ḡolāms*, whether eunuchs or not, had much influence and commanded much respect. The eunuchs especially were quite powerful because of their close association with the shah and their easy access to him (Chardin, VII, p. 472). Many of the *ḡolāms* obtained high rank and station. Ḵᵛāja Lo'lo', a Greek eunuch at Abū Saʿīd's court, was also one of his most powerful amirs (Ebn Baṭṭūṭa, II, p. 340). When Shah ʿAbbās I died, of the ninety-two powerful amirs twenty-one were *ḡolām-e šāh*. Many *ḡolāms* were also governors of key provinces (see Röhrborn, pp. 33-37). The shah also allowed them to acquire property and wealth. "The reward which the king gives to the male slaves is that, according as they have served him well, the king lends one 20, another 30, another 60,000 ducats at 20 per cent [or some other rate], he receiving the interest from it from year to year, while they afterwards lend the money out at 50, 70, and 80 per cent to gentlemen of the Court against good guarantees such as goods and houses" (Anonymous, I, p. 48). If the borrowers did not pay the *ḡolāms*, "they sell up the houses or property, nor is there any recourse for getting them back" (ibid., p. 49). The so-called "houseborn *ḡolāms*" (*ḡolām-e ḵānazād*) were especially influential, since they enjoyed the shah's favor more than any other servant (Ḥosaynī Monšī, I, fol. 131a). Not only did royal slaves occupy positions of responsibility, but also slaves owned by men of less exalted rank. Ebn Baṭṭūṭa (II, p. 285) visited a convent near Šūštar, which was completely managed by the four slaves owned by the shaikh.

2. The Qajar period (1800-1925).

Sources of supply. Slaves in Qajar Iran were obtained either through sale or through warfare. Poor parents also contributed to the slave pool by selling their children; these sales took place in Armenia, in southern Iran, and in Kurdistan (Polak, I, p. 248; Drouville, II, pp. 75-76). Bassett (p. 287) comments that "it might be thought that this sale is intended to be a form of marriage only; but the fact is that the girls are purchased to be domestics." Regular warfare, such as the Russo-Iranian wars, tribal incursions (*čapows*), slave raids, as well as punitive expeditions, especially against the Turkmen, were the major source of white slaves, mainly in northern Iran. In the first instance Armenian, Georgian, and Circassian slaves were obtained. Slave girls were "passed off by the Toorkmans and Khiva merchants as Kalmoeks, but generally they are Kuzzauks... purchased by the Persian" (Amanat, p. 20). In the second, the objectives were mainly Muslim Iranians captured in particular through Turkmen raids (see, e.g., Kinneir, pp. 26, 27; Amanat, pp. 39, 43f.; Ferrier, p. 81). The Turkmen felt little compunction in enslaving the Shiʿite population of Iran, whom they sold to the Ḵīva merchants, if they did not require them for themselves. However, they were not above capturing Sunni coreligionists either. Consul Abbott reports that the Ghoklans also raided the Yomūts and that those whom they took were usually disposed of to the Iranians (Amanat, p. 50).

In the south the situation was slightly different. Slaves were mainly blacks, imported through the Persian Gulf by Arab and Persian traders or overland by pilgrims returning from Mecca or Karbalāʾ. (There were also some slaves coming in from Damascus; Sheil, p. 242; Jaubert, p. 286.) Because of this point of origin, Persians called slaves colloquially *ḥājī* (Mostawfī, I, p. 213). In southeast Iran, slaves were produced either by parents' selling their children out of poverty or by the raids of slavers. The market was both in Arabia and in Afghanistan; "most of the slave girls employed as domestics in the houses of the gentry at Kandahar were brought from the outlying districts of Ghayn" (Sīstān) (Bellew, pp. 252, 292). Around 1900, slave raids were mounted by some local chieftains in Makrān. The Muslim slaves were sold mainly to Arabia; 450 per year went through the port of Jāsk alone. By 1905, the export of slaves from Makrān seems to have come to a stop again. There were also parents who were forced to sell children into slavery in Kermān and the Bandar-e ʿAbbās area toward the turn of the century (Lorimer, I/2, pp. 2510-11; see also Issawi, p. 126, n. 14).

Employment of slaves. Slaves were either used for domestic work or as pleasure objects, military men, administrative staff, or field laborers. Eunuchs were employed as harem guards. The main purpose of the Iranian élite's purchasing slaves was to display their wealth. The larger one's staff of servants and slaves, the more important one seemed. Moreover, the wives of the grandees demanded slave girls for domestic work in the *andarūn* (q.v.). Beautiful slave girls could become their masters' concubines and even marry them. Boys also were used as pleasure objects (Polak, I, p. 238; Drouville, II, p. 79). Some Europeans, although not allowed by Iranian law, also kept slaves in their houses, who could leave any moment they wished, claiming that, as Muslims, they were not compelled to serve Christians (Polak, I, pp. 254-55).

Most authors maintain that slaves in Iran never had to do field labor and only did light housework (e.g., Polak, I, p. 248; Sheil, p. 241; Sykes, p. 68). However, that only held true for those owned by the urban élite; slaves owned by the Turkmen tribes, especially those of Bukhara and Ḵīva, were used to herd their flocks and till their land (Vambéry, pp. 192-93). In southeast Iran, in Sīstān, Baluchistan, and Kermān, slaves were almost exclusively held for agricultural labor. According to a British consul "in Beluchistan there are several hamlets inhabited by slaves, who till the Government's property around Bampūr" (DCR 1671, Kermān 1894-95, p. 2; see also Goldsmid, I, p. 234). Abbott reports that in Sīstān "the cultivators of the soil, are for the most part,

Slaves both black and white," while he also reports that a tribe near Jabal Bārez had many members who were "a cross race, between Black Slaves and the People of the Country" (Amanat, pp. 164, 172).

Slave soldiers. A special kind of slaves were the *ḡolām-e šāh*, or the royal slaves. These formed the shah's bodyguard, and consisted mainly of young white slaves from the Caucasus, intermingled with sons from élite families. In the first quarter of the 13th/19th century this body amounted to some 3 to 4,000 men. This function "being one of honour as well as of contingent emolument, it is eagerly sought even by the highest ranks" Fraser (p. 254; cf. Kinneir, p. 32) observes. These *ḡolāms* also were used for other government work, and even reached the highest occupations in the country. Well-known examples are Manūčehr Khan Moʿtamed-al-Dawla, governor of Fārs, and K̲osrow Khan, who was governor of several provinces (Kermān among them) during his lifetime (Polak, I, p. 260). After the influx of white slaves came to a halt, the *ḡolām* corps was recruited from among freeborn Iranians.

Eunuchs. To guard a man's honor, i.e., his wives, was the task of eunuchs, either natural ones or gelded freemen and slaves. In the latter case the slaves were already castrated when imported and mostly bought when young. Eunuchs were predominantly black, especially when it became more difficult and then impossible to get white slaves. The last white eunuch died in 1856, according to Polak (I, p. 256). However, at the end of the 13th/19th century Nāṣer-al-Dīn Shah's harem had more than ninety eunuchs, both black and white (Moʿayyer-al-Mamālek, pp. 20, 21; this also contains pictures of both black and white eunuchs and further details on arrangements inside the harem). The eunuchs were called *k̲ᵛāja* or *āḡā*, and in the shah's harem they were under a *k̲ᵛājabāšī* or *āḡābāšī*. Nāṣer-al-Dīn Shah's *k̲ᵛājabāšī*, Baṣīrbāšī, was very influential and took advantage of his position, which cost him his life (Polak, I, p. 259). Eunuchs, who had played an influential role in the early part of the century, lost their position of influence after 1860, according to Polak. This coincided with their dwindling number. However, the shah's *k̲ᵛājabāšī* was still a very influential person (Moʿayyer-al-Mamālek, p. 21). Increasingly, élite families, due to the high cost of eunuchs, used old men to guard their wives. Even Nāṣer-al-Dīn Shah used old men to serve as gardeners and doormen inside the royal harem (Polak, I, p. 261; Moʿayyer-al-Mamālek, p. 21). Eunuchs occasionally came into being when a convicted criminal was condemned to gelding; if one survived the sentence, a bright future awaited him, since his well-paid services were sought eagerly (Polak, I, pp. 256, 261). Inside the royal harem also, beautiful female slaves were employed, who were uniformly Turkmen and Kurdish captives of war. They lived in a separate courtyard and were under a female chief called *aqal (aḡūl) bega k̲ānom*, who paid them wages. The slave girls served both as domestic help and as *ṣīḡas* (concubines; see MOTʿA). Finally, young boys (*ḡolām-bačča*) below the age of puberty were used as playmates and servants in the harems (Tāj-al-Salṭana, pp. 15, 17, 21, 52).

Classification of slaves. Black slaves were divided into two or three categories. According to Polak (I, p. 248). Zangīs and Ḥabašīs were the principal groups. The Zangīs were slaves imported from Zanzibar and its hinterland; the Ḥabašīs, or Ethiopians, were slaves imported from Abyssinia, Somalia and the southern Sudan. Sheil (p. 243) states that there are three kinds of black slaves: "Bambassees, Nubees, and Habeshees." The origin of the term Bambassee is not known, but it refers to Polak's Zangīs, and may be a mispronunciation of Mombassa, the port of origin of many of these slaves. The Nubees, or Nubians, were slaves from Nubia and Somalia, who were darker than Ethiopian slaves. "The Bombassees are in great disrepute as being ferocious, treacherous and lazy. The Nubees and Habeshees are highly esteemed as being mild, faithful, brave and intelligent" (Sheil, p. 243; Polak, I, p. 248). Wills (1886, p. 326), who confirms these Iranian sentiments, distinguishes between Habashis, Souhalis (Somalians), and Bombassis (cf. Kelly, pp. 414-18). There seems to have been no special classification for white slaves. The seemingly negative cultural image of the black slave (see Southgate) appears not to have been a social barrier in actual practice. Intermarriage took place, and the black slave had some marginal influence on Iranian culture. The popular and comical characters, Kākā Sīāh and Mīrzā Fīrūz, of the Iranian theater are cases in point (Bayżāʾī, pp. 172ff.). In the Persian Gulf area, where blacks thrived relatively well in Iran, they kept their old African custom of exorcism (see ZĀR) alive (Sāʿedī, *Ahl-e hawā*). In general, however, slaves were well integrated into society; they spoke Persian (although with an accent) and forgot their own languages and adopted Islam, thereby completing the assimilation process (Polak, I, p. 251).

Prices of slaves. Kinneir (p. 26) notes that the price of a slave varies according to the supply of the market and that "while I was in Tauris, in 1810, a young and beautiful Georgian girl could be purchased for about eighty pounds sterling." Unskilled male slaves were not expensive, according to Drouville (II, p. 79), but female slaves were more expensive, sometimes up to 600 tomans. They were easy to get in Erevan, where beautiful virgins were 60 to 100 tomans per person. A female Yomūt slave was offered at 30 tomans, while Cossack slave girls were worth 30 to 60 tomans in Astarābād around 1845 (Amanat, p. 50). Around 1860, the price of a boy was 12-18 ducats; for a beautiful Ḥabašī girl it was 70 ducats (Polak, II, p. 254). The price of eunuchs was much higher, in general three times that of a normal slave, as the mortality rate as a result of gelding was high (Polak, II, pp. 255-56). Wills reports that around 1870 the price of a Bombassi boy was $12 and that of a healthy girl of twelve a third more. As much as $80 or $100 might be given for a healthy young Ḥabašī girl (Wills, 1883, pp. 75-76; see also idem, 1886, p. 326, for other prices). At the turn of the century, one author observed that due to obstacles to the slave trade "negroes and negresses are expensive" (Sykes, p. 69). In

Sīstān the price of a strong young male slave was on average between 50 and 80 tomans; female slaves were cheaper (Issawi, p. 126; Lorimer, I/2, p. 2511).

Number of slaves. According to Malcolm (II, p. 594), slaves were not numerous in Iran. Similar observations were made by Bassett (p. 287), who stated around 1840 that "at this time white slaves are rare... black slaves are the more numerous." Lady Sheil observed that "slaves are not numerous in northern Persia judging by the few seen in the streets, doubtless there are more in the South," particularly in the coastal areas. She estimated the number of slaves imported at 2 to 3,000 per year (pp. 241-42; for more estimates see Issawi, pp. 125-26). The fact that in their outward appearances slaves, in general, "cannot be distinguished from other people" (Malcolm, II, p. 594), as well as the fact that most observers had a limited geographical point of observation, may have influenced the estimates of the slaves. However, Polak (I, p. 252) states that often male slaves wore more colorful clothes than native Iranians. Also the fact that the slave trade was a low-key activity may have contributed to our lack of information on the prevalence of slavery. "Slave dealers frequent the principal cities, and buy and sell slaves, but the demand is not so great as to support a public market" (Bassett, p. 287). Slave traders took parties of slaves from one town to the other. In the south, Bushire and Shiraz were important clearing centers. The governor of Shiraz regularly sent slaves to the shah and important courtiers (Polak, II, p. 254; Wills, 1886, p. 326). Slaves were kept in private houses, where they were stripped naked and could be inspected by purchasers (Bassett, p. 288). Probably because of the low life expectancy of the black slaves (victims of tuberculosis, they seldom lived longer than thirty), the importation of slaves continued at the same low, but consistent level throughout the 13th/19th century. Also marriage among slaves often did not produce offspring and the children often did not survive puberty (Polak, I, p. 248; see also Lorimer, I/2, p. 2494, on the state of health of slaves arriving in the Persian Gulf). Wills (1883, p. 74) says: "notwithstanding the careful patrolling of the Persian Gulf by our gunboats slaves are imported at a rate which keeps abreast of the demand. There are no longer slave-dealers and no slave markets in Persia."

Treatment of slaves. In general slaves were well treated in Iran. "Persia is the Paradise" for slaves according to Sykes (p. 68). Treatment in Afghanistan also seems to have been quite humane (Ali Shah, pp. 51-52). Because slaves were expensive, and in most cases a luxury, they were given light housework. Also, because they had no ties in Iran other than their masters, slaves were generally more trusted and more favored by their owners than other, free servants. Slaves, like servants, were often considered members of the family, and not despised on account of their servile condition (Malcolm, II, p. 594; Sykes, p. 68; Polak, II, p. 248; DCR 1671, p. 2). Slaves were set free on such family occasions as births or marriages or on demise of the owner. The owner saw to it that a male slave married one of his female slaves; children born from such a union were raised with the owner's children and became very trusted slaves of the family (Polak, I, p. 248). When maltreated, slaves had the right to complain (Gasteiger-Chan, p. 151) and could demand to be sold to another. However, to sell a household slave was a blow to one's dignity; even for the rare sale, it was difficult to find a buyer, who would be wary of buying a recalcitrant slave. It also happened, in cases of maltreatment, that slaves in the same town demonstrated in front of the house of the maltreated slave's owner to demand justice (Polak, I, p. 248; Wills, 1886, p. 326). Nevertheless, maltreatment occurred "where there is unlimited power on one hand," but it was rare (Sheil, pp. 243-44). Several slaves in the 1840s took refuge in the British legation to escape punishment. Slaves employed as field labor were in a less fortunate position. In southeastern Iran, "Their condition is extremely pitiable as, having no rights, they are kept on the verge of starvation and in rags. Nominally they receive one-third of the produce of the soil, but even this meagre percentage is subject to considerable official reductions" (DCR 1671, p. 2). A similar condition was the fate of slaves of the Turkmen who were kept as chattel and "would be half-clothed and half-starved, and at night be tethered to a stout wooden staple by a chain which they were forced to drag about with them all day" (Sykes, p. 110; Ferrier, p. 80; Vambéry, pp. 192-93, 331, 337; Ross, pp. 45, 47, 62, 65-66, 69, 82-85, 113, 122, 126). Polak (I, p. 248) is more positive about the treatment of slaves by the Turkmen, alleging that slaves would regain freedom after a few years and settle among them. There is conflicting evidence about the treatment of the slaves aboard the slaving vessels. Lorimer (I/2, p. 2494) cites a glaring case of barbarian treatment by Arab slave merchants; however, according to Issawi (p. 126), "almost all sources agree that the transport of slaves from Africa was relatively humane." Slaves were allowed to acquire property, and often got considerable wealth. However, they chose not to buy themselves free, in most cases (Sykes, p. 69).

Suppression of slavery. The suppression of the slave trade took about a century. Because, according to the tenets of Islam, slavery is a lawful practice, even though Islam also favors emancipation of slaves, it was only through pressure from foreign powers that the slave trade was put down. The first phase of the Russian conquest of the Caucasus was immediately felt in the slave business. Russia forbade the sale of Caucasian (Armenian, Georgian, and Circassian) males and females to Iran. This trade was still continued in the Persian part of the Caucasus either through the sale of children by indigent parents or, more frequently, through Persian incursions (*čapow*) into "infidel" areas. Girls and boys were also smuggled out of Russian territory into Iran. The effect of the Russian interdiction was nevertheless felt, for Drouville states that the occurrence of slavery was less than before. He, however, also states that the level of sales was almost the same as before (Drouville, II, pp. 74, 76). A big change was brought about by the Treaty of Torkamānčāy of 1243/1828, which gave Russia total control over the Caucasus. Thenceforth slaves from the Caucasus became a scarce article. Moreover, most of the slaves who had been captured during the 1210/1796 Caucasus campaign by Āḡā Moḥammad Khan (q.v.), as well as those soldiers captured during the Perso-Russian wars, were returned to Russia. This was the result of Article XIII of the treaty, which required the mutual return of captives. Implementation of this article led to the murder of the Russian poet and dramatist A. S. Greboyedov, sent as envoy to Iran, when he kept in the Russian legation two Georgian women from the house of Allāhyār Khan Āṣaf-al-Dawla who had embraced Islam and borne him children. A similar article had been included in the Perso-Ottoman Peace Treaty of 1747 to regulate the return of prisoners of war (Hertslet, p. 162). After 1210/1828, there was still some smuggling of slaves from Russian territory. But the Russian embassy would demand the immediate return of such slaves (Polak, I, p. 248). Russia also had a positive influence on the suppression of slavery when it extended its sphere of influence to the eastern shores of the Caspian. Its naval base on the island of Āšūrāda (q.v.) enabled it to stop shipping and provided military support (Amanat, p. 39; Sheil, p. 243). Further Russian conquests in central Asia, culminating in the conquest of the central Asian khanates, brought slavery on the northern Iranian border to a halt. Kidnapping in Iranian territory continued to be carried on by the Turkmen and Baluch due to lack of government control. A similar situation existed in West Azerbaijan, where Kurdish tribesmen robbed, killed, and captured people at will. This situation was brought under control by Reżā Khan, the future Reżā Shah.

In southern Iran the situation was not different. The effect of British efforts to stop the slave trade through its treaties with the sultan of Masqaṭ and other Persian Gulf rulers also was felt in Iran. (For detailed discussion of this issue see Kelly, chaps. 9 and 13; Lorimer, I/2, pp. 2475ff.). In 1848 Nāṣer-al-Dīn Shah forbade the future transportation of black slaves to Iran by sea. In 1851, Iran and Great Britain signed a treaty, allowing British vessels to search Iranian ships for slaves. This treaty was extended till 1873 by Article 13 of the 1857 peace treaty between Great Britain and Iran.

These treaties, however, did not have a major impact on the level of the slave trade. It was only through more intense naval patrolling after 1870 that the slave trade decreased. In 1882, a new treaty gave Great Britain further rights. Slaves found on Iranian ships were to be set free, while the court case against the Iranian transporter had to be conducted in the presence of British consular agents. Iran also participated in the Brussels Conference on the suppression of the slave trade. As a result Iran forbade the trade in slaves, as well as the import of slaves either by sea or land in 1890 (Hertslet, pp. 12, 13, 40, 42, 54-56, 58). Despite these measures, "many slaves were still introduced by the pilgrims from Mecca" (Sykes, p. 69), as well as by sea with the connivance of the Iranian local authorities (Lorimer, I/2, pp. 2509-10). The slave trade had virtually stopped by 1910; some slavery continued to exist for a time but disappeared altogether by the end of the Qajar period. The Iranian constitutions of 1906 and of 1979 do not recognize the status of slave, while through its adherence to the 1926 Geneva Convention, as well as to the 1948 Universal Declaration of Human Rights, Iran has officially committed itself to the abolition of slavery.

In Afghanistan slavery traffic was quite active in the northwest, where 400 to 500 were sold annually in Qandahār, while in Šoḡnān it was "the only article of commerce" at the end of the 19th century (Wheeler, pp. 102-03; Hamilton, p. 168). Slavery was abolished by Amir ʿAbd-al-Raḥmān in 1895 (Hamilton, p. 169), although it still was carried on in some areas of the country. In 1933 a reformist Afghan noted with some pride that "slavery is no longer allowed and a transgressor is severely dealt with" (Muhammad Ali, p. 189). Afghanistan as a member of the United Nations also subscribes to the abolition of slavery.

Bibliography: *Accounts and Papers*, Diplomatic and Consular Reports (DCR), no. 1671, Tehran (re: consulate Kermān), 1894. Abū Bakr Qoṭbī Aharī, *Tārīḵ-e Šayḵ Oways*, ed. J. B. van Loon, The Hague, 1954. S. I. Ali Shah, *Modern Afghanistan*, London, n.d. A. Amanat, *Cities and Trade: Consul Abbott on the Economy and Society of Iran 1847-1866*, London, 1983. Anonymous, *A Chronicle of the Carmelites in Persia*, 2 vols., London, 1939. G. Barbaro and A. Contarini, *Travels to Tana and Persia*, tr. W. Thomas and E. Roy, London, 1873. J. Bassett, *Persia the Land of the Imams*, New York, 1886. H. W. Bellew, *From the Indus to the Tigris*, London, 1874. B. Bayżāʾī, *Namāyeš dar Īrān*, Tehran, 1344 Š./1965. C. de Bruijn, *Reizen over Moskovie, door Persie en Indie...*, Amsterdam, 1714; the English and French translations of this book appear under the name Le Brun. J. Chardin, *Voyages*, ed. L. Langlès, 10 vols., Paris, 1811. R. G. de Clavijo, *Narrative of the Embassy of Ruy Gonzalez de Clavijo to the Court of Timur AD 1403-06*, Hakluyt Society 26, London, 1859. G. Drouville, *Voyage en Perse pendant les années 1812 et 1813*, 2 vols., Paris, 1819, J. P. Ferrier, *Caravan Journeys and Wanderings in Persia, Afghanistan, Turkistan and Beloochistan*, London, 1857, repr. London etc., 1976. Ebn Baṭṭūṭa, tr. Gibb, II. J. B. Fraser, *Historical and Descriptive Account of Persia*, New York, 1842. A. Gasteiger-Chan, *Van Tehran nach Beludschistan*, Innsbruck, 1881. J. Goldsmid, *Eastern Persia. An Account of the Persian Boundary Commission*, London, 1876. I. A. Hamilton, *Afghanistan*, Boston, 1910. Th. Herbert, *Travels in Persia 1627-1629*, ed. W. Foster, New York, 1929. E. Hertslet, *Treaties Concluded between Great-Britain and Persia*, London, 1891. Ch. Issawi, *The Economic History of Iran*, Chicago, 1972. E. Kaempfer, *Am Hofe des persischen Grosskönigs*, ed. W. Hinz, Leipzig, 1940. J. B. Kelly, *Britain and the Persian Gulf*,

London, 1968. J. M. Kinneir, *A Geographical Memoir of the Persian Empire*, London, 1813. J. Malcolm, *The History of Persia* II, London, 1815. Muhammad Ali, *Progressive Afghanistan*, Lahore, 1933. V. Minorsky, *Persia in AD 1478-91*, London, 1957. Dūst-ʿAlī Moʿayyer-al-Mamālek, *Yāddāšthā-ī az zendagānī-e kosūṣī-e Nāṣer-al-Dīn Šāh*, Tehran, 1351 Š./1972. Maḥmūd Ḥosaynī Monšī, *Tārīḵ-e Aḥmadšāhī*, ed. Sayyed Moradof, 2 vols., Moscow, 1974. ʿA. Mostawfī, *Šarḥ-e zendagānī-e man*, 3 vols., Tehran, n.d. Moḥammad b. Hendūšāh Naḵjavānī, *Dastūr al-kāteb fī taʿyīn al-marāteb*, ed. A. A. Alizade, 3 vols., Moscow, 1974. *A Narrative of Italian Travels*, ed. C. Grey, Hakluyt 49, London, 1873. J. E. Polak, *Persien, das Land und seine Bewohner*, 2 vols., Leipzig, 1865. J. R. Perry, *Karim Khan Zand. A History of Persia 1747-1779*, Chicago, 1979. R. M. Röhrborn, *Provinzen und Zentralgewalt Persiens im 16. und 17. Jahrhundert*, Berlin, 1966. F. E. Ross, ed., *Central Asia. Personal Narrative of General Josiah Harlan 1823-41*, London, 1939. Ḡ.-Ḥ. Sāʿedī, *Ahl-e hawā*, Tehran, 1342 Š./1963. Lady Sheil, *Glimpses of Life and Manners in Persia*, London, 1856. M. Southgate, "The Negative Images of Blacks in Some Medieval Iranian Writings," *Iranian Studies* 17, 1984, pp. 3-36. E. Sykes, *Persia and Its People*, New York, 1910. Tāj-al-Salṭana, *Ḵāṭerāt*, ed. M. Etteḥādīya and S. Saʿdvandīān, Tehran, 1361 Š./1982. J. Thévenot, *Travels*, London, 1686, II. A. Vambéry, *Travels in Central Asia*, London, 1864. S. Wheeler, *The Ameer Abdur Rahman*, London, 1895. C. J. Wills, *Persia as It Is*, London, 1883. Idem, *In the Land of the Lion and the Sun*, London, 1886.

(W. FLOOR)

v. MILITARY SLAVERY IN ISLAMIC IRAN

Military slavery may have been known in the Sasanian period, but, as the Sasanian army was based essentially on the free, mailed cavalryman, any slaves within it can only have been in the little-regarded following of infantrymen, in which conscripted peasants and other socially inferior elements played the main part.

It was the extension of Arab arms during the first two or three centuries of Islam into such regions as the Caucasus and Transoxania, giving access to a vast reservoir of potential slave manpower in the south Russian and inner Asian steppes, and into eastern Afghanistan and the fringes of India that provided the Muslim rulers and governors of Iran with their slaves, although, as noted above (see iii), outlying and as yet unconverted regions of Iran itself, such as Daylam and Ḡūr, also provided slaves until as late as the opening of the 5th/11th century. But it was the Turks of the Eurasian steppes who were prized most of all as slave soldiers. The harsh environment of their homeland inured them to hardship; they were prized for their loyalty to their Muslim masters, having totally abandoned their pagan past; above all, the ancestral equestrian abilities of their race, as mounted spearmen and archers who could shoot accurately from the saddle, soon made them an essential element in many Islamic armies, these military techniques supplementing those of other bodies of troops with special skills, such as the Daylami mountaineer infantrymen, with their javelins and battle-axes, the infantrymen of Sīstān, and the lightly armed Arab cavalry skirmishers.

From the caliphate of Hārūn al-Rašīd (170-93/786-809) onward, Turkish slaves began to be employed as guards in the caliphal armies in Iraq, so that, as the 3rd/9th century progressed, Turkish *mamlūks* or *ḡolāms* became the mainstay of the ʿAbbasid army (see D. Ayalon, *The Military Reforms of Caliph al-Muʿtaṣim, Their Background and Consequences*, unpubl. communication to the International Congress of Orientalists, New Delhi, 1964, printed in offset, Jerusalem, 1963; idem, "Preliminary Remarks on the *Mamlūk* Military Institution in Islam," in *War, Technology and Society in the Middle East*, ed. V. J. Parry and M. E. Yapp, London, 1975, pp. 51-58). It was not therefore surprising that the successor states to the caliphate in the Iranian world, probably beginning with the Taherid governors of Khorasan, should follow this lead. Indeed, the Taherids played a vital, linking role in the purveying of Turks from the central Asian slave markets to Iraq (see above), and very probably utilized them in their personal guard at their court in Nīšāpūr, even though direct evidence here is lacking.

Nevertheless, we do have specific information about the use of Turkish slave troops from the ensuing period of the Saffarids of Sīstān. Yaʿqūb b. Layṯ employed an élite force of 2,000 *ḡolāms*, whom he fitted out with gold and silver shields, swords, and maces which he had captured in Nīšāpūr when he overthrew the last Taherid governor there, Moḥammad b. Ṭāher b. ʿAbd-Allāh, in 259/873 (thus implying that the Taherids had already recruited a similar guard which had used this ceremonial equipment). Furthermore, in the 4th/10th century, certain Saffarid amirs in Sīstān were using Indian and possibly even some black (*zanjī*) slave troops (Masʿūdī, *Morūj*, Paris ed., VIII, pp. 49-50; ed. Pellat, sec. 3168; *Tārīḵ-e Sīstān*, p. 222; tr. Gold, p. 176; C. E. Bosworth, "The Armies of the Ṣaffārids," *BSOAS* 31, 1968, pp. 545-47). The Samanids of Transoxania and Khorasan controlled the corridor into inner Asia by which many of the Turkish slaves were imported into the Islamic world, and by the early 4th/10th century Turkish *ḡolāms* already formed the nucleus of the Samanid army, with the top commands held by *ḡolām* generals such as Qaratigin Esfījābī (q.v.; d. 317/929) and with Amir Naṣr b. Aḥmad (301-31/914-43) said to have 10,000 *ḡolāms*. An account of the reception in Bukhara of a reputed Chinese embassy describes the ceremonial parading of élite Turkish slave troops with gold or gilded and silver weapons and equipment (Qāżī Ebn al-Zobayr, *Ketāb al-ḏaḵāʾer wa'l-toḥaf*, tr. in Bosworth, "An Alleged Embassy from the Emperor of China to the Amir Naṣr b. Aḥmad: A Contribution to Sâmânid Military History," *Yād-nāma-ye Īrānī-e*

Mīnorskī, ed. M. Mīnovī and Ī. Afšār, Tehran, 1348 Š./1969, pp. 5-6, 9-11). It was the hope of the amirs that loyal Turkish troops would counterbalance the influence of the indigenous Iranian landowning classes' opposition to the Samanids' centralizing policies; but in fact Naṣr's father Aḥmad b. Esmāʿīl had been murdered by his *ḡolāms* in 301/914, and in the last decades of Samanid power it was overmighty Turkish slave generals like Begtuzun and Fāʾeq Ḵāṣṣa (q.v.) who deliberately brought about the disintegration of the state (see Barthold, *Turkestan*[3], pp. 246-68). At this time, too, the Daylami Buyids, when they took over northern and western Iran and Iraq, speedily felt a need for the recruitment of Turkish slave cavalrymen, who thenceforth became as important, or at times, more important than the tribal Daylami infantrymen. This caused tensions within the army over pay and privileges, for the Buyid amirs, distancing themselves from their fellow tribesmen, seem often to have favored the Turks as the more loyal element (Meskawayh and Ebn al-Aṯīr, passim, cited in Bosworth, "Military Organisation under the Būyids of Persia and Iraq," *Oriens* 18-19, 1965-66, pp. 153-59; H. Busse, *Chalif und Grosskönig: Die Buyiden im Iraq (945-1055)*, Beirut and Wiesbaden, 1969, pp. 329ff.).

It was from the Samanids' slave guards that there arose in Afghanistan and eastern Iran, out of the ruins of the Samanid state, the most powerful and territorially extensive empire thitherto known in the eastern Islamic world, that of the Turkish Ghaznavids. The founder, Sebüktigin (q.v.), was originally a slave soldier in the guard of the Samanids' Turkish commander-in-chief Alptigin (q.v.; concerning this slave guard, its training, and its ranks, we have a detailed—but probably idealized—account in Neẓām-al-Molk's *Sīar al-molūk* (*Sīāsat-nāma*), chap. xxvii, ed. Darke[1], Tehran, 2535 = 1353 Š./1974, pp. 135-50, tr. idem, *The Book of Government*, London, 1960, pp. 107-21; cf. Barthold, *Turkestan*[3], p. 227, and Bosworth, *The Ghaznavids*, pp. 102-03, 107). The multiracial Ghaznavid army was built around a slave core, mainly of Turks brought in from central Asia, through the intermediary of the Qarakhanids, who by then controlled Transoxania and eastern Turkestan, but also—following Saffarid precedent—of Indians, for Sultan Maḥmūd of Ḡazna and his successors were now able to tap the vast resources of slave manpower in India. At the heart of the forces was the sultan's palace guard, the *ḡolāmān-e sarāy*; it is presumably these troops who are depicted on what remains of the mural paintings of the complex of Ghaznavid palaces at Laškarī Bāzār (q.v.) in southern Afghanistan, according with the literary descriptions of such Ghaznavid historians as Bayhaqī and Gardīzī that these élite guards had uniforms of rich brocade and bejeweled belts and weapons when employed on ceremonial occasions (cited in Bosworth, *The Ghaznavids*, pp. 98ff., and see the references in idem, "Lashkar-i Bāzār" in *EI*[2]).

In the Saljuq period, the various atabeg (*atābak*) lines which developed during the 6th/12th century in such regions of Iran as Azerbaijan, Jebāl, Fārs, and Ḵūzestān sprang from the Turkish slave commanders who acted as tutors and guardians (*atābaks*, q.v.) for young Saljuq princes and who had been granted appanages in the outlying provinces of the empire. For, once the empire of the Great Saljuqs had been made firm under Alp Arslān and Malekšāh (qq.v.), the sultans had found it necessary to supplement and to counterbalance the tribal contingents of their own people, the Oghuz Turks, with professional paid troops, these being in large measure Turkish slaves purchased from central Asia but also slaves of Armenian, Greek, Georgian, and Negro origin (see Bosworth, in *Camb. Hist. Iran* V, pp. 78ff., 198-200). The employment of a professional slave army, usually in greater part Turkish, was taken over by the dynasties succeeding to the Saljuq heritage in Iran, such as the Ḵᵛārazmšāhs and the Ghurids. The Kᵛārazmšāhs' use of pagan Turkish troops recruited directly from the outer steppes contributed much to the shahs' unpopularity within Iran, for the historian Rāvandī states that their excesses were far worse than those of the Christian Georgians and Franks or of the infidel Qara Ḵetāy (*Rāḥat al-ṣodūr*, cited in Bosworth, op. cit., p. 183); while it was the Turkish slave troops of the Ghurids who retained their professional solidarity after the demise of the Ghurid sultanate in Afghanistan, and, as the Moʿezzīya (thus named after the great Moʿezz-al-Dīn or Šehāb-al-Dīn Moḥammad b. Sām, 569-602/1173-1206) and as similar groups, set up in northern India various Muslim principalities, notably the line of so-called "Slave Kings" in Delhi.

The irruption of the Mongols brought a new set of military traditions into the Iranian world, primarily those of a tribal Mongol-Turkish cavalry army backed up by an impressed horde of local population as auxiliaries to be employed in sieges and as cannon fodder in general (see B. Spuler, *Mongolen*[1], pp. 413-19). But, like other steppe invaders, the Mongol Il-khanids were gradually assimilated to the pervading culture and practices of Iran, and among their Turkmen epigones such as the Qara Qoyunlū and Āq Qoyunlū, the institution of the professional slave soldier reappears. Thus in an *ʿarż-nāma* or description of a review of the army and administration (cf. ʿARŻ, DĪVĀN-E) of the Āq Qoyunlū sultan Uzun Ḥasan (857-82/1453-78) are mentioned 3,900 *qolloḡčīs* or "servants," who were clearly slave soldiers (V. Minorsky, "A Civil and Military Review in Fārs in 881/1476," *BSOS* 10, 1939-42, pp. 155, 164).

Although the military basis of the theocratic Safavid state was originally the Qezelbāš (q.v.) tribal division of the eastern Anatolian and Azerbaijan Turkmen adherents of the Ṣafawīya Sufi order, their exclusive position as the troops upholding the régime was challenged when Shah Ṭahmāsb I (r. 930-84/1524-76) launched his four campaigns into the Caucasus region between 947/1540 and 960/1553, bringing back large numbers of Christian Georgian, Armenian, and Circassian prisoners as slaves (see H. H. Roemer, in *Camb. Hist. Iran* VI, pp. 245-46). These speedily became a rival force in the state to the

Qezelbāš. Under Moḥammad Ḵodā-banda in 994/1586, a Georgian nobleman convert became *lala* or tutor to the prince Ṭahmāsb b. ʿAbbās, a position corresponding to that of the Saljuq atabeg and an office previously held by a Qezelbāš amir. With the advent of Shah ʿAbbās I (r. 996-1038/1588-1629), the new elements, converted to Islam at least nominally, were formally constituted as the royal household slaves, *ḡolāmān-e ḵāṣṣa-ye šarīfa* or *qūllar* (the parallel here in nomenclature with the Ottoman *qapï qullarï* "slaves of the porte," among whom were the famed Janissaries, is notable). These were either still in slave legal status or were the sons of slaves, were specially trained for military or civil palace duties, and received their pay directly from the royal treasury. It was obvious that their prime allegiance would be to the shah their master and that they could therefore be used, if occasion arose, as a rival force in the state against the Qezelbāš Turkmen, just as the Great Saljuqs had at times been compelled to use their professional troops against the Oghuz tribesmen. Shah ʿAbbās's military *qūllar* served as mounted cavalrymen, bearing muskets, although handguns had been used, on a limited scale, in the Safavid army since Ṭahmāsb's time, very soon after the defeat of Čālderān (q.v.) at the hands of the Ottomans, with their superior firepower, and Shah ʿAbbās's special corps of musketeers (*tofangčīān*) seems to have been composed mainly of native Iranians. By 1006/1598, the Georgian Allāhverdī Khan could be appointed by the shah commander-in-chief of the Safavid forces (*sardār-e laškar*, later *sepahsālār*), and he was followed by an Armenian *ḡolām*, Qarčaqay Khan (R. M. Savory, *Iran under the Safavids*, Cambridge, 1980, pp. 64-66, 78-82, 92, 184; Roemer, in *Camb. Hist. Iran* VI, pp. 265-66; Savory, ibid., pp. 363-65). Even during the decline of the Safavids in the later 17th century, Chardin numbered the military *ḡolām*s at 10,000, and Tavernier assessed them at 18,000 (*Travels*, tr., London, 1684, I, pp. 224-25). According to the early 18th-century manual of Safavid administration, the *Tadkerat al-molūk* of Mīrzā Samīʿā, for the whole body of *ḡolāmān*, headed by the influential *qūllar āḡāsī*, there was a special vizier and a special financial officer (*mostawfī*) of the department of the *ḡolām*s (*Tadhkirat al-Mulūk, a Manual of Ṣafavid Administration*, tr. Minorsky, GMS 16, London, 1943, introd. p. 33; tr. pp. 56-57, 73, comm. pp. 127-28, 141).

During the 19th century, slavery gradually disappeared in Iran, though *ḡolām*s, a considerable proportion of them Georgians, still formed the royal bodyguard under the Qajar Fatḥ-ʿAlī Shah (r. 1797-1834); but, by the later part of his reign, the need was being felt for the formation of a modern professional army to withstand the encroachments on Persian territory of such powers as imperial Russia.

Bibliography: See also, for the early period, Bosworth, "The Turks in the Islamic Lands up to the Mid-11th Century," separatum from the (so far unpublished) *Philologiae Turcicae Fundamenta* III, Wiesbaden, 1970, p. 20; idem, "Barbarian Incursions: The Coming of the Turks into the Islamic World," in *Islamic Civilisation 950-1150*, ed. D. S. Richards, Oxford, 1973, pp. 1-16; idem, "Ghulām. ii. Persia," in *EI*².

(C. E. BOSWORTH)

vi. REGULATIONS GOVERNING SLAVERY IN ISLAMIC JURISPRUDENCE

Slavery is designated in *feqh* (i.e., religious law, although not in the Koran or *ḥadīṯ*) as *reqq* "weakness." The weakness in question is extrinsic to the person of the slave and results from his legal debarment (*ḥejr*) from ownership, guardianship, giving witness and exercising judgeship. Certain other rights and obligations are also materially affected by servitude. Matters concerning slavery never formed a separately organized topic in *feqh*, with the exception of manumission (*ʿetq*); the relevant regulations are scattered in books on *jehād*, trade (under the subheading *bayʿ al-ḥayawān* "the sale of animate beings"), marriage, fixed punishments (*ḥodūd*), and retribution and blood money (*qeṣāṣ wa dīa*). This distribution of the subject matter reflects the hybrid, even contradictory legal status of the slave; he was both an item of property and a person with a claim to certain rights. All schools of *feqh* tended, before modern times, to regard slavery as a permanent feature of Muslim society; the ethical emphasis of the Koran and Sunna on the desirability of emancipation never became fully reflected in law. This article summarizes the provisions of the Hanafite and Shafiʿite schools—the two Sunni schools that have had a historical presence in Iran—and those of Shiʿite (Jaʿfarī) jurisprudence.

The original source of all slavery is warfare, the enslavement of enemy captives being one of the options open to the Muslim ruler or commander. According to some jurists, slavery originally had a punitive aspect, in that the non-Muslim enemy by failing to use his intelligence to perceive the truth of Islam had assimilated himself to nonrational beings and therefore deserved to be treated as such (Boḵārī, II, p. 282). It follows from this that a Muslim may not be enslaved, although a slave embracing Islam after his capture is not automatically emancipated and his descendants may inherit his servile status. A minor captured from the enemy without parents or guardian automatically becomes Muslim, as does the foundling (*moltaqeṭ*) abducted from Dār al-Ḥarb, but both remain slaves. However, a slave voluntarily quitting Dār al-Ḥarb for Muslim territory is automatically emancipated on his arrival.

After the battle of Ḥonayn, the Prophet is said to have forbidden the enslavement of male Arab polytheists. The prohibition was regarded as specific to the occasion by Abū Bakr and as general in force by ʿOmar. Sunni schools of law followed the judgment of ʿOmar (although the question soon became theoretical), and Shiʿite *feqh* rejected it (see tradition of Moḥammad al-Bāqer in Ḥorr ʿĀmelī, VI/1, p. 17).

Heresy and rebellion (varyingly understood by different sects) might also lead to enslavement. *Fatwās* issued by the Ottomans in the course of their wars against Safavid Iran occasionally provided for enslavement of the wives and children of Shiʿites (Uzunçarşılı, IV/1, pp. 175-76, but see *fatwā* of Abu'l-Soʿūd Efendi prohibiting the enslavement of the Shiʿites of Nakjavān in Düzdağ, p. 111), and Shiʿites kidnapped from Khorasan were routinely sold as slaves in Bukhara (Vambéry, II, p. 59). Shiʿite *feqh* does not appear to have responded in kind. The enslavement of rebels against legitimate authority (*boḡāt*/ *ahl al-baḡy*) was prohibited in imitation of the exemple of clemency set by ʿAlī b. Abī Ṭāleb on his conquest of Basra. The case will be different with the Twelfth Imam; on his return, he will enslave the dependents of all who oppose his authority (Ḥorr ʿĀmelī, VI/1, pp. 56-59).

War against the non-Muslim enemy continued to be the theoretical justification for the acquisition of slaves, but the war was often fictive and consisted of little more than raids into enemy territory by professional slavers. The jurists never condemned this degeneration of *jehād*, although some scrupulous Hanafites, at a fairly late date, recommended the masters of female slaves to enter into a form of marriage with them (*nekāḥ tanazzohī*) in order to avoid the risk of adultery. For the Shiʿite imams, the fact that the pseudo-*jehād* of slavers was conducted under the auspices of a usurpative (*ẓālem*) authority appears to have been immaterial. Jaʿfar al-Ṣādeq drew up a kind of code of professional ethics for the slaver (*nakkās*; Ḥorr ʿĀmelī, VI/3, pp. 31-32), and Mūsā al-Kāẓem, all of whose thirty-seven children were born to slave mothers (Shaykh Mofīd, pp. 457-58), strongly recommended the purchase of women for concubinage (Ḥorr ʿĀmelī, VII/1, p. 191). Moḥammad al-Bāqer, Mūsā al-Kāẓem, and ʿAlī al-Reżā all explicitly permitted the purchase of slaves from the various nationalities—Slav, Turkish, Khazar, Daylamite, and Nubian—that were available on the market, including castrated males (Ḥorr ʿĀmelī, VI/1, pp. 17, 99-100, VI/3, p. 27; Ḥellī, II, p. 59). Jaʿfar al-Ṣādeq recommended against the purchase of African (Zanj) slaves, making an exception of the Nubians, a party of whom would one day assist the Mahdī (Ḥorr ʿĀmelī, VII/1, p. 56).

The devotional duties of the Muslim slave are in general the same as those of his free counterpart. According to a tradition of the Prophet, the prayers offered by an absconding (*ābeq*) slave are invalid (*Ṣaḥīḥ Moslem*, Ketāb al-Īmān no. 131); Nawawī considers this to apply to nonobligatory prayers only. Being without property, the slave is exempt from paying *zakāt* and performing the *ḥajj*, unless his master wishes to facilitate the latter for him. His master is obliged to pay *ṣadaqat al-feṭr* at the end of Ramażān on his behalf. The slave is not required to participate in *jehād*; if he volunteers, he must have the permission of his master (ʿAlī b. Abī Ṭāleb appears, however, to have accepted a slave volunteer without obtaining the master's permission; Ḥorr ʿĀmelī, VI/1, p. 15). The female slave is not required to cover herself as fully as the free woman when performing prayer, and no blame attaches to her if she permits parts of her body to be viewed by prospective purchasers.

Humane treatment of slaves is enjoined by the Prophet in a number of frequently quoted traditions, especially that which calls on the master to dress and feed the slave as if he were a member of his own family (Ḡazālī, II, pp. 199-201). *Feqh* contents itself with stipulating that the master must provide the slave with the necessities of life (*nafaqa*) at a level comparable to that enjoyed by the slaves of similarly situated owners. If he fails to do so, a judge may compel him to sell the slave; the same applies in the case of mistreatment amounting to grievous bodily harm. It is, in any event, desirable (*mostaḥabb*) to emancipate the slave as expiation for beating him, even lightly and with apparent justification. All schools are agreed on these matters.

As an item of property, the slave can be sold, given away, rented or inherited, and be owned either individually or jointly. He cannot own property; and items he brings with him at the time of sale belong automatically to the buyer unless it can be reasonably inferred that the seller was unaware of them, in which case they must be returned to him. A slave may be permitted (*maʾḏūn*) by his master to engage in commercial transactions. According to Hanafite *feqh*, the permission must be unrestricted in nature: the slave keeps his earnings and is responsible for his debts; if he fails to meet them, his master must sell him and pay off his debts from the proceeds. Shiʿite law agrees with these provisions, but stipulates that the master may demand a fixed proportion (*żarība*) of the slave's earnings (Ḥorr ʿĀmelī, VI/3, pp. 34-35). Shafeʿites regard the permission to trade as restricted in scope: whatever the slave earns belongs to the master, who is also responsible for the debts he incurs. All schools are of the view that the permission given to the *maʾḏūn* may be revoked at any time; it is not to be regarded as a form of incipient manumission.

The slave's status materially affects his or her ability to marry. A free man may marry a female slave (not, however, one he owns himself, unless he emancipates her first, a procedure praised in *ḥadīṯ*), and a free woman may marry a male slave. The consent of the owner of the slave partner in such "mixed" unions is necessary for their validity, and in the case of sale, a new owner may either confirm or dissolve the marriage. A master who consents to the marriage of his female slave renounces thereby his right of concubinage with her. The offspring of marriages between free persons and slaves are free. Finally, a male slave may marry a female slave, again after consent is obtained. The offspring of such a union share the servile status of the parents; if they are owned by different masters, they become the joint property of both masters, according to the Sunnis, and the property of the mother's owner, according to Shiʿite *feqh*. A master may compel two of his slaves to marry each other, having "coercive guardianship" (*welāyat al-ejbār*) over them, and he can also force the male partner in such a union to repudiate his wife. Hanafite and

Shafeʿite *feqh* are agreed that a slave can marry only two wives; Shiʿite *feqh* makes this limitation only in the case of free wives, permitting the slave to marry up to four slave women (Ḥorr ʿĀmelī, p. 520). Since slaves are barred from ownership, the owner must provide for the dowry and upkeep owed by his slave to his wife, and he also takes possession of the dowry given to a slave wife owned by him.

An owner has unrestricted right of concubinage (*estefrāš*) with his unmarried female slaves; if, however, he owns both a mother and her daughter, or two sisters, he can choose only one of the two for his bed. A period of restraint (*estebrāʾ*; see *EI*², s.v.) of forty-five days must be observed after the purchase of the slave, unless she has not reached puberty, has entered menopause, or has just completed a menstrual period. Unlike a wife, a concubine has no claim of sexual satisfaction on her master, but Shiʿite *feqh* recommends coitus with a female slave at least once every forty days in order to protect her against the temptation of fornication. Coitus interruptus (*ʿazl*), discouraged (*makrūh*) in the case of a wife, is unobjectionable with a concubine, in the view of both Shiʿite and Shafeʿite *feqh*. Shiʿite regulations also permit the simultaneous bedding of two concubines, a practice forbidden with wives (Ḥorr ʿĀmelī, p. 93; Ḥellī, II, p. 317). Shiʿite *feqh* differs sharply from the Sunni schools in permitting the owner of a female slave to assign sexual enjoyment of her to a third party, by way either of gift or of rental. This provision appears to contradict Koran 24:33. The offspring of such a liaison belongs to the owner of the woman. In the case of joint ownership of a female slave by two or more men, the Sunni schools deny the right of concubinage to all the owners; Shiʿite *feqh* permits it, although with reluctance. If two or more owners of a slave woman have coitus with her during a single menstrual cycle during which she becomes pregnant, paternity is established by lot (Ḥorr ʿĀmelī, VII/1, p. 566).

In partial compensation for his disabilities, the slave receives a lesser penalty than the free man or woman for certain offenses—generally a half, when the punishment can be fixed quantitatively. A slave who commits fornication or drinks alcohol receives half the number of lashes that are given a free man, and a married slave, male or female, who is guilty of adultery is not subject to lapidation. If the slave commits an offense calling for the payment of blood money, it must be paid by his master, who may also turn him over to the claimant in full or part payment. If conversely a slave is killed or suffers bodily injury, only Hanafite *feqh* makes the offender liable to retribution (*qeṣāṣ*); other schools provide for the payment of blood money—fixed at rates lower than those applicable to a free person—to the owner.

Manumission (*ʿetq*) is strongly recommended by the Koran. It serves as expiation for the violation of a solemn oath (5:89), manslaughter (4:92), and the form of repudiation of a wife known as *ẓehār* (58:3-4); is one of the purposes on which *zakāt* may be spent (9:60); and is generally enjoined as a means of drawing nearer to God (2:177, 90:11-13). The Prophet emancipated all his male slaves (Hamidullah, 1975, p. 632), and his promise that for every limb of a slave set free God will save from the fire a limb of the liberator is quoted in all the books of *feqh*. (Ṣadūq, p. 37, fixes the ratio at one limb of the liberator for every two limbs of a female slave set free.) Manumission may take place in fulfillment of a vow; otherwise it is a voluntary and unilateral procedure on the part of the owner, immediate in its effect and irrevocable.

Both Hanafite and Shafeʿite *feqh* recognizes as valid an implied act of manumission, or even one originating in drunkenness; Shiʿite *feqh* insists on the pronouncement or writing of an explicit formula of manumission while in a state of sobriety. A formula of manumission related from Jaʿfar al-Ṣādeq stipulates that the former slave should agree to perform his devotional duties, be loyal to "the friends of God" (i.e., the imams), and dissociate himself from His enemies (Ṣadūq, p. 37). Shiʿite *feqh* forbids the manumission of the non-Muslim slave; discourages manumission of the non-Shiʿite Muslim (*al-moslem al-mok̲ālef*) slave; and recommends manumission of the Shiʿite (*moʾmen*) slave, particularly after seven years of servitude (Ḥellī, III, p. 108). All jurists agree that a slave contracting leprosy is automatically freed, but physical defects such as blindness, being cross-eyed, and lameness to the point of immobility may serve as bars to emancipation.

Complexities arise when one among two or more owners of a slave decides to emacipate him. Hanafite *feqh* holds that free and servile statuses are indivisible (Bok̲ārī, II, p. 282): Abū Ḥanīfa believed that the slave must therefore continue in bondage until the claims of all his owners are satisfied, while Abū Yūsof and Šaybānī declared that the slave must be freed immediately, although the non-emancipating co-owners retain a right to compensation (ibid., p. 283). In either case, satisfaction of their claims is to be made either by the emancipating owner or by the slave himself, working to accumulate the necessary amount (a process known as *estesʿāʾ*). Shafeʿites regard it as possible for a slave to be partially emancipated, whether singly or plurally owned, one consequence of partial emancipation being that he acquires the right to ownership (ibid.). Shiʿite *feqh* agrees that partial manumission is possible, even to the extent of a single limb being emancipated (Sayyed Mortażā, p. 176); it otherwise coincides with the position of Abū Yūsof and Šaybānī.

Another path to freedom is *mokātaba*, a contractual agreement between the slave and his master whereby the former (*mokātab*) gradually purchases his freedom from the latter (*mokāteb*). Recommended by Koran 24:33, the acceptance of such an arrangement by the owner was regarded as obligatory by ʿOmar (Hamidullah and Aydın, p. 131). If slave and master are unable to agree on a price for freedom, the amount may be set by a judge. *Mokātaba* is irrevocable in its effects except that—according to Shiʿite *feqh*—the contract may provide for repossession of the slave if he fails to complete payment during the stipulated period, together with the forfeiture of all money paid. A *mokātab* cannot be sold, and a master has no right to concubinage with a female slave who has entered on *mokātaba*.

A master may will that the slaves he holds be emancipated on his death, a transaction known as *tadbīr*. Hanafites regard *tadbīr* as irrevocable and forbid the sale of a slave awaiting this form of emancipation (ibid.). Shafeʿites regard *tadbīr* as revocable only in connection with the sale of a slave; Shiʿites, as revocable without restriction, by way of analogy with a will. All schools regard the slave, in the case of *tadbīr*, as part of the disposable third of his master's estate: Shafeʿite and Shiʿite *feqh* therefore regard it as permissible to sell him to a new owner if this is needed to cover the debts of his deceased master. Shiʿite regulations prohibit the *tadbīr* of a non-Muslim slave (Sayyed Mortażā, p. 178).

The female slave who bears her master a child (*omm al-walad*) forms a special case; according to most Sunni opinion, she, too, attains freedom on the death of her master. The Egyptian Mārīa who bore the Prophet a short-lived son would seem to furnish the obvious precedent for the emancipation of the *omm al-walad*, but the Companions were divided on the matter, and it was some time before a categorically affirmative *ejmāʿ* on the subject crystallized (Boḵārī, II, p. 248). The Shiʿite position is more nuanced. ʿAlī b. Abī Ṭāleb is said to have permitted the sale of the *omm al-walad* if she had been bought on credit and the purchaser was unable to complete payment; Mūsā al-Kāẓem allowed greater latitude, proclaiming that the *omm al-walad*, like any other slave, could be sold, inherited, or given away (Ḥorr ʿĀmelī, VI/3, p. 51). The permissibility of such disposal of the woman was sometimes made dependent on the child's having died or attained maturity. If the child survives his father, the mother is emancipated only insofar as her value is equal to the child's share of the estate; if it exceeds that share, she must compensate the other heirs with the fruits of her labor (Ḥellī, III, p. 140).

Bibliography: A. General discussions, dealing largely or exclusively with Sunni *feqh*: Ö. N. Bilmen, *Hukuki islamiye ve ıstılahatı fikhiye kamusu*, Istanbul, 1969, IV, pp. 31-71; R. Brunschvig, "ʿAbd," in *EI*²; M. Hamidullah and M. A. Aydın, "Kölelik," in *Türkiye diyanet vakfı İslam ansiklopedisi* (specimen fascicle), Istanbul, 1986, pp. 126-32. B. Hanafite sources: ʿAlāʾ-al-Dīn ʿAbd-al-ʿAzīz Boḵārī, *Kašf al-asrār*, Istanbul, 1308/1890, I, p. 315; II, pp. 281-84; III, p. 248; Moḥammad b. ʿAlī Jazāʾerī, *Majmaʿ al-anhor be šarḥ moltaqa'l-abḥor*, Istanbul, 1264/1848, pp. 315-41, 715-22, 877-85. C. Shafeʿite sources: ʿAbd-Allāh Ḥażramī, *al-Moqaddema al-hażramīya fī feqh al-sāda al-šāfeʿīya*, Delhi, n.d., pp. 105-07; Zayn-al-ʿĀbedīn Malībārī, *Eršād al-ʿebād*, Singapore, n.d., pp. 74-75. D. Shiʿite sources: Moḥammad b. Ḥasan Ḥorr ʿĀmelī, *Wasāʾel al-Šīʿa*, ed. ʿAbd-al-Raḥīm Rabbānī Šīrāzī, Tehran, 1385/1965, VI/1, pp. 15-18, 89-90; VI/3, pp. 26-52; VII/1, pp. 13, 54-59, 77-78, 93, 100-02, 106, 150, 179, 191, 391, 497-590; VII/2, pp. 175, 181, 239, 391, 550, 582; Jaʿfar b. Ḥasan Moḥaqqeq Ḥellī, *Šarāʿeʿ al-Eslām*, ed. ʿAbd-al-Ḥosayn Moḥammad-ʿAlī, Najaf, 1389/1969, I, pp. 317-18, 336-37; II, pp. 55-61, 69-70, 77, 101, 188, 309-17, 354; III, pp. 105-40; tr., A. Querry, *Droit musulman: recueil de lois concernant les musulmans schyites*, Paris, 1871, I, pp. 332-33, 352-53, 420-28, 439-40, 446, 471, 554, 695-708; II, pp. 105-40; Shaikh Mortażā, *Ketāb al-enteṣār*, in *al-Jawāmeʿ al-feqhīya*, Qom, n.d., pp. 176-80 (lists fourteen points on which Shiʿite regulations differ from those of all four Sunni schools); Shaykh Abū ʿAbd-Allāh Moḥammad Mofīd, *al-Eršād*, tr. I. K. A. Howard, *The Book of Guidance*, London, 1981; Shaikh Ṣadūq Ebn Bābawayh, *al-Moqneʿ*, in *al-Jawāmeʿ al-feqhīya*, pp. 36-39; Hossein Modarressi Tabatabaʾi, *An Introduction to Shiʿi Law*, London, 1984, p. 197 (lists five monographs on slavery); Sayyed Moḥammad Kāẓem Ṭabāṭabāʾī Yazdī, *al-ʿOrwat al-woṯqā*, Tehran, 1392/1972, pp. 642-46. E. Other sources: M. Ertuğrul Düzdağ, *Şeyhülislam Ebussuud Efendi Fetvaları*, Istanbul, 1983; Muhammad Hamidullah, *The Muslim Conduct of State*, 7th edition, Lahore, 1977, pp. 216-21; idem, *Le Prophète de l'Islam*, 2nd ed., Beirut, 1975, II, 629-32; Abū Ḥāmed Ḡazālī, *Eḥyāʾ ʿolūm al-dīn*, Beirut, n.d.; İsmail Hakkı Uzunçarşılı, *Osmanlı tarihi*, Ankara, 1956; Arminius Vambéry, *Geschichte Bocharas*, Stuttgart, 1872.

(H. ALGAR)

BARḎAʿA or BARDAʿA (Arm. Partav, Georgian Bardavi, Mid. Pers. Pērōzāpāt; see Marquart, *Ērānšahr*, pp. 117-18), the chief town until the 4th/10th century of the Islamic province of Arrān (q.v.), the classical Caucasian Albania, situated two or three *farsaḵs* (i.e., 8-12 miles) south of the Kor river on its affluent the Ṯarṯūr (modern Terter). Its site now lies at the western extremity of the Šervān steppe in Soviet Azerbaijan.

Barḏaʿa was strategically situated on the edge of the lowlands of the lower Kor-Araxes (Aras) valley, adjacent to the mountains of eastern Transcaucasia; from it there ran routes to Dvin (Dabīl), Tiflis, and Bāb-al-Abwāb (Darband). It was already a frontier strong point under the Sasanians, having been fortified by Qobād I against the Huns and other steppe peoples who swept down through the Caucasus (see Balāḏorī, *Fotūḥ*, pp. 194-95), a role which it inherited in early Islamic times, when it became a bastion of Muslim arms against the Khazar Turks, being repeatedly mentioned in the accounts of Arab-Khazar warfare, e.g., during the great Khazar invasions of 104/722-23 and 112/730; it was perhaps at Barḏaʿa that the marriage was celebrated of the Khazar princess and the Arab governor Yazīd b. Osayd Solamī, the lady's early death providing the pretext for the further Khazar invasion under Rās Ṭarḵān during the decade 140-50/757-67 (see D. M. Dunlop, *The History of the Jewish Khazars*, Princeton, 1954, pp. 62, 69, 72, 179-81). At a somewhat later date, it further became a frontier point against the Christian Georgians and Abkāz (q.v.).

The Arab and Persian geographers of the 4th/10th century describe Barda'a as a town with a citadel, a congregational mosque where the treasury of Arrān was kept, several gates, and flourishing markets, including the Sunday market of Korakī (from Greek *kuriakos*, the Lord's Day); at this time Barda'a, like Arrān in general, retained a substantial proportion of Christians, and Ebn Ḥawqal (*Ṣūrat al-arż*, p. 348, tr., II, p. 342) lists certain princes of the Barda'a region in his own time (later 4th/10th century) who were clearly Christian (cf. V. Minorsky, *Abū-Dulaf Mis'ar ibn Muhalhil's Travels in Iran (circa A.D. 950)*, Cairo, 1955, pp. 74-75). The fertile rural environs produced much fruit (with a particularly noted variety of figs), nuts, and also the dyestuff madder (*rūnās*), which was exported as far as India. In the Kor and other nearby rivers, the sturgeon (*sormāhī* from Persian *šūrmāhī*, salt fish) and other tasty fish were caught; and there was extensive production of textiles, including silks (see Ebn Ḥawqal, pp. 337-39, 347, 349, tr. Kramers, II, pp. 330-32, 340, 342; Maqdesī, [Moqaddasī], p. 375; *Ḥodūd al-'ālam*, tr. Minorsky, pp. 143-44, secs. 36.21, 36.30; R. B. Serjeant, *Islamic Textiles. Material for a History up to the Mongol Conquest*, Beirut, 1972, p. 69).

Barda'a fell into Arab hands during 'Oṯmān's caliphate, probably before 32/652, when Salmān b. Rabī'a Bāhelī accepted the town's surrender after a short siege, tribute being levied on a similar basis as at Baylaqān (q.v.; Balāḏorī, *Fotūḥ*, p. 201). Barda'a's fortifications were strengthened by the governor of Armenia, in the face of Khazar threats, during 'Abd-al-Malek's caliphate, either by Ḥātem b. No'mān Bāhelī or the latter's son 'Abd-al-'Azīz, or by Moḥammad b. Marwān b. Ḥakam (ibid., p. 203). The most notable event in its subsequent history was the descent upon it and occupation for several months by the Scandinavian-Slavic Rūs, who sailed up the Kor from the Caspian and encamped at the village of Mobārakī just outside Barda'a. Only after their numbers had been decimated by plague was the Mosaferid ruler of Azerbaijan Marzobān b. Moḥammad able to drive them out (Ebn Meskawayh, *Tajāreb* II, pp. 62-67, tr. V, pp. 67-74; D. S. Morgoliouth, "The Russian Seizure of Bardha'ah in 943 A.D.," *BSO(A)S* 1, 1918, pp. 82-95; Dunlop, pp. 239-41). This may have been a factor in the apparent comparative decline of Barda'a in the second half of the 4th/10th century, attested by Ebn Ḥawqal and Maqdesī, although these sources imply that the chief factor was the extortions and oppressions there of the Deylamite Mosaferids and possibly raids by the Yazīdī Šervānšāhs and the Shaddadids of Ganja, who in 383/993, for instance, took possession of Barda'a and Baylaqān. At all events, Barda'a evidently at this time lost ground to Baylaqān. It is sporadically mentioned in Saljuq times (e.g., as being attacked in 457/1065 by the Abkāz or Alans) and in the Mongol period, when it was still significant enough for coins to be minted there by members of the Il-khanid family and their governors (including as late as 756/1355; see Spuler, *Mongolen*[1], pp. 129, 131, 133, 135). Thereafter, however, it lapsed into its present status as a village, now called Barda, among the ruins of its former glories.

Bibliography: See also Yāqūt, *Boldān*, Beirut, 1374-76/1955-57, I, pp. 379-81. Le Strange, *Lands*, pp. 177-78, 230. V. Minorsky, *Studies in Caucasian History*, London, 1953, pp. 17, 65, 117. Idem, *A History of Sharvān and Darband in the 10th-11th Centuries*, Cambridge, 1958, pp. 11, 18, 58, 73, 76 and index. *EI*² I, pp. 1040-41.

(C. E. BOSWORTH)

BARDAŠĪR, the old name of the city of Kermān (q.v.).

BARDESANES (Syr. Bar Dayṣān, Ar. Ebn Dayṣān), gnostic thinker (154-222) who occupies a position between the Syriac gnostic systems of the first two centuries A.D. and the Iranian gnostic system of Mani of the third century.

1. Sources. Bardesanes' own works are now known only through second-hand accounts by primarily Syriac authors, some of which include short quotations. The most important of these second-hand accounts are the antiheretical writings of church father Ephrem (306-73), who wrote against the teachings of Marcion, Bardesanes, and Mani. According to Ephrem (*Hymns* 53.6, tr. p. 182), Bardesanes wrote 150 hymns, from which he often quotes. Accounts of, possibly also quotations from or paraphrases of, a cosmological treatise are preserved in the works of Ephrem, Barḥadbešabbā (end 6th cent.), Theodore bar Konai (late 8th cent., q.v.), John of Dara (1st half 9th cent.), and Moses bar Kepha (813-903). Accounts of an ethnographic work which includes information about India and Indian religions are preserved by Porphyrius (234-ca. 303) and Hieronymus (ca. 347-ca. 419; cf. Drijvers, pp. 173ff.). Of Bardesanes' history of Armenia, mentioned by Moses of Khorene (see Drijvers, pp. 207f.) and his polemics against Marcion and other heresies nothing is extant. The names of two of Bardesanes' works are known from Ephrem (see Drijvers, p. 163): the *Book of Mysteries* (*Hymns* 56.9, tr. p. 192; this book was known to Mani, who wrote one of the same name) and the treatise *Of Domnus*, a book of anti-Platonist polemics, against which Ephrem wrote an entire treatise (*Prose Refutations* II, pp. 1-48, tr. pp. i-xxii). Ebn al-Nadīm (*Fehrest*, p. 402, tr. Dodge, p. 806) mentions three books by Bardesanes: *Light and Darkness (al-Nūr wa'l-Ẓolma)*, *The Spirituality of Truth* (*Rūḥānīya al-Ḥaqq*), and *The Moving and the Static* (*al-Motaḥarrek wa'l-jamād*).

The principal sources for Bardesanes' life are his contemporary Julius Africanus and the much later Agapius (Maḥbūb b. Qosṭanṭīn) of Mabbug (1st half of 10th century), Michael the Syrian (1126-99), and Bar Hebraeus (Ebn al-'Ebrī, 1225/6-86).

The *Book of the Law of the Countries*, written by one of Bardesanes' pupils, discusses the relation between destiny and free will and contains both primary and secondary source material. Though it contains traditions going back to Bardesanes, its apparent admixture of later elements disqualifies the work as a possible basis for reconstructing Bardesanes' system (see Ehlers, pp. 337-39). Western sources such as Eusebius of Caesarea (d. 339) and Epiphanius of Salamis (ca. 315-403) contain apparently authentic elements, but their references to Bardesanes' teaching appear to be based on the writings of his followers. The Arabic sources, e.g., Agapius, Māterīdī, Ebn al-Nadīm, Šahrestānī, are probably based on (lost) Syriac sources and, judging by their largely correct accounts of Manicheism, can be assumed to preserve some authentic traditions; they emphasize the dualistic character of Bardesanes' system and stress the inactive quality of darkness.

2. Life. According to Michael the Syrian (text, pp. 109-11, tr. pp. 183ff.) Bardesanes' parents, Nuḥāmā and Naḥšīram, had fled "Persia" in the year 475 (a mistake for 465 = A.D. 154; see Drijvers, pp. 186ff.) because of a revolt against the ruler in their native country. Bardesanes' Syriac name Bar Dayṣān is explained by a story that he was born on the bank of the Dayṣān (the river of Edessa), hence literally "Son of Dayṣān." This story is repeated by Ebn al-Nadīm (loc. cit.), whereas Mas'ūdī (*Tanbīh*, p. 130) reports another tradition which said that Bardesanes was not born there but was a foundling picked up on the banks of the river. The *Chronicle of Edessa* (p. 147, tr. p. 90) gives Bardesanes' birth date as 11 Tammuz 465. After Bardesanes' birth his parents moved to Hierapolis-Mabbug, where Bardesanes was educated by a "pagan" priest. Julius Africanus (*Kestoi* 29) reports that he once saw Bardesanes performing feats of archery at the court of King Abgar the Great of Edessa (177-212). Ephrem's statement that the devil "adorned Bardesanes with attire and jewels" (*Hymns* 1.12, tr. p. 4; in contrast to Marcion's asceticism and Mani's pale complexion) may also refer to Bardesanes' high social position. Finally the *Life* of Aberkios, who during his travels in the east preaching against Marcion once met him (Drijvers, p. 170), refers to Bardesanes' high birth and wealth. We may note that Africanus calls him a Parthian, but the sources do not provide firm enough evidence for a Parthian origin of Bardesanes. The Iranian elements in Bardesanes' system, however, are more easily explained if we assume an Iranian origin.

According to Michael, Bardesanes was converted to Christianity by Bishop Hystaspes, whom he once happened to hear in Edessa. He was intitiated into the mysteries of the Christians and made a deacon. Bardesanes himself founded a community, which soon became the chief Christian group in and around Edessa, replacing the Marcionites, at whom they aimed harsh polemics. Though Bardesanes accepted both the Old and New Testaments as holy scriptures his followers included many additional revelations in their holy books (Barḥadbešabbā; Drijvers, p. 104, and cf. pp. 111f.). Bardesanes wrote both hymns and prose works (see above), the reason for casting his teaching in the form of hymns with musical accompaniment being, according to Ephrem, his wish to appeal to young people (*Hymns* 1.17, 53-5-6, tr. pp. 5-6, 182).

There is also a tradition that Bardesanes later abandoned Christianity, becoming a "pagan" according to Agapius or a Valentinian according to Michael (Drijvers, pp. 188f.). This association of Bardesanes with the teaching of Valentine is also mentioned by Hippolytus (d. 235; Drijvers, p. 168), Eusebius (ibid., pp. 169f.), and Epiphanius (ibid., p. 178). It may be significant here that these were Western authors who were likely to have been more familiar with the Valentinian system, taught by Valentine himself in Rome ca. 135-60, than with other heresies and who may have been struck by certain strong but superficial resemblances between the two teachings (see further below).

According to Michael (loc. cit.) and Bar Hebraeus (*Chronicon* I, col. 47), Bardesanes died in 533 = A.D. 222, when he was 68 years old.

After the death of Bardesanes the community founded by him remained dominant in Edessa until Bishop Rabbūla (d. 435), an ardent persecutor of Marcionites and Bardesanites, destroyed the cult places of the Bardesanites (Bedjan, IV, pp. 431f.) and established his own "orthodox" church in Edessa after 400. The community was obviously not strong enough to withstand Rabbūla and half a millennium or so later we find the Bardesanites scattered in various parts of the Sasanian empire: according to Ebn al-Nadīm (loc. cit.) in the "swamps" of Iraq, in Khorasan, and in Ṣīn "China."

3. Teaching. Bardesanes' theological system must be reconstructed by carefully sifting the information provided by the secondary sources. The following outline of Bardesanes' cosmology is based on the Syriac sources (Ephrem, Barḥadbešabbā, Moses bar Kepha, John of Dara, and Bar Konai; see Drijvers, pp. 96-121, 130-43).

Cosmology. From eternity there were six beings (*ītyē*; on the meaning of Syr. *ītyā* see the discussion in Ehlers, pp. 340-43). According to Ephrem (*Hymns* 3.6, tr. p. 13), the six corresponded to the six directions: "he placed (*sām*) [them] in the four quarters of the winds, one... in the depth and one other on high." In the heights was the Lord God, located in the middle of Space (*Prose Refutations* I, pp. 132, 135, tr. pp. xcv-xcvii). In the middle were four beings: light, wind, fire, and water. In the beginning the light was in the east and the wind in the north. They were made up of atoms (*perdē*; II, pp. 214-19, tr. ci-ciii) and were light and heavy or fine and coarse (II, p. 159, tr. p. lxxiv; cf. Barḥadbešabbā in Drijvers, p. 100), of different colors, smells, tastes, and textures (II, pp. 223-24, tr. p. cvi), corresponding to the five senses. According to Ephrem "the Stranger (*nukrāyā*) [i.e., God] blew His life into the beings and girded (*ḥzaq*) them" (II, p. 158, tr. p. lxxiii).

The sixth substance, darkness, was in the depths. It was the heaviest of all the elements (I, p. 54, tr. p. lv) and is characterized as sleeping and powerless (I, p. 56, tr. p. lvi) and cold (II, p. 226, tr. p. cvii), a point stressed by the Arabic sources as constituting an important difference between Bardesanes and Mani (Vajda, pp. 23-31).

Whether the first being, God, is to be identified with the Father of Life whose consort is the Mother of Life (see below), implying that the uppermost level of being was peopled by several entities (as in other gnostic systems and in Manicheism), is not clear.

The four beings, weak and erring, were then shaken, either by chance or by destiny, and began to stir and knock against one another. According to Bar Konai, it was the wind blowing with its force that caused the elements to make contact and start mingling. Then, according to Ephrem (*Prose Refutations* II, p. 226, tr. p. cvii), "the heat caused the cold to disappear and its smoke (*tennānā*) rose up (*'ṭar*)" while, according to Bar Konai, the fire began to burn in a forest (*'b'*) and a dark smoke gathered (*qṭar*) that caused confusion, making the beings mingle and fight with each other. There is also the image of the darkness rising and making an assault (*s'ā*) on "the heels and the skirts of the upper Light" (ibid.), and Moses says that "the darkness made an assault (*s'ā*) from the depths to rise up and mingle with and among them" (Drijvers, p. 100). However, the attack is clearly provoked by the disturbances above the darkness and not by the darkness itself, as in Manicheism. The beings fled before the oncoming darkness, seeking refuge with God and asking Him to save them from it (or the disfiguring color caused by the darkness; Moses bar Kepha). Their Lord then sent to them the Word of Intention, which separated the darkness from the pure beings (according to Bar Konai, he ordered the wind to lie down and turn its blast against the confusion), and the darkness was thrown into the abyss. This Word, which is said to be the Logos (Barḥadbešabbā) or Christ (Moses, John), then erected each substance in its place and order and from the mingling that had taken place It made this world. Ephrem (*Prose Refutations* II, p. 220, tr. p. civ) also says that, according to Bardesanes, it was the power of the First Word which remained in created things that made everything, but he also quotes a different opinion among the Bardesanites that God sent down the atoms of spirit, force, and thought to the darkness to create order and that some of these were mixed with those others (of darkness). The world thus established was given a finite time to exist (Barḥadbešabbā) and was placed "in the middle," so that no further mingling of the darkness and the four beings might take place (Moses).

Few other details of Bardesanes' cosmology are known. The following have been preserved in Ephrem's hymns. According to the followers of Bardesanes the Father and Mother of Life brought forth the Son of Life (*Hymns* 55.1, tr. p. 187; Drijvers, p. 144): "Something streamed down from that Father of Life and the Mother became pregnant... and bore... the Son of Life." Another fragment (55.2, tr. p. 187) ascribed to Bardesanes makes it clear that the Son of Life is Christ: "(Bardesanes) called our Lord the child that was produced by two, through sexual union." The Holy Spirit brought forth two daughters, "the blush of the earth and the image in the water" (55.3, tr. p. 187). The Father and the Mother measured and laid out Paradise, founded it by their sexual union, and planted it with their numerous divine descendants (55.8, 10, tr. pp. 189f.). It is not clear whether these divine descendants may be compared with the Aeons who in Gnosticism and Manicheism populate the Realms of Light. It would seem that Bardesanes' system also contained the notion that the Sons of Darkness fashioned (human) bodies in the likeness of an image shown them by the Primal Man (*Prose Refutations* I, p. 123, tr. pp. xc-xci), comparable with the Archons who in the other systems are instrumental in the creation of man (see, e.g., Jonas, 1963, p. 202; for the Manichean version of this event, see ĀSRĒŠTĀR). The much later Michael the Syrian (loc. cit.) reports that there were three spiritual and four material elements of which man was composed and from which 360 worlds originated. (Numbers like 360, or 366 as Bar Hebraeus has it, Drijvers, p. 192, are known from other gnostic speculations; thus according to Basilides there were 365 heavens; Jonas, 1963, p. 43.)

Anthropology and soteriology. According to Ephrem, man consists of reason (*madd'ā*) or spirit, soul, and body, reason being hidden in the soul, which is subtle compared to the body but corporeal compared to reason (*Prose Refutations* II, p. 157, tr. p. lxxiii). Body and soul are separate parts of man (*Carmina Nisibena* 51.4, tr. p. 61). The soul, it too made from the *ītyē* (*Hymns* 53.4, tr. p. 182), wears the body like a garment (*Carmina Nisibena* 51.9, tr. p. 61; cf. *Prose Refutations* I, p. 8, tr. xxxii). The bodies, hailing from the darkness (*Hymns* 53.4, tr. p. 182), being fashioned by the Sons of Darkness compelled by an image shown them by the Primal Man (presumably of his own beauty; *Prose Refutations* I, p. 123, tr. p. xc), are not resurrected (*Carmina Nisibena* 51.4, tr. p. 60; *Hymns* 53.4, tr. p. 182). According to Ephrem, the soul is composed of seven parts (*Hymns* 53.4, tr. p. 182; *Prose Refutations* I, p. 8, tr. xxvii), but it is not clear whether the number seven here is connected with the seven planets.

There is also little information about the process of salvation. The cosmological accounts state that what was mixed is now in the process of being purified and distilled by conception and birth (Moses) and this process will continue until the world comes to an end. Whatever has not been purified within the period set for the world, the Word will purify at the end of time (Barḥadbešabbā). However, we do not know exactly in what manner salvation is achieved. Later sources disparagingly emphasize sexual union as a means of purification, especially for women (Michael and Agapius; Drijvers, p. 190), but no doubt such statements are tainted by antiheretical feeling. However, sexual union must have played some part in Bardesanes' soteriology. A passage in Ephrem (*Prose Refutations* I, p. 27, tr. pp. xli-xlii) concerning the Father and Mother of Life and their relationship to the sun and the moon may be of relevance here: According to Ephrem Bardesanes called the moon "an earth and a womb which is filled from a sublime and elevated stream which floods those who are below and beneath." Comparison with the salvatory function of the waxing and waning of the moon in Manicheism, with which Ephrem contrasts the Bardesanite myth (loc. cit.), would suggest a similar interpretation of the latter. Note also Ephrem's statement that Bardesanes compared (*mattel*) the Father and Mother of Life with the sun and moon (*Hymns* 55.10, tr. p. 189), and the later biographers of Bardesanes (Agapius, Michael, and Bar Hebraeus; Drijvers, p. 149) maintain that, according to him, the Mother of Life would undress every month to go in to the Father of Life to unite with him, from which union seven sons were born, in analogy with the waning of the moon.

About the soul's return Ephrem states that the souls were at first held back at the "Crossing," also called the "Bridal Chamber of Light" (*Prose Refutations* II, pp. 164-65, tr. pp. lxxvi-lxxvii). This hindrance was caused by Death, which Adam brought into the world through his sin, but then our Lord brought in Life, so that every soul, in every place and every depth, that has kept His word shall not taste Death but cross over the "Crossing" and be brought into the Kingdom. The body on the other hand, composed of atoms from the four beings and from darkness, returns to dust, dissolved into the original substance (ibid., p. 143, tr. p. lxvi). Moreover, Bardesanes, like Mani after him, insisted that the entire cosmos, the sea and the dry land, the heaven and the earth, must be purified (ibid., p. 204, tr. p. xcvii).

Astrology and free will. Bardesanes' system, like other gnostic systems, contained a fair share of astrological speculation. His interest in astrology is mentioned by Ephrem (*Hymns* 51.13, tr. p. 177): "he preaches the signs of the Zodiac, observes the hour (of birth), teaches the seven (planets), and inquires about the times," and in *Hymns* 1.18 (tr. p. 6) it is said that Bardesanes and his followers read books about the zodiac rather than the prophets. The *Book of the Law of the Countries* repeatedly emphasizes the free will of man; however, the more reliable Barḥadbešabbā states clearly that the followers of Bardesanes made nought of freedom [of will] (*ḥērūṯā mᵉbaṭṭᵉlīn*; cf. Ehlers, p. 339).

Bardesanes and Gnosticism. Bardesanes' system contains Gnostic elements that cannot be overlooked. As in gnostic systems as well as Manicheism, the presupposition for salvation is gnosis; cf. Ephrem (*Prose Refutations* II, p. 206, tr. p. xcviii), who states that in the schools of Bardesanes and Mani the creation is purified by knowledge and faith, and the tripartite arrangement of the original elements agrees in principle with several other Gnostic systems (Ehlers, p. 345). It is not clear whether Bardesanes' system contained the notion of the captured or mingled light as an expatriate, abandoned far away from home, typical of Gnosticism, including Manicheism. Only one passage in Ephrem (*Hymns* 55.6, tr. p. 188) contains a similar notion, in which apparently the Holy Spirit complains "My God and Lord, Thou hast left me alone." Some mythical elements common to both the Syriac Gnosticism, Bardesanes, and Manicheism probably derive in part from old Mesopotamian religion (Sumerian and Babylonian). Among these are the names Father of Life, Mother of Life, and Son of Life, the founding and planting of the Paradise Garden by the Father and Mother, and the idea of the Bridal Chamber of Light (Widengren, pp. 14f.).

Bardesanes attacks Marcion vehemently, rejecting his teaching of the two gods—the hidden or alien good God and the God of creation, the demiurge (see, e.g., Jonas, 1963, pp. 141ff.)—and probably also his asceticism, with its condemnation of marriage and reproduction (cf. Jonas, 1963, p. 145).

The various traditions that connect Bardesanes with the Valentinian speculation (see above) are probably based upon some striking similarities between the two systems. On the whole, however, the systems differ strongly from one another. A brief summary (based on Jonas, 1963, p. 174) of the main principles of Valentine's (fl. mid-2nd century) teaching may serve to illustrate the similarities between his and Bardesanes' systems (as well as an example of how evil is explained in Syriac Gnostic systems): From eternity there were in the invisible and nameless heights a perfect aeon (Fore-Father, Abyss) and his consort the Ennoia (Thought). The Aeon wanted to create from himself the beginning of all things and inserted his emission like a seed into the womb of the Ennoia, who conceived and bore the Mind (Nous, Father) and his consort Truth. These two then generated Word and Life; a further series of emanations produced a large number of aeons and finally the Sophia. The Sophia, in her desire to find the perfect aeon (Abyss) plunges into it but is stopped by the Limit (Horos) hiding the Aeon from his emanations (except Truth and Life), which returns her to her own kind. Her desire and the passion to which it led are separated from her and cast by the Limit outside of the other emanations as a formless spiritual substance, an "abortion" brought forth without conception, hypostasized as a separate being, the lower Sophia. All these events and the Sophia's remorse have created disturbances among the aeons, who pray to the Father for the emanation of Christos and the Holy Spirit, who are to restore the serenity among the aeons and give form to the formless substance. After perfect repose has been reestablished, all together they produce the aeon Jesus, who is to bring salvation to the formless substance. The world is then created by a demiurge of the typical Gnostic kind (cf. Jonas, 1963, p. 191), shaped by the Sophia. Here we may note the following similarities between the two systems: 1. In the Valentinian system the perfect aeon is the unknown god (known only by his first emanation, Mind and Truth) corresponding to the Stranger in that of Bardesanes (Ephrem, *Prose Refutations* II, p. 158)—a concept common to all Gnostic systems; 2. the importance of male and female couples in the Valentinian scheme and the similarity with Ephrem's description of the Father and Mother of Life's bringing forth the Son of Life (see above); 3. the importance of the Limit, which in the Valentinian speculation separates the aeons from the formless substance and the Boundary, which in Bardesanes' system separates the five higher elements from the sixth, and darkness below (*Prose Refutations* I, pp. 54-56; cf. Ehlers, p. 345 and n. 43); 4. the prayer to the Father corresponds to the element's taking refuge with the All-highest (and more closely to corresponding events in Manichean cosmology); 5. in the Valentinian system the Christos starts the creation process by giving form to the formless substance, though the creation is mainly performed at a later stage by the demiurge, and in Bardesanes' system it is the Word of Thought (Logos, Christ) sent by God that creates the visible world; 6. in the Valentinian system gnosis is brought to the historical Jesus by the Christos and the aeon Jesus who descend upon him at his baptism in the river Jordan; in Bardesanes' system it is again the Word of Thought (Logos, Christ) that starts the work of purification and salvation.

Bardesanes and Iran. There are, however, some fundamental differences between Bardesanes' system and the Syriac gnostic systems as exemplified in the Valentinian speculation, which characterize Bardesanes' system as an Iranian gnostic system. (On these two kinds of systems see Jonas, 1963, pp. 236f.) The feature of Bardesanes' system which places it firmly in the Iranian tradition is the coexistence from eternity of the two opposite principles of light and darkness, located in the heights and the depths respectively, and the disturbance of the original peace and harmony through an intermingling of the two principles. In details, however, the two systems differ considerably. Thus, in Bardesanes' system darkness is lifeless and inactive, and contact is caused by disturbances among the four lighter elements, which bring them all the way down to the boundary, thus awakening the sleeping darkness which rises and intermingles with the light elements. Mani, however, represents darkness as something evil and active, full of strife, which of itself rises and, arriving at the border, sees the light and wants to possess it and so attacks it. Mani's Father of Light therefore calls forth from Himself a series of emanations who are to fight the darkness, and during this fight some of the light is imprisoned in the darkness. It has not been determined where Bardesanes got the concept of the lifeless darkness from; it may, however, be related to the similar concept of *hulē* which is found in some Gnostic systems (Ehlers, p. 347) and which both Marcion and Bardesanes employed, according to Ephrem (*Hymns* 14.7-8, tr. p. 51) with n. 5; *Prose Refutations* I, p. 141, tr. p. c).

Another element which may derive from Iranian cosmologies is that of Space, in the middle of which God was located; this recalls the role played by Space in Zoroastrian (Zurvanite) tradition (cf. also Mani's Light Ether, coeternal with the Light Father). Similarly, an element of Bardesanes' system from Iranian religion not utilized by Mani appears to be the role he assigns to the wind, at once one of the light elements and the cause of the disturbance. This may reflect the dual nature of Vayu in Zoroastrian (Zurvanite) speculations.

Other elements. According to Drijvers (p. 151) the comparison of the Mother of Life with a fish (see above) may betray some connection with the cult of Atargatis, goddess of fertility honored in Hierapolis, where Bardesanes according to Michael was educated by a pagan priest (see above).

Bardesanes' system also contains elements borrowed from atomistic speculations. According to Ephrem (*Prose Refutations* II, pp. 214-20, tr. pp. ci-civ; cf. Ehlers, pp. 346f.), the beings (*ītyē*) consisted of minuscule, indissoluble particles (*perdē*). The characterization of the elements as "heavy/light" or "coarse/fine" is also known from Greek atomism (Ehlers, loc. cit.).

Bardesanes and Manicheism. Though Bardesanes' system is both similar and dissimilar to Manicheism, the lack of information makes it difficult to assess in detail how his system may have influenced Mani's: On the one hand, Bardesanes' Father of Life and Space resembles Mani's Father of Greatness (Father of Light, Lord of Paradise, Pater Ingenitus, Malek Jenān al-Nūr, etc.) who exists from eternity with four other Greatnesses, among them the Pure Ether (Mid. Pers. *'ndrw'z*, Sogd. *'wswycβry'*, Aer Ingenitus, al-Jaww); Bardesanes' Mother of Life has the same name as Mani's Mother of Life, the Father of Greatness's first emanation; Bardesanes' Paradise, which the Father of Life and the Mother of Life founded, recalls the name Lord of Paradise for Mani's Father of Greatness; Bardesanes' four *ītyē*, which God is said to have girded, at least superficially correspond to Mani's five elements (breeze, wind, light, water, fire), the sons of the First Man, whom he put on as a weapon and an armor (in both systems these four/five beings are mixed with darkness); and, finally, Bardesanes' Word of Intention spoken by God resembles the Cry uttered by the Spiritus Vivens, which cuts open the darkness and reveals the vanquished First Man and his sons (for details see, e.g., Asmussen, pp. 12ff.).

On the other hand, for a Gnostic system, that of Bardesanes, unlike Mani's, appears extremely simple, but this impression may be due to lack of source material. In Bardesanes' system the *ītyē* are weak and erring and themselves cause their downfall by waking the sleeper in the abyss. In Mani's system the First Man and his sons are sent out from the Paradise of Light to fight the attacking darkness but are defeated. Where Mani had recourse to the Gnostic notion of emanation to explain the creation of divine beings, Bardesanes apparently used sexual procreation. In this positive view of sexuality Bardesanes differs sharply from both Manicheism and other Gnostic systems (e.g., Marcionism, which advocated strict asceticism; see Jonas, 1963, p. 144). In Manicheism sexuality and reproduction are viewed as evil, as they perpetrate the imprisonment of the particles of light in matter by dividing them into smaller pieces, rendering the salvation process still more difficult. All the emanations proceeding from the Father of Greatness are therefore represented as asexual. However, in Bardesanes' system the Father and Mother of Life unite in a sexual manner, producing the Son of

Life, and salvation is thought to be brought about through conception and birth.

Conclusion: Bardesanes' system is a syncretistic one containing elements from Syriac Gnosticism, Iranian cosmological speculations, and Greek atomism. In stressing the existence of the two principles of light and darkness from eternity and the intermingling of the two principles as the origin of the creation and the beginning of the process of salvation, concepts adapted from Iranian religious speculations, he may have provided a partial model for Mani's system.

Bibliography: For a complete bibliography of sources and studies see Drijvers, 1966; for later publications also Davids, Ehlers, Vajda. The following bibliography contains only select titles. Sources: 1. Syriac. Bar Hebraeus, *Chronicon ecclesiasticum*, ed. J. B. Abbeloos and T. Lamy, 2 vols., Louvain, 1872-77. Theodore bar Konai, in CSCO, 2nd ser., 65-66, Paris, 1910-12. Barḥadbešabbā, ed. F. Nau, in *Patrologia Orientalis* XXIII, Paris, 1932. P. Bedjan, *Acta Martyrum et Sanctorum*, 7 vols., Paris, 1890-97. *Chronicon Edessenum*, ed. L. Hallier, *Untersuchungen über die edessenische Chronik mit dem syrischen Text nebst einer Übersetzung*, Texte und Untersuchungen zur Geschichte der altkristlichen Literatur 9/1, Leipzig, 1892. Ephrem, *Des heiligen Ephraem des Syrers Carmina Nisibena* II, ed. E. Beck, CSCO 240: Scriptores Syri 102, Louvain, 1963. Idem, *Des heiligen Ephraem des Syrers Hymnen contra Haereses (Hymns)*, ed. E. Beck, CSCO 169-70: Scriptores Syri 76-77, Louvain, 1957. Idem, *S. Ephraim's Prose Refutations of Mani, Marcion and Bardaisan*, ed. C. W. Mitchell, I, London, 1912, II, completed by A. A. Bevan and F. C. Burkitt, London, 1921. John of Dara, ed. A. Baumstark, "Iwannîs von Dârâ über Bardaiṣân," *Oriens Christianum*, 3rd ser., 8, 1933, p. 62-71. Michael the Syrian, ed. J. B. Chabot, *Chronique de Michel le Syrien* I-III, Paris, 1899-1910. *The Book of the Law of the Countries*, ed. F. Nau, in *Patrologia Syriaca* 1/2, Paris, 1907, cols. 536-611.

2. Arabic. The Arabic sources are conveniently put together in Vajda, 1966. Many of them are also found in S. Ḥ. Taqīzāda and A. Afšār Šīrāzī, *Mānī wa dīn-e ū be-enżemām-e motūn-e ʿarabī o fārsī dar bāra-ye Mānī o Mānawīyāt*, Tehran, 1335 Š./1956; see index s.vv. Ebn Dayṣān, Dayṣān.

3. Greek. Epiphanius, *Panarion*, ed. K. Holl. II, Die griechischen christlichen Schriftsteller der ersten Jahrhunderte (GCS) 31, Leipzig, 1922. Eusebius, *Historia ecclesiastica* I, ed. E. Schwarz, GCS 9^1, Leipzig, 1903. Hippolytus, *Refutatio omnium haeresium*, ed. P. Wendland, GCS 26, Leipzig, 1916. Julius Africanus, ed. and tr. J. R. Vielleford, Florence, 1970. Porphyrius, *Excerpta*, in Stobaeus, *Anthologium* 1-4, ed. C. Wachsmuth and O. Hense, Berlin, 1884-1912.

Secondary literature: A. Abel, "Dayṣāniyya," in EI^2 II, p. 199 (assumes that *The Book of the Laws of the Countries* was written by Bardesanes). J. P. Asmussen, *Xᵘāstvānīft: Studies in Manicheism*, Copenhagen, 1965. J. M. Davids, "Zur Kosmologie Bardaisans," *ZDMG* 120, 1970, pp. 32-42. H. J. W. Drijvers, *Bardaison of Edessa*, Assen, 1966. This is to date the most comprehensive study of the sources on Bardesanes. It also contains a detailed description and evaluation of earlier studies. The author concludes that Bardesanes' system does not fall within the definition of Gnosticism; however, the author's definition is probably more at fault than Bardesanes' system; see Ehlers, 1970. B. Ehlers, "Bardesanes von Edessa—ein syrischer Gnostiker," *Zeitschrift für Kirchengeschichte*, 1970, pp. 334-51 (criticism of Drijvers, 1966, with important clarification of Bardesanes' position within Gnosticism). H. Jonas, *Gnosis und spätantiker Geist* I, 2nd ed., Göttingen, 1954. Idem, *The Gnostic Religion*, enlarged ed., Boston, 1963. H. H. Schaeder, "Bardesanes von Edessa," *Zeitschrift für Kirchengeschichte* 51, 1932, pp. 21-74. G. Vajda, "Le témoignage d'al-Māturīdī sur la doctrine des Manichéens, des Daisanites et des Marcionites," *Arabica* 13, 1966, pp. 1-38, 113-28. G. Widengren, *Mesopotamian Elements in Manichaeism (King and Saviour II)*, Uppsala Universitets Årsskrift, 1946, no. 3. [See Addenda and corrigenda.]

(P. O. SKJÆRVØ)

BARDIYA, the younger son of Cyrus the Great. The name is derived from proto-Iranian **bardz-* "be high." In the Elamite version of the Behistun (Bīsotūn) inscription he is called Pirtiya, but the Akkadian version and private documents from Babylonia have the Median form Barziya. He is called Smerdis by Herodotus (3.30), Mardos by Aeschylus (*Persae* 774), Mergis by Justin (1.9), and Merphis by Hellanicus (Jacoby, *Fragmente* I, p. 449). On the other hand, Ctesias (*Persica* 29.8) calls the minor son of Cyrus Tanyoxarces (Old Persian **tanu-wazraka* "large bodied"; cf. also Xenophon, *Cyropaedia* 8.7,11 where he is called Tanaoxares). Both names, Bardiya and Tanyoxarces, imply that the prince was of exceptional physical strength, and it seems probable that Tanyoxarces was a nickname of Bardiya.

According to the Behistun inscription (1.29-30), Cambyses and Bardiya had the same father and mother. Herodotus (3.2 and 30) also says that they were full brothers, their mother being Cassandane (q.v.), daughter of Pharnaspes, an Achaemenid. Ctesias's assertion (29.2) that the wife of Cyrus and mother of his sons was Amytis, daughter of the last Median king Astyages, is apparently wrong.

Darius in his Behistun inscription (DB 1.30-33) says that Cambyses, after becoming king but before his departure to Egypt, slew Bardiya and that the assassination was kept a secret from the people. However, according to Herodotus (3.10), Bardiya (Smerdis) went to Egypt with Cambyses and spent some time there. Later Cambyses sent him back to Susa out of envy, because Bardiya alone could draw the bow brought from the Ethiopian king. Then Cambyses had a dream in which he saw his brother sitting on the royal throne. As a result of this dream Cambyses sent his trusted counselor Prexaspes from Egypt to Susa with the order to kill Smerdis. Herodotus gives two versions of the murder. According to the first, Smerdis was killed in a hunting field near Susa; the other version says that Prexaspes drowned him in the Erythrean Sea. The murder was kept secret and was known only to Patizeithes, a Magian whom Cambyses had left in charge of the royal palace before he went to Egypt, and a few others. This Magian had a brother, who looked very much like the dead Bardiya and even happened to have from birth the same name. Patizeithes persuaded him to raise a rebellion against Cambyses and proclaim himself king, claiming to be the real son of Cyrus. For some time he was able to pass himself off as the dead Bardiya (see Herodotus, 3.61-62).

In the Behistun inscription (DB 1.36, etc.) this impostor is called "Gaumāta the Magian" (*maguš*; the Akkadian version adds "a Mede," see DB 1.15). The name has been preserved by Justin (1.9) in the form Cometes as the name of the Usurper's brother. Justin says that it was Cometes who killed the prince Mergis and that the assassination took place after the death of Cambyses. As seen from the Behistun inscription, Gaumāta rose in revolt against Cambyses on March 11, 522 B.C., claiming to be Bardiya. As Herodotus (3.62-65) narrates further, news came from Persia to Cambyses when he was in Syria on his way back home that his younger brother had usurped the throne. However, Prexaspes assured Cambyses that he had slain Bardiya. Then Cambyses died in the spring of 522 B.C., confessing to the murder of his brother. But after the death of Cambyses Prexaspes consistently denied that Bardiya was dead. Finally Darius records in the Behistun inscription (1.48-61) that on 29 September 522 B.C. he slew Gaumāta with the help of six noble Persians and became king.

According to Ctesias (29.8-14) Cyrus on his deathbed appointed Bardiya (Tanyoxarces) governor (*despotēs* "lord") of the Bactrians, Choramnians (i.e., Chorasmians), Parthians, and Carmanians. When Bardiya flogged a Magian, Sphendadates by name, for some misdeed, Sphendadates in revenge told Cambyses that his brother was plotting against him. Then at the order of Cambyses Bardiya drank bull's blood and died. Sphendadates, who was very similar in appearance to Bardiya, dressed in the prince's clothes and pretended to be the minor son of Cyrus. After Cambyses' death he became king. Five years after the assassination, the mother of Bardiya learned from a eunuch that her son was dead and that the king was really Sphendadates. Before that time the disappearance of the prince passed quite unnoticed by everybody except Cambyses' accomplices Izabates, Artasyras, and Bagapates. Ctesias agrees with the Behistun inscription in dating the assassination of the prince before Cambyses' expedition against Egypt, which was conquered in the summer of 525 B.C. Since it took some time for Cambyses' army to get there, and the assassination became known only in September, 522 B.C. (see DB 1.55-57; cf. Herodotus, 3.68), Ctesias might be right in dating the death of the prince to 526 B.C.

If we believe Xenophon (*Cyropaedia* 8.7.11, 8.8.2), at his father's death Bardiya (Tanaoxares) had been designated satrap of the Medes, Armenians, and Cadusians. When Cyrus died his sons started quarreling (see also Plato, *Leges* 3.694-95; and *Epistulae* 7.332 A).

Some modern scholars (e.g., Olmstead) believe that the man who revolted against Cambyses was his true brother and lawful heir and that Darius killed him, calling him Gaumāta and inventing the story of the false Bardiya in order to justify his own seizure of the kingship. However, this must remain hypothetical (see GAUMĀTA).

According to the Behistun inscription (DB 3.21-28) in 522 B.C. a Persian, Vahyazdāta by name, raised a rebellion against Darius, also claiming to be Bardiya, son of Cyrus.

Bardiya left a daughter, Parmys by name, whom Darius married when he became king in order to legitimize his position (see Herodotus, 3.88).

Bibliography: Given in the text; see also W. Brandenstein and M. Mayrhofer, *Handbuch des Altpersischen*, Wiesbaden, 1964, pp. 110, 114. M. A. Dandamaev, *Persien unter den ersten Achämeniden*, Wiesbaden, 1976, pp. 108-58. Idem, *Politicheskaya istoriya Akhemenidskoĭ derzhavy*, Moscow, 1985, pp. 64-85. I. Gershevitch, "The False Smerdis," *Acta Antiqua Academiae Scientiarum Hungaricae* 27/4, Budapest, 1979, pp. 337-51. Kent, *Old Persian*, p. 200. F. W. König. *Der Falsche Bardiya: Dareios der Grosse und die Lügenkönige*, Vienna, 1938. A. T. Olmstead, *History of the Persian Empire*, Chicago, 1948, pp. 107-10. J. Wiesehöfer, *Der Aufstand Gaumātas und die Anfänge Dareios' I.*, Bonn, 1978.

(M. A. DANDAMAYEV)

BAṚĒC(Ī), a Pashtun tribe in southern Afghanistan. Like neighboring Tarīn and Dorrānī, the Baṛēc are part of the Šarḵbūn branch of the Saṛbanī Pashtun. Genealogists divide the tribe into two distinct sections, Dā'ūdzī and Ḥosaynzī, which are further subdivided respectively into five and six senior lineages, although only three are still represented today: the Badalzī among the Dā'ūdzī; and the Zakōzī and the Mandōzī among the Ḥosaynzī (Ḵᵛāja Neʿmat-Allāh, II, pp. 43 and 123f., n. 40; and *Gazetteer of Afghanistan* V, p. 89). The missing lineages might have taken part in the large migration of the Ḵaršbūn branch of the Pashtun toward the northeast where they lost their individuality (Ḵᵛāja Neʿmat-Allāh, II, p. 124, n. 40). What is certain but not conclusive, however, is that several lineage names (for instance, Malīzī and Dawlatzī) are found among both the Baṛēc and the Yūsofzī. The Baṛēc have assimilated three Šērānī (q.v.) lineages, which are still recognized as such (*Gazetteer of Afghanistan* V, pp. 89, 451). At the end of the nineteenth century, the tribal chieftaincy was held by the Mandōzī, who had taken it back from the Badalzī at the time of Nāder Shah.

The Baṛēc are a small tribe. Converging population estimates from the past (2500-3000 families according to Elphinstone, p. 426; 4000 according to Ḥayāt Khan, p. 81; and 15,000 souls according to O. Duke in *Gazetteer of Afghanistan* V, p. 88) do not fit well with contemporary estimates which, though uncertain, can justifiably be made at from ten to twenty thousand persons.

The Baṛēc are geographically concentrated in Šōrābak (Šōrāwak) district (q.v.) where, on the eastern edge of the Rēgestān desert and along the middle course of the Lōṛa river, they make up the majority of the population. According to their own traditions, they moved there during the 10th/16th century from the opposite edge of the desert (*Gazetteer of Afghanistan* V, pp. 92, 448f.). This is consistent with written sources (Hotak, English tr., p. 39; Russian tr., p. 41). Vestiges of the tribe's previous settlements, three Baṛēc villages survive to this day in the lower Helmand valley: one near the Bost ruins and the other two (Palālak and Lanḍay, both occupied by Zakōzī) below Dēšū. Over the centuries the rest of the tribe has kept up close contacts with these villages. On the other hand, gradual movements, reportedly during the 12th/18th century, took place from Šōrābak toward the lower Lōṛa where, around and below Nūškī in Pakistani Baluchistan, one finds three Mandōzī lineages (Hughes-Bullet, pp. 288f.) numbering about 5,000 persons in 1951 (Scholz, p. 36).

Location of the Baṛēc at the southern extremity of Pashtun territory and at the limits of the Baluch has allowed multiple contacts with the latter and Brahui, including intermarriages, as well as linguistic or even genealogical assimilation, especially in the isolated sections of the lower Helmand and lower Lōṛa valleys. In the 13th/19th century, Baṛēc mercenaries served in the army of the khan of Kalāt. Traditional relations with neighboring Pashtun tribes frequently involved conflict; Baṛēc territory was often raided by the Acəkzī (q.v.), and they competed with the Pīšīn Tarīn for the waters of the Lōṛa (*Gazetteer of Afghanistan* V, pp. 90f.).

The Baṛēc are, nowadays, the only Pashtun tribe in southern Afghanistan without a nomadic component. However, they used to practice, as is typical of people living on the fringes of deserts, a form of short-distance seminomadism during the spring (Elphinstone, p. 427); and in some cases there were short summertime migrations toward the heights of Sarlat (*Gazetteer of Afghanistan* V, p. 443). More recent information is lacking since the Šōrāwak district was not covered by the Afghan Nomad Survey of 1357 Š./1978, but pastoralism has probably not vanished. The Baṛēc still rear large herds of camels. They used to breed dromedaries both for themselves and for travelers in caravans plying the route between Qandahār and Sind province. Their major activity is irrigated farming, especially to produce staple cereals.

Pastures and fields are collective, hence inalienable, property. *Wēš*, the annual redistribution of fields among tribesmen, is still practiced. Though among the Zakōzī and Mandōzī every male regardless of age has the right to a share (*ḵōla wēš*), the Badalzī reserve this right (*mlātaṛ wēš*) for males who are old enough to fight, traditionally twelve years old, the age at which Pashtun boys receive their first rifles (Rešād, pp. 24ff.). The *wēš* practiced nowadays has been considerably modified: in Baṛēc villages in the lower Helmand, each family's share has been fixed and hereditary for several generations (Snoy, pp. 129f.), while, in the more conservative Šōrāwak district, shares (*ās wēš*) are no longer granted to horse owners as used to be done because of the strategic usefulness of their mounts during tribal hostilities (Rešād, pp. 25ff.).

The traditional abode of the Baṛēc is a kind of twig hut (*koḍəla*), which is described in *Gazetteer of Afghanistan* V, p. 91.

Bibliography: M. Elphinstone, *An Account of the Kingdom of Caubul*, London, 1815; repr. Graz, 1969. M. Hotak, *Pəṭa ḵazāna*, Eng. tr. H. G. Koshan, Kabul, 1358 Š./1979; Russ. tr. D. M. Ludin, Kabul, 1361 Š./1982. R. Hughes-Bullet, *Baluchistan District Gazetteer Series* IV: *Bolan and Chagai*, Karachi, 1906, reproduced in *Baluchistan through the Ages*, n.p., 1906, repr. Quetta, 1979, II. M. Ḥayāt Khan, *Ḥayāt-e Afḡān*, tr. H. Priestley, *Afghanistan and Its Inhabitants*, Lahore, 1874; repr. 1981. Ḵᵛāja Neʿmat-Allāh, *Maḵzan-e afḡānī*, tr. B. Dorn, *History of the Afghans*, London, 1836, repr. London, 1965, and Karachi, 1976. P. Rešād, "Baṛēcī aw Šōrāwak," in *Šayḵ Bostān Baṛēc*, Kabul, 1360 Š./1981, pp. 9-26. F. Scholz, *Belutschistan (Pakistan). Eine sozialgeographische Studie des Wandels in einem Nomadenland seit Beginn der Kolonialzeit*, Göttinger Geographische Abhandlungen 63, Göttingen, 1974, p. 36. P. Snoy, "Ethnologische Feldforschung in Afghanistan," *Jahrbuch des Südasien-Instituts der Universität Heidelberg* 3, 1968-69, pp. 127-30.

(D. BALLAND)

BARĒLVĪ, SAYYED **AḤMAD ŠAHĪD,** Indo-Muslim saint, author of Persian works, known for his reformist ideas, military ventures, and eventual martyrdom (1201-46/1786-1831). He was born into a pious Muslim family at Rae Bareli; after elementary education at home, he went to Lucknow in search of employment and then proceeded to Delhi, where in 1222/1807-08 he was initiated into Sufism by Shah ʿAbd-al-ʿAzīz b. Shah Walī-Allāh Dehlavī (q.v., d. 1239/1823). For seven years he served in the army of Nawwāb Amīr Khan, later the ruler of Tonk. Returning to Delhi, he gradually gained spiritual eminence, and many distinguished persons were initiated by him, including two relatives of Shah ʿAbd-al-ʿAzīz, Shah Moḥammad Esmāʿīl and Shah ʿAbd-al-Ḥayy, who became his principal disciples. He gained many more followers during missionary tours in north India. In 1237/1821, he set out with a large party to perform the pilgrimage to Mecca, returning home in 1240/1824 (Sayyed Moḥammad ʿAlī, *Maḵzan-e aḥmadī*, Agra, 1299/1824). Sayyed Aḥmad's ideas during this period have been lucidly presented in *Ṣerāṭ-e mostaqīm* (Lahore, n.d.), a Persian digest of his conversations compiled by Shah Moḥammad Esmāʿīl and Shah ʿAbd-al-Ḥayy in 1232/1817-18. He strongly affirms the profession of God's Unity (*tawḥīd*), uncompromisingly denounces all innovations (*bedʿat*), and advocates outer as well as inner holy war (jihad). Further, many references in his letters indicate Sayyed Aḥmad's awareness of the growing foreign political domination of Hindustan and the need to oppose it (*Makātīb-e Sayyed Aḥmad Barēlvī*, Patna University ms., pp. 36, 102, 129, and passim). In 1242/1826, accompanied by a large party of volunteers, he "migrated" from British India to the northwestern frontier tribal area, chosen for both religious and tactical reasons. The increasingly large segment of India under British control had been declared *dār al-ḥarb* as early as 1217/1801, so it was considered incumbent on Muslims to leave British India whenever possible (ʿAbd-al-ʿAzīz b. Walī-Allāh, *Fatāwā-ye ʿAzīzī*, Delhi, 1311/1893, I, p. 116). More importantly, Sayyed Aḥmad had been assured support by the area's battle-hardened Pathan chiefs, some of whom were nominally subservient to the Sikh kingdom. Though his primary interest was to combat the British, Sayyed Aḥmad became entangled in wars against Sikh commanders and local Pathan chiefs; his differences with the latter stemmed largely from his reformist ideas. He died while fighting a Sikh force at Balakot on 25 Ḏu'l-qaʿda 1246/8 May 1831. When his corpse was not immediately found, some of his followers developed the belief that he had not died but only disappeared temporarily; tracts were even written predicting his coming as Mahdi, though the belief faded with time (Walāyat ʿAlī, *Rasāʾel-e tesʿa*, Delhi, n.d., pp. 46-78; Q. Ahmad, *The Wahhabi Movement in India*, Calcutta, 1966, pp. 76-78).

Sayyed Aḥmad's actions and the movement resulting from them have to be viewed against the background of both the social and political disintegration of late eighteenth century India and the ideas and activities of Shah Walī-Allāh (d. 1176/1763). The latter's impact on Sayyed Aḥmad is evident in many respects, both substantive and procedural. For instance, Sayyed Aḥmad, like Shah Walī-Allāh, was considerably influenced by Sufi ideas and practices. He initiated people into Sufism first according to the four prevalent orders and then according to his own, the *Ṭarīqa-ye moḥammadīya* (Moḥammad Jaʿfar Thānesarī, *Tawārīḵ-e ʿajība*, Sadhaura, n.d., pp. 22-23). His *Ṣerāṭ-e mostaqīm* is composed on the lines of the Indo-Persian *malfūẓāt* (compilation of conversations); it discusses various mystical terms and practices, also dwelling upon jihad, which is not generally discussed in such works. He conceived of it mainly in religious and moral terms, but he was not oblivious to its political implications (*Makātīb*, pp. 28, 50, 131). He noted that "while rulers and statesmen have fallen into obscurity, foreigners from distant lands have become masters of Indian territories; it is the vendors of merchandise who have obtained sovereignty" (ibid., p. 102). He realized the importance of controlling the levers of political power in order to implement his reformist program (ibid., p. 188), but envisaged his task as the restoration of Indo-Muslim polity to a certain level and then a return to spiritual pursuits (ibid., pp. 81, 131).

Certain of Sayyed Aḥmad's ideas resembled those of Moḥammad b. ʿAbd-al-Waḥḥāb, the founder of the Wahhabi movement in Arabia, partly because of a common emphasis on the Koran and the Hadiths. But the Sufi influence, the brief spell of Mahdist fervor, and the strong political undercurrent are not evident in the Arabian antecedent. Due to the similarities, however, and the supposed influence of Arabian Wahhabism, Sayyed Aḥmad's adherents have come to be dubbed, incorrectly and misleadingly, Wahhabis or neo-Wahhabis (see, e.g., M. Mujeeb, *The Influence of Islam on Indian Society*, Meerut, 1972, pp. 84-85). The followers of Sayyed Aḥmad called themselves *mowaḥḥedīn* or *moḥammadīn* (*Rasāʾel-e tesʿa*, pp. 2, 70) and later *ahl-e ḥadīṯ*. The vigorous movement initiated by Sayyed Aḥmad evoked great sympathy among South Asian Muslims; though ultimately a failure, it drew attention to the threat of foreign domination and made a sustained effort to counter the British. Appealing to the masses rather than merely the élite of the Indo-Muslim community, it brought about significant social reforms. Negatively, its failure in the political field inspired alternative courses of action, including that which was to be advocated by his namesake, Sir Sayyed Aḥmad Khan, thus marking the beginning of the modernization of Indo-Muslim society.

Bibliography: See also Jaʿfar ʿAlī Naqwī, *Manẓūrat al-soʿadāʾ fī aḥwāl al-ḡozāt wa'l-šohadāʾ* or *Tārīḵ-e aḥmadī* (in Persian), mss. at Tonk and Lahore (covering the phase after Aḥmad's migration). Sayyed Aḥmad Khan, *Āṯār al-ṣanādīd* (Urdu), Delhi, 1941; repr. Karachi, 1974. Ḡolām-Rasūl Mehr, *Sayyed Aḥmad Šahīf* (Urdu), Karachi, 1954. M. A. Bari, "A Nineteenth-Century Muslim Reform Movement," in *Arabic and Islamic Studies in Honor of Hamilton A. R. Gibb*, ed. G. Makdisi, Cambridge, Mass., 1965, pp. 84-102. Storey, 1/2, pp. 1141-42. *EI*² I, pp. 282-83. *Urdu Encyclopaedia of Islam* II, Lahore, 1966, pp. 137-43.

(Q. AHMAD)

BARƎSMAN. See BARSOM.

BĀREZĀNĪ. See BĀRZĀNĪ.

BARF "snow" (from OIr. **vafra-* "snow," root *vap-* "to toss in the air, to pile up," cf. OInd. *vápati* "to disperse, to scatter," *vapra-* "heap, mound"; Pokorny, I, p. 1149; Mayrhofer, *Etymological Sanskrit Dictionary* III, pp. 144-45). This word and forms derived from it designate the snow in all western and most eastern Iranian languages and dialects; some East Iranian languages, Khotanese, Sogdian, Pashto, and Yidgha-Munji, have feminine forms derived from **vafrā-*, possibly an old collective plural (see Bailey, *Dictionary of Khotan Saka*, pp. 305-06). Other words for snow are found in Wakhi, which has *zəm* (cf. Av. *zyam-* "win-

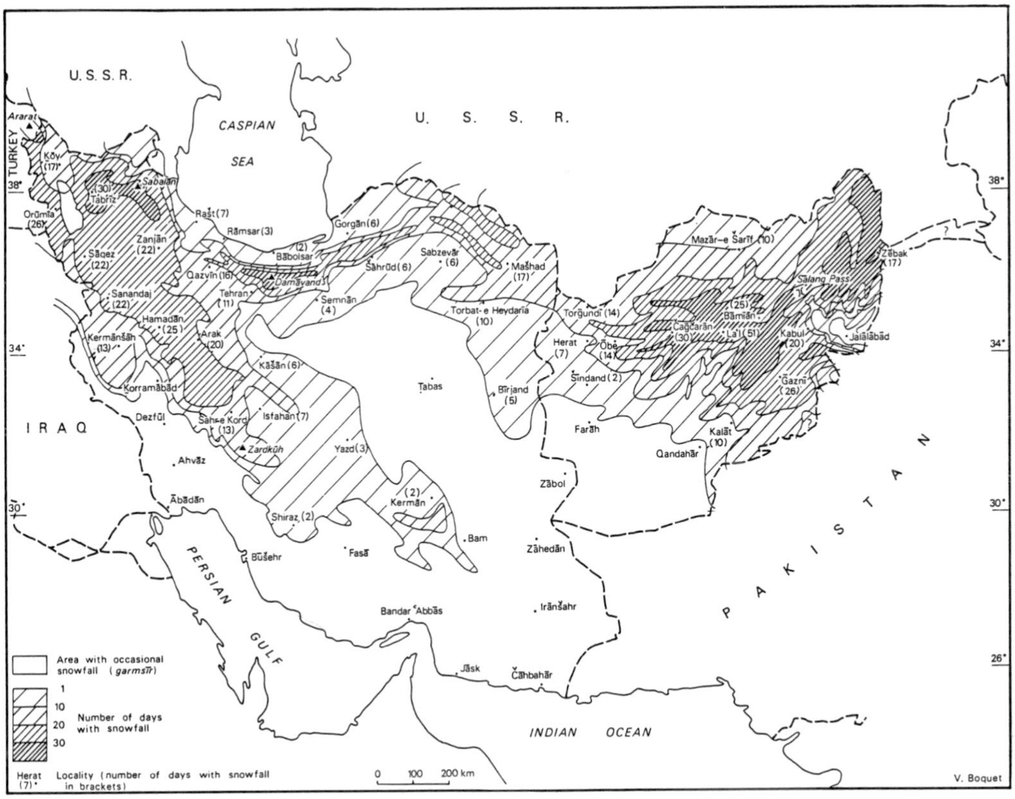

Figure 23. Snow in Iran and Afghanistan: Mean number of days in the year with snowfall

ter"), Shughni, which has *žinij* (cf. Av. *snaēža-* < OIr. **snaija-*), and Ossete, which has a loanword, Digor *met* and Iron *mit*.

If all Iranian languages have at least one word and sometimes several to designate snow, it is because snow is known in all the areas where these languages are currently spoken. There is a very clear contrast, however, between the southern part, which is largely inhospitable to habitation and where snow is only a negligible meteorological phenomenon, and the more densely settled northern part, where snow is, on the other hand, a major component of the climate, the landscape, and the framework of daily life.

On the tropical margins of the Irano-Afghan plateau, snow is in fact exceptional below an altitude of 1,000 meters. Not that it cannot fall in abundance there, but then it is a memorable event and as such duly recorded by local chroniclers (e.g., *Tārīḵ-e Sīstān*, pp. 174, 293). As a rule, snow falls rarely, once every ten or twenty years, and melts as soon as it touches the ground. From the Nangrahār basin in the east (a single day of snow has been recorded at Jalālābād between 1972 and 1983), to Ḵūzestān in the west (also one day of snow, at Dezfūl, between 1960 and 1979) and passing through the endorheic basins of Sīstān, Jāz Mūrīān, Lūt, and the Dašt-e Kavīr (two days of snow at Zaranj between 1969 and 1983, four at Zābol), the isarithm for one day of snow a year constitutes a good criterion for delimiting the type of geographic milieu traditionally called in Persian "warm lands" (*garmsīr*). When not too arid, warm lands offer nomads good winter pasturage precisely because they are never covered with snow (Figure 23). In the far south, on the shore of the Persian Gulf, precipitation in the form of snow is still rarer.

In the remaining two-thirds of the territory of Iran and Afghanistan snow is a common occurrence. The high average altitude and the continental climate favor the conversion into snow of most winter precipitation there and ensure its remaining on the ground; however, the frequency and abundance of snowfalls, on the one hand, and the duration and thickness of the snow cover, on the other, show great variations both in space and time.

The principal factors determining spatial variations in snowfall are altitude and latitude. Altitude appears to be the more important factor, to the degree that the snowfall map, like that of total precipitation, largely replicates the relief map (see Figure 23). The close correlation between altitude and snowfall can be illustrated by a section along the valley of the Harīrūd between Herat and Laʿl (Table 36) or, better still, along a single mountain slope.

The role of latitude is no less obvious; at identical altitudes of 1,300-1,350 meters, two days of snow a year on the average are received at Terīn Kōt (32° 37N), fourteen days at Ōbe (34° 22N), twenty days at Dar(r)a-ye Ṣūf (35° 55N), and twenty-eight days at Darwāz (38° 26N). Because of this fact, the snowfall isarithms drop lower toward the north; in Afghanistan the isarithm for twenty days of snow a year, which is at an altitude of 1,800 meters at Kabul (34° 33N), thus passes along the northern slopes of the central mountains (Qādes, Dara-ye Ṣūf) at 1,300 meters and along those of the Hindu Kush (Tāloqān, 36° 44N) at 800 meters. In western Iran the oblique course of the Zagros chain imposes on this snowfall gradient a northwest-southeast orientation, with, on average, thirty days of snow a year at Tabrīz (1,349 meters, 38° 08 N), twenty at Arak (1,753 meters, 34° 60 N), seven at Isfahan (1,570 meters, 32° 19 N), and three at Yazd (1,230 meters, 31° 54 N).

On a regional level, the extreme continental climate of lower central Asia disturbs the regularity of this pattern. Because the low-lying plains of Afghan Turkistan and northern Khorasan lie in a zone of very stable winter anticyclonic air, they are so dry that, despite their high latitude, snowfalls are infrequent and the snow cover does not last long below altitudes of 1,200-1,500 meters. This also explains why nomadic wintering is possible in such an area, which is obviously not warm land (see, for example, Mazār-e Šarīf, Table 36).

Finally, the role of exposure must be mentioned; it is especially significant in intramontane basins, which are sheltered from moist western winds (the principal carriers of snow) and, for this reason, enjoy abnormally light snowfall: Bāmīān, at an elevation of 2,550 meters, records only twenty-five days with snowfall a year and Zēbāk (2,600 meters) in Badaḵšān only seventeen; furthermore, since the beginning of meteorological observation, the depth of snow cover has never exceeded 11 centimeters at the latter station (70 centimeters at Bāmīān).

Temporal variations in snowfall. These are expressed in both the great irregularity in snowfall from year to year and in the unequal duration of the snowy season. In both instances, altitude remains the determining factor; the lower the altitude and therefore the rarer the snow, the greater the annual variation (Table 36, column 2) and the shorter the snowy season (Table 37).

Up to an altitude of about 2,500 meters, snowfall is spread over five or six months (November to March or April), except along a narrow transitional zone at the edge of the warm lands, where the snow season does not exceed three months (December-February). Occasional snowfalls can, however, take place as early as October, especially in northern latitudes (Afghan Turkistan, northern Khorasan). The snow showers of spring are particularly feared because of the irreparable damage that the snow can cause to young trees. At these moderate altitudes, the maximum snowfall and minimum temperature always coincide; they generally occur in January, except on the Caspian littoral, where both tend to shift into February because of the maritime climate, which moderates early winter temperatures and thus counteracts snowy precipitation. In any case, the snowy season is everywhere interspersed with thaws (described as *barf-ḵōrak* "snow eaters" if they are rainy), which periodically bring about melting of the normally thin snow cover (20-30 centimeters' normal thickness, with records above one meter). The intermittent presence of snow on the ground is thus the rule here, even though its cumulative duration can be high (an average of six weeks at Kabul, with recorded extremes of eighty-seven days in 1974-75 and of six days in 1978-79).

Above an altitude of 2,500 meters snowfall conditions change radically. First of all, the snowy season lasts longer, up to more than half the year; it snows frequently until May, and the maximum snowfall occurs toward the end of winter, approaching, even coinciding with, the maximum monthly precipitation. Above 3,000 meters, only the two or three hottest months of the year are without snowfall. On the high southern slopes of the Hindu Kush, exposed to the Indian monsoon (south Sālang), as on the summits of the Alborz (Demāvand, 'Alamkūh, Sabalān) and the Zagros (Zardkūh), which exceed 4,000 meters, it can snow at any time, including high summer. It is also above 2,500 meters that winter precipitation falls exclusively in solid form and that the persistence of the cold brings with it an uninterrupted snow cover lasting several months. The depth of the snow exceeds 50 centimeters between 2,500 and 3,000 meters and a full meter at higher elevations; drifts can reach more than 10 meters, as on the high plain of Kūhrang in the central Zagros (Preu, p. 54), and as a result avalanches are common.

Finally, at very high altitudes there are perennial snowfields and local glaciers. The snow line is located around 4,150 meters on the northern slopes of the Alborz (Taḵt-e Solaymān) and on the northeast face of Demāvand, 4,500 meters in Azerbaijan (Sabalān), and 4,000-4,200 meters in the central Zagros (Zardkūh, Šīrkūh). In more continental and drier Afghanistan the snowline rises toward 4,600-4,800 meters on the northern slopes of the central Hindu Kush (in the region of the Sālang pass) and 5,000-5,200 meters in its eastern (high Monjān valley, Pamirs) and western (Kūh-e Bābā) parts. On certain well-sheltered shady slopes, however, small cliff glaciers and firns are found at considerably lower altitudes, e.g., 4,200 and 3,500 meters respectively in the Sālang region. On the southern slopes, the snowline is about 400 meters above the levels cited.

Overall, the glaciated area is limited; there are no more than about 3,000 square kilometers of glaciers in Afghanistan (Pulyarkin, p. 6) and still fewer in Iran, where there is only a single valley glacier, the 'Alamčāl glacier in the Taḵt-e Solaymān massif (Alborz), which is nearly 4 kilometers long at an altitude between 3,900 and 4,200 meters. Flanked entirely by moraines and covered with rocks for almost its entire length, it moves very slowly. It is fed mostly by avalanches and the accumulation of wind-drifted snow.

During the cold periods of the Quaternary, the

Table 36

SNOW PROFILES IN AFGHANISTAN
(Year of record: September-August. Number of years of record variable)

Stations (with elevation)	Mean number of days with snowfall (in brackets, minimum and maximum recorded)	Mean number of days with snow on the ground (in brackets, minimum and maximum recorded)	Maximum snow depth recorded (with date)
I. *The latitudinal effect*			
S-N profile along the 62° E meridian:			
Šīndand (1150 m)	2 (0-4)	1 (0-7)	14 cm (15.1.77)
Herat (965 m)	7 (0-23)	7 (0-16)	45 cm (12.1.69)
Torḡundī (680 m)	14 (9-18)	20 (0-40)	44 cm (22.1.77)
Afghan Turkestan:			
Mazār-e Šarīf (380 m)	10 (2-23)	11 (3-36)	45 cm (25.1.77)
II. *The altitudinal effect*			
W-E profile between 34° and 35° N:			
Harīrūd valley			
Herat (965 m)	7 (0-23)	7 (0-16)	45 cm (12.1.69)
Ōbē (1300 m)	14 (11-18)	20 (9-34)	70 cm (15.12.80)
Čaḡčarān (2230 m)	30 (15-46)	77 (35-96)	62 cm (14.2.75)
Laʿl (2800 m)	51 (19-74)	115 (79-142)	99 cm (25.1.77)
South Sālang (3170 m)	78 (49-107)	172 (156-214)	520 cm (15.1.66)
North Sālang (3365 m)	98 (62-128)	193 (170-231)	460 cm (2.1.66)

Table 37

MONTHLY DISTRIBUTION OF DAYS WITH SNOWFALL ACCORDING TO ALTITUDINAL BELTS IN IRAN AND AFGHANISTAN

Altitude	Number of stations recorded	Mean annual number of days with snowfall	Monthly distribution of days with snowfall (%)							
			O	N	D	J	F	M	A	My
Iran:										
0-1000 m	9	6	—	3	15	38	30	13	1	—
1000-2000 m	20	12	—	4	19	36	25	13	3	—
2000-2500 m	1	13	—	3	25	35	22	11	4	—
Total	30	10	—	4	18	36	26	13	3	—
Afghanistan:										
0-1000 m	20	13	—	5	16	40	26	13	—	—
1000-2000 m	18	16	—	2	19	36	29	14	—	—
2000-2500 m	12	27	—	3	18	30	28	18	3	—
2500-3000 m	6	35	—	7	15	20	23	23	11	1
above 3000 m	3	71	5	8	13	17	17	18	14	8
Total	59	22	1	5	16	30	25	17	5	1

The figures have been rounded. Stations with less than one snowfall in the year have been omitted.

snow line was located about 1,000 meters lower than the present line, and glaciers had descended as far as 2,300 meters on the northern slopes of the central Hindu Kush, an area which is today entirely within the zone of permanent settlement. The line had even dipped below 2,000 meters on the northern piedmont of the Kermān mountains.

The significant snowfall on the Irano-Afghan highlands imposes serious constraints on their inhabitants. In the mountains, avalanches (*bahman* in Iran, *barfkōč* in Afghanistan) represent a real danger. Because of the generally heavy but brief snowfall and the usually large, bare, and rectangular mountain slopes, which do not hold snow well, avalanches of powdery snow are the most frequent. Avalanches can occur during snowfalls, notably when there is a storm; but they occur most often soon after the snow stops, when it begins to melt and thus becomes heavier on the surface. This type of avalanche can be triggered across wide areas, completely sweeping a slope over more than 1,000 meters. On the other hand, spring avalanches of heavy snow are rarer and channeled through fairly narrow corridors; these are unleashed when the first thaw or interlude of mild, rainy weather loosens the masses of snow accumulated during the winter on the summits of the slopes. In general, avalanches pose a serious threat only at well-defined times of the year; they are rare during the cold, clear, sunny periods of the winter.

In order to shelter caravans from snowstorms and to permit them to wait out series of consecutive avalanches, small "mountain caravansaries" (Siroux, pp. 35ff.) used to be built on the principal routes across the Alborz. Winter traffic, however, always has been quite limited in the mountains, because snow closes the passes from December to April in the Alborz and from October to May in the Hindu Kush. The modern highway network built for automobile traffic has resulted in the construction of tunnels to ensure the permanence of the great road links across the mountains. The one-way tunnel through the Kendovān pass (2,750 meters) was dug in 1937 on the Tehran-Čālūs road. Since 1982, it has been augmented to the east by the tunnels between Tehran and Sārī on the Fīrūzkūh road. In the Hindu Kush, the two-way Sālang tunnel (3,360 meters) between Kabul and Afghan Turkistan was not opened till 1343 Š./1964. Several modern routes have also been provided with protection against avalanches (e.g., the Harāz road between Tehran and Amol in 1964 and the Sālang road). Though, thanks to modern equipment, state authorities can clear the major roads, the same is not true of the secondary road system, which is put back into service each year only after the thaw, often by the users themselves.

The great difficulties in communication caused by snowfall explain why, in winter, village life comes to a standstill in the mountains. Once the livestock are shut up in the stables, peasant communities turn in on themselves and live, for long months, totally cut off from the outside world. Even within the villages the narrow lanes are blocked by snow cleared off the flat roofs, so that tunnels must sometimes be dug out to permit passage from one house to another (Iven, p. 41). Nor are the large cities spared; in Tehran, as in Kabul, it is not rare for heavy snowfall to paralyze traffic and social life totally. This situation seems to reflect not only objective technical difficulties but also mental attitudes rooted in the more or less distant rural past of the great majority of city dwellers.

On the other hand, the heavy mountain snowfall offers decisive advantages for rural life. Snow constitutes an important reservoir of water for the soil and vegetation, while at the same time providing insulation against frost. In contrast to the rainfall, which runs off, melted snow soaks deep into the ground, which is very advantageous for the pasturage and unirrigated cereals. Dry-farmed wheat, whether the winter wheat of Iran or the spring wheat of Afghanistan, given sufficient winter snowfall, can grow properly, even if the spring rains fail. Farther down, along the valleys and on the piedmonts, melting snow swells the rivers and refills the aquifers, which favors spring and even summer irrigation. Overall, it is on winter snowfall, rather than on spring rains, that the level of agricultural production in most of Iran and Afghanistan depends. Popular wisdom aptly celebrates the benefits of snow in a series of sayings, of which the most widespread in Afghanistan conforms to the following pattern: *Kabul* (or whatever other locality) *bī zar šawa(d), bī barf našawa(d)*, "Kabul can live without gold, but not without snow."

Snow itself also plays an important economic role. For centuries it was the sole means of cooling drinks and making sherbets in the large towns of Iran and Afghanistan. Two types of supply traditionally coexisted: In winter snow was collected in urban or suburban snow pits (*barfdān*) or snow caves (*barf-ambār*), where it was preserved until summer; at the same time, the closest mountain firns were exploited, which gave rise to a thriving snow trade from antiquity onward. The towns in Iran and Afghanistan were thus supplied with snow by caravans, traveling for the most part by night to bring snow from neighboring mountains (a maximum distance of 50 to 60 kilometers). Today the construction of commercial ice factories and the spread of refrigerators have ruined this trade (it disappeared around 1960 at Kermānšāh and Tehran). In the central Alborz, however, snow continued to be used until about 1975 to cool drinks and fruit on festive occasions. Industrial backwardness and limited electrification explain why the snow trade has declined much less in Afghanistan than in Iran; quite recently several large commercial truck delivery routes, originating in the firns of the Sālang pass and radiating out toward Kabul, Jalālābād, and Mazār-e Šarīf have developed.

Another kind of economic exploitation of snow in the form of winter sports for tourists was introduced quite recently in Iran. This business exists only on the southern slopes of the Tehran Alborz, where, after the construction of a snow bowl at Āb-e ʿAlī (ca. 1960), the Iranian Ski Federation undertook the building of genuine ski resorts. First built was the one at Šemšak (1966); then came one at Dīzīn (1970). Both are well-equipped and attract a growing number of sportsmen. The Towčāl massif, which dominates Tehran, has had mechanical ski lifts since 1980. There is nothing comparable in Afghanistan, where the Kabul bourgeoisie is content with the simpler pleasures of tobogganing at Qarḡa, at the gates of the capital, and where the foreign colony introduced cross-country skiing in the 1970s.

Iranian civilization, in the broad sense, has been ambivalent in relation to snow. Numerous expressions in the spoken language refer to snow, and a rich vocabulary exists for describing its different forms (Dehḵodā, s.v. *barf*); this vernacular vocabulary, often very little known, grows richer, as is logical, the higher the terrain. The word for snow also occurs in the formation of different toponyms (i.e., Barfak, a form in which the suffix *-ak* has a locative sense: "place where there is a great deal of snow"; Barfa, a form probably derived from the preceding one; Barfīān and Barfrīz, forms resulting from commercial exploitation of snow; etc.). The frequent mountain names in Kūh-e Sefīd or Sefīdkūh (Pashto, Spīngar) also refer to it indirectly. It has an important place in folklore related to winter, especially to its beginning, *šab-e čella*. Children also know how to take advantage of it to diversify their games (*barfī kardan* and *barf jangī* "snow fights"; van Oudenhoven, pp. 56, 68). Finally, snow constitutes a recurrent literary theme, notably in classical poetry.

Iranian material culture, on the other hand, shows many signs of failure to adapt to snow. The ubiquity of houses with flat terraced or slightly gabled roofs is a particularly striking example. To prevent roofs from collapsing and water from leaking in, snow must be rapidly cleared away whenever there is a heavy snowfall. This is an arduous task, not without risks, which, in towns, is often performed by laborers hired especially for this purpose (*barfī* in Iran, *barf-pāk* in Kabul). Even the most exposed high mountain villages are unacquainted with any form of protection against avalanches. The traditional clothing and means of transport also show no signs of adaptation, except for the existence of special shoes (*mūšag*) and particularly snowshoes, which have been noted among the Hazāra of Šahrestān and their neighbors the Taymanī of Ḡōr (Šahrestānī, pp. 181, 73). It is doubtless significant that the term denoting these last (respectively *čawḡāl* in Šahrestān and *čawḡān* in Taymanī country) is of Turkish, not Iranian origin.

Bibliography: The basic documentation comes from national meteorological yearbooks. The figures are based on the period 1960-1979 (with a few gaps) for Iran and for Afghanistan on all the data from the beginning of observations (which varies, depending on the station) up to and through 1983. Supplementary data have been drawn from the compilation by M. Alex, *Klimadaten ausgewählter Stationen des Vorderen Orients*, Supplement to Tübinger Atlas des Vorderen Orients, Series A, no. 14, Wiesbaden, 1985.

The data on snow are always very superficial. The absence of any information on the intensity of snowfalls and their cumulative depth prevents calculation of even an approximate proportion of snow in the total monthly or annual precipitation. Furthermore, the exact duration of snow cover on the ground has been recorded only since 1974 in Afghanistan and not at all in Iran. Finally, the single consistently usable figure for the majority of weather stations is the number of days with snowfall. Despite its crude character, it has been used to construct the snowfall map and to define the different types of snowfall systems.

The lack of data doubtless explains why snowfall remains one of the least known chapters in Irano-Afghan climatology. The classic climatic monographs accord it only a few, generally imprecise lines, and none provides a map. Among the most useful on this subject, despite their dates, are: E. Stenz, "Precipitation, Evaporation and Aridity in Afghanistan," *Acta Geophysica Polonica* 5, 1957, pp. 245-66; and, for its very detailed notes, H.-E. Iven, *Das Klima von Kabul*, Breslau, 1933. The accounts of travelers do not fail to comment on the difficulties encountered because of snow, and an examination of them, as well as of historical chronicles and even diplomatic reports, is very suggestive. A first use of such accounts, still very incomplete, has been made in C. Melville, "Meterological Hazards and Disasters in Iran: A Preliminary Survey to 1950," *Iran* 22, 1984, pp. 113-50 (see especially pp. 136-39). Among studies specifically devoted to snow A. Roch, "Avalanche Danger in Iran," *Journal of Glaciology* 3, 1961, pp. 979-83, and N. Rostaqī and R. V. Tskhvitava, *Arzyābī-e moqaddamātī dar mawred-e ḏaḵāyer-e barfī-e kūhhā-ye Afḡānestān*, Kabul, 1358 Š./1979, can be cited.

The question of the present snow line and its shifts in the Quaternary is better known, thanks to a number of geomorphological observations. One should begin with the two survey articles by C. Rathjens, "Fragen der horizontalen und vertikalen Landschaftsgliederung im Hochgebirgssystem des Hindukusch," and G. Schweizer, "Klimatisch bedingte geomorphologische und glaziologische Züge der Hochregion vorderasiatischer Gebirge (Iran und Ostanatolien)," conveniently brought together in C. Troll, ed., *Geoecology of the High-Mountain Regions of Eurasia*, Erdwissenschaftliche Forschung 4, Wiesbaden, 1972, pp. 205-20, 221-36. To the bibliography provided, one can add C. P. Péguy, "Les glaciers de l'Elbourz," *Bulletin de l'Association de géographes français* 284-85, 1959, pp. 44-49; and P. Bout et al., "Observations de géographie physique en Iran septentrional," *Mémoires et documents du C.D.C.G.* 8, 1961, pp. 9-101. Supplementary observations can be found in M. Kuhle, *Beiträge zur Quartärmorphologie SE-iranischer Hochgebirge: Die quartäre Vergletscherung des Kuh-i-Jupar*, Göttinger Geographische Abhandlungen 67, Göttingen, 1976; and C. Preu, *Die quartäre Vergletscherung der inneren Zardeh-Kuh-Gruppe (Zardeh-Kuh-Massiv), Zagros/Iran*, Augsburger Geographische Hefte 4, Augsburg, 1984. An estimate of the present glaciated surface in Afghanistan is given in V. A. Pulyarkin, *Afghanistan: Ekonomicheskaya geografiya*, Moscow, 1964.

Studies on relations between man and snow are also very few. For Iran the essential reference is A. Enjavī, *Jašnhā wa ādāb wa moʿtaqadāt-e zemestān*, Tehran, 1975. For Afghanistan, the subject has only been touched on by Ḡ.-Ḥ. Yagāna, "Zemestān-e mardom-e Ḡōr," *Farhang-e mardom* 6/2, 1362

Š./1983, pp. 165-88, which is useful only for its dialectological information, which should be supplemented by that of Š. ʿA. A. Šahrestānī, *Qāmūs-e lahja-ye darī-e hazāragī*, Kabul, 1361 Š./1983. N. J. A. van Oudenhoven, *Common Afghan Street Games*, Lisse, 1979, describes snow games. On mountain caravansaries, see M. Siroux, *Caravansérails d'Iran et petites constructions routières*, Mémoires de l'Institut Français d'Archéologie Orientale 81, Cairo, 1949. The question of the trade in snow is the only one to have been treated in depth. The general features are outlined in X. de Planhol, "Lineamenti generali del commercio della neve nel Mediterraneo e nel Medio Oriente," *Bollettino della Società Geografica Italiana*, ser. 10, vol. 2, fasc. 7-12, 1973, pp. 315-39. For more details, one should turn to B. Hourcade, "Le ramassage de la neige en haute vallée de Djadj-e Roud (Elbourz central, Iran)," *Revue de géographie alpine* 63/1, 1975, pp. 147-49; X. de Planhol, "Le commerce de la neige en Afghanistan," *Revue de géographie alpine* 62/2, 1974, pp. 269-76; X. de Planhol and F. Denizot, "La neige qui vient du Salang," *Afghanistan Journal* 4/2, 1977, pp. 74-75; and R. A. Watson, "The Snow Sellers of Mangalat, Iran," *Anthropos* 59, 1964, pp. 904-10.

The development of winter sports in the Tehran Alborz has been studied by E. Ehlers, T. Kröger, and T. Rahnemaee, "Formen nationalen Fremdenverkehrs in einem islamischen Land: Das vorrevolutionäre Iran," *Orient* (Hamburg) 24/1, 1983, pp. 95-133, especially pp. 108-14.

The place of the snow theme in classical Persian poetry can be appreciated from a reading of C.-H. de Fouchécour, *La description de la nature dans la poésie lyrique persane du XIe siècle*, Paris, 1969, passim. On snow in popular customs of Khorasan see ʿA. Qaysarī, "Marāsem-e awwalīn barf-e sāl," *Āyanda* 12/9-10, 1365 Š./1986-87, pp. 570-78.

(D. BALLAND, B. HOURCADE, AND C. M. KIEFFER)

BĀRFORŪŠĪ, MOLLĀ **MOḤAMMAD-ʿALĪ,** important figure in early Babism (1239-65/1823-49). He is generally referred to in Babi sources as Ḥażrat-e Qoddūs or Esm-Allāh al-Āḵer and in Bahai works as Noqṭa-ye Oḵrā (in contrast to Noqṭa-ye Ūlā, a title of the Bāb). Born the son of a farmer in Bārforūš (Bābol), he studied there, in Sārī, and in Mašhad before going to Karbalāʾ in 1256/1840-41, where he studied for some four years under Sayyed Kāẓem Raštī (q.v.), head of the Shaikhi school (q.v.). In 1260/1844, he became the last of the group of Shaikhis who accepted Sayyed ʿAlī-Moḥammad Šīrāzī (see BĀB) as Raštī's successor and *bāb al-emām*. Leaving Shiraz in September, 1844, he accompanied Sayyed Moḥammad-Salī on the *ḥajj*, returning with him to Būšehr in May, 1845. Bārforūšī went ahead alone to Shiraz, where, following an incident in the Šamšīrgarān mosque, he and two fellow Babis were arrested and expelled from the town. Going to Kermān, he met and tried unsuccessfully to convert Ḥājī Mollā Moḥammad Karīm Khan Kermānī (q.v.), who was already seeking leadership of the Shaikhi school for himself, after which he returned to Māzandarān, where he remained in comparative seclusion for some two years. In 1847, he went to Mašhad, where Mollā Moḥammad-Ḥosayn Bošrūʾī (q.v.) had already established an important center for the propagation of Babism, and assisted the latter in his activities there. Following the outbreak of difficulties with the local authorities, Bārforūšī again set off for Māzandarān, where he played a major role in organizing the gathering of leaders of the sect in the village of Badašt, at which the abrogation of the Islamic *Šarīʿa* and the advent of the *qīāma* were announced. Following this, he was imprisoned for some time in Sārī, but succeeded in effecting his escape in order to join the Babi defenders at the shrine of Shaikh Ṭabarsī near Bārforūš. Here, he was accorded high honors by Bošrūʾī and his followers, being regarded as the Qāʾem (Hidden Imam) in person, in tandem with Bošrūʾī himself. According to one source (ʿAbbās Effendi ʿAbd-al-Bahāʾ, *Makātīb-e ʿAbd-al-Bahāʾ* II, Cairo, 1330/1912, p. 254; cf. p. 252), he even claimed to be God in a work written during this period. Following the surrender of the Babi survivors at Shaikh Ṭabarsī, he was taken to Bārforūš and put to death there on 23 Jomādā II 1265/16 May 1849. His grave there was until recently in the possession of the Bahais, who regard it as a shrine. Few of the apparently voluminous writings of Bārforūšī have survived.

Bibliography: Details may be found in the general historical works listed under BABISM; brief biographies exist in M. A. Malek Ḵosravī *Tārīḵ-e šohadā-ye amr* I, Tehran, 130 *Badīʿ*/1352 Š./1973-74, pp. 58-82, 404-14, and passim. Mīrzā Asad-Allāh Fāżel Māzandarānī, *Ketāb-e ẓohūr al-ḥaqq* III, Cairo, n.d., pp. 405-30. See also idem, *Asrār al-āṯār*, 5 vols., Tehran, 124-29 *Badīʿ*/1347-53 Š./1968-74, IV, pp. 477-88. On Bārforūšī's messianic role, see Ḥājī Mīrzā Jānī Kāšānī, ed. E. G. Browne, *Kitāb-i-Nuqṭatu'l-Kāf*, London, 1910, pp. 152, 199, 202. On works by Bārforūšī see D. M. MacEoin, *Early Babi Doctrine and History: A Survey of Source Materials* (forthcoming). See also Eʿteżād-al-Salṭana, *Fetna-ye Bāb*, ed. ʿA.-Ḥ. Navāʾī, Tehran, 1362 Š./1983, index, s.v. M.-ʿA. Bārforūšī.

(D. M. MACEOIN)

BARG-E BŪ (or *deraḵt-e ġār*; Eng. laurel and sweet bay), *Laurus nobilis*, the most popular species of the family Lauracea, the one used for laurel wreaths. The tree is common in Persian gardens. It has stiff, dull green leaves, which, when dry, are used to flavor food, and edible purple, sweet, and fragrant fruits. The oil extracted from the fruit has a spicy odor and is officinal. The tree contains essential oil (1.25 percent in the leaves); the fruit contains fatty oil (28 percent in the pulp, 72 percent in the seeds).

The laurel family has alternate, simple, often evergreen, exstipulate leaves; panicles or umbels of flowers; and one-seeded drupes or berries. The species is mostly represented in Brazil and southwestern

Asia. Trees of the genus *Laurus* are native to the Mediterranean region. They are characterized by dark, evergreen leaves, inconspicuous, dioecious flowers in little axillary umbels and small, succulent, purple, cherry-like berries. They are usually about 5-6 m tall but may attain three times this height.

Bibliography: *Encyclopaedia Americana* III, 1963, p. 358; XVII, 1952, p. 97. H. P. Kelsey and W. A. Dayton, *Standardized Plant Names*, Harrisburg, Pa., 1942, p. 329. I. V. Palivin, "Lauraceae," in *Flora of U.S.S.R.* VII, 1937, p. 572. A. Parsa, *Flore de l'Iran*, Tehran, IV, 1949, p. 1191; VII, 1959, p. 85; VIII, 1960, p. 110. Ḥ. Ṯābetī, *Jangalhā, deraḵtān o deraḵtčahā-ye Īrān*, 2nd ed., Tehran, 1355 Š./1976.

(A. PARSA)

BARGOSTVĀN, armor, specifically horse armor, a distinctive feature of Iranian warfare from very early times on. The earliest known chamfron has been excavated at Ḥasanlū from a 9th-century B.C. stratum (M. A. Littauer and J. H. Crouvel, "Ancient Iranian Horse Helmets?" *Iranica Antiqua* 19, 1984, pp. 41-52 pl. VIII, esp. pp. 48-49). Evidence for horse defenses made from iron ringlets, however, appears considerably later at Dura Europos. The site, within the sphere of Iranian influence, has been dated by R. Ghirshman (*Parthes et Sassanides*, Paris, 1962, pl. 63, p. 52) and others to second and third century A.D. A rough sketch on a wall distinctly depicts a horseman in combined mail and lame body armor mounted on a war horse in a mail caparison. Later, in the fifth or late sixth to early seventh century A.D., depending on which date is given to the rock relief at Ṭāq-e Bostān near Kermānšāh (Bāḵtarān; ibid., pp. 192-93 and pl. 235), we have a unique instance in antiquity of a king in full armor mounting a horse wearing what appears to be a heavy defense (made of iron ringlets?) covered by a layer of fabric of sorts, with tassels.

In early Islamic times the word *bargost(o)vān* seems to have referred essentially to chain-mail defenses. Its earliest entry in a Persian dictionary, the 8th/14th century *Ṣeḥāḥ al-fors* by Moḥammad b. Hendūšāh Naḵjavānī (2nd ed., ʿA.-ʿA. Ṭāʿatī, Tehran, 2535 = 1355 Š./1976, p. 233) loosely defines it as "a defense [Persian *pūšeš*, used with that specialized meaning] thrown on horses in wartime." But early poetry is more informative. In the *Šāh-nāma*, its invention is attributed to Jamšēd in a passage praising his ability to make iron soft "by Kayanian glory" (*be-farr-e kayī*; ed. Mohl, I, p. 39; Moscow, I, p. 39). It is frequently associated with the *jowšan*, which we know to be a coat of mail. When Gēv leaves the battlefield after defeating the Turanians, their *bargostvān*s are ripped apart (*čāk-čāk*, used of iron, not fabric; *Šāh-nāma*, ed. Mohl, III, p. 202).

In pitched battle the way to deal with the *bargostvān* is to use a *ḵadang* wood arrow. As Hajīr shoots a volley of such arrows at Andarīmān, one of them goes through the saddle and the *bargostvān*, killing the horse (ibid., III, p. 546). Farroḵī Sīstānī (*Divān*, ed. M. Dabīrsīāqī, Tehran, 1349 Š./1970, p. 334, vv. 6729-30) compares the asters with "... silver studs which for the sake of fiery battle / Are stuck on the bluish ringlets (*ḡeybahā*) of the *bargostvān*." ʿOnṣorī at about the same time (ed. M. Dabīrsīāqī, Tehran, 1342 Š./1963, p. 253 v. 2382) writes these punning lines: "How would water stay in a sieve? So do stay / His arrows in the ringlets of the coat of mail (*jowšan*) and the *bargostvān*." ʿAbd-al-Wāseʿ Jabalī, who died in 555/1160, coined this vivid image showing that the ringlets could still be left apparent in his day: "Until the moment when from so much blood on the body of his Šabdēz (name of Ḵosrow II's mount in the *Šāh-nāma*)/The ringlets of the *bargostvān* became studded with garnets" (ʿAbd-al-Wāseʿ Jabalī, *Dīvān*, ed. Ḏ. Ṣafā, I, *Qaṣāyed*, Tehran, 1339 Š./1960, p. 301, where it is incorrectly noted; accurate version in Sorūrī, *Majmaʿ al-fors*, ed. M. Dabīrsīāqī, 3 vols., Tehran, 1338 Š./1959; I, p. 183). A famous line by Saʿdī confirms that chain mail *bargostvān*, which continued to be associated with the *jowšan*, was in common use in the 7th/13th century: "As for thee, thou art in no need of *jowšan* and *bargostovān*/On battle day, thou wrapst thyself in the mail [*zereh*] of the hair" (*Ḡazalīyāt-e Saʿdī*, ed. M. ʿA. Forūḡī, Tehran, 1342 Š./1963, p. 16).

It is difficult to ascertain at which stage a second type of *bargostvān* made of iron lames joined with mail and a variant made of iron scales appeared in Iran. The evidence of literary metaphors shows that they were in use at least as early as the 6th/12th century. When describing animals the anonymous author of the *Sendbād-nāma* (quoted under *bargostvān* by Dehḵodā) remarks that "the fish does not don [its] mail garment [*zereh*] nor the tortoise [its] *bargostvān*" in reference to the scale-like appearance of mail and the lamellar pattern of tortoise shell with its deep grooves separating roughly rectangular patches. The image recurs in the mid-8th/14th century in a panegyric to Shaikh Abū Esḥāq, the ruler of Fārs: "And for fear of your might, in the depths of the Indian Ocean—The fish forever wears [its] mail garment [*zereh*] and the tortoise its *bargostvān*" (ʿObayd Zākānī, *Kollīyāt*, ed. ʿA. Eqbāl, Tehran, 1352 Š./1963, p. 14). It is this lamellar type of horse armor that Giosafat Barbaro (q.v.), the Venetian ambassador to the court of Uzun Ḥasan, describes in a passage to which attention was drawn (with incorrect identification of the shah) by Hans Stöcklein (*Survey of Persian Art* VI, p. 2560, citing W. Thomas, translator of J. Barbaro and A. Contarini, *Travels to Tana and Persia*, London, 1873, p. 66).

The two types would appear to have been used concurrently, judging from literature as well as miniature painting (on which see below). However, the lamellar type alone survives through a handful of specimens in Istanbul, Paris (Musée de l'Armée), New York (The Metropolitan Museum of Art), and Bern (Kunsthistorisches Museum, Charlottenfels) which have been assigned various dates (14th, 15th, 16th century) and provenances, ranging from Iran and Turkey to Mamluk Egypt. A systematic study of the extant material (some of which is composite, as those in The Metropolitan Museum) must be undertaken before putting forward any regional attributions.

A fourth type of *bargostvān* was constructed on the same lines as the *kažāgand*—a defense only recently identified (A. S. Melikian-Chirvani, "The Westward Journey of the Kazhagand," *The Arms and Armour Society* 12/1, June, 1983, pp. 8-35), mail covered with silk waste (Persian *kaj/kaž*) glued on and concealed from sight by brocaded silk (*dībā*) with a silk lining inside. The full name *bargostvān-e kajīn* or *kažīn*, literally "the silk-waste *bargostvān*," was commonly shortened to either *bargostvān* or *kajīm*. The latter form is entered by Jamāl-al-Dīn Ḥosayn Enjū Šīrāzī in the *Farhang-e jahāngīrī* (ed. R. ʿAfīfī, 3 vols., Mašhad, 1351 Š./1972-1354 Š./1975, I, p. 715) as "a *bargostvān* padded inside with silk waste." Under *ğayba* (ibid., II, p. 2323), the lexicographer specified that it is used for making *kajīm*. It is to this type that references such as Bayhaqī's in the 5th/11th century may apply. When describing elephants in the Ghaznavid army, the Iranian historian mentions "the males with brocade *bargostvāns*..." (*Tārīḵ-e Bayhaqī*, ed. Adīb, p. 424, quoted by Dehḵodā). Things had not substantially changed on 21 Rajab 823/28 July 1420 when, in the battle opposing the Timurid army of Šāhroḵ and the Turkmen led by Qarā Yūsof, the former had "war elephants equipped with (their) armament and *kajīm*" (Ḥasan Rūmlū [Tehran], p. 128). A serious investigation has yet to be conducted through book painting to determine whether statistical evidence points to prevalence of any one type at a given time and, perhaps, in a given area. From a survey of the limited number of combat scenes adequately reproduced in color, it is clear that different types would be used simultaneously. In a double page from a *Ẓafar-nāma* described by authors as having been painted at Shiraz in 1436 (this writer has not seen the colophon) a *bargostvān* made of iron scales is mounted by Tīmūr, while the horses of an amir charging on and two other warriors wear defenses made from iron lames (*The Treasures of Islam*, Geneva, 1985, p. 59). In a *Šāh-nāma* page from a manuscript said to have been illustrated in Gīlān in 1494 (ibid., p. 63), scale armor may be seen on one horse. Lamellar horse defenses, constructed like the lamellar cuirasses (*derʿ*) worn by horsemen, also appear. Thirty years or so later, the *Šāh-nāma* executed for Shah Ṭahmāsb includes some very precise representations of lamellar horse defenses (ibid., pl. 52.1; 53.4), as well as of quilted defenses, stiff and heavy (with chain mail sewn inside or padding only?). Some other representations show shaped pieces of (varnished?) material that is likely to be highly resistant rhinoceros (*karg*) from which leather horse armor mentioned in Persian literature was made. The body of textual and visual evidence of which these are but selected examples makes it clear that the *bargostvān* played an important role in Iranian military tradition from pre-Islamic times down to the Safavid period. The value set upon horse defenses may be inferred from these lines in Šaraf-al-Dīn Bedlīsī's *Šaraf-nāma* (V. Veliamine-Zernof, ed., *Scheref-Nameh ou histoire des Kourdes par Scheref, prince de Bidlis*, St. Petersburg, 1862, II [Persian], p. 252): " At the time when Shah Esmāʿīl (II) entrusted this writer with inspecting the treasury (*ḵazīna*), the central reserve (*bayt-al-māl*), and the other possessions of the late shah (Ṭahmāsb), there were in the armory... the arms and outfit (*asleḥa wa yarāq*) for thirty thousand horsemen, consisting of cuirasses (*jobba*), coats of mail (*jowšan*), *kajīm*, and *bargostvān*."

J. W. Allan's recent assertion (*Persian Metal Technology 700-1300 A.D.*, Oxford, 1979, p. 96) à propos of "horse-armour" (Persian *bargostvān*, Arabic *tajāfīf* [*sic*]; the writer inexplicably uses the plural of Arabic *tijfāf*) to the effect that "the emphasis on speed and mobility in the Islamic period probably led this item of equipment to fall into disuse in Iran: there are certainly very few references to horse-armour in Iran after the [Arab] conquests (though see Fakhr-i Mudabbir [*sic*] pp. 216, 260-1)" cannot be maintained, considering the multiple evidence of Iranian lexicography, poetry, history, and book painting to the contrary.

See also ARMOR; ASB.

Bibliography: Given in the text.

(A. S. MELIKIAN-CHIRVANI)

BĀRHANG (also *bārtang*), plantain, is a general, imprecise name for about 27 species of *Plantago* L. (family Plantaginaceae; see Parsa, IV, pp. 240-67) in Iran, particularly *P. major* L., the greater plantain, *P. Lanceolata* L. (= *P. minor* L.), the lesser plantain, *P. ovata* Forsk., and *P. psyllium* L., fleawort.

Unmistakably, the rich pharmacognosy of *Plantago* was incorporated into Islamic medicine from Greek sources: Medical-botanical authors of the Islamic era (e.g., Ebn Sīnā, II, p. 203, Heravī, pp. 299-300) repeat more or less fully the descriptions and therapeutic indications found in Galen and, more especially, in Dioscorides, with some minor additions or modifications; even the commonest Arabic name for the plantain (also the standard name in Persian sources), *lesān al-ḥamal* (lit. "lamb tongue"), is a calque of its Greek name *arnóglōsson* (two other, uncommon, Arabic synonyms, *ḏū sabʿat ażlāʿ* and *kaṯīr al-ażlāʿ*, are translations of Dioscorides' *heptapleuron* "seven-ribbed" and *polupleuron* "many-ribbed," respectively, the reference being to the number of veins in each leaf blade of *P. major*). One of the common Arabic names for *P. psyllium*, *ḥašīšat al-barāğīṯ* (lit. "fleas' herb"), is an adaptation of Dioscorides' *psullion* (lit. "flea-like)," alluding to the resemblance in shape and color of its seeds to fleas.

The Iranian names for *Plantago*, however, do not show any trace of the Greek terminology. In addition to *bārhang/bārtang* for the (greater) plantain, we have *esparza/esfarza* (in current use in Iran, perhaps originally a dialectal Isfahani term), *ḵargūšak* (lit. "the little donkey ear," mentioned by Bīrūnī, p. 331 of the Ar. text), and the now obsolete (dialectal?) Persian *asb-/esba-ğūl/ğol* (or *asp-/espa-*, lit. "horse ear;" this name, or variants thereof, however, seems to be still in use in Indian *bāzārs*; see Dymock et al., III, pp. 126-27) for *P. psyllium*. (For some other names of the plantain—

Arabic, Persian, etc.—see Dehḵodā, *Loḡat-nāma*, s.vv. *bārtang* and *bārhang*, and Parsa, VIII, pp. 144-45.)

Galen mentions a few and Dioscorides about thirty medicinal properties and uses of *Plantago*. As to its "active nature," Galen (as quoted by Ebn al-Bayṭār, pt. 4, p. 107; tr. pp. 435f.) states that the plantain embodies both "cold moistness" and astringency. Of the various uses recommended by Dioscorides (as quoted by Ebn al-Bayṭār, ibid., pp. 107-08) the following may be mentioned here: Eating cooked plantain with vinegar and salt helps against intestinal ulcers and chronic diarrhea; (in a poultice) it is good for suppurative wounds, deep wounds, scrofula in the neck, tonsillitis, burns, etc.; eating cooked plantain helps cure epilepsy and asthma; the expressed juice of the leaves is good for oral inflammations, earache, hemoptysis and some other pulmonary ailments; chewing the cooked roots soothes toothache; eating its cooked roots and leaves is a remedy against pains in the kidneys and the bladder (for the cumulative traditional Greek, Arab, Persian, and Indian pharmacognosy of the *Lesān al-ḥamal*, see ʿAqīlī Ḵorāsānī, pp. 381-82).

There has been some confusion about the provenance of *esbaḡūl/esfarza* seeds. For instance, some authorities (e.g., Dymock et al., op. cit.; Chopra, 1930) have identified them as those of *P. ovata* Forsk, while the majority of the authors consider them to be those of *P. psyllium* L. The confusion is mainly due to the resemblance (in shape and some medical properties) of the various seeds involved. However, the synonymy of Gk. *psullion* = Ar. *ḥašīšat al-barāḡīṯ* = Syr./Ar. *bazr gaṭūnā/bezr qoṭūnā* = Pers. *esbaḡūl/esfarza*, found in some classical sources, seems to corroborate the latter view. According to Dioscorides (4.69), *psullion* is good for arthritis, headache, edema, tumors, erysipelas, and for clearing ulcers and running ears. These properties are reflected in Islamic sources (Arabic and Persian) under the standard heading *bezr qaṭūnā* (arabicized from Syriac).

Nowadays it seems that the therapeutic utilization of the common plantain and the fleawort in Iran and some neighboring countries is limited to the use of the dried ripe seeds in a few cases, especially against diarrhoea and dysentery (in India, Iran, Iraq). This is probably the oldest recognized main use of the plantain, since Pliny already states that both the greater and the lesser plantains are very effective against "rheumatismi" (25.39) or "intestinal complaints" (26.47; cf. Dymock et al., op. cit., p. 128). In Iran, plantain seeds in an infusion with the mucilaginous seeds of three other plants—*Sisymbrium alliaria* Scop., quince, and *Cordia mixa* L.—are used as a demulcent and expectorant in some pulmonary ailments; this popular traditional compound is called *č(ah)ār-toḵm(a)*, lit. "the four seeds." The *esbaḡūl/esfarza* seeds are used in the treatment of chronic dysentery (in the Indian subcontinent), as a coolant (*mobarred*), (in a poultice) against erysipelas (*bād-e sorḵ*), and to speed up the maturation of boils and abscesses (in Iran).

Bibliography: M.-Ḥ. ʿAqīlī Ḵorāsānī, *Maḵzan al-adwīa*, Tehran, 1276/1859-60, repr. 1349 Š./1970. Abū Rayḥān Bīrūnī, *Al-Bīrūnī's Book on Pharmacy and Materia Medica*, ed. and tr. Hakim Mohammed Said, Karachi, 1973. R. N. Chopra, "*Plantago Ovata*—Ispaghul—in Chronic Diarrhœas and Dysenteries," *Indian Medical Gazette* 65, 1930, p. 628. Idem, *Chopra's Indigenous Drugs of India*, 2nd revised ed., Calcutta, 1958, pp. 379-85. Dioscorides, *The Greek Herbal of Dioscorides*, Eng. tr. John Goodyear (A.D. 1655), ed. R. T. Gunther, New York, 1959, p. 70. W. Dymock, C. J. H. Warden, and D. Hooper, *Pharmacographia Indica*, 3 vols., London etc., 1890-93, repr. Karachi, 1972, III, pp. 127-29. Ebn al-Bayṭār, *al-Jāmeʿ*, 4 pts. in 2 vols., Būlāq, 1291/1874. Ebn Sīnā, *Qānūn dar ṭebb* II, tr. ʿAbd-al-Raḥmān Šarafkandī, Tehran, 1362 Š./1983-84. Mowaffeq-al-Dīn ʿAlī Heravī, *Ketāb al-abnīa ʿan ḥaqāʾeq al-adwīa*, ed. A. Bahmanyār and Ḥ. Maḥbūbī Ardakānī, Tehran, 1346 Š./1967-68. Muhammad Najmal-Ghani Khan, *Ḵazāʾen al-adwīa* I, 1st ed., Lucknow, 1971, pp. 660-61, s.v. *Bārtung kē bīj* (*bārhang* seeds). A. Parsa, *Flore de l'Iran*, Tehran, IV, 1949, and VIII, 1960.

(HAKIM M. SAID)

BARĪD, the official postal and intelligence service of the early Islamic caliphate and its successor states. The service operated by means of couriers mounted on mules or horses or camels or traveling on foot. In this way, official letters and despatches were delivered to the central *dīvān* in Damascus or Baghdad or such provincial capitals as Shiraz, Bukhara, and Ḡazna; and, since this was an official institution, with its personnel drawing their salaries from the central or provincial exchequers, it was only exceptionally that private correspondence was carried. The use of such a communications network dates back in the Iranian world to the Achaemenids, with their relay service along the "Royal Roads" such as the one from Sardis to Susa (cf. Herodotus, 5.52-3; *Camb. Hist. Iran* II/1, pp. 276-77), and was perpetuated by the Sasanians. Hence Ḵᵛāja Neẓām-al-Molk was correct (*Sīar al-molūk* [*Sīāsat-nāma*], chap. 10, ed. Darke[1], Tehran, 2535 = 1353 Š./1974, p. 79, tr. Darke, *The Book of Government*, London, 1960, p. 66) in tracing the institution back beyond Islamic times and in stressing the vital necessity of it for enabling the ruler to acquire information about happenings in remote provinces of the empire and, especially, to control governors and officials who might be tempted, because of their distance from the capital, into rebellion.

Popular etymology derived the term *barīd* from *borīda-donb* "having docked tails," but it derives in reality from late Latin *veredus* "post-horse," showing Byzantine influences in the evolution of the Islamic *barīd* system. However, the technical terminology of the system does contain some Persian elements, e.g., *forāneq* "man who carries the despatch bags" (from Pers. *parvāna*; see, further, the section on the technical terms of the postal service in Ḵᵛārazmī's *Mafātīḥ al-*

ʿolūm, ed. G. van Vloten, Leiden, 1895, pp. 63-64, Germ. tr. E. Wiedemann, in *Sb. der Phys.-Med. Soz. in Erlangen* 42, 1910, pp. 308-10 = *Aufsätze zur arabischen Wissenschaftsgeschichte*, Hildesheim, 1970, I, pp. 674-76, Eng. tr. with comm. C. E. Bosworth, in "Abū ʿAbdallāh al-Khwārazmī on the Technical Terms of the Secretary's Art," *JESHO* 12, 1969, pp. 141-43 = *Medieval Arabic Culture and Administration*, London, 1982, XV).

In early Islamic Iran, the stages (*sekka*, *rebāṭ*) of the *barīd* service were two *farsaḵs* (5 miles) apart, a comparatively short interval, since runners were employed as well as mounted couriers. The routes followed by these messengers are known to us from the itineraries and listings of staging posts, which form a considerable part of the classical Arabic geographical works, starting with that of Ebn Ḵordāḏbeh (mid-3rd/8th century; q.v.), who at one stage of his official career was *ṣāḥeb al-barīd* in Jebāl. The provincial postal-service directors (*aṣḥāb al-barīd*) were directly responsible to the caliph, as being the chief sources of intelligence, and, if a provincial governor or ruler raised a rebellion in his region, one of his first acts would be to endeavor to arrest the *ṣāḥeb al-barīd* and prevent his sending news back to the capital. Thus in 207/813, when the governor of Khorasan Ṭāher Ḏu'l-Yamīnayn (q.v.) omitted the caliph al-Ma'mūn's name from the *ḵoṭba* or Friday sermon, this being tantamount to an act of defiance, the caliph's *ṣāḥeb al-barīd*, Kolṯūm b. Ṯābet, felt certain that he would be killed when it became known to Ṭāher that he had written to Baghdad with the news (Ṭabarī, III, p. 1064).

The provincial dynasties which arose in the Iranian lands with the decline of the ʿAbbasids imitated the central government in their use of postal and intelligence services. The Samanids had *dīvān*s for the *ṣāḥeb al-barīd* and for the *mošref* ("overseer," i.e., intelligence gatherer) in their capital, Bukhara, from the time of Amir Naṣr II b. Aḥmad (301-31/914-43) onward (Naršaḵī, p. 36, reading here *dīvān-e ešrāf* for *dīvān-e šaraf*; tr. Frye, p. 26; Barthold, *Turkestan*[2], pp. 229-31), while the Ghaznavid *barīd* and *ešrāf* systems were held to be of paramount importance in what was, at its zenith in the early 5th/11th century, a far-flung empire; not infrequently, the office of *ṣāḥeb al-barīd* was a stepping-stone to that of vizier (see M. Nazim, *The Life and Times of Sulṭān Maḥmūd of Ghazna*, Cambridge, 1933, pp. 144-46; Spuler, *Iran*, pp. 333-34; Bosworth, *The Ghaznavids*, pp. 93-97). Under the earlier Saljuqs, with their looser, more decentralized system of government, the *barīd* system was apparently no longer maintained at its earlier level of efficiency or was even allowed to lapse altogether. Neẓām-al-Molk mourned this fact, regarding such a system as vital for his ideal, authoritarian monarch (*Sīar al-molūk*, chaps. 10, 13, 14, ed. Darke[1], pp. 79-89, 94-110. tr. Darke, pp. 66-74, 78-91; cf. *Camb. Hist. Iran* V, pp. 76, 267). It by no means disappeared, however, from Iran, for the Mongols, as a highly mobile aristocracy of cavalrymen, with an empire enormous in extent, were aware of the utility of a relay and courier system. Jengiz Khan ordered the establishment of post stations (Tk. *yam*, Rubruck's *iam*, and Marco Polo's *yanb*), and the subject populations were heavily afflicted by the duty of providing horses (Tk. *olaḡ*) for the messengers (Tk. *elči*; see P. Pelliot, "Sur *yam* ou *jam*, 'relai postal'," *T'oung-pao* 27, 1930, pp. 192-95; Spuler, *Mongolen*[1], pp. 422-26; *Camb. Hist. Iran* V, p. 536; and see OLĀḠ). The system continued, but apparently with declining efficiency, under the Il-khanids, although with the looser forms of political organization under the ensuing Turkmen dynasties in Iran, the *olaḡ* system gradually fell into disuse.

Bibliography: Given in the text. See also R. Levy, *The Social Structure of Islam*, Cambridge, 1957, pp. 299-302. D. Sourdel, "Barīd," in *EI*[2], pp. 1045-46.

(C. E. BOSWORTH)

BARĪDŠĀHĪ, a dynasty of Indo-Muslim kings of the Deccan plateau that ruled from 897/1491-92 to 1028/1619 in one of the five successor states to the Bahmanid kingdom (748-944/1347-1538, see BAHMANIDS. Though their state was small compared to their successor states, especially the ʿĀdelšāhī (q.v.) dynasty of Bijapur, the Neẓāmšāhī dynasty of Ahmadnagar, and the Qoṭbšāhī dynasty of Golkonda, the Barīdšāhī rulers enjoyed one advantage and strength, which was their inheritance of the former Bahmanid capital, the city of Bīdar (q.v.), to whose rich heritage of Indo-Muslim monuments they added a number of important ones of their own. The sequence of their rule is as follows:

Qāsem Barīd	897/1491-92–910/1504-05
Amir Barīd	910/1504-05–950/1543-44
ʿAlī Barīd Shah	950/1543-44–988/1580-81
Ebrāhīm Barīd Shah	988/1580-81–995/1586-87
Qāsem Barīd Shah II	995/1586-87–998/1589-90
Amir Barīd Shah II (usurped)	998/1589-90–1010/1601-02
Mīrzā ʿAlī Barīd Shah (usurped)	1010/1601-02–1018/1609-10
Amir Barīd Shah III	1018/1609-10–1028/1619

The dynasty was named after Qāsem Barīd, a Persianized Turk from the Caucasus who in his youth had been sold as a slave to Sultan Moḥammad Bahmanī III (r. 867-87/1463-82). Having distinguished himself in suppressing several Maratha rebellions, Qāsem rose steadily in power and prestige even as the Bahmanid state underwent serious decline. In 897/1491-92, a time when other Bahmanid nobles were declaring independent kingdoms in their respective fiefs, Qāsem acquired de facto control of the capital city by virtue of his elevation to the office of Bahmanid prime minister (*amīr-e jomla*). Although he never styled himself king, Qāsem did assume the kingdom's regalia, and permitted only nominal sovereignty to continue in the hands of weak Bahmanid successors. His transition from an imported slave to the founder of a new dynasty is both a legacy and an illustration of a pattern of political evolution typical of early Islamic Iran.

After Qāsem's death in 910/1504-05, his son Amir Barīd inherited his power, and like his father declined to crown himself king. Instead, he placed the last four Bahmanid kings on the throne, promptly murdering those he felt might form alliances that would threaten him. In his foreign relations Amir Barīd shrewdly curried the favor of his more powerful neighbors, but he failed to stay clear of the expanding 'Adelšāhīs of Bijapur, against whom his military efforts generally proved unsuccessful, and occasionally humiliating. The kingdom's last moment of political glory occurred in 972/1565, when Barīdšāhī troops under the command of Amir Barīd's son and successor, 'Alī, played a distinguished role in the battle of Talikota (where a confederacy of the four Deccani sultanates overthrew the Hindu kingdom of Vijayanagar). But after 'Alī's death in 988/1580-81 a succession of rulers, two of whom usurped power by force, watched the kingdom dwindle as its three neighbors steadily encroached upon Barīdšāhī domains. Finally, in 1028/1619, after a feeble resistance from the Bīdar commanders, Sultan Ebrāhīm II of Bijapur annexed the city and its adjoining territories, thus finally extinguishing the Barīdšāhī dynasty.

Sectarian tensions affecting Barīdšāhī relations with its neighbors were greatly influenced by contemporary developments taking place in Iran. As a result of the socio-religious movements that had carried the Safavid dynasty to power in the beginning of the 10/16th century, many Iranian adventurers, soldiers, Sufis, and literati migrated from Iran to the Deccan. Some of them, such as Šāh Ṭāher of Qazvīn, brought to India the same Shi'ite fervor that had figured so prominently in the Safavid revolution. Having acquired a reputation in Iran as a learned Shi'ite scholar, Šāh Ṭāher had been appointed by shah Esmā'īl I Ṣafawī to teach in Kāšān. His patron, however, soon grew jealous of the scholar's great popularity, and, when suspicions arose concerning his alleged Isma'ili affiliations, Šāh Ṭāher was forced to ffee Iran for India in 926/1520. There he sought royal patronage at the courts of the new successor states of the Bahmanids, and eventually settled in Ahmadnagar where he played an important role in expanding the Shi'ite sect. In 950/1543-44, when 'Alī Barīd was crowned king of the Barīdšāhīs in Bīdar, the new king's uncle made derogatory remarks respecting the Shi'ite sect to Šāh Ṭāher in the presence of the Neẓāmšāhī envoy from neighboring Ahmadnagar. Upon returning to Ahmadnagar the angered diplomat urged his own patron to punish the new Barīdšāhī king, who as a consequence was forced to surrender three forts to his more powerful neighbor.

The Barīdšāhī dynasty achieved its greatest cultural splendor in the middle of the 10th/16th century, under the thirty-seven-year rule of 'Alī Barīd. The first Barīdšāhī to adopt the title king, 'Alī presided over the apogee of Barīdšāhī architecture, the most important specimens of which were his own tomb and the Rangīn Maḥal, a lovely palace splendidly adorned with wood carving and mother-of-pearl work. Both monuments reflect considerable Persian influence and were important in establishing the transition from the heavy fortlike style so characteristic of the earlier Bahmanid kings to the lighter and more graceful style that later culminated in neighboring Bijapur and Golconda. The upper story of 'Alī's tomb, for example, is decorated with many small niches, a style evidently imported by architects from Iran. There, the motif can be found in the palace of 'Ālī Qāpū (q.v.) in Isfahan and, prior to that, in the mosque of Ardabīl.

Bibliography: *Free Ferešta*, ed. N. Kishor, Lucknow, 1864-65, pp. 176-77; tr. Briggs, III, pp. 299-303. H. K. Sherwani and P. M. Joshi, eds., *History of Medieval Deccan*, 2 vols., Hyderabad, 1973, I, pp. 298-350; II, pp. 268-78. H. K. Sherwani and J. Burton-Page, "Barīd-Shāhīs," in *EI*² I, pp. 1047-48. Sayyed 'Alī Ṭabāṭabā'ī, *Borhān-e ma'āṯer*, Delhi, 1936, pp. 251-95. G. Yazdani, *Bidar: Its History and Monuments*, Oxford, 1947, pp. 11-14, 25-27, 148-76.

(R. M. EATON)

BARIKĀNU, a town in Media, which was conquered and forced to pay a tribute by the Assyrian king Sargon II ca. 716 B.C. During his eighth campaign in 714 B.C. Sargon II marched against Media, among other countries, and accepted the tribute of horses, mules, oxen, and sheep from Satarpanu, the ruler of Barikānu. The same locality with its ruler Satarpanu is referred to as a "country" in an inscription of Sargon II composed in 713 B.C.

See also SATARPANU.

Bibliography: L. D. Levine, *Two Neo-Assyrian Stelae from Iran*, Royal Ontario Museum. Art and Archaeology, occasional paper 23, 1972, p. 42. F. Thureau-Dangin, "Une relation de la huitième campagne de Sargon," *Musée du Louvre, Département des Antiquités Orientales, Textes cunéiformes* 3, Paris, 1912, p. 10. H. Winckler, *Die Keilschrifttexte Sargons II*, Leipzig, 1889, p. 448.

(M. A. DANDAMAYEV)

BARIŠ NASK, one of the lost *nask*s of the *Hāδa-mąθra* group (see AVESTA), analyzed in *Dēnkard* 8.9. According to the Persian *Rivāyat*s, this *nask* contained originally sixty *karda*s, but only twelve were recovered after the time of Alexander. According to the summary of the *Bariš nask* in the *Dēnkard*, it contained matter concerning almost everything between heaven and earth, with perhaps a fair share of practical questions and advice not only on such matters as kings and judges and their authority, but also on such theological topics as body and soul, heaven and hell, and the afterlife. No extant Avestan texts or fragments have been identified as belonging to the *Bariš nask*. Darmesteter pointed out that the subjects treated in the *Bariš nask* recall parts of the *Mēnōy ī xrad* and that some of the Avestan Tahmuras fragments and some Avestan citations in the commentary of the Pahlavi *Vīdēvdād* could be from the

Bariš nask. The origin and meaning of *bariš* is unknown. The word can also be read as *brēh* "fate, destiny."

Bibliography: J. Darmesteter, *Le Zend-Avesta*, Paris, 1892-93, repr. 1960, III, pp. xv-xvii. *Dēnkard*, ed. M. J. Dresden, Wiesbaden, 1966, pp. 112-10, fols. 68.14-71.12 of the Meherji Rana copies of the lost portions of the manuscript. J. P. de Menasce, in *Camb. Hist. Iran* III/2, pp. 1160, 1180-81. W. E. West, *Pahlavi Texts* IV, SBE 37, pp. 20-23 (summary of the *nasks*), pp. 423, 430, 434 (quotations from the Persian *Rivāyats*).

(P. O. Skjærvø)

BARḴᵛARDĀR TORKMĀN, Mīrzā, author of *Aḥsan al-sīar*, a history of Shah Esmāʿīl Ṣafawī, completed in either 930/1523-24 (Williams, 1916, p. 298) or 937/1530-31 (Williams, 1918, p. viii). The work was apparently compiled in four volumes of which only the fourth is known. It includes: 1. a preface (pp. 1-6) in which the author states that as a Shiʿite he wants to "combat some of the errors" (ibid.) in the contemporary work *Ḥabīb al-sīar* of Ḵᵛāndamīr; 2. a lengthy narrative history (pp. 6-280) of the reign of Shah Esmāʿīl; 3. a section on the poets and "philosophers" of his time (pp. 280-305); and 4. a compilation (pp. 305-411) of "curious stories, geographical descriptions and the like, borrowed from Khwandamir, the *Maṭlaʿ al-Saʿdaīn*, and other works."

Bibliography: The only useful source on the author and his work is the very brief mention given by L. F. Rushbrook Williams in his article, "A New Authority on Babur?" *Journal of the Asiatic Society of Bengal*, N.S., 12, 1916, pp. 297-98. Idem, *An Empire Builder of the Sixteenth Century*, London, 1918, preface.

(R. D. McChesney)

BARKĪĀROQ, Rokn-al-Dīn Abu'l-Moẓaffar b. Malekšāh, Great Saljuq sultan (r. 485-98/1092-1105). Barkīāroq (properly, Berk-yaruq, Tk. "firm, strong brightness," see Clauson, *An Etymological Dictionary of Pre-Thirteenth Century Turkish*, pp. 361-62, 761-63) was the eldest of Malekšāh's sons, but still only thirteen on his father's death. The fact that Malekšāh left no adult sons goes a considerable way toward explaining why the mighty edifice of his empire now began to crumble, so that Barkīāroq's reign conventionally marks the opening stages of the decline of Great Saljuq unity in Iran and the Fertile Crescent. Moreover, the older Turkish tribal traditions of a patrimonial share-out of territories, in the absence of a single, mature, dominant, and experienced leader, reasserted themselves now, just as they had done twenty years previously around the time of Malekšāh's father Alp Arslān (q.v.).

When Malekšāh died, his widow Terken (Torkān) Ḵātūn attempted to place her four-year-old son Maḥmūd on the throne in Isfahan. Barkīāroq was proclaimed ruler at Ray by the rival party of the Neẓāmīya, the sons and partisans of the great vizier Neẓām-al-Molk (q.v.), as the candidate most likely to be able to hold his father's heritage together. Terken Ḵātūn and Maḥmūd conveniently died in 487/1094, and Barkīāroq was able through military force to dispose of the claims to power of other ambitious members of the Saljuq family, namely his uncle, Arslān Arḡūn in Khorasan and, more seriously, another uncle, Tutuš (Totaš) b. Alp Arslān (q.v.) of Damascus (487-88/1094-95). Barkīāroq was now reasonably firmly established in Iraq and Jebāl, i.e., western Iran, but he had to leave the sons of Tutuš in Syria and his half-brother Moḥammad Tapar (q.v.) in Azerbaijan and Arrān, the latter now receiving the support of his (Moḥammad's) full brother Sanjar (q.v.) and of Barkīāroq's former vizier Moʾayyed-al-Molk b. Neẓām-al-Molk.

The remaining years of Barkīāroq's reign were filled with continuous warfare and campaigns against Moḥammad, with the allegiance of the great Turkish amirs constantly changing, their underlying aim being that no one ruler should be able to secure complete domination. The sultan was driven to desperate expedients to raise money for his armies, including, reportedly, the confiscation of private property for *eqṭāʿ*s and, when his fortunes were especially low, the employment of Ismaʿili troops in his forces, leading to accusations that Barkīāroq personally favored them. By 497/1104, war-weary and already ill, Barkīāroq, although in control of western and central Iran and Iraq, agreed to a division of power with Moḥammad, who was to have northwestern Iran, Jazīra, and Syria, while Sanjar was to remain in Khorasan acknowledging only Moḥammad as his overlord. Whether these arrangements would have lasted is unknown, since Barkīāroq died only a few months later at the age of 25, and Moḥammad was able to succeed to thirteen years of uninterrupted sultanate.

Barkīāroq has inevitably suffered in comparison with his father, and the sources are lukewarm about him while being enthusiastic about Moḥammad. Yet the problems which he had faced had been formidable. The seeds of the trend toward decentralization and loosening of the fabric of the Great Saljuq empire had already been sown in his father's time; and Barkīāroq's sultanate is indeed notable for the beginnings of the Turkman atabegates and principalities which later were a feature of the lands from Kermān to Anatolia and Syria.

Bibliography: Primary sources: Bondārī, *Zobdat al-noṣra wa nokbat al-ʿoṣra*, ed. M. T. Houtsma in *Recueil de textes relatifs à l'histoire des Seljoucides* II, Leiden, 1889, pp. 82ff. Rāvandī, *Rāḥat al-ṣodūr wa āyat al-sorūr*, ed. M. Eqbāl, II, London, 1921, pp. 138-52. Ẓahīr-al-Dīn Nīšāpūrī, *Saljūq-nāma*, Tehran, 1332 Š./1954, pp. 35-39. Ṣadr-al-Dīn Ḥosaynī, *Akbār al-dawla al-saljūqīya*, pp. 75-79. *Mojmal al-tawārīḵ*, ed. Bahār, pp. 408-10. Ebn al-Jawzī, *al-Montaẓam fī taʾrīḵ al-molūk wa'l-omam*, 7 vols., Hyderabad, 1357-59/1938-41, IX, pp. 60-144. Ebn al-Aṯīr (Beirut), X, pp. 214-16, 219-20, 222, 224, 229, 232-35, 244-48, 262-64, 281-82, 287-91, 293-98, 303-

10, 313-20, 322-23, 329-35, 359-62, 369-72, 380-82. Secondary sources: C. Defrémery, "Recherches sur le règne du sultan seldjoukide Barkiarok (485-498 de l'hégire 1092-1104 de l'ère chrétienne)," *JA*, sér. 5, 1, 1853, pp. 425-58; 2, 1953, pp. 217-322. M. F. Sanaullah, *The Decline of the Saljūqid Empire*, Calcutta, 1938, pp. 91-113. C. L. Klausner, *The Seljuk Vezirate. A Study of Civil Administration 1055-1194*, Cambridge, Mass., 1973, passim. C. E. Bosworth, in *Camb. Hist. Iran* V, pp. 102-13. C. Cahen, in *EI*[2] "Barkyāruḳ."

(C. E. Bosworth)

BARLAAM AND IOSAPH, Persian *Belawhar o Būdāsaf*, a Greek Christian or Christianized novel of Buddhist origins which throughout the Middle Ages and until quite recently was almost universally attributed to St. John of Damascus (ca. 675-ca. 749), e.g., in the *Martyrologium* of Pope Sixtus the Fifth (1585-90), s.d. 27 November. All the manuscripts are later than 1500. Being extremely popular it received various accretions (e.g., the lost Greek *Apology of Aristides*, see Eusebius of Caesarea, *Historia ecclesiastica* 4.3) and was often translated: into Arabic (in the 13th century) whence into Ethiopic (in the 16th century), Armenian, Latin, and from Latin into the main European languages. The book won great favor in Germany through Rudolf von Ems' epic version of it (ca. 1230) and in Scandinavia in the same century through the Old Norse translation ordered by King Haakon Haakonsøn. It was used in the *Legenda aurea* by the Dominican Jacobus de Voragine (late 13th cent.) and in the *Gesta Romanorum* and thereby gained widespread popularity in Europe. Finally, William Shakespeare borrowed from it the *Tale of the Caskets* for his *Merchant of Venice*.

The Greek version relates the story of an Indian king who learns from his astrologers that his son Iosaph will be converted to Christianity and in order to prevent him from seeing the distress and misery of human life locks him up in a palace. The plan fails, however, and the prince both sees sick, blind, and old people and witnesses death and so begins to ponder the vanity of life. When God sends him the pious hermit Barlaam, the prince is converted to Christianity. In vain his father tries to win him back, but the prince renounces the throne, converts his father and his people, and retires as a hermit. After his death he works many miracles.

The novel is a syncretic compilation of Buddha stories ultimately derived from such works as Aśvaghoṣa's *Buddhacarita* (Career of the Buddha; 1st-2nd cents.), the *Lalitavistara* (an early Mahāyāna text), the *Mahāvastu* (from the canon of the Mahāsaṅgikas), and the Pali *Jātaka* tales (see Lang, in *EI*[2], p. 1216).

The name Iosaph is a corrupt arabicized form of *bodhisattva* (q.v.), in which the initial *b* was misread as *y*. The form is similar to and probably derives from the Manichean form Bwdysdf. The fact that fragments of the tale have been preserved in Manichean texts in Uigur, Parthian, and Persian in Manichean script from Turfan proves that it was the Manicheans who transmitted this Indian tale to the West (Henning, p. 92; Lang, "The Life," pp. 389-90; Asmussen, pp. 16-17). From Manichean Middle Persian the story was then translated into Arabic. In this connection we may note that Ebn al-Nadīm (*Fehrest*, p. 305.20-21), describing ʿAbbasid Baghdad as a cosmopolitan center and the main town of the western Manichean church, connects the translator Ebn al-Moqaffaʿ and his circle with the *Ketāb Belawhar wa Būḏāsaf*. (Ebn al-Moqaffaʿ's interest in Manicheism is referred to by Bīrūnī, Masʿūdī, and the *Tārīḵ-e gozīda*; see Asmussen, pp. 14-15; Lang in *EI*[2], p. 1216). This translation is now lost but it gave rise to several other Arabic versions, some abridged, and served as the basis for a free rendering into Hebrew by Ebn Chisdai (*Book of the King's Son and the Ascetic*, ca. 1200), which was translated into Judeo-Persian by Elisha ben Samuel (*Šāhzāda wa ṣūfī*), and was itself translated into Georgian in the ninth century. From this Georgian translation (*Life of the Blessed Iodasap*ʿ) a second Georgian translation was made (*The Wisdom of Balahvar*) and also a Greek translation by St. Euthymius the Georgian, an Athonite monk, who added the *Apology of Aristides* (Lang, "The Life," pp. 405f.; *The Wisdom*, pp. 62f.). It was this Greek version that became the mother text of all later Christian versions (see above).

Bibliography: J. P. Asmussen, "Der Manichäismus als Vermittler literarischen Gutes," *Temenos* 2, Helsinki, 1966, pp. 5ff. F. C. Conybeare, "The Barlaam and Josaphat Legend in the Ancient Georgian and Armenian Literatures," *Folk-Lore* 7, 1896, pp. 101ff. A. A. Gvakharia, *The Persian Versions of "Balavariani" ("Budasaf = Yodasaf and Balahvar")*, Tiflis, 1985. W. B. Henning, "Persian Poetical Manuscripts from the Time of Rūdakī," in *A Locust's Leg. Studies in Honour of S. H. Taqizadeh*, ed. W. B. Henning and E. Yarshater, London, 1962, pp. 89ff. E. G. Khintibidze, *On Mt. Athos Georgian Literary School*, Tiflis, 1982. D. M. Lang, "St. Euthymius the Georgian and the Barlaam and Ioasaph Romance," *BSOAS* 17/2, 1955, pp. 306ff. Idem, "The Life of the Blessed Iodasaph: A New Oriental Christian Version of the Barlaam and Ioasaph Romance (Jerusalem, Greek Patriarchal Library: Georgian MS 140)," *BSOAS* 20, 1957, pp. 389ff. Idem, *The Wisdom of Balahvar*, London, 1957 (with extensive bibliography pp. 125-28). Idem, "Bilawhar wa-Yūdāsaf," in *EI*[2] I, pp. 1215-17. Idem, *The Balavariani* (*Barlaam and Josaphat*). *A Tale from the Christian East Translated from the Old Georgian*, London, 1966. R. L. Wolff, "The Apology of Aristides—A Re-Examination," *Harvard Theological Revue* 30, 1937, pp. 233ff. Idem, "Barlaam and Ioasaph," ibid., 32, 1939, pp. 131ff. E. Rehatsek, "Book of the King's Son and the Ascetic," *JRAS*, 1890, pp. 119ff. G. R. Woodward and H. Mattingly, St. John Damascene, *Barlaam and Ioasaph*. The Loeb Classical Library, London and Cambridge, Mass., 1914.

(J. P. Asmussen)

BARLEY, Persian *jow* (from OIran. **yawa-*, cf. Av. *yauua-* "grain," Pahl. *jōrdā* "barley"), Pashto *wərbəša*.

i. *In Iran.*

ii. *In Afghanistan.*

i. In Iran

The cultivation of barley in Iran, like that of wheat, goes back to the origin of agriculture itself. Both botanical and archeological data locate the beginning of the "neolithic revolution" in the Fertile Crescent, i.e., a semiarid area stretching from Palestine to the Zagros through the Taurus foothills, where both wild barley, *Hordeum spontaneum*, and a wide-grain kind of wild wheat, *Triticum dicoccoides* can still be found (H. Helbaek, "Domestication of Food Plants in the Old World," *Science* 130, 1959, pp. 365-72). Most of the paleobotanical surveys made on several prehistoric sites on the Iranian plateau up to the fifth millennium B.C. show the existence of cultivated barley (O. Meder, *Klimaökologie und Siedlungsgang auf dem Hochland von Iran in vor- und frühgeschichtlicher Zeit*, Marburger Geographische Schriften 80, Marburg am Lahn, 1979, pp. 109-13). Barley cultivation is believed to have spread from there to the irrigated plains of Mesopotamia and Egypt, and then to Europe and other places (R. Ghirshman, *Iran*, London, 1954, p. 35).

Since those times, barley has been throughout history one of the two staple crops in the Iranian world, as a constant staple but subordinate to wheat, and is still mainly grown as a subsistence crop (H. Bowen-Jones, "Agriculture," in *Camb. Hist. Iran* I, p. 568; the map 33 of G. Stöber, —*Die Afshār. Nomadismus im Raum Kermān (Zentralirān)*, Marburger Geographische Schriften 76, Marburg am Lahn, 1978, clearly shows the geographical coincidence of barley and wheat cultivation).

Barley is grown throughout Iran and Afghanistan, either as a rainfed (*deym*) or irrigated (*ābī*) crop, and can be winter barley (*pāyīza*, "autumnal," often *jow-e torš* "sour barley") sown in November and harvested between May and July, or spring barley (*bahāra*, generally *jow-e šīrīn* "sweet barley") sown between February and April and harvested in summer. Cultivation techniques (see for instance P. H. T. Beckett, "Agriculture in Central Persia," *Tropical Agriculture* 34, 1957, pp. 9-28, and H. E. Wulff, *The Traditional Crafts of Persia*, Cambridge, Mass., and London, 1966, pp. 262-77) are quite similar for barley and wheat. The fields are plowed and sown with various types of traditional plows (*k̲īš*, *gāv-āhan*), or more and more with a tractor. Mature barley is harvested with a sickle (*dās*); green barley can be uprooted as fodder. Threshing is done in three traditional ways: by driving teams of draft animals over the threshing ground, with a wain (*čark̲-e k̲arman-kūbī*) or threshing board (*vāl*), and also with a tractor pulling a disk plow or threshing machine.

The greater part of barley acreage is devoted to unirrigated cultivation, using the dry-farming technique of plowed fallow, in regions where the mean amount of annual precipitation generally exceeds 300 mm (see the discussion of the limits of rainfed cultivation in Iran in H. Bobek, "Die Verbreitung des Regenfeldbaus in Iran," in *Festschrift L. Sölch*, Vienna, 1951, pp. 9-30). Most of the barley fields are in highlands, i.e., Azerbaijan, the northwestern and central Zagros, Alborz, and the chains of northern Khorasan, and all the central Afghan mountains, together with their northern loess-covered piedmont (Ch. Jentsch, "Die landwirtschaftlichen Produktionsflächen in Afghanistan und naturräumliche Möglichkeiten ihrer Erweiterung," in W. Kraus, ed., *Steigerung der landwirtschaftlichen Produktion und ihre Weiterverarbeitung in Afghanistan*, Afghanische Studien 6, Meisenheim am Glan, 1972, pp. 80-82 and inset map). Though winter barley can be found up to 2,000 m in the central Alborz (E. Ehlers, "Anbausysteme in den Höhenregionen des mittleren Elburz/Iran," in C. Rathjens, C. Troll, and H. Uhlig, eds., *Vergleichende Kulturgeographie der Hochgebirge des südlichen Asien/Comparative Cultural Geography of the High-Mountain Regions of Southern Asia*, Erdwissenschaftliche Forschung 5, Wiesbaden, 1973, pp. 66-67), spring barley grows in the highest permanent villages, for instance, above 1,900 m in eastern Azerbaijan (M. Bazin, *Le Tâlech: Une région ethnique au nord de l'Iran*, Paris, 1980, II, p. 97), as well as in summer temporary settlements such as the *yeylāq* of the Ṭāleš seminomads in the northwestern Alborz (ibid., II, p. 23) or the cold region (*sarḥadd*) of more or less sedentarized Afšār nomads in southeastern Iran (G. Stöber, op. cit., pp. 94-95). Such rainfed fields are regularly left fallow.

Irrigated cultivation of barley occurs in limited spots in the above-mentioned mountainous regions but is prevalent in central and eastern Iran and in the peripheral oases of Afghanistan. The fields are watered once or twice before the winter rains and three or four times in spring. Water needs have been estimated between 4,000 cubic meters per hectare around Borūjerd and 7,500 in the Zāyandarūd area (M. Atai, "Economic Report on Cultivation in the Region of the Sixth Province," *Taḥqīqāt-e eqteṣādī* 11-12, 1967, Eng. ed., p. 97), where barley is integrated into quite varied schemes of crop rotation (M. Bazin, *La vie rurale dans la région de Qom*, Paris, n.d. [1974], fig. 26 pp. 47-48).

Yields of barley are slightly lower than those of wheat, and there is of course a sharp contrast between irrigated and unirrigated lands. The latter give very low and irregular yields. Data from the years 1926 to 1933 compiled by M. Atai ("Economics of Cereals in Kuzistan," *Taḥqīqāt-e eqteṣādī* 3-4, 1962, pp. 56-91; idem, "Economic Report on Agriculture in the Isfahan and Yazd Areas," ibid., 9-10, 1965, pp. 144ff.; art. cit., 1967, pp. 81ff.) for several provinces of Iran range from 350 to 400 kg per hectare. The mean yield in Iran increased only to 502 kg per hectare in 1973, and the best yields obtained in the northwestern provinces never exceed 1,000 kg per hectare (Figure 24). Irrigated fields give much higher yields, with 1,400 to 1,817 kg per hectare in 1926-33 for the same provinces, and an average of

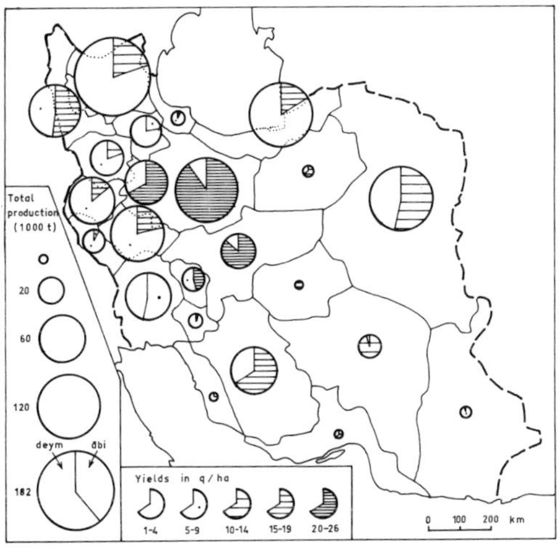

Figure 24. Barley production in Iran by *ostān* 1973

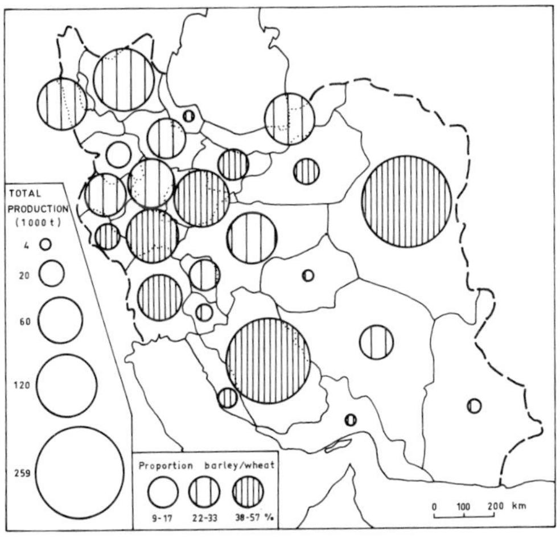

Figure 25. Barley production in Iran by *ostān* 1982

1,445 kg per hectare in 1973; the highest yields are reached in central Iran with 2,663 kg per hectare in Isfahan.

Barley is mostly a subsistence crop given to livestock, especially to sheep and horses, and provides little surplus for marketing. Before land reform in Iran, the crop was divided on the threshing ground between the tenant and the landlord. According to the factors of production supplied by each, the farmer's share could go from 1/4 to 4/5 (see detailed data for Isfahan in M. Atai, 1965, table 20, p. 128). After land reform, some of the former sharecroppers could bring barley to the market; a part of it was sold to the country's small brewing industry, and the bulk to specialized cereal traders (*ʿallāf*), who supply herders with supplementary grain for their fodder resources. As a whole, the barley production of Iran and Afghanistan is only marginally sufficient for domestic needs. In the late 1970s, the scarcity of available barley led to a sharp increase of its price in Iran, in such a way that many herders (for instance in northern Khorasan, cf. M.-H. Pâpoli-Yazdi, *Le nomadisme et le semi-nomadisme dans le Nord du Khorâssân: Etude de géographie humaine*, thèse lettres, Paris, 1983) were compelled to sell part of their flocks and horses. Efforts made after the 1979 revolution to raise the production in Iran seem to have been successful, with a conspicuous increase in Fārs and Khorasan (Figure 25), but it is difficult to see in these figures a long-term trend, since barley, because of its subordinate position vis-à-vis wheat, suffers from greater instability in acreage and production.

Bibliography: Given in the text.

(M. Bazin)

ii. In Afghanistan

Wild barleys (*jaw-e daštī*), including *Hordeum spontaneum* Koch. which is regarded as the sole ancestor of all cultivated forms, are widespread throughout northeastern Iran and northern Afghanistan as far as the Hindu Kush (Aitchison, 1890, p. 101; Vavilov and Bukinich, 1929, pp. 292f.). Owing to their sporadic distribution, which is strictly limited to human habitats, it seems, however, impossible to view these areas as an original cradle of barley cultivation (Zohary, 1969, p. 53). The probable western (Fertile Crescent ?) origin of Afghan barleys is moreover underlined by the local name of one of their forms, *jaw-e makkaʾī* (barley from Mecca), which has been recorded in Faryāb (Aitchison, 1890, p. 101).

Barley is widely grown in Afghanistan (Figure 26; see also Toepfer, 1972, for various agricultural surveys at the village level). The cultivated forms (*Hordeum vulgare*) are mainly winter and spring, four- or six-rowed, hulled species, most of them having a yellow grain color. Two-row species are much rarer. Naked varieties with blue grain color have been observed in the easternmost Afghan Hindu Kush (Edelberg and Jones, 1979, p. 52; Sakamoto et al., 1980, pp. 35f.). While hulled barley is grown both as an irrigated and non-irrigated crop, naked barley is always irrigated in Afghanistan.

In total acreage barley comes third after wheat and maize, occupying approximately 310,000-320,000 ha (some 8-9 percent of the whole area under cultivation) The estimated annual production fluctuates between 300,000 and 400,000 tons of grain, with a decennial average of 324,000 tons (1353-62 Š./1974-83). The corresponding yield is thus not far from 1 tn/ha, though more than 2 tn/ha can be expected from the best-irrigated fields (Wald, 1969, p. 43).

No regional statistical breakdown of barley production is available. An estimate of acreages cultivated in 1395 Š./1966 can be extracted only from the results of the agricultural census of the following year (Davydov, 1976, pp. 124f., from which the figures in Figure 26

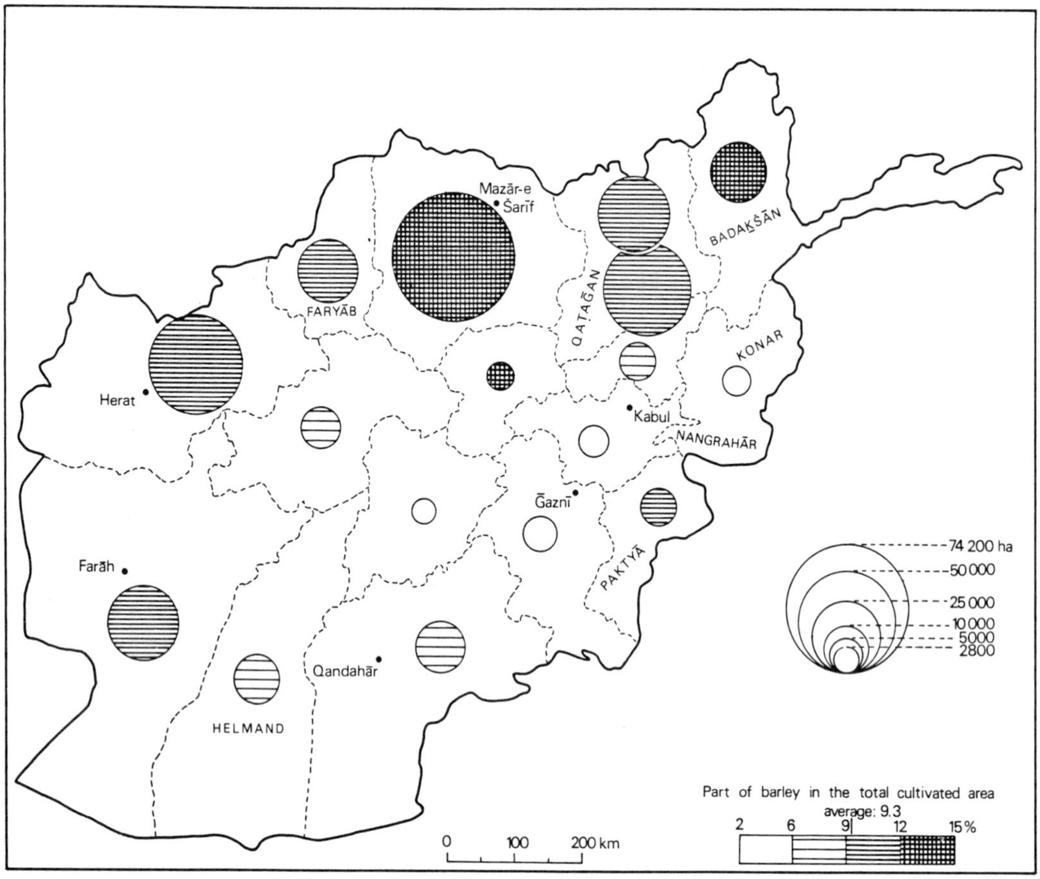

Figure 26. Geographical distribution of barley cultivation in Afghanistan (1345 Š./1966)
Source: Davydov, 1976, pp. 124-25.

have been taken). With 177,100 ha (11.5 percent of their agricultural lands) devoted to barley, the eight provinces of northern Afghanistan from Faryāb to Badak̲šān stand as the chief producing area, well above western Afghanistan (72,100 ha: 10.5 percent of agricultural lands). The remaining part of the country, in which barley occupies less than 5.5 percent of all cultivated areas, accounts for only 62,800 ha.

As a fast-growing cereal, barley is coarser and less esteemed than slower-growing wheat and maize. Its place in cropping systems shows, nevertheless, great variations which, on a broad scale of analysis, conforms to a model of three altitudinal belts.

At lower elevations, up to 2,000-2,200 m, barley remains a secondary winter (*tīrmāhī* "autumnal") irrigated (*ābī*) crop, mostly confined to areas too poor, too dry, or too saline to produce a satisfactory wheat crop—hence the former's low yield. Most of the production is used for feeding horses and donkeys, sometimes cows, rarely sheep. As human food, its consumption is restricted to the poorer people, who mix wheat and barley flour to make bread. In the same regions, spring (*bahārī*) irrigated barley may also follow winter wheat after the latter's harvest; it is sometimes sown along with vetch (*šāk̲al*) or alfalfa (*rešqa*) and is then always cut green as fodder. Recent improvements in the use of water and fertilizer have brought wheat to the better barley lands and have tended to reduce winter barley cultivation accordingly.

As elevation rises and the growing season shortens, winter barley cultivation increases, as its rapid growth permits double cropping of cereals (e.g., barley and maize or barley and millet) at altitudes where winter wheat does not. The relative importance of barley in mountain irrigated infields is thus one clear indicator of human pressure on the land; the higher the latter, the greater the former. Spring rainfed (*lalmī*) barley appears simultaneously on suitable slopes (outfields).

Finally, spring barley, both *ābī* and *lalmī*, remains the only cereal that can ripen in the cooler conditions and shorter growing seasons of the highest permanent fields. Above 2,900-3,200 m, it is the staple crop for human consumption. Barley fields have been recorded up to 3,450 m in the Hindu Kush (Grötzbach, 1972, p. 160) and even up to 3,700 m in the Pamir (Naumann, 1974, pp. 100), that is, some 300 m above the respective altitudinal limits of wheat but still more than 1,000 m below the absolute altitudinal limit of barley cultivation so far reported in the world (4,750 m in western Tibet, according to Chinese scientists quoted by Uhlig, 1980, p. 305). In high Nūrestān and adjoining regions, spring *ābī* barley is often sown mixed with leguminous plants such as peas (*mošong*) or horse beans (*bāqolī*), both being used to prepare a mixed flour from which bread is made (Scheibe, 1937, p. 112; von Moos, 1980, p. 26).

There is no industrial utilization of barley in Afghanistan.

Bibliography: J. E. T. Aitchison, *Notes on the Products of Western Afghanistan and of North-Eastern Persia*, Edinburgh, 1890. A. C. Davydov, *Sotsial'no-èkonomicheskaya struktura derevni Afganistana*, Moscow, 1976. L. Edelberg and S. Jones, *Nuristan*, Graz, 1979. E. Grötzbach, *Kulturgeographischer Wandel in Nordost-Afghanistan seit dem 19. Jahrhundert*, Afghanische Studien 4, Meisenheim am Glan, 1972. I. von Moos, *Die wirtschaftlichen Verhältnisse im Munjan-Tal und der Opiumgebrauch der Bevölkerung*, Bibliotheca Afghanica, Schriftenreihe 1, Liestal, 1980. C. M. Naumann, "Pamir und Wakhan," *Afghanistan Journal* 1/4, 1974, pp. 91-104. S. Sakamoto et al., "Variation and Geographical Distribution of Cultivated Plants and their Wild Relatives Native to Afghanistan," in Y. Tani, ed., *Preliminary Report of Field Survey on the Agrico-Pastoral Peoples in Afghanistan 1978*, Kyoto, 1980, pp. 35-66. A. Scheibe, ed., *Deutsche im Hindukusch*, Berlin, 1937. H. Toepfer, *Wirtschafts- und sozialgeographische Fallstudien in ländlichen Gebieten Afghanistans*, Bonner Geographische Abhandlungen 46, Bonn, 1972. H. Uhlig, "Der Anbau an den Höhengrenzen der Gebirge Süd- und Südostasiens," in C. Jentsch and H. Liedtke, eds., *Höhengrenzen in Hochgebirgen*, Arbeiten aus dem Geographischen Institut der Universität des Saarlandes 29, Saarbrücken, 1980, pp. 279-310. N. I. Vavilov and D. D. Bukinich, *Zemledel'cheskiĭ Afganistan*, Leningrad, 1929. H.-J. Wald, *Landnutzung und Siedlung der Pashtunen im Becken von Khost*, Schriften des Deutschen Orient-Instituts, Materialien und Dokumente, Opladen, 1969. K. Yamashita, ed., *Cultivated Plants and their Relatives*, Results of Kyoto University Scientific Expedition to the Karakoram and Hindukush 1955, 1, Kyoto, 1965. D. Zohary, "The Progenitors of Wheat and Barley in Relation to Domestication and Agricultural Dispersal in the Old World," in P. J. Ucko and G. W. Dimbleby, eds., *The Domestication and Exploitation of Plants and Animals*, London, 1969, pp. 47-66.

(D. BALLAND)

BARM-E DELAK, a site with a spring about 10 km southeast of Shiraz, where three panels bearing two Sasanian rock reliefs are carved in the mountain at a height of about 6.5 m above the ground. The place has been visited and described by several European travelers since the 17th century: for example, Tavernier, between 1632 and 1665; Kaempfer, the first to sketch the reliefs, in 1685; Flandin and Coste, who made some remarkable drawings, in 1840-41; and Andreas and Stolze, who took the first photographs of the site, at the end of the 19th century. Sarre and later Erdmann published the first scientific studies of the site.

1. The larger relief (Plate VI) measures 1.8 to 2.1 m (height) by 2.6 m and shows a man with a flower in his right hand which he presents to a woman, presumably his wife; the woman extends her right hand to the flower and her left hand, hidden in the sleeve, is brought to her mouth. A badly damaged Pahlavi inscription is carved under the arm of the male figure (Gropp proposed two variant readings of the inscription). The identification of the persons depicted in the relief and its overall purpose are still matters of debate. Various suggestions as to the identity of the two figures have been proposed: Sarre recognized in the relief scene the investiture of the queen by the god Ohrmazd (Ahura Mazdā), but this interpretation was rightly rejected by Erdmann, who proposed that the scene depicts the transmission of a fertility symbol by a great dignitary to the queen. More recently Hinz interpreted the scene as showing Prince Narseh (later Narseh I, 292-301), son of Šāpūr I (239-70), offering a flower to his niece Ardašīr-Anāhīd, wife of Bahrām II (274-97), Šāpūr I's grandson and Narseh's nephew, who took the throne after his father Bahrām I (271-74), Narseh's brother; thus the flower would be a symbol of reconciliation. According to de Waele, who compared the relief to the one at Sarāb-e Qandīl, it shows a prince obtaining a flower from an Anāhīd priestess, while Lukonin recognized in the woman Bahrām II's wife Šāpūrduxtak, and in the man Prince Ardašīr, chiliarch (*hazārbed*) and son of Pābak. However, the man, although not wearing a crown, can also be a king, since the relief obviously does not represent an investiture scene or celebrate a great victory; Frye has suggested that the man is Bahrām II himself.

2. The smaller, badly weathered relief (Plate VII) covers two panels, the left panel measuring 2.75 (height) by 1.25 m, the right panel 2.08 by 1.25 m. It depicts two persons, King Bahrām II to the left and a high official to the right, separated by unworked rock and a deep fissure. Bahrām II is easily identified by his crown with eagle wings and *korymbos*. His right hand is brought to his mouth in a sign of veneration; the left hand rests on the hilt of a sword. The man to the right, facing the king, is represented in a nearly identical gesture and wears a high rounded hat. Erdmann, who sees in the unworked rock the outlines of a fire altar, thinks this is the high priest and according to Hinz it is none other than the famous high priest Kartēr (Kirdēr).

Bibliography: F. C. Andreas and F. Stolze, *Persepolis*, Berlin, 1882, pl. 145. K. Erdmann, "Die sasanidischen Felsreliefs von Barm-i Dilak," *ZDMG* 99, 1949, pp. 50-57. E. Flandin and P. Coste. *Voyage en Perse. Perse ancienne*, Paris, 1851, pp. 66, 67, pl. 56. R. N. Frye, "The Tang-i Qandil and Barm-i Dilak Reliefs," *Bulletin of the Asia Institute of Pahlavi University* 1-4, Shiraz, 1976, pp. 35-44. Idem, *The*

PLATE VI

Barm-e Delak I

History of Ancient Iran, Munich, 1984, p. 304. G. Gropp, "Bericht über eine Reise in West- und Südiran," *AMI*, N.S. 3, 1970, pp. 201, 202, fig. 15. W. Hinz, *Altiranische Funde und Forschungen*, Berlin, 1969, pp. 217-28, figs. 136-39. E. Kaempfer, *Amoenitatum exoticarum Politico-physico-medicarum... Descriptiones Rerum Persicarum et Ulterioris Asiae*, Lemgoviae (Lemgo), 1712, pp. 361f. V. Lukonin, "The Complex of Barm-i Dilak," in *Iran v III vĕke* (Iran in the third century), Moscow, 1979, pp. 28-34, 110-113 (Eng. summary), figs. 10, 20, 21. Idem in *Camb. Hist. Iran* III, pp. 129, 881. F. Sarre and E. Herzfeld, *Iranische Felsreliefs*, Berlin, 1910, pp. 187, 188, pl. XXXII. Mīrzā Forṣat Šīrāzī, *Āṯār-e ʿAjam*, Bombay, 1354/1935, pp. 13-14. J. B. Tavernier, *Les six voyages de Jean Baptiste Tavernier qu'il a faits en Turquie, en Perse et aux Indes*, Paris, 1679, 1st pt., bk. 5, pp. 736-37. E. de Waele, "Sur le bas-relief sassanide de Tang-e Qandil et la 'bas-relief au couple' de Barm-i Dilak," *Revue des archéologues et historiens d'art de Louvain* 11, 1978, pp. 9-32.

(L. Vanden Berghe)

BARMAKIDS or Barāmeka, a well-known family of secretaries and viziers during the time of the early ʿAbbasids, stemming from the region of Balḵ where Barmak, the ancestor of the family, according to early Muslim authors was the high priest of the Zoroastrian fire temple of Nowbahār (Yāqūt, IV, p. 819; Ebn Ḵallekān, Cairo, III, p. 198; Beirut, IV, p. 29); however, the name Nowbahār is likely to be from Buddhist Sanskrit *nava-vihāra* "new monastery," and the eponym of the family, Barmak, may ultimately derive from Sanskrit *pramukha* "chief" (H. W. Bailey, *BSOAS* 11, 1943, p. 3). Muslim relations with the Balḵ region go back to the early phase of Islamic conquests during the time of Moʿāwīa, but no tie between a member of the Barmakids and a Muslim caliph can be established before the reign of Hešām b. ʿAbd al-Malek (105-25/723-42). Attempts to date this tie back to the time of the third caliph, ʿOṯmān (r. 23-35/644-56), seem unconvincing.

In his *Aḵbār al-Barāmeka*, ʿOmar b. al-Azraq, the early historian of that family, relates that Barmak was received with great respect by Hešām when he came to his court with 500 followers. Barmak was converted to Islam. He must have stayed many years at Roṣāfa, the residence of Hešām, where his son Ḵāled grew up with the caliph's son Maslama. Barmak appears to have been a physician, for, when Maslama married, Barmak advised him to take a certain medicine that would enable him to beget a child. Barmak was also endowed

PLATE VII

Barm-e Delak II

with the gift of prophecy; when he saw Moḥammad b. ʿAlī b. ʿAbd-Allāh b. ʿAbbās passing, he told his son Ḵāled that the caliphate would be transferred to the ʿAbbasids, and advised him to promote their cause in the future if he could (Ebn al-ʿAdīm, *Boḡyat al-ṭalab*, III, p. 22; V, pp. 337ff.). Barmak afterward left Syria for Gorgān where he met Yazīd b. Barāʾ and arranged a marriage between Yazīd's daughter and his son Ḵāled.

It was Ḵāled's fortune to participate in the ʿAbbasid mission (*daʿwa*) and to become one of the twenty members who were selected after the twelve syndics (*naqībs*) to propagate the cause of the Hashemites. His activities covered Gorgān, Tabarestān, and Ray, where he would go around posing as a merchant of cattle and slaves (*Boḡya*, loc. cit.). When the armies of Abū Moslem left Khorasan for the west, Ḵāled was, with Qaḥṭaba, entrusted with the distribution of plunder. After being wounded, he was well received by Saffāḥ, who at first thought, because of his eloquence, that he was an Arab. The caliph appointed him the manager of both the *dīvān* of the army (*jond*) and the *dīvān* of the land tax (*ḵarāj*). The registers used in the first *dīvān* were in the form of scrolls, and Ḵāled was the first one to replace the scrolls with ledgers (*dafāter*). Soon Ḵāled won the confidence of the caliph and became his principal adviser. His wife suckled Saffāḥ's daughter Rayṭa, and the caliph's wife suckled Ḵāled's daughter Omm Yaḥyā.

In the time of al-Manṣūr (r. 136-58/754-75), the rivalry between the vizier Abū Ayyūb and Ḵāled drove the latter away from the capital to Fārs where he served as governor. Ḵāled managed to drive rebellious Kurds from Fārs and proved to be a wise and generous governor, eulogized by poets. His generosity evidently exposed him once again to the intrigues of the vizier, for he instigated the caliph to recall Ḵāled and to take three million dirhams from him as restitution. The matter was soon settled, and Ḵāled remained for some time with al-Manṣūr, to whom he gave advice about the plan of the future capital and whom he dissuaded from ruining the Ayvān-e Kesrā (q.v.). Around 150/767 Ḵāled was appointed governor of Ṭabarestān, where he stayed for seven years. In 158/774, when a revolt broke out in Mosul, Ḵāled was commissioned to put it down and to become the city's governor; he stayed there until the death of al-Manṣūr, which occurred a few months later.

During the time of al-Mahdī, Ḵāled was given Šammasīya as a fief (*eqṭāʿ*), in a part of which, later called Sowayqa Ḵāled, he chose to build his residential quarters. Nearby his son Yaḥyā and Yaḥyā's two sons, Fażl and Jaʿfar, built their palaces.

Ḵāled's son Yaḥyā gained prominence first as an assistant to his father in governing Ray, then as a tutor of the prince Hārūn, then as the secretary and treasurer to Hārūn during the latter's campaign against Byzantium. In 163/779, as deputy governor of Fārs, he managed to abolish taxes paid on trees. Kāled died in 165/781-82, shortly after Hārūn returned from his campaign.

In the short reign of al-Hādī (r. 169-70/785-86) Yaḥyā was thrown into prison because he stood firmly against al-Hādī's attempts to remove Hārūn from succession to the caliphate. After al-Hādī's sudden death Yaḥyā was released from prison and in 170/786 became Hārūn al-Rašīd's vizier; the following year he received control of the caliphal seal. The height of Barmakid power was reached under al-Rašīd; in fact, there was no essential activity in the caliphate in which the "triumvirate" of Yaḥyā, Fażl, and Ja'far did not involve themselves. They received help from other Barmakids whenever necessary. Moḥammad b. Kāled was the caliph's chamberlain until he was dismissed from office in 179/795. Mūsā b. Yaḥyā was the leader of an army which put down a rebellion in Syria in 176/792. The main roles, however, were played by the three leaders, who, in spite of their power, did not act against the wishes of the caliph.

Yaḥyā remained in power for seventeen years. In 178/794 he was entrusted with all the administrative matters in the state. His son Fażl, the "foster" brother of Hārūn, was appointed governor of the East and Ja'far governor of the West in 176/792. Fażl also put down the revolt of Yaḥyā b. 'Abd-Allāh and was appointed governor of Khorasan where he proved to be an able and beloved administrator; he left Khorasan a year later after having had many mosques built. He remained in the caliph's favor until 183/799 when he was dismissed from all his offices. The dismissal of Fażl did not, however, presage the tragic end of the whole family; Ja'far remained unrivaled in his great position. In 180/796, he suppressed a revolt in Syria, gave the seal to his father, and was appointed head of the caliphal bodyguard and manager of the postal service, the mints, and the textile factory (*dīvān al-ṭerāz*). It is not clear what exactly took place between 183/799 and the pilgrimage of the caliph in 186/802 to turn him against his "viziers," but he did order that Ja'far be killed in 187/803. Fażl and his brothers were arrested, Yaḥyā put under surveillance, and the property of all the Barmakids (except Moḥammad b. Kāled) confiscated.

The end of the Barmakids has eluded satisfactory explanation. It is not enough to say, as the historians imply, that Hārūn grew exceedingly covetous in his later years; that raising his many children was very costly; that the luxury of the Barmakids and their favorites and clients provoked his envy; and that the intrigues of Fażl b. al-Rabī', who succeeded Moḥammad b. Kāled as chamberlain, and others turned the caliph against them. These and other reasons are suggestive but not convincing; there has thus been a popular tendency to seek other explanations. The stories of Ja'far's supposed marriage to 'Abbāsa (much embroidered in the sources) and of the censers used in the Ka'ba (mentioned in the sources en passant, possibly because the heathen object would recall the Buddhist background of the family) have been circulated as the events which led to the final disaster. Popular imagination has produced many other stories about the tragic end of the Barmakids, such as the dialogue between the mother of Ja'far and Hārūn (*al-'Eqd* V, pp. 62-65) and the story of the man who used to frequent the ruined halls of the Barmakids and lament their fate (*al-Faraj ba'd al-šedda* III, pp. 166-72).

The generosity of the Barmakids also became proverbial; to this day, an unstinting host of banquets and festivals is called "Barmakī." The eloquence (*balāḡa*) of Yaḥyā and his son Ja'far won the admiration of their contemporaries. They were also genuine patrons of poets and writers; under their auspices a special office was established for the support of poets. Ja'far's palace became the residence of caliphs. On the whole they set a tradition in different aspects of cultural as well as political life. The *nesba* Barmakī was applied to their descendants, such as the poet Jaḥẓa, and to people who lived in a quarter of Baghdad called al-Barmakīya. Today Barmakī designates a certain gypsy-like group which roams in Egypt and Syria (cf. *EI*[2] I, p. 1036).

Bibliography: Works containing information about the Barmakids include all major Arabic sources dealing with the early 'Abbasids until 187/803, e.g., Ya'qūbī, Ṭabarī, Mas'ūdī's *Morūj*, Ebn al-Aṯīr (see the indexes in the editions of these authors), and books of *adab* on poets of the period such as Jāḥeẓ's *al-Bayān wa'l-tabyīn*, ed. A. Hārūn, Cairo, 1960. Moḥammad b. Yazīd Mobarrad, *al-Kāmel*, ed. M.-A. Ebrāhīm, Cairo, 1956. *Aḡānī* (Cairo). Abū Bakr Moḥammad Ṣūlī, *Ketāb al-awrāq fī akbār Āl 'Abbās wa aš'ārehem*, ed. H. Dunne, Cairo, 1934-35. Ebn 'Abd-Rabbeh, *al-'Eqd al-farīd*, ed. A. Amīn, et al., Cairo, 1965. See also Ebn Badrūn, *Šarḥ al-Bassāma*, Cairo, n.d., pp. 222-42. Abū Esḥāq Ebrāhīm Raqīq, *al-Moktār men qoṭb al-sorūr*, ed. A. Manṣūr, Tunis, 1976. Abū Esḥāq Ebrāhīm Ḥosri, *Zahr al-ādāb wa ṯamar al-albāb*, ed. A.-M. Bījawī, Cairo, 1969. Abū 'Alī Moḥassen Tanūkī's *al-Faraj ba'd al-šedda*, ed. A. Šāljī, Beirut, 1978; *Neswār al-moḥāżera wa akbār al-moḏākara*, ed. A. Šāljī, Beirut, 1971-73; and *al-Mostajād men fa'alāt al-ajwād*, ed. Kord-'Alī, Damascus, 1946, contain anecdotes about the Barmakids. Biographical sources: *Ta'rīk Baḡdād* VII, p. 152. Ebn Kallekān, ed. 'Abbās, I, pp. 328-46, 472-75. Ṣalāḥ-al-Dīn Kalīl Ṣafadī, *al-Wāfī be'l-wafayāt*, ed. Š. Fayṣal, Wiesbaden, 1981, XI, pp. 156-67. Šams-al-Dīn Moḥammad b. Ṭūlūn, *Enbā' al-'omarā'*, Berlin, Staatsbibliothek, ms. no. 704, fols. 29, 46. Kāled: Ebn Kallekān, VI, p. 219; Kamāl-al-Dīn Abu'l-Qāsem b. 'Adīm, *Boḡyat al-ṭalab fī ta'rīk Ḥalab*, ms. Ahmed III (Istanbul), no. 2925, V, p. 336. Fażl: *Ta'rīk Baḡdād* XII, p. 334; Ebn Kallekān, ed. 'Abbās, IV, pp. 27-36; Ebn Taḡrīberdī, *al-Nojūm al-ẓāhera*, Cairo, II, p. 14; Ḏahabī, *Ketāb 'ebar fī akbār al-bašar*, ed. S. Monajjed, Kuwait, I, p. 309; Ebn al-'Emād, *Šaḏarāt fī akbār man dahab*, Cairo, 1350, I, p. 330. Yaḥyā: *Ta'rīk Baḡdād* XIV, p. 128. Ebn Kallekān, I, pp. 331-38, VI, pp. 219-29; Yāqūt,

Odabā', Cairo, 1936-38, XX, p. 5; Marzobānī, *Mo'jam al-šo'arā'*, Cairo, 1960, p. 488. Geographical sources, especially about Nowbahār: Ebn al-Faqīh, pp. 232-35; Yāqūt, IV, p. 817; Qazvīnī, *Āṯār al-belād*, Beirut, 1960, p. 330; Ḥemyarī, *al-Rawż al-me'ṭār*, ed. I. Abbas, Beirut, 1975, pp. 584-85 (see the index under individual Barmakids). Studies: L. Bouvat, "Les Barmécides d'après les historiens arabes et persans," *RMM* 12, 1912, pp. 1-131; Pers, tr. 'A.-Ḥ. Meykada, *Barmakīān*. S. Nadvi, "The Origin of the Barmakids," *Islamic Culture* 6, 1932, pp. 19-28. D. Sourdel, *Le vizirat 'abbaside de 749 à 936*, Damascus, 1959, I, pp. 127-81. *EI*[1] s.vv. "Dja'far," "al-Faḍl," and "Yaḥyā b. Khālid."

(I. ABBAS)

BĀRMĀN, the son of Vīsa, one of the Turanian heroes mentioned in the *Šāh-nāma* as a member of the army that Afrāsīāb led into Iran during the reign of Nowḏar. In hand to hand combat, Bārmān killed the aged Qobād, the son of Kāva. Some time later Bārmān himself died at the hands of Qāran, Qobād's brother. During the reigns of Kay Kāvūs and Kay Kosrow, another Turanian hero appeared with this name, evidently the son of Vīsa and brother of Pīrān, though he is not explicitly identified in the *Šāh-nāma* episode. This Bārmān was put, together with Hūmān, at the head of an army of 12,000 men which Sohrāb led into Iran. They were instructed by Afrāsīāb to prevent Sohrāb from recognizing his own father Rostam. Later, in the reign of Kay Kosrow, Bārmān faced the Iranian hero Rohhām, the son of Gōdarz, in the episode of the twelve challenges (*davāzdah rok*) and was killed by him.

Bibliography: *Šāh-nāma* (Moscow) II, p. 15 vv. 143ff.; III, index.

(DJ. KHALEGHI-MOTLAGH)

BARMĀYA, the name of a cow associated with Ferēdūn and eventually killed by Żaḥḥāk. The form Barmāya is found only in the *Šāh-nāma*, while an earlier form, Barmāyūn, is found, e.g., in the poetry of Farālāvī and Daqīqī (Lazard, *Premiers poètes*, pp. 43, 143), in the *Loḡat-e fors* (ed. M. Dabīrsīāqī, Tehran, 1336 Š./1957, p. 161), and in Ṯa'ālebī's *Ḡorar* (pp. 31, 35). This form corresponds to Avestan *barəmāyaona*, the epithet of an ox (*Yt.* 17.55; see K. Geldner, *Zeitschrift für vergleichende Sprachforschung* 24, 1879, p. 147) and indicates that the form Barmāya was created by Ferdowsī in place of Barmāyūn for metrical reasons.

The *Šāh-nāma* (Moscow, I, pp. 57-60), on the one hand, states that Barmāya suckled Ferēdūn for three years, but on the other seems to imply that Barmāya was born after Ferēdūn. Perhaps the original tale was that Ferēdūn and Barmāya were born at the same time and that Ferēdūn was suckled by Barmāya's mother. In the *Dēnkard* (book 9, ed. Madan, pp. 814-15, tr. West in *Pahlavi Texts* IV, SBE 37, pp. 218, 220) *gušn ī barmāyūn* occurs, meaning "bull," but in the *Bundahišn* (tr. Anklesaria, chap. 35.10, pp. 294-95; TD_2, p. 229.11) Barmāyūn is the name of Ferēdūn's brother, who also appears in the *Šāh-nāma* (I, p. 65 v. 256) with the same name (in some manuscripts, Pormāya); this demonstrates a relationship between the name of this bull and Ferēdūn's brother, perhaps also based on an original tale that had Ferēdūn and Barmāya/Barmāyūn born at the same time. It should also be noticed that in the chapter on the race and genealogy of the Kayān in the *Bundahišn* all of Ferēdūn's ancestors have names ending in -gāw (Pur-gāw, Sōg-gāw, Bōr-gāw, Syāh-gāw, Spēd-gāw, etc.; tr. Anklesaria, pp. 294-95; TD_2, p. 229).

Lending additional strength to the conjecture that Ferēdūn and Barmāya/Barmāyūn were born at the same time is the ancient belief that the births of prophets, certain kings, and famous heroes were accompanied by marvels. Since the birth of Barmāya, who was said to be a cow "of exceeding beauty, with a multicolored pelt the likes of which had never been seen before," represented such a miraculous event and at the same time augured well for Ferēdūn's birthday, one can surmise that the cow's birth was the marvel that accompanied the hero's birth. Thus when Ferēdūn fought with the snake-shouldered tyrant Żaḥḥāk, he was avenging not only the murder of his father, Ābtīn (q.v.), but also that of Barmāya (*Šāh-nāma* I, p. 57). The cow-headed mace that Ferēdūn took into battle against the tyrant is a possible allusion to his bovine birthmate.

Bibliography: Given in the text. See also J. Kāleqī-Moṭlaq, "Barmāya yā Pormāya?" *Īrān-nāma* 5/2, 1365 Š./1987, pp. 376-77. J. Matīnī, "Rewāyāt-e moktalef dar-bāra-ye dawrān-e kūdakī o javānī-e Ferīdūn," *Īrān-nāma* 4/1, 1364 Š./1985, pp. 87-132. Š. Meskūb, "Ferīdūn-e farrok," *Īrān-nāma* 5/1, 1364 Š./1985, pp. 26-27.

(DJ. KHALEGHI MOTLAGH)

BARNĀMA-RĪZĪ "planning." Among the countries of the Middle East Iran has a relatively long history of economic development planning. By the time of the revolution in 1357 Š./1979, five development plans of various durations had been implemented in Iran over a thirty-year period; and these planning efforts had been preceded by less formal types of state intervention in the country's mixed public and private economy.

The earliest economic policies aiming at planned economic development in modern Iran date back to the final decade of Reżā Shah's reign (1304-20 Š./1925-41). These uncoordinated public policies, however, did not constitute development planning as the term has come to be understood after World War II. The overall aim of the prewar policies was modernization, with the more specific economic objectives of achieving industrialization and developing the country's infrastructural facilities, while almost no attention was given to the agricultural sector (A. Banani, *The Modernization of Iran, 1921-1941*, Stanford, 1961, pp. 112-45; Z. Y. Hershlag, *Introduction to the Modern Economic History of the Middle East*, Leiden, 1964, pp. 194-207). The industrial policy of the period was basically determined on the basis of a vaguely expressed desire for self-sufficiency in a number of consumer goods. Consequently, much attention was given to import substitution and to the protection of the newly established state-owned industrial enterprises; foreign trade in fact became a state monopoly. The traditions of centralization in Iran's public administration and in the official decision-making processes also go back to the prewar years.

The Allied occupation of Iran and the abdication of Reżā Shah in 1320 Š./1941 ushered in a period of political unrest and economic chaos. During the immediate postwar years, the idea of reconstructing and developing the Iranian economy through government initiative gained fresh ground in the country. Early in 1325 Š./1946, a commission was formed at the Ministry of Finance for the purpose of development planning; and it produced a draft plan, containing essentially some broad financial allocations. Soon afterward, a Supreme Planning Board was created to formulate a more definitive plan. The Board prepared an ambitious plan, envisaging 62 billion rials ($1.9 billion) in public investments, which could not be financed domestically, without identifying adequate investment projects. Consequently, when the Iranian government made an informal loan application to the then newly founded International Bank for Reconstruction and Development, the consideration of the loan was made conditional on the inclusion of a sufficient number of projects in the plan and on their feasibility. An American firm of consulting engineers, Morrison-Knudsen, was hired to generate the required list of projects. This firm completed its work by Mordād, 1326 Š./August, 1947 (Morrison-Knudsen International Company, Inc., *Report on Program for the Development of Iran*, San Francisco, 1947), giving the government a choice of three alternative investment programs, ranging from $1.2 billion (for 240 projects) to $260 million (for 24 projects). The actual size and the method of financing the program were left to the government. These issues were settled in a subsequent report prepared by Mošarraf Nafīsī, with the cooperation of other members of the Supreme Planning Board. This report, submitted in Āḏar, 1326 Š./December, 1947, provided the basis for Iran's First Seven-Year Development Plan Act, which was eventually ratified by the Majles in Bahman, 1327 Š./February, 1949. Meanwhile, the government had hired the services of Overseas Consultants, a consortium of eleven American consulting firms, to evaluate the adequacy of the First Plan in the light of Iran's investment requirements. The detailed study of these foreign advisers proved invaluable for some time as a guide to planning in Iran (see Overseas Consultants, Inc., *Report on the Seven Year Development Plan for the Plan Organization of the Imperial Government of Iran*, New York, 1949, 5 vols.).

As the initial planning efforts were taking shape, it was decided that Iran's development activities should be supervised by a new government agency. Accordingly, the Plan Organization (Sāzmān-e Barnāma) was set up in 1327 Š./1949. The Plan Organization was to have a certain degree of independence so as to insulate it from the chronic governmental inefficiencies; but it was not to be an executive body. Its chief functions were to design development plans and to supervise and coordinate their execution. Aside from exceptional cases, the implementation of development programs and projects was to be the responsibility of the appropriate ministries. In practice, the Plan Organization deviated from the intent of the First Plan Act and directly executed most of the projects, a practice maintained also during the Second Plan. This was because the ministries had proved incapable of executing development projects, while the Plan Organization had failed to develop its supervisory and coordinating functions. Initially, the organizational structure of the Sāzmān-e Barnāma was specified only in broad terms; it had a managing director, a high council, a board of control, and a technical bureau charged with appraising the feasibility of the individual projects.

The First Plan, consisting merely of a partial investment program for the public sector, called for public investment expenditures of 21 billion rials (about $650 million), later raised to 26.3 billion rials in 1331 Š./1952, to be undertaken during a seven-year period starting in Mehr, 1327 Š./September, 1948. All of the country's oil revenues were to be set aside for financing the First Plan. The implementation of the First Plan, however, never gained any momentum. The first two years of the plan period were chiefly devoted to the setting up of the Plan Organization and the related administrative matters. Subsequently, for more than three years following the nationalization of the oil industry and the cessation of activities in that industry in 1330 Š./1951, the Plan Organization lost its main source of finance and could not effectively execute the planned investments. Therefore, the results of the First Plan turned out to be very disappointing; actual public investment expenditures amounted to 4.1 billion rials, or only sixteen percent of the planned total, during the "nominal" plan period. Meanwhile, with the resumption of activities in the oil sector in 1333 Š./1954, the government decided to adopt a new development plan, a plan that would also be more in line with Iran's increased oil revenues under the Oil Consortium Agreement.

The Second Plan, for the seven-year period from Mehr, 1334 Š./September, 1955 through Šahrīvar, 1341 Š./September, 1962, was prepared in a few months. Like its predecessor, it was not a comprehensive plan; it did not concern itself with the overall rate and pattern of development in the economy. The partial nature of the Second Plan was due not merely to its exclusion of the private sector, but also to its failure to embrace all the development activities of the public sector. It consisted of that portion of the public investments which was to be controlled by the Plan Organization; this accounted for only about one-half of the total public investments during the plan period. This line of demarcation reflected an arbitrary arrangement for allocating a certain share of the country's oil revenues to the Plan

Organization for financing the Second Plan. The design of the Second Plan did not follow from any particular planning methodology, and most of the investment decisions were made in an arbitrary fashion and without reference to any specific investment criterion. At the time, the lack of statistical data and familiarity with planning techniques were among the major problems of plan formulation in Iran. The investment program of the Second Plan, both in terms of its size and allocations, was revised several times, mainly due to the underestimation of the project costs. Originally, the planned public investments amounted to 70 billion rials (about $930 million); this figure was finally raised to 84 billion rials in 1336 Š./1957. The sectoral allocations of the Second Plan revealed a heavy emphasis, more pronounced in the final revision, on the development of infrastructure and social overhead capital; transport facilities and dams, for instance, accounted for almost two-thirds of the planned expenditures. By contrast, directly productive activities, in both agriculture and industry, received low priorities. Furthermore, the Second Plan was dominated by a relatively small number of capital-intensive projects, as the planners had continued to face a shortage of well-designed investment projects. The Second Plan had all the shortcomings of an unintegrated investment program prepared on a piecemeal basis and without clearly defined development objectives.

In the absence of quantitative targets, the results of the Second Plan cannot be measured in any precise manner. However, a comparison between the actual and the revised planned expenditures indicates a high degree of plan fulfillment, about ninety percent; the same applies to the sectoral investments. But this success is more apparent than real, because the revised investment program itself represented a drastic reduction in the scope of the original program so as to bring the plan more in line with actual developments. During the Second Plan, as previously, the planning machinery did not follow the traditional administrative setup of the government. The formulation and execution of the plan remained largely the responsibility of the Plan Organization, although the Second Plan Act had assigned important implementation functions to the ministries. Moreover, the specific duties of the various units of the Plan Organization continued to be undefined. However, in 1336 Š./1957, a planning unit was established for the first time in the Sāzmān-e Barnāma. This was the Economic Bureau, later renamed the Division of Economic Affairs, which for a few years also received the technical assistance of a team of foreign economists known as the Harvard Advisory Group. The Economic Bureau undertook a valuable mid-term review of the Second Plan and by 1340 Š./1961 had formulated a framework for the Third Plan; later it expanded into the Planning Division which played a crucial part in designing the Fourth and the Fifth Plans.

The Third Plan, covering the five-and-a-half-year period from Mehr, 1341 Š./September, 1962 through Esfand, 1346 Š./March, 1968, was Iran's first comprehensive development plan. The Plan Organization was to prepare, with the assistance of the ministries, a draft plan, called the "plan frame," of the Third Plan. The ministries were then to proceed with the task of designing specific investment projects. Eventually, the detailed projects, together with the plan frame and statements on general economic policies, were to appear in a single document that would constitute the Third Plan. The actual process of planning did not go far beyond the stage of the plan frame. Therefore, the Third Plan essentially came to consist of an investment program for the public sector, covering tentative sectoral allocations and broad programs for the major sectors, together with some forecasts for the private sector; it did not specify how private investments were to be realized. But the Third Plan Law introduced a major change regarding plan implementation, a change that was observed also in connection with the Fourth and the Fifth Plans. Thenceforth, all development projects, after being approved by the Plan Organization, were to be implemented directly by the ministries and the regular government agencies.

The Third Plan frame was based on an overall growth target, an average annual rate of increase of six percent in real gross national product (GNP). A number of secondary objectives were also specified in general terms. Originally, the Third Plan envisaged some 348 billion rials ($4.6 billion) in development outlays, consisting of fixed investments and certain supplementary expenditures; the public and the private shares were set at 190 and 158 billion rials, respectively. Since the oil revenues increased more rapidly than anticipated, the size of the public sector program was eventually raised to 230 billion rials by 1345 Š./1966, while nothing more was said regarding the investments of the private sector. Indeed, the Third Plan proved to be very open-ended in respect to the private sector. No formal planning model was used in preparing the Third Plan; the essential method of planning adopted was one of trial and error, or planning in stages, reflecting the absence of much of the statistical data required by more complex techniques. The sectoral allocations of the plan frame represented a sort of balanced growth strategy, envisaging a balance between investments in social overhead capital and directly productive activities. Agriculture, industry and services were equally emphasized; and about sixty percent of the public development outlays in these sectors were to be absorbed by relatively less capital-intensive projects.

In practice, the Third Plan's growth target was surpassed, as the measured growth rate amounted to nine percent per annum. The Third Plan frame had specified no sectoral production targets, except for agriculture. The planned annual rate of 4.1 percent for agriculture, however, was not attained. The government's agricultural policy had, in fact, changed drastically at the beginning of the plan period. A major land reform program, not foreseen in the plan frame, had replaced the measures planned for increasing agricultural production (see Plan Organization, *Third Plan Frame: Agriculture*, Tehran, 1961). During the Third Plan period, public development outlays actually amounted to 205 billion rials, implying an almost 90 percent fulfillment of the revised target. But private investments, amounting to 249 billion rials, were far in excess of the magnitude specified in the plan frame. The revised sectoral investment targets of the public sector were also attained with a high degree of success, except for manufacturing which showed a forty percent shortfall. In industry, too, actual developments deviated significantly from the industrial policy of the plan frame, which in the light of Iran's comparative advantages stressed the development of small and medium-scale industries (see Plan Organization, *Third Plan Frame: Industries and Mines*, Tehran, 1961). Starting in 1344 Š./1965, the government established a number of new, highly capital-intensive, and complex industries, including steel, machine tools, tractors, and petrochemicals. Such heavy industries absorbed the largest share of the industrial investments, as well as the country's scarce skilled manpower resources, during the Fourth and the Fifth Plan periods.

During the Third Plan period, a drastic change occurred in Iran's budgeting system. Until then, the preparation of the government's ordinary budget had been the responsibility of the Ministry of Finance, while the Plan Organization had developed its own budgetary procedures and had prepared the country's development budget. There was, however, some overlapping between the two budgets. In 1343 Š./1964, the budgetary functions of the Ministry of Finance were transferred to the new Central Budget Bureau established in the Plan Organization, which since that time has prepared Iran's annual budget, covering both current and capital transactions (F. Daftary, "Development Planning and Budgeting in Iran," in CENTO, *Seminar on Budget Administration*, Ankara, 1973, pp. 221-32). Moreover, as a major step toward improving the availability of statistical information, the Statistical Center of Iran, affiliated with the Plan Organization, was set up in 1344 Š./1965.

The Fourth Plan, covering the five-year period from Farvardīn, 1347 Š./March, 1968 through Esfand, 1351 Š./March, 1973, was the first comprehensive plan designed entirely by Iranians. The plan was based on an overall growth target, to increase real GNP at an average annual rate of nine percent. A number of secondary objectives regarding employment, income distribution, balance of payments, and the general level of prices were also stated. The total size of the Fourth Plan was originally set at 810 billion rials ($10.8 billion), ninety-two percent of which was to be financed domestically mainly through oil revenues. The public and the private sector programs were set at 443.5 and 366.5 billion rials respectively. The figure for the public sector was increased several times, being finally fixed at 555 billion rials. Once again, the plan was rather open-ended in terms of private investments and the policies required for calling forth the appropriate responses from that sector. As in the case of the Third Plan, the essential method of formulating the Fourth Plan was one of trial and error. The task of planning was broken into a number of stages and the process started by estimating total investment requirements on the basis of the overall growth target. Sectoral investment allocations were determined on the basis of sectoral production targets. The outstanding feature of the Fourth Plan's sectoral allocations was the high priority given to services, especially to transport and communications, while agriculture received a low emphasis in comparison with industry. According to the final revision, agriculture, manufacturing and mining, and transport and communications were respectively allocated 8.4, 20.9, and 23.6 percent of total development outlays of the public sector; other services subsectors were to absorb another 20.2 percent.

The growth of the Iranian economy was rather impressive during the Fourth Plan period. The real rate of growth in GNP amounted to 11.6 percent per annum, indicating an overfulfillment of the planned rate by about two percentage units. With the exception of agriculture and construction, all the sectoral value-added growth targets were either attained or surpassed. Agriculture, with 3.9 percent per annum, had the lowest growth rate, while oil, industry, and services grew at the average annual rate of 14-15 percent each. Concerning other objectives of the Fourth Plan, employment increased by 1.2 million persons, as against the target of 966 thousand. During the first three years of the plan period the general level of prices remained relatively stable, while in the final two years prices rose at about six percent per annum. Total fixed investments amounted to 789 billion rials (at 1338 Š./1959 prices) during the plan period; and public development outlays amounted to 507 billion rials, implying a ninety-one percent plan fulfillment. Sectoral investment targets were also attained with a similar degree of success.

The Fifth Plan, covering the five-year period from Farvardīn, 1352 Š./March, 1973 through Esfand, 1356 Š./March, 1978, was destined to be the last development plan executed during the reign of Moḥammad Reżā Shah (1320-57 Š./1941-78). Much effort was devoted to preparing this plan; alternative growth paths were investigated and the ministries participated actively in the planning process. Furthermore, several foreign advisory teams assisted the Plan Organization in connection with the more specialized planning tasks, including a team organized by the Battelle Memorial Institute, an American entity, to initiate regional planning in Iran. During the Fourth Plan period, the Plan Organization had already established, without much success, provincial offices throughout the country, as a first step toward decentralization in planning. A number of more sophisticated quantitative techniques were used in the preparation of the Fifth Plan, at various stages and to different degrees, including econometric models and linear programming techniques. Subsequently, a Planometrics Bureau was set up in the Plan Organization to develop more such mathematical models of planning as well as long-range perspective plans for the Iranian economy. The Fifth Plan also specified, for the first time, the sectoral composition of private investments.

The Fifth Plan Law, ratified by the Majles in Esfand, 1351 Š./March, 1973, introduced certain important changes into the planning machinery and the structure of the Plan Organization, which thenceforth came to be called the Plan and Budget Organization (Sāzmān-e Barnāma wa Būja), taking account of the integration of the tasks of planning and budgeting and of the ordinary and development budgets of the country. The head of the organization was given the rank of minister of state, and as such he would be a member of both the Council of Ministers and the Supreme Economic Council created earlier. The duties of the Plan Organization's High Council were transferred to the Supreme Economic Council, headed by the prime minister and with the membership of selected ministers. Furthermore, the internal organization of the planning agency was revised and expanded to encompass eight major divisions, including those for planning, budgeting, regionalization, technical affairs, coordination and supervision, and information.

The Fifth Plan was to assign high priorities to social welfare programs, better distribution of income, and in general to the qualitative improvements in the economy. As planning proceeded, however, the government's excessive concern with quantitative changes and physical growth re-asserted itself to a large extent. Originally, the Fifth Plan envisaged an average annual growth rate of 11.4 percent in real gross domestic product (GDP). To achieve this growth target, total fixed investment requirements were placed at 2,461 billion rials (about $37 billion), of which the public and the private sectors were to account for 1,549 and 912 billion rials, respectively. Agriculture, oil, industry, and services were to absorb 6, 19, 52, and 23 percent of planned total investments. With the unprecedented increase in the prices of crude oil during 1973-74, the estimate of Iran's oil revenues for the entire plan period was raised to almost $100 billion, instead of the original figure of $25 billion. Under the direct commands of the monarch, the government decided to disburse a major portion of the increased revenues, without considering the various types of non-capital constraints which had been examined in designing the original Fifth Plan. In 1353 Š./1974, the Fifth Plan was revised hastily and drastically. As a result, the annual growth rate target for GNP was more than doubled to 25.9 percent, and the production targets for agriculture, oil, industry, and services were increased to annual rates of 7, 51, 18 and 16 percent, respectively. The total size of the plan was also doubled to 4,699 billion rials (about $70 billion), with the public and the private shares amounting to 3,119 and 1,580 billion rials. The sectoral pattern of investment in the revised plan, however, did not deviate significantly from the original pattern. Clearly, the attributes of optimality, internal consistency, and realism, in planning and resource allocation, had become greatly undermined by the monarch's desire to embark on grandiose designs. In fact, development planning, requiring severe discipline and commitment, was practically abandoned in the final years of the Fifth Plan period; and no serious attempts were undertaken to formulate the sixth plan, whose implementation should have started in Farvardīn, 1357 Š./March, 1978.

The results of the revised Fifth Plan were never fully collected and published. Its overly ambitious nature, however, had become evident in practice. The decision to utilize Iran's relatively abundant financial resources, without due attention to the country's physical limits of absorptive capacity, including the administrative ability to design and execute sound development projects, proved to be catastrophic. Shortages and bottlenecks of various kinds, especially in terms of skilled manpower, raw materials, cement, and infrastructural capacity (notably ports and transport facilities), prevented realization of the revised goals. The average annual rate of growth of real GDP actually amounted to 6.9 percent, and in all the major sectors the growth rates fell short of the targets. The increased aggregate expenditures, in view of the supply shortages, generated excess demand and inflationary pressures in the economy, with consumer and wholesale prices rising at the average annual rates of 13 and 15 percent, respectively, during the plan period. There were drastic failures also in terms of the objectives for employment and income distribution. Total public investment outlays, amounting to about 2,300 billion rials at constant prices, fell short of the revised plan's target, but private investments, almost 1,890 billion rials, exceeded the revised target.

The oil revenues, providing substantial financial and foreign exchange resources, have created exceptionally favorable growth potentialities for Iran. These revenues make it possible for the country to finance large investment programs and achieve high growth rates, without having to witness, at least in principle, the so-called orthodox ailments of development: serious inflationary pressures and balance of payments problems. During 1341-56 Š./1962-77, coinciding with the Third, Fourth, and Fifth Plan periods, growth of the Iranian economy was indeed significant; the country's GDP increased at the real average annual rate of almost ten percent, and per capita income rose from about $175 to over $1,500. The oil revenues, however, proved to be a mixed blessing, as they undermined the necessity of sound planning, and increased the dependence of Iran on foreign economies. Furthermore, in the past the benefits of oil-generated economic growth in Iran were not distributed equitably to improve the existing unfavorable trend in the distribution of national income and wealth among households and geographical regions, as well as between rural and urban areas (see M. H. Pesaran, "Income Distribution and Its Major Determinants in Iran," in J. W. Jacqz, ed., *Iran: Past, Present and Future*, Aspen, 1976, pp. 267-86). These problems, together with the relative stagnation of the agricultural sector prompting the large-scale migration of the villagers to the cities, contributed to the socio-economic grievances underlying the 1979 revolution.

In the immediate years following the 1979 revolution, the Plan and Budget Organization, which remained intact, advocated a new type of planning, one in which the people themselves would participate directly, for the primary purpose of improving the standard of living of the underprivileged and the lower income groups in the society. Meanwhile, the sphere of government intervention in the economy had increased drastically through nationalization, confiscation, and the creation of a number of public foundations, while there had appeared spiral inflationary pressures as well as stagnation in most sectors. By 1361 Š./1982, the government of the Islamic Republic of Iran had apparently prepared a five-year development plan, which was never made public. Since then no other plans or drafts of plans have been formulated. As of Tīr, 1366 Š./July, 1987, the country is without a development plan.

Bibliography: The following documents produced by the Plan (and Budget) Organization are the main sources on planning in Iran: *Review of the Second Seven Year Plan Program of Iran*, Tehran, 1960. *Gozāreš-e ejrā-ye barnāma-ye haft-sāla-ye dovvom*, Tehran, 1343 Š./1964. *Outline of the Third Plan (1341-1346)*, Tehran, 1961. *Gozāreš-e ʿamalkard-e barnāma-ye sevvom*, Tehran, 1347 Š./1968. *Fourth National Development Plan, 1968-1972*, Tehran, 1968. *Summary of the Fifth National Development Plan, 1973-1978*, Tehran, 1973. *Summary of Iran's Fifth National Development Plan, 1973-1978*, revised Tehran, 1975. Much valuable information on the results of the plans and on actual developments are also to be found in Bank Markazi Iran, *Annual Report and Balance Sheet*, for various years. Idem, *Ḥesābhā-ye mellī-e Īrān, 1338-56*, Tehran, 1360 Š./1981.

Secondary sources: J. Amuzegar, *Iran: An Economic Profile*, Washington, D.C., 1977, pp. 159-77 and 247-58. G. B. Baldwin, *Planning and Development in Iran*, Baltimore, 1967. J. Bharier, *Economic Development of Iran, 1900-1970*, London, 1971, pp. 42-61 and 84-101. F. Daftary, *Economic Development and Planning in Iran, 1955-1967*, Ph.D. thesis, University of California, Berkeley, 1971, pp. 329-507. Idem, "Development Planning in Iran: A Historical Survey," *Iranian Studies* 6, 1973, pp. 176-228. R. E. Looney, *Iran at the End of the Century*, Lexington, Mass., 1977, pp. 5-79 and 123-30. H. Mehner, "Development and Planning in Iran after World War II," in G. Lenczowski, ed., *Iran under the Pahlavis*, Stanford, 1978, pp. 167-99. H. Motamen, "Development Planning in Iran," *Middle East Economic Papers* 3, 1956, pp. 98-111. P. B. Olsen and P. N. Rasmussen, "An Attempt at Planning in a Traditional State: Iran," in E. E. Hagen, ed., *Planning Economic Development*, Homewood, Ill., 1963, pp. 223-51. J. Price Gittinger, *Planning for Agricultural Development: The Experience of Iran*, Washington, D.C., 1965.

(F. Daftary)

BARNAVĪ, ʿALĀʾ-AL-DĪN ČEŠTĪ. See ČEŠTĪYA.

BARQ (lightning), the name of three Persian newspapers.

1. A daily newspaper founded in Tehran in Šawwāl, 1328/October, 1910, by Sayyed Żīāʾ-al-Dīn Ṭabāṭabāʾī (q.v.) as a replacement for his newspaper *Šarq*, which had been suppressed. Like *Šarq* it consisted of three pages in Persian and one in French, and its tone was revolutionary. It was also suppressed, in Rabīʿ II, 1329/April, 1911, and immediately replaced by *Raʿd*, which in due course suffered the same fate. In Ḏu'l-qaʿda, 1331/October, 1913, *Barq* reappeared briefly, and in the following month changed its name to *Raʿd*, which continued until 1335/1917, when Sayyed Żīāʾ was tried and although aquitted found it politic to leave the country for a while. On his return *Raʿd* reappeared but the title *Barq* was not used again. Sayyed Żīāʾ became the first prime minister immediately after the 1921 coup d'état, spearheaded by Reżā Khan (later Reżā Shah).

2. A thrice-weekly newspaper concerned with social questions, founded by Ḡolām-Ḥosayn Moṣāḥab in Tehran in Ordībehešt, 1322/May, 1943, but suppressed some months later. It reappeared briefly in Ḵordād, 1325/June, 1946 as a substitute for the right-wing *Āzād*.

3. A women's journal founded in the 1330s/1950s by Amīn Moʾayyad.

Bibliography: E. G. Browne, *The Press and Poetry of Modern Persia*, Cambridge, 1914, p. 54. M. Ṣadr Hāšemī, *Jarāyed wa majallāt-e Īrān*, 4 vols., Isfahan, 1327-32 Š./1948-53, II, pp. 11-14. ʿA. Āryanpūr, *Az Ṣabā tā Nīmā* II, Tehran, 1351 Š./1973, p. 108. Ḡ.-Ḥ. Ṣāleḥyār, *Čehra-ye maṭbūʿāt-e moʿāṣer*, Tehran, 1351 Š./1973, p. 253. L. P. Elwell-Sutton, "The Iranian Press, 1941-47," *Iran* 6, 1968, p. 81.

(L. P. Elwell-Sutton)

BARQ, the modern Persian term for electricity, borrowed from Arabic *barq* "lightning, flash of lightning." Pashto uses *brēṣ̌nā* "lightning."

i. *In Iran.*
ii. *In Afghanistan.*

i. In Iran

The history and evolution of production. The almost exclusive use of wood and charcoal as energy sources hampered Iran's economic development in the pre-20th century period. Government and private investors' efforts to create an industrial base had to face this issue, which often led to high investment cost, followed by energy-supply, operational, and financial problems. The new 19th-century industries in general used wood or coal boilers and later oil. It was only in 1297/1880 that (coal-based) gasworks were installed in Tehran at a cost of £30,000 at the instigation of Ḥosayn Khan Sepahsālār. Because of the lack of suitable coal, operations stopped a few years later. The machinery was bought by an Iranian who resold it in 1309/1891 to the "Compagnie générale belge pour éclairage et chauffage en Perse." This company bought more machinery, but no progress was made and the works were closed down (Issawi, pp. 306, 308).

The electrification of individual government buildings appears to have begun during the reign of Nāṣer-al-Dīn Shah (ca. 1304/1887) with the state armory (Eʿtemād-al-Salṭana, p. 93) and the shah's residence in Tehran (Tāj-al-Salṭana, p. 53).

It was only in 1318/1900 that the first electrical plant (of 6.6 kw) was built in Iran, in the city of Mašhad. Two years later a second one (of 19 kw) was built in the same city. This plant was financed by Moẓaffar-al-Dīn Shah at a cost of 8,000 tomans; the plant was imported from Russia by Ḥāji Bāqer Mīlānī, known as Rezayof. Both plants were used to illuminate the shrine of Emām Reżā and part of the street which is known as Bālā Ḵīābān and which lies between the plant and the shrine (Issawi, p. 310; Bank Melli Iran, p. 536). In 1321/1903, an electrical plant was erected in Rašt, which functioned irregularly and was closed down after a while. In 1323/1905, an electrical plant of 93 kw was erected in Tabrīz (ibid.).

Tehran. It was only in 1326/1908 that Ḥājj Ḥosayn Amīn-al-Żarb erected an electrical plant (of 300 kw) in Tehran for his brick factory. It was bought in Germany and was also used to light government buildings. The plant was located on Ḵīābān-e Barq, the present-day Ḵīābān-e Amīr Kabīr. Another smaller plant of 2 kw was erected shortly thereafter on Ark Street; this was also used for lighting government buildings (mainly the area around the Meydān-e Sepah, formerly Tūpḵāna). All these plants used coal as fuel (Baladīya, p. 123).

Sale of electricity by Amīn-al-Żarb in Tehran was per lamp; the cost of the previous night's consumption was collected the next day from the consumers. Rates differed per type of customer and the duration of power consumption. The municipality of Tehran paid 50 percent less than private consumers. Moreover, for both categories of consumers the rates were reduced as their number of connected lamps increased (Baladīya, p. 123). In 1308 Š./1929, there were 7 electrical plants in Tehran, with a capacity of 630 kw, that supplied street lighting. The number of street lamps in use rose from 1,408 in 1924 to 3,082 in 1929. In addition there were small plants to supply private homes and industries. Their installed capacity was estimated to be about 400 kw, thus a total of 1,000 kw in Tehran (Baladīya, p. 123), which by 1313 Š./1934 had risen to 1,500 kw. In 1934, the municipality (*šahrdārī*) took over electricity production in Tehran in view of large unmet demand. Prior to early 1934, electricity had been available only until midnight; shortly thereafter it became available until 2:00 a.m. When new equipment arrived in that same year, electricity became available 24 hours a day (US Legation no. 864.14 [23 Sept 1934, vol. 238]).

National situation. Between 1908 and 1925 no additional electrical plants were erected in Iran, but after that period considerable investment took place, so that by 1309 Š./1930 there were electrical plants in 29 towns. By 1315 Š./1936 there were about 100 electrical plants, private and government-owned, throughout Iran, ranging from small to big plants (*Sāl-nāma-ye Pārs*, 1315 Š./1936-37, p. 220). The majority (138 in 1939) of these plants ran on diesel oil, five steam plants used coal, and the two steam plants in Zābol used wood and regularly lay idle due to fuel shortages (Bank Melli Iran, p. 542; FO 371/23263, f. 152). Total installed capacity (thermal and hydroelectric) was 20 mw in 1939 (excluding Anglo-Iranian Oil Company production), which was produced by a total of 149 plants in 61 towns (Bank Melli Iran, p. 542). The first hydroelectric plants were built in the 1920s, the first at Marāḡa; the last of this group, built near Asadābād (Hamadān) in the early 1930s, had an installed capacity of 375 kw and was designed to supply power to a cotton spinning and weaving factory, the plans for which were never realized (FO 371/21900, ff. 100-01). Total installed hydroelectric capacity was 902 kw in 1939.

Parallel to the first generation of semipublic electric plants was the Anglo-Persian Oil Company's own electrification policy. APOC began to wire its workshops, offices, and lodgings in 1908 and continued to do so as oil fields were discovered. By 1920, all the industrial petroleum sites in Ḵūzestān were electrified; this province was thus given a lead in electrification that it has never relinquished. It is claimed that, in this pioneer phase of the electrification of Iran, industry preceded or accompanied electrical wiring and not the reverse.

Although new investments in the power sector after 1943 had increased Iran's installed capacity to 90 mw by 1948 (exclusive of 100 mw of AIOC), use of electricity in Iran was still very low compared to neighboring countries. In 1948 per capita kwh-production was 12, compared with 32 kwh in Turkey and 64 kwh in Lebanon. Of the 90 mw installed capacity only some 23 percent was used by the domestic and public sector. The remainder was used by the industrial sector. Of this countries. In 1948 per capita kwh production was 12, percent by a coal steam plant (in Tehran), and 8 percent hydroelectrically.

In most cases, power was generated by more than one plant in a city, which resulted in high operating costs. Except for Tehran and a few larger cities, electricity was not supplied on a 24-hour basis. In the smaller cities four to six hours in the evening was the usual practice, in larger cities 12 to 15 hours, with all-night service but no service during most of the daylight hours. This was due to the fact that industrial establishments usually had their own generating plants that only supplied other customers after factory hours. Outside the industrial sector, electricity was almost exclusively used for lighting; therefore it was uneconomical to invest in new capacity for other purposes. Finally, because the reliability of the systems was low, plant owners did not want to become too reliant on the system. As a consequence, service suffered both in quantity and quality (*Seven Year Development Plan* IV, pp. 189-92). In 1954 one third of the commercial production of electricity was in private hands; at Tehran there were twenty-seven private generators and only two belonging to the state and the municipality. This decentralized low-voltage system experienced losses as high as 50 percent of production, which was a handicap to manufacturers who had to have their factories wired themselves at very high cost.

After 1947 the state took the initiative in a new policy of financing large-scale projects such as the great hydroelectric dams, the first of which was the Karaj dam in 1948, and large steam plants, which were connected by high-tension lines. An effort was made to develop installations outside the Tehran region, in which 61 percent of national production was concentrated in 1956. It was not until the Third Development Plan, however, that this policy became truly coordinated and systematic: In 1963 the Iranian Power Authority (IPA/Sāzmān-e Barq) was created as an autonomous organization responsible for electricity. However, the need was felt for an organization with wider authority and broader functions. Thus, in 1964 the Ministry of Water and Power (Wezārat-e Āb o Barq) was created to

Table 38

DEVELOPMENT OF ELECTRICAL PRODUCTION IN IRAN

Year	Installed capacity (thousands of kw)	Production (billions of kwh)	Installed capacity per person (kw)
1904	0.4		
1928	10.0		
1932	10.5		
1939	21.3		
1945	22.1		
1948		0.20	
1954	125.0*		
1956		0.16	
1962	400.0	0.75	
1967	1,559.0	4.20	58
1972	3,354.0	5.00	108
1977	7,105.0	18.90	205
1978	8,589.0	19.80	238
1979	9,504.0	21.90	255
1980	11,228.0	22.40	293
1981	11,832.0	24.90	299
1982	11,908.0	28.80	292
1983	12,522.0	33.00	298
1984	13,019.0	36.60	300

*Excluding private production.

Source: Before 1967, estimates after J. Bahrier and scattered sources; after 1967, Ministry of Energy.

replace IPA. It was reorganized in 1974 and renamed the Ministry of Energy (Wezārat-e Nīrū; Markaz-e Āmār, p. 1).

In 1965 the power industry was nationalized to permit its consolidation and to allow the large-scale expansion of generating and transmission facilities. During the Third Plan period (1963-68), a start was made with the development of a nationwide grid system through the construction of transmission facilities in K̲ūzestān and Tehran provinces (Wezārat-e Nīrū, p. 10). By 1967, all generating capacity was in the public sector except for those in industrial plants, and since 1973 there has been little private investment in power generation, because in the beginning of that year the ministry required all industries to use public power. As a result, the private sector controlled an installed capacity of only 1,600 mw, supplying 7 percent of national production in 1984 (ibid.). In 1969 the TAVANIR (Šerkat-e Sahāmī-e Tawlīd o Enteqāl-e Nīrū) was created, which is responsible for planning, generation, transmission, and distribution of power in the public sector. It controls the nine regional power companies (Šerkat-e Barq-e Manṭaqa) and the K̲ūzestān Water and Power Authority, but it is not involved in hydrogeneration (Markaz-e Āmār, s.v.). The construction, maintenance, and operation of hydroelectric power stations are the responsibility of the regional water authorities under the Ministry of Energy. The Atomic Energy Organization of Iran (Sāzmān-e Nīrū-ye Ātomī), established in 1973, is responsible for the purchase, installation, and operation of all nuclear power plants. It is an independent agency responsible to the prime minister.

Production thus doubled every five years until 1978 (Table 38): 0.2 billion kwh in 1948, 4.1 in 1967, 18.9 in 1977. High-tension lines were built to link the great hydraulic plants to urban industrial centers: The 400-kw grid begun in 1973 exceeded 4,300 km in 1984; the 230-, 132-, and 63-kw grids, which totaled 1,800 km in 1967, reached 24,600 km in 1984.

Since 1980 the increase in production has continued at a sustained rate, but that of installed capacity has leveled off because of the slowdown in a number of projects (Tabrīz, Ṭūs, Nekā, the Lār dam) and lack of investment. In 1979 the nuclear plants at Būšehr and Ahvāz were abandoned, although it had been predicted that nuclear energy would furnish more than 20 percent of the country's electricity by 1983. Installed capacity per person dropped for the first time in 1982 (Wezārat-e Nīrū, p. 10); the drop led to a lowering of tension and cuts in current that mainly affect urban industries and populations, which had been favored since 1970. The new policy, on the contrary, is aimed at favoring the rural areas, which previously had been deliberately neglected; in 1966 only 4 percent of rural families had electric service. Since 1979, numerous villages have been connected to the grid or supplied from small plants; 16,800 villages had been electrified by 1984, versus 4,400 in 1978 (ibid., p. 44).

Present production (Figure 27). In 1984, total pro-

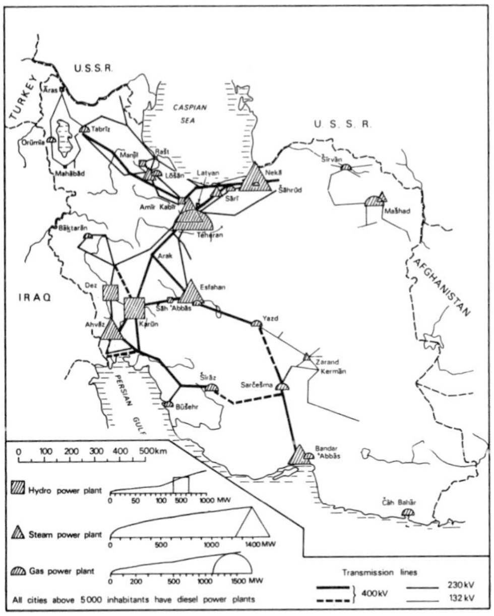

Figure 27. Electricity-generating stations and transmission lines in Iran

duction in Iran reached 36.6 billion kwh (of which 2.5 billion were produced by the private sector) for an installed capacity of 13,000 mw. The chief generating method was steam produced by fuel-burning plants. The fifteen steam plants scattered throughout the whole country furnished 50 percent of production in 1984, versus 35 percent in 1979. Large-scale urban plants produced 200 to 600 mw; the largest one in Iran, at Nekā in Māzandarān, produced 1,740 mw. The thirty-eight plants operating with gas turbines have been built for the most part in the last ten years on twenty-four urban or industrial sites, notably in Fārs and along the large gas pipelines; they are generally of medium size (from 50 to 100 mw as a rule) and produce 24.2 percent of the electricity. Hydroelectric production (15.7 percent) is stagnant because of the lack of new equipment. In this last category, however, Iran possesses a remarkable array of eight large dams intended for both irrigation and the production of electricity (Table 39). These remarkable and prestigious monuments (the Kārūn and Dez dams in particular) have been very controversial because of their cost, their questionable usefulness for irrigation, and the rapidity with which they become clogged with alluvial deposits.

Production by diesel engines (3.2 percent of the total) is under the regional power authorities, not TAVANIR; it is small in quantity but plays a considerable role in rural areas and small towns. At present all the towns of Iran with more than 5,000 inhabitants have diesel generators, and in many villages groups of residents have banded together to buy small generators that operate only in the evenings.

The geographical distribution of electric power production corresponds to that of the population and of industry (Figure 27). The entire country is served by an interconnected grid that is especially well developed in the western provinces, except for Kurdistan, which is far behind in this sphere. Between the Tehran region and Ḵūzestān, which consume 60 percent of the country's electricity, a dense grid of high- and medium-tension lines has been constructed to serve the main industrial centers of Iran. Toward the east two secondary grids have recently been connected to the principal grid: the northern Khorasan grid around Mašhad and the Kermān-Yazd-Bandar-e 'Abbās grid, centered on the coal mines of Zarand and the copper mines of Sarčašma. The undersupplied areas of eastern and southern Afghanistan extend across the border into Baluchistan and southern Khorasan in Iran. The thin population density and the dispersal of urban centers cause considerable energy losses (about 33 percent), despite the development of 400-kilowatt lines linking the large towns.

Iranian households consumed more than 35 percent of production in 1984; their total consumption had

Table 39

RESERVOIR DAMS IN IRAN (1984)

Name	River	Year of completion	Capacity of reservoir (in millions of m³)	Installed capacity (in mw)
Amīr Kabīr	Karaj	1340 Š./1961	205	90
Manjīl	Safīdrūd	1342 Š./1963	1,800	87
Latīān	Jājrūd	1348 Š./1969	95	22
Šāh 'Abbās	Zāyandarūd	1349 Š./1970	1,450	55
Aras	Aras	1350 Š./1971	1,350	22
Dez	Dez	1350 Š./1971	3,440	520
Mahābād	Mahābād	1351 Š./1972	230	6
Kārūn	Kārūn	1356 Š./1977	2,900	1,000
Lār	Rūd-e Lār*	1362 Š./1983	960	100*

*Not yet in operation.

doubled since 1979, while that of industry (31 percent of the total), of commerce (22 percent), and of agriculture (6 percent) remained steady. Average production per person reached 785 kwh, with an average consumption per subscriber of 4,220 kw. Despite recent policy, the imbalance between the supply for towns, where more than 90 percent of the houses had been electrified by 1976, and for the country, 14 percent of which is electrified, remains very large (National Census).

The future of electrical production does not seem to lie in large dams, for reasons of general policy, cost, and lack of suitable sites; by contrast, it is possible to develop the construction of small irrigation dams that generate electricity as a by-product. Nuclear energy does not seem to be a viable solution to the country's future needs, despite revival of the nuclear program in 1982. The main future source of primary energy is without question natural gas, which is already widely distributed in northern Khorasan and Fārs for direct use or to power small electrical plants.

Activities connected with electricity represent an important segment of the economy in Iran; the different public services overseeing electrical production and distribution employ 53,000 people. Manufacturers of small electrical goods (electrical appliances, bulbs, wire, small engines, etc.) employ more than 25,000 people, primarily in the Tehran region but also at Rašt and Shiraz, and produce 50 percent of the nation's needs. For heavy equipment, Iran depends entirely on foreign technology and goods (Markaz-e Āmār, s.v.).

Bibliography: Baladīya-ye Ṭehrān, *Dovvomīn sāl-nāma-ye eḥṣāʾīya-ye šahr-e Ṭehrān*, Tehran, 1310 Š./1931. J. Bharier, *Economic Development in Iran 1900-1970*, London, 1971. Bank Melli Iran, "l'Eclairage en Iran," *Bulletin de la Banque Mellie Iran* 41, 1939, pp. 535-49. M.-Ḥ. Eʿtemād-al-Salṭana, *al-Maʾāṯer wa'l-āṯār*, Tehran, 1307/1889-90. W. M. Floor, *Industrialization in Iran, 1900-1941*, Durham, 1984. M.-ʿA. Golrīz, *Mīnū-dar yā Bāb al-Janna-ye Qazvīn*, Tehran, 1337 Š./1958, pp. 712-13 (on the electrification of Qazvīn). M. Ḥejāzī, *Mīhan-e mā*, Tehran, 1338 Š./1959-60, pp. 617-18. Ch. Issawi, *The Economic History of Iran*, Chicago, 1972. Markaz-e Āmār-e Īrān, *Sāl-nāma-ye sāl-e 1362 [Š./1983]*, Tehran, 1363 Š./1984 (s.v. *barq*). B. Mosavar-Rahmani, *Energy Policy in Iran, Domestic Choices and International Implications*, New York, 1981. Overseas Consultants Inc., *Report on [the] Seven Year Development Plan for the Plan Organization* IV, New York, 1949, pp. 189-93. *Sāl-nāma-ye Pārs*, 1315 Š./1936. Statistical Center of Iran, *National Census of Population and Housing*, n.p., 1353 Š./1974 (entire country). Idem, *Statistical Yearbook*. US Government, *Iran, A Survey of US Business Opportunities*, Washington, D.C., 1977, pp. 105-17. Tāj-al-Salṭana, *Ḵāṭerāt*, ed. M. Etteḥādīya and S. Saʿdvandīān, Tehran, 1361 Š./1982. Wezārat-e Nīrū, Omūr-e Barq, *Sanʿat-e barq dar Īrān dar sāl-e 1363 [Š./1984]*, Tehran, n.d. (Daftar-e Barnāmarīzī-e Barq, Bakš-e Omūr-e Barq).

(W. Floor and B. Hourcade)

ii. In Afghanistan

Compared to Iran, Afghanistan is a very modest producer of electricity. Annual production is on the order of a billion kwh (1.039 billion in 1362 Š./1983-84), which represents a theoretical output of about 70 kwh per inhabitant, one of the lowest in the world. This last figure, however, has very little meaning in a country where only 5 percent of the population has access to electricity (about 100,000 households in 1977).

Another difference between the two countries lies in the means by which electricity was introduced and the development of the electrical infrastructure achieved. In Afghanistan, it is the public authorities who played the leading role from the beginning, thus illustrating a type of planned economic development that is quite original.

Except for a handful of small diesel generators installed in several royal palaces beginning in 1894, the true beginnings of electrification in Afghanistan go back to 1918, when the American engineer A. C. Jewett completed the construction of the first electrical plant in the country on behalf of an English firm. Established at Jabal al-Serāj, on the Sālangrūd about 65 km north of Kabul, it consists of a hydro plant with a capacity of 1,500 kw. Begun in 1911, the plant was a risky venture; the three turbines, as well as the rest of the heavy machinery, had to be brought by land from Peshawar on nine wagons drawn by elephants, which took two and a half months to make the journey, and workmen had to be recruited by means of three-month forced-labor contracts (*hašt-nafarī*; Bell, pp. 194ff.). The plant originally supplied electricity to the royal palace and the main public buildings of Kabul, as well as to the state workshops, which had operated until then on wood fuel. The power station at Jabal al-Serāj later underwent two enlargements but today supplies only the town of Jabal al-Serāj, which owes its industrial character (cement, textiles) to the plant.

During the period 1920-40 only limited progress in electrification of Afghanistan was recorded. Electricity was introduced at Qandahār, then at Herat, thanks to two tiny hydro plants finished in 1314 Š./1935 and in 1315 Š./1936 respectively, one built on an irrigation canal branching off of the Arḡandāb (Bābā Walī, 266 kw), the other on the Harīrūd (Jalwārča, 80 kw). The electrification of Kabul was enhanced by a small diesel plant of 1,300 kw for industrial use. Thus by 1940 installed capacity in the entire country hardly surpassed 3 mw, and private consumption was practically nonexistent.

The process of distributing electricity to the households of the capital was actually initiated only in the following year (1941), with the opening of the hydro plant at Čak-e Wardak (capacity: 3.360 kw), constructed on the upper Lōgar, 83 km southwest of Kabul, by the German firm Siemens. At the same time, the textile and food-processing industries that were being established in the Qaṭaḡan constructed their own plants to cover their energy needs: a stream-powered hydro plant at Pol-e Komrī, which also supplies the town (1320 Š./1941, 4,800 kw), a coal-fired plant for the sugar factory of Baḡlān (1322 Š./1943, 1,200 kw), and several diesel plants belonging to the Spīnzar cotton company around Qondūz. In 1335 Š./1956 generating capacity had thus risen to 16 mw, for a production of 36 million kwh.

It was then that the decisive policy of the first two five-year plans (1335-46 Š./1956-67) began; at the end of the period, the country's generating capacity had risen to 226 mw.

Though not all of the projects included in the plans could be realized, because of lack of funds, the electrical-production sector did not suffer a lowering of its budgetary priority. It absorbed about 10 percent of aggregate actual investment, a considerable amount, which ensured an average annual increase in production of nearly 60 percent in that period (286 million kwh in 1346 Š./1967). The emphasis was placed on hydroelectricity, the potential of which is very important in Afghanistan, being variously estimated, according to the sources, at between 2,500 and 36,000 mw, with the actual figure doubtless lying between these two. But the extreme seasonal irregularity of the riverine flow imposes reliance on the expensive technology of reservoir dams. Financial constraints have limited the harnessing process to the Kābolrūd alone, a river that is both more accessible and closest to the demographic center and principal energy market in the country. Thus downstream from the capital, on both sides of the confluence with the Panjšēr, a series of four hydro plants with a total generating capacity of 200 mw has been built: the Darūnta and Naḡlū dams built with Soviet aid, the Sarōbī dam and the Māhīpar stream-powered plant built with West German aid (Figure 28, Table 40). The Darūnta dam, which supplies Jalālābād with electricity, is the only dam connected with an important modern irrigation project. The other dams are devoted exclusively to production of electricity for the Kabul agglomeration and for the important center of textile manufacture at Golbahār, which are linked by a grid of 110-kilovolt lines.

Since 1967 the drive toward construction has slowed noticeably. The only heavy installations completed have been, on the one hand, two 36-mw turbines at the Kajakay dam on the Helmand—a project planned since the completion of the dam in 1331 Š./1952 but delayed several times—and, on the other hand, the construction

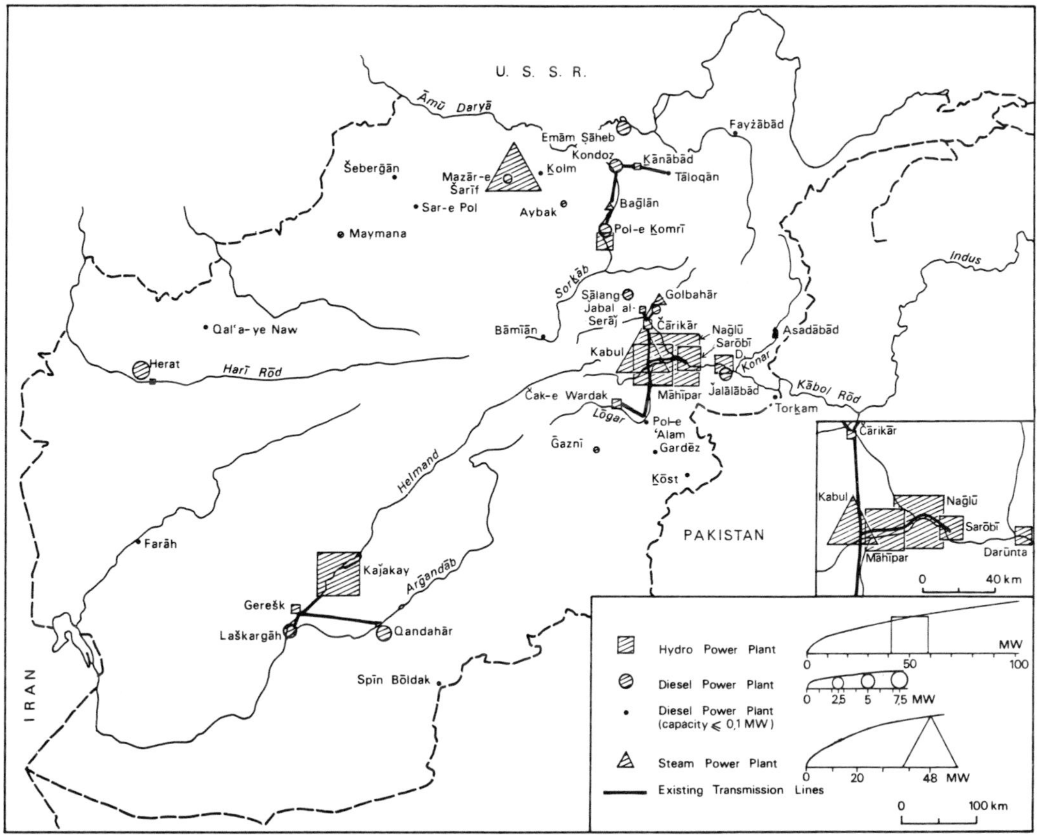

Figure 28. Electricity-generating stations and transmission lines in Afghanistan

Table 40

MAJOR HYDRO POWER PLANTS IN AFGHANISTAN

Dam	River	Year of completion	Capacity of reservoir (million m^3)	Height of waterfall (m)	Capacity of production (mw)
Sarōbī	Kābolrūd	1336 Š./1957	5	50	22
Darūnta	Kābolrūd	1343 Š./1965	40.5	18	11.5
Naḡlū	Kābolrūd	1346 Š./1967	530	70	100
Māhīpar	Kābolrūd	1345 Š./1966	no reservoir	323 (water pipe)	66
Kajakay	Helmand	1355 Š./1976	1,700	(not available)	72

The year of completion must be understood as the year of first production. Full capacity of production has often been reached in several stages.

of two large suburban steam plants at Emām Bokrī (Dehādī) southwest of Mazār-e Šarīf (48 mw) and at Pol-e Čarḵī east of Kabul (45 mw), the first running on natural gas extracted from the nearby fields of Jowzjān and the second, planned to stop load shedding due to poor hydraulic conditions in dry years and in summer, running on fuel imported by road from the U.S.S.R. Under these conditions, installed capacity only doubled between 1967 and 1980 and since then has remained at around 420 mw.

Present electrification efforts are directed toward renovation of existing plants to improve productivity and toward modernization of the transmission and distribution networks. The latter have remained entirely in embryonic form (aggregate length of lines: ca. 5,000 km), as there is no interconnection among the different regional production centers (Figure 28). They are mostly overhead and antiquated, leading to heavy line losses from clandestine tapping, as well as from the poor condition of the meters and of the lines themselves, which have been estimated at up to 53 percent of production in 1971 and up to 41 percent as late as 1983. The indispensable program of rehabilitation is being accomplished in the Kabul region with the aid of the German Democratic Republic, while in the north of the country, the establishment of a first grid of high-tension lines (220 kilovolts) interconnected with the Soviet network has been under way since 1981; completion is scheduled for 1991, and there is a possibility of subsequent extension to Kabul.

The organization of the Afghan electricity sector has been subject to many revisions during the twentieth century. Production and distribution had originally been entrusted to the Ministry of Commerce. In about 1933-34 these functions were assumed by the newly established Ministry of Public Works. A turning point came in 1319 Š./1940, when the private firm Tanwīrāt, soon pashtunized as Də Brēṣ̌nā Lōy Šerkat, was created. This firm obtained the concession for construction of several public plants, but the discovery of financial irregularities in 1955 forced the state to take control. Finally, a reorganization of several public agencies in the production-and-distribution sector took place in 1345 Š./1966. From it emerged the Də Afḡānestān Brēṣ̌nā Mo'assesa, a state enterprise, at first attached to the Ministry of Mines and Industry, then in 1356 Š./1977 to the Ministry of Water and Energy, and, finally, since 1361 Š./1982 to the new Ministry of Electrical Energy (Wezārat-e Anaržī-e Barq). This agency does not have a monopoly on either production or distribution of electricity in the country; it operates only 87 percent of the country's generating capacity, and its share of actual production is still smaller, having shrunk continuously since 1978 (80 percent in 1978, 75 percent in 1981, and 72 percent in 1983). The remainder is divided between two types of independent producer: on the one hand, private producers geared toward industrial use but also supplying 2,500 households, with a capacity of 14 mw (3 percent of national capacity), and, on the other, public producers directed by various other ministries, with a maximum capacity of 43 mw of generating capacity (10 percent of national capacity). The entire electrical sector (production, distribution, and consumption) employed only 3,507 people in 1362 Š./1983, of whom 1,983 were in Kabul.

Of a total generating capacity of 419 mw divided among 40 plants, hydroelectricity accounts for 70 percent (294 mw), steam power 23 percent (97 mw), and diesel power 7 percent (28 mw). The development of this distribution ratio over the last fifteen years has been marked by a diminution in the relative importance of hydroelectricity, which reached an effective maximum of 95 percent of generating capacity around 1970. During the same period, steam-powered electricity experienced the most spectacular growth.

Electricity is far from being available everywhere in Afghanistan; certain provinces such as Orozgān and Paktīkā are totally without it, while in the other provinces only the urban centers, about thirty in all, are electrified. It should be noted that only the largest among them (Kabul, Qandahār, Mazār-e Šarīf) have a permanent supply of electricity, at least in certain quarters, which explains their attraction as locations for new industries. In all other towns electric service is limited to two or three hours a day, from nightfall to about 10:00 p.m., and the number of customers within a particular locality is extremely small (public buildings like cinemas, hospitals, police stations, hotels, restaurants; private homes of high civilian and military officials, as well as of local notables); industries established in such centers continue to depend on their own electrical production. Rural electrification does not exist apart from a few electrified villages in the immediate vicinity of Kabul and Laškargāh.

The electrification of the entire country, which has been a declared goal of every Afghan government since 1955, is thus almost as far from becoming a reality as ever. Present plans are for harnessing new streams (the Harīrūd at Salma, the Balḵāb at Čašma-ye Šafā, the Kokča) and for multiplying small local plants, especially in the gas-producing region of the north; however, in the prevailing political context, most of these plans are not feasible. Since 1980, only two new plants have been opened: one at Fayżābād, the other at Asadābād, both quite modest in size. In fact, electricity is at stake in the present political struggle. The anti-government guerrillas regularly blow up the pylons of the transmission lines and sometimes damage the plants themselves. The distribution of electricity has thus become very erratic. At Kabul cuts in current have been chronic since 1982 and were particularly frequent and long-lasting in 1983. In the face of such disorganization, individuals adapt according to their means; the great majority of the population has recourse to paraffin lamps, which had fallen into disuse in Kabul but the sale of which has experienced a spectacular boom in recent years. The more privileged equip themselves with small domestic gasoline generators, which have become a typical feature of the urban landscape, while many manufacturers and merchants have furnished their factories and shops with emergency generators themselves.

Bibliography: The most recent account of electricity in Afghanistan can be found in Ḥ. Amīn *Jografīā-ye ṣan'atī-e Afgānestān*, Kabul, 1360 Š./1981, pp. 24-45. With its abundant historical and technical data, it is a useful supplement to the more economical analysis of H. J. Arens, *Die Stellung der Energiewirtschaft im Entwicklungsprozess Afghanistans*, Afghanische Studien 13, Meisenheim am Glan, 1974, summarized by the author himself in "Die Energieversorgung in Afghanistan," *Afghanistan Journal* 21, 1975, pp. 12-19. It is necessary to consult recent economic annuals and the Afghan press in order to bring the figures up to date.

For a historical perspective, one should consult Ḥ. Amīn, "Barq wa enkešāf-e ān dar Afgānestān," *Jogrāfīā* (Kabul) 51, 1346 Š./1967, pp. 15-35; and F. M. Fedāyī, *Enkešāfāt-e barq-e Afgānestān dar čehel sāl-e aḵīr*, Kabul, 1337 Š./1958. Very valuable data are found in M. Ali, *A New Guide to Afghanistan*, 3rd ed., Kabul, 1958 (correct: 1959), pp. 63-66. The work by M. J. Bell, ed., *An American Engineer in Afghanistan: From the Letters and Notes of A. C. Jewett*, Minneapolis, 1948, provides a first-hand account, filled with humor, of the difficulties in constructing the very first electrical plant in Afghanistan. S. Ḵalīlī, ed., *Sarōbī*, Kabul, n.d. (ca. 1957), gives a detailed account in Persian, but in a more bureaucratic style, of the stages in the construction of the first large dam on the Kābolrūd.

(D. Balland)

BARQĀNĪ, ABŪ BAKR AḤMAD b. Moḥammad b. Aḥmad b. Ḡāleb (b. 336/948, d. 425/1034), a traditionist (*moḥaddeṯ*), philologist, and lawyer of the Shafi'ite school, highly praised for his industry, erudition, and reliability. Born at Barqān in Ḵᵛārazm, he commenced his studies in his homeland and then left to pursue them at Baghdad. After an absence on a study tour which took him to Jorjān (Gorgān), Esfarā'īn, Nīšāpūr, Herāt, and Marv, he returned to Baghdad, and he did further study at Damascus and Cairo; but he chose Baghdad for his permanent abode and taught there until his death. Noteworthy among his many teachers were Moḥammad b. Aḥmad Abū 'Alī b. al-Ṣawwāf (d. 359/970), Moḥammad b. Ja'far b. al-Hayṯam Bondār (d. 360/970), 'Alī b. 'Omar Abu'l-Ḥasan Dāraqoṭnī (d. 385/995) at Baghdad, Aḥmad b. Ebrāhīm Abū Bakr Esmā'īlī (d. 371/981) at Jorjān, Moḥammad b. Aḥmad Abū 'Amr Ḥīrī (d. ca. 376/987) at Nīšāpūr. His most illustrious pupil was Aḥmad b. 'Alī Abū Bakr Ḵaṭīb Bagdādī (d. 463/1071), the author of the *Ta'riḵ Bagdād*. His best-known literary work is a *mosnad* in which he has combined the *Ṣaḥīḥ*s of Boḵārī and Moslem (Sezgin, *GAS* I, p. 229). He also made collections of traditions transmitted by Sofyān Ṯawrī (d. 161/778) and others.

Bibliography: Brockelmann, *GAL*, S. I, p. 259. Moḥammad Ḏahabī, *Taḏkerat al-ḥoffāẓ*, 3rd ed., Hyderabad, 1376/1957, III, pp. 1074-76. Idem, *al-'Ebar fī ḵabar man gabar* III, Kuwait, 1961, pp. 156-57. Ebn al-Jawzī, *al-Montaẓam* VIII, pp. 79-80. Ḵalīl b. Aybak Ṣafadī, *al-Wāfī be'l-wafayāt* VII, ed. E. 'Abbās, Wiesbaden, 1969, p. 331. Sam'ānī, ed. Yamānī, II, pp. 168-69. Sobkī, *Ṭabaqāt*, 2nd ed., IV, pp. 47-48. *Ta'rīḵ Bagdād* IV, pp. 373-76. Zereklī, *A'lām*² I, p. 205. Kaḥḥāla, II, p. 74.

(H. Schützinger)

BARR, Kaj, Danish orientalist (b. 26 June 1896 in Copenhagen, d. 4 January 1970). Kaj Barr began his studies at the Technical High School of Denmark in 1914, but gradually turned to foreign languages. In order to study the history of the natural sciences and mathematics, he taught himself Greek and Latin, but also interested himself in Oriental languages, especially Arabic, and linguistics. In 1917 he passed the entrance examinations to the University of Copenhagen and obtained his M.A. in classical languages in 1925. He earned a living as an assistant on the new edition of Hesych being prepared at the Royal Danish Academy, while concentrating more and more on the study of Iranian philology. His teachers were Arthur Christensen in Copenhagen and C. F. Andreas in Göttingen (qq.v). In 1935 he was appointed lecturer (associate professor) of classical philology and in 1945 professor of Iranian philology at the University of Copenhagen as the successor of A. Christensen. The same year he became a member of the Royal Danish Academy of Sciences and Letters.

By that time Barr was already recognized as one of the leading Iranian scholars in Europe, and in 1933 he undertook the publication of an edition of the fragments of a Pahlavi Psalter discovered at Turfan from F. C. Andreas's papers (see ANDREAS, iii). The published edition is in every respect exemplary and bears the stamp of Barr's original contribution in the glossary with its detailed commentary (F. C. Andreas and Kaj Barr, *Bruchstücke einer Pehlevi-Übersetzung der Psalmen*, SPAW, 1933, pp. 91-152).

He then collaborated with A. Christensen and W. B. Henning to publish Andreas's notes on Iranian dialects. Barr's responsibility was the editing of the notes on a series of Kurdish dialects (from Garrūs, Senna, Kermānšāh, Korūn, and Kalūn-Abdū). To this part of the book Barr contributed important independent research, notably on the development of intervocalic *m* to *w* in Kurdish dialects, the Iranian passive construction of the past tenses (on which see also his important remarks in Lingvistkredsen i København's *Aarsberetning for 1934*, pp. 13-14, where he emphasized the importance of the opposition "intransitive: transitive" in the verbal systems of Iranian languages) and the plural suffix *-gäl*. The book was published in 1939 (A. Christensen, K. Barr, and W. B. Henning, *Iranische Dialektaufzeichnungen aus dem Nachlass von C. F. Andreas*, Abh. der Gesellschaft der Wissenschaften zu Göttingen, Phil-hist. Kl., 3rd ser., 11, Berlin, 1939).

In 1936 Barr published a manuscript fragment from Turfan containing a Pahlavi glossary, which is important for the understanding of the graphic development of the so-called phonetic complements of Aramaic heterograms in Book Pahlavi ("Remarks on the Pahlavi Ligatures [x_1] and [x_2]," *BSOAS* 8, 1936, pp. 391-403). From 1937 he edited vols. VII-XII of the *Codices Avestici et Pahlavici Bibliothecae Universitatis Hafniensis*. In 1943 he published his "Bidrag til sigøjnerdialekternes grammatik" (Contributions to the grammar of Gypsy dialects, in *In Memoriam Kr. Sandfeld*, Copenhagen, 1943, pp. 31-46), which discusses the conjunction *te* in Gypsy dialects and its possible connection with Sogdian *'ty* and *-ty* "and" and Iranian elements in the Nūrī dialect.

In 1945 Barr left the exclusively linguistic field, turning to the history of Iranian religion. One of his objectives was to determine the exact import and contents of such Zoroastrian terms and concepts as *aša* ("Principia Zarathustriaca," in *Øst og Vest, Afhandlinger tilegnede Professor Dr. Phil. Arthur Christensen*, Copenhagen, 1945, pp. 130-39) and *drəgu-, driγu-* (in *Studia Orientalia Ioanni Pedersen... Dicata*, Copenhagen, 1953, pp. 21-40). He also discussed the presence of the three divine gifts *xvarr, fravahr*, and *tan gōhr* in Zarathustra (in *Festskrift til L. L. Hammerich*, Copenhagen, 1952, pp. 26-36), influenced by Dumézil's tripartition thesis.

His excellent translation of parts of the Avesta for the Danish series of *Verdensreligionernes Hovedværker* (The chief works of the world's religions): *Avesta*, Copenhagen, 1954), being in Danish, unfortunately remains inaccessible to most students of the Avesta. Here and in the introduction to his unfinished contribution on Zoroastrianism ("Zarathustrismen I") for the Danish *Illustreret Religionshistorie*, Barr summed up his views on the history and nature of Zoroastrianism (*Illustrated History of Religions*, ed. J. P. Asmussen and J. Læssøe, vol. 2, Copenhagen, 1968, pp. 233-77; Germ. tr., "Die Religion der alten Iranier," in *Handbuch der Religionsgeschichte* II, ed. idem with C. Colpe, Göttingen, 1972, pp. 265-318).

From 1964 Barr was president of the Union Internationale des Orientalistes, and in 1969 he received an honorary doctorate from the University of Copenhagen.

Bibliography: J. P. Asmussen in *Festskrift udgivet af Københavns universitet*, November, 1970. L. L. Hammerich, *Oversigt over Videnskabernes Selskabs virksomhed*, Copenhagen, 1971.

(J. P. ASMUSSEN)

BARRA, or Bāru, an Iranian loanword designating a tax in Babylonian texts, borrowed from Old Iranian *bar-* "to carry" (cf. Gk. *phóros*). The word appears nearly seventy times between 442 and 417 B.C. in the archives of the house of Murašū in different spellings (*bar-ra, ba-a-ri, ba-ar-ra*) intended to indicate the long vowel. It occurs almost exclusively in tax receipts, in enumerations of the following kind: "x minas of silver, y measures of beer, barley, or flour, total taxes: the soldier of the king, the flour of the king, the *bāru*, and all sorts of payments for the house of the king." The context and the fact that taxable lands were always fiefs attest that the *bāru* was an obligation for military purposes, payable in kind but especially in silver, and that it was probably the least important of the three mentioned taxes. Aside from the receipts there exists a suspension of tenancy for nonpayment of "the flour of the king and of the *bāru*."

Despite the *Chicago Assyrian Dictionary* (s.vv. *allāku, bāru*, and *zabālu* 1, b) and W. von Soden, *Akkadisches Handwörterbuch*, Wiesbaden, 1959- (s.v. *bāru*), the homonym *bāru*, cited in H. H. Figulla (p. 48 lines 2, 4, 7, 10, 14; and p. 49 lines 2, 4, 5, 7, 11, 16), refers to a "litter" carried at royal succession ceremonies and must be another Iranian loanword (also from the base *bar-* "to carry").

Bibliography: G. Cardascia, *Les archives des Murašû*, Paris, 1951, pp. 98ff. M. A. Dandamaev, "Svobodnye naemnye rabotniki v pozdneĭ Babilonii," *Assiriologiya i egiptologiya. Sbornik stateĭ*, Leningrad, 1964, pp. 31-50. W. Eilers, *Orientalistische Literaturzeitung*, 1934, col. 96, n. 4. H. H. Figulla, *Ur Excavation Texts* 4, Philadelphia, 1949, p. 12.

(G. CARDASCIA)

BARRASĪHĀ-YE TĀRĪḴĪ, a journal of historical studies of Iran published in Tehran during 1966-78. Its publication in March of 1966 by the public relations office of the Iranian Armed Forces under General B. Āryānā was undertaken in pursuance of a decree issued by Shah Moḥammad Reżā Pahlavī, who on December 6, 1965, had ordered a series of cultural activities, among them the preparation of a new history of Iran by the Pahlavi Library and the organizing of an international congress of Iranologists in Tehran the following year.

The journal had a ceremonial board of governors on which the chancellor (*raʾīs*) of Tehran University and a number of high-ranking army officers sat, but it was actually supervised by a six-member board of editors and run by an editor-director. For the first five years, Colonel Jahāngīr Qāʾem-maqāmī, a historian of the Qajar period, was the editor-director of the journal; subsequently the post was held by Colonel Yaḥyā Šahīdī, Qāʾem-maqāmī again, and Major Moḥammad Kašmīrī. The contributors were, however, mostly civilians, including some university professors.

As expected, the journal had a nationalistic slant, and much was made in its pages of the glories of ancient Iran. Nevertheless, the scholarly bent of Qāʾem-maqāmī and some of the contributors made for the publication of some useful bias-free research. While the articles on pre-Islamic Iran were generally derivative, some of the articles relating to Islamic Iran, particularly those bearing on the eighteenth and nineteenth centuries and descriptive geography, were well researched and original. The journal also published a number of historical documents (letters, decrees, etc.) pertaining to the modern history of Iran, especially in volume 8 (1351 Š./1972-73).

From 1971 the journal began a biannual English edition, *Historical Studies of Iran*, and a French edition, *Études historiques sur l'Iran*. A number of articles appearing in the journal were reprinted separately, and a special issue of *Barrasīhā-ye tārīḵī* was published in 1971 to coincide with the celebrations commemorating the 2500 years of monarchy in Iran.

The journal had a circulation of 2,500-2,600, and there were 250-420 pages per issue in 17 × 24 cm format, printed on very fine paper. It included both black-and-white and color illustrations and was printed in the Armed Forces printing office in Tehran. A yearly subscription initially cost 100 rials for the military and 170 for civilians; in the last year of publication the figures were 600 and 1,200 respectively. Outside of Iran, the yearly cost was first 6 dollars, which by the eleventh year had increased to 20 dollars. The journal ceased publication in 1978, following the events that led to the 1979 revolution.

(N. PARVĪN)

BARŠABBĀ, legendary bishop of Marv and founder of the Christian church in eastern Iran. The only completely preserved versions of the legend are found in Arabic sources, in the "Chronicle of Seʿert" (ed. with French tr. by A. Scher, *Patrologia Orientalis* 5, Paris, 1909, pp. 253-58; German tr. and valuable historical commentary by E. Sachau, "Die Christianisierungs-Legende von Merw," *Abhandlungen zur semitischen Religionskunde und Sprachwissenschaft W. W. Grafen von Baudissin... überreicht*, Giessen, 1918, pp. 399-409 and by P. Kawerau, *Christlich-arabische Chrestomathie aus historischen Schriftstellern des Mittelalters* II, CSCO 385, Louvain, 1977, pp. 81-90) and, in abbreviated form in the *Ketāb al-mejdal* of Mārī b. Solaymān (H. Gismondi, *Maris Amri et Slibae de Patriarchis Nestorianorum Commentaria* I, Rome, 1897, pp. 26-27 of Ar. text, p. 23 of Lat. tr.). According to these sources, Baršabbā was one of (rather, a descendant of) the Christians deported by Šāpūr I from Syria to western Iran. He converted Šīrrān (for Šīrzād?), the sister and wife of Šāpūr (i.e., Šāpūr II, as shown by a reference to the peace treaty with Jovian, A.D. 363), who sent her to Marv in order to remove her from the influence of Baršabbā; the latter, however, followed the queen to Marv and became its first bishop. After his death and burial, Baršabbā was miraculously resurrected and lived for a further fifteen years.

The account of Baršabbā in the Arabic sources evidently derives from a Syriac life. Fragments of this, and of a Sogdian translation, have been discovered at Bulayïq near Turfan and published by F. W. K. Müller and W. Lentz, "Soghdische Texte II," *SPAW*, 1934, pp. 522-28, 559-64. The name of the queen (lacking in the Sogd. fragments) is given in the Syriac text in the shortened form Šīr. Although these versions are more verbose than the Arabic, they contain little additional information. However, it is interesting that the Sogdian text credits Baršabbā with the foundation of monasteries in an area stretching from Fārs to Gorgān, Ṭūs, Abaršahr, Saraḵs, Marv al-Rūd, Balḵ, Herāt, and Sīstān.

According to Bīrūnī (*Āṯār al-bāqīa*, p. 299; *Chronology*, p. 296), the liturgical calendar of the Melkite church in Ḵᵛārazm included on the 21st of June the commemoration of "the priest Baršabbā" (misspelled *Bršy'*) "who brought Christianity to Marw about two hundred years after Christ." This festival was also observed by the Nestorians in Chinese Turkestan, as is witnessed by the Sogdian gospel lectionary C5 (see W. Sundermann, *Altorientalische Forschungen* 3, 1975, pp. 70-71, 73).

It is doubtful whether the legend of Baršabbā has any historical basis. A bishop of Marv of this name is historically attested in A.D. 424 (see J. B. Chabot, *Synodicon Orientale*, Paris, 1902, p. 43), and it is not unlikely that the legend is a pious fiction woven around his name as a result of local patriotism. In any case, to judge from the geographical distribution of the sources, it seems that Baršabbā was venerated only in the far east of Iran and beyond.

Bibliography: See also J. M. Fiey, "Chrétientés syriaques du Ḵorāsān et du Ségestān," *Le Muséon* 86, 1973, pp. 75-104.

(N. SIMS-WILLIAMS)

BARṢAUMĀ, a 5th-century bishop of Nisibis of Aramaic extraction, according to some sources originally from Bēt Qardū. Nothing is known of Barṣaumā prior to his studies at the School of Edessa. Here he belonged to the ardent supporters of Ḥībā, the head of the diophysite party, who became bishop of Edessa in 435. After the completion of his studies, he went to Nisibis. In his minor preaching post, he built up his reputation through his skills in exegesis, which elevated him to the episcopal see. The date of 435 for this event given in the Nestorian sources is not trustworthy.

His episcopal see was important for the Persian empire, as Nisibis was the point of contact between Persia and Byzantium. Arab nomads from both empires created ceaseless conflicts since they often met in the surrounding desert, and Barṣaumā, due to his strong loyalty to the Persian rulers and his abilities, was the right man for such a position. According to the words of the *marzbān* to the emperor, quoted by Barṣaumā himself: "The bishop of Nisibis is an expert in these affairs of the boundaries" (*Synodicon orientale*, p. 529). Beside using him in mediating services in conflicts, Pērōz valued the services of his trusted servant for diplomatic missions in negotiations with the Byzantines. His deep attachment to the Sasanian state, however, caused him difficulties in his proper episcopal domain. As a man with great ambitions and strong character, he found it difficult to accept superior authority, and this attachment thus led him into endless conflicts.

His political ambitions in ecclesiastical matters went in several directions. As a convinced Nestorian, he worked tirelessly for a reorientation of the theological tenets. He believed that his church should follow this course, as it was in the interest of the Sasanian state to wean the church away from the West. A new creed could accomplish this. Further, he pressed for a reorientation of the basic ethical ideals, a reshaping of Christian life, and a transformation of the inner countenance of the Persian church. The ancient tenets upheld by the spiritual elite of ascetics stood in opposition to the Zoroastrian tenets of Sasanian society. How he became a pioneer and advocate of a complete reorientation is illustrated by his marriage to a former nun ("daughter of the covenant"), Mamai. To be sure, the new trend was a blow to the ascetic forces. In this campaign for change, however, Barṣaumā could count on Pērōz and the power of the state.

Barṣaumā organized powerful forces working toward complete reshaping of Christianity in Persia along these lines, but the mounting tensions around him exploded into an episcopal revolt. In April, 484, he convened against the canons a group of bishops at Bēt Lāpaṭ. Through this convocation he launched severe accusations against Catholicos Bābōe (q.v.), who was trying to withstand the tremendous pressures for change in the history of the church in Persia. Thus Barṣaumā became deeply involved in the fight against the catholicos and his bishops, who rallied around him. However, all did not go without setbacks. His radical ideas, complications in curbing the influence of the ascetic elements, and perhaps also his intrigues aroused more suspicion after the tragic end of the catholicos. Thus Aqāq, not Barṣaumā, was elected to the vacant see. His submission to the decisions of the Synod of Bēt ʿAdrai in 485 concerning 1. the annulment of the accusations against Bābōē, 2. recognition of Aqāq, and 3. acceptance of penitence (*Synodicon orientale*, pp. 531-32) can be seen as due to the sobering effect that the death of Pērōz, his protector, had on him. Barṣaumā, however, was not a man to respect these conditions, and conflicts with Aqāq continued.

While Barṣaumā's aspirations in the church at large caused complications, his activities locally led to very important accomplishments in the founding of the School of Nisibis, which was to become a celebrated center of learning. His cooperation with Narsai (q.v.) must be regarded as vital in turning the vision and project into reality. Thanks to his material support, drawn from the resources of the church, and his strong hand in the organization, legislation, and administration of the community this intellectual center was established and lasted for generations (see SCHOOL OF NISIBIS). Barṣaumā saw in this center a hearth of spiritual culture, where the Antiochian traditions and Nestorian theology were cultivated, and an instrument for disseminating Nestorianism. He was correct in both views.

In comparison to his impact as a reformer, Barṣaumā's contribution to literature is quite insignificant. Beside his six letters (*Synodicon orientale*, pp. 531-39) there are only some small pieces in the genre of liturgy. He died at an advanced age sometime before 496 since, in this year, Hōšeʿ II had already been his successor for some time.

Bibliography: A Baumstark, *Geschichte der syrischen Literatur*, Bonn, 1922, pp. 108-09. S. Gero, *Barṣauma of Nisibis and Persian Christianity in the Fifth Century*, Louvain, 1981. J. Labourt, *Le christianisme dans l'empire perse sous la dynastie sassanide*, Paris, 1904, pp. 131-52. *Synodicon orientale*, ed. J. B. Chabot, Paris, 1902, pp. 525-39. A. Vööbus, *Les messaliens et les réformes de Barçauma de Nisibe*, Pinneberg, 1947. Idem, *History of the School of Nisibis*, Louvain, 1965.

(A. VÖÖBUS)

BARSĪĀN (also Bersīān, locally called Bīsyūn), a village in the *dehestān* of Barā'ān 45 km southeast of Isfahan on the north bank of the Zāyandarūd; it is situated on the old caravan route from Isfahan which, following the river, passed through Barsīān, Varzana, Ḵargūšī, Yazd, and further on to Ṭabas and Mašhad, and which provided the locality—which prospered quickly in Saljuq times—with its commercial underpinnings. According to Mostawfī (*Nozhat al-qolūb*, p. 51, tr. p. 58), Barsīān is in the seventh district of the Isfahan area. An expression of its former prosperity is its mosque (M. B. Smith, *Ars Islamica* 4, 1937, pp. 7ff.), which exhibits three main construction phases (Kleiss,

AMI, N.S. 5, 1972, pp. 214f.). The oldest component is the original free-standing Saljuq minaret, which is dated 491/1097-98). Built next to the minaret in 528/1134 was the domed Saljuq mosque. The structure has a dome diameter of 10.3 m and is in the form of a pavilion open on four sides. The central chamber was surrounded by an arcade which was removed in modern times. The domed chamber is significant in the art history of Iran for its decorative brickwork and its stucco mihrab (dated 498/1105), comparable to features found in the older north domed chamber (Gonbad-e ḵākī) of Isfahan's Masjed-e Jomʿa (Friday mosque; 481/1088) and to those in apparently Mongol domed mosques in the neighboring villages of Kāj, Daštī, and Ezīran. Early in the Safavid era under Shah Ṭahmāsb I (r. 930-84/1524-76), a two-*ayvān* courtyard was appended to Barsīān's domed mosque. As discernible from the foundation, it was erected with sun-dried brick covered by baked brick; its upper wall sections, for the most part, have been destroyed. The kind of façade that was used on the entire structure is no longer discernible. The space inside of the Saljuq domed chamber is articulated by three-quarter brick colonettes with ornamental mortar plugs in the joints.

Barsīān is the second caravan stop southeast of Isfahan. A Safavid caravansary, renovated in Qajar times, occupies the site today. It is a medium-sized structure 51.5 × 40 m with two axial *ayvān*s on the courtyard, one of them at the inner end of the domed entrance block, which is of baked brick. Four stables are located in the front and rear parts of the building; the entrances are in the oblique corner walls of the courtyard. The sleeping quarters are ranged round the courtyard, each entered through a small *ayvān*. North of the caravansary are the remains of a Safavid bath, which belonged to it (Kleiss, art. cit., pp. 223f.). East of the Saljuq domed mosque of Barsīān is a 40 × 40 m earthwork fort encircled by a trench, which appears to have served as a fortified way station and outer gateway to the caravansary (Siroux, *Anciennes voies et monuments*, p. 38).

The ten-sided fortress Nāranj Qalʿa has been dated to the Saljuq period (Siroux, pp. 88f.); at one time it sported ten circular towers and also served as a road station. Nāranj Qalʿa is also surrounded by a trench. The presence of the square earthwork fort, the ten-sided Saljuq Nāranj Qalʿa, and the caravansary attest Barsīān's significant place on the main route which ran from Isfahan to Yazd from early Islamic/Saljuq times until well into the Safavid period, shifted in Qajar times northward, and today runs through Nāʾīn.

Bibliography: A. Rafīʿī Mehrābādī, *Āṯār-e mellī-e Esfahān*, n.p., 1352 Š./1974, pp. 814ff., 827.

(W. Kleiss)

BARSḴĀN, or Barsḡān, a place in central Asia, on the southern shores of the Ïsïq-Göl, in the region known as Semirechye or Yeti-su "the land of the seven rivers," in what is now the Kirgiz SSR of the Soviet Union. In the medieval Islamic sources, the name seems also to have been applied, by a process of extension, to the tribe of Turks living in its vicinity. The author of *Ḥodūd al-ʿālam*, (tr. Minorsky, pp. 98, 116, cf. pp. 292-93 and map v at p. 279) describes this "upper" (i.e., farthest) Barsḵān (to be distinguished from a "lower" one in Transoxania; see Yāqūt, *Boldān*, Beirut, I, pp. 383-84) as a prosperous town, whose chief (*dehqān*) was from the Qarluq but whose inhabitants gave their preferential allegiance to the Toghuz-Oghuz, and he also states that there was a "river of Barsḵān," presumably the Ču, which flows out of the Ïsïq-Göl. The place is mentioned several times by Maḥmūd Kāšḡarī, who spells it Barsḡān, locates it in the territory of the Čegel tribe and says that it is named after a son of the mythical hero Afrāsīāb (q.v.; *Dīvān loḡāt al-Tork*, tr. Besim Atalay, Ankara, 1939-41, I, pp. 392-93, III, pp. 135, 417-18 and passim; a legend about the origin of Barsḵān from the semilegendary exploits of Alexander the Great is given also by Gardīzī, *Zayn al-akbār*, ed. Ḥabībī, pp. 265-66, in his section on Barsḵān; cf. also Barthold, *Four Studies on the History of Central Asia*, tr. V. and T. Minorsky, Leiden, 1962, III, p. 181).

Part of Barsḵān's historical fame comes from the fact that Sebüktigin (q.v.), founder of the Ghaznavid dynasty in eastern Afghanistan, came from there, having been captured in tribal warfare and sold as a slave, according to the *Pand-nāma* attributed to Sebüktigin and reproduced by the later historian Moḥammad Šabānkāraʾī (see Bosworth, *Ghaznavids*, p. 39 and *Later Ghaznavids*, pp. 134, 144). The Qarakhanid tribal confederation which took over Transoxania from the Samanids in the 5th/11th century seems to have arisen from the Qarluq and Čegel of the Barsḵān region, and, in the middle years of the 5th/11th century, Barsḵān was ruled by a Qarakhanid prince called Yïnaltigin (Barthold, *Four Studies* I, pp. 89-90). In later times, however, it disappears from historical mention.

Bibliography: Given in the text.

(C. E. Bosworth)

BARSOM (Av. *barəsman*), sacred twigs that form an important part of the Zoroastrian liturgical apparatus. The word *barsom* is the Middle Persian form of the Avestan *barəsman*, which is derived from the root *barəz*, Sanskrit *bṛh* "to grow high." The *barəsman* twigs were twigs of the *haoma* plant or the pomegranate used in certain ceremonies. They are first laid out and then tied up in bundles. The number varies according to the ceremony to be performed. Today brass or silver wires are used in place of twigs. These are about 9 inches long and one-eighth of an inch in diameter. Each such wire is called a *tāe*. The Avestan phrase *barəsman star* recalls the *barhiṣ stru* of the Vedas; probably these are historically related (see Mayrhofer, *Dictionary* II, pp. 415-16). Some writers have identified the *barəsman* with the *kusha* grass, but this is not correct, because the *barəsman* is never used as a seat for the divine beings (cf. Modi, p. 265).

In Zoroastrianism as in Brahmanism the number of

these twigs varies according to the ceremony. The *Šāyest-nē šāyest* (chap. 14.2) enjoins that neither more nor less than the requisite number should be used. The celebration of the Yasna requires 23 twigs of which 21 form a bundle. One twig is placed on the foot of the *māh-rūy*, i.e., the moon-faced or the crescent-like stand, which is otherwise known as the *barsomdān*. This twig is called *zorno tāe*, i.e., the twig of the saucer containing the *zōhr* or *zaoθra* water. The other, i.e., the twenty-third, twig is placed on the saucer containing the *jīvām*, i.e., the mixture of water and milk. The celebration of the Vendidad or Vidēvdāt ceremony requires 35 twigs of which 33 form a bundle and the other two are used as above. The celebration of the Vispered requires 35 twigs, that of the Yaziš̌n or Yasna of the Rapiθwin on Rōz Ordībehešt, Māh Fravardīn 15 twigs. The celebration of the *bāj* (q.v.) in honor of the departed souls uses 5 twigs. In the case of the ceremony of Nāvar, i.e., the initiation into priesthood, the recital of the *Mīnō Nāvar bāj* requires 7 twigs.

According to the *Nirangistan* (*Avesta*, tr. Darmesteter, III, p. 137) the minimum number to be used in the ritual is three, the minimum thickness of each twig is to be equal to that of a hair, the maximum length to be one *aēša* and the maximum breadth one *yava*. The *Vendidad* (19.19) also gives the length of one *aēša* and the breadth of one *yava*. Darmesteter takes *aēša* to be the length of a plowshare and the *yava* to be the breadth of a barley-corn (II, p. 265 n. 43). In the rituals the *barsom* twigs or brass or silver wires are placed on the above-mentioned two crescent-shaped metallic stands, known as *barsomdān*.

The second *hād* of the *Yasna* shows that the *barsom* was considered to be an essential requisite in the liturgical service of the Yasna. The *Vendidad* (14.8) speaks of it as one of the requisites of an Āθravan (q.v.). The *barsom* is so sacred that the very tree whose twigs are used is an object of praise. All the religious rites of the inner liturgical service of the Zoroastrians are celebrated with the *barsom*.

In the longest grace before meals, wherein certain chapters of the *Yasna* are recited, the *barsom* is a requisite. But it seems that in ancient times the *barsom* was absolutely required even in the simple forms of grace recited before meals. The reciter held it in his hand during these recitals. We learn from Ferdowsī that the last Sasanian king, Yazdegerd, when he hid himself in the house of a miller during his flight, asked for the *barsom* to say his grace before the meals. This gave a hint to the enemy searching for Yazdegerd, and he was treacherously assassinated by his general Māhōy Sūrī (*Šāh-nāma*, Moscow, IX, p. 353).

The object of holding the *barsom* and repeating prayers is to praise the Creator for the support accorded by nature and for the gift of the produce of the earth, which supplies the means of existence to the human and the animal world. The object of selecting the *barsom* from the twigs of a tree is to take it as a representative of the whole vegetable kingdom, for which benedictions and thanks to the Creator are offered, and there is

further proof to show that the performance of the *barsom* ritual is intended to express gratitude to the Creator for His boundless gifts. Thus the *Vendidad* (19.17-18) says, "Zaraθuštra asked Ahura Mazdā: O Divine Creator! In what way may I praise Thee? Ahura Mazdā replied: O Spitama Zaraθuštra! Go near a tree grown out of the earth and repeat thus: Homage unto thee, O beautiful, flourishing, strong and Mazdā-created tree." (In the next paragraph a reference to the method of cutting the *barsom* twig by a holy person is given.) This quotation shows that the *barsom* represents the vegetable creation of God and that the *barsom* ceremony is meant as a means of celebrating the praise of God for the vegetable kingdom. The ceremonial practice of keeping the *barsom* under water for a time (Āb-Zōhr, q.v.), thus bending its strength through moisture, reminds us of rainfall, the growth of crops, watering of plants, gathering of produce, and fertility of the soil, as Darmesteter has clearly pointed out (I, p. lxxxv). Further, we read in history that during the Sasanian period people used to hold the *barsom* in the hand, prior to saying grace and taking meals, and on this occasion they used to render thanks for His blessings.

According to the *Mēnōg ī xrad* (chap. 57.28), the celebration of the ceremony which symbolizes the act of praising Ohrmazd for His creation destroys the power of the demons or the evil influence. According to the *Dēnkard* (book VIII, chap. 26.24; Madan, II, pp. 731-32) the celebration of the praise of Ohrmazd with this ceremonial on a day of battle helps the soldiers and is like throwing a well-aimed arrow.

According to the old method, a Yōšdāsrgar priest who had performed the *xūb* ceremony, performed the ritual of preparing the *barsom*. He had to draw water from a well in the fire temple and purify a water pot by means of it. With this pure water collected in a ceremoniously purified pot, he went before the tree whose twigs were to be used in the ritual and washed with his right hand the twig to be cut. Then holding the *barsomčīn* knife in the right hand and the pot of pure water in the left, he took the *bāj* with the *xšnūman* (propitiatory formula) for *urvara* "plants, trees"— *frasastayaēča urvarā̊ vaŋhuyā̊ Mazda-δātayā̊ ašaonyā̊*—"for the glorification of the tree, good, created by Mazdā and holy," and he cut off the twig for the ritual with the recitation of an *Ašəm vohū*. With the word *ašəm* he cut off and rejected the partly dried tip of the end. With the word *vohū* he touched the stem, and with the word *vahištəm* he cut it off. At the end of the recital he paid his homage to the good vegetable creation of Ahura Mazdā thus: *nəmō urvaire vaŋuhī Mazda-δāte ašaone* "homage unto thee, O good holy tree, created by Mazdā!" With the cutting of each twig the above ritual is repeated. He then goes to the *yazišn-gāh*.

Today, a Yōšdāsrgar priest with the *xūb* makes the brass or silver wires pure together with all the metallic utensils required for the Yazišn ceremony. He then holds the requisite number of wires, all but one, in his hand. Then, holding the remaining *tāe* in his hand, with the usual recital of three *Ašəm vohū*s and a *Fravarānē*, he takes the *bāj* with the *xšnūman* of *Šahrevar*, the Amašaspand, who presides over metals. Then, during the recital of the *Ašəm vohū*, touching both the ends of the bundle of wires in his left hand, with the *āb-zōhr* wire in his right hand, he finishes the *bāj*. While finishing the *bāj* he touches again both the ends of the bundle of *barsom* wires in his left hand with the *zōhr* wire in his right hand.

Bibliography: Given in the text. See also M. Boyce, *Zoroastrians. Their Religious Beliefs and Practices*, London, 1979 (see index). Idem *Zoroastrianism* I, p. 167; II (see index). J. J. Modi, *Religious Ceremonies and Customs of the Parsees*, 2nd ed., Bombay, 1937, pp. 261-69.

(M. F. KANGA)

BARSOM YAŠT, in the liturgical manuscripts of the Avesta the name of the second *hād* (chapter) of the *Yasna*. According to Darmesteter (I, p. 7), *Yasna* 2 as well as the following *Yasna* 3-4 (*Srōš darūn*) complement *Yasna* 1, which announces to the gods the sacrifice. *Yasna* 2 draws their attention to the libation (*zaoθra*) and the *barəsman*, *Yasna* 3 to other offerings, and in *Yasna* 4 the offerings are consecrated to the gods. *Yasna* 2-3 are characterized by the formula *āyese yešti* "I seek/call (hither) NN by means of the sacrifice," Pahlavi translation *xwāhēm ō ēn yazišn* "I call (hither) to this worship," contrasting with the formulas *niuuaēδaiiemi hankāraiiemi* "I dedicate, I accomplish" (this sacrifice for NN) of *Yasna* 1 and *pairica dadəmahī āca vaēδaiiamahī* "we present, we dedicate" of *Yasna* 3. The objects of the call in *Yasna* 2 are first the libation and the *barsom*, then Ahura Mazdā, the Aməša Spəntas, and the other divine beings.

See BARSOM.

(P. O. SKJÆRVØ)

BARTANGĪ, a member of the Šuḡnī (q.v.) group or Šuḡnī-Rōšānī group of the East Iranian Pamir languages. The other members are: Šuḡnī, Bajūī, Rōšānī, Ḵūfī, Orōšōrī, and Sariqōlī [qq.v.]. Bartangī is spoken in the Gorno-Badakhshanskaya Avtonomnaya Oblast' of Soviet Tajikistan in the middle part of the Bartang valley (i.e., Bār-tāng "upper defile," cf. Edel'man, 1975, p. 44), which joins the Panj (Oxus) valley from the east and was formerly one of the poorest and most inaccessible parts of the Pamirs. The number of Bartangī speakers was reported in 1932 to be 2,000 (Zarubin, 1937, p. 4). The two dialects of Bartangī, which differ in minor details (Sokolova, 1960, p. 1), are Basidī and Siponjī. (For the name Siponj see Dodykhudoev, 1976, p. 143.) The names of the other villages in Bartang are given in Karamkhudoev, 1973, p. 9, and Edel'man, 1975, p. 50. In the upper part of the Bartang valley Orōšōrī is spoken. Bartangī has no written literature, the language of the schools and the mass media being Tajiki or Russian.

Bartangī was unknown to Iranists until 1914. The first material was collected by R. Gauthiot and I. I. Zarubin (cf. the latter's report, 1918). Gauthiot (1916, p. 64) referred to his new findings not as Bartangī but as "parlers rochânis occidentaux." This was criticized by Sköld (1936, p. 14). For further details of the history of research on the Šuḡnī group see Lentz, 1933, pp. 25ff., and Sokolova and Gryunberg, 1962.

The first text in Bartangī, a specimen of folk poetry, was published by Zarubin in 1924. The text corpus available now is still limited: Zarubin, 1937 (poetry; one prose text in Bartangī and Rōšānī); Sokolova, 1953 (a text with versions in Šuḡnī, Rōšānī, Ḵūfī, and Bartangī); Sokolova, 1960 (twelve texts with a copious glossary, a list of morphemes, and a Russian-Bartangī index). Comparative word lists are in Sköld, 1936. Some Bartangī words are also to be found in Andreev's monumental ethnographical work (1953-58) and in stray references in Soviet works on other Pamir languages. The most detailed descriptive grammar of Bartangī is by Karamkhudoev (1973, after some preparatory articles). It is written in an adapted Cyrillic script. It contains also conversational sentences and other text material.

Some of the salient characteristics of Bartangī are mentioned or discussed in works dealing with East Iranian or the Pamir languages and in important annotated bibliographies (e.g., Morgenstierne, 1958; Livshits, 1962; Sokolova, 1966; Pakhalina, 1969, 1975; Redard, 1970; Dodykhudoev, 1971-72; Oranskiĭ, 1975, 1979; Edel'man and Rastorgueva, 1975; Edel'man and Efimov, 1978).

Within the Šuḡnī group, Bartangī is most closely related to Orōšōrī. Some of the main differences are: Bartangī *tū*: Orōšōrī *tu* "you" (2nd sing.); the morpheme of ordinal numbers, Bartangī *-um*: Orōšōrī *-ēm*; the plural morpheme, Bartangī *-ēn* (< *-ānām*): Orōšōrī *-īf* (< *-ēv* < *-aibiš*); absence of the ergative construction in Orōšōrī, etc. (cf. Edel'man, 1976, p. 89). Bartangī is separated from Rōšānī by some differences of grammar and vocabulary (cf. Sokolova, 1960, pp. 4ff.). On the whole, however, Bartangī is nearer to Rōšānī than to Šuḡnī, especially with regard to the vowel system; cf., e.g., Šuḡnī *čīd*, Rōšānī *čod*, Bartangī *čod* (< *kata-*) "house." For other correspondences see Sokolova, 1953, pp. 130ff.

The vowel phonemes of Bartangī are: *i, ī, ē, ö, a, ā, o, u, ū* (on their phonetic realization see Sokolova, 1953, pp. 128ff.). Mid-rounded *ö* (phonetically long) is peculiar to Bartangī and Orōšōrī. The system of consonants is the same for the whole Šuḡnī group: plosives (*p, b, t, d, k, g, q*); affricates (*c = ts, j = dz, č, ǰ*); fricatives (*f, v, θ, δ, x̌, γ̌, x, γ, h*); sibilants (*s, z, š, ž*); sonants (*w, y, m, n, r, l; w* sometimes has an allophone *β*: Sokolova, 1953, p. 158).

The diachronic details of the phonetic development in the Šuḡnī group are intricate. The history of the vocalism has been analyzed by Sokolova, 1967. Morgenstierne (1973a, p. 108) has shown that the original distinction between Old Iranian final *-ă* and *-ā* can still be traced in the Šuḡnī group. Umlaut caused by *ī, ā* has become functionally relevant in morphophonemics, where other vowel alternations also occur, e.g., *čöd* "house," plur. *čadḗn* (cf. Morgenstierne, 1928, p. 37). Diachronic study of the consonants (the most systematic work is by Edel'man, 1980) reveals differences within the Šuγnī group mainly regarding the representation of old *-š-* and of old *r* + consonant, e.g., Šuγnī *zinaγ̌*, Rōšānī *zinaw*, Bartangī *zināw* (< **snušā-*) "daughter-in-law"; Šuγnī *pēx̌c-*, Bartangī *pāws-* (< **pṛsa-*) "to ask"; Šuγnī *mūd*, Bartangī and Rōšānī *mūg* (< *mūḍ* < **mṛta-*) "died." (For the development of old *rt*, *ṛt*, cf. Dodykhudoev, 1964; Morgenstierne, 1970, p. 338; Edel'man, 1963). A considerable part of the vocabulary of the Šuγnī group is of unknown or uncertain origin. Collections of etymologies are found, e.g., in Sokolova, 1967, but the most recent etymological standard work is that by Morgenstierne, 1974.

In their morphology the members of the Šuγnī group differ in minor details only. The function of the old cases has been taken over by prepositions and postpositions. Case-differentiated forms are restricted to the pronouns. For details see Payne, 1980, p. 162. The demonstrative pronouns are marked for three degrees of distance and go back to old **ima-*, **aita-*, and **awa-* (Morgenstierne, 1942, p. 258). The derivation of some of the personal pronouns, e.g., Bartangī *tamā́(š)* "you" (2nd plur.) is problematic (cf. Edel'man, 1971: Pakhalina, 1975a; Kuiper, *IIJ* 18, 1976, p. 99). Nouns have the plural allomorphs *-ēn*, *-yōn*, *-gōn*, *-ārj*, *-ōrj* (of doubtful origin: Pakhalina, 1975, p. 232). Adjectives have special feminine forms, e.g., Bartangī *rōšt*, fem. *rāšt* "red." The vigesimal system is used in counting (Edel'man, 1975b).

The verbal system is based on two stems: the present stem (from the Old Iranian present) and the past stem (derived from the old participle in *-ta*). The personal endings of the present tense are: 1. *-um*, 2. *-i/zero*, 3. *-t/d* in the singular and 1. *-an*, 2. *-at/af*, 3. *-an* in the plural. In the past tenses intransitive verbs have gender and number agreement in Bartangī (*sāw-* "to go," *niθ-* "to sit"):

present	past masc.	fem./plur.	perf. masc.	fem.	plur.
sāw-	*sud*	*sad*	*suč*	*sic*	*sač*
niθ-	*nöst*	*nāst*	*nösč*	*nesc*	*nāsč*

The internal vowel alternations arise as a result of umlauting, e.g., *sud* "went" < **cyuta-*, *sad* < **cyutā*. The perfect goes back to the participle in **-taka*, fem. **-tačī* (with *ī*-umlaut). The pluperfect, different from Rōšānī, is formed analytically from the perfect and the past of "to be," e.g., *wīnč vud* "had seen." In the past tenses person and number agreement is marked by moving clitic particles (see Payne, 1980, p. 165). Various verbal nouns occur: infinitive in *-ōw*; participles in *-īn*; *-ōč*, fem. *-ēc*; *-ön*, fem, *-ān*; *-öj*, fem. *-ēj*, e.g. *nivišöj* "intending to write." An analytical passive is formed with the auxiliary "go," e.g., *čöd wiröx̌čak sud* "the house was built" (Karamkhudoev, 1973, p. 174).

The syntax of the Šuγnī group needs much further investigation. Only in Bartangī and Rōšānī are there remnants of an optional ergative construction for pronominal agents in transitive past tenses, e.g., Bartangī *āz-um* (or ergatively: *mun-um*) *tār kitōb vuj* "I have brought you a book" (cf. Payne, 1980). More widespread than in Rōšānī is the tendency in Bartangī to use *az* as direct object marker, e.g., *mun-um az tā wīnt* "I saw you" (Payne, 1980, p. 163). In the order of words the defining part precedes the defined, e.g., Bartangī *pōdx̌ō puc* "king's son," *xušrūy γāc* "beautiful girl," *mun vōrj* "my horse." For more information on syntax see Sokolova, 1966, p. 389, and Edel'man, 1974.

It is a matter of controversy whether Bartangī should be called a "dialect" or a "language" (Edel'man, 1976, p. 85, and 1980a, pp. 139ff.). If "dialect" is used in a sociolinguistic sense with the meaning "unwritten or of little cultural prestige," the term would be appropriate for Bartangī. Moreover, as speakers of Bartangī, Orōšōrī, Rōšānī, and Šuγnī can understand each other, one may say that they speak "regional dialects." On the other hand, "dialect" also seems justified from a historical point of view (Lentz, 1933, p. 14).

Synchronically, the question "dialect of which language?" poses ethnic problems, as no generally recognized standard form exists. Even speakers of the most closely related Orōšōrī would never accept that they speak a "dialect" of Bartangī, and the reverse also holds true. (For the native classification see Sköld, 1936, p. 14). It is accordingly preferable to call Bartangī, Orōšōrī, Rōšānī, and Šuγnī "languages" and members of a genetically closely related "language group" (for this term cf., e.g., Heger, 1976) corresponding to the Russian expression "yazykovaya gruppa."

Bibliography: M. S. Andreev, *Tadzhiki doliny Khuf*, 2 vols., Stalinabad, 1953-58. R. Kh. Dodykhudoev, *Materialy po istoricheskoĭ fonetike shugnanskogo yazyka*, Dushanbe, 1962. Idem, "Ob otrazhenii drevneiranskoĭ gruppy *rt* v shugnanskom yazyke," in *Iranskaya filologiya, trudy nauchnoĭ konferentsii 1962*, Leningrad, 1964. Idem, "Die Pamir-Sprachen. Zum Problem der Konvergenz," *Mitteilungen des Instituts für Orientforschung* 17, 1971-72, pp. 463-70. Idem, *Pamirskaya mikrotoponimiya* (*issledovanie i materialy*), Dushanbe, 1975. Idem, "Pamirskie etimologii, Roshorv, Sipondzh," in *Iranskoe yazykoznanie. Istoriya, etimologiya, tipologiya*, Moscow, 1976, pp. 136-45. D. I. Edel'man, "Problema tserebral'nykh v vostochnoiranskikh yazykakh," *Voprosy yazykoznaniya*, 1963, pp. 67-81. Idem, "Sovremennoe sostoyanie izucheniya pamirskikh yazykov," ibid., 1964, pp. 128-32. Idem, "K voprosu o slovoobrazovanii mestoimeniĭ v indoiranskikh yazykakh," in *Indiĭskaya i iranskaya filologiya. Voprosy leksiki*, Moscow, 1971, pp. 151-60. Idem, "O konstruktsiyakh predlozheniya v iranskikh yazykakh," *Voprosy yazykoznaniya*, 1974, pp. 23-33. Idem, "Geograficheskie nazvaniya Pamira," in *Strany i narody vostoka* 16, Moscow, 1975, pp. 41-61. Idem, "Les verbes 'être' et 'avoir' dans les langues iraniennes," in *Mélanges linguistiques offerts à Émile*

Benveniste, Paris, 1975a, pp. 151-58. Idem, "K genezisu vigezimal'noĭ sistemy chislitel'nykh," *Voprosy yazykoznaniya*, 1975b, pp. 30-37 (cf. Oranskiĭ, *Narody Azii i Afriki*, 1970, p. 200). Idem, "Problema 'yazyk ili dialekt' pri otsutstvii pis'mennosti (na materiale pamirskikh yazykov)," in *Lingvisticheskaya geografiya, dialektologiya i istoriya yazyka*, Erevan, 1976, pp. 85-93. Idem, "K istorii yazgulyamskikh i shugnano-rushankikh ukazatel'nykh mestoimeniĭ," in *Iranskoe yazykoznanie. Istoriya, etimologiya, tipologiya*, Moscow, 1976, pp. 85-96. Idem, "History of the Consonant Systems of the North-Pamir Languages," *IIJ* 22, 1980, pp. 287-310. Idem, "K probleme 'yazyk ili dialekt' v usloviyakh otsutstviya pis'mennosti," in *Teoreticheskie osnovy klassifikatsii yazykov mira*, Moscow, 1980a, pp. 127ff. Idem, "Areal'nye cherty v severnopamirskoĭ morfologii," in *Iranskoe yazykoznanie, ezhegodnik 1980*, Moscow, 1981, pp. 67-76. D. I. Edel'man and V. A. Efimov, "Novoiranskie yazyki. Vostochnaya gruppa," in *Yazyki Azii i Afriki. Indoevropeĭskie yazyki* II, Moscow, 1978, pp. 198-253. D. I. Edel'man, V. S. Rastorgueva et al., *Opyt istoriko-tipologicheskogo issledovaniya iranskikh yazykov*, 2 vols., Moscow, 1975. R. Gauthiot, "De la réduction de la flexion nominale en iranien," *Mémoires de la société linguistique de Paris* 20, 1916, pp. 61-70. W. Geiger, "Die Pamir-Dialekte," in *Grundriss der iranischen Philologie* I/2, Strassburg, 1898-1901, pp. 288-344. K. Heger, "'Sprache' und 'Dialekt' als linguistisches und soziolinguistisches Problem," in *Zur Theorie des Dialekts*, ed. J. Göschel et al., Zeitschrift für Dialektologie und Linguistik, Beiheft 16, Wiesbaden, 1976, pp. 215-35. D. Karamshoev, "Novoe v pamirskoĭ filologii," *Voprosy yazykoznaniya*, 1977, pp. 126-33. Idem, *Kategoriya roda v pamirskikh yazykakh*, Dushanbe, 1978. Idem, "Vozniknovenie i razvitie otymennykh pokazateleĭ roda v shugnano-rushanskoĭ gruppe," in *Iranskoe yazykoznanie, ezhegodnik 1980*, Moscow, 1981, pp. 77-93. N. Karamkhudoev, *Bartangskiĭ yazyk. Fonetika i morfologiya*, Dushanbe, 1973. W. Lentz, *Pamir-Dialekte* I: *Materialien zur Kenntnis der Schugni-Gruppe*, Göttingen, 1933. V. A. Livshits, "Iranskie yazyki narodov Sredneĭ Azii," in *Narody Azii i Kazakhstana* I, Moscow, 1962, pp. 131-58. G. Morgenstierne, "Notes on Shughni," *NTS* 1, 1928, pp. 32-83. Idem, "Iranica I. The Demonstrative Pronouns in Shughni," *NTS* 12, 1942, pp. 258-60. Idem, "Neu-iranische Sprachen," in *HO* I, IV/1, 1958, pp. 155-78. Idem, "The Development of Iranian *r* + Consonant in the Shughni Group," in *W. B. Henning Memorial Volume*, ed. M. Boyce and I. Gershevitch, London, 1970, pp. 334-42. Idem, "The Development of *r* + Sibilant in Some Eastern Iranian Languages," in *Irano-Dardica*, Wiesbaden, 1973, pp. 84-93 (reprinted with additions from *TPS*, 1948). Idem, "Final *-a* and *-ā* in Iranian," ibid., pp. 108-09. Idem, *Etymological Vocabulary of the Shughni Group*, Wiesbaden, 1974. Idem, "Indo-European *dheugh-* and *deuk-* in Indo-Iranian," in *Monumentum H. S. Nyberg* II, Leiden, 1975, pp. 77-80 (on Shughni group *δůj-* "to milk," *wiδůj-* "to peel," etc.). Y. M. Oranskiy, *Die neuiranischen Sprachen der Sowjet-Union*, tr. from Russian by W. Winter, The Hague, 1975. Idem, "Indo-Iranica IV: Tadjik (régional) *buruǰ* 'bouleau'," in *Mélanges linguistiques offerts à Émile Benveniste*, Paris, 1975a, pp. 435-40 (p. 437 on Bartangi *vōwzn* "birch"). Idem, *Iranskie yazyki v istoricheskom osveshchenii*, Moscow, 1979. T. N. Pakhalina, *Pamirskie yazyki*, Moscow, 1969. Idem, "Sravnitel'nyĭ obzor pamirskikh yazykov," in *Strany i narody vostoka* 16, Moscow, 1975, pp. 222-50. Idem, "Eléments indo-aryens dans les langues iraniennes orientales," in *Mélanges linguistiques offerts à Émile Benveniste*, Paris, 1975a, pp. 441-45. Idem, "Ob indoariĭskikh elementakh v sisteme lichnykh mestoimeniĭ vostochnoiranskikh yazykov," in *Iranskoe yazykoznanie. Istoriya, ètimologiya, tipologiya*, Moscow, 1976, pp. 79-84. Idem, "O roli i-umlauta v istorii razvitiya vokalizma iranskikh yazykov," *Voprosy yazykoznaniya*, 1977, pp. 89-96. J. R. Payne, "The Decay of Ergativity in Pamir Languages," *Lingua* 51, 1980, pp. 147-86. Idem, "Pamir Languages," in *Corpus Linguarum Iranicarum*, ed. R. Schmitt, Wiesbaden, 1989. A. K. Pisarchik, "Terminy obrashcheniya 'lo' i 'ro' v shugnano-rushanskoĭ gruppe yazykov," *Izvestiya tadzhikskogo filiala Akademii Nauk SSSR* 15, 1949, pp. 59-67. G. Redard, "Other Iranian Languages," in *Current Trends in Linguistics* VI, 1970, pp. 103ff. W. Skalmowski, "Transitive Verb Constructions in the Pamir and Dardic Languages," *Studia Indoeuropejskie, Polska Akademia Nauk, Oddział w Krakowie Prace Komisji Językoznawstwa* **37**, Kraków, 1974, pp. 205-12. H. Sköld, *Materialien zu den iranischen Pamirsprachen*, Lund, 1936. V. S. Sokolova, *Ocherki po fonetike iranskikh yazykov* II, Moscow and Leningrad, 1953. Idem, *Bartangskie teksty i slovar'*, Moscow and Leningrad, 1960. Idem, "K utochneniyu klassifikatsii shugnano-rushanskoĭ gruppy pamirskikh yazykov," in *Iranskiĭ sbornik k semidesyatiletiyu professora I. I. Zarubina*, Moscow, 1963, pp. 71-80. Idem, "Shugnano-rushanskaya yazykovaya gruppa," in *Yazyki narodov SSSR* I, Moscow, 1966, pp. 362-97. Idem, *Geneticheskie otnosheniya yazgulyamskogo yazyka i shugnanskoĭ yazykovoĭ gruppy*, Leningrad, 1967. Idem, *Geneticheskie otnosheniya mundzhanskogo yazyka i shugnano-yazgulyamskoĭ yazykovoĭ gruppy*, Leningrad, 1973. Idem, "K rekonstruktsii vostochnoiranskogo vokalizma," in *Iranskoe yazykoznanie, ezhegodnik 1980*, Moscow, 1981, pp. 14-36. V. S. Sokolova, and A. L. Gryunberg, "Istoriya izucheniya bespis'mennykh iranskikh yazykov," in *Ocherki po istorii izucheniya iranskikh yazykov*, Moscow, 1962, pp. 118ff. P. Tedesco, "*a*-Stämme und *aya*-Stämme im Iranischen," *ZII* 2, 1923, pp. 284-315. Idem, "Ostiranische Nominalinflexion," *ZII* 4, 1926, pp. 94-166. I. I. Zarubin, "Materialy i zametki po etnografii gornykh tadzhikov," in *Sbornik Muzeya*

Antropologii i Etnografii imeni Petra Velikago... V, Petrograd, 1918, pp. 97-148. Idem, "Obrazets pripamirskoĭ narodnoĭ pezii," *Doklady Rossiĭskoĭ Akademii Nauk*, 1924, pp. 82-85. Idem, *Bartangskie i rushanskie teksty i slovar'*, Moscow and Leningrad, 1937.

(G. Buddruss)

BARTHÉLEMY, ADRIEN, French Orientalist, born in Paris on 24 August 1859, died at Emancé (Rambouillet) on 18 December 1949. He was a devoted linguist, who learned Sanskrit, Avestan, Turkish, Persian, and Arabic at a very young age. Early in his career he became interested in Persian grammar, and after 1878 he was a student of J. Darmesteter at the Ecole des Hautes Etudes; in 1887, he published the results of a study prepared under the latter's guidance in Paris, with the title *Gujastak Abalish: Relation d'une conférence théologique présidée par le Calife Ma'moun, texte pehlvi... avec traduction, commentaire et lexique*, which consists of a very detailed study of the text (from manuscripts Suppl. pers. 33 and 46 in the Bibliothèque Nationale and Haug 22 in Munich) and a glossary. In the same year he published, also in Paris, a translation with commentary of *Arta Viraf Namak: Descente d'Arta Viraf aux enfers*..., which appeared in the series Bibliothèque Orientale Elzévirienne (vol. 54).

A career in diplomacy took him away from Iranian studies and led him to begin a monumental dictionary of eastern Arabic dialects. While posted as French vice-consul at Rašt from June, 1903 to April, 1905, however, he conducted research on the phonology of Iranian dialects, specifically Ṭālešī and Gīlakī, but his notes, like his Pahlavi-French and Mazdean Persian dictionaries, remain unpublished.

After returning to France, he taught Arabic at the Ecole des Langues Orientales and the Ecole Pratique des Hautes Etudes from 1906 to 1929; his work evinces an exceptional rigor in the fields of dialectology and linguistics.

Bibliography: A. Barthélemy, *Dictionnaire Arabe-Français. Dialectes de Syrie: Alep, Damas, Liban, Jérusalem*, complementary fascicle, Paris, 1969, pp. 57-68. J. Basset, "Nécrologie," *JA* 239, 1951, pp. 239-41.

(F. Richard)

BARTHOLD, VASILIĬ VLADIMIROVICH, Russian Orientalist (1869-1930). He was born on 15 November 1869 in St. Petersburg, to a Russianized German family; his baptized name was Wilhelm, which he used in his works published in west European languages. In the years 1887-91 he studied at the Faculty of Oriental Languages of the University of St. Petersburg, mainly under the noted Russian Arabist Victor Rosen, and specialized in the history of the Middle East. Upon graduation he spent two years in western Europe, traveling, studying Oriental manuscripts, and attending the lectures of August Müller and Eduard Meyer in Halle and of T. Nöldeke in Strasbourg. In 1896 he began to teach at the University of St. Petersburg as Privatdozent, in 1901 he became extraordinary professor, in 1906 professor. He worked there until the end of his life. In 1900 he defended his thesis "Turkestan in the Age of the Mongol Conquest," for which he obtained the degree of Doctor of History of the Orient. In 1910 he was elected corresponding member and in 1913 academician of the Imperial Academy of Sciences in St. Petersburg, later the Academy of Sciences of the U.S.S.R. He lived all his life in St. Petersburg/Leningrad, frequently traveling to Central Asia, the Caucasus, western Europe, and the Middle East (Turkey and Egypt). He lectured at the Universities of Moscow, Tashkent (1925, 1927), Baku (1924), Istanbul (1926), and London (King's College, 1923). During his career, beside his university teaching, he held numerous positions in various scholarly institutions and societies, of which the most important were those of secretary (1905-13) and head (*upravlyayushchiĭ*, 1918-22) of the Oriental Branch of the Russian Archeological Society, secretary of the Russian Committee for the Study of Central and East Asia (1903-21), and chairman of the board (*kollegiya*) of Orientalists attached to the Asiatic Museum (1921-30). He was the editor of *Zapiski Vostochnogo otdeleniya Russkogo Arkheologicheskogo obshchestva* (Transactions of the oriental branch of the Russian archeological society, 1908-12), of *Zapiski Kollegii vostokovedov pri Aziatskom muzee Rossiĭskoĭ Akademii nauk* (Transactions of the board of orientalists, 1925-30), and of three short-lived periodicals: *Mir islama* (The world of Islam, 1912), *Musul'manskiĭ mir* (The Muslim world, 1917), and *Iran* (1-3, 1927-29). Barthold died from uremia in Leningrad on 19 August 1930.

Barthold's scholarly output was enormous: from the publication of his first article in 1892 till his death, he published 670 works (including 247 articles in *The Encyclopaedia of Islam*), and 14 of his works were published posthumously; about a dozen works prepared by him for publication still remain as manuscripts in his archives. He had an excellent philological training and a thorough knowledge of the three "classical" languages of the Islamic world, Arabic, Persian, and Turkish. But his main interest was in history; in the words of Minorsky, Barthold's "fundamental characteristic was that he was not an 'Oriental philologist' making inroads into history, but a 'historian' equipped with Oriental languages" (preface to Barthold's *Four Studies on the History of Central Asia*, tr. V. and T. Minorsky, 3 vols., Leiden, 1956, p. ix). Barthold wrote in his autobiography: "It seemed to me quite natural that a Russian Orientalist-historian should be attracted by a region which was geographically and historically closer to Russia than the other eastern countries, the region where a Russian scholar had at his disposal material which was much less available to a west European scholar" (*Sochineniya* IX, pp. 789-90). This region was Central Asia, and Barthold was the first who put the study of the history of Central Asia on a firm scholarly basis and actually founded this branch of

Oriental studies. But he never studied Central Asia in isolation. He perceived the process of world history as one of a convergence of individual societies through "the expansion of culture of one or several advanced peoples upon an ever vaster geographical region" (*Sochineniya* IX, p. 234). Therefore he paid great attention to the interaction of diverse cultural elements which, in his opinion, shaped Central Asian history, especially ancient Iranian, nomadic Turko-Mongolian, and Islamic civilizations. For Barthold, the study of these three civilizations also had an importance of its own, and he devoted a great number of works to Iranology, Turkology, and Islamology.

Some of Barthold's works deal (completely or partially) with pre-Islamic Central Asia and Iran. These works are now more outdated than his other works, because of the accumulation of archeological material and the progress in the study of Middle Iranian languages during the last five decades. But many of his general observations, as well as conclusions made on the basis of the study of Arabic sources which he was often the first to utilize, are still valid. Among his ideas which found brilliant confirmation in later research was that of the importance of Iranian Buddhism in the culture of Iran and Central Asia (see *Sochineniya* VII, pp. 469-72). His careful evaluation of the relative historical roles of the eastern and western regions of the Iranian world (*Sochineniya* VII, pp. 417-37) is also important. One of the recurrent themes of his studies bearing on the pre-Islamic Iranian world was the relation between the Iranian landed aristocracy (*dehqān*s) and urban culture; he linked the development of civilization with the flourishing of urban life brought by Islam and the decline of the *dehqān*s (cf. especially *Sochineniya* VII, pp. 359-73).

Barthold's greatest contribution to the study of Central Asia and Iran was in medieval history, from the early Islamic through the Timurid periods. His first monumental work, *Turkestan v èpokhu mongol'skogo nashestviya* (Turkestan in the age of the Mongol invasion, first published in 1898-1900; the title of the revised English edition of 1923 was changed to *Turkestan Down to the Mongol Invasion*), contains a detailed survey of the historical geography of Central Asia and a study of its political and, to some extent, social history from the Arab conquest to the Mongol invasion. It laid a firm foundation for our knowledge of this period in the history of Central Asia and eastern Iranian lands in general, on which all subsequent research has been based, and it is still indispensable. Barthold returned to the same period later in several articles devoted to specific historical problems, such as the history of the Arab conquests in Central Asia (*Sochineniya* II/2, pp. 380-87), the history of the Saffarids (*Sochineniya* VII, pp. 337-53), the history of the peasant movements in Iran (ibid., 438-49), and the system of taxation in Iran under the Mongols (*Sochineniya* IV, pp. 313-38).

The Timurid period attracted Barthold's attention while he was working on his *Turkestan*. His monograph "Ulugh Bek and His Time" (written in 1915, published in 1918) was, in a sense, a continuation of *Turkestan*, and, in turn, had its continuation in the monograph "Mīr ʿAlī Shīr and Political Life" (1926; see both in *Sochineniya* II/2; translated into English by V. and T. Minorsky in *Four Studies on the History of Central Asia* II and III). Beside these two works, which, like *Turkestan* for the earlier period, gave for the first time a critical scholarly analysis of the sources and provided basis for further research, Barthold devoted to the same period about a dozen more articles. They deal especially with the sources for Timurid history, and among them are also a long article "On the Burial of Timur" (*Sochineniya* II/2, pp. 423-54; English translation by J. M. Rogers in *Iran* 12, 1974, pp. 65-88), where, beside its main topic, some important questions about the cultural history of Iran and Central Asia are discussed, and "The Popular Movement in Samarkand in 1365" (*Sochineniya* II/2, pp. 362-77), in which Barthold was the first to study the *sarbedār* movement.

Barthold recognized also the importance of the study of the later period of the history of Central Asia—that of the Uzbek khanates of the 16th-19th centuries. He noticed that this period belonged to the least developed fields of the history of the Orient, "which is to be explained not by the lack of sources, but rather by the indifference of researchers" (*Sochineniya* II/2, p. 400). He himself discovered and described a number of manuscript sources related to this period. He also contributed to this field several studies and reviews dealing with the history of the Central Asian khanates shortly before the Russian conquest (*Sochineniya* II/2, pp. 320-21, 333-58, 400-13, 419-22) and an article on the Uzbek court ceremonial of the seventeenth century (ibid., pp. 388-99). Beside this, certain aspects of the modern period of Central Asian history are discussed in great detail in his general works dealing with the historical geography and the history of irrigation of Central Asia: "Accounts of the Aral Sea and Lower Reaches of the Amu-Darya," *Sochineniya* III, pp. 75-93; "On the History of Irrigation in Turkestan," ibid., 97-233; and especially "A History of the Cultural Life of Turkestan," *Sochineniya* II/1, pp. 268-433—the only work where he examined Central Asian history under Russian rule.

In the 1920s Barthold published general surveys of the history of the Tajiks (1925; Eng. tr., J. M. Rogers, *Afghan Studies* 3-4, 1982), Kirghiz (1927), and Turkmens (1929), as well as his "Twelve Lectures on the History of the Turks of Central Asia" (first published in Turkish in 1927, German translation in 1935, French translation in 1945; Russian original published in 1968, in *Sochineniya* V). The latter is still in many respects an unsurpassed general survey of the medieval history of Turkic peoples, which is of great value also for Iranologists.

Barthold's contribution to the study of history and culture of Iran and Iranian philology is also significant. His "Historico-Geographical Survey of Iran," published in 1903 (*Sochineniya* VII, pp. 31-225; English translation in 1984, see below), is still the only study of this kind; in it Barthold systematically examines the available archeological and literary evidence on each historical province of Iran from antiquity until modern times. The term Iran is understood in this work in a broader sense, as all regions of the Middle East inhabited by peoples speaking Iranian languages, from Mesopotamia to the Indus (excluding Central Asia, which Barthold more often referred to as Turkestan). Barthold's "Iran: A Historical Survey" (1926; see *Sochineniya* VII, pp. 229-334; English translation published in 1939 in Bombay) gives an excellent general introduction to Iranian studies, discussing the place of Iran and Iranian culture in world history, geography and ethnography of Iran, historical literature in Persian (probably the best concise survey of the subject available until now), and European and Russian study of Iran and Iranian culture. Beside these two monographs, Barthold devoted more than twenty articles (not counting those in *The Encyclopaedia of Islam*) to the study of various problems of the political, social, and cultural history of Iran. Among these must be noted "On the History of the Persian Epic" (1915, see *Sochineniya* VII, pp. 383-408; translated into German in *ZDMG* 98, 1944, pp. 121-57), where he proved the East Iranian origin of Persian epic poetry.

In his research Barthold utilized not only written sources, but also archeological evidence. Twice (in 1893-94 and 1904) he participated himself in archeological explorations in Central Asia, but he came to the conclusion that he was not fit for archeological field work. Still, he maintained his interest in archeology and played an important role in directing archeological work in Central Asia. More than two dozen of his articles are devoted to archeological subjects (see *Sochineniya* IV). The most fruitful, however, was his study of written, mainly narrative, sources in Arabic, Persian, and Turkic languages. As Barthold noted in his "Autobiography" (*Sochineniya* IX, p. 791), "in the field of history of the Orient, due to abundance of material that has not been used, in reading manuscripts one often feels the same delight as a pioneer discovering a new world in excavations of ancient cities." And, indeed, Barthold did prodigious pioneering work studying Arabic, Persian, and Turkic manuscript sources, many of which he discovered himself. Among Persian historical works which became known thanks to Barthold were *Tārīḵ-e Jaʿfarī* (i.e., *Tārīḵ-e kabīr*) by Jaʿfarī (see Storey-Bregel, p. 349), *Baḥr al-asrār* by Maḥmūd b. Walī (ibid., p. 1135), *Fatḥ-nāma* by Šādī (ibid., p. 1120), *ʿĀlāmārā-ye nāderī* by Moḥammad Kāẓem (ibid., p. 914), *Toḥfat al-tawārīḵ-e ḵānī* by ʿEważ Moḥammad (ibid., p. 1058), *Sobḥānqolī-nāma* by Moḥammad Salāḥ Balḵī (ibid., p. 1143), history of Abu'l-Fayż Khan by ʿAbd-al-Raḥmān Ṭāleʿ (ibid., p. 1149), *Maḵāzen al-taqwā fī tārīḵ Boḵārā* by Ḥosayn Mīrī (ibid., p. 1163), *Ẓafar-nāma-ye Ḵodāyār-ḵānī* by ʿAbd al-Ḡafūr (ibid., p. 1192). Many others were for the first time analyzed in detail by Barthold. He published the text of *Ḥodūd al-ʿālam* in a facsimile edition, and some of his works contain long extracts from Persian texts edited by him (the most important are: extracts from numerous sources included in the first part of the Russian edition of *Turkestan*; chapter on Turks from Gardīzī's *Zayn al-akbār*, see *Sochineniya* VIII, pp. 23-62; the last section of *Tārīḵ-e Jaʿfarī*, see *Sochineniya* VII, pp. 561-74). Probably the greatest contribution made by Barthold was to the study of Persian sources for the Mongol and especially the Timurid periods.

Finally, Barthold was also an outstanding historian of Oriental studies. His "History of the Study of the Orient in Europe and in Russia" (1st ed. 1911, 2nd ed. 1925, see *Sochineniya* IX, pp. 199-482; German translation in 1913, French translation in 1947) is an excellent general work on the exploration of Asia and the evolution of Oriental studies, which has still not been replaced by any work of comparable scope. Among his seventeen articles devoted to the detailed analysis of works of other scholars, three deal with Iranologists: K. Saleman, V. A. Zhukovskiĭ, and J. Marquart (see *Sochineniya* IX, pp. 599-618, 689-703, 779-88).

Bibliography: V. V. Bartol'd, *Sochineniya* (Collected works), vols. I-IX (vol. II in two parts), Moscow, 1963-77. This edition includes 511 works (among them 228 articles from *The Encyclopaedia of Islam* in Russian translation). Translations into Western languages continue to appear, the most recent being *An Historical Geography of Iran*, Princeton, 1984. Complete annotated bibliography of Barthold's published works and a description of his archives preserved in Leningrad are found in a volume containing two works: I. I. Umnyakov, *Annotirovannaya bibliografiya trudov akademika V. V. Bartol'da*, and N. N. Tumanovich, *Opisanie arkhiva akademika V. V. Bartol'da*, Moscow, 1976; reviewed by Yu. Bregel, "The Bibliography of Barthold's Works and the Soviet Censorship," *Survey* 24/3, 1979, pp. 91-107. The bibliography includes the section "Literature on Barthold" containing 141 titles (up to 1976). For additional bibliography of Soviet works on Barthold published in 1968-81, see B. V. Lunin, *Zhizn' i deyatel'nost' akademika V. V. Bartol'da*, Tashkent, 1981, pp. 212-16. Cf. Yu. Bregel, "Barthold and Modern Oriental Studies," *IJMES* 12, 1980, pp. 385-403.

(YU. BREGEL)

BARTHOLOMAE, CHRISTIAN, German scholar of Iranian and Indo-European studies (1855-1925).

1. *Life*. Bartholomae was born the son of a forester in Forst ob Limmersdorf (today Forstleithen near Limmersdorf), Upper Franconia, on 21 January 1855. After receiving his general education in Bayreuth he first studied the classical languages at Munich and Erlangen universities under, among others, Friedrich von Spiegel. Later he went to the university of Leipzig, at the time the undisputed center of linguistic studies, in order to study Sanskrit and comparative philology. There Heinrich Hübschmann exercised such a deep and decisive influence on Bartholomae and his scientific develop-

ment that he later, in the preface to his *Das altiranische Verbum* mentioned only Hübschmann, who had won him for Iranian studies, among his teachers. Bartholomae, who was to become an outstanding Indo-European scholar, did not advance rapidly in his academic career. It took five years after receiving the state doctorate (*Habilitation*) at the university of Halle for him to be appointed as extraordinary professor there in 1884. The following year he went to Münster, Westphalia, and only in 1898 was he appointed to a full professorship at the university of Giessen. In 1909 he moved to the university of Strassburg (as the successor to Hübschmann), but later the same year he left for Heidelberg, where he taught as professor of comparative philology and Sanskrit until his retirement in 1924. Bartholomae was an ordinary member of the Heidelberg Academy of Sciences and from before the war also a corresponding member of the (Imperial) Russian Academy of Sciences. He died on the island of Langeoog on 9 August 1925.

2. *Works.* Bartholomae devoted the main part of his life and work to Iranian linguistics, his chief endeavor being directed toward the integration of Iranian into the framework of Indo-European languages. With great energy and endurance he met the challenge of the Old Iranian texts, both the Avesta and the Old Persian inscriptions, breaking new ground in the linguistic investigation of these texts, establishing their phonological development and morphological structure. Bartholomae was strongly conscious of the need for combining the indigenous Indian Parsi tradition with both classical Western philological methods and those of comparative linguistics in the interpretation of the Avestan texts and in this way did much to relieve the pressure on Zoroastrian studies to base themselves exclusively upon the Zoroastrian tradition. The progress of Iranian studies around the turn of the century, especially of Iranian linguistics, is thus most clearly reflected in Bartholomae's publications on Old Iranian, from *Das altiranische Verbum* (1878) to the *Altiranisches Wörterbuch* (1904) with its supplementary volume (1906).

Bartholomae's first book, *Das altiranische Verbum*, was intended as the Iranian counterpart to several studies by Berthold Delbrück (mainly his *Das altindische Verbum*) and was therefore the first comprehensive presentation of the morphology and syntax of the Old Iranian verb to be written. In his *Handbuch der altiranischen Dialekte* (1883) he presented a more extensive and systematic comparative study of the phonology and morphology of the three old Indo-Iranian or Aryan languages (Avestan, Old Persian, and Old Indo-Aryan). The phonological part of this study, in which Iranian forms were derived from the original common Indo-Iranian forms, set a new standard for the linguistic analysis of both Indo-Iranian and Indo-European.

A decade later, however, this pioneering work was superseded by two other momentous studies by Bartholomae: "Vorgeschichte der iranischen Sprachen" (Prehistory of the Iranian languages, 1895) and "Awestasprache und Altpersisch" (Avestan and Old Persian, 1896), both in W. Geiger and E. Kuhn's *Grundriss der iranischen Philologie*. These two studies treat in detail the history of the phonology and morphology of the two Old Iranian languages, from Indo-European, via Indo-Iranian and proto-Iranian down to the individual historical languages. Bartholomae, with his by now long and profound experience with Old Iranian and Aryan linguistics and with complete command of the Iranian linguistic material, dealt with these subjects with such penetrating understanding and so thoroughly that his contributions have not yet been replaced. In the succinct and concise "Vorgeschichte," which is a detailed and precise comparative grammar of Old Iranian, he compared Old Iranian and Old Indo-Aryan phonology and morphology in order to reconstruct their common Indo-Iranian basis. Step by step he traced the changes of the Indo-European word forms (stem formations as well as inflectional forms) down to Proto-Iranian on the one hand, and on the other related the proto-Iranian state of the phonology and morphology to the Indo-European sources. In "Awestasprache und Altpersisch," starting from proto-Iranian, he described in parallel the phonological and morphological changes of Avestan and Old Persian. The syntax, however, is almost totally neglected in these studies; and it was left to Bartholomae's pupil H. Reichelt to fill this gap in Old Iranian grammar with his *Awestisches Elementarbuch* (Heidelberg, 1909).

What these two articles are to Old Iranian grammar, Bartholomae's *Altiranisches Wörterbuch* is to Old Iranian lexicography. Bartholomae spent over ten years compiling this work, which has been called "one of the best and most complete dictionaries written of any language" (M. J. Dresden), deservedly gaining the sobriquet of a *chalkénteros*. In it Bartholomae claimed to have collected and commented summarily on the entire Old Iranian linguistic material (both Avestan and Old Persian), as far as it was accessible in text editions. It was intended to replace F. Justi's *Altbactrisches Wörterbuch* (Leipzig, 1864), which had been the main source for Iranian lexicography, but had been made obsolete by K. F. Geldner's new edition of the Avesta (Stuttgart, 1885-95) and by the deeper understanding of the Pahlavi tradition achieved by scholars like M. Haug, E. W. West, and J. Darmesteter. Bartholomae added to the work of his predecessors by taking fully into consideration the tradition of the Parsi scholars, even where he regarded it as unreliable, and by supplementing Geldner's edition, which in fact contained fewer Avestan texts than N. L. Westergaard's *Zendavesta* (Copenhagen, 1854), by incorporating numerous smaller texts and fragments which were less accessible, sometimes even unpublished, and often had not yet been critically edited. Moreover, Bartholomae did not depend solely upon the text as edited by Geldner, but upon the manuscript tradition itself as given in Geldner's critical apparatus, which at times contains better readings than those printed in Geldner's text. On the whole the *Wörterbuch* is characterized by a felicitous combination of philological and linguistic approaches. In it Bartholomae propagated the use of the same transliteration system for Avestan which was employed in the *Grundriss* and which from then became the standard one and only recently is being replaced by the more systematic and faithful transliteration system of Karl Hoffmann. What Bartholomae intended his *Wörterbuch* to be was a summary of all the knowledge of his time, and so he did not confine himself merely to collecting the results of previous scholars but presented a lot of his own findings as well. One of the most useful features of the book is the reverse index (col. 1901ff.). The concordance of textual repetitions (pp. X-XXI) has in the meantime been replaced by B. Schlerath's *Awesta-Wörterbuch. Vorarbeiten* II: *Konkordanz*, Wiesbaden, 1968.

Each entry in this epochal dictionary is scrupulously exact and rests on intimate knowledge of Old Iranian. It specifies the language a word belongs to (j. = Young Avestan, g. = Gathic or Old Avestan, p. = Old Persian), then gives the forms and their meanings, all the attestations partly with translation, and in the notes discusses special questions of interpretation, etymology (briefly), the word's later development, the Pahlavi and Sanskrit renderings of the word, and occasionally discusses points of textual criticism. The alphabetical arrangement is that of Sanskrit dictionaries (except that *v* precedes *r*) and ignores unetymological anaptyctic and epenthetic vowels and the like.

The *Altiranisches Wörterbuch* was for decades and still remains the basis for all work on the Avesta and the Avestan language. It is still one of the essential tools of every Iranian scholar and is indispensible for any investigation of ancient Iranian literature. Its usefulness has by no means been impaired by the special indexes now available for many individual, mainly Old Avestan texts, nor by the new dictionary of Avestan proper names (M. Mayrhofer, "Die avestischen Namen," in *Iranisches Personennamenbuch* I/1, Vienna, 1977). It was and still is a model dictionary for any Indo-European language because of both its completeness and its critical examination and precise understanding of the vocabulary. Whatever imperfections remain in the book are due to the imperfect understanding of the texts at this early stage.

It is a matter of opinion whether the inclusion in the *Altiranisches Wörterbuch* of the vocabulary of the Old Persian inscriptions, which was easily accessible in Weissbach and Bang's edition, was really necessary. It is one of the points on which the *Wörterbuch* was severely criticized, it being alleged that the inclusion of the Old Persian material was a poor arrangement. Today, after the publication of Kent's *Old Persian* (New Haven, 1950, 2nd ed. 1953) and the discovery of numerous new inscriptions, the *Wörterbuch* plays only a minor role for Old Persian.

The Gathas, being the oldest Avestan texts, naturally commanded Bartholomae's special interest. He worked on these texts for the first time in 1879, when he published a text edition and a metrical and grammatical analysis of them; then, after the publication of the *Wörterbuch*, he published a translation of the Gathas (1905), combining the translations of individual Gathic words and phrases quoted in the dictionary. By the same method, Bartholomae's pupil F. Wolff later compiled a translation of the entire Avestan corpus on the basis of the *Wörterbuch* (F. Wolff, *Avesta. Die heiligen Bücher der Parsen*, Strassburg, 1910). Bartholomae expressed his view of Zarathustra's life and work in his rectorial speech *Zarathuštra's Leben und Lehre* (published Heidelberg, 1919; the speech was in fact not delivered owing to the circumstances prevailing in November, 1918).

It was not until 1904, after the appearance of the *Wörterbuch*, that Iranian studies was suddenly confronted with a wholly new situation in the epochal first publications of the manuscripts from Turfan oasis and elsewhere in Chinese Turkistan. Bartholomae at once realized the immense importance of these findings for the study of the Old Iranian languages and immediately began to investigate them. At any rate Bartholomae had already planned supplementary volumes to his dictionary in order to provide additional material and the results of new research, and he was soon able to publish such a supplementary volume (*Zum Altiranischen Wörterbuch*, 1906), containing among other things studies bearing on certain aspects of the new Middle Iranian, mainly Middle Persian, evidence, primarily on the notation of vowels in the Turfan manuscripts. As its subtitle *Nacharbeiten und Vorarbeiten* (Additional and preliminary studies) indicates, this book reflects a shift in Bartholomae's work from Old Iranian to Middle Persian.

From 1904 Bartholomae concentrated his research on Middle Persian. He eagerly familiarized himself first with these new texts from Turfan, then also with Book Pahlavi, the language of the Zoroastrian scriptures. Before this time he had used the Pahlavi translation, but only as a means to explain the Avesta; now the study of Pahlavi became a goal in itself, since the Turfan texts with their less ambiguous writing system offered welcome evidence for the interpretation of the graphically extremely ambiguous Book Pahlavi. Bartholomae's aim was again to make a thorough study of Middle Persian, thereby rendering it more accessible for Iranian historical linguistics. We need not wonder, therefore, that his two series of Middle Persian studies, *Zur Kenntnis der mitteliranischen Mundarten* and *Zum sasanidischen Recht* (both published by the Heidelberg Academy of Sciences) became an essential stimulus for Middle Iranian studies. Bartholomae did not yet attempt a comprehensive presentation of Middle Persian grammar or a lexicon, considering this to be premature, and therefore confined himself to the study of individual texts. Of Pahlavi texts he studied the Sasanian law book *Mādayān ī hazār dādestān*, which had been published shortly before by J. J. Modi (1901) on the basis of one single defective and carelessly written manuscript. Here he focused on the philological interpretation of the text and translated and commented on only a selection of its juridical decisions. His transcription of the Pahlavi script was based on purely historical principles, and for words of unknown or uncertain interpretation or pronunciation he employed the same mechanical transliteration he had used in the *Wörterbuch*, in which one Latin letter corresponded to each Pahlavi letter, e.g., *d* for the Pahlavi letters *y/d/g*, *n* for the Pahlavi letters *w/r/n*, etc.

While occupied with these Middle Iranian studies, Bartholomae compiled a detailed catalogue of the Zoroastrian manuscripts and related collections of the Bavarian State Library in Munich (from the estates of M. J. Müller, M. Haug, and F. Windischmann), the largest collection of its kind in Germany. This catalogue (*Die Zendhandschriften*, 1915) includes not only "Zend" manuscripts (as its title incorrectly suggests), but all kinds of Zoroastrian (Parsi) literature including texts in Middle Persian (Pahlavi, Pazand, and Parsi), New Persian, Sanskrit, and Gujarati. Müller's manuscripts were copies this scholar had made in the 1830s from manuscripts in Paris (already catalogued by E. Blochet in his rather scanty *Catalogue des manuscrits mazdéens*, Besançon, 1900), but Haug's manuscripts, which had been brought from India by Haug himself, were in part of great scholarly value, and Bartholomae describes in minute detail their material and formal conditions as well as their contents, giving extensive extracts of the texts themselves. Various points of textual criticism, lexicography (e.g., the many rare words in ms. M 51a.10), etymology, etc., make this book a rich source of information.

Outside the strictly Iranian field Bartholomae dealt with general problems of both Indo-European comparative linguistics and other Indo-European languages. The so-called "Bartholomae's Law" (q.v.) was first formulated in his *Arische Forschungen* I, 1882, pp. 3ff.

3. *Evaluation.* Bartholomae was a sensible and objective scholar, whose judgment was usually cautious and prudent. Influenced by the Neogrammarians (K. Brugmann and his followers) and characterized by ardor and love for his subject and exceptional patience, he eagerly worked at the same corpus of texts for more than two decades. Thus he was able to publish several major reference books of fundamental importance for the understanding of the Old Iranian languages and literature, while embodying in them in a way typical of him countless secondary results of his special research. In the first place it was the mystery of the Avestan language that he unraveled by his bold initiative, and this he did so thoroughly that most previous studies fell into oblivion, some perhaps unjustly.

Of Bartholomae's work, the most criticized is undoubtedly his translation of the *Gathas*; he has been blamed for a total disregard for morphology, syntax, and especially word order (see, e.g., H. Humbach, *Die Gathas des Zarathustra* I, Heidelberg, 1959, pp. 66ff.). The reasons for the defects in Bartholomae's translation must be sought first in the fact that it followed the Pahlavi version and the tradition laid down by his predecessors among Western scholars too closely, and second in the manner in which it was put together, i.e., from the translations of individual words and phrases in the *Wörterbuch* (see above). Had he rid himself of these ties to the past and approached the problem of translation more systematically and from a purely linguistic point of view the result might have been different.

The principal merit of Bartholomae's life work was unquestionably his illumination of the linguistic aspect of the Old Iranian languages and his finding a firm place for them within the discipline of Indo-European comparative linguistics. The sum of his investigations is laid down in his two articles in the *Grundriss* and in his *Wörterbuch.* These three contributions contain a complete exposition of Avestan and Old Persian phonology, morphology, and vocabulary, and are the culmination of Bartholomae's researches on these subjects. But it must be emphasized that, when looking at Iranian, Bartholomae always viewed Indo-Iranian as a unity. This point of view becomes clear in his "Vorgeschichte der iranischen Sprachen" (1895), his three volumes of *Arische Forschungen*, and in numerous other studies containing the word *arisch* (Aryan) in the title (e.g., "Arica" in 19 issues of *IF* 1-42, 1892-1924; see also the comprehensive review articles of A. Fick and J. Wackernagel in *ZDMG* 48, 1894, pp. 504-31; 50, 1896, pp. 674-735). How strong Bartholomae's influence was on subsequent generations of scholars, becomes obvious from the fact that no attempt at a systematic description of proto-Indo-Iranian was made until 1980 (A. Erhart, *Struktura indoíránských jazyků* [The structure of the Indo-Iranian languages], Brno, 1980), although, considering the progress made in Iranian linguistics, such a work was long overdue. Bartholomae's *Wörterbuch* is still the only comprehensive dictionary of any Old or Middle Iranian language (other than Old Persian); thus the compilation of a vocabulary of words of common Indo-Iranian stock remains a desideratum.

Bibliography: Works: *Das altiranische Verbum in Formenlehre und Syntax dargestellt*, Munich, 1878. *Die Gāθā's und heiligen Gebete des altiranischen Volkes* (*Metrum, Text, Grammatik und Wortverzeichniss*), Halle, 1879. *Arische Forschungen*, 3 vols., Halle, 1882-87. *Handbuch der altiranischen Dialekte* (*Kurzgefasste vergleichende Grammatik, Lesestücke und Glossar*), Leipzig, 1883. *Beiträge zur Flexionslehre der indogermanischen Sprachen, insbesondere der arischen Dialekte*, Gütersloh, 1888. *Studien zur indogermanischen Sprachgeschichte*, 2 vols., Halle, 1890-91. *Arisches und linguistisches*, Göttingen, 1891. "Vorgeschichte der iranischen Sprachen," in Geiger and Kuhn, *Grundriss der iranischen Philologie* I, pp. 1-151. "Awestasprache und Altpersisch," ibid., pp. 152-248. *Altiranisches Wörterbuch*, Strassburg, 1904. *Die Gatha's des Awesta. Zarathushtra's Verspredigten*, Strassburg, 1905. *Zum Altiranischen Wör-*

terbuch. Nacharbeiten und Vorarbeiten, Strassburg, 1906. *Über ein sasanidisches Rechtsbuch*, Heidelberg, 1910. *Die Zendhandschriften der K. Hof- und Staatsbibliothek in München. Beschrieben von Christian Bartholomae*, Munich, 1915. *Zur Kenntnis der mitteliranischen Mundarten*, 6 vols., Heidelberg, 1916-25. *Zum sasanidischen Recht*, 5 vols., Heidelberg, 1918-23. *Zur Buchenfrage*, Heidelberg, 1918. *Zur Etymologie und Wortbildung der indogermanischen Sprachen*, Heidelberg, 1919. *Zarathuštra's Leben und Lehre*, Heidelberg, 1919, 2nd ed. 1924. *Die Frau im sasanidischen Recht*, Heidelberg, 1924.

Obituaries: H. Junker, *Indogermanisches Jahrbuch* 11, 1927, pp. 562-73 (with a portrait as frontispiece of vol. 12, 1928). A. A. Freĭman, *Iran* 1, 1927, pp. 201-14. A. Götze, *Biographisches Jahrbuch für Altertumskunde* 48, 1928 (in *Jahresbericht über die Fortschritte der klassischen Altertumswissenschaft* 219, 1929), pp. 73-81. See also F. J. Meier, *Neue Deutsche Biographie* 1, 1953, p. 609b; A. Scherer, *Ruperto-Carola* 7/17, 1955, pp. 74-75.

Bibliography: See the obituary by Junker, pp. 567-73, to which must be added "Iranisches," *ZII* 4, 1926, pp. 173-93; and Engl. tr. (by L. Bogdanov) "Notes on Sasanian law" and "Notes on a Sasanian Law-Book," *Journal of the K. R. Cama Oriental Institute* 18, 1931 to 30, 1936.

(R. SCHMITT)

BARTHOLOMAE'S LAW, the name given to a rule of phonetic assimilation in the Indo-Iranian and probably also the proto-Indo-European languages first noted by Christian Bartholomae in 1882. The law is as follows: When a voiced aspirate consonant is followed by a voiceless one, the latter becomes voiced, taking over the former's aspiration. This is best illustrated from Vedic, in which the aspiration is preserved, e.g., when the morpheme *-tá-* (as in *bhṛ-tá-* "carried") is added to the root *dabh-* "to betray" (< **dhabh-*, see GRASSMANN'S LAW) the result is **dabh-tá-*, which gives *dabdhá-*; likewise *b(h)udh-* "to wake" > **budh-tá-* > *buddhá-*. The Vedic rule can be formulated as $*D^hT > DD^h$. Bartholomae's law is also manifested in the Iranian languages, where it explains the development of **ubh-ta-* > **ubdha-* "woven" (= Ved. *ubdhá-* "surrounded," Skt. *-vábhi-* "weaving") > Iranian **ubda-* in Young Avestan *ubdaēna-* "made of woven material," or **au̯gh-ta* "he said" (cf. Gk. *eúkhomai*) > **au̯gdha* > Old Avestan *aogədā*. It is important to bear in mind that the law covers combinations with *-s-*; thus **au̯gh-sa* "you say" > **au̯gžha* > Old Avestan *aoγžā*; **d(h)ibh-s-* (cf. Ved. *dabh-* "to betray," *dips-* "to intend to betray") > **dhibžh* > Old Avestan *diβžaidiiai* "to deceive, cheat." Also noteworthy are phonetic changes such as **-dh-t-*>**-ddh-*> (Ir. **-dd-*>) Ir. *-zd-*: e.g., Ved. *vṛddhá-* "increased" (cf. *vardh-* = Av. *varəd-* "to multiply") = Young Avestan *vərəzda-*; Indo-Iranian **dha-dh-tai* "he puts" > **dhaddhai̯* > Old Avestan *dazdē* (see below); Indo-Iranian **-žh-t-* > **-ždh-*, as in **g(h)ṛžh-ta* "he complained" (cf. Av. *garəz-* = Ved. *garh-* "to complain" or "reproach") > **g(h)ṛždha* > Old Avestan *gərəžda*.

In the later Old Iranian languages (Young Avestan, Old Persian), however, common morphemes such as the *-ta-* of the participle or the *-ta* of the 3rd singular of the middle voice (secondary ending) are reintroduced by analogy (almost always in Young Avestan, always in Old Persian; also in Vedic *dhatté*, for **daddhe*, "he puts" against Old Avestan *dazdē*, see above), e.g., Vedic *baddhá-* "bound" (from **b(h)adh-tá-*) against Young Avestan and Old Persian *basta-*; Old Avestan *aogədā* (see above) against Young Avestan *aoxta*; Vedic *dabdhá-* (see above) against Young Avestan *dapta-* "betrayed;" Vedic *drugdhá-* "harmed" (cf. Ved. *drógha-* "deceitful," OPers. *drauga-* "treason") against OPers. *duruxta-* "lied," etc.

The fact that this phenomenon is found in attested languages as ancient as Old Persian lends weight to the theory that a similar tendency to analogical balancing may be the reason why Bartholomae's Law generally does not apply in the other Indo-European languages. On the other hand its demonstrable effects on non-Indo-Iranian languages (see Mayrhofer, p. 116) indicate that it was probably operative in proto-Indo-European.

Bibliography: C. Bartholomae, *Arische Forschungen* I, Halle, 1882, pp. 3ff. Idem, "Vorgeschichte der iranischen Sprachen," in *Grundriss*, pp. 20ff. (very good collection of examples). N. E. Collinge, *The Laws of Indo-European*, Amsterdam and Philadelphia, 1985, pp. 7ff. (with bibliography pp. 10f.). M. Mayrhofer, "Lautlehre," in *Indogermanische Grammatik* I/2, Heidelberg, 1986, pp. 115ff. (with bibliographical data).

(M. MAYRHOFER)

BĀRŪ, (or Bāra), fortress in general, defensive wall, rampart. The word is not attested in the oldest sources and goes back at most only to the Sasanian period (communication from W. Eilers). The concept must be distinguished from various other old types of fortification used in Iran to protect parts of fortresses.

Defensive walls and earthworks dating from the start of human settlement in Iran still survive. Their forms evolved in parallel with the development of offensive and defensive weapons. In prehistoric and early historic times, the type of fortification generally depended on requirements imposed by the location of the castle or village and the natural features of the terrain. In all periods, fortifications were as far as possible placed on high ground in order to exploit difficulties of approach presented by a hill or mountain slope and to give the defenders a vantage point and view from above. Structural designs were determined by general knowledge and experience of attack and defense rather than by local traditions. In all periods well-tried and proven methods of fortification were chosen. In the early historic period, ancient Persian fortification technique shows signs of influence from Mesopotamia (Frankfort, p. 215), Anatolia (Kleiss, 1976, p. 28), and other neighboring countries. The same readiness to adopt techniques found effective elsewhere can be traced throughout the architectural history of Iran, right down to the adoption of the "French style" for design of fortresses and city walls in the early 13th/19th century, notably at K̲ʷoy and Tehran (Kleiss, 1980, p. 167).

Another factor influencing fortification design was the local building material. In arid parts of the Iranian plateau and in the K̲ūzestān plain adjoining Mesopotamia, dried or baked brick prevailed, while in mountainous regions use of stone, at least for foundations, was usual, though even there upper parts of defensive walls from the prehistoric and early historic periods are often of unbaked brick. Earthworks in the strict sense appeared only in the modern period, under European influence in the 12th/18th and early 13th/19th centuries (Kleiss, 1980, p. 167). The use of timber in combination with stone and earth, common in prehistoric and early historic fortifications in Europe (e.g., in the form of the "murus gallicus"), was unknown in Iran, mainly because of the shortage of wood. Even in the timber-rich Caspian region of Gīlān and Māzandarān, no remains of prehistoric or early historic defensive structures of wood and earth have yet been found.

Throughout Iranian history, fortification was primarily a matter of protecting castles, which served both as residences of kings or lords and as strongholds where local people, with their livestock, could take refuge. From the start of the historic period in the first millennium B.C., village perimeters were also fortified, at first mainly for protection from robbers and wild beasts, later increasingly for defense against enemies. Scattered through the country are remains of strongly fortified village or castle settlements dating from as early as the third millennium B.C. (Kleiss, 1979, p. 27).

Fortifications were also built to protect strategic sectors such as passes and valleys, and their outlines are sometimes visible as walls or banks on the ground; unpublished observations indicate that in a few cases they may go back to the Achaemenid period.

Large-scale frontier fortification, like that of the Roman *limes*, is matched in Iran by the so-called "Wall of Alexander," remains of which survive east of the Caspian Sea in Gorgān. This was a mud-brick wall with forts at regular intervals. In the light of recent research (Kīānī, p. 11) it seems probable that the attribution to Alexander is incorrect and that the wall was built in the Parthian period.

Bibliography: H. Frankfort, *The Art and Architecture of the Ancient World*, Harmondsworth, 1954, pp. 215f. M. Y. Kīānī, *Parthian Sites in Hyrcania*, Berlin, 1982, pp. 11ff. W. Kleiss, in H. J. Kellner, ed., *Urartu, ein wiederentdeckter Rivale Assyriens*, Munich, 1976, pp. 28f. Idem, "Ravaz und Yakhvali, zwei befestigte Plätze des 3. Jahrtausends," *AMI* 12, 1979, pp. 27ff. Idem, "Europäische Befestigungsarchitektur in Iran," *AMI* 13, 1980, pp. 167ff.

See also FORTIFICATION.

(W. KLEISS)

BARUCH (Baruk̲, Bāruk̲ in Ar. sources), the son of Neriah, was the scribe and disciple of the prophet Jeremiah, who lived at the time of the Babylonian occupation of Judah and the first Jewish exile to Babylonia (586 B.C.). Despite the relatively modest position which this Baruch might be supposed to have had according to the biblical account, he became a major figure of popular legends, and several extra-canonical biblical books were composed, of which he was the supposed author. Since he accompanied Jeremiah in his exile to Babylonia, a medieval Jewish tradition (attested from the tenth century A.D.) placed his tomb on the Euphrates, not far from the tomb of the prophet Ezekiel; these tombs served as centers for Jewish pilgrimage from Iraq and Iran in the Middle Ages, and there were reports of various miracles produced at Baruch's tomb.

Baruch is of interest to Iranian studies chiefly because he was identified with Zoroaster by the Syriac authors Išoʿdād of Marv (3rd/9th cent.) and Solomon of Baṣra (7th/13th cent.), an identification perpetuated by some of the Arabic historians (see the material collected by Richard Gottheil, "References to Zoroaster in Syriac and Arabic literature," in *Classical Studies in Honour of Henry Drisler*, New York, 1894, pp. 24-32, as well as Joseph Bidez and Franz Cumont, *Les Mages hellénisés. Zoroastre, Ostanès et Hystaspe d'après la tradition grecque*, Paris, 1938, repr. Paris, 1973, I, pp. 49ff., and the texts referred to and published in the second volume).

The identification of Zoroaster with the disciple of Jeremiah is puzzling, and the explanations put forward for it have not been quite convincing. It has been pointed out, for example, that an action attributed to Jeremiah was to hide the fire of the Jerusalem Temple, so that it should not be soiled by the Babylonians, and in this he could have something in common with the prophet of ancient Iran and his concern with fire. The analogy seems both remote and unsatisfactory, because this would make Zoroaster the equivalent of Jeremiah, not of Baruch. The latter, however, had become in Jewish apocryphal literature a figure of such great mystical wisdom, being credited as the author of a number of visionary revelations involving mystical flights to heaven, that the equation with Zoroaster, the great seer of Iran, might not have seemed too far-fetched.

The important thing about this identification is that in certain Christian circles in Iran, perhaps also among Jews, and possibly also among Muslims, efforts were made to create a common denominator between the two sets of traditions, the Judeo-Christian on the one hand, and the Iranian on the other. Similar attempts at harmonizing and equating figures from the two traditions are found, for example, with regard to Yima (Jamšēd), whose legend partly coincides with that of the prophet Isaiah; Gayōmard, who is expressly identified with a variety of biblical figures; and other persons of Iranian mythology and history.

Bibliography: See also A. Ben Yaakov, *Qevarim qedošim be-Bavel*, Jerusalem, 1973, pp. 38ff. J. Neusner, "Barukh ben Neriah and Zoroaster," *Journal of Bible and Religion* 32, 1964, pp. 359-60.

(SH. SHAKED)

BĀRŪT (also *bārūṭ* and *bārūd*) "gunpowder" is a loanword from Arabic; it passed from Turkish into Persian usage. This is also clear from the subsidiary Arabic term for gunpowder, *dawā'* or "remedy," which in fact is the first word used in Arabic to denote gunpowder. In India and Afghanistan, where the word *bārūt* was borrowed from the Persian, the subsidiary term *dārū* "remedy" is also used. Similar usage is also found in Iran where, for example, the Jaft tribe in Kurdistan refer to gunpowder as *darmān* "remedy;" the same word is also used in that sense by the Baluch (Schlimmer, pp. 469-70). The author of *Borhān-e qāṭe'* (ed. Mo'īn, I, p. 216) explains that *bārūt or namak-e čīnī* (Chinese salt) is *dārū-ye tofang* "powder for the musket" and adds that in Syriac it is the name given to *šūra* (niter, saltpeter), the principle element of *bārūt*.

The earliest use of the word in Persian probably dates from the last quarter of the 9th/15th century. According to an 11th/17th-century text, "*bārūt* and other war supplies were stored in the Ostūnāvand fortress" in 908/1503 (*'Ālamārā-ye ṣafawī*, p. 88). The same text, for the next year, also refers to the fact that there was *bārūt* stored in the citadel of Šūštar (p. 90). Similar information is offered by Lāhījānī (p. 78) and *Tārīḵ-e ḵāndān-e Mar'ašī* (p. 64). Nevertheless, *bārūt* is not a word that is frequently used in the historical texts, and the same holds for the arms necessary to use *bārūt effectively*.

Guns and cannon, and thus gunpowder, probably were first introduced in Iran during Uzun Ḥasan Āq Qoyunlū's reign; in 1473 he asked Venice for "artillery, arquebuses, and gunners" (Woods, p. 128). According to an early 11th/17th-century source, the requested military personnel and cannon were sent; the Venetians sent "100 artillerymen of experience and capacity, for in the matter of their artillery the Persian armies suffered greatly from a paucity of cannon, while on the other hand the Turkish armies in Asia were very well equipped in this arm, and they could effect much damage in their attack" (*Don Juan of Persia*, p. 98).

Minorsky, however, in his *Persia in A.D. 1479* (pp. 89, 115-16) doubts whether the Āq Qoyunlū had the use of firearms, although in Appendix II of the book he seems to accept it as a fact. It is possible that the sultan's personal troops had been the only group permitted to use firearms in the late 9th/15th century (Woods, p. 8). Two events indicate that cannon may have been used by the Āq Qoyunlū. According to Venetian sources the Āq Qoyunlū captured Ottoman artillery in 977/1472. The captured firearms were later used in the winter campaign against the Mamluks (Woods, pp. 129, 270 n. 109). In 890/1485, the Āq Qoyunlū used artillery against the infidel Samtzkhe in Georgia. The Persian account of this campaign is ambiguous about the nature of the artillery used; only once does the author use *tūp* "cannon," while using the term *ra'd* (*ostād-e ra'd*; *dīg-e ra'd*), which spewed dragon-like fire, a few times. *Ra'd* usually refers to a grenade launcher or a pyrotechnic device used to hurl flammable material into the enemy's camp. However, the text also mentions that rocks (*sang*) were hurled into the fortress, thus referring to a cannon (Abīvardī, pp. 51, 53-54). Another instance where the Āq Qoyunlū used cannon is reported to have occurred at Tiflis in 1489 (Woods, p. 285, n. 75). Finally, the Safavids in 913/1507, during the siege of Ḥeṣn Kayfā in Dīārbakr, used "a mortar of bronze, of four spans, which they brought from Mirdin [Mārdīn] ... This mortar was cast in that country at the time Jacob Solṭān (Ya'qūb Solṭān Āq Qoyunlū, d. 896/1490; *A Narrative of Italian Travels in Persia*, p. 153).

The pre-1500 use of gunpowder and firearms seems likely in view of the fact that Shah Esmā'īl Ṣafawī used handguns and cannon in his fight for the throne of Iran. Qāżī Aḥmad Qomī (mistakenly) states that during the battle between the Āq Qoyunlū Alvand Shah and Shah Esmā'īl (907/1501) a gun (*tofang*) was heard for the first time in Iran (Glassen, p. 212), although he also refers to an earlier instance in 905/1499 (Glassen, p. 183; *tofang-e ra'd-āhang*). This is also confirmed by the 11th/17th-century *'Ālamārā-ye ṣafawī* (p. 68). Thereafter, the use of (hand)guns (*tofang*) is attested by several sources (Ḥasan Rūmlū, pp. 171, 186, 206, 212, 221; *'Ālamārā-ye ṣafawī*, pp. 96, 102, 272, 290, 335, 483, 493, 519).

Gunpowder of varying quality was produced in many cities in Iran. In Isfahan, several gunpowder makers (*bārūtsāz*) were employed in the arsenal (*tūpḵāna*; *Taḏkerat al-molūk*, p. 95). According to Thevenot the gunpowder produced in Lār was of good quality (II, p. 132). However, according to Du Mans (p. 208) the gunpowder makers did not purify their saltpeter or sulfur adequately or mix these with the correct amount of charcoal.

Gunpowder is also used in the traditional Iranian craft of stone quarrying. Quarrymen (*kūhborr*, *sang-šekan*) pour ordinary powder into holes bored in the stone surface and plug them with cotton wads. They ignite these charges with saltpeter fuses (*fatīla*) to blast away the superficial layers of rock and thereby reach the valuable formations below the surface (Wulff, p. 127).

Bibliography: Ḥ. Abīvardī, *Čārtaḵt*, ed. Ī. Afšār, *FIZ* 15, 1347 Š./1968. *'Ālamārā-ye ṣafawī*, ed. Y. Šokrī, Tehran, 1350 Š./1971. *Don Juan of Persia*, ed. and tr. G. Le Strange, London, 1926. R. Du Mans, *Estat de la Perse*, Paris, 1890. E. Glassen, *Die frühen Safawiden nach Qāżī Aḥmad Qumī*, Freiburg, 1970. V. Minorsky, *Persia in A.D. 1479: An Abridged Translation of Faḍlullah B. Rūzbihān Khunjī's Tārīḵ-i 'Ālamārā-yi Amīnī*, London, 1957. *A Narrative of Italian Travels in Persia in the 15th and 16th Centuries*, London, 1873. J. L. Schlimmer, *Terminologie médico-pharmaceutique*, Tehran, 1349 Š./1970. Mīr Teymūr Mar'ašī, *Tārīḵ-e ḵāndān-e Mar'ašī Māzandarānī*, ed. M. Sotūda, Tehran, 2536 = 1356 Š./1977. 'Alī b. Ḥosayn Lāhījānī, *Tārīḵ-e ḵānī*, ed. M. Sotūda, Tehran, 1352 Š./1973. P. de Thevenot, *The Travels of*

Monsieur de Thevenot into the Levant, London, 1686. J. Woods, *The Aqqoyunlu: Clan, Confederation, Empire*, Chicago, 1976. H. E. Wulff, *The Traditional Crafts of Persia*, Cambridge, Mass., 1960.

(W. FLOOR)

BARZAN, part of a town, quarter (*maḥalla*), street, (*kūča*). The word is listed in the old dictionaries and is preserved in the common expression *kūy o barzan* "street and quarter." *Loḡat-e fors* (ed. Dabīrsīāqī, p. 153) quotes Rūdakī's verse *parnīān gašt bāḡ o barzan o kūy* "the garden, quarter, and street became (like) colored silk" and Šams-e Faḵrī (p. 368) defines the word as *sar-e kūča o maḥallat*. Under Reżā Shah *barzan* became the official designation of municipal divisions of a city (Barzan-e 1, 2, etc.).

Barzan is a Northwest-Iranian form in Persian, corresponding to the genuine Southwest-Iranian form seen in Old Persian *vardana-* or *vṛdana* (neut.) "town" and Pahl. *vālan* "community, settlement." The corresponding Avestan forms are Gathic *vərəzə̄nā̆-* (fem. and neut.), Young Avestan *varəzāna-* (neut.), "community" (a meaning Bartholomae deduced from the Pahlavi gloss *hamsāyak* "neighbor," see *AirWb.*, col. 1425, last note). Gathic *vərəzə̄na-* corresponds to Old Indian *vṛjána-* (neut.) "surroundings, place, community," also with zero grade of the root syllable (cf. *vərəzə̄nya-* "belonging to the community," corresponding to Rigvedic *vṛjanyà*, Mayrhofer, *Dictionary* III, p. 243), while Young Avestan *varəzāna-* has the full grade of the root syllable (the long *ā* in *-āna* is found only in the YAv. form) also found in Pahlavi *vālan* (< **vardan*), Persian *barzan*, and Khotanese **balysana-* (see below). The Old Persian form is graphically ambiguous: *vardana-* or *vṛdana-*.

Old Persian *vardana* "town" (Akkadian URU) contrasts in the inscriptions with *āvahana* "*settlement" (Akk. *ālum*, Elam. *hu-ma-nu-iš*; see, e.g., Brandenstein and Mayrhofer, p. 109) and *didā* "fortress" (Akk. *bīrtum*). The latter survived in Persian in the forms *dez* (genuine "Northwest" form < **dizā-*) and *dež* (a pseudo-archaic form). In Darius's Bīsotūn inscription nine *vardana*s "towns" are named, situated in Persis: Kuganakā (DB 2.9), Raxā (3.4f.), (H)uvādaičaya (3.51), Tāravā (3.22); Parthia: Patigrabanā (3.4f.), Višpa^{h}uzātiš (2.95f.); and Media: Ku^{n}duruš (2.65f.), Māruš (2.22).

Old Indian *vardhana-* (neut.) "town" must be one of the loanwords from Old Persian in Indian dating from the Achaemenid period (J. Wackernagel, *Kleine Schriften*, Göttingen [1956], pp. 384f.; Mayrhofer, *Dictionary* III, p. 158; others are *lipi-* "script" from OPers. *dipi-*, *mudrā-* "seal").

Further derivation of **v(a)rzanā̆-* remains problematic. Connection with Av. *varəz-* (fem.), which according to *AirWb.*, col. 1378, means "habitation" but according to later research should be equated with OInd. *ūrj-* "libation," is doubtful (cf. Kellens, pp. 361-64) and the root *varəz-* "to fend off" (*AirWb.*, cols. 1378, 1424f., cf. Gk. *wérgein*, *eirgein* "to constrict, close off," Pokorny, p. 1168) may be *vərəz-* "to work, make." The Pahlavi translations render Av. *vərəzə̄na-* by *varzišn* or *vālan* and *vālanīh* (often written *vʾln*, *vʾlnʾyh*, which Bartholomae transcribed as *vālūn-īh*), glossed as *hamsāyak* "neighbor" in *Y.* 33.4. This gloss recalls Khotanese *balysania-* (i.e., *balzania-*) "neighboring" (i.e., country), rendering (Buddhist) Sanskrit *sāmantaka* in the *Suvarṇabhāsasūtra* (Bailey, *Dictionary*, p. 272).

Semantically Iranian *vṛzana-* and Old Persian *vardana-* belong to an Indo-European group of words whose meaning has evolved from "town" to "fence," cf., e.g., Germanic *gard*, in Norwegian "farm" (note also *-gard* in names of towns) and "fence" and English *town* (cf. Swedish *-tun* in names of towns, Norwegian *tun* "central courtyard of a farm") but German *Zaun* "fence." Correspondingly, one would expect Middle Iranian *varzan*, *vālan* to designate fortified settlements, like Persian *kalāt*, Arabic *qalʿa*. The semantic narrowing of Persian *barzan* "*maḥalla*" is similar to that of Old Iranian *dahyu-* "land" > Persian *deh* "village" and Old Iranian *xšaθra* "realm" > Persian *šahr* "town." Compare also Akkadian *mātum* > Aramaic *māṯā* "village," Arabic *welāya* > Persian *welāyat* "marketplace" (see Eilers, 1977, p. 285).

In modern Iranian place names the forms Varzan and Varzana are common. We find Varzan west of Tehran (Razmārā, *Farhang* I, p. 230), in Rūdbār (ibid., III, p. 316), in the Dašt-e Kavīr (Adle, p. 82 n. 62); and Varzana in Dastjerd near Qom, possessing a large, abundantly irrigated estate (*Tārīḵ-e Qom*, p. 68; Razmārā, I, p. 230), in Bandpey, Bābol (ibid., III, p. 317), 24 km southeast of Golpāyagān (ibid., VI, p. 364), in the Gāvḵānī swamp, shortly before the mouth of the Zāyandarūd (ibid., X, p. 202; Schwarz, *Iran* V, p. 659), in Jāst (*Tārīḵ-e Qom*, p. 138); in the *ṭassūj* of Jahrūd we find both Varzan and Varzana (pp. 119, 120, 122); there were a *qarya* Varzan in the *ṭassūj* of Dwrʾḵyr (p. 142) and a "Varzana-ye bāʾera" (lit. "dilapidated V.") in Farāhān (p. 141). Note also Varzana-ye Ayyūb in the *rostāq* of Sāva, *ṭassūj* of Fīstīn (pp. 86, 114, 140), Varzana-ye Aznāh in Sāva (p. 140), Varzana-ye Āša in Ṭabraš (i.e., Tabrīš/Tabreš, present-day Tafrīš/Tafreš; p. 139), and Arabicized Varzat al-Fāleq in Sāva (p. 140) and Varzat al-Ṣarm in Vāzakrūd (p. 137). Eilers (1954, p. 353) mentions the possibility that the place names Golnābād (a ruined town east of Isfahan near the road to Sagzī and a place between Kermān and Yazd) might contain a dialect form *Golan < **vṛdan*; cf. Vardanābād in the *ṭassūj* of Qāsāq (*Tārīḵ-e Qom*, p. 114).

Bibliography: Ch. Adle, "Contribution à la géographie historique de Damghan," *Le monde iranien et l'islam* 1, 1971, pp. 69-104 (with illustrations and maps). *Borhān-e qāṭeʿ*, ed. M. Moʿīn, I, pp. 254f. W. Brandenstein and M. Mayrhofer, *Handbuch des altpersischen*, Wiesbaden, 1964. W. Eilers, "Der Name Demawand," *Archiv Orientální* 22, 1954, pp. 267-374. Idem, "Einige Prinzipien toponymischer Übertragung," *Onoma* 21, 1977, pp. 277-317. Horn, *Etymologie*, p. 46. Hübschmann, *Neupersische Studien*, p. 26), and in *Grundriss* I/1, p. 91 (both wrongly separate *barzan* from *vardana*). J. Kellens,

Les noms-racines de l'Avesta, Wiesbaden, 1974. Ḥasan b. Moḥammad b. Ḥasan Qomī, *Tārīḵ-e Qom*, Pers. tr. Ḥasan b. ʿAlī b. Ḥasan b. ʿAbd-al-Malek Qomī, ed. J. Ṭehrānī, Tehran, 1313 Š./1934, repr. 1361 Š./1982. Šams-e Faḵrī Eṣfahānī, *Meʿyār-e jamālī*, 4th pt.: *Vāža-nāma-ye fārsī*, ed. Ṣ. Kīā, Tehran, 1337 Š./1958.

(W. Eilers)

BĀRZĀNĪ, the name of a Kurdish tribe from Bārzān, a town in the former Hakkārī-Bahdīnān territory of northeastern Iraq (44° east longitude, 36° 50′ north latitude). Originally followers of the Naqšbandī order, the tribesmen now have little awareness of this past.

The shaikhs of Bārzān came to prominence in the wake of lawlessness and disorder following suppression of the semi-independent Kurdish principalities in the middle of the 13th/19th century. Information on the early Bārzānis is shrouded in Kurdish oral history. The first reference is to Bāzīrān (*Šaraf-nāma* I, p. 107). The leading shaikhs of the 13th/19th century were Shaikh Tāj-al-Dīn (also known as ʿAbd-al-Raḥmān) and Shaikh ʿAbd-al-Salām I.

Recorded history starts with Shaikh ʿAbd-al-Salām II (1885?-1914), who was probably the most formidable Kurdish tribal leader the Young Turks had to face. To the dismay of the Ottomans, he had largely succeeded in overcoming his Zebārī rivals. When in 1913 he hoisted the banner of revolt against Süleyman Nazif (Solaymān Naẓīf), the *wālī* of Mosul, he was defeated but able to escape to Urmia. Upon his return to Iraq he was captured and hanged in 1914 (according to other sources in 1916).

ʿAbd-al-Salām II was succeeded by his brother Shaikh Aḥmad Bārzānī (1889?-1969) as the religious leader of Bārzān who harrassed first the British and later the Hashemite monarchy. Apart from intermittent skirmishes with his Naqšbandī rivals, he challenged the authority of the mandatory power in 1919-20 by acts of violence. In the 1920s Shaikh Aḥmad demonstrated his religious eccentricity by proclaiming himself the incarnation of the divinity, which his followers accepted. In 1931 and in 1933 the Iraqi government was forced to take measures against him, but he evaded punishment by crossing into Turkey, where he stayed until a 1935 amnesty allowed him to return. However, he was obliged to reside first in Kirkuk and later in Sulaimaniya. The situation in the Second World War enabled him and his younger brother Mollā Moṣṭafā Bārzānī (1904-79) to escape from seclusion to Bārzān by way of Iran in 1943.

Mollā Moṣṭafā's strength was due to the military capabilities of his tribe and his own leadership as well as the support of the nontribal rural and urban population, especially the Kurdish intelligentsia and the middle class. From his tribal seat in Bārzān he pressed the government to promise improvement of cultural and social services. When these promises were not honored, serious fighting ensued. Outnumbered, he had to retreat and make his way to Iran. After having failed to reach an agreement with the Iranian government concerning political asylum, Mollā Moṣṭafā and his armed followers rallied to the emerging army of the Mahābād Republic (an autonomist Kurdish movement centered in Mahābād), where he was made one of four generals. The collapse of the Kurdish Republic in December, 1946, marked the beginning of a twelve-year uneventful asylum in the Soviet Union which he reached after a forced march with a small band of followers.

The overthrow of the Hashemite monarchy in 1958 offered Mollā Moṣṭafā the chance to return triumphantly to Baghdad. For two years Kurdish influence under General ʿAbd-al-Karīm Qāsem grew, not least because of internal power struggles and Kurdish support of army units loyal to Qāsem. The political honeymoon between Qāsem and Mollā Moṣṭafā was, however, of short duration because of increasing government interference in Kurdish affairs. When the Qāsem regime began to assert its authority over Kurdistan in earnest, Mollā Moṣṭafā returned to Bārzān. By 1961 the deteriorating political situation had led to open war with the disgruntled Kurds. The nine-year war ended in 1970 with a cease-fire and an agreement on granting the Kurds autonomy, and Mollā Moṣṭafā emerged as a charismatic Kurdish leader. But the reprieve was to last only four years, characterized by further clashes, repression, and Arabization of Kurdistan, as well as the internationalization of the Kurdish problem. In his old age Mollā Moṣṭafā was reduced to a pawn in the Iran-Iraq border disputes, in particular over the Šaṭṭ-al-ʿArab issue. When Iraq and Iran settled their differences at the expense of the Kurds in 1975, Molla Moṣṭafā had to seek refuge in Iran, never to return to the political scene. He died in 1979 in the United States.

Mollā Moṣṭafā's youngest sons, Edrīs (1944-87) and Masʿūd (b. 1946), have played minor roles in the Kurdish movement since the late 1960s. At the fifth congress of the Ḥezb-e Demokrāt-e Kordestān-e Īrān (Kurdish Democratic Party of Iran; KDPI) in Āḏar, 1360 Š./December, 1981, the Bārzānīs were reprehended for siding with the Islamic Republic against the autonomist movement of the Iranian Kurds (*Gozāreš-e Komīta-ye Markazī be-Kongra-ye panjom-e Ḥezb-e Demokrāt-e Kordestān-e Īrān, 1360*, p. 19). In May, 1983, the Turkish government carried retaliatory measures against Bārzān in response to an attack by armed "terrorist" groups who had killed a number of Turkish soldiers. These measures were largely a reaction to the activities of Edrīs and Masʿūd Bārzānī. The same year the Iraqi government forcibly transferred the entire Bārzānī tribe, mostly women and children, to an unknown place (Kurdish Students in Europe, *Saddam Hussein in the Light of Koshtapa Events: A Genuine Report on the Situation of the Barzani Kurds under the Iraqi President Saddam Hussein*, March, 1985). A cousin of Masʿūd, Moḥammad-Ḵāled, was later used by the Iranian government to found a new Kurdish Ḥezb-Allāh party (van Bruinessen, p. 24).

Bibliography: F. D. Andrews, ed., *The Lost*

Peoples of the Middle East, Salisbury, N.C., 1982. E. Ardalān, *Asrār-e Bārzān*, Tehran, 1325 Š./1946. *Bayn Kāžīk wa'l-Bārzānī*, n.p., 1969 (Selselat al-waṯā'eq al-kāžīkīya be'l-loḡa al-'arabīya 2). M. Brīfkānī, *Ḥaqā'eq ta'rīḵīya 'an al-qażīya al-bārzānīya*, Baghdad, 1953. M. van Bruinessen, *MERIP* 141, July-August, 1986. G. Chaliand, ed., *Les Kurdes et le Kurdistan*, Paris, 1981. Ṣ. Damlūjī, *Emārat Bahdīnān al-kordīya*, Mosul, 1952. W. Eagleton, Jr., *The Kurdish Republic of 1946*, London, 1963. E. Ghareeb, *The Kurdish Question in Iraq*, Syracuse, 1981. M. Jīāwūk, *Ma'sāt Bārzān al-maẓlūma*, Baghdad, 1954. W. Jwaideh, *The Kurdish Nationalist Movement: Its Origins and Development*, Ph.D. dissertation, Syracuse University, 1960. C. Kutschera, *Le mouvement national kurde*, Paris, 1979. *Memorandum sur la situation des Kurdes et leurs revendications*, Paris, 1948. Ḥ. Moṣṭafā, *al-Bārzānīyūn wa ḥarakāt Bārzān, 1932-1947*, Beirut, 1963. J. Nebez, *Kurdistan und seine Revolution*, Munich, 1972. B. Nikitine, "Les Kurdes racontés par eux-mêmes," *L'Asie française* 25/231, May, 1925, pp. 148-57. M. Pārsādūst, *Zamīnahā-ye tārīḵī-e eḵtelāfāt-e Īrān o 'Erāq*, Tehran, 1986, pp. 174-84. N. Pesyān, *Marg būd bāzgašt ham būd*, Tehran, 1328 Š./1949. Idem, *Az Mahābād-e ḵūnīn tā karānahā-ye Aras*, Tehran, 1328 Š./1949. M. Qaradāḡī, *Bārzān wa nehēnīkānī*, Baghdad, 1959. M. Šīrzād, *Nežāl al-akrād*, Cairo, 1946. M. Towfīqverdī (Tōfīq Wirdī), *Čawūnī Bārzānīānī qāramān bō Sūvīat* (The moving of heroic Barzānīs to the Soviet [Union]), Baghdad, 1961.

(W. BEHN)

BARZĪN (from Pahlavi Burzēn), the name of several figures in the *Šāh-nāma*.

Barzīn, a wealthy *dehqān* who lived at the time of Bahrām Gōr; he had three daughters (Māhāfarīd, Farānak, and Šanbalīd) skilled respectively in singing poetry, playing the harp, and dancing for Bahrām Gōr when he was their father's guest. Ultimately, all three were married to the king (*Šāh-nāma* [Moscow] VII, pp. 340-46).

Barzīn Garšāsp, Iranian hero descended from Jamšēd (*Šāh-nāma* IV, p. 302 v. 22b); he lived from the reign of Nowḏar until the reign of Kay Ḵosrow. He took part in the Māzandarān and Hāmāvarān campaigns.

Jahn Barzīn, according to Iranian legend a man from Damāvand and the first artisan, who was ordered by Ferēdūn to construct the Ṭāqdīs throne (*Šāh-nāma* IX, p. 220), for which he was awarded the governorship of Āmol and Sārī.

Ḵarrād Barzīn (both names related to two fire temples of the same name, Justi, *Namenbuch*, p. 178), a commander and adviser to Hormoz IV (r. 578-90) and adviser and chancery secretary to his son Ḵosrow II Parvēz (r. 590-628). Ḵarrād, who sprang from people perhaps living on the Caspian coast (*Šāh-nāma* VIII, p. 362 vv. 790-93), led Hormoz's army at the beginning of his reign in the war against the Ḵazarān and aided Bahrām Čōbīn (q.v.) in his war with the Turks (ibid., p. 334 vv. 330-35). However, with the rise of Bahrām, Ḵarrād seems to have lost his position and thus deeply resented his rival; he is said to have played a major role in turning Hormoz against Bahrām (ibid., pp. 349-51, 361-90, 402-07). He was later closely allied to Ḵosrow II Parvēz in his struggle with Bahrām and accompanied Ḵosrow when he fled to Rūm (Antiochia). From there he led a delegation sent by Ḵosrow to request aid from the Byzantine emperor Maurice (r. 582-602; ibid., IX, pp. 19ff.). After the defeat of Bahrām and his flight to Central Asia, Ḵarrād was sent by Ḵosrow to the *ḵāqān* of the Turks, where he successfully carried out a plot to kill Bahrām (ibid., pp. 155-69). Ḵarrād remained Ḵosrow's close adviser until the end of his reign. After Ḵosrow was deposed by his son, Šērōya (Qobād II, 628), Ḵarrād, an old man, was forced to visit the former king in prison and deliver his son's message (ibid., pp. 255-59, 275). Ḵarrād is considered one of the great statesmen of the time of Hormoz and Ḵosrow II, for he was very effective in stabilizing the political situation to the advantage of both monarchs.

Rām Barzīn, a Zoroastrian priest of the time of Qobād (r. 488-531; *Šāh-nāma* VIII, p. 50 v. 363b).

Rām Barzīn, general of Ḵosrow I Anōšīravān (r. 531-78) and guardian of the city of Madā'en, who in 550 or 551 put down the revolt of Anōšazād (q.v.), Ḵosrow's son (*Šāh-nāma* VIII, p. 104-09). Rām Barzīn is apparently the same person as Fabrizos, whom the Byzantine historian Procopius (*Bella* 4.10 in Nöldeke, *Geschichte der Perser*, p. 473) mentions in his account of the Anōšazād incident. He is also apparently the same person who in the time of Ḵosrow I, after the year 541, was the Persian ruler of Lāzīstān (= Lazike, classical Colchis; Procopius, 2.29.30).

Šādān Barzīn, one of the Zoroastrian *dehqān*s of Ṭūs and an author of the 4th/10th-century *Šāh-nāma* that was translated from Pahlavi into Persian by order of Abū Manṣūr 'Abd-al'-Razzāq (q.v.), commander (*sepahsālār*) of Ṭūs, in Moḥarram, 346/April, 957 (*Moqaddama-ye qadīm-e Šāh-nāma-ye abū-manṣūrī*, ed. M. Qazvīnī, in *Bīst maqāla* II, Tehran, 1313 Š./1934, p. 35). Šādān Barzīn also translated the report of Borzūya's bringing the *Kalīla wa Demna* from India (*Šāh-nāma* VIII, p. 247; Th. Nöldeke, *Das iranische Nationalepos*, Berlin and Leipzig, 1920, pp. 16f.).

Sīmā Barzīn, Zoroastrian priest who lived during the reign of Ḵosrow I Anōšīravān (r. 531-78) and was killed by order or Hormoz IV (r. 578-90). According to the *Šāh-nāma* (VIII, pp. 323-26), this man was the only member of the elite of Ḵosrow's time to favor Hormoz as Ḵosrow's successor. Ṯa'ālebī (*Ḡorar*, pp. 638f.) attributes this act of support to Bahrām Āḏarmāhān; however, according to the *Šāh-nāma*, Āḏarmāhān (Āḏarmahān) was one of the opponents of Hormoz's succession.

(DJ. KHALEGHI-MOTLAGH)

BAŠĀKERD (also Bašāgerd), a roughly rectangular mountainous district (*dehestān*) east of Mīnāb and north of Jāsk. Bašākerd proper is bounded on the west by the district of Rūdān and the coastal strip known as Bīābān, by Fannūč in Baluchistan to the east, by Manūjān to the north and by the western extension of the coastal plain of Baluchistan to the south. It covers some 4,000 square miles. Its major feature is the Kūh-e Bašākerd that stretches some 90 miles east-southeast from the Mārz range in the north to the Rapč river in the east. The name is often used to designate a larger area from as far north as Manūjān and east to Rامešk.

Bašākerd may be a plural of the form Baškard (or Bašgard), which is also used. For Bešgard the *Borhān-e Qāṭeʿ* (ed. Moʿīn, I, p. 284) gives the meaning "area with abundant game" (*šekārgāh*). Schwarz suggests (p. 245) that Bašākerd may be derived from Bās, which is mentioned as a settlement to the northwest of it by Moqaddasī (pp. 52.18, 461.3, 466.15, 473.7). It is worth noting also that *baš* is Baluchi for the "summer rain" which is a significant feature of the area's unpredictable monsoonal seasonality: *baš*, when it occurs, is a disaster for the date harvest but a bonus for the flocks—the two main economic activities of the district.

The topography and the natural conditions are similar to Makrān to the immediate east (see detailed description in BALUCHISTAN, i). The entire district is mountainous. The highest peak of the Bašākerd range is Kūh-e Kūrān at 7,090 ft. Many ranges, surprisingly rough considering their moderate height, rise above terraced plains. J. V. Harrison describes them as "basin shaped or synclinal, and their solid structure is hidden under a litter of harsh angular sandstone blocks loosely set in sand and dust" (p. 2). The dominant color is a dull olive-grey, here and there penetrated by rocks of other colors. Benches or terraces along the river courses increase in height from about 1,200 ft in the south on the western side of the district to 4,500 in the north. Information on the flora and fauna may be found in Gabriel. Game was abundant in the last century, but is depleted now. Settlement, which is sparse, is confined to the narrow riverbeds.

Little is known of the history of the district. The name Bašākerd does not appear in the medieval geographers, though it is generally considered to be the designation of Kūh-e Qofṣ (e.g., Tomaschek, 1883, p. 184). It is included in the province of Fārs by Fasāʾī (II, pp. 180-81). The earliest first-hand description comes from the first Western traveler, Floyer, who visited Angūrān/Angohrān (locally Angōhrān), Sardašt, Šahrbāvek, Jağdān (Joğdān), Darpahn, and Senderk (Sanderk) from Jāsk in 1876. He found a Raʾīs ʿAlī, in control of the district, enjoying a close relationship with a Mīr Yūsof, who ruled Jāsk to the south (1883, p. 152). Before 1874 the district had been "virtually independent" (Curzon, *Persian Question* II, p. 258). According to Floyer it was divided into six "provinces," each of which paid allegiance to a Sayf-Allāh Khan who occupied the central fort at Angohrān. In 1874, in pursuit of a blood feud, Sayf-Allāh Khan violated the accepted code of honor by the heinous crime of killing a guest, which provided an occasion for the Kermān government to interfere. After a seige that lasted a year Sayf-Allāh Khan went into exile, leaving the district to Raʾīs ʿAlī (who was a relative of the murdered man) under the patronage of Kerman (p. 196). Floyer describes the partly ruined fort as a massive triangular structure, 180 by 60 yards, situated on a hill. He saw immense date plantations, plus wheat, maize, pomegranates, and other crops (p. 246). In one place on his route he passed about three thousand sheep and goats, including the breed that produces down (*kork*), which fetched a good price in Bandar-e ʿAbbās (p. 247).

Fifty years later Gabriel and his wife saw the same places as Floyer (except Šahrbāvek) and explored in addition the direct route from Darpahn to Angohrān. Gabriel (1928, p. 235) mentions that a Barakat Khan, who was prominent in Bīābān and Bašākerd at the time when the Baluch challenged Reżā Shah in 1307 Š./1928, was taken to Tehran, while his son, ʿAbd-Allah Khan, escaped into the Sarḥadd. (A Mir Barakat Khan from Bīābān is listed by Jahānbānī, pp. 19, 47, as commanding 200 riflemen and 1,000 families.) Barakat seems to have returned by the time of Gabriel's visit. A few years later, in 1932-33, Harrison reached Garāhven from Jāsk, and in 1937 made a trip north of Angohrān as far as Šāhkahān, across the western spurs of the Mārz range. Angohrān at that time comprised 100 reed huts, and the population of the district was estimated at 8,000 families (*Persia*, p. 392). Razmārā (*Farhang* VIII, p. 49) has 108 villages and estimates only 400 people in Angohrān and 6,700 total population; he lists it as a part of the *bakš* of Kahnūj and the *šahrestān* of Jīroft in the province of Kermān.

In 1956 the linguist Gershevitch spent three months in the district. In addition to the places visited by the travelers mentioned above, he went to the Bīverc/Bīvarj area northwest of Angohrān. At this time Angohrān was the residence of Šāhverdī Khan, a great grandson of Allāhverdī Khan, the father of Sayf-Allāh Khan who was still remembered as the famous guest murderer. The fort was in ruins. Gershevitch includes some interesting details in his brief article, including a description of distinctive round huts (p. 218). In general, living conditions, social organization, and cultural institutions appear to differ very little from those of the Baluch to the east. What little cultivation is possible depends on drystone dams, some of which reach a height of 16 ft, built across narrow gorges to trap both soil and water. Dates and citrous are the most abundant crops, but small patches of other fruit, vegetables, and grains are also found. Animal products, which are exported to Bandar-e ʿAbbās, provide the basis of the economy. Baškardis are Shiʿite Muslims, and their society is stratified like that of Makrān (see BALUCHISTAN, i); the women wear masks as in the Persian Gulf.

See also BAŠKARDI.

Bibliography: E. A. Floyer, *Unexplored Baluchistan*, London, 1882. A. Gabriel, *Im Weltfernen Orient*, Berlin and Munich, 1929. I. Gershevitch, "Travels in Bashkardia," *Journal of the Royal Central Asiatic Society* 46, 1959, pp. 213-24. J. V. Harrison, "Coastal Makran," *Geographical Journal* 97/1, 1941, pp. 1-17. A. Jahānbānī, *'Amalīyāt-e qošūn dar Balūčestān az Mordād tā Bahman 1307*, Tehran, 1336 Š./1957. Kayhān, *Jog̱rāfīā* I, p. 57; II, p. 250. *Persia*, Geographical Handbook Series, Naval Intelligence Division, London, 1945, pp. 102-03, 104, 342, 391-92. W. Tomaschek, "Zur historischen Topographie von Persien, I," Sb. der Königl. Akademie der Wissenschaften, Phil.-hist. Cl. 102, 1883, pp. 145-231.

(B. SPOONER)

BASAWAL, the site of a Buddhist cave temple complex in eastern Afghanistan, first visited and described in 1878 by William Simpson and completely measured and partly excavated in 1965 by the Kyoto University Archeological Mission; it extends about 3 km along the schist cliff facing to the south and on the left bank of the Kābolrūd and is named for a village on the opposite side located some 50 km east of Jalālābād. The caves, 150 in all, are partly hewn out in two rows and arranged in seven groups, which presumably correspond to the seven monastic institutions of Buddhist times. Each group consists of three kinds of caves: 1. Residential caves with barrel-vaulted ceilings, oblong in plan, are the simplest and most numerous. 2. Caves roofed with cloister vaults on a square plan are few in number; they were once decorated with stucco or clay sculpture on the walls and with painted buddhas or bodhisattvas on the four sides of their pyramidal ceilings. 3. Most exceptional in both plan and number are caves on a square plan of huge dimensions with central square pillars, around which circumambulatory rites may have been performed. In the central area of the site, in particular, caves are supplemented with open-air buildings of various dimensions, some of which were cleared to reveal a shrine where images in clay, terra cotta, and stucco were found almost in situ. The clay head of a prince with mustache sculpted in the round is worthy of special attention, particularly in relation to clay sculptures from Kama Daka, Haḍḍa, Ḡaznī, Bāmīān, and from beyond Afghan territory; however, the dating of the Basawal head and of the caves themselves remains uncertain.

Bibliography: W. Simpson, "The Buddhist Caves of Afghanistan," *JRAS*, N.S. 14, pp. 319-31. S. Mizuno, ed., *Basawal and Jalalabad/Kabul*, Kyoto, 1971. M. Taddei, "Wall Paintings from Tapa Sardar, Ghazni," *South Asian Archaeology 1979*, Berlin, 1981, pp. 429-39.

(SH. KUWAYAMA)

BĀṢERĪ, a pastoral nomadic tribe of Fārs belonging to the Ḵamsa confederacy. Traditional location and area are best understood through the tribal concept of the *īl-rāh*, the tribal road and schedule. Winter pastures (*garmsīr*) were between Jahrom and Lār; by Nowrūz the tribe used to gather on the plain of Manṣūrābād near Lār, which served as winter residence of the khan. During spring they migrated past Jahrom, Ḵafr, Sarvestān, Marvdašt to the area around Dašt-e Morḡāb (ancient Pasargadae), whence they dispersed in June into summer quarters (*sarḥadd*) around Kūh-e Bol near Ābāda. The autumn migration returned along the same route during September-November, utilizing stubble on harvested lands. Distance covered each year was about 1,000 km, with striking and repitching of tents about 120 days a year.

The population in 1958 was 3,000 tents or 16,000 persons, all of Shi'ite persuasion. They speak standard Persian of the variety spoken in Shiraz. Some are bilingual and speak Turkish as well. Groups related to this main body of Bāṣerī are found west of Isfahan under the Darašūrī khans of the Qašqā'ī confederation, to whom they defected around 1277/1860 (according to their oral tradition). The Būgard Bāṣerī are found in northwest Fārs along the Qašqā'ī-Boir Aḥmad border. Scattered Bāṣerī groups are also found near Semnān, which is sometimes represented as the tribe's original homeland. On the other hand, many individuals and camps presently counted as Bāṣerī derive from other tribes like Nafar, Bahārlū, Arab, Qašqā'ī, and even settled villages.

The basic unit in Bāṣerī society is the tent (*ḵūna*) occupied by a nuclear or extended family. Several tents form a herding unit to be viable in terms of labor force and assemble a sizable, but manageable, herd (200-500 animals). Except during winter dispersal, camps comprise ten to forty tents organized in several herding units. Tribesmen are aligned in thirteen patriclans (*tīra*), often subdivided into segments (*awlād*), each with a headman (*kadḵodā*).

The nomads keep sheep, intermingled with 10-20 percent goats, and use donkeys for transport. Their economy is based on the sale of pastoral products, i.e., wool, clarified butter, and lambskins. Buttermilk, dried curds, and meat are consumed; other staples such as flour, rice, sugar, and tea are purchased, as are most items of household equipment and cloth other than tents. Animals are individual property, whereas pasture rights are held collectively with temporary usufruct allocated to *awlād*s. Some Bāṣerī own agricultural land as private property, which they let on sharecropping contracts to tenants.

The ecological, economic, demographic, and political relations of South Persian tribes are highly dynamic, especially when they, like the Bāṣerī, occupy an *īl-rāh* in close contact with other tribes and passing through densely settled lands. Nomad households and camps readily shift their tribal allegiance depending on the quality of leadership and security provided by competing khans. Thus the Bāṣerī have grown by assimilation while other, once larger, tribes have disappeared. The nomad and animal populations of the region as a whole are also subject to fluctuations. Households pursue herd management policies that generally succeed in producing growth in flocks, and good hygiene and nutrition produce human population growth. The balancing of animal population and the carrying capacity of pastures seems to depend on cycles of disease and natural catastrophe rather than human agency. But such losses, and unequal gains, together with fluctuation in prices and terms of trade for pastoral products, result in the impoverishment of some households. These people are forced to seek employment in towns and villages. Thus the growth of the human population is to some extent relieved through sedentarization of the poorest. The richest, who tend to invest some of their surplus in land, also tend to become sedentarized as landowners. As a result, the Bāṣerī maintain a relative economic homogeneity.

The Bāṣerī khans are drawn from the Żargāmī family, originally of the Kolomba'ī *tīra*. The income of the khan derives from private lands, private flocks, and the right to tax the tribesmen's herds (one to three per hundred animals). It is through chieftainship that the tribe functions as a political body. The khan represents the tribe and adjudicates internal disputes. Succession is among the closest agnates of the deceased khan, by acclamation and fiat.

The K̲amsa confederation, composed of the Arab tribes of Šaybānī and Jabbāra in Fārs, and the Turkish tribes of Aynālū, Bahārlū (qq.v.), and Nafar beside the Bāṣerī, was formed in 1278/1861-62 by the government and placed under the leadership of 'Alī-Moḥammad Qawām-al-Molk, a wealthy merchant of Shiraz. It served both as a counterweight to the powerful Qašqā'ī confederation, adjoining it to the northwest, and as a means to secure trade routes to Shiraz from the ports of K̲ārak and Bandar-e 'Abbās. Thus, from their palace at Nāranjestān in Shiraz, the Qawām family ruled a tribal confederation of up to 16,000 tents (ca. 1914), until this political structure was shattered by Reżā Shah in the 1310s Š./1930s.

Recent history. The Bāṣerī grew from a nucleus of sections called Waysī (Kolomba'ī, 'Abdolī, Labū Mūsā, Farhādī, Jūčīn, Īl-e K̲āṣṣ) to encompass also the 'Alī-Mīrzā'ī under Ḥājī Moḥammad Khan in the late 13th/19th century. Ways, the eponymous ancestor, is said to have come from Khorasan, while 'Alī-Mīrzā is supposed to have been a native of Fārs. Growth in numbers and influence continued under Ḥājī Moḥammad's son Parvīz Khan (r. 1293-1314 Š./1914-35). During his last years and the first years of his son Moḥammad Khan (r. 1314-25 Š./1935-46) Reżā Shah sought by highly repressive means to settle all the tribes, and most Bāṣerī were prevented from migrating, which resulted in severe losses in both flocks and people. With the weakening of government control after Reżā Shah's abdication and the occupation of Iran by the Allied forces in 1320 Š./1941, the tribesmen resumed pastoral migrations and tribal autonomy. Resistance to government control under Moḥammad-Reżā Shah (r. 1320-57 Š./1941-79) was temporarily resolved by the abdication of Moḥammad Khan in favor of his younger brother Ḥasan-'Alī Khan (r. 1325-35 Š./1946-56) until the tribe was finally placed under army administration in 1335 Š./1956. Government schemes for sedentarization, increasing encroachment of cultivation on pastures in the spring-autumn zone, and enhanced economic opportunities in the sedentary sector led to the discontinuation of the long, collective migration and extensive sedentarization. Some nomads continued to send flocks and shepherds to the south in the winter; others stabled and fed their animals in the upper mountain zone through the most severe months. After the revolution of 1357 Š./1978-79, however, some Bāṣerī groups are reported to have resumed their migrations.

See also K̲AMSA.

Bibliography: F. Barth, "The Land Use Pattern of Migratory Tribes of South Persia," *Norsk geografisk tidsskrift* 17, 1959-60, pp. 1-11. Idem, *Nomads of South Persia: The Basseri Tribe of the Khamseh Confederacy*, Oslo, 1961; 2nd ed., London and New York, 1965; most recent ed., Prospect Heights, Ill., 1986. Idem, "Capital, Investment and the Social Structure of a Pastoral Nomad Group in South Persia," in R. Firth and B. S. Yamey, eds., *Capital, Saving, and Credit in Peasant Societies*, London, 1964.

(F. BARTH)

BĀŠGĀH-E AFSARĀN (officers' club), an impressive building on the northwestern corner of the former Cossacks' parade ground in Tehran. The club was designed by Gevorkian, a French architect of Armenian descent who was general manager of government buildings. Gevorkian also supervised the main part of the construction work but abruptly left Iran before it was finished. The construction department of Bank Melli was given the task of completing the building. The building was dedicated by Reżā Shah on 3 Esfand 1317 Š./1939. Some of the main halls were furnished with rugs commissioned from the master weaver 'Am(ū)oqlī. The famous Pearl Cannon (Tūp-e Morvārīd) was transferred from Arg Square to the southern courtyard of the Officers' Club. While General Fereydūn Jam was chief of staff, the club underwent major repairs and restoration, as well as some redecoration. In 1331-32 Š./1952-53 it was a center of covert activities against Prime Minister Moḥammad Moṣaddeq.

(M. ṢĀNE'Ī)

BĀŠGĀH-E ARĀMENA (the Armenian club), a non-profit, non-political club, founded 1 January 1918 by Armenians in Tehran in accordance with legal provisions allowing religious communities and foreign citizens to establish clubs or associations with exclusive membership rights. The purpose of the club was to promote congeniality and solidarity among members and to provide edifying and entertaining programs for them. Necessary funds were secured through the sale of shares and membership fees. The Bāšgāh was originally located on South Qawām-al-Salṭana Avenue, later at the Čahārrāh-e Yūsofābād, before it was finally, in the mid-1960s, transferred to a building of its own on K̲ārg Avenue.

The club is run by a board of directors consisting of a chairman and two auditors (*bāzras*). Membership on the board is honorary and for two years and is renewable. The manager (who is paid) is chosen by the board, becomes an ex officio member of it, and looks after the daily activities of the club. The two auditors are elected by the general assembly, which convenes once every year. The board has to submit yearly reports on the activities and expenses of the club to the general assembly for approval. Auditors are required to submit separate annual reports for the same purpose.

In the 1930s a new club, Bāšgāh-e Javānān-e Arāmena (Armenian youth club), was founded by a number of Armenian youths; it organized social, artistic, and cultural activities but a few years later merged with the older club. A result of this merger was the establishment of a library at the Bāšgāh under the leadership of young members, who paid only one-fourth of the regular dues.

Until a couple of years after the revolution of 1357 Š./1978-79 this club was one of the main cultural centers in Tehran: it arranged exhibitions (e.g., of traditional Armenian women's costumes, paintings, and sculptures), dance and musical performances, lectures (often in Armenian), and various evening entertainments. Muslim guests also attended these programs until the Islamic government in mid-1359 Š./1980 restricted its activities and prohibited it from receiving Muslim guests and visitors.

The club ran a restaurant which was well known in Tehran for its excellent cuisine and for its friendly atmosphere and service. It offered facilities for people interested in such pastimes as card games, table tennis, and billiards.

Similar but smaller clubs existed in other cities with substantial Armenian communities, such as Isfahan and Tabrīz.

('A.-A. SA'ĪDĪ SĪRJĀNĪ)

BĀŠGĀH-E MEHRAGĀN (Mehragān Club), an organization founded in 1952 in Tehran by the executive committee of the Iran Teachers Association (Jāme'a-ye Mo'allemān-e Īrān, q.v.); membership in the club was open to teachers, students, and other intellectuals in Tehran and eventually in the provinces where branches were established, Prior to the founding of the club, *Mehragān* (q.v.) was also used as the name of a newspaper founded by the Iran Teachers Association in 1948 and edited by Moḥammad Deraḵšeš.

The Mehragān Club sponsored seminars on language and literature and other subjects under the guidance of a committee which included a number of noted scholars. As a rule the club published the lectures it sponsored, e.g., the lectures of Moḥsen Haštrūdī and a five-lecture series given by Sayyed Ḥasan Taqīzāda and published as *Kaṭāba: tārīḵ-e awā'el-e enqelāb wa mašrūṭīyat-e Īrān*, Tehran, 1338 Š./1959, an important publication on the Constitutional Revolution in spite of its brevity. The club was also a center for art and photography exhibitions and functioned as a theater.

Early in 1340 Š./1961, the executive committee of the Iran Teachers Association called on teachers all over the country to strike in protest against low wages and difficult working conditions. The teachers went on strike on 12 Ordībehešt/3 May and gathered in Bahārestān square to stage demonstrations, during which a teacher, Dr. Ḵān-'Alī, was killed, three other teachers were injured, and the head of the association, Moḥammad Deraḵšeš, was arrested. The refusal of Dr. Jahānšāh Ṣāleḥ, minister of education, to accommodate the teachers' demand stiffened the teachers' resolve, and the strike continued until the Šarīf Emāmī government was forced to resign. In the cabinet of the new government that was formed by 'Alī Amīnī, Deraḵšeš, at that time head of the club and of the Teachers Association and the strike organizer, became minister of education. During the years he held that post the Mehragān Club prospered; however, after the fall of this government the new government under Asad-Allāh 'Alam (1962) ordered the cessation of the club's activities; its headquarters and the newspaper *Mehragān* were closed, and the Teachers' Association went underground.

The Bāšgāh-e Mehragān is the locus of some events in Jamāl Mīr Ṣādeqī's novel *Bādhā ḵabar az taḡyīr-e faṣl mīdādand* (Tehran, 1363 Š./1985, pp. 142ff.).

(Ḥ. MAḤMŪDĪ)

BASILIUS OF CAESAREA or Basilius the Great (ca. A.D. 330-79), bishop in Caesarea in Cappadocia from 370, after Eusebius. Basilius was born in Caesarea into a distinguished family in the history of the early church. He, his younger brother Gregory of Nyssa, and Gregory of Nazianzus are the famous "three Cappadokian Fathers." In Caesarea he began to study rhetoric and philosophy, and later proceeded to Constantinople (ca. 346) and Athens, where Gregory of Nazianzus was his fellow student. In the history of the Christian church he is particularly known as an ardent antagonist of Arianism (the fundamental tenet of which was that the Son of God is a creature, although of an extraordinary kind, and with the adherents of which Basilius did not accept communion) and the founder of organized monasticism.

Among Basilius's numerous works only his *Letters*, numbering 365, partly written to himself, are of importance for Iranian studies. Letter XL (Loeb ed., I, pp. 232-33), a letter from the emperor Julian (the Apostate) to Basilius, mentions the empire of Persia and the Sasanian Šāhpūr (Sapor), "that descendant of Dareios," but this letter is unanimously and rightly regarded as spurious and was so regarded even in Byzantine times. Of greater value is Letter CCLVIII (Loeb ed., IV, pp. 34ff.), written in 377 to Bishop Epiphanius of Salamis in Cyprus. At the end of this letter Basilius is dealing with the Magusaeans (*magousaioi*; cf. Syriac *magušāyā* "magicus," e.g., in the Syriac Acts of Martyrs and Ephraem Syrus), identified in the same letter with the Magi (*magoi*), "colonists having long ago been introduced to our country [i.e., Cappadokia] from Babylon." Basilius mentions inter alia the importance they ascribe to oral tradition, their rejection of the slaying of animals, their unlawful marriages (i.e., next-of-kin marriages, *xwēdōdah*), and their belief in fire as God (i.e., the usual theme also in Oriental Christian anti-Zoroastrian polemics; cf. *mox-rapašt* "worshipping ashes" in Armenian texts). The last lines of Basilius's letter, however, reflect unusual, but probably genuine, Zurvanite traditions: "But regarding their descent from Abraham, no one of the Magi has up to the present told us any myths (*emythológēsen*) about that, but they ascribe to themselves a certain Zarnouas (*Zar[n]ouán tina*) as the beginning of the (human) race (the microcosm)," i.e., Zurvān/Time as macrocosm is the source of man. Also, according to Šahrestānī (tr. T. Haarbrücker, pt. 1, Halle, 1850, p. 276) "the Great Zurvān" (or, in the opinion of others, Gayōmart) was the first origin of man, as the Armenian Moses of Khorene has it, although confusing three distinct myths. The role of Abraham hinted at in Basilius's letter is seen again in the *Farhang-e jahāngīrī*, where Zurvān is identified with Abraham.

Among the numerous lost works of Basilius is his *Against the Manicheans* (attested by Iulian of Aeclanum [in Augustine]).

Bibliography: Saint Basil, *The Letters* I-IV, ed. R. J. Deferrari; IV, ed. M. R. P. McGuire, London and Cambridge. Mass., 1926-. I. F. Blue, "The Zarvanite System," in *Indo-Iranian Studies in Honour of Shams-ul-Ulema Dastur Darab Peshotan Sanjana*, London, Leipzig, and Bombay, 1925, p. 66. C. Clemen, *Fontes Historiae Religionis Persicae*, Bonn, 1920, p. 86. Idem, *Die griechischen und lateinischen Nachrichten über die persische Religion*, Giessen, 1920, pp. 53, 132. W. S. Fox and R. E. K. Pemberton, *Passages in Greek and Latin Literature Relating to Zoroaster and Zoroastrianism*, K. R. Cama Oriental Institute Publication, no. 4, Bombay, 1928, p. 94. R. C. Zaehner, *Zurvan: A Zoroastrian Dilemma*, Oxford, 1955, pp. 133, 138, 144, 266, 449.

(J. P. Asmussen)

BAŠKARDI (Bašākerdī), collective designation for numerous dialects spoken in southeastern Iran from Bandar-e ʿAbbās eastward, forming a transition from the dialects spoken in Fārs and Lārestān to Baluchi.

History of research. Words and sentences from Baškardi dialects were quoted for the first time by R. A. Floyer in his book *Unexplored Balūchistan* (pp. 467ff.). Floyer had visited Baškard in 1876, traveling from Jāsk on the Persian Gulf coast through Angohrān, Sardašt, Šahrbāvek (thus Gershevitch, 1959b—cf. Floyer, p. 197—but elsewhere "Šāhbāvek"), Jaḡdān, Darpahn, and Sanderk. The few Baškardi words quoted by Floyer received no attention from Iranian scholars until G. Morgenstierne quoted them in his article "Balochi Miscellanea" (1948, pp. 253-54). In 1956 I. Gershevitch and his wife were visiting Iran and at the suggestion of Morgenstierne undertook to travel to Baškard and adjacent regions to gather linguistic material. Gershevitch reported on the journey in a lecture delivered to the Royal Central Asian Society on 8 April 1959 and has since quoted words and grammatical forms from the Baškardi and related dialects in a number of articles. In 1972 P. O. Skjærvø collected a small amount of material in the town of Mīnāb and on the island of Hormoz, which was published in 1975.

Location. The term Baškardi should properly be used only for the dialects spoken in Baškard (the local name for the official Bašākerd, q.v.). However, North Baškardi appears to be part of a larger dialect area extending far to the north and northwest of Baškard; therefore the dialects in this area will be discussed here as well. Baškard borders on Baluchi-speaking areas to the west, south, and east. More distant neighbors of Baškardi are Lārestāni (Lār.) to the west and Kumzāri (Kumz.) across the Gulf on the Musandam peninsula (on Baškardi, Lārestāni, and Kumzāri in comparative perspective see Skjærvø, forthcoming).

Dialects. In Gershevitch's articles the following subdivisions of Baškardi and related dialects are distinguished (see, e.g., 1970, pp. 163ff.): 1. Dialects outside of Baškard proper include Rūdbāri (Rdb.), i.e., the dialects of Rūdbār (northwest of Baškard proper, center Kahnūj), as spoken by the Jūsī and Dīnār Bor tribes; Bandari, i.e., the Avazi (Evazi) dialect of Bandar-e ʿAbbās (B.-A.), spoken by Bandaris from Evaz in Lārestān; the dialect of Hormoz island (Horm.) may belong to this group; Mīnābi (Mīn); and Rūdāni of Berentīn (northeast of Mīnāb); 2. North Baškardi (NBš.), east and south(east) of Mīnāb, surrounding the Mārz range, includes the dialects from Rāmešk, Gerōn, and Darza to the east; Sardašt. Angohrān, Bīvraj (Bīverč), and Bešnū to the southwest; Dūrkān, Gešmīrān, and Mārīč to the north; 3. South Baškardi (SBš.), to the south of the North Baškardi area, includes the dialects from Šāhbāvek, Garāhven, Pīrōv, Pārmōnt, and Gwāfr; some of these Gershevitch calls Pīzgi dialects (Gershevitch, 1957, p. 318, refers to "the Pīzgī dialects of Šāhbāvek and Pārmōnt," and 1967, p. 323, to the "Pīzgī dialects spoken in the Kūh-i Āhven and Garāhven districts").

Linguistic position. Baškardi belongs to the so-called Southwest Iranian languages (see M. Mayrhofer, in *Compendium Linguarum Iranicarum*, ed. R. Schmitt, Wiesbaden, 1988, forthcoming, and G. Windfuhr, ibid.), characterized by the development of proto-Iranian **dz*, **θr*, and **št* > *d*, *s*, and *st*, respectively, e.g., SBš. *domestān* 'winter' (cf. Kumzāri *dimestān*, Man. Mid. Pers. *dmyst'n*), *dərāyen* or *drāʾen* 'hail' (cf. OInd. *hrādúnī*, Sogd. *zyδn*; Gershevitch, 1962a, p. 81); NBš, *aves*, SBš. *yōpes* "pregnant' (cf. Lārestāni *aos*, Pers. *ābes-tan*; Gershevitch, 1979, p. 149); Horm. *räst-* 'to send' (cf. Pers. *ferest-* but *ferešta* 'angel' from Man. Parth. *fryštg*). Phonetically Baškardi thus ranges itself more closely with its western neighbors Lārestāni and Kumzāri, which exhibit the same phonetic developments, than with Baluchi, in which **ts/dz* > *s/z*, but **θr* > *s* (see BALUCHISTAN, iii).

In both North and South Baškardi the Old Iranian present tense forms serve as present-future tense while there is a new continuous present tense (corresponding to Pers., e.g., *mī-konam*) formed from the infinitive with a prefix and the enclitic forms of 'to be'. The North Baškardi formations are more similar to those found in Lārestāni than to those of South Baškardi, cf. Lār. *a-*

kerdā-em (infinitive *kerda*), NBš. *a-kerdén-om*, but SBš. *be-kertén-īn* or *be-kért-īn* 'I am doing'.

Among the differences between North and South Baškardi the following phonetic characteristics may be noted (see examples below): Intervocalic *t* remains in South Baškardi (as in Baluchi) but becomes *r* in North Baškardi (as in Kumzāri). Intervocalic *p* remains in South Baškardi (as in Baluchi) but becomes *w* in North Baškardi (as in Kumzāri, Lārestāni, and all other Fārs dialects). OIr. **w* becomes *v* in South Baškardi but *g*(*w*) in North Baškardi (as in Baluchi, Parāčī and Ōrmuṛī, and exceptionally in the dialect of Ḵūr in the Dašt-e Kavīr).

The published material is too limited to tell what isoglosses North and South Baškardi may have in common that would define them as a "Baškardi" group against the neighboring dialects of Mīnāb, Rūdbār, Bandar-e ʿAbbās, etc. From what has been published it would seem that North Baškardi is more closely related to its western relatives than to South Baškardi.

Historical phonology. Following are some important phonological developments characteristic of the Baškardi dialects.

Vowels. In South Baškardi OIr. *a* in originally closed syllables > *ō* or *ū* (cf. Kumz. *a* > *ō*), e.g., *sūrt* 'cold' (Pers. *sard*), *doxūrt* 'shears' (< **do-kart*, cf. Av. *karəta-* 'knife'; Gershevitch, 1957, p. 318), *bāhr, bohr* 'spade' (< **badra-*, cf. Pers. *bēl*, Pers. dialects also *bāl*; Gershevitch, 1962a, p. 78), *oréhnč* 'three days hence' (cf. Īrānšahri *agrinti*; Gershevitch, 1964, p. 86 with n. 26). It thus coincides with SBš. *ō*/*ū* < older *ā*, e.g., *pū* 'foot' (NBš. *pā*; Gershevitch, 1962a, p. 83), *sōr*/*sūr* 'year' (NBš. *sāl*; Gershevitch, 1964a, passim), *pōr*/*pūr* 'last year' (Pers. *pār-sāl*, NBš. *pār*, cf. SBš. *pyār*, NBš. *pīrār* 'two years ago'; ibid., p. 86), *yōrt* 'flour' (Pers. *ārd*; Gershevitch, 1979, p. 149), *yōpes* 'pregnant' (< **āpuθrā*, NBš. *avés* [ibid.], cf. Lār. *aos*). Initially *ā* commonly becomes SBš. *yǎ* or *yō* (*vā* or *vō*), e.g., *yōrt* 'flour', *yōpes* 'pregnant', *yāš* or *vāš* 'millstone' (Mīn., Horm. *āš*, Bal. *āšš*, cf. Pers. *ās-īā*, all from < **ārθra-*; Gershevitch, ibid., and 1963, p. 15), *yāhmōn* 'sky' (< **āšmān*, cf. Bal. *āžmān*; Gershevitch, 1964c, p. 12 n. 3), *yas* 'fire' (< **āça-* < **āθra-*, cf. Bal. *ās*; Gershevitch, 1979, p. 149), *yamah* 'we' (< *ǎmāh*), *wox-o* (Floyer) 'you have come' (< **āht-x-* < **āgataka-*). In both North and South Baškardi *ān* > *ōn*, e.g., NBš. *jōn* 'body' (a meaning common in Iranian languages, see Gershevitch, 1962a, p. 83, 1962b, p. 82), NBš. *sālōntár* 'the year after next' (Gershevitch, 1964a, p. 86).

OIr. *i* and *u* > Bš. *e*, e.g., SBš *verx, vorx* 'leopard' (Gershevitch, 1959, p. 215), NBš. *avés*, SBš. *yōpes* 'pregnant', SBš, *drāʾen* 'hail' (see above). OIr. *ī* sometimes > *e*, e.g., NSBš. *deh* 'yesterday' (Gershevitch, 1964a, p. 85, cf. Pers. *dī-rūz*, Bal. *zī*). OIr. *ai* and *au* > NBš. *ī* and *ū*, and both > SBš. *ī* or *e* (Gershevitch, 1971, p. 277), e.g., NBš. *espīr*, SBš. *espīt* 'white' (Gershevitch, p. 227), NSBš. *parīr* 'the day before yesterday' (Gershevitch, 1964a, p. 78), NBš. *rūz*, SBš. *res* 'sun; day' (Gershevitch, 1962a, p. 84 n. 1, 1964a, passim), NBš. *aʾūš*, SBš. *omjīš* (*omjēšk*) 'the day after tomorrow' (< **-auša-*; Gershevitch, 1964a, pp. 84-85 nn.), *pā-xwāves* 'barefoot' (Av. *x˅ā.aoθra-* 'barefoot', Gershevitch, 1962a, pp. 83-84). Thus Bš. *e* can be the descendant of virtually any OIr. vowel (see also Gershevitch, 1971, p. 267: SBš. *e* < *a*/*i*). In North Baškardi and the (north) western dialects, *ū* remained or became *ü*/*ǖ*. In the dialects of Rāmešk and Gerōn, *ī* and *ū* were diphthongized to *īe* and *ǖe*, e.g., *parīer* 'the day before yesterday', *perǖešōn-* 'to sell' (Gershevitch, 1964a, passim, and 1971, p. 290 n. 46).

For OIr. *r̥* note SBš. *hors* 'bear' (Floyer *hirsh*, on which see Gershevitch, 1969a, p. 192) and Horm., Mīn. *poläng 'palang'* (= Bal., see Skjærvø, p. 125).

Consonants. North and South Baškardi differ sharply in their development of intervocalic OIr. surd stops *p*, *t*. In South Baškardi intervocalic *p* and *t* remain, while in North Baškardi they become *v*/*w* and *r*, respectively, e.g., SBš. *yāp*, NBš. *yǎu* 'water' (Kumz. *hāw*), SBš. *p-* 'to come' (< **upa-i-*), NBš. *nauk*, Horm., Mīn. *nöᵘk* 'grandson' (< **napaka-*; Gershevitch, 1973, p. 83), SBš. *katam* (Floyer), NBš. *karōn* 'which' (cf. Kumz. *kāram*), SBš. *espīt*, NBš. *espīr* 'white' (Kumz. *spīr*), Horm., Mīn. *domār* 'bridegroom, *dāmād*'.

In the western dialects and North Baškardi intervocalic *d* (*t*) is sometimes found instead or *r*, probably influenced by Persian, e.g., Horm. *dād* 'gave' (cf. Kumz. *dar*), Horm. *zed* 'struck' (cf. Kumz. *zurd*, but NBš. *zar*, Gershevitch, 1977, p. 65), but also NBš. *būd, būt* (Gershevitch, 1962a, p. 83, 1977, p. 64; cf. Kumz. *bur* 'he was', *burxat* 'he had been' = Bal. *būtagat*).

Before *i* or *y*, *t* is palatalized in South Baškardi, e.g., *oréhnč* 'three days hence', *mōš* 'man' (< **martiya*, Morgenstierne).

The development of intervocalic *k* varies considerably. One outcome of OIr. intervocalic *k* is NSBš. *x*, e.g., SBš. *verx, vorx* 'leopard', *jax* 'sissoo' (NBš. *jag*), *sax* 'stone', *rax* 'vein', *doxūrt* 'scissors' (Gershevitch, 1957, p. 318), Horm. *grīx* 'weeping' (Pers. *gerya*), and in the *aka*-participle: *wox-o* 'you have come' (Floyer). Final *-γ* is found in Horm., Mīn. *tāzeγ* 'yogurt', *gännūγ* 'mad'. Note also the development of unaccented *-aka* suffixes > *-k*/*g* in NBš. *nauk, sāg* (Gershevitch, 1972, p. 125), Horm., Mīn. *nöᵘk* 'grandson', Mīn. *gowg* 'daughter-in-law, *ʿarūs*' (cf. Lār. *baū, bei*), Horm., Mīn. *gwäsk* 'calf', *mošk* 'mouse' (cf. Lār. *mošk*), *türg* 'jackal'.

The OIr. spirants show some peculiar developments. Thus OIr. *f* > SBš. (Pīzgi) *hv*, e.g., *vahv-* 'to weave' and the place names (Kūh-e) Āhven (Floyer, pp. 183, 194: Aphen) and Garāhven (J. V. Harrison, *Geographical Journal*, 1941, p. 5: Garifin; possibly related to Av. *āfant-*, see Gershevitch, 1967a, pp. 322f.); *fr-* > *pr-* in Rāmeški *perǖešōn-* 'to sell' (< **frōš-ān-*, cf. Kumz. *fōšin-*); OIr. *ft* > NBš. *wt*, SBš. *pt*, e.g., SBš. *rapt*, NBš. *röᵘt* 'went', SBš. *haptōr*, NBš. *höᵘtar* (beside *kaftarg*) 'hyena' (Gershevitch, 1971, p. 287). OIr. *xt* > NBš. *ht* and *t*, but SBš. **kt*, e.g., Horm., Mīn. *do*, NBš. *doh*(*t*), SBš. *dek* (cf. Kumz. *ditk*). Note secondary **xt* > *ht* in NBš. *yaht-* 'came' (< **āxta* < **āgata-*). OIr. *xw* is preserved, e.g., Horm., Mīn. *xwāh* 'sister', SBš. *pā-xwāves* 'barefoot'. Initial *x* has become *k* in the word for 'cock': Horm., Mīn. *korūs*, Floyer *kirus* (Bal. *kurōs*, Ḵūri *kerūs*).

The affricate *č* becomes *s* in South Baškardi, e.g., *res* 'sun; day'. Note also *nj* > *nz* in *berenz* 'rice' (Gershevitch, 1959, p. 223), Bš. *renz* < **ranj* < Ar. *rajm* (ibid.), Mīn. *temzon-* 'to stretch' (Gershevitch, 1971, p. 290). It is lost in final position in SBš. *a*, NBš. *ei* 'from' (< **hača*). Final consonants have also been lost in *ka* 'somebody', NBš. *pa* (SBš. *pas*) 'after', *pī* 'before' (SBš. *pes* < **paθya*, cf. OPers. *pašiya*; Gershevitch, 1970b, p. 84 n. 6).

OIr. initial *w* remains as *v* in South Baškardi but becomes *g*(*w*) in North Baškardi (as in Baluchi), e.g., NBš. *gwav-*, SBš. *vahv-* 'to weave', Mīn. *gowg* 'daughter-in-law', *gwäk* 'frog', Horm., Mīn. *gwäsk* 'calf', SBš. *vask*, Mīn. *gōᵘz* 'bee, wasp, *zanbūr*' (Bal. *gwabz*, Lori *bawz*, see Skjærvø, p. 123), SBš. *vīz*, NBš. *gwaron* 'ram' (Gershevitch, 1977, p. 64), SBš. *vark* 'lamb' (Gershevitch, 1962a, p. 78 n. 2), NBš. *gīn-* 'to see' (Floyer), SBš. *verx*, *vorx* 'leopard, *palang*'.

OIr. *rd* becomes SBš. *r* (Gershevitch, 1964c, p. 26), e.g., *sōr* 'year', *der* 'heart', while *rt* remains, e.g., *sūrt* 'cold', *yōrt* 'flour'. To OPers., etc., *rs* corresponds Bš. *rh* in *tehr-* 'to fear' (Gershevitch, 1964c, p. 12 n. 1).

OIr. *šm* becomes Baškardi (*h*)*m* (*čehm*, cf. Kumz. *čōm*, Bal. *čamm*), *yāhmōn* 'sky' (cf. Bal. *āžmān*, Gershevitch, 1964c, p. 12 n. 3).

Morphology. Very little of the morphology of Baškardi is known. See Skjærvø, pp. 116-19, for some points of Mīnābi and Hormozi morphology and Gershevitch, 1970a and 1987 for the verb. The plural ending *-on* is seen in NSBš. *laharon* 'huts', Rdb. *pā'on* 'feet', *-ūn* in the NBš. pronoun *ā'ūn* 'they, those'. Morgenstierne mentioned the SBš. "indefinite" article *-o*, which, if correct, may be from **ēw*.

Pronouns. Independent personal pronouns and demonstrative pronouns include NBš. *mon* 'I', *yamah* 'we', *ā* 'he, that', *ā'ūn* 'they, those'; SBš. *men* 'I', *hamī* 'this'; Mīn. *ī* 'this'. The enclitic pronouns used as possessive pronouns and as agent are NBš. *-(o)m*, *-(e)t*, *-i/-e/-h-*, *-mōn/-mūn*, *-tōn/-tūn*, *-šōn/-šūn*, SBš. sing. = NBš., plur.: *-an*, *-(o)x*, *-(e)š*; note also Mīn. *me-m* (*to-d*, *o-y*, *mā-mo*, *šomā-ed*, *īšōn-šo*) *goft* 'I (etc.) said'.

Verbal system. From the published material it is seen that the Baškardi dialects have a general present/future tense and a continuous present formed from the past stem (more precisely, the infinitive) as in Lārestāni and Tati dialects (see AZERBAIJAN, viii). The present prefix for both present tenses is NBš. *ä-* (Horm. in the continuous present also *nä-*). South Baškardi has *a-* (which together with an initial *a-* produces *ā-* or *ei-*) in the present/future tense but *be-* in the continuous present tense, e.g., NBš. *a-kerden-om* (Horm. *čāy näxwardeni* 'he is drinking tea'), SBš. *be- kerten-īn*. The negative *na-* merges with *a-* to produce *nā-* in Mīn. (*nāxwarī*, *nākešom*), cf. Floyer *nāgīnan* 'I do not see'. The subjunctive has *be-*, but in South Baškardi also *e-*.

The perfect tense is formed in South Baškardi by *-x-* to the past stem (< **-ak*, cf. Kumz. *-x-*, Bal, *-k-*), in North Baškardi by *-eh-* to the past stem (3rd sing. *-i*). In the pluperfect SBš. *-at-*, NBš. *-ar-* is added to the perfect stem (cf. Kumz. and Bal. *-at-*: Kumz. *burxat* 'he had been', Bal. *ništat* = Pers. *nešasta būd*); note also Mīn. *hästäre* 'he was' (Bal. *hastat*).

Personal endings: NBš. sing. *-om*, *-i*, *-e/-et*(*i*); plur. Horm., Mīn. *-im*, *-i*, *-en*; NBš. *-īn*, *-ī*(*d*), *-end*(*i*), SBš. *-īn*, *-e*, *-et*, *-om*, *-āht*, *-e*(*h*)*n*. The construction of the past tenses of transitive verbs is of the ergative type. The endings of the past tenses are identical with the enclitic forms of 'to be' (see below). (On the agential pronouns see above.)

The only relatively well known forms are the general present tense forms of verbs, especially the "shortened" 3rd sing. forms, to which Gershevitch devoted an entire article. The following list of verbal forms is based on Gershevitch, 1970a and 1987, and Skjærvø.

'To be'; present NBš. *-om*, *-ī̆*, *-o*, *-īn/-īm*, *-ī*, *-en/-end*(*i*); SBš. *-īn*, *-o/-ū*, *ϕ*, *-om/-ām*, *-ah*(*t*), *-e*(*h*)*n*; Mīn. Horm. *om*, *-i*, *-ä/-e*(*n*)*/-i*, 3rd plur. *-en*, *-n*; 3rd sing. *hä* 'there is'; preterite 3rd sing. *hästäre* (with the SBš. form *-ō* cf. Pahlavi Psalter *HWEw/hō/*?)—*b-*, *bah-* 'to become' (1st-3rd sing. present): NBš. *abahom*, *abahai* (or *abom*, *abi*), *abū*(*t*); Rdb. *abaham*, *abahei*, *abī*; SBš. *abīn*, *abe*, *abī*; 3rd sing. subj. NBš. *bobū*; imperative NBš. *bǎ*; preterite 1st sing. Horm. *būdom*, 3rd sing. NBš. *būd*, *būt*.—*bar-* 'to carry': Mīn. Ber. *abát*, SBš. *abū*, *abū-h-e* 'he carries it'.—*bast-* 'to bind': preterite NBš. *bast-*, SBš. *bāst-*; perfect NBš. *basteh-*, SBš. *bāx-*; pluperf. NBš. *bastar-*, SBš. *bāxat-*.—*čin-* 'to collect': present SBš. 3rd sing. *ačī*.—*de*(*y*)*-*, SBš. *adeh-* 'to give': present B.-A. *adam* (Horm. *ädäm*), *adey*, *adeyt*; SBš. (*a* + *a-* > *ā-*, *ei-*) *ādehīn*, *ādehe* (*ādī*, *eidī*), *ādī*; preterite NBš. *dā*(*r*)*-*; Horm. *-om dād* (cf. Kumz. *dar-iš* 'he gave').—*derūst-* 'to say': SBš. preterite.—**dōn-* 'to know': possibly in Mīn. *ädont-a* 'he is wise' (cf. Bal. *nazānt* 'ignorant', etc., see Skjærvø, p. 121).—*go-* 'to say': present NBš. *agom*, 3rd sing. *agū*; Mīn. *ägäm*, 3rd sing. *äge*, 1st plur. *ägem*; imperative NBš. *bógo*; continuous present Mīn. *ägofteno*, *i*, *-e*; preterite Horm. *me-om go*, Mīn. *me-m goft*, *to-d goft*, *o-y goft*, *mā-mo goft*, *šomā-ed goft*, *īšōn-šo goft*.—*ger-* 'to take': present Horm. *ägerom*, Mīn. 3rd sing. *agent*; preterite Horm. *me-om ge*.—*geryaw-* 'to weep': Rdb. imperative *bégeryew*, preterite *geryéut* (Gershevitch, 1970a, p. 174 n. 34).—*gīn-* 'to see': present 1st sing. Floyer (NBš.) *nāgīnan*; preterite NBš. *dīst-*, SBš. *dīt-*; perf. NBš. *dīsteh-*, SBš. *dīx-*.—*hāx-* 'to leave': pluperfect SBš. *hāxat-*.— *j-*, *jū-* 'to eat': present SBš. *ajōn* (*ajō'n*, *ajūn*), *ajū*, *ajūt* (*ajū-h-an* 'he will eat us'), *ajom*, *ajāht*, *ajehn*; perfect SBš. *jūx-*.—*kan-* 'to do': present 1 sing. Horm. *äkonom*, 3rd sing. NBš. *akant*, Mīn. *äkon*, B.-A. (present stem *kon-*) and Ber. (present stem *kar-*) 3rd sing. *akot*, SBš. *akī*; 3rd sing. subj. Mīn. *bokond*; continuous present NBš. *akerdénom*, SBš. *bekért*(*én*)*īn* (Morgenstierne, 1958, p. 178 n. '*be-kert-*(*en-*)*om*' is wrong); preterite NBš. *kerd-*, SBš. *kert-*; perfect NBš. *kerdeh-*, SBš. *kex-*; pluperfect NBš. *kerda*(*r*), SBš. *kexat*, Mīn. preterite *-om ke*, *nä-m kerden*, *-i ke*.—*kaš-* 'to pull, smoke': present 1st sing. *nākešom*; pluperfect NBš. *kašidar-*.—*mer* 'to die': present 3rd sing. Mīn. *amet*.—*nen-* 'to sit': present 1st sing. Horm. *anīnom*, 3rd sing. NBš. *anent*, SBš. *anī*; imperative Horm. *beniŋ*, Mīn. *benin*; preterite Horm. *néštom* 'I sat down'; pluperf. Mīn. *néštare* 'he was sitting'.—SBš. *p-* 'to come': present 1st sing. *apīn*, 3rd sing. *apī*; perfect 2nd sing. *woxo* (Floyer, cf. Bal. *ātk-*).—NBš. *ra-, re-*, SBš. *r-*, *ra(y)-*, *rav-* 'to go': present NBš. *arrám, arrė'i, arrū(t), arre'īn, arreyī, arrán*; N(?)Bš. 2nd sing. *arāi* (Floyer), 3rd. sing. *arrō, arrū*; imperative NBš. *berra*, N(?)Bš. *rra* (Floyer); preterite Horm., Mīn. *röwt-om, -i, -(en), -im, -i, -en.*—*räst-* 'to send': Horm. present *ärästom*; preterite *om rästā*.—NBš. *ron-* 'to cover' (a ewe): 3 sing. *arroneti*; cont. present *arondéni*; preterite *rond-i*.—*ss-* 'to take': present Horm. *ässäm*.—*škan-* 'to break': present NBš. 3rd sing. *aškant*.—*tün-* 'can': Mīn. continuous past tense (?) 3rd sing. *nö-y-ätünästä* 'he could not'.—*ūst-* 'to stand': present Horm. *ūstom*.—*verest-*'to rise': imperative Mīn. *verest*; preterite Horm. *vərostādom*.—*xow-* 'to sleep': subjunctive Mīn. 3rd sing. *boxovet;* Horm. imperative *boxow*; preterite 1st sing. *xöwtom*.—*xwar-* SBš. 'to drink', Mīn. 'to eat': 1st sing. Mīn. *äxwarəm*, 3rd sing. Mīn. Ber. *axwát*, SBš. *axō*, Mīn. 2 plur. negative *nā́xwarī*; cont. present Horm. *äxwardenom*, 3rd sing. *näxwardeni* 'he is drinking'; preterite NBš. *xward-*, SBš. *xūrt-*, Horm. *-om xwä, -et xwä*; perfect NBš. *xwardeh-*, SBš. *xūx-*.—*yā̆-* 'to come': NBš. *ayāóm, ayā(t)*; Horm. *ätom*; imperative Mīn. *bódo* (Floyer *budu*); preterite NBš. *yaht-* (Gershevitch, 1979, p. 149); Horm., Mīn. *(hō)nd-* (cf. Lār. *hōnda*).—*zan-* 'to strike': present Horm. *äzänom*, 3rd sing. NBš. *azan(t)*, Horm. *äzän*, B.-A. *azot*, Ber. present stem *zar-*, 3rd sing. *azāt*, Mīn. *azant*, SBš. *azī*; continuous present Mīn. *äzädenom*, 3rd sing. *-e*; imperative B.-A., Ber. *bezo*; preterite Horm. *-om zed*, NBš. *zar-*.—Rdb. *zay-* 'to bear' (a child): 3rd sing. *azey*.—'Must' is Mīn. *m'ävā, t'ävā*, Horm. *om-tōa*, all with the subjunctive.

Particles. Noteworthy forms of prepositions are *e* (*ei*) 'from', *vā* 'to' (Mīn. *vā-xöw* 'to sleep', *to-vā* 'to you').

Lexicon. Gershevitch, 1959, contains a number of vocables pertaining to material culture: *pīš* 'dwarf palm', *verx*, *vorx* 'leopard', *jag* 'sissoo' (p. 215); *šahr*, designation for the cultivated oasis; *lahar*, the so-called beehive hut (p. 217); *tūp*, round and domed permanent hut; *kavār*, "flat-roofed kiosks consisting of a square wooden frame which is covered, lightly at the sides, with *pīsh* branches" (p. 218); *kapar*, a similar structure found in Bandar-e ʿAbbās; *ādūr-band* or *xār-xāna*, "a large tumulus-shaped heap of camel-thorn (*ādūr*)" used for air-conditioning purposes; *kat*, small, square chambers for storing dates; *balūč-kāra* 'freemen' (p. 219); *balūč* 'shepherd'; *renz*, stone heaps placed on mountain passes (pp. 222-23); *berenz* 'rice'.

Gershevitch, 1964a, contains an exhaustive list of temporal adverbs in the Baškardi dialects (Mīn. forms from Skjærvø):

'Today': SBš. *homre(s)*; NBš. *omrūz*; Mīn. *hōruz, ämruz*.
'Yesterday': SBš. *deh*; NBš. *deh, dūš*; Mīn. *dūš*.
'The day before y.': SBš. *parīr*; NBš. *parīr*.
'Three days ago': SBš. *pes-parīr*; NBš. *pīš-parīr, pas-parīr*, Mīn. *päš-p.*, Rām. *pašta-parīer, pīešter-parīer*.
'Four days ago': SBš. *pestom-parīr*; NBš. *pīštom-parīr*.
'Tomorrow': SBš. *beribūn, borbūm*; NBš. *bandī*; Min. *sabā*.
'Day after tomorrow': SBš: *omfīš, omješk*; NBš. *a'ūš*; Mīn. *pässabā*.
'Three days hence': SBš. *orehnč*; NBš. *paraūš*.
'Four days hence': SBš. *pas-o., paster-o., pašter-o.*; NBš. *pīštom-p., pas-p., pašteri, parter*.
'This year': SBš. *homsār*; NBš. *homsāl*; Mīn. *hōsāl*.
'Last year': SBš. *pōr, pūr*; NBš. *pār*.
'Two years ago': SBš. *pyār*; NBš. *pīrār*.
'Three years ago': SBš. *pes-pyār*; NBš. *pīš-pīrār, pas-pīrārsāl*; Mīn. *päš-p.*
'Four years ago': NBš. *pīštom-pīrār, pašta-p.*
'Next year': SBš. *sōr-de, sōr-nau, navinsōr*; NBš. *sāl-e degar*.
'Two years hence': SBš. *oddā'isōr, nauterin-sōr*; NBš. *sālōntar*.

Note also Mīn. *hōšü* and *ämšü* 'tonight', *düšü* 'last night'.

Sentences.

Floyer: *man hīč nāgīnan* 'I see nothing' [note that the NBš. 1st sing. in Gershevitch's material is *-om*], *ba-dil-i Anguhran arāi* 'are you going to Angohran?' *bu-du ba-dil* 'come inside!', *katam mail woxo* 'where have you come from?', *rra lahar* 'go home!', *rra ī mail* 'come here!'.

Gershevitch, 1962a: NBš. *sar-om/et ei-dar-i* (*būd*) 'I am/you are (was/were) bareheaded', *ā sar-i ei-dar-e, ā'ūn sar-šūn ei-dar-e* 'he is/they are bareheaded'; *jōn-šōn ei-dar-a* 'they are naked'; SBš. *sar a-dar-īn* 'I am bareheaded', *pū a-dar-om* 'we are barefoot'; Rdb. *pā'on-om ei-leid-en* 'I am barefoot'. Gershevitch, 1970a, p. 166: SBš. (Garāhven) *sax ajū-h-an* 'the dog will eat us'. Gershevitch, 1977: NBš. (Darpahn) *gwaron sovār abūt arronéti tā aves bobū* 'the ram mounts; he covers (the ewe) so that she becomes pregnant', *gwaron arondeni* 'the ram is mounting', *sovār būt rōnd-i* 'he mounted, he covered'. Gershevitch, 1987: NBš. *mon-et dīst-om*, SBš. *men-et dīt-īn* 'you saw me'; NBš. *lahar(-e) to-m dīst, lahar-et dīst-om, lahar-om dīst-i* 'I saw your hut', *laharon-mōn dīsteh-en*, SBš. *laharon-an dīx-en* 'we have seen the huts'; NBš. *čāhī-šōn xwardi*, SBš. *čāhīy-eš xūx* 'they have drunk tea'; NBš. *čāhī-tōn xwardeh-en* 'you have drunk their tea'; *agar čelim-šōn kašidar-īm* 'if they had smoked our waterpipe'; *javāb-šōn dār(-īn)* 'they answered him (us)'; *kīmat gā-om dārih-i* 'I have given you the price of the cow'; SBš. *šehm-eš peim kert-om* 'they prepared our supper', *sad-o-panjāh dōn pah-eš jūx-om* 'they have eaten 150 goats of ours'; *yamah derūst-ehn-an ke* 'we told them'; *hamī verx avādīy-e na-hāxat-om* 'this leopard had not left us livestock'.

Skjærvø: Mīn. *bodo kār-om hä* 'come! I want to talk to you' (lit. 'come! I have business'), *gāb-e mīnābī äzädene* 'he speaks Mīnābī', *čāi äxwardenəm* 'I am drinking tea', *šomā čāi näxwarī* 'don't you drink tea?', *bäle äxwarəm* 'yes I do', *röwten boxovet* 'he went to sleep', *köwtäm pā-m därd-i ke* 'I fell; my foot hurt', *mā čīz-i nä m-kerden* 'I did not do anything'. Horm. *dūš čāi-om/et xwä* 'yesterday I/you drank tea', *čāi näxwardeni* 'he is drinking tea', *mä dūš kār-om ke* 'yesterday I worked'.

Bibliography: (Words not mentioned in the text are quoted below.) R. A. Floyer, *Unexplored Balūchistan*, London, 1882 (*jade* 'homestead', *hirsh* 'bear', *lahar* 'hut', *xum, rum* 'date'). I. Gershevitch, "Sissoo at Susa," *BSOAS* 19, 1957, pp. 317-20; review of M. J. Dresden, *The Jātakastava or "Praise of the Buddha's Former Births,"* in *Bibliotheca Orientalis*, 1958, pp. 262-63 (NBš. *kūč-, kuht* 'to dig', p. 263a); "Travels in Bashkardia," *Royal Central Asiatic Society Journal* 46, 1959, pp. 213-24; "Outdoor Terms in Iranian," in W. B. Henning and E. Yarshater, eds., *A Locust's Leg. Studies in Honour of S. H. Taqizadeh*, London, 1962a, pp. 76-84 (Bš. *xāk* '*zamīn*'; SBš. *vark* 'lamb', NBš. *nox. nūög*, Rdb. *nawök* 'hollowed-out tree-trunks used for irrigation purposes', Bš. [<Bal.] *gīdā(h), gīda* 'grass', SBš. *dōr* 'udder', NBš. *pā-eidari* 'barefoot', *jōn-eidari* 'naked', Bš. *lard*, Rūdb. *leid* 'outside'); "The Sogdian Word for 'Advice', and Some Muγ Documents," *Central Asiatic Journal* 7, 1962b, pp. 77-95; apud J. Elfenbein, *A Vocabulary of Marw Baluchi*, Naples, 1963, pp. 15 (Bš. *yaš, waš* 'millstone'), 30 (Bš. *deh'dé* 'continually'), 31 (Bš. *dulăx* 'dust'), 74 (Bš. *šan-/šand* 'to strike'); "Iranian Chronological Adverbs," in G. Redard, ed., *Indo-Iranica. Mélanges présentés à Georg Morgenstierne*, Wiesbaden, 1964a, pp. 78-88 (on the time words see above; NBš. *pešte* 'earlier, before', p. 78; *paster* 'later', NBš. *de*, SBš. *de, dĭ* 'also'; SBš. *daγā 'dīgar'*, p. 86 nn. 28, 30); "Etymological Notes on Persian *mih, naxčīr, bēgāne*, and *bīmār*," in *Dr. J. M. Unvala Memorial Volume*, Bombay, 1964b, pp. 89-94 (Bš. *šekāl* 'mountain sheep', p. 91); "Dialect Variation in Early Persian," *TPS*, 1964c [1965], pp. 1-29 (*gohort* 'big', Bš. *gozer* 'big', p. 12 nn. 1-4; SBš. *mīšekāl/r* 'archer', B.-A. *melāl*, Rdb. NBš. *menāl* 'eyelash', p. 26, nn. 1-2); *The Avestan Hymn to Mithra*, Cambridge, 1967a; apud M. Schwartz, *Studies in the Texts of the Sogdian Christians*, Ph.D. dissertation, Berkeley, 1967b (N[?] Bš. *mard, bāmard, bādoxt*, p. 28; *xwan zan-* 'to weep' [of children], p. 251); apud R. E. Emmerick, *Saka Grammatical Studies*, Oxford, 1968, p. 103 (Bš. *šen* 'to separate, tear asunder'); "Amber at Persepolis," in *Studia Classica et Orientalia Antonino Pagliaro Oblata*, Rome, 1969a, II, pp. 167-251; "Iranian Nouns and Names in Elamite Garb," *TPS*, 1969b [1970], pp. 165-200 (NBš. *sōsk, sūsk* small partridge '*tīhū*', p. 182); "The Crushing of the Third Singular Present," in M. Boyce and I. Gershevitch, eds., *W. B. Henning Memorial Volume*, London, 1970a, pp. 161-74; "Island Bay and the Lion," *BSOAS* 33, 1970b, pp. 82-91; review of D. N. MacKenzie, *The "Sūtra of the Causes and Effects of Actions" in Sogdian, Indogermanische Forschungen* 75, 1970c, pp. 303-06 (*kūč-* 'to dig'); "Iranian Words Containing *-ăn-*," in C. E. Bosworth, ed., *Iran and Islam, in Memory of the Late Vladimir Minorsky*, Edinburgh, 1971, pp. 267-91 (SBš. *šen* 'kid'; SBš. *nav-insōr* 'next year', p. 274; SBš. *šōn kan-* 'to send'); "Notes on the Toponyms *Āsh* and *Nisā*," *Iran* 10, 1972, pp. 124-25; "Genealogical Descent in Iranian," *Bulletin of the Iranian Culture Foundation* 1/2, 1973, pp. 71-86 (Bš. *narauk*, Rām. *varrauk* 'great-grandson', p. 73; Bš *kar(r)anauk* 'great-great-grandson'); apud G. Morgenstierne, *Etymological Vocabulary of the Shughni Group*, Wiesbaden, 1974 (Bš. *dūn* 'two', p. 30b is wrong; *do dūn* is 'two' plus the numerative *dūn*, Mīn. *don*, Bal. *dān*, Pers. *dāna*); "Višāpa," in *Voprosy iranskoĭ i obshcheĭ filologii*, Tiflis, 1977, pp. 62-69 (NBš. [Darpahn] *šāft* 'to cover' (a ewe by the ram), NBš. *ārăn-/ārand, ārăr*, SBš. [Pārmōnt] *yīran-/irānt, yīrānst* 'to comb', pp. 64-65); "The Alloglottography of Old Persian," *TPS*, 1979, pp. 114-90; *Philologia Iranica*, ed., N. Sims-Williams, Wiesbaden, 1985; "A Bahuvrīhic Past-Tense Construction," *Cahiers Ferdinand de Saussure* 41 (*Cahier dédié à Georges Redard*), 1987, pp. 75-86 (*šehm* 'supper', *peim* 'ready', *dōn* numerative, *pah* 'goat', *avādī* 'livestock'). G. Morgenstierne, "Balochi Miscellanea," *AO* 5, 1948, pp. 253-92. Idem, "Neu-iranische Sprachen," in *HO* I, IV, 1, pp. 155-178. (A few words are quoted from Morgenstierne's lectures.) S. Ḥ. Rażawī, "Lahja-ye maḥallī-e Bandar-e 'Abbās (moqaddama)," *Awwalīn našrīya-ye farhang-e ḥawza-ye banāder wa jazāyer-e Bahr-e 'Oman wa Kalīj-e Fārs*, n.d., pp. 59-62 (contains verbal paradigms, all of which agree with forms given by Gershevitch, esp. 1970a, and Skjærvø [note 'to give': *adem, adey, adeyt, adeym, adeyn, adan*]; a vocabulary of 17 words contains the following words not in Skjærvø: *pos* 'small boy', *moḡ* 'date tree', *konūk* 'hole', *kondorūk* 'turpentine' [Pers. *saqqez*], *estāla* 'star' [with *r* > *l* as in Lārestāni]; for 'frog' and 'eyebrow' Rażawī has *gak* and *borm* [Skjærvø *gwäk* and *borg*]). P. O. Skjærvø, "Notes on the Dialects of Minab and Hormoz," *Norwegian Journal of Linguistics* (*NTS*) 29, 1975, pp. 113-28. Idem, "Languages of South-East Iran: Lārestānī, Kumzārī, Baškardī," in R. Schmitt, ed., *Compendium Linguarum Iranicarum*, Wiesbaden, forthcoming.

(P. O. SKJÆRVØ)

BASKERVILLE, HOWARD C., a teacher at the American mission in Tabrīz, killed April 19, 1909, at the age of 25 in a sally during the siege of Tabrīz.

A graduate of Princeton University (B.A., 1907), he arrived to teach science and English under a two-year contract at the Memorial School of the American Presbyterian Mission in Tabrīz shortly before the battle for the city began. Through Mīrzā Ḥosayn Šarīfzāda, a leading constitutionalist and a fellow teacher at the Memorial School he got acquainted with the Constitutional movement and many of its adherents. The assassination of Šarīfzāda in 1908 and the desperate shortage of food supplies in the besieged city, where people were dying of starvation, especially after the blockade of the city was completed by Febrary 3, as well as his sympathy for the Constitutionalists, led him to enlist in their ranks and become an ardent supporter of the popular cause. After resigning from his post he started drilling Persian volunteers together with W. A.

Moore, an Irishman and representative of several British papers in Persia. Baskerville's group, Fawj-e Najāt (Detachment of salvation) used to be trained in the courtyards of the citadel (*arg*). The U.S. State Department advised the Board of Foreign Missions in New York to have him recalled, and Baskerville was asked by the American consul in Tabrīz, William F. Doty, to give back his American passport.

With the danger of famine growing day by day the two "Europeans" advised sorties and carried out reconnaissance operations through the Royalist lines, mapping their positions. The final attempt to break the blockade took place on the night of April 19 against Qarā-Malek, a suburb of Tabrīz which was held by the Royalists and where food was stored. Two contradictory accounts of this last sortie, during which Baskerville was killed, have been preserved. An article published in *The Times* ("The Siege of Tabriz. From an Occasional Correspondent," July 3, 1909) thinly veils the identity of its author, W. A. Moore, who writes in a disparaging manner on the Persians taking part in the sally. He blames the setback on Sattār Khan, who failed to send in his previously offered support. Kasrawī, publishing the detailed report of Mehdī ʿAlawīzāda, one of Baskerville's comrades-in-arms who participated in the sortie, denies that Moore had taken part in the operation and points out that, because of Baskerville's lack of military experience, the plan had from the beginning not met with the approval of Sattār Khan (Kasrawī, pp. 894-97). Baskerville, who almost immediately assaulted the Royalist position, was shot through the heart around 6:00 p.m. The funeral at the American cemetery of Tabrīz on the following day turned into a great rally; Baskerville's men, groups of *fedāʾī*s, Armenians, Georgians, American residents of Tabrīz, and a great number of the inhabitants paid him the last honors.

Bibliography: E. G. Browne, *The Persian Revolution of 1905-1909*, London and Edinburgh, 2nd ed., 1966, pp. 269, 272, 440f. D. Fraser, *Persia and Turkey in Revolt*, Edinburgh and London, 1910, pp. 72ff. A. Kasrawī, *Tārīḵ-e mašrūṭa-ye Īrān*, vol. 2, Tehran, 2537 = 1357 Š./1978, pp. 891-900. M. Rechti, "L'agonie de Tauris," *Revue du Monde Musulman* 8, 1909, pp. 263-69. W. M. Shuster, *The Strangling of Persia*, New York, 1912; repr. 1968, pp. xli, xlvii. U.S. National Archives, State Department Numerical File 5931, Jan. 23, Apr. 1, 5, 6, 7, 14, 26, 1909. A. Yeselson, *United States-Persian Diplomatic Relations 1883-1921*, New Brunswick, New Jersey, 1956, pp. 99-102.

(K. EKBAL)

BĀSMA (also *bāṣma*, *basma*, and *baṣma*), a Turkish word which originally referred to a design applied (with an etching stylus, a wooden block press known as a *qāleb-e taḵtaʾī*, etc.) in ink, silver and gold foil, and the like to paper, cloth, and other such materials. It is similar in type to designs used in decorating Isfahani cloth (*qalamkārī*) or to those used in marking ordinary printed cloth (*čīt*). The noun *bāsma* and the verb *bāsma kardan* apparently entered Persian after the Mongol invasion, replacing the terms *mohr* and *mohr kardan*; the term *bāsmacī* was applied to those who stamped the cloth. Thus in the *Taḏkerat al-molūk*, which was apparently written during the years 1137-42/1724-29, one finds *bāsmačī* with this meaning, alongside goldbeater (*zarkūb*), gilder (*moḏahheb*), and papermaker (*kāḡaḏgar*). With the spread of the printing industry in Iran, the similarity between the act of applying *bāsma* designs and that of printing led to the adoption of the term for *ṭabʿ* and *čāp* (impression); likewise, the term *bāsma-ḵāna* came to be used for *maṭbaʿa* and *čāp-ḵāna* (printshop, press), *bāsmačī* for "printer," and *bāsmakārī* for "printing." The term *baṣma-ḵāna* was employed to mean "press' for the first time in Iran during the Safavid period, at the beginning of the 17th century. The *bāsma-ḵāna* entry in the trilingual dictionary by a Carmelite father in Iran named Angelo à St. Joseph, *Gazophylacium Linguae Persarum* (p. 415), which was completed in 1081/1670 and published in 1096/1684, defines the term as *kār-ḵāna-ye baṣmajī, maṭbaʿ*.

The terms *bāsma*, *bāsma-ḵāna*, *bāsmačī*, and *bāsmakārī*, meaning respectively "print," "press," printer," and "printing industry," began to be popularized for a second time in 19th-century Iran through influence from Azerbaijan and Tabrīz. The *bāsma-ḵāna* of Tabrīz was in operation until the death of ʿAbbās Mīrzā (1249/1833) and the Tehran press (*maṭbaʿ-e ḥorūfī*) until 1261/1845, when both were replaced by lithographic forms of printing.

Bibliography: M. Dabīrsīāqī, "Nokta-ī šenīdanī az āḡāz-e ṣanʿat-e čāp dar oṯmānī," *Soḵan* 26/4, 1355 Š./1976, pp. 449-54. Dehḵodā, s.v. *čāp*. M. Mīnovī, "Awwalīn kār-e maʿrefat," *Yaḡmā* 6/5-9 (especially no. 8), 1332 Š./1953, pp. 313-18. Moḥammad-Mahdī Khan, *Sanglax*, ed. G. Clauson, GMS, London, 1960, s.v. *basma*. *Taḏkerat al-molūk*, ed. M. Dabīrsīāqī, Tehran, 1335 Š./1956, p. 71; ed. Minorsky, p. 100.

(M. DABĪRSĪĀQĪ)

BAṢRA (Ar. al-Baṣra), town located near the Šaṭṭ al-ʿArab river in southern Iraq, a predominantly Arab town possessing a rich political, cultural, and economic history. This article concentrates mainly on describing the town's many significant ties with Iran.

Foundation and early history. Basra was initially established in about 17/638 as an encampment and garrison (Ar. *meṣr*, plur. *amṣār*) for the Arab tribesmen constituting the armies of the early caliphs. After campaigning in southern Iraq for several years and defeating the Sasanian forces there, the Muslims' commander, ʿOtba b. Ḡazwān, set up camp on the site of an old Persian settlement called Vaheštābāḏ Ardašīr which was destroyed by the Arabs, who called its ruins Ḵorayba (Yāqūt, II, p. 429). The site was near the modern village of Zobayr, not far from the port town of Obolla (class. Apologos). The new town was connected to the Šaṭṭ al-ʿArab by means of canals, particularly the Nahr al-Obolla, and in its earliest days consisted of rough huts made of reeds taken from the nearby marshes of southern Iraq. These were later augmented by mud-brick buildings and walls as the town grew, but even in much later times the poorer quarters still consisted of reed houses, as travelers' accounts, such as that of Pedro Teixeira (1604), reveal (Teixeira, p. 28).

Because of its role as an important garrison town, Basra figured prominently in the political history of the early Islamic state, since outside Arabia itself the predominantly Arabian ruling elite of the new state was closely concentrated in the *amṣār*. We therefore find Basra and its population frequently mentioned in accounts of such episodes as the first and second civil wars, which mainly took the form of struggle among contending groups within the ruling elite for control of just such military and administrative centers as Basra.

In its early days, the town served as the staging point from which further conquests in Iran and the east were launched. Its armies were instrumental in the rapid initial conquests of the Iranian districts of Ḵūzestān Fārs, Sīstān (Sejestān), Badḡīs, and Khorasan during the 640s and 650s, especially under the commanders Abū Mūsā Aš'arī and 'Abd-Allāh b. 'Āmer b. Korayz (qq.v.). Its role as garrison and starting point for these conquests meant that it also became the place from which many of these far-flung provinces were administered, and from which they were pacified after the inevitable rebellions that followed the conquests. We know that in the years immediately following the establishment of the town, the governors of Basra supervised the countryside they ruled via a number of lesser strong points located at Forāt, Sorraq, Jondī-Šāpūr, Manāḏer, Sūq al-Aḥwāz (Ahvāz), and Kowar al-Dejla, where small garrisons and tax agents were situated; it seems likely that similar procedures may have been followed in districts farther east as these were acquired by the Muslims. The more distant regions of Fārs, Sīstān, Khorasan, and those parts of Media called Māh al-Baṣra were, during the Omayyad period, usually part of the administrative responsibility of Basra, whose governor managed them by means of sub-governors. The tax administration during the Omayyad period operated through the agency of the Iranian *dehqāns* or landed squires, who were placed in charge of the collection of taxes on their districts, which they handed over to the authorities of the new state. At various times during the Omayyad period, the governorship of Basra was combined with that of its sister city Kūfa in central Iraq (which, like Basra, had large areas of Iran as administrative dependencies) in the hands of one governor, such as 'Abd-al-Malek's powerful viceroy, Ḥajjāj b. Yūsof. For roughly a century, in other words, Basra served as the administrative capital of considerable parts of Iran as well as of southern Iraq.

The population of early Basra was, as noted above, predominantly Arab. Of the many tribes represented in its population, the most important at that time were the Tamīm and the various clans of Bakr b. Wā'el, both of which had dominated areas near the site of Basra on the eve of the Islamic era. Tribes from the Ḥejāz, such as Qorayš, Kenāna, and Qays 'Aylān, were less numerous in Basra, and because of the greater distance to their traditional homelands they became increasingly marginal within the Arab population of the city. The tribes of 'Abd-al-Qays and Azd, from eastern Arabia and 'Omān respectively, begin to show up in Basra a bit after its initial foundation and seem to have increased in importance some decades later, probably due to continuing immigration. The juxtaposition in one place of so many Arab tribes, some of whom were traditionally hostile to one another, was doubtless partly responsible for the turbulent history of early Basra, although socio-economic and religious discontents of fairly recent origin were clearly at stake in some of the many uprisings there. To keep things in perspective, however, it should perhaps be noted here that Basra's early history was less turbulent than that of Kūfa, which had a tribal population of even greater diversity.

Although the Arab element was the dominant one in Basra's early population, however, the Arab settlers from the beginning had to share the city with many settlers from other ethnic groups. The commercial activities that focused on Basra (and its predecessor, Obolla) had drawn from various points around the Indian Ocean basin (Indians, Malays, and Blacks), and there was also a sizable Iranian component in the population. The Iranians of early Basra found themselves there for various reasons. A few had been *asāwera* (q.v.), the Sasanian cavalrymen who had joined the Muslims at the time of the conquest of Iraq and had settled in the new town as allies of the Arabs of Tamīm. Others doubtless came from villages in the vicinity of Basra, some of which—particularly in the direction of Ḵūzestān—had Iranian populations. The largest group of Iranians in early Basra, however, probably consisted of captives and recent converts to Islam (*mawālī*), who were serving or allied to their Arab masters or patrons.

Basra's administrative position meant that it was, with Kūfa, one of the main sources of (or conduits for) Arab immigration into Iran during the first centuries of the Islamic era. The first immigrants were mostly sent to serve as garrison troops to support Arab/Muslim domination of Iran, and went in such numbers over the years that in certain areas they had an enduring cultural and even linguistic impact; indeed, Arabic dialects are still spoken to this day around the city of Marv, the most important of the subordinate garrisons, by distant descendants of the early Arab settlers. Because of the close social, administrative, and other ties that existed between the Basrans themselves and these Arab immigrants to Iran, the tribal divisions and antagonisms that afflicted the population of Basra came to be reflected also in Marv and other garrisons in Iran, making the life of these eastern garrisons as turbulent as that of their restive parent. In Omayyad Khorasan, for example, the hostility between the tribal confederations of Bakr b. Wā'el and Tamīm, on the one hand, and the clans of Azd, on the other, were to a large extent reflections of similar tensions in Basra. In other areas of Iran, the tribes of Qays predominated.

From the ʿAbbasids to the Ottomans. The accession of the ʿAbbasid dynasty in 132/749 occurred just when Basra was beginning to enter its most vibrant period of cultural activity; during the 2nd-4th/8th-10th centuries, the city was the intellectual crossroads of the Islamic world (the cultural language of which was still exclusively Arabic), and was the home of renowned theologians, poets, Arabic grammarians, historians, and other writers. Some of these cultural figures were of Iranian descent, including the early paragon of piety Ḥasan al-Baṣrī; Sebawayh, one of the founders of the study of Arabic grammar; the famed poets Baššār b. Bord and Abū Nowās; the Muʿtazilite theologian ʿAmr b. ʿObayd; the early Arabic prose stylist Ebn al-Moqaffaʿ; and probably some of the authors of the noted encyclopaedia of the E̲kwān al-Ṣafāʾ. It was also during this period that Basra seems to have enjoyed its greatest economic prosperity, doubtless in part because the foundation of the new ʿAbbasid capital at Baghdad increased the demand for luxury goods and many other articles of the Indian Ocean trade, which passed from the Persian Gulf into Iraq via Basra and its nearby neighbor, Obolla. Although the town of Sīrāf on the coast of Fārs, and not Basra, was the main terminus of international trade in the Persian Gulf at this time, we should not underestimate Basra's commercial importance. Most of the goods transported between Sīrāf or other Gulf ports and Baghdad probably had to be transferred to different vessels at Basra or Obolla, because most ships suitable for the open waters of the Gulf would have difficulty negotiating the shallow, marshy course of the lower Tigris or Euphrates in southern Iraq. Basra and its environs produced vast quantities of excellent dates that were exported even as far as China. And we know that in the 2nd/8th century there were at least a few merchants residing in Basra who were regularly involved in the China trade. Moreover, Basra's commercial importance relied on more than the sea-borne commerce through the Persian Gulf. The city also had a certain amount of commercial contact with Ahvāz and thereby with other parts of K̲ūzestān by river, and one can assume that this engendered some overland commerce via K̲ūzestān with the Iranian plateau. More important yet was the overland trade with Syria and Arabia, particularly Yamāma and the Ḥejāz; indeed, Basra was unique as an entrepôt where the products carried by the Arabian caravan trade, including camels and sheep, could be found together with the commodities of the Gulf and Indian Ocean trade. The importance of Basran merchants in the Arabian trade network is suggested by a third/tenth-century text informing us that most of the merchants in the large Yemeni town of Ṣaʿda were Basrans (Qodāma b. Jaʿfar, *Ketāb al-k̲arāj*, BGA 6, p. 189).

If the shift of the imperial center from Omayyad Damascus to ʿAbbasid Baghdad (and, after the 830s, to Sāmarrā) brought palpable economic benefits to Basra, however, it also coincided with, and may have caused, profound changes in the political and social life of the city. Its rapid growth, spurred by burgeoning commerce, resulted in a more cosmopolitan population, and one far less dominated than previously by Arab tribal values and tribal divisions. The relative proximity of the ʿAbbasid capital to Kūfa and Basra led to a decline in the independence and political importance of the two Iraqi *amṣār*, both because the regime could exercise more immediate control over them and because the rapid growth of the new caliphal court refocused the attention of everyone in the region on the town farther north. In particular, the old links between Basra and its former administrative dependencies in Iran were decisively broken under the ʿAbbasids, as Iranians and Arabs living in Iran now looked to Baghdad (or Sāmarrā) as the relevant political center. When the ʿAbbasids' real power declined in the 3rd-4th/9th-10th centuries, Basra gradually became the political backwater it was to remain ever after—a provincial town whose political life was shaped more by local Arab tribes than by the power of the central government to which it ostensibly owed obedience. The Tamīm tribe, which had dominated Basra and the countryside around it during the city's early days, had been fairly well controlled by the Omayyad caliphs through their extensive connections with Arab tribal society; but the Tamīm's successors to local preeminence, such as the K̲afāja tribe in the 5th/11th and 6th/12th centuries and the Montafeq tribe (11th-14th/17th-20th centuries), proved much more difficult to contain. When they did not plunder or seize Basra, expelling the government's representatives, they frequently forced the "authorities" (Saljuqs, Ottomans) to recognize them as virtual rulers of the town. From about the tenth century on, then, the political history of Basra cannot be properly understood without an appreciation of the role of these powerful Arab tribes and their relation to the city.

The decline of caliphal power also permitted the emergence of various kinds of rebellions and uprisings against the authorities, in Basra and southern Iraq as elsewhere in the ʿAbbasid domains. The turbulence of the Ẓoṭṭ (ca. 205-20/820-35) seems to have had primarily social origins, whereas the uprising of the Zanj (255-69/869-83), who seized Basra and plundered it, and of the Qarmaṭīs, who plundered it in 923, seem to have had both social and religious roots. For a time the town came under the control of the Barīdīs, a family of local origin that reigned in K̲ūzestān and southern Iraq in the mid-tenth century, first as governors for the powerless late ʿAbbasids and then as independent princes, until they were expelled in 336/947 by the first Buyids. The tenth century also saw outbreaks of violence in Basra between the city's Sunni population and its Shiʿite minority.

The rule of the Daylamite Buyid dynasty, which seized control of the ʿAbbasid government in the 4th/10th century, reaffirmed to some extent Basra's ties with parts of Iran, especially Fārs, the locus of one of the main centers of Buyid power. The town was thereby drawn into the power struggles within the Buyid dynasty itself. Generally, Basra was ruled by various

Buyid princes more or less loyal to the great Buyid prince in Baghdad, who stationed a Daylamite garrison in the town, and it was also the home of an important fleet used by the Buyids to project their power across the Gulf of Oman and to suppress piracy. But it was a turbulent time; not only did sectarian violence continue (exacerbated, no doubt, by the fact that the Buyids were themselves Shiʿites); there were also several rebellions by Buyid princes or Daylamite officers against the reigning prince (*amīr al-omarāʾ*) and attempts to seize the city by outside groups such as the Qarmaṭīs, who tried to profit from disarray among the warring Buyid princes by launching an attack (unsuccessfully) against the city in the 370s/980s.

All this turbulence in Basra and surrounding areas of southern Iraq and Ḵūzestān caused a sharp decline both in commerce and in the population and general prosperity of Basra, starting in the late 4th/10th century. Although the Arab geographer Ebn Ḥawqal (mid-4th/10th century) still found the city constructed mostly of brick, mentioned its burgeoning commerce (which, unfortunately, he passes over as too well known to warrant description), and praised the palaces, gardens, and plentiful fruit and date trees found along the Nahr al-Obolla, his copyist notes that when he saw the city in 537/1142 most quarters were in ruins, the old city ramparts were far outside the inhabited areas, and the number of residents in the remaining quarters was greatly reduced. He attributed these changes to the repression and tyranny of governors and to the annual or bienniel incursions of the powerful Ḵafāja bedouins (Ebn Ḥawqal, pp. 235-38). In addition, however, one must point to a shift in commercial routes and conditions as causes of Basra's decline. The 5th/11th century seems to have seen a shift in the commerce between the Indian Ocean and the Mediterranean basin from the Persian Gulf to the Red Sea route. On the other hand, the demise of the Buyid dynasty, which had kept close watch on the trade routes from central Iran to the Persian Gulf coast entrepôts of Hormoz and Sīrāf, meant that these routes were made more risky for commerce by a resurgence of the unruly Šabānkāra Kurds. As a result, some trade from the Iranian plateau now became directed instead toward Basra during the early Saljuq period (late 5th/11th century). It may have been in recognition of this renewed economic link between Basra and southwestern Iran that the first Saljuqs combined Basra with Ḵūzestān to form a single administrative district.

But this commercial boost was to be short-lived and relatively small; for one thing, the collapse of the Buyids had also allowed the emergence of an aggressive nest of pirates at Qays, who preyed on Persian Gulf shipping and thereby reduced its volume. By the time the Mongol armies arrived in Iraq in the mid-7th/13th century, Basra was but a shadow of its former self; it surrendered without a struggle to the armies of Hülegü (Holāgū) Khan in 656/1258 and seems to have caused the new overlords few problems. For the Il-khans, as for their successors the Jalayerids, the Qara Qoyunlūs, and the Āq Qoyunlūs whose attentions were concentrated mostly on northwestern Iran, northern Mesopotamia, and eastern Anatolia, Basra was little more than a distant outpost of their fleeting empires.

The Mongol and Turkman periods (mid-8th/13th to early 11th/16th centuries) were virtually the last during which Basra maintained any integral contacts with Iran. There continued to be an important Iranian element in the population of Basra. Ebn Baṭṭūṭa, who visited the town in the 8th/14th century, described it as consisting of three quarters—the Hoḏayl quarter, the Banū Ḥarām quarter, and the Iranian quarter (*maḥallat al-ʿAjam*; Ebn Baṭṭūṭa, *Reḥla*, p. 186; Ebn al-Aṯīr, *Lobāb*, s.v. Banū Ḥarām). If the first two reveal that Basra was still predominantly an Arab town, the existence of an Iranian quarter clearly reveals the legacy of long centuries of intimate contact between Basra and the Iranian plateau. The demise of the original city became complete in 900/1495, when the original site of Basra was abandoned because of a dearth of fresh water and the population moved to a new location, the site of modern Basra, about twenty-five km to the east of the original town (near the old Obolla).

From the Ottomans to modern times. After a brief period of rule by the Safavids following Shah Esmāʿīl's conquest of Iraq (914-41/1508-34), Basra submitted to the Ottomans and entered a new era in its history. The generally hostile relations between the Ottomans and their rivals on the Iranian plateau meant a sharper border demarcation between Ottoman-controlled Iraq and Iran than had thitherto existed, and this must have contributed to a gradual attenuation of the Iranian contact with Basra and its population. It became more and more a purely Arab provincial town, often restless under its Ottoman overlords, but important to them as an outlet to the Persian Gulf for goods from Iraq and the north. The town was by turns an island of Ottoman rule and official stability, in the turbulence of southern Iraq's restive nomadic Arab tribes and piratical marshmen, and an independent fief controlled by powerful governors or rebellious Janissaries, who took advantage of their distance from the Ottoman provincial capital at Baghdad, their ties with the Montafeq and other tribes, or the uncertainty of communication through the marshes north of Basra to make themselves independent. The most important of these local rulers was doubtless Afrāsīāb, a local man who seized control of Basra in the early 11th/17th century, and his descendants, who continued to control Basra for almost half a century, despite repeated efforts by the Ottomans to dislodge them. The end of the 12th/18th century and the 13th/19th century saw a great resurgence of the Montafeq tribe, which repeatedly threatened Basra and cost the Ottomans great effort to control.

Despite this instability, Basra remained in the Ottoman cultural orbit. Its only real brush with the politics of the Iranian plateau occurred in the 1770s, during the invasion of Iraq launched by Karīm Khan Zand, when Basra was blockaded and finally forced to surrender in 1190/1776 and a Persian garrison was installed. But the

Zands, like the Ottomans, found it impossible to control the town without the backing of the Montafeq tribe, and upon Karīm Khan's death in 1193/1779 the governor, his brother Ṣādeq Khan, withdrew from the city. After a brief period of direct control by the Montafeq tribe, Basra returned once again to the Ottoman fold.

The Ottoman centuries saw a resurgence of seafaring activity in the Persian Gulf, this time with Europeans playing the leading roles, and Basra soon became an important base for Portuguese, Dutch, English, and French agents as well as for Indian merchants and Arab merchants from Oman and elsewhere. The (British) East India Company established a factory in Basra in the 1130s/1720s. The many European travelers who passed through Basra during the 11th/17th and 12th/18th centuries described it as a decidedly Arab town, fairly prosperous, with merchants from many parts of the Persian Gulf, Arabia, and Mesopotamia gathered there, but little mention is made of commerce with the cities of the Iranian plateau. Pedro Teixeira (1604), for example, speaks of commerce with Hormoz as well as shipping up the Tigris to Baghdad, and Tavernier (1639) mentions Dutch, English, Portuguese, and Indian merchants, as well as traders from Constantinople, Smyrna (İzmir), Aleppo (Ḥalab), Damascus, Cairo, Diyarbakr (Dīārbakr), Mosul, and Baghdad (Teixeira, pp. 26-28; Tavernier, I, bk. 2, pp. 198-200).

The instability that had plagued southern Iraq and acted as a drain on Basra's commercial potential for so many centuries began to give way in the late 13th/19th and early 14th/20th centuries under the impact of such reform measures as the *tapu* land-registration system, introduced by the Ottomans in the 1860s and 1870s, and the creation of modern armed forces by the Ottomans and their successors in Iraq. Together these measures broke the ability of the Montafeq shaikhs to organize effective, large-scale resistance and gave the state an edge too over the elusive marshmen, who had for so long preyed on commerce between Basra and the north. In the 14th/20th century, under British Mandate and the government of independent Iraq, Basra has undergone a rapid transformation into a modern city, with important civic, commercial, and industrial improvements, including a modern port, airport, communications, and public services. It is now the main focus of Iraq's export trade, especially for Basra's traditional prize product, dates (much of the petroleum from the oilfields of southern Iraq is transported by pipeline to estuaries on the Persian Gulf coast), and is one of the leading port cities and commercial entrepôts of the Persian Gulf.

Bibliography: Because of Basra's general importance, it is impossible to give a complete list of the vast number of sources that provide information about the city. Its political and cultural significance during the early and medieval Islamic periods caused it to be mentioned in virtually every Arabic chronicle (Ṭabarī, Balāḏorī, Yaʿqūbī, etc.), as well as in most of the works of Arab geographers and travelers (Eṣṭaḵrī, Ebn Ḥawqal, Hamadānī, Yāqūt, Ebn Baṭṭūṭa, etc.). Primary sources specifically mentioned in this article are cited in the following editions: Ebn Baṭṭūṭa, *Reḥla*, Beirut 1964; Ebn al-Aṯīr, *al-Lobāb fī tahḏīb al-ansāb*, Beirut, 1873; Ebn Ḥawqal, BGA 2, Leiden, 1938-39; Qodāma b. Jaʿfar, *Ketāb al-ḵarāj*, BGA 6, Leiden, 1889. A concise survey of Basra's early history, with a very complete list of primary sources, is provided in Charles Pellat's *Le milieu baṣrien et la formation de Ǧāḥiẓ*, Paris, 1953. An even more detailed examination of economic and social developments in the town's early years is provided by Ṣāleḥ Aḥmad ʿAlī, *al-Tanẓīmāt al-ejtemāʿīya wa'l-eqteṣādīya fi'l-Baṣra fi'l-qarn al-awwal al-hejrī*, Beirut, 1969, with an equally complete bibliography of early sources. A convenient summary of the early Islamic conquests in Iran, including those campaigns organized and supported from Basra, can be found in ʿA. Zarrīnkūb, "The Arab Conquest in Iran and Its Aftermath," in *Camb. Hist. Iran* IV, pp. 1-56. On settlement see F. M. Donner, "Tribal Settlement in Basra during the First Century A. H.," in T. Khalidi, ed., *Land Tenure and Social Transformation in the Middle East*, Beirut, 1984, pp. 97-120. A detailed examination of the rebellion of the Zanj, with a thorough bibliography of relevant sources, is Alexandre Popovic, *La révolte des esclaves en Iraq au IIIe/IXe siècle*, Paris, 1976. For the Buyid period, some information and much bibliography can be gleaned from H. Busse, *Chalif und Grosskönig: Die Buyiden im Iraq (945-1055)*, Beirut, 1969. Similarly, some information and sources for the Mongol period can be retrieved from D. Krawulsky, *Īrān—das Reich der Īl-ḫāne*, Wiesbaden, 1978. For information on the broader currents of trade in the Persian Gulf region in the Middle Ages, two works are especially helpful. One is Ḥasan b. Yazīd Sīrāfī's *Aḵbār al-Ṣīn wa'l-Hend*, ed. and tr. J. Sauvaget, *Relation de la Chine et de l'Inde: Rédigée en 851*, Paris 1948; the other is J. Aubin, "La ruine de Sîrâf et les routes du Golfe Persique au XIe et XIIe siècles," *Cahiers de civilisation médiévale* 2, 1959, pp. 295-301. For the Ottoman period, pending a careful examination of the Ottoman archival documents for Basra (which do not appear to have been explored to date), the most important sources of information are the many travelers' accounts, a complete list of which can be found in S. H. Longrigg's *Four Centuries of Modern Iraq*, Oxford, 1925, which can also be consulted for the outlines of Basra's history during this period. Travelers' accounts cited in this article are *The Travels of Pedro Teixeira..*, tr. and annotated by W. F. Sinclair, London, 1902; *Les six voyages de Jean-Baptiste Tavernier...*, Paris, 1681.

For the modern period see S. H. Longrigg, *Iraq, 1900-1950*, London, 1953.

(F. M. DONNER)

BASSĀM-E KORD, the Kharijite (fl. mid-3rd/9th century), one of the first poets in the New Persian language, active at the court of the Saffarids. The epithet "Kord" (spelled Kūrd in the *Tārīḵ-e Sīstān*) apparently meant "shepherd" and does not seem to have any connection with the western Iranian tribes who came to be known as the Kurds. Bassām had belonged to the Kharijite faction in Sīstān, against whom the Saffarid Ya'qūb b. Lay̱t (d. 265/878) fought at the start of his career, finally defeating them and killing their leader 'Ammār in 251/865. Some time after this battle, Bassām and several other Kharijites approached Ya'qūb for peace. After joining Ya'qūb's retinue, Bassām, who was a cultured man (*adīb*), followed the example set by Moḥammad b. Waṣīf Sīstānī, Ya'qūb's secretary, in writing poetry in Persian. Five verses of his poem congratulating Ya'qūb on his defeat of the Kharijites and 'Ammār's death are preserved in the *Tārīḵ-e Sīstān*.

Bibliography: *Tārīḵ-e Sīstān*, pp. 209-12. Ṣafā, *Adabīyāt* I, 2nd ed., 1335 Š./1956, pp. 166-67, 169. Lazard, *Premiers poètes* I, p. 18; II, p. 16. Rypka, *Hist. Iran. Lit.*, p. 136. Ch. Rempis, "Die ältesten Dichtungen in Neupersisch," *ZDMG* 101, 1951, pp. 220-40.

(Z. SAFA)

BAŠŠĀR-E MARḠAZĪ (possibly Bešgar; see Bahār, I, p. 378 n. 1), a Persian poet of the 4th/10th century, apparently from Marv in Khorasan. No information about his career has come down. Reżāqolī Khan Hedāyat (*Majma' al-foṣaḥā'* I, p. 440) mistook him for the famous Arabic poet of Iranian extraction Baššār b. Bord (put to death in 167/783). All of Baššār's poetry is lost except for a *qaṣīda* of thirty-one verses in praise of wine. The poem, recorded in part by Hedāyat (loc. cit.), was first published in its complete form by Rašīd Yāsamī, who had found it in a manuscript. It is thoroughly Samanid in tone and style, and its influence can be discerned in a well-known *mosammaṭ* (*ḵīzīd o ḵaz ārīd* . . .) by Manūčehrī Dāmḡānī (d. 432/1040).

Bibliography: Ṣafā, *Ganj-e soḵan* I, 7th ed., Tehran, 1363 Š./1984, pp. 76-78. Idem, *Adabīyāt* I, 2nd ed., Tehran, 1335 Š./1956, pp. 351-52. Nafīsī, *Naẓm o naṯr*, p. 24. M.-T. Bahār, *Sabk-šenāsī* I, Tehran, 1337 Š./1958. M. Moṣaffā, *Pāsdārān-e soḵan* I, Tehran, n.d., pp. 70-74. Rašīd Yāsamī, "Qaṣīda-ye Baššār-e Marḡazī," *Īrānšahr* 2, 1302 Š./1923, pp. 599-605.

(Z. SAFA)

BAST (sanctuary, asylum), the designation of certain sanctuaries in Iran that are considered inviolable and were often used by people seeking refuge (*bast nešastan, bast-nešīnī*) from prosecution (even common criminals), called *bastīs*. The word is probably derived from OIr. (OPers., Av.) *upastā-* "help, assistance," cf. Mid. Pers. *apastām* "reliance," Arm. lw. *apastan* "refuge, shelter" (see *AirWb.*, col. 396; Nyberg, *Manual* II, p. 24; Hübschmann, *Armenische Grammatik*, p. 104). Arabic *taḥaṣṣon*, asylum in a fortified place, is sometimes used in Iran.

Concepts of asylum and sanctuary are linked with widely spread beliefs and customs. Religious asylum was practiced by Jews. Greeks, and Romans. The Roman Catholic church made it a universal institution. In Islam, the customary right of asylum derives from the notions of "safeguard" or "protection" (see "'Ahd," "Amān," "Ḏhimma," "Ḥimāya," in *EI*² and "'Ār," ibid., suppl.; see also L. Gardet, *La cité musulmane*, Paris, 1961, pp. 75ff.). From "honoring the guest" (*ekrām al-żayf*) derived the Bedouin concept of the right of asylum (*eqrā'*; ibid., pp. 78, 280; see also "Dakẖīl" and "Djiwār," in *EI*²), which usually prevailed over "the duty of just war" (L. Massignon, *Opera minora*, Beirut, 1969, III, pp. 539ff.). Religious asylum is provided in a holy precinct (*ḥaram*), the prototype of which is the Ka'ba, where human beings as well as animals and plants find sanctuary (see "Ka'ba," in *EI*², with reference to Jewish precedents; cf. Koran 3:96). The notion of *ḥaram* space was extended to holy places such as the "shrines" of the imams (see "'Atabāt," in *EI*², suppl., and EIr.; Pers. *āstān/āstāna* is used in Iran) and the tombs (*mazārāt*) of holy persons such as *emāmzādas*, Sufi saints, or learned men (*ḵānaqāh, takīa, rebāṭ, zāwia*) visited by pilgrims.

Although this custom is of great antiquity, its beginnings in Iran remain unclear. The existence in Sasanian times of an official "protector of the poor" (*drigōšān yātagōv*) does not imply a right of asylum or an institution (see J. de Menasce, "Le protecteur des pauvres dans l'Iran sassanide," in *Mélanges Massé*, Tehran, 1963, pp. 1-6). Territorial asylum (which appeared with the creation of modern states in sixteenth-century Europe) seems to have been used early in Islamic Iran, along with religious asylum, whereas extraterritorial asylum appeared gradually with the development of diplomatic missions.

The vizier Šams-al-Dīn Moḥammad Ṣāḥeb-e Dīvān's retreat for a few days into the sanctuary of Fāṭema Ma'ṣūma at Qom (Rašīd-al-Dīn, *Jāme' al-tawārīḵ*, Baku, III, p. 200) must be interpreted as taking *bast*. Claimants to the throne, tribal chiefs, generals, and nobles who had fallen out with their overlords often found political-territorial asylum under a rival king or ruler (e.g., Safavid princes seeking refuge under the Ottomans).

With the establishment of a strong central government under the Safavids and the concomitant rise in religious fervor, the practice of taking asylum in religious or royal holy places became common. Under *bast* protection, *bastīs* found temporary accommodation and subsistence and could negotiate the terms of immunity with their prosecutors. The concept of the inviolability of a sacred space used for *bast* is often symbolized by a chain stretched across the gate or threshold of the precincts. Immunity is guaranteed by touching the chain and getting into the first courtyard (Massé, pp. 404ff.; Curzon, I, p. 347). The first Safavid shrine to be recognized as *bast* was the tomb of Shaikh Ṣafī-al-Dīn at Ardabīl. This was granted as a boon to Solṭān 'Alī by Tīmūr in 806/1404 (W. Hinz, *Irans Aufstieg zum Nationalstaat im fünfzehnten Jahrhundert*, Berlin and Leipzig, 1936, p. 15; *Taḏkerat al-molūk*, pp. 189f.). Some places, such as the Ardabīl mosque and the mausoleum of Fāṭema Maʿṣūma at Qom, seem to have been special refuges for debtors (Massé, pp. 406f., quoting Tavernier; Gemelli Carreri, *Giro del mondo*, Naples, 1699-1700, II, pp. 75f.). The royal palace of ʿĀlī Qāpū (q.v.) at Isfahan, whose threshold was particularly sacred, provided *bast* to those who took refuge in its cells (Massé, pp. 405f. quoting Tavernier, Della Valle, Bedik, Thévenot, Chardin, Oléarius, etc.). The Čehel Sotūn palace was also a *bast* (Masse, p. 406, quoting Struys). Other places, objects, and animals associated with royalty provided *bast*. Among them we find the royal kitchens, stables, and horses (the *bastī* had to stand near the horse's head or tail; Malcolm, II, p. 559 n.; see also Curzon, I, p. 155 n.; *bast* was later extended to horses in diplomatic missions, when the *bastī*s would take refuge under the horse; Massé, p. 406), the Pearl Cannon (Tūp-e Morvārīd) in Tehran, and thence the royal artillery (Massé, p. 405; Browne, tr., *Tarikh-i jadid*, p. 152).

Residences of renowned *mojtahed*s were also considered *bast*, even after their owners' deaths (Malcolm, II, pp. 443f.). The whole quarter of Bīdābād in Isfahan was a *bast* because a leading *mojtahed* lived there (Massé, p. 405, quoting De Bode). Mosques of *emāmzāda*s and other saints were also used as refuges (e.g., Šāh Čerāḡ in Shiraz, Sayyed Ḥamza in Tabrīz, Ḥājī Mīr Yaʿqūb in Ḵoy; see Massé, p. 407).

Extraterritorial rights granted to Russia and Britain by the Treaty of Torkamānčāy (1828) and an additional firman in 1840 enabled British diplomats to extend their protection to an increasing number of Persians or other subjects, which eventually led to the use of the legations, consulates, and embassy residences, and even the Indo-European Telegraph Department's stations as *bast*s (Wright, pp. 41ff.). Resort to telegraph stations was encouraged by the popular belief that the telegraph wires ended at the foot of the throne in Tehran (Curzon, I, p. 175).

Bast as a form of political protest was used early by social groups. In the reign of Shah ʿAbbās II, in 1066/1657, members of the guilds and craftsmen took *bast* inside the *dawlat-ḵāna* at Isfahan. Through the mediation of a *mojtahed*, they obtained the dismissal of an oppressive watchman (*dārūḡa*) from the Shah and, later, of the *dīvān-begī* (M. Keyvani, *Artisans and Guild Life in the Later Safavid Period*, Berlin, 1982, p. 157, quoting *ʿAbbās-nāma* and *Ḵold-e barīn*). Although political *bast* was extended considerably in the 13th/19th century with the development of diplomatic missions and telegraph stations (see Lambton, pp. 136, 141f.), the biggest *bast*s took place during the Constitutional Revolution (1905-11). In April, 1905, Tehran retailers, bankers, and merchants took refuge at Shah ʿAbd-al-ʿAẓīm in Ray (see Gilbar, p. 296). In December, 1905, the clergy (*ʿolamāʾ*), theology students (*ṭollāb*), and *bāzārī*s also took *bast* at Shah ʿAbd-al-ʿAẓīm, after being expelled from the Masjed-e Šāh in Tehran (Malekzāda, II, pp. 47ff.; Algar, pp. 246f.). The most celebrated *bast* took place in the British Legation at Tehran. During three weeks (19 July-10 August 1906), between 12,000 and 16,000 Tehrani demonstrators camped in the gardens while about one thousand *ʿolamāʾ* migrated to Qom. This led to the granting of a Constitution and a National Assembly (Browne, *Revolution*, pp. 118ff.; Malekzāda, II, pp. 161ff.; Algar, pp. 250f.; Wright, p. 47; Gilbar, p. 299). There were also important *bast*s in Tabrīz (British consulate: September, 1906; Turkish consulate: June, 1909; see Browne, *Revolution*, p. 130). The anti-Constitutionalist Shaikh Fażl-Allāh Nūrī took *bast* with some followers in Shah ʿAbd-al-ʿAẓīm for ninety days to express his disapproval of constitutional government (Malekzāda, IV, p. 212; Abdul-Hadi Hairi, *Shīʿism and Constitutionalism in Iran*, Leiden, 1977, p. 192). Like others involved in large-scale political protest, *bastī*s enjoyed various forms of support; in addition to British diplomatic protection, Constitutionalists were given financial aid by wealthy Iranian bankers and merchants (Gilbar, p. 299).

There were many attempts to restrict *bast*. In cases of great offense, attempts were made to starve out the *bastī*s (Massé, p. 407, quoting Morier). Violating or breaking of *bast* by force brought about a malediction or a curse upon trespassers. Troops broke *bast* at Mašhad in 1934 (see R. M. Savory, in G. Lenczowski, ed., *Iran under the Pahlavis*, Stanford, 1978, pp. 97f.). Authoritative reduction of *bast* was undertaken by Amīr(-e) Kabīr, who objected to the use of mosques to shelter armed followers of the *ʿolamāʾ* in Isfahan, Tabrīz, and Tehran. He also tried to suppress extraterritorial *bast* (Algar, pp. 129ff., F. Ādamīyat, *Amīr-e Kabīr o Īrān*, Tehran, 1354 Š./1975, pp. 432ff.). There were renewed attempts to suppress *bast* after Nāṣer-al-Dīn Shah's first visit to Europe (Curzon, I, p. 460). One of the most portentous violations of *bast* occurred in January, 1891, when Jamāl-al-Dīn Asadābādī "Afḡānī" was violently expelled from Shah ʿAbd-al-ʿAẓīm (Algar, pp. 199ff.; Pakdaman, pp. 141ff., 321ff., letter to Amīn-al-Żarb). The Majles, which was bombarded by the troops of Moḥammad-ʿAlī Shah (June, 1908), was also considered a *bast*. Moṣaddeq took refuge in it in 1953 (see P. Avery, *Modern Iran*, London, 1965, p. 436).

Although only Muslims benefited, in principle, from *bast*, there were exceptions for Christians, Jews, and Zoroastrians (see, e.g., Curzon, I, p. 155; on *ḏemmī*s' protection, see Lambton, p. 141). *Bast* protection was extended to ritually pure animals (Massé, p. 405; Algar, pp. 134f.; on pilgrim animals, see B. A. Donaldson, *The Wild Rue*, London, 1938, p. 68). Safety was not guaranteed to Babis who had been promised *bast* immunity (Browne, tr., *Tarikh-i jadid*, pp. 152f.). Jules Richard, a Frenchman who promoted photography in Iran, converted to Shiʿism after being involved in a scandal and took *bast* at Shah ʿAbd-al-ʿAẓīm in 1857 (see Ch. Adle, *Studia Iranica* 12, 1983, p. 257).

In Afghanistan, religious *bast* was practiced until the Communist revolution. Places such as the sanctuary of Mazār-e Šarīf, and the tombs of Sultan Maḥmūd and of the poet Sanā'ī at Ḡaznī were reckoned as *basts*. But the most celebrated *basts* were located at Qandahār and Herat (Farhādī).

At Qandahār, the Masjed-e Ḵerqa contains a fragment of a cloak attributed to the Prophet Moḥammad. This was brought from central Asia by Aḥmad Shah Dorrānī, whose tomb lies nearby. In September, 1881, Amir 'Abd-al-Raḥmān ordered that 'Abd-al-Raḥīm Āḵūnd Kākar—who had, together with other mullahs, proclaimed a *takfīr-nāma* against him—be "pulled out" of that sanctuary. He then killed him with his own hands (Munshi Sultan Mahomed Khan, ed., *The Life of Abdur Rahman Amir of Afghanistan*, London, 1900, I, p. 216). In December, 1959, there was a large-scale protest against the unveiling of women encouraged by Dā'ūd's government. Obvious manifestations of modernization (a local cinema, a girl's school, government buildings) were attacked. Ṣeddīq Wazīrī, governor of Qandahār, was replaced by General Khan Moḥammad Khan, who used force to soothe the revolt (Reštīya). According to the official version, landowners and *arbābs* wanted to take *bast* in the Masjed-e Ḵerqa for their usual protest against taxation. Riots were said to have resulted from the government's refusal to acknowledge *bast* (this official version is followed by L. Dupree, *Afghanistan*, Princeton, 1973, pp. 536f.). Near Herat, *bast* was traditionally provided at the sanctuary of Ḵ̌āja 'Abd-Allāh Anṣārī (q.v.) located at Gāzargāh (on the shrine, see F. Saljūqī, *Gāzargāh*, Kabul, 1962 and 1976, and *Āryānā* (special issue), 1355 Š./1976; Golombek, *The Timurid Shrine at Gazar Gah*, Toronto, 1969). During the civil war of 1929, various places were used as *bast* in Sunni-Shi'ite conflicts at Herat (Gāzargāh, Mūy-e Mobārak, Ḵerqa-ye Šarīf; Farhādī).

Bibliography: Official sources provide scant information on *bast*; we must rely mainly on observations made by foreign residents and travelers. H. Algar, *Religion and State in Iran 1785-1906*, Berkeley and Los Angeles, 1969. E. G. Browne, *The Persian Revolution 1905-1909*, London, 1910, repr. London, 1966. Idem, tr., *The Tarikh-i jadid or New History of Mirza Ali Muhammad the Bab*, Cambridge, 1893. J. Chardin, *Voyages du Chevalier Chardin en Perse et autres lieux de l'Orient*, ed. Langlès, Paris, 1811, VII, pp. 368ff. G. N. Curzon, *Persia and the Persian Question*, London, 1892, repr. 1966. R. Farhādī, personal communication, 1984. G. G. Gilbar, "The Big Merchants (*tujjār*) and the Persian Constitutional Revolution of 1906," *Asian and African Studies* 11, 1977, pp. 275-303. A. K. S. Lambton, "Social Change in Persia in the Nineteenth Century," ibid., 15, 1981, pp. 123-48. M. Malekzāda, *Tārīḵ-e enqelāb-e mašrūṭīyat-e Īrān*, Tehran, 7 vols. J. Malcolm, *The History of Persia*, London, 1815. H. Massé, *Croyances et coutumes persanes*, Paris, 1938, II, pp. 404-07. H. Pakdaman, *Djamal-ed-din Assad Abadi dit Afghani*, Paris, 1969. S. Q. Reštīya, personal communication, 1984, R. M. Savory, "Bast," in *EI*². D. Wright, *The English amongst the Persians*, London, 1977. [Idem, *The Persians among the English*, London, 1985, pp. 185-204. See Addenda.]

(J. Calmard)

BASṬĀM, BASṬĀMĪ. See BESṬĀM, BESṬĀMĪ.

BASTANEGĀR, a *gūša* in the instrumental repertory (*radīf*) of classical Persian music. The term appears for the first time in the treatise of Ṣafī-al-Dīn Ormavī where it is defined as one of the *maqāms* more commonly known as Eṣfahānak or Gavāšt/Gavešt (Wright, p. 62-63). Its scale was: G Ap Sip C̱ *Dp E*b *E*p (182, 204, 112, 139, 128, 49 cents; p = *koron* on half flat), C̱ being the finalis.

In 'Abd-al-Qāder Marāḡī b. Ḡaybī's *Maqāṣed-al-alḥān* (p. 75), as well as in later writings, Bastanegār is one of the eighteen *jomūʿ* and twenty-four *šoʿbas*, and a variant of Rū-ye-ʿErāq. In the *Bahjat al-rūḥ* (p. 55) it is described this way: "start with the first note of Māya (probably *E*p), then go to Segāh and Nahoft and return to Māya." *Borhān-e qāṭeʿ* calls it a combination of Ḥeṣār, Ḥejāz, and Segāh (ed. Moʿīn, I, p. 279). Later, in the Turkish-Arabic tradition, its name is attached to a typical scale: (*B*p *C*) *D E F G*b *A B*b *C*. It is still found in the Azerbaijani *maqām* as an important modulation of Čahārgāh on a different scale *C D*b *E F G*b *A* centered on *E* and ending on *C*. These forms have very little in common.

In its actual Persian form, Bastanegār has been reduced to a secondary and small *gūša* with the character of a melodic pattern moving up and down, rather than of a mode. It is played in two forms: a slow one in a non-measured rhythm (also called *naḡma*), and a faster in 3/16. According to the principal versions of the *radīf*, the first form is found in the context of Afšārī and Bayāt-e Tork, the second, more common, in Zābol and Moḵālef (both belonging to Čahārgāh and Segāh), Kord, Ḥejāz, Afšārī, ʿErāq (M. Maʿrūfī, *Radīf-e haft dastgāh-e mūsīqī-e īrānī/Les systèmes de la musique traditionelle de l'Iran (radif)*, Tehran, 1973; oral transmission of ʿA. A. Šahnāzī and Mīrzā ʿAbd-Allāh).

Bibliography: ʿAbd-al-Qāder Marāḡī b. Ḡaybī's *Maqāṣed al-alḥān*, ed. T. Bīneš, Tehran, 2536 = 1356 Š./1977. *Bahjat al-rūḥ* (an apochryph of ʿAbd-al-Mo'men b. Ṣafī-al-Dīn), ed. H. L. Rabino de Borgomale, Tehran, 1346 Š./1967. Šīrvānī al-Mo'men, *Resāla fīʿelm al-mūsīqī*, tr. d'Erlanger, *Traité anonyme dédié au Sultan Osmânli Muhammad II (XVe s.)*, La musique arabe 4, Paris, 1939. O. Wright, *The Modal System of Arab and Persian Music, A.D. 1250-1300*, London, 1978.

(J. During)

BASTŪR (Mid. Pers. Bastwar, Av. Bastauuairi), a hero of the Iranian national epic, son of Zarēr, King Goštāsp's brother. In the Avesta Bastauuairi is mentioned once (*Yt.* 13.103) when his *fravaši* is praised together with that of the other members of Goštāsp's house, who were the first followers of Zoroaster. In the great religious battle between Goštāsp and the Turanian king Arjāsp, Zarēr was commander-in-chief of the Iranian army (*Ayādgār ī Zarērān* in *Pahlavi Texts*, pp. 2-14, pars. 14, 17, 48, 55, 64, etc.; *Šāh-nāma*, Moscow, VI, p. 96 v. 444), while the command of the rear guard was entrusted to Bastūr (ibid., v. 451); but, according to Ṯaʿālebī (*Ḡorar*, p. 270), he was in charge of the left wing. After Zarēr perished at the hand of Bīdarafš (Pahl. Widrafš), Arjāsp's brother, Bastūr volunteered to avenge his father. Goštāsp first refused Bastūr's demand because of his infancy (*Ayādgār ī Zarērān*, pars. 79-81, cf. *Šāh-nāma*, p. 111 v. 667, *Ḡorar*, p. 274), but later, at the recommendation of Jāmāsp, the king's minister, gave his consent (*Ayādgār ī Zarērān*, par. 90; *Šah-nāma*, vv. 697ff.; *Ḡorar*, p. 274). According to the *Ayādgār ī Zarērān* (par. 105) and Ṯaʿālebī (*Ḡorar*, p. 275) Bastūr fought with Bīdarafš and killed him during a terrible battle, whereas in the *Šāh-nāma* Bīdarafš was killed by Esfandīār, Goštāsp's eldest son (*Šāh-nāma*, p. 115, v. 726), though Bastūr fought with Bīdarafš (*Šāh-nāma*, p. 114, v. 717). Bastūr took part also in Goštāsp's second battle with Arjāsp (*Šah-nāma*, pp. 143 v. 123, 159 v. 395). Etymologically the name probably means "with fastened breast guard" (M. Mayrhofer, *Iranisches Personennamenbuch* I/1, Vienna, 1977, p. 31). The Persian form Bastūr is often corrupted into Nastūr in Arabic and Persian manuscripts (Ṭabarī, I, 2, p. 677; *Šāh-nāma*).

Bibliography: See also A. Christensen, *Les Kayanides*, Copenhagen, 1931, p. 24. Justi, *Namenbuch*, p. 65. Markwart, *Provincial Capitals*, Rome, 1931, pp. 49-50.

(A. TAFAŻŻOLĪ)

BĀṬĀS, a village in Iraq on the Arbīl-Ravāndūz highway, center of the Ḥarīr subdistrict (*nāḥīa*) of Arbīl province. To the northeast of the village a rock relief, no longer in good preservation, stands on the cliff wall of the long valley some 80 m above the floor. It was discovered in 1899 by C. F. Lehmann-Haupt (see his *Armenien einst und jetzt* II/1, Berlin, 1926, pp. 278-81).

Set in a rectangular recess, the relief depicts a man in a posture of prayer (Figure 29). He has short hair and is wearing a pointed tiara with a headband or diadem. His clothes are a pleated robe, tucked up by means of a strap suspended between the legs, and an overcoat going down in pleats to the knees. Also more or less discernible are a belt, a scabbard, and shoes. The right hand is raised in prayer; the now vanished left hand held a long staff which rests on the ground and was once capped with a device of four superimposed balls. It is uncertain whether anything was carved in the rock above the right hand. Most probably this space was left blank; it was certainly not filled (as some have supposed, e.g. Lehmann-Haupt, op. cit., p. 281) with Hittite or Urartian hieroglyphs. (For detailed description of the relief and full bibliography, see R. M. Boehmer and H. von Gall, *Baghdader Mitteilungen* 6, 1973, pp. 65ff.).

There are good grounds for the opinion that the relief depicts Izates II, the king of Adiabene (ca. 36-62 A.D.), who was converted to Judaism. He is likely to have ordered the carving after the unexpected retreat of the Parthian king of kings, Vologases I (see BALĀŠ), who had marched against him but had been forced to abandon the campaign when nomadic Dahi and Sacae invaded the northeast of the Parthian empire.

Figure 29. Relief at Bāṭās, Iraq (drawing by H. von Gall)

Below the relief and close to the highway are some visible remains of stone walls. In addition to Parthian potsherds of the 1st/2nd century A.D., Islamic potsherds of the 13th/14th century have been found near the surface in this area. Approximately 1 km from Bāṭās a mound called Tell Tlai rises from the valley plain. Lehmann-Haupt took it to be "an Assyrian outpost" (*Mitteilungen der Vorderasiatisch-Aegyptischen Gesellschaft* 21, 1916, [1917], p. 124), and a superficial probe yielded potsherds of the Early Babylonian, Late Assyrian, Hellenistic-Parthian, and Islamic periods, including the 13th/14th century (see E. M. Boehmer, *Sumer* 30, 1974, pp. 101ff.).

Bibliography: Given in the text.

(R. M. BOEHMER)

BĀṬEN (inner, hidden), the opposite of *ẓāher* (outer, visible). Both can be predicated of living beings; in the Koran (57:3) God is *al-ẓāher wa'l-bāṭen*. Most frequently, however, *bāṭen* or *ẓāher* is associated with the concept *ʿelm* (knowledge). There are two ways in which knowledge can be hidden: (1) If it is not within everybody's reach and (2) if it relates to aspects of things beyond the reach of the senses. This distinction was explained by Ebn Taymīya (d. 728/1328) in his *Resāla fī ʿelm al-bāṭen wa'l-ẓāher* (p. 230.13-15) as follows: "ʿ*Elm al-bāṭen* can sometimes be knowledge of inner things, such as knowledge of intuitions and moods existing in the heart, and it can also be knowledge of extrasensory things of which prophets were apprised. On the other hand, *'elm al-bāṭen* can mean knowledge which is hidden from most people's understanding (*yabṭon 'an fahm akṯar al-nās*)." Both senses of the concepts *bāṭen* and *'elm al-bāṭen* gained currency, mainly in Shi'ite and Sufi circles.

Shi'ite ideas. The belief that things have an imperceptible inner nature (*bāṭen*) and that knowledge of this (*'elm al-bāṭen*) is a higher form of knowledge first arose among the Shi'ite radicals (*ḡolāt*, sing. *ḡālī*) at Kūfa in the 2nd/8th century. The Kaysānīya and Ḥarbīya sects held that God's *bāṭen* (or *ma'nā* "meaning") is eternal and that his *ẓāher* has been manifested in 'Alī, Moḥammad, and their descendants. Others, citing Koran 57:3, described God's *ẓāher* as the human body in which the *bāṭen*, i.e., the holy spirit (*rūḥ al-qodos*), is incarnated. *Bāṭen* and *ẓāher* were predicated not only of God but also of humans and the creation around them. Some of the *ḡolāt* distinguished between the *ẓāher* in humans, which is terrestrial, and the *bāṭen* in humans, which is eternal (*azalī*). The eternal part of a human was often called *al-joz' al-elāhī*, which may perhaps be rendered as "the divine spark."

Among the various beliefs of the *ḡolāt*, the one which acquired most notoriety and longest-lasting influence was their doctrine of the inner and outer meaning of the Koran and the Islamic law (*Šarī'a*). The appellation Bāṭenīya given to later offshoots of the *ḡolāt* such as the Isma'ilis referred to this doctrine. As metaphors for the *ẓāher* and *bāṭen* of the Koran and the *Šarī'a*, the words *qešr* (shell) and *lobb* (kernel) were used. According to the doctrine, humans can have knowledge of the inner as well as the outer meaning of God's book and law. Shi'ites of the various schools which arose (*ḡolāt*, Qarmatians, Isma'ilis, the Ekẖwān-al-Ṣafā) all believed the imam to be endowed, through divine afflatus (*elhām*), with knowledge of the *bāṭen* and consequent ability to explain the inner, true meaning of the Koran and the law through allegorical interpretation (*ta'wīl*). One of the first to treat Koranic themes as allegories was the Kufan *ḡālī* Moḡīra b. Sa'īd (put to death 119/737). Furthermore, the imam was believed to possess extrasensory knowledge of inner natures and future events (*ḡayb*). Believers loyal to the imam would gain salvation through the *'elm al-bāṭen* which he would impart to them, and possession of this knowledge of the inner truth would confer exemption from duty to obey the law and cause the soul to rise to the level of the angels. These beliefs were voiced mainly by *ḡolāt* and are likely to have been influenced by gnostic legacies from late antiquity.

Among the critics of the Shi'ite doctrine of *al-bāṭen* and *'elm al-bāṭen*, Ebn Ḥazm, Ḡazālī, the Zaydite Moḥammad Daylamī, and the Hanbalites Ebn al-Jawzī and Ebn Taymīya deserve mention. Ebn Ḥazm viewed *ta'wīl* as a dangerous threat to the understanding of clear texts. For Ḡazālī the greatest danger in the doctrine of knowledge not accessible to all was the resulting blind acceptance (*taqlīd*) of the authority of the imam. For Ebn al-Jawzī and Ebn Taymīya *'elm al-bāṭen* was an inadmissible innovation; like all Hanbalites, they believed that God has given his last word to humans by transmitting through the Koran and the Sunna all that He wished them to learn, and that this final revelation is intelligible to anybody without special knowledge.

Sufi ideas. While the ideas of the *ḡolāt* and other Shi'ites first emerged at Kūfa, the source of Sufi thinking about *al-bāṭen* and *'elm al-bāṭen* can be traced to Basra. The *bāṭen*, as understood by the early Basran mystics, is man's inner self, the complex of emotions which stir his soul (cf. Ebn Taymīya's definitions). Study of the human soul and inner self was pursued in Ḥasan Baṣrī's circle, particularly by his mystic pupils. A major role in this development appears to have been played by his pupil 'Abd-al-Wāḥed b. Zayd. The basis for *'elm al-bāṭen*, as thus defined, was found in a *ḥadīṯ qodsī* (saying of God Himself). This *ḥadīṯ* was said to have been transmitted by 'Abd-al-Wāḥed b. Zayd to his pupils Aḥmad Hojaymī and Aḥmad b. Ḡassān and to have been made known to him by Ḥasan Baṣrī, who had heard it from Ḥoḏayfa b. al-Yamān (one of the Prophet's companions), who had heard it from Moḥammad, who had heard it from God. Basran *'elm al-bāṭen* consists of knowledge of ways to train the soul and is a psychic discipline attainable by anybody through his own mental effort—not, like Kufan *'elm al-bāṭen*, a body of knowledge conferred by afflatus on a chosen individual. The mystic *'elm al-bāṭen* is expounded in fully developed form in the writings of Ḥāreṯ Moḥāsebī (3rd/9th century). In the east, Ḥakīm Termeḏī (d. ca. 300/910) built this concept of *'elm al-bāṭen* into his theosophical system. Heresiographers such as Ka'bī branded the Sufis of the 3rd/9th century simply as *aṣḥāb al-bāṭen*. In the Sufi manuals written in the 4th/10th century by Kalābāḏī, Sarrāj, and Abū Ṭāleb Makkī, *'elm al-bāṭen* is an essential component of the orthodox Sufism which these authors propound. In addition to the concept of *'elm al-bāṭen* as knowledge of means to train the soul, a second concept now entered Sufi thinking, namely the interpretability of the Koran and the Sunna from within. It was held that understanding of the inner self enables the mystic to understand the inner meaning of God's book and law. This method of interpretation from within was often described as *estenbāṭ* (inference). The biggest collection of such exegesis from the early medieval period is the *Ḥaqā'eq al-tafsīr* of Solamī (d. 412/1021).

From the 4th/10th century onward, a different tendency, already discernible among some of the earlier Sufis, becomes more and more prominent. *'Elm al-bāṭen* is no longer held to be attainable through human effort but is assumed (as by the Shi'ites) to be God-given knowledge. For example, the unknown author of *Adab al-molūk* (late 4th/10th century) describes *'elm al-bāṭen* as knowledge conferred on Sufis through divine afflatus. Ḡazālī in his *Eḥyā' 'olūm al-dīn* distinguishes two categories of *'elm al-bāṭen*: *'elm taṣqīl al-qalb* (knowledge of ways to polish the heart), which is a pedagogic discipline, and *'elm al-mokāšafa*, which is God-given illumination of the heart. Ebn al-'Arabī draws a similar distinction. The two meanings were not always clearly differentiated, with the result that misunderstandings and misrepresentations could arise, mainly in works by writers unsympathetic to Sufism.

The most serious criticism, voiced above all by the Hanbalites Ebn al-Jawzī and Ebn Taymīya, concerned the claim of many Sufis to possession of an *ʿelm al-bāṭen* of the second category, which in the view of the critics meant possession of a "private revelation."

See also BĀṬENĪYA; ISMAʿILISM; MAZDAKISM; ẒĀHER; ZAND; and ZENDĪQ.

Bibliography: Shiʿites, sources: Ašʿarī, *Maqālāt*, ed. Ritter, pp. 6-9. M. Daylamī, *Bayān madhab al-bāṭenīya wa-boṭlāneh manqūl men ketāb Qawāʿed ʿaqāʾed āl Moḥammad*, ed. R. Strothmann, Istanbul, 1939, pp. 4, 7-10, 16, 21, 30, 36f., 39, 44, 48f., 61-63, 80. Ebn Ḥazm, *Feṣal*, tr. I. Friedlander, "The Heterodoxies of the Shiites in the Presentation of Ibn Ḥazm," *JAOS* 28-29, 1907-08, see index s.v. *Bâṭinijja*. ʿAbd-al-Raḥmān Ebn al-Jawzī, *Talbīs Eblīs*, Cairo, 1928, pp. 102ff. A. Ebn Taymīya, *Resāla fī ʿelm al-bāṭen wa'l-ẓāher*, in *Majmūʿat al-rasāʾel al-monīrīya* I, Beirut, 1970, pp. 229-52. Ekwān al-Ṣafāʾ, *Rasāʾel*, 4 vols., Beirut, 1957, III, pp. 486, 488, 511. *Feraq al-šīʿa*, ed. Ritter, pp. 63, 82. M. Ḡazālī, *al-Monqed men al-żalāl*, ed. F. Jabre, Beirut, 1969, pp. 28ff. Idem, *Fażāʾeḥ al-bāṭenīya*, ed. ʿA. Badawī, Cairo, 1964, pp. 11ff. Abu'l-Ḥosayn ʿAbd-al-Raḥīm Kayyāṭ, *Ketāb al-enteṣār*, ed. H. S. Nyberg, Cairo, 1927, p. 136. *Ketāb al-haft wa'l-aẓella*, ed. A. Tamer and I. A. Khalifé, Beirut, 1970, pp. 29, 31, 61f., 87-89, 94f., 98, 100f., 107, 135, 191f., 194. M. Mofīd, *Awāʾel al-maqālāt*, Tabrīz, 1371/1951-52, pp. 37-41. Jaʿfar b. Ḥarb Nāšeʾ, *Oṣūl al-neḥal*, ed. J. van Ess, *Frühe muʿtazilitische Häresiographie. Zwei Werke des Nāšiʾ al-Akbar (gest. 293 H.)*, Beirut, 1971, p. 41. *Omm al-ketāb*, ed. W. Ivanow, "Ummu'l-kitāb," *Der Islam* 23, 1936, pp. 1-132, par. 106. S. Qomī, *Ketāb al-maqālāt wa'l feraq*, ed. J. Maškūr, Tehran, 1963, pp. 55f., 60, 62f. M. Šahrestānī, *Melal*, 2 vols., Beirut, 1975, I, pp. 147, 149-51, 189, 192. R. Strothmann, *Esoterische Sonderthemen bei den Nusairi*, Berlin, 1958, pars. 198, 248, 260, 263-64, 266, 269, 299-301.

Shiʿites, literature: R. Arnaldez, *Grammaire et théologie chez Ibn Ḥazm de Cordoue*, Paris, 1981, pp. 65f. J. van Ess, *Die Erkenntnislehre des ʿAḍud-addīn al-Īcī*, Wiesbaden, 1966, pp. 278ff. R. Freitag, *Seelenwanderung in der islamischen Häresie*, Berlin, 1985, see index of terms s.v. *bāṭin*. I. Goldziher, *Streitschrift des Gazālī gegen die Bāṭinijja-Sekte*, Leiden, 1916. Idem, *Die Ẓâhiriten*, Hildesheim, 1967. H. Halm, "Das 'Buch der Schatten.' Die Mufaḍḍal-Tradition der Ġulāt und die Ursprünge des Nuṣairiertums," *Der Islam* 55, 1978, pp. 219-66. Idem, *Die islamische Gnosis. Die extreme Schia und die ʿAlawiten*, Zurich and Munich, 1982, see index of terms s.vv. bāṭin, geheim. Idem, *Kosmologie und Heilslehre der frühen Ismāʿīlīya*, Wiesbaden, 1978, see index of terms s.vv. bāṭin, ʿilm al-bāṭin.

Sufism, sources: *Adab al-molūk*, ed. B. Radtke, Beirut, 1988, pp. 34-36. Ebn al-Jawzī, *Talbīs Eblīs*, pp. 321ff. Ebn Taymīya, *Resāla*, pp. 229-52. M. Ḡazālī, *Eḥyāʾ ʿolūm al-dīn* I, *bāb* 2. M. Kalābādī, *al-Taʿarrof le-madhab ahl al-taṣawwof*, Cairo, 1969, pp. 105f. Abū Ṭāleb Makkī, *Qūt al-qolūb*, 4 vols., Cairo, 1932, II, pp. 22-24, 40. Ḥ. Moḥāsebī, *al-Reʿāya le-ḥoqūq Allāh*, ed. M. Smith, GMS, N.S. 15, London, 1940. Abū Naṣr Sarrāj, *al-Lomaʿ fi'l-taṣawwof*, ed. R. A. Nicholson, GMS 22, Leiden and London, 1914, pp. 23f. Abū Ḥafṣ ʿOmar Sohravardī, *ʿAwāref al-maʿāref*, tr. R. Gramlich, *Die Gaben der Erkenntnisse des ʿUmar as-Suhrawardi. ʿAwārif al-maʿārif*, Freiburger Islamstudien 6, Wiesbaden, 1978, pp. 26ff. M. Solamī, *Ḥaqāʾeq al-tafsīr*, see Sezgin, *GAS* I, pp. 671-72. Ḥakīm Termedī, *Daqāʾeq al-ʿolūm*, ms. Ismail Saib I, Ankara, no. 1571, fols. 10bff.

Sufism, literature: A. Affifi, *The Mystical Philosophy of Muhyid Din-Ibnul Arabi*, Cambridge, 1937, pp. 105ff. J. van Ess, *Die Gedankenwelt des Ḥāriṯ al-Muḥāsibī*, Bonn, 1961. F. Meier, "Ein wichtiger Handschriftenfund zur Sufik," *Oriens* 20, 1967, pp. 60-106. B. Radtke, *Al-Ḥakīm al-Tirmiḏī*, Freiburg, 1980, see index s.v. *ʿilm al-bāṭin*. Idem, "Theologen und Mystiker in Ḫurāsān und Transoxanien," *ZDMG* 136, 1986, pp. 536-69 (esp. pp. 551ff.). H. Ritter, "Studien zur Geschichte der islamischen Frömmigkeit I. Ḥasan al-Baṣrī," *Der Islam* 21, 1933, pp. 1-83. K. M. al-Šaybī, *al-Ṣela bayn al-taṣawwof wa'l-tašayyoʿ*, Cairo, 1969 (only to be used as a collection of material).

(B. RADTKE)

BĀṬENĪYA, a generic term for all groups and sects which distinguished the *bāṭen* and the *ẓāher* of the Koran and the Islamic law (*Šarīʿa*). The Arabic word *bāṭen* (inner, hidden, q.v.) was used to denote non-literal meanings of Koranic verses and Islamic legal commands and prohibitions, its opposite, the Arabic word *ẓāher* (outer, visible), to denote literal or obvious meanings presented by the wording of the texts or the implementation of the laws. This distinction was fundamental to the thinking of a number of mainly Shiʿite sects, whose origins are traceable to 2nd/8th century Iraq. Christian, Jewish, and Gnostic influences on their thinking cannot be ruled out but are hard to prove in particular cases.

The first Islamic sect which professed to find allusions to the imamate of ʿAlī b. Abī Ṭāleb and his descendants in certain verses of the Koran was the Kaysānīya (q.v.), who expected ʿAlī's third son Moḥammad b. al-Ḥanafīya (d. 81/100) to come forth as the Mahdī. In particular, one branch of this sect, under the leadership of Moḥammad b. Ḥarb at Madāʾen, based its teachings on this type of Koranic exegesis (e.g., 95:1; see Qomī, p. 30). During the 2nd/8th century the Shiʿite radicals (*ḡolāt*, sing. *ḡālī*) in Iraq switched their allegiance to the imams of the line of Ḥosayn, the second son of ʿAlī, and they credited these imams with ability to impart secret knowledge, holding that the Prophet Moḥammad only transmitted the outer (*ẓāher*) wording of the divine revelation (*tanzīl*), whereas ʿAlī as his heir and executor (*waṣī*) possessed knowledge of its inner (*bāṭen*) meaning. It was also believed that ʿAlī's successors, i.e., the imams, kept possession of the knowledge of the *bāṭen* and that they entrusted the interpretation (*taʾwīl*) of the outer working to only a small number of initiates. The word pair *tanzīl taʾwīl* was first used in this sense by the Kufan *ḡālī* Abū Manṣūr ʿEjlī, who claimed to be the plenipotentiary of the fifth imam, Moḥammad al-Bāqer (d. 114/732 or 117/735; Nawbaḵtī, pp. 34f.; Qomī, pp. 46f.).

Two literary sources, both originally written at Kūfa, show how the Kufan *ḡolāt* identified their own secret doctrines with what they took to be inner meanings of the Koran. One is the *Omm al-ketāb*, preserved only in a Persian translation. The other is the *Ketāb al-haft wa'l-aẓella*, written probably by Moḥammad b. Senān, a Kufan *ḡālī* contemporary with the imams ʿAlī al-Reżā (d. 203/818) and Moḥammad al-Jawād (d. 220/835). In these texts the interpretation (*taʾwīl*) or unveiling (*kašf*) of the *bāṭen* is not an achievement of scholarly effort and human exegesis but a divine disclosure made known by the imams to a small number of initiates. Both texts therefore belong to the genre of apocalyptic literature. In the *Omm al-ketāb* the imam Moḥammad al-Bāqer tells secrets of the *bāṭen* to a select group of pupils; in the *Haft wa'l-aẓella* the imam Jaʿfar al-Ṣādeq initiates his confidant Mofażżal Joʿfī into hidden meanings.

For the Kufan *ḡolāt*, perception of the *bāṭen* usually implied complete neglect of the *ẓāher*. The outer commands and prohibitions of the *Šarīʿa* had no importance for a person acquainted with their inner meanings. Such a person therefore ceased to be bound by them and became exempt from all the ritual and legal obligations of the religion. Antinomianism (*ebāḥa*) of this type was expressed in a widely repeated saying that Koranic commands and prohibitions are really "men who must be followed or avoided" (e.g. Qomī, p. 47), i.e., that they are only allusions to imams and enemies of imams, their literal meanings being unimportant. This argument entered into the teachings of the Kufan *ḡālī* Abu'l-Ḵaṭṭāb (put to death ca. 138/755), who based it on the Koranic verse (4:28): "God wishes to make (burdens) lighter for you" (Qomī, p. 52). The Ḵaṭṭābīya described Moḥammad, the bringer of the *ẓāher*, as "speaking" (*nāṭeq*) and ʿAlī, the keeper of the *bāṭen*, as "silent" (*ṣāmet*; Qomī, pp. 50-52; for examples of Ḵaṭṭābīya *taʾwīl*, see pp. 54f.).

The *ḡolāt* sects in Iraq encountered strong opposition from the Twelver Shiʿites and at the end of the 3rd/9th century split into two groups: the Esḥāqī (named after Esḥāq al-Aḥmar, d. 286/899 at Baghdad) and the Noṣayrī (named after Moḥammad b. Noṣayr). The latter still survives. The sect's teachings were carried by wandering shaikhs to the coastal mountains of Syria, where its adherents today call themselves ʿAlawīs (q.v.). They are the only remaining heirs to the centuries-old legacy of the Kufan *ḡolāt*. It is by them that the *Ketāb al-haft wa'l-aẓella* has been handed down. As initiates acquainted with the *bāṭen*, they consider themselves exempt from all ritual obligations and therefore refrain from formal prayers, pilgrimage to Mecca, fasting in Ramażān, etc. (see Halm, 1982, pp. 315ff.).

Beside, but apart from, the extreme Bāṭenīs of the *ḡolāt* sects, who believed the *ẓāher* to be invalidated by the *bāṭen*, stood the moderate Bāṭenīs of the Ismaʿili sects, whose missionary activity (*daʿwa*) began in Iraq in the middle years of the 3rd/9th century. The distinction between *ẓāher* and *bāṭen* was likewise central to Ismaʿili doctrine, according to which six "speakers" (*nāṭeq*) in the course of human history successively brought a *Šarīʿa* (i.e., a combined system of religion and law). The six were Adam, Noah, Abraham, Moses, Jesus, and Moḥammad. Assigned to each of these was an "heir-executor" (*waṣī*; also termed *asās* "foundation"), respectively Abel (or Seth), Shem, Ishmael, Aaron (or Joshua), Simon Peter, and ʿAlī. Only a small circle of initiates knew the secret of the *bāṭen*—which was identical with the Ismaʿili doctrine of the Mahdī and his coming (*qīāma*)—and the few knowers were bound by their initiatory oath (*mīṯāq*) to keep the *bāṭen* secret and to adhere strictly to the *ẓāher*, i.e., to the commands and prohibitions of the *Šarīʿa*. Believers would not be exempted from this obligation (*taklīf*) until the last day (*yawm al-qīāma*), when the Mahdī would come forth, order abolition (*rafʿ*) of the *Šarīʿa*, and reinstate the original religion of Adam, namely pure monotheism (*tawḥīd*) without laws, commands, and prohibitions.

The earliest Ismaʿili literature consists mainly of *taʾwīl* works in which justification is found in verses of the Koran for every detail of Ismaʿili doctrine: e.g., the *Ketāb al-rošd wa'l-hedāya*, ascribed to the missionary (*dāʿī*) Ebn Hawšab Manṣūr al-Yaman (d. 302/915), or the *Ketāb al-kašf*, a collection of six tracts from the first phase of the Esmaʿili *daʿwa* said to have been compiled by Jaʿfar b. Manṣūr Yaman. Inner meanings of sets of words or chapters of the Koran and prescribed rituals are expounded in numerous Ismaʿili monographs bearing titles such as *Taʾwīl ḥorūf al-moʿjam*, *Taʾwīl al-basmala*, *Taʾwīl Sūrat al-nesā*, *Taʾwīl al-ṣalāt wa'l-ṣawm*, *Taʾwīl al-zakāt* (Poonawala, pp. 73, 144, 317, 331). Nevertheless the "outer" *Šarīʿa* was always binding on Ismaʿilis. For them, *ẓāher* and *bāṭen* were inseparable, as shown for example in the two chief works of the Fatimid jurist Qāżī Noʿmān (d. 363/974), namely his great compendium of law *Daʿāʾem al-Eslām* (ed. A. A. Fyzee, 2nd ed., Cairo, 1963-67), which is the foundation of Ismaʿili jurisprudence, and the subsequent *Taʾwīl al-Daʿāʾem* (ed. Moḥammad Aʿẓamī, Cairo, 1968-72). In Egypt the Fatimid caliphs, in their role as imams of the Ismaʿilis, always strictly applied the *Šarīʿa*. This is confirmed by their readiness to build mosques (al-Azhar, al-Ḥākem, and others) at Cairo and by their concern for the holy places at Mecca and Medina. They only allowed the *bāṭen* to be explained by a *dāʿī* to oath-bound initiates at weekly teaching sessions (*majāles al-ḥekma*; Maqrīzī, *Ḵeṭaṭ*, Būlāq, 1853, I, p. 391). Several written accounts of such sessions are known (Poonawala, index, p. 509, s.v. *majāles*). Only on rare occasions did the inherent antinomianism of the Isma'ili doctrine lead to heretical adjuration of the law, as in the disturbances of the Druzes at Cairo in 408-11/1017-21 during the Fatimid caliph al-Ḥākem's reign, or the proclamation of the *qīāma* at the fortress of Alamūt in 559/1164.

Polemics against the Bāṭenīs and their methods came not only from Sunnites such as Ḡazālī (d. 505/1111) but, above all, from Shi'ites such as the Ja'farī (Twelver) authors Nowbaḵtī and Qomī in their books on sects and the Zaydite author Moḥammad b. Ḥasan Daylamī (who wrote ca. 707/1308).

See also BĀṬEN; ISMA'ILISM.

Bibliography: Nawbaḵtī, *Feraq al-Šī'a* (*Die Sekten der Schi'a*), ed. H. Ritter, Istanbul, 1931. Sa'd b. 'Abd-Allāh Qommī (Qomī), *Ketāb al-maqālāt wa'l-feraq*, ed. J. Maškūr, Tehran 1342 Š./1963. *Omm al-ketāb*, ed. W. Ivanow, *Der Islam* 23, 1936, pp. 1-132; Italian tr. (*Ummu'l-kitāb*) by P. Filippani-Ronconi, Naples, 1966. *Ketāb al-haft wa'l-aẓella*, ed. M. Ḡāleb, Beirut, 1964; ed. 'Ā. Tāmer and I. A. Khalifé, Beirut, 1970. Ḥasan b. Faraj b. Ḥawšab Manṣūr al-Yaman, *Ketāb al-rošd wa'l-hedāya*, ed. Moḥammad Kāmel Ḥosayn, in *Collectanea of the Ismaili Society*, Cairo, 1948, pp. 185-213. Ja'far b. Manṣūr al-Yaman, *Ketāb al-kašf*, ed. R. Strothmann, London, 1952; ed. M. Ḡāleb, Beirut, 1404/1984. *Al-Majāles al-mostanṣerīya*, ed. Moḥammad Kāmel Ḥosayn, Cairo, n.d. Ḡazālī, *Fażā'eḥ al-Bāṭenīya* (*Streitschrift des Ġazālī gegen die Bāṭinijja-Sekte*), ed. and tr. I. Goldziher, Leiden, 1916. Moḥammad b. Ḥasan Daylamī, *Bayān maḏhab al-Bāṭenīya wa boṭlāneh* (*Die Geheimlehre der Batiniten*), excerpt from *Qawā'ed 'aqā'ed āl Moḥammad*, ed. R. Strothmann, Leipzig and Istanbul, 1939. H. Halm, "Das Buch der Schatten. Die Mufaḍḍal-Tradition der Ḡulāt und die Ursprünge des Nuṣairiertums," *Der Islam* 55, 1978, pp. 219-66; 58, 1981, pp. 15-86. Idem, *Die islamische Gnosis. Die extreme Schia und die 'Alawiten*, Zurich and Munich, 1982. Idem, *Kosmologie und Heilslehre der frühen Ismā'īlīya*, Wiesbaden, 1978. Moḥammad b. Mālek Ḥammādī Yamanī, *Kašf asrār al-Bāṭenīya*, ed. Moḥammad Zāhed Kawṯarī, 2nd ed., Cairo, 1375/1955. I. K. Poonawala, *Biobibliography of Ismā'īlī Literature*, Malibu, 1977.

(H. HALM)

BATHHOUSES (*ḥammām*, *garmāba*)

i. *General.*
ii. *The layout of rural bath structures.*

i. GENERAL

Pre-Islamic Iran. Bathhouses existed prior to the Islamic period in the Iranian cultural area. However, their number seems to have been limited due to the Zoroastrian religion's reverence for the holy element of water. This may explain why Yāqūt (I, p. 199; Spuler, p. 266), quoting the authority of an Arab physician, states that the Sasanians did not know the use of baths. Nevertheless, archeological finds in Ḵᵛārazm, for example, show the existence of cellars under houses, which were cooled by water basins in which the inhabitants may have bathed, though these cellars could be simple *sardābs* (Spuler, p. 286; Le Strange, p. 337). Other sources also confirm the existence of baths in pre-Islamic Iran. For example, King Vologeses (484-88) incurred the wrath of the Zoroastrian priests by building public baths, for in this way people would pollute the holy element, water. Kavād (488-531), after having enjoyed a bath in Amida after his conquest of that city, ordered the construction of such baths throughout his empire (Mez, p. 365). Finally, Ferdowsī relates that Ḵosrow II Parvēz (d. 628), prior to his assassination, took a bath (Boyce, p. 143). This evidence indicates that Yāqūt was probably only partly right.

Islamic Iran, medieval period. With the conversion of the population of Iran to Islam, ritual purity (*ṭahārat*, q.v.), e.g., through washing one's body (*ḡosl* and *wożū'*), became a requirement of religious life. Thenceforth bathing became an integral part of life. Besides, baths were frequented not only for purity and hygienic reasons, but also for medical purposes. Physicians prescribed taking the waters against a great variety of ailments (Spuler, p. 267).

We find therefore baths and hot springs mentioned frequently after the 3rd/9th century. Around 870 a local notable built a bathhouse in Eskejkat (Bukhara; Naršaḵī, p. 18). In the 10th century the use of hot springs is often mentioned for all kinds of physical ailments (Spuler, p. 266; Schwarz, VII, p. 869). A hot spring in Isfahan was believed to be only working during the month of Tīr (Schwarz, VII, p. 857). In Afrāsīāb near Samarkand the existence of a shower has been confirmed (*Bulletin of The Metropolitan Museum of Art* 37/4, 1942). Also baths are mentioned in Barḏa'a, hot springs in Tiflis, a famous sulfur spring in Ḥolwān (the present Sar-e pol-e Ḏohāb), and numerous baths in Borūjerd and near Ardabīl and Qazvīn (see ĀB-E GARM). Dowraq was also famous for its sulfur springs; while Arrajān was known for its soap manufacturing (Le Strange, pp. 177, 181, 191, 198, 242, 268). Sīrāf, on the Persian Gulf coast, also boasted a public bath (Whitehouse, pp. 78-80). Baths are also mentioned in the 5th/11th century in the Kermān area (Spuler, pp. 442, 501). Also in Ani, in Christian Armenia, many bathhouses existed at that time (Minorsky, p. 105).

Ḏemmīs had to wear distinctive signs (a necklace or *ṭawq*) made of iron, copper, or clay to identify themselves in a bathhouse to avoid a situation of uncleanliness for Muslims (Spuler, p. 294).

Number of baths. In the 3rd/9th century Baghdad boasted 5,000 baths, 100 years later 10,000, but it had only 2,000 baths in the 6th/12th century. However, these figures must be taken with a grain of salt (Mez, pp. 365-66). In the Safavid era cities like Isfahan boasted countless public bathhouses. Rich Persians and Europeans had, of course, their own private baths (Kaempfer, p. 155). Although some efforts have been made to list surviving historical monuments in various

Iranian cities in the absence of archeological research, we have no data on the number of bathhouses in the most important urban centers in Iran prior to the 19th century. We are better served for the latter period, although the data base is not always very reliable.

In 1890 there were 72 bathhouses in Isfahan, which were of different quality and cleanliness; this is possibly an estimate, because only 31 public baths have been identified as remaining historical monuments (Taḥwīldār, p. 40; Mehrābādī, pp. 405-08). However, around 1920 there were some 85 bathhouse keepers (*ḥammāmī*s; Janāb, *Ketāb al-Eṣfahān*, p. 78). The author of the *Neṣf-e Jahān* records that there were four classes of bathhouses in Isfahan, in descending order of quality and beauty (pp. 79f.). In Kermān there were 32 public baths (Goldsmid, *Eastern Persia* I, p. 191), but 51 bathhouses according to Wazīrī (p. 31) around 1870. The difference may be explained by the fact that Goldsmid only enumerated the most important ones, while Wazīrī counted them all. In Qazvīn there were 35 bathhouses in 1299/1880 (Golrīz, p. 404). Forṣat (pp. 504-06) enumerates at least 40 public baths in Shiraz around 1880, while Rabino reports of Kermānšāh in 1903 that "there are about 30 public baths, of which 5 or 6 are of a higher standard, but they are not made great use of by the working classes, who, not being of the Shiah persuasion, do not attach so great importance to bathing" (M 590, p. 6). In 1916 in Solṭānābād there were 30 public baths, two of which were new and had showers. One of the latter was reserved for Europeans (Wakīlī, p. 415). In Tehran the number of public baths (*ḥammām-e ʿomūmī*) grew from 146 in 1269/1852 to 182 in 1320/1902. Allowing for the growth of the city proper this meant that the number of baths per house grew from 1 per 148 houses to 1 per 89 houses between 1852 and 1902 (Etteḥādīya, pp. 204, 208). In 1925 there were not more than 151 public baths (*Second Yearbook*, p. 74), a situation that has worsened considerably in the present time in those parts of the city that do not have piped water and shower facilities (B. D. Clark and V. Costello, "The Urban System and Social Pattern in Iranian Cities," *Transactions of British Geographers* 59, 1973, p. 117).

Bathhouse staff. Personnel connected with bathhouses, referred to as *jamāʿat-e salmānīān* (the barbers' guild) in a firman by Shah ʿAbbās I (1038/1628) included the following: bathhouse keepers (*ḥammāmīān*); barbers (*salmānīān*); shavers (*dallākān*, also called *ḥallāq*), bath stokers (*tūntābān*), dyers of beards (*rangbandān*); wardrobe keepers (*jāmadārān*, also called *fūtadār*, Golčīn-e Maʿānī, p. 158), and bloodletters (*faṣṣādān*; Ḵākī, p. 48; Jazāʾerī, p. 107). Bath attendants who shaved heads (*sartarāšān*), masseurs (*āsījānān*), cuppers (*ḥajjāmān*), in addition to *ḥammāmī*s and *dallāks*, are mentioned in Timurid times (Roemer, p. 90). This shows no great change from the 10th century, when the following staff was mentioned: *ḥammāmī, qayyem* (robe keeper), *zabbāl* (dung man), *waqqād* (stoker), and *saqqā* (water carrier; Mez, p. 366). These occupations were considered to be of a low status. Nevertheless, the barber (*salmānī*) was one of the "blessed guildsmen" (*aṣnāfīān-e moqaddas*) among the *fotowwa* (q.v.) orders (Floor, p. 110). At the Safavid court, where the shah had his own private baths, there was a *ḵāṣṣatarāšbāšī* (chief of the court barbers), a *ḥammāmībāšī* (chief of the bath keepers; Āṣaf, p. 105). Kaempfer mentions the *salmānīḵāna* (barbers' department) among the *boyūtāt* (p. 125).

Social role of bathhouses. Bathhouses played an important role in social life. The bath was frequented for religious, hygienic, and medical reasons and for socializing and relaxation. It was also often a place for passing information and spreading rumors. Such was its place in society that the author of the *Qābūs-nāma* devoted one chapter of his book to the subject of good advice on proper behavior in a bath, as well as on its proper use (chap. 16). Similar sentiments are echoed in medical books such as the *Qānūnča* by Moḥammad Čaḡmīnī (pp. 75-77). A great many tales, proverbs, popular beliefs, and superstitions exist about the *ḥammām*, in which often the supernatural, especially *jenns*, play an important role (Šahrī, pp. 274f.; Taḥwīldār, pp. 20-21). Their use was universal and frequent, according to most observers. "The great amusement of the Persian women of every rank is the bath. Generally three or four hours in the week are passed by the very poorest in the hammam. The middle classes make parties to go to the hammam, and assist each other in the various processes of shampooing, washing with the keesa or rough glove, and washing the hair with pipe clay of Shiraz. As for the wealthier they have baths in their own houses, and use them almost daily. The public baths are open free of charge and without distinction to rich and poor. A few coppers are given to the delaks, or bath attendants, male or female. These pay for fuel, draw water, etc." (Wills, p. 334; see also Šahrī, pp. 274f. for social activities in the *ḥammām*). However, it would seem that the poor did not frequent the baths as regularly as Wills would have us believe. Apart from Rabino's observation, there is also the fact that they were unable to afford this expense on a daily basis.

Architecture and design. With few exceptions, there is neither any study of old existing public baths, nor archeological studies. Even the architectural aspect of the baths is missing from the readily available graphic descriptions of the baths by European travelers. Therefore, it is not yet possible to compare public baths in different parts of Iran or to analyze their technical and architectural development through the ages. We have a detailed study of a public bath (built before 441/1050) excavated in Sīrāf. However, it may be questioned whether its design, a rectangular building with maximum dimensions of 17 × 11.5 m, followed the classical example, as the archeological team seems to imply. One entered the Sīrāf bath through a rectangular room, probably the apodyterium. The bath also had a room with drains and a latrine in addition to an unheated frigidarium. On each side of the latter there are two rooms with a hypocaust under most of the floor, showing they were tepidaria. Finally, the bath had a caldarium, with a complete hypocaust heated by a furnace. Outside the building there was the stoking area and a small fuel store. Water for the *ḥammām* was drawn from an outside well or conduit. There does not exist any case study of later *ḥammāms*. There exist only some brief notes by Schroeder in Pope (p. 998) on a pre-Saljuq *ḥammām* in Negār (south of Kermān); further on a bath in Kāšān, of which Coste (plate 45) published a plan; and finally a plan of Ḥammām-e Šāh in Isfahan, dating from the time of Shah ʿAbbās I (r. 996-1038/1588-1629), in Gaube and Wirth (p. 158, fig. 52). [See also ii, below.] The following description of the physical outlay of a public bath, therefore, is based on graphic descriptions rather than on architectural or archeological data. Iconographic material, as represented by miniatures, also is rare. An example by an artist of the school of Behzād has been published by Gray (p. 117).

Layout of bathhouses and contemporary bathing practices. The bathhouse itself was below ground level in order to retain heat in winter or cold in summer. Its roof was even with the ground level. In Qara Qoyunlū Tabrīz an Italian traveler noted that each palace had its own bath, which was paneled with tiles in minute and beautiful designs (Contarini, p. 167; see also *Tārīḵ-e Yazd*, p. 40). Ebn Baṭṭūṭa gives a detailed description of *ḥammāms* in Baghdad, but he does not mention any decorations. He comments favorably, however, on the service given, for "I have never seen such an elaboration as all this in any city other than Baghdad" (*The Travels of Ebn Battutta*, tr. H. Gibb, [Cambridge 1962], pp. 329-30). The entrance of a bathhouse was often decorated, in the 13th/19th century frequently with scenes from the *Šāh-nāma*. This custom is probably of pre-Islamic origin, either Hellenistic (Mez, p. 366) or Iranian. It was a pre-Islamic Iranian custom to decorate the inside of houses and buildings (e.g., Naršaḵī, tr. Frye, pp. 27, 49; Ghirshman, p. 274).

A bathhouse consists, in general of at least three sections enclosed on all sides, lighted by small rectangles in the roof and/or by oil lamps. The atmosphere in the bath becomes progressively hotter and more humid as one proceeds toward the steam room (*garm-ḵāna*), where people experience intense perspiration. The first, or undressing, room, which is reached by a corridor (*rāhrow*), is called *sar(-e) ḥammām, raḵtkān, jāma-ḵāna*, or *sar-e bīna*. It generally is a large vaulted room (covered with tiles showing flowers, birds and other figures) with wooden benches, or benches of stone all around, which are covered with mats and carpets. It has a fountain in the middle while the walls are embellished with pictorial art, sometimes scenes from the *Šāh-nāma*. A client undresses in this room and puts on a loincloth (*long*) covering him from the waist to the knees; he takes tea, smokes, talks, and hears the news of the day. Each person takes his own linen and toilet articles. Well-to-do people take 2-3 servants to help them, as well as to guard their clothes, for sometimes clothes or shoes are stolen. Before entering the next room one is supposed to go to the toilet (*mostarāḥ, lawle'īn-ḵāna*), if need be. Hair of the genitals and anus are also removed so that unclean substances will not cling to them. To that end a depilatory (*nūra, zarnīḵ*, or *wājebī*), a mixture of quick-lime and orpiment, is used; it is a dangerous mixture, for "if you do not wash it away as the hair begins to fall, you are often burned in a most dreadful manner" (Waring, pp. 45f.). This procedure, called *kīsakašī*, is followed by soaping (*ṣābūnzanī*), after which the client takes a shower; in older times he took a plunge in the pool in the steam room.

On entering the second section one greets those present. This steam room (*garm-ḵāna*) is usually square or octagonal; the one Chardin visited was 6-8 feet in diameter. The floor is of marble or tiles and is steam-heated by means of covered flues. Traditionally there was a large water-filled basin (*ḵazīna*) resting on a large metal-topped stove (*tūn*) under which a fire slowly burned. (In the last few decades, due to official sanction against their use in public baths, *ḵazīnas* have been replaced by showers [*dūš*].) The fuel used was brushwood mixed primarily with dung cakes and some leaves. In the 17th century, according to Chardin, it was forbidden to use firewood due to scarcity of wood in Iran. But the main reason that it was not used was its high price. Moreover, with dung cakes the temperature could be kept more even. For the total ablution (*ḡosl*) it sufficed to immerse oneself a few times in this basin. This room is often pillared, the walls showing famous heroes from the *Šāh-nāma*.

Here a *dallāk* throws water on the hot tiles to wash the floor and to make steam. He then places a loincloth or towel on the floor, on which the client lies down, and makes a pillow with another towel on which he can put his head. First the client receives a massage (*moštmāl-e dāḵelī*). Then the *dallāk* dyes the hair of head and beard, after having washed it first. The hair is colored with *ḥennā* (q.v.) and left for one hour. After that the hair is washed with lukewarm water. Often the palms, soles, and nails are hennaed, while with pumice (*sang-e pā*) the soles and palms are smoothed. During the drying period head and beard are shaved (*sar-o rīš-tarāšī*); if desired nails are clipped. Women keep their hair; men after about 1850 kept two locks on both sides of their ears and one on top of their head (Polak, I, p. 359). Wearers of turbans shaved their heads entirely.

In the 11th/17th century, "soap [was] made of grease or tallow instead of oyl, and that [made] it to have a bad scent, and with the least sweating to breed lice in their linen" according to Thevenot (II, p. 88). Chardin confirms this (IV, p. 149), adding that the soap, made of fat and ashes, is soft, does not bleach well, and is expensive. "Therefore soap is imported from Turkey, especially from Aleppo, which has the best soap in the Orient, may be in the world."

The third section is the bath proper, called *qolletayn* in the 11th/17th century (Chardin, V, p. 197). About 10 persons could enter the *ḵazīna* at the same time and wash themselves at ease. In general, there were two baths, one hot bath and one cold bath (Francklin, pp. 70-72). Sometimes there was a third, lukewarm bath, which was especially favored by children. But if one is late, Chardin observes, "the water is covered with a thick fat cover of soap foam. It is disgusting but Iranians are accustomed to it. They just put it aside when they want to go under. It is easy to contract a contagious disease this way." The water for the *ḥammām*s was generally supplied by wells or conduits; in Isfahan all *ḥammām*s were supplied by wells (Eṣfahānī, p.80). The water in the baths was not always regularly refreshed, often not more than once or twice a year, because according to religious law water does not become unclean (*najes*) this way. Rose-scented earth (*gel-e gol*) was therefore commonly used in the baths to accommodate the customers (*Overseas Consultants* 2, p. 13). Public baths were therefore unclean and disease-ridden (Mostawfī, I, p. 168; Polak, I, p. 361). A local Tehrani wit is reported to have quipped that the water was daily refreshed by urine (Šahrī, p. 243). The very poor seized the opportunity to wash their rags in the public bath at the same time they bathed (Wills, p. 334). Of course, non-Muslims were not permitted to use the baths.

At least once, sometimes twice a year, Persians had themselves cupped (*gar-tarāšī*, *rag-zanī*, or *ḥejāmat*; see BLEEDING) in the bathhouses, because it was generally believed that this was healthy (Šahrī, pp. 257-59). As a number of persons are in the bath at one time, part of the time is passed in talking and smoking and sometimes sleeping. On coming out the client gets a white towel and returns to the first room, where his body is massaged (*moštmāl-e bīrūnī*) during some 15 minutes, which is different from the first massage. After drying and some relaxation the client takes his clothes and leaves. Outside the *ḥammām* there are all kinds of fruit and juice sellers to cater to the needs of the refreshed customers.

Classification of bathhouses. There were private and public baths. The former served the owners' needs and were in general inside the owners' houses. Public baths were often built for or by pious foundations (*awqāf*). In Šamsābād, Arslān Khan (1063-72) "built an imperial bath. Another bath, which had no equal, was at the gate of the court, and was given as endowment to the local *madrasa*" (Naršaḵī, pp. 40-41, tr. p. 30). Many *emāmzādas* and other *waqf* property derived part of their income from the revenues of bathhouses they owned and operated. This income paid for part of the upkeep of the buildings, salaries of the staff, and other expenditures (Kaempfer, pp. 107, 116). Many *ḥammām*s were found next to *bāzār*s, caravansaries, or *madrasas* (Ja'farī, pp. 33, 36, 45, 88; Mehrābādī, pp. 405f.; Eṣfahānī, pp. 79f.). There were also male and female public bathhouses; usually situated next to each other, but there also existed baths that were used by both sexes at different times of the day. Before daybreak a shell (*ḥalazūn*; Šahrī, p. 264) or long horn (*būq-e jawāz*) is blown to announce that the bath is ready. Men come to the baths from daybreak until 4 o'clock in the afternoon, then women until sunset. In the latter case the staff is female. If the 1925 statistics for Tehran are reliable, men were better served than women. The 107 male public baths had a total staff of 102 bath keepers (*ostād*), 423 attendants (*kārgar*) and 58 assistants (*pādow*), or an average staff of 5.4 per *ḥammām*. The data for the 41 female *ḥammām*s were 11 keepers, 11 attendants, and 24 assistants, or 1 per bath. This figure seems too low to run all 41 baths.

According to Waring, five days were allotted to men and only two to women; according to Polak, only the mornings were for women. To announce that the bathhouse was open for men, two old loincloths were hung flanking the entrance door or the entrance from the street. The sign for women was a thick curtain hung in front of the door. The entrance for male baths was in the street itself, while for women it was at the end of a lane.

Cost of a bath. According to Šahrī the cost for a bath was as follows, depending on the elaborateness of the bath, at the turn of the 14th/20th century: major ablutions (*ḡosl* + *ṭahīr* + *čālaḥawż*) only 6 *šāhī*s; depilation 2 *šāhī*s; soaping 5 *šāhī*s; trimming hair and beard 4 *šāhī*s; cupping 8 *šāhī*s; massage 5 *šāhī*s. In general for 20 *šāhī*s (1 *qerān*) a customer could get a bath. The bathhouse keeper did not ask for the specific amount and left it to the customer to pay the exact amount or throw in a tip (Šahrī, p. 263). Mostawfī (II, p. 169) gives slightly lower figures, but they are in agreement with Šahrī's data. An *ostād* who rented a *ḥammām* and invested 200 *tomans* in furniture, loincloths, fuel, etc., earned an average of 7-8 *qerān*s a day on his investment. The price for a normal bath was 100 *dīnār*s; with a shave it came to 5 *šāhī*s, and the services of the *jāmadār* and *dallāk-e ābgīr* raised the cost to 10 *šāhī*s. Well-to-do customers paid 1 *qerān*, of which 3/4 was a tip. Fuel was obtained from neighboring caravansaries and stables. For a sack of 15 *man*s (90 kg) the bathhouse keeper paid at least 10 *šāhī*s toward the end of the 13th/19th century (Mostawfī, I, p. 169). The rich had their private baths at home. It was expensive to keep a bath, for the fire had to be kept going; therefore the less rich rented a bath and supplied fuel from their own gardens and stables (Chardin, pp. 193-97; Waring, pp. 445-46; Polak, I, pp. 355-61). "The whole bath can always be hired for a few kerans" (Wills, p. 334). There were also the so-called *ḥammāmī-e andarūnī*, who were hired to fire up a few private bathhouses. Their monthly income came to 2-7 *toman*s, depending on the size of the bathhouses (Mostawfī, I, p. 169).

Village bathhouses. In the rural areas only big villages appear to have had bathhouses. According to Planck, peasants washed themselves three times per month during summer time in the irrigation ditches. During the winter they went to the *ḥammām* of nearby villages and/or heated water in their huts and washed themselves on the spot (Planck, p. 50; Petrosian, pp. 21, 31, 43, 103; Petrosian's book is also important for information on the general hygienic conditions in villages). In the 1960s bathhouses became more common, as well as showers. The water was regularly refreshed from nearby water sources, and sometimes small snakes got into the *ḵazīna* (Āl-e Aḥmad, p. 37, with a drawing of the layout of a village *ḥammām*; Ṣafīnežād, p. 61; Bazin, p. 84; Sahami, p. 39). If it was a big *ḥammām* there were two *kazīnas*, one with cold and one with warm water. The *ḥammāmī*, who was appointed by the *kadkoda* (village headman) or the *arbāb* (landowner), was paid in kind by the villagers. Rates were different for married men, bachelors, women, and children (Ṭāhbāz, p. 31; Porkārān, p. 26). When the *arbāb* wanted to use the bathhouse it was declared out of bounds (*qoroq*) to the general public (Ṭāhbāz, p. 30). The *ḥammāmī* and his wife not only had to take care of the bathhouse but also its fuel (Porkārān, p. 26).

Bibliography: J. Āl-e Aḥmad. *Owrāzān*, Tehran, 1337 Š./1958. Moḥammad Hāšem Āṣaf, *Rostam al-tawārīk*, ed. M. Moširī, Tehran, 1352 Š./1973. Ḡ.-Ḥ. Bagī'ī *Angīza*, Shiraz, n.d., pp. 17-21 (this autobiographical work contains a description of taking a bath in a bathhouse in Mašhad). M. Bazin, *La vie rurale dans la région de Qom*, Paris, n.d. M. Boyce, *Zoroastrians*, London, 1979. Moḥammad b. Maḥmūd b. 'Omar Čaḡmīnī, *Qānūnča*, ed. M.-T. Mīr, Shiraz, 1350 Š./1971. J. Chardin, *Voyages*, 10 vols., ed. L. Langlès, Paris, 1811. P. Coste, *Monuments modernes de la Perse*, Paris, 1867. M. Dawlatābādī, *Kelīdar* III, Tehran, n.d. [1363 Š./1984?], pp. 917ff. (detailed description of taking a bath in a village bathhouse). W. Floor, "Guilds and *futuvvat* in Iran," *ZDMG* 134/1, 1984, pp. 106-14. William Francklin, *Observations Made on a Tour from Bengal to Persia in the Years 1786-7*, London, 1790. H. Gaube and E. Wirth, *Der Bazar von Isfahan*, Wiesbaden, 1979. A. Golčīn-e Ma'ānī, *Šahrāšūb dar še'r-e fārsī*, Tehran, 1346 Š./1967. M.-'A. Golrīz, *Mīnūdar yā Bāb al-Jennat-e Qazvīn*, Tehran 1337 Š./1958. B. Gray, *Persian Painting*, Geneva, 1961. T. Herbert, *Some Years Travels*, ed. W. Foster, London, 1928. Moḥammad b. Maḥmūd b. Moḥammad-Reżā Eṣfahānī, *Neṣf jahān fī ta'rīf al-Eṣfahān*, ed. M. Sotūda, Tehran, 1340 Š./1961. Ja'far b. Moḥammad Ja'farī, *Tārīk-e Yazd*, ed. Ī. Afšār, Tehran, 1338 Š./1960. Āqā Mīr Sayyed 'Alī Janāb, *Ketāb al-Eṣfahān*, Isfahan, 1303 Š./1924. E. Kaempfer, *Am Hofe des Persischen Grosskönigs*, ed. W. Hinz, Leipzig, 1940. Sayyed Moḥammad-Karīm Khan Kermānī, *Majma' al-rasā'el-e fārsī*, 2nd ed., Kermān, n.d., pp. 118-202. Le Strange, *Lands*. J. Matīnī, "Ḡazālī dar pīšgāh-e farhang-e Īrān," *Īrān-nāma* 4/4, 1365 Š./1986, pp. 694-722 (pp. 709-15 on drawings of scenes from the *Šāh-nāma* in public baths). 'Abd-Allāh Marvarīd, *Šaraf-nāma*, ed. H. R. Roemer, Wiesbaden, 1952. A. Rafī'ī Mehrābādī, *Āṯār-e mellī-e Eṣfahān*, Tehran, 1352 Š./1973. Mostawfī, *Šarḥ-e zendagānī*. A. Mez, *Die Renaissance des Islam*, Heidelberg, 1922. V. Minorsky, *Studies in Caucasian History*, London, 1953. N. Najmī, *Dār al-Kelāfa*, Tehran, 1350 Š./1971. Ḥ. Narāqī, "Ḥammām-e tārīkī-e Bāḡ-e Šāh-e Fīn dar Kāšān," *Honar o mardom*, N.S. 101, 1349 Š./1970, pp. 9-23. Naršakī, ed. Rażawī; tr. Frye. Overseas Consultants Inc., *Report on Seven Year Development Plan for the Plan Organization of the Imperial Government of Iran*, 5 vols., New York, 1949. A. Petrosian et al., *The Health and Related Characteristics of Four Selected Village and Tribal Communities in Fars Ostan, Iran*, Shiraz, 1964. U. Planck, *Die sozialen und ökonomischen Verhältnisse in einem iranischen Dorf*, Opladen, 1962. J. Polak, *Persien, das Land und seine Bewohner*, 2 vols., Leipzig, 1865. A. U. Pope, *A Survey of Persian Art*, Oxford, 1939. H. Porkārān, *Fašandak*, Tehran, 1341 Š./1962. C. Sahami, *Le Guilan*, Clermont-Ferrand, n.d. J. Ṣafīnežād, *Ṭālebābād*, Tehran, 1345 Š./1966. J. Šahrī, *Gūša-i az tārīk-e ejtemā'ī-e Tehrān-e qadīm*, Tehran, 1357 Š./1978, pp. 236-88 (a comprehensive description of traditional *ḥammāms* in Tehran and all the practices, customs, rituals, beliefs, and superstitions associated with public bathhouses). Schwarz, *Iran*. Spuler, *Iran*. S. Ṭāhbāz, *Yūš*, Tehran, 1342 Š./1963. Jean de Thévenot, *The Travels of Monsieur Thévenot into the Levant*, 3 vols., London, 1686 (reprint 1971). S. Waring, *A Tour to Sheeraz*, London, 1807. R. Wakīlī Ṭabāṭabā'ī Tabrīzī, *Tārīk-e 'Erāq-e 'Ajam*, ed. M. Sotūda in *FIZ* 14, p. 415. D. Whitehouse, "Excavations at Siraf, Fourth and Fifth Interim Report," *Iran* 9, 1971, pp. 1-19; 10, 1972, pp. 63-87. C. J. Wills, *In the Land of the Lion and the Sun*, London, 1883.

(W. FLOOR)

ii. THE LAYOUT OF RURAL BATH STRUCTURES

A few related bath structures from different settings will be presented here: a village bath, the baths of a royal hunting lodge, and the bath in a caravansary, as well as a bath belonging to a complex that also included a caravansary, a palatial structure, and a large village. (For urban and other baths before the Qajar period see ii above, with bibliography.)

The bath structures to be discussed all belong to the general category of steam baths, rather than hot springs. They are unfortunately largely in ruins, and, as their superstructures have generally collapsed, the structural details are almost entirely lost. All were vaulted structures built of brick (especially the vaults), rubble concrete, or a mixture of rubble and bricks; wooden construction could not be used because of extreme moisture from the steam. Furthermore, these buildings included only those rooms that have been considered, since antiquity, necessary for an Oriental-style bath, so that among them not a single latrine facility could be recognized. Nevertheless, all examples contained, in independent or partly combined form, the basic complex of apodyterium (dressing and resting room), tepidarium (transitional, or cool, room, usually combined with the apodyterium), and caldarium/sudatorium (hot room), with associated hot-water pools. The ancient frigidarium (cold room) plays no part in the Oriental steam bath, which also does not include the unroofed cold swimming pool of antiquity. The latter would be contradictory to the moral ideas of Islam, as well as to the purpose of the Oriental bath.

A modest community bath of the 18th-19th centuries was preserved until quite recently outside the deserted

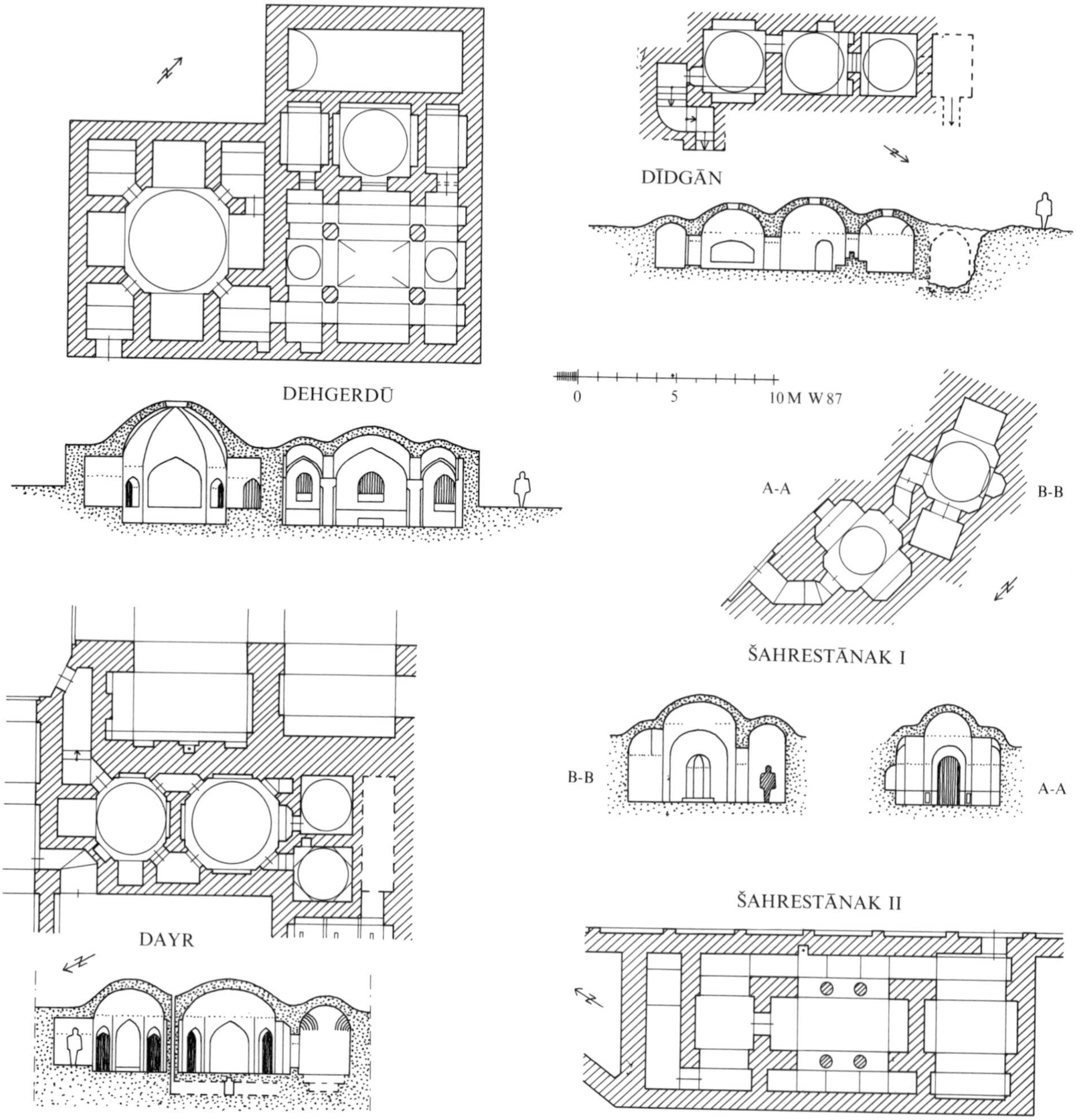

Figure 30. Typical bathhouse structures (W. Kleiss)

village of Dīdgān in Fārs. The village itself was in a former caravansary built of mud brick at the point where the road from Shiraz branches to Ābāda and Yazd. This bath was built almost completely underground. A bent staircase passage led down into a domed apodyterium with two large wall niches for the bathers' clothing (Figure 30). This dressing room opened into the tepidarium through a doorway set in one corner, so that it was difficult to catch a glimpse from one room to another. The maximum dimensions of the rooms were 3.40 × 3.20 m. The tepidarium, with only one small wall niche, also functioned partly as a caldarium; an axial passage led directly from it to the hot-water pool. Only this pool was heated, from a subterranean heating chamber outside the building; this chamber is now badly destroyed. There was no system for heating the floor and walls. The small scale of the installation makes it clear that men and women could use it only at separate times.

More noteworthy architecturally is the bath of Dehgerdū, preserved in ruined condition on the shorter caravan route from Isfahan to Shiraz, on the stretch between Īzadḵᵛāst and Marvdašt (Figure 30). It is much too large and spacious for a normal village bath. Stylistic features point to a construction date in the seventeenth century. The building was set only about half below ground, so that the visible part must have been impressive, especially as it stood apart from other buildings. It consisted essentially of only three rooms plus the heating chamber. An octagonal domed room 5.40 m in diameter with eight radial spaces—four tall *ayvān*s alternating with four enclosed corner rooms—served as apodyterium. From the southeast corner a passage led to the tepidarium, which was divided by four octagonal stone piers into a central space and an ambulatory. Three hot-water pools were installed on the northwest side of the tepidarium, which thus had already taken on half the function of the caldarium. Only these three pools, were heated, from below. The bath at Dehgerdū forms part of a complex containing a caravansary, a ruined building resembling a palace, and a large fortified village; its impressive architecture suggests that it must have been intended for important travelers on this caravan route, even including the Safavid court.

Aside from the Qajar palace baths, there were two in the hunting lodge of Nāṣer-al-Dīn Shah Qājār in Šahrestānak, northwest of Tehran. The lodge was laid out in about 1878 and has since been largely destroyed. The smaller bath, which was accessible only from the main courtyard of the palace, was an elegant two-room installation with walls lined with tiles and a western extension for the heating chamber. It consisted of an apodyterium and a caldarium, the latter with a statue niche on the west wall (Figure 30, Šahrestānak I). This bath could have been for the occasional use of the ruler or his hunting guests. There was also a somewhat larger bath off the domestic courtyard of the palace, which probably served the sovereign's entourage (Figure 30, Šahrestānak II). It also consisted of only two rooms and a hot-water pool, which was heated from the north. All the fittings have been destroyed; the function of the installation is nevertheless clearly recognizable from the water-resistant plaster on the walls.

Finally, there was a bath within the Dayr caravansary (Dayr-e Gač) on the old road direct from Verāmīn to Qom (Figure 30), a rare example of a bathhouse inside a caravansary. The large caravansary at Dayr must have been built in Safavid times inside a Saljuq *rebāṭ*. The bath was in the southwest corner and opened on a court, which led to the latrines and from which the bath was also heated. It consisted of two octagonal domed rooms with a maximum diameter of 4.50 m, which were heated by a hot-water duct under the floor. The two hot-water pools were on the south side of the tepidarium. The bath was built entirely of brick and was about half underground. Its rooms reached a height of 4.10 m, and the domes were without windows.

(W. KLEISS)

BĀTMAN, a measure of weight, the same as *mann* (q.v.) but more common in Central Asia, especially in modern times. The earliest information about *bātman* goes back to the 14th century; but most data are from the 17th-19th centuries. There was a great variety of *bātman*s in different regions of Central Asia. Beside the regional differences, separate varieties of *bātman* were apparently used for weighing different goods. All Central Asian *bātman*s were based on the *meṯqāl* (as distinct from Middle Eastern, including Iranian, *mann*s, which were based on the *derham*). Theoretically the *bātman* consisted of 40 *sīr* (with smaller fractional units), but the most frequently used portions were *dūnīmsīr* = 1/16 of a *bātman*, *čāryak* = 1/4 of a *dūnīmsīr*, and *unsīr* = 1/4 of a *bātman* (in Ḵᵛārazm). An analysis of indigenous and European sources done by E. A. Davidovich allowed her to establish more than two dozen different Central Asian *bātman*s (or *mann*s) differentiated by the names of the regions where they were in use, though some are identical in weight.

In Bukhara, two groups of *mann*s, or *bātman*s, existed originally: (a) units of "small weight," based on a *meṯqāl* of 4.8 g: *mann-e šarīʿ* = 180 *meṯqāl* = 0.864kg (recorded in the 14th and 18th centuries); *mann-e ṭāqī* = 5 *mann-e šarīʿ* = 4.32 kg (close to it, the *bātman* of Karšī [18th century] = 10 Russian pounds = about 4.0 kg); and a *bātman* = 1375 *meṯqāl* = 6.6 kg (18th century); (b) units of "big weight" (*sang-e bozorg*), based on a *meṯqāl* of 5.0 g: a *bātman* = 5120 *meṯqāl* = 25.6 kg; also a *bātman* five times greater of 128 kg; and a *mann* of Samarkand = 4000 *meṯqāl* = 20 kg (16th century). Another group of *bātman*s was based on the Russian *pud* (1 *bātman* = 16 *pud* = 262.088 kg, and 1 *bātman* = 8 *pud* = 131.044 kg), but they were artificially calculated in *meṯqāl* of 4.8 g; they appeared in the 16th or 17th centuries due to the development of trade with Russia, but were widely used also in internal trade (in the 19th century the *bātman* of 8 *pud* was chiefly used). In other places in Transoxiana (Samarkand, Jīzak, Ura-Tübe) and in Farḡāna, the 16-*pud* and especially the 8-*pud* *bātman*s were also used in the 19th century.

Beside these, the following main *bātman*s were recorded in other regions of Central Asia:

1. Ḵ˘ārazm: 1 *bātman* = 4.095 kg (17th century), 3.788 kg and 7.371 kg (18th century). According to Mo'nes (*Ferdows al-eqbāl*, Institute of Oriental Studies, Leningrad, ms. C-571, fol. 122b), in the 1770s, 1 *bātman* of Khiva was 3 1/2 times heavier than those of Tabrīz, that is, 10.5 kg. In the 19th century, much heavier *bātmans*, mainly of two weights: 20 kg (in Khiva, Hazārasp, and elsewhere, calculated at 4416 Khwarezmian *meṯqāl*s of 4.53 g) and 40 kg (in Urgenč, Ḵānqāh, Qongrat, etc.).

2. Jīzak, Ḵojand, Awlīā'-Atā (19th century): 1 *bātman* = 12 *pud* = 196.56 kg.

3. Farḡāna (19th century): beside the 8-*pud bātman*, also 1 *bātman* = 10 *pud* (163.8 kg) and 10.5 *pud* (171.99 kg).

4. Tashkent and Chimkent (19th century): 1 *bātman* = 10.5 *pud* (171.99 kg).

In the mountainous regions of the khanate of Bukhara numerous different *bātman*s were noted.

Bibliography: E. A. Davidovich, *Istoriya monetnogo dela Sredneĭ Azii XVII-XVIII vv.*, Dushanbe, 1964, pp. 293-317. Idem *Materialy po metrologii srednevekovoĭ Sredneĭ Azii*, Moscow, 1970 (published with the Russian translation of W. Hinz, *Islamische Masse und Gewichte*: *Musul'manskie mery i vesa s perevodom v metricheskuyu sistemu*), pp. 85-94.

(YU. BREGEL)

BATRAKATAŠ, place name which appears on the Elamite fortification tablets found at Persepolis, apparently the same as Pasargadae.

The name is found in various spellings: h.bat-ra-qa-taš (PF 44, 62, 774, 908, 1134, 1942; Fort. 1016, 6575, 7090), h.ba-iš-ra-qa-da (PF 43), h.ba-iš-sir-qa-da (PF 42), h.bat-ra-qa-da (PF 63). These variants point to an original Old Persian form *Pāθra-gadā, for which various etymological interpretations have been suggested. Gershevitch (p. 168) suggested identifying **gadā* with Old Iranian *gadā-* "club" (Av. *gaδā-*). For **pāθra-* Hinz (1975, p. 190, cf. idem, *Orientalia* 39, 1970, p. 425, and *ZDMG* 120, 1970, p. 376) preferred comparing Old Iranian *pāθra-* "protection," rather than Vedic *pajrá* "solid, strong, stout," as proposed by Gershevitch (loc. cit.). However, Hinz's suggestion that the second part of the name may contain Old Iranian *kata* "house, home" is unlikely, since one would expect intervocalic *-t-* to be spelled with double *-dd-* or *-tt-* in at least some of the Elamite transcriptions, although a meaning "protective house" or the like would be more suitable for the name of a city than, e.g., "protective club, strong club," etc.

The name strongly resembles Pasargadai, the Greek name of Cyrus the Great's capital (Hallock, p. 676) and the Elamite tablets support the identification of the two names, as they show that there were a royal treasury and royal stores at Batrakataš. It was also the seat of a priest who received rations for divine sacrifices. There was no agricultural cultivation, as barley for rations was brought from a place called Ha-da-ráš (*Haδahra) and wine from Ha-in-da-ra-ti-iš (*Antarantīš), Ra-šá-nu-iz-za (*Rašnuča), and Ti-ra-iz-zí-iš (Shiraz?). Batrakataš was administered together with another place, called Ra-ut-ku-iš (*Ratguš).

Bibliography: I. Gershevitch, "Iranian Nouns and Names in Elamite Garb," *TPS*, 1969 [1970], pp. 165-200. R. T. Hallock, *Persepolis Fortification Tablets*, Chicago, 1969. W. Hinz, *Altiranisches Sprachgut der Nebenüberlieferungen*, Wiesbaden, 1975. W. Hinz and H. Koch, *Elamisches Wörterbuch*, Archäologische Mitteilungen aus Iran, suppl. vol. no. 17, Berlin, 1987.

(H. KOCH)

BATS (Pers. *šabpara, mūš(-e)kūr*; Ar. *ḵoffāš*). Surveys of the Iranian bat (Mammalia: Chiroptera) fauna have been published by Blanford (1876), Misonne (1959), Lay (1967), E'temād (1969), and DeBlase (1980). DeBlase (1980) recognized thirty-eight species of Chiroptera from within the political boundaries of Iran, and this study is the primary basis for this article.

Pteropodidae: *Rousettus aegyptiacus* is known from Baluchistan, Qešm island, and three sites near Jahrom in Fārs. These records, together with occurrence in Pakistan and southern Arabia, indicate that it ranges across southern Iran wherever dates and other fruits are grown.

Rhinopomatidae: *Rhinopoma microphyllum* is the largest species of *Rhinopoma* in Iran, where both the nominate subspecies and *R. m. harrisoni* (Schlitter and DeBlase, 1974) occur. The two smaller forms have been frequently confused. DeBlase et al. (1973) have identified specimens and documented distribution for the following: *R. hardwickei arabium*, *R. muscatellum muscatellum*, and *R. m. seianum*. All three of these species are known from the hotter, lower southwestern side of the Zagros Mountains. *R. m. microphyllum* and *R. m. muscatellum* are also known from Baluchistan and *R. M. seianum* occurs, in Iran, only in the Sīstān area.

Emballonuridae: Both species of *Tahpozous* known from Iran are rather rare. *T. p. perforatus* is known only from two specimens collected along the southern coastal plain near the Strait of Hormoz. Its distribution in Oman and Pakistan, however, suggests a wider range in Iran. *T. nudiventris magnus* is common in the Tigris-Euphrates lowland of Iraq and has been documented at four localities on the Ḵūzestān plain in Iran. It has also been reported from near Urmia (Reżā'īya) in West Azerbaijan and Varāmīn, 37 km southeast of Tehran. These two locations, well east of the Zagros ridge, indicate that the species is considerably more widely distributed.

Rhinolophidae: *Rhinolophus ferrumequinum irani* is known from numerous localities across northern Iran, and south and east through the Zagros Mountains of western Iran to near Kermān, and one, Būšehr, on the south coastal plain. I have examined no specimens documenting this latter record and think the habitat rather doubtful for this species. There are no records from Iran east of the central deserts but its occurrence in adjacent areas of Afghanistan and Pakistan indicates that it could be expected there. *R. bocharicus* is known in Iran only from a single specimen from Čelmīr in Khorasan (Farhang-Azad, 1969, p. 730). DeBlase (1980, p. 95) examined this specimen and found it to be an immature with barely ossified wing epiphyses; however, its measurements fall within those of other *R. bocharicus* adults. *R. bocharicus* is known from the USSR along the Afghanistan border and from northern Afghanistan. It is possible that the Čelmīr specimen is of this species, but it is also quite likely that it is merely an immature *R. ferrumequinum*. It should be compared to immature specimens of both of these species. *Rhinolophus hipposideros midas* is known from several localities in the Zagros mountains, from Azerbaijan to Fārs, and from one site on the Makrān coast. However, its presence in the USSR all along the Iranian border on both sides of the Caspian and in Afghanistan indicate that it very likely occurs in much of the rest of the country. The specimens of *R. hipposideros* from the Caspian coastal lowland of Iran are distinctly darker than *R. h. midas*. DeBlase (1980, pp. 104-06) has tentatively assigned these to *R. h. minimus*; however, he points out that this isolated population is completely surrounded by *R. h. midas* and thus is unlikely to be the same subspecies that occurs in countries west of Iran. DeBlase (1972) has shown that *Rhinolophus euryale* and *R. mehelyi* have frequently been confused in Iran and elsewhere. Both of these species are known from several areas in the Transcaucasus of the USSR and from scattered sites in the Zagros Mountains of western Iran. *R. euryale* also occurs along both sides of the Iran-Soviet border east of the Caspian. DeBlase (1980, p. 112) tentatively assigns all Iranian specimens of *R. euryale* to the nominate subspecies. *Rhinolophus b. blasii* is known from several locations scattered over most of Iran, however; it is not known to occur on the Caspian coastal plain, the arid coastal lowlands of the south, from Baluchistan, or from the Sīstān area. *Asellia tridens murraiana* ranges across much of southern Iran. *Triaenops persicus persicus* was described from Shiraz and has been reported from only three other localities in Iran, two sites near Būšehr along the Persian Gulf coast and one from Baluchistan. This species is not common anywhere in its range, which reaches its easternmost limit in Iran.

Vespertilionidae: *Myotis mystacinus* is documented from fourteen locations scattered across northern Iran. *M. emarginatus* has been reported from four scattered locations in the southern Zagros, two along the Caspian coast, two along the Soviet border in northeastern Iran, and two from near the Pakistan border in central Baluchistan. *M. nattereri* is known from three sites, one in northwestern Azerbaijan, near Mākū; one in northeastern Azerbaijan at the Qoṭūrsū cave at Mt. Sabalān; and one near Kūhrang village in the central Zagros. *M. bechsteini* is known only from an adult female collected in the eastern Alborz. This specimen represents the southern and eastern distribution limits for this species. *Myotis blythi omari* is considerably larger than the other species of *Myotis* and is much more common. It has been collected at twenty-nine localities scattered through most of northern and western Iran. *M. capaccinii bureschi* is known from six locations, all clustered in Fārs near Persepolis and Šāhpūr Cave near Kāzerūn. This species ranges from Morocco to Japan but occurs in large numbers only in scattered pockets. This seems to be the pattern in Iran as well. *Vespertilio m. murinus* is known only from three single specimens taken at widely separated locations in the central Zagros, the eastern Alborz, and the central basin near Qom. DeBlase (1980, p. 184) has shown that *Eptesicus walli* Thomas is a junior synonym of *E. nasutus pellucens*. *E. nasutus* is known in Iran only from the Ḵūzestān plain and from a single record at Mīnāb near the Strait of Hormoz, though it probably occurs all along the southern costal plain and in Baluchistan. The Ḵūzestān specimens are *E. n. pellucens*, and the Mīnāb specimen is tentatively assigned to the nominate form, *E. n. nasutus* (DeBlase 1980, p. 183). Harrison (1963, p. 303) reported *Eptesicus bobrinskoi* from Qoṭūrsū in east Azerbaijan. His seven specimens are the only ones known from Iran or from anywhere outside the USSR. *Eptesicus nilssoni* was collected by Lay (1967, p. 145) in the central Alborz. This relatively rare bat ranges throughout the northern Palearctic and should be expected to occur throughout the northern, less arid slope of the Alborz. The next two species of *Eptesicus* are considerably larger than the three discussed above. *Eptesicus bottae*, the smaller of the two, is known from two locations in northwestern Iran between the Alborz and Zagros Mountains, from near the Soviet border in northeastern Iran, and from scattered locations in the southern Zagros. DeBlase (1980, p. 193) has shown that all of the northern records are assignable to *E. b. ognevi*, that the specimens from the southern Zagros are identical to ones from the Zagros in northern Iraq and in Turkey and should be considered to be *E. b. anatolicus*, and that *E. b. hingstoni*, while not yet reported from the Ḵūzestān plain, is likely to be found there. *Eptesicus s. serotinus* ranges through the Caucasus and Transcaucasus into Iranian Azerbaijan and east through the Alborz. *E. s. turcomanus* occurs in northeastern Iran and in the adjacent Transcaspian area of the USSR. *E. serotinus shiraziensis* is known only from a very few specimens collected near Shiraz, in the southern Zagros. This form has not been reported by any of the collectors working in that area in the past sixty-five years and could now be extinct. *Nyctalus l. leisleri* is known from four locations across northern Iran and one from the southern Zagros. This latter record indicates that the species ranges south through the Zagros as well as through the northern mountains. *N. n. noctula* is known from several locations on the Caspian coastal plain of Iran and the adjacent slopes of the Alborz. *N. l. lasiopterus* has been reported in Iran only once, a single specimen from "near Rūdsar" on the Caspian coastal plain (Eʿtemād, 1970, p. 547). It probably has an Iranian distribution similar to that of *N. noctula.* Neuhauser and DeBlase (1971) have shown that *Pipistrellus p. pipistrellus* occurs only along the Caspian coastal plain and the relatively lush northern face of the Alborz range, while *P. p. aladdin* ranges the length of the Zagros mountains and occurs in northeastern Iran as well as in adjacent parts of the USSR and Afghanistan. It is likely that this latter subspecies also occurs along the more arid south face of the Alborz between the two documented areas. *P. kuhli* is probably the most common bat in Iran. It is known from many locations, and virtually all ecosystems in the southern and central portions of the country, including the greatest penetration documented of the central deserts. There are records from Lake Urmia and Tabrīz, but it is conspicuously absent from most of the northern part of the country and quite rare in those northern regions where it has been reported. The species has not been found alive on the Caspian coastal plain and, based on ecology, should not be expected to occur there. However, a fresh specimen was found dead in the street at Bandar-e Pahlavī. It is likely that this had fallen from a vehicle that had hit it and carried it over the Alborz from the southern slope (DeBlase, 1980, p. 220). *P. savii* is a rather rare bat known only from four locations in three widely separated areas of Iran: Čelmīr in northern Khorasan, Mākū and Lake Urmia in Azerbaijan, and Sardašt, southwestern Lordegān, in the *šahrestān* of Šahr-e Kord in the southern Zagros. DeBlase (1980, p. 230) referred all of these specimens to the form *P. s. caucasicus.* Neuhauser and DeBlase (1974) have shown that *Barbastella leucomelas darjelingensis* occurs at the eastern end of the Alborz, and DeBlase (1980, p. 233) reports another specimen of this form from the same area. These are the westernmost records for this form. DeBlase (1980, p. 233) refers the other Iranian specimens of this species, two from near Tehran and one from Semnān, to the nominate form *B. l. leucomelas. Otonycteris hemprichi* is known from two localities in Khorasan and numerous ones in adjacent areas of the USSR and Afghanistan. It also occurs in Saudi Arabia and thus may be expected in much of Iran as well. *Plecotus austriacus* is known from five widely scattered points in Iran: near Mt. Sabalān in northeastern Azerbaijan; three areas in the central Zagros; and one in southeastern Baluchistan. *Miniopterus schreibersi pallidus* is known from numerous locations throughout the mountainous areas of northern and western Iran and, considering its distribution in Afghanistan, probably occurs in the eastern mountains as well. It does occur on the Caspian coastal plain, but is not known from the Ḵūzestān plain, the southern coastal strip, or from Baluchistan.

Molossidae: *Tadarida teniotis* is reported from two widely separated locations on the southern coastal plain, Būšehr and Mīnāb; from Čelmīr in northeastern Khorasan; and from the Alborz mountains southeast of the Caspian Sea. It probably occurs in nearly all parts of Iran. *Tadarida aegyptiaca* is known from a single specimen from the Persian Gulf coast in southern Iran (DeBlase, 1971, p. 12). Since the species is known from the southern Arabian peninsula and from Africa, as well as from Afghanistan and Pakistan, it is likely that it occurs throughout southern Iran, at least along the coast.

Zoogeography. Although thirty-eight species of bats are known from Iran, the record remains sketchy and incomplete. Only two species, *Myotis blythi* and *Pipistrellus kuhli*, are known from more than thirty locations, and only eleven more are known from more than ten locations. Twenty-one of the species are known from five or fewer localities, and six of these have been reported from a single site. Of the thirty-eight species of bats now documented from Iran, none is restricted to the political boundaries of the Iranian nation, and none is restricted to the main physiographic feature of the area, the Iranian Plateau. The Iranian bat fauna is strongly Palearctic in its affinity. Twenty-seven species are entirely, or almost entirely, restricted to the Palearctic faunal region. Of the remaining eleven species one, *Miniopterus schreibersi*, ranges widely through all four faunal regions in the eastern hemisphere. One species, *Barbastella leucomelas*, ranges widely in both the Palearctic and Oriental faunal regions, and two other species, *Rhinolophus blasii* and *Pipistrellus kuhli*, range widely in both the Palearctic and the Ethiopian faunal regions. *Triaenops persicus* has a rather restricted range but seems to be more widely distributed in the Ethiopian region than in the Palearctic. The remaining six species, *Rousettus aegyptiacus, Rhinopoma microphyllum, R. hardwickei, Taphozous perforatus, T. nudiventris*, and *Tadarida aegyptiaca*, range widely through the Ethiopian region and through India but are found in the Palearctic only in a restricted portion of southwestern Asia. Three of these, *R. microphyllum, R. hardwickei*, and *T. nudiventris*, continue through India well into the Oriental region.

DeBlase (1980) has shown that all but two Iranian bat species fall into one of three geographic groups in Iran. Nineteen species are primarily "northern" in their distribution, nine species are primarily "southern," and eight are wide-ranging in both north and south. And, using the Index of Faunistic Congruence, DeBlase (1980, pp. 267-73) has shown that as a whole the bat fauna of Iran is quite similar to that of Caucasia, the Levant, Anatolia, Transcaspia, and Afghanistan. The bat fauna of northern Iran is most similar to those of Caucasia, Transcaspia, Anatolia, Mediterranean Europe, and the Levant. The index of congruence for northern Iran is higher with eleven of the nineteen comparative regions than it is with southern Iran. The bat fauna of southern Iran is most similar to those of Oman, Egypt, Saudi Arabia, the Levant, Mesopotamia, and Afghanistan. This southern bat fauna has a higher index of congruence with nine of the comparative regions than with northern Iran. These figures further emphasize that the Iranian bat fauna is primarily Palearctic in its affinities and consists of two relatively distinct species complexes.

Bibliography: W. T. Blanford, *Eastern Persia. An Account of the Journeys of the Persian Boundary*

Commission 1870-71-72 II: *The Zoology and Geology*, London, 1876. A. F. DeBlase, "New Distributional Records of Bats from Iran," *Fieldiana. Zoology* 58/3, 1971, pp. 9-14. Idem, "*Rhinolophus euryale* and *R. mehelyi* (Chiroptera: Rhinolophicae) in Egypt and Southwest Asia," *Israel Journal of Zoology* 21, 1972, pp. 1-12. Idem, *The Bats of Iran. Systematics, Distribution, Ecology*, Fieldiana. Zoology, N.S. 4. A. F. DeBlase, D. A. Schlitter, and H. N. Neuhauser, "Taxonomic Status of *Rhinopoma muscatellum* Thomas (Chiroptera: Rhinopomatidae) from Southwest Asia," *Journal of Mammalogy* 54/4, 1973, pp. 831-41. E. E'temād, (The bats of Iran and the keys to identify them), Tehran, 1348 Š./1969 (with Eng. summary). Idem, "A Note on the Occurrence of the Giant Noctule *Nyctalus lasiopterus* Schreber, 1780, in Iran (Chiroptera: Vespertilionidae," *Mammalia* 34/3, 1970, p. 547. A. Farhang-Azad, "Bats from North Khorasan, Iran," *Mammalia* 33/4, 1969, pp. 730-32. D. L. Harrison, "Report on a Collection of Bats (Microchiroptera) from N. W. Iran," *Zeitschrift für Saugetierkunde* 28/2, 1963, pp. 301-08. D. M. Lay, "A Study of the Mammals of Iran Resulting from the Street Expedition of 1962-63," *Fieldiana. Zoology* 54, 1967, pp. 1-282. X. Misonne, *Analyse zoogéographique des mammifères de l'Iran*, Mémoires de l'Institut royal des sciences naturelles de Belgique, 2nd ser., 59, 1959. H. N. Neuhauser and A. F. DeBlase, "The Status of *Pipistrellus aladdin* Thomas from Central Asia," *Mammalia* 35/2, 1971, pp. 273-82. Idem, "Notes on Bats (Chiroptera: Vespertilionidae) New to the Faunal Lists of Afghanistan and Iran," *Fieldiana. Zoology* 65/2, 1974, pp. 85-96. D. A. Schlitter and A. F. DeBlase, "Taxonomy and Geographic Distribution of *Rhinopoma microphyllum* (Chiroptera: Rhinopomatidae) in Iran with the Description of a New Subspecies," *Mammalia* 38/4, 1974, pp. 657-65.

(A. F. DEBLASE)

BAṬṬAI YAZDĀNĪ, the founder or reformer of the Kantheans, a sect related to the Mandeans. According to the account of the Nestorian heresiographer Theodore Bar Konai, Baṭṭai was originally a slave of a chief of the Kanthean sect, Papa, son of Klilaye, from Gaukai in Babylonia. He ran away and went into hiding first among the Jews and then among the Manicheans. Later he returned to the Kantheans and reordered some of their discourses and mysteries of their magic. When the Sasanian king Pērōz (r. 459-84) proscribed all religions aside from Zoroastrianism, Baṭṭai reformed the Kanthean religion, "flattering the Magians and worshiping the stars." His followers adopted the worship of fire and placed it in their homes. Baṭṭai changed his name to the Persian Yazdānī, or Yazdānīz. He borrowed from the Jews the prohibition on eating pork, from the Pentateuch the name of the Lord God, and from the Christians the sign of the cross, which he placed on the left shoulders of his followers. His adherents say that the cross is the secret of the border between the Father of Greatness and the lower world. Bar Konai goes on describing their doctrine and quotes a Kanthean text agreeing almost literally with a passage of the Mandean Ginza. Michael the Syrian reports among the events of the reign of Pērōz's successor Balāš (r. 484-88) that the sect of the Kantheans appeared in Persia (*Chronique de Michel le Syrien*, ed. J.-B. Chabot, Paris, 1899-1910, IV, p. 255, tr. II, p. 151).

In Bar Konai's account, the Kanthean sect, named after their temple Kanthā, existed before Baṭṭai, and the Mandeans, named Maškenaye after their temple Maškenā, split off from it. It is evident, however, that the Mandean religion, as represented in the Ginza, is closer to the early baptist religion known to have existed centuries before Baṭṭai than the reform movement of the latter influenced by the Magians. If indeed there was a Kanthean sect which was reformed by Baṭṭai, it would have to be the result of an earlier schism. While the opinion of H. H. Schaeder that the sect of the Kantheans was merely a concoction of Christian heresiography is no longer tenable since its survival until the early ʿAbbasid age is attested by Islamic sources, the person and activity of Baṭṭai are mentioned only by Bar Konai. An alternative reading of the name of Yazdānī as Yazwānī has been proposed by S. H. Taqizadeh, who has suggested that the name of the Yazūqean sect attacked in the Ginza for its fire worship may be derived from it.

Bibliography: Theodore Bar Konai, *Liber Scholiarum*, ed. A. Scher, Leipzig, 1910, II, pp. 342-44; tr. R. Hespel and R. Draguet, Louvain, 1982, pp. 255-57. H. Pognon, *Inscriptions Mandaïtes des coupes de Khouabir*, Paris, 1898, pp. 11-13, 220-24. H. H. Schaeder, "Die Kantäer," *Welt des Orients* 1, 1947-52, pp. 288-98. S. H. Taqizadeh, "An Ancient Persian Practice Preserved by Non-Iranian People," *BSO(A)S* 9, 1937-39, p. 619. W. Madelung, "Abū'Īsā al-Warrāq über die Bardesaniten, Marcioniten und Kantäer," in *Studien zur Geschichte und Kultur des Vorderen Orients: Festschrift für Bertold Spuler zum siebzigsten Geburtstag*, ed. H. R. Roemer and A. Noth, Leiden, 1981, pp. 221-24.

(W. MADELUNG)

BAUR, FERDINAND CHRISTIAN (21 June 1792–2 December 1860), German theologian and scholar of Manicheism. Born at Schmiden near Stuttgart, he was the son of a Protestant pastor. In the course of training for the ministry, he attended the theological colleges at Blaubeuren and Maulbronn (1805-09). Next he studied theology, philosophy, and ancient languages at the University of Tübingen (1809-14). Publication of his first scholarly writings in 1817 drew attention to his abilities and led to his appointment to a professorship at Blaubeuren in the same year. While there he came under the influence of Schleiermacher's philosophy of religion, but after his appointment to the University of Tübingen in 1826 he increasingly adopted Hegel's dialectical method of reasoning and historical interpretation. The first example of Baur's application of this method to early Christian history is his essay "Die Christuspartei in der korinthischen Gemeinde, der Gegensatz des petrinischen und paulinischen Christentums in der ältesten Kirche, der Apostel Petrus in Rom" (*Tübinger Zeitschrift für Theologie* 3, 1831, pp. 61-206). This may be regarded as the position paper of the Tübingen school of New Testament researchers, in whose view the transmitted texts show evidence of historical development through the process of thesis, antithesis, and synthesis.

Baur is described as an impressive university teacher, but in his last years he was to witness the downfall of his school. In Prussia advocates of Baur's undogmatic historical approach encountered bureaucratic obstacles and found themselves compelled either to follow the officially approved line in their teaching or to choose other careers. It must be added that too rigid or biased application of Baur's method to canonical texts had in some cases given rise to distortions and errors. With Baur's death in 1860 his school also expired.

In the same year 1831 in which the essay on early Christian history came out, Baur published his second momentous work *Das manichäische Religionssystem nach den Quellen neu untersucht und entwickelt*. In it the Hegelian critical method for which Baur later became so well known is not used. This book earned a scholarly reputation in a much wider sphere than the circle of Lutheran theologians. It is a general survey of the Manichean teaching, admirably methodical, based on all the then available sources, with sound assessment of their worth, and still valid on most important points. It has been the model for all subsequent accounts of this religion.

Most important was Baur's view of Manicheism as a religion born at the watershed of the ancient and Christian worlds. He considered Manicheism to be the last great assemblage of ancient pre-Christian "nature spirit" beliefs which expressed religious consciousness "in figurative disguise," focusing it on man's imprisonment in the universe rather than on his inner life and seeing each individual's soul as a reflection of the "common world-soul." Manicheism therefore played the same role as neo-Platonism did in Greco-Roman society (pp. 487ff.). Baur rightly concluded that Manicheism was not a Christian heresy but a world religion *sui generis* (pp. 368ff.) and that it set forth an Oriental doctrine.

At the same time Baur was aware that Manichean syncretism flowed from many different sources. With regard to Zoroaster's teachings, Baur rightly attached great importance to the shared dualism of the Zoroastrians and the Manicheans and held that in this respect Manicheism had "its deepest roots" in Zoroastrianism, but he also recognized the great differences between them and refuted the then common opinion that Manicheism was merely a combination of Zoroastrianism and Christianity (pp. 404ff.). Against this he regarded Buddhism as an important formative influence, finding evidence in a wide range of shared features (pp. 433ff.). That theory was contested by contemporary critics and has not been borne out by subsequent research, which credits Buddhism with at most a minor role in the genesis of Manicheism.

It should be noted, however, that Baur had in mind not only a direct influence of Buddhism on Mani but also an indirect influence through the channel of gnosticism. He saw evidence of this in the story of Simon Magus in the pseudo-Clementine homilies (pp. 467ff.). His citations really amounted to no more than speculative surmises. Nevertheless recent research has, perhaps surprisingly, lent force to Baur's conclusion that certain details of the homilies point to "a source which appears to have been the same or at least very nearly the same as the source from which Manicheism flowed" (p. 486). It is now known from the so-called Mani Codex at Cologne that Mani was bred in a Judeo-Christian Elkesaite environment. This disclosure of course necessitates revision of Baur's appraisal of the importance of Christianity in the formation of the Manichean system (pp. 368ff.). More was involved in Mani's relationship to Christianity than " a form of the old nature religion clad in the language of Christianity" (p. 404).

Bibliography: F. Ch. Baur, *Das manichäische Religionssystem nach den Quellen neu untersucht und entwickelt*, Tübingen, 1831 (repr. 1928). J. H. Genthe, *Mit den Augen der Forschung. Kleine Geschichte der neutestamentlichen Wissenschaft*, Berlin, 1976, pp. 107-12. H. Mulert in *Neue deutsche Biographie* I, Berlin, 1963, pp. 670-71 (with recent literature). J. Ries, *Introduction aux études manichéennes* II, Louvain and Paris, 1959, pp. 365-72. H. Schmidt and J. Haussleiter in A. Hauck, ed., *Realencyklopädie für protestantische Theologie und Kirche* II, Leipzig, 1897, pp. 467-83 (contains citations of older writings concerning Baur as a person and as a theologian).

(W. SUNDERMANN)

BAVĀNĀTĪ, MĪRZĀ MOḤAMMAD-BĀQER, also called Ebrāhīm Jān Moʿaṭṭar and known as Mr. Bakir of Persia, Persian man of letters, poet, instructor of Persian in London, and self-styled prophet. He was born in Šeydān in Bavānāt, Fārs, most likely between the years 1230-35/1814-20 and died in 1310/1892-93 (Aḥmad; Shaikh Mofīd, s.v. Moʿaṭṭar; Šoʿāʿ-al-Molk, p. 445). He left his home village at the age of twelve and went to Shiraz, where he received traditional education and learned English. Possessing an inquiring mind and a restless nature, he soon delved into a variety of beliefs and faiths, professing to several during the course of his life. He was raised a Shiʿite but early in his youth followed the path of a dervish and affected the title Ḵodāʾī (Godly); later he gravitated to Christianity, calling himself Maẓhar-e ʿĪsā (The manifestation of Jesus; *Merʾāt al-faṣāḥa*, cited in Afšār, p. 11); then he adopted atheism only to convert to Judaism later; finally he devised a religious system of his own, an amalgam of Christianity and Islam, which he branded

Islamo-Christianity. He devoted most of his energy, time, and money to elaborating his religious system in Persian poems written "in the most bizarre style" and in countless tracts and leaflets in English, which he often distributed on the streets of London, for which he was once severely beaten by the mob (Browne, 1893, pp. 12-13; Pīrzāda, p. 210).

After spending years traveling the world and having mastered several languages (including Hebrew), Bavānātī found himself employed for a time as translator at the British consulate in Būšehr (Bushire). In Būšehr he befriended the young Jamāl-al-Dīn Asadābādī (see AFḠĀNĪ), who had stopped there in 1272/1856-57 on his way to India. Bavānātī's anti-Islamic statements had forced him to flee from Shiraz, and on his way to Būšehr, in Borāzjān, his life had been saved by Asadābādī (Afšār, p. 12; Keddie, pp. 24-25). Around 1880 he went to London and began teaching Persian. Among his students in London were the two brothers Ḥosaynqolī and ʿAbbāsqolī Nawwāb Šīrāzī and Edward G. Browne; in Iran Mīrzā Ḥasan Khan Mošīr-al-Dawla and Mīrzā Ḥosayn Khan Moʾtamen-al-Molk Pīrnīa were reported to have studied with him (Ādamīyat, quoting the son of Bavānātī). Toward the end of 1884 his daughter's poor health forced him to leave London for Beirut, where he stayed for a few years before he returned to Iran.

Bavānātī kept his ties with Sayyed Jamāl-al-Dīn Asadābādī and, in 1307/1889-90, for this association and on the charge of atheism was imprisoned in Tehran; he was freed through the intervention of Mīrzā ʿAlī-Aṣḡar Khan Amīn-al-Solṭān. Three of his letters (one in Arabic and two in Persian) to Sayyed Jamāl-al-Dīn have survived and are to be found in the Majles Library (published in Afšār, pp. 14-18). He is also the author of a versified commentary on twenty-six *sūra*s of the Koran, entitled *Rawżāt-e landanī wa fawḥāt-e anjomanī kenāyat az Qorʾān-e moʿaṭṭar*; the autograph manuscript is partly preserved in Cambridge (Browne, 1932, pp. 2-4) and partly in the library of the University of Tehran. Scattered fragments exist of his poetry, which, generally of very poor quality and almost incomprehensible, is filled with fantastic amalgams of bizarre imagery with all sorts of random allusions to history, mythology, legendary lore, political events of the time, mystic visions, etc. His most famous works to be published in England were the *Šomaysa-ye landanīya* and *Sodayra-ye nāsūtīya* (1882). His work can also be seen in an English-Persian dictionary compiled by A. N. Wollaston (London, 1889) on which he collaborated. He may also be the author of *Meftāḥ al-ʿerfān fī tartīb ṣowar al-Qorʾān* (Browne, 1932, p. 292).

Bavānātī was totally dedicated to the preaching of his so-called Islamo-Christian religious system. He did not care for money, avoided the company of the wealthy and the powerful, but at the same time, given to extreme loquacity and an uncontrolled bent toward argumentation, he often offended everybody around him by insulting their most cherished beliefs. Browne had characterized him as "a most remarkable and eccentric individual, impossible not to respect and like" (1893, pp. 12-15; *Press and Poetry*, p. 168).

Bibliography; M.-Ḥ. Roknzāda Ādamīyat, *Dānešmandān o soḵansarāyān-e Fārsī* I, Tehran, 1337 Š./1958, pp. 420ff. Ī. Afšār, *Sawād o bayāż* I, Tehran, 1343 Š./1964, pp. 1-45. Idem and A. Mahdawī, *Asnād o madārek-e čāp našoda dar bāra-ye Sayyed Jamāl-al-Dīn maʿrūf be Afḡānī*, Tehran, 1343 Š./1964. Aḥmad Dīvānbīgī Šīrāzī, *Ḥadīqat al-šoʿarāʾ*, ed. ʿA. Navāʾī, Tehran, 1366 Š./1987, III, pp. 1636-41. E. G. Browne, *Press and Poetry*, pp. 168-74 (picture of Bavānātī). Idem, *A Descriptive Catalogue of the Oriental Manuscripts Belonging to the late E. G. Browne*, completed by R. A. Nicholson, Cambridge, 1932, p. 37. N. Keddie, *Sayyid Jamāl-al-Dīn "al-Afghānī": A Political Biography*, Berkeley, etc., 1972. Ḥājī Moḥammad-ʿAlī Pīrzāda Nāʾīnī, *Safar-nāma*, ed. Ḥ. Farmānfarmāʾīān, Tehran, 1342 Š./1963, pp. 207-15. ʿAbd-al-Ḥosayn Navāʾī, "Īn īrānī-e ʿajīb," *Eṭṭelāʿāt-e māhāna* 3/1, 1329 Š./1950, pp. 15-18. Shaikh Mofīd Šīrāzī, *Merʾāt al-faṣāḥa*, MS belonging to Jaʿfar Solṭān-al-Qorāʾī. Moḥammad-Ḥosayn Šoʿāʿ-al-Molk Šīrāzī, *Taḏkera-ye šoʿāʿīya*, MS, Ketāb-ḵāna-ye Malek. Tehran, no. 3839, pp. 444-52. S./Ḥ. Taqīzāda, "Sayyed Jamāl-al-Dīn," *Kāva* 2/3, N.S., 1921, p. 10.

(Ī. AFŠĀR)

BĀVĪ (or Bābūʾī), a Luri-speaking tribe of the Kohgīlūya (Kūh[-e] Gīlūye). According to Ḥasan Fasāʾī, it is an offshoot of the Arab Bāwīya tribe of Ḵūzestān (*Fārs-nāma* II, p. 270), but V. Minorsky suggests that the name Bāvī could also have come from a mountain by that name south of Ḵorramābād ("Lur," in *EI*[2] V, p. 822).

According to tribal legend, the Bāvīs opposed Nāder Shah, and were transplanted to Khorasan as a result. There, their chief, Hāšem Khan, was at first made a governor by Nāder and then blinded by him. After Nāder's death in 1160/1747, the tribe, under the leadership of Hāšem Khan's son, returned to the Kohgīlūya (C. A. de Bode, *Travels in Luristan and Arabistan*, London, 1845, I, p. 278).

The Bāvīs reached the apex of their power and influence during the reign of Karīm Khan Zand. In 1173/1759-60, their chief, Heybat-Allāh Khan, son of Masīḥ Khan, was made the governor of the districts of the Čahār Boniča tribes (Boir Aḥmadī, Čorām, Došmanzīārī, Novī), of the Līrāvīs, and of the Tayyebī and Bahmaʾī (q.v.) tribes. After he died, his son, Moḥammad-Taqī Khan replaced him as the chief magistrate (*kalāntar*) of the Bāvī and Bāšt districts (Fasāʾī, II, p. 270; M. Bāvar, *Kūhgīlūya wa īlāt-e ān*, Gačsārān, 1324 Š./1945, p. 111).

In general, the Bāvīs have been a small tribe surrounded by more powerful and more belligerent neighbors, such as the Mamasanīs and the Boir Aḥmadīs. The latter, in particular, proved to be a constant threat. For example, in 1273/1856-57 Allāhkaram Khan Bāvī, the *kalāntar* of the Bāvīs, and his son were treacherously murdered by the men of Ḵodākaram Khan, the *kalāntar* of the Boir Aḥmadī, and then the Boir Aḥmadis plundered the entire Bāvī district (Fasā'ī, II, p. 270). And again in early 1309 Š./1930, Sartīp Khan Boir Aḥmadī slew the Bāvī chief, Asad-Allāh Khan, and then plundered his fort and possessions (Bāvar, p. 113).

The Bāvīs are now sedentary. They dwell in the *dehestān* of Pošt-e Kūh Bāšt Bābū'ī, and their principal center is the large village of Bāšt, 60 km east of Behbahān (Razmārā, *Farhang* VI, pp. 36, 76). The population of the Bāvīs was estimated at upwards of 4,000 families by de Bode (p. 277), at 1,200 families by M. L. Sheil (*Glimpses of Life and Manners in Persia*, London, 1856, p. 399), at more than 1,500 families by Fasā'ī (II, p. 270), and at 1,200 families by G. Demorgny ("Les réformes administratives en Perse: Les tribus du Fars," pt. 1, *RMM* 22, March, 1913, p. 112) and by M. Kayhān (*Joḡrāfīā* II, p. 88).

According to Kayhān, the Bāvī clans were: 'Alīšāhī, Gašīn, Mūsā'ī, Barāftābī, and Qal'a'ī (or 'Amala; *Joḡrāfīā* II, p. 88).

Bibliography: Given in text. See also M. Żarrābī, "Ṭawāyef-e Kohgīlūya," *FIZ* 9, 1340 Š./1961-62, pp. 300-01.

(P. Oberling)

BĀWĪYA, a Shi'ite tribe of Ḵūzestān. They range east and south of Ahvāz, between the Kārūn and Jarrāḥī rivers, to the south of Band-e Qīr and north of Māred. Estimated at 20,000 individuals in the early years of this century, of which 18,500 were nomadic, and 2,320 families in the 1930s, they were formerly camel breeders but have progressively sedentarized and diversified their livestock. They are organized in six sections with fifteen clans (Lorimer, *Gazetteer* II, pp. 119, 293-96; Oppenheim, IV, pp. 25, 90; Field, pp. 190-91; *Persia*, pp. 378-380).

They claim a proud lineage, which includes the pre-Islamic hero Mohalhel, but their early history is obscure. They apparently originated in the Banī Rabī'a of Iraq and moved into Iran in the late 10th/16th century along with the Banī Lām (q.v.). Their territory was immediately northwest of that of the Banī Ka'b (q.v.), with whom they have had a long association and rivalry, including occasional hostilities. In the winter of 1914-15, in common with several other of the Ḵūzestān tribes, they attacked the British force occupying Ahvāz, with which Shaikh Ḵaz'al of the Ka'b was in alliance. Since the late 1940s they have entirely sedentarized, in some sixty villages (Oppenheim, III, p. 356, IV, pp. 89-91).

Splinter groups of Bāwīya have dispersed among other tribes in both Iraq and Iran; there is a Bāwīya subsection of the 'Arab, a constituent tribe of the Ḵamsa confederacy ('Azzāwī, IV, pp. 191-92; Oppenheim, IV, p. 92).

Bibliography: (Great Britain) Admiralty, *Persia*, Geographical Handbook Series, Oxford, 1945. 'A. 'Azzāwī, *'Ašā'er al-'Erāq*, 4 vols., Baghdad, 1947. H. Field, *Contributions to the Anthropology of Iran*, Chicago, 1939. M. Freiherr von Oppenheim, *Die Beduinen*, ed. W. Caskel, 4 vols., Wiesbaden, 1967.

(J. Perry)

BÄX FÄLDISI̱N "horse dedication" (from *bäx* "horse" and *fäldisi̱n* "to dedicate or consecrate to the dead"), a funeral rite practiced by the Ossetes until recent times.

At the burial of a chieftain or other prominent man a horse was dedicated to the soul of the dead as a means of conveyance to paradise (*dzänät*). Before the interment a kind of funeral sermon was declaimed, where a detailed description of the journey through the land of the dead (*märdti̱ bästä*) was given. The ceremony included also dedication of the widow to the needs of the deceased in the other world. On its way, the soul has to cross a narrow bridge, consisting of a single beam or hair. At either side of the bridge the soul is usually met by Aminon, the judge (or doorkeeper) of the netherworld, who questions it about its good and evil deeds; in some texts the meeting with Aminon is omitted. Having crossed the bridge, the soul encounters a parade of people who either suffer punishment or receive reward for their actions in life. There is no distinction between heaven and hell; the good and the bad get their deserts indiscriminately in the same place. A common means of punishment is ice; thus the unrighteous judges sit on ice chairs, at ice tables, with sticks of ice in their hands. In the end the soul arrives at paradise, where it is received by Barasti̱r, the lord of the netherworld. In some texts the bridge is placed immediately before the arrival in paradise.

After the funeral a horse race (*dug'*) was arranged; sometimes this took place at a commemorative festival that was celebrated at some fixed date (e.g., seven or forty days, or one year) after the funeral itself. Great importance was attached to the funeral banquet, where it was usual to entertain hundreds of people for days, often with disastrous financial consequences for the family of the deceased.

Bäx fäldisi̱n sermons were first recorded about the middle of the 19th century, and a number of texts have since been published. There is some variation regarding details, but in all essentials both the structure of the texts and the eschatological notions they reflect are the same. The archaic language, characterized by conventional formulas and set phrases that recur practically unaltered in the various texts, testifies to an old tradition that has been orally transmitted from generation to generation. In the eschatology, Christian and Islamic notions mingle with each other and with autochthonous Ossetic and north Caucasian beliefs, and it is therefore often difficult to distinguish between ancient Iranian (Scytho-Sarmatian) elements and later accretions. However, the Iranian origin of both the ceremonies and the basic ideas behind them is indisputable.

Similar ceremonies were found all over the north Caucasus and among the east Georgian mountain tribes (the Khevsurs, Pshavs, Tushes). Funeral sermons of the *bäx fäldisi̱n* type are, however, recorded only among the Ossetes.

The eschatological notions of the *bäx fäldisin* sermons recur in the legends about the *katabasis* of Soslan, the Nart hero. In order to win the heart of Aciruxs, the Sun's daughter, Soslan needs the help of his dead wife, Beduxa, and must therefore descend to the netherworld, a deed that is normally beyond human power. On his way he meets the same visions, examples of rewards and punishments, as the soul of the *bäx fäldisin* sermons. These visions are explained to him by Beduxa. It is reasonable to believe that both in the sermons and in the Soslan legend some orally transmitted visionary traditions are reflected, and that they are somehow related to shamanistic practices (shamanism has been widespread in the north Caucasus and among the east Georgian highlanders until modern times).

The symbolic dedication of the horse (and the widow) has no doubt replaced an older custom of bloody sacrifice. This is borne out by the testimony of ancient Greek authors (see especially Herodotus, 4. 71-73), as well as by the finds made in the barrows of southern Russia and the Ponto-Caspian steppes, where both human and equine sacrifices are well attested. The change in funeral customs, which must have taken place in the early Middle Ages, can probably be ascribed to Christian (and perhaps Islamic) influence; the gradual concentration of the Ossetes (Alans) in the mountainous area of the central Caucasus, where horse pastures are relatively poor, may also have contributed to the development.

See also ASB, iii.

Bibliography: The Ossetic funeral rites are treated by B. Gatiev in *Sbornik svedeniĭ o kavkazskikh gortsakh* 9/3, Tiflis, 1876, pp. 2-18. V. F. Miller in *Osetinskie etyudy* II, Moscow, 1882, pp. 294-97; cf. also ibid., pp. 287-88, 245-47 (Barastir, Aminon). M. Kovalewsky in *Coutume contemporaine et loi ancienne. Droit coutumier ossétien*, Paris, 1893, pp. 50-63. R. Bleichsteiner in *Rossweihe und Pferderennen im Totenkult der kaukasischen Völker*, Wiener Beiträge zur Kulturgeschichte und Linguistik 4, Salzburg and Vienna, 1936, pp. 413-95. A. Kh. Magometov in *Kul'tura i byt osetinskogo naroda*, Ordzhonikidze, 1968, pp. 375-87. See also G. Dumézil. *Légendes sur les Nartes*, Paris, 1930, pp. 158-61 and pp. 200-02. Idem, *Romans de Scythie et d'alentour*, Paris, 1978, pp. 249-61. The funeral rites of the east Georgian highlanders are described by G. Charachidze in *Le système religieux de la Géorgie païenne*, Paris, 1968, pp. 303-404. *Bäx fäldisin* texts were published by A. Schiefner in *Bulletin de l'Académie impériale des sciences de Saint-Pétersbourg* 5, 1863, cols. 449-53, 6, 1863, cols. 453-58; by V. F. Miller in *Osetinskie etyudy* I, Moscow, 1881, pp. 108-15 (commentaries pp. 132-34). A collection of texts is found in *Iron adämi sfäldistad* II, Ordzhonikidze, 1961, pp. 396-417. Regarding early literature, see also the bibliographies in G. Dumézil and R. Bleichsteiner, opp. cit. The Ossetic funeral rites are discussed in their Iranian context by G. Widengren, *Die Religionen des Iran*, Stuttgart, 1965, pp. 165-70. *Soslan's katabasis*: a variant of the legend, is found in *Narti kaddžitä*, Dzäudžiqäu, 1946, pp. 115-35; French tr. by G. Dumézil in *Le livre des héros*, Paris, pp. 116-34; regarding other variants, see idem, *Légendes sur les Nartes*, Paris, 1930, pp. 103-05. On the Greek literary sources and the archeological finds of the Scytho-Sarmatian tombs, see E. H. Minns, *Scythians and Greeks*, Cambridge, 1913, pp. 87-97, 149-240. S. M. Rostovtzeff, *Iranians and Greeks in South Russia*, New York, 1921 (repr. 1969). Idem, *Skythien und der Bosporus* I, Berlin, 1931. T. T. Rice, *The Scythians*, London, 1957, pp. 92-124. B. N. Grakov, *Skify*, Moscow, 1971 (German tr. *Die Skythen*, Berlin, 1980), esp. chap. 8.

(F. THORDARSON)

BAYĀN, a noun common to Arabic and Persian meaning "statement," "exposition," "explanation." From an early date onward, it also encompassed the various arts of expression in speech and writing. As a critical term, *bayān* refers especially to clarity of expression (*ḥosn-e bayān*); this quality was reckoned among the essential characteristics of eloquence. In time, *bayān* became more or less synonymous with *balāḡa* and *faṣāḥa*. Often *ʿelm-e bayān* merely denotes rhetoric as a whole.

Although these general notions always remained with *bayān*, the term acquired a more technical definition in the 7th/13th century, when the rhetorical disciplines concerned with Arabic literature were redefined. The new system developed from ideas about the functioning of syntax and figurative speech in literature, which more than a century earlier had been expounded, without much coherence, in the *Dalāʾel eʿjāz al-Qorʾān* and the *Asrār al-balāḡa* by ʿAbd-al-Qāher Jorjānī (d. ca. 471/1078). The literary disciplines were arranged into a scholastic system by Sakkākī (555-626/1160-1228) in his work on the classification of sciences, *Meftāḥ al-ʿolūm*, and then popularized through digests from Sakkākī's work made by Jalāl-al-Dīn Moḥammad Qazvīnī, known also as Ḵaṭīb Demašq (d. 739/1338), Saʿd-al-Dīn Taftazānī (d. 792/1390), and others. In the terminology which henceforth dominated Arabic literary theory, *ʿelm al-balāḡa*, the science of rhetoric, consisted of three branches: (1) *ʿelm al-maʿānī*, the semantics of Arabic syntax; (2) *ʿelm al-bayān*, the theory of figurative speech proper; and (3) *ʿelm al-badīʿ*, the remaining forms of rhetorical embellishment.

ʿElm al-bayān is usually defined as a theory of the different ways to express a given thought with greater or lesser clarity (cf., e.g., Sakkākī, *Meftāḥ*, Cairo, 1317/1899, p. 167). It is based on the various modes by which a concept could be indicated. Indication by means of the conventional or literal meanings of words (*dalāla ważʿīya*) falls outside the definition just mentioned, because it does not allow any variation in the clarity of the expression. The true object of *bayān* is therefore figurative speech, which again can be divided into two types: signification by implication (*tażammon*) and signification on the basis of an association (*eltezām*), i.e., by means of a notion which is not inherent in the concept itself but is somehow related to it. The main items discussed under this heading are simile (*tašbīh*), trope (*majāz*), and metonymy (*kenāya*). The treatment of simile includes the analysis of the aspect (*wajh*) of the comparison and its purpose (*ḡaraż*). Among tropes, a further distinction is made between metaphor (*este'āra*), which involves a comparison, and "free trope" (*majāz-e morsal*), constructed on the basis of an abstract relationship such as that between the part and the whole, the cause and its effect, or the position (*maḥall*) and the thing which occupies it (*ḥāll*). The treatment of these subjects in *'elm-e bayān* differed significantly from that applied to them in older textbooks following the tradition inaugurated by the *Ketāb al-badīʿ* of Ebn al-Moʿtazz in the 3rd/9th century, where they were not distinguished from other figures of speech. One of *'elm-e bayān*'s advantages over the earlier tradition was that its methods led to a more explicit treatment of literary citations used in evidence.

The Persian study of rhetoric originated in the older Arabic tradition, for which the model had been set by Ebn al-Moʿtazz's *Ketāb al-badīʿ*. The most influential Persian works, the *Ḥadāʾeq al-seḥr* by Rašīd-e Vaṭvāṭ and the *Moʿjam* by Šams-e Qays-e Rāzī, were both written before the system of Sakkākī and his followers was introduced. This explains why *'elm-e bayān* as an independent and systematic theory of figurative speech was not widely accepted in Persian literary scholarship. Most later textbooks were still designed as mere lists of figures of speech, which, at most, drew a distinction between figures based on meaning and those based on sound. This does not mean, however, that Persian literati remained ignorant of the scholastic system. Among the scholars who took a leading role in its early development were many Iranians. In Persian-speaking countries, the system became an integral part of higher education through the teaching of Arabic and its literature. The influence of the scholastic approach also did not leave the study of Persian literature itself untouched. In 880/1475 Maḥmūd Gāwān, an Iranian vizier at the Bahmanid court of the Deccan, dealt with *'elm-e bayān* separately in the introduction to a work on Persian epistolography, *Manāẓer al-enšāʾ*, (cf. the description in G. Flügel, *Die arabischen, persischen und türkischen Handschriften der K.-K. Hofbibliothek zu Wien*, Vienna, 1865, I, pp. 237-40). Another early example of the application of *'elm-e bayān* is the *Resāla dar este'āra wa ḥaqīqat wa majāz* by 'Eṣām-al-Dīn Ebrāhīm Esferāʾenī (died at Samarqand in 944/1537), a monograph on tropes which in the 18th century was translated as least twice into Arabic (cf. C. Brockelmann, *GAL*, S. II, p. 571). The following works seem to have been written on the same principles: *Bayān-e badīʿ* by Mīrzā Abū Ṭāleb (about 1670); *Anwār al-balāḡa* by Āqā Moḥammad Hādī Motarjem (d. 1120/1708-09); *Mawhebat-e 'oẓmā* and *'Aṭīa-ye kobrā* by Serāj-al-Dīn Akbarābādī Ārzū (1101-69/1689-1755); *Toḥfat al-safar le-nūr al-baṣar* by 'Alī-Akbar Nawāb Šīrāzī Besmel (1187-1263/1773-1846); and *Nokbat al-bayān* by Mollā Mahdī Narāqī (d. 1209/1794-95) (Monzawî, *Noskahā* III, pp. 2125-51, passim), none of which achieved popularity. A more successful specimen of the Persian *'elm al-bayān* treatise was included in the textbook of rhetoric and prosody called *Ḥadāʾeq al-balāḡa* by Mīr Šams-al-Dīn Faqīr-e Dehlavī (1141-83/1728-69). It was printed several times on the Indian subcontinent (for the first time in 1814 at Calcutta), but it is best known in the French adaptation by Joseph Garcin de Tassy (*Rhétorique et prosodie des langues de l'Orient musulman*, Paris, 1873, repr. Amsterdam, 1970, pp. 1-77). Faqīr closely followed the pattern of the Arabic textbooks, but his book is of intrinsic interest to the Persianist because nearly all of its quotations are from Persian poetry.

Bibliography: A. F. Mehren, *Die Rhetorik der Araber*, Copenhagen and Vienna, 1853, pp. 20-42, 53ff. *EI*² s.vv. Bayān, al-Maʿānī wa'l-Bayān, Madjāz. 'A. Zarrīnkūb, *Šeʿr-e bīdorūḡ, šeʿr-e bīneqāb*, 3rd ed., Tehran, 2536 = 1356 Š./1977, pp. 53-63. Storey, *Persian Literature* III/1, Leiden, 1984, pp. 176-206.

(J. T. P. de Bruijn)

BAYĀN (declaration, elucidation), term applied to the writings of the Bāb (q.v.) in general (*Bayān-e fārsī* 3:17, p. 102; 6:1, pp. 184-85) and to two late works in particular, the *Bayān-e fārsī* and *al-Bayān al-'arabī*. The Bāb's first full-length work was a *tafsīr* of the *sūra al-Baqara*, begun in late 1259/1843 or early 1260/1844 and finished several months later; the original manuscript of the second half was stolen during the Bāb's *ḥajj* journey of 1260-61/1844-45, but several copies of the first part have survived. This portion at least contains little of a strikingly heterodox nature, although the *tafsīr* itself is highly interpretative. More important is the *tafsīr* on the *sūra Yūsof*, known as the *Qayyūm al-asmāʾ* or *Aḥsan al-qeṣaṣ* or simply the *Tafsīr* par excellence. Dating of this work is somewhat problematic, but there is internal evidence that it was begun in 1260/1844 and completed later that year or in early 1261/1845; other accounts state that it was finished by June, 1844, and it is certain that disciples of the Bāb carried copies of the entire work or large portions of it when they left Shiraz that summer. The Bāb himself states that this work was widely distributed during the first year of his career (*Bayān-e fārsī* 4:18, p. 148). Divided into 111 *sūras* (each devoted to a verse of the *sūra Yūsof*), this is a work of some 400 pages composed in a style similar to that of the Koran. It is described as having been sent down by God to the Hidden Imam and subsequently revealed by him to the Bāb (for details, see MacEoin *From Shaykhism to Babism: A study in Charismatic Renewal in Shīʿi Islam*, Ph.D. dissertation, Cambridge University, 1979, p. 159). Early copies, dated 1845 and 1846, are extant in Haifa and Tehran. The Bāb penned several shorter works during the year between the announcement of his claims in May, 1844, and his return to Būšehr from the *ḥajj* in May, 1845. There has been confusion as to what these works were, but they can be identified from detailed references in the *Ketāb al-fehrest*, written by the Bāb in

Būšehr in Jomādā II, 1261/June, 1845. This short work lists the *Do'ā-ye ṣaḥīfa*, *Ṣaḥīfa bayn al-ḥaramayn*, *Tafsīr besmellāh*, *Ketāb al-rūḥ*, *Ṣaḥīfat a'māl al-sana*, thirty-eight letters to individuals, twelve *kotbas* delivered on the *ḥajj* journey, and replies to forty-one questions. The titles are also given of several works stolen in February, 1845, between Medina and Jedda. The *Do'ā-ya ṣaḥīfa* seems to have been contemporary with the *Qayyūm al-asmā'* and may be referred to in it (fol. 67b). It is also known as the *Ṣaḥīfa-ye makzūna* and contains fourteen prayers for use on specific days or festivals; at least seven mss. are extant. The *Ṣaḥīfa bayn al-ḥaramayn* was written between Mecca and Medina for Mīrzā Moḥīṭ Kermānī and Sayyed 'Alī Kermānī, two leading Shaikhis from Karbalā' also on the *ḥajj*. Only about 100 short pages long, it is an unsystematic collection of replies to questions together with prayers; it contains a particularly interesting passage detailing the daily routine of the seeker (*sālek*; pp. 66-84). Several mss. are extant, including two dated 1261/1845, in Haifa and Tehran. Several mss. exist of a *Tafsīr ḥorūf al-besmellāh*, which appears to be identical with the *Tafsīr besmellāh* referred to and which is a short allegorical commentary. The *Ketāb al-rūḥ*, composed at sea on the return journey from the *ḥajj*, was highly regarded by the Bāb, who described it as "the greatest of all books" (Māzandarānī, *Asrār* IV, p. 44); it was seized at the time of the Bāb's arrest in June, 1845, and thrown into a well in Shiraz, from which it was later rescued in a seriously damaged condition. Some five incomplete mss. are in existence. It is said to have consisted originally of 700 *sūras* (*Ketāb al-fehrest*). The *Ṣaḥīfat a'māl al-sana* seems to have been written in Būšehr after the Bāb's return from the *ḥajj*, between May and June, 1845. It contains fourteen sections interspersed with unnumbered sections and deals with the observances and prayers for important dates in the Muslim calendar. Only two mss. of this breviary are known to exist. Not mentioned by name in the *Ketāb al-fehrest* is another work composed during the *ḥajj*, the *Kaṣā'el-e sab'a*, which includes seven interesting but scarcely radical rules prescribed for the Bāb's followers at this juncture. It is known to the present writer only through quotations in later works, but at least one ms. appears to exist in private hands.

Of considerable importance are two works probably composed shortly after the Bāb's return to Shiraz in July, 1845. These are two related treatises, the *Ṣaḥīfa-ye 'adlīya* and the *Resāla forū' al-'adlīya*, the former dealing with *oṣūl al-dīn* and the latter with certain *forū'* of Shi'ite *feqh*. The first consists of five *abwāb*: 1. on the mention of God, 2. in explanation of the Balance, 3. on the knowledge of God and his *awlīā'*, 4. on the return to God, 5. on the prayer of devotion to God. It appears to have been the first Persian work of the Bāb's (see pp. 3-4) and is of particular importance in helping us form a clear picture of his thought at this juncture, especially since it seems to represent his first effort at addressing a wider audience than the Shaikhi *'olamā'*. For details of some of its contents, see BĀB. Some dozen mss. are extant. The second of these works is less common but has the distinction of being the earliest of the Bāb's works to have been translated (from Arabic to Persian between 1262/1846 and 1263/1847). It consists of seven chapters (*abwāb*): 1. a short prayer for all the imams (*zīāra jāme'a ṣaḡīra*, 2. on daily prayer (*ṣalāt*), 3. on the regulations for prayer (*aḥkām al-ṣalāt*), 4. on the alms tax (*zakāt*), 5. on *koms*, 6. on jihad, 7. on borrowing (*dayn*), all dealt with in the traditional manner. Only three mss. are known to the present writer. Another important work from this period is a *tafsīr* on the *Sūrat al-kawṯar*, a commentary of over 200 pages written for Sayyed Yaḥyā Dārābī (q.v.) during a visit he made to Shiraz to interview the Bāb, possibly on behalf of Moḥammad Shah. This commentary consists largely of highly abstract and insubstantial speculations on the verses, words, and letters of the *sūra* in question. Of greater interest are numerous Hadiths quoted in a section toward the end, which indicate the Bāb's familiarity with works of tradition and his concern with prophecies relating to the advent of the Qā'em. There is evidence that this work was highly regarded by the Bāb's followers and widely distributed by them. Some ten mss. are extant, including one in Cambridge and one in London. During this period, the Bāb wrote several short *tafsīrs*, including those on the *Āyat al-nūr*, the *Sūrat al-qadr*, the *Sūrat al-tawḥīd*, and various Hadiths; he also continued to pen replies to queries from a large number of correspondents and to write brief treatises on topics such as compulsion and free will (*jabr* and *tafwīż*), predestination (*qadar*), and even grammar and syntax (*naḥw wa ṣarf*). Mss. of most of this material are extant.

Only two works of any importance may be ascribed to the period of the Bāb's residence in Isfahan from September, 1846, to March, 1847: a *tafsīr* on the *Sūra wa'l-'aṣr* and a *resāla* on the topic of the *nobowwa kāṣṣa* of Moḥammad. The first of these was written for the *emām-e jom'a* of Isfahan, Mīr Sayyed Moḥammad: some 100 pages in length, it was, apparently, penned in the space of about one day. Eight mss. are known, including one in Cambridge. The second was composed in two hours for Manūčehr Khan Mo'tamed-al-Dawla, governor of Isfahan. It is a short work of some fifty pages designed as an apologetic for the prophethood of Moḥammad. Some seven mss. are extant. Several surviving minor works—mostly letters—may also be dated from this period.

The style and content of the Bāb's works change markedly in the three-year period Rabī' II, 1263/March, 1847–Ramażān, 1266/July, 1850) of his imprisonment in Azerbaijan, when his claims and doctrines underwent a major transition (see BĀB). The most important work of this period and, indeed, the central book of the Babi canon, is the *Bayān-e fārsī*, a lengthy but incomplete work of nine *wāḥeds* (units) each of nineteen *abwāb* (chapters), except for the last, which has only ten. It was originally intended to complete this work in nineteen *wāḥeds*, an aim which seems to have been frustrated by the Bāb's death. (A continuation entitled *Motammem-e Bayān* was later written by Mīrzā Yaḥyā Ṣobḥ-e Azal and has been published.) The

Bayān-e fārsī was begun toward the end of the Bāb's stay in Mākū and contains a full expression of his doctrine as elaborated between then and his execution, together with the basic laws and regulations of the Babi *Šarīʿa*. Its contents have been discussed in a number of places, to which reference may be made (Rosen, III, pp. 1-32; Browne, 1889, pp. 918-33; idem, *Nuqṭatu'l-kāf*, London, 1910, pp. LIV-XCV; Wilson, "The Bayan"). A lithograph edition of this work, based on several mss., was published in Tehran about 1946 by the Azalī Babis, but copies of it are now rare. A. L. M. Nicolas published a French translation between 1911 and 1914. Preliminary materials for a collated edition based on six mss. may be found among the Browne papers in Cambridge University Library. Some fifty mss. are known to this writer, including two in Cambridge, two in Leningrad, two in London, two in Paris, and a defective but important copy in the hand of the Bāb's amanuensis, Sayyed Ḥosayn Yazdī, preserved by the Bahais in Haifa. The much shorter Arabic *Bayān* was also written in Mākū and, like the Persian *Bayān*, is incomplete, with only eleven *wāḥed*s. Each *wāḥed* has ninteen *abwāb*, but these latter are each little more than a verse in length, the overall effect being one of great compression with little or no logic in the sequence of subjects, dictated by the fact that this work is basically little more than a statement of the principal doctrines and regulations of the Persian *Bayān*. Gobineau's statement (*Religions et philosophies dans l'Asie centrale*, 10th ed., Paris, 1957, pp. 279-80) that there are three *Bayān*s, two in Arabic, is unfounded. Much rarer than its Persian equivalent, this work exists in some thirteen mss. (one an autograph), two of which are in Paris. It has been lithographed from the holograph ms. by the Azalī Babis in Tehran (n.d.), printed (in ʿAbd-al-Razzāq Ḥasanī, *al-Bābīyūn wa'l-Bahāʾīyūn*, Sidon, 1957, pp. 81-107), and twice translated into French (Gobineau, *Religions*, appendix: "Ketab-è Hukkam," pp. 409-82 [incomplete and inaccurate]; Nicolas—see bibliography). A related work, composed in the last period of the Bāb's life, is the *Haykal al-dīn*, originally written in two copies, one in the hand of the Bāb, one in that of Sayyed Ḥosayn Yazdī, both of which appear to have been lost. Other copies have since been located, however, and the text has been published in lithograph together with the Arabic *Bayān*. It is a compendium in eight *wāḥed*s of the laws of the Bāb and, although it parallels the contents of the Arabic *Bayān* in most particulars, it frequently gives fresh or modified regulations. Another short but important work is the Persian *Dalāʾel-e sabʿa*, supported, like the Persian *Bayān*, by an even briefer Arabic version. There has been disagreement as to the date of its composition, but clear internal evidence indicates that it was written at the end of 1264/1848 in Mākū. There has also been some controversy as to the identity of the recipient addressed in the text (the two main theories favoring either Sayyed Ḥosayn Yazdī or Mollā Moḥammad-Taqī Heravī), but all that can be said with certainty is that this individual was either not a believer or was a believer with doubts, had been a pupil of Sayyed Kāẓem Raštī (q.v.), and had met Mollā Moḥammad Ḥosayn Bošrūʾī (q.v.). This work provides seven "proofs" of the Bāb's mission, discusses his claim to *qāʾemīya*, cites numerous Hadiths of a prophetic nature, and refers by name to several of the Bāb's followers. Thirteen mss. are known to me, of which two are in Cambridge, one in London, and one in Paris. A lithograph edition has been published. An extremely lengthy work of this period is the *Ketāb al-asmāʾ* (also *Tafsīr al-asmāʾ* and *Ketāb asmāʾ koll šayʾ*), which consists largely of lengthy variations on the names of God, interspersed with doctrinal statements. It has been ascribed to the later Čahrīq period. Normally found in two volumes, the entire work consists of nineteen *wāḥed*s of nineteen *abwāb* each, but defective copies are almost standard. Its popularity is clear from the large number of extant mss., twenty-six of which are known to me (three in Cambridge, seven in London, four in Paris). Another of the Bāb's last works, similar in character to the last, is the *Ketāb-e panj šaʾn* or *Šoʾūn-e ḵamsa*. This originally consisted of seventeen sections of five passages each, arranged according to the "five grades" in which the Bāb stated his works to have been written (*Bayān-e fārsī* 3:17; 6:1; 9:2): *āyāt*, *monājāt*, *ḵotba* (= *ṣowar ʿelmīya*), *tafsīr*, and *fārsī*. The work was written over a seventeen-day period during Jomādā I, 1266/March-April, 1850, completed sections being sent, apparently, to individuals named in them. Eleven mss. are extant, one in Cambridge, two in London, and one in Paris. Numerous letters and *zīārat-nāma*s from this period are also extant, as are examples of talismans (*dawāʾer*, *hayākel*) in the Bāb's hand or containing passages from his writings.

It is impossible to comment adequately on the Bāb's style without extensive quotation in the original languages, but some general remarks will be in order. Although there are major changes in style and form, the striking characteristic of the Bāb's writing at all periods is its opacity and the syntactical contortions of the language, something true of both Persian and Arabic works. The Bāb's Arabic grammar is consistently bad (a point often referred to in Muslim criticisms but dismissed by Babis as the prerogative of a prophet), as a result of which some passages are incomprehensible: The reader must be guided for the most part by context and a developed feeling for the style than by strict reliance on grammar or syntax. Works like the *Bayān* are couched in an eccentric Persian style which often conceals the author's meaning, while others, such as the *Ketāb al-asmāʾ*, are unconnected and repetitive to an exaggerated degree. Much of this apparent incoherence seems to be a result of the considerable speed at which the Bāb composed (or "revealed") his works, a point to which he frequently alludes as evidence of divine inspiration. This inspirational quality—which may owe much to the disconnected nature of the Koran—becomes increasingly marked in the later works, where it is not infrequently linked to ideas and images of an exciting, vivid, and highly original nature. The effort required to penetrate the obscurities of the style of the persian *Bayān* in particular is often rewarded by access to fresh insights, and it cannot be denied that the more developed works display an unusual genius that thoroughly justifies their study.

All of the writings of the Bāb were recorded in the first instance in his own hand or in that of one of a number of amanuenses, of whom Sayyed Ḥosayn Yazdī (a "Letter of the Living") was by far the most important. These original texts appear to have been written in some form of "revelation script" (*ḵaṭṭ-e waḥy*), a form of shorthand devised to accommodate the Bāb's rapid dictation; few examples of these appear to have survived, however. Transcription of these originals was carried out to a large extent under the supervision of the Bāb himself, principally by Mollā ʿAbd-al-Karīm Qazvīnī and Shaikh Ḥasan Zonūzī. Numerous copies were made from these transcriptions during the Bāb's lifetime, an activity encouraged in the Persian *Bayān*, which makes the possession of a *ṣaḥīfa* of at least 1,000 verses obligatory for all Babis and gives instructions regarding the preparation of copies of the *Bayān* itself. There is evidence for wide distribution of copies of at least the major works of the Bāb before 1266/1850, but it is also clear that large numbers of manuscripts must have perished in the disturbed conditions of this and the immediately succeeding period. Those Babis who left Iran for Baghdad in 1853 seem to have carried a substantial number of texts with them and to have made efforts in later years to assemble copies of scriptural works in Iran for transfer to Iraq. Toward the end of the 13th/19th century, the British scholar Edward G. Browne was instrumental in having numerous Babi mss. transcribed for himself, largely by Azalī scribes; these now form an important part of the Browne collection in Cambridge University Library. Other Babi mss. were also acquired by the British Museum (now British Library), the Bibliothèque Nationale, and the Oriental Languages Institute in Petrograd. An important private collection belonging to the French scholar A. L. M. Nicolas was dispersed by sale in Paris in 1969; it seems that most (but not all) of it was purchased by the Bahai World Center in Israel. By far the largest and most important collections of Babi mss. are those in the national Bahai archives of Iran in Tehran and the international Bahai archives in Haifa. The former collection is extensive but uncatalogued and remains inaccessible owing to the conditions pertaining for the Bahais in Iran; its significance is considerable, however, in that it contains much extremely rare, even unique material. The latter is at present imperfectly catalogued and not freely accessible, although I am told that this situation may improve following the expansion of library facilities in coming years. There are also large numbers of mss. in the private collections of Azalī families in Iran, but these remain scattered and, for the most part, inaccessible. The Azalīs in Tehran have issued lithograph editions of a number of works of the Bāb, copies of which have become quite rare. The publication of properly edited complete texts of major works remains a sine qua non of future scholarship in this field.

Bibliography:The only detailed study of this subject to date is the present writer's *Early Bābī Doctrine and History: A Survey of Source Materials*, Los Angeles, 1987. See also idem, "Nineteenth-Century Bābī Talismans," *Studia Iranica* 14, 1985, pp. 77-98. The works of E. G. Browne on this subject are still invaluable: "The Bābīs of Persia II: Their Literature and Doctrines," *JRAS* 21, 1889, pp. 881-1009; "A Catalogue and Description of 27 Bābī Manuscripts," ibid., 24, 1892, pp. 433-99, 637-710; "Some Remarks on the Bābī Texts Edited by Baron Victor Rosen . . . ," ibid., 24, 1892, pp. 259-332; "Further Notes on Bābī Literature," in *Materials for the Study of the Bābī Religion*, Cambridge, 1918, esp. pp. 198-208; "Writings of the Bāb and Ṣubḥ-i-Ezel," in *A Traveller's Narrative Written to Illustrate the Episode of the Bāb*, 2 vols., Cambridge, 1891, I, pp. 335-47; completed by R. A. Nicholson, *A Descriptive Catalogue of the Oriental MSS Belonging to the Late E. G. Browne*, Cambridge, 1932, section F. Baron Victor Rosen's articles are also worth referring to: *Collections scientifiques de l'Institut des Langues Orientales du Ministère des Affaires Étrangères* I: *Manuscrits arabes*, St. Petersburg, 1877, pp. 179-212; III: *Manuscrits persans*, ibid., 1886, pp. 1-51; VI: *Manuscrits arabes*, ibid., 1891, pp. 141-255. The Azalī Babis in Tehran have published the following works of the Bāb: *Ṣaḥīfa-ye ʿadlīya*, n.d.; *Bayān-e fārsī*, n.d.; *Dalāʾel-e sabʿa ʿarabī wa fārsī*, n.d.; *al-Bayān al-ʿarabī* with *Ketāb-e haykal al-dīn* and *Tafsīr-e do āya az Haykal al-dīn*, n.d.; *Qesmat-ī az alwāḥ-e ḵaṭṭ-e Noqṭa-ye Ūlā wa Āqā Sayyed Ḥosayn Kāteb*, n.d.; *Majmūʿa-ī az āṯār-e Noqṭa-ye Ūlā wa Ṣobḥ-e Azal*, n.d.. The Bahais have published *Montaḵabāt-e āyāt az āṯār-e Ḥażrat-e Noqṭa-ye Ūlā*, Tehran, 134 *Badīʿ*/1356 Š./1977), together with an English translation by Habib Taherzadeh, *Selections from the Writings of the Bāb* (Haifa, 1976), a heavily edited selection of passages from major works.

The following mss. are among the most important: *Tafsīr Sūrat al-Baqara*, Cambridge University Library [CUL], Browne Or. Ms. F. 8; *Tafsīr Sūrat al-kawṯar*, CUL, Browne Or. Ms. F. 10; *Qayyūm al-asmāʾ*, CUL, Browne Or. Ms. F. 11; Arabic letters, CUL, Browne Or. Ms. F. 21 and 28 (item 7); *Resāla fi'l-solūk*, Iran National Bahai Archives [INBA]4011. C, pp. 123-27; *Ketāb al-rūḥ*, TBA, 4011. C, pp. 61-100, 7005.C; *Ḵoṭba fī Jedda*, INBA, 5006.C, pp. 330-35; *Ketāb ṣaḥīfat aʿmāl al-sana*, INBA, 5006.C, pp. 262-78; *Resāla forūʿ al-ʿAdlīya*, INBA, 5010.C, pp. 86-119; *Ketāb al-fehrest*, INBA, 6003.C, pp. 285-93; *al-Ṣaḥīfa al-makzūna*, INBA, 6009.C, pp. 1-171, CUL, Add. 3704(6).

Several translations of works of the Bāb into French were produced by A. L. M. Nicolas: *Le livre des sept preuves*, Paris, 1902 (*Dalāʾel-e sabʿa*); *Le Beyan arabe*, Paris, 1905; *Le Beyan persan*, 4 vols., Paris, 1911-14. See also S. G. Wilson, "The Bayan of the Bab," *The Princeton Theological Review* 13, October, 1959, pp. 633-54; M. Afnān, "Ketāb-e Bayān: Omm al-ketāb-e dawr-e Bābī," *Āhang-e Badīʿ*, 18 *Badīʿ*/1342 Š./1963, 2, pp. 54-64; idem, "Majmūʿa-ī az āṯār-e mobāraka-ye Ḥażrat-e Noqṭa-ye Ūlā," ibid., 11/12, pp. 412-16, 443.

(D. M. MacEoin)

BAYĀNĪ, MEHDĪ (Mahdī; 1285-1346 Š./1906-68), specialist in Persian manuscripts and calligraphy and pioneer in the field of Persian librarianship. Though born in Hamadān, he was the scion of a long line of *dīvān* secretaries and fiscal officers (*mostawfī*) from Farāhān. He was related to Mīrzā Salmān Farāhānī, secretary and confidant of Abu'l-Qāsem Khan Nāṣer-al-Molk Hamadānī, whose title Bayān-al-Salṭana is apparently the origin of the family name (Bayānī, *Aḥwāl o āṯār-e ḵ ͮošnevīsān*, 2nd ed., Tehran, 1363 Š./1984, introd. by Ḥ. Maḥbūbī Ardakānī, p. 3). Bayānī received his early education and training in calligraphy at the Aqdasīya and Ašrāf primary schools and, after graduating from the secondary school Dār al-Fonūn, enrolled in the Dār al-Moʿallemīn-e ʿĀlī (later Dāneš-sarā-ye ʿĀlī; higher teachers' college). In 1324 Š./1945, Bayānī received a doctorate in Persian literature from the University of Tehran.

Bayānī spent his early career as a teacher of Persian language and literature while working at the same time in the library of Dāneš-sarā-ye ʿĀlī; later he became the head of the Ministry of Education's public library (Ketāb-ḵāna-ye ʿOmūmī-e Maʿāref; 1312-16 Š./1933-37); as the founder and director of the Ketāb-ḵāna-ye Mellī, Iran's first national library, he directed the transferring of the books in the Maʿāref Library to the national library (1316-19 Š./1937-40; see Anjoman-e Maʿāref). He became the director of education for the province of Isfahan in 1319-20 Š./1940-41. In 1335 Š./1956, he was appointed head of the Royal Library (Ketāb-ḵāna-ye Salṭanatī, q.v.), a post which he held until he died on 18 Bahman 1346 Š./7 February 1968. While serving as chief imperial librarian, Bayānī also taught courses on the evolution of Persian scripts and on codicology. Bayānī was a long-time member of the Iran-Soviet Cultural Society and edited the journal *Payām-e now* (q.v.). He also founded a society for the support and publicizing of calligraphers and the calligraphic arts (Anjoman-e ḥemāyat-e ḵaṭṭ o ḵaṭṭāṭān). His biographical dictionary of Iranian calligraphers, *Aḥwāl o āṯār-e ḵ ͮošnevīsān*, is one of the most important research tools in Persian codicology. Bayānī's pioneering efforts in the fields of bibliography and manuscript identification, evaluation, and collection have yielded valuable catalogues of major holdings in Iran.

Among his other published works are: *Rāhnamā-ye ganjīna-ye Qorʾān*, with Mahdī Bahrāmī, Tehran, 1328 Š./1949. *Fehrest-e ḵoṭūṭ-e ḵ ͮoš-e Ketāb-ḵāna-ye Mellī*, 1328 Š./1949. *Nomūna-ye ḵoṭūṭ-e ḵ ͮoš-e Ketāb-ḵāna-ye Salṭanatī-e Īrān*, Tehran, 1329 Š./1950. *Aḥwāl o āṯār Mīr ʿEmād*, Tehran, 1331 Š./1952. *Fehrest-e Ketāb-ḵāna-ye Salṭanatī: Dīvānhā*, Tehran, 1347-48 Š./1968-69.

Bibliography: Ī. Afšār, *Sawād-o-bayāż* II, Tehran, 1350 Š./1971, pp. 546-51. Idem, "Wafāt-e Doktor Mahdī Bayānī," *Rāhnamā-ye ketāb* 11/1-3, 1347 Š./1968, pp. 115-18.

(M. Dabīrsīāqī)

BAYĀT, an important Turkish tribe.

Name and origin. Bayāt was one of the twenty-two Oghuz tribes listed in Maḥmūd Kāšḡarī's *Dīvān loḡāt al-tork* (comp. 464-76/1072-83). The tribe had a traditional brand mark and its totem was the falcon. The form Bayāt is used also by Faḵr-al-Dīn Mobārakšāh (603/1206; p. 48) and later authors such as Ḥasan Rūmlū (984/1576), Eskandar Beg (1025/1616), and Moḥammad-Kāẓem (1145/1733) and in the *Taḏkerat al-molūk* (ca. 1137/1725). The form Bāyāt is found only in Rašīd-al-Dīn's *Jāmeʿ al-tawārīḵ* (early 8th/14th century). The name's etymology is uncertain; it is the regular plural of *bayan* "rich" and may come from the probably Mongol Žuan-žuan. In that case Rašīd-al-Dīn's statement (p. 45) that it means fortunate (*bā-dawlat*) would happen to be correct.

In the 10th/16th century the name, most often in the form Bayad, occurs in forty-two toponyms in the Ottoman tax records. This number, though much smaller than those of names such as Kayï, Afšār, and Kïnïk, falls in the middle of the scale of toponymic occurrences of Oghuz tribal names in the tax records, the range being from four to ninety-four toponyms per tribe. Bayāt tribesfolk spread far into western Anatolia, their principal areas of settlement being in the provinces of Konya, Bursa, Afyon, Balıkesir and Kütahya. Today the name in forms such as Bayat, Bayatlar, Bayatlı is found in thirty-two mainly western Anatolian toponyms (see *Köylerimiz* and *Türkiye'de meskûn yerler kılavuzu*). The name also appears in toponyms in Iran (Bayāt, Bayātān, Bayātlū, Bayātlar); Razmāra lists two of these near Arāk, one near Zanjān, one near Urmia (Reżāʾīya), one in Ḵūzestān at Dašt-e Mīšān, one near Borūjerd, and one in Khorasan near Daragaz (*Farhang* II, p. 45, IV, p. 101, VI, p. 66, IX, p. 66). In Soviet territory, five places in Azerbaijan, four in Turkmenistan, and one in Uzbekistan close to the Turkmenistan border bear the names Bayat, Bayat-Khadzhi, and Bayat-Sindzhap and are listed in Defense Mapping Agency, *Official Standard Names Gazetteer* (cf. idem, 1984, pp. 209-10). In addition, Bayāt is the name of a village south of Baghdad and of small tribal groups in northern Syria and in Turkmenistan on the Āmū Daryā (ca. 39°N, 63°E). Oberling mentions a clan named Bayāt belonging to the Qašqāʾī tribe of Fārs (p. 30).

Cultural contributions. Dede Qorqut, the famous sage of the Oghuz Turks after whom an early Ottoman epic is named, came from the Bayāt tribe. So too did Fożūlī (d. 963/1556), the much admired bilingual (Turkish and Persian) poet. Ḥasan b. Maḥmūd, one of the earliest Turkish historians (9th/15th century), bore the surname Bayātī. The tribe has given its name to a mode in Turkish and Iranian music (see BAYĀT). It was also renowned for its breed of horses (Sümer, "Bayatlar," p. 374).

Early history. A substantial proportion of the Bayāt people must have entered Iran in the train of the Saljuq invaders in the first half of the 5th/11th century. There are mentions of a *nā'eb* (deputy commander) named Sonqor Bayātī at Baṣra in 513/1119 (Ebn al-Aṯīr, Beirut, X, p. 559) and of a castle in Lorestān which from about this time onward bore the name Bayāt. Jovaynī's history (comp. in 658/1260) mentions a Bayāt district in connection with events in Lorestān and Kurdistan (ed. Qazvīnī, III, pp. 283, 471). Another section of the Bayāts remained in the Syr Daryā region; they were among the Oghuz rebels who captured the Saljuq sultan Sanjar in 548/1153. Under the pressure of the Mongol invasion in the 7th/13th century they fled, together with other Oghuz tribes, to Syria and Anatolia.

The Bayāt tribes of Syria, Anatolia, and Iraq. The presence of Bayāt, Afšār, and Begdīlū (qq.v.) tribes in Syria and southeastern Anatolia is attested in sources from the 8th/14th century. They played an important part in the establishment of the Dulkadïr (Ḏu'l-Qadr) state and spread into the Sivas-Yozgat region. Another section continued to live between Aintab and Aleppo and later joined the Āq Qoyunlū (q.v.) confederacy. In the 10th/16th century and thereafter, Bayāt tribal groups were scattered over a vast expanse from Anatolia through Syria and Iraq to eastern Iran. In Syria their strength declined rapidly. The available information, derived mainly from Ottoman tax records, which give names of clans, numbers of households, and numbers of individuals, indicates that Bayāt groups then lived in the following regions (outside Iran). 1. The Bayāts of Aleppo and Aintab, who were gradually reduced to the level of a small tribe through emigration of many of their members to Anatolia and Iran. Today their main surviving groups are named Pahlavānlū and Rayḥānlū. Small Bayāt groups recorded as having lived around Damascus, Ḥamā, and Tripoli must have been offshoots of the Aleppo Bayāts. 2. Two Bayāt groups lived in the Diyarbakır (Dīār Bakr) region under the Boz *ulus*. 3. Much more important were the Šām Bayātī (Şam Bayadı) in Anatolia, who as their name indicates had migrated from Syria; being subjects of the Dulkadïr state, they were also called Dulkadïrlï Bayāt. For the most part they settled around Gedük in the Yozgat district, where they were known as the Boz Ok. Later they became Shi'ites and joined the Safavids. Other Šām Bayātī groups found abodes in the Yeni-Il (north of Malatya), around Amasya where they were known as the Ulu-Yörük, around Ankara, around Maraş, and as far afield as Kütahya and Antalya. Information about the times and circumstances of their migrations is scarce, the only recorded fact (Oğuzlar, p. 232) being that the Boz *ulus* and Yeni-Il Bayāts moved to central Anatolia in 1022/1613. Nevertheless the 11th/16th-century and present-day toponyms show that Bayāt tribespeople must have played a considerable part in the conquest and colonization of Anatolia. 4. The Bayāts of Iraq, consisting of thirteen clans, lived mainly around Kirkuk. They are still there today, some pursuing their old way of life but most now working in sedentary occupations.

The Bayāt tribes of Iran. The Bayāt presence in Iran is not attested before the 10th/16th century, when two separate groups are mentioned. The "genuine" or Āq (White) Bayāt tribe lived mainly around Kazzāz (34°N 49° 26′E., southeast of Hamadān) and then had 10,000 tents (Defense Mapping Agency, *Names Gazetteer*, p. 6; idem, 1984, s.v. "Bayāt"). Although pre-16th-century evidence is lacking, it seems probable that these Bayāts came from northern Syria with the Āq Qoyunlū. In Shah Ṭahmāsb's reign *begs* from the tribe were governors of Hamadān and districts on the Ottoman frontier, and in Shah 'Abbās I's reign Bayāt amirs and troops were sent to Azerbaijan, with the results that Bayāts settled in that province also. At the same time small groups established themselves at Darband and Šābrān. The Āq Bayāt tribe produced a large number of prominent amirs, whose names are mentioned in the chronicles of Ḥasan Rūmlū and Eskandar Beg and elsewhere. Although the Bayāts are reckoned in the *Taḏkerat al-molūk* (pp. 16-17, 193) to be less powerful than the Šāmlū and the Ḏu'l-Qadr, they are put fifth by Don Juan of Persia (1604), who himself belonged to this tribe, among the thirty-two noble families and clans "in whose hands the government is placed," being "most noble and comparable to dukes." Many Bayāt amirs were appointed to high positions outside the tribal area, e.g., Gadā-'Alī Solṭān to the governorship of Mākū in Shah 'Abbās I's reign, others to similar posts in the Īravān (Erevan) district, and Ḥosayn-'Alī Beg to the leadership of an embassy to Spain in 1006/1598 (Sümer, 1950, p. 385). The second main group, distinguished by the name Qara (Black) Bayāt, lived in Khorasan, for the most part around Nīšāpūr. Moḥammad-Kāẓem calls them the Nīšāpūri Bayāts. They were much involved with the Turkman tribes of Ḵ͏ᵛārazm. When Shah Esmā'īl I conquered Khorasan, they acknowledged Safavid sovereignty. The Uzbek ruler 'Abd-Allāh Khan (991-1006/1583-98), who seized much of Khorasan, placed them under the authority of his son 'Abd-al-Mon'em Khan (ibid, p. 387). Nevertheless they remained loyal to the Safavids and rendered such valuable services to Shah 'Abbās I that he rewarded them with a promise of tax exemption. Qara Bayāt amirs continued to hold the governorship of Nīšāpūr in Nāder Shah's reign and thereafter. In addition, there was a third Bayāt group, known as the Bayāt-e Šām or Bayāt-e Qājār, evidently, a branch of the Šām Bayātī of Syria and Anatolia. They must have come to Iran with the Qajar tribe in the wake of the Āq Qoyunlū. In the 10th/16th century the Qajars lived in Azerbaijan, mainly around Ganja and Barḏa'a; it is not clear which of the Qajar amirs were of Bayāt descent. In the 12th/18th century a village near Ganja bore the name of the Bayāt-e Šām and a certain Moḥammad-'Alī Khan, who belonged to this tribe, was an amir in the service of 'Ādel Shah Afšār. Under the Qajars, particularly in Fatḥ-'Alī

Shah's reign (1212-50/1797-1834), several amirs from the tribe rose to prominence.

The total strength of the Bayāts of Iran in the Safavid period was estimated at 40,000 families. Sedentarization of the Bayāt tribes began well before Reżā Shah's reign, in some cases (e.g., the Bayāts of Mākū) at the instigation of hereditary local chiefs (Oberling, 1974). Today they are entirely sedentary and live mainly around Zanjān.

Bibliography: General works: Faruk Sümer, "Bayatlar," *Istanbul Üniversitesi Edebiyat Fakültesi türk dili ve edebiyat dergisi*, 1950, pp. 374-98; idem, "Bayat," in *Türk ansiklopedisi* V, pp. 439-11; idem, *Oğuzlar (Türkmenler)*, 2nd ed., Ankara, 1972, pp. 222-37; idem, *Safevî devletinin kuruluşu ve gelişmesinde Anadolu türkmenlerinin rolü*, Ankara, 1972, pp. 192-93. Early history: Maḥmūd al-Kāšḡarī, ed. R. Dankoff and J. Kelly, *Compendium of the Turkic Dialects*, 3 vols., Cambridge, Mass., 1982 (cf. I, p. 102). Ḵᵛāja Rašīd-al-Dīn Fażl-Allāh, *Tārīḵ-e oḡūz*, ed. K. Jahn, *Die Geschichte der Oğuzen des Rašīd ad-Dīn*, Vienna, 1969, p. 45. Faḵr-al-Dīn Mobārakšāh, *Tārīḵ-e Mobārakšāh*, ed. E. Denison Ross, London, 1927, p. 48. Jovaynī, ed. Qazvīnī, I, p. 25. Place names: *Köylerimiz*, Istanbul, 1933, p. 92. *Türkiye'de meskûn yerler kılavuzu*, Ankara, 1946, p. 135. Defense Mapping Agency, *Official Standard Names Gazetteer*, no. 42 (U.S.S.R), Washington, D.C., I, A-B, p. 345. Idem, *Gazetteer of Iran*, 2 vols., 2nd ed., November, 1984. P. Oberling, *The Qashqā'i Nomads of Fārs*, The Hague, 1974, pp. 30, 226. Iranian sources: Ḥasan Rūmlū, ed. Seddon; Eskandar Beg, tr. Savory, pp. 226, 1311-12. *Taḏkerat al-molūk*, ed. Minorsky (e.g., pp. 16-17, 193). N. D. Miklukho-Maklay, ed., Moḥammad Kāẓem, *Nāma-ye ʿālamārā-ye nāderī*, 3 vols., Moscow, 1960-66 (II, p. 30a: Bayāt-e Andḵodī; III, p. 131b: Bayāt-e Bāzārī; and pp. 6a, 111a: Bayāt-e Nīšāpūrī).

(G. Doerfer)

BAYĀT or bayātī, one of the old modes of the Irano-Arabic musical tradition, mentioned for the first time by Šayḵ Ṣafadī (9th/15th century; Shiloah, p. 304) and by ʿAbd-al-Qāder b. Ḡaybī Marāḡī (d. 1435; pp. 64, 72) as one of the twenty-four *šoʿbas* sometimes called Nowrūz-e bayātī. According to the old sources quoted by Forṣat-e Šīrāzī (p. 20) it started on Ḥosaynī, then Ḥejāz and Rakab, then ended in Segāh and Neyrīz. In *Bahjat al-rūḥ* it appears as one of the twenty-four *šoʿbas* derived from the *maqām* Kūček; its old name was Nowrūz-e Aṣl (ibid., p. 80), a definition that is still quite relevant to the Arabic contemporary form.

Bayātī is a very important *maqām* of Arabic and Turkish classical music as well as popular traditions; it seems to have preserved its original form with the characteristic tetrachord (*jens*): *D* Ep *F G* (p = *koron* or half-flat), also called Ḥosaynī, and extended in *G A* Bb *C*.

As a distinct mode, its name has disappeared from Persian music, but it survives in the taxonomy of the *āvāz*, Bayāt-e Eṣfahān, Bayāt-e Tork (Zand), Bayāt-e Kord (qq.v.), and of the important *gūšas* of Bayāt-e Šīrāz, Bayāt-e ʿAjam, and Bayāt-e Rājeʿ. In this terminology, Bayāt refers to the modal context in which these modes are performed, i.e., their lower tetrachord characterized by the notes *C D E*p with the finalis on *D*. This interpretation, although ignored by Persian theoreticians, relies on comparative and historical musical analyses. In Azerbaijan, too, it is found only in that context and in a rare *maqām* called Čobān Bayātī, close to Bayāt-e Kord.

Bibliography: *Bahjat al-rūḥ* (an apocryph of ʿAbd-al-Mo'men b. Ṣafī-al-Din), ed. H. L. Rabino de Borgomale, Tehran, 1346 Š./1967. ʿAbd-al-Qāder b. Ḡaybī Marāḡī, *Maqāṣed al-alḥān*, ed. T. Bīneš, Tehran, 2536 = 1356 Š./1977. A. Shiloah, *The Theory of Music in Arabic Writings (c. 900-1900): Descriptive Catalogue of Manuscripts in Libraries of Europe and the U.S.A.*, Munich, 1979. Forṣat-e Šīrāzī, *Boḥūr al-alḥān*, Bombay, 1332/1914; ed. ʿA. Zarrīnqalam, Tehran, 1345 Š./1966.

(J. During)

BAYĀT-E EṢFAHĀN, or āvāz-e eṣfahān, a musical system based on a specific collection of modal pieces (*gūšahā*) which are performed in a particular order. According to the late 13th/19th-century author Forṣat Šīrāzī (apud Ṣafwat, p. 81), Eṣfahān was listed as one of the pieces of the modal system (*dastgāh*) of Homāyūn. In the twentieth century it has developed from a *gūša* of Homāyūn into a nearly independent *dastgāh*. Its smaller repertoire and cadential references to Homāyūn support the theory that it is a sub-*dastgāh* (*āvāz*, *naḡma*) of Homāyūn. Some theorists (Farhat, p. 164; Caron and Safvate, p. 89) believe it to be an independent *dastgāh*; others believe it to be derived from the *dastgāh* Šūr (During, p. 118).

The introductory part (*darāmad*) is in the mode of Eṣfahān. The scale degrees are F G Ap B C D Eb. The recitation tone (*šāhed*) is on C, the initial pitch (*āḡāz*) may be on C or G, the cadential pitch (*īst*) may be C or Ap, and the final pitch is on G, although earlier in the century it concluded on F.

Like other *dastgāhs*, Eṣfahān's scale and modal configuration have changed over time. The mood of Eṣfahān has been described as mystical and profound, expressing a mixture of happiness and melancholy. Its current similarity to the Western minor scale has made it a much-used mode in popular and semiclassical music, where Western minor tuning is used and the Ap eliminated (Zonis, p. 87).

The important *gūšas* of Bayāt-e Eṣfahān are the Darāmad, Jāmadarān, Bayāt-e Rājeʿ, ʿOššāq, Šāhḵatā'ī, Sūz-o-godāz, and Maṯnawī. Bayāt-e Rājeʿ is one of the most important *gūšas*, and has a slightly different modal character than the Darāmad. ʿOššāq, also very important, represents a distinct modulation. Šāhḵatā'ī, which is modally close to ʿOššāq, expresses the high pitch area (*awj*) of the *dastgāh*, cadencing to Eṣfahān at its conclusion. Both Sūz-o-godāz and Maṯnawī have modal configurations similar to Eṣfahān.

Bibliography: N. Caron and D. Safvate, *Iran: Les traditions musicales*, Berlin, 1966, pp. 88-91. J. During, *La musique iranienne: Tradition et évolution*, Paris, 1984, pp. 118-19. H. Farhat, *The Dastgah Concept in Persian Music*, Ph.D. dissertation, University of California, Los Angeles, 1965, I, pp. 164-75; II, pp. 355-58. M. Forṣat Šīrāzī, *Boḥūr al-alḥān*, ed. ʿA. Zarrīnqalam, Tehran, 1345 Š./1966. M. Karīmī (coll.), *Radīf-e āvāzī-e mūsīqī-e sonnatī-e Īrān*, transcribed and analyzed by M.-T. Masʿūdīya (Massoudieh), Tehran, 1357 Š./1978, pp. 83-97. R. Ḵāleqī, *Naẓar-ī be-mūsīqī* II, Tehran, 1352 Š./1973, pp. 207-14. K. Khatschi, *Der Dastgah: Studien zur neuen persischen Musik*, Regensburg, 1962, pp. 102-03. M. Maʿrūfī, *Radīf-e haft dastgāh-e mūsīqī-e īrānī*, Tehran, 1352 Š./1973 (s.v. Bayāt-e Eṣfahān). M. Sadeghi, *Improvisation in Nonrhythmic Solo Instrumental Contemporary Persian Art Music*, M. A. thesis, California State University, Los Angeles, 1971, pp. 35, 60, 62-63. D. Ṣafwat, *Ostādān-e mūsīqī-e Īrān wa alḥān-e mūsīqī-e īrānī*, Tehran, 1350 Š./1971, pp. 74-99. E. Zonis, *Classical Persian Music: An Introduction*, Cambridge, Mass., 1973, pp. 86-88.

(M. CATON)

BAYĀT-E KORD, or KORD-E BAYĀT, a part of the modal system (*dastgāh*) of Šūr in Persian music. The name Kord refers to its possible origin in Kurdish folklore. In addition to being performed as a part of Šūr, it is performed independently or even as a part of the *āvāz* Daštī. Although it is distinctive in character, it is seldom performed and today is known only by traditional masters.

The scale of the mode of Bayāt-e Kord is G Ap (*koron* or half-flat) Bb C D Eb F. The recitation tone (*šāhed*) is D, the initial pitch (*āḡāz*) is C, and the cadential pitch (*īst*) is Bb. Although this mode resembles that of Daštī, the *šāhed* does not include the variable pitch Dp. Reference to Šūr comes only at the end of Bayāt-e Kord with a final resolution to G.

Kord is located near the end of the *dastgāh* Šūr and is played after the *gūša* (piece) Ḥosaynī. Beside the *gūša* Bayāt-e Kord itself, the *gūša*s Rāḥ-e Rūḥ and Majlesafrūz are performed in that mode. As a whole Bayāt-e Kord is considered relatively simple, with the melody centering around the *šāhed*. The mood it conveys is considered similar to that of Šūr and is sweet and clear.

Bibliography: N. Caron and D. Safvate, *Iran: Les traditions musicales*, Berlin, 1966, p. 62. J. During, *La musique iranienne: Tradition et évolution*, Paris, 1984, p. 114. H. Farhat, *The Dastgah Concept in Persian Music*, Ph.D. dissertation, University of California, Los Angeles, 1965, I, pp. 50, 61-63; II, pp. 289-90. M. Maʿrūfī, *Radīf-e haft dastgāh-e mūsīqī-e īrānī*, Tehran, 1352 Š./1973 (s.v. Šūr, nos. 56-64). M. Sadeghi, *Improvisation in Nonrhythmic Solo Instrumental Contemporary Persian Art Music*, M. A. thesis, California State University, Los Angeles, 1971, p. 62. D. Ṣafwat, *Ostādān-e mūsīqī-e Īrān wa alḥān-e mūsīqī-e īrānī*, Tehran, 1350 Š./1971, pp. 74-99. E. Zonis, *Classical Persian Music: An Introduction*, Cambridge, Mass., 1973, p. 79.

(M. CATON)

BAYĀT-E TORK, a musical system (*āvāz, naḡma*) and one of the branches of the modal system (*dastgāh*) of Šūr (q.v.) in traditional classical music. It is also known as Āvāz-e Tork and Bayāt-e Zand for the Zand tribe in the region of Fārs. It is believed that the name Tork refers to the Turkic tribes of southern Iran, where many songs are found composed in this mode (Farhat, I, p. 82). The call to prayer (*aḏān*) and a number of prayers (*monājāt*) and poems (*maṯnawī*) performed on religious occasions are sung in this mode.

Although it is considered as originating within the *dastgāh* Šūr, its modal scheme is distinct from Šūr. The basic scale of Tork is F G Ap (*koron* or half-flat) Bb, C D and Eb. The primary reference pitch, or *šāhed*, is on the fourth scale degree, Bb, which is retained throughout the *dastgāh*, giving it, according to many musicians (Farhat, p. 85; Ḵāleqī, p. 156), a uniform or even monotonous character. Each piece (*gūša*) may end on the first or fourth degree of the scale, the more common one in recent times being the fourth degree, giving Tork the flavor of the Western major mode with a slightly flatted seventh degree. Indeed, some pieces in the current repertoire are believed to be borrowed from the *dastgāh* Māhūr (q.v.), such as Šekasta.

Important pieces (*gūšahā*) in Bayāt-e Tork include the Darāmad, Dogāh, Rūḥolarwāh (Rūh al-arwāḥ), Jāmadarān, Mahdī Żar(r)ābī, Šekasta, Qaṭār, Qarāʾī, and Maṯnawī. Rūḥolarwāh and Mahdī Żarrābī conclude on the second degree of the scale (G). Since that is the cadential pitch for Šūr these two pieces provide a link with that mode. Qaṭār is one of the more important pieces and Qarāʾī represents the high pitch area (*awj*) at the end of the *dastgāh*. Qaṭār is very common in the music of the Kurds in Iran (Barkešlī, p. 121). Šekasta is considered to be a modulation, modally resembling Afšārī (q.v., Caron and Safvate, p. 73). Although traditionally similar in expressive character to Šūr, the modern performance of Tork is felt to be lighter in mood, due to its closer relationship to the *dastgāh* Māhūr.

Bibliography: N. Caron and D. Safvate, *Iran: Les traditions musicales*, Berlin, 1966, pp. 70-74. M. Barkešlī, *Modāwamat dar oṣūl-e mūsīqī-e Īrān: Gāmhā wa dastgāhhā-ye mūsīqī-e īrānī*, Tehran, 2535 = 1353 Š./1974. J. During, *La musique iranienne: Tradition et évolution*, Paris, 1984, pp. 113-14. H. Farhat, *The Dastgah Concept in Persian Music*, Ph.D. dissertation, University of California, Los Angeles, 1965, I, pp. 82-91; II, pp. 309-16. M. Forṣat Šīrāzī, *Boḥūr al-alḥān*, ed. ʿA. Zarrīnqalam, Tehran, 1345 Š./1966. M. Karīmī (coll.), *Radīf-e āvāzī-e mūsīqī-e sonnatī-e Īrān*, transcribed and analyzed by M.-T. Masʿūdīya (Massoudieh), Tehran, 1357 Š./1978, pp. 32-43. R. Ḵāleqī, *Naẓar-ī be mūsīqī* II, Tehran, 1352 Š./1973, pp. 153-

57. K. Khatschi, *Der Dastgah: Studien zur neuen persischen Musik*, Regensburg, 1962, pp. 97-98. M. Ma‘rūfī, *Radīf-e haft dastgāh-e mūsīqī-e īrānī*, Tehran, 1352 Š./1973 (s.v. Bayāt-e Tork). M. Sadeghi, *Improvisation in Nonrhythmic Solo Instrumental Contemporary Persian Art Music*, M. A. thesis, California State University, Los Angeles, 1971, pp. 35, 59, 62-63. D. Ṣafwat, *Ostādān-e mūsīqī-e Īrān wa alḥān-e mūsīqī-e īrānī*, Tehran, 1350 Š./1971, pp. 74-99. E. Zonis, *Classical Persian Music: An Introduction*, Cambridge, Mass., 1973, pp. 77-79.

(M. Caton)

BAYATI̱, GAPPO (Ger.: Georg-Gappo Baiew), b. 9 September (old style 28 August) 1869, d. 24 April 1939, Ossetic man of letters. He was born in Vladikavkaz (now Ordzhonikidze) of a prominent north Caucasian family. He entered upon his literary career about the turn of the century, and became in the last decades before the October Revolution a distinguished figure in the political and cultural life of the Ossetes and one of the foremost pioneers of Ossetic literature. Among his earliest publications are *Gälabu* ("Butterfly," 1900), a collection of poems including some written by himself; *Iron ämbisändtä ämä uciucitä* ("Ossetic proverbs and riddles," 1900); *Farn* ("Peace," 1901), a collection of folktales and poems, including his own; and *Iron arg'äudtä* ("Ossetic folktales," 1901). During the civil strife of 1905-07 he sided with the czarist regime, and in the following years favored a democratic-monarchical form of government; in 1917 he joined the anti-Bolshevist forces. After the establishment of Soviet power in the Caucasus, he emigrated to Germany and settled in Berlin, where he taught Ossetic at the Oriental Seminar of the university and at the Ausland-Hochschule (Dozent, 1926-39) and dedicated himself to the propagation of knowledge of Ossetic and Caucasian culture. In 1922, he published a new edition of Khetägkati̱ K'osta's (q.v.) *Iron fändir*, containing the poet's biography, and in 1928 his translation of the Book of Daniel appeared. He also wrote several papers on Caucasian matters. He died in Berlin.

See also BIBLE, viii.

Bibliography: Nafi Dzhusoĭty, *Istoriya osetinskoĭ literatury* I, Tbilisi, 1980, pp. 111-20.

(F. Thordarson)

BAYĀŻ, literally "white," usually designating a small paper notepad with covers often made of leather which opens lengthwise and was carried around in inside pockets. Terms such as *moraqqa‘*, *safīna*, *jong*, *jarīda*, *kaškūl*, *dastūr*, *gol-dasta*, *ganjīna*, *teḏkār*, *majmū‘a*, and *ta‘līqāt* have occasionally been used in a similar sense. The interest of *bayāż* lies in the fact that several such books kept in various libraries contain notes by people of distinction. These notes sometimes contain lines of poetry, aphorisms, ethical and philosophical maxims, and amusing phrases. Some are listed in manuscript catalogues. Following are some important *bayāż*es: Tehran University Library possesses a *bayāż* dated 845/1441-42 (no. 2043), one by Moḥammad-Ja‘far Ḥosaynī dated 1068/1657-58 and 1092/1681 (no. 2145), one containing *zīārat-nāma*s and *monājāt* written in 1253/1837-38 (no. 1396), and one containing the handwriting of about 100 different scholars (no. 2144). Leningrad Oriental Library ms. no. A 688 is a *bayāż* called *Safīna-ye Ṣā'eb*. British Library Or. 4937 (Rieu, *Persian Manuscripts*, Suppl. no. 400) is a *bayāż* by Mīrzā ‘Abd-al-‘Aẓīm Qazvīnī Eṣfahānī, dated 1080/1669-70.

Bibliography: Ketāb-ḵāna-ye Markazī-e Dānešgāh-e Tehrān, *Majalla-ye ketāb-dārī* 7, 1318/1900, pp. 66-111. *Farḵonda-payām*, ed. Ḡ.-Ḥ. Yūsofī, Mašhad, 1359 Š./1980, pp. 148, 213. See also *al-Ḏarī‘a* III, p. 166, and M. Bayānī, *Ketāb-šenāsī-e ketābhā-ye ḵaṭṭī*, Tehran, 1353 Š./1974, p. 14.

(M.-T. Dānešpažūh)

BAYAZIT (Bāyazīd; Osm. Bayezid), a stronghold located three kilometers southeast of the modern village of Doğubayazit and approximately twenty-five kilometers southwest of Mt. Ararat, important in the defense of Anatolia against invasion from Iran. Situated in the province of Ağrı near the eastern border of the Turkish republic, Bayazit straddles the once-strategic road from Erzurum to Tabrīz. The name Bayazit, which was attached to the settlement by the sixteenth century, may have been derived from the Ottoman Sultan Bāyazīd I (1389-1403) or the brother of Sultan Aḥmad (1382-1410), the Jalayerid prince Bāyazīd. Before the Ottoman epoch the site was referred to by its Armenian name, Daroynk‘.

Fragments of Urartian walls and a relief from the 8th (?) century B.C. are still visible at the base of the fortress. In the mid-fourth century A.D. the Sasanians failed to capture the Armenian stronghold and royal treasury at Bayazit. Until the mid-8th century, princes of the Bagratid dynasty resided at Bayazit and rebuilt the fortress. In the early 10th century Bayazit was held briefly by Amir Yūsof of Azerbaijan only to be recaptured by King Gagik Arcruni. In 1020, the Byzantines took possession of the fortress and town, only to surrender both fifty years later to the Saljuqs. Tīmūr Leng briefly occupied the Bayazit region. It was not until the mid-16th century, after Sultan Solaymān concluded his Persian campaign, that this settlement was attached nominally to the *īālat* of Erzurum. In view of the Persian threat, the Ottomans assigned the defense of the town to the local Kurdish beys. In 1735, Persian troops destroyed part of the settlement but could not take the fortress. The Russians occupied Bayazit briefly in 1828, 1854, 1877, and 1914.

Bayazit is composed of three distinct but adjacent units: to the west at the base of an ascending canyon are the remains of the uninhabited town; to the east on the north flank of the road an impressive medieval fortress (Karaköse Kale) surrounds a towering outcrop; and on the south flank are the Armenian cemetery and the saray of İshak (Esḥāq) Paşa. The widely dispersed village of Bayazit, originally an Armenian settlement, was populated entirely by Kurds in 1930, when the Turkish army destroyed it during the Kurdish rebellion. The fortress of Bayazit has recently been the subject of a survey. The consistent use of rounded towers, finely drafted rusticated masonry, displaced entrances, and irregular plan of the walls indicate that most of this fort is of Armenian construction. Immediately below the fortress outcrop is the small mosque of Selim. The fabled saray of İshak Paşa is possessed of every convenience, including a lavishly decorated bathhouse, mosque, and harem. Constructed in the eighteenth century by Armenian, Georgian, and Persian artisans under the direction of Mahmud Paşa, the saray suffered considerable damage during the Russian occupations. In 1956, it was partially restored by the Turkish government.

Bibliography: W. E. D. Allen and P. Muratoff, *Caucasian Battlefields*, Cambridge, 1953, pp. 20, 29, 34, 42f., 74, 82, 133-50, 224, 244, 475. "Bayazet," *Haykakan Sovetakan Hanragitaran* 2, Erevan, 1976, pp. 262f. Awlīā' Čalabī (Evliya Çelebi), *Sīāḥat-nāma* IV, Istanbul, 1314/1896-97, p. 177. R. W. Edwards, "The Fortress at Doğubeyazit (Daroynk')," *Revue des études arméniennes* 18, 1984, pp. 435-59 (esp. the extensive bibliography in notes 1-33). 'A. Jawād (E. Cevat), *Tārīk̲ wa jog̲rāfīā log̲atī* I, Istanbul, 1313/1895-96, p. 153. Ḥājī K̲alīfa (Haci Halifa), *Jahānnomā* (*Cihannüma*), Istanbul, 1145/1732-33, pp. 417ff. P. Jaubert, *Voyage en Arménie et en Perse*, Paris, 1821, pp. 29-43, 58-93. "Lettre de M. Sartiges à M. Ard. de Longpérier sur un bas-relief de Bayazid," *Revue archéologique* 7/2, 1850, pp. 520-22. J. Markwart, "Die Genealogie der Bagratiden und das Zeitalter des Mar Abas und Ps. Moses Xorenac'i," *Caucasica* 6/2, 1930, pp. 11-14. A. Schweiger-Lerchenfeld, *Armenien, Ein Bild seiner Natur und seiner Bewohner*, Jena, 1878, pp. 1-8. C. Texier, *Description de l'Arménie, la Perse et la Mésopotamie* I, Paris, 1842, pp. 151f., pls. 29-34, 130-42. H. Tozer, *Turkish Armenia and Eastern Asia Minor*, London, 1881, pp. 384-91.

(R. W. Edwards)

BĀYBŪRTLŪ (also Bāybūrdlū), a Turkic tribe of northwestern Iran whose only vestiges seem to be the names of a few historical personalities. Its name implies that it came from Bāybūrt, or Bāybord, 100 miles northwest of Erzurum, in eastern Anatolia. It was one of the tribes which formed the mainstay of the early Safavids (G. Le Strange, ed. and tr., *Don Juan of Persia*, London, 1926, pp. 45-46). A leader of this tribe, Qarāja Elyās Bāybūrtlū, was one of Shah Esmā'īl I Ṣafawī's field commanders at the battle of Šarūr near Nak̲čavān (beginning of 907/mid-1501), in which Esmā'īl decisively defeated the Āq Qoyunlū Alvand Mīrzā, the ruler of Azerbaijan (British Museum MS, Or. 3248, fol. 69b, apud G. Sarwar, *History of Shāh Ismā'īl Ṣafawī*, Aligarh, 1939, p. 38). The tribe also produced two eminent personalities during the reign of Shah 'Abbās I: 1. Šāhverdī Bīg Bāybordlū, who was very close (*yasāvol-e ṣoḥbat*) to the Shah (Eskandar Beg, II, pp. 853, 871, tr. Savory, pp. 1084-85); 2. Morād Khan Sultan Bāybūrdlū, who was an amir and governor of Arasbār (ibid., p. 1086, tr. Savory, p. 1312).

Bibliography: Given in the text.

(P. Oberling)

BĀYDŪ (Baidu, on coins Badu), a son of Ṭarag̲āy and grandson of Hülegü (Holāgū), reigned as il-khan in Iran from Jomādā I to D̲u'l-qa'da, 694/March-October, 1295.

In 690/1291, during the election which ended with the choice of Gayk̲ātū, Bāydū had been approached by some of the Mongol amirs but was thwarted by Gayk̲ātū's quick arrival at the gathering; he was then approximately 35 years old and had taken part in the Syria campaign in 1281. He was then held in preventive detention at the royal court and insulted by the new il-khan when the latter was drunk. After 684/1284 he was governor of Baghdad and Dīārbakr (Rašīd-al-Dīn, p. 199; Spuler, p. 291) and entrusted with the task of quelling a rebellion in Mesopotamia. He took the opportunity to rally various forces and launch a rebellion against Gayk̲ātū, whose prestige was shaken by the collapse of the government's finances following the introduction of paper money (*čāv*) in 693/1294. The rival armies met near Hamadān, and Gayk̲ātū reached the battlefield in person on 3 Jomādā I 694/21 March 1295. After the defection of Amir Tag̲āčār he lost the battle and planned to withdraw to Asia Minor, where he had once been the viceroy, but decided to return to Tabrīz first and was caught; on Bāydū's order he was put to death on 6 Jomādā I 694/24 March 1295. Bāydū evidently adhered to traditional Mongol conceptions, though, as an enemy of Ḡāzān, he also relied on Christian counselors.

Bāydū assumed the sovereign power and executed a number of Gayk̲ātū's supporters but from the start had to face a strong adversary in the person of Ḡāzān, a son of Arg̲ūn (r. 683-90/1284-91). Ḡāzān, with the help of his trusted general Nowrūz, mustered his forces in Khorasan, and both armies marched on Ray. Nothing came of Bāydū's attempts to weaken Ḡāzān's resolve through the offer of a shared rulership and to suborn Nowrūz through the promise of promotion to the vizierate. Ḡāzān presented counterdemands, and a meeting between the two rivals was of no avail. The forces backing Ḡāzān were augmented by the adhesion of former supporters of Gayk̲ātū. While a body of Ḡāzān's troops under Nowrūz marched into Mesopotamia and Ḡāzān himself announced his intention to embrace Islam and to safeguard the heirs of the amirs whom Bāydū had executed, Bāydū retreated toward Caucasia and was overtaken and captured near Nak̲čavān; he was executed on Tuesday, 23 D̲u'l-qa'da 694/4 October 1295. Some of his associates were also put to death on Ḡāzān's orders. Ḡāzān was enthroned at Tabrīz on 29 D̲u'l-ḥejja 694/9 November 1295 and formally converted to (Sunni) Islam on the same date.

Bibliography: J. A. Boyle in *Camb. Hist. Iran* V, pp. 375-79. 'A. Eqbāl, *Tārīk̲-e mofaṣṣal-e Īrān* I, 2nd ed., Tehran, 1341 Š./1962, pp. 250-58. D. P. Little, *An Introduction to Mamluk Historiography...*, Freiburger Islamstudien 2, Wiesbaden, 1970. A. Melkonian, *Die Jahre 1287-1291 in der Chronik al-Yunīnīs*, Ph.D. dissertation, Freiburg-im-Breisgau, 1975 (ed., tr., and comm.). Rašīd-al-Dīn, *Jāmeʿ al-tawārīḵ*, (Baku). B. Spuler, *Mongolen*[4], esp. pp. 77-79 (with source references).

(B. SPULER)

BAYHAQ, a town of Khorasan in the Islamic period, also known as Sabzavār. Bayhaq is properly the name of a rural area (*rostāq*) lying between the district of Nishapur (Neyšābūr) and the eastern borders of Qūmes, of which Sabzavār and Ḵosrowjerd, separated by two *farsaḵ*s only, were the main urban centers. The early geographers are sparing in their descriptions of the town of Bayhaq-Sabzavār; it is described as producing corn and fruit and some silk textiles, and the center of its markets was covered over with timber arches. The *rostāq* was 25 *farsaḵ*s across and comprised, according to Yāqūt, 321 villages (but only 40 in its dependencies, according to Mostawfī a century or so later; see Moqaddasī, p. 318; *Ḥodūd al-ʿālam*, tr. Minorsky, p. 102; Yāqūt, *Boldān*, Beirut, I, pp. 537-38; *Nozhat al-qolūb*, pp. 149-50, tr. Le Strange, p. 148; Le Strange, *Lands*, p. 391). Bayhaq's comparatively low walls were raised in height by the Saljuq vizier Neẓām al-Molk in 464/1071-72, soon afterward dismantled by Arslān Arḡun b. Alp Arslān (Ebn Fondoq, *Tārīḵ-e Bayhaq*, ed. Aḥmad Bahmanyār, Tehran, 1317 Š./1938, p. 53), but, as subsequent events showed, must have been speedily rebuilt (see further, below).

Bayhaq's great strategic importance lay in its position on the great highway which skirted the northern fringes of the Dašt-e Kavīr and connected Ray and the west with Nishapur and Khorasan. Its cultural significance stemmed from the great number of *ʿolamāʾ* and literary men which the town produced ("innumerable," in Yāqūt's words; see also Samʿānī [Leiden], fol. 101a-b, ed. Hyderabad, II, pp. 412-15), such as the historian of the Ghaznavids Abu'l-Fażl Bayhaqī (q.v.), said to have been born in the village of Ḥāreṯābād, and several noted traditionists and lawyers, such as the Shafiʿite *faqīh* Aḥmad b. Ḥosayn Bayhaqī (d. 458/1066). Its religious and social significance lay in the fact that a considerable number of ʿAlid *sayyed*s emigrated thither in the Taherid period, usually from Nishapur (Ebn Fondoq, pp. 54-65, 254-55), gradually making Bayhaq a center of Shiʿism, so that Mostawfī (8th/14th century) could describe the inhabitants of Bayhaq as being all Twelver Shiʿite (*Nozhat al-qolūb*, p. 150, tr. p. 148).

We know more about the early Islamic history of Bayhaq than of any other Iranian town of comparable modest size, thanks to the local history, completed in 563/1167-68, by a local scholar ʿAlī b. Zayd, called Ebn Fondoq (see Storey, I, pp. 354, 1295-96; Storey-Bregel, II, pp. 1040-42; Q. S. K. Husaini, "Life and Works of Zahiru 'd-Din al-Bayhaqi...," *Islamic Culture* 28, 1954, pp. 297-318; idem, "The Tarikh-i-Bayhaq of Zahiru 'd-Din...al-Baihaqi," *Islamic Culture* 33, 1959, pp. 188-202; and see BAYHAQĪ, ABU'L-ḤASAN ʿALĪ). From this work, we learn of the surrender of the town in 30/650-51 to the Arab general ʿAbd-Allāh b. ʿĀmer b. Korayz (q.v.), after initial resistance, on a basis of the payment of tribute. In the time of ʿAbd-Allāh b. Ṭāher (q.v.; early 3rd/9th century), the district contained 395 villages, 321 of which were *ḵarāj*-paying, yielding a *ḵarāj* revenue of 178,796 dirhams and tithe or *ʿošr* from 24 villages of 57,800 dirhams (Ebn Fondoq, p. 34). In 213/828, during the prolonged Kharijite rebellion of Ḥamza b. Āḏarak (q.v.), Bayhaq was sacked by these sectaries, who destroyed the Friday mosque (ibid., pp. 44-45). The factional strife (*ʿaṣabīya*) which racked much of Khorasan in the succeeding centuries was evident in Bayhaq, a religious element of which was the rivalry between the adherents of the Karrāmīya movement (q.v.) and the orthodox Sunnite and Shiʿite groups (ibid., pp. 51, 267, 269). When the Oghuz under Ṭoḡrïl Beg appeared in Khorasan in the 420s/1030s, Bayhaq suffered both from the Turkmen depredations—so that no sowing of crops outside the town walls was possible for seven years—and from the armies of their Ghaznavid opponents (ibid., pp. 268, 273-74). During the disorders in Khorasan attendant on the decline and disappearance of Saljuq power there in the second half of the 6th/12th century, Bayhaq was again affected; thus it was besieged and sacked in 548-49/1153-54 by the Ḵᵛārazmšāh Atsïz b. Moḥammad's brother Yinaltigin, and in 561-62/1165-67 by the Turkish commander Ay Aba, opponent of the Ḵᵛārazmšāh Il-Arslān (ibid., pp. 271, 284). When the Mongols appeared in Khorasan in 617/1220, Bayhaq was taken by Börkey Noyan, with a reported (but doubtless exaggerated) number of 70,000 killed (Jowaynī, tr. Boyle, I, pp. 175-76), but it must have revived, and under the Il-khanids coins begin to be minted at Sabzavār from the reign of Abaqa (663-80/1265-82) onward, the series continuing through the periods of the Sarbadarids and Timurids to the Safavids, the latest attested date for minting being 935/1528-29 (see Spuler, *Mongolen*[1], pp. 130, 303; E. von Zambaur, *Die Münzprägungen des Islam, zeitlich und örtlich geordnet*, Wiesbaden, 1968, p. 138). Thus Sabzavār was obviously enjoying some prosperity at least during these times, and the Sabzavār district was indeed the home of the Sarbadarids, who ruled in Khorasan during the middle years of the 8th/14th century (see D. Krawulsky, *Ḫorāsān zur Timuridenzeit nach dem Tārīḫ-e Ḥāfeẓ-e Abrū...* I: *Edition und Einleitung*, Wiesbaden, 1982, pp. 79-80). Under the Safavids, fighting took place at Sabzavār between the Uzbeks and the shahs, and it suffered especially in 989/1581 from Moḥammad Shah's army and in 1004/1595-96 from the Uzbek ʿAbd-al-Moʾmen Khan (Eskandar Beg, tr. Savory, I, p. 423, II, pp. 686-87).

The modern town of Sabzavār had a population in ca. 1951 of 28,151 (Razmārā, *Farhang* IX, pp. 207-08) and 200,994 in 1345 Š./1966 (*Rāhnamā-ye šahrestānhā-ye Īrān*, ed. E. E. ʿArabānī, Tehran, 1345 Š./1967, p. 386); administratively, it falls within a district (*baḵš*) of the same name in the province (*ostān*) of Khorasan. See also SABZAVĀR.

Bibliography: Given in the text. See also for European travelers passing through Bayhaq, A. Gabriel, *Die Erforschung Persiens*, Vienna, 1952, index s.v. Sabzewar.

(C. E. BOSWORTH)

BAYHAQĪ, ABU'L-FAŻL MOḤAMMAD B. ḤOSAYN, secretary at the Ghaznavid court and renowned Persian historian, b. 385/995 at Ḥāreṯābād in Bayhaq (modern Sabzavār in Khorasan), d. Ṣafar, 470/August-September, 1077.

Life. In his youth Bayhaqī studied in Nīšāpūr, at that time an important cultural center; he later joined the secretariat (*dīvān-e resālat*) of Maḥmūd of Ḡazna (Roknī; Nāzim, pp. 142-44; Bosworth, 1963, p. 91), where for nineteen years he worked under Abū Naṣr Moškān (q.v.), becoming his assistant and protégé (Bayhaqī, p. 795). He was given the task of composing or preparing fair copies of important letters at court (ibid., pp. 845-52). He thus observed at close quarters the reigns of Maḥmūd (in part), Amīr Moḥammad, Mas'ūd I b. Maḥmūd, Mawdūd, Mas'ūd II, Bahā'-al-Dawla 'Alī b. Mas'ūd, 'Ezz-al-Dawla 'Abd-al-Rašīd, the usurper Ṭoḡrel, Amīr Farroḵzād b. Mas'ūd (see below), and Ẓahīr-al-Dawla Ebrāhīm, a period extending from 412/1021-22 to 470/1077. Owing to his vantage point near the center of power, he was very well informed about current events. After the death of Abū Naṣr Moškān in 431/1039, Mas'ūd appointed Bayhaqī as deputy to Abū Sahl Zūzanī (or Zawzanī; q.v.), the new head of the secretariat. Abū Naṣr had in fact recommended to the sultan that Bayhaqī be chosen as his successor, and the vizier Aḥmad b. 'Abd-al-Ṣamad had also praised Bayhaqī in the sultan's presence. Mas'ūd is reported to have said in private that, but for his youth, Bayhaqī, who was at that time forty-six years old, would have been named head of the secretariat.

Abū Sahl was not as adept in the affairs of the secretariat as his predecessor had been, and his ways were entirely different; nor was his deputy immune to his bad temper. Bayhaqī therefore wrote a confidential letter of resignation to the sultan, asking for another assignment. Mas'ūd, however, encouraged Bayhaqī to carry on and ordered his vizier to instruct Abū Sahl that Bayhaqī should receive proper treatment at the secretariat. Abū Sahl thus treated Bayhaqī with respect as long as Mas'ūd lived; later, however, his conduct changed again. Bayhaqī did encounter difficulties after Mas'ūd's death in 432/1041 (ibid., pp. 800-01), perhaps partly because of shortcomings of his own, which he himself occasionally acknowledges.

During the reign of 'Abd-al-Rašīd (441-44/1049-52) Bayhaqī was appointed head of the secretariat, only to be removed shortly afterward. According to Ebn Fondoq (p. 177), he was imprisoned by the judge (*qāżī*) of Ḡazna on the charge of having failed to pay the marriage portion (*mahr*) due to a wife, but 'Awfī claims in his *Jawāme' al-ḥekāyāt* (pt. 3, chap. 18) that the cause of his imprisonment was the machinations of his enemies. On the sultan's orders a slave by the name of Tūmān (or Nūyān, or Yūnān?) plundered Bayhaqī's property. When Ṭoḡrel—a runaway slave of the house of Maḥmūd—came to power and put 'Abd-al-Rašīd to death (444/1052), he imprisoned the sultan's servants in a fortress, to which Bayhaqī was also transferred from the magistrate's jail. Ṭoḡrel's rule lasted only fifty days, however; he was then killed, and the Ghaznavids returned to power. Bayhaqī was released.

According to Ebn Fondoq (p. 175), he served as secretary under Sultan Farroḵzād (444-51/1052-59) and at the end of the latter's reign retired from court service and settled down in Ḡazna to write his history. From Bayhaqī's own occasional comments on Farroḵzād's rule in the extant part of his book (pp. 116, 132, 137, 163, 175, 221, 253, 314, 318, 332, 358, 377, 480, 483), however, it does not seem that he worked at Farroḵzād's court. In fact, he clearly states that during those years he was working on his history. According to Ṣadr-al-Dīn Ḥosaynī in *Aḵbār al-dawla al-saljūqīya* (Chronicles of the Saljuq state; p. 29), Bayhaqī drafted the peace treaty (*ketāb al-ṣolḥ*) between the Saljuq Čaḡrī Beg and the Ghaznavids toward the end of Farroḵzād's reign; he may thus have been invited back to work after his disgrace and incarceration during the reign of 'Abd-al-Rašīd (see Bosworth, 1977, pp. 48, 52). In any event the contents of *Tārīḵ-e Bayhaqī* clearly show that in his old age, until his death in 470/1077, the author devoted himself entirely to writing.

Known works. By far the best-known of Bayhaqī's works is *Tārīḵ-e Bayhaqī*, the only extant portion of which covers the reign of Mas'ūd I (421-32/1030-41; page references to this work are cited from 'A.-A. Fayyāż's 1355 edition). In the sources, however, Bayhaqī's history is also known as *Tārīḵ-e nāṣerī*, *Tārīḵ-e āl-e Maḥmūd* (Ebn Fondoq, pp. 20, 175; 'Awfī, loc. cit., and *Lobāb al-albāb*, p. 28; Jūzjānī, I, pp. 225, 247, 248), *Jāme' al-tawārīḵ*, and *Jāme' fī ta'rīḵ Sebok-tegīn* (*Kašf al-ẓonūn*). Furthermore, the author himself called his work *Maqāmāt-e maḥmūdī* (p. 188; see below) and *Tārīḵ-e yamīnī* (pp. 27, 169), by which he clearly meant a "history of the years of Amīr Maḥmūd" (388-421/998-1030; p. 130).

Ebn Fondoq (pp. 20, 175) says that *Tārīḵ-e āl-e Maḥmūd*, which was written in Persian, covered the period from the earliest days of Seboktegīn to the beginning of the reign of Sultan Ebrāhīm (451-92/1059-99) and filled more than thirty books "with eloquence and lucidity." He had seen some of these volumes in the library of Saraḵs, others in the private collection of Ḵātūn Mahd 'Erāq in Nīšāpūr, and a few in various other places, but he had never seen the complete work. From all these comments and from indications in the work itself, it may be surmised that Bayhaqī had written a complete dynastic history of the Ghaznavids, the first book of which was called, or came to be known as, *Tārīḵ-e nāṣerī* after Nāṣer-al-Dīn Seboktegīn, the founder of the dynasty. This surmise is confirmed by the fact that 'Awfī, in his *Jawāme' al-ḥekāyāt* (pt. 1, chap. 21, and pt. 2, chap. 7) relates two episodes from the *Tārīḵ-e nāṣerī* pertaining to Amīr Seboktegīn's early years and before the birth of Maḥmūd. The next three books, *Tārīḵ-e yamīnī*, or *Maqāmāt-e maḥmūdī*, must have dealt mainly with Maḥmūd's era. Again it is Ebn Fondoq who points out (pp. 175-77) that Bayhaqī reported sixty-seven snowfalls in Nīšāpūr in 400/1009-10, followed by a famine in 401/1010-11, and related some points of conduct that had to be observed by the sultan's servants. The extant portion of the work (bks. 5-10) is a treatment of Mas'ūd's time and is known as *Tārīḵ-e mas'ūdī*, though most printed editions are entitled simply *Tārīḵ-e Bayhaqī*. Even from this extant portion of the history, however, certain sections are missing. For example, book 9 ends with an account of Mas'ūd's defeat by the Saljuqs and his intention to go to India; the author then announces (p. 900) that book 10 will contain two chapters dealing with Ḵ'ārazm and Jebāl, Mas'ūd's march to India, and the end of his days. What remains of book 10, however, contains only the chapter on Ḵ'ārazm, drawn from *al-Mosāmara fī akbār Ḵ'ārazm*, a lost work by Abū Rayḥān Bīrūnī (q.v.). A portion of book 5 may also be missing.

As for the period after Mas'ūd's death, Bayhaqī notes in his report of a flood in Ḡazna and the repair of the city and its fortress by the Saffarid 'Amr b. Layṯ, that these events had already been described by Maḥmūd Warrāq in his detailed history, written in 450/1058 but carrying the narrative down to 409/1018-19, and from that point Bayhaqī began the first-hand portion of his account (p. 342), which comes to a close in 451/1059, early in the reign of Sultan Ebrāhīm. The thirty books of his history thus covered at least forty-two years of the Ghaznavid era: the first four books comprising *Tārīḵ-e nāṣerī* and *Tārīḵ-e yamīnī*, books 5 through 10 comprising *Tārīḵ-e mas'ūdī* (the only extant portion, though parts of bks. 5 and 10 also seem to be missing), and books 11 through 30 covering the nineteen years of the second reign of Amīr Moḥammad b. Maḥmūd, the reigns of Mas'ūd II, Bahā'-al-Dawla 'Alī, 'Abd-al-Rašīd, and Farroḵzād, to the beginning of that of Ebrāhīm (432-51/1041-59). Bayhaqī mentions Farroḵzād's death at a young age and Ebrāhīm's succession on 19 Ṣafar 451/6 April 1059, adding that on that day the author himself was busy writing his book (p. 483).

In view, of the length of the extant portion, the complete work must have been monumental. In the 6th/12th century, 'Awfī cited in his *Jawāme' al-ḥekāyāt* some passages from *Tārīḵ-e Bayhaqī*, as did Jūzjānī in his *Ṭabaqāt-e nāṣerī* in the 7th/13th century; some volumes of the great history must thus still have been accessible in those times. Sa'īd Nafīsī has compiled two volumes (*Dar pīrāmūn-e Tārīḵ-e Bayhaqī*) containing all passages in later works that are explicitly cited from *Tārīḵ-e Bayhaqī*, as well as passages that he considers to have been taken from Bayhaqī's lost books; this compilation contains much useful information on Bayhaqī and the Ghaznavids.

Editions. The extant portion of *Tārīḵ-e Bayhaqī* has been published in several editions: (1) The Calcutta edition (1862), edited by W. H. Morley and W. N. Lees and published by the Asiatic Society of Bengal, containing no notes or indexes; (2) the lithographed edition by Aḥmad Adīb Pīšāvarī (Tehran, 1305/1887-88), with annotations including definitions of words and explanations of historical and geographical names, occasional variant readings, but mainly general comments on moral and philosophical issues as they occurred to the author; (3) *Tārīḵ-e mas'ūdī ma'rūf be Tārīḵ-e Bayhaqī*, edited by Nafīsī (Tehran, 1319 Š./1940), containing only half the text; (4) *Tārīḵ-e Bayhaqī*, edited by 'A.-A. Fayyāż and Q. Ḡanī (Tehran, 1324 Š./1945), containing the complete text, with an introduction, notes, and indexes; (5) *Tārīḵ-e mas'ūdī*, edited by Nafīsī (Tehran, 1319-32 Š./1940-53), with copious notes in three volumes; (6) *Tārīḵ-e Bayhaqī*, edited by Fayyāż (Mašhad, 1350 Š./1971; 2nd ed., Mašhad, 1355 Š./1976), with an introduction and incomplete notes and, in the second edition, a glossary of words and phrases prepared by M.-J. Yāḥaqqī (pp. 1021-90); (7) *Tārīḵ-e Bayhaqī*, edited by 'A. Eḥsānī (Tehran, 1358 Š./1980) and based on Fayyāż's edition; (8) *Gozīda-ye tārīḵ-e Bayhaqī* (selections from the Tārīḵ-e Bayhaqī), edited by M. Dabīrsīāqī, Tehran, 1348 Š./1970; (9) an edition of the complete work with glossaries and indexes, as well as a selection, prepared by Ḵ. Ḵaṭīb Rahbar is in press.

Tārīḵ-e Bayhaqī has also been translated into other languages. An Arabic version entitled *Ta'rīḵ al-Bayhaqī* was prepared by Yaḥyā al-Ḵaššāb and Ṣādeq Naš'at and published in Cairo in 1376/1956. A. K. Arends published a Russian translation, *Istoriya Masuda (1030-41)*, in Tashkent in 1962 (2nd ed., Moscow, 1969).

Some scholars have considered Bayhaqī's *Maqāmāt* or *Maqāmāt-e maḥmūdī*, which some historians also call *Maqāmāt-e Bū Naṣr Moškān*, to be a separate work. Bayhaqī himself (p. 188) reported that he had given the text of the agreement and mutual oath (*sowgand-nāma*) between Aḥmad b. Ḥasan Maymandī (q.v.) and Sultan Mas'ūd in his *Maqāmāt-e maḥmūdī*, by which, however, he meant that part of his monumental history dealing with the era of Maḥmūd of Ḡazna. In another place (p. 794), he says that details of Abū Naṣr Moškān's life and works are given in the *Maqāmāt* (*Maqāmāt-e maḥmūdī* in Adīb's edition); it can be inferred that this work is none other than *Maqāmāt-e maḥmūdī*, and it seems only logical that Moškān's life and works and the accounts of events attributed to him should have been included in the part of Bayhaqī's history devoted to Maḥmūd's era, just as the account of Moškān's activity during Mas'ūd's reign (421-31/1030-40) is given in the part known as *Tārīḵ-e mas'ūdī*. Sayf-al-Dīn 'Aqīlī, the author of *Āṯār al-wozarā'*, however, refers in a number of places to a work called *Maqāmāt-e Bū Naṣr Moškān* and its author Abu'l-Fażl Bayhaqī (pp. 8, 154, 161, 178, 186) and reproduces (pp. 180-86) from it the agreement that Bayhaqī says was in *Maqāmāt-e maḥmūdī* (see above). As J. Moḥaddeṯ Ormavī, the editor of *Āṯār al-wozarā'*, has pointed out (p. 178 n. 1), the author's source was actually *Maqāmāt-e maḥmūdī*. Furthermore, the material quoted from *Maqāmāt-e Bū Naṣr Moškān* by 'Awfī in his *Jawāme' al-ḥekāyāt* (e.g., in pt. 1, chap. 12) is so close to that in *Āṯār al-wozarā'* (pp. 154ff.) that it is clear that both authors drew from the same source. Nafīsī surmised that the *Maqāmāt* (essays) dealt with various matters connected with Maḥmūd of Ḡazna that Bayhaqī had heard from Abū Naṣr Moškān and that was the reason why the work was entitled *Maqāmāt-e maḥmūdī* and later came to be known as *Maqāmāt-e Bū Naṣr Moškān* (Nafīsī, 1342 Š./1963, I, p. 95; *EI*[2] I, p. 1131); however, they may have dealt with other matters as well. Ḥ. Moayyad, too, concluded about *Maqāmāt-e Bū Naṣr Moškān* that it was "apparently a collection of all accounts coming from and/or related to his master" (*EIr*. I, p. 353). It is apparent, however, that in the extant books of his history, too, Bayhaqī quotes his mentor, copies from his writings (e.g., pp. 89-96), and praises his command of the Arabic and Persian languages (pp. 88, 387). In fact, Bayhaqī's own style was influenced by that of his mentor—a fact borne out by a comparison between their writings. It is thus clear that *Maqāmāt-e maḥmūdi* was not a separate work but a portion of Bayhaqī's great history.

Ebn Fondoq (p. 175) mentions another work by Bayhaqī, *Zīnat al-kottāb*, adding that there is no book to match it in its field. From the title we may conclude that it dealt with the art of *enšā'* (i.e., writing letters, firmans, etc.). Bayhaqī himself was probably referring to this book when, reporting the events of 425/1034 (p. 550), he wrote that "very elegant" letters were sent from Mas'ūd's secretariat to Turkestan, which "are recorded in a treatise of my compilation but, if added to the present work, they would have made the narrative far too long." No trace of this work remains.

In a small collection in the Malek public library (Ketāb-ḵāna-ye Mellī-e Malek) there is a manuscript, catalogued as no. 474, which bears the date 656/1258. A few pages of this manuscript (25a-30b) contain a chapter from the writings of "Abu'l-Fażl, the disciple of Abū Manṣūr [Abū Naṣr?] Moškān, secretary to Sultan Maḥmūd." It consists of 373 Persian words matched with Arabic equivalents. The late 'Alī-Aṣḡar Ḥekmat published this chapter verbatim in his anthology of Persian prose, *Pārsī-e naḡz* (Polished Persian; Tehran, 1329 Š./1940, pp. 383-98). An edited version was published separately by Ṣ. Kīā under the original title of the treatise, *Čand soḵan ke dabīrān dar qalam ārand* (A few words that secretaries employ; Tehran, 1355 Š./1977).

Finally, Ebn Fondoq (pp. 177-78) cites four lines of Arabic verse, two of which he says were written by Abu'l-Fażl Bayhaqī while in prison during the short reign of Ṭoḡrel. Ṣalāḥ-al-Dīn Ṣafadī cites the same lines in *al-Wāfī be'l-wafayāt* (III, p. 20), presumably copied from Ebn Fondoq.

The importance of Tārīḵ-e Bayhaqī. Bayhaqī owes his reputation to the remaining parts of his history, which constitutes an important source for all aspects of Ghaznavid history in that period. With characteristic intellectual curiosity and zeal, the author expended enormous time and effort in gathering his materials and composing his work (see pp. 130-31, 422-24, 787). As a result *Tārīḵ-e Bayhaqī* is equally valuable as a work of historiography and as a work of literature.

Historiographic importance. An accurate and well-documented history of any period is generally best written after the participants have had time to gain some perspective. Although Bayhaqī personally witnessed many of the events he described and, during his long service at the Ghaznavid court, compiled a wealth of notes (pp. 190, 290, 381, 389, 734), he began writing his history only after many years had passed and he had achieved an emotional distance from earlier affections and animosities (pp. 189, 221-22). The nature of his historiographic method can be gleaned from his criticism, on one hand, of earlier histories written by the servants of rulers and marred by their biased judgments (p. 129) and, on the other, of historians who limited themselves to bare accounts of wars and victories (p. 451). Many writers of Arab histories before Bayhaqī's time had selected and composed their materials following the method of scholars of religious tradition: determining the accuracy of each tradition by establishing the correct sequence of reporters by whom it had been transmitted. Bayhaqī also used this approach in presenting his sources (see, e.g., pp. 253, 256, for two episodes involving Amir Seboktegīn; p. 510, for the account by a female entertainer named Zarrīn of the dowry of Bākālījār's daughter, whom Mas'ūd had married; p. 549, for a description of the decoration of the royal harem on the occasion of the wedding of Qadar Khan's daughter Šāhḵātūn with Amir Mas'ūd; and pp. 130ff., for a profile of Mas'ūd as a young man, as reported by Ḵ[v]āja Abū Sa'īd 'Abd-al-Ḡaffār). But, whereas these historians for the most part simply passed on variant accounts of each event, Bayhaqī displayed a more critical attitude. An author like Ṭabarī, for example, when confronted with variant accounts, did not evaluate their relative accuracy but contented himself with repeating each as it had come to him. As a consequence, his history, though valuable because of its tremendous scope, is not always reliable. Bayhaqī, on the other hand, made an effort to distinguish, in the vast amount of material at his disposal, between what was sound and what was unsound, according to what he knew about the identity and credentials of the respective sources. His extensive knowledge of historical literature (pp. 129,243) and his critical scrutiny of the works of earlier authors led him to develop a method based on the following principles. He reported events "from observation" or "from judicious listening to a reliable person" (pp. 904-05). Indeed, Bayhaqī did report most events from his own direct observation (pp. 151-52, 190, 201, 290, 293, 325, 328, 372, 659, 692, 734, 837, 840), but, when he relied on informants, he preferred those who had personally witnessed the events they described or had proved themselves trustworthy reporters in other contexts (pp. 130-31, 422-24). Furthermore, he cited all his sources, analyzing their credibility (e.g., pp. 130-31, 253, 256, 510, 549, 906, 909) and assessing which might be accepted (pp. 131, 530, 904-05) and which were of dubious value (pp. 515, 548, 794). Owing to this approach the precision of his work was unprecedented.

Bayhaqī was a thorough and highly perceptive reporter, who overlooked nothing worth relating and probed each question from every conceivable angle so that no aspect was left in doubt (p. 11). He cited many important documents (pp. 1-4, 89-96, 102-05, 268-81, 391-402, 417-21, 439-51, 846-53) and did not hesitate even to include confidential negotiations and agreements (pp. 13-14, 58-60, 69-70, 74-76, 98-99, 227-28, 337-38, 343-46, 417, 613, 634), thus disclosing secrets and exposing rivalries and conspiracies (pp. 159-62, 173, 283-85, 298-301, 304, 325-26, 402-17, 561) that might otherwise have been lost to historians. His attention to detail led him to provide a number of intimate glimpses into the private lives and behavior of his contemporaries (pp. 4-5, 80-81, 87-88, 145-49, 149-50), as well as accounts of customs, ceremonies, and rites. He describes, for example, how Ḥasanak presented himself before the tribunal (*dīvān*; 228-31); how confidential correspondence was guarded (pp. 29, 410); which titles were used in correspondence and the nuances of various modes of address for officials (pp. 7, 453, 501); and the illiteracy of General Begtoḡdī, commander of the palace guard (p. 388; for further discussion of the richness of detail in Bayhaqī's work, see Yūsofī, 1357 Š./1978, I, pp. 18-27). Even people of inferior standing (e.g., p. 600) are sometimes mentioned, and minor episodes are often included as substantiation for the author's arguments. He is precise about the dates, sometimes even the hours, when certain events took place (pp. 26-27, 295, 310, 319, 697) and occasionally gives statistics as well (p. 47). In his brief profiles of individuals information on each subject's background, disposition, mentality, method of work, and career progression is normally included (pp. 225-28, 313-16, 329-31, 522-24).

Bayhaqī demonstrated profound knowledge of his own society and the problems of his age and analyzed the causes of events with exceptional penetration (Yūsofī, op. cit., I, pp. 27-31). Yet he was unfailingly fair and objective in his judgments (e.g., pp. 27-28, 221-22, on Abū Sahl Zūzanī; p. 68, on Amir ʿAlī Qarīb; p. 298, on the general Ḡāzī; pp. 88, 179-80, 501-02, 785, 792, 799, on Abū Naṣr Moškān; and pp. 128-29, 800-01 on himself; for further information on Bayhaqī's commitment to truth and his historiographic method, see Yūsofī, op. cit., I, pp. 3-49; Zaryāb; Savory). What Bayhaqī has to say about events previous to his own time may sometimes be questionable, as when he quotes an earlier source to the effect that Ašnās and Afšīn are the same person (p. 168); in fact Ašnās, a Turk, was an important official at the court of the ʿAbbasid caliph al-Moʿtaṣem whereas Afšīn was a famous Iranian general in the caliph's service. But the main value of his history lies in the information it contains about the Ghaznavid period.

Because of Bayhaqī's carefully considered judgments and his critical remarks on Masʿūd and others (pp. 76, 77, 222, 223, 283, 298, 339, 340, 456-59, 479, 531-32, 600, 602, 663) his book is a many-faceted and informative history, rather than simply an arid recital of events. Furthermore the text is permeated with wisdom (pp. 112-28), moral ideas, and profound observations (pp. 234-35, 247, 308, 466, 480-86), often arising from perceived parallels with past events (pp. 31-39, 126-28, 168-72, 213-21, 236-43, 249-67, 456-59, 525, 533-43, 581-83, 617-19, 671-78, 865-68, 888-89). Persian and Arabic verses are quoted abundantly throughout the book (pp. 67, 71-72, 83-84, 152-53, 234-35, 244-45, 290, 308-10, 361-71, 466-67, 480-83, 487-97, 525, 788-89, 796-98, 854-62), a practice that may seem inappropriate (e.g., pp. 425-28) or redundant to the modern reader. But Bayhaqī wished to "adorn the history" (pp. 39, 169), to "teach moral lessons" (p. 243), and to "affect hearts" (p. 678), and it is fair to say that he achieved his ends: He has written a reliable history that is also delightful to read.

As literature. Bayhaqī was one of the most gifted and graceful writers of Persian prose. In the age in which Bayhaqī worked the position of court scribe (*dabīr*) was a highly regarded one (see Kaykāvūs b. Eskandar, pp. 207-15; *Čahār maqāla*, ed. Qazvīnī, pp. 19-41). Such a scribe had to be highly proficient in both Arabic and Persian and adept at composition of various types of letters. High intelligence, quick wit, and good sense were also required, as the state administration depended on experienced secretaries (see Bayhaqī, p. 88). It was not unusual for an able and judicious court secretary to become a vizier (see Kaykāvūs, p. 215). From his history it is clear that Bayhaqī had total command of Persian and Arabic, an elegant writing style, and great erudition. He was eminently qualified to serve as a secretary at the courts of his time.

Although strictly committed to the quest for truth, Bayhaqī wrote with a novelist's flair, as may be seen in passages about Masʿūd's *k*ᵛ*īš-kāna* in Herat (pp. 145-49), the story of Bū Bakr Ḥaṣīrī and Aḥmad b. Ḥasan Maymandī (pp. 197-207), the hanging of Ḥasanak (pp. 221-35), and the imprisonment of Amir Yūsof (pp. 322-29). This quality arises partly from the depth of his delineation of character and his description of what he knows about each individual's thoughts and behavior, as in his characterizations of Abū Sahl Zūzanī (pp. 27, 188-89, 222), Amir Yūsof (p. 322), Sultan Masʿūd (passim), Abū Naṣr Moškān (pp. 179-80, 501, 785, 792, 794, 795, 799), Aḥmad b. Ḥasan Maymandī (pp. 188, 191, 208, 465), Aḥmad b. ʿAbd-al-Ṣamad (p. 479), and even of lesser figures. Nor does he overlook outward appearance and dress, as in the stories of Amir Moḥammad in captivity (pp. 4-5) and Ḥasanak (p. 229). Large assemblies are also evocatively described, as in his accounts of the magnificent welcome given to Masʿūd by the inhabitants of Nīšāpūr and Ḡazna (pp. 41, 333-34) and of the sultan's army on the march to Marv in 431/1039-40 (p. 824). Bayhaqī is particularly adept at setting the scene for each episode, vividly describing faces and figures, garments, and weapons: the hanging of the vizier Ḥasanak (pp. 232-34), Aḥmad b. Abī Do'ād's mounted visit to Afšīn's house and Bū Dolaf's captivity there (pp. 216-17), the Ḡazna flood (pp. 340-42), the forests along the road to Āmol (pp. 189, 593), the natural beauty of Gorgān (p. 580), the sultan's enthronement and his audience (*bār*, q.v.; pp. 20, 41-42, 51-52, 334, 372, 382, 438, 597, 688-89, 697-98, 713-15) celebrations, various ceremonies, occasions when towns were decorated with lights (*čerāḡānī*, see ČERĀḠ; pp. 17, 49, 333, 384, 548), the arrangement of the seats of the shah and his courtiers and men of state on ceremonial occasions (pp. 20, 41-42, 51-52, 62-63, 173, 196-97, 199, 313, 382, 384, 476-77, 656; see also COURT), the manner in which *dīvān*s were arranged in the royal palace (pp. 175, 335, 378, 585, 645, 652).

Bayhaqī's dramatic gift for recounting clashes among personalities and personal reactions to events is another example of his literary skill, especially noteworthy in passages on the relations between the statesmen of Maḥmūd's era (*pedarīān*) and those of the era of his son Mas'ūd (*pesarīān*), the courtiers' reaction to the news that Aḥmad b. Ḥasan Maymandī had been named grand vizier (pp. 188, 192), and the encounter between Abū Sahl Zūzanī and Ḥasanak before the tribunal (pp. 229-30).

The book is rich in beautifully composed dialogue: Amir 'Alī Qarīb's sincere talk with Abū Naṣr Moškān before his departure for Herat (pp. 58-60); Altūntāš's speech before Sultan Mas'ūd at the arrival of Amir 'Alī Qarīb at Herat and Mas'ūd's reply (pp. 63-64); and the clash between Zūzanī and Ḥasanak at the tribunal (pp. 230-31).

Bayhaqī was an accomplished writer, who could adapt his style to suit his material, ranging from complete, detailed reports to episodes recounted with great economy but nevertheless enriched with charming imagery. Furthermore, like an able novelist, he brings together a diverse array of characters and events within an overall structure. The inclusion of instructive aphorisms at the end of each historical episode and sometimes elsewhere in the narrative is another attractive feature of Bayhaqī's book.

Bayhaqī's vast vocabulary in the Persian language permitted him an astounding range of expression (see pp. 1021-90; Zarrīnčīān). Furthermore, like all writers of taste and ability, he invented and combined many elegant words and phrases, thus lending a unique polish to his own style and enriching the Persian language as a whole. His complete understanding of the meanings and the nuances of words and his precision in using them enabled him to avoid loading his prose with synonyms and redundancies; he was always concise and to the point. Bayhaqī's prose is thus both dynamic and harmonious, with distinct high and low pitches and variation between deliberate and more animated tempos. It is also in harmony with the substance, serving to reinforce the ideas expressed. (For a discussion of the power of Bayhaqī's prose and its various manifestations, see Yūsofī, in *Yād-nāma*; idem, 1356 Š./1978, I, pp. 203-35.)

Bayhaqī, like all his educated contemporaries, was thoroughly familiar with Arabic literature. Arabic words and occasionally entire Arabic phrases are incorporated into his prose; sometimes even his Persian phraseology is influenced by Arabic (for the grammatical and lexical peculiarities of Bayhaqī's prose, see Bahār, *Sabk-šenāsī* II, pp. 66-95, esp. pp. 70-73, 85-87, on Arabic elements).

Bibliography: N. Ahmad, "A Critical Examination of Baihaqī's Narration of the Indian Expeditions During the Reign of Mas'ūd of Ghazna," in *Yād-nāma*, pp. 34-83 (also in *Afghanistan* 24/4, 1972, pp. 68-92). S. 'Aqīlī (or 'Oqaylī), *Āṯār al wozarā'*, ed. M. J. Moḥaddeṯ Ormavī, Tehran, 1337 Š./1959. A. K. Arends, "Aṯar-e mafqūd-e Abū Rayḥān Bīrūnī dar bāra-ye tārīḵ-e Ḵ'ārazm, ṭebq-e manābe'-e *Tārīḵ-e Bayhaqī*," *Payām-e novīn* 1/5, 1337-38 Š./1958-59, pp. 95-96. 'Awfī, *Jawāme' al-ḥekāyāt wa lawāme' al-rewāyāt*. Idem, *Lobāb*, ed. Nafīsī, pp. 567, 622-23 nn. Ḥ. Baḥr-al-'Olūmī, "*Tārīḵ-e Bayhaqī* yā ā'īna-ye 'ebrat," in *Yād-nāma*, pp. 53-67. S. H. Barani, "Abul Fazl Baihaqī," *Indo-Iranica* 5/1, 1951-52, pp. 5-11. W. Barthold, "Baihaḳī," in *EI*[1], pp. 592-93. Idem, *Turkestan*[3], pp. 21-24; Pers. tr., K. Kešāvarz, *Torkestān-nāma*, Tehran, 1352 Š./1973, I, pp. 76-79. M.-E. Bāstānī Pārīzī, "Yād-e Kermān dar *Tārīḵ-e Bayhaqī*," in *Yād-nāma*, pp. 39-52. Š. Bayānī, "Zan dar *Tārīḵ-e Bayhaqī*," in *Yād-nāma*, pp. 68-90. T. Bīneš, "Raveš-e 'elmī dar ketāb-e Bayhaqī," in *Yād-nāma*, pp. 91-102. Bosworth, *Ghaznavids*. Idem, *Later Ghaznavids*. Idem, "Early Sources for the First Four Ghaznavid Sultans (977-1041)," *Islamic Quarterly* 7/1-2, 1963, pp. 10-14, repr. in idem, *The Medieval History of Iran, Afghanistan and Central Asia*, London, 1977, no. XIII. Idem, "The Poetical Citations in Baihaqī's *Ta'rīkh-i Mas'ūdī*," in *XX. Deutscher Orientalistentag... 1977 in Erlangen. Vorträge, ZDMG*, Suppl. IV, Wiesbaden, 1980, pp. 41-56. M.-T. Dānešpažūh, "Bayhaqī-e fīlsūf," in *Yād-nāma*, pp. 174-81. Ebn Fondoq, *Tārīḵ-e Bayhaq*, ed. A. Bahmanyār, 2nd ed., Tehran, n.d. Elliot, *History of India* II, pp. 53-154. 'A. Eqbāl Āštīānī, "Ḵ'āja Abu'l-Fażl Bayhaqī," *Oṣūl-e ta'līm o tarbīat* 2/6, pp. 1-10, repr. in *Majmū'a-ye maqālāt-e 'Abbās Eqbāl Āštīānī*, ed. M. Dabīrsīāqī, Tehran, 1350 Š./1971, pp. 60-74. Idem, "Yak ṣafḥa az mojalladāt-e mafqūda-ye *Tārīḵ-e Bayhaqī*," *Armaḡān* 13/1, pp. 25-35, repr. in *Majmū'a-ye maqālāt*, pp. 282-89. M.-'A. Eslāmī Nodūšan, "Jahānbīnī-e Abu'l-Fażl Bayhaqī," in *Yād-nāma*, pp. 1-38, repr. in *Jām-e jahānbīn*, 3rd ed., Tehran, 1349 Š./1970, pp. 303-345. Idem, "Yak sarnevešt-e momtāz. Ḥasanak-e Wazīr," in *Jām-e jahānbīn*, 3rd ed., Tehran, 1349 Š./1970, pp. 295-302. G. Fallāḥ Rastegār, "Ādāb o rosūm o tašrīfāt-e darbār-e Ḡazna az ḵelāl-e *Tārīḵ-e Bayhaqī*," in *Yād-nāma*, pp. 412-67. Ḥ. Farzām, "Arzeš-e aḵlāqī-e *Tārīḵ-e Bayhaqī*," in *Yād-nāma*, pp. 293-411. 'A.-A. Fayyāż, "Nosḵahā-ye *Tārīḵ-e Bayhaqī*," in *Yād-nāma*, pp. 530-607. R. Gelpke, *Sultān Mas'ūd I von*

Ġazna. Die drei ersten Jahre seiner Herrschaft (421/1030-424/1033), Munich, 1957. A. Ḥabīb-Allāhī, "Ma'āḵeḏ-e aš'ār-e 'arabī-e *Tārīḵ-e Bayhaqī* wa mo'arrefī-e gūyandagān-e ānhā," in *Yād-nāma*, pp. 744-77. 'A. Ḥabībī, "Raveš-e tārīḵ-negārī-e do mowarreḵ-e bozorg (Bayhaqī wa Jūzjānī)," *Āryānā* 4, 1324-25 Š./1945-46, pp. 807-15. Idem, "Šāh-bahār-e Bayhaqī," *Yaḡmā* 18/2, 1344 Š./1965, pp. 57-60. Idem, "Taḥqīq-e barḵī az amāken-e *Tārīḵ-e Bayhaqī*," in *Yād-nāma*, pp. 137-52 (see also *Āryānā* 28/4, 1348-49 Š./1969-70, pp. 1-12; *Yaḡmā* 23, 1349 Š./1970, pp. 457-60). Idem, "Bayhaqī wa Afḡān Šāl," *Āryānā* 28/2, pp. 1-4 (see also *Yaḡmā* 21, 1347 Š./1968, pp. 231-36). Y. Hashėmi, "The Lacunae in Baihaqī," *Journal of the Pakistan Historical Society* 16, 1968, pp. 136-44. Ḡ.-S. Homāyūn, "Čand noqta-ye tāza dar bāra-ye *Tārīḵ-e Bayhaqī*," in *Yād-nāma*, pp. 778-98 (see also *Adab* 8/3-4, 1339 Š./1960, pp. 107-25). Ṣ. Ḥosaynī, *Aḵbār al-dawla al-saljūqīya*, ed. M. Eqbāl, Lahore, 1933. Jūzjānī (Jawzjānī), *Ṭabaqāt*, ed. 'A. Ḥabībī, Kabul, 1343 Š./1964. Ḵ. Ḵalīlī, "Dar aṭrāf-e ḥawāšī-e Āqā-ye Sa'īd Nafīsī bar *Tārīḵ-e Bayhaqī*," *Āryānā* 1/2, 1321-22 Š./1942-43, pp. 19-24. Ḵ. Ḵaṭīb Rahbar, "Ṭarḥ o tawżīḥ-e čand moškel az *Tārīḵ-e Bayhaqī*," in *Yād-nāma*, pp. 153-73. Kaykāvūs b. Eskandar, *Qābūs-nāma*, ed. Ḡ.-Ḥ. Yūsofī, 3rd ed., Tehran, 1364 Š./1985. A. de Biberstein Kazimirski, introduction to *Menoutchehri, poète persan du 11ème siècle de notre ère, du 5ème de l'hégire*, Paris, 1887, pp. 17-131. G. I. Kozlov, "Abu-'l-Fazl Beihaki," *Kratkie soobshcheni-ya Instituta Narodov Azii* 30, 1961. G. Lazard, "Un mémorialiste persan: Beyhaqi," in *Mélanges Labande*, Poitiers, 1974, pp. 471-78. A. K. Luther, "Bayhaqī and the Later Seljuq Historians. Some Comparative Remarks," in *Yād-nāma*, pp. 14-33. J. Matīnī, "Sīmā-ye Mas'ūd Ḡaznavī dar *Tārīḵ-e Bayhaqī*," ibid., pp. 530-607. Ī. Mehrdād, "Dar bāra-ye dāstānhā-ye Bayhaqī," *Kāva*, N.S. 6, pp. 31-35. M. Mīnovī, "'Ebrat-e tārīḵ," *Yaḡmā* 8, 1334 Š./1955, pp. 145-53, 193-203. Idem, "Tork o tāzīk dar 'aṣr-e Bayhaqī," in *Yād-nāma*, pp. 713-26. Idem, "The Persian Historian Bayhaqī," in *Historians of the Middle East*, ed. B. Lewis and P. M. Holt, London, 1962, pp. 138-40. M. Moḥaqqeq, "Barḵī az eṣṭelāḥāt-e edārī o dīvānī dar *Tārīḵ-e Bayhaqī*," in *Yād-nāma*, pp. 608-31. M. Moḥīṭ Ṭabāṭabā'ī, "Hazāra-ye mīlād-e Abu'l-Fażl Bayhaqī," *Yaḡmā* 23, pp. 385-92. S. Nafīsī, "Āṯār-e gom-šoda-ye Abu'l-Fażl Bayhaqī," *Mehr* 3, 1314-15 Š./1935-36, pp. 573-80, 674-81, 789-99, 905-13, 984-88, 1120-28, 1212-18; 4, 1315-16 Š./1936-37, pp. 125-36, 369-80, 489-96, 549-56, 665-72, 805-12, 961-64. Idem, *Āṯār-e gom-šoda-ye Abu'l-Fażl Bayhaqī*, Tehran, 1315 Š./1936. Idem, "Bayhaḳī," in *EI*² I, pp. 1130-31. Idem, *Dar pīrāmūn-e Tārīḵ-e Bayhaqī*, 2 vols., Tehran, 1342 Š./1963. M. Nāzim, *The Life and Times of Sulṭān Maḥmūd of Ghazna*, Cambridge, 1931. 'A. Nūrānī Weṣāl, "Šaḵṣīyat-e Āltūntāš dar naẓar-e Bayhaqī dar dawra-ye Solṭān Mas'ūd Ḡaznavī," in *Yād-nāma*, pp. 727-43. M. Parvīn Gonābādī, "Nokāt-ī rāje' be *Tārīḵ-e Bayhaqī*," in *Yād-nāma*, pp. 103-19. J. Reżā'ī, "Bū Sahl Zūzanī dar *Tārīḵ-e Bayhaqī*," ibid., pp. 220-31. Ṣ. Reżāzāda Šafaq, "Abu'l-Fażl Bayhaqī wa tārīḵ-e ū," *Armaḡān* 11, 1309 Š./1930, pp. 859-65; 12, 1310 Š./1931, pp. 70-78, 84-96; 26, 1336 Š./1957, pp. 97-102, 145-54, 199-208. M.-M. Roknī, "Dīvān-e resālat o ā'īn-e dabīrī az ḵelāl-e *Tārīḵ-e Bayhaqī*," in *Yād-nāma*, pp. 233-72. Ṣafā, *Adabīyāt* II, pp. 890-92. M. Šafī'ī, "Terāžedīhā-ye *Tārīḵ-e Bayhaqī*," in *Yād-nāma*, pp. 374-92. N. Šāh-Ḥosaynī, "Kūšānīān o *Tārīḵ-e Bayhaqī*," in *Yād-nāma*, pp. 354-63. Ṣalāh-al-Dīn Ṣafadī, *al-Wāfī be'l-wafayāt*, ed. H. Ritter, 2nd ed., Damascus, 1961. Ż. Sajjādī, "Taḥqīq dar amṯāl o aš'ār-e fārsī-e *Tārīḵ-e Bayhaqī*," in *Yād-nāma*, pp. 273-332. Ḡ.-R. Salīm, "Tawjīh-e tamṯīlhā-ye *Tārīḵ-e Bayhaqī*," in *Yād-nāma*, pp. 253-333. R. M. Savory, "Abu'l Fażl Bayhaqī as an Historiographer," in *Yād-nāma*, pp. 84-128. M. R. Waldman, "Semiotics and Historical Narrative," *Papers in Comparative Studies* 1, 1981, pp. 167-68. Idem, *Toward a Theory of Historical Narrative. A Case Study in Perso-Islamicate Historiography*, Columbus, Ohio, 1980. *Yād-nāma-ye Abu'l-Fażl Bayhaqī*, ed. J. Matīnī, Mašhad, 1350 Š./1971. Ḡ.-Ḥ. Yūsofī, *Farroḵī Sīstānī. Baḵš-ī dar šarḥ-e aḥwāl o rūzgār o še'r-e ū*, Mašhad, 1341 Š./1962. Idem, "Honar-e nevīsandagī-e Bayhaqī," in *Yād-nāma*, pp. 799-829. Idem, *Barghā-ī dar āḡūš-e bād*, Tehran, 1356 Š./1978. Idem, *Dīdār-ī bā ahl-e qalam*, 2nd ed., Mašhad, 1357 Š./1978. Idem, *Kāḡaḏ-e zar*, Tehran, 1363 Š./1984. Ḡ.-R. Zarrīnčīān, "Sayr-ī dar *Tārīḵ-e Bayhaqī*," B. A. dissertation, University of Mašhad, 1346 Š./1968. 'A. Zaryāb Ḵo'ī, "Tārīḵ-negārī-e Bayhaqī," *MDA Mašhad* 7, 1350 Š./1962, pp. 760-71.

(Ḡ.-Ḥ. Yūsofī)

BAYHAQĪ, ABU'L-ḤASAN MOḤAMMAD

b. Šo'ayb 'Ejlī Naysābūrī (d. 324/936), a jurist who helped promote the spread of the Shafi'ite school of Islamic law in Khorasan. After initial training at Nīšāpūr under traditionists such as Abū Bakr b. Ḵozayma and Būšanjī, he went to Baghdad and studied law under Moḥammad b. Jarīr Ṭabarī (d. 310/923; q.v.) and Aḥmad b. 'Omar b. Sorayj (d. 306/918-19), who was the principal exponent of Shafi'ite jurisprudence in Iraq at that time. After returning to Khorasan, Bayhaqī joined the circle of Abu'l-Fażl Bal'amī (d. 329/940), the learned vizier of the Samanids, who tried in vain to make him accept an appointment to the judiciary as *qāżī* at Čāč (Tashkent) or Ray. Bayhaqī propagated the Shafi'ite system through his teaching and his rulings (*fatwās*) and disputations, not through any writings of his own. Among his pupils were Abu'l-Walīd Ḥaṣṣān Naysābūrī (d. 349/960), who founded the first Shafi'ite *madrasa* at Nīšāpūr, and Abū Sahl Moḥammad b. Solaymān Ṣo'lūkī (d. 369/980), who after Bayhaqī's death in 324/936 became the chief Shafi'ite jurisconsult at Nīšāpūr. The notion that Abu'l-Ḥasan Moḥammad Bayhaqī was the founder of the Bayhaqīya *madrasa* at

Nīšāpūr, as Ebn Fondoq asserts, arose through a misunderstanding.

Bibliography: Sobkī, *Ṭabaqāt al-Šāfeʿīya al-kobrā*, ed. M. M. Ṭanāḥī and ʿA. M. Ḥelū, III, Cairo, 1384/1965, p. 173 (cf. pp. 226, 306, 345), based on the *Taʾrīḵ Naysābūr* of Ḥākem Naysābūrī. Ebn Fondoq (ʿAlī b. Zayd) Bayhaqī, *Tārīḵ-e Bayhaq*, ed. A. Bahmanyār, Tehran, 1317 Š./1938, p. 158. R. W. Bulliet, *The Patricians of Nishapur*, Cambridge, Mass., 1972, p. 251. H. Halm, *Die Ausbreitung der šāfiʿitischen Rechtschule von den Anfängen bis zum 8./14. Jahrhundert*, Wiesbaden, 1974, pp. 45-47.

(H. HALM)

BAYHAQĪ, EBRĀHĪM B. MOḤAMMAD, Arabic littérateur, known solely through his one book, the *Ketāb al-maḥāsen wa'l-masāwī*. Nothing is known of him except for what can be gleaned from this, though his forebears presumably had some connection with Bayhaq (q.v.) in Khorasan; he apparently wrote in the caliphate of al-Moqtader (295-320/908-32), and Brockelmann surmised that he may have belonged to the circle of Ebn al-Moʿtazz (d. 296/908; *GAL*, S. I, p. 249). His *adab* book deals with the good and bad aspects of historical events, moral characteristics, ways of behavior, etc., juxtaposing them antithetically and illustrating his argument with numerous literary and historical anecdotes, some with Iranian settings, e.g., on such Sasanian emperors as Anōšīravān and Ḵosrow Parvēz and on the Barmakids (qq.v.). From the general tendencies of much of the material chosen by him and from his personal attitudes, Bayhaqī emerges as a moderate Shiʿite, perhaps a Zaydī (Geries, pp. 74-79). He drew extensively on the work of his predecessor Jāḥeẓ (q.v.), and especially from the *Ketāb al-ḥayawān*, and was in turn much utilized by the unknown author of the *Ketāb al-maḥāsen wa'l-ażdād*, who, in Geries' opinion and *pace* van Vloten's tentative opting for a common source, drew directly from Bayhaqī's work (G. van Vloten, *Le livre des beautés et des antithèses*, Leiden, 1898, preface, pp. IX-XI; Geries, pp. 102-10). Otherwise, Bayhaqī's book seems to have been little known after his own time, with the author barely mentioned by later sources.

Bibliography: See also Ibrahim Geries, *Un genre littéraire arabe: al-Maḥâsin wa-l-masâwî*, Paris, 1977, pp. 71-101. Editions: *Dr. Friedrich Schwally, ed., Kitāb al-Maḥāsin val-Masāvī*, Giessen, 1900-02, 3 pts. (index in O. Rescher, *Index und Stellennachweise zu Fr. Schwally's Baihaqî-Ausgabe*, Stuttgart, 1923); Moḥammad Abu'l-Fażl Ebrāhīm, ed., Cairo, 1380/1961, 2 vols. (both based on the two extant mss. of Leiden and Calcutta).

(C. E. BOSWORTH)

BAYHAQĪ, ẒAHĪR-AL-DĪN ABU'L-ḤASAN ʿALĪ B. ZAYD (ca. 490-565/1097-1169), also known as Ebn Fondoq, an Iranian polymath of Arab descent, author of the *Tārīḵ-e Bayhaq*. What is known of Bayhaqī's life stems from the autobiographical section of his lost work on the history of Iran (410-560/1020-1165) *Mašāreb al-tajāreb* (preserved in Yāqūt, *Odabāʾ* V, pp. 208-13), from scattered remarks in his extant works, and from the reminiscences of ʿEmād-al-Dīn Eṣfahānī whose father was a long-time friend of the author in Ray (ibid., p. 214).

Bayhaqī was a descendant of one of the Prophet's companions, Ḵozayma b. Ṯābet Ḏu'l-Šahādatayn whose descendants had settled around Bost. The eponym of the family, Ḥākem Abū Solaymān Fondoq, was sent to Sabzavār as a judge by the Ghaznavid Sultan Maḥmūd (r. 388-421/998-421; see *Tārīḵ-e Bayhaq*, ed. A. Bahmanyār, Tehran, 1348/1929-30, pp. 101-02). Most of Bayhaqī's forefathers were judges or imams (ibid., p. 2). He was born in Sabzavār, the main city of the Bayhaq district, where his father's estates were located. In his introduction to *Tārīḵ-e Bayhaq* (p. *yb*, n. 1), Moḥammad Qazvīnī shows that 499/1106, the date given by Yāqūt, is based on a misreading; as Bayhaqī himself states (pp. 76-77), he was a schoolboy when the vizier Faḵr-al-Molk b. Neẓām-al-Molk was murdered (500/1106-07). Bayhaqī's broad education in literature and the sciences began in Nīšāpūr. In 507/1113-14, accompanied by his father, Bayhaqī visited the renowned ʿOmar Ḵayyām (*Tatemmat Ṣewān al-ḥekma*, ed. M. Šafīʿ, Lahore, 1935, p. 116), and in 517/1123, he went to Marv where he completed his studies in *feqh* with the Hanafite jurist Abū Saʿd Yaḥyā b. Ṣāʿed. In 521/1127, he returned to Nīšāpūr where his studies were "interrupted by marriage" (Yāqūt, p. 209). Bayhaqī spent the next few years serving his father-in-law the governor of Ray Šehāb-al-Dīn Moḥammad b. Masʿūd, who in 526/1132 secured for him the position of *qāżī* of Bayhaq. Bayhaqī may have made enemies in his new post; but, whatever the case, he soon grew tired of it and resigned. He then repaired to his father-in-law's home in Ray to devote himself to the study of mathematics and astrology. In 529/1135, Bayhaqī returned to Nīšāpūr but did not remain long; a year later, to improve his understanding of astrology, the restless scholar was off to Saraḵs where he squandered all of his money (Yāqūt, *Odabāʾ* V, pp. 210f.). He spent 532-36/1138-42 in Nīšāpūr. After an attempt to establish himself in Bayhaq failed "because of his relatives' envy" (ibid.), Bayhaqī finally returned to Nīšāpūr where he "threw his walking-stick away" (ibid.) and settled down to life in the seminary and the mosque. Bayhaqī enjoyed the favor of court circles, in particular, the patronage of the vizier Ṭāher b. Faḵr-al-Molk. In 543/1148, when Demetrius, king of Georgia, posed certain questions (of unknown purport) in Syriac (*soryānī*) and Arabic via an envoy to Sultan Sanjar, the sultan had Bayhaqī respond to them (*Tārīḵ-e Bayhaq*, p. 163). According to Yāqūt (ibid., p. 208), Bayhaqī died in 565/1169-70.

In his *Mašāreb al-tajāreb* (Yāqūt, *Odabāʾ* V, pp. 211ff.), Bayhaqī enumerates seventy-one of his own works, among which are four Persian works: *Rasāʾel*, *ʿOqūd al-mażāḥeq*, *Naṣāʾeḥ al-kobarāʾ*, and *Qeṣaṣ al-anbīāʾ*, as well as his *Tārīḵ-e Bayhaq* and an astrological treatise *Jawāmeʿ al-aḥkām al-nojūm* (Storey, II/1, p. 48).

Bayhaqī's works encompass all the learning of his time: Koranic, doctrinal, and legal studies, algebra, astrology and astronomy, including the use of the astrolabe, medicine, and pharmacology. Many are works of philology, including treatises on grammer and rhetoric, commentaries on *Nahj al-balāḡa*, on the poems of Boḥtorī and Abū Tammām, and on Ḥarīrī's *Maqāmāt*. Specimens of Bayhaqī's own poetry have survived as excerpts from his now lost anthology *Wešāḥ domyat al-qaṣr*, a continuation of Bāḵarzī's well-known *Domyat al-qaṣr*.

Apart from the *Jawāme' al-aḥkām* and scattered poems, Bayhaqī's only extant works are historical. Preserved in part in other historians' works (e.g., those of Yāqūt, Ebn al-Aṯīr, Ebn Abī Oṣaybe'a, Jovaynī, and Ḥamd-Allāh Mostawfī) is Bayhaqī's *Mašāreb al-tajāreb*, a sequel to 'Otbī's *Tārīḵ-e yamīnī* (*Tārīḵ-e Bayhaq*, p. 20). His *Tatemmat Ṣewān al-ḥekma*, a sequel to Abū Solaymān Sejestānī's *Ṣewān al-ḥekma*, and the history of his native region, *Tārīḵ-e Bayhaq*, which is modeled on an earlier, nonextant work by 'Alī b. Abī Ṣāleḥ Ḵ ̌ārī, have survived intact.

Neither a chronicle nor an analytical history, *Tārīḵ-e Bayhaq* is of the genre of works called *manāqeb*, largely prosopographies written in praise of a particular region and of the learned men who were born or resided there. After brief sections on the geography and history of Bayhaq, *Tārīḵ-e Bayhaq* describes its prominent families, compiled by the author himself (p. 21): sayyeds (pp. 54ff.); various ruling dynasties (pp. 66ff.); the house of Ḵ ̌āja Neẓām-al-Molk and the Mohallabids; and Bayhaqī's immediate family the Ḥākemī/Fondoqīs (pp. 101ff.). The major part of the work is devoted to the region's notables, beginning with scholars and divines (pp. 137ff.), followed by the heads of the 'Alids (*noqabā'*; pp. 253ff.), Persian poets (pp. 255ff.), and the grandees (pp. 264ff.). The work concludes with a brief catalogue of significant battles (pp. 266ff.) and a series of oddities found in Bayhaq (pp. 276ff.).

Bibliography: M.-T. Bahār, *Sabkšenāsī* II, 3rd ed., Tehran, 1349 Š./1970, pp. 365-71. Brockelmann, *GAL* I, p. 324; S. I., p. 557. D. M. Dunlop, "al-Bayhaḳī," in *EI*² I, pp. 1131-32. Aḥmad Faṣīḥ Ḵ ̌āfī, *Mojmal-e faṣīḥī* II, ed. M. Farroḵ, Mašhad, 1341 Š./1962, p. 242. M. Mo'īn, *Majmū'a-ye maqālāt* I, ed. M. Mo'īn, Tehran, 1364 Š./1985, pp. 148-49. Storey, I/1, pp. 353-54; I/2, pp. 1105-06, 1350.

(H. HALM)